VOX

SPANISH
and
ENGLISH
Student Dictionary

Second Edition

D0709112

New York   Chicago   San Francisco   Lisbon   London   Madrid   Mexico City
Milan   New Delhi   San Juan   Seoul   Singapore   Sydney   Toronto

The **McGraw·Hill** Companies

Copyright © 2013 by Larousse Editorial. All rights reserved. Printed in the United States of America. Except as permitted under the United States Copyright Act of 1976, no part of this publication may be reproduced or distributed in any form or by any means, or stored in a database or retrieval system, without the prior written permission of the publisher.

1 2 3 4 5 6 7 8 9 10 11 12 13   QLM/QLM   1 9 8 7 6 5 4 3 2

ISBN   978-0-07-180837-8
MHID   0-07-180837-X

Library of Congress Cataloging-in-Publication Data

Vox Spanish and English student dictionary. — 2nd. ed.
    p. cm. — (Vox dictionaries)
  ISBN 978-0-07-180837-8 (alk. paper)
  1. Spanish language—Dictionaries—English.   2. English language—Dictionaries—Spanish.   I. Title: Spanish and English dictionary.
  PC4640.V697   2012
  463'.21—dc23

                                                        2012032970

Dirección editorial: Jordi Induráin Pons
Coordinación editorial: Ma José Simón Aragón, Jordi Tebé Soriano
Asesoría pedagógica: Lluís Figueras Havidich, Ma Rosa Raméntol Estela
Realización: dos més dos edicions, s.l.
Ilustraciones: Juanjo Barco (Alins ilustración), Estudi Farrés
Cartografía: Santi Maicas
Diseño de cubierta: Francesc Sala

McGraw-Hill books are available at special quantity discounts to use as premiums and sales promotions or for use in corporate training programs. To contact a representative, please e-mail us at bulksales@mcgraw-hill.com.

This book is printed on acid-free paper.

Table of Contents

INTRODUCTION

Maybe you are already in the habit of using a dictionary, or maybe this is the first time you've looked at one. Whatever the case, it will be useful for you to read these pages to discover all that you can learn from it. First some figures: you'll find 30,000 words or entries (17,000 of them English) and 70,000 translations. Of course, there are bigger dictionaries, but, unlike this one, they are not specially designed for your grade or language level. Let time take its course and the day will come when you'll be ready for them; for the moment, you're better off with the words our experts and panel of teachers have selected to meet your specific needs. That way, you'll learn gradually and solidly, improving your knowledge day by day.

Almost without realizing it, you learn new vocabulary every day: in class, watching a film, listening to a song, or surfing the Internet. Sometimes you can deduce the meaning of a new word because it belongs to the same family as another one you have already studied, but sometimes it isn't so easy. This is when you should reach for your dictionary: you'll find the meaning of the new word, examples of how to use it, and other information that, with your teacher's help, will allow you to improve your Spanish.

Maybe you've wondered what it would be like to speak only Spanish to your teachers and classmates. In these pages, you'll find a selection of phrases organized by subject that you can practice. No doubt you'll enjoy learning expressions that you'd like to be able to use in Spanish, but which you can't find in your books! Your teachers will help you to get the most out of these words and phrases.

And now that you know your dictionary better, get as much out of it as you can. *¿Estás preparado?*

HOW TO USE
THIS DICTIONARY

Perhaps you think that a dictionary does nothing
more than show you the translation of a word.
Well, we're going to show you all that you can do with it,
because some of it's bound to be new to you:

▶ Have you seen a word that was spelled differently from the way
you thought? Every day we use lots of words, but sometimes
we don't know how to spell them or we feel lazy about looking
them up. Remember every word that you look up, it will help you
to build up a solid vocabulary base.

appearance [əˈpɪərəns] n **1** (becoming
visible) aparición f. **2** (before a court, etc)
comparecencia. **3** (look) apariencia.

aparcamiento nm **1** (acción) parking. **2**
(en la calle) place to park, parking
place…

arithmetic [(n) əˈrɪθmətɪk; (adj) ærɪθ-
ˈmetɪk] n aritmética.
▶ adj aritmético,-a.

aproximación nf **1** (gen) approximation. **2** (acercamiento) bringing together; (de países) rapprochement.

▶ Do you see the square brackets [ ] immediately after the English
headword? Here you will find the exact pronunciation of the
English headword. Maybe there are some symbols that you don't
understand, but we'll explain what they mean in another section.

achievement [əˈtʃiːvmənt] n **1** (completion) realización f. **2** (attainment)
logro. **3** (feat) hazaña, proeza.

► Have you seen the abbreviation that comes right after the Spanish headword? This tells you the part of speech of the headword: if it's a feminine or masculine noun, a transitive or intransitive verb, and so on. Your language teachers will have taught you what these words mean. Here you can put into practice what they have explained to you: sometimes a word can be a noun and an adjective and have different meanings. You should pay attention to a word's part of speech so that you don't make mistakes when you are translating.

behind [bɪ'haɪnd] *prep* detrás de.
► *adv* **1** detrás, atrás. **2** *(late)* atrasado,-a.
► *n fam (buttocks)* trasero.

alemán,-ana *adj* German.
► *nm & nf (persona)* German.
► *nm* alemán *(idioma)* German.

► Have you noticed that in some entries there are numbers? These show you the different meanings of the word. The number **1** indicates the commonest meaning, but the others are important too; all of them can help you to find the translation you're looking for.

capital ['kæpɪtəl] *n* **1** *(of country, etc)* capital *f.* **2** FIN capital *m: starting capital* capital inicial. **3** *(letter)* mayúscula: *write it in capitals* escríbelo con mayúsculas.

ampliar *vt* **1** to enlarge, extend. **2** ARQUIT to build an extension onto. **3** *(fotografía)* to enlarge. **4** *(capital)* to increase. **5** *(estudios)* to further. **6** *(tema, idea)* to develop, expand on.

► There are some words that are used only in a certain expression, or which require a certain preposition. Others have some peculiarity, such as an irregular plural. Because of this, you must be sure to read everything in the entry. You're bound to learn something new that will help you to understand what the word means and how it's used.

capability [keɪpə'bɪlɪtɪ] *n* capacidad *f* (to, para/de).
► *pl* capabilities.

absorto,-a *adj* **1** *(pasmado)* amazed, bewildered. **2** *(ensimismado)* absorbed (en, in).

► Have you seen a box with the letters COMP ? This means that the
  word is often used with another word and that together they have a
  different meaning. Have you see the letters LOC too? Now you can
  learn phrases and expressions with this word and see what verbs
  normally go with it.

elementary [elɪ'mentərɪ] *adj* **1** *(basic)*
elemental, básico,-a. **2** *(easy)* fácil,
sencillo,-a. COMP **elementary educa-**
tion enseñanza primaria.
faithfully ['feɪθfʊlɪ] *adv* fielmente.
LOC **yours faithfully** *(in letter)* atentamente.

accidente *nm* **1** accident: *sufrir un acci-*
dente to have an accident. **2** *(terreno)*
unevenness. LOC **por accidente** by
chance. COMP **accidente de trabajo** industrial accident. **‖ accidente de tráfi-**
co road accident. **‖ accidentes geo-**
gráficos geographical features.

► Have you seen some letters (for example, GB) after one of the
  numbers that indicate the different meanings? They tell you
  whether the word is used only in British English, in the United
  States, Canada, or Australia. If there are other letters after these,
  these tell you the field the word is used in, for example cookery
  or medicine.

dresser ['dresəʳ] *n* **1** GB *(in kitchen)* aparador *m*. **2** US *(chest of drawers)* tocador *m*.
fail [feɪl] *n* EDUC suspenso.
► *vt* **1** *(let down)* fallar, decepcionar;
(desert) fallar, faltar. **2** EDUC suspender.

ADN *abrev* MED (ácido desoxirribonucleico) desoxyribonucleic acid;
(abreviatura) DNA.
adobar *vt* **1** CULIN to marinate, marinade. **2** *(pieles)* to tan.

► If you see a box with this symbol ☒, read it carefully; this
  information is very interesting. Some Spanish words look very
  similar to English words, but they do not always mean the same
  thing and you can make a mistake.

fabric ['fæbrɪk] *n* **1** *(material)* tela, tejido. **2** *(structure)* fábrica, estructura.
☒ Fabric no significa 'fábrica', que se
traduce por **factory**.

▶ Sometimes a dictionary is like a mini-encyclopedia. If you see a text with a shaded background and a globe symbol, here you will find information about customs and culture.

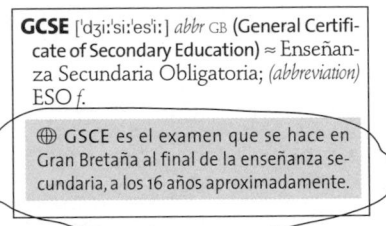

> **GCSE** [ˈdʒiːˈsiːˈesiː] *abbr* GB (General Certificate of Secondary Education) ≈ Enseñanza Secundaria Obligatoria; *(abbreviation)* ESO *f*.
>
> ⊕ GSCE es el examen que se hace en Gran Bretaña al final de la enseñanza secundaria, a los 16 años aproximadamente.

▶ Have you looked up a word you didn't know and found an arrow and another word you didn't know? Well, you're in luck! You're going to learn two new words. The arrow means that to find the meaning of the word, you have to go to another more important word which it comes from or is related to. You will find what you're looking for at the second word.

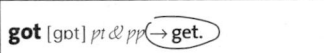

> **got** [gɒt] *pt & pp*→ **get**.

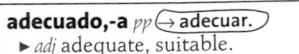

> **adecuado,-a** *pp*→ **adecuar**.
> ▶ *adj* adequate, suitable.

▶ You will also find a lot of other information about words: their plural, if they are irregular or not, or explanations about how to use them. So that you can find this information quickly, it is marked with an ① or a ✎.

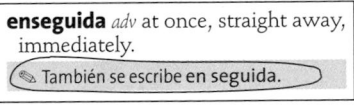

> **enseguida** *adv* at once, straight away, immediately.
> ✎ También se escribe en seguida.

We hope that this explanation has been helpful to you and that you will use it. Now you are ready and can start to use your dictionary.

ABBREVIATIONS USED IN THIS DICTIONARY

abr	abreviatura, abbreviation	*fam*	familiar use, uso familiar
adj	adjective, adjetivo	*fig*	figurative use, uso figurado
abbr	abbreviation, abreviatura		
adv	adverb, adverbio	FIN	finance, finanzas
AER	aeronautics, aeronáutica	FÍS	física, physics
AGR	agriculture, agricultura	*fml*	formal use, uso formal
AM	American Spanish, español americano	*fut*	future, futuro
		GB	British English, inglés británico
ANAT	anatomy, anatomía		
ARCH	architecture, arquitectura	*gen*	in general, en general
arg	argot, slang	GEOG	geography, geografía
ARQ	arquitectura, architecture	GEOL	geology, geología
ART	art, arte	*ger*	gerund, gerundio
art	article, artículo	GRAM	grammar, gramática
art def	artículo definido, definite article	HIST	history, historia
		imperat	imperative, imperativo
art indef	artículo indefinido, indefinite article	*imperf*	imperfect, imperfecto
		indef art	indefinite article, artículo indefinido
AUTO	automobiles, automóvil		
AV	aviation, aviación	*indic*	indicative, indicativo
BIOL	biology, biología	*inf*	infinitive, infinitivo
BOT	botany, botánica	INFORM	informática, computing
CHEM	chemistry, química	*interj*	interjection, interjección
CINEM	cinema, cinematografía	*iron*	ironic, irónico
COM	comercio, commerce	*irón*	irónico, ironic
COMM	commerce, comercio	JUR	law, derecho
comp	comparative, comparativo	LING	linguistics, lingüística
COMPUT	computing, informática	LIT	literature, literatura
conj	conjunction, conjunción	*loc*	locución, phrase
contr	contraction, contracción	MAR	maritime, marítimo
COST	costura, sewing	MAT	matemáticas, mathematics
CULIN	cookery, cocina	MATH	mathematics, matemáticas
def art	definite article, artículo definido	MED	medicine, medicina
		METEOR	meteorology, meteorología
DEP	deporte, sport		
EDUC	education, educación	MIL	military, militar
ELEC	electricity, electricidad	MUS	music, música
etc	etcetera, etcétera	MÚS	música, music
euf	uso eufemístico, euphemistic use	*n*	noun, nombre
		neut	neuter, neutro
euph	euphemistic use, uso eufemístico	*nf*	feminine noun, nombre femenino

nf pl	plural feminine noun, nombre femenino plural	*v aux*	auxiliary verb, verbo auxiliar
nm	masculine noun, nombre masculino	*vi*	intransitive verb, verbo intransitivo
nm o nf	masculine or feminine noun, nombre de género ambiguo	*vpr*	pronominal verb, verbo pronominal
nm & nf	masculine and feminine noun, nombre de género común	*vt*	transitive verb, verbo transitivo
nm pl	masculine plural noun, nombre masculino plural	*vt insep*	inseparable transitive phrasal verb, verbo preposicional transitivo inseparable
npl	plural noun, nombre plural	*vt sep*	separable transitive phrasal verb, verbo preposicional transitivo separable
pej	pejorative, peyorativo		
pers	person, persona		
pey	peyorativo, pejorative		
phr	phrase, locución	ZOOL	zoology, zoología
PHYS	physics, física	≈	approximately equivalent to, aproximadamente equivalente a
POL	politics, política		
pp	past participle, participio pasado	→	see, véase
pref	prefix, prefijo	►	different part of speech, cambio de categoría gramatical
prep	preposition, preposición		
pres	present, presente		
pron	pronoun, pronombre	◆	phrasal verb
pt	past, pasado	LOC	block of idioms and phrases, bloque de frases y locuciones
QUÍM	química, chemistry		
RAD	radio		
REL	religion, religión	COMP	block of compound nouns, bloque de compuestos
SEW	sewing, costura		
sím	símbolo, symbol		
sing	singular	①	note about some type of irregularity, nota sobre algún tipo de irregularidad morfológica
sl	slang, argot		
SP	sport, deporte		
subj	subjunctive, subjuntivo		
superl	superlative, superlativo	✎	note about a peculiarity of the headword, nota sobre alguna particularidad de la palabra
symb	symbol, símbolo		
TEAT	teatro, theatre		
TÉC	técnica, technical		
TECH	technical, técnica	☒	note about a false friend, nota sobre un «falso amigo»
THEAT	theatre, teatro		
TV	television, televisión		
US	American English, inglés norteamericano	⊕	cultural note, nota de tipo cultural

ENGLISH
SPANISH

A, a [eɪ] *n* **1** *(the letter)* A, a. **2** MUS la.
[COMP] **A road** carretera principal.

a [eɪ, *unstressed* ə] *indef art* **1** un, una: *a man and a woman* un hombre y una mujer. **2** *(not translated)*: *I'm a history teacher* soy profesor de historia; *two and a half litres* dos litros y medio. **3** *(per)* por: *three times a week* tres veces por semana; *£3 a kilo* tres libras el kilo. **4** *(a certain)* un tal, una tal: *a Mr Fletcher would like to see you* un tal Sr. Fletcher quiere verle.

✎ Se usa delante de las palabras que empiezan con sonido no vocálico. Consulta también **an**.

aback [ə'bæk] *adv* hacia atrás. [LOC] **to be taken aback** asombrarse.

abacus ['æbəkəs] *n* ábaco.

abandon [ə'bændən] *vt* abandonar.

abate [ə'beɪt] *vi (gen)* reducirse; *(storm, anger)* amainar; *(wind)* cesar.
▶ *vt (reduce)* reducir; *(stop)* acabar con.

abattoir ['æbətwɑːʳ] *n* matadero.

abbey ['æbɪ] *n* abadía.

abbot ['æbət] *n* abad *m*.

abbreviate [ə'briːvɪeɪt] *vt* abreviar.

abbreviation [əbriːvɪ'eɪʃᵊn] *n* **1** *(shortening)* abreviación *f*. **2** *(shortened form)* abreviatura.

abdicate ['æbdɪkeɪt] *vi* abdicar.

abdomen ['æbdəmən] *n* abdomen *m*.

abdominal [æb'dɒmɪnᵊl] *adj* abdominal. [COMP] **abdominal muscles** músculos abdominales.

abduct [æb'dʌkt] *vt* raptar, secuestrar.

abhor [əb'hɔːʳ] *vt* aborrecer, detestar.
ⓘ *pt & pp* abhorred, *ger* abhorring.

abide [ə'baɪd] *vt (bear, stand)* soportar, aguantar: *I can't abide that woman* no aguanto a esa mujer.
◆ **to abide by** *vt insep (promise)* cumplir con; *(rules, decision)* acatar.

ability [ə'bɪlɪtɪ] *n* **1** *(capability)* capacidad *f*, aptitud *f*. **2** *(talent)* talento.
ⓘ *pl* abilities.

ablation [ə'bleɪʃᵊn] *n* ablación *f*.

ablaze [ə'bleɪz] *adj* ardiendo, en llamas.

able ['eɪbᵊl] *adj* **1** que puede: *those able to escape did so* aquéllos que podían se escaparon. **2** *(capable)* hábil, capaz, competente: *he's a very able administrator* es un gestor muy competente. [LOC] **to be able to** poder.

✎ En pasado, **to be able to** se emplea en vez de **could** para expresar una capacidad relacionada con un acontecimiento concreto: *we weren't able to go* no pudimos ir.

abnormal [æb'nɔːmᵊl] *adj* **1** *(not normal)* anormal. **2** *(unusual)* inusual.

aboard [ə'bɔːd] *adv (ship, plane)* a bordo; *(train)* en el tren; *(bus)* en el autobús.
▶ *prep (ship, plane)* a bordo de; *(train, bus)* en. [LOC] **to go aboard 1** *(ship, plane)* embarcar, subir a bordo. **2** *(train, bus)* subir.

abode [ə'bəʊd] *n* [LOC] **of no fixed abode** sin domicilio fijo.

abolish [ə'bɒlɪʃ] *vt* **1** abolir, suprimir. **2** JUR derogar.

abominable [ə'bɒmɪnəbᵊl] *adj* abominable; *(terrible)* terrible, horrible. [COMP] **the Abominable Snowman** el Yeti.

aborigine [æbə'rɪdʒɪnɪ] *n* aborigen *mf*.

abort [ə'bɔːt] *vi* abortar.
▶ *vt* **1** *(foetus)* abortar. **2** *(mission, program, etc)* abortar.

abortion [ə'bɔ:ʃ°n] *n* **1** *(of foetus)* aborto. **2** *(of mission, etc)* interrupción *f.*

abound [ə'baund] *vi* abundar.

about [ə'baut] *prep* **1** *(concerning)* sobre, acerca de: *to speak about...* hablar de…; *what is the book about?* ¿de qué trata el libro? **2** *(showing where)* por, en; *(around)* alrededor de: *he's somewhere about the house* está por algún rincón de la casa.
▶ *adv* **1** *(approximately)* alrededor de: *at about three o'clock* a eso de las tres; *it cost about £500* costó unas quinientas libras. **2** *fam (almost)* casi: *she's about finished* está a punto de acabar. **3** *(near)* por aquí, por ahí: *there was nobody about* no había nadie. [LOC] **to be about to ...** estar a punto de… ▮ **how/what about + *noun*** ¿qué te parece + *sustantivo*? *how about a pizza?* ¿qué te parece si tomamos una pizza? ▮ **how/what about + *-ing*** ¿y si + *subj*? *how about going to Paris?* ¿y si fuéramos a París?

above [ə'bʌv] *prep* **1** *(higher than)* por encima de: *above our heads* por encima de nuestras cabezas. **2** *(more than)* más de, más que: *above 5,000 people* más de 5.000 personas.
▶ *adv* **1** arriba, en lo alto: *the palace, seen from above* el palacio, visto desde arriba. **2** *(in writing)* arriba: *see above* véase arriba. [LOC] **above all** sobre todo.

above-board [əbʌv'bɔ:d] *adj* legítimo,-a, legal.

abreast [ə'brest] *adv* [LOC] **to walk abreast** caminar uno al lado de otro; **to keep abreast of things** estar al tanto de las cosas.

abridge [ə'brɪdʒ] *vt* resumir, abreviar.

abroad [ə'brɔ:d] *adv (position)* en el extranjero; *(movement)* al extranjero.

abrupt [ə'brʌpt] *adj* **1** *(sudden)* repentino,-a. **2** *(rude)* brusco,-a, arisco,-a. **3** *(slope)* empinado,-a.

ABS ['eɪ'biː'es] *abbr* (anti-lock braking system) sistema *m* de antibloqueo; *(abbreviation)* ABS.

abscess ['æbses] *n (gen)* absceso; *(on gum)* flemón *m.*

abscond [əb'skɒnd] *vi* fugarse.

abseil ['æbseɪl] *vi* hacer rappel.

absence ['æbs°ns] *n* **1** *(of person)* ausencia. **2** *(of thing)* falta, carencia.

absent [*(adj)* 'æbs°nt; *(vb)* æb'sent] *adj* **1** ausente. **2** *(expression)* distraído,-a.

absentee [æbs°n'ti:] *n* ausente *mf.*

absenteeism [æbs°n'ti:ɪz°m] *n* absentismo.

absent-minded [æbs°nt'maɪndɪd] *adj* distraído,-a, despistado,-a.

absolute ['æbsəlu:t] *adj* **1** *(gen)* absoluto,-a. **2** *(total)* total: *there was absolute silence* hubo silencio total. [COMP] **absolute zero** cero absoluto.

absolutely [æbsə'lu:tlɪ] *adv* completamente, totalmente.
▶ *interj (agreement)* ¡por supuesto!, ¡desde luego!: *I think we should sell. What about you John? – Oh, absolutely!* creo que deberíamos vender. ¿Y tú John? –Oh, ¡por supuesto!

absolution [æbsə'lu:ʃ°n] *n* absolución *f.*

absolutism ['æbsəlu:tɪz°m] *n* absolutismo.

absolve [əb'zɒlv] *vt* absolver (of/from, de).

absorb [əb'zɔ:b] *vt* **1** *(liquids, etc)* absorber; *(shock)* amortiguar. **2** *(time)* ocupar.

absorption [əb'zɔ:pʃ°n] *n* absorción *f.*

abstain [əb'steɪn] *vi* abstenerse (from, de).

abstemious [æb'sti:mɪəs] *adj* abstemio,-a, sobrio,-a.

abstention [əb'stenʃ°n] *n* abstención *f.*

abstinence ['æbstɪnəns] *n* abstinencia.

abstract [*(adj-n)* 'æbstrækt; *(vb)* æb'strækt] *adj (not concrete)* abstracto,-a.
▶ *n (summary)* resumen *m.*

absurd [əb'sɜ:d] *adj* absurdo,-a.

abundance [ə'bʌndəns] *n* abundancia.

abundant [ə'bʌndənt] *adj* abundante.

abuse [*(n)* ə'bju:s; *(vb)* ə'bju:z] *n* **1** *(verbal)* insultos *mpl*; *(physical)* malos tratos *mpl.* **2** *(misuse)* abuso.
▶ *vt* **1** *(verbally)* insultar; *(physically)* maltratar. **2** *(misuse)* abusar de.

abyss [ə'bɪs] *n* abismo.

abysmal [ə'bɪsm°l] *adj* pésimo,-a.

AC ['eɪ'si:] *abbr* ELEC (alternating current) corriente *f* alterna; *(abbreviation)* CA *f.*

academic [ækə'demɪk] *adj* **1** *(gen)* académico,-a. **2** *(theoretical)* teórico: *it's a*

purely academic question es una cuestión puramente teórica.
► *n (scholar)* académico,-a; *(lecturer)* profesor,-ra universitario,-a. COMP
academic year año académico.

academy [əˈkædəmɪ] *n* **1** academia. **2** *(in Scotland)* instituto de enseñanza media.
ⓘ *pl* **academies**.

accelerate [ækˈseləreɪt] *vt* acelerar.
► *vi* acelerarse.

acceleration [ækseləˈreɪʃ°n] *n* aceleración *f*.

accelerator [əkˈseləreɪtəʳ] *n* acelerador *m*.

accent [*(n)* ˈæksənt; *(vb)* ækˈsent] *n* acento.
► *vt* acentuar.

accentuate [ækˈsentʃʊeɪt] *vt* acentuar.

accentuation [æksentʃʊˈeɪʃ°n] *n* acentuación *f*.

accept [əkˈsept] *vt* aceptar, admitir.

acceptable [əkˈseptəb°l] *adj* aceptable, admisible.

acceptance [əkˈseptəns] *n* **1** *(act of accepting)* aceptación *f*. **2** *(approval)* acogida.

access [ˈækses] *n* acceso.
► *vt* COMPUT acceder a, entrar en. COMP
access code código de acceso. ▌**access road** carretera de acceso.

accessibility [æksesɪˈbɪlɪtɪ] *n* accesibilidad *f*.

accessible [ækˈsesɪb°l] *adj* **1** accesible. **2** *(person)* asequible, tratable.

accessory [ækˈsesərɪ] *n* **1** *(gadget)* accesorio. **2** JUR *(accomplice)* cómplice *mf*.
► *n pl* **accessories** *(bag, gloves, etc)* complementos *mpl*.
ⓘ *pl* **accessories**.

accident [ˈæksɪdənt] *n* accidente *m*.
LOC **by accident** por casualidad.

accidental [æksɪˈdent°l] *adj* fortuito,-a.

acclaim [əˈkleɪm] *n* **1** *(welcome)* aclamación *f*. **2** *(praise)* elogios *mpl*, alabanza.
► *vt* **1** *(welcome)* aclamar. **2** *(praise)* elogiar, alabar.

acclimatize [əˈklaɪmətaɪz] *vt* aclimatar.
► *vi* aclimatarse.

accommodate [əˈkɒmədeɪt] *vt* alojar.

accommodation [əkɒməˈdeɪʃ°n] *n* alojamiento.

accomplice [əˈkɒmplɪs] *n* cómplice *mf*.

accomplish [əˈkɒmplɪʃ] *vt* lograr.

accomplishment [əˈkɒmplɪʃmənt] *n* **1** *(act of achieving)* realización *f*. **2** *(achievement)* logro.
► *n pl* **accomplishments** *(skills)* aptitudes *fpl*, dotes *fpl*, habilidades *fpl*.

accord [əˈkɔːd] *n (agreement)* acuerdo: *the Oslo accords* los acuerdos de Oslo. LOC
of one's own accord espontáneamente, por propia voluntad.
► *vt (award)* conceder, otorgar.

✗ To accord no significa 'acordar', que se traduce por **to agree**.

accordance [əˈkɔːd°ns] LOC **in accordance with** de acuerdo con.

according [əˈkɔːdɪŋ] *prep* **according to**
1 según: *according to Philip/the paper/my watch* según Philip/el periódico/mi reloj. **2** *(consistent with)* de acuerdo con: *it went according to plan* salió tal como se había previsto.

accordion [əˈkɔːdɪən] *n* acordeón *m*.

account [əˈkaʊnt] *n* **1** *(in bank)* cuenta. **2** *(report)* relación *f*, relato, informe *m*: *he gave us an account of his experiences* nos contó sus experiencias. LOC **on account of** por, a causa de: *don't leave on my account* no te vayas por mí. ▌**on no account** bajo ningún concepto. ▌**to keep the accounts** llevar las cuentas. ▌**to take into account** tener en cuenta. COMP **accounts department** sección *f* de contabilidad.
◆ **to account for** *vi* explicar.

accountable [əˈkaʊntəb°l] *adj* LOC **to be accountable to SB for STH** ser responsable ante ALGN de ALGO.

accountant [əˈkaʊntənt] *n* contable *mf*.

accumulate [əˈkjuːmjʊleɪt] *vt* acumular.
► *vi* acumularse.

accumulation [əkjuːmjʊˈleɪʃ°n] *n* acumulación *f*.

accumulator [əˈkjuːmjʊleɪtəʳ] *n* acumulador *m*.

accuracy [ˈækjʊrəsɪ] *n* **1** *(of numbers, instrument, information)* exactitud *f*, precisión *f*. **2** *(of shot)* certeza.

accurate ['ækjurət] *adj* **1** *(numbers, etc)* exacto,-a, preciso,-a. **2** *(instrument)* de precisión. **3** *(shot)* certero,-a.

accusation [ækjuː'zeɪʃ^ən] *n* acusación *f*.

accuse [ə'kjuːz] *vt* acusar (of, de).

accused [ə'kjuːzd] *n* **the accused** *(man)* el acusado; *(woman)* la acusada.

accustom [ə'kʌstəm] *vt* acostumbrar (to, a).

accustomed [ə'kʌstəm^əd] *adj* LOC **to be accustomed to** esar acostumbrado a.

ace [eɪs] *n* **1** *(gen)* as *m*. **2** *(tennis)* ace *m*.

acetic [ə'siːtɪk] *adj* acético,-a. COMP **acetic acid** ácido acético.

acetone ['æsɪtəʊn] *n* acetona.

acetylene [ə'setɪliːn] *n* acetileno.

ache [eɪk] *n* dolor *m*.

► *vi* doler: *my head aches* me duele la cabeza, tengo dolor de cabeza.

> ✎ Ache se usa para formar palabras compuestas como **headache** *(dolor de cabeza)*, **toothache** *(dolor de muelas)*, **earache** *(dolor de oídos)* o **stomach-ache** *(dolor de estómago)*.

achieve [ə'tʃiːv] *vt* **1** *(finish)* realizar, llevar a cabo. **2** *(attain)* lograr, conseguir.

achievement [ə'tʃiːvmənt] *n* **1** *(completion)* realización *f*. **2** *(attainment)* logro. **3** *(feat)* hazaña, proeza.

Achilles [ə'kɪliːz] *n* Aquiles. COMP **Achilles' heel** *fig* talón *m* de Aquiles. ‖ **Achilles' tendon** ANAT tendón *m* de Aquiles.

acid ['æsɪd] *adj* **1** CHEM ácido,-a. **2** *(taste)* agrio,-a. COMP **acid rain** lluvia ácida.

► *n* CHEM ácido,-a.

acknowledge [ək'nɒlɪdʒ] *vt* **1** *(admit)* admitir, reconocer. **2** *(be thankful)* agradecer, expresar agradecimiento por. LOC **to acknowledge receipt of** acusar recibo de.

acknowledgement [ək'nɒlɪdʒmənt] *n* **1** *(recognition)* reconocimiento. **2** *(thanks)* muestra de agradecimiento. COMP **acknowledgement of receipt** acuse *m* de recibo.

acknowledgment [æk'nɒlɪdʒmənt] *n* → **acknowledgement.**

acne ['æknɪ] *n* acné *f*.

acorn ['eɪkɔːn] *n* bellota.

acoustic [ə'kuːstɪk] *adj* acústico,-a.

acoustics [ə'kuːstɪks] *n (science)* acústica.

► *n pl (sound conditions)* acústica *f sing*.

acquaint [ə'kweɪnt] *vt* informar (with, de). LOC **to acquaint** SB **with** STH familiarizarse con ALGO. ‖ **to be acquainted with** SB conocer a ALGN, tener trato con ALGN.

acquaintance [ə'kweɪntəns] *n (person)* conocido,-a: *an acquaintance of mine un conocido mío*. LOC **to make** SB**'s acquaintance** conocer a ALGN.

acquiesce [ækwɪ'es] *vi* consentir (in, en), conformarse (in, con).

acquire [ə'kwaɪə^r] *vt* adquirir.

acquisition [ækwɪ'zɪʃ^ən] *n* adquisición *f*.

acquit [ə'kwɪt] *vt* absolver, declarar inocente.

ⓘ *pt & pp* **acquitted**, *ger* **acquitting**.

acquittal [ə'kwɪt^əl] *n* absolución *f*.

acre ['eɪkə^r] *n* acre *m*.

> ✎ Un acre equivale a 40,47 hectáreas.

acrobat ['ækrəbæt] *n* acróbata *mf*.

acrobatic [ækrə'bætɪk] *adj* acrobático,-a.

acronym ['ækrənɪm] *n* sigla.

acropolis [ə'krɒpəlɪs] *n* acrópolis *f*.

across [ə'krɒs] *prep* **1** *(movement)* a través de, de un lado a otro de: *to swim across a river* cruzar un río nadando/a nado. **2** *(position)* al otro lado de: *they live across the road* viven enfrente.

► *adv* de un lado a otro: *it's 4 metres across* mide 4 metros de lado a lado.

> ✎ Con verbos como **walk, run, swim**, etc, se suele traducir por 'cruzar' o 'atravesar'.

acrylic [ə'krɪlɪk] *adj* acrílico,-a.

act [ækt] *n* **1** acto, acción *f*. **2** THEAT acto. **3** *(of parliament)* ley *f*. COMP **act of God** fuerza mayor.

► *vi* **1** *(do something)* actuar. **2** *(behave)* portarse, comportarse: *she acts like a little girl* se comporta como una niña. **3** *(in theatre)* actuar, hacer teatro; *(in cinema)* actuar, hacer cine.

▶ *vt* hacer el papel de: *she's acting (the part of) Portia* ella hace el papel de Portia.
◆ **to act as** *vt insep* hacer de: *I had to act as interpreter* tuve que hacer de intérprete.

acting ['æktɪŋ] *adj* en funciones.
▶ *n* **1** THEAT *(profession)* teatro. **2** *(performance)* interpretación *f*, actuación *f*.

actinium [æk'tɪnɪəm] *n* actinio.

action ['ækʃ°n] *n* **1** *(gen)* acción *f*. **2** JUR demanda. COMP **action replay** repetición *f* de la jugada. ▌ **action stations** zafarrancho de combate.

ⓧ Action no significa 'acción' (de una empresa), que se traduce por share.

activate ['æktɪveɪt] *vt (mechanism, bomb)* activar.

activation [æktɪ'veɪʃ°n] *n (of mechanism, bomb)* activación *f*.

active ['æktɪv] *adj* activo,-a. COMP **the active voice** la voz activa.

activism ['æktɪvɪz°m] *n* activismo.

activist ['æktɪvɪst] *n* activista *mf*.

activity [æk'tɪvɪtɪ] *n* actividad *f*.
ⓘ *pl* **activities**.

actor ['æktər] *n* actor *m*.

actress ['æktrəs] *n* actriz *f*.

actual ['æktʃuəl] *adj* real, verdadero,-a.

ⓧ Actual no significa 'actual', que se traduce por present, current o up-to-date.

actually ['æktjuəlɪ] *adv* **1** en realidad, realmente, de hecho: *I haven't actually decided what to do yet* en realidad, todavía no he decidido qué hacer. **2** *(indicating surprise)* incluso, hasta: *she actually accused me of stealing her bag* hasta me acusó de robarle el bolso.

ⓧ Actually no significa 'actualmente', que se traduce por nowadays, at present.

acupuncture ['ækjupʌnktʃə] *n* acupuntura.

acupuncturist ['ækjupʌnktʃərɪst] *n* acupunturista *mf*.

acute [ə'kjuːt] *adj* **1** *(gen)* agudo,-a. **2** *(angle)* agudo,-a. **3** *(hearing, etc)* muy

fino,-a, muy desarrollado,-a. COMP **acute accent** acento agudo. ▌ **acute triangle** triángulo acutángulo.

AD ['eɪ'diː] *abbr* (Anno Domini) después de Cristo; *(abbreviation)* d.J.C.

ad [æd] *n fam* anuncio.

Adam ['ædəm] *n* Adán *m*. COMP **Adam's apple** nuez *f* (de la garganta).

adamant ['ædəmənt] *adj* firme, inflexible. LOC **to be adamant about** STH mantenerse firme en ALGO.

adapt [ə'dæpt] *vt* adaptar.
▶ *vi* adaptarse.

adaptable [ə'dæptəb°l] *adj (person)* capaz de adaptarse.

adaptation [ædəp'teɪʃ°n] *n* adaptación *f*.

adapter [ə'dæptər] *n* ELEC → **adaptor**.

adaptor [ə'dæptər] *n* ELEC ladrón *m*.

add [æd] *vt* **1** *(gen)* añadir, agregar. **2** *(numbers)* sumar.
◆ **to add to** *vt insep* aumentar.
◆ **to add up** *vt sep (numbers)* sumar.
▶ *vi fig* cuadrar: *there's something funny going on; it doesn't add up* pasa algo raro; es que no cuadra.

addend ['ædənd] *n* MAT sumando.

adder ['ædər] *n* ZOOL víbora.

addict ['ædɪkt] *n* **1** adicto,-a. **2** *fam (fanatic)* fanático,-a.

addicted [ə'dɪktɪd] *adj* adicto,-a.

addiction [ə'dɪkʃ°n] *n* adicción *f*.

addictive [ə'dɪktɪv] *adj* que crea adicción: *nicotine is addictive* la nicotina crea adicción.

addition [ə'dɪʃ°n] *n* **1** adición *f*, añadidura. **2** MATH adición *f*, suma. LOC **in addition to** además de.

additional [ə'dɪʃən°l] *adj* adicional.

additive ['ædɪtɪv] *n* aditivo.

additive-free ['ædɪtɪv'friː] *adj* sin aditivos.

address [ə'dres] *n* **1** *(on letter)* dirección *f*, señas *fpl*. **2** *(speech)* discurso, alocución *f*.
▶ *vt* **1** *(problem)* abordar. **2** *(person)* dirigirse a. COMP **address book** libro de direcciones. ▌ **form of address** tratamiento.

adductor [ə'dʌktər] *n* ANAT aductor,-ra.

adenoids ['ædənɔɪdz] *n pl* adenoides *mpl*, vegetaciones *fpl*.

adept [ə'dept] *adj* experto,-a, diestro,-a.

❌ Adept no significa 'adepto, seguidor', que se traducen por **follower, supporter**.

adequate ['ædɪkwət] *adj* **1** *(enough)* suficiente. **2** *(satisfactory)* satisfactorio,-a.

adhere [əd'hɪər] *vi* *(stick)* adherirse, pegarse.

adherent [əd'hɪərənt] *adj* adherente.

adhesive [əd'hiːsɪv] *adj* adhesivo,-a.
▶ *n* adhesivo.

adipose ['ædɪpəʊz] *adj* adiposo,-a.

adjacent [ə'dʒeɪsənt] *adj* adyacente.
COMP **adjacent angles** ángulos adyacentes.

adjective ['ædʒɪktɪv] *n* adjetivo.

adjoin [ə'dʒɔɪn] *vt* lindar con.
▶ *vi* colindar.

adjoining [ə'dʒɔɪnɪŋ] *adj* **1** *(building)* contiguo,-a. **2** *(land)* colindante.

adjourn [ə'dʒɜːn] *vt* aplazar, suspender.
▶ *vi* suspenderse.

adjournment [ə'dʒɜːnmənt] *n* aplazamiento, suspensión *f*.

adjust [ə'dʒʌst] *vt* ajustar, arreglar.
▶ *vi* *(person)* adaptarse.

adjustable [ə'dʒʌstəbəl] *adj* regulable.
COMP **adjustable spanner** llave *f* inglesa.

adjustment [ə'dʒʌstmənt] *n* **1** ajuste *m*, arreglo. **2** *(person)* adaptación *f*. **3** *(change)* cambio.

administer [əd'mɪnɪstər] *vt* **1** *(control)* administrar. **2** *(give)* administrar, dar; *(laws, punishment)* aplicar.

administration [ədmɪnɪs'treɪʃən] *n* **1** administración *f*. **2** *(of law, etc)* aplicación *f*.

administrator [əd'mɪnɪstreɪtər] *n* administrador,-ra.

admirable ['ædmɪrəbəl] *adj* admirable.

admiral ['ædmərəl] *n* almirante *m*.

admiration [ædmɪ'reɪʃən] *n* admiración *f*.

admire [əd'maɪər] *vt* admirar.

admirer [əd'maɪərər] *n* *(gen)* admirador,-ra; *(suitor)* pretendiente *mf*.

admissible [əd'mɪsɪbəl] *adj* admisible.

admission [əd'mɪʃən] *n* **1** *(gen)* admisión *f*; *(to hospital)* ingreso. **2** *(price)* entrada. **3** *(acknowledgement)* reconocimiento.

admit [əd'mɪt] *vt* **1** *(allow in)* admitir; *(to hospital)* ingresar. **2** *(acknowledge)* reconocer.
ⓘ *pt & pp* **admitted**, *ger* **admitting**.

admittance [əd'mɪtəns] *n* entrada. LOC «**No admittance**» «Prohibida la entrada».

admittedly [əd'mɪtɪdlɪ] *adv* es verdad que, lo cierto es que.

admonish [əd'mɒnɪʃ] *vt* amonestar.

ado [ə'duː] *n* LOC **without further ado** sin más preámbulos.

adobe [ə'dəʊbɪ] *n* adobe *m*.

adolescence [ædə'lesəns] *n* adolescencia.

adolescent [ædə'lesənt] *adj* adolescente.
▶ *n* adolescente *mf*.

adopt [ə'dɒpt] *vt* adoptar.

adoption [ə'dɒpʃən] *n* adopción *f*.

adoptive [ə'dɒptɪv] *adj* adoptivo,-a.

adore [ə'dɔːr] *vt* adorar.

adorn [ə'dɔːn] *vt* adornar.

adrenalin [ə'drenəlɪn] *n* adrenalina.

Adriatic [eɪdrɪ'ætɪk] *adj* adriático,-a. COMP **the Adriatic (Sea)** el (mar) Adriático.

adrift [ə'drɪft] *adj* a la deriva.

adulate ['ædjʊleɪt] *vt* adular.

adult ['ædʌlt] *adj* **1** *(gen)* adulto,-a. **2** *(film, etc)* para adultos.
▶ *n* adulto,-a.

adulterate [ə'dʌltəreɪt] *vt* adulterar.

adultery [ə'dʌltərɪ] *n* adulterio.

advance [əd'vɑːns] *n* **1** *(gen)* avance *m*. **2** *(payment)* anticipo. LOC **in advance 1** *(gen)* antes. **2** *(rent, etc)* por adelantado.
▶ *vt* **1** *(gen)* avanzar. **2** *(money, date)* adelantar.

advantage [əd'vɑːntɪdʒ] *n* **1** ventaja. **2** *(benefit)* provecho. LOC **to take advantage of 1** *(thing)* aprovechar. **2** *(person)* aprovecharse de.

advantageous [ædvən'teɪdʒəs] *adj* ventajoso,-a, provechoso,-a.

adventure [əd'ventʃəʳ] *n* aventura. COMP **adventure playground** parque *m* infantil.

adverb ['ædvɜːb] *n* adverbio.

adversary ['ædvəsərɪ] *n* adversario,-a. ① *pl* adversaries.

adversative [æd'vɜːsətɪv] *adj* adversativo,-a.

adverse ['ædvɜːs] *adj* desfavorable.

adversity [əd'vɜːsɪtɪ] *n* adversidad *f*. ① *pl* adversities.

advert ['ædvɜːt] *n* fam anuncio.

advertise ['ædvətaɪz] *vt* anunciar.
▶ *vi* hacer publicidad.

advertisement [əd'vɜːtɪsmənt] *n* anuncio.
▶ *n pl* **advertisements** *(on television)* publicidad *f*, anuncios *mpl*.

🗙 Advertisement no significa 'advertencia', que se traduce por warning.

advertiser ['ædvətaɪzəʳ] *n* anunciante *mf*.

advertising ['ædvətaɪzɪŋ] *n* publicidad *f*. COMP **advertising agency** agencia de publicidad. ▮ **advertising campaign** campaña publicitaria.

advice [əd'vaɪs] *n* consejos *mpl*. COMP **a piece of advice** un consejo.

advise [əd'vaɪz] *vt* aconsejar.

🗙 To advise no significa 'avisar', que se traduce por to warn.

adviser [əd'vaɪzəʳ] *n* consejero,-a.

advocate [*(n)* 'ædvəkət; *(vb)* 'ædvəkeɪt] *n* **1** *(supporter)* partidario,-a. **2** *(lawyer)* abogado,-a defensor,-ra.
▶ *vt* abogar por, propugnar.

Aegean [ɪ'dʒiːən] *adj* egeo,-a. COMP **the Aegean (Sea)** el (mar) Egeo.

aerial ['eərɪəl] *adj* aéreo,-a.
▶ *n* antena.

aerobe ['eərəʊb] *n* aerobio.

aerobics [eə'rəʊbɪks] *n* aerobic *m*, aeróbic *m*.

aerodrome ['eərədrəʊm] *n* aeródromo.

aerodynamics [eərəʊdaɪ'næmɪks] *n* aerodinámica.

aeronautics [eərə'nɔːtɪks] *n* aeronáutica.

aeroplane ['eərəpleɪn] *n* aeroplano, avión *m*.

aerosol ['eərəsɒl] *n* aerosol *m*.

aerostatic [eərə'stætɪk] *adj* aerostático,-a.

aesthetic [iːs'θetɪk] *adj* estético,-a.

aesthetics [iːs'θetɪks] *n* estética.

affair [ə'feəʳ] *n* **1** *(matter)* asunto: *that's your affair* eso es asunto tuyo. **2** *(case)* caso: *the Watergate affair* el caso Watergate. COMP **current affairs** actualidad *f sing*.

affect [ə'fekt] *vt* **1** *(gen)* afectar. **2** *(feign)* fingir, afectar: *he affected indifference* fingió indiferencia.

affection [ə'fekʃən] *n* afecto, cariño.

affectionate [ə'fekʃənət] *adj* afectuoso,-a, cariñoso,-a.

affiliate [ə'fɪlɪət] *n* afiliado,-a.
▶ *vt* afiliar.
▶ *vi* afiliar.

affinity [ə'fɪnɪtɪ] *n* afinidad *f*. ① *pl* affinities.

affirm [ə'fɜːm] *vt* afirmar, asegurar.

affirmation [æfə'meɪʃən] *n* afirmación *f*.

affirmative [ə'fɜːmətɪv] *adj* afirmativo,-a.

affix [ə'fɪks] *vt* *(stamp)* poner; *(poster)* fijar.

afflict [ə'flɪkt] *vt* afligir.

affluence ['æfluəns] *n* riqueza, prosperidad *f*.

affluent ['æfluənt] *adj* rico,-a.

afford [ə'fɔːd] *vt* permitirse, costear: *I can't afford to pay £750 for a coat* no puedo (permitirme) pagar 750 libras por un abrigo.

afforestation [əfɒrɪ'steɪʃən] *n* repoblación *f* forestal.

affricate ['æfrɪkət] *n* africada.

Afghan ['æfgæn] *adj* afgano,-a.
▶ *n* **1** *(person)* afgano,-a. **2** *(language)* afgano.

Afghanistan [æfgænɪ'stæn] *n* Afganistán *m*.

afield [ə'fiːld] *adv* LOC **far afield** lejos: *they went as far afield as Canada* llegaron hasta Canadá.

afloat [əˈfləʊt] *adj* a flote.

afoot [əˈfʊt] *adv* en marcha, en proceso.

afraid [əˈfreɪd] *adj* temeroso,-a. LOC **to be afraid 1** *(frightened)* tener miedo. **2** *(sorry)* temer, sentir, lamentar: *I'm afraid so/not* me temo que sí/no. ▌**to be afraid of** STH/SB tener miedo de ALGO/ALGN.

afresh [əˈfreʃ] *adv* de nuevo: *he had to start afresh* tuvo que volver a empezar.

África [ˈæfrɪkə] *n* África. COMP **South Africa** Sudáfrica.

African [ˈæfrɪkən] *adj* africano,-a. ▸ *n* africano,-a. COMP **South African** sudafricano,-a.

Afro [ˈæfrəʊ] *adj & n (hairstyle)* afro.

Afro-American [æfrəʊəˈmerɪkən] *adj* afroamericano,-a. ▸ *n* afroamericano,-a.

⊕ Afro-American es el término más adecuado para referirse a los estadounidenses cuyos antepasados eran originarios del África subsahariana y que, en su mayoría, fueron llevados como esclavos a América entre los siglos XVI y XIX.

after [ˈɑːftər] *prep* **1** *(time)* después de: *after class* después de la clase. **2** *(following)* detrás de: *the police are after us* la policía nos está persiguiendo. **3** US *(past)* y: *it's a quarter after four* son las cuatro y cuarto. ▸ *adv* después: *the day after* el día después. ▸ *conj* después que, después de que: *after he left, I went to bed* después de que se marchara, me acosté. ▸ *n pl* **afters** GB *fam* postre *m*.

afterbirth [ˈɑːftəbɜːθ] *n* placenta.

after-effect [ˈɑːftərɪfekt] *n* efecto secundario, secuela.

afterlife [ˈɑːftəlaɪf] *n* más allá *m*.

afternoon [ɑːftəˈnuːn] *n* tarde *f*: *in the afternoon* por la tarde.

after-sales service [ɑːftəˈseɪlzsɜːvɪs] *n* servicio posventa.

aftershave [ˈɑːftəʃeɪv] *n* loción *f* para después del afeitado.

aftertaste [ˈɑːftəteɪst] *n* regusto.

afterwards [ˈɑːftəwədz] *adv* después, luego.

again [əˈgen, əˈgeɪn] *adv* **1** *(once more)* otra vez, de nuevo: *play me that song again* tócame esa canción otra vez. **2** *(in questions)*: *where do you live again?* ¿dónde has dicho que vives? LOC **again and again** repetidamente. ▌**now and again** de vez en cuando.

against [əˈgenst, əˈgeɪnst] *prep* **1** *(gen)* contra: *against the wall* contra la pared; *Leeds played against Liverpool* Leeds jugó contra Liverpool. **2** *(opposed to)* en contra de: *I voted against the proposal* voté en contra de la propuesta.

age [eɪdʒ] *n* edad *f*. LOC **of age** mayor de edad. ▌**under age** menor de edad. ▸ *vt & vi* envejecer.

aged [eɪdʒd] *adj* de (tantos años de) edad: *a boy aged ten* un muchacho de diez años. COMP **the aged** los ancianos *mpl*.

agency [ˈeɪdʒənsɪ] *n* **1** *(commercial)* agencia: *a travel/advertising/employment agency* una agencia de viajes/publicidad/empleo. **2** *(governmental, etc)* organismo. ① *pl* agencies.

agenda [əˈdʒendə] *n* orden *m* del día.

✖ Agenda no significa 'agenda', que se traduce por diary.

agent [ˈeɪdʒənt] *n* agente *mf*.

aggravate [ˈægrəveɪt] *vt* **1** *(make worse)* agravar. **2** *fam (annoy)* irritar, molestar.

aggression [əˈgreʃən] *n* **1** *(act)* agresión *f*. **2** *(feeling)* agresividad *f*.

aggressive [əˈgresɪv] *adj* **1** *(gen)* agresivo,-a. **2** *(dynamic)* emprendedor,-ra.

aggressor [əˈgresər] *n* agresor,-ra.

aghast [əˈgɑːst] *adj* horrorizado,-a.

agile [ˈædʒaɪl] *adj* ágil.

agility [əˈdʒɪlɪtɪ] *n* agilidad *f*.

agitate [ˈædʒɪteɪt] *vt* agitar.

agnostic [ægˈnɒstɪk] *adj* agnóstico,-a. ▸ *n* agnóstico,-a.

ago [əˈgəʊ] *adv* hace: *ten days ago* hace diez días; *it happened a long time ago* ocurrió hace mucho tiempo.

✎ Ago se usa siempre con el verbo en pasado. Consulta también for, since.

agonise [ˈægənaɪz] *vi* → agonize.

agonize ['ægənaɪz] *vi* agonizar.
agony ['ægənɪ] *n* **1** *(pain)* dolor *m* muy agudo. **2** *(anguish)* angustia.
ⓘ *pl* agonies.

❌ Agony no significa 'agonía (antes de morir)', que se traduce por **dying breath**.

agora ['ægərə] *n* ágora.
ⓘ *pl* agoras o agorae ['ægəraɪ, 'ægəriː].
agree [ə'griː] *vi* **1** *(be in agreement)* estar de acuerdo (with, con): *do you agree with me?* ¿estás de acuerdo conmigo? **2** *(reach an agreement)* ponerse de acuerdo (on, en): *they can't agree on a name for the baby* no se ponen de acuerdo en el nombre del bebé. **4** *(food, climate, etc)* sentar bien (with, -): *the prawns didn't agree with me* las gambas no me sentaron bien.
▶ *vt (grammatically)* concordar (with, con).
agreeable [ə'griːəbəl] *adj* **1** *(pleasant)* agradable. **2** *(in agreement)* conforme.
agreement [ə'griːmənt] *n* **1** acuerdo: *the two men reached an agreement* los dos hombres llegaron a un acuerdo. **2** *(grammatical)* concordancia.
agricultural [ægrɪ'kʌltʃərəl] *adj* agrícola.
agriculture ['ægrɪkʌltʃəʳ] *n* agricultura.
agronomy [ə'grɒnəmɪ] *n* agronomía.
aground [ə'graʊnd] *adj* encallado,-a.
ᴸᴼᶜ **to run aground** encallar.
ahead [ə'hed] *adv (in front)* delante: *there's a police checkpoint ahead* hay un control de policía aquí delante; *we finished ahead of schedule* acabamos antes de lo previsto. ᴸᴼᶜ **go ahead!** ¡adelante!
aid [eɪd] *n (help)* ayuda; *(rescue)* auxilio.
ᶜᴼᴹᴾ **humanitarian aid** ayuda humanitaria.
▶ *vt* ayudar, auxiliar.
AIDS [eɪdz] *n* (Acquired Immune Deficiency Syndrome) sida *m*.
aileron ['eɪlərɒn] *n* alerón *m*.
ailing ['eɪlɪŋ] *adj* enfermo,-a.
ailment ['eɪlmənt] *n* dolencia, achaque *m*.
aim [eɪm] *n* **1** *(marksmanship)* puntería: *his aim is good* tiene buena puntería. **2** *(objective)* meta, objetivo: *what's your aim in life?* ¿qué objetivo tienes en la vida?

▶ *vt* **1** *(gun)* apuntar (at, a). **2** *(attack)* dirigir (at, a).
ain't [eɪnt] *contr fam* → am not, is not, are not, has not, have not.
air [eəʳ] *n* aire *m*. ᴸᴼᶜ **by air 1** *(send letter)* por avión. **2** *(travel)* en avión. ᶜᴼᴹᴾ **air hostess** azafata. **air lane** ruta aérea. **air pressure** presión *f* atmosférica. **air rifle** escopeta de aire comprimido. **air terminal** terminal *f* aérea. **air traffic controller** controlador,-ra aéreo,-a.
▶ *vt* **1** *(gen)* airear. **2** *(room)* ventilar.
airbag ['eəbæg] *n* airbag *m*.
airbase ['eəbeɪs] *n* base *f* aérea.
air-bed ['eəbed] *n* GB colchón *m* de aire.
air-conditioned [eəkən'dɪʃ°nd] *adj* con aire acondicionado, refrigerado,-a.
air-conditioning [eəkən'dɪʃ°nɪŋ] *n* aire *m* acondicionado.
aircraft ['eəkrɑːft] *n (gen)* aeronave *f*; *(plane)* avión *m*.
ⓘ *pl* aircraft.
aircraft-carrier ['eəkrɑːtkæriəʳ] *n* portaaviones *m inv*.
airfield ['eəfiːld] *n* campo de aviación.
airforce ['eəfɔːs] *n* fuerza aérea, fuerzas *fpl* aéreas.
airline ['eəlaɪn] *n* línea aérea.
airliner ['eəlaɪnəʳ] *n* avión *m* de pasajeros *(grande)*.
airmail ['eəmeɪl] *n* correo aéreo.
airplane ['eəpleɪn] *n* US aeroplano, avión *m*.
airport ['eəpɔːt] *n* aeropuerto.
airship ['eəʃɪp] *n* dirigible *m*.
airsick ['eəsɪk] *adj* mareado,-a. ᴸᴼᶜ **to be airsick** marearse.
airspace ['eəspeɪs] *n* espacio aéreo.
airstrip ['eəstrɪp] *n* pista de aterrizaje.
airtight ['eətaɪt] *adj* hermético,-a.
airway ['eəweɪ] *n* **1** *(route)* ruta aérea, vía aérea. **2** *(airline)* línea aérea.
airy ['eərɪ] *adj* **1** *(ventilated)* bien ventilado,-a. **2** *(light)* ligero,-a.
ⓘ *comp* airier, *superl* airiest.
aisle [aɪl] *n* **1** *(between seats, shelves, etc)* pasillo. **2** *(section of church)* nave *f* lateral.
aitch [eɪtʃ] *n* hache *f*.

ajar [ə'dʒɑːʳ] *adj* entreabierto,-a.

akimbo [ə'kɪmbəʊ] *adv* en jarras.

akin [ə'kɪn] *adj* parecido,-a (to, a).

alabaster ['æləbɑːstəʳ] *n* alabastro.

alarm [ə'lɑːm] *n* **1** *(device)* alarma. **2** *(fear)* temor *m*, alarma. [COMP] **alarm clock** despertador *m*.
  ► *vt* alarmar, asustar.

alarmism [ə'lɑːmɪzᵊm] *n* alarmismo.

Albanian [æl'beɪnɪən] *adj* albanés,-esa.
  ► *n* **1** *(person)* albanés,-esa. **2** *(language)* albanés *m*.

albatross ['ælbətrɒs] *n* albatros *m*.

albino [æl'biːnəʊ] *adj* albino,-a.
  ► *n* albino,-a.
  ⓘ *pl* albinos.

album ['ælbəm] *n* álbum *m*.

albumen ['ælbjʊmɪn, US æl'bjuːmən] *n* **1** *(white of egg)* clara de huevo. **2** *(in plants)* albumen *m*.

albumin ['ælbjʊmɪn, US æl'bjuːmən] *n* albúmina.

alcohol ['ælkəhɒl] *n* alcohol *m*.

alcohol-free ['ælkəhɒlfriː] *adj* sin alcohol.

alcoholism ['ælkəhɒlɪzᵊm] *n* alcoholismo.

aldehyde ['ældɪhaɪd] *n* aldehído.

ale [eɪl] *n* cerveza.

alert [ə'lɜːt] *adj* **1** *(quick to act)* alerta, vigilante. **2** *(lively)* vivo,-a.
  ► *n* alarma.
  ► *vt* alertar, avisar.

A-level ['eɪlevᵊl] *abbr* GB (Advanced level) ≈ segundo curso de bachillerato.

alfalfa [æl'fælfə] *n* alfalfa.

algae ['æ.ldʒiː] *n pl* algas *fpl*.
  ⓘ *sing* alga ['ælgə].

algebra ['ældʒɪbrə] *n* álgebra.

algebraic [ældʒɪ'breɪɪk] *adj* algebraico,-a.

Algeria [æl'dʒɪərɪə] *n* Argelia.

Algerian [æl'dʒɪərɪən] *adj* argelino,-a.
  ► *n* argelino,-a.

algorithm ['ælgərɪðᵊm] *n* algoritmo.

alias ['eɪlɪəs] *adv* alias.
  ► *n* alias *m*.

alibi ['ælɪbaɪ] *n* coartada.

alien ['eɪlɪən] *adj* **1** *(foreign)* extranjero,-a. **2** *(extraterrestrial)* extraterrestre. **3** *(strange)* extraño,-a, ajeno,-a: *his ideas are alien to me* sus ideas me son ajenas.
  ► *n* **1** *(foreigner)* extranjero,-a. **2** *(extraterrestrial)* extraterrestre *mf*.

alight [ə'laɪt] *adj* encendido,-a, ardiendo.

align [ə'laɪn] *vt* alinear (with, con).

alike [ə'laɪk] *adj (the same)* iguales; *(similar)* parecidos,-as: *they are alike in all respects* son iguales en todo.
  ► *adv* igual: *they dress alike* visten igual.

alimentary [ælɪ'mentᵊrɪ] *adj* alimenticio,-a. [COMP] **alimentary canal** tubo digestivo.

alimony ['ælɪmənɪ] *n* pensión *f* alimenticia.

alive [ə'laɪv] *adj* vivo,-a.

alkaline ['ælkəlaɪn] *adj* alcalino,-a.

all [ɔːl] *adj (singular)* todo,-a; *(plural)* todos,-as: *all the chairs* todas las sillas; *all day/month/year* todo el día/mes/año.
  ► *pron* **1** *(everything)* todo, la totalidad *f*: *all was lost in the fire* se perdió todo en el incendio. **2** *(everybody)* todos *mpl*, todo el mundo: *all of them helped/they all helped* ayudaron todos.
  ► *adv* completamente, totalmente: *she was dressed all in leather* iba vestida toda de cuero. [LOC] **after all 1** *(despite everything)* después de todo. **2** *(it must be remembered)* no hay que olvidarlo. **‖ all over** en todas partes. **‖ to be all over** acabar: *in ten minutes it was all over* en diez minutos todo había acabado. **‖ all right 1** *(acceptable)* bien, bueno,-a: *the film's all right, but I've seen better ones* la película no está mal, pero las he visto mejores. **2** *(well, safe)* bien: *are you all right?* ¿estás bien? **3** *(accepting suggestion)* vale, bueno: *are you coming? –all right* ¿te vienes? –vale. **‖ all that** tan: *he's not all that fast* no es tan rápido. **‖ all the + comp** tanto + *adj/adv*, aún + *adj/adv*: *all the better* tanto mejor. **‖ all the time** todo el rato, siempre. **‖ at all** en absoluto. **‖ in all** en total. **‖ not at all** no hay de qué.

Allah ['ælə] *n* Alá *m*.

alleged [ə'ledʒd] *adj* presunto,-a.

allegory ['ælɪgərɪ] *n* alegoría.
  ⓘ *pl* allegories.

allergic [əˈlɜːdʒɪk] *adj* alérgico,-a (**to**, a).
allergy [ˈælədʒɪ] *n* alergia.
 ① *pl* allergies.
alleviate [əˈliːvɪeɪt] *vt* aliviar, mitigar.
alley [ˈælɪ] *n* callejuela, callejón *m*.
alliance [əˈlaɪəns] *n* alianza.
allied [ˈælaɪd] *adj* **1** POL aliado,-a. **2** *(related)* relacionado,-a, afín.
alligator [ˈælɪɡeɪtə'] *n* caimán *m*.
alliteration [əlɪtəˈreɪʃ°n] *n* aliteración *f*.
allocate [ˈæləkeɪt] *vt (money)* destinar; *(time, space, job, etc)* asignar.
allocation [æləˈkeɪʃ°n] *n* **1** *(distribution)* asignación *f*; *(of money)* distribución *f*. **2** *(money given)* cuota.
allot [əˈlɒt] *vt* asignar.
 ① *pt & pp* allotted, *ger* allotting.
all-out [ɔːˈlaʊt] *adj* total.
allow [əˈlaʊ] *vt* **1** *(permit)* permitir, dejar. **2** *(set aside)* conceder, dar, dejar. **3** *(admit)* admitir, reconocer.
 ◆ **to allow for** *vt insep* tener en cuenta.
allowance [əˈlaʊəns] *n* **1** *(from government)* subsidio, prestación *f*. **2** *(from employer)* dietas *fpl*, asignación *f*. **3** US *(pocket money)* paga semanal. LOC **to make allowances for 1** *(take into account)* tener en cuenta. **2** *(be permissive)* tener paciencia con.
alloy [ˈælɔɪ] *n* aleación *f*.
all-purpose [ɔːˈlpɜːpəs] *adj* multiuso.
all-star [ˈɔːlstɑː'] *adj* estelar: *an all-star cast* un reparto estelar.
all-terrain [ɔːlˈterreɪn] *adj* todo terreno.
allude [əˈluːd] *vi* aludir (**to**, a).
allure [əˈljʊə'] *n* atractivo, encanto.
 ► *vt* atraer, seducir.
alluring [əˈljʊərɪŋ] *adj* seductor,-ra.
allusion [əˈluːʒ°n] *n* alusión *f*.
alluvial [əˈluːvɪəl] *adj* aluvial.
ally [ˈælaɪ] *n* aliado,-a.
 ① *pl* allies.
 ► *vt* aliar (**with**, con).
 ► *vi* aliarse (**with**, con).
 ① *pt & pp* allied, *ger* allying.
almighty [ɔːlˈmaɪtɪ] *adj* todopoderoso,-a.
 ► *n* the Almighty el Todopoderoso.

almond [ˈɑːmənd] *n* almendra. COMP almond tree almendro.
almost [ˈɔːlməʊst] *adv* casi.
alone [əˈləʊn] *adj (unaccompanied)* solo,-a.
 ► *adv (only)* solo, solamente. LOC **to leave STH alone** no tocar ALGO. I **to leave SB alone** dejar a ALGN en paz.
along [əˈlɒŋ] *prep* **1** por, a lo largo de: *we walked along the riverbank* caminamos por la orilla del río. **2** *(in)* en: *his office is along this corridor* su despacho está en este pasillo.
 ► *adv* adelante, hacia adelante: *move along, please* circulen, por favor. LOC **along with** junto con. I **come along 1** *(sing)* ven. **2** *(plural)* venid.
alongside [əlɒŋˈsaɪd] *prep* al lado de.
 ► *adv* al costado, al lado.
aloof [əˈluːf] *adj* distante.
 ► *adv* a distancia.
alopecia [æləˈpiːʃə] *n* alopecia.
aloud [əˈlaʊd] *adv* en voz alta.
alpha [ˈælfə] *n* alfa. COMP alpha ray rayo alfa.
alphabet [ˈælfəbet] *n* alfabeto, abecedario.
alphabetical [ælfəˈbetɪk°l] *adj* alfabético,-a. LOC **in alphabetical order** por orden alfabético.
alphanumeric [ælfənjuˈmerɪk] *adj* alfanumérico,-a.
alpine [ˈælpaɪn] *adj* alpino,-a.
Alps [ælps] *n pl* the Alps los Alpes *mpl*.
already [ɔːlˈredɪ] *adv* ya: *they've already left* ya se han ido.
also [ˈɔːlsəʊ] *adv* también.
altar [ˈɔːltə'] *n* altar *m*.
altarpiece [ˈɔːltəpiːs] *n* retablo.
alter [ˈɔːltə'] *vt (gen)* cambiar; *(clothes)* arreglar.
 ► *vi* cambiar, cambiarse.
alteration [ɔːltəˈreɪʃ°n] *n* modificación *f*.
 ► *n pl* alterations reformas *fpl*.
alternate [*(adj)* ɔːlˈtɜːnət; *(vb)* ɔːlˈtɜːneɪt] *adj* alterno,-a.
 ► *vt* alternar.
 ► *vi* alternarse.

alternating [ˈɔːltɜːneɪtɪŋ] COMP alternating current corriente *f* alterna.

alternative [ɔːˈltɜːnətɪv] *adj* alternativo,-a.
▶ *n (option)* opción *f*, alternativa.

alternator [ˈɔːltəneɪtəʳ] *n* alternador *m*.

although [ɔːlˈðəʊ] *conj* aunque.

altimeter [ˈæltɪmiːtəʳ] *n* altímetro.

altitude [ˈæltɪtjuːd] *n* altitud *f*, altura.

altogether [ɔːltəˈgeðəʳ] *adv* **1** *(completely)* del todo. **2** *(on the whole)* en conjunto. **3** *(in total)* en total.

altruism [ˈæltruɪzᵊm] *n* altruismo.

aluminium [æljuˈmɪnɪəm] *n* aluminio. COMP **aluminium foil** papel *m* de aluminio, papel *m* de plata.

aluminum [əˈluːmɪnəm] *n* US aluminio.

alveolar [ælvɪˈəʊləʳ] *adj* alveolar. COMP **alveolar sacs** ANAT sacos alveolares.

alveolus [ælˈvɪələs] *n* alveolo, alvéolo.
① *pl* **alveoli** [ælˈvɪəlaɪ].

always [ˈɔːlweɪz] *adv* siempre.

am [æm] *pres* → **be**.

a.m. [ˈeɪˈem] *abbr* **(ante meridiem)** de la mañana.

amass [əˈmæs] *vt* acumular.

amateur [ˈæmətəʳ] *adj* aficionado,-a.
▶ *n* aficionado, -a.

amateurism [ˈæmətʃərɪzᵊm] *n* amateurismo.

amaze [əˈmeɪz] *vt* asombrar, pasmar.

amazement [əˈmeɪzmənt] *n* asombro, pasmo.

amazing [əˈmeɪzɪŋ] *adj* asombroso,-a, pasmoso,-a.

Amazon [ˈæməzᵊn] *n* **the Amazon 1** *(river)* el Amazonas *m*. **2** *(basin)* Amazonia.

ambassador [æmˈbæsədəʳ] *n* embajador,-ra.

amber [ˈæmbəʳ] *n* ámbar *m*.
▶ *adj* ámbar.

ambience [ˈæmbɪəns] *n* ambiente *m*.

ambiguity [æmbɪˈgjuːɪtɪ] *n* ambigüedad *f*.
① *pl* **ambiguities**.

ambiguous [æmˈbɪgjuəs] *adj* ambiguo,-a.

ambition [æmˈbɪʃᵊn] *n* ambición *f*.

ambitious [æmˈbɪʃəs] *adj* ambicioso,-a.

ambulance [ˈæmbjʊləns] *n* ambulancia.

ambush [ˈæmbʊʃ] *n* emboscada.
▶ *vt* poner una emboscada a.

ameba [əˈmiːbə] *n* US → **amoeba**.

ameliorate [əˈmiːlɪəreɪt] *vt* mejorarse.
▶ *vi* mejorar.

amelioration [əmiːlɪəˈreɪʃᵊn] *n* mejora.

amen [ɑːˈmen] *interj* amén.

amenable [əˈmiːnəbᵊl] *adj* tratable, bien dispuesto,-a.

amend [əˈmend] *vt (law)* enmendar; *(error)* corregir.

amendment [əˈmendmənt] *n* enmienda.

amenities [əˈmiːnɪtɪz] *n pl* servicios *mpl*, prestaciones *fpl*.

America [əˈmerɪkə] *n* América. COMP **Central America** América Central, Centroamérica. ❙ **Latin America** América Latina, Latinoamérica. ❙ **North America** América del Norte, Norteamérica. ❙ **South America** América del Sur, Sudamérica.

✎ Los estadounidenses suelen referirse a su propio país (Estados Unidos), como America y a ellos, como Americans.

American [əˈmerɪkən] *adj* **1** *(gen)* americano,-a. **2** *(from USA)* estadounidense. COMP **American football** fútbol *m* americano.
▶ *n* **1** *(gen)* americano,-a. **2** *(from USA)* estadounidense *mf*.

⊕ En Estados Unidos, llaman football al fútbol americano (más parecido al rugby que al fútbol europeo) y denominan soccer a lo que nosotros llamamos «fútbol».

americium [æməˈrɪsɪəm] *n* americio.

amethyst [ˈæməθɪst] *n* amatista.

amiable [ˈeɪmɪəbᵊl] *adj* afable, amable.

amicable [ˈæmɪkəbᵊl] *adj* amistoso,-a, amigable.

amid [əˈmɪd] *prep* en medio de, entre.

amidst [əˈmɪdst] *prep* → **amid**.

amine [əˈmiːn] *n* amina.

amino acid [æmiːnəʊ'æsɪd] *n* aminoácido.

amiss [ə'mɪs] *adv* mal. LOC **to take amiss** tomar a mal.

ammonia [ə'məʊnɪ] *n* amoníaco.

ammunition [æmjʊ'nɪʃʰn] *n* municiones *fpl*.

amnesia [əm'niːzɪə] *n* amnesia.

amnesty ['æmnəstɪ] *n* amnistía.
ⓘ *pl* amnesties.

amniotic [æmnɪ'ɒtɪk] *adj* amniótico,-a.

amoeba [æ'miːbə] *n* ameba.
ⓘ *pl* amoebae [ə'miːbiː].

amok [ə'mɒk] LOC **to run amok** volverse loco,-a y causar destrozos.

among [ə'mʌŋ] *prep* entre.

amongst [ə'mʌŋst] *prep* → **among**.

amorphous [ə'mɔːfəs] *adj* amorfo,-a.

amount [ə'maʊnt] *n* cantidad *f*.
◆ **to amount to** *vt insep* **1** ascender a. **2** *fig* equivaler a.

amp [æmp] *n* (*abbr of* ampere) amperio, ampere *m*.

ampere ['æmpeəʳ] *n* amperio.

amphetamine [æm'fetəmiːn] *n* anfetamina.

amphibian [æm'fɪbɪən] *n* anfibio.

amphibious [æm'fɪbɪəs] *adj* anfibio,-a.

amphitheater ['æmfɪθɪətəʳ] *n* US anfiteatro.

amphitheatre ['æmfɪθɪətəʳ] *n* anfiteatro.

amphora ['æmfərə] *n* ánfora.
ⓘ *pl* amphoras o amphorae ['æmfəriː].

ample ['æmpʰl] *adj* **1** (*enough*) bastante. **2** (*plenty*) más que suficiente. **3** (*large, generous*) amplio,-a.

amplification [æmplɪfɪ'keɪʃʰn] *n* amplificación *f*.

amplifier ['æmplɪfaɪəʳ] *n* amplificador *m*.

amplify ['æmplɪfaɪ] *vt* **1** (*sound*) amplificar. **2** (*statement*) ampliar.
ⓘ *pt & pp* amplified, *ger* amplifying.

amplitude ['æmplɪtjuːd] *n* amplitud *f*.

amputate ['æmpjʊteɪt] *vt* amputar.

amputation [æmpjʊ'teɪʃʰn] *n* amputación *f*.

amuck [ə'mʌk] *adv* → **amok**.

amulet ['æmjʊlət] *n* amuleto.

amuse [ə'mjuːz] *vt* entretener, divertir.

amusement [ə'mjuːzmənt] *n* **1** (*enjoyment*) diversión *f*, entretenimiento. **2** (*pastime*) pasatiempo. COMP **amusement arcade** salón *m* de juegos. **I amusement park** parque *m* de atracciones.

amusing [ə'mjuːzɪŋ] *adj* entretenido,-a, divertido,-a.

an [ən, æn] *indef art* **1** un, una. **2** (*per*) por.

✎ Se usa delante de las palabras que empiezan con sonido vocálico. Consulta también a.

anabolism [ə'næbəlɪzʰm] *n* anabolismo.

anachronistic [ænə'krɒnɪk] *adj* anacrónico,-a.

anaconda [ænə'kɒndə] *n* anaconda.

anaemia [ə'niːmɪə] *n* anemia.

anaemic [ə'niːmɪk] *adj* anémico,-a.

anaerobic [æneə'rəʊbɪk] *adj* anaerobio,-a.

anaesthesia [ænəs'θiːzɪə] *n* anestesia.

anaesthetic [ænəs'θetɪk] *adj* anestésico,-a.
▶ *n* anestésico.

anaesthetise [ə'niːsθətaɪz] *vt* → **anaesthetize**.

anaesthetize [ə'niːsθətaɪz] *vt* anestesiar.

anagram ['ænəgræm] *n* anagrama *m*.

anal ['eɪnʰl] *adj* anal.

analgesic [ænəl'dʒiːzɪk] *adj* analgésico,-a.
▶ *n* analgésico.

analog ['ænəlɒg] *adj-n* US → **analogue**.

analogue ['ænəlɒg] *adj* analógico,-a.
▶ *n* análogo.

analogy [ə'nælədʒɪ] *n* analogía, semejanza.
ⓘ *pl* analogies.

analyse ['ænəlaɪz] *vt* analizar.

analysis [ə'nælɪsɪs] *n* análisis *m*.
ⓘ *pl* analyses [ə'nælɪsiːz].

analyst ['ænəlɪst] *n* analista *mf*.

anarchism ['ænəkɪzʰm] *n* anarquismo.

anarchist ['ænəkɪst] *n* anarquista *mf*.

anarchy ['ænəkɪ] *n* anarquía.
ⓘ *pl* anarchies.

anatomy [əˈnætəmɪ] *n* anatomía.
ⓘ *pl* anatomies.

ancestor [ˈænsəstəʳ] *n* antepasado.

anchor [ˈæŋkəʳ] *n* ancla.
▶ *vt* **1** *(ship)* anclar. **2** *(make secure)* sujetar.

anchovy [ˈæntʃəvɪ] *n (salted)* anchoa; *(fresh)* boquerón *m*.
ⓘ *pl* anchovies.

ancient [ˈeɪnʃ°nt] *adj* **1** antiguo,-a; *(monument)* histórico,-a. **2** *fam* viejísimo,-a. [COMP] **ancient history** historia antigua.

✎ Ancient no se emplea en el sentido de 'anterior' con el que a menudo se usa «antiguo» en español *(mi antiguo jefe)*. La palabra inglesa para este sentido de «antiguo» es **former** *(my former boss)*.

and [ænd, *unstressed* ənd] *conj* **1** y; *(before i- and hi-)* e: *black and white* blanco y negro; *opinions and ideas* opiniones e ideas. **2** *(with infinitives)*: *go and look for it* ve a buscarlo; *wait and see what happens* espera a ver lo que pasa. **3** *(expressing repetition, increase)*: *it rained and rained* no paró de llover. **4** *(with numbers)*: *a hundred and twenty* ciento veinte; *two thousand and eighty four* dos mil ochenta y cuatro. **5** *(in sums)* más: *four and six are ten* cuatro más seis son diez.

Andes [ˈændiːz] *n pl* **the Andes** los Andes *mpl*.

Andorra [ænˈdɔːrə] *n* Andorra.

Andorran [ænˈdɔːrən] *adj* andorrano,-a.
▶ *n* andorrano,-a.

android [ˈændrɔɪd] *n* androide *m*.

anecdote [ˈænɪkdəʊt] *n* anécdota.

anemia [əˈniːmɪə] *n* US → anaemia.

anemic [əˈniːmɪk] *adj* US → anaemic.

anemometer [ænɪˈmɒmɪtəʳ] *n* anemómetro.

anemone [əˈnemənɪ] *n* BOT anémona.

anesthesia [ænəsˈθiːzɪə] *n* → anaesthesia.

anesthetic [ænəsˈθetɪk] *adj-n* → anaesthetic.

anesthetize [əˈniːsθətaɪz] *vt* → anaesthetize.

angel [ˈeɪndʒ°l] *n* ángel *m*.

anger [ˈæŋgəʳ] *n* cólera, ira, furia.
▶ *vt* encolerizar, enojar, enfurecer.

angina [ænˈdʒaɪnə] [*also* **angina pectoris**] *n* angina de pecho.

❎ Angina no significa 'anginas', que se traduce por **sore throat**.

angiosperm [ˈændʒɪəspɜːm] *n* angiosperma.

angle¹ [ˈæŋg°l] *n* ángulo.

angle² [ˈæŋg°l] *vi* pescar con caña.

anglepoise lamp [ˈæŋg°lpɔɪzlæmp] *n* flexo.

angler [ˈæŋgləʳ] *n* pescador,-a.

Anglican [ˈæŋglɪkən] *adj* anglicano,-a.
▶ *n* anglicano,-a.

angling [ˈæŋglɪŋ] *n* pesca con caña.

Anglo-Saxon [æŋgləʊˈsæks°n] *adj* anglosajón,-ona.
▶ *n* **1** *(person)* anglosajón,-ona. **2** *(language)* anglosajón *m*.

Angola [æŋˈgəʊlə] *n* Angola.

Angolan [æŋˈgəʊlən] *adj* angoleño,-a.
▶ *n* angoleño,-a.

angry [ˈæŋgrɪ] *adj* enojado,-a, enfadado,-a.
ⓘ *comp* angrier, *superl* angriest.

angstrom [ˈæŋgstrəm] *n* ángstrom *m*.

anguish [ˈæŋgwɪʃ] *n* angustia.

angular [ˈæŋgjʊləʳ] *adj* angular.

anhydride [ænˈhaɪdraɪd] *n* anhídrido.

animal [ˈænɪm°l] *adj* animal.
▶ *n* animal *m*.

animate [*(adj)* ˈænɪmət; *(vb)* ˈænɪmeɪt] *adj* animado,-a, vivo,-a.
▶ *vt* **1** animar. **2** *fig* estimular.

animation [ænɪˈmeɪʃ°n] *n* **1** animación *f*. **2** *(life)* vida, marcha.

animator [ˈænɪmeɪtəʳ] *n* animador,-ra.

animism [ˈænɪmɪz°m] *n* animismo.

anion [ˈænaɪən] *n* anión *m*.

anise [ˈænɪs] *n (plant)* anís *m*.

ankle [ˈæŋk°l] *n* tobillo.

annelid [ˈænəlɪd] *n* anélido.

annexe [ˈænəks] *n* anexo, anejo.

annihilate [əˈnaɪəleɪt] *vt* aniquilar.

anniversary [ænɪˈvɜːsərɪ] *n* aniversario.
ⓘ *pl* anniversaries.

announce [ə'naʊns] *vt* anunciar.

announcement [ə'naʊnsmənt] *n* anuncio.

announcer [ə'naʊnsə^r] *n (on TV, radio)* presentador,-ra, locutor,-ra.

annoy [ə'nɔɪ] *vt* molestar, fastidiar.

annoying [ə'nɔɪɪŋ] *adj* molesto,-a.

annual ['ænjʊəl] *adj* anual.

annul [ə'nʌl] *vt* anular.
ⓘ *pt & pp* annulled, *ger* annulling.

annular ['ænjʊlə^r] *adj* anular.

anode ['ænəʊd] *n* ánodo.

anomaly [ə'nɒməlɪ] *n* anomalía.
ⓘ *pl* anomalies.

anonymous [ə'nɒnɪməs] *adj* anónimo,-a.

anopheles [ə'nɒfəli:z] *n* anofeles *m*.

anorak ['ænəræk] *n* anorak *m*.

anorexia [ænə'reksɪə] *n* anorexia.

another [ə'nʌðə^r] *adj* otro,-a.
► *pron* otro,-a.

answer ['ɑ:nsə^r] *n* respuesta, contestación *f*.
► *vt & vi* responder, contestar.
◆ **to answer back** *vt sep & vi* replicar.
◆ **to answer for** *vt insep* **1** *(guarantee)* responder por, garantizar. **2** *(accept responsibility)* responder de.

answering machine ['ɑ:nsərɪŋməʃi:n] *n* contestador *m* automático.

answerphone ['ɑ:nsəfəʊn] *n* contestador *m* automático.

ant [ænt] *n* hormiga. COMP **ant hill** hormiguero.

Antarctic [ænt'ɑ:ktɪk] *adj* antártico,-a.
► *n* **the Antarctic** la Antártida. COMP **Antarctic Circle** Círculo polar antártico.

Antarctica [ænt'ɑ:ktɪkə] *n* Antártida.

anteater ['ænti:tə^r] *n* oso hormiguero.

antecedent [æntɪ'si:d^ənt] *n* antecedente *m*.

antediluvian [æntɪdɪ'lu:vɪən] *adj* antediluviano,-a.

antenatal [æntɪ'neɪt^əl] *adj* prenatal.

antenna [æn'tenə] *n* **1** [*pl* antennae [æn'teni:]] *(of insect)* antena. **2** [*pl* antennas] *(aerial)* antena.

anterior [æn'tɪərɪə^r] *adj* anterior.

anthem ['ænθəm] *n* motete *m*.

anther ['ænθə^r] *n* antera.

anthology [æn'θɒlədʒɪ] *n* antología.
ⓘ *pl* anthologies.

anthracite ['ænθrəsaɪt] *n* antracita.

anthropology [ænθrə'pɒlədʒɪ] *n* antropología.

antibiotic [æntɪbaɪ'ɒtɪk] *adj* antibiótico,-a.
► *n* antibiótico.

antibody ['æntɪbɒdɪ] *n* anticuerpo.
ⓘ *pl* antibodies.

anticipate [æn'tɪsɪpeɪt] *vt* **1** *(expect)* esperar. **2** *(get ahead of)* adelantarse a. **3** *(foresee)* anticiparse a, prever.

anticipation [æntɪsɪ'peɪʃ^ən] *n* **1** *(expectation)* expectación *f*. **2** *(foresight)* previsión *f*.

anticline ['æntɪklaɪn] *n* anticlinal *m*.

anticlockwise [æntɪ'klɒkwaɪz] *adj* en el sentido contrario a las agujas del reloj.

anticyclone [æntɪ'saɪkləʊn] *n* anticiclón *m*.

antidote ['æntɪdəʊt] *n* antídoto.

antifreeze ['æntɪfri:z] *n* anticongelante *m*.

antigen ['æntɪdʒen] *n* antígeno.

Antilles [æn'tɪli:z] *n pl* Antillas *fpl*.

antimony ['æntɪmənɪ] *n* antimonio.

antipodes [æn'tɪpədi:z] *n pl* antípodas *fpl*.

antipyretic [æntɪpaɪ'retɪk] *n* antipirético.

antique [æn'ti:k] *adj* antiguo,-a. COMP **antique shop** tienda de antigüedades.
► *n* antigüedad *f*.

antiquity [æn'tɪkwɪtɪ] *n* antigüedad *f*.
ⓘ *pl* antiquities.

antiseptic [æntɪ'septɪk] *adj* antiséptico,-a.
► *n* antiséptico.

antiviral [æntɪ'vaɪr^əl] *adj* MED antivirus.

antivirus [æntɪ'vaɪrəs] *adj* INFORM antivirus.

antlers ['æntlə^r] *n pl* cornamenta *f sing*.

antonym ['æntənɪm] *n* antónimo.

anus ['eɪnəs] *n* ano.

anvil ['ænvɪl] *n* yunque *m*.

anxiety [æŋ'zaɪətɪ] *n* ansiedad *f*.
ⓘ *pl* anxieties.

anxious ['æŋkʃəs] *adj* **1** *(worried)* preocupado,-a (**about**, por). **2** *(desirous)* ansioso,-a.

any ['enɪ] *adj* **1** *(in questions)* algún,-una: *are there any biscuits left?* ¿queda alguna galleta? **2** *(negative)* ningún,-una: *he hasn't bought any milk/biscuits* no ha comprado leche/galletas; *without any difficulty* sin ninguna dificultad. **3** *(no matter which)* cualquier,-ra: *any old rag will do* cualquier trapo sirve.

▶ *pron* **1** *(in questions)* alguno,-a: *there are foxes round here, have you seen any?* hay zorros por aquí, ¿has visto alguno? **2** *(negative)* ninguno,-a: *they're very cheap, but I haven't sold any* son muy baratos, pero no he vendido ninguno. **3** *(no matter which)* cualquiera: *any of these books will do* cualquiera de estos libros sirve.

▶ *adv no suele traducirse*: *I don't work there any more* ya no trabajo allí; *do you want any more?* ¿quieres más?.

✎ En preguntas y frases negativas, con los sustantivos contables en singular no se usa any sino a o an.

anybody ['enɪbɒdɪ] *pron* **1** *(in questions)* alguien: *has anybody seen my car?* ¿ha visto alguien mi coche? **2** *(negative)* nadie: *there isn't anybody in the room* no hay nadie en la sala. **3** *(no matter who)* cualquiera: *anybody would tell you the same* cualquiera te diría lo mismo.

anyhow ['enɪhaʊ] *adv* **1** → **anyway**. **2** *(carelessly)* de cualquier forma, de cualquier manera.

anyone ['enɪwʌn] *pron* → **anybody**.

anyplace ['enɪpleɪs] *adv* US → **anywhere**.

anything ['enɪθɪŋ] *pron* **1** *(in questions)* algo, alguna cosa: *is there anything left?* ¿queda algo? **2** *(negative)* nada: *there isn't anything left* no queda nada. **3** *(no matter what)* cualquier cosa: *anything will do* cualquier cosa sirve; *they can cost anything from £5 to £5,000* el precio va desde cinco libras a cinco mil.

anyway ['enɪweɪ] *adv* **1** *(in any case)* de todas formas, de todos modos. **2** *(in conversation)* bueno, bueno pues, total, en cualquier caso: *anyway, as I was saying, ...* bueno pues, como te decía, ...

anywhere ['enɪweər] *adv* **1** *(in questions - situation)* en algún sitio, en alguna parte; *(- direction)* a algún sitio, a alguna parte: *have you seen my keys anywhere?* ¿has visto mis llaves en alguna parte?; *are you going anywhere this weekend?* ¿vas a algún sitio el fin de semana? **2** *(negative - situation)* en ningún sitio, en ninguna parte; *(- direction)* a ningún sitio, a ninguna parte: *I can't find him anywhere* no lo encuentro en ninguna parte; *we're not going anywhere* no vamos a ningún sitio. **3** *(no matter where - situation)* donde sea, en cualquier sitio; *(- direction)* a donde sea, a cualquier sitio: *I'd live anywhere as long as it's with you* viviría en cualquier sitio mientras sea contigo; *she'd travel anywhere to see Bruce* viajaría a cualquier sitio para ver a Bruce.

aorta [eɪˈɔːtə] *n* aorta.

apart [əˈpɑːt] *adv* **1** *(not together)* separado,-a; *(distant)* alejado,-a. **2** *(in pieces)* en piezas. [LOC] **apart from** aparte de. ‖ **to fall apart** deshacerse. ‖ **to tell apart** distinguir.

apartheid [əˈpɑːtheɪt] *n* apartheid *m*.

apartment [əˈpɑːtmənt] *n* piso, apartamento. [COMP] **apartment block / apartment building** bloque *m* de pisos.

apathetic [æpəˈθetɪk] *adj* apático,-a.

apathy ['æpəθɪ] *n* apatía.

ape [eɪp] *n* simio.
▶ *vt* imitar.

Apennines ['æpənaɪnz] *n* **the Apennines** los (montes) Apeninos *mpl*.

aperitif [əperɪˈtiːf] *n* aperitivo.

aperture ['æpətʃər] *n* abertura.

❌ Aperture no significa 'apertura (de una tienda)', que se traduce por opening.

apex ['eɪpeks] *n* ápice *m*; *(of triangle)* vértice *m*.
ⓘ *pl* apexes o apices.

apiculture ['eɪpɪkʌltʃər] *n* apicultura.

apiece [əˈpiːs] *adv* cada uno,-a: *she gave us three apiece* nos dio tres a cada uno.

apocalypse [əˈpɒkəlɪps] *n* apocalipsis *m*.

apogee ['æpədʒiː] *n* apogeo.

apologise [əˈpɒlədʒaɪz] vi → apologize.

apologize [əˈpɒlədʒaɪz] vi disculparse, pedir perdón.

apology [əˈpɒlədʒɪ] n **1** (for mistake) disculpa. **2** fml (of beliefs) apología.
ⓘ pl apologies.

apoplexy [ˈæpəpleksɪ] n apoplejía.
ⓘ pl apoplexies.

apophthegm [ˈæpəθem] n apotema.

apostle [əˈpɒsl] n apóstol m.

apostrophe [əˈpɒstrəfɪ] n apóstrofo.

apothegm [ˈæpəθem] vt → apophthegm.

appal [əˈpɔːl] vt horrorizar.
ⓘ pt & pp appalled, ger appalling.

Appalachians [æpəˈleɪʃəns] n the Appalachians los (montes) Apalaches mpl.

appall [əˈpɔːl] vt US → appal.

appalling [əˈpɔːlɪŋ] adj **1** (horrific) horroroso,-a. **2** (bad) malísimo,-a.

apparatus [æpəˈreɪtəs] n **1** (equipment) aparatos mpl; (piece of equipment) aparato. **2** (structure) aparato.

apparent [əˈpærənt] adj **1** (obvious) evidente. **2** (seeming) aparente.

apparently [əˈpærəntlɪ] adv **1** (obviously) evidentemente. **2** (seemingly) aparentemente.

appeal [əˈpiːl] n **1** (request) ruego, llamamiento; (plea) súplica. **2** (attraction) atractivo. **3** JUR apelación f.
▶ vi **1** (request) pedir, solicitar; (plead) suplicar. **2** (attract) atraer: it doesn't appeal to me no me atrae. **3** JUR apelar (against, -), recurrir (against, -).

appealing [əˈpiːlɪŋ] adj **1** (moving) suplicante. **2** (attractive) atractivo,-a.

appear [əˈpɪər] vi **1** (become visible) aparecer. **2** (before a court, etc) comparecer (before, ante). **3** (seem) parecer.

appearance [əˈpɪərəns] n **1** (becoming visible) aparición f. **2** (before a court, etc) comparecencia. **3** (look) apariencia.

appendices [əˈpendɪsiːz] n pl → appendix.

appendicitis [əpendɪˈsaɪtɪs] n apendicitis f.

appendix [əˈpendɪks] n **1** [pl appendices] (in book) apéndice m. **2** [pl appendixes] MED apéndice m.

appetite [ˈæpɪtaɪt] n apetito.

appetizer [ˈæpɪtaɪzər] n aperitivo.

appetizing [ˈæpɪtaɪzɪŋ] adj apetitoso,-a.

applaud [əˈplɔːd] vi (clap) aplaudir.
▶ vt **1** (clap) aplaudir. **2** (praise) alabar.

applause [əˈplɔːz] n aplauso.

apple [ˈæpl] n manzana. COMP apple pie tarta de manzana. ‖ apple tree manzano. ‖ the Big Apple Nueva York.

applet [ˈæplət] n COMPUT applet m.

appliance [əˈplaɪəns] n **1** (device) aparato. **2** (fire engine) coche m de bomberos.

applicable [ˈæplɪkəbl] adj aplicable.

applicant [ˈæplɪkənt] n (for job) candidato,-a, solicitante mf.

application [æplɪˈkeɪʃən] n **1** (for job) solicitud f. **2** (of ointment, theory, etc) aplicación f. **3** (effort) diligencia.

apply [əˈplaɪ] vt aplicar.
▶ vi **1** (be true) aplicarse, ser aplicable. **2** (for job) solicitar.
ⓘ pt & pp applied, ger applying.

appoint [əˈpɔɪnt] vt **1** (person for job) nombrar. **2** (day, date, etc) fijar, señalar.

appointment [əˈpɔɪntmənt] n **1** (meeting - with lawyer, etc) cita; (- with hairdresser, dentist, doctor) hora. **2** (person for job) nombramiento.

apposition [æpəˈzɪʃən] n aposición f.

appraisal [əˈpreɪzl] n valoración f, evaluación f.

appraise [əˈpreɪz] vt valorar, evaluar.

appreciate [əˈpriːʃɪeɪt] vt **1** (be thankful for) agradecer. **2** (understand) entender, comprender. **3** (value) valorar, apreciar.
▶ vi revalorizarse, valorizarse.

appreciation [əpriːʃɪˈeɪʃən] n **1** (thanks) agradecimiento, gratitud f. **2** (understanding) comprensión f. **3** (appraisal) evaluación f. **4** (increase in value) apreciación f, aumento en valor.

apprehend [æprɪˈhend] vt **1** (arrest) detener, capturar. **2** (understand) comprender.

apprehension [æprɪˈhenʃən] n **1** (arrest) detención f, captura. **2** (fear) aprensión f, temor m, recelo.

apprehensive [æprɪˈhensɪv] adj (fearful) aprensivo,-a.

apprentice [ə'prentɪs] n aprendiz,-za.
approach [ə'prəutʃ] n 1 (coming near) aproximación f, acercamiento; (arrival) llegada. 2 (way in) acceso, entrada. 3 (to problem) enfoque m.
▸ vi (come near) acercarse, aproximarse.
▸ vt 1 (come near) acercarse a, aproximarse a. 2 (tackle - problem) enfocar, abordar; (- person) dirigirse a. COMP approach road vía de acceso.
appropriate [ə'prəupriət] adj apropiado,-a, adecuado,-a, indicado,-a.
approval [ə'pru:vəl] n aprobación f. LOC on approval a prueba.
approve [ə'pru:v] vt aprobar.

☒ To approve no significa 'aprobar (un examen)', que se traduce por to pass.

---

approximate [(adj) ə'prɒksɪmət; (vb) ə'prɒksɪmeɪt] adj aproximado,-a.
▸ vi aproximarse (to, a).
apricot ['eɪprɪkɒt] n (fruit) albaricoque m. COMP apricot tree albaricoquero.
April ['eɪprɪl] n abril m. COMP April Fool's Day el día 1 de abril (≈ día de los Santos Inocentes).

✎ Para ejemplos de uso, consulta May.

apron ['eɪprən] n 1 (garment - domestic) delantal m; (- workman's) mandil m. 2 (at airport) pista de estacionamiento.
apse [æps] n ábside m.
apt [æpt] adj 1 (suitable) apropiado,-a; (remark) acertado,-a. 2 (liable to) propenso,-a.
APT ['eɪ'pi:'ti:] abbr GB (Advanced Passenger Train) ≈ AVE m.
aptitude ['æptɪtju:d] n aptitud f.
aquarium [ə'kweərɪəm] n acuario.
① pl aquaria o aquariums.
Aquarius [ə'kweərɪəs] n Acuario.
aquatic [ə'kwætɪk] adj acuático,-a.
aqueduct ['ækwɪdʌkt] n acueducto.
aquifer ['ækwɪfəʳ] n acuífero.
Arab ['ærəb] adj árabe.
▸ n (person) árabe mf.
Arabia [ə'reɪbɪə] n Arabia.
Arabian [ə'reɪbɪən] adj árabe, arábigo,-a.

▸ n árabe mf. COMP Arabian Peninsula Península Arábiga. ❙ Arabian Sea Mar m Arábigo.
Arabic ['ærəbɪk] adj Árabe.
▸ n (language) Árabe m. COMP arabic numerals números mpl arábigos.
arachnid [ə'ræknɪd] n arácnido.
aragonite [ə'rægənaɪt] n aragonito.
arbitrary ['ɑ:bɪtrərɪ] adj arbitrario,-a.
arbitrate ['ɑ:bɪtreɪt] vt & vi arbitrar.
arc [ɑ:k] n arco.
arcade [ɑ:'keɪd] n pasaje m. COMP shopping arcade galerías fpl comerciales.
arch [ɑ:tʃ] n 1 (gen) arco; (vault) bóveda. 2 (of foot) empeine m.
▸ vt 1 (back, eyebrows) arquear, enarcar. 2 (vault) abovedar.
archaeological [ɑ:kɪə'lɒdʒɪkəl] adj arqueológico,-a.
archaeologist [ɑ:kɪ'ɒlədʒɪst] n arqueólogo,-a.
archaeology [ɑ:kɪ'ɒlədʒɪ] n arqueología.
archaic [ɑ:'keɪɪk] adj arcaico,-a.
archaism ['ɑ:keɪɪzəm] n arcaísmo.
archangel [ɑ:'keɪndʒəl] n arcángel m.
archbishop [ɑ:tʃ'bɪʃəp] n arzobispo.
archeological [ɑ:kɪə'lɒdʒɪkəl] adj US → archaeological.
archeologist [ɑ:kɪ'ɒlədʒɪst] n US → archaeologist.
archeology [ɑ:kɪ'ɒlədʒɪ] n US → archaeology.
archer ['ɑ:tʃəʳ] n arquero.
archery ['ɑ:tʃərɪ] n tiro con arco.
archipelago [ɑ:kɪ'pelɪgəu] n archipiélago.
① pl archipelagos o archipelagoes.
architect ['ɑ:kɪtekt] n arquitecto,-a.
architecture ['ɑ:kɪtektʃəʳ] n arquitectura.
archives ['ɑ:kaɪvz] n pl archivo m sing.
archivist ['ɑ:kaɪvɪst] n archivero,-a.
Arctic ['ɑ:ktɪk] adj ártico,-a.
▸ n the Arctic el Ártico. COMP the Arctic Circle el Círculo Polar Ártico. ❙ the Arctic Ocean el océano Ártico.
ardor ['ɑ:dəʳ] n US → ardour.
ardour ['ɑ:dəʳ] n ardor m.

arduous ['ɑːdjuəs] *adj* arduo,-a.
are [ɑːʳ, əʳ] *pres* → be.
area ['eərɪə] *n* 1 *(extent)* área, superficie *f.* 2 *(region)* región *f*; *(of town)* zona. 3 *(field)* campo.
arena [ə'riːnə] *n* 1 *(stadium)* estadio, 2 *(in amphitheatre)* arena. 3 *fig* ámbito.

☒ Arena no significa 'arena', que se traduce por sand.

aren't [ɑːnt] *contr* → are not.
Argentina [ɑːdʒən'tiːnə] *n* Argentina.
Argentine ['ɑːdʒəntaɪn] *adj* argentino,-a.
▶ *n* the Argentine Argentina.
Argentinian [ɑːdʒən'tɪnɪən] *adj* argentino,-a.
▶ *n* argentino,-a.
argon ['ɑːgɒn] *n* argón *m.*
argot ['ɑːgəʊ] *n* jerga.
argue ['ɑːgjuː] *vi* 1 *(quarrel)* discutir (with, con). 2 *(reason)* argüir, argumentar, sostener.
argument ['ɑːgjumənt] *n* 1 *(quarrel)* discusión *f*, disputa. 2 *(reasoning)* argumento. [LOC] **to have an argument with** se discutir con ALGN.
arid ['ærɪd] *adj* árido,-a.
aridity [ə'rɪdɪtɪ] *n* aridez *f.*
Aries ['eəriːz] *n* Aries.
arise [ə'raɪz] *vi* surgir (from, de).
ⓘ *pt* arose [ə'rəʊz], *pp* arisen [ə'rɪzən].
aristocracy [ærɪs'tɒkrəsɪ] *n* aristocracia.
ⓘ *pl* aristocracies.
aristocrat ['ærɪstəkræt, US ə'rɪstəkræt] *n* aristócrata *mf.*
arithmetic [*(n)* ə'rɪθmətɪk; *(adj)* ærɪθ'metɪk] *n* aritmética.
▶ *adj* aritmético,-a.
arithmetical [ærɪθ'metɪkəl] *adj* aritmético,-a. [COMP] **arithmetical progression** progresión *f* aritmética.
ark [ɑːk] *n* arca.
arm [ɑːm] *n* 1 ANAT brazo. 2 *(of coat, etc)* manga. 3 *(of chair)* brazo.
▶ *vt* armar.
▶ *n pl* arms *(weapons)* armas *fpl.*
armadillo [ɑːmə'dɪləʊ] *n* armadillo.
ⓘ *pl* armadillos.

armchair [ɑːm'tʃeəʳ] *n* sillón *m.*
Armenia [ɑːmiːnɪə] *n* Armenia.
Armenian [ɑːmiːnɪən] *adj* armenio,-a.
▶ *n* 1 *(person)* armenio,-a. 2 *(language)* armenio.
armistice ['ɑːmɪstɪs] *n* armisticio.
armor ['ɑːməʳ] *n* US → armour.
armour ['ɑːməʳ] *n* 1 armadura. 2 *(on vehicle)* blindaje *m.*
armpit ['ɑːmpɪt] *n* sobaco, axila.
armrest ['ɑːmrest] *n* brazo.
army ['ɑːmɪ] *n* ejército.
ⓘ *pl* armies.
aroma [ə'rəʊmə] *n* aroma *m.*
aromatic [ærə'mætɪk] *adj* aromático,-a.
arose [ə'rəʊz] *pt* → arise.
around [ə'raʊnd] *adv* 1 *(near, in the area)* alrededor: *is there anybody around?* ¿hay alguien cerca? 2 *(from place to place)*: *they cycle around together* van juntos en bicicleta. 3 *(approximately)* alrededor de: *it costs around £5,000* cuesta unas cinco mil libras.
▶ *prep* 1 *(near)*: *there aren't many shops around here* hay pocas tiendas por aquí. 2 *(all over)*: *there were clothes around the room* había ropa por toda la habitación. 3 *(in a circle or curve)* alrededor de: *he put his arms around her* la rodeó con los brazos. 4 *(at)* sobre, cerca de: *they came around seven* vinieron sobre las siete.
arouse [ə'raʊz] *vt* 1 *(awake)* despertar. 2 *(sexually)* excitar.
arrange [ə'reɪndʒ] *vt* 1 *(gen)* arreglar; *(furniture, etc)* colocar, ordenar. 2 *(plan)* planear, organizar. 3 *(marriage)* concertar.
arrangement [ə'reɪndʒmənt] *n* 1 *(agreement)* acuerdo, arreglo. 2 MUS arreglo.
▶ *n pl* arrangements *(plans)* planes *mpl*; *(preparations)* preparativos *mpl.*
array [ə'reɪ] *n* 1 *(selection)* surtido. 2 *(series)* serie *f.* 3 COMPUT matriz *f.*
arrears [ə'rɪəz] *n pl* atrasos *mpl.*
arrest [ə'rest] *n* arresto, detención *f.*
arrival [ə'raɪvəl] *n* llegada.
arrive [ə'raɪv] *vi* llegar.
arrogant ['ærəgənt] *adj* arrogante.
arrow ['ærəʊ] *n* flecha.
arsenal ['ɑːsənəl] *n* arsenal *m.*

arsenic ['ɑ:sⁿnɪk] *n* arsénico.

arson ['ɑ:sⁿn] *n* incendio provocado.

arsonist ['ɑ:sənɪst] *n* pirómano,-a.

art [ɑ:t] *n (painting, etc)* arte *m*.
▶ *n pl* **arts** *(branch of knowledge)* letras *fpl*. COMP **art deco** art deco *m*. ▮ **art gallery 1** *(museum)* pinacoteca. **2** *(commercial)* galería de arte. ▮ **art nouveau** art nouveau *m*, modernismo.

artefact ['ɑ:tɪfækt] *n* artefacto.

arterial [ɑ:'tɪərɪəl] *adj* **1** ANAT arterial. **2** *(road)* principal, importante.

artery ['ɑ:terɪ] *n* ANAT arteria.
ⓘ *pl* arteries.

artesian well [ɑ:ti:zɪən'wel] *n* pozo artesiano.

arthritis [ɑ:θ'raɪtəs] *n* artritis *f*.

arthropod ['ɑ:θrəpɒd] *n* artrópodo.

artichoke ['ɑ:tɪtʃəʊk] *n* alcachofa.

article ['ɑ:tɪkⁿl] *n* artículo. COMP **article of clothing** prenda de vestir. ▮ **definite article** artículo determinado. ▮ **indefinite article** artículo indeterminado. ▮ **leading article** editorial *m*.

articulate [*(adj)* ɑ:'tɪkjʊlət; *(vb)* ɑ:'tɪkjʊleɪt] *adj (person)* que se expresa con facilidad; *(speech)* claro,-a.
▶ *vt* **1** articular. **2** *(pronounce)* pronunciar.

articulated [ɑ:'tɪkjʊleɪtɪd] *adj* articulado,-a. COMP **articulated lorry** camión *m* articulado.

articulation [ɑ:tɪkjʊ'leɪʃⁿn] *n* articulación *f*.

artifact ['ɑ:tɪfækt] *n* US → **artefact**.

artificial [ɑ:tɪ'fɪʃⁿl] *adj* artificial.

artillery [ɑ:'tɪlərɪ] *n* artillería.

artisan [ɑ:'tɪzæn] *n* artesano,-a.

artist ['ɑ:tɪst] *n* **1** artista *mf*. **2** *(painter)* pintor,-ra.

artistic [ɑ:'tɪstɪk] *adj* artístico,-a.

artwork ['ɑ:twɜ:k] *n* ilustraciones *fpl*.

as [æz, *unstressed* əz] *prep* como: *he works as a clerk* trabaja de oficinista.
▶ *adv (in comparatives)*: *eat as much as you like* come tanto como quieras.
▶ *conj* **1** *(while)* mientras; *(when)* cuando: *as he painted, he whistled* mientras pintaba, silbaba; *as he grew older he became more tolerant* a medida que iba envejeciendo se

volvía más tolerante. **2** *(because)* ya que, como: *as there were no seats we had to stand* como no había asientos tuvimos que estar de pie. **3** *(although)* aunque: *tall as he was, he still couldn't reach the shelf* aunque era alto no podía alcanzar el estante. LOC **as far as** hasta. ▮ **as far as I know** que yo sepa. ▮ **as for** en cuanto a. ▮ **as if** como si. ▮ **as long as** mientras. ▮ **as of** desde. ▮ **as soon as** tan pronto como. ▮ **as though** como si. ▮ **as well as** además de. ▮ **as yet** hasta ahora, de momento.

asbestos [æs'bestəs] *n* amianto.

ascend [ə'send] *vt* ascender, subir a.
▶ *vi* ascender, subir.

ascendancy [ə'sendənsɪ] *n* predominio, supremacía.
ⓘ *pl* ascendancies.

ascension [ə'senʃⁿn] *n* ascensión *f*.

ascent [ə'sent] *n* **1** *(slope)* subida. **2** *(climb)* ascensión *f*.

ascribe [əs'kraɪb] *vt* atribuir (**to**, a).

aseptic [ə'septɪk] *adj* aséptico,-a.

asexual [eɪ'sekʃʊəl] *adj* asexual.

ash¹ [æʃ] *n* ceniza. COMP **Ash Wednesday** miércoles *m* de ceniza.
ⓘ *pl* ashes.

ash² [æʃ] *n (tree)* fresno.
ⓘ *pl* ashes.

ashamed [ə'ʃeɪmd] *adj* avergonzado,-a.

ashbin ['æʃbɪn] *n* US cubo de la basura.

ashtray ['æʃtreɪ] *n* cenicero.

Asia ['eɪʃə, 'eɪʒə] *n* Asia.

Asian ['eɪʃⁿn, 'eɪʒⁿn] *adj* asiático,-a.
▶ *n* asiático,-a.

Asiatic [eɪʃɪ'ætɪk, eɪʒɪ'ætɪk] *adj* asiático,-a.

aside [ə'saɪd] *adv* al lado, a un lado.
LOC **aside from** aparte de.

ask [ɑ:sk] *vt* **1** *(inquire)* preguntar. **2** *(request)* pedir: *we have to ask permission* debemos pedir permiso. **3** *(invite)* invitar, convidar: *he asked her to go out with him* la invitó a salir con él.
◆ **to ask after** *vt insep* preguntar por.
◆ **to ask for** *vt insep (thing)* pedir; *(person)* preguntar por.
◆ **to ask out** *vt sep* invitar a salir.

asleep [əˈsliːp] *adj (person)* dormido,-a. LOC **to fall asleep** dormirse.

asparagus [æsˈpærəgəs] *n (plant)* espárrago; *(shoots)* espárragos *mpl.* COMP **an asparagus tip** una punta de espárrago.

aspect [ˈæspekt] *n* **1** *(gen)* aspecto. **2** *(of building)* orientación *f.*

asphalt [ˈæsfælt] *n* asfalto.

asphyxia [əsˈfɪksɪə] *n* asfixia.

asphyxiate [əsˈfɪksɪeɪt] *vt* asfixiar.

aspic [ˈæspɪk] *n* CULIN gelatina.

aspire [əsˈpaɪəʳ] *vi* aspirar (to, a).

aspirin® [ˈæspɪrɪn] *n* aspirina®.

ass [æs] *n (animal)* burro,-a, asno,-a; *(person)* burro,-a, imbécil *mf.*

assail [əˈseɪl] *vt* **1** *(physically)* atacar. **2** *(doubts, problems, etc)* asaltar.

assailant [əˈseɪlənt] *n* atacante *mf.*

assassin [əˈsæsɪn] *n* asesino,-a.

assassinate [əˈsæsɪneɪt] *vt* asesinar.

assassination [əsæsɪˈneɪʃ°n] *n* asesinato.

> ✎ Assassin, assassinate y assassination sólo se emplean cuando se trata del asesinato de un personaje importante. En los demás casos, se usan las palabras murderer, murder.

assault [əˈsɔːlt] *n* **1** MIL asalto, ataque *m.* **2** JUR agresión *f.*
▶ *vt* JUR *(gen)* agredir; *(sexually)* abusar de.

assemble [əˈsembəl] *vt* **1** *(bring together)* reunir. **2** *(put together)* montar. **3** COMPUT ensamblar.
▶ *vi* reunirse.

assembly [əˈsemblɪ] *n* **1** *(meeting)* reunión *f.* **2** *(group, body)* asamblea. **3** TECH *(putting together)* montaje *m; (unit)* unidad *f.* COMP **assembly hall** sala de actos. ‖ **assembly line** cadena de montaje.
ⓘ *pl* assemblies.

assent [əˈsent] *n* asentimiento.
▶ *vi* asentir (to, a).

assert [əˈsɜːt] *vt* aseverar, afirmar.

assertion [əˈsɜːʃ°n] *n* afirmación *f.*

assess [əˈses] *vt* **1** *(value)* tasar, valorar. **2** *(calculate)* calcular. **3** *fig* evaluar.

assessment [əˈsesmənt] *n* **1** *(valuation)* tasación *f*, valoración *f.* **2** *(calculation)* cálculo. **3** *fig* evaluación *f.*

asset [ˈæset] *n* calidad *f* positiva, ventaja.
▶ *n pl* **assets** COMM activo *m sing.*

assign [əˈsaɪn] *vt* asignar, atribuir.

assignment [əˈsaɪnmənt] *n* **1** *(mission)* misión *f.* **2** *(task)* tarea.

assimilate [əˈsɪmɪleɪt] *vt* asimilar.
▶ *vi* asimilarse.

assist [əˈsɪst] *vt & vi* ayudar.

> ✖ To assist no significa 'asistir, ir', que se traducen por to attend, to go.

assistance [əˈsɪstəns] *n* ayuda.

assistant [əˈsɪstənt] *n* **1** *(helper)* ayudante *mf.* **2** *(in shop)* dependiente *mf.*

associate [*(adj-n)* əˈsəʊʃɪət; *(vb)* əˈsəʊʃɪeɪt] *adj* **1** *(company)* asociado,-a. **2** *(member)* correspondiente.
▶ *n (partner)* socio,-a.
▶ *vt* asociar.
▶ *vi* relacionarse (with, con).

association [əsəʊʃɪˈeɪʃ°n] *n* asociación *f.*

associative [əˈsəʊʃɪətɪv] *adj* asociativo,-a.

associativity [əsəʊʃɪəˈtɪvɪtɪ] *n* propiedad *f* asociativa.

assonance [ˈæsənəns] *n* asonancia.

assorted [əˈsɔːtɪd] *adj* surtido,-a, variado,-a.

assortment [əˈsɔːtmənt] *n* surtido, variedad *f.*

assume [əˈsjuːm] *vt* **1** *(suppose)* suponer. **2** *(power, responsibility)* tomar, asumir. **3** *(attitude, expression)* adoptar.

assurance [əˈʃʊərəns] *n* **1** *(guarantee)* garantía. **2** *(confidence)* seguridad *f*, confianza. **3** *(insurance)* seguro. COMP **life assurance** seguro de vida.

assure [əˈʃʊəʳ] *vt* asegurar.

asterisk [ˈæstərɪsk] *n* asterisco.

asteroid [ˈæstərɔɪd] *n* asteroide *m.*

asthma [ˈæsmə] *n* asma.

astonish [əsˈtɒnɪʃ] *vt* asombrar, sorprender.

astonishing [əsˈtɒnɪʃɪŋ] *adj* asombroso,-a, sorprendente.

astonishment [əsˈtɒnɪʃmənt] *n* asombro.

astound [əsˈtaʊnd] *vt* asombrar.

astral [ˈæstrəl] *adj* astral.

astray [əˈstreɪ] *adv* extraviado,-a. LOC **to go astray 1** *(err)* descarriarse. **2** *(be lost)* extraviarse.

astrolabe [ˈæstrəleɪb] *n* astrolabio.

astrologer [əsˈtrɒlədʒəʳ] *n* astrólogo,-a.

astrology [əsˈtrɒlədʒɪ] *n* astrología.

astronaut [ˈæstrənɔːt] *n* astronauta *mf*.

astronomer [əsˈtrɒnəməʳ] *n* astrónomo,-a.

astronomical [æstrəˈnɒmɪkəl] *n* astronómico,-a.

astronomy [əsˈtrɒnəmɪ] *n* astronomía.

astute [əsˈtjuːt] *adj* astuto,-a, sagaz.

asylum [əˈsaɪləm] *n* **1** *(political)* asilo, refugio. **2** *(for mentally ill)* manicomio.

asymmetric [æsɪˈmetrɪk] *adj* asimétrico,-a. COMP **asymmetric bars** barras *fpl* asimétricas.

at¹ [æt, *unstressed* ət] *prep* **1** *(position)* en, a: *at home/school/work/church* en casa/el colegio/el trabajo/la iglesia; *she's at the dentist's* ha ido al dentista. **2** *(time)* a: *at two o'clock* a las dos; *at night* por la noche. **3** *(direction, violence)* a, contra: *she's always shouting at them* no para de gritarles. **4** *(with numbers)* a: *at 50 miles an hour* a 50 millas la hora,. **5** *(state)*: *he's at breakfast/lunch/dinner* está desayunando/comiendo/cenando; *men at work* hombres trabajando. **6** *(ability)*: *he's good at French* va bien en francés. LOC **at first** al principio. ∎ **at last!** ¡por fin! ∎ **at least** por lo menos. ∎ **at most** como máximo. ∎ **at the moment** ahora.

at² [æt] *n* *(Internet)* arroba

ate [et, eɪt] *pt* → **eat**.

atheism [ˈeɪθɪɪzəm] *n* ateísmo.

atheist [ˈeɪθɪɪst] *n* ateo,-a.

Athens [ˈæθənz] *n* Atenas.

athlete [ˈæθliːt] *n* atleta *mf*.

athletic [æθˈletɪk] *adj* **1** atlético,-a. **2** *(sporty)* deportista.

athletics [æθˈletɪks] *n* atletismo.

Atlantic [ətˈlæntɪk] *adj* atlántico,-a. COMP **the Atlantic (Ocean)** el (océano) Atlántico.

atlas [ˈætləs] *n* atlas *m inv*.

atmosphere [ˈætməsfɪəʳ] *n* **1** atmósfera. **2** *(ambience)* ambiente *m*, atmósfera.

atmospheric [ætməsˈferɪk] *adj* atmosférico,-a. COMP **atmospheric pressure** presión *f* atmosférica.

atoll [ˈætɒl] *n* atolón *m*.

atom [ˈætəm] *n* átomo. COMP **atom bomb** bomba atómica.

atomic [əˈtɒmɪk] *adj* atómico,-a.

atrium [ˈeɪtrɪəm] *n* atrio.
  ① *pl* atriums o atria [ˈeɪtrɪə].

atrocity [əˈtrɒsɪtɪ] *n* atrocidad *f*.
  ① *pl* atrocities.

attach [əˈtætʃ] *vt* **1** *(fasten)* sujetar. **2** *(tie)* atar. **3** *(stick)* pegar. **4** *(document)* adjuntar.

attachment [əˈtætʃmənt] *n* **1** TECH accesorio. **2** *(to an e-mail)* anexo. **3** *(fondness)* cariño, apego.

attack [əˈtæk] *n* *(gen)* ataque *m*; *(terrorist)* atentado.
  ► *vt* **1** atacar.

attain [əˈteɪn] *vt* **1** *(goal)* lograr. **2** *(rank, age)* llegar a.

attempt [əˈtempt] *n* *(try)* intento, tentativa.
  ► *vt* intentar.

attend [əˈtend] *vt* **1** *(be present at)* asistir a: *all her friends attended the funeral* todos sus amigos asistieron al funeral. **2** *(care for)* atender, cuidar.
  ► *vi* asistir.
  ◆ **to attend to** *vt insep* **1** ocuparse de. **2** *(in shop)* despachar.

attendance [əˈtendəns] *n* **1** *(being present)* asistencia. **2** *(people present)* asistentes *mpl*.

attendant [əˈtendənt] *n* *(in car park, museum)* vigilante *mf*; *(in cinema)* acomodador,-ra.

attention [əˈtenʃən] *n* atención *f*.
  ► *interj* **attention!** MIL ¡firmes! LOC **to pay attention** prestar atención.

attentive [əˈtentɪv] *adj* **1** *(paying attention)* atento,-a. **2** *(helpful)* solícito,-a.

attic ['ætɪk] *n* desván *m*.

attire [ə'taɪəʳ] *n* atuendo, atavío.

attitude ['ætɪtjuːd] *n* **1** *(way of thinking)* actitud *f*. **2** *(pose)* postura, pose *f*.

attorney [ə'tɜːnɪ] *n* US abogado,-a. COMP Attorney General GB ≈ Ministro,-a de Justicia.

attract [ə'trækt] *vt* atraer.

attraction [ə'trækʃən] *n* atracción *f*.

attractive [ə'træktɪv] *adj* **1** *(person)* atractivo,-a. **2** *(offer)* interesante, tentador,-ra.

attribute [*(n)* æ'trɪbjuːt *(vb)* ə'trɪbjuːt] *n* atributo.
► *vt* atribuir.

attribution [ætrɪ'bjuːʃən] *n* atribución *f*.

attributive [ə'trɪbjutɪv] *adj* atributivo,-a.

atypical [eɪ'tɪpɪkəl] *adj* atípico,-a.

aubergine ['əʊbəʒiːn] *n* berenjena.

auction ['ɔːkʃən] *n* subasta.
► *vt* subastar.

audacious [ɔː'deɪʃəs] *adj* **1** *(daring)* audaz, intrépido,-a. **2** *(rude)* descarado,-a, osado,-a.

audible ['ɔːdɪbəl] *adj* audible.

audience ['ɔːdɪəns] *n* *(spectators)* público; *(radio)* audiencia; *(television)* telespectadores *mpl*.

audio-visual [ɔːdɪəʊ'vɪzjuəl] *adj* audiovisual.

audit ['ɔːdɪt] *n* auditoría.
► *vt* auditar.

audition [ɔː'dɪʃən] *n* prueba.

auditor ['ɔːdɪtəʳ] *n* auditor,-ra.

auditorium [ɔːdɪ'tɔːrɪəm] *n* auditorio.
ⓘ *pl* auditoriums o auditoria [ɔːdɪ'tɔːrɪə].

augment [ɔːg'ment] *vt fml* aumentar.
► *vi fml* aumentarse.

augmentative [ɔːg'mentətɪv] *adj* aumentativo,-a.

August ['ɔːgəst] *n* agosto.

✎ Para ejemplos de uso, consulta May.

aunt [ɑːnt] *n* tía.

auntie ['ɑːntɪ] *n fam* tía, tita.

au pair [əʊ'peəʳ] *n* au pair *f*. COMP au pair girl au pair *f*.

aura ['ɔːrə] *n* aura.

auricle ['ɒrɪkəl] *n* **1** *(of heart)* aurícula. **2** *(of ear)* aurícula, pabellón *m* de la oreja.

aurora [ɔː'rɔːrə] *n* aurora. COMP aurora australis aurora austral. ▍ aurora borealis aurora boreal.

auscultate ['ɔːskʌlteɪt] *vt* auscultar.

auscultation [ɔːskʌl'teɪʃən] *n* auscultación *f*.

austere [ɒs'tɪəʳ] *adj* austero,-a.

austerity [ɒs'terɪtɪ] *n* austeridad *f*.

Australia [ɒ'streɪlɪə] *n* Australia.

Australian [ɒ'streɪlɪən] *adj* australiano,-a.
► *n* australiano,-a.

Austria ['ɒstrɪə] *n* Austria.

Austrian ['ɒstrɪən] *adj* austríaco,-a, austriaco,-a.
► *n* austríaco,-a, austriaco,-a.

authentic [ɔː'θentɪk] *adj* auténtico,-a.

author ['ɔːθəʳ] *n* autor,-ra, escritor,-ra.

authoritarian [ɔːθɒrɪ'teərɪən] *adj* autoritario,-a.

authority [ɔː'θɒrɪtɪ] *n* **1** *(gen)* autoridad *f*. **2** *(permission)* autorización *f*, permiso.
ⓘ *pl* authorities.

authorisation [ɔːθəraɪ'zeɪʃən] *n* → authorization.

authorise ['ɔːθəraɪz] *vt* → authorize.

authorization [ɔːθəraɪ'zeɪʃən] *n* autorización *f*.

authorize ['ɔːθəraɪz] *vt* autorizar.

autism ['ɔːtɪzəm] *n* autismo.

autistic [ɔː'tɪstɪk] *adj* autista.

auto ['ɔːtəʊ] *n* US *fam* coche *m*.
ⓘ *pl* autos.

autobiography [ɔːtəbaɪ'ɒgrəfɪ] *n* autobiografía.
ⓘ *pl* autobiographies.

autograph ['ɔːtəgrɑːf] *n* autógrafo.
► *vt* autografiar.

automatic [ɔːtə'mætɪk] *adj* automático,-a. COMP automatic pilot piloto automático.

automation [ɔːtə'meɪʃən] *n* automatización *f*.

automobile [ˈɔːtəməbiːl] *n* automóvil *m*, coche *m*.

autonomous [ɔːˈtɒnəməs] *adj* autónomo,-a.

autonomy [ɔːˈtɒnəmɪ] *n* autonomía.
ⓘ *pl* autonomies.

autopsy [ˈɔːtɒpsɪ] *n* autopsia.
ⓘ *pl* autopsies.

autumn [ˈɔːtəm] *n* otoño.

auxiliary [ɔːgˈzɪljərɪ] *adj* auxiliar. COMP **auxiliary verb** verbo auxiliar.

available [əˈveɪləbəl] *adj* disponible.

avalanche [ˈævəlɑːnʃ] *n* **1** alud *m*. **2** *fig* avalancha.

avarice [ˈævərɪs] *n* avaricia.

avenge [əˈvendʒ] *vt* vengar.

avenue [ˈævənjuː] *n* **1** *(street)* avenida. **2** *(means)* vía.

average [ˈævərɪdʒ] *n* promedio, media. LOC **above average** por encima de la media. ▌**below average** por debajo de la media. ▌**on average** por término medio.
▶ *adj* **1** medio,-a. **2** *(not special)* corriente, regular.
▶ *vt* hacer un promedio de: *I average 10 kilometres an hour* hago un promedio de 10 kilómetros por hora.

aversion [əˈvɜːʒən] *n* aversión *f*.

avert [əˈvɜːt] *vt* *(avoid)* evitar. LOC **to avert one's eyes** apartar la vista.

aviary [ˈeɪvjərɪ] *n* pajarera.
ⓘ *pl* aviaries.

aviation [eɪvɪˈeɪʃən] *n* aviación *f*.

aviator [ˈeɪvɪeɪtər] *n* aviador,-ra.

avid [ˈævɪd] *adj* ávido,-a.

avocado [ævəˈkɑːdəʊ] [also **avocado pear**] *n* aguacate *m*.
ⓘ *pl* avocados.

avoid [əˈvɔɪd] *vt* **1** evitar. **2** *(question)* eludir. **3** *(person)* esquivar.

awake [əˈweɪk] *adj* despierto,-a.
▶ *vi* **1** despertar. **2** despertarse.
ⓘ *pt* awoke [əˈwəʊk], *pp* awoken [əˈwəʊkən].

awaken [əˈweɪkən] *vt-vi* → awake.
ⓘ *pt & pp* awakened.

award [əˈwɔːd] *n* **1** *(prize)* premio; *(medal)* condecoración *f*; *(trophy)* tro-feo. **2** *(grant)* beca. **3** *(damages)* indemnización *f*.
▶ *vt* **1** *(prize, grant)* otorgar, conceder. **2** *(damages)* adjudicar.

aware [əˈweər] *adj* **1** consciente. **2** *(informed)* informado,-a, enterado,-a. LOC **to be aware of** ser consciente de. ▌**to become aware of** darse cuenta de.

away [əˈweɪ] *adv* **1** lejos, fuera, alejándose: *he lives 4 km away* vive a 4 km (de aquí); *the wedding is 6 weeks away* faltan 6 semanas para la boda. **2** *(indicating continuity)*: *they worked away all day* trabajaron todo el día. LOC **to go away** irse, marcharse. ▌**to put away** guardar. ▌**to run away** irse corriendo.

awe [ɔː] *n* sobrecogimiento.

awful [ˈɔːfʊl] *adj* **1** *(shocking)* atroz, horrible. **2** *fam* *(very bad)* fatal, horrible, espantoso,-a.

awfully [ˈɔːfʊlɪ] *adv* *fam* terriblemente.

awhile [əˈwaɪl] *adv* un rato.

awkward [ˈɔːkwəd] *adj* **1** *(clumsy - person)* torpe; *(- expression)* poco elegante. **2** *(difficult)* difícil; *(uncooperative)* poco cooperativo,-a: *it's an awkward place to get to* es difícil llegar hasta allí. **3** *(embarrassing)* embarazoso,-a, delicado,-a. **5** *(uncomfortable)* incómodo,-a.

awning [ˈɔːnɪŋ] *n* toldo.

awoke [əˈwəʊk] *pt* → awake.

awoken [əˈwəʊkən] *pp* → awake.

ax [æks] *n* US → axe.

axe [æks] *n* hacha.

axiom [ˈæksɪəm] *n* axioma *m*.

axis [ˈæksɪs] *n* eje *m*.

axle [ˈæksəl] *n* eje *m*.

axon [ˈæksəm] *n* axón *m*.

Azerbaijan [æzəbaɪˈdʒɑːn] *n* Azerbaiyán *m*.

Azerbaijani [æzəbaɪˈdʒɑːnɪ] *adj* azerbaiyano,-a, azerí.
▶ *n* **1** *(person)* azerbaiyano,-a, azerí *mf*. **2** *(language)* azerí *m*, azerbaiyano.

azimuth [ˈæzɪməθ] *n* acimut *m*.

Aztec [ˈæztek] *adj* azteca.
▶ *n* **1** *(person)* azteca *mf*. **2** *(language)* azteca *m*.

B

B, b [biː] *n* **1** *(the letter)* B, b *f.* **2** *(musical note)* si *m.* COMP **B road** carretera secundaria.

babble ['bæbəl] *vi* balbucear.
► *vt* farfullar.
► *n* murmullo, rumor *m.*

baboon [bə'buːn] *n* mandril *m,* babuino.

baby ['beɪbɪ] *n* **1** bebé *m.* **2** *(of animal)* cría. LOC **to have a baby** dar a luz, tener un niño. COMP **baby carriage** US cochecito de niño. ‖ **baby tooth** diente *m* de leche.
ⓘ *pl* babies.

baby-sit ['beɪbɪsɪt] *vi* hacer de canguro, cuidar niños.
ⓘ *pt & pp* baby-sat ['beɪbɪsæt], *ger* babysitting.

baby-sitter ['beɪbɪsɪtər] *n* canguro *mf.*

baby-walker ['beɪbɪwɔːkər] *n* andador *m,* tacataca *m,* tacatá *m.*

bachelor ['bætʃələr] *n* soltero. COMP **bachelor flat** piso de soltero.

❌ Bachelor no significa 'bachiller', que no tiene una traducción directa en inglés.

bacillus [bə'sɪləs] *n* bacilo.
ⓘ *pl* bacilli [bə'sɪlaɪ].

back [bæk] *n* **1** *(of person)* espalda. **2** *(of animal, book)* lomo. **3** *(of chair)* respaldo. **4** *(of hand)* dorso. **5** *(sport - player)* defensa *mf; (- position)* defensa.
► *adj* trasero,-a, de atrás.
► *adv (at the rear)* atrás; *(towards the rear)* hacia atrás. LOC **back to front** al revés.
► *vt* **1** *(support)* apoyar, respaldar. **2** *(finance)* financiar.
◆ **to back away** *vi* retirarse.
◆ **to back off** *vi* apartarse.
◆ **to back out** *vi* volverse atrás.

◆ **to back up** *vt sep (support)* apoyar; *(vehicle)* dar marcha atrás a.

✎ Cuando se combina con un verbo, la partícula **back** da el sentido de contrapartida a la acción normal del verbo. Así, to answer back, to be back, to come back, to give back, to phone back... significan 'contestar', 'estar de vuelta', 'volver', 'devolver', 'volver a llamar'...

backache ['bækeɪk] *n* dolor *m* de espalda.

backbone ['bækbəʊn] *n* columna vertebral.

backbreaking ['bækbreɪkɪŋ] *adj (work)* agotador,-ra.

backcloth ['bækklɒθ] *n* telón *m* de fondo.

backdated [bæk'deɪtɪd] *adj* con efecto retroactivo.

backer ['bækər] *n* **1** FIN promotor,-ra. **2** *(guarantor)* fiador,-ra. **3** *(supporter)* partidario,-a.

backfire [bæk'faɪər] *vi* fallar: *our plan backfired* nos salió el tiro por la culata.

background ['bækgraʊnd] *n* **1** fondo. **2** *fig (origins)* orígenes *mpl,* antecedentes *mpl.* COMP **background knowledge** conocimientos *mpl* previos. ‖ **background music** música de fondo.

backhand ['bækhænd] *n* revés *m.* COMP **backhand shot** revés *m.*

backhanded [bæk'hændɪd] *adj (compliment)* equívoco,-a.

backhander [bæk'hændər] *n fam* soborno.

backing ['bækɪŋ] *n* **1** *(support)* apoyo, respaldo. **2** MUS acompañamiento.

backlash ['bæklæʃ] *n* reacción *f* violenta y repentina.
ⓘ *pl* backlashes.

backlog ['bæklɒg] *n* acumulación *f* de trabajo, trabajos *mpl* pendientes.

backpack ['bækpæk] *n* US mochila.
▶ *vi* viajar por un país o continente: *my sister's backpacking around Europe* mi hermana está de viaje por Europa.

back-seat ['bæksi:t] *n* asiento trasero.

backside ['bæksaɪd] *n fam* trasero.

backslash ['bækslæʃ] *n* barra inversa.

backslide ['bækslaɪd] *vi* reincidir.
ⓘ *pt & pp* **backslid** ['bækslɪd].

backstage [bæk'steɪdʒ] *n* **1** *(area)* bastidores *mpl*. **2** *(dressing-rooms)* camerinos *mpl*.

backstroke ['bækstrəʊk] *n (swimming)* espalda.

backtrack ['bæktræk] *vi* **1** *(retrace one's steps)* desandar lo andado, volverse atrás. **2** *(reverse opinion)* desdecirse.

backup ['bækʌp] *n* **1** *(moral support)* apoyo. **2** COMPUT copia de seguridad. COMP **backup file** archivo de seguridad.

backward ['bækwəd] *adj* **1** hacia atrás. **2** *(child)* atrasado,-a. **3** *(shy)* tímido,-a.
▶ *adv* → **backwards**.

backwards ['bækwədz] *adv* **1** hacia atrás. **2** *(the wrong way)* al revés: *he always does things backwards* siempre hace las cosas al revés.

backyard [bæk'jɑːd] *n* patio de atrás.

bacon ['beɪkən] *n* tocino, bacón *m*.

bacteria ['bæktɪərɪə] *n pl* bacterias *fpl*.
ⓘ *sing* **bacterium**.

bacterium [bæk'tɪərɪəm] *n* bacteria.
ⓘ *pl* **bacteria**.

bad [bæd] *adj* **1** malo,-a; *(before masc noun)* mal: *he made a bad decision* tomó una mala decisión. **2** *(rotten)* podrido,-a. **3** *(serious)* grave: *they had a bad accident* tuvieron un accidente grave. **4** *(naughty)* malo,-a, travieso,-a. **5** *(aches, illnesses)* fuerte, intenso,-a: *he's got a bad headache* tiene un fuerte dolor de cabeza. LOC **to be bad at** *(skill, subject)* ser malo,-a en: *he's bad at English* es malo en inglés. ‖ **to come to a bad end** acabar mal. ‖ **to have a bad leg** tener la pierna lisiada. COMP **bad cheque** cheque *m* sin fondos.
ⓘ *comp* **worse**, *superl* **worst**.

▶ *adv* mal. LOC **to feel bad** encontrarse mal. ‖ **to look bad 1** *(person)* tener mala cara. **2** *(situation)* pintar mal.
▶ *n* lo malo. LOC **too bad!** ¡mala pata!, ¡qué lástima!

baddy ['bædɪ] *n fam* malo,-a de la película.
ⓘ *pl* **baddies**.

bade [beɪd] *pt* → **bid**.

badge [bædʒ] *n* **1** insignia, distintivo. **2** *(metallic)* chapa. COMP **lapel badge** pin *m*.

badger ['bædʒəʳ] *n* tejón *m*.

badly ['bædlɪ] *adv* **1** mal: *he behaved badly at the party* se portó mal en la fiesta. **2** *(seriously)* gravemente: *he was badly hurt in the bombing* fue gravemente herido en el atentado. **3** *(very much)* mucho,-a: *he badly needs your help* tiene mucha necesidad de tu ayuda.

bad-mannered [bæd'mænəd] *adj* maleducado,-a.

bad-tempered [bæd'tempəd] *adj (permanently)* de mal genio; *(temporarily)* malhumorado,-a, de mal humor.

baffle ['bæfəl] *vt* **1** *(perplex)* dejar perplejo,-a, desconcertar. **2** *(frustrate)* frustrar.

bag [bæg] *n* **1** *(paper, plastic)* bolsa; *(large)* saco. **2** *(handbag)* bolso. **3** *(for school)* cartera.
▶ *n pl* **bags** *(under eyes)* ojeras *fpl*. LOC **bags of** montones de.

baggage ['bægɪdʒ] *n* equipaje *m*.

baggy ['bægɪ] *adj* holgado,-a, ancho,-a.
ⓘ *comp* **baggier**, *superl* **baggiest**.

bagpipes ['bægpaɪps] *n pl* gaita *f sing*.

bail¹ [beɪl] *n* fianza. LOC **to be on bail** estar en libertad bajo fianza.
◆ **to bail out** *vt sep* **1** pagar la fianza a. **2** *fig* sacar de un apuro.

bail² [beɪl] *vt (water)* achicar.

bailiff ['beɪlɪf] *n (court officer)* alguacil *m*.

bait [beɪt] *n* cebo.
▶ *vt* **1** cebar. **2** *(torment)* atosigar. LOC **to take the bait** picar.

bake [beɪk] *vt* cocer (en el horno).
▶ *vi* cocerse.

baked [beɪkt] *adj* cocido al horno. COMP **baked apple** manzana al horno. I **baked beans** alubias *fpl* guisadas en salsa de tomate. I **baked potato** patata asada.

baker ['beɪkəʳ] *n (of bread)* panadero,-a; *(of cakes)* pastelero,-a.

bakery ['beɪkərɪ] *n (for bread)* panadería; *(for cakes)* pastelería.
ⓘ *pl* bakeries.

baking ['beɪkɪŋ] *n* cocción *f.* COMP **baking powder** levadura en polvo. I **baking soda** bicarbonato sódico.

balaclava [bælə'klɑːvə] *n* pasamontañas *m.*

balance ['bæləns] *n* **1** equilibrio. **2** *(scales)* balanza. **3** *(of account, etc)* saldo. **4** *(remainder)* resto.
▶ *vi* **1** mantenerse en equilibrio. **2** FIN cuadrar.

balanced ['bælənst] *adj* equilibrado,-a.

balcony ['bælkənɪ] *n* **1** balcón *m.* **2** *(in theatre)* anfiteatro; *(gallery)* gallinero.
ⓘ *pl* balconies.

bald [bɔːld] *adj* **1** calvo,-a. **2** *(tyre)* desgastado,-a. **3** *(style)* escueto,-a. **4** *(statement)* directo,-a, franco,-a.

Balearic [bælɪ'ærɪk] *adj* balear, baleárico,-a. COMP **the Balearic Islands** las (islas) Baleares.

ball [bɔːl] *n* **1** *(gen)* pelota; *(football, etc)* balón *m*; *(golf, billiards)* bola. **2** *(of paper)* bola; *(of wool)* ovillo. **3** *(of eye)* globo ocular. **4** *(dance)* baile *m*, fiesta. LOC **to play ball 1** US *(sport)* jugar a la pelota. **2** *(cooperate)* cooperar, colaborar. COMP **gala ball** baile *m* de etiqueta.

ballad ['bæləd] *n* balada.

ball-and-socket ['bɔːlən'sɒkɪt] COMP **ball-and-socket joint** articulación *f* de rótula.

ballast ['bæləst] *n (boat, balloon)* lastre *m.*

ballerina [bælə'riːnə] *n* bailarina.

ballet ['bæleɪ] *n* ballet *m.*

ballistics [bə'lɪstɪks] *n* balística.

balloon [bə'luːn] *n* **1** globo. **2** *(in cartoon)* bocadillo. **3** *(glass)* copa grande.

☒ Balloon no significa 'balón', que se traduce por ball.

ballot ['bælət] *n* **1** *(vote)* votación *f.* **2** *(votes recorded)* número de votos escrutados. LOC **to take a ballot on** STH someter algo a votación. COMP **ballot box** urna. I **ballot paper** papeleta.

ballpoint ['bɔːlpɔɪnt] [también **ballpoint pen**] *n* bolígrafo.

ballroom ['bɔːlruːm] *n* sala de baile. COMP **ballroom dancing** baile *m* de salón.

balm [bɑːm] *n* bálsamo.

balmy ['bɑːmɪ] *adj* **1** *(weather)* suave. **2** *(soothing)* balsámico,-a.
ⓘ *comp* balmier, *superl* balmiest.

balsam ['bɔːlsəm] *n* → balm.

balsamic [bɔːl'sæmɪk] *adj* balsámico,-a.

Baltic ['bɔːltɪk] *adj* báltico,-a. COMP **the Baltic (Sea)** el (mar) Báltico.

bamboo [bæm'buː] *n* bambú *m.*

ban [bæn] *n* prohibición *f.*
▶ *vt* prohibir.
ⓘ *pt & pp* banned, *ger* banning.

banal [bə'nɑːl] *adj* banal, trivial.

banality [bə'nælɪtɪ] *n* banalidad *f.*
ⓘ *pl* banalities.

banana [bə'nɑːnə] *n* **1** *(fruit)* plátano, banana. **2** *(tree)* bananero, AM banano.

band [bænd] *n* **1** *(gen)* banda; *(pop)* conjunto; *(jazz)* orquesta. **2** *(strip)* tira. **3** *(around arm)* brazalete *m.* **4** *(wrapper)* faja. **5** PHYS banda, frecuencia. **7** TECH correa.

bandage ['bændɪdʒ] *n* venda, vendaje *m.*
▶ *vt* vendar.
◆ **to bandage up** *vt sep* vendar.

Band-Aid® ['bændeɪd] *n* tirita®.

B and B ['biːən'biː] *abbr (bed and breakfast)* casa de huéspedes que ofrece habitación con desayuno incluido.

⊕ Los B and B son una alternativa por lo general más asequible a los hoteles. Tradicionalmente, estos establecimientos solían estar situados en casas grandes cuyos dueños obtenían así una fuente adicional de ingresos. Hoy en día, el concepto se ha ampliado y hay B and B para todos los gustos y bolsillos.

bandit ['bændɪt] *n* bandido,-a.

bandstand ['bændstænd] *n* quiosco de música.

bandwidth ['bændwɪdθ] *n* ancho de banda.

bandy ['bændɪ] *vt* SP *(ball)* pasarse. LOC **to bandy sb's name about** difamar ALGN, hablar mal de ALGN.
ⓘ *pt & pp* bandied, *ger* bandying.

bandy-legged ['bændɪləgᵈd] *adj* patizambo,-a.

bang [bæŋ] *n* 1 *(blow)* golpe *m*. 2 *(noise)* ruido; *(of gun)* estampido; *(explosion)* estallido; *(of door)* portazo.
▶ *vt* golpear, dar golpes en.
▶ *adv fam* justo: *bang in the middle* justo en medio. LOC **to bang the door** dar un portazo.
▶ *n pl* bangs US flequillo.

banger ['bæŋər] *n* 1 *(firework)* petardo. 2 GB *fam (sausage)* salchicha. 3 *fam (car)* tartana, trasto.

bangle ['bæŋgəl] *n* brazalete *m*.

banish ['bænɪʃ] *vt (expel)* desterrar.

banishment ['bænɪʃmənt] *n* destierro, exilio.

banister ['bænɪstər] *n* barandilla.

bank¹ [bæŋk] *n* banco. COMP **bank holiday** GB festivo, día festivo.
▶ *vt (deposit money)* ingresar, depositar.

bank² [bæŋk] *n* 1 *(of river)* ribera; *(edge)* orilla: *on the banks of the Manzanares* a orillas del Manzanares. 2 *(mound)* loma; *(embankment)* terraplén *m*.
▶ *vt* 1 *(soil, earth)* amontonar. 2 *(river)* encauzar.

bankbook ['bæŋkbʊk] *n* libreta de ahorro, cartilla de ahorro.

banker ['bæŋkər] *n* banquero,-a.

banking ['bæŋkɪŋ] *n* banca.

banknote ['bæŋknəʊt] *n* billete *m* de banco.

bankruptcy ['bæŋkrʌptsɪ] *n* quiebra, bancarrota.
ⓘ *pl* bankruptcies.

banner ['bænər] *n* 1 *(flag)* bandera. 2 *(placard)* pancarta. 3 *(on web page)* banner *m*, anuncio.
▶ *adj* US excelente, de primera. COMP **banner headlines** grandes titulares *mpl*.

banns [bænz] *n pl* amonestaciones *fpl*.

banquet ['bæŋkwɪt] *n* banquete *m*.

banter ['bæntər] *n* bromas *fpl*, guasa.
▶ *vi* bromear, estar de guasa.

baptise [bæp'taɪz] *vt* → **baptize**.

baptism ['bæptɪzəm] *n* bautismo.

baptize [bæp'taɪz] *vt* bautizar.

bar [baːr] *n* 1 *(iron, gold)* barra. 2 *(in prison)* barrote *m*. 3 *(soap)* pastilla. 4 *(obstacle)* obstáculo. 5 *(counter)* barra, mostrador *m*. 6 *(room)* bar *m*. 7 *(in court)* tribunal *m*: *the prisoner at the bar* el acusado, la acusada. COMP **bar chart** gráfica de barras.
▶ *vt* 1 *(door)* atrancar; *(road, access)* cortar. 2 *(ban)* prohibir, vedar; *(from a place)* prohibir la entrada. 3 *(prevent)* impedir.
ⓘ *pt & pp* barred, *ger* barring.
▶ *prep* excepto, salvo: *they all came, bar his parents* acudieron todos, excepto sus padres.
▶ *n* **the Bar** JUR el colegio de abogados.

barbarian [baː'beərɪən] *adj* bárbaro,-a.
▶ *n* bárbaro,-a.

barbecue ['baːbəkjuː] *n* barbacoa.
▶ *vt* asar a la parrilla.
ⓘ *ger* barbecuing.

barbed [baːbd] *adj* 1 con púas, punzante. 2 *fig* mordaz, incisivo,-a.

barber [baː'baːr] *n* barbero. COMP **barber's shop** barbería.

barbiturate [baː'bɪtʃərət] *n* barbitúrico.

bare [beər] *adj* 1 *(naked)* desnudo,-a; *(head)* descubierto,-a. 2 *(land)* raso,-a; *(tree, plant)* sin hojas. 3 *(empty)* vacío,-a; *(unfurnished)* sin muebles. 4 *(scant)* escaso,-a. 5 *(worn)* gastado,-a, raído,-a.
▶ *vt* desnudar; *(uncover)* descubrir.

barefaced ['beəfeɪst] *adj* descarado,-a.

barefoot ['beəfʊt] *adj* descalzo,-a.
▶ *adv* descalzo,-a.

barely ['beəlɪ] *adv* apenas.

bargain ['baːgən] *n* 1 *(agreement)* trato, acuerdo. 2 *(good buy)* ganga.
▶ *vi* 1 *(negotiate)* negociar. 2 *(haggle)* regatear. COMP **bargain offer** oferta especial. **bargain price** precio de oferta, precio de saldo.

barge [baːdʒ] *n* gabarra, barcaza.

baritone ['bærɪtəʊn] *n* barítono.
barium ['beərɪʌm] *n* bario.
bark¹ [ba:k] *n* **1** *(of dog)* ladrido. **2** *(cough)*
tos *f* fuerte.
▸ *vi* ladrar.
bark² [ba:k] *n (of tree)* corteza.
barley ['ba:lɪ] *n* cebada.
barmaid ['ba:meɪd] *n* camarera.
barman ['ba:mən] *n* camarero, barman *m*.
ⓘ *pl* **barmen** ['ba:men].
barn [ba:n] *n (for grain)* granero.
barnacle ['ba:nəkəl] *n* percebe *m*.
barnyard ['ba:nja:d] *n* corral *m*.
barometer [bə'rɒmɪtə'] *n* barómetro.
baron ['bærən] *n* barón *m*.
baroness ['bærənəs] *n* baronesa.
baroque [bə'rɒk] *adj* barroco,-a.
▸ *n* barroco.
barrack ['bɒrək] *vt (jeer)* abuchear.
barracks ['bærəks] *n pl* cuartel *m*.

> ✎ Puede considerarse singular o plural:
> *where is/are the barracks* ¿dónde está el
> cuartel.

barrage ['bæra:ʒ] *n* presa, embalse *m*.
barrel ['bærəl] *n* **1** *(of beer)* barril *m*; *(of
wine)* tonel *m*, cuba. **2** *(of gun)* cañón *m*.
3 *(of pen)* depósito. **4** TECH tambor *m*.
barren ['bærən] *adj* **1** *(land, woman)* estéril. **2** *(meagre)* escaso,-a.
barricade [bærɪ'keɪd] *n* barricada.
▸ *vt* poner barricadas en.
barrier ['bærɪə'] *n* barrera. COMP **barrier
reef** banco de coral, arrecife *m*.
barrister ['bærɪstə'] *n* abogado,-a
(capacitado,-a para actuar en tribunales superiores).
barrow ['bærəʊ] *n (wheelbarrow)* carretilla; *(for carrying goods)* carro.
barstool ['ba:stu:l] *n* taburete *m* de bar.
bartender ['ba:tendə'] *n* US camarero,
barman *m*.
barter ['ba:tə'] *n* trueque *m*.
▸ *vt* trocar.
basalt ['bæsɔ:lt] *n* basalto.
base¹ [beɪs] *n* **1** *(gen)* base *f*. **2** ARCH *(of
column)* basa, base *f*. **3** *(of word)* raíz *f*.
▸ *vt* basar.

base² [beɪs] *adj* **1** bajo,-a, vil. **2** *(metal)*
común, de baja ley.
baseball ['beɪsbɔ:l] *n* béisbol *m*.
baseline ['beɪslaɪn] *n* **1** SP *(tennis)* línea
de saque. **2** *(diagram)* línea cero. **3** ART
punto de fuga.
basement ['beɪsmənt] *n* sótano.
bash [bæʃ] *vt fam* golpear, aporrear.
▸ *n* **1** *fam (blow)* golpe *m*. **2** *fam (try)* intento.
bashful ['bæʃful] *adj* vergonzoso,-a,
tímido,-a, modesto,-a.
basic ['beɪsɪk] *adj* **1** básico,-a. **2** *(elementary)* elemental, para principiantes.
basil ['bæzəl] *n* BOT albahaca.
basilica [bə'zɪlɪkə] *n* basílica.
basin ['beɪsən] *n* **1** *(bowl)* cuenco; *(washbowl)* palangana. **2** *(washbasin)* lavabo.
3 GEOG cuenca.
basis ['beɪsɪs] *n* base *f*, fundamento.
LOC **on the basis of ... 1** *(according to)* según. **2** *(in accordance with)* de acuerdo
con. **3** *(starting from)* a partir de. **2** *(because of)* por, a causa de.
ⓘ *pl* **bases** ['beɪsi:z].

> ✎ En ocasiones, **basis** puede traducirse
> al español mediante un adverbio: *on a
> temporary/regular/weekly basis* temporal-
> mente/regularmente/semanalmente.

bask [ba:sk] *vi* tumbarse al sol.
basket ['ba:skɪt] *n* **1** cesta, cesto. **2**
(basketball) canasta, cesta. **3** *(of balloon)*
barquilla.
basketball ['ba:skɪtbɔ:l] *n* baloncesto.
Basque [ba:sk] *adj* vasco,-a.
▸ *n* **1** *(person)* vasco,-a. **2** *(language)* vasco, euskera *m*.
bas-relief [bæsrɪ'li:f] *n* bajorrelieve *m*.
bass¹ [beɪs] *n* **1** MUS *(singer)* bajo. **2** MUS
(notes) graves *mpl*. **3** MUS *(guitar)* bajo.
▸ *adj* MUS bajo,-a.
bass² [bæs] *n (fish)* róbalo, lubina; *(freshwater)* perca.
bassoon [bə'su:n] *n* fagot *m*.
bastard ['ba:stəd] *adj & n* bastardo,-a.
baste [beɪst] *vt* CULIN rociar, bañar.
bastion ['bæstɪən] *n* baluarte *m*.
bat¹ [bæt] *n* ZOOL murciélago.

bat² [bæt] *n* SP bate *m*; *(table tennis)* pala.
▶ *vi* batear.
① *pt & pp* batted, *ger* batting.

batch [bætʃ] *n (gen)* lote *m*, remesa; *(of bread, etc)* hornada.

bath [bɑːθ] *n* 1 baño. 2 *(tub)* bañera.
▶ *vi* bañarse.
▶ *n pl* baths piscina *f sing* municipal.
LOC **to have a bath / take a bath** bañarse. ‖ **to run a bath** preparar un baño.

bathe [beɪð] *vt* 1 MED *(cut, wound)* lavar. 2 *(eyes)* bañarse. 3 *fig (with light)* bañar.
▶ *vi (in sea)* bañarse.

⊕ La diferencia entre los verbos bath y bathe es que este último se emplea para referirse a un baño en el mar, un río o un lago, es decir, sin un objetivo higiénico.

bather ['beɪðəʳ] *n* bañista *mf*.

bathing ['beɪðɪŋ] *n* baño. LOC "No bathing" «Prohibido bañarse». COMP **bathing costume** traje *m* de baño. ‖ **bathing suit** traje *m* de baño.

bathrobe ['bɑːθrəʊb] *n* albornoz *m*.

bathroom ['bɑːθruːm] *n* cuarto de baño.

bathtub ['bɑːθtʌb] *n* US bañera.

bathyscaph ['bæθɪskæf] *n* batiscafo.

baton ['bætən, 'bætɒn] *n* 1 *(truncheon)* porra. 2 MUS batuta. 3 SP testigo.

batrachian [bə'treɪkjən] *adj* batracio,-a.
▶ *n* batracio.

battalion [bə'tæljən] *n* batallón *m*.

batter¹ ['bætəʳ] *n* CULIN rebozado.

batter² ['bætəʳ] *vt (person)* golpear, apalear; *(bruise)* magullar; *(object)* maltratar, estropear.

batter³ ['bætəʳ] *n* SP *(baseball, cricket)* bateador,-ra.

battery ['bætərɪ] *n* 1 ELEC *(wet)* batería; *(dry)* pila. 2 MIL *(of artillery)* batería. 3 *(series)* batería.
① *pl* batteries.

battle ['bætəl] *n* batalla.
▶ *vi* pelearse, batirse.

battlefield ['bætəlfiːld] *n* campo de batalla.

battleship ['bætəlʃɪp] *n* acorazado.

bauble ['bɔːbəl] *n* 1 *(trinket)* baratija. 2 *(Christmas decoration)* bola de Navidad.

bawl [bɔːl] *vi* chillar, gritar.

bay¹ [beɪ] *n* GEOG bahía; *(large)* golfo.
COMP **Bay of Biscay** golfo de Vizcaya.

bay² [beɪ] *n (tree)* laurel *m*.

bay³ [beɪ] *vi (howl)* aullar.

bay⁴ [beɪ] *n* 1 ARCH *(recess)* hueco, nicho. 2 *(in factory)* nave *f*.

bayonet ['beɪənət] *n* MIL bayoneta.

bazaar [bə'zɑːʳ] *n* bazar *m*.

BBC ['biːbiːˈsiː] *abbr* (British Broadcasting Corporation) compañía británica de radiodifusión; *(abbreviation)* BBC *f*.

BC ['biːˈsiː] *abbr* (before Christ) antes de Cristo.

be [biː] *vi* 1 *(permanent or essential characteristic)* ser: *she's clever* es inteligente. 2 *(nationality, origin)* ser: *John's English* John es inglés. 3 *(occupation)* ser: *we are both teachers* los dos somos profesores. 4 *(ownership, authorship)* ser: *it's my pencil* es mi lápiz. 5 *(composition)* ser: *this cupboard is oak* este armario es de roble. 6 *(use)* ser: *this product is for tiles* este producto es para baldosas. 7 *(location)* estar: *Whitby is on the coast* Whitby está en la costa. 8 *(temporary state)* estar: *your supper's cold* tu cena está fría; *how are you?* ¿cómo estás? 9 *(age)* tener: *Philip is 22* Philip tiene 22 años. 10 *(price)* costar, valer: *a single ticket is £9.50* un billete de ida cuesta 9,50 libras. 11 *(ner)* tener: *he's hot/cold* tiene calor/frío; *he's right* tiene razón. LOC **to be about to + inf** estar para + *inf*, estar a punto de + *inf*: *the train is about to arrive* el tren está a punto de llegar.
▶ *aux* 1 be + *pres part (action in progress or near future)* estar: *it is raining* está lloviendo; *the train is coming* viene el tren; *I am going on Thursday* iré el jueves. 2 to be + *pp (passive)* ser: *she was arrested at the border* fue detenida en la frontera, la detuvieron en la frontera. 3 be + *to* + *inf (future)*: *the King is to visit Egypt* el Rey visitará Egipto. LOC **there is / there are** hay.
◆ **to be after** *vi* querer, estar buscando: *what are you after?* ¿qué estás buscando?
◆ **to be off** *vi (leave)* salir, marcharse; *(be stale, bad)* estar pasado,-a.
◆ **to be in** *vi* 1 *(at home)* estar en casa. 2 *(in fashion)* estar de moda.

◆ **to be out** *vi (away)* no estar, estar fuera: *John's out at the moment* John no está en estos momentos.

◆ **to be away** *vi* estar fuera.

◆ **to be back** *vi* estar de vuelta, haber vuelto.

● **to be over** *vi* haber acabado.

ⓘ *pres 1ª pers* am, *2ª pers sing y todas las del pl* are, *3ª pers sing* is; *pt 1ª y 3ª pers sing* was, *2ª pers sing y todas del pl* were; *pp* been.

beach [biːtʃ] *n* playa.

ⓘ *pl* beaches.

beacon ['biːkən] *n* **1** *(fire)* almenara. **2** *(light)* baliza. **3** *(lighthouse)* faro.

bead [biːd] *n* **1** *(on rosary, necklace)* cuenta; *(glass)* abalorio. **2** *(of liquid)* gota.

beak [biːk] *n* pico.

beaker ['biːkəʳ] *n* **1** taza alta. **2** *(for measuring, playing dice)* cubilete *m*. **3** CHEM vaso de precipitación.

beam [biːm] *n* **1** *(wooden)* viga. **2** *(of light)* rayo. **3** *(width of ship)* manga. **4** *(smile)* sonrisa radiante. **5** PHYS haz *m*.
▶ *vi* **1** *(shine)* brillar. **2** *(smile)* sonreír.
▶ *vt* irradiar, emitir. COMP **electron beam** haz *m* de electrones.

bean [biːn] *n* **1** *(vegetable)* alubia, judía, haba. **2** *(of coffee)* grano.

beansprout ['biːnspraʊt] *n* brote *m* de soja.

bear¹ [beəʳ] *n* ZOOL oso. COMP **bear cub** ZOOL osezno. ▌ **grizzly bear** oso pardo. ▌ **the Great Bear** la Osa Mayor. ▌ **the Little Bear** la Osa Menor.

bear² [beəʳ] *vt* **1** *(gen)* llevar. **2** *(show signs of)* mostrar, revelar. **3** *(weight)* soportar, aguantar; *(responsibility, cost)* asumir. **4** *(fruit)* producir. **5** FIN *(interest)* devengar.
ⓘ *pt* bore [bɔːʳ], *pp* borne [bɔːⁿ].

bearable ['beərəbəl] *adj* soportable, llevadero,-a.

beard [bɪəd] *n* **1** *(on face)* barba. **2** *(of corn)* arista, raspa.

bearded ['bɪədɪd] *adj* barbudo,-a.

bearing ['beərɪŋ] *n* **1** *(posture)* porte *m*. **2** *(relevance)* relación *f*. **3** *(importance)* trascendencia. **4** TECH cojinete *m*. **5** ARCH soporte *m*, columna. **6** MAR rumbo, orientación *f*.

bearskin ['beəskɪn] *n (hat)* birretina.

beast [biːst] *n* bestia, animal *m*.

beastly ['biːstlɪ] *adj* **1** bestial. **2** *(unpleasant)* antipático,-a. **3** *sl (damn)* dichoso,-a, maldito,-a.
ⓘ *comp* beastlier, *superl* beastliest.

beat [biːt] *n* **1** *(of heart)* latido. **2** *(noise)* golpe *m*, ruido; *(of rain)* tamborileo; *(of wings)* aleteo. **3** MUS ritmo. **4** *(of policeman)* ronda.
▶ *adj fam* agotado,-a, rendido,-a.
▶ *vt* **1** *(hit)* golpear; *(metals)* martillear; *(person)* azotar; *(drum)* tocar. **2** CULIN batir. **3** *(defeat)* vencer, derrotar; *(in competition)* ganar.
▶ *vi* **1** *(heart)* latir. **2** *(wings)* batir.
◆ **to beat down** *vt sep* **1** *(door)* derribar, echar abajo. **2** *(price)* conseguir un precio más bajo.
◆ **to beat up** *vt sep* dar una paliza a.
ⓘ *pt* beat, *pp* beaten ['biːtən].

beater ['biːtəʳ] *n* **1** CULIN batidora. **2** *(in hunting)* ojeador,-ra.

beating ['biːtɪŋ] *n* **1** *(thrashing)* paliza. **2** *(defeat)* derrota. **3** *(of heart)* latidos *mpl*.

beautician [bjuːˈtɪʃən] *n* esteticista *mf*.

beautiful ['bjuːtɪfʊl] *adj* **1** *(person, object, place)* hermoso,-a, bonito,-a, precioso,-a; *(person)* guapo,-a. **2** *(wonderful)* maravilloso,-a, magnífico,-a. **3** *(delicious)* delicioso,-a.

beauty ['bjuːtɪ] *n* belleza. COMP **beauty spot 1** *(on face)* lunar *m*. **2** *(place)* lugar *m* pintoresco.
ⓘ *pl* beauties.

beaver ['biːvəʳ] *n* castor *m*.

became [bɪˈkeɪm] *pt* → become.

because [bɪˈkɒz] *conj* porque.
▶ *prep* **because of** a causa de: *they were late because of the snow* llegaron tarde a causa de la nieve.

become [bɪˈkʌm] *vi* **1** *(with noun)* convertirse en, hacerse, llegar a ser: *to become a doctor/teacher* hacerse médico,-a/maestro,-a; *to become friends* hacerse amigos. **2** *(change into)* convertirse en, transformarse en: *chrysalises become butterflies* las crisálidas se transforman en mariposas. **3** *(irrevocable state)* volverse; *(temporary state)* ponerse; *(involuntary state)* quedarse: *to become mad* volverse loco,-a, *to become fat* engordar; *to become sad* ponerse triste.

ⓘ *pt* **became** [brˈkeɪm], *pp* **become**.

becoming [brˈkʌmɪŋ] *adj* **1** *(dress, etc)* que sienta bien, favorecedor,-ra. **2** *(behaviour, language)* apropiado,-a.

bed [bed] *n* **1** cama. **2** *(for animals)* lecho. **3** *(of flowers)* arriate *m*, macizo. **4** *(of river)* lecho, cauce *m*; *(of sea)* fondo. **5** GEOL capa, yacimiento. ⌊ᴏᴄ⌋ **to go to bed** acostarse. ▌**to put SB to bed** acostar a ALGN. ▌**to make the bed** hacer la cama. ⌊ᴄᴏᴍᴘ⌋ **bunk bed** litera. ▌**double bed** cama de matrimonio. ▌**single bed** cama individual. ▌**twin beds** camas *fpl* separadas. ▌**bed and board** pensión *f* completa. ▌**bed and breakfast** alojamiento con desayuno incluido.

✎ Consulta B and B.

bedbug [ˈbedbʌg] *n* chinche *f*.
bedclothes [ˈbedkləʊðz] *n pl* ropa de cama.
bedding [ˈbedɪŋ] *n* **1** ropa de cama. **2** *(for animals)* lecho.
bedpan [ˈbedpæn] *n* cuña, orinal *m* de cama.
bedridden [ˈbedrɪdən] *adj* postrado,-a en cama.
bedroom [ˈbedruːm] *n* dormitorio, habitación *f*.
bedside [ˈbedsaɪd] *n* cabecera.
bedsit [bedˈsɪt] *n* estudio.

⊕ El **bedsit** es un tipo de alojamiento de alquiler asequible típico del Reino Unido. Consiste en una sola habitación que hace de dormitorio, sala de estar y comedor. Se suele compartir el baño con otras personas y a veces se tiene derecho a cocina.

bedsore [ˈbedsɔː] *n* MED llaga, úlcera.
bedspread [ˈbedspred] *n* cubrecama.
bedtime [ˈbedtaɪm] *n* la hora de acostarse.
bee [biː] *n* abeja.
beech [biːtʃ] *n* *(wood)* haya. ⌊ᴄᴏᴍᴘ⌋ **beech grove** hayal *m*, hayedo. ▌**beech tree** haya.
bee-eater [ˈbiːiːtər] *n* abejaruco.

beef [biːf] *n* **1** *(meat)* carne *f* de buey, carne *f* de vaca. **2** *(animal)* buey *m*, vaca; *(cattle)* ganado vacuno. ⌊ᴄᴏᴍᴘ⌋ **corned beef** carne *f* de vaca en conserva.
beefburger [ˈbiːfbɜːgər] *n* hamburguesa.
beefeater [ˈbiːfiːtər] *n* alabardero de la Torre de Londres.
beefsteak [ˈbiːfsteɪk] *n* bistec *m*.
beehive [ˈbiːhaɪv] *n* colmena.
beekeeper [ˈbiːkiːpər] *n* apicultor,-ra.
beekeeping [ˈbiːkiːpɪŋ] *n* apicultura.
beeline [ˈbiːlaɪn] *n* línea recta. ⌊ᴏᴄ⌋ **to make a beeline for...** irse directamente a…
been [biːn, bɪn] *pp* → **be**.
beep [biːp] *n* pitido.
▶ *vi* pitar, tocar el pito. ⌊ᴏᴄ⌋ **to beep the horn** tocar el claxon.
beer [bɪər] *n* cerveza.
beeswax [ˈbiːzwæks] *n* cera de abejas.
beet [biːt] *n* remolacha.
beetle [ˈbiːtəl] *n* escarabajo.
beetroot [ˈbiːtruːt] *n* **1** [*pl* **beet**] remolacha azucarera. **2** US [*pl* **beets**] remolacha.
before [brˈfɔː] *prep* **1** *(earlier)* antes de. **2** *(in front of)* delante de; *(in the presence of)* ante; *(for the attention of)* ante: *he's before me in the queue* va delante de mi en la cola; *he appeared before the judge* compareció ante el juez. **3** *(rather than)* antes que. **4** *(ahead)* por delante. **5** *(first)* primero: *ladies before gentlemen* las señoras primero.
▶ *conj* **1** *(earlier than)* antes de + *inf*, antes de que + *subj*: *don't forget to say goodbye before you go* no te olvides de despedirte antes de irte. **2** *(rather than)* antes de + *inf*: *he would starve before he asked them for money* preferiría morir de hambre antes de pedirles dinero.
▶ *adv* **1** *(earlier)* antes. **2** *(previous)* anterior. **3** *(already)* ya: *we've seen it before* ya lo hemos visto.
beforehand [brˈfɔːhænd] *adv* **1** *(earlier)* antes. **2** *(in advance)* de antemano, con antelación: *payment must be made a month beforehand* los pagos deben efec-

tuarse con un mes de antelación. **3** *(before)* antes: *they arrived two hours beforehand* llegaron dos horas antes.

befriend [bɪˈfrend] *vt* ofrecer su amistad a.

beg [beg] *vt* **1** mendigar. **2** *(ask for)* pedir. **3** *lit (beseech)* suplicar, rogar. [LOC] **I beg your pardon** ¿cómo ha dicho?
▸ *vi* **1** mendigar. **2** *(dog)* sentarse *(con las patas delanteras levantadas)*.
ⓘ *pt & pp* begged, *ger* begging.

began [bɪˈgæn] *pt* → begin.

beggar [ˈbegəʳ] *n* **1** mendigo,-a, pordiosero,-a. **2** *fam* tipo, individuo,-a: *he's a funny beggar* es un tipo raro.

begin [bɪˈgɪn] *vt* empezar, comenzar.
ⓘ *pt* began [bɪˈgæn], *pp* begun [bɪˈgʌn], *ger* beginning.

beginner [bɪˈgɪnəʳ] *n* principiante *mf*.

beginning [bɪˈgɪnɪŋ] *n* **1** principio, comienzo. **2** *(cause)* origen *m*, causa.

begrudge [bɪˈgrʌdʒ] *vt* **1** *(envy)* envidiar. **2** *(disapprove)* desaprobar.

beguile [bɪˈgaɪl] *vt* **1** *(seduce)* seducir, atraer; *(bewitch)* embrujar. **2** *(cheat)* engañar.

begun [bɪˈgʌn] *pp* → begin.

behalf [bɪˈhɑːf] *phr* on behalf of *(acting for)* en nombre de, de parte de; *(in favour of)* por, en favor de; *(for the benefit of)* para, en beneficio de.

behave [bɪˈheɪv] *vi* **1** *(people)* comportarse, portarse. **2** *(equipment, machinery)* funcionar bien: *this computer won't behave* este ordenador no funciona bien.

behavior [bɪˈheɪvjəʳ] *n* US → behaviour.

behaviour [bɪˈheɪvjəʳ] *n* **1** *(of person)* conducta, comportamiento. **2** *(of equipment, machine)* funcionamiento. **3** *(treatment)* trato.

behead [bɪˈhed] *vt* decapitar.

behind [bɪˈhaɪnd] *prep* detrás de.
▸ *adv* **1** detrás, atrás. **2** *(late)* atrasado,-a. **3** *(with payment)* retrasado,-a: *he's behind with the payments* está retrasado en los pagos.
▸ *n fam (buttocks)* trasero.

behindhand [bɪˈhaɪndhænd] *adv* en retraso, retrasado,-a.

beige [beɪʒ] *n* beige *m*.
▸ *adj* (de color) beige.

being [ˈbiːɪŋ] *n* **1** *(living thing)* ser *m*. **2** *(existence)* existencia. [LOC] **being as** ya que, puesto que: *being as they arrived late …* puesto que llegaron tarde … ‖ **for the time being** por ahora, de momento. [COMP] **human being** ser *m* humano.

Belarus [ˈbelərʌs] *n* Bielorrusia.

belated [bɪˈleɪtɪd] *adj fam* tardío,-a.

belay [bɪˈleɪ] *vt (boat)* amarrar; *(rope in mountaineering)* asegurar, fijar.

belch [beltʃ] *n* eructo.
▸ *vi* eructar. [LOC] **to belch (out)** vomitar, arrojar: *the burning building belched out smoke* el edificio en llamas arrojaba humo.

beleaguer [bɪˈliːgəʳ] *vt* **1** *(beseige)* sitiar, cercar. **2** *(harass)* perseguir, hostigar.

belfry [ˈbelfrɪ] *n* campanario.
ⓘ *pl* belfries.

Belgian [ˈbeldʒən] *adj* belga.
▸ *n* belga *mf*.

Belgium [ˈbeldʒəm] *n* Bélgica.

belie [bɪˈlaɪ] *vt* **1** *(contradict)* mostrar como falso. **2** *(misrepresent)* no reflejar, ocultar. **3** *(fail to justify)* defraudar.

belief [bɪˈliːf] *n* **1** *(gen)* creencia. **2** *(opinion)* opinión *f*. **3** *(confidence)* confianza: *he has no belief in the legal system* no tiene confianza en el sistema jurídico. [LOC] **to the best of my belief** que yo sepa. ‖ **it is beyond belief** parece mentira.

believable [bɪˈliːvəbəl] *adj* creíble, verosímil.

believe [bɪˈliːv] *vt* **1** *(accept as true, think)* creer. **2** *(suppose)* suponer.
▸ *vi* **1** creer (in, en). **2** *(trust)* confiar (in, en). **3** *(support, be in favour of)* ser partidario,-a (in, de). **4** REL tener fe. [LOC] **it is believed that** se cree que.

believer [bɪˈliːvəʳ] *n* **1** creyente *mf*. **2** *(supporter)* partidario,-a.

belittle [bɪˈlɪtəl] *vt* menospreciar.

bell [bel] *n* **1** *(church, etc)* campana. **2** *(handbell)* campanilla. **3** *(on bicycle, door, etc)* timbre *m*. **4** *(on toy, hat)* cascabel *m*. **5** *(cowbell)* cencerro. **6** *(flower)* campanilla. [LOC] **to ring the bell** tocar el timbre.

B

bell-bottoms [belˈbɒtəmz] *n pl* pantalones *mpl* acampanados.

bellboy [ˈbelbɔɪ] *n* botones *m*.

bellhop [ˈbelhɒp] *n* US botones *m*.

belligerent [bɪˈlɪdʒərənt] *adj* beligerante.

bellow [ˈbeləʊ] *n* bramido.
▶ *vi* bramar.
▶ *n pl* **bellows** fuelle *m sing*.

belly [ˈbelɪ] *n* **1** *(person)* vientre *m*, barriga. **2** *(animal)* panza. [COMP] **belly button** ombligo. ▌ **belly laugh** carcajada.
ⓘ *pl* **bellies**.

bellyache [ˈbelɪeɪk] *n fam* dolor *m* de barriga.
▶ *vi fam* quejarse.

bellybutton [ˈbelɪbʌtən] *n fam* ombligo.

belong [bɪˈlɒŋ] *vi* **1** pertenecer (to, a), ser (to, de). **2** *(be a member of a club)* ser socio,-a (to, de); *(be a member of a political party)* ser miembro (to, de). **3** *(have suitable qualities)* ser apto,-a (in, para).

belongings [bɪˈlɒŋɪŋz] *n pl* pertenencias *fpl*, bártulos *mpl*.

beloved [*(adj)* bɪˈlʌvd; *(n)* bɪˈlʌvɪd] *adj* querido,-a, amado,-a.
▶ *n* amado,-a.

below [bɪˈləʊ] *prep* **1** debajo de, bajo. **2** por debajo (de). **3** *(lower than)* bajo. [LOC] **below sea level** por debajo del nivel del mar.
▶ *adv* **1** abajo. **2** de abajo. [LOC] **see below** véase abajo.

belt [belt] *n* **1** cinturón *m*. **2** TECH correa. **3** *(area)* zona.
▶ *vt fam (hit)* arrear un tortazo.
◆ **to belt along** *vi fam* ir a todo gas.
◆ **to belt up** *vi fam* cerrar el pico.

bemused [bɪˈmjuːzd] *adj* perplejo,-a.

bench [bentʃ] *n* **1** banco. **2** JUR tribunal *m*. **3** SP banquillo. [LOC] **to be on the bench** ser juez,-za.
ⓘ *pl* **benches**.

bend [bend] *n* **1** *(in road, etc)* curva. **2** *(in pipe)* ángulo.
▶ *vt* **1** doblar, curvar. **2** *(head)* inclinar; *(back)* doblar, encorvar; *(knee)* doblar, flexionar.
▶ *vi* **1** doblarse, combarse: *the legs of the chair bent when he sat down* las patas de la silla se combaron cuando se sentó. **2** *(head)* inclinarse; *(back)* encorvarse. **3** *(road)* torcer.
◆ **to bend down** *vi* agacharse.
◆ **to bend over** *vi* inclinarse.
ⓘ *pt & pp* **bent** [bent].

beneath [bɪˈniːθ] *prep* **1** bajo, debajo de. **2** por debajo de: *the underground line runs beneath our house* la línea de metro va por debajo de nuestra casa. **3** *fig* indigno,-a de, no digno,-a de: *it's beneath you to behave like this* es indigno de ti comportarte de esta manera.
▶ *adv* de abajo: *she lives in the flat beneath* vive en el piso de abajo.

benefactor [ˈbenɪfæktə] *n* benefactor *m*.

beneficial [benɪˈfɪʃəl] *adj* beneficioso,-a, provechoso,-a.

beneficiary [benɪˈfɪʃərɪ] *n* beneficiario,-a.
ⓘ *pl* **beneficiaries**.

benefit [ˈbenɪfɪt] *n* **1** *(advantage)* beneficio, provecho. **2** *(good)* bien *m*. **3** *(allowance)* subsidio. **4** *(charity performance)* función *f* benéfica; *(charity game)* partido benéfico.
▶ *vt* beneficiar.
▶ *vi* beneficiarse (from, de).
ⓘ *pt & pp* **benefited** (US **benefitted**), *ger* **benefiting** (US **benefitting**).

benevolence [bɪˈnevələns] *n* benevolencia.

benevolent [bɪˈnevələnt] *adj* benévolo,-a. [COMP] **benevolent society** sociedad *f* benéfica.

beneficence [bɪˈnefɪsəns] *n* beneficencia.

benign [bɪˈnaɪn] *adj* benigno,-a.

bent [bent] *pt & pp* → **bend**.
▶ *adj* **1** torcido,-a, doblado,-a. **2** *sl (corrupt)* corrupto,-a.
▶ *n (innate ability)* facilidad *f*, don *m*: *she's got a bent for maths* tiene facilidad para las matemáticas.

benzene [ˈbenziːn] *n* CHEM benceno.

benzine [ˈbenziːn] *n* CHEM bencina.

bequest [bɪˈkwest] *n* legado.

bereaved [bɪˈriːvd] *adj* desconsolado,-a, afligido,-a: *his bereaved wife* su desconsolada esposa.

bereavement [bɪ'riːvmənt] *n* **1** *(loss)* pérdida. **2** *(mourning)* duelo.

beret ['bereɪ] *n* boina.

berry ['berɪ] *n* baya.
ⓘ *pl* berries.

> ✎ Hay muchas frutas cuyo nombre se forma con berry, ya que se trata de bayas. Por ejemplo: blackberry *(mora)*, gooseberry *(grosella espinosa)*, raspberry *(frambuesa)* o strawberry *(fresón)*.

berserk [bə'zɜːk] *adj* enloquecido,-a.

berth [bɜːθ] *n* **1** *(in harbour)* amarradero. **2** *(on ship)* camarote *m*, litera.
> ▶ *vi* atracar.

beryl ['berəl] *n* GEOL berilo.

beryllium [bə'rɪlɪəm] *n* CHEM berilio.

beseech [bɪ'siːtʃ] *vt lit* implorar, suplicar.
ⓘ *pt & pp* besought [bɪ'sɔːt] o beseeched.

beset [bɪ'set] *vt* **1** *(attack, harass)* acosar, asaltar. **2** *(hem in, surround)* acorralar, cercar.
ⓘ *pt & pp* beset, *ger* besetting.

beside [bɪ'saɪd] *prep* **1** al lado de. **2** *(compared to)* frente a, comparado,-a con. LOC **to be beside os** estar fuera de sí. ▌ **that's beside the point** esto no viene al caso.

besides [bɪ'saɪdz] *prep (as well as)* además de, aparte de.
> ▶ *adv* además.

besiege [bɪ'siːdʒ] *vt* **1** MIL sitiar. **2** *fig* asediar, inundar.

besought [bɪ'sɔːt] *pt & pp* → beseech.

best [best] *adj (superl of* good*)* mejor. LOC **the best part of** casi: *it cost me the best part of £5,000* me costó casi 5.000 libras. COMP **best man** padrino de boda. **the best one** el mejor, la mejor.
> ▶ *adv* **1** *(superl of* well*)* mejor. **2** *(to a greater extent)* más: *of all the girls she is the one he likes best* de todas las chicas ella es la que le gusta más. LOC **best before ...** consumir preferentemente antes de …
> ▶ *n* **1** lo mejor: *the best is yet to come* lo mejor aún está por venir. **2** *(person)* el mejor, la mejor: *she's the best in the class at maths* es la mejor de la clase en mates. **3** *(in*

sport) plusmarca. LOC **all the best! 1** ¡que te vaya bien! **2** *(in letter)* un saludo. ▌ **it's for the best** más vale que sea así.

bestial ['bestɪəl] *adj* bestial, brutal.

bestow [bɪ'stəʊ] *vt (honour, award)* otorgar (**on**, a); *(favour)* hacer (**on**, a), *(title)* conferir (**on**, a).

best-seller [best'selə'] *n* best seller *m*, superventas *m*.

bet [bet] *n* apuesta. LOC **to make a bet** hacer una apuesta.
> ▶ *vt & vi* apostar.
ⓘ *pt & pp* bet o betted, *ger* betting.

beta ['biːtə] *n* beta. COMP **beta rays** rayos *mpl* beta.

betray [bɪ'treɪ] *vt* **1** traicionar. **2** *(secret)* revelar. **3** *(show signs of)* dejar ver, acusar. **4** *(deceive)* engañar.

betrayal [bɪ'treɪəl] *n* **1** traición *f*. **2** *(deceit)* engaño.

better¹ ['betə'] *adj* **1** *(comp of* good*)* mejor: *his new novel is better than his last one* su última novela es mejor que la anterior. **2** *(more healthy)* mejor: *he's feeling better today* hoy se encuentra mejor. LOC **to get better** recuperarse, mejorarse. ▌ **better and better** cada vez mejor.
> ▶ *adv* **1** *(comp of* well*)* mejor. **2** *(to a greater extent)* más: *I like this one better* me gusta más éste. LOC **had better + inf** más vale que + *subj*: *we'd better be going* más vale que nos vayamos. ▌ **to like STH/SB better** preferir ALGO/a ALGN.
> ▶ *vt* **1** *(improve)* mejorar: *he has bettered their working conditions* ha mejorado sus condiciones de trabajo. **2** *(surpass)* superar: *he bettered his own record* superó su propio récord.
> ▶ *n pl* **betters** superiores *mpl*: *you must listen to your betters* debes escuchar a tus superiores.

betting ['betɪŋ] *n* apuestas *fpl*. LOC **what's the betting that he "(she, it, etc)...?** ¿qué te apuestas a que …?: *what's the betting that he arrives late?* ¿qué te apuestas a que llega tarde? COMP **betting shop** GB administración *f* de apuestas hípicas.

between [bɪ'twiːn] *prep* entre: *choose a number between one and ten* escoge un número entre uno y diez.

► *adv* [también **in between**] de en medio: *we could see the sea if it wasn't for the houses (in) between* podríamos ver el mar si no fuera por las casas de en medio.

bevel ['bevəl] *n* bebida.

beverage ['bevərɪdʒ] *n* bebida.

bevy ['bevɪ] *n (of birds)* bandada.
ⓘ *pl* bevies.

beware [bɪ'weər] *vi* tener cuidado (of, con): *beware of the dog!* ¡cuidado con el perro!

bewilder [bɪ'wɪldər] *vt* desconcertar, dejar perplejo,-a.

bewitch [bɪ'wɪtʃ] *vt* **1** hechizar, embrujar. **2** *fig* hechizar, fascinar.

beyond [bɪ'jɒnd] *prep* **1** más allá de: *they live beyond the mountains* viven más allá de las montañas. **2** *(outside)* fuera de: *it's beyond my jurisdiction* está fuera de mi jurisdicción. ⃞LOC **it's beyond doubt** es indudable, es seguro, no cabe duda.
► *adv* más allá, más lejos.
► *n* **the beyond** el más allá.

bias ['baɪəs] *n* **1** *(prejudice)* parcialidad *f*, prejuicio. **2** *(inclination)* tendencia, predisposición *f*. **3** *(in statistics)* margen *f* de error.
► *vt* predisponer, influenciar.
ⓘ *pt & pp* biased o biassed, *ger* biasing o biassing.

biased ['baɪəst] *adj* parcial.

bib [bɪb] *n* **1** *(for baby)* babero. **2** *(top of apron, overall)* peto.

Bible ['baɪbəl] *n* Biblia.

bibliography [bɪblɪ'ɒgrəfɪ] *n* bibliografía.
ⓘ *pl* bibliographies.

bicarbonate [baɪ'kɑ:bənət] *n* CHEM bicarbonato.

biceps ['baɪseps] *n* bíceps *m*.

bicker ['bɪkər] *vi* discutir, porfiar.

bicycle ['baɪsɪkəl] *n* bicicleta. ⃞LOC **to ride a bicycle** montar en bicicleta. ⃞COMP **bicycle pump** bomba de bicicleta.

bid [bɪd] *n* **1** *(at auction)* puja. **2** *(attempt)* intento. **3** *(offer)* oferta.
► *vi (at auction)* pujar (for, por).
ⓘ *pt & pp* bid, *ger* bidding.

bidder ['bɪdər] *n* postor,-ra, pujador,-ra, licitador,-ra.

bidding ['bɪdɪŋ] *n* **1** *(at auction)* puja, oferta. **2** *(order)* orden *f*.

bide [baɪd] *vt* **to bide one's time** esperar el momento oportuno.
ⓘ *pt* bided o bode [bəʊd], *pp* bided, *ger* biding.

bidet ['bi:deɪ] *n* bidé *m*.

bifocal [baɪ'fəʊkəl] *adj* bifocal.
► *n pl* bifocals lentes *fpl* bifocales.

bifurcate ['baɪfəkeɪt] *vi* bifurcarse.

big [bɪg] *adj* **1** *(size, importance)* grande; *(before sing noun)* gran. **2** *(older)* mayor.
ⓘ *comp* bigger, *superl* biggest.

bigamy ['bɪgəmɪ] *n* bigamia.

big-head ['bɪghed] *n* sabihondo,-a, creído,-a.

big-hearted [bɪg'hɑːtɪd] *adj* de buen corazón, generoso,-a.

bigmouth ['bɪgmaʊθ] *n* bocazas *mf*.

bigot ['bɪgət] *n* fanático,-a.

⃠ Bigot no significa 'bigote', que se traduce por **moustache**.

bigotry ['bɪgətrɪ] *n* fanatismo.

bigwig ['bɪgwɪg] *n fam* pez *m* gordo.

bike [baɪk] *n* **1** *fam (bicycle)* bici *f*. **2** *(motorcycle)* moto *f*.

bikeway ['baɪkweɪ] *n* carril-bici *m*.

bikini® [bɪ'ki:nɪ] *n* biquini® *m*, bikini® *m*.

bilateral [baɪ'lætərəl] *adj* bilateral.

bile [baɪl] *n* bilis *f*, hiel *f*. ⃞COMP **bile duct** conducto biliar.

biliary ['bɪlɪərɪ] *adj* biliar.

bilingual [baɪ'lɪŋgwəl] *adj* bilingüe.

bilirubin [bɪlɪ'ru:bɪn] *n* bilirrubina.

bill¹ [bɪl] *n* **1** factura; *(in restaurant)* cuenta. **2** *(law)* proyecto de ley. **3** US *(banknote)* billete *m*. **4** *(poster)* cartel *m*. ⃞COMP **bill of exchange** letra de cambio. ‖ **Bill of Rights** declaración *f* de derechos.
► *vt* **1** facturar, pasar la factura. **2** THEAT programar.

bill² [bɪl] *n* **1** *(of bird)* pico. **2** *(headland)* cabo, promontorio.

billboard ['bɪlbɔ:d] *n* US valla publicitaria.

billfold ['bɪlfəʊld] *n* US billetero, cartera.

billing ['bɪlɪŋ] *n* **1** *(invoicing)* facturación *f*. **2** THEAT *orden de aparición en cartel*.

billion ['bɪlɪən] *n* **1** mil millones *mpl*. **2** GB *(formerly)* billón *m*.

✎ En el uso actual, tanto en EE UU como en Gran Bretaña, un billion equivale a mil millones. Antiguamente, el billion británico tenía el mismo significado que en español, es decir, 'un millón de millones'

billionaire [bɪlɪə'neəʳ] *n* multimillonario,-a.

billow ['bɪləʊ] *n* **1** *(of water)* ola. **2** *(of smoke)* nube *f*.
▸ *vt* **1** *(sea)* ondear. **2** *(sail)* hincharse.

billy goat ['bɪlɪgəʊt] *n* macho cabrío.

bin [bɪn] *n* **1** *(for rubbish)* cubo de la basura; *(for paper)* papelera. **2** *(large container)* recipiente *m*.

binary ['baɪnərɪ] *adj* binario,-a. COMP **binary fission** bipartición *f*, fisión *f* binaria.

bind [baɪnd] *n fam* fastidio, molestia.
▸ *vt* **1** *(tie up)* atar; *(cereals, corn)* agavillar. **2** CULIN *(sauce)* ligar. **3** *(book, etc)* encuadernar. **4** *(bandage)* vendar. **5** *(require)* obligar.
ⓘ *pt & pp* bound [baʊnd].

binder ['baɪndəʳ] *n* **1** *(file)* carpeta. **2** *(of books)* encuadernador,-ra.

binding ['baɪndɪŋ] *n* **1** *(of book)* encuadernación *f*. **2** SEW ribete *m*. **3** *(of skis)* fijación *f*.
▸ *adj* obligatorio,-a (on, para).

binge [bɪndʒ] *n (drinking)* borrachera; *(eating)* atracón *m*.
▸ *vi* atiborrarse, hartarse de comida.

bingo ['bɪŋgəʊ] *n* bingo.
ⓘ *pl* bingos.

binnacle ['bɪnəkəl] *n* bitácora.

binoculars [bɪ'nɒkjʊləz] *n pl* prismáticos *mpl*, gemelos *mpl*.

biochemistry [baɪəʊ'kemɪstrɪ] *n* bioquímica.

biodegradable [baɪəʊdɪ'greɪdəbəl] *adj* biodegradable.

biography [baɪ'ɒgrəfɪ] *n* biografía.
ⓘ *pl* biographies.

biological [baɪə'lɒdʒɪkəl] *adj* biológico,-a.

biologist [baɪ'ɒlədʒɪst] *n* biólogo,-a.

biology [baɪ'ɒlədʒɪ] *n* biología.

biomass ['baɪəʊmæs] *n* biomasa.

biomechanics [baɪəʊmɪ'kænɪks] *n* biomecánica.

biometry [baɪ'ɒmətrɪ] *n* biometría.

bionic [baɪ'ɒnɪk] *adj* biónico,-a.

biophysics [baɪəʊ'fɪzɪks] *n* biofísica.

biopsy ['baɪɒpsɪ] *n* biopsia.
ⓘ *pl* biopsies.

biorhythm ['baɪərɪðəm] *n* biorritmo.

biosphere ['baɪəsfɪəʳ] *n* biosfera.

biotope ['baɪətəp] *n* biotopo.

biped ['baɪped] *adj* bípedo,-a.
▸ *n* bípedo.

biplane ['baɪpleɪn] *n* biplano.

bipolar [baɪ'pəʊləʳ] *adj* bipolar.

birch [bɜːtʃ] *n* **1** *(tree)* abedul *m*. **2** *(rod)* vara de abedul.
▸ *vt* azotar.

bird [bɜːd] *n* **1** *(large)* ave *f*; *(small)* pájaro. **2** GB *sl (girl)* chica. **3** *sl (person)* tipo. COMP **bird of prey** ave *f* de rapiña, ave *f* de presa.

birdcage ['bɜːdkeɪdʒ] *n* jaula de pájaro.

birdie ['bɜːdɪ] *n* **1** *(little bird)* pajarito. **2** *(in golf)* birdie *m*.

birdseed ['bɜːdsiːd] *n* BOT alpiste *m*.

bird's-eye view [bɜːdzaɪ'vjuː] *n* vista panorámica.

bird-watcher ['bɜːdwɒtʃəʳ] *n* ornitólogo,-a *(cuya afición es observar las aves)*.

Biro® ['baɪrəʊ] [also written biro] *n fam* boli *m*.
ⓘ *pl* Biros.

birth [bɜːθ] *n* **1** nacimiento. **2** MED parto. **3** *(descent)* linaje *m*. LOC **to give birth to 1** *(child)* dar a luz a. **2** *fig* dar lugar a. COMP **birth certificate** partida de nacimiento. ‖ **birth control** control *m* de la natalidad. ‖ **birth rate** tasa de natalidad.

birthday ['bɜːθdeɪ] *n* cumpleaños *m*.

birthmark ['bɜːθmɑːk] *n* mancha de nacimiento, antojo.

birthplace ['bɜːθpleɪs] *n* lugar *m* de nacimiento.

biscuit ['bɪskɪt] *n* galleta.

bisection [baɪ'sekʃən] *n* bisección *f*.

bisectrix [baɪ'sektrɪks] *n* bisectriz *f*.
ⓘ *pl* bisectrices [baɪ'sektrɪsiːz].

bisexual [baɪ'seksjʊəl] *adj* bisexual.
▶ *n* bisexual *mf*.

bishop ['bɪʃəp] *n* **1** obispo. **2** *(chess)* alfil *m*.

bison ['baɪsən] *n* bisonte *m*.

bissextile [baɪ'sekstaɪl] *adj* bisiesto,-a.

bit¹ [bɪt] *n* **1** *(small piece)* trozo, pedacito. **2** *(small amount)* poco. **3** *fam (time)* un poco, un ratito. LOC **a bit** *fam (rather)* algo, un poco. ‖ **a bit of** algo de. ‖ **quite a bit / a good bit** *fam* bastante. **to come to bits** hacerse pedazos, romperse.

bit² [bɪt] *n* **1** *(of bridle)* bocado. **2** *(of drill)* broca.

bit³ [bɪt] *n* COMPUT bit *m*.

bit⁴ [bɪt] *pt* → bite.

bite [baɪt] *n* **1** *(act)* mordisco. **2** *(of insect)* picadura. **3** *(of dog, etc)* mordedura. **4** *(of food)* bocado.
▶ *vt* **1** morder. **2** *(insect, snake)* picar. **3** *(grip)* agarrar.
▶ *vi* **1** morder. **2** *(insect, snake)* picar. **3** *(fish)* picar.
ⓘ *pt* bit, *pp* bitten ['bɪtən].

biting ['baɪtɪŋ] *adj* **1** *(wind)* cortante, penetrante. **2** *(comment)* mordaz.

bitten ['bɪtən] *pp* → bite.

bitter ['bɪtə'] *adj* **1** *(gen)* amargo,-a; *(fruit)* ácido,-a, agrio,-a. **2** *(weather)* glacial. **3** *(person)* amargado,-a. **4** *(fight)* enconado,-a.
▶ *n* cerveza amarga.

bitterly ['bɪtəlɪ] *adv* **1** con amargura, amargamente: *she complained bitterly* se quejó amargamente. **2** *(very)* muy: *it's bitterly cold* hace un frío glacial.

bitterness ['bɪtənəs] *n* **1** *(gen)* amargura; *(of fruit)* acidez *f*. **2** *(of weather)* crudeza. **3** *(resentment)* rencor *m*, resentimiento.

bittersweet ['bɪtəswi:t] *adj* agridulce.

bitumen ['bɪtjʊmɪn] *n* betún *m*.

bivalent [baɪ'veɪlənt] *adj* bivalente.

bivalve ['baɪvælv] *adj* bivalvo,-a.
▶ *n* bivalvo.

bizarre [bɪ'zɑ:'] *adj* **1** raro,-a, extraño,-a.

blab [blæb] *vi* **1** *fam (gossip)* cotillear, chismear. **2** *fam (talk constantly)* rajar, parlotear.
ⓘ *pt & pp* blabbed, *ger* blabbing.

black [blæk] *adj* **1** negro,-a. **2** *(dirty)* sucio,-a. **3** *(threatening)* amenazador,-ra. LOC **a bit** black and white blanco y negro. COMP **black economy** economía sumergida.
▶ *n* **1** *(colour)* negro. **2** *(person)* negro,-a.
▶ *vt* **1** *(make black)* ennegrecer. **2** *(boycott)* boicotear.
◆ **to black out** *vt sep* **1** *(windows of house)* tapar; *(electrical supply)* apagar el alumbrado. **2** *(cause power cut)* dejar sin luz, causar un apagón.
▶ *vi (faint)* desmayarse.

blackberry ['blækbərɪ] *n* zarzamora, mora. COMP **blackberry bush** zarza.
ⓘ *pl* blackberries.

blackbird ['blækbɜ:d] *n* mirlo.

blackboard ['blækbɔ:d] *n* pizarra.

blackcurrant [blæk'kʌrənt] *n* grosella negra.

blacken ['blækən] *vt* **1** ennegrecer. **2** *fig (defame)* manchar.

blackhead ['blækhed] *n* espinilla.

blackjack ['blækdʒæk] *n* *(card game)* veintiuna.

blackleg ['blækleg] *n* esquirol *m*.

blacklist ['blæklɪst] *n* lista negra.

blackmail ['blækmeɪl] *n* chantaje *m*.
▶ *vt* hacer chantaje a, chantajear.

blackmailer ['blækmeɪlə'] *n* chantajista *mf*.

blackout ['blækaʊt] *n* **1** *(through electrical fault)* apagón *m*; *(in wartime)* oscurecimiento general de una ciudad. **2** *(fainting)* pérdida de conocimiento, desmayo.

blacksmith ['blæksmɪθ] *n* herrero. COMP **blacksmith's forge** herrería.

blackthorn ['blækθɔ:n] *n* BOT endrino.

bladder ['blædə'] *n* **1** vejiga. **2** *(in tyre, football)* cámara de aire.

blade [bleɪd] *n* **1** *(of sword, knife, etc)* hoja. **2** *(of ice skate)* cuchilla. **3** *(of propeller, fan, oar, hoe)* pala. **4** *(of grass)* brizna.

blame [bleɪm] *n* culpa.
▶ *vt* culpar, echar la culpa a.

blanch [blɑːntʃ] *vt* CULIN escaldar.
► *vi* palidecer.

bland [blænd] *adj* soso,-a.

🗵 Bland no significa 'blando', que se traduce por **soft**.

blank [blæŋk] *adj* **1** *(page, etc)* en blanco. **2** *(look, etc)* vacío,-a. **3** *(cassette, tape)* virgen. COMP **blank cheque** cheque *m* en blanco.
► *n* **1** *(on paper)* espacio en blanco. **2** *(bullet)* bala de fogueo.

blanket [ˈblæŋkɪt] *n* **1** manta, AM frazada. **2** *(layer)* capa, manto: *a blanket of snow* una capa de nieve.

blare [bleəˈ] *n* **1** *(loud noise)* estruendo, fragor *m*. **2** *(of trumpet)* trompetazo.
► *vi* resonar, sonar.
◆ **to blare out** *vi* sonar muy fuerte.

blaspheme [blæsˈfiːm] *vi* blasfemar (against, contra).

blasphemy [ˈblæsfəmɪ] *n* blasfemia.
ⓘ *pl* blasphemies.

blast [blɑːst] *n* **1** *(of wind)* ráfaga. **2** *(of water, air, etc)* chorro. **3** *(of horn)* toque *m*. **4** *(of trumpet)* trompetazo. **5** *(explosion)* explosión *f*, voladura. **6** *(shock wave)* onda expansiva. **7** *(reprimand)* bronca.
► *vt* **1** *(explode)* volar, hacer volar. **2** *(criticize)* criticar. **3** *(reprimand)* echar una bronca. **4** *(ruin, spoil)* echar a perder, dar al traste con. **5** *(shoot)* pegar un tiro a. **6** *(shrivel, wither)* marchitar.

blasted [ˈblɑːstɪd] *adj* maldito,-a, dichoso,-a.

blast-off [ˈblɑːstɒf] *n* *(of rocket, missile)* despegue *m*.

blatant [ˈbleɪtənt] *adj* descarado,-a.

blaze [bleɪz] *n* **1** *(fire)* incendio. **2** *(flame)* llamarada. **3** *(of light)* resplandor *m*. **4** *(outburst)* arranque *m*, acceso.
► *vi* **1** *(fire)* arder. **2** *(sun)* brillar con fuerza. **3** *(light)* resplandecer.

blazer [ˈbleɪzəˈ] *n* americana de sport, blazer *m*.

bleach [bliːtʃ] *n* lejía.
► *vt* blanquear.

bleachers [ˈbliːtʃəz] *n pl* US gradas *fpl*.

bleak [bliːk] *adj* **1** *(countryside)* desolado,-a. **2** *(weather)* desapacible. **3** *(future)* poco prometedor,-ra. **4** *(welcome, reception)* frío,-a.

bleary [ˈblɪərɪ] *adj* **1** *(from tears)* nubloso,-a. **2** *(from tiredness)* legañoso,-a.
ⓘ *comp* blearier, *superl* bleariest.

bleat [bliːt] *n* balido,
► *vi* balar.

bled [bled] *pt & pp →* bleed.

bleed [bliːd] *vi* MED sangrar.
ⓘ *pt & pp* bled [bled].

bleep [bliːp] *n* pitido.
► *vi* pitar.
► *vt* localizar con un busca.

bleeper [ˈbliːpəˈ] *n* busca *m*, buscapersonas *m*.

blemish [ˈblemɪʃ] *n* **1** desperfecto, imperfección *f*.
► *vt* **1** *(spoil)* estropear, desmejorar. **2** *fig (reputation)* manchar, tiznar. LOC **without a blemish** *fig* intachable.

blench [blentʃ] *vi* **1** *(recoil)* retroceder. **2** *(flinch)* pestañear, inmutarse.

blend [blend] *n* mezcla, combinación *f*.
► *vt* **1** *(mix)* mezclar, combinar. **2** *(match)* matizar, armonizar.

blender [ˈblendəˈ] *n* CULIN batidora, minipímer® *m*.

bless [bles] *vt* bendecir. LOC **bless you!** *(on sneezing)* ¡Jesús!

blessed [ˈblesɪd] *adj* **1** *(holy)* bendito,-a, santo,-a. **2** *(content, happy)* bienaventurado,-a.

blessing [ˈblesɪŋ] *n* bendición *f*.

blew [bluː] *pt →* blow.

blight [blaɪt] *n* **1** *(mildew)* tizón *m*. **2** *(calamity)* plaga.

blind [blaɪnd] *adj* ciego,-a.
► *n* *(on window)* persiana.
► *vt* **1** cegar, dejar ciego,-a. **2** *(dazzle)* deslumbrar.

blindfold [ˈblaɪndfəʊld] *n* venda.
► *vt* vendar los ojos a.
► *adv* con los ojos vendados.

blink [blɪŋk] *n* **1** parpadeo. **2** *(gleam, glimmer)* destello. LOC **on the blink** *fam* averiado,-a.

blinkers [ˈblɪŋkəz] *n pl* anteojeras *fpl*.

bliss [blɪs] *n* felicidad *f*, dicha.

blister ['blɪstər] n **1** (on skin) ampolla. **2** (on paint, surface) burbuja.

blizzard ['blɪzəd] n tempestad f de nieve, ventisca.

bloated ['bləʊtɪd] adj hinchado,-a.

blob [blɒb] n **1** (drop) gota. **2** (smudge) borrón m. **3** (of colour) mancha.

bloc [blɒk] n POL bloque m.

block [blɒk] n **1** bloque m. **2** (of wood, stone) taco. **3** (group of buildings) manzana. **6** (obstruction) obstrucción f. COMP block letters mayúsculas fpl. ‖ block of flats bloque m de pisos. ‖ note block taco, bloc m de notas.
▸ vt **1** (pipe, etc) obstruir, atascar. **2** (streets, etc) bloquear.

blockade [blɒ'keɪd] n MIL bloqueo.
▸ vt bloquear.

blockage ['blɒkɪdʒ] n obstrucción f, atasco.

blockbuster ['blɒkbʌstər] n **1** fig (novel) best seller m, éxito de ventas. **2** fig (film) película de acción.

bloke [bləʊk] n GB fam tipo, tío.

blond [blɒnd] [suele escribirse blonde cuando se refiere a una mujer] adj rubio,-a.
▸ n rubio,-a.

blonde [blɒnd] adj-n → blond.

blood [blʌd] n **1** sangre f. **2** (ancestry) parentesco, alcurnia. COMP blood pressure tensión f arterial. ‖ blood vessel vaso sanguíneo.

bloodhound ['blʌdhaʊnd] n sabueso.

bloodshed ['blʌdʃed] n derramamiento de sangre.

bloodstream ['blʌdstriːm] n corriente f sanguínea.

bloodthirsty ['blʌdθɜːstɪ] adj sanguinario,-a, ávido,-a de sangre.
① comp bloodthirstier, superl bloodthirstiest.

bloody ['blʌdɪ] adj **1** (battle) sangriento,-a. **2** sl (damned) puñetero,-a, mierda de.
① comp bloodier, superl bloodiest.

bloody-minded [blʌdɪ'maɪndɪd] adj **1** (stubborn) tozudo,-a, terco,-a. **2** (bad-tempered) de malas pulgas.

bloom [bluːm] n **1** (flower) flor f. **2** (on fruit) pelusa.
▸ vi florecer.

bloomer ['bluːmər] n GB fam metedura de pata, pifia.

blossom ['blɒsəm] n flor f.
▸ vi florecer.
◆ to blossom out vi alcanzar su plenitud.

✎ Blossom se refiere a las flores de los árboles; para el resto de flores, se emplea la palabra flower.

blot [blɒt] n (of ink) borrón m; (on reputation) mancha.
▸ vt **1** (stain) manchar. **2** (dry) secar.
◆ to blot out vt sep **1** (hide) ocultar. **2** (memory) borrar.
① pt & pp blotted, ger blotting.

blotch [blɒtʃ] n mancha.
▸ vi **1** (become stained) mancharse. **2** (skin) salir manchas.

blotting-paper ['blɒtɪŋpeɪpər] n papel m secante.

blouse [blaʊz] n blusa.

blow¹ [bləʊ] n golpe m.

blow² [bləʊ] vi **1** (wind) soplar. **2** (instrument) tocar, sonar; (whistle) pitar. **3** (fuse) fundirse. **4** (tyre) reventarse.
▸ vt fam (money) despilfarrar, malgastar.
◆ to blow away vt sep **1** arrastrar. **2** fam fig mandar al otro barrio.
◆ to blow in vt sep derribar.
◆ to blow off vi (lid, hat) salir volando.
◆ to blow out vt sep **1** (flame) apagar; (candle) soplar. **2** (cheeks) hinchar.
◆ to blow over vt sep derribar.
▸ vi **1** derrumbarse. **2** (storm) amainar.
◆ to blow up vt sep **1** (explode) (hacer) volar: they blew up the building hicieron volar el edificio. **2** (inflate) hinchar. **3** (photograph) ampliar.
▸ vi **1** (explode) explotar. **2** (lose one's temper) salirse de sus casillas.
① pt blew [bluː], pp blown [bləʊn].

blowhole ['bləʊhəʊl] n **1** (of whale) orificio nasal. **2** (hole, air vent) respiradero.

blowlamp ['bləʊlæmp] n soplete m.

blown [bləʊn] pp → blow.

blowout [ˈbləʊaʊt] n **1** AUTO reventón m, pinchazo. **2** sl comilona, atracón m.

blowtorch [ˈbləʊtɔːtʃ] n soplete m.

blow-up [ˈbləʊʌp] n (photograph) ampliación f.

blue [bluː] adj **1** azul. **2** (sad) triste. **3** (depressed) deprimido,-a. **4** (obscene) verde: a blue joke un chiste verde.
▶ n azul m.
▶ n pl **blues** MUS blues m.
▶ n pl **the blues** la depresión f.

bluebell [ˈbluːbel] n BOT campanilla.

blueberry [ˈbluːbərɪ] n BOT arándano.
ⓘ pl blueberries.

blue-collar [ˈbluːkɒləʳ] adj obrero,-a.

blueprint [ˈbluːprɪnt] n fig anteproyecto.

blues [bluːz] n pl → blue.

blunder [ˈblʌndəʳ] n metedura de pata.
▶ vi meter la pata.

blunt [blʌnt] adj **1** (knife) desafilado,-a; (pencil) despuntado,-a. **2** fig (person) que no tiene pelos en la lengua.
▶ vt desafilar, embotar; (pencil) despuntar. COMP **blunt angle** MATH ángulo obtuso.

blur [blɜːʳ] n borrón m, mancha.

blurb [blɜːb] n fam pej información f publicitaria.

blurred [blɜːd] adj **1** borroso,-a. **2** fig (memories) vago,-a, confuso,-a.

blurt [blɜːt] LOC **to blurt** STH **out** soltar ALGO bruscamente, espetar algo.

blush [blʌʃ] n rubor m, sonrojo.
▶ vi ruborizarse, sonrojarse.

blusher [ˈblʌʃəʳ] n colorete m.

blustery [ˈblʌstərɪ] adj (windy) ventoso,-a.

boa [ˈbəʊə] n ZOOL boa.

boar [bɔːʳ] n ZOOL verraco.

board [bɔːd] n **1** (piece of wood) tabla, tablero. **2** (food) comida, pensión f. **3** (committee) junta, consejo. **4** (company) compañía: the gas board la compañía del gas. LOC **on board** MAR a bordo. I **to take on board 1** (responsibility) asumir. **2** (concept, idea) abarcar. COMP **board and lodging** pensión completa. I **board of directors** junta directiva. I **board of trade** US cámara de comercio.

▶ vt (ship, etc) subirse a, embarcar en.
▶ vi (lodge) alojarse; (at school) ser interno,-a.

boarder [ˈbɔːdəʳ] n **1** (gen) huésped mf. **2** (at school) interno,-a.

boarding [ˈbɔːdɪŋ] n **1** (ship, plane, etc) embarque m. **2** (lodging) pensión f, alojamiento. COMP **boarding card** tarjeta de embarque. I **boarding house** casa de huéspedes. I **boarding school** internado.

boast [bəʊst] n jactancia.
▶ vi jactarse (about, de), presumir (about, de).
▶ vt fig presumir de.

boat [bəʊt] n barco, nave f; (small) bote m, barca; (large) buque m, navío; (launch) lancha.

boatswain [ˈbəʊsən] n contramaestre m.

boatyard [ˈbəʊtjɑːd] n astillero.

bob¹ [bɒb] n **1** (jerking movement) sacudida; (bouncing movement) rebote m. **2** (curtsy) reverencia.
▶ vi **1** (jerk) moverse a sacudidas; (bounce) rebotar. **2** (curtsy) hacer una reverencia.

bobbin [ˈbɒbɪn] n (for textiles, wire, etc) carrete m, bobina; (for lace) bolillo, palillo.

bobby [ˈbɒbɪ] n GB fam poli m.
ⓘ pl bobbies.

ⓦ Este término, aunque hoy poco utilizado, se usa para referirse a los agentes de policía del Reino Unido. El nombre proviene del fundador del cuerpo, sir Robert Peel, ya que Bobby es el diminutivo de Robert.

bobsleigh [ˈbɒbsleɪ] n bobsleigh m.

bode [bəʊd] pt → bide.
▶ vt (foretell) presagiar, augurar. LOC **to bode ill/well** ser de buen/mal agüero.

bodice [ˈbɒdɪs] n corpiño.

body [ˈbɒdɪ] n **1** cuerpo. **2** (corpse) cadáver m. **3** (organization) organismo, entidad f, ente m; (association) agrupación f. **4** (of wine) cuerpo. **5** (of people) grupo, conjunto. **6** AUTO (of car) carrocería. **7** AV fuselaje m.
ⓘ pl bodies.

body-blow [ˈbɒdɪbləʊ] n revés m.

body-building ['bɒdɪbɪldɪŋ] *n* SP culturismo.

bodyguard ['bɒdɪgɑːd] *n* guardaespaldas *m*.

bodywork ['bɒdɪwɜːk] *n* carrocería.

bog [bɒg] *n* **1** pantano, cenagal *m*. **2** *sl (toilet)* meódromo.
◆ **to bog down** *vt sep* atascar.

bogey ['bəʊgɪ] *n (golf)* bogey *m*.

bogus ['bəʊgəs] *adj* **1** *(fake)* falso,-a, apócrifo,-a. **2** *(fictitious)* ficticio,-a. **3** *(sham)* simulado,-a, fingido,-a.

boil[1] [bɔɪl] *n* MED furúnculo, forúnculo.

boil[2] [bɔɪl] *vt (liquid)* hervir; *(food)* hervir, cocer; *(egg)* pasar por agua, cocer.
▸ *vi* **1** *(liquid)* hervir; *(food)* hervir, cocerse. **2** *fig (undulate, seethe)* bullir.
◆ **to boil down to** *vt insep fig* reducirse a.

boiler ['bɔɪlər] *n* **1** caldera. **2** *(fowl)* gallina *(que solo sirve para el caldo)*.

boiling ['bɔɪlɪŋ] *adj* hirviendo, hirviente. COMP **boiling point** punto de ebullición.

boisterous ['bɔɪstərəs] *adj* **1** *(noisy, rowdy)* bullicioso,-a, alborotador,-ra. **2** *(weather)* borrascoso,-a; *(sea)* agitado,-a.

bold [bəʊld] *adj* **1** *(brave)* valiente. **2** *(daring)* audaz, atrevido,-a. **3** *(cheeky)* descarado,-a, fresco,-a. **4** *(vivid)* vivo,-a. **5** *(print)* en negrita.

Bolivia [bəˈlɪvɪə] *n* Bolivia.

Bolivian [bəˈlɪvɪən] *adj* boliviano,-a.
▸ *n* boliviano,-a.

bolster ['bəʊlstər] *n* **1** *(pillow)* cabezal *m*, travesaño. **2** TECH soporte *m*.
▸ *vt* reforzar.

bolt [bəʊlt] *n* **1** *(on door, etc)* cerrojo; *(small)* pestillo. **2** *(screw)* perno, tornillo. **3** *(lightning)* rayo.
▸ *vt* **1** *(lock)* cerrar con cerrojo, cerrar con pestillo. **2** *(screw)* sujetar con pernos, sujetar con tornillos. **3** *fam (food)* engullir.
▸ *vi (person)* escaparse; *(horse)* desbocarse.

bolus ['bəʊləs] *n* bolo alimenticio.

bomb [bɒm] *n* **1** bomba. **2** US *(failure)* fracaso.
▸ *vt* MIL bombardear; *(terrorist)* colocar una bomba en.
▸ *vi* US *fam (fail)* fracasar.

bombard [bɒmˈbɑːd] *vt* bombardear.

bombardment [bɒmˈbɑːdmənt] *n* bombardeo.

bombastic [bɒmˈbæstɪk] *adj* rimbombante, ampuloso,-a.

bomber ['bɒmər] *n* **1** MIL bombardero. **2** *(terrorist)* terrorista *mf* que coloca bombas.

> ✕ Bomber no significa 'bombero', que se traduce por **fireman**.

bombing ['bɒmɪŋ] *n* **1** MIL bombardeo. **2** *(terrorist act)* atentado con bomba.

bombshell ['bɒmʃel] *n* **1** *fig* bomba. **2** MIL *(artillery bomb)* obús *m*. **3** *fam (attractive woman)* mujer *f* explosiva.

bona fide [bəʊnəˈfaɪdɪ] *adj* genuino,-a, auténtico,-a.

bond [bɒnd] *n* **1** *(link)* lazo, vínculo: *bonds of friendship* vínculos de amistad. **2** FIN bono, obligación *f*. **3** JUR fianza. **4** *(agreement)* pacto, compromiso.
▸ *vt* **1** *(stick, join)* pegar, unir. **2** *(deposit in customs)* depositar.
▸ *vi (stick, join)* pegarse, unirse.

bondage ['bɒndɪdʒ] *n* esclavitud *f*, servidumbre *f*.

bone [bəʊn] *n* **1** hueso. **2** *(of fish)* espina, raspa; *(of whale)* barba. **3** *(of corset)* ballena.
▸ *vt (meat)* deshuesar; *(fish)* quitar la espina.
▸ *n pl* **bones** *(remains)* huesos *mpl*, restos *mpl* mortales. COMP **bone marrow** médula ósea.
◆ **to bone up on** *vt insep* empollar.

bonfire ['bɒnfaɪər] *n* hoguera. COMP **Bonfire night** GB *la noche del cinco de noviembre; se celebra con hogueras y fuegos artificiales.*

> ⊕ Es la noche del 5 de noviembre que se celebra en Inglaterra con hogueras y fuegos artificiales. Conmemora el intento fallido en el año 1605, de Guy Fawkes y otros conspiradores, de volar el edificio del parlamento. También se llama **Guy Fawkes Night**.

bonkers ['bɒŋkəz] *adj* GB *sl* chalado,-a.

bonnet ['bɒnɪt] *n* **1** *(child's, woman's)* gorro, gorra. **2** *(maid's)* cofia. **3** AUTO capó *m*.

bonus ['bəʊnəs] *n* **1** *(gratuity)* plus *m*, sobresueldo, prima. **2** *(benefit)* beneficio.
ⓘ *pl* bonuses.

bony ['bəʊnɪ] *adj* **1** *(thin)* esquelético,-a. **2** *(with a lot of bone)* huesudo,-a. **3** *(like bone)* óseo,-a. **4** *(meat)* lleno,-a de huesos; *(fish)* lleno,-a de espinas.
ⓘ *comp* bonier, *superl* boniest.

bonze [bɒnz] *n* bonzo.

boo [buː] *n* abucheo.
▶ *vi* abuchear.

booby ['buːbɪ] *n* alcatraz *m*.
ⓘ *pl* boobies.

booby-trap ['buːbɪtræp] *n* trampa explosiva.

book [bʊk] *n* **1** libro. **2** *(of tickets)* taco; *(of matches)* cajetilla.
▶ *vt* **1** *(table, room, holiday)* reservar; *(entertainer, speaker)* contratar. **2** *(police)* multar; *(football)* advertir, amonestar.
▶ *n pl* **books** COMM libros *mpl*, cuentas *fpl*. LOC **to be booked up 1** *(hotel, restaurant)* estar completo. COMP **savings book** libreta de ahorro.
◆ **to book in** *vt sep (in hotel)* hacer la reserva.
▶ *vi* registrarse.

bookcase ['bʊkkeɪs] *n* librería, estantería.

booking ['bʊkɪŋ] *n* *(table, room, holiday)* reserva; *(entertainer, speaker)* contratación *f*. COMP **booking office** taquilla.

bookkeeping ['bʊkkiːpɪŋ] *n* contabilidad *f*, teneduría de libros.

bookmaker ['bʊkmeɪkəʳ] *n* GB corredor,-ra de apuestas.

bookmark ['bʊkmɑːk] *n* *(for book)* punto de libro; *(electronic)* marcador.
▶ *vt (electronically)* agregar un marcador.

bookseller ['bʊkseləʳ] *n* librero,-a.

bookshelf ['bʊkʃelf] *n* estante *m*.
▶ *n pl* **bookshelves** estantería.
ⓘ *pl* bookshelves.

bookshop ['bʊkʃɒp] *n* librería.

bookstand ['bʊkstænd] *n* **1** *(stall)* quiosco de periódicos. **2** *(bookrest)* atril *m*.

bookstore ['bʊkstɔːʳ] *n* US librería.

bookworm ['bʊkwɜːm] *n fig* ratón *m* de biblioteca.

boom¹ [buːm] *n (noise)* estampido.
▶ *vi* tronar, retumbar.
▶ *interj* ¡bum!

boom² [buːm] *n* **1** MAR botalón *m*. **2** *(of microphone)* jirafa. **3** *(of crane)* brazo. **4** *(barrier)* barrera.

boom³ [buːm] *n fig (prosperity, increase)* boom *m*, auge *m*.

boomerang ['buːməræŋ] *n* **1** bumerán *m*. **2** *fig* resultado contraproducente.

boost [buːst] *n* **1** *(incentive)* incentivo, estímulo. **2** *(promotion)* promoción *f*, fomento. **3** *(increase)* aumento.
▶ *vt* **1** *(create an incentive)* incentivar, estimular. **2** *(promote)* promocionar, fomentar. **3** *(increase)* aumentar.

booster ['buːstəʳ] *n* **1** ELEC elevador *m* de voltaje. **2** RAD repetidor *m*. **3** TECH motor *m* auxiliar de propulsión. COMP **booster injection** MED revacunación *f*.

boot [buːt] *n* **1** *(footwear)* bota. **2** GB *(of car)* maletero, portaequipajes *m*. **3** *(kick)* patada.
▶ *vt* **1** *(kick)* dar una patada a. **2** COMPUT cargar el sistema operativo.
◆ **to boot out** *vt sep* echar, echar a patadas.

bootblack ['buːtblæk] *n* US limpiabotas *m*, AM lustrabotas *m*.

booth [buːð] *n* **1** cabina. **2** *(at fair)* puesto. COMP **telephone booth** locutorio.

bootleg ['buːtleg] *n (illegal recording)* grabación *f* pirata.

bootlegger ['buːtlegəʳ] *n* contrabandista *mf* de licores.

booty ['buːtɪ] *n* botín *m*.
ⓘ *pl* booties.

booze [buːz] *n fam* trinque *m*, alcohol *m*.
▶ *vi fam* mamar.

bop [bɒp] *n* **1** *fam (dance)* baile *m*. **2** *fam (thump)* cachete *m*.
▶ *vi fam (dance)* bailar.
ⓘ *pt & pp* bopped, *ger* bopping.

border ['bɔːdəʳ] n **1** (of country) frontera. **2** (edge) borde m. **3** (in sewing) ribete m, orla. **4** (of flowers, plants) arriate m.
◆ **to border on** vt insep **1** lindar con. **2** fig rayar en.

bore¹ [bɔːʳ] pt → bear.

bore² [bɔːʳ] n **1** (of gun) ánima, alma; (calibre) calibre m. **2** (hole) taladro.
▶ vt & vi perforar, taladrar.

bore³ [bɔːʳ] n (person) pelmazo,-a, pesado,-a; (thing) lata, rollo, tostón m.
▶ vt aburrir, fastidiar.

bored [bɔːd] adj aburrido,-a. LOC **to get bored** aburrirse.

boredom ['bɔːdəm] n aburrimiento.

borer ['bɔːrəʳ] n **1** (tool) taladro, barrena. **2** (machine) taladradora.

boric ['bɔːrɪk] adj CHEM bórico,-a. COMP **boric acid** ácido bórico.

boring ['bɔːrɪŋ] adj aburrido,-a.

born [bɔːn] adj nato,-a: she's a born leader es una líder nata. LOC **to be born** nacer.

borne [bɔːn] pp → bear².

borough ['bʌrə] n **1** (district) barrio, distrito. **2** (town, city) ciudad f.

borrow ['bɒrəʊ] vt pedir prestado,-a, tomar prestado,-a: can I borrow your pen? ¿me dejas tu boli?; you can borrow it if you like te lo presto si quieres.

Bosnia ['bɒznɪə] n Bosnia.

Bosnian ['bɒznɪən] adj bosnio,-a.
▶ n bosnio,-a.

bosom ['buzəm] n **1** pecho. **2** (centre) seno: in the bosom of the family en el seno de la familia. COMP **bosom friend** amigo,-a del alma.

boss [bɒs] n jefe,-a.
◆ **to boss around** vt sep mangonear.

bosun ['bəʊsən] n MAR contramaestre m.

botanic [bə'tænɪk] adj botánico,-a.

botanical [bə'tænɪkəl] adj botánico,-a. COMP **botanical gardens** jardín m botánico.

botany ['bɒtənɪ] n botánica.

botch [bɒtʃ] n chapuza.
▶ vt [also **to botch up**.] (bungle) pifiarla, fastidiarla.

both [bəʊθ] adj ambos,-as, los dos, las dos.

▶ pron ambos,-as, los dos, las dos: both of us nosotros,-as dos; both of you vosotros,-as dos; both of them los dos, las dos, ambos,-as. LOC **both ... and** tanto ... como: both she and her sister are teachers tanto ella como su hermana son profesoras.
▶ adv a la vez: it's both cheap and good es bueno y barato a la vez.

bother ['bɒðəʳ] n **1** (nuisance) molestia, fastidio. **2** (problems) problemas mpl.
▶ vt **1** (be a nuisance) molestar, fastidiar. **2** (worry) preocupar.
▶ vi **1** (take trouble) molestarse, tomar la molestia. **2** (worry) preocuparse.

Botswana [bɒt'swɑːnə] n Botsuana.

Botswanan [bɒt'swɑːnən] adj botsuanés,-esa, botsuano,-a.
▶ n botsuanés,-esa, botsuano,-a.

bottle ['bɒtəl] n **1** botella; (small) frasco; (for baby) biberón m; (for gas) bombona. **2** sl (nerve) agallas fpl.
▶ vt (wine, etc) embotellar; (fruit) envasar.

bottle-bank ['bɒtəlbæŋk] n contenedor m de vidrio.

bottled ['bɒtəld] adj (wine, etc) embotellado,-a; (fruit) envasado,-a. COMP **bottled gas** gas m butano.

bottom ['bɒtəm] n **1** (gen) fondo; (of bottle) culo; (of hill, steps, page) pie m; (of ship) quilla. **2** (of dress) bajo; (of trousers) bajos mpl. **3** (buttocks) trasero, culo. **4** (last) último,-a. **5** (underneath) parte f inferior, parte f de abajo.
▶ adj **1** (position) de abajo. **2** (number, result) más bajo,-a.

bottomless ['bɒtəmləs] adj sin fondo, insondable.

boudoir ['buːdwɑːʳ] n tocador m.

bough [baʊ] n rama.

bought [bɔːt] pt & pp → buy.

bouillon ['buːjɒn] n CULIN caldo.

boulder ['bəʊldəʳ] n canto rodado.

boulevard ['buːləvɑːd] n bulevar m.

bounce [baʊns] n bote m.
▶ vi (ball) rebotar, botar.
▶ vt **1** (cheque) ser rechazado por el banco. **2** (ball) hacer botar.

bouncer ['baʊnsəʳ] n sl gorila m.

bound¹ [baʊnd] *pt & pp* → bind.
▸ *adj* **1** *(tied)* atado,-a. **2** *(forced)* obligado,-a. **3** *(book)* encuadernado,-a. **LOC** **to be bound to** ser seguro que.

bound² [baʊnd] *adj (destined)* destinado,-a: *he knew he was bound to succeed* sabía que estaba destinado a tener éxito. **LOC** **to be bound for** ir con destino, navegar con rumbo a. ▎ **-bound** con rumbo a: *Paris-bound* con rumbo a París.

bound³ [baʊnd] *n (jump)* salto, brinco.
▸ *vi* saltar.

boundary [ˈbaʊndərɪ] *n* límite *m*, frontera. **COMP** **boundary stone** hito, mojón *m*.
ⓘ *pl* boundaries.

boundless [ˈbaʊndləs] *adj* sin límites.

bounds [baʊndz] *n pl (border)* frontera; *(boundary)* límites *mpl*.

bouquet [buːˈkeɪ] *n* **1** *(flowers)* ramo. **2** *(wine)* aroma *m*, buqué *m*.

bourgeois [ˈbʊəʒwɑːʳ] *adj* burgués,-esa.
▸ *n* burgués,-esa.

bourgeoisie [bʊəʒwɑːˈziː] *n* burguesía.

bout [baʊt] *n* **1** *(period)* rato. **2** MED *(of flu, measles, etc)* ataque *m*. **3** *(boxing)* combate.

boutique [buːˈtiːk] *n* boutique *f*, tienda.

bovine [ˈbəʊvaɪn] *adj* bovino,-a.
▸ *n* bovino.

bow¹ [bəʊ] *n* **1** *(for arrows)* arco. **2** *(of violin)* arco. **3** *(knot)* lazo. **COMP** **bow saw** sierra de arco.

bow² [baʊ] *n* MAR proa.

bow³ [baʊ] *n (with body)* reverencia.
▸ *vt* inclinar: *he bowed his head* inclinó la cabeza.

bowel [ˈbaʊəl] *n* intestino.
▸ *n pl* **bowels** *(entrails)* entrañas *fpl*.

bowl [bəʊl] *n* **1** *(for food, etc)* cuenco, fuente *f*, bol *m*; *(large drinking bowl)* tazón *m*. **2** *(for washing)* palangana, barreño. **3** *(of toilet)* taza.

bow-legged [bəʊˈlegd, bəʊˈlegɪd] *adj* patizambo,-a.

bowler¹ [ˈbəʊləʳ] *n (hat)* bombín *m*.

bowler² [ˈbəʊləʳ] *n (cricket)* lanzador,-ra.

bowling [ˈbəʊlɪŋ] *n* bolos *mpl*. **COMP** **bowling alley** bolera.

bow-tie [bəʊˈtaɪ] *n* pajarita.

box¹ [bɒks] *n* **1** caja; *(large)* cajón *m*. **2** *(of matches)* cajetilla. **3** THEAT palco. **4** *(for sentry)* garita. **5** *(of coach)* pescante *m*. **6** GB *fam (telly)* tele *f*. **COMP** **box number** número de apartado de correos. ▎ **box office** taquilla. ▎ **post-office box** apartado de correos.

box² [bɒks] *vi* boxear.

boxcar [ˈbɒkskɑːʳ] *n* US furgón *m*.

boxer [ˈbɒksəʳ] *n* **1** boxeador,-ra. **2** *(dog)* bóxer *m*.

boxing [ˈbɒksɪŋ] *n* boxeo. **COMP** **Boxing Day** GB *el día 26 de diciembre*.

⊕ El 26 de diciembre es festivo en Gran Bretaña. Las tiendas inician las rebajas, se disputan partidos de fútbol y se celebran carreras de caballos.

boy [bɔɪ] *n (baby)* niño; *(child)* chico, muchacho; *(youth)* joven *m*.

boycott [ˈbɔɪkɒt] *n* boicoteo, boicot *m*.
▸ *vt* boicotear.

boyfriend [ˈbɔɪfrend] *n* **1** *(fiancé)* novio. **2** *(male friend)* amigo.

boyhood [ˈbɔɪhʊd] *n* infancia, niñez *f*.
▸ *adj* de la infancia.

bra [brɑː] *n* sostén *m*, sujetador *m*.

brace [breɪs] *n* **1** *(clamp)* abrazadera. **2** ARCH *(support)* riostra. **3** *(drill)* berbiquí *m*. **4** *(on teeth)* aparato.
▸ *n pl* **braces** tirantes *mpl*.

bracelet [ˈbreɪslət] *n* pulsera, brazalete *m*.

bracken [ˈbrækən] *n* BOT helechos *mpl*.

bracket [ˈbrækɪt] *n* **1** *(round)* paréntesis *m*. **2** *(for shelf)* escuadra, soporte *m*. **3** *(group, category)* grupo, categoría *m*. **COMP** **square bracket** corchete *m*.

brag [bræg] *n* jactancia, fanfarria.
▸ *vi* jactarse (**about**, de).
ⓘ *pt & pp* bragged, *ger* bragging.

braggart [ˈbrægət] *n* fanfarrón,-ona.

braid [breɪd] *n* **1** *(on clothing)* galón *m*. **2** *(plait)* trenza.

Braille [breɪl] *n* braille *m*.

brain [breɪn] *n (organ)* cerebro, seso.

▶ *n pl* **brains 1** *(intellect)* cerebro, seso, inteligencia. **2** *(as food)* sesos *mpl*. [LOC] **to have brains** ser un cerebro, ser inteligente. [LOC] **brain death** muerte *f* cerebral. ▍ **brain drain** fuga de cerebros. ▍ **brain scan** electroencefalograma *m*.

brain-dead ['breɪndɛd] *adj* clínicamente muerto,-a.

brainstorming ['breɪnstɔːmɪŋ] *n* reunión *f* creativa, lluvia de ideas.

brainy ['breɪnɪ] *adj fam* inteligente, sesudo,-a.
ⓘ *comp* **brainier**, *superl* **brainiest**.

braise [breɪz] *vt* CULIN freír y luego cocer a fuego lento.

brake [breɪk] *n* freno. [COMP] **brake arm** palanca del freno. ▍ **brake block** pastilla de freno. ▍ **brake fluid** líquido de freno.
▶ *vt* frenar, hacer frenar.

bramble ['bræmbəl] *n* BOT zarzamora, mora. [COMP] **bramble bush** zarza.

bran [bræn] *n* salvado.

branch [brɑːntʃ] *n* **1** *(tree)* rama. **2** *(of family)* ramo. **3** *(road, railway)* ramal *m*; *(stream, river)* brazo. **4** *(of shop)* sucursal *f*; *(of bank)* oficina, sucursal *f*. **5** *(field of science, etc)* ramo. **6** *(of candelabra)* brazo.
▶ *vi (road)* bifurcarse.

brand [brænd] *n* **1** marca. **2** *(type)* clase *f*, tipo.

brand-new [brænd'njuː] *adj* flamante, de estreno.

brandy ['brændɪ] *n* brandy *m*.
ⓘ *pl* **brandies**.

brass [brɑːs] *n* **1** latón *m*. **2** *sl (money)* pasta. **3** MUS metales *mpl*.
▶ *adj* de cobre.

brassiere ['bræzɪəʳ] *n* sujetador *m*, sostén *m*.

brat [bræt] *n fam pej* mocoso,-a.

brave [breɪv] *adj* valiente.
▶ *n* guerrero indio.
▶ *vt* **1** *(defy)* desafiar. **2** *(confront)* afrontar, hacer frente a.

bravo [brɑː'vəʊ] *interj* ¡bravo!

brawl [brɔːl] *n* reyerta, pelea.
▶ *vi* pelearse.

bray [breɪ] *vi* **1** *(donkey, ass)* rebuznar. **2** *(laugh)* carcajearse.

Brazil [brə'zɪl] *n* Brasil.

Brazilian [brə'zɪlɪən] *adj* brasileño,-a.
▶ *n* brasileño,-a.

breach [briːtʃ] *n* **1** *(opening)* brecha, abertura. **2** *(in promise, undertaking)* incumplimiento; *(in law)* violación *f*, infracción *f*. **3** *(in relationship)* ruptura.

bread [brɛd] *n* pan *m*. [COMP] **wholemeal bread** pan *m* integral.

bread-and-butter ['brɛdənbʌtəʳ] *adj (commonplace)* rutinario,-a, corriente y moliente.

breadth [brɛdθ] *n* **1** *(broadness)* ancho, anchura. **2** *(space)* extensión *f*, amplitud *f*.

break [breɪk] *n* **1** *(in leg, etc)* rotura. **2** *(in relationship)* ruptura. **3** *(in meeting)* descanso, pausa; *(at school)* recreo. [LOC] **to take a break** tomarse un descanso. ▍ **without a break** sin descanso, sin parar. ▍ **at break of day** al amanecer.
▶ *vt* **1** romper. **2** *(record)* batir.
▶ *vi* **1** romperse. **2** *(storm)* estallar.
◆ **to break away** *vi (escape)* escaparse, darse a la fuga; *(leave family, job)* irse.
◆ **to break down** *vt sep* **1** *(door)* derribar, echar abajo. **2** *(resistance)* vencer.
▶ *vi* **1** *(car)* averiarse; *(driver)* tener una avería. **2** *(burst into tears)* romper a llorar. **3** *(talks, negotiations)* fracasar.
◆ **to break in** *vi (force entry)* entrar por la fuerza.
◆ **to break off** *vt sep* **1** *(relationship)* romper. **2** *(discussions, negotiations)* interrumpir.
◆ **to break out** *vi* **1** *(prisoners)* escaparse. **2** *(war, fire, etc)* estallar.
◆ **to break up** *vt sep (chair, table, etc)* romper; *(ship, boat)* desguazar.
▶ *vi* **1** *(couple)* separarse. **2** *(gathering, meeting)* disolverse. **3** *(school)* empezar las vacaciones.
ⓘ *pt* **broke** [brəʊk], *pp* **broken** ['brəʊkən].

breakable ['breɪkəbəl] *adj* frágil, rompible.

breakage ['breɪkɪdʒ] *n* rotura.

breakdown ['breɪkdaʊn] *n* **1** *(of car, machine)* avería. **2** MED crisis *f* nerviosa. **3** *(in negotiations)* ruptura. **4** *(chemical analysis)* análisis *m*. [COMP] **breakdown service** (servicio de) asistencia en carretera. ▌ **breakdown van / breakdown truck** grúa.

breakfast ['brekfəst] *n* desayuno. LOC **to have breakfast** desayunar.

▶ *vi* desayunar.

break-in ['breɪkɪn] *n* entrada forzada.

breaking ['breɪkɪn] *n* **1** *(of leg, object)* rotura. **2** *(of relationship)* ruptura.

break-out ['breɪkaʊt] *n (from prison)* fuga.

breakthrough ['breɪkθruː] *n* avance *m* importante.

break-up ['breɪkʌp] *n (of relationship, negotiations)* ruptura; *(of couple)* separación *f*.

breakwater ['breɪkwɔːtəʳ] *n* rompeolas *m*.

bream [briːm] *n (river fish)* brema. COMP **gilt-head bream** dorada. ▌ **red bream** besugo.

breast [brest] *n* **1** *(chest)* pecho; *(of woman)* pecho, seno. **2** *(of chicken, etc)* pechuga.

breastbone ['brestbəʊn] *n* ANAT esternón *m*.

breast-feed ['brestfiːd] *vt* amamantar, dar el pecho a.

ⓘ *pt & pp* breast-fed ['brestfed].

breaststroke ['breststrəʊk] *n (swimming)* braza.

breath [breθ] *n* **1** *(of person)* aliento. **2** *(of air)* soplo. **3** *(breathing)* resuello, respiración *f*. LOC **out of breath** sin aliento. COMP **breath test** GB prueba del alcohol.

Breathalyser® ['breθəlaɪzəʳ] *n* alcoholímetro.

breathe [briːð] *vt (air, etc)* respirar.

▶ *vi* **1** *(air, etc)* respirar. **2** *(be alive)* respirar, vivir: *is he still breathing?* ¿respira aún? LOC **to breathe in** aspirar. ▌ **to breathe out** espirar.

breathing ['briːðɪŋ] *n* respiración *f*.

bred [bred] *pt & pp* → breed.

breeches ['brɪtʃɪz] *n pl* **1** *(knee-length trousers)* calzones *mpl*. **2** *fam (trousers)* pantalones *mpl*.

breed [briːd] *n (of animal)* raza; *(of plant)* variedad *f*.

▶ *vt (animals)* criar.

▶ *vi (animals)* reproducirse.

ⓘ *pt & pp* bred [bred].

breeze [briːz] *n* METEOR brisa.

brew [bruː] *n* **1** *(tea, etc)* infusión *f*. **2** *(potion)* brebaje *m*.

▶ *vt* **1** *(beer)* elaborar. **2** *(tea, etc)* preparar.

▶ *vi* **1** *(tea, etc)* reposar. **2** *(storm)* prepararse, acercarse.

brewer ['bruːəʳ] *n* fabricante *mf* de cerveza, cervecero,-a. COMP **brewer's yeast** levadura de cerveza.

brewery ['bruːərɪ] *n* fábrica de cerveza, cervecería.

ⓘ *pl* breweries.

briar ['braɪəʳ] *n* BOT *(heather)* brezo.

bribe [braɪb] *n* soborno.

▶ *vt* sobornar.

bribery ['braɪbərɪ] *n* soborno.

bric-a-brac ['brɪkəbræk] *n* baratijas *fpl*.

brick [brɪk] *n* **1** ladrillo. **2** *(toy)* cubo (de madera).

bricklayer ['brɪkleɪəʳ] *n* albañil *m*.

bridal ['braɪdəl] *adj* nupcial. COMP **bridal gown** vestido de novia.

bride [braɪd] *n* novia, desposada. COMP **the bride and groom** los novios.

bridegroom ['braɪdgruːm] *n* novio.

✎ Bridegroom o groom sólo se emplean para referirse al novio durante el día de la boda.

bridesmaid ['braɪdzmeɪd] *n* dama de honor.

bridge [brɪdʒ] *n* **1** puente *m*. **2** *(of nose)* caballete *m*.

bridle ['braɪdəl] *n* brida.

▶ *vt (horse)* embridar.

▶ *vi* mostrar desagrado (at, por).

brief [briːf] *adj (short)* breve; *(concise)* conciso,-a; *(scanty)* diminuto,-a.

▶ *n* **1** *(report)* informe *m*. **2** JUR expediente *m*. **3** MIL instrucciones *fpl*.

▶ *vt* **1** *(inform)* informar (about, sobre). **2** *(instruct)* dar instrucciones a.

briefcase ['briːfkeɪs] *n* maletín *m*, cartera.

briefing ['briːfɪŋ] *n* reunión *f* informativa, briefing *m*.

brigade [brɪˈɡeɪd] *n* MIL brigada.

▶ *vt* MIL formar una brigada con.

bright [braɪt] *adj* **1** *(gen)* brillante. **2** METEOR *(sky, day)* claro,-a, despejado,-a;

(sunny) soleado,-a, de sol. **3** *(colour)* vivo,-a. **4** *(cheerful)* alegre, animado,-a.

◆ **to brighten up** *vt sep* **1** METEOR despejar. **2** *(room, house)* dar un aspecto más alegre a. **3** *(enliven)* alegrar, animar.

brightness ['braɪtnəs] *n* **1** *(light)* luminosidad *f*. **2** *(of sun)* resplandor *m*. **3** *(of day)* claridad *f*. **4** *(of colour)* viveza. **5** *(cleverness)* inteligencia.

brilliant ['brɪljənt] *adj* **1** *(gen)* brillante. **2** *(colour)* vivo,-a. **3** *fam* estupendo,-a, fantástico,-a.

brim [brɪm] *n* **1** *(of cup, glass, etc)* borde *m*. **2** *(of hat)* ala.

▶ *vi* rebosar (with, de): *he was brimming with pride* rebosaba de orgullo.

brine [braɪn] *n* salmuera.

bring [brɪŋ] *vt* **1** traer. **2** *(lead)* llevar, conducir.

◆ **to bring about** *vt sep* *(accident, change, etc)* provocar, causar.

◆ **to bring back** *vt sep* **1** *(book, record, etc)* devolver. **2** *(past experience, childhood, etc)* recordar, hacer recordar.

◆ **to bring down** *vt sep* **1** *(chair, book, etc)* bajar. **2** *(door, house, government)* derribar. **3** *(prices, temperature)* hacer bajar.

◆ **to bring forward** *vt sep* **1** *(meeting, appointment)* adelantar. **2** *(theme, question)* presentar, plantear.

◆ **to bring in** *vt sep* **1** *(person)* hacer pasar. **2** *(coal, food, etc into house)* traer. **3** JUR *(verdict)* emitir, pronunciar.

◆ **to bring off** *vt sep* *(victory, result)* conseguir, lograr.

◆ **to bring on** *vt sep* *(illness)* provocar.

◆ **to bring out** *vt sep* *(record)* sacar al mercado, sacar; *(book)* publicar.

◆ **to bring to** *vt sep* hacer volver en sí.

◆ **to bring up** *vt sep* **1** *(chair, book, etc)* subir. **2** *(child)* criar, educar. **3** *(subject, topic)* plantear. **4** *(vomit)* devolver.

ⓘ *pt & pp* brought [brɔːt].

brink [brɪŋk] *n* borde *m*.

brisk [brɪsk] *adj* enérgico,-a.

bristle ['brɪsəl] *n* cerda.

▶ *vi* **1** *(hair)* erizarse, ponerse de punta. **2** *(show annoyance)* mosquearse.

Britain ['brɪtən] *n* Gran Bretaña. COMP **Great Britain** Gran Bretaña.

British ['brɪtɪʃ] *adj* británico,-a.

▶ *n pl* **the British** los británicos *mpl*.

Briton ['brɪtən] *n* británico,-a.

brittle ['brɪtəl] *adj* quebradizo,-a, frágil.

broach [brəʊtʃ] *n* **1** *(drill bit)* broca. **2** *(roasting-spit)* espetón *m*.

broad [brɔːd] *adj* **1** *(street, avenue)* ancho,-a; *(surface, water, plateau)* extenso,-a. **2** *fig (field of study, debate)* amplio,-a. **3** *(measurement)* de ancho. **4** *(general)* general. **5** *(main)* principal. **6** *(accent)* marcado,-a, cerrado,-a. **7** *(vowel)* abierto,-a.

broadcast ['brɔːdkɑːst] *n (by TV, radio)* emisión *f*.

▶ *vt* **1** *(by TV, radio)* emitir, transmitir. **2** *(make known)* difundir.

ⓘ *pt & pp* broadcast.

broadcasting ['brɔːdkɑːstɪŋ] *n* **1** RAD radiodifusión *f*. **2** TV transmisión *f*.

broaden ['brɔːdən] *vt* ensanchar.

broadly ['brɔːdlɪ] *adv* en términos generales.

broad-minded [brɔːd'maɪndɪd] *adj* liberal, tolerante.

broccoli ['brɒkəlɪ] *n* brécol *m*, brócoli *m*.

brochette [brə'ʃet] *n* brocheta.

brochure ['brəʊʃə'] *n* folleto.

broil [brɔɪl] *vt* US asar a la parrilla.

broiler ['brɔɪlə'] *n* **1** CULIN pollo. **2** *(gridiron)* parrilla.

broke [brəʊk] *pt* → **break**.

▶ *adj fam* sin un duro, sin blanca.

broken ['brəʊkən] *pp* → **break**.

▶ *adj* **1** *(plate, window, etc)* roto,-a. **2** *(machine)* estropeado,-a. **3** *(bone)* fracturado,-a. **4** *(person)* destrozado,-a. **6** *(language)* chapurreado,-a: *he speaks broken Spanish* chapurrea el español.

broker ['brəʊkə'] *n* COMM corredor,-ra, agente *mf* de Bolsa.

brolly ['brɒlɪ] *n* GB *fam* paraguas *m*.

ⓘ *pl* brollies.

bromine ['brəʊmaɪn] *n* CHEM bromo.

bronchial ['brɒŋkɪəl] *adj* ANAT bronquial. COMP **bronchial tubes** ANAT bronquios *mpl*.

bronchitis [brɒŋ'kaɪtəs] *n* MED bronquitis *f*.

bronchus ['brɒŋkəs] n bronquio.
ⓘ pl bronchi ['brɒŋkaɪ].

brontosaurus [brɒntə'sɔːrəs] n brontosaurio.

bronze [brɒnz] n bronce m. COMP the Bronze Age HIST la Edad del Bronce.
▶ vi (get a suntan) broncearse.

brooch [brəʊtʃ] n broche m.

brood [bruːd] n 1 (birds) nidada. 2 fam fig (children) prole f.
▶ vi 1 (hen) empollar. 2 fig (worry) apurarse, preocuparse.

brook [brʊk] n arroyo, riachuelo.

broom [bruːm] n 1 (for sweeping) escoba. 2 BOT hiniesta.

broomstick ['bruːmstɪk] n 1 (handle) palo de escoba. 2 (of witch) escoba.

Bros [brɒs] abbr (Brothers) Hermanos mpl; (abbreviation) Hnos: Jones Bros Hnos Jones.

broth [brɒθ] n CULIN caldo.

brothel ['brɒθəl] n burdel m.

brother ['brʌðəʳ] n 1 (gen) hermano. 2 US fam (friend) colega m, tío: what's happening brother? ¿qué pasa tío?

brotherhood ['brʌðəhʊd] n hermandad f, cofradía.

brother-in-law ['brʌðərɪnlɔː] n cuñado.
ⓘ pl brothers-in-law ['brʌðərɪnlɔː].

brought [brɔːt] pt & pp → bring.

brow [braʊ] n 1 (eyebrow) ceja. 2 (forehead) frente f. 3 (of hill) cresta.

browbeat ['braʊbiːt] vt intimidar.
ⓘ pt browbeat, pp browbeaten ['braʊbiːtən].

brown [braʊn] adj 1 marrón. 2 (hair, etc) castaño,-a. 3 (skin) moreno,-a.
▶ vi CULIN dorarse.

brownie ['braʊnɪ] n US pastelito de chocolate y nueces.

browse [braʊz] vi 1 (grass) pacer. 2 (person in shop) mirar.
◆ to browse through vt insep (book, magazine) hojear.

browser ['braʊzəʳ] n (Internet) navegador m, explorador m.

bruise [bruːz] n morado, magulladura, contusión f.
▶ vt magullar, contusionar.
▶ vi magullarse.

bruiser ['bruːzəʳ] n fam gorila m, matón m.

brunch [brʌnʃ] n brunch m.

✎ El brunch es una especie de copioso desayuno que se toma a última hora de la mañana y hace asimismo las veces de almuerzo.

brunette [bruː'net] n morena.
▶ adj moreno,-a.

brush [brʌʃ] n 1 (for teeth, clothes, etc) cepillo. 2 (artist's) pincel m; (house painter's) brocha. 3 (unpleasant encounter) roce m: he had a brush with the police tuvo un roce con la policía.
▶ vt 1 (gen) cepillar. 2 (touch lightly) rozar.
◆ to brush away vt sep (dirt, dust) quitar, limpiar.
◆ to brush up vt sep (knowledge) refrescar, repasar.
◆ brush-off ['brʌʃɒf] n (rebuff, snub) desaire m.

brushwood ['brʌʃwʊd] n 1 (twigs) broza. 2 (undergrowth) maleza.

brusque [brʌsk] adj brusco,-a.

Brussels ['brʌsəlz] n Bruselas. COMP Brussels sprouts coles fpl de Bruselas.

brutal ['bruːtəl] adj brutal, cruel.

brute [bruːt] n bruto,-a, bestia mf.
▶ adj brutal, bruto,-a.

❎ Brute no se utiliza en el sentido de '(importe) bruto', que se traduce por gross.

bubble ['bʌbəl] n (in liquid) burbuja; (of soap) pompa.

bubonic [bjuː'bɒnɪk] adj MED bubónico,-a. COMP bubonic plague peste f bubónica.

buck¹ [bʌk] n (rabbit, hare) macho; (deer) ciervo; (goat) macho cabrío.
▶ adj (animal) macho.

buck² [bʌk] n US fam dólar m.

bucket ['bʌkɪt] n cubo.

buckle ['bʌkəl] n (on shoe, belt) hebilla.
▶ vt (belt) abrochar.
▶ vi 1 (metal, object) torcerse, combarse. 2 (knees) doblarse.

bucolic [bjuː'kɒlɪk] adj bucólico,-a.

bud¹ [bʌd] n (on tree, plant) brote m, yema; (of flower) botón m, capullo.

bud² [bʌd] *n* US *fam* colega *mf*.

Buddhism ['budɪzəm] *n* REL budismo.

budding ['bʌdɪŋ] *adj* en ciernes.

buddy ['bʌdɪ] *n* US *fam* amigote *m*, colega *mf*.
ⓘ *pl* buddies.

budge [bʌdʒ] *vt* **1** *(move)* mover. **2** *(make change opinion)* hacer cambiar de opinión.

budgerigar ['bʌdʒərɪgɑːʳ] *n* ZOOL periquito.

budget ['bʌdʒɪt] *n* presupuesto.
► *adj (good-value)* bien de precio.
► *vt* **to budget for** presupuestar.

budgie ['bʌdʒɪ] *n* ZOOL *fam* periquito.

buff [bʌf] *n* **1** *(leather)* piel *f* de ante. **2** *(colour)* color *m* de ante. **3** *(enthusiast)* aficionado,-a.

buffalo ['bʌfələʊ] *n* ZOOL búfalo.
ⓘ *pl* buffalo o buffaloes.

buffer ['bʌfəʳ] *n* **1** *(for train)* tope *m*. **2** COMPUT memoria intermedia. **3** CHEM regulador *m*.

buffet ['bʌfeɪ] *n* **1** *(bar)* bar *m*; *(at station)* bar *m*, cantina. **2** *(meal)* bufé *m* libre, bufé *m*. **3** *(sideboard)* aparador *m*.

bug [bʌg] *n* **1** *(insect)* bicho. **2** *fam (microbe)* microbio. **3** *(microphone)* micrófono oculto. **4** *fam (interest)* afición *f*. **5** *(in computer program)* error *m*.
► *vt* **1** *fam* ocultar micrófonos en. **2** US *(annoy)* molestar, fastidiar: *what's bugging her?* ¿qué mosca le ha picado?
ⓘ *pt & pp* bugged, *ger* bugging.

bugle ['bjuːgəl] *n* MUS corneta.

build [bɪld] *n* *(physique)* constitución *f*, complexión *f*: *a strong build* una complexión fuerte.
► *vt* construir.
ⓘ *pt & pp* built [bɪlt].

builder ['bɪldəʳ] *n* **1** *(owner of company)* constructor,-ra. **2** *(bricklayer)* albañil *m*.

building ['bɪldɪŋ] *n* **1** edificio. **2** *(action)* construcción *f*, edificación *f*. COMP **building society** sociedad *f* hipotecaria. ▮ **the building industry / the building trade** la construcción.

build-up ['bɪldʌp] *n* **1** *(increase)* aumento: *a build-up in pollution* un aumento de la contaminación. **2** *(of gas)* acumulación *f*.

built [bɪlt] *pt & pp* → build.

built-in [bɪlt'ɪn] *adj* **1** *(as component)* incorporado,-a. **2** *(recessed)* empotrado,-a.

built-up [bɪlt'ʌp] *adj* urbanizado,-a.

bulb [bʌlb] *n* **1** BOT bulbo. **2** ELEC bombilla.

Bulgaria [bʌl'geərɪə] *n* Bulgaria.

Bulgarian [bʌl'geərɪən] *adj* búlgaro,-a.
► *n* búlgaro.

bulge [bʌldʒ] *n* bulto.

bulimia [bjuː'liːmɪə] *n* bulimia.

bulk [bʌlk] *n* **1** *(mass)* masa, bulto; *(amount, quantity)* volumen *m*, cantidad *f*. **2** *(greater part)* mayor parte *f*.

bulk-buying ['bʌlkbaɪɪŋ] *n* compra en grandes cantidades.

bull¹ [bʊl] *n* **1** toro. **2** *(elephant, whale, etc)* macho. **3** FIN alcista *mf*.
► *adj* **1** *(elephant, whale, etc)* macho. **2** FIN alcista, en alza.

bull² [bʊl] *n* REL *(papal)* bula.

bulldog ['bʊldɒg] *n* bulldog *m*.

bulldozer ['bʊldəʊzəʳ] *n* bulldozer *m*.

bullet ['bʊlɪt] *n* bala.

bulletin ['bʊlɪtɪn] *n* **1** *(publication)* boletín *m*. **2** *(medical, etc)* parte *m*.

bulletproof ['bʊlɪtpruːf] *adj* antibalas. COMP **bulletproof vest** chaleco antibalas.

bullfight ['bʊlfaɪt] *n* corrida de toros.

bullfighter ['bʊlfaɪtəʳ] *n* torero,-a.

bullfighting ['bʊlfaɪtɪŋ] *n* los toros *mpl*; *(art)* tauromaquia.

bullion ['bʊljən] *n* *(gold)* oro en lingotes; *(silver)* plata en lingotes.

bullock ['bʊlək] *n* buey *m*.

bullring ['bʊlrɪŋ] *n* plaza de toros.

bull's-eye ['bʊlzaɪ] *n* **1** *(target)* diana. **2** *(score)* acierto. **3** MAR *(porthole)* portilla. LOC **to score a bull's-eye** dar en el blanco.

bullshit ['bʊlʃɪt] *n* taboo *(nonsense)* chorradas *fpl*.

bully ['bʊlɪ] *n* matón,-ona.
ⓘ *pl* bullies.

bum¹ [bʌm] *n* GB *fam (bottom)* culo.

bum² [bʌm] *n* **1** US *fam (tramp)* vagabundo,-a. **2** US *fam (idler)* vago,-a, holgazán,-ana.

▸ *vt fam (scrounge)* gorrear, sablear.

bumblebee [ˈbʌmbəlbiː] *n* ZOOL abejorro.

bummer [ˈbʌməʳ] *n fam* lata, latazo.

bump [bʌmp] *n* **1** *(blow)* golpe *m*, batacazo. **2** *(on head)* chichón *m*; *(swelling)* hinchazón *m*; *(lump)* bulto. **4** *(dent)* abolladura. **5** *(on road)* bache *m*.
▸ *vt* **1** darse un golpe en: *he bumped his head* se dio un golpe en la cabeza. **2** dar un golpe a.
▸ *vi* **1** chocar (into, con), topar (into, contra). **2** *(collide)* chocar, colisionar.
◆ **to bump into** *vt insep fam* encontrar por casualidad, tropezar con.
◆ **to bump off** *vt sep sl* liquidar.

bumper [ˈbʌmpəʳ] *n* parachoques *m*.
▸ *adj* abundante.

bumpy [ˈbʌmpɪ] *adj* **1** *(surface)* desigual, accidentado,-a. **2** *(road)* lleno,-a de baches.
ⓘ *comp* bumpier, *superl* bumpiest.

bun [bʌn] *n* **1** *(bread)* panecillo; *(sweet)* bollo. **2** *(cake)* ma(g)dalena. **3** *(hair)* moño.

bunch [bʌntʃ] *n* **1** manojo. **2** *(flowers)* ramo. **3** *(fruit)* racimo. **4** *fam (group of people)* grupo; *(gang)* pandilla.

bundle [ˈbʌndəl] *n* **1** *(clothes)* fardo, bulto. **2** *(wood)* haz *m*. **3** *(papers, banknotes)* fajo. **4** *(keys)* manojo.

bung [bʌŋ] *n* *(stopper)* tapón *m*.

bungalow [ˈbʌŋgələʊ] *n* bungalow *m*.

bungle [ˈbʌŋgəl] *vt* chapucear.

bungler [ˈbʌŋgələʳ] *n* chapucero,-a.

bunion [ˈbʌnjən] *n* MED juanete *m*.

bunk [bʌŋk] *n* *(bed)* litera.

bunk-bed [ˈbʌŋkbed] *n* litera.
ⓘ *pl* bunk-beds.

bunker [ˈbʌŋkəʳ] *n* **1** MIL búnker *m*. **2** *(golf)* búnker *m*.

bunny [ˈbʌnɪ] *n fam* conejito.
ⓘ *pl* bunnies.

buoy [bɔɪ] *n* boya, baliza.

buoyant [ˈbɔɪənt] *adj* **1** flotante. **2** *(cheerful)* animado,-a. **3** *(optimistic)* optimista.

burden [ˈbɜːdən] *n* carga.
▸ *vt* cargar.

bureau [ˈbjʊərəʊ] *n* **1** *(desk)* escritorio. **2** US *(office)* oficina. **3** US *(agency)* agen-

cia. **4** US *(chest of drawers)* cómoda. **5** US departamento del estado.
ⓘ *pl* bureaus o bureaux [ˈbjʊərəʊ].

bureaucracy [bjʊəˈrɒkrəsɪ] *n* burocracia.
ⓘ *pl* bureaucracies.

burger [ˈbɜːgəʳ] *n* hamburguesa.

burglar [ˈbɜːgləʳ] *n* ladrón,-ona.

burglary [ˈbɜːglərɪ] *n (gen)* robo.
ⓘ *pl* burglaries.

burgle [ˈbɜːgəl] *vt* robar.

burial [ˈberɪəl] *n* entierro. COMP **burial ground** cementerio.

burn¹ [bɜːn] *n* quemadura.
▸ *vt* quemar.
▸ *vi* **1** arder.
◆ **to burn down** *vt sep* incendiar.
◆ **to burn out** *vi* **1** *(fire)* extinguirse. **2** *(fuse, bulb)* fundirse.
ⓘ *pt & pp* burnt [bɜːnt] o burned.

burn² [bɜːn] *n (stream)* arroyo.

burner [ˈbɜːnəʳ] *n* quemador *m*.

burning [ˈbɜːnɪŋ] *adj* **1** *(on fire)* en llamas, ardiendo. **2** *(sun)* abrasador,-ra, de justicia; *(heat)* achicharrante. **3** *(desire, need)* ardiente. COMP **burning issue / burning question** cuestión *f* candente.

burnt [bɜːnt] *pt & pp* → burn.

burnt-out [ˈbɜːntaʊt] *adj* **1** *(building, car)* carbonizado,-a. **2** *fig (person)* quemado,-a, caduco,-a.

burp [bɜːp] *n fam* eructo.
▸ *vi fam* eructar.

burrow [ˈbʌrəʊ] *n* madriguera.

bursary [ˈbɜːsərɪ] *n (scholarship)* beca.
ⓘ *pl* bursaries.

burst [bɜːst] *n* **1** *(of balloon, pipe)* reventón *m*; *(of tyre)* pinchazo, reventón *m*. **2** *(explosion)* estallido, explosión *f*. **3** *(of applause)* salva. **4** *(of gunfire)* ráfaga.
▸ *vi (balloon, pipe)* reventarse; *(tyre)* pincharse, reventarse.
ⓘ *pt & pp* burst.

bury [ˈberɪ] *vt* enterrar.
ⓘ *pt & pp* buried, *ger* burying.

bus [bʌs] *n* **1** autobús *m*, bus *m*. **2** COMPUT bus *m*. COMP **bus conductor** cobrador. ‖ **bus conductress** cobradora. ‖ **bus lane** carril *m* de autobuses. ‖ **bus route** línea de autobús. ‖ **bus shelter**

parada de autobús cubierta. ∎ **bus station** estación f de autobuses. ∎ **bus stop** parada de autobús.

bush [bʊʃ] n 1 *(plant)* arbusto. 2 *(land)* breña.
▶ n pl **bushes** matorral m, maleza.

Bushman ['bʊʃmən] n & adj bosquimano,-a.
① pl **Bushmen** ['bʊʃmen].

bushy ['bʊʃɪ] adj espeso,-a, tupido,-a.
① comp **bushier**, superl **bushiest**.

business ['bɪznəs] n 1 *(commerce)* negocios mpl: *the business world* el mundo de los negocios. 2 *(firm)* negocio, empresa: *he's got a small business on the coast* tiene un pequeño negocio en la costa. 3 *(affair)* asunto, tema m: *I've got business to discuss with the manager* tengo asuntos que tratar con el director. LOC **it's my "(your, etc)" business to ...** me *(te, etc)* incumbe .... ∎ **to go out of business** quebrar. ∎ **to run a business** llevar un negocio. ∎ **to set up a business** montar un negocio. ∎ **mind your own business!** ¡no te metas donde no te llaman! LOC **business card** tarjeta de presentación, tarjeta comercial. ∎ **business trip** viaje m de negocios.

businesslike ['bɪznəslaɪk] adj formal, serio,-a.

businessman ['bɪznəsmən] n hombre m de negocios, empresario.
① pl **businessmen** ['bɪznəsmen].

businesswoman ['bɪznəswʊmən] n mujer m de negocios, empresaria.
① pl **businesswomen** ['bɪznəswɪmɪn].

busker ['bʌskər] n GB músico callejero,-a.

bust¹ [bʌst] n busto.

bust² [bʌst] adj fam roto,-a. LOC **to go bust** fam quebrar.
▶ vt fam romper.
▶ vi romperse.
① pt & pp **bust** [bʌst] o **busted**.

bustard ['bʌstəd] n avutarda.

bustle ['bʌsəl] n bullicio, ajetreo.

busy ['bɪzɪ] adj 1 *(person)* ocupado,-a, atareado,-a. 2 *(street, place)* concurrido,-a. 3 *(day)* ajetreado,-a. 4 US *(telephone)* comunicando: *the line was busy* estaba comunicando. LOC **to get busy 1** fam *(work)* ponerse a trabajar. 2 *(hurry)* darse prisa.
① comp **busier**, superl **busiest**.

busybody ['bɪzɪbɒdɪ] n entremetido,-a, fisgón,-ona.
① pl **busybodies**.

but [bʌt] conj 1 pero: *it's cold, but dry* hace frío, pero no llueve; *I'd like to, but I can't* me gustaría, pero no puedo. 2 *(after negative)* sino: *not two, but three* no dos, sino tres. 3 *(after negative with verb)* sino que: *she told him not to wait, but to go home* le dijo que no se esperara, sino que se fuera para casa. LOC **but for** de no ser por, si no fuera por: *but for him, we would have failed* de no ser por él, habríamos fracasado.
▶ adv (nada) más que, no ... sino, solamente, solo,: *he spoke nothing but the truth* no dijo nada más que la verdad.
▶ prep excepto, salvo, menos: *everyone but me* todos menos yo; *I can meet you any day but Friday* te puedo ver cualquier día excepto el viernes.
▶ n pero: *there are no buts about it* no hay pero que valga.

butane ['bjuːteɪn] n CHEM butano. COMP **butane bottle** bombona (de butano). ∎ **butane gas** gas m butano.

butcher ['bʊtʃər] n carnicero,-a.

butcher's ['bʊtʃəz] n carnicería.

butchery ['bʊtʃərɪ] n carnicería.

butt¹ [bʌt] n *(with head)* cabezazo.

butt² [bʌt] n 1 *(of rifle)* culata. 2 *(of cigarette)* colilla. 3 US fam *(bottom)* culo.

butt³ [bʌt] n *(target)* blanco.

butt⁴ [bʌt] n 1 *(barrel)* tonel m. 2 *(for water)* aljibe m.

butter ['bʌtər] n mantequilla.
▶ vt untar con mantequilla. COMP **butter dish** mantequera. ∎
◆ **to butter up** vt sep fam dar coba a.

buttercup ['bʌtəkʌp] n BOT botón m de oro, ranúnculo.

butterfingers ['bʌtəfɪŋgəz] n manazas mf, torpe mf.

butterfly ['bʌtəflaɪ] n 1 mariposa. 2 SP *(swimming)* mariposa.
① pl **butterflies**.

buttock ['bʌtək] n **1** (of person) nalga. **2** (of animal) anca.
▶ n pl **buttocks** (bottom) trasero, nalgas fpl.

button ['bʌtən] n **1** (on clothing, machine) botón m; (on doorbell) pulsador m, botón m: press the button pulse el botón. **2** BOT (bud) botón m, yema.
▶ vi abrocharse.
▶ vt **to button (up)** abrochar, abrocharse: button (up) your coat abróchate el abrigo.

buttonhole ['bʌtənhəʊl] n ojal m.

buttress ['bʌtrəs] n ARCH contrafuerte m.

butty ['bʌtɪ] n fam bocata m.
ⓘ pl butties.

buy [baɪ] n compra.
▶ vt **1** comprar: they've just bought a new flat acaban de comprar un piso nuevo. **2** (bribe) sobornar. **3** fam (accept, believe) tragárselo: he's so gullible he bought it es tan ingenuo que se lo tragó.
ⓘ pt & pp bought [bɔːt].

buyer ['baɪəʳ] n comprador,-ra.

buying power ['baɪɪŋpaʊəʳ] n poder m adquisitivo.

buzz [bʌz] n **1** zumbido. **2** (of voices) murmullo. **3** fam telefonazo, toque m: give me a buzz dame un toque.
▶ vi zumbar.

buzzard ['bʌzəd] n ratonero.

buzzer ['bʌzəʳ] n timbre m.

buzzing ['bʌzɪŋ] n zumbido.

buzz-saw ['bʌzsɔː] n sierra circular.

buzz-word ['bʌzwɜːd] n palabra pegadiza, palabra que está de moda.

by [baɪ] prep **1** (agent) por: painted by Constable pintado por Constable. **2** (means) por: by air/sea por avión/mar; by car/train en coche/tren; by hand a mano; by heart de memoria. **3** (showing difference) por: I won by 3 points gané por tres puntos; better by far muchísimo mejor. **4** (not later than) para: I need it by ten lo necesito para las diez. **5** (during) de: by day/night de día/noche. **6** (near) junto a, al lado de: sit by me siéntate a mi lado. **7** (according to) según: by the rules según las reglas. **8** (measurements) por: 6 metres by 4 6 metros por 4. **9** (rate) por: paid by the hour pagado por horas. **10** MATH por: 12 divided by 3 12 dividido por 3. **11** (progression) a: day by day día a día; little by little poco a poco. **12** (in sets) en: two by two de dos en dos. **13** (introducing gerund) : you can find out by reading the papers te enterarás leyendo los periódicos. LOC **to go by** pasar delante. I **by** so solo,-a.
▶ adv al lado, delante. LOC **to go by** pasar delante.

bye [baɪ] interj fam ¡adiós!, ¡hasta luego!

bye-bye ['baɪbaɪ] interj fam ¡adiós!, ¡hasta luego! LOC **to say bye-bye** fam decir adiós. I **to go to bye-byes** ir a dormir, ir a la cama.

Byelorussia [bjeləʊ'rʌʃə] n → Belarus.

bygone ['baɪgɒn] adj pasado,-a: a bygone age tiempos pasados.
▶ n (object) antigualla. LOC **in bygone times** antiguamente. I **let bygones be bygones** lo pasado, pasado está.

bylaw ['baɪlɔː] n ley f municipal.

bypass ['baɪpɑːs] n **1** AUTO variante f. **2** TECH tubo de desviación. **3** MED bypass m.
▶ vt **1** (traffic, road) desviar. **2** (avoid) esquivar, evitar.

by-product ['baɪprɒdʌkt] n **1** subproducto, derivado. **2** fig consecuencia.

byre ['baɪəʳ] n establo.

by-road ['baɪrəʊd] n carretera secundaria.

bystander ['baɪstændəʳ] n espectador,-ra, curioso,-a.

byte [baɪt] n COMPUT byte m.

by-way ['baɪweɪ] n **1** (road) carretera secundaria. **2** (remote path) camino poco frecuentado.

byword ['baɪwɜːd] n **1** arquetipo, mayor mf exponente. **2** (proverb) refrán m, proverbio. LOC **to be a byword in** ser sinónimo de: their products are a byword in luxury sus productos son sinónimo de lujo.

Byzantine [bɪ'zæntaɪn] n bizantino,-a.
▶ adj bizantino,-a.

Byzantium [bɪ'zæntɪəm] n Bizancio.

C

C, c [si:] *n* **1** *(the letter)* C, c *f*. **2** MUS do.

c. [ˈsentʃərɪ] *abbr* **(circa)** hacia; *(abbreviation)* h.: *Ramses III c. (800 BC)* Ramsés III (h. 800 a. d. C.).

cab [kæb] *n* **1** *(taxi)* taxi *m*. **2** *(in vehicle)* cabina. COMP **cab driver** taxista *mf*. **cab rank** parada de taxis.

cabaret [ˈkæbəreɪ] *n* cabaret *m*.

cabbage [ˈkæbɪdʒ] *n* col *f*, repollo, berza.

cabin [ˈkæbɪn] *n* **1** *(wooden house)* cabaña. **2** *(on ship)* camarote *m*. **3** *(on plane)* cabina. COMP **cabin crew** personal *m* de cabina.

> **X** Cabin no significa 'cabina (telefónica)', que se traduce por **phone box**.

cabinet [ˈkæbɪnət] *n* **1** *(furniture - gen)* armario; *(glass fronted)* vitrina. **2** POL gabinete *m* (ministerial), consejo de ministros. COMP **cabinet meeting** consejo de ministros.

cable [ˈkeɪbəl] *n* **1** *(rope, wire)* cable *m*. **2** *(telegram)* cable *m*, telegrama *m*. COMP **cable television** televisión por cable.

cacao [kəˈkɑːəʊ] *n* BOT cacao.

cache [kæʃ] *n* **1** *(store)* alijo. **2** *(computer memory)* caché *m*. COMP **cache memory** memoria caché.

cackle [ˈkækəl] *n* **1** *(of hen)* cacareo. **2** *(of person)* risotada, carcajada.
> *vi* **1** *(of hen)* cacarear. **2** *(of person)* reírse a carcajadas.

cacophony [kəˈkɒfənɪ] *n* cacofonía.

cactus [ˈkæktəs] *n* cactus *m*.
> ① *pl* cacti [ˈkæktaɪ] o cactuses.

caddie [ˈkædɪ] *n* *(in golf)* cadi *m*. COMP **caddie car / caddie cart** carrito de golf.

cadence [ˈkeɪdəns] *n* cadencia.

cadet [kəˈdet] *n* cadete *m*.

cadge [kædʒ] *vt fam* gorronear.
> *vi fam* gorronear (from/off, a).

cadger [ˈkædʒəʳ] *n fam* gorrón,-ona.

cadmium [ˈkædmɪəm] *n* cadmio.

caecum [ˈsiːkəm] *n* ANAT intestino ciego.
> ① *pl* caeca [ˈsiːkə].

Caesarean [sɪˈzeərɪən] [also **Caesarean section**] *n* cesárea.

caesium [ˈsiːzɪəm] *n* cesio.

café [ˈkæfeɪ] *n* cafetería, café *m*.

cafeteria [kæfəˈtɪərɪə] *n* *(in factory, college, etc)* cafetería, cantina; *(restaurant)* autoservicio, self-service *m*.

caffeine [ˈkæfiːn] *n* cafeína.

cage [keɪdʒ] *n* *(gen)* jaula.
> *vt* enjaular.

cagey [ˈkeɪdʒɪ] *adj fam* reservado,-a, cauteloso,-a, precavido,-a.
> ① *comp* cagier, *superl* cagiest.

cagoule [kəˈguːl] *n* chubasquero.

cajole [kəˈdʒəʊl] *vt* engatusar.

cake [keɪk] *n* **1** CULIN pastel *m*, tarta, torta. **2** *(of soap)* pastilla.

calamity [kəˈlæmɪtɪ] *n* calamidad *f*.
> ① *pl* calamities.

calcite [ˈkælsaɪt] *n* calcita.

calcium [ˈkælsɪəm] *n* calcio.

calculate [ˈkælkjəleɪt] *vt & vi* calcular.

calculation [kælkjəˈleɪʃən] *n* cálculo.

calculator [ˈkælkjəleɪtəʳ] *n* calculadora.

calculus [ˈkælkjələs] *n* **1** MATH cálculo matemático. **2** [*pl* **calculi** [ˈkælkjəlaɪ]] MED cálculo.

calendar [ˈkælɪndəʳ] *n* calendario.

calf¹ [kɑːf] *n* ZOOL *(of cattle)* ternero,-a, becerro,-a; *(of whale)* ballenato; *(of other animals)* cría.
> ① *pl* calves.

calf² [kɑːf] n ANAT pantorrilla.
ⓘ pl **calves.**

caliber ['kælɪbəʳ] n US → **come.**

calibre ['kælɪbəʳ] n calibre m.

caliph ['keɪlɪf, 'kælɪf] n califa f.

call [kɔːl] n **1** (shout, cry) grito, llamada. **2** (by telephone) llamada (telefónica). **4** (demand) demanda; (need) motivo. ⃞LOC **to be on call** estar de guardia. ‖ **to give sb a call** llamar a ALGN. ⃞COMP **call box** GB cabina telefónica.
▸ vt **1** (shout) llamar. **2** (by telephone) llamar. **3** (summon - meeting, strike, election) convocar; (announce - flight) anunciar.
▸ vi **1** (shout) llamar. **2** (by phone) llamar. **3** (visit) pasar, hacer una visita: I called round at Martin's this afternoon he pasado por casa de Martin esta tarde. **4** (train) parar (at, en). ⃞LOC **to call for** STH/ SB pasar a recoger ALGO/a ALGN.
◆ **to call back** vi (by phone) volver a llamar; (visit) volver a pasar.
◆ **to call on** vt insep visitar, ir a ver a.
◆ **to call out** vt sep (summon - fire brigade) llamar; (doctor) hacer venir; (workers) llamar a la huelga.

caller ['kɔːləʳ] n **1** (visitor) visita, visitante mf. **2** (by telephone) persona que llama.

calligraphy [kə'lɪgrəfɪ] n caligrafía.

calling ['kɔːlɪŋ] n (vocation) vocación f, llamada; (profession) profesión f. ⃞COMP **calling card** US tarjeta de visita.

callous ['kæləs] adj duro,-a, insensible.

⊠ Callous no significa 'callos', que se traduce por tripe.

callus ['kæləs] n callo.
ⓘ pl **calluses.**

calm [kɑːm] adj **1** (sea, weather) en calma, tranquilo,-a. **2** (person) tranquilo, -a, calmado,a: keep calm! ¡tranquilo!
▸ n **1** (of sea, weather) calma f. **2** (peace and quiet) tranquilidad f.
▸ vt calmar, tranquilizar, sosegar.
◆ **to calm down** vt tranquilizar, calmar.
▸ vi tranquilizarse, calmarse.

Calor Gas® ['kæləgæs] n (gas m) butano.

caloric [kə'lɒrɪk] adj calórico,-a.

calorie ['kælərɪ] n caloría.

calvary ['kælvərɪ] n calvario.

calves [kɑːvz] npl → **calf.**

calyx ['keɪlɪks, 'kælɪks] n cáliz m.
ⓘ pl **calices o calixes.**

Cambodia [kæm'bəʊdɪə] n Camboya.

Cambodian [kæm'bəʊdɪən] adj camboyano,-a.
▸ n **1** (person) camboyano,-a. **2** (language) camboyano.

camcorder ['kæmkɔːdəʳ] n videocámara.

came [keɪm] pt → **come.**

camel ['kæməl] n ZOOL camello,-a.

camellia [kə'miːlɪə] n BOT camelia.

camera ['kæmᵊrə] n cámara.

cameraman ['kæmᵊrəmən] n cámara mf.

Cameroon [kæmə'ruːn] n Camerún m.

Cameroonian [kæmə'ruːnɪən] adj & n camerunés,-esa.

camomile ['kæməmaɪl] n BOT manzanilla, camomila.

camouflage ['kæməflɑːʒ] n camuflaje m.

camp [kæmp] n **1** (gen) campamento. **2** (group, faction) bando.
▸ vi acampar.

campaign [kæm'peɪn] n campaña.
▸ vi hacer una campaña (for, en favor de).

camper ['kæmpəʳ] n **1** (person) campista mf. **2** (vehicle) caravana.

campfire ['kæmpfaɪəʳ] n fogata, hoguera.

camping ['kæmpɪŋ] n camping m. ⃞LOC «No camping» «Prohibido acampar». ‖ **to go camping** ir de camping. ⃞COMP **camping site** camping m, campamento.

campus ['kæmpəs] n campus m.
ⓘ pl **campuses.**

can¹ [kæn] n **1** (tin - for food, drinks) lata, bote m. **2** (container - for oil, petrol, etc) bidón m.

can² [kæn] aux **1** (gen) poder: can you come tomorrow? ¿puedes venir mañana?. **2** (know how to) saber: he can speak Chinese sabe hablar chino; can you swim? ¿sabes nadar?. **3** (be allowed to) poder, estar permitido,-a: you can't smoke here no se puede fumar aquí; you can go now ya te puedes ir. **4** (with verbs of perception or mental activity): she couldn't see anything no veía nada; I can smell burning huele a quemado.
ⓘ pt & cond **could** [kʊd].

Canada [ˈkænədə] n Canadá.
Canadian [kəˈneɪdɪən] adj canadiense.
  ► n (person) canadiense mf.
canal [kəˈnæl] n canal m.
canapé [ˈkænəpeɪ] n canapé m.
canary [kəˈneərɪ] n canario.
  ① pl canaries.
cancel [ˈkænsəl] vt 1 (gen) cancelar. 2 (stamp) matasellar. 3 (delete) tachar. 6 MATH eliminar.
  ① pt & pp cancelled (US canceled), ger cancelling (US canceling).
cancellation [kænsəˈleɪʃən] n 1 (gen) cancelación f. 2 (of stamp) matasellos m.
cancer [ˈkænsəʳ] n MED cáncer m.
  ► n Cancer (constellation, sign) Cáncer m.
cancerous [ˈkænsərəs] adj canceroso,-a.
candid [ˈkændɪd] adj franco,-a, sincero,-a. COMP candid camera cámara indiscreta.

🗙 Candid no significa 'cándido', que se traduce por ingenuous.

candidacy [ˈkændɪdəsɪ] n candidatura.
  ① pl candidacies.
candidate [ˈkændɪdət] n candidato,-a.
candidature [ˈkændɪdətʃəʳ] n candidatura.
candle [ˈkændəl] n (gen) vela; (in church) cirio.
candlestick [ˈkændəlstɪk] n (gen) candelero, palmatoria.
candy [ˈkændɪ] n US (sweets) caramelos mpl, golosinas fpl; (a sweet) caramelo.
  ① pl candies.
candyfloss [ˈkændɪflɒs] n GB algodón m de azúcar.
cane [keɪn] n 1 BOT caña. 2 (stick) bastón m. 3 (furniture) mimbre m.
canine [ˈkeɪnaɪn] adj ZOOL canino,-a. COMP canine tooth (diente m) canino, colmillo.
canister [ˈkænɪstəʳ] n (for tea, coffee, etc) bote m, lata.
canned [kænd] adj enlatado,-a. COMP canned food conservas fpl.
cannelloni [kænəˈləʊnɪ] n pl canelones mpl, canalones mpl.
cannibal [ˈkænɪbəl] n caníbal mf.

canning [ˈkænɪŋ] n enlatado. COMP canning factory fábrica de conservas. I canning industry industria conservera.
cannon [ˈkænən] n 1 MIL cañón m. 2 (in billiards) carambola.
  ① pl cannon o cannons.
cannonball [ˈkænənbɔːl] n bala de cañón.
cannot [ˈkænɒt] aux = can not.
canoe [kəˈnuː] n canoa, piragua.
canonization [kænənaɪˈzeɪʃən] n canonización.
can-opener [ˈkænəʊpənəʳ] n abrelatas m.
can't [kɑːnt] aux = can not.
canteen [kænˈtiːn] n 1 (restaurant) cantina, comedor m. 2 (set of cutlery) juego de cubiertos. 3 (flask) cantimplora.
cantilever [ˈkæntɪliːvəʳ] n ARCH voladizo. COMP cantilever bridge puente m voladizo.
canton [ˈkæntɒn] n cantón m.
canvas [ˈkænvəs] n 1 (cloth) lona. 2 ART lienzo.
canvass [ˈkænvəs] vi POL hacer propaganda electoral (for, a favor de), hacer campaña (for, a favor de).
canyon [ˈkænjən] n GEOG cañón m.
canyoning [ˈkænjənɪŋ] n barranquismo.
cap [kæp] n 1 (type of hat) gorra. 2 (cover - of pen) capuchón m; (- of bottle) tapón m, chapa. 3 GEOG casquete m.
capability [keɪpəˈbɪlɪtɪ] n capacidad f (to, para/de).
  ① pl capabilities.
capable [ˈkeɪpəbəl] adj 1 (able) capaz (of, de): he's capable of breaking the world record es capaz de batir el récord mundial. 2 (competent) competente, capaz: a very capable person una persona muy competente.
capacity [kəˈpæsɪtɪ] n capacidad f.
  ① pl capacities.
cape¹ [keɪp] n (garment) capa.
cape² [keɪp] n cabo. COMP Cape Verde Cabo Verde.
caper¹ [ˈkeɪpəʳ] n alcaparra.
caper² [ˈkeɪpəʳ] n 1 (jump) brinco. 2 fam (prank) travesura, broma.
capillary [kəˈpɪlərɪ] n capilar m.
  ① pl capillaries.

capital [ˈkæpɪtᵊl] n **1** (of country, etc) capital f. **2** FIN capital m: starting capital capital inicial. **3** (letter) mayúscula: write it in capitals escríbelo con mayúsculas.
▶ adj **1** (gen) capital. **2** (letter) mayúscula: capital A A mayúscula. COMP **capital goods** bienes mpl de equipo.

capitalism [ˈkæpɪtᵊlɪzᵊm] n capitalismo.

capitol [ˈkæpɪtᵊl] n capitolio.

capitulation [kəpɪtjəˈleɪʃᵊn] n capitulación f.

Capricorn [ˈkæprɪkɔːn] n (constellation, sign) Capricornio.

capsicum [ˈkæpsɪkəm] n pimiento.

capsize [kæpˈsaɪz] vi zozobrar.
▶ vt hacer zozobrar.

capsule [ˈkæpsjuːl] n cápsula.

captain [ˈkæptɪn] n capitán,-ana.

caption [ˈkæpʃᵊn] n **1** (under picture) leyenda, pie m de foto. **2** CINEM subtítulo.

captivate [ˈkæptɪveɪt] vt cautivar, fascinar.

captivating [ˈkæptɪveɪtɪŋ] adj encantador,-ra, cautivador,-ra.

captive [ˈkæptɪv] adj & n cautivo,-a.

captivity [kæpˈtɪvɪti] n cautiverio, cautividad f.

capture [ˈkæptʃər] n (seizure - of person) captura, apresamiento; (of town) toma, conquista.
▶ vt **1** (seize - person) capturar, apresar; (- town) tomar. **2** fig (attract) captar.

car [kɑːr] n **1** AUTO coche m, automóvil m. **2** US (railway carriage) vagón m, coche m. LOC **to go by car** ir en coche.

caramel [ˈkærəmel] n **1** CULIN (burnt sugar) azúcar m quemado. **2** (toffee) caramelo.

carapace [ˈkærəpeɪs] n caparazón m.

carat [ˈkærət] n quilate m.

caravan [ˈkærəvæn] n caravana.

caravel [ˈkærəvel] n carabela.

carbohydrate [kɑːbəʊˈhaɪdreɪt] n hidrato de carbono, carbohidrato.

carbon [ˈkɑːbᵊn] n CHEM carbono. COMP **carbon dioxide** dióxido de carbono. **carbon monoxide** monóxido de carbono. **carbon paper** papel m carbón.

⊠ Carbon no significa 'carbón', que se traduce por coal.

carbonated [ˈkɑːbᵊneɪtɪd] adj (fizzy) gaseoso,-a, con gas.

Carboniferous [kɑːbəˈnɪfᵊrəs] adj GEOL carbonífero,-a. COMP **the Carboniferous period** el carbonífero.

carburettor [kɑːbəˈretər] n carburador m.

carcass [ˈkɑːkəs] n res f muerta.

carcinogenic [kɑːsɪnəˈdʒenɪk] adj MED cancerígeno,-a, carcinógeno,-a.

card [kɑːd] n **1** (gen) tarjeta. **2** (greetings card) tarjeta de felicitación, felicitación f. **3** (of membership, identity) carnet m, carné m. **4** (stiff paper) cartulina. **5** carta, naipe m.

cardboard [ˈkɑːdbɔːd] n cartón m.

cardiac [ˈkɑːdɪæk] adj cardíaco,-a. COMP **cardiac arrest** paro cardíaco. **cardiac sphincter** cardias.

cardigan [ˈkɑːdɪgən] n rebeca.

cardinal [ˈkɑːdɪnᵊl] adj (most important) capital, fundamental, principal.
▶ n REL cardenal m. COMP **cardinal number** número cardinal. **cardinal point** punto cardinal. **cardinal sin** pecado capital.

cardiologist [kɑːdɪˈɒlədʒɪst] n cardiólogo,-a.

cardiology [kɑːdɪˈɒlədʒi] n cardiología.

care [keər] n **1** (gen) cuidado: take care when driving at night (ten) cuidado al conducir de noche; I left the baby in the care of my mother dejé al bebé al cuidado de mi madre. **2** (worry, grief) preocupación f.
▶ vi (be worried, be concerned) preocuparse (about, por); importar: I don't care no me importa, me da igual.
▶ vt (feel concern, mind) importar: no-one cares if you're late a nadie le importa si llegas tarde. LOC «Handle with care» «Frágil». **take care!** **1** (be careful) ¡ten cuidado! **2** (look after yourself) ¡cuídate! COMP **medical care** asistencia médica.
◆ **to care for** vt insep **1** (look after) cuidar, atender. **2** (like) gustar; (feel affection for) querer, sentir cariño por.

career [kəˈrɪər] n **1** (profession) carrera. **2** (working life) vida profesional.

carefree [ˈkeəfriː] adj despreocupado,-a, libre de preocupaciones.

careful ['keəful] *adj* **1** *(cautious)* prudente, cuidadoso,-a: *a careful driver* un conductor prudente. **2** *(painstaking)* cuidadoso,-a. LOC **to be careful** tener cuidado.

carefully ['keəfulɪ] *adv* **1** *(cautiously)* con cuidado, con precaución: *drive carefully* conduce con cuidado. **2** *(with great attention)* cuidadosamente.

careless ['keələs] *adj (inattentive, thoughtless - person)* descuidado; *(driving)* negligente.

caress [kə'res] *n* caricia.
▸ *vt* acariciar.

caretaker ['keəteɪkər] *n* conserje *m*, portero,-a.

cargo ['kɑːgəu] *n (goods)* carga; *(load)* cargamento.
ⓘ *pl* cargoes o cargos.

✗ Cargo no significa 'cargo (empleo)', que se traduce por position.

Caribbean [kærɪ'bɪən, US kə'rɪbɪən] *adj* caribeño,-a. COMP **the Caribbean (Sea)** el (mar) Caribe.

caribou ['kærɪbuː] *n* caribú *m*.

caricature ['kærɪkətjuər] *n* caricatura.

caries ['keərɪz] *n* caries *f*.

carnage ['kɑːnɪdʒ] *n* carnicería.

carnal ['kɑːnəl] *adj* carnal.

carnation [kɑː'neɪʃən] *n* clavel *m*.

carnival ['kɑːnɪvəl] *n* carnaval *m*.

carnivore ['kɑːnɪvɔːr] *n* carnívoro,-a.

carnivorous [kɑː'nɪvərəs] *adj* carnívoro,-a.

carol ['kærəl] *n* villancico.

carotene ['kærətiːn] *n* caroteno.

carousel [kærə'sel] *n* **1** US *(roundabout)* tiovivo, caballitos *mpl*, carrusel *m*. **2** *(for baggage)* cinta transportadora. **3** *(for slides)* carrete *m* de diapositivas.

carp¹ [kɑːp] *n (fish)* carpa.

carp² [kɑːp] *vi (complain)* quejarse (about/at, de).

carpenter ['kɑːpɪntər] *n* carpintero,-a.

carpentry ['kɑːpɪntrɪ] *n* carpintería.

carpet ['kɑːpɪt] *n* **1** *(gen)* alfombra; *(fitted)* moqueta. **2** *fig* alfombra.

✗ Carpet no significa 'carpeta', que se traduce por folder.

carriage ['kærɪdʒ] *n* **1** HIST *(horse-drawn)* carruaje *m*. **2** GB *(railway vehicle)* vagón *m*, coche *m*. **3** *(of typewriter)* carro. **4** *(cost of transport)* porte *m*, transporte *m*.

carriageway ['kærɪdʒweɪ] *n* GB calzada.

carrier ['kærɪər] *n* **1** *(company, person)* transportista *mf*. **2** AV compañía aérea, línea aérea. **3** MED *(of disease)* portador,-ra. COMP **aircraft carrier** MAR portaaviones *m*. I **carrier pigeon** paloma mensajera.

carrion ['kærɪən] *n* carroña.

carrot ['kærət] *n* zanahoria.

carrousel [kærə'sel] *n* **1** *(roundabout)* tiovivo, carrusel. **2** *(for baggage reclaim)* cinta.

carry ['kærɪ] *vt* **1** *(gen)* llevar. **2** *(goods, load, passengers)* transportar. **3** *(disease)* ser portador,-ra de. **4** *(blame, responsibility)* cargar con. **5** *(entail, involve)* conllevar **8** MATH llevar(se).

◆ **to carry forward / carry over** *vt sep* llevar a la columna siguiente, llevar a la página siguiente: *carry this figure forward to the next page* lleva esta cifra a la página siguiente.

◆ **to carry off** *vt sep* **1** *(part, action, duty)* realizar con éxito, salir airoso,-a de: *she carried the speech off well* salió airosa del discurso. **2** *(prize)* llevarse, hacerse con.

◆ **to carry on** *vt insep* continuar con, seguir con.

◆ **to carry through** *vt sep (plan, etc)* llevar a cabo.

ⓘ *pt & pp* carried, *ger* carrying.

carry-out ['kærɪaut] *n* **1** US *(food)* comida para llevar. **2** *(drink)* bebida para llevar.

carsick ['kɑːsɪk] *adj* mareado,-a (al ir en coche). LOC **to get carsick** marearse en coche.

cart [kɑːt] *n* **1** *(horse-drawn)* carro, carreta; *(handcart)* carretilla. **2** US *(for shopping)* carrito, carro.

cartel [kɑː'tel] *n* cártel *m*.

Cartesian [kɑː'tiːzɪən] *adj* cartesiano,-a.

Carthaginian [kɑːθə'dʒɪnɪən] *adj* cartaginense.
▸ *n* cartaginense *mf*.

cartilage ['kɑːtɪlɪdʒ] *n* cartílago.

cartography [kɑː'tɒgrəfɪ] *n* cartografía.

carton [ˈkɑːtˀn] *n (of cream, yoghurt)* bote *m; (of milk, juice, cigarettes)* cartón *m; (of cereals, etc)* caja.

❎ Carton no significa 'cartón', que se traduce por cardboard.

cartoon [kɑːˈtuːn] *n* **1** *(drawing)* viñeta, chiste *m; (strip)* tira cómica, historieta. **2** *(animated)* dibujos *mpl* animados.

cartridge [ˈkɑːtrɪdʒ] *n* **1** MIL cartucho. **2** *(for pen)* recambio.

carve [kɑːv] *vt* **1** *(wood, stone)* tallar; *(statue, etc)* esculpir; *(initials)* grabar. **2** *(meat)* cortar, trinchar.

cascade [kæsˈkeɪd] *n* cascada.

case¹ [keɪs] *n* **1** *(gen)* caso. **2** JUR *(lawsuit)* causa, litigio, pleito. ⸤LOC⸥ in case ... por si..., en caso de que... ‖ in no case bajo ninguna circunstancia.

case² [keɪs] *n* **1** *(suitcase)* maleta. **2** *(box)* caja, cajón *m; (small, hard container)* estuche *m; (soft container)* funda.

cash [kæʃ] *n* dinero (en) efectivo, metálico.
▶ *vt (cheque)* cobrar, hacer efectivo.

cashier [kæˈʃɪər] *n* cajero,-a.

cashmere [kæʃˈmɪər] *n* cachemira.

casino [kəˈsiːnəʊ] *n* casino.
ⓘ *pl* casinos.

cask [kɑːsk] *n* tonel *m*, barril *m*.

❎ Cask no significa 'casco (para la cabeza)', que se traduce por helmet.

casket [ˈkɑːskɪt] *n* **1** *(box)* cofre *m*. **2** *(coffin)* ataúd *m*.

casserole [ˈkæsərəʊl] *n* **1** *(dish)* cazuela. **2** *(food)* guiso, guisado.

cassette [kəˈset] *n* casete *f*.

cast [kɑːst] *n* **1** THEAT reparto. **2** TECH *(mould)* molde *m; (product)* pieza.
▶ *vt* **1** *(gen)* lanzar. **2** *(shadow, light)* proyectar. **3** *(vote)* emitir. **4** THEAT *(part, role)* asignar el papel a. ⸤LOC⸥ to be cast away naufragar. ‖ to cast a spell on STH/SB hechizar ALGO/a ALGN.
◆to cast about for / cast around for *vt insep* buscar, andar buscando.
◆to cast out *vt sep fml* expulsar.
ⓘ *pt & pp* cast.

castaway [ˈkɑːstəweɪ] *n* náufrago,-a.

caste [kɑːst] *n* casta.

caster [ˈkɑːstər] *n (wheel)* ruedecilla.

Castilian [kæˈstɪliən] *adj* castellano,-a.
▶ *n* **1** *(person)* castellano,-a. **2** *(language)* castellano.

casting [ˈkɑːstɪŋ] *n* **1** TECH *(process)* fundición *f; (object)* pieza fundida. **2** THEAT *(selection)* selección *f*, casting *m*.

cast-iron [ˈkɑːstaɪən] *adj* de hierro fundido, de hierro colado.

castle [ˈkɑːsˀl] *n* **1** *(gen)* castillo. **2** *(chess)* torre *f*.
▶ *vi (chess)* enrocar.

castor¹ [ˈkɑːstər] *n →* caster.

castor² [ˈkɑːstər] *n* ⸤COMP⸥ castor oil aceite *m* de ricino.

castrate [kæˈstreɪt] *vt* castrar, capar.

casual [ˈkæʒjʊəl] *adj* **1** *(chance - visit, visitor)* ocasional; *(- meeting)* fortuito,-a, casual. **2** *(superficial)* superficial, *(reader)* ocasional. **3** *(informal)* informal.

casually [ˈkæʒjʊəlɪ] *adv* **1** *(dress)* de manera informal. **2** *(unconcernedly)* despreocupadamente.

❎ Casually no significa 'casualmente', que se traduce por by chance.

casualty [ˈkæʒjʊəltɪ] *n (of accident)* herido,-a; MIL baja
ⓘ *pl* casualties.

❎ Casualty no significa 'casualidad', que se traduce por chance.

cat [kæt] *n (domestic)* gato,-a; *(lion, tiger)* felino,-a

Catalan [ˈkætəlæn] *adj* catalán,-ana.
▶ *n* **1** *(person)* catalán,-ana. **2** *(language)* catalán *m*.

catalogue [ˈkætəlɒg] *n* catálogo.
▶ *vt* catalogar.

catalyst [ˈkætəlɪst] *n* catalizador *m*.

catapult [ˈkætəpʌlt] *n* **1** *(gen)* catapulta. **2** *(toy)* tirachinas *m*.

cataract [ˈkætərækt] *n* **1** *(waterfall)* catarata. **2** MED catarata.

catarrh [kəˈtɑːr] *n* catarro.

catastrophe [kəˈtæstrəfɪ] *n* catástrofe *f*.

catch [kætʃ] *n* **1** *(of ball)* parada. **2** *(of fish)* presa. **4** *(fastener on door)* pestillo.

► *vt* **1** *(gen)* coger, agarrar; *(fish)* pescar. **2** *(train, plane - take)* coger, tomar: *I just caught the last train* cogí el último tren con el tiempo justo. LOC **to catch a cold** resfriarse, coger un resfriado.

◆ **to catch on** *vi* **1** *(understand)* entender, darse cuenta (to, de). **2** *(become popular)* ponerse de moda, imponerse.

◆ **to catch out** *vt sep* *(doing something wrong)* pillar, sorprender; *(trick)* hacer que uno caiga.

◆ **to catch up** *vt sep* *(person)* alcanzar.
ⓘ *pt & pp* **caught** [kɔːt].

catching [ˈkætʃɪŋ] *adj* contagioso,-a.

catchword [ˈkætʃwɜːd] *n* eslogan *m*.

catechism [ˈkætəkɪzəm] *n* catecismo.

categoric [kætəˈgɒrɪk] *adj* categórico,-a.

category [ˈkætəgərɪ] *n* categoría.
ⓘ *pl* **categories**.

cater [ˈkeɪtəʳ] *vi* *(food)* proveer comida (for, para).

◆ **to cater for** *vt insep* *(needs, interests, tastes)* atender a, satisfacer.

caterer [ˈkeɪtərəʳ] *n* proveedor,-ra.

catering [ˈkeɪtərɪŋ] *n* *(business, course)* hostelería; *(service)* catering *m*.

caterpillar [ˈkætəpɪləʳ] *n* oruga.

cathedral [kəˈθiːdrəl] *n* catedral *f*.

catheter [ˈkæθətəʳ] *n* catéter *m*.

cathode [ˈkæθəʊd] *n* cátodo. COMP **cathode ray** rayo catódico.

Catholic [ˈkæθəlɪk] *adj & n* REL católico,-a.

Catholicism [kəˈθɒlɪsɪzəm] *n* REL catolicismo.

cattle [ˈkætəl] *n pl* ganado (vacuno).

caught [kɔːt] *pt & pp* → **catch**.

cauldron [ˈkɔːldrən] *n* caldero.

cauliflower [ˈkɒlɪflaʊəʳ] *n* coliflor *f*.

cause [kɔːz] *n* **1** *(gen)* causa **2** *(reason, grounds)* razón *f*, motivo.
► *vt* causar.

caustic [ˈkɔːstɪk] *adj* cáustico,-a. COMP **caustic soda** sosa cáustica.

cauterize [ˈkɔːtəraɪz] *vt* cauterizar.

caution [ˈkɔːʃən] *n* **1** *(care, prudence)* cautela, precaución *f*, prudencia. **2** *(warning)* aviso, advertencia.
► *vt* **1** *(warn)* advertir. **2** GB *(judge, etc)* amonestar.

cautious [ˈkɔːʃəs] *adj* cauteloso,-a, prudente, cauto,-a.

cavalry [ˈkævəlrɪ] *n* caballería.
ⓘ *pl* **cavalries**.

cave [keɪv] *n* cueva. COMP **cave painting** pintura rupestre.

◆ **to cave in** *vi* *(roof, etc)* hundirse, derrumbarse; *(opposition, etc)* ceder.

caveman [ˈkeɪvmæn] *n* cavernícola *m*, hombre *m* de las cavernas.

cavern [ˈkævən] *n* caverna.

caviar [ˈkævɪɑːʳ] *n* caviar *m*.

caving [ˈkeɪvɪŋ] *n* espeleología.

cavity [ˈkævɪtɪ] *n* **1** *(hole)* cavidad *f*. **2** *(in tooth)* caries *f*.
ⓘ *pl* **cavities**.

caw [kɔː] *n* graznido.
► *vi* graznar.

cayman [ˈkeɪmən] *n* caimán *m*.

CD [ˈsiːˈdiː] *abbr* (compact disc) disco compacto; *(abbreviation)* CD *m*.

CD-ROM [ˈsiːˈdiːˈrɒm] *abbr* (compact disc read-only memory) CD-ROM *m*.

cease [siːs] *vt* suspender. LOC **to cease fire** MIL cesar el fuego.
► *vi* cesar.

cease-fire [siːsˈfaɪəʳ] *n* alto el fuego.

ceaseless [ˈsiːsləs] *adj* incesante.

cecum [ˈsiːkəm] *n* US → **caecum**.

cedar [ˈsiːdəʳ] *n* BOT cedro.

ceiling [ˈsiːlɪŋ] *n* **1** *(of room)* techo. **2** *(upper limit)* tope *m*, límite *m*.

celebrate [ˈselɪbreɪt] *vt & vi* celebrar.

celebrated [ˈselɪbreɪtɪd] *adj* célebre, famoso,-a.

celebration [selɪˈbreɪʃən] *n* *(event)* fiesta, festejo; *(activity)* celebración *f*.
► *n pl* **celebrations** festividades *fpl*, festejos *mpl*.

celebrity [səˈlebrɪtɪ] *n* celebridad *f*, personaje *m* famoso.
ⓘ *pl* **celebrities**.

celery [ˈselərɪ] *n* apio.

celestial [sɪˈlestɪəl] *adj* **1** *(heavenly)* celestial. **2** *(of the skies)* celeste.

cell [sel] *n* **1** *(in prison, monastery)* celda. **2** *(of honeycomb)* celdilla. **3** *(of organism)* célula. **4** ELEC *(in battery)* pila.

cellar ['selə^r] *n* **1** *(basement)* sótano. **2** *(for wine)* bodega.

cellist ['tʃelɪst] *n* violoncelista *mf*.

cello ['tʃeləʊ] *n* violoncelo.
ⓘ *pl* cellos.

Cellophane® ['seləfeɪn] *n* celofán® *m*.

cellphone ['selfəʊn] *n* US teléfono móvil.

cellular ['seljələ^r] *adj* celular. COMP cellular telephone teléfono móvil.

cellulite ['seljʊlaɪt] *n (fat)* celulitis *f*.

celluloid® ['seljələɪd] *n* celuloide® *m*.

cellulose ['seljələʊs] *n* celulosa.

Celsius ['selsɪəs] *adj* Celsius: *30 degrees Celsius* 30 grados Celsius.

Celt [kelt] *n* celta *mf*.

cement [sɪ'ment] *n* **1** *(in building)* cemento. **2** *(glue)* adhesivo; *(for filling teeth)* empaste *m*. COMP cement mixer hormigonera.

cemetery ['semətrɪ] *n* cementerio.
ⓘ *pl* cemeteries.

censor ['sensə^r] *n* censor,-ra.
▶ *vt* censurar.

censorship ['sensəʃɪp] *n* censura.

censure ['senʃə^r] *n fml* censura.
▶ *vt fml* censurar.

census ['sensəs] *n* censo, padrón *m*.

cent [sent] *n* centavo, céntimo.

centenary [sen'ti:nərɪ] *n* centenario.
ⓘ *pl* centenaries.

centennial [sen'tenɪəl] *n* US centenario.

center ['sentə^r] *n & vb* US → **centre**.

centigrade ['sentɪgreɪd] *adj* centígrado,-a.

centigram ['sentɪgræm] *n* centigramo.

centilitre ['sentɪli:tə^r] *n* centilitro.

centimetre ['sentɪmi:tə^r] *n* centímetro.

centipede ['sentɪpi:d] *n* ciempiés *m*.

central ['sentrəl] *adj* **1** *(government, bank, committee)* central. **2** *(of, at or near centre)* céntrico,-a. COMP central nervous system sistema *m* nervioso central.

centre ['sentə^r] *n* centro.
▶ *vt (put in centre)* centrar.
▶ *vi (focus on)* centrarse (on/upon, en).

centrifugal [sentrɪ'fju:g^əl] *adj* centrífugo,-a.

centripetal [sen'trɪpɪt^əl] *adj* centrípeto,-a.

century ['sentʃərɪ] *n* siglo: *the twentieth century* el siglo veinte.
ⓘ *pl* centuries.

ceramic [sə'ræmɪk] *adj* de cerámica.
▶ *n* cerámica.

ceramics [sə'ræmɪks] *n (art)* cerámica; *(objects)* objetos *mpl* de cerámica.

cereal ['sɪərɪəl] *n (plant, grain)* cereal *m*; *(breakfast food)* cereales *mpl*.

cerebellum [serɪ'beləm] *n* cerebelo.

cerebral ['serɪbrəl] *adj* cerebral. COMP cerebral palsy parálisis *f* cerebral.

cerebrum ['serəbrəm] *n* cerebro.

ceremony ['serɪmənɪ] *n* ceremonia.
ⓘ *pl* ceremonies.

certain ['sɜ:t^ən] *adj* **1** *(gen)* seguro,-a: *she's certain to pass* seguro que aprobará. **2** *(specific, particular)* cierto,-a. **4** *(named)* tal: *a certain Pedro Díaz* un tal Pedro Díaz.

certainly ['sɜ:t^ənlɪ] *adv* **1** *(definitely, surely)* seguro. **2** *(when answering questions)* desde luego, por supuesto.

certainty ['sɜ:t^əntɪ] *n* certeza, seguridad *f*.
ⓘ *pl* certainties.

certificate [sə'tɪfɪkət] *n (gen)* certificado: *birth certificate* partida de nacimiento.

certify ['sɜ:tɪfaɪ] *vt* certificar.
ⓘ *pt & pp* certified, *ger* certifying.

cervical ['sɜ:vɪk^əl] *adj* **1** *(of neck)* cervical. **2** *(of uterus)* del (cuello del) útero. COMP cervical cancer cáncer *m* de útero. ‖ cervical vertebrae vértebras cervicales.

cervix ['sɜ:vɪks] *n* **1** *fml (neck)* cerviz *f*, cuello. **2** *(uterus)* cuello del útero.
ⓘ *pl* cervixes o cervices.

cesium ['si:zɪəm] *n* US → **caesium**.

cesspit ['sespɪt] *n* pozo negro.

cetacean [sɪ'teɪʃ^ən] *adj* cetáceo,-a.
▶ *n* cetáceo.

chafe [tʃeɪf] *vt* **1** *(make sore)* rozar, excoriar. **2** *(make warm)* frotar, friccionar.
▶ *vi* irritarse.

chain [tʃeɪn] *n* **1** *(metal rings)* cadena. **2** *(of shops, hotels, etc)* cadena; *(of events)* cadena, serie *f*. COMP chain reaction reacción en cadena. ‖ mountain chain cordillera, cadena montañosa.
▶ *vt* encadenar, atar.

chair [tʃeəʳ] n (gen) silla; (with arms) sillón m, butaca. ⎡LOC⎤ **to address the chair** dirigirse al presidente, dirigirse a la presidencia. ⎡COMP⎤ **chair lift** telesilla.
▸ vt (meeting) presidir.

chairman [ˈtʃeəmən] n presidente m.
ⓘ pl chairmen [ˈtʃeəmen].

chairmanship [ˈtʃeəmənʃɪp] n presidencia.

chairperson [ˈtʃeəpɜːsən] n presidente,-a.

chairwoman [ˈtʃeəwʊmən] n presidenta.
ⓘ pl chairwomen [ˈtʃeəwɪmɪn].

chaise longue [ʃeɪzˈlɒŋ] n diván m.

chalet [ˈʃæleɪ] n chalet m, chalé m.

chalice [ˈtʃælɪs] n cáliz m.

chalk [tʃɔːk] n 1 (mineral) creta, roca caliza. 2 (for writing) tiza.
◆ **to chalk up** vt insep fam (victory, success) apuntarse.

challenge [ˈtʃælɪndʒ] n reto, desafío.
▸ vt 1 (invite to compete) retar, desafiar. 2 (statement) poner en duda, cuestionar.

challenger [ˈtʃælɪndʒəʳ] n (for title, leadership) aspirante mf; (opponent, rival) contrincante mf, rival mf.

challenging [ˈtʃælɪndʒɪŋ] adj (task, job, problem) que supone un reto; (idea) estimulante; (look, tone) desafiante.

chamber [ˈtʃeɪmbəʳ] n 1 (gen) cámara. 2 (of gun) recámara.

chambermaid [ˈtʃeɪmbəmeɪd] n camarera (de hotel).

chameleon [kəˈmiːlɪən] n camaleón m.

champagne [ʃæmˈpeɪn] n (French) champán m, champaña; (Catalan) cava m.

champion [ˈtʃæmpɪən] n 1 campeón, -ona. 2 fig (defender) defensor,-ra, paladín,-ina.
▸ adj premiado,-a.
▸ vt fig defender, abogar por.

championship [ˈtʃæmpɪənʃɪp] n SP campeonato.

chance [tʃɑːns] n 1 (fate, fortune) azar m, casualidad f. 2 (opportunity) oportunidad f, ocasión f: you won't get another chance like this no se te presentará otra oportunidad como ésta. 3 (possibility,

likelihood) posibilidad f. ⎡LOC⎤ **by chance** por casualidad.
▸ adj (meeting, discovery, occurrence) fortuito,-a, casual.
▸ vt (risk) arriesgar.

chancellor [ˈtʃɑːnsələʳ] n 1 POL canciller m. 2 GB (of university) rector,-ra. ⎡COMP⎤ **Chancellor of the Exchequer** GB ministro,-a de Hacienda.

chancy [ˈtʃɑːnsɪ] adj fam arriesgado,-a.
ⓘ comp chancier, superl chanciest.

chandelier [ʃændəˈlɪəʳ] n araña.

change [tʃeɪndʒ] n 1 (gen) cambio. 2 (of clothes) muda. 3 (coins) cambio, monedas fpl; (money returned) cambio, vuelta.
▸ vi cambiar, cambiarse.

changeable [ˈtʃeɪndʒəbəl] adj variable.

changeless [ˈtʃeɪndʒləs] adj inmutable.

changing [ˈtʃeɪndʒɪŋ] adj cambiante. ⎡COMP⎤ **changing room** vestuario.
▸ n MIL cambio, relevo.

channel [ˈtʃænəl] n 1 (gen) canal m. 2 (on television) canal m, cadena.

chant [tʃɑːnt] n 1 REL canto litúrgico, cántico. 2 (of crowd) eslogan m, consigna.

chaos [ˈkeɪɒs] n caos m.

chaotic [keɪˈɒtɪk] adj caótico,-a.

chap [tʃæp] n fam tío, tipo.

chapel [ˈtʃæpəl] n capilla.

chaplain [ˈtʃæplɪn] n capellán m.

chapter [ˈtʃæptəʳ] n capítulo.

char [tʃɑːʳ] vt chamuscar, carbonizar.
ⓘ pt & pp charred, ger charring.

character [ˈkærəktəʳ] n 1 (gen) carácter m. 2 (in film, book, play) personaje m.

characteristic [kærəktəˈrɪstɪk] adj característico,-a.
▸ n característica.

characterize [ˈkærəktəraɪz] vt (gen) caracterizar; (describe character of) calificar (as, de).

chard [tʃɑːd] n acelgas fpl.

charge [tʃɑːdʒ] n 1 (price) precio; (fee(s)) honorarios mpl. 2 (responsibility) cargo. 3 JUR cargo, acusación f. 4 MIL (attack) carga. 5 (explosive) carga explosiva. 6 ELEC carga.
▸ vt 1 (ask as a price - customer, amount) cobrar; (record as debit) cargar. 2 JUR

acusar (with, de). **3** ELEC cargar. **4** MIL cargar contra, atacar.

charger [ˈtʃɑːdʒəʳ] n **1** ELEC cargador m. **2** (horse) corcel m.

chariot [ˈtʃærɪət] n cuadriga, carro.

charisma [kəˈrɪzmə] n carisma m.

charitable [ˈtʃærɪtəbªl] adj **1** (person) caritativo,-a. **2** (organization) benéfico,-a.

charity [ˈtʃærɪtɪ] n **1** (gen) caridad f. **2** (organization) institución f benéfica.
ⓘ pl charities.

charlatan [ˈʃɑːlətªn] n embaucador,-a.

❎ Charlatan no significa 'charlatán (que habla mucho)', que se traduce por chatterbox.

charm [tʃɑːm] n **1** (quality) encanto. **2** (object) amuleto. **3** (spell) hechizo.
▶ vt encantar.

charmer [ˈtʃɑːməʳ] n **1** (charming person) persona encantadora. **2** (of snakes) encantador,-ra.

charming [ˈtʃɑːmɪŋ] adj (delightful) encantador,-ra.

chart [tʃɑːt] n **1** (table) tabla; (graph) gráfico; (map) carta, mapa m. **2** (navigational) carta de navegación.
▶ vt (make a map of) trazar un mapa de; (plan, plot on map) trazar.
▶ n pl the charts MUS la lista de éxitos, el hit parade m.

charter [ˈtʃɑːtəʳ] n **1** (gen) estatutos mpl; (of town) fuero. **2** (constitution) carta. **3** (hiring of plane, etc) fletamiento.
▶ vt **1** (grant rights, privileges to) aprobar los estatutos de. **2** (hire plane, boat, etc) fletar, alquilar.

chartered [ˈtʃɑːtəd] adj (qualified) colegiado,-a. COMP chartered accountant contable mf diplomado,-a.

chase [tʃeɪs] n (gen) persecución f; (hunt) caza.
▶ vt (gen) perseguir; (hunt) cazar.

chasm [ˈkæzªm] n **1** GEOG sima. **2** fig abismo.

chassis [ˈʃæsɪ] n chasis m.
ⓘ pl chassis.

chaste [tʃeɪst] adj **1** (pure) casto,-a, puro,-a. **2** (not ornate) sobrio,-a, sencillo,-a.

chastise [tʃæsˈtaɪz] vt fml castigar.

chastity [ˈtʃæstɪtɪ] n castidad f.

chat [tʃæt] n **1** (in general) charla. **2** (on Internet) charla, chat m.

chatter [ˈtʃætəʳ] n **1** (rapid talk) cháchara, parloteo. **2** (of teeth) castañeteo.
▶ vi **1** (talk rapidly) chacharear, parlotear, cotorrear. **2** (teeth) castañetear.

chatterbox [ˈtʃætəbɒks] n fam parlanchín,-ina, charlatán,-ana.

chatty [ˈtʃætɪ] adj (person) hablador,-ra, parlanchín,-ina.
ⓘ comp chattier, superl chattiest.

chauffeur [ˈʃəʊfəʳ] n chófer mf, chofer mf.

chauvinism [ˈʃəʊvɪnɪzªm] n chovinismo.

cheap [tʃiːp] adj **1** (gen) barato,-a. **2** (of poor quality, shoddy) ordinario,-a. **3** (contemptible - trick, gibe, crook) vil, bajo,-a; (vulgar - joke, remark) de mal gusto.
▶ adv barato.

cheapen [ˈtʃiːpªn] vt **1** (in price) abaratar. **2** (degrade) degradar, rebajar.

cheat [tʃiːt] n **1** (gen) tramposo,-a; (swindler) estafador,-ra. **2** (trick) trampa; (swindle) estafa, timo.
▶ vt (trick, deceive) engañar; (swindle) estafar, timar.
▶ vi (gen) hacer trampa(s); (in exam) copiar.

check [tʃek] n **1** (gen) revisión f, control m; (of machine) verificación f, inspección f; (of results, facts, information) comprobación f, verificación f. **2** (stop, restraint) control m, freno. **3** US → cheque. **4** US (bill) cuenta, nota. **5** (chess) jaque m.
▶ vi (make sure) comprobar, verificar.
◆ to check in vi (at airport) facturar el equipaje; (at hotel) registrarse.
▶ vt sep facturar.
◆ to check out vi pagar la cuenta e irse, dejar el hotel.
▶ vt sep (facts, information) verificar, comprobar; (place) ir a ver; (person) hacer averiguaciones sobre.

checked [tʃekt] adj a cuadros.

checkers [ˈtʃekəz] n pl US damas fpl.

checkmate [ˈtʃekmeɪt] n (jaque m) mate m.
▶ vt dar (jaque) mate a.

checkout [ˈtʃekaʊt] n (in supermarket) caja.

checkpoint [ˈtʃekpɔɪnt] n control m.

checkroom ['tʃekruːm] *n* US guardarropa.

check-up ['tʃekʌp] *n (by doctor)* chequeo, reconocimiento médico.

cheek [tʃiːk] *n* **1** ANAT mejilla. **2** *fam (nerve, impudence)* descaro, cara.

cheekbone ['tʃiːkbəʊn] *n* pómulo.

cheeky ['tʃiːkɪ] *adj (person)* descarado,-a, fresco,-a; *(remark)* impertinente.
ⓘ *comp* cheekier, *superl* cheekiest.

cheer [tʃɪər] *n* **1** *(shout of joy)* viva *m*, vítor *m*, hurra *m*. **2** *(happiness)* alegría.
▶ *vt* **1** *(applaud with shouts)* vitorear, aclamar. **2** *(gladden)* animar, alegrar.
◆ **to cheer up** *vt sep* animar, alegrar.
▶ *vi* animarse, alegrarse: *cheer up!* ¡ánimo!

cheerful ['tʃɪəfʊl] *adj* alegre.

cheerio [tʃɪərɪ'əʊ] *interj* GB *fam* ¡adiós!, ¡hasta luego!

cheerleader ['tʃɪəliːdər] *n* animador, -ra (de un equipo deportivo).

cheers [tʃɪəz] *interj* **1** *fam (as toast)* ¡salud! **2** *fam (thanks)* ¡gracias! **3** *fam (goodbye)* ¡adiós!, ¡hasta luego!

cheese [tʃiːz] *n* queso.

cheetah ['tʃiːtə] *n* guepardo.

chef [ʃef] *n* chef *m*, jefe,-a de cocina.

chemical ['kemɪkəl] *adj* químico,-a.
▶ *n* sustancia química.

chemist ['kemɪst] *n* **1** CHEM químico, -a. **2** GB *(pharmacist)* farmacéutico,-a.
COMP **chemist's (shop)** GB farmacia.

chemistry ['kemɪstrɪ] *n* química.

chemotherapy [kiːməʊ'θerəpɪ] *n* quimioterapia.

cheque [tʃek] *n* cheque *m*, talón *m*.

chequebook ['tʃekbʊk] *n* talonario de cheques.

chequered ['tʃekəd] *adj* **1** *(cloth, pattern)* a cuadros. **2** *fig (past, history, career)* con altibajos, accidentado,-a.

chequers ['tʃekəz] *n pl* damas *fpl*.

cherish ['tʃerɪʃ] *vt* **1** *(person)* apreciar, querer. **2** *(hope, memory, illusion)* abrigar.

cherry ['tʃerɪ] *n (fruit)* cereza, guinda; *(wood)* cerezo. COMP **cherry tree** cerezo.
ⓘ *pl* cherries.

chess [tʃes] *n* ajedrez *m*: *a game of chess* una partida de ajedrez.

chessboard ['tʃesbɔːd] *n* tablero de ajedrez.

chessmen ['tʃesmən] *n pl* piezas *fpl* de ajedrez.

chest [tʃest] *n* **1** *(large)* arca, arcón *m*; *(small)* cofre *m*. **2** ANAT pecho.

chestnut ['tʃesnʌt] *n* **1** BOT *(tree, wood)* castaño; *(nut)* castaña. **2** *(colour)* castaño. **3** *(horse)* alazán,-ana.
▶ *adj (colour)* castaño,-a; *(horse)* alazán,-ana.

chew [tʃuː] *vt (food)* mascar, masticar; *(nails, pencil)* morder.

chewing gum ['tʃuːɪŋgʌm] *n* chicle *m*.

chic [ʃiːk] *adj* chic, elegante.
▶ *n* elegancia.

chick [tʃɪk] *n* polluelo.

chicken ['tʃɪkɪn] *n* **1** *(hen)* gallina; *(food)* pollo. **2** *fam (coward)* gallina *mf*.
▶ *adj fam* gallina.

chickenpox ['tʃɪkɪnpɒks] *n* varicela.

chickpea ['tʃɪkpiː] *n* garbanzo.

chicory ['tʃɪkərɪ] *n* achicoria, chicoria.

chief [tʃiːf] *n (gen)* jefe,-a; *(of party)* líder *mf*; *(of tribe)* cacique *m*.
▶ *adj* principal.

chiefly ['tʃiːflɪ] *adv (mainly)* principalmente; *(especially)* sobre todo.

chieftain ['tʃiːftən] *n* cacique *m*, jefe,-a.

chiffon ['ʃɪfɒn] *n* gasa.

chilblain ['tʃɪlbleɪn] *n* sabañón *m*.

child [tʃaɪld] *n* **1** *(boy)* niño; *(girl)* niña. **2** *(son)* hijo; *(daughter)* hija.
ⓘ *pl* children.

childbirth ['tʃaɪldbɜːθ] *n* parto.

childhood ['tʃaɪldhʊd] *n* infancia.

childish ['tʃaɪldɪʃ] *adj (of a child)* infantil; *(immature)* pueril, infantil.

childlike ['tʃaɪldlaɪk] *adj* infantil.

children ['tʃɪldrən] *n pl* → child.

chili ['tʃɪlɪ] *n* US → chilli.

chill [tʃɪl] *n* MED *(cold)* resfriado; *(shiver)* escalofrío.
▶ *adj (wind, etc)* frío,-a.
▶ *vt* enfriar.

chilli ['tʃɪlɪ] *n* chile *m*.

chilling ['tʃɪlɪŋ] *adj* **1** glacial. **2** *fig* espeluznante, escalofriante.

chilly ['tʃɪlɪ] *adj (gen)* frío,-a.
ⓘ *comp* chillier, *superl* chilliest.

chime [tʃaɪm] *n (bells)* carillón *m*; *(sound of bells)* repique *m*; *(of clock)* campanada; *(of doorbell)* campanilla.
▶ *vi (bells)* sonar, repicar; *(clock)* dar la hora, sonar.

chimney ['tʃɪmnɪ] *n* chimenea.

✎ Chimney sólo se refiere al conducto por donde sale el humo. El hogar se traduce por fireplace.

chimpanzee [tʃɪmpæn'ziː] *n* chimpancé *m*.

chin [tʃɪn] *n* barbilla, mentón *m*.

china ['tʃaɪnə] *n* **1** *(white clay)* loza; *(fine)* porcelana. **2** *(crockery)* vajilla, objetos *mpl* de porcelana, loza.

China ['tʃaɪnə] *n* China.

Chinese [tʃaɪ'niːz] *adj* chino,-a.
▶ *n* **1** *(person)* chino,-a. **2** *(language)* chino.

chink¹ [tʃɪŋk] *n* grieta, abertura.

chink² [tʃɪŋk] *n (noise)* tintineo.
▶ *vt* hacer tintinear, hacer sonar.

chip [tʃɪp] *n* **1** GB *(fried potato)* patata frita. **2** US patata frita (de bolsa). **3** COMPUT chip *m*. **4** *(of wood)* astilla; *(of stone)* lasca. **5** *(flaw - in plate, glass)* desportilladura. **6** *(in gambling)* ficha.
▶ *vt* **1** GB *(potatoes)* cortar. **2** *(china, glass)* desportillar; *(paint)* desconchar.
ⓘ *pt & pp* chipped, *ger* chipping.

chipboard ['tʃɪpbɔːd] *n* aglomerado, madera aglomerada.

chiropodist [kɪ'rɒpədɪst] *n* podólogo, -a, pedicuro,-a, callista *mf*.

chirp [tʃɜːp] *vi (insect)* chirriar; *(bird)* gorjear.

chisel ['tʃɪzəl] *n (for stone)* cincel *m*.
▶ *vt (stone)* cincelar; *(wood, metal)* labrar, tallar.
ⓘ *pt & pp* chiselled (US chiseled), *ger* chiselling (US chiseling).

chit [tʃɪt] *n fam (note)* nota.

chitchat ['tʃɪttʃæt] *n fam* palique *m*, cháchara.

chives [tʃaɪvz] *n pl* BOT cebollino, cebolleta.

chloride ['klɔːraɪd] *n* cloruro.

chlorine ['klɔːriːn] *n* cloro.

chloroform ['klɒrəfɔːm] *n* cloroformo.

chlorophyll ['klɒrəfɪl] *n* clorofila.

chock [tʃɒk] *n* calzo, cuña.

chock-a-block [tʃɒkə'blɒk] *adj fam* hasta los topes, de bote en bote.

chock-full [tʃɒk'fʊl] *adj fam* hasta los topes.

chocolate ['tʃɒkələt] *n* **1** *(substance)* chocolate *m*: *a bar of chocolate* una chocolatina, una tableta de chocolate. **2** *(individual sweet)* bombón *m*.

choice [tʃɔɪs] *n* **1** *(act)* elección *f*, opción *f*. **2** *(person, thing chosen)* elección *f*. **3** *(variety, range)* surtido, selección *f*.
▶ *adj* **1** *(top quality)* selecto,-a, de primera calidad.

choir ['kwaɪə'] *n* coro.

choke [tʃəʊk] *vt* **1** *(person)* ahogar, asfixiar, estrangular. **2** *(block - pipe, drain, etc)* atascar, obstruir.
▶ *n* estárter *m*.

❌ Choke no significa 'choque', que se traduce por collision.

cholera ['kɒlərə] *n* cólera *m*.

cholesterol [kə'lestə'rɒl] *n* colesterol *m*.

choose [tʃuːz] *vt* **1** *(select)* escoger, elegir; *(elect)* elegir. **2** *(decide)* decidir, optar por.
ⓘ *pt* chose [tʃəʊz], *pp* chosen ['tʃəʊzən], *ger* choosing.

choosy ['tʃuːzɪ] *adj fam* exigente.
ⓘ *comp* choosier, *superl* choosiest.

chop [tʃɒp] *n* **1** *(blow)* tajo, golpe *m*; *(with axe)* hachazo. **2** CULIN chuleta.
▶ *vt* cortar (up, -).
◆ to chop down *vt sep (tree, etc)* talar.
◆ to chop off *vt sep* cortar.
ⓘ *pt & pp* chopped, *ger* chopping.

choppy ['tʃɒpɪ] *adj (sea)* picado,-a.
ⓘ *comp* choppier, *superl* choppiest.

chopsticks ['tʃɒpstɪks] *n pl* palillos *mpl*.

choral ['kɔːrəl] *adj* coral. COMP choral society coral *f*, orfeón *m*.

chorale [kə'rɑːl] *n* coral *f*.

chord¹ [kɔːd] *n* **1** MATH cuerda. **2** ANAT → cord.

chord² [kɔːd] *n* MUS acorde *m*.

chore [tʃɔːʳ] *n (job)* quehacer *m*, tarea; *(boring job)* lata.

choreography [kɒrɪˈɒgrəfɪ] *n* coreografía.

chorister [ˈkɒrɪstəʳ] *n* corista *mf*.

chorus [ˈkɔːrəs] *n* **1** *(choir)* coro. **2** *(of song)* estribillo.

chose [tʃəʊz] *pt* → choose.

chosen [ˈtʃəʊzᵊn] *pp* → choose.
▸ *adj* elegido,-a, escogido,-a.

Christ [kraɪst] *n* Cristo, Jesucristo.

christening [ˈkrɪsᵊnɪŋ] *n (ritual)* bautismo; *(celebration)* bautizo.

Christian [ˈkrɪstɪən] *adj & n* cristiano,-a.

Christmas [ˈkrɪsməs] *n* Navidad *f*, Navidades *fpl*. COMP **Christmas Eve** Nochebuena. ▐ **Christmas Day** día *m* de Navidad.

chrome [krəʊm] *n* cromo.

chromosome [ˈkrəʊməsəʊm] *n* cromosoma *m*.

chronic [ˈkrɒnɪk] *adj* **1** *(disease, person, problem)* crónico,-a. **2** GB *fam (terrible)* malísimo,-a, terrible.

chronicle [ˈkrɒnɪkᵊl] *n* crónica.

chronological [krɒnəˈlɒdʒɪkᵊl] *adj* cronológico,-a.

chronology [krəˈnɒlədʒɪ] *n* cronología.

chronometer [krəˈnɒmɪtəʳ] *n* cronómetro.

chrysalis [ˈkrɪsəlɪs] *n* crisálida.
ⓘ *pl* chrysalises.

chrysanthemum [krɪˈsænθəməm] *n* crisantemo.

chubby [ˈtʃʌbɪ] *adj (person)* regordete,-a, gordinflón,-ona.
ⓘ *comp* chubbier, *superl* chubbiest.

chuck [tʃʌk] *vt* **1** *fam (throw)* tirar. **2** *fam (give up)* dejar, plantar.
◆ **to chuck away** *vt sep (rubbish)* tirar; *(money)* derrochar.

chuckle [ˈtʃʌkᵊl] *vi* reírse (entre dientes).
▸ *n* risita.

chum [tʃʌm] *n fam* compinche *mf*.

church [tʃɜːtʃ] *n* iglesia. COMP **Church of England** Iglesia Anglicana.

churchyard [ˈtʃɜːtʃjɑːd] *n* cementerio, camposanto.

churn [tʃɜːn] *n* **1** GB *(for milk)* lechera. **2** *(for butter)* mantequera.
▸ *vt* **1** *(butter)* hacer; *(milk, cream)* batir. **2** *(water, earth)* agitar (up, -), revolver (up, -).
◆ **to churn out** *vt sep* producir en serie, hacer como churros.

chute [ʃuːt] *n (slide)* tobogán *m*.

cicada [sɪˈkɑːdə] *n* cigarra.

cider [ˈsaɪdəʳ] *n* sidra.

cigar [sɪˈgɑːʳ] *n* puro, cigarro.

cigarette [sɪgəˈret] *n* cigarrillo.

cinder [ˈsɪndəʳ] *n* ceniza, pavesa.

Cinderella [sɪndəˈrelə] *n* (la) Cenicienta.

cinema [ˈsɪnəmə] *n* cine *m*.

cinnamon [ˈsɪnəmən] *n* canela.

cipher [ˈsaɪfəʳ] *n* **1** *(code)* código, clave *f*. **2** *(zero)* cero; *(numeral)* cifra.

circle [ˈsɜːkᵊl] *n* círculo.
▸ *vt (encircle)* rodear, cercar; *(move in a circle)* dar vueltas alrededor de.

circuit [ˈsɜːkɪt] *n* **1** *(route, journey round)* recorrido; *(of running track)* vuelta. **2** ELEC circuito. **3** SP *(series of tournaments)* circuito.

circular [ˈsɜːkjələʳ] *adj* circular.

circulate [ˈsɜːkjəleɪt] *vi* circular.
▸ *vt* hacer circular.

circulation [sɜːkjəˈleɪʃᵊn] *n* **1** *(gen)* circulación *f*. **2** *(of newspaper, magazine)* tirada.

circulatory [sɜːkjəˈleɪtərɪ] *adj* circulatorio,-a.

circumcision [sɜːkəmˈsɪʒᵊn] *n* circuncisión *f*.

circumference [səˈkʌmfᵊrəns] *n* circunferencia.

circumflex [ˈsɜːkəmfleks] *n* circunflejo.

circumstance [ˈsɜːkəmstəns] *n (condition, fact)* circunstancia.
▸ *n pl* **circumstances** *(financial position)* situación *f* económica.

circus [ˈsɜːkəs] *n* **1** *(entertainment)* circo. **2** GB *(in town)* glorieta, plaza redonda.

cistern [ˈsɪstən] *n* cisterna.

cite [saɪt] *vt* citar.

citizen [ˈsɪtɪzᵊn] *n* ciudadano,-a.

citizenship [ˈsɪtɪzᵊnʃɪp] *n* ciudadanía.

citric [ˈsɪtrɪk] *adj* cítrico,-a.

city ['sɪtɪ] n ciudad f. COMP **city council** GB ayuntamiento, municipio. ‖ **the City** GB el centro financiero de Londres.
ⓘ pl **cities**.

⊕ La City de Londres es el barrio original a partir del cual creció la actual metrópoli. Hoy en día, concentra las sedes de las grandes empresas y es unos de los centros económicos más importantes del mundo.

civic ['sɪvɪk] adj (duty, pride) cívico,-a; (leader, event) municipal.

civics ['sɪvɪks] n educación f cívica.

civil ['sɪvəl] adj **1** (of citizens) civil. **2** (polite) cortés,-esa, educado,-a. COMP **civil servant** funcionario,-a. ‖ **the Civil Service** la administración pública.

civilian [sɪ'vɪljən] adj civil. LOC **in civilian dress** de paisano.
▶ n civil mf.
▶ n pl **civilians** población f sing civil.

civility [sɪ'vɪlɪtɪ] n cortesía.

civilization [sɪvɪlaɪ'zeɪʃ°n] n civilización f.

civilize ['sɪvɪlaɪz] vt civilizar.

clad [klæd] pt & pp → **clothe**.
▶ adj vestido,-a.

claim [kleɪm] n **1** (demand - for insurance) reclamación f; (for benefit, allowance) solicitud f. **2** (assertion) afirmación f.
▶ vt **1** (gen) reclamar. **2** (apply for) solicitar. **3** (of disaster, accident, etc) cobrar. **4** (assert) afirmar, sostener, decir.
▶ vi presentar un reclamación.

claimant ['kleɪmənt] n **1** (of benefit, allowance) solicitante mf; (of insurance) reclamante mf. **2** (to throne) pretendiente mf. **3** JUR demandante mf.

clam [klæm] n almeja.

clamber ['klæmbəʳ] vi trepar gateando (over, a).

clammy ['klæmɪ] adj (weather) bochornoso,-a; (hands) pegajoso,-a.
ⓘ comp **clammier**, superl **clammiest**.

clamor ['klæməʳ] n US → **clothe**.

clamour ['klæməʳ] n clamor m.
▶ vi clamar.

clamp [klæmp] n abrazadera.
▶ vt sujetar con abrazaderas.

◆ **to clamp down on** vt insep poner freno a, tomar medidas drásticas contra.

clan [klæn] n clan m.

clandestine [klæn'destɪn] adj clandestino,-a.

clang [klæŋ] n sonido metálico (fuerte).
▶ vi sonar.

clap [klæp] n **1** (noise) ruido seco. **2** (applause) aplauso. **3** (slap) palmada.
▶ vt **1** (applaud) aplaudir. **2** (slap) dar una palmada a.

◆ **to clap on** vt sep (add) agregar.

clapperboard ['klæpəbɔːd] n claqueta.

clapping ['klæpɪŋ] n aplausos mpl.

claret ['klærət] n (wine) clarete m.

clarify ['klærɪfaɪ] vt aclarar.
ⓘ pt & pp **clarified**, ger **clarifying**.

clarinet [klærɪ'net] n clarinete m.

clarity ['klærɪtɪ] n claridad f.

clash [klæʃ] n **1** (fight) enfrentamiento, choque m; (disagreement, argument) desacuerdo. **2** (conflict - of interests) conflicto; (- of personalities, cultures, opinions) choque m. **3** (loud noise) sonido.
▶ vi **1** (opposing forces - fight) chocar; (- disagree) discutir, enfrentarse (with, a). **2** (interests) estar en conflicto. **3** (dates, events) coincidir. **4** (colours) desentonar (with, con). **5** (cymbals) sonar.

clasp [klɑːsp] n (on necklace) broche m; (on belt) cierre m, hebilla.
▶ vt agarrar, sujetar.

class [klɑːs] n clase f.
▶ vt clasificar, catalogar.

classic ['klæsɪk] adj clásico,-a.
▶ n (novel, film, play) clásico.
▶ n pl **classics** (literature) clásicos mpl; (languages) clásicas fpl.

classical ['klæsɪk°l] adj (gen) clásico,-a.

classification [klæsɪfɪ'keɪʃ°n] n clasificación f.

classified ['klæsɪfaɪd] adj **1** (categorized) clasificado,-a. **2** (secret) secreto,-a, confidencial.

classify ['klæsɪfaɪ] vt clasificar.
ⓘ pt & pp **classified**, ger **classifying**.

classmate ['klɑːsmeɪt] n compañero,-a de clase.

classroom ['klɑːsruːm] n aula, clase f.

classy [ˈklɑːsɪ] *adj sl* con clase.
ⓘ *comp* classier, *superl* classiest.

clatter [ˈklætəʳ] *n* ruido.
▶ *vi* hacer ruido.

clause [klɔːz] *n* **1** *(in document)* cláusula. **2** LING oración *f*.

claustrophobia [klɔːstrəˈfəʊbɪə] *n* claustrofobia.

claustrophobic [klɔːstrəˈfəʊbɪk] *adj* claustrofóbico,-a.

clavichord [ˈklævɪkɔːd] *n* clavicordio.

clavicle [ˈklævɪkəl] *n* clavícula.

claw [klɔː] *n* **1** *(of lion, tiger, etc)* garra, zarpa; *(of cat)* uña; *(of bird)* garra; *(of crab, lobster)* pinza.
▶ *vi (scratch)* arañar (at, -).

clay [kleɪ] *n* arcilla.

clean [kliːn] *adj* limpio,-a.
▶ *vt (gen)* limpiar.
▶ *vi* limpiarse.
◆ **to clean out** *vt sep* **1** *(room, etc)* limpiar a fondo. **2** *fam (take all money)* dejar limpio,-a, dejar sin blanca.
◆ **to clean up** *vt sep* **1** *(room, mess, etc)* limpiar. **2** *fam (money, fortune)* hacer, sacar.
▶ *vi* **1** *(room, etc)* limpiar. **2** *fam (make money)* forrarse, barrer con todo.

clean-cut [kliːnˈkʌt] *adj (outline, feature)* bien definido,-a, nítido,-a; *(person, appearance)* limpio,-a, muy cuidado,-a.

cleaner [ˈkliːnəʳ] *n* **1** *(person)* encargado, -a de la limpieza. **2** *(product)* limpiador *m*.
▶ *n* **cleaner's** *(place, shop)* tintorería.

cleanse [klenz] *vt* limpiar (of, de).

cleanser [ˈklenzəʳ] *n (detergent)* producto de limpieza; *(lotion for skin)* leche *f* limpiadora, crema limpiadora.

cleansing [ˈklenzɪŋ] *n* limpieza.

clear [klɪəʳ] *adj* **1** *(glass, plastic, liquid)* transparente; *(sky, day, etc)* despejado,-a. **2** *(not blocked - road, desk)* despejado,-a; *(free - time)* libre. **3** *(picture, outline)* nítido, -a. **4** *(voice, sound, explanation)* claro,-a.
▶ *adv* **1** *(clearly - speak)* claramente; *(hear)* bien. **2** *(not touching)* a distancia.
▶ *vt* **1** *(table)* quitar; *(floor, road)* despejar; *(pipe, drain)* desatascar; *(building, room - of people)* desalojar, desocupar;

(house, room - of furniture) vaciar. **2** *(accused person)* absolver, exculpar; *(one's name)* limpiar. **3** *(debt)* liquidar, saldar. **4** *(obstacle)* salvar. **5** SP *(ball)* despejar.
◆ **to clear away** *vt sep (dishes, etc)* recoger, quitar.1
◆ **to clear off** *vi fam* largarse.
▶ *vt sep (debt)* liquidar.
◆ **to clear out** *vi fam* largarse.
▶ *vt sep (cupboard, drawers, room)* vaciar; *(old things)* tirar.
◆ **to clear up** *vt sep* **1** *(mystery, crime)* resolver, esclarecer; *(issue, misunderstanding)* aclarar; *(loose ends)* atar. **2** *(tidy)* recoger.
▶ *vi* **1** *(tidy)* ordenar. **2** *(weather)* despejar, mejorar.

clearance [ˈklɪərəns] *n* **1** SP despeje *m*. **2** *(permission)* autorización *f*. [COMP] **clearance sale** liquidación *f*.

clear-cut [klɪəˈkʌt] *adj* claro,-a, bien definido,-a.

clear-headed [ˈklɪəˈhedɪd] *adj* lúcido,-a, despejado,-a.

clearing [ˈklɪərɪŋ] *n (in wood)* claro.

clearness [ˈklɪənəs] *n* claridad *f*.

clear-sighted [klɪəˈsaɪtɪd] *adj* perspicaz, lúcido,-a.

clef [klef] *n* MUS clave *f*: bass/treble clef clave de fa/de sol.

cleft [kleft] *adj (chin, lip)* partido,-a.
▶ *n* hendidura, grieta.

clementine [ˈkleməntaɪn] *n* clementina.

clench [klentʃ] *vt* **1** *(teeth, fist)* apretar. **2** *(grip)* apretar, agarrar.

clergy [ˈklɜːdʒɪ] *n* clero.

clergyman [ˈklɜːdʒɪmən] *n* clérigo.
ⓘ *pl* clergymen [ˈklɜːdʒɪmən].

clerical [ˈklerɪkəl] *adj* **1** REL clerical, eclesiástico,-a. **2** *(of a clerk)* de oficina, administrativo,-a.

clerk [klɑːk, US klɜːrk] *n* **1** *(office worker)* oficinista *mf*, administrativo,-a. **2** US *(in a shop)* dependiente,-a *mf*.

clever [ˈklevəʳ] *adj* **1** *(person - intelligent)* listo,-a, inteligente; *(skilful)* hábil. **2** *(idea, plan, gadget)* ingenioso,-a; *(move)* hábil.

cliché [ˈkliːʃeɪ] *n* cliché *m*, tópico.

click [klɪk] n (sound - gen) clic m; (of tongue, fingers) chasquido.
- ▸ vt (tongue, fingers) chasquear.
- ▸ vi **1** (make noise) hacer clic. **2** (understand, realize) caer en la cuenta, darse cuenta de.

client ['klaɪənt] n cliente,-a.

cliff [klɪf] n acantilado, precipicio.

cliffhanger ['klɪfhæŋəʳ] n situación f de suspense.

climate ['klaɪmət] n **1** GEOG clima m. **2** fig clima m, situación f.

climatic [klaɪ'mætɪk] adj climático,-a.

climatological [klaɪmətə'lɒdʒɪkəl] adj climatológico,-a.

climatology [klaɪmə'tɒlədʒɪ] n climatología.

climax ['klaɪmæks] n clímax m.

climb [klaɪm] n **1** (gen) subida. **2** SP escalada.
- ▸ vt subir (a).
- ▸ vi trepar.
- ◆ **to climb down** vi **1** (descend) bajar. **2** fig (admit mistake, withdraw) ceder, volverse atrás.

climber ['klaɪməʳ] n **1** SP alpinista mf, escalador,-ra. **2** BOT enredadera.

climbing ['klaɪmɪŋ] n SP alpinismo, montañismo.

clinch [klɪntʃ] n **1** fam (embrace) abrazo apasionado. **2** SP (in boxing) cuerpo a cuerpo.
- ▸ vt fam (deal) cerrar; (argument) resolver; (title) hacerse con.
- ▸ vi SP (in boxing) abrazarse.

cling [klɪŋ] vi **1** (hold tightly) agarrarse (to, a). **2** (stick - clothes) pegarse, ceñirse; (- smell) pegarse.
- ① pt & pp clung [klʌŋ].

clingfilm ['klɪŋfɪlm] n film m transparente.

clinic ['klɪnɪk] n **1** (private, specialized) clínica. **2** (in state hospital) ambulatorio, dispensario.

clink [klɪŋk] n (noise) tintineo.
- ▸ vt hacer tintinear.
- ▸ vi tintinear.

clip¹ [klɪp] n **1** (with scissors) tijeretada. **2** (of film) fragmento. **3** fam (blow) cachete m.
- ▸ vt **1** (cut - gen) cortar; (ticket) picar; (animals) esquilar. **2** (cut out) recortar. **3** fam (hit) dar un cachete a.
- ① pt & pp clipped, ger clipping.

clip² [klɪp] n **1** (for papers, etc) clip m; (for hair) pasador m, clip m. **2** (brooch) broche m, alfiler m de pecho.

clipboard ['klɪpbɔːd] n INFORM portapapeles m.

clippers ['klɪpəz] n pl (for nails) cortaúñas m sing; (for hair) maquinilla f sing.

clipping ['klɪpɪŋ] n (cutting) recorte m de periódico, recorte m de prensa.

clique [kliːk] n pej camarilla.

clitoris ['klɪtərɪs] n clítoris m.

cloak [kləʊk] n **1** (garment) capa. **2** fig (cover) capa, manto.

cloakroom ['kləʊkruːm] n **1** (gen) guardarropa. **2** GB euph (toilet) lavabo, servicios mpl.

clock [klɒk] n reloj m (de pared).
- ▸ vt **1** (time - athlete, race) cronometrar. **2** (register - speed, time) registrar, hacer.
- ◆ **to clock in/on** vi fichar (al llegar al trabajo).
- ◆ **to clock out/off** vi fichar (al salir del trabajo).
- ◆ **to clock up** vt insep (miles, hours) hacer.

clockwise ['klɒkwaɪz] adv en el sentido de las agujas del reloj.

clog [klɒg] n (shoe) zueco.
- ▸ vt [also clog up] obstruir, atascar.
- ▸ vi [also clog up] obstruirse, atascarse.
- ① pt & pp clogged, ger clogging.

cloister ['klɔɪstəʳ] n claustro.

clone [kləʊn] n clon m.
- ▸ vt clonar.

close¹ [kləʊz] n **1** (end) fin m, final m. **2** (precincts) recinto.
- ▸ vt cerrar.
- ▸ vi **1** (gen) cerrar, cerrarse. **2** (end) concluir, terminar.
- ◆ **to close up** vi **1** (of wound) cicatrizar, cerrarse. **2** (shop, etc) cerrar.

close² [kləʊs] adj **1** (near) cercano,-a (to, a), próximo,-a (to, a). **2** (friend) íntimo,-a; (relation, family) cercano,-a.
- ▸ adv **1** (in position) cerca. **2** (in time) cerca.

closed [kləʊzd] adj cerrado,-a.

close-knit [kləʊsˈnɪt] *adj* unido,-a.

closely [ˈkləʊslɪ] *adv* **1** *(connect)* estrechamente, muy. **2** *(resemble)* mucho. **3** *(carefully - watch, listen)* atentamente; *(follow)* de cerca; *(question)* a fondo.

closet [ˈklɒzɪt] *n* US armario.

close-up [ˈkləʊsʌp] *n* primer plano.

closing [ˈkləʊzɪŋ] *n* cierre *m*.

closure [ˈkləʊʒəʳ] *n* *(gen)* cierre *m*; *(debate)* clausura.

clot [klɒt] *n* **1** *(of blood)* coágulo. **2** GB *fam* tonto,-a, bobo,-a.
▶ *vt* coagular.
▶ *vi (blood)* coagularse; *(cream)* cuajar.
ⓘ *pt & pp* clotted, *ger* clotting.

cloth [klɒθ] *n* **1** *(fabric)* tela; *(thick)* paño. **2** *(rag)* trapo.
✎ Consulta también clothes.

clothe [kləʊð] *vt* **1** *(dress, provide clothes for)* vestir (**in/with**, de). **2** *(cover)* revestir (**in**, de), cubrir (**in**, de).
ⓘ *pt & pp* clothed o clad [klæd], *ger* clothing.

clothes [kləʊðz] *n pl* ropa *f sing*.

clothing [ˈkləʊðɪŋ] *n* ropa.

cloud [klaʊd] *n* nube *f*.
◆ to cloud over *vi (sky)* nublarse; *(face, eyes)* empañarse.

cloudy [ˈklaʊdɪ] *adj* **1** *(sky, weather, day)* nublado,-a. **2** *(liquid)* turbio,-a.
ⓘ *comp* cloudier, *superl* cloudiest.

clout [klaʊt] *n* **1** *fam* tortazo. **2** *fam (influence)* influencia, peso.

clove¹ [kləʊv] *n (spice)* clavo.

clove² [kləʊv] *n (of garlic)* diente *f*.

clover [ˈkləʊvəʳ] *n* trébol *m*.

cloverleaf [ˈkləʊvəliːf] *n* BOT hoja de trébol.

clown [klaʊn] *n* payaso, clown *m*.

club [klʌb] *n* **1** *(gen)* club *m*. **2** *(stick)* porra. **3** SP *(in golf)* palo. **5** *(in cards - English pack)* trébol *m*; *(- Spanish pack)* basto.

cluck [klʌk] *n* cloqueo.
▶ *vi* cloquear.

clue [kluː] *n* pista.

clump [klʌmp] *n* **1** *(of trees)* grupo; *(of plants)* mata, macizo. **2** *(of earth)* terrón *m*.

clumsy [ˈklʌmzɪ] *adj* **1** *(gen)* torpe. **2** *(tool, shape)* pesado,-a y difícil de manejar; *(furniture)* mal diseñado,-a.
ⓘ *comp* clumsier, *superl* clumsiest.

clung [klʌŋ] *pt & pp* → cling.

cluster [ˈklʌstəʳ] *n (of trees, stars, buildings, people)* grupo; *(of berries, grapes)* racimo; *(of plants)* macizo.
▶ *vi* agruparse, apiñarse (**round**, alrededor de/en torno a).

clutch [klʌtʃ] *n* **1** AUTO embrague *m*. **2** *(grasp, grip)* agarrón *m*.
▶ *vt (seize)* agarrar; *(hold tightly)* estrechar, apretar.

clutter [ˈklʌtəʳ] *n (things)* cosas *fpl*, trastos *mpl*; *(untidy state)* desorden *m*.
▶ *vt* [also to clutter up] llenar, atestar, abarrotar.

cm [ˈsiːˈem] *symb* (**centimetre**) centímetro; *(symbol)* cm.

coach [kəʊtʃ] *n* **1** GB *(bus)* autocar *m*. **2** *(carriage)* carruaje *m*, coche *m* de caballos. **3** *(on train)* coche *m*, vagón *m*. **4** EDUC *(tutor)* profesor,-ra particular. **5** SP *(trainer)* entrenador,-ra.
▶ *vt* **1** EDUC dar clases particulares a, preparar. **2** SP entrenar.

coagulate [kəʊˈægjəleɪt] *vt* coagular.
▶ *vi* coagularse.

coagulation [kəʊægjəˈleɪʃªn] *n* coagulación *f*.

coal [kəʊl] *n* carbón *m*, hulla.

coalition [kəʊəˈlɪʃªn] *n* coalición *f*.

coarse [kɔːs] *adj* **1** *(fabric)* basto,-a; *(skin)* áspero,-a; *(sand, salt)* grueso,-a. **2** *(language, joke)* grosero,-a, vulgar.

coast [kəʊst] *n* costa, litoral *m*.
▶ *vi (in car)* ir en punto muerto; *(on bicycle)* ir sin pedalear.

coastal [ˈkəʊstªl] *adj* costero,-a.

coastguard [ˈkəʊstgɑːd] *n* guardacostas *mf*.

coat [kəʊt] *n* **1** *(overcoat)* abrigo; *(short)* chaquetón *m*. **2** *(of paint)* capa, mano *f*; *(of dust)* capa. **3** *(of animal)* pelo, pelaje *m*.
▶ *vt* **1** cubrir (**in/with**, de).

coating [ˈkəʊtɪŋ] *n* **1** CULIN capa, baño. **2** *(of paint, dust, wax)* capa; *(of metal)* revestimiento.

coax [kəʊks] *vt (person)* engatusar.

coaxial [kəʊˈæksəl] *adj* coaxial.

cob [kɒb] *n (of corn)* mazorca (de maíz).

cobble [ˈkɒbəl] *n* adoquín *m*.
▶ *vt (street)* adoquinar.

cobblestone [ˈkɒbəlstəʊn] *n* adoquín *m*.

cobweb [ˈkɒbweb] *n* telaraña.

cocaine [kəˈkeɪn] *n* cocaína.

coccyx [ˈkɒksɪks] *n* coxis *m*, cóccix *m*.
ⓘ *pl* coccyxes o coccyges.

cochineal [kɒtʃɪˈniːl] *n* cochinilla.

cochlea [ˈkɒklɪə] *n* caracol *m* del oído.

cock [kɒk] *n* **1** *(rooster)* gallo; *(any male bird)* macho. **2** *(on firearm)* percutor *m*.

cockle [ˈkɒkəl] *n* berberecho.

Cockney [ˈkɒknɪ] *adj* del barrio obrero del este de Londres.
▶ *n* **1** *(person)* persona del barrio obrero del este de Londres. **2** *(dialect)* dialecto que se habla en el barrio obrero del este de Londres.

cockpit [ˈkɒkpɪt] *n (in plane)* cabina del piloto, carlinga; *(in racing car)* cabina.

cockroach [ˈkɒkrəʊtʃ] *n* cucaracha.

cocktail [ˈkɒkteɪl] *n* cóctel *m*.

cocoa [ˈkəʊkəʊ] *n (powder)* cacao; *(drink)* chocolate *m*.

coconut [ˈkəʊkənʌt] *n* coco.

cocoon [kəˈkuːn] *n* capullo.
▶ *vt fig* envolver, arropar.

cod [kɒd] *n* bacalao.
ⓘ *pl* cod.

code [kəʊd] *n* **1** *(gen)* código. **2** *(telephone)* prefijo; *(postal)* código (postal).
▶ *vt* poner en clave, cifrar.

codification [kəʊdɪfɪˈkeɪʃən] *n* codificación *f*.

codify [ˈkəʊdɪfaɪ] *vt* codificar.
ⓘ *pt & pp* codified, *ger* codifying.

coeducation [kəʊedjəˈkeɪʃən] *n* enseñanza mixta.

coefficient [kəʊɪˈfɪʃənt] *n* coeficiente *m*.

coexist [kəʊɪgˈzɪst] *vi* coexistir.

coffee [ˈkɒfɪ] *n* café *m*.

coffeepot [ˈkɒfɪpɒt] *n* cafetera.

coffer [ˈkɒfər] *n* arca, cofre *m*.

coffin [ˈkɒfɪn] *n* ataúd *m*, féretro.

cog [kɒg] *n* **1** *(on wheel)* diente *m*. **2** *fig* pieza.

cogent [ˈkəʊdʒənt] *adj* convincente, contundente.

cognac [ˈkɒnjæk] *n* coñac *m*.

cognitive [ˈkɒgnɪtɪv] *adj* cognitivo,-a.

coherent [kəʊˈhɪərənt] *adj* coherente.

coil [kɔɪl] *n* **1** *(of rope, wire)* rollo; *(of cable)* carrete *m*; *(of hair)* rizo, moño; *(of smoke)* espiral *m*, voluta. **2** *(single loop)* vuelta, lazada. **3** TECH bobina.
▶ *vt* [also to coil up] enrollar.

coin [kɔɪn] *n* moneda.
▶ *vt* acuñar.

coincide [kəʊɪnˈsaɪd] *vi* coincidir (with, con).

coincidence [kəʊˈɪnsɪdəns] *n* coincidencia, casualidad *f*.

Coke® [kəʊk] *n* Coca Cola®.

coke [kəʊk] *n (coal)* coque *m*.

colander [ˈkʌləndər] *n* colador *m*.

cold [kəʊld] *adj* frío,-a.
▶ *n* **1** *(weather)* frío. **2** MED resfriado, catarro, constipado. COMP cold cuts US embutidos *mpl*, fiambres *mpl*.

cold-blooded [kəʊldˈblʌdɪd] *adj* **1** ZOOL de sangre fría. **2** *fig (person)* frío,-a, insensible; *(crime)* a sangre fría.

coleslaw [ˈkəʊlslɔː] *n* ensaladilla de col y zanahoria.

colic [ˈkɒlɪk] *n* cólico.

coliseum [kɒlɪˈsiːəm] *n* coliseo.

collaborate [kəˈlæbəreɪt] *vi* colaborar (with, con).

collaborator [kəˈlæbəreɪtər] *n* **1** colaborador,-ra. **2** *(with enemy)* colaboracionista *mf*.

collage [ˈkɒlɑːdʒ] *n* ART collage *m*.

collapse [kəˈlæps] *n* **1** *(falling down)* derrumbamiento; *(falling in)* hundimiento. **2** *(failure, breakdown)* fracaso. **3** *(prices, currency)* caída en picado; *(business, company)* quiebra. **4** MED colapso.
▶ *vi* **1** *(building, bridge, etc)* derrumbarse, desplomarse; *(roof)* hundirse, venirse abajo. **2** MED *(person)* sufrir un colapso.
▶ *vt (table)* plegar.

collapsible [kəˈlæpsəbəl] *adj* plegable.

collar [ˈkɒləʳ] n **1** (of shirt, etc) cuello. **2** (for dog) collar m. **3** TECH collar m, abrazadera.
▸ vt fam pescar, pillar.

⊠ Collar no significa 'collar (de persona)', que se traduce por **necklace**.

collarbone [ˈkɒləbəʊn] n clavícula.

collateral [kəˈlætˀrəl] adj colateral. LOC **collateral damage** daños mpl colaterales.

colleague [ˈkɒliːg] n colega mf, compañero,-a.

collect [kəˈlekt] vt **1** (glasses, plates, belongings, etc) recoger; (information, data) reunir, recopilar. **2** (stamps, records, etc) coleccionar. **3** (taxes) recaudar; (rent) cobrar. **4** (pick up, fetch) ir a buscar, recoger.
▸ vi **1** (dust, water) acumularse; (people) reunirse, congregarse. **2** (for charity) recaudar dinero, hacer una colecta.

collection [kəˈlekʃˀn] n **1** (of stamps, paintings, etc) colección f; (of poems, short stories) recopilación f; (of people) grupo m. **2** (range of new clothes) colección f. **3** (for charity) colecta. **4** (of mail, of refuse) recogida. **5** (of taxes) recaudación f; (of rent) cobro.

collective [kəˈlektɪv] adj colectivo,-a.
▸ n (enterprise) cooperativa.

collector [kəˈlektəʳ] n **1** (of stamps, etc) coleccionista mf. **2** (of rent, debts, tickets) cobrador,-ra.

college [ˈkɒlɪdʒ] n **1** (for higher education) escuela, instituto mf. **2** US (university) universidad f, facultad f. **3** GB (within university) colegio universitario.

⊠ College no significa 'colegio (de niños)', que se traduce por **school**.

collide [kəˈlaɪd] vi chocar.

colliery [ˈkɒljərɪ] n mina de carbón.
ⓘ pl collieries.

collision [kəˈlɪʒˀn] n (between cars, trains, etc) colisión f, choque m; (between ships) abordaje m.

colloquial [kəˈləʊkwɪəl] adj coloquial.

cologne [kəˈləʊn] n colonia.

Colombia [kəˈlʌmbɪə] n Colombia.

Colombian [kəˈlʌmbɪən] adj & n colombiano,-a.

colon¹ [ˈkəʊlən] n ANAT colon m.

colon² [ˈkəʊlən] n LING dos puntos mpl.

colonel [ˈkɜːnˀl] n coronel m.

colonial [kəˈləʊnɪəl] adj colonial.
▸ n colono,-a.

colonialism [kəˈləʊnɪəlɪzˀm] n colonialismo.

colonist [ˈkɒlənɪst] n (inhabitant) colono; (colonizer) colono,-a, colonizador,-ra.

colonize [ˈkɒlənaɪz] vt colonizar.

colony [ˈkɒlənɪ] n (gen) colonia.
ⓘ pl colonies.

color [ˈkʌləʳ] n US → **colour**.

colossal [kəˈlɒsˀl] adj colosal.

colossus [kəˈlɒsəs] n coloso.

colour [ˈkʌləʳ] n color m.
▸ adj (television, film, etc) en color.
▸ vt **1** (with pen, paint, crayon) pintar, colorear; (dye) teñir. **2** fig (affect negatively, influence) influir en.
▸ vi **1** (blush) ruborizarse, sonrojarse, ponerse rojo,-a. **2** (of leaves) ponerse amarillo,-a; (fruit) coger color.
▸ n pl **colours** GB (worn by team, school) colores mpl; MIL (flag) bandera, enseña.
◆ **to colour in** vt sep pintar, colorear.

colour-blind [ˈkʌləblaɪnd] adj daltónico,-a.

coloured [ˈkʌləd] adj de color, de colores.

colourful [ˈkʌləful] adj **1** (full of colour, bright) lleno,-a de color, vistoso,-a; (brightly coloured) de colores vivos. **2** (person) pintoresco,-a.

colouring [ˈkʌlərɪŋ] n **1** (substance, dye) colorante m. **2** (person's skin, hair and eye colour) color m. **3** (of animal's skin, fur, plumage) color m.

colourless [ˈkʌlələs] adj **1** (without colour) incoloro,-a, sin color; (pale) pálido,-a. **2** fig (dull, uninteresting) soso,-a, anodino,-a, gris.

colt [kəʊlt] n potro.

column [ˈkɒləm] n (gen) columna.

columnist [ˈkɒləmnɪst] n columnista mf.

coma [ˈkəʊmə] n MED coma m. LOC **to go into a coma** caer en coma, entrar en coma.

comb [kəʊm] n **1** (for hair) peine m. **2** (for wool, cotton) carda. **3** (of bird) cresta. **4** (of honeycomb) panal m.
 ► vt **1** (hair) peinar. **2** (wool, cotton) cardar, peinar. **3** (search - area) rastrear, peinar.

combat ['kɒmbæt] n combate m.
 ► vt combatir, luchar contra.

combination [kɒmbɪ'neɪ[ə]n] n combinación f.

combine [(vb) kəm'baɪn; (n) 'kɒmbaɪn] vt combinar.
 ► vi (gen) combinarse; (teams, forces) unirse; (companies) fusionarse.
 ► n COMM grupo industrial, asociación f.

combined [kəm'baɪnd] adj combinado,-a, conjunto,-a.

combustible [kəm'bʌstɪb[ə]l] adj combustible, inflamable.

combustion [kəm'bʌstʃ[ə]n] n combustión f.

come [kʌm] vi **1** (gen) venir. **2** (arrive, reach) llegar. **3** (happen) suceder.
 ► vt (behave, play the part) hacerse: don't come the innocent with me no te hagas el inocente conmigo.

◆ **to come about** vi (happen) ocurrir, suceder.

◆ **to come across** vt insep (thing) encontrar, tropezar con.
 ► vi **1** (be understood) ser comprendido, -a. **2** (make an impression) causar una impresión.

◆ **to come after** vt insep seguir.

◆ **to come along** vi **1** (progress) ir, marchar. **2** (hurry up) darse prisa. **3** (arrive) venir, llegar; (appear) aparecer.

◆ **to come back** vi **1** (return) volver (from, de). **2** (remember) volver a la memoria. **3** (return to topic, question, idea) volver (to, a); (reply, retort) replicar, contestar.

◆ **to come before** vt insep **1** JUR comparecer ante. **2** (be more important than) ser más importante que.

◆ **to come down** vi **1** (gen) bajar; (collapse) caerse, hundirse, venirse abajo; (fall - rain, snow) caer. **2** (plane - land) aterrizar; (- fall) caer.

◆ **to come down with** vt insep (illness) caer enfermo,-a de, contraer, coger.

◆ **to come in** vi (enter) entrar.

◆ **to come on** vi **1** (make progress) avanzar. **2** (hurry up) darse prisa.

◆ **to come out** vi **1** (leave) salir (of, de); (tooth, hair) caerse; (stain) salir, quitarse; (colour, dye) desteñirse. **2** (sun, moon, stars) salir. **3** (new book, record, magazine, figures) salir, publicarse; (film) estrenarse.

◆ **to come through** vt insep (operation, accident) sobrevivir, salir con vida de; (illness) recuperarse de; (difficult period) pasar por, atravesar.

◆ **to come up to** vt insep **1** (equal) alcanzar, llegar a, estar a la altura de. **2** (approach - in space) acercarse a; (- in time) ser casi.

◆ **to come up with** vt insep (idea) tener, ocurrirse; (solution) encontrar; (plan) idear; (proposal) presentar, plantear.

◆ **to come upon** vt insep encontrarse con, encontrar.
 ⓘ pt came [keɪm], pp come[kʌm], ger coming.

comeback ['kʌmbæk] n **1** fam (of person) reaparición f, vuelta, retorno. **2** (way of obtaining compensation) reclamación f. **3** (reply) réplica, respuesta.

comedian [kə'miːdɪən] n cómico, humorista m.

comedienne [kəmiːdɪ'en] n cómica, humorista.

comedy ['kɒmədɪ] n comedia.
 ⓘ pl comedies.

comet ['kɒmɪt] n cometa m.

comfort ['kʌmfət] n **1** (well-being) comodidad f, confort m, bienestar m. **2** (thing, luxury) comodidad f. **3** (consolation) consuelo.
 ► vt consolar.

comfortable ['kʌmf[ə]təb[ə]l] adj **1** (furniture, clothes, etc) cómodo,-a. **2** (life) desahogado,-a, acomodado,-a.

comforting ['kʌmfətɪŋ] adj reconfortante.

comic ['kɒmɪk] adj cómico,-a.
 ► n **1** (comedian) cómico,-a, humorista mf. **2** (magazine) tebeo, cómic m.

coming ['kʌmɪŋ] adj (gen) próximo,-a; (generation) venidero,-a, futuro,-a.
 ► n llegada.

comma ['kɒmə] n coma. LOC inverted comma comilla.

command [kə'mɑːnd] n **1** (order) orden f. **2** (control, authority) mando. **3** (knowledge, mastery) dominio. **4** INFORM comando, instrucción f.
▸ vt **1** (order) mandar, ordenar. **2** MIL (have authority over) estar al mando de, comandar.

commander [kə'mɑːndəʳ] n **1** MIL comandante m. **2** MAR capitán m de fragata.

commanding [kə'mɑːndɪŋ] adj **1** (voice, manner, appearance) autoritario,-a. **2** (position) dominante, de superioridad.

commandment [kə'mɑːndmənt] n REL mandamiento.

commando [kə'mɑːndəʊ] n comando.
ⓘ pl commandos o commandoes.

commemorate [kə'meməreɪt] vt conmemorar.

commend [kə'mend] vt (praise) alabar (for, por), elogiar (for, por); (recommend) recomendar.

comment ['kɒment] n comentario, observación f. LOC no comment sin comentarios.
▸ vt comentar, observar.

commentary ['kɒmənt°rɪ] n **1** (spoken description) comentario, comentarios mpl. **2** (set of written remarks) comentario, crítica.
ⓘ pl commentaries.

commentator ['kɒmənteɪtəʳ] n comentarista mf.

commerce ['kɒmɜːs] n comercio.

commercial [kə'mɜːʃ°l] adj comercial.
▸ n (advertisement) anuncio, spot m publicitario.

commercialization [kə'mɜːʃ°laɪzeɪʃ°n] n comercialización f.

commercialize [kə'mɜːʃ°laɪz] vt comercializar.

commission [kə'mɪʃ°n] n **1** COMM comisión f. **2** (piece of work) encargo.
▸ vt (order) encargar.

commissioner [kə'mɪʃ°nəʳ] n **1** (public official) comisario. **2** (member of a commission) comisionado,-a.

commit [kə'mɪt] vt **1** (crime, error, sin) cometer. **2** (send to prison, etc) internar. **3** (bind) comprometer, obligar; (pledge) asignar, consignar, destinar.
ⓘ pt & pp committed, ger committing.

commitment [kə'mɪtmənt] n **1** (undertaking, obligation) compromiso, obligación f; (responsibility) responsabilidad f. **2** (dedication) dedicación f, entrega.

committed [kə'mɪtɪd] adj (to a cause) comprometido,-a; (dedicated) dedicado,-a, entregado,-a.

committee [kə'mɪtɪ] n comité m.

commode [kə'məʊd] n cómoda.

commodity [kə'mɒdɪtɪ] n **1** COMM producto, artículo, mercancía. **2** FIN materia prima.
ⓘ pl commodities.

> ✕ Commodity no significa 'comodidad', que se traduce por comfort.

common ['kɒmən] adj **1** (ordinary, average) corriente. **2** (usual, not scarce) común, corriente. **3** (shared, joint) común. **4** pej (vulgar) ordinario,-a.
▸ n (land) tierras fpl comunales.

commoner ['kɒmənəʳ] n plebeyo,-a.

commonplace ['kɒmənpleɪs] adj común, corriente.
▸ n (platitude) lugar m común, tópico.

Commons ['kɒmənz] n pl the Commons GB los Comunes. COMP the House of Commons la Cámara de los Comunes.

> ⊕ La Cámara de los Comunes británica es el equivalente al Congreso español y es el órgano legislativo más importante del Reino Unido.

Commonwealth ['kɒmənwelθ] n GB Commonwealth f.

> ⊕ La Commonwealth es una organización compuesta por 53 naciones con fuertes vínculos con el Reino Unido por haber pertenecido en algún momento de su historia al Imperio británico.

commotion [kə'məʊʃ°n] n (scandal) escándalo; (noise, excitement) alboroto, jaleo; (confusion) confusión f.

communal ['kɒmjənəl] *adj (shared)* comunal; *(of a community)* comunitario,-a.

commune ['kɒmjuːn] *n* comuna.

communicate [kə'mjuːnɪkeɪt] *vt* **1** *(make known, convey)* comunicar. **2** MED transmitir, contagiar.
▸ *vi* comunicarse (with, con).

communication [kəmjuːnɪ'keɪʃən] *n* **1** *(gen)* comunicación *f*. **2** *(message)* comunicado.
▸ *n pl* **communications** comunicaciones *fpl*.

communicative [kə'mjuːnɪkətɪv] *adj* comunicativo,-a.

communion [kə'mjuːnjən] *n fml* comunión *f*.
▸ *n* **Communion** REL Comunión *f*.

communiqué [kə'mjuːnɪkeɪ] *n* comunicado.

communism ['kɒmjənɪzəm] *n* comunismo.

communist ['kɒmjənɪst] *adj* comunista.
▸ *n* comunista *mf*.

community [kə'mjuːnɪtɪ] *n* comunidad *f*.
ⓘ *pl* **communities**.

commute [kə'mjuːt] *vi* desplazarse diariamente al lugar de trabajo.
▸ *vt* conmutar.

commuter [kə'mjuːtəʳ] *n* persona que se desplaza diariamente a su lugar de trabajo. COMP **the commuter belt** los barrios *mpl* periféricos.

compact [*(adj-vb)* kəm'pækt; *(n)* 'kɒmpækt] *adj (gen)* compacto,-a; *(style)* conciso,-a.
▸ *n* **1** *(for powder)* polvera de bolsillo. **2** US coche *m* utilitario.
▸ *vt* compactar, comprimir.

companion [kəm'pænjən] *n* **1** *(partner, friend)* compañero,-a. **2** *(person employed)* persona de compañía. **3** *(either of pair or set)* compañero,-a, pareja.

companionship [kəm'pænjənʃɪp] *n* compañerismo, camaradería.

company ['kʌmpənɪ] *n* **1** *(companionship)* compañía. **2** *(visitors)* visita. **3** *(business)* empresa, compañía, sociedad *f*. **4** THEAT compañía. **5** MIL compañía.
ⓘ *pl* **companies**.

comparable ['kɒmpərəbəl] *adj* comparable (to, a) (with, con).

comparative [kəm'pærətɪv] *adj* **1** *(relative)* relativo,-a. **2** *(making a comparison)* comparado,-a. **3** LING comparativo,-a.
▸ *n* LING comparativo.

compare [kəm'peəʳ] *vt* comparar (to/ with, con).

comparison [kəm'pærɪsən] *n* comparación *f*.

compartment [kəm'pɑːtmənt] *n (in wallet, fridge, desk)* compartimento; *(in train)* departamento, compartimento.

compass ['kʌmpəs] *n* **1** *(magnetic)* brújula, compás *m: the points of the compass* los puntos cardinales. **2** [se usa como *sing* or *pl*] *(for drawing)* compás *m: a pair of compasses, a compass* un compás. COMP **compass rose** rosa de los vientos.

compassion [kəm'pæʃən] *n* compasión *f*.

compassionate [kəm'pæʃənət] *adj* compasivo,-a.

compatibility [kəmpætə'bɪlɪtɪ] *n* compatibilidad *f*.

compatible [kəm'pætɪbəl] *adj* compatible (with, con).

compatriot [kəm'pætrɪət] *n* compatriota *mf*.

compel [kəm'pel] *vt* **1** *(force)* obligar. **2** *fig (inspire)* infundir, inspirar.
ⓘ *pt & pp* **compelled**, *ger* **compelling**.

compensate ['kɒmpənseɪt] *vt* **1** *(recompense, indemnify)* indemnizar (for, por), compensar (for, por). **2** *(counterbalance)* compensar.
▸ *vi* compensar (for, -).

compensation [kɒmpən'seɪʃən] *n* **1** *(money, damages)* indemnización *f* (for, por). **2** *(way of compensating)* compensación *f* (for, por).

compere ['kɒmpeəʳ] *n* GB presentador, -ra.
▸ *vt* GB presentar.

compete [kəm'piːt] *vi (try to win)* disputarse; *(take part in)* competir, participar.

competence ['kɒmpɪtəns] *n* **1** *(ability)* competencia, capacidad *f*, aptitud *f: a fair level of competence in German* un buen nivel de alemán. **2** JUR *(legal author-ity)* competencia.

> ☒ Competence no significa 'competencia (en el mercado)', que se traduce por competition.

competent ['kɒmpɪtənt] *adj* **1** *(person)* competente; *(work, novel, etc)* aceptable, bastante bien. **2** JUR competente.

competition [kɒmpə'tɪʃ[ə]n] *n* **1** *(gen)* concurso; *(race, sporting event)* competición *f*. **2** *(rivalry)* competencia.

competitive [kəm'petɪtɪv] *adj* competitivo,-a.

competitor [kəm'petɪtər] *n* **1** COMM *(rival)* competidor,-ra, rival *mf*. **2** SP *(in race, etc)* participante *mf*; *(opponent)* contrincante *mf*. **3** *(in quiz, etc)* concursante *mf*, participante *mf*; *(in competitive examination)* opositor,-ra.

compilation [kɒmpɪ'leɪʃ[ə]n] *n* **1** *(gen)* compilación *f*. **2** *(record, etc)* recopilación *f*.

compile [kəm'paɪl] *vt* **1** *(produce book, list, etc)* compilar; *(collect information)* recopilar. **2** COMPUT compilar.

complain [kəm'pleɪn] *vi* quejarse (about/of, de).

complaint [kəm'pleɪnt] *n* **1** *(gen)* queja (about, de); *(formal)* reclamación *f*. **2** MED enfermedad *f* (leve), achaque *m*.

complement ['kɒmplɪmənt] *n* *(gen)* complemento (to, de).
> ▸ *vt* complementar.

complementary [kɒmplɪ'ment[ə]rɪ] *adj* *(gen)* complementario,-a.

complete [kəm'pliːt] *adj* **1** *(entire)* completo,-a. **2** *(finished)* acabado,-a, terminado,-a.
> ▸ *vt* **1** *(make whole)* completar. **2** *(finish)* acabar, terminar. **3** *(fill in - form)* rellenar.

completion [kəm'pliːʃ[ə]n] *n* *(act, state)* finalización *f*, terminación *f*.

complex ['kɒmpleks] *adj* complejo,-a.
> ▸ *n* complejo.

complexion [kəm'plekʃ[ə]n] *n* *(quality of skin)* cutis *m*; *(colour or tone of skin)* tez *f*.

> ☒ Complexion no significa 'complexión (física)', que se traduce por constitution.

complexity [kəm'pleksɪtɪ] *n* complejidad *f*.
> ① *pl* complexities.

complicate ['kɒmplɪkeɪt] *vt* complicar.

complicated ['kɒmplɪkeɪtɪd] *adj* complicado,-a.

complication [kɒmplɪ'keɪʃ[ə]n] *n* complicación *f*.
> ▸ *n pl* complications MED complicaciones *fpl*.

complicity [kəm'plɪsɪtɪ] *n* complicidad *f* (in, en).

compliment ['kɒmplɪmənt] *vt* felicitar (on, por).
> ▸ *n* *(praise)* cumplido, halago.
> ▸ *n pl* compliments saludos *mpl*, felicitaciones *fpl*.

comply [kəm'plaɪ] *vi* *(order)* obedecer (with, -), cumplir (with, con); *(request)* acceder (with, a); *(law)* acatar (with, -); *(standards)* cumplir (with, con).
> ① *pt & pp* complied, *ger* complying.

component [kəm'pəʊnənt] *adj* componente.
> ▸ *n* **1** *(gen)* componente *m*. **2** AUTO pieza.

compose [kəm'pəʊz] *vt* **1** *(music, poem)* componer; *(letter)* redactar. **2** *(constitute)* componer. **3** *(one's thoughts)* poner en orden.
> ▸ *vi* MUS componer.

composed [kəm'pəʊzd] *adj* *(calm)* sereno,-a, sosegado,-a, tranquilo,-a.

composer [kəm'pəʊzər] *n* compositor,-ra.

composite ['kɒmpəzɪt] *adj* compuesto,-a.
> ▸ *n* combinación *f*, conjunto.

composition [kɒmpə'zɪʃ[ə]n] *n* **1** *(gen)* composición *f*. **2** *(essay)* redacción *f*. **3** *(substance)* mezcla.

compost ['kɒmpɒst] *n* abono orgánico, abono vegetal, compost *m*.

composure [kəm'pəʊʒər] *n* calma, serenidad *f*, compostura.

compound¹ [*(adj-n)* 'kɒmpaʊnd; *(vb)* kəm'paʊnd] *adj* compuesto,-a.
> ▸ *n* **1** CHEM compuesto. **2** *(substance)* mezcla. **3** LING palabra compuesta.

▸ *vt* **1** *(mix)* componer, combinar, mezclar. **2** *(worsen, exacerbate - problem)* agravar; *(- difficulty)* aumentar.

compound² ['kɒmpaʊnd] *n (enclosed area)* recinto.

comprehend [kɒmprɪ'hend] *vt* **1** *(understand)* comprender. **2** *fml (include)* comprender, abarcar.

comprehensible [kɒmprɪ'hensəbəl] *adj* comprensible.

comprehension [kɒmprɪ'henʃən] *n* comprensión *f*.

comprehensive [kɒmprɪ'hensɪv] *adj (thorough)* detallado,-a, global, completo,-a; *(broad)* amplio,-a, extenso,-a.

✗ Comprehensive no significa 'comprensivo (tolerante)', que se traduce por understanding.

compress [*(n)* 'kɒmpres, *(vb)* kəm'pres] *n* compresa.
▸ *vt* **1** *(air, straw)* comprimir. **2** *(text, argument, speech)* condensar.

compressibility [kəmpresɪ'bɪlɪtɪ] *n* compresibilidad *f*.

compression [kəm'preʃən] *n* compresión *f*.

compressor [kəm'presər] *n* compresor *m*.

comprise [kəm'praɪz] *vt (consist of, be made up of)* comprender, constar de; *(constitute, form)* componer, constituir.

compromise ['kɒmprəmaɪz] *n* acuerdo mutuo, solución *f* de compromiso.
▸ *vi* llegar a un acuerdo, transigir.
▸ *vt (endanger, weaken)* comprometer.

✗ Compromise no significa 'compromiso (obligación o promesa de matrimonio)', que se traducen por commitment y engagement.

compulsion [kəm'pʌlʃən] *n* **1** *(force)* obligación *f*, coacción *f*. **2** *(urge)* compulsión *f*.

compulsive [kəm'pʌlsɪv] *adj* **1** *(compelling, fascinating)* fascinante, irresistible, absorbente. **2** *(obsessive)* obsesivo,-a.

compulsory [kəm'pʌlsərɪ] *adj (subject, military service)* obligatorio,-a; *(retirement, redundancy)* forzoso,-a.

computation [kɒmpjʊ'teɪʃən] *n* cálculo, cómputo.

compute [kəm'pju:t] *vt* computar, calcular.

computer [kəm'pju:tər] *n* ordenador *m*, computadora.

computerization [kəmpju:tərəɪ'zeɪʃən] *n (of data)* computerización *f*; *(of system, business)* informatización *f*.

computerize [kəm'pju:təraɪz] *vt (data)* computarizar, computerizar; *(system, business)* informatizar.

computing [kəm'pju:tɪŋ] *n* informática.

comrade ['kɒmreɪd] *n* POL camarada *mf*, compañero,-a.

con¹ [kɒn] *n fam* estafa, timo.
▸ *vt fam (money)* estafar, timar; *(person)* embaucar, engañar.
① *pt & pp* conned, *ger* conning.

con² [kɒn] *n (disadvantage)* contra *m*.

✎ Consulta también pro.

concave ['kɒnkeɪv] *adj* cóncavo,-a.

concavity [kɒn'kævɪtɪ] *n* concavidad *f*.

conceal [kən'si:l] *vt (gen)* ocultar; *(facts)* encubrir; *(feelings)* disimular.

concede [kən'si:d] *vt* **1** *(admit)* reconocer, admitir. **2** *(allow, give away)* conceder.
▸ *vi* ceder, rendirse.

conceit [kən'si:t] *n (pride)* vanidad *f*.

conceivable [kən'si:vəbəl] *adj* concebible, imaginable.

conceive [kən'si:v] *vt* **1** *(gen)* concebir. **2** *(understand)* entender.

concentrate ['kɒnsəntreɪt]
▸ *vt (gen)* concentrar (on, en).
▸ *vi* **1** *(person)* concentrarse (on, en).

concentration [kɒnsən'treɪʃən] *n* concentración *f* (on, en).

concentric [kən'sentrɪk] *adj* concéntrico,-a.

concept ['kɒnsept] *n* concepto.

conception [kən'sepʃən] *n* **1** *(of child, idea, plan)* concepción *f*. **2** *(idea)* concepto, idea, noción *f*.

concern [kən'sɜ:n] *n* **1** *(worry)* preocupación *f*, inquietud *f*. **2** *(interest)* interés *m*; *(affair)* asunto. **3** COMM *(company, business)* negocio.

▶ *vt* **1** *(affect, involve)* afectar, concernir. *(interest)* interesar. **2** *(worry)* preocupar. **3** *(book, film, article, etc)* tratar de.

concerned [kənˈsɜːnd] *adj (worried)* preocupado,-a (about/for, por).

concerning [kənˈsɜːnɪŋ] *prep* referente a, con respecto a, en cuanto a.

concert [ˈkɒnsət] *n* concierto.

concerted [kənˈsɜːtɪd] *adj* concerta-do,-a, coordinado,-a.

concerto [kənˈtʃeətəʊ] *n* concierto.
ⓘ *pl* concertos o concerti [kənˈtʃeətiː].

✎ Concerto se refiere específicamente a conciertos de música clásica para uno o varios instrumentos solistas y una orquesta.

concession [kənˈseʃ°n] *n* concesión *f* (to, a).

concessionaire [kənseʃəˈneəʳ] *n* concesionario,-a.

conciliate [kənˈsɪlɪeɪt] *vt & vi* conciliar.

concise [kənˈsaɪs] *adj* conciso,-a.

concision [kənˈsɪʒ°n] *n* concisión *f*.

conclude [kənˈkluːd] *vt* **1** *(end)* concluir, finalizar. **2** *(settle - deal)* cerrar; *(- agreement)* llegar a; *(- treaty)* firmar. **3** *(deduce)* concluir, llegar a la conclusión de.
▶ *vi* concluir, terminar.

conclusion [kənˈkluːʒ°n] *n* conclusión *f*.

conclusive [kənˈkluːsɪv] *adj* concluyente.

concoct [kənˈkɒkt] *vt* **1** *(dish, sauce, drink)* confeccionar, preparar. **2** *(story, excuse, explanation)* inventar, inventarse.

concord [ˈkɒŋkɔːd] *n* **1** *fml (harmony)* concordia. **2** LING concordancia.

concourse [ˈkɒŋkɔːs] *n (hall)* vestíbulo; *(in station)* explanada.

❌ Concourse no significa 'concurso (competición)', que se traduce por competition.

concrete [ˈkɒŋkriːt] *adj* **1** *(definite, not abstract)* concreto,-a. **2** *(made of concrete)* de hormigón.
▶ *n* hormigón *m*.

concur [kənˈkɜːʳ] *vi (agree)* estar de acuerdo, coincidir.
ⓘ *pt & pp* concurred, *ger* concurring.

concurrence [kənˈkʌrəns] *n* acuerdo, coincidencia.

concussion [kənˈkʌʃ°n] *n* MED conmoción *f* cerebral.

condemn [kənˈdem] *vt* condenar.

condemnation [kɒndemˈneɪʃ°n] *n* condena.

condensation [kɒndenˈseɪʃ°n] *n* CHEM *(process)* condensación *f*; *(on glass)* vaho.

condense [kənˈdens] *vt* condensar.

condenser [kənˈdensəʳ] *n* condensador *m*.

condescend [kɒndɪˈsend] *vi* **1** *(deign)* condescender, dignarse. **2** *(patronize)* tratar con condescendencia.

condescending [kɒndɪˈsendɪŋ] *adj (attitude, answer)* condescendiente.

condiment [ˈkɒndɪmənt] *n* condimento.

condition [kənˈdɪʃ°n] *n* **1** *(state)* condición *f*, estado. **2** *(requirement, provision)* condición *f*. **3** MED afección *f*, enfermedad *f*.
▶ *vt* **1** *(determine, accustom)* condicionar. **2** *(treat - hair)* acondicionar, suavizar.

conditional [kənˈdɪʃən°l] *adj* condicional.
▶ *n* the conditional LING el condicional *m*.

conditioner [kənˈdɪʃ°nəʳ] *n (for hair)* acondicionador *m*, suavizante *m*.

condolences [kənˈdəʊlənsɪz] *n pl* pésame *m sing*.

condom [ˈkɒndəm] *n* condón *m*, preservativo.

condominium [kɒndəˈmɪnɪəm] *n* **1** POL condominio. **2** US *(apartment block)* bloque *m* de pisos; *(apartment)* apartamento, piso.

condone [kənˈdəʊn] *vt (person)* aprobar, consentir.

condor [ˈkɒndɔːʳ] *n* cóndor *m*.

conducive [kənˈdjuːsɪv] *adj* propicio,-a (to, para).

conduct [*(n)* ˈkɒndəkt; *(vb)* kɒnˈdʌkt] *n* **1** *(behaviour)* conducta, comportamiento. **2** *(management)* dirección *f*, gestión *f*, administración *f*.
▶ *vt* **1** *(direct - survey, campaign)* llevar a cabo, realizar; *(- business)* administrar.

2 *(lead, guide)* conducir, guiar. **3** *(transmit - heat, etc)* conducir. **4** MUS dirigir.
▸ *vi* MUS dirigir.

conduction [kən'dʌkʃ°n] *n* PHYS conducción *f*.

☒ Conduction no significa 'conducción (de un vehículo)', que se traduce por driving.

conductivity [kən'dʌktɪvɪtɪ] *n* conductividad *f*.

conductor [kən'dʌktəʳ] *n* **1** *(of heat, electricity)* conductor *m*. **2** *(of orchestra)* director,-ra de orquesta. **3** *(on bus)* cobrador,-ra. **4** US *(on train)* jefe,-a de tren.

☒ Conductor no significa 'conductor (de un vehículo)', que se traduce por driver.

conductress [kən'dʌktrəs] *n (on bus)* cobradora.

conduit ['kɒndjʊɪt] *n* conducto.

cone [kəʊn] *n* **1** *(shape, for traffic)* cono. **2** *(for ice cream)* cucurucho. **3** BOT *(fruit of pine tree)* piña.

confectioner [kən'fekʃ°nəʳ] *n* confitero,-a, pastelero,-a.

confectionery [kən'fekʃ°nrɪ] *n* dulces *mpl*.

confederacy [kən'fed°rəsɪ] *n* confederación *f*.
ⓘ *pl* confederacies.

confederation [kənfedə'reɪʃ°n] *n* confederación *f*.

confer [kən'fɜːʳ] *vt (award, grant, bestow)* conferir, conceder.
▸ *vi (consult, discuss)* consultar (with, con) (about/on, sobre).
ⓘ *pt & pp* conferred, *ger* conferring.

conference ['kɒnf°rəns] *n* **1** *(large event, convention)* congreso. **2** *(meeting)* reunión *f*, junta.

☒ Conference no significa 'conferencia (discurso)', que se traduce por lecture.

confess [kən'fes] *vt & vi* confesar.
confessed [kən'fest] *adj* declarado,-a.
confession [kən'feʃ°n] *n* confesión *f*.
confessional [kən'feʃ°nəl] *n* confesionario.
confessor [kən'fesəʳ] *n* REL confesor *m*.
confetti [kən'fetɪ] *n* confeti *m*.

confidant ['kɒnfɪdænt] *n* confidente *m*.
confidante ['kɒnfɪdænt] *n* confidenta.
confide [kən'faɪd] *vt* confiar.
◆ **to confide in** *vi* confiar en.

confidence ['kɒnfɪdəns] *n* **1** *(trust, faith)* confianza (in, en), fe *f* (in, en). **2** *(self-confidence)* confianza, seguridad *f*. **3** *(secrecy)* confianza. **4** *(secret)* confidencia.

confident ['kɒnfɪd°nt] *adj* **1** *(certain)* seguro,-a. **2** *(self-confident)* seguro,-a de sí mismo,-a.

confidential [kɒnfɪ'denʃ°l] *adj* confidencial.

confine [kən'faɪn] *vt* **1** *(person)* confinar, recluir; *(animal)* encerrar. **2** *(limit, restrict)* limitar.

confinement [kən'faɪnmənt] *n* **1** *(imprisonment)* reclusión *f*. **2** MED *(in childbirth)* parto.

confines ['kɒnfaɪnz] *n pl* límites *mpl*, confines *mpl*.

confirm [kən'fɜːm] *vt* confirmar.

confirmation [kɒnfə'meɪʃ°n] *n* confirmación *f*.

confirmed [kən'fɜːmd] *adj (inveterate)* empedernido,-a.

confiscate ['kɒnfɪskeɪt] *vt* confiscar.

conflict [*(n)* 'kɒnflɪkt; *(vb)* kən'flɪkt] *n* conflicto.
▸ *vi* chocar (with, con), estar en conflicto (with, con).

conflicting [kən'flɪktɪŋ] *adj (evidence, accounts)* contradictorio,-a; *(opinions, interests)* contrario,-a, opuesto,-a.

confluence ['kɒnfluəns] *n* confluencia.

conform [kən'fɔːm] *vi* **1** *(comply with rules, standards, regulations)* ajustarse (to/with, a), cumplir (to/with, con). **2** *(agree, be consistent with)* conformarse (to/with, con), concordar (with, con). **3** *(fit in, behave like other people)* ser conformista.

conformist [kən'fɔːmɪst] *adj* conformista.
▸ *n* conformista *mf*.

conformity [kən'fɔːmɪtɪ] *n* conformidad *f*.

confront [kən'frʌnt] *vt* hacer frente a, enfrentarse a.

confuse [kən'fjuːz] *vt* confundir.

confused [kən'fju:zd] *adj* **1** *(person)* confundido,-a. **2** *(mind, ideas, account)* confuso,-a.

confusing [kən'fju:zɪŋ] *adj* confuso,-a.

confusion [kən'fju:ʒən] *n* confusión *f*.

congeal [kən'dʒi:l] *vi (blood)* coagularse; *(fat)* solidificarse.

congenial [kən'dʒi:nɪəl] *adj* agradable.

congenital [kən'dʒenɪtəl] *adj* MED congénito,-a.

congested [kən'dʒestɪd] *adj* congestionado,-a.

congestion [kən'dʒestʃən] *n* congestión *f*.

conglomerate [*(n)* kən'glɒmərət; *(vb)* kən'glɒməreɪt] *n* **1** COMM conglomerado (de empresas). **2** GEOL conglomerado.

congratulate [kən'grætjəleɪt] *vt* felicitar (on, por).

congratulation [kən'grætjəleɪʃənz] *n* felicitación *f*.
▶ *interj* **congratulations!** ¡felicidades! *fpl*, ¡enhorabuena!

congregate ['kɒŋgrɪgeɪt] *vi* congregarse.

congregation [kɒŋgrɪ'geɪʃən] *n* REL *(people gathered)* fieles *mpl*; *(parishioners)* feligreses *mpl*.

congress ['kɒŋgres] *n* congreso.
▶ *n* **Congress** US el Congreso.

congruent ['kɒŋgruənt] *adj* MATH congruente.

conic ['kɒnɪk] *adj* cónico,-a.

conifer ['kɒnɪfər] *n* conífera.

conjecture [kən'dʒektʃər] *n* conjetura, suposición *f*.
▶ *vi* hacer conjeturas.

conjugal ['kɒndʒəɡəl] *adj* conyugal.

conjugate ['kɒndʒəɡeɪt] *vt* conjugar.
▶ *vi* conjugarse.

conjugation [kɒndʒə'ɡeɪʃən] *n* conjugación *f*.

conjunction [kən'dʒʌŋkʃən] *n* conjunción *f*. LOC **in conjunction with** conjuntamente con.

conjure ['kʌndʒər] *vi* hacer magia, hacer juegos de manos.

◆ **to conjure up** *vt sep (evoke - memories)* evocar, traer a la memoria; *(summon - spirits)* invocar.

🗙 Conjure no significa 'conjura (conspiración)', que se traduce por plot.

conjurer ['kʌndʒərər] *n* mago,-a, prestidigitador,-ra.

connect [kə'nekt] *vt* **1** *(gen)* conectar. **2** *(associate)* relacionar, asociar. **3** *(on telephone)* poner (with, con).

connection [kə'nekʃən] *n* **1** *(gen)* conexión *f*. **2** *(train, plane)* conexión *f*, enlace *m*.
▶ *n pl* **connections** *(professional)* contactos *mpl*; *(relatives)* familia, parientes *mpl*.

connector [kə'nektər] *n* conector *m*.

connoisseur [kɒnə'sɜ:r] *n* entendido,-a, conocedor,-ra.

connotation [kɒnə'teɪʃən] *n* connotación *f*.

conquer ['kɒŋkər] *vt (country, mountain, heart)* conquistar; *(enemy, fear)* vencer.

conqueror ['kɒŋkərər] *n* conquistador,-ra, vencedor,-ra.

conquest ['kɒŋkwest] *n* conquista.

consanguinity [kɒnsæŋ'gwɪnɪti] *n* consanguinidad *f*.

conscience ['kɒnʃəns] *n* conciencia.

conscientious [kɒnʃɪ'enʃəs] *adj (work)* concienzudo,-a; *(person)* aplicado,-a, serio,-a.

conscientiousness [kɒnʃɪ'enʃəsnəs] *n* escrupulosidad *f*.

conscious ['kɒnʃəs] *adj* **1** MED consciente. **2** *(aware)* consciente. **3** *(intentional, deliberate)* deliberado,-a.

conscript [*(n)* 'kɒnskrɪpt; *(vb)* kən'skrɪpt] *n* recluta.
▶ *vt* reclutar.

conscription [kən'skrɪpʃən] *n* servicio militar obligatorio.

consecrate ['kɒnsɪkreɪt] *vt* consagrar.

consecutive [kən'sekjətɪv] *adj* consecutivo,-a.

consensus [kən'sensəs] *n* consenso.

consent [kən'sent] *n* consentimiento.
▶ *vi* consentir (to, en), acceder (to, en).

consequence ['kɒnsɪkwəns] n **1** (result) consecuencia. **2** (importance) importancia, trascendencia.

consequent ['kɒnsɪkwənt] adj consiguiente.

conservation [kɒnsə'veɪʃ°n] n conservación f.

conservationist [kɒnsə'veɪʃ°nɪst] n ecologista mf.

conservatism [kən'sɜ:vətɪz°m] n POL conservadurismo.

conservative [kən'sɜ:vətɪv] adj **1** (traditional) conservador,-ra. **2** (cautious) cauteloso,-a, prudente.
▶ n (traditionalist) conservador,-ra.
▶ adj **Conservative** POL conservador,-ra.
▶ n **Conservative** POL conservador,-ra.

conservatoire [kən'sɜ:vətwɑː'] n conservatorio.

conservatory [kən'sɜ:vətrɪ] n **1** MUS conservatorio. **2** (greenhouse) invernadero.
ⓘ pl conservatories.

conserve [kən'sɜ:v] vt (nature, wildlife, etc) conservar, proteger; (save) conservar, ahorrar.
▶ n CULIN (jam) confitura.

consider [kən'sɪdə'] vt considerar.

considerable [kən'sɪd°rəb°l] adj considerable.

considerate [kən'sɪd°rət] adj considerado,-a, atento,-a.

consideration [kənsɪdə'reɪʃ°n] n **1** (gen) consideración f. **2** (factor to consider) factor m a tener en cuenta.

considering [kən'sɪdərɪŋ] prep teniendo en cuenta.
▶ conj teniendo en cuenta que.
▶ adv después de todo.

consign [kən'saɪn] vt **1** COMM (send - goods) consignar. **2** fml (entrust) confiar.

consignment [kən'saɪnmənt] n COMM remesa, envío.

consist [kən'sɪst] vi **1** fml (have as chief element) consistir (in, en). **2** (comprise, be composed of) constar (of, de), estar compuesto,-a (of, de).

consistency [kən'sɪstənsɪ] n (of actions, behaviour, policy) coherencia, lógica. **2** (of mixture) consistencia.

consistent [kən'sɪstənt] adj (of person, behaviour, beliefs) coherente (with, con), consecuente (with, con); (denial, improvement) constante.

consolation [kɒnsə'leɪʃ°n] n consuelo.

console¹ ['kɒnsəʊl] n (electrical) consola; (video games) consola.

console² [kən'səʊl] vt consolar.

consolidate [kən'sɒlɪdeɪt] vt **1** (gen) consolidar. **2** COMM (merge) fusionar.

consolidation [kənsɒlɪ'deɪʃ°n] n **1** (gen) consolidación f. **2** COMM fusión f.

consommé ['kɒnsɒmeɪ] n consomé m.

consonant ['kɒns°nənt] n consonante f.

conspicuous [kəns'pɪkjʊəs] adj (clothes) llamativo,-a; (mistake, difference, lack) evidente, obvio,-a.

conspiracy [kən'spɪrəsɪ] n conspiración f: a conspiracy to murder una conspiración de asesinato.
ⓘ pl conspiracies.

conspirator [kən'spɪrətə'] n conspirador,-ra.

conspire [kən'spaɪə'] vi conspirar.

constable ['kʌnstəb°l] n policía mf, guardia mf, agente mf (de policía).

constabulary [kən'stæbjələrɪ] n GB policía.
ⓘ pl constabularies.

constant ['kɒnstənt] adj **1** (gen) constante. **2** (unchanging) constante.
▶ n constante f.

constellation [kɒnstə'leɪʃ°n] n constelación f.

consternation [kɒnstə'neɪʃ°n] n consternación f.

constipated ['kɒnstɪpeɪtɪd] adj estreñido,-a.

❎ To be constipated no significa 'estar constipado (acatarrado)', que se traduce por to have a cold.

constipation [kɒnstɪ'peɪʃ°n] n estreñimiento.

❎ Constipation no significa 'constipado (catarro)', que se traduce por cold.

constituency [kən'stɪtjʊənsɪ] n circunscripción f, distrito electoral.
ⓘ pl constituencies.

constituent [kəns'tɪtjuənt] *adj* constituyente.
▶ *n (component)* componente *m*.

constitute ['kɒnstɪtjuːt] *vt* constituir.

constitution [kɒnstɪ'tjuːʃªn] *n* **1** *(gen)* constitución *f*. **2** *(of person)* constitución *f*, complexión *f*.

constitutional [kɒnstɪ'tjuːʃªnªl] *adj* constitucional.

constrain [kəns'treɪn] *vt* **1** *(oblige, force)* constreñir, obligar, forzar. **2** *(restrict, hold back)* contener.

constraint [kən'streɪnt] *n* **1** *(compulsion, coercion)* coacción *f*, obligación *f*. **2** *(restriction)* restricción *f*, limitación *f*.

constrict [kən'strɪkt] *vt* **1** *(blood vessels)* estrangular; *(breathing, movement)* dificultar; *(neck)* apretar, oprimir. **2** *fig (action, behaviour)* limitar, coartar.

construct [kəns'trʌkt] *vt* construir.

construction [kən'strʌkʃªn] *n* **1** *(gen)* construcción *f*. **2** *fig (meaning)* interpretación *f*.

constructive [kən'strʌktɪv] *adj* constructivo,-a.

constructor [kən'strʌktəʳ] *n* constructor,-ra.

construe [kən'struː] *vt* interpretar.

consul ['kɒnsªl] *n* cónsul *mf*.

consulate ['kɒnsjələt] *n* consulado.

consult [kən'sʌlt] *vt* consultar.
▶ *vi* consultar.

consultant [kən'sʌltənt] *n* **1** *(expert, advisor)* asesor,-ra, consultor,-ra. **2** GB *(doctor)* especialista *mf*.

consultation [kɒnsəl'teɪʃªn] *n* consulta.

consulting [kən'sʌltɪŋ] *adj (architect, engineer)* asesor,-ra, consultor,-ra. COMP
consulting room MED consulta.

consume [kən'sjuːm] *vt* consumir.

consumer [kən'sjuːməʳ] *n* consumidor,-ra.

consummate [*(adj)* 'kɒnsəmət; *(vb)* 'kɒnsəmeɪt] *adj fml* consumado,-a.
▶ *vt fml* consumar.

consumption [kən'sʌmpʃªn] *n* consumo.

contact ['kɒntækt] *n* contacto. COMP
contact lenses lentes *fpl* de contacto.
▶ *vt* ponerse en contacto con.

contagion [kən'teɪdʒªn] *n* contagio.

contagious [kən'teɪdʒəs] *adj* contagioso,-a.

contain [kən'teɪn] *vt* contener.

container [kən'teɪnəʳ] *n* **1** *(receptacle)* recipiente *m*; *(packaging)* envase *m*. **2** *(for transporting goods)* contenedor *m*, contáiner *m*.

containment [kən'teɪnmənt] *n* contención *f*.

contaminate [kən'tæmɪneɪt] *vt* contaminar.

contamination [kəntæmɪ'neɪʃªn] *n* contaminación *f*.

contemplate ['kɒntempleɪt] *vt* contemplar.

contemporaneous [kɒntempə'reɪnɪəs] *adj fml* contemporáneo,-a.

contemporary [kən'tempªrərɪ] *adj* contemporáneo,-a.
▶ *n* contemporáneo,-a.
ⓘ *pl* contemporaries.

contempt [kən'tempt] *n* desprecio, desdén *m*, menosprecio.

contemptible [kən'temptəbªl] *adj* despreciable.

contend [kən'tend] *vi* **1** *(compete)* contender, competir. **2** *(deal with, struggle against)* enfrentarse a, lidiar con.
▶ *vt (claim, state)* sostener, afirmar.

contender [kən'tendəʳ] *n* contendiente *mf* (for, por).

content¹ ['kɒntent] *n* contenido.
▶ *n pl* **contents** contenido *m sing*.

content² [kən'tent] *adj* contento,-a, satisfecho,-a: *he's content to watch the match at home* se conforma con ver el partido en casa.
▶ *n* contento.
▶ *vt* contentar, satisfacer.

contented [kən'tentɪd] *adj* contento,-a, satisfecho,-a.

contention [kən'tenʃªn] *n* **1** *(opinion, assertion)* opinión *f*. **2** *(dispute, disagreement)* discusión *f*, controversia.

contentious [kən'tenʃəs] *adj* polémico,-a.

contest [*(n)* 'kɒntest; *(vb)* kən'test] *n* **1** *(competition - gen)* concurso; *(- sports)* competición f; *(- boxing)* combate m. **2** *(struggle, attempt)* contienda, lucha.

▶ vt **1** *(championship, seat)* competir por, luchar por, disputarse; *(election)* presentarse como candidato,-a a. **2** *(dispute)* refutar, rebatir. **3** JUR *(appeal against)* impugnar.

🗶 To contest no significa 'contestar', que se traduce por to answer.

contestant [kən'testənt] n *(in competition, quiz, game)* concursante mf; *(for post, position)* candidato,-a, aspirante mf.

context ['kɒntekst] n contexto.

contiguous [kən'tɪgjuəs] adj contiguo,-a.

continent ['kɒntɪnənt] n continente m.

continental [kɒntɪ'nentəl] adj continental.

▶ adj Continental GB europeo,-a.

contingency [kən'tɪndʒənsɪ] n contingencia. COMP **contingency plan** plan m de emergencia.

contingent [kən'tɪndʒənt] adj contingente.

▶ n contingente m.

continual [kən'tɪnjuəl] adj continuo,-a, constante.

continuation [kəntɪnju'eɪʃən] n continuación f.

continue [kən'tɪnju:] vt & vi continuar, seguir.

continuous [kən'tɪnjuəs] adj continuo,-a.

contort [kən'tɔ:t] vt *(face)* contraer.

▶ vi contraerse.

contortion [kən'tɔ:ʃən] n contorsión f.

contour ['kɒntuər] n contorno.

contraband ['kɒntrəbænd] n contrabando.

contraception [kɒntrə'sepʃən] n anticoncepción f.

contraceptive [kɒntrə'septɪv] adj anticonceptivo,-a.

▶ n anticonceptivo.

contract [*(n)* 'kɒntrækt; *(vb)* kən'trækt] n *(gen)* contrato; *(for public work, services)* contrata.

▶ vt **1** *(place under contract)* contratar. **2** *(make smaller)* contraer. **3** fml *(debt, habit, illness)* contraer.

contraction [kən'trækʃən] n contracción f.

contractor [kən'træktər] n contratista mf.

contradict [kɒntrə'dɪkt] vt & vi contradecir.

contradiction [kɒntrə'dɪkʃən] n contradicción f.

contradictory [kɒntrə'dɪktərɪ] adj contradictorio,-a.

contraption [kən'træpʃən] n fam cacharro, artefacto, artilugio.

contrary [*(adj)* 'kɒntrərɪ; *(n)* kɒn'treərɪ] adj **1** *(opposite)* contrario,-a. **2** *(stubborn)* terco,-a, obstinado,-a, tozudo,-a.

▶ n **the contrary** lo contrario.

contrast [*(n)* 'kɒntrɑ:st; *(vb)* kɒn'trɑ:st] n contraste m.

▶ vt & vi contrastar.

contribute [kən'trɪbju:t] vt **1** *(money)* contribuir (to, a; towards, para); *(ideas, information)* aportar. **2** *(article, poem, etc)* escribir.

▶ vi **1** *(gen)* contribuir (to, a; towards, para); *(in discussion)* participar (to, en). **2** *(to newspaper, magazine, etc)* colaborar (to, en), escribir (to, para).

contributor [kən'trɪbjətər] n **1** *(to charity, appeal, etc)* donante mf. **2** *(to newspaper, magazine, etc)* colaborador,-ra.

contrive [kən'traɪv] vt **1** *(way, device)* idear, inventar; *(meeting)* arreglar; *(meal, dress, etc)* improvisar. **2** *(manage)* conseguir.

contrived [kən'traɪvd] adj artificial.

control [kən'trəul] vt controlar.

▶ n **1** *(power, command)* poder m, dominio, mando; *(authority)* autoridad f. **2** *(restriction, means of regulating)* control m. **3** *(place, people in control)* control m. **4** *(switch, button)* botón m, mando. COMP **control tower** torre f de emergencia.

▶ n pl **controls** *(of vehicle)* mandos mpl.

controller [kən'trəulər] n **1** *(financial)* interventor,-ra. **2** *(in broadcasting)* director,-ra de programación.

controversy [kən'trɒvəsɪ] n controversia, polémica.

ⓘ pl **controversies**.

contusion [kən'tju:ʒªn] *n* contusión *f*.

convalesce [kɒnvəˈles] *vi* convalecer.

convalescence [kɒnvəˈlesªns] *n* convalecencia.

convalescent [kɒnvəˈlesªnt] *adj* convaleciente.

convenience [kənˈvi:nɪəns] *n* conveniencia, comodidad *f*. COMP **convenience food** plato precocinado.

convenient [kənˈvi:nɪənt] *adj (time, arrangement)* conveniente, oportuno,-a; *(thing)* práctico,-a, cómodo,-a.

convent ['kɒnvənt] *n* convento.

convention [kənˈvenʃªn] *n* convención *f*, congreso.

converge [kənˈvɜ:dʒ] *vi (lines, roads)* convergir (on, en), converger (on, en); *(people)* reunirse.

conversant [kənˈvɜ:sªnt] *adj* familiarizado,-a (with, con), versado,-a (with, en).

conversation [kɒnvəˈseɪʃªn] *n* conversación *f*.

converse ['kɒnvɜ:s] *adj* opuesto,-a, contrario,-a.

conversion [kənˈvɜ:ʃn] *n* conversión *f* (to, a; into, en).

convert [*(vb)* kənˈvɜ:t; *(n)* 'kɒnvɜ:t] *vt (gen)* convertir (into, en; to, a).
► *n* REL converso,-a.

convertible [kənˈvɜ:təbªl] *adj (gen)* convertible; *(car)* descapotable.
► *n* AUTO descapotable *m*.

convex ['kɒnveks] *adj* convexo,-a.

convey [kənˈveɪ] *vt* **1** *(goods, people, electricity)* transportar, conducir; *(sound)* transmitir, llevar. **2** *(opinion, feeling, idea)* comunicar, transmitir.

conveyance [kənˈveɪəns] *n* **1** *(transport)* transporte *m*. **2** *fml (vehicle)* vehículo. **3** JUR traspaso, transferencia.

conveyor belt [kənˈveɪəˈbelt] *n* cinta transportadora.

convict [*(n)* 'kɒnvɪkt; *(vb)* kənˈvɪkt] *n* presidiario,-a, recluso,-a.
► *vt* JUR declarar culpable, condenar.

conviction [kənˈvɪkʃªn] *n* **1** *(belief)* convicción *f*, creencia. **2** JUR condena (for, por).

convince [kənˈvɪns] *vt* convencer.

convincing [kənˈvɪnsɪŋ] *adj* convincente.

convoy ['kɒnvɔɪ] *n* convoy *m*.

cook [kʊk] *n* cocinero,-a.
► *vt (food)* guisar, cocinar; *(meals)* preparar, hacer.

cooker ['kʊkəʳ] *n (stove)* cocina.

cookery ['kʊkərɪ] *n* cocina: *Spanish cookery* cocina española. COMP **cookery book** libro de cocina.

cookie ['kʊkɪ] *n* **1** US *(biscuit)* galleta. **2** *(in computing)* cookie *m & f*, galleta.

cooking ['kʊkɪŋ] *n* cocina: *home cooking* cocina casera.

cool [ku:l] *adj* **1** *(gen)* fresco,-a. **2** *(unfriendly, reserved)* frío,-a. **3** *(calm)* tranquilo,-a, sereno,-a. **4** *fam (great)* guay.

coop [ku:p] *n* gallinero.

cooperate [kəʊˈɒpəreɪt] [also written co-operate] *vi* cooperar, colaborar.

coordinate [*(vb)* kəʊˈɔ:dɪneɪt; *(n)* kəʊˈɔ:dɪnət] [also written co-ordinate] *vt* coordinar.
► *n* MATH coordenada.

coordination [kəʊɔ:dɪˈneɪʃªn] [also written co-ordination] *n* coordinación *f*.

cop [kɒp] *n sl (policeman)* poli *mf*.

cope [kəʊp] *vi* arreglárselas, poder.

copious ['kəʊpɪəs] *adj* copioso,-a, abundante.

copper ['kɒpəʳ] *n* **1** *(metal)* cobre *m*. **2** GB *fam (coin)* penique *m*, pela, perra. **3** *sl (policeman)* poli *mf*.

copse [kɒps] *n* arboleda, bosquecillo.

copulate ['kɒpjəleɪt] *vi* copular.

copy ['kɒpɪ] *n* **1** *(reproduction)* copia. **2** *(of book, magazine, etc)* ejemplar *m*.
① *pl* copies.
► *vi* copiar.

copycat ['kɒpɪkæt] *n fam* copión,-ona.
► *adj (crime)* inspirado,-a en otro.

copyright ['kɒpɪraɪt] *n* copyright *m*, derechos *mpl* de autor.

coral ['kɒrªl] *n* coral *m*.

cord [kɔ:d] *n* **1** *(string, rope)* cuerda. **2** ELEC cable *m*. **3** *(corduroy)* pana.

cordon ['kɔ:dªn] *n* cordón *m*.

corduroy ['kɔ:dərɔɪ] *n* pana.

core [kɔːʳ] *n* **1** *(gen)* núcleo. **2** *(of apple, pear, etc)* corazón *m*.

coriander [kɒrɪˈændəʳ] *n* cilantro.

cork [kɔːk] *n* *(material)* corcho.

corkscrew [ˈkɔːkskruː] *n* sacacorchos *m*.

corm [kɔːm] *n* bulbo.

corn¹ [kɔːn] *n* *(gen)* cereales *mpl*; *(wheat)* trigo; *(oats)* avena; *(maize)* maíz *m*.

corn² [kɔːn] *n* MED callo.

corncob [ˈkɔːnkɒb] *n* mazorca de maíz.

cornea [ˈkɔːnɪə] *n* córnea.

corned beef [kɔːndˈbiːf] *n* carne *f* en conserva.

corner [ˈkɔːnəʳ] *n* **1** *(of street)* esquina; *(bend in road)* curva; *(of table, etc)* esquina, punta. **2** *(of room, cupboard, etc)* rincón *m*; *(of mouth)* comisura; *(of eye)* rabillo; *(of page, envelope)* ángulo. **3** SP *(kick - in football)* córner *m*, saque *m* de esquina.
▶ *vt* arrinconar, acorralar; *(person)* arrinconar.

cornet [ˈkɔːnɪt] *n* **1** MUS corneta. **2** GB *(for ice-cream)* cucurucho.

cornflakes [ˈkɔːnfleɪks] *npl* copos de maíz.

cornice [ˈkɔːnɪs] *n* cornisa.

corolla [kəˈrɒlə] *n* corola.

coronation [kɒrəˈneɪʃᵊn] *n* coronación *f*.

coroner [ˈkɒrənəʳ] *n* juez *mf* de instrucción.

corporal [ˈkɔːpᵊrəl] *n* MIL cabo.

corporate [ˈkɔːpᵊrət] *adj* **1** *(collective)* colectivo,-a. **2** *(of a corporation)* de la empresa, de la compañía.

corporation [kɔːpəˈreɪʃᵊn] *n* corporación *f*.

corps [kɔːʳ] *n* cuerpo.
ⓘ *pl* corps [kɔːz].

corpse [kɔːps] *n* cadáver *m*.

corpus [ˈkɔːpəs] *adj* **1** *(of texts)* corpus *m*. **2** ANAT cuerpo. COMP ANAT **corpus callosum** cuerpo calloso.

corpuscle [ˈkɔːpəsᵊl] *n* corpúsculo, glóbulo.

correct [kəˈrekt] *adj* correcto,-a.
▶ *vt* corregir.

correspond [kɒrɪsˈpɒnd] *vi* **1** *(gen)* corresponderse (with, con). **2** *(write)* escribirse (with, con).

correspondence [kɒrɪsˈpɒndᵊns] *n* correspondencia.

correspondent [kɒrɪsˈpɒndᵊnt] *n* corresponsal *mf*.

corridor [ˈkɒrɪdɔːʳ] *n* pasillo.

corrode [kəˈrəud] *vt* corroer.
▶ *vi* corroerse.

corrosion [kəˈrəuʒᵊn] *n* **1** *(process)* corrosión *f*. **2** *(substance)* herrumbre *f*, orín *m*.

corrupt [kəˈrʌpt] *adj* corrompido,-a, corrupto,-a.
▶ *vt* corromper; *(bribe)* sobornar.

corruption [kəˈrʌpʃᵊn] *n* corrupción *f*.

corset [ˈkɔːsɪt] *n* corsé *m*.

cortex [ˈkɔːteks] *n* corteza.

cos [ˈkəusaɪn] *abbr* **(cosine)** coseno; *(abbreviation)* cos.

cosine [ˈkəusaɪn] *n* MATH coseno.

cosmetic [kɒzˈmetɪk] *adj* cosmético,-a.
COMP **cosmetic surgery** cirugía estética.

cosmic [ˈkɒzmɪk] *adj* cósmico,-a.

cosmonaut [ˈkɒzmənɔːt] *n* cosmonauta *mf*.

cosmopolitan [kɒzməˈpɒlɪtᵊn] *adj* cosmopolita.

cosmos [ˈkɒzmɒs] *n* cosmos *m*.

cost [kɒst] *vt* costar, valer.
ⓘ *pt & pp* cost [kɒst].
▶ *n* *(price)* coste *m*, precio. COMP **cost of living** coste de la vida.

costal [ˈkɒstəl] *adj* costal.

co-star [ˈkəustɑːʳ] *n* coprotagonista *mf*.

Costa Rica [kɒstəˈriːkə] *n* Costa Rica.

Costa Rican [kɒstəˈriːkən] *adj* costarricense.
▶ *n* *(person)* costarricense *mf*.

cost-effective [kɒstɪˈfektɪv] *adj* rentable.

costly [ˈkɒstlɪ] *adj* costoso,-a.
ⓘ *comp* costlier, *superl* costliest.

costume [ˈkɒstjuːm] *n* traje *m*.
▶ *n pl* **costumes** THEAT vestuario.

cosy [ˈkəuzɪ] *adj* **1** *(room, house, atmosphere)* acogedor,-ra. **2** *(chat)* íntimo,-a y agradable.
ⓘ *comp* cosier, *superl* cosiest.

cot [kɒt] *n* **1** *(for baby)* cuna. **2** US *(camp bed)* cama de campaña.

cotton ['kɒtᵊn] *n* **1** *(cloth, plant)* algodón *m*. **2** *(thread)* hilo (de coser).
▸ *adj (shirt, etc)* de algodón. COMP **cotton bud** bastoncillo de algodón. ‖ **cotton wool** algodón *m* hidrófilo.

couch [kaʊtʃ] *n (sofa)* canapé *m*, sofá *m*.

couchette [kuːˈʃet] *n* litera.

✎ Couchette se refiere específicamente a las literas de los trenes. Las literas que puede haber en una casa se llaman **bunk beds**.

cougar ['kuːgəʳ] *n* puma *m*.

cough [kɒf] *n* tos *f*.
▸ *vi* toser.

could [kʊd] *pt* → can.

council ['kaʊnsᵊl] *n* **1** *(elected group)* consejo. **2** GB *(of town, city)* ayuntamiento. **3** REL concilio.

councillor ['kaʊnsᵊləʳ] *n* concejal,-la.

counsel ['kaʊnsᵊl] *n* **1** *(advice)* consejo. **2** JUR abogado,-a.

counsellor ['kaʊnsᵊləʳ] *n* **1** *(adviser)* consejero,-a, asesor,-ra. **2** US *(lawyer)* abogado,-a.

count¹ [kaʊnt] *n (act of counting)* recuento; *(of votes)* escrutinio; *(total)* total *m*, suma.
▸ *vt* **1** *(gen)* contar. **2** *(consider)* considerar.

✗ To count no significa 'contar (relatar)', que se traduce por **to tell**.

count² [kaʊnt] *n (nobleman)* conde *m*.

countable ['kaʊntəbᵊl] *adj* contable.

countdown ['kaʊntdaʊn] *n* cuenta atrás.

counter ['kaʊntəʳ] *n* **1** *(in shop)* mostrador *m*; *(individual)* ventanilla. **2** *(in board games)* ficha.

counteract [kaʊntəˈrækt] *vt* contrarrestar.

counterattack ['kaʊntᵊrətæk] *n* contraataque *m*.
▸ *vt* contraatacar.

counterclockwise [kaʊntəˈklɒkwaɪz] *adj* US en sentido contrario a las agujas del reloj.

counterfeit ['kaʊntəfɪt] *adj* falso,-a, falsificado,-a.
▸ *n* falsificación *f*.
▸ *vt* falsificar.

counterfoil ['kaʊntəfɔɪl] *n* matriz *f*.

counterpart ['kaʊntəpɑːt] *n* homólogo,-a.

counterproductive [kaʊntəprəˈdʌktɪv] *adj* contraproducente.

countess ['kaʊntəs] *n* condesa.

countless ['kaʊntləs] *adj* incontable, innumerable.

country ['kʌntrɪ] *n* **1** *(state, nation)* país *m*; *(people)* pueblo. **2** [no se usa en *pl*] *(rural area)* campo. **3** [no se usa en *pl*] *(region, area of land)* región *f*, zona, territorio. **1** [también **country music**] MUS música country, country *m*.
ⓘ *pl* countries.
▸ *adj (rural - life, lane)* rural; *(- house)* de campo.

countryman ['kʌntrɪmən] *n* **1** *(man from country)* campesino. **2** *(compatriot)* compatriota *m*.
ⓘ *pl* countrymen ['kʌntrɪmən].

countryside ['kʌntrɪsaɪd] *n (area)* campo, campiña; *(scenery)* paisaje *m*.

countrywoman ['kʌntrɪwʊmən] *n* **1** *(woman from the country)* campesina. **2** *(compatriot)* compatriota.
ⓘ *pl* countrywomen ['kʌntrɪwɪmɪn].

county ['kaʊntɪ] *n* condado.
ⓘ *pl* counties.

coup [kuː] *n* golpe *m*. COMP **coup d'état** golpe *m* de estado.

couple ['kʌpᵊl] *n* **1** *(two things)* par *m*; *(a few)* unos,-as. **2** *(two people)* pareja.
▸ *vt* conectar, acoplar.

coupon ['kuːpɒn] *n* **1** COMM *(for discount, free gift, etc)* cupón *m*, vale *m*. **2** GB *(for competition, football pools)* boleto.

courage ['kʌrɪdʒ] *n* coraje *m*, valor *m*, valentía.

courageous [kəˈreɪdʒəs] *adj* valiente.

courgette [kuəˈʒet] *n* calabacín *m*.

courier ['kʊərɪəʳ] *n* **1** *(messenger)* mensajero,-a. **2** *(guide)* guía *mf* turístico,-a.

course [kɔːs] *n* **1** *(gen)* curso; *(of ship)* rumbo. **2** EDUC *(year - long)* curso; *(- short)* cursillo; *(at university)* carrera; *(individual subject)* asignatura. **3** *(of meal)* plato. **4** SP *(for golf)* campo. LOC **of course** desde luego, por supuesto. COMP **main course** segundo plato.

court [kɔ:t] n **1** JUR (place, people) tribunal m; (building) juzgado. **2** (royal) corte f. **3** SP (tennis, squash, etc) pista, cancha. **4** (courtyard) patio.

courteous ['kɜ:tɪəs] adj cortés.

courtesy ['kɜ:təsɪ] n **1** (good manners) cortesía, educación f. **2** (polite act or remark) favor m, atención f.
ⓘ pl courtesies.

courthouse ['kɔ:thaʊs] n juzgado.

courtroom ['kɔ:truːm] n sala de justicia, tribunal m.

courtyard ['kɔ:tjɑːd] n patio.

cousin ['kʌzən] n primo,-a.

cove [kəʊv] n cala, ensenada.

covenant ['kʌvənənt] n JUR (formal agreement) convenio, pacto; (clause) cláusula, provisión f.

cover ['kʌvər] n **1** (lid) tapa, cubierta. **2** (thing that covers - gen) funda. **3** (outside pages - of book) cubierta, tapa; (of magazine) portada. **4** (insurance) cobertura. **5** (shelter, protection) abrigo, protección f.
▶ vt **1** (place over - gen) cubrir (with, de); (- floor, wall) revestir (with, de); (- sofa) tapizar; (- book) forrar. **2** (with lid, hands) tapar. **3** (hide) tapar.

coverage ['kʌvərɪdʒ] n cobertura.

coveralls ['kʌvərɔːlz] n pl US → overalls.

covering ['kʌvərɪŋ] n (protective) cubierta, envoltura; (layer) capa.

covert ['kʌvət] adj secreto,-a.

cover-up ['kʌvərʌp] n encubrimiento.

covet ['kʌvət] vt codiciar.

cow [kaʊ] n vaca.

coward ['kaʊəd] n cobarde mf.

cowardly ['kaʊədlɪ] adj cobarde.

cowboy ['kaʊbɔɪ] n vaquero.

cox [kɒks] n timonel mf.

coy [kɔɪ] adj tímido,-a, recatado,-a.

coyote [kaɪˈəʊtɪ] n coyote m.

cozy ['kəʊzɪ] adj US → cosy.
ⓘ comp cozier, superl coziest.

crab [kræb] n (shellfish) cangrejo.

crack [kræk] vt **1** (break - cup, glass, etc) rajar; (- bone) fracturar, romper. **2** (break open - safe) forzar; (- egg, nut) cascar; (- bottle) abrir, descorchar. **3** (hit) pegar, golpear.
▶ vi **1** (break - cup, glass) rajarse, resquebrarse; (- rock, plaster, paint, skin) agrietarse. **2** (relationship, system) venirse abajo; (person) sufrir una crisis nerviosa.
▶ n **1** (in cup, glass) raja; (in ice, wall, ground, pavement, etc) grieta. **2** (slit, narrow opening) rendija. **3** (of whip) restallido, chasquido.
▶ adj (troops, regiment, shot) de primera.

cracked [krækt] adj fam (mad, crazy) chiflado,-a, chalado,-a.

cracker ['krækər] n **1** (biscuit) galleta seca. **2** (firework) petardo m.

cracking ['krækɪŋ] adj fam (shot, goal) de primera; (pace) muy rápido,-a.

crackle ['krækəl] n (of twigs, etc) crujido, chasquido.
▶ vi (twigs, etc) chasquear; (fire) chisporrotear, crepitar; (radio, telephone) hacer ruido.

cradle ['kreɪdəl] n cuna f.
▶ vt (baby) acunar (en los brazos), mecer.

craft [krɑːft] n **1** (occupation) oficio. **2** (art) arte m; (skill) habilidad f, destreza. **3** (boat) embarcación f.
▶ vt trabajar.

craftsman ['krɑːftsmən] n artesano.
ⓘ pl craftsmen ['krɑːftsmən].

craftswoman ['krɑːftswʊmən] n artesana.
ⓘ pl craftswomen ['krɑːftswɪmɪn].

crafty ['krɑːftɪ] adj (person) astuto,-a; (child) pillo,-a; (method, idea, etc) hábil.
ⓘ comp craftier, superl craftiest.

crag [kræg] n peña, risco, peñasco.

cram [kræm] vt (stuff, fill) atestar (with, de), atiborrar (with, de).
▶ vi fam (learn for exam) empollar.
ⓘ pt & pp crammed, ger cramming.

cramp[1] [kræmp] n MED calambre m.
▶ n pl cramps (gen) retortijones mpl.

cramp[2] [kræmp] vt obstaculizar.

cranberry ['krænbərɪ] n arándano.
ⓘ pl cranberries.

crane [kreɪn] n **1** ZOOL grulla común. **2** (machine) grúa.

cranium ['kreɪnɪəm] n cráneo.
ⓘ pl craniums o crania ['kreɪnɪə].

crank [kræŋk] n **1** *(crankshaft)* cigüeñal m. **2** *(starting handle)* manivela.

crash [kræʃ] n **1** *(noise)* estrépito; *(of thunder)* trueno, estallido. **2** *(collision)* choque m, accidente m. **3** COMM *(collapse)* quiebra.

crate [kreɪt] n caja, cajón m.
▶ vt embalar.

crater [ˈkreɪtəʳ] n cráter m.

crave [kreɪv] vt ansiar, tener ansias de.

craving [ˈkreɪvɪŋ] n *(gen)* ansia (for, de), ansias fpl (for, de); *(in pregnancy)* antojo (for, de).

crawfish [ˈkrɔːfɪʃ] n → crayfish.

crawl [krɔːl] vi **1** *(move slowly - person, snake)* arrastrarse; *(- baby)* gatear. **2** *(car, traffic)* ir a paso de tortuga.
▶ n SP *(in swimming)* crol m.

crayfish [ˈkreɪfɪʃ] n cangrejo de río.
ⓘ pl crayfish.

crayon [ˈkreɪɒn] n lápiz m de cera.

craze [kreɪz] n *(fashion)* moda; *(game, sport, hobby, etc)* manía.

crazy [ˈkreɪzɪ] adj fam loco,-a.
ⓘ comp crazier, superl craziest.

creak [kriːk] vi *(floorboard, stairs, joints)* crujir, hacer un crujido; *(door, hinge)* chirriar.

cream [kriːm] n **1** *(of milk)* nata, crema (de leche). **2** *(cosmetic)* crema; *(medical)* pomada, crema.

crease [kriːs] n **1** *(wrinkle)* arruga; *(fold)* pliegue m; *(ironed)* raya. **2** SP *(in cricket)* línea.

create [kriːˈeɪt] vt **1** *(gen)* crear. **2** *(cause)* producir, causar.

creation [kriːˈeɪʃ⁰n] n creación f.

creature [ˈkriːtʃəʳ] n **1** *(animal)* criatura. **2** *(human being)* ser m.

credentials [krɪˈdenʃ⁰lz] n pl **1** *(qualifications)* credenciales fpl. **2** *(documents)* cartas fpl credenciales.

credible [ˈkredɪb⁰l] adj creíble.

credit [ˈkredɪt] n **1** *(praise, approval)* mérito, reconocimiento. **2** *(belief, trust, confidence)* crédito. **3** FIN *(gen)* crédito; *(in accountancy)* haber m; *(on statement)* saldo acreedor. **5** EDUC crédito.
▶ n pl **credits** *(of film, programme)* ficha técnica.

creditor [ˈkredɪtəʳ] n acreedor,-ra.

creed [kriːd] n credo.

creek [kriːk] n **1** GB cala. **2** US riachuelo, arroyo.

creep [kriːp] vi **1** *(move quietly)* moverse sigilosamente, deslizarse. **2** *(move with the body close to the ground)* arrastrarse, reptar.
ⓘ pt & pp crept [krept].

creeper [ˈkriːpəʳ] n (planta) trepadora.

cremate [krɪˈmeɪt] vt incinerar.

crematorium [kreməˈtɔːrɪəm] n (horno) crematorio.
ⓘ pl crematoriums o crematoria [kreməˈtɔːrɪə].

crepe [kreɪp] n crepe m.

crept [krept] pt & pp → creep.

crescent [ˈkres⁰nt] n *(shape)* medialuna.
▶ adj creciente. COMP **crescent moon** luna creciente.

cress [kres] n berro.

crest [krest] n **1** *(of cock)* cresta. **2** *(of hill)* cima, cumbre f; *(of wave)* cresta.

crestfallen [ˈkrestfɔːl⁰n] adj abatido,-a.

crevice [ˈkrevɪs] n grieta, raja.

crew¹ [kruː] n **1** *(of ship, etc)* tripulación f. **2** *(working team)* equipo.

crew² [kruː] pt → crow.

crib [krɪb] n **1** *(manger)* pesebre m; *(Nativity scene)* belén m, pesebre m. **2** *(for baby)* cuna. **3** *(for cheating)* chuleta.
▶ vt plagiar, copiar.
ⓘ pt & pp cribbed, ger cribbing.

crick [krɪk] n *(in neck)* tortícolis f.

cricket¹ [ˈkrɪkɪt] n *(insect)* grillo.

cricket² [ˈkrɪkɪt] n SP cricket m.

cried [kraɪd] pp → cry.

crime [kraɪm] n crimen m.

criminal [ˈkrɪmɪn⁰l] adj criminal.
▶ n delincuente mf, criminal mf.

cringe [krɪndʒ] vi encogerse, agacharse.

crinkle [ˈkrɪŋk⁰l] n arruga.
▶ vt arrugar.

cripple [ˈkrɪp⁰l] n lisiado,-a, tullido,-a.
▶ vt **1** *(person)* dejar cojo,-a, lisiar. **2** fig *(industry, country)* paralizar.

crisis [ˈkraɪsɪs] n crisis f.
ⓘ pl crises [ˈkraɪsiːs].

crisp [krɪsp] *adj* **1** *(pastry, biscuits, etc)* crujiente; *(lettuce)* fresco,-a. **2** *(weather, air)* frío,-a y seco,-a.
▸ *n* GB patata frita *(de bolsa o churrería)*.

✎ Son las patatas de bolsa o de churrería que se comen frías, pues las que se comen calientes se llaman **chips** en inglés británico y **french fries** en inglés americano.

crisscross ['krɪskrɒs] *vt* entrecruzar.
critic ['krɪtɪk] *n* *(reviewer)* crítico,-a.
critical ['krɪtɪkəl] *adj* crítico,-a.
criticism ['krɪtɪsɪzəm] *n* crítica.
criticize ['krɪtɪsaɪz] *vt* criticar.
croak [krəʊk] *n* **1** *(of raven)* graznido; *(of frog)* canto. **2** *(of person)* voz *f* ronca.
Croatia [krəʊ'eɪʃə] *n* Croacia.
Croatian [krəʊ'eɪʃən] *adj* croata.
▸ *adj* *(person)* croata *mf*; *(language)* croata *m*.

crochet ['krəʊʃeɪ] *n* ganchillo.
crockery ['krɒkəri] *n* loza, vajilla.
crocodile ['krɒkədaɪl] *n* cocodrilo.
crocus ['krəʊkəs] *n* azafrán *m*.
crony ['krəʊni] *n* *fam* compinche *mf*.
ⓘ *pl* cronies.
crook [krʊk] *n* **1** cayado, gancho. **2** *fam (criminal)* sinvergüenza *mf*, delincuente *mf*.
▸ *vt (finger, arm)* doblar.
crop [krɒp] *n* **1** *(plant)* cultivo; *(harvest)* cosecha. **2** *(group, batch)* tanda. **3** *(hairstyle)* corte *m* al rape.
cross [krɒs] *n* **1** *(gen)* cruz *f*. **2** BIOL *(hybrid)* cruce *m*.
▸ *vt (street, river, bridge,)* cruzar, atravesar; *(arms, legs)* cruzar.
▸ *vi (walk across)* cruzar *(over, -)*; *(intersect, pass each other)* cruzarse.
crossbar ['krɒsbɑːʳ] *n (of goal)* travesaño, larguero; *(of bicycle)* barra.
crossing ['krɒsɪŋ] *n* **1** MAR travesía. **2** *(intersection, crossroads)* cruce *m*. COMP border crossing paso fronterizo.
cross-reference [krɒs'refərəns] *n* remisión *f*.
▸ *vt* remitir.
crossroads ['krɒsrəʊdz] *n* encrucijada, cruce *m*.

crossword ['krɒswɜːd] [también **crossword puzzle**] *n* crucigrama *m*.
crotch [krɒtʃ] *n* entrepierna.
crotchet ['krɒtʃɪt] *n* MUS negra.
crouch [kraʊtʃ] [también **crouch down**] *vi (person)* agacharse, ponerse en cuclillas; *(cat)* agazaparse.
crow¹ [krəʊ] *n (bird)* cuervo.
crow² [krəʊ] *vi (cock)* cantar, cacarear.
ⓘ *pt* crowed o crew [kruː], *pp* crowed.
crowbar ['krəʊbɑːʳ] *n* palanca.
crowd [kraʊd] *n* **1** *(large number of people)* multitud *f*, muchedumbre *f*, gentío; *(at match, concert, etc)* público. **2** *(particular group)* gente *f*; *(clique)* pandilla.
crowded ['kraʊdɪd] *adj* abarrotado,-a de gente, concurrido,-a.
crown [kraʊn] *n* **1** *(of king, queen)* corona. **2** ANAT *(of head)* coronilla; *(of tooth)* corona. **3** *(top - of hat, tree)* copa.
crucial ['kruːʃəl] *adj* crucial.
crucifix ['kruːsɪfɪks] *n* crucifijo.
crucify ['kruːsɪfaɪ] *vt* crucificar.
ⓘ *pt & pp* crucified, *ger* crucifying.
crude [kruːd] *n* **1** *(manners, style)* tosco,-a, grosero,-a; *(joke)* grosero,-a, ordinario,-a. **2** *(oil)* crudo,-a.

✖ Crude no significa 'crudo (sin hacer)', que se traduce por **raw**.

cruel ['kruːəl] *adj* cruel.
ⓘ *comp* crueller, *superl* cruellest.
cruelty ['kruːəlti] *n* crueldad *f* (to, hacia).
ⓘ *pl* cruelties.
cruise [kruːz] *vi* MAR hacer un crucero.
▸ *n* crucero.
cruiser ['kruːzəʳ] *n* **1** *(warship)* crucero. **2** *(pleasure boat)* yate *m*.
crumb [krʌm] *n* miga, migaja.
crumble ['krʌmbəl] *vt (gen)* desmenuzar, deshacer; *(bread)* desmigajar.
crumple ['krʌmpəl] *vt (clothes)* arrugar; *(paper)* estrujar.
crunch [krʌntʃ] *vt* **1** *(food)* mascar. **2** *(with feet, tyres)* hacer crujir.
crusade [kruː'seɪd] *n* cruzada.
crush [krʌʃ] *vt* **1** *(squash - gen)* aplastar; *(squeeze)* estrujar;. **2** *(smash, pound - gen)* triturar; *(- ice)* picar.

▶ *n* **1** *(of people)* aglomeración *f*. **2** GB *(soft drink)* refresco.

crust [krʌst] *n* corteza.

crustacean [krʌˈsteɪʃ°n] *n* crustáceo.

crutch [krʌtʃ] *n* **1** *(for walking)* muleta.

crux [krʌks] *n* quid *m*, meollo.

cry [kraɪ] *vt* **1** *(shout, call)* gritar. **2** *(weep)* llorar.
ⓘ *pt & pp* cried, *ger* crying.

crying [ˈkraɪɪŋ] *n* *(weeping)* llanto.

crypt [krɪpt] *n* cripta.

crystal [ˈkrɪst°l] *n* cristal *m*.

crystallize [ˈkrɪst°laɪz] *vt* cristalizar.

cub [kʌb] *n* ZOOL cachorro,-a

cube [kjuːb] *n* **1** *(shape)* cubo; *(of sugar)* terrón *m*; *(of ice)* cubito; *(of cheese, meat, etc)* dado. **2** MATH cubo. COMP cube root raíz *f* cúbica.
▶ *vt* MATH elevar al cubo.

cubic [ˈkjuːbɪk] *adj* cúbico,-a.

cubism [ˈkjuːbɪz°m] *n* cubismo.

cuckoo [ˈkuku:] *n* cuco.
ⓘ *pl* cuckoos.

cucumber [ˈkjuːkʌmbə'] *n* pepino.

cuddle [ˈkʌd°l] *vt* abrazar, acariciar.

cue¹ [kjuː] *n* **1** *(for actor)* pie *m*; *(for musician)* entrada. **2** *(signal)* señal *f*. **3** *(example)* ejemplo.

cue² [kjuː] *n* *(in billiards, etc)* taco. COMP cue ball bola blanca.

cuff¹ [kʌf] *n* **1** *(of sleeve)* puño. **2** US *(of trousers)* dobladillo.
▶ *n pl* cuffs *sl* esposas *fpl*.

cuff² [kʌf] *vt* dar un bofetada a.
▶ *n* bofetada, cachete *m*, bofetón *m*.

cufflinks [ˈkʌflɪŋks] *n pl* gemelos *mpl*.

cuisine [kwɪˈziːn] *n* cocina.

cul-de-sac [ˈkʌldəsæk] *n* calle *f* sin salida.

culminate [ˈkʌlmɪneɪt] *vi* culminar.

culottes [kjuːˈlɒts] *n pl* falda pantalón *f sing*.

culprit [ˈkʌlprɪt] *n* culpable *mf*.

cult [kʌlt] *n* *(gen)* culto; *(sect)* secta.

cultivate [ˈkʌltɪveɪt] *vt* cultivar.
ⓘ *pt & pp* cupped, *ger* cupping.

culture [ˈkʌltʃə'] *n* **1** *(gen)* cultura. **2** *(growth)* cultivo.

cumbersome [ˈkʌmbəsəm] *adj* **1** *(thing)* incómodo,-a, voluminoso,-a, pesado,-a. **2** *(procedure)* torpe, engorroso,-a.

cumin [ˈkʌmɪn] *n* comino.

cunning [ˈkʌnɪŋ] *adj* astuto,-a
▶ *n* astucia.

cup [kʌp] *n* **1** *(for drinking)* taza. **2** SP *(trophy)* copa.

cupboard [ˈkʌbəd] *n* armario.

curator [kjuˈreɪtə'] *n* *(of museum)* conservador,-ra.

curb [kɜːb] *n* **1** *(for horse)* barbada. **2** *(control)* freno. **3** US bordillo.

curd [kɜːd] *n* *(from milk)* cuajada. COMP curd cheese requesón *m*.

curdle [ˈkɜːd°l] *vi* *(form curds)* cuajarse; *(go bad)* cortarse.

cure [kjuə'] *vt* curar.
▶ *n* cura.

cure-all [ˈkjuərɑ:l] *n* panacea.

curfew [ˈkɜːfjuː] *n* toque *m* de queda.

curiosity [kjuərɪˈɒsətɪ] *n* curiosidad *f*.
ⓘ *pl* curiosities.

curious [ˈkjuərɪəs] *adj* **1** *(inquisitive)* curioso,-a. **2** *(strange, odd)* curioso,-a, extraño,-a; *(interesting)* interesante.

curl [kɜːl] *vt* rizar.
▶ *vi* rizarse.
▶ *n* *(of hair)* rizo; *(ringlet)* bucle *m*, tirabuzón *m*; *(of smoke)* espiral *f*, voluta.

curly [ˈkɜːlɪ] *adj* rizado,-a.
ⓘ *comp* curlier, *superl* curliest.

currant [ˈkʌrənt] *n* **1** *(dried grape)* pasa (de Corinto). **2** *(fruit)* grosella.

currency [ˈkʌrənsɪ] *n* FIN moneda. COMP foreign currency divisa.
ⓘ *pl* currencies.

current [ˈkʌrənt] *adj* **1** *(present, existing - gen)* actual; *(- month, year)* en curso; *(most recent - issue)* último,-a. **2** *(generally accepted)* corriente, común, habitual, general. COMP current account cuenta corriente.
▶ *n* *(gen)* corriente *f*.

currently [ˈkʌrəntlɪ] *adv* **1** *(at present)* actualmente, en la actualidad. **2** *(commonly)* comúnmente.

curriculum [kəˈrɪkjələm] *n* EDUC plan *m* de estudios. COMP curriculum vitae currículum *m*, historial *m*.

curry ['kʌrɪ] n CULIN curry m.
ⓘ pl curries.

curse [kɜːs] n **1** (evil spell) maldición f. **2** (oath) palabrota.

cursor ['kɜːsəʳ] n cursor m.

curt [kɜːt] adj seco,-a, brusco,-a.

curtain ['kɜːtⁿɪn] n **1** (gen) cortina. **2** THEAT telón m.

curvature ['kɜːvətʃəʳ] n (of surface) curvatura. **2** MED encorvamiento.

curve [kɜːv] n (gen) curva.
▶ vi (of road, river, ball) describir una curva, torcer.

cushion ['kʊʃⁿn] n (gen) cojín m; (large) almohadón m.
▶ vt fig suavizar, amortiguar.

custard ['kʌstəd] n (cold, set) natillas fpl; (hot, liquid) crema. COMP custard apple chirimoya.

custom ['kʌstəm] n costumbre f: it's a typical Spanish custom es una típica costumbre española.

customary ['kʌstəmərɪ] adj (habitual) acostumbrado,-a, habitual.

customer ['kʌstəməʳ] n cliente mf.

customize ['kʌstəmaɪz] vt hacer por encargo, hacer a la medida.

custom-made [kʌstəm'meɪd] adj (clothes, etc) hecho,-a a medida.

customs ['kʌstəmz] n aduana.
✎ Puede ser tanto singular como plural.

cut [kʌt] n **1** (ge) corte m; (knife wound) cuchillada. **3** (share) parte f, tajada. **4** (reduction - in budget, services, wages) recorte m; (- in level, number, price) reducción f. **6** ELEC corte m, apagón m.
▶ vt **1** (gen) cortar **2** (reduce - level, number) reducir; (- budget, spending) recortar; (- price) rebajar, reducir.
◆ to cut down vt sep (tree) talar, cortar; (kill) matar.
◆ to cut off vt sep **2** (disconnect, discontinue) cortar: our phone's been cut off nos han cortado el teléfono. **3** (isolate, separate) aislar: she felt cut off se sentía aislada.
◆ to cut out vt sep **1** (from newspaper) recortar; (in sewing) cortar. **2** (exclude) suprimir, eliminar.
ⓘ pt & pp cut, ger cutting.

cutaneous [kjuː'teɪnɪəs] adj cutáneo,-a.

cute [kjuːt] adj **1** (sweet) mono,-a, rico, -a; (good-looking) guapo,-a, lindo,-a. **2** US (clever) listo,-a.

cutlery ['kʌtlərɪ] n cubiertos mpl, cubertería.

cutlet ['kʌtlət] n CULIN chuleta.

cutout ['kʌtaʊt] n **1** (shape) recortable m. **2** (device, switch) cortacircuitos m.

cutter ['kʌtəʳ] n (tool) cúter m.

cutting ['kʌtɪŋ] n **1** (from newspaper) recorte m. **2** BOT esqueje m.

cuttlefish ['kʌtⁿlfɪʃ] n jibia, sepia.

cyanide ['saɪənaɪd] n cianuro.

cybernetics [saɪbə'netɪks] n cibernética.

cycle ['saɪkⁿl] n **1** (series of events, of songs, etc) ciclo; (of washing machine) programa m. **2** (bicycle) bicicleta; (motorcycle) moto f. COMP cycle lane/path/way carril m bici. ‖ cycle track velódromo.
▶ vi ir en bicicleta.

cyclic ['sɪklɪk, 'saɪklɪk] adj cíclico,-a.

cyclical ['sɪklɪkⁿl, 'saɪklɪkⁿl] adj cíclico,-a.

cycling ['saɪklɪŋ] n ciclismo.

cyclist ['saɪklɪst] n ciclista mf.

cyclone ['saɪkləʊn] n ciclón m.

cygnet ['sɪgnət] n pollo de cisne.

cylinder ['sɪlɪndəʳ] n **1** (gen) cilindro. **2** (for gas) bombona.

cylindrical [sɪ'lɪndrɪkⁿl] adj cilíndrico,-a.

cymbal ['sɪmbⁿl] n címbalo, platillo.

cynic ['sɪnɪk] n cínico,-a.

cynical ['sɪnɪkⁿl] adj cínico,-a.

cynicism ['sɪnɪsɪzⁿm] n cinismo.

cypress ['saɪprəs] n ciprés m.

Cypriot ['sɪprɪət] adj chipriota,-a.
▶ n **1** (person) chipriota mf. **2** (language) chipriota m.

Cyprus ['saɪprəs] n Chipre m.

cyst [sɪst] n quiste m.

cystitis [sɪ'staɪtɪs] n cistitis f.

czar [zɑːʳ] n zar m.

Czech [tʃek] adj checo,-a.
▶ n **1** (person) checo,-a. **2** (language) checo. COMP Czech Republic República Checa.

Czechia ['tʃekɪə] n Chequia.

D

D, d [di:] *n* **1** *(the letter)* D, d *f*. **2** MUS re *m*.

'd [əd] *aux* **1** → **would.** *I'd go* iría. **2** → **had:** *he'd seen* había visto. **3** *fam* → **did.** *what'd you do?* ¿qué hiciste?

dab [dæb] *n (of paint)* toque *m*; *(of perfume)* gota; *(of butter)* poquito.
▸ *vi* dar ligeros toques (at, en).
▸ *n pl* **dabs** GB *sl* huellas *fpl* dactilares.

dabble ['dæbªl] *vi (in activity)* aficionarse (in, a), tener escarceos (in, con).
▸ *vt (in water)* chapotear.

dad [dæd] *n fam* papá *m*.

daddy ['dædɪ] *n fam* papá *m*, papi *m*.
ⓘ *pl* daddies.

daffodil ['dæfədɪl] *n* narciso.

dagger ['dægəʳ] *n* **1** *(weapon)* daga, puñal *m*. **2** *(obelisk)* cruz *f*.

daguerreotype [də'gerəutaɪp] *n* daguerrotipo.

dahlia ['deɪljə] *n* dalia.

daily ['deɪlɪ] *adj (newspaper, prayers)* diario,-a; *(routine)* diario,-a, cotidiano,-a.
▸ *adv* diariamente, a diario.
▸ *n (newspaper)* diario.
ⓘ *pl* dailies.

dainty ['deɪntɪ] *adj* **1** *(delicate - thing)* delicado,-a, fino,-a; *(- person)* precioso,-a, delicado,-a, refinado,-a.
ⓘ *comp* daintier, *superl* daintiest.
▸ *n pl* **dainties** *(small cakes)* pastelitos *mpl*.

dairy ['deərɪ] *n* **1** *(on farm)* vaquería. **2** *(shop)* lechería; *(company)* central *f* lechera. COMP **dairy products** productos lácteos. ‖ **dairy products** productos lácteos.
ⓘ *pl* dairies.

✎ No hay que confundir las palabras dairy con diary, que significa 'diario, agenda'.

dairymaid ['deərɪmeɪd] *n* lechera.

dairyman ['deərɪmən] *n* lechero.
ⓘ *pl* dairymen['deərɪmən].

dais [deɪz] *n* tarima.
ⓘ *pl* daises.

daisy ['deɪzɪ] *n* margarita.
ⓘ *pl* daisies.

daltonism ['dɔ:ltənɪzªm] *n* daltonismo.

dam¹ [dæm] *n* **1** *(barrier)* dique *m*. **2** *(reservoir)* embalse *m*, presa.
◆ **to dam up** *vt sep* **1** *(river)* represar, embalsar. **2** *(emotions)* reprimir, contener.
ⓘ *pt & pp* dammed, *ger* damming.

dam² [dæm] *n* ZOOL madre *f*.

damage ['dæmɪdʒ] *n (gen)* daño; *(to reputation, cause, health)* perjuicio, daños *mpl*; *(destruction)* destrozos *mpl*, daños *mpl*.

dame [deɪm] *n* **1** US *fam* mujer *f*, tía. **2** *(in pantomime)* vieja *(representada por un hombre)*.
▸ *n* **Dame** GB *(title)* título honorífico concedido a una mujer.

damn [dæm] *interj fam* ¡mecachis!, ¡caray!
▸ *adj fam* maldito,-a, condenado,-a.
▸ *adv fam* muy, sumamente: *you were damn lucky* tuviste mucha suerte.
▸ *vt* **1** REL condenar. **2** *(curse)* maldecir: *damn it!* ¡maldita sea!

damned [dæmd] *adj* **1** *fam* maldito,-a, condenado,-a. **2** REL condenado,-a.

damp [dæmp] *adj (gen)* húmedo,-a; *(wet)* mojado,-a. COMP **damp course** aislante *m* hidrófugo.
▸ *n* humedad *f*.

dampen ['dæmpªn] *vt* **1** *(make damp)* humedecer. **2** *fig (enthusiasm, ardour, etc)* hacer perder, apagar, enfriar; *(person's spirits)* desanimar.

damsel ['dæmzəl] *n* doncella.

dance [dɑːns] *n (gen)* baile *m*; *(classical, tribal)* danza.
▸ *vi* bailar.

dancer ['dɑːnsəʳ] *n* bailarín,-ina; *(flamenco)* bailaor,-ra.

dandelion ['dændɪlaɪən] *n* diente *m* de león.

dandruff ['dændrʌf] *n* caspa.

dandy ['dændɪ] *n* dandy *m*, petimetre *m*.
ⓘ *pl* dandies.
▸ *adj* US *fam* estupendo,-a.

danger ['deɪndʒəʳ] *n (peril, hazard)* peligro; *(risk)* riesgo.

dangerous ['deɪndʒərəs] *adj (gen)* peligroso,-a; *(risky)* arriesgado,-a; *(illness)* grave.

dangle ['dæŋgəl] *vt (hang)* colgar; *(swing)* balancear.
▸ *vi* colgar, pender.

Danish ['deɪnɪʃ] *adj* danés,-esa.
▸ *n (language)* danés *m*.
▸ *n pl* **the Danish** los daneses *mpl*.

dank [dæŋk] *adj* húmedo,-a y frío,-a.

dare [deəʳ] *vi* atreverse **(to**, a), osar **(to**, -).
▸ *vt (challenge)* desafiar.
▸ *n* desafío, reto.

daredevil ['deədevəl] *n* atrevido,-a, temerario,-a.

daring ['deərɪŋ] *adj (bold, brave)* audaz, osado,-a, atrevido,-a.
▸ *n* osadía, atrevimiento, audacia.

dark [dɑːk] *adj* **1** *(without light)* oscuro,-a. **2** *(hair, skin)* moreno,-a; *(eyes)* negro,-a. **3** *(gloomy)* triste, sombrío,-a. **4** *(sinister)* siniestro,-a, tenebroso,-a. **5** *(secret)* misterioso,-a.
▸ *n* **1** *(darkness)* oscuridad *f*. **2** *(nightfall)* anochecer *m*.

darken ['dɑːkən] *vt* **1** oscurecer, hacer más oscuro,-a. **2** *fig* entristecer, ensombrecer.

darkness ['dɑːknəs] *n* oscuridad *f*.

darling ['dɑːlɪŋ] *n (lover)* querido,-a, amor *m*, cariño; *(popular person)* niño,-a mimado,-a.
▸ *adj* **1** *(loved)* querido,-a. **2** *fam (charming)* precioso,-a, encantador,-ra, mono,-a.

darn [dɑːn] *n* zurcido.
▸ *vt (sock, etc)* zurcir.

darnel ['dɑːnəl] *n* cizaña.

dart [dɑːt] *n* **1** *(object)* dardo, flechilla. **2** *(rush)* movimiento rápido. **3** SEW *(fold)* pinza.
▸ *vt (look, glance)* lanzar; *(tongue)* disparar.
▸ *vi (move quickly - person)* precipitarse; *(- butterfly, etc)* revolotear.

dartboard ['dɑːtbɔːd] *n* diana, blanco de tiro.

dash [dæʃ] *n* **1** *(sudden run)* carrera. **2** *(small amount)* poco; *(of salt, spice)* pizca; *(of liquid)* chorrito, gota. **3** *(horizontal mark)* raya; *(hyphen)* guion *m*; *(in Morse code)* raya. **4** *(style, panache)* elegancia; *(energy, vitality)* brío, dinamismo. **5** US *(dashboard)* salpicadero.
▸ *vt* **1** *(hit)* lanzar, arrojar; *(smash)* romper, estrellar. **2** *(hopes)* truncar.

dashboard ['dæʃbɔːd] *n* salpicadero.

data ['deɪtə] *n pl* datos *mpl*, información *f*.
ⓘ *sing* datum.

database ['deɪtəbeɪs] *n* COMPUT base *f* de datos.

date¹ [deɪt] *n* **1** *(in time)* fecha. **2** *(appointment)* cita, compromiso: *I've got a date with David tonight* tengo una cita con David esta noche. **3** US *(person)* ligue *m*, amigo,-a, pareja. **4** *(performance, booking)* actuación *f*.
▸ *vt* **1** *(write a date on)* fechar. **2** *(determine the date of)* datar. **3** *(show the age of)* demostrar la edad de. **4** US *fam (go out with)* salir con.
▸ *vi* **1** *(have existed since)* datar **(from**, de), remontarse **(back to**, a). **2** *(go out of fashion)* pasar de moda. **3** US *(go out together)* salir juntos, ser novios.

date² [deɪt] *n (fruit)* dátil *m*.

dated ['deɪtɪd] *adj* anticuado,-a.

dative ['deɪtɪv] *n* LING dativo.

datum ['deɪtəm] *n* dato.
ⓘ *pl* data.

daub [dɔːb] *n* **1** *(small bit, smear)* mancha. **2** *(bad painting)* pintarrajo.
▸ *vt* embadurnar.

daughter ['dɔːtəʳ] *n* hija.

daughter-in-law ['dɔːtərɪnlɔː] *n* nuera.

daunt [dɔ:nt] *vt (frighten)* intimidar; *(dishearten)* desanimar, desalentar.

dauphin ['dɔ:fɪn] *n* delfín *m*.

dawn [dɔ:n] *n* alba, aurora, amanecer *m*.
▶ *vi* amanecer, alborear, clarear.

day [deɪ] *n* día *m*. LOC **the day after tomorrow** pasado mañana. ▌**the day before tomorrow** anteayer. COMP **day off** día libre.
▶ *n pl* **days** *(period)* época, tiempos *mpl*.

daybreak ['deɪbreɪk] *n* amanecer *m*, alba.

daydream ['deɪdri:m] *n* ensueño, ensoñación *f*.
▶ *vi* soñar despierto,-a, fantasear.

daytime ['deɪtaɪm] *n* día *m*.
▶ *adj (flight)* diurno,-a.

daze [deɪz] *n* aturdimiento.
▶ *vt* aturdir.

D-day ['di:deɪ] *n* **1** *(in war)* día *m* D. **2** *(important date)* el día *m* señalado.

deacon ['di:kən] *n* diácono.

deactivate [di:'æktɪveɪt] *vt* desactivar.

dead [ded] *adj* **1** *(not alive)* muerto,-a. **2** *(obsolete - language)* muerto,-a; *(- custom)* desusado,-a, en desuso; *(finished with - topic, issue, debate)* agotado,-a, pasado,-a; *(- glass, bottle)* terminado,-a, acabado,-a. **3** *(numb)* entumecido,-a, dormido,-a. **4** *(not functioning - telephone)* desconectado,-a, cortado,-a; *(- machine)* averiado,-a; *(- battery)* descargado,-a, gastado,-a; *(- match)* gastado,-a. **5** *fam (very tired)* muerto,-a. **6** *(dull, quiet, not busy)* muerto,-a. **7** *(sounds)* sordo,-a; *(colours)* apagado,-a. **8** SP *(ball)* muerto,-a. **9** *(total)* total, completo,-a, absoluto,-a.
▶ *adv* **1** *(completely, absolutely)* completamente, sumamente; *(as intensifier)* muy: *I'm dead sure* estoy segurísimo. **2** *(exactly)* justo: *we arrived dead on time* llegamos puntualísimos.
▶ *n* **the dead** los,-las muertos,-as.

deaden ['dedən] *vt (pain)* calmar, aliviar; *(noise, blow)* amortiguar.

deadline ['dedlaɪn] *n (date)* fecha límite, fecha tope, plazo de entrega; *(time)* hora límite, hora tope.

deadlock ['dedlɒk] *n* punto muerto, impasse *m*.

deaf [def] *adj* sordo,-a.
▶ *n* **the deaf** los sordos *mpl*.

deaf-aid ['defeɪd] *n* audífono.

deafen ['defən] *vt* ensordecer.

deaf-mute ['defmju:t] *n* sordomudo,-a.

deafness ['defnəs] *n* sordera.

deal [di:l] *n* **1** *(agreement)* trato, acuerdo, pacto; *(financial)* acuerdo. **2** *(treatment)* trato. **3** *(amount)* cantidad *f*. **4** *(in card games)* reparto.
▶ *vt* **1** *(cards)* repartir, dar. **2** *(drugs)* traficar.
◆ **to deal with** *vt insep* **1** COMM *(trade with)* tratar con, tener relaciones comerciales con. **2** *(tackle - problem, etc)* abordar, ocuparse de; *(- task)* encargarse de; *(- person)* tratar (con), lidiar con.
ⓘ *pt & pp* **dealt** [delt].

dealer ['di:lər] *n* **1** COMM comerciante *mf*, negociante *mf*; *(illegal - in drugs)* traficante *mf*; *(- in stolen goods)* perista *mf*. **3** FIN corredor,-ra de bolsa, corredor,-ra de valores.

dealt [delt] *pt & pp* → **deal**.

dean [di:n] *n* **1** REL deán *m*. **2** EDUC decano,-a.

deanery ['di:nərɪ] *n* decanato.

dear [dɪər] *adj* **1** *(loved - person)* querido,-a; *(- thing)* preciado,-a. **2** *(as form of address)* querido,-a. **3** *fam (in letter)* querido,-a; *(more formally)* apreciado,-a, estimado,-a. **4** *(expensive)* caro,-a.
▶ *interj* ¡Dios mío!
▶ *adv* caro.

dearly ['dɪəlɪ] *adv* **1** *(very much)* mucho. **2** *(at a cost)* caro.

death [deθ] *n* **1** *(gen)* muerte *f*; *(decease, demise)* fallecimiento, defunción *f*. **2** *(end - of custom, institution)* fin *m*. COMP **death penalty** pena de muerte.

deathtrap ['deθtræp] *n fam* lugar peligroso.

debacle [deɪ'bɑ:kəl] *n* debacle *m*.

debate [dɪ'beɪt] *n* debate *m*.
▶ *vt* **1** *(discuss)* debatir, discutir. **2** *(consider, think over)* considerar, dar vueltas a.

debit ['dɛbɪt] *n* FIN débito.
▸ *vt* cargar en cuenta.

debrief [di:'bri:f] *vt* interrogar.

debris ['deɪbri:] *n (ruins)* escombros *mpl*; *(wreckage)* restos *mpl*.

debt [det] *n (something owed)* deuda; *(indebtedness)* endeudamiento.

debtor ['detə'] *n* deudor,-ra.

debug [di:'bʌg] *vt* **1** *(computer programme, system)* depurar. **2** *(room, building, etc)* quitar los micrófonos ocultos de.
ⓘ *pt & pp* debugged, *ger* debugging.

debunk [di:'bʌŋk] *vt fam (person)* desmitificar, desenmascarar; *(idea, belief)* desacreditar, desprestigiar.

debut ['deɪbju:] *n* debut *m*.

decade ['dekeɪd] *n* década, decenio.

decadence ['dekədəns] *n* decadencia.

decaffeinated [di:'kæfɪneɪtɪd] *adj* descafeinado,-a.

decagon ['dekəgɒn] *n* decágono.

decagonal [dɪ'kægənəl] *adj* decagonal.

decahedron [dekə'hi:drən] *n* decaedro.

decalitre ['dekəli:tə'] *n* decalitro.

decanter [dɪ'kæntə'] *n* decantador *m*.

decapitation [dɪkæpɪ'teɪʃən] *n* decapitación *f*.

decapod ['dekəpɒd] *n* decápodo.

decasyllable [dekə'sɪləbəl] *n* decasílabo.

decathlete [dɪ'kæθli:t] *n* decatleta *m*.

decathlon [dɪ'kæθlɒn] *n* decatlón *m*.

decay [dɪ'keɪ] *n* **1** *(of organic matter)* descomposición *f*; *(of teeth)* caries *f*. **2** *(of building)* deterioro, desmoronamiento. **3** *fig (of culture, values)* decadencia.

decease [dɪ'si:s] *n* fallecimiento, defunción *f*.

deceit [dɪ'si:t] *n (trick)* engaño; *(deceiving)* falsedad *f*.

deceive [dɪ'si:v] *vt* engañar.

decelerate [di:'seləreɪt] *vi* reducir la velocidad, desacelerar.

December [dɪ'sembə'] *n* diciembre *m*.

✎ Para ejemplos de uso, consulta May.

decency ['di:sənsɪ] *n* **1** *(seemliness)* decencia, decoro. **2** *(politeness)* buena educación *f*, cortesía, consideración *f*.
ⓘ *pl* decencies.

decennial [dɪ'senɪəl] *n* decenal.

decent ['di:sənt] *adj* decente.

decentralize [di:'sentrəlaɪz] *vt* descentralizar.

deception [dɪ'sepʃən] *n (trick)* engaño; *(deceiving)* falsedad *f*.

⊠ Deception no significa 'decepción', que se traduce por disappointment.

deceptive [dɪ'septɪv] *adj* engañoso,-a: *appearances can be deceptive* las apariencias engañan.

decibel ['desɪbel] *n* decibelio.

decide [dɪ'saɪd] *vt* decidir.

deciduous [dɪ'sɪdjʊəs] *adj* de hoja caduca.

decigram ['desɪgræm] *n* decigramo.

decilitre ['desɪli:tə'] *n* decilitro.

decimal ['desɪməl] *n* decimal *m*. COMP decimal point coma decimal.

decimate ['desɪmeɪt] *vt* diezmar.

decimation [desɪ'meɪʃən] *n* reducción *f* catastrófica, acción de diezmar.

decimetre ['desɪmi:tə'] *n* decímetro.

decipher [dɪ'saɪfə'] *vt* descifrar.

decision [dɪ'sɪʒən] *n* **1** *(choice, verdict)* decisión *f*. **2** *(resolution)* resolución *f*, decisión *f*, determinación *f*.

decisive [dɪ'saɪsɪv] *adj* **1** *(conclusive - gen)* decisivo,-a; *(- victory)* contundente. **2** *(firm, resolute - person)* decidido,-a, resuelto,-a; *(- reply, action)* firme.

deck [dek] *n* **1** *(of ship)* cubierta. **2** *(of bus, coach)* piso. **3** US *(of cards)* baraja. **4** *(of record player)* plato. **5** US *(raised roofless area)* terraza.

deckchair ['dektʃeə'] *n* tumbona.

declaim [dɪ'kleɪm] *vt* declamar.
▸ *vi* declamar.

declamation [deklə'meɪʃən] *n* declamación *f*.

declarant [dɪ'kleərənt] *n* declarante *mf*.

declaration [deklə'reɪʃən] *n* declaración *f*.

declare [dɪ'kleə'] *vt* **1** *(gen)* declarar; *(opinion)* manifestar. **2** *(at customs)* declarar.

declassify [dɪ'klæsɪfaɪ] *vt* desclasificar.
ⓘ *pt & pp* declassified, *ger* declassifying.

D

declination [deklɪˈneɪʃ°n] *n* declinación *f*, variación *f*. COMP **magnetic declination** variación *f* magnética.

decline [dɪˈklaɪn] *n* **1** *(decrease)* disminución *f*, descenso. **2** *(deterioration - gen)* deterioro, declive *m*, decadencia; *(in health)* deterioro, empeoramiento.

decode [diːˈkəʊd] *vt* decodificar, descodificar.

decompose [diːkəmˈpəʊz] *vt* descomponer.
▶ *vi* **1** descomponerse, pudrirse. **2** CHEM descomponerse.

decomposer [diːkəmˈpəʊzəʳ] *n* saprótrofo.

decompress [dɪkəmˈpres] *vt* someter a descompresión.

decompression [dɪkəmˈpreʃ°n] *n* descompresión *f*.

decongestion [diːkənˈdʒetʃ°n] *n* descongestión *f*.

decontaminate [diːkənˈtæmɪneɪt] *vt* descontaminar.

decor [ˈdeɪkɔːʳ] *n* **1** *(furnishings)* decoración *f*. **2** THEAT decorado.

decorate [ˈdekəreɪt] *vt* **1** *(adorn, make beautiful)* decorar (with, con), adornar (with, con). **2** *(paint)* pintar; *(wallpaper)* empapelar. **3** *(honour)* condecorar (for, por).

decoration [dekəˈreɪʃ°n] *n* **1** *(act, art)* decoración *f*. **2** *(ornament)* adorno. **3** *(medal)* condecoración *f*.

decorator [ˈdekəreɪtəʳ] *n* *(designer)* decorador,-ra, interiorista *mf*; *(painter)* pintor,-ra; *(wallpaperer)* empapelador,-ra.

decoy [ˈdiːkɔɪ] *n* **1** *(bird)* cimbel *m*; *(in hunting)* señuelo, reclamo. **2** *fig (lure)* señuelo, carnada, gancho.

decrease [dɪˈkriːs] *n* disminución *f*, descenso.
▶ *vt* disminuir, reducir.

decreasing [dɪˈkriːsɪŋ] *adj* decreciente.

decree [dɪˈkriː] *n* **1** *(command)* decreto. **2** US *(judgement)* sentencia.
▶ *vt* decretar.

decriminalize [diːˈkrɪmɪn°laɪz] *vt* despenalizar.

dedicate [ˈdedɪkeɪt] *vt* dedicar.

dedicatory [ˈdedɪkət°rɪ] *adj* dedicatorio,-a.

deduce [dɪˈdjuːs] *vt* deducir (from, de).

deduct [dɪˈdʌkt] *vt* *(gen)* descontar, deducir; *(from taxes)* desgravar.

deduction [dɪˈdʌkʃ°n] *n* **1** *(subtraction)* deducción *f*, descuento; *(from taxes)* desgravación *f*. **2** *(reasoning)* deducción *f*.

deed [diːd] *n* **1** *lit (act)* acto, acción *f*, obra; *(feat)* hazaña, proeza. **2** JUR escritura.

deejay [ˈdiːdʒeɪ] *n* pinchadiscos *mf*, discjockey *mf*.

deep [diːp] *adj* **1** *(river, hole, well, etc)* hondo,-a, profundo,-a. **2** *(shelf, wardrobe)* de fondo; *(hem, border)* ancho,-a. **3** *(sound, voice)* grave, bajo,-a; *(note)* grave; *(breath)* hondo,-a.
▶ *adv* **1** *(to a great depth)* profundamente. **2** *(far from the outside)* lejos. **3** *(far in time, late)* tarde.

deepen [ˈdiːp°n] *vt* **1** *(well, channel, river)* profundizar, hacer más profundo,-a. **2** *(knowledge)* profundizar, ahondar; *(sympathy)* aumentar; *(colour, emotion)* intensificar; *(sound, voice)* hacer más grave.

deep-freeze [ˈdiːpˈfriːz] *n* congelador *m*.
▶ *vt* *(at home)* congelar; *(commercially)* ultracongelar.
ⓘ *pt* deep-froze [diːpˈfrəʊz], *pp* deep-frozen [diːpˈfrəʊz°n].

deep-sea [ˈdiːpsiː] *n* *(fishing, diving)* de altura.

deer [dɪəʳ] *n* ciervo, venado.
ⓘ *pl* deer.

default [dɪˈfɔːlt] *n* **1** *(failure to act)* omisión *f*, negligencia. **2** *(failure to pay)* incumplimiento de pago, mora, demora.
▶ *vi* **1** *(fail to act)* faltar a sus compromisos, incumplir un acuerdo. **2** *(fail to pay)* no pagar (on, -), demorarse (on, en).

defeat [dɪˈfiːt] *n* **1** *(of army, team)* derrota; *(of motion, bill)* rechazo. **2** *fig (of hopes, plans)* fracaso.
▶ *vt* **1** *(gen)* derrotar, vencer. **2** *fig (hopes, plans)* frustrar.

defect [*(n)* ˈdiːfekt; *(vb)* dɪˈfekt] *n* *(gen)* defecto; *(flaw)* desperfecto, tara.

▸ *vi (party, team)* desertar, pasarse al bando contrario; *(country)* huir.

defective [dɪ'fektɪv] *adj* **1** *(faulty)* defectuoso,-a; *(flawed)* con desperfectos; *(incomplete, lacking)* deficiente. **2** LING defectivo,-a

defence [dɪ'fens] *n* defensa.

defend [dɪ'fend] *vt* defender.
▸ *vi* SP jugar de defensa.

defendant [dɪ'fendənt] *n* JUR *(in civil case)* demandado,-a; *(in criminal case)* acusado,-a.

defender [dɪ'fendər] *n* **1** *(gen)* defensor,-ra. **2** SP defensa *mf*.

defense [dɪ'fens] *n* US → **defence**.

defensive [dɪ'fensɪv] *adj* defensivo,-a.

defer¹ [dɪ'fɜːr] *vt (postpone)* aplazar, posponer, retrasar.
① *pt & pp* **deferred**, *ger* **deferring**.

defer² [dɪ'fɜːr] *vi (submit to)* deferir (to, a).
① *pt & pp* **deferred**, *ger* **deferring**.

defiance [dɪ'faɪəns] *n* desafío.

defiant [dɪ'faɪənt] *adj* desafiante.

deficiency [dɪ'fɪʃənsɪ] *n* **1** *(lack)* deficiencia; *(shortage)* escasez *f*, falta, déficit *m*. **2** *(fault, shortcoming)* defecto, deficiencia.
① *pl* **deficiencies**.

deficient [dɪ'fɪʃənt] *adj* deficiente.

deficit ['defɪsɪt] *n* déficit *m*.

define [dɪ'faɪn] *vt* definir.

definite ['defɪnət] *adj* **1** *(final, fixed - gen)* definitivo,-a; *(- opinions)* fijo,-a. **2** *(clear, distinct)* claro,-a.

definitely ['defɪnətlɪ] *adv* **1** *(without doubt)* sin duda, seguramente. **2** *(definitively)* definitivamente.
▸ *interj* ¡desde luego!, ¡claro que sí!

definition [defɪ'nɪʃən] *n* definición *f*.

definitive [dɪ'fɪnɪtɪv] *adj* **1** *(final, conclusive)* definitivo,-a. **2** *(ultimate - study, etc)* de mayor autoridad.

deflate [dɪ'fleɪt] *vt (balloon, tyre)* desinflar, deshinchar.

deflation [dɪ'fleɪʃən] *n* **1** *(of balloon, tyre)* desinflamiento. **2** *(economic)* deflación *f*.

deflect [dɪ'flekt] *vt* desviar.
▸ *vi* desviarse.

deforest [diː'fɒrɪst] *vt* deforestar.

deform [dɪ'fɔːm] *vt* deformar.

deformation [diːfɔː'meɪʃən] *n* deformación *f*.

deformed [dɪ'fɔːmd] *adj* deforme.

defraud [dɪ'frɔːd] *vt* estafar.

> ☒ To **defraud** no significa 'defraudar (decepcionar)', que se traduce por to **disappoint**.

defrost [diː'frɒst] *vt* **1** *(freezer, food)* descongelar. **2** US *(windscreen)* desempañar.

deft [deft] *adj* diestro,-a, hábil.

defunct [dɪ'fʌŋkt] *adj* difunto,-a.

defy [dɪ'faɪ] *vt* **1** *(gen)* desafiar; *(disobey - law, order, authority)* desobedecer, desacatar. **2** *(make impossible)* ser imposible.
① *pt & pp* **defied**, *ger* **defying**.

degenerate [*(adj-n)* dɪ'dʒenərət; *(vb)* dɪ'dʒenəreɪt] *adj* degenerado,-a.
▸ *n* degenerado,-a.
▸ *vi* degenerar (Into, en).

degenerative [dɪ'dʒenərətɪv] *adj* degenerativo,-a.

degradation [degrə'deɪʃən] *n* degradación *f*.

degrade [dɪ'greɪd] *vt* degradar.

degree [dɪ'griː] *n* **1** *(unit of measurement)* grado. **2** *(extent, level, point)* nivel *m*, punto; *(amount)* algo. **3** EDUC título.

dehumanize [diː'hjuːmənaɪz] *vt* deshumanizar.

dehydrate [diːhaɪ'dreɪt] *vt* deshidratar.
▸ *vi* deshidratarse.

de-icing [diː'aɪsɪŋ] *n* deshielo.

deification [diːɪfɪ'keɪʃən] *n* deificación *f*.

deign [deɪn] *vi* dignarse (to, a).

deity ['deɪtɪ] *n* deidad *f*.
① *pl* **deities**.

dejection [dɪ'dʒekʃən] *n* abatimiento, desaliento, desánimo.

delay [dɪ'leɪ] *n* retraso.
▸ *vt* **1** *(gen)* aplazar, retrasar. **2** *(make late - flight, train)* retrasar, demorar; *(person)* entretener.

delayed [dɪ'leɪd] *adj* con retraso.

delegate [*(adj-n)* 'delɪgət; *(vb)* 'delɪgeɪt] *n* delegado,-a.
▸ *vt (duties, responsibility, etc)* delegar (to, en).

delegation [delɪ'geɪʃən] *n* delegación *f*.

delete [dɪ'liːt] *vt (remove)* eliminar, suprimir; *(cross out)* tachar.

deliberate [*(adj)* dɪ'lɪbªrət; *(vb)* dɪ'lɪbəreɪt] *adj* **1** *(intentional)* deliberado,-a, intencionado,-a; *(studied)* premeditado,-a. **2** *(slow, unhurried)* pausado,-a, lento,-a; *(careful)* reflexivo,-a.
▶ *vi* deliberar (on, sobre).

delicacy ['delɪkəsɪ] *n* **1** *(softness, tenderness)* delicadeza. **2** *(fragility)* fragilidad *f*. **3** *(food)* exquisitez *f*.
ⓘ *pl* delicacies.

delicate ['delɪkət] *adj* **1** *(fine - gen)* delicado,-a; *(- embroidery, handiwork)* fino,-a, esmerado,-a. **2** *(easily damaged)* frágil. **3** *(sensitive - instrument)* sensible; *(- sense of smell, taste)* fino,-a.

delicatessen [delɪkə'tesªn] *n* charcutería.

delicious [dɪ'lɪʃəs] *adj* delicioso,-a.

delight [dɪ'laɪt] *n* **1** *(great pleasure, joy)* placer *m*, gusto, alegría, deleite *m*. **2** *(source of pleasure)* encanto, delicia, placer *m*.
▶ *vi* deleitarse (in, en/con).

delighted [dɪ'laɪtɪd] *adj (person)* encantado,-a, contentísimo,-a; *(smile, shout, look)* de alegría.

delinquency [dɪ'lɪŋkwənsɪ] *n* **1** *(behaviour)* delincuencia. **2** *(act)* delito.

delinquent [dɪ'lɪŋkwənt] *adj* **1** *(youth)* delincuente; *(activity)* delictivo,-a. **2** FIN *(person)* moroso,-a.
▶ *n* delincuente *mf*.

delirious [dɪ'lɪrɪəs] *adj* **1** MED delirante. **2** *fig (happy)* loco,-a de alegría.

deliver [dɪ'lɪvəʳ] *vt* **1** *(gen)* entregar; *(distribute)* repartir (a domicilio). **2** *(hit, kick, push)* dar; *(shot, fast ball)* lanzar. **3** *(say)* pronunciar. **4** *(produce, provide, fulfil)* cumplir. **5** MED *(baby)* asistir en el parto de, atender en el parto de.

delivery [dɪ'lɪvªrɪ] *n* **1** *(act - gen)* entrega, reparto; *(- of mail)* reparto. **2** *(consignment)* partida, remesa. **3** *(manner of speaking)* modo de hablar. **4** *(of baby)* parto. **5** *(throwing, launching - of ball, missile)* lanzamiento. COMP **delivery note** albarán de entrega.
ⓘ *pl* deliveries.

delta ['deltə] *n* **1** GEOG delta *m*. **2** *(Greek letter)* delta.

deltoid ['deltɔɪd] *adj* deltoides.
▶ *n* deltoides *m*.

delude [dɪ'luːd] *vt* engañar.

deluge ['deljuːdʒ] *n* **1** *(rain)* diluvio; *(flood)* inundación *f*. **2** *fig* avalancha, alud *m*.

delusion [dɪ'luːʒªn] *n* **1** *(false belief)* falsa ilusión *f*; *(mistaken idea)* error *m*. **2** *(act, state)* engaño.

de luxe [də'lʌks] *adj* de lujo.

demagogue ['deməgɒg] *n* demagogo,-a.

demagogy ['deməgɒgɪ] *n* demagogia.

demand [dɪ'mɑːnd] *n* **1** *(request)* solicitud *f*, petición *f*; *(claim)* exigencia; *(for pay rise, rights, etc)* reclamación *f*. **2** COMM demanda. **3** *(note, warning)* aviso.
▶ *vt (call for, insist on)* exigir; *(rights, conditions, etc)* reclamar.

demanding [dɪ'mɑːndɪŋ] *adj* **1** *(person - gen)* exigente; *(awkward)* difícil. **2** *(tiring - job, etc)* agotador,-ra.

dementia [dɪ'menʃɪə] *n* demencia.

demise [dɪ'maɪz] *n* **1** *(death)* fallecimiento, defunción *f*. **2** *fig (end)* desaparición *f*, *(failure)* fracaso.

demist [diː'mɪst] *vt* desempañar.

demo ['deməʊ] *n* **1** *(recording, tape)* maqueta. **2** *fam (demonstration)* manifa *f*, manifestación *f*. **3** INFORM demo.
ⓘ *pl* demos.

demobilize [diː'məʊbɪlaɪz] *vt* desmovilizar.

democracy [dɪ'mɒkrəsɪ] *n* democracia.
ⓘ *pl* democracies.

democrat ['deməkræt] *n* demócrata *mf*.

demography [dɪ'mɒgrəfɪ] *n* demografía.

demolish [dɪ'mɒlɪʃ] *vt* derribar, demoler, echar abajo.

demolition [demə'lɪʃªn] *n* demolición *f*, derribo.

demon ['diːmən] *n* demonio, diablo.

demonstrate ['demənstreɪt] *vt* demostrar.
▶ *vi (protest)* manifestarse.

demonstration [deməˈstreɪʃ°n] n **1** *(act of showing)* demostración f, muestra. **3** *(march)* manifestación f.

demonstrative [dɪˈmɒnstrətɪv] adj **1** *(person - showing feelings)* abierto,-a, expresivo,-a. **3** LING demostrativo,-a.

demonstrator [ˈdemənstreɪtəʳ] n POL manifestante mf.

demoralize [dɪˈmɒr°laɪz] vt desmoralizar.

den [den] n **1** *(of animals)* guarida. **2** *(secret meeting-place)* antro. **3** fam *(room)* cuarto; *(for study)* estudio.

denarius [dɪˈneərɪəs] n denario.
① pl **denarii** [dɪˈneərɪɪ].

denaturize [diːˈneɪtʃəraɪz] vt desnaturalizar.

dendrite [ˈdendraɪt] n dendrita.

denial [dɪˈnaɪəl] n **1** *(of accusation)* mentís m, desmentido **2** *(of principle)* negación f. **3** *(of rights, justice)* denegación f. **4** *(of request)* negativa, rechazo.

denim [ˈdenɪm] n tela vaquera.
► n pl **denims** vaqueros mpl, tejanos mpl.

Denmark [ˈdenmɑːk] n Dinamarca.

denominate [dɪˈnɒmɪneɪt] vt denominar.

denomination [dɪnɒmɪˈneɪʃ°n] n **1** REL confesión f. **2** *(standard of value)* valor m. **3** *(classification)* denominación f.

denominator [dɪˈnɒmɪneɪtəʳ] n MATH denominador m.

denounce [dɪˈnaʊns] vt denunciar.

dense [dens] adj denso,-a.

density [ˈdensɪtɪ] n *(gen)* densidad f.
① pl **densities**.

dent [dent] n *(in car, metal)* abolladura.
► vt *(car, metal)* abollar.

dentist [ˈdentɪst] n dentista mf.

dentistry [ˈdentɪstrɪ] n odontología.

denture [ˈdentʃəʳ] n *(plate)* prótesis f dental.
► n pl **dentures** dentadura f sing postiza.

deny [dɪˈnaɪ] vt **1** *(repudiate - accusation, fact)* negar; *(rumour, report)* desmentir; *(charge)* rechazar. **2** *(refuse - request)* denegar; *(- rights, equality)* privar de; *(- access)* negar.
① pt & pp **denied**, ger **denying**.

deodorant [diːˈəʊdərənt] n desodorante m.

deoxyribonucleic [diːɒksɪraɪbəʊnjuː-ˈkleɪk] n desoxirribonucleico,-a.

depart [dɪˈpɑːt] vi fml partir, salir.

department [dɪˈpɑːtmənt] n **1** *(in shop)* sección f; *(in company, organization)* departamento, sección f; *(in government)* ministerio. **2** fam *(responsibility)* campo, esfera, terreno.

departure [dɪˈpɑːtʃəʳ] n **1** *(of person)* partida, marcha; *(of plane, train, etc)* salida. **2** fig *(divergence)* desviación f; *(venture, type of activity)* innovación f.

depend [dɪˈpend] vi depender.
◆ **to depend on** vt confiar en.

depict [dɪˈpɪkt] vt **1** *(portray visually, in music)* pintar, representar, retratar. **2** *(describe in writing)* describir, retratar.

deplore [dɪˈplɔːʳ] vt deplorar.

deploy [dɪˈplɔɪ] vt **1** MIL desplegar. **2** *(use effectively)* utilizar, hacer uso de.

deport [dɪˈpɔːt] vt deportar.

deportee [diːpɔːˈtiː] n deportado,-a.

depose [dɪˈpəʊz] vt **1** *(remove from power - leader, president)* deponer, destituir; *(- king)* destronar. **2** JUR declarar, deponer.

deposit [dɪˈpɒzɪt] n **1** *(sediment)* sedimento, depósito; *(layer)* capa. **2** *(mining - of gold, etc)* yacimiento. **3** FIN *(payment into account)* depósito, ingreso.

☒ Deposit no significa 'depósito (recipiente)', que se traduce por **tank**.

depot [ˈdepəʊ] n *(storehouse)* almacén m.

depreciate [dɪˈpriːʃɪeɪt] vi FIN depreciarse.
► vt FIN depreciar, amortizar.

depress [dɪˈpres] vt **1** *(make sad)* deprimir. **2** *(reduce - prices, sales, wages)* reducir, disminuir. **3** fml *(press down)* pulsar, apretar.

depression [dɪˈpreʃ°n] n depresión f.

depressive [dɪˈpresɪv] adj depresivo,-a.

deprive [dɪˈpraɪv] vt privar (of, de).

depth [depθ] n *(of hole, swimming pool, mine, etc)* profundidad f; *(of cupboard, shelf)* fondo; *(of hem, border)* ancho.

deputation [depjʊ'teɪʃ°n] *n* delegación *f*.

deputy ['depjətɪ] *n* **1** *(substitute)* sustituto,-a, suplente *mf*. **2** POL diputado,-a. **3** US ayudante *mf* del shérif. COMP **deputy head** EDUC subdirector,-ra. ① *pl* deputies.

derby ['dɑ:bɪ] *n* **1** SP *(between two local teams)* derby *m*. **2** US *(horse race)* carrera (de caballos). **3** US *(bowler hat)* bombín *m*, sombrero (de) hongo. ① *pl* derbies.

derelict ['derɪlɪkt] *adj (building)* abandonado,-a, en ruinas.

deride [dɪ'raɪd] *vt* burlarse de, ridiculizar, reírse de.

derive [dɪ'raɪv] *vt (get, obtain)* sacar, recibir.
▶ *vi* **1** LING *(word)* derivar, derivarse (from, de). **2** *(stem from - problem, attitude)* provenir (from, de).

dermatitis [dɜ:mə'taɪtɪs] *n* dermatitis *f*.

dermis ['dɜ:mɪs] *n* dermis *f*.

derogatory [dɪ'rɒgət°rɪ] *adj (remark, attitude, article)* despectivo,-a; *(meaning, sense)* peyorativo,-a.

derrick ['derɪk] *n* **1** *(crane)* grúa. **2** *(tower over oil well)* torre *f* de perforación.

descend [dɪ'send] *vt* descender, bajar.

descent [dɪ'sent] *n (by plane, climbers, etc)* descenso, bajada; *(slope)* pendiente *f*, declive *m*.

describe [dɪ'skraɪb] *vt* **1** *(depict in words)* describir. **2** *(call, characterize)* calificar, definir. **3** *(move in shape)* describir; *(draw)* trazar.

desert¹ ['dezət] *n* desierto.

desert² [dɪ'zɜ:t] *vt (family, person, place)* abandonar; *(political party, idea)* desertar (from, de).

deserve [dɪ'zɜ:v] *vt* merecer, merecerse.

desiccation [desɪ'keɪʃ°n] *n* desecación *f*.

design [dɪ'zaɪn] *n* **1** ART *(gen)* diseño, dibujo. **2** *(plan, drawing)* plano, proyecto; *(sketch)* boceto; *(of dress)* patrón *m*; *(of product, model)* modelo. **3** *fig (purpose, intention)* plan *m*, intención, proyecto.
▶ *vt* **1** *(gen)* diseñar, proyectar; *(fashion, set, product)* diseñar; *(course, programme)* planear, estructurar. **2** *(develop for a purpose)* concebir, idear; *(intend, mean)* pensar, destinar.

designate [*(vb)* 'dezɪgneɪt; *(adj)* 'dezɪgnət] *vt* **1** *fml (indicate, mark, show)* indicar, señalar. **2** *(appoint)* designar, nombrar.

desire [dɪ'zaɪə°] *n* deseo.
▶ *vt fml* desear.

desist [dɪ'zɪst] *vi fml* desistir (from, de).

desk [desk] *n* **1** *(in school)* pupitre *m*; *(in office)* escritorio. **2** *(service area)* mostrador *m*. **3** *(newspaper office)* sección *f*.

desktop [desktɒp] *n* escritorio. COMP **desktop computer** ordenador de sobremesa. ▌ **desktop publishing** autoedición.

desolate ['desələt] *adj* **1** *(place)* deshabitado,-a, desierto,-a. **2** *(person - sad)* triste, desconsolado,-a; *(lonely)* solitario,-a.
▶ *vt* desolar.

despair [dɪs'peə°] *n* desesperación *f*.
▶ *vi* desesperar (of, de), desesperarse (of, por).

desperado [despə'rɑ:dəʊ] *n* forajido,-a.

desperate ['desp°rət] *adj (reckless, risky)* desesperado,-a.

despicable [dɪ'spɪkəb°l] *adj (person, act)* despreciable, vil; *(behaviour)* indigno,-a.

despise [dɪ'spaɪz] *vt* despreciar, menospreciar.

despite [dɪ'spaɪt] *prep* a pesar de: *she went to work despite having a bad cold* se fue a trabajar a pesar de estar muy resfriada.

despondent [dɪ'spɒndənt] *adj* desalentado,-a, desanimado,-a, abatido,-a.

despot ['despɒt] *n* déspota *mf*.

dessert [dɪ'zɜ:t] *n* postre *m*.

destabilize [di:'steɪbəlaɪz] *vt* desestabilizar.

destination [destɪ'neɪʃ°n] *n* destino.

destined ['destɪnd] *adj* **1** *(intended, meant)* destinado,-a. **2** *(fated)* condenado,-a, destinado,-a. **3** *(bound)* con destino (for, a).

destiny ['destɪnɪ] *n* destino, sino.
ⓘ *pl* **destinies**.

❌ Destiny no significa 'destino (punto de llegada)', que se traduce por **destination**.

destitute ['destɪtjuːt] *adj* indigente, mísero,-a.

❌ To destitute no significa 'destituir', que se traduce por **to dismiss**.

destroy [dɪ'strɔɪ] *vt* destruir.

destruction [dɪ'strʌkʃ⁰n] *n* destrucción *f*.

detach [dɪ'tætʃ] *vt* **1** *(separate, remove)* separar, quitar; *(unstick)* despegar: *you can detach the collar from the coat* se puede quitar el cuello del abrigo. **2** MIL destacar.

detached [dɪ'tætʃt] *adj* **1** *(separated - gen)* separado,-a, suelto,-a. **2** *(person, manner - impartial)* objetivo,-a, imparcial, *(- aloof)* distante, indiferente. COMP **detached house** vivienda unifamiliar.

detail ['diːteɪl] *n* detalle *m*, pormenor *m*.
▶ *vt* **1** *(describe)* detallar. **2** MIL destacar.
▶ *n pl* **details** *(information)* información *f*; *(particulars)* datos *mpl*.

detain [dɪ'teɪn] *vt* **1** *(hold - in custody)* detener. **2** *(delay)* entretener, demorar.

detainee [diːteɪ'niː] *n* detenido,-a.

detect [dɪ'tekt] *vt* **1** *(gen)* detectar. **2** *(discover - crime, criminal, fraud)* descubrir.

detective [dɪ'tektɪv] *n* *(private)* detective *mf*; *(in police force)* agente *mf*, oficial *mf*.

detector [dɪ'tektər] *n* detector *m*.

detente ['deɪtɒnt] *n* distensión *f*.

detention [dɪ'tenʃ⁰n] *n* **1** JUR *(of suspect)* detención *f*, arresto. **2** EDUC *(of pupil)* castigo.

deter [dɪ'tɜːr] *vt* **1** *(person - dissuade)* disuadir (from, de). **2** *(prevent, stop)* impedir.
ⓘ *pt & pp* **deterred**, *ger* **deterring**.

detergent [dɪ'tɜːdʒənt] *n* detergente *m*.

deteriorate [dɪ'tɪərɪəreɪt] *vi* *(economy, health, situation, relations, material)* deteriorarse; *(weather, work)* empeorar.

deterioration [dɪtɪərɪə'reɪʃ⁰n] *n* *(gen)* empeoramiento; *(of material)* deterioro.

determination [dɪtɜːmɪ'neɪʃ⁰n] *n* determinación *f*.

determine [dɪ'tɜːmɪn] *vt* determinar.

determined [dɪ'tɜːmɪnd] *adj* *(person)* decidido,-a, resuelto,-a; *(attempt, effort)* enérgico,-a, persistente.

❌ Determined no significa 'determinado (cierto)', que se traduce por **particular**.

determiner [dɪ'tɜːmɪnər] *n* LING determinante *m*.

deterrent [dɪ'terənt] *adj* disuasivo,-a, disuasorio,-a.
▶ *n* fuerza disuasoria, fuerza disuasiva.

detest [dɪ'test] *vt* detestar, odiar, aborrecer: *I detest cooking* odio cocinar.

detonate ['detəneɪt] *vi* estallar, detonar, explotar.
▶ *vt* hacer estallar, hacer explotar.

detonation [detə'neɪʃ⁰n] *n* detonación *f*.

detour ['diːtuər] *n* *(in traffic)* desvío.

detract [dɪ'trækt] *vt* **to detract from** *(achievement)* quitar mérito(s) a, restar valor a; *(beauty)* deslucir.

detractor [dɪ'træktər] *n* detractor,-ra.

detritus [dɪ'traɪtəs] *n* **1** GEOL detrito, detritus *m*. **2** *(debris)* deshechos *mpl*.

deuce [djuːs] *n* *(in tennis)* cuarenta *mpl* iguales.

devaluation [diːvæljuː'eɪʃ⁰n] *n* FIN devaluación *f*, desvaloración *f*.

devalue [diː'væljuː] *vt* **1** FIN *(currency)* devaluar, desvalorizar. **2** *(person, achievement)* subvalorar.

devastate ['devəsteɪt] *vt* **1** *(city, area, country)* devastar. **2** *fam fig (person)* anonadar, apabullar.

devastation [devə'steɪʃ⁰n] *n* devastación *f*.

develop [dɪ'veləp] *vt* **1** *(gen)* desarrollar; *(foster - trade, arts)* fomentar, promover. **2** *(acquire - habit, quality, feature)* contraer, adquirir; *(- talent, interest)* mostrar; *(get - illness, disease)* contraer. **3** *(exploit - resources)* explotar; *(- site, land)* urbanizar. **4** *(film, photograph)* revelar.
▶ *vi* **1** *(gen)* desarrollarse; *(- system)* perfeccionarse. **2** *(evolve - emotion)* conver-

tirse (**into**, en), transformarse (**into**, en); *(plot, novel)* desarrollarse. **3** *(appear - problem, complication, symptom)* aparecer, surgir; *(situation, crisis)* producirse. **4** *(of film, photograph)* salir.

developer [dɪˈveləpəʳ] *n* **1** *(of land, property - company)* promotora inmobiliaria, empresa constructora; *(- person)* constructor,-ra. **2** *(for photographs)* revelador *m*.

developing [dɪˈveləpɪŋ] *adj (country)* en vías de desarrollo.

development [dɪˈveləpmənt] *n* **1** *(gen)* desarrollo; *(- of skill, system)* perfección *f*; *(fostering)* fomento, promoción *f*; *(evolution)* evolución *f*. **2** *(invention - of product)* creación *f*. **4** *(event, incident)* acontecimiento, suceso; *(advance)* avance *m*, conquista. **5** *(of resources)* explotación *f*; *(of site, land, etc)* urbanización *f*.

deviance [ˈdiːvɪəns] *n* desviación *f*.

deviant [ˈdiːvɪənt] *adj* anormal.
▶ *n* pervertido,-a.

deviate [ˈdiːvɪeɪt] *vi* desviarse (**from**, de).

device [dɪˈvaɪs] *n* **1** *(object, equipment)* aparato, artefacto; *(mechanism)* mecanismo, dispositivo. **2** *(scheme, trick)* ardid *m*, estratagema.

devil [ˈdevəl] *n* diablo, demonio.

devious [ˈdiːvɪəs] *adj* tortuoso,-a, sinuoso,-a.

devise [dɪˈvaɪz] *vt (plan, scheme)* idear, concebir, crear; *(object, tool)* inventar.

devoid [dɪˈvɔɪd] *adj* carente (**of**, de), desprovisto,-a (**of**, de).

devote [dɪˈvəʊt] *vt (time, effort)* dedicar, consagrar.

devoted [dɪˈvəʊtɪd] *adj (loyal - friend)* fiel (**to**, a), leal (**to**, a); *(- couple)* unido,-a; *(- follower, supporter)* ferviente; *(selfless)* abnegado,-a: *your devoted daughter* tu hija que te quiere.

devotion [dɪˈvəʊʃən] *n* **1** *(loyalty)* lealtad *f*, fidelidad *f*; *(love)* cariño, afecto, amor *m*. **2** *(to work, research, cause)* dedicación *f*, entrega. **3** REL *(devoutness)* devoción *f*.

devour [dɪˈvaʊəʳ] *vt* devorar.

dew [djuː] *n* rocío.

dexterity [dekˈsterɪtɪ] *n (manual)* destreza, maña; *(intellectual)* habilidad *f*.

diabetes [daɪəˈbiːtiːz] *n* diabetes *f*.
ⓘ *pl* diabetes.

diabolical [daɪəˈbɒlɪkəl] *adj* **1** *(evil)* diabólico,-a. **2** GB *fam (extremely bad)* espantoso,-a, atroz.

diabolo [dɪˈæbələʊ] *n* diábolo.

diacritic [daɪəˈkrɪtɪk] *adj* diacrítico,-a.
▶ *n* signo diacrítico.

diadem [ˈdaɪədem] *n* diadema.

diaeresis [daɪˈerəsɪs] *n* diéresis *fpl*.
ⓘ *pl* diaereses [daɪˈerəsiːz].

diagnose [ˈdaɪəgnəʊz] *vt* MED diagnosticar.

diagnosis [daɪəgˈnəʊsɪs] *n* MED diagnóstico.
ⓘ *pl* diagnoses [daɪəgˈnəʊsiːs].

diagonal [daɪˈægənəl] *adj (line)* diagonal; *(path)* en diagonal.
▶ *n* diagonal *f*.

diagram [ˈdaɪəgræm] *n (gen)* diagrama *m*; *(graph)* gráfico, gráfica; *(of process, system)* esquema *m*.

dialect [ˈdaɪəlekt] *n* dialecto.

dial [ˈdaɪəl] *n* **1** *(of clock)* esfera. **2** *(of radio)* dial *m*.
▶ *vt* marcar. COMP **dialling code** prefijo (telefónico). ▌**dialling tone** señal *f* de llamada.

dialogue [ˈdaɪəlɒg] *n* diálogo.

diameter [daɪˈæmɪtəʳ] *n* diámetro.

diamond [ˈdaɪəmənd] *n* **1** *(stone)* diamante *m*, brillante *m*. **2** *(shape)* rombo. **3** *(in cards)* diamante *m*.

diaper [ˈdaɪəpəʳ] *n* US pañal *m*.

diaphragm [ˈdaɪəfræm] *n* diafragma *m*.

diarrhoea [daɪəˈrɪə] *n* diarrea.

diary [ˈdaɪərɪ] *n* **1** *(of thoughts, events, etc)* diario. **2** *(for appointments)* agenda.
ⓘ *pl* diaries.

❌ Diary no significa 'diario (periódico)', que se traduce por **newspaper**.

diastole [daɪˈæstəlɪ] *n* diástole *f*.

dice [daɪs] *n* dado.
ⓘ *pl* dice.

dichotomy [daɪˈkɒtəmɪ] *n* dicotomía.
ⓘ *pl* dichotomies.

dictate [*(vb)* dɪk'teɪt; *(n)* 'dɪkteɪt] *vt* **1** *(letter, etc)* dictar. **2** *(state, lay down - law, demands, trends)* ordenar; *(terms, conditions)* imponer.
▸ *vi (read out)* dictar.
▸ *n* mandato.

dictation [dɪk'teɪʃən] *n* dictado.

dictator [dɪk'teɪtəʳ] *n* dictador,-ra.

dictatorship [dɪk'teɪtəʃɪp] *n* dictadura.

dictionary ['dɪkʃənərɪ] *n* diccionario.
ⓘ *pl* dictionaries.

did [dɪd] *pt* → do.

didn't [dɪdənt] *pt* → do.

didactic [dɪ'dæktɪk] *adj* didáctico,-a.

die [daɪ] *vi* morir, morirse.
◆ to die away *vi (noise)* desvanecerse, irse apagando; *(breeze)* amainar.

die-hard ['daɪhɑːd] *n* intransigente *mf*.

dieresis [daɪ'erəsɪs] *n* US → diaeresis.

diesel ['diːzəl] *n* **1** *(fuel)* gasóleo, gasoil *m*. **2** *(car)* coche *m* diesel.

diet ['daɪət] *n* **1** *(food)* dieta (alimenticia), alimentación *f*. **2** *(restricted food)* régimen *m*, dieta. ⌐LOC⌐ **to be on a diet** estar a régimen. ❙ **to go on a diet** ponerse a régimen.
▸ *adj (food)* de régimen, bajo,-a en calorías.
▸ *vi* estar a régimen, estar a dieta, hacer régimen, hacer dieta.

differ ['dɪfəʳ] *vi* **1** *(be unlike)* ser distinto,-a (from, de), ser diferente (from, de), diferir (from, de). **2** *(disagree)* discrepar (about/on, en).

difference ['dɪfərəns] *n* diferencia.

different ['dɪfərənt] *adj* diferente (from, de), distinto,-a (from, de).

differential [dɪfə'renʃəl] *adj* diferencial.
▸ *n* **1** FIN diferencial *m*. **2** [también **differential gear**] AUTO diferencial *m*.

differentiate [dɪfə'renʃɪeɪt] *vt* diferenciar (from, de), distinguir (from, de).
▸ *vi* distinguir (between, entre).

difficult ['dɪfɪkəlt] *adj* difícil.

difficulty ['dɪfɪkəltɪ] *n* dificultad *f*.
ⓘ *pl* difficulties.

diffuse [*(adj)* dɪ'fjuːs; *(vb)* dɪ'fjuːz] *adj (light, gas)* difuso,-a.
▸ *vt (light, heat, news)* difundir.

diffusion [dɪ'fjuːʒən] *n* difusión *f*.

dig [dɪg] *n* **1** *(poke, prod)* codazo. **2** *fam (gibe)* pulla; *(hint)* indirecta. **3** *(by archaeologists)* excavación *f*.
▸ *vt (ground, garden)* cavar (en); *(by machine - tunnel, trench)* excavar; *(by hand - hole)* hacer, cavar; *(site)* excavar.
◆ to dig into *vt insep* **1** *(investigate, examine)* investigar. **2** *(resources, savings, reserves)* echar mano de.
◆ to dig out *vt sep (trapped person, car)* sacar, desenterrar.
ⓘ *pt & pp* dug, *ger* digging.

digest [*(n)* 'daɪdʒest; *(vb)* dɪ'dʒest] *n (summary)* resumen *m*, compendio.
▸ *vt* digerir.

digestion [dɪ'dʒestʃən] *n* digestión *f*.

digestive [daɪ'dʒestɪv] *adj* digestivo,-a.

digger ['dɪgəʳ] *n* excavadora.

digit ['dɪdʒɪt] *n* **1** MATH dígito. **2** ANAT *(finger)* dedo; *(thumb)* pulgar *m*.

digital ['dɪdʒɪtəl] *adj* **1** *(watch, display, recording)* digital. **2** ANAT dactilar, digital.

dignify ['dɪgnɪfaɪ] *vt* dignificar.
ⓘ *pt & pp* dignified, *ger* dignifying.

dignitary ['dɪgnɪtərɪ] *n* dignatario,-a.
ⓘ *pl* dignitaries.

dignity ['dɪgnɪtɪ] *n* dignidad *f*.

dilapidated [dɪ'læpɪdeɪtɪd] *adj (furniture)* desvencijado,-a, en mal estado; *(building)* ruinoso,-a; *(car)* desvencijado,-a, destartalado,-a.

☒ Dilapidated no significa 'dilapidado (malgastado)', que se traduce por wasted.

dilate [daɪ'leɪt] *vt* dilatar.

dilation [daɪ'leɪʃən] *n* dilatación *f*.

dilemma [dɪ'lemə] *n* dilema *m*.

diligence ['dɪlɪdʒəns] *n* diligencia.

dill [dɪl] *n* eneldo.

dilute [daɪ'luːt] *vt* **1** *(liquid, concentrate)* diluir. **2** *fig (criticism, effect, influence)* atenuar, suavizar.
▸ *adj* diluido,-a.

dilution [daɪ'luːʃən] *n* dilución *f*.

dim [dɪm] *adj* **1** *(light)* débil, tenue; *(room, corridor, corner)* oscuro,-a. **2** *fam (person)* tonto,-a, corto,-a (de luces).
ⓘ *comp* dimmer, *superl* dimmest.

▸ *vt (light)* atenuar, bajar; *(eyes)* nublar, empañar; *(memory)* borrar, difuminar.
ⓘ *pt & pp* dimmed, *ger* dimming.

dime [daɪm] *n* US moneda de diez centavos.

dimension [dɪˈmenʃən] *n* dimensión *f*.
▸ *n pl* **dimensions** dimensiones *fpl*.

diminish [dɪˈmɪnɪʃ] *vt* disminuir, reducir.

diminution [dɪmɪˈnjuːʃən] *n* disminución *f*, reducción *f*.

diminutive [dɪˈmɪnjətɪv] *adj* **1** diminuto,-a. **2** LING diminutivo,-a.
▸ *n* LING diminutivo.

dimmer [ˈdɪmər] [también **dimmer switch**] *n* regulador *m* de intensidad (de la luz).

dimple [ˈdɪmpəl] *n* hoyuelo.

din [dɪn] *n (of voices)* barullo, alboroto; *(of traffic)* estruendo, ruido.

dine [daɪn] *vi fml (gen)* comer (on, -); *(in evening)* cenar (on, -).
◆ **to dine out** *vi* cenar fuera.

diner [ˈdaɪnər] *n* **1** *(person)* comensal *mf*. **2** US restaurante *m* barato.

dinghy [ˈdɪŋɡɪ] *n* bote *m*.
ⓘ *pl* dinghies.

dingy [ˈdɪndʒɪ] *adj (dark, depressing - room, house, street)* lúgubre, deprimente, sórdido,-a; *(drab - colour, wall, curtains)* deslucido,-a; *(dirty)* sucio,-a.
ⓘ *comp* dingier, *superl* dingiest.

dining car [ˈdaɪnɪŋkɑːr] *n* vagón *m* restaurante.

dining room [ˈdaɪnɪŋruːm] *n* comedor *m*.

dinner [ˈdɪnər] *n (at midday)* comida; *(in evening)* cena. LOC **to have dinner** cenar. COMP **dinner jacket** esmoquin *m*, smoking *m*.

⊕ En los países anglosajones la cena se sirve mucho más temprano que en España (entre las 17 h 30 y las 19 h) y es la comida más importante del día.

dinosaur [ˈdaɪnəsɔːr] *n* dinosaurio.

diocese [ˈdaɪəsɪs] *n* diócesis *f*.

dioxide [daɪˈɒksaɪd] *n* dióxido.

dip [dɪp] *n* **1** *(downward slope)* declive *m*, pendiente *f*; *(drop - in prices, temperature, sales, production, profits)* caída, descen-

so. **2** *fam (quick swim)* chapuzón *m*. **3** CULIN *(sauce)* salsa.
▸ *vt* **1** *(put into liquid - pen, brush, bread)* mojar; *(- hand, spoon)* meter. **2** *(lower - head)* agachar, bajar.
▸ *vi* bajar.
ⓘ *pt & pp* dipped, *ger* dipping.

diphthong [ˈdɪfθɒŋ] *n* LING diptongo.

diploma [dɪˈpləʊmə] *n* diploma *m*.

diplomacy [dɪˈpləʊməsɪ] *n* diplomacia.

diplomat [ˈdɪpləmæt] *n* **1** *(ambassador, etc)* diplomático,-a. **2** *(tactful person)* persona diplomática.

diplomatic [dɪpləˈmætɪk] *adj* diplomático,-a.

dire [ˈdaɪər] *adj* **1** *(desperate, extreme)* extremo,-a, urgente. **2** *(serious, ominous)* serio,-a, grave. **3** *(terrible, dreadful)* terrible, atroz.

direct [dɪˈrekt, daɪˈrekt] *adj* **1** *(gen)* directo,-a. **2** *(exact, complete)* exacto,-a. **3** *(straightforward - person)* franco,-a, sincero,-a; *(- question)* directo,-a; *(- answer)* claro,-a.
▸ *adv (go, write, phone)* directamente; *(broadcast)* en directo.
▸ *vt* **1** *(gen)* dirigir. **2** *(show the way)* indicar el camino a.

direction [dɪˈrekʃən, daɪˈrekʃən] *n* dirección *f*.
▸ *n pl* **directions** instrucciones *fpl* de uso. LOC **to ask for directions** preguntar cómo se va.

directive [dɪˈrektɪv] *n* directiva, directriz *f*.

director [dɪˈrektər, daɪˈrektər] *n* director,-ra.

directory [dɪˈrektərɪ, daɪˈrektərɪ] *n* **1** *(telephone)* guía telefónica, listín *m* (de teléfonos); *(book, lost, index)* directorio, guía. **2** [también **street directory**] callejero.
ⓘ *pl* directories.

dirt [dɜːt] *n* **1** *(dirtiness)* suciedad *f*. **2** *(earth)* tierra. **3** *fam (scandal, gossip)* chismes *mpl*, trapos *mpl* sucios.

dirty [ˈdɜːtɪ] *adj* **1** *(gen)* sucio,-a; *(stained)* manchado,-a. COMP **dirty word** palabrota.
ⓘ *comp* dirtier, *superl* dirtiest.
▸ *vt* ensuciar.

disability [dɪsə'bɪlɪtɪ] *n (state)* invalidez *f*, discapacidad *f*, minusvalía; *(handicap)* desventaja, handicap *m*.
ⓘ *pl* disabilities.

disabled [dɪs'eɪbªld] *adj* minusválido,-a. COMP **disabled access** acceso para minusválidos.
▸ *n pl* **the disabled** los minusválidos.

disadvantage [dɪsəd'vɑ:ntɪdʒ] *n (drawback)* desventaja; *(obstacle)* inconveniente *m*.

disadvantaged [dɪsəd'vɑ:ntɪdʒd] *adj* desfavorecido,-a.
▸ *n pl* **the disadvantaged** los desfavorecidos *mpl*.

disagree [dɪsə'gri:] *vi* **1** *(not agree)* no estar de acuerdo (on, en), (with, con), disentir (with, de), discrepar (with, de), (on, en). **3** *(food)* sentar mal (with, a); *(weather)* no convenir (with, a).

disagreeable [dɪsə'grɪəbªl] *adj* desagradable.

disagreement [dɪsə'gri:mənt] *n* **1** *(difference of opinion)* desacuerdo; *(argument)* discusión *f*, riña, altercado. **2** *(lack of similarity)* discrepancia.

disappear [dɪsə'pɪəʳ] *vi* desaparecer.

disappearance [dɪsə'pɪərəns] *n* desaparición *f*.

disappoint [dɪsə'pɔɪnt] *vt* decepcionar, defraudar, desilusionar.

disappointed [dɪsə'pɔɪntɪd] *adj* decepcionado,-a.

disappointment [dɪsə'pɔɪntmənt] *n* desilusión *f*, decepción *f*.

disapprove [dɪsə'pru:v] *vt* desaprobar (of, -).

disarm [dɪs'ɑ:m] *vt* **1** *(gen)* desarmar; *(bomb)* desactivar.

disarmament [dɪs'ɑ:məmənt] *n* desarme *m*.

disaster [dɪ'zɑ:stəʳ] *n* desastre *m*.

disbelief [dɪsbɪ'li:f] *n* incredulidad *f*.

disc [dɪsk] *n* disco. COMP **disc jockey** pinchadiscos *m sing*.

discard [dɪs'kɑ:d] *vt* desechar, deshacerse de.

discern [dɪ'sɜ:n] *vt* percibir, distinguir.

discernment [dɪ'sɜ:nmənt] *n* (buen) criterio, discernimiento.

discharge [*(n)* 'dɪstʃɑ:dʒ; *(vb)* dɪs'tʃɑ:dʒ] *n* **1** descarga. **2** *(of prisoner)* liberación *f*, puesta en libertad; *(of patient)* alta. **3** *(of worker)* despido.
▸ *vt* **1** *(give, send out - sewage, waste, oil)* verter; *(smoke, fumes)* despedir; *(- electric current)* descargar. **2** *(prisoner)* liberar, poner en libertad; *(patient)* dar de alta. **3** *(dismiss)* despedir.

disciple [dɪ'saɪpªl] *n* discípulo,-a.

disciplinary ['dɪsɪplɪnərɪ] *adj* disciplinario,-a.

discipline ['dɪsɪplɪn] *n* **1** *(behaviour)* disciplina. **2** *(punishment)* castigo.

disclose [dɪs'kləʊz] *vt* **1** *(make known)* revelar, dar a conocer. **2** *(show)* mostrar, dejar ver.

disco ['dɪskəʊ] *n fam* disco *f*, discoteca.
ⓘ *pl* discos.

discomfort [dɪs'kʌmfət] *n* **1** incomodidad *f*. **2** inquietud *f*, desasosiego.

disconnect [dɪskə'nekt] *vt (from mains)* desconectar; *(gas, electricity, etc)* cortar.

disconsolate [dɪs'kɒnsələt] *adj* desconsolado,-a.

discontent [dɪskən'tent] *n* descontento.

discontinue [dɪskən'tɪnju:] *vt (service)* suspender, interrumpir; *(model)* dejar de fabricar.

discotheque ['dɪskətek] *n fml* discoteca.

discount [*(n)* 'dɪskaʊnt; *(vb)* dɪs'kaʊnt] *n* descuento.
▸ *vt (goods)* rebajar; *(price)* reducir; *(amount, bill of exchange)* descontar.

discourage [dɪs'kʌrɪdʒ] *vt* **1** *(dishearten)* desanimar, desalentar. **2** *(dissuade)* disuadir (from, de).

discouragement [dɪs'kʌrɪdʒmənt] *n* desaliento, desánimo.

discover [dɪ'skʌvəʳ] *vt (find - gen)* descubrir; *(mistake, loss, fact)* descubrir, darse cuenta de.

discoverer [dɪ'skʌvərəʳ] *n* descubridor,-ra.

discovery [dɪ'skʌvərɪ] *n* descubrimiento.
ⓘ *pl* discoveries.

discredit [dɪsˈkredɪt] n *(dishonour, disgrace)* descrédito.

discreet [dɪˈskriːt] adj *(gen)* discreto,-a; *(distance)* prudencial.

discrepancy [dɪˈskrepənsɪ] n discrepancia.
ⓘ pl discrepancies.

discrete [dɪsˈkriːt] adj diferenciado,-a, distinto,-a.

❌ Discrete no significa 'discreto', que se traduce por discreet.

discretion [dɪˈskreʃᵊn] n **1** *(quality of being discreet)* discreción f; *(prudence)* prudencia. **2** *(judgement)* criterio, juicio.

discriminate [dɪˈskrɪmɪneɪt] vi *(treat differently)* discriminar (against, a; between, entre).
▸ vt *(see a difference)* distinguir (from, de), discriminar.

discrimination [dɪskrɪmɪˈneɪʃᵊn] n **1** *(bias)* discriminación f. **2** *(distinction)* diferenciación f, distinción f. **3** *(judgement)* discernimiento, criterio.

discus [ˈdɪskəs] n *(object)* disco.
▸ n the discus *(event, sport)* el lanzamiento de disco.
ⓘ pl discuses o disci [ˈdɪskaɪ].

discuss [dɪˈskʌs] vt *(talk about - person)* hablar de; *(- subject, topic)* hablar de, tratar; *(- plan, problem)* discutir.

❌ To discuss no significa 'discutir (pelearse)', que se traduce por to argue.

discussion [dɪˈskʌʃᵊn] n discusión f, debate m.

❌ Discussion no significa 'discusión (pelea)', que se traduce por argument.

disdain [dɪsˈdeɪn] n desdén m, desprecio.
▸ vt desdeñar, despreciar.

disease [dɪˈziːz] n enfermedad f.

disembark [dɪsɪmˈbɑːk] vt desembarcar.

disembarkation [dɪsɪmbɑːˈkeɪʃᵊn] n *(of people)* desembarco; *(of goods)* desembarque m.

disenchanted [dɪsɪnˈtʃɑːntɪd] adj desencantado,-a, desilusionado,-a.

disenchantment [dɪsɪnˈtʃɑːntmənt] n desencanto, desilusión f.

disengage [dɪsɪnˈgeɪdʒ] vt **1** *(free - gen)* soltar (from, de); *(gears, mechanism)* desconectar. **2** MIL *(troops)* retirar (from, de).

disentangle [dɪsɪnˈtæŋgᵊl] vt *(unravel)* desenredar, desenmarañar.

disfavour [dɪsˈfeɪvəʳ] n desaprobación f.

disfigure [dɪsˈfɪgəʳ] vt *(face, person)* desfigurar; *(building, town, landscape)* afear, estropear.

disgrace [dɪsˈgreɪs] n **1** *(loss of favour)* desgracia; *(loss of honour)* deshonra, deshonor m. **2** *(shame)* escándalo, vergüenza.
▸ vt **1** *(bring shame on)* deshonrar. **2** *(discredit)* desacreditar.

disgraceful [dɪsˈgreɪsfʊl] adj vergonzoso,-a: it's disgraceful es vergonzoso, es una vergüenza.

disguise [dɪsˈgaɪz] n disfraz m. LOC in disguise disfrazado,-a.
▸ vt *(person)* disfrazar (as, de); *(voice, handwriting)* disimular.

disgust [dɪsˈgʌst] n *(revulsion)* asco, repugnancia; *(strong disapproval)* indignación f.
▸ vt *(revolt)* repugnar, dar asco a; *(disapprove)* indignar.

❌ To disgust no significa 'disgusto', que se traduce por displeasure o sorrow.

disgusting [dɪsˈgʌstɪŋ] adj asqueroso,-a, repugnante.

dish [dɪʃ] n **1** *(plate)* plato; *(for serving)* fuente f. **2** CULIN *(food)* plato. **3** TV antena parabólica.
▸ n pl dishes *(crockery)* platos mpl, vajilla f sing. LOC to do the dishes lavar los platos.

dishcloth [ˈdɪʃklɒθ] n trapo, bayeta.

dishearten [dɪsˈhɑːtᵊn] vt descorazonar, desanimar, desalentar.

dishevel [dɪˈʃevᵊl] vt despeinar.
ⓘ pt & pp dishevelled *(US disheveled)*, ger dishevelling *(US disheveling)*.

dishonest [dɪsˈɒnɪst] adj *(person, answer)* deshonesto,-a, poco honrado,-a; *(means, etc)* fraudulento,-a.

dishonour [dɪsˈɒnər] *n* deshonra, deshonor *m*.
▸ *vt* deshonrar.

dishonourable [dɪsˈɒnərəbəl] *adj* deshonroso,-a.

dishwasher [ˈdɪʃwɒʃər] *n (machine)* lavaplatos *m*, lavavajillas *m*; *(person)* lavaplatos *mf*.

disillusion [dɪsɪˈluːʒən] *vt* desilusionar.

disinfect [dɪsɪnˈfekt] *vt* desinfectar.

disinfection [dɪsɪnˈfekʃən] *n* desinfección *f*.

disinherit [dɪsɪnˈherɪt] *vt* desheredar.

disintegration [dɪsɪntɪˈɡreɪʃən] *n* desintegración *f*.

disinter [dɪsɪnˈtɜːr] *vt fml* desenterrar.
① *pt & pp* disinterred, *ger* disinterring.

disk [dɪsk] *n (gen)* disco. COMP disk drive COMPUT disquetera.

diskette [dɪsˈket] *n* COMPUT disquete *m*.

dislike [dɪsˈlaɪk] *n* aversión *f*, antipatía.

dislocation [dɪsləˈkeɪʃən] *n* MED dislocación *f*.

dislodge [dɪsˈlɒdʒ] *vt* **1** *(object)* sacar. **2** *(person)* desalojar (from , de).

disloyal [dɪsˈlɔɪəl] *adj* desleal (to, a/con).

dismal [ˈdɪzməl] *adj* sombrío,-a, deprimente, lúgubre.

dismantle [dɪsˈmæntəl] *vt (take apart - machinery)* desmontar; *(- furniture)* desarmar.

dismay [dɪsˈmeɪ] *n* consternación *f*.
▸ *vt* consternar.

☒ To dismay no significa 'desmayo', que se traduce por faint.

dismiss [dɪsˈmɪs] *vt* **1** descartar, desechar. **2** *(sack)* despedir.

dismissal [dɪsˈmɪsəl] *n* **1** descarte *m*, abandono. **2** *(sacking - of employee)* despido; *(- of official, minister)* destitución *f*.

dismissive [dɪsˈmɪsɪv] *adj* desdeñoso,-a.

dismount [dɪsˈmaʊnt] *vi* desmontarse (from, de), apearse (from, de).

disobedience [dɪsəˈbiːdɪəns] *n* desobediencia.

disobedient [dɪsəˈbiːdɪənt] *adj* desobediente.

disobey [dɪsəˈbeɪ] *vt* desobedecer.

disorder [dɪsˈɔːdər] *n* desorden *m*.

disordered [dɪsˈɔːdəd] *adj* desordenado,-a.

disorganisation [dɪsɔːɡənaɪˈzeɪʃən] *n* → disorganization.

disorganization [dɪsɔːɡənaɪˈzeɪʃən] *n* desorganización *f*.

disorganize [dɪsˈɔːɡənaɪz] *vt* desorganizar.

disorganized [dɪsˈɔːɡənaɪzd] *adj* desorganizado,-a.

disorientate [dɪsˈɔːrɪənteɪt] *vt* desorientar.

disorientation [dɪsɔːrɪənˈteɪʃən] *n* desorientación *f*.

disown [dɪsˈəʊn] *vt* renegar de, repudiar.

disparity [dɪˈspærɪtɪ] *n fml (inequality)* disparidad *f*; *(difference)* discrepancia.
① *pl* disparities.

dispatch [dɪˈspætʃ] *n* **1** mensaje, despacho. **2** *(journalist's report)* noticia, reportaje *m*.
▸ *vt* **1** *(send)* enviar, expedir. **2** *(finish quickly)* despachar.

☒ To dispatch no significa 'despachar (despedir)', que se traduce por to dismiss.

dispel [dɪˈspel] *vt* disipar.
① *pt & pp* dispelled, *ger* dispelling.

dispensary [dɪˈspensərɪ] *n (in hospital)* dispensario; *(in school)* enfermería.
① *pl* dispensaries.

dispense [dɪˈspens] *vt* **1** *(distribute)* distribuir, repartir. **2** JUR *(justice)* administrar. **3** *fml (public service)* suministrar, administrar.
◆ **to dispense with** *vt insep* prescindir de, pasar sin.

dispenser [dɪˈspensər] *n* máquina expendedora.

disperse [dɪˈspɜːs] *vt* dispersar.

dispersed [dɪsˈpɜːst] *adj* disperso,-a.

D

displace [dɪs'pleɪs] vt **1** (gen) desplazar; (bone) dislocar. **2** (replace) sustituir, reemplazar.

display [dɪ'spleɪ] n **1** exposición f, muestra. **2** COMPUT visualización f.
► vt **1** exhibir, exponer. **5** COMPUT visualizar.

displease [dɪs'pliːz] vt fml disgustar.

displeasure [dɪs'pleʒəʳ] n disgusto.

disposable [dɪ'spəʊzəbªl] adj desechable, de usar y tirar.

disposal [dɪ'spəʊzªl] n **1** eliminación f. **2** disponibilidad f.

dispose [dɪ'spəʊz] vt **1** disponer, colocar. **2** fml predisponer (to/towards, hacia).
◆ **to dispose of** vt insep **1** tirar, deshacerse de.

☒ To dispose no significa 'disponer de (tener)', que se traduce por to have.

disposition [dɪspə'zɪʃªn] n **1** fml carácter m. **2** disposición f.

dispossess [dɪspə'zes] vt desposeer, despojar.

disproportionate [dɪsprə'pɔːʃªnət] adj desproporcionado,-a (to, a).

disprove [dɪs'pruːv] vt (theory) refutar, rebatir.

disputable [dɪ'spjuːtəbəl] adj discutible.

dispute [(n) 'dɪspjuːt; (vb) dɪ'spjuːt] n discusión f.
► vi discutir.

disqualification [dɪskwɒlɪfɪ'keɪʃªn] n descalificación f.

disqualify [dɪs'kwɒlɪfaɪ] vt descalificar.
① pt & pp disqualified, ger disqualifying.

disregard [dɪsrɪ'gɑːd] n indiferencia (for, hacia); despreocupación f.
► vt (danger, difficulty) ignorar, despreciar.

disrespect [dɪsrɪ'spekt] n falta de respeto.

disrespectful [dɪsrɪ'spektfʊl] adj irrespetuoso,-a; irreverente.

disrupt [dɪs'rʌpt] vt interrumpir.

disruption [dɪs'rʌpʃªn] n (of meeting) interrupción f; (of traffic) problemas mpl.

disruptive [dɪs'rʌptɪv] adj perjudicial, nocivo,-a; perturbador,-ra.

dissatisfaction [dɪssætɪs'fækʃªn] n insatisfacción f, descontento.

dissatisfied [dɪs'sætɪsfaɪd] adj insatisfecho,-a, descontento,-a.

dissect [dɪ'sekt, daɪ'sekt] vt diseccionar.

disseminate [dɪ'semɪneɪt] vt fml divulgar, difundir, diseminar.

dissemination [dɪsemɪ'neɪʃªn] n fml diseminación f, difusión f.

dissent [dɪ'sent] n desacuerdo, disconformidad f.
► vi disentir, discrepar.

dissenting [dɪ'sentɪŋ] adj discrepante.

dissertation [dɪsə'teɪʃªn] n **1** (formal discourse) disertación f. **2** EDUC (for lower degree, master's) tesina; (for PhD) tesis f (doctoral).

dissidence ['dɪsɪdªns] n disidencia.

dissident ['dɪsɪdənt] adj disidente.
► n disidente mf.

dissimilar [dɪ'sɪmɪləʳ] adj diferente (to, de), distinto,-a (to, de/a).

dissimilarity [dɪsɪmɪ'lærɪtɪ] n diferencia.

dissimulate [dɪ'sɪmjəleɪt] vt fml disimular; ocultar, encubrir.
► vi fml disimular.

dissipate ['dɪsɪpeɪt] vt dispersar; difundir.
► vi disiparse, desvanecerse.

dissipated ['dɪsɪpeɪtɪd] adj disoluto,-a, disipado,-a.

dissociate [dɪ'səʊʃɪeɪt] vt (separate) disociar (from, de), separar (from, de).

dissolve [dɪ'zɒlv] vt disolver.

dissuade [dɪ'sweɪd] vt disuadir (from, de).

dissuasion [dɪ'sweɪʒªn] n disuasión f.

dissuasive [dɪ'sweɪsɪv] adj disuasorio,-a.

distance ['dɪstəns] n (gen) distancia. LOC **from a distance** desde lejos. **in the distance** a lo lejos.
► vt distanciar.

distant ['dɪstənt] adj lejano,-a, distante.

distaste [dɪsˈteɪst] *n* aversión *f*, desagrado.

distasteful [dɪsˈteɪstfʊl] *adj (idea, task)* desagradable; *(joke, remark)* de mal gusto.

distend [dɪˈstend] *vt* dilatar, hinchar.
▸ *vi* dilatarse, hincharse.

distil [dɪsˈtɪl] *vt* destilar.
ⓘ *pt & pp* distilled, *ger* distilling.

distill [dɪsˈtɪl] *vt* US → distil.

distillation [dɪstɪˈleɪʃən] *n* destilación *f*.

distiller [dɪsˈtɪlər] *n* destilador,-ra.

distillery [dɪsˈtɪləri] *n* destilería.
ⓘ *pl* distilleries.

distinct [dɪˈstɪŋkt] *adj* distinto,-a (from, a), diferente (from, de).

distinction [dɪˈstɪŋkʃən] *n* **1** diferencia, distinción *f*. **3** GB ≈ matrícula de honor.

distinctive [dɪˈstɪŋktɪv] *adj* distintivo,-a, característico,-a; personal, inconfundible.

distinctly [dɪˈstɪŋktlɪ] *adv* con claridad.

ⓧ Distinctly no significa 'de forma distinta', que se traduce por differently.

distinguish [dɪˈstɪŋgwɪʃ] *vt* distinguir.
▸ *vi* distinguir (between, entre).

distinguished [dɪˈstɪŋgwɪʃt] *adj* distinguido,-a.

distort [dɪˈstɔːt] *vt* deformar.

distortion [dɪˈstɔːʃən] *n* deformación *f*.

distract [dɪˈstrækt] *vt* distraer (from, de).

distracting [dɪˈstræktɪŋ] *adj (noise)* molesto,-a; *(presence)* que distrae.

distraction [dɪˈstrækʃən] *n* distracción *f*. **2** desconsuelo, aflicción *f*.

distraught [dɪˈstrɔːt] *adj* afligido,-a.

distress [dɪˈstres] *n (mental)* aflicción *f*, angustia; *(physical)* dolor *m*; *(exhaustion)* agotamiento. COMP **distress call** señal de socorro.
▸ *vt (upset)* afligir; *(grieve)* consternar.

distressing [dɪˈstresɪŋ] *adj* penoso,-a, angustioso,-a.

distribute [dɪˈstrɪbjuːt] *vt* distribuir.

distribution [dɪstrɪˈbjuːʃən] *n* distribución *f*.

distributor [dɪˈstrɪbjətər] *n* distribuidor,-ra.

district [ˈdɪstrɪkt] *n (of town, city)* distrito, barrio; *(of country)* región *f*, zona.

distrust [dɪsˈtrʌst] *n* desconfianza, recelo.
▸ *vt* desconfiar de, no fiarse de.

disturb [dɪˈstɜːb] *vt* molestar.

disturbed [dɪˈstɜːbd] *adj* perturbado,-a.

disturbing [dɪˈstɜːbɪŋ] *adj* inquietante.

disuse [dɪsˈjuːs] *n* desuso.

ditch [dɪtʃ] *n (gen)* zanja; *(at roadside)* cuneta; *(for irrigation)* acequia.
▸ *vt fam* deshacerse de.
▸ *vi* AV hacer un aterrizaje forzoso.

dither [ˈdɪðər] *vi* vacilar, titubear.

ditto [ˈdɪtəʊ] *n (in list)* ídem *m*.

diuretic [daɪjəˈretɪk] *adj* diurético,-a.

diurnal [daɪˈɜːnəl] *adj* diurno,-a.

divan [dɪˈvæn] *n (couch)* diván *m*, canapé *m*.

dive [daɪv] *n* **1** *(into water)* zambullida; *(in competition)* salto (de trampolín); *(underwater)* buceo; *(whale)* inmersión *f*. **2** *(of plane, bird)* picado.
▸ *vi* [US *pt* dove [dəʊv]] **1** *(into water)* zambullirse, tirarse (de cabeza); *(in competition)* saltar; *(underwater)* bucear; *(whale)* sumergirse. **2** *(birds, planes)* bajar en picado. **3** *(move suddenly)* precipitarse hacia.
◆ **to dive in** *vi* zambullirse, tirarse de cabeza.

diver [ˈdaɪvər] *n* buzo, submarinista *mf*.

diverge [daɪˈvɜːdʒ] *vi (gen)* divergir; *(roads)* bifurcarse.

divergence [daɪˈvɜːdʒəns] *n* divergencia.

divergent [daɪˈvɜːdʒənt] *adj* divergente.

diverse [daɪˈvɜːs] *adj* diverso,-a, variado,-a.

diversification [daɪvɜːsɪfɪˈkeɪʃən] *n* **1** *(variety)* variedad *f*. **2** COMM diversificación *f*.

diversify [daɪˈvɜːsɪfaɪ] *vt* diversificar.
ⓘ *pt & pp* diversified, *ger* diversifying.

D

diversion [daɪˈvɜːʃªn] n desvío, desviación f.

diversity [daɪˈvɜːsɪtɪ] n diversidad f.

divert [daɪˈvɜːt] vt 1 desviar. 2 divertir.

divest [daɪˈvest] vt despojar, privar (of, de).

divide [dɪˈvaɪd] vt dividir, separar.
▸ vi dividirse, bifurcarse.
▸ n fml división f, diferencia.

divided [dɪˈvaɪdɪd] adj (opinion) dividido,-a.

dividend [ˈdɪvɪdend] n dividendo.

divider [dɪˈvaɪdəʳ] n (in file) separador m; (in room) mampara.

dividers [dɪˈvaɪdəz] n pl compás m de punta (fija).

divine [dɪˈvaɪn] adj divino,-a.

diviner [dɪˈvaɪnəʳ] n zahorí m.

diving [ˈdaɪvɪŋ] n 1 buceo, submarinismo. 2 (in competition) saltos mpl (de trampolín). COMP **diving board** trampolín m. ▎ **diving mask** gafas f pl de bucear.

divinity [dɪˈvɪnɪtɪ] n 1 (quality, state) divinidad f. 2 (subject) teología.
① pl divinities.

divisible [dɪˈvɪzəbəl] adj divisible.

division [dɪˈvɪʒªn] n división f, reparto.

divisor [dɪˈvaɪzəʳ] n divisor m.

divorce [dɪˈvɔːs] n divorcio.
▸ vi divorciarse.

divorced [dɪˈvɔːst] adj divorciado,-a.

divulge [daɪˈvʌldʒ] vt divulgar, revelar.

DIY [ˈdiːˈaɪˈwaɪ] abbr GB (do-it-yourself) bricolaje m.

dizziness [ˈdɪzɪnəs] n mareo, vértigo.

dizzy [ˈdɪzɪ] adj 1 (person) mareado,-a. 2 (speed, pace) vertiginoso,-a; (height) de vértigo.
① comp dizzier, superl dizziest.

DJ¹ [ˈdiːˈdʒeɪ] abbr GB fam (dinner jacket) esmoquin m, smoking m.

DJ² [ˈdiːˈdʒeɪ] abbr (disc jockey) pinchadiscos m, disc-jockey m.

DNA [ˈdiːˈenˈeɪ] abbr (deoxyribonucleic acid) ácido desoxirribonucleico; (abbreviation) ADN m.

do [duː] vt 1 (gen) hacer. 2 (as job) dedicarse. 3 (be sufficient for) ser suficiente; (be satisfactory for, acceptable to) ir bien a. 4 fam (cheat, swindle) estafar, timar. LOC **how do you do?** (greeting) buenos días, buenas tardes; (answer) mucho gusto.

✎ Do es el verbo auxiliar que se emplea en inglés con la mayoría de los verbos para formar las preguntas (do you like dancing? ¿te gusta bailar?; does she live in Spain? ¿vive en España?) y formar las frases negativas (I don't want to go no quiero ir; he doesn't play tennis no juega a tenis). También sirve para sustituir al verbo principal en las respuestas (did you see the film? – no I didn't ¿viste la película – no, no la vi) y para otros usos, como en las question tags o como manera de enfatizar una afirmación.

◆ **to do away with** vt insep abolir, suprimir.
◆ **to do for** vt insep (manage) arreglárselas para conseguir.
◆ **to do in** vt sep fam matar, agotar.
◆ **to do up** vt sep 1 fam (fasten, belt) abrochar(se). 2 (wrap) envolver. 3 (dress up) arreglar.
◆ **to do with** vt insep (need) venir bien a.
◆ **to do without** vi arreglárselas sin.
① pt did [dɪd], pp done [dʌn], ger doing.

doc [dɒk] n fam doctor,-ra.

docile [ˈdəʊsaɪl] adj dócil.

dock¹ [dɒk] n 1 MAR (gen) muelle m; (for cargo) dársena f. 2 JUR banquillo (de los acusados).
▸ vt (ship) atracar (at, a); (spaceship) acoplar.
▸ n pl docks puerto.

dock² [dɒk] vt 1 (animal's tail) cortar. 2 (wages) descontar dinero de.

docker [ˈdɒkəʳ] n estibador,-ra, cargador,-ra.

dockland [ˈdɒklænd] n zona del puerto, zona portuaria.

⊕ En Londres Docklands es la antigua zona portuaria cerca del río Támesis donde se han establecido muchas grandes empresas, sobre todo del sector financiero.

dockside ['dɒksaɪd] *n* dársena.

dockyard ['dɒkjɑːd] *n* astillero.

doctor ['dɒktər] *n* médico,-a, doctor,-ra.
▶ *vt pej* falsificar, amañar.

doctorate ['dɒktərət] *n* doctorado.

doctrine ['dɒktrɪn] *n* doctrina.

document ['dɒkjəmənt] *n* documento.
▶ *vt* documentar.

documentary [dɒkjə'mentərɪ] *adj* documental.
▶ *n* documental *m*.
① *pl* documentaries.

documentation [dɒkjəmən'teɪʃən] *n* documentación *f*.

dodder ['dɒdər] *vi fam* andar tambaleándose.

doddery ['dɒdərɪ] *adj fam* chocho,-a.

doddle ['dɒdəl] COMP it's a doddle *fam* es pan comido, está chupado.

dodecagon [dəʊ'dekəgɒn] *n* dodecágono.

dodecahedron [dəʊdekə'hiːdrən] *n* dodecaedro.

dodecasyllable [dəʊdekə'sɪləbəl] *n* dodecasílabo.

dodge [dɒdʒ] *n* **1** *(quick movement)* regate *m*. **2** *fam (trick)* truco, treta, artimaña.
▶ *vt* esquivar.

dodgems ['dɒdʒəmz] *n pl* coches *mpl* de choque, autos *mpl* de choque.

dodgy ['dɒdʒɪ] *adj* **1** *fam (risky)* arriesgado,-a. **2** *fam (person)* que no es de fiar.
① *comp* dodgier, *superl* dodgiest.

doe [dəʊ] *n (of deer)* gama; *(of rabbit)* coneja.

does [dʌz] *pres* → do.

doesn't ['dʌzənt] *contr (does + not)* → do.

dog [dɒg] *n* perro,-a.
▶ *vt (pursue)* perseguir.
① *pt & pp* dogged, *ger* dogging.

dogged ['dɒgɪd] *adj* terco,-a, obstinado,-a.

doggie ['dɒgɪ] *n* → doggy.

doggy ['dɒgɪ] *n* perrito,-a.
① *pl* doggies.

doghouse ['dɒghaʊs] *n US* caseta del perro.

dogma ['dɒgmə] *n* dogma *m*.

dogmatic [dɒg'mætɪk] *adj* dogmático,-a.

dogmatism ['dɒgmətɪzəm] *n* dogmatismo.

dog-tired ['dɒgtaɪəd] *adj* rendido,-a, hecho,-a polvo.

doh [dəʊ] *n MUS* do.

do-it-yourself [duːɪtjɔː'self] *n* bricolaje *m*.

dole [dəʊl] *n* the dole GB *fam* el subsidio de desempleo, el paro.
◆ to dole out *vt sep* repartir, dar.

doll [dɒl] *n* muñeca.
◆ to doll up *vt sep fam* poner guapo,-a.

dollar ['dɒlər] *n* dólar *m*.

dolly ['dɒlɪ] *n (doll)* muñeca.
① *pl* dollies.

dolmen ['dɒlmən] *n* dolmen *m*.

dolphin ['dɒlfɪn] *n* delfín *m*.

domain [də'meɪn] *n* **1** *(lands)* dominios *mpl*. **2** *(in computing)* dominio. **3** *(sphere of knowledge)* campo, esfera; *(area of activity)* ámbito.

dome [dəʊm] *n ARCH (roof)* cúpula; *(ceiling)* bóveda.

domestic [də'mestɪk] *adj* **1** doméstico,-a: domestic animal animal doméstico. **2** hogareño,-a, casero,-a. **3** *(news, flight)* nacional; *(trade, policy)* interior; *(affairs, policy, market)* interno,-a.

domesticate [də'mestɪkeɪt] *vt* domesticar.

domicile ['dɒmɪsaɪl] *n JUR* domicilio.

dominance ['dɒmɪnəns] *n* dominio.

dominant ['dɒmɪnənt] *adj* dominante.

dominate ['dɒmɪneɪt] *vt* dominar.
▶ *vi (predominate)* predominar.

domination [dɒmɪ'neɪʃən] *n* dominación *f*.

domineer [dɒmɪ'nɪər] *vi* avasallar.

domineering [dɒmɪ'nɪərɪŋ] *adj* dominante.

Dominica [dɒmɪ'niːkə] *n* Dominica.

Dominican [də'mɪnɪkən] *adj* dominicano,-a.
▶ *n* dominicano,-a. COMP **Dominican Republic** República Dominicana.

dominion [dəˈmɪnjən] n dominio.
domino [ˈdɒmɪnəʊ] n ficha de dominó.
  ▶ n pl **dominoes** (game) dominó m.
  ① pl **dominoes**.
donate [dəʊˈneɪt] vt donar.
donation [dəʊˈneɪʃ°n] n 1 (act) donación f. 2 (gift) donativo.
done [dʌn] pp → do.
  ▶ adj 1 (finished) terminado,-a, hecho,-a. 2 bien visto,-a.
donkey [ˈdɒŋkɪ] n burro,-a, asno.
donor [ˈdəʊnəʳ] n donante m.
don't [dəʊnt] aux (do + not) → do.
donut [ˈdəʊnʌt] n → doughnut.
doodle [ˈduːd°l] vi garabatear.
  ▶ n garabato.
doom [duːm] n (fate) destino; (ruin) fatalidad f; (death) muerte f.
  ▶ vt (destine) destinar; (condemn) condenar.
door [dɔːʳ] n 1 (gen) puerta. 2 (entrance) puerta, entrada.
doorbell [ˈdɔːbel] n timbre m.
doorknob [ˈdɔːnɒb] n pomo.
doorman [ˈdɔːmən] n portero.
doormat [ˈdɔːmæt] phr felpudo.
doorstep [ˈdɔːstep] n 1 peldaño, umbral m. 2 GB fam (thick slice of bread) rebanada gruesa de pan.
doorstop [ˈdɔːstɒp] n cuña, tope.
door-to-door [dɔːtəˈdɔː] adj de puerta en puerta, a domicilio.
doorway [ˈdɔːweɪ] n entrada, portal m.
dope [dəʊp] vt 1 fam (food, drink) adulterar con drogas, poner droga en. 2 SP (athlete, horse) dopar, drogar.
doping [ˈdəʊpɪŋ] n dopaje m, doping m.
dormant [ˈdɔːmənt] adj 1 (volcano) inactivo,-a; (animal, plant) aletargado,-a. 2 fig (idea, emotion, rivalry) latente.
dormer [ˈdɔːməʳ] [también dormer window] n buhardilla.
dormitory [ˈdɔːmɪt°rɪ] n 1 (in boarding school, hostel) dormitorio. 2 US residencia de estudiantes, colegio mayor.
  ① pl **dormitories**.
  ❌ Dormitory no significa 'dormitorio (de una casa)', que se traduce por bedroom.

dormouse [ˈdɔːmaʊs] n lirón m.
  ① pl **dormice** [ˈdɔːmaɪs].
dorsal [ˈdɔːsəl] adj dorsal.
dosage [ˈdəʊsɪdʒ] n (amount) dosis f; (on medicine bottle) posología.
dose [dəʊs] n dosis f.
  ▶ vt medicar.
doss [dɒs] n fam (short sleep) cabezada.
  ◆ to **doss down** vi GB fam echarse a dormir.
dossier [ˈdɒsɪeɪ] n expediente m, dossier m.
dot [dɒt] n (spot) punto.
  ▶ vt 1 (letter) poner el punto a. 2 (scatter) esparcir, salpicar.
  ① pt & pp **dotted**, ger **dotting**.
dote [dəʊt] vi to **dote on** adorar.
dotted [ˈdɒtɪd] adj (line) de puntos.
dotty [ˈdɒtɪ] adj GB fam chiflado,-a.
  ① comp **dottier**, superl **dottiest**.
double [ˈdʌb°l] adj doble. COMP **double bass** contrabajo. ▌ **double bed** cama de matrimonio. ▌ **double room** habitación doble.
  ▶ n doble.
  ▶ vt 1 (increase twofold) doblar, duplicar. 2 (fold in half) doblar por la mitad.
  ▶ n pl **doubles** (tennis) partido de dobles.
  ◆ to **double back** vi volver sobre sus pasos.
  ◆ to **double up** vt sep doblar.
  ▶ vi 1 (with pain, laughter) doblarse; (with laughter) partirse, mondarse. 2 (share) compartir la habitación.
double-click [dʌb°lˈklɪk] vi hacer doble clic.
double-cross [dʌb°lˈkrɒs] vt fam engañar, traicionar.
double-dealing [dʌb°lˈdiːlɪŋ] n doble juego.
double-decker [dʌb°lˈdekəʳ] n [también double-decker bus] GB autobús m de dos pisos.

⊕ Double-decker es cualquier vehículo de dos pisos. Sin embargo el **double-decker** por antonomasia es el clásico autobús londinense que se retiró del servicio en 2005.

double-edged [dʌbəl'edʒd] *adj* de doble filo.

double-park [dʌbəl'pɑːk] *vt* aparcar en doble fila.

doubt [daʊt] *n (gen)* duda; incertidumbre *f*.
▶ *vi* dudar.

doubtful ['daʊtfʊl] *adj* dudoso,-a, incierto,-a.

doubtless ['daʊtləs] *adv* sin duda, indudablemente.

dough [dəʊ] *n* **1** CULIN masa. **2** *sl (money)* pasta.

doughnut ['dəʊnʌt] *n* rosquilla, donut® *m*.

Douro ['dʊərəʊ] *n* el Duero.

douse [daʊs] *vt* **1** *(extinguish - light, candle)* apagar. **2** *(soak)* mojar, empapar.

dove¹ [dʌv] *n (in bird)* paloma (blanca).

dove² [dəʊv] *pt* US → **dive**.

dovecote ['dʌvkəʊt] *n* palomar *m*.

dowdy ['daʊdɪ] *adj pej* sin gracia, sin estilo.
ⓘ *comp* dowdier, *superl* dowdiest.

down¹ [daʊn] *prep* **1** *(to a lower level)* (hacia) abajo. **2** *(at a lower level)* abajo. **3** *(along)* por: *cut it down the middle* córtalo por la mitad.
▶ *adv* **1** *(to lower level)* (hacia) abajo. **2** *(on paper, in writing)*: *she wrote his phone number down* apuntó su teléfono.
▶ *vt* **1** *(knock over, force to ground)* derribar, tumbar. **2** *fam (drink)* beberse rápidamente: *he downed the glass in one* se bebió el vaso de un trago.

down² [daʊn] *n (on bird)* plumón *m*; *(on peach)* pelusa; *(on body)* vello.

downcast ['daʊnkɑːst] *adj* abatido,-a.

downer ['daʊnər] *n* **1** *fam (drug)* calmante *m*, sedante *m*. **2** *(blow, depressing experience)* palo.

downfall ['daʊnfɔːl] *n* **1** *fig (of person)* perdición *f*, ruina. **2** *(of regime, dictator, etc)* caída.

downgrade [daʊn'greɪd] *vt* **1** *(demote)* bajar de categoría. **2** *(make seem unimportant)* restar importancia a.

downhearted [daʊn'hɑːtɪd] *adj* desanimado,-a, desmoralizado,-a.

downhill [daʊn'hɪl] *adv* cuesta abajo.
▶ *n (in skiing)* descenso.

download ['daʊnləʊd] *vt* bajar; *(internet)* descargar.

downpour ['daʊnpɔːr] *n* chaparrón *m*, aguacero.

downright ['daʊnraɪt] *adj fam* descarado,-a.
▶ *adv fam* muy, absolutamente.

downs [daʊnz] *n pl* GB colinas *fpl*.

Down's syndrome ['daʊnz sɪndrəʊm] *n* MED síndrome *m* de Down.

downstairs [daʊn'steəz] *adv (down the stairs)* abajo.
▶ *adj (room)* (del piso) de abajo.
▶ *n* planta baja.

downstream [daʊn'striːm] *adv* río abajo.

downtown [daʊn'taʊn] *adj* US céntrico,-a.
▶ *n* US centro de la ciudad.

downward ['daʊnwəd] *adj (movement)* descendente; *(direction, pressure)* hacia abajo.

downwards ['daʊnwədz] *adv* hacia abajo.

downy ['daʊnɪ] *adj* aterciopelado,-a.
ⓘ *comp* downier, *superl* downiest.

dowry ['daʊərɪ] *n* dote *f*.
ⓘ *pl* dowries.

doze [dəʊz] *n* cabezada.
▶ *vi* dormitar, echar una cabezada.
◆ **to doze off** *vi* quedarse dormido,-a.

dozen ['dʌzən] *n* docena.

dozy ['dəʊzɪ] *adj* **1** *(sleepy)* adormilado,-a. **2** GB *fam (stupid)* tonto,-a.
ⓘ *comp* dozier, *superl* dozier.

Dr ['dɒktər] *abbr* (**Doctor**) Doctor,-ra; *(abbreviation)* Dr., Dra.

drab [dræb] *adj* **1** *(colour)* apagado,-a; *(appearance)* soso,-a, sin gracia. **2** *(dreary - life)* monótono,-a, gris.

draft [drɑːft] *n* **1** *(rough copy - of letter, speech, etc)* borrador *m*; *(of plot)* esbozo; *(of plan, project)* anteproyecto. **2** FIN *(bill of exchange)* letra de cambio, giro. **3** US *(conscription)* (reclutamiento para el)

servicio militar obligatorio. **4** US →
draught.
▸ *adj (version, copy)* preliminar.
draftsman ['drɑːftsmən] *n* US →**draughtsman**.

drag [dræg] *n (hindrance)* estorbo (on,
para), carga (on, para).
▸ *vt (pull, cause to trail)* arrastrar, llevar a
rastras.
◆ **to drag on** *vi* alargarse, prolongarse, hacerse interminable.
◆ **to drag out** *vt sep* alargar, prolongar.
◆ **to drag up** *vt sep (revive, recall)* sacar a
relucir.
① *pt & pp* **dragged,** *ger* **dragging**.

dragon ['drægºn] *n* **1** *(mythology)* dragón *m*. **2** *fam (woman)* bruja.

dragonfly ['drægənflaɪ] *n* libélula.
① *pl* **dragonflies**.

drain [dreɪn] *n* desagüe *m*, alcantarilla.
▸ *vt* **1** *(empty)* vaciar; *(- wound, blood)*
drenar. **2** *(rice, pasta, vegetables, etc)* escurrir.
▸ *vi* **1** *(discharge - pipes, rivers)* desaguar. **2**
(dry out) escurrir (off, -), escurrirse (off, -).
3 *fig (strength, energy, etc)* irse agotando.
▸ *n pl* **the drains** *(of town)* el alcantarillado *m sing*; *(of building)* las tuberías *fpl*
del desagüe.
◆ **to drain away** *vi (liquid - empty)* va-
ciarse.

drainage ['dreɪnɪdʒ] *n* **1** drenaje, desagüe *m*. **2** *(drains - of town)* alcantarillado; *(of building)* desagüe *m*. COMP **drainage basin** cuenca hidrográfica.

drainpipe ['dreɪnpaɪp] *n (pipe)* tubo de
desagüe.

drake [dreɪk] *n* pato (macho).

drama ['drɑːmə] *n* **1** THEAT *(play)* obra
de teatro; *(plays, literature)* teatro, drama *m*. **2** *(as school subject)* expresión *f*
corporal; *(at drama school)* arte *m* dramático.

dramatic [drəˈmætɪk] *adj* dramático,-a,
teatral, emocionante.

dramatist ['dræmətɪst] *n* dramatur-
go,-a.

drank [dræŋk] *pt* → **drink**.

drape [dreɪp] *vt* **1** *(decorate)* drapear;
(cover) cubrir (in/with, con). **2** *(part of
body)* descansar, acomodar.
▸ *n pl* **drapes** US *(curtains)* cortinas *fpl*.

drastic ['dræstɪk] *adj* drástico,-a.

draught [drɑːft] *n* **1** *(of cold air)* corriente *f* (de aire). **2** *(swallow of beer, etc)* trago. **3** *(medicine)* pócima. **4** *(piece in game)*
dama, pieza.
▸ *n pl* **draughts** GB damas *fpl*.

draughtboard ['drɑːftbɔːd] *n* tablero
de damas.

draughtsman ['drɑːftsmən] *n* **1** *(artist)*
delineante *mf*. **2** GB *(in game)* ficha de
damas.
① *pl* **draughtsmen** ['drɑːftsmən].

draughtswoman ['drɑːftswumən] *n*
ARCH delineante.
① *pl* **draughtswomen** ['drɑːftswɪmɪn].

draw [drɔː] *n* **1** *(raffle, lottery)* sorteo. **2**
SP *(tie - gen)* empate *m*. **3** *(attraction)*
atracción *f*.
▸ *vt* **1** *(sketch - picture)* dibujar; *(- plans)*
trazar. **2** *(move)* llevar. **3** *(pull out, take
out - gen)* sacar, extraer; *(bow)* tensar. **4**
SP *(tie)* empatar. **5** *(attract)* atraer. **6** *(produce, elicit)* provocar, obtener; *(- praise)*
conseguir.
◆ **to draw back** *vi* **1** *(move away)* retirarse, retroceder. **2** *(pull out)* echarse
atrás, volverse atrás.
◆ **to draw in** *vi* **1** *(of days)* acortarse. **2**
(train) llegar.
◆ **to draw off** *vt sep (liquid)* sacar, extraer.
◆ **to draw on** *vt insep (make use of - experience, etc)* recurrir a, hacer uso de; *(- money, savings)* utilizar, recurrir a.
▸ *vi (approach - winter, night, etc)* acercarse.
◆ **to draw up** *vt sep (draft - contract, treaty,
etc)* preparar, redactar; *(- list)* hacer; *(-
plan)* esbozar.
▸ *vi (of vehicle)* detenerse, pararse.
① *pt* **drew** [druː], *pp* **drawn** [drɔːn].

drawback ['drɔːbæk] *n* inconveniente
m, desventaja.

drawbridge ['drɔːbrɪdʒ] *n* puente *m*
levadizo.

drawer ['drɔːəʳ] *n* **1** *(in furniture)* cajón *m*.
2 *(draughtsperson)* dibujante *mf*.

drawing ['drɔːɪŋ] *n* dibujo: *she's good at drawing* dibuja muy bien. LOC **to go back to the drawing board** volver a empezar, empezar de nuevo. COMP **drawing board** tablero de dibujo. ▌**drawing pin** GB chincheta. ▌**drawing room** sala de estar, salón *m*.

drawn [drɔːn] *pp* → **draw**.
▶ *adj* **1** *(face - tired, haggard)* ojeroso,-a, cansado,-a; *(- worried)* preocupado,-a. **2** SP *(match, etc)* empatado,-a.

dread [dred] *n* terror *m*, pavor *m*.
▶ *vt* temer, tener terror a: *he's dreading the exam* el examen le da terror.

dreadful ['dredfʊl] *adj* **1** *(shocking)* terrible, espantoso,-a, atroz. **2** *fam (awful)* fatal, horrible, malísimo,-a: *how dreadful!* ¡qué horror!

dream [driːm] *n* **1** *(while asleep)* sueño: *I had a bad dream* tuve una pesadilla; *sweet dreams!* ¡felices sueños! **2** *(daydream)* ensueño, sueño: *he lives in a dream* vive en las nubes. **3** *(hope, fantasy)* sueño (dorado), deseo, ilusión *f*: *the house of your dreams* la casa de tus sueños.
▶ *adj (imaginary)* imaginario,-a; *(ideal)* ideal, de ensueño: *your dream holiday* las vacaciones de tus sueños.
▶ *vt* **1** *(while asleep)* soñar: *I dreamt that I was flying* soñé que volaba. **2** *(imagine)* imaginarse: *I never dreamt you'd actually do it* nunca me imaginé que lo harías de verdad.
▶ *vi* **1** *(while asleep)* soñar (about/of, con); *(daydream)* soñar (despierto,-a): *I dreamt about you last night* soñé contigo anoche; *dream on* sigue soñando. **2** *(imagine)* soñar (of, con); *(contemplate)* soñar despierto: *I dream of having my own business* sueño con tener mi propia empresa.
◆ **to dream up** *vt sep fam pej (excuse)* inventarse; *(plan)* idear.
① *pt & pp* dreamed o dreamt [dremt].

dreamer ['driːmər] *n* soñador,-ra.

dreamt [dremt] *pt & pp* → **dream**.

dreary ['drɪərɪ] *adj* **1** *(gen)* triste, deprimente. **2** *fam (dull, uninteresting)* pesado,-a, aburrido,-a.
① *comp* drearier, *superl* dreariest.

dredge¹ [dredʒ] *vt & vi (river, lake, etc)* dragar, rastrear.

dredge² [dredʒ] *vt* CULIN *(with sugar)* espolvorear; *(with flour)* enharinar, rebozar.

drench [drentʃ] *vt* empapar. LOC **to be/get drenched** empaparse. ▌**to be drenched to the skin** estar calado,-a hasta los huesos.

dress [dres] *n* **1** *(for women)* vestido. **2** *(clothing)* ropa, vestimenta.
▶ *adj (shirt, suit)* de etiqueta. COMP **dress rehearsal** THEAT ensayo general.
▶ *vt* **1** *(person)* vestir. **2** MED *(wound)* vendar. **3** CULIN *(poultry, crab)* aderezar, preparar; *(salad)* aliñar. **4** *(shop window)* arreglar, decorar; *(Christmas tree)* decorar, adornar; *(hair)* arreglar.
▶ *vi (gen)* vestirse; *(formally)* vestirse de etiqueta. LOC **to get dressed** vestirse.
◆ **to dress down** *vt sep (scold)* regañar; *(rebuke)* echar una bronca.
▶ *vi (dress informally)* vestirse informalmente.
◆ **to dress up** *vi (in fancy dress)* disfrazarse (as, de); *(dress formally)* ponerse de tiros largos.
▶ *vt sep fig (truth, facts, etc)* disfrazar.

dresser ['dresər] *n* **1** GB *(in kitchen)* aparador *m*. **2** US *(chest of drawers)* tocador *m*.

dressing ['dresɪŋ] *n* **1** *(gen)* apósito; *(bandage)* vendaje *m*. **2** *(act of getting dressed)* el vestir(se) *m*. **3** CULIN *(for salad)* aliño. **4** US *(stuffing)* relleno. COMP **dressing gown** bata. ▌**dressing room** THEAT camerino. ▌**dressing table** tocador *m*.

dressmaker ['dresmeɪkər] *n (woman)* modista *f*, modisto; *(man)* modista *m*, modisto.

dressmaking ['dresmeɪkɪŋ] *n* costura.

drew [druː] *pt* → **draw**.

dribble ['drɪbəl] *n* **1** *(saliva)* saliva, baba. **2** *(of water, blood)* gotas *fpl*, hilo, chorrito. **3** SP dribling *m*.
▶ *vi* **1** *(baby)* babear. **2** *(liquid)* gotear.
▶ *vt* driblar, regatear.

dried [draɪd] *pp* → **dry**.
▶ *adj (fruit)* seco,-a; *(milk)* en polvo.

drier ['draɪər] *n* → **dryer**.

drift [drɪft] *n* **1** *(of snow)* ventisquero; *(of sand)* montón *m*. **2** MAR *(flow of water)* deriva. **3** *(movement)* movimiento; *(tendency)* tendencia.**4** *(meaning, gist)* significado, sentido, idea: *do you get my drift?* ¿entiendes lo que quiero decir?
▶ *vi* **1***(float on water)* ir a la deriva. **2** *(pile up - of snow, sand, leaves, etc)* amontonarse.

drill¹ [drɪl] *n* **1** *(handtool)* taladro; *(large machine)* barreno, perforadora; *(dentist's)* fresa; *(drill head, bit)* broca. **2** MIL instrucción *f*. **3** EDUC *(exercise)* ejercicio. **4** *(rehearsal, practice)* simulacro; *(procedures to be followed)* procedimiento: *fire drill* simulacro de incendio; *safety drill* instrucciones de seguridad.
▶ *vt* **1** *(wood, metal, etc)* taladrar, perforar; *(hole)* hacer, perforar. **2** MIL instruir.
▶ *vi* **1** *(for oil, coal)* perforar. **2** MIL entrenarse. LOC **to drill STH into SB** inculcarle ALGO a ALGN.

drill² [drɪl] *n (material)* dril *m*.

drink [drɪŋk] *n (gen)* bebida; *(alcoholic drink)* copa, trago; *(soft drink)* refresco: *let's go for a drink!* ¡vamos a tomar algo!, ¡vamos a tomar una copa!
▶ *vt (gen)* beber, tomar: *you haven't drunk your tea* no te has bebido el té; *what do you want to drink?* ¿qué quieres beber?LOC **to drink a toast to SB** brindar por ALGN. ‖ **to drink to STH/SB** brindar por ALGO/ALGN. ‖ **to have STH to drink** tomar(se) ALGO.
▶ *vi* beber: *she doesn't drink (alcohol)* no bebe (alcohol); *don't drink and drive* si bebes, no conduzcas.
◆ **to drink in** *vt sep (scene, sights, sounds, etc)* apreciar, empaparse de; *(success)* saborear.
ⓘ *pt* **drank** [dræŋk], *pp* **drunk** [drʌŋk].

drinkable ['drɪŋkəbəl] *adj (water)* potable; *(wine, beer, etc)* aceptable.

drinker ['drɪŋkəʳ] *n* bebedor,-ra.

drinking ['drɪŋkɪŋ] *n (alcohol)* bebida; *(action)* beber *m*. COMP **drinking fountain** fuente *f* de agua potable. ‖ **drinking water** agua potable.

drip [drɪp] *n* **1** *(drop of liquid)* goteo; *(sound)* gotear *m*. **2** MED gota a gota *m*:

they put him on a drip le pusieron el gota a gota. **3** *fam (person)* soso,-a.
▶ *vi (fall in drops)* gotear, caer; *(fall heavily)* chorrear: *the tap drips* el grifo gotea.
▶ *vt* dejar caer gota a gota.
ⓘ *pt & pp* **dripped**, *ger* **dripping**.

drive [draɪv] *n* **1** *(trip)* paseo en coche; *(journey)* viaje *m*: *we went for a drive* dimos una vuelta en coche; *it's a two-hour drive* es un viaje de dos horas. **2** *(road)* calle *f*. **3** SP *(golf, tennis)* drive *m*. **4** *(campaign)* campaña: *sales drive* promoción; *membership drive* campaña para atraer socios; *a no-smoking drive* una campaña antitabaco. **5** *(energy, initiative)* energía. **6** *(propulsion system)* transmisión *f*, propulsión *f*; *(of wheeled vehicle)* tracción *f*: *front-wheel drive* tracción delantera; *four-wheel drive* tracción en las cuatro ruedas.
▶ *vt* **1** *(operate - vehicle)* conducir: *he drives a bus* es conductor de autobús. **2** *(take - person)* llevar (en coche). **3** *(cause to move - person)* hacer, obligar a; *(- animal)* arrear. **4** *(provide power for, keep going)* hacer funcionar, mover: *the river drives the waterwheel* el río mueve el molino. **5** *(force, compel to act)* forzar, obligar; *(cause to be in state)* llevar: *you're driving me crazy* me estás volviendo loco.
▶ *vi (vehicle)* conducir: *can you drive?* ¿sabes conducir?; *he's learning to drive* está aprendiendo a conducir; *I drove here* vine en coche.
◆ **to drive at** *vt insep* insinuar.
◆ **to drive away** *vt sep (fend off - attacker, animal)* ahuyentar; *(throw out)* alejar.
◆ **to drive off** *vt sep* ahuyentar.
▶ *vi (car, driver)* irse.
◆ **to drive out** *vt sep* expulsar.
ⓘ *pt* **drove** [drəʊv], *pp* **driven** ['drɪvᵊn].

drivel ['drɪvᵊl] *n* tonterías *fpl*, bobadas *fpl*, memeces *fpl*.

driven ['drɪvᵊn] *pp* → **drive**.

driver ['draɪvəʳ] *n* **1** *(of bus, car)* conductor,-ra; *(of taxi)* taxista *mf*; *(of lorry)* camionero,-a; *(of racing car)* piloto *mf*; *(of train)* maquinista *mf*: *he's a very good driver* conduce muy bien. **2** SP *(golf club)* madera número 1. COMP **driver's licence** US carnet *m* de conducir, permiso de conducir.

driving ['draɪvɪŋ] *n* AUTO conducción *f*: *we shared the driving* nos turnamos para conducir.
► *adj* COMP **driving licence** carnet *m* de conducir, permiso de conducir. ‖ **driving school** autoescuela. ‖ **driving test** examen *m* de conducir.

drizzle ['drɪzªl] *n* llovizna.
► *vi* lloviznar.

droll [drəʊl] *adj (amusing)* gracioso,-a, chistoso,-a; *(odd, quaint)* curioso,-a.

dromedary ['drɒmədªrɪ] *n* dromedario.
ⓘ *pl* dromedaries.

drone¹ [drəʊn] *n (bee)* zángano.

drone² [drəʊn] *n* **1** *(noise)* zumbido. **2** *(monotonous talk)* cantinela, sonsonete *m*.
► *vi (bee, plane, engine)* zumbar.

drool [druːl] *n* **1** *(of baby)* baba, babas *fpl*. **2** *(drivel)* tonterías *fpl*, bobadas *fpl*.
► *vi (of baby, dog)* babear.

droop [druːp] *n (of shoulders)* caída, inclinación *f*,.
► *vi* **1** *(head)* inclinarse, caerse; *(shoulders)* encorvarse; *(eyelids)* cerrar. **2** *(flower)* marchitarse; *(branches)* inclinarse.

drop [drɒp] *n* **1** *(of liquid)* gota: *she carried the cup without spilling a drop* llevó la taza sin derramar ni una gota; *we could do with a drop of rain* nos iría bien un poco de lluvia. **2** *(sweet)* pastilla, caramelo. **3** *(descent, distance down)* desnivel *m*, caída. **4** *(fall - gen)* caída; *(in temperature)* descenso.
► *vt* **1** *(let fall - accidentally)* caérsele a uno: *he dropped the glass* se le cayó el vaso; *don't drop it!* ¡que no se te caiga!. **2** *(let fall - deliberately)* dejar caer, tirar; *(let go of)* soltar; *(launch - bomb, supplies)* lanzar: *she dropped her handkerchief by his chair* dejó caer su pañuelo al lado de su silla; *drop it!* ¡suéltalo! **3** *(lower - gen)* bajar; *(- speed)* reducir. **4** *fam (set down - passenger)* dejar (off, -); *(- delivery)* dejar, pasar a dejar (off, -): *where shall I drop you?* ¿dónde quieres que te deje? **5** *(give up, abandon)* dejar, abandonar. **6** *(omit, leave out - in speaking)* no pronunciar, comerse; *(in writing)* omitir: *don't drop your "h"s* no te comas las «haches». **7** SP *(player from team)* echar, sacar, no seleccionar; *(lose)* perder. LOC **to drop**

dead caerse muerto,-a. ‖ **to drop SB a line / drop SB a note** escribir cuatro/unas líneas a ALGN.
► *vi* **1** *(fall - object)* caer, caerse; *(- person)* dejarse caer, tirarse. **2** *(prices, temperature, voice)* bajar; *(wind)* amainar; *(speed)* reducirse, disminuir. **3** *(lapse)* dejar: *let it drop!* ¡déjalo ya!, ¡basta ya!
◆ **to drop away** *vi* **1** *(support, interest)* disminuir. **2** *(ground)* caer.
◆ **to drop by** *vi* pasar.
► *vt insep* pasar por.
◆ **to drop in** *vi (visit)* pasar.
◆ **to drop off** *vi* **1** *fam (fall asleep)* dormirse. **2** *(sales, interest, etc)* disminuir.
◆ **to drop out** *vi (of school, etc)* dejar los estudios; *(of group)* dejar el grupo; *(of race, competition)* abandonar; *(of society)* marginarse.
ⓘ *pt & pp* dropped, *ger* dropping.

droplet ['drɒplət] *n* gotita.

drought [draʊt] *n* sequía.

drove [drəʊv] *pt → drive*.
► *n* **1** *(of cattle)* manada. **2** *(of people)* multitud *f*.

drown [draʊn] *vt* **1** *(gen)* ahogar. **2** *(submerge - place)* inundar, anegar.
► *vi* ahogarse.

drowse [draʊz] *vi* dormitar.

drowsy ['draʊzɪ] *adj (person, look)* somnoliento,-a: *these tablets make me drowsy* estas pastillas me dan sueño. LOC **to feel drowsy** tener sueño.
ⓘ *comp* drowsier, *superl* drowsiest.

drug [drʌg] *n* **1** *(medicine)* medicamento. **2** *(narcotic)* droga: *hard/soft drugs* drogas duras/blandas. LOC **to be on/do/take drugs** drogarse. COMP **drug addict** drogadicto,-a, toxicómano,-a. ‖ **drug dealer** traficante *mf* de drogas. ‖ **drug pusher** camello *mf*.
► *vt* **1** *(person, animal)* drogar. **2** *(food, drink)* adulterar con drogas.
ⓘ *pt & pp* drugged, *ger* drugging.

druggist ['drʌgɪst] *n* US farmacéutico,-a.

drugstore ['drʌgstɔːʳ] *n* US *establecimiento donde se puede comprar medicamentos, cosméticos, periódicos y otras cosas*.

D

drum [drʌm] n **1** *(instrument)* tambor m. **2** *(container)* bidón m. **3** TECH tambor.
▶ vi **1** tocar el tambor.
ⓘ pt & pp **drummed**, ger **drumming**.
▶ n pl **drums** *(set)* batería.

drummer ['drʌmə^r] n *(in marching band)* tambor mf; *(in pop group, jazz band)* batería mf.

drumstick ['drʌmstɪk] n **1** MUS baqueta, palillo (de tambor). **2** CULIN muslo (de ave).

drunk [drʌŋk] pp → **drink**.
▶ adj borracho,-a. LOC **to get drunk** emborracharse.

drunkard ['drʌŋkəd] n borracho,-a.

drunken ['drʌŋkən] adj borracho,-a.

dry [draɪ] adj **1** seco,-a. COMP **dry dock** dique m seco. ‖ **dry goods 1** GB comestibles mpl no perecederos. **2** US artículos mpl de mercería. ‖ **dry land** tierra firme.
ⓘ comp **drier**, superl **driest**.
▶ vt secar.
▶ vi secarse (off, -).
ⓘ pt & pp **dried**, ger **drying**.

dry-clean [draɪ'kliːn] vt limpiar en seco.

dry-cleaner's [draɪ'kliːnəz] n tintorería, tinte m.

dryer ['draɪə^r] n *(for clothes)* secadora; *(for hair)* secador m.

dryness ['draɪnəs] n sequedad f.

dual ['djuːəl] adj *(gen)* doble. COMP **dual carriageway** GB carretera de doble calzada.

dub¹ [dʌb] vt *(soundtrack)* doblar (into, a).
ⓘ pt & pp **dubbed**, ger **dubbing**.

dub² [dʌb] vt *(give nickname)* apodar.
ⓘ pt & pp **dubbed**, ger **dubbing**.

dub³ [dʌb] n MUS dub m.

dubbing ['dʌbɪŋ] n *(of soundtrack)* doblaje m.

duchess ['dʌtʃəs] n duquesa.

duck¹ [dʌk] n pato,-a.

duck² [dʌk] vi *(bend down)* agacharse; *(hide)* esconderse: *she ducked behind the sofa* se escondió detrás del sofá.

duckling ['dʌklɪŋ] n patito.

duct [dʌkt] n conducto.

ductile ['dʌktaɪl] adj dúctil.

ductility [dʌk'tɪləti] n ductilidad f.

dud [dʌd] n **1** fam *(object)* trasto inútil, engañifa; *(person)* desastre m, inútil mf. **2** *(grenade, bomb, firework, etc)* granada, bomba, fuego artificial, etc. que no estalla.
▶ adj *(defective)* defectuoso,-a; *(worthless, useless)* inútil,; *(valueless - note, coin)* falso,-a; *(grenade, bomb, firework)* que no estalla. COMP **dud cheque** cheque m sin fondos.

due [djuː] adj *(expected)* esperado,-a: *her new book is due out in December* su nuevo libro saldrá en diciembre; *the train is due (in) at five o'clock* el tren debe llegar a las cinco. LOC **due to** debido a. COMP **due date** (fecha de) vencimiento.
▶ n merecido.
▶ adv derecho hacia: *due north* derecho hacia el norte.
▶ n pl **dues** cuota.

duel ['djuːəl] n duelo.
▶ vi batirse en duelo (with, con).
ⓘ pt & pp **duelled** (US **dueled**), ger **duelling** (US **dueling**).

duet [djuː'et] n dúo.

dug [dʌg] pt & pp → **dig**.

duke [djuːk] n duque m.

dull [dʌl] adj **1** *(boring - job)* monótono,-a, pesado,-a; *(- person, life, film)* pesado,-a, aburrido,-a, soso,-a; *(- place, town)* aburrido,-a. **2** *(not bright - colours)* apagado,-a; *(weather, day)* gris, triste, feo,-a. **3** *(sound, pain)* sordo,-a. **4** *(slow-witted)* torpe, lerdo,-a.
▶ vt *(pain)* aliviar, calmar; *(sound)* amortiguar; *(hearing)* embotar.

duly ['djuːlɪ] adv **1** fml *(properly)* debidamente. **2** *(as expected)* como era de esperar.

dumb [dʌm] adj **1** *(unable to speak)* mudo,-a. **3** US fam *(stupid)* tonto,-a.

dummy ['dʌmɪ] n **1** *(in shop window, dressmaker's)* maniquí m. **2** *(fake)* imitación f. **3** GB *(for baby)* chupete m. **4** fam imbécil mf.
ⓘ pl **dummies**.

dump [dʌmp] n vertedero, basurero.
▶ vt *(drop, unload - rubbish)* verter, descargar; *(leave)* dejar, poner: *he dumped*

his dirty washing on the floor dejó su ropa sucia en el suelo.

dumping ['dʌmpɪŋ] *n* vertido. [LOC] «No dumping» «Prohibido arrojar basuras».

dune [djuːn] [también **sand dune**] *n* duna.

dung [dʌŋ] *n* estiércol *m*.

dungarees [dʌŋɡə'riːz] *n (garment)* peto; *(overalls)* mono.

dungeon ['dʌndʒən] *n* mazmorra.

duo ['djuːəʊ] *n* dúo.
ⓘ *pl* duos.

duodena [djuː ə'diːnə] *n pl* → **duodenum**.

duodenum [djuː ə'diːnəm] *n* duodeno.
ⓘ *pl* duodenums o duodena [djuː ə'diːnə].

dupe [djuːp] *n* ingenuo,-a.
▶ *vt* engañar, embaucar.

duplex ['djuːpleks] *n* US *(house)* casa adosada; *(flat, apartment)* dúplex *m*.

duplicate [*(adj)*'djuːplɪkət; *(n)*'djuːplɪkeɪt] *adj* duplicado, a.
▶ *n* copia, duplicado. [LOC] in duplicate por duplicado.
▶ *vt* duplicar, hacer copias de.

durable ['djʊərəbəl] *adj* duradero,-a.

duration [djʊə'reɪʃən] *n* duración *f*.

during ['djʊərɪŋ] *prep* durante: *I lived in France during the war* viví en Francia durante la guerra; *she's out at work during the day* trabaja fuera de casa durante el día.

dusk [dʌsk] *n* anochecer *m*. [LOC] at dusk al anochecer.

dust [dʌst] *n* polvo.
▶ *vt* quitar el polvo a.

dustbin ['dʌstbɪn] *n* GB cubo de la basura. [COMP] dustbin man basurero.

dustcart ['dʌstkɑːt] *n* camión *m* de la basura.

duster ['dʌstər] *n (for dusting)* paño, trapo (del polvo); *(for blackboard)* borrador *m*.

dustman ['dʌstmən] *n* GB basurero.

dustpan ['dʌstpæn] *n* recogedor *m*.

Dutch [dʌtʃ] *adj* holandés,-esa, neerlandés,-esa. [LOC] to go Dutch (with sb) pagar a escote.
▶ *n (language)* holandés *m*.

Dutchman ['dʌtʃmən] *n* holandés *m*, neerlandés *m*.
ⓘ *pl* Dutchmen ['dʌtʃmən].

Dutchwoman ['dʌtʃwʊmən] *n* holandesa.
ⓘ *pl* Dutchwomen ['dʌtʃwɪmɪn].

duty ['djuːtɪ] *n* **1** *(obligation)* deber *m*, obligación *f*: *I feel it's my duty to go* creo que es mi obligación ir. **2** *(task)* función *f*, cometido: *her duties include dealing with the public* sus funciones incluyen atender al público. **3** *(service)* guardia, servicio. **4** *(tax)* impuesto. [LOC] to be off duty **1** *(doctor, nurse, etc)* no estar de guardia. **2** *(police, firefighter, etc)* no estar de servicio. ▌ to be on duty **1** *(doctor, nurse, etc)* estar de guardia. **2** *(police, firefighter, etc)* estar de servicio. [COMP] customs duties derechos *mpl* de aduana, aranceles *mpl*.
ⓘ *pl* duties.

duty-free ['djuːtɪfriː] *adj & adv* libre de impuestos. [COMP] duty-free shop duty-free *m*, tienda libre de impuestos.

duvet ['duːveɪ] *n* GB edredón *m*. [COMP] duvet cover funda de edredón.

DVD ['diːviːdiː] *n* (Digital Video Disc) DVD *m*. [COMP] DVD player lector *m* de DVD.

dwarf [dwɔːf] *n* enano,-a.
ⓘ *pl* dwarfs o dwarves [dwɔːz].
▶ *adj* enano,-a.

dwell [dwel] *vi fml* habitar, vivir.
ⓘ *pt & pp* dwelt [dwelt].

dweller ['dwelər] *n* habitante *mf*.

dwelling ['dwelɪŋ] *n fml* morada.

dwelt [dwelt] *pt & pp* → **dwell**.

dye [daɪ] *n* tinte *m*, tintura, colorante *m*.
▶ *vt* teñir.

dying ['daɪɪŋ] *adj* moribundo,-a.

dyke [daɪk] *n (bank)* dique *m*, barrera; *(causeway)* terraplén *m*.

dynamic [daɪ'næmɪk] *adj* dinámico,-a.

dynamics [daɪ'næmɪks] *n* dinámica.

dynamite ['daɪnəmaɪt] *n* dinamita.

dynamo ['daɪnəməʊ] *n* dinamo *f*.
ⓘ *pl* dynamos.

dynasty ['dɪnəstɪ] *n* dinastía.
ⓘ *pl* dynasties.

dyne [daɪn] *n* dina.

dysentery ['dɪsəntrɪ] *n* disentería.

dyslexia [dɪs'leksɪə] *n* dislexia.

dyslexic [dɪs'leksɪk] *adj* disléxico,-a.

dystrophy ['dɪstrəfɪ] *n* distrofia.

E

E, e [iː] *n* **1** *(the letter)* E, e *f*. **2** MUS mi *m*.

each [iːtʃ] *adj* cada: *each day* cada día, todos los días.
▶ *pron* cada uno,-a: *they each have their own car* cada uno tiene su coche.
▶ *adv* cada uno,-a: *apples cost 15p each* las manzanas cuestan 15 peniques la pieza.

✎ Each y every tienen significados muy similares. Each se emplea cuando se considera cada cosa por separado. Every, cuando se considera cada cosa en función del todo del que forma parte.

eager [ˈiːgəʳ] *adj (anxious)* ávido,-a (to, de), ansioso,-a (to, de); *(desirous)* deseoso,-a (to, de).

eagle [ˈiːgəl] *n* **1** *(bird)* águila. **2** *(in golf)* eagle *m*.

eaglet [ˈiːglət] *n* aguilucho.

ear¹ [ɪəʳ] *n* **1** ANAT oreja. **2** *(sense)* oído. ⸤COMP⸥ **ear canal** conducto auditivo. ‖ **ear flap** orejera. ‖ **ear lobe** lóbulo. ‖ **ear, nose and throat specialist** otorrinolaringólogo,-a.

ear² [ɪəʳ] *n (of cereal)* espiga.

earache [ˈɪəreɪk] *n* dolor *m* de oídos.

eardrum [ˈɪədrʌm] *n* tímpano.

earflap [ˈɪəflæp] *n* orejera.

earl [ɜːl] *n* conde *m*.

early [ˈɜːlɪ] *adj* **1** *(before expected)* temprano,-a, pronto,-a: *we were early* llegamos temprano. **2** *(initial)* primero,-a: *take the early train* coge el primer tren de la mañana. **3** *(near beginning)*: *in the early 1960's* a principios de los sesenta.
ⓘ *comp* **earlier**, *superl* **earliest**.
▶ *adv* **1** *(before expected)* temprano, pronto; *(soon)* pronto: *she got up early* se levantó temprano. **2** *(in good time)* con tiempo, con anticipación: *we got there early to get a good seat* llegamos con tiempo para coger buen sitio.

earn [ɜːn] *vt* ganar, ganarse: *how much do you earn a month?* ¿cuánto ganas al mes?

✎ Cuando se habla de dinero, la diferencia entre earn y win (ambos, 'ganar') es que earn se refiere al dinero que se gana trabajando y win al que se obtiene por azar, como en la lotería.

earner [ˈɜːnəʳ] *n* **1** *(person)* persona que gana dinero: *I'm the only earner in the family* soy el único de la familia que gana un sueldo. **2** *(thing)* cosa rentable.

earnest [ˈɜːnɪst] *adj* serio,-a, formal.

earnings [ˈɜːnɪŋz] *n pl* **1** *(personal)* ingresos *mpl*. **2** *(of company)* ganancias *fpl*.

earphones [ˈɪəfəʊnz] *n pl* auriculares *mpl*.

earplug [ˈɪəplʌg] *n* tapón *m* para los oídos.

earring [ˈɪərɪŋ] *n* pendiente *m*.

earth [ɜːθ] *n* **1** *(gen)* tierra. **2** GB toma de tierra, tierra. **3** GB *(of fox, badger)* madriguera.

✎ Cuando se refiere al planeta Tierra se suele escribir con mayúscula: Earth.

earthen [ˈɜːðən] *adj* **1** *(of earth)* de tierra. **2** *(of baked clay)* de barro, de arcilla.

earthquake [ˈɜːθkweɪk] *n* terremoto.

earthworm [ˈɜːθwɜːm] *n* lombriz *f*.

earwax [ˈɪəwæks] *n* cerumen *m*, cera.

earwig [ˈɪəwɪg] *n* tijereta.

ease [iːz] *n* **1** *(lack of difficulty)* facilidad *f*. **2** *(natural manner)* soltura, naturalidad *f*. **3** *(freedom from pain)* alivio. **4** *(leisure, affluence)* comodidad *f*, desahogo.

► vt 1 *(relieve, alleviate)* aliviar (of, de), calmar. 2 *(improve)* mejorar, facilitar; *(make easier)* facilitar.

► vi 1 *(pain)* aliviarse, calmarse; *(tension, etc)* disminuir. 2 *(become easier)* mejorar.

◆ **to ease off / ease up** vi 1 *(pain)* aliviarse, calmarse; *(tension, etc)* disminuir; *(rain)* amainar. 2 *(slow down)* ir más despacio.

◆ **to ease up on** vt insep fam *(go easy, be more moderate)* aflojar, no pasarse con.

easel ['i:zəl] n caballete m.

easily ['i:zɪlɪ] adv 1 *(without difficulty)* fácilmente, con facilidad. 2 *(by far)* con mucho; *(without doubt)* sin duda.

east [i:st] adj *(gen)* este, oriental; *(wind)* del este.
► adv hacia el este.
► n este m.
► n **the East** *(Asia)* Oriente m; *(Eastern Europe)* el Este m.

Easter ['i:stə'] n 1 REL Pascua (de Resurrección). 2 *(holiday)* Semana Santa.

easterly ['i:stəlɪ] adj 1 *(to the east)* al este, hacia el este. 2 *(from the east)* del este.
► n viento del este.
ⓘ pl **easterlies**.

eastern ['i:stən] adj oriental, del este.

eastward ['i:stwəd] adj hacia el este.

eastwards ['i:stwədz] adv hacia el este.

easy ['i:zɪ] adj 1 *(not difficult)* fácil, sencillo. 2 *(comfortable)* cómodo,-a, holgado,-a. 3 *(unworried, relaxed)* tranquilo,-a.
ⓘ comp **easier**, superl **easiest**.
► adv con cuidado, con calma.

easy-going [i:zɪˈgəʊɪŋ] adj *(relaxed)* tranquilo,-a; *(easy to please)* fácil de complacer, poco exigente.

eat [i:t] vt comer.
► vi comer.
◆ **to eat away** vt sep *(mice)* roer; *(termites)* carcomer; *(acid)* corroer.
◆ **to eat out** vi *(lunch)* comer fuera; *(dinner)* cenar fuera.
◆ **to eat up** vt sep 1 *(finish food)* comerse: *eat it all up!* ¡cómetelo todo!. 2 *(consume)* consumir, tragar, devorar.
ⓘ pt **ate** [et, eɪt], pp **eaten** ['i:tən].

eaten ['i:tən] pp → eat.

eavesdrop ['i:vzdrɒp] vi escuchar a escondidas (on, -).
ⓘ pt & pp **eavesdropped**, ger **eavesdropping**.

ebb [eb] n reflujo.
► vi 1 *(water)* bajar. 2 fig disminuir.

ebonite ['ebənaɪt] n ebonita.

ebony ['ebənɪ] n ébano.

eccentric [ɪkˈsentrɪk] adj excéntrico,-a.
► n *(person)* excéntrico,-a.

echinoderm [ɪˈkaɪnəʊdɜ:m] n equinodermo.

echo ['ekəʊ] n eco.
ⓘ pl **echoes**.
► vt 1 repetir *(back, -)*. 2 fig *(words)* repetir, imitar; *(opinions)* hacerse eco de.

eclectic [ɪˈklektɪk] adj fml ecléctico,-a.
► n ecléctico,-a.

eclipse [ɪˈklɪps] n eclipse m.
► vt eclipsar.

ecofriendly [ekəʊˈfrendlɪ] adj que no perjudica el medio ambiente.

ecological [i:kəˈlɒdʒɪkəl] adj ecológico,-a. COMP **ecological footprint** huella ecológica.

ecologist [ɪˈkɒlədʒɪst] n ecologista mf.

ecology [ɪˈkɒlədʒɪ] n ecología.

economic [ekəˈnɒmɪk, i:kəˈnɒmɪk] adj 1 *(gen)* económico,-a. 2 *(profitable)* rentable.

economically [ekəˈnɒmɪklɪ, i:kəˈnɒmɪklɪ] adv económicamente: *economically speaking* en términos económicos.

economics [ekəˈnɒmɪks, i:kəˈnɒmɪks] n 1 *(science)* economía. 2 EDUC económicas fpl, ciencias fpl económicas.

economist [ɪˈkɒnəmɪst] n economista mf.

economize [ɪˈkɒnəmaɪz] vi economizar (on, en), ahorrar (on, en).

economy [ɪˈkɒnəmɪ] n 1 *(saving)* economía, ahorro. 2 *(science)* economía.
ⓘ pl **economies**.

ecosystem ['i:kəʊsɪstəm] n ecosistema m.

Ecuador ['ekwədɔ:'] n Ecuador m.

Ecuadorian [ekwəˈdɔ:rɪən] adj ecuatoriano,-a.
► n ecuatoriano,-a.

eczema ['eksɪmə] n eccema m.

edema [ɪˈdi:mə] n US → oedema.

Eden ['iːdən] n el Edén m.

edge [edʒ] n **1** (of cliff, wood, etc) borde m. **2** (of coin, step, etc) canto. **3** (of knife) filo. **4** (of water) orilla. **5** (of town) afueras fpl. **6** (of paper) margen m.
▶ vt **1** (supply with border) bordear. **2** SEW ribetear.
◆ **to edge away** vi alejarse poco a poco.
◆ **to edge forward** vi avanzar lentamente, avanzar poco a poco.

edible ['edɪbəl] adj comestible.

edict ['iːdɪkt] n **1** edicto. **2** JUR decreto.

edit ['edɪt] vt **1** (prepare for printing) preparar para la imprenta. **2** (correct) corregir; (put together) editar. **3** (run newspaper, etc) dirigir. **4** (film, programme) montar, editar.
◆ **to edit out** vt sep cortar.

edition [ɪ'dɪʃən] n edición f.

editor ['edɪtər] n **1** (of book) editor,-ra; (writer) redactor,-ra; (proofreader) corrector,-ra. **2** (of newspaper, etc) director,-ra. **3** (of film, programme) montador,-ra.

editorial [edɪ'tɔːrɪəl] adj editorial.
▶ n editorial m. COMP **editorial staff** redacción f.

educate ['edjukeɪt] vt educar.

educated ['edjukeɪtɪd] adj culto,-a, cultivado,-a.

> ☒ **Educated** no significa 'educado (de buenos modales)', que se traduce por polite.

education [edju'keɪʃən] n **1** (system of teaching) educación f, enseñanza. **2** (training) formación f, preparación f. **3** (acquisition of knowledge) estudios mpl, formación f académica. **4** (theory of teaching) pedagogía. **5** (knowledge, culture) cultura.

> ☒ **Education** no significa 'educación (buenos modales)', que se traduce por manners.

educational [edju'keɪʃənəl] adj educativo,-a.

eel [iːl] n anguila.

eerie ['ɪərɪ] adj misterioso,-a.

effect [ɪ'fekt] n efecto.
▶ vt fml efectuar, provocar.
▶ n pl **effects** (property) efectos mpl.

effective [ɪ'fektɪv] adj **1** (successful) eficaz. **2** (real, actual) efectivo,-a. **3** (operative) vigente. **4** (impressive) impresionante; (striking) llamativo,-a.

effervescent [efə'vesənt] adj efervescente.

efficiency [ɪ'fɪʃənsɪ] n **1** (of person) eficiencia, competencia. **2** (of system, product) eficacia. **3** (of machine) rendimiento.

efficient [ɪ'fɪʃənt] adj **1** (person) eficiente, competente. **2** (system, product) eficaz. **3** (machine) de buen rendimiento.

effigy ['efɪdʒɪ] n efigie f.
ⓘ pl **effigies**.

effort ['efət] n **1** (exertion) esfuerzo. **2** (attempt, struggle) intento, tentativa. **3** (achievement) obra.

egg¹ [eg] n **1** (laid by birds, etc) huevo. **2** BIOL (ovum) óvulo. COMP **boiled egg** huevo pasado por agua.

egg² [eg] vt **to egg on** animar, incitar.

eggplant ['egplɑːnt] n US berenjena.

eggshell ['egʃel] n cáscara de huevo.

ego ['iːgəu] n ego.
ⓘ pl **egos**.

egocentric [iːgəu'sentrɪk] adj egocéntrico,-a.

egoism ['iːgəuɪzəm] n egoísmo.

egoist ['iːgəuɪst] n egoísta mf.

Egypt ['iːdʒɪpt] n Egipto.

Egyptian [ɪ'dʒɪpʃən] adj egipcio,-a.
▶ n **1** (person) egipcio,-a. **2** (language) egipcio.

eider ['aɪdər] [also eider duck] n eider m.

eiderdown ['aɪdədaun] n edredón m.

eight [eɪt] adj ocho.
▶ n ocho.

✎ Consulta también **six**.

eighteen [eɪ'tiːn] adj dieciocho.
▶ n dieciocho.

✎ Consulta también **six**.

eighteenth [eɪ'tiːnθ] adj decimoctavo,-a.
▶ adv en decimoctavo lugar.

▶ *n* **1** *(in series)* decimoctavo,-a. **2** *(fraction)* decimoctavo; *(one part)* decimoctava parte *f*.

✎ Consulta también sixth.

eighth [eɪtθ] *adj* octavo,-a.
▶ *adv* en octavo lugar.
▶ *n* **1** *(in series)* octavo,-a. **2** *(fraction)* octavo; *(one part)* octava parte *f*.

✎ Consulta también sixth.

eightieth ['eɪtɪɪθ] *adj* octogésimo,-a.
▶ *adv* en octogésimo lugar.
▶ *n* **1** *(in series)* octogésimo,-a. **2** *(fraction)* octogésimo; *(one part)* octogésima parte *f*.

✎ Consulta también sixtieth.

eighty ['eɪtɪ] *adj* ochenta.
▶ *n* ochenta.

✎ Consulta también sixty.

either ['aɪðə', 'i:ðə'] *pron* **1** *(affirmative)* cualquiera: *either of them* cualquiera de los dos. **2** *(negative)* ni el uno ni el otro, ni la una ni la otra, ninguno de los dos, ninguna de las dos: *I can't stand either* no aguanto ni el uno ni el otro.
▶ *adj* **1** cualquier. **2** *(both)* cada, los dos, las dos, ambos,-as. **3** *(neither)* ninguno de los dos, ninguna de las dos.
▶ *conj* **1** *(affirmative)* o: *he'll arrive either today or tomorrow* llegará u hoy o mañana. **2** *(negative)* ni: *I didn't go to either the wedding or the party* no fui ni a la boda ni a la fiesta.
▶ *adv* *(after negative)* tampoco: *Ann didn't come either* tampoco vino Ann.

ejaculation [ɪdʒækʊ'leɪʃən] *n* **1** *(ejection)* eyaculación *f*. **2** *(exclamation)* exclamación *f*.

eject [ɪ'dʒekt] *vt* expulsar, echar.
▶ *vi* AV eyectar(se).

ejection [ɪ'dʒekʃən] *n* **1** *(gen)* expulsión *f*. **2** *(from plane)* eyección *f*.

elaborate [*(adj)* ɪ'læbərət; *(vb)* ɪ'læbəreɪt] *adj* **1** *(detailed, extensive)* detallado,-a. **2** *(ornate, intricate)* muy trabajado,-a, esmerado,-a. **3** *(complex, intricate)* complicado,-a.
▶ *vt* *(work out in detail, refine)* elaborar.

▶ *vi* *(discuss in detail)* explicar detalladamente; *(expand)* ampliar, dar más detalles.

elaboration [ɪlæbə'reɪʃən] *n* **1** *(working out in detail)* elaboración *f*. **2** *(additional detail)* complicación *f*, detalle *m*.

elastic [ɪ'læstɪk] *adj* elástico,-a. COMP
elastic band goma elástica.

elasticity [ɪlæ'stɪsətɪ] *n* elasticidad *f*.

Elastoplast® [ɪ'læstəplɑːst] *n* tirita®.

elbow ['elbəʊ] *n* **1** ANAT codo. **2** *(bend)* recodo.

elder ['eldə'] *adj* mayor.
▶ *n* **1** mayor *m*. **2** REL anciano,-a.

elderly ['eldəlɪ] *adj* mayor, anciano,-a.
▶ *n* **the elderly** los ancianos *mpl*.

eldest ['eldɪst] *adj* mayor.
▶ *n* el mayor, la mayor.

elect [ɪ'lekt] *adj* electo,-a.
▶ *vt* **1** *(vote for)* elegir. **2** *(choose, decide)* decidir.

election [ɪ'lekʃən] *n* elección *f*.
▶ *adj* electoral.

elector [ɪ'lektə'] *n* elector,-ra.

electoral [ɪ'lektərəl] *adj* electoral. COMP
electoral college colegio electoral. **electoral roll / electoral register** censo electoral.

electorate [ɪ'lektərət] *n* electorado.

electric [ɪ'lektrɪk] *adj* eléctrico,-a.

electrical [ɪ'lektrɪkəl] *adj* eléctrico,-a.

electrician [ɪlek'trɪʃən] *n* electricista *mf*.

electricity [ɪlek'trɪsɪtɪ] *n* electricidad *f*.

electrocute [ɪ'lektrəkjuːt] *vt* electrocutar.

electrode [ɪ'lektrəʊd] *n* electrodo.

electrolysis [ɪlek'trɒləsɪs] *n* electrólisis *f*.

electrolyte [ɪ'lektrəlaɪt] *n* electrolito, electrólito.

electromagnet [ɪlektrəʊ'mægnɪt] *n* electroimán *m*.

electromagnetism [ɪlektrəʊ'mægnɪtɪzəm] *n* electromagnetismo.

electromagnetic [ɪlektrəʊmæg'netɪk] *adj* electromagnético,-a.

electron [ɪ'lektrɒn] *n* electrón *m*. COMP
electron microscope microscopio electrónico.

E

electronic [ɪlek'trɒnɪk] *adj* electrónico,-a.

electronics [ɪlek'trɒnɪks] *n (science, technology)* electrónica.
▸ *n pl (circuits and devices)* componentes *mpl* electrónicos.

elegance ['elɪgəns] *n* elegancia.

elegant ['elɪgənt] *adj* elegante.

element ['elɪmənt] *n* **1** CHEM elemento. **2** *(necessary part of a whole)* parte *f*, componente *m*. **3** ELEC resistencia. **4** *(group, section)* fracción *f*.
▸ *n pl* **elements 1***(weather)* los elementos *mpl*. **2***(basics)* rudimentos *mpl*.

elementary [elɪ'mentərɪ] *adj* **1** *(basic)* elemental, básico,-a. **2** *(easy)* fácil, sencillo,-a. COMP **elementary education** enseñanza primaria.

elephant ['elɪfənt] *n* elefante *m*. COMP **elephant seal** elefante *m* marino.

elevate ['elɪveɪt] *vt fml (raise)* elevar; *(promote)* ascender, promover.

elevated ['elɪveɪtɪd] *adj fml (fine, noble)* elevado,-a, noble.

elevation [elɪ'veɪʃən] *n* **1** *fml (gen)* elevación *f*. **2** *fml (in rank)* ascenso. **3** *(height)* altitud *f*, altura. **4** ARCH alzado.

elevator ['elɪveɪtəʳ] *n* **1** US ascensor *m*. **2** *(machine)* montacargas *m*.

eleven [ɪ'levən] *adj* once.
▸ *n* once *m*.

✎ Consulta también **six**.

eleventh [ɪ'levənθ] *adj* undécimo,-a.
▸ *adv* en undécimo lugar.
▸ *n* **1** *(in series)* undécimo,-a, onceno,-a. **2** *(fraction)* onceavo, undécimo; *(one part)* onceava parte *f*, undécima parte *f*.

✎ Consulta también **sixth**.

elicit [ɪ'lɪsɪt] *vt* **1** *fml (facts, information)* sonsacar, obtener. **2** *(reaction, response)* provocar.

elide [ɪ'laɪd] *vt* elidir.
▸ *vi* elidirse.

eligible ['elɪdʒəbəl] *adj* **1** *(qualified, suitable)* idóneo,-a, apto,-a. **2** *(desirable)* deseable.

eliminate [ɪ'lɪmɪneɪt] *vt* eliminar.

elision [ɪ'lɪʒən] *n* elisión *f*.

elite [eɪ'li:t] *n* elite *f*.
▸ *adj* exclusivo,-a, selecto,-a.

elk [elk] *n* alce *m*.

ellipse [ɪ'lɪps] *n* elipse *f*.

ellipsis [ɪ'lɪpsɪs] *n* elipsis *f*.
① *pl* **ellipses** [ɪ'lɪpsi:z].

elliptic [ɪ'lɪptɪk] *adj* elíptico,-a.

elm [elm] *n* olmo.

elongated ['i:lɒŋgeɪtɪd] *adj* alargado,-a.

eloquence ['eləkwəns] *n* elocuencia.

eloquent ['eləkwənt] *adj* elocuente.

else [els] *adv* más, otro,-a: *anything else?* ¿algo más?; *where else have you been?* ¿en qué otro(s) sitio(s) has estado?

elsewhere [els'weəʳ] *adv* en otro sitio, en otra parte.

elude [ɪ'lu:d] *vt* **1** *(escape from)* escaparse de. **2** *(avoid)* eludir. **3** *(not remember)* no recordar, no acordarse; *(not understand)* no entenderse.

elusive [ɪ'lu:sɪv] *adj* **1** *(difficult to capture)* huidizo,-a, esquivo,-a. **2** *(difficult to remember)* difícil de recordar; *(difficult to understand)* difícil de entender.

e-mail ['i:meɪl] *n* correo electrónico.

emancipate [ɪ'mænsɪpeɪt] *vt* emancipar.

emancipation [ɪmænsɪ'peɪʃən] *n* emancipación *f*.

embankment [ɪm'bæŋkmənt] *n* **1** *(wall, earth, etc)* terraplén *m*. **2** *(river bank)* dique *m*.

embargo [em'bɑ:gəʊ] *n* embargo.
① *pl* **embargoes**.
▸ *vt* **1** *(prohibit)* prohibir. **2** *(seize)* embargar.
① *pt & pp* **embargoed**, *ger* **embargoing**.

embark [ɪm'bɑ:k] *vt* embarcar.
◆ **to embark on** *vt insep* emprender.

embarrass [ɪm'bærəs] *vt (make ashamed)* avergonzar, hacer pasar vergüenza a; *(make awkward)* desconcertar.

embarrassed [ɪm'bærəst] *adj (behaviour, action)* embarazoso,-a; *(person)* avergonzado,-a, molesto,-a.

☒ **Embarrassed** no significa 'embarazada', que se traduce por **pregnant**.

embarrassing [ɪmˈbærəsɪŋ] *adj* embarazoso,-a, violento,-a, desconcertante.

embarrassment [ɪmˈbærəsmənt] *n* **1** *(state)* vergüenza, desconcierto. **2** *(person, object)* vergüenza, estorbo. **3** *(event, situation)* disgusto, vergüenza.

embassy [ˈembəsɪ] *n* embajada.
ⓘ *pl* embassies.

embed [ɪmˈbed] *vt (jewels, stones)* incrustar; *(weapon, nails)* clavar (in, en).
ⓘ *pt & pp* embedded, *ger* embedding.

embellish [ɪmˈbelɪʃ] *vt* adornar, embellecer.

ember [ˈembəʳ] *n* brasa, ascua.

emblem [ˈembləm] *n* emblema *m*.

emblematic [embləˈmætɪk] *adj* emblemático,-a.

emboss [ɪmˈbɒs] *vt (leather, metal)* repujar; *(initials)* grabar en relieve.

embrace [ɪmˈbreɪs] *n* abrazo.
▶ *vt* **1** *(hug)* abrazar, dar un abrazo a. **2** *(include)* abarcar, incluir. **3** *fml (accept - opportunity, etc)* aprovechar; *(- offer)* aceptar. **4** *fml (adopt - religion, etc)* convertirse a; *(- new idea)* abrazar.

embroidery [ɪmˈbrɔɪdəəɪ] *n* SEW bordado.

embryo [ˈembrɪəu] *n* embrión *m*.
ⓘ *pl* embryos.
▶ *adj* embrionario,-a.

emerald [ˈemərəld] *n* esmeralda *f*.
▶ *adj* (de color) esmeralda.

emerge [ɪˈmɜːdʒ] *vi* **1** *(come out)* emerger, aparecer, salir. **2** *(become known)* resultar.

emergence [ɪˈmɜːdʒəns] *n* aparición *f*.

emergency [ɪˈmɜːdʒənsɪ] *n* **1** emergencia. **2** MED urgencia.
ⓘ *pl* emergencies.
▶ *adj* de emergencia, de urgencia.

emergent [ɪˈmɜːdʒənt] *adj* **1** *(emerging)* emergente. **2** *(of countries, nations)* en vías de desarrollo.

emery [ˈeməɪ] *n* esmeril *m*.

emigrant [ˈemɪgrənt] *n* emigrante *mf*.

emigrate [ˈemɪgreɪt] *vi* emigrar.

emigration [emɪˈgreɪʃən] *n* emigración *f*.

eminence [ˈemɪnəns] *n* eminencia.

eminent [ˈemɪnənt] *adj* **1** *(of person)* eminente. **2** *(of qualities)* destacado,-a.

emir [eˈmɪəʳ] *n* emir *m*.

emirate [ˈemɪrət] *n* emirato. COMP
United Arab Emirates Emiratos *mpl* Árabes Unidos.

emissary [ˈemɪsərɪ] *n* emisario,-a.
ⓘ *pl* emissaries.

emission [ɪˈmɪʃən] *n* emisión *f*.

⊠ Emission no significa 'emisión (de televisión)', que se traduce por programme.

emit [ɪˈmɪt] *vt (signal, heat, light, smoke)* emitir, producir; *(sound, noise)* producir; *(smell)* despedir; *(cry)* dar.
ⓘ *pt & pp* emitted, *ger* emitting.

emoticon [ɪˈmɒtɪkɒn] *n* COMPUT emoticón *m*, emoticono.

emotion [ɪˈməʊʃən] *n* **1** *(feeling)* sentimiento. **2** *(strong feeling)* emoción *f*.

emotional [ɪˈməʊʃənəl] *adj* **1** *(connected with feelings)* emocional, afectivo,-a. **2** *(moving)* conmovedor,-ra, emotivo,-a. **3** *(sensitive)* emotivo,-a, sentimental.

emotive [ɪˈməʊtɪv] *adj* emotivo,-a.

emperor [ˈempərəʳ] *n* emperador *m*.

emphasis [ˈemfəsɪs] *n* énfasis *m*.
ⓘ *pl* emphases [ˈemfəsiːs].

emphasize [ˈemfəsaɪz] *vt* enfatizar.

emphatic [emˈfætɪk] *adj* **1** *(forceful - tone, gesture)* enfático,-a, enérgico,-a. **2** *(insistent - refusal, rejection, assertion)* categórico,-a, rotundo,-a.

empire [ˈempaɪəʳ] *n* imperio: *the British Empire* el Imperio Británico.

empirical [emˈpɪrɪkəl] *adj* empírico,-a.

employ [ɪmˈplɔɪ] *n* *fml* empleo.
▶ *vt* **1** *(give work to)* emplear; *(appoint)* contratar. **2** *fml (make use of, use)* emplear, usar. **3** *(occupy)* ocupar.

employed [ɪmˈplɔɪd] *adj* **1** *(in work)* empleado,-a. **2** *(busy)* ocupado,-a.

employee [emˈplɔɪiː, emplɔɪˈiː] *n* empleado,-a.

employer [emˈplɔɪəʳ] *n* **1** *(manager, boss)* empresario,-a; *(of domestic worker)* patrón,-ona. **2** *(company, organization)* empresa, organismo.

employment [em'plɔɪmənt] *n* **1** *(work)* trabajo; *(availability of work)* empleo. **2** *(use)* empleo, uso.

empress ['emprəs] *n* emperatriz *f*.

empty ['emptɪ] *adj* **1** *(gen)* vacío,-a; *(place)* desierto,-a; *(house)* desocupado,-a, deshabitado,-a; *(seat, table, place)* libre. **2** *fam (hungry)* hambriento,-a.
ⓘ *comp* emptier, *superl* emptiest.
▶ *vt* vaciar.
▶ *n pl* empties envases *mpl*, cascos *mpl*.

emulsifier [ɪ'mʌlsɪfaɪəʳ] *n* emulsionante *m*.

emulsify [ɪ'mʌlsɪfaɪ] *vt* emulsionar.
ⓘ *pt & pp* emulsified, *ger* emulsifying.

emulsion [ɪ'mʌlʃən] *n* emulsión *f*.

enable [ɪ'neɪbəl] *vt* permitir.

enact [ɪ'nækt] *vt* **1** *(law)* promulgar. **2** *(play)* representar.

enamel [ɪ'næməl] *n* esmalte *m*.
▶ *vt* esmaltar.
ⓘ *pt & pp* enamelled *(US* enameled*)*, *ger* enamelling *(US* enameling*)*.

encephalic [ensɪ'fælɪk] *adj* encefálico,-a.

enchant [ɪn'tʃɑːnt] *vt* **1** *(delight)* encantar, cautivar. **2** *(cast spell on)* hechizar.

enchanted [ɪn'tʃɑːntɪd] *adj* encantado,-a.

enchanting [ɪn'tʃɑːntɪŋ] *adj* encantador,-ra.

enchantment [ɪn'tʃɑːntmənt] *n* **1** *(delight)* encanto. **2** *(spell)* hechizo.

encircle [ɪn'sɜːkəl] *vt* rodear, cercar.

enclitic [en'klɪtɪk] *adj* enclítico,-a.

enclose [ɪn'kləʊz] *vt* **1** *(surround)* encerrar; *(with wall or fence)* cercar, rodear. **2** *(include in letter)* adjuntar.

enclosure [ɪn'kləʊʒəʳ] *n* **1** *(land)* cercado; *(area)* recinto. **2** *(with letter)* anexo, documento adjunto.

encode [ɪŋ'kəʊd] *vt* codificar.

encore ['ɒŋkɔːʳ] *interj* ¡otra!.
▶ *n* repetición *f*, bis *m*.

encounter [ɪn'kaʊntəʳ] *n* encuentro.
▶ *vt (meet)* encontrar, encontrarse con; *(be faced with)* tropezar con.

encourage [ɪn'kʌrɪdʒ] *vt* **1** *(cheer, inspire)* animar, alentar. **2** *(develop, stimulate)* fomentar, favorecer, estimular.

encouragement [ɪn'kʌrɪdʒmənt] *n* **1** *(act)* aliento, ánimo. **2** *(development)* fomento, estímulo.

encrypt [en'krɪpt] *vt* cifrar.

encyclopaedia [ensaɪklə'piːdɪə] *n* enciclopedia.

encyclopedia [ensaɪklə'piːdɪə] *n* enciclopedia.

end [end] *n* **1** *(extremity - of rope)* cabo; *(- of street)* final *m*; *(- of table, sofa)* extremo; *(- of stick, tail)* punta; *(- of box)* lado. **2** *(final part, finish)* fin *m*, final *m*. **3** *(aim)* objeto, objetivo, fin *m*. **4** *(of cigarette)* colilla.
▶ *adj* final, último,-a.
▶ *vt* **1** *(conclude)* acabar, terminar. **2** *(stop)* terminar, poner fin a, acabar con.
◆ **to end in** *vi* acabar en.
◆ **to end off** *vt sep* acabar.
◆ **to end up** *vi* acabar, terminar.

endanger [ɪn'deɪndʒəʳ] *vt* poner en peligro.

endangered [ɪn'deɪndʒəd] *adj* en peligro. [COMP] **endangered species** especie *f* en peligro (de extinción).

endeavor [ɪn'devəʳ] *n* US → endeavour.

endeavour [ɪn'devəʳ] *n fml* esfuerzo, empeño.
▶ *vi* esforzarse, intentar, procurar.

endemic [en'demɪk] *adj* endémico,-a.

ending ['endɪŋ] *n* **1** final *m*, conclusión *f*, desenlace *m*. **2** LING terminación *f*.

endive ['endaɪv] *n* **1** GB escarola. **2** US endibia.

endless ['endləs] *adj* interminable.

endocarp ['endəʊkɑːp] *n* endocarpio.

endocrine ['endəʊkrɪn] *adj* endocrino,-a. [COMP] **endocrine gland** glándula endocrina.

endorse [ɪn'dɔːs] *vt* **1** *(of cheque, etc)* endosar. **2** *(approve)* aprobar, apoyar.

endow [ɪn'daʊ] *vt* **1** *(bless)* dotar. **2** *(give money)* dotar (de fondos).

endurance [ɪn'djʊərəns] *n* resistencia, aguante *m*.
▶ *adj* de resistencia.

endure [ɪn'djʊəʳ] *vt* soportar, aguantar.

▶ vi *(continue to exist, survive)* durar.
enemy ['enəmɪ] *n* enemigo,-a.
ⓘ *pl* enemies.
▶ *adj* enemigo,-a.
energetic [enə'dʒetɪk] *adj* enérgico,-a.
energy ['enədʒɪ] *n* energía.
▶ *n pl* **energies** *(efforts)* energías *fpl*, fuerzas *fpl*.
ⓘ *pl* energies.
enforce [ɪn'fɔːs] *vt* **1** *(force to obey)* hacer cumplir. **2** *(impose)* imponer.
engage [ɪn'ɡeɪdʒ] *vt* **1** *(hire)* contratar. **2** *(take up, occupy)* ocupar, entretener. **3** *(attract)* llamar, atraer, captar. **5** AUTO *(gear)* engranar, meter; *(clutch)* apretar. **6** TECH engranar con.
engaged [ɪn'ɡeɪdʒd] *adj* **1** *(to be married)* prometido,-a. **2** *(busy)* ocupado,-a.
engagement [ɪn'ɡeɪdʒmənt] *n* **1** *(to be married)* petición *f* de mano; *(period)* noviazgo. **2** *(appointment)* compromiso, cita. **3** MIL combate *m*. **4** *(employment)* contrato, empleo.
engaging [ɪn'ɡeɪdʒɪŋ] *adj* atractivo,-a.
engine ['endʒɪn] *n* **1** motor *m*. **2** *(of train)* máquina, locomotora. COMP **engine driver** maquinista *mf*.
engineer [endʒɪ'nɪər] *n* **1** *(graduate)* ingeniero,-a; *(technician)* técnico,-a. **2** US maquinista *mf*.
▶ *vt (contrive)* maquinar, tramar, urdir.
engineering [endʒɪ'nɪərɪŋ] *n* ingeniería.
England ['ɪŋɡlənd] *n* Inglaterra.
English ['ɪŋɡlɪʃ] *adj* inglés,-esa.
▶ *n (language)* inglés *m*.
Englishman ['ɪŋɡlɪʃmən] *n* inglés *m*.
ⓘ *pl* Englishmen.
English-speaking ['ɪŋɡlɪʃspiːkɪŋ] *adj* de habla inglesa.
Englishwoman ['ɪŋɡlɪʃwʊmən] *n* inglesa.
ⓘ *pl* Englishwomen ['ɪŋɡlɪʃwɪmɪn].
engrave [ɪn'ɡreɪv] *vt* grabar.
engrossed [ɪn'ɡrəʊst] *adj* absorto,-a (in, en).
engulf [ɪn'ɡʌlf] *vt* envolver.
enhance [ɪn'hɑːns] *vt* **1** *(beauty, taste)* realzar; *(quality, chances)* mejorar; *(power, value)* aumentar. **2** COMPUT procesar.

enigma [ɪ'nɪɡmə] *n* enigma *m*.
enigmatic [enɪɡ'mætɪk] *adj* enigmático,-a.
enjoy [ɪn'dʒɔɪ] *vt* **1** *(get pleasure from)* disfrutar de; *(like)* gustarle a uno. **2** *(benefit from)* gozar de.
enjoyment [ɪn'dʒɔɪmənt] *n* placer *m*.
enlarge [ɪn'lɑːdʒ] *vt* **1** *(gen)* extender, aumentar; *(photograph)* ampliar.
enlargement [ɪn'lɑːdʒmənt] *n* **1** *(photograph)* ampliación *f*. **2** extensión *f*.
enlighten [ɪn'laɪtən] *vt* **1** *(free from ignorance)* iluminar, ilustrar. **2** *(inform)* informar, instruir.
enlightenment [ɪn'laɪtənmənt] *n* **1** *fml (act)* aclaración *f*, explicación *f*. **2** *(liberalism)* tolerancia.
▶ *n* the Enlightenment la Ilustración *f*.
enliven [ɪn'laɪvən] *vt* avivar, animar.
enormous [ɪ'nɔːməs] *adj* enorme.
enough [ɪ'nʌf] *adj* bastante, suficiente.
▶ *adv* bastante, suficientemente.
enquire [ɪŋ'kwaɪər] *vt* preguntar.
▶ *vi* **1** preguntar, informarse. **2** JUR investigar (into, -).
enquiry [ɪŋ'kwaɪərɪ] *n* **1** pregunta. **2** JUR investigación *f*.
ⓘ *pl* enquiries.
enrage [ɪn'reɪdʒ] *vt* enfurecer.
enrich [ɪn'rɪtʃ] *vt* enriquecer.
enrol [ɪn'rəʊl] *vt* matricular, inscribir.
▶ *vi* matricularse, inscribirse.
ⓘ *pt & pp* enrolled, *ger* enrolling.
enroll [ɪn'rəʊl] *n* US → enrol.
enrollment [ɪn'rəʊlmənt] *n* US → enrolment.
enrolment [ɪn'rəʊlmənt] *n* matrícula, inscripción *f*.
ensemble [ɒn'sɒmbəl] *n* conjunto.
ensue [ɪn'sjuː] *vi* **1** *(follow)* seguir. **2** *(result)* resultar (from, de).
ensure [ɪn'ʃʊər] *vt* **1** *(make sure)* asegurarse. **2** *(assure)* asegurar.
entail [ɪn'teɪl] *vt* *(involve, mean)* suponer, implicar; *(make necessary)* ocasionar.
entangle [ɪn'tæŋɡəl] *vt* enredar.
enter ['entər] *vt* **1** *(gen)* entrar en. **3** *(participate)* participar en; *(register)* inscribirse en. **4** *(write down, record)* anotar, apuntar.

E

enterprise ['entəpraɪz] *n* **1** *(venture)* empresa, proyecto. **2** *(initiative)* iniciativa. **3** *(firm)* empresa.

entertain [entə'teɪn] *vt* **1** *(amuse)* entretener, divertir. **2** *fml (suggestion, etc)* considerar, tener en cuenta; *(doubts, etc)* abrigar. **3** *(invite)* recibir, invitar.
▸ *vi (act as host)* tener invitados.

> ☒ To entertain no significa 'entretener (distraer)', que se traduce por to occupy.

entertaining [entə'teɪnɪŋ] *adj* divertido,-a, entretenido,-a.

entertainment [entə'teɪnmənt] *n* **1** *(amusement)* entretenimiento, diversión *f*. **2** THEAT espectáculo, función *f*.

enthral [ɪn'θrɔːl] *vt* cautivar.
ⓘ *pt & pp* enthralled, *ger* enthralling.

enthrall [ɪn'θrɔːl] *vt* US → enrol.

enthrone [ɪn'θrəʊn] *vt* entronizar.

enthusiasm [ɪn'θjuːzɪæzəm] *n* entusiasmo (about/for, por).

enthusiast [ɪn'θjuːzɪæst] *n* entusiasta *mf*.

enthusiastic [ɪnθjuːzɪ'æstɪk] *adj* **1** *(reaction)* entusiástico,-a, caluroso,-a. **2** *(person)* entusiasta.

entice [ɪn'taɪs] *vt* persuadir, tentar.

entire [ɪn'taɪər] *adj* entero,-a.

entitle [ɪn'taɪtəl] *vt* **1** *(give right to)* dar derecho (to, a). **2** *(book, etc)* titular.

entity ['entɪtɪ] *n* entidad *f*.
ⓘ *pl* entities.

entourage [ɒntʊ'rɑːʒ] *n* séquito.

entrails ['entreɪlz] *n pl* entrañas *fpl*, tripas *fpl*, vísceras *fpl*.

entrance ['entrəns] *n* **1** *(gen)* entrada; *(door, gate)* puerta; *(hall)* vestíbulo, hall *m*. **2** *(admission)* entrada, admisión *f*; *(to school, university)* ingreso.

entrant ['entrənt] *n* *(competitor)* participante *mf*; *(applicant)* aspirante *mf*.

entrepreneur [ɒntrəprə'nɜːr] *n (business person)* empresario,-a.

entrust [ɪn'trʌst] *vt* confiar.

entry ['entrɪ] *n* **1** *(entrance)* entrada; *(joining)* ingreso. **2** *(right to enter)* admisión *f*. **3** US *(door, gate)* puerta. **4** *(item in accounts)* asiento; *(in diary)* anotación *f*; *(in dictionary)* entrada. **5** *(in competition - participant)* participante *mf*.
ⓘ *pl* entries.

entryphone ['entrɪfəʊn] *n* portero automático.

enumerate [ɪ'njuːməreɪt] *vt* enumerar.

enunciate [ɪ'nʌnsɪeɪt] *vt* **1** *(pronounce)* pronunciar, articular. **2** *(express)* expresar, enunciar.

envelop [ɪn'veləp] *vt* envolver.

envelope ['envələʊp] *n* *(of letter)* sobre *m*; *(covering)* envoltura.

enviable ['envɪəbəl] *adj* envidiable.

envious ['envɪəs] *adj* *(person)* envidioso,-a; *(look, etc)* de envidia.

environment [ɪn'vaɪrənmənt] *n* **1** *(ecology)* medio ambiente *m*: *we need to protect the environment* hemos de proteger el medio ambiente. **2** *(surroundings)* ambiente *m*, entorno; *(habitat)* hábitat *m*.

environmental [ɪnvaɪrən'mentəl] *adj* **1** *(ecological)* del medio ambiente, ambiental: *environmental pollution* contaminación del medio ambiente. **2** *(of surroundings)* ambiental.

environs [ɪn'vaɪrənz] *n pl* alrededores *mpl*.

envisage [ɪn'vɪzɪdʒ] *vt* **1** *(foresee)* prever. **2** *(imagine)* imaginarse.

envoy ['envɔɪ] *n* enviado,-a.

envy ['envɪ] *n* envidia (at/of, de).
ⓘ *pl* envies.
▸ *vt* envidiar, tener envidia de.
ⓘ *pt & pp* envied, *ger* envying.

enzyme ['enzaɪm] *n* enzima *m & f*.

ephemeral [ɪ'femərəl] *adj* efímero,-a.

epic ['epɪk] *adj* épico,-a.

epicentre ['episentər] *n* epicentro.

epidemic [epɪ'demɪk] *n* epidemia.
▸ *adj* epidémico,-a.

epidermis [epɪ'dɜːmɪs] *n* epidermis *f*.

epiglottis [epɪ'glɒtɪs] *n* epiglotis *f*.

epigraph ['epɪgrɑːf] *n* epígrafe *m*.

epilepsy ['epɪlepsɪ] *n* epilepsia.

epileptic [epɪ'leptɪk] *adj* epiléptico,-a.
▸ *n* epiléptico,-a.

epilogue ['epɪlɒg] *n* epílogo.

episode ['epɪsəʊd] *n* **1** episodio. **2** *(of series)* capítulo.

epitaph ['epɪtɑːf] *n* epitafio.
epithelial [epɪ'θiːlɪəl] *adj* epitelial.
epithet ['epɪθet] *n* epíteto.
epoch ['iːpɒk] *n* época.
equal ['iːkwəl] *adj* **1** *(identical)* igual; *(same)* mismo,-a. **2** *(capable)* capaz.
► *n* igual *mf*.
► *vt* **1** MATH ser igual a, equivaler a. **2** *(match)* igualar.
equality [ɪ'kwɒlɪtɪ] *n* igualdad *f*.
① *pl* equalities.
equalize ['iːkwəlaɪz] *vi* SP empatar.
► *vt* igualar.
equanimity [ekwə'nɪmɪtɪ] *n* ecuanimidad *f*.
equate [ɪ'kweɪt] *vt* equiparar (with, con), comparar (with, con).
equation [ɪ'kweɪʒən] *n* **1** MATH ecuación *f*. **2** *fml (relationship)* relación *f*. COMP **simple equation** ecuación *f* de primer grado.
equator [ɪ'kweɪtəʳ] *n* ecuador *m*.
equestrian [ɪ'kwestrɪən] *adj* ecuestre.
► *n (man)* jinete *m*; *(woman)* amazona.
equidistant [iːkwɪ'dɪstənt] *adj* equidistante.
equilateral [iːkwɪ'lætərəl] *adj* equilátero,-a. COMP **equilateral triangle** triángulo equilátero.
equilibrium [iːkwɪ'lɪbrɪəm] *n* equilibrio.
equine ['ekwaɪn] *adj* equino,-a.
equinox ['iːkwɪnɒks] *n* equinoccio.
equip [ɪ'kwɪp] *vt* **1** *(fit out, supply)* equipar (with, con), proveer (with, de). **2** *(prepare)* preparar (for/to, para).
① *pt & pp* equipped, *ger* equipping.
equipment [ɪ'kwɪpmənt] *n* **1** *(materials)* equipo, material *m*. **2** *(act of equipping)* equipamiento.
equitable ['ekwɪtəbəl] *adj fml* equitativo,-a.
equivalence [ɪ'kwɪvələns] *n* equivalencia.
equivalent [ɪ'kwɪvələnt] *adj* equivalente.
► *n* equivalente *m*.
era ['ɪərə] *n* era, época.
eradicate [ɪ'rædɪkeɪt] *vt* erradicar.

eradication [ɪrædɪ'keɪʃən] *n* erradicación *f*.
erase [ɪ'reɪz] *vt* borrar.
eraser [ɪ'reɪzəʳ] *n* goma de borrar.
erect [ɪ'rekt] *adj* **1** *(upright)* derecho,-a, erguido, a. **2** ANAT erecto,-a.
► *vt (build)* erigir, levantar; *(put up - tent)* armar; *(- flagstaff)* izar.
erection [ɪ'rekʃən] *n* erección *f*.
ergonomic [ɜːgə'nɒmɪk] *adj* ergonómico,-a.
erode [ɪ'rəʊd] *vt* **1** *(rock, soil)* erosionar. **2** *(metal)* corroer, desgastar.
erosion [ɪ'rəʊʒən] *n* **1** *(of rock, soil)* erosión *f*. **2** *(of metal)* corrosión *f*.
erotic [ɪ'rɒtɪk] *adj* erótico,-a.
errand ['erənd] *n* encargo, recado.
error ['erəʳ] *n* error *m*, equivocación *f*.
erupt [ɪ'rʌpt] *vi* **1** *(volcano)* entrar en erupción. **2** *fig (war, violence, fire)* estallar. **3** MED *(rash, spots, etc)* brotar, salir; *(tooth)* salir.
eruption [ɪ'rʌpʃən] *n* **1** *(volcano)* erupción *f*. **2** *fig (war, anger)* estallido. **3** *(disease)* brote *m*, epidemia; *(rash, spots, etc)* erupción *f*.
escalator ['eskəleɪtəʳ] *n* escalera mecánica.
escalope ['eskəlɒp] *n* escalope.
escapade ['eskəpeɪd, eskə'peɪd] *n* aventura.
escape [ɪ'skeɪp] *n* **1** *(flight)* fuga, huida (from, de). **2** *(of gas)* fuga, escape *m*.
► *vi* **1** *(get free, get away)* escaparse, fugarse, huir. **2** *(gas, etc)* escapar.
► *vt* **1** *(avoid)* escapar a, librarse de. **2** *(be forgotten or unnoticed)* no recordar.
escort [*(n)* e'skɔːt; *(vb)* ɪ'skɔːt] *n* **1** acompañante *mf*. **2** MIL escolta.
► *vt* **1** acompañar: *I'll escort you home* te acompañaré a casa. **2** MIL escoltar.
Eskimo ['eskɪməʊ] *n* **1** *(person)* esquimal *mf*. **2** *(language)* esquimal *m*.
① *pl* Eskimos o Eskimo.
► *adj* esquimal.
esophagus [ɪ'sɒfəgəs] *n* US → **oesophagus**.
esoteric [esəʊ'terɪk] *adj* esotérico,-a.
espadrille [espə'drɪl] *n* alpargata.
especial [ɪ'speʃəl] *adj* especial.

especially [ɪˈspeʃəlɪ] *adv* especialmente, sobre todo.

espresso [esˈpresəʊ] *n* café *m* exprés.
ⓘ *pl* espressos.

essay [ˈeseɪ] *n* **1** *(school)* redacción *f*; *(university)* trabajo. **2** *(literary)* ensayo. **3** *fml (attempt)* intento.
▶ *vt fml* intentar.

essence [ˈesəns] *n* esencia.

essential [ɪˈsenʃəl] *adj* esencial.
▶ *n (necessary thing)* necesidad *f* básica.
▶ *n pl* **essentials** lo esencial *m sing*, lo fundamental *m sing*.

establish [ɪˈstæblɪʃ] *vt* **1** *(gen)* establecer. **2** *(find out, determine)* determinar, averiguar.

established [ɪˈstæblɪʃt] *adj* **1** *(practice, custom)* consolidado,-a. **2** *(person - set up)* establecido,-a; *(- well known)* reconocido,-a. **3** *(fact)* comprobado,-a.

establishment [ɪˈstæblɪʃmənt] *n* **1** *(setting up)* establecimiento, fundación *f*. **2** *(premises)* establecimiento; *(business)* negocio. **3** *(staff)* plantilla, personal *m*.
▶ *n* the Establishment GB el sistema.

estate [ɪˈsteɪt] *n* **1** *(land)* finca. **2** GB *(with houses)* urbanización *f*. **3** *(money and property)* propiedad *f*, bienes *mpl*; *(inheritance)* herencia.

☒ Estate no significa 'estado', que se traduce por state o condition.

esteem [ɪˈstiːm] *vt* estimar.
▶ *n* aprecio, estima.

esthetic [iːsˈθetɪk] *adj* US → aesthetic.

estimate [*(n)* ˈestɪmət; *(vb)* ˈestɪmeɪt] *n* **1** *(calculation - of amount, size)* cálculo, estimación *f*; *(- of value, cost)* valoración *f*, estimación *f*; *(- for work)* presupuesto. **2** *(judgement)* evaluación *f*, juicio, opinión *f*.
▶ *vt* **1** *(calculate)* calcular. **2** *(judge, form opinion about)* pensar, creer, estimar.
▶ *vi (for work)* hacer un presupuesto (for, de).

☒ To estimate no significa 'estimar (querer)', que se traduce por to respect.

estimation [estɪˈmeɪʃən] *n* **1** opinión *f*, juicio. **2** *(esteem)* estima, aprecio.

Estonia [eˈstəʊnɪə] *n* Estonia.

Estonian [eˈstəʊnɪən] *adj* estonio,-a.
▶ *n* **1** *(person)* estonio,-a. **2** *(language)* estonio.

estrogen [ˈiːstrədʒən] *n* US → oestrogen.

estuary [ˈestjʊərɪ] *n* estuario.
ⓘ *pl* estuaries.

etching [ˈetʃɪŋ] *n* aguafuerte *m & f*.

eternal [ɪˈtɜːnəl] *adj* **1** *(everlasting)* eterno,-a. **2** *fam (unceasing)* incesante. **3** *(immutable)* inmutable.

eternity [ɪˈtɜːnətɪ] *n* eternidad *f*.

ether [ˈiːθəʳ] *n* éter *m*.

ethic [ˈeθɪk] *n* ética.

ethical [ˈeθɪkəl] *adj* ético,-a, moral.

ethics [ˈeθɪks] *n (science)* ética.
▶ *n pl (moral correctness)* moralidad *f*.

Ethiopia [iːˈθɪəʊpɪə] *n* Etiopía.

Ethiopian [iːˈθɪəʊpɪən] *adj* etíope.
▶ *n* **1** *(person)* etíope *mf*, etiope *mf*. **2** *(language)* etíope *m*.

ethnic [ˈeθnɪk] *adj* étnico,-a. COMP **ethnic minority** minoría étnica.

ethnography [eθˈnɒɡrəfɪ] *n* etnografía.

ethnology [eθˈnɒlədʒɪ] *n* etnología.

ethyl [ˈiːθaɪl, ˈeθɪl] *n* CHEM etilo. COMP **ethyl alcohol** alcohol *m* etílico.

etiquette [ˈetɪket] *n* protocolo, etiqueta.

☒ Etiquette no significa 'etiqueta (rótulo)', que se traduce por label.

etymological [etɪməˈlɒdʒɪkəl] *adj* etimológico,-a.

etymology [etɪˈmɒlədʒɪ] *n* etimología.
ⓘ *pl* etymologies.

eucalyptus [juːkəˈlɪptəs] *n* eucalipto.
COMP **eucalyptus tree** eucalipto.

EU [ˈiːˈjuː] *abbr* (European Union) Unión *f* Europea; *(abbreviation)* UE *f*.

euphemism [ˈjuːfəmɪzəm] *n* eufemismo.

euro [ˈjʊərəʊ] *n* euro.

Europe [ˈjʊərəp] *n* Europa.

European [jʊərəˈpɪən] *adj* europeo,-a.
▶ *n (person)* europeo,-a. COMP **European Economic Community** Comunidad *f* Económica Europea. **European Parliament** Parlamento Europeo. **European Union** Unión *f* Europea.

euthanasia [juːθəˈneɪzɪə] *n* eutanasia.

evacuate [ɪˈvækjueɪt] *vt* **1** *(people)* evacuar. **2** *(place)* desalojar; *(mil)* desocupar.

evacuation [ɪvækjuˈeɪʃən] *n* **1** *(of people)* evacuación *f*. **2** *(of place)* desalojo.

evade [ɪˈveɪd] *vt* **1** evadir, eludir.

evaluate [ɪˈvæljueɪt] *vt (assess)* evaluar, juzgar; *(estimate value)* valorar, calcular (el valor de), tasar.

evaluation [ɪvæljuˈeɪʃən] *n* evaluación *f*.

evaporate [ɪˈvæpəreɪt] *vt* evaporar.
▶ *vi* evaporarse.

evaporation [ɪvæpəˈreɪʃən] *n* evaporación *f*.

evasion [ɪˈveɪʒən] *n* **1** *(gen)* evasión *f*. **2** *(excuse, etc)* evasiva.

evasive [ɪˈveɪsɪv] *adj* evasivo,-a.

eve [iːv] *n* víspera, vigilia. [LOC] **on the eve of** sth en vísperas de ALGO.

even [ˈiːvən] *adj* **1** *(level, flat)* llano,-a, plano,-a, *(smooth)* liso,-a: *this surface isn't even* esta superficie no es plana. **2** *(regular, steady)* uniforme, regular, constante. **3** *(evenly balanced)* igual, igualado,-a. **4** *(number)* par. **5** *(placid character)* apacible. **7** *(on the same level as)* a nivel (with, de).
▶ *adv* **1** hasta, incluso, aun: *it's always sunny, even in winter* siempre hace sol, incluso en invierno. **2** *(with negative)* siquiera, ni siquiera: *she never even said hello* ni siquiera me saludó. **3** *(before comparative)* aun, todavía: *she's even more beautiful than I remembered* es aun más guapa de lo que recordaba. [LOC] **even if** aun si, aunque. ‖ **even so** aun así. ‖ **even though** aunque, aun cuando.
▶ *vt* **1** *(level)* nivelar, allanar. **2** *(score)* igualar; *(situation)* equilibrar.
◆ **to even out** *vt sep (make level)* nivelar; *(make equal)* igualar; *(spread equally)* repartir equitativamente.

evening [ˈiːvənɪŋ] *n (early)* tarde *f*; *(late)* noche *f*. [LOC] **good evening!** ¡buenas tardes!, ¡buenas noches!

✎ Evening comprende la parte final de la tarde y el principio de la noche, antes de que anochezca del todo.

evenly [ˈiːvənlɪ] *adv* **1** *(uniformly)* uniformemente. **2** *(fairly, equally)* equitativamente, igualmente. **3** *(of voice)* en el mismo tono,.

event [ɪˈvent] *n* **1** *(happening)* suceso, acontecimiento. **2** SP prueba.

eventual [ɪˈventʃuəl] *adj* **1** *(final, ultimate)* final. **2** *(resulting)* consiguiente. **3** *(possible)* posible.

❌ Eventual no significa 'provisional', que se traduce por temporary.

E

eventually [ɪˈventʃuəlɪ] *adv* finalmente, con el tiempo.

ever [ˈevər] *adv* **1** *(in negative sentences)* nunca, jamás. **2** *(in questions)* alguna vez. **3** *(always)* siempre. **4** *(after comparative and superlative)* nunca. **5** *(emphatic use)*: *how ever did you lose your coat?* ¿cómo has podido perder el abrigo? [LOC] **for ever** para siempre.

evergreen [ˈevəɡriːn] *adj* BOT de hoja perenne.
▶ *n* árbol *m* de hoja perenne.

everlasting [evəˈlɑːstɪŋ] *adj* **1** *(eternal, lasting for ever)* eterno,-a. **2** *(lasting for a long time)* duradero,-a.

every [ˈevrɪ] *adj* **1** *(each)* cada; *(all)* todos,-as: *every day* cada día, todos los días. **3** *(all possible)*: *we encourage people to help in every way* animamos a la gente a que ayude de cualquier manera. [LOC] **every other day** un día sí un día no, cada dos días.

✎ Consulta también each.

everybody [ˈevrɪbɒdɪ] *pron* todos,-as, todo el mundo.

everyday [ˈevrɪdeɪ] *adj (day-to-day)* diario,-a; *(ordinary)* corriente, cotidiano,-a: *for everyday use* para uso diario.

everyone [ˈevrɪwʌn] *pron* → **everybody**.

everyplace [ˈevrɪpleɪs] *adv* → US **everywhere**.

everything [ˈevrɪθɪŋ] *pron* todo.

everywhere [ˈevrɪweər] *adv* **1** *(place)* en todas partes, por todas partes: *he's been everywhere* ha estado en todas partes. **2** *(movement)* a todas partes.

evidence ['evɪdəns] *n* **1** *(proof)* prueba, pruebas *fpl*. **2** *(sign, indication)* indicio, indicios *mpl*, señal *f*. **3** JUR *(testimony)* testimonio, declaración *f*.
▸ *vt* **1** *(prove)* demostrar, probar. **2** *(give proof of)* justificar.

evident ['evɪdənt] *adj* evidente.

evil ['i:vəl] *adj* **1** *(gen)* malo,-a. **2** *(foul-smell)* fétido,-a, repugnante; *(- temper, weather)* terrible, de perros. **4** *(unlucky)* aciago,-a, de mal agüero.
▸ *n (wickedness)* mal *m*, maldad *f*.

evoke [ɪ'vəʊk] *vt* **1** *(bring to mind)* evocar. **2** *fml (produce, cause)* provocar.

evolution [i:və'lu:ʃən] *n* evolución *f*.

evolve [ɪ'vɒlv] *vt* **1** *(develop)* desarrollar. **2** *(give off)* desprender.
▸ *vi* evolucionar.

ewe [ju:] *n* oveja.

exact [ɪg'zækt] *adj* **1** *(precise)* exacto,-a. **2** *(meticulous)* meticuloso,-a. **3** *(accurate)* preciso,-a. **4** *(specific, particular)* justo.
▸ *vt (demand, insist on)* exigir (**from**, a).

exacting [ɪg'zæktɪŋ] *adj* exigente.

exaggerate [ɪg'zædʒəreɪt] *vt* exagerar.

exalt [ɪg'zɔːlt] *vt* **1** *fml (elevate)* exaltar, elevar. **2** *(praise, extol)* ensalzar.

exam [ɪg'zæm] *n fam* examen *m*.

examination [ɪgzæmɪ'neɪʃən] *n* **1** EDUC examen *m*. **2** *(inspection)* inspección *f*, examen *m*; *(of house, room)* registro. **3** MED reconocimiento. **4** JUR interrogatorio.

examine [ɪg'zæmɪn] *vt* **1** *(inspect)* inspeccionar, examinar; *(check)* comprobar; *(consider)* examinar, estudiar. **2** *(customs)* registrar. **3** EDUC examinar (in/on, de). **4** MED hacer un reconocimiento a. **5** JUR interrogar.

examiner [ɪg'zæmɪnəʳ] *n* examinador,-ra.

example [ɪg'zɑːmpəl] *n (gen)* ejemplo. **exasperate** [ɪg'zɑːspəreɪt] *vt* exasperar, irritar. LOC **for example** por ejemplo.

excavate ['ekskəveɪt] *vt* excavar.

excavation [ekskə'veɪʃən] *n* excavación *f*.

excavator ['ekskəveɪtəʳ] *n (machine)* excavadora.

exceed [ɪk'si:d] *vt* exceder.

excel [ɪk'sel] *vt (surpass)* superar.
▸ *vi (be very good at)* destacar (at/in, en), sobresalir (at/in, en).
ⓘ *pt & pp* **excelled**, *ger* **excelling**.

excellence ['eksələns] *n* excelencia.

excellent ['eksələnt] *adj* excelente.
▸ *interj fam* ¡estupendo!, ¡fantástico!.

except [ɪk'sept] *prep* excepto, salvo.
▸ *vt fml* excluir, exceptuar.

exception [ɪk'sepʃən] *n* excepción *f*.

exceptional [ɪk'sepʃənəl] *adj* excepcional.

excerpt ['eksɜːpt] *n* extracto.

excess [ɪk'ses] *n* **1** exceso. **2** COMM excedente *m*.
▸ *adj* excedente, sobrante.

excessive [ɪk'sesɪv] *adj* excesivo,-a.

exchange [ɪks'tʃeɪndʒ] *n* **1** *(gen)* cambio. **2** *(of ideas, information, etc)* intercambio. **3** *(of prisoners)* canje *m*. **4** FIN cambio. **5** EDUC *(reciprocal visit)* intercambio.
▸ *vt* **1** *(gen)* cambiar. **2** *(ideas, information, etc)* intercambiar. **3** *(prisoners)* canjear.

exchequer [ɪks'tʃekəʳ] *n (treasury)* tesoro público.
▸ *n* **the Exchequer** Hacienda.

excite [ɪk'saɪt] *vt* **1** *(enthuse, thrill)* emocionar, apasionar. **2** *fml (bring about)* provocar. **3** *(stimulate)* excitar.

excited [ɪk'saɪtɪd] *adj* **1** emocionado,-a, ilusionado,-a. **2** *(sexually)* excitado,-a.

excitement [ɪk'saɪtmənt] *n* **1** *(strong feeling)* emoción *f*, entusiasmo, ilusión *f*. **2** *(commotion)* agitación *f*, conmoción *f*, revuelo.

exciting [ɪk'saɪtɪŋ] *adj* emocionante.

exclaim [ɪk'skleɪm] *vt* exclamar, gritar.
▸ *vi* exclamar.

exclamation [eksklə'meɪʃən] *n* exclamación *f*. COMP **exclamation mark** signo de admiración. ▮ **exclamation point** US signo de admiración.

exclude [ɪk'sklu:d] *vt* **1** *(leave out, not include)* excluir, no incluir. **2** *(debar, prevent from entering)* no admitir.

excluding [ɪk'sklu:dɪŋ] *prep (excepting)* excepto, con excepción de.

exclusive [ɪk'sklu:sɪv] *adj* **1** *(gen)* exclusivo,-a. **2** *(press)* en exclusiva.
▶ *n (press)* exclusiva.

excrement ['ekskrɪmənt] *n* excremento.

excrete [ɪk'skri:t] *vt* excretar.

excretory [ɪk'skrəi:təər] *adj* excretor,-ra. COMP **excretory system** sistema excretor.

excruciating [ɪk'skru:ʃeɪtɪŋ] *adj* **1** insoportable. **2** *euph* fatal, horrible.

excursion [ɪk'skɜ:ʒən] *n (outing)* excursión *f*, viaje *m*.

excuse [(n) ɪk'skju:s; (vb) ɪk'skju:z] *n* **1** *(apology)* disculpa. **2** *(pretext)* excusa.
▶ *vt* **1** perdonar, disculpar. **2** *(justify)* justificar. **3** *(exempt)* eximir.

execute ['eksɪkju:t] *vt* **1** *(put to death)* ejecutar. **2** *(carry out)* ejecutar; *(orders)* cumplir; *(tasks)* realizar. **3** *(music, etc)* interpretar.

execution [eksɪ'kju:ʃən] *n* **1** *(carrying out)* ejecución *f*; *(of order)* cumplimiento; *(of task)* realización *f*. **2** *(putting to death)* ejecución *f*. **4** *(of music, etc)* interpretación *f*.

executioner [eksɪ'kju:ʃənəʳ] *n* verdugo.

executive [ɪg'zekjətɪv] *adj* ejecutivo,-a.
▶ *n (person)* ejecutivo,-a; *(committee)* ejecutiva.
▶ *n* **the executive** el (poder) ejecutivo.

exemplify [ɪg'zemplɪfaɪ] *vt* ejemplificar.
ⓘ *pt & pp* **exemplified**, *ger* **exemplifying**.

exempt [ɪg'zempt] *adj* exento,-a, libre (from, de).
▶ *vt* eximir, dispensar (from, de).

exemption [ɪg'zempʃən] *n* exención *f* (from, de).

exercise ['eksəsaɪz] *n* ejercicio. COMP **exercise book** cuaderno.
▶ *vt* **1** *(employ, make use of)* ejercer, emplear. **2** *(give exercise to - dog)* sacar de paseo; *(- horse)* entrenar.
▶ *vi* hacer ejercicio, entrenarse.

exert [ɪg'zɜ:t] *vt* ejercer.

exhalation [ekshəl'eɪʲən] *vt* exhalación *f*.

exhale [eks'heɪl] *vt (breathe out)* exhalar.
▶ *vi (give off)* despedir.

exhaust [ɪg'zɔ:st] *n* **1** *(pipe)* (tubo de) escape *m*. **2** *(fumes)* gases *mpl* de combustión.
▶ *vt* **1** *(gen)* agotar. **2** *(empty)* vaciar.

exhausted [ɪg'zɔ:stɪd] *adj* agotado,-a.

exhausting [ɪg'zɔ:stɪŋ] *adj* agotador,-ra.

exhaustive [ɪg'zɔ:stɪv] *adj* exhaustivo,-a.

E

exhibit [ɪg'zɪbɪt] *n* ART objeto expuesto.
▶ *vt* **1** *(display, show)* exponer, presentar. **2** *fml (manifest)* manifestar, mostrar.
▶ *vi (of artist)* exponer.

exhibition [eksɪ'bɪʃən] *n* **1** *(art, etc)* exposición *f*. **2** *(display)* demostración *f*, muestra.

exhibitionist [eksɪ'bɪʃənɪst] *n* exhibicionista *mf*.

exhilarating [ɪg'zɪləreɪtɪŋ] *adj (invigorating)* estimulante; *(exciting)* emocionante.

exhume [eks'hju:m] *vt* exhumar.

exile ['eksaɪl] *n* **1** *(action)* destierro, exilio. **2** *(person)* desterrado,-a, exiliado,-a.
▶ *vt* desterrar, exiliar.

exist [ɪg'zɪst] *vi* **1** *(gen)* existir. **2** *(subsist)* subsistir (on, a base de).

existence [ɪg'zɪstəns] *n* existencia.

existent [ɪg'zɪstənt] *adj* existente.

exit ['eksɪt] *n* **1** *(gen)* salida. **2** THEAT mutis *m*.
▶ *vi* THEAT hacer mutis.

❌ **Exit** no significa 'éxito', que se traduce por **success**.

exodus ['eksədəs] *n* éxodo.

exorbitant [ɪg'zɔ:bɪtənt] *adj* exorbitante.

exorcism ['eksɔ:sɪzəm] *n* exorcismo.

exotic [eg'zɒtɪk] *adj* exótico,-a.

expand [ɪk'spænd] *vt* **1** *(enlarge - business)* ampliar; *(- number)* aumentar, incrementar. **2** *(gas, metal)* dilatar, expandir.
▶ *vi* **1** *(grow larger)* crecer, aumentar. **2** *(metal)* dilatarse; *(gas)* expandirse. **3** *(spread out)* extenderse.

◆ **to expand on** *vt insep* ampliar, desarrollar.

expanse [ɪk'spæns] *n* extensión *f*.

expansion [ɪk'spænʃən] *n* **1** crecimiento, aumento. **2** *(gas, metal)* dilatación *f*, expansión *f*. **3** *(trade)* desarrollo.

expansive [ɪk'spænsɪv] *adj* **1** *(friendly, talkative)* hablador,-ra, comunicativo,-a. **2** *(able to expand)* expansivo,-a.

expect [ɪk'spekt] *vt* **1** *(anticipate)* esperar: *I never expected to win* no esperaba ganar. **2** *(demand)* esperar, contar con. **3** GB *fam (suppose)* suponer, imaginar.

expectancy [ɪk'spektənsɪ] *n (anticipation)* expectación *f*, expectativa; *(hope)* ilusión *f*.

expectation [ekspek'teɪʃən] *n (hope, firm belief)* esperanza.
  ▶ *n pl* **expectations** *(confident feelings)* expectativas *fpl*.

☒ Expectation no significa 'expectativa', que se traduce por **excitement**.

expedient [ɪk'spiːdɪənt] *adj* conveniente, oportuno,-a.
  ▶ *n* expediente *m*, recurso.

expedition [ekspɪ'dɪʃən] *n* **1** *(gen)* expedición *f*. **2** *fml (speed)* aceleración *f*, prontitud *f*.

expel [ɪk'spel] *vt* expulsar.
  ⓘ *pt & pp* expelled, *ger* expelling.

expend [ɪk'spend] *vt* **1** *fml (spend, use)* gastar, emplear. **2** *fml (use up, exhaust)* agotar.

expendable [ɪk'spendəbəl] *adj fml* prescindible.

expenditure [ɪk'spendɪtʃəʳ] *n* gasto, desembolso.

expense [ɪk'spens] *n* gasto, desembolso.
  ▶ *n pl* **expenses** gastos *mpl*.

expensive [ɪk'spensɪv] *adj* caro,-a.

experience [ɪk'spɪərɪəns] *n* experiencia.
  ▶ *vt (sensation, situation, etc)* experimentar; *(difficulty)* tener; *(loss)* sufrir.

experienced [ɪk'spɪərɪənst] *adj* experimentado,-a, con experiencia.

experiment [ɪk'sperɪmənt] *n* experimento.

  ▶ *vi* experimentar, hacer experimentos.

experimental [ɪksperɪ'mentəl] *adj* experimental.

expert ['ekspɜːt] *n* experto,-a (at/in/on, en).
  ▶ *adj* experto,-a.

expertise [ekspɜː'tiːz] *n (skill)* pericia, habilidad *f*; *(knowledge)* conocimiento (práctico).

expire [ɪk'spaɪəʳ] *vi* **1** *(come to end)* terminar, acabarse; *(die)* expirar, morir. **2** *(run out - contract)* vencer; *(- passport, ticket)* caducar. **3** MED *(breathe out)* espirar.

expiry [ɪk'spaɪərɪ] *n* **1** *(ending)* expiración *f*, terminación *f*. **2** *(of contract, bill of exchange)* vencimiento; *(of passport, driving licence, etc)* caducidad *f*.

explanation [eksplə'neɪʃən] *n* explicación *f*.

explicit [ɪk'splɪsɪt] *adj* explícito,-a.

explode [ɪk'spləʊd] *vt* **1** *(blow up - bomb, etc)* hacer estallar, hacer explotar. **2** *(refute - theory)* refutar; *(- rumour)* desmentir.
  ▶ *vi* **1** *(blow up)* estallar, explotar. **2** *(react violently)* reventar, explotar, estallar.

exploit [*(n)* 'eksplɔɪt; *(vb)* ɪk'splɔɪt] *n* hazaña, proeza.
  ▶ *vt* **1** *(work, develop fully)* explotar. **2** *(use unfairly)* aprovecharse de, explotar.

exploitation [eksplɔɪ'teɪʃən] *n* explotación *f*.

exploration [eksplə'reɪʃən] *n* exploración *f*.

explore [ɪk'splɔːʳ] *vt* **1** *(gen)* explorar. **2** *(examine)* examinar.
  ▶ *vi* explorar.

explorer [ɪk'splɔːrəʳ] *n* explorador,-ra.

explosion [ɪk'spləʊʒən] *n* **1** *(gen)* explosión *f*, estallido. **2** *(violent outburst)* ataque *m*, arrebato.

explosive [ɪk'spləʊsɪv] *adj* explosivo,-a.

exponent [ɪk'spəʊnənt] *n* **1** *(gen)* exponente *m*; *(supporter)* defensor,-ra (of, de), partidario,-a (of, de). **2** *(performer)* intérprete *mf*; *(expert)* experto,-a. **3** MATH exponente *m*.

exponential [ekspə'nenʃəl] *adj* MATH exponencial.

export [(n) 'ekspɔːt; (vb) ɪk'spɔːt] *n* **1** (trade) exportación *f*. **2** (article) artículo de exportación.
▶ *vt* exportar.

exporter [ek'spɔːtə^r] *n* exportador,-ra.

expose [ɪk'spəʊz] *vt* **1** (uncover, make visible) exponer. **2** (make known - secret, etc) revelar, descubrir; (- person) desenmascarar. **3** fig (lay open) exponerse. **4** (photo) exponer.

exposure [ɪk'spəʊʒə^r] *n* **1** (being exposed) exposición *f*. **2** (revelation, disclosure) revelación *f*, descubrimiento. **3** (in photography - picture) fotografía; (- time) exposición *f*. **4** (position of house, etc) situación *f*, orientación *f*. **5** (publicity) publicidad *f*; (coverage) cobertura.

express [ɪk'spres] *adj* **1** (explicit) expreso,-a, claro,-a. **2** (fast - mail) urgente; (- train, coach) expreso.
▶ *adv* urgente.
▶ *n* (rail) (tren *m*) expreso.
▶ *vt* **1** expresar. **2** fml (juice) exprimir.

expression [ɪk'spreʃən] *n* **1** (gen) expresión *f*; (manifestation) manifestación *f*. **2** MATH expresión *f*.

expressive [ɪk'spresɪv] *adj* expresivo,-a.

expressway [ɪk'spresweɪ] *n* US autopista.

expulsion [ɪk'spʌlʃən] *n* expulsión *f*.

exquisite [ek'skwɪzɪt, 'ekskwɪzɪt] *adj* **1** (delicate, etc) exquisito,-a, perfecto,-a. **2** fml (of emotion) intenso,-a; (of power to feel) delicado,-a.

extend [ɪk'stend] *vt* **1** (enlarge) ampliar; (lengthen - line, road) prolongar, alargar. **2** (over time) prolongar, alargar; (deadline) prorrogar. **3** (stretch out - arm, hand) alargar, tender; (- leg) estirar; (- wing) desplegar, extender.
▶ *vi* **1** (in space) continuar, extenderse, llegar hasta. **2** (in time) prolongarse, alargarse, durar. **3** (become extended - ladder, etc) extenderse. **4** (include, affect) incluir, abarcar, extenderse a.

extension [ɪk'stenʃən] *n* **1** (widening) ampliación *f*, extensión *f*. **2** (of line, road, etc) prolongación *f*. **5** (telephone line) extensión *f*; (telephone) supletorio.

extensive [ɪk'stensɪv] *adj* **1** (area) extenso,-a, amplio,-a. **2** (wide-ranging) vasto,-a, amplio,-a, extenso,-a; (thorough) exhaustivo, minucioso,-a. **3** (very great in effect, widespread) importante, múltiple.

E

extensor [ɪk'stensə^r] *n* extensor.

extent [ɪk'stent] *n* **1** (expanse) extensión *f*. **2** (range, scale, scope) amplitud *f*, alcance *m*. **3** (point) punto.

extenuate [ɪk'stenjʊeɪt] *vt* fml atenuar.

exterior [ɪk'stɪərɪə^r] *adj* exterior, externo,-a: *exterior walls* paredes exteriores.
▶ *n* **1** exterior *m*. **2** (of person) aspecto externo, apariencia.

exterminate [ɪk'stɜːmɪneɪt] *vt* exterminar.

extermination [ɪkstɜːmɪ'neɪʃən] *n* exterminación *f*, exterminio.

external [ek'stɜːnəl] *adj* externo,-a, exterior. COMP **external ear** oído externo.

extinct [ɪk'stɪŋkt] *adj* **1** (of animal) extinguido,-a. **2** (of volcano) extinguido,-a, apagado,-a.

extinction [ɪk'stɪŋkʃən] *n* extinción *f*.

extinguish [ɪk'stɪŋgwɪʃ] *vt* extinguir.

extinguisher [ɪk'stɪŋgwɪʃə^r] *n* extintor *m*.

extort [ɪk'stɔːt] *vt* (money) sacar, conseguir a la fuerza; (promise, confession) arrancar, obtener.

extortion [ɪk'stɔːʃən] *n* extorsión *f*.

extra ['ekstəə] *adj* (additional) extra, más, otro,-a; (spare) de sobra; (on top) aparte.
▶ *adv* (more than usually) extra, muy; (additional) aparte.
▶ *n* **1** (additional thing) extra *m*, complemento; (additional charge) suplemento; (luxury) lujo. **2** CINEM extra *mf*. **3** (press) edición *f* especial.

extract [(n) 'ekstrækt; (vb) ɪk'strækt] *n* extracto.

▶ *vt* **1** *(pull out)* extraer, sacar. **2** *(obtain - confession, promise, etc)* arrancar, obtener; *(- information, passage, quotation)* extraer, sacar. **3** *(produce)* extraer, sacar.

extraction [ɪk'strækʃən] *n* **1** *(gen)* extracción *f.* **2** *(of tooth)* extracción *f.* **3** *(descent)* origen *m.*

extractor [ɪk'stræktəʳ] *n* extractor *m.* COMP **extractor fan** extractor *m* de humos.

extradite ['ekstrədaɪt] *vt* extraditar, extradir.

extradition [ekstrə'dɪʃən] *n* extradición *f.*

extramarital [ekstrə'mæəɪtəl] *adj* extramatrimonial.

extraordinary [ɪk'strɔːdənəɪ] *adj* extraordinario,-a.

extrasensory [ekstrə'sensəəɪ] *adj* extrasensorial.

extraterrestrial [ekstrətə'restrɪəl] *adj* extraterrestre.
▶ *n* extraterrestre *mf.*

extravagance [ɪk'strævəgəns] *n* *(spending)* derroche *m*, despilfarro, lujo; *(behaviour)* extravagancia.

extravagant [ɪk'strævəgənt] *adj* **1** *(wasteful - person)* derrochador,-ra, despilfarrador,-ra; *(- thing)* ineficaz, ineficiente. **2** *(extreme)* extravagante. **3** *(luxurious)* lujoso,-a.

extreme [ɪk'striːm] *adj* **1** *(gen)* extremo,-a. **2** *(severe, unusual)* excepcional.
▶ *n* extremo.

extremism [ɪk'striːmɪzəm] *n* extremismo.

extremist [ɪk'striːmɪst] *n* extremista *mf.*

extremity [ɪk'stremɪtɪ] *n* **1** *fml (furthest point)* extremo. **2** *fml (extreme degree, situation)* situación *f* extrema.
▶ *n pl* **extremities** ANAT extremidades *fpl.*
ⓘ *pl* extremities.

extricate ['ekstrɪkeɪt] *vt fml* librar, sacar. LOC **to extricate os** lograr salir (from, de).

extrinsic [ɪk'strɪnzɪk] *adj* extrínseco,-a.

extrovert ['ekstrəvɜːt] *adj* extrovertido,-a.
▶ *n* extrovertido,-a.

exuberance [ɪg'zjuːbəəəns] *n* *(vigour)* exuberancia; *(high spirits)* euforia.

exuberant [ɪg'zjuːbəəənt] *adj* **1** *(of person)* eufórico,-a. **2** *(of plants)* exuberante.

exude [ɪg'zjuːd] *vt* **1** *fml (of sweat, etc)* exudar, rezumar. **2** *fig (of feeling)* rebosar: *she exudes confidence* rebosa de confianza.
▶ *vi (of sweat, etc)* exudar, rezumar.

exultant [ɪg'zʌltənt] *adj* exultante.

eye [aɪ] *n* **1** ANAT ojo. **2** *(sense)* vista. **3** *(of needle, potato, storm)* ojo.
▶ *vt (observe)* mirar, observar; *(look at longingly)* echar el ojo a.

eyeball ['aɪbɔːl] *n* globo ocular.

eyebolt ['aɪbəʊlt] *n* armella, hembrilla.

eyebrow ['aɪbrəʊ] *n* ceja.

eye-catching ['aɪkætʃɪŋ] *adj* llamativo,-a.

eyelash ['aɪlæʃ] *n* pestaña.

eyelid ['aɪlɪd] *n* párpado.

eyeliner ['aɪlaɪnəʳ] *n* lápiz *m* de ojos.

eyesight ['aɪsaɪt] *n* vista.

eyesore ['aɪsɔːʳ] *n* monstruosidad *f.*

eyestrain ['aɪstreɪn] *n* vista cansada.

eyetooth [aɪ'tuːθ] *n* colmillo.

eyewash ['aɪwɒʃ] *n* **1** MED colirio. **2** *fam (nonsense)* tonterías *fpl*: *it's all eyewash!* ¡eso son disparates!.

eyewitness ['aɪwɪtnəs] *n* testigo presencial, testigo ocular.

F

F, f [ef] *n* **1** *(the letter)* F, f *f*. **2** MUS fa *m*.

F [ˈfærənhaɪt] *abbr* **(Fahrenheit)** Fahrenheit; *(abbreviation)* F.

fable [ˈfeɪbəl] *n* fábula.

fabric [ˈfæbrɪk] *n* **1** *(material)* tela, tejido. **2** *(structure)* fábrica, estructura.

> ⊠ Fabric no significa 'fábrica', que se traduce por factory.

fabulous [ˈfæbjələs] *adj* fabuloso,-a.

façade [tɔˈsɑːd] *n* fachada.

face [feɪs] *n* **1** *(gen)* cara. **2** *(surface)* superficie *f*. **3** *(of dial)* cuadrante *m*. **4** *(of watch)* esfera. LOC **face down** boca abajo. ▌ **face up** boca arriba.

▸ *vt* **1** *(look towards)* mirar hacia. **2** *(look onto)* estar orientado,-a hacia, dar a. **3** *(be opposite to)* estar enfrente de. **4** *(confront)* presentarse, plantearse; *(deal with)* enfrentarse a. **5** *(tolerate)* soportar.

◆ **to face up to** *vt insep* afrontar, enfrentar, enfrentarse a.

faceless [ˈfeɪsləs] *adj* anónimo,-a.

facelift [ˈfeɪslɪft] *n* **1** lifting *m*. **2** *fig (building)* lavado de cara.

facet [ˈfæsɪt] *n* faceta.

facial [ˈfeɪʃəl] *adj* facial.

facilitate [fəˈsɪlɪteɪt] *vt* facilitar.

facility [fəˈsɪlɪtɪ] *n* facilidad *f*.

▸ *n pl* **facilities 1** *(equipment)* instalaciones *fpl*, servicios *mpl*. **2** *(means)* facilidades *fpl*.

ⓘ *pl* facilities.

fact [fækt] *n* **1** *(event, happening)* hecho. **2** *(the truth)* realidad *f*. LOC **as a matter of fact** en realidad. ▌ **in fact** de hecho.

faction [ˈfækʃən] *n* facción *f*.

factor [ˈfæktəʳ] *n* factor *m*.

factorize [ˈfæktəraɪz] *vt* descomponer en factores.

factory [ˈfæktərɪ] *n* fábrica.

ⓘ *pl* factories.

faculty [ˈfækəltɪ] *n* **1** *(power, ability)* facultad *f*. **2** *(at university)* facultad *f*. **3** US *(at university)* profesorado.

ⓘ *pl* faculties.

fad [fæd] *n* **1** *(fashion)* moda pasajera. **2** *(personal)* manía.

fade [feɪd] *vt* *(colour)* descolorar, descolorir, desteñir.

◆ **to fade away** *vi* **1** *(become less intense, strong, etc)* desvanecerse, esfumarse. **2** *(die)* morirse.

faecal [ˈfiːkəl] *adj* fecal.

faeces [ˈfiːsiːz] *n pl* heces *fpl*.

fag [fæg] *n* **1** GB *fam (cigarette)* pitillo. **2** *sl (drag)* lata, rollo.

Fahrenheit [ˈfærənhaɪt] *adj* Fahrenheit.

fail [feɪl] *n* EDUC suspenso.

▸ *vt* **1** *(let down)* fallar, decepcionar; *(desert)* fallar, faltar. **2** EDUC suspender.

▸ *vi* **1** *(neglect)* dejar de. **2** *(not succeed)* fracasar, no hacer algo. **3** *(crops)* fallar, echarse a perder. **4** *(stop working)* fallar. **5** *(light)* acabarse, irse apagando. **6** *(become weak)* debilitarse, fallar. **7** COMM *(become bankrupt)* quebrar, fracasar.

failing [ˈfeɪlɪŋ] *n* *(fault)* defecto, fallo; *(weakness)* punto débil.

▸ *prep* a falta de.

fail-safe [ˈfeɪlseɪf] *adj* *(device, mechanism)* de seguridad; *(plan)* infalible.

failure [ˈfeɪljəʳ] *n* **1** *(lack of success)* fracaso. **2** COMM quiebra. **3** EDUC suspenso. **4** *(person)* fracasado,-a. **5** *(breakdown)* fallo, avería. **6** *(of crops)* pérdida.

faint [feɪnt] *adj* **1** *(sound, voice)* débil, tenue. **2** *(colour)* pálido,-a. **3** *(slight - memory, etc)* vago,-a.
▸ *n* mareo.
▸ *vi* desmayarse (from, de).

fair¹ [feəʳ] *adj* **1** *(just)* justo,-a; *(impartial)* imparcial; *(reasonable)* razonable. **2** *(considerable)* considerable. **3** *(idea, guess, etc)* bastante bueno,-a. **4** *(weather)* bueno,-a. **5** *(hair)* rubio,-a; *(skin)* blanco,-a.

fair² [feəʳ] *n* **1** *(market)* mercado, feria. **2** *(show)* feria; *(funfair)* parque *m* de atracciones.

fairground ['feəɡraʊnd] *n* *(site)* recinto ferial; *(show)* feria; *(funfair)* parque *m* de atracciones.

fairly ['feəlɪ] *adv* **1** *(justly)* justamente. **2** *(moderately)* bastante. **3** *(completely)* completamente.

fairway ['feəweɪ] *n* **1** *(golf)* calle *f*. **2** *(sea)* canal *m* navegable.

fairy ['feərɪ] *n* hada. [COMP] **fairy story/ tale** cuento de hadas.
ⓘ *pl* fairies.

faith [feɪθ] *n* **1** fe *f*. **2** *(trust, confidence)* confianza (in, en), fe *f* (in, en). **3** REL fe *f*.

faithful ['feɪθfʊl] *adj* **1** *(loyal)* fiel (to, a), leal (to, a/con). **2** *(accurate)* exacto,-a.

faithfully ['feɪθfʊlɪ] *adv* fielmente. [LOC] **yours faithfully** *(in letter)* atentamente.

fake [feɪk] *n* **1** falsificación *f*. **2** *(person)* impostor,-ra, farsante *mf*.
▸ *adj* falso,-a, falsificado,-a.
▸ *vt* **1** *(falsify)* falsificar. **2** *(pretend)* fingir: *she faked illness* fingió estar enferma.

falcon ['fɔːlkən] *n* halcón *m*.

fall [fɔːl] *n* **1** *(act of falling)* caída. **2** *(of rock)* desprendimiento; *(of snow)* nevada. **3** *(decrease)* baja, descenso, disminución *f*. **4** *(defeat)* caída. **5** US *(autumn)* otoño.
▸ *vi* **1** *(gen)* caer, caerse. **2** *(decrease)* bajar, descender. **3** *(be defeated)* caer; *(be killed)* perecer. [LOC] **to fall asleep** quedarse dormido. ‖ **to fall in love** enamorarse.
▸ *n pl* **falls** *(waterfall)* cascada *f* sing, cataratas *fpl*.
◆ **to fall apart** *vi* romperse, deshacerse, caerse a pedazos.
◆ **to fall back** *vi (retreat)* retroceder, retirarse.

◆ **to fall back on** *vt insep (resort to)* recurrir a.
◆ **to fall behind** *vi (be overtaken)* retrasarse, rezagarse.
◆ **to fall down** *vi* **1** *(gen)* caer, caerse. **2** *(fail)* fallar.
◆ **to fall for** *vt insep* **1** *(be tricked)* dejarse engañar por, picar. **2** *fam (fall in love)* enamorarse de.
◆ **to fall off** *vi* **1** *(decrease in quantity)* bajar, disminuir; *(in quality)* empeorar. **2** *(become detached)* desprenderse, caerse.
◆ **to fall out** *vi (quarrel)* reñir (with, con), pelearse (with, con).
▸ *vi (drop)* caerse.
◆ **to fall over** *vt insep* caer, tropezar con.
ⓘ *pt* fell [fel], *pp* fallen ['fɔːlən].

fallen ['fɔːlən] *pp* → fall.
▸ *adj (not virtuous)* perdido,-a.

Fallopian tube [fələʊpɪən'tjuːb] *n* trompa de Falopio.

fallout ['fɔːlaʊt] *n* lluvia radiactiva.

fallow ['fæləʊ] *adj* en barbecho.

false [fɔːls] *adj* **1** *(untrue)* falso,-a. **2** *(artificial)* postizo,-a. [COMP] **false alarm** falsa alarma. ‖ **false start** salida nula. ‖ **false teeth** dentadura postiza.

falsify ['fɔːlsɪfaɪ] *vt* **1** *(alter falsely)* falsificar. **2** *(misrepresent)* falsear.
ⓘ *pt & pp* falsified, *ger* falsifying.

falter ['fɔːltəʳ] *vi (person)* vacilar, titubear; *(voice)* fallar.

fame [feɪm] *n* fama.

familiar [fə'mɪlɪəʳ] *adj* **1** *(well-known)* conocido,-a (to, a). **2** *(aware)* familiarizado,-a (with, con). **3** *(intimate)* íntimo,-a.

☒ Familiar no significa 'familiar (de la familia)', que se traduce por family.

familiarity [fəmɪlɪ'ærɪtɪ] *n* familiaridad *f*.

familiarize [fə'mɪlɪəraɪz] *vt (become acquainted)* familiarizar (with, con).

family ['fæmɪlɪ] *n* familia.
ⓘ *pl* families.
▸ *adj* familiar. [COMP] **family name** apellido.

famine ['fæmɪn] *n* hambruna, hambre *f*.

famous ['feɪməs] *adj* famoso,-a (for, por).

famously ['feɪməslɪ] *adv* fam estupendamente.

fan [fæn] *n* **1** *(object)* abanico. **2** ELEC ventilador *m.* **3** *(follower)* aficionado,-a; *(of pop star, etc)* admirador,-ra, fan *mf.* **4** *(of football)* hincha *mf.*
▶ *vt (face)* abanicar; *(elec)* ventilar.
ⓘ *pt & pp* fanned, *ger* fanning.

fanatic [fəˈnætɪk] *n* fanático,-a.
▶ *adj* fanático,-a (about, de).

fancier [ˈfænsɪəʳ] *n* aficionado,-a.

fanciful [ˈfænsɪfʊl] *adj* **1** *(idea)* imaginario,-a, fantástico,-a. **2** *(extravagant)* caprichoso,-a, estrafalario,-a.

fancy [ˈfænsɪ] *n* **1** *(imagination)* fantasía, imaginación *f.* **2** *(whim)* capricho, antojo.
ⓘ *pl* fancies.
▶ *adj* **1** *(jewels, goods, etc)* de fantasía. **2** *(high-class, posh)* elegante, de lujo.
▶ *vt* **1** *(want)* apetecer, querer. **2** *(find attractive)* encontrar atractivo,-a. **3** *(think)* creer, suponer.
ⓘ *pt & pp* fancied, *ger* fancying.

fanfare [ˈfænfeəʳ] *n* fanfarria.

fang [fæŋ] *n* colmillo.

fantastic [fænˈtæstɪk] *adj* fantástico,-a.

fantasy [ˈfæntəsɪ] *n* fantasía.
ⓘ *pl* fantasies.

FAQ [ˈefeɪˈkjuː] *n* (frequently asked questions) preguntas frecuentes.

far [fɑːʳ] *adj* **1** *(distant)* lejano,-a, remoto,-a. **2** *(more distant)* opuesto,-a, extremo,-a.
ⓘ *comp* farther o further, *superl* farthest o furthest.
▶ *adv* **1** *(a long way)* lejos. **2** *(a long time)* lejos. **3** *(much)* mucho. LOC **as far as** hasta: *as far as I am concerned* por lo que a mí se refiere. ‖ **far away** lejos. ‖ **so far** hasta ahora.

faraway [ˈfɑːrəweɪ] *adj* lejano,-a, remoto,-a; *(look)* distraído,-a.

farce [fɑːs] *n* farsa.

fare [feəʳ] *n* *(price)* tarifa, precio del billete; *(boat)* pasaje *m.*
▶ *vi (progress, get on)* desenvolverse.

✎ Fare se refiere sólo a los billetes de transporte público.

farewell [feəˈwel] *interj* ¡adiós!
▶ *n* despedida.

farm [fɑːm] *n* granja.
▶ *adj* agrícola, de granja.

▶ *vt* **1** *(use land)* cultivar, labrar. **2** *(breed animals)* criar.
▶ *vi (grow crops)* cultivar la tierra.

farmer [ˈfɑːməʳ] *n* granjero,-a, agricultor,-ra.

farmhouse [ˈfɑːmhaʊs] *n* granja.

farming [ˈfɑːmɪŋ] *n* agricultura. LOC **farming industry** industria agropecuaria.

farmland [ˈfɑːmlænd] *n* tierra de cultivo.

farmyard [ˈfɑːmjɑːd] *n* corral *m.*

far-reaching [fɑːˈriːtʃɪŋ] *adj* de gran alcance.

farrier [ˈfærɪəʳ] *n* herrero.

far-sighted [fɑːˈsaɪtɪd] *adj* previsor,-ra.

fart [fɑːt] *n* **1** *fam* pedo. **2** *(fool)* carcamal *m*, carroza *m.*
▶ *vi* tirarse un pedo.

farther [ˈfɑːðəʳ] *adj* comp → far: *Santander is farther than Murcia* Santander está más lejos que Murcia.

farthest [ˈfɑːðɪst] *adj* → far: *Pluto is the farthest planet from the Sun* Plutón es el planeta más alejado del Sol.
▶ *adv* → far: *who lives farthest from the school?* ¿quién vive más lejos de la escuela?

fascinate [ˈfæsɪneɪt] *vt* fascinar.

fascinating [ˈfæsɪneɪtɪŋ] *adj* fascinante.

fascination [fæsɪˈneɪʃən] *n* fascinación *f.*

fascism [ˈfæʃɪzəm] *n* fascismo.

fascist [ˈfæʃɪst] *n* fascista *mf.*
▶ *adj* fascista.

fashion [ˈfæʃən] *n* **1** *(style)* moda. **2** *(way)* modo. LOC **in fashion** de moda. ‖ **out of fashion** pasado de moda.
▶ *vt (clay)* formar; *(metal)* labrar.

fashionable [ˈfæʃənəbəl] *adj* de moda.

fast¹ [fɑːst] *adj* **1** *(gen)* rápido,-a. **2** *(tight, secure)* firme, seguro,-a. **3** *(clock)* adelantado,-a.
▶ *adv* **1** rápidamente, deprisa. **2** *(securely)* firmemente; *(thoroughly)* profundamente.

fast² [fɑːst] *n* ayuno.
▶ *vi* ayunar.

fasten [ˈfɑːsən] *vt* **1** *(attach)* fijar, sujetar. **2** *(tie)* atar. **3** *(box, door, window)* cerrar; *(belt, dress)* abrochar.
▶ *vi (box, door, etc)* cerrarse; *(dress, etc)* abrocharse.

fastener ['fɑːsənəʳ] n cierre m.

fastidious [fæˈstɪdɪəs] adj quisquilloso,-a, melindroso,-a.

☒ Fastidious no significa 'fastidioso (molesto)', que se traduce por **annoying**.

fat [fæt] adj gordo,-a.
① comp **fatter**, superl **fattest**.
▶ n 1 (of meat) grasa; (of person) carnes fpl. 2 (for cooking) manteca; (lard) lardo.

fatal ['feɪtəl] adj 1 (causing disaster) fatal, funesto,-a; (serious) grave. 2 (causing death) mortal. 3 (fateful) fatídico,-a.

☒ Fatal no significa 'fatal (muy malo)', que se traduce por **awful**.

fatality [fəˈtælɪtɪ] n víctima mortal.
① pl **fatalities**.

fate [feɪt] n 1 (destiny) destino. 2 (person's lot) suerte f.

fated ['feɪtɪd] adj predestinado,-a.

fateful ['feɪtful] adj fatídico,-a.

father ['fɑːðəʳ] n 1 (male parent) padre m. 2 (priest) padre m.
▶ vt engendrar.

father-in-law ['fɑːðərɪnlɔː] n suegro.

fatherland ['fɑːðəlænd] n patria.

fatherly ['fɑːðəlɪ] adj paternal.

fatigue [fəˈtiːg] n 1 fatiga, cansancio. 2 TECH fatiga.
▶ vt fml fatigar, cansar.

fat-soluble [fætˈsɒljəbəl] adj liposoluble.

fatten ['fætən] vt 1 (animal) cebar (up, -). 2 (person) engordar (up,-).

fattening ['fætənɪŋ] adj que engorda: biscuits are fattening las galletas engordan.

fatty ['fætɪ] adj (also greasy) graso,-a.
① comp **fattier**, superl **fattiest**.
▶ n fam pej gordinflón,-ona.
① pl **fatties**.

faucet ['fɔːsɪt] n US grifo.

fault [fɔːlt] n 1 (gen) defecto. 2 (blame) culpa. 4 (mistake) error m, falta. 5 (in earth) falla. 6 (in tennis, etc) falta.
▶ vt criticar, encontrar defectos a.

☒ Fault no significa 'falta (carencia)', que se traduce por **lack**.

faultless ['fɔːltləs] adj perfecto,-a, intachable, impecable.

faulty ['fɔːltɪ] adj defectuoso,-a.
① comp **faultier**, superl **faultiest**.

fauna ['fɔːnə] n fauna.

faux pas [fəʊˈpɑː] n metedura de pata.
① pl **faux pas**.

favor ['feɪvəʳ] n-vt US → **favour**.

favorite ['feɪvərɪt] n US → **favorite**.

favour ['feɪvəʳ] n 1 (kindness) favor m. 2 (approval) aprobación f, favor m. 3 (favouritism) parcialidad f, favoritismo.
▶ vt 1 (prefer) preferir, inclinarse por. 2 (benefit, aid) favorecer.

favourable ['feɪvərəbəl] adj favorable (to/towards, a).

favourite ['feɪvərɪt] n favorito,-a.
▶ adj favorito,-a.

favouritism ['feɪvərɪtɪzəm] n favoritismo.

fawn [fɔːn] n 1 ZOOL cervato. 2 (colour) beige m.
▶ adj beige.
◆ to fawn on vt insep adular, lisonjear.

fax [fæks] n fax m.
▶ vt enviar por fax. COMP **fax machine** fax m.

fear [fɪəʳ] n miedo, temor m.
▶ vt temer, tener miedo a.
▶ vi temer, tener miedo.
◆ to fear for vt insep temer por: I fear for the children's safety temo por la seguridad de los niños.

fearful ['fɪəful] adj 1 (frightened) temeroso,-a (of, de). 2 (terrible) terrible, espantoso,-a.

fearless ['fɪələs] adj audaz.

fearsome ['fɪəsəm] adj temible.

feasibility ['fiːzəbɪlɪtɪ] n viabilidad f.

feasible ['fiːzəbəl] adj 1 (viable) factible, viable. 2 (plausible) verosímil.

feast [fiːst] n 1 festín m, banquete m. 2 fam comilona. 3 REL fiesta de guardar, día m de fiesta.
▶ vi banquetear, festejar.

feat [fiːt] n proeza, hazaña.

feather ['feðəʳ] n pluma.

feature ['fiːtʃəʳ] n 1 (of face) rasgo, facción f. 2 (characteristic) rasgo, característica. 3 (press) artículo especial, especial m.
COMP **feature (film)** largometraje m.

▶ vt *(have)* tener; *(film)* tener como protagonista: *this car features the latest safety devices* este coche incorpora los últimos dispositivos de seguridad.

▶ vi *(appear)* figurar (in, en): *his name featured in the police report* su nombre figuró en el informe policial.

February [ˈfebrʊərɪ] *n* febrero.

✎ Para ejemplo de uso, consulta May.

fecal [ˈfiːkəl] *adj* US → **faecal**.

feces [ˈfiːsiːz] *n* US → **faeces**.

fed [fed] *pt & pp* → **feed**. `LOC` **to be fed up with** *fam* estar harto,-a de.

federal [ˈfedərəl] *adj* federal.

federation [fedəˈreɪʃən] *n* federación *f*.

fee [fiː] *n* **1** *(doctor's, etc)* honorarios *mpl*; *(for tuition)* derechos *mpl* (de matrícula). **2** *(membership)* cuota, cuota de socio. `COMP` **registration fee** matrícula.

feeble [ˈfiːbəl] *adj* **1** *(person)* débil. **2** *(light, sound)* tenue, débil. **3** *(argument, excuse)* de poco peso.

feed [fiːd] *n* **1** comida. **2** *fam* comilona. **3** *(for cattle)* pienso. **4** TECH alimentación *f*.

▶ vt **1** alimentar: *could you feed our cat while we're away?* ¿podrías dar de comer a nuestro gato mientras estamos fuera? **2** *(breastfeed)* dar de mamar a; *(bottle-feed)* dar el biberón a. **3** TECH alimentar, suministrar. **4** *(insert)* introducir; *(coins)* meter.

▶ vi *(people)* comer, alimentarse (on, de); *(animals)* pacer.

◆ **to feed up** *vt sep (animal)* cebar; *(person)* engordar.

ⓘ *pt & pp* fed [fed].

feedback [ˈfiːdbæk] *n* **1** TECH retroalimentación *f*, retroacción *f*. **2** *fig* reacción *f*, respuesta.

feeder [ˈfiːdər] *n* **1** TECH alimentador *m*. **2** *(road)* ramal *m*, carretera.

feel [fiːl] *n* **1** *(sense, texture)* tacto. **2** *(atmosphere)* aire *m*, ambiente *m*.

▶ vt **1** *(touch)* tocar, palpar. **2** *(search with fingers)* buscar. **3** *(sense, experience)* sentir, experimentar. **4** *(believe)* creer.

▶ vi **1** *(be)* sentir(se), encontrarse. **2** *(seem)* parecer: *it feels like leather* parece piel. **3** *(perceive, sense)* sentir: *she could feel all eyes upon her* sentía que todos la miraban. **4** *(opinion)* opinar, pensar: *how do you feel about exams?* ¿qué opinas de los exámenes?

◆ **to feel for** *vt insep (have sympathy for)* compadecer a, compadecerse de.

ⓘ *pt & pp* felt [felt].

feeler [ˈfiːlər] *n* antena.

feeling [ˈfiːlɪŋ] *n* **1** *(emotion)* sentimiento, emoción *f*. **2** *(sensation)* sensación *f*. **3** *(sense)* sensibilidad. **4** *(impression)* impresión *f*: *I have the feeling that …* tengo la impresión de que …

▶ *adj* sensible, compasivo,-a.

▶ *n pl* **feelings** sentimientos *mpl*.

feet [fiːt] *n pl* → **foot**.

feign [feɪn] *vt* fingir, aparentar: *she feigned illness to get off school* fingió estar enferma para no ir a la escuela.

feint [feɪnt] *n fml (fencing)* finta; *(boxing)* treta, estratagema.

▶ *adj (paper)* rayado,-a.

feldspar [ˈfeldspɑːr] *n* feldespato.

feline [ˈfiːlaɪn] *adj* felino,-a.

▶ *n* felino,-a.

fell¹ [fel] *vt* **1** *(tree)* talar. **2** *(enemy)* derribar.

fell² [fel] *pt* → **fall**.

fellow [ˈfeləʊ] *n* **1** *fam (chap)* tipo, tío: *old fellow* viejo amigo; *poor fellow!* ¡pobrecito! **2** *(companion, comrade)* compañero,-a, camarada *mf*. **3** *(member)* socio,-a.

fellowship [ˈfeləʊʃɪp] *n* **1** *(group)* asociación *f*, sociedad *f*. **2** *(companionship)* compañerismo, camaradería. **3** EDUC *(scholarship)* beca.

felspar [ˈfelspɑːr] *n* feldespato.

felt¹ [felt] *pt & pp* → **feel**.

felt² [felt] *n* fieltro.

▶ *adj* de fieltro.

felt-tip [ˈfelttɪp] [also **felt-tip pen**] *n* rotulador *m*.

female [ˈfiːmeɪl] *n* **1** hembra. **2** *(woman)* mujer *f*; *(girl)* chica.

▶ *adj* **1** femenino,-a. **2** ZOOL hembra.

feminine [ˈfemɪnɪn] *adj* femenino,-a.

▶ *n* femenino,-a.

feminism [ˈfemɪnɪzəm] *n* feminismo.

feminist [ˈfemɪnɪst] *n* feminista *mf*.

femoral [ˈfiːmərəl] *adj* femoral.

femur ['fiːməʳ] *n* fémur *m*.

fence [fens] *n* valla, cerca. LOC **to sit on the fence** ver los toros desde la barrera.
► *vi* **1** SP practicar la esgrima. **2** *(land)* cercar.

fencing ['fensɪŋ] *n* **1** SP esgrima. **2** *(structure)* cercado.

fend [fend] *vi* **to fend for os** valerse por uno mismo,-a.
◆ **to fend off** *vt sep (blow)* parar, desviar; *(question)* esquivar; *(attack)* rechazar, defenderse de.

fender ['fendəʳ] *n* **1** *(for fire)* pantalla. **2** US *(on automobile)* parachoques *m*.

fennel ['fenəl] *n* hinojo.

ferment [*(n)* 'fɜːment] [*(vb)* fəˈment] *n* **1** *(substance)* fermento. **2** *(unrest)* agitación *f*.
► *vt & vi* fermentar.

fermentation [fɜːmenˈteɪʃən] *n* fermentación *f*.

fern [fɜːn] *n* helecho.

ferocious [fəˈrəʊʃəs] *adj* feroz.

ferocity [fəˈrɒsɪtɪ] *n* ferocidad *f*.

ferret ['ferɪt] *n* hurón *m*.
◆ **to ferret out** *vt sep* descubrir.

ferrous ['ferəs] *adj* ferroso,-a.

ferry ['ferɪ] *n (small)* barca de pasaje; *(large)* transbordador *m*, ferry *m*.
① *pl* **ferries**.
► *vt* transportar.
① *pt & pp* **ferried**, *ger* **ferrying**.

ferryboat ['ferɪbəʊt] *n* → **ferry**.

fertile ['fɜːtaɪl] *adj* fértil.

fertility [fəˈtɪlɪtɪ] *n* fertilidad *f*.

fertilization [fɜːtəlaɪˈzeɪʃən] *n* **1** *(soil)* fertilización *f*. **2** *(egg)* fecundación *f*.

fertilize ['fɜːtɪlaɪz] *vt* **1** *(soil)* fertilizar, abonar. **2** *(egg)* fecundar.

fertilizer ['fɜːtɪlaɪzəʳ] *n* fertilizante *m*, abono.

ferule¹ ['feruːl] *n* férula.

fervent ['fɜːvənt] *adj* fervoroso,-a.

fervor ['fɜːvəʳ] *n* US → **fervour**.

fervour ['fɜːvəʳ] *n* fervor *m*.

fester ['festəʳ] *vi* **1** MED supurar, enconarse. **2** *fig* amargarse.

festival ['festɪvəl] *n* **1** *(event)* festival *m*. **2** *(celebration)* fiesta.

fetal ['fiːtəs] *n* US → **foetal**.

fetch [fetʃ] *vt* **1** *(go and get)* ir por, ir a buscar, buscar; *(bring)* traer. **2** *fam (sell for)* venderse por, alcanzar.
◆ **to fetch up** *vi* ir a parar.

fête [feit] *n (party)* fiesta; *(fair)* feria.
► *vt* festejar.

fetid ['fetɪd] *adj* fétido,-a.

fetish ['fetɪʃ] *n* fetiche *m*.

fetter ['fetəʳ] *vt* **1** encadenar. **2** *fig* estorbar, poner trabas a.
► *n pl* **fetters** grilletes *mpl*, cadenas *fpl*.

fetus ['fiːtəs] *n* US → **foetus**.

feud [fjuːd] *n* enemistad *f* (duradera): *there's been a feud between the two families for years* hace años que existe una enemistad entre ambas familias.
► *vi* disentir, reñir, pelear.

⊠ **Feud** no significa 'feudo (dominio)', que se traduce por **fief**.

feudal ['fjuːdəl] *adj* feudal.

feudalism ['fjuːdəlɪzəm] *n* feudalismo.

fever ['fiːvəʳ] *n* fiebre *f*.

feverish ['fiːvərɪʃ] *adj* febril.

few [fjuː] *adj* **1** *(not many)* poco,-a, pocos,-as: *very few cars* muy pocos coches. **2** *(some)* uno,-as cuantos,-as, algunos,-as: *in the next few days* en los próximos días.
► *pron* **1** *(not many)* pocos,-as: *many try but few succeed* muchos lo intentan pero pocos lo consiguen. **2** *(some)* unos,-as cuantos,-as, algunos,-as: *there are a few left* quedan unos cuantos.

fiancé [frˈænseɪ] *n* prometido, novio.

fiancée [frˈænseɪ] *n* prometida, novia.

fiasco [frˈæskəʊ] *n* fiasco, fracaso.
① *pl* **fiascos**.

fib [fɪb] *n fam* bola, trola.
► *vi fam* contar bolas, contar trolas.
① *pt & pp* **fibbed**, *ger* **fibbing**.

fibre ['faɪbəʳ] *n* fibra. COMP **fibre optics** fibra óptica. ‖ **man-made fibre** fibra artificial.

fibreglass ['faɪbəglɑːs] *n* fibra de vidrio.

fibrosis [faɪˈbrəʊsɪs] *n* fibrosis *f*.

fibrous ['faɪbrəs] *adj* fibroso,-a.

fibula ['fɪbjələ] *n* peroné *m*.

fickle ['fɪkəl] *adj* inconstante, voluble.

fiction ['fɪkʃən] *n* **1** *(novels)* novela, narrativa. **2** *(invention)* ficción *f.*

fictitious [fɪk'tɪʃəs] *adj* ficticio,-a.

fiddle ['fɪdəl] *n* **1** *fam* violín *m.* **2** *fam (fraud)* estafa, trampa.
▶ *vi* **1** tocar el violín. **2** *fam (play)* juguetear **(with,** con**)**.
▶ *vt fam (cheat)* amañar, falsificar.
◆ **to fiddle about / fiddle around** *vi fam* perder el tiempo.

fiddler ['fɪdlər] *n* **1** *fam (violinist)* violinista *mf.* **2** *fam (cheat)* tramposo,-a.

fidelity [fɪ'delɪtɪ] *n* fidelidad *f.*

fidget ['fɪdʒɪt] *n* persona inquieta.
▶ *vi (move about)* moverse, no poder estar(se) quieto,-a; *(play about)* jugar **(with,** con**)**.

fief [fi:f] *n* feudo.

field [fi:ld] *n* **1** *(gen)* campo. **2** *(for mining)* yacimiento. **3** *(subject, area)* campo, terreno. **4** SP *(competitors)* competidores *mpl; (horses)* participantes *mpl.*

fierce [fɪəs] *adj* **1** *(gen)* feroz. **2** *fig (heat, competition, etc)* fuerte, intenso,-a; *(argument)* acalorado,-a.

fiery ['faɪərɪ] *adj* **1** *(colour)* encendido,-a, rojo,-a. **2** *(burning)* ardiente. **3** *(food)* muy picante; *(drink)* muy fuerte.
① *comp* **fierier,** *superl* **fieriest.**

fifteen [fɪf'ti:n] *adj* quince.
▶ *n* quince *m.*

✎ Consulta también **six.**

fifteenth [fɪf'ti:nθ] *adj* decimoquinto,-a.
▶ *adv* en decimoquinto lugar.
▶ *n* **1** *(in series)* decimoquinto,-a. **2** *(fraction)* decimoquinto; *(one part)* decimoquinta parte *f.*

✎ Consulta también **sixth.**

fifth [fɪfθ] *adj* quinto,-a.
▶ *adv* quinto, en quinto lugar.
▶ *n* **1** *(in series)* quinto,-a. **2** *(fraction)* quinto; *(one part)* quinta parte *f.*

✎ Consulta también **sixth.**

fiftieth ['fɪftɪəθ] *adj* quincuagésimo,-a.
▶ *adv* en quincuagésimo lugar.
▶ *n* **1** *(in series)* quincuagésimo,-a. **2** *(fraction)* quincuagésimo; *(one part)* quincuagésima parte *f.*

✎ Consulta también **sixtieth.**

fifty ['fɪftɪ] *adj* cincuenta.
▶ *n* cincuenta *m.*

✎ Consulta también **sixty.**

fifty-fifty ['fɪftɪ'fɪftɪ] *adv fam* mitad y mitad, a medias.

fig [fɪg] *n* higo. COMP **fig tree** higuera.

fight [faɪt] *n* **1** *(struggle)* lucha. **2** *(physical violence)* pelea; *(quarrel)* riña; *(argument)* disputa. **3** *(boxing)* combate *m.*
▶ *vi* **1** *(quarrel)* pelear(se) **(about/over,** por**)**, discutir **(about/over,** por**)**. **2** *(in boxing)* pelear **(against,** contra**)**. **3** *(with physical violence)* pelearse **(with,** con**)** **(against,** contra**)**, luchar **(with,** con**)** **(against,** contra**)**.
▶ *vt* **1** *(bull)* lidiar. **2** *(engage in - battle)* librar; *(war)* hacer; *(election)* presentarse a. **3** *(with physical violence)* pelearse, luchar.
◆ **to fight back** *vi* defenderse, resistir.
▶ *vt sep (tears)* contener.
◆ **to fight off** *vt sep* vencer, rechazar.
① *pt & pp* **fought** [fɔ:t].

fighter ['faɪtər] *n* **1** *(war)* combatiente *mf.* **2** *(boxing)* boxeador,-ra. **3** *fig* luchador,-ra.

fig-leaf ['fɪgli:f] *n* hoja de parra.

figurative ['fɪgərətɪv] *adj* figurado,-a.

figure ['fɪgər] *n* **1** *(number, sign)* cifra, número. **2** *(money, price)* cantidad *f,* precio. **3** *(in art, shape, human form)* figura. **4** *(personality)* figura, personaje *m.*
▶ *vi (appear)* figurar, constar.
▶ *vt* US *(think)* suponer, imaginarse.
◆ **to figure out** *vt sep fam (gen)* comprender, enterarse; *(problem)* resolver, calcular.

filament ['fɪləmənt] *n* filamento.

file [faɪl] *n* **1** *(tool)* lima. **2** *(folder)* carpeta. **3** *(archive)* archivo, expediente *m.* **4** COMPUT archivo. **5** *(line)* fila.
▶ *vt* **1** *(smooth)* limar. **2** *(put away)* archivar; *(in card index)* fichar. **3** JUR presentar.
▶ *vi (walk in line)* desfilar.

filigree ['fɪlɪgri:] *n* filigrana.

fill [fɪl] *vt* **1** *(make full)* llenar (with, de). **2** *(time)* ocupar. **3** *(cover)* cubrir. **4** CULIN rellenar. **5** *(tooth)* empastar. **6** *(hold a position)* ocupar; *(appoint)* cubrir. **7** *(fulfil)* satisfacer.
▶ *vi* llenarse (with, de).
◆ **to fill in** *vt sep* **1** *(space, form)* rellenar. **2** *(inform)* poner al corriente (on, de).
◆ **to fill in for** *vt insep* sustituir a.
◆ **to fill up** *vt sep* llenar.
▶ *vi* llenarse.

fillet [ˈfɪlɪt] *n* filete *m*.

filling [ˈfɪlɪŋ] *n* **1** *(in tooth)* empaste *m*. **2** CULIN relleno. COMP **filling station** gasolinera.

film [fɪlm] *n* **1** CINEM película, filme *m*, film *m*. **2** *(coating of dust, etc)* capa, película. **3** *(of photos)* carrete *m*, rollo.
▶ *vt* **1** CINEM rodar, filmar; *(tv programme)* grabar. **2** *(event)* filmar.
▶ *vi* CINEM rodar.

filter [ˈfɪltər] *n* filtro.
▶ *vt* filtrar.

filth [fɪlθ] *n* **1** *(dirt)* suciedad *f*, porquería. **2** *fig (obscenity)* obscenidades *fpl*, porquerías *fpl*.

filthy [ˈfɪlθɪ] *adj* **1** *(dirty)* sucio,-a, asqueroso,-a. **2** *(obscene)* obsceno,-a, grosero,-a, asqueroso,-a.
ⓘ *comp* **filthier**, *superl* **filthiest**.

fin [fɪn] *n* aleta.

final [ˈfaɪnəl] *adj* final.
▶ *n* SP final *f*.
▶ *n pl* **finals** *(at university)* exámenes *mpl* finales.

finale [fɪˈnɑːlɪ] *n* final *m*.

finalist [ˈfaɪnəlɪst] *n* finalista *mf*.

finality [faɪˈnælətɪ] *n* carácter *m* definitivo.

❌ Finality no significa 'finalidad (objetivo)', que se traduce por **purpose**, **aim**.

finalize [ˈfaɪnəlaɪz] *vt (plans, arrangements)* ultimar; *(date)* fijar.

finally [ˈfaɪnəlɪ] *adv* **1** *(at last)* por fin, al final. **2** *(lastly)* por último, finalmente.

finance [ˈfaɪnæns] *n (management of money)* finanzas *fpl*.
▶ *vt* financiar.
▶ *n pl* **finances** *(money available)* fondos *mpl*.

financial [faɪˈnænsɪəl] *n* financiero,-a, económico,-a.

find [faɪnd] *n (act, thing found)* hallazgo.
▶ *vt* **1** *(gen)* encontrar. **2** JUR declarar.
◆ **to find out** *vt sep* **1** *(enquire)* preguntar, averiguar; *(discover)* descubrir, enterarse de.
▶ *vi* **1** *(enquire)* informarse (about, sobre), averiguar. **2** *(discover)* enterarse (about, de), (llegar a) saber.
ⓘ *pt & pp* **found** [faʊnd].

finding [ˈfaɪndɪŋ] *n* **1** *(of inquiry)* conclusión *f*, resultado. **2** JUR fallo, veredicto.

✎ Se usa en plural con el mismo significado.

fine¹ [faɪn] *adj* **1** *(gen)* fino,-a. **2** *(high-quality)* excelente. **3** *(weather)* bueno,-a. **4** *(healthy)* bien. **5** *fam (all right)* bien.
▶ *adv* **1** *(in small bits)* fino, finamente. **2** *fam (very well)* muy bien.

fine² [faɪn] *n (punishment)* multa.
▶ *vt* multar.

finger [ˈfɪŋgər] *n* dedo.
▶ *vt* tocar.

fingernail [ˈfɪŋgəneɪl] *n* uña.

fingerprint [ˈfɪŋgəprɪnt] *n* huella digital, huella dactilar.

fingertip [ˈfɪŋgətɪp] *n* punta del dedo, yema del dedo.

finish [ˈfɪnɪʃ] *n* **1** fin *m*, final *m*. **2** SP llegada, meta. **3** *(for surface)* acabado.
▶ *vt* acabar, terminar.
◆ **to finish up** *vi (end up)* ir a parar a/en.

finite [ˈfaɪnaɪt] *adj* finito,-a.

Finland [ˈfɪnlənd] *n* Finlandia.

Finn [fɪn] *n (person)* finlandés,-esa.

Finnish [ˈfɪnɪʃ] *adj* finlandés,-esa.
▶ *n (language)* finlandés *m*.

fiord [fɪˈɔːd] *n* fiordo.

fir [fɜːr] *n* abeto.

fire [faɪər] *n* **1** *(gen)* fuego. **2** *(blaze)* incendio, fuego. **3** *(heater)* estufa. **4** MIL fuego. LOC **to be on fire** estar ardiendo. ❙ **to catch fire** prenderse. COMP **fire brigade** los bomberos. ❙ **fire engine** coche de bomberos. ❙ **fire escape** escalera de incendios. ❙ **fire extinguisher** extintor *m*. ❙ **fire hydrant** boca de incendios. ❙ **fire station** parque *m* de bomberos.

▶ *vt (weapon)* disparar; *(rocket)* lanzar. **2**
fam (dismiss) despedir.
▶ *vi* **1** *(shoot)* disparar (at, sobre), hacer
fuego. **2** AUTO encenderse.
▶ *interj* ¡fuego!

firearm ['faɪərɑːm] *n* arma de fuego.

firebreak ['faɪəbreɪk] *n* cortafuego.

firecracker ['faɪəkrækə'] *n* petardo.

firefighter ['faɪəfaɪtə'] *n* bombero *mf*.

firefly ['faɪəflaɪ] *n* luciérnaga.
① *pl* fireflies.

fireman ['faɪəmən] *n* bombero.
① *pl* firemen ['faɪəmən].

fireplace ['faɪəpleɪs] *n* **1** *(structure)* chimenea. **2** *(hearth)* hogar *m*.

fireproof ['faɪəpruːf] *adj* a prueba de
fuego.

firewall ['faɪəwɔːl] *n* cortafuego.

firewood ['faɪəwʊd] *n* leña.

fireworks ['faɪəwɜːks] *n pl* fuegos *mpl*
artificiales, fuegos *mpl* de artificio.

firing ['faɪərɪŋ] *n* tiroteo.

firm¹ [fɜːm] *n (business)* empresa.

> ✗ Firm no significa 'firma (escrita)', que
se traduce por signature.

firm² [fɜːm] *adj* **1** *(strong, solid, steady)* firme, sólido,-a. **2** *(strict, strong)* duro,-a. **3**
FIN *(steady)* firme, estable.

first [fɜːst] *adj* primero,-a.
▶ *adv* **1** *(before anything else)* primero. **2**
(for the first time) por primera vez. **3** *(in
preference to)* antes. LOC **at first** al principio. **❙ first of all** primero.
▶ *n* **1** la primera vez. **2** *(gear)* primera: *I
can't put it into first* no puedo meter primera.

first-aid [fɜːst'eɪd] *adj* de primeros
auxilios. COMP **first-aid kit** botiquín *m*.

first-born ['fɜːstbɔːn] *adj* primogénito,-a.
▶ *n* primogénito,-a.

first-class ['fɜːstklɑːs] *adj* **1** de primera
clase. **2** *fig* de primera, excelente.
▶ *adv* en primera.

first-hand [fɜːst'hænd] *adj* de primera
mano.

firstly ['fɜːstlɪ] *adv* en primer lugar.

first-rate ['fɜːstreɪt] *adj* de primera.
▶ *adv* de primera.

fiscal ['fɪskəl] *adj* fiscal.

fish [fɪʃ] *n* **1** pez *m*. **2** CULIN pescado. COMP
fish farm piscifactoría. **❙ fish finger** pali-
to de pescado rebozado. **❙ fish shop**
pescadería.
① *pl* fish o fishes.
▶ *vi* pescar (for, -).

> ✎ Cuando significa 'pez', fish es un nom-
bre contable y su plural es fish, aunque
también se puede emplear la forma menos frecuente fishes. Cuando significa
'pescado', es incontable y, por lo tanto, no
tiene plural.

fishbowl ['fɪʃbəʊl] *n* pecera.

fisherman ['fɪʃəmən] *n* pescador *m*.
① *pl* fishermen ['fɪʃəmən].

fish-hook ['fɪʃhʊk] *n* anzuelo.

fishing ['fɪʃɪŋ] *n* pesca. LOC **to go fishing**
ir de pesca. COMP **fishing line** sedal *m*. **❙
fishing net** red *f* de pesca. **❙ fishing rod**
caña de pescar.

fishmonger ['fɪʃmʌŋgə'] *n* GB pescadero,-a. COMP **fishmonger's** pescadería.

fission ['fɪʃən] *n* fisión *f*.

fissure ['fɪʃə'] *n* fisura, grieta.

fist [fɪst] *n* puño.

fistful ['fɪstfʊl] *n* puñado.

fit¹ [fɪt] *n* **1** MED ataque *m*, acceso. **2** *(of
laughter, rage)* ataque *m*.

fit² [fɪt] *adj* **1** *(suitable, appropriate)*
adecuado,-a, apropiado,-a; *(qualified
for)* capacitado,-a, capaz. **2** *(in good
health)* sano,-a, bien de salud; *(physically)*
en forma. **3** *fam (ready)* a punto de.
① *comp* fitter, *superl* fittest.
▶ *n* **1** *(of clothes)* : *it's a perfect fit* me va perfectamente. **2** *(in space)*: *it'll be a tight fit*
vamos a estar muy apretados.
▶ *vt* **1** *(be right size for)* sentar bien, quedar bien. **2** *(try (clothing) on sb)* probar. **3**
(key) abrir. **4** *(install)* instalar, poner. **5**
(adapt) ajustar, adaptar, adecuar.
◆ **to fit in** *vi* **1** *(get on)* llevarse bien, integrarse. **2** *(suit)* encajar; *(harmonize)*
pegar, quedar bien; *(tally)* cuadrar.

► *vt sep* **1** *(physically)* hacer sitio para. **2** *(in timetable)* hacer un hueco para. **3** *(harmonize)* encajar, cuadrar.

ⓘ *pt & pp* fitted, *ger* fitting.

fitness ['fɪtnəs] *n* **1** *(health)* buena forma física, buen estado físico. **2** *(suitability)* capacidad *f* (for, para).

fitted ['fɪtɪd] *adj (cupboard)* empotrado,-a; *(room)* amueblado,-a. COMP fitted carpet moqueta.

fitting ['fɪtɪŋ] *adj (appropriate, proper)* apropiado,-a, adecuado,-a.

► *n* SEW prueba.

► *n pl* **fittings 1** *(accessories)* accesorios *mpl*. **2** *(furnishings)* muebles, cortinas y alfombras.

five [faɪv] *n* cinco.

► *adj* cinco.

✎ Consulta también six.

fix [fɪks] *n* **1** *fam (difficult situation)* apuro, aprieto. **2** *(position of ship, aircraft)* posición *f*. **3** *(dishonest arrangement)* tongo.

► *vt* **1** *(gen)* fijar. **2** *(decide)* decidir; *(date, meeting, etc)* fijar. **3** *(organize)* arreglar, organizar. **4** *(dishonestly)* amañar. **5** *(repair)* arreglar.

◆ **to fix on** *vt insep (decide, select - person)* decidir, optar por, escoger; *(- date)* fijar.

◆ **to fix up** *vt sep* **1** *(accommodate, provide with)* proveer (with, de), conseguir. **2** *(organize)* arreglar, organizar. **3** *(repair, redecorate)* arreglar; *(install)* poner.

fixation [fɪk'seɪʃən] *n* obsesión *f*.

fixture ['fɪkstʃəʳ] *n* SP encuentro.

► *n pl* **fixtures** *(furniture)* muebles *mpl* empotrados.

fizz [fɪz] *n* burbujeo, efervescencia.

► *vi* burbujear.

fizzle ['fɪzəl] *vi* burbujear.

◆ **to fizzle out** *vi* esfumarse, perder fuerza, quedar en nada.

fizzy ['fɪzɪ] *adj (gen)* gaseoso,-a, con gas; *(wine)* espumoso,-a.

ⓘ *comp* fizzier, *superl* fizziest.

fjord [fɪ'ɔːd] *n* fiordo.

flabbergasted ['flæbəgɑːstɪd] *adj* pasmado,-a, atónito,-a.

flabby ['flæbɪ] *adj (part of body)* fofo,-a.

ⓘ *comp* flabbier, *superl* flabbiest.

flaccid ['flæksɪd] *adj* fláccido,-a.

flag¹ [flæg] *n (paving slab)* → flagstone.

flag² [flæg] *n* **1** *(gen)* bandera. **2** MAR pabellón *m*. **3** *(for charity)* banderita.

◆ **to flag down** *vt sep* hacer señales para que un coche se detenga.

flagellum [flə'dʒələm] *n* flagelo.

ⓘ *pl* flagellums o flagella [flə'dʒələ].

flagpole ['flæɡpəʊl] *n* asta de bandera.

flagship ['flæɡʃɪp] *n* buque *m* insignia.

flagstone ['flæɡstəʊn] *n (large)* losa; *(small)* loseta.

flair [fleəʳ] *n* talento, don *m*, facilidad *f*.

flake [fleɪk] *n* **1** *(of snow, oats)* copo. **2** *(of skin, soap)* escama. **3** *(of paint)* desconchón *m*, trozo desprendido.

► *vi* **to flake away/off** *(gen)* descamarse; *(paint)* desconcharse.

flamboyant [flæm'bɔɪənt] *adj* llamativo,-a, extravagante.

flame [fleɪm] *n* llama.

► *vi* **1** *(burn)* arder. **2** *(glow, shine)* brillar. **3** *(become angry)* montar en cólera.

flame-thrower ['fleɪmθrəʊəʳ] *n* lanzallamas *m*.

flamingo [flə'mɪŋɡəʊ] *n* flamenco.

ⓘ *pl* flamingos o flamingoes.

flammable ['flæməbəl] *adj* inflamable.

flan [flæn] *n* CULIN tarta rellena.

⊠ Flan no significa 'flan', que se traduce por crème caramel.

flange [flændʒ] *n (on wheel)* pestaña; *(on pipe)* reborde *m*.

flank [flæŋk] *n* **1** *(of animal)* ijada, ijar *m*. **2** MIL flanco. **3** *(of building, mountain, etc)* lado, falda.

flannel ['flænəl] *n (material)* franela.

flap [flæp] *n* **1** *(of envelope, pocket)* solapa. **2** *(of tent)* faldón *m*. **3** *(of plane)* alerón *m*.

► *vt (wings)* batir; *(arms)* agitar.

► *vi* **1** *(wings)* aletear. **2** *(flag, sails)* ondear. **3** *fam* inquietarse.

ⓘ *pt & pp* flapped, *ger* flapping.

flare [fleəʳ] *n* **1** *(flame)* llamarada. **2** *(signal)* bengala.

► *vi* **1** llamear. **2** *fig* estallar, encenderse.

◆ **to flare up** *vi (blow up, erupt)* estallar, encenderse; *(get angry)* enfadarse, montar en cólera.

flared ['fleəd] *adj* acampanado,-a.

flash [flæʃ] *n* **1** *(of light)* destello, centelleo; *(of lightning)* relámpago. **2** *(from firearm)* fogonazo. **3** *fig* destello, rayo. **4** *(photography)* flash *m*.
► *vi* brillar, destellar.
► *vt (shine light)* dirigir, lanzar; *(- torch)* encender, dirigir.

flashback ['flæʃbæk] *n* flashback *m*.

flashlight ['flæʃlaɪt] *n* **1** *(torch)* linterna. **2** *(photo)* flash *m*.

flashy ['flæʃɪ] *adj* llamativo,-a.
① *comp* flashier, *superl* flashiest.

flask [flæsk] *n* **1** frasco. **2** CHEM matraz *m*.

flat¹ [flæt] *n (apartment)* piso.

flat² [flæt] *adj* **1** *(level, even)* llano,-a, plano,-a; *(smooth)* liso,-a. **2** *(shoes)* sin tacón. **3** *(tyre, ball, etc)* desinflado,-a. **4** *(battery)* descargado,-a. **5** *(drink)* sin gas. **6** MUS *(key)* bemol; *(voice, instrument)* desafinado,-a.
① *comp* flatter, *superl* flattest.
► *n* **1** *(plain)* llano, llanura. **2** *(of hand)* palma. **3** MUS bemol *m*. **4** US *(tyre)* pinchazo.

flatly ['flætlɪ] *adv* **1** *(categorically)* categóricamente, rotundamente. **2** *(voice)* con voz monótona.

flatten ['flætən] *vt* **1** *(make flat)* allanar, aplanar *(out, -)*; *(smooth)* alisar. **2** *(crush)* aplastar; *(knock down)* derribar, tumbar; *(knock over)* atropellar.

flatter ['flætəʳ] *vt* **1** *(praise)* halagar, adular. **2** *(suit)* favorecer.

flattering ['flætərɪŋ] *adj* **1** *(words)* lisonjero,-a, halagüeño,-a. **2** *(clothes, etc)* favorecedor,-ra.

flattery ['flætərɪ] *n* adulación *f*, halagos *mpl*.

flaunt [flɔːnt] *vt* hacer alarde de, hacer ostentación de.

flautist ['flɔːtɪst] *n* flautista *mf*.

flavor ['fleɪvəʳ] *n* US → flavour.

flavour ['fleɪvəʳ] *n* sabor *m*, gusto.
► *vt* sazonar, condimentar (with, con).

flavouring ['fleɪvərɪŋ] *n* condimento.

flaw [flɔː] *n* **1** *(fault - in material, product, etc)* defecto, tara. **2** *(failing - in character)* defecto; *(- in argument)* error *m*.

flawless ['flɔːləs] *adj* sin defecto, impecable, perfecto,-a.

flax [flæks] *n* lino.

fleck [flek] *n* mota, punto.

fled [fled] *pt* → flee.

flee [fliː] *vt (run away)* huir de.
► *vi* **1** *(run away, escape)* huir. **2** *(vanish)* desaparecer.
① *pt & pp* fled [fled].

fleece [fliːs] *n* **1** *(sheep's coat, fabric)* lana. **2** *(sheared)* vellón *m*.

fleet [fliːt] *n* **1** *(of ships)* flota. **2** *(of vehicles)* flota, parque *m* móvil.

fleeting ['fliːtɪŋ] *adj* fugaz, efímero,-a.

flesh [fleʃ] *n* **1** *(of animals, humans)* carne *f*. **2** *(of fruit)* carne *f*, pulpa.

flew [fluː] *pt* → fly¹.

flex [fleks] *n* GB cable *m*.
► *vt (body, joints)* doblar; *(muscles)* flexionar.

flexibility [fleksɪˈbɪlɪtɪ] *n* flexibilidad *f*.

flexible ['fleksəbəl] *adj* flexible.

flexor ['fleksəʳ] *n* flexor.

flexitime ['fleksɪtaɪm] *n* horario flexible.

flick [flɪk] *n* **1** *(jerk)* movimiento rápido, movimiento brusco. **2** *(of fingers)* capirotazo; *(of whip)* latigazo, chasquido; *(of tail)* coletazo. **3** *(of pages)* hojeada.
◆ **to flick away** *vt sep* quitar, sacudirse.
◆ **to flick through** *vt insep* hojear.

flicker ['flɪkəʳ] *n* **1** *(of flame, eyelids)* parpadeo; *(of light)* titileo, parpadeo. **2** *fig (slight sign)* señal *f*, muestra; *(faint emotion)* chispa, pizca.
► *vi* **1** *(gen)* parpadear; *(shadow)* bailar. **2** *(eyelids)* parpadear. **3** *(smile)* esbozarse.

flies [flaɪs] *pt* → fly³.

flight [flaɪt] *n* **1** *(journey by air)* vuelo: *our flight has been delayed* nuestro vuelo se ha retrasado. **2** *(path)* trayectoria. **3** *(flock of birds)* bandada. **4** *(of stairs)* tramo. **5** *(escape)* huida, fuga. [COMP] **flight attendant** auxiliar *mf* de vuelo.

flimsy ['flɪmzɪ] *adj* **1** *(thin)* fino,-a, ligero,-a. **2** *(structure)* poco sólido,-a. **3** *fig (unconvincing)* flojo,-a, pobre, poco convincente.
① *comp* flimsier, *superl* flimsiest.

flinch [flɪntʃ] *vi* **1** *(wince)* estremecerse. **2** *(shun)* retroceder (from, ante).

F

fling [flɪŋ] n **1** *(throw)* lanzamiento. **2** *(wild time)* juerga. **3** *(affair)* aventura (amorosa), romance m.
▸ vt **1** *(throw)* arrojar, tirar, lanzar. **2** *(move)* echar, lanzar. **3** *(say)* lanzar.
ⓘ *pt & pp* flung [flʌŋ].

flint [flɪnt] n **1** *(stone)* sílex m; *(piece)* pedernal m. **2** *(of lighter)* piedra.

flip [flɪp] n **1** *(light blow)* golpecito. **2** *(somersault)* voltereta (en el aire).
▸ interj fam ¡ostras!
▸ vt **1** *(toss - gen)* echar, tirar al aire; *(-coin)* echar a cara o cruz. **2** *(turn over)* dar la vuelta a.
▸ vi fam *(get angry)* perder los estribos; *(go mad)* volverse loco,-a.
ⓘ *pt & pp* flipped, ger flipping.

flip-flop ['flɪpflɒp] n chancla.

flipper ['flɪpəʳ] n aleta.

flirt [flɜːt] n coqueto,-a, ligón,-ona.
▸ vi *(coquette)* flirtear (with, con), coquetear (with, con).

float [fləʊt] n **1** *(for fishing)* boya, flotador m. **2** *(for swimming)* flotador m. **3** *(vehicle - in procession)* carroza; *(- for delivery)* furgoneta.
▸ vi *(gen)* flotar.

flock [flɒk] n **1** *(of sheep, goats)* rebaño; *(of birds)* bandada. **2** fam *(crowd)* multitud f, tropel m.

flood [flʌd] n **1** *(overflow of water)* inundación f. **2** *(of river)* riada.
▸ vt **1** *(gen)* inundar, anegar; *(engine)* ahogar. **2** fig *(with calls, applications, etc)* llover, inundar (with, de).
▸ vi **1** *(river)* desbordarse. **2** fig *(cover, fill)* invadir, inundar.

floodgate ['flʌdgeɪt] n compuerta.

flooding ['flʌdɪŋ] n inundación f.

floodlight ['flʌdlaɪt] n foco.

floor [flɔːʳ] n **1** *(surface)* suelo. **2** GEOG fondo. **3** *(storey)* piso, planta. **4** *(dance)* pista.

✖ Floor no significa 'flor', que se traduce por flower.

flop [flɒp] n fam fracaso.
▸ vi **1** *(fall clumsily)* abalanzarse, arrojarse (into, en); *(sit or lie clumsily)* tumbarse, dejarse caer. **2** fam *(fail)* fracasar.
ⓘ *pt & pp* flopped, ger flopping.

floppy ['flɒpɪ] adj blando,-a, flexible.
COMP **floppy disk** COMPUT disco flexible, disquete m.
ⓘ comp floppier, superl floppiest.

flora ['flɔːrə] n flora.

florist ['flɒrɪst] n florista mf. COMP **florist's (shop)** floristería.

flounce [flaʊns] n SEW volante m.

flounder ['flaʊndəʳ] n *(fish)* platija.
▸ vi **1** *(struggle, move with difficulty)* forcejear. **2** fig *(hesitate, dither)* vacilar.

flour [flaʊəʳ] n harina.
▸ vt enharinar.

flourish ['flʌrɪʃ] n **1** *(gesture)* ademán m, gesto exagerado. **2** *(signature)* rúbrica.
▸ vt *(wave about)* agitar, blandir.
▸ vi **1** *(be successful)* florecer, prosperar. **2** *(plant)* crecer bien.

flow [fləʊ] n **1** *(gen)* flujo. **2** *(of river)* corriente f. **3** *(of traffic)* circulación f.
▸ vi **1** *(gen)* fluir. **2** *(pour out - blood)* manar; *(- tears)* correr. **3** *(tide)* subir. **4** *(traffic)* circular.
◆ **to flow into** vi *(river)* desembocar en: *the Ebro flows into the sea at Amposta* el Ebro desemboca en el mar en Amposta.

flower [flaʊəʳ] n flor f.
▸ vi florecer.

flowerbed ['flaʊəbed] n parterre m, macizo.

flowerpot ['flaʊəpɒt] n maceta, tiesto.

flown [fləʊn] pp → fly.

flu [fluː] n gripe f: *he's got (the) flu* tiene la gripe.

fluctuate ['flʌktjʊeɪt] vi fluctuar.

fluency ['fluːənsɪ] n **1** fluidez f. **2** *(of language)* dominio (in, de).

fluent ['fluːənt] adj **1** *(gen)* fluido,-a. **2** *(language)* fluido,-a: *he speaks fluent English* habla inglés con soltura.

fluff [flʌf] n **1** *(down, material)* pelusa, lanilla. **2** fam *(mistake, blunder)* pifia, fallo.
▸ vt fam *(do badly, fail)* hacer mal.

fluffy ['flʌfɪ] adj **1** *(feathery)* mullido,-a. **2** *(toys)* de peluche.
ⓘ comp fluffier, superl fluffiest.

fluid ['fluːɪd] adj **1** *(not solid)* fluido,-a, líquido,-a. **2** *(smooth, graceful)* natural, con soltura. **3** *(not fixed)* flexible.
▸ n fluido, líquido.

fluke [fluːk] *n fam* chiripa.

flung [flʌŋ] *pt & pp* → fling.

fluorescent [fluəˈresənt] *adj* fluorescente. COMP **fluorescent light/lamp** fluorescente *m*.

flurry [ˈflʌrɪ] *n* **1** *(of wind)* ráfaga; *(of snow)* nevisca. **2** *fig (burst)* nerviosismo.
ⓘ *pl* flurries.

flush¹ [flʌʃ] *n (in cards)* color *m*.

flush² [flʌʃ] *n* **1** *(blush)* rubor *m*. **2** *(of emotion)* acceso, arrebato. **3** *(of toilet)* cisterna.
▸ *vt* **1** *(cause to blush)* ruborizar, sonrojar. **2** *(clean)* limpiar con agua. **3** *(toilet)* tirar (de) la cadena.
▸ *vi* **1** *(blush)* ruborizarse. **2** *(toilet)* funcionar.

fluster [ˈflʌstər] *vt* poner nervioso, a.
▸ *n* confusión *f*, agitación *f*.

flute [fluːt] *n* flauta.

flutter [ˈflʌtər] *n* **1** *(excitement)* agitación *f*, emoción *f*. **2** *(of wings)* aleteo. **3** *(of eyelashes)* pestañeo. **4** *fam (bet)* apuesta.
▸ *vt* **1** *(eyelashes)* parpadear. **2** *(wings)* aletear.
▸ *vi* **1** *(flag)* ondear. **2** *(wings)* aletear. **3** *(flit)* revolotear. **4** *(heart)* palpitar.

fluvial [ˈfluːvɪəl] *adj* fluvial.

fly¹ [flaɪ] *vi* **1** volar. **2** *(go by plane)* ir en avión. **3** *(flag, hair)* ondear. **4** *fam (flee)* largarse.
▸ *vt* **1** *(plane)* pilotar. **2** *(send by plane)* transportar. **3** *(kite)* hacer volar. **4** *(flag)* enarbolar.
ⓘ *pt* flew [fluː], *pp* flown [fləʊn], *ger* flying.
▸ *n pl* flies *(on trousers)* bragueta *f sing.*
◆ **to fly away / off** *vi* irse volando.

fly² [flaɪ] *adj* GB *fam (smart)* astuto,-a.
ⓘ *comp* flier, *superl* fliest.

fly³ [flaɪ] *n* mosca.
ⓘ *pl* flies.

flying [ˈflaɪɪŋ] *n* **1** AV aviación *f*. **2** *(action)* vuelo.
▸ *adj* **1** *(soaring)* volante; *(animal, machine)* volador,-ra, que vuela. **2** *(quick)* rápido,-a.

flyover [ˈflaɪəʊvər] *n* GB paso elevado.

foal [fəʊl] *n* potro,-a.
▸ *vi* parir.

foam [fəʊm] *n* espuma.

foamy [ˈfəʊmɪ] *adj* espumoso,-a.
ⓘ *comp* foamier, *superl* foamiest.

fob [fɒb] *vt* engañar, engatusar.
ⓘ *pt & pp* fobbed, *ger* fobbing.

focal [ˈfəʊkəl] *adj* focal.

focus [ˈfəʊkəs] *n* **1** foco. **2** *(centre)* centro.
ⓘ *pl* focuses o foci [ˈfəʊsaɪ].
▸ *vt* **1** *(camera, etc)* enfocar (on, -). **2** *fig (concentrate)* fijar (on, en), centrar (on, en).
ⓘ *pt & pp* focused o focussed, *ger* focusing o focussing.

fodder [ˈfɒdər] *n* pienso, forraje *m*.

foetal [ˈfiːtəl] *adj* fetal.

foetus [ˈfiːtəs] *n* feto.

fog [fɒg] *n* niebla.
▸ *vt* **1** *(mirror, etc)* empañar. **2** *(photo)* velar. **3** *fig* complicar.
▸ *vi* empañarse (up/over, -).
ⓘ *pt & pp* fogged, *ger* fogging.

foggy [ˈfɒgɪ] *adj* **1** de niebla: *it's foggy* hay niebla. **2** *(confused)* confuso,-a.
ⓘ *comp* foggier, *superl* foggiest.

foglamp [ˈfɒglæmp] *n* faro antiniebla.

foil¹ [fɔɪl] *vt (prevent, frustrate)* frustrar.

foil² [fɔɪl] *n* **1** *(metal paper)* papel *m* de plata. **2** *(contrast)* contraste *m*.

fold¹ [fəʊld] *n (for sheep)* redil *m*, aprisco.

fold² [fəʊld] *n* **1** *(crease)* pliegue *m*, doblez *m*. **2** GEOG pliegue *m*.
▸ *vt* **1** doblar, plegar (up, -). **2** *(wrap)* envolver.
▸ *vi* **1** doblarse, plegarse. **2** *(go bankrupt)* quebrar.

folder [ˈfəʊldər] *n* carpeta.

folding [ˈfəʊldɪŋ] *adj* plegable.

folk [fəʊk] *n pl* gente *f sing.*
▸ *adj* popular.
▸ *n pl* folks *fam (family)* familia *f sing*; *(friends)* amigos *mpl*.

folklore [ˈfəʊklɔːr] *n* folklor(e) *m*.

follicle [ˈfɒlɪkəl] *n* folículo.

follow [ˈfɒləʊ] *vt* **1** *(gen)* seguir. **2** *(pursue)* perseguir. **3** *(take interest in)* seguir, estar al corriente de.
▸ *vi* **1** *(gen)* seguir. **2** *(understand)* entender. **3** *(be logical)* resultar, derivarse.
◆ **to follow up** *vt sep* **1** *(develop)* profundizar en. **2** *(investigate)* investigar.

following ['fɒləʊɪŋ] *adj* siguiente
▸ *prep* después de.
▸ *n (supporters)* seguidores *mpl*.
folly ['fɒlɪ] *n fml* locura, desatino.
① *pl* follies.
fond [fɒnd] *adj* **1** *(loving)* cariñoso,-a. **2** *(indulgent)* indulgente. **3** *(hope, belief)* vano,-a.
fondle ['fɒndəl] *vt* acariciar.
fondness ['fɒndnəs] *n* **1** cariño (for, a). **2** *(liking)* afición *f* (for, a/por).
font [fɒnt] *n* pila (bautismal).
food [fuːd] *n* comida, alimento.
foodstuffs ['fuːdstʌfs] *n pl* alimentos *mpl*, productos *mpl* alimenticios.
fool [fuːl] *n* **1** tonto,-a, loco,-a. **2** *(jester)* bufón,-ona. LOC to make a fool of poner en ridículo a. ∥ to play the fool hacer el tonto.
▸ *vt* engañar.
▸ *vi* bromear.
◆ to fool about / fool around *vi* **1** *(be stupid)* hacer el tonto, hacer el payaso. **2** *(waste time)* perder el tiempo neciamente.
foolish ['fuːlɪʃ] *adj* **1** *(silly)* tonto,-a. **2** *(stupid)* estúpido,-a; *(unwise)* imprudente. **3** *(ridiculous)* ridículo,-a.
foolproof ['fuːlpruːf] *adj* **1** *(plan, method, idea)* infalible. **2** *(machine)* seguro,-a.
foot [fʊt] *n* **1** ANAT pie *m*. **2** *(measurement)* pie *m*. **3** *(bottom)* pie *m*. **4** *(of animal)* pata. LOC on foot a pie.
① *pl* feet.
football ['fʊtbɔːl] *n* **1** *(game)* fútbol *m*. **2** *(ball)* balón *m*. COMP football player futbolista *mf*. ∥ football pools quinielas.

⊕ En inglés americano football a secas se refiere al 'fútbol americano'; el 'fútbol' tal como se conoce en Europa se suele llamar soccer.

football ['fʊtbɔːlər] *n* futbolista *mf*.
footlights ['fʊtlaɪts] *n pl* candilejas *fpl*.
footloose ['fʊtluːs] *adj* libre.
footnote ['fʊtnəʊt] *n* nota a pie de página.
footpath ['fʊtpɑːθ] *n* sendero, camino.
footprint ['fʊtprɪnt] *n* huella, pisada.
footstep ['fʊtstep] *n* paso, pisada.

footwear ['fʊtweər] *n* calzado.
for [fɔːr] *prep* **1** *(intended)* para. **2** *(purpose)* para: what's this for? ¿para qué sirve esto? **3** *(destination)* para. **4** *(in order to help, on behalf of)* por: do it for me hazlo por mí. **5** *(because of, on account of)* por, a causa de. **6** *(past time)* durante; *(future time)* por; *(specific point in time)* para. **7** *(distance)*: I walked for five miles caminé cinco millas. **8** *(in exchange, as replacement of)* por. **9** *(in favour of, in support of)* por, a favor de. **10** *(despite)* a pesar de, para; *(considering, contrast)* para: she's very tall for her age es muy alta para su edad. **11** *(as)* de, como, por. **12** *(in order to obtain)* para: for further details ... para más información…
▸ *conj* **6** *fml lit* ya que, puesto que.
forage ['fɒrɪdʒ] *n (food)* forraje *m*.
forbade [fɔː'beɪd] *pt* → forbid.
forbid [fə'bɪd] *vt* **1** *(prohibit)* prohibir. **2** *(make impossible)* impedir.
① *pt* forbade [fɔː'beɪd], *pp* forbidden [fɔː'bɪdən], *ger* forbidding.
forbidden [fə'bɪdən] *pp* → forbid.
forbidding [fə'bɪdɪŋ] *adj (stern)* severo,-a; *(unfriendly)* formidable.
force [fɔːs] *n* **1** *(strength, power, violence)* fuerza. **2** PHYS fuerza. **3** MIL cuerpo.
▸ *vt (oblige)* forzar, obligar.
forceful ['fɔːsfʊl] *adj (person, manner)* enérgico,-a; *(speech)* contundente; *(argument)* convincente.
forceps ['fɔːseps] *n pl* fórceps *m inv*.
ford [fɔːd] *n* vado.
▸ *vt* vadear.
forearm ['fɔːrɑːm] *n* antebrazo.
foreboding [fɔː'bəʊdɪŋ] *n* presentimiento.
forecast ['fɔːkɑːst] *n* pronóstico, previsión *f*.
▸ *vt* pronosticar.
① *pt & pp* forecast o forecasted.
forefinger ['fɔːfɪŋgər] *n (dedo)* índice *m*.
forefront ['fɔːfrʌnt] *n* vanguardia.
forego[1] [fɔː'gəʊ] *vt (precede)* preceder.
① *pt* forewent [fɔː'went], *pp* foregone ['fɔːgɒn], *ger* foregoing.
forego[2] [fɔː'gəʊ] *vt* → forgo.
① *pt* forewent [fɔː'went], *pp* foregone ['fɔːgɒn], *ger* foregoing.

foregoing [fɔːˈɡəʊɪŋ] *adj* precedente.
foregone [ˈfɔːɡɒn] *pp* → **forego**.
▸ *adj* inevitable.
foreground [ˈfɔːɡraʊnd] *n* primer plano, primer término.
forehead [ˈfɒrɪd, ˈfɔːhed] *n* frente *f*.
foreign [ˈfɒrɪn] *adj* **1** *(from abroad)* extranjero,-a. **2** *(dealing with other countries)* exterior. **3** *(strange)* ajeno,-a, extraño,-a.
foreigner [ˈfɒrɪnəʳ] *n* extranjero,-a.
foreman [ˈfɔːmən] *n* **1** *(of workers)* capataz *m*. **2** *(of jury)* presidente *m* del jurado.
ⓘ *pl* **foremen** [ˈfɔːmən].
foremost [ˈfɔːməʊst] *adj* principal.
forename [ˈfɔːneɪm] *n* nombre *m* (de pila).
forensic [fəˈrensɪk] *adj* forense.
forerunner [ˈfɔːrʌnəʳ] *n* precursor,-ra.
foresaw [fɔːˈsɔː] *pt* → **foresee**.
foresee [fɔːˈsiː] *vt* prever.
ⓘ *pt* **foresaw** [fɔːˈsɔː], *pp* **foreseen** [fɔːˈsiːn], *ger* **foreseeing**.
foreseen [fɔːˈsiːn] *pp* → **foresee**.
foresight [ˈfɔːsaɪt] *n* previsión *f*.
foreskin [ˈfɔːskɪn] *n* prepucio.
forest [ˈfɒrɪst] *n* **1** *(gen)* bosque *m*. **2** *(jungle)* selva.
▸ *adj* forestal.
forestall [fɔːˈstɔːl] *vt* **1** *(preempt)* anticiparse a. **2** *(prevent)* prevenir.
forestry [ˈfɒrɪstrɪ] *n* silvicultura.
foretell [fɔːˈtel] *vt* predecir, pronosticar.
ⓘ *pt & pp* **foretold** [fɔːˈtəʊld].
forethought [ˈfɔːθɔːt] *n* **1** previsión *f*. **2** JUR premeditación *f*.
foretold [fɔːˈtəʊld] *pt & pp* → **foretell**.
forever [fəˈrevəʳ] *adv* **1** *(all the time)* siempre. **2** *(for good)* para siempre.
forewarn [fɔːˈwɔːn] *vt* prevenir.
forewent [fɔːˈwent] *pp* → **forego**.
foreword [ˈfɔːwɜːd] *n* prólogo.
forfeit [ˈfɔːfɪt] *n* **1** *(penalty)* pena, multa. **2** *(in games)* prenda.
▸ *vt* perder, perder (el derecho de).
forgave [fəˈɡeɪv] *pt* → **forgive**.
forge [fɔːdʒ] *n* **1** *(apparatus)* fragua. **2** *(smithy)* forja.

▸ *vt* **1** *(counterfeit)* falsificar. **2** *(metal)* forjar, fraguar.
forgery [ˈfɔːdʒərɪ] *n* falsificación *f*.
ⓘ *pl* **forgeries**.
forget [fəˈɡet] *vt* **1** *(gen)* olvidar, olvidarse de. **2** *(leave behind)* dejar.
ⓘ *pt* **forgot** [fəˈɡɒt], *pp* **forgotten** [fəˈɡɒtən], *ger* **forgetting**.
▸ *vi* olvidarse de, no recordar.
forgive [fəˈɡɪv] *vt* **1** *(pardon)* perdonar. **2** *(let off debt)* perdonar.
ⓘ *pt* **forgave** [fəˈɡeɪv], *pp* **forgiven** [fəˈɡɪvən].
forgiven [fəˈɡɪvən] *pp* → **forgive**.
forgiveness [fəˈɡɪvnəs] *n* perdón *m*.
forgo [fɔːˈɡəʊ] *vt* renunciar a, sacrificar.
ⓘ *pt* **forwent** [fɔːˈwent], *pp* **forgone** [ˈfɔːɡɒn], *ger* **forgoing**.
forgone [fɔːˈɡɒn] *pp* → **forgo**.
forgot [fəˈɡɒt] *pt* → **forget**.
forgotten [fəˈɡɒtən] *pp* → **forget**.
fork [fɔːk] *n* **1** *(for eating)* tenedor *m*. **2** AGR horca, horquilla. **3** *(in road, river, etc)* bifurcación *f*.
▸ *vi* **1** *(road, river, etc)* bifurcarse. **2** *(person, car)* torcer, girar.
▸ *n pl* **forks** *(on bike)* horquilla.
forlorn [fəˈlɔːn] *adj* **1** *(forsaken)* abandonado,-a. **2** *(desolate)* triste. **3** *(hopeless)* desesperado,-a.
form [fɔːm] *n* **1** *(shape, mode, etc)* forma. **2** *(kind)* clase *f*, tipo. **3** *(formality)* formas *fpl*; *(behaviour)* educación *f*. **4** *(physical condition)* forma. **5** *(mood, spirit)* humor *m*. **6** *(document)* formulario, impreso, hoja. **7** EDUC *(age group)* curso; *(class)* clase *f*.
▸ *vt* **1** *(mould)* moldear; *(make)* hacer, formar. **2** *(be, constitute)* formar, constituir. **3** *fig (idea)* hacerse, formarse.
formal [ˈfɔːməl] *adj* **1** *(gen)* formal. **2** *(dress, dinner)* de etiqueta.

❌ **Formal** no significa 'formal (serio)', que se traduce por **serious**.

formality [fɔːˈmælɪtɪ] *n* *(correctness)* formalidad *f*; *(convention)* ceremonia.
ⓘ *pl* **formalities**.
format [ˈfɔːmæt] *n* formato.
▸ *vt* COMPUT formatear.
ⓘ *pt & pp* **formatted**, *ger* **formatting**.

formation [fɔːˈmeɪʃən] *n* **1** *(gen)* formación *f*. **2** *(establishment)* creación *f*.

former [ˈfɔːməʳ] *adj* **1** *(earlier)* antiguo,-a; *(person)* ex. **2** *(of two)* primero,-a.
▸ *pron* **the former** aquél, aquélla.

formerly [ˈfɔːməlɪ] *adv* *(previously)* antiguamente, antes.

formidable [ˈfɔːmɪdəbəl] *adj* **1** *(impressive)* formidable. **2** *(daunting)* temible, imponente.

> ☒ Formidable no significa 'formidable (magnífico)', que se traduce por **wonderful**.

formula [ˈfɔːmjələ] *n* fórmula.
ⓘ *pl* **formulas** o **formulae** [ˈfɔːmjuliː].

formulate [ˈfɔːmjəleɪt] *vt* formular.

formulation [fɔːmjəˈleɪʃən] *n* formulación *f*.

fort [fɔːt] *n* fuerte *m*.

forth [fɔːθ] *adv* *(onwards)* en adelante.

forthcoming [fɔːθˈkʌmɪŋ] *adj* **1** *fml (happening in near future)* próximo,-a. **2** *(available)* disponible. **3** *(communicative)* comunicativo,-a, dispuesto,-a a hablar.

fortieth [ˈfɔːtɪəθ] *adj* cuadragésimo,-a.
▸ *adv* en cuadragésimo lugar.
▸ *n* *(fraction)* cuadragésimo; *(one part)* cuadragésima parte *f*.

✎ Consulta también **sixtieth**.

fortification [fɔːtɪfɪˈkeɪʃən] *n* fortificación *f*.

fortify [ˈfɔːtɪfaɪ] *vt* **1** MIL fortificar. **2** *(strengthen)* fortalecer.
ⓘ *pt & pp* **fortified**, *ger* **fortifying**.

fortnight [ˈfɔːtnaɪt] *n* GB quincena, quince días *mpl*.

fortress [ˈfɔːtrəs] *n* fortaleza.

fortunate [ˈfɔːtʃənət] *adj* afortunado,-a.

fortunately [ˈfɔːtʃənətlɪ] *adv* afortunadamente, por suerte.

fortune [ˈfɔːtʃən] *n* **1** *(fate)* fortuna; *(luck)* suerte *f*. **2** *(money)* fortuna.

fortune-teller [ˈfɔːtʃənteləʳ] *n* adivino,-a.

forty [ˈfɔːtɪ] *adj* cuarenta.
▸ *n* cuarenta *m*.

✎ Consulta también **sixty**.

forum [ˈfɔːrəm] *n* foro.

forward [ˈfɔːwəd] *adv* [como adverbio, también **forwards**] **1** *(gen)* hacia adelante. **2** *(time)* en adelante.
▸ *adj* **1** *(position)* delantero,-a, frontal; *(movement)* hacia delante. **2** *(future)* a largo plazo. **3** *(advanced)* adelantado,-a, precoz. **4** *(too bold, too eager)* atrevido,-a, descarado,-a, fresco,-a.
▸ *vt* **1** *(send on to new address)* remitir; *(send goods)* enviar, expedir. **2** *fml (further, advance)* adelantar, fomentar.

forwent [fɔːˈwent] *pt* → **forgo**.

fossil [ˈfɒsəl] *n* fósil *m*.
▸ *adj* fósil.

foster [ˈfɒstəʳ] *vt* **1** *(child)* acoger temporalmente. **2** *(encourage)* fomentar, promover.
▸ *adj* adoptivo,-a.

fought [fɔːt] *pt & pp* → **fight**.

foul [faul] *adj* **1** *(dirty, disgusting)* asqueroso,-a; *(smell)* fétido,-a. **2** *(language)* grosero,-a, obsceno,-a.
▸ *n* SP falta (on, contra).
▸ *vt* **1** *(dirty)* ensuciar; *(pollute)* contaminar. **2** *(snag)* enredar. **3** SP cometer una falta contra.

found¹ [faund] *vt* *(metals)* fundir.

found² [faund] *vt* **1** *(establish)* fundar. **2** *(base)* basar (on, en).

found³ [faund] *pt & pp* → **find**.

foundation [faunˈdeɪʃən] *n* **1** *(act, organization)* fundación *f*. **2** *(basis)* fundamento, base *f*. **3** *(make-up)* base *f*.
▸ *n pl* **foundations** cimientos *mpl*.

founder¹ [ˈfaundəʳ] *vi* **1** *(plan, etc)* fracasar, malograrse. **2** *(ship)* hundirse. **3** *(horse)* dar un traspié.

founder² [ˈfaundəʳ] *n* fundador,-ra.

foundry [ˈfaundrɪ] *n* fundición *f*.
ⓘ *pl* **foundries**.

fountain [ˈfauntən] *n* **1** fuente *f*. **2** *(jet)* surtidor *m*, chorro.

four [fɔːʳ] *adj* cuatro.
▸ *n* cuatro.

✎ Consulta también **six**.

fourteen [fɔːˈtiːn] *adj* catorce.
▸ *n* catorce *m*.

✎ Consulta también **six**.

fourteenth [fɔːˈtiːnθ] *adj* decimocuarto,-a.

▸ *adv* en decimocuarto lugar.

▸ *n* **1** *(in series)* decimocuarto,-a. **2** *(fraction)* decimocuarto; *(one part)* decimocuarta parte *f*.

✎ Consulta también sixth.

fourth [fɔːθ] *adj* cuarto,-a.

▸ *adv* cuarto, en cuarto lugar.

▸ *n* **1** *(in series)* cuarto,-a. **2** *(fraction)* cuarto; *(one part)* cuarta parte *f*.

✎ Consulta también sixth.

fowl [faʊl] *n* ave *f* de corral.

ⓘ *pl* fowl.

fox [fɒks] *n* zorro,-a.

▸ *vt* **1** *fam (trick)* engañar. **2** *(confuse)* dejar perplejo,-a, confundir, despistar.

foxy [ˈfɒksɪ] *adj fam* astuto,-a.

ⓘ *comp* foxier, *superl* foxiest

foyer [ˈfɔɪeɪ, ˈfɔɪəʳ] *n* vestíbulo.

fraction [ˈfrækʃən] *n* **1** *(division)* fracción *f*. **2** *(small part, bit)* poquito.

fractional [ˈfrækʃənəl] *adj* **1** *(in fractions)* fraccionario,-a. **2** *(very small)* muy pequeño,-a, ínfimo,-a.

fracture [ˈfræktʃəʳ] *n* fractura.

▸ *vt* fracturar.

▸ *vi* fracturarse.

fragile [ˈfrædʒaɪl] *adj* **1** frágil. **2** *fig (health)* delicado,-a.

fragility [frəˈdʒɪlɪtɪ] *n* fragilidad *f*.

fragment [*(n)* ˈfrægmənt; *(vb)* frægˈment] *n* fragmento.

▸ *vi* fragmentarse.

fragmentation [frægmənˈteɪʃən] *n* fragmentación *f*.

fragrance [ˈfreɪgrəns] *n* fragancia.

fragrant [ˈfreɪgrənt] *adj* fragante.

frail [freɪl] *adj* **1** frágil, delicado,-a. **2** *(morally weak)* débil.

frame [freɪm] *n* **1** *(of building, machine, tent)* armazón *f*. **2** *(of bed)* armadura. **3** *(of bicycle)* cuadro. **4** *(of spectacles)* montura. **5** *(of window, door, picture, etc)* marco. **6** CINEM fotograma *m*. **7** *(of comic)* viñeta.

▸ *vt* **1** *(picture)* enmarcar. **2** *(door)* encuadrar.

framework [ˈfreɪmwɜːk] *n* **1** armazón *f*. **2** *fig* estructura, sistema *m*, marco.

franc [fræŋk] *n* franco.

France [frɑːns] *n* Francia.

franchise [ˈfræntʃaɪz] *n* **1** COMM concesión *f*, franquicia. **2** *(vote)* derecho de voto.

frank [fræŋk] *adj* franco,-a.

▸ *vt* franquear.

frantic [ˈfræntɪk] *adj* **1** *(hectic)* frenético,-a. **2** *(anxious)* desesperado,-a.

fraternal [frəˈtɜːnəl] *adj* fraternal.

fraternity [frəˈtɜːnɪtɪ] *n* **1** *(brotherhood)* fraternidad *f*. **2** *(society)* asociación *f*. **3** REL hermandad *f*, cofradía. **4** US *(university)* club *m* de estudiantes.

ⓘ *pl* fraternities.

fraud [frɔːd] *n* **1** *(act)* fraude *m*. **2** *(person)* impostor,-ra, farsante *mf*.

fraught [frɔːt] *adj* **1** *(filled, charged)* lleno,-a (with, de), cargado,-a (with, de). **2** *fam (worried)* nervioso,-a, alterado,-a, tenso,-a.

fray¹ [freɪ] *vi* **1** *(cloth)* deshilacharse, raerse. **2** *(tempers, nerves, etc)* crisparse.

fray² [freɪ] *n* contienda, lucha.

freak [friːk] *n* **1** *(monster)* monstruo; *(strange person)* bicho raro. **2** *fam (fan)* fanático,-a. **3** *(eccentric)* estrafalario,-a.

▸ *adj (unusual)* insólito,-a; *(unexpected)* inesperado,-a.

◆ to freak out *vt sep* flipar, alucinar.

freckle [ˈfrekəl] *n* peca.

free [friː] *adj* **1** *(gen)* libre. **2** *(without cost)* gratuito,-a, gratis; *(exempt)* libre (from, de).

▸ *adv* **1** *(gratis)* gratis. **2** *(loose)* suelto,-a.

▸ *vt* **1** *(liberate, release - person)* poner en libertad, liberar; *(- animal)* soltar. **2** *(rid)* deshacerse (of/from, de), librarse (of/from, de). **3** *(loosen, untie)* soltar, desatar.

freedom [ˈfriːdəm] *n* libertad *f*.

freehand [ˈfriːhænd] *adj* a mano alzada.

freelance [ˈfriːlɑːns] *adj* independiente, autónomo,-a.

▸ *n* persona que trabaja por cuenta propia.

▸ *vi* trabajar por cuenta propia.

freestyle ['fri:staɪl] n (swimming) estilo libre.

freeway ['fri:weɪ] n US autopista.

freewheel [fri:'wi:l] vi (cycle) ir a rueda libre; (car) ir en punto muerto.

freeze [fri:z] n 1 METEOR helada. 2 COMM congelación f.
▶ vt (gen) congelar.
▶ vi 1 (liquid) helarse; (food) congelarse. 2 METEOR helar.
ⓘ pt froze [frəʊz], pp frozen [frəʊzən], ger freezing.

freezer ['fri:zər] n congelador m.

freeze-up ['fri:zʌp] n helada.

freight [freɪt] n 1 (transport) transporte m. 2 (goods) carga, flete m. 3 (price) flete m.
▶ vt transportar.

freighter ['freɪtər] n (ship) buque m de carga; (aircraft) avión m de carga.

French [frentʃ] adj francés,-esa.
▶ n (language) francés m.
▶ n pl the French los franceses mpl.

Frenchman ['frentʃmən] n francés m.
ⓘ pl Frenchmen ['frentʃmən].

Frenchwoman ['frentʃwʊmən] n francesa.
ⓘ pl Frenchwomen ['frentʃwɪmɪn].

frenzy ['frenzɪ] n frenesí m.
ⓘ pl frenzies.

frequency ['fri:kwənsɪ] n frecuencia.
ⓘ pl frequencies.

frequent [(adj) 'fri:kwənt; (vb) frɪ'kwent] adj frecuente.
▶ vt frecuentar.

fresco ['freskəʊ] n fresco.
ⓘ pl frescos o frescoes.

fresh [freʃ] adj 1 (gen) fresco,-a. 2 (water) dulce. 3 (air) puro,-a.

freshen ['freʃən] vt refrescar.
▶ vi refrescarse.

freshly ['freʃlɪ] adv recién: freshly baked bread pan recién hecho.

freshness ['freʃnəs] n 1 (brightness) frescura. 2 (cool) frescor m. 3 (newness) novedad f. 4 fam (cheek) descaro.

freshwater ['freʃwæɔ:tər] adj de agua dulce: freshwater fish pez de agua dulce.

fret¹ [fret] vi preocuparse (about/at/over, por).
▶ vt (wear away) raer, desgastar.
ⓘ pt & pp fretted, ger fretting.
▶ n (worry) preocupación f.

fret² [fret] n (on guitar) traste m.

friar [fraɪər] n fraile m.

fricative ['frɪkətɪv] adj fricativo,-a.
▶ n fricativa.

friction ['frɪkʃən] n 1 (conflict) fricción f, roces mpl. 2 (rubbing) rozamiento, roce m.

Friday ['fraɪdɪ] n viernes m.

📝 Para ejemplos de uso, consulta Saturday.

fridge [frɪdʒ] n nevera, frigorífico.

fried [fraɪd] pt & pp → fry.
▶ adj frito,-a.

friend [frend] n 1 amigo,-a, compañero,-a. 2 (helper, supporter) amigo,-a (of/to, de).

friendly ['frendlɪ] adj 1 (person) simpático,-a, amable. 2 (atmosphere) acogedor,-ra. 3 (smile, manner, etc) amable.
ⓘ comp friendlier, superl friendliest.

friendship ['frendʃɪp] n amistad f.

frieze [fri:z] n 1 (painted) friso. 2 (wallpaper) cenefa.

frigate ['frɪgət] n fragata.

fright [fraɪt] n 1 (shock) susto. 2 (fear) miedo.

frighten ['fraɪtən] vt asustar, espantar.

frightfully ['fraɪtfʊlɪ] adv fam muchísimo.

frigid ['frɪdʒɪd] adj 1 (sexually) frígido,-a. 2 (icy) glacial, muy frío,-a.

frill [frɪl] n (on dress) volante m.
▶ n pl frills (decorations) adornos mpl.

fringe [frɪndʒ] n 1 (decorative) fleco. 2 (of hair) flequillo. 3 (edge) borde m.

frisk [frɪsk] vt (search) registrar, cachear.
▶ vi (frolic) brincar, retozar.

frisky ['frɪskɪ] adj (child, animal) juguetón,-ona; (adult) vivo,-a, vital.
ⓘ comp friskier, superl friskiest.

fritter ['frɪtər] n CULIN buñuelo.

frivolity [frɪ'vɒlətɪ] n frivolidad f.
ⓘ pl frivolities.

frizzy ['frɪzɪ] adj crespo,-a, rizado,-a.
ⓘ comp frizzier, superl frizziest.

frock [frɒk] n vestido.

frog [frɒg] n rana.

frolic ['frɒlɪk] vi juguetear, retozar.
▶ n aventura.

from [frɒm] *prep* **1** *(starting at)* de; *(train, plane)* procedente de: *the train from Madrid* el tren procedente de Madrid. **2** *(origin, source)* de, desde. **9** *(because of)* por, a causa de. **10** *(considering, according to)* según, por. **11** *(indicating difference)* de; *(when distinguishing)* entre. **12** *(indicating position)* desde. LOC **from now on** de ahora en adelante, a partir de ahora.

front [frʌnt] *n* **1** *(forward part)* parte *f* delantera, frente *m*. **2** METEOR frente *m*. **3** *(facade)* fachada. **4** MIL frente *m*. **5** *(promenade)* paseo marítimo.
► *adj* delantero,-a, de delante.
► *vi (face)* dar (on/onto, a).
► *vt* **1** *(lead, head)* encabezar. **2** *(present)* presentar.

frontalis [frənˈtalɪs] *n* músculo frontal.

frontier [ˈfrʌntɪəʳ] *n* frontera.
► *adj* fronterizo,-a.

front page [ˈfrʌntpeɪdʒ] *adj* de portada, de primera plana.

frost [frɒst] *n* **1** *(covering)* escarcha. **2** *(freezing)* helada.
► *vt* helar, cubrir de escarcha.

frostbite [ˈfrɒstbaɪt] *n* congelación *f*.

frosted [ˈfrɒstɪd] *adj* **1** *(glass)* esmerilado,-a. **2** CULIN recubierto,-a de azúcar glas, escarchado,-a.

frosty [ˈfrɒstɪ] *adj* **1** METEOR *(cold with frost)* de helada; *(very cold)* helado,-a, muy frío,-a. **2** METEOR *(covered with frost)* escarchado,-a, cubierto,-a de escarcha. **3** *fig (unfriendly)* glacial.
① *comp* **frostier**, *superl* **frostiest**.

froth [frɒθ] *n (gen)* espuma.

frown [fraʊn] *n* ceño.
► *vi* fruncir el ceño.

froze [frəʊz] *pt* → **freeze**.

frozen [ˈfrəʊzən] *pp* → **freeze**.
► *adj* **1** *(water, ground)* helado,-a. **2** *(food)* congelado,-a.

fructose [ˈfrʌktəʊz] *n* fructosa.

frugal [ˈfruːgəl] *adj* frugal.

fruit [fruːt] *n* **1** *(food)* fruta. **2** BOT fruto. **3** *(result, reward)* fruto.
► *adj* de fruta. COMP **fruit juice** zumo de fruta. ‖ **fruit salad** macedonia.
► *vi* dar fruto.

fruitful [ˈfruːtfʊl] *adj* fructífero,-a.

frustrate [frʌˈstreɪt] *vt* **1** *(thwart)* frustrar. **2** *(upset)* frustrar.

frustration [frʌˈstreɪʃən] *n* frustración *f*.

fry¹ [fraɪ] *vt* freír.
► *vi* **1** freírse. **2** *fig (in sun)* asarse, achicharrarse.
① *pt & pp* **fried**, *ger* **frying**.

fry² [fraɪ] *n pl (fish)* alevines *mpl*.

fryer [fraɪəʳ] *n (frying pan)* sartén *f*.

frying pan [ˈfraɪɪŋpæn] *n* sartén *f*.

ft [ˈfʊt, ˈfiːt] *abbr (foot, feet)* pie *m*, pies *mpl*.

fuel [fjʊəl] *n* **1** *(gen)* combustible *m*. **2** *(for motors)* carburante *m*.
► *vt* **1** *(plane)* abastecer de combustible; *(car)* echar gasolina. **2** *fig (make worse)* empeorar; *(encourage)* alimentar.

fugitive [ˈfjuːdʒɪtɪv] *n (from danger, war, etc)* fugitivo,-a; *(from justice)* prófugo,-a.
► *adj* fugitivo,-a.

fulcrum [ˈfʊlkrəm] *n* fulcro.

fulfil [fʊlˈfɪl] *vt* **1** *(promise, duty)* cumplir. **2** *(task, plan, ambition)* realizar. **3** *(role, function, order)* efectuar, desempeñar. **4** *(need, desire, wish)* satisfacer.
① *pt & pp* **fulfilled**, *ger* **fulfilling**.

fulfill [fʊlˈfɪl] *vt* US → **fulfil**.

fulfilled [fʊlˈfɪld] *pt & pp* → **fulfill**.
► *adj* realizado,-a, satisfecho,-a.

full [fʊl] *adj* **1** *(gen)* lleno,-a. **2** *(week, day)* cargado,-a, movido,-a. **3** *(entire, complete)* completo,-a. **4** *(highest or greatest possible)* máximo,-a. LOC **full time** a jornada completa. COMP **full board** pensión *f* completa. ‖ **full stop** punto.
► *adv (directly)* justo, de lleno.

full-length [fʊlˈleŋθ] *adj* **1** *(mirror, portrait)* de cuerpo entero. **2** *(garment)* largo,-a. **3** *(film)* de largo metraje.

full-scale [fʊlˈskeɪl] *adj* **1** *(actual size)* de tamaño natural. **2** *(complete, total)* completo,-a, total.

full-time [fʊlˈtaɪm] *adj* a tiempo completo, de jornada completa.
► *adv* a tiempo completo.

fumble [ˈfʌmbəl] *vt* dejar caer.
► *vi* **to fumble for** buscar a tientas.
► *vi* **to fumble with** hacer torpemente.

fume [fjuːm] vi **1** (produce smoke, etc) echar humo. **2** fig (show anger) echar humo, subirse por las paredes.
▶ n pl **fumes** humos mpl.

❌ To fume no significa 'fumar', que se traduce por to smoke.

fumigate [ˈfjuːmɪɡeɪt] vt fumigar.

fun [fʌn] n **1** (enjoyment, pleasure) diversión f: it'll be good fun when we go camping lo pasaremos muy bien cuando nos vayamos de camping. **2** (amusement) gracia f: it's no fun staying in alone on Saturday night no tiene gracia quedarse solo en casa el sábado por la noche.
▶ adj (humorous, amusing) divertido,-a.

function [ˈfʌŋkʃən] n **1** (purpose, use, duty) función f. **2** (ceremony) acto, ceremonia; (reception) recepción f. **3** MATH función f.
▶ vi funcionar. LOC **to fulfil a function** desempeñar una función. COMP **function key** tecla de función.

functional [ˈfʌŋkʃənəl] adj **1** (operational) funcional. **2** (practical, useful) práctico,-a.

fund [fʌnd] n **1** (sum of money) fondo. **2** (supply) fuente f.
▶ vt **1** (finance) patrocinar. **2** (debt) consolidar.
▶ n pl **funds** (financial resources) fondos mpl.

fundamental [fʌndəˈmentəl] adj fundamental.
▶ n pl **fundamentals** (essential part, basic rule) fundamentos mpl, reglas fpl básicas.

fundamentalist [fʌndəˈmentəlɪst] adj REL fundamentalista, integrista.
▶ n REL fundamentalista mf, integrista mf.

funeral [ˈfjuːnərəl] n entierro, funeral m.
▶ adj fúnebre.

funfair [ˈfʌnfeəʳ] n GB feria, parque m de atracciones.

fungus [ˈfʌŋɡəs] n hongo.
ⓘ pl **funguses** o **fungi** [ˈfʌndʒaɪ].

funicular [fjuːˈnɪkjələʳ] n funicular m.

funk [fʌŋk] n MUS funky m.

funky [ˈfʌŋkɪ] adj **1** MUS funky. **2** fam (fashionable) guay, chulo,-a.
ⓘ comp **funkier**, superl **funkiest**.

funnel [ˈfʌnəl] n **1** (for liquid) embudo. **2** (chimney) chimenea.

▶ vi verterse.
▶ vt fig (channel) encauzar.

funny [ˈfʌnɪ] adj **1** (amusing) gracioso,-a, divertido,-a: I don't find your remarks at all funny tus comentarios no son nada graciosos. **2** (strange) raro,-a, extraño,-a, curioso,-a: the funny thing is that ... lo curioso es que ... **3** fam (slightly ill) rarillo,-a, malito,-a; (slightly mad) chiflado,-a: I feel funny no me encuentro bien.
ⓘ comp **funnier**, superl **funniest**.

fur [fɜːʳ] n **1** (of living animal) pelo, pelaje m. **2** (of dead animal) piel f. **3** (garment) abrigo de piel. **4** (on tongue) sarro.
▶ adj de piel. COMP **fur coat** abrigo de pieles.

furious [ˈfjʊərɪəs] adj (very angry) furioso,-a: she'll be furious if we break anything se pondrá furiosa si rompemos algo; he's got a furious temper tiene muy mal genio.

furnace [ˈfɜːnəs] n horno.

furnish [ˈfɜːnɪʃ] vt **1** (house, etc) amueblar (with, de): I'd like to rent a furnished flat quisiera alquilar un piso amueblado. **2** fml (supply - material) suministrar, proveer; (- information, etc) facilitar, proporcionar.

furnishings [ˈfɜːnɪʃɪŋz] n pl muebles, cortinas y alfombras.

furniture [ˈfɜːnɪtʃəʳ] n mobiliario, muebles mpl: I need some new furniture necesito unos muebles nuevos.

furrow [ˈfʌrəʊ] n **1** AGR surco. **2** (wrinkle) arruga.
▶ vt **1** AGR surcar. **2** (forehead) arrugar.

furry [ˈfɜːrɪ] adj **1** (hairy) peludo,-a. **2** (scaly) sarroso,-a.
ⓘ comp **furrier**, superl **furriest**.

further [ˈfɜːðəʳ] adj **1** (farther) más lejos: she lives further down the road vive más abajo de la calle. **2** (more, additional) más, adicional; (new) nuevo,-a: I have just one further question tengo una pregunta más; this office will remain closed until further notice esta oficina permanecerá cerrada hasta nuevo aviso; for further information, please contact ... para más información, póngase en contacto con ...
▶ adv **1** (farther) más lejos: is it much further? ¿queda mucho más?; don't go any further no vayas más lejos. **2** (more, to a

greater degree) más: *the police want to take the matter further* la policía quiere investigar más el asunto; *I'd like to go further into this subject* me gustaría estudiar el tema más a fondo. **3** *fml (besides)* además: *further, I'd like to complain about the lack of parking spaces* además, quisiera quejarme de la falta de aparcamientos.
► *vt (advance, promote)* fomentar, promover: *he would have gone to any lengths to further his career* hubiera hecho cualquier cosa para promover su propia carrera. ⌊LOC⌋ **this must not go any further** esto tiene que quedar entre nosotros, esto no tiene que salir de aquí. ‖ **further to** con referencia a, referente a: *further to your letter of the 6th inst* con referencia a su carta del día 6 del corriente. ⌊COMP⌋ **further education** estudios *mpl* superiores.

✎ Consulta también **far.**

furthermore [fɜːðə'mɔːʳ] *adv fml* además.

furthest ['fɜːðɪst] *adj* → **far, farthest, further.**
► *adv* → **far, further.**

furtive ['fɜːtɪv] *adj* furtivo,-a.

fury ['fjʊərɪ] *n* furia. ⌊LOC⌋ **to be in a fury** estar furioso,-a. ‖ **to fly into a fury** ponerse hecho,-a una furia.
ⓘ *pl* furies.

fuse [fjuːz] *n* **1** ELEC fusible *m*, plomo: *the fuses blew* saltaron los fusibles, se fundieron los plomos. **2** *(wick)* mecha; *(detonator)* espoleta. ⌊LOC⌋ **to blow a fuse 1** *(appliance)* saltar el fusible de, fundirse el plomo de. **2** *(person)* estallar, explotar. ⌊COMP⌋ **fuse box** caja de fusibles.
► *vt* **1** *(cause to stop working, melt)* fundir- **2** *fig (merge)* fusionar.
► *vi* **1** *(stop working, melt)* fundirse: *the lights have fused* se han fundido los plomos. **2** *fig (merge)* fusionarse: *the two companies fused* las dos empresas se fusionaron.

fuselage ['fjuːzəlɑːʒ] *n* fuselaje *m*.

fusillade [fjuːzə'leɪd] *n* tiroteo,.

fusion ['fjuːʒən] *n* fusión *f*.

fuss [fʌs] *n* **1** *(commotion, nervous excitement)* alboroto, jaleo. **2** *(angry scene, dispute)* escándalo, problemas *mpl*; *(complaints)* quejas *fpl*.
► *vt (pester, annoy, bother)* molestar: *stop fussing me* no me molestes.
► *vi* **1** *(worry, fret)* preocuparse, inquietarse: *don't fuss, we'll get there on time* no te preocupes, llegaremos a tiempo. **2** *(pay excessive attention to)* preocuparse excesivamente (over, de). ⌊LOC⌋ **to make a fuss / kick up a fuss** *(complain strongly)* armar un escándalo, montar una escena. ‖ **to make a fuss of sb** deshacerse por ALGN.

fussy ['fʌsɪ] *adj* **1** *(concerned with details)* quisquilloso,-a, exigente. **2** *(nervous about small things)* nervioso,-a. **3** *(too elaborate)* recargado,-a.
ⓘ *comp* **fussier,** *superl* **fussiest.**

fusty ['fʌstɪ] *adj* **1** *(musty)* mohoso,-a, rancio,-a; *(stale)* que huele a cerrado. **2** *(old-fashioned)* chapado,-a a la antigua.
ⓘ *comp* **fustier,** *superl* **fustiest.**

futile ['fjuːtaɪl] *adj* vano,-a, inútil: *a futile attempt to save him* un intento inútil de salvarlo.

future ['fjuːtʃəʳ] *adj* futuro,-a: *my future husband* mi futuro marido; *we arranged to meet at some future time* quedamos para vernos en un futuro. ⌊COMP⌋ **future tense** futuro.
► *n* **1** futuro, porvenir *m*: *the future is promising* el futuro es prometedor. **2** *(verb tense)* futuro. ⌊LOC⌋ **in future** en el futuro, de aquí en adelante. ‖ **in the future** en el futuro. ‖ **in the distant future** en un futuro lejano. ‖ **in the near future** en un futuro próximo. ‖ **in the not too distant future** en un futuro no muy lejano.

fuzz [fʌz] *n (fluff)* pelusa; *(fine hair)* vello.

fuzzy ['fʌzɪ] *adj* **1** *(frizzy)* rizado,-a, crespo,-a; *(fluffy)* con pelusilla. **2** *(blurred)* borroso,-a, movido,-a.
ⓘ *comp* **fuzzier,** *superl* **fuzziest.**

F

G

G, g [giː] *n* **1** *(the letter)* G, g *f*. **2** MUS sol *m*.

g [græm] *symb* **(gram, gramme)** gramo; *(abbreviation)* g.

gab [gæb] *n* labia, palique *m*. LOC **to have the gift of the gab** tener el pico de oro.
▶ *vi* charlar, parlotear.
ⓘ *pt & pp* **gabbed**, *ger* **gabbing**.

gabardine ['gæbədiːn] *n* gabardina.

gabble ['gæbªl] *n* chapurreo.
▶ *vt* farfullar, charlotear.

gadfly ['gædflaɪ] *n* ZOOL tábano.
ⓘ *pl* **gadflies**.

gadget ['gædʒɪt] *n fam* aparato, artilugio, chisme *m*.

Gaelic ['geɪlɪk] *adj* gaélico,-a.
▶ *n (language)* gaélico.

gaffe [gæf] *n* metedura de pata.

gag [gæg] *n* **1** *(cover for the mouth)* mordaza. **2** *(joke)* chiste *m*, gag *m*, broma.
▶ *vt* amordazar.
▶ *vi* tener náuseas.
ⓘ *pt & pp* **gagged**, *ger* **gagging**.

gaily ['geɪlɪ] *adv* alegremente.

gain [geɪn] *n* **1** *(achievement)* logro. **2** *(profit)* ganancia. **3** *(increase)* aumento.
▶ *vt* **1** *(achieve)* lograr, conseguir. **2** *(obtain)* ganar. **3** *(increase)* aumentar. **4** *(clock)* adelantar.
▶ *vi* **1** *(clock)* adelantar. **2** *(shares)* subir.

gait [geɪt] *n* andares *mpl*.

gaiter ['geɪtəʳ] *n* polaina.

galactic [gəˈlæktɪk] *adj* galáctico,-a.

galaxy ['gæləksɪ] *n* galaxia.
ⓘ *pl* **galaxies**.

gale [geɪl] *n (wind)* vendaval *m*; *(storm)* tempestad *f*.

gall¹ [gɔːl] *n fig* descaro, caradura. COMP **gall bladder** vesícula biliar.

gall² [gɔːl] *vt* irritar, molestar.

gallant ['gælənt] *adj* **1** *(brave)* valiente. **2** *(chivalrous)* galante.

galleon ['gælɪən] *n* galeón *m*.

gallery ['gælərɪ] *n* **1** *(gen)* galería. **2** *(in theatre)* gallinero.
ⓘ *pl* **galleries**.

galley ['gælɪ] *n* **1** *(ship)* galera. **2** *(kitchen on ships)* cocina.

gallon ['gælən] *n* galón *m*.

> ✎ Equivale en GB a 4,55 litros y en US 3,78 litros.

gallop ['gæləp] *n* galope *m*.
▶ *vi* galopar.

gallows ['gæləʊz] *n pl* horca *sing*, patíbulo *sing*.

galore [gəˈlɔːʳ] *adj* en abundancia.

galvanize ['gælvənaɪz] *vt* galvanizar.

gamble ['gæmbªl] *n* **1** *(risky undertaking)* empresa arriesgada. **2** *(risk)* riesgo. **3** *(bet)* jugada, apuesta.
▶ *vt* jugar(se).
▶ *vi* **1** *(bet)* apostar. **2** *(take a risk)* arriesgarse, confiar.

gambler ['gæmbləʳ] *n* jugador,-ra.

gambling ['gæmblɪŋ] *n* juego.

game [geɪm] *n* **1** juego. **2** *(match)* partido. **3** *(of cards, chess, etc)* partida. **4** *(hunting)* caza. COMP **game reserve** coto de caza.
▶ *adj* dispuesto,-a, listo,-a.
▶ *n pl* **games** GB educación *f sing* física.

gamekeeper ['geɪmkiːpəʳ] *n* guardabosque *mf*.

gammon ['gæmən] *n* GB jamón *m (ahumado o curado a la sal)*.

gamut ['gæmət] *n* gama, serie *f*.

gander ['gændəʳ] *n* ganso.

gang [gæŋ] *n* **1** *(criminals)* banda. **2** *(youths)* pandilla.

gangplank ['gæŋplæŋk] *n* plancha.

gangrene ['gæŋgri:n] *n* gangrena.

gangster ['gæŋstə'] *n* gángster *m*.

gangway ['gæŋweɪ] *n* **1** GB *(aisle, passage)* pasillo. **2** *(on ship)* pasarela.

gaol [dʒeɪl] *n* GB cárcel *f*.

✎ Consulta también jail.

gap [gæp] *n* **1** *(hole)* abertura, hueco. **2** *(crack)* brecha. **3** *(empty space)* espacio. **4** *(blank)* blanco. **5** *(time)* intervalo.

gape [geɪp] *vi* **1** abrirse. **2** *(stare)* mirar boquiabierto,-a.

garage ['gærɑ:ʒ, 'gærɪdʒ] *n* **1** garaje *m*. **2** *(for repairs)* taller *m* mecánico. **3** *(for petrol, etc)* gasolinera.

garbage ['gɑ:bɪdʒ] *n* **1** US basura. **2** GB desperdicios *mpl*. **3** *fig* tonterías *fpl*, majaderías *fpl*, sandeces *fpl*.

garbled ['gɑ:bəld] *adj* confuso,-a.

garden ['gɑ:dən] *n* jardín *m*.
▶ *vi* cuidar el jardín.

gardener ['gɑ:dənə'] *n* *(gen)* jardinero,-a; *(of vegetables)* hortelano,-a.

gargle ['gɑ:gəl] *vi* hacer gárgaras.

gargoyle ['gɑ:gɔɪl] *n* gárgola.

garish ['geərɪʃ] *adj (colour)* chillón,-ona, llamativo,-a; *(light)* cegador,-ra, deslumbrante.

garland ['gɑ:lənd] *n* guirnalda.

garlic ['gɑ:lɪk] *n* ajo.

garment ['gɑ:mənt] *n (clothes)* prenda.

garnet ['gɑ:nɪt] *n* granate *m*.

garnish ['gɑ:nɪʃ] *n* guarnición *f*.
▶ *vt* guarnecer.

garrison ['gærɪsən] *n* guarnición *f*.

garter ['gɑ:tə'] *n* liga.

gas [gæs] *n* **1** *(substance)* gas *m*. **2** US gasolina. **3** *(anaesthetic)* anestesia. **4** US *fig* algo divertido. COMP **gas chamber** cámara de gas. ▌ **gas mask** máscara antigás. ▌ US **gas station** gasolinera.
ⓘ *pl* gases o gasses.
▶ *vt* asfixiar con gas.
▶ *vi fam* charlotear.

gaseous ['gæsɪəs] *adj* gaseoso,-a.

gash [gæʃ] *n* cuchillada.

gasket ['gæskɪt] *n* junta.

gasoline ['gæsəli:n] *n* US gasolina.

gasp [gɑ:sp] *vi* **1** *(in astonishment)* quedar boquiabierto,-a. **2** *(to pant)* jadear.

gassy ['gæsɪ] *adj* gaseoso,-a.
ⓘ *comp* gassier, *superl* gassiest.

gastric ['gæstrɪk] *adj* gástrico,-a.

gastronomy [gæs'trɒnəmɪ] *n* gastronomía.

gate [geɪt] *n* **1** *(door)* puerta, verja. **2** *(at airport)* puerta; *(at stadium)* entrada. **3** GB *(attendance)* asistencia.

gateau ['gætəʊ] *n* pastel *m*, tarta.
ⓘ *pl* gateaux ['gætəʊz].

gatecrash ['geɪtkræʃ] *vt fam* colarse en.
▶ *vi fam* colarse.

gateway ['geɪtweɪ] *n* entrada, puerta.

gather ['gæðə'] *vt* **1** *(collect)* juntar. **2** *(call together)* reunir. **3** *(pick up)* recoger. **4** *(taxes)* recaudar. **5** *(gain)* ganar, cobrar.
▶ *vi* **1** *(come together)* reunirse, juntarse. **2** *(build up)* acumularse. **3** *(form)* formarse.

gathering ['gæðərɪŋ] *n* reunión *f*.

gauche [gəʊʃ] *adj (awkward)* torpe, desmañado,-a; *(tactless)* sin tacto.

gaudy ['gɔ:dɪ] *adj* chillón,-ona.
ⓘ *comp* gaudier, *superl* gaudiest.

gauge [geɪdʒ] *n* **1** *(device)* indicador *m*, calibrador *m*. **2** *(measure)* medida estándar. **3** *(railways)* ancho de vía.
▶ *vt* **1** *(measure)* medir, calibrar. **2** *fig* apreciar, calcular.

gaunt [gɔ:nt] *adj* **1** *(lean)* demacrado,-a. **2** *fig (desolate)* lúgubre; *(grim)* siniestro,-a.

gauze [gɔ:z] *n* gasa.

gave [geɪv] *pt* → give.

gay [geɪ] *adj* **1** *fam (homosexual)* gay. **2** *(happy, lively)* alegre. **3** *(bright)* vistoso,-a.

gaze [geɪz] *n* mirada fija.
▶ *vi* mirar fijamente.

gazelle [gə'zel] *n* gacela.

gazette [gə'zet] *n* GB boletín oficial.

GCSE ['dʒi:'si:'es'i:] *abbr* GB (General Certificate of Secondary Education) ≈ Enseñanza Secundaria Obligatoria; *(abbreviation)* ESO *f*.

⊕ GCSE es el examen que se hace en Gran Bretaña al final de la enseñanza secundaria, a los 16 años aproximadamente.

GDP [ˌdʒiːˈdiːˈpiː] *abbr* (gross domestic product) producto interior bruto; *(abbreviation)* PIB *m*.

gear [gɪəʳ] *n* **1** TECH engranaje *m*. **2** AUTO marcha, velocidad *f*. **3** *(equipment)* equipo. **4** *fam (belongings)* efectos *mpl* personales, pertenencias *fpl*; *(clothes)* ropa. COMP **gear lever** palanca de cambios.

gearbox [ˈgɪəbɒks] *n* caja de cambios.

gearshift [ˈgɪəʃɪft] *n* AUTO US palanca de cambio.

gearstick [ˈgɪəstɪk] *n* AUTO palanca de cambio.

geese [giːs] *n pl* → goose.

gel [dʒel] *n* **1** gel *m*. **2** *(for hair)* gomina, fijador *m*.

gelatine [ˈdʒeləti:n] *n* gelatina.

gem [dʒem] *n* **1** *(jewel)* gema. **2** *fig (person, thing)* joya, alhaja.

Gemini [ˈdʒemɪnaɪ] *n* Géminis *m*.

gender [ˈdʒendəʳ] *n* género.

gene [dʒiːn] *n* gene *m*, gen *m*. COMP **gene pool** banco genético.

genera [ˈdʒenərə] *n pl* → genus.

general [ˈdʒenʳrəl] *adj* general. COMP **general election** elecciones *fpl* generales. ‖ **general knowledge** cultura general.
▸ *n* MIL general *m*.

generalize [ˈdʒenʳrəlaɪz] *vt & vi* generalizar.

generate [ˈdʒenəreɪt] *vt (gen)* generar.

generation [dʒenəˈreɪʃʰn] *n* generación *f*.

generator [ˈdʒenəreɪtəʳ] *n* generador *m*.

generic [dʒəˈnerɪk] *adj* genérico,-a.

generosity [dʒenəˈrɒsəti] *n* generosidad *f*.

generous [ˈdʒenʳrəs] *adj* generoso,-a.

genetic [dʒəˈnetɪk] *adj* genético,-a. COMP **genetic code** código genético.

genetically [dʒəˈnetɪklɪ] *adv* genéticamente. LOC **genetically modified** transgénico,-a.

genetics [dʒəˈnetɪks] *n* genética.

genial [ˈdʒiːnɪəl] *adj* afable, amable.

☒ Genial no significa 'genial (brillante)', que se traduce por **brilliant**.

genital [ˈdʒenɪtʰl] *adj* genital.
▸ *n pl* **genitals** (órganos *mpl*) genitales *mpl*.

genitive [ˈdʒenɪtɪv] *adj* genitivo,-a.
▸ *n* genitivo.

genius [ˈdʒiːnɪəs] *n* **1** *(person)* genio. **2** *(gift)* don *m*.
ⓘ *pl* **geniuses**.

☒ Genius no significa 'genio (carácter)', que se traduce por **temper**.

genocide [ˈdʒenəsaɪd] *n* genocidio.

genome [ˈdʒiːnəʊm] *n* genoma *m*.

genotype [ˈdʒenətaɪp] *n* genotipo.

genre [ˈʒɑːnrə] *n* género.

gent [dʒent] *n fam* caballero, señor *m*.

gentle [ˈdʒentʰl] *adj* **1** *(person)* bondadoso,-a, dulce, tierno,-a. **2** *(breeze, movement, touch, etc)* suave. **3** *(hint)* discreto,-a. **4** *(noble)* noble.
ⓘ *comp* **gentler**, *superl* **gentlest**.
▸ *n pl* **gents** servicio de caballeros.

gentleman [ˈdʒentʰlmən] *n* caballero, señor *m*.
ⓘ *pl* **gentlemen** [ˈdʒentʰlmən].

gently [ˈdʒentlɪ] *adv* **1** *(smoothly)* suavemente. **2** *(slowly)* despacio, poco a poco. **3** *(kindly)* amablemente.

genuine [ˈdʒenjuɪn] *adj* **1** *(authentic, true)* genuino,-a, auténtico,-a, verdadero,-a. **2** *(sincere)* sincero,-a.

genus [ˈdʒiːnəs] *n* género.
ⓘ *pl* **genera** [ˈdʒenərə].

geographic [dʒɪəˈgræfɪk] *adj* geográfico,-a.

geography [dʒɪˈɒgrəfɪ] *n* geografía.

geological [dʒɪəˈlɒdʒɪkəl] *adj* geológico,-a.

geology [dʒɪˈɒlədʒɪ] *n* geología.

geometric [dʒɪəˈmetrɪk] *adj* geométrico,-a.

geometry [dʒɪˈɒmətrɪ] *n* geometría.

geranium [dʒəˈreɪnɪəm] *n* geranio.

geriatric [dʒerɪˈætrɪk] *adj* geriátrico,-a.

germ [dʒɜːm] *n* germen *m*.

German [ˈdʒɜːmən] *adj* alemán,-ana.
▸ *n* **1** *(person)* alemán,-ana. **2** *(language)* alemán *m*.

Germany [ˈdʒɜːmənɪ] *n* Alemania.

germinate [ˈdʒɜːmɪneɪt] *vi* germinar.
▸ *vt* hacer germinar.

germination [dʒɜ:mɪˈneɪʃ°n] *n* germinación *f*.

gerund [ˈdʒerənd] *n* gerundio.

gestation [dʒesˈteɪʃ°n] *n* BIOL gestación *f*.

gesticulate [dʒesˈtɪkjəleɪt] *vi* gesticular.

gesture [ˈdʒestʃəʳ] *n* **1** ademán *m*, gesto. **2** *fig (token)* detalle *m*, gesto, muestra.
▶ *vi* hacer gestos, hacer ademanes.

☒ Gesture no significa 'gesto (de la cara)', que se traduce por **grimace**.

get [get] *vt* **1** *(obtain)* obtener, conseguir: *I want to get a job* quiero conseguir un trabajo; *he got a bank loan* le concedieron un crédito bancario; *what did you get in maths?* ¿qué sacaste en mates?. **2** *(receive)* recibir: *I got your letter yesterday* recibí tu carta ayer. **3** *(buy)* comprar: *where did you get your jeans?* ¿dónde compraste tus vaqueros? **4** *(fetch)* traer: *get the car* traiga el coche. **5** *(catch illnesses, means of transport)* coger: *she got the flu* cogió la gripe. **6** *(receive signal)* captar, recibir, coger. **7** *(ask)* pedir, decir; *(persuade)* persuadir, convencer: *get your brother to help you* pídele a tu hermano que te ayude. **8** *(have sth done)* hacer algo a uno: *she loves getting her hair done* le encanta que le arreglen el pelo.
▶ *vi* **1** *(become)* ponerse, volverse: *she gets very angry if we're late* se pone furiosa si llegamos tarde. **2** *(go)* ir: *how do you get there?* ¿cómo se va hasta allí? **3** *(arrive)* llegar: *how did you get home?* ¿cómo llegaste a casa? **4** *(come to)* llegar a. **5** *(start)* empezar a. LOC **to get dressed** vestirse. **| to get lost** perderse. **| to get married** casarse. **| to get old** envejecer, hacerse viejo. **| to get ready** prepararse. **| to get wet** mojarse.

◆ **to get across** *vt insep (cross - street, road)* cruzar; *(- bridge)* atravesar.
▶ *vi* hacerse entender.

◆ **to get ahead** *vi* adelantar, progresar.

◆ **to get along** *vi* **1** *(manage)* arreglárselas, apañárselas. **2** *(leave)* marcharse, irse.

◆ **to get along with** *vt insep* **1** *(person)* llevarse (bien) con. **2** *(progress)* marchar.

◆ **to get around** *vi* **1** *(person)* moverse; *(travel)* viajar. **2** *(news)* difundirse.
▶ *vt insep (avoid)* evitar, sortear.

◆ **to get around to** *vi* encontrar tiempo para.

◆ **to get away** *vi* escaparse, irse.
▶ *vt sep* alejar, quitar, sacar.

◆ **to get away with** *vt insep* salir impune de.

◆ **to get back** *vi* **1** *(return)* volver, regresar. **2** *(move backwards)* moverse hacia atrás, retroceder.
▶ *vt sep (recover)* recuperar: *did you get your money back?* ¿te devolvieron el dinero?

◆ **to get behind** *vi* atrasarse.

◆ **to get by** *vi* **1** *(manage)* arreglárselas. **2** *(pass)* pasar.

◆ **to get down** *vt sep* **1** *(depress)* deprimir, desanimar. **2** *(gen)* bajar. **3** *(write down)* apuntar, anotar. **4** *(swallow)* tragar.
▶ *vi (descend)* bajarse.

◆ **to get down to** *vi* ponerse a.

◆ **to get in** *vi* **1** *(arrive)* llegar. **2** *(enter)* entrar; *(car)* subir; *(be elected)* ser elegido,-a.
▶ *vt sep* **1** *(insert)* meter. **2** *(harvest)* cosechar; *(washing)* recoger; *(supplies)* comprar. **3** *(summon)* llamar.

◆ **to get into** *vt insep* **1** *(arrive)* llegar a. **2** *(enter)* entrar en; *(car)* subir a.

◆ **to get off** *vt sep (remove)* quitarse.
▶ *vt insep (vehicle, horse, etc)* bajarse de.
▶ *vi* **1** bajarse. **3** *(begin)* comenzar. **4** *(escape)* escaparse.

◆ **to get off with** *vt insep fam* ligar con.

◆ **to get on** *vt insep (vehicle)* subir a, subirse a; *(bicycle, horse, etc)* montar a.
▶ *vi* **1** *(make progress)* progresar, avanzar, ir. **2** *(succeed)* tener éxito. **3** *(be friendly)* llevarse bien, avenirse, entenderse. **4** *(continue)* seguir, continuar. **5** *(grow old)* hacerse mayor, envejecerse.

◆ **to get out** *vt sep (thing)* sacar; *(stain)* quitar.
▶ *vi* **1** *(leave)* salir. **2** *(of car, etc)* bajar de, bajarse de. **3** *(escape)* escapar(se). **4** *(news, rumours, etc)* llegar a saberse, hacerse público,-a.

◆ **to get out of** *vt insep (avoid)* librarse de.
▶ *vi (stop)* dejar, perder la costumbre.

◆ **to get over** *vt insep* **1** *(illness)* recuperarse de. **2** *(recover from)* sobreponerse a; *(forget)* olvidar. **3** *(obstacle)* salvar; *(difficulty)* vencer.
▶ *vt sep (idea, etc)* comunicar, hacer comprender.

◆ **to get over with** *vt sep* acabar con.

G

◆ **to get round** *vt insep* **1** *(obstacle)* salvar. **2** *(law, regulation)* evitar, soslayar. **3** *(person)* convencer, persuadir.
▶ *vi (news)* difundirse, hacerse público,-a, llegar a saber.

◆ **to get through** *vi* **1** *(gen)* llegar. **2** *(on phone)* conseguir hablar (to, con). **3** *(communicate)* hacerse comprender (to, a).
▶ *vt insep* **1** *(finish)* acabar, terminar. **2** *(consume)* consumir; *(money)* gastar; *(drink)* beber. **3** *(exam)* aprobar.

◆ **to get together** *vi (people)* reunirse, juntarse.
▶ *vt sep* **1** *(people)* juntar, reunir. **2** *(assemble)* montar; *(money)* recoger, reunir.

◆ **to get up** *vi* **1** *(rise)* levantarse; *(climb up)* subir. **2** *(become stronger - wind, storm)* levantarse.

◆ **to get up to** *vt insep* **1** hacer: *what have you been getting up to?* ¿qué has estado haciendo? **2** *(reach)* llegar a.
ⓘ *pt* got [got], *pp* got [got] (US gotten ['gotᵊn]), *ger* getting.

getaway ['getəweɪ] *n fam* fuga, huida.

get-together ['gettəgeðəʳ] *n fam (meeting)* reunión *f*; *(party)* fiesta.

getup ['getʌp] *n fam* atavío, atuendo.

geyser ['giːzəʳ, US 'gaɪzəʳ] *n* **1** *(natural spring)* géiser *m*. **2** *(water heater)* calentador *m* de agua.

ghastly ['gɑːstlɪ] *adj* **1** espantoso,-a, horrible, horroroso,-a. **2** *(pale)* pálido,-a, mortecino,-a.
ⓘ *comp* ghastlier, *superl* ghastliest.

gherkin ['gɜːkɪn] *n* pepinillo.

ghetto ['getəʊ] *n* gueto.
ⓘ *pl* ghettos o ghettoes.

ghost [gəʊst] *n* fantasma *m*, espectro.
COMP ghost train tren *m* de la bruja.

ghostwrite ['gəʊstraɪt] *vt (literature)* hacer de negro, escribir para otro.

giant ['dʒaɪənt] *n* gigante,-a.
▶ *adj* gigante, gigantesco,-a.

gibberish ['dʒɪbərɪʃ] *n* galimatías *m*.

Gibraltar [dʒɪ'brɔːltəʳ] *n* Gibraltar *m*.

Gibraltarian [dʒɪbrɔː'teərɪən] *adj* gibraltareño,-a.

giddy ['gɪdɪ] *adj (dizzy)* mareado,-a.
ⓘ *comp* giddier, *superl* giddiest.

gift [gɪft] *n* **1** *(present)* regalo, obsequio. **2** *(talent)* don *m*. **3** REL ofrenda. **4** JUR donación *f*. COMP gift shop tienda de regalos.

gifted ['gɪftɪd] *adj* dotado,-a.

gigabyte ['gɪgəbaɪt] *n* (giga)byte *m*.

gigantic [dʒaɪ'gæntɪk] *adj* gigantesco,-a.

giggle ['gɪgᵊl] *n* **1** risita, risa tonta. **2** GB *fam* broma, diversión *f*.

gild [gɪld] *vt* dorar.

gill [gɪl] *n (of fish)* agalla, branquia.

gilt [gɪlt] *adj* dorado,-a.
▶ *n* dorado.

gin [dʒɪn] *n* ginebra.

ginger ['dʒɪndʒəʳ] *n (spice)* jengibre *m*.
▶ *adj (hair)* rojo,-a; *(person)* pelirrojo,-a.

◆ **to ginger up** *vt sep* animar, estimular.

gingerbread ['dʒɪndʒəbred] *n* pan *m* de jengibre.

gipsy ['dʒɪpsɪ] *n* gitano,-a.
ⓘ *pl* gipsies.

giraffe [dʒɪ'rɑːf] *n* jirafa.

girdle ['gɜːdᵊl] *n* **1** *(clothes)* faja. **2** *fig* cinturón *m*.
▶ *vt fig* rodear.

girl [gɜːl] *n* **1** chica, muchacha, joven *f*; *(small)* niña. **2** *(daughter)* hija.

girlfriend ['gɜːlfrend] *n* **1** *(partner)* novia. **2** *(friend)* amiga, compañera.

girlish ['gɜːlɪʃ] *adj (of girl)* de niña; *(effeminate)* afeminado,-a.

giro ['dʒaɪrəʊ] *n* GB giro.
ⓘ *pl* giros.

gist [dʒɪst] *n (general idea)* idea general, sentido general; *(fundamental idea)* lo esencial.

give [gɪv] *n (flexibility)* elasticidad *f*, flexibilidad *f*.
▶ *vt* **1** *(gen)* dar, entregar. **2** *(as a gift)* dar, regalar: *he gave her a dress* le regaló un vestido. **3** *(perform a concert, etc)* dar; *(speech)* pronunciar. **4** *(dedicate)* dedicar, consagrar. LOC **to give way** ceder el paso.
▶ *vi (yield)* ceder; *(cloth, elastic)* dar de sí.

◆ **to give away** *vt sep* **1** *(gen)* distribuir, repartir; *(present)* regalar; *(prize)* entregar. **2** *(betray)* delatar, traicionar; *(disclose)* revelar, descubrir.

◆ **to give back** *vt sep (return)* devolver.

◆ **to give in** *vi (admit defeat)* darse por vencido,-a, rendirse; *(yield)* ceder.
▶ *vt sep (hand in)* entregar.

◆ **to give off** *vt sep (smell, heat, etc)* despedir, desprender, emitir.

◆ **to give onto** *vi* dar a.

◆ **to give over** *vt sep (hand over)* entregar; *(allocate)* dedicar, asignar.
▶ *vi fam (stop)* dejar de.

◆ **to give up** *vt sep* **1** *(renounce)* dejar; *(idea)* abandonar, renunciar a. **2** *(devote)* dedicar. **3** *(surrender)* entregarse.
▶ *vi (admit defeat)* darse por vencido,-a, rendirse.

◆ **to give up on** *vt insep* abandonar, desistir.
ⓘ *pt* gave [geɪv], *pp* given ['gɪvªn], *ger* giving.

given ['gɪvªn] *pp* → **give**.
▶ *adj* **1** *(fixed)* dado,-a, determinado,-a. **2** *(prone)* dado,-a, propenso,-a.
▶ *prep* **1** *(considering)* dado,-a, teniendo en cuenta. **2** *(if)* si.

glacial ['gleɪʃªl] *adj* **1** GEOL glaciar. **2** *(icy)* glacial.

glacier ['glæsɪəʳ, 'gleɪʃəʳ] *n* GEOL glaciar *m*.

glad [glæd] *adj (pleased)* contento,-a, alegre; *(happy)* feliz.
ⓘ *comp* gladder, *superl* gladdest.

gladden ['glædªn] *vt* alegrar.

gladiator ['glædɪeɪtəʳ] *n* HIST gladiador *m*.

gladly ['glædlɪ] *adv* de buena gana, con mucho gusto.

glamorous ['glæmərəs] *adj* **1** atractivo,-a. **2** *(charming)* encantador,-ra.

glamour ['glæməʳ] *n* **1** atractivo. **2** *(charm)* encanto.

glance [glɑːns] *n* vistazo, ojeada.
▶ *vi* echar un vistazo (at, a).

gland [glænd] *n* ANAT glándula.

glare [gleəʳ] *n* **1** *(light)* luz *f* deslumbrante. **2** AUTO deslumbramiento. **3** *(look)* mirada furiosa, mirada hostil.
▶ *vi* **1** *(dazzle)* deslumbrar. **2** *(look)* lanzar una mirada furiosa.

glass [glɑːs] *n* **1** *(material)* vidrio, cristal *m*. **2** *(for drinking)* vaso; *(with stem)* copa. **3** GB barómetro.
ⓘ *pl* glasses.
▶ *n pl* glasses gafas *fpl*.

glassware ['glɑːsweəʳ] *n* cristalería.

glaze [gleɪz] *n (for pottery)* vidriado; *(lustre)* brillo, lustre *m*; *(varnish)* barniz *m*, esmalte *m*.
▶ *vt* **1** *(pottery)* vidriar, esmaltar. **2** *(windows)* poner cristales a. **3** CULIN glasear.

gleam [gliːm] *n* **1** destello, rayo. **2** *fig* rayo, resquicio, vislumbre *m*.
▶ *vi* brillar, destellar, relucir.

glean [gliːn] *vt* **1** AGR espigar. **2** *fig* recoger, cosechar.

glide [glaɪd] *n* **1** deslizamiento. **2** AV planeo, vuelo sin motor. **3** LING semivocal *f*.
▶ *vi* **1** deslizarse. **2** AV planear.

glider ['glaɪdəʳ] *n* AV planeador *m*.

glimmer ['glɪməʳ] *n (light)* luz *f* tenue.
▶ *vi* brillar con luz tenue.

glimpse [glɪmps] *n* visión *f* fugaz.
▶ *vt* vislumbrar, entrever.

glisten ['glɪsªn] *vi* brillar, relucir.

glitter ['glɪtəʳ] *n* brillo.
▶ *vi* brillar, relucir.

global ['gləʊbªl] *adj* **1** mundial. **2** *(total)* global. COMP **global warming** calentamiento global.

globalization [gləʊzbəlaɪ'zeɪʃªn] *n* globalización *f*.

globe [gləʊb] *n* globo

✕ Globe no significa 'globo (de niño)', que se traduce por balloon.

globe-trotter ['gləʊbtrɒtəʳ] *n fam* trotamundos *mf*.

globule ['glɒbjuːl] *n* glóbulo.

gloom [gluːm] *n* **1** *(darkness)* penumbra *f*. **2** *(sadness)* tristeza, melancolía. **3** *(hopelessness)* desolación *f*, pesimismo.

gloomy ['gluːmɪ] *adj* **1** *(dark)* lóbrego,-a, oscuro,-a, tenebroso,-a. **2** *(sad)* melancólico,-a, triste; *(depressing)* deprimente. **3** *(pessimistic)* pesimista. **4** *(weather)* gris, encapotado,-a.
ⓘ *comp* gloomier, *superl* gloomiest.

glorious ['glɔːrɪəs] *adj* **1** glorioso,-a. **2** *(wonderful)* espléndido,-a, magnífico,-a.

glory ['glɔːrɪ] *n* **1** *(gen)* gloria. **2** *fig* esplendor *m*.
ⓘ *pl* glories.

G

gloss [glɒs] n **1** lustre m, brillo. **2** *(explanation)* glosa. **3** *fig* oropel m.

▸ vt *(text)* glosar, comentar.

◆ **to gloss over** vt insep *(play down)* paliar, suavizar; *(hide)* encubrir; *(ignore)* pasar por alto.

glossary ['glɒsərɪ] n glosario.

ⓘ pl glossaries.

glove [glʌv] n guante m. COMP **glove compartment** guantera.

glow [gləʊ] n **1** *(of lamp)* luz f; *(of jewel)* brillo. **2** *(of fire)* calor m vivo; *(of sky)* arrebol m; *(of fire, metal, etc)* incandescencia. **3** *(of face)* rubor m. **4** *fig* sensación f de bienestar, satisfacción f.

▸ vi **1** *(jewel, sun, etc)* brillar; *(of metal)* estar al rojo vivo; *(fire)* arder. **2** *fig* rebosar de.

glucose ['gluːkəʊz] n glucosa.

glue [gluː] n cola, pegamento.

▸ vt encolar, pegar.

gluten ['gluːtən] n gluten m.

gluteal ['gluːtəl] adj glúteo,-a.

gluteus ['gluːtɪəs] n glúteo.

glutton ['glʌtᵊn] n glotón,-ona.

glycerine ['glɪsəˌriːn] n glicerina.

GMT ['dʒiːˈemˈdiː] abbr (Greenwich Mean Time) hora media de Greenwich; *(abbreviation)* GMT.

gnat [næt] n ZOOL mosquito.

gnaw [nɔː] vt **1** *(bite)* roer. **2** *fig (worry)* corroer.

gnome [nəʊm] n gnomo.

GNP ['dʒiːˈenˈpiː] abbr (gross national product) producto nacional bruto; *(abbreviation)* PNB m.

gnu [nuː] n ñu m.

go [gəʊ] n **1** *(energy)* energía, empuje m. **2** *(turn)* turno: it's my go me toca a mí. **3** *(try)* intento: I'd like to have a go at hang gliding me gustaría intentar vuelo con ala delta. **4** *(start)* principio.

▸ vi **1** *(gen)* ir: to go on holiday irse de vacaciones. **2** *(leave)* marcharse, irse; *(bus, train, etc)* salir: let's go! ¡vámonos. **3** *(vanish)* desaparecer. **4** *(function)* funcionar, marchar: his business is going very well su negocio marcha muy bien. **5** *(become)* volverse, ponerse, quedarse: to go deaf quedarse

sordo,-a. **6** *(fit)* entrar, caber: the bed won't go into the room la cama no cabrá en la habitación. **7** *(break)* romperse, estropearse; *(yield)* ceder; *(blow)* fundirse. **8** *(progress)* ir, marchar, andar: things aren't going too well for him no le van muy bien las cosas. **9** *(be available)* quedar, haber: is there any more meat going? ¿queda algo de carne?. **10** *(make a noise, gesture, etc)* hacer: go like this with your head haz así con la cabeza. **11** *(time - pass)* pasar; *(- be remaining)* faltar: the years went by slowly los años pasaron lentamente; only two weeks to go solo faltan dos semanas. **16** *(say)* decir: as the saying goes según el dicho.

▸ vt **1** *(make a noise)* hacer: it goes tick-tock hace tic-tac. **2** *(travel)* hacer, recorrer.

▸ interj go! *(starting races)* ¡ya!: ready, steady, go! ¡preparados, listos, ya!.

◆ **to go after** vt insep *(pursue)* perseguir, andar tras.

◆ **to go ahead** vi *(proceed)* proceder: go ahead! ¡adelante!.

◆ **to go along with** vt insep estar de acuerdo con.

◆ **to go around** vi → to go round.

◆ **to go away** vi marcharse.

◆ **to go back** vi *(return)* volver, regresar; *(date from)* datar de, remontarse a.

◆ **to go back on** vt insep *(break)* romper, no cumplir.

◆ **to go by** vi *(time)* pasar.

▸ vt insep *(rules)* atenerse a, seguir; *(instinct)* dejarse llevar por; *(appearances)* juzgar por.

◆ **to go down** vi **1** *(gen)* bajar; *(tyre)* deshincharse; *(sun)* ponerse; *(ship)* hundirse. **2** *(be received)* ser acogido,-a.

◆ **to go for** vt insep **1** *(attack)* atacar. **2** *(fetch)* ir a buscar. **3** *fam (like)* gustar. **4** *fam (be valid)* valer para.

◆ **to go in** vi entrar.

◆ **to go in for** vt insep *(enter - race, competition)* participar en; *(- exam)* presentarse a; *(- career)* dedicarse a; *(like, agree with)* ser partidario,-a de.

◆ **to go into** vt insep **1** *(gen)* entrar en. **2** *(investigate)* investigar. **3** *(crash)* chocar contra.

◆ **to go off** vi **1** *(leave)* marcharse. **2** *(bomb)* estallar; *(alarm)* sonar; *(gun)* dispararse. **3** *(food)* estropearse, pasarse; *(milk)* cortarse. **4** *(stop operating)* apagarse.

▶ *vt insep (stop liking)* perder el gusto por, perder el interés por.

◆ **to go on** *vi* **1** *(continue)* seguir, continuar. **2** *(happen)* pasar, ocurrir. *what's going on?* ¿qué pasa?. **3** *(complain)* quejarse (**about**, de); *(talk at length)* hablar sin parar. **4** *(light, etc)* encenderse. **5** *(age)* estar a punto de cumplir: *she's ten going on eleven* está a punto de cumplir los once años.

◆ **to go out** *vi* **1** *(leave)* salir: *he goes out a lot* sale mucho. **2** *(fire, light)* apagarse.

◆ **to go over** *vt insep (check, revise)* revisar, repasar.

◆ **to go over to** *vt insep* **1** *(betray)* pasarse a. **2** *(change to)* cambiar a, pasar a.

◆ **to go round** *vi* **1** *(gyrate)* dar vueltas, girar. **2** *(visit)* pasar por casa de, visitar.

◆ **to go through** *vt insep* **1** *(undergo)* pasar por, sufrir, padecer. **2** *(examine)* examinar; *(search)* registrar; *(spend)* gastar; *(explain)* explicar.

▶ *vi (act, law)* ser aprobado,-a.

◆ **to go through with** *vt insep* llevar a cabo.

◆ **to go under** *vi* **1** *(ship)* hundirse. **2** *fig* fracasar.

◆ **to go up** *vi* **1** *(gen)* subir; *(approach)* acercarse. **2** *(curtain in theatre)* levantarse. **3** *(explode)* estallar; *(burst into flames)* prenderse fuego.

① *pt* went [went], *pp* gone [gɒn], *ger* going.

goal [gəʊl] *n* **1** SP *(area)* meta, portería. **2** SP *(point)* gol *m*, tanto. **3** *(aim)* fin *m*, objetivo, meta.

goalkeeper ['gəʊlkiːpəʳ] *n* portero,-a, guardameta *mf*.

goat [gəʊt] *n (female)* cabra; *(male)* macho cabrío.

goatee [gəʊtiː] *n (beard)* perilla.

gobble ['gɒbəl] *vt* engullir, zamparse.

god [gɒd] *n (deity, idol)* dios *m*.

▶ *n* God Dios *m*.

godchild ['gɒdtʃaɪld] *n* ahijado,-a.

① *pl* godchildren ['gɒdtʃɪldrən].

goddaughter ['gɒddɔːtəʳ] *n* ahijada.

goddess ['gɒdəs] *n* diosa.

godfather ['gɒdfɑːðəʳ] *n* padrino.

godmother ['gɒdmʌðəʳ] *n* madrina.

godparents ['gɒdpeərənts] *n pl* padrinos *mpl*.

godsend ['gɒdsend] *n* regalo llovido del cielo.

godson ['gɒdsʌn] *n* ahijado.

goggle ['gɒgəl] *vi* quedarse atónito,-a.

goggles ['gɒgəlz] *n pl* gafas *fpl* protectoras.

going ['gəʊɪŋ] *n* **1** *(departure)* ida, salida. **2** *(pace)* paso, ritmo. **3** *(path, road)* estado del camino.

▶ *adj* **1** *(price, rate)* actual, corriente. **2** *(business)* que marcha bien.

gold [gəʊld] *n (metal)* oro.

▶ *adj* **1** *(colour)* dorado,-a. **2** *(made of gold)* de oro.

golden ['gəʊldⁿn] *adj* **1** de oro. **2** *(colour)* dorado,-a. **3** *(hair)* rubio,-a.

goldfinch ['gəʊldfɪntʃ] *n* jilguero.

goldfish ['gəʊldfɪʃ] *n* pez *m* de colores.

① *pl* goldfish ['gəʊldfɪʃ].

goldsmith ['gəʊldsmɪθ] *n* orfebre *mf*.

golf [gɒlf] *n* golf *m*.

▶ *vi* jugar al golf. COMP **golf course** campo de golf.

golfer ['gɒlfəʳ] *n* jugador,-ra de golf.

gone [gɒn] *pp* → **go**.

▶ *adj* **1** *(time)* pasado,-a. **2** *(dead)* muerto,-a.

gong [gɒŋ] *n* **1** gong *m*. **2** *fam fig (award, prize)* galardón *m*.

good [gʊd] *adj* **1** bueno,-a; *(before m sing noun)* buen. **2** *(healthy)* sano,-a. **3** *(kind)* amable. **4** *(useful)* servible. LOC **for good** para siempre. COMP **Good Friday** Viernes *m* Santo.

① *comp* better, *superl* best.

▶ *n* bien *m*: *its for your own good* es por tu propio bien.

▶ *n pl* goods *(property)* bienes *mpl*; COMM *(in shop)* género *m sing*, artículos *mpl*; COMM *(merchandise)* mercancías *fpl*.

goodbye [gʊdˈbaɪ] [also written goodbye] *n* adiós *m*.

▶ *interj* ¡adiós!

good-for-nothing ['gʊdfənʌθɪŋ] *n* golfo.

good-hearted [gʊd'hɑːtɪd] *adj* de buen corazón.

good-humoured [gʊd'hjuːməd] *adj* de buen humor, campechano,-a.

good-looking [gʊd'lʊkɪŋ] *adj* guapo,-a, bien parecido,-a.

good-natured [gʊd'neɪtʃəd] *adj* bondadoso,-a.

goodness ['gʊdnəs] *n* **1** *(virtue)* bondad *f.* **2** *(in food)* lo nutritivo.

goodwill [gʊd'wɪl] *n* buena voluntad *f.*

goose [guːs] *n* ganso, oca.
ⓘ *pl* geese.

gooseberry ['gʊzbrɪ, 'guːsbᵊrɪ] *n* **1** BOT grosella espinosa. **2** GB *fam fig (person)* carabina.
ⓘ *pl* gooseberries.

gooseflesh ['guːsfleʃ] *n* piel *f* de gallina.

gore¹ [gɔːʳ] *n* sangre *f* derramada.

gore² [gɔːʳ] *vt* dar una cornada a.

gorge [gɔːdʒ] *n (mountain pass)* desfiladero; *(ravine)* barranco.

gorgeous ['gɔːdʒəs] *adj* **1** magnífico,-a, espléndido,-a. **2** *(person)* guapísimo,-a.
▶ *n fam* guapo,-a.

gorilla [gə'rɪlə] *n* ZOOL gorila *m.*

go-slow [gəʊ'sləʊ] *n* huelga de celo.

gospel ['gɒspᵊl] *n* **1** REL evangelio. **2** MUS música gospel.

gossip ['gɒsɪp] *n* **1** *(talk)* cotilleo, chismorreo. **2** *(person)* cotilla *mf*, chismoso,-a. **COMP** gossip column crónica de sociedad.
▶ *vi* cotillear, chismorrear.

got [gɒt] *pt & pp* → get.

Gothic ['gɒθɪk] *adj* **1** godo,-a. **2** *(language, architecture, type)* gótico,-a.

gotten ['gɒtᵊn] *pp* US → get.

gourmet ['gʊəmeɪ] *n* gastrónomo,-a, gurmet *mf.*

govern ['gʌvᵊn] *vt* **1** gobernar, dirigir. **2** LING regir. **3** *(determine)* dictar.
▶ *vi* **1** gobernar. **2** *(predominate)* predominar, prevalecer.

government ['gʌvᵊnmənt] *n* gobierno.
▶ *adj* **1** *(of government)* del gobierno, gubernamental. **2** *(of a governor)* del gobernador.

governmental [gʌvᵊn'mentᵊl] *adj* gubernamental.

governor ['gʌvᵊnəʳ] *n* **1** *(town, state, bank)* gobernador,-ra. **2** *(prison)* director,-ra. **3** *(school)* administrador,-ra. **4** GB *fam (employer)* jefe *m.*

gown [gaʊn] *n* **1** vestido largo. **2** *(judge's, academic's)* toga. **3** *(surgeon's)* bata.

GP ['dʒiː'piː] *abbr* (general practitioner) médico,-a de cabecera.
ⓘ *pl* GPs.

grab [græb] *vt* **1** *(seize, snatch)* coger, agarrar, asir. **2** *(capture, arrest)* pillar, coger. **3** *fam* entusiasmar.
ⓘ *pt & pp* grabbed, *ger* grabbing.

grace [greɪs] *n* **1** gracia, elegancia. **2** *(deportment)* garbo. **3** *(courtesy)* delicadeza, cortesía. **4** *(blessing)* bendición *f.* **5** REL gracia. **6** *(delay)* plazo.
▶ *vt* **1** *(adorn)* adornar. **2** *(honour)* honrar.

✖ Grace no significa 'gracia (chiste)', que se traduce por **joke**.

gracious ['greɪʃəs] *adj* **1** gracioso,-a. **2** *(polite)* cortés. **3** *(kind)* amable. **4** *(benevolent)* benévolo,-a.
▶ *interj* ¡Dios mío!.

✖ Gracious no significa 'gracioso (divertido)', que se traduce por **funny**.

grade [greɪd] *n* **1** *(degree, level)* grado. **2** *(quality)* calidad *f.* **3** *(class, category)* clase *f*, categoría. **4** *(rank)* rango, grado. **5** *(mark)* nota. **6** US *(gradient)* pendiente *f.* **7** US *(form)* clase *f.*
▶ *vt* **1** *(sort, classify)* clasificar. **2** *(road)* nivelar. **3** *(student)* calificar, poner una nota. **4** *(colours)* degradar.
◆ **to grade up** *vt sep* subir de categoría.
◆ **to grade down** *vt sep* bajar de categoría.

gradual ['grædjʊəl] *adj* gradual.

graduate [*(n)* 'grædjʊət; *(vb)* 'grædjʊeɪt] *n* EDUC *(after 3-year course)* diplomado,-a; *(after 5-year course)* licenciado,-a.
▶ *vt* *(grade, classify)* graduar.

▶ *vi (after 3-year course)* diplomarse (in, en); *(after 5-year course)* licenciarse (in, en).

graduation [grædjuˈeɪ[ə]n] *n* **1** EDUC graduación *f*. **2** TECH graduación *f*.

graft [grɑ:ft] *n (of plant, tissue)* injerto.
▶ *vt* injertar (onto, en).

grain [greɪn] *n* **1** *(gen)* grano. **2** *(cereals)* cereales *mpl*. **3** *(in wood)* veta, fibra; *(in stone)* filón *m*, veta; *(of leather)* flor *f*.
▶ *vt (give granular texture)* granular.

grammar ['græmə'] *n* gramática. LOC **grammar school** instituto de enseñanza media.

gramme [græm] *n* gramo.

granary ['grænərɪ] *n* granero.
ⓘ *pl* granaries.

grand [grænd] *adj* **1** *(splendid)* grandioso,-a, espléndido,-a, magnífico,-a. **2** *(impressive)* impresionante. **3** *(important - person)* distinguido,-a, importante. **4** *fam (great)* fenomenal. COMP **grand piano** piano de cola.

grandchild ['grænt[aɪld] *n* nieto,-a.
ⓘ *pl* grandchildren [grən't[ɪldrən].

granddad ['grændæd] *n fam* abuelo.

granddaughter ['grændɔ:tə'] *n* nieta.

grandfather ['grændfɑ:ðə'] *n* abuelo.

grandma ['grænmɑ:] *n fam* abuela.

grandmother ['grænmʌðə'] *n* abuela.

grandpa ['græmpɑ:] *n fam* abuelo.

grandparents ['grændpeərənts] *n pl* abuelos *mpl*.

grandson ['grændsʌn] *n* nieto.

granite ['grænɪt] *n* granito.
▶ *adj* de granito.

granny ['grænɪ] *n fam* abuela.
ⓘ *pl* grannies.

grant [grɑ:nt] *n* **1** EDUC beca. **2** *(subsidy)* subvención *f*. **3** JUR *(rights, property)* cesión *f*.
▶ *vt* **1** conceder, otorgar. **2** JUR ceder, transferir. LOC **to take STH for granted** dar ALGO por sentado.

granule ['grænju:l] *n* gránulo.

grape [greɪp] *n* uva.

grapefruit ['greɪpfru:t] *n* pomelo.
ⓘ *pl* grapefruits o grapefruit.

grapevine ['greɪpvaɪn] *n (gen)* parra; *(vine)* vid *f*.

graph [grɑ:f] *n* gráfica, gráfico. COMP **graph paper** papel cuadriculado.

graphic ['græfɪk] *adj* **1** *(gen)* gráfico,-a. **2** *(vivid)* muy gráfico,-a, vívido,-a.

graphite ['græfaɪt] *n* grafito.

grasp [grɑ:sp] *vt* **1** *(seize - with hands)* agarrar, asir; *(opportunity, offer)* aprovechar. **2** *(understand)* comprender, captar.

grass [grɑ:s] *n (plant)* hierba, yerba; *(lawn)* césped *m*; *(pasture)* pasto; *(dried)* paja.

grasshopper ['grɑ:shɒpə'] *n* saltamontes *m*.

grassy ['grɑ:sɪ] *adj* cubierto,-a de hierba.
ⓘ *comp* grassier, *superl* grassiest.

grate¹ [greɪt] *vt* **1** CULIN rallar. **2** *(scrape - gen)* rascar; *(- teeth)* hacer rechinar.

grate² [greɪt] *n (metal frame)* rejilla; *(fireplace)* chimenea.

grateful ['greɪtful] *adj (person)* agradecido,-a; *(letter, smile)* de agradecimiento.

grater ['greɪtə'] *n* rallador *m*.

gratification [grætɪfɪ'keɪ[ə]n] *n* gratificación *f*, satisfacción *f*, placer *m*.

gratify ['grætɪfaɪ] *vt* **1** *(satisfy - desire, etc)* satisfacer. **2** *(give pleasure to)* complacer, gratificar.
ⓘ *pt & pp* gratified, *ger* gratifying.

gratitude ['grætɪtju:d] *n* gratitud *f*, agradecimiento.

gratuitous [grə'tju:ɪtəs] *adj* gratuito,-a.

❌ Gratuitous no significa 'gratuito (gratis)', que se traduce por free.

grave¹ [greɪv] *n* tumba, sepultura.

grave² [greɪv] *adj* **1** *(gen)* grave. **2** [grɑ:v] *(accent)* grave.

gravel ['græv[ə]l] *n* grava, gravilla, guijo.

gravestone ['greɪvstəun] *n* lápida.

graveyard ['greɪvjɑ:d] *n* cementerio.

gravity ['grævɪtɪ] *n* **1** PHYS gravedad *f*. **2** *(seriousness)* gravedad *f*; *(of person, manner)* gravedad *f*, circunspección *f*.

gray [greɪ] *adj* US → grey.

graze¹ [greɪz] *n* rasguño, roce *m*.

graze² [greɪz] *vt (sheep, cattle)* pastar, pastorear, apacentar.

grease [gri:s] *n (gen)* grasa.
▶ *vt (part of car, machine, device)* engrasar.

greasy ['gri:sɪ] adj 1 (oily - hands) grasiento,-a. 3 fam pej (smarmy) pelota. ⓘ comp greasier, superl greasiest.

great [greɪt] adj 1 (gen) grande; (before sing noun) gran. 2 fam (excellent, wonderful) estupendo,-a, fantástico,-a, sensacional, fabuloso,-a.
▶ adv fam muy bien, estupendamente, fenomenal.

great-grandchild [greɪt'græntʃaɪld] n bisnieto,-a, biznieto,-a.
ⓘ pl great-grandchildren [greɪtgrən'tʃɪldrən].

great-grandfather [greɪt'grændfɑ:ðəʳ] n bisabuelo.

great-grandmother [greɪt'grænmʌðəʳ] n bisabuela.

Greece [gri:s] n Grecia.

greed [gri:d] n 1 (for money, power) codicia, avaricia. 2 (for food) gula, glotonería.

greedy ['gri:dɪ] adj 1 (for money, power) codicioso,-a. 2 (for food) glotón,-ona. ⓘ comp greedier, superl greediest.

Greek [gri:k] adj griego,-a.
▶ n 1 (person) griego,-a. 2 (language) griego.

green [gri:n] adj 1 (colour) verde. 2 (environment friendly) ecológico,-a. 4 (pale) pálido,-a 5 (inexperienced) novato,-a, verde; (gullible) ingenuo,-a, crédulo,-a. 6 (jealous) envidioso,-a.
▶ n 1 (colour) verde m. 2 (stretch of grass) césped m; (in golf) green m; (in village) césped público .
▶ n pl greens (vegetables) verduras fpl.
▶ n pl the Greens POL los verdes mpl.

greenfly ['gri:nflaɪ] n pulgón m.
ⓘ pl greenflies.

greengrocer ['gri:ngrəʊsəʳ] n verdulero,-a. LOC greengrocer's (shop) verdulería.

greenhouse ['gri:nhaʊs] n invernadero. COMP greenhouse effect efecto invernadero.

Greenland ['gri:nlənd] n Groenlandia.

Greenlander ['gri:nləndəʳ] n groenlandés,-esa.

greet [gri:t] vt 1 (wave at, say hello to) saludar; (welcome) dar la bienvenida a; (receive) recibir. 2 (react) acoger, recibir. 3 fig (meet) llegar, presentarse.

greeting ['gri:tɪŋ] n saludo.
▶ n pl greetings saludos mpl, recuerdos mpl.

gregarious [gre'geərɪəs] adj gregario,-a, sociable.

gremlin ['gremlɪn] n duende m.

Grenada [grə'neɪdə] n Granada.

grenade [grə'neɪd] n granada.

grew [gru:] pt → grow.

grey [greɪ] adj 1 (colour) gris; (hair) cano,-a; (sky) nublado,-a, gris. 2 (gloomy) triste, gris.
▶ n 1 (colour) gris m. 2 (horse) caballo tordo. LOC to go grey encanecer.

greyhound ['greɪhaʊnd] n galgo.

grid [grɪd] n 1 (grating) reja, parrilla, rejilla. 2 ELEC (network) red f nacional de tendido eléctrico. 3 (on map) cuadrícula.

griddle ['grɪdəl] n CULIN plancha.

grief [gri:f] n dolor m, pena.

grieve [gri:v] vt afligir, apenar, dar pena a, entristecer.
▶ vi apenarse, afligirse.

grill [grɪl] n CULIN (over cooker) gratinador m, grill m; (on charcoal) parrilla. 4 → grille.

grille [grɪl] n reja.

grim [grɪm] adj 1 (serious) austero,-a, severo,-a; (look) ceñudo,-a. 2 (unpleasant) horroroso,-a, pesimista; (- prospect, outlook) nefasto,-a, desalentador,-ra; (- reality) crudo,-a, duro,-a. 3 (gloomy - landscape, place) lúgubre, sombrío,-a. ⓘ comp grimmer, superl grimmest.

grimace ['grɪməs] n mueca.

grin [grɪn] n (genuine) sonrisa (abierta); (mocking) sonrisa burlona.
▶ vi sonreír (abiertamente). ⓘ pt & pp grinned, ger grinning.

grind [graɪnd] vt 1 (mill) moler; (crush) machacar, triturar; (lens, mirror) pulir; (knife, blade) afilar. 2 US (mince - beef) picar. 3 (teeth) rechinar. 4 (press down hard on) incrustar, aplastar; (press in) meter.
▶ vi 1 (crush) triturarse. 2 (make harsh noise) rechinar. 3 US (swot) empollar. ⓘ pt & pp ground [graʊnd].
▶ n 1 fam (work) trabajo pesado; (effort) paliza. 2 US fam (swot) empollón,-ona.
◆ to grind down vt sep oprimir.
◆ to grind out vt sep (music) tocar.

grinder ['graɪndə'] n (machine - for coffee) molinillo; (person - for knives, etc) afilador,-ra.

grindstone ['graɪnstəʊn] n muela, piedra de afilar.

gringo ['grɪŋgəʊ] n pej gringo,-a.
ⓘ pl gringos.

grip [grɪp] n 1 (tight hold) asimiento. 2 (of tyre) adherencia, agarre m. 3 fig (control, force) control m, dominio. 4 SP (way of holding) la forma en que uno coge la raqueta, etc; (part of handle) asidero, empuñadura. 5 (hairgrip) horquilla.
▶ vt 1 (hold tightly - gen) agarrar, asir, sujetar. 2 (adhere to) tener agarre, agarrarse, adherirse. 3 fig (film, story, play) captar el interés de, captar la atención de.
▶ vi adherirse.
ⓘ pt & pp gripped, ger gripping.

grit [grɪt] n 1 (fine) arena; (coarse) gravilla; (dirt) polvo. 2 fam (determination) valor m, agallas fpl.

grizzly ['grɪzlɪ] [also grizzly bear] n oso pardo.

groan [grəʊn] n 1 gemido, quejido. 2 (creak) crujido.
▶ vi 1 (in pain) gemir, quejarse; (with disapproval) gruñir. 2 (creak) crujir.

grocer ['grəʊsə'] n tendero,-a. COMP grocer's (shop) tienda de comestibles.

groceries ['grəʊsərɪz] n pl comestibles mpl.

grocery ['grəʊsərɪ] n US tienda de ultramarinos, tienda de comestibles.
ⓘ pl groceries.

groggy ['grɒgɪ] adj fam grogui.
ⓘ comp groggier, superl groggiest.

groin [grɔɪn] n ANAT ingle f.

groom [gruːm] n 1 (bridegroom) novio. 2 (for horses) mozo de cuadra.

✎ Se usa para referirse al novio sólo durante el día de la boda. Es la forma abreviada de bridegroom.

groove [gruːv] n 1 (gen) ranura; (for door) guía; (in column) acanaladura. 2 (on record) surco.

groovy ['gruːvɪ] adj fam guay, genial.
ⓘ comp groovier, superl grooviest.

grope [grəʊp] vi andar a tientas.

gross [grəʊs] adj 1 (flagrant - injustice) flagrante; (- ignorance) craso,-a; (- error) grave. 2 (fat) muy gordo,-a, obeso,-a. 3 (behaviour, manners) grosero,-a, tosco,-a; (- language) soez; (disgusting) asqueroso,-a. 4 FIN (total) bruto,-a.
▶ vt (person) obtener unos ingresos brutos de; (film, etc) recaudar.

grotesque [grəʊˈtesk] adj grotesco,-a.

grotto ['grɒtəʊ] n gruta.
ⓘ pl grottoes o grottos.

ground¹ [graʊnd] n 1 (surface of earth) suelo; (soil, earth) tierra; (terrain, land) campo, terreno. 2 US (electrical) tierra. 3 ART (background) fondo. 4 (matter, subject) aspecto, punto. COMP ground floor planta baja.
▶ n pl grounds (reason, justification) razón f, motivo; (of coffee) poso, posos mpl; (gardens) jardines mpl; (area of land) terreno.

ground² [graʊnd] pt & pp → grind.
▶ adj 1 (coffee) molido,-a. 2 US (beef) picado,-a.

grounding ['graʊndɪŋ] n base f, conocimientos mpl.

groundwork ['graʊndwɜːk] n trabajo preliminar, trabajo preparatorio.

group [gruːp] n grupo.
▶ vt agrupar.

grouper ['gruːpə'] n mero.

groupie ['gruːpɪ] n fam grupi mf.

grow [grəʊ] vi 1 (gen) crecer. 2 (increase) aumentar. 3 (become) hacerse, volverse. 4 (begin gradually) llegar a. LOC to grow old envejecer.
▶ vt 1 (crop, plant, flower) cultivar. 2 (beard, etc) dejarse (crecer); (hair, nails) dejarse crecer.
◆ to grow into vt insep (become) convertirse en, hacerse.
◆ to grow on vt insep llegar a gustar.
◆ to grow up vi 1 (become adult) hacerse mayor; (spend childhood) criarse, crecer. 2 (spring up) surgir, nacer, desarrollarse.
ⓘ pt grew [gruː], pp grown [grəʊn].

grower ['grəʊə'] n (farmer) cultivador,-ra.

growl [graʊl] n gruñido.
▶ vi gruñir.

grown [grəʊn] pp → grow.
▶ adj adulto,-a.

grown-up ['grəʊnʌp] *adj* mayor, adulto,-a.

► *n* persona mayor.

growth [grəʊθ] *n* **1** *(gen)* crecimiento; *(increase)* aumento; *(development)* desarrollo. **2** MED *(tumour)* bulto, tumor *m*. **3** *(of beard)* barba.

grub [grʌb] *n* *(larva)* larva, gusano.

► *vi* **1** *(by digging)* escarbar, hurgar. **2** *fig* rebuscar.

ⓘ *pt & pp* grubbed, *ger* grubbing.

grudge [grʌdʒ] *n* rencor *m*.

► *vt* **1** *(begrudge, resent)* dar a regañadientes, dar de mala gana. **2** *(envy)* envidiar.

grumble ['grʌmbəl] *n* **1** *(complaint)* queja. **2** *(of thunder)* estruendo.

► *vi* **1** *(moan, complain)* refunfuñar, quejarse *(about,* de*)*. **2** *(rumble - thunder)* retumbar; *(- stomach)* hacer ruido.

grumpy ['grʌmpɪ] *adj* gruñón,-ona, malhumorado,-a, de mal humor.

ⓘ *comp* grumpier, *superl* grumpiest.

grunge [grʌndʒ] *n* MUS grunge *m*.

grunt [grʌnt] *n* gruñido.

► *vi* gruñir.

guarantee [gærən'tiː] *n* *(gen)* garantía; *(certificate)* certificado de garantía.

► *vt* **1** *(gen)* garantizar; *(assure, promise)* asegurar. **2** *(debt)* avalar, garantizar.

guard [gɑːd] *n* **1** *(sentry, soldier)* guardia *mf*; *(security guard)* guarda *mf*, guarda jurado,-a, guarda de seguridad; *(prison officer)* carcelero,-a. **2** *(duty)* guardia. **3** GB *(on train)* jefe,-a de tren. **4** *(on machine)* dispositivo de seguridad; *(on gun)* seguro. LOC **to be on guard** estar de guardia. ‖ **to stand guard** montar guardia.

► *vt* **1** *(watch over)* vigilar; *(protect - person, reputation)* proteger; *(keep - secret)* guardar. **2** *(control - tongue)* cuidar, controlar.

☒ To guard no significa 'guardar (en un sitio)', que se traduce por to put away.

guardian ['gɑːdɪən] *n* **1** *(defender)* guardián,-ana, defensor,-ra. **2** JUR *(of child)* tutor,-ra.

guava ['gwɑːvə] *n* *(fruit)* guayaba.

guess [ges] *n* *(conjecture)* conjetura; *(estimate)* cálculo. LOC **to have a guess** adivinar.

► *vt* **1** *(gen)* adivinar. **2** US *fam (suppose)* suponer, pensar, creer.

► *vi* adivinar.

guesswork ['geswɜːk] *n* conjeturas *fpl*, suposiciones *fpl*.

guest [gest] *n* **1** *(at home, restaurant, etc)* invitado,-a; *(in hotel)* cliente,-a, huésped,-da. **2** *(on TV programme)* invitado,-a.

guesthouse ['gesthaʊs] *n* casa de huéspedes, pensión *f*.

guestroom ['gestruːm] *n* cuarto de (los) invitados.

Guiana [gar'ænə, gɪ'ɑːnə] *n* Guayana.

guidance ['gaɪdəns] *n* *(help, advice)* orientación *f*, consejos *mpl*.

guide [gaɪd] *n* **1** *(person)* guía *mf*. **2** *(book)* guía. **3** *(indicator)* guía, modelo. COMP **guide dog** perro lazarillo.

► *vt* **1** *(show the way)* guiar; *(lead)* conducir. **2** *(advise, influence)* orientar, aconsejar.

guidebook ['gaɪdbʊk] *n* guía.

guideline ['gaɪdlaɪn] *n* pauta, directriz *f*.

guiding ['gaɪdɪŋ] *adj* que guía, que sirve de guía.

guild [gɪld] *n* *(of workers)* gremio; *(association)* asociación *f*, agrupación *f*.

guillotine ['gɪlətiːn] *n* guillotina.

► *vt* *(person, paper)* guillotinar.

guilt [gɪlt] *n* **1** JUR culpabilidad *f*. **2** *(blame)* culpa; *(remorse)* remordimiento.

guilty ['gɪltɪ] *adj* culpable *(of,* de*)*. LOC **to find SB guilty** declarar culpable a ALGN.

ⓘ *comp* guiltier, *superl* guiltiest.

Guinea ['gɪnɪ] *n* Guinea. COMP **Equatorial Guinea** Guinea Ecuatorial. ‖ **New Guinea** Nueva Guinea.

guinea ['gɪnɪ] *n* *(coin)* guinea. COMP **guinea fowl** gallina de Guinea, pintada. ‖ **guinea pig** conejillo de Indias, cobaya.

Guinea-Bissau [gɪnɪbɪ'saʊ] *n* Guinea Bissau.

Guinean ['gɪnɪən] *adj* guineano,-a.

► *n* guineano,-a.

guitar [gɪ'tɑːr] *n* guitarra.

guitarist [gɪ'tɑːrɪst] *n* guitarrista *mf*.

gulf [gʌlf] *n* **1** GEOG golfo. **2** *fig* abismo. COMP **Gulf of Mexico** golfo de Méjico. ‖ **Persian Gulf** golfo Pérsico. ‖ **Gulf Stream** corriente *f* del Golfo.

gull [gʌl] *n* gaviota.

gulley ['gʌlɪ] *n* → gully.

gullible ['gʌlɪbºl] *adj* crédulo,-a.

gully ['gʌlɪ] *n* **1** GEOG *(small valley, ravine)* barranco, torrentera. **2** *(deep ditch, waterway, channel)* surco, cauce *m*.
ⓘ *pl* gullies.

gulp [gʌlp] *n (of drink)* trago; *(of air)* bocanada: *he drank his glass in one gulp* se bebió todo el vaso de un trago.
► *vt (drink)* beberse de un trago (down, -); *(food)* engullir (down, -).
► *vi (swallow air)* tragar aire; *(with fear)* tragar saliva.
◆ **to gulp back** *vt insep* tragarse.

gum¹ [gʌm] *n* ANAT encía.

gum² [gʌm] *n* **1** *(natural substance)* goma, resina. **2** *(chewing gum)* chicle *m*. **3** *(glue)* goma (de pegar), pegamento.
► *vt* pegar (con goma).
ⓘ *pt & pp* gummed, *ger* gumming

gumboil ['gʌmbɔɪl] *n* flemón *m*.

gumboot ['gʌmbuːt] *n* bota de agua.

gumtree ['gʌmtriː] *n* gomero, árbol *m* del caucho.

gun [gʌn] *n* **1** *(gen)* arma de fuego; *(handgun)* pistola, revólver *m*; *(rifle)* rifle *m*, fusil *m*; *(shotgun)* escopeta; *(cannon)* cañón *m*. **2** SP pistola.

gunboat ['gʌnbəʊt] *n (lancha)* cañonera.

gunfire ['gʌnfaɪəʳ] *n (gen)* fuego, disparos *mpl*; *(shooting)* tiroteo; *(shellfire)* cañoneo, cañonazos *mpl*.

gunman ['gʌnmən] *n* pistolero.
ⓘ *pl* gunmen ['gʌnmən].

gunner ['gʌnəʳ] *n* artillero.

gunpoint ['gʌnpɔɪnt] LOC **at gunpoint** a punta de pistola.

gunpowder ['gʌnpaʊdəʳ] *n* pólvora.

gunshot ['gʌnʃɒt] *n* disparo, tiro.

guru ['guːruː] *n* gurú *m*.

gush [gʌʃ] *n* chorro, borbotón *m*.
► *vi* **1** *(liquid)* salir a borbotones. **2** *(person)* ser efusivo,-a: *everyone was gushing over her new baby* todos se deshacían en elogios con su nuevo bebé.
► *vt* chorrear, derramar.

gust [gʌst] *n* **1** *(of wind)* ráfaga, racha; *(of rain)* chaparrón *m*. **2** *fig (of anger)* arrebato: *gust of laughter* carcajada.
► *vi* soplar.

gut [gʌt] *n* **1** ANAT intestino. **2** *fam (belly)* barriga, tripa.
► *n pl (entrails)* entrañas *fpl*, tripas *fpl*; *fam (courage)* agallas *fpl*: *it takes guts to do what you did* hay que tener agallas para hacer lo que hiciste.

gutter ['gʌtəʳ] *n (in street)* arroyo, cuneta; *(on roof)* canal *m*, canalón *m*. COMP **gutter press** prensa amarilla.

guy [gaɪ] *n* **1** *fam (man)* tipo, tío: *he's a great guy* es un tío estupendo; *a tough guy* un tipo duro. **2** US *fam (person)* tío,-a: *come on you guys* venga tíos. COMP **Guy Fawkes Night** → Bonfire night.

Guyana [gaɪˈænə] *n* Guyana, Guayana.

Guyanan [gaɪˈænən] *adj-n* → Guyanese.

guzzle ['gʌzºl] *vt fam (eat)* zamparse, engullirse; *(drink)* chupar, tragar.
► *vi fam (eat)* engullir; *(drink)* chupar, tragar.

gym [dʒɪm] *n* **1** *fam (gymnasium)* gimnasio. **2** *(gymnastics)* gimnasia.

gymkhana [dʒɪmˈkɑːnə] *n* gymkhana.

gymnasium [dʒɪmˈneɪzɪəm] *n* gimnasio.
ⓘ *pl* gymnasiums o gymnasia [dʒɪmˈneɪzɪə].

gymnast ['dʒɪmnæst] *n* gimnasta *mf*.

gymnastics [dʒɪmˈnæstɪks] *n* gimnasia.

gymnosperm ['dʒɪmnəʊspɜːm] *n* gimnospermo.

gynaecological [gaɪnəkəˈlɒdʒɪkºl] *adj* ginecológico,-a.

gynaecologist [gaɪnɪˈkɒlədʒɪst] *n* ginecólogo,-a.

gynaecology [gaɪnɪˈkɒlədʒɪ] *n* ginecología.

gypsum ['dʒɪpsəm] *n* yeso.

gypsy ['dʒɪpsɪ] *n* gitano,-a.
ⓘ *pl* gypsies.
► *adj* gitano,-a.

gyroscope ['dʒaɪrəskəʊp] *n* giroscopio, giróscopo.

G

H, h [eɪtʃ] *n (the letter)* H, h *f*.
habit ['hæbɪt] *n* **1** *(custom)* hábito, costumbre *f*. **2** REL *(garment)* hábito.
habitable ['hæbɪtəbəl] *adj* habitable.
habitat ['hæbɪtæt] *n* hábitat *m*.
habitual [hə'bɪtʃuəl] *adj* **1** *(usual)* habitual. **2** *(liar, etc)* empedernido,-a.
hack [hæk] *vt* **1** *(cut)* cortar. **2** COMPUT *(cut)* cortar.
hacker ['hækə'] *n fam (in computers)* pirata *mf*.
had [hæd] *pt & pp* → have.
haddock ['hædək] *n (fish)* eglefino.
hadn't ['hæd] *pt* → have.
haematoma [hi:mə'təʊmə] *n* hematoma *mf*.
haemorrhage ['hemərɪdʒ] *n* hemorragia.
haggis ['hægɪs] *n* CULIN *plato típico escocés hecho con las asaduras del cordero*.
haggle ['hægəl] *vi* regatear (**over**, -).
hail¹ [heɪl] *n (greeting)* saludo; *(shout)* grito.
▶ *vi* **1** *(call a taxi)* llamar. **2** *(acclaim)* aclamar.
hail² [heɪl] *n* **1** METEOR granizo. **2** *fig* lluvia.
▶ *vi* METEOR granizar.
hailstone ['heɪlstəʊn] *n* granizo.
hailstorm ['heɪlstɔ:m] *n* granizada.
hair [heə'] *n* **1** *(on head)* cabello, pelo. **2** *(on body)* vello. **3** *(horse's mane)* crin *f*.
hairbrush ['heəbrʌʃ] *n* cepillo para el pelo.
haircut ['heəkʌt] *n* corte *m* de pelo. LOC **to have a haircut** cortarse el pelo.
hairdresser ['heədresə'] *n* peluquero,-a. COMP **hairdresser's** peluquería.
hairdryer ['heədraɪə'] *n* secador *m* (de pelo).

hairspray ['heəspreɪ] *n* laca para el pelo.
hairstyle ['heəstaɪl] *n* peinado.
hairy ['heərɪ] *adj* **1** peludo,-a. **2** *fig (scary)* espeluznante, espantoso,-a.
ⓘ *comp* hairier, *superl* hairiest.
Haiti ['heɪtɪ] *n* Haití *m*.
Haitian ['heɪʃⁿn] *adj* haitiano,-a.
▶ *n* haitiano,-a.
hake [heɪk] *n (fish)* merluza; *(young)* pescadilla.
half [hɑ:f] *n* **1** mitad *f*: *a kilo and a half* un kilo y medio. **2** SP *(period)* parte *f*, mitad *f*, tiempo. **3** *(beer)* media pinta.
ⓘ *pl* halves.
▶ *adj* medio,-a: *he´s been gone for half an hour* lleva fuera media hora. COMP **half board** media pensión *f*. ▌ **half term** *vacaciones que se hacen a mitad de trimestre*.
▶ *adv* medio, a medias: *she´s half Spanish* es medio española. LOC **half past** y media: *it's half past two* son las dos y media.

⊕ **Half term** es una semana de vacaciones que los colegios británicos tienen a mediados de cada trimestre.

half-day [hɑ:f'deɪ] *n* media jornada.
half-mast [hɑ:f'mɑ:st] *phr* **at half-mast** a media asta.
half-note ['hɑ:fnəʊt] *n* US blanca.
half-time [hɑ:f'taɪm] *n* SP descanso, media parte *f*.
halfway ['hɑ:fweɪ] *adj* medio,-a, intermedio,-a.
▶ *adv* a medio camino.
hall [hɔ:l] *n* **1** *(entrance)* vestíbulo, entrada. **2** *(for concerts, etc)* sala. **3** *(mansion)* casa solariega, mansión *f*. **4** US *(corridor)* pasillo, corredor *m*.
hallo [hə'ləʊ] *interj* → hello.

Halloween [hæləʊˈiːn] n víspera de Todos los Santos.

🌐 Halloween es la fiesta de la víspera de Todos los Santos. Los niños se disfrazan y van de casa en casa. Cuando les abren la puerta dicen «trick or treat!» (truco o trato) y la gente les da golosinas.

hallucinate [həˈluːsɪneɪt] vi alucinar.
hallway [ˈhɔːlweɪ] n US vestíbulo.
halo [ˈheɪləʊ] n 1 (round moon, etc) halo. 2 REL aureola.
ⓘ pl haloes o halos.
halogen [ˈhælədʒen] n halógeno.
halt [hɔːlt] n 1 alto, parada. 2 (railway) apeadero.
▶ vt parar, detener, interrumpir.
halve [hɑːv] vt 1 (cut in two) partir en dos. 2 (reduce) reducir a la mitad. 3 (share) compartir. 4 (golf) empatar.
halves [hɑːvz] n pl → halt.
ham [hæm] n (food) jamón m.
hamburger [ˈhæmbɜːgər] n (food) hamburguesa.

✎ Lo más habitual es llamar burger a la hamburguesa.

hamlet [ˈhæmlət] n aldea.
hammer [ˈhæmər] n 1 (tool, bone) martillo. 2 (gun) percutor m.
▶ vt 1 (gen) martillar, martillear; (nail) clavar. 2 fam (beat) dar una paliza, machacar.
hammock [ˈhæmək] n 1 hamaca. 2 MAR coy m.
hamster [ˈhæmstər] n ZOOL hámster m.
hand [hænd] n 1 mano f. 2 (worker) trabajador,-ra, operario,-a; (sailor) tripulante mf, marinero,-a. 3 (of clock) manecilla, aguja. 4 (handwriting) letra. 5 (of cards) mano f, cartas fpl. 6 (applause) aplauso. LOC at hand a mano. ‖ hands up! ¡manos arriba! ‖ on the one hand por un lado ‖ by hand a mano ‖ on the other hand por otro lado ‖ to lend a hand echar una mano.
◆ to hand back vt sep devolver.
◆ to hand in vt sep (work, etc) entregar; (resignation, etc) presentar, notificar.

◆ to hand on vt sep (traditions, etc) transmitir, heredar; (give) pasar, dar.
◆ to hand out vt sep (distribute) repartir, distribuir; (give - gen) dar; (- punishment) aplicar.
◆ to hand over vt sep (give) entregar; (one's possessions, etc) ceder.
handbag [ˈhændbæg] n bolso.
handball [ˈhændbɔːl] n SP balonmano.
handbook [ˈhændbʊk] n (guidebook) guía; (reference book) manual m.
handbrake [ˈhændbreɪk] n freno de mano.
handcuff [ˈhændkʌf] vt esposar.
▶ n pl handcuffs esposas fpl.
handful [ˈhændfʊl] n puñado.
handicap [ˈhændɪkæp] n 1 (physical) discapacidad f; (mental) deficiencia, disminución f psíquica. 2 (in sport) handicap m. 3 fig obstáculo
▶ vt obstaculizar, impedir.
ⓘ pt & pp handicapped, ger handicapping.
handicapped [ˈhændɪkæpt] adj 1 (physically) minusválido,-a, discapacitado,-a, disminuido,-a físico,-a; (mentally) disminuido,-a psíquico,-a. 2 fig desfavorecido,-a.
handicraft [ˈhændɪkrɑːft] n 1 (job, art) artesanía; (objects) objetos mpl de artesanía. 2 (manual skill) habilidad f manual.
handkerchief [ˈhæŋkətʃiːf] n pañuelo.
ⓘ pl handkerchiefs o handkerchieves.
handle [ˈhændəl] n 1 (of door) pomo, manilla. 2 (of drawer) tirador m. 3 (of cup) asa. 4 (of knife) mango. 5 (lever) palanca. 6 (crank) manivela.
▶ vt 1 (gen) manejar, manipular. 2 (people) tratar. 3 (tolerate) aguantar. 4 (control) controlar, dominar. 5 (manage) poder con, tener la capacidad para.
handlebar [ˈhændəlbɑːr] n manillar m.
handmade [hændˈmeɪd] adj hecho,-a a mano.
handout [ˈhændaʊt] n 1 (leaflet) folleto, prospecto; (political) octavilla. 2 EDUC material m. 3 (press) nota de prensa.

handshake [ˈhændʃeɪk] *n* apretón *m* de manos.

handsome [ˈhænsəm] *adj* **1** *(man)* apuesto, guapo; *(woman)* bella, guapa. **2** *(elegant)* elegante. **3** *(generous)* considerable, generoso,-a.

hands-on [ˈhændzɒn] *adj (for computers)* práctico,-a.

handstand [ˈhændstænd] *n* LOC **to do a handstand** hacer el pino.

handwriting [ˈhændraɪtɪŋ] *n* letra, escritura.

handy [ˈhændɪ] *adj* **1** *(person)* hábil. **2** *(close at hand)* a mano, cercano,-a. **3** *(useful)* práctico,-a, cómodo,-a, útil.
① *comp* handier, *superl* handiest.

handyman [ˈhændɪmæn] *n* manitas *mf*.
① *pl* handymen [ˈhændɪmən].

hang [hæŋ] *vt* **1** [*pt & pp* hung [hʌŋ]] *(gen)* colgar. **2** [*pt & pp* hung [hʌŋ]] *(wallpaper)* colocar. **3** [*pt & pp* hanged.] JUR ahorcar.
▶ *n (of dress, etc)* caída.
◆ **to hang about / hang around** *vi* **1** esperar. **2** *(waste time)* perder el tiempo.
▶ *vt insep* frecuentar.
◆ **to hang back** *vi* **1** quedarse atrás. **2** *fig* vacilar.
◆ **to hang down** *vi* colgar, caer.
◆ **to hang on** *vi* **1** *(hold tight)* agarrarse. **2** *(wait)* esperar.
◆ **to hang out** *vt sep (washing)* tender.
▶ *vi fam* soler estar.
◆ **to hang up** *vt sep* colgar.

hangar [ˈhæŋəʳ] *n* hangar *m*.

hanger [ˈhæŋəʳ] *n* percha *f*.

hang-glider [ˈhæŋɡlaɪdəʳ] *n* ala delta.

hang-gliding [ˈhæŋɡlaɪdɪŋ] *n* ala *m* delta.

hangover [ˈhæŋəʊvəʳ] *n* **1** *(after too much drinking)* resaca. **2** *(remains)* resto, vestigio.

happen [ˈhæpən] *vi* **1** *(occur)* ocurrir, pasar, suceder. **2** *(by chance)* dar la casualidad de.

happening [ˈhæpənɪŋ] *n* acontecimiento.

happily [ˈhæpɪlɪ] *adv* **1** *(in a happy way)* felizmente, con alegría. **2** *(luckily)* afortunadamente.

happiness [ˈhæpɪnəs] *n* felicidad *f*, alegría.

happy [ˈhæpɪ] *adj* **1** *(cheerful)* feliz, alegre, dichoso,-a, afortunado,-a. **2** *(glad)* contento,-a, satisfecho,-a. LOC **happy birthday!** ¡feliz cumpleaños!
① *comp* happier, *superl* happiest.

harass [ˈhærəs] *vt* **1** acosar, hostigar. **2** *(military)* hostilizar, hostigar. **3** *(worries, problems)* atormentar, agobiar.

harassment [ˈhærəsmənt] *n* acoso, hostigamiento.

harbor [ˈhɑːbəʳ] *n* US → harbour.

harbour [ˈhɑːbəʳ] *n* puerto.
▶ *vt* **1** *(criminal)* encubrir. **2** *(doubts)* abrigar. **3** *(suspicions)* tener; *(contain, hide)* contener, esconder.

hard [hɑːd] *adj* **1** *(gen)* duro,-a; *(solid)* sólido,-a. **2** *(difficult)* difícil. **3** *(harsh)* severo,-a. **4** *(work)* arduo,-a, agotador,-ra. **5** *(final decision)* definitivo,-a, irrevocable; *(person)* severo,-a, inflexible. **6** LING fuerte. LOC **hard of hearing** duro,-a de oído. ‖ **to work hard** trabajar mucho. COMP **hard court** pista dura. ‖ **hard disk** disco duro. ‖ **hard labour** trabajos forzados.
▶ *adv (forcibly)* fuerte; *(diligently)* mucho, concienzudamente, con ahínco.

harden [ˈhɑːdən] *vt* **1** endurecer. **2** *fig* insensibilizar.

hardly [ˈhɑːdlɪ] *adv (scarcely)* apenas, casi; *(not easily)* difícilmente.

hardness [ˈhɑːdnəs] *n* dureza.

hardware [ˈhɑːdweəʳ] *n* **1** *(goods)* artículos *mpl* de ferretería. **2** COMPUT hardware *m*, soporte *m* físico. COMP **hardware store** ferretería.

hard-working [ˈhɑːdˈwɜːkɪŋ] *adj* trabajador,-ra.

hare [heəʳ] *n* ZOOL liebre *f*.
▶ *vi* correr muy deprisa.

haricot bean [ˈhærɪkəʊbiːn] *n* alubia, judía.

harm [hɑːm] *n* mal *m*, daño.
▶ *vt* dañar, perjudicar. LOC **to do SB harm** hacerle daño a ALGN. ‖ **there's no harm in...** no se pierda nada...

harmful [ˈhɑːmfʊl] *adj* dañino,-a, nocivo,-a, perjudicial.

harmless ['hɑːmləs] *adj* inocuo,-a, inofensivo,-a.

harmonic [hɑːˈmɒnɪk] *adj* armónico,-a.

harmony ['hɑːmənɪ] *n* armonía.
ⓘ *pl* harmonies.

harp [hɑːp] *n* MUS arpa.

harpist ['hɑːpɪst] *n* MUS arpista *mf*.

harpoon [hɑːˈpuːn] *n* arpón *m*.
► *vt* arponear.

harsh [hɑːʃ] *adj* **1** *(cruel)* cruel, duro,-a, severo,-a. **2** *(sound)* discordante. **3** *(rough)* áspero,-a.

harvest ['hɑːvɪst] *n* **1** *(gen)* cosecha, siega. **2** *(grapes)* vendimia.
► *vt* **1** cosechar, recoger. **2** *(grapes)* vendimiar.

harvester ['hɑːvɪstər] *n* **1** *(person)* segador,-ra. **2** *(machine)* segadora, cosechadora.

has [hæz] *pres* → have.

haste [heɪst] *n* prisa, precipitación *f*.

hasten ['heɪsən] *vi* darse prisa.

hastily ['heɪstɪlɪ] *adv (quickly)* de prisa.

hat [hæt] *n* sombrero.

hatch [hætʃ] *n* **1** *(on ship)* escotilla. **2** *(of chickens, brood)* pollada.
► *vt* **1** *(eggs)* empollar, incubar. **2** *fig (plot, plan)* idear, tramar.
► *vi* salir del cascarón, salir del huevo.

hate [heɪt] *n* odio.
► *vt* **1** *fam (detest)* odiar, detestar, aborrecer. **2** *fam (regret)* lamentar, sentir.

hatred ['heɪtrəd] *n* odio.

haul [hɔːl] *n* **1** *(distance)* recorrido, camino. **3** *(fish)* redada. **4** *(loot)* botín *m*.
► *vt* **1** *(drag)* tirar de, arrastrar. **2** *(boat)* halar; *(car, caravan, etc)* remolcar.

haunt [hɔːnt] *n (of people)* sitio preferido; *(of criminals, animals)* guarida.
► *vt* **1** *(frequent - gen)* frecuentar; *(- ghost)* aparecer en, rondar por. **2** *(memory, thought)* obsesionar, perseguir.

haunted ['hɔːntɪd] *adj* encantado,-a.

have [hæv] *vt* **1** *(gen)* tener, poseer. **2** *(food)* comer, tomar; *(drink)* beber, tomar. **3** *(treatment)* recibir: *she's having physiotherapy* acude a fisioterapia. **4** *(invite)* recibir, invitar. **5** *(borrow)* pedir prestado, dejar. **6** *(party, meeting)* cele-

brar, tener, dar. **7** *(cause to happen)* hacer, mandar: *he had the house painted* hizo pintar la casa. **8** *fam (cheat)* timar.
LOC **have got** tener: *he's got two sisters* tiene dos hermanas; *we haven't got any sugar* no tenemos azúcar. **▮ to have breakfast** desayunar. **▮ to have dinner** cenar. **▮ to have just** acabar de: *I have just seen him* acabo de verlo. **▮ to have lunch** comer, almorzar. **▮ to have a bath** bañarse. **▮ to have a shower** ducharse. **▮ to have a swim** darse un baño.
► *aux* haber: *I have seen her* la he visto.
◆ **to have on** *vt sep* **1** *(wear)* llevar puesto,-a. **2** *(tease)* tomar el pelo a.
◆ **to have out** *vt sep (tooth)* sacarse; *(appendix)* operarse de.
ⓘ *3rd pers pres sing* has [hæz], *pt & pp* had [hæd], *ger* having.

✎ Have es el verbo auxiliar que se emplea en inglés para conjugar los tiempos perfectos.

haven ['heɪvən] *n* **1** *fig* refugio, asilo. **2** *(harbour)* puerto.

havoc ['hævək] *n* estragos *mpl*.

hawk¹ [hɔːk] *n* halcón *m*.

hawk² [hɔːk] *vt* **1** *(in the street)* vender en la calle; *(door to door)* vender de puerta en puerta. **2** *(gossip, news)* divulgar, pregonar, difundir.
► *vi* carraspear.

hay [heɪ] *n* BOT heno. COMP **hay fever** fiebre *f* del heno.

hazard ['hæzəd] *n* **1** *(risk)* riesgo, peligro. **2** *(in sports in general)* obstáculo.
► *vt* **1** *fml* arriesgar, poner en peligro. **2** *fml (guess, remark)* aventurar, atreverse a hacer.

hazardous ['hæzədəs] *adj* arriesgado,-a, peligroso,-a, aventurado,-a.

haze [heɪz] *n* **1** neblina. **2** *fig* confusión *f*, vaguedad *f*.
► *vt* US hacer una novatada a.

hazel ['heɪzəl] *n* BOT avellano.
► *adj* (de color de) avellana.

hazelnut ['heɪzəlnʌt] *n* BOT avellana.

hazy ['heɪzɪ] *adj* con neblina.

he [hi:] *pron* **1** él: *he's my brother* (él) es mi hermano. **2** *(gen)* el que, quien.
▸ *n* **1** *(male animals)* macho. **2** *(man)* hombre *m*, varón *m*.

head [hed] *n* **1** *(gen)* cabeza; *(mind)* mente *f*. **2** *(on tape recorder, video)* cabezal *m*. **3** *(of bed, table)* cabecera. **4** *(of page)* principio. **5** *(on beer)* espuma. **6** *(cape)* cabo, punta. **7** *(of school, company)* director,-ra.
▸ *adj* principal, jefe.
▸ *vt* **1** *(company, list, etc)* encabezar. **2** *(ball)* rematar de cabeza, dar un cabezazo a, cabecear.
◆ **to head for** *vt insep* dirigirse hacia.
◆ **to head off** *vi* marcharse, irse.
▸ *vt sep (divert)* interceptar; *(avoid)* evitar.

headache ['hedeɪk] *n* dolor *m* de cabeza.

head-first [hed'fɜ:st] *adv* de cabeza.

head-hunter [hed'hʌntə'] *n* **1** cazador,-ra de cabezas, jíbaro,-a. **2** *fam fig* cazatalentos *mf*.

heading ['hedɪŋ] *n* **1** *(of chapter)* encabezamiento, título. **2** *(letterhead)* membrete *m*.

headlamp ['hedlæmp] *n* AUTO faro.

headlight ['hedlaɪt] *n* AUTO faro.

headline ['hedlaɪn] *n* titular *m*.

headmaster [hed'mɑ:stə'] *n* director *m*.

headmistress [hed'mɪstrəs] *n* directora.

headphones ['hedfəʊnz] *n pl* auriculares *mpl*, cascos *mpl*.

headquarters ['hedkwɔ:təz] *n* **1** *(of an organization)* sede *f*; *(main office)* oficina central. **2** *(of a firm)* domicilio social. **3** MIL cuartel *m* general.

✎ Headquarters puede considerarse tanto singular como plural: *our headquarters is/are in New York* nuestra sede está en Nueva York.

headteacher [hed'ti:'] *adj* director,-a.

headword ['hedwɜ:d] *n* entrada.

heal [hi:l] *vt* **1** *(disease, patient)* curar; *(wound)* cicatrizar, curar. **2** *fig* curar, remediar.

▸ *vi* **1** *(wounds)* cicatrizar, cicatrizarse; *(people)* curarse,. **2** *fig* remediarse.
◆ **to heal up** *vi* curarse, cicatrizarse.

health [helθ] *n* **1** salud *f*. **2** *(service)* sanidad *f*. **3** *fig* prosperidad *f*. COMP **health care** sanidad *f*. ‖ **health centre** centro de salud. ‖ **health food** alimentos *mpl* naturales.

healthy ['helθɪ] *adj* **1** *(gen)* sano,-a. **2** *(good for health)* saludable. **3** *(appetite)* bueno,-a. **4** *(prosperous)* próspero,-a; *(disposition)* sensato,-a.
ⓘ *comp* healthier, *superl* healthiest.

heap [hi:p] *n* montón *m*.

hear [hɪə'] *vt* **1** *(gen)* oír. **3** *(lecture)* asistir a; *(a news item)* saber. **3** JUR *(case)* ver; *(witness, defendant)* oír.
ⓘ *pt & pp* heard [hɜ:d].

heard [hɜ:d] *pt & pp* → hear.

hearer ['hɪərə'] *n* oyente *mf*.

hearing ['hɪərɪŋ] *n* **1** *(sense)* oído. **2** *(act of hearing)* audición *f*. **3** JUR audiencia, vista.

heart [hɑ:t] *n* **1** ANAT corazón *m*. **2** *(centre of feeling)* corazón *m*. **3** *(courage)* valor *m*, corazón *m*. **4** *(of lettuce, etc)* cogollo; *(of place)* corazón *m*, centro; *(of question)* fondo, quid *m*, meollo. LOC **to learn by heart** aprender de memoria. ‖ **to take heart** animarse. ‖ **to learn by heart** aprender de memoria. COMP **heart attack** ataque *m* de corazón.
▸ *n pl* **hearts** *(cards)* corazones *mpl*; *(Spanish cards)* copas *fpl*.

heartbeat ['hɑ:tbi:t] *n* latido del corazón.

heartburn ['hɑ:tbɜ:n] *n* ardor *m* de estómago.

hearten ['hɑ:tⁿn] *vt* animar, alentar.

heartless ['hɑ:tləs] *adj* cruel, insensible.

heat [hi:t] *n* **1** *(gen)* calor *m*. **2** *(heating)* calefacción *f*. **3** SP eliminatoria, serie *f*. **4** ZOOL celo.
▸ *vt* **1** calentar. **2** *fig* acalorar.
◆ **to heat up** *vi (warm up)* calentarse; *(to raise excitement, etc)* acalorarse.

heater ['hi:tə'] *n* calentador *m*.

heather ['heðə'] *n* BOT brezo.

heating ['hi:tɪŋ] *n* calefacción *f*.

heatstroke [ˈhiːtstrəʊk] *n* MED insolación *f*.

heatwave [ˈhiːtweɪv] *n* ola de calor.

heave [hiːv] *n (pull)* tirón *m*; *(push)* empujón *m*.
▸ *vt* **1** *(pull)* tirar; *(lift)* levantar. **2** *(push)* empujar. **3** *fam (throw)* lanzar, arrojar.

heaven [ˈhevən] *n* **1** cielo. **2** *fam* gloria, paraíso.
▸ *n pl* **heavens** cielo.

heavily [ˈhevɪlɪ] *adv* **1** *(fall, move, step, etc)* pesadamente; *(rain)* fuertemente, mucho. **2** *(sleep, etc)* profundamente; *(drink)* con exceso, mucho; *(breathe)* con dificultad *f*.

heavy [ˈhevɪ] *adj* **1** *(gen)* pesado,-a. **2** *(rain, blow)* fuerte, pesado,-a. **3** *(traffic)* denso,-a. **4** *(sleep)* profundo,-a. **5** *(crop)* abundante. **6** *(atmosphere)* cargado,-a. **7** *(loss, expenditure)* grande, considerable. COMP **heavy metal** rock *m* duro, heavy metal *m*.
ⓘ *comp* **heavier**, *superl* **heaviest**.

heavy-duty [ˈhevɪˈdjuːtɪ] *adj (clothes, shoes, etc)* de faena, resistente; *(equipment, machinery, etc)* reforzado,-a, robusto,-a, para grandes cargas.

heavyweight [ˈhevɪweɪt] *n* **1** SP peso pesado. **2** *fig* peso pesado.

Hebrew [ˈhiːbruː] *adj* hebreo,-a.
▸ *n* **1** *(person)* hebreo,-a. **2** *(language)* hebreo.

hectare [ˈhektɑːr] *n* hectárea.

hectic [ˈhektɪk] *adj* agitado,-a, ajetreado,-a, movido,-a.

he'd [hiːz] *contr* **1** he had. **2** he would.

hedge [hedʒ] *n* **1** seto vivo. **2** *fig* protección *f*, barrera.
▸ *vi* contestar con evasivas.
▸ *vt* **1** cercar, separar con un seto. **2** *fig (protect)* proteger, guardar; *(protect os against)* protegerse.

hedgehog [ˈhedʒhɒg] *n* ZOOL erizo.

heel [hiːl] *n* **1** ANAT talón *m*. **2** *(on shoe)* tacón *m*; *(of sock)* talón *m*.
▸ *vt* **1** poner tacón a. **2** *(in rugby)* talonear. **3** MAR inclinar.
▸ *vi* MAR escorar.

height [haɪt] *n* **1** *(gen)* altura. **2** *(altitude)* altitud *f*. **3** *(of person)* estatura. **4** GEOG cumbre *f*, cima.

heir [eər] *n* heredero.

heiress [ˈeəres] *n* heredera.

held [held] *pt & pp* → **hold**.

helicopter [ˈhelɪkɒptər] *n* helicóptero.

heliport [ˈhelɪpɔːt] *n* helipuerto.

helium [ˈhiːlɪəm] *n* CHEM helio.

helix [ˈhiːlɪks] *n* hélice *f*.

hell [hel] *n* infierno.

he'll [hiːl] *contr* **1** he will. **2** he shall.

hello [heˈləʊ] *interj* **1** ¡hola! **2** *(on telephone - answering)* ¡diga!; *(- calling)* ¡oiga! **3** *(to get sb's attention)* ¡oiga!, ¡oye!

helm [helm] *n* MAR timón *m*.

helmet [ˈhelmɪt] *n* casco.

help [help] *n* **1** *(gen)* ayuda. **2** *(servant)* asistenta, criada.
▸ *interj* ¡socorro!
▸ *vt* **1** *(gen)* ayudar. **2** *(be of use)* ayudar, servir. **3** *(to relieve)* aliviar. **4** *(avoid)* evitar.
◆ **to help out** *vt sep* ayudar.

helper [ˈhelpər] *n* **1** ayudante,-a *mf*, auxiliar *mf*. **2** *(collaborator)* colaborador,-ra.

helpful [ˈhelpfʊl] *adj* **1** *(thing)* útil, práctico,-a,. **2** *(person)* amable.

helping [ˈhelpɪŋ] *n* ración *f*, porción *f*.
▸ *adj* ayuda.

helpless [ˈhelpləs] *adj* **1** *(unprotected)* desamparado,-a, indefenso,-a, desvalido,-a. **2** *(powerless)* impotente, incapaz, inútil.

hem [hem] *n* SEW dobladillo.
▸ *vt* hacer un dobladillo en.
ⓘ *pt & pp* **hemmed**, *ger* **hemming**.

hematoma [hiːməˈtəʊmə] *n* US → **haematoma**.

hemisphere [ˈhemɪsfɪər] *n* hemisferio.

hemorrhage [ˈhemərɪdʒ] *n* US → **haemorrhage**.

hen [hen] *n (chicken)* gallina; *(female bird)* hembra.

hence [hens] *adv* **1** *fml (so)* por eso, por lo tanto, de ahí. **2** *(from now)* de aquí a, dentro de.

henceforth [hensˈfɔːθ] *adv fml* de ahora en adelante.

henhouse [ˈhenhaʊs] *n* gallinero.

henna ['henə] n BOT alheña.

heptagon ['heptəgən] n heptágono.

heptagonal [hep'tægənəl] adj heptagonal.

her [hɜːʳ] pron 1 (direct object) la: I love her la quiero. 2 (indirect object) le; (with other third person pronouns) se: give it to her dáselo. 3 (after preposition) ella: go with her vete con ella. 4 fam (as subject) ella: listen, that's her! ¡escucha, es ella!
▶ adj su, sus; (emphatic) de ella.

heraldic [he'rældɪk] adj heráldico,-a.

herb [hɜːb] n hierba.

herbaceous [hɜː'beɪʃəs] adj herbáceo,-a.

herbal ['hɜːbəl] adj de hierbas.

herbicide ['hɜːbɪsaɪd] n herbicida m.

herbivore ['hɜːbɪvɔːʳ] n ZOOL herbívoro,-a.

herd [hɜːd] n 1 (cattle) manada; (goats) rebaño; (pigs) piara. 2 fam (people) montón m, multitud f.

here [hɪəʳ] adv aquí. LOC **here you are** aquí tienes.

hereby [hɪə'baɪ] adv fml por la presente.

hereditary [hɪ'redɪtərɪ] adj hereditario,-a.

heredity [hɪ'redɪtɪ] n herencia.

heresy ['herəsɪ] n herejía.
ⓘ pl **heresies.**

heritage ['herɪtɪdʒ] n herencia, patrimonio.

hermaphrodite [hɜː'mæfrədaɪt] adj hermafrodita.

hernia ['hɜːnɪə] n hernia.

hero ['hɪərəʊ] n 1 (gen) héroe m. 2 (in novel) protagonista m.
ⓘ pl **heroes.**

heroic [hɪ'rəʊɪk] adj heroico,-a.

heroin ['herəʊɪn] n (drug) heroína.

heroine ['herəʊɪn] n 1 heroína. 2 (in novel) protagonista.

herpes ['hɜːpiːz] n herpe m, herpes m.

herring ['herɪŋ] n arenque m.
ⓘ pl **herring o herrings.**

hers [hɜːz] pron (sing) (el) suyo, (la) suya; (pl) (los) suyos, (las) suyas; (emphatic) de ella: this pencil is hers este lápiz es suyo.

herself [hɜː'self] pron 1 (reflexive use) se: she washed herself se lavó. 2 (emphatic) ella misma: she made it all herself lo hizo todo ella misma. LOC **by herself** sola.

hertz [hɜːts] n hertz m, hercio m.

he's [hiːz] contr 1 he is. 2 he has.

hesitate ['hezɪteɪt] vi vacilar, dudar.

hesitation [hezɪ'teɪʃən] n duda, indecisión.

heterogeneous [hetərəʊ'dʒiːnɪəs] adj heterogéneo,-a.

heterosexual [hetərəʊ'seksjʊəl] adj heterosexual.

heterotrophic [hetərəʊ'trɒfɪk] adj heterotrófico,-a.

hexagon ['heksəgən] n hexágono.

hexagonal [hek'sægənəl] adj hexagonal.

hi [haɪ] interj fam ¡hola!

hibernate ['haɪbəneɪt] vi hibernar.

hiccough ['hɪkʌp] n-vi → hiccup.

hiccup ['hɪkʌp] n hipo: to have hiccups tener hipo.

hid [hɪd] pt & pp → hide.

hidden ['hɪdən] pp → hide.
▶ adj 1 escondido,-a. 2 fig oculto,-a.

hide¹ [haɪd] n (concealed place) escondite m.
▶ vt (conceal) esconder; (obscure) ocultar, tapar.
ⓘ pt hid [hɪd], pp hid [hɪd] o hidden ['hɪdən].

hide² [haɪd] n 1 piel f, cuero. 2 fig (of a person) pellejo.

hide-and-seek [haɪdən'siːk] n escondite m.

hideous ['hɪdɪəs] adj 1 (terrible) horroroso,-a, atroz. 2 (ugly) horrendo,-a, espantoso.

hide-out ['haɪdaʊt] n escondrijo, escondite m, guarida.

hierarchic [haɪə'rɑːkɪk] adj jerárquico,-a.

hierarchy ['haɪərɑːkɪ] n jerarquía.
ⓘ pl **hierarchies.**

hieroglyphics [haɪərə'glɪfɪks] n pl jeroglíficos mpl.

hi-fi ['haɪfaɪ] n hifi m, alta fidelidad f.

high [haɪ] adj 1 alto,-a, elevado. 2 (important) alto,-a, importante; (strong) fuerte. 3 (very good) bueno,-a. 4 (going rotten - food) pasado,-a; (- game) manido,-a. **5** *(of time)* pleno,-a. ⟨COMP⟩ **high jump** salto de altura. ∎ **high school** instituto (de bachillerato). ∎ **high street** calle mayor. ∎ **high tide** marea alta.

⊕ El **high school** es el equivalente a los institutos de bachillerato, sobre todo en Estados Unidos.

high-class [haɪˈklɑːs] *adj (classy)* de categoría; *(superior)* de calidad *f*.

higher [ˈhaɪər] *adj* **1** → high. **2** superior. **3** *(bigger)* más alto,-a; *(number, velocity, etc)* mayor. ⟨COMP⟩ **higher education** enseñanza superior.

high-heeled [ˈhaɪhiːld] *adj* de tacón alto.

highlight [ˈhaɪlaɪt] *vt* **1** destacar, hacer resaltar. **2** *(with pen)* marcar *(con un rotulador fosforescente)*.
▸ *n* **1** ART toque *m* de luz. **2** *(hairdressing)* reflejo. **3** *fig (especially in show business)* atracción *f* principal; *(most outstanding)* punto culminante; *(aspect or feature)* característica notable.

highly [ˈhaɪlɪ] *adv (very)* muy; *(favourably)* muy bien.

Highness [ˈhaɪnəs] *n* Alteza *mf*.

high-pitched [ˈhaɪpɪtʃt] *adj (sound, voice)* agudo,-a; *(roof)* empinado,-a.

high-tech [haɪˈtek] *adj* de alta tecnología.

highway [ˈhaɪweɪ] *n* **1** US autovía. **2** JUR vía pública.

hijack [ˈhaɪdʒæk] *n* secuestro.
▸ *vt* secuestrar.

hijacker [ˈhaɪdʒækər] *n* secuestrador,-a.

hijacking [ˈhaɪdʒækɪŋ] *n* secuestro.

hike [haɪk] *n* **1** *(walk)* excursión *f* a pie. **2** *fam* aumento de precio.
▸ *vi* ir de excursión, hacer una excursión.
▸ *vt fam* aumentar los precios.

hiker [ˈhaɪkər] *n* excursionista.

hiking [ˈhaɪkɪŋ] *n* excursionismo a pie.

hilarious [hɪˈleərɪəs] *adj* graciosísimo,-a, hilarante, divertidísimo,-a.

hill [hɪl] *n* **1** colina, cerro. **2** *(slope)* cuesta.

hillside [ˈhɪlsaɪd] *n* ladera.

hilltop [ˈhɪltɒp] *n* cumbre *f*, cima.

him [hɪm] *pron* **1** *(direct object)* lo: *I love him* lo quiero. **2** *(indirect object)* le; *(with other pronouns)* se: *give him the money* dale el dinero; *give it to him* dáselo. **3** *(after preposition)* él: *we went with him* fuimos con él. **4** *fam (as subject)* él: *it's him!* ¡es él!

himself [hɪmˈself] *pron* **1** *(reflexive)* se; *(alone)* solo, por sí mismo: *he cut himself* se cortó; *he did it by himself* lo hizo solo. **2** *(emphatic)* él mismo, sí mismo, en persona.

hinder [ˈhɪndər] *vt* dificultar, entorpecer, estorbar, impedir.

Hindu [hɪnˈduː, ˈhɪnduː] *n* hindú *mf*.
▸ *adj* hindú.

Hinduism [ˈhɪnduɪzəm] *n* hinduismo.

hinge [hɪndʒ] *n* **1** TECH gozne *m*, bisagra. **2** *(for stamps)* fijasello. **3** *fig* eje *m*.
▸ *vi* girar sobre goznes.

hint [hɪnt] *n* **1** insinuación *f*, indirecta. **2** *(advice)* consejo, sugerencia. **3** *(clue)* pista. **4** *(trace)* pizca. **5** *(sign)* sombra.
▸ *vt (imply)* insinuar, aludir a.

hip¹ [hɪp] *n* ANAT cadera.

hip² [hɪp] ⟨LOC⟩ **hip hip hooray!** ¡hurra!

hippie [ˈhɪpɪ] *n fam* hippie *mf*.

hippo [ˈhɪpəʊ] *n fam* hipopótamo.

hippopotamus [hɪpəˈpɒtəməs] *n* ZOOL hipopótamo.

hippy [ˈhɪpɪ] *n fam* hippie *mf*.
ⓘ *pl* hippies.

hire [ˈhaɪər] *n* alquiler *m*.
▸ *vt* **1** *(rent)* alquilar. **2** *(employ)* contratar.
◆ **to hire out** *vt sep (equipment, vehicles, etc)* alquilar; *(people)* contratar.

his [hɪz] *adj* **1** su, sus: *his dog* su perro. **2** *(emphatic)* de él.
▸ *pron* (el) suyo, (la) suya, (los) suyos, (las) suyas.

Hispanic [hɪsˈpænɪk] *adj* hispánico,-a.
▸ *n* US hispano,-a, latino,-a.

hiss [hɪs] *n* **1** *(gen)* siseo. **2** *(air, snake, steam, etc)* silbido. **3** *(protest)* silbido.
▸ *vt* **1** sisear, silbar. **2** *(in protest)* pitar, abuchear.

historic [hɪˈstɒrɪk] *adj* histórico,-a.

historical [hɪˈstɒrɪkəl] *adj* histórico,-a.

H

history [ˈhɪstˤrɪ] *n* **1** *(in general)* historia. **2** COMPUT historial *m*.
ⓘ *pl* histories.

☒ History no significa 'historia (relato)', que se traduce por story.

hit [hɪt] *n* **1** *(blow)* golpe *m*. **2** *(success)* éxito, acierto. **3** *(shot)* impacto. **4** *(visit to web page)* acceso. **5** *fig (damaging remark)* pulla.
▸ *vt* **1** *(strike)* golpear, pegar. **2** *(crash into)* chocar contra. **3** *(affect)* afectar, perjudicar. **4** *(reach)* alcanzar.
◆ **to hit back** *vi (strike in return)* devolver golpe por golpe; *(reply to criticism)* defenderse.
ⓘ *pt & pp* hit, *ger* hitting.

hitch [hɪtʃ] *n* obstáculo, dificultad *f*.
▸ *vt (tie)* enganchar, atar.
▸ *vi fam* hacer autoestop, ir a dedo, hacer dedo.

hitchhike [ˈhɪtʃhaɪk] *vi* hacer autoestop.

hitchhiking [ˈhɪtʃhaɪkɪŋ] *vi* autoestop *m*, dedo.

HIV [ˈeɪtʃaɪˈviː] *abbr* (human immunodeficiency virus) virus *m* de inmunodeficiencia humana; *(abbreviation)* VIH *m*.

hive [haɪv] *n* **1** colmena. **2** *fig* lugar *m* muy activo.

hoard [hɔːd] *n* **1** *(provisions)* reserva. **2** *(money)* tesoro escondido.
▸ *vt* **1** *(objects)* acumular. **2** *(money)* atesorar.

hoarse [hɔːs] *adj* ronco,-a, áspero,-a.

hoax [həʊks] *n (trick)* trampa, engaño; *(joke)* broma pesada.
▸ *vt* engañar a, gastar una broma a.

hob [hɒb] *n (of cooker)* encimera; *(next to fireplace)* repisa.

hobble [ˈhɒbˤl] *vi (limp)* cojear, andar con dificultad *f*.
▸ *vt* **1** *(tie)* trabar, manear. **2** *fig* poner trabas a, obstaculizar.

hobby [ˈhɒbɪ] *n* afición *f*, hobby *m*, pasatiempo favorito.
ⓘ *pl* hobbies.

hockey [ˈhɒkɪ] *n* SP hockey *m*.

hoe [həʊ] *n* azada, azadón *m*.
▸ *vt (earth)* azadonar, cavar; *(weeds)* sachar.

hog [hɒg] *n* **1** cerdo, puerco, marrano. **2** *fam pej (not a nice person)* indeseable *mf*.
▸ *vt* acaparar.
ⓘ *pt & pp* hogged, *ger* hogging.

hoist [hɔɪst] *n* **1** *(crane)* grúa. **2** *(lift)* montacargas *m*.
▸ *vt* **1** levantar, subir. **2** *(flag)* izar.

hold [həʊld] *n* **1** *(place to grip)* asidero. **2** *(in ship, plane)* bodega. LOC **to get hold of** **1** *(grab)* agarrar, coger. **2** *(obtain)* hacerse con, encontrar.
▸ *vt* **1** *(keep in one's hand)* aguantar, sostener: *hold my bag* aguántame el bolso. **2** *(opinion)* sostener. **3** *(contain)* dar cabida a, tener capacidad para: *the stadium holds a lot of people* el estadio tiene capacidad para mucha gente. **4** *(meeting)* celebrar; *(conversation)* mantener: *political parties often hold meetings in parks* los partidos políticos celebran a menudo sus mítines en los parques. LOC **to hold SB** abrazar a ALGN.
◆ **to hold back** *vt sep* **1** *(suspect)* retener. **2** *(information)* ocultar; *(restrain)* contener; *(feelings)* reprimir; *(keep)* guardar.
▸ *vi (hesitate)* vacilar, no atreverse; *(abstain)* abstenerse.
◆ **to hold down** *vt sep (control)* dominar; *(job)* desempeñar.
◆ **to hold forth** *vi* hablar largo y tendido.
◆ **to hold off** *vt sep* mantener alejado,-a.
▸ *vi (refrain)* refrenarse.
◆ **to hold on** *vi* **1** *(grip tightly)* agarrarse fuerte, agarrarse bien. **2** *(wait)* esperar; *(on phone)* no colgar.
◆ **to hold over** *vt sep* aplazar.
◆ **to hold up** *vt sep* **1** *(rob)* atracar, asaltar. **2** *(delay)* retrasar. **3** *(raise)* levantar. **4** *(support)* aguantar, sostener.
▸ *vi* aguantar, resistir.
◆ **to hold with** *vt insep* estar de acuerdo con.
ⓘ *pt & pp* held [held].

holder [ˈhəʊldəʳ] *n* **1** *(owner)* poseedor, -ra; *(of passport)* titular *mf*. **2** *(container)* recipiente *m*, receptáculo. **3** *(bearer - gen)* portador,-ra; *(- of bonds)* tenedor,-ra.

4 *(handle)* asidero. **5** *(tenant - on land)* arrendatario,-a; *(- of a flat)* inquilino,-a.

hold-up ['həʊldʌp] *n* **1** *(robbery)* atraco; *(of train, etc)* asalto. **2** *(delay)* retraso. **3** AUTO atasco.

hole [həʊl] *n* **1** *(gen)* agujero; *(in ground, golf)* hoyo. **2** *(in road)* bache *m*. **3** *(of rabbits)* madriguera; *(cavity)* cavidad *f*. **4** *fam (town)* pueblucho de mala muerte. **5** *fam (place to live)* cuchitril *m*; *(unsavoury place)* antro. **6** *(a tight spot)* aprieto, apuro.
  ▶ *vt* **1** *(make holes - small)* agujerear; *(large)* hacer un boquete en. **2** *(at golf)* meter en el hoyo.

holiday ['hɒlɪdeɪ] *n* **1** *(one day)* fiesta, día *m* de fiesta, día *m* festivo. **2** *(period)* vacaciones *fpl*. LOC **to be on holiday** estar de vacaciones. ‖ **to go on holiday** irse de vacaciones.
  ▶ *vi* GB *(gen)* pasar las vacaciones; *(in summer)* veranear.

Holland ['hɒlənd] *n* Holanda.

hollow ['hɒləʊ] *adj* **1** *(sound, thing)* hueco,-a. **2** *(cheeks, etc)* hundido,-a. **3** *fig (laugh)* falso,-a; *(promise)* vacío,-a.
  ① *comp* **hollower**, *superl* **hollowest**.
  ▶ *n* **1** hueco. **2** GEOG hondonada.

holly ['hɒlɪ] *n* acebo.
  ① *pl* **hollies**.

holocaust ['hɒləkɔ:st] *n* holocausto.

holy ['həʊlɪ] *adj* **1** REL *(sacred)* santo,-a, sagrado,-a. **2** *(blessed)* bendito,-a.
  ① *comp* **holier**, *superl* **holiest**.

home [həʊm] *n* **1** *(house)* hogar *m*, casa. **2** *fml* domicilio. **3** *(institution)* asilo. **4** *(country, village, etc)* patria, tierra. **5** ZOOL hábitat *m*. LOC **at home** en casa.
  ▶ *adj* **1** casero,-a. **2** POL *(del)* interior. **3** *(native)* natal.

homeland ['həʊmlænd] *n* *(gen)* patria; *(birthplace)* tierra natal.

homeless ['həʊmləs] *adj* sin hogar, sin techo.

home-made ['həʊm'meɪd] *adj* casero,-a, de fabricación casera, hecho,-a en casa.

homemaker ['həʊm'meɪkər] *n* ama de casa.

homesick ['həʊmsɪk] *adj* nostálgico,-a.

homesickness ['həʊmsɪknəs] *n* añoranza, morriña, nostalgia.

homework ['həʊmwɜ:k] *n* deberes *mpl*.

homogeneous [hɒmə'dʒi:nɪəs] *adj* homogéneo,-a.

homograph ['hɒməgræf] *n* homógrafo.

homonym ['hɒmənɪm] *n* homónimo.

homosexual [həʊməʊ'seksjʊəl] *adj & n* homosexual.

honest ['ɒnɪst] *adj* **1** *(trustworthy)* honrado,-a, honesto,-a. **2** *(frank)* sincero,-a, franco,-a. **3** *(fair)* justo,-a.
  ▶ *adv* *fam* de verdad.

honestly ['ɒnɪstlɪ] *adv* **1** *(fairly)* honradamente. **2** *(frankly)* sinceramente, francamente. **3** *(truthfully)* de verdad, a decir verdad.
  ▶ *interj* *(question)* ¿de verdad?; *(exclamation)* ¡hay que ver!

honesty ['ɒnɪstɪ] *n* honradez *f*.

honey ['hʌnɪ] *n* **1** miel *f*. **2** US *fam (dear)* cariño, cielo.

honeycomb ['hʌnɪkəʊm] *n* panal *m*.

honeymoon ['hʌnɪmu:n] *n* luna de miel, viaje *m* de novios.

honor ['ɒnər] *n* US → **honour**.

honour ['ɒnər] *n* **1** *(virtue)* honor *m*, honra. **2** *(title)* Su Señoría.
  ▶ *vt* **1** *(respect)* honrar. **2** *(cheque)* pagar, aceptar; *(promise, word, agreement)* cumplir.

hood [hʊd] *n* **1** *(of clothes)* capucha. **2** *(on pram, etc)* capota. **3** US *(car bonnet)* capó *m*. **4** *(of hawk)* capirote *m*.

hoof [hʊf] *n* *(of sheep, cow, etc)* pezuña; *(of horse)* casco.
  ① *pl* **hoofs** o **hooves**.

hook [hʊk] *n* **1** *(gen)* gancho. **2** *(for fishing)* anzuelo.
  ▶ *vt* **1** *(catch)* enganchar. **2** *(fishing)* pescar, coger. **3** *(in boxing)* pegar un gancho.
  ◆ **to hook up** *vt sep (connect)* conectar.

hooligan ['hu:lɪgən] *n* gamberro,-a.

hoop [hu:p] *n* *(gen)* aro; *(of barrel)* fleje *m*; *(of wheel)* llanta.

hoot [hu:t] *n* **1** *(of owl)* ululato, grito. **2** *(of car)* bocinazo. **3** *fam (funny thing)* cosa divertida; *(funny person)* persona divertida.

hooter ['huːtər] n 1 *(siren)* sirena. 2 *(on car)* bocina, claxon m. 3 GB *(nose)* narizota, napias fpl.

Hoover® ['huːvər] n GB aspiradora.

hooves ['huːvz] pl → hoof.

hop¹ [hɒp] n 1 salto, brinco. 2 *fam (dance)* baile m. 3 AV *fam* vuelo corto.
► vi saltar, dar brincos, dar saltos.
► vt 1 US *fam (train, etc)* coger. 2 AV cruzar.
① pt & pp hopped, ger hopping.

hop² [hɒp] n *(plant)* lúpulo.

hope [həʊp] n *(gen)* esperanza; *(false)* ilusión f.
► vt esperar.

hopeful ['həʊpfʊl] adj 1 *(promising)* esperanzador,-ra, prometedor,-ra, alentador,-ra. 2 *(confident)* optimista.

hopefully ['həʊpfʊlɪ] adv 1 *(confidently)* con esperanza, con ilusión, con optimismo. 2 *fam (all being well)* ojalá.

hopeless ['həʊpləs] adj 1 desesperado,-a. 2 *fam (useless)* inútil.

hopelessly ['həʊpləslɪ] adv sin esperanza, con desesperación, desesperadamente.

horizon [həˈraɪzən] n horizonte m.

horizontal [hɒrɪˈzɒntəl] adj horizontal.

hormonal [hɔːˈməʊnəl] adj hormonal.

hormone ['hɔːməʊn] n hormona.

horn [hɔːn] n 1 ZOOL asta, cuerno. 2 AUTO bocina, claxon m. 3 MUS cuerno, trompa.

horoscope ['hɒrəskəʊp] n horóscopo.

horrible ['hɒrɪbəl] adj *(gen)* horrible, horroroso,-a; *(person)* antipático,-a.

horrid ['hɒrɪd] adj *(horrible)* horroroso,-a, horrible; *(unkind)* antipático,-a, odioso,-a; *(child)* inaguantable, insoportable.

horrific [həˈrɪfɪk] adj horrendo,-a, horroroso,-a.

horrify ['hɒrɪfaɪ] vt horrorizar, espantar.
① pt & pp horrified, ger horrifying.

horrifying ['hɒrɪfaɪɪŋ] adj escalofriante.

horror ['hɒrər] n horror m, terror m.
COMP horror film película de terror.

hors d'oeuvre [ɔːˈdɜːvr] n CULIN entremés m.
① pl hors d'oeuvre o hors d'oeuvres.

horse [hɔːs] n 1 ZOOL caballo. 2 *(in gym)* potro. 3 TECH caballete m. 4 *sl (heroin)* caballo. COMP horse riding equitación f.

horseback ['hɔːsbæk] adj & adv a caballo. LOC on horseback a caballo.

horsepower ['hɔːspaʊər] n 1 AUTO caballo de vapor, caballo. 2 potencia.

horseshoe ['hɔːsʃuː] n herradura.

hose¹ [həʊz] n *(pipe)* manguera.
① pl hose.
► vt regar, lavar.

hose² [həʊz] n pl *(socks)* calcetines mpl; *(stockings)* medias fpl.

hosepipe ['həʊzpaɪp] n manguera.

hospitable [hɒˈspɪtəbəl] adj hospitalario,-a, acogedor,-ra.

hospital ['hɒspɪtəl] n hospital m.

hospitality [hɒspɪˈtælɪtɪ] n hospitalidad f.

host¹ [həʊst] n 1 *(person)* anfitrión,-ona; *(place)* sede f. 2 *(TV presenter)* presentador,-ra. 3 *(animal, plant)* huésped m.
► vt 1 TV presentar. 2 celebrar,.

host² [həʊst] n *(large number)* multitud f.

Host [həʊst] n REL hostia.

hostage ['hɒstɪdʒ] n rehén mf.

hostel ['hɒstəl] n residencia, hostal m.

hostess ['həʊstəs] n 1 *(at home)* anfitriona. 2 *(on plane, etc)* azafata. 3 *(in club)* camarera. 4 TV presentadora.

hostile ['hɒstaɪl] adj hostil, enemigo,-a.

hostility [hɒˈstɪlɪtɪ] n hostilidad f.
① pl hostilities.

hot [hɒt] adj 1 *(gen)* caliente. 2 METEOR caluroso,-a, cálido,-a. 3 *(food - spicy)* picante.
① comp hotter, superl hottest.

hotel [həʊˈtel] n hotel m.

hotline ['hɒtlaɪn] n línea directa.

hound [haʊnd] n perro de caza.
► vt *(harass)* acosar, perseguir.

hour [aʊər] n hora f.

hourly ['aʊəlɪ] adj cada hora.
► adv a cada hora, por horas.

house [(n) haʊs; (vb) haʊz] n 1 *(gen)* casa; *(official use)* domicilio. 2 POL cámara. 3 THEAT sala. 4 *(company)* empresa, casa.
COMP House of Commons Cámara de los Comunes. ▌ House of Lords Cáma-

ra de los Lores. ▮ **House of Representatives** Cámara de Representantes. ▮ **Houses of Parliament** Parlamento.

▸ vt **1** *(gen)* alojar, albergar; *(supply housing)* proveer de vivienda. **2** *(store)* guardar, almacenar; *(fit)* dar cabida a.

⚓ Tanto el Reino Unido como Estados Unidos disponen, al igual que nosotros, de un sistema legislativo bicameral, con unas cámaras bajas (equivalentes al Congreso de los diputados), que se llaman **House of Commons** en el Reino Unido y **House of Representatives** en Estados Unidos, y unas cámaras altas (similares a nuestro Senado), que se llaman **House of Lords** en el Reino Unido y **Senate** en Estados Unidos.

housemaster ['hausmɑːstəʳ] *n* EDUC tutor *m*.

housemistress ['hausmɪstrəs] *n* EDUC tutora.

housewife ['hauswaɪf] *n* ama de casa.
ⓘ *pl* **housewives** ['hauswaɪvz].

housework ['hauswɜːk] *n* quehaceres *mpl* domésticos.

housing ['hauzɪŋ] *n* **1** vivienda. **2** TECH bastidor *m*, caja.

hover ['hɒvəʳ] *vi* **1** *(aircraft)* permanecer inmóvil *(en el aire)*. **2** *(bird)* cernerse, revolotear. **3** *(move around)* rondar. **4** *(hesitate)* dudar, vacilar.

hovercraft ['hɒvəkrɑːft] *n* aerodeslizador *m*.
ⓘ *pl* **hovercraft**.

how [hau] *adv* **1** *(in questions - direct)* ¿cómo?; *(- indirect)* cómo: *tell me how to do it* dime cómo se hace. **2** *(in exclamations)* qué: *how odd!* ¡qué extraño!, ¡qué raro! ▮LOC▮ **how about...?** ¿qué te parece si...? ▮ **how are you?** ¿cómo estás? ▮ **how many** cuántos,-as ▮ **how much** cuánto

✎ La expresión **How do you do?** se emplea en inglés formal cuando se encuentran dos personas por primera vez. La respuesta es la misma **How do you do?** El equivalente en español sería 'encantado'.

however [hau'evəʳ] *adv* **1** *(nevertheless)* sin embargo, no obstante. **2** *(with adj)* por: *however hard it may be* por difícil que sea; *however much* por más que, por mucho que.

howl [haul] *n (cry)* aullido.
▸ *vi* aullar.
◆ **to howl down** *vt sep* abuchear.

HP ['eɪtʃ'piː] *abbr* (horsepower) caballos *mpl* de vapor; *(abbreviation)* cv *mpl*.

HQ ['eɪtʃ'kjuː] *abbr* **1** (headquarters) cuartel *m* general. **2** *fig* centro de operaciones.

HTML ['eɪtʃ'tiː'em'el] *abbr* (hypertext markup language) HTML.

hub [hʌb] *n* **1** AUTO cubo. **2** *fig* centro, eje *m*.

hubcap ['hʌbkæp] *n* AUTO tapacubos *m*.

huddle ['hʌdəl] *n* grupo.
▸ *vi* **1** *(crouch)* acurrucarse, apiñarse, amontonarse. **2** *(cluster)* apiñarse.

hug [hʌg] *n* abrazo.
▸ *vt* **1** abrazar. **2** *fig (kerb, coast)* pegarse a, ceñirse a.
ⓘ *pt & pp* **hugged**, *ger* **hugging**.

huge [hjuːdʒ] *adj* enorme, inmenso,-a.

hull [hʌl] *n* **1** *(of ship)* casco. **2** BOT *(shell)* cáscara; *(pod)* vaina.
▸ *vt (peas, beans, etc)* desvainar.

hullo [hʌ'ləu] *interj* → **hello**.

hum [hʌm] *n (of bees, engine)* zumbido.
▸ *vi* **1** *(bees, engine, etc)* zumbar. **2** *(sing)* tararear, canturrear. **3** *(bustling with activity)* hervir.
▸ *vt (tune)* tararear, canturrear.
ⓘ *pt & pp* **hummed**, *ger* **humming**.

human ['hjuːmən] *adj* humano,-a. ▮COMP▮ **human being** ser *m* humano.
▸ *n* ser *m* humano, humano.

humanitarian [hjuːmænɪ'teərɪən] *adj* humanitario,-a, filantrópico,-a.
▸ *n* filántropo,-a.

humanity [hjuː'mænɪtɪ] *n* **1** *(virtue)* humanidad *f*. **2** *(mankind)* género humano, raza humana.
ⓘ *pl* **humanities**.

humanize ['hjuːmənaɪz] *vt* humanizar.

humble ['hʌmbəl] *adj* humilde.
▸ *vt* humillar.
ⓘ *comp* **humbler**, *superl* **humbliest**.

humerus ['hju:mərəs] *n* ANAT *(bone)* húmero.
ⓘ *pl* humeri ['hju:mərai].

humid ['hju:mɪd] *adj* húmedo,-a.

> ❌ Humid no significa 'húmedo (impregnado de agua)', que se traduce por damp, wet.

humidity [hju:'mɪdɪtɪ] *n* humedad *f*.
humiliate [hju:'mɪlɪeɪt] *vt* humillar.
humiliation [hju:mɪlɪ'eɪʃ°n] *n* humillación *f*.
hummingbird ['hʌmɪŋbɜ:d] *n* colibrí *m*.
humor ['hju:məʳ] *n* US → humour.
humorous ['hju:mərəs] *adj* **1** *(funny)* gracioso,-a, divertido,-a. **2** *(writer)* humorístico,-a, humorista.
humour ['hju:məʳ] *n* **1** humor *m*. **2** *(of a joke)* gracia. **3** *(whim)* capricho.
> ▶ *vt* complacer, seguir el humor a.

> ❌ Humour no significa 'humor (estado de ánimo)', que se traduce por mood.

hump [hʌmp] *n* **1** *(on back)* giba, joroba. **2** *(hillock)* montículo.
> ▶ *vt* **1** GB *fam (carry)* cargar.

humus ['hju:məs] *n* AGR mantillo, humus *m*.
hunchback ['hʌntʃbæk] *n* *(person)* jorobado,-a.
hundred ['hʌndrəd] *n* cien.
> ▶ *n pl* hundreds *(many)* centenares *mpl*, cientos *mpl*.

hundredth ['hʌndrədθ] *adj* centésimo,-a.
> ▶ *adv* en centésimo lugar.

hung [hʌŋ] *pt & pp* → hang.
Hungarian [hʌŋ'geərɪən] *adj* húngaro,-a.
> ▶ *n* **1** *(person)* húngaro,-a. **2** *(language)* húngaro.

Hungary ['hʌŋgərɪ] *n* Hungría.
hunger ['hʌŋgəʳ] *n* **1** hambre *f*. **2** *fig* sed *f*. [COMP] **hunger strike** huelga de hambre.
> ◆ **to hunger after / hunger for** *vt insep* ansiar, anhelar, tener hambre de.

hungry ['hʌŋgrɪ] *adj* **1** hambriento,-a. **2** *fig* ávido,-a, sediento,-a. [LOC] **to be hungry** tener hambre.
ⓘ *comp* hungrier, *superl* hungriest.

hunt [hʌnt] *n* **1** *(gen)* caza, cacería. **2** *(search)* búsqueda.
> ▶ *vt* cazar.
> ◆ **to hunt down** *vt sep (corner)* acorralar, perseguir; *(to find)* dar con, encontrar.
> ◆ **to hunt out / hunt up** *vt sep (to find)* encontrar; *(to look for)* buscar.

hunter ['hʌntəʳ] *n* **1** cazador,-ra *mf*. **2** ZOOL caballo de caza. **3** *(watch)* saboneta.
hunting ['hʌntɪŋ] *n* *(gen)* caza; *(expedition)* cacería, montería.
hurdle ['hɜ:d°l] *n* **1** SP valla. **2** *fig* obstáculo.
> ▶ *vt* SP *(barrier)* saltar.

hurdling ['hɜ:dlɪŋ] *n* SP carrera de vallas.
hurl [hɜ:l] *vt* **1** lanzar, arrojar, tirar. **2** *(insults)* soltar.
hurrah [hʊ'rɑ:] *interj* ¡hurra!: *hurrah for Peter!* ¡viva Peter!
> ▶ *vt* vitorear, aclamar.

hurray [hʊ'reɪ] *interj* ¡hurra!
hurricane ['hʌrɪkən, 'hʌrɪkeɪn] *n* huracán *m*.
hurry ['hʌrɪ] *n* prisa: *are you in a hurry for the report?* ¿le corre prisa el informe? [LOC] **to be in a hurry** tener prisa.
> ▶ *vi* apresurarse, darse prisa.
> ◆ **to hurry up** *vi* darse prisa.
ⓘ *pt & pp* hurried, *ger* hurrying.

hurt [hɜ:t] *n* **1** *(harm)* daño, dolor *m*, mal *m*. **2** *(wound)* herida. **3** *fig* daño, perjuicio.
> ▶ *adj* **1** *(physically)* herido,-a. **2** *(offended)* dolido,-a.
> ▶ *vt* **1** *(cause injury)* lastimar, hacer daño; *(to wound)* herir: *he has hurt his arm* se ha hecho daño en el brazo. **2** SP lesionar. **3** *(offend)* herir, ofender: *you hurt her feelings* la has ofendido, le has herido los sentimientos.
> ▶ *vi* **1** doler: *my eyes hurt* me duelen los ojos. **2** *fam* venir mal, ir mal.
ⓘ *pt & pp* hurt.

husband ['hʌzbənd] *n* marido, esposo.
hush [hʌʃ] *n* quietud *f*, silencio.
> ▶ *vt* callar, silenciar.

► *interj* ¡silencio! ¡cállate! ¡cállese! ¡chito! COMP **hush money** *fam* soborno *(que se paga para que alguien no hable)*.

◆ **to hush up** *vt sep (affair)* echar tierra a; *(person)* hacer callar.

hustle ['hʌsəl] *n* bullicio. COMP **hustle and bustle** ajetreo

hut [hʌt] *n* **1** cabaña. **2** *(in garden)* cobertizo. **3** MIL barraca.

hyacinth ['haɪəsɪnθ] *n* BOT jacinto.

hyaena [haɪˈiːnə] *n* hiena.

hybrid ['haɪbrɪd] *adj* híbrido,-a.
► *n* híbrido.

hydrant ['haɪdrənt] *n* boca de riego.

hydrate [haɪˈdreɪt] *vt* hidratar.

hydraulic [haɪˈdrɔːlɪk] *adj* hidráulico,-a. COMP **hydraulic brake** freno hidráulico.

hydrocarbon [haɪdrəʊˈkɑːbən] *n* CHEM hidrocarburo.

hydrochloric [haɪdrəˈklɒrɪk] *adj* clorhídrico,-a. COMP **hydrochloric acid** ácido clorhídrico.

hydroelectric [haɪdrəʊɪˈlektrɪk] *adj* hidroeléctrico,-a. COMP **hydroelectric power station** central *f* hidroeléctrica.

hydrogen ['haɪdrədʒən] *n* CHEM hidrógeno. COMP **hydrogen bomb** bomba de hidrógeno.

hydrography [haɪˈdrɒɡrəfɪ] *n* hidrografía.

hydrology [haɪˈdrɒlədʒɪ] *n* hidrología.

hydroplane ['haɪdrəpleɪn] *n* hidroavión *m*, hidroplano.

hydrosphere ['haɪdrəsfər] *n* hidrosfera.

hydroxide [haɪˈdrɒksaɪd] *n* hidróxido.

hyena [haɪˈiːnə] *n* ZOOL hiena.

hygiene ['haɪdʒiːn] *n* higiene *f*.

hygienic [haɪˈdʒiːnɪk] *adj* higiénico,-a.

hymn [hɪm] *n* himno. COMP **hymn book** cantoral *m*.

hyperbola [haɪˈpɜːbələ] *n* hipérbola.
① *pl* **hyperbole** [haɪˈpɜːbəlɪ] o **hyperbolas**.

hyperbole [haɪˈpɜːbəlɪ] *n* hipérbole *f*.

hyperlink ['haɪpəlɪŋk] *n* hiperenlace.

hypermarket ['haɪpəmɑːkɪt] *n* GB hipermercado.

hypertension [haɪpəˈtenʃən] *n* MED hipertensión *f*.

hypertext ['haɪpətekst] *n* hipertexto.

hyphen ['haɪfən] *n* guion *m*.

hypnosis [hɪpˈnəʊsɪs] *n* MED hipnosis *f*.

hypnotise ['hɪpnətaɪz] *vt* → **hypnotize**.

hypnotize ['hɪpnətaɪz] *vt* hipnotizar.

hypochondriac [haɪpəˈkɒndrɪæk] *n* hipocondríaco,-a.
► *adj* hipocondríaco,-a.

hypocrisy [hɪˈpɒkrɪsɪ] *n* hipocresía.

hypocrite ['hɪpəkrɪt] *n* hipócrita *mf*.

hypotension [haɪpəʊˈtenʃən] *n* MED hipotensión *f*.

hypotenuse [haɪˈpɒtənjuːz] *n (geometry)* hipotenusa.

hypothesis [haɪˈpɒθəsɪs] *n* hipótesis *f*.
① *pl* **hypotheses** [haɪˈpɒθəsiːz].

hypothetic [haɪpəˈθetɪk] *adj* hipotético,-a.

hysteria [hɪˈstɪərɪə] *n* histeria.

hysterical [hɪˈsterɪkəl] *adj* histérico,-a.

H

I

I, i [aɪ] *n (the letter)* I, i *f*.

I [aɪ] *pron* yo.

Iberian [aɪˈbɪərɪən] *adj (modern)* ibérico,-a; *(historically)* ibero,-a, íbero,-a.
► *n* **1** *(person - now)* ibérico,-a; *(- historically)* ibero,-a, íbero,-a. **2** *(language)* ibero, íbero. COMP **Iberian Peninsula** Península Ibérica.

ice [aɪs] *n* **1** *(frozen water)* hielo. **2** *(ice-cream)* helado. COMP **ice cube** cubito de hielo. ▮ **ice hockey** hockey *m* sobre hielo. ▮ **ice lolly** polo. ▮ **ice ring** pista de hielo.

iceberg [ˈaɪsbɜːg] *n* **1** iceberg *m*. **2** *fig* persona fría.

icebreaker [ˈaɪsbreɪkəʳ] *n* rompehielos *m inv*.

ice-cream [ˈaɪskriːm] *n* helado.

Iceland [ˈaɪslənd] *n* Islandia.

Icelander [ˈaɪsləndəʳ] *n (person)* islandés,-esa.

Icelandic [aɪsˈlændɪk] *adj* islandés,-esa.
► *n (language)* islandés *m*.

ice-skate [ˈaɪsskeɪt] *vi* patinar sobre hielo.

ice-skating [ˈaɪskeɪtɪŋ] *n* patinaje *m* sobre hielo.

icicle [ˈaɪsɪkəl] *n* carámbano.

icing [ˈaɪsɪŋ] *n* cobertura.

icon [ˈaɪkən] *n* icono.

iconography [aɪkəˈnɒgrəfɪ] *n* iconografía.

icy [ˈaɪsɪ] *adj* **1** *(very cold - hand, etc)* helado,-a; *(- wind)* glacial. **2** *(covered with ice)* cubierto,-a de hielo. **3** *fig* glacial.
ⓘ *comp* **icier,** *superl* **iciest**.

ID [aɪˈdiː] *abbr* **(**identification**)** identificación *f*. COMP **ID card** documento nacional de identidad, DNI *m*.

I'd [aɪd] *contr* **1** I would. **2** I had.

idea [aɪˈdɪə] *n* **1** *(gen)* idea; *(opinion)* opinión *f*, *(intuition)* impresión *f*, sensación *f*. **3** *(concept)* concepto.
► *n* **the idea** *(aim, purpose)* idea, intención *f*, objetivo.

ideal [aɪˈdiːl] *adj* ideal, perfecto,-a.
► *n* **1** *(perfect example)* ideal *m*. **2** *(principle)* principio, ideal *m*.

idealize [aɪˈdɪəlaɪz] *vt* idealizar: *we tend to idealize the past* tendemos a idealizar el pasado.

identical [aɪˈdentɪkəl] *adj* **1** *(exactly alike)* idéntico,-a **(to/with,** a**)**. **2** *(the same)* mismísimo,-a.

identification [aɪdentɪfɪˈkeɪʃən] *n* **1** *(gen)* identificación *f*. **2** *(papers)* documentación *f*.

identify [aɪˈdentɪfaɪ] *vt* **1** *(gen)* identificar. **2** *(associate)* asociar **(with,** con**)**, relacionar **(with,** con**)**.
ⓘ *pt & pp* **identified,** *ger* **identifying**.

Identikit® [aɪˈdentɪkɪt] COMP **Identikit picture** retrato robot.

identity [aɪˈdentɪtɪ] *n* identidad *f*. COMP **identity card** carnet *m* de identidad.
ⓘ *pl* **identities**.

ideogram [ˈɪdɪəʊgræm] *n* ideograma *m*.

ideological [aɪdɪəˈlɒdʒɪkəl] *adj* ideológico,-a.

ideology [aɪdɪˈɒlədʒɪ] *n* ideología.
ⓘ *pl* **ideologies**.

idiom [ˈɪdɪəm] *n* **1** *(phrase)* locución *f*, modismo, frase *f* hecha. **2** *(language)* lenguaje *m*, idioma *m*; *(style)* estilo.

❌ **Idiom** no significa 'idioma', que se traduce por **language**.

idiomatic [ɪdɪəˈmætɪk] *adj* idiomático,-a.

idiot ['ɪdɪət] *n* **1** *fam* idiota *mf*, tonto,-a. **2** MED idiota *mf*.

idle ['aɪdªl] *adj* **1** *(lazy)* perezoso,-a, vago,-a. **2** *(not working - person)* parado,-a, desempleado,-a; *(- machinery)* parado,-a; *(- money)* improductivo,-a.
ⓘ *comp* idler, *superl* idlest
▶ *vi (waste time)* gandulear, holgazanear, perder el tiempo.

idol ['aɪdªl] *n* ídolo.

idolatry [aɪ'dɒlətrɪ] *n* idolatría.
ⓘ *pl* idolatries.

i.e. ['aɪ'iː] *abbr* (id est) esto es, a saber; *(abbreviation)* i.e.

if [ɪf] *conj* **1** *(supposing)* si: *if it rains, we'll stay at home* si llueve, nos quedaremos en casa; *you can come if you want* puedes venir si quieres. **2** *(whether)* si: *do you know if she got the job?* ¿sabes si consiguió el trabajo? **3** *(used after verbs expressing feelings)* que: *do you mind if I open the window?* ¿te importa que abra la ventana? **4** *(but)* aunque, pero: *it's good, if a little slow at times* es bueno pero algo lento a veces. **5** *(in exclamations)*: *well, if it isn't Jimmy Jazz!* vaya, ¡pero si es Jimmy Jazz!
LOC *if I were you* yo que tú, yo en tu lugar. ▮ *if only (present or future time)* ¡ojalá!, ¡si al menos...!

igloo ['ɪglʊ:] *n* iglú *m*.
ⓘ *pl* igloos.

igneous ['ɪgnɪəs] *adj* ígneo,-a.

ignition [ɪg'nɪʃªn] *n* **1** ignición *f*. **2** AUTO encendido, arranque *m*.

ignorance ['ɪgnərəns] *n* ignorancia.

ignorant ['ɪgnərənt] *adj* **1** *(unaware)* ignorante (of, de). **2** *fam (rude)* descortés, maleducado,-a.

ignore [ɪg'nɔː'] *vt* **1** *(order, warning)* no hacer caso de, hacer caso omiso de; *(behaviour, fact)* pasar por alto. **2** *(person)* hacer como si no existiese.

✘ To **ignore** no significa 'ignorar (no saber)', que se traduce por **not to know**.

iguana [ɪ'gwɑːnə] *n* iguana.

ilium ['ɪlɪəm] *n* ilion *m*, íleon *m*.

ill [ɪl] *adj* **1** *(sick)* enfermo,-a. **2** *(harmful, unpropitious)* malo,-a.
▶ *n fml (harm, evil)* mal *m*.

▶ *adv* **1** *(badly)* mal. **2** *(unfavourably)* mal. **3** *(with difficulty)* mal, a duras penas.
▶ *n pl* ills *(problems, misfortunes)* desgracias *fpl*.

I'll [aɪl] *contr* **1** I will. **2** I shall.

illegal [ɪ'liːgªl] *adj* ilegal.

illegality [ɪlɪ'gælɪtɪ] *n* ilegalidad *f*.
ⓘ *pl* illegalities.

illegible [ɪ'ledʒɪbªl] *adj* ilegible.

illegitimate [ɪlɪ'dʒɪtɪmət] *adj* ilegítimo,-a.

illicit [ɪ'lɪsɪt] *adj* ilícito,-a.

illiterate [ɪ'lɪtªrət] *adj* **1** *(unlettered)* analfabeto,-a. **2** *(uneducated)* ignorante, inculto,-a. **3** *(poor style)* inculto,-a, pobre.
▶ *n (unlettered person)* analfabeto,-a.

ill-mannered [ɪl'mænəd] *adj* maleducado,-a, descortés.

illness ['ɪlnəs] *n* enfermedad *f*.
ⓘ *pl* illnesses.

illogical [ɪ'lɒdʒɪkªl] *adj* ilógico,-a.

illuminate [ɪ'luːmɪneɪt] *vt* iluminar.

illuminated [ɪ'luːmɪneɪtªd] *adj (manuscript)* iluminado,-a.

illumination [ɪluːmɪ'neɪʃªn] *n* **1** *(light)* iluminación *f*. **2** *(clarification)* aclaración.

illusion [ɪ'luːʒªn] *n* ilusión *f*, falsa impresión *f*.

✘ **Illusion** no significa 'ilusión (esperanza)', que se traduce por **hope**.

illusionist [ɪ'luːʒªnɪst] *n* ilusionista *mf*.

illustrate ['ɪləstreɪt] *vt* ilustrar.

illustrated ['ɪləstreɪt] *adj* ilustrado,-a.

✘ **Illustrated** no significa 'ilustrado (culto)', que se traduce por **learned**.

illustration [ɪləs'treɪʃªn] *n* **1** *(gen)* ilustración *f*. **2** *(example)* ejemplo.

illustrative ['ɪləstrətɪv] *adj* **1** *(gen)* ilustrativo,-a, ilustrador,-ra. **2** *(example)* aclaratorio,-a.

I'm [aɪm] *contr* I am.

image ['ɪmɪdʒ] *n* **1** *(gen)* imagen *f*. **2** *(reputation)* imagen *f*, fama, reputación *f*.

imaginary [ɪ'mædʒɪnərɪ] *adj* imaginario,-a, inventado,-a.

imagination [ɪmædʒɪ'neɪʃ°n] *n (gen)* imaginación *f; (inventiveness)* inventiva.

imaginative [ɪ'mædʒɪnətɪv] *adj (person)* imaginativo,-a, de gran inventiva; *(creation)* lleno,-a de imaginación, lleno,-a de fantasía.

imagine [ɪ'mædʒɪn] *vt* **1** *(visualize)* imaginar. **2** *(suppose)* suponer, imaginar(se), figurarse.

imam [ɪ'mɑːm] *n* imán *m*.

imbalance [ɪm'bæləns] *n* desequilibrio.

IMF ['aɪ'em'ef] *abbr* (International Monetary Fund) Fondo Monetario Internacional; *(abbreviation)* FMI *m*.

imitate ['ɪmɪteɪt] *vt (gen)* imitar, copiar; *(for fun)* imitar.

imitation [ɪmɪ'teɪʃ°n] *n* **1** *(gen)* imitación *f*, copia; *(for fun)* imitación *f*. **2** *(reproduction)* reproducción *f*.
▸ *adj* de imitación.

immaterial [ɪmə'tɪərɪəl] *adj* **1** *(unimportant)* irrelevante. **2** *(incorporeal)* inmaterial, incorpóreo,-a.

immature [ɪmə'tjʊəʳ] *adj* **1** *(gen)* inmaduro,-a; *(- plant)* joven. **2** *(childish)* inmaduro,-a, pueril.

immediate [ɪ'miːdɪət] *adj* **1** *(instant)* inmediato,-a; *(urgent)* urgente. **2** *(nearest)* inmediato,-a, más próximo,-a. **3** *(direct)* primero,-a, principal.

immediately [ɪ'miːdɪətlɪ] *adv (instantly, at once)* inmediatamente, de inmediato, en seguida, en el acto.

immense [ɪ'mens] *adj* inmenso,-a, enorme.

immensely [ɪ'menslɪ] *adv* enormemente, sumamente.

immersion [ɪ'mɜː'ʃ°n] *n* **1** inmersión *f*, sumersión *f*. **2** *fig* absorción *f*.

immigrant ['ɪmɪgrənt] *adj* inmigrante.
▸ *n* inmigrante *mf*.

immigrate ['ɪmɪgreɪt] *vi* inmigrar.

immigration [ɪmɪ'greɪʃ°n] *n* inmigración *f*.

imminent ['ɪmɪnənt] *adj* inminente.

immoral [ɪ'mɒrªl] *adj* inmoral.

immortal [ɪ'mɔː'tªl] *adj* **1** *(god, soul, etc)* inmortal. **2** *fig (fame, memory, etc)* imperecedero,-a, perdurable.
▸ *n* inmortal *mf*.

immortality [ɪmɔː'tælɪtɪ] *n* inmortalidad *f*.

immune [ɪ'mjuːn] *adj* **1** *(gen)* inmune (to, a). **2** *(exempt)* exento,-a.

immunity [ɪ'mjuːnɪtɪ] *n* **1** *(gen)* inmunidad *f*. **2** *(exemption)* exención *f*.

immunize ['ɪmjənaɪz] *vt* inmunizar (against, contra).

immunodeficient [ɪmjʊnəʊdɪ'fɪʃ°nt] *adj* inmunodeficiente.

immunodeficiency [ɪmjʊnəʊdɪ'fɪʃ°n-sɪ] *n* inmunodeficiencia.

immunology [ɪmjuː'nɒlədʒɪ] *n* inmunología.

impact [*(n)* 'ɪmpækt; *(vb)* ɪm'pækt] *n* **1** *(gen)* impacto; *(crash)* choque *m*. **2** *(impression, effect)* efecto, impresión *f*, impacto.
▸ *vt* US *(have impact on)* impresionar.

impartial [ɪm'pɑː'ʃªl] *adj* imparcial.

impatience [ɪm'peɪʃ°ns] *n* **1** *(eagerness)* impaciencia, ansiedad *f*. **2** *(irritation)* impaciencia, irritación *f*.

impatient [ɪm'peɪʃ°nt] *adj* **1** *(eager)* impaciente, ansioso,-a. **2** *(irritable)* irritable. **3** *fml (intolerant)* intolerante.

impeachment [ɪm'piː.tʃmənt] *n* JUR *(accusation)* acusación *f*, denuncia; *(trial)* proceso.

impeccable [ɪm'pekəbªl] *adj (gen)* impecable, perfecto,-a.

impending [ɪm'pendɪŋ] *adj* inminente.

imperative [ɪm'perətɪv] *adj* **1** *(indispensable)* imprescindible. **2** *(authoritative)* imperativo,-a, imperioso,-a. **3** LING imperativo,-a.

imperfect [ɪm'pɜːfekt] *adj* **1** *(gen)* imperfecto,-a; *(goods, sight)* defectuoso,-a. **2** LING imperfecto,-a.
▸ *n* the imperfect LING el imperfecto.

imperfection [ɪmpə'fekʃ°n] *n (gen)* imperfección *f; (defect)* defecto, tara, tacha; *(blemish)* mancha.

imperial [ɪmˈpɪərɪəl] *adj* **1** *(gen)* imperial. **2** *(weight, measure)* del sistema métrico *británico*.

imperialism [ɪmˈpɪərɪəlɪzᵊm] *n* imperialismo.

imperialist [ɪmˈpɪərɪəlɪst] *n* imperialista *mf*.

impersonal [ɪmˈpɜːsᵊnəl] *adj* impersonal.

impersonate [ɪmˈpɜːsᵊneɪt] *vt* **1** *(imitate to deceive)* hacerse pasar por. **2** *(imitate to entertain)* imitar.

impertinent [ɪmˈpɜːtɪnənt] *adj* impertinente, descarado,-a.

implant [*(vb)* ɪmˈplɑːnt; *(n)* ˈɪmplɑːnt] *vt* **1** MED implantar, injertar. **2** *(ideas, etc)* inculcar (in, en).
▸ *n* MED implantación *f*, injerto.

implement [*(n)* ˈɪmpləmənt; *(vb)* ˈɪmplɪment] *n* *(instrument)* instrumento, utensilio; *(tool)* herramienta.
▸ *vt* *(plan, suggestion, etc)* llevar a cabo, poner en práctica, *(law, policy)* aplicar.

implementation [ɪmpləmənˈteɪʃᵊn] *n* *(of plan, etc)* puesta en práctica, desarrollo; *(of law, etc)* aplicación *f*.

implicate [ˈɪmplɪkeɪt] *vt* implicar, (in, en).

implication [ɪmplɪˈkeɪʃᵊn] *n* implicación *f*.

implicit [ɪmˈplɪsɪt] *adj* **1** *(implied)* implícito,-a, tácito,-a. **2** *(absolute)* absoluto,-a, incondicional.

implied [ɪmˈplaɪd] *adj* implícito,-a, tácito,-a.

imply [ɪmˈplaɪ] *vt* **1** *(involve, entail)* implicar, suponer, presuponer. **2** *(mean)* significar, querer decir; *(hint)* insinuar, dar a entender.
ⓘ *pt & pp* implied.

impolite [ɪmpəˈlaɪt] *adj* maleducado,-a, descortés.

import [ˈɪmpɔːt] *n* **1** *(article)* artículo de importación. **2** *(activity)* importación *f*.
▸ *vt* importar.

❎ To import no significa 'importar (tener importancia)', que se traduce por to matter.

importance [ɪmˈpɔːtᵊns] *n* importancia.

important [ɪmˈpɔːtᵊnt] *adj* **1** *(gen)* importante. **2** *(influential)* de categoría.

importation [ɪmpɔːˈteɪʃᵊn] *n* importación *f*.

importer [ɪmˈpɔːtəʳ] *n* importador,-ra.

impose [ɪmˈpəʊz] *vt* *(gen)* imponer (on, a).
◆ to impose on *vt insep* *(take advantage of)* abusar de, aprovecharse de.

impossible [ɪmˈpɒsɪbᵊl] *adj* *(gen)* imposible.

impotence [ˈɪmpətᵊns] *n* impotencia.

impoverishment [ɪmˈpɒvᵊrɪʃmənt] *n* empobrecimiento.

imprecise [ɪmprəˈsaɪs] *adj* impreciso,-a, inexacto,-a.

imprecision [ɪmprəˈsɪʒᵊn] *n* imprecisión *f*, falta de precisión.

impress [ɪmˈpres] *vt* **1** *(cause respect)* impresionar. **2** *(emphasize, stress)* subrayar, convencer, recalcar. **3** *fig* grabar.

impression [ɪmˈpreʃᵊn] *n* **1** *(gen)* impresión *f*. **2** *(imitation)* imitación *f*. **3** *(imprint, mark)* marca, señal *f*, impresión *f*; *(in wax, plaster)* molde *m*; *(of foot, etc)* huella. **4** *(reprint)* impresión *f*, edición *f*.

impressionism [ɪmˈpreʃᵊnɪzᵊm] *n* ART impresionismo.

impressionist [ɪmˈpreʃᵊnɪst] *adj* ART impresionista.
▸ *n* **1** ART impresionista. **2** *(mimic)* imitador,-ra.

impressive [ɪmˈpresɪv] *adj* impresionante.

imprison [ɪmˈprɪzᵊn] *vt* encarcelar, meter en la cárcel.

imprisonment [ɪmˈprɪzᵊnmənt] *n* encarcelamiento.

improbable [ɪmˈprɒbəbᵊl] *adj* **1** *(event)* improbable. **2** *(story, explanation)* inverosímil.

improper [ɪmˈprɒpəʳ] *adj* **1** *(behaviour)* impropio,-a; *(method, conditions)* inadecuado,-a. **3** *(language)* indecente. **2** *(proposal)* deshonesto,-a.

improve [ɪmˈpruːv] *vt* **1** *(quality, etc)* mejorar. **2** *(skill, knowledge)* perfeccionar. **3** *(mind)* cultivar. **4** *(property)* hacer mejoras en. **5** *(increase)* aumentar.
▸ *vi* *(get better)* mejorar, mejorarse.

◆ **to improve on** *vt insep (better)* superar.

improvement [ɪmˈpruːvmənt] *n* **1** *(gen)* mejora, mejoramiento; *(in health)* mejoría. **2** *(in knowledge)* perfeccionamiento. **3** *(increase)* aumento.

improvise [ˈɪmprəvaɪz] *vt* improvisar.

imprudent [ɪmˈpruːdᵊnt] *adj fml (unwise)* imprudente; *(rash)* precipitado,-a.

impudent [ˈɪmpjudᵊnt] *adj* insolente, fresco,-a, descarado,-a.

impulse [ˈɪmpʌls] *n* **1** *(sudden urge)* impulso, capricho; *(stimulus, drive)* impulso, estímulo, ímpetu *m*. **2** TECH impulso.

impulsive [ɪmˈpʌlsɪv] *adj* impulsivo,-a, irreflexivo,-a.

impunity [ɪmˈpjuːnɪtɪ] *n* impunidad *f*.

impure [ɪmˈpjʊəʳ] *adj* **1** *(contaminated)* contaminado,-a; *(adulterated)* adulterado,-a. **2** *(morally - act)* impuro,-a; *(- thought)* impúdico,-a, deshonesto,-a.

in¹ [ɪn] *prep* **1** *(place)* en, dentro de: *it's in the box* está en la caja. **2** *(motion)* en, a: *we arrived in Bonn* llegamos a Bonn. **3** *(time - during)* en, durante: *in 1980* en 1980. **4** *(time - within)* en, dentro de. **5** *(wearing)* en, vestido,-a de: *the woman in black* la mujer vestida de negro. **6** *(state, condition)* en. **7** *(ratio, measurement, number)* varias traducciones: *in twos* de dos en dos; *she's in her thirties* tiene treinta y tantos años. **8** *(profession)* en: *she's in television* trabaja en la televisión. **9** *(weather, light)* varias traducciones: *walking in the rain* caminando bajo la lluvia. **10** *(after superlative)* de: *the tallest in the class* el más alto de la clase. ⸤LOC⸥ **in all** en total.

▶ *adv* **1** *(motion)* dentro. **2** *(tide)* alto,-a. **3** *(fashionable)* de moda: *hats are in* los sombreros están de moda. **4** *(on sale, obtainable)* disponible.

▶ *n pl* **ins and outs** *(details)* detalles *mpl*, pormenores *mpl*.

▶ *phr* **to be in** *(at home)* estar en casa; *(at work)* estar.

inability [ɪnəˈbɪlɪtɪ] *n* incapacidad *f*.

inaccessible [ɪnækˈsesəbᵊl] *adj* inaccesible.

inaccuracy [ɪnˈækjərəsɪ] *n* **1** *(gen)* inexactitud *f*. **2** *(error)* error *m*, incorrección *f*.
① *pl* **inaccuracies**.

inaccurate [ɪnˈækjərət] *adj (gen)* inexacto,-a; *(incorrect)* incorrecto,-a, erróneo,-a.

inactive [ɪnˈæktɪv] *adj* inactivo,-a.

inactivity [ɪnækˈtɪvtɪ] *n* inactividad *f*.

inadequate [ɪnˈædɪkwət] *adj* **1** *(not sufficient)* insuficiente; *(not appropriate)* inadecuado,-a. **2** *(person)* incapaz, incompetente. **3** *(defective)* defectuoso,-a, imperfecto,-a.

inanimate [ɪnˈænɪmət] *adj* inanimado,-a.

inappropriate [ɪnəˈprəuprɪət] *adj (unsuitable - clothes, behaviour)* poco apropiado,-a, no apropiado,-a; *(- time, remark)* inoportuno,-a, inconveniente.

inarticulate [ɪnɑːˈtɪkjʊlət] *adj* **1** *(person)* incapaz de expresarse. **2** *(speech, words, writing)* mal expresado,-a, incoherente. **3** *(cry, sound)* inarticulado,-a. **4** *(joints)* inarticulado,-a.

inattentive [ɪnəˈtentɪv] *adj (not paying attention)* poco atento,-a, distraído,-a; *(not attentive)* poco atento,-a.

inaudible [ɪnˈɔːdəbᵊl] *adj* inaudible, imperceptible.

inaugural [ɪˈnɔːgjʊrəl] *adj* inaugural, de inauguración, de apertura.

inaugurate [ɪˈnɔːgjʊreɪt] *vt* **1** *(building, exhibition, etc)* inaugurar. **2** *(president, etc)* investir.

inauguration [ɪnɔːgjʊˈreɪʃᵊn] *n* **1** *(of building, etc)* inauguración *f*. **2** *(of president, etc)* investidura, toma de posesión.

inborn [ˈɪnbɔːn] *adj* innato,-a.

inbox [ˈɪnbɒks] *n* bandeja de entrada.

inbred [ˈɪnbred] *adj* **1** *(innate)* innato,-a. **2** *(produced by inbreeding)* endogámico,-a.

Inc [ɪnˈkɔːpəreɪtɪd] *abbr* US (Incorporated) ≈ sociedad *f* anónima; *(abbreviation)* S.A.

incantation [ɪnkænˈteɪʃᵊn] *n* conjuro, ensalmo.

incapable [ɪnˈkeɪpəbᵊl] *adj* **1** *(unable)* incapaz. **2** *(incompetent)* incompetente.

3 *(helpless)* impotente, imposibilitado,-a.

incapacity [ɪnkəˈpæsɪtɪ] *n* incapacidad *f.*

incense¹ [ˈɪnsens] *n* incienso.

incense² [ɪnˈsens] *vt (make angry)* enfurecer, poner furioso,-a.

incentive [ɪnˈsentɪv] *n* incentivo, estímulo, aliciente *m.*

incest [ˈɪnsest] *n* incesto.

inch [ɪntʃ] *n* **1** *(measurement)* pulgada. **2** *(small amount)* poco, pelo, ápice *m.*
ⓘ *pl* inches.

✎ Equivale a 2,54 cm.

incidence [ˈɪnsɪdⁿs] *n* **1** *(occurrence)* frecuencia, extensión *f.* **2** PHYS incidencia.

incident [ˈɪnsɪdⁿnt] *n (event)* incidente *m; (violent episode)* altercado.

incidentally [ɪnsɪˈdentⁿlɪ] *adv* **1** *(by the way)* a propósito, por cierto, dicho sea de paso. **2** *(by chance)* por casualidad.

incinerate [ɪnˈsɪnəreɪt] *vt* incinerar, quemar.

incineration [ɪnsɪnəˈreɪʃⁿn] *n* incineración *f,* quema.

incision [ɪnˈsɪʒⁿn] *n* incisión *f.*

incisive [ɪnˈsaɪsɪv] *adj* **1** *(comment, wit)* incisivo,-a, mordaz. **2** *(mind)* penetrante.

incisor [ɪnˈsaɪzəʳ] *n* (diente *m*) incisivo.

inclination [ɪnklɪˈneɪʃⁿn] *n* **1** *(tendency)* inclinación *f,* tendencia; *(disposition)* disposición *f,* propensión *f.* **2** *(slope)* inclinación *f,* pendiente *f.* **3** *(bow)* inclinación *f.*

incline [*(n)* ˈɪnklaɪn; *(vb)* ɪnˈklaɪn] *n* pendiente *f,* inclinación *f,* cuesta.
▶ *vt* **1** *(bend forward)* inclinar. **2** *fml (persuade, influence)* inclinar, predisponer.
▶ *vi* **1** *(slope)* inclinarse, estar inclinado,-a. **2** *(tend)* tender a, tener tendencia a.

inclined [ɪnˈklaɪnd] *adj* **1** *(disposed, encouraged)* dispuesto,-a (to, a). **2** *(tending to)* propenso,-a. **3** *(having natural ability)* dotado,-a. **4** *(sloping)* inclinado,-a.

include [ɪnˈkluːd] *vt* incluir.

including [ɪnˈkluːdɪŋ] *prep* incluso, incluyendo.

inclusion [ɪnˈkluːʒⁿn] *n* inclusión *f.*

inclusive [ɪnˈkluːsɪv] *adj* inclusive.

incognito [ɪnkɒgˈniːtəʊ] *adv* de incógnito.

incoherence [ɪnkəʊˈhɪərəns] *n* incoherencia.

incoherent [ɪnkəʊˈhɪərənt] *adj* incoherente.

income [ˈɪnkʌm] *n (from work)* ingresos *mpl,* renta; *(from investment)* réditos *mpl.* COMP **income tax** impuesto sobre la renta.

incompatibility [ɪnkəmpætəˈbɪlɪtɪ] *n* incompatibilidad *f.*
ⓘ *pl* incompatibilities.

incompatible [ɪnkəmˈpætəbⁿl] *adj* incompatible (with, con).

incompetence [ɪnˈkɒmpətⁿns] *n* incompetencia, ineptitud *f,* incapacidad *f.*

incompetent [ɪnˈkɒmpətⁿnt] *adj* incompetente, inepto,-a, incapaz.
▶ *n* incompetente *mf,* inepto,-a.

incomplete [ɪnkəmˈpliːt] *adj* **1** *(not whole)* incompleto,-a; *(not finished)* inacabado,-a, sin terminar. **2** *(partial)* parcial.

incomprehensible [ɪnkɒmprɪˈhensəbⁿl] *adj* incomprensible.

inconceivable [ɪnkənˈsiːvəbⁿl] *adj* **1** inconcebible. **2** *fam* imposible, increíble.

inconclusive [ɪnkənˈkluːsɪv] *adj* **1** *(debate, vote, etc)* no decisivo,-a. **2** *(evidence, result, etc)* no concluyente.

inconsequent [ɪnˈkɒnsɪkwənt] *adj* **1** *(not following logically)* inconsecuente. **2** *(inconsequential)* de poca importancia, sin trascendencia.

inconsiderate [ɪnkənˈsɪdⁿrət] *adj* desconsiderado,-a, inconsiderado,-a, poco atento,-a.

inconsistent [ɪnkənˈsɪstⁿnt] *adj* **1** *(not agreeing with, at variance with)* inconsecuente; *(contradictory)* contradictorio, -a. **2** *(changeable - weather)* variable; *(- person)* inconstante, voluble, irregular; *(- behaviour)* imprevisible, irregular.

inconstant [ɪnˈkɒnstᵊnt] *adj* **1** *(person)* inconstante, veleidoso,-a, mudable. **2** *(not fixed)* variable.

incontinence [ɪnˈkɒntɪnᵊns] *n* incontinencia.

inconvenience [ɪnkənˈviːnɪəns] *n (gen)* inconveniente *m*; *(trouble, difficulty)* molestia, dificultad *f*; *(hindrance)* estorbo, obstáculo; *(discomfort)* incomodidad *f*: *I'm sorry to cause you so much inconvenience* siento causarle tanta molestia.
▸ *vt (annoy)* causar molestia a, molestar; *(cause difficulty)* incomodar.

inconvenient [ɪnkənˈviːnɪənt] *adj* **1** *(gen)* inconveniente, molesto,-a, incómodo,-a; *(place)* mal situado,-a; *(time)* mal, inoportuno,-a; *(arrangement)* poco práctico,-a. **2** *(fact)* incómodo,-a.

incorporate [ɪnˈkɔːpəreɪt] *vt* **1** *(make part of, include in)* incorporar (**in/into**, a), incluir (**in/into**, en); *(include, contain)* incluir, contener. **2** US *(company)* constituir, constituir en sociedad.
▸ *adj* US *(company)* constituido,-a, constituido,-a en sociedad.

☒ To incorporate no significa 'incorporarse (levantarse)', que se traduce por to sit up.

incorrect [ɪnkəˈrekt] *adj* **1** *(wrong, untrue)* incorrecto,-a, erróneo,-a, equivocado,-a. **2** *(- dress)* impropio,-a, inadecuado,-a.

increase [*(n)* ˈɪnkriːs; *(vb)* ɪnˈkriːs] *n (gen)* aumento, incremento; *(in price, temperature)* subida, alza.
▸ *vt (gen)* aumentar, incrementar; *(temperature)* subir.

increasing [ɪnˈkriːsɪŋ] *adj* creciente.

increasingly [ɪnˈkriːsɪŋlɪ] *adv* cada vez más.

incredible [ɪnˈkredɪbᵊl] *adj (unbelievable)* increíble, inverosímil; *(amazing)* fantástico,-a.

incredulous [ɪnˈkredjələs] *adj* incrédulo,-a.

increment [ˈɪnkrɪmənt] *n* aumento, incremento.

incriminate [ɪnˈkrɪmɪneɪt] *vt* incriminar.

incubate [ˈɪnkjʊbeɪt] *vt* incubar.
▸ *vi (of eggs)* incubar; *(of bird)* empollar.

incubation [ɪnkjʊˈbeɪᵊn] *n* incubación *f*.

incubator [ˈɪnkjʊbeɪtəʳ] *n* incubadora.

incurable [ɪnˈkjʊərəbᵊl] *adj* **1** *(disease)* incurable. **2** *fig (loss)* irremediable; *(habit, optimist)* incorregible.
▸ *n* enfermo,-a incurable.

indebted [ɪnˈdetɪd] *adj* **1** *(in debt)* endeudado,-a. **2** *fig (grateful)* agradecido,-a.

indecent [ɪnˈdiːsᵊnt] *adj* **1** *(obscene)* indecente, indecoroso,-a, obsceno,-a. **2** *(improper)* impropio,-a, indebido,-a, injustificado,-a; *(undue)* excesivo,-a.

indecisive [ɪndɪˈsaɪsɪv] *adj* **1** *(hesitant)* indeciso,-a, irresoluto,-a. **2** *(inconclusive)* poco concluyente, no concluyente, no decisivo,-a.

indeed [ɪnˈdiːd] *adv* **1** *(yes, certainly)* efectivamente, en efecto: *are you Mr Fox? yes, indeed* ¿es el Sr Fox? sí, efectivamente. **2** *(intensifier)* realmente, de veras, de verdad: *thank you very much indeed* muchísimas gracias. **3** *fml (in fact)* realmente, en realidad, de hecho; *(what is more)* es más.

indefinite [ɪnˈdefɪnət] *adj* **1** *(vague, not precise)* indefinido,-a, vago,-a, impreciso,-a. **2** *(not fixed - period of time, amount, number)* indefinido,-a, indeterminado,-a.

indefinitely [ɪnˈdefɪnətlɪ] *adv* indefinidamente.

indemnity [ɪnˈdemnɪtɪ] *n* **1** *(insurance, guarantee)* indemnidad *f* (**against**, contra). **2** *(compensation)* indemnización *f* (**for**, por), reparación *f*, compensación *f*.
① *pl* indemnities.

indent [*(vb)* ɪnˈdent; *(n)* ˈɪndent] *vt (text)* sangrar.
▸ *vi* GB *(order)* hacer un pedido (**for**, de), encargar (**for**, -).
▸ *n* GB *(order)* pedido.

indentation [ɪndenˈteɪʃᵊn] *n* **1** *(in text)* sangría. **2** *(notch in edge, mark)* mella, muesca.

independence [ɪndɪˈpendəns] *n* independencia (**from**, de).

independent [ɪndɪˈpendənt] *adj (gen)* independiente.
▸ *n* POL (candidato,-a) independiente *mf*.

in-depth [ɪnˈdepθ] *adj* minucioso,-a, exhaustivo,-a, a fondo.

indeterminate [ɪndɪˈtɜːmɪnət] *adj* indeterminado,-a.

India [ˈɪndɪə] *n* (la) India. COMP **India rubber** caucho.

index [ˈɪndeks] *n* índice. COMP **index finger** dedo índice.
ⓘ *pl* **indexes** o **indices** [ˈɪndɪsiːz].

Indian [ˈɪndɪən] *adj* indio,-a, hindú *mf*.
▸ *n* indio,-a, hindú. COMP **the Indian Ocean** el océano Índico.

indicate [ˈɪndɪkeɪt] *vt* indicar, señalar, marcar.
▸ *vi* AUTO poner el intermitente.

indication [ɪndɪˈkeɪʃən] *n (gen)* indicio, señal *f*, indicación *f*.

indicative [ɪnˈdɪkətɪv] *adj* **1** *fml* indicativo,-a (of, de). **2** LING indicativo,-a.
▸ *n* LING indicativo.

indicator [ˈɪndɪkeɪtəʳ] *n* **1** *(gen)* indicador *m*. **2** AUTO intermitente *m*.

indices [ˈɪndɪsiːz] *n pl* → **index**.

indictment [ɪnˈdaɪtmənt] *n* **1** JUR acusación *f*, sumario. **2** *fig (criticism)* crítica.

indifference [ɪnˈdɪfərəns] *n* indiferencia (to, ante).

indifferent [ɪnˈdɪfərənt] *adj* **1** *(gen)* indiferente (to, a). **2** *(mediocre, average)* mediocre, regular, pobre.

✖ Indifferent no significa 'indiferente (irrelevante)', que se traduce por immaterial.

indigestion [ɪndɪˈdʒestʃən] *n* indigestión *f*, empacho.

indignation [ɪndɪgˈneɪʃən] *n* indignación *f* (about/over, por) (at, ante/por).

indigo [ˈɪndɪgəʊ] *n* añil *m*.

indirect [ɪndɪˈrekt] *adj* indirecto,-a.

indirectly [ɪndɪˈrektlɪ] *adv* indirectamente.

indissoluble [ɪndɪˈsɒljəbəl] *adj fml (cannot be dissolved)* indisoluble; *(cannot be broken)* inseparable.

individual [ɪndɪˈvɪdjʊəl] *adj* **1** *(single, separate)* por separado. **2** *(for one person)* individual. **3** *(particular, personal)* personal, propio,-a. **4** *(different, unique)* personal, original.
▸ *n* **1** *(person)* individuo, persona. **2** *fam* individuo, tipo, tío,-a.

individualism [ɪndɪˈvɪdjʊəlɪzəm] *n* individualismo.

individualist [ɪndɪˈvɪdjʊəlɪst] *n* individualista *mf*.

individually [ɪndɪˈvɪdjʊəlɪ] *adv (separately)* individualmente, por separado; *(one by one)* uno por uno.

indivisible [ɪndɪˈvɪzəbəl] *adj* indivisible.

indoor [ˈɪndɔːʳ] *adj* **1** *(aerial, plant, photography, etc)* interior; *(clothes, etc)* de estar por casa. **2** SP *(swimming pool, running track)* cubierto,-a.

indoors [ɪnˈdɔːz] *adv (inside house)* dentro (de casa); *(at home)* en casa; *(inside building)* a cubierto, dentro.

induction [ɪnˈdʌkʃən] *n* **1** *(initiation - gen)* admisión *f*, ingreso; *(- of priest)* instalación *f*. **2** US *(recruitment)* reclutamiento. **3** *(logic)* inducción *f*.

inductive [ɪnˈdʌktɪv] *adj* inductivo,-a.

indulgence [ɪnˈdʌldʒəns] *n* **1** *(luxury)* (pequeño) lujo; *(bad habit)* vicio. **2** *(of desire, whim)* satisfacción *f*, complacencia; *(partaking - of food, drink)* abuso; *(of person)* consentimiento; *(of child)* mimo. **3** REL indulgencia.

industrial [ɪnˈdʌstrɪəl] *adj* industrial.

industrialize [ɪnˈdʌstrɪəlaɪz] *vt* industrializar.
▸ *vi* industrializarse.

industrious [ɪnˈdʌstrɪəs] *adj (hard-working)* trabajador,-ra, laborioso,-a; *(diligent)* diligente, aplicado,-a.

industry [ˈɪndəstrɪ] *n* **1** *(gen)* industria. **2** *fml (hard work)* diligencia.
ⓘ *pl* **industries**.

inefficiency [ɪnɪˈfɪʃənsɪ] *n* **1** *(gen)* ineficacia. **2** *(of person)* incompetencia, ineficiencia, ineptitud *f*.

inefficient [ɪnɪˈfɪʃənt] *adj* **1** *(gen)* ineficaz. **2** *(person)* incompetente, ineficiente, poco eficiente.

inept [ɪˈnept] *adj (person)* inepto,-a, incapaz; *(remark)* torpe.

inequality [ɪnɪˈkwɒlətɪ] *n* desigualdad *f*.
ⓘ *pl* inequalities.

inequity [ɪnˈekwətɪ] *n* injusticia.
ⓘ *pl* inequities.

inertia [ɪˈnɜːʃə] *n* **1** PHYS inercia. **2** *(lethargy)* inercia, letargo, apatía.

inevitable [ɪnˈevɪtəbəl] *adj* **1** *(unavoidable)* inevitable. **2** *fam (usual)* sempiterno,-a, consabido,-a, de siempre.

inexact [ɪnɪgˈzækt] *adj* inexacto,-a.

inexpensive [ɪnɪkˈspensɪv] *adj* barato,-a, económico,-a.

inexperience [ɪnɪkˈspɪərɪəns] *n* inexperiencia, falta de experiencia.

inexpert [ɪnˈekspɜːt] *adj (person)* inexperto,-a (at, en).

inexplicable [ɪnɪkˈsplɪkəbəl] *adj* inexplicable.

inexpressive [ɪnɪkˈspresɪv] *adj* inexpresivo,-a.

infant [ˈɪnfənt] *n* **1** *(baby)* bebé *m*, niño,-a; *(at infant school)* niño,-a, párvulo,-a. **2** GB menor *mf* de edad.
COMP **infant school** escuela primaria.

infanticide [ɪnˈfæntɪsaɪd] *n* **1** *(crime)* infanticidio. **2** *(person)* infanticida *mf*.

infantry [ˈɪnfəntrɪ] *n* infantería.

infect [ɪnˈfekt] *vt* **1** *(wound, cut, etc)* infectar; *(food, water, etc)* contaminar; *(person)* contagiar. **2** *fig (emotions)* contagiar. **3** *(poison)* envenenar.

infection [ɪnˈfekʃən] *n* **1** *(of wound, cut, etc)* infección *f*; *(of food, water, etc)* contaminación *f*; *(with illness)* infección *f*, contagio. **2** *(disease)* infección *f*.

infectious [ɪnˈfekʃəs] *adj* infeccioso,-a, contagioso,-a.

inferior [ɪnˈfɪərɪər] *adj* inferior (to, a).
▶ *n* inferior *mf*.

inferiority [ɪnfɪərɪˈɒrətɪ] *n* inferioridad *f*.

infertility [ɪnfəˈtɪlətɪ] *n* esterilidad *f*.

infidel [ˈɪnfɪdəl] *n* infiel *mf*.

☒ Infidel no significa 'infiel (con la pareja, un amigo)', que se traduce por **unfaithful**.

infidelity [ɪnfɪˈdelətɪ] *n* infidelidad *f*.
ⓘ *pl* infidelities.

infiltration [ɪnfɪlˈtreɪʃən] *n* infiltración *f*.

infinite [ˈɪnfɪnət] *adj (endless)* infinito,-a; *(very great)* sin límites.
▶ *n* the Infinite Dios *m*.

infinitesimal [ɪnfɪnɪˈtesɪməl] *adj* infinitesimal, infinitésimo,-a.

infinitive [ɪnˈfɪnɪtɪv] *n* LING infinitivo.

infinity [ɪnˈfɪnɪtɪ] *n* **1** *(gen)* infinidad *f*. **2** MATH infinito.

infirmary [ɪnˈfɜːmərɪ] *n* **1** *(hospital)* hospital *m*. **2** *(in school, etc)* enfermería.
ⓘ *pl* infirmaries.

inflammable [ɪnˈflæməbəl] *adj* **1** inflamable. **2** *fam fig* explosivo,-a.

inflammation [ɪnfləˈmeɪʃən] *n* inflamación *f*.

inflate [ɪnˈfleɪt] *vt* **1** inflar, hinchar. **2** *fig* inflar, hinchar, exagerar. **3** *(economy)* inflar.

inflation [ɪnˈfleɪʃən] *n* inflación *f*.

inflexible [ɪnˈfleksɪbəl] *adj* inflexible.

inflict [ɪnˈflɪkt] *vt* **1** *(grief, suffering, pain)* causar (on, a); *(blow)* dar a, asestar a, propinar a; *(defeat, punishment)* infligir (on, a), imponer (on, a); *(grief, suffering, pain)* causar (on, a). **2** *fig (view, etc)* imponer (on, a).

influence [ˈɪnfluəns] *n (gen)* influencia.
▶ *vt (decision, etc)* influir en/sobre; *(person)* influenciar.

influential [ɪnfluˈenʃəl] *adj* influyente.

influenza [ɪnfluˈenzə] *n* gripe *f*.

info [ˈɪnfəu] *n fam* información *f*.

inform [ɪnˈfɔːm] *vt* informar, notificar.

informal [ɪnˈfɔːməl] *adj (speech)* informal, familiar; *(discussion)* informal.

☒ Informal no significa 'informal (poco serio)', que se traduce por **unreliable**.

information [ɪnfəˈmeɪʃən] *n (gen)* información *f*; *(facts)* datos *mpl*.

informative [ɪnˈfɔːmətɪv] *adj* informativo,-a.

infrared [ɪnfrəˈred] *adj* infrarrojo,-a.

infrastructure [ˈɪnfrəstrʌktʃər] *n* infraestructura.

infringe [ɪnˈfrɪndʒ] *vt (law, rule, etc)* infringir, transgredir, violar; *(copyright,* *agreement, etc)* no respetar; *(liberty, rights)* violar, usurpar.

infuriate [ɪn'tjʊərɪeɪt] *vt* enfurecer, poner furioso,-a, sacar de quicio.

ingenious [ɪn'dʒiːnɪəs] *adj (person, thing)* ingenioso,-a; *(idea)* genial.

ingenuity [ɪndʒɪ'njuːɪtɪ] *n* ingenio, ingeniosidad *f*, inventiva.

ingredient [ɪn'griːdɪənt] *n* **1** CULIN ingrediente *m*. **2** *fig* componente *m*, elemento.

inhabit [ɪn'hæbɪt] *vt* habitar, vivir en, ocupar, poblar.

inhabitable [ɪn'hæbɪtəbəl] *adj* habitable.

❎ Inhabitable no significa 'inhabitable', que se traduce por uninhabitable.

inhabitant [ɪn'hæbɪtənt] *n* habitante *mf*.

inhalation [ɪnhə'leɪʃən] *n* inhalación *f*.

inhale [ɪn'heɪl] *vt (air)* aspirar, respirar; *(gas, vapour)* inhalar.

inherit [ɪn'herɪt] *vt* heredar (from, de).

inheritance [ɪn'herɪtəns] *n (money, property, etc)* herencia (from, de); *(succession)* sucesión *f*.

inheritor [ɪn'herɪtər] *n* heredero,-a.

inhibit [ɪn'hɪbɪt] *vt* **1** *(person)* inhibir, cohibir. **2** *(hold back - attempt)* inhibir. **3** *(prevent)* impedir, restringir.

inhuman [ɪn'hjuːmən] *adj* inhumano,-a.

initial [ɪ'nɪʃəl] *adj* inicial, primero,-a.

▸ *n* inicial *f*, letra inicial.

▸ *n pl* **initials** *(of name)* iniciales *fpl*; *(of abbreviation)* siglas *fpl*.

initially [ɪ'nɪʃəlɪ] *adv* al principio.

initiate [*(vb)* ɪ'nɪʃɪeɪt; *(n)* ɪ'nɪʃɪət] *vt* **1** *(gen)* iniciar; *(reform, plan, etc)* promover. **2** JUR entablar. **3** *(admit, introduce)* admitir (into, en).

▸ *n* iniciado,-a.

initiative [ɪ'nɪʃɪətɪv] *n* iniciativa.

inject [ɪn'dʒekt] *vt* **1** *(drug, etc)* inyectar; *(person)* poner una inyección a, pinchar. **2** *fig (new ideas, enthusiasm, etc)* infundir; *(money, resources, etc)* invertir.

injection [ɪn'dʒekʃn] *n* **1** inyección *f*.

injure ['ɪndʒər] *vt* **1** herir, lesionar, lastimar. **2** *fig (feelings)* herir; *(health, reputation, etc)* perjudicar.

injured ['ɪndʒəd] *adj* **1** *(hurt)* herido,-a, lesionado,-a, lastimado,-a. **2** *fig (offended - feeling)* herido,-a; *(- look, tone, etc)* ofendido,-a.

▸ *n pl* **the injured** los heridos.

injury ['ɪndʒərɪ] *n* **1** herida, lesión *f*. **2** *fig (to feelings, etc)* daño; *(to reputation)* agravio.

① *pl* **injuries.**

❎ Injury no significa 'injuria', que se traduce por insult.

injustice [ɪn'dʒʌstɪs] *n* injusticia.

ink [ɪŋk] *n* tinta.

▸ *vt* entintar.

inkblot ['ɪŋkblɒt] *n* borrón *m*.

inkjet printer ['ɪŋkdʒet 'prɪntər] *n* impresora de chorro de tinta.

inkpad ['ɪŋkpæd] *n* tampón *m* de entintar, almohadilla.

inland [*(adj)* 'ɪnlənd; *(adv)* ɪn'lænd] *adj* (del) interior.

▸ *adv (travel)* tierra adentro, hacia el interior; *(live)* en el interior. COMP **Inland Revenue** GB Hacienda.

inn [ɪn] *n (with lodgings)* posada, fonda, mesón *m*; *(in country)* venta; *(pub)* taberna.

innate [ɪ'neɪt] *adj* innato,-a.

inner ['ɪnər] *adj* **1** *(room, region, etc)* interior; *(organization)* interno,-a. **2** *(feelings, etc)* interior, íntimo,-a.

innocence ['ɪnəsəns] *n* inocencia.

innocent ['ɪnəsnt] *adj (gen)* inocente; *(harmless)* inocuo,-a, inofensivo,-a; *(naive)* ingenuo,-a.

innovate ['ɪnəveɪt] *vi* innovar.

innumerable [ɪ'njuːmərəbəl] *adj* innumerable.

inopportune [ɪn'ɒpətjuːn] *adj* inoportuno,-a.

inorganic [ɪnɔː'gænɪk] *adj* inorgánico,-a.

input ['ɪnpʊt] *n (of power)* entrada; *(of money, resources)* inversión *f*; *(of data)* input *m*.

▸ *vt* COMPUT entrar, introducir.

① *pt & pp* **input** o **inputted.**

inquire [ɪnˈkwaɪəʳ] *vi fml* preguntar, informarse.
◆ **to inquire into** *vt insep* investigar.
inquiry [ɪnˈkwaɪrɪ] *n* **1** *fml (question)* pregunta. **2** *(investigation)* investigación *f*.
ⓘ *pl* **inquiries**.
inquisition [ɪnkwɪˈzɪʃən] *n* investigación *f*, inquisición *f*. COMP **the Inquisition** HIST la Inquisición *f*.
inquisitive ɪnkwɪˈzɪtɪv] *adj (person)* curioso,-a.
inroads [ˈɪnrəʊds] *n pl (raid)* incursión *f* *sing*.
▶ *fig (encroachment)* intrusión *f*.
insalubrious [ɪnsəˈluːbrɪəs] *adj fml* insalubre.
insane [ɪnˈseɪn] *adj* **1** *(person)* loco,-a, demente; *(act)* insensato,-a. **2** *fam (idea, etc)* loco,-a. LOC **to go insane** volverse loco,-a.

☒ Insane no significa 'insano', que se traduce por **unhealthy**.

inscription [ɪnˈskrɪpʃən] *n (gen)* inscripción *f*; *(in book)* dedicatoria.
insect [ˈɪnsekt] *n* insecto.
insecticide [ɪnˈsektɪsaɪd] *n* insecticida *m*.
insecure [ɪnsɪˈkjʊəʳ] *adj* inseguro,-a.
insecurity [ɪnsɪˈkjʊərɪtɪ] *n* inseguridad *f*.
inseminate [ɪnˈsemɪneɪt] *vt* inseminar.
insensitive [ɪnˈsensətɪv] *adj* insensible.
insert [*(vb)* ɪnˈsɜːt; *(n)* ˈɪnsɜːt] *vt (gen)* introducir en, meter en; *(comment, clause, paragraph, etc)* incluir (in, en), insertar (in, en); *(advertisement)* poner (in, en).
▶ *n (in book, newspaper)* encarte *m*; *(in clothing)* añadido.
inside [ɪnˈsaɪd] *n* **1** interior *m*, parte *f* interior. **2** *(driving on left)* la izquierda; *(driving on right)* la derecha.
▶ *adv (position)* dentro; *(movement)* adentro. LOC **inside out** del revés.
▶ *prep* dentro de.
▶ *n pl* **insides** *fam* entrañas *fpl*, tripas *fpl*.
insight [ˈɪnsaɪt] *n* **1** *(deep understanding, perception)* perspicacia, penetración *f*. **2** *(sudden understanding)* idea.

insignificant [ɪnsɪgˈnɪfɪkənt] *adj* insignificante.
insincere [ɪnsɪnˈsɪəʳ] *adj* poco sincero,-a, insincero,-a, falso,-a.
insinuate [ɪnˈsɪnjʊeɪt] *vt* **1** *(hint, suggest)* insinuar, dar a entender. **2** *(worm, install)* insinuarse (into, en).
insist [ɪnˈsɪst] *vt* **1** *(declare firmly)* insistir en. **2** *(demand forcefully)* exigir.
insolence [ˈɪnsələns] *n* insolencia.
insolent [ˈɪnsələnt] *adj* insolente.
insoluble [ɪnˈsɒljəbəl] *adj* **1** *(of substances)* insoluble, indisoluble. **2** *fig* sin solución, insoluble.
insomnia [ɪnˈsɒmnɪə] *n* insomnio.
inspect [ɪnˈspekt] *vt (gen)* inspeccionar, examinar, revisar.
inspection [ɪnˈspekʃən] *n* **1** *(gen)* inspección *f*, examen, revisión *f* **2** *(of luggage)* registro.
inspector [ɪnˈspektəʳ] *n (gen)* inspector,-ra; *(on train)* revisor,-ra; *(in police)* inspector,-ra de policía.
inspiration [ɪnspɪˈreɪʃən] *n* **1** *(gen)* inspiración *f*. **2** *fam (good idea)* genialidad *f*.
inspire [ɪnˈspaɪəʳ] *vt* **1** *(gen)* inspirar. **2** *(encourage)* estimular, animar, mover. **3** *(fill with - fear)* infundir; *(- confidence, respect)* inspirar.

☒ To inspire no significa 'inspirar (aire)', que se traduce por **to breathe, to inhale**.

install [ɪnˈstɔːl] [also **instal**] *vt* **1** *(equipment, etc)* instalar. **2** *(person)* instalar, colocar.
installation [ɪnstəˈleɪʃən] *n* instalación *f*.
installment [ɪnˈstɔːlmənt] *n* US→ **instalment**
instalment [ɪnˈstɔːlmənt] *n* **1** *(of payment)* plazo. **2** *(of book, story, etc)* entrega; *(of collection)* fascículo.
instance [ˈɪnstəns] *n* ejemplo, caso. LOC **for instance** por ejemplo.
▶ *vt* poner por caso, citar como ejemplo.

☒ Instance no significa 'instancia (formulario)', que se traduce por **form**.

instant [ˈɪnstənt] *n* instante *m*, momento.

▶ adj **1** (at once) inmediato,-a. **2** (coffee, etc) instantáneo,-a. **3** fml (urgent) urgente. **4** COMM (of the present month) del corriente.

instantly ['ɪnstəntlɪ] adv al instante, inmediatamente.

instead [ɪn'sted] adv en cambio, en su lugar: Mrs Jones couldn't do the class so I did it instead la Señora Jones no pudo dar la clase así que yo la di en su lugar.
▶ prep **instead of** en vez de, en lugar de: we should eat more fish instead of meat deberíamos comer más pescado en lugar de carne.

instinct ['ɪnstɪŋkt] n instinto.

instinctive [ɪn'stɪŋktɪv] adj instintivo,-a.

institute ['ɪnstɪtjuːt] n **1** (gen) instituto, centro. **2** (professional body) colegio, asociación f; (educational) escuela.
▶ vt fml (organize, establish) instituir, establecer, fundar; (initiate - enquiry) iniciar, empezar, (- proceedings) entablar.

institution [ɪnstɪ'tjuːʃ°n] n **1** (gen) institución f **3** (home) asilo; (asylum) hospital m psiquiátrico, manicomio; (orphanage) orfanato.

instruct [ɪn'strʌkt] vt **1** (teach) instruir, enseñar; (inform) informar. **2** (order) ordenar, mandar, dar instrucciones. **3** JUR (solicitor, barrister) dar instrucciones a; (jury) instruir.

instruction [ɪn'strʌkʃ°n] n **1** (teaching) instrucción f, enseñanza. **2** (order) orden f, mandato.

instructor [ɪn'strʌktər] n (gen) instructor,-ra; (of driving) profesor,-ra; (of sport) monitor,-ra.

instrument ['ɪnstrəmənt] n instrumento.

insufficient [ɪnsə'fɪʃ°nt] adj insuficiente.

insulate ['ɪnsjəleɪt] vt **1** TECH aislar (against/from, de). **2** fig (protect) proteger (against, contra), (from, de).

insulation [ɪnsjə'leɪʃ°n] n TECH aislamiento.

insulator ['ɪnsjəleɪtər] n TECH aislante m, aislador m.

insulin ['ɪnsjəlɪn] n insulina.

insult [(n) 'ɪnsʌlt; (vb) ɪn'sʌlt] n insulto.
▶ vt insultar, ofender, injuriar.

insurance [ɪn'ʃuərəns] n **1** seguro. **2** fig (safeguard) salvaguarda, protección f, garantía.

insure [ɪn'ʃuər] vt **1** asegurar (against, contra). **2** US (ensure) asegurar.

insurgent [ɪn'sɜːdʒənt] adj insurgente, insurrecto,-a.

insurrection [ɪnsə'rekʃ°n] n insurrección f.

intact [ɪn'tækt] adj intacto,-a.

intake ['ɪnteɪk] n **1** (of food, etc) consumo; (of breath) inhalación f. **2** TECH (of air, water) entrada; (of electricity, gas, water) toma. **3** (number of people) número de personas inscritas.

integer ['ɪntɪdʒər] n MATH entero, número entero.

integral ['ɪntɪgrəl] adj **1** (intrinsic, essential) integral, esencial, fundamental. **2** (built-in) incorporado,-a. **3** MATH integral.

integrity [ɪn'tegrətɪ] n **1** (honesty) integridad f, honradez f. **2** (completeness) totalidad f.

intellect ['ɪntəlekt] n **1** (intelligence) intelecto, inteligencia. **2** (person) intelectual mf.

intellectual [ɪntə'lektjuəl] adj intelectual.
▶ n intelectual mf.

intelligence [ɪn'telɪdʒ°ns] n **1** (gen) inteligencia. **2** (information) información f, espionaje m.

intelligent [ɪn'telɪʒ°nt] adj inteligente.

intend [ɪn'tend] vt **1** (plan, mean, have in mind) tener la intención de, tener el propósito de, proponerse, pensar, querer. **2** (destine for) ir dirigido,-a a.

intense [ɪn'tens] adj **1** (gen) intenso,-a, fuerte; (stare) penetrante. **2** (emotions) profundo,-a, grande, vivo,-a. **3** (person) muy serio,-a.

intensify [ɪn'tensɪfaɪ] vt (search, campaign) intensificar; (effort) redoblar; (production, pollution, pain) aumentar.
ⓘ pt & pp intensified, ger intensifying.

intensity [ɪn'tensɪtɪ] n **1** intensidad f. **2** (of person) seriedad f.
ⓘ pl intensities.

intensive [ɪnˈtensɪv] *adj* **1** *(course, training, etc)* intensivo,-a. **2** *(search)* minucioso,-a; *(study)* profundo,-a. COMP **intensive care** cuidados *mpl* intensivos.

intention [ɪnˈtenʃ°n] *n (purpose, aim, plan, determination)* intención *f*, propósito.

interact [ɪntərˈækt] *vi* **1** *(people)* relacionarse, interaccionar. **2** CHEM reaccionar.

interaction [ɪntərˈækʃ°n] *n* interacción *f*.

interactive [ɪntərˈæktɪv] *adj* interactivo,-a.

inter-city [ɪntəˈsɪti] *adj* interurbano,-a, de largo recorrido.

intercom [ˈɪntəkɒm] *n* interfono.

interconnection [ɪntəkəˈnekʃ°n] *n* interconexión *f*.

intercontinental [ɪntəkɒntɪˈnent°l] *adj* intercontinental.

intercostal [ɪntəˈkɒst°l] *adj* intercostal.

intercourse [ˈɪntəkɔːs] *n* **1** *(dealings)* trato. **2** *(sexual)* coito, relaciones *fpl* sexuales.

interest [ˈɪntrəst] *n* **1** *(gen)* interés *m*. **2** *(hobby)* afición *f*, interés *m*. **3** *(advantage, benefit)* provecho, beneficio. **4** COMM *(share, stake)* participación *f*, interés *m*. **5** FIN *(money)* interés *m*, rédito. ► *vt* interesar.

interested [ˈɪntrəstɪd] *adj* interesado,-a (in, en).

interesting [ˈɪntrəstɪŋ] *adj* interesante.

interface [ˈɪntəfeɪs] *n* **1** COMPUT interface *f*, interfaz *f*. **2** *fig* terreno común.

interfere [ɪntəˈfɪəʳ] *vi (meddle)* entrometerse (in, en), inmiscuirse (in, en).

interference [ɪntəˈfɪərəns] *n* **1** *(meddling)* intromisión *f*, entrometimiento, injerencia. **2** *(with broadcast)* interferencia.

interior [ɪnˈtɪərɪəʳ] *adj* interior. ► *n* interior *m*, parte *f* interior.

interjection [ɪntəˈdʒekʃ°n] *n* **1** *(part of speech)* interjección *f*. **2** *(comment)* interposición *f*.

intermediate [ɪntəˈmiːdɪət] *adj* intermedio,-a.

internal [ɪnˈtɜːn°l] *adj* interno,-a.

international [ɪntəˈnæʃ°nəl] *adj* internacional.

internationalize [ɪntəˈnæʃnəlaɪz] *vt* internacionalizar.

Internet [ˈɪntənet] *n* Internet *f*.

interpret [ɪnˈtɜːprət] *vt (gen)* interpretar; *(understand)* interpretar, entender.

interpretation [ɪntɜːprəˈteɪʃ°n] *n* interpretación *f*.

interpreter [ɪnˈtɜːprətəʳ] *n* intérprete *mf*.

interrogate [ɪnˈterəgeɪt] *vt* interrogar.

interrogation [ɪnterəˈgeɪʃ°n] *n* interrogatorio.

interrogative [ɪntəˈrɒgəætɪv] *adj fml* interrogativo,-a. ► *n* LING *(word)* palabra interrogativa; *(phrase)* oración *f* interrogativa.

interrupt [ɪntəˈrʌpt] *vt* interrumpir. ► *vi* interrumpir.

interruption [ɪntəˈrʌpʃ°n] *n* interrupción *f*.

interstate [ˈɪntəsteɪt] *adj (esp us)* interestatal, entre estados.

interval [ˈɪntəv°l] *n* **1** *(in time, space)* intervalo (between, entre). **2** *(in play, film, etc)* intermedio, descanso; *(in play)* entreacto. **3** *(pause, break)* pausa; *(silence)* silencio; *(rest)* descanso. **4** MUS intervalo.

intervene [ɪntəˈviːn] *vi* **1** *(person)* intervenir (in, en). **2** *(event, etc)* sobrevenir, ocurrir. **3** *fml (time)* transcurrir, mediar.

⊠ To intervene no significa 'intervenir (operar)', que se traduce por to operate on.

interview [ˈɪntəvjuː] *n (gen)* entrevista; *(press)* entrevista. ► *vt* entrevistar, hacer una entrevista a, entrevistarse con.

interviewee [ɪntəvjuːˈiː] *n* entrevistado,-a.

interviewer [ˈɪntəvjuːəʳ] *n* entrevistador,-ra.

intervocalic [ɪntəvəˈkælɪk] *adj* intervocálico,-a.

intestinal [ɪnˈtestɪn°l] *adj* intestinal.

intestine [ɪn'testɪn] *n* intestino. COMP
large intestine intestino grueso. ‖ **small intestine** intestino delgado.

intimate¹ ['ɪntɪmət] *adj* **1** *(gen)* íntimo,-a; *(link, etc)* estrecho,-a. **2** *(knowledge)* profundo,-a.
▶ *n (friend)* amigo,-a íntimo,-a.

intimate² ['ɪntɪmeɪt] *vi fml* insinuar, dar a entender.

☒ To intimate no significa 'intimar (conocerse mejor)', que se traduce por to become close.

intimidate [ɪn'tɪmɪdeɪt] *vt* intimidar.

into ['ɪntu] *prep* **1** *(indicating movement)* en, dentro de, a; *(in direction of)* a, hacia; *(against)* contra, con. **2** *(time, age)* hasta. **3** *(indicating change)* en, a: *he turned water into wine* transformó el agua en vino. **4** MATH entre: *what's four into twenty?* ¿cuánto son veinte entre cuatro?

intolerant [ɪn'tɒlərənt] *adj* intolerante, intransigente.

intonation [ɪntə'neɪʃən] *n* entonación *f*.

intoxicate [ɪn'tɒksɪkeɪt] *vt* **1** *fml* embriagar, emborrachar. **2** *fig* embriagar.

☒ To intoxicate no significa 'intoxicar', que se traduce por to poison.

intoxication [ɪntɒksɪ'keɪʃən] *n* embriaguez *f*.

☒ Intoxicate no significa 'intoxicación', que se traduce por poisoning.

intranet ['ɪntrənet] *n* red *f* local.
intransitive [ɪn'trænsɪtɪv] *adj* LING intransitivo,-a.
intrauterine [ɪntrə'juːtəraɪn] *adj* MED intrauterino,-a.
introduce [ɪntrə'djuːs] *vt* **1** *(person, programme)* presentar. **2** *(bring in - gen)* introducir; *(- new product, etc)* presentar, lanzar; *(law, procedure, etc)* instituir. **3** *(to hobby, habit)* iniciar (to, en). **4** *(bring up)* proponer, sugerir, plantear. **5** *fml (insert)* introducir, meter, insertar.
introduction [ɪntrə'dʌkʃən] *n* **1** *(of person, programme)* presentación *f*. **2** *(to book, speech, etc)* introducción *f*. **3** *(- of new product, etc)* presentación *f*, lanzamien-

to; *(- of law, procedure, etc)* introducción *f*, institución *f*. **4** *(first experience)* iniciación *f*. **5** MUS introducción *f*.

introvert ['ɪntrəvɜːt] *n* introvertido,-a.
intruder [ɪn'truːdər] *n* intruso,-a.
intuition [ɪntjuː'ɪʃən] *n* intuición *f*.
intuitive [ɪn'tjuːɪtɪv] *adj* intuitivo,-a.
invade [ɪn'veɪd] *vt (gen)* invadir.
invader [ɪn'veɪdər] *n* invasor,-ra.
invalid¹ ['ɪnvəlɪd] *n (disabled person)* inválido,-a, minusválido,-a; *(sick person)* enfermo,-a.
invalid² [ɪn'vælɪd] *adj (gen)* inválido,-a, no válido,-a, nulo,-a; *(out of date)* caducado,-a.
invalidate [ɪn'vælɪdeɪt] *vt (result, rule, etc)* invalidar, anular; *(argument)* refutar, demostrar el error de.
invasion [ɪn'veɪʒən] *n (gen)* invasión *f*.
invent [ɪn'vent] *vt* inventar, inventarse.
invention [ɪn'venʃən] *n* **1** *(gen)* invento, invención *f*; *(lying)* invención *f*, mentira. **2** *(capacity for inventing)* inventiva.
inventive [ɪn'ventɪv] *adj* inventivo,-a.
inventor [ɪn'ventər] *n* inventor,-ra.
inventory ['ɪnvəntrɪ] *n* inventario.
ⓘ *pl* inventories.
inversion [ɪn'vɜːʒən] *n* inversión *f*.

☒ Inversion no significa 'inversión (de dinero)', que se traduce por investment.

invert [ɪn'vɜːt] *vt* invertir. COMP **inverted commas** comillas.

☒ To invert no significa 'invertir (dinero)', que se traduce por to invest.

invertebrate [ɪn'vɜːtɪbrət] *adj* invertebrado,-a.
invest [ɪn'vest] *vt* **1** *(money)* invertir (in, en). **2** *(time, effort, etc)* emplear (in, en), invertir (in, en). **3** *fml (right, rank, power, etc)* investir (with, con), conferir (with, -), otorgar (with, -). **4** *fml (quality, characteristic, etc)* revestir (with, con), envolver (with, de). **5** MIL *dated* sitiar, cercar.
investigate [ɪn'vestɪgeɪt] *vt (crime)* investigar; *(cause, possibility)* examinar, estudiar.
▶ *vi fam (check)* mirar.

investigation [ɪnvestɪˈgeɪʃ⁰n] *n (of crime)* investigación *f* (into, sobre); *(of cause, possibility)* examen *m* (into, de), estudio (into, de).

investigator [ɪnˈvestɪgeɪtəʳ] *n* investigador,-ra.

investment [ɪnˈvestmənt] *n* **1** *(of money)* inversión *f*. **2** *(investiture)* investidura.

investor [ɪnˈvestəʳ] *n* inversor,-ra, inversionista *mf*.

invidious [ɪnˈvɪdɪəs] *adj* **1** *(task, job, etc)* odioso,-a, ingrato,-a. **2** *(comparison, choice, etc)* injusto,-a.

> ☒ Invidious no significa 'envidioso', que se traduce por envious.

invisible [ɪnˈvɪzəb⁰l] *adj* invisible.

invitation [ɪnvɪˈteɪʃ⁰n] *n* invitación *f*.

invite [*(vb)* ɪnˈvaɪt; *(n)* ˈɪnvaɪt] *vt* **1** *(guest, etc)* invitar, convidar; *(candidate, participant)* pedir, invitar. **2** *(comment, suggestion, etc)* solicitar. **3** *(criticism, disaster, etc)* provocar, incitar.

invoice [ˈɪnvɔɪs] *n* COMM factura.

invoke [ɪnˈvəʊk] *vt* invocar.

involuntary [ɪnˈvɒləntərɪ] *adj* involuntario,-a.

involve [ɪnˈvɒlv] *vt* **1** *(entail)* suponer, implicar, conllevar; *(give rise to)* acarrear, ocasionar. **2** *(include, affect, concern)* tener que ver con, afectar a. **3** *(implicate)* implicar, involucrar, meter.

inward [ˈɪnwəd] *adj* interior.
▸ *adv* hacia dentro.

inwards [ˈɪnwədz] *adv* hacia dentro.

iodine [ˈaɪədiːn] *n* yodo.

ion [ˈaɪən] *n* ion *m*.

ionize [ˈaɪənaɪz] *vt* ionizar.

ionosphere [aɪˈɒnəsfɪəʳ] *n* ionosfera.

IQ [ˈaɪˈkjuː] *abbr* (intelligence quotient) coeficiente *m* de inteligencia; *(abbreviation)* CI *m*.

Iran [ɪˈrɑːn] *n* Irán.

Iraq [ɪˈrɑːk] *n* Irak.

Ireland [ˈaɪələnd] *n* Irlanda. COMP **Northern Ireland** Irlanda del norte.

iris [ˈaɪ⁰rɪs] *n* **1** *(of eye)* iris *m inv*. **2** BOT lirio.

Irish [ˈaɪrɪʃ] *adj* irlandés,-esa.

Irishman [ˈaɪrɪʃmən] *n* irlandés *m*.
① *pl* Irishmen [ˈaɪrɪʃmən].

Irishwoman [ˈaɪrɪʃwʊmən] *n* irlandesa.
① *pl* Irishwomen [ˈaɪrɪʃwɪmɪn].

iron [ˈaɪən] *n* **1** *(metal)* hierro. **2** *(appliance)* plancha. **3** *(for golf)* hierro, palo de hierro.
▸ *adj* de hierro.
▸ *vt (clothes)* planchar.
▸ *n pl* **irons** *(fetters)* grilletes *mpl*.
◆ **to iron out** *vt sep* **1** *(clothes)* planchar. **2** *fig (problem, difficulty, etc)* resolver, solucionar.

ironing [ˈaɪ⁰rənɪŋ] *n* planchado. LOC **to do the ironing** planchar. COMP **ironing board** tabla de planchar.

ironic [aɪˈrɒnɪk] *adj* irónico,-a.

ironmonger [ˈaɪənmʌngəʳ] *n* GB ferretero,-a. COMP **ironmonger's (shop)** ferretería.

ironmongery [ˈaɪənmʌngərɪ] *n* GB ferretería.

irony [ˈaɪ⁰rənɪ] *n* ironía.
① *pl* ironies.

irregular [ɪˈregjələʳ] *adj* **1** *(gen)* irregular; *(uneven)* desigual. **2** *(unusual, abnormal)* raro,-a, anormal; *(against the rules)* inadmisible. **3** *(troops)* irregular.

irrelevant [ɪˈrelɪvənt] *adj* **1** *(unimportant - fact, detail, etc)* irrelevante. **2** *(out of place)* que no viene al caso: *that's irrelevant* eso no tiene nada que ver, eso no viene al caso.

irresistible [ɪrɪˈzɪstəb⁰l] *adj* **1** *(temptation, impulse, etc)* irresistible: *an irresistible urge* un impulso irrefrenable. **2** *(person, thing)* irresistible.

irresponsibility [ɪrɪspɒnsəˈbɪlətɪ] *n* irresponsabilidad *f*, falta de seriedad.

irresponsible [ɪrɪˈspɒnsəb⁰l] *adj* irresponsable, poco serio,-a.

irrigable [ˈɪrɪgəb⁰l] *adj* irrigable, regadío,-a.

irrigate [ˈɪrɪgeɪt] *vt* **1** AGR regar, irrigar. **2** MED irrigar.

irrigated [ˈɪrɪgeɪtɪd] *vt* **1** AGR irrigado,-a. **2** MED irrigar.

irrigation [ɪrɪˈgeɪʃ⁰n] *n* AGR riego, irrigación *f*. COMP **irrigation channel** acequia, canal *m* de riego. **I irrigation farming** cultivo de regadío. **I irrigation system** sistema *m* de regadío.

irritate ['ɪrɪteɪt] *vt* **1** *(annoy)* irritar, molestar, fastidiar. **2** MED *(cause discomfort)* irritar; *(make inflamed)* inflamar.

irritating ['ɪrɪteɪtɪŋ] *adj* **1** *(annoying)* irritante, molesto,-a, fastidioso,-a, pesado,-a. **2** MED irritante.

irritation [ɪrɪ'teɪʃ°n] *n* **1** MED irritación *f*. **2** *(cause of annoyance)* molestia, fastidio. **3** *(anger)* mal humor *m*, enfado, irritación *f*.

is [ɪz] *pres* → **be**.

Islam ['ɪzlɑːm] *n* islam *m*.

Islamic [ɪz'læmɪk] *adj* islámico,-a.

island ['aɪlənd] *n* isla.
▶ *adj* isleño,-a. COMP **safety island** US isla de peatones, isleta, refugio. **I traffic island** isla de peatones, isleta, refugio.

Isle [aɪl] *n* isla.

islet ['aɪlət] *n* islote *m*.

isobar ['aɪsəbɑːʳ] *n* isobara.

isolate ['aɪsəleɪt] *vt* aislar (**from**, de): *scientists have isolated the germ* los científicos han aislado el microbio.

isolated ['aɪsəleɪtɪd] *adj* **1** *(solitary)* aislado,-a, apartado,-a: *an isolated house* una casa aislada; *I live a very isolated life* llevo una vida muy solitaria. **2** *(single)* aislado,-a, único,-a, excepcional: *an isolated case* un caso aislado.

isosceles [aɪ'sɒsəliːz] *adj* isósceles. COMP **isosceles triangle** triángulo isósceles.

isotherm ['aɪsəθɜːm] *n* isotermo.

isotope ['aɪsətəʊp] *n* isótopo.

Israel ['ɪzrɪəl] *n* Israel.

Israeli [ɪz'reɪlɪ] *adj* israelí.
▶ *n* israelí *mf*.

Israelite ['ɪzrɪəlaɪt] *adj* israelita.
▶ *n* israelita *mf*.

issue ['ɪʃuː] *n* **1** *(subject, topic)* tema *m*, cuestión *f*, asunto. **2** *(of newspaper, magazine, etc)* número. **3** *(of stamps, shares, back notes, etc)* emisión *f*; *(of book)* publicación *f*. **4** *(of passport, licence)* expedición *f*. **5** *(of equipment, supplies, etc)* distribución *f*, reparto, suministro.

6 *fml (emergence - of water, blood)* flujo. **7** *fml (children)* descendencia. **8** *fml (result, outcome)* resultado, consecuencia, desenlace *m*.
▶ *vt* **1** *(book, article)* publicar. **2** *(stamps, shares, banknotes, etc)* emitir. **3** *(passport, visa)* expedir. **4** *(equipment, supplies, etc)* distribuir, repartir, suministrar, proporcionar. **5** *(order, instruction)* dar; *(statement, warning)* dar, hacer público; *(writ, summons)* dictar, expedir; *(decree)* promulgar; *(warrant)* expedir.
▶ *vi* **1** *fml (liquid, blood)* fluir, manar; *(smell, etc)* salir. **2** *fml (result)* resultar (**from**, de), provenir (**from**, de), derivar(se) (**from**, de).

isthmus ['ɪsməs] *n* istmo.

it [ɪt] *pron* **1** *(subject)* él, ella, ello: *where's my supper? it's in the oven!* ¿dónde está mi cena? ¡está en el horno!; *whose is this coat? it's mine!* ¿de quién es este abrigo? ¡es mío!; *is it a boy or a girl?* ¿es niño o niña?; *who's that? who is it? it's me!* ¿quién eres? ¿quién es? ¡soy yo! **2** *(object - direct)* lo, la; *(- indirect)* le: *I doubt it* lo dudo; *I've just got this letter. Can you read it for me?* acabo de recibir esta carta. ¿Me la puedes leer?; *do you like skiing? yes, I love it* ¿te gusta esquiar? sí, me encanta; *she went up to the horse and patted it* se acercó al caballo y lo acarició; *can you manage that bag? Give it to me* ¿puedes con esa bolsa? Dámela. **3** *(after prep)* él, ella, ello: *a vase with flowers in it* un florero con flores dentro; *the train was still there so I ran for it* el tren aún estaba allí así que corrí para cogerlo; *you're not frightened of it, are you?* no le tienes miedo, ¿verdad?; *tell me about it* explícamelo, cuéntamelo. **4** *(abstract)* ello: *let's get on with it* vamos a por ello. **5** *(impersonal)* no se traduce: *it's cold* hace frío; *it's too early* es demasiado temprano; *it's six o'clock* son las seis; *it's Wednesday* es miércoles; *it's cloudy* está nublado; *it's not far* no está lejos; *it's impossible* es imposible; *it's important* es importante; *it's worth it* vale la pena; *it doesn't matter* no importa; *what's it like?* ¿cómo es?; *it cost a fiver* costó cinco libras; *it's true* es verdad; *it seems (that) she failed* parece que suspendió.

Italian [ɪˈtælɪən] *adj* italiano,-a.
▶ *n* **1** *(person)* italiano,-a. **2** *(language)* italiano.

italic [ɪˈtælɪks] *adj* (letra) cursiva.

itch [ɪtʃ] *n* **1** MED picazón *f*, picor *m*. **2** *fam fig (strong desire)* deseo, anhelo, ansia: *an itch to travel* un deseo de viajar.
▶ *vi* picar: *my feet itch* me pican los pies; *I'm itching all over* me pica todo; *this blanket itches* esta manta pica.

it'd [ˈɪtəd] *contr* **1** it had. **2** it would.

item [ˈaɪtəm] *n* **1** *(on list)* artículo, cosa; *(in collection)* pieza. **2** *(on agenda)* asunto, punto. **3** *(on bill)* partida, asiento. **4** *(in show)* número. COMP **item of clothing** prenda de vestir.
▶ *adv* también.

itinerary [aɪˈtɪnˀrərɪ] *n* itinerario, ruta. ① *pl* itineraries.

it'll [ˈɪtˀl] *contr* it will.

its [ɪts] *adj* (one thing) su; (more than one thing) sus: *the cat cleaned its paws* el gato se limpió las patas; *the baby's in its pram* el bebé está en su cochecito; *the film has its good points* la película tiene sus puntos buenos.

it's [ɪts] *contr* **1** → it is. **2** → it has.

itself [ɪtˈself] *pron* **1** *(reflexive)* se: *the bird preened itself* el pájaro se arregló las plumas; *Barcelona has opened itself up to the sea* Barcelona se ha abierto al mar. **2** *(emphatic)* en sí: *the house itself is quite old* la casa en sí es bastante vieja; *the job itself isn't that difficult* el trabajo en sí no es muy difícil; *she is politeness itself* es la cortesía personificada. **3** *(after prep)* sí: *the committee wants to keep all the profits for itself* el comité quiere guardar todos los beneficios para sí; *each dog has a kennel to itself* cada perro tiene su propia casita; *the idea in itself isn't bad* la idea en sí no está mal; *the first course was a meal in itself* el primer plato ya era una comida de por sí. LOC **by itself** solo,-a: *it switches off by itself* se apaga solo, se apaga automáticamente; *the baby did it all by itself* el niño lo hizo él solo.

I've [aɪv] *contr* I have.

ivory [ˈaɪvərɪ] *n (substance)* marfil *m*; *(colour)* color *m* marfil.
▶ *adj* de marfil.
▶ *n pl* **ivories** *(objects)* objetos *mpl* de marfil; *(piano keys)* teclas *fpl*. LOC **an ivory tower** una torre de marfil. COMP **Ivory Coast** Costa de Marfil.

ivy [ˈaɪvɪ] *n* hiedra, yedra. COMP **Ivy League** *ocho prestigiosas universidades privadas del nordeste de los Estados Unidos.*

⊕ La **Ivy League** reúne a las ocho universidades más prestigiosas de Estados Unidos que, además, son de las más antiguas. Un título de cualquiera de estos centros suele ser sinónimo de una excelente formación académica.

J

J, J [dʒeɪ] *n (the letter)* J, j *f.*

jab [dʒæb] *n* **1** pinchazo; *(with elbow)* codazo. **2** *fam (of pain)* pinchazo: *a flu jab* una inyección contra la gripe. **3** *(in boxing)* gancho.
 ▶ *vt* pinchar; *(with elbow)* dar un codazo a.
 ⓘ *pt & pp* jabbed, *ger* jabbing.

jack [dʒæk] *n* **1** AUTO gato. **2** *(in cards)* jota; *(Spanish pack)* sota. **3** *(in bowls)* boliche *m.* **4** ELEC enchufe *m.* LOMP **jack plug** ELEC jack *m*, clavija.

jackal ['dʒækɔːl] *n* chacal *m.*

jacket ['dʒækɪt] *n* **1** *(in general)* chaqueta; *(of suit)* americana; *(leather, etc)* cazadora. **2** *(of book)* sobrecubierta. **3** US *(of record)* funda. COMP **jacket potato** patata asada *(con su piel).*

jackknife ['dʒæknaɪf] *n* navaja.

jackpot ['dʒækpɒt] *n* (premio) gordo. LOC **to hit the jackpot** tocarle a ALGN el gordo.

Jacuzzi® [dʒ'kuːzɪ] *n* jacuzzi® *m.*

jade [dʒeɪd] *n* jade *m.*

jagged ['dʒægɪd] *adj* irregular, dentado,-a.

jaguar ['dʒægjuər] *n* jaguar *m.*

jail [dʒeɪl] *n* cárcel *f*, prisión *f.*
 ▶ *vt* encarcelar: *he was jailed for life* lo condenaron a cadena perpetua.

jailer ['dʒeɪlər] *n* carcelero,-a.

jailhouse ['dʒeɪlhaʊs] *n* US cárcel *f.*

jam¹ [dʒæm] *n* mermelada, confitura. COMP **jam jar** bote *m* de mermelada.

jam² [dʒæm] *n (tight spot)* aprieto, apuro. LOC **to get into a jam** meterse en un apuro. COMP **jam session** sesión improvisada de jazz o rock.

 ▶ *vt* **1** *(fill)* abarrotar, atestar: *thousands of people jammed the streets* miles de personas abarrotaban las calles. **2** *(cram)* embutir, meter a la fuerza: *she jammed all her things into the bag* embutió todas sus cosas en la bolsa. **3** *(block)* bloquear: *the switchboard was jammed with calls of complaint* las llamadas de protesta bloquearon la centralita.
 ⓘ *pt & pp* jammed, *ger* jarring.

Jamaica [dʒə'meɪkə] *n* Jamaica.

Jamaican [dʒə'meɪkən] *adj* jamaicano,-a.
 ▶ *n* jamaicano,-a.

jangle ['dʒæŋgəl] *vi* sonar de un modo discordante.
 ▶ *vt* hacer sonar de un modo discordante.
 ▶ *n* sonido discordante.

January ['dʒænjʊərɪ] *n* enero.

✎ Para ejemplos de usos, consulta May.

Japan [dʒə'pæn] *n* (el) Japón *m.*

Japanese [dʒæpə'niːz] *adj* japonés,-esa.
 ▶ *n* **1** *(person)* japonés,-esa. **2** *(language)* japonés *m.*

jar [dʒɑːr] *n* **1** *(glass)* tarro, bote *m*: *a jar of strawberry jam* un tarro de mermelada de fresa. **2** *(earthenware)* vasija, tinaja. **3** *(shake, shock)* sacudida: *it gave me a bit of a jar* me chocó bastante. **4** *fam (drink)* copa: *let's go and have a few jars!* ¡vamos a tomar unas copas!

jargon ['dʒɑːgən] *n* jerga, jerigonza.

jasmine ['dʒæzmɪn] *n* jazmín *m.*

jaundice ['dʒɔːndɪs] *n* ictericia.

jaunty ['dʒɔːntɪ] *adj* garboso,-a.
 ⓘ *comp* jauntier, *superl* jauntiest.

javelin ['dʒævəlɪn] *n* jabalina. LOC **to throw the javelin** lanzar la jabalina.

COMP **javelin competition** lanzamiento de jabalina.

jaw [dʒɔː] n **1** ANAT mandíbula. COMP **upper jaw** maxilar m superior. **I lower jaw** maxilar m inferior. **2** ZOOL mandíbula, quijada, carrillera.
▸ vi fam (talk) charlar.

jazz [dʒæz] n jazz m. LOC **and all that jazz** y demás, y toda la pesca, y todo el rollo.
▸ adj de jazz, jazzístico,-a. COMP **jazz band** conjunto de jazz.
◆ **to jazz up** vt sep (in general) hacer más alegre, dar vida a; (party) animar.

jealous ['dʒeləs] adj **1** celoso,-a. **2** (envious) envidioso,-a. LOC **to be jealous of** SB tener celos de ALGN, estar celoso,-a de ALGN. **I to make** SB **jealous** poner celoso,-a a ALGN.

jealousy ['dʒeləsɪ] n **1** celos mpl. **2** (envy) envidia.
ⓘ pl jealousies.

jeans [dʒiːnz] n pl vaqueros mpl, tejanos mpl.

jeep® [dʒiːp] n jeep® m, todoterreno.

jeer [dʒɪəʳ] vi (mock) burlarse (at, de), mofarse (at, de).
▸ vt (boo) abuchear.
▸ vi (boo) abuchear.
▸ n pl jeers (booing) abucheos mpl; (mocking) burlas fpl, mofas fpl, befas fpl.

jelly ['dʒelɪ] n **1** (in general) jalea. **2** (fruit) gelatina.
ⓘ pl jellies.

jellyfish ['dʒelɪfɪʃ] n medusa.
ⓘ pl jellyfishes.

jeopardy ['dʒepədɪ] n peligro. LOC **to be in jeopardy** estar en peligro, peligrar. **I to put in jeopardy** poner en peligro, hacer peligrar.

jerk [dʒɜːk] n **1** (pull) tirón m; (jolt) sacudida. **2** fam imbécil mf, subnormal mf. LOC **with a jerk** bruscamente.
▸ vt dar una sacudida a, tirar de.
▸ vi dar una sacudida.

jerrycan ['dʒerɪkæn] n bidón m.

jersey ['dʒɜːzɪ] n jersey m, suéter m.

jest [dʒest] n broma. LOC **In jest** en broma.
▸ vi bromear.

jester ['dʒestəʳ] n HIST bufón m.

Jesus ['dʒiːzəs] n Jesús m, Jesucristo. COMP **Jesus Christ** Jesucristo.

jet [dʒet] n **1** (aircraft) reactor m. **2** (stream) chorro. **3** (outlet) boquilla, mechero. COMP **jet engine** reactor m, propulsor m a chorro. **I jet foil** deslizador m. **I jet lag** jet lag m, desarreglo horario. **I jet set** la jet set f, la jet f. **I jet propulsion** propulsión f a chorro.

jetty ['dʒetɪ] n (stone) malecón m; (wooden) embarcadero.
ⓘ pl jetties.

Jew [dʒuː] n REL judío,-a.

jewel ['dʒuːəl] n **1** joya, alhaja. **2** (stone) piedra preciosa. **3** (in watch) rubí m.

jewelled ['dʒuːəld] adj adornado,-a con piedras preciosas.

jeweller ['dʒuːələʳ] n joyero,-a.

jewellery ['dʒuːəlrɪ] n joyas fpl.

Jewish ['dʒuːɪʃ] adj judío,-a.

jigsaw ['dʒɪɡsɔː] n **1** (saw) sierra de vaivén. **2** (puzzle) rompecabezas m, puzzle m.

jingle ['dʒɪŋɡəl] n **1** tintineo. **2** TV tonadilla publicitaria.
▸ vi tintinear.
▸ vt hacer sonar.

jinx [dʒɪŋks] n **1** (person) gafe mf. **2** (bad luck) mala suerte f: there's a jinx on this computer este ordenador está gafado.
▸ vt gafar.

job [dʒɒb] n **1** (employment) empleo, (puesto de) trabajo: what's your job? ¿en qué trabajas? **2** (piece of work) trabajo; (task) tarea: he did a good job (of work) hizo un buen trabajo. LOC **it's a good job that ...** menos mal que... **I on the job** trabajando. **I out of a job** parado, -a. **I to make the best of a bad job** poner a mal tiempo buena cara. COMP **job centre** oficina de empleo. **I job hunting** búsqueda de trabajo.

jobless ['dʒɒbləs] adj parado,-a.

jockey ['dʒɒkɪ] n jockey m.

jog [dʒɒɡ] n **1** (push) empujoncito, sacudida. **2** (pace) trote m.
▸ vt empujar, sacudir.

► *vi* hacer footing. LOC **at a jog trot** a trote corto. ‖ **to go for a jog** (ir a) hacer footing.

◆ **to jog along** *vi* **1** andar a trote corto. **2** *fig* ir tirando.

ⓘ *pt & pp* jogged, *ger* jogging.

jogging ['dʒɒgɪŋ] *n* footing *m*. LOC **to go jogging** hacer footing.

join [dʒɔɪn] *vt* **1** *(bring together)* juntar, unir. **2** *(connect)* unir, conectar: *the two cities are joined by a bridge* las dos ciudades están unidas por un puente. **3** *(company, etc)* incorporarse a: *Mr Osuna joined the company last year* el Sr Osuna se incorporó a la empresa el año pasado. **4** *(armed forces)* alistarse en; *(police)* ingresar en. **5** *(club)* hacerse socio,-a de. **6** *(party)* afiliarse a, ingresar en. **7** *(be with sb)* reunirse con, unirse a: *would you like to join us for the evening?* ¿les gustaría pasar la tarde con nosotros? LOC **join the club!** ¡ya somos dos *etc*! ‖ **to join forces** aunar esfuerzos. ‖ **to join hands** cogerse de las manos.

► *vi* **1** juntarse, unirse. **2** *(rivers)* confluir; *(roads)* juntarse, empalmar.

◆ **to join in** *vi* participar.

◆ *vt insep* *(debate)* intervenir en.

◆ **to join up** *vi* alistarse.

joiner ['dʒɔɪnəʳ] *n* carpintero *que se dedica a puertas, ventanas, etc*.

joint [dʒɔɪnt] *n* **1** junta, unión *f*. **2** ANAT articulación *f*. **3** *sl (drugs)* porro. LOC **to put out of joint** *(elbow, shoulder, etc)* dislocar: *she put her shoulder out of joint* se dislocó el hombro.

► *adj* colectivo,-a, mutuo,-a. COMP **joint account** cuenta conjunta, cuenta indistinta. ‖ **joint owner** copropietario,-a.

► *vt* CULIN descuartizar.

jointed ['dʒɔɪntɪd] *adj* **1** articulado,-a. **2** *(chicken, etc)* cortado,-a a piezas.

jointly ['dʒɔɪntlɪ] *adv* conjuntamente.

joke [dʒəʊk] *n* **1** chiste *m*: *shall I tell you a joke?* ¿te cuento un chiste? **2** *(practical)* broma: *John can't take a joke* John no aguanta una broma. **3** *(person)* payaso. LOC **to make a joke of** STH reírse de ALGO. ‖ **to play a joke on** SB gastar una

broma a ALGN. ‖ **to tell a joke** contar un chiste.

► *vi* bromear. LOC **you must be joking!** ¡venga ya!

joker ['dʒəʊkəʳ] *n* **1** bromista *mf*: *some joker put salt in the sugar* algún gracioso ha puesto sal en el azúcar. **2** *(card)* comodín *m*. **3** *fam* idiota *mf*. COMP **the joker in the pack** un elemento desconocido.

jolly ['dʒɒlɪ] *adj (cheerful)* alegre, animado,-a: *she was a very jolly person* era una persona muy animada.

ⓘ *comp* jollier, *superl* jolliest.

► *adv* GB *fam* muy: *it's jolly difficult* es la mar de difícil; *they played jolly well* jugaron fenomenal.

◆ **to jolly along** *vt sep* dar ánimos a, animar.

ⓘ *pt & pp* jollied, *ger* jollying.

jolt [dʒəʊlt] *n* **1** sacudida. **2** *(fright)* susto.

► *vt* sacudir.

► *vi* dar tumbos.

Jordan ['dʒɔːdən] *n* **1** *(country)* Jordania.

Jordanian [dʒɔːˈdeɪnɪən] *adj* jordano,-a.

► *n* jordano,-a.

jot [dʒɒt] *n* pizca: *there isn't a jot of truth in it* no hay pizca de verdad en esto; *I don't care a jot* me importa un bledo.

► *vt* apuntar, anotar.

◆ **to jot down** *vt sep* apuntar.

ⓘ *pt & pp* jotted, *ger* jotting.

joule [dʒuːl] *n* julio.

journal ['dʒɜːnəl] *n* **1** *(magazine)* revista. **2** *(diary)* diario.

journalism ['dʒɜːnəlɪzəm] *n* periodismo.

journalist ['dʒɜːnəlɪst] *n* periodista *mf*.

journey ['dʒɜːnɪ] *n* viaje *m*: *it's a 100 mile journey* es un viaje de 100 millas.

► *vi* viajar.

joy [dʒɔɪ] *n* **1** alegría, júbilo: *her face was a picture of joy* estaba radiante de alegría; *he's a joy to work with* da gusto trabajar con él. **2** *fam (satisfaction)* satisfacción *f*; *(luck)* suerte *f*; *(success)* éxito: *you can complain all you like, but you'll get no joy* quéjate todo lo que quieras, pero no te servirá de nada.

joyful ['dʒɔɪfʊl] *adj* jubiloso,-a, alegre.

joystick ['dʒɔɪstɪk] n **1** AV palanca de mando. **2** COMPUT joystick m.

jubilation [dʒuːbɪ'leɪʃ°n] n júbilo.

❌ Jubilation no significa 'jubilación', que se traduce por retirement.

jubilee ['dʒuːbɪliː] n **1** festejos mpl. **2** (anniversary) aniversario.

Judaism ['dʒuːdeɪɪzəm] n judaísmo.
▶ n vibración f (violenta).

judge [dʒʌdʒ] n **1** (man) juez m; (woman) juez f, jueza. **2** (in competition) jurado, miembro del jurado.
▶ vt **1** (court case) juzgar. **2** (calculate) calcular: it's hard to judge how much we need es difícil calcular cuánto necesitamos.

judgement ['dʒʌdʒmənt] [también se escribe judgment.] n **1** (ability) (buen) juicio, (buen) criterio. **2** (opinion) juicio, opinión f: my personal judgement is that ... mi opinión es que ...; in my judgement ... a mi juicio... **3** (decision) fallo. **4** (criticism) crítica.

judicial [dʒuː'dɪʃ°l] adj judicial. COMP judicial inquiry investigación f judicial.

judo ['dʒuːdəu] n yudo, judo.

jug [dʒʌg] n **1** jarra, jarro. **2** sl (prison) chirona.

juggle ['dʒʌg°l] vi **1** hacer juegos malabares (with, con). **2** fig (figures, etc) jugar (with, con).

juggler ['dʒʌg°lə'] n malabarista mf.

jugular ['dʒʌgjələ'] adj yugular. COMP jugular vein vena yugular.
▶ n yugular f. LOC to go for the jugular saltarle a ALGN a la yugular.

juice [dʒuːs] n **1** (gen) jugo. **2** (of fruit) zumo, AM jugo. **3** fam (petrol) gasolina; (electricity) fuerza, luz f. COMP juice extractor licuadora.

juicy ['dʒuːsɪ] adj **1** jugoso,-a. **2** fam (gossip, etc) picante, escabroso,-a.
ⓘ comp juicier, superl juiciest.

jukebox ['dʒuːkbɒks] n máquina de discos.

July [dʒuː'laɪ] n julio.

✎ Para ejemplos de usos, consulta May.

jumble ['dʒʌmb°l] n revoltijo, mezcolanza. COMP jumble sale rastrillo benéfico.
▶ vt desordenar.

jumbo ['dʒʌmbəu] adj gigante.
▶ n [Also jumbo jet.] (plane) jumbo.

jump [dʒʌmp] n **1** salto: a parachute jump un salto en paracaídas. **2** (in prices, etc) salto, aumento importante, disparo: there's been a tremendous jump in profits ha habido un aumento importante de los beneficios. **3** (fence) valla, obstáculo: the horse refused at the first jump el caballo se plantó en el primer obstáculo. COMP jump seat asiento plegable. ‖ jump suit mono.
▶ vi **1** saltar. **2** (rise sharply) dar un salto: inflation jumped 2% last month la inflación dio un salto de un 2% el mes pasado. LOC to jump to conclusions llegar a conclusiones precipitadas.
▶ vt saltar: he tried to jump the wall, but it was too high intentó saltar el muro, pero era demasiado alto. LOC to jump rope US saltar a la comba. ‖ to jump the gun precipitarse, adelantarse. ‖ to jump the lights saltarse el semáforo en rojo. ‖ to jump the queue colarse.
◆ to jump at vt insep aceptar sin pensarlo: when they offered him the job, he jumped at it cuando le ofrecieron el trabajo lo aceptó sin pensar.

jumper¹ ['dʒʌmpə'] n **1** GB jersey m. **2** US (dress) pichi m.

jumper² ['dʒʌmpə'] n SP saltador,-ra.

junction ['dʒʌŋkʃ°n] n **1** (railways) empalme m. **2** (roads) cruce m. **3** (motorway - entry) acceso; (- exit) salida.

June [dʒuːn] n junio.

✎ Para ejemplos de usos, consulta May.

jungle ['dʒʌŋg°l] n selva, jungla.

junior ['dʒuːnɪə'] adj **1** (in rank) subalterno,-a. **2** (in age) menor, más joven. **3** US (after name) hijo.
▶ n **1** (in rank) subalterno,-a. **2** (in age) menor mf: she is three years my junior tiene tres años menos que yo. **3** GB alumno,-a de EGB. **4** US hijo: where's your mom, Junior? ¿dónde está tu mamá,

hijo? COMP **junior college** US *colegio universitario para los dos primeros cursos.* ‖ **junior high school** US instituto de enseñanza secundaria. ‖ **junior school** GB escuela primaria.

junk [dʒʌŋk] *n* trastos *mpl.* COMP **junk food** comida basura. ‖ **junk mail** correo basura. ‖ **junk shop** chamarilería.

Jupiter ['dʒuːpɪtəʳ] *n* Júpiter *m.*

Jurassic [dʒuˈræsɪk] *adj* jurásico,-a.

jury ['dʒʊərɪ] *n* jurado.
  ① *pl* juries.

just¹ [dʒʌst] *adj* **1** *(fair)* justo,-a. **2** *(justifiable)* fundado,-a, justificado,-a. **3** *(deserved)* merecido,-a. LOC **to get one's just desserts** llevar su merecido.

just² [dʒʌst] *adv* **1** *(exactly)* exactamente, precisamente, justo: *this is just what I needed* esto es justo lo que necesitaba. **2** *(only)* solamente, solo: *no sugar for me, please, just milk* no quiero azúcar, gracias, solo leche. **3** *(barely)* apenas, por poco: *I ran all the way and (only) just caught the bus* fui corriendo y cogí el autobús por poco. **4** *(right now)* en este momento: *I'm just finishing it* lo acabo ahora mismo. **5** *(simply)* sencillamente:

we could just stay here and wait for her pues, sencillamente podríamos quedarnos aquí y esperarla. **6** *(for emphasis)*: *he's just as clever as you are* él es tan inteligente como tú. **7** *(used to interrupt)*: *just shut up, will you?* ¡cállese, por favor! **8** *fam (really)* realmente, verdaderamente: *the weather's just marvellous* hace un tiempo realmente maravilloso. LOC **just about** prácticamente. ‖ **just in case** por si acaso. ‖ **just like that!** ¡sin más! ‖ **just so 1** *(tidy)* ordenado,-a, arreglado,-a. **2** *(as a reply)* sí, exactamente. ‖ **just then** en ese momento. ‖ **just the same 1** *(not different)* exactamente igual. **2** *(nevertheless)* sin embargo, no obstante.
  ▸ *phr* **to have just +** *pres part* acabar de + *infin*: *he has just telephoned* acaba de telefonear.

justice ['dʒʌstɪs] *n* **1** justicia. **2** *(judge - man)* juez *m;* *(- woman)* juez *f,* jueza. LOC **to bring to justice** llevar ante los tribunales. ‖ **to do justice to** SB hacer justicia a ALGN.

justify ['dʒʌstɪfaɪ] *vt* justificar.
  ① *pt & pp* justified, *ger* justifying.

J

K

K, k [keɪ] *n (the letter)* K, k *f*.

kaleidoscope [kəˈlaɪdəskəup] *n* caleidoscopio.

kangaroo [kæŋɡəˈruː] *n* canguro.
ⓘ *pl* **kangaroos**.

karaoke [kærɪˈəʊkɪ] *n* karaoke *m*.

karate [kəˈrɑːtɪ] *n* kárate *m*.

karstic [ˈkɑːstɪk] *adj* kárstico,-a.

Kazakh [kæˈzæk] *adj* kazajio,-a.
▶ *n* **1** *(person)* kazajio,-a. **2** *(language)* kazajio.

Kazakhstan [kæzækˈstæn] *n* Kazajstán.

keen [kiːn] *adj* **1** *(eager)* entusiasta, aficionado,-a: *he's a very keen pupil* es un alumno muy entusiasta. **2** *(sharp - mind, senses, etc)* agudo,-a, vivo,-a; *(- look)* penetrante; *(- wind)* cortante; *(- edge, point)* afilado,-a. **3** *(feeling)* profundo, a, intenso,-a. **4** *(competition)* fuerte, reñido,-a. **5** *(price)* competitivo,-a. ‖LOC‖ **to be keen on sth** ser aficionado,-a a ALGO, gustarle ALGO a ALGN. ‖ **to be keen on sb** gustarle ALGN a ALGN. ‖ **to take a keen interest in** mostrar un gran interés por.

keep [kiːp] *n* **1** *(board)* sustento, mantenimiento: *to earn one's keep* ganarse el pan. **2** *(of castle)* torreón *m*, torre *f* del homenaje.
▶ *vt* **1** *(not throw away)* guardar. **2** *(not give back)* quedarse con: *keep the change* quédese con el cambio. **3** *(have)* tener; *(carry)* llevar. **4** *(look after, save)* guardar: *can you keep me a loaf of bread for Friday?* ¿me guarda una barra de pan para el viernes?. **5** *(put away, store)* guardar: *where do you keep the glasses?* ¿dónde guardas los vasos? **6** *(secret)* guardar: *can you keep a secret?* ¿sabes guardar un secreto? **7** *(with adj, verb, etc)* mantener: *these doors must be kept locked* estas puertas deben mantenerse cerradas.
▶ *vi* **1** *(do repeatedly)* no dejar de; *(do continuously)* seguir, continuar: *she was exhausted but kept swimming* estaba agotada pero siguió nadando. **2** *(stay fresh)* conservarse. **3** *(continue in direction)* continuar, seguir: *keep left/right* circula por la izquierda/derecha. **4** *(with adj, verb, etc)* quedarse, permanecer: *we must keep calm* debemos mantener la calma. ‖LOC‖ **to keep going** seguir (adelante). ‖ **to keep one's head** no perder la cabeza. ‖ **to keep quiet** callarse, no hacer ruido. ‖ **to keep sb from doing sth** impedir que ALGN haga ALGO. ‖ **to keep sth from sb** ocultar ALGO a ALGN.
◆ **to keep off** *vi (stay away)* mantenerse a distancia; *(of rain)* no llover: *if the rain keeps off, we'll be able to play tennis* si no llueve, podremos jugar a tenis.
▶ *vt sep (make stay away)* no dejar entrar, no dejar acercarse; *(avoid)* no tocar, no hablar de: *"Keep off the grass"* «No pisar la hierba».
◆ **to keep out** *vt sep* no dejar entrar, no dejar pasar.
▶ *vi* no entrar.
◆ **to keep up** *vt sep* **1** *(gen)* mantener, seguir. **2** *(from sleeping)* mantener despierto,-a, tener en vela.
▶ *vi* **1** *(not fall behind)* aguantar el ritmo. **2** *(stay in touch)* mantenerse al día.
ⓘ *pt & pp* **kept** [kept].

keeper [ˈkiːpəʳ] *n* **1** *(in zoo)* guardián, -ana. **2** *(in park)* guarda *mf*. **3** *(in museum)* conservador,-ra; *(in archives)* archivador,-ra.

kennel [ˈkenəl] *n* caseta del perros.
▶ *n pl* **kennels** *(boarding)* residencia *f sing* canina.

Kenya ['kenjə] *n* Kenia.

Kenyan ['kenjən] *adj* keniano,-a.
▸ *n* keniano,-a.

kerb [kɜːb] *n* bordillo.

kept [kept] *pt & pp* → keep.

kernel ['kɜːnˀl] *n* **1** *(of nut, fruit)* semilla.
2 *fig* núcleo, grano.

kerosene ['kerəsiːn] *n* US queroseno.

ketchup ['ketʃəp] *n* ketchup *m*, catsup *m*.

kettle ['ketˀl] *n* tetera *(para hervir agua)*:
will you put the kettle on to make some tea?
¿quieres poner el agua a hervir para hacer té? LOC **that's a different kettle of fish** eso es harina de otro costal.

key [kiː] *n* **1** *(of door, car, etc)* llave *f*. **2** *(of clock, mechanical)* llave *f*. **3** *fig (to problem, map, code)* clave *f*; *(to exercises)* respuestas *fpl*. **4** *(on computer, piano, etc)* tecla. **5** MUS *(on wind instrument)* llave *f*, pistón *m*; *(set of notes)* clave *f*; *(tone, style)* tono.
▸ *adj* clave, principal: *tourism is the country's key industry* el turismo es la industria principal del país. COMP **key ring** llavero.
◆ **to key in** *vt sep* introducir, teclear:
she keyed in the data introdujo los datos.

keyboard ['kiːbɔːd] *n* teclado. COMP **keyboard player** teclista *mf*.
▸ *n pl* **keyboards** teclados *mpl*.

keyhole ['kiːhəʊl] *n* ojo de la cerradura.

khaki ['kɑːkɪ] *n* caqui *m*.
▸ *adj* caqui.

kick [kɪk] *n* **1** *(by person)* puntapié *m*, patada. **2** SP golpe *m*, tiro. **3** *(by animal)* coz *f*. **4** *fam (pleasure)* diversión *f*, emoción *f*: *he gets a kick out of playing basketball* se divierte jugando al baloncesto.
▸ *vt* **1** *(hit ball)* dar un puntapié a, golpear con el pie; *(score)* marcar. **2** *(hit person)* dar una patada a; *(move legs)* patalear. **3** *(by animal)* dar coces a, cocear.
◆ **to kick off** *vi* SP sacar, hacer el saque inicial; *(begin)* empezar, comenzar.
▸ *vt sep* **1** *(begin)* empezar, comenzar, iniciar. **2** *(remove - shoes)* quitarse.
◆ **to kick out** *vt sep* echar.

kick-off ['kɪkɒf] *n* SP saque *m* inicial.

kid¹ [kɪd] *n* **1** *fam* crío,-a, niño,-a, chico,-a, chaval,-la. **2** *(animal)* cabrito. **3** *(leather)* cabritilla. LOC **to treat sb with**

kid gloves tratar a ALGN con guantes de seda.
▸ *adj (brother, sister)* menor.

kid² [kɪd] *vt* **1** *(deceive, tease)* tomar el pelo a, engañar. **2** *(fool os)* engañarse a sí mismo, hacerse ilusiones.
▸ *vi* estar de broma: *you're kidding!* ¡estás de broma!, ¡no me digas!; *no kidding!* ¡en serio!

kidnap ['kɪdnæp] *vt* secuestrar, raptar.
① *pt & pp* **kidnapped**, *ger* **kidnapping**.

kidnapper ['kɪdnæpəʳ] *n* secuestrador,-ra.

kidnapping ['kɪdnæpɪŋ] *n* secuestro.

kidney ['kɪdnɪ] *n* riñón *m*. COMP **kidney machine** riñón *m* artificial.

kill [kɪl] *n (act)* matanza; *(animal)* pieza.
▸ *vt* **1** matar, asesinar. **2** *fig (hope, conversation, etc)* destruir, acabar con; *(pain)* aliviar. **3** *(hurt)* doler mucho: *my back's killing me* me duele mucho la espalda. LOC **to kill os** matarse, suicidarse. | **to kill os laughing** morirse de risa. | **to kill time** pasar el rato, matar el tiempo. | **to kill two birds with one stone** matar dos pájaros de un tiro. |
◆ **to kill off** *vt sep* exterminar, rematar.

killer ['kɪləʳ] *n (person)* asesino,-a; *(thing)* mortal, que mata. COMP **killer whale** orca.

killing ['kɪlɪŋ] *n* matanza; *(of person)* asesinato. LOC **to make a killing** ganar una fortuna, hacer el negocio del siglo.
▸ *adj fig* agotador,-ra, duro,-a.

kiln [kɪln] *n* horno.

kilo ['kiːləʊ] *n* kilo.
① *pl* **kilos**.

kilobyte ['kɪləbaɪt] *n* kilobyte.

kilocalorie ['kɪləkælərɪ] *n* kilocaloría.

kilogram ['kɪləɡræm] *n* kilogramo.

kilogramme ['kɪləɡræm] *n* US → kilogram.

kilometer [kɪ'lɒmɪtəʳ] *n* US → kilometer.

kilometre [kɪ'lɒmɪtəʳ] *n* kilómetro.

kilt [kɪlt] *n* falda escocesa.

kimono [kɪ'məʊnəʊ] *n* quimono.
① *pl* **kimonos**.

K

kin [kɪn] *n* parientes *mpl*, familia. COMP **next of kin** pariente *m* más próximo.

kind [kaɪnd] *adj (person)* amable: *she is the sweetest, kindest person I know* es la persona más dulce y amable que conozco; *that's very kind of you* eres muy amable.
▸ *n (sort)* tipo, género, clase *f: what kind of ...?* ¿qué clase de …? LOC **to be two of a kind** ser tal para cual. ‖ **to pay in kind 1** pagar en especie. **2** *(treatment)* pagar con la misma moneda.
▸ *adv* **kind of** bastante, algo, un poco: *it's kind of difficult* es un poco difícil; *have you finished? – Kind of ...* ¿has acabado? –Más o menos; *... and that kind of thing ...* y cosas por el estilo.

kindergarten [ˈkɪndəgɑːtˀn] *n* parvulario, guardería.

kind-hearted [kaɪndˈhɑːtɪd] *adj* bondadoso,-a.

kindly [ˈkaɪndlɪ] *adj* amable.
ⓘ *comp* **kindlier**, *superl* **kindliest**.
▸ *adv* **1** con amabilidad: *she very kindly lent me £5* tuvo la amabilidad de prestarme cinco libras. **2** *(please)* por favor: *kindly shut up!* ¡haz el favor de callarte!

kindness [ˈkaɪndnəs] *n* **1** bondad *f*, amabilidad *f*. **2** *(favour)* favor *m*.

kinetics [kɪˈnetɪks] *n* cinética.

king [kɪŋ] *n* rey *m*. COMP **the king and queen** los reyes *mpl*. ‖ **the Three Kings** los Reyes *mpl* Magos.

kingdom [ˈkɪŋdəm] *n* reino.

kingfisher [ˈkɪŋfɪʃəʳ] *n* martín pescador *m*.

king-size [ˈkɪŋsaɪz] *adj* extragrande, extralargo,-a.

kiosk [ˈkiːɒsk] *n* **1** quiosco. **2** *(telephone)* cabina telefónica.

kipper [kɪpəʳ] *n* arenque *m*.

Kiribati [kɪrɪˈbætɪ] *n* Kiribati.

kiss [kɪs] *n* beso.
ⓘ *pl* **kisses**.
▸ *vt* besar, dar un beso a: *he kissed her on the cheek* le dio un beso en la mejilla.
▸ *vi* besarse, darse un beso.

kit [kɪt] *n* **1** *(equipment, gear)* equipo, equipaje *m*. **2** *(clothes)* ropa. **3** *(model)* maqueta, kit *m*.
◆ **to kit out** *vt sep* equipar.

kitchen [ˈkɪtʃɪn] *n* cocina. COMP **kitchen garden** huerto.

kite [kaɪt] *n* **1** *(bird)* milano. **2** *(toy)* cometa: *to fly a kite* hacer volar una cometa.

kitten [ˈkɪtˀn] *n* gatito,-a. LOC **to have kittens** tener un ataque: *I nearly had kittens!* ¡por poco me da un ataque!

kitty [ˈkɪtɪ] *n* **1** *fam (cat)* minino,-a. **2** *(in card games)* bote *m*; *(for bills, drinks)* fondo común.
ⓘ *pl* **kitties**.

kiwi [ˈkiːwiː] *n* **1** *(bird)* kiwi *m*. **2** *(fruit)* kiwi *m*.

klaxon [ˈklæksˀn] *n* claxon *m*.

knack [næk] *n* maña, truco. LOC **to get the knack of doing** STH cogerle el tranquillo a ALGO.

knapsack [ˈnæpsæk] *n* mochila.

knead [niːd] *vt* amasar.

knee [niː] *n* **1** ANAT rodilla: *on one's knees* de rodillas. **2** *(of trousers)* rodillera.
▸ *vt* dar un rodillazo a.

kneecap [ˈniːkæp] *n* rótula.

kneel [niːl] *vi* arrodillarse.
ⓘ *pt & pp* **knelt** [nelt].

kneepad [ˈniːpæd] *n* rodillera.

knelt [nelt] *pt & pp* → **kneel**.

knew [njuː] *pt* → **know**.

knickers [ˈnɪkəz] *n pl* bragas *fpl*: *she bought three pairs of knickers* compró tres bragas.

knife [naɪf] *n (gen)* cuchillo; *(folding)* navaja.
ⓘ *pl* **knives**.
▸ *vt* apuñalar, acuchillar.

knight [naɪt] *n* **1** *arch* caballero. **2** *(chess)* caballo. **3** caballero, *(hombre que lleva el título de Sir)*. COMP **knight in shining armour** príncipe *m* azul.

knit [nɪt] *vt* tejer.
▸ *vi* **1** hacer punto, hacer media. **2** MED soldarse. **3** *fig* unirse. LOC **to knit one's brow** fruncir.
ⓘ *pt & pp* **knit** o **knitted**, *ger* **knitting**.

knitting [ˈnɪtɪŋ] *n (material)* punto; *(activity)* labor *f* de punto. COMP **knitting machine** tricotosa. ‖ **knitting needle** aguja de tejer.

knives [naɪvz] *pl* → **knife**.

knitwear [ˈnɪtweəʳ] *n* género de punto.

knob [nɒb] *n* **1** *(on door - large)* pomo; *(- small)* tirador *m*. **2** *(on stick)* puño. **3** *(natural)* bulto, protuberancia. **4** *(on radio, etc)* botón *m*.

knock [nɒk] *n* **1** *(blow)* golpe *m*. **2** *(on door)* llamada: *was that a knock at the door?* ¿han llamado a la puerta? **3** *fig (bad luck)* revés *m*.

▸ *vt* **1** *(to hit)* golpear, darse un golpe en. **2** *fam (criticize)* criticar, hablar mal de: *the newspapers are forever knocking the England manager* los periódicos siempre critican al entrenador de la selección inglesa.

▸ *vi* **1** *(at door)* llamar: *please knock before entering* por favor, llamen antes de entrar. **2** *(of car engine)* golpear, martillear.

◆ **to knock down** *vt sep* **1** *(building)* derribar. **2** *(person - with a car)* atropellar; *(- with a blow)* derribar. **3** *(price)* rebajar.

◆ **to knock out** *vt sep* **1** *(make unconscious)* dejar sin conocimiento; *(put to sleep)* dejar dormido,-a; *(boxing)* dejar K.O. **2** *(from competition)* eliminar.

◆ **to knock over** *vt sep* **1** *(overturn)* volcar, tirar. **2** *(run over)* atropellar.

knockdown ['nɒkdaʊn] *adj* rebajado. [COMP] **knockdown price** precio de saldo.

knocker ['nɒkər] *n* **1** aldaba. **2** *(critic)* detractor,-ra.

knockout ['nɒkaʊt] *n* **1** SP knock-out *m*, fuera de combate *m*. **2** *fam* maravilla: *it's a knockout!* ¡es alucinante!

knot [nɒt] *n* **1** *(gen)* nudo. **2** *(people)* corrillo, grupo.

▸ *vt* anudar.

ⓘ *pt & pp* **knotted**, *ger* **knotting**.

know [nəʊ] *vt* **1** *(be acquainted with)* conocer: *do you know Colin?* ¿conoces a Colin? **2** *(recognize)* reconocer: *I'd know him if I saw him again* lo reconocería si lo volviera a ver. **3** *(have knowledge of)* saber: *I don't know the answer* no sé la respuesta. [LOC] **as far as I know** que yo sepa. ▪ **don't I know it!** ¡y me lo dices a mí?, ¡ni que lo digas! ▪ **how should I know?** ¿yo qué sé? ▪ **if only I'd known!** ¡haberlo sabido! ▪ **not that I know of** que yo sepa, no. ▪ **you never know** nunca se sabe. ▪ **I know what!** ¡ya lo tengo! ▪ **to be in the know** estar enterado,-a.

▪ **you know best** tú sabes mejor que yo, sabes lo que más te conviene. ▪ **to know better** tener más juicio. ▪ **to know by sight** conocer de vista. ▪

◆ **to know about** *vt insep* **1** saber de, entender de.

◆ **to know of** *vt insep* saber de, haber oído hablar de.

ⓘ *pt* **knew** [nju:], *pp* **known** [nəʊn].

know-all ['nəʊɔːl] *n* sabelotodo *mf*.

know-how ['nəʊhaʊ] *n* saber hacer *m*, conocimiento práctico.

knowledge ['nɒlɪdʒ] *n* **1** *(learning, information)* conocimientos *mpl*: *his knowledge of football is amazing* sus conocimientos de fútbol son increíbles. **2** *(awareness)* conocimiento: *at that time I had no knowledge of what was happening* entonces no tenía conocimiento de lo que estaba pasando. [LOC] **to my knowledge** que yo sepa. ▪ **to be common knowledge that …** ser notorio que …, todo el mundo sabe que … ▪ **it has come to my knowledge that …** he llegado a saber que … ▪ **to have a good knowledge of sth** conocer algo bien.

knowledgeable ['nɒlɪdʒəbəl] *adj* entendido,-a: *he's very knowledgeable about music* es muy entendido en música.

known [nəʊn] *pp* → **know**.

knuckle ['nʌkəl] *n* nudillo.

◆ **to knuckle down** *vi fam* ponerse a trabajar en serio.

◆ **to knuckle under** *vi* pasar por el aro.

koala [kəʊˈɑːlə] *n* koala *m*.

Koran [kɔːˈrɑːn] *n* Alcorán *m*, Corán *m*.

Korea [kəˈrɪə] *n* Corea. [COMP] **North Korea** Corea del Norte. ▪ **South Korea** Corea del Sur.

Korean [kəˈrɪən] *adj* coreano,-a.

▸ *n* **1** *(person)* coreano,-a. **2** *(language)* coreano. [COMP] **North Korean** norcoreano,-a. ▪ **South Korean** surcoreano,-a.

kudos ['kjuːdɒs] *n* prestigio.

Kurd [kɜːd] *adj* kurdo,-a.

▸ *n (person)* kurdo,-a.

Kurdish ['kɜːdɪʃ] *adj* kurdo,-a.

▸ *n (language)* kurdo.

Kuwait [kʊˈweɪt] *n* Kuwait.

Kuwaiti [kʊˈweɪtɪ] *adj* kuwaití.

▸ *n* kuwaití *mf*.

K

L, l [el] *n (the letter)* L, l *f.*

l ['liːtə'] *symb* (litre, US liter) litro; *(symbol)* l.

lab [læb] *n fam (abbr of* laboratory*)* laboratorio.

label ['leɪbᵊl] *n* **1** etiqueta. **2** *(record company)* casa discográfica.
▶ *vt* **1** etiquetar, poner etiqueta a. **2** *fig* calificar (as, de).
ⓘ *pt & pp* labelled (US labeled)*, ger* labelling (US labeling*)*.

laboratory [ləˈbɒrətəri, US ˈlæbrətɔːrɪ] *n* laboratorio.
ⓘ *pl* laboratories.

labor ['leɪbə'] *n* US → labour.

⊕ El Labor Day es el día del trabajo en Estados Unidos. Se celebra del primer lunes de septiembre y marca el final del verano y el inicio del curso escolar.

labour ['leɪbə'] *n* **1** *(work)* trabajo. **2** *(task)* labor *f*, tarea, faena. **3** *(workforce)* mano *f* de obra. **4** *(childbirth)* parto.
COMP labour camp campo de trabajos forzados. ‖ Labour Day día del trabajo. ‖ labour force mano *f* de obra.
▶ *vi* **1** *(work hard)* trabajar duro. **2** *(move slowly)* avanzar penosamente; *(engine)* funcionar con dificultad.
▶ *n* Labour GB los laboristas *mpl*, el Partido Laborista.

laborer ['leɪbərə'] *n* US → labourer.

labourer ['leɪbərə'] *n* peón *m*, jornalero,-a, bracero. COMP farm labourer peón *m* agrícola.

labyrinth ['læbərɪnθ] *n* laberinto.

lace [leɪs] *n* **1** *(material)* encaje *m*. **2** *(shoestring)* cordón *m*.
▶ *vt (pull string through)* poner los cordones a.

lachrymal ['lækrɪmᵊl] *adj* lagrimal, lacrimal.

lack [læk] *n* falta, carencia, escasez *f*: *she has no lack of self-confidence* no le falta confianza en sí misma. LOC for lack of por falta de.
▶ *vt* carecer de.

lacquer ['lækə'] *n* laca.
▶ *vt (metal, wood)* lacar; *(hair)* poner laca a.

lacrimal ['lækrɪmᵊl] *adj* → lachrymal.

lactic ['læktɪk] *adj* láctico,-a.

lactose ['læktəʊs] *n* lactosa.

lad [læd] *n* **1** GB *fam* muchacho, chaval *m*, chico. **2** GB *fam* diablillo, pillo: *John's a bit of a lad.* John es un poco pillo. **3** *(stable boy)* mozo de cuadra.

ladder ['lædə'] *n* **1** escalera (de mano). **2** GB *(in stocking)* carrera. **3** *fig* escala. COMP rope ladder escalera de cuerda.
▶ *vi* GB hacerse una carrera.
▶ *vt* GB hacerse una carrera en.

laden ['leɪdᵊn] *adj* cargado,-a (with, de). LOC to be fully laden estar lleno,-a hasta el tope.

ladies ['leɪdɪz] *n* GB *(toilet)* lavabo (de señoras). COMP ladies room US lavabo (de señoras).

ladle ['leɪdᵊl] *n* cucharón *m*.
▶ *vt* servir con cucharón.
◆ to ladle out *vt sep* repartir.

lady ['leɪdɪ] *n* señora; *(of high social position)* dama.
ⓘ *pl* ladies.

ladybird ['leɪdɪbɜːd] *n* mariquita.

ladybug ['leɪdɪbʌg] *n* US mariquita.

lag [læg] *n* **1** retraso. **2** GB *sl* preso. COMP time lag retraso.

lager ['lɑːgə'] *n* cerveza rubia.

laid [leɪd] *pt & pp* → lay².

lain [leɪn] *pp* → **lie².**

lake [leɪk] *n* lago.

lama ['lɑ:mə] *n* lama *m.*

lamb [læm] *n* **1** *(animal)* cordero,-a. **2** *(meat)* carne *f* de cordero. **3** *fam (person)* cordero,-a: *poor lamb!* ¡pobrecito,-a!

lame [leɪm] *adj* **1** cojo,-a; *lame in one leg* cojo,-a de una pierna. **2** *fig* débil; *(excuse)* poco convincente; *(business)* fallido,-a. COMP **lame duck** inútil *mf.*

lamp [læmp] *n* **1** lámpara. **2** *(on car, train)* faro.

lamppost ['læmppəʊst] *n* (poste *m* de) farol *m.*

lampshade ['læmpʃeɪd] *n* pantalla (de lámpara).

land [lænd] *n* **1** *(gen)* tierra: *by land and sea* por tierra y por mar. **2** *(soil)* suelo, tierra. **3** *(country, region)* tierra: *in foreign lands* en tierras extranjeras. **4** *(property)* terreno, tierras *fpl.* LOC **land ahoy!** ¡tierra a la vista! COMP **farm land** tierras *fpl* de cultivo. ❙ **land-agent** GB encargado,-a de una granja.
▶ *vi* **1** *(plane, etc)* aterrizar, tomar tierra; *(bird)* posarse. **2** *(disembark)* desembarcar. **3** *(fall)* caer.
◆ **to land in** *vt sep* causar, traer: *he's bound to land you in trouble* seguro que te traerá problemas.
◆ **to land up** *vi* acabar.

landing ['lændɪŋ] *n* **1** *(plane)* aterrizaje *m.* **2** *(on stairs)* descansillo, rellano. **3** *(of people)* desembarco. COMP **crash landing** aterrizaje *m* de emergencia. ❙ **landing field** pista de aterrizaje. ❙ **landing gear** tren *m* de aterrizaje.

landlady ['lændleɪdɪ] *n (of flat)* propietaria, dueña; *(of house)* casera.
ⓘ *pl* landladies.

landlord ['lændlɔ:d] *n* **1** *(of flat)* propietario, dueño; *(of house)* casero.

landowner ['lændəʊnə'] *n* propietario,-a, terrateniente *mf*, hacendado,-a.

landscape ['lændskeɪp] *n* paisaje *m.* COMP **landscape gardener** jardinista *mf*, arquitecto,-a paisajista. ❙ **landscape painter** paisajista *mf.*
▶ *vt* ajardinar.

lane [leɪn] *n* **1** *(in country)* camino, sendero; *(in town)* callejuela, callejón *m.* **2**

(on road) carril *m.* **3** *(in athletics, swimming)* calle *f.*

language ['læŋgwɪdʒ] *n* **1** *(faculty, way of speaking)* lenguaje *m.* **2** *(tongue)* idioma *m*, lengua. **3** *(school subject)* lengua. LOC **to use bad language** ser mal hablado,-a. COMP **language laboratory** laboratorio de idiomas. ❙ **language school** escuela de idiomas.

lantern ['læntən] *n* linterna, farol *m.*

Laos [lauz, laus] *n* Laos.

Laotian ['laʊʃɪən] *adj* laosiano,-a.
▶ *n* laosiano,-a.

lap¹ [læp] *n* regazo; *(knees)* rodillas *fpl*; *(skirt)* falda.

lap² [læp] *n* **1** SP vuelta. **2** *fig (stage)* etapa.
▶ *vt* SP *(overtake)* doblar.
▶ *vi (go round)* dar la vuelta.
ⓘ *pt & pp* lapped, *ger* lapping.

lap³ [læp] *vt* **1** *(animal)* beber a lengüetadas. **2** *(waves)* lamer, besar.
ⓘ *pt & pp* lapped, *ger* lapping.

lapel [lə'pel] *n* solapa.

Lapland ['læplænd] *n* Laponia.

lapse [læps] *n* **1** *(in time)* intervalo, lapso. **2** *(slip)* desliz *m.* **3** *(when speaking)* lapsus *m*; *(of memory)* fallo.

laptop ['læptɒp] [also **laptop computer**] *n* ordenador *m* portátil.

lard [lɑ:d] *n* manteca de cerdo.

larder ['lɑ:də'] *n* despensa.

large [lɑ:dʒ] *adj* **1** grande; *(before sing noun)* gran; *(sum, amount)* importante; *(meal)* abundante. **2** *(family)* numeroso,-a. **3** *(extensive)* amplio,-a, extenso,-a. LOC **at large** *(as a whole)* en general. ❙ **by and large** por lo general.

large-scale ['lɑ:dʒskeɪl] *adj* **1** de gran escala. **2** *(map)* a gran escala.

lark¹ [lɑ:k] *n (bird)* alondra.

lark² [lɑ:k] *n fam (bit of fun)* broma.
◆ **to lark about / lark around** *vi fam* hacer el indio.

larva ['lɑ:və] *n* larva.
ⓘ *pl* larvae ['lɑ:vi:].

laryngitis [lærɪn'dʒaɪtəs] *n* laringitis *f.*

larynx ['lærɪŋks] *n* laringe *f.*
ⓘ *pl* larynxes o larynges ['lærɪdʒi:z].

L

lasagna [ləˈzɑːnjə] n lasaña.
laser [ˈleɪzər] n láser m.
lash [læʃ] n **1** (blow with whip) latigazo, azote m; (with tail) coletazo. **2** (whip) látigo; (thong) tralla. **3** (eyelash) pestaña.
ⓘ pl lashes.
▶ vt **1** (in general) azotar. **2** (fasten) sujetar.
◆ **to lash out** vi **1** arremeter (against/at, contra). **2** (splurge) gastarse un montón (de dinero) (on, en).
lass [læs] n fam chica, chavala.
ⓘ pl lasses.
lasso [læˈsuː] n lazo.
ⓘ pl lassos o lassoes.
last [lɑːst] adj **1** (final) último,-a. **2** (most recent) último,-a: the last time la última vez. **3** (past) pasado,-a; (previous) anterior: last Monday el lunes pasado; the night before last anteanoche.
▶ adv **1** por última vez: when he last came to see me cuando vino a verme por última vez. **2** (at the end) en último lugar; (in race) en última posición. LOC at last al fin, por fin. ‖ at long last por fin.
▶ n (person) el/la último,-a; (thing) lo último: are you the last? ¿eres tú el último? LOC last but one penúltimo,-a.
▶ vi (continue) durar; (hold out) aguantar, resistir.
▶ vt durar.
◆ **to last out** vi resistir, aguantar.
lasting [ˈlɑːstɪŋ] adj duradero,-a.
lastly [ˈlɑːstlɪ] adv por último, finalmente.
latch [lætʃ] n pestillo: come in, the door's on the latch entra, el pestillo no está echado.
late [leɪt] adj **1** (not on time) tardío,-a: you're ten minutes late llegas diez minutos tarde. **2** (far on in time) tarde: in late May a finales de mayo. **3** euph (dead) difunto,-a, fallecido,-a. **4** (former) anterior. **5** (last-minute) de última hora. LOC to get late hacerse tarde.
▶ adv **1** tarde: I stayed up late last night anoche me acosté muy tarde. **2** (recently) recientemente: as late as yesterday ayer mismo. LOC of late últimamente.

lately [ˈleɪtlɪ] adv últimamente, recientemente.
later [ˈleɪtər] adj **1** más tardío,-a: we'll discuss that at a later date hablaremos de eso más adelante. **2** (more recent) más reciente.
▶ adv **1** más tarde: five minutes later cinco minutos más tarde; see you later! ¡hasta luego! **2** (afterwards) después, luego. LOC later on más adelante, más tarde.
lateral [ˈlætərəl] adj lateral.
latest [ˈleɪtɪst] adj último,-a, más reciente.
▶ n lo último. LOC at the latest como máximo.
latex [ˈleɪteks] n látex m.
lather [ˈlɑːðər] n **1** (of soap) espuma. **2** (sweat) sudor m.
▶ vt enjabonar.
Latin [ˈlætɪn] adj latino,-a.
▶ n **1** (person) latino,-a. **2** (language) latín m. COMP Latin American latinoamericano,-a.
latitude [ˈlætɪtjuːd] n latitud f.
latter [ˈlætər] adj **1** (last) último,-a: the latter days of his life were very happy los últimos días de su vida fueron muy felices. **2** (second) segundo,-a.
▶ pron the latter éste,-a, este,-a último,-a.
lattice [ˈlætɪs] n celosía, enrejado.
Latvia [ˈlætvɪə] n Letonia.
Latvian [ˈlætvɪən] adj letón,-ona.
▶ n **1** (person) letón,-ona. **2** (language) letón m.
laugh [lɑːf] vi reír, reírse: it makes me laugh me da risa. LOC he who laughs last laughs longest quien ríe último ríe mejor. ‖ to laugh one's head off fam partirse de risa, troncharse de risa, desternillarse de risa.
▶ n risa: we had a really good laugh nos reímos muchísimo.
◆ **to laugh at** vt insep reírse de.
◆ **to laugh off** vt sep tomar a risa.
laughter [ˈlɑːftər] n risas fpl: a fit of laughter un ataque de risa.
launch [lɔːntʃ] vt **1** lanzar: it will be launched on the market next year se lanzará al mercado el año que viene. **2** (ship)

botar; *(lifeboat)* echar al mar. **3** *(film, etc)* estrenar; *(book)* presentar. **4** *(company)* fundar. **5** *(scheme, attack)* iniciar. COMP **launch pad** plataforma de lanzamiento.
▶ *n (boat)* lancha.
ⓘ *pl* launches.

launching [ˈlɔːntʃɪŋ] *n* **1** lanzamiento. **2** *(of ship)* botadura. **3** *(of film)* estreno; *(of book)* presentación *f.* COMP **launching pad** plataforma de lanzamiento.

launder [ˈlɔːndəʳ] *vt* **1** *(clothes)* lavar (y planchar). **2** *fig (money)* blanquear.

launderette [lɔːnˈdᵊret] *n* lavandería automática.

laundry [ˈlɔːndrɪ] *n* **1** *(place)* lavandería. **2** *(dirty)* ropa sucia, colada; *(clean)* ropa limpia, ropa lavada. LOC **to do the laundry** lavar la ropa.
ⓘ *pl* laundries.

lava [ˈlɑːvə] *n* lava.

lavatory [ˈlævətᵊrɪ] *n* **1** váter *m.* **2** *(room)* lavabo, baño.
ⓘ *pl* lavatories.

lavender [ˈlævɪndəʳ] *n* espliego, lavanda.
▶ *adj (colour)* de color lavanda.

law [lɔː] *n* **1** ley *f.* **2** EDUC derecho. LOC **against the law** contra la ley. **∥ by law** por ley. **∥ to keep within the law** obrar según la ley. COMP **law and order** orden *m* público. **∥ law court** tribunal *m* de justicia.

lawful [ˈlɔːfʊl] *adj* legal.

lawn [lɔːn] *n* césped *m.*

lawnmower [ˈlɔːnməʊəʳ] *n* cortacésped *m & f.*

lawsuit [ˈlɔːsjuːt] *n* pleito, juicio.

lawyer [ˈlɔːjəʳ] *n* abogado,-a.

laxative [ˈlæksətɪv] *adj* laxante.
▶ *n* laxante *m.*

lay¹ [leɪ] *adj* **1** REL laico,-a, seglar. **2** *(non-professional)* lego,-a, no profesional.

lay² [leɪ] *vt* **1** *(gen)* poner, colocar; *(spread out)* extender. **2** *(bricks, carpet)* poner; *(cable, pipe)* tender; *(foundations, basis)* echar; *(bomb)* colocar. **3** *(prepare)* preparar; *(curse)* lanzar. **4** *(eggs)* poner.

5 *(bet)* apostar. **6** *(charge)* formular. LOC **to lay the table** poner la mesa.
▶ *vi (hen)* poner huevos.
◆ **to lay by** *vt sep* guardar; *(money)* ahorrar.
◆ **to lay down** *vt sep* **1** *(let go)* dejar, soltar. **2** *(give up)* entregar. **3** *(establish)* imponer, fijar.
◆ **to lay off** *vt sep (worker)* despedir.
▶ *vt insep fam (stop)* dejar en paz.
▶ *vi fam* parar: *lay off!* ¡ya está bien!, ¡para ya!
◆ **to lay on** *vt sep (provide)* suministrar.
▶ *vt insep (burden)* cargar.
◆ **to lay out** *vt sep* **1** *(spread out)* tender, extender. **2** *(arrange)* disponer, colocar. **3** *(present)* presentar, exponer. **4** *(town, etc)* hacer el trazado de; *(garden)* diseñar.
◆ **to lay over** *vi* US *(gen)* hacer una parada (at/in, en); *(plane)* hacer escala (at/in, en).
ⓘ *pt & pp* laid [leɪd].

lay³ [leɪ] *pp* → lie².

lay-by [ˈleɪbaɪ] *n* área de descanso.
ⓘ *pl* lay-bys.

layer [ˈleɪəʳ] *n* **1** capa. **2** *(of rock)* estrato. **3** *(hen)* gallina ponedora.

layout [ˈleɪaʊt] *n* **1** *(arrangement)* disposición *f;* *(presentation)* presentación *f.* **2** *(printing)* composición *f,* formato. **3** *(plan)* trazado.

laze [leɪz] *vi* gandulear, holgazanear.
◆ **to laze about / laze around** *vi* hacer el vago.

laziness [ˈleɪzɪnəs] *n* pereza.

lazy [ˈleɪzɪ] *adj* **1** gandul,-la, vago,-a, perezoso,-a. **2** *(river)* perezoso,-a.
ⓘ *comp* lazier, *superl* laziest.

lazybones [ˈleɪzɪbəʊnz] *n* perezoso,-a, gandul,-la.
ⓘ *pl* lazybones.

lb [paʊnd] *abbr* (pound) libra.
ⓘ *pl* lb o lbs.

lead¹ [led] *n* **1** *(metal)* plomo. **2** *(in pencil)* mina. LOC **to swing the lead** *fam* hacer el vago.

lead² [liːd] *vt* **1** *(guide)* llevar, conducir: *our tour guide led the way to the cathedral* la guía nos llevó a la catedral. **2** *(be leader*

L

of) liderar, dirigir. **3** *(be first in)* ocupar el primer puesto en. **4** *(influence)* llevar: *he is easily led* se deja llevar fácilmente.
► *vi* **1** *(road)* conducir, llevar (to, a). **2** *(command)* tener el mando. **3** *(go first)* ir primero,-a.
ⓘ *pt & pp* led [led].
► *n* **1** *(front position)* delantera. **2** SP liderato; *(difference)* ventaja. **3** THEAT primer papel *m*.

leader ['liːdəʳ] *n* **1** POL líder *mf*, dirigente *mf*. **2** *(in race)* líder *mf* (of/in, de).

leadership ['liːdəʃɪp] *n* **1** *(position)* liderato, liderazgo. **2** *(qualities)* dotes *mpl* de mando. **3** *(leaders)* dirección *f*.

lead-free ['ledfriː] *adj* sin plomo.

leading ['liːdɪŋ] *adj* destacado,-a, principal.

leaf [liːf] *n* **1** *(of plant)* hoja. **2** *(of book)* hoja, página.
ⓘ *pl* leaves [liːˈvz].

leaflet ['liːflət] *n* *(folded)* folleto; *(single sheet)* octavilla, hoja suelta.
► *vi* GB repartir folletos, repartir octavillas.

league [liːg] *n* liga. LOC **to be in league with** SB estar conchabado,-a con ALGN.

leak [liːk] *vi* **1** *(container)* tener un agujero; *(pipe)* tener un escape. **2** *(roof)* gotear. **3** *(gas, fluid)* escaparse.
► *n* **1** *(hole)* agujero. **2** *(in roof)* gotera. **3** *(of gas)* fuga, escape *m*; *(of liquid)* escape *m*. **4** *fig (of information, etc)* filtración *f*.
◆ **to leak out** *vi* **1** *(gas, fluid)* escaparse. **2** *fig* filtrarse.

leakage ['liːkɪdʒ] *n* fuga, escape *m*.

leaky ['liːkɪ] *adj* **1** *(container)* agujereado,-a; *(pipe)* con un escape. **2** *(roof)* que tiene goteras. **3** *(pipe)* que tiene escapes.
ⓘ *comp* leakier, *superl* leakiest.

lean¹ [liːn] *adj* **1** *(person)* delgado,-a, flaco,-a. **2** *(meat)* magro,-a. **3** *(harvest)* malo,-a, escaso,-a; *(year)* malo,-a, pobre: *it was a lean year for car sales* fue un mal año para la venta de coches.
► *n* *(meat)* carne *f* magra.

lean² [liːn] *vi* **1** inclinarse. **2** *(for support)* apoyarse (on, en) (against, contra).
► *vt* apoyar.
◆ **to lean on** *vt insep* **1** *(depend on)* depender de. **2** *(pressure)* presionar a.
◆ **to lean towards** *vt insep* estar a favor de, tirar hacia.
ⓘ *pt & pp* leaned o leant [lent].

leaning ['liːnɪŋ] *adj* inclinado,-a.
► *n* inclinación *f*, tendencia.

leant [lent] *pt & pp* → **lean²**.

leap [liːp] *vi* saltar, brincar.
ⓘ *pt & pp* leaped o leapt [lept].
► *n* **1** salto, brinco. COMP **leap year** año bisiesto.

leapfrog ['liːpfrɒg] *n* pídola.
► *vt* *fig (skip)* saltarse.
ⓘ *pt & pp* leapfrogged, *ger* leapfrogging.

leapt [lept] *pt & pp* → **leap**.

learn [lɜːn] *vt* **1** aprender: *I'd love to learn (how) to ice-skate* me encantaría aprender a patinar sobre hielo. **2** *(find out about)* enterarse de, saber.
► *vi* **1** aprender. **2** *(find out)* enterarse (about/of, de).
ⓘ *pt & pp* learned o learnt [lɜːnt].

learned ['lɜːnəd] *adj* erudito,-a.

learner ['lɜːnəʳ] *n* estudiante *mf*. COMP **learner driver** conductor,-a en prácticas.

learnt [lɜːnt] *pt & pp* → **learn**.

leash [liːʃ] *n* correa.

leasing ['liːsɪŋ] *n* **1** arrendamiento, arriendo. **2** FIN leasing *m*.

least [liːst] *adj* menor, menos: *he makes the least money* es el que gana menos dinero.
► *adv* menos: *when you least expect it* cuando menos lo esperas.
► *n* lo menos: *it's the least I can do* es lo menos que puedo hacer. LOC **at (the) least** por lo menos.

leather ['leðəʳ] *n* piel *f*, cuero.
► *adj* de piel, de cuero.

leave¹ [liːv] *vt* **1** *(go away from)* dejar, abandonar; *(go out of)* salir de: *she left home when she was 16* se marchó de casa a los 16 años. **2** *(stop being with)* irse de, marcharse de. **3** *(forget)* dejarse, olvi-

dar, olvidarse. **4** *(allow to remain)* dejar: *please leave the door open* por favor, deja la puerta abierta. **5** *(cause to remain)* dejar: *the glass left a ring on the table* el vaso dejó un cerco en la mesa. **6** *(bequeath)* dejar, legar. **7** MATH dar: *two from six leaves four* seis menos dos dan cuatro.
▸ *vi* marcharse, irse, partir: *he left for Rome this morning* esta mañana salió hacia Roma.
◆ **to leave off** *vt insep* dejar de: *there was so much noise that I had to leave off studying* había tanto ruido que tuve que dejar de estudiar.
▸ *vi* acabar, terminar.
◆ **to leave out** *vt sep* omitir, excluir.
① *pt & pp* left, *ger* leaving.

leave² [liːv] *n* **1** *(time off)* permiso. **2** *(permission)* permiso. LOC **to be on leave** MIL estar de permiso.

leaven ['levᵊn] *n* levadura.

leaves [liːvz] *pl* ▸ **leaf.**

Lebanese [lebəˈniːz] *adj* libanés,-esa.
▸ *n* libanés,-esa.
▸ *n pl* **the Lebanese** los libaneses *mpl.*

Lebanon ['lebənən] *n* Líbano.

lectern ['lektən] *n* atril *m*; *(in church)* facistol *m.*

lecture ['lektʃər] *n* **1** conferencia. **2** *(in university)* clase *f.* **3** *(telling-off)* reprimenda, sermón *m.*
▸ *vi* **1** dar una conferencia (on, sobre). **2** *(in university)* dar clase.
▸ *vt (scold)* sermonear, echar una reprimenda a.

☒ Lecture no significa 'lectura', que se traduce por reading.

lecturer ['lektʃərər] *n* **1** conferenciante *mf.* **2** *(in university)* profesor,-ra.

☒ Lecturer no significa 'lector', que se traduce por reader.

led [liːvz] *pp & pt* ▸ **lead².**

ledge [ledʒ] *n* **1** *(shelf)* repisa; *(of window)* antepecho, alféizar *m.* **2** *(of rock)* saliente *m.*

lee [liː] *n* **1** MAR sotavento, socaire *m.* **2** *(shelter)* abrigo. LOC **in the lee of** al abrigo de.

leech [liːtʃ] *n* sanguijuela.

leek [liːk] *n* puerro.

left¹ [left] *adj* **1** izquierdo,-a. **2** POL de izquierdas: *the left wing of the party* el ala izquierda del partido.
▸ *adv* a la izquierda, hacia la izquierda.
▸ *n* **1** izquierda: *keep to the left* manténgase a la izquierda. **2** *(punch)* golpe *m* de la izquierda. LOC **on the left** a mano izquierda.

left² [left] *pt & pp* ▸ **leave¹.** LOC **to be left** quedar: *is there any milk left?* ¿queda leche? I **to be left over** sobrar, quedar. COMP **left luggage office** consigna.

left-hand ['lefthænd] *adj* izquierdo,-a: *the shop is on the left-hand side* la tienda está a mano izquierda.

leftover ['leftəuvər] *adj* sobrante, restante.
▸ *n pl* **leftovers** sobras *fpl*, restos *mpl.*

leg [leg] *n* **1** ANAT pierna; *(of animal)* pata. **2** CULIN *(lamb, etc)* pierna; *(chicken, etc)* muslo. **3** *(of furniture)* pata, pie *m.* **4** *(of trousers)* pernera. **5** *(stage)* etapa. LOC **to pull sb's leg** *fam* tomarle el pelo a ALGN.

legal ['liːgᵊl] *adj* **1** legal, lícito,-a. **2** *(relating to the law)* jurídico,-a, legal: *the legal profession* la abogacía. LOC **to take legal action** entablar un pleito (against, contra).

legalize ['liːgᵊlaɪz] *vt* legalizar.

legend ['ledʒᵊnd] *n* leyenda.

legendary ['ledʒᵊndᵊrɪ] *adj* legendario,-a.

leggings ['legɪŋz] *n pl (whole leg)* mallas *fpl*; *(below knee)* polainas *fpl.*

legible ['ledʒəbᵊl] *adj* legible.

legion ['liːdʒᵊn] *n* legión *f.*

legionary ['liːdʒᵊnərɪ] *n* legionario.
① *pl* legionaries.

legionnaire [liːdʒəˈneər] *n* legionario. COMP **legionnaire's disease** enfermedad *f* del legionario.

legislation [ledʒɪsˈleɪʃᵊn] *n* legislación *f.*

legislative ['ledʒɪslətɪv] *adj* legislativo,-a.

legitimate [lɪˈdʒɪtɪmət] *adj* legítimo,-a.

L

legume ['legjʊːm] n legumbre f.

leisure ['leʒər, US 'liːʒər] n ocio, tiempo libre. LOC at leisure 1 *(with free time)* en su tiempo libre. 2 *(calmly)* tranquilamente. COMP leisure centre centro recreativo.

lemon ['lemən] n limón m.
▶ adj *(colour)* de color limón. COMP lemon squeezer exprimidor m. ‖ lemon tree limonero.

lemonade [leməˈneɪd] n 1 *(fizzy - plain)* gaseosa; *(- lemony-flavoured)* limonada. 2 *(still)* limonada.

lend [lend] vt 1 dejar, prestar: *could you lend me some money?* ¿me dejas un poco de dinero? 2 *fig (add)* dotar de, prestar. LOC to lend os to sth prestarse a ALGO, prestarse para ALGO. ‖ to lend (sb) a hand echar una mano (a ALGN).
ⓘ pt & pp lent [lent].

length [leŋθ] n 1 longitud f. 2 *(of time)* duración f. 3 *(piece)* trozo; *(of cloth)* largo. 4 *(of road)* tramo; *(of swimming pool)* largo.

lengthen ['leŋθən] vt 1 *(skirt, etc)* alargar. 2 *(lifetime)* prolongar.
▶ vi 1 *(skirt, etc)* alargarse. 2 *(lifetime)* prolongarse; *(days)* crecer.

lengthy ['leŋθɪ] adj *(in general)* largo,-a.
ⓘ comp lengthier, superl lengthiest.

lens [lenz] n 1 *(of glasses)* lente m & f. 2 *(of camera)* objetivo. 3 ANAT cristalino.
ⓘ pl lenses.

lent [lent] pt & pp → lend.

lentil ['lentəl] n lenteja.

Leo ['liːəʊ] n Leo.

leopard ['lepəd] n leopardo.

leotard ['liːətɑːd] n malla.

Lesotho [lɪˈsuːtuː] n Lesotho.

less [les] adj menos.
▶ pron menos: *the less you buy, the less you'll spend* cuánto menos compres, menos gastarás. LOC no less nada menos.
▶ adv menos: *less and less* cada vez menos; *he was being less than sincere* no fue nada sincero. LOC much less menos aún.
▶ prep menos.

lessen ['lesən] vt disminuir, reducir.
▶ vi disminuir, reducirse.

lesser ['lesər] adj menor.

lesson ['lesən] n 1 *(class)* clase f. 2 *(warning)* lección f.

let [let] vt *(allow)* dejar: *he lets the children watch cartoon videos* a los niños les deja mirar vídeos de dibujos animados. LOC to let sb alone dejar a ALGN en paz, no molestar a ALGN. ‖ to let sb know hacer saber a ALGN, avisar a ALGN.
▶ aux que + subjuntivo: *let him come* que venga; *let's go!* ¡vamos!, ¡vámonos!
▶ vt GB *(rent)* alquilar: *«House to let»* «Se alquila casa».
▶ n GB *(renting)* alquiler m.
◆ to let down vt sep 1 *(lower)* bajar. 2 *(lengthen)* alargar. 3 *(deflate)* desinflar. 4 *(disappoint)* fallar, defraudar.
◆ to let in vt sep dejar entrar: *her father let me in* me abrió su padre.
◆ to let into vt sep 1 dejar entrar a: *this key will let you into the garage* con esta llave podrás entrar en el garaje. 2 *(reveal)* revelar.
◆ to let off vt sep 1 *(leave off)* dejar. 2 *(bomb)* hacer explotar; *(fireworks)* hacer estallar. 3 *(person - forgive)* perdonar; *(- let leave)* dejar marcharse; *(- free)* dejar en libertad.
◆ to let on vi fam *(tell)* decir, descubrir.
▶ vt insep fam *(pretend)* hacer ver.
◆ to let out vt sep 1 *(in general)* dejar salir; *(release)* soltar (from, de). 2 *(utter)* soltar.
◆ to let through vt sep dejar pasar.
◆ to let up vi parar.
◆ to let up on vt insep fam dejar en paz.
ⓘ pt & pp let, ger letting.

let's [lets] v aux → let.

letter ['letər] n 1 *(of alphabet)* letra. 2 *(message)* carta. LOC to the letter al pie de la letra. COMP capital letter mayúscula. ‖ letter box buzón m. ‖ small letter minúscula.

lettuce ['letɪs] n lechuga.

leukaemia [luːˈkiːmɪə] n leucemia.

leukemia [luːˈkiːmɪə] n US → leukaemia.

leukocyte ['luːkəsaɪt] n leucocito.

level ['levəl] *adj* **1** *(horizontal)* llano,-a, plano,-a. **2** *(even)* a nivel, nivelado,-a; *(spoonful, etc)* raso,-a: *the table's not level* la mesa no está nivelada. **3** *(equal)* igual, igualado,-a. **4** *(steady)* estable; *(voice)* llano,-a. COMP **level crossing** paso a nivel.
▶ *n* **1** nivel *m*: *above sea level* sobre el nivel del mar. **2** *(flat ground)* llano, llanura. LOC **to be on a level with** estar al mismo nivel que.
▶ *vt* **1** *(make level, survey)* nivelar. **2** *(raze)* arrasar, rasar. **3** *(aim)* apuntar.
▶ *adv* a ras (with, de).
① *pt & pp* levelled *(US* leveled*)*, *ger* levelling *(US* leveling*)*.

lever ['li:vər] *n* **1** palanca. **2** *(in lock)* guarda.

levy ['levi] *vt* recaudar; *(fine)* imponer.
① *pt & pp* levied, *ger* levying.
▶ *n* recaudación *f*; *(of fine)* imposición *f*.
① *pl* levies.

lexical ['leksɪkəl] *adj* léxico, a.

liable ['laɪəbəl] *adj* **1** *(likely, susceptible)* propenso,-a (to, a): *the car is liable to stall* el coche tiende a calarse. **2** *(susceptible)* susceptible (to, a).

liar ['laɪər] *n* mentiroso,-a, embustero,-a: *he's such a liar!* ¡menudo embustero está hecho!

liberal ['lɪbərəl] *adj* **1** *(in general)* liberal. **2** *(abundant)* abundante.

Liberal ['lɪbərəl] *adj* POL liberal.
▶ *n* POL liberal *mf*.

liberalize ['lɪbərəlaɪz] *vt* liberalizar.

liberation [lɪbəˈreɪʃən] *n* liberación *f*.

Liberia [laɪˈbɪəriə] *n* Liberia.

Liberian [laɪˈbɪəriən] *adj* liberiano,-a.
▶ *n* liberiano,-a.

liberty ['lɪbəti] *n* libertad *f*.
① *pl* liberties. LOC **at liberty** en libertad, libre (to, de). ‖ **to take liberties with sb/sth** tomarse libertades con ALGN/ALGO.

Libra ['li:brə] *n* Libra *m*.

librarian [laɪˈbreəriən] *n* bibliotecario,-a.

library ['laɪbrəri] *n* **1** biblioteca. **2** *(collection)* colección *f*. COMP **newspaper library** hemeroteca.
① *pl* libraries.

⊠ Library no significa 'librería (tienda)', que se traduce por bookshop, ni 'librería (mueble)', que se traduce por bookcase.

libretto [lɪˈbretəʊ] *n* libreto.
① *pl* librettos o libretti [lɪˈbreti:].

Libya ['lɪbiə] *n* Libia.

Libyan ['lɪbiən] *adj* libio,-a.
▶ *n* libio,-a.

lice [laɪs] *pl* → louse.

licence ['laɪsəns] *n* **1** *(permit)* licencia, permiso. **2** *(freedom)* libertad *f*; *(excessive freedom)* licencia. COMP **licence number** matrícula.

license ['laɪsəns] *n* US → licence.
▶ *vt* autorizar, dar licencia a.

licensed ['laɪsənst] *adj* autorizado,-a.

lichen ['laɪkən, 'lɪtʃən] *n* liquen *m*.

lick [lɪk] *vt* **1** lamer. **2** *fam (defeat - team)* vencer a, derrotar; *(- problem)* superar, solucionar. LOC **to lick one's lips** relamerse.
▶ *n* **1** lamedura, lengüetada. **2** *fam (of paint)* mano *f*.

licorice ['lɪkərɪs, 'lɪkərɪʃ] *n* regaliz *m*.

lid [lɪd] *n* **1** *(cover)* tapa. **2** *(of eye)* párpado. LOC **to take the lid off sth** *fig* destapar ALGO.

lie¹ [laɪ] *vi* mentir.
① *pt & pp* lied, *ger* lying.
▶ *n* mentira. LOC **to tell lies** mentir.

lie² [laɪ] *vi* **1** *(adopt a flat position)* acostarse, tumbarse. **2** *(be situated)* estar (situado,-a), encontrarse. **3** *(be buried)* yacer. **4** *(remain)* quedarse, permanecer.
◆ **to lie back** *vi* recostarse.
◆ **to lie down** *vi* acostarse, tumbarse, echarse.
◆ **to lie up** *vi* guardar cama.
① *pt* lay [leɪ], *pp* lain [leɪn], *ger* lying.

Liechtenstein ['lɪktənstaɪn] *n* Liechtenstein.

lie-down ['laɪdaʊn] *n* siesta.

lieutenant [lefˈtenənt, US lu:ˈtenənt] *n* **1** MIL teniente *m*. **2** *(non-military)* lugarteniente *m*.

life [laɪf] *n* **1** vida. **2** *(of battery)* duración *f*. LOC **it's a matter of life and death** es

cuestión de vida o muerte. ∎ **not on your life!** *fam* ¡ni hablar! ∎ **to come to life** cobrar vida. ∎ **to lose one's life** perder la vida. ∎ **to take one's own life** suicidarse, quitarse la vida. ∎ **to take sb's life** matar a ALGN. COMP **life belt / life buoy** salvavidas *m*. ∎ **life jacket** chaleco salvavidas. ∎ **life style** estilo de vida.
ⓘ *pl* **lives** [laɪvz].

lifeboat [ˈlaɪfbəʊt] *n* **1** *(on shore)* lancha de socorro. **2** *(on ship)* bote *m* salvavidas.

lifeguard [ˈlaɪfgɑːd] *n* socorrista *mf*.

lifelong [ˈlaɪflɒŋ] *adj* de toda la vida.

life-saver [ˈlaɪfseɪvəʳ] *n* socorrista *mf*.

lifestyle [ˈlaɪfstaɪl] *n* estilo de vida.

lifetime [ˈlaɪftaɪm] *n* **1** vida: *in her lifetime* en su vida. **2** *fam* eternidad *f*.

lift [lɪft] *vt* **1** *(in general)* levantar, coger. **2** *(by plane)* transportar.
▶ *vi (of movable parts)* levantarse:.
▶ *n* GB ascensor *m*. LOC **to give sb a lift 1** *(in car)* llevar a ALGN en coche. **2** *(cheer up)* animar.

liftoff [ˈlɪftɒf] *n* despegue *m*.

ligament [ˈlɪgəmənt] *n* ligamento.

light¹ [laɪt] *n* **1** *(gen)* luz *f*. **2** *(lamp)* luz *f*, lámpara; *(traffic light)* semáforo. **3** *(for cigarette, fire)* fuego. LOC **in (the) light of** GB en vista de, teniendo en cuenta. ∎ **to come to light** salir a luz. ∎ **to throw light on** STH aclarar ALGO. COMP **light bulb** bombilla. ∎ **light switch** interruptor *m* de la luz. ∎ **light year** año luz.
▶ *vt* **1** *(ignite)* encender. **2** *(illuminate)* iluminar, alumbrar.
ⓘ *pt & pp* **lighted** o **lit** [lɪt].
▶ *adj (colour)* claro,-a; *(complexion)* blanco,-a. **2** *(bright)* con mucha claridad.

light² [laɪt] *adj* **1** *(not heavy)* ligero,-a; *(rain)* fino,-a; *(breeze)* suave. **2** *(sentence, wound)* leve. COMP **light aircraft** avioneta.

lighten¹ [ˈlaɪtⁿn] *vt* **1** *(colour)* aclarar. **2** *(room)* iluminar.
▶ *vi (colour)* aclararse.

lighten² [ˈlaɪtⁿn] *vt (make less heavy)* aligerar.
▶ *vi (mood, etc)* alegrarse.

lighter [ˈlaɪtəʳ] [also **cigarette lighter**] *n* encendedor *m*, mechero.

lighthouse [ˈlaɪthaʊs] *n* faro.

lighting [ˈlaɪtɪŋ] *n* **1** *(in general)* iluminación *f*. **2** *(system)* alumbrado.

lightly [ˈlaɪtlɪ] *adv* **1** *(not heavily)* ligeramente. **2** *(not seriously)* a la ligera.

lightning [ˈlaɪtⁿnɪŋ] *n* rayo; *(flash only)* relámpago.

lights-out [ˈlaɪtsaʊt] *n* la hora de apagar las luces.

lightweight [ˈlaɪtweɪt] *n (boxing)* peso ligero.

lignite [ˈlɪgnaɪt] *n* lignita.

like¹ [laɪk] *prep* **1** *(the same as)* como: *the flat looks like new* el piso está como nuevo. **2** *(typical of)* propio,-a de: *it isn't like her to make a scene* no es propio de ella armar un escándalo. LOC **to look like** SB parecerse a ALGN. ∎ **something like that** ALGO así, ALGO por el estilo.
▶ *adj* **1** *(such as)* como. **2** *fml* parecido,-a.
▶ *conj fam* como.
▶ *n* ALGO parecido: *I've never seen the like of it* nunca he vista cosa igual.

like² [laɪk] *vt* **1** *(enjoy)* gustar. **2** *(want)* querer, gustar: *I'd like a cup of coffee* me gustaría tomar un café. LOC **to like** STH **better** preferir ALGO.
▶ *vi* querer: *if you like* si quieres.
▶ *n pl* **likes** gustos *mpl*.

likeable [ˈlaɪkəbəl] *adj* simpático,-a.

likelihood [ˈlaɪklɪhʊd] *n* probabilidad *f*.

likely [ˈlaɪklɪ] *adj* probable: *he's likely to leave late* es probable que salga tarde.
▶ *adv* probablemente. LOC **as likely as not** *fam* lo más seguro.
ⓘ *comp* **likelier**, *superl* **likeliest**.

likeness [ˈlaɪknəs] *n* **1** *(similarity)* semejanza, parecido. **2** *(portrait)* retrato.

likewise [ˈlaɪkwaɪz] *adv* **1** *(the same)* lo mismo, igualmente: *to do likewise* hacer lo mismo.

liking [ˈlaɪkɪŋ] *n (for thing)* gusto, afición *f*; *(for person)* simpatía; *(for friend)* cariño.

lilac [ˈlaɪlək] *n* **1** BOT lila. **2** *(colour)* lila *m*.
▶ *adj (de color)* lila.

lily [ˈlɪlɪ] *n* lirio, azucena.
ⓘ *pl* **lilies**.

limb [lɪmb] n **1** ANAT miembro. **2** *(branch)* rama.
- **to limber up** vi SP entrar en calor.
  ▸ vt sep calentar.
lime [laɪm] n **1** *(citrus fruit)* lima. **2** *(citrus tree)* limero. **3** *(linden)* tilo.
limestone [ˈlaɪmstəʊn] n piedra caliza.
limit [ˈlɪmɪt] n límite m. LOC **that's the limit!** *fam* ¡eso es el colmo! ‖ **to be off limits** estar en zona prohibida (**to**, para). ‖ **within limits** dentro de ciertos límites.
  ▸ vt limitar, restringir (**to**, a)
limitation [lɪmɪˈteɪʃən] n limitación f.
limousine [lɪməˈziːn] n limusina.
limp¹ [lɪmp] vi cojear.
  ▸ n cojera.
limp² [lɪmp] adj **1** *(floppy)* flojo,-a, fláccido,-a; *(lettuce)* mustio,-a. **2** *(weak)* débil.
limpet [ˈlɪmpɪt] n lapa.
linden [ˈlɪndən] n tilo.
line [laɪn] n **1** *(in general)* línea: *in a straight line* en línea recta. **2** *(drawn on paper)* raya. **3** *(of text)* línea, renglón m; *(of poetry)* verso: *new line* punto y aparte. **4** *(row)* fila, hilera. **5** US *(queue)* cola. **6** *(cord)* cuerda, cordel m; *(fishing)* sedal m; *(wire)* cable m. **7** *(route)* vía. LOC **all along the line 1** *(from the beginning)* desde el principio. **2** *(in detail)* con todo detalle. ‖ **in line with** *fig* conforme a. ‖ **to stand in line** US hacer cola. COMP **dotted line** línea de puntos. ‖ **line drawing** dibujo lineal.
  ▸ vt **1** *(draw lines on)* dibujar rayas en. **2** *(mark with wrinkles)* arrugar. **3** *(form rows along)* bordear.
- **to line up** vi ponerse en fila; *(in queue)* hacer cola.
linen [ˈlɪnɪn] n **1** *(material)* lino, hilo. **2** *(sheets, etc)* ropa blanca, lencería. COMP **bed linen** ropa de cama. ‖ **table linen** mantelería.
liner [ˈlaɪnər] n *(mar)* transatlántico.
linesman [ˈlaɪnzmən] n juez mf de línea, linier m.
  ① pl linesmen [ˈlaɪnzmən].

line-up [ˈlaɪnʌp] n *(of people)* alineación f, formación f.
lingerie [ˈlɑːnʒəriː] n fml lencería.
linguist [ˈlɪŋgwɪst] n **1** lingüista mf. **2** *(fam)* políglota mf.
linguistic [lɪŋˈgwɪstɪk] adj lingüístico,-a.
linguistics [lɪŋˈgwɪstɪks] n lingüística.
lining [ˈlaɪnɪŋ] n forro.
link [lɪŋk] n **1** *(in chain)* eslabón m. **2** *(connection)* enlace m. **3** fig vínculo, lazo.
  ▸ vt **1** unir, conectar. **2** fig vincular, relacionar.
linkage [ˈlɪŋkɪdʒ] n conexión f.
lintel [ˈlɪntəl] n dintel m.
lion [ˈlaɪən] n león m.
lioness [ˈlaɪənəs] n leona.
  ① pl lionesses.
lip [lɪp] n **1** labio. **2** *(of cup, etc)* borde m.
lipid [ˈlɪpɪd] n lípido.
lip-read [ˈlɪpriːd] vt leer en los labios.
  ▸ vi leer en los labios.
  ① pt & pp lip-read [ˈlɪpred].
lipstick [ˈlɪpstɪk] n *(stick)* barra de labios, lápiz m de labios; *(substance)* pintura de labios.
liquefaction [lɪkwɪˈfækʃən] n licuefacción f, licuación f.
liquefy [ˈlɪkwɪfaɪ] vt licuar.
  ▸ vi licuarse.
  ① pt & pp liquefied, ger liquefying.
liqueur [lɪˈkjʊər, US lɪˈkɜːr] n licor m.
liquid [ˈlɪkwɪd] n **1** líquido.
  ▸ adj **1** líquido,-a.
liquidate [ˈlɪkwɪdeɪt] vt liquidar.
liquor [ˈlɪkər] n US licor m.
liquorice [ˈlɪkərɪs, ˈlɪkərɪʃ] n regaliz m.
lira [ˈlɪərə] n lira.
  ① pl liras o lire [ˈlɪərə].
list [lɪst] n lista.
  ▸ vt hacer una lista de: *he listed the contents of the house* hizo una lista de las cosas que había en la casa.
listen [ˈlɪsən] vi escuchar (**to**, -): *listen to me!* ¡escúchame!
- **to listen in** vi *(radio)* escuchar (**to**, -).
- **to listen out** vi fam estar a la escucha, estar en escucha (**for**, de).
listener [ˈlɪsənər] n **1** *(in general)* oyente mf. **2** RAD radioyente mf.

L

| listing 222 |

listing ['lɪstɪŋ] *n* listado.

lit [lɪt] *pt & pp* → **light**.

liter ['liːtə'] *n* US → **litre**.

literacy ['lɪt°rəsɪ] *n* **1** *(ability to read)* alfabetización *f*. **2** *(knowledge)* conocimientos *mpl*, nociones *fpl*.

literal ['lɪt°rəl] *adj* literal.

literary ['lɪt°rərɪ] *adj* literario,-a.

literature ['lɪt°rətʃə'] *n* **1** literatura. **2** *(bibliography)* bibliografía.

lithium ['lɪθɪəm] *n* litio.

lithograph ['lɪθəgrɑːf] *n* litografía.

lithosphere ['lɪθəsfɪə'] *n* litosfera.

Lithuania [lɪθjuˈeɪnɪə] *n* Lituania.

Lithuanian [lɪθjuˈeɪnɪən] *adj* lituano,-a.
► *n* **1** *(person)* lituano,-a. **2** *(language)* lituano.

litre ['liːtə'] *n* litro.

litter ['lɪtə'] *n* **1** *(rubbish)* basura, desperdicios *mpl*; *(paper)* papeles *mpl*. **2** *(of kittens, etc)* camada. COMP **litter bin** GB papelera.

little ['lɪt°l] *adj* **1** *(small)* pequeño,-a: *a little cup* una tacita. **2** *(not much)* poco,-a: *a little milk* un poco de leche. COMP **little finger** dedo meñique.
ⓘ *comp* **less**, *superl* **least**.
► *pron* poco: *more tea? -just a little, please* ¿quieres más té? -un poco, por favor.
► *adv* poco: *I'm a little (bit) tired* estoy un poco cansada. LOC **little by little** poco a poco.

liturgy ['lɪtədʒɪ] *n* liturgia.
ⓘ *pl* **liturgies**.

live¹ [lɪv] *vi* vivir: *he lives in the country* vive en el campo.
► *vt* vivir: *the old woman had lived a life of luxury* la vieja había llevado una vida llena de lujos. LOC **to live it up** *fam* pasárselo bomba.
◆ **to live down** *vt sep* lograr que se olvide.
◆ **to live in** *vi* *(student)* estar internado,-a; *(servant)* vivir con la familia.
◆ **to live off** *vt insep* vivir de.
◆ **to live on** *vi* sobrevivir; *(memory)* seguir vivo,-a.
◆ **to live through** *vt insep* sobrevivir.

live² [laɪv] *adj* **1** *(not dead)* vivo,-a: *it's a real live snake* es una serpiente de verdad. **2** *(still burning)* vivo,-a, candente; *(issue)* candente. **3** *(broadcast)* en directo: *a live concert* un concierto en directo.
► *adv* en directo, en vivo.

livelihood ['laɪvlɪhʊd] *n* sustento.

lively ['laɪvlɪ] *adj* **1** vivo,-a, animado,-a; *(interest)* entusiasmado,-a. **2** *(colour)* vivo,-a.
ⓘ *comp* **livelier**, *superl* **liveliest**.

liven ['laɪv°n] *vt* **to liven up** animar.
► *vi* **liven up** animarse.

liver ['lɪvə'] *n* ANAT hígado.

lives [laɪvz] *pl* → **life**.

livestock ['laɪvstɒk] *n* ganado. LOC **livestock farming** ganadería.

living ['lɪvɪŋ] *adj* vivo,-a: *every living creature* todo bicho viviente.
► *n* vida: *what do you do for a living?* ¿cómo te ganas la vida? COMP **living room** salón *m*, sala de estar. ‖ **living thing** ser *m* vivo.

lizard ['lɪzəd] *n* lagarto; *(small)* lagartija.

'll [l] *v aux* → **will**, **shall**.

llama ['lɑːmə] *n* ZOOL llama.

load [ləʊd] *n* **1** *(in general)* carga: *a lorry shed its load on the motorway yesterday* ayer un camión perdió su carga en la autopista. **2** *(weight)* peso. LOC **a load of ...** / **loads of ...** *fam* montones de…, un montón de…
► *vt* cargar (**with**, de): *they loaded up the van with furniture* cargaron la furgoneta de muebles.
► *vi* cargar.
◆ **to load down** *vt sep* cargar (**with**, de); *(with worries, etc)* agobiar (**with**, de/por).

loaf [ləʊf] *n* pan *m*; *(French)* barra; *(sliced)* pan *m* de molde.
ⓘ *pl* **loaves** [ləʊvz].

loan [ləʊn] *n* *(of money)* préstamo, crédito. LOC **on loan** prestado,-a.

loathe [ləʊð] *vt* odiar, aborrecer.

loaves [ləʊvz] *pl* → **loaf**.

lobby ['lɒbɪ] *n* **1** *(hall)* vestíbulo. **2** POL grupo de presión.
ⓘ *pl* **lobbies**.

▶ *vi* presionar (**for**, para) (**against**, en contra de).

▶ *vt* POL presionar, ejercer presión sobre.

lobe [ləub] *n* lóbulo.

lobster ['lɒbstə'] *n* bogavante *m*.

local ['ləʊkəl] *adj* **1** *(in general)* local. **2** *(person)* del barrio, de la zona.

▶ *n* **1** *fam (person)* vecino,-a. **2** GB *fam* bar *m*, pub *m* *(del barrio)*. **3** US *(train)* tren *m* de cercanías; *(bus)* autobús *m*.

⊠ Local no significa 'local (establecimiento)', que se traduce por premises.

locality [ləʊˈkælɪtɪ] *n fml* localidad *f*.
ⓘ *pl* localities.

locate [ləʊˈkeɪt] *vt* **1** *fml (find)* localizar. **2** *fml (situate)* situar, ubicar.

location [ləʊˈkeɪʃⁿn] *n* **1** lugar, ubicación *m*. **2** CINEM exteriores *mpl*.

loch [lɒk] *n* *(in Scotland)* lago.

lock¹ [lɒk] *n* **1** *(gen)* cerradura; *(padlock)* candado. **2** *(in canal)* esclusa. **3** *(in wrestling)* llave *f*.

▶ *vt* *(with key)* cerrar con llave; *(with padlock)* cerrar con candado.

▶ *vi* **1** *(door, etc)* cerrarse (con llave).

lock² [lɒk] *n* *(of hair)* mecha, mechón *m*.

locker ['lɒkə'] *n* armario, taquilla.

locksmith ['lɒksmɪθ] *n* cerrajero.

locomotion [ləʊkəˈməʊʃⁿn] *n* locomoción *f*.

locomotive [ləʊkəˈməʊtɪv] *n* locomotora.

▶ *adj* locomotor,-ra.

locomotor [ləʊkəˈmətə'] *adj* locomotor,-a.

locust ['ləʊkəst] *n* langosta.

✎ La palabra locust se refiere al insecto; el marisco se llama lobster.

lodge [lɒdʒ] *n* **1** *(in general)* casita; *(hunter's)* refugio. **2** *(porter's)* portería. **3** *(masonic)* logia.

▶ *vi* **1** *(as guest)* alojarse, hospedarse. **2** *(become fixed)* quedarse atrapado,-a.

▶ *vt* *(complaint)* presentar.

lodger ['lɒdʒə'] *n* huésped,-da.

lodging ['lɒdʒɪŋ] *n* alojamiento. COMP lodging house casa de huéspedes.

loft [lɒft] *n* desván *m*, buhardilla.

▶ *vt* SP lanzar al aire.

log [lɒg] *n* **1** tronco; *(for fire)* leño. **2** *(on ship)* cuaderno de bitácora; *(on plane)* diario de vuelo. **3** MATH *fam (abbr of logarithm)* logaritmo.

▶ *vt* **1** registrar, anotar. **2** *(cover)* recorrer.

◆ **to log in** *vi* COMPUT entrar (en el sistema).

◆ **to log out** *vi* COMPUT salir (del sistema).

ⓘ *pt & pp* logged, *ger* logging.

logarithm ['lɒgərɪðⁿm] *n* logaritmo.

logic ['lɒdʒɪk] *n* lógica.

logical ['lɒdʒɪkⁿl] *adj* lógico,-a: *the logical thing would be to say yes* lo lógico sería decir que sí.

logistics [ləˈdʒɪstɪks] *n* logística.

logo ['ləʊgəʊ] *n* logotipo.
ⓘ *pl* logos.

loin [lɔɪn] *n* CULIN *(of pork)* lomo; *(of beef)* solomillo.

lollipop ['lɒlɪpɒp] *n* **1** pirulí *m*, piruleta. **2** GB *(iced)* polo.

lolly ['lɒlɪ] *n* **1** GB *fam* pirulí *m*, piruleta. **2** GB *fam (iced)* polo.
ⓘ *pl* lollies.

loneliness ['ləʊnlɪnəs] *n* soledad *f*.

lonely ['ləʊnlɪ] *adj* **1** *(person)* solo,-a. **2** *(place)* solitario,-a, aislado,-a.
ⓘ *comp* lonelier, *superl* loneliest.

lonesome ['ləʊnsⁿm] *adj* US→ lonely.

long¹ [lɒŋ] *adj* largo,-a: *a long journey* un largo viaje. COMP long jump salto de longitud.

▶ *adv* mucho tiempo: *it takes a long time to climb the mountain* se tarda mucho en escalar la montaña. LOC as long as *(while)* mientras. ▌ long ago hace mucho tiempo.

long² [lɒŋ] *phr* to long to do STH tener muchos deseos de hacer ALGO.

◆ **to long for** *vt insep (yearn)* anhelar; *(nostalgically)* añorar.

long-distance [lɒŋˈdɪstⁿns] *adj* de larga distancia.

L

longing ['lɒŋɪŋ] *n (yearning)* ansia, anhelo; *(nostalgia)* nostalgia.

longitude ['lɒndʒɪtjuːd] *n* longitud *f*.

long-life ['lɒŋlaɪf] *adj (battery)* de larga duración; *(milk)* UHT, uperizado,-a.

long-range ['lɒŋreɪndʒ] *adj* **1** *(distance)* de largo alcance. **2** *(plans, forecast)* a largo plazo.

long-term [lɒŋ'tɜːm] *adj* a largo plazo, de largo plazo.

long-wearing [lɒŋ'weərɪŋ] *adj* US duradero,-a, resistente.

loo [luː] *n* GB *fam* váter *m*.
ⓘ *pl* loos.

look [lʊk] *vi* **1** mirar (at, -). **2** *(seem)* parecer: *he looks tired* parece cansado. LOC **look out!** ¡cuidado!
▶ *vt* mirar: *I can't look him in the face* no puedo mirarle a la cara. **2** *(seem)* parecer: *he doesn't look his age* no aparenta la edad que tiene.
▶ *n* **1** *(glance)* mirada: *have a look at this* mira esto. **2** *(appearance)* aspecto, apariencia. **4** *(fashion)* moda: *I'm not into the punk look* no me va la moda punk.
▶ *interj* ¡mira!
◆ **to look after** *vt insep (deal with)* ocuparse de, atender a; *(take care of)* cuidar (de).
◆ **to look at** *vt insep* **1** *(consider)* mirar, considerar. **2** *(examine)* mirar.
◆ **to look back** *vi* mirar atrás.
◆ **to look for** *vt insep* buscar: *what are you looking for?* ¿qué buscas?
◆ **to look forward to** *vt insep* esperar (con ansia).
◆ **to look on** *vt insep* considerar.
◆ **to look like** *vt insep* parecerse a: *he looks like his father* se parece a su padre.
◆ **to look out** *vi (be careful)* ir con cuidado.
◆ **to look through** *vt insep (check)* revisar (bien); *(quickly)* ojear.
◆ **to look up** *vi fam (improve)* mejorar.
▶ *vt sep* **1** *(in dictionary, etc)* consultar, buscar.

lookalike ['lʊkəlaɪk] *n fam* doble *mf*, sosia *m*.

loom¹ [luːm] *n* telar *m*.

loom² [luːm] *vi* vislumbrarse; *(causing fear)* amenazar.
◆ **to loom up** *vi* surgir.

loony ['luːnɪ] *adj fam* chiflado,-a, chalado,-a.
ⓘ *comp* loonier, *superl* looniest.

loop [luːp] *n (in string, etc)* lazo.
▶ *vi* formar un lazo. LOC **to loop the loop** rizar el rizo.

loose [luːs] *adj* **1** *(in general)* suelto,-a. **2** *(not tight)* flojo,-a; *(clothes)* holgado,-a.
▶ *vt lit* soltar.

loose-fitting [luːs'fɪtɪŋ] *adj* holgado,-a, amplio,-a.

loosen ['luːsən] *vt (gen)* soltar, aflojar; *(belt)* desabrochar.
▶ *vi* **1** soltarse, aflojarse.
◆ **to loosen up** *vi (relax)* relajarse.

loot [luːt] *n* botín *m*.

lord [lɔːd] *n* **1** señor *m*. **2** GB *(title)* lord *m*. **3** *(judge)* señoría *mf*. LOC **good Lord!** ¡ay Dios!, ¡Dios mío! COMP **the Lord** REL el Señor.

lorry ['lɒrɪ] *n* GB camión *m*.
ⓘ *pl* lorries.

lose [luːz] *vt* **1** *(in general)* perder: *don't lose it* no lo pierdas. **2** *(clock)* atrasar.
▶ *vi* **1** *(in general)* perder: *Liverpool lost to United* el Liverpool perdió ante el United. **2** *(clock)* atrasarse. LOC **to lose one's way** perderse. ❙ **to lose sight of** STH perder ALGO de vista.
ⓘ *pt & pp* lost [lɒst], *ger* losing.

loser ['luːzər] *n* perdedor,-ra.

loss [lɒs] *n* **1** *(in general)* pérdida. **2** MIL *(death)* baja.
ⓘ *pl* losses.

lost [lɒst] *pt → lose.*
▶ *adj* perdido,-a. LOC **to get lost** perderse. COMP **lost property** objetos perdidos.

lost-and-found [lɒstən'faʊnd] [also lost-and-found department] *n* US oficina de objetos perdidos.

lot [lɒt] *n* **1** *(large number)* cantidad *f*: *he talks a lot* habla mucho. **2** *(group)* grupo: *the next lot of passengers* el próximo grupo de pasajeros. **3** *(fate)* suerte *f*. LOC **thanks a lot!** ¡muchísimas gracias!
▶ *n* **the lot** todo,-a, todos,-as.

▶ *phr* **lots of** mucho,-a, muchos,-as, cantidad de: *there were lots of people* había mucha gente.

lotion ['ləʊʃºn] *n* loción *f*.

lottery ['lɒtºrɪ] *n* lotería.
ⓘ *pl* lotteries.

loud [laʊd] *adj* **1** *(sound)* fuerte. **2** *(voice)* alto,-a. **3** *(colour)* chillón,-ona.
▶ *adv* fuerte, alto. [LOC] **out loud** en voz alta.

loudly ['laʊdlɪ] *adv (speak)* alto; *(shout)* fuerte; *(complain)* a voz en grito.

loudness ['laʊdnəs] *n (of sound)* fuerza, intensidad *f*; *(noisiness)* bullicio.

loudspeaker [laʊd'spiːkəʳ] *n* altavoz *m*.

lounge [laʊndʒ] *n* salón *m*. [COMP] **lounge suit** *fam* traje *m*.
▶ *vi* **1** *(on sofa, etc)* repantigarse. **2** *(idle)* holgazanear.

lounger ['laʊndʒəʳ] *n (chair)* tumbona.

louse [laʊs] *n* **1** piojo. **2** *fam* canalla *mf*.
ⓘ *pl* lice.

lousy ['laʊzɪ] *adj* **1** *fam* fatal, malísimo,-a: *he felt lousy* se encontraba fatal.
ⓘ *comp* lousier, *superl* lousiest.

lovable ['lʌvəbºl] *adj* adorable.

love [lʌv] *n* **1** *(in general)* amor *m*; *(affection)* cariño; *(liking)* afición *f* (**for**, a). **2** GB *fam (person)* guapo,-a, chato,-a. **3** *(regards)* recuerdos *mpl*: *(give my) love to your parents* muchos recuerdos a tus padres. [LOC] **to be in love with** estar enamorado,-a de. ▮ **to fall in love** enamorarse. ▮ **to make love** hacer el amor (**to**, a). [COMP] **love affair** aventura amorosa, lío.
▶ *vt* **1** amar, querer: *do you love him?* ¿lo quieres? **2** *(like a lot)* encantarle a uno, gustarle a uno mucho: *I love playing tennis* me encanta jugar a tenis.

lovely ['lʌvlɪ] *adj* **1** *(wonderful)* estupendo,-a, maravilloso,-a. **2** *(beautiful)* hermoso,-a, precioso,-a; *(charming)* encantador,-ra.
ⓘ *comp* lovelier, *superl* loveliest.

lover ['lʌvəʳ] *n* amante *mf*.:

loving ['lʌvɪŋ] *adj* cariñoso,-a: *your loving son, Paul* tu hijo que te quiere, Paul.

low [ləʊ] *adj* **1** *(in general)* bajo,-a; *(neckline)* escotado,-a: *low clouds* nubes bajas. **2** *(battery)* gastado,-a. **3** *(depressed)* deprimido,-a, abatido,-a. **4** MUS grave. [LOC] **to keep a low profile** ser discreto,-a. [COMP] **low tide** marea baja. ▮ **the Low Countries** los Países Bajos.
▶ *adv* bajo: *we're running low on petrol* se nos acaba la gasolina.
▶ *n (low level)* punto bajo.

low-calorie [ləʊ'kælərɪ] *adj* bajo,-a en calorías, hipocalórico,-a.

lower ['ləʊəʳ] *adj* inferior. [COMP] **lower case** caja baja, minúscula.
▶ *vt* **1** *(in general)* bajar; *(price)* rebajar. **2** *(flag)* arriar.

lower-class [ləʊə'klɑːs] *adj* de clase baja.

lowest ['ləʊɪst] *adj* más bajo,-a; *(price, speed)* mínimo,-a.
▶ *n* mínimo: *at the lowest* como mínimo.

low-fat [ləʊ'fæt] *adj* de bajo contenido graso.

loyal ['lɔɪəl] *adj* leal, fiel.

loyalty ['lɔɪəltɪ] *n* lealtad *f*, fidelidad *f*.
ⓘ *pl* loyalties.

lozenge ['lɒzɪndʒ] *n* **1** pastilla. **2** *(geometry)* rombo.

LP ['el'piː] *abbr* (long player) elepé *m*; *(abbreviation)* LP.

lubricant ['luːbrɪkənt] *n* lubricante *m*.

lucerne [luː'sɜːn] *n* GB alfalfa.

luck [lʌk] *n* suerte *f*. [LOC] **bad luck! / hard luck! / tough luck!** ¡mala suerte! ▮ **good luck! / best of luck!** ¡suerte! ▮ **to be in luck** estar de suerte. ▮ **to try one's luck** probar fortuna.

luckily ['lʌkɪlɪ] *adv* afortunadamente.

lucky ['lʌkɪ] *adj (in general)* afortunado,-a; *(timely)* oportuno,-a: *how lucky you were!* ¡qué suerte tuviste! [COMP] **lucky charm** amuleto.
ⓘ *comp* luckier, *superl* luckiest.

lucrative ['luːkrətɪv] *adj* lucrativo,-a.

ludo ['luːdəʊ] *n* GB parchís *m*.

luggage ['lʌgɪdʒ] *n* GB equipaje *m*. [COMP] **luggage rack** portaequipajes *m*. ▮ **luggage van** furgón *m* de equipaje.

L

lukewarm ['lu:kwɔ:m] *adj* tibio,-a, templado,-a.

lullaby ['lʌləbaɪ] *n* canción *f* de cuna, nana.

ⓘ *pl* lullabies.

lumbar ['lʌmbəʳ] *adj* lumbar.

luminous ['lu:mɪnəs] *adj* luminoso,-a.

lump [lʌmp] *n* **1** *(chunk)* pedazo, trozo; *(in sauce)* grumo. **2** *(swelling)* bulto, protuberancia; *(in throat)* nudo. **3** *(of sugar)* terrón *m*. **4** *fam (idiot)* burro,-a.

lumpy ['lʌmpɪ] *adj* lleno,-a de bultos; *(sauce)* grumoso,-a.

ⓘ *comp* lumpier, *superl* lumpiest.

lunar ['lu:nəʳ] *adj* lunar. COMP lunar landing alunizaje *m*. ▌ lunar month mes *m* lunar.

lunatic ['lu:nətɪk] *adj* loco,-a.

▸ *n* loco,-a, lunático,-a. COMP lunatic asylum manicomio. ▌ the lunatic fringe los fanáticos *mpl*.

lunch [lʌntʃ] *n* comida, almuerzo: *we'll have lunch at one* comeremos a la una. COMP business lunch almuerzo de trabajo. ▌ lunch break hora de comer. ▌ lunch hour hora de comer.

▸ *vi fml* comer, almorzar.

lunchtime ['lʌntʃtaɪm] *n* hora de comer, hora de almorzar.

lung [lʌŋ] *n* pulmón *m*: *her little girl has a good pair of lungs!* ¡su hijita tiene buenos pulmones! COMP lung cancer cáncer *m* de pulmón.

lurk [lɜ:k] *vi* **1** *(wait)* estar al acecho. **2** *(hide)* esconderse.

lust [lʌst] *n* **1** *(sexual)* lujuria. **2** *(greed)* codicia; *(strong desire)* ansia.

lute [lu:t] *n* laúd *m*.

Luxembourg ['lʌksᵊmbɜ:g] *n* Luxemburgo.

Luxembourger ['lʌksᵊmbɜ:gəʳ] *n* luxemburgués,-esa.

luxuriant [lʌgˈzjʊərɪənt] *adj* **1** *(vegetation)* exuberante; *(hair)* abundante.

luxurious [lʌgˈzjʊərɪəs] *adj* lujoso,-a.

luxury ['lʌkʃərɪ] *n* lujo.

ⓘ *pl* luxuries.

lychee ['laɪtʃi:] *n* lichi *m*.

lying ['laɪɪŋ] *adj (deceitful)* mentiroso,-a.

▸ *n (lies)* mentiras *fpl*.

lymph [lɪmf] *n* linfa.

lymphatic [lɪmˈfætɪk] *adj* linfático,-a.

lynch [lɪntʃ] *vt* linchar.

lynx [lɪŋks] *n* lince *m*.

lyre [laɪəʳ] *n* lira.

lyric ['lɪrɪk] *adj* lírico,-a.

▸ *n* poema *m* lírico.

▸ *n pl* lyrics *(of song)* letra *f sing*.

M, m [em] *n (the letter)* M, m *f*.

mac [mæk] *n* GB *fam (mackintosh)* impermeable *m*.

macaroni [mækə'rəʊnɪ] *n* macarrones *mpl*.

macaw [mə'kɔ:] *n* guacamayo, ara *m*.

mace [meɪs] *n (club, staff)* maza.

macerate ['mæsəreɪt] *vt* macerar.
▶ *vi* macerarse.

machine [mə'ʃi:n] *n* **1** *(gen)* máquina. **2** *(organization, system)* organización *f*, aparato. COMP **machine gun** ametralladora.
▶ *n pl* **machines** *(machinery)* maquinaria *f sing*.

machinery [mə'ʃi:nərɪ] *n* **1** *(machines)* maquinaria. **2** *(workings)* mecanismo.

mackerel ['mækərəl] *n* caballa.

mackintosh ['mækɪntɒʃ] *n* impermeable *m*.

macro ['mækrəʊ] *n* COMPUT macro *f*.

macroeconomics [mækrəʊi:kə'nɒmɪks] *n* macroeconomía.

macroscopic [mækrə'skɒpɪk] *adj* macroscópico,-a.

mad [mæd] *adj* **1** *(insane)* loco,-a: *she's quite mad* está completamente loca. **2** *fam (person)* loco,-a; *(crazy - idea, plan)* disparatado,-a, descabellado,-a. **3** *fam (enthusiastic)* loco,-a **(about,** por), chiflado,-a: *he's mad about her* está loco por ella. **4** *fam (angry)* enfadado,-a, furioso,-a **(at/with,** con). LOC **to drive SB mad / send SB mad** volver a ALGN loco,-a, traer loco,-a a ALGN. ‖ **to get mad** enfadarse. ‖ **to go mad** volverse loco,-a, enloquecer.
ⓘ *comp* **madder,** *superl* **maddest.**

Madagascan [mædə'gæskⁿn] *adj* malgache.
▶ *n (person)* malgache *mf*.

Madagascar [mædə'gæskəʳ] *n* Madagascar.

madam ['mædəm] *n fml* señora.

made [meɪd] *pt & pp* → **make**.
▶ *adj (produced)* hecho,-a, fabricado,-a: *made in England* hecho,-a en Inglaterra. LOC **to be made from** STH estar hecho, -a de ALGO. ‖ **to be made of** STH ser de ALGO, estar hecho,-a de ALGO, estar compuesto,-a de ALGO.

madly ['mædlɪ] *adv* como un loco.

madness ['mædnəs] *n* **1** *(insanity)* locura, demencia. **2** *(foolishness)* locura: *it is madness to drive in this weather* es una locura conducir con el tiempo que hace.

magazine [mægə'zi:n] *n* **1** *(periodical)* revista. **2** *(on TV, radio)* magacín *m*, magazine *m*. COMP **magazine rack** revistero.

maggot ['mægət] *n* larva, gusano.

magic ['mædʒɪk] *n* magia.
▶ *adj* mágico,-a. COMP **magic wand** varita mágica.

magical ['mædʒɪkⁿl] *adj* mágico,-a.

magician [mə'dʒɪʃⁿn] *n* **1** *(conjurer)* prestidigitador,-ra, ilusionista *mf*. **2** *(wizard)* mago,-a.

magistrate ['mædʒɪstreɪt] *n* JUR magistrado,-a, juez *mf*.

magma ['mægmə] *n* magma.

magnesite ['mægnesɪt] *n* magnesita.

magnesium [mæg'ni:zɪəm] *n* magnesio.

magnet ['mægnət] *n* imán *m*.

magnetic [mæg'netɪk] *adj* **1** *(force, etc)* magnético,-a. **2** *fig (personality, charm)* carismático,-a.

magnetism ['mægnɪtɪzⁿm] *n* magnetismo.

magnetized ['mægnɪtaɪzd] *adj* magnetizado,-a. **2** *fig (person)* magnetizar, cautivar.

magnification [mægnɪfɪ'keɪʃ°n] *n* **1** *(increase)* aumento, ampliación *f*. **2** *(power of lens, etc)* aumento.

magnificent [mæg'nɪfɪs°nt] *adj (splendid)* magnífico,-a, espléndido,-a.

magnify ['mægnɪfaɪ] *vt* **1** *(enlarge)* aumentar, ampliar. **2** *fig (exaggerate)* exagerar, agrandar.
ⓘ *pt & pp* magnified, *ger* magnifying.

magnifying glass ['mægnɪfaɪɪŋglɑːs] *n* lupa.
ⓘ *pl* magnifying glasses.

magnitude ['mægnɪtjuːd] *n (size)* magnitud *f*; *(importance)* magnitud *f*, envergadura.

magnolia [mæg'nəʊlɪə] *n* **1** *(tree)* magnolio, magnolia. **2** *(flower)* magnolia.

magpie ['mægpaɪ] *n* urraca.

mahogany [mə'hɒgənɪ] *n (wood, tree)* caoba; *(colour)* color *m* caoba.

maid [meɪd] *n (servant)* criada, sirvienta; *(in hotel)* camarera.

maiden ['meɪd°n] *n (unmarried woman, girl)* doncella.
▸ *adj (first of its kind - speech, voyage)* inaugural.

mail [meɪl] *n* **1** *(system)* correo: *send it by mail* envíalo por correo. **2** *(letters, etc)* correo, cartas *mpl*, correspondencia.
▸ *vt (send)* mandar por correo.

mailbox ['meɪlbɒks] *n* buzón *m*.

mailman ['meɪlmæn] *n* US cartero.
ⓘ *pl* mailmen ['meɪlmæn].

maim [meɪm] *vt* mutilar, lisiar.

main [meɪn] *adj (most important)* principal: *be careful when you cross the main road* ten cuidado al cruzar la carretera principal. COMP **main course** plato principal, segundo plato. ▮ **main road** carretera principal.

mainframe ['meɪnfreɪm] [also mainframe computer] *n* unidad *f* central, ordenador *m* central.

mainland ['meɪnlənd] *n* continente o isla grande en contraposición a una isla cercana más pequeña.

mainly ['meɪnlɪ] *adv (chiefly)* principalmente, sobre todo; *(mostly)* en su mayoría.

maintain [meɪn'teɪn] *vt* **1** *(preserve, keep up - gen)* mantener; *(- silence, appearances)* guardar. **2** *(support financially)* mantener, sostener.

maintenance ['meɪntənəns] *n* **1** *(gen)* mantenimiento. **2** *(upkeep of family)* manutención *f*.

maize [meɪz] *n* maíz *m*.

majesty ['mædʒəstɪ] *n* majestad *f*.
ⓘ *pl* majesties.

major ['meɪdʒəʳ] *adj* **1** *(more important, greater)* mayor, principal: *tourism is the major industry* el turismo es la industria principal. **2** *(important - gen)* importante; *(- issue)* de gran envergadura; *(- illness)* grave. **3** MUS *(key, scale)* mayor.
▸ *n* **1** MIL comandante *m*.

majorette [meɪdʒər'et] *n* majorette *f*.

majority [mə'dʒɒrɪtɪ] *n* mayoría: *the great majority of students* la gran mayoría de los estudiantes. LOC **to be in a/the majority** ser mayoría.
ⓘ *pl* majorities.
▸ *adj* mayoritario,-a.

make [meɪk] *n (brand)* marca: *what make is your watch?* ¿de qué marca es tu reloj?
▸ *vt* **1** *(produce - gen)* hacer; *(construct)* construir; *(manufacture)* fabricar; *(create)* crear; *(prepare)* preparar: *she made some sandwiches* hizo unos bocadillos, preparó unos bocadillos; *stop making all that noise!* ¡dejad de hacer tanto ruido! **2** *(carry out, perform)* hacer: *I must make a phone call* tengo que hacer una llamada. **3** *(cause to be)* hacer, poner, volver: *the gift made him happy* el regalo lo hizo feliz. **4** *(force, compel)* hacer, obligar; *(cause to do)* hacer: *they make me go to bed early* me obligan a acostarme temprano. **5** *(be, become)* ser, hacer; *(cause to be)* hacer, convertir en: *she'll make a good singer* será buena cantante, tiene madera de cantante.
▸ *vi (to be about to)* hacer como, simular: *he made as if to kiss her* hizo como si la besara. LOC **to make sense** tener sentido. ▮ **to make sure (of STH)** asegurarse (de ALGO).

◆ **to make for** *vt insep* **1** *(move towards)* dirigirse hacia. **2** *(result in, make possible)* contribuir a, crear, conducir a.

◆ **to make out** *vt sep* **1** *(write - list, receipt)* hacer; *(- cheque)* extender, hacer; *(- report)* redactar. **2** *(see)* distinguir, divisar; *(writing)* descifrar. **3** *(understand)* entender, comprender.

▶ *vt insep fam (pretend, claim)* pretender, hacerse pasar por.

◆ **to make up** *vt sep* **1** *(invent)* inventar. **2** *(put together)* hacer; *(assemble)* montar; *(bed, prescription)* preparar; *(page)* componer; *(clothes, curtains)* confeccionar, hacer. **3** *(complete)* completar. **4** *(constitute)* componer, formar, integrar; *(represent)* representar. **5** *(cosmetics)* maquillar.

▶ *vi* **1** maquillarse, pintarse. **2** *(become friends again)* hacer las paces, reconciliarse.

① *pt & pp* made, *ger* making.

maker ['meɪkəʳ] *n (of product)* fabricante *mf*; *(of film, etc)* creador,-ra.

make-up ['meɪkʌp] *n* **1** *(cosmetics)* maquillaje *m: she never wears make-up* nunca se maquilla, nunca se pone maquillaje. **2** *(composition, combination)* composición *f*. **3** *(of person)* carácter *m*.

malaria [mə'leərɪə] *n* malaria, paludismo.

Malawi [mə'lɑːwɪ] *n* Malawi.

Malawian [mə'lɑːwɪən] *adj* malawiano,-a.

▶ *n* malawiano,-a.

Malaysia [mə'leɪzɪə] *n* Malaysia, Malasia.

Malaysian [mə'leɪzɪən] *adj* malasio,-a.

▶ *n* malasio,-a.

Maldives ['mɔːldaɪvz] *n* Maldivas.

Maldivian [mɔːl'dɪvɪən] *adj* maldivo,-a.

▶ *n* maldivo,-a.

male [meɪl] *adj* **1** *(animal, plant)* macho; *(person, child)* varón; *(sex, hormone, character, organ)* masculino,-a. **2** *(manly)* varonil, viril.

▶ *n (man, boy)* varón *m*; *(animal, plant)* macho.

Mali ['mɑːlɪ] *n* Malí.

Malian ['mɑːlɪən] *adj* maliense.

▶ *n* maliense *mf*.

mall [mæl, mɔːl] *n* US *(covered)* centro comercial; *(street)* zona comercial.

malleability ['mælɪəbɪlɪtɪ] *n* **1** *(metal)* maleabilidad *f*. **2** *fig (person)* docilidad *f*.

malleable ['mælɪəbəl] *adj* **1** *(metal)* maleable. **2** *fig (person)* dócil.

mallet ['mælət] *n* mazo.

malnutrition [mælnjuː'trɪʃ°n] *n* desnutrición *f*.

malt [mɔːlt] *n (grain)* malta.

Malta ['mɔːltə] *n* Malta.

Maltese [mɔːl'tiːz] *adj* maltés,-esa.

▶ *n* **1** *(person)* maltés,-esa. **2** *(language)* maltés *m*.

▶ *n pl* the Maltese los malteses *mpl*.

maltreatment [mæl'triːtmənt] *n* malos tratos *mpl*.

mammal ['mæm°l] *n* mamífero.

mammary ['mæmərɪ] *adj* mamario,-a.

COMP mammary gland mama.

mammography [mæ'mɒgrəfɪ] *n* mamografía.

① *pl* mammographies.

mammoth ['mæməθ] *n* ZOOL mamut *m*.

mammy ['mæmɪ] *n fam* mamá.

① *pl* mammies.

man [mæn] *n* **1** *(adult male)* hombre *m*, señor *m: an old man* un hombre mayor, un señor mayor, un viejo. **2** *(human being, person)* ser *m* humano, el hombre *m: all men are born equal* todos los hombres nacen iguales. **3** *(husband)* marido, hombre *m*; *(boyfriend)* novio; *(partner)* pareja: *man and wife* marido y mujer.

① *pl* men.

manage ['mænɪdʒ] *vt* **1** *(run - business, company)* dirigir; *(- property)* administrar: *she manages a shop* es la encargada de una tienda, lleva una tienda. **2** *(handle, cope with - child, person)* llevar, manejar; *(- animal)* domar; *(- work, luggage, etc)* poder con. **3** *(succeed)* conseguir, lograr: *we managed it!* ¡lo conseguimos! **4** *(have room for, have time for)* poder.

▶ *vi* **1** poder: *can you manage?* ¿puedes? **2** *(financially)* arreglárselas, apañarse.

manager ['mænɪdʒəʳ] *n* **1** *(of company, bank)* director,-ra, gerente *mf*. **2** *(of shop, restaurant)* encargado,-a; *(of depart-*

ment) jefe,-a. **3** *(of actor, group, etc)* representante *mf*, manager *mf*. **4** SP *(of football team)* entrenador *m*, míster *m*.

mandarin ['mændərın] *n* **1** mandarina. **2** GB *pej (government official)* mandarín *m*.
▸ *n* Mandarin *(language)* mandarín *m*.

mandatory ['mændət^orɪ] *adj (compulsory)* obligatorio,-a.

mandible ['mændɪb^ol] *n* mandíbula.

mane [meɪn] *n (of horse)* crin *f*; *(of lion)* melena.

maneuver [mə'nu:vər] *n & v* US → **manoeuvre**.

manganese ['mæŋgəni:z] *n* manganeso.

manger ['meɪndʒər] *n* pesebre *m*.

mangle ['mæŋg^ol] *vt* **1** *(cut to pieces)* destrozar, despedazar; *(crush)* aplastar.

mango ['mæŋgəʊ] *n* mango.
ⓘ *pl* mangoes o mangos.

mangrove ['mæŋgrəʊv] *n* manglar *m*.

maniac ['meɪnɪæk] *n* **1** *fam (wild person)* loco,-a. **2** *fam (fan)* entusiasta *mf*, fanático,-a.

manifestation [mænɪfe'steɪʃ^on] *n fml* manifestación *f*.

✗ Manifestation no significa 'manifestación (de protesta)', que se traduce por demonstration.

manifesto [mænɪ'festəʊ] *n* manifiesto.
ⓘ *pl* manifestos o manifestoes.

manioc ['mænɪɒk] *n* mandioca, yuca.

manipulate [mə'nɪpjəleɪt] *vt* **1** *(work - machine)* manejar; *(- knob, lever)* accionar. **2** *(control, influence)* manipular.

mankind [mæn'kaɪnd] *n* la humanidad *f*, el género humano, los hombres *mpl*.

man-made [mæn'meɪd] *adj* **1** *(lake, etc)* artificial. **2** *(fabric, etc)* sintético,-a.

mannequin ['mænɪkɪn] *n* **1** *(dummy)* maniquí *m*. **2** *dated (model)* modelo *f*.

manner ['mænər] *n* **1** *(way, method)* manera, modo: *in this manner* de esta manera. **2** *(way of behaving)* forma de ser, comportamiento, aire *m*: *she has a pleasant manner* tiene una forma de ser agradable. LOC **in a manner of speaking** por decirlo así, hasta cierto punto.

▸ *n pl* **manners** *(social behaviour)* maneras *fpl*, modales *mpl*; *(customs)* costumbres *fpl*. COMP **bad manners** falta de educación. **I good manners** buenos modales *mpl*.

manoeuvre [mə'nu:vər] *n* maniobra.
▸ *vt* **1** *(gen)* maniobrar. **2** *(person)* manipular, manejar.
▸ *vi* maniobrar.

manometer [mæ'nɒmɪtər] *n* manómetro.

manor ['mænər] *n* señorío. COMP **manor house** casa solariega.

manpower ['mænpaʊər] *n* mano *f* de obra.

mansion ['mænʃ^on] *n (gen)* casa grande; *(country)* casa solariega.

mantelpiece ['mænt^olpi:s] *n* repisa de chimenea.

mantis ['mæntɪs] *n* mantis *f*.
ⓘ *pl* mantis.

manual ['mænjʊəl] *adj* manual.
▸ *n* manual *m*.

manufacture [mænjə'fæktʃər] *n (gen)* fabricación *f*; *(of clothing)* confección *f*; *(of foodstuffs)* elaboración *f*.
▸ *vt* **1** *(gen)* fabricar; *(clothing)* confeccionar; *(foodstuffs)* elaborar. **2** *fig (excuse, etc)* inventar.

manufactured [mænjə'fæktʃərəd] *adj* manufacturado,-da.

manufacturer [mænjə'fæktʃərər] *adj* fabricante *mf*.

manure [mə'njʊər] *n* abono, estiércol *m*.

manuscript ['mænjəskrɪpt] *n* **1** *(historic handwritten book)* manuscrito. **2** *(original copy of text)* original *m*, texto original.

many ['menɪ] *adj* mucho,-a, muchos,-as: *many people never go abroad* mucha gente nunca va al extranjero.
ⓘ *comp* more, *superl* most. LOC **as many ... as** tantos,-as... como. **I how many?** ¿cuántos,-as? **I not many** pocos,-as, no muchos,-as. **I too many** demasiados,-as.
▸ *pron* muchos,-as: *I don't want many* no quiero muchos.

✎ Many se usa sobre todo en las frases negativas y en las preguntas; en las frases afirmativas se usa más a lot of.

map [mæp] *n (of country, region)* mapa *m*; *(of town, bus, tube)* plano. `COMP` **map of the world** mapamundi *m*.
▶ *vt (area)* trazar un mapa de.
ⓘ *pt & pp* mapped, *ger* mapping.

maple ['meɪpəl] *n (tree, wood)* arce *m*.

marathon ['mærəθɒn] *n* maratón *m*.
▶ *adj fig* maratoniano,-a, larguísimo,-a.

marble ['mɑːbəl] *n* **1** *(stone, statue)* mármol *m*. **2** *(glass ball)* canica.
▶ *n pl* **marbles** *(game)* canicas *fpl*. ART mármoles *mpl*.

March [mɑːtʃ] *n* marzo.

✎ Para ejemplos de uso, consulta **May**.

march [mɑːtʃ] *n* **1** MIL marcha. **2** *(walk)* caminata. **3** *(demonstration)* manifestación *f*. **4** MUS marcha.
▶ *vi* **1** MIL marchar, hacer una marcha. **2** *(walk)* caminar, marchar.
▶ *vt* hacer marchar.

mare [meəʳ] *n* yegua.

margarine [mɑːdʒəˈriːn] *n* margarina.

marge [mɑːdʒ] *n* GB *fam* margarina.

margin ['mɑːdʒɪn] *n* **1** *(gen)* margen *m*. **2** *(difference, leeway)* margen *m*: *there is no margin for error* no hay margen de error.

marginal ['mɑːdʒɪnəl] *adj* **1** *(small, minor)* menor, pequeño,-a, mínimo,-a. **2** *(artist)* marginal.

marihuana [mærɪˈhwɑːnə] *n* marihuana.

marina [məˈriːnə] *n* puerto deportivo.

marinate ['mærɪneɪt] *vt* adobar.

marine [məˈriːn] *n (life, flora, etc)* marino,-a, marítimo,-a.
▶ *adj (law, stores, etc)* marítimo,-a.
▶ *n* soldado de infantería de marina.
▶ *n pl* **the Marines** GB la infantería de marina.

marionette [mærɪəˈnet] *n* marioneta, títere *m*.

marital ['mærɪtəl] *adj (relations, problems)* matrimonial, marital; *(bliss)* conyugal. `COMP` **marital status** estado civil.

maritime ['mærɪtaɪm] *adj* marítimo,-a.

mark [mɑːk] *n* **1** *(imprint, trace)* huella; *(from blow)* señal *f*; *(stain)* mancha: *there's a mark on this blouse* esta blusa tie-

ne una mancha. **2** *(sign, symbol)* marca, señal *f*: *I've put a mark by the things I'm interested in* he señalado las cosas que me interesan. **3** EDUC nota, calificación *f*: *he got a good mark in maths* sacó una buena nota en mates. `LOC` **on your marks, get set, go!** ¡preparados, listos, ya!
▶ *vt* **1** *(gen)* marcar. **2** EDUC *(correct)* corregir; *(grade - student)* poner nota a; *(- exam, essay, etc)* puntuar, calificar.
▶ *vi (stain)* mancharse.
◆ **to mark down** *vt sep* **1** *(reduce price of)* rebajar el precio de. **2** *(reduce marks of)* bajar la nota de. **3** *(note in writing)* apuntar.
◆ **to mark out** *vt sep* **1** *(area)* marcar, delimitar; *(boundary)* marcar, trazar. **2** *(choose)* señalar, seleccionar.

market ['mɑːkɪt] *n* **1** *(selling fruit, vegetables, etc)* mercado; *(selling clothes, etc)* mercadillo; *(marketplace)* plaza: *I always go to the market on Saturdays* siempre voy a la plaza los sábados. **2** *(trade)* mercado: *the property market* el mercado inmobiliario. `LOC` **to be on the market** estar en venta. `COMP` **market day** día *m* de mercado. ▌ **market garden** GB huerta. ▌ **market price** precio de mercado.

marketing ['mɑːkɪtɪŋ] *n* marketing *m*, mercadotecnia.

marketplace ['mɑːkɪtpleɪs] *n* mercado; *(square)* plaza.

marksman ['mɑːksmən] *n* tirador *m*.
ⓘ *pl* marksmen ['mɑːksmən].

marmalade ['mɑːməleɪd] *n* mermelada (de cítricos).

✎ La palabra **marmalade** sólo se refiere a las mermeladas de cítricos y en especial a la de naranja. Las demás mermeladas se llaman **jam**.

maroon [məˈruːn] *adj* granate.
▶ *n* (color *m*) granate *m*.

marquee [mɑːˈkiː] *n (large tent)* carpa.

marriage ['mærɪdʒ] *n* **1** *(state, institution)* matrimonio. **2** *(act, wedding)* boda, casamiento, enlace *m* matrimonial. `LOC` **to take sb in marriage** casarse con ALGN. `COMP` **marriage bureau** agencia matrimonial. ▌ **marriage certificate** certificado de matrimonio.

M

married ['mærɪd] *adj* **1** *(person, status)* casado,-a (to, con): *a married couple* un matrimonio. **2** *(life, bliss)* matrimonial, conyugal.

marrow ['mærəʊ] *n* **1** ([also bone marrow] ANAT *(of bone)* tuétano, médula. *fig (inner meaning)* meollo. **2** [also vegetable marrow] GB calabacín *m* grande.

marry ['mærɪ] *vt* **1** *(take in marriage)* casarse con. **2** *(unite in marriage)* casar.
▶ *vi* **1** casarse. **2** *fig* unirse. LOC **to get married** casarse (to, con).
ⓘ *pt & pp* **married**, *ger* **marrying**.

Mars [ma:z] *n* Marte *m*.

marsh [ma:ʃ] *n* **1** *(bog)* pantano. **2** *(area)* zona con pantanos, pantanal *m*.

marshal ['ma:ʃəl] *n* **1** MIL mariscal *m*. **2** *(at sports event, demonstration)* oficial *mf*, organizador,-ra.

martial ['ma:ʃəl] *adj* marcial.

Martian ['ma:ʃən] *n* marciano,-a.
▶ *adj* marciano,-a.

martyr ['ma:tər] *n* **1** mártir *mf*. **2** *fam* víctima *f* (to, de).

martyrdom ['ma:tədəm] *n* martirio.

marvel ['ma:vəl] *n* **1** *(wonder)* maravilla: *it's a marvel no-one was hurt* es un milagro que no hubiera heridos. **2** *(person)* maravilla. LOC **to do marvels / work marvels** hacer maravillas.
▶ *vi* **1** *fml* maravillarse (at, con), asombrarse (at, de).
ⓘ *pt & pp* **marvelled** (US **marveled**), *ger* **marvelling** (US **marveling**).

marvellous ['ma:vələs] *adj* maravilloso,-a, magnífico,-a, estupendo,-a.

marzipan ['ma:zɪpæn] *n* mazapán *m*.

mascara [mæ'ska:rə] *n* rímel *m*.

⊠ Mascara no significa 'máscara', que se traduce por mask.

mascot ['mæskɒt] *n* mascota.

masculine ['ma:skjəlɪn] *adj* masculino,-a.
▶ *n* LING masculino.

mash [mæʃ] *n* CULIN *fam* puré *m* de patatas.
▶ *vt* **1** *(beat, crush)* triturar (up, -), machacar (up, -). **2** CULIN *(potatoes)* hacer un puré de. COMP **mashed potatoes** puré *m* de patatas.

mask [ma:sk] *n* *(gen)* máscara; *(disguise)* careta, carátula; *(around eyes)* antifaz *m*. COMP **diving mask** gafas *fpl* de bucear.
▶ *vt* *(gen)* enmascarar.

masked [ma:skt] *adj* enmascarado,-a. COMP **masked ball** baile *m* de disfraces, baile *m* de máscaras.

masking tape ['ma:skɪŋteɪp] *n* cinta adhesiva.

masochism ['mæsəkɪzəm] *n* masoquismo.

masochist ['mæsəkɪst] *n* masoquista.
▶ *adj* masoquista.

mason ['meɪsən] *n* *(builder)* albañil *m*.

mass [mæs] *n* **1** *(large quantity)* montón *m*, masa; *(of people)* masa, multitud *f*, muchedumbre *f*: *a mass of books* un montón de libros. **2** *(majority)* mayoría.
▶ *vi* *(crowd)* congregarse, reunirse en gran número.
▶ *vt* reunir.
▶ *adj* masivo,-a, multitudinario,-a, de masas: *there was a mass meeting* se celebró un mitin multitudinario. COMP **mass media** medios *mpl* de comunicación (de masas).
▶ *n pl* **masses** *fam* *(lots)* cantidad *f*, montones *mpl*, mogollón *m*.

Mass [mæs] *n* REL misa.

massage ['mæsa:ʒ] *n* masaje *m*.
▶ *vt* **1** *(person, body)* dar un masaje a; *(part of body)* dar un masaje en.

masseter ['mæsətər] *n* masetero.

masseur [mæ'sɜ:r] *n* masajista *m*.

masseuse [mæ'sɜ:z] *n* masajista.

massif [mæ'si:f] *n* macizo.

massive ['mæsɪv] *adj* **1** *(huge)* enorme, gigantesco,-a. **2** *(solid, weighty)* sólido,-a, macizo,-a.

mast [ma:st] *n* **1** MAR mástil *m*, palo. **2** *(transmitter)* torre *f*, poste *m*.

master ['ma:stər] *n* **1** *(of slave, servant, dog)* amo; *(of household)* señor *m*; *(owner)* dueño. **2** MAR *(of ship)* capitán *m*; *(of fishing boat)* patrón *m*. **3** GB *(teacher - infant school)* maestro, profesor *m*; *(- secondary)* profesor *m*. COMP **master bedroom** dormitorio principal. ▌**master copy** original *m*.
▶ *n* **Master's (degree)** EDUC máster *m*.

► *adj (expert, skilled)* maestro,-a, experto,-a.
► *vt (learn - subject, skill)* llegar a dominar; *(- craft)* llegar a ser experto,-a en.
mastermind ['mɑ:stəmaɪnd] *n (person)* cerebro, genio.
masterpiece ['mɑ:stəpi:s] *n* obra maestra.
mastodon ['mæstədɒn] *n* mastodonte *m*.
masturbation [mæstə'beɪʃ°n] *n* masturbación *f*.
mat [mæt] *n* **1** *(rug)* alfombrilla; *(doormat)* felpudo. **2** *(rush mat)* estera; *(beach mat)* esterilla. **3** SP colchoneta.
match¹ [mætʃ] *n (light)* cerilla, fósforo.
match² [mætʃ] *n* **1** SP *(football, hockey, etc)* partido, encuentro. **2** *(equal)* igual *mf*: *when it comes to chess, she's no match for you* ella no puede competir contigo al ajedrez. **3** *(marriage)* casamiento, matrimonio. **4** *(clothes, colour, etc)* juego, combinación *f*.
ⓘ *pl* matches.
► *vt* **1** *(equal)* igualar: *nobody can match him* nadie lo iguala. **2** *(go well with)* hacer juego (con), combinar (con): *her shoes match her dress* los zapatos hacen juego con el vestido. **3** *(be like, correspond to)* corresponder a, ajustarse a.
► *vi* **1** *(go together)* hacer juego, combinar. **2** *(tally)* coincidir, concordar. **3** *(people)* llevarse bien, avenirse.
matchbox ['mætʃbɒks] *n* caja de cerillas.
ⓘ *pl* matchboxes.
matching ['mætʃɪŋ] *adj* que hace juego, a juego.
mate [meɪt] *n* **1** *(school friend, fellow worker, etc)* compañero,-a, colega *mf*; *(friend)* amigo,-a, colega *mf*, compinche *mf*. **2** *(assistant)* ayudante *mf*, aprendiz,-za. **3** ZOOL pareja; *(male)* macho; *(female)* hembra.

✎ Mate entra también en la formación de palabras como classmate (compañero de clase), flatmate (persona con la que se comparte un piso), roommate (persona con la que se comparte una habitación) o teammate (compañero de equipo).

material [mə'tɪərɪəl] *n* **1** *(physical substance)* materia, material *m*: *raw material* materia prima; *building materials* materiales de construcción. **2** *(cloth)* tela, tejido.
► *adj* **1** *(physical)* material. **2** *(important)* importante.
materialism [mə'tɪərɪəlɪz°m] *n* materialismo.
maternity [mə'tɜ:nɪtɪ] *n* maternidad *f*.
math [mæθ] *n fam* US mates *fpl*.
mathematical [mæθə'mætɪk°l] *adj* matemático,-a.
mathematician [mæθ°mə'tɪʃ°n] *n* matemático,-a.
mathematics [mæθ°'mætɪks] *n* matemáticas *fpl*.
maths [mæθs] *n fam* mates *fpl*.
mating ['meɪtɪŋ] *n* ZOOL acoplamiento, apareamiento. COMP **mating call** reclamo. ❙ **mating season** época de celo.
matrix ['meɪtrɪks] *n* matriz *f*.
ⓘ *pl* matrixes o matrices ['meɪtrɪsi:z].
matter ['mætə'] *n* **1** *(affair, subject)* asunto, cuestión *f*: *it's a personal matter* es un asunto personal. **2** *(trouble, problem)* problema *m*: *what's the matter?* ¿qué pasa? **3** PHYS *(physical substance)* materia, sustancia. **4** *(type of substance, things of a particular kind)* materia. LOC **as a matter of fact** en realidad, de hecho. ❙ **to be another matter** ser otra cosa.
► *vi (be important)* importar (to, a): *it doesn't matter* no importa, es igual, da igual. LOC **no matter** no importa: *no matter what* pase lo que pase; *no matter what I say* diga lo que diga.
matting ['mætɪŋ] *n* estera.
mattress ['mætrəs] *n* colchón *m*.
ⓘ *pl* mattresses.
mature [mə'tʃʊə'] *adj (gen)* maduro,-a.
► *vt* madurar.
► *vi & vt* madurar.
maturity [mə'tʃʊərətɪ] *n* madurez *f*.
Mauritania [mɒrɪ'teɪnɪə] *n* Mauritania.
Mauritanian [mɒrɪ'teɪnɪən] *adj* mauritano,-a.
► *n* mauritano,-a.
mausoleum [mɔ:sə'lɪəm] *n* mausoleo.
mauve [məʊv] *adj* malva.
► *n* malva *m*.

M

maverick ['mævᵊrɪk] *n* inconformista *mf*, independiente *mf*.
▶ *adj* inconformista, independiente.

maxilla 'mæksɪlə] *n* maxilar *m*.
ⓘ *pl* maxillae.

maximum ['mæksɪməm] *adj* máximo,-a.
▶ *n* máximo, máximum *m*. LOC **to the maximum** al máximo.

May [meɪ] *n* mayo: *his birthday is on the twentieth of May* su cumpleaños es el veinte de mayo; *at the beginning/end of May* a principios/finales de mayo; *in the middle of May* a mediados de mayo; *last May* en mayo del año pasado; *next May* en mayo del año que viene.

may [meɪ] *aux* **1** *(possibility, probability)* poder, ser posible: *he may come* es posible que venga, puede que venga; *you may laugh, but I think it's serious* tú bien puedes reír, pero yo creo que es grave. **2** *(permission)* poder: *may I help you?* ¿en qué puedo servirle?; *may I go?* ¿puedo irme? **3** *(wish)* ojalá: *may it be so* ojalá sea así.

✎ Cuando **may** expresa una posibilidad se puede traducir por 'quizá', 'quizás', 'a lo mejor', 'tal vez' o 'puede que'; cuando se usa para pedir o conceder permiso se traduce sencillamente por 'poder'. Consulta también **might**.

maybe ['meɪbiː] *adv* quizá, quizás, tal vez: *maybe it'll rain* tal vez llueva; *maybe you're right* quizás tengas razón, a lo mejor tienes razón.

mayday ['meɪdeɪ] *n* señal *f* de socorro, S.O.S. *m*.

mayonnaise [meɪəˈneɪz] *n* mayonesa, mahonesa.

mayor [meəʳ] *n* (*man*) alcalde *m*; (*woman*) alcaldesa.

mayoress ['meəres] *n* alcaldesa.

maze [meɪz] *n* laberinto.

me¹ [miː] *n* MUS mi *m*.

me² [miː] *pron* **1** *(as object of verb)* me: *follow me* sígueme; *give it to me* dámelo; *he looked at me* me miró. **2** *(after prep)* mí: *it's for me* es para mí; *are you talking to me?* ¿me lo dices a mí? **3** *(emphatic)* yo: *it's me!* ¡soy yo!; *it's me, David* soy David.

meadow ['medəʊ] *n* prado, pradera.

meal¹ [miːl] *n (flour)* harina.

meal² [miːl] *n (gen)* comida: *three meals a day* tres comidas al día. LOC **to have a meal 1** *(lunch)* comer. **2** *(supper)* cenar.

✎ **Meal** se refiere a cualquiera de las tres comidas principales que se toman a lo largo del día.

mealtime ['miːltaɪm] *n* hora de comer.

mean¹ [miːn] *adj* **1** *(miserly, selfish - person)* mezquino,-a, tacaño,-a, agarrado,-a. **2** *(unkind)* malo,-a, antipático,-a; *(petty)* mezquino,-a; *(ashamed)* avergonzado,-a. **3** *fam (skilful, great)* excelente, de primera, genial. LOC **to be no mean** ser todo,-a un,-a: *she's no mean singer* es una cantante genial.

mean² [miːn] *vt* **1** *(signify, represent)* significar, querer decir; *(to be a sign of, indicate)* ser señal de, significar: *what does «mug» mean?* ¿qué significa «mug»?, ¿qué quiere decir «mug»? **2** *(have in mind)* pensar, tener la intención de: *she didn't mean to do it* lo hizo sin querer. **3** *(involve, entail)* suponer, implicar; *(have as result)* significar: *that means we can't go on holiday* eso significa que no podemos irnos de vacaciones. LOC **to be meant for 1** *(be intended for)* ser para. **2** *(be destined for)* estar dirigido,-a a, ir dirigido,-a a: *these shoes are meant for light walking* estos zapatos son para pasear.
ⓘ *pt & pp* meant [ment].

mean³ [miːn] *adj (average)* medio,-a: *mean temperature* temperatura media.
▶ *n* **1** *(average)* promedio. **2** MATH media. **3** *(middle term)* término medio.

meander [mɪˈændəʳ] *vi* **1** *(river, etc)* serpentear. **2** *(person)* vagar, deambular, andar sin rumbo fijo. **3** *fig (conversation)* divagar.
▶ *n (of river, etc)* meandro.

meaning ['miːnɪŋ] *n* **1** *(sense)* sentido, significado. *what's the meaning of «draft»?* ¿qué significa «draft»?, ¿qué quiere decir «draft»? **2** *(significance, importance)* sentido; *(purpose, intention)* intención *f*: *a glance full of meaning* una mirada llena de intención.

meaningless ['mi:nɪŋləs] *adj* **1** *(word, phrase, etc)* sin sentido. **2** *(futile)* sin sentido, inútil, vano,-a.

means [mi:nz] *n (way, method)* medio, manera: *there's no means of escape* no hay escapatoria, no hay manera de escapar; *a means of transport* un medio de transporte. ▶ *n pl (resources)* medios *mpl* de vida, recursos *mpl*. [LOC] **a means to an end** un medio de conseguir un objetivo, un medio para lograr un fin. I **by all means** naturalmente, por supuesto. I **by means of** por medio de, mediante. I **by no means / not by any means** de ninguna manera, de ningún modo. I **to live beyond one's means** vivir por encima de sus posibilidades.
ⓘ *pl* means.

meant [mæri'hwɑ:nə] *pp & pt* → **mean**.

meantime ['mi:ntaɪm] *adv* mientras tanto, entretanto. [LOC] **in the meantime** mientras tanto.

meanwhile ['mi:nwaɪl] *adv* mientras tanto, entretanto.

measles ['mi:zᵊlz] *n* MED sarampión *m*.

measurable ['meʒᵊrəbᵊl] *adj* mensurable.

measure ['meʒər] *n* **1** *(system)* medida: *liquid measure* medida para líquidos. **2** *(indicator)* indicador *m*: *it's a measure of her popularity* es un indicador de su popularidad. **3** *(ruler)* regla. **4** *(measured amount, unit)* medida. **5** *(amount, degree, extent)* grado, cantidad *f*: *some measure of happiness* cierta felicidad. **6** *(method, step, remedy)* medida, disposición *f*: *safety measures* medidas de seguridad. [LOC] **in large measure** en gran parte, en gran medida. I **in some measure** hasta cierto punto, en cierta medida. I **to take measures** tomar medidas, adoptar medidas.
▶ *vt* **1** *(area, object, etc)* medir. **2** *(person)* tomar las medidas de. **3** *fig (assess)* evaluar; *(consider carefully)* sopesar, pensar bien.
▶ *vi (be)* medir: *it measures 3 feet by 6 feet* mide 1 metro por 2 metros.

☒ Measure no significa 'mesura', que se traduce por **moderation**.

⊕ Tanto los británicos como los americanos utilizan un sistema de medidas diferente del sistema métrico decimal, que es el que empleamos nosotros. En la páginas centrales de este diccionario encontrarás las equivalencias entre estos dos sistemas de medición.

measurement ['meʒəmənt] *n* **1** *(act)* medición *f*. **2** *(length, etc)* medida.

measuring ['meʒᵊrɪŋ] *n (act)* medición *f*. [COMP] **measuring tape** cinta métrica, metro.

meat [mi:t] *n* carne *f*: *I prefer meat to fish* me gusta más la carne que el pescado. [COMP] **cold meat / cooked meat** fiambre *m*.

meatball ['mi:tbɔ:l] *n* albóndiga.

mechanic [mə'kænɪk] *n (person)* mecánico,-a.

mechanical [mə'kænɪkᵊl] *adj* mecánico,-a.

mechanics [mə'kænɪks] *n (science)* mecánica. [COMP] **the mechanics** *(working parts)* el mecanismo. *(processes)* el funcionamiento.

mechanism ['mekənɪzᵊm] *n* mecanismo.

medal ['medᵊl] *n* medalla.

medallist ['medəlɪst] *n* medalla *mf*, campeón,-ona.

media ['mi:dɪə] *n pl* **the media** los medios *mpl* de comunicación.

✎ Consulta también **media**.

mediaeval [medɪ'i:vᵊl] *adj* medieval.

median ['mi:dɪən] *adj* MATH mediano,-a. ▶ *n* MATH *(line)* mediana; *(quantity)* valor *m* mediano.

mediator ['mi:dɪeɪtər] *n* mediador,-ra.

medical ['medɪkᵊl] *adj (treatment, care, examination)* médico,-a; *(book, student)* de medicina.
▶ *n fam (check-up)* chequeo, reconocimiento médico, revisión *f* médica.

medicinal [mə'dɪsɪnᵊl] *adj* medicinal.

medicine ['medɪsᵊn] *n* **1** *(science)* medicina. **2** *(drugs, etc)* medicina, medicamento.

medieval [medɪ'i:vᵊl] *adj* medieval.

mediocrity [mi:dɪ'ɒkrətɪ] *n* mediocridad *f*.

M

meditation [medɪˈteɪʃᵊn] *n* meditación *f*.

Mediterranean [medɪtəˈreɪnɪən] *adj* mediterráneo,-a.
▶ *n* the Mediterranean el Mediterráneo.

medium [ˈmiːdɪəm] *adj (average)* mediano,-a, regular, normal. `COMP` **medium wave** onda media.
▶ *n* **1** [*pl* media] *(means)* medio. **2** [*pl* media.] *(environment)* medio (ambiente). **3** [*pl* media] *(middle position)* punto medio, término medio. **4** [*pl* mediums] *(spiritualist)* médium *mf*.

medium-sized [ˈmiːdɪəmˈsaɪzd] *adj (thing)* de tamaño mediano.

meet [miːt] *vt* **1** *(by chance)* encontrar, encontrarse con: *she met an old friend* se encontró con un viejo amigo. **2** *(by arrangement)* reunirse con, quedar con; *(informally)* ver: *I'm meeting Rob tomorrow* he quedado con Rob para mañana. **3** *(meet for first time)* conocer: *I met him at a party* lo conocí en una fiesta. **4** *(collect)* ir a buscar, pasar a buscar; *(await arrival of)* esperar; *(receive)* ir a recibir: *he'll meet me at the station* me vendrá a buscar a la estación.
▶ *vi* **1** *(by chance)* encontrarse: *we'll meet again* nos volveremos a encontrar. **2** *(by arrangement)* reunirse, verse, quedar,; *(formally)* entrevistarse: *we arranged to meet on Saturday* quedamos para el sábado., **3** *(get acquainted)* conocerse: *I think we've already met* creo que ya nos conocemos.
ⓘ *pt & pp* met [met].
▶ *n* **1** SP encuentro.

meeting [ˈmiːtɪŋ] *n* **1** *(gen - prearranged)* reunión *f*; *(- formal)* entrevista; *(- date)* cita. **2** *(chance encounter)* encuentro. **3** *(of club, committee, etc)* reunión *f*; *(of assembly)* sesión *f*; *(of shareholders, creditors)* junta. **4** POL *(rally)* mitin *m*. `COMP` **meeting place** lugar *m* de encuentro, lugar *m* de reunión.

megabyte [ˈmegəbaɪt] *n* COMPUT megabyte *m*, megaocteto.

megalith [ˈmegəlɪθ] *n* megalito.

megaphone [ˈmegəfəʊn] *n* megáfono, altavoz *m*.

megawatt [ˈmegəwɒt] *n* megavatio.

melamine [ˈmeləmiːn] *n* melamina.

melodramatic [melədrəˈmætɪk] *adj* melodramático,-a.

melody [ˈmelədɪ] *n* melodía.
ⓘ *pl* melodies.

melon [ˈmelən] *n (honeydew, etc)* melón *m*; *(watermelon)* sandía.

melt [melt] *vt* **1** *(ice, snow, butter, etc)* derretir. **2** *(metal)* fundir (down, -). **3** *(sugar, chemical)* disolver. **4** *fig* ablandar.
▶ *vi* **1** *(ice, snow)* derretirse (away, -). **2** *(metal)* fundirse. **3** *(sugar, chemical)* disolverse.
◆ **to melt away** *vi* **1** *(money, crowd, person)* desaparecer. **2** *fig (confidence, etc)* desvanecerse, esfumarse; *(anger)* disiparse, desaparecer.

melting [ˈmeltɪŋ] *n (of metal)* fundición *f*; *(of snow)* derretimiento. `COMP` **melting point** punto de fusión. ❙ **melting pot** crisol *m*.

member [ˈmembəʳ] *n* **1** *(gen)* miembro *mf*; *(of club)* socio,-a; *(of union, party)* afiliado,-a: *the youngest member of the family* el miembro más joven de la familia. **2** POL *(of Parliament)* diputado,-a; *(of European Parliament)* eurodiputado,-a. **3** ANAT miembro.
▶ *adj (country, state)* miembro,-a.

membership [ˈmembəʃɪp] *n* **1** *(of club - state)* calidad *f* de socio,-a, pertenencia; *(- entry)* ingreso. **2** *(of political party, union - state)* afiliación *f*; *(- entry)* ingreso. **3** *(members - of club)* miembros *mpl*, socios *mpl*; *(- of political party)* afiliados *mpl*.

membrane [ˈmembreɪn] *n* membrana.

memo [ˈmeməʊ] *n* **1** *(official)* memorándum *m*. **2** *(personal note)* nota, apunte *m*. `COMP` **memo pad** bloc *m* de notas.
ⓘ *pl* memos.

memorandum [meməˈrændəm] *n* **1** *(official note)* memorándum *m*, memorando. **2** *(personal note)* nota, apunte *m*.
ⓘ *pl* memorandums o memoranda [meməˈrændə].

memorial [məˈmɔːrɪəl] *adj (plaque, etc)* conmemorativo,-a.
▶ *n (monument)* monumento conmemorativo; *(ceremony)* homenaje *m*.

⊕ El **Memorial Day** es una fiesta que se celebra en Estados Unidos el último lunes de mayo en honor de todos los soldados muertos en las distintas guerras en las que ha participado el país americano.

memorize ['meməraɪz] vt memorizar, aprender de memoria.

memory ['memərɪ] n **1** (ability, computers) memoria: she's got a good memory for names tiene buena memoria para los nombres. **2** (recollection) recuerdo. LOC **to lose one's memory** perder la memoria. ‖ **within living memory** que se recuerde.

ⓘ pl **memories**.

men [men] pl → **man**.

menace ['menəs] n **1** (threat) amenaza (to, para); (danger) peligro (to, para). **2** fam (nuisance - person) pesado,-a; (- thing) lata, molestia.

▶ vt amenazar (with, de).

mend [mend] vt **1** (repair - gen) reparar, arreglar; (sew) coser; (patch) remendar; (darn) zurcir: can you mend my watch? ¿me puedes arreglar el reloj? **2** (improve) mejorar. LOC **to be on the mend** ir mejorando.

▶ n (patch) remiendo; (darn) zurcido.

meninges [meˈnɪdʒəs] n pl MED meninges fpl.

meningitis [menɪnˈdʒaɪtəs] n MED meningitis f.

meniscus [mɪˈnɪskəs] n menisco.

ⓘ pl **meniscuses** o **menisci** [mɪˈnɪskaɪ].

menopause ['menəpɔːz] n menopausia.

menstrual ['menstruəl] adj menstrual. COMP **menstrual cycle** ciclo menstrual. ‖ **menstrual period** regla, período.

menstruation [menstruˈeɪʃⁿn] n menstruación f, regla.

menswear ['menzweəʳ] n ropa de caballero, ropa de hombres.

mental ['mentⁿl] adj mental: mental effort esfuerzo mental; mental health salud mental; mental arithmetic cálculo mental. COMP **mental age** edad f mental. ‖ **mental handicap** disminución f psíquica. ‖

mental home / mental hospital (hospital m) psiquiátrico.

mentality [menˈtælətɪ] n mentalidad f.

ⓘ pl **mentalities**.

mention ['menʃⁿn] n mención f: she made no mention of your visit no mencionó tu visita.

▶ vt mencionar, hacer mención de, aludir a: he never mentioned the money no mencionó el dinero. LOC **don't mention it!** ¡de nada!, ¡no hay de qué!

menu ['menjuː] n **1** carta, menú m. **2** COMPUT menú m. COMP **menu bar** barra de menús.

ⓘ pl **menus**.

meow [mɪˈaʊ] n maullido, miau m.

▶ vi maullar.

mercenary ['mɜːsⁿnərɪ] adj mercenario,-a.

▶ n mercenario,-a.

ⓘ pl **mercenaries**.

merchandise ['mɜːtʃⁿndaɪz] n mercancías fpl, géneros mpl.

▶ vt (sell) vender, poner en venta; (promote) promocionar.

merchant ['mɜːtʃⁿnt] n (trader) comerciante mf; (dealer, businessperson) negociante mf. COMP **merchant bank** banco comercial. ‖ **merchant navy** marina mercante.

Mercury¹ ['mɜːkjərɪ] n (planet) Mercurio.

mercury² ['mɜːkjərɪ] n (metal) mercurio.

mercy ['mɜːsɪ] n **1** (compassion) misericordia, clemencia, piedad f: have mercy upon me! ¡tenga piedad de mí! **2** fam (good fortune) suerte f, milagro; (blessing) bendición f.

LOC **to be at the mercy of** SB/STH estar a la merced de ALGN/ALGO.

ⓘ pl **mercies**.

▶ adj de ayuda, de socorro. COMP **mercy killing** eutanasia.

mere [mɪəʳ] adj mero,-a, simple, puro,-a.

▶ adj **merest** (slightest) el/la más mínimo,-a.

merge [mɜːdʒ] vt (combine - gen) unir (with, a), combinar (with, con); (- road) empalmar (into, con); (- river) desem-

M

bocar (into, en); *(- firms, businesses)* fusionar.

meridional [mə'rɪdɪənªl] *adj* meridional.

meringue [mə'ræŋ] *n* merengue *m*.

merit ['merɪt] *n* mérito.
▶ *vt (deserve)* merecer.

mermaid ['mɜːmeɪd] *n* sirena.

merry ['merɪ] *adj* **1** *(cheerful)* alegre; *(amusing)* divertido,-a, gracioso,-a. **2** *fam (slightly drunk)* alegre, achispado, -a. [LOC] **merry Christmas!** ¡felices Navidades!
ⓘ *comp* **merrier**, *superl* **merriest**.

merry-go-round ['merɪɡəʊraʊnd] *n* tiovivo, caballitos *mpl*.

mess [mes] *n* **1** *(untidy state)* desorden *m*, revoltijo: *your room is a complete mess!* ¡tu habitación está toda desordenada! **2** *(confusion, mix-up)* confusión *f*, lío, follón *m*; *(person, thing)* desastre *m*: *what a mess!* ¡vaya lío!
▶ *vt (untidy)* desordenar; *(dirty)* ensuciar.
◆ **to mess about / mess around** *vi* **1** *(idle)* gandulear; *(kill time)* pasar el tiempo; *(potter about)* entretenerse. **2** *(act the fool)* hacer el primo, tontear.
◆ **to mess up** *vt sep* **1** *fam (untidy)* desordenar; *(dirty)* ensuciar. **2** *(spoil)* estropear, echar a perder.

message ['mesɪdʒ] *n* **1** *(communication)* recado, mensaje *m*: *could you give her a message?* ¿podrías darle un recado? **2** *(of story, film, etc)* mensaje *m*. [LOC] **to get the message** *(understand)* entender, darse cuenta.

messenger ['mesɪndʒəʳ] *n* mensajero,-a. [COMP] **messenger boy** recadero.

Messiah [mə'saɪə] *n* REL Mesías *m*.

messy ['mesɪ] *adj* **1** *(untidy)* desordenado,-a, en desorden; *(- dirty)* sucio,-a. **2** *(confused)* complicado,-a, enredado,-a; *(awkward)* difícil; *(unpleasant)* desagradable.
ⓘ *comp* **messier**, *superl* **messiest**.

met [met] *pp & pt* → **meet**.

metabolism [mə'tæbəlɪzªm] *n* metabolismo.

metal ['metªl] *n* metal *m*.
▶ *adj* metálico,-a, de metal.

metallic [mə'tælɪk] *adj* metálico,-a. [COMP] **metallic paint** pintura metalizada.

metallurgy [mə'tælədʒɪ] *n* metalurgia.

metamorphic [metə'mɔːfɪk] *adj* metamórfico,-a

metamorphosis [metə'mɔːfəsɪs] *n* metamorfosis *f*.
ⓘ *pl* **metamorphoses** [metə'mɔːfəsiːz].

metaphor ['metəfəʳ] *n* metáfora.

metaphysics [metə'fɪzɪks] *n* metafísica.

metatarsus [metə'tɑːsəs] *n* metatarso.
ⓘ *pl* **metatarsi** [metə'tɑːsaɪ].

meteorite ['miːtɪəraɪt] *n* meteorito.

meteorological [miːtɪərə'lɒdʒɪkªl] *adj* meteorológico,-a.

meteorologist [miːtɪə'rɒlədʒɪst] *n* meteorólogo,-a.

meteorology [miːtɪə'rɒlədʒɪ] *n* meteorología.

meter ['miːtəʳ] *n* **1** US → **metre**. **2** contador *m*.
▶ *vt* medir.

methacrylate [meθ'ækrɪleɪt] *n* metacrilato.

methane ['miːθeɪn] *n* metano.

method ['meθəd] *n* **1** *(manner, way)* método, forma. **2** *(system, order)* sistema *m*, orden *m*, lógica.

metonymy [me'tɒnɪmɪ] *n* metonimia.

metre ['miːtəʳ] *n* **1** *(measure)* metro. **2** *(in poetry)* metro. [COMP] **cubic metre** metro cúbico.

metric ['metrɪk] *adj* métrico,-a. [COMP] **metric system** sistema métrico. ‖ **metric ton** tonelada métrica.

metropolis [mə'trɒpəlɪs] *n* metrópoli *f*, metrópolis *f*.
ⓘ *pl* **metropolises**.

metropolitan [metrə'pɒlɪtªn] *adj* metropolitano,-a.

mew [mjuː] *vi* maullar.
▶ *n* maullido.

Mexican ['meksɪkªn] *adj* mejicano,-a.
▶ *n* mejicano,-a.

Mexico ['meksɪləʊ] *n* Méjico.

mi [miː] *n* MUS mi *m*.

miaow [miː'aʊ] *n* maullido.
▶ *vi* maullar.

mica [ˈmaɪkə] n mica.

mice [maɪs] pl → **mouse**.

micro [ˈmaɪkrəʊ] n fam microordenador m.
ⓘ pl micros.

microbe [ˈmaɪkrəʊb] n microbio.

microbiology [maɪkrəʊbaɪˈɒlədʒɪ] n microbiología.

microchip [ˈmaɪkəʊtʃɪp] n microchip m.

microclimate [ˈmaɪkrəʊklaɪmət] n microclima mf.

microfilm [ˈmaɪkrəʊfɪlm] n microfilme m.

micron [ˈmaɪkrɒn] n micra.

microphone [ˈmaɪkrəfəʊn] n micrófono.

microprocessor [maɪkrəʊˈprəʊsesəʳ] n microprocesador m.

microscope [ˈmaɪkrəskəʊp] n microscopio.

microscopic [maɪkrəˈskɒpɪk] adj microscópico,-a.

microwave [ˈmaɪkrəweɪv] n microonda. ⸻COMP⸻ **microwave oven** horno de microondas, microondas m inv.
▶ vt cocinar en el microondas.

midday [mɪdˈdeɪ] n mediodía m.
▶ adj de mediodía. ⸻LOC⸻ **at midday** al mediodía.

middle [ˈmɪdəl] adj (central) de en medio, central; (medium) mediano,-a, medio,-a: he's the middle son él es el hijo mediano. ⸻LOC⸻ **in the middle of nowhere** en el quinto pino. ⸻COMP⸻ **middle age** mediana edad f. ▌**middle class** clase f media. ▌**middle finger** dedo corazón. ▌**the Middle Ages** la Edad Media.
▶ n 1 (centre) medio, centro: there's a pond in the middle of the garden hay un estanque en medio del jardín. 2 (halfway point of period, activity) mitad f: in the middle of a storm en medio de una tormenta. 3 fam (waist) cintura.

⸺ El apellido se traduce por surname o family name y el nombre de pila, por Christian name o first name. Casi todo el mundo tiene dos Christian names, aunque se utilice sólo uno. Ese segundo nombre de pila es el middle name, que se suele escribir sólo con la inicial.

middle-aged [mɪdəlˈeɪdʒd] adj de mediana edad.

middle-class [mɪdəlˈklɑːs] adj de la clase media.

middleman [ˈmɪdəlmən] n intermediario.
ⓘ pl middlemen [ˈmɪdəlmen].

middleweight [ˈmɪdəlweɪt] n (boxing) peso medio.

midnight [ˈmɪdnaɪt] n medianoche f: we got home at midnight llegamos a casa a medianoche.

midwife [ˈmɪdwaɪf] n comadrona, partera, matrona.
ⓘ pl midwives [ˈmɪdwaɪvz].

might [maɪt] aux 1 (possibility) poder: it might rain podría llover. 2 (in suggestions or requests) poder: you might try the hardware shop podrías probar en la ferretería. 3 (permission) poder: he asked if he might come in pidió permiso para entrar. ⸻LOC⸻ I **might have known!** ¡debí imaginármelo!, ¡típico! ▌I **might (just) as well** más vale que.

⸺ Como expresa una posibilidad también se puede traducir por 'quizá', 'quizás', 'a lo mejor', 'tal vez' o 'puede que'. Consulta también may.

mighty [ˈmaɪtɪ] adj 1 (very strong) muy fuerte; (powerful) potente. 2 (great, imposing) enorme.
ⓘ comp mightier, superl mightiest.
▶ adv US fam (very) muy.

migraine [ˈmaɪgreɪn] n jaqueca, migraña.

migrant [ˈmaɪgrənt] adj migratorio,-a.
▶ n (person) emigrante mf; (bird) ave f migratoria.

migrate [maɪˈgreɪt] vi migrar.

migration [maɪˈgreɪʃən] n migración f.

migratory [ˈmaɪgrətərɪ] adj migratorio,-a.

mike [maɪk] n fam micro.

mild [maɪld] adj 1 (person, character) apacible, afable, dulce. 2 (climate, weather) benigno,-a, templado,-a, suave, blando,-a; (soap, detergent) suave. 3 (protest, attempt) ligero,-a; (punishment, fever) leve;

(illness, attack) ligero,-a, leve; *(criticism, rebuke)* suave, leve.

mile [maɪl] *n* milla (1,6 kms).
➤ *n pl* **miles** *(much)* mucho, muchísimo: *I'm miles better* estoy mucho mejor; *it's miles away* está muy lejos.

mileage ['maɪlɪdʒ] *n* **1** AUTO *(miles travelled by a car)* ≈ kilómetros *mpl*, kilometraje *m*. **2** *fam fig (benefit, advantage, use)* jugo, partido.

mileometer [maɪ'lɒmɪtəʳ] *n* AUTO cuentakilómetros *m*.

milestone ['maɪlstəʊn] *n* **1** hito, mojón *m*. **2** *fig* hito.

militant ['mɪlɪtənt] *adj* POL militante.
➤ *n* POL militante *mf*.

military ['mɪlɪt°rɪ] *adj* militar.
➤ *n* **the military** los militares, las fuerzas armadas.

milk [mɪlk] *n (gen)* leche *f*. COMP **milk shake** batido. ▌ **milk tooth** diente *m* de leche.
➤ *adj (bottle, production)* de leche; *(product)* lácteo,-a.

milkman ['mɪlkmən] *n* lechero, repartidor *m* de la leche.
ⓘ *pl* **milkmen** ['mɪlkmen].

milky ['mɪlkɪ] *adj* **1** *(liquid, jewel)* turbio,-a. **2** *(coffee, tea)* con mucha leche; *(substance)* lechoso,-a. **3** *(colour)* pálido,-a. COMP **Milky Way** Vía Láctea.
ⓘ *comp* milkier, *superl* milkiest.

mill [mɪl] *n* **1** *(machinery)* molino. **2** *(for coffee, pepper, etc)* molinillo. **3** *(factory)* fábrica.
➤ *vt (crush, grind)* moler.

millennium [mɪ'lenɪəm] *n* milenio, milenario.
ⓘ *pl* **millenniums** o **millennia** [mɪ'lenɪə].

millet ['mɪlɪt] *n* mijo.

millimetre ['mɪlɪmiːtəʳ] *n* milímetro.

million ['mɪljən] *n* millón *m*: *one million dollars* un millón de dólares.
➤ *n pl* **millions** *fam (lots)* millones *mpl*.

millionaire [mɪljə'neəʳ] *n* millonario,-a.

millionth ['mɪljənθ] *adj* millonésimo,-a.
➤ *n* millonésima parte, millonésimo.

millipede ['mɪlɪpiːd] *n* milpiés *m inv*.

millstone ['mɪlstəʊn] *n* muela, rueda de molino.

mime [maɪm] *n* **1** *(art)* mimo. **2** *(performance)* pantomima, representación *f* de mimo.
➤ *vt (express by mime)* expresar haciendo mímica.

mimic ['mɪmɪk] *n* imitador,-ra.
➤ *vt (copy)* imitar, remedar.
ⓘ *pt & pp* mimicked, *ger* mimicking.

mince [mɪns] *n* GB *(meat)* carne *f* picada.
COMP **mince pie** pastelito.
➤ *vt (chop, cut)* picar.

mind [maɪnd] *n* **1** *(intellect)* mente *f*. **2** *(mentality)* mentalidad *f*. **3** *(brain, thoughts)* cabeza, cerebro: *her mind was very confused* estaba confusa.
➤ *vt* **1** *(heed, pay attention to)* hacer caso de; *(care about)* importar, preocupar: *I mind what people say* me importa lo que dice la gente. **2** *(be careful with)* tener cuidado con: *mind the step!* ¡cuidado con el escalón! **3** *(look after - child)* cuidar, cuidar de; *(- house)* vigilar; *(- shop)* atender; *(- seat, place)* guardar. **4** *(object to, be troubled by)* tener inconveniente en, importar: *I don't mind staying* no tengo inconveniente en quedarme. **5** *(fancy, quite like)* venir bien: *I wouldn't mind a coffee* me vendría bien un café.
➤ *vi* **1** *(be careful)* tener cuidado: *mind (out)!* ¡cuidado!, ¡ojo! **2** *(object to)* importar, molestar: *do you mind if I open the window?* ¿le importa que abra la ventana?
LOC **never mind 1** *(it doesn't matter)* no importa, da igual. **2** *(don't worry)* no te preocupes. **3** *(let alone)* ni hablar de. ▌ **to be out of one's mind** estar loco,-a. ▌ **to change one's mind** cambiar de opinión, cambiar de parecer. ▌ **to make up one's mind** decidirse. ▌ **to SB's mind** en la opinión de ALGN.

mine¹ [maɪn] *n (gen)* mina.
➤ *vt* **1** *(coal, gold, etc)* extraer; *(area)* explotar. **2** MIL sembrar minas en, minar.
➤ *vi* explotar una mina.

mine² [maɪn] *pron* (el) mío, (la) mía, (los) míos, (las) mías, lo mío: *hey! that's mine!* ¡ey! ¡eso es mío!; *a friend of mine* un/una amigo,-a mío,-a.

miner ['maɪnəʳ] *n* minero,-a.

mineral ['mɪn°rəl] *adj* mineral.
 ► *n* mineral *m*. COMP **mineral water** agua mineral. ‖ **mineral oil** GB petróleo.

miniature ['mɪnɪtʃəʳ] *n* miniatura.
 ► *adj* (en) miniatura.

minibus ['mɪnɪbʌs] *n* microbús *m*.
 ① *pl* minibuses.

minicab ['mɪnɪkæb] *n* GB taxi *m*.

minicomputer [mɪnɪkəm'pjuːtəʳ] *n* microordenador *m*.

minimal ['mɪnɪm°l] *adj* mínimo,-a.

minimum ['mɪnɪməm] *adj* mínimo,-a.
 ► *n* mínimo: *a minimum of 20 people* un mínimo de 20 personas.

mining ['maɪnɪŋ] *n* minería, explotación *f* de minas: *coal mining* extracción de carbón.
 ► *adj* (area, town, industry) minero,-a.
 COMP **mining engineer** ingeniero,-a de minas.

miniseries [mɪnɪ'sɪəriːz] *n* TV miniserie *f*.

miniskirt ['mɪnɪskɜːt] *n* minifalda.

minister ['mɪnɪstəʳ] *n* **1** (gen) ministro,-a (for, de). **2** GB (priest) pastor,-ra.
 ► *vi* atender (to, a), cuidar (to, a).

ministry ['mɪnɪstrɪ] *n* (gen) ministerio.
 ► *n* the ministry
 ① *pl* ministries. GB (priesthood) el clero.

minor ['maɪnəʳ] *adj* **1** (unimportant) menor; (secondary) secundario,-a. **2** MUS menor.
 ► *n* JUR menor *mf*.

minority [maɪ'nɒrɪtɪ] *n* **1** minoría. **2** JUR minoría de edad.
 ① *pl* minorities.
 ► *adj* minoritario,-a.

mint¹ [mɪnt] *n* FIN (place) casa de la moneda.
 ► *vt* (coins, words) acuñar.

mint² [mɪnt] *n* **1** BOT menta. **2** (sweet) caramelo de menta.

minus ['maɪnəs] *prep* **1** MATH menos: *four minus three equals one* cuatro menos tres es igual a uno. **2** METEOR bajo cero: *minus five degrees* cinco grados bajo cero.
 ► *adj* negativo,-a. COMP **minus sign** signo de menos *m*.

 ► *n* **1** MATH menos *m*. **2** (disadvantage) desventaja *m*.

minuscule ['mɪnəskjuːl] *adj* minúsculo.

minute¹ [maɪ'njuːt] *adj* (tiny) diminuto,-a, minúsculo,-a.

minute² ['mɪnɪt] *n* **1** (of time) minuto: *it's a five minute walk* es un paseo de cinco minutos. **2** fam (moment) momento; (instant) instante *m*: *I'll be back in a minute* ahora vuelvo, vuelvo en un momento.
 ► *n pl* **minutes** (notes) acta *f sing*, actas *fpl*. LOC **(at) any minute now** en cualquier momento. ‖ **at the last minute** en el último momento, a última hora.

miracle ['mɪrək°l] *n* (gen) milagro.

mirage [mɪ'rɑːʒ] *n* espejismo.

mirror ['mɪrəʳ] *n* (gen) espejo: *stop looking at yourself in the mirror* deja de mirarte en el espejo. COMP **driving mirror** espejo (retrovisor).
 ► *vt* reflejar.

misbehave [mɪsbɪ'heɪv] *vi* portarse mal, comportarse mal.

miscarriage [mɪs'kærɪdʒ] *n* MED aborto (espontáneo).

miscarry [mɪs'kærɪ] *vi* **1** MED abortar (espontáneamente), tener un aborto. **2** (plans, etc) fracasar, frustrarse, malograrse.
 ① *pt & pp* miscarried, ger miscarrying.

miscellaneous [mɪsɪ'leɪnɪəs] *adj* (mixed, varied) variado,-a, vario,-a, diverso,-a, misceláneo,-a.

mischief ['mɪstʃɪf] *n* **1** (naughtiness) travesura, diablura: *I know you're up to some mischief* sé que estás haciendo alguna travesura. **2** fml daño, mal *m*.

miserable ['mɪz°rəb°l] *adj* **1** (person - unhappy) abatido,-a, triste, deprimido, -a; (- bad-tempered) antipático,-a. **2** (place, etc) deprimente, triste; (weather) horrible. **3** (paltry) miserable, mezquino,-a; (pathetic) lamentable.

misery ['mɪzərɪ] *n* **1** (wretchedness, unhappiness) desgracia, desdicha, tristeza. **2** (suffering) sufrimiento, dolor *m*, suplicio. **3** (poverty) pobreza, miseria.
 ① *pl* miseries.

M

misfortune [mɪsˈfɔːtʃˀn] n infortunio, desgracia, mala fortuna.

miss¹ [mɪs] n señorita.

> ✎ Miss se emplea delante del apellido de una mujer soltera.

miss² [mɪs] n *(catch, hit, etc)* fallo; *(shot)* tiro errado.

▸ vt **1** *(not to hit, score, etc)* fallar: *he missed a penalti* falló un penalti. **2** *(not catch)* perder: *I missed the bus* perdí el autobús. **3** *(not experience)* perderse: *don't miss this concert!* ¡no te pierdas este concierto! **4** *(not see)* perderse: *she doesn't miss anything* no se le escapa nada. **5** *(not attend - meeting, etc)* no asistir a; *(- class, work)* faltar a. **7** *(long for - person)* echar de menos; *(- place)* añorar: *she misses her family* echa de menos a su familia.

▸ vi **1** *(catch, kick, etc)* fallar; *(shot)* errar el tiro. **2** *(engine)* fallar. **3** *(fail)* fallar.

◆ **to miss out** vt sep *(omit, fail to include)* saltarse, omitir; *(overlook, disregard)* pasar por alto, dejarse.

▸ vi *(lose opportunity)* dejar pasar, perderse.

missile [ˈmɪsaɪl] n **1** *(explosive weapon)* misil m. **2** *(object thrown)* proyectil m.

missing [ˈmɪsɪŋ] adj **1** *(object - lost)* perdido,-a, extraviado,-a. **2** *(person - disappeared)* desaparecido,-a; *(- absent)* ausente: *she's been missing for a week* hace una semana que desapareció. LOC **to be missing** faltar. COMP **missing person** desaparecido,-a.

mission [ˈmɪʃˀn] n misión f.

missionary [ˈmɪʃˀnərɪ] n misionero,-a.

ⓘ pl missionaries.

misspell [mɪsˈspel] vt escribir mal.

ⓘ pt & pp misspelled o misspelt [mɪsˈspelt], ger misspelling.

misspend [mɪsˈspend] vt malgastar.

ⓘ pt & pp misspent [mɪsˈspent].

mist [mɪst] n **1** *(gen)* neblina; *(sea)* bruma; *(haze)* calima. **2** *(on window, mirror, etc)* vaho.

mistake [mɪsˈteɪk] n *(error)* equivocación f, error m; *(in test)* falta; *(oversight)* descuido: *there must be some mistake* debe haber algún error. LOC **by mistake 1** *(in error)* por error. **2** *(unintentionally)* sin querer. ▮ **to make a mistake** equivocarse, cometer un error.

▸ vt **1** *(misunderstand)* entender mal. **2** *(confuse)* confundir (**for**, con).

ⓘ pt mistook [mɪsˈtʊk], pp mistaken [mɪsˈteɪkˀn].

mistaken [mɪsˈteɪkˀn] pp → mistake.

▸ adj *(wrong, incorrect)* equivocado,-a, erróneo,-a. LOC **to be mistaken** equivocarse.

mister [ˈmɪstəʳ] n señor m.

mistletoe [ˈmɪsˀltəʊ] n muérdago.

mistook [mɪsˈtʊk] pt → mistake.

mistreat [mɪsˈtriːt] vt maltratar, tratar mal.

mistress [ˈmɪstrəs] n **1** *(owner - gen)* dueña, ama, señora; *(of dog)* ama, dueña. **2** *(lover)* amante f. **3** GB maestra, profesora.

mistrust [mɪsˈtrʌst] n desconfianza, recelo.

▸ vt desconfiar de.

misty [ˈmɪstɪ] adj **1** METEOR neblinoso,-a: *it's misty* hay neblina. **2** *(window, glasses, etc)* empañado,-a.

ⓘ comp mistier, superl mistiest.

misunderstand [mɪsʌndəˈstænd] vt *(gen)* entender mal; *(misinterpret)* malinterpretar.

ⓘ pt & pp misunderstood [mɪsʌndəˈstʊd].

misunderstanding [mɪsʌndəˈstændɪŋ] n malentendido (**about**, sobre).

mite [maɪt] n *(insect)* ácaro, acárido.

miter [ˈmaɪtəʳ] n US → mitre.

mitigating [ˈmɪtɪgeɪtɪŋ] adj mitigador,-ra. COMP **mitigating circumstances** JUR circunstancias fpl atenuantes.

mitre [ˈmaɪtəʳ] n **1** REL mitra. **2** TECH inglete m.

mitten [ˈmɪtˀn] n *(fingers covered)* manopla; *(fingers exposed)* mitón m.

mix [mɪks] n **1** *(mixture - gen)* mezcla. **2** CULIN preparado.

▸ vt **1** *(combine)* mezclar, combinar: *mix the sugar with the butter* mezclar el azúcar con la mantequilla. **2** *(make, prepare - plaster, cement)* amasar; *(- cocktail, salad, medicine)* preparar.

▶ vi **1** *(substances)* mezclarse. **2** *(clothes, colours, food)* combinar bien, ir bien juntos,-as. **3** *(people - come together)* mezclarse con la gente; *(- get on)* llevarse bien (with, con).

◆ **to mix up** *vt sep* **1** *(ingredients)* mezclar bien. **2** *(confuse)* confundir. **3** *(mess up, put in disorder)* desordenar, revolver.

mixed [mɪkst] *adj* **1** *(of different kinds)* variado,-a: *mixed biscuits* galletas surtidas. **2** *(ambivalent)* desigual. **3** *(for both sexes)* mixto,-a.

mixer ['mɪksə^r] *n (for food)* batidora.

mixture ['mɪkstʃə^r] *n (gen)* mezcla.

mix-up ['mɪksʌp] *n fam (confusion)* lío, confusión *f*; *(misunderstanding)* malentendido.

mm ['mɪlɪmiːtə^r] *symb (millimetre)* milímetro; *(abbreviation)* mm.

moan [məʊn] *n* **1** *(groan)* gemido, quejido. **2** *(complaint)* queja, protesta.
▶ vi **1** *(groan)* gemir. **2** *(complain)* quejarse (about, de), protestar (about, por).

moaner ['məʊnə^r] *n* quejica *m & f*.

moat [məʊt] *n* foso.

mobile ['məʊbaɪl] *adj (object, troops, etc)* móvil, movible. COMP **mobile home** caravana, remolque *m*. ❚ **mobile phone** teléfono móvil.
▶ *n (hanging ornament)* móvil *m*.

mock [mɒk] *adj* **1** *(object)* de imitación. **2** *(feeling)* fingido,-a, simulado,-a; *(modesty)* falso,-a.
▶ vt *(laugh at, make fun of)* burlarse de, mofarse de.
▶ vi burlarse (at, de).

mockery ['mɒkəri] *n* **1** *(ridicule)* burla, mofa. **2** *(farce)* farsa; *(travesty)* parodia. LOC **to make a mockery of** STH poner ALGO en ridículo.

modal ['məʊdəl] *adj* modal. COMP **modal auxiliary** auxiliar *m* modal. ❚ **modal verb** verbo modal.

model ['mɒdəl] *n* modelo.
▶ *adj* **1** *(miniature)* en miniatura, a escala; *(toy)* de juguete. **2** *(exemplary)* ejemplar; *(ideal)* modelo.
▶ vt *(clay, etc)* modelar.
ⓘ *pt & pp* **modelled** (US **modeled**), *ger* **modelling** (US **modeling**).

modem ['məʊdem] *n* COMPUT modem *m*.

moderate ['mɒdərət] *adj* **1** *(average)* mediano,-a, regular: *moderate size* tamaño mediano. **2** *(not extreme)* moderado,-a; *(reasonable)* razonable. **3** *(talent, ability, performance)* mediocre, regular.
▶ vt moderar.
▶ vi moderarse.

moderation [mɒdə'reɪʃ^ən] *n* moderación *f*.

modern ['mɒd^ən] *adj* **1** *(up-to-date)* moderno,-a. **2** *(history, literature, etc)* contemporáneo,-a. COMP **modern language** lengua moderna.

modernize ['mɒd^ənaɪz] *vt* modernizar.
▶ vi modernizarse.

modest ['mɒdɪst] *adj* **1** *(gen)* modesto,-a, humilde. **2** *(improvement, increase)* modesto,-a; *(- price)* módico,-a.

modesty ['mɒdɪsti] *n* **1** *(humility)* modestia, humildad *f*. **2** *(chastity)* pudor *m*, recato.

modify ['mɒdɪfaɪ] *vt (change)* modificar.
ⓘ *pt & pp* **modified**, *ger* **modifying**.

module ['mɒdjuːl] *n* módulo.

moist [mɔɪst] *adj (damp)* húmedo,-a; *(slightly wet)* ligeramente mojado,-a: *a moist sponge cake* un bizcocho tierno.

moisture ['mɔɪstʃə^r] *n* humedad *f*.

mold [məʊld] *n* → **mould**.

mole¹ [məʊl] *n (on skin)* lunar *m*.

mole² [məʊl] *n* **1** ZOOL topo. **2** *fam (spy)* topo *mf*, espía *mf*.

molecular [mə'lekjələ^r] *adj* molecular.

molecule ['mɒlɪkjuːl] *n* molécula.

molest [mə'lest] *vt* **1** *(attack - person)* atacar, asaltar; *(- dog)* perseguir, atacar. **2** *(sexually)* abusar sexualmente.

> ✖ To molest no significa 'molestar', que se traduce por **to bother**.

mollusc ['mɒləsk] *n* molusco.

molt [məʊlt] *n* US → **moult**.

mom [mɒm] *n* US *fam* mamá *f*.

moment ['məʊmənt] *n (instant)* momento, instante *m*: *just a moment* un momentito; *I didn't believe that story for a moment* no me creí ese cuento ni por un momento. LOC **at any moment** de un

M

momento a otro, en cualquier momento. **I at the moment** en este momento. **I at the last moment** a última hora. **I for the moment** de momento, por el momento. **I in a moment** dentro de un momento.

mommy ['mɒmɪ] *n* US *fam* mamá.
ⓘ *pl* mommies.

Monaco ['mɒnəkəʊ] *n* Mónaco.

monarch ['mɒnək] *n* monarca *m*.

monarchy ['mɒnəkɪ] *n* monarquía.
ⓘ *pl* monarchies.

monastery ['mɒnəstˀrɪ] *n* monasterio.
ⓘ *pl* monasteries.

Monday ['mʌndɪ] *n* lunes *m inv*.

✎ Para ejemplos de uso, consulta Saturday.

Monegasque ['mɒnəgæsk] *n* monegasco,-a.

monetary ['mʌnɪtˀrɪ] *adj* monetario,-a.

money ['mʌnɪ] *n* **1** *(gen)* dinero: *how much money have you got?* ¿cuánto dinero tienes? **2** *(currency)* moneda. [LOC] **to make money 1** *(person)* ganar dinero, hacer dinero. **2** *(business)* dar dinero. **I to put money on** STH apostar por ALGO.

moneybox ['mʌnɪbɒks] *n* hucha.
ⓘ *pl* moneyboxes.

Mongol ['mɒŋgɒl] *n* mongol,-la, mogol,-la.

Mongolia [mɒŋ'gəʊlɪə] *n* Mongolia.

Mongolian [mɒŋ'gəʊlɪən] *adj* mongol, -la, mogol,-la.
▸ *n* **1** *(person)* mongol,-la, mogol,-la. **2** *(language)* mongol *m*, mogol *m*.

monitor ['mɒnɪtˀr] *n* **1** *(screen)* monitor *m*. **2** *(school pupil)* responsable *mf*, encargado,-a.
▸ *vt (check)* controlar; *(follow)* seguir de cerca; *(watch)* observar.

monk [mʌŋk] *n* monje *m*.

monkey ['mʌŋkɪ] *n* **1** *(gen)* mono,-a; *(long-tailed)* mico,-a. [COMP] **monkey nut** cacahuete *m*. **I monkey wrench** llave *f* inglesa.

monogamy [mə'nɒgəmɪ] *n* monogamia.

monographic [mɒnə'græfɪk] *adj* monográfico,-a.

monolith ['mɒnəlɪθ] *n* monolito.

monologue ['mɒnəlɒg] *n* monólogo.

monopoly [mə'nɒpəlɪ] *n* monopolio.
ⓘ *pl* monopolies.

monorail ['mɒnəʊreɪl] *n* monorraíl *m*, monocarril *m*.

monotheism ['mɒnəʊθiːzˀm] *n* monoteísmo.

monotonous [mə'nɒtənəs] *adj* monótono,-a.

monotony [mə'nɒtənɪ] *n* monotonía.

monoxide [mə'nɒksaɪd] *n* monóxido.

monsoon [mɒn'suːn] *n* **1** *(wind)* monzón *m*. **2** *(rainy season)* estación *f* lluviosa. [COMP] **monsoon rains** lluvias *fpl* monzónicas.

monster ['mɒnstˀr] *n (gen)* monstruo.
▸ *adj fam (huge)* enorme, gigantesco,-a.

Montenegrin [mɒntɪ'niːgrɪn] *adj* montenegrino,-a.
▸ *n* montenegrino,-a.

Montenegro [mɒntɪ'niːgrəʊ] *n* Montenegro.

month [mʌnθ] *n* mes *m*: *I'm going on holiday at the end of the month* me voy de vacaciones a final de mes.

monthly ['mʌnθlɪ] *adj* mensual.
▸ *adv* mensualmente, cada mes.
▸ *n (magazine)* revista mensual.

monument ['mɒnjəmənt] *n* monumento (to, a).

monumental [mɒnjə'mentˀl] *adj* **1** *(gen)* monumental. **2** *fam (lie, blunder, etc)* garrafal, monumental.

moo [muː] *n (of cow)* mugido.
▸ *vi* mugir.
◆ **to mooch about / mooch around** *vi* dar vueltas, deambular.
ⓘ *pt & pp* mooed, *ger* mooing.

mood¹ [muːd] *n* LING modo.

mood² [muːd] *n* **1** *(humour)* humor *m*: *her moods change very quickly* cambia de humor de repente. [LOC] **to be in a good/ bad mood** estar de buen/mal humor.

moon [muːn] *n* luna: *full moon* luna llena. [LOC] **to be over the moon** estar en el séptimo cielo.

moonlight ['muːnlaɪt] *n* claro de luna, luz *f* de luna.

Moor [muər] n moro,-a.

moor¹ [muər] n (heath) brezal m.

moor² [muər] vt (with rope) amarrar; (with anchor) anclar.
▶ vi (with anchor) anclar; (with rope) echar amarras.

mooring ['muərɪŋ] n (place) amarradero.
▶ n pl moorings (ropes, etc) amarras fpl.

Moorish ['muərɪʃ] adj moro,-a.

moorland ['muərlənd] n páramo.

moose [muːs] n alce m.

mop [mɒp] n 1 (for floor) fregona. 2 fam (of hair) mata de pelo.
▶ vt 1 (floor) fregar, limpiar. 2 (brow, tears) enjugarse (with, con), secarse.
◆ to mope about / mope around vi andar abatido,-a, andar deprimido,-a.
ⓘ pt & pp mopped, ger mopping.

moped ['məupɛd] n ciclomotor m.

moral ['mɒrəl] adj moral.
▶ n (of story) moraleja.
▶ n pl morals moral f sing, moralidad f sing.

☒ Moral no significa 'moral (estado de ánimo)', que se traduce por morale.

morale [məˈrɑːl] n moral f, estado de ánimo.

morality [məˈrælɪtɪ] n moralidad f, moral f.

morally ['mɒrəlɪ] adv moralmente.

more [mɔːr] adj más: more than half an hour más de media hora.
▶ pron más: we need some more necesitamos más. LOC the more ..., the more ... cuanto más ..., más ... ❙ what is more además, lo que es más.
▶ adv más: it's more expensive es más caro. LOC more and more cada vez más. ❙ more or less 1 (approximately) más o menos. 2 (almost) casi.

✎ Consulta también many y much.

moreover [mɔːˈrəuvər] adv fml además, por otra parte.

morgue [mɔːg] n depósito de cadáveres.

morning ['mɔːnɪŋ] n (gen) mañana; (early) madrugada: at eight o'clock in the morning a las ocho de la mañana; the following morning a la mañana siguiente.

LOC good morning! ¡buenos días! ❙ in the morning (tomorrow before noon) mañana por la mañana.
▶ adv mornings por la mañana, por las mañanas.

Moroccan [məˈrɒkən] adj marroquí, -ina.
▶ n marroquí,-ina.

Morocco [məˈrɒkəu] n Marruecos.

morose [məˈrəus] adj malhumorado, -a, hosco,-a, taciturno,-a.

☒ Morose no significa 'moroso', que se traduce por defaulting.

morpheme ['mɔːfiːm] n LING morfema m.

morphine ['mɔːfiːn] n morfina.

morphological [mɔːfəˈlɒdʒɪkəl] adj morfológico,-a.

morphology [mɔːˈfɒlədʒɪ] n (gen) morfología.

Morse [mɔːs] n Morse m. COMP Morse code alfabeto Morse.

mortal ['mɔːtəl] adj (gen) mortal.
▶ n mortal mf.

mortality [mɔːˈtælɪtɪ] n mortalidad f.

mortgage ['mɔːgɪdʒ] n hipoteca.
▶ adj hipotecario,-a.
▶ vt hipotecar.

mosaic [məˈzeɪɪk] adj mosaico.

Moslem ['mʌzləm] adj musulmán, -ana.
▶ n musulmán,-ana.

mosque [mɒsk] n mezquita.

mosquito [məsˈkiːtəu] n mosquito.
COMP mosquito bite picadura de mosquito. ❙ mosquito net mosquitero, mosquitera.
ⓘ pl mosquitoes o mosquitos.

moss [mɒs] n BOT musgo.

most [məust] adj 1 (greatest in quantity) más: Simon's got the most points Simon tiene más puntos. 2 (majority) la mayoría de, la mayor parte de: most people live in flats la mayoría de la gente vive en pisos.
▶ adv más: the most difficult question la pregunta más difícil.
▶ pron 1 (greatest part) la mayor parte: it rained most of the time llovió durante la mayor parte del tiempo. 2 (greatest number

M

or amount) lo máximo. **3** *(the majority of people)* la mayoría.
► *adv* **1** *(superlative)* más: *the most beautiful girl* la chica más guapa. **3** *(very)* muy, de lo más: *it was most kind of you* ha sido muy amable de su parte; *a most delightful evening* una tarde muy agradable. **3** US *(almost)* casi. ᴸᴼᶜ **for the most part** por lo general. **I most of all** sobre todo.

✎ Consulta también **many** y **much**.

mostly ['məʊstlɪ] *adv* **1** *(mainly)* principalmente, en su mayor parte. **2** *(generally)* generalmente; *(usually)* normalmente.

moth [mɒθ] *n* mariposa nocturna. ᶜᴼᴹᴾ **clothes moth** polilla.

mother ['mʌðəʳ] *n* madre *f*: *a single mother* una madre soltera.
► *vt* **1** *(care for)* cuidar como una madre; *(rear)* criar. **2** *(spoil)* mimar. ᶜᴼᴹᴾ **Mother Nature** la Madre *f* Naturaleza. **I mother ship** buque *m* nodriza. **I mother tongue** lengua materna.

mother-in-law ['mʌðərɪnlɔ:] *n* suegra. ① *pl* mothers-in-law.

mother-of-pearl [mʌðərəv'pɜ:l] *n* madreperla, nácar *m*.

motif [məʊ'ti:f] *n* **1** *(pattern, design)* motivo. **2** *(in music, literature - theme)* tema *m*.

motion ['məʊʃ³n] *n* **1** *(movement)* movimiento. **2** *(gesture)* gesto, ademán *m*. **3** POL *(proposal)* moción *f*. ᴸᴼᶜ **in motion** en movimiento. **I in slow motion** CINEM a cámara lenta. ᶜᴼᴹᴾ **motion picture** película. **I motion pictures** el cine *m*.

motivate ['məʊtɪveɪt] *vt* motivar.

motive ['məʊtɪv] *n* **1** *(reason)* motivo. **2** JUR móvil *m*.
► *adj* motor,-ra, motriz. ᶜᴼᴹᴾ **motive force / motive power** fuerza motriz.

motocross ['məʊtəkrɒs] *n* SP motocross *m*.

motor ['məʊtəʳ] *n* **1** *(engine)* motor *m*. **2** GB *fam (car)* coche *m*, automóvil *m*. ᶜᴼᴹᴾ **motor racing** carreras *fpl* de coches. **I motor vehicle** vehículo a motor.
► *adj* **1** TECH motor,-ra. **2** BIOL motor,-ra, motriz.

motorbike ['məʊtəbaɪk] *n fam* motocicleta, moto *f*.

motorboat ['məʊtəbəʊt] *n* lancha motora, motora.

motorcycle ['məʊtəsaɪk³l] *n* motocicleta, moto *f*.

motorcycling ['məʊtəsaɪk³lɪŋ] *n* motociclismo.

motorcyclist ['məʊtəsaɪk³lɪst] *n* motociclista *mf*, motorista *mf*.

motorist ['məʊtərɪst] *n* automovilista *mf*, conductor,-ra (de coche).

motorway ['məʊtəweɪ] *n* GB autopista.

motto ['mɒtəʊ] *n* lema *m*.
① *pl* mottos o mottoes.

mould¹ [məʊld] *n (growth)* moho.

mould² [məʊld] *n* **1** *(cast)* molde *m*. **2** *fig (type)* carácter *m*, temple *m*.
► *vt* **1** *(figure)* moldear; *(clay)* modelar.

moult [məʊlt] *vi* ZOOL mudar.
► *n* ZOOL muda.

mound [maʊnd] *n* **1** *(small hill)* montículo. **2** *(pile, heap)* montón *m*.

mount¹ [maʊnt] *n (mountain)* monte *m*.

mount² [maʊnt] *n* **1** *(horse, etc)* montura. **2** *(for machine, gun, trophy)* soporte *m*, base *f*; *(for photo, picture)* fondo; *(for jewel)* engaste *m*, engarce *m*; *(for slide)* marquito.
► *vt* **1** montar. *(stairs)* subir.
► *vi* **1** *(go up)* subir, ascender.
◆ **to mount up** *vi (accumulate)* amontonarse, acumularse.

mountain ['maʊnt³n] *n* **1** GEOG montaña. **2** *fig (large amount)* montaña, montón *m*. ᶜᴼᴹᴾ **mountain bike** bicicleta de montaña. **I mountain range** cordillera, sierra.
► *adj* de montaña.

mountaineer [maʊntə'nɪəʳ] *n* montañero,-a, alpinista *mf*, AM andinista *mf*.

mountaineering [maʊntə'nɪərɪŋ] *n* montañismo, alpinismo, AM andinismo.

mountainous ['maʊnt³nəs] *adj* **1** *(region)* montañoso,-a. **2** *(huge)* enorme, gigantesco,-a.

mourn [mɔːn] *vt (person)* llorar la muerte de; *(thing)* llorar, añorar.

mourning ['mɔ:nɪŋ] n luto, duelo. LOC **to be in mourning for** SB estar de luto por ALGN.

mouse [maʊs] n (gen) ratón m.
ⓘ pl **mice.**

mousse [mu:s] n CULIN mousse f.

moustache [məs'ta:ʃ] n bigote m.

mouth [(n) maʊθ; (vb) maʊð] n **1** ANAT boca. **2** (of river) desembocadura; (of bottle) boca; (of tunnel, cave) boca, entrada. **3** (person to feed) boca. LOC **to keep one's mouth shut** mantener la boca cerrada, no decir nada. COMP **mouth organ** armónica.

mouthful ['maʊθfʊl] n **1** (of food) bocado; (of drink) trago; (of air) bocanada. **2** fam (long word, phrase) trabalenguas m.

mouth-to-mouth [maʊθtə'maʊθ] [also **mouth-to-mouth resuscitation**] n boca a boca m.

movable ['mu:vəbəl] adj movible, móvil.

move [mu:v] n **1** (act of moving, movement) movimiento: he watched my every move observó todos mis movimientos. **2** (to new home) mudanza; (to new job) traslado. **3** (in game) jugada; (turn) turno: whose move is it? ¿a quién le toca jugar? **4** (action, step) paso, acción f, medida; (decision) decisión f; (attempt) intento.
▶ vt **1** (gen) mover; (furniture, etc) cambiar de sitio, trasladar; (transfer) trasladar; (out of the way) apartar: you've moved the furniture! ¡habéis cambiado los muebles de sitio! **2** (affect emotionally) conmover. **3** (in games) mover, jugar.
▶ vi **1** (gen) moverse; (change - position) trasladarse, desplazarse; (- house) mudarse; (- post, department) trasladarse: she was so scared she couldn't move tenía tanto miedo que no podía moverse.
◆ **to move away** vi **1** (move aside, etc) alejarse, apartarse. **2** (change house) mudarse de casa.
◆ **to move in** vi **1** (into new home) instalarse. **2** (prepare to take control, attack, etc) acercarse.
◆ **to move over** vt sep (step aside) apartarse.
▶ vi (make room) correrse, moverse.

movement ['mu:vmənt] n **1** (act, motion) movimiento; (gesture) gesto, ademán m. **2** (of goods) traslado; (of troops) desplazamiento; (of population) movimiento. **3** (political, literary) movimiento. **4** (trend) tendencia, corriente f.
▶ n pl **movements** (activities) movimientos mpl, actividades fpl.

movie ['mu:vɪ] n US película.
▶ n pl **the movies** el cine m sing. LOC **to go to the movies** ir al cine.

moving ['mu:vɪŋ] adj **1** (that moves) móvil; (in motion) en movimiento, en marcha. **2** (causing motion) motor,-ra, motriz. **3** (causing action, motivating) instigador,-ra, promotor,-ra. **4** (emotional) conmovedor,-ra.

mow [məʊ] vt (lawn) cortar, segar; (corn, wheat) segar.
ⓘ pt **mowed**, pp **mowed** o **mown** [məʊn].

mower ['məʊəʳ] n (for lawn) cortacésped m & f; (for fields) segadora.

mown [məʊn] pp → **mow.**

Mozambique [məʊzæm'bi:k] n Mozambique.

Mozambiquean [məʊzæm'bi:kən] adj mozambiqueño,-a.
▶ n mozambiqueño,-a.

MP ['em'pi:] abbr (member of Parliament) diputado,-a.

mph ['em'pi:'eɪtʃ] abbr (miles per hour) millas por hora.

Mr abbr (Mister) señor; (abbreviation) sr.

Mrs abbr señora; (abbreviation) sra.

Ms abbr (Miss) señorita; (abbreviation) srta.

much [mʌtʃ] adj mucho,-a: we haven't got much bread no tenemos mucho pan; he didn't have much time no tenía mucho tiempo; we've made too much jam hemos hecho demasiada mermelada; why is there so much traffic? ¿por qué hay tanto tráfico?; take as much time as you need tómate tanto tiempo como necesites; how much money have you got? ¿cuánto dinero tienes?
ⓘ comp **more**, superl **most.**
▶ pron mucho: there's not much to do round here no hay mucho que hacer por aquí; how much is it? ¿cuánto vale? LOC **a bit much** un poco demasiado, un po-

M

co excesivo,-a. ▌ **as much 1** *(equal)* equivalente a. **2** *(the same)* lo mismo.
▶ *adv* mucho: *he felt much better* se encontraba mucho mejor.

✎ Much se emplea sobre todo en las frases negativas e interrogativas, en las frases afirmativas se emplea a lot.

mucus ['mjuːkəs] *n* mucosidad *f*.
mud [mʌd] *n* *(gen)* barro, lodo; *(thick)* fango.
muddle ['mʌdəl] *n* **1** *(mess)* desorden *m*: *everything's in a muddle* todo está en desorden. **2** *(confusion, mix-up)* confusión *f*, embrollo, lío.
▶ *vt* [also **to muddle up]** *(untidy)* revolver, desordenar; *(confuse mentally)* liar, confundir, embarullar; *(confuse, mix up)* confundir.
◆ **to muddle through** *vi* arreglárselas.
muddy ['mʌdɪ] *adj* **1** *(gen)* fangoso,-a, barroso,-a, lodoso,-a. **2** *(colour)* sucio,-a. **3** *(thinking, idea, etc)* confuso,-a, turbio,-a.
① *comp* muddier, *superl* muddiest.
mudguard ['mʌdgɑːd] *n* guardabarros *m inv*.
muesli ['mjuːzlɪ] *n* muesli *m*.
muffin ['mʌfɪn] *n* **1** GB *panecillo redondo que se come tostado y con mantequilla.* **2** US *tipo de magdalena.*
mug [mʌg] *n* *(large cup)* taza alta, tazón *m*.
mugger ['mʌgəʳ] *n* atracador,-ra, asaltante *mf*.
mugging ['mʌgɪŋ] *n* atraco, asalto.
mule [mjuːl] *n* ZOOL mulo,-a.
mullet ['mʌlɪθ] ᴄᴏᴍᴘ **grey mullet** mújol *m*. ▌ **red mullet** salmonete *m*.
multicultural [mʌltɪ'kʌltʃərəl] *adj* multicultural.
multilateral [mʌltɪ'lætərəl] *adj* multilateral.
multinational [mʌltɪ'næʃnəl] *adj* multinacional.
▶ *n* multinacional *f*.
multiple ['mʌltɪpəl] *adj* múltiple.
▶ *n* MATH múltiplo.

multiple-choice [mʌltɪpəl'tʃɔɪs] *adj* tipo test.
multiplex ['mʌltɪpleks] *adj* **1** *(cinema)* multicines *mpl*. **2** TECH múltiple.
multiplication [mʌltɪplɪ'keɪʃən] *n* multiplicación *f*. ᴄᴏᴍᴘ **multiplication sign** signo de multiplicar. ▌ **multiplication table** tabla de multiplicar.
multiply ['mʌltɪplaɪ] *vt* MATH multiplicar (by, por).
① *pt & pp* multiplied, *ger* multiplying.
▶ *vi* multiplicarse.
multipurpose [mʌltɪ'pɜːpəs] *adj* multiuso *inv*.
mum [mʌm] *n* GB *fam* mamá *f*.
mumble ['mʌmbəl] *vt* *(gen)* decir entre dientes, mascullar; *(prayer)* musitar.
▶ *vi* hablar entre dientes, farfullar.
mummify ['mʌmɪfaɪ] *vt* momificar.
① *pt & pp* mummified, *ger* mummifying.
mummy¹ ['mʌmɪ] *n* *(dead body)* momia *f*.
① *pl* mummies.
mummy² ['mʌmɪ] *n* GB *fam (mother)* mamá *f*.
① *pl* mummies.
mumps [mʌmps] *n* MED paperas *fpl*.
mundane [mʌn'deɪn] *adj* **1** *(worldly)* mundano,-a. **2** *pej (banal)* rutinario,-a, banal.
municipal [mjuː'nɪsɪpəl] *adj* municipal.
municipality [mjuːnɪsɪ'pælɪtɪ] *n* municipio.
① *pl* municipalities.
mural ['mjʊərəl] *n* pintura mural, mural *m*.
murder ['mɜːdəʳ] *n* **1** asesinato, homicidio. **2** *fam fig (difficult experience)* pesadilla. ᴄᴏᴍᴘ **murder story** novela negra, novela policíaca.
▶ *vt* **1** *(kill)* asesinar, matar. **2** *fam fig (be angry with)* matar.
murderer ['mɜːdərəʳ] *n* asesino, homicida *mf*.
murmur ['mɜːməʳ] *n* **1** *(of voice)* murmullo, susurro. **2** *(of traffic)* rumor *m*; *(of insects)* zumbido; *(of wind)* murmullo; *(of water)* susurro. **3** MED soplo.
▶ *vt* murmurar: *they murmured their approval* hubo un murmullo de aprobación.

▶ *vi* **1** murmurar, susurrar. **2** *(complain)* quejarse (**against/at**, de).

❌ To murmur no significa 'murmurar (hablar mal)', que se traduce por to gossip.

muscle ['mʌsəl] *n* **1** ANAT músculo. **2** *(muscle power)* fuerza. **3** *fig (strength, power)* poder *m*, fuerza. LOC **to not move a muscle** no inmutarse.

◆ **to muscle in** *vi (situation)* entrometerse (**on**, en); *(place)* introducirse por la fuerza.

muscular ['mʌskjələ'] *adj* **1** *(pain, tissue)* muscular. **2** *(person)* musculoso,-a.

musculature ['mʌskjələtʃə'] *n* **1** musculatura. **2** *(person)* musculoso,-a.

muse¹ [mjuːz] *vi* meditar (**on/over**, -), reflexionar (**on/over**, sobre).

muse² [mjuːz] *n* musa.
▶ *n pl* **the Muses** las Musas *fpl*.

museum [mjuːˈzɪəm] *n* museo.

mushroom ['mʌʃruːm] *n* **1** BOT seta, hongo. **2** CULIN *(button mushroom)* champiñón *m*; *(wild)* seta. COMP **mushroom cloud** hongo nuclear.

✎ La palabra mushroom se usa para designar cualquier seta u hongo comestible; las setas no comestibles se llaman toadstools.

music ['mjuːzɪk] *n* música. COMP **music box** caja de música. **music centre** equipo de música. **music hall** teatro de variedades. **music score** partitura. **music stand** atril *m*.

musical ['mjuːzɪkəl] *adj* **1** *(gen)* musical. **2** *(person - gifted)* dotado,-a para la música; *(- fond of music)* aficionado,-a a la música, melómano,-a. COMP **musical box** caja de música. **musical instrument** instrumento musical.
▶ *n* musical *m*.

musician [mjuːˈzɪʃən] *n* músico,-a.

musk [mʌsk] *n (substance)* almizcle *m*.

musket ['mʌskɪt] *n* mosquete *m*.

musketeer [mʌskəˈtɪə'] *n* mosquetero.

Muslim ['mʌzlɪm] *adj* musulmán,-ana.
▶ *n* musulmán,-ana.

muslin ['mʌzlɪn] *n* muselina.

mussel ['mʌsəl] *n* mejillón *m*.

must¹ [mʌst] *aux* **1** *(necessity, obligation)* deber, tener que: *I must leave now* tengo que marcharme ahora; *must you play your music so loud?* ¿es necesario poner la música tan fuerte? **2** *(probability)* deber de: *she must be tired* debe de estar cansada; *but someone must have seen her* pero alguien debe de haberla visto. LOC **if I must** si no hay más remedio. **if you must know, ...** si te empeñas en saberlo, …
▶ *n (need)* necesidad *f*: *it's an absolute must for all film buffs* es imprescindible para todos los cinéfilos.

mustache [məsˈtɑːʃ] *n* US → moustache.

mustard ['mʌstəd] *n (gen)* mostaza. COMP **mustard gas** gas *m* mostaza.

mutant ['mjuːtənt] *n* mutante *mf*.
▶ *adj* mutante.

mutation [mjuːˈteɪʃən] *n* mutación *f*.

mute [mjuːt] *adj (dumb, silent)* mudo,-a. COMP **deaf mute** sordomudo,-a.
▶ *n* **1** LING mudo,-a. **2** *(dumb person)* mudo,-a. **3** MUS sordina.

mutilate ['mjuːtɪleɪt] *vt* mutilar.

mutilation [mjuːtɪˈleɪʃən] *n* mutilación *f*.

mutiny ['mjuːtɪnɪ] *n* motín *m*, amotinamiento, sublevación *f*, rebelión *f*.
ⓘ *pl* mutinies.
▶ *vi* amotinarse.
ⓘ *pt & pp* mutinied, *ger* mutinying.

mutter ['mʌtə'] *n* murmullo, refunfuño.
▶ *vt (mumble)* murmurar, mascullar, decir entre dientes, refunfuñar.
▶ *vi* **1** *(mumble)* murmurar, hablar entre dientes. **2** *(complain)* refunfuñar, rezongar, quejarse.

mutton ['mʌtn] *n* carne *f* de oveja.

mutual ['mjuːtʃʊəl] *adj* **1** *(help, love, etc)* mutuo,-a, recíproco,-a. **2** *(friend, interest, etc)* común.

mutually ['mjuːtʃʊəlɪ] *adv* mutuamente.

muzzle ['mʌzəl] *n* **1** *(snout)* hocico. **2** *(guard)* bozal *m*. **3** *(of gun)* boca.

M

▸ vt **1** *(dog)* poner un bozal a. **2** *fig (person, press, etc)* amordazar.

muzzy ['mʌzɪ] *adj* **1** *(blurred)* borroso,-a. **2** *(groggy)* atontado,-a, espeso,-a.
ⓘ *comp* muzzier, *superl* muzziest.

my [maɪ] *adj* mi, mis: *my book* mi libro; *my records* mis discos; *one of my friends* un amigo mío.
▸ *interj* ¡caramba!, ¡caray!

myopia [maɪ'əupɪə] *n* miopía.

myopic [maɪ'ɒpɪk] *adj* miope.

myrtle ['mɜːtəl] *n* BOT arrayán *m*, mirto.

myself [maɪ'self] *pron* **1** *(reflexive)* me: *I cut myself* me corté; *I helped myself* me serví. **2** *(after preposition)* mí (mismo,-a): *I kept it for myself* lo guardé para mí; *I said to myself* me dije a mí mismo. **3** *(emphatic)* yo mismo,-a: *I did it by myself* lo hice yo mismo,-a. ⎡LOC⎤ **all by myself 1** *(alone)* solo,-a. **2** *(without help)* yo solo,-a. ▮ **to myself** *(private)* para mí solo,-a.

mysterious [mɪ'stɪərɪəs] *adj* misterioso,-a.

mysteriously [mɪ'stɪərɪəslɪ] *adv* misteriosamente.

mystery ['mɪstərɪ] *n* misterio.
ⓘ *pl* mysteries.

mystic ['mɪstɪk] *adj* místico,-a.
▸ *n* místico,-a.

mystical ['mɪstɪkəl] *adj* místico,-a.

myth [mɪθ] *n* **1** *(ancient story)* mito. **2** *(fallacy)* falacia.

mythical ['mɪθɪkəl] *adj* **1** *(of a myth)* mítico,-a. **2** *(not real, imagined)* imaginario,-a, fantástico,-a.

mythological [mɪθə'lɒdʒɪkəl] *adj* mitológico,-a.

mythology [mɪ'θɒlədʒɪ] *n* mitología.

N, n [en] *n (the letter)* N, n *f*.

N [nɔːθ] *abbr* **(north)** norte *m; (abbreviation)* N.

naff [næf] *adj fam* hortera.

nag [næg] *vt* **1** *(annoy)* molestar, fastidiar. **2** *(complain)* dar la tabarra a.
▶ *vi* quejarse.
ⓘ *pt & pp* **nagged**, *ger* **nagging**.

nail [neɪl] *n* **1** *(on finger, toe)* uña: *to bite/cut/trim one's nails* morderse/cortarse/arreglarse las uñas. **2** *(metal)* clavo
▶ *vt* **1** clavar, fijar con clavos. **2** *fam* pillar, coger. [COMP] **nail clippers** cortaúñas *m*. ▮ **nail polish** esmalte *m* para las uñas. ▮ **nail varnish** esmalte *m* para las uñas. ▮ **nail varnish remover** quitaesmaltes *m*.
◆ **to nail down** *vt sep* **1** *(thing)* clavar, sujetar con clavos. **2** *fig (person)* conseguir que ALGN se comprometa: *I couldn't nail him down to a price* no pude conseguir que me concretara un precio.

naive [naɪˈiːv] *adj* ingenuo,-a.

naked [ˈneɪkɪd] *adj* desnudo,-a.

name [neɪm] *n* **1** *(first name)* nombre *m; (surname)* apellido: *his name's Richard* se llama Richard; *what's your name?* ¿cómo te llamas? **2** *(fame)* fama, reputación *f*: *she made her name in the theatre* se hizo famosa en el teatro.
▶ *vt* **1** llamar: *they named the child Dominic after his uncle* al niño le pusieron Dominic por su tío. **2** *(appoint)* nombrar: *he was named Minister of Transport* lo nombraron Ministro de Transportes.
[LOC] **in the name of...** en nombre de…
[COMP] **big name** pez *m* gordo. ▮ **name day** santo.

namely [ˈneɪmlɪ] *adv* a saber.

Namibia [nəˈmɪbɪə] *n* Namibia.

Namibian [nəˈmɪbɪən] *adj* namibio,-a.
▶ *n* namibio,-a.

nanny [ˈnænɪ] *n* **1** *(carer)* niñera. **2** GB *fam (grandmother)* yaya, abuela.
ⓘ *pl* **nannies**.

nap [næp] *n* siesta.
▶ *vi* dormir la siesta. [LOC] **to have a nap / take a nap** echar la siesta.
ⓘ *pt & pp* **napped**, *ger* **napping**.

nape [neɪp] *n* nuca, cogote *m*.

napkin [ˈnæpkɪn] *n* servilleta. [COMP] **napkin ring** servilletero.

nappy [ˈnæpɪ] *n* GB pañal *m*.
ⓘ *pl* **nappies**.

narcissus [nɑːˈsɪsəs] *n* narciso.
ⓘ *pl* **narcissi** o **narcissuses**.

narcotic [nɑːˈkɒtɪk] *adj* narcótico,-a.
▶ *n* narcótico.

narrate [nəˈreɪt] *vt* narrar.

narrative [ˈnærətɪv] *adj* narrativo,-a.
▶ *n* **1** narración *f*. **2** *(genre)* narrativa.

narrator [nəˈreɪtəʳ] *n* narrador,-ra.

narrow [ˈnærəʊ] *adj* **1** estrecho,-a: *a narrow road* una carretera estrecha. **2** *(restricted)* reducido,-a, restringido,-a: *a narrow circle of friends* un círculo reducido de amigos. **3** *(by very little)* escaso,-a: *by a narrow majority* por una escasa mayoría.
ⓘ *comp* **narrower**, *superl* **narrowest**.
▶ *vt* **1** *(make narrower)* estrechar. **2** *(reduce)* reducir, acortar: *Leeds narrowed Hull's lead to only 1 point* el Leeds redujo la ventaja del Hull a 1 solo punto.

nasal [ˈneɪzˀl] *adj* **1** nasal. **2** *(way of speaking)* gangoso,-a.

nasty [ˈnɑːstɪ] *adj* **1** *(unpleasant)* desagradable, repugnante, horrible: *what a nasty smell!* ¡qué olor más desagradable! **2** *(malicious)* malintencionado,-a; *(unkind)*

antipático,-a: *she was really nasty to everyone* se mostró muy antipática con todos. **3** *(dangerous)* peligroso,-a: *this bend is really nasty* esta curva es muy peligrosa. **4** *(tricky)* peliagudo,-a: *it's quite a nasty little problem* es un problemita bastante peliagudo. **5** *(serious)* grave: *a nasty cold* un resfriado de cuidado.
ⓘ *comp* **nastier,** *superl* **nastiest.**

nation ['neɪʃən] *n* **1** *(country)* nación *f*, país *m*. **2** *(ethnic group)* pueblo, nación *f*.

national ['næʃnəl] *adj* nacional. COMP **national anthem** himno nacional.
► *n* súbdito,-a, ciudadano,-a.

nationalism ['næʃnəlɪzm] *n* nacionalismo.

nationalist ['næʃnəlɪst] *adj* nacionalista.
► *n* nacionalista *mf*.

nationality [næʃ'nælɪtɪ] *n* nacionalidad *f*.
ⓘ *pl* **nationalities.**

native ['neɪtɪv] *adj* **1** *(place)* natal; *(language)* materno,-a: *her native country* su país natal; *his native tongue is Danish* su lengua materna es el danés; *we need a native speaker of English* necesitamos un hablante de inglés que sea nativo. **2** *(plant, animal)* originario,-a: *it's native to Australia* es originario de Australia; *native varieties of grape* variedades autóctonas de vid.
► *n* **1** natural *mf*, nativo,-a: *she's a native of Orense* es natural de Orense. **2** *(original inhabitant)* indígena *mf*. COMP **Native American** indio,-a americano,-a.

Ⓦ Se llama **Native American** a los descendientes de las tribus aborígenes que habitaban Estados Unidos antes de la llegada de los europeos. Se trata de una multitud de pueblos con lenguas y tradiciones diferentes que fueron diezmados durante la colonización y, posteriormente, recluidos en reservas.

nativity [nə'tɪvɪtɪ] *n* natividad *f*.
ⓘ *pl* **nationalities.**

NATO ['neɪtəʊ] [also written Nato] *abbr* **(North Atlantic Treaty Organization)** Organización *f* del Tratado del Atlántico Norte; *(abbreviation)* OTAN *f*.

natural ['nætʃərəl] *adj* natural. **3** *(usual)* natural, normal: *it's only natural to feel afraid* es normal tener miedo. COMP **natural childbirth** parto natural. **I natural gas** gas *m* natural. **I natural history** historia natural. **I natural resources** recursos *mpl* naturales. **I natural science** ciencias *fpl* naturales. **I natural selection** selección *f* natural.

naturally ['nætʃrəlɪ] *adv* **1** *(by nature)* por naturaleza. **2** *(unaffectedly)* con naturalidad. **3** *(not artificially)* de manera natural. **4** *(of course)* naturalmente, por supuesto.

nature ['neɪtʃər] *n* **1** *(gen)* naturaleza. **2** *(character)* carácter *m*, forma de ser: *it's in her nature to be like that* es así por naturaleza. LOC **by nature** por naturaleza. COMP **nature conservation** conservación *f* de la naturaleza. **I nature reserve** reserva natural. **I nature study** ciencias *fpl* naturales.

naughty ['nɔːtɪ] *adj* **1** travieso,-a, malo,-a. **2** *(risqué)* atrevido,-a.
ⓘ *comp* **naughtier,** *superl* **naughtiest.**

Nauru ['naʊruː, 'nɑːʊːruː:] *n* Nauru.

Nauruan [naʊ'ruːən] *adj* nauruano,-a.
► *n* nauruano,-a.

nausea ['nɔːzɪə] *n* **1** *(physical)* náusea. **2** *(disgust)* asco, repugnancia.

nauseating ['nɔːzɪeɪtɪŋ] *adj* **1** *(physically)* nauseabundo,-a. **2** *(disgusting)* asqueroso,-a, repugnante.

nautical ['nɔːtɪkəl] *adj* náutico,-a. COMP **nautical mile** milla náutica.

Navajo ['nævəhəʊ] *adj-n* → **Navaho.**

naval ['neɪvəl] *adj* naval. COMP **naval battle** batalla naval. **I naval base** base *f* naval.

navel ['neɪvəl] *n* ombligo.

navigate ['nævɪgeɪt] *vt* **1** *(river, sea)* navegar por. **2** *(steer - ship)* gobernar; *(- plane)* pilotar.
► *vi (when sailing, flying)* dirigir; *(when driving)* guiar: *you drive, I'll navigate* tú conduce, yo te guiaré.

navigation [nævɪ'geɪʃən] *n* navegación *f*.

navigator ['nævɪgeɪtər] *n* MAR navegante *mf*.

navy ['neɪvɪ] *n* marina de guerra, armada. COMP **navy blue** azul marino.
ⓘ *pl* navies.

Nazi ['nɑːtsɪ] *adj* nazi.
▶ *n* nazi *mf*.

Nazism ['nɑːtsɪzəm] *n* nazismo.

Neanderthal [nɪ'ændɑːˈl] *adj* de Neanderthal. COMP **Neanderthal man** hombre *m* de Neanderthal.

near [nɪəʳ] *adj* **1** cercano,-a: *where is the nearest bank?* ¿dónde está el banco más cercano?; *a near relative* un pariente cercano. **2** *(time)* próximo,-a: *in the near future* en un futuro próximo.
ⓘ *comp* nearer, *comp* nearest.
▶ *adv* cerca: *I live quite near (by)* vivo bastante cerca.
▶ *prep* **1** cerca de: *it's near the market* está cerca del mercado. **2** [also near to.] a punto de: *she was near to crying* estuvo a punto de llorar.
▶ *vt* acercarse a: *we are nearing the day when...* nos acercamos al día en que…

nearby [(*adj*) 'nɪəbaɪ, (*adv*) nɪə'baɪ] *adj* cercano,-a: *a nearby hotel* un hotel cercano.
▶ *adv* cerca: *is there one nearby?* ¿hay alguno cerca?

nearly ['nɪəlɪ] *adv* casi. LOC **not nearly** ni mucho menos, ni con mucho: *there's not nearly enough time to finish* el tiempo para acabar es del todo insuficiente.

neat [niːt] *adj* **1** *(room)* ordenado,-a; *(garden)* bien arreglado,-a. **2** *(person)* pulcro,-a; *(in habits)* ordenado,-a. **3** *(writing)* claro,-a. **4** *(clever)* ingenioso,-a, apañado,-a. **5** *(drinks)* solo,-a. **6** US fantástico,-a, estupendo,-a, chulo,-a, guay.

neatness ['niːtnəs] *n* esmero.

necessarily [nesə'serɪlɪ] *adv* **1** necesariamente. **2** *(inevitably)* inevitablemente, forzosamente.

necessary ['nesɪsˈeʳrɪ] *adj* **1** necesario,-a. **2** *(inevitable)* inevitable, forzoso,-a. LOC **to do the necessary** hacer lo necesario.
▶ *n pl* **necessaries** lo necesario, cosas *fpl* necesarias.

necessity [nɪ'sesɪtɪ] *n* **1** necesidad *f*: *it's a necessity* es indispensable. **2** *(item)* requisito indispensable.
ⓘ *pl* necessities.

neck [nek] *n* cuello. LOC **to be in STH up to one's neck** estar metido,-a en ALGO hasta el cuello. **‖ to break one's neck** desnucarse. **‖ to risk one's neck** jugarse el tipo.

necklace ['nekləs] *n* collar *m*.

neckline ['neklaɪn] *n* escote *m*. LOC **with a low neckline** muy escotado,-a.

nectarine ['nektərɪn] *n* nectarina.

née [neɪ] *adj* de soltera: *Mrs Hastings, née Lawley* la Sra. Hastings, de soltera Lawley.

need [niːd] *n* **1** necesidad *f*: *there's no need for all of you to come with me* no hace falta que me acompañéis todos; *I have enough to satisfy my needs* tengo suficiente para satisfacer mis necesidades. **2** *(poverty)* necesidad *f*, infortunio: *to help SB in time of need* ayudar a ALGN en tiempos de necesidad. LOC **if need be** si hace falta. **‖ to be in need of** necesitar. **‖ to have need of** necesitar, tener necesidad de.
▶ *vt* necesitar: *you'll need a pencil* necesitarás un lápiz; *I need to see you* tengo que verte.
▶ *aux* hacer falta: *need we all go?* ¿hace falta que vayamos todos?; *need you drive so fast?* ¿tienes que conducir tan deprisa?; *you needn't come in tomorrow* no hace falta que vengas mañana; *you needn't have bought me a present* no hacía falta que me compraras ningún regalo.

needle ['niːdˈl] *n* **1** *(gen)* aguja. **2** GB *fam (friction)* pique *m*. **3** US *fam (injection)* inyección *f*. **4** *(leaf)* hoja: *pine needles* hojas de pino. LOC **it's like looking for a needle in a haystack** es como buscar una aguja en un pajar.
▶ *vt fam* pinchar.

needless ['niːdləs] *adj* innecesario,-a.

needn't ['niːdənt] *v* → need.

negative ['negətɪv] *adj* negativo,-a.
▶ *n* **1** LING negación *f*. **2** *(answer)* negativa. **3** *(photograph)* negativo.

neglect [nɪ'glekt] *n* **1** *(of thing)* descuido, desatención *f*: *the house was in a state of neglect* la casa estaba totalmente descuidada, la casa se encontraba en un estado de abandono. **2** *(of duty)* incumplimiento.

▶ *vt* **1** *(not take care of)* tener abandonado,-a, desatender: *I've been neglecting my friends recently* tengo abandonados a mis amigos. **2** *(fail to attend to)* descuidar: *with so much sport you've been neglecting your academic work* con tanto deporte tienes los estudios muy descuidados. **3** *(forget to do)* olvidar: *she neglected to lock the safe* olvidó cerrar la caja con llave.

neglected [nɪ'glektɪd] *adj* descuidado,-a.

negligence ['neglɪdʒəns] *n* negligencia.

negotiate [nɪ'gəʊʃɪeɪt] *vt* negociar.

negotiation [nɪgəʊʃɪ'eɪʃ°n] *n* negociación *f*: *the agreement is under negotiation* el acuerdo se está negociando.

negotiator [nɪ'gəʊʃɪeɪtəʳ] *n* negociador,-ra.

neigh [neɪ] *n* relincho.
▶ *vi* relinchar.

neighbor ['neɪbəʳ] *n* US → neighbour.

neighbour ['neɪbəʳ] *n* **1** vecino,-a. **2** *(fellow man)* prójimo,-a.

neighbourhood ['neɪbəhʊd] *n* **1** vecindad *f*, barrio. **2** *(people)* vecindario. COMP **neighbourhood watch** grupo de vigilancia vecinal.

neither ['naɪðəʳ, 'niːðəʳ] *adj* ninguno de los dos, ninguna de las dos: *neither boy knew the answer* ninguno de los dos chicos sabía la respuesta.
▶ *pron* ninguno de los dos, ninguna de las dos: *neither is here* ninguno de los dos está aquí.
▶ *adv* **1** ni: *he's neither fat nor thin* no es ni gordo ni delgado. **2** tampoco: *I don't like it and neither does my wife* no me gusta a mí, y a mi mujer tampoco. LOC **neither... nor...** ni... ni...: *she neither smokes nor drinks* ni fuma ni bebe.

neolithic [nəʊ'lɪθɪk] *adj* neolítico,-a.

neon ['niːɒn] *n* neón *m*. COMP **neon light** luz *f* de neón. ▌ **neon sign** rótulo con tubos de neón.

Nepal [nə'pɔːl] *n* Nepal.

Nepalese [nepə'liːz] *adj* nepalés,-esa, nepalí.
▶ *n* **1** *(person)* nepalés,-esa, nepalí *mf*. **2** *(language)* nepalés *m*, nepalí *m*.

Nepali [nə'pɔːlɪ] *adj* → Nepalese.

nephew ['nevjuː] *n* sobrino.

Neptune ['neptjuːn] *n* Neptuno.

nerve [nɜːv] *n* **1** nervio. **2** *(daring)* valor *m*. **3** *(cheek)* descaro, cara: *what a nerve!* ¡qué cara! LOC **to be a bundle of nerves** estar hecho,-a un manojo de nervios. ▌ **to get on sb's nerves** crispar los nervios a ALGN. ▌ **to lose one's nerve** rajarse. COMP **nerve cell** neurona. ▌ **nerve centre** centro neurálgico. ▌ **nerve gas** gas *m* nervioso.

nervous ['nɜːvəs] *adj* **1** nervioso,-a. **2** *(afraid)* miedoso,-a; *(timid)* tímido,-a. **3** *(apprehensive)* aprensivo,-a. COMP **nervous breakdown** crisis *f* nerviosa. ▌ **nervous system** sistema *m* nervioso. ▌ **nervous wreck** manojo de nervios.

nest [nest] *n* **1** nido; *(hen's)* nidal *m*. **2** *(wasp's)* avispero; *(animal's)* madriguera. **3** *fig* nido, refugio.
▶ *vi* anidar, nidificar.
▶ *vt* COMPUT anidar.

net¹ [net] *n* red *f*.
▶ *vt* coger con red.
Ⓘ *pt & pp* netted, *ger* netting.

net² [net] *adj* FIN neto,-a: *they made a net profit of £1.5M* tuvieron beneficios netos de un millón y medio de libras. COMP **net result** resultado final. ▌ **net weight** peso neto.

nether ['neðəʳ] *adj lit* inferior, de abajo.

Netherlander ['neðəlændəʳ] *n* neerlandés,-esa.

Netherlands ['neðələndz] *n* **the Netherlands** los Países *mpl* Bajos.

netsurfer ['netsɜːfəʳ] *n* internauta *mf*.

nettle ['net°l] *n* ortiga. LOC **to grasp the nettle** coger el toro por los cuernos. COMP **nettle rash** urticaria.

network ['netwɜːk] *n* red *f*.
▶ *vt* COMPUT conectar en red.

neuron ['njʊərɒn] *n* neurona.

neuter ['njuːtəʳ] *adj* neutro,-a.
▶ *n* LING neutro.

neutral ['njuːtrəl] *adj (in general)* neutro,-a: *a neutral colour/shampoo* un color/champú neutro. **2** POL neutral: *a neutral country* un país neutral. **3** *(impartial)* neu-

tral, imparcial: *a neutral judgment* un juicio imparcial.
▶ *n* AUTO punto muerto: *leave the car in neutral* deja el coche en punto muerto.

neutron ['njuərɒn] *n* neutrón *m*.

never ['nevər] *adv* nunca, jamás: *I have never been there* jamás he estado allí; *we never go there any more* ya no vamos allí nunca; *never have I heard such rubbish* en mi vida he oído tales tonterías; *he never so much as thanked me* ni siquiera me dio las gracias. LOC **never again** nunca más. **I never mind!** ¡no importa!

never-ending [nevə'rendɪŋ] *adj* interminable.

nevertheless [nevəðə'les] *adv* sin embargo.

new [njuː] *adj* **1** nuevo,-a: *a new car* un coche nuevo; *new bread* pan recién hecho. **2** *(baby)* recién nacido,-a: *she's got a new baby* acaba de tener un hijo. LOC **what's new?** ¿qué hay de nuevo? COMP **new moon** luna nueva. **I New Testament** Nuevo Testamento. **I new wave** nueva ola. **I New World** Nuevo Mundo. **I New Year** Año Nuevo. **I New Year's Day** día *m* de Año Nuevo. **I New Year's Eve** Nochevieja. **I New York** Nueva York. **I New Zealand** Nueva Zelanda. **I New Zealander** neozelandés,-esa.

newborn ['njuːbɔːn] *adj* recién nacido,-a.

newcomer ['njuːkʌmər] *n* recién llegado,-a.

Newfoundland ['njuːfəndlənd] *n* Terranova.

news [njuːz] *n* noticias *fpl*. LOC **bad news travels fast** las malas noticias corren deprisa. **I it's news to me** *fam* ahora me entero. **I no news is good news** la falta de noticias son buenas noticias. **I to break the news to sb** dar la noticia a ALGN. COMP **a piece of news** una noticia. **I news agency** agencia de noticias. **I news bulletin** boletín *m* de noticias. **I news conference** conferencia de prensa. **I news item** noticia.

newsagent ['njuːzeɪdʒənt] *n* vendedor,-ra de periódicos. COMP

newsagent's (shop) quiosco, puesto de periódicos.

newsdealer ['njuːzdiːlər] *n* US vendedor,-ra de periódicos.

newsflash ['njuːzflæʃ] *n* noticia de última hora.

newsgroup ['njuːzgruːp] *n* grupo de discusión.

newsletter ['njuːzletər] *n* hoja informativa, boletín *m*.

newspaper ['njuːspeɪpər] *n* diario, periódico.

newsstand ['njuːzstænd] *n* quiosco, puesto de periódicos.

newt [njuːt] *n* tritón *m*.

newton ['njuːtən] *n* newton *m*.

next [nekst] *adj* **1** *(following - in order)* próximo,-a, siguiente; *(- in time)* próximo,-a, que viene: *the next street on the left* la próxima calle a la izquierda; *it's on the next page* está en la página siguiente; *not this stop, the next* esta parada no, la siguiente; *next Thursday (Friday, etc)* el próximo jueves *(viernes, etc)*, el jueves *(viernes, etc)* que viene; *next week/month/year* la semana/el mes/el año que viene. **2** *(room, house, etc)* de al lado: *they live in the next house* viven en la casa de al lado.
▶ *adv* luego, después, a continuación: *what did you say next?* ¿qué dijiste luego?; *what do you want to do next?* ¿qué quieres hacer ahora?
▶ *prep* **next to** al lado de: *it's next to the cinema* está al lado del cine. LOC **next to nothing** casi nada. **I next door** al lado, la casa de al lado: *they live next door* viven (en la casa de) al lado.

next-door ['nekstdɔːr] *adj* de al lado, de la casa de al lado: *my next-door neighbours* los vecinos de al lado.

NGO ['en'dʒiː'əu] *abbr* (Non-Governmental Organization) Organización *f* no gubernamental; *(abbreviation)* ONG *f*.

nibble ['nɪbəl] *n* **1** *(action)* mordisco. **2** *(piece)* bocadito.
▶ *vi* picar.

Nicaragua [nɪkə'rægjuə] *n* Nicaragua.

Nicaraguan [nɪkə'rægjuən] *adj* nicaragüense.
▶ *n* nicaragüense.

N

nice [naɪs] *adj* **1** *(person)* amable, simpático: *he's such a nice boy!* ¡es un chico tan simpático! **2** *(thing)* bueno,-a, agradable: *nice day today, isn't it?* hace buen día, ¿verdad? **3** *(food)* delicioso,-a, bueno,-a. **4** *(pretty)* bonito,-a, mono,-a, guapo,-a.

nicely ['naɪslɪ] *adv* **1** *(well)* bien: *she was very nicely dressed* iba muy bien vestida. **2** *(properly)* bien: *behave nicely, dear* compórtate bien, cariño. **3** *fam (very well)* perfecto, estupendo: *Friday would suit me nicely* el viernes me iría perfecto.

nickel ['nɪkəl] *n* **1** níquel *m.* **2** US moneda de cinco centavos.

nickname ['nɪkneɪm] *n* apodo.
▸ *vt* apodar: *he was nicknamed "Lanky"* lo apodaron «Lanky».

niece [niːs] *n* sobrina.

Niger [niːˈʒeər] *n* Níger.

Nigeria [naɪˈdʒɪərɪə] *n* Nigeria.

Nigerian [naɪˈdʒɪərɪən] *adj* nigeriano,-a.
▸ *n* nigeriano,-a.

night [naɪt] *n* noche *f.* LOC **all night long** toda la noche. **I at night** de noche. **I by night** de noche. **I last night** anoche. **I late at night** a altas horas de la noche. **I night and day** noche y día. **I to have a bad night** pasar una mala noche. **I to have a good night 1** *(sleep well)* dormir bien. **2** *(have fun)* pasárselo bien. **I to have a late night** acostarse tarde. **I to have a night out** salir por la noche. COMP **night shift** turno de noche. **I night watchman** vigilante *m* nocturno.

nightdress ['naɪtdres] *n* camisón *m.*
ⓘ *pl* nightdresses.

nightfall ['naɪtfɔːl] *n* anochecer *m.*

nightie ['naɪtɪ] *n* camisón *m.*

nightgown ['naɪtgaʊn] *n* camisón *m.*

nightingale ['naɪtɪŋgeɪl] *n* ruiseñor *m.*

nightmare ['naɪtmeər] *n* pesadilla.

nighttime ['naɪttaɪm] *n* noche *f.*

nil [nɪl] *n* **1** cero, nada: *costs have been reduced to practically nil* los costes se han reducido prácticamente a cero. **2** SP cero: *Lincoln beat Grantham two goals to nil* Lincoln ganó a Grantham por dos goles a cero.

nine [naɪn] *adj* nueve.
▸ *n* nueve *m.*

✎ Consulta también six.

nineteen [naɪnˈtiːn] *adj* diecinueve.
▸ *n* diecinueve *m.*

✎ Consulta también six.

nineteenth [naɪnˈtiːnθ] *adj* decimonono,-a.
▸ *adv* en decimonono lugar.
▸ *n* **1** *(in series)* decimonono,-a. **2** *(fraction)* decimonono; *(one part)* decimonona parte *f.*

✎ Consulta también sixth.

ninetieth ['naɪntɪəθ] *adj* nonagésimo,-a.
▸ *adv* en nonagésimo lugar.
▸ *n* **1** *(in series)* nonagésimo,-a. **2** *(fraction)* nonagésimo; *(one part)* nonagésima parte *f.*

✎ Consulta también sixtieth.

ninety ['naɪntɪ] *adj* noventa.
▸ *n* noventa *m.*

✎ Consulta también sixty.

ninth [naɪnθ] *adj* nono,-a, noveno,-a.
▸ *adv* en nono lugar, en noveno lugar.
▸ *n* **1** *(in series)* nono,-a, noveno,-a. **2** *(fraction)* noveno; *(one part)* novena parte *f.*

✎ Consulta también sixth.

nip [nɪp] *n* **1** *(pinch)* pellizco: *she gave him a nip* le pegó un pellizco. **2** *(bite)* mordisco, mordedura: *the dog gave me a nip on the ankle* el perro me pegó un mordisco en el tobillo. **3** *(drink)* trago: *a nip of whisky* un trago de whisky.
▸ *vt* **1** *(pinch)* pellizcar: *a crab nipped my finger* un cangrejo me pellizcó el dedo. **2** *(bite)* morder *(con poca fuerza)*: *the dog nipped me* el perro me mordió.
ⓘ *pt & pp* nipped, *ger* nipping.

nipple ['nɪpəl] *n* **1** *(female)* pezón *m.* **2** *(male)* tetilla. **3** *(teat)* tetilla. **4** TECH pezón *m.*

nit [nɪt] *n* **1** liendre *f.* **2** GB *fam* imbécil *mf.*

niter ['naɪtər] *n* US→ nitre.

nitre ['naɪtər] *n* salitre *m.*

nitrogen ['naɪtrədʒən] *n* nitrógeno.

no [nəʊ] *adv* no: *have you seen it? –no!* ¿lo has visto? –¡no!; *he's no better than a thief* no es más que un ladrón. LOC **no way!** ¡ni hablar!

▶ adj ninguno,-a; (before masc sing) ningún: I have no time no tengo tiempo; «No smoking» «Prohibido fumar»; «No motorcycles» «Motos no».

▶ n no: there were two noes, nine yeses and one abstention hubo dos noes, nueve síes y una abstención.

nobility [nəʊˈbɪlɪtɪ] n nobleza.

noble [ˈnəʊbəl] adj noble.
ⓘ comp nobler, superl noblest.
▶ n noble mf.

nobleman [ˈnəʊbəlmən] n noble m.
ⓘ pl noblemen [ˈnəʊbəlmən].

noblewoman [ˈnəʊbəlwʊmən] n noble f.
ⓘ pl noblewomen [ˈnəʊbəlwɪmɪn].

nobody [ˈnəʊbədɪ] pron nadie: nobody went to the party no fue nadie a la fiesta.
▶ n don nadie m.

nod [nɒd] n 1 saludo con la cabeza. 2 (in agreement) señal f de asentimiento.
▶ vi 1 saludar con la cabeza. 2 (agree) asentir (con la cabeza).
ⓘ pt & pp nodded, ger nodding.

noise [nɔɪz] n ruido, sonido.
▶ n pl noises comentarios mpl. LOC to make a noise hacer ruido. COMP big noise fam pez m gordo.

noisy [ˈnɔɪzɪ] adj ruidoso,-a.
ⓘ comp noisier, superl noisiest.

nomad [ˈnəʊmæd] n nómada mf.

no-man's-land [ˈnəʊmænzlænd] n tierra de nadie.

nominal [ˈnɒmɪnəl] adj 1 nominal. 2 (price) simbólico,-a.

nominate [ˈnɒmɪneɪt] vt 1 nombrar: he was nominated team captain lo nombraron capitán del equipo. 2 (propose) proponer: I nominate Neil as captain yo propongo a Neil como capitán.

nonconformist [nɒnkənˈfɔːmɪst] adj disidente.

none [nʌn] pron ninguno,-a: none of the keys opens the door ninguna de las llaves abre la puerta; none of them could do it nadie supo hacerlo; I wanted nutmeg, but they had none quería nuez moscada, pero no tenían.
▶ adv de ningún modo: he's none the worse for his ordeal no le ha afectado esa mala experiencia. LOC none but únicamente, solamente, solo: none but the strongest survived sobrevivieron solo los más fuertes..

nonsense [ˈnɒnsəns] n tonterías fpl: don't talk nonsense! ¡no digas tonterías!

nonstick [nɒnˈstɪk] adj antiadherente.

nonstop [nɒnˈstɒp] adj 1 (continuous) continuo,-a. 2 (flight, etc) directo,-a, sin escalas.
▶ adv sin parar.

noodle [ˈnuːdəl] n fideo.

noon [nuːn] n mediodía m.

no-one [ˈnəʊwʌn] [also written no one] pron nadie: no-one went to the party no fue nadie a la fiesta.

no-place [ˈnəʊpleɪs] adv US→ nowhere.

nor [nɔːʳ] conj 1 ni: neither you nor I ni tú ni yo; I neither know nor care ni lo sé ni me importa. 2 tampoco: nor do I yo tampoco.

Nordic [ˈnɔːdɪk] adj nórdico,-a.

normal [ˈnɔːməl] adj normal.

normally [ˈnɔːməlɪ] adv normalmente.

normality [nɔːˈmælɪtɪ] n normalidad f.

north [nɔːθ] n norte m: to the north of London al norte de Londres; in the north of Scotland en el norte de Escocia.
▶ adj del norte: I live in north London vivo en el norte de Londres.
▶ adv al norte, hacia el norte: we're travelling north viajamos hacia el norte; they've moved north se han trasladado al norte; it's north of Cambridge está al norte de Cambridge. COMP North Pole Polo Norte.

northeast [nɔːθˈiːst] n nordeste m, noreste m.
▶ adj del nordeste.
▶ adv al nordeste, hacia el nordeste.

northern [ˈnɔːðən] adj norte, del norte.

northwest [nɔːθˈwest] n noroeste m.
▶ adj del noroeste.
▶ adv al noroeste, hacia el noroeste.

Norway [ˈnɔːweɪ] n Noruega.

Norwegian [nɔːˈwiːdʒən] adj noruego,-a.
▶ n 1 (person) noruego,-a. 2 (language) noruego.

nose [nəʊz] n 1 nariz f. 2 (of animal) hocico. 3 (sense) olfato. 4 (of car, etc) morro.

N

LOC **to blow one's nose** sonarse. ▍ **to get up sb's nose** GB *fam* fastidiar a ALGN. ▍ **under sb's very nose / right under sb's nose** ante las propias narices de ALGN.

nosebleed ['nəʊzbliːd] *n* hemorragia nasal.

nostril ['nɒstrəl] *n* fosa nasal.

nosy ['nəʊzɪ] *adj fam* curioso,-a, entrometido,-a.

ⓘ *comp* **nosier,** *superl* **nosiest.**

not [nɒt] [la forma contracta es n't: isn't, aren't, doesn't.] *adv* no: *I did not steal it* no lo robé; *she told me not to tell anyone* me dijo que no lo dijera a nadie; *I hope/suppose not* espero/supongo que no; *are you coming or not?* ¿vienes o no? LOC **not likely!** ¡ni hablar! ▍ **not that...** no es que...: *where is he?, not that I mind, of course* ¿dónde está?, no es que me importe, claro está. ▍ **not to say...** por no decir…

✎ Not acompaña al auxiliar del verbo en las oraciones negativas. En el inglés hablado y en los textos escritos informales se suele contraer a -n't: *she isn't English; he doesn't like it.* También se usa para la forma negativa de los verbos subordinados.

notary ['nəʊtərɪ] *n* notario,-a.
ⓘ *pl* **notaries.**

note [nəʊt] *n* **1** MUS nota; *(key)* tecla. **2** *(message)* nota. **3** *(money)* billete *m*.
▶ *vt* **1** *(notice)* notar, advertir: *I noted a certain reluctance on John's part* noté cierta reticencia por parte de John. **2** *(pay special attention)* fijarse en: *note that the plural of «child» is «children»* fijaos en que el plural de «child» es «children». **3** *(write down)* apuntar, anotar.
▶ *n pl* **notes** apuntes *mpl*.
◆ **to note down** *vt sep* apuntar.

ⓧ Note no significa 'nota (calificación)', que se traduce por **mark**.

notebook ['nəʊtbʊk] *n* **1** *(book)* libreta, cuaderno. **2** *(computer)* ordenador *m* portátil.

notepad ['nəʊtpæd] *n* bloc *m* de notas.

nothing ['nʌθɪŋ] *n* nada: *there's nothing left* no queda nada; *it's nothing special* no es nada del otro jueves. LOC **for nothing**

fam gratis. ▍ **nothing but...** únicamente…, solo…

▶ *adv* de ningún modo, de ninguna manera: *it's nothing like a pheasant* no se parece en nada a un faisán.

notice ['nəʊtɪs] *n* **1** *(sign)* letrero: *there's a notice which says «No parking»* hay un letrero que pone «Prohibido aparcar». **2** *(announcement)* anuncio: *there's a notice in the paper about a lost dog* hay un anuncio en el diario acerca de un perro extraviado. **3** *(warning)* aviso: *they gave him a month's notice to quit the flat* le dieron un plazo de un mes para abandonar el piso. LOC **to take no notice of** no hacer caso de. ▍ **until further notice** hasta nuevo aviso. ▍ **without notice** sin previo aviso.
▶ *vt* notar, fijarse en, darse cuenta de.
▶ *vi fam (show)* verse: *don't worry, the stain doesn't notice* no te preocupes, la mancha no se ve.

ⓧ Notice no significa 'noticia', que se traduce por **news**.

noticeable ['nəʊtɪsəbᵊl] *adj* que se nota, evidente.

noticeboard ['nəʊtɪsbɔːd] *n* tablón *m* de anuncios.

notify ['nəʊtɪfaɪ] *vt* notificar, avisar.
ⓘ *pt & pp* **notified,** *ger* **notifying**

notion ['nəʊʃᵊn] *n* noción *f*, idea, concepto.
▶ *n pl* **notions** US mercería *f sing*.

notorious [nəʊ'tɔːrɪəs] *adj pej* célebre: *a notorious criminal* un conocido criminal.

ⓧ Notorious no significa 'notorio (conocido)', que se traduce por **well-known**.

nougat ['nuːgɑː] *n* turrón *m* blando.

nought [nɔːt] *n* cero: *nought point sixty-six* cero coma sesenta y seis. COMP **noughts and crosses** tres en raya *m*.

noun [naʊn] *n* nombre *m*, sustantivo. COMP **noun phrase** sintagma *m* nominal.

nourish ['nʌrɪʃ] *vt* nutrir, alimentar.

nourishing ['nʌrɪʃɪŋ] *adj* nutritivo,-a.

novel¹ ['nɒvᵊl] *adj* original, novedoso,-a: *what a novel idea!* ¡qué idea más original!

novel² ['nɒvᵊl] *n* novela.

novelist ['nɒvᵊlɪst] *n* novelista *mf*.

novelty ['nɒvªltɪ] *n* **1** novedad *f*: *the novelty soon wore off* pronto dejó de ser novedad. **2** *(trinket)* chuchería.
ⓘ *pl* novelties.

November [nəʊˈvembəʳ] *n* noviembre *m*.

✎ Para ejemplos de uso, consulta May.

novice ['nɒvɪs] *n* **1** novato,-a. **2** REL novicio,-a.

now [naʊ] *adv* **1** *(at the present)* ahora; *(used contrastively)* ya: *where do you work now?* ¿dónde trabajas ahora?; *I'm ready now* ya estoy listo. **2** *(immediately)* ya, ahora mismo: *do it now!* ¡hazlo ya! **3** *(in past)* ya, entonces. **4** *(introductory)* bueno, vamos a ver, veamos: *now, let's begin* bueno, empecemos. LOC **by now** ya: *she'll be in Mexico by now* ya debe de estar en Méjico. ∎ **for now** por el momento. ∎ **from now on** de ahora en adelante. ∎ **just now 1** *(at this moment)* en estos momentos, ahora mismo. **2** *(a short while ago)* hace un momento, ahora mismo: *I can't help you just now* ahora mismo no puedo ayudarte; ∎ **now and then** de vez en cuando. ∎ **right now** ahora mismo.
▶ *conj* [also now that] ahora que, ya que: *now (that) we're all here, we can begin* ya que estamos todos, podemos empezar.

nowadays ['naʊədeɪz] *adv* hoy día, hoy en día, actualmente.

nowhere ['nəʊweəʳ] *adv (position)* en ninguna parte, en ningún sitio, en ningún lugar; *(direction)* a ninguna parte, a ningún sitio: *where are you going? – nowhere special* ¿dónde vas? –a ningún sitio en especial; *there's nowhere to hide* no hay donde esconderse. LOC **in the middle of nowhere** en el quinto pino. ∎ **nowhere near** muy lejos de.

nozzle ['nɒzªl] *n (of hose)* boquilla; *(of oilcan)* pitorro; *(large calibre)* tobera.

nuclear ['njuːklɪəʳ] *adj* nuclear. COMP **nuclear bomb** bomba nuclear. ∎ **nuclear energy** energía nuclear. ∎ **nuclear fission** fisión *f* nuclear. ∎ **nuclear fusion** fusión *f* nuclear. ∎ **nuclear power** energía nuclear. ∎ **nuclear power station** central *f* nuclear. ∎ **nuclear reactor** reactor *m* nu-

clear. ∎ **nuclear waste** residuos nucleares. ∎ **nuclear weapon** arma nuclear.

nucleus ['njuːklɪəs] *n* núcleo.
ⓘ *pl* nuclei [njuːˈklɪaɪ].

nude [njuːd] *adj* desnudo,-a.
▶ *n* desnudo.

nudge [nʌdʒ] *n* **1** *(with elbow)* codazo. **2** empujón *m* suave.
▶ *vt* dar un codazo a.

nuisance ['njuːsªns] *n* **1** molestia, fastidio, lata. **2** *(person)* pesado,-a. LOC **to make a nuisance of os** dar la lata.

numb [nʌm] *adj* entumecido,-a, insensible. LOC **to be numb with cold** estar helado,-a de frío.

number ['nʌmbəʳ] *n* número. LOC **a number of...** varios,-as... ∎ **any number of...** muchísimos,-as... ∎ **without number** un sinfín de... COMP **number plate** placa de matrícula..
◆ **to number off** *vi* numerarse.

numeral ['njuːmərəl] *n* número, cifra.

numerous ['njuːmərəs] *adj* numeroso,-a.

nun [nʌn] *n* monja, religiosa.

nurse [nɜːs] *n* **1** enfermero,-a. **2** *(children's)* niñera.
▶ *vt* **1** *(look after)* cuidar. **2** *(suckle)* amamantar. **3** *(hold)* acunar. **4** *(feeling)* guardar.

nursery ['nɜːsªrɪ] *n* **1** *(in house)* cuarto de los niños. **2** *(kindergarten)* guardería. **3** *(for plants)* vivero. COMP **nursery rhyme** canción *f* infantil, poema *m* infantil. ∎ **nursery school** parvulario.
ⓘ *pl* nurseries.

nut [nʌt] *n* **1** BOT fruto seco. **2** TECH tuerca. **3** *fam (head)* coco. **4** *fam (nutcase)* chalado,-a, chiflado,-a.

nutcrackers ['nʌtkrækəz] *n pl* cascanueces *m inv*.

nutmeg ['nʌtmeg] *n* nuez *f* moscada.

nutrient [njuːˈtrɪənt] *n* nutriente *m*.

nutrition [njuːˈtrɪʃªn] *n* nutrición *f*.

nutritious [njuːˈtrɪʃəs] *adj* nutritivo,-a.

nutshell ['nʌtʃel] *n* cáscara. LOC **in a nutshell** en pocas palabras.

nylon® ['naɪlɒn] *n* nailon *m*.
▶ *n pl* **nylons** medias *fpl* de nailon.

nymph [nɪmf] *n* ninfa.

N

O, o [əʊ] *n (the letter)* O, o *f*.

O [əʊ] *n (as number)* cero.

oak [əʊk] *n* **1** BOT roble *m*. **2** *(wood)* roble *m*.
► *adj* de roble.

oar [ɔːʳ] *n* remo.

oarsman [ˈɔːzmən] *n* remero.
ⓘ *pl* oarsmen [ˈɔːzmən].

oasis [əʊˈeɪsɪs] *n* oasis *m*.
ⓘ *pl* oases [əʊˈeɪsiːz].

oats [əʊts] *n pl* avena.

oath [əʊθ] *n* **1** JUR juramento. **2** *(swearword)* palabrota, juramento. LOC **on my oath** lo juro. ‖ **to be on oath / be under oath** estar bajo juramento.

obedience [əˈbiːdɪəns] *n* obediencia.

obedient [əˈbiːdɪənt] *adj* obediente.

obelisk [ˈɒbəlɪsk] *n* obelisco.

obese [əʊˈbiːs] *adj* obeso,-a.

obesity [əʊˈbiːsɪtɪ] *n* obesidad *f*.

obey [əˈbeɪ] *vt* **1** *(gen)* obedecer; *(orders)* acatar. **2** *(law)* cumplir.
► *vi (gen)* obedecer.

object [*(n)* ˈɒbdʒekt; *(vb)* əbˈdʒekt] *n* **1** *(thing)* objeto, cosa. **2** *(aim, purpose)* objetivo, fin *m*. **3** *(focus of feelings)* objeto: *he was an object of ridicule* fue objeto de burlas. **4** LING complemento: *direct/indirect object* complemento directo/indirecto. COMP **object glass / object lens** objetivo.
► *vt* objetar.
► *vi* **1** *(oppose)* oponerse (to, a), poner reparos (to, a).

objection [əbˈdʒekʃ⁽ə⁾n] *n* objeción *f*, reparo, inconveniente.

objective [əbˈdʒektɪv] *adj* objetivo,-a.
► *n* **1** *(purpose)* objetivo, fin *m*. **2** *(lens)* objetivo.

objectivity [əbˈdʒektɪvɪtɪ] *n* objetividad *f*.

obligation [ɒblɪˈgeɪ⁽ə⁾n] *n* obligación *f*.

oblige [əˈblaɪdʒ] *vt* **1** *(compel)* obligar: *I felt obliged to attend* me veía obligado a asistir. **2** *(do a favour)* hacer un favor a, ayudar a. LOC **much obliged!** ¡muy agradecido,-a!
► *vi (do a favour)* hacer un favor, ayudar.

oblong [ˈɒblɒŋ] *adj* oblongo,-a, alargado,-a.
► *n* rectángulo.

oboe [ˈəʊbəʊ] *n* oboe *m*.

obscene [ɒbˈsiːn] *adj* obsceno,-a, indecente.

obscenity [əbˈsenɪtɪ] *n* obscenidad *f*.
ⓘ *pl* obscenities.

obscure [əbˈskjʊəʳ] *adj* **1** *(unclear)* oscuro,-a, poco claro,-a. **2** *(vague, indistinct)* vago,-a, confuso,-a; *(hidden)* recóndito,-a.

❌ Obscure no significa 'oscuro (un color)', que se traduce por **dark**.

obsequious [əbˈsiːkwɪəs] *adj* servil.

❌ Obsequious no significa 'obsequioso', que se traduce por **obliging**.

observant [əbˈzɜːv⁽ə⁾nt] *adj* observador,-ra.

observation [ɒbzəˈveɪ⁽ə⁾n] *n* **1** *(watching, study)* observación *f*; *(surveillance)* vigilancia. **2** *(remark)* observación *f*, comentario.

observatory [əbˈzɜːvət⁽ə⁾rɪ] *n* observatorio.
ⓘ *pl* observatories.

observe [əbˈzɜːv] *vt* **1** *(see, watch)* observar, ver; *(in surveillance)* vigilar. **2** *(law)* cumplir, respetar. **3** *fml (say)* señalar.
► *vi* observar.

obsess [əbˈses] *vt* obsesionar.

obsession [əb'seʃən] *n* obsesión *f* (with/about, con).

obsessive [əb'sesɪv] *adj* obsesivo,-a.
► *n* obsesivo,-a.

obstacle ['ɒbstək°l] *n* **1** obstáculo. **2** *fig* obstáculo, impedimento. COMP **obstacle race** carrera de obstáculos.

obstetrics [ɒb'stetrɪks] *n* obstetricia, tocología.

obstinate ['ɒbstɪnət] *adj* obstinado,-a.

obstruct [əb'strʌkt] *vt* **1** (block - gen) obstruir; (- pipe, etc) atascar, bloquear; (- view) tapar. **2** (make difficult) dificultar.

obstruction [əb'strʌkʃən] *n* **1** (gen) obstrucción *f*. **2** (hindrance) estorbo, obstáculo.

obtain [əb'teɪn] *vt* obtener, conseguir.

obtuse [əb'tjuːs] *adj fml* (stupid) obtuso,-a. COMP **obtuse angle** ángulo obtuso.

obvious ['ɒbvɪəs] *adj* (clear) obvio,-a: for obvious reasons por razones obvias.

obviously ['ɒbvɪəslɪ] *adv* obviamente, evidentemente.

occasion [ə'keɪʒ°n] *n* **1** (time) ocasión *f*; (event) acontecimiento. **2** (opportunity) ocasión *f*, oportunidad *f*: if the occasion arises si se presenta la ocasión. LOC **on occasion** de vez en cuando. ‖ **on the occasion of** con motivo de. ‖ **to rise to the occasion** estar a la altura de las circunstancias, dar la talla.

occasional [ə'keɪʒ°nəl] *adj* (not frequent) esporádico,-a, eventual.

occasionally [ə'keɪʒ°nəlɪ] *adv* de vez en cuando, ocasionalmente.

occipital [ɒk'spɪt°l] *adj* occipital.

occult ['ɒkʌlt] *adj* oculto,-a.

❌ Occult no significa 'oculto (escondido)', que se traduce por **hidden**.

occupant ['ɒkjəpənt] *n* (gen) ocupante *mf*; (tenant) inquilino,-a.

occupation [ɒkjə'peɪʃ°n] *n* **1** (job) ocupación *f*, profesión *f*. **2** (pastime) pasatiempo. **3** (act, state of occupying) ocupación *f*.

occupied ['ɒkjəpaɪd] *adj* ocupado,-a.

occupy ['ɒkjəpaɪ] *vt* ocupar.
ⓘ *pt & pp* occupied, ger occupying.

occur [ə'kɜːʳ] *vi* **1** (happen - event, incident) ocurrir, suceder; (- change) producirse. **2** *fml* (be found, exist) existir, darse. **3** (come to mind) ocurrir, ocurrirse: it never occurred to me to ask no se me ocurrió preguntar.
ⓘ *pt & pp* occurred, ger occurring.

occurrence [ə'kʌrəns] *n* **1** (event, incident) suceso. **2** *fml* (frequency) incidencia, frecuencia; (existing amount) cantidad *f*.

❌ Occurrence no significa 'ocurrencia', que se traduce por **idea**.

ocean ['əʊʃ°n] *n* océano.
► *adj* oceánico,-a: **ocean currents** corrientes oceánicas.

oceanic [əʊʃɪ'ænɪk] *adj fml* oceánico,-a.

oceanography [əʊʃən'ɒgrəfɪ] *n* oceanografía.

ocher ['əʊkəʳ] *adj* US → ochre.

ochre ['əʊkəʳ] *adj* (de color) ocre.
► *n* ochre *m*.

o'clock [ə'klɒk] *adv* : it's one o'clock es la una; at three o'clock a las tres.

octagon ['ɒktəgən] *n* octágono, octógono.

octagonal [ɒk'tægən°l] *adj* octagonal, octogonal.

octahedron [ɒktə'hiːdrən] *n* octaedro.

October [ɒk'təʊbəʳ] *n* octubre *m*.
Para ejemplos de uso, consulta May.

octopus ['ɒktəpəs] *n* pulpo.
ⓘ *pl* octopuses.

odd [ɒd] *adj* **1** (strange) extraño,-a, raro,-a: the odd thing is that... lo raro es que... **2** (number) impar. **3** (approximately) y pico: thirty odd people unas treinta y pico personas. **4** (shoe, glove, etc) suelto,-a, desparejado,-a. LOC **to be the odd man out 1** (be over) estar de más. **2** (be different) ser la excepción. COMP **odd jobs** trabajillos *mpl*.
► *n pl* **odds 1** (probability, chances) probabilidades *fpl*: the odds are that... lo más probable es que... **2** (in betting) apuestas *fpl*. LOC **against (all) the odds** contra todo pronóstico.

odontology [ɒdɒn'tɒlədʒɪ] *n* odontología.

odor ['əʊdəʳ] *adj* US → odour.

odorless ['əʊdələs] *adj* US → odourless.

odour ['əʊdəʳ] n (smell) olor m; (fragrance) perfume m, fragancia.

odourless ['əʊdələs] adj inodoro,-a.

odyssey ['ɒdɪsɪ] n odisea.

oesophagus [iː'sɒfəgəs] n esófago.
ⓘ pl oesophagi [iː'sɒfəgaɪ].

oestrogen ['iːstrədʒən] n estrógeno.

of [ɒv, unstressed əv] prep **1** (belonging to) de: a friend of mine un amigo mío. **2** (made from) de: Spanish-leather shoes zapatos de piel española. **3** (containing) de: a bag of crisps una bolsa de patatas. **4** (showing a part, a quantity) de: a kilo of apples un kilo de manzanas. **5** (partitive use) de: the two of us nosotros dos. **6** (dates, distance) de: the 7th of August el 7 de agosto. **7** (apposition) de: the city of London la ciudad de Londres. **8** (by) de: the works of Shakespeare las obras de Shakespeare. **9** (with, having) de: a child of five un niño de cinco años. **10** (after superlative) de: best of all was the food lo mejor de todo fue la comida.

off [ɒf] prep **1** (movement) de: he got off the bus bajó del autobús. **2** (indicating removal) de: he cut a branch off the tree cortó una rama del árbol. **3** (distance, situation) diferentes traducciones: a narrow street off the main road una callejuela que sale a la carretera; the ship sank off Malpica el barco se hundió a la altura de Malpica. **4** (away from) diferentes traducciones: the ship went off course el barco se desvió de su rumbo; we're a long way off finding a cure estamos lejos de encontrar una cura. **5** (not wanting) : I'm off coffee ya no tomo café. **6** (not at work) : she comes off duty at 10.00pm acaba el turno a las 10.00. **7** fam (from) a: I bought it off Eva se lo compré a Eva.
▸ adv **1** (departure): he ran off se fue corriendo; I'm off me voy. **2** (showing distance) a: the village is three miles off el pueblo está a tres millas. **3** (reduced in price) menos: 70% off! ¡70% menos! **4** (disconnected, not working) diferentes traducciones: turn the light off apaga la luz; she turned the tap off cerró el grifo. **7** (free, on holiday) libre: can I have the afternoon off? ¿puedo tomarme la tarde libre? ‖LOC‖ off and on / on and off de vez en cuando, a ratos. ‖ right off / straight off acto seguido.

▸ adj **1** (event) cancelado,-a, suspendido,-a: the wedding's off la boda se ha suspendido. **2** (not turned on - gas, water) cerrado,-a; (- electricity) apagado,-a. ‖COMP‖ off season temporada baja.

offence [ə'fens] n **1** JUR delito, infracción f: a traffic offence una infracción de tráfico. **2** (insult) ofensa. ‖LOC‖ to take offence at sth ofenderse por algo, sentirse ofendido,-a por algo.

offend [ə'fend] vt **1** (insult, hurt) ofender: she'll be offended if we don't go se ofenderá si no vamos.
▸ vi **1** fml (do wrong to) atentar (against, a). **2** JUR fml (commit crime) cometer un delito.

offender [ə'fendəʳ] n **1** JUR (gen) infractor,-ra; (criminal) delincuente mf. **2** (culprit) culpable mf.

offensive [ə'fensɪv] adj **1** (insulting) ofensivo,-a, insultante. **2** (disgusting - gen) repugnante; (- smell) desagradable. **3** (attacking) ofensivo,-a.
▸ n MIL ofensiva.

offer ['ɒfəʳ] vt **1** (gen) ofrecer: she offered us a coffee nos ofreció un café. **2** (show willingness) ofrecerse (to, para): he offered me a lift to the airport se ofreció para llevarme al aeropuerto. **3** (propose) proponer, sugerir.
▸ n **1** (gen) oferta, ofrecimiento; (proposal) propuesta. **2** COMM oferta. ‖LOC‖ to be on offer **1** (at reduced price) estar de oferta. **2** (available) disponible.

office ['ɒfɪs] n **1** (room) despacho, oficina; (building) oficina; (staff) oficina. **2** GB ministerio: the Foreign Office el Ministerio de Asuntos Exteriores. **3** (post, position) cargo. ‖LOC‖ to hold office ocupar un cargo. ‖COMP‖ office block edificio de oficinas. ‖ office boy recadero. ‖ office junior auxiliar mf de oficina. ‖ office worker oficinista mf.

officer ['ɒfɪsəʳ] n **1** MIL oficial mf. **2** (police officer) agente mf. **3** (in government) funcionario,-a. **4** (of club, society) directivo,-a.

official [ə'fɪʃəl] adj (gen) oficial.
▸ n funcionario,-a, oficial mf.

❎ Official no significa 'oficial (militar)', que se traduce por **officer**.

officially [ə'fɪʃ°lɪ] *adv* oficialmente.

officious [ə'fɪʃəs] *adj (too eager)* oficioso,-a; *(interfering)* entrometido,-a.

⊠ Officious no significa 'oficioso (no oficial', que se traduce por unofficial.

off-licence ['ɒflaɪs°ns] *n* GB tienda de bebidas alcohólicas.

offshoot ['ɒfʃuːt] *n* BOT retoño, vástago.

offshore [ɒf'ʃɔːʳ] *adj* **1** *(at sea)* a poca distancia de la costa. **2** *(breeze)* terral, de tierra. **3** *(overseas)* en el extranjero.
▶ *adv* mar adentro.

offside [ɒf'saɪd] *adj* **1** SP fuera de juego. **2** GB *(part of vehicle)* del lado del conductor.
▶ *adv* SP en fuera de juego.
▶ *n* GB *(of vehicle)* lado del conductor.

offspring ['ɔːfsprɪŋ] *n* **1** *fml (child)* descendiente *mf*; *(children)* descendencia, prole *f*. **2** *(animal - one)* cría; *(- several)* crías *fpl*.
① *pl* offspring.

off-the-record [ɒfðə'rekɔːd] *adj* extraoficial, confidencial.

often ['ɒf°n, 'ɒft°n] *adv (frequently)* a menudo, con frecuencia: *we often go to the theatre* vamos al teatro a menudo.

oh [əʊ] *interj* ¡oh!, ¡ay!, ¡vaya!: *oh, really?* ¿de veras?; *oh, look!* ¡eh, mira!

ohm [əʊm] *n* ohmio, ohm *m*.

oil [ɔɪl] *n* **1** *(gen)* aceite *m*: *sunflower oil* aceite de girasol. **2** *(petroleum)* petróleo: *crude oil* crudo. **3** ART *(painting)* óleo, pintura al óleo.
▶ *vt* engrasar, lubricar, lubrificar.
▶ *n pl* oils *(paints)* óleo: *she paints in oils* pinta al óleo. COMP oil painting cuadro al óleo, óleo. ▌oil rig plataforma petrolífera. ▌oil slick marea negra. ▌oil tanker petrolero. ▌oil well pozo petrolífero.

oilcan ['ɔɪlkæn] *n* aceitera.

oilcloth ['ɔɪlklɒθ] *n* hule *m*.

oilfield ['ɔɪlfiːld] *n* yacimiento petrolífero.

oily ['ɔɪlɪ] *adj* **1** *(food)* aceitoso,-a, grasiento,-a; *(skin, hair)* graso,-a. **2** *pej (manner)* empalagoso,-a.
① *comp* oilier, *superl* oiliest.

ointment ['ɔɪntmənt] *n* ungüento, pomada.

okay [əʊ'keɪ] *interj* ¡vale!, ¡de acuerdo!
▶ *adj* correcto,-a, bien: *are you okay?* ¿estás bien?
▶ *adv* bien, bastante bien: *he's doing okay at school* va bien en el colegio.
▶ *n* visto bueno, aprobación *f*.

old [əʊld] *adj* **1** *(gen)* viejo,-a: *an old man* un anciano, un hombre mayor; *the old part of the city* el casco antiguo de la ciudad; *he's an old friend* es un viejo amigo. **2** *(former)* antiguo,-a: *in my old job* en mi antiguo trabajo. LOC how old are you? ¿cuántos años tienes?, ¿qué edad tienes? ▌to be... years old tener... años. COMP old age vejez *f*. ▌the Old World el viejo mundo.
▶ *n* the old las personas *fpl* mayores, los ancianos *mpl*.

older ['əʊldəʳ] *adj* **1** *(comparative)* → old. **2** *(elder)* mayor.

old-fashioned [əʊld'fæʃ°nd] *adj (outdated - gen)* anticuado,-a, pasado,-a de moda; *(- person)* chapado,-a a la antigua.

olfactory ['ɒlfækt°rɪ] *adj* olfativo,-a, olfatorio,-a. COMP olfactory epithelium epitelio olfativo. ▌olfactory nerve nervio olfativo.

oligarchy ['ɒlɪgɑːkɪ] *n* oligarquía.
① *pl* oligarchies.

olive ['ɒlɪv] *n* **1** *(tree, wood)* olivo. **2** *(fruit)* aceituna, oliva. **3** *(colour)* verde *m* oliva. COMP olive grove olivar. ▌olive oil aceite *m* de oliva. ▌olive tree olivo.
▶ *adj (paint)* color aceituna; *(skin)* aceitunado,-a.

Olympiad [ə'lɪmpɪæd] *n* Olimpíada, Olimpiada.

Olympic [ə'lɪmpɪk] *adj* olímpico,-a.
▶ *n pl* the Olympics los Juegos Olímpicos, la Olimpíada *f sing*. COMP Olympic Games Juegos *mpl* Olímpicos.

omega ['əʊmɪgə] *n* omega.

omelette ['ɒmlət] *n* tortilla. COMP plain omelette tortilla francesa.

omit [əʊ'mɪt] *vt* **1** *(not include, leave out)* omitir, suprimir; *(forget to include)* olvi-

O

dar incluir. **2** *(fail to do)* omitir, dejar de; *(forget)* olvidarse.
ⓘ *pt & pp* omitted, *ger* omitting.

omnivore [ˈɒmnɪvɔːʳ] *n* omnívoro.

omnivorous [ɒmˈnɪvərəs] *adj* ZOOL *fml* omnívoro,-a.

on [ɒn] *prep* **1** *(covering or touching)* sobre, encima de, en: *it's on the table* está encima de la mesa. **2** *(supported by, hanging from)* en: *she put the picture on the wall* colgó el cuadro en la pared. **3** *(to, towards)* a, hacia: *on the right/left* a la derecha/izquierda. **4** *(at the edge of)* en: *a village on the coast* un pueblo de la costa. **5** *(days, dates, times)* no se traduce: *on Saturday* el sábado. **6** *(at the time of, just after)* al: *on arriving* al llegar. **7** *(as means of transport)* a, en: *on foot* a pie; *on the train* en el tren. **8** *(regarding, about)* sobre, de: *a book on art* un libro de arte. **9** *(in possession of)* con: *have you got any money on you?* ¿llevas dinero?
► *adv* **1** *(not stopping)* sin parar: *she kept on talking* siguió hablando. **2** *(movement forward)* diferentes traducciones: *walk on until you get to the church* sigue hasta que llegues a la iglesia; *it's time we were moving on* es hora de que nos vayamos. **3** *(clothes - being worn)* puesto,-a: *she had a cap on* llevaba puesta una gorra. **4** *(working)* diferentes traducciones: *who left the TV on?* ¿quién dejó la TV encendida?; *don't leave the tap on!* ¡no dejes el grifo abierto! **5** *(happening)* diferentes traducciones: *what time is the film on?* ¿a qué hora ponen la película?; *have we got anything on this weekend?* ¿tenemos plan para este fin de semana? [LOC] **and so on** y así sucesivamente. **from that day on** a partir de aquel día.
► *adj* **1** *(in use)* diferentes traducciones: *is the heating on?* ¿está puesta la calefacción?; *all the lights were on* todas las luces estaban encendidas. **2** *(happening)* diferentes traducciones: *the strike's on* la huelga sigue convocada; *is the party still on?* ¿se hace la fiesta?; *the match is on after all* después de todo, el partido se celebra. **3** *(performing)* diferentes traducciones: *you're on next!* ¡sales tú el próximo!; *they're bringing the sub on* hacen salir a jugar al suplente. [LOC] **it's not on** no hay derecho, eso no vale. **you're on!** ¡trato hecho!

once [wʌns] *adv* **1** *(one time)* una vez: *once a week* una vez por semana. **2** *(formerly)* antes, en otro tiempo: *I was a cook once* antes era cocinero. [LOC] **at once 1** *(at the same time)* a la vez. **2** *(immediately)* en seguida, inmediatamente, ahora mismo. **once again** otra vez. **once and for all** de una vez para siempre, de una vez por todas. **once in a while** de vez en cuando. **once more** una vez más. **once upon a time** érase una vez.
► *conj* una vez que, en cuanto: *once everyone gets here, we can start* una vez que lleguen todos, podemos empezar.
► *n* vez *f*: *just this once* solo esta vez.

oncoming [ˈɒnkʌmɪŋ] *adj* **1** *(traffic)* que viene en dirección contraria. **2** *(event, season)* venidero,-a, futuro,-a.

one [wʌn] *adj* **1** *(stating number)* un, una: *I've got one brother* tengo un hermano. **2** *(unspecified, a certain)* un, una, algún, -una: *one day in January* un día de enero. **3** *(only, single)* único,-a: *it's my one chance* es mi única oportunidad. **4** *(same)* mismo, -a: *in one direction* en la misma dirección.
► *pron* **1** *(thing)* uno,-a: *a red one* uno,-a rojo,-a; *this one* éste,-a. **2** *(person)* él, la: *he's the one who I was telling you about* es él de quien te estaba hablando. **3** *(any person, you)* uno, una: *one can't think of everything* uno no puede pensar en todo. [LOC] **one after another** uno,-a detrás de otro,-a. **one and only** el uno al otro. **one at a time** de uno en uno. **one by one** de uno,-a en uno,-a.
► *n (number)* uno: *my son is one today* mi hijo cumple un año hoy.

oneself [wʌnˈself] *pron* **1** *(reflexive)* se; *(emphatic)* uno,-a mismo,-a; *(after prep)* sí mismo,-a: *to wash oneself* lavarse. **2** *(alone)* solo,-a: *one can't do everything oneself* uno no puede hacerlo todo solo. [LOC] **(all) by oneself** solo,-a. **to oneself** para sí, para sí solo,-a.

one-way [ˈwʌnweɪ] *adj* **1** *(street)* de sentido único, de dirección única. **2** *(ticket)* de ida.

onion [ˈʌnɪən] *n* cebolla.

online [ˈɒnlaɪn] *adj* COMPUT en línea.
► *adv* COMPUT en línea.

onlooker ['ɒnlʊkə^r] *n* espectador,-ra, curioso,-a.

only ['əʊnlɪ] *adj (sole)* único,-a: *the only problem is that...* el único problema es que... **COMP** **only child** hijo,-a único,-a.
▶ *adv* **1** *(just, merely)* solo, solamente: *he's only a child* solo es un niño. **2** *(exclusively)* solo, solamente, únicamente: *only my mother knows* mi madre es la única que lo sabe. **LOC** **not only... but also** no solamente... sino también. **only just 1** *(a moment before)* acabar de. **2** *(almost not, scarcely)* por poco. **only too...** muy...
▶ *conj* pero: *it's like yoghurt, only better* es como el yogur, pero mejor.

onshore [ɒn'ʃɔː^r] *adj (on land)* en tierra.
▶ *adv (towards land)* tierra adentro.

onto ['ɒntʊ] *prep* **1** *(movement)* a, en: *it fell onto the floor* cayó al suelo. **2** *(new subject)* a: *let's move onto a different subject* cambiemos de tema.

onwards ['ɒnwədz] *adv* GB adelante, hacia adelante: *from now onwards* de ahora en adelante.

ooze¹ [uːz] *vi* rezumar.
▶ *vt* **1** rezumar. **2** *fig* rebosar.

ooze² [uːz] *n* cieno, lodo.

opacity [əʊ'pæsɪtɪ] *n* **1** *(non-transparency)* opacidad *f*. **2** *(obscurity)* oscuridad *f*.

opal ['əʊp^əl] *n* ópalo.

opaque [əʊ'peɪk] *adj* **1** *(not transparent)* opaco,-a. **2** *(difficult to understand, obscure)* obscuro,-a, oscuro,-a, poco claro,-a.

open ['əʊp^ən] *adj* **1** *(gen)* abierto,-a; *I can't keep my eyes open* no puedo mantener los ojos abiertos. **2** *(not covered)* descubierto,-a: *an open car* un coche descapotable. **COMP** **open day** jornada de puertas abiertas. **open letter** carta abierta. **open season** temporada de caza.
▶ *n* SP *(competition)* open *m*.
▶ *vt* abrir: *open your mouth* abre la boca. **LOC** **to open fire** abrir fuego (on/at, contra).
▶ *vi* **1** *(gen)* abrir, abrirse: *the door opened* la puerta se abrió. **2** *(spread out, unfold)* abrirse: *the roses are opening* las rosas se están abriendo. **3** *(start - conference, play, book)* comenzar, empezar;

(film) estrenarse. **4** *(begin business)* abrir.
▶ *adj* **open to** *(susceptible)* susceptible a, expuesto,-a a; *(receptive)* abierto,-a a.
▶ *n* **the open** *(the outdoors, open air)* campo, aire *m* libre.
♦ **to open into / open onto** *vt insep* dar a: *the back door opens onto the patio* la puerta trasera da al patio.

open-air ['əʊp^əneə^r] *adj* al aire libre.

opener ['əʊp^ənə^r] *n* abridor *m*.

opening ['əʊp^ənɪŋ] *n* **1** *(ceremony - gen)* inauguración *f*, comienzo. **2** *(first night)* estreno. **3** *(process of opening, unfolding)* apertura. **4** *(hole)* abertura; *(space)* hueco; *(gap)* brecha; *(clearing)* claro. **5** *(chance)* oportunidad *f* (for, para). **6** *(vacancy)* vacante *f* (for, para). **COMP** **opening hours** horario de apertura. **opening night** noche *f* de estreno.
▶ *adj (initial)* inicial.

openly ['əʊp^ənlɪ] *adv (not secretly)* abiertamente; *(publicly)* públicamente, en público.

open-minded [əʊp^ən'maɪndɪd] *adj* abierto,-a, de actitud abierta.

openness ['əʊp^ənnəs] *n (frankness)* franqueza; *(receptiveness)* actitud *f* abierta.

opera ['ɒp^ərə] *n* ópera.

operate ['ɒpəreɪt] *vt* **1** *(machine, etc)* hacer funcionar, manejar,. **2** *(manage, run - business)* dirigir, llevar.
▶ *vi* **1** *(function - machine, etc)* funcionar. **2** *(carry on trade)* operar; *(work)* trabajar. **3** MED operar (on, a), intervenir (on, a).

operating ['ɒpəreɪtɪŋ] *adj* COMM *(losses, costs)* de explotación. **COMP** **operating room** US quirófano. **operating system** COMPUT sistema *m* operativo. **operating theatre** GB quirófano.

operation [ɒpə'reɪʃ^ən] *n* **1** MED operación *f*, intervención *f*. **2** *(of machine - gen)* funcionamiento; *(- by person)* manejo; *(of system)* uso. **3** *(activity)* operación *f*; *(planned campaign)* campaña. **4** MIL operación *f*. **5** MATH operación *f*.

operator ['ɒpəreɪtə^r] *n* **1** *(of equipment, machine)* operario,-a. **2** *(of switchboard)* operador,-ra, telefonista *mf*.

O

ophthalmologist [ɒfθæl'mɒlədʒɪst] *n* oftalmólogo,-a, oculista *mf*.

opinion [ə'pɪnɪən] *n* **1** *(belief)* opinión *f*, parecer *m*. **2** *(evaluation, estimation)* opinión *f*, concepto. LOC **in my opinion** en mi opinión, a mi juicio. COMP **opinion poll** encuesta.

opium ['əupɪəm] *n* opio.

opponent [ə'pəunənt] *n* adversario,-a, oponente *mf*.

opportunity [ɒpə'tjuːnɪtɪ] *n* **1** *(gen)* oportunidad *f*, ocasión *f*. **2** *(prospect)* perspectiva.
ⓘ *pl* opportunities.

oppose [ə'pəuz] *vt* oponerse a.

opposite ['ɒpəzɪt] *adj* **1** *(facing)* de enfrente: *she lives on the opposite side of the road* vive al otro lado de la calle. **2** *(contrary, different)* opuesto,-a, contrario,-a.
▶ *prep* enfrente de, frente a: *the building opposite the cinema* el edificio enfrente del cine.
▶ *adv* enfrente: *the family who live opposite* la familia que vive enfrente.
▶ *n* lo contrario, lo opuesto: *the opposite of big is small* lo contrario a grande es pequeño.

opposition [ɒpə'zɪʃ⁰n] *n* **1** *(resistance)* oposición *f*, resistencia. **2** *(rivals - in sport)* adversarios *mpl*; *(- in business)* competencia.
▶ *n* the Opposition POL la oposición *f*.

oppress [ə'pres] *vt* oprimir.

oppression [ə'preʃ⁰n] *n* opresión *f*.

oppressor [ə'presə^r] *n* opresor,-ra.

opt [ɒpt] *vi* optar (for, por).
◆ **to opt out** *vi* *(person)* abandonar, dejar de participar.

optic ['ɒptɪk] *adj* óptico,-a.

optical ['ɒptɪk⁰l] *adj* óptico,-a.

optician [ɒp'tɪʃ⁰n] *n* óptico,-a, oculista *mf*. COMP **optician's (shop)** óptica.

optics ['ɒptɪks] *n* óptica.

optimism ['ɒptɪmɪz⁰m] *n* optimismo.

optimist ['ɒptɪmɪst] *n* optimista *mf*.

optimistic [ɒptɪ'mɪstɪk] *adj* optimista.

option ['ɒpʃ⁰n] *n* **1** *(choice)* opción *f*, posibilidad *f*. **2** EDUC *(optional subject)* asignatura optativa.

optional ['ɒpʃ⁰nəl] *adj* opcional.

or [ɔː^r] *conj* **1** *(alternative - gen)* o; *(- before word beginning with o or ho)* u: *tea or coffee* té o café. **2** *(with negative)* ni: *she can't sing or dance* no sabe cantar ni bailar. **3** *(otherwise)* o: *come on, or we'll be late!* ¡date prisa o llegaremos tarde! LOC **or so** más o menos.

oral ['ɔːr⁰l] *adj* **1** *(spoken - gen)* oral; *(tradition)* transmitido,-a oralmente. **2** MED *(contraceptive)* oral; *(hygiene)* bucal.
▶ *n* *(exam)* examen *m* oral.

orange ['ɒrɪndʒ] *n* **1** *(fruit)* naranja. **2** *(colour)* naranja *m*. COMP **orange blossom** azahar *m*. ▌ **orange juice** zumo de naranja. ▌ **orange tree** naranjo.
▶ *adj* naranja, de color naranja.

orang-utan [ɔː'ræŋuː'tæn] *n* orangután *m*.

orbicularis [ɔːbɪkə'lærɪs] *adj* **1** ANAT orbicular. **2** *fml lit (sphere)* esfera; *(sun)* el sol *m*; *(moon)* la luna.

orbit ['ɔːbɪt] *n* **1** *(of satellite)* órbita. **2** *(area of influence)* órbita, esfera de influencia, ámbito. LOC **to go into orbit** entrar en órbita.
▶ *vt* girar alrededor de, orbitar alrededor de.

orbital ['ɔːbɪt⁰l] *adj* orbital, orbitario,-a. COMP **orbital road** carretera de circunvalación.

orchard ['ɔːtʃəd] *n* huerto.

orchestra ['ɔːkɪstrə] *n* orquesta.

orchid ['ɔːkɪd] *n* BOT orquídea.

order ['ɔːdə^r] *n* **1** *(gen)* orden *m*: *in alphabetical/chronological order* por orden alfabético/cronológico. *she put her affairs in order* puso sus asuntos en orden. **2** *(fitness for use)* condiciones *fpl*, estado: *the car's in good working order* el coche funciona bien. **3** *(obedience, authority, discipline)* orden *m*, disciplina. **4** *(rules, procedures, etc)* orden *m*, procedimiento. **5** *(command)* orden *f*. **6** COMM *(request, goods)* pedido: *the waiter took our order* el camarero tomó nota de lo que queríamos. **7** *(group, society)* orden *f*; *(badge, sign worn)* condecoración *f*, orden *f*: *the monastic orders* las órdenes monásticas. LOC **in order that** para que, a fin de que. ▌ **in order to** para, a fin de. ▌ **out of order** *(not working)* que

no funciona. COMP **order book** libro de pedidos. **order form** hoja de pedido.
▶ vt **1** *(command)* ordenar, mandar. **2** *(ask for)* pedir, encargar: *I've ordered a cake for his birthday* he encargado un pastel para su cumpleaños. **3** *(arrange, put in order, organize)* ordenar, poner en orden.
▶ vi *(request to bring, ask for)* pedir.

ordinal ['ɔ:dɪnᵊl] *adj* ordinal.
▶ n ordinal m.

ordinarily ['ɔ:dənᵊrɪlɪ] *adv* generalmente.

ordinary ['ɔ:dɪnᵊrɪ] *adj (usual, normal)* normal, usual, habitual; *(average)* normal, común. COMP **ordinary seaman** marinero.

☒ Ordinary no significa 'ordinario (vulgar)', que se traduce por **vulgar**.

ordinate ['ɔ:dɪnət] *n* MATH ordenada.

ore [ɔ:ʳ] *n* mineral *m*, mena.

☒ Ore no significa 'oro', que se traduce por **gold**.

oregano [ɒrɪ'gɑ:nəʊ] *n* orégano.

organ ['ɔ:gᵊn] *n* órgano.

organic [ɔ:'gænɪk] *adj* **1** *(living)* orgánico,-a. **2** *(without chemicals)* biológico,-a, ecológico,-a.

organism ['ɔ:gənɪzᵊm] *n* organismo.

organization [ɔ:gənaɪ'zeɪʃᵊn] *n* organización *f*.

organize ['ɔ:gənaɪz] *vt* organizar, ordenar.
▶ vi organizar.

organized ['ɔ:gənaɪzd] *adj (gen)* organizado,-a.

organizer ['ɔ:gənaɪzəʳ] *n* organizador, -ra.

orgy ['ɔ:dʒɪ] *n (wild party)* orgía.
ⓘ *pl* orgies.

Orient ['ɔ:rɪənt] *n* **the Orient** el oriente *m*.

oriental [ɔ:rɪ'entᵊl] *adj* oriental.
▶ n oriental *mf*.

orientate ['ɔ:rɪənteɪt] *vt* orientar.

orientation [ɔ:rɪən'teɪʃᵊn] *n* orientación *f*.

origin ['ɒrɪdʒɪn] *n* origen *m*.
▶ n *pl* **origins** origen *m sing*.

original [ə'rɪdʒɪnᵊl] *adj* original, originario,-a, primero,-a.
▶ n original *m*.

originally [ə'rɪdʒɪnəlɪ] *adv* **1** *(in the beginning)* originariamente, en un principio. **2** *(in a new way)* con originalidad.

originate [ə'rɪdʒɪneɪt] *vt (create)* originar, crear, dar lugar a.
▶ vi *(arise)* tener su origen (in, en), originarse (in, en), provenir (in, de).

ornament ['ɔ:nəmənt] *n (decoration)* ornamento, adorno; *(object)* adorno.

ornithology [ɔ:nɪ'θɒlədʒɪ] *n* ornitología.

orography [ɒ'rɒgrəfɪ] *n* orografía.

orphan ['ɔ:fᵊn] *n* huérfano,-a.
▶ vt dejar huérfano,-a. LOC **to be orphaned** quedar huérfano,-a.

orphanage ['ɔ:fᵊnɪdʒ] *n* orfanato.

orthodox ['ɔ:θədɒks] *adj* ortodoxo,-a.

orthography [ɔ:'θɒgrəfɪ] *n* ortografía.

orthopaedic [ɔ:θəʊ'pi:dɪk] *adj* MED ortopédico,-a.

osmosis [ɒz'məʊsɪs] *n* ósmosis *f*, osmosis *f*.

osseous ['ɒsɪəs] *adj* óseo,-a.

ostensible [ɒ'stensɪbᵊl] *adj (apparent)* aparente; *(alleged)* pretendido,-a, fingido,-a.

☒ Ostensible no significa 'ostensible', que se traduce por **obvious**.

O

ostrich ['ɒstrɪtʃ] *n* avestruz *m*.

other ['ʌðəʳ] *adj* **1** *(additional)* otro,-a: *I have one other idea* tengo otra idea. **2** *(different)* otro,-a: *people from other countries* gente de otros países. **3** *(second, remaining)* otro,-a: *it's on the other side of the street* está al otro lado de la calle. LOC **every other day** un día sí, otro no. **the other day** el otro día.
▶ pron otro,-a. LOC **one after the other** uno tras otro.
▶ prep **other than** *(except)* aparte de, salvo: *there was nobody other than the teacher* aparte del profesor, no había nadie.

otherwise ['ʌðəwaɪz] *adv* **1** *(differently)* de otra manera, de manera distinta: *she couldn't do otherwise* no podía obrar

de otra manera. **2** *(apart from that, in other respects)* aparte de eso, por lo demás.
► *conj (if not)* si no, de no ser así, de lo contrario.
► *adj* distinto,-a.

otitis [əʊˈtaɪtɪs] *n* otitis *f*.

otter [ˈɒtəʳ] *n* nutria.

ouch [aʊtʃ] *interj* ¡ay!

ought [ɔːt] *aux* ought to **1** *(moral obligation)* deber: *you ought to have helped them* debiste ayudarles. **2** *(recommendation)* deber, tener que. **3** *(expectation)* deber de: *they ought to be home by now* seguramente ya estarán en casa.

ounce [aʊns] *n* **1** *(weight)* onza. **2** *fam (small quantity)* pizca.

✎ La onza equivale a 28,35 gramos.

our [aʊəʳ] *adj* nuestro,-a: *our house* nuestra casa; *our children* nuestros hijos.

ours [aʊəz] *pron* (el) nuestro, (la) nuestra: *a friend of ours* un amigo nuestro.

ourselves [aʊəˈselvz] *pron* **1** *(reflexive)* nos: *we made ourselves comfortable* nos pusimos cómodos. **2** *(emphatic)* nosotros,-as mismos,-as: *we did it ourselves* lo hicimos nosotros mismos.

out [aʊt] *adv* **1** *(gen)* fuera, afuera: *could you wait out there?* ¿podrías esperar allí fuera?; *she ran out* salió corriendo. **2** *(expressing distance)* en: *they live out in the country* viven en el campo. **3** *(expressing removal)* diferentes traducciones: *I've had a tooth out* me han sacado una muela; *she got out a handkerchief* sacó un pañuelo. **4** *(available, existing)* diferentes traducciones: *the film comes out next month* la película se estrenará el mes que viene; *it's the best sandwich out* es el mejor bocadillo que hay. **5** *(protruding)* que se sale: *a nail sticking out* un clavo que sobresale. **6** *(clearly, loudly)* en voz alta: *he called out to me* me llamó en voz alta.
► *prep* out of **1** *(gen)* fuera de: *out of danger* fuera de peligro; *they are out of the cup* han quedado fuera de la copa. **2** *(from among)* de: *she got five out of ten in French* sacó (un) cinco sobre diez en francés. **3** *(without)* sin: *out of money* sin dinero. **6** *(using, made from)* de: *made out of wood* hecho,-a de madera.

outboard motor [aʊtbɔːˈdməʊtəʳ] *n* MAR motor *m* fueraborda, fueraborda *m*.

outbreak [ˈaʊtbreɪk] *n* **1** *(of violence, fighting)* brote *m*. **2** *(of disease)* brote *m*, epidemia; *(of spots)* erupción *f*.

outburst [ˈaʊtbɜːst] *n* **1** *(of emotion)* explosión *f*, arrebato *m*. **2** *(of activity)* explosión *f*.

outcast [ˈaʊtkɑːst] *n* marginado,-a.

outclass [aʊtˈklɑːs] *vt* superar.

outcome [ˈaʊtkʌm] *n* resultado.

outdated [aʊtˈdeɪtɪd] *adj* anticuado,-a.

outdoor [aʊtˈdɔːʳ] *adj (gen)* exterior.

outdoors [aʊtˈdɔːz] *adv* fuera, al aire libre.

outer [ˈaʊtəʳ] *adj* exterior, externo,-a.
COMP **outer space** espacio exterior. ‖ **outer suburbs** afueras *fpl*.

outgrow [aʊtˈgrəʊ] *vt (clothes, etc)* hacerse demasiado grande para: *he's outgrown his shoes* se le han quedado pequeños los zapatos.
ⓘ *pt* outgrew [aʊtˈgruː], *pp* outgrown [aʊtˈgrəʊn].

outing [ˈaʊtɪŋ] *n (trip)* salida, excursión *f*.

outlaw [ˈaʊtlɔː] *n* forajido,-a, proscrito,-a.
► *vt* prohibir, declarar ilegal.

outlet [ˈaʊtlet] *n* **1** *(opening - gen)* salida; *(for water)* desagüe *m*. **2** *fig (for emotions)* válvula de escape. **3** COMM *(shop)* punto de venta.

outline [ˈaʊtlaɪn] *n* **1** *(outer edge)* contorno; *(shape)* perfil *m*. **2** *(draft)* bosquejo, esquema *m*; *(summary)* resumen *m*.
► *vt* **1** *(draw lines of)* perfilar; *(sketch)* bosquejar. **2** *(summarize)* resumir.

outnumber [aʊtˈnʌmbəʳ] *vt* superar en número, ser más que.

out-of-date [aʊtəvˈdeɪt] *adj (fashion)* pasado,-a de moda; *(technology)* desfasado,-a, obsoleto,-a; *(food, ticket)* caducado,-a.

output [ˈaʊtpʊt] *n* **1** *(gen)* producción *f*; *(of machine)* rendimiento. **2** COMPUT salida.

outrageous [aʊtˈreɪdʒəs] *adj* **1** *(shocking - gen)* escandaloso,-a; *(crime)* atroz; *(language)* injurioso,-a. **2** *(unconventional)* extravagante.

outside [(n) aʊt'saɪd; (prep) 'aʊtsaɪd] n **1** (exterior part) exterior m, parte f exterior: from the outside desde fuera. **2** GB (when driving) derecha.

▶ prep **1** (gen) fuera de. **2** (beyond) más allá de, fuera de: outside working hours fuera del horario laboral. **3** (other than) aparte de, fuera de.

▶ adv (gen) fuera, afuera.

▶ adj **1** (exterior) exterior. **2** (external) externo,-a. **3** (remote) remoto,-a. LOC at the outside como máximo, como mucho.

outsider [aʊt'saɪdəʳ] n **1** (person- stranger) extraño,-a, forastero,-a, desconocido,-a. **2** (unlikely winner - athlete, etc) competidor,-ra con pocas probabilidades de ganar.

outskirts ['aʊtskɜːts] n pl afueras fpl, alrededores mpl, extrarradio m sing.

outstanding [aʊt'stændɪŋ] adj **1** (excellent) destacado,-a, notable, sobresaliente; (exceptional) excepcional, extraordinario,-a, singular. **2** (gen) sin pagar, pendiente.

outstretched [aʊt'stretʃt] adj extendido,-a.

outward ['aʊtwəd] adj **1** (appearance) exterior; (sign) externo,-a, show. **2** (journey, flight) de ida.

outwards ['aʊtwədz] adv (gen) hacia fuera, hacia afuera; (attention, etc) hacia el exterior.

oval ['əʊvəl] adj oval, ovalado,-a.
▶ n óvalo.

ovary ['əʊvərɪ] n ovario.
ⓘ pl ovaries.

ovation [əʊ'veɪʃən] n ovación f.

oven ['ʌvən] n horno.

over ['əʊvəʳ] adv **1** (down) diferentes traducciones: the boy fell over el niño se cayó; I knocked the glass over tiré la copa (de un golpe). **2** (from one side to another) diferentes traducciones: turn over the page dar la vuelta a la página; he bent over se inclinó. **3** (across) diferentes traducciones: let's cross over crucemos al otro lado; over here/there aquí/allí. **5** (too much) de más: it's 50 grams over pesa 50 gramos de más. LOC over here aquí. ▮ over there allí.

▶ prep **1** (gen) encima de: a sign over the door un letrero encima de la puerta; he wore a jacket over his sweater llevaba una americana encima del jersey. **2** (across); (on the other side of) al otro lado de: he lives over the border vive al otro lado de la frontera. **3** (during) durante: over the past 25 years durante los últimos 25 años. **4** (throughout) por: we travelled all over Italy viajamos por toda Italia. **5** (more than) más de: she's over thirty tiene más de treinta años. **6** (about) por: an argument over money una discusión por dinero. LOC all over en todas partes. ▮ over and above además de.

▶ adj (ended) acabado,-a, terminado, -a: the game is over la partida ha acabado.

overact [əʊvər'ækt] vi exagerar, sobreactuar.

overall [(adj) 'əʊvərɔːl; (adv) əʊvər'ɔːl] adj (general) global, total.

▶ adv (generally, on the whole) en conjunto, por lo general.

▶ n GB (work coat) guardapolvo, bata.

▶ n pl overalls mono m sing.

overambitious [əʊvəræm'bɪʃəs] adj demasiado ambicioso,-a.

overboard ['əʊvəbɔːd] adv por la borda. LOC to fall overboard caer al agua. ▮ to go overboard pasarse.

overbooking [əʊvə'bʊkɪŋ] n sobrecontratación f.

overcame [əʊvə'keɪm] pt → overcome.

overcoat ['əʊvəkəʊt] n abrigo.

overcome [əʊvə'kʌm] vt **1** (defeat) vencer. **2** (overwhelm) agobiar, abrumar, invadir, apoderarse de, vencer: he was overcome by sleep el sueño se apoderó de él.
ⓘ pt overcame [əʊvə'keɪm], pp overcome [əʊvə'kʌm].

overdose ['əʊvədəʊs] n sobredosis f.

overflow [(n) 'əʊvəfləʊ; (vb) əʊvə'fləʊ] n **1** (of river, etc) desbordamiento. **2** (pipe) tubo de desagüe; (hole) rebosadero.

▶ vi **1** (river) desbordarse; (bath, etc) rebosar. **2** (people) rebosar. **3** (be full of) rebosar (with, de). LOC to be full to overflowing estar lleno,-a hasta el borde.

▶ vt (liquid) salirse de.

overhead [(adj) 'əʊvəhed; (adv) əʊvə'hed] adj (cable) aéreo,-a; (railway) elevado,-a.
► adv arriba, por encima de la cabeza.

overhear [əʊvə'hɪəʳ] vt oír por casualidad.
ⓘ pt & pp overheard [əʊvə'hɜːd].

overheard [əʊvə'hɜːd] pt & pp → overhear.

overland [(adj) 'əʊvəlænd; (adv) əʊvə'lænd] adj por tierra.
► adv por tierra.

overlap [əʊvə'læp] vi superponerse, solaparse.
ⓘ pt & pp overlapped, ger overlapping.
► n superposición f, coincidencia.

overlook [əʊvə'lʊk] vt 1 (not notice) pasar por alto;. 2 (excuse) disculpar. 3 (have a view of) tener vistas a.

overnight [əʊvə'naɪt] adv 1 (during the night) durante la noche; (at night) por la noche: it rained overnight llovió durante la noche. 2 fam (suddenly) de la noche a la mañana.
► adj 1 (during the night) de la noche; (for the night) de una noche. 2 fam (sudden) repentino,-a.

oversaw [əʊvə'sɔː] pt → oversee.

overseas [əʊvə'siːz] adj (person) extranjero,-a; (trade) exterior.
► adv en ultramar.

oversee [əʊvə'siː] vt supervisar.
ⓘ pt oversaw [əʊvə'sɔː], pp overseen [əʊvə'siːn].

overseen [əʊvə'siːn] pp → oversee.

oversized [əʊvə'saɪzd] adj demasiado grande.

oversleep [əʊvə'sliːp] vi quedarse dormido,-a, no despertarse a tiempo.
ⓘ pt & pp overslept [əʊvə'slept].

overslept [əʊvə'slept] pt & pp → oversleep.

overtake [əʊvə'teɪk] vt 1 GB (a vehicle) adelantar, pasar, AM rebasar: we overtook a sports car adelantamos un coche deportivo. 2 (surpass) superar. 3 (happen suddenly to) adelantarse a; (surprise) sorprender.
ⓘ pt overtook [əʊvə'teɪkən], pp overtaken [əʊvə'tʊk].

overtaken [əʊvə'teɪkən] pp → overtake.

overtime ['əʊvətaɪm] n (extra work, extra hours) horas fpl extras.

overtook [əʊvə'tʊk] pt → overtake.

overturn [əʊvə'tɜːn] vt 1 (vehicle) volcar; (boat) hacer zozobrar; (furniture) dar la vuelta a. 2 (government) derrocar. 3 fig (ruling) anular.
► vi (vehicle) volcar; (boat) zozobrar.

overview ['əʊvəvjuː] n perspectiva general.

overweight [əʊvə'weɪt] adj (thing) demasiado pesado,-a; (person) demasiado gordo,-a.

overwhelm [əʊvə'welm] vt 1 (physically - defeat) arrollar, aplastar. 2 fig (emotionally) abrumar.

overwhelming [əʊvə'welmɪŋ] adj (defeat, victory) aplastante, arrollador,-ra; (generosity) abrumador,-ra.

ovine ['əʊvɪn] adj ovino,-a.

oviparous [əʊ'vɪpərəs] adj ovíparo,-a.

ovulate ['ɒvjəleɪt] vi ovular.

ovulation [ɒvjə'leɪʃən] n ovulación f.

ovule ['ɒvjuːl] n óvulo.

owe [əʊ] vt (gen) deber: you owe me 10 pounds me debes 10 libras.

owing ['əʊɪŋ] adj (due) debido,-a.
► prep owing to debido a, a causa de.

owl [aʊl] n búho, lechuza.

own [əʊn] adj propio,-a: they grow their own vegetables cultivan sus propios verduras.
► pron propio,-a: would you like to borrow mine or do you have your own? ¿quieres que te deje el mío o ya tienes uno propio? LOC on one's own 1 (alone) solo,-a. 2 (without help) uno,-a mismo,-a.
► vt (possess) poseer, ser dueño,-a de.
◆ to own up vi confesarlo.

owner ['əʊnəʳ] n dueño,-a, propietario,-a.

ox [ɒks] n buey m.
ⓘ pl oxen [ɒks'ən].

oxen ['ɒksən] npl → ox.

oxidation [ɒksɪ'deɪʃən] n oxidación f.

oxide ['ɒksaɪd] n óxido.

oxygen ['ɒksɪdʒən] n oxígeno.

oyster ['ɔɪstəʳ] n (shellfish) ostra.

ozone ['əʊzəʊn] n ozono. COMP ozone layer capa de ozono.

ozone-friendly ['əʊzəʊnfrendlɪ] adj que no daña la capa de ozono.

P

P, p [piː] *n (the letter)* P, p *f*.

pace [peɪs] *n* **1** *(rate, speed)* marcha, ritmo, velocidad *f*. **2** *(step)* paso.
▸ *vt* **1** *(room, floor)* ir de un lado a otro de. **2** *(set speed for)* marcar el ritmo a.

pacemaker ['peɪsmeɪkəʳ] *n* **1** SP liebre *f*. **2** MED marcapasos *m*.

pachyderm ['pækɪdɜːm] *n* paquidermo.

pacifism ['pæsɪfɪzᵊm] *n* pacifismo.

pacifist ['pæsɪfɪst] *n* pacifista *mf*.

pacify ['pæsɪfaɪ] *vt* **1** *(person)* calmar, tranquilizar. **2** *(country)* pacificar.
ⓘ *pt & pp* pacified, *ger* pacifying.

pack [pæk] *n* **1** *(parcel)* paquete *m*; *(bundle)* fardo, bulto; *(rucksack)* mochila. **2** US *(packet - gen)* paquete *m*; *(of cigarettes)* paquete *m*, cajetilla. **3** GB *(of cards)* baraja. **4** *pej (of thieves)* banda, partida. **5** *(of lies)* sarta. **6** *(of wolves, dogs)* manada; *(of hounds)* jauría.
▸ *vt* **1** *(goods)* empaquetar, envasar. **2** *(suitcase)* hacer; *(clothes, etc)* poner, meter. **3** *(fill)* atestar, abarrotar, llenar: *the disco was packed with young people* la discoteca estaba abarrotada de jóvenes. **4** *(press down)* apretar.
▸ *vi* **1** *(suitcase, etc)* hacer las maletas, hacer el equipaje: *he hasn't packed yet* aún no ha hecho las maletas. **2** *(people)* apiñarse, apretarse, meterse.
◆ **to pack up** *vi* **1** *(stop, give up)* dejarlo. **2** *(machine)* estropearse; *(car)* averiarse.
▸ *vt sep (belongings - in case)* meter en la maleta; *(gather together)* recoger.

package ['pækɪdʒ] *n* **1** *(parcel)* paquete *m*. **2** *(proposals)* paquete *m*; *(agreement)* acuerdo. COMP **package holiday** viaje *m* organizado.
▸ *vt (goods)* empaquetar, envasar.

packaging ['pækɪdʒɪŋ] *n* embalaje *m*.

packed [pækt] *adj (with people)* lleno,-a, abarrotado,-a, repleto,-a; *(with facts, information, etc)* lleno,-a.

packet ['pækɪt] *n* **1** *(small box - gen)* paquete *m*, cajita; *(of cigarettes)* paquete *m*, cajetilla; *(envelope)* sobre *m*. **2** *fam (large amount of money)* dineral *m*.

packing ['pækɪŋ] *n (material)* embalaje *m*.

pact [pækt] *n* pacto.

pad [pæd] *n* **1** *(cushioning)* almohadilla, cojinete *m*. **2** *(inkpad)* tampón *m*. **3** *(of paper)* taco, bloc *m*. **4** *(of animal)* almohadilla. **5** *(platform)* plataforma. COMP **knee pad** rodillera. **sanitary pad** compresa.
▸ *vt (chair, etc)* acolchar, rellenar, guatear; *(garment)* poner hombreras a.
ⓘ *pt & pp* padded, *ger* padding.

paddle¹ ['pædᵊl] *n (oar)* pala, remo.
▸ *vt (boat, canoe)* remar con pala.
▸ *vi* remar con pala.

paddle² ['pædᵊl] *vi (walk or play in water)* mojarse los pies, chapotear.
▸ *n* chapoteo.

paddling pool ['pædᵊlɪŋpuːl] *n* piscina para niños, piscina infantil.

padlock ['pædlɒk] *n* candado.
▸ *vt* cerrar con candado.

padre [pɑːdreɪ] *n (priest)* padre *m*.

paediatrician [piːdⁱætrɪʃᵊn] *n* pediatra *mf*.

paedophile ['piːdəfaɪl] *n* pedófilo,-a.

pagan ['peɪgᵊn] *adj* pagano,-a.
▸ *n* pagano,-a.

page¹ [peɪdʒ] *n* **1** *(of book)* página; *(of newspaper)* plana, página. LOC **on the front page** en primera plana.

page² [peɪdʒ] *n* **1** *(boy servant, at wedding)* paje *m*; *(in hotel, club)* botones *m*. **2** HIST escudero.

pagoda [pə'gəʊdə] *n* pagoda.
paid [peɪd] *pp & pt* → **pay**.
► *adj (purchase, holiday)* pagado,-a; *(work)* remunerado,-a.
pail [peɪl] *n* cubo.
pain [peɪn] *n* **1** *(physical)* dolor *m*: *I've got a pain in my stomach* me duele el estómago. **2** *(mental suffering)* sufrimiento, dolor *m*. **3** *(annoying thing)* lata, fastidio; *(person)* pesado,-a, pelmazo. LOC **to be a pain in the neck** ser un,-a pesado,-a.
► *vt* doler, dar pena a, apenar.
► *n pl* **pains** *(effort)* esfuerzos *mpl*.

☒ Pain no significa 'pena (tristeza)', que se traduce por **grief**, **sorrow**.

painful ['peɪnfʊl] *adj (physically)* doloroso,-a; *(mentally)* angustioso,-a.
painkiller ['peɪnkɪlə'] *n* calmante *m*.
painless ['peɪnləs] *adj* **1** *(without pain)* indoloro,-a, sin dolor. **2** *(without distress)* sencillo,-a, sin complicaciones.
paint [peɪnt] *n* pintura: *a tin of paint* una lata de pintura. LOC **"Wet paint"** «Recién pintado».
► *vt (gen)* pintar: *we're going to paint the walls yellow* vamos a pintar las paredes de amarillo.
► *vi* pintar: *she paints in oils* pinta al óleo.
paintbrush ['peɪntbrʌʃ] *n* **1** *(for walls, etc)* brocha. **2** *(artist's)* pincel *m*.
painter ['peɪntə'] *n* **1** ART pintor,-ra. **2** *(decorator)* pintor,-ra de brocha gorda.
painting ['peɪntɪŋ] *n* **1** ART *(picture)* pintura, cuadro. **2** *(activity)* pintura.
pair [peə'] *n* **1** *(of shoes, socks, gloves, etc)* par *m*; *(of cards)* pareja: *a pair of brown eyes* dos ojos castaños. **2** *(of people, animals)* pareja. LOC **in pairs** de dos en dos. COMP **a pair of scissors** unas tijeras. ∎ **a pair of trousers** unos pantalones.
► *vt (people)* emparejar; *(animals)* aparear.
► *vi (animals)* aparearse.
pajamas [pə'dʒæməz] *n pl* US → **pyjamas**.
Pakistan [pɑːkɪ'stɑːn] *n* Pakistán *m*.
Pakistani [pɑːkɪ'stɑːnɪ] *adj* pakistaní.
► *n* pakistaní *mf*.
pal [pæl] *n fam* amigo,-a, colega *mf*.
palace ['pæləs] *n* palacio.

Palaeolithic [pælɪəʊ'lɪθɪk] *adj* paleolítico,-a.
palate ['pælət] *n (gen)* paladar *m*.
pale [peɪl] *adj (complexion, skin)* pálido,-a; *(colour)* claro,-a, pálido,-a; *(light)* débil. LOC **to turn pale** ponerse pálido,-a.
► *vi* palidecer.
Paleolithic [pælɪəʊ'lɪθɪk] *adj* US → **Palaelothic**.
Palestine ['pælɪstaɪn] *n* Palestina.
Palestinian [pælɪ'stɪnɪən] *adj* palestino,-a.
► *n* palestino,-a.
palette ['pælət] *n* paleta.
palfrey ['pɔːlfrɪ] *n* palafrén *m*.
palm¹ [pɑːm] *n* BOT *(tree)* palmera; *(leaf)* palma. COMP **palm tree** palmera.
palm² [pɑːm] *n* ANAT palma.
pamphlet ['pæmflət] *n* folleto.
pan [pæn] *n (saucepan)* cacerola, cazuela, cazo; *(cooking pot)* olla.
Panama ['pænəmə] *n* Panamá *m*.
Panamanian [pænə'meɪnɪən] *adj* panameño,-a.
► *n* panameño,-a.
pancake ['pænkeɪk] *n* tortita, crepe *f*.
pancreas ['pæŋkrɪəs] *n* páncreas *m*.
panda ['pændə] *n (oso)* panda *m*.
pane [peɪn] *n* cristal *m*, vidrio.
panel ['pænəl] *n* **1** *(of door, wall, car body, etc)* panel *m*; *(on ceiling)* artesón *m*. **2** *(of controls, instruments)* tablero. **3** *(group of people)* panel *m*; *(team)* equipo.
panic ['pænɪk] *n* pánico: *panic spread throughout the crowd* el pánico cundió entre la gente. LOC **to get into a panic** dejarse llevar por el pánico.
► *vt* infundir pánico a.
► *vi* entrarle el pánico a, aterrarse.
ⓘ *pt & pp* panicked, *ger* panicking.
panic-stricken ['pænɪkstrɪkⁿn] *adj* preso,-a de pánico, aterrorizado,-a.
panorama [pænə'rɑːmə] *n (view)* panorama *m*.
panoramic [pænə'ræmɪk] *adj* panorámico,-a.
pant [pænt] *vi* jadear, resoplar.
pantheon ['pænθɪən] *n* ARCH panteón *m*.
panther ['pænθə'] *n* pantera.

pantomime ['pæntəmaɪm] n 1 (mime) pantomima. 2 GB (play) representación musical navideña basada en cuentos de hadas.

⊕ Es una representación teatral cómica y musical que se hace por Navidades y que suele contar historias tradicionales como, por ejemplo, Aladdin (Aladino y la lámpara maravillosa), Puss in Boots (El gato con botas) o Cinderella (La Cenicienta).

pantry ['pæntrɪ] n despensa.
ⓘ pl pantries.

pants [pænts] n pl 1 GB (underpants - men's) calzoncillos mpl; (- women's) bragas fpl. 2 US (trousers) pantalón m, pantalones mpl.

papaya [pə'paɪə] n papaya.

paper ['peɪpər] n 1 (material) papel m: take a sheet of paper coge una hoja de papel. 2 (newspaper) periódico, diario. 3 (examination) examen m. 4 (essay, written work) trabajo (escrito); (for conference) ponencia. ⌐LOC⌐ on paper por escrito. ⌐COMP⌐ paper mill fábrica de papel. ‖ paper money papel m moneda. ‖ paper shop quiosco.
▸ vt empapelar.
▸ n pl papers (documents) documentos mpl.

☒ Paper no significa 'papel (en el teatro o el cine)', que se traduce por role, part.

paperclip ['peɪpəklɪp] n clip m.

paprika ['pæprɪkə] n pimentón m dulce.

Papua ['pæpjʊə] n Papúa. ⌐COMP⌐ Papua New Guinea Papúa Nueva Guinea.

Papuan ['pæpjʊən] adj papú,-úa.
▸ n papú,-úa.

parabola [pə'ræbələ] n MATH parábola.

parachute ['pærəʃuːt] n paracaídas m.
▸ vi saltar en paracaídas.

parade [pə'reɪd] n 1 (procession) desfile m: fashion parade desfile de modelos. 2 MIL desfile m.
▸ vt 1 hacer desfilar. 2 (flaunt - knowledge, wealth) alardear, hacer alarde de.
▸ vi 1 (gen) desfilar. 2 MIL pasar revista.

☒ Parade no significa 'parada (detención)', que se traduce por stop.

paradise ['pærədaɪs] n paraíso.

paradox ['pærədɒks] n paradoja.

paraffin ['pærəfɪn] n GB queroseno. ⌐COMP⌐ paraffin wax parafina.

paragraph ['pærəgrɑːf] n párrafo. ⌐COMP⌐ full stop, new paragraph punto y aparte.

Paraguay [pærə'gwaɪ] n Paraguay.

Paraguayan [pærə'gwaɪən] adj paraguayo,-a.
▸ n paraguayo,-a.

parallel ['pærəlel] adj 1 paralelo,-a (to/ with, a). 2 fig (similar) paralelo,-a (to/with, a), análogo,-a (to/with, a).
▸ n 1 MATH paralela. 2 GEOG paralelo. 3 (similarity) paralelo, paralelismo.

paralyse ['pærəlaɪz] vt (gen) paralizar.

paralysis [pə'ræləsɪs] n 1 MED parálisis f. 2 fig paralización f.

paralytic [pærə'lɪtɪk] adj MED paralítico,-a.
▸ n MED paralítico,-a.

parameter [pə'ræmɪtər] n parámetro.

paranoia [pærə'nɔɪə] n paranoia.

paraplegia [pærə'pliːdʒə] n MED paraplejía.

parasite ['pærəsaɪt] n parásito,-a.

parasol [pærə'sɒl] n sombrilla.

paratrooper ['pærətruːpər] n MIL paracaidista mf.

parcel ['pɑːsəl] n 1 (package) paquete m. 2 (piece of land) parcela. ⌐LOC⌐ parcel post servicio de paquetes postales.

parchment ['pɑːtʃmənt] n pergamino.

pardon ['pɑːdən] n 1 (forgiveness) perdón m. 2 JUR indulto. ⌐LOC⌐ I beg your pardon! fml ¡perdone! ‖ I beg your pardon? fml ¿cómo dice?
▸ vt 1 (forgive) perdonar: pardon me for interrupting perdone que le interrumpa. 2 JUR indultar. ⌐COMP⌐ pardon? (for repetition) ¿cómo dice?, ¿cómo? ‖ pardon me! (sorry) ¡perdón!, ¡perdone!, ¡Vd. perdone!

parent ['peərənt] n (father) padre m; (mother) madre f.
▸ n pl parents padres mpl.

☒ Parent no significa 'pariente', que se traduce por relative.

parietal [pə'raɪətəl] adj parietal.

P

parish ['pærɪʃ] *n* **1** REL parroquia. **2** GB *(civil)* municipio.

parishioner [pə'rɪʃ°nər] *n* feligrés,-esa.

park [pɑːk] *n* parque *m*, jardín *m* público.
▸ *vt (car)* aparcar, estacionar: *I'm parked opposite* he aparcado enfrente.
▸ *vi* aparcar, estacionar.

parking ['pɑːkɪŋ] *n (act)* estacionamiento. LOC **"No parking"** «Prohibido aparcar». COMP **parking meter** parquímetro.

parliament ['pɑːləmənt] *n (assembly)* parlamento.
▸ *n* **Parliament** GB *(body)* Parlamento; *(period)* legislatura.

parlor ['pɑːlər] *adj* US → parlour.

parlour ['pɑːlər] *n* **1** US *(shop)* salón *m*, tienda. **2** *dated (room in house)* salón *m*. COMP **parlour game** juego de salón.

parody ['pærədɪ] *n* parodia.
ⓘ *pl* parodies.
▸ *vt* parodiar.
ⓘ *pt & pp* parodied, *ger* parodying.

parole [pə'rəʊl] *n* libertad *f* condicional.
▸ *vt* poner en libertad condicional.

parquet ['pɑːkeɪ] *n* parqué *m*.

parrot ['pærət] *n* loro, papagayo.

parsimonious [pɑːsɪ'məʊɪəs] *adj fml* mezquino,-a, tacaño,-a.

❌ Parsimonious no significa 'parsimonioso (lento)', que se traduce por **slow**.

parsley ['pɑːslɪ] *n* perejil *m*.

parsnip ['pɑːsnɪp] *n* chirivía.

part [pɑːt] *n* **1** *(gen)* parte *f*: *we spent part of the day on the beach* pasamos parte del día en la playa. **2** *(component)* pieza. **3** *(of serial, programme)* capítulo. **4** *(measure)* parte *f*. **5** *(in play, film)* papel *m*: *she plays the part of Scarlett* hace el papel de Scarlett. **6** *(role, share, involvement)* papel *m*, parte *f*: *I want no part in your dodgy deals* no quiero saber nada de tus negocios sucios. LOC **for my part** por mi parte, en cuanto a mí. ‖ **in part** en parte. ‖ **the best part of / the better part of** la mayor parte de, casi todo,-a. ‖ **to play a part in** desempeñar un papel en.
▸ *adv* en parte.
▸ *adj* parcial.
▸ *vt (separate)* separar (from, de).

▸ *vi* **1** *(separate)* separarse; *(say goodbye)* despedirse: *they parted as friends* se separaron amistosamente. **2** *(open - lips, curtains)* abrirse.
▸ *n pl* **parts** *(area)* zona, parajes *mpl*.
◆ **to part with** *vt insep* desprenderse de, separarse de.

partial ['pɑːʃəl] *adj* **1** *(not complete)* parcial. **2** *(biased)* parcial. LOC **to be partial to** STH ser aficionado,-a a ALGO.

participant [pɑː'tɪsɪpənt] *n (gen)* participante *mf*; *(in competition)* concursante *mf*.

participate [pɑː'tɪsɪpeɪt] *vi* participar (in, en).

participation [pɑːtɪsɪ'peɪʃ°n] *n* participación *f*.

participle ['pɑːtɪsɪp°l] *n* participio.

particle ['pɑːtɪk°l] *n* partícula.

particular [pə'tɪkjʊlər] *adj* **1** *(special)* particular, especial: *for no particular reason* por nada en especial. **2** *(specific)* concreto, particular. **3** *(fussy)* exigente, especial.
▸ *n pl* **particulars** *(of event, thing)* detalles *mpl*; *(of person)* datos *mpl* personales.

❌ Particular no significa 'particular (privado)', que se traduce por **private**.

particularly [pə'tɪkjʊlərlɪ] *adv* especialmente, particularmente.

partly ['pɑːtlɪ] *adv* en parte.

partner ['pɑːtnər] *n* **1** *(in an activity)* compañero,-a; *(in dancing, tennis, cards, etc)* pareja. **2** COMM socio,-a, asociado,-a. **3** *(spouse)* cónyuge *mf*; *(husband)* marido; *(wife)* mujer *f*; *(in relationship)* pareja, compañero,-a.

partnership ['pɑːtnəʃɪp] *n* **1** COMM *(company)* sociedad *f*. **2** *(working relationship)* asociación *f*.

partridge ['pɑːtrɪdʒ] *n* perdiz *f*.
ⓘ *pl* partridges o partridge.

part-time [pɑːt'taɪm] *adj (work, job)* de media jornada, a tiempo parcial.
▸ *adv* media jornada, a tiempo parcial.

part-timer [pɑːt'taɪmər] *n* trabajador, -ra a tiempo parcial.

party ['pɑːtɪ] *n* **1** *(celebration)* fiesta: *birthday party* fiesta de cumpleaños. **2** POL partido. **3** *(group)* grupo.
ⓘ *pl* parties.

▸ *adj* **1** *(dress)* de fiesta; *(mood, atmosphere)* festivo,-a. **2** POL *(member, leader)* del partido.

▸ *vi (go to parties)* ir a fiestas; *(have fun)* divertirse.

ⓘ *pt & pp* partied, *ger* partying.

pass [pɑːs] *n* **1** GEOG *(in mountains - gen)* puerto, paso (de montaña); *(narrow)* desfiladero. **2** *(official permit)* pase *m*, permiso. **3** *(in exam)* aprobado. **4** SP pase *m*.

COMP **bus pass** abono de autobús.

▸ *vt* **1** *(go past - gen)* pasar; *(person)* cruzarse con: *I passed her in the street* me crucé con ella en la calle. **2** *(overtake)* adelantar. **3** *(cross - border, frontier)* pasar, cruzar. **4** *(give, hand)* pasar: *pass me that screwdriver* pásame ese destornillador. **5** SP *(ball)* pasar. **6** *(exam, test, examinee)* aprobar; *(bill, law, proposal, motion)* aprobar; *(censor)* pasar. **7** *(time)* pasar.

▸ *vi* **1** *(go past - gen)* pasar; *(procession)* desfilar; *(people)* cruzarse: *I was just passing* pasaba por aquí. **2** *(overtake)* adelantar. **3** *(move, go)* pasar: *we passed through Zaragoza* pasamos por Zaragoza. **4** SP hacer un pase. **5** *(exam, test)* aprobar; *(bill, motion)* ser aprobado,-a. **6** *(happen)* ocurrir, acontecer, suceder: *it came to pass that ...* sucedió que…

◆ **to pass away** *vi (die)* pasar a mejor vida.

◆ **to pass by** *vi* pasar: *she watched the people passing by* miraba pasar a la gente.

▸ *vt sep* pasar de largo.

◆ **to pass out** *vi* **1** *(faint)* desmayarse. **2** MIL graduarse.

▸ *vt sep (distribute)* repartir.

passage ['pæsɪdʒ] *n* **1** *(in street)* pasaje *m*; *(alleyway)* callejón *m*; *(narrow)* pasadizo. **2** *(in building - corridor)* pasillo. **3** *(way, movement - gen)* paso; *(of vehicle)* tránsito, paso. **4** *(of time)* paso, transcurso. **5** MAR *(journey)* travesía, viaje *m*; *(fare)* pasaje *m*. **6** *(writing, music)* pasaje *m*.

passenger ['pæsɪndʒəʳ] *n* pasajero,-a.

passer-by [pɑːsə'baɪ] *n* transeúnte *mf*.

ⓘ *pl* passers-by.

passion ['pæʃn] *n* pasión *f*. COMP **passion fruit** granadilla, maracuyá *m*.

passionate ['pæʃ°nət] *adj* apasionado,-a.

passionately ['pæʃ°nətlɪ] *adv* apasionadamente, fervientemente.

passive ['pæsɪv] *adj (gen)* pasivo,-a.

▸ *n* LING voz *f* pasiva.

passivity [pæ'sɪvɪtɪ] *n* pasividad *f*.

passport ['pɑːspɔːt] *n* pasaporte *m*.

password ['pɑːswɜːd] *n* contraseña.

past [pɑːst] *adj* **1** *(gone by in time)* pasado, -a; *(former)* anterior. **2** *(gone by recently)* último,-a: *the past few days* los últimos días. **3** *(finished, over)* acabado,-a, terminado,-a: *summer is past* el verano ha terminado. **4** LING pasado,-a. COMP **past participle** participio pasado. **past tense** pasado.

▸ *n* **1** *(former times)* pasado: *in the past* en el pasado, antes, antiguamente. **2** *(of person)* pasado; *(of place)* historia.

▸ *prep* **1** *(farther than, beyond)* más allá de; *(by the side of)* por (delante de): *it's just past the cinema* está un poco más allá del cine. **2** *(in time)* y: *it's five past six* son las seis y cinco. **3** *(older than)* más de: *he's past forty* pasa de los cuarenta (años). **4** *(beyond the limits of)*: *it's past my comprehension* me resulta incomprensible.

▸ *adv*: *a few joggers ran past* pasaron unos haciendo footing.

pasta ['pæstə] *n* pasta, pastas *fpl*.

paste [peɪst] *n* **1** *(mixture)* pasta; *(glue)* engrudo. **2** CULIN pasta, paté *m*.

▸ *vt (stick)* pegar; *(put paste on)* encolar.

pasteboard ['peɪstbɔːd] *n* cartón *m*.

pastel ['pæst°l] *n* **1** *(chalk)* pastel *m*; *(drawing)* dibujo al pastel. **2** *(colour)* color *m* pastel.

▸ *adj (drawing)* al pastel; *(colour, tone, shade, etc)* pastel.

✗ Pastel no significa 'pastel (tarta)', que se traduce por **cake, pie**.

pastime ['pɑːstaɪm] *n* pasatiempo.

pastry ['peɪstrɪ] *n* **1** *(dough)* masa. **2** *(cake)* pasta, bollo.

ⓘ *pl* pastries.

pasture ['pɑːstʃəʳ] *n* pasto.

pasty[1] ['pæstɪ] *n* CULIN empanadilla.

ⓘ *pl* pasties.

pasty[2] ['peɪstɪ] *adj* **1** *(pale)* pálido,-a. **2** *(like paste)* pastoso,-a.

ⓘ *comp* pastier, *superl* pastiest.

P

pat [pæt] n **1** (tap) golpecito, palmadita; (touch) toque m; (caress) caricia. **2** (of butter) porción f.
▶ vt (tap) dar palmaditas a; (touch) tocar; (caress) acariciar.
ⓘ pt & pp patted, ger patting.

patch [pætʃ] n **1** (to mend clothes) remiendo, parche m. **2** (over eye) parche m. **3** (area on surface - gen) trozo, lugar m, zona; (- of colour, damp, etc) mancha. **4** (plot of land) parcela.
▶ vt (mend) remendar; (put patch on) poner un parche a.

patchwork ['pætʃwɜːk] n **1** labor f de retales. **2** fig (of fields) mosaico.
▶ adj de retales.

pâté ['pæteɪ] n paté m.

patella [pə'telə] n rótula.

patent ['peɪtʰnt] n COMM patente f.
▶ adj (obvious) patente, evidente. COMP patent leather charol m.
▶ vt COMM patentar.

paternity [pə'tɜːnɪtɪ] n paternidad f.

path [pɑːθ] n **1** (track) camino, sendero: keep to the path seguir el camino. **2** (course of bullet, missile) trayectoria; (of flight) rumbo. LOC to be on the right path ir bien encaminado,-a.

pathetic [pə'θetɪk] adj patético,-a.

pathology [pə'θɒlədʒɪ] n patología.

pathway ['pɑːθweɪ] n camino, sendero.

patience ['peɪʃns] n **1** (quality) paciencia: I lost my patience perdí la paciencia. **2** (card game) solitario.

patient ['peɪʃʰnt] adj (person - gen) paciente; (long-suffering) sufrido,-a: be patient with him ten paciencia con él.
▶ n paciente mf, enfermo,-a.

patiently ['peɪʃʰntlɪ] adv pacientemente.

patio ['pætɪəʊ] n patio.
ⓘ pl patios.

patriarch ['peɪtrɪɑːk] n patriarca m.

patrician [pə'trɪʃʰn] adj patricio,-a.
▶ n patricio.

patrimony ['pætrɪmənɪ] n patrimonio.

patriot ['peɪtrɪət] n patriota mf.

patriotic [pætrɪ'ɒtɪk] adj patriótico,-a.

patrol [pə'trəʊl] n patrulla. LOC to be on patrol patrullar, estar de patrulla.

▶ vt (area) patrullar por, estar de patrulla en.
ⓘ pt & pp patrolled (US patroled), ger patrolling (US patroling).

patron ['peɪtrən] adj **1** (customer) cliente, -a habitual, parroquiano,-a. **2** (sponsor) patrocinador,-ra, mecenas m. COMP patron saint patrón m.

☒ Patron no significa 'patrón (jefe)', que se traduce por boss.

pattern ['pætʰn] n **1** (decorative design) diseño, dibujo; (on fabric) diseño, estampado. **2** (way something develops) orden m, estructura: behaviour pattern patrón de conducta. **3** (example, model) ejemplo, modelo. **4** (for sewing, knitting) patrón m; (sample) muestra.

pause [pɔːz] n **1** (gen) pausa; (silence) silencio; (rest) descanso. **2** MUS pausa.
▶ vi (gen) hacer una pausa; (stop moving) detenerse.

pavement ['peɪvmənt] n GB acera. **2** US calzada, pavimento.

paving ['peɪvɪŋ] n pavimento. COMP paving stone baldosa, losa.

paw [pɔː] n **1** ZOOL (foot) pata; (claw - of big cats) zarpa, garra. **2** fam (person's hand) manaza.

pawn [pɔːn] n **1** (in chess) peón m. **2** (unimportant person) juguete m, marioneta, títere m.

pawnshop ['pɔːnʃɒp] n casa de empeños.

pawpaw ['pɔːpɔː] n papaya.

pay [peɪ] n (wages) paga, sueldo, salario. COMP pay phone teléfono público.
▶ vt **1** (gen) pagar; (bill, debt) pagar, saldar: I paid him 10 pounds to mend my bike le pagué 10 libras para que me arreglara la bici. **2** (make, give - attention) prestar; (homage, tribute) rendir; (respects) presentar, ofrecer; (compliment, visit, call) hacer. **3** FIN (make, give - interest, dividends) dar. **4** (be worthwhile) compensar, convenir: it'll pay you to keep your mouth shut te conviene no decir ni pío. LOC to pay attention prestar atención.
▶ vi **1** (gen) pagar: you don't have to pay to go in no hay que pagar para entrar. **2** fig

(suffer) pagar (**for,** -): *he'll pay for this!* ¡me las pagará! **3** *(be profitable - business, etc)* ser rentable, ser factible. **4** *(be worthwhile)* compensar, convenir. ⌐ᴏᴄ⌐ **to get paid** cobrar. ▌ **to pay in advance** pagar por adelantado. ▌ **to pay cash / pay in cash** pagar al contado, pagar en efectivo.

◆ **to pay back** *vt sep* **1** *(money)* devolver, reembolsar; *(loan, mortgage)* pagar. **2** *fig (take revenge on)* hacer pagar a: *I'll pay you back for this!* ¡te haré pagar por esto!

◆ **to pay off** *vt sep* **1** *(debt)* saldar, liquidar, cancelar; *(loan)* pagar; *(mortgage)* acabar de pagar. **2** *(worker)* dar el finiquito a.

▶ *vi (be successful)* dar resultado; *(prove worthwhile)* valer la pena.

ⓘ *pt & pp* paid [peɪd].

payment ['peɪmənt] *n* **1** *(paying)* pago. **2** *(instalment)* plazo.

payroll ['peɪrəʊl] *n* nómina.

pea [piː] *n* guisante *m*.

peace [piːs] *n* **1** *(not war)* paz *f*. **2** *(tranquility)* paz *f*, tranquilidad *f*: *I just want a bit of peace and quiet* solo quiero un poco de paz y de tranquilidad. ⌐ᴏᴄ⌐ **at peace / in peace** en paz. ▌ **to make one's peace with sb** hacer las paces con ALGN.

peaceful ['piːsful] *adj* **1** *(non-violent)* pacífico,-a. **2** *(calm)* tranquilo,-a.

peacefully ['piːsfulɪ] *adv* *(quietly)* tranquilamente; *(non violently)* pacíficamente.

peacetime ['piːstaɪm] *n* tiempos *mpl* de paz.

peach [piːtʃ] *n* **1** *(fruit)* melocotón *m*. **2** *(colour)* (color *m*) melocotón *m*.

▶ *adj* de color melocotón. ⌐ᴄᴏᴍᴘ⌐ **peach tree** melocotonero.

peacock ['piːkɒk] *n* pavo real.

peak [piːk] *n* **1** ɢᴇᴏɢ *(of mountain)* pico; *(summit)* cima, cumbre *f*. **2** *fig (highest point)* cumbre *f*, punto álgido; *(climax)* apogeo. **3** *(of cap)* visera. ⌐ᴏᴄ⌐ **peak hours** horas *fpl* punta.

▶ *adj (maximum)* máximo,-a.

▶ *vi* alcanzar el punto máximo.

peaked [piːkt] *adj (cap)* con visera.

peanut ['piːnʌt] *n* cacahuete *m*.

▶ *n pl* **peanuts** *(small amount)* una miseria.

pear [peəʳ] *n (fruit)* pera. ⌐ᴄᴏᴍᴘ⌐ **pear tree** peral *m*.

pearl [pɜːl] *n* perla.

peasant ['pezənt] *adj* campesino,-a, rural.

▶ *n* **1** *(gen)* campesino,-a. **2** *pej (uncultured person)* inculto,-a, palurdo,-a.

pebble ['pebəl] *n* guija, guijarro, china.

peck [pek] *n (of bird)* picotazo; *(kiss)* besito.

▶ *vt (bird)* picotear; *(kiss)* dar un besito a.

▶ *vi (bird)* picotear (**at,** -).

pectin ['pektɪn] *n* pectina.

pectoral ['pektərəl] *adj* pectoral.

peculiar [prˈkjuːlɪəʳ] *adj* **1** *(strange)* extraño,-a, raro,-a; *(unwell)* indispuesto,-a. **2** *(particular)* característico,-a (**to,** de), propio,-a (**to,** de).

pedagogy ['pedəgɒdʒɪ] *n* pedagogía.

pedal ['pedəl] *n (gen)* pedal *m*. ⌐ᴄᴏᴍᴘ⌐ **pedal bin** cubo de la basura con pedal.

▶ *vi* pedalear.

ⓘ *pt & pp* pedalled (ᴜs pedaled), *ger* pedalling (ᴜs pedaling).

pedalo ['pedələʊ] *n* patín *m*.

ⓘ *pl* pedalos o pedaloes.

peddle ['pedəl] *vt* ᴄᴏᴍᴍ vender de puerta en puerta.

pederast ['pedəræst] *n* pederasta *m*.

pedestal ['pedɪstəl] *n* pedestal *m*.

pedestrian [pəˈdestrɪən] *n* peatón, -ona. ⌐ᴄᴏᴍᴘ⌐ **pedestrian crossing** paso de peatones. ▌ **pedestrian precinct** zona peatonal.

▶ *adj (dull)* pedestre.

pediatrician [piːdɪˈætrɪʃən] *n* ᴜs → **paediatrician**.

pedigree ['pedɪgriː] *n (of animals)* pedigrí *m*; *(of people)* linaje *m*.

▶ *adj* de raza.

pedophile ['piːdəfaɪl] *n* ᴜs → **paedophile**.

pee [piː] *n fam* pis *m*, pipí *m*.

▶ *vi fam* hacer pis, hacer pipí.

peel [piːl] *n (skin - gen)* piel *f*; *(- of orange, lemon, etc)* corteza, cáscara, monda, mondadura.

▶ *vt* pelar, quitar la piel de.

P

► *vi (skin)* pelarse; *(paint)* desconcharse; *(wallpaper)* despegarse.

peeler ['pi:lə^r] [also potato peeler] *n* pelapatatas *m*.

peep¹ [pi:p] *n (look)* ojeada, vistazo.
► *vi* espiar, mirar a hurtadillas.

peep² [pi:p] *n (noise)* pío: *I don't want to hear another peep out of you!* ¡que no te oiga decir ni pío!

peephole ['pi:phəul] *n* mirilla.

peer [pɪə^r] *vi (look closely)* mirar detenidamente (at, -).

peg [peg] *n* **1** *(for hanging clothes on)* percha, colgador *m*. **2** TECH clavija.
► *vt* **1** *(clothes)* tender (out, -); *(tent)* fijar con estacas (down, -). **2** *(prices)* fijar, estabilizar.
ⓘ *pt & pp* **pegged,** *ger* **pegging.**

pejorative [pə'dʒɒrətɪv] *adj* peyorativo,-a, despectivo,-a.

pelican ['pelɪkən] *n* pelícano.

pelvis ['pelvɪs] *n* pelvis *f*.

pen¹ [pen] *n (gen)* pluma; *(ballpoint)* bolígrafo *m*.
► *vt (write - gen)* escribir.
ⓘ *pt & pp* **penned,** *ger* **penning.**

✎ Pen es el nombre general que se da a cualquier instrumento que escriba con tinta, por ejemplo, la estilográfica (**fountain pen**), el bolígrafo (**ballpoint pen**) o el rotulador (**felt tip pen**).

pen² [pen] *n* corral *m*.

penal ['pi:n^əl] *adj* penal.

penalty ['pen^əltɪ] *n* **1** *(gen)* pena, castigo; *(fine)* multa. **2** SP *(gen)* castigo (máximo); *(football)* penalti *m*. **3** *(disadvantage)* desventaja, inconveniente *m*.
ⓘ *pl* **penalties.**

pence [pens] *n* → **penny**

pencil ['pens^əl] *n* lápiz *m*: *write in pencil* escribir con lápiz. COMP **pencil case** plumero, estuche *m* de lápices. ▌**pencil sharpener** sacapuntas *m*.

pending ['pendɪŋ] *adj (waiting to be decided or settled)* pendiente; *(imminent)* próximo,-a, inminente.
► *prep (while awaiting)* en espera de.

penetrate ['penɪtreɪt] *vt* **1** *(gen)* penetrar en; *(clothing)* atravesar, traspasar; *(organization)* infiltrarse en. **2** *(understand)* penetrar, entender.
► *vi (sink in)* causar impresión.

penfriend ['penfrend] *n* amigo,-a por correspondencia.

penguin ['peŋgwɪn] *n* pingüino.

penicillin [penɪ'sɪlɪn] *n* penicilina.

peninsula [pə'nɪnsjulə] *n* península.

penis ['pi:nɪs] *n* ANAT pene *m*.
ⓘ *pl* **penises** o **penes** ['pi:ni:s].

penknife ['pennaɪf] *n* cortaplumas *m*, navaja.
ⓘ *pl* **penknives** ['pennaɪvz].

pennant ['penənt] *n* banderín *m*.

penny ['penɪ] *n* **1** GB penique *m*: *a fifty pence piece* una moneda de cincuenta peniques. **2** US centavo.
ⓘ *pl* **penises** o **pence** [pens].

pennyroyal [penɪ'rɔɪəl] *n* poleo.

pension ['penʃ^ən] *n* pensión *f*.

pensioner ['penʃ^ənə^r] *n* jubilado,-a, pensionista *mf*.

pentagon ['pentəgən] *n* pentágono.

⊕ El Pentagon (Pentágono) es la sede de la secretaría de Defensa de los Estados Unidos y es sinónimo del poderío militar del país. Fue uno de los objetivos de los famosos atentados perpetrados con aviones de pasajeros el 11 de septiembre de 2001.

pentathlon [pen'tæθlən] *n* pentatlón *m*.

penthouse ['penthaus] *n* ático.

penultimate [pɪ'nʌltɪmət] *adj* penúltimo,-a.

people ['pi:p^əl] *n pl* **1** *(gen)* gente *f*, personas *fpl*: *a lot of people* mucha gente; *over a hundred people* más de cien personas; *people say that...* dicen que..., se dice que... **2** *(citizens)* ciudadanos *mpl*; *(inhabitants)* habitantes *mpl*. COMP **old people** los viejos *mpl*, los ancianos *mpl*, la gente *f* mayor. ▌**the common people** la gente *f* corriente. ▌**young people** los jóvenes *mpl*, la juventud *f*, la gente *f* joven.
► *n (nation, race)* pueblo, nación *f*.
► *vt* poblar.

✎ Consulta también **person**.

pepper ['pepər] n **1** (spice) pimienta. **2** (vegetable) pimiento.
▶ vt CULIN echar pimienta a.

peppermint ['pepəmɪnt] n **1** BOT menta. **2** (sweet) caramelo de menta.

per [pɜːʳ] prep por: 100 miles per hour 100 millas por hora. LOC **as per** de acuerdo con, según. **I per annum** por año, al año. **I per cent** por ciento.

perceive [pə'siːv] vt (see) percibir, ver; (notice) notar; (realize) darse cuenta de.

☒ To perceive no significa 'percibir (dinero)', que se traduce por receive.

percentage [pə'sentɪdʒ] n porcentaje m.

perception [pə'sepʃən] n **1** (sense) percepción f. **2** (insight) perspicacia, agudeza. **3** (way of understanding) idea.

perch¹ [pɜːtʃ] n (fish) perca.
① pl perch o perches.

perch² [pɜːtʃ] n **1** (for bird) percha. **2** (high position) posición f elevada, posición f privilegiada; (pedestal) pedestal m.
▶ vi (bird) posarse (on, en); (person) sentarse (on, en).

percolator ['pɜːkəleɪtəʳ] n cafetera eléctrica.

percussion [pə'kʌʃən] n percusión f.

percussionist [pə'kʌʃ°nɪst] n percusionista nf.

perennial [pə'renɪəl] adj perenne.

perfect [(adj) 'pɜːfɪkt; (vb) pə'fekt] adj **1** (gen) perfecto,-a. **2** (absolute, utter - fool) perdido,-a, redomado,-a; (- gentleman) consumado,-a; (- waste of time) auténtico,-a: he's a perfect stranger to me me es totalmente desconocido. **3** LING perfecto,-a.
▶ n LING perfecto.
▶ vt perfeccionar.

perfection [pə'fekʃən] n **1** (state, quality) perfección f. **2** (act) perfeccionamiento. LOC **to do** STH **to perfection** hacer ALGO a la perfección.

perfectionist [pə'fekʃ°nɪst] n perfeccionista mf.

perfectly ['pɜːfektlɪ] adv **1** (exactly, faultlessly) perfectamente. **2** (absolutely) totalmente.

perform [pə'fɔːm] vt **1** (task) ejecutar, llevar a cabo; (function) desempeñar,

hacer, cumplir. **2** (piece of music) interpretar, tocar; (song) cantar; (play) representar, dar; (role) interpretar.
▶ vi **1** (actor) actuar; (singer) cantar; (musician) tocar, interpretar; (dancer) bailar. **2** (machine) funcionar, marchar; (person) trabajar.

performance [pə'fɔːməns] n **1** (of task) ejecución f, realización f; (of function, duty) ejercicio. **2** (session - at theatre) representación f, función f; (- of circus, show, etc) número, espectáculo. **3** (action - of song, of musician) interpretación f; (- of play) representación f; (- of actor) interpretación f, actuación f. **4** (of machine) funcionamiento.

performer [pə'fɔːməʳ] n (gen) artista mf, actor m, actriz f; (musician) intérprete mf.

perfume ['pɜːfjuːm] n perfume m.
▶ vt perfumar.

perhaps [pə'hæps] adv quizá, tal vez: perhaps they've got lost quizá se hayan perdido.

perimeter [pə'rɪmɪtəʳ] n perímetro.

period ['pɪərɪəd] n **1** (length of time) período, periodo. **2** (epoch) época. **3** GEOL período. **4** EDUC (lesson) clase f. **5** (menstruation) regla, período. **6** US (full stop) punto.
▶ adj (dress, furniture) de época.

periodic [pɪərɪ'bdɪk] adj periódico,-a. COMP **periodic table** CHEM tabla periódica.

periodical [pɪərɪ'bdɪk°l] adj periódico,-a.
▶ n publicación f periódica.

peripheral [pə'rɪfər°l] adj **1** (zone, etc) periférico,-a. **2** (secondary) secundario,-a.

periphery [pə'rɪfərɪ] n **1** (of city) periferia. **2** (of society) margen m.

periscope ['perɪskəʊp] n periscopio.

perish ['perɪʃ] vi **1** (die) perecer, fallecer. **2** (decay) estropearse.
▶ vt (rubber) deteriorar.

perishable ['perɪʃəb°l] adj perecedero,-a.

peritonitis [perɪtə'naɪtəs] n MED peritonitis f.

perm [pɜːm] n fam (in hair) permanente f.

permanent ['pɜːmənənt] adj **1** (lasting - gen) permanente; (dye, ink) indeleble; (damage) irreparable. **2** (job, address) fijo,-a.

P

permission [pəˈmɪʃ°n] *n (gen)* permiso; *(authorization)* autorización *f*. ⌷LOC⌷ **to ask for permission to do** STH pedir permiso para hacer ALGO.

permit [*(n)* ˈpɜːmɪt; *(vb)* pɜːˈmɪt] *n* permiso.
► *vt (gen)* permitir; *(authorize)* autorizar: *he was not permitted access to the meeting* no se le permitió la entrada a la reunión.
► *vi* permitir: *weather permitting* si el tiempo lo permite.
ⓘ *pt & pp* **permitted**, *ger* **permitting**.

permutation [pɜːmjuˈteɪʃ°n] *n* **1** MATH permutación *f*. **2** GB *fam (in football pools)* combinación *f*.

perpendicular [pɜːpənˈdɪkjələʳ] *adj* **1** MATH perpendicular **(to**, a). **2** *(upright)* vertical.
► *n* perpendicular *f*.

perpetuity [pɜːprˈtjuːtɪ] *n* perpetuidad *f*.

perplexity [pəˈpleksɪtɪ] *n* perplejidad *f*.

persecution [pɜːsɪˈkjuːʃ°n] *n* persecución *f*.

perseverance [pɜːsɪˈvɪərəns] *n* perseverancia.

persistent [pəˈsɪstənt] *adj* **1** *(person)* insistente. **2** *(cough, pain, fog)* persistente; *(rain)* continuo,-a, persistente; *(denials, rumours, warnings)* continuo,-a, constante, repetido,-a.

person [ˈpɜːs°n] *n* **1** *(gen)* persona: *he's a really nice person* es una persona muy simpática. **2** LING persona. ⌷LOC⌷ **in person** personalmente.

✎ El plural más usual es **people**, pero **persons** se emplea en el lenguaje jurídico.

personal [ˈpɜːs°nəl] *adj* **1** *(private)* personal, privado,-a: *for personal reasons* por motivos personales. **2** *(own)* particular, personal. **3** *(individual)* personal. **4** *(physical - appearance)* personal; *(hygiene)* íntimo,-a, personal. **5** *(in person)* en persona. ⌷LOC⌷ **to get personal** hacer alusiones personales. ⌷COMP⌷ **personal computer** ordenador personal.

personality [pɜːs°ˈnælɪtɪ] *n* **1** *(nature)* personalidad *f*. **2** *(famous person)* personaje *m*.
ⓘ *pl* **personalities**.

personally [ˈpɜːs°nəlɪ] *adv* **1** *(in person)* personalmente, en persona. **2** *(for my part)* personalmente. **3** *(as a person)* como persona. ⌷LOC⌷ **to take** STH **personally** ofenderse.

personify [pɜːˈsɒnɪfaɪ] *vt* personificar.
ⓘ *pt & pp* **personified**, *ger* **personifying**.

perspective [pəˈspektɪv] *n* **1** ART perspectiva. **2** *fig (view, angle)* perspectiva.

persuade [pəˈsweɪd] *vt* persuadir, convencer: *she's easily persuaded* se deja convencer fácilmente.

persuasion [pəˈsweɪʒ°n] *n* **1** *(act)* persuasión *f*. **2** *(ability)* persuasiva.

perturb [pəˈtɜːb] *vt* perturbar.

Peru [pəˈruː] *n* Perú.

Peruvian [pəˈruːvɪən] *adj* peruano,-a.
► *n (person)* peruano,-a.

perversion [pəˈvɜːʃ°n] *n* **1** *(sexual)* perversión *f*. **2** *(distortion)* tergiversación *f*, distorsión *f*.

perversity [pəˈvɜːsɪtɪ] *n (wickedness)* perversidad *f*; *(stubbornness)* terquedad *f*.
ⓘ *pl* **perversities**.

pessimist [ˈpesɪmɪst] *n* pesimista *mf*.

pessimistic [pesɪˈmɪstɪk] *adj* pesimista.

pest [pest] *n* **1** plaga: *greenfly and other pests* pulgones y otras plagas. **2** *fam (person)* pelma *mf*, pesado,-a; *(thing)* lata, rollo.

☒ Pest no significa 'peste (mal olor)', que se traduce por **stink**.

pester [ˈpestəʳ] *vt* molestar.

pesticide [ˈpestɪsaɪd] *n* pesticida.

pet [pet] *n (tame animal)* animal *m* de compañía, mascota. ⌷COMP⌷ **teacher's pet** enchufado,-a.
► *adj* **1** *(kind person)* sol, cielo; *(term of affection)* cariño, cielo. **2** *(tame)* domesticado,-a. **3** *(favourite - theory, subject, etc)* favorito,-a. ⌷COMP⌷ **pet name** nombre *m* cariñoso. ▌**pet shop** tienda de animales.
► *vt (animal)* acariciar.
► *vi fam* tocarse y besuquearse.
ⓘ *pt & pp* **petted**, *ger* **petting**.

petal [ˈpet°l] *n* pétalo.

petiole [ˈpetɪəʊl] *n* pecíolo.

petition [pəˈtɪʃ°n] *n* **1** petición *f*, solicitud *f*. **2** JUR demanda.

▶ *vt* presentar una solicitud a.
▶ *vi* solicitar (for, -).

petrochemical [petrəʊˈkemɪkəl] *adj* petroquímico,-a.

petrol [ˈpetrəl] *n* gasolina. COMP **petrol pump** surtidor *m* de gasolina. I **petrol station** gasolinera.

🅇 Petrol no significa 'petróleo', que se traduce por oil.

petroleum [pəˈtrəʊliəm] *n* petróleo. COMP **petroleum jelly** vaselina.

petticoat [ˈpetɪkəʊt] *n (underskirt)* enaguas *fpl*; *(slip)* enagua, combinación *f*.

petty [ˈpetɪ] *adj* **1** *(trivial)* insignificante, sin importancia. **2** *(mean)* mezquino, -a. COMP **petty cash** dinero para gastos *mpl* menores.
ⓘ *comp* pettier, *superl* pettiest.

petulant [ˈpetjʊlənt] *adj* malhumorado,-a.

🅇 Petulant no significa 'petulante', que se traduce por vain.

pew [pjuː] *n* banco de iglesia.

phalange [ˈfælændʒ] *n* falange *f*.

phallus [ˈfæləs] *n* falo.

phantom [ˈfæntəm] *n (ghost)* fantasma *m*.
▶ *adj (imaginary)* ilusorio,-a.

Pharaoh [ˈfeərəʊ] *n* faraón *m*.

pharmaceutical [fɑːməˈsjuːtɪkəl] *adj* farmacéutico,-a.

pharmacist [ˈfɑːməsɪst] *n* farmacéutico,-a.

pharmacy [ˈfɑːməsɪ] *n* farmacia.
ⓘ *pl* pharmacies.

✎ Cuando se trata del establecimiento donde se expenden medicamentos, la palabra más usual es chemist's.

pharyngitis [færɪnˈdʒaɪtɪs] *n* faringitis *f*.

pharynx [ˈfærɪŋks] *n* faringe *f*.

phase [feɪz] *n (gen)* fase *f*; *(stage)* etapa.
▶ *vt* escalonar, realizar por etapas.

pheasant [ˈfezənt] *n* faisán *m*.

phenomenon [fɪˈnɒmɪnən] *n* fenómeno.
ⓘ *pl* phenomenons o phenomena [fɪˈnɒmɪnə].

philately [fɪˈlætəlɪ] *n* filatelia.

philharmonic [fɪləˈmɒnɪk] *adj* filarmónico,-a.

Philippine [ˈfɪlɪpiːn] *adj* filipino,-a.

Philippines [ˈfɪlɪpiːnz] *n* Filipinas.

philology [fɪˈlɒlədʒɪ] *n* filología.

philosopher [fɪˈlɒsəfəʳ] *n* filósofo,-a.

philosophical [fɪləˈsɒfɪkəl] *adj* filosófico,-a.

philosophy [fɪˈlɒsəfɪ] *n* filosofía.

phobia [ˈfəʊbɪə] *n* fobia.

Phoenician [fəˈniːʃən] *adj* fenicio,-a.
▶ *n* **1** *(person)* fenicio,-a. **2** *(language)* fenicio.
▶ *n* fenicio,-a.

phone [fəʊn] *n fam* teléfono. COMP **phone book** listín *m*, guía telefónica. I **phone box** cabina telefónica. I **phone call** llamada telefónica. I **phone number** número de teléfono.
▶ *vt* llamar (por teléfono), telefonear.
▶ *vi* llamar (por teléfono), telefonear.

phonecard [ˈfəʊnkɑːd] *n* tarjeta telefónica.

phonetic [fəˈnetɪk] *adj* fonético,-a.

phonetics [fəˈnetɪks] *n* fonética.

phosphorus [ˈfɒsfərəs] *n* fósforo.

photo [ˈfəʊtəʊ] *n fam* foto *f*.

photocopier [ˈfəʊtəʊkɒpɪəʳ] *n* fotocopiadora.

photocopy [ˈfəʊtəʊkɒpɪ] *n* fotocopia.
ⓘ *pl* photocopies.
▶ *vt* fotocopiar.
ⓘ *pt & pp* photocopied, *ger* photocopying.

photoelectric [fəʊtəʊɪˈlektrɪk] *adj* fotoeléctrico,-a. COMP **photoelectric cell** célula fotoeléctrica, fotocélula.

photograph [ˈfəʊtəgrɑːf] *n* fotografía, foto *f*: *colour photograph* fotografía en color. LOC **to take a photograph of** STH/SB fotografiar ALGO/a ALGN, hacer/sacar/tomar una fotografía de ALGO/ALGN.
▶ *vt* fotografiar.

photographer [fəˈtɒgrəfəʳ] *n* fotógrafo,-a.

photographic [fəʊtəˈgræfɪk] *adj* fotográfico,-a.

photography [fəˈtɒgrəfɪ] *n* fotografía.

photosynthesis [fəʊtəʊˈsɪnθəsɪs] *n* fotosíntesis *f*.

P

phrasal verb [freɪzəˈlˈvɜːb] *n* verbo compuesto.

✎ Los **phrasal verbs** son verbos seguidos de una partícula (adverbio, preposición) cuyo significado es muy distinto del significado del verbo por si solo. Existen multitud de **phrasal verbs** y su traducción suele plantear bastantes problemas a los estudiantes de inglés. En algunos casos, el verbo es separable, es decir, se pueden colocar complementos entre el verbo y la partícula, y en otros no.

phrase [freɪz] *n* **1** LING frase *f*, locución *f*. **2** *(expression)* frase *f*, expresión *f*.
▶ *vt (express)* expresar.

physical [ˈfɪzɪkəl] *adj* **1** *(gen)* físico,-a, material. **2** *(of physics)* físico,-a. **3** *fam euph (rough)* duro,-a: *it was a very physical game* fue un partido muy duro. LOC **physical education** educación *f* física. ‖ **physical geography** geografía física.
▶ *n (medical examination)* reconocimiento médico.

physician [fɪˈzɪʃən] *n* médico,-a.
physicist [ˈfɪzɪsɪst] *n* físico,-a.
physics [ˈfɪzɪks] *n* física.
physiology [fɪzɪˈɒlədʒɪ] *n* fisiología.
physiotherapist [fɪzɪəʊˈθerəpɪst] *n* fisioterapeuta *mf*.
physiotherapy [fɪzɪəʊˈθerəpɪ] *n* fisioterapia.
pianist [ˈpɪənɪst] *n* pianista *mf*.
piano [pɪˈænəʊ] *n (instrument)* piano.
ⓘ *pl* pianos.
piccolo [ˈpɪkələʊ] *n* flautín *m*.
ⓘ *pl* piccolos.
pick¹ [pɪk] *n (tool)* pico, piqueta.
pick² [pɪk] *n (choice)* elección *f*, selección *f*: *take your pick* elige el que quieras, escoge el que quieras. COMP **the pick of the bunch** el/la mejor de todos,-as.
▶ *vt* **1** *(choose - gen)* elegir, escoger; *(team)* seleccionar. **2** *(flowers, fruit, cotton, etc)* coger, recoger. **3** *(remove pieces from - gen)* escarbar, hurgar; *(spots)* tocarse. **4** *(remove from - hair, etc)* quitar. **5** *(open - lock)* forzar, abrir con una ganzúa. **6** *(of birds)* picotear.

◆ **to pick on** *vt insep (victimize)* meterse con; *(choose for task)* elegir, escoger.
◆ **to pick up** *vt sep* **1** *(lift)* levantar; *(from floor)* recoger; *(take)* coger; *(stitch)* coger; *(telephone)* descolgar: *don't forget to pick up all your litter* no os olvidéis de recoger toda la basura. **2** *(learn - language)* aprender; *(- habit)* adquirir, coger; *(- news, gossip)* descubrir, enterarse de. **3** *(illness, cold)* pescar, pillar. **4** *(acquire, get)* conseguir, encontrar. **5** *(collect - person)* recoger, pasar a buscar; *(- hitchhiker)* coger; *(- thing)* recoger: *I'll pick you up at 9.00 pm* te vendré a buscar a las nueve.

pickaxe [ˈpɪkæks] *n* GB pico, piqueta.
picket [ˈpɪkɪt] *n* **1** *(industry)* piquete *m*. **2** *(stick)* estaca.
pickle [ˈpɪkəl] *vt* encurtir, conservar en vinagre.
▶ *n pl* **pickles** *(vegetables)* encurtidos *mpl*.
pickpocket [ˈpɪkpɒkɪt] *n* carterista *mf*.
pick-up [ˈpɪkʌp] *n (on record player)* brazo (del tocadiscos). COMP **pick-up truck** furgoneta, camioneta.
picnic [ˈpɪknɪk] *n* picnic *m*.
▶ *vi (go on a picnic)* ir de picnic; *(eat)* hacer un picnic.
ⓘ *pt & pp* picnicked, *ger* picnicking.
picnicker [ˈpɪknɪkə] *n* excursionista *mf*.
picture [ˈpɪktʃə] *n* **1** *(painting)* pintura, cuadro; *(portrait)* retrato; *(drawing)* dibujo, grabado; *(illustration)* ilustración *f*, lámina; *(photograph)* fotografía, foto *f*: *he painted her picture* la retrató; *I took a picture of them* les saqué una foto. **2** *(account, description)* descripción *f*; *(mental picture)* imagen *f*, idea, impresión *f*. **3** TV *(quality of image)* imagen *f*. **4** GB *(film)* película. LOC **to take a picture** hacer una foto. COMP **picture book** libro ilustrado. ‖ **picture window** ventanal *m*.
▶ *vt* **1** *(imagine)* imaginarse: *I can't picture them married* no me los imagino casados. **2** *(paint)* pintar; *(draw)* dibujar.
▶ *n pl* **the pictures** GB el cine: *we went to the pictures* fuimos al cine.
pie [paɪ] *n* CULIN *(sweet)* pastel *m*, tarta; *(savoury)* pastel *m*, empanada.
piece [piːs] *n* **1** *(bit - large)* trozo, pedazo; *(small)* cacho; *(of broken glass)* fragmento.

2 *(part, component)* pieza, parte f: *a thirty-piece dinner service* una vajilla de treinta piezas. **3** *(coin)* moneda. **4** *(in board games)* ficha. **5** *(in newspaper)* artículo. **6** *(item, example of)* pieza: *a piece of advice* un consejo; *a piece of chalk* una tiza; *a piece of furniture* un mueble; *a piece of news* una noticia; *a piece of paper* un papel; *a piece of work* un trabajo. LOC **in one piece** *(unharmed)* sano,-a y salvo,-a. ‖ **to be in pieces 1** *(broken)* estar hecho,-a pedazos. **2** *(dismantled)* estar desmontado,-a. ‖ **to break STH in pieces** hacer ALGO pedazos.

pier [pɪər] n **1** *(landing place)* muelle m, embarcadero. **2** ARCH *(pillar)* pilar m, estribo.

pierce [pɪəs] vt **1** *(make hole in)* perforar, agujerear; *(go through)* atravesar, traspasar. **2** *(of light, sound)* penetrar, traspasar.

piercing ['pɪəsɪŋ] adj *(sound)* agudo,-a; *(scream)* desgarrador,-ra; *(look)* penetrante; *(wind)* cortante.

piety ['paɪətɪ] n piedad f.

pig [pɪg] n **1** ZOOL cerdo, puerco, marrano. **2** pej *(ill-mannered person)* cerdo, puerco, cochino; *(glutton)* glotón,-ona, tragón,-ona, comilón,-ona.

pigeon ['pɪdʒɪn] n *(bird)* paloma; *(for eating)* pichón m.

pigeonhole ['pɪdʒɪnhəʊl] n casilla.
  ▸ vt encasillar.

piggy ['pɪgɪ] n cerdito. COMP **piggy bank** hucha (en forma de cerdito).
  ① pl **piggies**.

piglet ['pɪglət] n cerdito, cochinillo.

pigment ['pɪgmənt] n pigmento.

pigsty ['pɪgstaɪ] n pocilga.
  ① pl **pigsties**.

pigtail ['pɪgteɪl] n coleta.

pilchard ['pɪltʃəd] n sardina.

pile¹ [paɪl] n **1** *(heap)* montón m, pila. **2** fam *(a lot of)* montón m, pila: *I've got a pile of essays to mark* tengo que corregir un montón de redacciones.
  ▸ vt **1** *(form a pile)* amontonar, apilar. **2** *(fill)* llenar, colmar: *the sink was piled high with dishes* el fregadero estaba lleno de platos.
  ▸ n pl **piles of** montones mpl de.

pile² [paɪl] n ARCH pilote m, pilar m.

pilgrim ['pɪlgrɪm] n peregrino,-a.

pilgrimage ['pɪlgrɪmɪdʒ] n peregrinación f.

pill [pɪl] n *(gen)* píldora, pastilla.

pillow ['pɪləʊ] n almohada.

pillowcase ['pɪləʊkeɪs] n funda de almohada.

pilot ['paɪlət] n **1** AV piloto mf. **2** MAR práctico mf. **3** *(TV or radio programme)* programa m piloto. COMP **pilot light** piloto.
  ▸ adj piloto, experimental.
  ▸ vt **1** *(ship, etc)* pilotar. **2** *(guide)* dirigir. **3** *(test)* poner a prueba.

pimento [pɪˈmentəʊ] n pimiento morrón.
  ① pl **pimentos**.

pimp [pɪmp] n chulo, proxeneta mf.

pimple ['pɪmpəl] n *(spot)* grano.

pin [pɪn] n **1** *(gen)* alfiler m. **2** *(badge, brooch)* insignia, pin m, alfiler m. **3** TECH *(peg, dowel)* clavija, espiga. **4** ELEC polo: *a two-pin plug* una clavija de dos patillas. COMP **pins and needles** hormigueo.
  ▸ vt **1** *(garment, hem, seam)* prender (con alfileres); *(papers, etc together)* sujetar (con un alfiler); *(notice on board, etc)* clavar (up, -); *(hair)* recoger (up,-). **2** *(person)* inmovilizar; *(arms)* sujetar.
  ▸ n pl **pins** fam *(legs)* patas fpl.
  ◆ **to pin up** vt sep clavar (con chinchetas), sujetar (con alfileres).
  ① pt & pp **pinned**, ger **pinning**.

pinafore ['pɪnəfɔːr] n *(apron)* delantal m. COMP **pinafore dress** pichi m.

pinball ['pɪnbɔːl] n flipper m.

pincer ['pɪnsər] n *(of crab, etc)* pinza.
  ▸ n pl **pincers** *(tool)* tenaza, tenazas fpl.

pinch [pɪntʃ] n **1** *(nip)* pellizco. **2** *(small amount)* pizca.
  ▸ vt **1** *(nip)* pellizcar; *(shoes)* apretar. **2** fam *(steal)* birlar, afanar, robar.

☒ To **pinch** no significa 'pinchar', que se traduce por **to prick**.

pine¹ [paɪn] n BOT *(tree, wood)* pino.
  ▸ adj de pino. COMP **pine cone** piña. ‖ **pine nut** piñón m.
  ◆ **to pine away** vi consumirse, morirse de pena.

pineapple ['paɪnæpəl] n piña.

P

ping-pong ['pɪŋpɒŋ] *n* tenis *m* de mesa, ping-pong *m*.

pinion['pɪnɪən] *n* TECH piñón *m*.

pink [pɪŋk] *adj* (de color) rosa, rosado,-a. LOC **to go pink / turn pink** ponerse colorado,-a.
  ► *n* **1** *(colour)* (color *m*) rosa *m*. **2** BOT clavel *m*, clavellina.

pint [paɪnt] *n* *(measurement)* pinta.
  ► *n* **a pint** *fam (of beer)* una cerveza, una jarra. LOC **to go for a pint** ir a tomar una cerveza.

✎ En Gran Bretaña equivale a 0,57 litros; en Estados Unidos equivale a 0,47 litros.

pioneer [paɪə'nɪə^r] *n* pionero,-a.
  ► *vt (policy, industry)* promover; *(technique)* iniciar.

pious ['paɪəs] *adj* piadoso,-a.

pip¹ [pɪp] *n (seed)* pepita.

pip² [pɪp] *n (sound)* señal *f* (corta).

pipe [paɪp] *n* **1** *(for water, gas, etc)* tubería, cañería, conducto. **2** *(for smoking)* pipa: *he smokes a pipe* fuma en pipa.
  ► *n pl* **pipes** gaita *f sing*.

pipeline ['paɪplaɪn] *n (for water)* tubería, cañería; *(for gas)* gasoducto; *(for oil)* oleoducto.

piper ['paɪpə^r] *n* gaitero,-a.

piping ['paɪpɪŋ] *n* tubería, cañería.

piracy ['paɪ^ərəsɪ] *n* piratería.

piranha [pɪ'rɑːnə] *n (fish)* piraña.

pirate ['paɪ^ərət] *n* pirata *m*.
  ► *adj* pirata.
  ► *vt* piratear.

pirouette [pɪru'et] *n* pirueta.

Pisces ['paɪsiːz] *n* piscis.
  ► *vi* hacer piruetas, piruetear.

pistachio [pɪs'tɑːʃɪəʊ] *n* pistacho. COMP **pistachio tree** pistachero.
  ① *pl* pistachios.

pistil ['pɪstɪl] *n* pistilo.

pistol ['pɪst^əl] *n* pistola.

piston ['pɪst^ən] *n* TECH pistón *m*, émbolo.

pit¹ [pɪt] *n* **1** *(hole)* hoyo, foso; *(grave)* fosa. **2** *(mine)* mina, pozo. **3** *(mark - on metal, glass)* señal *f*, marca; *(- on skin)* pi-

cadura, cicatriz *f*. **4** THEAT *(for orchestra)* foso de la orquesta.
  ► *n pl* **the pits** *(in motor racing)* los boxes *mpl*.

pit² [pɪt] *n* US *(seed)* pepita; *(stone)* hueso.

pitch¹ [pɪtʃ] *n* **1** MUS *(of sound)* tono; *(of instrument)* diapasón *m*. **2** SP *(field)* campo, terreno; *(throw)* lanzamiento. **3** *(degree, level)* grado, punto, extremo. **4** *(position, site)* lugar *m*, sitio; *(in market)* puesto. **5** MAR *(movement)* cabezada. **6** *(slope of roof)* pendiente *f*.
  ► *vt* **1** MUS *(note, sound)* entonar. **2** *fig (aim, address)* dirigir (at, a); *(set)* dar un tono a. **3** *(throw)* tirar, arrojar; *(in baseball)* lanzar. **4** *(tent)* plantar, montar; *(camp)* montar.
  ► *vi* **1** *(fall)* caerse. **2** *(ship, plane)* cabecear. **3** SP *(in baseball)* lanzar.

pitch² [pɪtʃ] *n (tar)* brea, pez *f*.

pitched [pɪtʃt] *adj (roof)* en pendiente, inclinado,-a. COMP **pitched battle** batalla campal.

pitcher¹ ['pɪtʃə^r] *n (of clay)* cántaro.

pitcher² ['pɪtʃə^r] *n* SP pítcher *mf*, lanzador,-ra.

pitchfork ['pɪtʃfɔːk] *n* AGR horca.

pith [pɪθ] *n* **1** *(of bone, plant)* médula; *(of orange)* piel *f* blanca. **2** *fig* meollo.

pitiful ['pɪtɪfʊl] *adj* **1** *(arousing pity - sight)* lastimoso,-a; *(cry)* lastimero,-a. **2** *(arousing contempt)* lamentable.

pituitary [pɪ'tjuːɪt^ərɪ] *adj* pituitario,-a. LOC **pituitary gland** glándula pituitaria.

pity ['pɪtɪ] *n* **1** *(compassion)* piedad *f*, compasión *f*: *she gave him some money out of pity* le dio dinero por compasión. **2** *(regret)* lástima, pena. LOC **for pity's sake!** ¡por amor de Dios! ❙ **what a pity!** ¡qué lástima!, ¡qué pena!
  ① *pl* pities.
  ► *vt (feel pity for)* compadecerse de, tener lástima de, dar lástima.
  ① *pt & pp* pitied, *ger* pitying.

pivot ['pɪvət] *n* **1** pivote *m*. **2** *fig* eje *m*.

pixel ['pɪksəl] *n* píxel *m*.

pizza ['piːtsə] *n* pizza.

pizzeria [piːtsə'rɪə] *n* pizzería.

placard ['plækɑːd] *n* pancarta.

place [pleɪs] n **1** *(particular position, part)* lugar m, sitio: *we visited lots of different places* fuimos a muchos sitios diferentes. **2** *(proper position)* lugar m, sitio; *(suitable place)* lugar m adecuado, sitio adecuado: *put the book back in its place* devuelve el libro a su sitio. **3** *(building)* lugar m, sitio; *(home)* casa, piso: *let's go to my place* vamos a mi casa. **4** *(in book)* página. **5** *(seat)* asiento, sitio; *(at table)* cubierto. **6** *(position, role, rank)* lugar m; *(duty)* obligación f: *if I were in your place* yo en tu lugar. **7** *(in race, contest)* puesto, lugar m, posición f; *(in queue)* turno. **8** *(job)* puesto; *(at university, on course)* plaza; *(on team)* puesto. LOC **all over the place** por todas partes, por todos lados. ∥ **in place** en su sitio. ∥ **in place of sə / in sb's place** en el lugar de ALGN. ∥ **out of place** fuera de lugar. ∥ **to take place** tener lugar.
▸ vt **1** *(put - gen)* poner; *(- carefully)* colocar: *she placed the vase on the shelf* puso el florero en el estante. **2** *(find home, job for)* colocar. **3** *(rank, class)* poner, situar. **4** *(remember - face, person)* recordar; *(- tune, accent)* identificar. LOC **to place an order** hacer un pedido.

placenta [plə'sentə] n placenta.
① pl **placentas** o **placentae** [plə'sentiː].

plague [pleɪg] n **1** *(of insects, etc)* plaga. **2** MED peste f.
▸ vt **1** *(pester)* acosar, asediar. **2** *(afflict)* afligir, asolar, plagar, atormentar.

plain [pleɪn] adj **1** *(clear)* claro,-a, evidente: *he made it quite plain* lo dejó muy claro. **2** *(straightforward)* franco,-a, directo,-a: *tell me in plain language* dímelo en lenguaje corriente. **3** *(simple, ordinary)* sencillo,-a; *(without pattern)* liso,-a. **4** *(unattractive)* poco agraciado,-a, feúcho,-a. **5** *(chocolate)* sin leche. LOC **in plain clothes** vestido,-a de paisano.
▸ adv **1** *(absolutely)* totalmente. **2** *(clearly)* claramente, francamente.
▸ n GEOG llanura.

plait [plæt] n trenza.
▸ vt trenzar.

plan [plæn] n **1** *(scheme, arrangement)* plan m, proyecto: *a change of plan* un cambio

de planes. **2** *(map, drawing, diagram)* plano; *(design)* proyecto; *(for essay)* esquema m.
▸ vt **1** *(make plans)* planear, proyectar, planificar; *(intend)* pensar, tener pensado: *they plan to get married next year* tienen planeado casarse el año que viene. **2** *(make a plan of - house, garden, etc)* hacer los planos de, diseñar; *(- economy, strategy)* planificar.
① pt & pp **planned**, ger **planning**.

plane¹ [pleɪn] n **1** MATH *(surface)* plano. **2** fig *(level, standard)* nivel m. **3** fam *(aircraft)* avión m: *they went by plane* fueron en avión.
▸ adj plano,-a.

plane² [pleɪn] n *(tool)* cepillo.
▸ vt cepillar.

plane³ [pleɪn] n *(tree)* plátano.

planet ['plænət] n planeta m.

planetarium [plænɪ'teərɪəm] n planetario.
① pl **planetariums** o **planetaria** [plænɪ'teərɪə].

plank [plæŋk] n *(of wood)* tablón m, tabla.

plankton ['plæŋktən] n plancton m.

planning ['plænɪŋ] n planificación f.

plant¹ [plɑːnt] n BOT planta.
▸ vt **1** *(flowers, trees)* plantar; *(seeds, vegetables)* sembrar; *(bed, garden, etc)* plantar (with, de). **2** *(bomb)* colocar; *(blow)* plantar; *(kiss)* dar, plantar. **3** *(ideas, doubt)* inculcar, meter.

plant² [plɑːnt] n *(factory)* planta, fábrica; *(machinery)* equipo, maquinaria.

plantation [plæn'teɪʃən] n *(for crops)* plantación f.

plasma ['plæzmə] n plasma m.

plaster ['plɑːstə] n **1** *(powder, mixture - gen)* yeso; *(for walls)* revoque m, enlucido. **2** MED escayola: *he's got his arm in plaster* tiene el brazo escayolado.
▸ vt **1** *(wall, ceiling)* enyesar, enlucir. **2** *(cover, spread)* cubrir (with, de).

plastic ['plæstɪk] adj **1** *(bag, cup, spoon, etc)* de plástico,-a. **2** *(malleable)* moldeable. COMP **plastic surgery** cirugía plástica. ∥ **the plastic arts** las artes fpl plásticas.
▸ n **1** plástico. **2** fam *(credit cards)* tarjetas de crédito.

Plasticine® ['plæstɪsiːn] n GB plastilina.

P

| plate | 286 |

plate [pleɪt] *n* **1** *(dish, plateful)* plato. **2** *(sheet of metal, glass)* placa; *(thin layer)* lámina. **3** *(illustration)* grabado, lámina. `COMP` number plate matrícula. **I** plate rack escurreplatos.

plateau ['plætəʊ] *n* **1** GEOG meseta. **2** *(state)* estancamiento.
ⓘ *pl* plateaus o plateaux ['plætəʊz].

platform ['plætfɔːm] *n* **1** *(gen)* plataforma; *(for speaker)* tribuna, estrado; *(for band)* estrado. **2** *(railway)* andén *m*, vía.

platinum ['plætɪnəm] *n* platino.

platonic [plə'tɒnɪk] *adj* platónico,-a.

platoon [plə'tuːn] *n* MIL pelotón *m*.

platypus ['plætɪpəs] *n* ornitorrinco.

play [pleɪ] *n* **1** *(recreation)* juego: *children at play* niños jugando. **2** SP *(action)* juego; *(match)* partido, jugada. **3** THEAT obra (de teatro), pieza (teatral).
▶ *vt* **1** *(game, sport)* jugar a. **2** SP *(compete against)* jugar contra; *(in position)* jugar de; *(ball)* pasar; *(card)* jugar; *(piece)* mover. **3** MUS tocar. **4** *(joke, trick)* gastar, hacer. **5** THEAT *(part)* hacer el papel de, hacer de; *(play)* representar, dar: *she plays the part of Juliet* hace de Julieta. `LOC` to play it cool hacer como si nada. **I** to play the game jugar limpio.
▶ *vi* **1** *(amuse oneself)* jugar (at, a), (with, con). **2** SP *(at game)* jugar. **3** THEAT *(cast)* actuar, trabajar; *(show)* ser representado,-a. **4** MUS tocar.
◆ **to play about** *vi* juguetear.
◆ **to play around** *vi* *(gen)* juguetear; *(have affairs)* tener líos.

player ['pleɪə'] *n* **1** SP jugador,-ra. **2** THEAT *(actor)* actor *m*; *(actress)* actriz *f*.

playful ['pleɪfʊl] *adj* juguetón,-ona, travieso,-a.

playground ['pleɪɡraʊnd] *n* patio de recreo.

playhouse ['pleɪhaʊs] *n* **1** *(theatre)* teatro. **2** *(for children)* casita.

playing card ['pleɪɪŋkɑːd] *n* carta, naipe *m*.

playing field ['pleɪɪŋfiːld] *n* campo deportivo.

playmate ['pleɪmeɪt] *n* compañero,-a de juego, amiguito,-a.

play-off ['pleɪɒf] *n* SP partido de desempate.

playpen ['pleɪpen] *n* parque *m* (para niños).

playtime ['pleɪtaɪm] *n* recreo.

plead [pliːd] *vi* suplicar (with, -).
▶ *vt* *(give as excuse)* alegar.

pleading ['pliːdɪŋ] *adj* *(tone, voice, look)* suplicante.
▶ *n* súplica, ruego.

pleasant ['plezᵊnt] *adj* **1** *(gen)* agradable; *(surprise)* grato,-a. **2** *(person)* simpático, -a, amable.
ⓘ *comp* pleasanter, *superl* pleasantest.

please [pliːz] *vt* *(make happy, be agreeable to)* agradar, gustar, complacer; *(satisfy)* contentar, complacer: *you can't please everyone* no se puede complacer a todos.
▶ *vi* **1** *(satisfy)* contentar, complacer, satisfacer. **2** *(choose, want, like)* querer: *you can do as you please* puedes hacer lo que quieras.
▶ *interj* por favor: *quiet, please* silencio, por favor.

pleased [pliːzd] *adj* *(happy)* contento,-a; *(satisfied)* satisfecho,-a. `LOC` pleased to meet you! ¡encantado,-a!, ¡mucho gusto!

pleasing ['pliːzɪŋ] *adj* agradable, grato,-a.

pleasure ['pleʒə'] *n* placer *m*: *it's a pleasure to be here* es un placer estar aquí. `LOC` my pleasure ha sido un placer. **I** to have the pleasure of... tener el placer de…, tener gusto de… **I** with pleasure con mucho gusto.

plebeian [plɪ'biːən] *adj* **1** HIST plebeyo, -a. **2** *pej* ordinario,-a.

plentiful ['plentɪfʊl] *adj* abundante.

plenty ['plentɪ] *n* abundancia.
▶ *pron* mucho,-a, muchos,-as: *we've got plenty of time* tenemos tiempo de sobra.

pliers ['plaɪəz] *n pl* alicates *mpl*, tenazas *fpl*.

plinth [plɪnθ] *n* *(of column, pillar)* plinto; *(of statue)* peana.

plod [plɒd] *vi* **1** *(walk slowly)* andar con paso lento. **2** *(work steadily)* hacer laboriosamente.
ⓘ *pt & pp* plodded, *ger* plodding.

plot¹ [plɒt] n **1** *(conspiracy)* conspiración f, complot m. **2** *(of book, film, etc)* trama, argumento.
► vt **1** *(plan secretly)* tramar, urdir. **2** *(course, position)* trazar.
► vi conspirar, tramar, maquinar.
ⓘ pt & pp **plotted**, ger **plotting**

plot² [plɒt]

plough [plaʊ] n AGR arado.
► vt *(land, etc)* arar.

plow [plaʊ] adj US → **plough**.

plug [plʌg] n **1** *(for bath, sink, etc)* tapón m. **2** ELEC *(on lead)* enchufe m, clavija; *(socket)* enchufe m, toma de corriente. **3** *(publicity)* publicidad f.
► vt **1** *(hole, etc)* tapar (up, -). **2** *(publicize)* dar publicidad a, promocionar.
◆ **to plug away** vt insep perseverar (at, en).
◆ **to plug in** vt sep enchufar.
► vi enchufarse.
◆ **to plug into** vt sep enchufar a.
ⓘ pt & pp **plugged**, ger **plugging**.

plug-in ['plʌgɪn] n plug-in m, conector m.

plum [plʌm] n **1** *(fruit)* ciruela. **2** *(colour)* color m ciruela. COMP **plum tree** ciruelo.
► adj fam fantástico,-a.

plumber ['plʌmə'] n fontanero,-a.

plumbing ['plʌmɪŋ] n **1** *(occupation)* fontanería. **2** *(system)* tubería, cañería.

plump [plʌmp] adj regordete, rollizo,-a.

plunder ['plʌndə'] n **1** *(action)* pillaje m, saqueo. **2** *(loot)* botín m.
► vt saquear, pillar.

plunge [plʌndʒ] n **1** *(dive)* zambullida, chapuzón m. **2** *(fall)* caída, descenso.
► vi **1** *(dive)* lanzarse, zambullirse; *(fall)* caer, hundirse. **2** *(drop - prices, etc)* caer en picado.
► vt *(immerse)* sumergir, hundir; *(thrust)* clavar, meter; *(in despair, poverty, etc)* sumir.

plural ['plʊər⁹l] adj plural.
► n plural m.

plus [plʌs] prep más: four plus five is nine cuatro más cinco son nueve.
► adj **1** *(ion, number)* positivo,-a. **2** *(and more)* más de, ALGO más de. **3** *(advantageous)* positivo,-a.
► n **1** MATH *(sign)* signo más. **2** *(advantage)* ventaja, factor m positivo, pro.

Pluto ['pluːtəʊ] n Plutón m.

plutonium [pluːtəʊnɪəm] n plutonio.
◆ **to ply with** vt sep *(drink, food)* no parar de ofrecer; *(questions)* asediar a, acosar a.

ply [plaɪ] n *(of wood)* chapa; *(of paper)* capa.
ⓘ pl **plies**.

plywood ['plaɪwʊd] n contrachapado.

pm ['piːem] abbr **(post meridiem)** de la tarde. it is 5.10 p.m. son las cinco y diez de la tarde.

pneumatic [njuːˈmætɪk] adj neumático,-a.

pneumonia [njuːˈməʊnɪə] n pulmonía.

poach [pəʊtʃ] vt CULIN *(fish)* hervir; *(eggs)* escalfar.

poacher ['pəʊtʃə'] n *(of game)* cazador,-ra furtivo,-a; *(of fish)* pescador,-ra furtivo,-a.

pocket ['pɒkɪt] n **1** *(gen)* bolsillo. **2** *(small area - of air)* bolsa; *(- of resistance)* foco.
► adj *(dictionary, camera, etc)* de bolsillo.
LOC **pocket money** *(for children)* paga, semanada.

pocketknife ['pɒkɪtnaɪf] n navaja.
ⓘ pl **pocketknives**.

pod [pɒd] n BOT vaina.

podium ['pəʊdɪəm] n podio.
ⓘ pl **podiums** o **podia** ['pəʊdɪə].

poem ['pəʊəm] n poema m, poesía.

poet ['pəʊət] n poeta mf.

poetic [pəʊˈetɪk] adj poético,-a.

poetry ['pəʊətrɪ] n poesía.

point [pɔɪnt] n **1** *(sharp end - of knife, nail, pencil)* punta. **2** *(place)* punto, lugar m: meeting point punto de encuentro. **3** *(moment)* momento, instante m: at this point en este momento. **4** *(state, degree)* punto, extremo. **5** *(on scale, graph, compass)* punto; *(on thermometer)* grado. **6** SP *(score, mark)* punto, tanto. **8** *(item, matter, idea, detail)* punto. **9** *(central idea, meaning)* idea, significado: you've missed the point no has captado la idea. **10** *(purpose, use)* sentido, propósito: what's the point? ¿para qué? **11** *(quality, ability)* cualidad f. **12** GEOG punta, cabo. **13** MATH *(in geometry)* punto (de intersección). **14** *(in decimals)* coma: five point six cinco coma seis. LOC **to come to the point** ir al grano. COMP **point of view** punto de vista.

▶ *vi* **1** *(show)* señalar: *the girl pointed at the clown* la niña señaló al payaso con el dedo. **2** *fig (indicate)* indicar.

▶ *vt* **1** *(with weapon)* apuntar. **2** *(direct)* señalar, indicar.

◆ **to point out** *vt sep* **1** *(show)* señalar. **2** *(mention)* señalar, hacer notar; *(warn)* advertir.

✎ En el sistema inglés, los millares se separan con una coma y los decimales con un punto, así que *tres mil ochocientos treinta y cinco* se escribiría 3,835 y *treinta y ocho coma veinticinco* se escribiría 38.25.

pointed ['pɔɪntɪd] *adj* puntiagudo,-a, en punta.

pointless ['pɔɪntləs] *adj (meaningless)* sin sentido; *(useless)* inútil.

poison ['pɔɪzªn] *n* veneno.

▶ *vt (harm, kill - person, animal)* envenenar; *(make ill)* intoxicar; *(river)* contaminar.

poisoning ['pɔɪzªnɪŋ] *n* envenenamiento.

poisonous ['pɔɪzªnəs] *adj* **1** *(plant, berry, snake)* venenoso,-a; *(drugs, gas)* tóxico, -a. **2** *fig* pernicioso,-a.

poke [pəʊk] *n (jab)* empujón *m*, golpe *m*; *(with elbow)* codazo; *(with sharp object)* pinchazo.

poker ['pəʊkəʳ] *n (card game)* póquer *m*.

Poland ['pəʊlənd] *n* Polonia.

polar ['pəʊləʳ] *adj* polar. COMP **polar bear** oso polar.

polarity [pəʊ'lærɪtɪ] *n* polaridad *f*.
ⓘ *pl* polarities.

Pole [pəʊl] *n* polaco,-a.

pole¹ [pəʊl] *n (stick, post)* poste *m*, pértiga. COMP **pole vault** salto con pértiga.

pole² [pəʊl] *n (electrical, geographical)* polo. LOC **to be poles apart** ser polos opuestos.

police [pə'liːs] *n pl (body)* policía *f sing*; *(officers)* policías *mpl*. COMP **police station** comisaría.

✎ Recuerda que el verbo que acompaña a police va en plural.

policeman [pə'liːsmən] *n* policía *m*, agente *m* de policía, guardia *m*.
ⓘ *pl* policemen [pə'liːsmən].

policewoman [pə'liːswʊmən] *n* policía, agente *f* de policía, guardia.
ⓘ *pl* policewomen [pə'liːswɪmɪn].

policy ['pɒlɪsɪ] *n* **1** POL política. **2** *(course of action, plan)* política, estrategia. **3** *(insurance)* póliza (de seguros).
ⓘ *pl* policies.

polish ['pɒlɪʃ] *n* **1** *(for furniture)* cera (para muebles); *(for shoes)* betún *m*; *(for floors)* cera, abrillantador *m* (de suelos); *(for nails)* esmalte *m*. **2** *(shine)* lustre *m*, brillo. **3** *fig (refinement)* refinamiento, brillo.

▶ *vt (floor, furniture)* sacar brillo a, encerar; *(shoes)* limpiar; *(silver, cutlery)* sacar brillo a; *(nails)* pintar con esmalte; *(stone)* pulir.

Polish ['pəʊlɪʃ] *adj* polaco,-a.

▶ *n* **1** *(person)* polaco,-a. **2** *(language)* polaco.

▶ *n pl* **the Polish** los polacos *mpl*.

polite [pə'laɪt] *adj* cortés, educado,-a, cumplido,-a, correcto,-a: *he was very polite to me* me trató con cortesía.
ⓘ *comp* politer, *superl* politest.

politely [pə'laɪtlɪ] *adv* cortésmente, educadamente, correctamente.

politeness [pə'laɪtnəs] *n* cortesía, educación *f*.

political [pə'lɪtɪkªl] *adj (gen)* político,-a.

politician [pɒlɪ'tɪʃªn] *n* político,-a.

politics ['pɒlɪtɪks] *n* **1** *(gen)* política: *he's active in politics* es militante (político). **2** *(science)* ciencias *fpl* políticas.

▶ *n pl (view, opinions)* ideas *fpl* políticas.

polka ['pɒlkə] *n (dance)* polca. COMP **polka dot** lunar *m*.

poll [pəʊl] *n* **1** *(voting)* votación *f*. **2** *(survey)* encuesta, sondeo.

▶ *vt* **1** *(votes - obtain)* obtener. **2** *(ask opinion)* sondear, encuestar.

▶ *n pl* **the polls** las elecciones *fpl*, los comicios *mpl*. LOC **to go to the polls** acudir a las urnas.

pollen ['pɒlən] *n* polen *m*.

pollination [pɒlɪ'neɪʒªn] *n* polinización *f*.

polling ['pəʊlɪŋ] *n* votación *f*. COMP **polling station** colegio electoral.

pollute [pə'luːt] *vt* contaminar.

pollution [pə'luːʃᵊn] *n* contaminación *f*.

polo ['pəʊləʊ] *n* SP polo.

polo-neck ['pəʊləʊnek] *adj (sweater)* de cuello alto, de cuello cisne.

polyester [pɒlɪ'estəʳ] *n* poliéster *m*.

polygamy [pɒ'lɪgəmɪ] *n* poligamia.

polygon ['pɒlɪgɒn] *n* polígono.

polytechnic [pɒlɪ'teknɪk] *n* escuela politécnica, politécnico.

pond [pɒnd] *n* estanque *m*.

pony ['pəʊnɪ] *n* póney *m*, poni *m*.
ⓘ *pl* ponies.

ponytail ['pəʊnɪteɪl] *n* cola de caballo.

pool¹ [puːl] *n* **1** *(of water, oil, blood, etc)* charco; *(of light)* foco. **2** *(pond)* estanque *m*; *(in river)* pozo.

pool² [puːl] *n* **1** *(common fund of money)* fondo común; *(in gambling)* bote *m*. **2** *(common supply of services)* servicios *mpl* comunes. **3** US *(snooker)* billar *m* americano.
▶ *vt (funds, money)* reunir, juntar; *(ideas, resources)* poner en común.
▶ *n pl* the pools las quinielas *fpl*.

poor [pʊəʳ] *adj* **1** *(person, family, country)* pobre. **2** *(inadequate)* pobre, escaso,-a; *(bad quality)* malo,-a; *(inferior)* inferior: *you've got a poor memory* tienes mala memoria. **3** *(unfortunate)* pobre: *poor Edward* el pobre Edward.
▶ *n pl* the poor los pobres *mpl*.

poorly ['pʊəlɪ] *adj (ill)* indispuesto,-a.
▶ *adv (badly)* mal: *poorly dressed* mal vestido,-a.

pop¹ [pɒp] *n* **1** *(of cork)* taponazo. **2** *fam (drink)* gaseosa.
▶ *vt* **1** *(burst)* hacer reventar; *(cork)* hacer saltar. **2** *(put)* poner, meter.
▶ *vi* **1** *(burst)* estallar, reventar; *(cork)* saltar. **2** *(go quickly)* ir rápidamente.
ⓘ *pt & pp* popped, *ger* popping.

pop² [pɒp] *n fam (music)* música pop.
COMP pop art pop-art *m*. ‖ pop star estrella del pop.

popcorn ['pɒpkɔːn] *n* palomitas *fpl* de maíz.

pope [pəʊp] *n* papa *m*.

poplar ['pɒpləʳ] *n* BOT álamo.

poppy ['pɒpɪ] *n* amapola.
ⓘ *pl* poppies.

popular ['pɒpjʊləʳ] *adj* **1** *(well-liked - gen)* popular; *(- person)* estimado,-a; *(- resort, restaurant)* muy frecuentado,-a; *(fashionable)* de moda: *she's popular with her workmates* les cae muy bien a sus compañeras de trabajo. **2** *(of or for general public)* popular; *(prices)* popular, económico,-a.

popularity [pɒpjʊ'lærɪtɪ] *n* popularidad *f*.

population [pɒpjʊ'leɪʃᵊn] *n* población *f*.

porcelain ['pɔːsᵊlɪn] *n* porcelana.
▶ *adj* de porcelana.

porch [pɔːtʃ] *n* **1** *(of church)* pórtico; *(of house)* porche *m*, entrada. **2** US *(veranda)* terraza.

porcine ['pɔːsaɪn] *adj* porcino,-a.

porcupine ['pɔːkjʊpaɪn] *n* puerco espín.

pore [pɔːʳ] *n* ANAT poro.

pork [pɔːk] *n* carne *f* de cerdo. COMP pork butcher charcutero,-a.

pornography [pɔː'nɒgrəfɪ] *n* pornografía.

porridge ['pɒrɪdʒ] *n* gachas *fpl* de avena.

port¹ [pɔːt] *n (harbour, town)* puerto.
▶ *adj* portuario,-a.

port² [pɔːt] *n (left side)* babor *m*.

portable ['pɔːtəbᵊl] *adj* portátil.

porter ['pɔːtəʳ] *n* **1** *(in hotel, block of flats)* portero,-a; *(in public building, school)* conserje *m*; *(in hospital)* camillero. **2** *(at station, airport)* mozo, maletero.

portion ['pɔːʃᵊn] *n (gen)* porción *f*, parte *f*; *(of food)* ración *f*.
◆ to portion out

portrait ['pɔːtreɪt] *n* retrato.

portray [pɔː'treɪ] *vt* **1** *(painting)* representar, retratar. **2** *(describe)* describir, retratar. **3** *(act)* interpretar.

portrayal [pɔː'treɪəl] *n* **1** *(painting)* representación *f*. **2** *(description)* descripción *f*. **3** *(acting)* interpretación *f*.

Portugal ['pɔːtjʊgᵊl] *n* Portugal.

P

Portuguese [pɔːtjuˈgiːz] *adj* portugués, -esa.

▶ *n* **1** *(person)* portugués,-esa. **2** *(language)* portugués *m*.

▶ *n pl* **the Portuguese** los portugueses *mpl*.

pose [pəʊz] *n* **1** *(position, stance)* postura, actitud *f*. **2** *pej (affectation)* pose *f*, afectación *f*.

▶ *vt (problem, question, etc)* plantear; *(threat)* representar.

▶ *vi* **1** *(for painting, photograph)* posar. **2** *pej (behave affectedly)* presumir, hacer pose. LOC **to pose as** hacerse pasar por.

posh [pɒʃ] *adj* **1** GB *fam (place, area)* elegante, de lujo; *(accent)* refinado,-a. **2** GB *fam (upper-class)* pijo,-a.

position [pəˈzɪʃən] *n* **1** *(place)* posición *f*. **2** *(right place)* sitio, lugar *m*: they manoeuvred the piano into position colocaron el piano en su lugar. **3** *(posture)* postura, posición *f*. **4** *(on scale, in competition)* posición *f*, lugar *m*, puesto; *(social standing)* categoría social, posición *f*. **5** *(job)* puesto. **6** *(situation, circumstances)* situación *f*, lugar *m*. **7** *(opinion, point of view)* postura, posición *f*. **8** SP posición *f*.

▶ *vt (put in place)* colocar, poner.

positive [ˈpɒzɪtɪv] *adj* **1** *(gen)* positivo,-a. **2** *(definite - proof, evidence)* concluyente, definitivo,-a; *(- refusal, decision)* categórico,-a; *(- instruction, order)* preciso,-a. **3** *(effective - criticism, advice)* constructivo,-a; *(- attitude, experience)* positivo,-a. **4** *(quite certain)* seguro,-a (**about**, de): I'm absolutely positive estoy segurísimo.

▶ *n* positivo.

possess [pəˈzes] *vt* **1** *(own)* poseer, tener. **2** *(take over - anger, fear)* apoderarse de.

possession [pəˈzeʃən] *n* **1** *(ownership)* posesión *f*, poder *m*. **2** *(thing owned)* bien *m*, posesión *f*.

possessive [pəˈzesɪv] *adj* **1** *(person)* posesivo,-a; *(selfish)* egoísta. **2** LING posesivo,-a.

▶ *n* LING posesivo.

possessor [pəˈzesər] *n* poseedor,-ra.

possibility [pɒsɪˈbɪlɪtɪ] *n* **1** *(likelihood)* posibilidad *f*. **2** *(something possible)* posibilidad *f*.

ⓘ *pl* possibilities.

possible [ˈpɒsɪbəl] *adj* posible. LOC **as much as possible** todo lo posible. **▮ as soon as possible** cuanto antes, lo antes posible.

▶ *n* posible candidato,-a.

possibly [ˈpɒsɪblɪ] *adv* **1** *(reasonably, conceivably)* posiblemente: you can't possibly have finished already! ¡no es posible que ya hayas acabado! **2** *(in requests)*: could you possibly give me a lift to the station? ¿me podría llevar a la estación? **3** *(perhaps)* posiblemente, quizás.

post¹ [pəʊst] *n (of wood)* estaca, poste *m*.

post² [pəʊst] *n* **1** *(job)* puesto, empleo; *(important position)* cargo. **2** MIL puesto.

▶ *vt* **1** MIL destinar, apostar. **2** *(employee)* destinar, mandar.

post³ [pəʊst] *n* GB *(mail)* correo; *(collection)* recogida; *(delivery)* reparto: it's in the post ya está enviado.

▶ *vt* **1** GB *(send - letter, parcel)* mandar por correo, echar al correo; *(put in postbox)* echar al buzón. COMP **post office** Correos, oficina de correos.

postage [ˈpəʊstɪdʒ] *n* franqueo, porte *m*.

postal [ˈpəʊstəl] *adj* postal.

postbag [ˈpəʊstbæg] *n* **1** *(sack)* saca (de correos). **2** GB *(letters)* correspondencia.

postbox [ˈpəʊstbɒks] *n* GB buzón *m*.

postcard [ˈpəʊstkɑːd] *n* tarjeta postal *f*.

postcode [ˈpəʊstkəʊd] *n* GB código postal.

poster [ˈpəʊstər] *n* póster *m*, cartel *m*.

postgraduate [pəʊstˈgrædjuət] *n* postgraduado,-a.

▶ *adj* de postgrado.

postman [ˈpəʊstmən] *n* cartero.

ⓘ *pl* postmen [ˈpəʊstmən].

postmark [ˈpəʊstmɑːk] *n* matasellos *m*.

▶ *vt* timbrar, matasellar.

postpone [pəsˈpəʊn] *vt* posponer.

posture [ˈpɒstʃər] *n* **1** *(position of body)* postura, pose *f*. **2** *(attitude)* postura.

▶ *vi* hacer poses, adoptar poses.

postwar [ˈpəʊstwɔːr] *adj* de la posguerra.

postwoman [ˈpəʊstwʊmən] *n* cartera.

ⓘ *pl* postwomen [ˈpəʊstwɪmɪn].

pot [pɒt] *n* **1** CULIN *(container)* pote *m*, tarro; *(for cooking)* olla, puchero; *(earthen-*

ware) vasija; *(teapot)* tetera; *(coffee pot)* cafetera. **2** *(of paint)* bote *m*. **3** *(flowerpot)* maceta, tiesto.
▶ *vt (plant)* plantar en una maceta.
▶ *n* **the pot** *(in card games)* el bote.

potassium [pəˈtæsɪəm] *n* potasio.

potato [pəˈteɪtəʊ] *n* patata.
ⓘ *pl* potatoes.

potential [pəˈtenʃ[ə]l] *adj* potencial.
▶ *n* potencial *m*.

potholer [ˈpɒθəʊləʳ] *n* GB espeleólogo,-a.

potholing [ˈpɒθəʊlɪŋ] *n* GB espeleología.

potter [ˈpɒtəʳ] *n* alfarero,-a.

pottery [ˈpɒtərɪ] *n* alfarería.

potty [ˈpɒtɪ] *n* orinal *m*.
ⓘ *pl* potties.

pouch [paʊtʃ] *n* **1** *(gen)* bolsa (pequeña); *(for tobacco)* petaca. **2** ZOOL bolsa abdominal.

poultry [ˈpəʊltrɪ] *n* aves *fpl* de corral.

pounce [paʊns] *n* salto.
▶ *vi* saltar (on, sobre), abalanzarse (on, sobre).

pound¹ [paʊnd] *vt* **1** *(crush)* machacar. **2** *(strike, beat)* aporrear, golpear.
▶ *vi* **1** *(strike, beat)* aporrear (at/on, -), golpear (at/on, -); *(of waves)* batir (against, contra). **2** *(heart)* palpitar, latir con fuerza.

pound² [paʊnd] *n* **1** FIN libra: *a five-pound note* un billete de cinco libras. **2** *(weight)* libra: *half a pound of tomatoes* media libra de tomates.

✎ Como medida de peso equivale a 454 gr.

pound³ [paʊnd] *n* *(enclosure - for dogs)* perrera; *(- for cars)* depósito.

pour [pɔːʳ] *vt* *(liquid)* verter, echar; *(substance)* echar; *(drink)* servir: *she poured the orange juice into a jug* vertió el zumo de naranja en una jarra.
▶ *vi* **1** *(blood)* manar, salir; *(water, sweat)* chorrear. **2** *fig* moverse en tropel. COMP **to pour (down/with rain)** llover a cántaros: *it's pouring* está lloviendo a cántaros.

pouring [ˈpɔːrɪŋ] *adj (rain)* torrencial.

poverty [ˈpɒvətɪ] *n (gen)* pobreza.

powder [ˈpaʊdəʳ] *n (dust)* polvo; *(cosmetic, medicine)* polvos *mpl*.
▶ *vt* **1** *(put powder on)* poner polvos, empolvar. **2** *(pulverize)* pulverizar, reducir a polvo.

power [ˈpaʊəʳ] *n* **1** *(strength, force)* fuerza; *(of sun, wind)* potencia, fuerza; *(of argument)* fuerza. **2** *(ability, capacity)* poder *m*, capacidad *f*: *it's beyond his power* no está en sus manos. **3** *(faculty)* facultad *f*. **4** *(control, influence, authority)* poder *m*; *(of country)* poderío, poder *m*: *the power of the media* el poder de los medios de comunicación. **5** *(nation)* potencia; *(person, group)* fuerza. **6** PHYS *(capacity, performance)* potencia; *(energy)* energía. **7** ELEC electricidad *f*, corriente *f*. **8** MATH potencia: *six to the power of four* seis elevado a la cuarta potencia.
▶ *vt* propulsar, impulsar: *it's powered by electricity* funciona con electricidad.

powerful [ˈpaʊəfʊl] *adj* **1** *(strong - athlete, body, current)* fuerte; *(- blow, engine, machine)* potente. **2** *(influential - enemy, nation, ruler)* poderoso,-a. **3** *(effective)* impactante.

powerless [ˈpaʊələs] *adj* impotente.

practical [ˈpræktɪkəl] *adj* **1** *(gen)* práctico,-a. **2** *(good with hands)* hábil.
▶ *n* *(lesson)* clase *f* práctica. COMP **practical joke** broma.

practically [ˈpræktɪk[ə]lɪ] *adv* **1** *(almost)* casi, prácticamente. **2** *(in a practical way)* de manera práctica.

practice [ˈpræktɪs] *n* **1** *(repeated exercise)* práctica; *(training)* entrenamiento: *I'm out of practice* me falta práctica. **2** *(action, reality)* práctica: *in practice* en la práctica. **3** *(custom, habit)* costumbre *f*. LOC **to be out of practice** haber perdido práctica.
▶ *vt & vi* US → **practise.**

practise [ˈpræktɪs] *vt* **1** GB *(do repeatedly - language, serve, scales)* practicar; *(song, act)* ensayar. **2** GB *(religion, belief, economy)* practicar. **3** GB *(profession)* ejercer.
▶ *vi* **1** GB *(gen)* practicar. **2** GB *(sports team)* entrenar; *(actors)* ensayar. **3** GB *(professionally)* ejercer (as, de/como).

pragmatic [præɡˈmætɪk] *adj* pragmático,-a.

prairie [ˈpreərɪ] *n* pradera, llanura.

praise [preɪz] *n* **1** alabanza, elogio, loa. **2** REL alabanza.
▶ *vt* **1** elogiar. **2** REL alabar.

pram [præm] *n* GB cochecito de niño.

prank [præŋk] *n (trick)* broma; *(of child)* travesura. LOC **to play a prank on** SB gastar una broma a ALGN.

prawn [prɔːn] *n (large)* langostino; *(medium)* gamba; *(small)* camarón *m*.

pray [preɪ] *vi* REL orar, rezar.

prayer [preər] *n* REL *(request)* oración *f*, rezo, plegaria; *(action)* oración *f*, rezo.

preach [priːtʃ] *vt* **1** REL *(gospel)* predicar; *(sermon)* dar, hacer. **2** *(advocate)* aconsejar.
▶ *vi* REL predicar.

preacher ['priːtʃər] *n* predicador,-ra.

precaution [prɪˈkɔːʃən] *n* precaución *f*.

precedent ['presɪdənt] *n* precedente *m*.

preceding [prɪˈsiːdɪŋ] *adj* anterior.

precinct ['priːsɪŋkt] *n* **1** *(of cathedral, hospital, etc)* recinto. **2** GB *(part of town)* zona.
▶ *n pl* **precincts** recinto *m sing*.

> ✖ Precinct no significa 'precinto', que se traduce por **seal**.

precious ['preʃəs] *adj* **1** *(jewel, stone, metal)* precioso,-a. **2** *(moment, memory, possession)* preciado,-a, querido,-a. COMP **precious little** poquísimo,-a.

> ✖ Precious no significa 'precioso (bonito)', que se traduce por **beautiful**.

precipice ['presɪpɪs] *n* precipicio.

precipitation [prɪsɪpɪˈteɪʃən] *n* **1** *fml (haste)* precipitación *f*. **2** METEOR precipitación.

precise [prɪˈsaɪs] *adj* preciso,-a.

precisely [prɪˈsaɪslɪ] *adv (exactly)* precisamente; *(accurately)* con precisión. LOC **precisely!** ¡exacto!, ¡eso es!

precision [prɪˈsɪʒən] *n* precisión *f*.

precocious [prɪˈkəʊʃəs] *adj* precoz.

precooked [priːˈkʊkt] *adj* precocinado,-a.

predator ['predətər] *n* ZOOL depredador *m*.

predecessor ['priːdɪsesər] *n* predecesor,-ra, antecesor,-ra.

predict [prɪˈdɪkt] *vt* predecir.

prediction [prɪˈdɪkʃən] *n* predicción *f*.

predominate [prɪˈdɒmɪneɪt] *vi* predominar.

prefect ['priːfekt] *n* **1** *(official)* prefecto. **2** GB *(in school)* monitor,-ra.

prefer [prɪˈfɜːr] *vt* preferir: *she prefers coffee to tea* prefiere el café al té.
ⓘ *pt & pp* **preferred**, *ger* **preferring**.

preferable ['prefərəbəl] *adj* preferible (to, a).

preference ['prefərəns] *n* preferencia (for, por).

prefix ['priːfɪks] *n* LING prefijo.

pregnancy ['pregnənsɪ] *n* embarazo.
ⓘ *pl* **pregnancies**.

pregnant ['pregnənt] *n (woman)* embarazada; *(animal)* preñada: *she's six months pregnant* está embarazada de seis meses.

preheat ['priːhiːt] *vt* precalentar.

prehistoric [priːhɪˈstɒrɪk] *adj* prehistórico,-a.

prehistory [priːˈhɪstərɪ] *n* prehistoria.

prejudice ['predʒədɪs] *n* **1** *(unfavourable bias)* prejuicio; *(favourable)* predisposición *f*.
▶ *vt* **1** *(influence, bias)* predisponer (against, contra), (in favour of, a favor de). **2** *(harm)* perjudicar.

prejudiced ['predʒʊdɪst] *adj* parcial.

premature [preməˈtjʊər] *adj (gen)* prematuro,-a.

premiere ['premɪeər] *n* estreno.

premises ['premɪsɪz] *n pl* local *m*. LOC **on the premises** dentro del local.

preoccupy [priːˈɒkjʊpaɪ] *vt (worry)* preocupar; *(think about too much)* pensar demasiado en.
ⓘ *pt & pp* **preoccupied**, *ger* **preoccupying**.

preparation [prepəˈreɪʃən] *n* **1** *(action)* preparación *f*. **2** *(substance)* preparado.
▶ *n pl* **preparations** preparativos *mpl* (for, para).

preparatory [prɪˈpærətərɪ] *adj* preparatorio,-a, preliminar.

prepare [prɪˈpeər] *vt (gen)* preparar; *(report)* redactar.
▶ *vi* prepararse (for, para).

prepared [prɪˈpeəd] *adj* **1** *(gen)* preparado,-a. **2** *(willing)* dispuesto,-a (to, a).

preposition [prepəˈzɪʃən] *n* preposición *f*.

prescribe [prɪs'kraɪb] vt **1** (medicine, drugs, etc) recetar; (holiday, rest) recomendar. **2** fml (order) prescribir.

prescription [prɪs'krɪpʃ°n] n receta (médica).

presence ['prez°ns] n **1** (gen) presencia; (attendance) asistencia. **2** (spirit) espíritu m.

present¹ ['prez°nt] adj **1** (in attendance) presente. **2** (current) actual. **3** LING presente.
▶ n (now) presente m, actualidad f. LOC **at present** actualmente, en este momento.
▶ n **the present** LING presente m. COMP **present continuous** presente continuo. I **present perfect** presente perfecto. I **present tense** presente.

present² [(vb) prɪ'zent; (n) 'prez°nt] vt **1** (make presentation) entregar, hacer entrega de; (give - as gift) regalar. **2** (offer - report, petition, bill, cheque) presentar; (- argument, ideas, case) presentar, exponer. **3** fml (offer - apologies, respects) presentar; (- compliments, greetings) dar. **4** (give - difficulty, problem) plantear; (constitute) suponer, constituir, ser. **5** (introduce) presentar. **6** (play) representar; (programme) presentar.
▶ n (gift) regalo; (formal) obsequio: he gave me a present me hizo un regalo.

presentation [prez°n'teɪʃ°n] n **1** (of awards, prizes, gifts) entrega. **2** (way of presenting) presentación f. **3** (of play) representación f.

presenter [prɪ'zentər] n (on radio) presentador,-ra, locutor,-ra; (on TV) presentador,-ra.

presently ['prez°ntlɪ] adv **1** GB (soon) pronto, enseguida. **2** US (at present) actualmente.

preservation [prezə'veɪʃ°n] n (of wildlife) conservación f, preservación f; (of food, works of art, buildings) conservación f.

preservative [prɪ'zɜ:vətɪv] n CULIN conservante m.

preserve [prɪ'zɜ:v] n CULIN (fruit) conserva; (jam) confitura, mermelada.
▶ vt conservar, proteger.

preset [pri:'set] vt programar.
ⓘ pt & pp preset, ger presetting.

presidency ['prezɪdənsɪ] n presidencia.
ⓘ pl presidencies.

president ['prezɪd°nt] n presidente,-a.

press [pres] n **1** (newspapers) prensa. **2** (machine) prensa, imprenta. **3** (act of pressing) presión f; (of hand) apretón m; (act of ironing) planchado. COMP **press agency** agencia de prensa. I **press conference** conferencia de prensa, rueda de prensa.
▶ vt **1** (push down - button, switch) pulsar, apretar, presionar; (- accelerator) pisar; (- key on keyboard) pulsar; (- trigger) apretar. **2** (squeeze - hand) apretar. **3** (crush - fruit) exprimir, estrujar; (- grapes, olives, flowers) prensar. **4** (clothes) planchar, planchar a vapor. **5** (record) imprimir. **6** (urge, put pressure on) presionar, instar; (insist on) insistir en, exigir.
▶ vi **1** (push) apretar, presionar. **2** (crowd) apretujarse, apiñarse. **3** (urge, pressurize) presionar, insistir; (time) apremiar.

pressing ['presɪŋ] adj urgente, apremiante.

pressure ['preʃər] n **1** (gen) presión f. **5** (stress) tensión f: he's under a lot of pressure está sometido a una gran presión. COMP **pressure cooker** olla a presión, olla exprés.

prestige [pres'ti:ʒ] n prestigio.

prestigious [pres'tɪdʒəs] adj prestigioso,-a.

presume [prɪ'zju:m] vt suponer, imaginarse, presumir: I presume so supongo que sí.
▶ vi **1** suponer. **2** (venture to) atreverse a.

☒ To presume no significa 'presumir (vanagloriarse)', que se traduce por to boast.

pretend [prɪ'tend] vt (feign) fingir, aparentar: the children pretended to be asleep los niños fingían estar dormidos.
▶ vi (feign) fingir.
▶ adj (make-believe) de mentirijillas.

☒ To pretend no significa 'pretender', que se traduce por to want to, to try to.

pretension [prɪ'tenʃ°n] n pretensión f.

pretentious [prɪ'tenʃəs] adj pretencioso,-a.

preterite ['pret°rɪt] n LING pretérito.

pretty ['prɪtɪ] adj (girl, baby) bonito,-a, guapo,-a, mono,-a; (thing) bonito,-a

P

mono,-a: *what a pretty little girl!* ¡qué niña más bonita!

ⓘ *comp* prettier, *superl* prettiest.

▶ *adv* bastante: *I'm pretty sure* estoy bastante seguro,-a. LOC **pretty much** más o menos. I **pretty well** casi.

prevailing [prɪˈveɪlɪŋ] *adj* predominante.

prevent [prɪˈvent] *vt (gen)* impedir; *(avoid - accident)* evitar; *(- illness)* prevenir. LOC **to prevent SB from doing STH** impedir a ALGN hacer ALGO.

prevention [prɪˈvenʃən] *n* prevención *f*.

preview [ˈpriːvjuː] *n* preestreno.

previous [ˈpriːvɪəs] *adj* previo,-a, anterior: *the previous day* el día anterior.

prey [preɪ] *n* 1 *(animal)* presa. 2 *fig* presa, víctima.

price [praɪs] *n* 1 *(gen)* precio; *(amount)* importe *m*; *(value)* valor *m*: *what's the price of this jacket?* ¿qué precio tiene esta chaqueta? 2 *fig (cost, sacrifice)* precio. LOC **at any price** a toda costa, cueste lo que cueste.

▶ *vt (fix price of)* tener un precio; *(value)* valorar, tasar; *(mark price on)* poner el precio a.

priceless [ˈpraɪsləs] *adj* que no tiene precio, inestimable.

pricey [ˈpraɪsɪ] *adj fam* caro,-a.

ⓘ *comp* pricier, *superl* priciest.

prick [prɪk] *n (pain)* pinchazo; *(hole)* agujero.

▶ *vt (with needle, pin, fork)* pinchar.

▶ *vi (pin, thorn)* pinchar; *(itch, sting)* escocer, picar.

prickly [ˈprɪklɪ] *adj* 1 *(plant)* espinoso,-a; *(animal)* con púas; *(wool, sweater)* que pica. 2 *(irritable, touchy)* enojadizo,-a, irritable, difícil.

ⓘ *comp* pricklier, *superl* prickliest.

pride [praɪd] *n* 1 *(gen)* orgullo; *(self-respect)* amor *m* propio. 2 *(arrogance)* soberbia, orgullo.

priest [priːst] *n* sacerdote *m*, cura *m*.

priestess [ˈpriːstes] *n* sacerdotisa.

priesthood [ˈpriːsθʊd] *n (clergy)* clero; *(office)* sacerdocio.

primary [ˈpraɪmərɪ] *adj* 1 *(main)* principal, fundamental. 2 *(first, basic)* primario,-a. COMP **primary school** escuela primaria.

primate [ˈpraɪmeɪt] *n* ZOOL primate *m*.

prime [praɪm] *adj* 1 *(main, chief)* principal, primero,-a. 2 *(first-rate - meat)* de primera (calidad); *(example, location)* excelente.

▶ *n (best time of life)* flor *f* de la vida. COMP **Prime Minister** primer,-a ministro,-a.

▶ *vt* 1 *(engine, pump, bomb)* cebar; *(surface, wood)* imprimar, preparar. 2 *fig (person)* preparar, enseñar.

primitive [ˈprɪmɪtɪv] *adj (man, tribe, culture)* primitivo,-a; *(tool, method, shelter)* rudimentario,-a, primitivo,-a.

prince [prɪns] *n* príncipe *m*.

princess [ˈprɪnses] *n* princesa.

ⓘ *pl* princesses.

principal [ˈprɪnsɪpəl] *adj* principal.

▶ *n* 1 EDUC director,-ra. 2 THEAT protagonista *mf*, primera figura.

principle [ˈprɪnsɪpəl] *n* 1 *(basic idea, rule, law)* principio; *(basis)* base *f*. 2 *(moral rule)* principio: *it's a matter of principle* es cuestión de principios.

print [prɪnt] *n* 1 *(lettering)* letra: *in large print* en letra grande. 2 *(photo)* copia. 3 *(printed fabric)* estampado. 4 *(mark - of finger, foot)* huella.

▶ *vt* 1 *(book, page, poster, etc)* imprimir; *(publish)* publicar, editar. 2 *(photo - negative)* imprimir; *(- copy)* sacar una copia de. 3 *(write clearly)* escribir con letra de imprenta. 4 *(fabric)* estampar. 5 *(make impression)* marcar.

◆ **to print out** *vt sep* imprimir.

printer [ˈprɪntər] *n (person)* impresor,-ra; *(machine)* impresora.

printing [ˈprɪntɪŋ] *n (act, process)* impresión *f*; *(industry)* imprenta. COMP **printing press** prensa.

print-out [ˈprɪntaʊt] *n* COMPUT impresión *f*.

prior [ˈpraɪər] *adj* anterior, previo,-a. LOC **prior to** antes de.

priority [praɪˈɒrɪtɪ] *n* prioridad *f*.

ⓘ *pl* priorities.

▶ *adj* prioritario,-a.

prism [ˈprɪzəm] *n* prisma.

prison ['prɪzªn] *n* prisión *f*, cárcel *f*: *he's in prison* está en la cárcel.

prisoner ['prɪzªnəʳ] *n (in jail)* preso,-a, recluso,-a; *(captive)* prisionero,-a.

privacy ['praɪvəsɪ] *n* privacidad *f*.

private ['praɪvət] *adj* **1** *(own, for own use - property, house, class)* particular; *(- letter, income)* personal. **2** *(confidential)* privado, -a, confidencial. **3** *(not state-controlled)* privado,-a. **4** *(not official)* privado,-a, personal. **5** *(person)* reservado,-a. COMP **private eye** detective *mf* privado,-a.
▸ *n* MIL soldado raso.

privatize ['praɪvətaɪz] *vt* privatizar.

privilege ['prɪvɪlɪdʒ] *n* privilegio.

prize [praɪz] *n (gen)* premio.
▸ *adj (having won a prize)* premiado,-a; *(excellent)* de primera, selecto,-a.

probability [prɒbə'bɪlɪtɪ] *n* probabilidad *f*.
ⓘ *pl* probabilities.

probable ['prɒbəbªl] *adj* probable.

probably ['prɒbəblɪ] *adv* probablemente: *it'll probably rain* es probable que llueva.

probation [prə'beɪʃªn] *n* **1** JUR libertad *f* condicional. **2** *(in employment)* período de prueba.

probe [prəʊb] *n* **1** MED sonda. **2** *(investigation)* investigación *f*.
▸ *vt* **1** MED sondar. **2** *(investigate - gen)* investigar; *(public opinion)* sondear.

ⓧ To **probe** no significa 'probar (demostrar o catar)', que se traducen por to **prove** o to **taste**.

problem ['prɒbləm] *n* problema *m*: *no problem!* ¡no hay problema!, ¡ningún problema!

procedure [prə'siːdʒəʳ] *n (set of actions)* procedimiento; *(step)* trámite *m*, gestión *f*.

proceed [prə'siːd] *vi* **1** *(continue)* seguir, continuar. **2** *(progress)* marchar. **3** *fml (go along)* avanzar, circular; *(go towards)* dirigirse a.

ⓧ To **proceed** no significa 'proceder (venir de)', que se traduce por to **come from**.

proceedings [prə'siːdɪŋz] *n pl* **1** *(events at meeting, ceremony, etc)* actos *mpl*. **2** JUR *(lawsuit)* proceso *sing*.

process ['prəʊses] *n* **1** *(set of actions, changes)* proceso: *the process of growing old* el envejecimiento. **2** *(method)* procedimiento, proceso.
▸ *vt* **1** *(raw material, food)* procesar, tratar; *(film)* revelar. **2** *(deal with)* ocuparse de, tramitar. **3** COMPUT procesar, tratar.

processing ['prəʊsesɪŋ] *n* **1** *(treatment)* procesamiento, tratamiento; *(of film)* revelado. **2** *(in business, law)* tramitación *f*. **3** COMPUT procesamiento.

procession [prə'seʃªn] *n* **1** *(gen)* desfile *m*. **2** REL procesión *f*.

processor ['prəʊsesəʳ] *n* **1** *(for food)* robot *m* de cocina. **2** COMPUT procesador *m*.

proclaim [prə'kleɪm] *vt* proclamar, declarar.

procure [prə'kjʊəʳ] *vt (obtain)* conseguir, obtener.

ⓧ To **procure** no significa 'procurar (intentar)', que se traduce por to **try**.

prodigy ['prɒdɪdʒɪ] *n* prodigio.
ⓘ *pl* prodigies.

produce [*(vb)* prə'djuːs; *(n)* 'prɒdjuːs] *vt* **1** *(gen)* producir, fabricar. **2** *(give birth to)* tener. **3** *(show)* enseñar, presentar. **4** *(cause)* producir, causar. **5** *(play)* poner en escena, dirigir.
▸ *n* productos *mpl*: *produce of Spain* productos de España.

producer [prə'djuːsəʳ] *n* **1** *(gen)* productor,-ra, fabricante. **2** *(play)* director,-ra de escena.

product ['prɒdʌkt] *n* producto.

production [prə'dʌkʃªn] *n* **1** *(gen)* producción *f*, fabricación *f*. **2** *(of film)* producción *f*; *(of play)* producción *f*, puesta en escena. COMP **production line** cadena de montaje.

productive [prə'dʌktɪv] *adj* productivo,-a.

productivity [prɒdʌk'tɪvɪtɪ] *n* productividad *f*.

profession [prə'feʃªn] *n (occupation)* profesión *f*: *he's a baker by profession* es panadero de profesión.

professional [prə'feʃªnəl] *adj (gen)* profesional.
▸ *n* profesional *mf*.

P

professor [prəˈfəsəʳ] *n* **1** GB catedrático, -a. **2** US profesor,-ra universitario,-a.

proficiency [prəˈfɪʃ°nsɪ] *n* competencia.

profile [ˈprəʊfaɪl] *n* **1** *(side view)* perfil *m*. **2** *(description)* perfil *m*; *(written)* reseña.

profit [ˈprɒfɪt] *n* **1** COMM ganancia, beneficio. **2** *fml (advantage)* provecho. LOC **to make a profit** sacar beneficios, tener ganancias.

profitable [ˈprɒfɪtəb°l] *adj* **1** COMM rentable. **2** *(beneficial)* provechoso,-a.

profit-making [ˈprɒfɪtmeɪkɪŋ] *adj (business)* rentable; *(charity)* con fines lucrativos.

profound [prəˈfaʊnd] *adj* profundo,-a.

program [ˈprəʊgræm] *n* COMPUT programa *m*.
▶ *vt* COMPUT programar.
ⓘ *pt & pp* programmed, *ger* programming.

programme [ˈprəʊgræm] *n (gen)* programa *m*; *(plan)* plan *m*.
▶ *vt (gen)* programar; *(activities)* planear.

programmer [ˈprəʊgræməʳ] *n* programador,-ra.

programming [ˈprəʊgræmɪŋ] *n* programación *f*.

progress [*(n)* ˈprəʊgres; *(vb)* prəʊˈgres] *n* *(advance)* progreso, avance *m*; *(development)* desarrollo.
▶ *vi* **1** *(advance)* progresar, avanzar, adelantar; *(develop)* desarrollar. **2** *(improve)* mejorar, hacer progresos. LOC **to be in progress** *(work)* estar en curso, estar en marcha.

progression [prəʊˈgreʃ°n] *n* **1** *(development)* evolución *f*, avance *m*. **2** *(series)* serie *f*.

prohibit [prəˈhɪbɪt] *vt* prohibir.

prohibition [prəʊɪˈbɪʃ°n] *n* prohibición *f*.

project [*(n)* ˈprɒdʒekt; *(vb)* prəˈdʒekt] *n* **1** *(gen)* proyecto. **2** EDUC trabajo, estudio.
▶ *vt* **1** *(gen)* proyectar. **2** *(extrapolate)* extrapolar.
▶ *vi* sobresalir, resaltar.

projectile [prəˈdʒektaɪl] *n* proyectil *m*.

projection [prəˈdʒek°n] *n* **1** *(gen)* proyección *f*. **2** *(protuberance)* saliente *m*, resalto.

proletariat [prəʊləˈteərɪət] *n* proletariado.

prologue [ˈprəʊlɒg] *n* prólogo.

prolong [prəˈlɒŋ] *vt* prolongar, alargar.

promenade [prɒməˈnɑːd] *n* **1** GB *(at seaside)* paseo marítimo. **2** *fml (walk)* paseo.

prominent [ˈprɒmɪnənt] *adj (important)* importante; *(projecting)* prominente, saliente.

promise [ˈprɒmɪs] *n* **1** *(pledge)* promesa. **2** *(expectation, hope)* esperanza, esperanzas *fpl*. LOC **to break a promise** romper una promesa. **I to keep a promise** mantener una promesa.
▶ *vt* **1** prometer: *you promised to help me* prometiste ayudarme. **2** *(seem likely)* prometer.
▶ *vi (gen)* prometer; *(swear)* jurar: *I promise* te lo prometo.

promote [prəˈməʊt] *vt* **1** *(in rank)* promover, ascender. **2** *(encourage)* promover, fomentar.

promotion [prəˈməʊ°n] *n* promoción *f*.

prompt [prɒmpt] *adj (quick)* pronto,-a, rápido,-a; *(punctual)* puntual.
▶ *adv* en punto.
▶ *vt* **1** *(cause, incite)* instar, incitar, mover. **2** THEAT apuntar.
▶ *n* THEAT *(line)* apunte *m*.

promptly [ˈprɒmptlɪ] *adv* rápidamente.

prone [prəʊn] *adj (face down)* boca abajo. LOC **to be prone to** STH ser propenso,-a a ALGO.

pronoun [ˈprəʊnaʊn] *n* LING pronombre *m*.

pronounce [prəˈnaʊns] *vt* **1** LING pronunciar. **2** *(declare)* declarar.
▶ *vi* pronunciarse (on, sobre).

pronunciation [prənʌnsɪˈeɪʃ°n] *n* pronunciación *f*.

proof [pruːf] *n* **1** *(evidence)* prueba. **2** *(trial copy, print)* prueba.

propaganda [prɒpəˈgændə] *n* propaganda.

❌ Propaganda no significa 'propaganda (publicidad)', que se traduce por **advertising**.

propagation [prɒpəˈgeɪʃ°n] *n* propagación *f*.

propane [ˈprəʊpeɪn] *n* propano.

propel [prəˈpel] *vt* propulsar, impulsar. ⓘ *pt & pp* **propelled**, *ger* **propelling**.

propeller [prəˈpeləʳ] *n* hélice *f*.

propelling pencil [prəpelɪŋˈpensªl] *n* portaminas *m*.

proper [ˈprɒpəʳ] *adj* **1** *(suitable)* adecuado,-a, apropiado,-a; *(correct)* correcto,-a. **2** *fam (real, genuine)* verdadero,-a, de verdad. **3** *fam (thorough)* auténtico,-a. **4** *(respectable)* correcto,-a, decente. ᴄᴏᴍᴘ **proper name / proper noun** nombre propio.

ⓧ Proper no significa 'propio (de uno)', que se traduce por **own**.

properly [ˈprɒpəlɪ] *adv* **1** *(properly)* bien, adecuadamente. **2** *(correctly)* bien; *(as one should)* como es debido.

property [ˈprɒpətɪ] *n* **1** *(possessions, ownership)* propiedad *f*. **2** *(buildings, land)* propiedad *f*, bienes *mpl*; *(estate)* finca, **3** *fml (building)* inmueble *m*. ⓘ *pl* **properties**.

prophecy [ˈprɒfəsɪ] *n* profecía. ⓘ *pl* **prophecies**.

prophet [ˈprɒfɪt] *n* profeta *m*.

prophetic [prəˈfetɪk] *adj* profético,-a.

proportion [prəˈpɔːʃªn] *n* **1** *(ratio)* proporción *f*. **2** *(part)* parte *f*; *(percentage)* porcentaje *m*. **3** *(correct relation)* proporción *f*. ▶ *n pl* **proportions** dimensiones *fpl*, proporciones *fpl*.

proportional [prəˈpɔːʃªnəl] *adj* proporcional (**to**, a).

proposal [prəˈpəʊzªl] *n* propuesta.

propose [prəˈpəʊz] *vt* **1** *(suggest)* proponer. **2** *(intend)* pensar. ▶ *vi* declararse, proponer matrimonio a.

prose [prəʊz] *n* ʟɪᴛ prosa.

prosecute [ˈprɒsɪkjuːt] *vt* ᴊᴜʀ procesar. ▶ *vi* ᴊᴜʀ *(bring a charge)* entablar una acción judicial; *(be prosecutor)* llevar la acusación.

prosecution [prɒsɪˈkjuːʃªn] *n* ᴊᴜʀ *(action)* procesamiento, acción *f* judicial. ▶ *n* **the prosecution** ᴊᴜʀ *(person)* la acusación.

prosecutor [ˈprɒsɪkjuːtəʳ] *n* ᴊᴜʀ fiscal *mf*, acusador,-ra.

prospect [*(n)* ˈprɒspekt; *(vb)* prəˈspekt] *n* **1** *(picture in mind)* perspectiva. **2** *(possibility, hope)* posibilidad *f*, probabilidad *f*. **3** *fml (wide view)* panorama *m*, vista, perspectiva. ▶ *vt* prospectar, explorar. ▶ *vi* buscar (**for**, -). ▶ *n pl* **prospects** perspectivas *fpl*.

ⓧ Prospect no significa 'prospecto', que se traduce por **leaflet**.

prosper [ˈprɒspəʳ] *vi* prosperar.

prosperity [prɒˈsperɪtɪ] *n* prosperidad *f*.

prosperous [ˈprɒspªrəs] *adj* próspero,-a.

prostate [ˈprɒsteɪt] *n* próstata.

prosthesis [ˈprɒsθəsɪs] *n* prótesis *f*.

prostitute [ˈprɒstɪtjuːt] *n* prostituta.

protect [prəˈtekt] *vt (gen)* proteger; *(interests)* proteger, salvaguardar.

protection [prəˈtekʃªn] *n (gen)* protección *f*; *(shelter)* protección *f*, amparo.

protective [prəˈtektɪv] *adj* protector,-ra.

protector [prəˈtektəʳ] *n* protector,-ra.

protein [ˈprəʊtiːn] *n* proteína.

protest [*(n)* ˈprəʊtest; *(vb)* prəˈtest] *n (gen)* protesta; *(complaint)* queja; *(demonstration)* manifestación *f* de protesta. ▶ *vt* protestar de. ▶ *vi* protestar (**about**, de), (**against**, contra), (**at**, por): *they protested about the working conditions* protestaron de las condiciones de trabajo.

Protestant [ˈprɒtɪstªnt] *adj* protestante. ▶ *n* protestante *mf*.

proton [ˈprəʊtɒn] *n* protón *m*.

proud [praʊd] *adj* orgulloso,-a: *I'm proud of you* estoy orgulloso de ti.

proudly [ˈpraʊdlɪ] *adv (with satisfaction)* orgullosamente, con orgullo; *(arrogantly)* arrogantemente, con arrogancia.

prove [pruːv] *vt* **1** *(show to be true)* probar, demostrar. **2** *(turn out to be)* demostrar. ⓘ *pt* **proved**, *pp* **proved** o **proven** [ˈpruːvən], *ger* **proving**.

ⓧ To prove no significa 'probar (comida)', que se traduce por **to taste**.

proven [ˈpruːvªn] *pp* → **prove**. ▶ *adj* probado,-a, comprobado,-a.

P

proverb [ˈprɒvɜ:b] n proverbio, refrán m.

provide [prəˈvaɪd] vt 1 (supply) proveer, suministrar, proporcionar: he provided us with all the information nos facilitó toda la información. 2 fig (answer, example) ofrecer, dar.

provided [prəˈvaɪdɪd] [also provided that] conj siempre que, con tal que.

province [ˈprɒvɪns] n 1 (region) provincia. 2 fig terreno, campo, competencia.

provincial [prəˈvɪnʃ°l] adj 1 (government) provincial; (town) de provincia(s). 2 pej provinciano,-a, pueblerino,-a.

provision [prəˈvɪʒ°n] n 1 (supply) suministro, abastecimiento. 2 (preparation) previsiones fpl.
▸ n pl **provisions** (food) provisiones fpl, víveres mpl.

provisional [prəˈvɪʒ°nəl] adj provisional.

provoke [prəˈvəʊk] vt 1 (make angry) provocar, irritar: he's not easily provoked no se irrita fácilmente. 2 (cause) provocar.

prowl [praʊl] vi merodear, rondar.
▸ vt merodear por, rondar por.
▸ n merodeo.

proximity [ˈprɒksɪmɪtɪ] n fml proximidad f.

prune [pru:n] n ciruela pasa.

psalm [sɑ:m] n salmo.

pseudonym [ˈsu:d°nɪm] n seudónimo.

psychedelic [saɪkɪˈdelɪk] adj psicodélico,-a.

psychiatric [saɪkɪˈætrɪk] adj psiquiátrico,-a.

psychiatrist [saɪˈkaɪətrɪst] n psiquiatra mf.

psychiatry [saɪˈkaɪətrɪ] n psiquiatría.

psychic [ˈsaɪkɪk] adj (mental) psíquico,-a.

psychoanalyst [saɪkəʊˈænəlɪst] n psicoanalista mf.

psychological [saɪkəˈlɒdʒɪk°l] adj psicológico,-a.

psychologist [saɪˈkɒlədʒɪst] n psicólogo,-a.

psychology [saɪˈkɒlədʒɪ] n psicología.

psychosis [saɪˈkəʊsɪs] n psicosis f.
ⓘ pl **psychoses** [saɪˈkəʊsi:z].

pub [pʌb] n bar m, pub m, taberna.

puberty [ˈpju:bətɪ] n pubertad f.

pubis [ˈpju:bɪs] n pubis m.

public [ˈpʌblɪk] adj público,-a. COMP **public convenience** servicios mpl, aseos mpl. ‖ **public holiday** fiesta nacional. ‖ **public house** bar m, pub m. ‖ **public school 1** GB colegio privado. 2 US colegio público.
▸ **the public** el público.

⊕ En el Reino Unido, los **public schools** son colegios privados de prestigio y de mucha tradición; suelen ser internados. Los colegios públicos británicos se llaman **state schools**. En Estados Unidos los **public schools** son, sencillamente, colegios públicos.

publication [pʌblɪˈkeɪʃ°n] n publicación f.

publicity [pʌˈblɪsɪtɪ] n publicidad f.

publish [ˈpʌblɪʃ] vt 1 (book, newspaper) publicar, editar. 2 (make known) divulgar.

publisher [ˈpʌblɪʃ[ə'] n (person) editor,-ra. (company) editorial f.

pudding [ˈpʊdɪŋ] n 1 CULIN (sweet) budín m, pudín m; (savoury) pastel m. 2 GB fam (dessert) postre m.

puddle [ˈpʌd°l] n charco.

Puerto Rican [pweətəʊˈri:k°n] adj puertorriqueño,-a, portorriqueño,-a.
▸ n puertorriqueño,-a, portorriqueño,-a.

Puerto Rico [pweətəʊˈri:kəʊ] n Puerto Rico.

puff [pʌf] n 1 (of wind, air) soplo, racha, ráfaga; (of smoke) bocanada. 2 (action) soplo, soplido; (at cigarette, pipe) calada, chupada.
▸ vt (blow - gen) soplar; (- smoke) echar.
▸ vi 1 (pipe, cigarette) chupar (at/on, -), dar caladas (at/on, a). 2 (pant) jadear, resoplar. 3 (train) echar humo, echar vapor.

puke [pju:k] vi fam devolver, vomitar.

pull [pʊl] n 1 (tug) tirón m. 2 (of moon, current) fuerza. 3 (attraction) atracción f; (influence) influencia.
▸ vt 1 (draw) tirar de; (drag) arrastrar: the horse was pulling a cart el caballo tiraba de una carreta. 2 (tug forcefully) tirar de, dar un tirón a: don't pull my hair! ¡no me tires del pelo! 3 (remove, draw out) sacar. 4 (damage - muscle) sufrir un tirón. 5

fam (attract - crowd, audience) atraer; *(boy, girl)* ligarse, ligar con.
▶ *vi* **1** *(tug)* tirar (at/on, de). **2** *(on pipe, cigarette)* chupar, dar caladas a. **3** *(of vehicle - veer)* tirar.
◆ **to pull down** *vt sep* derribar, tirar (abajo).
◆ **to pull in** *vt sep* **1** *(crowd)* atraer. **2** *(money)* sacar, ganar.
▶ *vi (train)* entrar en la estación; *(bus, car)* parar.
◆ **to pull out** *vt sep (gun, tooth, plug, etc)* sacar; *(troops)* retirar.
▶ *vi* **1** *(train)* salir de la estación; *(bus, car)* salir. **2** *(withdraw)* retirarse.

pulley ['pʊlɪ] *n* polea.

pullover ['pʊləʊvəʳ] *n* pullover *m*, jersey *m*.

pulmonary ['pʌlmənʳɪ] *adj* pulmonar.

pulse¹ [pʌls] *n* **1** ANAT pulso. **2** PHYS pulsación *f*.
▶ *vi* palpitar, latir.

pulse² [pʌls] *n* BOT legumbre *f*.

puma ['pjuːmə] *n* puma *m*.

pumice stone ['pʌmɪsstəʊn] *n* piedra pómez.

pump¹ [pʌmp] *n (machine)* bomba: *bicycle pump* bomba de aire, bombín *m*.
▶ *vt* bombear.
▶ *vi (of heart)* latir.
◆ **to pump up** *vt sep* inflar.

pump² [pʌmp] *n (plimsoll)* zapatilla de lona, playera; *(for dancing)* zapatilla de ballet.

pumpkin ['pʌmpkɪn] *n* calabaza.

punch¹ [pʌntʃ] *n* **1** *(blow)* puñetazo, golpe *m*; *(in boxing)* pegada. **2** *fig* fuerza, empuje *m*.
▶ *vt* dar un puñetazo a, pegar a.

punch² [pʌntʃ] *n (for making holes)* perforadora, taladro; *(in leather)* punzón *m*; *(for tickets)* máquina de picar billetes.
▶ *vt (make a hole in)* perforar; *(leather)* punzar; *(ticket)* picar.

punch³ [pʌntʃ] *n (drink)* ponche *m*.

punctual ['pʌŋktjʊəl] *adj* puntual.

punctuality ['pʌŋktjʊəlɪtɪ] *n* puntualidad *f*.

punctuate ['pʌŋktjʊeɪt] *vt* **1** LING puntuar. **2** *(interrupt)* interrumpir.

punctuation [pʌŋktjʊ'eɪʃ°n] *n* puntuación *f*. COMP **punctuation mark** signo de puntuación.

puncture ['pʌŋktʃəʳ] *n* pinchazo.
▶ *vt (tyre, ball, etc)* pinchar.

punish ['pʌnɪʃ] *vt* castigar.

punishment ['pʌnɪʃmənt] *n* castigo.

punk [pʌŋk] *n (person)* punk *mf*; *(music)* punk *m*.

pupil¹ ['pjuːpəl] *n* EDUC alumno,-a.

pupil² ['pjuːpəl] *n* ANAT pupila.

puppet ['pʌpɪt] *n* **1** títere *m*. **2** *fig* títere *m*. COMP **puppet show** teatro de títeres.

puppy ['pʌpɪ] *n* cachorro,-a.
ⓘ *pl* **puppies**.

purchase ['pɜːtʃəs] *n fml* compra.
▶ *vt fml* comprar, adquirir.

pure ['pjʊəʳ] *adj (gen)* puro,-a. *it was pure chance* fue pura casualidad.

purée ['pjʊəreɪ] *n* puré *m*.

purification [pjʊərɪfɪ'keɪʃ°n] *n* purificación *f*.

purify ['pjʊərɪfaɪ] *vt (gen)* purificar; *(water)* depurar, purificar.
ⓘ *pt & pp* **purified**, *ger* **purifying**.

puritan ['pjʊərɪt°n] *adj* puritano,-a.
▶ *n* puritano,-a.

purple ['pɜːpəl] *adj* morado,-a.
▶ *n* (color *m*) púrpura, (color *m*) morado.

purpose ['pɜːpəs] *n* **1** *(aim, intention)* propósito, intención *f*, fin *m*; *(reason)* razón *f*, motivo: *what is the purpose of your visit?* ¿cuál es el motivo de su visita? **2** *(use)* uso, utilidad *f*. **3** *(determination)* resolución *f*. LOC **to no purpose** inútilmente, en vano. ❘ **on purpose** a propósito, adrede, a posta.

purr [pɜːʳ] *n (of cat)* ronroneo.
▶ *vi (of cat)* ronronear.

purse [pɜːs] *n* **1** GB monedero, portamonedas *m*. **2** US bolso.
▶ *vt (lips)* fruncir.

pursue [pə'sjuː] *vt* **1** *(chase)* perseguir; *(follow)* seguir. **2** *(seek)* buscar; *(strive for)* esforzarse por conseguir, luchar por. **3** *(carry out - policy)* llevar a cabo; *(- mat-*

ter) investigar. **4** *(continue with)* seguir, dedicarse a, ejercer.

pursuit [pəˈsjuːt] *n* **1** *(chase)* persecución *f*; *(hunt)* caza. **2** *(search)* búsqueda; *(striving)* lucha. **3** *(activity)* actividad *f*.

pus [pʌs] *n* pus *m*.

push [pʊʃ] *n (shove)* empujón *m*.
► *vt* **1** *(gen)* empujar. **2** *(press - button, bell, etc)* pulsar, apretar.
► *vi* **1** *(shove)* empujar. **2** *(move forward)* abrirse paso. **3** *(pressurize)* presionar, exigir.

pushchair [ˈpʊʃtʃeəʳ] *n* GB cochecito de niño, sillita de niño.

push-up [ˈpʊʃʌp] *n* US flexión *f*.

pussycat [ˈpʊsɪkæt] *n fam* minino,-a, gatito,-a.

put [pʊt] *vt* **1** *(gen)* poner; *(place)* colocar; *(add)* echar, añadir; *(place inside)* meter, poner. **2** *(express)* expresar, decir: *you put that very well* lo has expresado muy bien. **3** *(calculate, estimate)* calcular: *I'd put the cost at 100 pounds* yo diría que cuesta 100 libras. LOC **to put STH right** arreglar ALGO. | **to put the blame on SB** echar la culpa a ALGN.
◆ **to put down** *vt sep* **1** *(set down - gen)* dejar; *(- phone)* colgar. **2** *(payment)* entregar, dejar (en depósito); *(deposit)* dejar. **3** *(rebellion)* sofocar. **4** *(write)* apuntar, anotar, escribir.
► *vi* AV aterrizar.
◆ **to put forward** *vt sep* **1** *(idea, theory, plan)* proponer, presentar. **2** *(clock, meeting, wedding)* adelantar.
◆ **to put in** *vt sep* **1** *(install, fit)* instalar, poner. **2** *(include, insert)* poner, incluir; *(say)* agregar. **3** *(enter, submit - claim, request, bid)* presentar. **4** *(spend time working)* trabajar, hacer.
► *vi (ship)* hacer escala.
◆ **to put off** *vt sep* **1** *(postpone)* aplazar, posponer. **2** *(distract)* distraer. **3** *(discourage)* desanimar, disuadir, quitar las ganas a.
◆ **to put on** *vt sep* **1** *(clothes)* poner, ponerse: *put your coat on* ponte el abrigo. **2** *(expression, attitude)* fingir, adoptar. **3** *(gain, increase)* aumentar. **4** *(present - show)* presentar, montar; *(- exhibition)* organizar. **5** *(switch on - light, television)* encender; *(- music, radio)* poner.
◆ **to put out** *vt sep* **1** *(fire, light, cigarette)* apagar. **2** *(put outside - cat, washing, rubbish)* sacar. **3** *(extend - hand)* tender, alargar; *(- tongue)* sacar; *(dislocate)* dislocar. **4** *(inconvenience)* molestar; *(upset, offend, annoy)* molestar, ofender. **5** *(publish, issue)* publicar; *(broadcast)* difundir.
◆ **to put up** *vt sep* **1** *(provide accommodation for)* alojar, hospedar. **2** *(erect - tent)* armar; *(- building, fence)* levantar, construir. **3** *(shelves, picture, decorations)* colocar; *(curtains, notice, poster)* colgar. **4** *(raise - hand)* levantar; *(flag)* izar; *(hair)* recoger; *(umbrella)* abrir. **5** *(increase - price, etc)* aumentar, subir. **6** *(present - candidate)* presentar, proponer.
► *vt insep* **1** *(resistence, struggle)* ofrecer, oponer: *they put up a good fight* ofrecieron mucha resistencia. **2** *(money)* poner, aportar.
◆ **to put up with** *vt insep* soportar, aguantar.
ⓘ *pt & pp* **put**, *ger* **putting**.

putt [pʌt] *n* tiro al hoyo.
► *vt* tirar al hoyo.

puzzle [ˈpʌzᵊl] *n* **1** *(jigsaw)* puzzle *m*; *(toy)* rompecabezas *m*; *(riddle)* adivinanza, acertijo; *(crossword)* crucigrama *m*. **2** *(mystery)* misterio, enigma *m*.
► *vt* dejar perplejo,-a, extrañar.
◆ **to puzzle out** *vt sep (problem)* resolver; *(mystery)* descifrar.

pygmy [ˈpɪgmɪ] *adj* pigmeo,-a, enano,-a.
► *n (small person)* pigmeo,-a, enano,-a.

pyjamas [pəˈdʒɑːməz] *n pl* pijama *m sing*.

pylon [ˈpaɪlᵊn] *n* **1** ELEC torre *f* (de tendido eléctrico). **2** ARCH pilón *m*, pilar *m*.

pylorus [ˈpaɪlərəs] *n* píloro.

pyramid [ˈpɪrəmɪd] *n* pirámide *f*.

pyrites [paɪˈraɪtiːz] *n* pirita.

pyromaniac [paɪrəʊˈmeɪnɪæk] *n* pirómano,-a.

pyrotechnics [paɪrəʊˈteknɪks] *n* pirotecnia.
► *n pl* fuegos *mpl* artificiales.

python [ˈpaɪθᵊn] *n* pitón *m*.

Q

Q, q [kjuː] *n (the letter)* Q, q *f.*

quack [kwæk] *vi* graznar.

Qatar [kæ'tɑːʳ] *n* Qatar.

quadriceps ['kwɒdrɪseps] *n* ANAT cuádriceps *m.*

quail [kweɪl] *n* codorniz *f.*

quake [kweɪk] *n fam* terremoto.

qualification [kwɒlɪfɪ'keɪʃ°n] *n* **1** *(for job)* requisito. **2** *(ability)* aptitud *f,* capacidad *f.* **3** *(paper)* diploma *m,* título **4** *(reservation)* reserva, salvedad *f.* **5** *(restriction)* limitación *f.*

☒ Qualification no significa 'calificación (nota)', que se traduce por mark.

qualified ['kwɒlɪfaɪd] *adj* **1** *(for job)* capacitado,-a. **2** *(with qualifications)* titulado,-a: *qualified nurse* enfermero,-a titulado,-a. **3** *(limited, modified)* limitado,-a, restringido,-a.

qualify ['kwɒlɪfaɪ] *vt* **1** *(entitle, make eligible)* capacitar, dar derecho. **2** *(modify)* modificar, matizar, puntualizar. **3** LING calificar.
ⓘ *pt & pp* qualified, *ger* qualifying.

quality ['kwɒlɪtɪ] *n* **1** *(degree of excellence)* calidad *f: of good quality* de buena calidad; *of poor quality* de poca calidad. **2** *(attribute)* cualidad *f: she has many qualities* tiene muchas cualidades. COMP **quality control** control *m* de calidad. ▮ **quality newspapers** prensa de calidad.
ⓘ *pl* qualities.

quantity ['kwɒntɪtɪ] *n* **1** cantidad *f.* **2** MATH cantidad *f.*
ⓘ *pl* quantities.

quarrel ['kwɒr°l] *n* **1** riña, disputa, pelea. **2** *(disagreement)* desacuerdo. **3** *(complaint)* queja: *I have no quarrel with him* no tengo ninguna queja de él, no tengo nada contra él. LOC **to pick a quar-**

rel with SB meterse con ALGN, buscar pelea con ALGN.
▶ *vi (argue)* reñir, pelearse, disputar, discutir: *she is always quarrelling with her mother* siempre está discutiendo con su madre.
ⓘ *pt & pp* quarrelled (US quarreled), *ger* quarrelling (US quarreling).

quarry ['kwɒrɪ] *n* **1** cantera. **2** *(in hunting)* presa.
ⓘ *pl* quarries.
▶ *vt* extraer.
ⓘ *pt & pp* quarried, *ger* quarrying.

quart [kwɔːt] *n* cuarto de galón.

✎ En Gran Bretaña equivale a 1,14 litros; en Estados Unidos equivale a 0,95 litro.

quarter ['kwɔːtəʳ] *n* **1** cuarto. **2** *(area)* barrio: *the old quarter* el casco antiguo. **3** *(time)* cuarto: *it's a quarter to one* es la una menos cuarto. **4** *(of moon)* cuarto. **5** *(three months)* trimestre *m.* **6** US *(amount)* veinticinco centavos; *(coin)* moneda de veinticinco centavos. COMP **first quarter** cuarto creciente. ▮ **last quarter** cuarto menguante.
▶ *n pl* **quarters** alojamiento *m sing.* COMP **at close quarters** desde muy cerca. ▮ **to give no quarter** no dar cuartel.

quartz [kwɔːts] *n* cuarzo. COMP **quartz watch** reloj *m* de cuarzo.

quay [kiː] *n* muelle *m.*

queen [kwiːn] *n* **1** reina. **2** *(cards, chess)* dama, reina; *(chess)* reina. COMP **queen bee** abeja reina. ▮ **Queen Mother** reina madre.

queer [kwɪəʳ] *adj* **1** raro,-a, extraño,-a. **2** *(ill)* malucho,-a. **3** *fam* gay. **4** *(mad)* loco,-a, chiflado,-a.

quench [kwentʃ] *vt* **1** *(thirst)* saciar. **2** *(fire)* apagar.

query [ˈkwɪərɪ] *n* **1** pregunta, duda. **2** LING signo de interrogación. **3** *fig* interrogante *m*.
ⓘ *pl* queries.
▸ *vt* **1** *(doubt)* poner en duda. **2** *(ask)* preguntar.
ⓘ *pt & pp* queried, *ger* querying.

quest [kwest] *n* búsqueda, busca. LOC **in quest of** en busca de: *in quest of the Holy Grail* en busca del Santo Grial.

question [ˈkwestʃən] *n* **1** pregunta. **2** *(in exam)* pregunta, problema *m*. **3** *(problem, issue)* cuestión *f*, problema *m*. **4** *(topic, matter)* cuestión *f*, asunto *m*. LOC **it's a question of** se trata de, es cuestión de: *it's a question of time* es cuestión de tiempo. ▌**out of the question** imposible, impensable. ▌**that is the question** de eso se trata. ▌**without question** sin rechistar: *she did it without question* lo hizo sin rechistar. COMP **question mark 1** *(punctuation mark)* signo de interrogación, interrogación *f*, interrogante *m*. **2** *(doubt)* interrogante *m*. ▌**question tag** coletilla.
▸ *vt* **1** hacer preguntas a, interrogar. **2** *(cast doubt on)* cuestionar, poner en duda.

questionnaire [kwestʃəˈneəʳ] *n* cuestionario.

queue [kjuː] *n* GB cola. LOC **to jump the queue** colarse.
▸ *vi* hacer cola.

quick [kwɪk] *adj* **1** *(fast)* rápido,-a: *let's have a quick look* echemos un vistazo. **2** *(clever)* espabilado,-a, listo,-a.

quickly [ˈkwɪklɪ] *adv (speed up)* rápido
▸ *vi (speed up)* acelerarse.

quicksand [ˈkwɪksænd] *n* arenas *fpl* movedizas.

quiet [ˈkwaɪət] *adj* **1** *(silent)* callado,-a, silencioso,-a: *he kept quiet all night* estuvo callado toda la noche. **2** *(peaceful, calm)* tranquilo,-a, sosegado,-a: *this is a very quiet village* éste es un pueblo muy tranquilo. **3** *(unobtrusive)* callado,-a, reservado,-a. **4** *(tranquil, without fuss)* tranquilo,-a. LOC **be quiet!** ¡cállate!
▸ *n* **1** *(silence)* silencio. **2** *(calm)* tranquilidad *f*, calma, sosiego.
▸ *vt* US calmar, silenciar: *she quieted the baby down* calmó a la criatura.

▸ *vi* US calmarse. LOC **on the quiet** a la chita callando, a hurtadillas: *he did it on the quiet* lo hizo en secreto.

quietly [ˈkwaɪətlɪ] *adv* **1** *(silently)* silenciosamente, sin hacer ruido; *(not loudly)* bajo: *she always speaks quietly* siempre habla en voz baja. **2** *(calmly)* tranquilamente. **3** *(discreetly)* discretamente, con discreción. **4** *(simply)* sencillamente, con sencillez.

quilt [kwɪlt] *n* edredón *m*.

quince [kwɪns] *n* membrillo.

quit [kwɪt] *vt* **1** dejar, abandonar: *he quit his job* dejó el trabajo. **2** *(stop)* dejar de: *she quit smoking* dejó de fumar.
▸ *vi* marcharse, irse.
ⓘ *pt & pp* quit, *ger* quitting.
✗ To quit no significa 'quitar', que se traduce por to remove.

quite [kwaɪt] *adv* **1** *(rather)* bastante: *they played quite well* jugaron bastante bien; *they're quite difficult exercises* son ejercicios bastante difíciles. **2** *(totally)* completamente, del todo: *I quite understand* lo entiendo perfectamente. **3** *(exceptional)* excepcional, increíble, original: *it's been quite a year* ha sido un año excepcional. **4** *(exactly)* exactamente: *it isn't quite what I was looking for* no es exactamente lo que buscaba.

quiver¹ [ˈkwɪvəʳ] *n* **1** *(tremble of lips, voice)* temblor *m*; *(of eyelids)* parpadeo; *(shiver)* estremecimiento.
▸ *vi* temblar, estremecerse.

quiz [kwɪz] *n* **1** *(competition)* concurso. **2** *(enquiry)* encuesta; *(exam)* examen *m*.
▸ *vt* preguntar, interrogar.

quotation [kwəʊˈteɪʃən] *n* **1** LING cita. **2** FIN cotización *f*. **3** COMM presupuesto. COMP **quotation marks** comillas *fpl*.

quote [kwəʊt] *n* **1** LING cita. **2** *(price - gen)* presupuesto; *(- for shares)* cotización *f*.
▸ *vt* **1** citar, entrecomillar. **2** *(price)* dar, ofrecer. **3** FIN cotizar.

quotient [ˈkwəʊʃənt] *n* **1** *(in mathematics)* cociente *m*. **2** *(degree)* coeficiente *m*, grado. COMP **intelligence quotient** coeficiente intelectual *m*, coeficiente *m* de inteligencia.

R

R, r [ɑː] *n* **1** *(the letter)* R, r *f*.
rabbit ['ræbɪt] *n* conejo.
raccoon [rə'kuːn] *n* mapache *m*.
race¹ [reɪs] *n* *(people)* raza.
race² [reɪs] *n* **1** SP carrera. **2** *(current)* corriente *f* fuerte; *(channel)* canal *m*. LOC **to run a race** participar en una carrera.
  ▶ *vt* **1** *(person)* competir con, echar una carrera a. **2** *(engine)* acelerar.
racecourse ['reɪskɔːs] *n* GB hipódromo.
racehorse ['reɪhɔːs] *n* caballo de carreras.
racial ['reɪʃəl] *adj* racial.
racing ['reɪsɪŋ] *n* carreras *fpl*.
  ▶ *adj* de carreras. COMP **racing car** coche *m* de carreras. ‖ **racing driver** piloto de carreras.
racism ['reɪsɪzəm] *n* racismo.
racist ['reɪsɪst] *adj* racista.
  ▶ *n* racista *mf*.
rack [ræk] *n* **1** estante *m*. **2** AUTO baca. **3** *(on train)* rejilla. **4** *(for torture)* potro.
racket¹ ['rækɪt] *n* SP raqueta.
racket² ['rækɪt] *n* **1** *(din)* alboroto, ruido. **2** *fam (fraud)* timo. **3** *fam (business)* asunto, negocio.
racoon [rə'kuːn] *n* mapache *m*.
racquet ['rækɪt] *n* raqueta.
radar ['reɪdɑːʳ] *n* radar *m*. COMP **radar trap** control *m* de velocidad por radar.
radiation [reɪdɪ'eɪʃən] *n* radiación *f*.
radiator ['reɪdɪeɪtəʳ] *n* radiador *m*.
radical ['rædɪkəl] *adj* radical.
  ▶ *n* radical *mf*.
radii ['reɪdɪaɪ] *n pl* → radius.
radio ['reɪdɪəu] *n* radio *f*. COMP **radio cassette** radiocasete *m*.
  ① *pl* radios.

radioactive [reɪdɪəu'æktɪv] *adj* radiactivo,-a. LOC **radioactive waste** residuos *mpl* radiactivos.
radioactivity [reɪdɪəuæk'tɪvɪtɪ] *n* radiactividad *f*.
radiography [reɪdɪ'ɒgrəfɪ] *n* radiografía.
  ① *pl* radiographies.
radiologist [reɪdɪ'ɒlədʒɪst] *n* radiólogo,-a.
radiology [reɪdɪ'ɒlədʒɪ] *n* radiología.
radish ['rædɪʃ] *n* rábano.
radium ['reɪdɪəm] *n* radio.
radius ['reɪdɪəs] *n* radio.
  ① *pl* radii ['reɪdɪaɪ].
radon ['reɪdɒn] *n* radón *m*.
raffle ['ræfəl] *n* rifa.
  ▶ *vt* rifar, sortear.
raft [rɑːft] *n* **1** balsa. **2** US *fam* montón *m*.
rag [ræg] *n* **1** harapo, andrajo,. **2** *(for cleaning)* trapo.
rage [reɪdʒ] *n* rabia, furor *m*, cólera.
  ▶ *vi* **1** *(person)* estar hecho,-a una furia. **2** *(fire, etc)* arder sin control; *(storm, sea)* rugir; *(debate, etc)* seguir candente.
ragout [ræ'guː] *n* ragú *m*.
raid [reɪd] *n* **1** MIL incursión *f*, ataque *m*. **2** *(by police)* redada. **3** *(robbery)* atraco.
  ▶ *vt* **1** MIL hacer una incursión en. **2** *(police)* hacer una redada en. **3** *(rob)* atracar, asaltar.
rail [reɪl] *n* **1** barra. **2** *(handrail)* pasamano, barandilla, baranda. **3** *(for train)* raíl *m*, carril *m*, riel *m*. **4** *(the railway)* ferrocarril *m*. LOC **by rail** por ferrocarril.
railing ['reɪlɪŋz] *n* verja.
railroad ['reɪlrəud] *n* US → railway.
  ▶ *vt* **1** *(person)* presionar. **2** *(measure, bill)* tramitar sin debate.

railway ['reɪlweɪ] *n* ferrocarril *m*. `COMP` **railway carriage** vagón *m*. ▪ **railway engine** locomotora. ▪ **railway line** vía férrea. ▪ **railway station** estación *f* de ferrocarril. ▪ **railway track** vía férrea.

rain [reɪn] *n* lluvia. `COMP` **rain forest** selva tropical. ▪ **rain gauge** pluviómetro.
▸ *vi* llover: *it's raining* está lloviendo.

rainbow ['reɪnbəʊ] *n* arco iris *m*.

raincoat ['reɪnkəʊt] *n* impermeable *m*.

raindrop ['reɪndrɒp] *n* gota de lluvia.

rainfall ['reɪnfɔːl] *n* **1** precipitación *f*. **2** *(quantity)* pluviosidad *f*.

rainforest ['reɪnfɑrɪst] *n* selva tropical.

rainy ['reɪnɪ] *adj* lluvioso,-a.
ⓘ *comp* **rainier**, *superl* **rainiest**.

raise [reɪz] *vt* **1** *(lift up)* levantar: *raise your hands* levantad la mano. **2** *(move to a higher position)* subir. **3** *(build, erect)* erigir, levantar. **4** *(increase)* subir, aumentar. **5** *(improve)* mejorar. **6** *(laugh, smile, etc)* provocar; *(doubt, fear)* suscitar. **7** *(children)* criar, educar; *(animals)* criar. **8** *(matter, point)* plantear. **9** *(funds)* recaudar.
▸ *n* US aumento de sueldo.

> ✎ Raise en el sentido de 'levantar' siempre va seguido de un complemento. Mientras que rise (subir), nunca lleva complemento.

raisin ['reɪzⁿn] *n* pasa.

rake [reɪk] *n* *(tool)* rastrillo.

rally ['rælɪ] *n* **1** *(public gathering)* reunión *f*; *(political)* mitin *m*; *(demonstration)* manifestación *f*. **2** *(car race)* rally *m*. **3** *(in tennis)* intercambio (de golpes).
ⓘ *pl* **rallies**.
▸ *vi* *(recover)* reponerse, recuperarse.
▸ *vt* *(bring together)* unir.
ⓘ *pt & pp* **rallied**, *ger* **rallying**.

ram [ræm] *n* ZOOL carnero.

ramp [ræmp] *n* **1** *(slope)* rampa. **2** *(steps)* escalerilla. **3** GB *(speed bump)* badén *m*. **4** US *(slip road)* vía de acceso.

ran [ræn] *pt* → **run**.

ranch [rɑːntʃ] *n* rancho, hacienda. `COMP` **ranch house 1** *(type of house)* bungalow *m*. **2** *(house on ranch)* hacienda.

random ['rændəm] *adj* aleatorio,-a. `LOC` **at random** al azar. `COMP` **random access memory** memoria de acceso directo.

rang [ræŋ] *pt* → **ring**.

range [reɪndʒ] *n* **1** *(choice)* gama, surtido; *(of products)* gama; *(of clothes)* línea. **2** *(reach)* alcance *m*. **3** *(of mountains)* cordillera, sierra. **4** US *(prairie)* pradera.
▸ *vi* **1** variar, oscilar: *they range from ... to...* van desde … hasta … **2** *(wander)* vagar (over, por).
▸ *vt* **1** *(arrange)* colocar, disponer. **2** *(travel)* recorrer, viajar por.

rank [ræŋk] *n* **1** *(line)* fila. **2** MIL *(in hierarchy)* graduación *f*, rango.
▸ *vi* *(be)* figurar, estar.
▸ *vt* *(classify)* clasificar, considerar.

ranking ['ræŋkɪŋ] *n* clasificación *f*, ranking *m*.

ransom ['rænsəm] *n* rescate *m*. `LOC` **to hold to ransom 1** pedir rescate por. **2** *fig* chantajear. `LOC` **ransom money** rescate *m*.
▸ *vt* rescatar.

rap [ræp] *n* **1** golpe *m* seco. **2** MUS rap *m*.
▸ *vi* **1** golpear. **2** MUS cantar rap.
ⓘ *pt & pp* **rapped**, *ger* **rapping**.

rape¹ [reɪp] *n* violación *f*.
▸ *vt* violar.

rape² [reɪp] *n* BOT colza.

rapid ['ræpɪd] *adj* rápido,-a.
▸ *n pl* **rapids** rápidos *mpl*.

rapper ['ræpəʳ] *n* cantante *mf* de rap, rapero,-a.

rare [reəʳ] *adj* **1** *(uncommon)* poco común, raro,-a. **2** *(air)* enrarecido,-a. **3** CULIN poco hecho,-a. `COMP` **rare earth** tierra rara. ▪ **rare gas** gas *m* raro.

> ✗ Rare no significa 'raro (extraño)', que se traduce por strange.

rarely ['reəlɪ] *adv* rara vez, pocas veces.

rascal ['rɑːskəl] *n* bribón *m*, pillo.

rash¹ [ræʃ] *n* **1** MED sarpullido, erupción *f* cutánea. **2** *(series)* sucesión *f*, serie *f*.

rash² [ræʃ] *adj* imprudente, precipitado,-a.

raspberry ['rɑːzbᵊrɪ] n **1** frambuesa. **2** fam (noise) pedorreta.
ⓘ pl raspberries.

rat [ræt] n **1** rata. **2** fam canalla m.

rate [reɪt] n **1** tasa, índice m **2** (speed) velocidad f, ritmo **3** (price) tarifa, precio. LOC **at any rate** (anyway) de todos modos. **2** (at least) por lo menos, al menos. **at the rate of** a razón de. **first/second rate** de primera/segunda (categoría). COMP **rate of exchange** tipo de cambio.
▸ vt **1** (consider) considerar **2** (deserve) merecer. **3** (fix value) tasar.
▸ n pl **rates** GB contribución f sing urbana.

rather ['rɑːðəʳ] adv **1** (a little) algo; (fairly) bastante; (very) muy. **2** (showing preference): I'd rather go out preferiría salir. **3** (more precisely) o mejor dicho: there was a river, or rather a stream había un río, o mejor dicho un arroyo

ratify ['rætɪfaɪ] vt ratificar.
ⓘ pt & pp ratified, ger ratifying.

ratings ['reɪtɪŋs] n pl TV índice m sing de audiencia.

ratio ['reɪʃɪəu] n razón f, relación f, proporción f.
ⓘ pl ratios.

ration ['ræʃᵊn] n ración f.
▸ vt racionar.
▸ n pl **rations** víveres mpl.

❌ Ration no significa 'ración (de comida)', que se traduce por portion.

rational ['ræʃᵊnəl] adj racional.

rattle ['rætᵊl] n **1** (object) carraca, matraca; (baby's) sonajero; (rattlesnake's) cascabel m. **2** (noise) ruido; (of train) traqueteo; (vibration) vibración f.
▸ vt hacer sonar, hacer vibrar.
▸ vi sonar, vibrar.

rattlesnake ['rætᵊlsneɪk] n serpiente f de cascabel.

ravage ['rævɪdʒ] vt devastar, asolar.
▸ n pl **ravages** estragos mpl.

rave [reɪv] n GB fiesta con música de baile y que puede durar toda la noche.

raven ['reɪvᵊn] n cuervo.

ravine [rəˈviːn] n barranco.

raw [rɔː] adj **1** (uncooked) crudo,-a. **2** (unprocessed) bruto,-a; (unrefined) sin refinar; (untreated) sin tratar. **3** (inexperienced) novato,-a. **4** (weather) crudo,-a.
COMP **raw material** materia prima.

ray¹ [reɪ] n (of light) rayo.

ray² [reɪ] n (fish) raya.

razor ['reɪzəʳ] n **1** (cutthroat) navaja de afeitar; (safety) maquinilla de afeitar. **2** (electric) máquina de afeitar. COMP **razor blade** hoja de afeitar.

reach [riːtʃ] n alcance m. LOC **beyond the reach of** fuera del alcance de. **out of reach of** fuera del alcance de. **within reach of 1** (at hand) al alcance de. **2** (near) cerca de
▸ vt **1** (arrive in/at, get to) llegar a. **2** (rise to, fall to) alcanzar. **3** (be able to touch) alcanzar, llegar a. **4** (contact) contactar, localizar. **5** (pass) alcanzar
▸ vi **1** (be long enough) llegar. **2** (extend) extenderse. **3** (take) extender la mano, tender la mano.

react [rɪˈækt] vi reaccionar.

reaction [rɪˈækʃᵊn] n reacción f.

reactor [rɪˈæktəʳ] n reactor m.

read [riːd] vt **1** (gen) leer. **2** (instrument) indicar, marcar. **3** (sign, notice) decir, poner.
◆ **to read out** vt sep leer en voz alta.
ⓘ pt & pp read [red].

readable ['riːdəbᵊl] adj **1** (handwriting) legible. **2** (style) ameno,-a.

reader ['riːdəʳ] n **1** (person - gen) lector,-ra; (- of proofs) corrector,-ra. **2** (at university) profesor,-ra adjunto,-a. **3** (apparatus) lector m.

readily ['redɪlɪ] adv **1** (easily) fácilmente. **2** (willingly) de buena gana.

reading ['riːdɪŋ] n **1** lectura. **2** (of bill, law) presentación f. **3** (of instrument) indicación f, lectura. **4** (interpretation) interpretación f.

readjust [riːəˈdʒʌst] vt reajustar.
▸ vi (readapt) readaptarse.

ready ['redɪ] adj **1** (prepared) preparado,-a, listo,-a. **2** (willing) dispuesto,-a. **3** (quick) rápido,-a; (easy) fácil. LOC **to get ready** prepararse. **to get STH ready**

R

preparar ALGO. ▌ **to make ready** preparar.

ready-made [redɪˈmeɪd] *adj* hecho,-a, confeccionado,-a.

reafforestation [rɪəfɒrɪˈsteɪ[ə]n] *n* GB reforestación *f*, repoblación *f* forestal.

reagent [riːˈeɪdʒənt] *n* reactivo.

real [rɪəl] *adj* **1** real, verdadero,-a. **2** *(genuine)* auténtico,-a. COMP **real estate** bienes *mpl* inmuebles.
► *adv* US *fam* muy

realise [ˈrɪəlaɪz] *vt* → realize.

reality [rɪˈælɪti] *n* realidad *f*.

realize [ˈrɪəlaɪz] *vt* **1** *(understand)* darse cuenta de, comprender. **2** *(know)* saber. **3** *(carry out)* realizar. **4** *(sell)* realizar, vender; *(fetch)* reportar

⊠ To realize no significa 'realizar', que se traduce por **to carry out**.

really [ˈrɪəli] *adv* **1** *(in fact)* en realidad. **2** *(very)* muy, realmente. **3** *(showing interest)* ¿ah sí?, ¿en serio? ¿de verdad?; *(showing surprise)* ¿de verdad?, ¡no me digas!; *(showing annoyance)* ¡vaya!

reap [riːp] *vt* cosechar.

rear[1] [rɪə[r]] *adj* trasero,-a, de atrás.
► *n* **1** *(back part)* parte *f* de atrás. **2** *(of room)* fondo. **3** *fam (of person)* trasero.

rearmament [riːˈɑːməmənt] *n* rearme *m*.

rearrange [riːəˈreɪndʒ] *vt* **1** *(objects)* colocar de otra manera. **2** *(event)* cambiar la fecha de, cambiar la hora de.

rear-view mirror [rɪəvjuːˈmɪrə] *n* retrovisor *m*.

reason [ˈriːz[ə]n] *n* **1** *(cause)* razón *f*, motivo. **2** *(faculty)* razón *f*.
► *vt* deducir, llegar a la conclusión de que
► *vi* razonar.

reasonable [ˈriːzənəb[ə]l] *adj* **1** *(gen)* razonable. **2** *(acceptable)* aceptable.

reasonably [ˈriːz[ə]nəbli] *adv* **1** *(gen)* razonablemente. **2** *(quite)* bastante.

reassure [riːəˈʃʊə[r]] *vt* **1** *(comfort)* tranquilizar. **2** *(assure again)* volver a asegurar.

rebate [ˈriːbeɪt] *n* **1** *(of tax)* devolución *f*. **2** *(discount)* descuento.

rebel [*(adj-n)* ˈreb[ə]l; *(vb)* rɪˈbel] *adj* rebelde.
► *n* rebelde *mf*.
► *vi* rebelarse (against, contra).
① *pt & pp* rebelled, *ger* rebelling.

rebellion [rɪˈbeliən] *n* rebelión *f*.

rebound [*(n)* ˈriːbaʊnd; *(vb)* rɪˈbaʊnd] *n* rebote *m*.
► *vi* rebotar.

recall [*(n)* riːˈkɔːl; *(vb)* rɪˈkɔːl] *n* **1** *(memory)* memoria. **2** *(withdrawal)* retirada.
► *vt* **1** *(remember)* recordar. **2** *(withdraw)* retirar.

receipt [rɪˈsiːt] *n* **1** *(document)* recibo. **2** *(act of receiving)* recepción *f*, recibo.
► *n pl* **receipts** COMM ingresos *mpl*, recaudación *f sing*.

receive [rɪˈsiːv] *vt* **1** *(gen)* recibir. **2** *(wound)* sufrir. **3** *(radio signal)* recibir. **4** *(stolen goods)* comerciar con
► *vt (welcome)* recibir, acoger.

receiver [rɪˈsiːvə[r]] *n* **1** *(of telephone)* auricular *m*. **2** *(of stolen goods)* perista *mf*. **3** JUR síndico,-a, síndico,-a de quiebras. **4** *(of radio signal)* receptor *m*. **5** *(in American football)* receptor,-ra.

recent [ˈriːs[ə]nt] *adj* reciente: *in recent months/years* en los últimos meses/años.

recently [ˈriːs[ə]ntli] *adv* **1** *(lately)* recientemente, últimamente. **2** *(a short time ago)* hace poco

reception [rɪˈsep[ə]n] *n* **1** *(gen)* recepción *f*. **2** *(welcome)* acogida. **3** *(party)* recepción *f*; *(after wedding)* banquete *m*. COMP **reception desk** recepción *f*.

receptionist [rɪˈsep[ə]nɪst] *n* recepcionista *m & f*.

recharge [riːˈtʃɑːdʒ] *vt* recargar.

rechargeable [riːˈtʃɑːdʒəb[ə]l] *adj* recargable.

recipe [ˈresəpi] *n* **1** receta. **2** *fig* fórmula. COMP **recipe book 1** *(personal collection)* recetario. **2** *(cookery book)* libro de cocina.

reckless [ˈrekləs] *adj* **1** *(hasty)* precipitado,-a. **2** *(careless)* imprudente, temerario,-a. COMP **reckless driving** conducción *f* temeraria.

reckon [ˈrek[ə]n] *vt* **1** *(estimate)* calcular. **2** *(calculate)* calcular. **3** *(regard)* considerar. **4** *(think)* creer, considerar.

reckoning ['rekˤnɪŋ] n cálculos mpl: by my reckoning, … según mis cálculos,…

recognise ['rekəgnaɪz] vt → **recognize**.

recognition [rekəg'nɪʃˤn] n reconocimiento.

recognize ['rekəgnaɪz] vt reconocer.

recollect [rekə'lekt] vt recordar.

☒ To recollect no significa 'recolectar', que se traduce por **to harvest**.

recollection [rekə'lekʃˤn] n recuerdo.

☒ Recollection no significa 'recolección', que se traduce por **harvest**.

recommend [rekə'mend] vt recomendar.

recommendation [rekəmen'deɪʃˤn] n recomendación f.

reconstruct [ri:kəns'trʌkt] vt reconstruir.

record [(n) 'rekɔ:d; (vb) rɪ'kɔ:d] n **1** (written evidence) constancia escrita **2** (note) relación f. **3** (facts about a person) historial m. **4** MUS disco. **5** SP récord m, marca, plusmarca. LOC **to break a record** batir un récord. COMP **medical record** historial m médico. ▌**record holder** plusmarquista mf. ▌**record player** tocadiscos m sing.
▸ vt **1** (write down) anotar, apuntar. **2** (voice, music) grabar. **3** (instrument, gauge) registrar
▸ adj récord.
▸ n pl **records** (files) archivos mpl

☒ Record no significa 'recordar', que se traduce por **to remember**.

recorded [rɪ'kɔ:dɪd] adj (written) anotado,-a; (on tape, etc) grabado,-a. COMP **recorded delivery** correo certificado.

recorder [rɪ'kɔ:dəʳ] n MUS flauta. COMP **cassette recorder** casete m.

recording [rɪ'kɔ:dɪŋ] n grabación f. COMP **recording studio** estudio de grabación.

recover [rɪ'kʌvəʳ] vt (gen) recuperar; (dead body) rescatar.
▸ vi recuperarse, reponerse.

recovery [rɪ'kʌvərɪ] n recuperación f.

recreation [rekrɪ'eɪʃˤn] n **1** (free time) esparcimiento. **2** (hobby) pasatiempo. **3** (in school) recreo.

recruit [rɪ'kru:t] n (soldier) recluta m.
▸ vt (soldier) reclutar.

recruitment [rɪ'kru:tmənt] n (of soldiers) reclutamiento; (of employees) contratación f.

recta ['rektə] n pl → **rectum**.

rectangle ['rektæŋgˤl] n rectángulo.

rectangular [rekt'æŋgjuləʳ] adj rectangular.

rectify ['rektɪfaɪ] vt rectificar.

rectum ['rektəm] n recto.
ⓘ pl rectums o recta ['rektə].

recur [rɪ'kɜ:ʳ] vi repetirse, reproducirse.
ⓘ pt & pp recurred, ger recurring.

☒ To recur no significa 'recurrir a', que se traduce por **to resort to, to turn to**.

recurrent [rɪ'kʌrənt] adj **1** MATH periódico,-a. **2** MED recurrente.

recycle [ri:'saɪkˤl] vt reciclar.

recycling [ri:'saɪkˤlɪŋ] n reciclaje m.

red [red] n **1** (colour) rojo. **2** (left-winger) rojo,-a.
▸ adj **1** rojo,-a **2** (hair) pelirrojo,-a.
ⓘ comp redder, superl reddest.

redbreast ['redbrest] n petirrojo.

redcurrant [red'kʌrənt] n grosella.

redemption [rɪ'dempʃˤn] n **1** (of debt) pago. **2** (of voucher) canje m. **3** REL redención f.

red-haired ['redheəd] adj pelirrojo,-a.

redhead ['redhed] n pelirrojo,-a.

redid [ri:'dɪd] pt → **redo**.

redo [ri:'du:] vt rehacer, volver a hacer.
ⓘ pt redid [ri:'dɪd], pp redone [ri:'dʌn], ger redoing.

redone [ri:'dʌn] pt → **redo**.

redskin ['redskɪn] n piel roja mf.

reduce [rɪ'dju:s] vt **1** (gen) reducir, disminuir. **2** (price, etc) rebajar.

reduction [rɪ'dʌkʃˤn] n (gen) reducción f; (fall) disminución f; (in price) rebaja.

redundancy [rɪ'dʌndənsɪ] n **1** (dismissal) despido. **2** (superfluity) superfluidad f. **3** LING redundancia.
ⓘ pl redundancies.

R

redundant [rɪˈdʌndənt] *adj* **1** *(dismissed)* despedido,-a. **2** *(superfluous)* superfluo,-a. **3** LING redundante.

redwood [ˈredwʊd] *n* secuoya.

reed [riːd] *n* **1** *(plant)* caña, junco. **2** MUS lengüeta.

reef [riːf] *n* arrecife *m*.

reel [riːl] *n* **1** *(of thread, cotton)* carrete *m*; *(of camera film)* carrete *m*, rollo; *(of cine film)* bobina; *(of wire, tape)* rollo. **2** *(for fishing)* carrete *m*.
◆ **to reel in** *vt sep (line)* recoger, cobrar; *(fish)* cobrar, sacar del agua.

refer [rɪˈfɜː] *vt (send)* mandar, enviar
▸ *vi* **1** *(allude to)* referirse (to, a). **2** *(mention, name)* hacer referencia (to, a).
① *pt & pp* referred, *ger* referring.

referee [refəˈriː] *n* SP árbitro,-a.
▸ *vt* arbitrar.

reference [ˈrefərəns] *n* **1** referencia, mención **2** *(for job)* referencias *fpl*. COMP reference book libro de consulta.

referendum [refəˈrendəm] *n* referéndum *m*.
① *pl* referendums o referenda [refəˈrendə].

refill [*(n)* ˈriːfɪl; *(vb)* riːˈfɪl] *n (for pen, etc)* recambio; *(for lighter)* carga.
▸ *vt (glass, pen)* volver a llenar; *(lighter)* recargar.

refinery [rɪˈfaɪnərɪ] *n* refinería.
① *pl* refineries.

reflect [rɪˈflekt] *vt* reflejar
▸ *vi (think)* reflexionar (on, sobre).
◆ **to reflect on** *vt insep* perjudicar

reflection [rɪˈflekʃən] *n* **1** *(image)* reflejo. **2** *(thought)* reflexión *f*. **3** *(aspersion)* descrédito. LOC on reflection, ... pensándolo bien, ...

reflector [rɪˈflektər] *n (gen)* reflector *m*; *(on car)* catafaro.

reflex [ˈriːfleks] *n* reflejo.
① *pl* reflexes.

reflexive [rɪˈfleksɪv] *adj* reflexivo,-a.

reforest [riːˈfɒrɪst] *vt* reforestar.

reforestation [riːfɒrɪˈsteɪʃən] *n* reforestación *f*, repoblación *f* forestal.

reform [rɪˈfɔːm] *n* reforma.
▸ *vt* reformar.

refraction [rɪˈfrækʃən] *n* refracción *f*.

refrain¹ [rɪˈfreɪn] *n* MUS estribillo.

☒ Refrain no significa 'refrán', que se traduce por proverb, saying.

refrain² [rɪˈfreɪn] *vi* abstenerse (from, de)

refresh [rɪˈfreʃ] *vt* refrescar.

refreshing [rɪˈfreʃɪŋ] *adj (gen)* refrescante; *(rest, sleep)* reparador,-ra.

refreshment [rɪˈfreʃmənt] *n* refresco.

refrigerator [rɪˈfrɪdʒəreɪtər] *n* frigorífico, nevera.

refuge [ˈrefjuːdʒ] *n* refugio.

refugee [refjuːˈdʒiː] *n* refugiado,-a.

refund [*(n)* ˈriːfʌnd; *(vb)* riːˈfʌnd] *n* reembolso.
▸ *vt* reembolsar.

refusal [rɪˈfjuːzəl] *n* **1** *(negative reply)* negativa, respuesta negativa. **2** *(rejection)* rechazo.

refuse¹ [ˈrefjuːs] *n* basura. COMP refuse collection recogida de basuras.

refuse² [rɪˈfjuːz] *vt* **1** *(reject)* rehusar, rechazar, no aceptar. **2** *(withhold)* negar, denegar, no conceder
▸ *vi* negarse (to, a)

regard [rɪˈɡɑːd] *n* respeto, consideración. LOC to hold in high regard tener en gran estima. ‖ without regard to sin hacer caso de.
▸ *vt* **1** *(consider)* considerar. **2** *(look at)* mirar. **3** *(heed)* hacer caso a.
▸ *n pl* regards recuerdos *mpl*.

regarding [rɪˈɡɑːdɪŋ] *prep* tocante a, respecto a.

regardless [rɪˈɡɑːdləs] *adv fam* a pesar de todo.
▸ *prep* regardless of *fam* sin tener en cuenta.

regime [reɪˈʒiːm] [also written régime] *n* régimen *m*.

regiment [ˈredʒɪmənt] *n* regimiento.
▸ *vt* **1** MIL regimentar. **2** *fig* disciplinar, reglamentar.

region [ˈriːdʒən] *n* región *f*.

regional [ˈriːdʒənəl] *adj* regional.

register [ˈredʒɪstər] *n (gen)* registro; *(in school)* lista. COMP register office registro civil.

▶ vt **1** *(put on record, list)* registrar; *(car, student)* matricular; *(birth, death, marriage)* inscribir en el registro. **2** *(show - reading)* indicar, marcar; *(- feeling)* mostrar, reflejar. **3** *(make known)* hacer constar. **4** *(letter)* certificar.
▶ vi **1** *(for classes)* matricularse; *(at congress, with doctor)* inscribirse; *(at hotel)* registrarse.

✕ To register no significa 'registrar (cachear)', que se traduce por to frisk.

registered ['redʒɪstəd] *adj* **1** *(person)* inscrito,-a; *(student)* matriculado,-a. **2** *(letter)* certificado,-a. **3** *(car, etc)* matriculado,-a; *(ship)* de bandera. comp **registered trademark** marca registrada.

registration [redʒɪs'treɪʃ°n] *n* **1** *(of birth, death, marriage)* inscripción *f*; *(of patent, etc)* registro. **2** *(enrolment)* inscripción *f*; *(of student)* matrícula. comp **registration number** AUTO matrícula.

registry ['redʒɪstrɪ] *n* registro. comp **registry office** registro civil

regret [rɪ'gret] *n* **1** *(remorse)* remordimiento. **2** *(sadness)* pesar *m*.
▶ vt **1** *(feel sorry)* lamentar, arrepentirse de. **2** *(express one's sadness)* lamentar. **3** *(miss)* echar de menos, echar en falta.
▶ *n pl* **regrets** excusas *mpl*

regular ['regjʊlə'] *adj*. **1** *(gen)* regular. **2** *(normal)* normal. **3** *(habitual)* habitual. **4** *(normal in size)* de tamaño normal. **5** US *(pleasant)* simpático,-a.
▶ *n fam* cliente *mf* habitual.

✕ Regular no significa 'regular (pasable)', que se traduce por so-so, not bad.

regularity [regjʊ'lærətɪ] *n* regularidad *f*.
regularly ['regjʊləlɪ] *adv* regularmente, con regularidad.
regulate ['regjʊleɪt] *vt* regular.
regulation [regjʊ'leɪʃ°n] *n* **1** *(control)* regulación *f*. **2** *(rule)* regla.
rehearsal [rɪ'hɜːs°l] *n* ensayo.
rehearse [rɪ'hɜːs] *vt* ensayar.
reign [reɪn] *n* reinado.
▶ *vi* reinar.
rein [reɪn] *n* rienda.
▶ *n pl* **reins** *(child's)* andadores *mpl*.

reindeer ['reɪndɪə'] *n* reno.
ⓘ *pl* reindeer o reindeers.

reject [*(n)* 'riːdʒekt; *(vb)* rɪ'dʒekt] *n* *(thing)* artículo defectuoso; *(person)* marginado,-a.
▶ vt *(gen)* rechazar, no aceptar; *(in law)* desestimar.

rejection [rɪ'dʒekʃ°n] *n* *(gen)* rechazo; *(negative reply)* respuesta negativa.
rejoice [rɪ'dʒɔɪs] *vi* alegrarse.
relapse [rɪ'læps] *n* **1** MED recaída. **2** *(crime)* reincidencia.
▶ vi **1** MED recaer. **2** *(crime)* reincidir. LOC **to suffer a relapse** tener una recaída.
relate [rɪ'leɪt] *vt* **1** *(tell)* relatar, contar. **2** *(connect)* relacionar (to, con).
▶ vi *(connect)* relacionarse.
related [rɪ'leɪtɪd] *adj* **1** *(connected)* relacionado,-a. **2** *(relatives)* emparentado,-a.
relation [rɪ'leɪʃ°n] *n* **1** *(connection)* relación *f*. **2** *(family)* pariente *mf*.
relationship [rɪ'leɪʃ°nʃɪp] *n* **1** *(connection)* relación *f*. **2** *(between people)* relaciones *fpl*.
relative ['relətɪv] *adj* relativo,-a.
▶ *n* pariente *mf*, familiar *mf*.
relatively ['relətɪvlɪ] *adv* relativamente.
relativity [relə'tɪvɪtɪ] *n* relatividad *f*.
relaunch [*(vb)* riː'lɔːntʃ; *(n)* 'riːlɔːntʃ] *vt* relanzar.
▶ *n* relanzamiento.
relax [rɪ'læks] *vt* **1** *(gen)* relajar. **2** *(grip, hold)* aflojar. **3** *(rules, control)* suavizar.
▶ vi **1** *(gen)* relajarse. **2** *(grip, hold)* aflojarse.
relaxation [riːlæk'seɪʃ°n] *n* **1** *(gen)* relajación *f*. **2** *(of grip, hold)* aflojamiento. **3** *(of rules, control)* suavización *f*.
relaxed [rɪ'lækst] *adj* **1** *(person)* relajado,-a. **2** *(atmosphere)* distendido,-a.
relaxing [rɪ'læksɪŋ] *adj* relajante.
relay ['riːleɪ] *n* **1** relevo. **2** ELEC relé *m*. comp **relay race** carrera de relevos. ‖ **relay station** estación *f* repetidora.
release [rɪ'liːs] *n* **1** *(setting free)* liberación *f*, puesta en libertad. **2** *(relief)* alivio. **3** *(of film)* estreno; *(of record)* lanzamiento. **4** *(of gas, etc)* emisión *f*.

R

5 *(new thing - film)* estreno, novedad *f* cinematográfica; *(- record)* nuevo disco, novedad *f* discográfica. **6** *(statement)* comunicado.
▶ *vt* **1** *(set free)* liberar, poner en libertad. **2** *(let go of)* soltar. **3** *(bring out - film)* estrenar; *(- record)* sacar. **4** *(gas, etc - give out)* emitir. **5** *(statement, information)* hacer público, dar a conocer.

relevant ['reləvənt] *adj* **1** *(connected)* pertinente. **2** *(important)* relevante.

reliable [rɪ'laɪəbəl] *adj* fiable.

relief [rɪ'li:f] *n* **1** *(from pain, etc)* alivio. **2** *(help)* auxilio, socorro, ayuda. **3** *(person)* relevo. **4** *(lifting of siege)* liberación *f*. **5** GEOG relieve *m*.

relieve [rɪ'li:v] *vt* **1** *(lessen)* aliviar. **2** *(take over from)* relevar. **3** *(help)* socorrer, ayudar. **4** *(lift siege of)* liberar.

religion [rɪ'lɪdʒən] *n* religión *f*.

religious [rɪ'lɪdʒəs] *adj* religioso,-a.

reload [ri:'ləʊd] *vt* *(gun)* volver a cargar; *(program, page)* recargar.

reluctant [rɪ'lʌktənt] *adj* reacio,-a.

reluctantly [rɪ'lʌktəntlɪ] *adv* muy a mi *(tu, su, etc)* pesar.

rely on [rɪ'laɪ ɒn] *vt* *(trust)* confiar en.
ⓘ *pt & pp* relied.

remade [ri:'meɪd] *pt & pp* → remake.

remain [rɪ'meɪn] *vi* **1** *(stay)* quedarse, permanecer. **2** *(be left)* quedar, sobrar. **3** *(continue)* seguir, continuar.
▶ *n pl* remains restos *mpl*.

remainder [rɪ'meɪndər] *n* resto.

remake [*(n)* 'ri:meɪk; *(vb)* ri:'meɪk] *n* nueva versión *f*.
▶ *vt* hacer una nueva versión de.
ⓘ *pt & pp* remade [ri:'meɪd].

remark [rɪ'mɑ:k] *n* observación *f*.
▶ *vt* **1** *(say)* observar, comentar. **2** *(notice)* advertir.
◆ **to remark on** *vt insep* comentar.

remarkable [rɪ'mɑ:kəbəl] *adj* **1** *(exceptional)* extraordinario,-a, excepcional. **2** *(odd)* extraño,-a; *(surprising)* sorprendente, curioso,-a.

remedy ['remədɪ] *n* remedio.
ⓘ *pl* remedies.
▶ *vt* remediar.

remember [rɪ'membər] *vt* **1** recordar, acordarse de. **2** *(commemorate)* recordar.
▶ *vi* acordarse, recordar.

✎ La diferencia entre **remember** y **remind** es que **remember** se refiere al acto de recordar algo (acordarse de) y **remind** se emplea cuando se le recuerda algo a alguien.

remind [rɪ'maɪnd] *vt* recordar.

✎ Consulta también **remember**.

reminder [rɪ'maɪndər] *n* **1** *(note)* recordatorio. **2** *(of payment due)* aviso. **3** *(keepsake)* recuerdo.

remorse [rɪ'mɔ:s] *n* remordimiento.

remote [rɪ'məʊt] *adj* **1** *(far away)* remoto,-a, lejano,-a. **2** *(lonely)* aislado,-a, apartado,-a. **3** *(person)* distante. COMP **remote control** mando a distancia.

removal [rɪ'mu:vəl] *n* **1** *(getting rid of)* eliminación *f*; *(surgically)* extirpación *f*. **2** *(moving)* traslado; *(to another house)* traslado, mudanza. **3** *(from post)* destitución *f*.

remove [rɪ'mu:v] *vt* **1** *(get rid of - gen)* quitar, eliminar; *(- surgically)* extirpar. **2** *(take out, take off)* quitar. **3** *(move)* trasladar. **4** *(dismiss)* destituir.
▶ *vi* *(change houses)* trasladarse.

renaissance [rə'neɪsəns] *n* renacimiento. COMP **the Renaissance** el Renacimiento.
▶ *adj* **Renaissance** renacentista.

rename [ri:'neɪm] *vt* renombrar.

rendezvous ['rɒndɪvu:] *n* **1** cita. **2** *(place)* lugar *m* de reunión.
ⓘ *pl* rendezvous.

renew [rɪ'nju:] *vt* **1** *(gen)* renovar; *(contract, permit, etc)* prorrogar. **2** *(start again)* reanudar. **3** *(replace)* sustituir.

renewable [rɪ'nju:əbəl] *adj* renovable. COMP **renewable energy** energía renovable.

renounce [rɪ'naʊns] *vt* renunciar a.

rent [rent] *n* **1** *(for flat, etc)* alquiler *m*. **2** *(for land)* arriendo.
▶ *vt* **1** *(flat)* alquilar. **2** *(land)* arrendar.
LOC **"For rent"** «Se alquila».

✖ Renta no significa 'renta (ingresos)', que se traduce por **income**.

rental ['rentªl] *n* **1** *(for flat, etc)* alquiler *m*. **2** *(for land)* arriendo.

rented ['rentɪd] *adj* de alquiler.

reorganise [ri:'ɔ:gənaɪz] *vt* → **reorganize**.

reorganize [ri:'ɔ:gənaɪz] *vt* reorganizar.

repaid [ri:'peɪd] *pt & pp* → **repay**.

repair [rɪ'peəʳ] *n* reparación *f*.
▶ *vt* reparar, arreglar.

repay [ri:'peɪ] *vt* devolver.
ⓘ *pt & pp* repaid, *ger* repaying.

repeat [rɪ'pi:t] *n* **1** *(gen)* repetición *f*. **2** *(on television)* reposición *f*.
▶ *vt & vi* repetir.

repel [rɪ'pel] *vt* **1** *(gen)* repeler. **2** *(disgust)* repugnar, repeler.
ⓘ *pt & pp* repelled, *ger* repelling.

repellent [rɪ'pelənt] *n* repelente *m*.
▶ *vt* arrepentirse de.

repetition [repə'tɪʃªn] *n* repetición *f*.

repetitive [rɪ'petɪtɪv] *adj* repetitivo,-a.

replace [rɪ'pleɪs] *vt* **1** *(put back)* devolver a su sitio. **2** *(substitute)* reemplazar, sustituir; *(change)* cambiar.

replacement [rɪ'pleɪsmənt] *n* **1** *(act)* sustitución *f*, reemplazo *m*. **2** *(person)* sustituto,-a. **3** *(thing)* otro,-a. **4** *(spare part)* recambio, pieza de recambio.

replay [*(n)* 'ri:pleɪ; *(vb)* ri:'pleɪ] *n* **1** *(of film sequence)* repetición *f* de la jugada. **2** *(match)* partido de desempate.
▶ *vt* **1** *(tape, film)* volver a poner. **2** *(match)* volver a jugar.

reply [rɪ'plaɪ] *n* respuesta, contestación *f*. ‖LOC‖ in reply to en respuesta a.
ⓘ *pl* replies.
▶ *vi* responder (to, a), contestar (to, a).
ⓘ *pt & pp* replied.

report [rɪ'pɔ:t] *n* **1** *(informative document)* informe *m*. **2** *(school report)* boletín *m* escolar, informe *m* escolar. **3** *(piece of news)* noticia. **4** *(news story)* reportaje *m*. **5** *(rumour)* rumor *m*. **6** *(of gun)* estampido.
▶ *vi* **1** *(give information)* informar (on, sobre). **2** *(go in person)* presentarse.
▶ *vt* **1** *(say, inform)* decir. **2** *(to authority)* informar de. **3** *(to police - crime)* denunciar; *(- accident)* dar parte de

reported speech [rɪpɔ:tɪd'spi:tʃ] *n* estilo indirecto.

reporter [rɪ'pɔ:təʳ] *n* reportero,-a.

represent [reprɪ'zent] *vt* representar.

representative [reprɪ'zentətɪv] *adj* representativo,-a.
▶ *n* **1** representante *mf*. **2** US diputado,-a.

reproach [rɪ'prəʊtʃ] *n* reproche *m*.
▶ *vt* reprochar (for, -).

reproduce [ri:prə'dju:s] *vt* reproducir.
▶ *vi* reproducirse.

reproduction [ri:prə'dʌkʃªn] *n* reproducción *f*.

reproductive [ri:prə'dʌktɪv] *adj* reproductor,-ra.

reptile ['reptaɪl] *n* reptil *m*.

republic [rɪ'pʌblɪk] *n* república.

republican [rɪ'pʌblɪkən] *adj* republicano,-a.
▶ *n* republicano,-a.

repugnant [rɪ'pʌgnənt] *adj* repugnante.

repulsion [rɪ'pʌlʒən] *vt* **1** *(reject)* rechazar. **2** *(drive back)* repulsar.

repulsive [rɪ'pʌlsɪv] *adj* repulsivo,-a.

reputation [repjʊ'teɪʃªn] *n* reputación *f*, fama. ‖LOC‖ to have a reputation for ... tener fama de…

request [rɪ'kwest] *n* **1** solicitud *f*, petición *f*. **2** *(on radio)* canción *f*.
▶ *vt* **1** *(gen)* pedir, solicitar; *(officially)* rogar. **2** *(on radio)* pedir.

require [rɪ'kwaɪəʳ] *vt* **1** requerir, exigir. **2** *(need)* necesitar, requerir. ‖LOC‖ to be required to do STH estar obligado,-a a hacer ALGO.

requirement [rɪ'kwaɪəmənt] *n* **1** *(demand)* requisito. **2** *(need)* necesidad *f*.

reran [ri:'ræn] *pt* → **rerun**.

rerun [*(n)* 'ri:rʌn; *(vb)* ri:'rʌn] *n* *(repetition)* repetición *f*; *(TV programme)* reposición *f*; *(film)* reestreno.
▶ *vt* *(repeat)* repetir; *(TV programme)* reponer; *(film)* reestrenar.
ⓘ *pt* reran [ri:'ræn], *pp* rerun [ri:'rʌn], *ger* rerunning.

resat ['ri:sɑt] *pt & pp* → **resit**.

rescue ['reskju:] *n* rescate *m*.
▶ *vt* rescatar (from, de).

research [rɪ'sɜ:tʃ] *n* investigación *f*.
▶ *vi* investigar (into, -).
▶ *vt* documentar.

R

researcher [rɪ'sɜːtʃəʳ] *n* investigador,-ra.

resemblance [rɪ'zembləns] *n* parecido, semejanza.

resemble [rɪ'zembªl] *vt* parecerse a.

resent [rɪ'zent] *vt* ofenderse por.

resentment [rɪ'zentmənt] *n* resentimiento, rencor *m*.

reservation [rezə'veɪʃªn] *n* reserva.

reserve [rɪ'zɜːv] *n* (*gen*) reserva.
▶ *vt* reservar.

reservoir ['rezəvwɑːʳ] *n* **1** (*lake*) embalse *m*. **2** (*store*) reserva.

reset [riː'set] *vt* **1** (*programmer, computer*) reinicializar; (*mechanism*) rearmar. **2** (*clock*) poner en hora. **3** (*bone*) componer. **4** (*book*) recomponer.
ⓘ *pt & pp* reset, *ger* resetting.

residence ['rezɪdəns] *n* residencia.

resident ['rezɪdªnt] *adj* residente.
▶ *n* (*gen*) residente *mf*; (*of area*) vecino, -a; (*in hotel*) huésped,-da.

residential [rezɪ'denʃªl] *adj* residencial.

residual [rɪ'zɪdjuəl] *adj* residual.

resign [rɪ'zaɪn] *vi* dimitir (from, de), presentar la dimisión.
▶ *vt* dimitir de. ⃝ᴏᴄ to resign os to sth resignarse a ALGO.

resignation [rezɪg'neɪʃªn] *n* **1** (*from post*) dimisión *f*. **2** (*acceptance*) resignación *f*. ⃝ᴏᴄ to hand in one's resignation presentar la dimisión.

resilience [rɪ'zɪliəns] *n* **1** (*flexibility*) elasticidad *f*. **2** (*strength*) fuerza, resistencia.

resin ['rezɪn] *n* resina.

resist [rɪ'zɪst] *vt* **1** (*not give in to*) resistir. **2** (*oppose*) oponer resistencia a.

resistance [rɪ'zɪstəns] *n* **1** (*gen*) resistencia. **2** (*opposition*) oposición *f*. ⃝ᴏᴄ to put up resistance oponer resistencia.

resistant [rɪ'zɪstənt] *adj* resistente.

resit [(*n*) 'riːsɪt; (*vb*) riː'sɪt] *n* examen *m* de repesca.
▶ *vt* volver a presentarse a.
ⓘ *pt & pp* resat [riː'sɪt], *ger* resitting.

resolution ['rezəluːʃən] *n* resolución *f*.

resort [rɪ'zɔːt] *n* **1** (*place*) lugar *m* de vacaciones. **2** (*recourse*) recurso.
▶ *vi* recurrir (to, a).

resource [rɪ'zɔːs] *n* recurso.

respect [rɪ'spekt] *n* **1** (*admiration, consideration*) respeto. **2** (*aspect*) respecto
▶ *vt* respetar.

respectable [rɪ'spektəbªl] *adj* **1** (*gen*) respetable. **2** (*decent*) decente.

respiration [respɪ'reɪʃən] *n* respiración *f*.

respiratory ['respªrətªrɪ] *adj* respiratorio,-a. ᴄᴏᴍᴘ respiratory system sistema *m* respiratorio.

respond [rɪ'spɒnd] *vi* responder.

response [rɪ'spɒns] *n* **1** (*gen*) respuesta. **2** (*reaction*) reacción *f*.

responsibility [rɪspɒnsɪ'bɪlɪtɪ] *n* responsabilidad *f*. ᴄᴏᴍᴘ to accept responsibility for responsabilizarse de.
ⓘ *pl* responsibilities.

responsible [rɪ'spɒnsəbªl] *adj* **1** (*gen*) responsable. **2** (*position*) de responsabilidad

rest¹ [rest] *n* **1** (*repose*) descanso, reposo. **2** (*peace*) paz *f*, tranquilidad *f*. **3** (*support*) soporte *m*; (*for head*) reposacabezas *m*; (*for arms*) apoyabrazos *m*.
▶ *vt* **1** (*relax*) descansar. **2** (*lean*) apoyar.
▶ *vi* **1** (*relax*) descansar. **2** (*be calm*) quedarse tranquilo,-a. **3** (*depend*) depender (on, de).
▶ *vt* (*lean*) apoyar.

✘ To rest no significa 'restar', que se traduce por to substract.

rest² [rest] *vi* quedar así.
▶ *n* the rest el resto.

restaurant ['restªrɒnt] *n* restaurante *m*.

restless ['restləs] *adj* inquieto,-a. ⃝ᴏᴄ to grow restless impacientarse.

restoration [restə'reɪʃªn] *n* **1** (*gen*) restauración *f*. **2** (*return*) devolución *f*.

restore [rɪ'stɔːʳ] *vt* **1** (*gen*) restaurar. **2** (*return*) devolver. **3** (*order*) restablecer.

restrain [rɪ'streɪn] *vt* contener.

restrict [rɪ'strɪkt] *vt* restringir, limitar.

restriction [rɪ'strɪkʃən] *n* (*limited*) restricción *f*.

result [rɪ'zʌlt] *n* **1** resultado. **2** (*consequence*) consecuencia.
▶ *vi* to result from resultar de.
◆ to result in *vt insep* producir.

resume [rɪˈzjuːm] vt **1** *(begin again)* reanudar. **2** *(take over again)* volver a asumir.
▶ vi continuar.

☒ To resume no significa 'resumir', que se traduce por **to summarize**.

résumé [ˈrezjuːmeɪ] n **1** *(summary)* resumen m. **2** US *(curriculum vitae)* currículo, currículum vitae m.

resuscitate [rɪˈsʌsɪteɪt] vt reanimar.

retail [ˈriːteɪl] n venta al detalle, venta al por menor.
▶ vt vender al detalle, vender al por menor.
▶ adv al detalle, al por menor.

retailer [ˈriːteɪləʳ] n detallista mf, minorista mf.

retain [rɪˈteɪn] vt **1** *(keep - power, moisture)* retener; *(- heat, charge)* conservar. **2** SP *(lead)* mantener; *(title)* revalidar. **3** *(possessions)* guardar. **4** *(remember)* retener, recordar. **5** *(hold back)* contener. **6** *(employ)* contratar.

retaliate [rɪˈtælɪeɪt] vi tomar represalias (**against**, contra).

retard [rɪˈtɑːd] vt retardar, retrasar.

retina [ˈretɪnə] n retina.
ⓘ pl retinas o retinae [ˈretɪniː].

retinue [ˈretɪnjuː] n séquito.

retire [rɪˈtaɪəʳ] vt *(from work)* jubilar.
▶ vi **1** *(from work)* jubilarse. **2** *(withdraw)* retirarse. **3** *(go to bed)* acostarse.

retired [rɪˈtaɪəd] adj jubilado,-a.

retirement [rɪˈtaɪəmənt] n jubilación f.

retrace [rɪˈtreɪs] vt desandar, volver sobre. ɪᴏᴄ **to retrace one's steps** volver sobre sus pasos.

retreat [rɪˈtriːt] n **1** *(withdrawal)* retirada. **2** *(place)* retiro, refugio.
▶ vi **1** *(withdraw)* retirarse. **2** *(back down)* dar marcha atrás.

retribution [retrɪˈbjuːʃən] n justo castigo.

☒ Retribution no significa 'retribución (pago)', que se traduce por **pay**.

retrospective [retrəˈspektɪv] adj **1** *(exhibition, etc)* retrospectivo,-a. **2** *(law)* retroactivo,-a.

return [rɪˈtɜːn] n **1** *(coming or going back)* vuelta, regreso. **2** *(giving back)* devolución f. **3** SP *(of ball)* devolución f; *(of service)* resto. **4** *(on keyboard)* retorno. **5** *(ticket)* billete m de ida y vuelta. ᴄᴏᴍᴘ **return ticket** billete m de ida y vuelta.
▶ vi **1** *(come back, go back)* volver, regresar. **2** *(reappear)* reaparecer.
▶ vt **1** *(give back)* devolver. **2** SP *(ball)* devolver; *(serve)* restar. **3** POL *(elect)* elegir. **4** *(verdict)* pronunciar. **5** *(interest)* producir.
▶ n pl **returns** resultados mpl electorales.

returnable [rɪˈtɜːnəbəl] adj retornable.

reunion [riːˈjuːnɪən] n reencuentro.

☒ Reunion no significa 'reunión', que se traduce por **meeting**.

reunite [riːjuːˈnaɪt] vt *(parts)* reunir.

reuse [riːˈjuːz] vt *(parts)* reutilizar.

reveal [rɪˈviːl] vt **1** *(make known)* revelar. **2** *(show)* dejar ver, mostrar.

☒ To reveal no significa 'revelar (una foto)', que se traduce por **to develop**.

revenge [rɪˈvendʒ] n venganza.
▶ vt vengar. ɪᴏᴄ **to revenge os** vengarse.

revenue [ˈrevənjuː] n ingresos mpl.

reverberation [rɪvɜːbəˈreɪʃən] vt resonar, retumbar.

reverse [rɪˈvɜːs] adj inverso,-a.
▶ n **1** *(back - of coin, paper)* reverso; *(- of cloth)* revés m. **2** AUTO marcha atrás. **3** *(setback)* revés m. ᴄᴏᴍᴘ **reverse gear** marcha atrás. ▌ **the reverse side 1** *(of coin, paper)* reverso. **2** *(of cloth)* revés m.
▶ vt **1** *(positions, roles)* invertir. **2** *(decision)* revocar. **3** *(vehicle)* dar marcha atrás a.
▶ vi AUTO poner marcha atrás, dar marcha atrás.
▶ n **the reverse** lo contrario.

revert [rɪˈvɜːt] vi **1** volver (**to**, a). **2** JUR revertir.

review [rɪˈvjuː] n **1** *(magazine, show)* revista. **2** MIL revista. **3** *(examination)* examen m. **4** *(of film, book, etc)* crítica.
▶ vt **1** *(troops)* pasar revista a. **2** *(examine)* examinar. **3** *(film, book, etc)* hacer una crítica de. ɪᴏᴄ **under review** bajo revisión.

R

revise [rɪ'vaɪz] *vt* **1** revisar. **2** *(correct)* corregir. **3** *(change)* modificar. **4** *(examination topic)* repasar.
▸ *vi (for exam)* repasar.

revision [rɪ'vɪʒ°n] *n* **1** revisión *f.* **2** *(correction)* corrección *f.* **3** *(change)* modificación *f.* **4** *(for exam)* repaso.

revival [rɪ'vaɪv°l] *n* **1** *(rebirth)* renacimiento. **2** *(of economy)* reactivación *f.* **3** *(of play)* reestreno.

revive [rɪ'vaɪv] *vt* **1** reanimar, reavivar, despertar. **2** *(economy)* reactivar. **3** *(play)* reestrenar. **4** MED reanimar.
▸ *vi* MED volver en sí.

revolt [rɪ'vəʊlt] *n (rising)* revuelta, rebelión *f.*
▸ *vi (rise)* sublevarse (**against**, contra), rebelarse (**against**, contra).
▸ *vt (disgust)* repugnar.

revolting [rɪ'vəʊltɪŋ] *adj* repugnante, asqueroso,-a.

revolution [revə'lu:ʃ°n] *n* revolución *f.*

revolutionary [revəl'u:ʃ°nərɪ] *adj* revolucionario,-a.
▸ *n* revolucionario,-a.

revolve [rɪ'vɒlv] *vi* girar.
▸ *vt* hacer girar.

revolver [rɪ'vɒlvəʳ] *n* revólver *m.*

revolving [rɪ'vɒlvɪŋ] *adj* giratorio,-a. COMP **revolving door** puerta giratoria.

reward [rɪ'wɔ:d] *n* recompensa.
▸ *vt* recompensar.

rewind [ri:'waɪnd] *vt* rebobinar.
ⓘ *pt & pp* **rewound** [ri:'waʊnd].

rewound [ri:'waʊnd] *pt & pp* → **rewind**.

rewrite [(vb) ri:'raɪt; (n) 'ri:raɪt] *vt* volver a escribir.
ⓘ *pt* **rewrote** [ri:'rəʊt], *pp* **rewritten** [ri:'rɪtən].
▸ *n* nueva versión *f.*

rewritten [ri:'rɪtən] *pp* → **rewrite**.

rewrote [ri:'rəʊt] *pt* → **rewrite**.

rheumatism ['ru:mətɪz°m] *n* reumatismo, reuma *m,* reúma *m.*

rhinoceros [raɪ'nɒsərəs] *n* rinoceronte *m.*
ⓘ *pl* **rhinoceroses** o **rhinoceros**.

rhizome ['raɪzəʊm] *n* rizoma *m.*

rhombus ['rɒmbəs] *n* rombo.
ⓘ *pl* **rhombuses** o **rhombi** ['rɒmbaɪ].

rhubarb ['ru:bɑ:b] *n* ruibarbo.

rhyme [raɪm] *n* rima.
▸ *vi* rimar (**with**, con).

rhythm ['rɪð°m] *n* ritmo.

rhythmic ['rɪðmɪk] *adj* rítmico,-a. COMP **rhythmic gymnastics** gimnástica rítmica.

rib [rɪb] *n* costilla. COMP **rib cage** caja torácica.

ribbon ['rɪb°n] *n* **1** cinta. **2** *(for hair)* lazo.

ribonucleic [raɪbəʊnju'kleɪk] *adj* ribonucleico,-a.

rice [raɪs] *n* arroz *m.* COMP **rice field** arrozal *m.* ▌ **rice pudding** arroz *m* con leche.

rich [rɪtʃ] *adj* **1** rico,-a. **2** *(luxurious)* suntuoso,-a, lujoso,-a. **3** *(fertile)* fértil. **4** *(food)* fuerte, pesado,-a.
▸ *n pl* **riches** riqueza *f sing.*

✗ Rich no significa 'rico (sabroso)', que se traduce por tasty.

richness ['rɪtʃnəs] *n* **1** *(wealth)* riqueza. **2** *(fertility)* fertilidad *f.* **3** *(of voice)* sonoridad *f.* **4** *(of colour)* viveza.

rid [rɪd] *vt* librar. LOC **to get rid of** deshacerse de.
ⓘ *pt & pp* **rid** o **ridded**, *ger* **ridding**.

ridden ['rɪdən] *pp* → **ride**.

riddle ['rɪd°l] *n* acertijo, adivinanza.
▸ *vt* **1** cribar. **2** *(with bullets)* acribillar.

ride [raɪd] *n* **1** *(on bicycle, horse)* paseo. **2** *(in car)* paseo, vuelta; *(on bus, train)* viaje *m,* trayecto.
▸ *vi* **1** *(on horse)* montar a caballo; *(on bicycle)* ir en bicicleta. **2** *(in vehicle)* viajar.
▸ *vt* **1** *(horse)* montar. **2** *(bicycle)* montar en, andar en.
ⓘ *pt* **rode** [rəʊd], *pp* **ridden** ['rɪdən], *ger* **riding**.

rider ['raɪdəʳ] *n* **1** *(on horse - man)* jinete *m,* *(woman)* amazona. **2** *(on bicycle)* ciclista *mf.* **3** *(on motorcycle)* motorista *mf.* **4** *(clause)* cláusula adicional.

ridge [rɪdʒ] *n* **1** GEOG cresta. **2** *(of roof)* caballete *m.*

ridiculous [rɪ'dɪkjʊləs] *adj* ridículo,-a.

ridicule ['rɪdɪkju:l] *n* ridículo.
▸ *vt* ridiculizar, poner en ridículo.

riding ['raɪdɪŋ] *n* equitación *f.*

rifle ['raɪf°l] *n* rifle *m,* fusil *m.*

rig [rɪg] *n* plataforma petrolífera.
▶ *vt* **1** MAR aparejar. **2** *fam (fix)* amañar.
ⓘ *pt & pp* **rigged**, *ger* **rigging**.

right [raɪt] *adj* **1** *(not left)* derecho,-a. **2** *(correct)* correcto,-a. **3** *(just)* justo,-a. **4** *(suitable)* apropiado,-a, adecuado,-a. **5** *fam (total)* auténtico,-a, total. **6** *fam (okay)* bien. ⃞ⓁⓄⒸ **all right!** ¡bien!, ¡conforme!, ¡vale! ▌ **right away** en seguida. ▌ **right now** ahora mismo. ▌ **to be right** tener razón. ▌ **to get it right** acertar. ▌ **to put right** arreglar, corregir. ⃞ⒸⓄᴹᴾ **right angle** ángulo recto. ▌ **right wing** POL derecha.
▶ *adv* **1** a la derecha. **2** *(correctly)* bien, correctamente. **3** *(exactly)* justo. **4** *(well)* bueno, bien.
▶ *n* **1** *(not left)* derecha. **2** *(entitlement)* derecho.
▶ *vt* **1** corregir. **2** MAR enderezar.

right-hand ['raɪthænd] *adj* derecho,-a.

right-handed [raɪt'hændɪd] *adj* diestro,-a.

right-wing ['raɪtwɪŋ] *adj* POL de derechas, derechista.

rigid ['rɪdʒɪd] *adj* rígido,-a.

rim [rɪm] *n* **1** *(gen)* borde *m*, canto. **2** *(of wheel)* llanta. **3** *(of spectacles)* montura.

rind [raɪnd] *n* corteza.

ring¹ [rɪŋ] *n* **1** *(for finger)* anillo, sortija. **2** *(hoop)* anilla, aro. **3** *(circle)* círculo; *(of people)* corro; *(of criminals)* red *f*. **4** *(of circus)* pista, arena. **5** *(for boxing)* ring *m*, cuadrilátero; *(for bullfighting)* ruedo. ⃞ⒸⓄᴹᴾ **ring road** cinturón *m* de ronda.
▶ *vt* **1** *(put a ring on)* anillar. **2** *(draw a ring round)* marcar con un círculo. **3** *(encircle)* rodear.

ring² [rɪŋ] *n* **1** *(of bell)* tañido, toque *m*; *(of doorbell)* llamada. **2** *(phone call)* llamada.
▶ *vi* **1** *(bell)* sonar. **2** *(ears)* zumbar.
▶ *vt* **1** *(call)* llamar. **2** *(bell)* tocar.
◆ **to ring off** *vt sep* colgar el teléfono.
◆ **to ring up** *vt sep* llamar por teléfono, telefonear.
ⓘ *pt* **rang** [ræŋ], *pp* **rung** [rʌŋ].

ringing ['rɪŋɪŋ] *n* **1** campaneo, repique *m*. **2** *(in ears)* zumbido.

rink [rɪŋk] *n* pista de patinaje. ⃞ⒸⓄᴹᴾ **ice rink** pista de hielo.

rinse [rɪns] *vt* **1** *(clothes, hair)* aclarar. **2** *(dishes, mouth)* enjuagar.
▶ *n* **1** *(of clothes)* aclarado. **2** *(of dishes)* enjuague *m*. **3** *(for hair)* tinte *m*.

riot ['raɪət] *n* **1** *(in street)* disturbio. **2** *(in prison)* motín *m*. ⃞ⒸⓄᴹᴾ **riot police** policía antidisturbios.
▶ *vi* **1** *(in street)* provocar disturbios. **2** *(in prison)* amotinarse.

rip [rɪp] *n* rasgón *m*, desgarrón *m*.
▶ *vt* rasgar, desgarrar.
ⓘ *pt & pp* **ripped**, *ger* **ripping**.

ripe [raɪp] *adj* maduro,-a.

rip-off ['rɪpɒf] *n fam* timo.

ripple ['rɪpəl] *n* **1** *(on water)* onda. **2** *(sound)* murmullo.
▶ *vt* rizar.
▶ *vi* rizarse.

rise [raɪz] *n* **1** ascenso, subida. **2** *(increase)* aumento. **3** *(slope)* subida, cuesta.
▶ *vi* **1** ascender, subir. **2** *(increase)* aumentar. **3** *(stand up)* ponerse de pie. **4** *(get up)* levantarse. **5** *(sun)* salir. **6** *(river)* nacer. **7** *(level of river)* crecer. **8** *(mountains)* elevarse.
ⓘ *pt* **rose** [rəʊz], *pp* **risen** ['rɪzən].

risen ['rɪzən] *pp* → **rise**.

rising ['raɪzɪŋ] *n (rebellion)* levantamiento.
▶ *adj* **1** *(prices)* en aumento. **2** *(sun)* naciente. **3** *(land)* en pendiente.

risk [rɪsk] *n* riesgo, peligro. ⃞ⓁⓄⒸ **to take a risk** correr un riesgo.
▶ *vt* arriesgar.

risky ['rɪskɪ] *adj* arriesgado,-a.
ⓘ *comp* **riskier**, *superl* **riskiest**.

ritual ['rɪtjʊəl] *adj* risorio.

rite [raɪt] *n* rito.

rival ['raɪvəl] *adj* competidor,-ra, rival.
▶ *n* competidor,-ra, rival *mf*.
▶ *vt* competir con, rivalizar con.

river ['rɪvər] *n* río.

river-bed ['rɪvəbed] *n* lecho.

riverside ['rɪvəsaɪd] *n* ribera, orilla.

rivet ['rɪvɪt] *n* remache *m*.
▶ *vt* **1** remachar. **2** *fig* fijar, absorber.

road [rəʊd] *n* **1** carretera. **2** *(way)* camino. ⃞ⒸⓄᴹᴾ **road sign** señal *f* de tráfico.

R

roadway [ˈrəʊdweɪ] n calzada.
roadworks [ˈrəʊdweːks] n pl obras.
roam [rəʊm] vt vagar por.
▶ vi vagar.
roar [rɔːʳ] n 1 (of bull, person) bramido. 2 (of lion, sea) rugido. 3 (of traffic) estruendo. 4 (of crowd) griterío, clamor m.
▶ vi 1 (bull, person) bramar. 2 (lion, sea) rugir.
roast [rəʊst] adj asado,-a. COMP roast beef rosbif m. I roast potato patata al horno.
▶ n asado.
▶ vt 1 (meat) asar. 2 (coffee, nuts, etc) tostar.
▶ vi asarse.
rob [rɒb] vt 1 robar. 2 (bank) atracar; (shop) asaltar, robar.
ⓘ pt & pp robbed, ger robbing.

✎ Rob no es lo mismo que steal: rob se usa con la persona robada o con un sitio que se atraca; steal se usa con el dinero u objetos robados. Consulta también steal.

robber [ˈrɒbəʳ] n atracador,-a.
robbery [ˈrɒbərɪ] n atraco.
robin [ˈrɒbɪn] n petirrojo.
robot [ˈrəʊbɒt] n robot m.
rock [rɒk] n 1 (gen) roca. 2 US piedra. 3 MUS rock m, música rock.
▶ vt 1 (chair) mecer. 2 (baby) acunar. 3 (upset) sacudir, convulsionar.
▶ vi (chair) mecerse.
rocket [ˈrɒkɪt] n 1 (missile) cohete m. COMP rocket launcher lanzacohetes m.
▶ vi (rise) dispararse.
rocking-chair [ˈrɒkɪntʃeəʳ] n mecedora.
rocky [ˈrɒkɪ] adj rocoso,-a.
ⓘ comp rockier, superl rockiest.
rod [rɒd] n 1 (thin) vara. 2 (thick) barra. 3 (for fishing) caña.
rode [rəʊd] pt → ride.
rodent [ˈrəʊdᵊnt] n roedor m.
roebuck [ˈrəʊbʌk] n corzo.
rogue [rəʊg] n bribón,-ona, pillo,-a.
role [rəʊl] n papel, interpretación m.
roll [rəʊl] n 1 (gen) rollo. 2 (of film) carrete m. 3 (list) lista. 4 (of bread) bollo, panecillo; (sandwich) bocadillo. COMP to call the roll pasar lista.

▶ vt 1 (ball, coin) hacer rodar. 2 (flatten) allanar, apisonar. 3 (into a ball) enroscar. 4 (paper) enrollar.
◆ to roll up vt sep 1 enrollar. 2 (into a ball) enroscar.
▶ vi enrollarse.
roller [ˈrəʊləʳ] n 1 (for painting) rodillo. 2 (wave) ola grande. 3 (for hair) rulo. COMP roller coaster montaña rusa. I roller skating patinaje m sobre ruedas.
rollerblades [ˈrəʊləbleɪdz] n pl patines mpl en línea.
ROM [rɒm] abbr (read-only memory) memoria solo de lectura; (abbreviation) ROM f.
Roman [ˈrəʊmən] adj romano,-a.
▶ n romano,-a. COMP Roman numeral número romano.
Romance [rəʊˈmæns] adj románico,-a.
romance [rəʊˈmæns] n 1 romance m. 2 (novel) novela romántica.
Romania [ruːˈmeɪnɪə] n Rumanía.
Romanian [ruːˈmeɪnɪən] adj rumano,-a.
▶ n 1 (person) rumano,-a. 2 (language) rumano.
romanise [ˈrəʊmənaɪz] vt romanizar.
romantic [rəʊˈmæntɪk] adj romántico,-a.
roof [ruːf] n 1 tejado; (tiled) techado. 2 (of mouth) cielo. 3 (of car, etc) techo. COMP flat roof azotea. I roof rack baca. I roof tiles tejas fpl.
▶ vt techar.
rooftop [ˈruːftɒp] n tejado.
rookie [ˈrʊkɪ] n fam novato,-a.
room [ruːm] n 1 habitación f, pieza. 2 (space) espacio, sitio, lugar m. COMP room temperature temperatura ambiente.
▶ vi 1 (lodge) alojarse. 2 (share a room) compartir una habitación.
roomy [ˈruːmɪ] adj espacioso,-a.
ⓘ comp roomier, superl roomiest.
rooster [ˈruːstəʳ] n gallo.
root¹ [ruːt] n raíz f.
▶ vt arraigar.
▶ vi arraigar.
rope [rəʊp] n (gen) cuerda; (thicker) soga.
▶ vt atar (con cuerdas), amarrar.
◆ to rope off vt sep acordonar.

rosary ['rəʊzərɪ] n rosario.
ⓘ pl **rosaries**.

rose¹ [rəʊz] n 1 (flower) rosa. 2 (bush) rosal m. 3 (colour) rosa m. 4 (of shower, etc) alcachofa. COMP **rose garden** rosaleda. ‖ **rose window** rosetón m.

rose² [rəʊz] pt → **rise**.

rosé ['rəʊzeɪ] n vino rosado.

rosebud ['rəʊzbʌd] n capullo de rosa.

rosebush ['rəʊzbʌʃ] n rosal m.

rosemary ['rəʊzmərɪ] n romero.

rot [rɒt] n 1 (decay) putrefacción f. 2 (rubbish) tonterías fpl.
▸ vt pudrir.
▸ vi pudrirse.
ⓘ pt & pp **rotted**, ger **rotting**.

rotate [rəʊ'teɪt] vt 1 (spin) hacer girar, dar vueltas a. 2 (alternate) alternar.
▸ vi 1 (spin) girar, dar vueltas. 2 (alternate) alternarse.

rotation [rəʊ'teɪʃən] n rotación f

rotten [rɒtən] adj podrido,-a.

rough [rʌf] adj 1 (not smooth) áspero,-a, basto,-a. 2 (road) lleno,-a de baches. 3 (edge) desigual. 4 (rude) rudo,-a. 5 (approximate) aproximado,-a.

roughly ['rʌflɪ] adv 1 (about) aproximadamente; (more or less) más o menos. 2 (not gently) bruscamente.

round [raʊnd] adj redondo,-a.
▸ n 1 (circle) círculo. 2 (series) serie f, tanda; (one of a series) ronda. 3 SP (stage of competition) ronda; (boxing) asalto; (of golf) partido. 4 (of drinks) ronda. 5 (of policeman, etc) ronda. 6 (for gun) cartucho. 7 (of bread) rebanada. COMP **round trip** viaje m de ida y vuelta. ‖ **round number** número redondo.
▸ adv 1 (in circles): it goes round and round da vueltas y vueltas. 2 (about) por ahí. 3 (to somebody's house) a casa.
▸ prep alrededor de.
▸ vt doblar.

roundabout ['raʊndəbaʊt] n 1 tiovivo. 2 AUTO rotonda.

route [ruːt] n 1 ruta, camino. 2 (of bus) línea, trayecto.
▸ vt mandar.

router ['ruːtəʳ] n COMPUT direccionador m, enrutador m.

routine [ruː'tiːn] n rutina.

row¹ [raʊ] n 1 (fight) riña, pelea. 2 (din, racket) jaleo.
▸ vi pelearse.

row² [rəʊ] n (line) fila, hilera.

row³ [rəʊ] vi (in a boat) remar.

rowing ['rəʊɪŋ] n remo. COMP **rowing boat** bote m de remos.

royal ['rɔɪəl] adj real.

royalty ['rɔɪəltɪ] n 1 realeza. 2 (people) miembros mpl de la familia real.
ⓘ pl **royalties**.
▸ n pl **royalties** (gen) royalties mpl; (of writer) derechos mpl de autor.

rub [rʌb] n friega.
▸ vt (gen) frotar; (hard) restregar.
▸ vi rozar.
◆ **to rub out** vt sep borrar.
▸ vi borrarse.
ⓘ pt & pp **rubbed**, ger **rubbing**.

rubber ['rʌbəʳ] n 1 caucho, goma. 2 (eraser) goma de borrar. COMP **rubber band** goma elástica. ‖ **rubber ring** flotador m.

rubbish ['rʌbɪʃ] n 1 (refuse) basura. 2 (nonsense) tonterías fpl. COMP **rubbish bin** cubo de la basura. ‖ **rubbish dump** vertedero, basurero.

rubella [ruː'belə] n rubéola.

ruby ['ruːbɪ] n rubí m.
ⓘ pl **rubies**.

rucksack ['rʌksæk] n mochila.

rudder ['rʌdəʳ] n timón m.

rude [ruːd] adj 1 (person) maleducado, -a, grosero,-a; (behaviour) grosero,-a; (word) malsonante. 2 (improper) grosero,-a. 3 (crude) rudo,-a, tosco,-a.

rug [rʌg] n alfombra, alfombrilla.

rugby ['rʌgbɪ] n rugby m.

ruin ['ruːɪn] n ruina.
▸ vt 1 arruinar. 2 (spoil) estropear.

ruined ['ruːɪnd] adj 1 arruinado,-a. 2 (spoilt) estropeado,-a. 3 (building) en ruinas.
◆ **to rule out** vt sep excluir, descartar.

ruler ['ruːləʳ] n 1 gobernante mf, dirigente mf. 2 (monarch) soberano,-a, monarca mf. 3 (instrument) regla.

R

ruling ['ruːlɪŋ] *adj (in charge)* dirigente; *(governing)* en el poder; *(reigning)* reinante.
▸ *n* JUR fallo.

rum [rʌm] *n* ron *m*.

Rumania [ruːˈmeɪnɪə] *n* → Romania.

Rumanian [ruːˈmeɪnɪən] *adj-n* → Romanian.

rumble ['rʌmbəl] *n (gen)* ruido sordo; *(of thunder)* estruendo.
▸ *vi (gen)* hacer un ruido sordo; *(thunder)* retumbar.

ruminant ['ruːmɪnənt] *adj* rumiante.
▸ *n* rumiante *m*.

run [rʌn] *n* 1 carrera. 2 *(trip)* viaje *m*; *(for pleasure)* paseo. 3 *(ski)* pista. 4 *(in stocking)* carrera. 4 *(in cricket)* carrera. 9 *(in printing)* tirada. 10 *(at cards)* escalera.
[LOC] **to go for a run** ir a correr.
▸ *vi* 1 *(gen)* correr. 2 *(flow)* correr. 3 *(operate)* funcionar. 4 *(trains, buses)* circular. 5 *(in election)* presentarse. 6 *(play)* estar en cartel; *(contract, etc)* seguir vigente. 7 *(colour)* correrse.
▸ *vt* 1 *(gen)* correr. 2 *(race)* correr en, participar en. 3 *(take by car)* llevar, acompañar. 4 *(manage)* dirigir, regentar. 5 *(organize)* organizar. 6 *(operate)* hacer funcionar. 7 *(pass, submit to)* pasar. 8 *(publish)* publicar. 9 *(water)* dejar correr.
◆ **to run after** *vt insep* perseguir.
◆ **to run away** *vi* 1 *(gen)* irse corriendo. 2 *(from home, etc)* fugarse, escaparse.
◆ **to run down** *vt sep* 1 *(knock down)* atropellar. 2 *(criticize)* criticar. 3 *(battery)* agotar.
▸ *vt insep* bajar corriendo.
▸ *vi* 1 bajar corriendo. 2 *(battery)* agotarse. 3 *(clock)* pararse.
◆ **to run into** *vt insep* 1 entrar corriendo en. 2 *(car)* chocar con. 3 *(meet)* tropezar con.
◆ **to run off** *vt sep (print)* imprimir.
▸ *vi* irse corriendo.
◆ **to run out** *vi* 1 salir corriendo. 2 *(be used up - gen)* acabarse; *(- stocks)* agotarse. 3 *(contract)* caducar.
ⓘ *pt* ran [ræn], *pp* run [rʌn], *ger* running

rung¹ [rʌŋ] *n* escalón *m*.

rung² [rʌŋ] *pp* → ring.

runner ['rʌnəʳ] *n* 1 corredor,-ra. 2 *(of sledge)* patín *m*; *(of skate)* cuchilla. 3 *(carpet)* alfombrilla. 4 *(on furniture)* tapete *m*. [COMP] **runner bean** judía verde.

running ['rʌnɪŋ] *n* 1 *(action)* el correr; *(sport)* atletismo. 2 *(management)* dirección *f*.
▸ *adj* 1 *(water)* corriente. 2 *(continuous)* continuo,-a.

runny ['rʌnɪ] *adj* 1 *(liquid)* líquido,-a; *(egg)* poco hecho..
ⓘ *comp* runnier, *superl* runniest.

run-up ['rʌnʌp] *n* 1 *(period before)* etapa preliminar. 2 *(before jumping, etc)* carrerilla.

runway ['rʌnweɪ] *n* pista de aterrizaje.

rural ['ruːrəl] *adj* rural.

rush¹ [rʌʃ] *n* 1 prisa. 2 *(movement)* movimiento impetuoso. [COMP] **rush hour** hora punta. ▎**rush job** trabajo urgente.
▸ *vt* 1 *(hurry - person)* apresurar, dar prisa a, meter prisa a. 2 *(send quickly)* enviar urgentemente. 3 *(attack)* abalanzarse sobre.
▸ *vi* ir deprisa, precipitarse.
◆ **to rush in** *vi* entrar corriendo.
◆ **to rush out** *vi* salir corriendo.

rush² [rʌʃ] *n (plant)* junco.

Russia ['rʌʃə] *n* Rusia.

Russian ['rʌʃən] *adj* ruso,-a.
▸ *n* 1 *(person)* ruso,-a. 2 *(language)* ruso.

rust [rʌst] *n* óxido, herrumbre *m*.
▸ *vt* oxidar.
▸ *vi* oxidar.

rustle ['rʌsəl] *n (of leaves, etc)* crujido; *(of silk)* frufrú *m*.
▸ *vt (leaves, etc)* hacer crujir.
▸ *vi (leaves, etc)* crujir.
▸ *vt (cattle)* robar.
▸ *vi (cattle)* robar ganado.

rusty ['rʌstɪ] *adj* 1 *(metal)* oxidado,-a. 2 *fig* oxidado,-a, olvidado,-a.
ⓘ *comp* rustier, *superl* rustiest.

ruthless ['ruːθləs] *adj* cruel, despiadado,-a.

Rwanda [ruˈændə] *n* Ruanda.

Rwandan [ruˈændən] *adj* ruandés,-esa.
▸ *n* ruandés,-esa.

rye [raɪ] *n* centeno. [COMP] **rye bread** pan *m* de centeno. ▎**rye grass** ballica.

S

S, s [es] *n (the letter)* S, s *f.*

saber ['seɪbəʳ] *n* US → sabre.

sabotage ['sæbətɑːʒ] *n* sabotaje *m.*
▶ *vt* sabotear.

saboteur [sæbə'tɜːʳ] *n* saboteador,-ra.

sabre ['seɪbəʳ] *n* sable *m.*

saccharin ['sækərɪn] *n* sacarina.

sachet ['sæʃeɪ] *n* bolsita, sobrecito.

sack¹ [sæk] *n (bag)* saco.
▶ *vt* GB *fam* despedir a, echar a. LOC **to get the sack** ser despedido,-a. **to give sb the sack** despedir a ALGN.

sack² [sæk] *vt* MIL saquear.
▶ *n* MIL saqueo.

> ❌ To sack no significa 'sacar', que se traduce por **to take out**.

sacrament ['sækrəmənt] *n* sacramento.

sacred ['seɪkrəd] *adj* sagrado,-a.

sacrifice ['sækrɪfaɪs] *n* **1** *(gen)* sacrificio. **2** *(offering)* ofrenda.
▶ *vt* sacrificar.

sacrum ['sækrəm] *n* ANAT sacro.
ⓘ *pl* sacra ['sækrə].

sad [sæd] *adj* **1** *(unhappy)* triste: *you look very sad* estás muy triste. **2** *(deplorable)* lamentable.
ⓘ *comp* sadder, *superl* saddest.

sadden ['sædən] *vt* entristecer.
▶ *vi* entristecerse.

saddle ['sædəl] *n (for horse)* silla (de montar); *(of bicycle, etc)* sillín *m.*
▶ *vt* ensillar (up, -).

sadism ['seɪdɪzəm] *n* sadismo.

sadist ['seɪdɪst] *n* sádico,-a.

sadly ['sædlɪ] *adv* tristemente.

sadness ['sædnəs] *n* tristeza.

safari [sə'fɑːrɪ] *n* safari *m.*

safe [seɪf] *adj* **1** *(gen)* seguro,-a; *(out of danger)* a salvo, fuera de peligro: *it's not safe to play in the road* es peligroso jugar en la calle. **2** *(unharmed)* ileso,-a, indemne. **3** *(not risky - method, investment, choice)* seguro,-a; *(subject)* no polémico,-a. LOC **safe and sound** sano,-a y salvo,-a.
▶ *n* caja fuerte, caja de caudales.

safe-conduct [seɪf'kɒndʌkt] *n* salvoconducto.

safely ['seɪflɪ] *adv* **1** *(for certain)* con toda seguridad: *we can safely say that...* podemos decir con toda seguridad que .... **2** *(without mishap)* sin contratiempos, sin accidentes. **3** *(securely)* de manera segura.

safety ['seɪftɪ] *n* seguridad *f.* COMP **safety belt** cinturón *m* de seguridad. **safety match** cerilla, fósforo. **safety pin** imperdible *m.*

saffron ['sæfrən] *n (plant, condiment)* azafrán *m.*

sag [sæg] *vi* **1** *(shelf, branch, beam, ceiling)* combarse; *(roof, bed)* hundirse. **2** *(demand, prices, etc)* caer, bajar. **3** *fig (spirits)* flaquear, decaer.
ⓘ *pt & pp* sagged, *ger* sagging.

sage¹ [seɪdʒ] *adj* sabio,-a.
▶ *n* sabio,-a.

sage² [seɪdʒ] *n* BOT salvia.

Sagittarius [sædʒɪ'teərɪəs] *n* Sagitario.

said [sed] *pt & pp* → say.

sail [seɪl] *n* **1** *(canvas)* vela. **2** *(of windmill)* aspa.
▶ *vt* **1** *(travel)* navegar; *(cross)* cruzar en barco: *she sailed the Atlantic single-handed* cruzó el Atlántico sola. **2** *(control ship)* gobernar. LOC **in full sail** a toda vela. **to set sail** zarpar, hacerse a la mar.
▶ *vi* **1** *(ship, boat)* navegar. **2** *(begin journey)* zarpar, hacerse a la mar.

S

sailing ['seɪlɪŋ] n **1** (skill) navegación f. **2** (sport) vela: we go sailing every weekend hacemos vela todos los fines de semana. **3** (departure) salida; (crossing) travesía. COMP **sailing boat** barco de vela, velero.

sailor ['seɪləʳ] n marinero.

saint [seɪnt] n (person) santo,-a.

sake [seɪk] n bien m: for your own sake por tu propio bien; for the kids' sake por los niños. LOC **for God's sake!** ¡por el amor de Dios!, ¡por Dios! ∎ **for Heaven's sake!** ¡por el amor de Dios!

salad ['sæləd] n ensalada. COMP **salad bowl** ensaladera. ∎ **salad dressing** aliño, aderezo.

salamander ['sæləmændəʳ] n salamandra.

salami [sə'lɑːmɪ] n salami m.

salary ['sælərɪ] n sueldo, salario.
ⓘ pl salaries.

sale [seɪl] n **1** (act, transaction) venta. **2** (special offer) rebajas fpl, liquidación f: I bought it in a sale lo compré en las rebajas.
▸ n pl **sales** (amount sold) venta, ventas fpl; (reductions) rebajas fpl. LOC **for sale** en venta. ∎ **"For sale"** (sign on house, etc) «Se vende». ∎ **on sale 1** (available) en venta, a la venta. **2** (reduced) rebajado,-a. COMP **clearance sale** liquidación f. ∎ **sale goods** artículos mpl rebajados. ∎ **sales assistant** dependiente,-a.

salesclerk ['seɪlzklɑːk] n US dependiente,-a.

salesman ['seɪlzmən] n **1** (gen) vendedor m; (in shop) dependiente m. **2** (travelling) representante m.
ⓘ pl salesmen ['seɪlzmən].

saleswoman ['seɪlzwumən] n **1** (gen) vendedora; (in shop) dependienta. **2** (travelling) representante f.
ⓘ pl saleswomen ['seɪlzwɪmɪn].

saline ['seɪlaɪn] adj salino,-a.

saliva [sə'laɪvə] n saliva.

salivary [sə'laɪvərɪ] adj salival.

salmon ['sæmən] n **1** (fish) salmón m. **2** (colour) color m salmón.
ⓘ pl salmon.

salmonella [sælmə'nelə] n **1** (bacteria) salmonella. **2** (food poisoning) intoxicación f.

saloon [sə'luːn] n **1** US taberna, bar m. **2** (public room) sala; (on ship) salón m.

salt [sɔːlt] n (gen) sal f. LOC **to be the salt of the earth** ser la sal de la tierra.▸ adj salado,-a.
▸ vt **1** (preserve, cure) salar. **2** (season) echar sal a.
▸ n pl **salts** sales fpl.

salted ['sɔːltɪd] adj salado,-a.

salpeter [sɔːlt'piːtəʳ] n US → saltpetre.

saltpetre [sɔːlt'piːtəʳ] n salitre m.

salty ['sɔːltɪ] adj salado,-a.
ⓘ comp saltier, superl saltiest.

salute [sə'luːt] n MIL saludo; (firing of guns) salva.
▸ vt MIL saludar.

❌ To salute no significa 'saludar (decir hola)', que se traduce por to say hello.

Salvadorian [sælvə'dɔːrɪən] adj salvadoreño,-a.
▸ n salvadoreño,-a.

samba ['sæmbə] n (dance) samba.

same [seɪm] adj **1** (not different) mismo,-a: the same day el mismo día. **2** (alike) mismo,-a, igual, idéntico,-a: he's wearing the same tie as you lleva una corbata igual que la tuya. LOC **at the same time 1** (simultaneously) a la vez, al mismo tiempo. **2** (however) sin embargo, aun así.
▸ pron **the same** lo mismo: it won't be the same without you no será lo mismo sin ti.
▸ adv **the same** igual, del mismo modo: they talk the same hablan igual. LOC COMP **all the same** a pesar de todo. ∎ **it's all the same to me** me da igual, me da lo mismo. ∎ **the same as** igual que, como. ∎ **the same to you** ¡igualmente!

Samoa [sə'məuə] n Samoa.

Samoan [sə'məuən] adj samoano,-a.
▸ n **1** (person) samoano,-a. **2** (language) samoano.

sample ['sɑːmpəl] n muestra.
▸ vt probar.

sanatorium [sænə'tɔːrɪəm] n sanatorio.
ⓘ pl sanatoriums o sanatoria [sænə'tɔːrɪə].

sanction ['sæŋkʃən] n sanción f.
▶ vt fml sancionar.

sanctuary ['sæŋktjʊərɪ] n **1** REL (sacred place) santuario. **2** (gen) refugio, protección f. **3** (for animals) reserva.
ⓘ pl sanctuaries.

sand [sænd] n (gen) arena.
▶ vt (smooth) lijar (down, -).
▶ n pl **sands** (beach) playa f sing; (sandbank) banco m sing de arena.

sandal ['sændəl] n sandalia.

sandbank ['sændbæŋk] n banco de arena.

sandcastle ['sænka:səl] n castillo de arena.

sander ['sændə'] n (machine) lijadora.

sandpaper ['sændpeɪpə'] n papel m de lija.
▶ vt lijar.

sandwich ['sænwɪdʒ] n (French bread) bocadillo; (sliced bread) sándwich m.
ⓘ pl sandwiches.

sandy ['sændɪ] adj **1** (beach, etc) arenoso,-a, de arena. **2** (hair) rubio,-a oscuro,-a.
ⓘ comp sandier, superl sandiest.

sane [seɪn] adj **1** (person) cuerdo,-a; (mind) sano,-a. **2** fig (solution, decision, etc) sensato,-a.

☒ Sane no significa 'sano (con salud)', que se traduce por healthy.

sang [sæŋ] pt → sing.

sanitary ['sænɪtərɪ] adj **1** (to do with health) sanitario,-a, de sanidad. **2** (hygienic) higiénico,-a. COMP **sanitary napkin** / **sanitary pad** / **sanitary towel** compresa.

sanitation [sænɪ'teɪʃən] n (public health) sanidad f (pública); (hygiene) higiene f.

sank [sæŋk] pt → sink.

Santa Claus [sæntə'klɔ:z] n Papá m Noel.

sap [sæp] n BOT savia.

sapphire ['sæfaɪə'] n zafiro.

sarcasm ['sɑ:kæzəm] n sarcasmo.

sarcastic [sɑ:'kæstɪk] adj sarcástico,-a.

sarcophagus [sɑ:'kɒfəgəs] n sarcófago.
ⓘ pl **sarcophaguses** o **sarcophagi** [sɑ:'kɒfəgaɪ].

sardine [sɑ:'di:n] n sardina. COMP **to be packed like sardines** estar como sardinas en lata.

sat [sæt] pt & pp → sit.

satanic [sə'tænɪk] adj satánico,-a.

satchel ['sætʃəl] n cartera (de colegial), mochila (de colegial).

satellite ['sætəlaɪt] n satélite m. COMP **satellite dish** TV antena parabólica. **satellite television** televisión f vía satélite.

satin ['sætɪn] n satén m, raso.
▶ adj (made of satin) de satén, de raso.

satisfaction [sætɪs'fækʃən] n satisfacción f.

satisfactory [sætɪs'fæktərɪ] adj **1** satisfactorio,-a. **2** EDUC suficiente.

satisfied ['sætɪsfaɪd] adj **1** satisfecho, -a, complacido,-a, contento,-a. **2** (convinced) convencido,-a.

satisfy ['sætɪsfaɪ] vt **1** (please, make happy) satisfacer, complacer, contentar; does nothing satisfy you? ¿no hay nada que te satisfaga? **2** (fulfil) satisfacer. **3** (convince) convencer.
ⓘ pt & pp satisfied, ger satisfying.

satisfying ['sætɪsfaɪŋ] adj (gen) satisfactorio,-a; (meal) bueno,-a, delicioso,-a.

satsuma [sæt'su:mə] n mandarina.

saturate ['sætʃəreɪt] vt saturar (with, de).

saturation [sætʃə'reɪʃən] n saturación f.

Saturday ['sætədɪ] n sábado: next Saturday el sábado que viene, el próximo sábado; on Saturday morning el sábado por la mañana; the following Saturday el sábado siguiente.

Saturn ['sætɜ:n] n Saturno.

sauce [sɔ:s] n CULIN salsa.

saucepan ['sɔ:spən] n cazo, cacerola.

saucer ['sɔ:sə'] n platillo.

Saudi ['saʊdɪ] adj saudí, saudita.
▶ n saudí mf, saudita mf. COMP **Saudi Arabia** Arabia Saudita.

sauna ['sɔ:nə] n sauna.

sausage ['sɒsɪdʒ] n salchicha.

sauté ['səʊteɪ] vt saltear.
ⓘ pt & pp sautéed o sautéd, ger sautéing.
▶ adj salteado,-a.

S

savage ['sævɪdʒ] *adj* **1** *(ferocious)* feroz; *(cruel)* cruel; *(violent)* violento,-a, salvaje: *a savage attack* un ataque duro. **2** *pej (primitive)* salvaje.

savanna [sə'vænə] *n* sabana.

save [seɪv] *vt* **1** *(gen)* salvar (from, de), rescatar (from, de): *you saved my life!* ¡me has salvado la vida! **2** *(not spend)* ahorrar: *I've saved $200 towards my holidays* he ahorrado 200 dólares para las vacaciones. **3** *(keep, put by - food, strength)* guardar, reservar; *(- stamps)* coleccionar. **4** SP *(goal)* parar. **5** COMPUT guardar, archivar.
▶ *vi (not spend)* ahorrar (up, -): *we're saving up to buy a flat* ahorramos para comprar un piso.
▶ *n* SP parada.

saving ['seɪvɪŋ] *n (of time, money)* ahorro, economía.
▶ *n pl* **savings** ahorros *mpl*. COMP **savings account** cuenta de ahorros.

savor ['seɪvəʳ] *n* US → savour.

savory ['seɪvərɪ] *adj* US → savoury.

savour ['seɪvəʳ] *vt* saborear.

savoury ['seɪvərɪ] *adj* **1** *(salty)* salado, -a; *(tasty)* sabroso,-a. **2** *(respectable, wholesome)* saludable, sano,-a.
▶ *n* entrante *m* salado, canapé *m*.

saw¹ [sɔ:] *n (tool)* sierra, serrucho.
▶ *vt* serrar.
▶ *vi* serrar, cortar.
ⓘ *pt* sawed, *pp* sawed o sawn [sɔ:n].

saw² [sed] *pt* → see.

sawdust ['sɔ:dʌst] *n* serrín *m*.

sawn [sɔ:n] *pp* → saw¹.

saxophone ['sæksəfəʊn] *n* saxofón *m*.

saxophonist [sæk'sɒfənɪst] *n* saxofonista *mf*, saxo *mf*.

say [seɪ] *vt* **1** *(gen)* decir: *what did he say?* ¿qué dijo?, ¿qué ha dicho? **2** *(prayer)* rezar; *(poem, lines)* recitar. **3** *(think)* pensar, opinar, decir: *I say we keep looking* creo que deberíamos seguir buscando. **5** *(suppose)* suponer, poner, decir: *come round at, say, 8.00 pm* pásate hacia las 8.00, ¿te parece? LOC **it is said that ...** dicen que ..., se dice que .... ‖ **not to say ...** por no decir .... ‖ **that is to say** es decir.
ⓘ *pt & pp* said [sed].

saying ['seɪɪŋ] *n* dicho, decir *m*.

scab [skæb] *n* MED costra, postilla.

scabies ['skeɪbiːz] *n* MED sarna.

scaffold ['skæfəʊld] *n* **1** *(framework)* andamio. **2** *(for execution)* patíbulo, cadalso.

scaffolding ['skæfəldɪŋ] *n* andamiaje *m*.

scald [skɔ:ld] *n* escaldadura.
▶ *vt* escaldar.

scale¹ [skeɪl] *n* **1** *(of fish, reptile)* escama. **2** *(on skin)* escama.

scale² [skeɪl] *n* **1** *(measure)* escala: *a metric scale* una escala métrica. **2** *(size, amount)* escala, magnitud *f*. **3** MUS escala. LOC **on a large scale** a gran escala. COMP **scale model** maqueta.

scale³ [skeɪl] *n (pan)* platillo.
▶ *vi* SP *(weigh)* pesar.
▶ *n pl* **scales** *(for weighing in shop, kitchen)* balanza; *(bathroom, large weights)* báscula.

scallop ['skɒləp] *n (mollusc)* vieira, concha de peregrino.

scalp [skælp] *n* ANAT cuero cabelludo.

scalpel ['skælpəl] *n* **1** *(surgeon's)* bisturí *m*; *(for dissecting)* escalpelo. **2** *(tool)* escoplo, gubia.

scamper ['skæmpəʳ] *vi* corretear.

scampi ['skæmpɪ] *n* colas *fpl* de cigala rebozadas.

scan [skæn] *vt* **1** *(examine)* escrutar, escudriñar. **2** *(glance at)* echar un vistazo a. **3** TECH *(with radar)* explorar. **4** MED, INFORM escanear.
ⓘ *pt & pp* scanned, *ger* scanning.
▶ *n* **1** TECH *(with radar)* exploración *f*. **2** MED *(gen)* exploración *f* ultrasónica; *(in gynaecology, etc)* ecografía.

scandal ['skændəl] *n* **1** *(outrage)* escándalo; *(disgrace)* vergüenza. **2** *(gossip)* chismorreo.

> ✕ Scandal no significa 'escándalo (alboroto)', que se traduce por **racket**.

scandalous ['skændələs] *adj* escandaloso,-a.

> ✕ Scandalous no significa 'escandaloso (ruidoso)', que se traduce por **noisy**.

scanner ['skænəʳ] *n* **1** TECH *(radar)* antena direccional. **2** MED, INFORM escáner *m*.

scapula ['skæpjʊlə] *n* ANAT escápula.

scar [skɑːʳ] n **1** cicatriz f. **2** fig marca, señal f.

scarce [skeəs] adj (not plentiful) escaso,-a.

scarcely ['skeəslɪ] adv (hardly) apenas: I scarcely know them apenas los conozco. **2** (surely not) ni mucho menos.

scare [skeəʳ] n **1** (fright) susto. what a scare you gave me! ¡vaya susto me has dado! **2** (widespread alarm) alarma, pánico.
▶ vt asustar, espantar: did I scare you? ¿te he asustado?
▶ vi asustarse, espantarse.

scarecrow ['skeəkrəʊ] n espantapájaros m.

scared ['skeəd] adj asustado,-a, espantado,-a. [loc] to be scared tener miedo (of, a/de): I'm scared of spiders tengo miedo a las arañas, las arañas me dan miedo.

scarf [skɑːf] n (small) pañuelo; (silk) fular m; (long, woollen) bufanda.
ⓘ pl scarfs o scarves [skɑːvz].

scarlet ['skɑːlət] adj escarlata.
▶ n escarlata m.

scary ['skeərɪ] adj fam (situation, etc) espantoso,-a; (film, story) de miedo, de terror.
ⓘ comp scarier, superl scariest.

scatter ['skætəʳ] vt **1** (crowd, birds) dispersar. **2** (papers, cushions, etc) esparcir, desparramar; (money) derrochar.
▶ vi dispersarse.

scenario [sɪˈnɑːrɪəʊ] n **1** (of film) guion m; (in theatre) argumento. **2** (situation) (posible) situación f, panorama m.
ⓘ pl scenarios.

☒ Scenario no significa 'escenario', que se traduce por stage.

scene [siːn] n **1** (place) lugar m, escenario; (sight, picture) escena. **2** (in play, book) escena. **3** (stage setting) decorado, escenario.

scenery ['siːnərɪ] n **1** (landscape) paisaje m. **2** THEAT (on stage) decorado.

scent [sent] n **1** (gen) olor m; (pleasant smell) aroma m. **2** (perfume) perfume m. **3** (track, trail) pista, rastro.
▶ vt **1** (animal) olfatear. **2** fig (suspect) intuir. **3** (perfume) perfumar (with, de).

scepter ['septəʳ] n US → sceptre.

sceptical ['skeptɪkəl] adj escéptico,-a.

sceptre ['septəʳ] n cetro.

schedule ['ʃedjuːl, US 'skedjuəl] n **1** (programme) programa m: a work schedule un programa de trabajo. **2** (list - gen) lista. **3** US (timetable) horario. [loc] on schedule **1** (flight) a la hora (prevista). **2** (work) al día. ▮ to be ahead of schedule ir adelantado,-a. ▮ to be behind schedule ir retrasado,-a.
▶ vt programar, fijar.

schematic [skiːˈmætɪk] adj esquemático,-a.

scheme [skiːm] n **1** (plan) plan m; (project) proyecto. **2** (system, order) sistema m, orden m; (arrangement) disposición f, combinación f: a colour scheme una combinación de colores. **3** (plot) complot m, conspiración f.
▶ vi (plot) conspirar, intrigar, confabularse.
▶ vt (plan deviously) tramar, maquinar.

☒ Scheme no significa 'esquema (resumen)', que se traduce por outline.

schism ['skɪzəm] n cisma m.

schizophrenia [skɪtsəʊˈfriːnɪə] n esquizofrenia.

schizophrenic [skɪtsəʊˈfrenɪk] adj esquizofrénico,-a.

scholar ['skɒləʳ] n **1** (learned person) erudito,-a; (specialist) especialista mf: Latin scholar latinista. **2** (scholarship holder) becario,-a. **3** (good learner) estudiante mf.

☒ Scholar no significa 'escolar (alumno)', que se traduce por pupil.

scholarship ['skɒləʃɪp] n **1** (grant, award) beca. **2** (learning) erudición f.

school[1] [skuːl] n **1** (gen) escuela, colegio: what are you going to do when you leave school? ¿qué harás cuando dejes el colegio? **2** (lessons) clase f: let's meet after school quedemos después de clase. **3** (university department) facultad f. **4** (group of artists, etc) escuela: the Dutch school of painting la escuela pictórica holandesa. [comp] school age edad f escolar.
▶ vt **1** (teach) enseñar; (train) educar, formar. **2** (discipline) disciplinar.

S

school² [skuːl] n (of fish) banco.

schoolbook ['skuːlbʊk] n libro de texto.

schoolboy ['skuːlbɔɪ] n alumno, escolar m.

schoolchild ['skuːltʃaɪld] n alumno,-a, escolar mf.
ⓘ pl schoolchildren ['skuːltʃɪldrən].

schoolgirl ['skuːlgɜːl] n alumna, escolar f.

school-leaver ['skuːlliːvəʳ] n alumno,-a que está a punto de dejar la escuela.

schoolteacher ['skuːltiːtʃəʳ] n (secondary school) profesor,-ra; (primary school) maestro,-a.

science ['saɪəns] n 1 (gen) ciencia. 2 (subject) ciencias fpl. COMP science fiction ciencia ficción.

scientific [saɪən'tɪfɪk] adj científico,-a.

scientist ['saɪəntɪst] n científico,-a.

scissors ['sɪzəz] n pl tijeras fpl. COMP a pair of scissors unas tijeras.

scold [skəʊld] vt reñir, regañar.

scone [skəʊn, skɒn] n CULIN bollo (que se suele comer con mantequilla, mermelada, nata, etc).

scoop [skuːp] n 1 (for flour, rice, etc) pala; (for ice-cream) cucharón m. 2 (amount) palada, cucharada. 3 (news story) primicia.
▶ vt 1 (take out) sacar con una pala. 2 (beat rival) vencer, pisar; (get news first) dar la primicia. 3 (win) ganar; (make profit) forrarse.

scooter ['skuːtəʳ] n (child's) patinete m, patineta; (motorized) escúter m, Vespa.

scope [skəʊp] n alcance m: that is beyond the scope of this report eso queda fuera del alcance de este informe.

scorch [skɔːtʃ] vt 1 (singe) chamuscar,. 2 (burn) quemar, abrasar.
▶ vi 1 (singe) chamuscarse. 2 GB fam (travel fast) ir a toda velocidad.

score [skɔːʳ] n 1 SP (gen) tanteo; (in golf, cards) puntuación f: what's the score? ¿cómo van? 2 (in exam, test) nota, calificación f. 3 MUS (written version) partitura; (of film, play, etc) música.
▶ vt 1 SP (goal) marcar, hacer, meter; (point) ganar; (run) hacer, realizar: he scored the winning goal marcó el gol decisivo. 2 (in exam, test) sacar, obtener,

conseguir. 3 (give points to) dar, puntuar: this question scores 10 points esta pregunta vale 10 puntos.
▶ vi SP (gen) marcar (un tanto); (goal) marcar (un gol); (point) puntuar, conseguir puntos.

scoreboard ['skɔːbɔːd] n marcador m.

scorer ['skɔːrəʳ] n 1 (scorekeeper) encargado,-a del marcador. 2 (goal striker) goleador,-ra.

scorn [skɔːn] n desdén m, desprecio.
▶ vt desdeñar, despreciar, menospreciar.

Scorpio ['skɔːpɪəʊ] n Escorpión mf.

scorpion ['skɔːpɪən] n escorpión m, alacrán m.

Scot [skɒt] n escocés,-esa.

Scotland ['skɒtlənd] n Escocia.

Scottish ['skɒtɪʃ] adj escocés,-esa.

scourer ['skaʊrəʳ] n estropajo.

scout [skaʊt] n 1 MIL (person) explorador,-ra; (plane) avión m de reconocimiento. 2 (boy) scout m.

scowl [skaʊl] vi fruncir el ceño.
▶ n ceño (fruncido).

scrabble ['skræbəl] vi (among stones, etc) escarbar; (in bag, etc) hurgar; (on floor, etc) rebuscar.

scramble ['skræmbəl] vi trepar (over, por) (up, a), subir gateando. (clamber) moverse rápidamente.
▶ vt 1 (mix, jumble) revolver, mezclar. 2 (eggs) revolver.

scrambled eggs [skræmbəld 'egz] n pl huevos revueltos.

scrap [skræp] n 1 (of paper, cloth, etc) trozo, pedazo; (of news, conversation) fragmento, migaja. 2 (of metal) chatarra. 3 (in negatives) pizca, ápice m.
▶ vt 1 (throw away) desechar; (cars, etc) desguazar. 2 fig (idea) descartar; (plan) abandonar.
ⓘ pt & pp scrapped, ger scrapping.
▶ n pl scraps (gen) restos mpl.

scrapbook ['skræpbʊk] n álbum m de recortes.

scrape [skreɪp] vt 1 (surface, paint, etc) raspar (away/off, -), rascar (away/off, -): he scraped the paint off the door raspó la pintura de la puerta. **2** *(graze skin)* arañarse. **3** *(rub against)* rozar, raspar, rascar.

▸ *vi* **1** *(grate)* chirriar. **2** *(rub against)* raspar, rozar. **3** *(economize)* hacer economías, ahorrar.

scratch [skrætʃ] *n* arañazo, rasguño: *there's a scratch on this record* este disco está rayado.

▸ *adj* **1** *(improvised)* improvisado,-a.
ⓘ *comp* scratchier, *superl* scratchiest.

▸ *vt* **1** *(with nail, claw)* arañar, rasguñar; *(paintwork, furniture, record)* rayar. **2** *(part of body)* rascar: *she scratched her leg* se rascó la pierna.

▸ *vi* **1** *(animal)* arañar, rascar, rasguñar; *(pen)* raspear; *(wool, sweater, towel)* raspar, picar. **2** *(itch)* rascarse.

scream [skriːm] *n* **1** *(of pain, fear)* grito, chillido, alarido; *(of laughter)* carcajada. **2** *fig (screech)* chirrido. **3** *fam (funny person)* persona divertida; *(funny thing)* cosa divertida: *your cousin's a scream* tu primo es la monda, tu primo es divertidísimo.

▸ *vi* **1** *(gen)* gritar, chillar,; *(wind, siren, etc)* aullar: *she screamed for help* pidió socorro a gritos; *he was screaming with laughter* se mondaba de risa, se tronchaba de risa. **2** *fig (need)* pedir (a gritos), clamar (a gritos).

screech [skriːtʃ] *n* *(of person)* grito, alarido, chillido; *(of tyres, brakes, birds, etc)* chirrido; *(of siren)* aullido. COMP **screech owl** lechuza.

▸ *vt* gritar, decir a gritos, chillar.

▸ *vi* *(person)* chillar; *(tyres, brakes, bird, etc)* chirriar; *(siren)* aullar; *(gate)* rechinar.

screen [skriːn] *n* **1** *(partition)* biombo, mampara. **2** *(for window)* mosquitera. **3** *(protection, cover)* cortina, pantalla. **4** *(of TV, for projection)* pantalla.

▸ *n* **the screen** la pantalla, el cine.

screenplay [ˈskriːnpleɪ] *n* guion *m*.

screensaver [ˈskriːnseɪvəʳ] *n* salvapantallas *m*.

screw [skruː] *n* **1** *(metal pin)* tornillo. **2** *(propeller)* hélice *f*. **3** *(turn)* vuelta.

▸ *vt* **1** *(fasten with screws)* atornillar; *(tighten)* enroscar, apretar: *screw the two pieces together* une las dos piezas con tornillos. **2** *(crumple)* arrugar. **3** *(cheat,*

swindle) timar; *(overcharge)* clavar; *(get money out of)* sacar.

▸ *vi* *(turn, tighten)* atornillarse, enroscarse.

screwdriver [ˈskruːdraɪvəʳ] *n* *(tool)* destornillador *m*.

scribble [ˈskrɪbəl] *n* garabato, garabatos *mpl*.

▸ *vt* garabatear, garrapatear.

scribe [skraɪb] *n* **1** *(copier)* escribiente *mf*, amanuense *mf*. **2** *(in Biblical times)* escriba *m*.

script [skrɪpt] *n* **1** *(of film, etc)* guion *m*. **2** *(writing)* escritura; *(text)* texto; *(handwriting)* letra.

scroll [skrəʊl] *n* COMPUT barra de desplazamiento.

◆ **to scroll down** *vi* COMPUT desplazarse hacia abajo.

◆ **to scroll up** *vi* COMPUT desplazarse hacia arriba.

scrooge [skruːdʒ] *n* *fam pej* tacaño,-a.

scrotum [ˈskrəʊtəm] *n* ANAT escroto.
ⓘ *pl* scrotums o scrota [ˈskrəʊtə].

scrounge [skraʊndʒ] *vi* *fam* gorrear (from/off, a), vivir de gorra.

▸ *vt* *(gen)* gorrear (from/off, a), gorronear (from/off, a): *he scrounges fags off his friends* gorronea pitillos a los amigos.

scrub¹ [skrʌb] *n* *(undergrowth)* maleza.

scrub² [skrʌb] *vt* **1** *(clean)* fregar bien, restregar. **2** *fam (cancel)* cancelar.
ⓘ *pt & pp* scrubbed, *ger* scrubbing.

scruffy [ˈskrʌfɪ] *adj* desaliñado,-a.
ⓘ *comp* scruffier, *superl* scruffiest.

scrupulous [ˈskruːpjʊləs] *adj* *(meticulous)* escrupuloso,-a.

scrutinize [ˈskruːtɪnaɪz] *vt* escudriñar.

scrutiny [ˈskruːtɪnɪ] *n* **1** *(examination)* examen *m* profundo. **2** GB *(of votes)* escrutinio. LOC **to be under scrutiny** ser analizado,-a.

scuba [ˈskjuːbə] *n* equipo de submarinismo. COMP **scuba diving** submarinismo, buceo con botellas de oxígeno.

sculptor [ˈskʌlptəʳ] *n* escultor,-ra.

sculpture [ˈskʌlptʃəʳ] *n* escultura.

▸ *vt* esculpir (in, en).

S

scythe [saɪð] *n* guadaña.

sea [siː] *n* **1** mar *m & f*: *we love swimming in the sea* nos encanta nadar en el mar. **2** *fig* mar *m*, multitud *f*: *a sea of faces* un mar de caras. LOC **at sea** en el mar. **I by sea** por mar, en barco. **I by the sea** a orillas del mar. **I out to sea** mar adentro. **I to go by sea** ir en barco. COMP **sea bird** ave *f* marina. **I sea lion** león marino. **I sea mile** milla marina. **I sea wall** dique *m*, rompeolas *m*.
▶ *adj* marítimo,-a, de mar.

seabed ['siːbed] *n* fondo marino.

seafood ['siːfuːd] *n* marisco, mariscos *mpl*.

seagull ['siːɡʌl] *n* gaviota.

seahorse ['siːhɔːs] *n* caballito de mar, hipocampo.

seal¹ [siːl] *n* ZOOL foca.

seal² [siːl] *n* **1** *(official stamp)* sello: *wax seal* sello de lacre. **2** *(on letter)* sello; *(on bottle, etc)* precinto.

seam [siːm] *n* **1** SEW costura. **2** GEOL *(of mineral)* veta, filón *m*: *coal seam* veta de carbón.

seaman ['siːmən] *n* marinero, marino.
ⓘ *pl* **seamen** ['siːmən].

search [sɜːtʃ] *n* *(gen)* búsqueda (for, de); *(of building)* registro; *(of person)* cacheo. LOC **in search of** en busca de. LOC **search warrant** orden *f* de registro.
▶ *vt* *(gen)* buscar (for, -); *(building, suitcase, etc)* registrar; *(person)* cachear, registrar: *they searched the house for clues* registraron la casa buscando pistas.
▶ *vi* *(gen)* buscar (through, entre); *(pockets)* registrar.

seashell ['siːʃel] *n* concha (de mar).

seashore ['siːʃɔː'] *n* *(coast)* orilla del mar.

seasick ['siːsɪk] *adj* mareado,-a.

seasickness ['siːsɪknəs] *n* mareo.

seaside ['siːsaɪd] *n* playa, costa. LOC COMP **seaside resort** lugar *m* de veraneo en la costa.

season ['siːzən] *n* *(of year)* estación *f*; *(time)* época; *(for sport, theatre, social activity)* temporada: *the tourist season* la temporada turística. LOC **to be in season 1** *(fresh food)* estar en sazón. **2** *(game)* ser temporada de: *strawberries are in season* es temporada de fresas. **I to go in season** ir en temporada alta. **I to go off/out of season** ir en temporada baja.
▶ *vt* **1** *(food)* sazonar (with, con), condimentar (with, con).

seasonal ['siːzənəl] *adj* estacional.

seasoning ['siːzənɪŋ] *n* CULIN condimento.

seat [siːt] *n* **1** *(chair - gen)* asiento; *(- in cinema, theatre)* butaca: *I'd like a window seat* quisiera un asiento al lado de la ventanilla. **2** *(place)* plaza; *(at theatre, opera, stadium)* localidad *f*. **3** POL *(in parliament)* escaño. LOC **to take a seat** sentarse, tomar asiento. COMP **seat belt** cinturón *m* de seguridad.
▶ *vt* **1** *(sit)* sentar. **2** *(accommodate)* tener sitio para; *(theatre, hall, etc)* tener cabida para. LOC **please be seated** siéntese/siéntense por favor. **I to seat os** sentarse.

seaweed ['siːwiːd] *n* alga (marina).

second¹ ['sekənd] *n* **1** *(time)* segundo: *Powell's time was 9.77 seconds* Powell hizo un tiempo de 9,77 segundos. **2** *fam* momento, momentito: *I'll be back in a second* enseguida vuelvo. COMP **second hand** *(of watch)* segundero. **I second name** apellido.

second² ['sekənd] *adj* *(gen)* segundo,-a; *(another)* otro,-a: *it's the second largest city in England* es la segunda ciudad más grande de Inglaterra. LOC **to have second helpings** repetir. **I to have second thoughts (about STH)** entrarle dudas a uno (sobre ALGO), cambiar de idea (sobre ALGO). COMP **second floor 1** GB segundo piso. **2** US primer piso. **I second name** apellido.
▶ *pron* segundo,-a.
▶ *n* **1** *(in series)* segundo,-a. **2** GB *(degree)* ≈ notable *m*.
▶ *adv* segundo, en segundo lugar: *he came second* llegó segundo, quedó en segundo lugar.

✎ Consulta también **sixth**.

secondary ['sekəndərɪ] *adj* secundario,-a. COMP **secondary school** colegio de enseñanza secundaria, instituto de bachillerato .

see

second-class [sekənd'klɑ:s] *adj* de segunda (clase).

second-degree [sekənddɪ'gri:] *adj* MED de segundo grado. COMP **second-degree burns** quemaduras *fpl* de segundo grado.

second-hand [sekənd'hænd] *adj* **1** *(used, not new)* de segunda mano, usado,-a, viejo,-a: *we bought a second-hand car* compramos un coche de segunda mano. ▶ *adv* **1** *(buy)* de segunda mano. **2** *(learn, find out)* por terceros.

secret ['si:krət] *adj* **1** *(gen)* secreto,-a: *this is my secret hiding-place* éste es mi escondite secreto. ▶ *n* **1** *(gen)* secreto; *(something confided)* secreto, confidencia. **2** *(method, key)* secreto, clave *f.* LOC **in secret** en secreto. **I to keep a secret** guardar un secreto.

secretary ['sekrətərɪ] *n* **1** secretario,-a. **2** *(non-elected official)* ministro,-a; *(representative below ambassador)* ministro,-a plenipotenciario,-a. ① *pl* **secretaries.**

secrete [sɪ'kri:t] *vt* **1** *(emit liquid)* secretar, segregar. **2** *fml (hide)* ocultar, esconder.

secretion [sɪ'kri:ʃən] *n (of liquid)* secreción *f.*

secretly ['si:krətlɪ] *adv* en secreto.

sect [sekt] *n* secta.

section ['sekʃən] *n* sección *f.*

sector ['sektə] *n (gen)* sector *m.*

secular ['sekjulə'] *adj (education)* laico,-a; *(art, music)* profano,-a.

☒ Secular no significa 'secular (antiguo)', que se traduce por **ancient.**

secure [sɪ'kjuə'] *adj* **1** *(job, income, etc)* seguro,-a; *(relationship, etc)* estable. **2** *(ladder, shelf, foothold)* firme; *(stronghold)* seguro,-a; *(base, foundation)* sólido,-a. ▶ *vt* **1** *(make safe)* asegurar; *(protect)* proteger *(from,* de), *(against,* contra). **2** *(fasten)* cerrar bien. **3** *(obtain)* obtener, conseguir.

☒ Secure no significa 'seguro', que se traduce por **sure.**

securely [sɪ'kjuəlɪ] *adv* bien.

security [sɪ'kjuərətɪ] *n* **1** *(safety, confidence)* seguridad *f.* **2** *(protection)* seguridad *f.* COMP **security guard** guarda *mf* de seguridad. **I security service** servicio de seguridad. **I security van** furgoneta blindada. ① *pl* **securities.**

sedan [sɪ'dæn] *n* US *(car)* berlina.

sedate [sɪ'deɪt] *vt* MED sedar.

sedative ['sedətɪv] *n* sedante *m*, calmante *m.* ▶ *adj* sedante.

sedentary ['sedəntərɪ] *adj* sedentario,-a.

sediment ['sedɪmənt] *n* sedimento.

sedimentary [sedɪ'mentərɪ] *adj* sedimentario,-a.

sedimentation [sedɪmen'teɪʃən] *n* sedimentación *f.*

seduction [sɪ'dʌkʃən] *n (sexual)* seducción *f.*

see [si:] *vt* **1** *(gen)* ver: *you can see the sea from here* desde aquí se ve el mar; *see page 123* véase la página 123. **2** *(meet, visit)* ver; *(receive)* ver, atender; *(go out with)* salir con: *I'm seeing Pat on Friday* he quedado con Pat el viernes. **3** *(understand)* comprender, entender, ver: *I can see your point* entiendo tu punto de vista. **4** *(visualize, imagine)* imaginarse, ver; *(envisage)* creer: *I can't see him working in a factory* no me lo imagino trabajando en una fábrica. **5** *(find out, discover)* ver; *(learn)* oír, leer: *I'll see what I can do* veré lo que puedo hacer. **6** *(ensure, check)* asegurarse de, procurar: *see that you arrive on time* procura llegar a la hora. **7** *(accompany)* acompañar: *he saw me home* me acompañó a casa. ▶ *vi* **1** *(gen)* ver: *she can't see without her glasses* no ve sin las gafas. **2** *(find out, discover)* ver: *we'll have to see* ya veremos. **3** *(understand)* entender, ver: *oh, I see* ah, ya veo. LOC **I'll be seeing you!** ¡hasta luego! **I let me see/let's see** a ver, vamos a ver. **I seeing is believing** ver para creer. **I see you around** ya nos veremos. **I see you later/soon/Monday!** ¡hasta luego/pronto/el lunes! **I you see 1** *(in explanations)* verás. **2** *(in questions)* ¿sabes?, ¿ves? ① *pt* **saw** [sɔ:], *pp* **seen** [si:n], *ger* **seeing.**

S

seed [siːd] *n* BOT *(gen)* semilla; *(of fruit)* pepita: *sunflower seeds* pipas.
▶ *vt* **1** *(plant seeds)* sembrar (**with**, de). **2** *(remove seed)* despepitar.

seek [siːk] *vt* **1** *(look for, try to obtain)* buscar: *the homeless seek food and shelter* la gente sin techo busca comida y alojamiento. **2** *(ask for)* pedir, solicitar. **3** *(attempt, try)* tratar de, intentar.
▶ *vi* *(look for, try to obtain)* buscar (**after/ for**, -), ir en busca de.
ⓘ *pt & pp* sought [sɔːt].

seem [siːm] *vi (appear)* parecer: *she seems nice* parece maja; *it seems like there's going to be a storm* parece que va a haber una tormenta. LOC **so it seems** eso parece.

seemingly ['siːmɪŋli] *adv* **1** *(used with adjective)* aparentemente. **2** *(used separately)* al parecer, según parece.

seen [siːn] *pp* → see.

seep [siːp] *vi* filtrarse.

seesaw ['siːsɔː] *n (for children)* balancín *m*, subibaja *m*.

see-through ['siːθruː] *adj* transparente.

segment ['segmənt] *n (gen)* segmento; *(of orange)* gajo.

seize [siːz] *vt* **1** *(grab)* asir, agarrar, coger: *he seized my arm* me agarró del brazo. **2** *(opportunity)* aprovechar. **3** *(take control of)* tomar, apoderarse de. **4** *(person - arrest)* detener; *(- take hostage)* secuestrar. LOC **to be seized with** STH *(pain, fear, panic, etc)* apoderarse ALGO de uno.

seldom ['seldəm] *adv* raramente, pocas veces: *we seldom eat out* pocas veces comemos fuera.

select [sɪ'lekt] *vt (thing)* escoger, elegir; *(team, player, candidate)* seleccionar.
▶ *adj* selecto,-a, escogido,-a.

selection [sɪ'lekʃən] *n* **1** *(people or things chosen)* selección *f*; *(choosing)* elección *f*. **2** *(range to choose from)* surtido, gama.

selective [sɪ'lektɪv] *adj* selectivo,-a.

self [self] *n* **1** ser *m*, uno,-a mismo,-a, sí mismo,-a: *he was his usual self again* volvió a ser él mismo. **2** *(in psychology)* yo: *my other self* mi otro yo.
ⓘ *pl* selves.

self-adhesive [selfəd'hiːsɪv] *adj* autoadhesivo,-a, autoadherente.

self-catering [self'keɪtərɪŋ] *adj* sin servicio de comidas.

self-confident [self'kɒnfɪdənt] *adj* seguro,-a de sí mismo,-a.

self-control [selfkən'trəʊl] *n* dominio de sí mismo,-a, autocontrol *m*.

self-defence [selfdɪ'fens] *n* defensa personal, autodefensa. LOC **to act in self-defence** actuar en defensa propia.

self-employed [selfɪm'plɔɪd] *adj* autónomo,-a, que trabaja por cuenta propia.

self-esteem [selfɪ'stiːm] *n* amor *m* propio.

self-government [self'gʌvənmənt] *n* autonomía, autogobierno.

self-help [self'help] *n* autoayuda.

selfish ['selfɪʃ] *adj* egoísta.

selfishness ['selfɪʃnəs] *n* egoísmo.

self-made [self'meɪd] *adj (man, woman)* que ha llegado donde está por sus propios esfuerzos, que se ha hecho a sí mismo,-a .

self-portrait [self'pɔːtreɪt] *n* autorretrato.

self-respect [selfrɪ'spekt] *n* amor *m* propio, dignidad *f*.

self-service [self'sɜːvɪs] *adj* de autoservicio.
▶ *n* autoservicio.

self-sufficient [selfsə'fɪʃənt] *adj* autosuficiente.

sell [sel] *vt* **1** *(gen)* vender: *he sold his bike to his neighbour* vendió la bici a su vecino. **2** *fam (convince)* convencer de.
▶ *vi (product)* venderse: *these plants sell at a pound each* estas plantas se venden a una libra cada una. LOC **to be sold out** estar agotado,-a.
◆ **to sell off** *vt sep* liquidar.
◆ **to sell out** *vi* **1** *(be disloyal)* claudicar, venderse. **2** COMM *(sell all of)* agotarse (**of**, -), acabarse (**of**, -).
▶ *vt sep* COMM *(sell all of)* agotar, agotar las existencias de.
ⓘ *pt & pp* sold [səʊld].

sell-by date ['selbaɪdeɪt] *n* fecha límite de venta, fecha de caducidad.

seller ['selə^r] *n (person)* vendedor,-ra.

Sellotape® ['seləteɪp] *n* celo®.

sell-out ['selaʊt] *n* **1** *(performance)* éxito de taquilla. **2** *fam (betrayal)* traición *f*, engaño.

semantic [sɪ'mæntɪk] *adj* semántico,-a.

semen ['si:mən] *n* semen *m*.

semester [sɪ'mestə^r] *n* semestre *m*.

semiautomatic [semɪɔ:tə'mætɪk] *adj* semiautomático,-a.

semicircle ['semɪsɜːkəl] *n* semicírculo.

semicolon [semɪ'kəʊlən] *n* punto y coma *m*.

semidetached [semɪdɪ'tætʃt] *adj* pareado,-a.
▶ *n (house)* casa pareada.

semifinal [semɪ'faɪnəl] *n* semifinal *f*.

semifinalist [semɪ'faɪnəlɪst] *n* semifinalista *mf*.

seminal ['semɪnəl] *adj* seminal.

semiskimmed [semɪ'skɪmd] *adj* semidesnatado, a, semidescremado,-a.

semolina [semə'li:nə] *n* sémola.

senate ['senət] *n* POL senado.

senator ['senətə^r] *n* senador,-ra.

send [send] *vt* **1** *(gen)* enviar, mandar; *(telex, telegram)* enviar, poner; *(radio signal, radio message)* transmitir, emitir: *he sent me some flowers* me mandó flores. **2** *(order to go)* mandar, enviar: *the doctor sent me to a specialist* el médico me mandó a un especialista. **3** *(cause to become)* volver, hacer: *the noise sent her mad* el ruido la volvió loca.
▶ *vi (send a message)* avisar.
◆ **to send away** *vt sep* despachar.
◆ **to send back** *vt sep* **1** *(goods, etc)* devolver. **2** *(person)* hacer volver.
◆ **to send for** *vt insep* **1** *(person)* llamar a, hacer llamar a. **2** *(thing)* pedir, encargar.
◆ **to send in** *vt sep (application, request)* mandar, enviar.
① *pt & pp* **sent** [sent].

sender ['sendə^r] *n* remitente *mf*.

Senegal [senɪ'gɔːl] *n* Senegal.

Senegalese [senɪgə'liːz] *adj* senegalés,-esa.
▶ *n* senegalés,-esa.
▶ *n pl* **the Senegalese** los senegaleses *mpl*.

senile ['siːnaɪl] *adj* senil.

senior ['siːnɪə^r] *adj* **1** *(in age)* mayor: *he's five years senior to me* es cinco años mayor que yo. **2** *(in rank)* superior; *(with longer service)* más antiguo,-a, de mayor antigüedad [COMP] **senior citizen** jubilado,-a.
▶ *n* **1** *(in age)* mayor *mf*; *(in rank)* superior *fm*. **2** GB *(pupil)* mayor *mf*. **3** US estudiante *mf* del último curso.

☒ To accord no significa 'acordar', que se traduce por **to agree**.

sensation [sen'seɪʃən] *n (gen)* sensación *f*; *(ability to feel)* sensibilidad *f*.

sensational [sen'seɪʃənəl] *adj* **1** *fam (wonderful)* sensacional. **2** *(exaggerated)* sensacionalista.

sensationalist [sen'seɪʃənəlɪst] *adj* sensacionalista.

sense [sens] *n* **1** *(faculty)* sentido: *sense of smell* sentido del olfato. **2** *(feeling - of well-being, loss)* sensación *f*; *(awareness, appreciation - of justice, duty)* sentido. **3** *(wisdom, judgement)* sentido común. **4** *(meaning - gen)* sentido; *(- of word)* significado, acepción *f*: *in every sense of the word* en todos los sentidos. [LOC] **in a sense** hasta cierto punto, en cierto sentido. ▌**in no sense** de ninguna manera. ▌**to make sense 1** *(have clear meaning)* tener sentido. **2** *(be sensible)* ser razonable, ser sensato,-a. ▌**to talk sense** hablar con juicio. [COMP] **sense of humour** sentido del humor.

senseless ['sensləs] *adj* **1** *(unconscious)* inconsciente. **2** *(foolish, pointless)* absurdo,-a, sin sentido, insensato,-a.

sensibility [sensɪ'bɪlətɪ] *n* sensibilidad *f*.
▶ *n pl* **sensibilities** susceptibilidad *f sing*.

sensible ['sensɪbəl] *adj* **1** *(person)* sensato,-a; *(behaviour, decision)* razonable, prudente; *(choice)* acertado,-a. **2** *(clothes)* cómodo,-a.

☒ Sensible no significa 'sensible', que se traduce por **sensitive**.

sensitive ['sensɪtɪv] *adj* **1** *(person - perceptive)* sensible (to, a), consciente (to, de). **2** *(person - touchy)* susceptible (to, a), pre-

S

ocupado,-a (**about**, por). **3** *(teeth, paper, instrument, film)* sensible (**to**,-a).

sensitivity [sensɪ'tɪvətɪ] *n* **1** *(gen)* sensibilidad *f* (**to**, a/frente a). **2** *(touchiness)* susceptibilidad *f* (**to**, a). **3** *(of skin, issue)* delicadeza.

sensor ['sensər] *n* TECH sensor *m*, detector *m*.

sent [sent] *pt & pp* → send.

sentence ['sentəns] *n* **1** *(gen)* frase *f*; *(in grammar)* oración *f*. **2** JUR sentencia, fallo.
▶ *vt* JUR condenar.

☒ Sentence no significa 'sentencia (máxima)', que se traduce por **saying**.

sentimental [sentɪ'mentəl] *adj* sentimental.

sentry ['sentrɪ] *n* centinela *m*.
ⓘ *pl* sentries.

sepal ['sepəl] *n* BOT sépalo.

separate [*(vb)* 'sepəreɪt; *(adj)* 'sepərət] *vt* separar (**from**, de).
▶ *vi* **1** *(gen)* separarse.
▶ *adj* **1** *(apart)* separado,-a: *keep the sheep separate from the goats* mantén a las ovejas separadas de las cabras. **2** *(not shared)* separado,-a, individual: *we had separate rooms* cada uno tenía su habitación. **3** *(different)* distinto,-a, diferente.

separately ['sepərətlɪ] *adv* por separado, aparte.

separation [sepə'reɪʃən] *n* separación *f*.

sepia ['si:pɪə] *adj* sepia.

September [səp'tembər] *n* septiembre *m*, setiembre *m*.

✎ Para ejemplos de uso, consulta **May**.

septic ['septɪk] *adj* séptico,-a.

septum ['septəm] *n* ANAT septo.
ⓘ *pl* septa ['septə].

sepulcher ['sepəlkər] *n* US → sepulchre.

sepulchre ['sepəlkər] *n* sepulcro.

sequel ['si:kwəl] *n* **1** *(result, consequence)* secuela. **2** *(book, film, etc)* segunda parte *f*.

sequence ['si:kwəns] *n* secuencia, orden *m*.

sequoia [sɪ'kwɔɪə] *n* secoya, secuoya.

Serb [sɜ:b] *n (person)* serbio,-a.
▶ *adj* serbio,-a.

Serbia ['sɜ:bɪə] *n* Serbia.

Serbian ['sɜ:bɪən] *n* **1** *(person)* serbio, -a. **2** *(dialect)* serbio.
▶ *adj* serbio,-a.

serf [sɜ:f] *n* siervo,-a.

sergeant ['sɑ:dʒənt] *n* **1** MIL sargento *mf*. **2** *(of police)* cabo *mf*.

serial ['sɪərɪəl] *adj* **1** consecutivo,-a, en serie. **2** *(in parts)* seriado,-a, en capítulos.
▶ *n (gen)* serie *f*, serial *m*.

series ['sɪəri:z] *n (gen)* serie *f*, sucesión *f*. ⓛⓞⓒ **in series** TECH en serie.
ⓘ *pl* series.

serious ['sɪərɪəs] *adj* **1** *(solemn, earnest)* serio,-a: *you can't be serious!* ¡no lo dices en serio! **2** *(causing concern, severe)* grave, serio,-a: *no serious damage was caused* no hubo daños importantes.

seriously ['sɪərɪəslɪ] *adv* **1** *(in earnest)* en serio. **2** *(severely)* seriamente, gravemente.

seriousness ['sɪərɪəsnəs] *n* **1** *(severity)* seriedad *f*. **2** *(earnestness, solemnity)* seriedad *f*. ⓛⓞⓒ **in all seriousness** hablando (muy) en serio.

sermon ['sɜ:mən] *n* sermón *m*.

serum ['sɪərəm] *n* MED suero.
ⓘ *pl* serums o sera ['sɪərə].

servant ['sɜ:vənt] *n* sirviente *mf*.

serve [sɜ:v] *vt* **1** *(work for)* servir (**as**, de). **2** *(customer)* servir: *dinner is served at 8.00 pm* se sirve la cena a les 8.00. **3** *(be useful to)* servir, ser útil: *it serves many different purposes* sirve para varias cosas. **4** *(provide with service)* prestar servicio a: *the new hospital will serve the whole region* el nuevo hospital prestará servicio a toda la región.
▶ *vi* **1** *(work for)* servir: *my father served in the army* mi padre sirvió en el ejército. **2** *(in shop)* atender; *(food, drink)* servir. **3** *(be useful to)* servir (**as**, de): *this will serve as an example* esto servirá de ejemplo.
▶ *n (tennis)* saque *m*.

server ['sɜ:vər] *n (computer)* servidor *m*.

service ['sɜ:vɪs] *n* **1** *(gen)* servicio. **2** *(maintenance of car, machine)* revisión *f*. **3** REL oficio. **4** *(tennis)* saque *m*, servicio.

▶ *adj (for use of workers)* de servicio: *service entrance* entrada de servicio. COMP **service area** área de servicio. ▌ **service charge 1** *(on bill)* servicio. **2** *(in banking)* comisión *f*. ▌ **service station** estación *f* de servicio.

▶ *n pl* **services** *(work, act, help)* servicios *mpl*.

serviette [sɜ:vɪˈet] *n* GB servilleta.

sesame [ˈsesəmɪ] *n* BOT sésamo, ajonjolí *m*.

session [ˈseʃən] *n* **1** *(gen)* sesión *f*. **2** EDUC *(term)* trimestre *m*.

set¹ [set] *n* **1** *(of golf clubs, brushes, tools, etc)* juego; *(books, poems)* colección *f*; *(of turbines)* equipo, grupo: *chess set* juego de ajedrez; *set of dishes* vajilla. **2** ELEC *(apparatus)* aparato: *they bought a TV set* compraron un televisor. **3** MATH conjunto. **4** SP *(tennis)* set *m*.

set² [set] *n* **1** *(in hairdressing)* marcado. **2** *(scenery)* decorado; *(place of filming)* plató *m*. **3** *(position, posture)* postura. COMP **set square** cartabón *m*, escuadra.

▶ *vt* **1** *(put, place)* poner, colocar. **2** *(prepare - trap)* tender, preparar; *(- table)* poner; *(- camera, video)* preparar; *(- clock, watch, oven, etc)* poner: *set the table for dinner* pon la mesa para la cena. **3** *(date, time)* fijar, señalar, acordar: *have you set a date for the wedding?* ¿has fijado una fecha para la boda? **4** *(price)* fijar; *(value)* poner. **5** *(exam, test, problem)* poner; *(homework)* mandar, poner. **6** *(story, action)* ambientar: *the novel is set in Madrid* la novela está ambientada en Madrid.

◆ **to set off** *vi (begin journey)* salir.

▶ *vt sep* **1** *(bomb)* hacer estallar; *(alarm)* hacer sonar; *(firework)* lanzar, tirar. **2** *(cause, start)* provocar.

① *pt & pp* set.

◆ **to set up** *vt sep* **1** *(business)* establecer, montar. **2** *(machine)* instalar.

setback [ˈsetbæk] *n* revés *m*, contratiempo.

settee [seˈti:] *n* sofá *m*.

settle¹ [ˈsetəl] *vt* **1** *(establish)* instalar, colocar; *(make comfortable)* poner cómodo,-a *he settled himself on the sofa* se puso cómodo en el sofá. **2** *(decide on, fix)* acordar, decidir, fijar. **3** *(sort out - problem, dispute)* resolver, solucionar; *(- differences)* resolver, arreglar; *(- score)* arreglar, ajustar: *we need to settle an argument* tenemos que resolver una discusión. **4** *(calm - nerves)* calmar; *(- stomach)* asentar.

▶ *vi* **1** *(make one's home in)* establecerse, instalarse. **2** *(make os comfortable)* ponerse cómodo,-a (into, en). **3** *(bird, fly, etc)* posarse. **4** *(sediment, dregs)* precipitarse. **5** *(calm down)* calmarse. **6** *(pay)* pagar, saldar la deuda.

◆ **to settle down** *vi* **1** *(establish a home)* instalarse, afincarse, establecerse; *(lead settled way of life)* empezar a llevar una vida asentada. **2** *(calm down)* calmarse, tranquilizarse. **3** *(get comfortable)* ponerse cómodo,-a.

◆ **to settle in** *vi* **1** *(get used to)* acostumbrarse, adaptarse. **2** *(move in)* instalarse.

settle² [ˈsetəl] *n (wooden bench)* banco.

settlement [ˈsetəlmənt] *n* **1** *(village)* poblado, pueblo, asentamiento; *(colony)* colonia. **2** *(agreement)* acuerdo, convenio.

setup [ˈsetʌp] *n* **1** *(arrangement, organization)* sistema *m*, situación *f*. **2** *fam (trick)* montaje *m*.

seven [ˈsevən] *adj* siete.
▶ *n* siete *m*.

✎ Consulta también **six**.

seventeen [sevənˈti:n] *adj* diecisiete.
▶ *n* diecisiete *m*.

✎ Consulta también **six**.

seventeenth [sevənˈti:nθ] *adj* decimoséptimo,-a.
▶ *adv* en decimoséptimo lugar.
▶ *n* **1** *(in series)* decimoséptimo,-a. **2** *(fraction)* decimoséptimo; *(one part)* decimoséptima parte *f*.

✎ Consulta también **sixth**.

seventh [ˈsevənθ] *adj* séptimo,-a.
▶ *adv* en séptimo lugar.
▶ *n* **1** *(in series)* séptimo,-a. **2** *(fraction)* séptimo; *(one part)* séptima parte *f*.

✎ Consulta también **sixth**.

seventieth [ˈsevəntɪəθ] *adj* septuagésimo,-a.

S

► *adv* en septuagésimo lugar.
► *n* **1** *(in series)* septuagésimo,-a. **2** *(fraction)* septuagésimo; *(one part)* septuagésima parte *f*.

✎ Consulta también **sixtieth**.

seventy ['sevəntɪ] *adj* setenta.
► *n* setenta *m*.

✎ Consulta también **sixty**.

several ['sevərəl] *adj (some)* varios,-as: *we've been there several times* hemos ido varias veces.
► *pron (some)* varios,-as.

severe [sɪ'vɪər] *adj* **1** *(person, punishment, treatment)* severo,-a. **2** *(pain)* agudo,-a; *(injury, illness, damage)* grave, serio,-a.

severity [sɪ'verətɪ] *n* **1** *(of person, punishment, criticism)* severidad *f*. **2** *(of pain)* agudeza, intensidad *f*; *(of illness, wound)* gravedad *f*.

sew [səu] *vt* coser (onto, a).
► *vi* coser.
◆ **to sew up** *vt sep* **1** *(hole, tear, etc)* coser; *(mend)* remendar. **2** *fam (arrange, settle)* arreglar, acordar: *you've got everything sewn up!* ¡lo tienes todo arreglado!
ⓘ *pt* sewed, *pp* sewed o sewn [səun].

sewage ['sjuːɪdʒ] *n* aguas *fpl* residuales.

sewer ['sjuər] *n* alcantarilla, cloaca.

sewing ['səuɪŋ] *n* costura. COMP **sewing machine** máquina de coser.

sewn [səun] *pp* → sew.

sex [seks] *n* sexo: *the opposite sex* el sexo opuesto. LOC **to have sex with SB** tener relaciones sexuales con ALGN.

sexism ['seksɪzəm] *n* sexismo.

sexist ['seksɪst] *adj* sexista.
► *n* sexista *mf*.

sexual ['seksjuəl] *adj* sexual.

sexuality [seksju'ælətɪ] *n* sexualidad *f*.

sexy ['seksɪ] *adj (sexually attractive)* sexy; *(erotic)* erótico,-a.
ⓘ *comp* sexier, *superl* sexiest.

shabby ['ʃæbɪ] *adj* **1** *(clothes)* gastado,-a, raído,-a, desharrapado,-a; *(furniture)* de aspecto lastimoso. **2** *(person)* mal vestido,-a, desaseado,-a.
ⓘ *comp* shabbier, *superl* shabbiest.

shack [ʃæk] *n* choza.

shade [ʃeɪd] *n* **1** *(shadow)* sombra: *a temperature of 30 degrees in the shade* una temperatura de 30 grados a la sombra. **2** *(for lamp)* pantalla; *(for eye)* visera; *(blind)* persiana. **3** *(of colour)* tono, matiz *m*.
► *vt* **1** *(shelter from light)* proteger de la luz. **2** ART *(darken)* sombrear (in, -).
► *vi (change gradually)* convertirse (into, en).
► *n pl* **shades** *fam* gafas *fpl* de sol.

shadow ['ʃædəu] *n* **1** *(dark shape)* sombra. **2** *(trace)* sombra, vestigio. **3** *(follower)* sombra.
► *adj* GB en la sombra.

shady ['ʃeɪdɪ] *adj* **1** *(place)* a la sombra; *(tree)* que da sombra. **2** *fam (person)* sospechoso,-a; *(deal, past)* turbio,-a.
ⓘ *comp* shadier, *superl* shadiest.

shaft [ʃɑːft] *n* **1** *(of axe, tool, golf club)* mango; *(of arrow)* astil *m*; *(of lance, spear)* asta. **2** *(of mine)* pozo; *(of lift)* hueco. **3** *(of light)* rayo.

shake [ʃeɪk] *n* **1** sacudida. **2** US *fam (milkshake)* batido.
► *vt* **1** *(move - carpet, person)* sacudir; *(- bottle, dice)* agitar: *shake well before use* agítese bien antes de usar. **2** *(upset, shock)* afectar, impresionar: *the news shook her badly* la noticia le afectó mucho. LOC **to shake hands** estrecharse la mano. ‖ **to shake one's head** negar con la cabeza.
► *vi (gen)* temblar: *she was shaking with fear* temblaba de miedo.
ⓘ *pt* shook [ʃuk], *pp* shaken ['ʃeɪkən].

shaken ['ʃeɪkən] *pp* → shake.
► *adj (liquid)* agitado,-a.

shaker ['ʃeɪkər] *n (for cocktails)* coctelera; *(for salt)* salero.

shaky ['ʃeɪkɪ] *adj* **1** *(hand, voice)* tembloroso,-a; *(writing)* temblón,-ona; *(step)* inseguro,-a. **2** *fig (argument, etc)* sin fundamento; *(government, currency)* débil.
ⓘ *comp* shakier, *superl* shakiest.

shall [ʃæl, *unstressed* ʃəl] *aux* **1** [usado con la primera persona del *sing* y el *pl*] *(future)*: *I shall go tomorrow* iré mañana; *I shan't mention any names* no daré nombres. **2** [usado con la primera persona del *sing* y el *pl*] *(questions, offers, suggestions)*: *shall I close the window?* ¿cierro la ventana?; *I'll carry it, shall I?* lo llevaré yo, ¿quieres?

3 *fml (emphatic, command)*: *you shall leave immediately* te irás enseguida.

shallow ['ʃæləʊ] *adj* **1** *(water, pond, etc)* poco profundo,-a; *(dish, bowl)* llano, -a, plano,-a. **2** *fig* superficial.
ⓘ *comp* shallower, *superl* shallowest.
► *n pl* **shallows** bajío *m sing.*

shame [ʃeɪm] *n* **1** *(disgrace, humiliation)* vergüenza; *(dishonour)* deshonra. **2** *(pity)* pena, lástima: *what a shame you couldn't go* qué pena que no pudieras ir.
► *vt* avergonzar, deshonrar.

shameful ['ʃeɪmfʊl] *adj* vergonzoso,-a.

shameless ['ʃeɪmləs] *adj* desvergonzado,-a.

shammy ['ʃæmɪ] *n* gamuza.
ⓘ *pl* shammies.

shampoo [ʃæm'puː] *n* **1** *(product)* champú *m.* **2** *(act)* lavado.
ⓘ *pl* shampoos.

shandy ['ʃændɪ] *n* GB cerveza con limonada.
ⓘ *pl* shandies.

shan't [ʃɑːnt] *aux* → shall.

shanty ['ʃæntɪ] *n (shack)* chabola.
ⓘ *pl* shanties.

shantytown ['ʃæntɪtaʊn] *n* chabolas *fpl*, barrio de chabolas.

shape [ʃeɪp] *n* **1** *(form, appearance)* forma: *in the shape of a heart* en forma de corazón. **2** *(outline, shadow)* figura. **3** *(state - of thing)* estado; *(- of person)* forma, condiciones *fpl*: *the team is in good shape* el equipo está en buena forma. **4** *(framework, character)* configuración *f.* ⎵LOC⎵ **in shape** *(fit)* en forma. ▌ **in the shape of 1** *(physically)* bajo la forma de. **2** *(figuratively)* en forma de. ▌ **to take shape** tomar forma.
► *vt* **1** *(gen)* dar forma a; *(clay)* modelar: *he shaped the dough into a ball* formó una bola con la masa. **2** *(character)* formar; *(future, destiny)* decidir, determinar.
◆ **to shape up** *vi* desarrollarse.

share [ʃeəʳ] *n* **1** *(portion)* parte *f.* **2** FIN acción *m*
► *vt* **1** *(have or use with others)* compartir: *can you share one book between two?* ¿podéis compartir un libro entre los dos?* **2** *(tell news, feelings, etc)* compartir. **3** *(divide)* repartir, dividir.
► *vi* compartir: *there's only one bed so you'll have to share* solo hay una cama, así que tendréis que compartirla.

shareholder ['ʃeəhəʊldəʳ] *n* accionista *mf.*

shareware ['ʃeəweəʳ] *n* programas *mpl* compartidos.

shark [ʃɑːk] *n* ZOOL tiburón *m.*

sharp [ʃɑːp] *adj* **1** *(knife, etc)* afilado,-a; *(needle, pencil)* puntiagudo,-a. **2** *(angle)* agudo,-a; *(bend)* cerrado,-a; *(slope)* empinado,-a. **3** *(outline)* definido,-a; *(photograph, etc)* nítido,-a; *(contrast)* marcado, -a. **4** *(mind, wit)* perspicaz; *(eyes, ears)* agudo,-a, bueno,-a: *keep a sharp eye on those two* ten bien vigilados a esos dos. **5** *(person - clever)* listo,-a, vivo,-a. **6** *(pain)* agudo,-a, fuerte; *(cry, noise)* agudo,-a, estridente; *(frost)* fuerte; *(wind)* cortante, penetrante. **7** *(taste)* ácido,-a; *(smell)* acre. **8** *(change, etc)* brusco,-a, repentino,-a, súbito,-a. **9** MUS *(key)* sostenido, -a; *(too high)* desafinado,-a.
► *adv* **1** *(exactly)* en punto: *at ten o'clock sharp* a las diez en punto. **2** *(abruptly)* bruscamente.

sharpen ['ʃɑːpən] *vt* **1** *(knife, claws)* afilar; *(pencil)* sacar punta a. **2** *fig (feeling, intelligence)* agudizar; *(desire)* avivar; *(appetite)* abrir.
► *vi (voice)* agudizarse.

sharpener ['ʃɑːpənəʳ] *n (for knife)* afilador *m*; *(for pencil)* sacapuntas *m.*

sharply ['ʃɑːplɪ] *adv* **1** *(abruptly, suddenly)* repentinamente. **2** *(acutely)* agudamente. **3** *(clearly)* marcadamente, claramente.

shatter ['ʃætəʳ] *vt* **1** *(break into small pieces)* romper, hacer añicos, hacer pedazos. **2** *fig (health)* destrozar, quebrantar, minar; *(nerves)* destrozar.

shave [ʃeɪv] *n* afeitado. ⎵LOC⎵ **to have a shave** afeitarse.
► *vt* **1** *(face, legs, underarms)* afeitar; *(head)* rapar. **2** *(wood)* cepillar.
► *vi (person)* afeitarse: *he shaves every morning* se afeita cada mañana.

shaver ['ʃeɪvəʳ] *n* máquina de afeitar.

S

shaving ['ʃeɪvɪŋ] n (of face) afeitado.
[COMP] **shaving brush** brocha de afeitar.
▌ **shaving cream** crema de afeitar. ▌
shaving foam espuma de afeitar.
▸ n pl **shavings** (wood) virutas fpl.

shawl [ʃɔːl] n chal m, mantón m.

she [ʃiː] pron ella: she's called Nina se llama Nina; she's happy está contenta.
▸ n (animal) hembra; (baby) niña.

she- [ʃiː] pref hembra: she-bear osa.

shear [ʃɪər] vt 1 (sheep) esquilar.
ⓘ pt sheared, pp sheared o shorn [ʃɔːn].
▸ n pl **shears** (gen) tijeras fpl (grandes);
(for hedges) podadera f sing.

shearer ['ʃɪərər] n esquilador,-ra.

shed¹ [ʃed] n (in garden, for bicycles) cobertizo.

shed² [ʃed] vt 1 (leaves, horns, skin) mudar; (clothes) quitarse, despojarse de;
(workers, jobs) deshacerse de; (load,
weight) perder: the snake sheds its skin la
serpiente muda la piel. 2 fig (inhibitions,
etc) liberarse de. 3 (water) repeler. 4
(blood, tears, etc) derramar.
ⓘ pt & pp shed, ger shedding.

she'd [ʃiːd] contr 1 she had. 2 she
would.

sheep [ʃiːp] n oveja.
ⓘ pl sheep.

sheepdog ['ʃiːpdɒg] n perro pastor.

sheepfold ['ʃiːpfəʊld] n redil m, aprisco.

sheer [ʃɪər] adj 1 (total, utter) total, absoluto,-a, puro,-a: by sheer coincidence por
pura casualidad. 2 (cliff) escarpado,-a;
(drop) vertical.

sheet [ʃiːt] n 1 (on bed) sábana: bottom/
top sheet sábana bajera/encimera. 2 (of
paper) hoja; (of metal) lámina, chapa;
(of glass) lámina, placa; (of tin) hoja.
[COMP] **sheet music** hojas pl de partitura, papel pautado.

shelf [ʃelf] n estante. [COMP] (set of)
shelves estantería.
ⓘ pl shelves.

shell [ʃel] n 1 (of egg, nut) cáscara; (of
pea) vaina; (of tortoise, lobster, etc) caparazón m; (of snail, oyster, etc) concha: the
children were collecting shells on the beach
los niños recogían conchas en la playa.
2 (of building) armazón m, esqueleto,

estructura; (of vehicle) armazón m; (of
ship) casco. 3 MIL (for explosives) proyectil m, obús m.

she'll [ʃiːl] contr 1 she will. 2 she shall.

shellfish ['ʃelfɪʃ] n (individual) marisco;
(as food) marisco, mariscos mpl.
ⓘ pl shellfish.

shelter ['ʃeltər] n 1 (protection) abrigo,
protección f, cobijo: the climbers sought
shelter from the storm los montañeros
buscaron abrigo para protegerse de la
tormenta. 2 (place) refugio, cobijo.
▸ vt (protect) proteger, resguardar;
these trees should shelter us from the rain
esos árboles nos resguardarán de la lluvia.
▸ vi (from weather, etc) resguardarse,
guarecerse; (from danger) refugiarse.

shelve [ʃelv] vt 1 (put on shelf) poner en el
estante, poner en la estantería. 2 fig
(postpone, abandon) aparcar, archivar.

shepherd ['ʃepəd] n pastor m.
▸ vt (guide, direct) guiar, conducir.

shelves [ʃelvz] pl → shelf.

sheriff ['ʃerɪf] n 1 US sheriff mf, alguacil,-la. 2 GB gobernador,-ra civil.

sherry ['ʃerɪ] n jerez m.
ⓘ pl sherries.

she's [ʃiːz] contr 1 she is. 2 she has.

shield [ʃiːld] n 1 (for protection) escudo. 2
TECH pantalla protectora. 3 (of animal)
caparazón m.
▸ vt (protect) proteger (from, de).

shift [ʃɪft] n 1 (change) cambio: a shift in
policy un cambio de política. 2 (of work,
workers) turno: the day/night shift el turno de día/de noche. [COMP] **shift key** tecla
de las mayúsculas.
▸ vt 1 (change) cambiar; (move) desplazar, mover: he shifted his feet movió sus
pies. 2 (transfer) traspasar, transferir. 3
US (change gear) cambiar.
▸ vi 1 (change) cambiar: the wind shifted
el viento cambió de dirección. 2 US
(change gear) cambiar de marcha.

shilling ['ʃɪlɪŋ] n chelín m.

shin [ʃɪn] n ANAT espinilla, canilla. [COMP]
shin guard / shin pad espinillera.

shinbone ['ʃɪnbəʊn] n ANAT tibia.

shine [ʃaɪn] n brillo, lustre m: *he gave his shoes a good shine* sacó brillo a sus zapatos.
▶ vi **1** *(sun, light, eyes)* brillar; *(metal, glass, shoes)* relucir, brillar; *(face)* resplandecer, irradiar: *her eyes shone with happiness* le brillaban los ojos de alegría. **2** fig *(excel)* sobresalir **(at, en)**, destacar **(at, en)**, brillar **(at, en)**: *he shines at tennis* destaca en tenis.
ⓘ *pt & pp* **shone** [ʃɒn].

shiny [ˈʃaɪnɪ] adj brillante.
ⓘ *comp* **shinier,** *superl* **shiniest.**

ship [ʃɪp] n *(gen)* barco, buque m, embarcación f. ᴄᴏᴍᴘ **passenger ship** buque m de pasajeros. ▌ **ship's company** tripulación f.
▶ vt *(send - gen)* enviar, mandar; *(- by ship)* enviar por barco: *we had our luggage shipped to England* mandamos nuestro equipaje a Inglaterra por barco.
ⓘ *pt & pp* **shipped,** *ger* **shipping.**

shipbuilding [ˈʃɪpbɪldɪŋ] n construcción f naval.

shipment [ˈʃɪpmənt] n *(act)* embarque m, envío, transporte m (marítimo).

shipowner [ˈʃɪpəʊnəʳ] n armador,-ra.

shipwreck [ˈʃɪprek] n naufragio. ʟᴏᴄ **to be shipwrecked** naufragar.

shipyard [ˈʃɪpjɑːd] n astillero.

shirk [ʃɜːk] vt *(duty, etc)* esquivar, eludir.

shirt [ʃɜːt] n *(gen)* camisa; *(for sport)* camiseta.

shirtsleeve [ˈʃɜːtsliːv] n manga de camisa. ʟᴏᴄ **in shirtsleeves** en mangas de camisa.

shiver [ˈʃɪvəʳ] n *(with cold)* escalofrío.
▶ vi *(with cold)* temblar, tiritar; *(with fear)* estremecerse.
▶ n pl **the shivers** escalofríos mpl.

shivery [ˈʃɪvərɪ] adj *(with cold)* estremecido,-a; *(feverish)* destemplado,-a.

shoal¹ [ʃəʊl] n *(underwater sandbank)* banco de arena.

shoal² [ʃəʊl] n *(of fish)* banco, cardumen m.
▶ n pl **shoals** fam montones mpl.

shock¹ [ʃɒk] n **1** *(jolt, blow)* choque m, impacto, golpe m; *(of explosion, etc)* sacudida; *(electric)* descarga. **2** *(upset, distress)* conmoción f, golpe m; *(fright, scare)* susto: *you gave me quite a shock* me has dado un buen susto. **3** ᴍᴇᴅ shock m, choque m. ᴄᴏᴍᴘ **shock absorber** amortiguador m. ▌ **shock therapy / shock treatment** electrochoque m.
▶ vt **1** *(upset)* conmocionar, conmover, afectar. **2** *(startle)* asustar, sorprender; *(scandalize)* escandalizar, horrorizar.
▶ vi impresionar, impactar.

shock² [ʃɒk] n *(of hair)* mata.

shocked [ʃɒkt] adj horrorizado,-a, escandalizado,-a.

shocking [ˈʃɒkɪŋ] adj **1** *(disgraceful, offensive)* chocante, escandaloso,-a, vergonzoso,-a. **2** fam *(very bad)* espantoso,-a, pésimo,-a.

shoe [ʃuː] n **1** zapato: *I need a new pair of shoes* necesito unos zapatos nuevos. **2** *(for horse)* herradura. ʟᴏᴄ **to put os in sb else's shoes** ponerse en el lugar de ALGN. ᴄᴏᴍᴘ **shoe polish** betún m.
▌ **shoe shop** zapatería.

shoebrush [ˈʃuːbrʌʃ] n cepillo para los zapatos.

shoehorn [ˈʃuːhɔːn] n calzador m.

shoelace [ˈʃuːleɪs] n cordón m (de zapato).

shoemaker [ˈʃuːmeɪkəʳ] n zapatero,-a.

shoeshine [ˈʃuːʃaɪn] n limpieza de zapatos. ᴄᴏᴍᴘ **shoeshine boy** limpiabotas m.

shone [ʃɒn] pt → **shine.**

shook [ʃʊk] pt → **shake.**

shoot [ʃuːt] n ʙᴏᴛ *(gen)* brote m, retoño, renuevo; *(of vine)* sarmiento.
▶ vt **1** *(person, animal)* pegar un tiro a, pegar un balazo a; *(hit, wound)* herir (de bala); *(kill)* matar de un tiro, matar a tiros; *(hunt)* cazar: *she was shot in the back* recibió un balazo en la espalda. **2** *(fire - missile)* lanzar; *(- arrow, bullet, weapon)* disparar; *(- glance)* lanzar: *they shot questions at her* la bombardearon a preguntas. **3** *(film)* rodar, filmar; *(photograph)* fotografiar. ʟᴏᴄ **to shoot pool** jugar al billar. ▌ **to shoot sb dead** matar a ALGN a tiros.

S

▸ *vi* **1** *(fire weapon)* disparar (**at**, a/sobre); *(hunt with gun)* cazar. **2** SP *(aim at goal)* tirar, disparar, chutar. **3** CINEM rodar, filmar. **5** BOT brotar.

◆ **to shoot down** *vt sep* **1** *(aircraft)* derribar, abatir; *(person)* matar a tiros. **2** *fig (argument, idea, etc)* rebatir.

① *pt & pp* **shot** [ʃɒt].

shooting [ˈʃuːtɪŋ] *n* **1** *(shots)* disparos *mpl*, tiros *mpl*; *(killing)* asesinato. **2** *(hunting)* caza. **3** CINEM rodaje *m*.

▸ *adj (pain)* punzante. COMP **shooting star** estrella fugaz.

shop [ʃɒp] *n* **1** *(gen)* tienda; *(business)* comercio, negocio: *I'm going to the shop* voy a la tienda. **2** *(workshop)* taller *m*. LOC **to keep shop** tener una tienda. COMP **repair shop** taller *m* de reparaciones. **I shop assistant** dependiente,-a. **I shop window** escaparate *m*.

▸ *vi (gen)* hacer la compra, comprar: *we usually shop on Saturday mornings* normalmente hacemos la compra los sábados por la mañana.

◆ **to shop around** *vi* ir de tienda en tienda y comparar precios.

① *pt & pp* **shopped**, *ger* **shopping**.

shopkeeper [ˈʃɒpkiːpəʳ] *n* tendero,-a.

shoplifter [ˈʃɒplɪftəʳ] *n* mechero,-a.

shoplifting [ˈʃɒplɪftɪŋ] *n* hurto (en las tiendas).

shopper [ˈʃɒpəʳ] *n* comprador,-ra.

shopping [ˈʃɒpɪŋ] *n (purchases)* compra, compras *fpl*; *(activity)* compra: *I had a bit of shopping to do* tuve que hacer unas compras. LOC **to do the shopping** hacer la compra. **I to go shopping** ir de compras. COMP **shopping bag** cesta de la compra. **I shopping basket** bolsa de la compra. **I shopping centre** centro comercial. **I shopping list** lista de la compra. **I shopping mall** US centro comercial. **I shopping precinct** zona comercial. **I shopping trolley** carrito (de la compra).

shore [ʃɔːʳ] *n (of sea, lake)* orilla; *(coast)* costa; *(beach)* playa. LOC **on shore** en tierra.

shorn [ʃɔːn] *pp* → **shear**.

short [ʃɔːt] *adj* **1** *(not long)* corto,-a; *(not tall)* bajo,-a: *he's got short hair* lleva el pe-

lo corto; *Jo is short for Joanne* Jo es el diminutivo de Joanne. **2** *(brief - of time)* breve, corto,-a: *the days are shorter in winter* los días son más cortos en invierno **3** *(deficient)* escaso,-a: *water was short* escaseaba el agua. **4** *(curt)* seco,-a, brusco,-a. LOC **for short** para abreviar. **I in short** en pocas palabras. **I short of** a menos que, salvo que. **I to be short of** STH andar escaso,-a de ALGO, estar falto,-a de ALGO: *I'm a bit short of money* ando ALGO escaso de dinero. **I to run short of** STH acabarse ALGO: *we're running short of coffee* se nos está acabando el café. COMP **short circuit** cortocircuito. **I short cut 1** *(route)* atajo. **2** *(method)* método fácil, fórmula mágica. **I short order** US comida rápida. **I short story** cuento.

▸ *adv (abruptly)* bruscamente: *the car stopped short* el coche se paró bruscamente.

▸ *n* **1** *(drink)* copa, chupito. **2** CINEM cortometraje *m*, corto. **3** ELEC cortocircuito.

shortage [ˈʃɔːtɪdʒ] *n* falta, escasez *f*.

shorten [ˈʃɔːtən] *vt* acortar.

▸ *vi* acortarse.

shorthand [ˈʃɔːthænd] *n* taquigrafía.

shortly [ˈʃɔːtlɪ] *adv* **1** *(soon)* dentro de poco, en breve: *shortly after/before* poco después/antes. **2** *(impatiently)* bruscamente.

shorts [ʃɔːts] *n pl* **1** pantalones *mpl* cortos, shorts *mpl*: *a pair of shorts* un pantalón corto. **2** US *(underpants)* calzoncillos *mpl*.

short-sighted [ˈʃɔːtsaɪtɪd] *adj* **1** MED miope, corto,-a de vista. **2** *(plan, policy, etc)* corto,-a de miras, estrecho,-a de miras.

short-sleeved [ˈʃɔːtsliːvd] *adj* de manga corta.

shot¹ [ʃɒt] *n* **1** *(act, sound)* tiro, disparo, balazo: *I thought I heard a shot* creo haber oído un disparo. **2** *(projectile)* bala, proyectil *m*. **3** *(person)* tirador,-ra. **4** SP *(in football)* chut *m*, chute *m*; *(in tennis, golf, cricket, etc)* golpe *m*; *(in basketball)* tiro. **5** *(attempt, try)* intento. **6** *fam (injection)* inyección *f*, pinchazo. **7** *(drink)* trago, chupito. **8** *(photo)* foto *f; (cinema)* toma. ⓛⓄⓒ **like a shot** *(without hesitation)* sin pensarlo dos veces, sin dudar.

shot² [sed] *pt & pp* → **shoot**.

shotgun ['ʃɒtgʌn] *n* escopeta.

should [ʃud] *aux* **1** *(duty, advisability, recommendation)* deber: *you should see the dentist* deberías ir al dentista. **2** *(probability)* deber de: *the clothes should be dry now* la ropa ya debe de estar seca. **3** *(subjunctive, conditional)*: *if you should see Janet by any chance* si por casualidad vieras a Janet. **4** *(conditional, 1st person)* : *I should like to ask a question* quisiera hacer una pregunta. **5** *(tentative statement)* : *I should think so* me imagino que sí. **6** *(disbelief, surprise)*: *how should I know!* ¡yo qué sé! ⓛⓄⓒ **I should have thought ...** hubiera pensado...

> ✎ Should, cuando expresa el condicional para la primera persona, equivale a would.

shoulder ['ʃəuldə'] *n* **1** ANAT hombro: *she looked over her shoulder* miró por encima del hombro. **2** *(of meat)* paletilla. **3** *(of hill, mountain)* ladera; *(of road)* arcén *m*, andén *m*. ⓛⓄⓒ **a shoulder to cry on** un paño de lágrimas. ▌ **to rub shoulders with** sb codearse con ALGN. ⒸⓄⓜⓅ **shoulder bag** bolso *(de bandolera)*. ▌ **shoulder blade** omóplato. ▌ **shoulder strap 1** *(of garment)* tirante *m*. **2** *(of bag)* correa.

▶ *n pl* **shoulders** ANAT hombros *mpl*, espalda *f sing*.

shout [ʃaut] *n* grito.

▶ *vt* gritar (out, -): *get out! he shouted* ¡fuera! gritó.

▶ *vi* gritar: *I don't like it when you shout at me* no me gusta que me grites.

◆ **to shout down** *vt sep* abuchear.

shouting ['ʃautɪŋ] *n* gritos *mpl*.

shove [ʃʌv] *n* empujón *m*: *we had to give the car a shove* tuvimos que dar un empujón al coche.

▶ *vt* **1** *(push)* empujar: *she shoved the plate away* apartó el plato de un empujón. **2** *(put casually)* meter.

▶ *vi* *(push)* empujar, dar empujones.

shovel ['ʃʌvəl] *n* **1** *(tool)* pala. **2** *(machine)* excavadora, pala mecánica.

show [ʃəu] *n* **1** THEAT *(entertainment)* espectáculo; *(performance)* función *f*: *let's go and see a show* vayamos a ver un espectáculo. **2** *(on TV, radio)* programa *m*, show *m*. **3** *(exhibition)* exposición *f*. **4** *(display)* muestra, demostración *f*: *a show of strength* una demostración de fuerza, una exhibición de fuerza. **5** *(outward appearance, pretence)* apariencia. ⓛⓄⓒ **the show must go on** el espectáculo debe continuar. ▌ **time will show** el tiempo lo dirá. ⒸⓄⓜⓅ **fashion show** desfile *m* de modelos. ▌ **quiz show** programa *m* concurso. ▌ **show business** el mundo del espectáculo.

▶ *vt* **1** *(gen)* enseñar: *I showed her my photos* le enseñé mis fotos. **2** *(point out)* indicar, señalar. **3** *(reveal - feelings)* demostrar, expresar; *(interest, enthusiasm, etc)* demostrar, mostrar: *she rarely shows his feelings* raras veces demuestra sus sentimientos. **4** *(allow to be seen)* dejar ver: *black doesn't show the dirt* el negro no deja ver la suciedad. **5** *(prove, demonstrate)* demostrar. **6** *(guide)* llevar, acompañar: *I'll show you to your room* te acompañaré a tu habitación. **7** *(painting, etc)* exponer, exhibir; *(film)* dar, poner, pasar, proyectar; *(slides)* pasar, proyectar; *(on TV)* dar, poner.

▶ *vi* **1** *(be perceptible)* verse, notarse: *the stain doesn't show* no se ve la mancha. **2** CINEM poner, dar, echar, proyectar, exhibir: *what's showing at the Odeon?* ¿qué dan en el Odeon?, ¿qué echan en el Odeon?

◆ **to show off** *vi (gen)* fanfarronear, presumir, lucirse; *(child)* hacerse el/la gracioso,-a.

▶ *vt sep* **1** *(set off)* hacer resaltar, realzar. **2** *(flaunt, parade)* hacer alarde de, presumir de.

◆ **to show up** *vt sep* **1** *(make visible)* hacer resaltar, hacer destacar. **2** *fam (embarrass)* dejar en ridículo, poner en evidencia.

▶ *vi* **1** *(be visible)* notarse, verse. **2** *fam (arrive)* acudir, presentarse, aparecer. ① *pt* **showed**, *pp* **showed** o **shown** [ʃəun].

S

shower ['ʃaʊəʳ] n **1** METEOR chubasco, chaparrón m. **2** (of stones, blows, insults, etc) lluvia. **3** (in bathroom) ducha. LOC to **have a shower / take a shower** ducharse. COMP **shower cap** gorro de baño. ‖ **shower gel** gel m de baño, gel m de ducha.
▸ vt **1** (sprinkle) espolvorear; (spray) rociar. **2** fig (bestow, heap) inundar, colmar, llover.
▸ vi **1** (rain) llover; (objects) caer, llover. **2** (in bath) ducharse.

showing ['ʃaʊɪŋ] n **1** (of film) pase m, sesión f, proyección f; (of paintings) exhibición f. **2** (performance) actuación f; (result) resultado.

showman ['ʃaʊmən] n **1** (manager) empresario (de espectáculos). **2** (entertainer) artista m, showman m.
ⓘ pl **showmen** ['ʃaʊmən].

shown [ʃaʊn] pp → show.

show-off ['ʃaʊɒf] n fam fanfarrón, -ona.

showroom ['ʃaʊruːm] n sala de exposiciones (de concesionario de coches).

showy ['ʃaʊɪ] adj (thing) llamativo,-a, vistoso,-a; (person) ostentoso,-a.
ⓘ comp **showier**, superl **showiest**.

shrank [ʃræŋk] pt → shrink.

shrapnel ['ʃræpnəl] n metralla.

shred [ʃred] n **1** (gen) triza; (of cloth) jirón m; (of paper) tira; (of tobacco) brizna, hebra. **2** fig (bit) pizca: not a shred of truth ni pizca de verdad. LOC to **tear** STH/ sb **to shreds** hacer trizas ALGO/a ALGN.
▸ vt (paper) hacer trizas, triturar; (vegetables - cut in strips) cortar en tiras; (- grate) rallar.
ⓘ pt & pp **shredded**, ger **shredding**.

shrew [ʃruː] n ZOOL musaraña.

shrewd [ʃruːd] adj **1** (person) astuto,-a, sagaz. **2** (decision) muy acertado,-a; (move) hábil, inteligente.

shrewdness ['ʃruːdnəs] n (gen) astucia, sagacidad f.

shriek [ʃriːk] n chillido, grito agudo.
▸ vi chillar, gritar. LOC to **shriek with laughter** reírse a carcajadas.
▸ vt chillar, gritar.

shrill [ʃrɪl] adj **1** (voice, words, people) agudo,-a, estridente; (sound, whistle) agudo,-a, estridente, penetrante. **2** (demand, protest, criticism) frenético,-a, estridente.
▸ vi (whistle) pitar; (phone, alarm) sonar; (person, voice) chillar.

shrimp [ʃrɪmp] n camarón m, gamba.

shrine [ʃraɪn] n REL (holy place) santuario, lugar m sagrado.

shrink [ʃrɪŋk] vt (clothes, etc) encoger.
▸ vi **1** (clothes) encoger, encogerse; (meat) achicarse, reducirse. **2** (savings, profits, etc) disminuir, reducirse. **3** (move back) retroceder, echarse atrás.
ⓘ pt **shrank** [ʃræŋk], pp **shrunk** [ʃrʌŋk].

shroud [ʃraʊd] n **1** REL mortaja, sudario. **2** fig (of mist, secrecy) velo.

Shrove Tuesday [ʃrəʊv'tjuːzdɪ] n martes m de carnaval.

shrub [ʃrʌb] n arbusto, mata.

shrug [ʃrʌg] vt encoger. LOC to **shrug one's shoulders** encogerse de hombros.
ⓘ pt & pp **shrugged**, ger **shrugging**.

shrunk [ʃrʌŋk] pp → shrink.

shudder ['ʃʌdəʳ] n **1** (of person) escalofrío. **2** (of machine, engine) vibración f, sacudida.
▸ vi **1** (person) estremecerse, temblar (with, de): I shudder to think of it me dan escalofríos solo de pensarlo. **2** (machinery, vehicle) vibrar, dar sacudidas.

shuffle ['ʃʌfəl] n **1** (walk) arrastre m. **2** (of cards) baraje m, barajadura.
▸ vt **1** (feet - drag) arrastrar; (- move) mover. **2** (cards) barajar; (papers) revolver.
▸ vi (walk) andar arrastrando los pies; (in seat) revolverse.

shut [ʃʌt] vt (gen) cerrar: shut your eyes cierra los ojos.
▸ vi (gen) cerrar, cerrarse.
◆ to **shut down** vt sep (factory, business) cerrar.
▸ vi (factory, business) cerrar.
◆ to **shut up** vt sep **1** (close) cerrar. **2** (confine) encerrar. **3** fam (quieten) callar, hacer callar.
▸ vi **1** (close) cerrar. **2** (keep quiet) callarse: shut up! ¡cállate!
ⓘ pt & pp **shut**, ger **shutting**.

shutdown [ˈʃʌtdaʊn] *n (of factory, etc)* cierre *m*.

shutter [ˈʃʌtəʳ] *n* **1** *(on window)* postigo, contraventana; *(of shop)* cierre *m*. **2** *(of camera)* obturador *m*.

shuttle [ˈʃʌtəl] *n* **1** AV puente *m* aéreo. **2** *(bus, train)* servicio regular de enlace. **3** *(in weaving)* lanzadera. [COMP] **shuttle service** servicio regular de enlace.

shuttlecock [ˈʃʌtəlkɒk] *n* volante *m*.

shy [ʃaɪ] *adj* **1** *(person)* tímido,-a, vergonzoso,-a: *don't be shy* no seas tímido, no tengas vergüenza. **2** *(animal)* asustadizo,-a.
ⓘ *comp* shyer o shier, *superl* shyest o shiest.
▶ *vi (horse)* espantarse (at, de), respingar, asustarse.

shyness [ˈʃaɪnəs] *n* timidez *f*.

sick [sɪk] *adj* **1** *(ill)* enfermo,-a. **2** *(nauseated, queasy)* mareado,-a. **3** *(fed up)* harto,-a; *(worried)* preocupado,-a: *I'm sick and tired of your moaning* estoy más que harto de tus quejas. [LOC] **to be sick** vomitar, devolver. ∎ **to feel sick** estar mareado,-a, tener náuseas. [COMP] **sick leave** baja por enfermedad.

sickle [ˈsɪkəl] *n* hoz *f*.

sickly [ˈsɪklɪ] *adj* **1** *(person)* enfermizo,-a. **2** *(smell, taste)* empalagoso,-a, dulzón, -ona; *(colour)* horrible, asqueroso,-a.
ⓘ *comp* sicklier, *superl* sickliest.

sickness [ˈsɪknəs] *n* **1** *(illness)* enfermedad *f*. **2** *(nausea)* náuseas *fpl*, ganas *fpl* de vomitar.

side [saɪd] *n* **1** *(gen)* lado; *(of coin, cube, record)* cara: *there's a garage at the side of the house* hay un garaje al lado de la casa; *write on one side of the paper only* solo escribir en una cara del papel. **2** *(of hill, mountain)* ladera, falda. **3** *(of body)* lado, costado: *she was lying on her side* estaba echada de lado. **4** *(edge - gen)* borde *m*; *(- of lake, river, etc)* orilla; *(- of page)* margen *m*. [LOC] **side by side** juntos,-as, uno,-a al lado del/de la otro,-a. ∎ **to keep on the right side of** SB tratar de llevarse bien con ALGN.
▶ *adj* lateral. [COMP] **side dish** guarnición *f*, acompañamiento. ∎ **side drum** tambor *m*. ∎ **side effect** efecto secundario. ∎ **side street** callejuela. ∎ **side view** vista de perfil.

sideboard [ˈsaɪdbɔːd] *n (furniture)* aparador *m*.

sideboards [ˈsaɪdbɔːdz] *n pl* patillas *fpl*.

sideburns [ˈsaɪdbɜːnz] *n pl* patillas *fpl*.

sidecar [ˈsaɪdkɑːʳ] *n* sidecar *m*.

sidelight [ˈsaɪdlaɪt] *n* AUTO luz *f* de posición.

sidereal [saɪˈdɪərɪəl] *adj* sideral.

sidewalk [ˈsaɪdwɔːk] *n* US acera.

sideways [ˈsaɪdweɪz] *adj (movement, step)* lateral; *(look, glance)* de soslayo, de reojo.
▶ *adv* de lado.

siege [siːdʒ] *n* **1** MIL sitio, cerco. **2** *(by criminals, journalists)* asedio. [LOC] **to be under siege** estar sitiado,-a.

Sierra Leone [sɪeərəlɪˈəʊn] *n* Sierra Leona.

Sierra Leonean [sɪeərəlɪˈəʊnən] *adj* sierraleonés,-esa.
▶ *n* sierraleonés,-esa.

sieve [sɪv] *n (fine)* tamiz *m*; *(coarse)* criba; *(for liquids)* colador *m*.
▶ *vt (fine)* tamizar; *(coarse)* cribar.

sigh [saɪ] *n (of person)* suspiro.
▶ *vi (person)* suspirar (**for**, por); *(wind)* susurrar, gemir: *she sighed with relief* suspiró aliviada.

sight [saɪt] *n* **1** *(gen)* vista: *his sight is failing* le está fallando la vista; *we waited until he was out of sight* esperamos hasta que hubo desaparecido; *it was her first sight of the countryside* fue la primera vez que veía el campo. **2** *(thing seen, spectacle)* espectáculo. [LOC] **in/within sight** a la vista. ∎ **to come into sight** aparecer. ∎ **to know** SB **by sight** conocer a ALGN de vista.
▶ *vt* ver, divisar.
▶ *adv* **a sight** *fam (a great deal)* mucho: *a sight better* mucho mejor.
▶ *n pl* **sights** *(of city)* monumentos *mpl*, lugares *mpl* de interés.

sightseeing [ˈsaɪtsiːɪŋ] *n* visita turística, turismo. [LOC] **to go sightseeing** visitar los monumentos y lugares de interés.

sign [saɪn] *n* **1** *(symbol)* signo, símbolo. **2** *(gesture)* gesto, seña; *(signal)* señal *f*:

S

wait until I give the sign espera hasta que dé la señal. LOC **as a sign of** como muestra de. COMP **sign language** lenguaje *m* por señas.

▶ *vt* **1** *(letter, document, cheque, etc)* firmar: *sign your name here, please* firme aquí, por favor. **2** *(player, group)* fichar (**on/up**, -). **3** *(gesture)* hacer una seña/señal.

▶ *vi* **1** *(write name)* firmar. **2** *(player, group)* fichar (**for/with**, por). **3** US *(use sign language)* comunicarse por señas, hablar por señas.

◆ **to sign up** *vt sep* *(soldier)* reclutar; *(worker)* contratar.

▶ *vi* *(soldier)* alistarse; *(student)* matricularse.

signal ['sɪgnəl] *n* señal *f*: *traffic signal* señal de tráfico.

▶ *adj* *(achievement, triumph, success, etc)* señalado,-a, destacado,-a, notable.

▶ *vt* **1** *(indicate)* indicar, señalar, marcar; *(forecast)* pronosticar. **2** *(gesture)* hacer señas, hacer una seña: *he signalled the waiter to bring the bill* le hizo una seña al camarero para que trajera la cuenta.

▶ *vi* **1** *(gesture)* hacer señas, hacer una seña. **2** AUTO poner el intermitente.

signature ['sɪgnɪtʃə^r] *n* *(name)* firma.

significance [sɪg'nɪfɪkəns] *n* **1** *(meaning)* significado. **2** *(importance)* importancia: *it's of no significance* no tiene importancia.

significant [sɪg'nɪfɪkənt] *adj* **1** *(meaningful - gen)* significativo,-a. **2** *(important)* importante, trascendente, considerable.

signify ['sɪgnɪfaɪ] *vt fml* significar.
ⓘ *pt & pp* **signified**, *ger* **signifying**.

signpost ['saɪnpəʊst] *n* poste *m* indicador.

silence ['saɪləns] *n* *(gen)* silencio: *we walked in silence* caminamos en silencio. LOC **to reduce SB to silence** dejar a ALGN sin habla.

▶ *vt* *(person)* acallar, hacer callar; *(protest, opposition, criticism)* apagar, silenciar.

silencer ['saɪlənsə^r] *n* silenciador *m*.

silent ['saɪlənt] *adj* **1** *(thing, place, taciturn person)* silencioso,-a. **2** *(not speaking)* callado,-a: *he was silent for a moment* se quedó callado un momento. **3** *(film, con-*

sonant) mudo,-a; *(prayer)* silencioso,-a. LOC **to be silent** callarse.

silhouette [sɪluː'et] *n* silueta.

silicon ['sɪlɪkən] *n* silicio.

silicone ['sɪlɪkəʊn] *n* silicona.

silk [sɪlk] *n* seda.
▶ *adj* de seda.

silken ['sɪlkən] *adj* *(like silk)* sedoso,-a; *(of silk)* de seda.

silkworm ['sɪlkwɜːm] *n* gusano de seda.

silky ['sɪlkɪ] *adj* *(cloth, hair, fur, etc)* sedoso,-a; *(voice)* aterciopelado,-a; *(skin)* suave.
ⓘ *comp* **silkier**, *superl* **silkiest**.

sill [sɪl] *n* *(of window)* alféizar *m*, antepecho.

silly ['sɪlɪ] *adj* **1** *(stupid)* tonto,-a, estúpido,-a: *how silly of me!* ¡qué tonto soy! **2** *(unimportant)* trivial, sin importancia.
ⓘ *comp* **sillier**, *superl* **silliest**.
▶ *n* tonto,-a, bobo,-a.

silver ['sɪlvə^r] *n* **1** *(metal)* plata: *sterling silver* plata de ley. **2** *(coins)* monedas *fpl* (de plata). **3** *(articles, ornaments, etc)* plata.
▶ *adj* **1** *(made of silver)* de plata. **2** *(in colour)* plateado,-a; *(hair)* canoso,-a, cano,-a. COMP **silver foil / silver paper** papel *m* de plata. ‖ **silver medal** medalla de plata. ‖ **silver screen** el cine *m*.
▶ *vt* *(metal)* dar un baño de plata a, platear.

similar ['sɪmɪlə^r] *adj* parecido,-a (**to**, a), similar (**to**, a), semejante (**to**, a): *those boys are very similar* esos chicos se parecen mucho.

similarity [sɪmɪ'lærətɪ] *n* *(likeness)* semejanza, parecido, similitud *f*.
ⓘ *pl* **similarities**.

simile ['sɪmɪlɪ] *n* símil *m*.

simmer ['sɪmə^r] *vt* CULIN hervir a fuego lento.
▶ *vi* CULIN hervir a fuego lento.

simple ['sɪmpəl] *adj* **1** *(gen)* sencillo,-a, simple: *a simple solution* una solución sencilla. **2** *(plain, pure, nothing more than)* sencillo,-a, puro,-a, mero,-a: *for the simple reason that...* por la sencilla razón que ...
ⓘ *comp* **simpler**, *comp* **simplest**.

simplicity [sɪmˈplɪsəti] n **1** (easiness, incomplexity) sencillez f, simplicidad f. **2** (lack of sophistication) sencillez f, naturalidad f.

simplify [ˈsɪmplɪfaɪ] vt simplificar.
ⓘ pt & pp simplified, ger simplifying.

simply [ˈsɪmplɪ] adv **1** (easily, plainly, modestly) simplemente, sencillamente: she lives very simply vive muy sencillamente. **2** (only) simplemente, solamente, solo; (just, merely) meramente: I simply don't know sencillamente, no lo sé. **3** (really, absolutely) francamente, realmente.

simulate [ˈsɪmjəleɪt] vt simular.

simultaneous [sɪməlˈteɪnɪəs] adj simultáneo,-a: simultaneous translation traducción simultánea.

sin [sɪn] n pecado.
▶ vi pecar (against, contra).
ⓘ pt & pp sinned, ger sinning.

since [sɪns] adv desde entonces: she arrived in 1988 and has lived here ever since llegó en 1988 y vive aquí desde entonces.
▶ prep desde: I've been here since four o'clock llevo aquí desde las cuatro.
▶ conj **1** (time) desde que: it's years since I went to the theatre hace años que no voy al teatro. **2** (because, seeing that) ya que, puesto que: since you're going to the shop ... ya que vas a la tienda ...

sincere [sɪnˈsɪər] adj sincero,-a.

sincerely [sɪnˈsɪəlɪ] adv sinceramente.
ᴸᴼᶜ Yours sincerely (in letter) (le saluda) atentamente.

sincerity [sɪnˈserətɪ] n sinceridad f.

sinew [ˈsɪnjuː] n tendón m.

sing [sɪŋ] vt (gen) cantar.
▶ vi (person, bird) cantar; (wind, kettle, bullet) silbar; (ears, insect) zumbar.
ⓘ pt sang [sæŋ], pp sung [sʌŋ].

singer [ˈsɪŋər] n (gen) cantante mf; (in choir) cantor,-ra: jazz singer cantante de jazz.

singing [ˈsɪŋɪŋ] n (act) canto, cantar m; (songs) canciones fpl: he loves singing in the shower le encanta cantar en la ducha.

single [ˈsɪŋɡəl] adj **1** (only one) solo,-a, único,-a: we heard a single scream oímos un solo grito. **2** (composed of one part) simple, sencillo,-a: single figures cifras de un solo dígito. **3** (for one person) indi-

vidual. **4** (separate, individual) cada: every single day todos los días. **5** (unmarried) soltero,-a. ᴸᴼᶜ in single file en fila india. ᶜᴼᴹᴾ single cream nata líquida. ▌ single parent **1** (mother) madre f soltera. **2** (father) padre m soltero. ▌ single room habitación f individual.
▶ n **1** GB (single ticket) billete m de ida, billete m sencillo. **2** (record) (disco) sencillo, single m.
▶ n pl singles SP (in tennis, badminton) individuales mpl.

single-parent [ˈsɪŋɡəlpeərənt] adj (family) monoparental.

singular [ˈsɪŋɡjʊlər] adj **1** (in grammar) singular. **2** fml (outstanding) extraordinario,-a.
▶ n LING singular m.

sinister [ˈsɪnɪstər] adj siniestro,-a.

sink [sɪŋk] n (in kitchen) fregadero, pila; (in bathroom) lavabo, lavamanos m.
▶ vt **1** (ship) hundir. **2** fig (hopes, plans) acabar con.
▶ vi **1** (gen) hundirse. **2** (sun, moon) ponerse.
ⓘ pt sank [sæŋk], pp sunk [sʌŋk].

sinner [ˈsɪnər] n pecador,-ra.

sip [sɪp] n sorbo.
▶ vt sorber, beber a sorbos.
ⓘ pt & pp sipped, ger sipping.

siphon [ˈsaɪfən] n (gen) sifón m.

sir [sɜːr] n **1** fml (gen) señor m: yes, sir sí, señor. **2** (title) sir m. ᴸᴼᶜ Dear Sir (in letter) muy señor mío, muy señores míos, estimado señor.

siren [ˈsaɪərən] n (gen) sirena.

sirloin [ˈsɜːlɔɪn] n solomillo.

sister [ˈsɪstər] n **1** (relative) hermana. **2** (comrade) hermana, compañera.

sister-in-law [ˈsɪstərɪnlɔː] n cuñada.
ⓘ pl sisters-in-law.

sit [sɪt] vt **1** (child, etc) sentar (down, -): she sat him down on the table lo sentó en la mesa. **2** (room, hall, etc) tener cabida para; (table) ser para. **3** GB (exam) presentarse a.
▶ vi **1** (action) sentarse (down, -): I sat next to Anna me senté junto a Anna. **2** (be seated) estar sentado,-a: they were sitting on the floor estaban sentados en el

suelo. **3** *(village, building)* estar, situarse; *(clothes)* sentar, quedar: *that dress sits well on you* aquel vestido te sienta bien.
▸ *vi fam (baby-sit)* hacer de canguro (for, a).
◆ **to sit back** *vi* **1** *(lean back)* recostarse; *(relax)* ponerse cómodo,-a. **2** *(take no active part)* cruzarse de brazos.
◆ **to sit out** *vt sep* **1** *(stay until end)* aguantar (hasta el final). **2** *(not dance)* no bailar.
◆ **to sit up** *vi* **1** *(in bed)* incorporarse (en la cama). **2** *(stay up late)* quedarse levantado,-a.
▸ *vt sep (child, etc)* sentar.
① *pt & pp* **sat** [sæt], *ger* **sitting**.

site [saɪt] *n (location)* situación *f*, emplazamiento, colocación *f*. COMP **archaeological site** yacimiento arqueológico.
▸ *vt* situar, ubicar, emplazar.

sit-in ['sɪtɪn] *n (protest)* sentada.

sitting ['sɪtɪŋ] *n (of meal)* turno; *(of committee, for portrait)* sesión *f*.
▸ *adj (position)* sentado,-a. COMP **sitting room** sala de estar.

situated ['sɪtjʊeɪtɪd] *adj (building, etc)* situado,-a, ubicado,-a.

situation [sɪtjʊ'eɪʃən] *n* **1** *(circumstances)* situación *f*: *we're in a difficult situation* estamos en una situación difícil. **2** *(location)* situación *f*, ubicación *f*.

sit-up ['sɪtʌp] *n* SP abdominal *m*.

six [sɪks] *adj* seis: *it costs six pounds* cuesta seis libras; *six hundred* seiscientos,-as; *six thousand* seis mil.
▸ *n* seis *m*: *she's six years old* tiene seis años; *it's six o'clock* son las seis.

sixteen [sɪks'tiːn] *adj* dieciséis.
▸ *n* dieciséis *m*.
✎ Consulta también **six**.

sixteenth [sɪks'tiːnθ] *adj* decimosexto,-a.
▸ *adv* en decimosexto lugar.
▸ *n* **1** *(in series)* decimosexto,-a. **2** *(fraction)* decimosexto; *(one part)* decimosexta parte *f*.
✎ Consulta también **sixth**.

sixth [sɪksθ] *adj* sexto,-a: *the sixth floor* la sexta planta, el sexto piso.
▸ *adv* sexto, en sexto lugar: *he came sixth* llegó en sexto lugar.
▸ *n* **1** *(in series)* sexto,-a; *(day)* el seis, el día seis: *the sixth of June* el seis de junio. **2** *(fraction)* sexto; *(one part)* sexta parte *f*. COMP **sixth form** GB ≈ segundo de bachillerato. ∎ **sixth form college** GB ≈ *instituto para estudiantes de segundo de bachillerato*.

sixtieth ['sɪkstɪəθ] *adj* sexagésimo,-a.
▸ *adv* en sexagésimo lugar.
▸ *n* **1** *(in series)* sexagésimo,-a. **2** *(fraction)* sexagésimo; *(one part)* sexagésima parte *f*.

sixty ['sɪkstɪ] *adj* sesenta: *there were about sixty people* había unas sesenta personas.
▸ *n* sesenta *m*.

size [saɪz] *n* **1** *(gen)* tamaño; *(magnitude)* magnitud *f*: *it's the size of an egg* es del tamaño de un huevo. **2** *(of clothes)* talla; *(of shoes)* número; *(of person)* talla, estatura: *she's a size 12* gasta la talla 12.

skate¹ [skeɪt] *n* patín *m*.
▸ *vi* patinar.

skate² [skeɪt] *n (fish)* raya.

skateboard ['skeɪtbɔːd] *n* monopatín *m*.

skater ['skeɪtəʳ] *n* patinador,-ra.

skating ['skeɪtɪŋ] *n* patinaje *m*. COMP **ice skating** patinaje *m* sobre hielo. ∎ **skating rink** pista de patinaje.

skeleton ['skelɪtən] *n* **1** *(of person, animal)* esqueleto. **2** *(of building, ship)* armazón *m*, estructura.

sketch [sketʃ] *n* **1** *(drawing)* dibujo; *(preliminary drawing)* bosquejo, esbozo. **2** *(outline, rough idea)* esquema *m*, esbozo.
▸ *vt (draw)* dibujar; *(preliminary drawing)* bosquejar, hacer un bosquejo de.
▸ *vi* hacer bosquejos, hacer bocetos.
◆ **to sketch in/out**

skewer ['skjʊəʳ] *n* CULIN pincho, brocheta.

ski [skiː] *n (equipment)* esquí *m*.
▸ *vi* esquiar. LOC **to ski down** bajar esquiando. COMP **ski jump** **1** *(slope)* pista de saltos, trampolín *m*. **2** *(competition)* saltos *mpl* de esquí. ∎ **ski lift** telesquí *m*.

ski resort estación *f* de esquí. **ski slope** pista de esquí.

skid [skɪd] *n* AUTO patinazo, derrapaje *m*. COMP **skid row** US barrios *mpl* bajos, barriadas *fpl*.

skier ['skɪəʳ] *n* esquiador,-ra

skies [skaɪz] *pl* → **sky**.

skiing ['skiːɪŋ] *n* esquí *m*.

skilful ['skɪlfʊl] *adj* (gen) diestro,-a, hábil. LOC **to be skilful at** STH ser hábil para ALGO.

skilfully ['skɪlfʊli] *adv* hábilmente.

skill [skɪl] *n* **1** (ability) habilidad *f*, destreza; (talent) talento, don *m*, dotes *fpl*. **2** (technique) técnica, arte *m*.
► *n pl* **skills** (expertise) capacidad *f sing*, aptitudes *fpl*: *a person with computer skills* una persona que sepa informática.

skilled [skɪld] *adj* **1** (specialized) cualificado,-a, especializado,-a. **2** (able) hábil, diestro,-a; (expert) experto,-a.

skillful ['skɪlfʊl] *adj* US → **skilful**.

skillfully ['skɪlfʊli] *adv* US → **skilfully**.

skimmed [skɪmd] *adj* (milk) desnatado,-a.

skimmer ['skɪməʳ] *n* (spoon) espumadera.

skin [skɪn] *n* **1** (of person) piel *f*; (of face) cutis *m*, piel *f*: *she has light/dark skin* tiene la piel clara/morena. **2** (of animal) piel *f*, pellejo. **3** (of fruit, vegetable) piel *f*. **4** (on paint) telilla, capa fina; (on milk, custard, etc) nata.

skinflint ['skɪnflɪnt] *n fam* tacaño,-a.

skinhead ['skɪnhed] *n* cabeza *mf* rapada, skin *mf*.

skinny ['skɪni] *adj fam* flaco,-a.
ⓘ *comp* **skinnier**, *superl* **skinniest**.

skip¹ [skɪp] *n* salto, brinco.
► *vi* **1** (move, jump) saltar, brincar; (with rope) saltar a la comba. **2** (jump, flit) saltar.
► *vt* (miss, omit) saltarse: *she skipped a few pages* se saltó unas páginas.
ⓘ *pt & pp* **skipped**, *ger* **skipping**.

skip² [skɪp] *n* (container) contenedor *m*.

skipper ['skɪpəʳ] *n* **1** MAR patrón,-ona, capitán,-ana. **2** SP capitán,-ana.

skipping ['skɪpɪŋ] *n* COMP **skipping rope** comba, cuerda de saltar.

skirt [skɜːt] *n* (garment) falda.

skirting ['skɜːtɪŋ] *n* [also **skirting board**] *n* GB zócalo, rodapié *m*.

skittle ['skɪtəl] *n* (wooden pin) bolo.
► *n pl* **skittles** bolos *mpl*, boliche *m sing*.

skull [skʌl] *n* **1** ANAT cráneo. **2** (symbol) calavera. COMP **skull and crossbones** bandera pirata.

skunk [skʌŋk] *n* ZOOL mofeta.

sky [skaɪ] *n* (gen) cielo; (firmament) firmamento.
ⓘ *pl* **skies**.

sky-blue ['skaɪbluː] *adj* azul celeste.

skylark ['skaɪlɑːk] *n* alondra.

skylight ['skaɪlaɪt] *n* tragaluz *m*, claraboya.

skyline ['skaɪlaɪn] *n* **1** (horizon) horizonte *m*. **2** (of city) perfil *m*.

skyscraper ['skaɪskreɪpəʳ] *n* rascacielos *m*.

slab [slæb] *n* (of stone) losa; (of cake) trozo; (of chocolate) tableta.

slack¹ [slæk] *adj* **1** (not taut) flojo,-a: *a slack rope* una cuerda floja. **2** (careless, lax) descuidado,-a. **3** (not busy - trade, demand) flojo,-a.
► *n* (part of rope, wire, etc) parte *f* floja.
◆ **to slack off**

slack² [slæk] *n* (coal) cisco.

slacken ['slækən] *vt* **1** (rope, grip) aflojar; (reins) soltar. **2** (speed) reducir, disminuir.
► *vi* (speed) reducirse, disminuir.

slalom ['slɑːləm] *n* SP slalom *m*, eslalon *m*.

slam [slæm] *n* (of lid, book, etc) golpe *m*; (of door) portazo.
► *vt* **1** (shut forcefully) cerrar de golpe: *she slammed the door in my face* me dio con la puerta en las narices. **2** (throw noisily) arrojar, lanzar. **3** *fig* (criticize) criticar duramente. **4** (defeat) dar una paliza a. LOC **to slam on the brakes** AUTO dar un frenazo. **to slam the phone down** colgar de golpe.
ⓘ *pt & pp* **slammed**, *ger* **slamming**.

slang [slæŋ] *n* argot *m*, jerga.
► *adj* de jerga, de argot.

S

slant [slɑ:nt] *n* **1** *(gen)* inclinación *f.* **2** *(point of view)* enfoque *m*, punto de vista.
▶ *vt* **1** *(slope)* inclinar. **2** *fig (news, report, etc)* presentar tendenciosamente.
▶ *vi (slope)* inclinarse.

slap [slæp] *n* *(gen)* palmada; *(smack)* cachete *m*; *(in face)* bofetada, bofetón *m*.
COMP **a slap in the face** *(rebuff)* un desaire, una bofetada.
▶ *adv* **1** *(straight)* de lleno: *we drove slap into a wall* dimos de lleno contra una pared. **2** *(right)* justo.
▶ *vt (gen)* pegar (con la mano).
ⓘ *pt & pp* **slapped**, *ger* **slapping**.

slash [slæʃ] *n* **1** *(with sword)* tajo; *(with knife)* cuchillada. **2** *fam (oblique)* barra oblicua.
▶ *vt* **1** *(with sword)* dar un tajo a; *(with knife)* acuchillar, rajar. **2** *fig (prices, wages)* rebajar, reducir: *prices slashed* precios de remate.

slate [sleɪt] *n (gen)* pizarra. LOC **to wipe the slate clean** hacer borrón y cuenta nueva.

slaughter ['slɔ:tər] *n* matanza.
▶ *vt (animals)* matar, sacrificar; *(people)* matar brutalmente.

slaughterhouse ['slɔ:təhaʊs] *n* matadero.

slave [sleɪv] *n* esclavo,-a. COMP **slave trade** trata de esclavos.

slavery ['sleɪvəri] *n* esclavitud *f.*

sledge [sledʒ] *n* GB trineo.
▶ *vi* ir en trineo.

sleep [sli:p] *n* sueño: *I'm going to have a little sleep* voy a dormir un poco. LOC **to go to sleep 1** *(fall asleep)* dormirse. **2** *(become numb)* dormirse, entumecerse.
▶ *vi (gen)* dormir: *I slept well* he dormido bien.
◆ **to sleep in** *vi (sleep late)* quedarse en la cama, dormir hasta tarde.
ⓘ *pt & pp* **slept** [slept].

sleeping ['sli:pɪŋ] *adj* durmiente, dormido,-a. COMP **sleeping bag** saco de dormir. ‖ **Sleeping Beauty** la Bella Durmiente. ‖ **sleeping car** coche cama *m.*

sleepless ['sli:pləs] *adj* insomne. LOC **to have a sleepless night** pasar la noche en blanco.

sleepy ['sli:pɪ] *adj* **1** *(drowsy)* soñoliento,-a. **2** *(quiet, not busy)* tranquilo,-a.
ⓘ *comp* **sleepier**, *superl* **sleepiest**.

sleet [sli:t] *n* aguanieve *f.*
▶ *vi* caer aguanieve.

sleeve [sli:v] *n* **1** *(of garment)* manga. **2** *(of record)* funda. LOC **to have STH up one's sleeve** guardarse una carta en la manga.

sleigh [sleɪ] *n* trineo. COMP **sleigh bell** cascabel *m.*

slender ['slendər] *adj* **1** *(person)* delgado,-a, esbelto,-a. **2** *fig (hope, chance)* ligero,-a, remoto,-a; *(income, majority)* escaso,-a.
ⓘ *comp* **slenderer**, *comp* **slenderest**.

slept [slept] *pt & pp* → **sleep**.

slice [slaɪs] *n* **1** *(of bread)* rebanada; *(thin - ham, etc)* lonja, loncha; *(- meat)* tajada; *(- salami, lemon, etc)* rodaja. **2** *(portion - of cake, pie)* porción *f*, trozo; *(- of melon, etc)* raja. **3** *fig (share)* parte *f*; *(proportion)* proporción *f.* COMP **sliced bread** pan *m* de molde.
▶ *vt* **1** *(cut up)* cortar a rebanadas, cortar a lonjas, cortar a rodajas: *she sliced up the ham* cortó el jamón en lonchas. **2** *(cut off)* cortar: *can you slice me a piece of cake?* ¿puedes cortarme un trozo de pastel?
◆ **to slick down** *vt sep (hair)* alisar.

slid [slɪd] *pt & pp* → **slide**.

slide [slaɪd] *n* **1** *(act of sliding)* deslizamiento, desliz *m*; *(slip)* resbalón *m.* **2** *(in playground)* tobogán *m.* **3** *(photo)* diapositiva. **4** *(of microscope)* platina, portaobjetos *m.* COMP **slide projector** proyector *m* de diapositivas.
▶ *vt (gen)* deslizar, pasar; *(furniture)* correr.
▶ *vi* **1** *(slip deliberately)* deslizar, deslizarse; *(slip accidentally)* resbalar: *she slid on the ice* resbaló en el hielo. **2** *(move quietly)* deslizarse: *the drawer slid open* el cajón se abrió con facilidad.
ⓘ *pt & pp* **slid** [slɪd].

slight [slaɪt] *adj* **1** *(small in degree)* pequeño,-a, ligero,-a; *(not serious, unim-*

portant) leve, insignificante: *a slight change of plan* un pequeño cambio de planes. **2** *(person)* menudo,-a. [LOC] **not in the slightest** en absoluto.

▶ *n (affront)* desaire *m*, desprecio.

slightly ['slaɪtlɪ] *adv (a little)* ligeramente, un poco, ALGO: *I know him slightly* apenas lo conozco. [LOC] **to be slightly built** ser de complexión menuda.

slim [slɪm] *adj* **1** *(person, build)* delgado,-a, esbelto,-a. **2** *(chance, hopes, prospect)* remoto,-a.

ⓘ *comp* slimmer, *superl* slimmest.

▶ *vi* adelgazar, hacer régimen: *I'm slimming* estoy a régimen.

ⓘ *pt & pp* slimmed, *ger* slimming.

sling [slɪŋ] *n* **1** MED cabestrillo. **2** *(catapult)* honda; *(child's)* tirador *m*. **3** *(device for lifting, carrying)* cuerda; *(for baby)* canguro.

▶ *vt* **1** *fam (throw)* tirar, arrojar: *sling it in the bin* tíralo a la basura. **2** *(lift, support)* colgar.

ⓘ *pt & pp* slung [slʌŋ].

slingshot ['slɪŋʃɒt] *n* tirachinas *m*.

slip [slɪp] *n* **1** *(slide)* resbalón *m*; *(trip)* traspiés *m*, tropezón *m*. **2** *(mistake)* error *m*, equivocación *f*; *(moral)* desliz *m*. **3** *(women's underskirt)* combinación *f*; *(petticoat)* enaguas *fpl*. [COMP] **a slip of the pen** un lapsus. ‖ **a slip of the tongue** un lapsus linguae.

▶ *vi* **1** *(slide)* resbalar; *(fall, get away, escape)* caer: *my foot slipped* se me fue el pie. **2** AUTO *(clutch, tyre)* patinar.

▶ *vt* **1** *(pass, give, put)* pasar, deslizar, dar a escondidas: *she slipped the note into her bag* disimuladamente metió la nota en el bolso. **2** *(overlook, forget)* escaparse.

◆ **to slip out** *vi (secret, comment, etc)* escaparse.

ⓘ *pt & pp* slipped, *ger* slipping.

slipper ['slɪpəʳ] *n* zapatilla.

slippery ['slɪpərɪ] *adj (surface)* resbaladizo,-a

ⓘ *comp* slipperier, *superl* slipperiest.

slit [slɪt] *n (opening)* abertura, hendedura; *(cut)* corte *m*, raja: *light came*

through the slits in the blind entraba la luz por las ranuras de la persiana.

▶ *vt (cut)* cortar, rajar, hender.

ⓘ *pt & pp* slit, *ger* slitting.

slither ['slɪðəʳ] *vi* deslizarse.

slogan ['sləʊgən] *n* eslogan *m*, lema *m*.

slope [sləʊp] *n* **1** *(incline)* cuesta, pendiente *f*; *(upward)* subida; *(downward)* bajada, declive *m*: *a steep slope* una cuesta empinada. **2** *(of mountain)* ladera, falda, vertiente *f*; *(of roof)* vertiente *f*.

▶ *vi* inclinarse.

sloppy ['slɒpɪ] *adj* **1** *(messy, careless - gen)* descuidado,-a; *(- manual work)* chapucero,-a; *(- appearance, dress)* desaliñado,-a, dejado,-a. **2** *(sentimental)* empalagoso,-a.

ⓘ *comp* sloppier, *superl* sloppiest.

slot [slɒt] *n* **1** *(for coin)* ranura; *(groove)* muesca; *(opening)* rendija, abertura. **2** *(programme)* espacio; *(position, place)* puesto, hueco. [COMP] **slot machine 1** *(vending machine)* distribuidor *m* automático. **2** *(for gambling)* máquina tragaperras.

▶ *vt (insert)* insertar, introducir: *slot the coin in the machine* insertar la moneda en la máquina.

ⓘ *pt & pp* slotted, *ger* slotting.

Slovak ['sləʊvæk] *adj* eslovaco,-a.

▶ *n* **1** *(person)* eslovaco,-a. **2** *(language)* eslovaco.

Slovakia [sləʊˈvækɪə] *n* Eslovaquia.

Slovene ['sləʊviːn] *adj* esloveno,-a.

▶ *n* **1** *(person)* esloveno,-a. **2** *(language)* esloveno.

Slovenia [sləʊˈviːnə] *n* Eslovenia.

slow [sləʊ] *adj* **1** *(gen)* lento,-a: *a slow recovery* una recuperación lenta. **2** *(clock, watch)* atrasado,-a: *my watch is slow* mi reloj va atrasado. **3** *(dull, not active)* aburrido,-a. **4** *(not quick to learn)* lento,-a, torpe; *(thick)* corto,-a de alcances: *he's a slow learner* le cuesta aprender. [COMP] **to be slow about/in doing** STH tardar en hacer ALGO.

▶ *adv* despacio, lentamente: *drive slow!* ¡conduce despacio!

▶ *vt (vehicle, machine)* reducir la marcha de.

S

▸ *vi* (gen) ir más despacio.

◆ **to slow down** *vt sep* hacer ir más despacio.

▸ *vi* (gen) ir más despacio.

slowdown ['sləʊdaʊn] *n* US (workers) huelga de celo.

slowly ['sləʊlɪ] *adv* despacio, lentamente.

sludge [slʌdʒ] *n* **1** (mud) fango, cieno, lodo, barro. **2** (sewage) aguas *fpl* residuales.

slug [slʌg] *n* ZOOL babosa.

slum [slʌm] *n* **1** (place, house, etc) casuca, casucha, tugurio. **2** *fam* (tip) pocilga.
▸ *vi fam* visitar los barrios bajos.
ⓘ *pt & pp* slummed, *ger* slumming.
▸ *n pl* **slums** (area) barrios *mpl* bajos.

slump [slʌmp] *n* (recession) crisis *f* económica; (drop in demand, etc) bajón *m*, baja repentina.

slung [slʌŋ] *pt & pp* → sling.

slurp [slɜːp] *vt* sorber ruidosamente.

sly [slaɪ] *adj* **1** (cunning) astuto,-a, ladino,-a; (deceitful) tramposo,-a. **2** (secretive, knowing) furtivo,-a: *a sly smile* una sonrisa maliciosa. **3** (mischievous, playful) travieso,-a, pícaro,-a. LOC **on the sly** a escondidas.
ⓘ *comp* slyer o slier, *superl* slyest o sliest.

smack¹ [smæk] *n* **1** (slap) bofetada, tortazo, azote *m*; (blow) golpe *m*. **2** *fam* (loud kiss) besote *m*, beso sonoro.
▸ *vt* **1** (slap) dar una bofetada a, abofetear, pegar a. **2** (strike) golpear.

smack² [smæk] *n* **1** (flavour) sabor *m*; (smell) olor *m*. **2** (hint, suggestion) pizca.

small [smɔːl] *adj* **1** (not large) pequeño, -a, chico,-a: *we live in a small flat* vivimos en un piso pequeño. **2** (in height) bajo,-a, pequeño,-a: *he's a small man* es un hombre bajito. **3** (young) joven, pequeño,-a: *when I was small* cuando era pequeño. LOC **in the small hours** a altas horas de la madrugada. COMP **small ads** anuncios *mpl* por palabras, pequeños anuncios *mpl*. ▮ **small change** cambio, monedas *fpl* sueltas. ▮ **small letter** letra minúscula. ▮ **small print** letra pequeña.
ⓘ *comp* smaller, *comp* smallest.

▸ *adv* pequeño: *cut it up small* córtalo en trocitos.

smallpox ['smɔːlpɒks] *n* viruela.

smart [smɑːt] *adj* **1** (elegant) elegante, fino,-a; (chic) fino,-a, de buen tono. **2** US (clever) listo,-a, inteligente; (sharp) agudo,-a, vivo,-a; (impudent) fresco,-a, descarado,-a: *he thinks he's so smart* se cree muy listo. **3** (quick, brisk) rápido,-a, ligero,-a.

smash [smæʃ] *n* **1** (noise) estrépito, estruendo. **2** (collision) choque *m* violento, colisión *f*. **3** (blow) golpe *m*. **4** SP (tennis) smash *m*, mate *m*. **5** (success, hit) exitazo, gran éxito. COMP **smash hit** gran éxito, exitazo.
▸ *vt* **1** (break) romper; (shatter) hacer pedazos, hacer añicos; (destroy - car, room, etc) destrozar: *the vandals smashed the place up* los vándalos destrozaron el local. **2** (hit forcefully) romper; (crash, throw violently) estrellar (into, contra). **3** (defeat) vencer, aplastar; (destroy) destrozar. **4** SP (in tennis) hacer un mate.
▸ *vi* **1** (break) romperse; (shatter) hacerse añicos: *the mirror smashed into tiny pieces* el espejo se hizo añicos. **2** (crash) estrellarse (into, contra), chocar (into, contra).

smashing ['smæʃɪŋ] *adj* GB *fam* estupendo,-a, fantástico,-a, genial, fenomenal.

smear [smɪəʳ] *n* **1** (smudge, stain) mancha. **2** *fig* (defamation) calumnia.
▸ *vt* **1** (spread - butter, ointment) untar; (-grease, paint) embadurnar: *he smeared butter on the bread* untó el pan con mantequilla. **2** (make dirty) manchar. **3** *fig* (defame) calumniar, difamar.

smell [smel] *n* **1** (sense) olfato. **2** (odour) olor *m*; (perfume) perfume *m*, aroma *m*.
▸ *vt* **1** oler. **2** *fig* olfatear.
▸ *vi* **1** oler. **2** (have particular smell) oler (a).
ⓘ *pt & pp* smelled o smelt [smelt].

smelly ['smelɪ] *adj* apestoso,-a, maloliente.

smelt¹ [smelt] *vt* (melt) fundir.

smelt² [smelt] *pp* → smell.

smile [smaɪl] *n* sonrisa.
▸ *vi* (gen) sonreír.

▶ *vt (say with a smile)* decir sonriendo.

◆ **to smile on** *vi* sonreír a.

smiley ['smaɪlɪ] *n* COMPUT emoticón *m*.

smith [smɪθ] *n* herrero,-a.

smog [smɒg] *n* niebla tóxica, smog *m*.

smoke [sməʊk] *n* **1** *(gen)* humo. **2** *fam (cigarette)* cigarrillo, cigarro, pitillo.

▶ *vt* **1** *(person)* fumar. **2** *(meat, fish)* ahumar.

▶ *vi* **1** *(person)* fumar. **2** *(fire, chimney, etc)* echar humo, humear.

smoker ['sməʊkəʳ] *n* **1** *(person)* fumador,-ra. **2** *(on train)* vagón *m* de fumadores.

smoking ['sməʊkɪŋ] *adj* humeante.

▶ *n* fumar *m*.

smoky ['sməʊkɪ] *adj* lleno,-a de humo.
ⓘ *comp* smokier, *comp* smokiest.

smooth [smuːð] *adj* **1** *(surface, texture, tyre)* liso,-a; *(skin)* suave; *(road)* llano,-a, uniforme; *(sea)* tranquilo,-a, en calma. **2** *(liquid mixture, sauce)* sin grumos. **3** *(wine, beer, etc)* suave.

▶ *vt (gen)* alisar; *(with sandpaper)* lijar; *(polish)* pulir.

smother ['smʌðəʳ] *vt* **1** *(asphyxiate)* asfixiar, ahogar. **2** *(put out - fire)* sofocar, extinguir, apagar. **3** *(stifle - yawn, cough, laughter)* contener, reprimir; *(suppress - opposition)* acallar. **4** *(cover)* cubrir (in/with, de); *(heap)* colmar (in/with, de).

▶ *vi (asphyxiate)* asfixiarse, ahogarse.

smudge [smʌdʒ] *n (stain - gen)* mancha; *(- of ink)* borrón *m*.

▶ *vt (gen)* manchar; *(writing)* emborronar.

▶ *vi (ink, paint, etc)* correrse.

smuggle ['smʌgəl] *vt* **1** *(illegally)* pasar de contrabando. **2** *(sneak)* pasar a escondidas.

smuggler ['smʌgləʳ] *n* contrabandista *mf*.

snack [snæk] *n (light meal)* bocado, piscolabis *m*, tentempié *m*, refrigerio; *(in afternoon)* merienda.

▶ *vi* comer, comerse. LOC **to have a snack** picar ALGO. COMP **snack bar** cafetería.

▶ *n pl* **snacks** *(gen)* cosas *fpl* para picar; *(in bar)* tapas *fpl*.

snail [sneɪl] *n* caracol *m*.

snake [sneɪk] *n (big)* serpiente *f*; *(small)* culebra.

▶ *vi fig (river, road, etc)* serpentear.

snap [snæp] *n* **1** *(sharp noise)* ruido seco; *(of fingers, branch)* chasquido. **2** *fam (snapshot)* foto *f*, instantánea.

▶ *vt* **1** *(break)* partir en dos, romper en dos. **2** *(close)* cerrar de golpe. **3** *(click)* chasquear. **4** *(say sharply)* decir bruscamente.

▶ *vi* **1** *(break)* romperse, partirse. **2** *fig (person)* perder los nervios, sufrir una crisis nerviosa. **3** *(speak sharply)* regañar (at, a), hablar con brusquedad (at, a).
ⓘ *pt & pp* snapped, *ger* snapping.

⊕ **Snap** es también un juego de cartas en el que los jugadores van poniendo cartas sobre la mesa, y si salen dos del mismo número el primero que cante snap se las lleva todas. El que se quede sin cartas es eliminado; gana el que queda cuando los demás están eliminados.

snapshot ['snæpʃɒt] *n* foto *f*, instantánea.

snarl [snɑːl] *n (growl)* gruñido.

▶ *vi (growl)* gruñir (at, a).

▶ *vt (say)* gruñir.

snatch [snætʃ]

vt **1** *(grab)* arrebatar, arrancar, coger; *(steal)* robar; *(kidnap)* secuestrar. **2** *(sleep, food, etc)* coger, pillar; *(opportunity, etc)* aprovechar.

▶ *vi* arrebatar, quitar.

sneak [sniːk] *n fam* acusica *mf*, acusón,-ona, chivato,-a, soplón,-ona.

▶ *vt (take out)* sacar (a escondidas); *(take in)* pasar (a escondidas), colar (de extranjis).

▶ *vi* **1** *(move)* moverse sigilosamente. **2** *(tell tales)* acusar (on, a), chivarse (on, de).

sneakers ['sniːkəz] *n pl* US zapatillas *fpl* de deporte.

sneer [snɪəʳ] *n* **1** *(look)* cara de desprecio; *(smile)* sonrisa burlona. **2** *(remark)* comentario desdeñoso.

S

▶ *vi (mock)* burlarse (at, de), mofarse (at, de); *(scorn)* desdeñar, despreciar.

sneeze [sni:z] *n* estornudo.

▶ *vi* estornudar.

sniff [snɪf] *n* **1** aspiración. **2** *(inhalation)* aspiración *f* (por la nariz), inhalación *f*.

▶ *vt* **1** *(person - gen)* oler; *(animal)* olfatear, husmear. **3** *(drugs)* esnifar.

◆ **to snip off** *vt sep* cortar con tijeras.

snob [snɒb] *n* esnob *mf*.

snooker ['snu:kəʳ] *n* snooker *m*.

snoop [snu:p] *vi* **1** *(search, investigate)* husmear, fisgar. **2** *(pry)* entrometerse, meterse (into, en).

▶ *n (person)* fisgón,-ona.

snooze [snu:z] *n fam* cabezada, siestecilla.

▶ *vi fam* dormitar, echar una cabezada.

snore [snɔːʳ] *n* ronquido.

▶ *vi* roncar.

snorkel ['snɔːkəl] *n (of swimmer)* tubo de respiración; *(of submarine)* esnórquel *m*.

▶ *vi* bucear con tubo de respiración.

ⓘ *pt & pp* snorkelled (US snorkeled), ger snorkelling (US snorkeling).

snorkelling ['snɔːkəlɪŋ] *n* buceo (con tubo de respiración).

snort [snɔːt] *vi* **1** *(make noise - person)* resoplar, bufar; *(- animal)* resoplar. **2** *(say angrily, etc)* bramar, gruñir.

▶ *vt (drugs)* esnifar.

▶ *n* **1** *(person)* resoplido, bufido; *(animal)* resoplido. **2** *fam (drink)* trago.

snout [snaut] *n* **1** *(of animal)* morro, hocico. **2** GB *fam (of person)* napias *mf*, narizotas *mf*. **3** *(of gun, bottle, etc)* morro. **4** GB *sl (tobacco)* tabaco. **5** GB *sl (informer)* soplón,-ona, chivato,-a.

snow [snəʊ] *n* **1** METEOR *(gen)* nieve *f*; *(snowfall)* nevada. **2** TV nieve *f*.

▶ *vi* nevar: *it's snowing* está nevando.

snowball ['snəʊbɔːl] *n* bola de nieve.

snowboard ['snəʊbɔːd] *n* snowboard.

snowdrop ['snəʊdrɒp] *n* BOT campanilla de invierno.

snowflake ['snəʊfleɪk] *n* copo de nieve.

snowman ['snəʊmæn] *n* muñeco de nieve.

snowplough ['snəʊplaʊ] *n* quitanieves *m*.

snowshoe ['snəʊʃuː] *n* raqueta (de nieve).

snowstorm ['snəʊstɔːm] *n* tormenta de nieve.

snowy ['snəʊɪ] *adj* de nieve, nevado,-a.

ⓘ *comp* snowier, *superl* snowiest.

◆ **to snuff out** *vt sep (rebellion)* sofocar; *(hopes)* acabar con.

so [səʊ] *conj* **1** *(therefore)* así que, por lo tanto, de manera que. **2** *(to express purpose)* para, para que.

▶ *adv* **1** *(introductory)* así que, pues, bueno: *so you've decided to come* así que has decidido venir. **2** *(very - before adj or adv)* tan; *(- before noun or with verb)* tanto,-a: *she's so bored* está tan aburrida. **3** *(unspecified number or amount, limit)* tanto,-a: *I can only do so much* no puedo hacer más. **4** *(thus, in this way)* así, de esta manera, de este modo: *he's about so tall* es así de alto. **5** *(to avoid repetition)* que sí: *I think/hope so* creo/espero que sí. **6** *(to express agreement, also)* también: *so am I/so do I/so can I/so have I* yo también.

▶ *adj (factual, true)* así: *it can't be so* no puede ser. LOC **and so on (and so forth)** y así sucesivamente. ‖ **if so** de ser así. ‖ **or so** más o menos. ‖ **so far** hasta ahora. ‖ **so long!** ¡hasta luego! ‖ **so many** tantos,-as. ‖ **so much** tanto. ‖ **so much for** STH: *so much for your advice!* ¡vaya consejo que me diste! ‖ **so that** para que. ‖ **so what?** ¿y qué?

soak [səʊk] *vt (put in liquid)* poner en remojo, remojar; *(saturate)* empapar.

▶ *vi* **1** *(washing, dried pulses)* estar en remojo. **2** *(bathe)* bañarse. **3** *(penetrate)* empapar, calar.

▶ *n* **1** remojón *m*. **2** *fam (drunkard)* borracho,-a.

soap [səʊp] *n* jabón *m*: *a bar/cake/tablet of soap* una pastilla de jabón. COMP **soap opera** culebrón *m*, telenovela. ‖ **soap powder** detergente *m* en polvo.

▶ *vt* enjabonar, jabonar.

soar [sɔːʳ] *vi* **1** *(bird, plane - fly)* volar; *(- rise)* remontar el vuelo, remontarse; *(- glide)* planear. **2** *fig (prices, costs, etc)* dispararse. **3** *(building)* elevarse, alzarse.

sob [sɒb] *n* sollozo.
▶ *vi* sollozar.
▶ *vt* decir sollozando, decir entre sollozos.
ⓘ *pt & pp* sobbed, *ger* sobbing.

sober [ˈsəʊbəʳ] *adj* **1** *(not drunk)* sobrio,-a. **2** *(person)* serio,-a, formal; *(attitude)* sobrio,-a, moderado,-a, sensato,-a. **3** *(colour)* discreto,-a, sobrio,-a.

so-called [ˈsəʊkɔːld] *adj* llamado,-a, supuesto,-a.

soccer [ˈsɒkəʳ] *n* fútbol *m*.

⊕ El **soccer** es la denominación que se utiliza en Estados Unidos para hablar nuestro fútbol. La palabra **football** está reservada al fútbol americano, uno de los deportes rey del país.

sociable [ˈsəʊʃəbəl] *adj* sociable.

social [ˈsəʊʃəl] *adj* **1** *(gen)* social. **2** *fam (sociable)* sociable.
▶ *n (informal meeting)* acto social, reunión *f* (social); *(party)* fiesta; *(dance)* baile *m*.

socialism [ˈsəʊʃəlɪzəm] *n* socialismo.

socialist [ˈsəʊʃəlɪst] *adj & n* socialista *mf*.

socialize [ˈsəʊʃəlaɪz] *vi (mix socially)* relacionarse, alternar; *(at party)* mezclarse con la gente, hacer vida social.
▶ *vt* **1** TECH *(adapt to society)* socializar. **2** US *(nationalize)* nacionalizar.

society [səˈsaɪətɪ] *n* **1** *(community, people)* sociedad *f*. **2** *(fashionable group, upper class)* (alta) sociedad *f*. **3** *(organization, club)* sociedad *f*, asociación *f*, club *m*, círculo. **4** *fml (company)* compañía.
ⓘ *pl* societies.

sociology [səʊsɪˈɒlədʒɪ] *n* sociología.

sock [sɒk] *n* calcetín *m*.

socket [ˈsɒkɪt] *n* **1** ANAT *(of eye)* cuenca, órbita; *(of joint)* glena. **2** ELEC *(for plug)* enchufe *m*, toma de corriente; *(for light bulb)* portalámparas *m*. COMP **socket wrench** llave *f* de tubo.

soda [ˈsəʊdə] *n* **1** CHEM sosa, soda. **2** *(soda water)* soda, sifón *m*. **3** US *(pop)* refresco. **4** *(ice-cream soda)* soda con helado y almíbar.

sodium [ˈsəʊdɪəm] *n* CHEM sodio. COMP **sodium bicarbonate** bicarbonato sódico.

sofa [ˈsəʊfə] *n* sofá *m*.

soft [sɒft] *adj* **1** *(not hard)* blando,-a; *(spongy)* esponjoso,-a; *(flabby)* fofo,-a. **2** *(skin, hair, fur, etc)* suave. **3** *(light, music, colour)* suave; *(words)* tierno,-a; *(breeze, steps, knock)* ligero,-a; *(outline)* difuminado,-a; *(voz)* baja. **4** *fam (easy)* fácil. COMP **soft copy** datos *mpl* contenidos en la memoria del ordenador. **‖ soft drink** refresco. **‖ soft palate** velo del paladar.

soft-boiled [ˈsɒftˈbɔɪld] *adj (egg)* pasado por agua.

soften [ˈsɒfən] *vt* suavizar, ablandar.
▶ *vi (leather, heart, butter)* ablandarse; *(skin)* suavizarse.

softener [ˈsɒfənəʳ] *n* suavizante *m*.

software [ˈsɒftweəʳ] *n* COMPUT software *m*.

soggy [ˈsɒgɪ] *adj* **1** *(wet)* empapado,-a, saturado,-a. **2** *(too soft)* pastoso,-a, gomoso,-a.
ⓘ *comp* soggier, *superl* soggiest.

soil [sɔɪl] *n* **1** *(earth)* tierra. **2** *fml (country, territory)* tierra.
▶ *vt* **1** *(dirty)* ensuciar; *(stain)* manchar. **2** *fig (reputation)* manchar.
▶ *vi* ensuciarse.

soiled [sɔɪld] *adj (dirty)* sucio,-a; *(stained)* manchado,-a.

solar [ˈsəʊləʳ] *adj* solar. COMP **solar cell** célula solar. **‖ solar corona** corona solar. **‖ solar energy** energía solar. **‖ solar plexus** plexo solar. **‖ solar year** año solar. **‖ the solar system** el sistema *m* solar.

sold [sləpt] *pt & pp* → **sell**.

solder [ˈsɒldəʳ] *n* soldadura.
▶ *vt* soldar.

soldier [ˈsəʊldʒəʳ] *n (not officer)* soldado; *(military man)* militar *m*. COMP **a soldier of fortune** un mercenario.

sole¹ [səʊl] *n (fish)* lenguado.

sole² [səʊl] *adj* **1** *(only, single)* único,-a. **2** *(exclusive)* exclusivo,-a.

sole³ [səʊl] *n* *(of foot)* planta; *(of shoe, sock)* suela.
▸ *vt* poner suela a.]

solicitor [sə'lɪsɪtə'] *n* **1** GB abogado,-a. **2** US oficial *mf* de justicia.

solid ['sɒlɪd] *adj* **1** *(not liquid or gas)* sólido,-a. **2** *(not hollow)* macizo,-a. **3** *(dense, compact)* compacto,-a. **4** *(unmixed)* puro,-a, macizo,-a. **5** *(strong)* sólido,-a, fuerte. **6** *(reliable)* sólido,-a, de confianza, de fiar. **7** *(unanimous)* unánime. **8** *(continuous)* seguido,-a, entero, -a; *(unbroken)* continuo,-a. **9** TECH *(three-dimensional)* tridimensional.
▸ *n (substance)* sólido.

solidarity [sɒlɪ'dærətɪ] *n* solidaridad *f*.

solidification [səlɪdɪfɪ'keɪ[ə]n] *n* solidificación *f*.

solidify [sə'lɪdɪfaɪ] *vt* solidificar.
▸ *vi* solidificarse.
ⓘ *pt & pp* **solidified**, *ger* **solidifying**.

solitary ['sɒlɪt*ə*rɪ] *adj* **1** *(alone)* solitario, -a. **2** *(secluded, remote)* apartado,-a, retirado,-a. **3** *(only, sole)* solo,-a, único,-a.

solitude ['sɒlɪtjuːd] *n* soledad *f*.

solo ['səʊləʊ] *n* **1** MUS solo. **2** AV vuelo en solitario. **3** *(card game)* solitario.
ⓘ *pl* **solos**.
▸ *adj* **1** MUS *(performance, album)* en solitario; *(instrument)* solo; *(piece)* para solista. **2** *(attempt, flight)* en solitario.
▸ *adv* **1** MUS *(play, sing)* solo,-a. **2** *(fly)* en solitario.

soloist ['səʊləʊɪst] *n* MUS solista *mf*.

solstice ['sɒlstɪs] *n* solsticio.

soluble ['sɒljəbəl] *adj* soluble.

solution [sə'ljuːʃən] *n* solución *m*.

solve [sɒlv] *vt* *(problem)* resolver, solucionar; *(case, equation)* resolver.

solvent ['sɒlvənt] *adj* **1** *(not in debt)* solvente. **2** *(that can dissolve)* soluble.
▸ *n* solvente *m*, disolvente *m*.

Somali [sə'mɑːlɪ] *adj* somalí.
▸ *n* somalí *mf*.

Somalia [sə'mɑːlɪə] *n* Somalia.

some [sʌm] *adj* **1** *(with plural noun)* unos, -as, algunos,-as; *(a few)* unos,-as

cuantos,-as, unos,-as pocos,-as: *there were some flowers on the table* había unas flores en la mesa. **2** *(with singular noun)* algún, alguna; *(a little)* algo de, un poco de: *would you like some coffee?* ¿quieres un poco de café? **3** *(certain)* cierto,-a, alguno,-a: *some days are better than others* algunos días son mejores que otros. **4** *(unknown, unspecified)* algún, alguna: *some day* un día de éstos. **5** *(quite a lot of)* bastante: *she's been gone some time* hace ya bastante tiempo que se ha ido. **6** *fam iron (none, not at all)* valiente, menudo,-a: *some help that was!* ¡valiente ayuda! **7** *fam (quite a lot, a fine)* menudo,-a: *that was some meal!* ¡menuda comida!
▸ *pron* **1** *(unspecified number)* unos,-as, algunos,-as: *I'll have to buy some potatoes* tendré que comprar patatas. **2** *(unspecified amount)* no se traduce: *if you want more paper, there's some in the drawer* si te hace falta más papel, hay en el cajón. **3** *(certain ones)* ciertos,-as, algunos,-as; *(a certain part)* algo, un poco, parte *f*: *some of my friends* algunos amigos míos.
▸ *adv* **1** *(approximately, about)* unos,-as, alrededor de, aproximadamente: *there were some twenty people* había unas veinte personas. **2** US *fam (rather, a little)* un poco: *they waited some* esperaron un poco.

somebody ['sʌmbədɪ] *pron* alguien: *somebody must have lost it* alguien debe haberlo perdido. ⓁⓄⒸ **somebody else** otro,-a, otra persona.

somehow ['sʌmhaʊ] *adv* **1** *(in some way)* de algún modo, de alguna manera. **2** *(for some reason)* por alguna razón.

someone ['sʌmwʌn] *pron* → **somebody**.

someplace ['sʌmpleɪs] *adv* US → **somewhere**.

somersault ['sʌməsɔːlt] *n* *(by acrobat)* salto mortal; *(by child)* voltereta; *(by car)* vuelta de campana.
▸ *vi* *(acrobat)* dar un salto mortal; *(child)* dar volteretas; *(car)* dar una vuelta de campana.

something ['sʌmθɪŋ] *pron* **1** algo. **2** *(a thing of value)* algo. **3** *(in vague or ill-defined statements)* algo.

▶ *adv*: it costs something like 100 pounds cuesta unas cien libras.

sometime ['sʌmtaɪm] *adv* algún día.
▶ *adj fml (former)* antiguo,-a, ex-.

sometimes ['sʌmtaɪmz] *adv* a veces, de vez en cuando.

somewhat ['sʌmwɒt] *adv* algo, un tanto.

somewhere ['sʌmweə^r] *adv* **1** *(in some place)* en alguna parte; *(to some place)* a alguna parte. **2** *(approximately)* más o menos, alrededor de.
▶ *pron* un lugar, un sitio. LOC **somewhere else 1** *(in)* en otra parte, en otro sitio. **2** *(to)* a otra parte, a otro sitio.

son [sʌn] *n* hijo.

song [sɒŋ] *n (gen)* canción *f*; *(art, of bird)* canto.

songbird ['sɒŋbɜːd] *n* pájaro cantor, ave *f* canora.

songbook ['sɒŋbʊk] *n* cancionero.

songwriter ['sɒŋraɪtə^r] *n* compositor, -ra (de canciones).

son-in-law ['sʌnɪnlɔː] *n* yerno.
ⓘ *pl* sons-in-law.

soon [suːn] *adv* **1** *(within a short time)* pronto, dentro de poco. **2** *(early)* pronto, temprano. **3** *(expressing preference, readiness, willingness)*: I'd (just) as soon eat in as... preferiría comer en casa que... LOC **as soon as** tan pronto como. **as soon as possible** cuanto antes. **soon afterwards** poco después.

sooner ['suːnə^r] *adv* **1** *(earlier)* más temprano. **2** *(rather)* antes. LOC **no sooner said than done** dicho y hecho. **sooner or later** tarde o temprano. **the sooner the better** cuanto antes mejor.

soot [sʊt] *n* hollín *m*.

soothe [suːð] *vt* **1** *(calm)* calmar, tranquilizar, aplacar; *(quieten)* acallar. **2** *(ease pain)* aliviar, calmar.

sorcerer ['sɔːsərə^r] *n* hechicero, brujo.

sorcery ['sɔːsəri] *n* hechicería, brujería.

sore [sɔː^r] *adj* **1** *(aching)* dolorido,-a; *(painful)* doloroso,-a; *(inflamed)* inflamado,-a. **2** US *fam (angry)* enfadado,-a (about, por), picado,-a (about, por).

3 *lit (great)* enorme, gran; *(serious)* grave; *(urgent)* urgente.
▶ *n* MED llaga, úlcera.

sorrow ['sɒrəʊ] *n* **1** *(grief)* pena, pesar *m*, dolor *m*. **2** *(cause of sadness)* disgusto.
▶ *vi* llorar (at/over/for, por).

sorry ['sɒri] *adj (pitiful, wretched)* triste, lamentable. LOC **to be sorry** *(grieved, feeling sadness)* sentir. **to feel sorry for** SB compadecer. **to say sorry** disculparse, pedir perdón.
ⓘ *comp* sorrier, *superl* sorriest.
▶ *interj* **1** *(apology)* ¡perdón!, ¡disculpe! **2** GB *(for repetition)* ¿perdón?, ¿cómo?

sort [sɔːt] *n* **1** *(type, kind)* clase *f*, tipo, género, suerte *f*; *(make, brand)* marca. **2** *fam (person)* tipo,-a, tío,-a. LOC **a sort of** una especie de. **of a sort / of sorts** una especie de. **nothing of the sort** nada semejante. **sort of** en cierto modo.
▶ *vt* **1** *(classify)* clasificar. **2** *(repair)* arreglar.
▶ *vi (check)* revisar (through, -).
◆ **to sort out** *vt sep* **1** *(classify)* clasificar; *(put in order)* ordenar, poner en orden. **2** *(separate)* separar (from, de). **3** *(solve - problem)* arreglar, solucionar; *(- misunderstanding)* aclarar. **4** *(arrange)* organizar, arreglar; *(set - date)* fijar. **5** *(deal with - person)* meter en vereda.

so-so ['səʊsəʊ] *adv fam* así así, regular.

sought [sɔːt] *pt & pp* → seek.

soul [səʊl] *n* **1** REL alma, espíritu *m*. **2** *(spirit)* espíritu *m*; *(feeling, character)* carácter *m*, personalidad *f*. **3** *(person)* alma, persona. **4** MUS soul *m*, música soul.

sound¹ [saʊnd] *adj* **1** *(healthy)* sano,-a. **2** *(solid)* sólido,-a, firme; *(in good condition)* en buen estado. **3** *(sensible)* sensato,-a, acertado,-a; *(valid)* sólido,-a, lógico,-a, razonable; *(responsible)* responsable, formal, de fiar; *(reliable, safe)* seguro,-a. **4** *(thorough)* completo,-a; *(severe)* severo,-a. **5** *(of sleep)* profundo,-a. LOC **to be sound asleep** estar dormido como un tronco.

sound² [saʊnd] *vt* **1** MAR sondar. **2** MED *(gen)* sondar; *(chest)* auscultar.
▶ *n* MED sonda.

S

sound³ [saund] n GEOG estrecho, brazo de mar.

sound⁴ [saund] n **1** *(gen)* sonido; *(noise)* ruido. **2** TV *(volume)* volumen m. **3** *(impression, idea)* idea. COMP **sound effects** efectos sonoros.
▶ vt **1** *(bell, horn, trumpet)* tocar, hacer sonar; *(alarm)* dar (la señal de); *(retreat)* tocar. **2** LING pronunciar.
▶ vi **1** *(bell, horn, alarm, etc)* sonar, resonar. **2** *(seem)* parecer; *(give impression)* sonar. **3** LING pronunciarse, sonar.

soundtrack ['saundtræk] n banda sonora.

soup [su:p] n CULIN *(gen)* sopa; *(clear, thin)* caldo, consomé m.

sour ['sauəʳ] adj **1** *(fruit)* ácido,-a, agrio, -a; *(milk)* cortado,-a, agrio,-a; *(wine)* agrio,-a. **2** *(person)* amargado,-a, avinagrado,-a; *(behaviour, expression)* agrio,-a, avinagrado,-a.
▶ vt **1** *(milk)* agriar, cortar. **2** *(person, relationship)* amargar.
▶ vi **1** *(milk)* agriarse, cortarse; *(wine)* agriarse. **2** *(person, character)* amargarse, avinagrarse.

source [sɔ:s] n **1** *(of river)* fuente f, nacimiento. **2** *(origin, cause)* fuente f, origen m.

south [sauθ] n sur m.
▶ adj sur, del sur, meridional. COMP **South American** sudamericano,-a. **the South Pole** el Polo Sur.
▶ adv *(direction)* hacia el sur; *(location)* al sur.
▶ n **the South** el Sur m, el sur m.

southeast [sauθi:st] n sudeste m.
▶ adj sudeste, del sudeste.
▶ adv *(direction)* hacia el sudeste; *(location)* al sudeste.

southern ['sʌðᵊn] adj del sur, meridional, austral. COMP **Southern Europe** Europa del Sur.

southward ['sauθwəd] adj hacia el sur, en dirección sur.
▶ adv al sur, hacia el sur.

southwards ['sauθwədz] adv *(direction)* hacia el sur; *(location)* al sur.

southwest [sauθwest] n suroeste m.
▶ adj suroeste, del suroeste.
▶ adv al suroeste, hacia el suroeste.

souvenir [su:vəˈnɪəʳ] n recuerdo *(of, de)*.

sovereign ['sɒvrɪn] n **1** soberano,-a. **2** GB *(coin)* soberano.
▶ adj soberano,-a.

sow¹ [sau] n ZOOL cerda, puerca.

sow² [səu] vt *(gen)* sembrar (with, de).
ⓘ pt **sowed**, pp **sowed** o **sown** [səun].

sown [səun] pp → **sow**.

soy [sɔɪ] n US soja.

soya ['sɔɪə] n GB soja. COMP **soya bean** soja.

spa [spa:] n **1** *(resort)* balneario; *(baths)* baños mpl, termas fpl. **2** US *(jacuzzi)* jacuzzi m. **3** US *(gymnasium)* gimnasio.

space [speɪs] n **1** PHYS espacio. **2** *(continuous expanse)* espacio. **3** *(room, unoccupied area)* espacio, sitio, lugar m. **4** *(gap, empty place)* espacio, hueco. **5** *(in time)* espacio, lapso. COMP **space lab** laboratorio espacial. **space probe** sonda espacial. **space ship** nave f espacial. **space shuttle** transbordador m espacial.

space-bar ['speɪsba:ʳ] n barra espaciadora m.

spacecraft ['speɪskra:ft] n nave f espacial.
ⓘ pl **spacecraft**.

spaceship ['speɪsʃɪp] n nave f espacial.

spade¹ [speɪd] n *(playing card - international pack)* pica; *(- Spanish pack)* espada.

spade² [speɪd] n *(for digging)* pala.

| ❌ Spade no significa 'espada', que se traduce por **sword**. |

spaghetti [spəˈgetɪ] n espagueti m.

Spain [speɪn] n España.

span¹ [spæn] pt → **spin**.

span² [spæn] n **1** *(of wings)* envergadura; *(of arch, bridge)* luz f, ojo; *(of hand)* palmo. **2** *(of time)* período, lapso.
▶ vt **1** *(cross)* atravesar, cruzar. **2** *(extend over)* abarcar, extenderse a.
ⓘ pt & pp **spanned**, ger **spanning**.

Spaniard ['spænjəd] n *(person)* español,-la.

Spanish ['spænɪʃ] *adj* español,-la. COMP
Spanish America Hispanoamérica. ▮
Spanish guitar guitarra clásica.
▶ *n* **1** *(person)* español,-la. **2** *(language)*
español *m*, castellano.
▶ *n pl* the Spanish los españoles *mpl*.

spanner ['spænəʳ] *n* llave *f* de tuerca.

spare [speəʳ] *adj* **1** *(reserve)* de repuesto; *(free)* libre; *(extra)* de sobra. **2** *(thin, lean)* enjuto,-a.
▶ *n (spare part)* recambio, repuesto.
COMP spare room habitación *f* de invitados. ▮ spare time tiempo libre. ▮
spare tyre **1** *(wheel)* rueda de recambio. **2** *(stomach)* michelín *m*. ▮ spare
wheel rueda de recambio.
▶ *vt* **1** *(do without)* prescindir de, pasar
sin. **2** *(begrudge)* escatimar. **3** *(save, relieve)* ahorrar, evitar.

spark [spɑːk] *n* **1** *(from fire, electrical)* chispa. **2** *(trace)* chispa, pizca. **3** *(cause, trigger)* chispazo. COMP spark plug bujía.
▶ *vi* echar chispas, chispear.

sparking plug ['spɑːkɪŋplʌg] *n* AUTO
bujía.

sparkle ['spɑːkəl] *n* **1** *(of diamond, glass)*
centelleo, destello, brillo; *(of eyes)* brillo. **2** *fig (liveliness)* viveza; *(wit)* brillo.
▶ *vi* **1** *(gen)* brillar; *(firework)* echar chispas, chispear. **2** *fig (person)* brillar, lucirse; *(conversation)* brillar.

sparkler ['spɑːkələʳ] *n* **1** *(firework)* bengala. **2** *fam (gem)* brillante *m*.

sparrow ['spærəu] *n* gorrión *m*.

sparse [spɑːs] *adj (vegetation)* escaso,-a,
poco denso,-a; *(population)* disperso,-a, esparcido,-a; *(hair)* ralo,-a; *(information)* escaso,-a.

spasm ['spæzəm] *n* **1** MED espasmo. **2**
(of coughing, laughing, etc) ataque *m*, acceso; *(of anger)* arrebato, acceso.

spat [spæt] *pt & pp* → **spit²**.

spatter ['spætəʳ] *vt (splash)* salpicar
(with, de); *(sprinkle)* rociar (with, de).
▶ *vi* salpicar.
▶ *n (spattered spot)* salpicadura, manchita; *(small amount)* pizca.

speak [spiːk] *vi* **1** *(gen)* hablar. **2** *(make
speech)* pronunciar un discurso. **3** *(on
phone)* hablar.

▶ *vt* **1** *(utter, say)* decir. **2** *(language)* hablar. LOC generally/roughly speaking
en términos generales. ▮ personally
speaking personalmente. ▮ speaking
of... a propósito de...
◆ to speak for *vt insep (state views, wishes
of)* hablar en nombre de.
◆ to speak out *vi (speak openly)* hablar
claro.
◆ to speak up *vi* **1** *(speak more loudly)*
hablar más fuerte. **2** *(give opinion)* defender.
ⓘ *pt* spoke [spəuk], *pp* spoken
[spəukən].

speaker ['spiːkəʳ] *n* **1** *(gen)* persona que
habla, el que habla, la que habla; *(in
dialogue)* interlocutor,-ra; *(in public)*
orador,-ra; *(lecturer)* conferenciante
mf. **2** *(of language)* hablante *mf*. **3** *(loudspeaker)* altavoz *m*.
▶ *n* the Speaker **1** GB el/la presidente,-a de la Cámara de los Comunes.
2 US el/la presidente,-a de la Cámara de
los Representantes.

spear [spɪəʳ] *n* **1** *(gen)* lanza; *(javelin)* jabalina; *(harpoon)* arpón *m*. **2** BOT punta.
▶ *vt (with fork)* pinchar; *(with harpoon)*
arponear; *(impale with spear)* atravesar
con una lanza.

special ['speʃəl] *adj* **1** *(not ordinary or usual)*
especial; *(exceptional)* extraordinario,
-a. **2** *(specific)* específico,-a, particular.
▶ *n* **1** *(train)* tren *m* especial. **2** *(TV programme)* programa *m* especial. **3** US
(special offer) oferta especial.

speciality [speʃɪˈælɪtɪ] *n* especialidad *f*.
ⓘ *pl* specialities.

specialize ['speʃəlaɪz] *vi* especiliazarse.

species ['spiːʃiːz] *n* especie *f*.
ⓘ *pl* species.

specific [spəˈsɪfɪk] *adj* **1** *(particular, not
general)* específico,-a; *(definite)* concreto,-a. **2** *(exact, detailed, precise)* preciso,-a; *(clear in meaning)* explícito,-a.
▶ *n* MED *(drug)* específico.
▶ *n pl* **specifics** *(particulars, details)* datos
mpl (concretos).

specify ['spesɪfaɪ] *vt* especificar, precisar, concretar.
ⓘ *pt & pp* specified, *ger* specifying.

S

specimen ['spesɪmən] *n* **1** *(sample)* espécimen *m*, muestra. **2** *(example)* ejemplar *m*. **3** *fam pej (person)* tipo,-a.

speck [spek] *n* **1** *(of dust, soot)* mota; *(stain)* manchita; *(dot)* punto negro. **2** *(trace)* pizca.

spectacle ['spektəkᵊl] *n (show, display)* espectáculo.
▶ *n pl* **spectacles** gafas *fpl*.

spectacular [spek'tækjələʳ] *adj* espectacular.

spectator [spek'teɪtəʳ] *n* espectador,-ra.
▶ *n pl* **the spectators** el público *m sing*.

specter ['spektəʳ] *n* US → spectre.

spectre ['spektəʳ] *n* espectro.

spectrum ['spektrəm] *n* **1** PHYS espectro. **2** *(range)* espectro, gama.
ⓘ *pl* **spectra** ['spektrə].

sped [sped] *pt & pp* → speed.

speech [spi:tʃ] *n* **1** *(faculty, act)* habla. **2** *(spoken language, way of speaking)* habla, manera de hablar. **3** *(formal talk)* discurso, alocución *f; (informal talk)* charla; *(lectura)* conferencia; *(lines in play)* diálogo. COMP **direct speech** estilo directo. **I indirect speech** estilo indirecto. **I part of speech** parte de la oración.
ⓘ *pl* **speeches**.

speed [spi:d] *n* **1** *(rate of movement)* velocidad *f; (quickness)* rapidez *f; (haste)* prisa. **2** *(sensitivity of film)* sensibilidad *f*, velocidad *f; (time of shutter)* tiempo de exposición, abertura. **3** *(gear)* marcha, velocidad *f*. **4** *sl (drug)* speed *m*, anfetas *fpl*. COMP **speed limit** límite *m* de velocidad.
▶ *vi* **1** *(go fast)* ir corriendo, ir a toda prisa, ir a toda velocidad. **2** *(break limit)* ir a exceso de velocidad.
1 *(hurry - process, matter)* acelerar. **2** *(take quickly)* hacer llegar rápidamente.
◆ **to speed up** *vt sep (process, matter, production)* acelerar; *(person)* apresurar, meter prisa a.
▶ *vi (vehicle)* acelerar; *(person, process, production)* acelerarse, apresurarse, darse prisa.
ⓘ *pt & pp* **speeded o sped** [sped].

speedboat ['spi:dbəʊt] *n* lancha rápida.

speeding ['spi:dɪŋ] *n* AUTO exceso de velocidad.

speedometer [spɪ'dɒmɪtəʳ] *n* velocímetro.

speedway ['spi:dweɪ] *n* **1** *(racing)* carreras *fpl* de moto. **2** *(track)* pista de carreras, circuito.

speedy ['spi:dɪ] *adj (quick)* rápido,-a, veloz; *(prompt)* pronto,-a, rápido,-a.
ⓘ *comp* **speedier**, *superl* **speediest**.

speleology [spi:lɪ'ɒlədʒɪ] *n* espeleología.

spell¹ [spel] *n (magical)* hechizo, encanto.

spell³ [spel] *vt* **1** *(orally)* deletrear; *(written)* escribir correctamente. **2** *fig (mean)* significar, representar; *(bring)* traer, acarrear; *(foretell)* anunciar, augurar, presagiar.
▶ *vi* saber escribir correctamente.
◆ **to spell out** *vt sep* **1** *(word)* deletrear. **2** *(explain in detail)* explicar con detalle, detallar, pormenorizar.
ⓘ *pt & pp* **spelled o spelt** [spelt].

spelling ['spelɪŋ] *n* ortografía. COMP **spelling mistake** falta de ortografía.

spelt [spelt] *pt & pp* → spell.

spend [spend] *vt* **1** *(money)* gastar (on, en). **2** *(pass time)* pasar. **3** *(devote time/energy)* dedicar (on, a), invertir (on, en). **4** *(use up, exhaust)* gastar, agotar.
▶ *vi (money)* gastar.
ⓘ *pt & pp* **spent** [spent].

spent [spent] *pt & pp* → spend.
▶ *adj* **1** *(used)* usado,-a, gastado,-a. **2** *(exhausted)* agotado,-a; *(finished)* acabado,-a.

sperm [spɜ:m] *n* esperma *mf*. COMP **sperm whale** cachalote *m*.

sphere [sfɪəʳ] *n* **1** *(shape)* esfera. **2** *(area, range, extent)* esfera, ámbito.

spherical ['sferɪkəl] *adj* esférico,-a.

sphincter ['sfɪŋktəʳ] *n* esfínter *m*.

sphinx [sfɪŋks] *n* esfinge *f*.

spice [spaɪs] *n* **1** especia. **2** *fig* sazón *m*, sal *f*, salsa, sabor *m*.
▶ *vt* **1** CULIN sazonar, condimentar. **2** *(story, etc)* echar salsa a (up, -).

spicy ['spaɪsɪ] *adj* **1** CULIN *(seasoned)* sazonado,-a, condimentado,-a; *(hot)* picante. **2** *fig (story, etc)* picante.
ⓘ *comp* spicier, *superl* spiciest.

spider ['spaɪdəʳ] *n* araña. COMP **spider's web** telaraña.

spied [spaɪd] *pt & pp* → spy.

spike¹ [spaɪk] *n* **1** *(sharp point)* punta, pincho; *(sharp-pointed object)* objeto puntiagudo. **2** *(on running shoe)* clavo.
► *vt* **1** *(with shoes)* clavar. **2** *(drink)* echar alcohol a.

spike² [spaɪk] *n* BOT espiga.

spill [spɪl] *vt (liquid)* derramar, verter; *(knock over)* volcar.
► *vi* **1** *(liquid)* derramarse, verterse. **2** *(people)* salir en tropel.
◆ **to spill over** *vi (liquid)* salirse, desbordarse; *(people)* rebosar; *(conflict)* extenderse.
ⓘ *pt & pp* spilled o spilt [spɪlt].

spilt [spɪlt] *pt & pp* → spill.

spin [spɪn] *n* **1** *(turn)* vuelta, giro, revolución *f*. **2** *(of washing machine)* centrifugado. **3** SP *(of ball)* efecto. **4** *(of plane)* barrena; *(of car)* patinazo. **5** *(ride, trip)* vuelta, paseo (en coche o en moto).
► *vt* **1** *(make turn)* hacer girar, dar vueltas a. **2** *(washing)* centrifugar. **3** *(ball)* darle efecto a. **4** *(cotton, wool, etc)* hilar; *(spider's web)* tejer.
► *vi* **1** *(turn)* girar, dar vueltas. **2** *(washing machine)* centrifugar. **3** *(cotton, wool, etc)* hilar. **4** *(plane)* caer en barrena; *(car)* patinar. **5** *(move rapidly)* girar(se), darse la vuelta.
ⓘ *pt* spun [spʌn] o span [spæn], *pp* spun [spʌn], *ger* spinning.

spinach ['spɪnɪdʒ] *n* **1** BOT espinaca. **2** CULIN espinacas *fpl*.

spinal ['spaɪnəl] *adj* espinal, vertebral. COMP **spinal column** columna vertebral. **‖ spinal cord** médula espinal.

spin-dryer [spɪn'draɪəʳ] *n* secador *m* centrífugo, centrifugadora.

spine [spaɪn] *n* **1** ANAT columna vertebral, espina dorsal, espinazo. **2** *(of book)* lomo. **3** ZOOL *(of hedgehog, etc)* púa. **4** BOT espina.

spinning ['spɪnɪŋ] *n (action)* hilado; *(art)* hilandería. COMP **spinning top** peonza, trompo. **‖ spinning wheel** rueca, torno de hilar.

spiny ['spaɪnɪ] *adj* espinoso,-a.
ⓘ *comp* spinier, *superl* spiniest.

spiral ['spaɪərəl] *n* espiral *f*.
► *adj* espiral, en espiral.
► *vi* **1** *(move in a spiral)* moverse en espiral. **2** *(increase rapidly)* dispararse.

spire [spaɪəʳ] *n* aguja.

spirit¹ ['spɪrɪt] *n* CHEM alcohol *m*.
► *n pl* **spirits** *(alcoholic drink)* bebidas *fpl* alcohólicas, licores *mpl*.

spirit² ['spɪrɪt] *n* **1** *(soul)* espíritu *m*, alma; *(ghost)* fantasma *m*. **2** *(person)* ser *m*, alma. **3** *(force, vigour)* vigor *m*, energía; *(personality)* carácter *m*; *(courage)* valor *m*.

spiritual ['spɪrɪtjʊəl] *adj* espiritual.
► *n (song)* espiritual *m* negro.

spit¹ [spɪt] *n* **1** CULIN asador *m*, espetón *m*. **2** GEOG *(of sand)* banco; *(of land)* punta, lengua.

spit² [spɪt] *n (saliva)* saliva, esputo.
► *vt (gen)* escupir.
► *vi* **1** *(gen)* escupir (at, a), (on, en). **2** *(rain)* chispear. **3** *(sputter)* chisporrotear.
◆ **to spit out** *vt sep* **1** *(gen)* escupir. **2** *fig (say sharply)* soltar.
ⓘ *pt & pp* spat [spæt].

spite [spaɪt] *n (ill will)* rencor *m*, ojeriza. LOC **in spite of** a pesar de, pese a
► *vt* fastidiar.

spiteful ['spaɪtfʊl] *adj (person)* rencoroso,-a, malévolo,-a; *(comment)* malicioso,-a.

spittle ['spɪtəl] *n* saliva, baba.

splash [splæʃ] *n* **1** *(noise)* chapoteo. **2** *(spray)* salpicadura, rociada. **3** *(small amount)* gota, chorrito, poco. **4** *fig (of light, colour, etc)* mancha.
► *vt* **1** *(gen)* salpicar (with, de), rociar (with, de). **2** *fam (of news, story, etc)* sacar, salir.
ⓘ *pl* splashes.
► *vi* **1** *(of liquid)* salpicar, esparcirse. **2** *(move noisily)* chapotear (about/around, -).
◆ **to splash down** *vi* amarar, amerizar.

S

◆ **to splash out** *vi fam* darse un lujo, gastarse un dineral.

spleen [spliːn] *n* ANAT bazo.

splendid ['splendɪd] *adj* **1** *(excellent)* estupendo,-a, maravilloso,-a. **2** *(magnificent)* espléndido,-a, magnífico,-a.

⊠ Splendid no significa 'espléndido (generoso)', que se traduce por lavish.

splinter ['splɪntəʳ] *n (of wood)* astilla; *(of metal, bone, stone)* esquirla; *(of glass)* fragmento.

split [splɪt] *n* **1** *(crack, cut, break)* grieta, raja. **2** *(tear - in garment)* desgarrón *m*, rasgón *m*; *(- in seam)* descosido. **3** *(division)* división *f*, ruptura. **4** *(division, sharing out)* reparto.

► *adj* **1** *(cracked)* partido,-a, rajado,-a; *(torn)* desgarrado,-a, rasgado,-a. **2** *(divided)* dividido,-a.

► *vt* **1** *(crack, break)* agrietar; *(cut)* partir. **2** *(tear - garment)* rajar, desgarrar; *(- seam)* descoser. **3** PHYS *(atom)* desintegrar. **4** *(divide, separate)* dividir (up, -).

► *vi* **1** *(crack)* agrietarse, rajarse; *(in two parts)* partirse. **2** *(tear - garment)* rajarse, desgarrarse; *(- seams)* descoserse. **3** *(divide)* dividirse (up, -).

◆ **to split up** *vt sep (friends, lovers)* separar. ► *vi (crowd, meeting)* dispersarse; *(couple)* separarse, romper.

ⓘ *pt & pp* split, *ger* splitting.

spoil [spɔɪl] *vt* **1** *(ruin)* estropear, echar a perder, arruinar. **2** *(invalidate)* anular. **3** *(make child selfish)* mimar, consentir; *(indulge)* complacer.

► *vi (food)* estropearse, echarse a perder.

ⓘ *pt & pp* spoiled o spoilt [spɔɪlt].

spoilt [spɔɪlt] *pp* → spoil.

► *adj* **1** *(food, etc)* estropeado,-a. **2** *(child)* mimado,-a, consentido,-a. **3** *(ballot paper)* nulo,-a.

spoke¹ [spəʊk] *n (of wheel)* radio, rayo.

spoke² [spəʊk] *pt* → speak.

spoken ['spəʊk°n] *pt & pp* → speak.
► *adj* hablado,-a, oral.

spokesman ['spəʊksmən] *n* portavoz *m*
ⓘ *pl* spokesmen ['spəʊksmən].

spokesperson ['spəʊkspɜːs°n] *n* portavoz *mf*.

ⓘ *pl* spokespersons o spokespeople ['spəʊkspiːp°l].

spokeswoman ['spəʊkswʊmən] *n* portavoz *f*.

ⓘ *pl* spokeswomen ['spəʊkswɪmɪn].

sponge [spʌndʒ] *n* **1** *(gen)* esponja. **2** GB *(cake)* bizcocho. COMP **sponge cake** bizcocho.

sponsor ['spɒnsəʳ] *n* **1** *(gen)* patrocinador,-ra, sponsor *mf*; *(for arts)* mecenas *mf*. **2** FIN avalador,-ra, garante *mf*.

► *vt* **1** *(gen)* patrocinar; *(studies, research)* subvencionar. **2** *(support)* apoyar, respaldar. **3** FIN avalar, garantizar.

spontaneous [spɒnˈteɪnɪəs] *adj* espontáneo,-a.

spooky ['spuːkɪ] *adj fam* escalofriante, espeluznante, horripilante.

ⓘ *comp* spookier, *superl* spookiest.

spool [spuːl] *n* carrete *m*, bobina.

spoon [spuːn] *n* cuchara.

spoonful ['spuːnfʊl] *n* cucharada.

ⓘ *pl* spoonfuls o spoonsful.

sport [spɔːt] *n* **1** *(gen)* deporte *m*. **2** *(person)* buena persona. **3** *(fun)* diversión *f*. **4** *fam (fellow)* amigo,-a.

► *vt (wear proudly)* lucir.

► *vi (frolic)* retozar, juguetear.

sports [spɔːts] *n pl* deportes *mpl*.

► *n (meeting)* competición *f* deportiva.

► *adj* deportivo,-a, de deportes. COMP **sports car** (coche *m*) deportivo. ‖ **sports centre/complex** polideportivo. ‖ **sports club** club deportivo. ‖ **sports commentator** comentarista deportivo. ‖ **sports event** evento deportivo. ‖ **sports ground** campo de deportes. ‖ **sports jacket** chaqueta (de) sport.

sportsman ['spɔːtsmən] *n* deportista *m*.
ⓘ *pl* sportsmen ['spɔːtsmən].

sportswear ['spɔːtsweəʳ] *n (for sport)* ropa de deporte; *(casual)* ropa (de) sport.

sportswoman ['spɔːtswʊmən] *n* deportista.

ⓘ *pl* sportswomen ['spɔːtswɪmɪn].

sporty ['spɔːtɪ] *adj* deportivo,-a, aficionado,-a a los deportes.

ⓘ *comp* sportier, *superl* sportiest.

spot [spɒt] *n* **1** *(dot)* punto; *(on fabric)* lunar *m*, mota; *(on animal)* mancha. **2** *(mark, stain)* mancha. **3** *(blemish, pimple)* grano. **4** *(place)* sitio, lugar *m*. **5** *(area of body)* punto; *(flaw)* mancha. **6** *(fix, trouble)* lío, aprieto, apuro. **7** *(place in broadcast)* espacio. **8** *fam (small amount)* poquito, poquitín *m*; *(drop)* gota. **9** *(position)* puesto. **10** *fam (spotlight)* foco. LOC **on the spot 1** *(at once, then and there)* en el acto, allí mismo. **2** *(at the place of the action)* en el lugar del los hechos. **3** *(without moving away)* en el lugar.
▸ *vt* **1** *(notice)* darse cuenta de, notar; *(see)* ver; *(recognize)* reconocer; *(find)* encontrar, descubrir; *(catch out)* pillar. **2** *(mark with spots)* motear; *(stain)* manchar, salpicar.
▸ *vi* GB *(rain)* chispear, lloviznar.
ⓘ *pt & pp* spotted, *ger* spotting.
▸ *adj (price, cash)* contante, al contado.

spotlight ['spɒtlaɪt] *n (lamp)* foco, proyector *m*, reflector *m*; *(beam)* luz *f* de foco.
▸ *vt* **1** iluminar, enfocar. **2** *(draw attention to)* poner de relieve, destacar.

spotted ['spɒtɪd] *adj (with dots)* con puntos; *(fabric)* de lunares; *(speckled)* moteado,-a; *(stained)* manchado,-a; *(animal)* con manchas.

spotty ['spɒtɪ] *adj (person, face, complexion)* con granos, lleno,-a de granos.
ⓘ *comp* spottier, *superl* spottiest.

spout [spaʊt] *n* **1** *(of jug)* pico; *(of fountain)* surtidor *m*, caño; *(of roof-gutter)* canalón *m*; *(of teapot)* pitorro. **2** *(jet of water)* chorro.

sprain [spreɪn] *n* MED torcedura.
▸ *vt* torcer.

sprang [sræŋ] *pt* → spring.

spray¹ [spreɪ] *n (of flowers)* ramillete *m*.

spray² [spreɪ] *n* **1** *(of water)* rociada; *(from sea)* espuma; *(from aerosol)* pulverización *f*. **2** *(aerosol)* spray *m*; *(atomizer)* atomizador *m*, vaporizador *m*. COMP **spray can** aerosol *m*. ∎ **spray paint** pintura spray.
▸ *vt (water)* rociar; *(crops)* fumigar; *(paint)* pintar a pistola.
▸ *vi (water)* rociar.

spread [spred] *vt* **1** *(lay out)* extender, tender; *(unfold)* desplegar; *(scatter)* esparcir. **2** *(butter, etc)* untar, extender; *(paint, glue, etc)* extender, repartir. **3** *(news, ideas, etc)* difundir, divulgar; *(rumour)* hacer correr; *(disease, fire)* propagar; *(panic, terror)* sembrar. **4** *(wealth, work, cost)* distribuir, repartir.
▸ *vi* **1** *(stretch out)* extenderse; *(open out, unfold)* desplegarse; *(widen)* ensancharse. **2** *(butter, etc)* extenderse. **3** *(news, ideas, etc)* difundirse, divulgarse; *(rumour)* correr; *(disease, fire)* propagarse. **4** *(in time)* extenderse.
ⓘ *pt & pp* spread.

spreadsheet ['spredʃiːt] *n* hoja de cálculo.

spring [sprɪŋ] *n* **1** *(season)* primavera. **2** *(of water)* manantial *m*, fuente *f*. **3** *(of mattress, seat)* muelle *m*; *(of watch, lock, etc)* resorte *m*; *(of car)* ballesta. **4** *(elasticity)* elasticidad *f*; *(active, healthy quality)* energía, brío. **5** *(leap, jump)* salto, brinco. COMP **spring onion** cebolleta.
▸ *vi* **1** *(jump)* saltar. **2** *(appear)* aparecer (de repente),
▸ *vt* **1** *(operate mechanism)* accionar. **2** *fig (news, surprise)* espetar (on, a), soltar. **3** *fam (help escape, set free)* soltar.
ⓘ *pt* sprang [spræŋ], *pp* sprung [sprʌŋ].

springboard ['sprɪŋbɔːd] *n* trampolín *m*.

sprinkle ['sprɪŋkəl] *vt* **1** *(with water)* rociar (with, de/con), salpicar (with, de/con). **2** *(with flour, sugar, etc)* espolvorear (with, de/con). **3** *fig* salpicar (with, de/con).

sprint [sprɪnt] *(dash)* carrera corta.
▸ *vi (dash)* correr a toda velocidad.

sprocket ['sprɒkɪt] *n* TECH diente *m* de engranaje. COMP **sprocket wheel** rueda dentada.

sprout [spraʊt] *n* BOT *(shoot)* brote *m*, retoño. COMP **(Brussels) sprouts** coles *fpl* de Bruselas.
▸ *vi* brotar, salir.
▸ *vt (leaves, shoots)* echar; *(beard, etc)* salir.

sprung [sprʌŋ] *pp* → spring.

spud [spʌd] *n fam* patata.

spun [spʌn] *pt & pp* → spin.

spur [spɜːʳ] *n* **1** *(horse rider's)* espuela. **2** ZOOL *(of cock)* espolón *m*.
▶ *vt* **1** *(horse)* espolear. **2** *fig (stimulate)* estimular, incitar.
ⓘ *pt & pp* spurred, *ger* spurring.

spy [spaɪ] *n (gen)* espía *mf*.
ⓘ *pl* spies.
▶ *vi* espiar (on, a).
ⓘ *pt & pp* spied, *ger* spying.

spyhole ['spaɪhəʊl] *n* mirilla.

squabble ['skwɒbəl] *n* riña, pelea.
▶ *vi* reñir, pelearse (over, por) (about, sobre).

squad [skwɒd] *n* **1** MIL pelotón *m*. **2** *(of police)* brigada. **3** SP *(team)* equipo; *(national)* selección *f*.

squadron ['skwɒdrən] *n (of soldiers)* escuadrón *m*; *(of planes)* escuadrilla; *(of ships)* escuadra.

square [skweəʳ] *n* **1** *(shape)* cuadrado; *(on fabric)* cuadro; *(on chessboard, graph paper, crossword)* casilla. **2** *(in town)* plaza; *(block of houses)* manzana. **3** MATH cuadrado. **4** *(tool)* escuadra.
▶ *adj* **1** *(in shape)* cuadrado,-a; *(forming right angle)* en ángulo recto, a escuadra. **2** MATH cuadrado,-a. **3** *fam (fair)* justo,-a, equitativo,-a; *(honest)* honesto,-a, franco,-a. **4** *(equal in points)* igual, empatado,-a; *(not owing money)* en paz. COMP
square **metre** metro cuadrado. ‖ square **root** raíz *f* cuadrada.
▶ *adv* directamente.

squared ['skweəd] *adj (paper)* cuadriculado,-a.

squash[1] [skwɒʃ] *n* **1** *(drink)* concentrado de frutas. **2** SP squash *m*.
▶ *vt* **1** *(crush, flatten)* aplastar, chafar. **2** *(squeeze)* apretar, apiñar.
▶ *vi* **1** *(crush, flatten)* aplastarse, chafarse. **2** *(squeeze)* apretujarse.

squash[2] [skwɒʃ] *n* BOT calabaza.

squat [skwɒt] *adj (person)* rechoncho,-a y bajo,-a, achaparrado,-a; *(building)* achaparrado,-a.
ⓘ *comp* squatter, *superl* squattest.
▶ *vi* **1** *(crouch)* agacharse, ponerse en cuclillas. **2** *(in building)* ocupar ilegalmente.
ⓘ *pt & pp* squatted, *ger* squatting.

squatter ['skwɒtəʳ] *n* ocupante *mf* ilegal, okupa *mf*.

squeak [skwiːk] *n (of mouse)* chillido; *(of wheel, hinge, etc)* chirrido, rechinamiento; *(of shoes)* crujido.
▶ *vi (mouse)* chillar; *(wheel, hinge, etc)* chirriar, rechinar; *(shoes)* chirriar.

squeal [skwiːl] *n* **1** *(of animal, person)* chillido, grito; *(of tyres, brakes)* chirrido.
▶ *vi* **1** *(animal, person)* chillar; *(tyres, brakes)* chirriar. **2** *fam (inform on)* cantar, chivarse.
▶ *vt (say)* decir chillando, gritar.

squeeze [skwiːz] *vt* **1** *(gen)* apretar; *(lemon, orange)* exprimir. **2** *(fit in)* meter. **3** *(force out)* extraer, sacar.

squeezer ['skwiːzəʳ] *n* exprimidor *m*.

squid [skwɪd] *n (gen)* calamar *m*; *(small)* chipirón *m*.
ⓘ *pl* squid o squids.

squint [skwɪnt] *n* **1** MED bizquera, estrabismo. **2** *fam (quick look)* vistazo, ojeada, miradita.
▶ *vi* **1** MED bizquear, ser bizco,-a. **2** *(in sunlight)* entrecerrar los ojos.

squire [skwaɪəʳ] *n* **1** HIST *(knight's armour-carrier)* escudero. **2** GB *fam* jefe *m*.

squirrel ['skwɪrəl] *n* ardilla.

Sri Lanka [sriːˈlæŋkə] *n* Sri Lanka.

stab [stæb] *n* **1** *(with knife)* puñalada, navajazo. **2** *(of pain)* punzada.
▶ *vt (with knife)* apuñalar, acuchillar.
ⓘ *pt & pp* stabbed, *ger* stabbing.

stability [stəˈbɪlɪti] *n* estabilidad *f*.

stabilizer ['steɪbəlaɪzəʳ] *n* **1** *(on plane, ship, bicycle)* estabilizador *m*. **2** *(in food)* estabilizante *m*.

stable[1] ['steɪbəl] *adj* **1** estable.
ⓘ *comp* stabler, *comp* stablest.

stable[2] ['steɪbəl] *n (for horses)* cuadra; *(for other animals)* establo.

stack [stæk] *n* **1** *(pile, heap)* montón *m*. **2** *(of grass, grain, etc)* almiar *m*. **3** *(chimney)* cañón de chimenea.
▶ *vt* **1** *(pile up)* apilar, amontonar; *(fill)* llenar. **2** *fam (in cards)* arreglar.
▶ *n pl* stacks *fam* montón *m*, montones *mpl*.
▶ *n pl* stacks *(in library)* estanterías *fpl*.

stadium ['steɪdɪəm] *n* estadio.
ⓘ *pl* stadiums o stadia ['steɪdɪə].

staff [stɑːf] *n* **1** *(personnel - gen)* personal *m*, plantilla; *(- teachers)* profesorado. **2** MIL estado mayor. **3** *(stick)* bastón *m*; *(of shepherd)* cayado; *(of bishop)* báculo; *(flagpole)* asta. **4** [*n* staves ['steɪvz]] MUS pentagrama *m*.

stag [stæg] *n* ZOOL ciervo, venado.

stage [steɪdʒ] *n* **1** *(point, period)* etapa, fase *f*. **2** *(of journey, race)* etapa; *(day's journey)* jornada. **3** *(in theatre)* escenario, escena; *(raised platform)* plataforma, tablado, estrado. **4** *fig (scene of action)* escena. **5** *(of rocket)* fase *f*. **6** *fam (stagecoach)* diligencia. LOC **by stages / in stages** por etapas.
▶ *vt* **1** THEAT poner en escena, montar. **2** *(hold, carry out)* llevar a cabo, efectuar; *(arrange)* organizar, montar.
▶ *n* **the stage** *(the theatre)* el teatro, las tablas *fpl*.

stagecoach ['steɪdʒkəʊtʃ] *n* diligencia.

stagger ['stægər] *vi (walk unsteadily)* tambalearse.
▶ *vt* **1** *(hours, work)* escalonar. **2** *(amaze)* asombrar, pasmar.
▶ *n (unsteady walk)* tambaleo.

stagnation [stæg'neɪʃən] *n (of water)* estancamiento; *(person)* anquilosamiento.

stain [steɪn] *n* **1** *(gen)* mancha. **2** *(dye)* tinte *m*, tintura.
▶ *vt* **1** *(gen)* manchar. **2** *(dye)* teñir. COMP **stain remover** quitamanchas *m*.
▶ *vi* mancharse.

stainless ['steɪnləs] *adj (spotless)* sin mancha. COMP **stainless steel** acero inoxidable.

stair [steər] *n* **1** *(single step)* escalón *m*, peldaño. **2** *lit* escalera.
▶ *n pl* **stairs** escalera *f sing*.

staircase ['steəkeɪs] *n* escalera.

stairway ['steəweɪ] *n* escalera.

stake [steɪk] *n* **1** *(bet)* apuesta. **2** *(investment, share)* interés *m*, participación *f*.
▶ *vt* **1** *(bet)* apostar, jugar(se); *(risk)* arriesgar, jugarse. **2** *(give financial support to)* invertir en.

stale [steɪl] *adj* **1** *(food - gen)* no fresco, -a, pasado,-a; *(- bread, cake)* duro,-a; *(tobacco)* rancio,-a; *(wine, beer)* picado, -a. **2** *(air)* viciado,-a; *(smell)* a cerrado. **3** *(news)* viejo,-a, pasado,-a; *(joke)* trillado,-a.

stalemate ['steɪlmeɪt] *n* **1** *(chess)* tablas *fpl*. **2** *fig* punto muerto, impasse *m*.

stalk [stɔːk] *n* **1** BOT *(of plant)* tallo; *(of fruit)* rabo, rabillo; *(of cabbage)* troncho. **2** ZOOL pedúnculo.

stall² [stɔːl] *n* **1** *(in market)* puesto, tenderete *m*; *(at fair)* caseta, barraca. **2** *(for animal - stable)* establo; *(- stable compartment)* compartimiento (en un establo). **3** *(row of seats)* sillería. **4** *(small room, compartment)* compartimiento.
▶ *vi* AUTO calarse, pararse.
▶ *n pl* **stalls** *(in theatre)* platea *f sing*.

stallion ['stælɪən] *n* semental *m*.

stamen ['steɪmən] *n* BOT estambre *m*.

stamina ['stæmɪnə] *n (endurance)* resistencia, aguante *m*.

stammer ['stæmər] *n* tartamudeo.
▶ *vi* tartamudear.
▶ *vt (say with a stammer)* decir tartamudeando, farfullar.

stamp [stæmp] *n* **1** *(postage)* sello; *(fiscal)* timbre *m*; *(trading stamp)* cupón *m*, vale *m*. **2** *(tool - gen)* sello; *(- rubber)* sello de goma, tampón *m*; *(- metal)* cuño, troquel *m*. **3** *(seal, mark)* sello. **4** *(with foot - act)* patada, pisotón *m*; *(- sound)* paso. COMP **stamp collecting** filatelia.
▶ *vt* **1** *(letter)* franquear. **2** *(passport, document)* sellar, marcar con sello; *(metal, coin)* acuñar, troquelar.

✖ Stamp no significa 'estampa', que se traduce por **picture**.

stand [stænd] *n* **1** *(position)* lugar *m*, sitio; *(attitude, opinion)* posición *f*, postura; *(defence, resistance)* resistencia. **2** *(of lamp, sculpture, etc)* pie *m*, pedestal *m*, base *f*. **3** *(stall - in market)* puesto, tenderete *m*; *(- at exhibition)* stand *m*; *(- at fair)* caseta, barraca. **4** *(for taxis)* parada. **5** SP *(in stadium)* tribuna. **6** US *(witness box)* estrado.

S

▶ *vi* **1** *(person - be on one's feet)* estar de pie, estar; *(- get up)* ponerse de pie, levantarse; *(- remain on one's feet)* quedarse de pie; *(- take up position)* ponerse. **2** *(measure - height)* medir; *(- value, level)* marcar, alcanzar. **3** *(thing - be situated)* estar, encontrarse.

▶ *vt* **1** *(place)* poner, colocar. **2** *fam (bear, tolerate)* aguantar, soportar. **3** *fam (invite)* invitar: *I'll stand you a drink* te invitaré a una copa. LOC **not to stand a chance** no tener ni la más remota posibilidad. ‖ **to stand clear (of** STH**)** apartarse (de algo). ‖ **to stand in the way of** impedir, obstaculizar, poner trabas a. ‖ **to stand to reason** ser lógico,-a. ‖ **to stand trial** ser procesado,-a.

◆ **to stand back** *vi (move back)* apartarse, echarse hacia atrás, alejarse; *(be objective)* distanciarse (**from**, de).

◆ **to stand by** *vi* **1** *(do nothing)* cruzarse de brazos, quedarse sin hacer nada. **2** *(be ready for action - gen)* estar preparado,-a, estar listo,-a; *(- troops)* estar en estado de alerta.

▶ *vt insep* **1** *(not desert)* no abandonar, respaldar, apoyar, defender. **2** *(keep to - decision)* atenerse a; *(- promise)* cumplir.

◆ **to stand for** *vt insep* **1** *(mean)* significar, querer decir; *(represent)* representar. **2** *(support, be in favour of)* defender, apoyar, ser partidario,-a de. **3** *(tolerate)* tolerar, permitir, consentir.

◆ **to stand in for** *vt insep (substitute, deputize)* sustituir, suplir.

◆ **to stand up** *vi* **1** *(get up)* ponerse de pie, levantarse; *(be standing)* estar de pie. **2** *(withstand)* resistir (**to**, -), soportar (**to**, -).

▶ *vt sep* **1** *(place upright)* poner en posición vertical. **2** *fam (fail to keep appointment)* dejar plantado,-a a, dar un plantón a.

◆ **to stand up for** *vt insep (defend)* defender; *(support)* apoyar.

① *pt & pp* **stood** [stʊd].

standard ['stændəd] *n* **1** *(level, degree)* nivel *m*; *(quality)* cualidad *f.* **2** *(criterion, yardstick)* criterio, valor *m.* **3** *(norm, rule)* norma, regla, estándar *m.* **4** *(flag)* estandarte *m*, bandera; *(of ship)* pabellón

m. **5** *(official measure)* patrón *m.* COMP **standard of living** nivel *m* de vida.

▶ *adj* normal, estándar.

▶ *n pl* **standards** *(moral principles)* principios *mpl*, valores *mpl*.

standardize ['stændədaɪz] *vt* normalizar, estandarizar.

standby ['stændbaɪ] *n* **1** *(person)* suplente *mf*, sustituto,-a, reserva *mf*. **2** *(thing)* recurso.

stank [stæŋk] *pt* → **stink**.

stanza ['stænzə] *n* estrofa.

staple¹ ['steɪpəl] *adj* **1** *(food, ingredient)* básico,-a; *(product, export)* principal. **2** *(usual)* típico,-a, de siempre.

▶ *n (main food)* alimento básico; *(main product)* producto principal; *(main thing)* elemento principal.

staple² ['steɪpəl] *n (fastener)* grapa.

▶ *vt* grapar.

stapler ['steɪpələʳ] *n* grapadora.

star [stɑːʳ] *n (gen)* estrella; *(person)* estrella, astro. COMP **Stars and Stripes** la bandera de los Estados Unidos.

▶ *vi* CINEM protagonizar (**in**, -).

① *pt & pp* **starred**, *ger* **starring**.

⊕ La bandera de Estados Unidos se conoce como **Stars and Stripes** (barras y estrellas) porque está compuesta por 13 barras horizontales rojas y lleva en una esquina 50 estrellas blancas sobre un fondo azul.

starboard ['stɑːbəd] *n* MAR estribor *m.*

starch [stɑːtʃ] *n (for laundry, in rice)* almidón *m*; *(in potatoes)* fécula.

▶ *vt (laundry)* almidonar.

stare [steəʳ] *n* mirada fija.

▶ *vi* mirar fijamente (**at**, -), clavar la vista (**at**, en).

starfish ['stɑːfɪʃ] *n* estrella de mar.

starlet ['stɑːlət] *n* aspirante *f* a estrella.

starling ['stɑːlɪŋ] *n* estornino.

start [stɑːt] *n* **1** *(gen)* principio, comienzo, inicio. **2** SP *(of race)* salida; *(advantage)* ventaja. **3** *(fright, jump)* susto, sobresalto.

▶ *vt* **1** *(begin - gen)* empezar, comenzar, iniciar; *(- conversation)* entablar. **2** *(cause to begin - fire, epidemic)* provocar; *(- argu-*

ment, fight, war, etc) empezar, iniciar. **3** *(set up - business)* montar, poner; *(- organization)* fundar, establecer, crear. **4** *(set in motion - machine)* poner en marcha; *(- vehicle)* arrancar, poner en marcha.
▶ *vi* **1** *(begin)* empezar, comenzar. **2** *(be set up - business)* ser fundado,-a, fundarse, crearse. **3** *(begin to operate)* ponerse en marcha; *(car)* arrancar.
◆ **to start off** *vi* **1** *(begin)* empezar, comenzar. **2** *(leave)* salir, ponerse en camino.
▶ *vt sep* empezar, ayudar a empezar.
◆ **to start up** *vt sep (car)* arrancar; *(engine)* poner en marcha; *(business)* montar, poner en marcha; *(conversation)* entablar.

starter ['stɑːtəʳ] *n* **1** SP *(official)* juez *mf* de salida. **2** SP *(competitor)* competidor,-ra, participante *mf*. **3** AUTO motor *m* de arranque. **4** CULIN *fam* primer plato, entrante *m*.

startle ['stɑːtəl] *vt* asustar, sobresaltar: *you startled me!* ¡me has asustado!

starvation [stɑːˈveɪʃən] *n* hambre *f*, inanición *f*.

starve [stɑːv] *vi (feel hungry)* pasar hambre; *(die)* morirse de hambre.
▶ *vt* **1** *(deprive of food)* privar de comida a, hacer pasar hambre a. **2** *fig* privar *(of, de)*.

starving ['stɑːvɪŋ] *adj* muerto,-a de hambre, famélico,-a.

state [steɪt] *n* **1** *(condition)* estado. **2** POL *(government)* estado. **3** *(country, division of country)* estado. **4** *(ceremony, pomp)* ceremonia, pompa, solemnidad *f*.
▶ *adj* POL estatal, del estado.
▶ *vt* **1** *(say, declare, express)* exponer, declarar, afirmar. **2** *(specify)* fijar.

stated ['steɪtɪd] *adj (specified)* indicado,-a, señalado,-a.

statement ['steɪtmənt] *n* **1** *(gen)* declaración *f*, afirmación *f*; *(official)* comunicado. **2** FIN estado de cuentas, extracto de cuenta. COMP **to make a statement** JUR prestar declaración.

statesman ['steɪtsmən] *n* estadista *m*, hombre *m* de estado.
ⓘ *pl* **statesmen** ['steɪtsmən].

static ['stætɪk] *adj* **1** TECH estático,-a. **2** *(not moving, not changing)* estacionario,-a. COMP **static electricity** electricidad *f* estática.
▶ *n (interference)* interferencias *fpl*, parásitos *mpl*.
▶ *n* **statics** PHYS estática.

station ['steɪʃən] *n* **1** *(railway)* estación *f* (de ferrocarril); *(underground)* estación *f* de metro; *(bus, coach)* estación *f*, terminal *f*. **2** *(radio)* emisora, estación *f*, radio *f*; *(TV)* canal *m*. **3** AGR granja. **4** *(social rank)* condición *f* social, posición *f* social.

stationary ['steɪʃənəri] *adj* estacionario,-a.

stationer ['steɪʃənəʳ] *n* dueño,-a de una papelería. COMP **stationer's (shop)** papelería.

stationery ['steɪʃənəri] *n (paper)* papel *m* de escribir; *(pen, ink, etc)* artículos *mpl* de escritorio.

statistics [stəˈtɪstɪks] *n (science)* estadística.
▶ *n pl (data)* estadísticas *fpl*.

statue ['stætjuː] *n* estatua.

statuette [stætjuˈet] *n* estatuilla.

stature ['stætʃəʳ] *n* **1** *(height)* estatura, talla. **2** *fig (standing)* talla.

statute ['stætjuːt] *n* estatuto.

staves [steɪvz] *n pl* → **staff**.

stay¹ [steɪ] *n* **1** *(prop, support)* sostén *m*, soporte *m*, puntal *m*. **2** *(in corset)* ballena.

stay² [steɪ] *n (time)* estancia, permanencia.
▶ *vi (remain)* quedarse, permanecer.
▶ *vt (continue to be)* seguir.
▶ *vi (reside temporarily)* alojarse, hospedarse.
▶ *vt fml (stop)* detener; *(delay)* aplazar, suspender; *(calm)* calmar.
◆ **to stay in** *vi* quedarse en casa, no salir.

steadily ['stedɪli] *adv* **1** *(grow, improve, rise)* constantemente, a un ritmo constante; *(rain, work)* sin parar. **2** *(gaze, stare)* fijamente; *(walk)* con paso seguro, decididamente; *(speak)* firmemente.

S

steady ['stedɪ] *adj* **1** *(table, ladder, etc)* firme, seguro,-a; *(gaze)* fijo,-a; *(voice)* tranquilo,-a, firme. **2** *(regular, constant - heartbeat, pace)* regular; *(- demand, speed, improvement, decline, increase)* constante; *(- flow, rain)* continuo,-a; *(rhythm)* regular, constante; *(- prices, currency)* estable. **3** *(regular - job)* fijo,-a, estable; *(- income)* regular, fijo,-a. **4** *(student)* aplicado,-a; *(worker, person)* serio,-a, formal.
ⓘ *comp* **steadier**, *superl* **steadiest**.
▶ *interj* ¡cuidado!, ¡ojo!
▶ *n (boyfriend)* novio; *(girlfriend)* novia.
▶ *vt* **1** *(hold firm - ladder, table, etc)* sujetar, sostener; *(stabilize)* estabilizar. **2** *(person, nerves)* calmar, tranquilizar.
ⓘ *pt & pp* **steadied**, *ger* **steadying**.

steak [steɪk] *n* **1** *(of beef)* bistec *m*, filete *m*; *(of salmon)* rodaja. **2** *(meat for stewing)* carne *f* de vaca para estofar.

steal [stiːl] *vt* robar, hurtar.
▶ *vi* **1** *(rob)* robar, hurtar. **2** *(move quietly, creep)* moverse con sigilo.
ⓘ *pt* **stole** [stəʊl], *pp* **stolen** ['stəʊlən].

steam [stiːm] *n* vapor *m*. COMP **steam engine 1** *(locomotive)* locomotora de vapor, máquina de vapor. **2** *(engine)* motor *m* de vapor. **steam iron** plancha de vapor.
▶ *vt* CULIN *(vegetables)* cocer al vapor.
▶ *vi (boat)* echar vapor; *(soup, drink, etc)* humear.

steamboat ['stiːmbəʊt] *n* vapor *m*.

steamer ['stiːmə'] *n* **1** MAR vapor *m*, buque *m* de vapor. **2** CULIN olla a vapor.

steamship ['stiːmʃɪp] *n* vapor *m*, buque *m* de vapor.

steel [stiːl] *n (gen)* acero.
▶ *adj (knife, girder, etc)* de acero. COMP **steel industry** industria del acero **steel mill** acerería, acería. **steel wool** estropajo de acero.

steelworks ['stiːlwɜːks] *n pl* acería, acerería.

steep¹ [stiːp] *vt (soak - washing)* remojar; *(- dried food)* poner en remojo; *(- fruit)* macerar.
▶ *vi (fruit)* macerarse.

steep² [stiːp] *adj* **1** *(hill, slope, stairs)* empinado,-a; *(rise, drop)* abrupto,-a,

brusco,-a. **2** *fam (price, fee)* excesivo,-a; *(demand)* excesivo,-a, poco razonable.

steeple ['stiːpəl] *n* aguja, chapitel *m*.

steeplechase ['stiːpəlʃeɪs] *n* carrera de obstáculos.

steer¹ [stɪə'] *n* buey *m*.

steer² [stɪə'] *vt (gen)* dirigir, guiar; *(vehicle)* conducir, dirigir; *(ship)* gobernar; *(conversation)* llevar.
▶ *vi (vehicle)* ir al volante; *(ship)* llevar el timón, estar al timón.

steering ['stɪərɪŋ] *n* dirección *f*. COMP **steering column** columna de (la) dirección. **steering lock 1** *(device)* seguro antirrobo. **2** *(when turning)* radio de giro. **steering wheel** volante *m*.

stem [stem] *n* **1** BOT *(of plant, flower)* tallo; *(of leaf)* pecíolo; *(of fruit)* pedúnculo. **2** *(of glass)* pie *m*; *(of tobacco pipe)* boquilla, caña. **3** LING raíz *f*, radical *m*.
▶ *vt (stop - gen)* frenar, detener, parar; *(- bleeding)* contener, parar.
ⓘ *pt & pp* **stemmed**, *ger* **stemming**.

stench [stentʃ] *n* hedor *m*, peste *f*, fetidez *f*.

stencil ['stensəl] *n* **1** *(template)* plantilla; *(design, pattern)* estarcido. **2** *(for typewriter)* cliché *m*, matriz *f*.

stenography [stə'nɒgrəfɪ] *n* US taquigrafía.

step [step] *n* **1** *(gen)* paso. **2** *(measure)* medida; *(formality)* gestión *f*, trámite *m*. **3** *(stair)* escalón *m*, peldaño; *(of vehicle)* estribo.
▶ *vi* **1** *(move, walk)* dar un paso, andar. **2** *(tread)* pisar.
▶ *n pl* **steps** GB *(stepladder)* escalera de tijera. *(outdoor)* escalinata; *(indoor)* escalera; *(of plane)* escalerilla.
ⓘ *pt & pp* **stepped**, *ger* **stepping**.

stepbrother ['stepbrʌðə'] *n* hermanastro.

stepchild ['steptʃaɪld] *n* hijastro,-a.
ⓘ *pl* **stepchildren** ['steptʃɪldrən].

stepdaughter ['stepdɔːtə'] *n* hijastra.

stepfather ['stepfɑːðə'] *n* padrastro.

stepladder ['steplædə'] *n* escalera de tijera.

stepmother ['stepmʌðə'] *n* madrastra.

stimulation

steppe [step] *n* GEOG estepa.

stepsister ['stepsɪstəʳ] *n* hermanastra.

stepson ['stepsʌn] *n* hijastro.

stereo ['steriəʊ] *n* estéreo.

stereotype ['steriətaɪp] *n* estereotipo.
▶ *vt* estereotipar.

sterile ['steraɪl] *adj* **1** *(barren)* estéril. **2** *(germfree)* esterilizado,-a.

sterility [stə'rɪlɪti] *n* esterilidad *f*.

sterilize ['sterəlaɪz] *vt* esterilizar.

sterling ['stɜːlɪŋ] *n* FIN libra esterlina, libras *fpl* esterlinas. LOC **the pound sterling** la libra esterlina.

stern¹ [stɜːn] *adj* severo,-a, austero,-a.

stern² [stɜːn] *n* MAR popa.

sternum ['stɜːnəm] *n* ANAT esternón *m*.
ⓘ *pl* **sternums** o **sterna** ['stɜːnə].

steroid ['sterɔɪd] *n* esteroide *m*.

stethoscope ['steθəskəʊp] *n* estetoscopio.

stew [stjuː] *n* CULIN estofado, guisado.
▶ *vt* *(meat)* estofar, guisar; *(fruit)* hacer una compota de.

steward ['stjuːəd] *n* **1** *(on ship)* camarero; *(on plane)* auxiliar *m* de vuelo. **2** *(manager of estate)* administrador *m*. **3** *(of club, hotel)* mayordomo. **4** GB *(in horse racing)* comisario de carreras; *(in athletics)* juez *m*; *(at demonstration, etc)* oficial *mf*.

stewardess ['stjuːədes] *n* *(on ship)* camarera; *(on plane)* azafata, auxiliar *f* de vuelo.
ⓘ *pl* **stewardesses**.

stick¹ [stɪk] *vt* **1** *(insert pointed object)* clavar, hincar. **2** *fam* poner, meter. **3** *(fix)* colocar, fijar; *(with glue)* pegar, fijar. **4** *fam* *(bear)* aguantar, soportar.
▶ *vi* **1** *(penetrate)* clavarse. **2** *(fix, become attached)* pegarse. **3** *(jam - drawer, key in lock)* atascarse; *(- machine part, lock)* atrancarse, encasquillarse; *(- vehicle in mud)* atascarse. **4** *(in cards)* plantarse.
◆ **to stick out** *vi* **1** *(project, protrude)* salir, sobresalir; *(be noticeable)* resaltar, destacarse. **2** *fam* *(be obvious)* ser obvio,-a, ser evidente.
▶ *vt sep* **1** *(tongue, hand)* sacar. **2** *(endure)* aguantar.
ⓘ *pt & pp* **stuck** [stʌk].

stick² [stɪk] *n* **1** *(piece of wood)* trozo de madera, palo; *(twig)* ramita; *(for punishment)* palo, vara. **2** *(for walking)* bastón *m*. **3** *(for plants)* rodrigón *m*, tutor *m*. **4** MUS *(baton)* batuta; *(drumstick)* palillo. **5** SP *(for hockey)* palo.

sticker ['stɪkəʳ] *n* **1** *(label)* etiqueta adhesiva; *(with slogan, picture)* pegatina. **2** *(person)* persona tenaz.

sticking ['stɪkɪŋ] COMP **sticking plaster** *(small)* tirita®; *(on roll)* esparadrapo.

sticky ['stɪki] *adj* pegajoso,-a. COMP **sticky tape** cinta adhesiva.
ⓘ *comp* **stickier**, *comp* **stickiest**.

stiff [stɪf] *adj* **1** *(hair, fabric)* rígido,-a, tieso,-a; *(card, collar, brush, lock)* duro,-a. **2** *(joint)* entumecido,-a; *(muscle)* agarrotado,-a. **3** *(door, window)* difícil de abrir, difícil de cerrar. **4** *(not liquid)* espeso,-a, consistente. **5** *(person, manner)* estirado,-a, tieso,-a; *(smile)* forzado,-a. **6** *fig* *(climb, test, etc)* difícil, duro,-a; *(breeze)* fuerte; *(sentence, punishment)* severo,-a. **7** *fam* *(price, fee)* excesivo,-a. **8** *fam* *(drink)* fuerte, cargado,-a. LOC **to be stiff** tener agujetas.

stifle ['staɪfəl] *vt* ahogar, sofocar.

still [stɪl] *adj* **1** *(not moving)* quieto,-a, inmóvil; *(stationary)* parado,-a; *(water)* manso,-a; *(air)* en calma. **2** *(tranquil, calm)* tranquilo,-a; *(peaceful)* sosegado,-a; *(subdued)* callado,-a, apagado,-a; *(silent)* silencioso,-a. **3** *(not fizzy - water)* sin gas; *(soft drink)* sin burbujas.
▶ *adv* **1** *(so far)* todavía, aún. **2** *(even)* aún, todavía. **3** *(even so, nevertheless)* a pesar de todo, con todo, no obstante, sin embargo. **4** *fml* *(besides, yet, in addition)* aún, todavía. **5** *(quiet, without moving)* quieto,-a. COMP **still life** ART naturaleza muerta *m*.

stilt [stɪlt] *n* zanco.

stilted ['stɪltɪd] *adj* afectado,-a.

stimulant ['stɪmjʊlənt] *n* estimulante *m*.

stimulate ['stɪmjəleɪt] *vt* *(activate)* estimular; *(encourage)* animar, alentar.

stimulating ['stɪmjəleɪtɪŋ] *adj* *(gen)* estimulante; *(inspiring)* inspirador,-ra.

stimulation [stɪmjə'leɪʃ°n] *n* *(stimulus)* estímulo; *(action)* estimulación *f*.

S

stimulus ['stɪmjələs] *n* estímulo.
ⓘ *pl* stimuli ['stɪmjəliː].

sting [stɪŋ] *n* **1** *(organ - of bee, wasp)* aguijón *m*; *(- of scorpion)* uña; *(- of plant)* pelo urticante. **2** *(action, wound)* picadura. **3** *(pain)* escozor *m*, picazón *f*. **4** *fig (of remorse)* punzada. **5** *US (trick)* timo, golpe *m*.
▶ *vt* **1** *(gen)* picar. **2** *fig (remark)* herir en lo más hondo; *(conscience)* remorder. **3** *(provoke)* incitar, provocar (into/to, a). **4** *(overcharge, swindle)* clavar.
▶ *vi* **1** *(insects, nettles, etc)* picar; *(substance)* escocer. **2** *(be painful)* escocer.
ⓘ *pt & pp* stung [stʌŋ].

stink [stɪŋk] *n* **1** *(smell)* peste *f*, hedor *m*, hediondez *f*, fetidez *f*. **2** *fam (fuss, trouble)* escándalo, lío, follón *m*.
▶ *vi* **1** apestar (of, a), heder (of, a). **2** *fam (seem bad or dishonest)* dar asco.
ⓘ *pt* stank [stæŋk] o stunk [stʌŋk], *pp* stunk [stʌŋk].

stinking ['stɪŋkɪŋ] *adj* apestoso,-a.

stipulate ['stɪpjəleɪt] *vt* estipular, especificar.

stipulation [stɪpjə'leɪʃ°n] *n* estipulación *f*, condición *f*.

stir [stɜːr] *vt* **1** *(liquid, mixture)* remover, revolver. **2** *(move slightly)* mover, agitar. **3** *(curiosity, interest, etc)* despertar, excitar; *(anger)* provocar; *(imagination)* avivar, estimular; *(emotions)* conmover.
▶ *vi* **1** *(move)* moverse, agitarse; *(wake up)* despertarse; *(get up)* levantarse. **2** *(feelings)* despertarse. **3** *fam (cause trouble)* armar lío, meter cizaña.
ⓘ *pt & pp* stirred, *ger* stirring.

stirring ['stɜːrɪŋ] *adj (moving)* conmovedor,-ra; *(rousing, exciting)* emocionante.

stirrup ['stɪrəp] *n* **1** *(for riding)* estribo. **2** *(on trousers)* trabilla. COMP **stirrup pump** bomba de mano.

stitch [stɪtʃ] *n* **1** *(in sewing)* puntada; *(in knitting)* punto. **2** MED punto (de sutura). **3** *(sharp pain)* punzada; *(when running, etc)* flato.
▶ *vt* **1** SEW coser (on, a), (up, -). **2** MED suturar (up, -).
▶ *vi* SEW coser.

stoat [stəʊt] *n* armiño.

stock [stɒk] *n* **1** *(supply)* reserva. **2** COMM *(goods)* existencias *fpl*, stock *m*; *(variety)* surtido. **3** FIN *(company's capital)* capital *m* social. **4** AGR *(livestock)* ganado. **5** CULIN *(broth)* caldo. LOC **in stock** en existencia. ‖ **out of stock** agotado,-a. COMP **stock exchange** bolsa. ‖ **stock market** mercado bursátil.
▶ *vt* COMM *(keep supplies of)* tener en stock; *(sell)* vender.
▶ *n pl* **stocks** FIN *(shares)* acciones *fpl*, valores *mpl*.

stockbroker ['stɒkbrəʊkər] *n* corredor,-ra de bolsa, agente *mf* de bolsa, bolsista *mf*.

stockholder ['stɒkhəʊldər] *n* US accionista *mf*.

stocking ['stɒkɪŋ] *n* media.

stoic ['stəʊɪk] *n* estoico,-a.

stoical ['stəʊɪk°l] *adj* estoico,-a.

stoicism ['stəʊɪsɪz°m] *n* estoicismo.

stole¹ [stəʊl] *pt* → steal.

stole² [stəʊl] *n (garment)* estola.

stolen ['stəʊlən] *pp* → steal.

stomach ['stʌmək] *n* **1** ANAT estómago. **2** *fam (belly)* barriga; *(abdomen)* abdomen *m*, vientre *m*.
▶ *vi fig (bear, endure)* aguantar, soportar, tragar; *(eat, drink)* tolerar.

stomachache ['stʌməkeɪk] *n* dolor *m* de estómago.

stoma ['stəʊmə] *n* estoma *m*.
ⓘ *pl* stomas o stomata ['stəʊmətə].

stomp [stɒmp] *vi fam* pisar fuerte.

stone [stəʊn] *n* **1** *(gen)* piedra. **2** *(on grave)* lápida. **3** *(of fruit)* hueso. **4** MED cálculo, piedra. **5** GB *(measure of weight) unidad de peso que equivale a 6,348 kg.*
▶ *adj* de piedra, pétreo,-a. COMP **Stone Age** Edad *f* de Piedra.
▶ *vt* **1** *(person)* apedrear, lapidar. **2** *(fruit)* deshuesar.

stoneware ['stəʊnweər] *n* gres *m*, cerámica de gres.

stonework ['stəʊnwɜːk] *n* mampostería.

stood [stʊd] *pt & pp* → stand.

stooge [stuːdʒ] *n* **1** THEAT comparsa *mf*. **2** *pej (person)* títere *mf*, pelele *mf*.

stool [stuːl] *n* **1** *(seat)* taburete *m*, banqueta. **2** MED *(faeces)* deposición *f*, heces *fpl*.

stoop¹ [stuːp] *n* US *(porch)* entrada.

stoop² [stuːp] *n* *(of person)* encorvamiento, encorvadura; *(of shoulders)* espaldas *fpl* encorvadas.
► *vi* **1** *(bend)* inclinarse (**down**, -), agacharse (**down**, -). **2** *(have a stoop)* andar encorvado,-a.

stop [stɒp] *n* **1** *(halt)* parada, alto. **2** *(stopping place)* parada. **3** *(on journey)* parada; *(break, rest)* descanso, pausa. **4** *(punctuation mark)* punto; *(in telegram)* stop *m*. **5** MUS *(on organ)* registro; *(knob)* botón *m* de registro; *(on wind instrument)* llave *f*. **6** *(in camera)* diafragma *m*.
► *vt* **1** *(halt - vehicle, person)* parar, detener; *(- machine, ball)* parar. **2** *(end, interrupt production)* parar; *(- inflation, advance)* parar, contener; *(- conversation, play)* interrumpir; *(- pain, etc)* poner fin a, acabar con. **3** *(pay, mark, holidays)* suspender; *(cheque)* cancelar; *(money from wages)* retener. **4** *(cease)* dejar de, parar de. **5** *(prevent)* impedir, evitar. **6** *(block - hole)* tapar, taponar (**up**, -); *(- gap)* rellenar (**up**, -); *(- tooth)* empastar (**up**, -). **7** MUS *(string, key)* apretar; *(hole)* cubrir.
► *vi* **1** *(halt)* parar, pararse, detener, detenerse. **2** *(cease)* acabarse, terminar, cesar. **3** GB *fam* *(stay)* quedarse.
◆ **to stop over** *vi* **1** *(interrupt journey)* parar; *(overnight)* pasar la noche, hacer noche. **2** *(on flight)* hacer escala.
ⓘ *pt & pp* **stopped**, *ger* **stopping**.

stopcock [ˈstɒpkɒk] *n* llave *f* de paso.

stopover [ˈstɒpəʊvəʳ] *n* *(stop)* parada; *(on flight)* escala; *(stay)* estancia.

stopper [ˈstɒpəʳ] *n* tapón *m*.

stopping [ˈstɒpɪŋ] *adj* GB *(of train)* que para en todas las estaciones.

stop-press [stɒpˈpres] *adj* *(news)* de última hora.

stopwatch [ˈstɒpwɒtʃ] *n* cronómetro.
ⓘ *pl* **stopwatches**.

storage [ˈstɔːrɪdʒ] *n* **1** *(act)* almacenaje *m*, almacenamiento. **2** *(place)* almacén *m*, depósito, guardamuebles *m*.

3 *(cost)* (gastos *mpl* de) almacenaje *m*. **4** COMPUT almacenamiento.

store [stɔːʳ] *n* **1** *(supply - gen)* reserva, provisión *f*; *(- of wisdom, knowledge)* reserva; *(- of jokes, etc)* colección *f*. **2** *(warehouse)* almacén *m*, depósito. **3** US *(shop)* tienda.
► *vt* **1** *(put away)* almacenar (**up**, -); *(keep)* guardar; *(amass)* acumular, hacer acopio de. **2** COMPUT almacenar. **3** *(put in storage)* guardar, almacenar, mandar a un depósito. **4** *fig (trouble, etc)* ir acumulando (**up**, -), ir almacenando (**up**, -). **5** *(fill with supplies)* abastecer (**with**, de).
► *n pl* **stores** *(provisions)* provisiones *fpl*, víveres *mpl*. MIL *(supplies, equipment)* pertrechos *mpl*; *(place)* intendencia *f sing*.

storehouse [ˈstɔːhaʊs] *n* almacén *m*, depósito.

storekeeper [ˈstɔːkiːpəʳ] *n* US tendero,-a.

storeroom [ˈstɔːruːm] *n* *(gen)* almacén *m*, depósito; *(for food)* despensa.

storey [ˈstɔːrɪ] *n* piso, planta.

stork [stɔːk] *n* cigüeña.

storm [stɔːm] *n* **1** *(thunderstorm)* tormenta; *(at sea)* tempestad *f*, temporal *m*; *(with wind)* borrasca. **2** *fig (uproar)* revuelo, escándalo; *(of missiles, insults)* lluvia, torrente *m*.

stormy [ˈstɔːmɪ] *adj* **1** *(weather)* tormentoso,-a. **2** *fig (meeting, discussion)* acalorado,-a; *(relationship)* tormentoso,-a, con muchos altibajos.
ⓘ *comp* **stormier**, *superl* **stormiest**.

story¹ [ˈstɔːrɪ] *n* US → **storey**.

story² [ˈstɔːrɪ] *n* **1** *(gen)* historia; *(tale)* cuento, relato; *(account)* relato. **2** *(anecdote)* anécdota; *(joke)* chiste *m*. **3** *(rumour)* rumor *m*; *(lie)* mentira, cuento. **4** *(newspaper article)* artículo; *(newsworthy item)* artículo de interés periodístico. **5** *(storyline, narrative, plot)* argumento, trama.
ⓘ *pl* **stories**.

storybook [ˈstɔːrɪbʊk] *n* libro de cuentos.

storyteller [ˈstɔːrɪteləʳ] *n* cuentista *mf*.

stout [staʊt] *adj* **1** *euph (fat)* corpulento,-a, robusto,-a. **2** *(strong)* sólido,-a, fuerte. **3** *(determined, resolute)* firme, resuelto,-a, tenaz; *(brave)* valiente.

S

► *n (beer)* cerveza negra.

stove [stəʊv] *n* **1** *(for heating)* estufa. **2** *(cooker)* cocina; *(cooking ring)* hornillo; *(oven)* horno.

straight [streɪt] *adj* **1** *(not curved - gen)* recto,-a; *(- hair)* liso,-a. **2** *(level, upright)* derecho,-a, recto,-a. **3** *(tidy, neat)* en orden. **4** *(honest - person)* honrado,-a, de confianza; *(sincere)* sincero,-a. **5** *(direct - question)* directo,-a; *(- refusal, rejection)* categórico,-a, rotundo,-a. **6** *(correct, accurate)* correcto,-a. **7** *(consecutive)* seguido,-a. **8** *(drink)* solo,-a.
► *adv* **1** *(in a straight line)* recto,-a. **2** *(not in a curve)* derecho,-a, recto,-a. **3** *(directly)* directamente. **4** *(immediately)* en seguida. **5** *(frankly)* francamente, con franqueza. **6** *(clearly)* claro, con claridad: LOC **straight away** en seguida. ‖ **straight off** en el acto. ‖ **straight up** en serio. ‖ **to go straight** *(criminal)* reformarse.

straightaway [streɪtə'weɪ] *adv* en seguida, inmediatamente.

straighten ['streɪt°n] *vt* **1** *(wire)* enderezar; *(- tie, skirt, picture)* poner bien, poner recto,-a; *(- hair)* estirar, alisar. **2** *(tidy)* ordenar (up, -), arreglar (up, -).
► *vi (road)* hacerse recto,-a.

straightforward [streɪt'fɔ:wəd] *adj* **1** *(honest)* honrado,-a; *(sincere, open)* sincero,-a, franco,-a, abierto,-a. **2** *(simple, easy)* sencillo,-a, simple; *(clear)* claro,-a.

strain¹ [streɪn] *n* **1** *(race, breed)* raza; *(descent)* linaje *m*; *(of plant, virus)* cepa. **2** *(streak)* vena.

strain² [streɪn] *n* **1** PHYS *(tension)* tensión *f*; *(pressure)* presión *f*; *(weight)* peso. **2** *(stress, pressure)* tensión *f*, estrés *m*; *(effort)* esfuerzo; *(exhaustion)* agotamiento. **3** *(tension)* tirantez *f*, tensión *f*. **4** MED torcedura, esguince *m*.
► *vt* **1** *(stretch)* estirar, tensar. **2** *(damage, weaken - muscle)* torcer(se), hacerse un esguince en; *(- back)* hacerse daño en; *(- voice, eyes)* forzar; *(ears)* aguzar; *(- heart)* cansar. **3** *(stretch - patience, nerves, credulity)* poner a prueba; *(resources)* estirar al máximo; *(- relations)* someter a demasiada tensión, crear tirantez en. **4** *(filter - liquid)* colar; *(- vegetables, rice)* escurrir.

strainer ['streɪnə'] *n* colador *m*.

strait [streɪt] *n* GEOG estrecho.
► *n pl* **straits** *(difficulties)* aprietos *mpl*, apuros *mpl*.

straitjacket ['streɪtdʒækɪt] *n* **1** camisa de fuerza. **2** *fig* control *m*, limitaciones *fpl*.

strand¹ [strænd] *n lit (beach)* playa.

strand² [strænd] *n* **1** *(of thread)* hebra, hilo; *(of rope, string)* ramal *m*; *(of hair)* pelo; *(of pearls)* sarta. **2** *fig (of story, argument)* hilo, línea.

strange [streɪndʒ] *adj* **1** *(odd, bizarre)* extraño,-a, raro,-a. **2** *(unknown)* desconocido,-a; *(unfamiliar)* nuevo,-a.
COMP **strange to say** aunque parezca mentira.

strangely ['streɪndʒlɪ] *adv* extrañamente.

stranger ['streɪndʒə'] *n (unknown person)* extraño,-a, desconocido,-a; *(outsider)* forastero,-a.

☒ Stranger no significa 'extranjero', que se traduce por **foreigner**.

strangle ['stræŋg°l] *vt* **1** *(kill)* estrangular. **2** *fig (stifle)* sofocar, ahogar.

stranglehold ['stræŋg°lhəʊld] *n* **1** SP *(wrestling)* llave *f* al cuello. **2** *pej (firm control)* poder *m*, dominio.

strap [stræp] *n (on watch, camera)* correa; *(on bag)* asa; *(on shoe)* tira; *(on dress, etc)* tirante *m*.
► *vt* **1** *(fasten)* atar con correa. **2** *(bandage)* vendar.
ⓘ *pt & pp* **strapped**, *ger* **strapping**.

strapless ['stræpləs] *adj* sin tirantes.

strapping ['stræpɪŋ] *adj (big, strong)* fornido,-a, robusto,-a.

stratagem ['strætədʒəm] *n* estratagema.

strategic [strə'ti:dʒɪk] *adj* estratégico,-a.

strategist ['strætədʒɪst] *n* estratega *mf*.

strategy ['strætədʒɪ] *n* estrategia.
ⓘ *pl* **strategies**.

stratosphere ['strætəsfɪə'] *n* estratosfera.

stratum ['strɑ:təm] *n* **1** GEOL estrato. **2** *(level, class)* estrato, nivel *m*.
ⓘ *pl* **strata** ['strɑ:tə].

straw [strɔ:] n **1** *(dried stalk(s))* paja. **2** *(for drinking)* paja, pajita.
‣ *adj* de paja.

strawberry ['strɔ:bᵊrɪ] n *(gen)* fresa; *(large)* fresón m. ⃞COMP **strawberry jam** mermelada de fresa. ‖ **strawberry tree** madroño.
ⓘ *pl* strawberries.

stray [streɪ] *adj* **1** *(lost)* perdido,-a, extraviado,-a; *(animal)* callejero,-a. **2** *(isolated, odd)* perdido,-a.
‣ *n (animal)* animal *m* extraviado.
‣ *vi* **1** *(get lost)* extraviarse, perderse; *(wander away)* desviarse, apartarse, alejarse; *(from group)* separarse, apartarse, alejarse. **2** *fig (digress, wander)* divagar, apartarse del tema, desviarse del tema.

stream [stri:m] n **1** *(brook)* arroyo, riachuelo. **2** *(current)* corriente *f*. **3** *(flow of liquid)* flujo, chorro, río; *(of blood, air)* chorro; *(of lava, tears)* torrente *m*; *(of light)* raudal *m*. **4** *fig (of people)* oleada, torrente *m*; *(of vehicles, traffic)* desfile *m* continuo, caravana; *(of abuse, excuses, insults)* torrente *m*, sarta. **5** GB *(class, pupils)* clase *f*, grupo, nivel *m* *(de alumnos seleccionados según su nivel académico)*.
‣ *vi* **1** *(flow, pour out)* manar, correr, chorrear; *(gush)* salir a chorros. **2** *fig (people, vehicles, etc)* desfilar. **3** *(hair, banner, scarf)* ondear.
‣ *vt* **1** *(liquid)* derramar. **2** GB poner en grupos según su nivel académico.

streamer ['stri:məʳ] n *(decoration)* serpentina; *(flag)* banderín m.

street [stri:t] n calle *f*. ⃞LOC **at street level** a nivel de la calle. ‖ **to walk the streets 1** *(homeless)* estar sin techo. **2** *(prostitute)* trabajar la calle. ⃞COMP **one-way street** calle de sentido único. ‖ **street cleaner** barrendero,-a. ‖ **street corner** esquina. ‖ **street directory** callejero. ‖ **street lamp** farola. ‖ **street lighting** alumbrado público. ‖ **street plan** plano de la ciudad. ‖ **street market** mercadillo. ‖ **street value** valor *m* (en el mercado).

streetcar ['stri:tkɑ:ʳ] n US tranvía.

streetlamp ['stri:tlæmp] n farol m, farola.

streetlight ['stri:tlaɪt] n farol m, farola.

strength [streŋθ] n **1** *(of person - physical)* fuerza, fuerzas *fpl*, fortaleza; *(- stamina)* resistencia, aguante *m*. **2** *(intellectual, spiritual)* fortaleza, entereza, firmeza. **3** *(of machine, object)* resistencia; *(of wind, current)* fuerza, *(of light, sound, magnet, lens)* potencia. **4** *(of solution)* concentración *f*; *(of drug)* potencia; *(of alcohol)* graduación *f*. **5** *(of currency)* valor *m*, fortaleza; *(of economy)* solidez *f*, fortaleza. **6** *(of argument, evidence, story)* fuerza, validez *f*, credibilidad *f*; *(of emotion, conviction, colour)* intensidad *f*; *(of protest)* energía. **7** *(strong point)* punto fuerte, virtud *f*; *(ability, capability)* capacidad *f*; *(advantage)* ventaja. **8** *(power, influence)* poder *m*, potencia. **9** *(force in numbers)* fuerza numérica, número.

strengthen ['streŋθᵊn] vt **1** *(wall, glass, defence, etc)* reforzar; *(muscle)* fortalecer. **2** *(character, faith, love)* fortalecer; *(support)* aumentar; *(relationship, ties)* consolidar, fortalecer; *(resolve, determination)* redoblar, intensificar.
‣ *vi* **1** *(muscle)* fortalecerse. **2** *(economy, currency)* reforzarse, fortalecerse; *(relationship)* consolidarse, reforzarse, fortalecerse; *(support, opposition, feeling)* intensificarse, aumentar.

stress [stres] n **1** MED tensión *f* (nerviosa), estrés *m*. **2** *(pressure)* presión *f*, tensión *f*. **3** TECH tensión *f*. **4** *(emphasis)* hincapié *m* (on, en), énfasis *m* (on, en). **5** LING *(on word)* acento (tónico). ⃞COMP **stress mark** acento.
‣ *vt* **1** *(emphasize)* hacer hincapié en, poner énfasis en, subrayar, enfatizar. **2** LING *(word)* acentuar.

stressed [strest] *adj* **1** MED *(person)* estresado,-a. **2** PHYS *(object)* tensado,-a.

stressful ['stresful] *adj* estresante, de mucho estrés.

stretch [stretʃ] n **1** *(of land, water)* extensión *f*; *(of road)* tramo, trecho. **2** *(elasticity)* elasticidad *f*. **3** *(act of stretching)* estiramiento. **4** *(period of time)* período, tiempo, intervalo; *(in prison)* condena. **5** SP *(of racetrack)* recta.
‣ *vt* **1** *(extend - elastic, clothes, rope)* estirar; *(- canvas)* extender; *(- shoes)* ensanchar;

S

(- arm, leg) alargar, estirar, extender; *(-wings)* desplegar, extender. **2** *(make demands on, make to use all abilities)* exigir a. **3** *(strain - money, resources)* estirar, emplear al máximo; *(- patience)* abusar; *(- meaning)* forzar, distorsionar.

▸ *vi* **1** *(elastic)* estirarse; *(fabric)* dar de sí; *(shoes)* ensancharse, dar de sí; *(person, animal - gen)* estirarse; *(person - when tired)* desperezarse. **2** *(extend - land, sea, etc)* extenderse (out, -); *(- in time)* alargarse, prolongarse. **3** *(reach)* llegar (to, para), alcanzar (to, para).

▸ *adj (material, jeans, etc)* elástico,-a.

◆ **to stretch out** *vi (person - gen)* estirarse; *(- lie down)* tumbarse.

▸ *vt sep* **1** *(arm, leg)* alargar, estirar, extender. **2** *(money, resources)* estirar.

❌ To stretch no significa 'estrechar', que se traduce por **to tighten**, **to narrow**.

stretcher ['stretʃəʳ] *n* camilla.

stretchy ['stretʃɪ] *adj* elástico,-a.
ⓘ *comp* stretchier, *superl* stretchier.

strew [struː] *vt lit (scatter)* esparcir, desparramar; *(lie scattered)* sembrar, cubrir.
ⓘ *pt* strewed, *pp* strewed o strewn [struːn].

strict [strɪkt] *adj* **1** *(severe - person)* severo,-a, estricto,-a; *(- discipline)* riguroso,-a, severo,-a, estricto,-a; *(- rule, law, order, etc)* estricto,-a, riguroso,-a, rígido,-a. **2** *(exact, precise)* estricto,-a, riguroso,-a; *(complete, total)* absoluto,-a.

strictly ['strɪktlɪ] *adv* **1** *(severely)* severamente, estrictamente, de manera estricta. **2** *(rigorously, rigidly)* estrictamente; *(categorically)* terminantemente. **3** *(exactly, precisely)* estrictamente, exactamente; *(completely)* totalmente, del todo. **4** *(exclusively)* exclusivamente. ⃞ **strictly speaking** en realidad.

stride [straɪd] *n* **1** *(long step)* zancada; *(gait)* paso, manera de andar. **2** *(advance, development)* progresos *mpl*.

▸ *vi* andar a zancadas.
ⓘ *pt* strode [strəʊd], *pp* stridden ['strɪdən].

▸ *n pl* **strides** *fam (trousers)* pantalón *m sing*, pantalones *mpl*.

stridden ['strɪdən] *pp* → **stride**.

strike [straɪk] *n* **1** *(by workers, students, etc)* huelga. **2** SP *(blow - gen)* golpe *m*; *(- in tenpin bowling)* pleno; *(- in baseball)* strike *m*. **3** *(find)* hallazgo; *(of oil, gold, etc)* descubrimiento. **4** MIL ataque *m*: air strike ataque aéreo.

▸ *vt* **1** *(hit)* pegar, golpear. **2** *(knock against, collide with)* dar contra, chocar contra; *(ball, stone)* pegar contra, dar contra; *(lightning, bullet, torpedo)* alcanzar. **3** *(disaster, earthquake)* golpear, sobrevenir; *(disease)* atacar, golpear. **4** *(gold, oil)* descubrir, encontrar, dar con; *(track, path)* dar con. **5** *(coin, medal)* acuñar. **6** *(match)* encender. **7** *(of clock)* dar, tocar. **8** MUS *(note)* dar; *(chord)* tocar. **9** *(bargain, deal)* cerrar, hacer; *(balance)* encontrar, hallar; *(agreement)* llegar a. **10** *(pose, attitude)* adoptar. **11** *(give impression)* parecer, dar la impresión de. **12** *(occur to)* ocurrírsele a; *(remember)* acordarse de. **13** *(render)* dejar. **14** *(cause fear, terror, worry)* infundir. **15** *(take down - sail, flag)* arriar; *(- tent, set)* desmontar. **16** *(cutting)* plantar.

▸ *vi* **1** *(attack - troops, animal, etc)* atacar; *(- disaster, misfortune)* sobrevenir, ocurrir; *(- disease)* atacar, golpear; *(- lightning)* alcanzar, caer. **2** *(workers, etc)* declararse en huelga, hacer huelga. **3** *(clock)* dar la hora.

◆ **to strike back** *vi* **1** *(gen)* devolver el golpe. **2** MIL contraatacar.

◆ **to strike down** *vt sep (by illness, disease)* abatir, fulminar.

◆ **to strike off** *vt sep* **1** *(name from list)* tachar. **2** JUR *(doctor, lawyer, etc)* inhabilitar para ejercer.

◆ **to strike on** *vt insep (discover)* dar con, encontrar.

◆ **to strike out** *vt sep (remove, cross out)* tachar.

▸ *vi* **1** *(attack, hit out)* arremeter (at, contra). **2** *(set off)* emprender el camino.

◆ **to strike up** *vt insep (friendship)* entablar, trabar; *(conversation)* entablar, iniciar.

▸ *vi (band)* empezar a tocar.
ⓘ *pt & pp* struck [strʌk].

strikebreaker ['straɪkbreɪkəʳ] *n* esquirol *mf*, rompehuelgas *mf*.

striker ['stɹaɪkəʳ] n **1** (worker) huelguista mf. **2** SP (football) delantero,-a; (cricket) bateador,-ra.

striking ['stɹaɪkɪŋ] adj **1** (eye-catching) llamativo,-a; (stunning) atractivo,-a. **2** (similarity, resemblance) sorprendente, asombroso,-a; (feature, etc) impresionante, destacado,-a. **3** (on strike) en huelga.

string [stɹɪŋ] n **1** (cord) cuerda, cordel m; (lace) cordón m; (of puppet) hilo. **2** (on instrument, racket) cuerda. **3** (of garlic, onions) ristra; (of pearls, beads) sarta, hilo. **4** (of vehicles) fila, hilera; (of hotels) cadena; (of events) serie f, cadena, sucesión f; (of lies, complaints) sarta; (of insults) retahíla. COMP **string orchestra** orquestra de cuerda. ‖ **string quartet** cuarteto de cuerda.
► vt **1** (beads) ensartar, enhebrar. **2** (guitar, racket) encordar. **3** (beans) quitar la hebra a.
① pt & pp **strung** [stɹʌŋ].
► n pl **the strings** MUS los instrumentos mpl de cuerda.

strip¹ [stɹɪp] vt **1** (person) desnudar, quitarle la ropa a; (bed) quitar la ropa de; (room, house) vaciar; (wallpaper, paint) quitar; (leaves, bark) arrancar. **2** (property, rights, titles) despojar (of, de). **3** (engine) desarmar, desmontar (down, -); (ship) desaparejar.
► vi (undress) desnudarse (off, -), quitarse la ropa; (perform striptease) hacer un strip-tease.
① pt & pp **stripped**, ger **stripping**.
► n (striptease) strip-tease m.

strip² [stɹɪp] n **1** (of paper, leather) tira; (of land) franja; (of metal) tira, cinta. **2** SP (colours, kit) equipo. **3** (airstrip) pista (de aterrizaje). **4** [also strip (cartoon)] historieta, tira cómica. COMP **strip lighting** alumbrado fluorescente. ‖ **strip mining** US explotación f a cielo abierto.

stripe [stɹaɪp] n **1** (gen) raya, lista. **2** MIL galón m. **3** (kind, type) tipo, clase f.
► vi pintar a rayas, dibujar a rayas.

striped [stɹaɪpt] adj rayado,-a, a rayas: a striped shirt una camisa a rayas.

stripy ['stɹaɪpɪ] adj rayado,-a, a rayas.
① comp **stripier**, superl **stripiest**.

strive [stɹaɪv] vi esforzarse, procurar.
① pt **strove** [stɹəʊv], pp **striven** ['stɹɪvən].

striven ['stɹɪvən] pt → **strive**.

strode [stɹəʊd] pt → **stride**.

stroke [stɹəʊk] n **1** (blow) golpe m. **2** (caress) caricia. **3** SP (in tennis, cricket, golf) golpe m, jugada; (in billiards) tacada; (in rowing) palada, (in swimming - movement) brazada; (- style) estilo. **4** SP (oarsman) cabo. **5** (of pen) trazo; (of brush) pincelada. **6** (of bell) campanada. **7** (of engine) tiempo; (of piston) carrera. **8** MED ataque m de apoplejía, derrame m cerebral. **9** (oblique) barra (oblicua).
► vt **1** (caress) acariciar. **2** (ball) dar un golpe a.

stroll [stɹəʊl] n paseo, vuelta.
► vi dar un paseo, dar una vuelta.

stroller ['stɹəʊləʳ] n **1** (pushchair) cochecito, sillita de niño. **2** (person) paseante mf.

strong [stɹɒŋ] adj **1** (physically - person) fuerte; (- consitution) robusto,-a. **2** (material, furniture, shoes, etc) fuerte, resistente. **3** (country, army) poderoso,-a, fuerte. **4** (beliefs, views, principles) firme; (faith) firme, sólido,-a; (support) mucho, firme. **5** (argument, evidence) contundente, convincente; (influence) grande; (protest) enérgico,-a. **6** (colour) fuerte, intenso,-a, vivo,-a; (smell, food, drink) fuerte; (tea, coffee) fuerte, cargado,-a; (light) brillante. **7** (resemblance, accent) fuerte, marcado,-a. **8** (chance, likelihood, probability) bueno,-a. **9** (wind, current) fuerte. **10** (good - team) fuerte; (- cast) sólido,-a. **11** (currency, etc) fuerte.
► adv fuerte.

strongbox ['stɹɒŋbɒks] n caja fuerte.

stronghold ['stɹɒŋhəʊld] n **1** MIL fortaleza. **2** fig baluarte m.

strongroom ['stɹɒŋruːm] n cámara acorazada.

stroppy ['stɹɒpɪ] adj GB fam borde, de mala uva.
① comp **stroppier**, superl **stroppiest**.

strove [stɹəʊv] pt → **strive**.

struck [stɹʌk] pt & pp → **strike**.

structural ['stɹʌktʃ(ə)ɹəl] adj (gen) estructural. COMP **structural engineer** ingeniero,-a de estructuras.

structure ['strʌktʃəʳ] n **1** *(organization, composition)* estructura. **2** *(thing constructed)* construcción f; *(building)* edificio.
▶ vt *(arguemnt, essay, report, etc)* estructurar; *(event)* planificar.

struggle ['strʌgᵊl] n *(gen)* lucha; *(physical fight)* pelea, forcejeo.
▶ vi **1** *(fight)* luchar; *(physically)* forcejear. **2** *(strive)* luchar (for, por), esforzarse (for, por); *(suffer)* pasar apuros; *(have difficulty)* costar, tener problemas.

strum [strʌm] vt rasguear.
▶ vi rasguear (on, -).
ⓘ pt & pp strummed, ger strumming.

strung [strʌŋ] pt & pp → string. [LOC] to be highly strung estar muy nervioso, -a, estar muy tenso,-a.

strut [strʌt] n **1** ARCH *(rod, bar)* puntal m, riostra. **2** *(way of walking)* contoneo, pavoneo.
▶ vi pavonearse, contonearse.
ⓘ pt & pp strutted, ger strutting.

stub [stʌb] n *(of cigarette)* colilla; *(of pencil, candle)* cabo; *(of cheque, etc)* matriz f.
▶ vt darse un golpe.
ⓘ pt & pp stubbed, ger stubbing.
◆ to stub out vt sep apagar.

stubborn ['stʌbᵊn] adj **1** *(person, animal)* terco,-a, testarudo,-a, tozudo,-a, obstinado, a; *(refusal, resistance)* obcecado,-a. **2** *(stain, cough, etc)* rebelde.

stubbornly ['stʌbᵊnlɪ] adv tercamente, cabezudamente.

stubby ['stʌbɪ] adj corto,-a y rechoncho,-a.
ⓘ comp stubbier, superl stubbiest.

stucco ['stʌkəʊ] n estuco.
ⓘ pl stuccoes o stuccos.

stuck [stʌk] pt & pp → stick.
▶ adj **1** *(unable to move)* atascado,-a. **2** *(trapped)* atrapado,-a; *(in routine)* estancado,-a. **3** fam *(stumped)* atascado,-a; *(in difficulties)* en apuros.

stuck-up [stʌk'ʌp] adj fam creído,-a, estirado,-a.

stud [stʌd] n semental m. [COMP] stud farm cuadra.

student ['stjuːdᵊnt] n **1** *(university)* estudiante mf, universitario,-a; *(school)* alumno,-a. **2** fml *(scholar)* estudioso,-a.
▶ adj estudiantil.

studio ['stjuːdɪəʊ] n **1** *(TV, radio)* estudio. **2** *(artist's)* estudio, taller m.
ⓘ pl studios.
▶ n pl studios CINEM estudios mpl.

studious ['stjuːdɪəs] adj **1** *(fond of studying)* estudioso,-a, aplicado,-a. **2** fml *(careful)* esmerado,-a; *(deliberate)* deliberado,-a.

study ['stʌdɪ] n **1** *(act of studying)* estudio; *(investigation, research)* investigación f, estudio. **2** *(room)* despacho, estudio.
ⓘ pl studies.
▶ vt **1** *(gen)* estudiar; *(university subject)* estudiar, cursar; *(investigate, research)* estudiar, investigar. **2** *(scrutinize)* estudiar, examinar.
▶ vi estudiar.
ⓘ pt & pp studied, ger studying.
▶ n pl studies *(work)* estudios mpl; *(subjects)* estudios mpl, asignaturas fpl.

stuff [stʌf] n **1** fam *(matter, material, substance)* materia, material m. **2** fam *(things, possesions)* cosas fpl, trastos mpl. **3** fam *(content)* cuento, rollo, cosas fpl.
▶ vt **1** *(fill - container, bag, box)* llenar (with, de); *(- cushion, toy, food)* rellenar (with, de); *(- hole)* tapar. **2** *(dead animal)* disecar. **3** *(push carelessly, shove)* meter, poner. **4** fam *(beat, thrash)* dar una paliza a. **5** sl *(sod)* meter.

stuffed [stʌft] adj **1** *(full)* relleno,-a; *(crammed)* atiborrado,-a. **2** *(animal)* disecado,-a.

stuffing ['stʌfɪŋ] n relleno.

stuffy ['stʌfɪ] adj **1** *(room)* mal ventilado,-a; *(atmosphere)* cargado,-a. **2** *(person)* estirado,-a, remilgado,-a; *(institution)* tradicional; *(ideas, manners)* formal, serio,-a, convencional.
ⓘ comp stuffier, superl stuffiest.

stumble ['stʌmbᵊl] n tropezón m, traspié m, trompicón m.
▶ vi **1** *(trip)* tropezar (on/over, con), dar un traspié. **2** *(walk unsteadily)* tambalearse. **3** *(while speaking)* atrancarse, atascarse.
◆ to stumble across / stumble on vt insep dar con, tropezar con.

stun [stʌn] vt **1** *(make unconscious)* dejar sin sentido; *(daze)* aturdir, atontar, pas-

mar. **2** (surprise) sorprender, dejar atónito,-a, dejar pasmado,-a; (shock) atolondrar, aturdir, dejar anonadado,-a.
ⓘ pt & pp **stunned**, ger **stunning**.

stung [stʌŋ] pt & pp → **sting**.

stunk [stʌŋk] pt & pp → **stink**.

stunning ['stʌnɪŋ] adj **1** (surprising) alucinante, apabullante; (shocking) asombroso,-a. **2** (beautiful, impressive) impresionante, imponente, fenomenal.

stunt¹ [stʌnt] vt (growth) atrofiar.

stunt² [stʌnt] n **1** (dangerous act) proeza; (in film) escena peligrosa. **2** (trick) truco, maniobra. COMP **stunt man** especialista m. **‖ stunt woman** especialista f.

stunted ['stʌntɪd] adj (tree, body) raquítico,-a; (growth) atrofiado,-a.

stupefy ['stjuːpɪfaɪ] vt **1** (alcohol, drugs) atontar, aturdir, aletargar. **2** (amaze) dejar pasmado,-a, dejar estupefacto,-a.
ⓘ pt & pp **stupefied**, ger **stupefying**.

stupid ['stjuːpɪd] adj **1** tonto,-a, bobo,-a, imbécil, estúpido,-a. **2** (senseless) atontado,-a. **3** fam (annoying) maldito,-a.
ⓘ comp **stupider**, comp **stupidest**.
▸ n tonto,-a, imbécil mf.

stupidity [stjuː'pɪdɪtɪ] n estupidez f, tontería.

stupidly ['stjuːpɪdlɪ] adv estúpidamente, tontamente.

stupor ['stjuːpəʳ] n estupor m.

sturdy ['stɜːdɪ] adj **1** (strong) robusto,-a, fuerte; (solid) sólido,-a. **2** (opposition, resistance, defence) enérgico,-a, férreo,-a, tenaz, inquebrantable.
ⓘ comp **sturdier**, superl **sturdiest**.

sturgeon ['stɜːdʒ°n] n esturión m.

stutter ['stʌtəʳ] n tartamudeo.
▸ vi tartamudear.
▸ vt decir tartamudeando, balbucear.

sty¹ [staɪ] n (for pigs) pocilga.
ⓘ pl **sties**.

sty² [staɪ] n → **stye**.
ⓘ pl **sties**.

stye [staɪ] n (in eye) orzuelo.

style [staɪl] n **1** (gen) estilo. **2** (type, model) modelo, diseño. **3** (of hair) peinado. **4** (fashion) moda. **5** fml (correct title) título. **6** BOT estilo.

▸ vt **1** (gen) diseñar; (hair) peinar. **2** fml (name, title) llamar.

stylish ['staɪlɪʃ] adj **1** (elegant) elegante, con mucho estilo. **2** (fashionable) a la moda, de última moda.

stylist ['staɪlɪst] n **1** (hairdresser) estilista mf, peluquero,-a. **2** (writer) estilista mf.

stylized ['staɪlaɪzd] adj estilizado,-a.

stylus ['staɪləs] n **1** (of record player) aguja. **2** (for writing) estilo.
ⓘ pl **styluses** o **styli**.

suave [swɑːv] adj (charming, polite) afable, cortés; (slick, ingratiating) zalamero,-a.

☒ Suave no significa 'suave', que se traduce por soft.

sub [sʌb] n **1** (submarine) submarino. **2** SP (substitute) sustituto,-a, suplente mf. **3** (subscription) cuota, subscripción f, suscripción f. **4** (subeditor) redactor,-ra **5** GB (advance from wages) anticipo.
▸ vi (act as substitute) sustituir (for, a).
▸ vt **1** GB (give an advance) anticipar, dar un anticipo. **2** (subedit) corregir, revisar.
ⓘ pt & pp **subbed**, ger **subbing**.

subconscious [sʌb'kɒnʃəs] adj subconsciente.
▸ n **the subconscious** el subconsciente m.

subcontinent [sʌb'kɒntɪnənt] n subcontinente m.

subcontract [(n) sʌb'kɒntrækt; (vb) sʌbkən'trækt] n subcontrato.
▸ vt subcontratar (to, a).

subculture ['sʌbkʌltʃəʳ] n subcultura.

subdivide [sʌbdɪ'vaɪd] vt subdividir (into, en).

subgroup ['sʌbgruːp] n subgrupo.

subhuman [sʌb'hjuːmən] adj infrahumano,-a.

subject [(n-adj) 'sʌbdʒekt; (vb) səb'dʒekt] n **1** (theme, topic) tema m. **2** EDUC asignatura. **3** (citizen) súbdito, ciudadano,-a. **4** LING sujeto. **5** (cause) objeto (of/for, de). **6** (of experiment) sujeto.
▸ vt (bring under control) someter, sojuzgar (to, a).
▸ adj (subordinate, governed) sometido,-a.

subject to (bound by) sujeto,-a a; (prone to - floods, subsidence) expuesto,-a a; (- change, delay) susceptible de, suje-

S

to,-a a; *(- illness)* propenso,-a a. COMP
subject matter 1 *(topic)* tema *m*, materia. **2** *(contents)* contenido.
▶ *prep* **subject to** *(conditional on)* previo,
-a, supeditado,-a a.
◆ **to subject to** *vt sep* someter a.
subjective [səb'dʒɛktɪv] *adj* subjetivo,-a.
subjunctive [səb'dʒʌŋktɪv] *adj* LING
subjuntivo,-a.
▶ *n* LING subjuntivo.
sublet [sʌb'let] *vt* realquilar, subarrendar.
▶ *vi* realquilar, subarrendar.
ⓘ *pt & pp* sublet, *ger* subletting.
sublime [sə'blaɪm] *adj* **1** *(beauty, music,
compliment, etc)* sublime. **2** *fam (food, performance)* maravilloso,-a, sensacional.
3 *pej (indifference, ignorance, etc)* sumo,-a,
supremo,-a, absoluto,-a, total.
▶ *n* **the sublime** lo sublime.
subliminal [sʌb'lɪmɪnəl] *adj* subliminal.
sub-machine-gun [sʌbmə'ʃiːngʌn] *n*
ametralladora, metralleta.
submarine ['sʌbməriːn] *n* submarino.
▶ *adj* submarino,-a.
submerge [səb'mɜːdʒ] *vt* sumergir (in,
en).
▶ *vi* sumergirse.
submission [səb'mɪʃən] *n* **1** *(subjection)*
sumisión *f* (to, a). **2** SP *(in wrestling)* rendición *f*. **3** *(presentation)* presentación *f*.
4 *(report)* informe *m*; *(proposal)* propuesta.
submit [səb'mɪt] *vt* **1** *(present)* presentar. **2** *(subject)* someter (to, a). **3** JUR
(suggest) sostener.
▶ *vi (admit defeat, surrender)* rendirse, ceder; *(to demand, wishes)* acceder.
ⓘ *pt & pp* submitted, *ger* submitting.
subnormal [sʌb'nɔːməl] *adj* **1** *(person)*
subnormal, retrasado,-a. **2** *(temperatures)* por debajo de lo normal.
subordinate [(adj-n) sə'bɔːdɪnət; (vb)
sə'bɔːdɪneɪt] *adj* **1** *(lower, less important)*
subordinado,-a (to, a), secundario,
-a. **2** LING subordinado,-a. COMP **subordinate clause** oración *f* subordinada.
▶ *n (person)* subordinado,-a,
subalterno,-a.
▶ *vt* subordinar (to, a), supeditar (to, a).

subordination [səbɔːdɪ'neɪʃən] *n* subordinación *f*.
subscribe [səb'skraɪb] *vi* **1** *(to newspaper,
etc)* suscribirse (to, a), abonarse (to,
a). **2** *(to charity)* hacer donaciones,
contribuir con donativos (to, a). **3** *(to
opinion, theory)* suscribir (to, -), estar de
acuerdo (to, con). **4** FIN *(shares)* suscribir (for, -).
▶ *vt* **1** *(contribute)* contribuir, donar. **2**
fml (sign) suscribir.
subscriber [səb'skraɪbər] *n (to newspaper,
etc)* suscriptor,-ra, abonado,-a; *(to telephone service, cable television)* abonado,-a.
subscription [səb'skrɪpʃən] *n (to newspaper,
etc)* suscripción *f*, abono; *(to club)* cuota;
(to charity) donativo, donación *f*.
subsection ['sʌbsekʃən] *n* JUR *(in document, text)* artículo.
subsequent ['sʌbsɪkwənt] *adj* subsiguiente, posterior. LOC **subsequent to**
posterior a.
subside [səb'saɪd] *vi* **1** *(land, building,
road)* hundirse. **2** *fig (person)* dejarse
caer. **3** *(storm, wind)* amainar; *(floods)*
decrecer, bajar; *(pain, fever)* disminuir;
(noise, applause) irse apagando; *(anger,
excitement)* calmarse.
subsidiary [səb'sɪdɪərɪ] *adj* **1** *(role, interest, issue)* secundario,-a. **2** *(income)* adicional, extra; *(payment, loan)* subsidiario,-a.
▶ *n* COMM filial *f*.
ⓘ *pl* subsidiaries.
subsidize ['sʌbsɪdaɪz] *vt (gen)* subvencionar; *(exports)* primar.
subsidy ['sʌbsɪdɪ] *n* subvención *f*, subsidio.
ⓘ *pl* subsidies.
subsist [səb'sɪst] *vi* subsistir.
subsistence [səb'sɪstəns] *n* subsistencia.
subsoil ['sʌbsɔɪl] *n* subsuelo.
substance ['sʌbstəns] *n* **1** *(matter)* sustancia. **2** *(real matter, solid content)* sustancia, solidez *f*. **3** *(essence, gist)* esencia,
sustancia. **4** *(wealth)* riqueza.
substantial [səb'stænʃəl] *adj* **1** *(solid)*
sólido,-a, fuerte. **2** *(large - sum, increase,
loss, damage)* importante, considerable; *(- difference, change)* sustancial, no-

table. **3** *(meal - large)* abundante; *(nourishing)* sustancioso,-a. **4** *(wealthy)* acaudalado,-a. **5** *fml (real, tangible)* sustancial.

substantiate [səb'stænʃɪeɪt] *vt (gen)* confirmar, corroborar; *(accusation)* probar.

substantive ['sʌbstəntɪv] *adj fml (research, information, evidence)* sustantivo, -a; *(matter, issue)* fundamental.
▶ *n* LING sustantivo.

substitute ['sʌbstɪtjuːt] *n* **1** *(person)* sustituto,-a, suplente *mf*. **2** *(thing)* sucedáneo (for, de).
▶ *vt* sustituir, reemplazar.
▶ *vi* sustituir, suplir (for, a).

substitution [sʌbstɪ'tjuːʃ°n] *n* sustitución *f*.

subterranean [sʌbtə'reɪnɪən] *adj* subterráneo,-a.

subtitle ['sʌbtaɪt°l] *n* subtítulo.
▶ *vt* subtitular, poner subtítulos a.

subtle ['sʌt°l] *adj* **1** *(person - tactful)* delicado,-a, discreto,-a. **2** *(colour, difference, hint, joke)* sutil; *(taste)* delicado,-a, ligero,-a; *(lighting)* tenue, sutil. **3** *(remark, mind)* agudo,-a, perspicaz; *(plan, argument, analysis)* ingenioso,-a; *(irony)* fino,-a.
ⓘ *comp* **subtler**, *comp* **subtlest**.

subtotal ['sʌb'təʊt°l] *n* subtotal *m*.

subtract [səb'trækt] *vt* restar (from, de).

subtraction [səb'trækʃ°n] *n* resta.

subtropical [sʌb'trɒpɪk°l] *adj* subtropical.

suburb ['sʌbɜːb] *n* barrio residencial.
COMP **the suburbs** las afueras *fpl*.

❌ Suburb no significa 'suburbio (barrio desfavorecido)', que se traduce por slums.

suburban [sə'bɜːb°n] *adj (area)* de los barrios residenciales; *(attitude)* convencional.

suburbia [sə'bɜːbɪə] *n* los barrios *mpl* residenciales.

subversion [sʌb'vɜːʃ°n] *n* subversión *f*.

subversive [sʌb'vɜːsɪv] *adj* subversivo,-a.
▶ *n (person)* elemento subversivo.

subway ['sʌbweɪ] *n* **1** GB *(underpass)* paso subterráneo. **2** US *(underground)* metro.

succeed [sək'siːd] *vi* **1** *(be successful - person)* tener éxito, triunfar; *(- plan, marriage)* salir bien; *(- strike)* surtir efecto, dar resultado. **2** *(manage)* lograr, conseguir. **3** *(throne)* subir (to, a); *(title)* heredar (to, -).
▶ *vt* **1** *(take place of)* suceder a. **2** *fml (follow after)* suceder a.

❌ To succeed no significa 'suceder', que se traduce por to happen.

succeeding [sək'siːdɪŋ] *adj* subsiguiente.

success [sək'ses] *n* **1** *(good result, achievement)* éxito. **2** *(successful person, thing)* éxito.

❌ Success no significa 'suceso', que se traduce por event.

successful [sək'sesful] *adj (person, career, film)* de éxito; *(plan, performance, attempt)* acertado,-a, logrado,-a; *(business)* próspero,-a; *(marriage)* feliz; *(meeting)* satisfactorio,-a, positivo, -a.

successfully [sʌk'sesfuli] *adv* con éxito, satisfactoriamente.

succession [sək'seʃ°n] *n* **1** *(act of following)* sucesión *f*. **2** *(series)* serie *f*, sucesión *f*. **3** *(to post, throne)* sucesión *f*.

successive [sək'sesɪv] *adj* sucesivo,-a, consecutivo,-a.

successor [sək'sesər] *n* sucesor,-ra.

succulent ['sʌkjələnt] *adj* **1** *(juicy)* suculento,-a. **2** BOT carnoso,-a.
▶ *n* BOT planta carnosa, suculenta.

such [sʌtʃ] *adj* **1** *(of that sort)* tal, semejante. **2** *(so much, so great)* tal, tanto,-a.
▶ *adv (so very)* tan.
▶ *pron (of that specified sort)* tal. LOC **as such 1** *(strictly speaking)* propiamente dicho. **2** *(that way)* como tal. **I in such a way that...** de tal manera que... **I such as** *(like, for example)* como. **I such as?** ¿por ejemplo?

suck [sʌk] *vt* **1** *(person - liquid)* sorber; *(- lollipop, pencil, thumb, etc)* chupar; *(insect - blood, nectar)* chupar, succionar. **2** *(vacuum cleaner)* aspirar (in, -); *(pump)* succionar, aspirar (in, -); *(plant)* absorber (up, -). **3** *(draw powerfully)* arrastrar.
▶ *vi* **1** *(person)* chupar (at/on, -); *(baby)* mamar (at, -); *(vacuum cleaner)* aspirar (up,-); *(pump)* succionar, aspirar.

S

sucker ['sʌkə'] n **1** ZOOL ventosa. **2** BOT chupón m, mamón m. **3** (rubber disc) ventosa.

suckle ['sʌkªl] vt amamantar, dar de mamar a.
▶ vi mamar.

sucrose ['sjuːkrəʊz] n sacarosa.

suction ['sʌkʃªn] n (sticking together) succión f; (of water, air) aspiración f. COMP **suction cup** ventosa. ‖ **suction pump** bomba de aspiración.

Sudan [suːˈdæn] [also the Sudan] n Sudán.

Sudanese [suːdəˈniːz] adj sudanés, -esa.
▶ n sudanés,-esa.
▶ n pl **the Sudanese** los sudaneses mpl.

sudden ['sʌdªn] adj **1** (quick) súbito,-a, repentino,-a. **2** (unexpected) inesperado,-a, imprevisto,-a. **3** (abrupt) brusco,-a. LOC **all of a sudden** de repente. COMP **sudden death** muerte f súbita.

suddenly ['sʌdªnlɪ] adv **1** (unexpectedly) de repente, de pronto. **2** (abruptly) bruscamente.

suds [sʌdz] n pl jabonaduras fpl, espuma f sing (de jabón).

sue [suː] vt JUR demandar.
▶ vi JUR entablar una demanda (for, por).

suede [sweɪd] n ante m, gamuza f.
▶ adj de ante, de gamuza.

suet ['suːɪt] n sebo.

suffer ['sʌfə'] vt **1** (gen) sufrir; (pain) padecer, sufrir; (hunger) padecer, pasar; (losses) sufrir, registrar. **2** (bear, tolerate) aguantar, soportar, tolerar.
▶ vi **1** (gen) sufrir. **2** (be affected - work, studies, etc) verse afectado,-a; (- health) resentirse: LOC **to suffer from 1** (illness) sufrir de, padecer. **2** (shock) sufrir los efectos de. **3** (effects) resentirse de.

sufferer ['sʌfªrə'] n enfermo,-a.

suffering ['sʌfªrɪŋ] n (affliction) sufrimiento, aflicción f; (grief) pena, dolor m; (pain) dolor m.

sufficient [səˈfɪʃªnt] adj suficiente, bastante. LOC **to be sufficient** bastar.

suffix ['sʌfɪks] n sufijo.

suffocate ['sʌfəkeɪt] vt asfixiar, ahogar.
▶ vi asfixiarse, ahogarse.

❌ To suffocate no significa 'sofocar (un incendio)', que se traduce por **to put out**.

suffocation [sʌfəˈkeɪʃªn] n asfixia, ahogo.

suffrage ['sʌfrɪdʒ] n sufragio.

sugar ['ʃʊgə'] n **1** azúcar m & f. **2** US fam (form of address) cariño, cielo. COMP **sugar beet** remolacha azucarera.
▶ vt azucarar.

sugar-coated [ʃʊgəˈkəʊtɪd] adj cubierto,-a de azúcar.

suggest [səˈdʒest] vt **1** (propose) sugerir, proponer; (advise) sugerir, aconsejar. **2** (imply) insinuar. **3** (indicate) indicar. **4** (evoke) evocar, sugerir.

suggestion [səˈdʒestʃªn] n **1** (proposal) sugerencia, propuesta. **2** (insinuation) insinuación f. **3** (indication, hint) indicio; (slight trace) sombra, traza, asomo, nota. **4** (in psychology) sugestión f.

suggestive [səˈdʒestɪv] adj (with sexual connotations) provocativo,-a, insinuante.

suicidal [suːɪˈsaɪdªl] adj suicida.

suicide ['suːɪsaɪd] n **1** (act) suicidio. **2** (person) suicida mf. **3** fig suicidio. COMP **to commit suicide** suicidarse.

suit [suːt] n **1** (man's) traje m; (woman's) traje m de chaqueta. **2** JUR pleito, juicio. **3** (in cards) palo.
▶ vt **1** (be convenient, acceptable) convenir a, venir bien a; (please) satisfacer, agradar, contentar. **2** (be right for) ir bien a, sentar bien a; (look good on) quedar bien a, favorecer. **3** (adapt) adaptar (to, a), ajustar (to, a).

suitable ['suːtəbªl] adj **1** (appropriate) adecuado,-a (for, para), apropiado, -a (for, para); (for job, post) adecuado,-a, indicado,-a, idóneo,-a. **2** (acceptable, proper) apropiado,-a, apto,-a. **3** (convenient) conveniente.

suitcase ['suːtkeɪs] n maleta.

suite [swiːt] n **1** (of furniture) juego. **2** (in hotel) suite f. **3** MUS suite f. **4** (retinue) séquito, comitiva. **5** COMPUT juego.

suited ['su:tɪd] *adj* apropiado,-a (for, para), adecuado,-a (for, para).

sulk [sʌlk] *vi* enfurruñarse, estar de mal humor.
▶ *n* malhumor *m*.

sulky ['sʌlkɪ] *adj (look, mood)* malhumorado,-a; *(person)* con tendencia a enfurruñarse.
ⓘ *comp* sulkier, *superl* sulkiest.

sullen ['sʌlən] *adj* **1** *(person, mood)* hosco,-a, arisco,-a, huraño,-a; *(face)* adusto,-a.

sully ['sʌlɪ] *vt* **1** *(dirty)* ensuciar. **2** *fig (tarnish, spoil)* manchar, mancillar.
ⓘ *pt & pp* sullied, *ger* sullying.

sultan ['sʌltⁿn] *n* sultán *m*.

sultry ['sʌltrɪ] *adj* **1** *(weather)* bochornoso,-a, sofocante. **2** *(person)* sensual.
ⓘ *comp* sultrier, *superl* sultriest.

sum [sʌm] *n* **1** MATH *(calculation)* cuenta; *(addition)* suma, adición *f*. **2** *(amount of money)* suma (de dinero), cantidad *f* (de dinero). **3** *(total amount)* suma, total *m*. COMP in sum en resumen. ‖ LOC the sum total total *m*.
▶ *n pl* sums aritmética *f sing*, cálculos *mpl*.
◆ to sum up *vt sep* **1** *(summarize)* resumir, hacer un resumen de, sintetizar. **2** *(size up - situation)* evaluar; *(- person)* catalogar.
▶ *vi (summarize)* resumir; *(of judge)* recapitular.
ⓘ *pt & pp* summed, *ger* summing.

summarize ['sʌməraɪz] *vt* resumir, hacer un resumen de.

summary ['sʌmərɪ] *n (gen)* resumen *m*.
ⓘ *pl* summaries.
▶ *adj* **1** JUR *(justice, punishment)* sumario,-a: summary trial juicio sumario. **2** *(immediate - dismissal)* inmediato,-a. **3** *(brief - account)* breve, corto,-a. LOC in summary en resumen.

summer ['sʌmər] *n* **1** *(gen)* verano. **2** *lit* abril *m*.
▶ *adj (gen)* de verano; *(summery)* veraniego,-a.

summertime ['sʌmətaɪm] *n* verano, estío.

summit ['sʌmɪt] *n* **1** *(of mountain, career)* cumbre *f*, cima. **2** *(meeting)* cumbre *f*.

summon ['sʌmən] *vt* **1** *(person)* llamar; *(meeting, parliament)* convocar. **2** JUR citar, emplazar.
◆ to summon up *vt insep* **1** *(courage)* armarse de; *(strength)* reunir, cobrar; *(support)* lograr, obtener; *(resources, help)* reunir, conseguir. **2** *(memories, thoughts)* evocar.

sumptuous ['sʌmptjuəs] *adj (gen)* suntuoso,-a; *(meal)* opíparo,-a.

sun [sʌn] *n (gen)* sol *m*.

sunbathe ['sʌnbeɪð] *vi* tomar el sol.

sunbeam ['sʌnbi:m] *n* rayo de sol.

sunbed ['sʌnbed] *n* cama solar.

sunburn ['sʌnbɜ:n] *n* quemadura de sol.

sunburnt ['sʌnbɜ:nt] *adj (burnt)* quemado,-a (por el sol); *(tanned)* bronceado,-a, moreno,-a.

Sunday ['sʌndɪ] *n* domingo.

📎 Para ejemplos de uso, consulta Saturday.

sundial ['sʌndaɪəl] *n* reloj *m* de sol.

sundown ['sʌndaʊn] *n* US puesta de(l) sol.

sun-dried ['sʌndraɪd] *adj* secado,-a al sol.

sunflower ['sʌnflaʊər] *n* girasol *m*. COMP sunflower seed semilla de girasol, pipa.

sung [sʌŋ] *pp* → sing.

sunglasses ['sʌnglɑ:sɪz] *n pl* gafas *fpl* de sol.

sunhat ['sʌnhæt] *n* pamela, sombrero de ala ancha.

sunk [sʌŋk] *pp* → sink.

sunken ['sʌnkən] *adj* **1** *(ship, treasure)* hundido,-a, sumergido,-a; *(eyes, cheeks)* hundido,-a. **2** *(terrace, bath)* a un nivel más bajo.

sunlight ['sʌnlaɪt] *n* sol *m*, luz *f* del sol.

sunlit ['sʌnlɪt] *adj* soleado,-a.

sunny ['sʌnɪ] *adj* **1** *(room, house, etc)* soleado,-a; *(day)* de sol. **2** *fig (person)* alegre, risueño,-a; *(future)* risueño,-a.
ⓘ *comp* sunnier, *superl* sunniest.

sunrise ['sʌnraɪz] *n (sun-up)* salida del sol; *(dawn)* amanecer *m*, alba *m*.

sunroof ['sʌnru:f] *n* **1** AUTO capota, techo corredizo. **2** *(on building)* azotea.

S

sunset ['sʌnset] *n (sundown)* puesta de(l) sol, ocaso; *(twilight)* crepúsculo, atardecer *m*.

sunshade ['sʌnʃeɪd] *n* **1** *(parasol)* sombrilla. **2** *(awning)* toldo.

sunshine ['sʌnʃaɪn] *n* **1** sol *m*, luz *f* de sol. **2** *fig* alegría. **3** GB *fam (friendly form of address)* corazón, majo,-a; *(sarcastic)* guapo,-a.

sunstroke ['sʌnstrəʊk] *n* insolación *f*.

suntan ['sʌntæn] *n* bronceado, moreno. COMP **suntan lotion** bronceador *m*.

sun-tanned ['sʌntænd] *adj* bronceado,-a, moreno,-a.

super ['suːpəʳ] *adj fam* genial, súper, fenomenal, de primera.
  ► *n* **1** GB *(superintendent)* comisario,-a de policía. **2** US *(superintendent)* portero,-a.

superb [suːˈpɜːb] *adj* estupendo,-a, magnífico,-a, espléndido,-a, soberbio,-a.

superbly [suˈpɜːblɪ] *adv* estupendamente, magníficamente, espléndidamente, soberbiamente.

supercilious [suːpəˈsɪlɪəs] *adj (condescending)* altanero,-a; *(disdainful)* desdeñoso,-a.

superficial [suːpəˈfɪʃ°l] *adj (gen)* superficial.

superfluous [suːˈpɜːfluəs] *adj (gen)* superfluo,-a; *(remark, comment)* de más.

superhuman [suːpəˈhjuːmən] *adj* sobrehumano,-a.

superintendent [suːpərɪnˈtendənt] *n* **1** *(person in charge - gen)* director,-ra, inspector,-ra, supervisor,-ra. **2** GB *(in police)* comisario,-a de policía. **3** US *(in apartment building)* portero,-a, conserje *mf*. **4** *(of park)* encargado,-a.

superior [suːˈpɪərɪəʳ] *adj* **1** *(gen)* superior (**to**, a). **2** *pej (attitude, tone, smile)* de superioridad.
  ► *n (senior)* superior *mf*.

superiority [suːpɪərɪˈɒrɪtɪ] *n* superioridad *f*.

superlative [suːˈpɜːlətɪv] *adj* **1** *(excellent)* superlativo,-a, de primera, excelente, excepcional. **2** LING superlativo,-a.
  ► *n* LING superlativo.

superman ['suːpəmæn] *n* superhombre *m*.
  ⓘ *pl* **supermen** ['suːpəmən].

supermarket [suːpəˈmɑːkɪt] *n* supermercado, autoservicio.

supernatural [suːpəˈnætʃ°rəl] *adj* sobrenatural.
  ► *n* **the supernatural** lo sobrenatural *m*.

superpower ['suːpəpaʊəʳ] *n* superpotencia.

supersonic [suːpəˈsɒnɪk] *adj* supersónico,-a.

superstar ['suːpəstɑːʳ] *n* superestrella.

superstition [suːpəˈstɪʃ°n] *n* superstición *f*.

superstitious [sjuːpəˈstɪʃəs] *adj* supersticioso,-a.

superstore ['suːpəstɔːʳ] *n* hipermercado.

superstructure ['suːpəstrʌktʃəʳ] *n* superestructura.

supertanker ['suːpətæŋkəʳ] *n* superpetrolero.

supervise ['suːpəvaɪz] *vt* **1** *(watch over)* vigilar. **2** *(keep check on)* supervisar; *(run)* dirigir.

supervision [suːpəˈvɪʒ°n] *n* supervisión *f*.

supervisor ['suːpəvaɪzəʳ] *n* **1** *(gen)* supervisor,-ra. **2** GB *(of thesis)* director,-ra de tesis.

superwoman ['suːpəwʊmən] *n* supermujer *f*.
  ⓘ *pl* **superwomen** ['suːpəwɪmɪn].

supper ['sʌpəʳ] *n* cena. LOC **to have supper** cenar.

supper-time ['sʌpətaɪm] *n* hora de cenar.

supplement [(*n*) 'sʌplɪmənt]; *(vb)* 'sʌplɪment] *n* **1** *(charge)* suplemento. **2** *(dietary)* complemento. **3** LIT suplemento.
  ► *vt* complementar.

supplementary [sʌplɪˈment°rɪ] *adj* **1** *(gen)* suplementario, a, adicional. **2** MATH suplementario,-a.

supplier [səˈplaɪəʳ] *n* COMM proveedor, -ra, abastecedor,-ra.

supply [səˈplaɪ] *n* **1** *(provision)* suministro. **2** COMM *(provision - to markets, areas, etc)* abastecimiento; *(- to individuals,* *houses, shops, etc)* suministro. **3** *(amount availabe)* reserva.

ⓘ *pl* supplies.

▶ *vt* **1** *(goods, materials)* suministrar. **2** *(a person, company, city, etc)* abastecer (with, de), proveer (with, de). **3** *(give - information, proof, facts)* facilitar, proporcionar. **4** MIL *(with provisions)* aprovisionar. **5** *fml (need, requirement)* satisfacer.

ⓘ *pt & pp* supplied, *ger* supplying.

▶ *n pl* supplies *(food)* provisiones *fpl*, víveres *mpl*; *(stock)* existencias *fpl*, stock *m*. MIL pertrechos *mpl*.

support [sə'pɔːt] *n* **1** *(physical - gen)* apoyo, sostén *m*; *(- thing worn on body)* protector *m*. **2** *(of building)* soporte *m*, puntal *m*. **3** *(moral)* apoyo, respaldo. **4** *(financial)* ayuda económica, apoyo económico; *(sustenance)* sustento; *(person)* sostén *m*. **5** *(supporters)* afición *f*. **6** *(evidence)* pruebas *fpl*.

▶ *vt* **1** *(roof, bridge, etc)* sostener; *(weight)* aguantar, resistir; *(part of body)* sujetar. **2** *(back, encourage)* apoyar, respaldar, ayudar; *(cause, motion, proposal)* apoyar, estar de acuerdo con. **3** SP *(follow)* seguir; *(encourage)* animar. **4** *(keep, sustain)* mantener, sustentar, sostener; *(feed)* alimentar. **5** *(corroborate, substantiate)* confirmar, respaldar, apoyar, respaldar. **6** *fml (endure)* soportar, tolerar.

❌ To support no significa 'soportar (sufrir)', que se traduce por to bear.

supporter [sə'pɔːtə^r] *n* **1** POL partidario,-a. **2** SP *(gen)* seguidor,-ra; *(fan)* hincha *mf*, forofo,-a.

▶ *n pl* supporters SP la afición *f sing*. COMP supporters' club peña deportiva.

supporting [sə'pɔːtɪŋ] *adj (part, role)* secundario,-a.

suppose [sə'pəʊz] *vt* **1** *(assume, imagine)* suponer, imaginarse. **2** *(in polite requests): I don't suppose you could lend me £10, could you?* no podrías dejarme 10 libras, ¿no? **3** *(believe)* creer. **4** *(postulate)* suponer. **5** *fml (presuppose)* suponer. LOC I suppose not supongo que no. I I suppose so supongo que sí.

▶ *conj* **1** *(hypothesis)* ¿y si…?, pongamos por caso, supongamos. **2** *(making suggestions)* ¿y si…?, ¿qué tal si…?

supposed [sə'pəʊzd] *adj* supuesto,-a. LOC to be supposed to **1** *(supposition, reputation)* se supone que, dicen que. **2** *(obligation, responsibility)* deber, tener que. **3** *(intention)* se supone que.

supposing [sə'pəʊzɪŋ] *conj* **1** *(hypothesis)* ¿y si…?, suponiendo. **2** *(making suggestions)* ¿y si…?, ¿qué tal si…?

suppository [sə'pɒzɪt^ərɪ] *n* supositorio.

ⓘ *pl* suppositories.

supremacy [suː'preməsɪ] *n* supremacía.

supreme [suː'priːm] *adj (highest)* supremo,-a, sumo,-a; *(greatest)* supremo,-a.

supremo [suː'priːməʊ] *n* GB *fam* gran jefe,-a.

ⓘ *pl* supremos.

surcharge ['sɜːtʃɑːdʒ] *n* recargo, sobretasa.

▶ *vt (person)* aplicar un recargo a.

sure [ʃʊə^r] *adj* **1** *(positive, certain)* seguro,-a (about/of, de); *(convinced)* convencido,-a. **2** *(certain, inevitable)* seguro,-a. **3** *(reliable)* seguro,-a.

▶ *adv* **1** *(of course)* claro, por supuesto. **2** US *(as intensifier)* realmente, de verdad.

surely ['ʃʊəlɪ] *adv* **1** *(doubtless)* seguramente, sin duda. **2** *(as intensifier): surely you haven't forgotten!* ¡no se te habrá olvidado! **3** *(in a sure manner)* con seguridad. **4** US *(certainly)* por supuesto, desde luego, claro (que sí).

surf [sɜːf] *n (waves)* olas *fpl*, oleaje *m*; *(foam)* espuma.

▶ *vi* hacer surf. LOC to surf the net navegar en Internet.

surface ['sɜːfɪs] *n* **1** *(gen)* superficie *f*; *(of road)* firme *m*. **2** *fig (exterior)* apariencia.

▶ *adj (gen)* superficial.

▶ *vt (cover road)* pavimentar; *(with asphalt)* asfaltar.

▶ *vi* **1** *(submarine, etc)* salir a la superficie; *(problems, etc)* aflorar, aparecer, surgir. **2** *(from bed)* asomarse, dejarse ver; *(after disappearance)* reaparecer.

surfboard ['sɜːfbɔːd] *n* tabla de surf.

surfer ['sɜːfə^r] *n* surfista *mf*.

surfing ['sɜːfɪŋ] *n* surf *m*.

S

surgeon ['sɜːdʒªn] *n* cirujano,-a.

surgery ['sɜːdʒərɪ] *n* **1** *(operating)* cirugía. **2** GB *(place)* consultorio, consulta; *(time)* consulta.

ⓘ *pl* surgeries.

surgical ['sɜːdʒɪkªl] *adj (instrument, treatment)* quirúrgico,-a.

Surinam [suərɪ'næm] *n* Surinam.

surmount [sɜː'maunt] *vt* **1** *(overcome)* superar, vencer. **2** ARCH rematar, coronar.

surname ['sɜːneɪm] *n* apellido.

surpass [sɜː'pɑːs] *vt (better)* superar; *(exceed)* superar, sobrepasar.

surplus ['sɜːpləs] *n (of goods, produce)* excedente *m*, sobrante *m*; *(of budget)* superávit *m*.
▶ *adj* sobrante, excedente.

surprise [sə'praɪz] *n* sorpresa.
▶ *adj (visit, result)* inesperado,-a; *(attack, party)* sorpresa.
▶ *vt* **1** *(cause surprise to)* sorprender. **2** *(catch unawares)* sorprender, coger desprevenido,-a.

surprised [sə'praɪzd] *adj (person)* sorprendido,-a; *(look)* de sorpresa.

surprising [sə'praɪzɪŋ] *adj* sorprendente.

surreal [sə'rɪəl] *adj* surrealista.

surrealism [sə'rɪəlɪzªm] *n* surrealismo.

surrealist [sə'rɪəlɪst] *n* surrealista *mf*.
▶ *adj* surrealista.

surrender [sə'rendəʳ] *n* **1** *(capitulation)* rendición *f*; *(submission)* sumisión *f*, claudicación *f*. **2** *(giving up - of arms)* entrega; *(- of rights)* renuncia.
▶ *vt* **1** MIL *(weapons, town)* rendir, entregar. **2** *fml (passport, ticket, etc)* entregar; *(claim, right, privilege)* renunciar a, ceder.
▶ *vi* rendirse, entregarse.

surround [sə'raund] *vt (encircle)* rodear (with, de).
▶ *n* marco, borde *m*.

surrounding [sə'raundɪŋ] *adj* circundante.
▶ *n pl* **surroundings** *(of town, city, etc)* alrededores *mpl fpl*. *(environment)* entorno, ambiente *m*.

surveillance [sɜː'veɪləns] *n* vigilancia.

survey [*(n)* 'sɜːveɪ; *(vb)* sə'veɪ] *n* **1** *(investigation - of opinion)* sondeo, encuesta; *(- of prices, trends, etc)* estudio; *(written report)* informe *m*. **2** *(of land)* inspección *f*, reconocimiento; *(in topography)* medición *f*. **3** *(general view)* visión *f* general, visión *f* de conjunto. **4** GB *(of house, building)* inspección *f*, peritaje *m*.
▶ *vt* **1** *(contemplate, look at)* contemplar, mirar. **2** *(study - gen)* examinar, analizar; *(- prices, trends, etc)* estudiar, hacer una encuesta sobre; *(investigate - people)* encuestar, hacer un sondeo de. **3** *(- land)* hacer un reconocimiento de; *(in topography)* medir. **4** *(house, building)* inspeccionar, hacer un peritaje de.

surveyor [sə'veɪəʳ] *n (of land)* agrimensor,-ra, topógrafo,-a; *(of house, building)* perito,-a.

survival [sə'vaɪvªl] *n* **1** *(gen)* supervivencia. **2** *(relic)* reliquia, vestigio (from, de).

survive [sə'vaɪv] *vi* **1** *(gen)* sobrevivir; *(custom, tradition)* sobrevivir, perdurar; *(book, painting)* conservarse. **2** *fam (cope, get by)* ir tirando, arreglárselas.
▶ *vt* **1** *(disaster)* sobrevivir a. **2** *(person)* sobrevivir a.

survivor [sə'vaɪvəʳ] *n* superviviente *mf*, sobreviviente *mf*.

suspect [*(adj-n)* 'sʌspekt; *(vb)* sə'spekt] *adj (suspicious)* sospechoso,-a; *(dubious, questionable)* dudoso,-a.
▶ *n (person)* sospechoso,-a.
▶ *vt* **1** *(believe guilty)* sospechar de; *(mistrust)* recelar de, desconfiar de, dudar de. **2** *(think true)* sospechar. **3** *(suppose, guess)* imaginarse, creer.

suspend [sə'spend] *vt* **1** *(stop temporarily)* suspender; *(postpone)* posponer, aplazar. **2** *(remove)* suspender. **3** *(hang)* suspender, colgar.

> ❌ To suspend no significa 'suspender (un examen)', que se traduce por to fail.

suspense [səs'spens] *n (anticipation)* incertidumbre *f*; *(intrigue)* suspense *m*, intriga.

suspension [sə'spenʃªn] *n* **1** *(halt)* suspensión *f*; *(postponement)* aplazamiento, postergación *f*. **2** *(of employee, player)* suspensión *f*; *(of pupil)* expulsión *f*. **3**

CHEM suspensión *f*. **4** TECH suspensión *f*. COMP **suspension points** puntos suspensivos.

suspicion [səˈspɪʃᵊn] *n* **1** *(gen)* sospecha; *(mistrust)* recelo, desconfianza; *(doubt)* duda; *(hunch)* presentimiento. **2** *(slight trace)* pizca, asomo, atisbo.

suspicious [səˈspɪʃəs] *adj* **1** *(arousing suspicion)* sospechoso,-a. **2** *(distrustful, wary)* desconfiado,-a, suspicaz.

sustain [səˈsteɪn] *vt* **1** *(keep alive - gen)* sustentar; *(- spirits, hope)* mantener. **2** *(maintain - gen)* sostener; *(- interest, conversation)* mantener; *(- work)* continuar. **3** MUS *(note)* sostener. **4** *fml (suffer - loss, injury, wound, etc)* sufrir. **5** *fml (hold up)* sostener. **6** JUR admitir.

sustainable [səˈsteɪnəbᵊl] *adj* sostenible.

suture [ˈsʌtʃəʳ] *n (thread)* hilo de sutura; *(stitch)* punto de sutura.
▸ *vt* suturar.

swab [swɒb] *n* **1** MED *(cotton wool)* algodón *m*; *(gauze)* gasa. **2** MED *(specimen)* frotis *m*, muestra. **3** *(cleaning cloth)* paño, bayeta, trapo; *(mop)* fregona.
▸ *vt* **1** MED *(wound)* limpiar. **2** MAR *(deck)* limpiar, fregar.
ⓘ *pt & pp* swabbed, *ger* swabbing.

swallow¹ [ˈswɒləʊ] *n (of drink, food)* trago.
▸ *vt* **1** *(food, etc)* tragar. **2** *fig (be taken in by)* tragarse.
▸ *vi* tragar.
◆ **to swallow up** *vt sep* **1** *(engulf)* tragarse, engullir. **2** *(use up)* consumir, tragarse, comerse, absorber.

swallow² [ˈswɒləʊ] *n (bird)* golondrina.

swam [swæm] *pt* → swim.

swamp [swɒmp] *n* pantano, ciénaga.
▸ *vt* **1** *(land)* inundar, anegar; *(boat)* hundir. **2** *fig (inundate)* inundar (with/ by, de); *(overwhelm)* agobiar, abrumar (with/by, de).

swan [swɒn] *n (bird)* cisne *m*.
▸ *vi* pavonearse.
ⓘ *pt & pp* swanned, *ger* swanning.

swap [swɒp] *n* canje *m*, cambalache *m*.
▸ *vt fam* cambiar, intercambiar.
▸ *vi* hacer un intercambio, cambiar.
ⓘ *pt & pp* swapped, *ger* swapping.

swarm [swɔːm] *n* **1** *(of bees)* enjambre *m*. **2** *fig (of people)* enjambre *m*, nube *f*, multitud *f*.
▸ *vi* **1** *(bees)* enjambrar. **2** *fig (people)* aglomerarse, apiñarse, arremolinarse.
◆ **to swarm with** *vt insep* rebosar de, estar plagado,-a de.

swathe¹ [sweɪð] *n* → swath.

swathe² [sweɪð] *vt (wrap)* envolver, vendar.
◆ **to swathe in** *vt sep fig* envolver.

sway [sweɪ] *n* **1** *(movement)* balanceo, vaivén *m*, movimiento. **2** *fig (influence)* dominio, influencia (over, sobre).
▸ *vt* **1** *(swing)* balancear, bambolear. **2** *fig (influence)* influir en, influenciar, convencer.
▸ *vi* **1** *(person, tree, ladder)* balancearse, bambolearse; *(tower)* bambolearse; *(crops)* mecerse; *(person - totter)* tambalearse. **2** *fig (waver)* vacilar (between, entre), oscilar (between, entre).

swear [sweəʳ] *vt* **1** *(declare formally)* jurar; *(vow)* juramentar. **2** *fam (state firmly)* jurar.
▸ *vi* **1** *(declare formally)* jurar, prestar juramento. **2** *(curse)* decir palabrotas, soltar tacos; *(blaspheme)* jurar, blasfemar.
◆ **to swear by** *vt insep fam* tener una fe absoluta en.
◆ **to swear in** *vt sep (in court)* tomarle juramento a.
◆ **to swear to** *vt insep* jurar.
ⓘ *pt* swore [swɔːʳ], *pp* sworn [swɔːn].

swearword [ˈsweəˈwɜːd] *n* palabrota.

sweat [swet] *n* **1** *(perspiration)* sudor *m*. **2** *fam (hard work)* paliza. **3** *fam (anxious state)* nerviosismo. COMP **sweat gland** glándula sudorípara.
▸ *vi* **1** *(perspire)* sudar. **2** *(cheese)* exudar humedad. **3** *(work hard)* sudar la gota gorda. **4** *fam (worry)* estar preocupado,-a, sufrir.
▸ *vt* GB *(cook gently)* rehogar.
◆ **to sweat out** *vt sep (illness, cold)* quitarse sudando; *(toxins)* eliminar.

sweater [ˈswetəʳ] *n* suéter *m*, jersey *m*.

sweatshirt [ˈswetʃɜːt] *n* sudadera.

Swede [swiːd] *n (person)* sueco,-a.

Sweden [ˈswiːdᵊn] *n* Suecia.

Swedish [ˈswiːdɪʃ] *adj* sueco,-a.

S

► *n (language)* sueco.

► *n pl* **the Swedish** los suecos *mpl*.

sweep [swiːp] *n* **1** *(with broom)* barrido. **2** *(of arm)* movimiento amplio, gesto amplio; *(with weapon)* golpe *m*. **3** *(curve)* curva; *(area, stretch)* extensión *f*. **4** *fig (range, extent)* abanico, alcance *m*. **5** *(by police, rescuers)* peinado, rastreo. **6** *fam (chimney cleaner)* deshollinador,-ra.

► *vt* **1** *(room, floor)* barrer; *(chimney)* deshollinar. **2** *(with hand)* quitar de un manotazo. **3** *(move over)* azotar, barrer. **4** *(remove by force)* arrastrar, llevarse. **5** *(pass over)* recorrer. **6** *fig (spread through)* recorrer, extenderse por. **7** *(touch lightly)* rozar, pasar por.

► *vi* **1** *(with broom)* barrer. **2** *(move quickly)* pasar rápidamente. **3** *(extend)* recorrer, extenderse.

◆ **to sweep aside** *vt sep* **1** *(objection, etc)* rechazar; *(suggestion)* descartar. **2** *(object)* apartar (bruscamente).

◆ **to sweep away** *vt sep* **1** *(privilege, etc)* erradicar. **2** *(by flood, storm)* arrastrar, llevarse.

◆ **to sweep up** *vt sep* **1** *(room, etc)* barrer; *(dust, etc)* (barrer y) recoger. **2** *(object, person)* recoger, levantar.

► *vi* barrer, limpiar.

① *pt & pp* **swept** [swept].

sweeping ['swiːpɪŋ] *adj* **1** *(broad)* amplio,-a; *(very general)* muy general. **2** *(overwhelming)* arrollador,-ra, aplastante; *(far-reaching)* radical; *(huge)* enorme. COMP **sweeping brush** escoba.

sweet [swiːt] *adj* **1** *(taste)* dulce; *(sugary)* azucarado,-a. **2** *(pleasant)* agradable; *(smell)* fragante, bueno,-a; *(sound, music, voice)* melodioso,-a, suave, dulce. **3** *(air)* limpio,-a; *(water)* dulce. **4** *(charming)* encantador,-ra, simpático,-a; *(cute)* rico,-a, mono,-a; *(gentle)* dulce. COMP **sweet corn** maíz *m* tierno. ❙ **sweet pea** guisante *m* de olor. ❙ **sweet pepper** pimiento morrón. ❙ **sweet potato** boniato, batata.

► *n* **1** GB *(candy)* caramelo, golosina; *(chocolate)* bombón *m*. **2** GB *(dessert)* postre *m*. **3** *(form of address)* cariño, cielo, amor *m*, vida.

sweet-and-sour ['swiːtᵊnsauəʳ] *adj* CULIN agridulce.

sweetcorn ['swiːtkɔːn] *n* maíz *m* tierno.

sweeten ['swiːtᵊn] *vt* **1** *(drink, etc)* endulzar, azucarar; *(air, breath)* refrescar. **2** *fig (person)* endulzar (el carácter de); *(temper)* aplacar, calmar. **3** *fam (make more attractive)* hacer más apetecible.

◆ **to sweeten up** *vt sep* ablandar.

sweetener ['swiːtᵊnəʳ] *n* **1** *(in food, drink)* edulcorante *m*, dulcificante *m*. **2** *fam (bribe)* soborno.

sweetheart ['swiːthɑːt] *n* **1** *(dear, love)* cariño, tesoro, amor *m*. **2** *(loved one)* novio,-a.

sweetness ['swiːtnəs] *n* *(taste)* dulzor *m*; *(smell)* fragancia; *(sound)* suavidad *f*; *(character)* dulzura, simpatía.

swell [swel] *n* **1** *(of sea)* marejada, oleaje *m*. **2** MUS *(crescendo)* crescendo.

► *vi* **1** *(gen)* hincharse (**up**, -); *(sea)* levantarse; *(river)* crecer, subir. **2** *(grow - in number)* crecer, aumentar; *(- louder)* hacerse más fuerte.

► *vt* **1** *(gen)* hinchar; *(river)* hacer crecer. **2** *(increase in number)* aumentar, engrosar.

① *pt & pp* **swelled** o **swollen** ['swəʊlən].

swelling ['swelɪŋ] *n* *(swollen place)* hinchazón *f*, bulto; *(condition)* tumefacción *f*.

swept [swept] *pt & pp* → **sweep**.

swerve [swɜːv] *n* **1** AUTO viraje *m* brusco, desvío brusco. **2** SP *(by player)* regate *m*; *(of ball)* efecto.

► *vi* **1** AUTO virar bruscamente, dar un viraje brusco. **2** SP *(player)* dar un regate, regatear; *(ball)* llevar efecto. **3** *fig (veer, deviate)* desviarse (**from**, de).

swift [swɪft] *adj* **1** *(runner, horse)* rápido, -a, veloz. **2** *(reaction, reply)* pronto,-a, rápido,-a.

► *n (bird)* vencejo común.

swim [swɪm] *n* baño. LOC **to go for a swim** ir a nadar. ❙ **to have a swim** bañarse, nadar.

► *vi* **1** *(gen)* nadar. **2** *(be covered in liquid)* nadar (**in**, en), flotar (**in**, en); *(be overflowing)* estar cubierto,-a (**with**, de), estar inundado,-a. **3** *(spin, whirl)* dar vueltas.

▶ vt *(cross river)* cruzar a nado, cruzar nadando; *(cover distance)* nadar, hacer; *(use particular stroke)* nadar.
ⓘ *pt* **swam** [swæm], *pp* **swum** [swʌm], *ger* **swimming**.

swimmer ['swɪməʳ] *n* nadador,-ra.

swimming ['swɪmɪŋ] *n* natación *f.* [LOC] **to go swimming** ir a nadar. [COMP] **swimming baths** piscina cubierta. ‖ **swimming costume** bañador *m.* ‖ **swimming pool** piscina. ‖ **swimming trunks** bañador *m* (de hombre).

swimsuit ['swɪmsuːt] *n* bañador *m.*

swimwear ['swɪmweəʳ] *n* bañadores *mpl.*

swindle ['swɪndəl] *n (fiddle)* estafa; *(con)* timo.
▶ vt estafar, timar.

swine [swaɪn] *n* **1** [*pl* **swine**] *arch (pig)* cerdo, puerco, cochino. **2** [*pl* **swines**] *fam (person)* cerdo,-a, canalla *mf,* marrano,-a.

swing [swɪŋ] *n* **1** *(movement)* balanceo, vaivén *m; (of pendulum)* oscilación *f,* vaivén *m; (of hips)* contoneo. **2** *(plaything)* columpio. **3** *(change, shift)* giro, viraje *m,* cambio. **4** SP *(in golf, boxing)* swing *m.* **5** MUS *(jazz style)* swing *m; (rhythm)* ritmo. [COMP] **swing bridge** puente *m* giratorio. ‖ **swing door** puerta giratoria.
▶ vi **1** *(hanging object)* balancearse, bambolearse; *(pendulum)* oscilar; *(arms, legs)* menearse; *(child on swing)* columpiarse; *(on a pivot)* mecerse. **2** *(drive)* girar, doblar; *(walk)* caminar con energía; *(jump)* saltar. **3** *(shift)* cambiar, oscilar, virar. **4** *(music, band)* tener ritmo; *(party)* estar muy animado,-a.
▶ vt **1** *(gen)* balancear. **2** *(cause to move)* hacer girar. **3** *(change)* cambiar. **4** *fam (arrange, achieve)* arreglar.
ⓘ *pt & pp* **swung** [swʌŋ].

swipe [swaɪp] *n* **1** *(blow)* golpe *m.* **2** *(verbal attack)* ataque *m.* [COMP] **swipe card** tarjeta magnética.
▶ vt **1** pegarle a, darle a. **2** *fam (pinch)* birlar, mangar, afanar.
▶ vi asestar un golpe (at, a), intentar darle (at, a).

swirl [swɜːl] *n* **1** *(gen)* remolino; *(of smoke, cream)* voluta; *(of skirt)* vuelo. **2** *(pattern)* espiral *f.*
▶ vi *(whirl)* arremolinarse; *(person)* girar, dar vueltas.
▶ vt arremolinar.

Swiss [swɪs] *adj* suizo,-a.
▶ *n* suizo,-a.
▶ *n pl* **the Swiss** los suizos *mpl.*

switch [swɪtʃ] *n* **1** ELEC interruptor *m,* conmutador *m.* **2** US *(on railway)* agujas *fpl.* **3** *(change, shift)* cambio; *(turnaround)* viraje *m.* **4** *(exchange, swap)* intercambio, trueque *m.*
▶ vt **1** *(change)* cambiar de; *(move)* trasladar; *(attention)* desviar. **2** *(exchange)* intercambiar. **3** *(setting)* poner; *(channel)* cambiar de. **4** *(train)* desviar, cambiar de vía.
▶ vi *(gen)* cambiar (**to,** a).
◆ **to switch off** vt sep *(light, TV, etc)* apagar; *(current, gas, electricity)* cortar, desconectar; *(engine)* parar.
▶ vi *(light, machine, heating)* apagarse; *(engine)* parar; *(person)* distraerse, desconectar, dejar de prestar atención.
◆ **to switch on** vt sep *(light, machine, engine)* encender; *(light, radio, TV)* poner.
▶ vi *(gen)* encenderse.
◆ **to switch over** vi *(gen)* cambiar (**to,** a); *(channel)* cambiar de canal.

switchboard ['swɪtʃbɔːd] *n* centralita.

Switzerland ['swɪtsələnd] *n* Suiza.

swivel ['swɪvəl] *vi* girarse, volverse.
ⓘ *pt & pp* **swivelled** (US **swiveled**), *ger* **swivelling** (US **swiveling**).
▶ vt *(head)* girar; *(chair)* hacer girar. [COMP] **swivel chair** silla giratoria.

swollen ['swəʊlən] *pp* → **swell.**
▶ *adj (ankle, face)* hinchado,-a; *(glands)* inflamado,-a; *(river, lake)* crecido,-a.

swoop [swuːp] *vi* **1** *(bird)* abalanzarse (down on, sobre), abatirse (down on, sobre); *(plane)* bajar en picado. **2** *fam (police)* hacer una redada (on, en).
▶ *n* **1** *(of bird, plane)* descenso (en picado). **2** *fam (by police)* redada.

sword [sɔːd] *n* espada.

swordfish ['sɔːdfɪʃ] *n* pez *m* espada.

swore [swɔːʳ] *pt* → **swear.**

S

sworn [swɔːn] *pp* → **swear**.

swot [swɒt] *n* empollón,-ona.
▸ *vi* empollar.
ⓘ *pt & pp* swotted, *ger* swotting.

swum [swʌm] *pp* → **swim**.

swung [swʌŋ] *pt & pp* → **swing**.

sybarite ['sɪbəraɪt] *n lit* sibarita *mf*.

syllable ['sɪləbəl] *n* sílaba.

syllabus ['sɪləbəs] *n* programa *m* de estudios.
ⓘ *pl* syllabuses o syllabi.

sylph [sɪlf] *n* sílfide *f*.

symbiosis [sɪmbɪ'əʊsɪs] *n* simbiosis *f*.

symbol ['sɪmbəl] *n* símbolo (of, de).

symbolize ['sɪmbəlaɪz] *vt* simbolizar.

symmetrical [sɪ'metrɪkəl] *adj* simétrico,-a.

symmetry ['sɪmɪtrɪ] *n* simetría.

sympathetic [sɪmpə'θetɪk] *adj* **1** *(showing pity, compassion)* compasivo,-a; *(understanding)* comprensivo,-a (to, con); *(kind)* amable. **2** *(showing agreement, approval)* favorable (to, a).

☒ Sympathetic no significa 'simpático', que se traduce por **nice**.

sympathize ['sɪmpəθaɪz] *vi* **1** *(show pity, commiserate)* compadecer, compadecerse (with, de); *(understand)* comprender (with, -). **2** *(support - cause)* simpatizar (with, con).

sympathizer ['sɪmpəθaɪzəʳ] *n* simpatizante *mf*.

sympathy ['sɪmpəθɪ] *n* **1** *(pity, compassion)* compasión *f*, lástima; *(condolences)* condolencia, pésame *m*. **2** *(understanding)* comprensión *f*; *(affinity)* afinidad *f*. **3** *(agreement, support)* acuerdo.
ⓘ *pl* sympathies.
▸ *n pl* **sympathies** *(condolences)* condolencia *f sing*, pésame *m sing*. *(loyalties, leanings)* simpatías *fpl*, tendencias *fpl*.

☒ Sympathy no significa 'simpatía (amabilidad)', que se traduce por **pleasantness**.

symphony ['sɪmfənɪ] *n* sinfonía. COMP **symphony orchestra** orquesta sinfónica.
ⓘ *pl* symphonies.

symposium [sɪm'pəʊzɪəm] *n* simposio.
ⓘ *pl* symposiums o symposia.

symptom ['sɪmptəm] *n* **1** MED síntoma *m*. **2** *(sign)* síntoma *m*, señal *f*, indicio.

synagogue ['sɪnəgɒg] *n* sinagoga.

synchronize ['sɪŋkrənaɪz] *vt* sincronizar.

syncopation [sɪŋkə'peɪʃən] *n* síncopa.

syndicalism ['sɪndɪkəlɪzəm] *n* sindicalismo.

syndicalist ['sɪndɪkəlɪst] *n* sindicalista *mf*.

syndicate ['sɪndɪkət] *n* **1** *(gen)* corporación *f*, agrupación *f*, empresa. **2** *(news agency)* agencia (de prensa).
▸ *vt (distribute)* distribuir; *(publish)* publicar.

☒ Syndicate no significa 'sindicato', que se traduce por **trade union**.

syndrome ['sɪndrəʊm] *n* síndrome *m*.

synonym ['sɪnənɪm] *n* sinónimo.

synopsis [sɪ'nɒpsɪs] *n* sinopsis *f*, resumen *m*.
ⓘ *pl* synopses.

syntactic [sɪn'tæktɪk] *adj* sintáctico,-a.

syntax ['sɪntæks] *n* sintaxis *f inv*.

synthesis ['sɪnθəsɪs] *n* síntesis *f inv*.
ⓘ *pl* syntheses.

synthesize ['sɪnθəsaɪz] *vt* sintetizar.

synthesizer ['sɪnθəsaɪzəʳ] *n* sintetizador *m*.

synthetic [sɪn'θetɪk] *adj* sintético,-a.
▸ *n* fibra sintética.

syphilis ['sɪfɪlɪs] *n* sífilis *f*.

Syria ['sɪrɪə] *n* Siria.

Syrian ['sɪrɪən] *adj* sirio,-a.
▸ *n* sirio,-a.

syringe [sɪ'rɪndʒ] *n* MED jeringa, jeringuilla.
▸ *vt* MED *(ear)* hacer un lavado de.

syrup ['sɪrəp] *n* **1** MED jarabe *m*. **2** CULIN almíbar *m*.

system ['sɪstəm] *n* **1** *(gen)* sistema *m*: **2** *(body)* cuerpo, organismo.

systematic [sɪstə'mætɪk] *adj* sistemático,-a, metódico,-a.

systematize ['sɪstɪmətaɪz] *vt* sistematizar.

systemize ['sɪstəmaɪz] *vt* sistematizar.

systole ['sɪstəlɪ] *n* sístole *m*.

T

T, t [ti:] *n (the letter)* T, t *f*.

tab [tæb] *n* **1** *(flap)* lengüeta; *(on can)* anilla. **2** *(label)* etiqueta. **3** US *(bill)* cuenta. **4** *(on computer)* tabulador *m*.

table ['teɪbᵊl] *n* **1** *(gen)* mesa. **2** *(chart)* tabla, cuadro. **3** SP clasificación *f*. COMP **table football** futbolín *m*. ▮ **table of contents** índice *m* de materias. ▮ **table tennis** tenis *m* de mesa, pingpong *m*.
▶ *vt* GB *(motion, report, etc)* presentar.
▶ *n pl* **tables** tablas *fpl* de multiplicar.

> ☒ Table no significa 'tabla (de madera)', que se traduce por **board, plank**.

tablecloth ['teɪbᵊlklɒθ] *n* mantel *m*.

tablespoon ['teɪbᵊlspuːn] *n* **1** cucharón *m*. **2** cuchara grande.

tablet ['tæblɪt] *n* **1** MED pastilla, comprimido. **2** *(of soap)* pastilla.

tabloid ['tæblɔɪd] *n* periódico de formato pequeño.

tabulate ['tæbjuleɪt] *vt* tabular.

tachycardia [tækɪ'kɑːdɪə] *n* taquicardia.

tack [tæk] *n* **1** *(nail)* tachuela. **2** MAR bordada, viraje *m*. **3** *(approach)* táctica. **4** SEW hilván *m*.

tackle ['tækᵊl] *n* **1** *(equipment)* equipo, aparejos *mpl*. **2** MAR polea, aparejo. **3** SP *(football)* entrada; *(rugby)* placaje *m*.
▶ *vt* **1** *(deal with - problem)* abordar, encarar; *(- task)* emprender; *(person)* hablar con. **2** SP *(football)* entrarle a; *(rugby)* placar.

tact [tækt] *n* tacto, discreción *f*.

> ☒ Tact no significa 'tacto (sentido)', que se traduce por **touch**.

tactful ['tæktfʊl] *adj* diplomático,-a.

tactic ['tæktɪk] *n* táctica.

tactical ['tæktɪkᵊl] *adj* táctico,-a.

tactics ['tæktɪks] *n pl* MIL táctica *f sing*.

tactless ['tæktləs] *adj (person)* falto,-a de tacto, poco diplomático,-a; *(remark, question)* indiscreto,-a.

tadpole ['tædpəʊl] *n* renacuajo.

Tadzhik ['tædʒɪk] *adj* tadjiko,-a.
▶ *n (person)* tadjiko,-a.
ⓘ *pl* Tadzhik.

Tadzhiki [tæ'dʒiːkɪ] *n (language)* tadjiko.

Tadzhikistan [tædʒiːkɪ'stæn] *n* Tadjikistán.

tag [tæg] *n* **1** *(label)* etiqueta. **2** *(phrase)* coletilla. **3** *(game)* el corre que te pillo.
▶ *vt* etiquetar.

Tahiti [tə'hiːtɪ] *n* Tahití.

Tahitian [tə'hiːʃᵊn] *adj* tahitiano,-a.
▶ *n* **1** *(person)* tahitiano,-a. **2** *(language)* tahitiano.

4 ['teɪfə] *n* taifa.

tail [teɪl] *n (gen)* cola; *(of some four-legged animals)* cola, rabo.
▶ *n pl* **tails** *(of coin)* cruz *f sing*.

tailback ['teɪlbæk] *n (traffic jam)* caravana, cola, retención *f*.

tailbone ['teɪlbəʊn] *n* cóccix *m*.

tailor ['teɪlər] *n* sastre,-a.

Taiwan [taɪ'wæn] *n* Taiwan.

Taiwanese [taɪwæ'niːz] *adj* taiwanés,-esa.
▶ *n* taiwanés,-esa.

take [teɪk] *n* CINEM toma.
▶ *vt* **1** *(gen)* llevar. **2** *(remove)* llevarse, quitar, coger. **3** *(hold, grasp)* tomar, coger. **4** *(accept - money, etc)* aceptar. **5** *(win prize, competition)* ganar. **6** *(medicine, drugs)* tomar. **7** *(subject)* estudiar; *(course of study)* seguir, cursar. **8** *(bus, train, etc)* tomar, coger. **9** *(time)* tardar, llevar. LOC **not to take no for an answer** no

aceptar una respuesta negativa. **I take it or leave it** lo tomas o lo dejas. **I to take place** ocurrir. **I to take STH for granted** dar ALGO por sentado.

► *vi* **1** *(work - dye)* coger; *(- fire)* prender; *(- cutting)* prender; *(- seed)* germinar. **2** *(fish)* picar. **3** *(in draughts, etc)* comer.

◆ **to take after** *vi* parecerse.

◆ **to take apart** *vt sep* **1** *(machine, etc)* desmontar, deshacer. **2** *(argument)* echar por tierra.

◆ **to take away** *vt sep* **1** *(remove)* llevarse, quitar. **2** *(subtract)* restar.
► *vi (food)* llevar.

◆ **to take back** *vt sep* **1** *(accept back)* recibir otra vez, aceptar algo devuelto; *(employee)* readmitir. **2** *(return)* devolver. **3** *(retract)* retirar, retractar. **4** *(in time)* hacer recordar.

◆ **to take off** *vt sep* **1** *(clothes)* quitarse. **2** *(remove, detach)* quitar, sacar. **3** *(force to go)* llevar. **4** *(have as holiday)* tomarse. **5** *(imitate)* imitar. **6** *(deduct, discount)* descontar, rebajar.
► *vi* **1** *(plane)* despegar. **2** *(leave hurriedly)* irse, marcharse. **3** *(become popular)* tener éxito, ponerse de moda.

◆ **to take over** *vt sep* **1** *(country, party, etc)* tomar (posesión de), apoderarse de; *(building)* ocupar. **2** *(company, business)* absorber, adquirir; *(job, post)* hacerse cargo de; *(duty, responsibility)* asumir.
ⓘ *pt* took [tʊk], *pp* taken ['teɪkən].

take-away ['teɪkəweɪ] *n* **1** *(food)* comida para llevar. **2** *(restaurant)* restaurante *m* de comida para llevar.

taken ['teɪkən] *pp* → **take**.
► *adj (seat)* ocupado,-a.

take-off ['teɪkə:f] *n* **1** *(aviation)* despegue *m*. **2** SP salto.

take-out ['teɪkaʊt] *n* US *(food)* comida para llevar.

takeover ['teɪkəʊvəʳ] *n* **1** POL toma de posesión. **2** *(of company)* adquisición *f*.

talc [tælk] *n* talco.

talcum powder ['tælkəmpaʊdəʳ] *n* polvos *mpl* de talco.

tale [teɪl] *n (story)* cuento.

talent ['tælənt] *n* **1** *(special ability)* talento, dotes *mpl*. **2** *(talented people)* gente *f* de talento, gente *f* dotada. **3** *fam (attractive people)* gente *f* guapa.

talented ['tæləntɪd] *adj* de talento.

talk [tɔ:k] *vi* **1** *(gen)* hablar (to, con/a). **2** *(negotiate)* negociar.
► *vt* hablar (about/of, de).
► *n* **1** *(conversation)* conversación *f*. **2** *(lecture)* charla, conferencia.
► *n pl* **talks** negociaciones *fpl*.

◆ **to talk back** *vi* contestar, contestar de mala manera.

◆ **to talk down** *vt insep* **1** *(person)* hacer callar. **2** *(aircraft)* dirigir por radio.

talkative ['tɔ:kətɪv] *adj* hablador,-ra, parlanchín,-ina, charlatán,-ana.

tall [tɔ:l] *adj* alto,-a. COMP **tall story** cuento chino.

tallow ['tæləʊ] *n* sebo.

talon ['tælən] *n* garra.

tambourine [tæmbə'ri:n] *n* pandereta.

tame [teɪm] *adj* **1** *(by nature)* manso,-a, dócil. **2** *(tamed)* domesticado,-a.
► *vt* domar, domesticar.

tampon ['tæmpɒn] *n* tampón *m*.

tan¹ [tæn] *n* **1** *(colour)* color *m* marrón claro. **2** *(suntan)* bronceado, moreno. LOC **to get a tan** ponerse moreno.
► *adj* marrón claro.
► *vt* **1** *(leather)* curtir. **2** *(skin)* broncear, poner moreno,-a.
► *vi* broncearse, ponerse moreno,-a.
ⓘ *pt & pp* tanned, *ger* tanning.

tangent ['tændʒənt] *n* tangente *f*.

tangerine [tændʒə'ri:n] *n* **1** *(fruit)* clementina, mandarina. **2** *(colour)* naranja.
► *adj* naranja.

tangle ['tæŋgəl] *n (confused mass)* enredo, embrollo; *(confusion)* enredo, lío.
► *vt* enredar, enmarañar.
► *vi* enredarse.

tank [tæŋk] *n* **1** *(for water)* depósito, tanque *m*; *(for fuel)* depósito. **2** MIL tanque *m*. COMP **think tank** grupo de expertos.

tanker ['tæŋkəʳ] *n* **1** *(ship)* buque *m* cisterna. **2** *(for oil)* petrolero. **3** *(lorry)* camión *m* cisterna.

tanned [tænd] *adj (person)* moreno,-a, bronceado,-a; *(leather)* curtido,-a.

tantrum ['tæntrəm] *n* berrinche *m*, rabieta.

Tanzania [tænzə'nɪə] *n* Tanzania.

Tanzanian [tænzə'nɪən] *adj* tanzano,-a.
► *n* tanzano,-a.

tap¹ [tæp] *n* **1** grifo. **2** *(light blow)* golpecito. **3** *(on phone)* micrófono de escucha. **4** *(on barrel)* espita; *(for gas)* llave *f*.
COMP **tap water** agua del grifo.
► *vt* **1** *(strike lightly)* dar un golpecito a. **2** *(on keyboard)* teclear, pulsar. **3** *(liquid)* sacar. **4** *(resources)* explotar, utilizar. **5** *(telephone)* pinchar, intervenir.
◆ **to tap out** *vt sep* **1** teclear, escribir a máquina. **2** *(in Morse code)* enviar.
ⓘ *pt & pp* tapped, *ger* tapping.
☒ Tap no significa 'tapa', que se traduce por lid.

tap² [tæp] *n* claqué *m*. COMP **tap dance** claqué *m*.

tape [teɪp] *n* **1** *(audio, visual)* cinta. **2** *(recorded material)* grabación *f*. **3** SP cinta de llegada. **4** *(sticky)* cinta adhesiva.
COMP **tape measure** cinta métrica. ▌ **tape recorder** magnetófono.
► *vt* **1** *(fasten)* pegar con cinta adhesiva. **2** *(record)* grabar.

tapestry ['tæpəstrɪ] *n* **1** *(art)* tapicería. **2** *(cloth)* tapiz *m*.
ⓘ *pl* tapestries.

tar [tɑːʳ] *n* **1** *(for roads, in cigarettes)* alquitrán *m*. **2** *(in soap, etc)* brea.
► *vt* alquitranar.
ⓘ *pt & pp* tarred, *ger* tarring.

target ['tɑːgɪt] *n* **1** *(of missile, goal, aim)* objetivo. **2** *(in shooting, of criticism)* blanco. **3** *(board)* diana.
► *vt* **1** *(aim at target)* apuntar. **2** *(cause to have effect on)* dirigir a, destinar a.
► *adj* *(date, figure)* fijado,-a; *(audience, market)* objetivo.

tariff ['tærɪf] *n* **1** *(list of fixed charges)* tarifa. **2** *(duty to be paid on imports)* arancel *m*.
► *adj* arancelario,-a.

tarmac ['tɑːmæk] *n* **1** asfalto. **2** *(area)* pista.
► *vt* asfaltar.

tarpaulin [tɑː'pɔːlɪn] *n* lona.

tarsus ['tɑːsəs] *n* ANAT tarso.
ⓘ *pl* tarsi.

tart [tɑːt] *adj* **1** *(sour)* acre, agrio,-a. **2** *(reply)* mordaz, áspero,-a, acre.
► *n* **1** *(pie)* tarta, pastel *m*.
◆ **to tart up** *vt sep* *(building)* renovar, remodelar; *(person)* emperifollar.

tartan ['tɑːtən] *n* tartán *m*.

tartar ['tɑːtəʳ] *n* **1** *(on teeth)* sarro. **2** *(in wine)* tártaro.

task [tɑːsk] *n* tarea, labor *f*.

Tasmania [tæz'meɪnɪə] *n* Tasmania.

Tasmanian [tæz'meɪnɪən] *adj* tasmano,-a.
► *n* tasmano,-a.

taste [teɪst] *n* **1** *(faculty)* gusto. **2** *(flavour)* sabor *m*. **3** *(small sample)* muestra, poquito; *(experience)* experiencia. **4** *(ability to make good judgements)* gusto; *(liking)* afición *f* (for, a), gusto (for, por). COMP **taste buds** papilas gustativas.
► *vt* **1** *(try food)* probar; *(wine)* catar, degustar. **2** *(eat, drink)* probar. **3** *(experience)* conocer. **4** *(perceive flavour)* notar.
► *vi* saber (of/like, a).

tasteful ['teɪstful] *adj* de buen gusto, elegante.

tasteless ['teɪstləs] *adj* **1** de mal gusto. **2** *(insipid)* insípido,-a, soso,-a.

tasty ['teɪstɪ] *adj* sabroso,-a, rico,-a.
ⓘ *comp* tastier, *superl* tastiest.

tattoo [tə'tuː] *n* **1** MIL retreta. **2** *(on skin)* tatuaje *m*.
ⓘ *pl* tattoos.
► *vt* tatuar.
ⓘ *pt & pp* tattooed, *ger* tattooing.

taught [tɔːt] *pt & pp* → **teach**.

taunt [tɔːnt] *n* mofa, pulla, insulto.
► *vt* *(mock)* burlarse de, mofarse de; *(provoke)* hostigar, provocar.

Taurus ['tɔːrəs] *n* Tauro.

taut [tɔːt] *adj* tirante, tenso,-a.

tavern ['tævəⁿn] *n* taberna, mesón *m*.

tax [tæks] *n* **1** impuesto, contribución *f*. **2** *fig (burden, strain)* carga (on, sobre), esfuerzo (on, para).
ⓘ *pl* taxes.
► *vt* **1** *(impose a tax on - goods, profits)* gravar; *(- business, person)* imponer contribuciones a. **2** *fig (strain, test)* poner a prueba.

T

taxation [tæk'seɪʃªn] *n (taxes)* impuestos *mpl*; *(system)* sistema *m* tributario.

tax-deductible ['tæksdɪ'dʌktəbªl] *adj* desgravable.

tax-free ['tæks'fri:] *adj* libre de impuestos, exento,-a de impuestos.

taxi ['tæksɪ] *n* taxi *m*. COMP **taxi driver** taxista *mf*.
ⓘ *pl* taxis.

taxonomy [tæk'sɒnəmɪ] *n* taxonomía.
ⓘ *pl* taxonomies.

taxpayer ['tækspeɪªr] *n* contribuyente *mf*.

tea [ti:] *n* **1** *(gen)* té *m*. **2** *(infusion)* infusión *f*.

tea-break ['ti:breɪk] *n* descanso *para tomar el té*.

teach [ti:tʃ] *vt (gen)* enseñar; *(subject)* dar clases. LOC **that'll teach you** así aprenderás.
▶ *vi* ser profesor,-ra, dar clases
ⓘ *pt & pp* taught [tɔ:t].

teacher ['ti:tʃər] *n* maestro,-a, profesor,-ra.

teaching ['ti:tʃɪŋ] *n* enseñanza.
▶ *adj* docente. COMP **teaching staff** profesorado.
▶ *n pl* **teachings** enseñanzas *fpl*.

teacup ['ti:kʌp] *n* taza para té.

teak [ti:k] *n* teca.

team [ti:m] *n* **1** *(gen)* equipo. **2** *(of horses)* tiro; *(of oxen)* yunta.
▶ *adj* de equipo.
▶ *vi* combinar (**with**, con).

teamwork ['ti:mwɜ:k] *n* trabajo de equipo.

teapot ['ti:pɒt] *n* tetera.

tear¹ [teər] *n (rip)* rasgón *m*, desgarrón *m*.
▶ *vt* **1** *(rip, make a hole)* rasgar, desgarrar; *(pull apart, into pieces)* romper, hacer pedazos. **2** *(remove by force)* arrancar.
▶ *vi* **1** romperse, rasgarse. **2** *(rush)* ir a toda velocidad, lanzarse, precipitarse. COMP **wear and tear** desgaste *m*.
◆ **to tear apart** *vt sep* **1** *(rip up)* despedazar, desgarrar; *(destroy)* destrozar. **2** *fig* destrozar, desgarrar.

◆ **to tear up** *vt sep (paper)* hacer pedazos; *(plant)* arrancar de raíz.
ⓘ *pt* **tore** [tɔ:ʳ], *pp* **torn** [tɔ:n].

tear² [tɪəʳ] *n* lágrima.

teardrop ['tɪəd rɒp] *n* lágrima.

tearoom ['ti:rum] *n* salón *m* de té.

tease [ti:z] *vt* **1** *(make fun of - playfully)* tomar el pelo a, burlarse de; *(- annoyingly, unkindly)* molestar. **2** *(wool, etc)* cardar.
▶ *vi* tomar el pelo.
▶ *n* **1** *(joker)* bromista *mf*. **2** *fam (flirt)* coqueta.

teasel ['ti:zªl] *n* cardencha.

teashop ['ti:ʃɒp] *n* salón *m* de té.

teaspoon ['ti:spu:n] *n* cucharilla.

teat [ti:t] *n* **1** ZOOL tetilla. **2** *(on bottle)* tetina.

teatime ['ti:taɪm] *n* hora del té, hora de la merienda.

technical ['teknɪkªl] *adj* técnico,-a. COMP **technical college** instituto de formación profesional.

technician [tek'nɪʃªn] *n* técnico,-a.

technique [tek'ni:k] *n* técnica.

technological [teknə'lɒdʒɪkªl] *adj* tecnológico,-a.

technology [tek'nɒlədʒɪ] *n* tecnología.
ⓘ *pl* technologies.

teddy bear ['tedɪbeəʳ] [also **teddy**] *n* osito de peluche.

tedious ['ti:dɪəs] *adj* tedioso,-a, aburrido,-a.

teenage ['ti:neɪdʒ] *adj* adolescente.

teenager ['ti:neɪdʒəʳ] *n* quinceañero,-a.

teens [ti:nz] *n pl* adolescencia.

tee-shirt ['ti:ʃɜ:t] *n* camiseta.

teeth [ti:θ] *n pl* → tooth.

teethe [ti:ð] *vi* echar los dientes.

teetotaller [ti:'təutªləʳ] *n* abstemio,-a.

telecommunications [telɪkəmju:nɪ-'keɪʃªnz] *n pl* telecomunicaciones *fpl*.

telegram ['telɪgræm] *n* telegrama *m*.

telegraph ['telɪgrɑ:f] *n* telégrafo.
▶ *vi* telegrafiar.

telepathy [tɪ'lepəθɪ] *n* telepatía.

telephone ['telɪfəun] *n* teléfono. COMP **telephone box** cabina telefónica. ▌**telephone call** llamada telefónica. ▌

telephone directory listín *m* telefónico. I **telephone number** número telefónico.
▸ *vt* telefonear, llamar por teléfono.
▸ *vi* hacer una llamada telefónica.

telephonist [təˈlefənɪst] *n* telefonista *mf*.

telephoto lens [telɪfəʊtəʊ'lenz] *n* teleobjetivo.

teleprinter [ˈtelɪprɪntəʳ] *n* teletipo.

telescope [ˈtelɪskəʊp] *n* telescopio.

telescopic [telɪˈskɒpɪk] *adj (aerial)* telescópico,-a; *(umbrella)* plegable.

televise [ˈtelɪvaɪz] *vt* televisar.

television [ˈtelɪvɪʒ°n] *n* **1** *(gen)* televisión *f*. **2** *(set)* televisor *m*.

telex® [ˈteleks] *n* télex *m*.
▸ *vt* enviar por télex.

tell [tel] *vt* **1** *(gen)* decir. **2** *(story, joke)* contar; *(truth, lies, secret)* decir. **3** *(talk about)* hablar de. **4** *fml* comunicar, informar. **5** *(distinguish)* distinguir.
◆ **to tell apart** *vt sep* (saber) distinguir.
◆ **to tell off** *vt sep* **1** regañar, reñir. **2** MIL destacar.
◆ **to tell on** *vt insep (inform on)* chivarse de.
ⓘ *pt & pp* told [təʊld].

teller [ˈteləʳ] *n (in bank)* cajero,-a.

telling-off [telɪŋˈɒf] *n fam* bronca.

telltale [ˈtelteɪl] *n* chivato,-a, acusica *mf*.
▸ *adj* revelador,-ra.

telly [ˈtelɪ] *n fam* tele *f*.
ⓘ *pl* tellies.

temper [ˈtempəʳ] *n* **1** *(mood)* humor *m*; *(nature)* genio. **2** *(of metal)* temple *m*.
▸ *vt* **1** *(metal)* templar. **2** *fig* atenuar.

tempera [ˈtempərə] *n* temple *m*. COMP **tempera paints** témperas.

temperate [ˈtemprrɪt] *adj (gen)* moderado,-a; *(climate)* templado,-a.

temperature [ˈtemp°rɪtʃəʳ] *n* temperatura. LOC **to have/run a temperature** tener fiebre.

tempered [ˈtempəd] *adj* templado,-a.

tempest [ˈtempɪst] *n* tempestad *f*.

template [ˈtempleɪt] *n* plantilla.

temple [ˈtemp°l] *n* **1** *(building)* templo. **2** ANAT sien *f*.

temporary [ˈtemp°rərɪ] *adj* temporal.

tempt [tempt] *vt* tentar.

temptation [tempˈteɪʃ°n] *n* tentación *f*.
LOC **to yield to temptation** caer en la tentación.

tempting [ˈtemptɪŋ] *adj* tentador,-ra.

ten [ten] *n* diez *m*.
▸ *adj* diez.

✎ Consulta también **six**.

tenable [ˈtenəb°l] *adj* **1** *(theory, etc)* sostenible, defendible. **2** *(post, office)*: *how long is the post tenable for?* ¿durante cuántos años se puede ocupar el puesto?

tenacity [təˈnæsɪtɪ] *n* tenacidad *f*.

tenant [ˈtenənt] *n* inquilino,-a.

tend [tend] *vt (person)* cuidar de, atender; *(other)* ocuparse de.
▸ *vi (have tendency)* tender (**to**, a), tener tendencia (**to**, a).
◆ **to tend to** *vt insep* ocuparse de.

tendency [ˈtendənsɪ] *n* tendencia.
ⓘ *pl* tendencies.

tender¹ [ˈtendəʳ] *adj* **1** *(meat, etc)* tierno, -a. **2** *(loving)* tierno,-a, cariñoso, a. **3** *(sore)* dolorido,-a. **4** *(delicate)* delicado,-a, sensible.
ⓘ *comp* tenderer, *comp* tenderest.

tender² [ˈtendəʳ] *n* COMM *(offer)* oferta.
▸ *vt* presentar, ofrecer.
▸ *vi* hacer una oferta (**for**, para).

tenderness [ˈtendənəs] *n* ternura.

tendon [ˈtendən] *n* tendón *m*.

tennis [ˈtenɪs] *n* tenis *m*. COMP **tennis court** pista de tenis. I **tennis player** jugador,-a de tenis.

tenon [ˈtenən] *n* espiga.
▸ *vt* despatillar.

tenor [ˈtenəʳ] *n* tenor *m*.

tense [tens] *adj* **1** *(anxious)* tenso,-a. **2** *(taut)* tirante, tenso,-a.
▸ *n (of verb)* tiempo verbal.
▸ *vt* tensar.

tension [ˈtenʃ°n] *n* tensión *f*.

tent [tent] *n* tienda de campaña.

tentacle [ˈtentək°l] *n* tentáculo.

tenth [tenθ] *adj* décimo,-a.
▸ *adv* en décimo lugar.
▸ *n (fraction)* décimo; *(one part)* décima parte *f*.

✎ Consulta también **sixth**.

T

tepee ['tiːpiː] *n* tipi *m*.

tepid ['tepɪd] *adj* tibio,-a.

term [tɜːm] *n* **1** EDUC trimestre *m*. **2** *(period of time)* período. **3** *(expression, word)* término.
▶ *n pl* **terms** *(sense)* términos *mpl*. COMM condiciones *fpl*, *(relations)* relaciones *fpl*.

terminal ['tɜːmɪnəl] *adj* terminal.
▶ *n* **1** ELEC borne *m*. **2** COMPUT terminal *m*. **3** *(at airport, etc)* terminal *f*.

terminate ['tɜːmɪneɪt] *vt* **1** *(gen)* terminar, poner fin a; *(contract)* rescindir. **2** *(pregnancy)* interrumpir.
▶ *vi* terminarse.

termini ['tɜːmɪnaɪ] *n pl* → **terminus**.

terminology [tɜːmɪˈnɒlədʒɪ] *n* terminología.

terminus ['tɜːmɪnəs] *n* término.
ⓘ *pl* **terminuses** o **termini** ['tɜːmɪnaɪ].

termite ['tɜːmaɪt] *n* termita.

terrace ['terəs] *n* **1** *(of house, café, bar, etc)* terraza. **2** *(on hillside)* terraza, bancal *m*.
▶ *n pl* **terraces** SP gradas *fpl*.

terraced house [terəstˈhaʊs] *n* casa adosada.

terrain [təˈreɪn] *n* terreno.

terrible ['terɪbəl] *adj* **1** terrible, espantoso,-a. **2** *fam (as intensifier)* mucho,-a.

terribly ['terɪblɪ] *adv* **1** terriblemente. **2** *fam (very)* muy.

terrific [təˈrɪfɪk] *adj* **1** *(wonderful)* fabuloso,-a, estupendo,-a. **2** *(huge)* tremendo,-a.

☒ Terrific no significa 'terrorífico', que se traduce por **terrifying**.

terrify ['terɪfaɪ] *vt* aterrar, aterrorizar.
ⓘ *pt & pp* **terrified**, *ger* **terrifying**.

terrifying ['terɪfaɪɪŋ] *adj* aterrador,-ra, espantoso,-a.

territory ['terɪtərɪ] *n* **1** *(gen)* territorio. **2** *(zone)* zona, área.
ⓘ *pl* **territories**.

terror ['terər] *n* **1** *(gen)* terror *m*, espanto. **2** *fam (child)* diablillo.

terrorism ['terərɪzəm] *n* terrorismo.

terrorist ['terərɪst] *n* terrorista *mf*.
▶ *adj* terrorista.

tertiary ['tɜːʃərɪ] *adj* terciario,-a.

test [test] *n* **1** *(trial)* prueba. **2** EDUC *(gen)* examen *m*; *(multiple choice)* test *m*. **3** MED análisis *m*. COMP **test tube** probeta.
▶ *vt* probar.

testicle ['testɪkəl] *n* testículo.

testify ['testɪfaɪ] *vt* JUR declarar.
▶ *vi* **1** *(bear witness)* dar fe (**to**, de). **2** JUR prestar declaración, testificar.
ⓘ *pt & pp* **testified**, *ger* **testifying**.

testimony ['testɪmənɪ] *n* testimonio.
ⓘ *pl* **testimonies**.

test-tube baby [testtjuːˈbeɪbɪ] *n* niño,-a probeta.

tetanus ['tetənəs] *n* tétanos *m inv*.

text [tekst] *n* texto.

textbook ['tekstbʊk] *n* libro de texto.

textile ['tekstaɪl] *adj* textil.
▶ *n* textil *m*.

texture ['tekstʃər] *n* textura.

Thai [taɪ] *adj* tailandés,-esa.
▶ *n* **1** *(person)* tailandés,-esa. **2** *(language)* tailandés *m*.

Thailand ['taɪlænd] *n* Tailandia.

Thames [temz] *n* el Támesis *m*.

than [ðæn, *unstressed* ðən] *conj* **1** que: *he is taller than you are* él es más alto que tú. **2** *(with numbers)* de: *more than fifty* más de cincuenta. **3** *(followed by clause)* de lo que: *this is easier than we thought* esto es más fácil de lo que pensábamos.

thank [θæŋk] *vt* dar las gracias a, agradecer. LOC **no, thank you** no, gracias. ❙ **thank you** gracias.

thankful ['θæŋkfʊl] *adj* agradecido,-a.

thankless ['θæŋkləs] *adj* ingrato,-a.

thanks [θæŋks] *interj* gracias: *thanks to* gracias a. LOC **no, thanks** no, gracias.
▶ *n pl (gratitude)* agradecimiento.

thanksgiving [θæŋksˈɡɪvɪŋ] *n* acción *f* de gracias. COMP **Thanksgiving Day** Día *m* de Acción de Gracias.

⊕ Thanksgiving Day (Día de Acción de Gracias) se celebra en Estados Unidos el cuarto jueves de noviembre. Recuerda el día de 1621 en que los colonos ingleses dieron gracias a Dios por la cosecha que les permitiría sobrevivir su segundo invierno en el Nuevo Mundo.

that [ðæt *unstressed* ðət] *adj* ese, esa; *(remote)* aquel, aquella.
ⓘ *pl* those.
▶ *pron* **1** ése *m*, ésa; *(remote)* aquél *m*, aquélla. **2** *(indefinite)* eso; *(remote)* aquello. **3** *(relative)* que, el/la que, el/la cual. [LOC] that is to say es decir. I that's it **1** *(that's all)* eso es todo. **2** *(that's right)* eso es. **3** *(that's enough)* se acabó. I that's right así es. I that's that se acabó. I who's that? *(on 'phone)* ¿quién es?
ⓘ *pl* those.
▶ *adv fam* tan, tanto,-a, tantos,-as.

thatch [θætʃ] *n* **1** *(straw)* paja; *(roof)* tejado de paja. **2** *(hair)* mata.

thaw [θɔ:] *n* deshielo.
▶ *vt* *(food)* descongelar; *(snow, ice)* derretir.
▶ *vi* **1** *(food)* descongelarse; *(snow, ice)* derretirse. **2** *(person)* ablandarse; *(relations)* distenderse, mejorar.
◆ to thaw out *vi* descongelarse.
▶ *vt sep* descongelar.

the [ðə] *[delante de una vocal se pronuncia* [ðɪ]; *con énfasis* [ði:]] *def art* **1** el, la; *(plural)* los, las. **2** *(per)* por: *we are paid by the hour* nos pagan por horas. **3** *(emphasis)* el, la, los, las: *you're not the Paul Newman, are you?* no serás el auténtico Paul Newman, ¿verdad?
▶ *adv (with comparatives)*: *the more you have, the more you want* cuanto más se tiene, más se quiere.

theater [ˈθɪətəʳ] *n* US → theatre.

theatre [ˈθɪətəʳ] *n* **1** *(gen)* teatro. **2** MED quirófano. **3** US cine *m*. **4** *(scene of action)* escenario.
▶ *adj* teatral, de teatro.

theft [θeft] *n* robo, hurto.

their [ðeəʳ] *adj* su; *(plural)* sus: *they took their children and their dog* se llevaron a sus hijos y al perro.

theirs [ðeəz] *pron* (el) suyo, (la) suya; *(plural)* (los) suyos, (las) suyas: *that house is theirs* aquella casa es suya.

them [ðem, *unstressed* ðəm] *pron* **1** *(direct object)* los, las; *(indirect object)* les; *(before another pronoun)* se: *the Smiths are coming, do you know them?* vienen los Smith, ¿los

conoces?; *take these flowers and give them to Mary* coge estas flores y se las das a Mary. **2** *(with preposition, stressed)* ellos, ellas: *don't speak to them* no hables con ellos. **3** *fam (used with singular meaning)* lo, la, le: *if anyone arrives, tell them to wait* si llega alguien, dile que espere.

thematic [θɪˈmætɪk] *adj* temático,-a.

theme [θi:m] *n* tema *m*. [COMP] theme park parque *m* temático.

themselves [ðəmˈselvz] *pron* **1** *(subject)* ellos/ellas mismos(as): *they made it themselves* lo hicieron ellos mismos. **2** *(object)* se: *they looked at themselves in the mirror* se miraron en el espejo. **3** *(after preposition)* sí mismos,-as: *they are old enough to look after themselves* son lo bastante mayores como para cuidar de sí mismos. [LOC] by themselves solos,-as: *don't leave the children by themselves* no dejes a los niños solos.

then [ðen] *adv* entonces, luego: *I was born in 1963, life was different then* nací en 1963, entonces la vida era distinta; *I'll have soup first and then steak* primero tomaré sopa y luego un filete.

theology [θɪˈɒlədʒɪ] *n* teología.

theorem [ˈθɪərəm] *n* teorema *m*.

theoretic [θɪəˈretɪk] *adj* teórico,-a.

theoretical [θɪəˈretɪkəl] *adj* teórico,-a.

theory [ˈθɪərɪ] *n* teoría. [LOC] in theory en teoría.
ⓘ *pl* theories.

therapist [ˈθerəpɪst] *n* terapeuta *mf*.

therapy [ˈθerəpɪ] *n* terapia, terapéutica: *she's having therapy* está recibiendo terapia.
ⓘ *pl* therapies.

there [ðeəʳ] *adv* **1** allí, allá, ahí: *I often go there on holiday* voy de vacaciones allí a menudo. **2** *(in discussion)* acerca de eso: *I agree with you there* estoy de acuerdo contigo en eso. [LOC] there and then en el momento. I there is/are, etc → be. I there you are aquí tiene. I there you go ya está.

thereafter [ðeəˈræftəʳ] *adv* a partir de entonces.

thereby [ˈðeəbaɪ] *adv* por eso, por ello.

T

therefore [ˈðeəfɔːʳ] *adv* por tanto, por lo tanto, por consiguiente.

thermal [ˈθɜːməl] *adj* **1** *(stream, bath, spring)* termal; *(underwear)* térmico,-a. **2** PHYS térmico,-a.
▸ *n* corriente *f* térmica.

thermometer [θeˈmɒmɪtəʳ] *n* termómetro.

thermos® [ˈθɜːmɒs] *n* termo.

thermostat [ˈθɜːməstæt] *n* termostato.

thesaurus [θɪˈsɔːrəs] *n* diccionario ideológico.

these [ðiːz] *adj* estos,-as: *these apples are cheaper than those* estas manzanas son más baratas que aquellas.
▸ *pron* éstos,-as: *which ones do you prefer? –these* ¿cuáles prefieres? –éstos.

they [ðeɪ] *pron* **1** *(plural)* ellos,-as: *where are the children? –they're in the garden* ¿dónde están los niños? –están en el jardín. **2** *fam (singular - substitutes* he *or* she*)* él, ella: *if anyone saw the accident, they should go to the police* si alguien vio el accidente, que vaya a la policía. LOC **they say that...** se dice que…

thick [θɪk] *adj* **1** *(solid things)* grueso,-a: *it's a thick book* es un libro grueso. **2** *(liquid, gas, vegetation, etc)* espeso,-a. **3** *(beard, eyebrows)* poblado,-a. **4** *(cloud, smoke, fog, forest)* denso,-a, espeso,-a. **5** *(fur, hedge)* tupido,-a. **6** *fam (stupid)* corto,-a, corto,-a de alcances; *(unable to think)* espeso,-a. **7** *(accent)* marcado,-a, cerrado,-a; *(of speech, voice)* poco claro,-a.
▸ *adv* espesamente, gruesamente.

thicken [ˈθɪk°n] *vt* espesar.
▸ *vi* espesarse, hacerse más denso,-a.

thickness [ˈθɪknəs] *n* **1** *(in size)* espesor *m*, grosor *m*. **2** *(density - of liquid)* espesura; *(- of fog)* densidad *f*. **3** *(layer)* capa.

thief [θiːf] *n (gen)* ladrón,-ona; *(mugger)* atracador,-ra.
ⓘ *pl* thieves [θiːvz].

thieves [θiːvz] *pl* → thief.

thigh [θaɪ] *n* muslo.

thighbone [ˈθaɪbəʊn] *n* fémur *m*.

thimble [ˈθɪmbªl] *n* dedal *m*.

thin [θɪn] *adj* **1** *(gen)* delgado,-a, fino,-a, **2** *(liquid - soup, sauce)* poco espeso,-a, claro,-a; *(- rain)* fino,-a. **3** *(audience, crowd)* poco numeroso,-a; *(response, attendance)* escaso,-a. **4** *(voice)* débil. **5** *(excuse, argument)* pobre, poco convincente.
ⓘ *comp* thinner, *superl* thinnest.
▸ *adv* finamente.
▸ *vt (paint)* diluir; *(sauce)* hacer menos espeso,-a.
▸ *vi* **1** *(fog, mist)* disiparse. **2** *(audience, crowd, traffic)* hacerse menos denso,-a, disminuir.
◆ **to thin down** *vi* adelgazar.
▸ *vt sep (sauce)* hacer menos espeso,-a, aclarar; *(paint)* diluir.
◆ **to thin out** *vt insep (crowd, traffic)* mermar, disminuir.
▸ *vt sep (crops, plants)* entresacar.

thing [θɪŋ] *n* **1** *(object)* cosa, objeto. **2** *(non-material)* cosa. **3** *(affair)* asunto. **4** *(person, creature)*: *you poor little thing!* ¡pobrecito! **5** *(with negative)* nada: *I can't understand a thing you're saying* no entiendo nada de lo que dices.
▸ *n* **the thing** *(what)* lo que: *the thing I like most in life* lo que más me gusta en la vida.
▸ *n pl* **things** *(belongings)* cosas *fpl*, ropa *f sing*, equipaje *m sing*.

think [θɪŋk] *vi* **1** *(gen)* pensar. **2** *(remember)* acordarse (of, de), recordar. **3** *(imagine)* imaginarse, pensar.
▸ *vt* **1** *(gen)* pensar. **2** *(believe)* creer. **3** *(remember)* recordar, acordarse de.
◆ **to think ahead** *vi* prevenir.
◆ **to think back** *vi* hacer memoria.
◆ **to think out** *vt sep (consider carefully)* estudiar, pensar bien.
ⓘ *pt & pp* thought [θɔːt].

thinking [ˈθɪŋkɪŋ] *n* **1** *(opinion)* opinión *f*, parecer *m*. **2** *(thought)* pensamiento.
▸ *adj* pensante, inteligente.

third [θɜːd] *adj* tercero,-a. COMP **third person** LING tercera persona.
▸ *adv (in series)* tercero, en tercer lugar.
▸ *n* **1** tercero,-a. **2** *(fraction)* tercio; *(one part)* tercera parte *f*.

✎ Consulta también sixth.

third-party [ˈθɜːdpɑːtɪ] *adj (insurance)* a terceros.

third-world ['θɜːdwɜːld] *adj (in general)* del tercer mundo; *(pejorative use)* tercermundista.

thirst [θɜːst] *n* sed *f*.

thirsty ['θɜːstɪ] *adj* **1** sediento,-a: *I'm thirsty* tengo sed. **2** *(work, etc)* que da sed. **3** *fig (eager)* ansioso,-a (**for**, por). [LOC] **to be thirsty** tener sed.
ⓘ *comp* thirstier, *superl* thirstiest.

thirteen [θɜːˈtiːn] *n* trece *m*.
▶ *adj* trece.

✎ Consulta también six.

thirteenth [θɜːˈtiːnθ] *adj* decimotercero,-a.
▶ *adv* en decimotercero lugar.
▶ *n (fraction)* decimotercero; *(one part)* decimotercera parte *f*.

✎ Consulta también sixth.

thirties ['θɜːtɪz] *n pl* **the thirties** los años *mpl* treinta. [LOC] **to be in one's thirties** tener treinta y tantos años.

✎ Consulta también sixties.

thirtieth ['θɜːtɪəθ] *adj* trigésimo,-a.
▶ *adv* en trigésimo lugar.
▶ *n (fraction)* trigésimo; *(one part)* trigésima parte *f*.

✎ Consulta también sixtieth.

thirty ['θɜːtɪ] *n* treinta *m*.
▶ *adj* treinta.

✎ Consulta también sixty.

this [ðɪs] *adj* este, esta: *whose is this book?* ¿de quién es este libro?
ⓘ *pl* these [ðiːs].
▶ *pron* **1** éste, ésta; *(indefinite)* esto: *I prefer this one* prefiero éste. **2** *(on 'phone)*: *this is Laura* soy Laura.
ⓘ *pl* these [ðiːs].
▶ *adv* tan, tanto,-a: *I didn't think it was this far* no creía que fuera tan lejos. [LOC] **this is** *(introducing)* te presento a.

thistle ['θɪsᵊl] *n* cardo.

thoracic [θəˈræsɪk] *adj* torácico,-a.

thorax ['θɔːræks] *n* tórax *m inv*.

thorn [θɔːn] *n* espina, pincho.

thorough ['θʌrə] *adj* **1** *(deep)* profundo,-a, a fondo. **2** *(careful)* cuidadoso,-a,

minucioso,-a. **3** *(person)* concienzudo,-a. **4** *(utter, complete)* total, verdadero,-a.

thoroughgoing ['θʌrəgəʊɪŋ] *adj* profundo,-a, minucioso,-a.

thoroughly ['θʌrəlɪ] *adv* **1** *(carefully)* a fondo, meticulosamente. **2** *(completely)* totalmente, absolutamente.

those [ðəʊz] *adj* esos,-as; *(remote)* aquellos,-as: *could you pass me those plates?* ¿me podrías pasar esos platos?
▶ *pron* ésos,-as; *(remote)* aquéllos,-as: *if these are my books, whose are those?* si estos libros son míos, ¿de quién son aquellos?

though [ðəʊ] *conj* aunque, si bien, a pesar de que: *though he doesn't earn very much, he loves his job* aunque no gana mucho, le encanta su trabajo.
▶ *adv* sin embargo, a pesar de todo: *it's expensive –it's worth it though* es caro –sin embargo, vale lo que cuesta. [LOC] **even though** como si. ▌**even though** aun cuando, a pesar de que.

thought [θɔːt] *pt & pp* → think.
▶ *n* **1** pensamiento **2** *(consideration)* consideración *f*. **3** *(idea, opinion)* idea, opinión *f*. **4** *(intention)* intención *f*.

thoughtful ['θɔːtfʊl] *adj* **1** *(considerate)* atento,-a, considerado,-a. **2** *(pensive)* pensativo,-a, meditabundo,-a. **3** *(considered)* serio,-a.

thoughtless ['θɔːtləs] *adj* **1** *(unthinking)* irreflexivo,-a, descuidado,-a. **2** *(inconsiderate)* desconsiderado,-a, poco considerado,-a.

thousand ['θaʊzᵊnd] *n* mil *m*: *there were thousands of people* había miles de personas.
▶ *adj* mil: *it costs a thousand euros* cuesta mil euros.

thousandth ['θaʊzᵊnθ] *adj* milésimo,-a.
▶ *adv* en milésimo lugar.
▶ *n (fraction)* milésimo; *(one part)* milésima parte *f*.

thrash [θræʃ] *vt* **1** *(beat)* azotar. **2** *(defeat)* derrotar, dar una paliza a. **3** *(arm, leg, etc)* sacudir.

thread [θred] *n* **1** SEW hilo, hebra. **2** *(of screw, bolt)* rosca. **3** *(of story)* hilo.
▶ *vt* **1** *(needle)* enhebrar. **2** *(beads)* ensartar.

threat [θret] *n* amenaza.

T

threaten ['θretᵊn] *vt* amenazar (with/to, con).
▶ *vi* amenazar.

threatening ['θretᵊnɪŋ] *adj* amenazador,-ra, intimidatorio,-a.

three [θriː] *n* tres *m*.
▶ *adj* tres. COMP **three quarters** tres cuartos. ❙ **Three Wise Men** los Reyes Magos.

✎ Consulta también **six**.

three-dimensional [θriːdɪˈmenʃənəl] *adj* tridimensional.

thresh [θreʃ] *vt* trillar.

thresher ['θreʃəʳ] *n (machine)* trilladora.

threshold ['θreʃəʊld] *n* **1** umbral *m*. **2** *fig* umbral *m*, límite *m*.

threw [θruː] *pt* → **throw**.

thrill [θrɪl] *n (excitement)* emoción *f*, ilusión *f*.
▶ *vt (excite)* entusiasmar, hacer ilusión a, ilusionar.
▶ *vi (de excited)* entusiasmarse.

thriller ['θrɪləʳ] *n (novel)* novela de suspense; *(film)* película de suspense; *(play)* obra de suspense.

thrilling ['θrɪlɪŋ] *adj* emocionante, apasionante.

throat [θrəʊt] *n* garganta.

thrombosis [θrɒmˈbəʊsɪs] *n* trombosis *f inv*.

throne [θrəʊn] *n* trono.

throttle ['θrɒtᵊl] *n* **1** válvula reguladora. **2** *fam* acelerador *m*. LOC **at full throttle** a toda pastilla.

through [θruː] *prep* **1** por, a través de. **2** *(because of)* por, a causa de. **3** *(from beginning to the end)* hasta el final de.
▶ *adv* **1** de un lado a otro. **2** *(to the end)* hasta el final. **3** GB *(on phone)* conectado,-a. **4** US terminado,-a, acabado,-a.
▶ *adj (train)* directo,-a; *(traffic)* de paso.

throughout [θruːˈaʊt] *prep* **1** por todo,-a, en todo,-a. **2** *(time)* a lo largo de.
▶ *adv* **1** *(all over)* por/en todas partes. **2** *(completely)* completamente. **3** *(time)* todo el tiempo.

throw [θrəʊ] *n* **1** lanzamiento, tiro. **2** *(of dice)* tirada, lance *m*; *(in game)* jugada, turno.
▶ *vt* **1** *(gen)* tirar, arrojar, lanzar. **2** *fig (kiss)* echar, tirar; *(glance, look)* lanzar, dirigir.
◆ **to throw away** *vt sep* **1** *(get rid of, discard)* tirar. **2** *(waste)* desaprovechar, perder; *(money)* malgastar, derrochar. **3** *(speech)* lanzar al aire.
◆ **to throw back** *vt sep* **1** *(ball, etc)* devolver. **2** *(bedclothes)* echar atrás.
◆ **to throw in** *vt sep* **1** *fam (include)* incluir gratis. **2** SP sacar de banda.
◆ **to throw out** *vt sep* **1** *(expel)* echar, expulsar. **2** *(reject)* rechazar. **3** *(discard)* tirar.
◆ **to throw up** *vi* vomitar, devolver.
ⓘ *pt* **threw** [θruː], *pp* **thrown** [θrəʊn].

throwaway ['θrəʊəweɪ] *adj* de usar y tirar.

throw-in ['θrəʊɪn] *n* SP saque *m* de banda.

thrown [θrəʊn] *pp* → **throw**.

thru [θruː] *prep-adv* US → **through**.
◆ **to thrust on** *vt sep* imponer.

thud [θʌd] *n* ruido sordo.
▶ *vi* caer con un ruido sordo.
ⓘ *pt & pp* **thudded**, *ger* **thudding**.

thumb [θʌm] *n* pulgar *m*.
▶ *vt* hacer autostop.
◆ **to thumb through** *vt insep* hojear.

thumbtack ['θʌmtæk] *n* US chincheta.

thump [θʌmp] *n (blow)* golpe *m*, puñetazo; *(sound)* golpazo.
▶ *vt* golpear, pegar un puñetazo.
▶ *vi (gen)* golpear; *(heart)* latir con fuerza; *(feet)* caminar con pasos pesados.

thunder ['θʌndəʳ] *n* trueno.
▶ *vi* tronar.
▶ *vt (shout)* bramar, rugir.

thunderstorm ['θʌndəstɔːm] *n* tormenta.

Thursday ['θɜːzdɪ] *n* jueves *m*.

✎ Para ejemplos de uso, consulta **Saturday**.

thus [ðʌs] *adv* **1** *(in this way, like this)* así, de este modo. **2** *(consequently)* así que, por lo tanto, por consiguiente. **3** *(to this extent)* hasta.

thwart [θwɔːt] *vt* desbaratar, frustrar.

thyme [taɪm] *n* tomillo.

thyroid ['θaɪrɔɪd] *n* tiroides *m*. COMP **thyroid gland** glándula tiroides.

Tibet [tɪˈbet] *n* Tíbet.

Tibetan [tɪˈbet³n] *adj* tibetano.
► *n* **1** *(person)* tibetano,-a. **2** *(language)* tibetano.

tibia [ˈtɪbɪə] *n* tibia.

tick¹ [tɪk] *n* ZOOL garrapata.

tick² [tɪk] *n* **1** *(noise)* tictac *m*, **2** *(mark)* marca, señal *f*.
► *vi (clock)* hacer tictac.
► *vt* señalar, marcar.

ticket [ˈtɪkɪt] *n* **1** *(for transport)* billete *m*. **2** *(for concert, cinema, etc)* entrada. **3** *(for library, etc)* carnet *m*. **4** *(label)* etiqueta. **5** *(for item deposited)* resguardo. **6** *fam (fine)* multa. **7** POL lista de candidatos. [COMP] **ticket collector** revisor,-a. ‖ **ticket inspector** revisor,-a. ‖ **ticket office** taquilla.

tickle [ˈtɪk³l] *n* cosquilleo.
► *vi (touch lightly)* hacer cosquillas; *(itch)* picar.

tidal [ˈtaɪd³l] *adj* de la marea. [COMP] **tidal wave 1** *(gen)* maremoto. **2** *†fig* oleada.

tide [taɪd] *n* **1** marea. **2** *fig (trend)* corriente *f*. [COMP] **high tide** pleamar *f*. ‖ **low tide** bajamar *f*.

tidy [ˈtaɪdɪ] *adj* **1** *(place)* ordenado,-a, bien arreglado. **2** *(person - appearance)* arreglado,-a; *(- habits)* metódico,-a.
ⓘ *comp* tidier, *superl* tidiest.
► *n* organizador *m*.
► *vt* [also tidy up] ordenar.
► *vi* [also tidy up] poner las cosas en orden.
◆ **to tidy away** *vt sep* recoger, guardar.
◆ **to tidy out** *vt sep* limpiar, ordenar.
ⓘ *pt & pp* tidied, *ger* tidying.

tie [taɪ] *n* **1** *(of shirt)* corbata. **2** *(for fastening)* cierre *m*. **3** *(rod, beam)* tirante *m*. **4** *fig (bond)* lazo, vínculo: *family ties are strong* los lazos del parentesco son fuertes. **5** *fig (restriction)* atadura. **6** SP *(draw)* empate *m*; *(match)* partido.
► *vt* **1** *(fasten)* atar; *(knot, bow)* hacer. **2** *fig* ligar, vincular, relacionar. **3** *(restrict)* atar. **4** MUS ligar.
► *vi* **1** *(fasten)* atarse. **2** SP empatar.
◆ **to tie down** *vt sep* **1** atar, sujetar. **2** *(restrict)* atar; *(commit oneself)* comprometerse.
◆ **to tie up** *vt sep* **1** *(fasten)* atar; *(boat)* amarrar. **2** *(link)* conectar, ligar, rela-

cionar. **3** *(occupy)* liar, ocupar. **4** FIN *(capital)* inmovilizar, invertir. **5** *(finalize)* finalizar, concluir, cerrar.
ⓘ *pt & pp* tied, *ger* tidying.

tier [tɪəʳ] *n* **1** *(in stadium)* grada. **2** *(of cake)* piso. **3** *(in hierarchy)* nivel *m*.

tiger [ˈtaɪgəʳ] *n* tigre *m*.

tight [taɪt] *adj* **1** *(firmly fastened)* apretado,-a, duro,-a. **2** *(taut)* tirante, tenso,-a. **3** *(clothes)* ajustado,-a, ceñido,-a. **4** *(not leaky)* hermético,-a, impermeable. **5** *(hold)* estrecho,-a, fuerte. **6** *(packed together)* apretado,-a. **7** *(strict - schedule)* apretado,-a; *(- security)* estricto,-a, riguroso,-a. **8** *fam (mean)* agarrado,-a, tacaño,-a. **9** *fam (drunk)* borracho,-a. **10** *(bend)* cerrado,-a.
► *adv* firmemente, fuerte.

tighten [ˈtaɪt³n] *vt* **1** *(gen)* apretar, ajustar; *(rope)* tensar. **2** *(make stricter - security)* hacer más estricto, reforzar; *(- credit)* restringir.
► *vi* **1** *(gen)* apretarse; *(rope, muscles)* tensarse.
◆ **to tighten up** *vt sep* intensificar, hacer más estricto,-a.
► *vi* ponerse más estricto,-a.

tightrope [ˈtaɪtrəʊp] *n* cuerda floja. [COMP] **tightrope walker** funámbulo.

tights [taɪts] *n pl* **1** *(gen)* pantys *mpl*, medias *fpl*. **2** *(thick)* leotardos *mpl*, mallas *fpl*.

tigress [ˈtaɪgrəs] *n* tigresa.

tile [taɪl] *n* *(wall)* azulejo; *(floor)* baldosa; *(roof)* teja.
► *vt* **1** *(wall)* alicatar, poner azulejos a. **2** *(floor)* embaldosar. **3** *(roof)* tejar.

till [tɪl] *prep* hasta.
► *conj* hasta que.
► *n* *(for cash)* caja.
► *vt* *(cultivate)* labrar, cultivar.

tiller [ˈtɪləʳ] *n* caña del timón.

tilt [tɪlt] *n* **1** inclinación *f*, ladeo. **2** *(with lance)* acometida.
► *vt* inclinar, ladear.
► *vi* **1** *(slope, shift)* inclinarse. **2** *(with lance)* acometer.

timber [ˈtɪmbəʳ] *n* **1** *(wood)* madera (de construcción). **2** *(beam)* viga. **3** *(trees)*

T

árboles *mpl* maderables. COMP **timber mill** aserradero.

▶ *interj* ¡cuidado, que cae!, ¡allá va!

time [taɪm] *n* **1** *(period)* tiempo. **2** *(short period)* rato. **3** *(of day)* hora. **4** *(age, period, season)* época. **5** *(occasion)* vez *f*. **6** *(suitable moment)* momento. **7** MUS compás *m*. **8** GB la hora de cerrar.

▶ *vt* **1** *(measure time)* medir la duración de, calcular; *(races, etc)* cronometrar. **2** *(schedule)* estar previsto,-a. LOC **(and) about time** ya era hora. ‖ **all the time** todo el tiempo. ‖ **at any time** en cualquier momento. ‖ **at no time** nunca. ‖ **at one time** en un tiempo. ‖ **at the same time** al mismo tiempo. ‖ **for the time being** de momento. ‖ **from time to time** de vez en cuando. ‖ **in time 1** *(in the long run)* con el tiempo. **2** *(not late)* a tiempo. ‖ **on time** puntual. ‖ **time after time** una y otra vez. ‖ **time's up** se acabó el tiempo. ‖ **to be ahead of one's time** adelantarse a su época. ‖ **to give SB a hard time** ponérselo difícil a ALGN. ‖ **to have a bad time** pasarlas negras. ‖ **to have a good time** pasarlo bien. ‖ **to take one's time 1** *(not hurry)* hacer ALGO con calma. **2** *(be slow)* tardar mucho. ‖ **to tell the time** decir la hora.

▶ *n pl* **times** veces *fpl*. LOC **at times** a veces. ‖ **to keep up with the times** estar al día.

timeless ['taɪmləs] *adj* eterno,-a.

timely ['taɪmlɪ] *adj* oportuno,-a.

timer ['taɪmər] *n* temporizador *m*.

time-share ['taɪmʃeər] *adj (property)* en multipropiedad.

timetable ['taɪmteɪbəl] *n* horario.

timid ['tɪmɪd] *n* tímido,-a.

timing ['taɪmɪŋ] *n* **1** *(time chosen)* momento escogido; *(judgement)* sentido de la oportunidad. **2** SP *(measurement of time)* cronometraje *m*.

tin [tɪn] *n* **1** *(metal)* estaño. **2** *(can)* lata, bote *m*. **3** *(for baking)* molde *m*.

▶ *vt* enlatar.

ⓘ *pt & pp* **tinned**, *ger* **tinning**.

tinfoil ['tɪnfɔɪl] *n* papel *m* de estaño.

tinkle ['tɪŋkəl] *n* tintineo.

▶ *vt* hacer tintinear.

▶ *vi* **1** *(ring)* tintinear. **2** GB *fam (urinate)* hacer pipí.

tinned [tɪnd] *adj* enlatado,-a. COMP **tinned food** comida de lata.

tin-opener ['tɪnəʊpənər] *n* abrelatas *m inv*.

tinsel ['tɪnsəl] *n* espumillón *m*.

tiny ['taɪnɪ] *adj* diminuto,-a.

ⓘ *comp* **tinier**, *superl* **tiniest**.

tip¹ [tɪp] *n (gen)* extremo, punta, cabo; *(of cigarette)* boquilla, filtro. LOC **from tip to toe** de pies a cabeza.

tip² [tɪp] *n* **1** *(gratuity)* propina. **2** *(advice)* consejo, truco; *(confidential information)* soplo, confidencia; *(prediction)* pronóstico.

▶ *vt* **1** *(give gratuity to)* dar una propina a. **2** *(predict)* pronosticar.

tip³ [tɪp] *n (for rubbish)* vertedero, basurero; *(dirty place)* porquería, desorden *m*.

▶ *vt* **1** *(lean, tilt)* inclinar, ladear. **2** *(pour)* verter; *(throw)* tirar; *(empty)* vaciar. **3** *(rubbish)* verter.

◆ **to tip over** *vi (overturn)* volcarse, caerse; *(boat)* zozobrar.

▶ *vt sep* volcar.

ⓘ *pt & pp* **tipped**, *ger* **tipping**.

tipsy ['tɪpsɪ] *adj* achispado,-a, piripi.

ⓘ *comp* **tipsier**, *superl* **tipsiest**.

tiptoe ['tɪptəʊ] *vi* caminar de puntillas. LOC **on tiptoe** de puntillas.

tire¹ [taɪər] *vt* cansar.

▶ *vi* cansarse *(of, de)*.

◆ **to tire out** *vt sep* agotar.

tire² [taɪər] *n* US → **tyre**.

tired [taɪəd] *adj* **1** *(weary)* cansado,-a. **2** *(fed up)* harto,-a *(of, de)*. LOC **to get tired** cansarse.

tireless ['taɪələs] *adj* incansable.

tiresome ['taɪəsəm] *adj* molesto,-a, pesado,-a.

tiring ['taɪərɪŋ] *adj* cansado,-a, agotador,-ra.

tissue ['tɪʃuː] *n* **1** *(cloth)* tisú *m*. **2** *(handkerchief)* pañuelo de papel, kleenex. **3** BIOL tejido. COMP **tissue paper** papel *m* de seda.

title ['taɪtəl] *n* título.

▶ *vt* titular.

▶ *n pl* **titles** *(film credits)* créditos *mpl*.

titleholder ['taɪtəlhəʊldəʳ] *n* campeón,-ona.

to [tʊ, *unstressed* tə] *prep* **1** *(with place)* a: *we're going to a concert* vamos a un concierto. **2** *(towards)* hacia: *the Labour party has moved to the right* el partido laborista se ha desplazado hacia la derecha. **3** *(as far as, until)* a, hasta: *from beginning to end* desde el principio hasta el final. **4** *(of time)* menos: *it's ten to two* son las dos menos diez. **5** *(with indirect object)* a: *I showed the letter to my mother* le enseñé la carta a mi madre. **6** *(indicating comparison)* a: *I prefer tea to coffee* prefiero el té al café. **7** *prep (ratio)* a: *they won by fourteen points to ten* ganaron por catorce puntos a diez. **8** *(in order to)* para, a fin de: *I worked overtime to earn some extra money* hice horas extras para ganar más dinero. **9** *(substituting infinitive)*: *would you like to dance? -I'd love to* ¿te gustaría bailar? -me encantaría.
▸ *adv (of door)* ajustada: *push the door to* ajusta la puerta. ⓁⓄⒸ **to and fro** ir y venir.

> ✎ Cuando se usa con la raíz del verbo para formar el infinitivo no se traduce: *I want to help you* quiero ayudarte.

toad [təʊd] *n* sapo.

toadstool ['təʊdstuːl] *n* hongo venenoso.

> ✎ Toadstool es el nombre en general de las setas no comestibles, las que sí se pueden comer se llaman mushrooms.

toast [təʊst] *n* **1** *(food)* pan *m* tostado, tostada. **2** *(drink)* brindis *m*.
▸ *vt* **1** *(cook)* tostar. **2** *(drink)* brindar por, beber a la salud de.

toaster ['təʊstəʳ] *n* tostadora.

tobacco [tə'bækəʊ] *n* tabaco.
ⓘ *pl* tobaccos o tobaccoes.

tobacconist's [təbækənɪsts] *n* estanco.

Tobago [tə'beɪgəʊ] *n* Tobago.

toboggan [tə'bɒgən] *n* trineo.

today [tə'deɪ] *n* hoy *m*.
▸ *adv* **1** hoy. **2** *(nowadays)* hoy en día.
◆ **to toddle off** *vi* marcharse, irse.

toddler ['tɒdləʳ] *n* niño,-a (que empieza a andar).

toe [təʊ] *n* **1** ANAT dedo del pie. **2** *(of shoe)* puntera; *(of sock)* punta.

toecap [təʊcæp] *n* puntera.

toenail ['təʊneɪl] *n* uña del dedo del pie.

toffee ['tɒfɪ] *n* caramelo.
◆ **to tog out / tog up** *vt sep* vestir.
▸ *vi* vestirse.

together [tə'geðəʳ] *adv* **1** *(gen)* juntos, -as. **2** *(simultaneously)* a la vez, al mismo tiempo. **3** *(nonstop)* seguido,-a. ⓁⓄⒸ **to bring together** reunir. Ⅰ **to come together** juntarse.Ⅰ **together with** junto con.
▸ *adj fam (confident, organized, capable)* seguro,-a de sí mismo,-a.

Togo ['təʊgəʊ] *n* Togo.

Togolese [təʊgə'liːz] *adj* togolés,-esa.
▸ *n* togolés,-esa.

toilet ['tɔɪlət] *n* **1** *(appliance)* váter *m*, inodoro; *(room)* lavabo, baño. **2** *(public)* servicios *mpl*, aseos *mpl*. **3** *(washing)* aseo personal, higiene *m* personal.
ⒸⓄⓂⓅ **toilet paper** papel *m* higiénico.

toiletries ['tɔɪlətrɪz] *n pl* artículos *mpl* de aseo.

token ['təʊkªn] *n* **1** *(sign, proof)* señal *f*, prueba. **2** *(memento, souvenir)* detalle *m*, recuerdo. **3** *(coupon)* vale *m*. **4** *(coin)* ficha. ⓁⓄⒸ **in token of** en recuerdo de.
▸ *adj* simbólico,-a.

told [təʊld] *pt & pp* → **tell**.

tolerance ['tɒlərəns] *n* tolerancia.

tolerant ['tɒlərənt] *adj* tolerante (of/ towards, con).

tolerate ['tɒləreɪt] *vt* tolerar, aguantar, soportar.

toll¹ [təʊl] *n* **1** *(payment)* peaje *m*. **2** *(loss)* mortalidad *f*, número de víctimas mortales. ⓁⓄⒸ **to take its toll on** afectar negativamente.

toll² [təʊl] *n (of bell)* tañido.
▸ *vt* tañer, doblar.
▸ *vi* doblar.

tollgate ['təʊlgeɪt] *n* peaje *m*.

tom [tɒm] *n* gato (macho).

tomahawk ['tɒməhɔːk] *n* hacha de guerra.

tomato [tə'mɑːtəʊ, US tə'meɪtəʊ] *n* tomate *m*.
ⓘ *pl* tomatoes.

tomb [tuːm] n tumba, sepulcro.

tombstone ['tuːmstəʊn] n lápida (sepulcral).

tomcat ['tɒmkæt] n gato (macho).

tomorrow [tə'mɒrəʊ] n mañana.
▶ adv mañana: *tomorrow morning/afternoon* mañana por la mañana/tarde; *see you tomorrow!* ¡hasta mañana!

ton [tʌn] n tonelada.
▶ n pl **tons** *fam* montones *mpl*.

tone [təʊn] n tono.

Tonga ['tɒŋgə] n Tonga.

Tongan ['tɒŋgən] adj tongano,-a.
▶ n **1** *(person)* tongano,-a. **2** *(language)* tongano.

tongs [tɒŋz] n pl tenacillas *fpl*, pinzas *fpl*.

tongue [tʌŋ] n **1** ANAT lengua. **2** *(language)* lengua, idioma m. **3** *(of shoe)* lengüeta. **4** *(of bell)* badajo. **5** *(of land, flame)* lengua. LOC **to stick one's tongue out** sacar la lengua. COMP **tongue twister** trabalenguas m.

tonic ['tɒnɪk] n **1** MED tónico. **2** MUS tónica. **3** *(drink)* tónica.
▶ adj tónico,-a. COMP **tonic water** tónica.

tonight [tə'naɪt] n esta noche f.
▶ adv esta noche f.

tonne [tʌn] n tonelada.

tonsil ['tɒnsəl] n amígdala.

tonsillitis [tɒnsə'laɪtəs] n amigdalitis f.

too [tuː] adv **1** *(excessively)* demasiado. **2** *(also)* también. **3** *(besides)* además. **4** *(very)* muy. LOC **too many** demasiados,-as. ▌**too much** demasiado,-a.

took [tʊk] pt → take.

tool [tuːl] n *(gen)* herramienta; *(instrument)* instrumento.
▶ vt *(book)* estampar; *(leather)* labrar.
▶ n pl **tools** *(gardening, etc)* útiles *mpl*.
◆ **to tool up** vt sep equipar.

toolbar ['tuːlbɑːʳ] n barra de herramientas.

toolbox ['tuːlbɒks] n caja de herramientas.

toolkit ['tuːlkɪt] n juego de herramientas.

tooth [tuːθ] n **1** *(gen)* diente m; *(molar)* muela; *(front tooth)* incisivo. **2** *(of comb)* púa. **3** *(of saw)* diente m.
① pl **teeth**.

toothache ['tuːθeɪk] n dolor m de muelas.

toothbrush ['tuːθbrʌʃ] n cepillo de dientes.

toothless ['tuːθləs] adj desdentado,-a.

toothpaste ['tuːθpeɪst] n pasta de dientes.

toothpick ['tuːθpɪk] n mondadientes m inv, palillo.

top¹ [tɒp] n **1** *(highest/upper part)* parte f superior. **2** *(far end - of street)* final m; *(- of table)* cabecera. **3** *(of mountain)* cumbre m. **4** *(of tree)* copa. **5** *(surface)* superficie f. **6** *(of bottle)* tapón m; *(of pen)* capuchón m. **7** *(highest position)*: *she was top of the class* fue la primera de la clase. **8** *(of list)* cabeza. **9** *(of car)* capota. **10** *(clothes)* top m; *(of bikini)* parte de arriba. **11** *(beginning)* principio. **12** *(gear)* directa.
▶ adj **1** *(highest)* de arriba, superior, más alto,-a. **2** *(best, highest, leading)* mejor, principal. **3** *(highest, maximum)* principal, máximo,-a. COMP **top brass** altos mandos *mpl*. ▌**top gear** directa.
▶ vt **1** *(cover)* cubrir, rematar. **2** *(remove top of plant/fruit)* quitar los rabillos. **3** *sl (kill)* cargarse. **4** *(come first, head)* encabezar. **5** *(better, surpass, exceed)* superar.
① pt & pp **topped**, ger **topping**.
▶ n pl **tops** *(of plant)* hojas *fpl*.

top² [tɒp] n peonza. LOC **to sleep like a top** dormir como un tronco.

topaz ['təʊpæz] n topacio.

topic ['tɒpɪk] n tema m.

> ☒ Tópico no significa 'tópico', que se traduce por **commonplace**.

topography [tə'pɒgrəfɪ] n topografía.

toponym ['tɒpənɪm] n topónimo.

topping ['tɒpɪŋ] n *(for pizza)* ingrediente m; *(for ice-cream)* cubierta.
▶ adj excelente.

topple ['tɒpəl] vt **1** *(overturn)* volcar. **2** *fig (overthrow)* derribar, derrocar.
▶ vi *(fall)* caerse; *(lose balance)* tambalearse, perder el equilibrio.

torch [tɔːtʃ] n **1** *(with naked flame)* antorcha. **2** *(electric)* linterna.
► vt quemar, prender fuego a.

tore [tɔːʳ] pt → **tear**.

torment [*(n)* 'tɔːmənt; *(vb)* tɔː'ment] n *(gen)* tormento; *(suffering)* angustia.
► vt **1** *(cause to suffer)* atormentar, torturar. **2** *(annoy)* molestar.

torn [tɔːn] pp → **tear**.

tornado [tɔː'neɪdəʊ] n tornado.
ⓘ pl **tornados** o **tornadoes**.

torpedo [tɔː'piːdəʊ] n torpedo.
ⓘ pl **torpedos** o **torpedoes**.

torrent ['tɒrənt] n torrente m.

torrential [təˈrenʃəl] adj torrencial.

torso ['tɔːsəʊ] n torso.
ⓘ pl **torsos**.

tort [tɔːt] n JUR agravio.

tortoise ['tɔːtəs] n tortuga (de tierra).

torture ['tɔːtəʳ] n tortura.

Tory ['tɔːrɪ] n GB conservador,-ra.
ⓘ pl **Tories**.
► adj GB conservador,-ra.

toss [tɒs] n **1** *(shake)* sacudida, movimiento. **2** *(of coin)* sorteo a cara o cruz.
► vt **1** *(move, shake)* mover, agitar, sacudir; *(pancake)* dar la vuelta a; *(salad)* mezclar. **2** *(throw)* arrojar, lanzar, tirar.
ⓁⓄⒸ **to toss a coin** echarlo a cara o cruz.
ⓘ pt & pp **tossed**, ger **tossing**.

total ['təʊtəl] adj *(overall)* total; *(complete)* completo,-a, rotundo,-a.
► n total m, suma. ⓁⓄⒸ **in total** en total.
► vt sumar.
► vi sumar, ascender a.

totalitarian [təʊtælɪ'teərɪən] adj totalitario,-a.

totally ['təʊtəlɪ] adv totalmente, completamente.

totem ['təʊtəm] n tótem m. ⲥⲟⲙⲣ **totem pole** tótem m.

touch [tʌtʃ] n **1** *(gen)* toque m; *(light touch)* roce m. **2** *(detail)* detalle m, toque m. **3** *(sense)* tacto. **4** *(connection)* contacto, comunicación f. **5** *(slight quantity)* poquito, pizca. **6** fam *(skill, ability)* habilidad f. **7** *(manner, style)* toque m, sello. **9** SP toque m. ⓁⓄⒸ **to be in touch with** STH estar al corriente de ALGO. ❙

to get in touch ponerse en contacto (with, con).
► vt **1** *(gen)* tocar; *(lightly)* rozar. **2** *(eat)* probar. **3** *(move)* conmover. **4** *(equal, rival)* igualar.
► vi tocarse.
◆ **to touch down** vi **1** *(plane)* aterrizar.
◆ **to touch on / touch upon** vi mencionar.
◆ **to touch up** vt sep ART retocar.

touching ['tʌtʃɪŋ] adj conmovedor,-ra.

touch-screen ['tʌtʃskriːn] n pantalla táctil.

tough [tʌf] adj **1** *(strong)* fuerte, resistente. **2** *(difficult)* duro,-a, arduo,-a. **3** *(rough, violent)* violento,-a. **4** *(severe)* duro,-a, severo,-a. **5** *(meat)* duro,-a.
► n tipo duro.

tour [tʊəʳ] n **1** viaje m, excursión f. **2** *(round building)* visita. **3** *(by performers)* gira; *(cycling)* vuelta.
► vt **1** *(gen)* recorrer, viajar por. **2** *(building)* visitar. ⲥⲟⲙⲣ **tour operator** agente m de viajes.
► vi *(by performers)* hacer una gira.

tourism ['tʊərɪzəm] n turismo.

tourist ['tʊərɪst] n turista mf.
► adj turístico,-a. ⲥⲟⲙⲣ **tourist class** clase f turista. ❙ **tourist office** oficina de turismo.

tournament ['tʊənəmənt] n torneo.

tow [təʊ] vt remolcar.
► n remolque m. ⓁⓄⒸ **on tow** de remolque.

toward [tə'wɔːd] prep US → **towards**.

towards [tə'wɔːdz] prep **1** *(in direction of)* hacia. **2** *(attitude)* con, para con. **3** *(payment)* para. **4** *(of time)* hacia, cerca de.

towel ['taʊəl] n toalla.

tower ['taʊəʳ] n **1** *(gen)* torre f. **2** *(of church)* campanario. ⲥⲟⲙⲣ **tower block** bloque m (de pisos).

town [taʊn] n **1** *(large)* ciudad f; *(small)* población f, municipio, pueblo. **2** *(city centre)* centro. **3** *(people)* ciudadanos mpl, ciudad f.
► adj urbano,-a, municipal. ⲥⲟⲙⲣ **town council** ayuntamiento. ❙ **town hall** ayuntamiento.

T

township ['taʊnʃɪp] *n* **1** *(gen)* municipio, pueblo. **2** *(in South Africa)* distrito segregado.

toxic ['tɒksɪk] *n* tóxico,-a.

toy [tɔɪ] *n* juguete *m*.
▶ *adj* **1** de juguete. **2** *(dog)* enano,-a. COMP **toy shop** juguete *m*.

toyshop ['tɔɪʃɒp] *n* juguetería.

trace [treɪs] *n* **1** *(mark, sign)* indicio, rastro. **2** *(small amount - material)* pizca, vestigio; *(- non-material)* dejo, asomo, nota. COMP **trace element** oligoelemento.
▶ *vt* **1** *(sketch)* trazar, esbozar. **2** *(copy)* calcar. **3** *(find)* encontrar, localizar; *(follow)* seguir la pista de. **4** *(describe development)* describir.

tracer ['treɪsər] *n* **1** MIL trazadora. **2** MED trazador *m*. COMP **tracer bullet** bala trazadora.

trachea [trəˈkiːə] *n* ANAT tráquea.

tracing ['treɪsɪŋ] *n* calco. COMP **tracing paper** papel *m* de calco.

track [træk] *n* **1** *(mark)* pista, huellas *fpl*, rastro; *(of wheels)* rodada. **2** *(of rocket, bullet, etc)* trayectoria. **3** *(path)* camino, senda, sendero. **4** SP pista. **5** *(for motor-racing)* circuito. **6** *(of railway)* vía; *(platform)* andén *m*. **7** *(on record, etc)* tema *m*, corte *m*, canción *f*. LOC **to be on the right track** ir por buen camino. **to keep track of** seguir. COMP **track and field** atletismo.
▶ *vt* **1** *(person, animal)* seguir la pista de. **2** TECH seguir la trayectoria de.
◆ **to track down** *vt sep* localizar.

tracksuit ['træksuːt] *n* chándal *m*.

tract¹ [trækt] *n* *(treatise)* tratado; *(pamphlet)* folleto.

traction ['trækʃən] *n* tracción *f*.

tractor ['træktər] *n* tractor *m*.

trade [treɪd] *n* **1** *(commerce)* comercio. **2** *(business)* negocio; *(industry)* industria. **3** *(occupation)* oficio, profesión *f*.
▶ *adj* comercial. COMP **trade gap** déficit *m* comercial. **trade fair** feria de muestras. **trade name** nombre *m* comercial. **trade union** sindicato. **trade winds** vientos *mpl* alisios.
▶ *vi* *(do business)* comerciar.
▶ *vt* *(exchange)* cambiar.

trademark ['treɪdmɑːk] *n* marca registrada, marca.

trader ['treɪdər] *n* comerciante *mf*.

tradesman ['treɪdzmən] *n* **1** *(businessman)* comerciante *m*; *(shopkeeper)* tendero. **2** *(deliveryman)* repartidor *m*.
ⓘ *pl* **tradesmen** ['treɪdzmən].

trading ['treɪdɪŋ] *n* comercio.

tradition [trəˈdɪʃən] *n* tradición *f*.

traditional [trədɪʃənəl] *adj* tradicional.

traffic ['træfɪk] *n* tráfico.
▶ *adj* de la circulación, del tráfico. COMP **traffic circle** US rotonda. **traffic jam** atasco, embotellamiento. **traffic lights** semáforo. **traffic warden** guardia *mf* de tráfico.
▶ *vi* traficar (in, con).

⊕ Un **traffic warden** es un especie de guardia urbano que vigila que los coches estén bien aparcados y regula el tráfico de las ciudades.

tragedy ['trædʒədɪ] *n* tragedia.
ⓘ *pl* **tragedies**.

tragic ['trædʒɪk] *adj* trágico,-a.

trail [treɪl] *n* **1** *(path)* camino, sendero. **2** *(track, mark, scent)* rastro, pista, huellas *fpl*. **3** *(of rocket, comet)* cola; *(of dust, vapour)* estela; *(of blood)* reguero.
▶ *vt* **1** *(follow)* seguir la pista de. **2** *(drag)* arrastrar.
▶ *vi* **1** *(lag behind)* ir rezagado,-a, quedarse atrás. **2** *(drag)* arrastrarse.

trailer ['treɪlər] *n* **1** AUTO remolque *m*. **2** US caravana. **3** CINEM tráiler *m*, avance *m*.

train [treɪn] *n* **1** *(transport)* tren *m*. **2** *(of dress)* cola. **3** *(line - of animals)* recua; *(- of vehicles)* convoy *m*.
▶ *vt* **1** SP entrenar, preparar. **2** *(teach)* enseñar. **3** *(animal)* amaestrar, adiestrar. COMP **train driver** maquinista *m*. **train station** estación *f* de tren.
▶ *vi* **1** SP entrenarse, prepararse. **2** *(teach)* estudiar. **3** MIL adiestrarse.

trained [treɪnd] *adj* **1** *(worker - skilled)* calificado,-a, cualificado,-a. **2** *(animal)* amaestrado,-a, adiestrado,-a.

trainee [treɪˈniː] n 1 (manual work) aprendiz,-za. 2 (professional work) persona que está haciendo prácticas.

trainer [ˈtreɪnəʳ] n 1 SP entrenador,-ra. 2 (of dogs) amaestrador,-ra; (of circus animals) domador,-ra; (of race horses) preparador,-ra. 3 (shoe) zapatilla de deporte.

training [ˈtreɪnɪŋ] n 1 formación f (profesional), capacitación f. 2 SP entrenamiento, preparación f física.
▸ vi MIL instrucción f.

traitor [ˈtreɪtəʳ] n traidor,-ra.

tram [træm] n tranvía m.

tramcar [ˈtræmkɑːʳ] n tranvía m.

tramp [træmp] n vagabundo,-a.

☒ Tramp no significa 'trampa', que se traduce por trap.

trample [ˈtræmpəl] vt pisotear.
▸ vi pisotear (on/over, -).

trampoline [ˈtræmpəliːn] n cama elástica.

tranquilliser [ˈtræŋkwɪlaɪzəʳ] n → tranquillizer.

tranquillizer [ˈtræŋkwɪlaɪzəʳ] n tranquilizante m, calmante m.

transcend [trænˈsend] vt 1 (go beyond) trascender. 2 (surpass) superar.

transept [ˈtrænsept] n crucero.

transfer [(n) ˈtrænsfɜːʳ; (vb) trænsˈfɜːʳ] n 1 FIN transferencia. 2 JUR (of property) traspaso. 3 (of employee) traslado. 4 SP (of player) traspaso; (player) fichaje m. 5 (drawing) cromo, calcomanía. 6 (of airline passenger) transbordo, trasbordo.
▸ vt 1 FIN transferir. 2 JUR (property) traspasar. 3 (employee, prisoner) trasladar. 4 SP (player) traspasar. 5 (data, information, phone call) pasar.
ⓘ pt & pp transferred, ger transferring.

transform [trænsˈfɔːm] vt transformar.
▸ vi transformarse (into, en), convertirse (into, en).

transistor [trænˈzɪstəʳ] n transistor.

transition [trænˈzɪʃən] n transición f.

transitive [ˈtrænsɪtɪv] adj transitivo,-a.

translate [trænsˈleɪt] vt 1 (gen) traducir (from, de) (into, a). 2 (express, explain) expresar. 3 (transform) transformar.
▸ vi (person) traducir; (word, book, etc) traducirse.

translation [trænsˈleɪʃən] n traducción f.

translator [trænsˈleɪtəʳ] n traductor,-ra.

translucent [trænzˈluːsənt] adj translúcido,-a.

transmission [trænzˈmɪʃən] n transmisión f.

transmit [trænzˈmɪt] vt transmitir (to, a).
ⓘ pt & pp transmitted, ger transmitting.

transmitter [trænzˈmɪtəʳ] n transmisor m.

transparency [trænsˈpeərənsɪ] n 1 (quality) transparencia. 2 (slide) diapositiva; (acetate) transparencia.
ⓘ pl transparencies.

transparent [trænsˈpeərənt] adj 1 transparente. 2 fig claro,-a, evidente.

transplant [(n) ˈtrænsplɑːnt; (vb) trænsˈplɑːnt] n trasplante m.
▸ vt trasplantar.

transport [(n) ˈtrænspɔːt; (vb) trænsˈpɔːt] n transporte m.
▸ vt 1 transportar. 2 HIST deportar.

trap [træp] n 1 (gen) trampa. 2 (vehicle) coche m ligero de dos ruedas. 3 (of drain) sifón m. LOC to set a trap tender una trampa.
▸ vt 1 (catch - gen) atrapar; (snare - animal) cazar; (imprison) entrampar; (part of body) pillar. 2 SP (in football) parar con el pie. 3 fig (trick) engañar, tender una trampa a. 4 (heat, light, etc) retener.
ⓘ pt & pp trapped, ger trapping.

trapdoor [ˈtræpdɔːʳ] n (gen) trampilla; (in theatre) escotillón m.

trapeze [trəˈpiːz] n (of circus) trapecio.

trapezium [trəˈpiːziəm] n trapecio.
ⓘ pl trapeziums o trapezia [trəˈpiːziə].

trapezoid [ˈtræpɪzɔɪd] n 1 GB trapecio m. 1 US trapezoide

trash [træʃ] n basura. COMP trash can 1 (on computer) papelera de reciclaje. 2 (for waste) US cubo de la basura.

trauma [ˈtrɔːmə] n trauma m.

T

travel ['træv^əl] *n* viajes *mpl*, viajar *m*. COMP
travel agency agencia de viajes. ▌**travel
sickness** mareo.
▶ *vt* viajar por, recorrer.
▶ *vi* **1** *(make a journey)* viajar; *(go)* ir. **2**
(move, go) ir. **3** *(go fast)* ir rápido, ir a
toda velocidad. **4** *(as salesperson)* ser
viajante, ser representante. **5** *(wine,
food, etc)* poderse transportar.
ⓘ *pt & pp* travelled *(US* traveled), *ger*
travelling *(US* traveling).
▶ *n pl* **travels** *(journeys)* viajes *mpl*.

traveler ['træv^ələ^r] *n* US → traveller.

traveller ['træv^ələ^r] *n* **1** *(gen)* viajero,-a.
2 *(representative)* viajante *mf*, represen-
tante *mf*. COMP **traveller's cheque** cheque
m de viaje.

trawler ['trɔːlə^r] *n* pesquero de arrastre.

tray [treɪ] *n* **1** *(for food)* bandeja. **2** *(for papers)* caja, cesta. **3** *(in photography)* cubeta.

treachery ['tretʃəri] *n* traición *f*.
ⓘ *pl* treacheries.

tread [tred] *n* **1** *(manner or sound of walking)*
paso, pasos *mpl*. **2** *(on stair)* escalón *m*.
▶ *vt* **1** *(gen)* pisar, pisotear. **2** *(walk on)*
andar por; *(make)* hacer.
ⓘ *pt* trod [trɒd], *pp* trodden ['trɒdən] o
trod [trɒd].

treason ['triːz^ən] *n* traición *f*.

treasure ['treʒə^r] *n* *(gen)* tesoro.

treasurer ['treʒərə^r] *n* tesorero,-a.

treasury ['treʒəri] *n* tesorería.
ⓘ *pl* treasuries.

treat [triːt] *n* **1** *(meal, drink)* convite *m*. **2**
(present) regalo. **3** *(pleasure)* placer *m*,
gusto, deleite *m*.
▶ *vt* **1** *(gen)* tratar. **2** *(invite)* invitar; *(give)*
regalar.

treatment ['triːtmənt] *n* **1** MED tratamiento, cura. **2** *(manner of treating)* trato. **3** *(process)* tratamiento.

❌ Treatment no significa 'tratamiento
(forma de dirigirse alguien)', que se traduce por form of address.

treaty ['triːti] *n* tratado.
ⓘ *pl* treaties.

treble ['treb^əl] *adj* **1** *(threefold)* triple. **2** MUS
de tiple. COMP **treble clef** clave *f* de sol.
▶ *n* MUS tiple *mf*.

▶ *vt* triplicar.
▶ *vi* triplicarse.

tree [triː] *n* árbol *m*.

tree-top ['triːtɒp] *n* copa.

trekking ['trekɪŋ] *n* senderismo.

tremble ['tremb^əl] *n* temblor *m*.
▶ *vi* temblar.

tremendous [trɪ'mendəs] *adj* **1** *(huge)*
tremendo,-a, inmenso,-a. **2** *fam*
(great) fantástico,-a, estupendo,-a.

trench [trentʃ] *n* **1** *(ditch)* zanja. **2** MIL
trinchera.

trend [trend] *n* **1** *(tendency)* tendencia
(to/towards, hacia), tónica. **2** *(fashion)*
moda.

trendy ['trendi] *adj fam* moderno,-a,
de moda.
ⓘ *comp* trendier, *superl* trendiest.

trespass ['trespəs] *n* **1** entrada ilegal.
2 REL pecado.
▶ *vi* **1** *(on land)* entrar sin autorización; *(in affairs)* entrometerse. **2** REL
pecar (against, contra). LOC "No tres-
passing" «Prohibido el paso».

❌ To trespass no significa 'traspasar',
que se traduce por to go through.

trespasser ['trespəsə^r] *n* intruso,-a.

tress [tres] *n* mechón *m*.
▶ *n pl* **tresses** melena *f sing*, cabellera *f sing*.

trestle ['tres^əl] *n* caballete *m*.

trial ['traɪəl] *n* **1** JUR proceso, juicio. **2**
(test) prueba. **3** *(suffering)* aflicción *f*,
sufrimiento; *(trouble)* molestia.
▶ *n pl* **trials** SP pruebas *fpl*.

triangle ['traɪæŋg^əl] *n* triángulo.

triangular [traɪ'æŋgjʊlə^r] *adj* triangular.

tribal ['traɪb^əl] *adj* tribal.

tribe [traɪb] *n* **1** tribu *f*. **2** *fam (family)*
tribu *f*, familia.

tribune ['trɪbjuːn] *n* **1** ARCH tribuna. **2**
(Roman magistrate) tribuno.

tributary ['trɪbjʊtəri] *n* afluente *m*.
ⓘ *pl* tributaries.
▶ *adj* tributario,-a.

tribute ['trɪbjuːt] *n* **1** *(homage)* homenaje *m*, tributo. **2** *(payment)* tributo.

triceps ['traɪseps] *n pl* tríceps *m inv*.

trick [trɪk] *n* **1** *(gen)* truco.**2** *(prank, joke)* broma. **3** *(cards won)* baza. LOC **to play a trick on SB** gastarle una broma a ALGN. ∎ **trick or treat** US *frase de los niños que en Halloween van por las casas pidiendo un regalo a cambio de no hacer una jugarreta.*
▶ *adj* de juguete, de mentira.
▶ *vt (deceive)* engañar, burlar.

trickle ['trɪkəl] *n* **1** goteo, hilo. **2** *fig* pequeña cantidad *f*, poco.
▶ *vi* **1** *(liquid)* gotear, salir gota a gota. **2** *fig* salir *(entrar, llegar, etc)* poco a poco.

tricky ['trɪkɪ] *adj* **1** *(person)* astuto,-a. **2** *(problem, situation - difficult)* difícil; *(- delicate)* delicado,-a.
ⓘ *comp* trickier, *superl* trickiest.

tricycle ['traɪsɪkəl] *n* triciclo.

trident ['traɪdənt] *n* tridente *m*.

trier [traɪəʳ] *n* persona que se esfuerza.

trifle ['traɪfəl] *n* **1** *(unimportant thing)* nimiedad *f*. **2** *(little money)* poco dinero. **3** GB postre de bizcocho. LOC **a trifle** un poco, algo.

trigger ['trɪgəʳ] *n* **1** *(of gun)* gatillo. **2** *(of camera, machine)* disparador *m*.

trigonometry [trɪgə'nɒmətrɪ] *n* trigonometría.

trillion ['trɪlɪən] *n* **1** billón *m*. **2** GB *(formerly)* trillón *m*.

✎ En el uso actual, tanto en EE UU como en Gran Bretaña, un trillion equivale al billón español, es decir, un millón de millones.

trim [trɪm] *adj* **1** *(neat, tidy)* (bien) arreglado,-a, ordenado,-a, cuidado,-a. **2** *(person, figure)* esbelto,-a, delgado,-a.
ⓘ *comp* trimmer, *superl* trimmest.
▶ *n* **1** *(cut)* recorte *m*. **2** *(decoration - on clothes)* adornos *mpl*; *(- along edges)* ribete *m*; *(upholstery)* tapicería.
▶ *vt* **1** *(make neat)* arreglar; *(cut - hair)* cortar, recortar; *(- hedge, etc)* podar. **2** *(reduce by cutting back)* recortar, reducir. **3** *(decorate)* adornar *(with, con)*; *(upholster)* tapizar.
◆ **to trim off** *vt sep* recortar, quitar.
ⓘ *pt & pp* trimmed, *ger* trimming.

trimmings ['trɪmɪŋz] *n pl* **1** CULIN *(accompaniments)* guarnición *f sing*. **2** *(deco-*

rations) adornos *mpl*. **3** *(after cutting)* recortes *mpl*.

Trinidad ['trɪnɪdæd] *n* Trinidad. COMP **Trinidad and Tobago** Trinidad y Tobago.

trip [trɪp] *n* **1** *(journey)* viaje *m*. **2** *(excursion)* excursión *f*.
▶ *vi* **1** *(stumble)* tropezar (over, con). **2** *(move lightly)* ir con paso ligero.
ⓘ *pt & pp* tripped, *ger* tripping.

tripe [traɪp] *n* **1** CULIN callos *mpl*. **2** *fam* tonterías *fpl*, bobadas *fpl*.

triple ['trɪpəl] *adj* triple.

triplet ['trɪplət] *n (child)* trillizo,-a.

triumph [traɪəmf] *n* **1** triunfo, éxito. **2** *(joy)* júbilo, alegría.
▶ *vi* triunfar (over, de/sobre), vencer.

trivial ['trɪvɪəl] *adj* trivial.

trod [trɒd] *pt* → tread.

trodden ['trɒdən] *pp* → tread.

troll [trəʊl] *n* duende *m*.

trolley ['trɒlɪ] *n* **1** *(in supermarket, at airport)* carro, carrito. **2** *(in hospital)* cama con ruedas. **3** *(for food)* mesita de ruedas. **4** US tranvía. COMP **trolley bus** trolebús *mf*. ∎ **trolley car** tranvía *mf*.

trombone [trɒm'bəʊn] *n* trombón *m*.

trophy ['trəʊfɪ] *n* trofeo.
ⓘ *pl* trophies.

tropic ['trɒpɪk] *n* trópico.
▶ *n pl* **the tropics** los trópicos *mpl*.

tropical ['trɒpɪkəl] *adj* tropical.

tropism [trə'pɪzəm] *n* tropismo.

troposphere ['trɒpəsfɪəʳ] *n* troposfera.

trot [trɒt] *n* trote *m*.
▶ *vi (gen)* trotar, ir al trote; *(on horse)* cabalgar al trote.
ⓘ *pt & pp* trotted, *ger* trotting.
▶ *n pl* **the trots** *fam* diarrea *f sing*.

trouble ['trʌbəl] *n* **1** *(problems)* problema *m*, problemas *mpl*. **2** *(inconvenience, bother)* molestia, esfuerzo. **3** *(unrest, disturbance)* conflictos *mpl*, disturbios *mpl*. LOC **to be in trouble** tener problemas. ∎ **to get in trouble** meterse en un lío.
▶ *vt* **1** *(cause worry, distress)* preocupar, inquietar. **2** *(hurt)* dar problemas a, doler. **3** *(bother)* molestar, incomodar.
▶ *vi* molestarse, preocuparse (about, por).

T

troublemaker ['trʌbºlmeɪkəʳ] n alborotador,-ra.

trough [trɒf] n (for drinking) abrevadero; (for eating) comedero, pesebre m.

trousers ['traʊzəz] n pl pantalón m sing, pantalones mpl.

trout [traʊt] n trucha.

trowel ['traʊəl] n 1 (bricklaying tool) paleta. 2 (garden tool) desplantador m.

truant ['truːənt] n (from school) persona que hace novillos. LOC **to play truant** hacer novillos.

truce [truːs] n tregua.

truck [trʌk] n 1 (lorry) camión m. 2 GB (railway wagon) vagón m.

trucker ['trʌkəʳ] n US camionero,-a.

true [truː] adj 1 (not false) verdadero,-a, cierto,-a. 2 (genuine, real) auténtico,-a, genuino,-a, real. 3 (faithful) fiel, leal. 4 (exact) exacto,-a. LOC **to come true** hacerse realidad.
► adv 1 (truthfully) sinceramente. 2 (accurately) bien.

truffle ['trʌfºl] n trufa.

truly ['truːlɪ] adv 1 (really) verdaderamente, de verdad, realmente. 2 (sincerely) sinceramente. 3 (faithfully) fielmente, lealmente. LOC **yours truly** (in letters) atentamente.

◆ **to trump up** vt sep inventar, falsificar.

trumpet ['trʌmpɪt] n MUS trompeta.
► vi 1 fanfarronear. 2 (elephant) barritar.

truncheon ['trʌntʃºn] n porra (de policía).

trunk [trʌŋk] n 1 (of tree, body) tronco. 2 (large case) baúl m. 3 (elephant's) trompa. 4 US (of car) maletero.

trunks [trʌŋks] n pl bañador m sing (de hombre).

trust [trʌst] n 1 (confidence) confianza. 2 (responsibility) responsabilidad f. 3 FIN (money, property) fondo de inversión.
► vt 1 (have faith in, rely on) confiar en, fiarse de. 2 (hope, expect) esperar.
► vi confiar (in, en), tener confianza (in, en).

trustful ['trʌstfʊl] adj confiado,-a.

trustworthy ['trʌstwɜːðɪ] adj 1 (person) digno,-a de confianza, honrado,-a. 2 (news, etc) fidedigno,-a.

truth [truːθ] n verdad f.

truthful ['truːθfʊl] adj 1 (account, etc) verídico,-a, veraz. 2 (person) sincero,-a, veraz.

try [traɪ] n 1 intento. 2 SP (rugby) ensayo.
ⓘ pl tries.
► vt 1 (attempt) intentar. 2 (test, use) probar, ensayar; (food) probar. 3 JUR juzgar, procesar.
► vi (make an attempt) intentar.
◆ **to try for** vi tratar de obtener.
◆ **to try on** vt sep (clothes) probarse.
◆ **to try out** vt sep probar, ensayar.
ⓘ pt & pp tried, ger trying.

tsar [zɑːʳ] n zar m.

tsarina [zɑːˈriːnə] n zarina.

tsetse fly ['tsetsɪflaɪ] n mosca tsetsé.

T-shirt ['tiːʃɜːt] n camiseta.

tub [tʌb] n 1 (for washing clothes) balde m. 2 (bath) bañera. 3 (food container) tarrina.

tuba ['tjuːbə] n tuba.

tube [tjuːb] n 1 (pipe, container) tubo. 2 AUTO cámara de aire.
► n **the tube** la televisión f.
► n **the Tube** (underground) el metro.

⊕ The Tube es el nombre con el que se conoce al metro de Londres.

tuck [tʌk] n 1 (fold) pliegue m. 2 GB (sweets, etc) golosinas fpl, chucherías fpl.

Tuesday ['tjuːzdɪ] n martes m inv.

✎ Para ejemplos de uso, consulta **Saturday**.

tuft [tʌft] n 1 (of feathers) penacho. 2 (of hair) mechón m. 3 (of grass) mata.

tug [tʌg] n 1 (pull) tirón m, estirón m. 2 (boat) remolcador m.
► vt 1 (pull) tirar de, dar un estirón de. 2 (boat) remolcar.
ⓘ pt & pp tugged, ger tugging.
► vi tirar (at, de).
ⓘ pt & pp tugged, ger tugging.

tuition [tjuːˈɪʃºn] n enseñanza, instrucción f. COMP **private tuition** clases fpl particulares. ❙ **tuition fees** EDUC matrícula.

tulip ['tjuːlɪp] n tulipán m.

tumble ['tʌmbºl] n caída, tumbo. COMP **tumble drier** secadora.
► vi 1 (fall) caerse. 2 (in acrobatics) dar volteretas.

tumbler ['tʌmbᵊləʳ] n **1** (glass) vaso. **2** (acrobat) volteador,-ra. **3** (toy) tentetieso.

tummy ['tʌmɪ] n barriga.
ⓘ pl tummies.

tumor ['tjuːməʳ] n US → tumour.

tumour ['tjuːməʳ] n barriga.

tuna ['tjuːnə] n atún m, bonito.
ⓘ pl tuna o tunas.

tune [tjuːn] n melodía. ⎡LOC⎤ **in tune** afinado,-a. **‖ out of tune** desafinado,-a.
▶ vt **1** MUS afinar. **2** (radio, etc) sintonizar. **3** (engine) poner a punto.

tuner ['tjuːnəʳ] n **1** (of piano) afinador, -ra. **2** (on radio) sintonizador m.

tungsten ['tʌŋstən] n tungsteno.

tunic ['tjuːnɪk] n túnica.

tuning ['tjuːnɪŋ] n **1** (of instrument) afinación f. **2** (of radio) sintonización f. **3** (of engine) puesta a punto. ⎡COMP⎤ **tuning fork** diapasón m.

Tunis ['tjuːnɪs] n Túnez.

Tunisia [tjuː'nɪsɪə] n Túnez.

Tunisian [tjuː'nɪsɪən] adj tunecino,-a.
▶ n tunecino,-a.

tunnel ['tʌnᵊl] n túnel m.
▶ vt excavar un túnel.
ⓘ pt & pp tunnelled (US tunneled), ger tunnelling (US tunneling).

turban ['tɜːbᵊn] n turbante m.

turbojet ['tɜːbəʊdʒet] n turborreactor m.

turbot ['tɜːbət] n rodaballo.
ⓘ pl turbot o turbots.

turbulence ['tɜːbjʊləns] n turbulencia.

turf [tɜːf] n césped m. ⎡COMP⎤ **the turf** las carreras de caballos, el turf m.
◆ **to turf out** vt sep fam poner de patitas en la calle, echar.

Turk [tɜːk] n (person) turco,-a.

Turkey ['tɜːkɪ] n Turquía.

turkey ['tɜːkɪ] n pavo. ⎡LOC⎤ **to talk turkey** hablar a las claras.

Turkish ['tɜːkɪʃ] adj turco,-a.
▶ n (language) turco.
▶ n pl **the Turkish** los turcos mpl.

turn [tɜːn] n **1** (gen) vuelta. **2** (change of direction) giro, vuelta; (bend) curva, recodo. **3** (chance, go) turno. **4** (change) cambio, giro.
⎡LOC⎤ **to turn a corner** doblar la esquina.

▶ vt **1** (rotate) girar, hacer girar. **2** (page) pasar, volver; (soil) revolver; (ankle) torcer. **3** (change) convertir, transformar; (milk) agriar; (stomach) revolver.
▶ vi **1** (revolve) girar, dar vueltas. **2** (change direction - person) girarse, volverse. **3** (become) hacerse, ponerse, volverse; (milk) agriarse, cortarse.
◆ **to turn back** vt sep **1** (make return) hacer volver. **2** (clock) retrasar.
▶ vi (return) volverse atrás.
◆ **to turn down** vt sep **1** (reject) rechazar; (request) denegar. **2** (radio, etc) bajar. **3** (fold) doblar.
◆ **to turn into** vt sep convertir.
◆ **to turn off** vt sep **1** (electricity) desconectar; (light, gas, appliance) apagar; (tap) cerrar. **2** (dislike) repugnar, dar asco a.
▶ vt insep (off road) salir de.
▶ vi **1** (switch off) apagarse. **2** (off road) salir.
◆ **to turn on** vt sep **1** (electricity) conectar; (light, gas, appliance) encender; (tap) abrir; (engine) poner en marcha, encender. **2** (attack) atacar, arremeter contra; (aim, point at) apuntar, dirigir. **3** fam (excite) excitar, entusiasmar.
▶ vt insep (hinge on) depender de, girar en torno a.
▶ vi encenderse.
◆ **to turn out** vt sep **1** (light) apagar. **2** (produce) producir, fabricar. **3** (empty) vaciar; (cake, jelly, etc) desmoldar. **4** (expel) expulsar, echar.
▶ vi **1** (prove to be, happen) salir, resultar. **2** (go out) salir; (attend) asistir, acudir; (crowds) salir a la calle.
◆ **to turn round** vi dar la vuelta.
◆ **to turn up** vi (arrive) llegar, presentarse; (appear) aparecer.
▶ vt sep **1** (fold upwards) doblar hacia arriba, levantar; (shorten) acortar. **2** (radio, gas, heat, etc) subir.
▶ vt insep (find) descubrir, encontrar.

turnabout ['tɜːnəbaʊt] n giro, cambio.

turning ['tɜːnɪŋ] n bocacalle f, esquina. ⎡COMP⎤ **turning lathe** torno.

turnip ['tɜːnɪp] n nabo.

turnover ['tɜːnəʊvəʳ] n **1** (sales, business) facturación f. **2** (movement of employees) movimiento; (of stock) rotación f. **3** CULIN pastelito relleno.

T

turnpike ['tɜːnpaɪk] *n* US autopista de peaje.

turquoise ['tɜːkwɔɪz] *n* **1** *(gem)* turquesa. **2** *(colour)* azul *m* turquesa.
► *adj* azul turquesa.

turtle ['tɜːtəl] *n* tortuga marina.

tusk [tʌsk] *n* colmillo.

tutor ['tjuːtəʳ] *n* **1** *(private teacher)* profesor,-ra particular. **2** *(at university)* profesor,-ra, tutor,-ra.
► *vt* dar clases particulares a (in, de).

Tuvalu [tuːvəˈluː] *n* Tuvalu.

tuxedo [tʌkˈsiːdəu] *n* US esmoquin *m*.
ⓘ *pl* tuxedos.

TV ['tiːˈviː] *abbr* (television) televisión *f*, tele *f*.

tweezers ['twiːzəz] *n pl* pinzas *fpl*.

twelfth [twelfθ] *adj* duodécimo,-a.
► *adv* en duodécimo lugar.
► *n (fraction)* duodécimo; *(one part)* duodécima parte *f*.

✎ Consulta también sixth.

twelve [twelv] *n* doce *m*.
► *adj* doce.

✎ Consulta también six.

twenties ['twentɪz] *n pl* the twenties los años *mpl* veinte. LOC to be in one's twenties tener veintitantos años.

✎ Consulta también sixties.

twentieth ['twentɪəθ] *adj* vigésimo,-a.
► *adv* en vigésimo lugar.
► *n (fraction)* vigésimo; *(one part)* vigésima parte *f*.

✎ Consulta también sixtieth.

twenty ['twentɪ] *n* veinte *m*.
► *adj* veinte.

✎ Consulta también sixty.

twice [twaɪs] *adv* dos veces. LOC twice over dos veces.

twig¹ [twɪg] *n* ramita.

twilight ['twaɪlaɪt] *n* crepúsculo.

twin [twɪn] *n* gemelo,-a, mellizo,-a.
► *adj* gemelo,-a, mellizo,-a. COMP twin bed cama doble.
► *vt* hermanar.
ⓘ *pt & pp* twinned, *ger* twinning.

twinkle ['twɪŋkəl] *n* **1** *(of light, stars)* centelleo. **2** *(in eye)* brillo.
► *vi* **1** *(lights, stars)* centellear, destellar. **2** *(eyes)* brillar.

twirl [twɜːl] *n* giro, vuelta.
► *vt* **1** girar rápidamente, dar vueltas a. **2** *(twist, fiddle with)* retorcer, juguetear con.
► *vi* girar rápidamente, dar vueltas.

twist [twɪst] *n* **1** *(in road)* recodo, vuelta. **2** *(action)* torsión *m*. **3** MED torcedura, esguince *m*. **4** *(dance)* twist *m*.
► *vt* **1** *(sprain)* torcer. **2** *(screw, coil)* retorcer. **3** *(turn, wind)* girar, dar vueltas a.
► *vi* **1** *(turn)* girarse. **2** *(wind, coil)* enroscarse, enrollarse. **3** *(road)* serpentear.

twitch [twɪtʃ] *n* **1** *(pull)* tirón *m*. **2** *(nervous tic)* tic *m* nervioso.
► *vt* mover.
► *vi* moverse nerviosamente.

twitter ['twɪtəʳ] *n* gorjeo.
► *vt* gorjear.

two [tuː] *n* dos *m*. LOC in two por la mitad. ▌ in twos de dos en dos. ▌ it takes two es cosa de dos. ▌ to put two and two together atar cabos. ▌ that makes two of us ya somos dos.
► *adj* dos.

tycoon [taɪˈkuːn] *n* magnate *m*.

type [taɪp] *n* **1** *(kind)* tipo, clase *f*. **2** *(letter)* letra, carácter *m*.
► *vt & vi* escribir a máquina.
◆ to type up *vt sep* pasar a máquina.

⊠ Type no significa 'tipo (persona)', que se traduce por guy.

typewriter ['taɪpraɪtəʳ] *n* máquina de escribir.

typhoid ['taɪfɔɪd] *n* fiebre *f* tifoidea.

typhus ['taɪfəs] *n* tifus *m*.

typical ['tɪpɪkəl] *adj* típico,-a.

typing ['taɪpɪŋ] *n* mecanografía.

typist ['taɪpɪst] *n* mecanógrafo,-a.

tyranny ['tɪrənɪ] *n* tiranía.
ⓘ *pl* tyrannies.

tyrant ['taɪərənt] *n* tirano,-a.

tyre [taɪəʳ] *n* neumático.

Tyrrhenian [tɪˈriːnɪən] *adj* tirreno,-a. COMP the Tyrrhenian Sea el (mar) *m* Tirreno.

tzar [zɑːʳ] *n* zar *m*, czar *m*.

U

U, u [juː] *n (the letter)* U, u *f.*
udder [ˈʌdəʳ] *n* ubre *f.*
UFO [ˈjuːˈefəʊ] *abbr (unidentified flying object)* ovni *m f,* objeto volador no identificado.
Uganda [juːˈgændə] *n* Uganda.
Ugandan [juːˈgændən] *adj* ugandés, -esa.
▶ *n* ugandés,-esa.
ugly [ˈʌglɪ] *adj* **1** feo,-a. **2** *(situation, etc)* desagradable. **3** *(custom, vice)* repugnante.
ⓘ *comp* uglier, *superl* ugliest.
Ukraine [juːˈkreɪn] *n* Ucrania.
Ukranian [juːˈkeɪnɪən] *adj* ucraniano,-a.
▶ *n* **1** *(person)* ucraniano,-a. **2** *(language)* ucraniano.
ulcer [ˈʌlsəʳ] *n* **1** *(external)* llaga. **2** *(in stomach)* úlcera.
ulna [ˈʌlnə] *n* cúbito.
ⓘ *pl* ulnae [ˈʌlniː].
ultimate [ˈʌltɪmət] *adj* **1** *(final)* final. **2** *(basic)* esencial, fundamental.
▶ *n* the ultimate *(good)* el último grito; *(bad)* el colmo.

❎ Ultimate no significa último', que se traduce por last.

ultrasound [ˈʌltrəsaʊnd] *n* ultrasonido.
ultraviolet [ʌltrəˈvaɪələt] *adj* ultravioleta.
umbilical [ʌmˈbɪlɪkˀl] *adj* umbilical.
[COMP] **umbilical cord** cordón *m* umbilical.
umbrella [ʌmˈbrelə] *n* **1** paraguas *m.* **2** *fig (protection)* manto *f; (patronage)* patrocinio.
umpire [ˈʌmpaɪəʳ] *n* árbitro,-a.

▶ *vt* arbitrar.

✎ El término umpire se emplea sobre todo para hablar de árbitros de deportes como el cricket o el tenis. La palabra usual para 'árbitro' es referee.

unable [ʌnˈeɪbˀl] *adj* incapaz.
unacceptable [ʌnəkˈseptəbˀl] *adj* inaceptable, inadmisible.
unaccountable [ʌnəˈkaʊntəbˀl] *adj* inexplicable.
unaccustomed [ʌnəˈkʌstəmd] *adj* desacostumbrado,-a.
unaffected [ʌnəˈfektɪd] *adj* **1** *(unchanged)* no afectado,-a. **2** *(for person)* afable, campechano. **3** *(indifferent)* inmutable. **4** *(style)* llano,-a.
unanimous [juːˈhænɪməs] *adj* unánime.
unashamed [ʌnəˈʃeɪmd] *adj* descarado,-a.
unattended [ʌnəˈtendɪd] *adj* **1** *(children)* sin vigilar. **2** *(not looked after)* desatendido,-a. **3** *(alone)* solo,-a.
unavailable [ʌnəˈveɪləbˀl] *adj* **1** no disponible. **2** *(busy)* ocupado,-a. **3** *(out of print)* agotado,-a. **4** *(not for sale)* que no está en venta.
unaware [ʌnəˈweəʳ] *adj* ignorante, inconsciente.
unbearable [ʌnˈbeərəbˀl] *adj* inaguantable, insoportable, intolerable.
unbeatable [ʌnˈbiːtəbˀl] *adj* **1** *(competition)* invencible. **2** *(price, quality)* insuperable, inigualable, inmejorable.
unbelievable [ʌnbɪˈliːvəbˀl] *adj* increíble.
unbiased [ʌnˈbaɪəst] *adj* imparcial.
unbiassed [ʌnˈbaɪəst] *adj* → unbiased.

unblock [ʌnˈblɒk] *vt* **1** *(pipe, drain)* desatascar. **2** *(street, road)* desobstruir. **3** *(nose)* destaponar.

unbreakable [ʌnˈbreɪkəbəl] *adj* **1** irrompible. **2** *fig* inquebrantable. **3** *(horse)* indomable.

unbutton [ʌnˈbʌtən] *vt* desabrochar.
▸ *vi fam* relajarse.

uncertain [ʌnˈsɜːtən] *adj* **1** *(not certain)* incierto,-a, dudoso,-a. **2** *(unspecified)* indeterminado,-a. **3** *(indecisive)* indeciso,-a. **4** *(changeable)* variable.

unchanged [ʌnˈtʃeɪndʒd] *adj* igual, sin alterar.

unchecked [ʌnˈtʃekt] *adj* **1** no comprobado,-a. **2** *(unrestrained)* libre, libremente.

uncivilized [ʌnˈsɪvəlaɪzd] *adj* **1** *(tribe)* salvaje. **2** *(not cultured)* inculto,-a. **3** *fig* poco ortodoxo,-a.

uncle [ˈʌŋkəl] *n* tío.

unclear [ʌnˈklɪər] *adj* confuso,-a.

uncoil [ʌnˈkɔɪl] *vt* desenrollar.
▸ *vi* **1** *(snake)* desenroscarse. **2** *(rope)* desenrollarse.

uncomfortable [ʌnˈkʌmfətəbəl] *adj* **1** *(physical)* incómodo,-a. **2** *(worrying)* inquietante. **3** *(unpleasant)* desagradable.

uncommon [ʌnˈkɒmən] *adj* **1** *(rare)* poco común. **2** *(strange)* insólito,-a; *(unusual)* extraordinario,-a. **3** *(excessive)* desmesurado,-a.

unconcerned [ʌnkənˈsɜːnd] *adj* despreocupado, indiferente.

unconscious [ʌnˈkɒnʃəs] *adj* **1** MED inconsciente. **2** *(unaware)* inconsciente. **3** *(not on purpose)* involuntario,-a.
▸ *n* **the unconscious** el inconsciente.

🗷 Unconscious no significa 'inconsciente (irresponsable)', que se traduce por thoughtless.

uncontrollable [ʌnkənˈtrəʊləbəl] *adj* **1** *(general)* incontrolable. **2** *(people)* ingobernable. **3** *(desire)* irresistible. **4** *(child)* indisciplinado,-a.

uncountable [ʌnˈkaʊntəbəl] *adj* incontable.

uncover [ʌnˈkʌvər] *vt* **1** destapar. **2** *(secret)* revelar, descubrir.

unction [ˈʌŋkʃən] *n* **1** REL *(act, ointment)* unción *f*. **2** *(balm)* ungüento.

uncultivated [ʌnˈkʌltɪveɪtɪd] *adj* **1** *(land)* yermo,-a, baldío,-a. **2** *(person)* inculto,-a.

undamaged [ʌnˈdæmɪdʒd] *adj* **1** *(goods)* sin desperfectos, intacto,-a. **2** *(person)* indemne, ileso,-a.

undefeated [ʌndɪˈfiːtɪd] *adj* invicto,-a.

undeniable [ʌndɪˈnaɪəbəl] *adj* innegable.

under [ˈʌndər] *prep* **1** *(below)* bajo, debajo de. **2** *(less than)* menos de. **3** *(controlled, affected, influenced by)* bajo. **4** *(suffering, subject to)* bajo. **5** *(according to)* conforme a, según. **6** *(known by)* con, bajo.
▸ *adv* **1** *(below)* debajo. **2** *(less)* menos.

undercarriage [ˈʌndəkærɪdʒ] *n* tren *m* de aterrizaje.

underclothes [ˈʌndəkləʊðz] *n pl* ropa *f* *sing* interior.

undercover [ʌndəˈkʌvər] *adj* clandestino,-a, secreto,-a,.
▸ *adv* en la clandestinidad.

underdeveloped [ʌndədɪˈveləpt] *adj* **1** subdesarrollado,-a. **2** *(of photo)* insuficientemente revelado,-a.

underestimate [*(n)* ʌndərˈestɪmət; *(vb)* ʌndərˈestɪmeɪt] *n* menosprecio.
▸ *vt* infravalorar, subestimar.

undergo [ʌndəˈgəʊ] *n* cúbito.
ⓘ *pt* **underwent** [ʌndəˈwent], *pp* **undergone** [ʌndəˈgɒn].

undergone [ʌndəˈgɒn] *pp* → undergo.

underground [*(adj-n)* ˈʌndəgraʊnd; *(adv)* ʌndəˈgraʊnd] *adj* **1** subterráneo, -a. **2** *fig* clandestino,-a. **3** *fig (cinema, music)* underground.
▸ *n* **1** *(railway)* metro. **2** *(resistance)* resistencia.
▸ *adv* **1** bajo tierra. **2** *fig (secretly)* en la clandestinidad, clandestinamente.

undergrowth [ˈʌndəgrəʊθ] *n* maleza, monte *m* bajo.

underline [ʌndəˈlaɪn] *vt* subrayar.

underneath [ʌndəˈniːθ] *prep* bajo, debajo de.
▸ *adv* abajo, debajo, por debajo.
▸ *adj* de abajo, inferior.
▸ *n* parte *f* inferior, fondo.

undernourished [ˌʌndə'nʌrɪʃt] *adj* desnutrido,-a, subalimentado,-a.

underpants ['ʌndəpænts] *n pl* calzoncillos *mpl*, eslip *m sing*.

understand [ˌʌndə'stænd] *vt* **1** entender. **2** *(believe)* tener entendido. **3** *(to get on with sb)* entenderse. **4** *(take for granted)* sobreentender.
ⓘ *pt & pp* understood [ˌʌndə'stʊd].

understanding [ˌʌndə'stændɪŋ] *n* comprensión.

understatement [ˌʌndə'steɪtmənt] *n* eufemismo.

understood [ˌʌndə'stʊd] *pt & pp* → understand.

undertake [ˌʌndə'teɪk] *vt (take on - job, task)* emprender; *(- responsibility)* asumir.
▸ *vi (promise)* comprometerse (to, a).
ⓘ *pt* undertook [ˌʌndə'tʊk], *pp* undertaken [ˌʌndə'teɪkən].

undertaken [ˌʌndə'teɪkən] *pp* → undertake.

undertaker ['ʌndəteɪkə'] *n* empresario,-a de pompas fúnebres.
▸ *n pl (undertaker's)* funeraria, pompas *fpl* fúnebres.

undertook [ˌʌndə'tʊk] *pt* → undertake.

undervalue [ˌʌndə'vælju:] *vt* subvalorar.

underwater [ˌʌndə'wɔ:tə'] *adj* submarino,-a, subacuático,-a.
▸ *adv* bajo el agua.

underwear ['ʌndəwɜ:ə'] *n* ropa interior.

underwent [ˌʌndə'went] *pt* → undergo.

underworld ['ʌndəwɜ:ld] *n (of criminals)* hampa, bajos fondos *mpl*, inframundo.

undesirable [ˌʌndɪ'zaɪərəbəl] *adj* indeseable.
▸ *n* indeseable *mf*.

undetermined [ˌʌndɪ'tɜ:maɪnd] *adj* indeterminado,-a, indefinido,-a.

undid [ʌn'dɪd] *pt* → undo.

undisputed [ˌʌndɪs'pju:tɪd] *adj* **1** *(unquestionable)* indiscutible, incuestionable. **2** *(unchallenged)* incontestable.

undo [ʌn'du:] *vt* **1** *(knot)* deshacer, desatar. **2** *(button)* desabrochar. **3** *(arrange-*

ment) anular. **4** *(destroy)* deshacer, destruir. **5** *(to set right)* enmendar, reparar.
ⓘ *pt* undid [ʌn'dɪd], *pp* undone [ʌn'dʌn].

undone [ʌn'dʌn] *pp* → undid.
▸ *adj (incomplete)* inacabado,-a.

undoubted [ʌn'daʊtɪd] *adj* indudable.

undress [ʌn'dres] *vt* desnudar.
▸ *vi* desnudarse.

undrinkable [ʌn'drɪŋkəbəl] *adj* imbebible.

uneasy [ʌn'i:zɪ] *adj* **1** *(worried)* intranquilo,-a, inquieto,-a, preocupado,-a; *(disturbing)* inquietante. **2** *(annoying)* incómodo,-a.
ⓘ *comp* uneasier, *superl* uneasiest.

unemployed [ˌʌnɪm'plɔɪd] *adj* parado,-a, sin trabajo, en paro.

unemployment [ˌʌnɪm'plɔɪmənt] *n* **1** paro, desempleo. **2** *(percentage)* número de parados.

unequal [ʌn'i:kwəl] *adj* **1** *(not the same)* desigual, distinto,-a; *(pulse)* irregular. **2** *(not adequate)* poco apto, inadecuado,-a.

unequivocal [ˌʌnɪ'kwɪvəkəl] *adj* inequívoco,-a, claro,-a.

uneven [ʌn'i:vən] *adj* **1** *(not level)* desigual; *(bumpy)* accidentado,-a. **2** *(varying)* irregular, variable. **3** *(road)* lleno,-a de baches. **4** *(unfairly matched)* desigual. **5** MATH impar.

unexpected [ˌʌnɪk'spektɪd] *adj* **1** inesperado,-a. **2** *(event)* imprevisto,-a.

unfair [ʌn'feə'] *adj* injusto,-a.

unfaithful [ʌn'feɪθfʊl] *adj* **1** *(husband, wife)* infiel. **2** *(friend)* desleal.

unfamiliar [ˌʌnfə'mɪlɪə'] *adj (unknown)* desconocido,-a.

unfashionable [ʌn'fæʃ[ə]nəbəl] *adj (fashion, trends, etc)* pasado,-a de moda; *(ideas, measures)* poco popular.

unfasten [ʌn'tɑ:sən] *vt* **1** *(vest, button)* desabrochar. **2** *(untie)* desatar. **3** *(open)* abrir.

unfavorable [ʌn'feɪv[ə]rəbəl] *adj* US → unfavourable.

unfavourable [ʌn'feɪv[ə]rəbəl] *adj* **1** *(gen)* desfavorable; *(criticism)* adverso, a. **2** *(winds)* contrario,-a.

U

unfinished [ʌnˈfɪnɪʃt] *adj* inacabado, -a, incompleto,-a, sin acabar.

unfit [ʌnˈfɪt] *adj* **1** *(person)* no apto,-a, incapaz. **2** *(physically)* incapacitado,-a, inútil. **3** *(injured)* lesionado,-a. **4** *(incompetent)* incompetente. LOC **to be unfit** no estar en forma.

unfold [ʌnˈfəʊld] *vt* **1** *(paper)* desplegar; *(sheet)* desdoblar. **2** *(newspaper)* abrir; *(map)* extender. **3** *(outline)* exponer; *(reveal)* revelar. **4** *(secret)* descubrir.
▶ *vi* **1** *(open up)* desdoblarse; *(landscape)* extenderse. **2** *(ideas, etc)* desarrollarse. **3** *(secret)* descubrirse, revelarse.

unforgettable [ʌnfəˈgetəbəl] *adj* inolvidable.

unfortunate [ʌnˈfɔːtʃənət] *adj* **1** *(person, event)* desgraciado,-a. **2** *(remark)* desafortunado,-a.

unfriendly [ʌnˈfrendlɪ] *adj* poco amistoso,-a, antipático,-a, hostil.
ⓘ *comp* **unfriendlier**, *superl* **unfriendliest**.

unfulfilled [ʌnfʊlˈfɪld] *adj* **1** *(not carried out)* incumplido,-a, frustrado,-a. **2** *(not satisfied)* insatisfecho,-a. **3** *(ambition)* frustrado,-a; *(dream)* irrealizado,-a.

ungrateful [ʌnˈgreɪtful] *adj* **1** *(unthankful)* desagradecido,-a. **2** *(thankless)* ingrato,-a.

unhappy [ʌnˈhæpɪ] *adj* **1** *(sad)* infeliz. **2** *(miserable)* desdichado,-a. **3** *(unsuitable)* desafortunado,-a, poco afortunado,-a.
ⓘ *comp* **unhappier**, *superl* **unhappiest**.

unharmed [ʌnˈhɑːmd] *adj* ileso,-a.

unhealthy [ʌnˈhelθɪ] *adj* **1** *(place)* malsano,-a, insalubre. **2** *(ill)* enfermizo, -a, enfermo,-a. **3** *fig (unnatural)* morboso,-a, malsano,-a.
ⓘ *comp* **unhealthier**, *superl* **unhealthiest**.

unhelpful [ʌnˈhelpful] *adj (advice)* inútil, vano,-a; *(person)* poco servicial.

unhurt [ʌnˈhɜːt] *adj* ileso,-a, indemne.

unicorn [ˈjuːnɪkɔːn] *n* unicornio.

uniform [ˈjuːnɪfɔːm] *adj* **1** uniforme. **2** *(temperature)* constante.
▶ *n* uniforme *m*.

unify [ˈjuːnɪfaɪ] *vt* unificar.
ⓘ *pt & pp* **unified**, *ger* **unifying**.

unimportant [ʌnɪmˈpɔːtənt] *adj* insignificante, sin importancia, poco importante.

uninhabited [ʌnɪnˈhæbɪtɪd] *adj* **1** deshabitado,-a. **2** *(deserted)* despoblado,-a.

uninteresting [ʌnˈɪntrəstɪŋ] *adj* sin interés.

union [ˈjuːnɪən] *n* **1** unión *f*. **2** *fig (marriage)* enlace *m*. **3** *(of workers)* sindicato. **4** TECH unión *f*.
▶ *adj* sindical, del sindicato. COMP **Union Jack** *la bandera del Reino Unido*.

⊕ La **Union Jack** es la bandera del Reino Unido y está formada por la combinación de las enseñas de Inglaterra, Escocia e Irlanda.

unionize [juːnjəˈnaɪz] *vt* sindicalizar.
▶ *vi* agremiarse, sindicalizarse.

unirrigated [ʌnˈɪrɪgeɪtəd] *adj* de secano.

unique [juːˈniːk] *adj* **1** *(singular)* único, -a. **2** *(outstanding)* extraordinario,-a.

unit [ˈjuːnɪt] *n* **1** unidad *f*. **2** *(furniture)* módulo, elemento. **3** MIL unidad *f*. **4** MATH unidad *f*. **5** TECH grupo. **6** *(centre)* centro; *(department)* servicio. **7** *(team)* equipo.

unite [juːˈnaɪt] *vt (join)* unir; *(assemble)* reunir.
▶ *vi* unirse, reunirse.

unity [ˈjuːnɪtɪ] *n (union)* unidad *f*; *(harmony)* armonía.

universal [juːnɪˈvɜːsəl] *adj* universal.

universe [ˈjuːnɪvɜːs] *n* universo.

university [juːnɪˈvɜːsətɪ] *n* universidad *f*.
ⓘ *pl* **universities**.
▶ *adj* universitario,-a.

unkempt [ʌnˈkempt] *adj* **1** *(general)* descuidado,-a. **2** *(hair)* despeinado,-a. **3** *(appearance)* desaliñado,-a.

unkind [ʌnˈkaɪnd] *adj* **1** *(unpleasant)* desconsiderado,-a. **2** *(cruel)* cruel; *(criticism)* despiadado,-a.

unknown [ʌnˈnəʊn] *adj* desconocido,-a.
▶ *n* lo desconocido.

unleash [ʌnˈliːʃ] *vt* **1** *(dog)* soltar. **2** *fig (free - gen)* liberar; *(- passions)* desatar. **3** *(fury)* provocar.

unless [ənˈles] *conj* a menos que, a no ser que.
▶ *prep* salvo, excepto.

unlike [ʌnˈlaɪk] *adj (different)* diferente a, distinto de; *(not characteristic)* impropio,-a.
▶ *prep* a diferencia de

unlikely [ʌnˈlaɪklɪ] *adj (improbable)* improbable, poco probable; *(unexpected, unusual)* inverosímil.
ⓘ *comp* unlikelier, *superl* unlikeliest.

unlimited [ʌnˈlɪmɪtɪd] *adj* ilimitado,-a.

unload [ʌnˈləʊd] *vt* **1** *(gen)* descargar. **2** *(get rid of)* deshacerse de.
▶ *vi* descargar.

unlock [ʌnˈlɒk] *vt* **1** *(door)* abrir (con llave). **2** *fig (secret)* revelar; *(enigma)* resolver.

unlucky [ʌnˈlʌkɪ] *adj* **1** *(unfortunate)* desafortunado,-a, desgraciado,-a. **2** *(fateful)* aciago,-a, nefasto,-a.
ⓘ *comp* unluckier, *superl* unluckiest.

unmarried [ʌnˈmærɪd] *adj* soltero,-a.

unmistakable [ʌnmɪsˈteɪkəbəl] *adj* inconfundible, inequívoco,-a.

unnecessary [ʌnˈnesəsərɪ] *adj* innecesario,-a.

unnoticed [ʌnˈnəʊtɪst] *adj* inadvertido,-a, desapercibido,-a.

unoccupied [ʌnˈɒkjʊpaɪd] *adj* **1** *(house)* deshabitado,-a. **2** *(person)* desocupado,-a. **3** *(post)* vacante. **4** *(area)* despoblado,-a. **5** *(seat)* libre. **6** MIL no ocupado,-a.

unofficial [ʌnəˈfɪʃəl] *adj* extraoficial, oficioso,-a.

unpack [ʌnˈpæk] *vt* **1** *(objects)* desempaquetar, desenvolver. **2** *(suitcase)* deshacer. **3** *(boxes)* desembalar.
▶ *vi* deshacer las maletas.

unpardonable [ʌnˈpɑːdənəbəl] *adj* imperdonable.

unpleasant [ʌnˈplezənt] *adj* **1** *(disagreeable, nasty)* desagradable, molesto,-a. **2** *(unfriendly)* antipático,-a. **3** *(words)* grosero,-a, mal educado,-a.

unplug [ʌnˈplʌg] *vt* desenchufar.
ⓘ *pt & pp* unplugged, *ger* unplugging.

unpopular [ʌnˈpɒpjələ*] *adj* impopular.

unpredictable [ʌnprɪˈdɪktəbəl] *adj* **1** imprevisible. **2** *(of person)* de reacciones imprevisibles. **3** *(whimsical)* antojadizo,-a.

unproductive [ʌnprəˈdʌktɪv] *adj* **1** *(inefficient)* improductivo,-a. **2** *fig (fruitless)* infructuoso,-a.

unprovable [ʌnˈpruːvəbəl] *adj* indemostrable.

unpublished [ʌnˈpʌblɪʃt] *adj* inédito,-a, no publicado,-a.

unreachable [ʌnˈriːtʃəbəl] *adj* inalcanzable.

unreadable [ʌnˈriːdəbəl] *adj* **1** *(handwriting)* ilegible. **2** *(book)* imposible de leer; *(understand)* incomprensible.

unreal [ʌnˈrɪəl] *adj* irreal.

unrealistic [ʌnrɪəˈlɪstɪk] *adj* poco realista.

unreasonable [ʌnˈriːzənəbəl] *adj* **1** irrazonable. **2** *(irrational)* irracional. **3** *(excessive)* desmesurado,-a; *(prices)* exorbitante. **4** *(hour)* inoportuno,-a.

unrecognizable [ʌnrekəgˈnaɪzəbəl] *adj* irreconocible.

unreliable [ʌnrɪˈlaɪəbəl] *adj* **1** *(person)* de poca confianza, poco formal, que no es de fiar. **2** *(information)* que no es de fiar, poco seguro,-a. **3** *(machine)* poco fiable, poco seguro,-a. **4** *(news)* poco fidedigno,-a.

unrest [ʌnˈrest] *n* **1** *(uneasiness)* malestar *m*. **2** *(restlessness)* inquietud *f*; *(political disturbance)* agitación *f*, disturbios *mpl*.

unroll [ʌnˈrəʊl] *vt* desenrollar.
▶ *vi* desenrollarse.

unsaddle [ʌnˈsædəl] *vt* **1** *(horse)* desensillar. **2** *(horseman)* desmontar.

unsafe [ʌnˈseɪf] *adj* **1** *(risky)* inseguro,-a, arriesgado,-a. **2** *(dangerous)* peligroso,-a.

unsatisfactory [ʌnsætɪsˈfæktərɪ] *adj* insatisfactorio,-a, poco satisfactorio,-a.

unsavory [ʌnˈseɪvərɪ] *adj* US → unsavoury.

unsavoury [ʌnˈseɪvərɪ] *adj* **1** *(taste, etc)* desagradable; *(tasteless)* insípido,-a. **2** *(morally not right)* deshonroso, a, infame, sospechoso,-a; *(person)* indeseable.

U

unscrew [ʌn'skruː] *vt* destornillar, desatornillar.

unseen [ʌn'siːn] *adj (invisible)* no visto, -a, invisible; *(unnoticed)* inadvertido,-a.

unselfish [ʌn'selfɪʃ] *adj* desinteresado,-a.

unsettled [ʌn'set³ld] *adj* **1** *(weather)* inestable. **2** *(person)* nervioso,-a, intranquilo; *(situation)* inestable. **3** *(country, etc)* agitado,-a. **4** *(question, matter)* pendiente; *(account, etc)* sin saldar. **5** *(land)* sin colonizar, sin poblar.

unshaven [ʌn'ʃeɪv³n] *adj* sin afeitar.

unsheathe [ʌn'ʃiːð] *vt* desenvainar.

unshrinkable [ʌn'ʃrɪŋkəb³l] *adj* inencogible, que no encoge.

unskilled [ʌn'skɪld] *adj* **1** *(worker)* no cualificado,-a. **2** *(job)* no especializado,-a. **3** *(untalented)* inexperto,-a.

unsolved [ʌn'sɒlvd] *adj* sin resolver.

unstable [ʌn'steɪb³l] *adj* inestable.

unsteady [ʌn'stedɪ] *adj* **1** *(not firm)* inseguro,-a, inestable; *(furniture)* cojo,-a, inestable. **2** *(voice, hand)* tembloroso, -a, poco firme. **3** *(weather conditions)* variable; *(pulse)* irregular.
ⓘ *comp* unsteadier, *superl* unsteadiest.

unstressed [ʌn'strest] *adj* LING átono,-a.

unsuccessful [ʌnsək'sesful] *adj* **1** fracasado,-a, sin éxito. **2** *(useless)* inútil, infructuoso,-a; *(examination)* suspendido,-a. **3** *(candidate in elections)* derrotado,-a, vencido,-a.

unsuited [ʌn'suːtɪd] *adj* **1** *(person)* no apto,-a; *(thing)* impropio,-a, inadecuado,-a. **2** *(people)* incompatible.

unsure [ʌn'ʃʊər] *adj* inseguro,-a, poco seguro,-a.

unsympathetic [ʌnsɪmpə'θetɪk] *adj* *(unfeeling)* poco compasivo, sin compasión *f*, indiferente; *(lacking understanding)* poco comprensivo,-a.

untamable [ʌn'teɪməb³l] *adj* indomable.

untangle [ʌn'tæŋg³l] *vt* desenredar.

untidy [ʌn'taɪdɪ] *adj* **1** *(room, person)* desordenado,-a. **2** *(scruffy)* desaliñado,-a, desaseado,-a; *(hair)* despeinado,-a.
ⓘ *comp* untidier, *superl* untidiest.

untie [ʌn'taɪ] *vt* **1** *(unfasten)* desatar. **2** *(liberate)* soltar, desligar.

until [ʌn'tɪl] *prep* hasta.
▶ *conj* hasta que.

untrue [ʌn'truː] *adj* **1** falso,-a. **2** *(unfaithful)* infiel, desleal. **3** *(inexact)* inexacto,-a, erróneo,-a.

unusable [ʌn'juːzəb³l] *adj* inservible.

unused *adj* **1** [ʌn'juːzd] *(new)* nuevo,-a, sin estrenar; *(not in use)* que no se utiliza. **2** [ʌn'juːst] *(unaccustomed)* desacostumbrado,-a.

unusual [ʌn'juːʒʊəl] *adj* **1** *(rare, strange)* insólito,-a, poco común. **2** *(different)* original; *(exceptional)* extraordinario,-a.

unveil [ʌn'veɪl] *vt* **1** *(uncover)* descubrir. **2** *fig (reveal)* descubrir, desvelar; *(secret)* revelar.

unwanted [ʌn'wɒntɪd] *adj* **1** *(child)* no deseado,-a. **2** *(advice, etc)* no solicitado,-a, no pedido,-a. **3** *(superfluous)* superfluo,-a.

unwelcome [ʌn'welkəm] *adj* **1** *(guest)* inoportuno,-a, molesto,-a; *(news)* desagradable. **2** *(uncomfortable)* incómodo,-a.

unwell [ʌn'wel] *adj (sick, ill)* indispuesto,-a, malo,-a.

unwilling [ʌn'wɪlɪŋ] *adj* reacio,-a, poco dispuesto,-a.

unwind [ʌn'waɪnd] *vt* desenrollar.
▶ *vi* **1** desenrollarse. **2** *fam (relax)* relajarse.
ⓘ *pt & pp* unwound [ʌn'waʊnd].

unwise [ʌn'waɪz] *adj* **1** *(foolish)* imprudente; *(senseless)* insensato,-a. **2** *(ill-advised)* desaconsejable, poco aconsejable.

unwound [ʌn'waʊnd] *pt & pp* → unwind.

unwrap [ʌn'ræp] *vt (present)* desenvolver; *(parcel, package)* abrir, deshacer.
ⓘ *pt & pp* unwrapped, *ger* unwrapping.

unzip [ʌn'zɪp] *vt* **1** bajar la cremallera de. **2** COMPUT descomprimir.
ⓘ *pt & pp* unzipped, *ger* unzipping.

up [ʌp] *adv* **1** *(upwards)* hacia arriba, arriba. **2** *(out of bed)* levantado,-a. **3** *(sun, moon):* the sun is up ha salido el sol. **4** *(roadworks)* levantado,-a, en obras. **5** *(towards)*

hacia. **6** *(northwards)* ir hacia el norte. **7** *(totally finished)* acabado,-a. **8** *(into pieces)* a trozos, a porciones, a raciones.
▶ *prep* **1** *(movement): to go up the stairs* subir la escalera. **2** *(position)* en lo alto de.
▶ *vt* subir, aumentar.
ⓘ *pt & pp* upped, *ger* upping.

up-and-coming [ˌʌpənˈkʌmɪŋ] *adj* prometedor,-ra, que promete mucho.

up-and-down [ˌʌpənˈdaʊn] *adj* **1** *(motion)* vertical; *(varying)* variable. **2** *(eventful)* accidentado,-a; *(period)* con altibajos.

upbringing [ˈʌpbrɪŋɪŋ] *n* educación *f*.

upcoming [ˈʌpkʌmɪŋ] *adj* próximo,-a.

update [*(n)* ˈʌpdeɪt; *(vb)* ʌpˈdeɪt] *n* actualización *f*, puesta al día.
▶ *vt* actualizar, modernizar.

upfront [ʌpˈfrʌnt] *adj* sincero,-a, franco,-a.

upgrade [*(vb)* ʌpˈgreɪd; *(n)* ˈʌpgreɪd] *vt* **1** *(promote)* ascender, subir de categoría. **2** *(improve)* mejorar.
▶ *n* mejora.

uphekd [ʌpˈhəeld] *pt & pp* → uphold.

uphill [*(adj)* ˈʌphɪl; *(adv)* ʌpˈhɪl] *adj* **1** ascendente. **2** *fig (task, struggle)* arduo,-a, difícil, duro,-a, penoso,-a.
▶ *adv* cuesta arriba.

uphold [ʌpˈhəʊld] *vt* **1** *(opinion)* sostener, mantener; *(to support)* apoyar. **2** *(defend)* defender. **3** *(confirm)* confirmar.
ⓘ *pt & pp* upheld [ʌpˈhəeld].

upholster [ʌpˈhəʊlstəʳ] *vt* tapizar.

upkeep [ˈʌpkiːp] *n (maintenance)* conservación *f*; *(costs)* gastos *mpl* de mantenimiento.

uplift [ʌpˈlɪft] *vt (lift up)* elevar, levantar; *(soul, voice)* inspirar, elevar, alzar.
▶ *n fig* edificación *f*, inspiración *f*.

upload [ʌpˈləʊd] *vt (Internet)* publicar en la red, subir a la red.

up-market [ˈʌpmɑːkɪt] *adj* de calidad *f* superior, de categoría.

upon [əˈpɒn] *prep fml* en, sobre.
Consulta también on.

upper [ˈʌpəʳ] *adj* **1** *(position)* superior. **2** *(in geography)* alto,-a; superior.
▶ *n (of shoe)* pala.

uppermost [ˈʌpəməʊst] *adj* **1** más alto,-a. **2** *fig* principal, dominante.

upright [ˈʌpraɪt] *adj* **1** derecho,-a, vertical. **2** *(honest)* recto,-a, honrado,-a.
▶ *adv* derecho, en posición *f* vertical.
▶ *n* SP poste *m*, palo.

uprising [ʌpˈraɪzɪŋ] *n* alzamiento, levantamiento, sublevación *f*.

uproar [ˈʌprɔːʳ] *n* alboroto, tumulto.

uproot [ʌpˈruːt] *vt* **1** *(plant, etc)* desarraigar, arrancar; *(people)* desarraigar. **2** *(eliminate)* eliminar, extirpar.

upset [*(adj-vb)* ʌpˈset; *(n)* ˈʌpset] *adj* **1** *(angry)* disgustado,-a, contrariado,-a. **2** *(mentally or physically)* trastornado,-a; *(worried)* preocupado,-a. **3** *(nerves)* desquiciado,-a; *(a little unwell)* indispuesto,-a. **4** *(stomach)* trastornado,-a. **5** *(overturned)* volcado,-a; *(spoiled)* desbaratado,-a.
▶ *n* **1** *(reversal)* revés *m*, contratiempo; *(slight ailment)* malestar *m*. **2** *(emotion, stomach, etc)* trastorno; *(plans, etc)* trastorno. **3** *(trouble, difficulty)* molestia *f*. **4** *(sport)* un resultado inesperado.
▶ *vt* **1** *(overturn)* volcar; *(capsize)* hacer zozobrar. **2** *(spill)* derramar. **3** *(shock)* trastornar. **4** *(person)* contrariar; *(worry)* preocupar; *(displease)* disgustar. **5** *(stomach)* sentar mal. **6** *(plans)* desbaratar. **7** *(to cause disorder)* desordenar, revolver.
ⓘ *pt & pp* upset [ʌpˈset], *ger* upsetting.

upsetting [ʌpˈsetɪŋ] *adj* desconcertante, inquietante, preocupante.

upside down [ˌʌpsaɪdˈdaʊn] *adv* **1** al revés. **2** *fig (disorder)* patas arriba.

upstairs [*(adv)* ʌpˈsteəz; *(n)* ˈʌpsteəz] *adv (direction)* al piso de arriba; *(position)* en el piso de arriba.
▶ *adj* de arriba.
▶ *n* piso de arriba, piso superior.

upstream [ʌpˈstriːm] *adv* **1** aguas arriba. **2** *(against the current)* a contracorriente.

upsurge [ˈʌpsɜːdʒ] *n* **1** *(increase)* aumento; *(anger)* acceso. **2** *fig (strong increase in feelings, etc)* resurgimiento; *(of violence)* ola.

up-to-date [ˌʌptəˈdeɪt] *adj* **1** al día. **2** *(modern)* moderno,-a, a la moda; *(informed)* al tanto, al corriente, al día.

U

upward ['ʌpwəd] *adj* hacia arriba.
> *adv* hacia arriba.
> *adj* COMM *(tendency)* al alza *m*.

upwards ['ʌpwədz] *adv* **1** hacia arriba.
2 *fam* algo más de.

uranium [jʊ'reɪnɪəm] *n* CHEM uranio.

Uranus [jʊ'reɪnəs] *n* Urano.

urban ['ɜ:bən] *adj* urbano,-a.

urbane [ɜ:'beɪn] *adj* cortés, urbano,-a.

ureter [jʊə'ri:tər] *n* uréter *m*.

urethra [jʊ'ri:θrə] *n* uretra.

urge [ɜ:dʒ] *n* impulso, deseo.
> *vt* **1** encarecer, preconizar, instar, insistir. **2** *(incite)* incitar; *(plead)* exhortar. **3** *(encourage)* animar.

urgency ['ɜ:dʒənsɪ] *n* urgencia.

urgent ['ɜ:dʒənt] *adj* urgente.

urinary ['jʊərɪnərɪ] *adj* urinario,-a.
COMP **urinary tract** tracto urinario.

urinate ['jʊərɪneɪt] *vi* orinar.

urine ['jʊərɪn] *n* orina.

urn [ɜ:n] *n* urna.

urology [jʊ'rɒlədʒɪ] *n* MED urología.

Ursa ['ɜ:rsə] *(constellation)* *n* la Osa.

Uruguay ['jʊərəgwaɪ] *n* Uruguay.

Uruguayan [jʊərə'gwaɪən] *adj* uruguayo,-a.
> *n* uruguayo,-a.

us [ʌs, ʌz] *pron* **1** nos; *(with preposition)* nosotros,-as. **2** *fam* me.

usable ['ju:zəbəl] *adj* utilizable, aprovechable.

usage ['ju:sɪdʒ] *n* **1** uso, manejo. **2** *(custom)* uso, costumbre *f*, usanza. **3** LING uso. **4** *(way of speaking)* habla *m*, lenguaje *m*.

use [*(n)* ju:s; *(vb)* ju:z] *n* **1** uso, empleo, utilización *f*. **2** *(handling)* manejo. **3** *(usefulness)* utilidad *f*. **4** *(right to use, power to use)* uso.
> *vt* **1** utilizar. **2** *(consume)* gastar, consumir. **3** *(exploit unfairly)* aprovecharse de. **4** *fam (need)* necesitar.

> *aux* **to use to** *(past habits)* soler, acostumbrar: *we used to go fishing in the lake* solíamos ir a pescar al lago.

✎ Como auxiliar, si la frase no indica una costumbre, se debe traducir con el imperfecto.

◆ **to use up** *vt sep* gastar, acabar.

useable ['ju:zəbəl] *adj* → usable.

used ['ju:st] *adj* **1** [ju:zd] *(second-hand)* usado,-a. **2** [ju:st] *(accustomed)* acostumbrado,-a. COMP **to be used to** estar acostumbrado,-a a. ▌ **to get used to** acostumbrarse a.

✎ Consulta también use.

useful ['ju:sfʊl] *adj* útil.

useless ['ju:sləs] *adj* **1** inútil. **2** *fam (person)* inepto,-a, incompetente.

user ['ju:zər] *n* usuario,-a.

usual ['ju:ʒʊəl] *adj* habitual, corriente.
> *n* **1** lo habitual. **2** *fam (drink, etc)* lo de siempre.

utensil [ju:'tensəl] *n* utensilio.

uterus ['ju:tərəs] *n* útero.
① *pl* uteruses o uteri ['ju:tərai].

utility [ju:'tɪlɪtɪ] *n* **1** utilidad *f*. **2** *(company)* empresa de servicio público.
① *pl* utilities.

utmost ['ʌtməʊst] *adj* sumo,-a, extremo,-a.
> *n* máximo.

utter ['ʌtər] *adj* completo,-a, total.
> *vt* **1** *(words)* pronunciar, articular; *(feelings)* expresar. **2** *(lies curses, etc)* soltar; *(shouts, cries, etc)* lanzar, dar. **3** *(theatre)* proferir; *(sounds)* emitir.

utterly ['ʌtəlɪ] *adv* totalmente.

uvula ['ju:vjʊlə] *n* úvula, campanilla.
① *pl* uvulas o uvulae ['ju:vjuli:].

Uzbek ['ʊzbek] *adj* uzbeco,-a.
> *n* **1** *(person)* uzbeco,-a. **2** *(language)* uzbeco.

Uzbekistan [ʊzbekɪ'stæn] *n* Uzbekistán.

V

V, v [viː] *n (the letter)* V, v *f*.

vacancy [ˈveɪk°nsɪ] *n* **1** *(job)* vacante *f*. **2** *(room)* habitación *f* libre. `LOC` "No vacancies" «Completo».
ⓘ *pl* vacancies.

vacant [ˈveɪk°nt] *adj* **1** *(gen)* vacío. **2** *(job)* vacante. **3** *(room)* libre. **4** *(mind, expression)* vacío,-a.

vacation [vəˈkeɪʃ°n] *n* vacaciones *fpl*.

vaccinate [ˈvæksɪneɪt] *vt* vacunar.

vaccination [vɒksɪˈneɪʃ°n] *n* vacunación *f*.

vaccine [ˈvæksiːn] *n* vacuna.

vacuum [ˈvækjʊəm] *n* **1** vacío. **2** *fam (vacuum cleaner)* aspiradora. `COMP` **vacuum cleaner** aspirador *m*. **❚ vacuum flask** termo.
▶ *vt* limpiar con aspiradora, pasar la aspiradora por.

vacuum-packed [ˈvækjʊəmpækt] *adj* envasado,-a al vacío.

vagina [vəˈdʒaɪnə] *n* vagina.
ⓘ *pl* vaginas o vaginae [vəˈdʒaɪniː].

vaginae [vəˈdʒaɪniː] *n pl* → vagina.

vague [veɪg] *adj* **1** *(imprecise)* vago,-a, impreciso,-a. **2** *(indistinct)* borroso,-a.

> ❌ Vague no significa 'vago (holgazán)', que se traduce por lazy.

vain [veɪn] *adj* **1** *(conceited)* vanidoso,-a. **2** *(hopeless)* vano,-a, inútil. `LOC` **in vain** en vano.

valence [ˈveɪləns] *n* US valencia.

valency [ˈveɪlənsɪ] *n* GB valencia.
ⓘ *pl* valencies.

valid [ˈvælɪd] *adj* **1** válido,-a. **2** *(ticket)* valedero,-a.

validate [ˈvælɪdeɪt] *vt fml* validar.

valley [ˈvælɪ] *n* valle *m*.

valor [ˈvælər] *n* US → valour.

valour [ˈvælər] *n* valor *m*, valentía.

> ❌ Valour no significa 'valor (valía)', que se traduce por value.

valuation [væljuˈeɪʃ°n] *n* **1** *(act)* valoración *f*. **2** *(price)* valor *m*.

value [ˈvæljuː] *n* valor *m*.
▶ *vt* **1** *(estimate value of)* valorar, tasar. **2** *(appreciate)* valorar, apreciar.

valve [vælv] *n* **1** *(in general)* válvula. **2** RAD lámpara. **3** ZOOL valva. **4** MUS llave *f*.

vampire [ˈvæmpaɪər] *n* urgencia.

van [væn] *n* **1** camioneta, furgoneta. **2** GB *(on train)* furgón *m*.

vanadium [vəˈneɪdɪəm] *n* vanadio.

Vandal [ˈvænd°l] *adj* vándalo,-a.
▶ *n* vándalo,-a.

vandalism [ˈvændəlɪzəm] *n* vandalismo.

vandalize [ˈvændəlaɪz] *n* urgencia.

vane [veɪn] *n* **1** *(weather, etc)* veleta. **2** *(of fan, etc)* aspa.

vanilla [vəˈnɪlə] *n* vainilla.

vanish [ˈvænɪʃ] *vi* desaparecer.

vanity [ˈvænɪtɪ] *n* vanidad.

vapor [ˈvæpər] *n* US → vapour.

vapour [ˈveɪpər] *n* **1** vapor *m*. **2** *(on windowpane)* vaho.

variable [ˈveərɪəb°l] *adj* variable.
▶ *n* variable *f*.

variant [ˈveərɪənt] *n* variante *f*.

varicose [ˈværɪkəʊs] *adj* varicoso,-a.
`COMP` **varicose veins** varices *fpl*.

varied [ˈveərɪd] *adj* variado,-a, diverso,-a.

variety [vəˈraɪətɪ] *n* **1** *(diversity)* variedad *f*. **2** *(assortment)* surtido.
ⓘ *pl* varieties.

various ['veərɪəs] adj 1 (different) diverso,-a, distinto,-a. 2 (several) varios,-as.

varnish ['vɑ:nɪʃ] n 1 (for wood, metals) barniz m. 2 (for nails) esmalte m.
▶ vt 1 (wood, metals) barnizar. 2 (nails) pintar.

vary ['veərɪ] vi variar.
▶ vt variar de.
① pt & pp **varied,** ger **varying.**

vascular ['væskjələʳ] adj vascular.

vas deferens ['væs 'defərenz] n ANAT conducto deferente.

vase [vɑ:z, US veɪz] n jarrón m, florero m.

vassal ['væsəl] n vasallo,-a.

vast [vɑ:st] adj (extensive) vasto,-a, inmenso,-a; (huge) inmenso,-a, enorme.

Vatican ['vætɪkən] adj vaticano,-a. COMP **Vatican City** Ciudad f del Vaticano.
▶ n **the Vatican** el Vaticano.

vault¹ [vɔ:lt] n 1 (ceiling) bóveda. 2 (in bank) cámara acorazada. 3 (for dead) panteón m; (in church) cripta. 4 (cellar) sótano; (for wine) bodega.

vault² [vɔ:lt] vt saltar.
▶ vi saltar.
▶ n (gymnastics) salto.

veal [vi:l] n ternera.

vector ['vektəʳ] n vector m.

vegetable ['vedʒtəbəl] n 1 (as food) verdura, hortaliza. 2 (as plant) vegetal m. 3 fam (person) vegetal m.

vegetarian [vedʒɪ'teərɪən] adj vegetariano,-a.
▶ n vegetariano,-a.

vegetation [vedʒɪ'teɪʃən] n vegetación f.

vehicle ['vi:əkəl] n 1 TECH vehículo. 2 fig medio, vehículo.

veil [veɪl] n velo.
▶ vt velar.

vein [veɪn] n 1 ANAT vena. 2 BOT vena, nervio. 3 (of mineral) veta, vena, filón m. 4 (mood) humor m, vena.

velum ['vi:ləm] n velo (del paladar).
① pl **vela** ['vi:lə].

velvet ['velvɪt] n terciopelo.

vena cava ['vi:nə 'keɪvə] n ANAT vena cava.

vending machine ['vendɪŋməʃi:n] n máquina expendedora.

vendor ['vendəʳ] n vendedor,-ra.

Venezuela [venə'zweɪlə] n Venezuela.

Venezuelan [venə'zweɪlən] adj venezolano,-a.
▶ n venezolano,-a.

vengeance ['vendʒəns] n venganza.

venous ['vi:nəs] adj venoso,-a.

ventilate ['ventɪleɪt] vt ventilar.

ventricle ['ventrɪkəl] n ventrículo.

venture ['ventʃəʳ] vt arriesgar, aventurar.
▶ vi arriesgarse.
▶ n aventura, empresa arriesgada.
COMP **business venture** empresa comercial. ‖ **joint venture** empresa conjunta. ‖ **venture capital** capital m riesgo.

venue ['venju:] n 1 (place) local m. 2 (scene) escenario.

Venus ['vi:nəs] n Venus f. COMP **Venus flytrap** dionea.

veranda [və'rændə] n porche m.

verb [vɜ:b] n verbo.

verbal ['vɜ:bəl] adj verbal. COMP **verbal noun** gerundio.

verdict ['vɜ:dɪkt] n 1 veredicto, fallo. 2 (opinion) opinión f, juicio.

verge [vɜ:dʒ] n 1 borde m, margen m. 2 (of road) arcén m.
◆ **to verge on** vt insep 1 (condition) rayar en. 2 (age) rondar.

verify ['verɪfaɪ] vt verificar, comprobar.
① pt & pp **verified,** ger **verifying.**

vermicelli [vɜ:mɪ'selɪ] n fideos mpl.

vermin ['vɜ:mɪn] n pl 1 (small animals) alimañas fpl. 2 (insects) bichos mpl, sabandijas fpl. 3 (people) gentuza f sing, chusma f sing.

verruca [və'ru:kə] n verruga.
① pl **verrucas o verrucae** [və'ru:ki:].

verse [vɜ:s] n 1 (poetry) versos mpl, poesía. 2 (set of lines) estrofa. 3 (song, set of lines) estrofa. 4 (in Bible) versículo.

☒ **Verse** no significa 'verso (parte del poema)', que se traduce por **line.**

version ['vɜ:ʒ°n] *n* **1** versión *f*. **2** MUS interpretación *f*. **3** AUTO modelo. `COMP` **stage version** THEAT adaptación *f* teatral.

versus ['vɜ:səs] *prep* **1** *(against)* contra. **2** *(as opposed to)* frente a.

vertebra ['vɜ:tɪbrə] *n* vértebra.
ⓘ *pl* vertebrae ['vɜ:tɪbri:].

vertebral ['vɜ:tɪbrəl] *adj* vertebral.

vertebrate ['vɜ:tɪbrət, 'vɜ:tɪbreɪt] *adj* vertebrado,-a.
▶ *n* vertebrado.

vertex ['vɜ:teks] *n* vértice *m*.
ⓘ *pl* vertexes o vertices ['vɜ:tɪsi:z].

vertical ['vɜ:tɪkəl] *adj* vertical.

very ['verɪ] *adv* **1** *(extremely)* muy. **2** *(emphatic)* muy.
▶ *adj* **1** *(extreme)* de todo. **2** *(precise)* mismo,-a, exacto,-a. `LOC` **the very best** el/la mejor, lo mejor,

vesicle ['vesɪk°l] *n* vesícula.

vessel ['ves°l] *n* **1** *(ship)* nave *f*, buque *m*. **2** *(container)* recipiente *m*, vasija. **3** ANAT vaso. `COMP` **cargo vessel** buque *m* de carga.

vest [vest] *n* **1** GB camiseta. **2** US chaleco.

vestibule ['vestɪbju:l] *n* **1** *(entrance hall)* vestíbulo, entrada. **2** ANAT vestíbulo.

vet [vet] *n fam* veterinario,-a.

veteran ['vet°rən] *adj* veterano,-a.
▶ *n* **1** veterano,-a. **2** *(soldier, etc)* excombatiente *mf*.

veterinary ['vet°rɪn°rɪ] *adj* veterinario,-a. `COMP` **veterinary surgeon** veterinario,-a.

veto ['vi:təʊ] *n* veto.
ⓘ *pl* vetoes.
▶ *vt* vetar; *(forbid)* prohibir, vedar.
ⓘ *pt & pp* vetoed, *ger* vetoing.

vexed [vekst] *adj* disgustado,-a. `COMP` **vexed question** tema *m* controvertido.

via ['vaɪə] *prep* **1** *(through)* vía, por. **2** *(by means of)* por medio de, a través de.

vibrate [vaɪ'breɪt, US 'vaɪbreɪt] *vi* vibrar (with, con).
▶ *vt* hacer vibrar.

vibration [vaɪ'breɪ[°n] *n* vibración *f*.

vicar ['vɪkə'] *n* párroco.

vice¹ [vaɪs] *n* vicio.

vice² [vaɪs] *n (tool)* torno de banco, tornillo de banco.

vice³ [vaɪs] *pref* vice-. `COMP` **vice admiral** MIL vicealmirante *m*. ▌ **vice chancellor** EDUC rector,-ra. ▌ **vice president** vicepresidente,-ta.

vicereine [vaɪs'reɪn] *n* virreina.

viceroy ['vaɪsrɔɪ] *n* virrey *m*.

vicinity [və'sɪnətɪ] *n* **1** inmediaciones *fpl*. **2** *fml* proximidad *f*.

vicious ['vɪʃəs] *adj* **1** *(cruel)* cruel; *(malicious)* malintencionado,-a. **2** *(violent)* virulento,-a, violento,-a. **3** *(dangerous)* peligroso,-a.

✖ Vicious no significa 'vicioso', que se traduce por depraved.

victim ['vɪktɪm] *n* víctima.

victory ['vɪkt°rɪ] *n* victoria, triunfo.
ⓘ *pl* victories.

victuals ['vɪt°lz] *n pl* vituallas *fpl*, víveres *mpl*.

vicuna [vɪ'kju:nə] *n* vicuña.

video ['vɪdɪəʊ] *n* **1** *(in general)* vídeo. **2** *(pop video)* videoclip *m*. `COMP` **video game** videojuego.
ⓘ *pl* videos.

videoconference [vɪdɪəʊk'kɒnfərəns] *n* videoconferencia.

videodisc ['vɪdɪəʊdɪsk] *n* videodisco.

videorecorder [vɪdɪəʊrɪ'kɔ:də'] *n* vídeo.

videotape ['vɪdɪəʊteɪp] *n* cinta de vídeo
▶ *vt* grabar en vídeo.

videotext ['vɪdɪəʊtekst] *n* videotexto.

Vietnam [vɪet'næm] *n* Vietnam.

Vietnamese [vɪetnə'mi:z] *adj* vietnamita.
▶ *n* **1** *(person)* vietnamita *mf*. **2** *(language)* vietnamita *m*.
▶ *n pl* **the Vietnamese** los vietnamitas *mpl*.

view [vju:] *n* **1** vista, panorama *m*. **2** *(opinion)* opinión *f*, parecer *m*.
▶ *vt* **1** *(consider)* considerar, ver. **2** *(regard, think about)* enfocar. **3** *(examine)* ver; *(visit)* visitar. **4** *(watch)* ver; *(critically)* visionar.

viewer ['vju:əʳ] n **1** TV telespecta-dor,-ra, televidente mf. **2** (photography) visionadora.

viewpoint ['vju:pɔɪnt] n punto de vista.

vignette [vɪn'jet] n **1** (artwork) viñeta. **2** (description) estampa.

vigor ['vɪgəʳ] n US → vigour.

vigour ['vɪgəʳ] n vigor m, energía.

Viking ['vaɪkɪŋ] adj vikingo,-a.
▶ n vikingo,-a.

villa ['vɪlə] n **1** (for holidays) chalet m; (in country) casa de campo. **2** (Roman) vi-lla. **3** GB (large house) villa, quinta.

village ['vɪlɪdʒ] n (gen) pueblo; (small) pueblecito. COMP **village idiot** el tonto del pueblo. ▌ **village life** la vida de pueblo.

villager ['vɪlɪdʒəʳ] n habitante m del pueblo, aldeano,-a.

villain ['vɪlən] n **1** (bad character) malo,-a, malo,-a de la película. **2** GB fam mal-vado,-a. LOC **the villain of the piece** fam el malo de la película.

vine [vaɪn] n **1** vid f. **2** (made to climb) pa-rra. COMP **vine grower** viticultor,-ra. ▌ **vine growing** viticultura. ▌ **vine leaf** hoja de parra. ▌ **vine shoot** sarmiento.

vinegar ['vɪnɪgəʳ] n vinagre m. COMP **vinegar bottle** vinagrera. ▌ **wine vine-gar** vinagre m de vino.

vineyard ['vɪnjəd] n viña, viñedo.

vintage ['vɪntɪdʒ] n cosecha.
▶ adj **1** (wine) de añada. **2** (classic) clásico,-a; (high-quality) glorioso,-a, maravilloso,-a. **3** fam lo mejor de. COMP **vintage car** coche m de época construido entre 1919 y 1930.

viola¹ [vaɪ'əʊlə] n MUS viola.

viola² [vaɪ'əʊlə] n BOT violeta.

violate ['vaɪəleɪt] vt violar; (law) infrin-gir, transgredir.

violation [vaɪə'leɪʃ°n] n violación f; (of law) infracción f, transgresión f.

violence ['vaɪələns] n violencia.

violet ['vaɪələt] n **1** BOT violeta f. **2** (colour) violeta m, violado,-a, violáceo,-a.
▶ adj (de color) violeta, violado,-a.

violin [vaɪə'lɪn] n violín m.

violinist [vaɪə'lɪnɪst] n violinista mf.

viper ['vaɪpəʳ] n víbora.

viral ['vaɪrəl] adj viral, vírico,-a.

virgin [vaɪə'lɪnɪst] adj virgen.
▶ n virgen f.

Virgo ['vɜ:gəʊ] n Virgo.

virtual ['vɜ:tʃuəl] adj virtual. COMP **vir-tual reality** realidad f virtual.

virtue ['vɜ:tʃu:] n **1** virtud f. **2** (advan-tage) ventaja. LOC **by virtue of** en vir-tud de. ▌ **in virtue of** en virtud de.

virus ['vaɪ°rəs] n virus m. COMP **virus in-fection** infección f vírica.
ⓘ pl viruses.

visa ['vi:zə] n visado, am visa. COMP **en-try visa** visado de entrada. ▌ **exit visa** visado de salida.

viscosity [vɪs'kɒsɪtɪ] n viscosidad f.

visibility [vɪzɪ'bɪlətɪ] n visibilidad f.

visible ['vɪzɪ'bəl] adj visible.

Visigoth ['vɪzɪgɒθ] n visigodo,-a.

Visigothic ['vɪzɪgɒθɪk] adj visigodo,-a.

vision ['vɪʒ°n] n **1** (gen) visión f. **2** (eye-sight) vista. LOC **a man of vision** un hombre con visión de futuro.

visit ['vɪzɪt] vt **1** (person) visitar, hacer una visita a. **2** (place) visitar, ir a.
▶ vi estar de visita.
▶ n visita. LOC **to pay sb a visit** hacer una visita a algn. ▌ **to visit with sb** US charlar con algn.

visiting ['vɪzɪtɪŋ] adj **1** (for visiting) de vi-sita. **2** (guest) visitante. COMP **visiting card** tarjeta de visita. ▌ **visiting hours** horas fpl de visita. ▌ **visiting lecturer** profesor,-ra invitado,-a. ▌ **visiting team** equipo visitante.

visitor ['vɪzɪtəʳ] n **1** (at home) invitado,-a, visita. **2** (tourist) turista mf, visitante mf. COMP **visitors' book** libro de visitas.

visor ['vaɪzəʳ] n visera.

visual ['vɪʒuəl] adj visual. COMP **visual aid** medio visual. ▌ **visual arts** artes mpl visuales. ▌ **visual display unit** pan-talla.

vital ['vaɪt°l] adj **1** vital. **2** (essential) esencial, imprescindible. COMP **vital organ** órgano vital. ▌ **vital signs** seña-les fpl de vida.

▶ *n pl* órganos *mpl* vitales. LOC **of vital importance** de suma importancia.

vitamin ['vɪtəmɪn, 'vaɪtəmɪn] *n* vitamina. COMP **vitamin C** vitamina C. ‖ **vitamin content** contenido vitamínico. ‖ **vitamin deficiency** avitaminosis *f.*

vitro ['vi:trəʊ] LOC **in vitro** in vitro.

viva ['vaɪvə] *n* GB *fam (abbr of* viva voce*)* examen *m* oral.

vivid ['vɪvɪd] *adj* **1** vivo,-a, intenso,-a. **2** *(description)* gráfico,-a. LOC **to have a vivid imagination** tener mucha imaginación.

viviparous [vɪ'vɪpərəs] *adj* vivíparo,-a.

vixen ['vɪksⁿn] *n* zorra.

V-neck ['vi:nek] *n* cuello de pico.

vocabulary [və'kjæbjʊlərɪ] *n* vocabulario.
ⓘ *pl* vocabularies.

vocal ['vəʊkⁿl] *adj* **1** vocal. **2** *fam (noisy)* escandaloso,-a. COMP **vocal cords** cuerdas *fpl* vocales.

vocational [vəʊ'keɪ∫ⁿnəl] *adj* profesional. COMP **vocational guidance** orientación *f* profesional.

vocative ['vɒkətɪv] *n* vocativo.
▶ *adj* vocativo,-a.

vogue [vəʊg] *n* boga, moda. LOC **to be all the vogue** estar muy en boga. COMP **to be in vogue** estar en boga.

voice [vɔɪs] *n* voz *f.* LOC **at the top of one's voice** a voz en grito. ‖ **in a loud voice** en voz alta. ‖ **in a low/soft voice** en voz baja, a media voz. ‖ **to lose one's voice** quedarse afónico,-a, quedarse sin voz. ‖ **to lower/raise one's voice** bajar/levantar la voz. ‖ **with one voice** de una voz, a una, a coro. COMP **voice box** laringe *f.* ‖ **voice offstage** THEAT voz *f* en off.
▶ *vt* **1** expresar. **2** LING sonorizar.

voiceless ['vɔɪsləs] *adj* **1** *(hoarse)* afónico,-a. **2** LING sordo,-a.

voice-over ['vɔɪsˌəʊvəʳ] *n* voz *f* en off.

void [vɔɪd] *adj* **1** vacío,-a (of, de): *void of interest* falto,-a de interés. **2** JUR nulo, -a, inválido,-a.
▶ *n* vacío.
▶ *vt* **1** *(empty)* vaciar. **2** JUR anular.

volcano [vɒl'keɪnəʊ] *n* volcán *m.*
ⓘ *pl* volcanos o volcanoes.

volley ['vɒlɪ] *n* **1** MIL descarga. **2** *fig (of stones)* aluvión *m; (of blows)* tanda; *(of applause)* salva. **3** *(tennis)* volea.
▶ *vi* **1** MIL lanzar una descarga. **2** *(tennis)* hacer una volea.
▶ *vt (sp)* volear.

volleyball ['vɒlɪbɔ:l] *n* voleibol *m.*

volt [vəʊlt] *n* voltio.

voltage ['vəʊltɪdʒ] *n* voltaje *m*, tensión *f.*

voltmeter ['vəʊltmi:təʳ] *n* voltímetro.

voluble ['vɒljəbⁿl] *adj* locuaz, hablador,-ra.

✕ Voluble no significa 'voluble', que se traduce por changeable.

volume ['vɒlju:m] *n* **1** volumen *m.* **2** *(book)* tomo. LOC **to speak volumes** decirlo todo. ‖ **to turn down/up the volume** bajar/subir el volumen.

voluntary ['vɒləntⁿrɪ] *adj* voluntario,-a. COMP **voluntary organization** organización *f* benéfica. ‖ **voluntary society** sociedad *f* benéfica. ‖ **voluntary work** obras *fpl* benéficas. ‖ **voluntary helper/worker** voluntario,-a.

volunteer [vɒlən'tɪəʳ] *n* voluntario,-a.
▶ *vt* ofrecer.
▶ *vi* **1** ofrecerse (for, para). **2** MIL alistarse como voluntario,-a (for, en).

vomit ['vɒmɪt] *n* vómito.
▶ *vi* vomitar, devolver.
▶ *vt* vomitar, devolver.

vote [vəʊt] *n* **1** voto. **2** *(voting)* voto, votación *f.* **3** *(right to vote)* sufragio.
▶ *vi* votar. COMP **vote of censure** voto de censura. ‖ **vote of confidence** voto de confianza.
▶ *vt* **1** votar. **2** *(elect)* elegir. **3** *fam* considerarse: *the party was voted a complete flop* la fiesta se consideró un desastre total. LOC **to be voted into/out of office** ganar/perder las elecciones. ‖ **to vote by a show of hands** votar a mano alzada. ‖ **to vote on sth / take a vote on sth** someter algo a votación.
◆ **to vote down** *vt sep* rechazar.
◆ **to vote through** *vt sep* aprobar.

voter ['vəʊtəʳ] *n* votante *mf.*

voucher ['vaʊt∫əʳ] *n* GB vale *m*, bono. JUR comprobante *m*, justificante *m.*

vow [vaʊ] *n* **1** promesa solemne. **2** REL voto. LOC **to take a vow of chastity/poverty** hacer voto de castidad/pobreza. ▌ **to take one's vows** pronunciar sus votos. COMP **vow of silence** voto de silencio.

vowel ['vaʊəl] *n* vocal *f*.

voyage ['vɔɪɪdʒ] *n* viaje *m*; *(by sea)* viaje *m* en barco; *(crossing)* travesía.
▶ *vi fml* viajar.

✎ Voyage se refiere a un viaje generalmente largo por mar o en el espacio. La palabra más usual para 'viaje' es journey.

vulgar ['vʌlgəʳ] *adj* **1** *(in poor taste)* de mal gusto. **2** *(coarse)* grosero,-a, ordinario,-a. **3** LING vulgar. COMP **vulgar fraction** fracción *f* común.

✖ Vulgar no significa 'vulgar (corriente', que se traduce por common.

vulgarity [vʌl'gærɪtɪ] *n* **1** *(poor taste)* mal gusto. **2** *(coarseness)* vulgaridad *f*, ordinariez *f*, grosería.

vulnerable ['vʌln°rəb°l] *adj* vulnerable.

vulture ['vʌltʃəʳ] *n* buitre *m*.

vulva ['vʌlvə] *n* vulva.
ⓘ *pl* vulvas o vulvae ['vʌlviː].

W, w [ˈdjʌbəlju:] *n (the letter)* W, w *f*.

W [west] *abbr* **(west)** oeste *m*; *(abbreviation)* O.

wade [weɪd] *vi* caminar por el agua.
▸ *vt* vadear.

wafer [ˈweɪfəʳ] *n (for ice cream)* barquillo; *(biscuit)* galleta de barquillo.

wage [weɪdʒ] *n* sueldo, salario.
▸ *n pl* **wages** sueldo *m sing*, salario *m sing*.

waggon [ˈwægən] *n* GB → **wagon**.

wagon [ˈwægən] *n* **1** *(cart)* carro; *(covered)* carromato. **2** GB *(railway truck)* vagón *m*. **3** US *(trolley)* carrito, mesa camarera.

wagon-lit [vægɒnˈliː] *n* coche-cama *m*.
ⓘ *pl* **wagons-lits**.

wail [weɪl] *n (of pain, grief)* lamento, gemido; *(of siren)* aullido.
▸ *vi* **1** *(person - cry)* gemir, llorar; *(- complain)* quejarse **(about/over, de)**, lamentarse **(about/over, de)**. **2** *(siren)* aullar, ulular; *(wind)* ulular.

waist [weɪst] *n* **1** ANAT cintura. **2** *(of garment)* talle *m*. **3** *(of guitar, etc)* parte estrecha.

waistcoat [ˈweɪskəʊt] *n* chaleco.

waistline [ˈweɪstlaɪn] *n* **1** ANAT cintura. **2** SEW talle *m*.

wait [weɪt] *n (gen)* espera; *(delay)* demora.
▸ *vi* esperar **(for, -)**, aguardar **(for, -)**. ⎣LOC⎤ **to wait at table** servir la mesa.
▸ *vt* esperar, aguardar.
◆ **to wait about / wait around** *vi* esperar, perder el tiempo.
◆ **to wait on** *vt insep* servir.

waiter [ˈweɪtəʳ] *n* camarero. ⎣COMP⎤ **head waiter** maitre *m*.

waiting [ˈweɪtɪŋ] *n* espera. ⎣COMP⎤ **waiting room** sala de espera.

waitress [ˈweɪtrəs] *n* camarera.
ⓘ *pl* **waitresses**.

wake [weɪk] *vt* despertar **(up, -)**.
▸ *vi* despertarse **(up, -)**.
◆ **to wake up to** *vt insep (become aware)* darse cuenta de.
ⓘ *pt* **woke** [wəʊk], *pp* **woken** [ˈwəʊkən].

Wales [weɪlz] *n* País *m* de Gales.

walk [wɔːk] *n* **1** *(gen)* paseo; *(distance)* camino; *(long)* caminata, excursión *f*; *(sport)* marcha. **2** *(path, route)* paseo, ruta; *(long)* excursión *f*. **3** *(gait)* modo de andar *mpl*.
▸ *vi* andar, caminar, pasear.
▸ *vt* **1** *(cover on foot)* ir a pie, ir andando, andar. **2** *(person)* acompañar; *(animal)* pasear.
◆ **to walk away** *vi* alejarse.
◆ **to walk into** *vt insep* **1** *(get caught)* caer en. **2** *(bump into)* tropezar con.
◆ **to walk out** *vi* **1** *(leave suddenly)* marcharse. **2** *(go on strike)* ir a la huelga.
◆ **to walk out on** *vt insep (abandon)* abandonar a.

walker [ˈwɔːkəʳ] *n* **1** *(gen)* paseante *mf*; *(hiker)* excursionista *mf*. **2** *(athlete)* marchador,-ra. **3** *(for babies)* andador *m*; *(for disabled)* andador *m*.

walkie-talkie [wɔːkɪˈtɔːkɪ] *n* walkie-talkie *m*.

walkman® [ˈwɔːkmən] *n* walkman® *m*.
ⓘ *pl* **walkmen** [ˈwɔːkmən].

wall [wɔːl] *n* **1** *(exterior)* muro; *(defensive, city)* muralla; *(garden)* tapia; *(sea)* dique *m*. **2** *(interior)* pared *f*; *(partition)* tabique *m*. **3** ANAT *(of artery, blood vessel)* pared *f*; *(of abdomen)* pared *f* abdominal. **4** SP barrera.

wallet ['wɒlɪt] *n* cartera.

wallpaper ['wɔːlpeɪpə'] *n* **1** papel *m* pintado. **2** *(for computer screen)* papel *m* tapiz.
▸ *vt* empapelar.

wally ['wɒlɪ] *n fam* idiota *mf*, inútil *mf*.
ⓘ *pl* wallies.

walnut ['wɔːlnʌt] *n (fruit)* nuez *f; (wood)* nogal *m*. COMP walnut tree nogal *m*.

walrus ['wɔːlrəs] *n* morsa.
ⓘ *pll* walruses.

waltz [wɔːls] *n* vals *m*.
ⓘ *pl* waltzes.

wand [wɒnd] *n* varita.

wander ['wɒndə'] *vi* **1** *(roam)* deambular, errar, vagar; *(stroll)* pasear, caminar. **2** *(stray)* apartarse, desviarse, alejarse; *(get lost)* extraviarse.
▸ *n* vuelta, paseo.

want [wɒnt] *n* **1** *(lack)* falta, carencia. **2** *(desire, need)* necesidad *f.*
▸ *vt* **1** *(gen)* querer. **2** *fam (need)* necesitar. **3** *fam (ought to)* deber. **4** *fml (lack)* necesitar, carecer de,.

wanted ['wɒntɪd] *adj* **1** *(for work)* necesario,-a. **2** *(by police)* buscado,-a.

war [wɔː'] *n* guerra.

ward [wɔːd] *n* **1** *(in hospital)* sala. **2** GB *(for elections)* distrito electoral.

warden ['wɔːdⁿn] *n* **1** *(of hostel, home)* encargado,-a. **2** US *(of prison)* alcaide *m*, director,-ra. **3** *(of university)* rector,-ra.

wardrobe ['wɔːdrəʊb] *n* **1** armario (ropero), guardarropa *m*. **2** *(clothes)* vestuario. **3** *(theatre)* vestuario.

warehouse ['weəhaʊs] *n* almacén *m*, depósito.
▸ *vt* almacenar, depositar.

warfare ['wɔːfeə'] *n* **1** *(war)* guerra. **2** *(conflict, struggle)* lucha, batalla.

warhead ['wɔːhed] *n* ojiva, cabeza.

warm [wɔːm] *adj* **1** *(climate, wind)* cálido,-a; *(day)* caluroso,-a, de calor. **2** *(hands, etc)* caliente; *(liquid)* tibio,-a, templado,-a. **3** *(clothing)* de abrigo, que abriga. **4** *(colour)* cálido,-a. **5** *(welcome, applause, etc)* cálido,-a, caluroso,-a. **6** *(character)* afectuoso,-a.
▸ *vt (gen)* calentar.

▸ *vi* calentarse.
◆ **to warm up** *vt sep* **1** *(food)* calentar, recalentar; *(engine)* calentar. **2** *(audience, party)* animar.
▸ *vi* **1** *(food, engine, etc)* calentarse. **2** *(audience, party)* animarse. **3** SP hacer ejercicios de calentamiento.

warm-blooded ['wɔːm'blʌdɪd] [se escribe warm blooded cuando no se usa para calificar a un nombre] *adj* de sangre caliente.

warmly ['wɔːmlɪ] *adv* **1** *(with heat)* con ardor. **2** *(thank)* con efusión; *(recommend)* con entusiasmo; *(welcome, greet)* calurosamente. **3** *(dress)* con ropa de abrigo.

warmth [wɔːmθ] *n* **1** *(heat)* calor *m*. **2** *fig* afecto, cordialidad *f.*

warm-up ['wɔːmʌp] *n* SP calentamiento, precalentamiento.

warn [wɔːn] *vt* **1** avisar (of, de), advertir (of, de), prevenir (about, sobre), (against, contra). **2** *(instead of punishing)* amonestar.

warning ['wɔːnɪŋ] *n* **1** *(of danger)* aviso, advertencia. **2** *(instead of punishment)* amonestación *f*. **3** *(advance notice)* aviso.
▸ *adj (shot, glance)* de aviso, de advertencia.

warrant ['wɒrənt] *n* **1** JUR orden *f* judicial, mandamiento judicial. **2** *(voucher)* bono, vale *m*. **3** *fml (justification)* justificación *f*. COMP warrant officer suboficial *m*.
▸ *vt* **1** *fml (justify)* justificar; *(deserve)* merecer, ser digno,-a de. **2** *(guarantee)* garantizar.

warranty ['wɒrəntɪ] *n* **1** COMM *(guarantee)* garantía. **2** *fml (authority)* autorización *f.*
ⓘ *pl* warranties.

warrior ['wɒrɪə'] *n* guerrero,-a.

warship ['wɔːʃɪp] *n* buque *m* de guerra.

wart [wɔːt] *n* verruga.

warthog ['wɔːthɒg] *n* jabalí *m* verrugoso.

wartime ['wɔːtaɪm] *n* tiempos *mpl* de guerra.
▸ *adj* de guerra.

was [wɒz, *unstressed* wəz] *pt* → be.

wash [wɒʃ] *n* **1** *(act)* lavado. **2** *(laundry)* ropa sucia, colada. **3** *(of ship)* estela; *(of water)* remolinos *mpl*; *(sound)* chapoteo.
▸ *vt* **1** *(gen)* lavar; *(dishes)* fregar. **2** *(carry)* llevar, arrastrar.
▸ *vi* **1** *(gen)* lavarse. **2** *(flow, lap)* batir.
◆ **to wash away** *vt sep* **1** *(destroy and carry away)* llevarse, arrastrar. **2** *(remove)* borrar.
◆ **to wash up** *vt sep* **1** fregar. **2** arrastrar a la playa.
▸ *vi* **1** fregar los platos. **2** US lavarse las manos y la cara, lavarse rápidamente.

washable [ˈwɒʃəbəl] *adj* lavable.

washbasin [ˈwɒʃbeɪsən] *n* *(fixed to wall)* lavabo; *(bowl)* palangana.

washbowl [ˈwɒʃbəʊl] *n* US palangana.

washer [ˈwɒʃəʳ] *n* **1** TECH *(metal)* arandela; *(rubber)* junta. **2** *fam (machine)* lavadora.

washing [ˈwɒʃɪŋ] *n* **1** *(action)* lavado, el lavar *m*. **2** *(dirty clothes)* colada, ropa sucia; *(clean clothes)* colada; *(clothes hanging out)* ropa tendida. ᴸᴼᶜ **to do the washing** hacer la colada. ᴸᴼᶜ **washing machine** lavadora. ‖ **washing powder** detergente *m*.

washing-up [wɒʃɪŋˈʌp] *n* **1** *(action)* fregado, el fregar *m*. **2** *(dishes)* platos *mpl*. ᴸᴼᶜ **to do the washing-up** fregar los platos. ᴄᴼᴹᴾ **washing-up liquid** lavavajillas *m*.

wasp [wɒsp] *n* avispa. ᴄᴼᴹᴾ **wasp's nest** avispero.

waste [weɪst] *n* **1** *(gen)* derroche *m*; *(of money, energy)* despilfarro; *(of time)* pérdida,. **2** *(matter)* desechos *mpl*, desperdicios *mpl*; *(rubbish)* basura.
▸ *adj* **1** *(unwanted)* desechado,-a. **2** *(land)* yermo,-a, baldío,-a.
▸ *vt* *(gen)* desperdiciar, malgastar; *(resources)* derrochar; *(time, chance)* desaprovechar, perder.

wastepaper basket [weɪstˈpeɪpə-bɑː-kɪt] *n* papelera.

watch [wɒtʃ] *n* **1** *(timepiece)* reloj *m*. **2** *(look-out)* vigilancia, guardia; *(person)* vigilante *mf*, guardia *mf*, centinela *mf*, guarda *mf*. **3** MAR *(period, body)* guardia; *(individual)* vigía. **4** HIST ronda.
ⓘ *pl* watches.
▸ *vt* **1** *(look at, observe)* mirar, observar; *(television, sport)* ver. **2** *(keep an eye on)* vigilar, observar; *(spy on)* espiar, vigilar. **3** *(be careful about)* tener cuidado con, cuidar de.
▸ *vi* *(look)* mirar, observar. ᴸᴼᶜ **watch out!** ¡cuidado!
◆ **to watch out for** *vt insep* **1** *(look out for, be alert)* estar alerta, estar pendiente de. **2** *(be careful of)* tener cuidado con.

watchdog [ˈwɒtʃdɒg] *n* **1** perro guardián. **2** *fig* guardián,-ana.

watcher [ˈwɒtʃəʳ] *n* observador,-ra, espectador,-ra.

water [ˈwɔːtəʳ] *n* **1** *(gen)* agua: *drinking water* agua potable; *mineral water* agua mineral; *running water* agua corriente, *spring water* agua de manantial. **2** *(tide)* marea. ᴄᴼᴹᴾ **water bottle** *(flask)* cantimplora. ‖ **water polo** waterpolo.‖ **water power** energía hidráulica. ‖ **water supply** abastecimiento de agua, suministro de agua. ‖ **water tank** depósito de agua. ‖ **water vapour** vapor *m* de agua. ‖ **water wheel 1** *(for power)* rueda hidráulica. **2** *(for irrigation)* noria.
▸ *vt* **1** *(plant, river)* regar. **2** *(animals)* abrevar.
◆ **to water down** *vt sep* **1** *(drink)* aguar, mezclar con agua. **2** *fig* descafeinar.

watercolor [ˈwɔːtəkʌləʳ] *n* → watercolour.

watercolour [ˈwɔːtəkʌləʳ] *n* acuarela.
▸ *n pl* **watercolours** acuarelas *fpl*.

watercress [ˈwɔːtkres] *n* berro.

waterfall [ˈwɔːtəfɔːl] *n* cascada, salto de agua, catarata.

watering [ˈwɔːtərɪŋ] *n* riego.

watermark [ˈwɔːtəmɑːk] *n* filigrana.

watermelon [ˈwɔːtəmelən] *n* sandía.

watermill [ˈwɔːtəmɪl] *n* molino de agua.

waterpark [ˈwɔːtəpɑːk] *n* parque *m* acuático.

waterpipe [ˈwɔːtəpaɪp] *n* cañería.

W

waterproof ['wɔːtəpruːf] *adj* **1** *(material)* impermeable. **2** *(watch)* sumergible.
▶ *n (coat)* impermeable *m*.
▶ *vt* impermeabilizar.

water-ski ['wɔːtəskiː] *n* esquí *m* acuático.
▶ *vi* hacer esquí acuático.

water-skiing ['wɔːtəskiːɪŋ] *n* esquí *m* acuático.

watersports ['wɔːtəspɔːts] *n pl* deportes *mpl* acuáticos.

watertight ['wɔːtətaɪt] *adj* **1** estanco,-a, hermético,-a. **2** *fig* irrefutable, irrebatible.

water-wheel ['wɔːtəwiːl] *n* **1** *(for power)* rueda hidráulica. **2** *(for irrigation)* noria.

waterworks ['wɔːtəwɜːks] *n* depuradora, planta de tratamiento de aguas.
▶ *n pl* GB *fam euph* aparato urinario.

watt [wɒt] *n* ELEC watt *m*, vatio.

wave [weɪv] *n* **1** *(in sea)* ola. **2** *(in hair)* onda. **3** PHYS onda. **4** *(of hand)* ademán *m*, movimiento; *(in greeting)* saludo con la mano. **5** *(steady increase)* ola, oleada. **6** *(influx)* oleada; *(sudden increase)* oleada, ola.
▶ *vi* **1** *(greet)* saludar (con la mano). **2** *(flag)* ondear; *(corn)* ondular. **3** *(hair)* ondular.
▶ *vt* **1** *(brandish)* agitar. **2** *(direct)* indicar con la mano. **3** *(hair)* marcar, ondular.

wavelength ['weɪvleŋθ] *n* RAD longitud *f* de onda.

wavy ['weɪvɪ] *adj* ondulado,-a.
ⓘ *comp* wavier, *superl* waviest.

wax [wæks] *n* **1** *(gen)* cera. **2** *(in ear)* cerumen *m*.
▶ *vt (polish)* encerar. COMP paraffin wax parafina. ‖ sealing wax lacre *m*. ‖ wax candle vela. ‖ wax crayons ceras *fpl*. ‖ wax paper papel *m* encerado.

way [weɪ] *n* **1** *(right route, road, etc)* camino. **2** *(direction)* dirección *f*. **3** *(distance)* distancia. **4** *(manner, method)* manera, modo.
▶ *adv fam* muy. LOC all the way **1** *(distance)* todo el viaje. **2** *(completely)* totalmente. ‖ by the way *(incidentally)* a propósito, por cierto. ‖ in a way en cierto modo, en cierta manera. ‖ in some ways en algunos aspectos. ‖ in this way *(thus)* de este modo, de esta manera. ‖ one way or the other *(somehow)* de algún modo, de una manera u otra, como sea. ‖ out of the way **1** *(remote)* apartado,-a, remoto,-a. **2** *(exceptional)* excepcional, particular, original. ‖ that way **1** *(direction)* por allá. **2** *(like that)* así. ‖ the right way round bien puesto. ‖ the wrong way round al revés. ‖ to be in the way estorbar, estar por en medio. ‖ to be on the way *(coming)* estar en camino, estar al llegar, avecinarse. ‖ to get out of the way apartarse. ‖ to find your way encontrar el camino. ‖ to give way **1** *(collapse)* ceder, hundirse. **2** *(yield)* ceder (to, a). **3** *(when driving)* ceder el paso. ‖ to loose your way perderse. LOC way in entrada. ‖ way out **1** *(exit)* salida. **2** *(solution)* solución *f*, remedio.
▶ *n pl* ways *(customs)* costumbres *fpl*; *(habits, behaviour)* manías *fpl*.

WC ['wɔːtəskiːɪŋ] *abbr* water closet váter *m*, retrete *m*.

we [wiː, *unstressed* wɪ] *pron* nosotros, -as.

weak [wiːk] *adj* **1** *(gen)* débil. **2** *(tea, coffee, etc)* aguado,-a, poco cargado,-a.
▶ *n pl* the weak los necesitados *mpl*, los inválidos *mpl*.

weaken ['wiːkən] *vt* **1** *(gen)* debilitar. **2** *(argument)* quitar fuerza a; *(morale)* socavar.
▶ *vi* **1** *(person)* debilitarse, desfallecer. **2** *(resolve, influence)* flaquear. **3** *(currency)* aflojar, caer. **4** *(give in)* ceder.

weakness ['wiːknəs] *n* **1** *(gen)* debilidad *f*, flaqueza. **2** *(lack of conviction)* falta de peso, pobreza. **3** *(defect, fault, flaw)* flaqueza, punto flaco.
ⓘ *pl* weaknesses.

wealth [welθ] *n* **1** *(riches)* riqueza. **2** *fig* abundancia, profusión *f*.

wealthy ['welθɪ] *adj* rico,-a, adinerado,-a, acaudalado,-a.
ⓘ *comp* wealthier, *superl* wealthiest.

weapon ['wepən] *n* arma.

wear [weəʳ] *n* **1** *(clothing)* ropa: *evening wear* traje de noche; *ladies' wear* ropa para señoras; *men's wear* ropa para hombres. **2** *(use)* uso: *for everyday wear* para todos los días. **3** *(deterioration)* desgaste *m*, deterioro. **4** *(capacity for being used)* durabilidad *f* COMP **wear and tear** desgaste *m*.
▶ *vt* **1** *(clothing, jewellery, etc)* llevar, vestir; *(shoes)* calzar. **2** *fam (accept, tolerate)* tolerar, aceptar, soportar. **3** *(damage by use)* desgastar.
▶ *vi* **1** *(become damaged by use)* desgastarse. **2** *(endure)* durar.
◆ **to wear out** *vt sep* **1** *(shoes, etc)* gastar, desgastar, romper con el uso. **2** *(person)* agotar, rendir.
▶ *vi (shoes, etc)* gastarse, desgastarse, romperse con el uso.
ⓘ *pt* **wore** [wɔːʳ], *pp* **worn** [wɔːn].

wearable ['weərəbəl] *adj* que se puede llevar, que se puede poner.

weary ['wɪərɪ] *adj* **1** *(exhausted)* cansado, -a, agotado,-a. **2** *(fed up)* cansado,-a, harto,-a.
ⓘ *comp* **wearier**, *superl* **weariest**.
▶ *vt* cansar.
▶ *vi* cansarse de.

weasel ['wiːzəl] *n* comadreja.

weather ['weðəʳ] *n (gen)* tiempo. COMP **weather forecast** parte *m* meteorológico.

weather-vane ['weðəveɪn] *n (clothing)* veleta.

weave [wiːv] *n* tejido.
▶ *vt* **1** *(gen)* tejer. **2** *fig (plot, story)* tramar, urdir.
ⓘ *pt* **wove** [wəʊv], *pp* **woven** [wəʊvən], *ger* **weaving**.

weaver ['wiːvəʳ] *n* tejedor,-ra.

web [web] *n* **1** *(spider's)* telaraña. **2** *fig* red *f*, sarta, embrollo. **3** *(of animals' feet)* membrana interdigital. **4** *(Internet)* web *f*.

webmaster ['webmɑːstəʳ] *n* administrador,-ra de web.

website ['websaɪt] *n* web *f*, sitio web.

wed [wed] *vt* casarse con.
ⓘ *pt & pp* **wedded** o **wed**, *ger* **wedding**.

we'd [wiːd] *contr* (we had, we would) → **have**, **would**.

wedding ['wedɪŋ] *n* boda, casamiento. COMP **wedding anniversary** aniversario de bodas. ❙ **wedding ring** anillo de bodas.

wedge [wedʒ] *n* **1** *(gen)* cuña, calza. **2** *(of cake, cheese)* trozo grande. **3** *(golf)* wedge *m*.
▶ *vt* **1** *(force apart)* acuñar, calzar. **2** *(pack tightly)* apretar.

Wednesday ['wenzdɪ] *n* miércoles *m inv*.
✎ Para ejemplos de uso, consulta **Saturday**.

weed [wiːd] *n* **1** BOT *(in garden)* mala hierba; *(in water)* algas *fpl*. **2** *fam pej (person)* debilucho,-a, canijo,-a.

weedkiller ['wiːdkɪləʳ] *n* herbicida *m*.

week [wiːk] *n* semana.

weekend ['wiːkend, wiːˈkend] *n* fin *m* de semana. COMP **long weekend** puente *m*.
▶ *vi* pasar el fin de semana.

weekly ['wiːklɪ] *adj* semanal.
▶ *adv* semanalmente, cada semana: *twice weekly* dos veces por semana.
▶ *n (press)* semanario.

weep [wiːp] *vi* **1** *fml (person)* llorar. **2** *(wound)* supurar.
ⓘ *pt & pp* **wept** [wept].

weigh [weɪ] *vt* **1** *(gen)* pesar. **2** *fig (consider carefully)* ponderar, sopesar (**up**, -); *(compare carefully)* contraponer (**with/against**, a).
▶ *vi* **1** *(gen)* pesar. **2** *(be important to, have influence on)* influir en, pesar.

weight [weɪt] *n* **1** *(gen)* peso. **2** *(of scales, clock, gym)* pesa; *(heavy object)* peso, cosa pesada. **3** *fig (burden, worry)* peso, carga. **4** *fig (importance, influence)* peso, importancia, influencia. LOC **to lose weight** perder peso, adelgazar. ❙ **to put on weight** engordar, ganar peso. COMP **weights and measures** pesos *mpl* y medidas.
▶ *vt* **1** *(make heavy)* cargar con peso, poner peso en, añadir peso a; *(fishing net)* lastrar. **2** *fig (statistics, etc)* ponderar.

weightlifter ['weɪtlɪftə'] *n* SP levanta-dor,-ra de pesas, halterófilo,-a.

weird [wɪəd] *adj* **1** *(bizarre)* raro,-a, ex-traño,-a. **2** *(eerie)* siniestro,-a.

welcome ['welkəm] *adj* **1** *(gen)* bien-venido,-a. **2** *(news, sight, etc)* grato,-a, agradable; *(change)* oportuno,-a, be-neficioso,-a. LOC **you're welcome** *(not at all)* no hay de qué, de nada.
▶ *interj* bienvenido,-a (**to**, a).
▶ *n* bienvenida, acogida.
▶ *vt* **1** *(greet)* acoger, recibir; *(officially)* dar la bienvenida a. **2** *(approve of, sup-port)* aplaudir, acoger con agrado.

welcoming ['welkəmɪŋ] *adj* *(smile)* aco-gedor,-ra; *(speech)* de bienvenida.

weld [weld] *n* soldadura.
▶ *vt* **1** soldar. **2** *fig* soldar, unir.
▶ *vi* soldarse.

welfare ['welfeə'] *n* **1** *(well-being)* bien-estar *m*; *(health)* salud *f*. **2** *(care, help)* protección *f*. **3** US *(money)* seguridad *f* social. COMP **welfare state** estado de bienestar. **‖ welfare worker** asistente *mf* social.

well' [wel] *n* **1** *(for water)* pozo. **2** *(of staircase)* hueco de la escalera; *(of lift)* hueco del ascensor. **3** GB *(in court)* área *de los abogados*.
▶ *vi* *(tears, blood)* brotar (**up**, -), manar (**up**, -).

well² [wel] *adj* **1** *(in good health)* bien. **2** *(satisfactory, right)* bien.
▶ *adv* **1** *(gen)* bien. **2** *(with modals)* bien. **3** *(much, quite)* bien. LOC **as well** *(also, too)* también. **‖ as well as** además de. **‖ very well** muy bien, bueno. **‖ well done!** ¡muy bien!, ¡así se hace! **‖ well I never!** ¡vaya!, ¡habráse visto! **‖ well off** *(comfortable, rich)* acomodado,-a.
▶ *interj* **1** *(gen)* bueno, bien, pues. **2** *(surprise)* ¡vaya!

well-balanced ['wel'bælənst] [se escribe well balanced cuando no se usa para cali-ficar a un nombre] *adj* equilibrado,-a.

well-behaved ['welbɪ'heɪvd] [se escribe well behaved cuando no se usa para calificar a un nombre] *adj* formal, educado,-a.

well-being [wel'biːɪŋ] *n* bienestar *m*.

well-done ['wel'dʌn] [se escribe well done cuando no se usa para calificar a un nombre] *adj* muy hecho,-a.

well-founded ['wel'faʊndɪd] [se escribe well founded cuando no se usa para calificar a un nombre.] *adj* bien fundado,-a.

wellington ['welɪŋtən] [a veces Wel-lington] *n* botas de agua.

well-known [wel'nəʊn] *adj* (bien) co-nocido,-a.

well-off ['wel'ɒf] [se escribe well off cuan-do no se usa para calificar a un nombre] *adj* rico,-a, acomodado,-a, pudiente.

Welsh [welʃ] *adj* galés,-esa.
▶ *n* *(language)* galés *m*.
▶ *n pl* **the Welsh** los galeses *mpl*.

Welshman ['welʃmən] *n* galés *m*.
ⓘ *pl* **Welshmen** ['welʃmən].

Welshwoman ['welʃwʊmən] *n* galesa.
ⓘ *pl* **Welshwomen** ['welʃwɪmɪn].

went [went] *pt* → go.

wept [wept] *pt & pp* → weep.

were [wɜː'] *pt* → be.

we're [wɪə'] *contr* (we are) → be.

werewolf ['wɪəwʊlf] *n* hombre *m* lobo.
ⓘ *pl* **werewolves** ['wɪəwʊlvz].

west [west] *n* oeste *m*, occidente *m*.
▶ *adj* occidental, del oeste. COMP **West Indies** las Antillas. **‖ West Indian** anti-llano,-a.
▶ *adv* al oeste, hacia el oeste.
▶ *n* **the West** POL Occidente *m*, los países *mpl* occidentales.

western ['westən] *adj* del oeste, occi-dental.
▶ *n* *(cinema)* western *m*.

westerner ['westənə'] *n* occidental *mf*.

westward ['westwəd] *adj* hacia el oes-te.

westwards ['westwəds] *adv* hacia el oeste.

wet [wet] *adj* **1** *(gen)* mojado,-a; *(damp)* húmedo,-a. **2** *(weather)* lluvioso,-a. **3** *(paint, ink)* fresco,-a. **4** *fam (person)* apocado,-a, soso,-a.
ⓘ *comp* **wetter**, *superl* **wettest**.
▶ *n* **1** *(damp)* humedad *f*. **2** *(rain)* lluvia. **3** *fam (person)* apocado,-a; *(politician)* moderado,-a.

► *vt* mojar, humedecer.

ⓘ *pt & pp* **wet** o **wetted**, *ger* **wetting**.

wetness ['wetnəs] *n* humedad *f*.

wetsuit ['wetsu:t] *n* traje *m* isotérmico.

we've [wi:v] *contr* (we have) → have.

whale [weɪl] *n* ballena.

whalebone ['weɪlbəʊn] *n* (barba de) ballena.

whaler ['weɪlər] *n* (gen) ballenero,-a.

whaling ['weɪlɪŋ] *n* caza de ballenas.
COMP **whaling industry** industria ballenera.

wharf [wɔ:f] *n* muelle *m*, embarcadero.

ⓘ *pl* **wharfs** o **wharves**.

wharves [wɔ:vz] *pl* → wharf.

what [wɒt] *adj* 1 (direct questions) qué: *what time is it?* ¿qué hora es?. 2 (indirect questions) qué: *I don't know what to do* no sé qué hacer. 3 (exclamations) qué: *what a man!* ¡qué hombre! 4 (all the) todo,-a. *what money we have is in the drawer* todo el aceite que tenemos está aquí.

► *pron* 1 (direct questions) qué: *what is it?* ¿qué es?. 2 (indirect questions) qué: *he didn't know what to say* no sabía qué decir. 3 lo que: *that's what he told me* eso es lo que me dijo. LOC **guess what?** ¿sabes qué? ▮ **what about...?** ¿qué te parece…?. ▮ **what for?** 1 (why) ¿por qué? 2 (for what purpose) ¿para qué? ▮ **what if...?** ¿y si…? ▮ **what is it?** 1 (what's wrong?) ¿qué pasa? 2 (definition) ¿qué es?

► *interj* ¡cómo!: *what! you've lost it!* ¡cómo! ¡lo has perdido!

whatever [wɒt'evər] *adj* 1 (any) cualquiera que. 2 (at all) en absoluto.

► *pron* 1 (anything, all that) (todo) lo que. 2 (no matter what): *whatever happens* pase lo que pase. 3 (surprise) qué. 4 *fam* (show indifference) lo que sea.

whatsoever [wɒtsəʊ'evər] *adj* en absoluto.

wheat [wi:t] *n* trigo.

wheatmeal ['wi:tmi:l] *n* COMP **wheatmeal flour** harina integral de trigo.

wheel [wi:l] *n* 1 rueda. 2 (steering wheel) volante *m*.

► *vt* (push) empujar.

► *vi* 1 girar. 2 (birds) revolotear.

► *n pl* **wheels** *fam* coche *m sing*.

wheelbarrow ['wi:lbærəʊ] *n* carretilla de mano.

wheelchair ['wi:ltʃeər] *n* silla de ruedas.

when [wen] *adv* 1 (direct questions) cuándo: *when did it happen?* ¿cuándo pasó? 2 (indirect questions) cuándo: *tell me when you're ready* dime cuándo estés listo. 3 (at which, on which) cuando, en que: *there are times when I can't cope* hay momentos en que no puedo más.

► *conj* 1 (at the time that) cuando: *when I arrived* cuando llegué yo. 2 (whenever) cuando, siempre que: *when I have a free moment* cuando tenga un momento libre. 3 (considering) cuando, si: *why do you want to move?* ¿por qué te quieres mudar? 4 (although) cuando, aunque: *they said it was red when in fact it was blue* dijeron que era roja cuando en realidad era azul.

► *pron* cuando: *that was when it broke* fue entonces cuando se rompió.

whenever [wen'evər] *conj* 1 (at any time, when) cuando quiera que. 2 (every time that) siempre que.

► *adv* (surprise) cuándo.

where [weər] *adv* 1 (direct question - place) dónde; (- direction) adónde: *where is it?* ¿dónde está?. 2 (indirect question) dónde, adónde: *tell me where it is* dime dónde está. 3 (at, in or which) donde, en que; (to which) adonde, a donde: *this is where it all happened* es aquí donde pasó todo.

► *conj* 1 donde: *where I come from we don't do that* de donde soy yo eso no se hace. 2 (when) cuando: *where possible* cuando sea posible.

whereabouts [(n) 'weərəbaʊts; (adv) weərə'baʊts] *n* paradero.

► *adv* (por) dónde.

whereas [weər'æz] *conj* 1 mientras que. 2 JUR considerando que.

whereby [weə'baɪ] *adv fml* por el/la/lo cual.

wherein [weə'rɪn] *adv* en donde.

whereupon ['weərəpɒn] *adv* con lo cual.

W

wherever [weər'evəʳ] *conj* **1** *(in any place, where)* dondequiera que. **2** *(everywhere)* dondequiera.

▶ *adv* **1** *(in questions)* dónde, adónde. **2** *(unspecified place)* en cualquier parte.

whether ['weðəʳ] *conj* **1** si. **2** *(no matter if)* aunque.

which [wɪtʃ] *adj* **1** *(direct questions)* qué, cuál, cuáles: *which size?* ¿qué tamaño/talla? **2** *(indirect questions)* qué: *I can't remember which department she's in* no recuerdo en qué sección trabaja.

▶ *pron* **1** *(questions)* cuál, cuáles: *which do you want?* ¿cuál quieres? **2** *(indirect questions)* cuál: *ask him which is his* pregúntale cuál es el suyo. **3** *(defining relative)* que; *(with preposition)* que, el/la que, el/la cual, los/las que, los/las cuales: *the shoes which I bought* los zapatos que compré. **4** *(non-defining relative)* el/la cual, los/las cuales: *two glasses, one of which was dirty* dos copas, una de las cuales estaba sucia. **5** *(referring to a clause)* lo que, lo cual: *he lost, which was sad* perdió, lo cual era triste.

whichever [wɪtʃ'evəʳ] *adj* **1** *(any one)* cualquier, el/la que. **2** *(no matter which)* cualquiera que, no importa. **3** *(interrogative)* cuál.

▶ *pron* **1** cualquiera, el/la que. **2** *(interrogative)* cuál.

while [waɪl] *n* *(time)* rato, tiempo: *we talked for a while* charlamos durante un rato.

▶ *conj* **1** *(when)* mientras: *somebody stole our car while we were on holiday* nos robaron el coche mientras estábamos de vacaciones. **2** *(although)* aunque: *while I sympathize with the cause, I cannot support your methods* aunque simpatizo con la causa, no puedo apoyar tus métodos. **3** *(whereas)* mientras que: *he prefers to go out, while I like staying in* él prefiere salir mientras que a mí me gusta quedarme en casa.

whim [wɪm] *n* antojo, capricho.

whimsical ['wɪmsɪkəl] *adj* *(person, idea, etc)* caprichoso,-a; *(smile)* enigmático,-a; *(story, etc)* fantástico,-a.

whip [wɪp] *n* **1** *(for animals)* látigo; *(for punishment)* azote *m*; *(for riding)* fusta. **2** CULIN *(desert)* batido.

▶ *vt* **1** *(person)* azotar; *(horse)* fustigar. **2** *(wind)* azotar. **3** CULIN *(ingredients)* batir; *(cream, egg whites)* montar. **4** GB *fam* *(steal)* birlar, mangar. **5** *(act quickly)* hacer algo deprisa.

ⓘ *pt & pp* whipped, *ger* whipping.

whipping ['wɪpɪŋ] *n* azotaina, paliza. COMP **whipping cream** nata para montar.

whirl [wɜːl] *n* **1** *(movement)* giro, vuelta. **2** *fig* torbellino.

▶ *vi* **1** *(move round)* girar, dar vueltas; *(of dust, leaves, etc)* arremolinarse. **2** *(move quickly)* ir como un relámpago.

whisk [wɪsk] *n* **1** *(quick movement)* movimiento brusco, sacudida. **2** CULIN *(hand)* batidor *m*; *(electric)* batidora.

▶ *vt* **1** *(of animal's tail)* sacudir (la cola). **2** CULIN batir. **3** *(take quickly)* llevar rápidamente.

whisker ['wɪskəʳ] *n* *(single hair)* pelo (de la barba).

▶ *n pl* whiskers *(man's)* patillas *fpl.* *(of cat, etc)* bigote *m*, bigotes *mpl*.

whiskey ['wɪskɪ] *n* → whisky.

whisky ['wɪskɪ] *n* whisky *m*.

ⓘ *pl* whiskies.

whisper ['wɪspəʳ] *n* **1** *(quiet voice)* susurro. **2** *(rumour)* rumor *m*, voz *f*.

▶ *vt* **1** *(gen)* susurrar, decir en voz baja. **2** *(rumour)* correr la voz, rumorearse.

whispering ['wɪspərɪŋ] *n* *(gen)* cuchicheo; *(of leaves)* murmullo.

whistle ['wɪsəl] *n* **1** *(instrument)* silbato, pito. **2** *(noise)* silbido, pitido; *(of train)* pitido; *(of wind)* silbido.

▶ *vt* *(tune)* silbar.

▶ *vi* *(person, kettle, wind)* silbar; *(referee, police, train)* pitar.

white [waɪt] *adj* **1** blanco,-a. **2** *(pale)* pálido,-a.

▶ *n* **1** blanco, color *m* blanco. **2** *(person)* blanco,-a. **3** *(of egg)* clara. **4** *(of eye)* blanco. COMP **white (blood) cell** glóbulo blanco. ▌**the White House** la Casa Blanca.

▶ *n pl* **whites** *(linen)* ropa *f sing* blanca; *(for tennis)* ropa *f sing* de jugar al tenis.

⊕ La **White House** es la residencia oficial del presidente de Estados Unidos y se usa como sinónimo del gobierno de este país.

white-collar [waɪtˈkɒləʳ] *adj* administrativo,-a; oficinista *mf*.

whiten [ˈwaɪtⁿn] *vt* blanquear, emblanquecer.

◆ **to whittle away** *vt sep* mermar, ir reduciendo, ir disminuyendo.

◆ **to whittle down** *vt sep* reducir.

whiz [wɪz] *n* → **whizz**.

whizz [wɪz] *n (sound)* zumbido, silbido.

▶ *vi* **1** *(make sound)* zumbar, silbar. **2** *(car, bullet)* pasar zumbando, pasar silbando; *(time)* pasar volando.

who [huː] *pron* **1** *(direct questions)* quién, quiénes: *who is it?* ¿quién es? **2** *(indirect questions)* quién, quiénes: *I don't know who they are* no sé quiénes son. **3** *(defining relative)* que: *you're the only one who can help me* eres el único que puede ayudarme. **4** *(non-defining relative)* que, quien, quienes, el/la cual, los/las cuales: *the workers, who were on strike,...* los trabajadores, los cuales estaban en huelga,…

whoever [huːˈevəʳ] *pron* **1** *(the person who)* quien, quienquiera que, el que. **2** *(no matter who)* quienquiera que, cualquiera que. **3** *(questions, exclamations)* quién?

whole [həʊl] *adj* **1** *(entire, all (the), the full amount of)* entero,-a, íntegro,-a, todo,-a. **2** *(intact, not broken)* intacto,-a, sano,-a; *(in one piece, complete)* entero, -a. COMP **whole number** número entero.

▶ *n* conjunto, todo. LOC **as a whole** en conjunto, en su totalidad. ❚ **on the whole** en general.

wholemeal [ˈhəʊlmiːl] *adj* integral.

wholesale [ˈhəʊlseɪl] *adj* **1** COMM al por mayor. **2** *(complete, indiscriminate)* total, general, masivo,-a, sistemático,-a, absoluto,-a, indiscriminado,-a.

▶ *adv* **1** COMM al por mayor. **2** *(on a large scale)* de modo general, en su totalidad, en masa, de manera sistemática.

▶ *n* COMM venta al por mayor.

whom [huːm] *pron* **1** *fml (direct questions)* a quién/quiénes: *to whom should I address it?* ¿a quién debería ir dirigido? **2** *fml (relative - defining)* que, quien, quienes; *(- after preposition)* quien, quienes, el cual, la cual, los cuales, las cuales: *pupils whom I have taught* alumnos a quienes he dado clase. **3** *(relative - non-defining)* quien, quienes, el cual, la cual, los cuales, las cuales: *our guest, of whom you must all have heard,...* nuestro invitado, de quien todos deben haber oído hablar,…

whopper [ˈwɒpəʳ] *n* **1** *fam (large thing)* cosa enorme, cosa descomunal. **2** *fam (lie)* trola, bola.

whose [huːz] *pron* **1** *(direct questions)* de quién/quiénes: *whose is this?* ¿de quién es esto? **2** *(indirect questions)* de quién/quiénes: *I don't know whose it is* no sé de quién es.

▶ *adj* **1** *(direct questions)* de quién/quiénes: *whose dog is this?* de quién es este perro? **2** *(indirect questions)* de quién/quiénes: *I wonder whose books these are* me pregunto de quién serán estos libros. **3** *(relative)* cuyo,-a, cuyos,-as: *the woman whose car was stolen* la mujer cuyo coche fue robado.

why [waɪ] *adv* **1** *(direct questions - for what reason)* por qué; *(- for what purpose)* para qué: *why didn't you go?* ¿por qué no fuiste? **2** *(indirect questions - for what reason)* por qué; *(- for what purpose)* para qué: *I asked him why he did it* le pregunté por qué lo hizo. **3** *(relative)* por eso: *that is why he left* por eso se fue. COMP **why not?** ¿por qué no?

▶ *interj* ¡vaya!, ¡anda!, ¡toma!

▶ *n* porqué *m*.

wick [wɪk] *n* mecha.

wicked [ˈwɪkɪd] *adj* **1** *(evil - person)* malvado,-a, malo,-a; *(- action)* malo,-a,

W

perverso,-a, inicuo,-a. **2** *(harmful)* peligroso,-a, dañino,-a, nocivo,-a. **3** *(mischievous)* travieso,-a, pícaro,-a. **4** *fam fig (very bad - gen)* malísimo,-a; *(-weather)* feo,-a, horrible; *(- temper, price)* terrible; *(- waste)* vergonzoso,-a; *(humour)* cruel.
▶ *n pl* **the wicked** los malos.

wicker [ˈwɪkəʳ] *n* mimbre *m*.
▶ *adj* de mimbre.

wide [waɪd] *adj* **1** *(broad)* ancho,-a; *(space, hole, gap)* grande. **2** *(having specified width)* de ancho. **3** *(large - area)* amplio,-a, extenso,-a; *(- knowledge, experience, repercussions)* amplio,-a; *(- coverage, range, support)* extenso,-a. **4** *(eyes, smile)* abierto,-a. **5** *(off target)* desviado,-a.
▶ *adv* **1** *(fully - gen)* completamente. **2** *(off target)* desviado.

wide-angle [ˈwaɪdæŋgəl] *adj* amplio,-a. COMP **wide-angle lens** objetivo gran angular.

widely [ˈwaɪdlɪ] *adv* **1** *(over wide area or range of things)* extensamente; *(generally)* generalmente. **2** *(to a large degree)* mucho.

widen [ˈwaɪdən] *vt* **1** *(road, etc)* ensanchar. **2** *fig (knowledge, etc)* ampliar, extender.
▶ *vi* **1** *(road, etc)* ensancharse; *(eyes)* abrirse. **2** *(project, etc)* extenderse; *(difference, gap)* aumentar.

widescreen [ˈwaɪdskriːn] *adj* TV pantalla panorámica.

widespread [ˈwaɪdspred] *adj (concern, confusion, unrest, use, belief)* generalizado,-a; *(damage, disease, news)* extenso,-a, extendido,-a. LOC **to become widespread 1** *(gen)* generalizarse. **2** *(illness, news)* extenderse, difundirse.

widow [ˈwɪdəʊ] *n* viuda.

widower [ˈwɪdəʊəʳ] *n* viudo.

width [wɪdθ] *n* **1** *(gen)* anchura. **2** *(of material)* ancho. **3** *(of swimming pool)* ancho.

wield [wiːld] *vt* **1** *(weapon, tool, etc)* empuñar, blandir, manejar. **2** *fig (power, control, etc)* ejercer.

wife [waɪf] *n* esposa, mujer *f*.
ⓘ *pl* **wives**.

wig [wɪg] *n* **1** *(gen)* peluca. **2** JUR peluquín *m*.

wild [waɪld] *adj* **1** *(gen)* salvaje. **2** *(plant, flower)* silvestre; *(vegetation)* salvaje. **3** *(country, landscape)* agreste. **4** *(weather - wind)* borrascoso,-a; *(- sea)* bravo,-a; *(- night)* tempestuoso,-a. **5** *(very excited - person)* loco,-a *(with, de)*, alocado,-a. **6** *(showing lack of thought - thoughts, talk)* disparatado,-a; *(- guess)* al azar; *(- idea, scheme)* descabellado,-a. **7** *fam (fantastic, crazy)* bárbaro,-a, salvaje. LOC **wild boar** jabalí *m*.
▶ *n* **the wild** estado salvaje, estado natural, naturaleza.

wildcat [ˈwaɪldkæt] *n* gato,-a montés. COMP **wildcat strike** huelga espontánea.

wildebeest [ˈwɪldəbiːst] *n* ñu *m*.

wildlife [ˈwaɪldlaɪf] *n* fauna. COMP **wildlife park** reserva natural.

will¹ [wɪl] *n* **1** *(control, volition)* voluntad *f*; *(free will)* albedrío. **2** JUR testamento, últimas *fpl* voluntades. LOC **against one's will** contra su voluntad. COMP **last will and testament** última voluntad *f*.
▶ *vt* **1** *(make or intend to happen by power of mind)* desear, querer. **2** *fml (intend, desire)* querer, ordenar, mandar. **3** JUR legar, dejar en testamento.

will² [wɪl] *aux* **1** *(future)*: *she will be here tomorrow* estará aquí mañana. **2** *(be disposed to, be willing to)*: *(no), I won't* no quiero. **3** *(requests)* querer: *will you do me a favour?* ¿quieres hacerme un favor? **4** *(general truths, custom)*: *accidents will happen* siempre habrá accidentes. **5** *(orders, commands)*: *will you be quiet!* ¡quieres callarte! **6** *(insistence, persistence)* insistir en: *she will play her music at full volume* insiste en poner la música a tope. **7** *(can, possibility)* poder: *this phone will accept credit cards* este teléfono va con tarjetas de crédito. **8** *(supposition, must, probability)* deber de: *that'll be John* será John, debe de ser John.

willing [ˈwɪlɪŋ] *adj* **1** *(without being forced)* complaciente, de gran voluntad, dispuesto,-a; *(eager)* entusiasta. **2**

(ready, prepared, disposed) dispuesto,-a **(to, a). 3** *(given/done gladly)* voluntario, -a. COMP **to show willing** dar pruebas de buena voluntad.

willingly ['wɪlɪŋlɪ] *adv* de buena gana, de buen grado.

willow ['wɪləʊ] *n* sauce *m*.

willpower ['wɪlpaʊəʳ] *n* (fuerza de) voluntad *f*.

wilt [wɪlt] *vt* marchitar, secar.
  ▶ *vi* **1** *(plant)* marchitarse, secarse. **2** *(person - become weak or tired)* debilitarse, decaer, languidecer; *(- lose confidence)* desanimarse.

wimp [wɪmp] *n fam pej* debilucho,-a, esmirriado,-a, canijo,-a.

win [wɪn] *n* victoria,
  ▶ *vt* **1** *(gen)* ganar; *(victory)* conseguir, ganar. **2** *(prize, cup, etc)* ganar, llevarse. **3** *(gain, obtain, achieve - gen)* conseguir, obtener, ganar; *(- friendship, respect)* granjearse; *(- sympathy, affection)* ganarse, granjearse; *(- support)* atraer, captar; *(- heart, love)* conquistar.
  ▶ *vi* ganar.
  ① *pt & pp* won, *ger* winning.

wind¹ [wɪnd] *n* **1** METEOR viento, aire *m*. **2** *(breath)* aliento. **3** *(flatulence)* gases *mpl*, flato; *(air)* gases *mpl* del estómago. **4** *pej (talk)* palabrería.
  ▶ *adj* MUS de viento. COMP **wind instrument** instrumento de viento.
  ▶ *vt* **1** dejar sin aliento, cortar la respiración. **2** *(baby)* hacer eructar.

wind² [waɪnd] *vt* **1** *(handle)* dar vueltas a, girar. **2** *(on reel)* arrollar, devanar. **3** *(tape, film)* bobinar. **4** *(clock)* dar cuerda a **(up, -). 5** *(bandage, scarf)* envolver; *(wool)* ovillar.
  ▶ *vi (road, river)* serpentear, zigzaguear; *(staircase)* formar una espiral.
  ① *pt & pp* wound [waʊnd].
  ▶ *n (bend)* curva, recodo, vuelta.

windlass ['wɪndləs] *n* torno.

windmill ['wɪndmɪl] *n* molino de viento.

window ['wɪndəʊ] *n* **1** *(gen)* ventana. **2** *(in vehicle, bank, theatre, etc)* ventanilla. **3** *(of shop)* escaparate *m*. **4** *(glass)* cristal *m*. **5** COMPUT ventana.

window-dressing ['wɪndəʊdresɪŋ] *n* **1** decoración *f* de escaparates, escaparatismo. **2** *fig* fachada, apariencias *fpl*.

windowpane ['wɪndəʊpeɪn] *n* cristal *m*.

windpipe ['wɪndpaɪp] *n* tráquea.

windscreen ['wɪndskriːn] *n* AUTO parabrisas *m inv*. COMP **windscreen wiper** limpiaparabrisas *m*.

windshield ['wɪndʃiːld] *n* US→ **windscreen**.

windsurf ['wɪndsɜːf] *vi* hacer windsurfing.

windsurfing ['wɪndsɜːfɪŋ] *n* windsurf *m*.

windy ['wɪndɪ] *adj* **1** *(day, weather)* ventoso,-a; *(place)* expuesto,-a al viento. **2** *(speech)* rimbombante.
  ① *comp* windier, *superl* windiest.

wine [waɪn] *n* **1** vino: *red/rosé/white wine* vino tinto/rosado/blanco. **2** *(colour)* (color *m*) morado, granate *m*.
  COMP **wine cellar** bodega. ❙ **wine grower** vinicultor,-ra. ❙ **wine taster** catavinos *mf*.

winery ['waɪnərɪ] *n* bodega.
  ① *pl* wineries.

wineskin ['waɪnskɪn] *n* odre *m*, bota.

wing [wɪŋ] *n* **1** *(gen)* ala. **2** AUTO aleta. **3** SP *(side)* banda; *(player)* extremo,-a.
  ▶ *vi* volar.
  ▶ *n pl* **wings** THEAT bastidores *mpl*.

winged [wɪŋd] *adj* alado,-a, con alas.

winger ['wɪŋəʳ] *n* SP extremo,-a.

wingspan ['wɪŋspæn] *n* envergadura.

wink [wɪŋk] *n* guiño.
  ▶ *vi* **1** *(person)* guiñar el ojo. **2** *(of light, star)* titilear, parpadear..
  ◆ **to wink at** *vt insep (pretend not to notice)* hacer la vista gorda.

winker ['wɪŋkəʳ] *n GB (indicator)* intermitente *m*.

winkle ['wɪŋkəl] *n* bígaro, bigarro.

winner ['wɪnəʳ] *n* **1** ganador,-ra, vencedor,-ra. **2** *fam (idea, etc)* éxito.

winning ['wɪnɪŋ] *adj* **1** *(person, team, etc)* ganador,-ra. **2** *(ticket, number, etc)* premiado,-a. **3** *(stroke, goal)* decisivo,-a. **4** *(smile, ways)* atractivo,-a, encantador,-ra.
  ▶ *n pl* **winnings** ganancias *fpl*.

W

winter ['wɪntər] *n* invierno.
▶ *vi fml* invernar, pasar el invierno.
COMP **winter solstice** solsticio de invierno.

wipe [waɪp] *vt (clean)* limpiar; *(dry)* enjugar.
▶ *vi (dishes)* enjugar.
▶ *n* **1** *(clean)* lavado, fregado. **2** *(cloth)* paño, trapo.
◆ **to wipe out** *vt sep* **1** *(destroy - army)* aniquilar; *(- population, species)* exterminar. **2** *(clean inside)* limpiar el interior de. **3** *(cancel - debts)* saldar, liquidar, cancelar; *(- profit)* borrar, anular.

wiper ['waɪpər] *n* AUTO limpiaparabrisas *m inv*.

wire ['waɪər] *n* **1** *(metal)* alambre *m*. **2** ELEC cable *m*, hilo. **3** *(fence)* alambrada, valla. **4** US telegrama *m*. COMP **wire cutters** cortaalambres *m inv*.
▶ *vt* **1** *(fasten, join)* atar con alambre. **2** *(house)* hacer la instalación eléctrica de; *(equipment, appliance)* conectar (a la toma eléctrica). **3** US *(telegram)* enviar un telegrama a; *(money)* mandar un giro telegráfico a.

wired ['waɪəd] *adj* conectado,-a.

wireless ['waɪələs] *n* **1** *(set)* radio *f*. **2** *(system)* radiofonía. COMP **wireless operator** radiotelegrafista *mf*.

wiring ['waɪrɪŋ] *n* cableado.

wisdom ['wɪzdəm] *n* **1** *(knowledge)* sabiduría, saber *m*. **2** *(good sense - of person)* cordura, (buen) juicio, tino; *(- of action)* prudencia, sabiduría, sensatez *f*. COMP **wisdom tooth** muela del juicio.

wise [waɪz] *adj* **1** *(learned, knowledgeable)* sabio,-a. **2** *(sensible, prudent - person)* prudente, sensato,-a; *(- action, remark)* prudente; *(- advice)* sabio,-a; *(- decision, choice, move)* atinado,-a, acertado,-a. COMP **the Three Wise Men** los Reyes Magos. ‖ **wise guy** sabelotodo.

✎ Consulta **three**.

◆ **to wise up** *vi (realize, become aware)* darse cuenta; *(become informed)* enterarse; *(wake up)* espabilarse.

wish [wɪʃ] *vt* **1** *(want)* querer, desear. **2** *fml (demand, want)* querer. **3** *(hope)* desear.
▶ *vi* **1** desear (for, -). **2** *fml (want)* querer.
▶ *n* deseo.
▶ *n pl* **wishes** *(greeting)* deseos *mpl*; *(in letter)* saludos *mpl*, recuerdos *mpl*.
◆ **to wish on** *vt sep*: *I wouldn't wish that on anyone* eso no se lo desearía a nadie.

wishful ['wɪʃful] *adj fml* de ensueño. COMP **wishful thinking** ilusiones *fpl*.

wisp [wɪsp] *n* **1** *(of grass, straw, etc)* brizna; *(of hair, wool, etc)* mechón *m*; *(of smoke, cloud)* voluta. **2** *(person)* persona menuda.

wistful ['wɪstful] *adj* pensativo,-a, nostálgico,-a, melancólico,-a.

wit [wɪt] *n* **1** *(clever humour)* agudeza, ingenio. **2** *(intelligence)* inteligencia. **3** *(person)* persona salada, chistoso,-a.

witch [wɪtʃ] *n* bruja. COMP **witch doctor** hechicero.
ⓘ *pl* **witches**.

witchcraft ['wɪtʃkrɑːft] *n* brujería.

witch-hunt ['wɪtʃhʌnt] *n* caza de brujas.

with [wɪð, wɪθ] *prep* **1** *(accompanying)* con: *come with me* ven conmigo. **2** *(having, possessing)* con, de; *(including, and also)* con, incluido: *the man with the beard* el hombre de la barba. **3** *(using, by means of)* con: *cut it with a knife* córtalo con un cuchillo. **4** *(cover, fill, contain)* de: *you fill it with water* lo llenas de agua. **5** *(agreeing, in support of)* con: *we're with you all the way!* ¡estamos contigo hasta el final! **6** *(against)* con: *I've had a row with Daniel* he discutido con Daniel. **7** *(because of, on account of)* de: *trembling with fear* temblando de miedo. **8** *(indicating manner)* con: *with pleasure* con mucho gusto. **9** *(in same direction as)* con: *with the flow* con la corriente. **10** *(at the same time and rate as)* con: *wine improves with age* el vino mejora con los años. **11** *(regarding, concerning)* con: *this has nothing to do with you* esto no tiene nada que ver contigo. **12** *(in the case of, as regards)* con respecto a, en cuanto a: *with Mrs Smith what happened was that...* en el caso de la Señora Smith lo que pasó fue que… **13** *(as an employee or client of)* en: *she's with the council now* trabaja en el ayuntamiento ahora. **14** *(remaining)*: *with only half an hour to go* cuando tan solo falta media hora. **15** *(despite, in spite of)* con: *with all his faults* con todos sus defectos. **16** *(in comparisons)* con: *if we compare this brand with a cheaper one* si comparamos esta marca con una más barata. **17** *(illness)* con: *he's in bed with flu* está en cama con la gripe. **18** *(according to)* según, de acuerdo con: *prices vary with the seasons* los precios varían según la temporada.

withdraw [wɪðˈdrɔː] *vt* **1** *(take out)* retirar, sacar. **2** *fml (retract, take back - statement)* retractarse de, retirar; *(- offer)* renunciar a; *(- charge, support)* retirar.
ⓘ *pt* withdrew [wɪðˈdruː], *pp* withdrawn [wɪðˈdrɔːn].
▶ *vi (retire, not take part in)* retirarse. `COMP`
to withdraw into oneself retraerse.

withdrawal [wɪðˈdrɔːəl] *n* **1** *(gen)* retirada. **2** *(of words)* retractación *f*. **3** *(psychology, behaviour)* retraimiento. `COMP`
withdrawal symptoms síndrome *m* de abstinencia.

withdrawn [wɪðˈdrɔːn] *pp* → withdraw.

withdrew [wɪðˈdruː] *pt* → withdraw.

wither [ˈwɪðəʳ] *vt* **1** *(plant)* marchitar, secar. **2** *(crush)* fulminar, aplastar, intimidar.
▶ *vi* **1** *(plant)* marchitarse (away, -), secarse (away, -). **2** *fig (hopes, etc)* desvanecerse, menguar.

within [wɪˈðɪn] *prep* **1** *fml (inside)* dentro de. **2** *(inside range or limits of)* al alcance de. **3** *(less than - distance)* a menos de. **4** *(less than - time)* dentro de.
▶ *adv fml* dentro, en el interior.

without [wɪˈðaʊt] *prep* **1** sin. **2** *arch* fuera de.
▶ *adv* **1** fuera. **2** sin.

withstand [wɪðˈstænd] *vt (gen)* resistir; *(pain)* aguantar, soportar.
ⓘ *pt & pp* withstood [wɪðˈstʊd].

withstood [wɪðˈstʊd] *pt & pp* → withstand.

witness [ˈwɪtnəs] *n* **1** *(person)* testigo *mf*. **2** *fml (testimony, evidence)* testimonio.
ⓘ *pl* witnesses.
▶ *vt* **1** *(see)* presenciar, ver. **2** *(document)* firmar como testigo. **3** *(be a sign or proof of)* testimoniar; *(look at the example of)* ver, notar, considerar.
▶ *vi* JUR *fml (give evidence, testify)* atestiguar (to, -), declarar (to, -).

witty [ˈwɪtɪ] *adj (person)* ingenioso,-a, agudo,-a, salado,-a; *(remark)* agudo, -a; *(speech)* gracioso,-a.
ⓘ *comp* wittier, *superl* wittiest.

wives [waɪvz] *n pl* → wife.

we'd [wiːd] *contr* (we had, we would) → have, would.

wizard [ˈwɪzəd] *n* **1** *(male witch)* brujo, hechicero. **2** *(genius)* lince *mf*, genio, experto, -a.

woeful [ˈwəʊfʊl] *adj* **1** *fml (very sad)* afligido,-a, apenado,-a, triste. **2** *(deplorable)* lamentable, deplorable, penoso,-a, malísimo,-a.

woke [wəʊk] *pt* → wake.

woken [ˈwəʊkən] *pp* → have, wake.

wolf [wʊlf] *n* lobo. `COMP` wolf cub lobezno.
ⓘ *pl* wolves.
▶ *vt* [also wolf down] tragarse, zamparse, devorar.

wolfhound [ˈwʊlfhaʊnd] *n* perro lobo.

wolfram [ˈwʊlfrəm] *n* wolframio, volframio, wolfram *m*.

wolves [wʊlvz] *pl* → wolf.

woman [ˈwʊmən] *n* mujer *f*, señora.
ⓘ *pl* women [ˈwɪmɪn].

womb [wuːm] *n* útero, matriz *f*.

women [ˈwɪmɪn] *n pl* → woman.

won [wʌn] *pt & pp* → win.

wonder [ˈwʌndəʳ] *n* **1** *(thing)* maravilla, milagro. **2** *(feeling)* admiración *f*, asombro.
▶ *adj* milagroso,-a.
▶ *vt* **1** *fml (be surprised)* sorprenderse, extrañarse. **2** *(ask oneself)* preguntarse. **3** *(polite request)*: *I wonder if you can help me* a ver si puede ayudarme.

W

► *vi* **1** *(reflect, ponder)* pensar (about, en); *(doubt)* tener dudas. **2** *fml (marvel)* asombrarse, maravillarse, admirarse. `COMP` **I shouldn't wonder if** + *indic* no me extrañaría que + *subj*. **I it's a wonder (that)** + *indic* es un milagro que + *subj*. **I no/little/small wonder (that)** + *indic* no es de extrañar que + *subj*.

wonderful [ˈwʌndəful] *adj* maravilloso,-a, estupendo,-a.

wont [wəunt] *n* costumbre *f*, hábito.

won't [wəunt] *contr* (will not) → **will**.

wood [wud] *n* **1** *(material)* madera. **2** *(for fire)* leña. **3** *(forest)* bosque *m*. **4** SP *(golf)* palo de madera; *(bowling)* bola.
► *n pl* **woods** bosque *m sing*.

wooden [ˈwudən] *adj* **1** de madera. **2** *fig (expression, style)* rígido,-a; *(movement)* tieso,-a; *(acting)* sin expresión.

woodland [ˈwudlənd] *n* bosque *m*, arbolado, monte *m*.

woodpecker [ˈwudpekəʳ] *n* pico, pájaro carpintero.

woodwork [ˈwudwɜːk] *n* **1** *(craft)* carpintería. **2** *(of building)* maderaje *m*, maderamen *m*.

woodworm [ˈwudwɜːm] *n* carcoma: *it has woodworm* está carcomido,-a.

woody [ˈwudɪ] *adj* **1** *(wooded)* arbolado,-a. **2** *(like wood)* leñoso,-a.
ⓘ *comp* **woodier**, *superl* **woodiest**.

wool [wul] *n* lana.
► *adj* **1** *(made of wool)* de lana. **2** COMM lanero,-a.

woolen [ˈwulən] *adj-n* US → **woollen**.

woollen [ˈwulən] *adj* **1** *(made of wool)* de lana. **2** COMM lanero,-a.
► *n pl* **woollens** géneros *mpl* de lana.

word [wɜːd] *n* **1** *(gen)* palabra: *tell me what happened in your own words* explícame con tus propias palabras lo que pasó. **2** *(message, news)* noticia: *word came that...* llegó noticia (de) que... **3** *(promise)* palabra: *I give you my word* te doy mi palabra. **4** *(command)* orden *f*: *wait until I give the word* espera hasta que dé la orden. **5** LING palabra, vocablo, voz *f*. **6 the word** *(rumour)* voz *f*, rumor *m*: *the word is that Macy is pregnant* corre la voz de que Macy

está embarazada. `LOC` **in a word** en una palabra. **I in other words** o sea, es decir. **I not in so many words** no exactamente. **I to keep one's word** cumplir su palabra. **I to put sth into words** expresar ALGO con palabras. **I word for word** palabra por palabra. `COMP` **a word of advice** un consejo. **I a word of warning** una advertencia. **I word processor** procesador *m* de textos.
► *n pl* **words** *(lyrics)* letra *f sing*. *(discussion, talk)* palabras *fpl*.
► *vt* expresar, formular, redactar: *a well-worded letter* una carta bien redactada.

wording [ˈwɜːdɪŋ] *n* redacción *f*, expresión *f*, palabras *fpl*, términos *mpl*.

wore [wɔːʳ] *pt* → **wear**.

work [wɜːk] *n* **1** *(gen)* trabajo. **2** *(employment)* empleo, trabajo. **3** *(building work, roadworks)* obras *fpl*. **4** *(product, results)* trabajo, obra. **5** *(literary, etc)* obra.
► *vt* **1** *(person)* hacer trabajar. **2** *(machine)* manejar; *(mechanism)* accionar. **3** *(mine, oil well)* explotar; *(land, fields)* trabajar, cultivar. **4** *(produce)* hacer. **5** *(wood, metal, clay)* trabajar; *(dough)* amasar. **6** *(make by work or effort)* trabajar. **7** *fam (arrange)* arreglar. **8** *(move gradually)*: *work the butter into the flour* vaya mezclando la mantequilla con la harina. `COMP` **to be in work** tener trabajo. **I to be out of work** estar en el paro. **I to get down/set to work** ponerse a trabajar. **I to get worked up** exaltarse.
► *vi* **1** *(gen)* trabajar. **2** *(machine, system)* funcionar. **3** *(medicine, cleaner)* surtir efecto; *(plan)* tener éxito. **4** *(move)*: *they eventually worked round to my way of thinking* finalmente coincidieron con mi parecer.
► *n pl* **works** *(factory)* fábrica *f sing*.
◆ **to work out** *vt sep* **1** *(calculation, sum)* calcular, hacer. **2** *(plan, scheme)* planear, elaborar, pensar; *(itinerary)* planear; *(details, idea)* desarrollar. **3** *(problem)* solucionar, resolver; *(solution)* encontrar. **4** *(person)* calar, entender.
► *vi* **1** *(calculation)* salir (at, por), resultar. **2** *(turn out well - things)* salir bien;

(- problem) resolverse. **3** SP hacer ejercicio.

workaholic [wɜ:kə'hɒlɪk] *n fam* adicto,-a al trabajo.

workbench ['wɜ:kbentʃ] *n* banco de trabajo.

workbook ['wɜ:kbʊk] *n* cuaderno, libreta de ejercicios.

workday ['wɜ:kdeɪ] *n* US día *m* laborable.

worker ['wɜ:kə'] *n (gen)* trabajador,-ra; *(manual)* obrero,-a, operario,-a; *(office)* oficinista *mf*, administrativo,-a. COMP **worker bee** abeja obrera.

workforce ['wɜ:kfɔ:s] *n (of company, factory, etc)* personal *m*, plantilla; *(of country)* población *f* activa.

working ['wɜ:kɪŋ] *adj* **1** *(clothes, conditions, surface)* de trabajo; *(week, day, life)* laborable. **2** *(population, partner, etc)* activo,-a; *(person, mother)* que trabaja. COMP **the working class** la clase trabajadora.
▶ *n (machine, model)* que funciona; *(part)* móvil.
▶ *adj* **1** *(majority)* suficiente. **2** *(hypothesis, etc)* de trabajo.
▶ *n (of machine)* funcionamiento; *(of pit)* explotación *f*.
▶ *n pl* **workings** *(of mine, quarry)* pozos *mpl*. *(mechanics)* funcionamiento.

working-class [wɜ:kɪŋ'klɑ:s] *adj (person)* de clase obrera, de clase trabajadora; *(area)* obrero,-a.

workman ['wɜ:kmən] *n (gen)* trabajador *m*; *(manual)* obrero, operario.
ⓘ *pl* **workmen** ['wɜ:kmən].

workmate ['wɜ:kmeɪt] *n* compañero, -a de trabajo.

workplace ['wɜ:kpleɪs] *n* lugar *m* de trabajo.

workshop ['wɜ:kʃɒp] *n* taller *m*.

worktop ['wɜ:ktɒp] *n* encimera.

world [wɜ:ld] *n* **1** *(earth)* mundo: *I'd love to travel round the world* me encantaría dar la vuelta al mundo. **2** *(sphere)* mundo: *the world of show business* el mundo del espectáculo. **3** *(life)* mundo, vida: *in this world* en esta vida. **4** *(people)* mundo: *in the eyes of the world* a los ojos del mundo. **5** *(large amount, large number)*: *this will make a world of difference to the disabled* esto cambiará totalmente la vida de los minusválidos. LOC **out of this world** fenomenal.
▶ *adj (population, peace)* mundial; *(politics, trade)* internacional: *world record* récord mundial; *world power* potencia mundial. COMP **World Bank** Banco Mundial. **I world champion** campeón,-ona mundial. **I World Cup** el Mundial, los Mundiales. **I world fair** exposición *f* internacional. **I world music** música étnica. **I World Wusic** guerra mundial.

worldwide ['wɜ:ldwaɪd] *adj* mundial, universal.
▶ *adv* mundialmente.

worm [wɜ:m] *n* **1** *(grub, maggot)* gusano; *(earthworm)* lombriz *f*. **2** *pej (person)* gusano, canalla. **3** TECH *(of screw)* tornillo.
▶ *vt* **1** *(make one's way)* deslizarse; *(insinuate)* insinuarse (into, en). **2** MED quitar las lombrices a, desparasitar.
▶ *n pl* **worms** MED lombrices *fpl*.

worn [wɔ:n] *pp* → **wear**.

worn-out ['wɔ:naʊt] [se escribe worn out cuando no se usa para calificar a un nombre] *adj* **1** *(thing)* gastado,-a, estropeado,-a. **2** *(person)* rendido,-a, agotado,-a.

worried ['wʌrɪd] *adj (person)* inquieto,-a, preocupado,-a (about, por); *(look, voice)* de preocupación.

worry ['wʌrɪ] *n (state, feeling)* preocupación *f*, inquietud *f*, intranquilidad *f*; *(problem)* preocupación *f*, problema *m*; *(responsibility)* responsabilidad *f*.
ⓘ *pl* **worries**.
▶ *vt* **1** inquietar, preocupar. **2** *(annoy, disturb)* molestar. **3** *(of dog)* acosar, perseguir.
▶ *vi* inquietarse, preocuparse (about/ over, por).
ⓘ *pt & pp* **worried**, *ger* **worrying**.

worrying ['wʌriɪŋ] *adj* inquietante, preocupante, desconcertante.

W

worse [wɜːs] *adj (comp of* **bad**) peor.
▶ *adv (comp of badly)* peor; *(more intensely)* más. ⌐LOC¬ **to be worse off 1** *(financially)* andar peor de dinero. **2** *(physically)* estar peor. ▌ **to get worse** empeorar. ▌ **to get worse and worse** ir de mal en peor. ▌ **to go from bad to worse** ir de mal en peor. ▌ **to make matters worse** por si fuera poco. ▌ **worse still** lo que es peor.
▶ *n* lo peor.

worsen [ˈwɜːsən] *vt* empeorar.
▶ *vi* empeorarse.

worship [ˈwɜːʃɪp] *n* **1** REL adoración *f*, veneración *f*, culto; *(service)* culto, oficio. **2** *(devotion, love)* amor *m*, culto, idolatría.
▶ *vt* **1** REL adorar, venerar. **2** *(idolize)* rendir culto a, idolatrar.
ⓘ *pt & pp* worshipped*, ger* worshipping.

worst [wɜːst] *adj (superl of* **bad**) peor.
▶ *adv (superl)* peor.
▶ *n (indefinite)* lo peor; *(person)* el/la peor, los/las peores. ⌐LOC¬ **at (the) worst** en el peor de los casos. ▌ **if the worst comes to the worst** si pasa lo peor.

worth [wɜːθ] *n* **1** *(in money)* valor *m*. **2** *(of person)* valía; *(of thing)* valor *m*.
▶ *adj* **1** *(having certain value)* que vale, que tiene un valor de. **2** *(deserving of)* que vale la pena, que merece la pena. ⌐LOC¬ **to get one's money's worth** sacarle jugo al dinero. ▌ **to be worth** SB's **while** valer la pena.

worthless [ˈwɜːθləs] *adj* **1** *(gen)* sin valor. **2** *(useless)* inútil, sin ningún valor. **3** *(person)* despreciable.

worthwhile [wɜːθˈwaɪl] *adj (gen)* que vale la pena, que merece la pena.

worthy [ˈwɜːðɪ] *adj* **1** *(deserving)* digno,-a (of, de), merecedor,-ra (of, de); *(winner, opponent, successor)* digno,-a. **2** *(action, cause)* meritorio,-a, bueno,-a, justo,-a.
ⓘ *comp* worthier*, superl* worthiest.

would [wʊd] *aux* **1** *(conditional)*: *I would love to* me encantaría. **2** *(polite requests)*: *would you be so kind as to close the window?* ¿me haría usted el favor de cerrar la ven-

tana? **3** *(offers, invitations)*: *would you like a drink?* ¿quieres tomar algo? **4** *(willingness)*: *he wouldn't help me* se negó a ayudarme, no quiso ayudarme. **5** *(giving advice)*: *I wouldn't dwell on it* yo que tú no pensaría en ello. **6** *(conjecture)*: *that would have been in 1978* eso debe haber sido en 1978. **7** *(past habit, custom)* soler: *we would often go out together* a menudo salíamos juntos. **8** *(insistence, persistence)*: *you would say that!* ¡es típico de ti decir eso!

wound¹ [wuːnd] *n* herida.
▶ *vt* herir.

wound² [waʊnd] *pt & pp* → **wind²**

wounded [ˈwuːndɪd] *adj* herido,-a.
▶ *n pl* **the wounded** los heridos.

wove [wəʊv] *pt* → **weave**.

woven [ˈwəʊvən] *pp* → **weave**.

wrap [ræp] *vt* **1** *(cover)* envolver. **2** *fig (surround, immerse)* envolver (in, de), rodear (in, de).
◆ **to wrap up** *vi* **1** *(wear warm clothes)* abrigarse. **2** *(shut up)* callarse, cerrar el pico.
▶ *vt sep (complete)* conseguir; *(conclude)* concluir, dar fin a.
ⓘ *pt & pp* wrapped*, ger* wrapping.

wrapper [ˈræpər] *n (of food)* envoltorio, envoltura; *(of book)* sobrecubierta.

wrapping [ˈræpɪŋ] *n* envoltura, envoltorio. ⌐COMP¬ **wrapping paper 1** *(plain)* papel *m* de envolver. **2** *(fancy)* papel *m* de regalo.

wrath [rɒθ] *n* cólera, ira.

wreak [riːk] *vt* causar, provocar, sembrar. ⌐COMP¬ **to wreak damage/havoc on** STH hacer estragos en ALGO.

wreath [riːθ] *n (of flowers)* corona.

wreck [rek] *n* **1** MAR *(action)* naufragio; *(ship)* barco naufragado o hundido. **2** *(of car, plane)* restos *mpl*; *(of building)* ruinas *fpl*, escombros *mpl*. **3** *fig (person)* ruina.
▶ *vt* **1** MAR *(ship)* hacer naufragar. **2** *(car, plane)* destrozar; *(machine)* desbaratar, estropear. **3** *fig (health, career)* arruinar; *(life, marriage)* destrozar; *(hopes)* destruir, echar por tierra; *(plans)* estropear, desbaratar; *(chances)* echar a perder.

wreckage ['rekɪdʒ] n **1** (of vehicle) restos mpl; (of building) ruinas fpl, escombros mpl. **2** fig ruina.

wrecked [rekt] adj **1** MAR (ship) naufragado,-a; (sailor) náufrago,-a. **2** (car, plane) destrozado,-a; (building) destruido,-a.
▶ n fig (life, career, hopes) arruinado,-a, destrozado,-a; (plans) estropeado,-a.
▶ adj fam fig (stoned) ciego,-a, colocado,-a, pasado,-a.

wrench [rentʃ] n **1** (pull) tirón m, arranque m. **2** MED torcedura. **3** fig separación f dolorosa. **4** GB (tool) llave f inglesa. **5** US (tool) llave f.
ⓘ pl wrenches.
▶ vt **1** (pull) arrancar (de un tirón), arrebatar. **2** MED torcer.

wrestle ['res°l] vi **1** (fight) luchar (with, con/contra). **2** fig (problem, conscience) luchar (with, con), lidiar (with, con).
▶ vt luchar contra.
▶ n lucha.

wrestler ['res°lə'] n SP luchador,-ra.

wrestling ['res°lɪŋ] n lucha.

wretch [retʃ] n **1** (unfortunate person) desdichado,-a, infeliz, desgraciado,-a. **2** fam (rascal) pillo,-a, pícaro,-a, granuja mf. **3** (bad person) canalla mf, malvado,-a.

wriggle ['rɪg°l] vi retorcerse, menearse, moverse.
▶ vt menear, mover.
▶ n meneo.

wriggly ['rɪg°lɪ] adj sinuoso,-a.
ⓘ comp wrigglier, superl wriggliest.

wring [rɪŋ] vt **1** (one's hands) torcer, retorcer; (bird's neck) retorcer. **2** (clothes) escurrir (out, -), retorcer (out, -). **3** fig (heart) partir. **4** fig (confession, truth, etc) sonsacar, arrancar, sacar.
ⓘ pt & pp wrung [rʌŋ].
▶ n (of clothes): give it a good wring escúrrelo bien.

wringer ['rɪŋə'] n escurridor m, rodillo.

wrinkle ['rɪŋk°l] n arruga.
▶ vt arrugar.
▶ vi arrugarse.

wrinkled ['rɪŋk°ld] adj arrugado,-a.

wrist [rɪst] n **1** ANAT muñeca. **2** (of clothes) puño.

wristband ['rɪstbænd] n **1** (of clothes) puño. **2** (sweatband) muñequera.

wristwatch ['rɪstwɒtʃ] n reloj m de pulsera.
ⓘ pl wristwatches.

write [raɪt] vt (gen) escribir; (article) redactar; (cheque) extender.
▶ vi (gen) escribir (about, sobre).
◆ to write back vi contestar (por carta).
◆ to write down vt sep (note) anotar, apuntar.
ⓘ pt wrote [rəʊt], pp written ['rɪt°n], ger writing.

writer ['raɪtə'] n **1** (by profession) escritor,-ra; (of book, letter) autor,-ra. **2** (of handwriting): she's a neat writer tiene buena letra.

writhe [raɪð] vi (physically) retorcerse, contorsionarse.

writing ['raɪtɪŋ] n **1** (script) escritura; (handwriting) letra. **2** (written work) composición f, trabajo. **3** (occupation) profesión f de escritor,-ra, trabajo literario; (activity) escribir m. ⎣LOC⎤ in writing por escrito. ⎣COMP⎤ writing desk escritorio. ❙ writing materials objetos mpl de escritorio. ❙ writing paper papel m de escribir.
▶ n pl writings obra, escritos mpl.

written ['rɪt°n] pp → write.
▶ adj escrito,-a. ⎣LOC⎤ the written word la palabra escrita. ⎣COMP⎤ written consent consentimiento por escrito. ❙ written exam examen m escrito.

wrong [rɒŋ] adj **1** (erroneous) erróneo,-a, equivocado,-a, incorrecto,-a: a wrong answer una respuesta incorrecta. **2** (mistaken) equivocado,-a: we proved him wrong demostramos que estaba equivocado. **3** (evil, immoral) malo,-a; (unacceptable, unfair) injusto,-a: stealing is wrong robar es malo. **4** (amiss) mal: is anything wrong? ¿pasa algo? **5** (unsuitable) inadecuado,-a, impropio,-a; (time) inoportuno,-a: she's the wrong person for the job no es la persona adecuada para el puesto, I think I said the wrong thing creo que

W

he dicho algo que no debía; *he was in the wrong place at the wrong time* estaba en el sitio equivocado en el momento inoportuno. LOC **to be in the wrong 1** *(mistaken)* estar equivocado,-a. **2** *(at fault)* tener la culpa. ▌**to be wrong** *(person)* estar equivocado,-a, no tener razón, equivocarse. ▌**to have/get the wrong number** *(tel)* confundirse de número, equivocarse de número. ▌**to get sb wrong** malinterpretar a ALGN. ▌**to get sth wrong** equivocarse, no acertar. ▌**to go wrong 1** *(things in general)* salir mal. **2** *(make a mistake)* equivocarse. **3** *(go wrong way)* equivo-

carse de camino. *(machine, device)* romperse, estropearse. *(plan)* fallar, fracasar. ▌**wrong side out** al revés. ▌**you can't go wrong** *(giving directions)* no tiene pérdida.
▸ *adv* mal, incorrectamente, equivocadamente.
▸ *n* **1** *(evil, bad action)* mal *m*. **2** *(injustice)* injusticia; *(offence)* agravio.
▸ *vt (treat unfairly)* ser injusto,-a con; *(judge unfairly)* juzgar mal; *(offend)* agraviar.

wrote [rəʊt] *pt* → write.

wrung [rʌŋ] *pt & pp* → wring.

wry [raɪ] *adj* irónico,-a, sardónico,-a.

X

X, x [eks] *n (the letter)* X, x *f*.
xenon ['zenɒn] *n* xenón *m*.
xenophobia [zenə'fəʊbɪə] *n* xenofobia.
xenophobic [zen'fəʊbɪk] *adj* xenófobo,-a.
xerography [zɪ'rɒgrəfɪ] *n* xerografía.
Xerox® ['zɪərɒks] *n* xerocopia, fotocopia.

▶ *vt* xerocopiar, fotocopiar.
X-ray ['eksreɪ] *n* **1** rayo X. **2** *(photograph)* radiografía.
▶ *vt* radiografiar.
xylene ['zaɪliʌn] *n* xileno.
xylography [zaɪ'lɒgrəfɪ] *n* xilografía.
xylophone ['zaɪləfəʊn] *n* xilófono.

Y, y [waɪ] *n (the letter)* Y, y *f.*

yacht [jɒt] *n* **1** yate *m.* **2** *(with sails)* velero, yate *m.* COMP **yacht club** club *m* náutico. ▮ **yacht race** regata.

yachting [ˈjɒtɪŋ] *n* deporte *m* de la vela, vela.

yak [jæk] *n* yac *m*, yak *m.*

yank [jæŋk] *n fam* tirón *m.*
▶ *vt fam* tirar de.
◆ **to yank out** *vt sep* arrancar, sacar de un tirón.

yard [jɑːd] *n* **1** *(measure)* yarda. **2** GB *(of house)* patio. **3** US *(of house)* jardín *m.* **4** *(industrial)* almacén *m.* **5** *(naut)* verga. COMP **Scotland Yard** *oficina central de la policía británica en Londres.*

✎ Una yarda equivale a 0,914 metros.

yarn [jɑːn] *n* **1** hilo. **2** *(story)* cuento. COMP **to spin a yarn 1** *(story)* contar un cuento. **2** *(lie)* venir con cuentos.

yawn [jɔːn] *vi* **1** bostezar. **2** *(gap, etc)* abrirse.
▶ *n* **1** bostezo. **2** *fam (boring event)* rollo.

year [jɪəʳ] *n* **1** año. **2** EDUC curso. LOC **all the year round** durante todo el año. ▮ **year in, year out** año tras año.

yearbook [ˈjɪəbʊk] *n* anuario.

yearly [ˈjɪəlɪ] *adj* anual.
▶ *adv* anualmente.

yearn [jɜːn] *vi (desire)* anhelar (for, -), ansiar (for, -); *(nostalgically)* añorar. LOC **to yearn to do** STH suspirar por hacer ALGO.

yearning [ˈjɜːnɪŋ] *n (desire)* anhelo (for, de); *(nostalgia)* añoranza (for, de).
▶ *adj* anhelante.

yeast [jiːst] *n* levadura.

yell [jel] *n* grito, alarido.
▶ *vi* gritar, dar alaridos.

yellow [ˈjeləʊ] *adj* **1** amarillo,-a. **2** *(cowardly)* cobarde.
▶ *n* amarillo.
▶ *vt* ponerse amarillo.
▶ *vi* amarillear. COMP **yellow card** *(sp)* tarjeta amarilla. ▮ **yellow fever** fiebre *f* amarilla. ▮ **yellow jersey** *(sp)* maillot *m* amarillo. ▮ **Yellow Pages** páginas amarillas. ▮ **yellow press** prensa sensacionalista.

yelp [jelp] *n* gañido.
▶ *vi* gañir.

Yemen [ˈjemən] *n* Yemen.

Yemeni [ˈjemənɪ] *adj* yemení.
▶ *n* yemení *mf.*

yeoman [ˈjəʊmən] *n* HIST pequeño terrateniente *m.* COMP **yeoman of the guard** alabardero de la Torre de Londres.

yes [jes] *adv* **1** sí. **2** *(answering person)* dime; *(answering phone)* ¿dígame? ▶ *n* sí *m.* LOC **to say yes** decir que sí.

yesterday [ˈjestədɪ] *adv* ayer.
▶ *n* ayer *m.* LOC **the day before yesterday** anteayer.

yesteryear [ˈjestəjɪəʳ] *adv lit* antaño.

yet [jet] *adv* **1** todavía, aún. **2** *(until now)* hasta la fecha, hasta ahora. **3** *(even)* aún, todavía. **4** *(expressing future possibility, hope, etc)* aún: *don't give up, you may win yet* no te rindas, aún puedes ganar. COMP **yet again** otra vez. ▮ **yet another…** otro,-a… más: *yet another gold medal for Broddle* otra medalla de oro más para Broddle.
▶ *conj* pero, aunque: *a cheap yet effective solution to the problem* una solución barata pero efectiva para el problema.

yew [juː] *n* tejo.

yield [jiːld] *n* **1** *(harvest)* cosecha. **2** FIN *(return)* rendimiento, rédito.

▸ *vt* **1** *(produce)* producir, dar. **2** *(give, hand over)* entregar. **3** FIN rendir.

▸ *vi* **1** *(surrender)* rendirse (**to**, ante), ceder (**to**, a). **2** *(break)* ceder. **3** US ceder el paso.

◆ **to yield up** *vt sep (secrets)* revelar.

yoghourt ['jɒgət] *n* → yoghurt.

yoghurt ['jɒgət] *n* yogur *m*. COMP yoghurt maker yogurtera.

yogurt ['jɒgət] *n* → yoghurt.

yoke [jəʊk] *n* **1** *(for carrying, pulling)* yugo. **2** *(pair of oxen)* yunta. **3** SEW canesú *m*.

▸ *vt* **1** *(oxen)* uncir. **2** *fig* unir.

yolk [jəʊk] *n* yema.

you [juː] *pron* **1** *(subject, familiar, singular)* tú: *and what did you say?* y tú, ¿qué dijiste? **2** *(subject, familiar, plural - men)* vosotros; *(- women)* vosotras: *you two, where are you going?* vosotros dos, ¿adónde vais? **3** *(subject, polite, singular)* usted, Vd., Ud.: *you must wait here until the doctor arrives* usted debe esperar aquí hasta que llegue el médico. **4** *(subject, polite, plural)* ustedes, Vds., Uds.: *you must both wait here* ustedes dos deben esperar aquí. **5** *(subject, impersonal)* se, uno: *you can go by coach or train* se puede ir en tren o en autocar. **6** *(object, familiar, singular)* te; *(with prep)* ti; *(if prep is con)* contigo: *I'm going with you* voy contigo. **7** *(object, familiar, plural)* os; *(with preposition)* vosotros,-as: *I'll go with you* iré con vosotros. **8** *(direct object, polite, singular - man)* lo, le; *(- woman)* la; *(with preposition)* usted: *good morning, sir, can I help you?* buenos días, señor, ¿puedo ayudarlo? **9** *(direct object, polite, plural - men)* los; *(- women)* las; *(with preposition)* ustedes: *I wanted to talk to you two ladies* quería hablar con ustedes dos. **10** *(indirect object, polite, singular)* le: *I'll send you a letter* le mandaré una carta. **11** *(indirect object, polite, plural)* les: *I sent both of you a card* les mandé una felicitación a los dos. **12** *(object, impersonal)*: *cyanide kills you* el cianuro mata.

young [jʌŋ] *adj (gen)* joven; *(brother, sister)* menor. LOC **to be young at heart** ser joven de espíritu. COMP **young lady 1** *(woman)* señorita. **2** *(girlfriend)* novia. ❙ **young man 1** *(man)* joven *m*, muchacho. **2** *(boyfriend)* novio. ❙ **young woman** joven *f*, muchacha.

▸ *n* **the young** *(humans)* los jóvenes *mpl*, la juventud *f*, la gente *f* joven; *(animals)* las crías *fpl*.

youngish ['jʌŋɪʃ] *adj* bastante joven, juvenil.

youngster ['jʌŋstər] *n* joven *mf*.

your [jɔːr] *adj* **1** *(familiar, singular)* tu, tus; *(plural)* vuestro,-a, vuestros,-as. **2** *(polite)* su, sus. **3** *fml (address)* Su: *Your Majesty* Su Majestad.

yours [jɔːz] *pron* **1** *(familiar, singular)* (el) tuyo, (la) tuya, (los) tuyos, (las) tuyas; *(plural)* (el) vuestro, (la) vuestra, (los) vuestros, (las) vuestras. **2** *(polite)* (el) suyo, (la) suya, (los) suyos, (las) suyas. **3** *(letters)* le saluda…: *Yours sincerely…* le saluda atentamente…

yourself [jɔːˈself] *pron* **1** *(familiar singular)* te; *(emphatic)* tú mismo,-a. **2** *(polite singular)* se; *(emphatic)* usted mismo,-a.

yourselves [jɔːˈselvz] *pron* **1** *(familiar plural)* os; *(emphatic)* vosotros,-as mismos,-as. **2** *(polite plural)* se; *(emphatic)* ustedes mismos,-as.

youth [juːθ] *n* **1** *(period)* juventud *f*. **2** *(young person)* joven *mf*. **3** *(young people)* juventud *f*, los jóvenes *mpl*. COMP **youth club** club *m* juvenil. ❙ **youth hostel** albergue *m* juvenil.

youthful ['juːθful] *adj* joven, juvenil.

yowl [jaʊl] *n* aullido.

▸ *vi* aullar.

yucca ['jʌkə] *n* yuca.

Yugoslav ['juːgəslɑːv] *n (person)* yugoslavo,-a.

Yugoslavia [juːgəˈslɑːvɪə] *n* Yugoslavia.

Yugoslavian [juːgəˈslɑːvɪən] *adj* yugoslavo,-a.

▸ *n* yugoslavo,-a.

yuppie ['jʌpɪ] *n* yuppie *mf*.

Y

Z

Z, z [zed] *n (the letter)* Z, z *f*.
Zaire [zɑ: 'ɪə] *n* Zaire.
Zairean [zɑ: 'ɪrɪən] *adj* zaireño,-a.
▶ *n* zaireño,-a.
Zambia ['zæmbɪə] *n* Zambia.
Zambian ['zæmbɪən] *adj* zambiano,-a.
▶ *n* zambiano,-a.
zap [zæp] *vt* **1** *fam (kill)* cargarse. **2** *(attack)* atacar.
▶ *vi (hurry)* apresurarse.
ⓘ *pt & pp* zapped, *ger* zapping.
▶ *n* marcha.
zeal [zi: l] *n* celo, entusiasmo.
zebra ['zi: brə, 'zebrə] *n* cebra. COMP zebra crossing paso de peatones, paso de cebra.
zebu ['zi: bu:, 'zi: bju:] *n* cebú *m*.
zed [zed] *n* GB zeta.
zee [zi:] *n* US zeta.
zenith ['zenɪθ] *n* cenit *m*.
zephyr ['zefər] *n* céfiro.
zeppelin ['zepəlɪn] *n* zepelín *m*.
zero ['zɪərəʊ] *n* cero.
ⓘ *pl* zeros o zeroes.
zest [zest] *n* **1** *(eagerness)* brío, entusiasmo. **2** *(spice)* emoción *f*. **3** *(of lemon, etc)* cáscara.
zigzag ['zɪgzæg] *n* zigzag *m*.
▶ *vi* zigzaguear.
ⓘ *pt & pp* zigzagged, *ger* zigzagging.

Zimbabwe [zɪm'bɑ: bweɪ] *n* Zimbabwe.
Zimbabwean [zɪm'bɑ: bwɪən] *adj* zimbabwense, zimbabuo,-a.
▶ *n* zimbabwense *mf*, zimbabuo,-a.
zinc [zɪŋk] *n* cinc *m*, zinc *m*.
zip [zɪp] *n* **1** cremallera. **2** *fam (energy)* vigor *m*, energía. **3** *fam (hiss)* zumbido.
▶ *vt* COMPUT comprimir. COMP zip code US código postal. ❙ zip fastener cremallera.
◆ to zip by *vt insep* pasar como un rayo.
▶ *vi* pasar como un rayo.
◆ to zip past *vt-vi* → zip by.
◆ to zip up *vt sep* cerrar con cremallera.
zipped [zɪpt] *adj* COMPUT comprimido,-a.
zipper ['zɪpər] *n* US cremallera.
zodiac ['zəʊdɪæk] *n* zodiaco, zodíaco.
zombie ['zɒmbɪ] *n* zombi *mf*, zombie *mf*.
zonal ['zəʊnəl] *adj* zonal.
zone [zəʊn] *n* zona.
▶ *vt* dividir en zonas.
zoo [zu:] *n* zoo *m*, parque *m* zoológico, zoológico.
ⓘ *pl* zoos.
zoological [ʒʊə'lɒdʒɪkəl] *adj* zoológico,-a.
zoologist [zʊ'ɒlədʒɪst] *n* zoólogo,-a.
zoology [zʊ'ɒlədʒɪ] *n* zoología.
zucchini [zu: 'ki: nɪ] *n* US calabacín *m*.
ⓘ *pl* zucchini o zucchinis.
zygote ['zaɪgəʊt] *n* cigoto.

LEARNING IN SPANISH

LA COMUNICACIÓN EN CLASE

- ► ¡Buenos días a todos!
- ► ¿Cómo estáis esta mañana?
- ► ¿Qué quiere decir...?
- ► ¿Cómo se pronuncia esta palabra?
- ► ¿Podrías repetir eso, por favor?
- ► ¿Podría hablar más despacio?
- ► Lo siento, no lo entiendo

COMMUNICATION IN CLASS

- ► Good morning everybody!
- ► How are you this morning?
- ► What does... mean?
- ► How do you pronounce this word?
- ► Could you repeat that, please?
- ► Could you speak more slowly?
- ► Sorry, I don't understand

PASANDO LISTA

- ► Voy a pasar lista
- ► ¿Dónde está Pedro? Hoy no ha venido...
- ► Kevin no ha venido porque está enfermo
- ► Marta no está porque ha ido al médico

TAKING THE ROLL

- ► I'm going to take the roll
- ► Where's Peter? –He's not here today...
- ► Kevin isn't here because he's ill
- ► Marta is absent because she's gone to the doctor's

Vocabulario / Vocabulary

lista de alumnos de clase	roll	silla	chair
		limpiar	clean
		borrar	rub off
tiempo climatológico	weather	leer	read
		responder	answer
caliente	hot	repartir	hand out
frío	cold	sacar	take out
estufa	heater	encender	switch on
aparato de aire acondicionado	air conditioner	apagar	switch off
		abrir	open
pizarra	blackboard	cerrar	close

PREGUNTANDO SOBRE COSAS QUE SE HACEN EN CLASE

- ¿Podrías limpiar la pizarra?
- ¿Podrías borrar esas frases?
- Por favor, levantad esas sillas

REQUESTING ACTIONS IN CLASS

- Would you clean the blackboard?
- Could you erase those sentences?
- Please, lift those chairs up

ORGANIZAR LA CLASE

- Sacad los libros de matemáticas, por favor
- ¿Podrías repartir estas hojas, por favor?
- Colocaos en grupos de 2,3,4...
- Voy a dividir la clase en dos grupos

ORGANIZING THE CLASS

- Take your math books out, please
- Could you hand out these papers, please?
- Put yourselves into groups of 2,3,4...
- I'm going to divide the class in two groups

PONER DEBERES

- En casa, leed este fragmento
- Revisad estos ejercicios
- Completad las siguientes actividades...

ASSIGNING HOMEWORK

- Read this passage at home
- Go over these exercises
- Complete the following activities...

HABLAR SOBRE LA LECCIÓN

- En unos minutos vamos a practicar...
- Al final de la clase vamos a leer una historia
- María, por favor, ¿podrías responder a esta pregunta?
- ¿Podrías traerme los diccionarios?
- ¿Podrías pasarme la goma?

TALKING ABOUT THE LESSON

- In a few minutes we're going to practice...
- At the end of the class we're going to read a story
- Mary, please, could you answer this question?
- Could you bring me the dictionaries?
- Could you pass me the eraser?

Vocabulario / Vocabulary

papel de lija	sandpaper
papel higiénico	toilet paper
papel de periódico	newspaper
papel de colores	colored paper
papel charol	glazed paper
maqueta	model
retrato	portrait
dibujo	drawing
contorno	outline
esquema	diagram
fondo	background
paisaje	landscape

Diseños / Patterns

tela vaquera	denim
liso	plain
a rayas	striped
a cuadros	checked
de lunares	spotted

Texturas / Textures

liso	smooth
rugoso	rough
suave	soft
áspero	coarse
duro	hard

marquetería
marquetry

tejer
knitting

cerámica
pottery

bordado
embroidery

costura
sewing

collage
collage

mosaicos
mosaics

decoración de huevos
egg decorating

encuadernado de libros
bookbinding

construcción de collares
beadwork

diseño de postales
cardmaking

FRASES COMUNICATIVAS EN CLASE DE MANUALIDADES

COMMUNICATIVE SENTENCES IN THE ARTS & CRAFTS CLASS

- ► Voto a buscar los ceras, por favor
- ► Fetch the crayons, please

- ► Que los responsables repartan los pinceles, por favor
- ► Students in charge, please, hand out the brushes

- ► ¡Arreglad ese desorden!
- ► Tidy up that mess!

- ► ¿Puedo sacar punta a los lápices de colores?
- ► May I sharpen the crayons?

- ► Hoy vamos a hacer dos talleres en clase
- ► Today we are going to do two workshops in class

- ► Traed toallas para secar la mesa
- ► Fetch some towels to dry the table

- ► Calcad la plantilla en la cartulina
- ► Trace round the template onto the card

- ► Colgad esos dibujos para que se sequen
- ► Hang up those printings to dry them

- ► Este pegamento se seca enseguida
- ► This glue sets right away

- ► Lavaos las manos antes de salir de clase
- ► Wash your hands before leaving the class

Verbos en la clase de manualidades

pegar	stick	**cortar**	cut out
calcar	trace	**doblar**	fold
sombrear	shade	**difuminar**	diffuse
mirar	look	**acabar**	finish
dibujar	draw	**crear**	create
colorear	color	**pulir**	polish
seguir	follow	**pintar**	paint
completar	complete	**hacer punto**	knit
comenzar de nuevo	start over	**bordar**	embroider
		coser	sew

FRASES COMUNICATIVAS EN CLASE DE MATEMÁTICAS

- ► ¿Puedes resolver esta multiplicación?
  - $7 \times 3 =$ (siete por tres igual a _ _ _ _)
- ► Dime el resultado de esta suma
- ► ¿Cuál es el dividendo de esta división?
  - ¿y el resto?
- ► ¿Cuántas caras tiene un hexágono?
- ► Dibuja una línea recta
- ► Coge una regla y comprueba esta medida
- ► ¿Cómo se leen estos números?
  - 6.5 seis coma cinco
  - $1\,{}^{2}/{}_{3}$ uno y dos tercios
  - 8^2 ocho al cuadrado
  - 5^3 cinco al cubo
  - 3^4 tres elevado a cuatro

COMMUNICATIVE SENTENCES IN THE MATH CLASS

- ► Can you solve this multiplication?
  - $7 \times 3 =$ (seven times three equals _ _ _ _)
- ► Tell me the answer to this sum
- ► What is the dividend of this division?
  - and the remainder?
- ► How many sides does a hexagon have?
- ► Draw a straight line
- ► Take a ruler and check this measurement
- ► How do you read these numbers?
  - six point five
  - one and two thirds
  - eight squared
  - five cubed
  - three to the power of four

Vocabulario / Vocabulary

operación	operation
resultado	result
problema	problem
conmutativa	commutative
asociativa	associative
distributiva	distributive
resto	remainder
divisor	divisor
cociente	quotient

Don't forget

In English we use a comma (,) to separate thousands, but in Spanish we use a period (.):

1.532.620   **1,532,620**

However, the Spanish use a comma to separate decimals, not a period, like we do:

23,45   **23.45**

+	más plus	$7 + 2 = 9$ **suma** / addition
−	menos minus	$7 - 2 = 5$ **resta** / subtraction
×	multiplicado por multiplied by	$7 \times 2 = 14$ **multiplicación** / multiplication
/	dividido entre divided by	$7 / 2 = 3,5$ **división** / division

=	es igual a is equal to	≠	no es igual a is not equal to
1/2	fracción fraction	3.<u>5</u>	parte decimal decimal part
()	paréntesis parenthesis	$\sqrt{}$	raíz cuadrada de square root of
%	porcentaje percentage	∅	conjunto vacío empty set
>	es mayor que is greater than	≥	es igual o mayor que is equal to or greater than
<	es menor que is less than	≤	es igual o menor que is equal to or less than
∈	pertenece a belongs to	π	pi pi

Números / Numbers

1	uno	one	21	veintiuno	twenty-one
2	dos	two	22	veintidós	twenty-two
3	tres	three	30	treinta	thirty
4	cuatro	four	31	treinta y uno	thirty-one
5	cinco	five	40	cuarenta	forty
6	seis	six	50	cincuenta	fifty
7	siete	seven	60	sesenta	sixty
8	ocho	eight	70	setenta	seventy
9	nueve	nine	80	ochenta	eighty
10	diez	ten	90	noventa	ninety
11	once	eleven	100	cien	one hundred
12	doce	twelve	101	ciento uno	one hundred one
13	trece	thirteen			
14	catorce	fourteen	200	doscientos	two hundred
15	quince	fifteen	300	trescientos	three hundred
16	dieciséis	sixteen			
17	diecisiete	seventeen	1.000	mil	one thousand
18	dieciocho	eighteen			
19	diecinueve	nineteen	1.000.000	un millón	one million
20	veinte	twenty			

Ordinales / Ordinal numbers

primero	first	undécimo	eleventh
segundo	second	duodécimo	twelfth
tercero	third	decimotercero	thirteenth
cuarto	fourth	decimocuarto	fourteenth
quinto	fifth	decimoquinto	fifteenth
sexto	sixth	vigésimo	twentieth
séptimo	seventh	vigésimo primero	twenty-first
octavo	eighth		
noveno	ninth	trigésimo	thirtieth
décimo	tenth	centésimo	hundredth

1.345.36**5**	unidad unit	**1/2**	medio a half
1.345.3**6**5	decenas tens	**1/3**	un tercio a third
1.345.**3**65	centenas hundreds	**1/4**	un cuarto a quarter
1.34**5**.365	millares thousands		
1.345.365	millones millions	**3/4**	tres cuartos three quarters

Medidas de longitud / Linear measures

1 milímetro	1 millimeter	= 0.04 inches
1 centímetro	1 centimeter	= 0.39 inches
1 metro	1 meter	= 1.09 yards
1 kilómetro	1 kilometer	= 1,093.61 yards / 0.62 miles

Medidas de capacidad / Measures of capacity

1 mililitro	1 mililiter	= 0.002 pints
1 centilitro	1 centiliter	= 0.02 pints
un litro	1 liter	= 2.113 pints

Pesos / Weights

1 gramo	1 gram	= 0,035 ounces
1 kilo	1 kilogram	= 2.204 pounds
1 tonelada	1 ton	= 2204 pounds

FRASES COMUNICATIVAS EN FÚTBOL Y BALONCESTO

- ► Venga, hagamos diez flexiones
- ► Botad el balón
- ► Haz una finta y lanza el balón
- ► Penalización por más de 3 segundos
- ► Parad el partido
- ► Id a la línea de tiros libres
- ► Bloquead el tiro
- ► ¡Pasos!
- ► Dobles
- ► Id al punto de penalty
- ► Id a la línea de banda
- ► Id a la línea de fondo
- ► Pasad el balón
- ► Coged el rebote
- ► Salto entre dos
- ► Detén el balón en la línea de medio campo

COMMUNICATIVE SENTENCES IN SOCCER AND BASKETBALL

- ► Come on! Let's do ten push-ups
- ► Bounce the ball
- ► Fake and shoot the ball
- ► Three-second violation
- ► Stop the game
- ► Go to the free-throw line
- ► Block the shot
- ► Traveling!
- ► Double dribble
- ► Go to the penalty spot
- ► Go to the side line
- ► Go to the end line
- ► Pass the ball
- ► Get the rebound
- ► Jump ball
- ► Stop the ball at the midfield line

pista de atletismo
athletic track

estadio
stadium

pabellón deportivo
arena

gradas
stands

pista de juego
pitch

terreno de juego
field

Verbos en la clase de educación física

caminar	walk	usar	blow a
hacer footing	jog	el silbato	whistle
nadar	swim	arrodillarse	kneel
bucear	dive	hacer una finta	fake
saltar	jump	hacer flexiones	do push-ups
placar	tackle		
patinar	skate	hacer el pino	do a handstand
esquiar	ski		
hacer esquí acuático	water-ski	botar	bounce
apuntar	aim	lanzar	throw
correr	run	coger	catch
golpear	punch	balancearse	swing
pedalear	cycle	escalar	climb
montar	ride	hacer estiramientos	stretch
chutar	hit (the ball)		
chutar	kick	flexionar hacia delante	bend over
saltar a la comba	jump rope		
caer	fall	flexionar hacia atrás	bend backwards

balón — ball

cuerda — rope

colchoneta — mat

palo de hockey — hockey stick

raqueta — racket

potro — vaulting-horse

bate — bat

silbato — whistle

FRASES COMUNICATIVAS

- ► ¡Mirad, está lloviendo a cántaros!

- ► Ayer un rayo cayó en la antena

- ► Vamos a mirar la estación meteorológica y comprobar la humedad

- ► ¡Estamos a dos grados bajo cero!

- ► ¡Hala! ¡Acaba de salir un arco iris!

- ► Se aproxima un frente frío

COMMUNICATIVE SENTENCES

- ► Look, it's pouring down rain!

- ► Yesterday, lightning struck the antenna

- ► Let's look at the weather station and check the humidity

- ► It's two degrees below zero!

- ► Wow, a rainbow has just appeared!

- ► A cold front is approaching

Estaciones / Seasons	
primavera	spring
verano	summer
otoño	fall
invierno	winter

Temperatura / Temperature	
cálido	hot
templado	warm
fresco	cool
frío	cold
helado	freezing

Vocabulario / Vocabulary			
soleado	sunny	atardecer	dusk
lluvioso	rainy	nubes	clouds
nevado	snowy	nieve	snow
ventoso	windy	lluvia	rain
nebuloso	foggy	granizo	hail
nublado	cloudy	niebla	fog
tormentoso	stormy	trueno	thunder
amanecer	dawn	arco iris	rainbow

FRASES COMUNICATIVAS EN EL LABORATORIO

COMMUNICATIVE SENTENCES AT THE LAB

- ► Examinad ese insecto con el microscopio
- ► Look at that insect under the microscope

- ► Ajustad el objetivo si está borroso
- ► Adjust the lens if it's blurred

- ► Tened mucho cuidado con esas probetas
- ► Be very careful with those test tubes

- ► Colocad bien los taburetes
- ► Put those stools back properly

- ► No os llevéis las batas a casa
- ► Don't take the lab coats home

- ► Conectad esos electrodos
- ► Connect those electrodes

El microscopio / The microscope	
prismáticos binoculares	prismatic binoculars
rueda de enfoque	focusing wheel
lente convexa	convex lens
lente cóncava	concave lens

Vocabulario / Vocabulary			
probeta	test tube	alambre	wire
llama	flame	electrodo	electrode
frasco	flask	imán	magnet
embudo	funnel	espátula	spatula
filtro de papel	filter paper	pipeta	pipette
pinzas	tongs	peso	weight
lupa	magnifying glass	batería	battery
		temporizador	timer
jeringuilla	syringe	microscopio	microscope
termómetro	thermometer	ocular	eyepiece
gasa	gauze	transparencia	slide
trípode	tripod	báscula	balance/ scales
bata de laboratorio	lab coat	objetivo	objective lens

La cara / The face

ojo	eye
nariz	nose
oreja	ear
boca	mouth
mejilla	cheek
barbilla	chin
frente	forehead
mandíbula	jaw
bigote	mustache
barba	beard
diente	tooth
labio	lip
lengua	tongue

El ojo / The eye

globo ocular	eyeball
ceja	eyebrow
párpado	eyelid
pestaña	eyelash
pupila	pupil
iris	iris

Los órganos / The organs

cerebro	brain
tráquea	windpipe
intestino	bowel
vejiga	bladder

Peinados / Hairstyles

rubio	blonde/fair	calvo	bald
moreno	dark	entradas	receding hairline
gris, canoso	gray		
liso	straight	trenzas	plaits
rizado	curly	coleta	ponytail
ondulado	wavy	flequillo	bangs
en punta	spiky		
a la altura	shoulder-		
de los hombros	length	perilla	goatee
largo	long	barba	stubble
corto	short	de 3 días	

FRASES COMUNICATIVAS

- ¿Cuántos huesos crees que tiene el cuerpo humano?
- ¿Eres miope/hipermétrope?
- ¿Te han operado alguna vez?

COMMUNICATIVE SENTENCES

- How many bones do you think the human body has?
- Are you near-/far-sighted?
- Have you ever had surgery?

FRASES COMUNICATIVAS EN CLASE DE INFORMÁTICA

COMMUNICATIVE SENTENCES IN THE COMPUTER SCIENCE CLASS

- ► Imprimid los textos después de corregirlos
- ► Print the texts after you've corrected them

- ► Encended los monitores
- ► Switch the monitors on

- ► Id a la carpeta 'Mis documentos' y abridla
- ► Go to the 'My documents' folder and open it

- ► Preparad una breve presentación visual
- ► Prepare a short visual presentation

- ► Ahora no hay conexión a Internet
- ► There's no Internet connection available now

Partes de un e-mail / Parts of an email

correo basura	spam
tema	subject
herramientas	tools
borrador	draft
archivo	file
adjuntar	attach
guardar	save
eliminar	delete
enviar	send
archivo adjunto	attachment
libreta de direcciones	address book

Vocabulario / Vocabulary

dominio	domain	palanca	joystick
enlace	link	de mando	
contraseña	password	impresora	inkjet printer
motor de	search	de inyección	
búsqueda	engine	impresora láser	laser printer
descarga	download	cartucho	cartridge

Meses / Months

enero	January
febrero	February
marzo	March
abril	April
mayo	May
junio	June
julio	July
agosto	August
septiembre	September
octubre	October
noviembre	November
diciembre	December

Días / Days

lunes	Monday
martes	Tuesday
miércoles	Wednesday
jueves	Thursday
viernes	Friday
sábado	Saturday
domingo	Sunday

Don't forget

In Spanish, never write days and months with a capital letter.

FRASES COMUNICATIVAS

COMMUNICATIVE SENTENCES

- ▶ ¿Qué fecha es hoy?
- ▶ What's today's date?

- ▶ El año 2013 no es un año bisiesto
- ▶ The year 2013 is not a leap year

- ▶ ¿Qué día de la semana es el 13?
- ▶ What day of the week is the 13th?

- ▶ El último fin de semana de marzo iremos de excursión
- ▶ We're going on a field trip on the last weekend in March

- ▶ Nos quedan 10 minutos
- ▶ We have 10 minutes left

- ▶ Tenemos que cambiar las pilas al reloj de pared
- ▶ We need to replace the batteries in the clock

- ▶ ¿Qué hora es?
- ▶ What's the time? / What time is it?

Vocabulario / Vocabulary

reloj de pulsera	watch	agujas del reloj	the hands of a clock
reloj de pared	clock	calendario	calendar
		año bisiesto	leap year

son las nueve en punto
it's nine o'clock

son las 9 y cinco
it's five past nine

son las 9 y diez
it's ten past nine

son las nueve y cuarto
it's a quarter past nine

son las nueve y media
it's half past nine

son las diez menos veinte
it's twenty to ten

son las diez menos cuarto
it's a quarter to ten

son las diez menos diez
it's ten to ten

09:15 **son las nueve y quince**
it's nine fifteen

09:10 **son las nueve y diez**
it's nine ten

09:30 **son las nueve treinta**
it's nine thirty

son las nueve y cuarenta **09:40**
it's nine forty

Carta informal / Informal letter

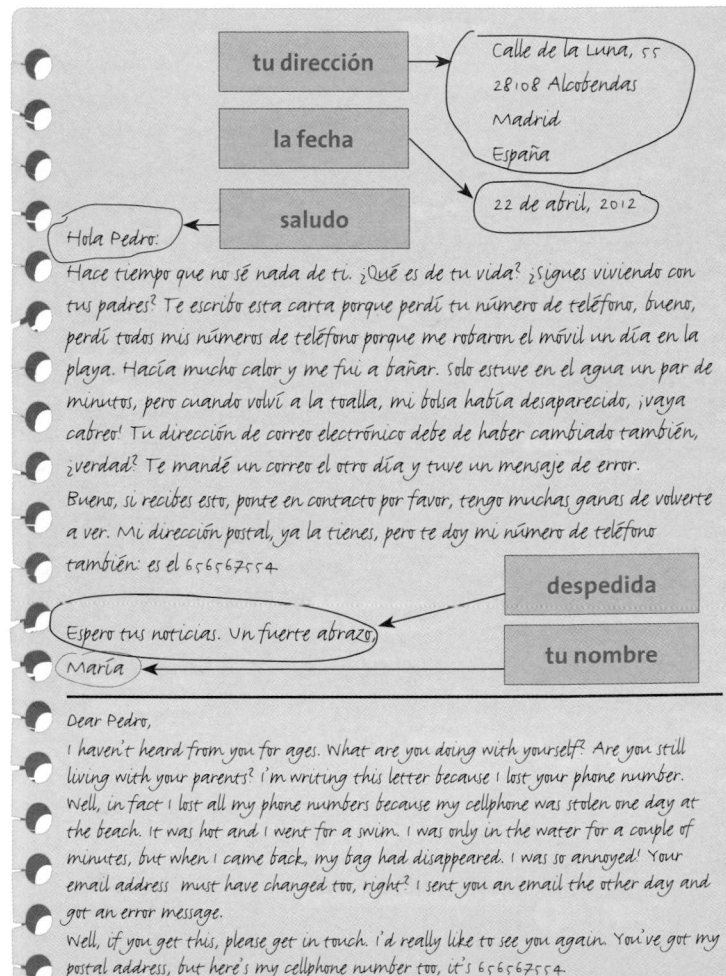

tu dirección → Calle de la Luna, 55
28108 Alcobendas
Madrid
España

la fecha → 22 de abril, 2012

saludo → Hola Pedro:

Hace tiempo que no sé nada de ti. ¿Qué es de tu vida? ¿Sigues viviendo con tus padres? Te escribo esta carta porque perdí tu número de teléfono, bueno, perdí todos mis números de teléfono porque me robaron el móvil un día en la playa. Hacía mucho calor y me fui a bañar. Solo estuve en el agua un par de minutos, pero cuando volví a la toalla, mi bolsa había desaparecido, ¡vaya cabreo! Tu dirección de correo electrónico debe de haber cambiado también, ¿verdad? Te mandé un correo el otro día y tuve un mensaje de error. Bueno, si recibes esto, ponte en contacto por favor, tengo muchas ganas de volverte a ver. Mi dirección postal, ya la tienes, pero te doy mi número de teléfono también: es el 65656 7554

despedida → Espero tus noticias. Un fuerte abrazo,

tu nombre → María

Dear Pedro,

I haven't heard from you for ages. What are you doing with yourself? Are you still living with your parents? I'm writing this letter because I lost your phone number. Well, in fact I lost all my phone numbers because my cellphone was stolen one day at the beach. It was hot and I went for a swim. I was only in the water for a couple of minutes, but when I came back, my bag had disappeared. I was so annoyed! Your email address must have changed too, right? I sent you an email the other day and got an error message.

Well, if you get this, please get in touch. I'd really like to see you again. You've got my postal address, but here's my cellphone number too, it's 65656 7554.

Looking forward to hearing from you.

Love,

María

FRASES ÚTILES EN CARTAS Y CORREOS ELECTRÓNICOS / USEFUL PHRASES IN LETTERS AND EMAILS

SALUDOS FORMALES
- Estimado Sr. García
- Apreciada Sra. Gutiérrez
- Muy Sr mío / Muy Sra. mía
- Muy Sres. míos

FORMAL GREETINGS
- Dear Mr. García
- Dear Mrs Gutiérrez
- Dear Sir / Dear Madam
- Dear Sirs

SALUDOS INFORMALES
- Querida Paloma
- Hola Felipe

INFORMAL GREETINGS
- Dear Paloma
- Hi Felipe, Dear Felipe

DESPEDIDAS FORMALES
- Le agradezco de antemano su atención
- Le saluda atentamente
- Reciba un cordial saludo
- Quedo a la espera de recibir sus noticias

FORMAL CLOSING PHRASES
- I thank you in advance for your attention
- Yours faithfully, Yours sincerely
- Yours faithfully, Yours sincerely
- I look forward to hearing from you.

DESPEDIDAS INFORMALES
- Saludos cordiales
- Un saludo / Saludos
- Un abrazo
- Hasta pronto

INFORMAL CLOSING PHRASES
- Kind regards
- Yours / Yours
- Best wishes
- See you soon

DESPEDIDAS ENTRE AMIGOS Y FAMILIARES
- Con cariño / Con amor
- Un (fuerte) abrazo
- Un beso / Besos
- Un besazo / Un besote

CLOSING PHRASES FOR FRIENDS AND FAMILY
- Yours affectionately / Love
- Best wishes / Love
- Love / Lots of love
- Love / Lots of love

OTRAS EXPRESIONES
- Me dirijo a Usted ...
- Dale recuerdos a ...
- Saludos a ...
- María te manda recuerdos

OTHER EXPRESSIONS
- I am writing to you ...
- Give my greetings to ...
- Give my love to ...
- María sends her greetings/love

Al teléfono

- ¿Puedo hablar con Juan? / ¿Está Juan?
- ¿Podría dejarle un mensaje, por favor?
- ¿De parte de quién?
- Hola, soy Belén
- Un momento, por favor
- Ahora no está
- Te has equivocado de número
- ¿Puede deletrear su nombre?
- Está comunicando / Comunica
- No hay línea
- Mi dirección de correo electrónico es I, N, F, O, 'arroba', A, B, C, 'punto' E, S

On the phone

- Can I speak to John, please? / Is John there, please?
- Could I leave a message for him, please?
- Who's calling?
- Hello, it's Belén speaking
- Hold on, please
- He/she's not in at the moment
- Wrong number / You've dialled the wrong number
- Could you spell your name?
- The line's engaged / The line's busy
- There's no tone
- My email address is info@abc.es

SMS / SMS		
xa	para	for
xo	pero	but
xq, xk	porque	because
ad+	además	what's more / also
nls	no lo sé	I don't know
tkm	te quiero mucho	I love you a lot
a2	adiós	bye
salu2	saludos	regards
tvl	te veo luego	see you later

In general, Spanish words are pronounced as they are written,
there is a closer correspondence between the pronunciation
and the written word than there is in English. So, if you learn
a few easy rules, you will be able to pronounce Spanish correctly
when you read it.

Of course, people from different countries have different
pronunciations, but the differences do not usually prevent
understanding. Here we give you both European and Latin American
Spanish, although the main differences in pronunciation,
as opposed to accent, are confined to the letters **c** and **z**.

VOCALES / VOWELS

Spanish has 5 pure vowels:

a	**casa** – similar to the *a* in *father*, but shorter
e	**Pepe** – similar to the *e* in *went*, but a little longer
i	similar to *ee* in *feel*, but a little shorter
o	similar to the *o* in British English *lost*
u	similar to *oo* in *root*

DIPTONGOS / DIPHTHONGS

ai	like the *y* in *pylon*.
au	like *ow* in *cow*.
ei	like *ay* in *day*.
eu	this does now exist in English, it is similar to a combination of *e* as in *get* and *w* as in *wet*.
oi /oy	like *oy* in *boy*.
ui /uy	like *wee* in *sweet*.
uo	similar to *wo* in *woke*.

CONSONANTES / CONSONANTS

b, v	these are pronounced exactly the same, but they do have two pronunciations: – at the start of a sentence and after **m**, like the *b* in *bubble* – in other positions, the lips vibrate, but do not close entirely. It's like an English *v*, but with the top and bottom lips instead of the top teeth and bottom lips.
c	– before **a**, **o** and **u**, like the *c* in *cat*. – before **e** and **i**, like *th* in *thin* [in American Spanish like *s* in *sister*]
d	– at the start of a sentence, and after **l**, like *d* in *dad*. – in all other positions, like *th* in *this*.

f	as in English.
g	– before **a**, **o** and **u**, like *g* in *gang*.
	– before **e** and **i**, like Scottish *ch* as in *loch*.
	– remember that in the combinations **gue** and **gui**, the **u** is not pronounced unless it is written with a diaresis (**ü**), so in **guerra**, the first syllable **gue** is pronounced like *ge* in *get*, and in **guitarra**, **gui** is pronounced like *gi* in *give*.
h	always silent.
j	like Scottish *ch* as in *loch*.
k	as in English.
l	as in English.
ll	like *lli* as in *billion* [in some pronunciations, like *y* in *yes*].
m	as in English.
n	as in English.
ñ	like *ny* as in *canyon*.
p	as in English.
qu	like *c* in *cat*
r	a single tap of the tongue behind the teeth.
rr	a strongly trilled *r*, as in Scottish pronunciation.
s	as in English.
t	as in English.
w	this only occurs in foreign words, it is pronounced like *b* and *v* (see above).
z	like *th* in *thin* [in American Spanish like *s* in *sister*].

Acentuación / Accentuation

To pronounce Spanish properly, you also need to know which syllable to stress, a change in stress can sometimes change the meaning of a word! Here are the basic rules:
– words ending in a consonant except **–n** or **–s** are stressed on the last syllable: co<u>mer</u> (to eat), ciu<u>dad</u> (city), continen<u>tal</u> (continental).
– words ending in a vowel or **–n** or **–s** are stressed on the next to last syllable: <u>co</u>men (they eat), ciu<u>da</u>des (cities), te<u>rra</u>za (terrace), ja<u>ra</u>be (syrup).

All words which are exceptions to these two rules have a written accent over the stressed vowel; the accent shows you where the stress falls, it does not change the quality of the vowel: <u>ár</u>bol (tree), <u>á</u>guila (eagle), aca<u>bé</u> (I finished), ja<u>món</u> (ham).

Spanish verbs are conjugated in three moods: the indicative, the subjunctive and the imperative. In the indicative and subjunctive there are simple tenses and compound tenses. Compound tenses for all verbs are formed with the auxiliary verb *haber*, which accompanies the invariable participle of the verb to be conjugated.

The following table shows the conjugation of compound tenses, which is, as stated above, the same for all verbs, the only difference being the participle which follows the auxiliary. Following on from that come the simple tenses; firstly the three regular conjugations and then the models for the conjugation of the irregular verbs.

Tiempos compuestos / Compound Tenses

AMAR / TEMER / PARTIR					
indicative			**subjunctive**		
Present Perfect	he	amado / temido / partido	Present Perfect	haya	amado / temido / partido
	has	amado / temido / partido		hayas	amado / temido / partido
	ha	amado / temido / partido		haya	amado / temido / partido
	hemos	amado / temido / partido		hayamos	amado / temido / partido
	habéis	amado / temido / partido		hayáis	amado / temido / partido
	han	amado / temido / partido		hayan	amado / temido / partido
Pluperfect	había	amado / temido / partido	Pluperfect	hubiera o hubiese	amado / temido / partido
	habías	amado / temido / partido		hubieras o hubieses	amado / temido / partido
	había	amado / temido / partido			
	habíamos	amado / temido / partido		hubiera o hubiese	amado / temido / partido
	habíais	amado / temido / partido			
	habían	amado / temido / partido			
Past Anterior	hube	amado / temido / partido		hubiéramos o hubiésemos	amado / temido / partido
	hubiste	amado / temido / partido			
	hubo	amado / temido / partido		hubierais o hubieseis	amado / temido / partido
	hubimos	amado / temido / partido			
	hubisteis	amado / temido / partido		hubieran o hubiesen	amado / temido / partido
	hubieron	amado / temido / partido			
Future Perfect	habré	amado / temido / partido	Future Perfect	hubiere	amado / temido / partido
	habrás	amado / temido / partido		hubieres	amado / temido / partido
	habrá	amado / temido / partido		hubiere	amado / temido / partido
	habremos	amado / temido / partido		hubiéremos	amado / temido / partido
	habréis	amado / temido / partido		hubiereis	amado / temido / partido
	habrán	amado / temido / partido		hubieren	amado / temido / partido
Future Perfect	habría	amado / temido / partido			
	habrías	amado / temido / partido			
	habría	amado / temido / partido			
	habríamos	amado / temido / partido			
	habríais	amado / temido / partido			
	habría	amado / temido / partido			

Tiempos simples / Simple Tenses

Modelos de conjugación de los verbos regulares / Models for the Conjugation of Regular Verbs

-AR VERB AMAR			
indicative		**subjunctive**	
Present	am–o	**Present**	am–e
	am–as / (vos) am–ás		am–es
	am–a		am–e
	am–amos		am–emos
	am–áis		am–éis
	am–an		am–en
Imperfect	am–aba	**Imperfect**	am–ara o am–ase
	am–abas		am–aras o am–ases
	am–aba		am–ara o am–ase
	am–ábamos		am–áramos o am–ásemos
	am–abais		am–arais o am–aseis
	am–aban		am–aran o am–asen
Preterite	am–é	**Future**	am–are
	am–aste		am–ares
	am–ó		am–are
	am–amos		am–áremos
	am–asteis		am–aréis
	am–aron		am–aren
Future	am–aré		
	am–arás		
	am–ará		
	am–aremos		
	am–aréis		
	am–arán		
Conditional	am–aría		
	am–arías		
	am–aría		
	am–aríamos		
	am–aríais		
	am–arían		
imperative		**non–personal forms**	
Imperativo	am–a (tú)	**Infinitve**	am–ar
	am–e (él/Vd.)		
	am–emos (nos.)	**Gerund**	am–ando
	am–ad (vos.)		
	am–en (ellos/Vds.)	**Past participle**	am–ado

-ER VERB TEMER			
indicative		**subjunctive**	
Present	tem–o	**Present**	tem–a
	tem–es / (vos) tem–és		tem–as
	tem–e		tem–a
	tem–emos		tem–amos
	tem–éis		tem–áis
	tem–en		tem–an
Imperfect	tem–ía	**Imperfect**	tem–iera o tem–iese
	tem–ías		tem–ieras o tem–ieses
	tem–ía		tem–iera o tem–iese
	tem–íamos		tem–iéramos o tem–iésemos
	tem–íais		tem–ierais o tem–ieseis
	tem–ían		tem–ieran o tem–iesen
Preterite	tem–í	**Future**	tem–iere
	tem–iste		tem–ieres
	tem–ió		tem–iere
	tem–imos		tem–iéremos
	tem–isteis		tem–iereis
	tem–ieron		tem–ieren
Future	tem–eré		
	tem–erás		
	tem–erá		
	tem–eremos		
	tem–eréis		
	tem–erán		
Conditional	tem–ería		
	tem–erías		
	tem–ería		
	tem–eríamos		
	tem–eríais		
	tem–erían		
imperative		**non-personal forms**	
Imperativo	tem–e (tú)	**Infinitve**	tem–er
	tem–a (él/Vd.)		
	tem–amos (nos.)	**Gerund**	tem–iendo
	tem–ed (vos.)		
	tem–an (ellos/Vds.)	**Past participle**	tem–ido

-IR VERB PARTIR			
indicative		**subjunctive**	
Present	part-o part-es / (vos)part-ís part-e part-imos part-ís part-en	**Present**	part-a part-as part-a part-amos part-áis part-an
Imperfect	part-ía part-ías part-ía part-íamos part-íais part-ían	**Imperfect**	part-iera *o* part-iese part-ieras *o* part-ieses part-iera *o* part-iese part-iéramos *o* part-iésemos part-ierais *o* part-ieseis part-ieran *o* part-iesen
Preterite	part-í part-iste part-ió part-imos part-isteis part-ieron	**Future**	part-iere part-ieres part-iere part-iéremos part-iereis part-ieren
Future	part-iré part-irás part-irá part-iremos part-iréis part-irán		
Conditional	part-iría part-irías part-iría part-iríamos part-iríais part-irían		
imperative		**non-personal forms**	
Imperativo	part-e (tú) part-a (él/Vd.) part-amos (nos.) part-id (vos.) part-an (ellos/Vds.)	**Infinitve** **Gerund** **Past participle**	part-ir part-iendo part-ido

ESPAÑOL

INGLÉS

A

A, a *nf (la letra)* A, a.

a *prep* **1** *(dirección)* to, on , in: *girar a la derecha* to turn (to the) right; *irse a casa* to go home; *subir al autobús* to get on the bus; *llegar a Barcelona* to arrive in Barcelona. **2** *(destino)* to, towards. **3** *(distancia)* away: *a diez kilómetros de casa* ten kilometres (away) from home. **4** *(lugar)* at, on: *a la entrada* at the entrance; *a la izquierda* on the left. **5** *(tiempo)* at: *a las once* at eleven; *a tiempo* in time; *al final* in the end. **6** *(modo)* by, in: *a ciegas* blindly; *a oscuras* in the dark. **7** *(instrumento)* by, in: *a mano* by hand; *a pie* on foot. **8** *(precio)* a: *a tres euros el kilo* three euros a kilo. **9** *(medida)* at: *a 90 kilómetros por hora* at 90 kilometres an hour. **10** *(finalidad)* to: *él vino a vernos* he came to see us. **11** *(complemento directo persona)*: *vi a Juanita* I saw Juanita. **12** *(complemento indirecto)* to: *dámelo* give it to me. **13** *verbo* + *a* + *inf* to: *aprender a nadar* to learn (how) to swim.

✎ Consulta también al.

ábaco *nm* abacus.

abad *nm* abbot.

abadesa *nf* abbess.

abadía *nf* abbey.

abajo *adv* **1** *(lugar)* below, down: *ahí abajo* down there. **2** *(en una casa)* downstairs. **3** *(dirección)* down, downward: *calle abajo* down the street.
▶ *interj* down with!: *¡abajo el dictador!* down with the dictator!

abalanzarse *vpr* **1** *(lanzarse)* to rush forward, spring forward. **2** **abalanzarse sobre** to rush at; *(león, tigre)* to pounce on; *(águila, etc)* to swoop down on.

abandonado,-a *pp* → abandonar.
▶ *adj* **1** abandoned: *un barco abandonado* an abandoned ship. **2** *(descuidado)* neglected: *tiene el despacho abandonado* his office hasn't been looked after. **3** *(desaseado)* untidy, unkempt.

abandonar *vt* **1** *(desamparar)* to abandon, forsake: *la suerte le ha abandonado* luck has forsaken him. **2** *(lugar)* to leave, quit: *abandonar el barco* to abandon ship. **3** *(descuidar)* to neglect. **4** *DEP (retirarse)* to withdraw from.
▶ *vpr* **abandonarse** to neglect os.

abanicar *vt* to fan.

abanico *nm* **1** fan. **2** *fig* range: *un abanico de posibilidades* a range of possibilities.

abaratar *vt* to reduce the price of, make cheaper.
▶ *vpr* **abaratarse** *(precio)* to come down; *(artículo)* to become cheaper.

abarcar *vt* **1** *(englobar)* to cover, embrace: *sus conocimientos abarcan el campo de la psicología* her knowledge covers the field of psychology. **2** *(abrazar)* to embrace.

abarrotado,-a *adj* packed (de, with).

abastecer *vt* to supply, provide.

abastecimiento *nm* supplying.

abasto LOC dar abasto *fam* to be sufficient for: *no doy abasto para corregir tantos ejercicios* I've got so many exercises to correct that I just can't cope.

abatible *adj* folding, collapsible: *asiento abatible* folding seat.

abatido,-a *pp* → abatir.
▶ *adj (deprimido)* dejected, depressed.

abatir *vt* **1** *(derribar)* to knock down, pull down. **2** *(matar)* to kill; *(herir)* to wound. **3** *(bajar)* to lower, take down.

abdicar *vt & vi* to abdicate, renounce.

abdomen *nm* abdomen.
abdominal *adj* abdominal.
▸ *nm pl* **abdominales** *(ejercicios)* sit-ups.
abductor *adj* abductor.
abecedario *nm* alphabet.
abedul *nm* birch tree, birch.
abeja *nf* bee. COMP **abeja obrera** worker bee. ‖ **abeja reina** queen bee.
abejorro *nm* bumblebee.
abertura *nf* 1 *(agujero)* opening, gap; *(grieta)* crack, slit. 2 *(en óptica)* aperture.
abeto *nm* fir tree, fir.
abierto,-a *pp* → **abrir**.
▸ *adj* 1 open, unlocked. 2 *(grifo)* (turned) on: *dejó el grifo abierto* she left the tap running. 3 *fig (sincero)* open, frank. 4 *(tolerante)* open-minded.
abisal *adj* abyssal.
abismo *nm* abyss.
ablación *nf* ablation.
ablandar *vt* 1 to soften. 2 *fig (persona)* to soothe, soften up, appease.
▸ *vpr* **ablandarse** to soften, get softer.
ablativo *nm* ablative (case).
abofetear *vt* to slap.
abogacía *nf* legal profession.
abogado,-a *nm & nf* lawyer, solicitor; *(tribunal supremo)* barrister. COMP **abogado de oficio** legal-aid lawyer. ‖ **abogado defensor** counsel for the defence. ‖ **abogado del diablo** devil's advocate.
abolición *nf* abolition.
abolir *vt* to abolish.
abolladura *nf (hundimiento)* dent; *(bollo)* bump.
abollar *vt* to dent.
abominable *adj* abominable, loathsome.
abonado,-a *pp* → **abonar**.
▸ *adj* 1 *(tierra)* fertilized. 2 FIN paid.
▸ *nm & nf (al teléfono, a revista)* subscriber; *(a teatro, tren, etc)* season ticket holder.
abonar *vt* 1 FIN to pay. 2 *(tierra)* to fertilize. 3 *(subscribir)* to subscribe.
▸ *vpr* **abonarse** *(a una revista)* to subscribe (a, to); *(al teatro, tren, etc)* to buy a season ticket (a, for).
abono *nm* 1 *(pago)* payment. 2 *(fertilizante)* fertilizer; *(acción)* fertilizing. 3 *(a revista)* subscription; *(a teatro, tren, etc)* season-ticket.

abordaje *nm* boarding. LOC **¡al abordaje!** stand by to board!
abordar *vt* 1 MAR *(chocar)* to run foul of, collide with; *(atacar)* to board. 2 *fig (persona)* to approach; *(asunto, tema)* to tackle.
aborigen *adj* aboriginal, native.
▸ *nm* aborigine, native.
aborrecer *vt* 1 to abhor, hate, detest. 2 *(aves)* to abandon.
abortar *vi (voluntariamente)* to abort, have an abortion; *(involuntariamente)* to miscarry, have a miscarriage.
▸ *vt (interrumpir)* to stop; *(frustrar)* to foil, thwart.
aborto *nm* 1 *(provocado)* abortion; *(espontáneo)* miscarriage. 2 *pey (persona)* ugly person, freak; *(cosa)* abortion.
abotonar *vt (ropa)* to button, button up.
▸ *vpr* **abotonarse** to do one's buttons up.
abovedado,-a *adj* vaulted, arched.
abrasador,-ra *adj* burning, scorching.
abrasar *vt (quemar)* to burn, scorch.
▸ *vi* to burn (up): *esta sopa abrasa* this soup is scalding hot.
▸ *vpr* **abrasarse** to burn. LOC **abrasarse de calor** *fig* to be sweltering.
abrazadera *nf* clamp, brace.
abrazar *vt* to embrace, hug.
abrazo *nm* hug, embrace. LOC **dar un abrazo a** ALGN to embrace SB. ‖ **un abrazo (de)** *(en carta)* with best wishes from.
abrebotellas *nm inv* bottle opener.
abrecartas *nm inv* letter-opener, paper knife.
abrelatas *nm inv* tin-opener, US can-opener.
abrevadero *nm* drinking trough.
abreviar *vt* 1 *(acortar)* to shorten, cut short. 2 *(texto)* to abridge; *(palabra)* to abbreviate.
abreviatura *nf* abbreviation.
abridor *nm* opener.
abrigar *vt* 1 *(contra el frío)* to wrap up; *(ropa)* to be warm. 2 *(proteger)* to shelter, protect. 3 *fig (sospechas)* to harbour (US harbor), have.

▶ *vpr* **abrigarse** *(uso reflexivo)* to wrap os up.

abrigo *nm* **1** *(prenda)* coat, overcoat. **2** *(refugio)* shelter. LOC **ropa de abrigo** warm clothing, warm clothes *pl*.

abril *nm* April.

※ Para ejemplos de uso, consulta marzo.

abrillantador *nm* polish.

abrillantar *vt* to polish, make shine, burnish.

abrir *vt* **1** *(gen)* to open. **2** *(cremallera)* to undo: *abrió la cremallera de la maleta* she undid the zip on the case, she unzipped the case. **3** *(luz)* to switch on, turn on; *(gas, grifo)* to turn on.
▶ *vpr* **abrirse 1** *(gen)* to open. **2** *(dar)* to open (a, onto), look (a, onto): *la casa se abre al mar* the house looks onto the sea. **3** *fig (sincerarse)* to open out. **4** *argot (largarse)* to clear off, be off LOC **abrir fuego** MIL to open fire. ▮ **abrir paso** to make way. ▮ **en un abrir y cerrar de ojos** *fam* in the twinkling of an eye.

abrochar *vt* **1** *(camisa)* to button (up); *(zapato)* to tie up. **2** *(botones)* to do up; *(broche, corchete)* to fasten: *abróchense los cinturones* please fasten your seat belts.

absceso *nm* abscess.

abscisa *nf* abscissa.

ábside *nm* apse.

absolución *nf* **1** REL absolution. **2** JUR acquittal.

absolutismo *nm* absolutism.

absoluto,-a *adj* absolute. LOC **en absoluto** not at all, by no means. ▮ **nada en absoluto** nothing at all.

absolver *vt* **1** REL to absolve. **2** JUR to acquit.

absorbente *adj* **1** absorbent. **2** *fig (trabajo)* absorbing; *(exigente)* demanding. **3** *fig (persona)* overbearing.
▶ *nm* absorbent.

absorber *vt* to absorb, soak up.

absorción *nf* absorption.

absorto,-a *adj* **1** *(pasmado)* amazed. **2** *(ensimismado)* absorbed (en, in).

abstemio,-a *adj* abstemious, teetotal.
▶ *nm & nf* teetotaller.

abstención *nf* abstention.

abstenerse *vpr* to abstain (de, from), refrain (de, from).

abstinencia *nf* abstinence. COMP **síndrome de abstinencia** withdrawal symptoms *pl*.

abstracción *nf* abstraction.

abstracto,-a *adj* abstract.

absurdo,-a *adj* absurd.

abuchear *vt* to boo, jeer at.

abuela *nf* grandmother; *(familiarmente)* grandma, granny.

abuelo *nm* grandfather; *(familiarmente)* granddad, grandpa.
▶ *nm pl* **abuelos** grandparents.

abundancia *nf* abundance, plenty.

abundante *adj* abundant, plentiful.

abundar *vi* to abound, be plentiful.

aburrido,-a *pp* → **aburrir**.
▶ *adj* **1** *(con ser)* boring, tedious. **2** *(con estar)* bored, weary; *(cansado)* tired of; *(harto)* fed up with.

aburrimiento *nm* boredom.

aburrir *vt* **1** to bore. **2** *(cansar)* to tire.
▶ *vpr* **aburrirse** to get bored (con/de/ por, with).

abusar *vi* **1** *(propasarse)* to go too far, abuse (de, -): *abusar de algn* to take unfair advantage of sb. **2** *(usar mal)* to misuse (de, -): *abusar de la comida* to eat too much.

abusivo,-a *adj* excessive, exorbitant.

abuso *nm* **1** abuse, misuse. **2** *(injusticia)* injustice.

a.C. *abrev* (antes de Cristo) before Christ; *(abreviatura)* BC.

acá *adv* **1** *(lugar)* here, over here. **2** *(tiempo)* now, at this time. LOC **de acá para allá** to and fro, up and down.

acabado,-a *pp* → **acabar**.
▶ *adj* **1** *(terminado)* finished; *(perfecto)* perfect, complete: *acabado,-a de hacer* freshly made. **2** *fig (malparado)* worn-out, spent: *una persona acabada* a has-been; *un actor acabado* a burnt-out actor.
▶ *nm* **acabado** finish.

acabar *vt* **1** *(gen)* to finish; *(completar)* to complete. **2** *(consumir)* to use up.

▶ *vi* **1** *(gen)* to finish, end; *acaba en punta* it has a pointed end. **2 acabar por** + *gerundio* to end up + *-ing*: *acabé por comprar el vestido* I ended up buying the dress.
▶ *vpr* **acabarse** to end, finish, come to an end; *(no quedar)* to run out. LOC **acabar bien** to have a happy ending. **I acabar con 1** *(destruir)* to destroy, put an end to. **2** *(terminar)* to finish, finish off. **I acabar de** + *inf* to have just + *pp*: *no lo toques, acabo de pintarlo ahora mismo* don't touch it, I've just painted it. **I acabar mal 1** *(cosa)* to end badly. **2** *(persona)* to come to a bad end. **I ¡se acabó!** that's it!

academia *nf* **1** *(institución)* academy. **2** *(escuela)* school, academy.

acalorado,-a *adj* **1** hot; *(cara)* flushed. **2** *fig (persona)* excited, worked up; *(debate)* heated, angry.

acampada *nf* camping.

acampar *vt & vi* to camp.

acantilado *nm* cliff.

acaparar *vt* **1** *(productos)* to hoard; *(mercado)* to corner, buy up. **2** *(monopolizar)* to monopolize, keep for os.

acariciar *vt* **1** to caress, fondle. **2** *(pelo, animal)* to stroke. **3** *fig (esperanzas, etc)* to cherish; *(idea, plan)* to have in mind.

ácaro *nm* mite.

acarrear *vt* **1** *(transportar)* to carry, transport. **2** *fig (producir)* to cause, bring, give rise to.

acaso *adv* perhaps, maybe: *acaso esté enfermo* maybe he's ill. LOC **por si acaso** just in case.

acatar *vt* **1** *(leyes, etc)* to obey, observe, comply with. **2** *(respetar)* to respect.

acatarrarse *vpr* to catch a cold.

acceder *vi* **1** *(consentir)* to consent (a, to), agree (a, to). **2** *(tener entrada)* to enter. **3** *(alcanzar)* to accede (a, to).

accesible *adj* accessible; *(persona)* approachable.

acceso *nm* **1** *(entrada)* access, entry. **2** *(de tos)* fit; *(de fiebre)* attack, bout. **3** INFORM access: *acceso aleatorio* random access.

accidental *adj* accidental: *no fue más que un encuentro accidental* it was nothing but a chance meeting.

accidente *nm* **1** accident: *sufrir un accidente* to have an accident. **2** *(terreno)* unevenness, irregularity. LOC **por accidente** by chance. COMP **accidente de trabajo** industrial accident. **I accidente de tráfico** road accident. **I accidentes geográficos** geographical features.

acción *nf* **1** action; *(acto)* act, deed. **2** COM share. **3** TEAT plot. LOC **entrar en acción** MIL to go into action. **I ponerse en acción** to start doing sth. COMP **película de acción** adventure film.

accionar *vt (máquina)* to drive, work, activate.

accionista *nm o nf* shareholder, stockholder.

acechar *vt* **1** *(vigilar)* to watch, spy on; *(esperar)* to lie in wait for. **2** *(caza)* to stalk.

acecho LOC **estar al acecho de 1** *(vigilar)* to be on the lookout for. **2** *(esperar)* to lie in wait for.

aceite *nm* oil. COMP **aceite de girasol** sunflower oil. **I aceite de maíz** corn oil. **I aceite de oliva** olive oil. **I aceite de ricino** castor oil.

aceitera *nf* **1** oil bottle. **2** AUTO oil can.
▶ *nf pl* **aceiteras** oil and vinegar set *sing*, cruet *sing*.

aceituna *nf* olive.

aceleración *nf* acceleration. COMP **poder de aceleración** AUTO acceleration.

acelerador,-ra *adj* accelerating.
▶ *nm* **acelerador** AUTO accelerator.

acelerar *vt* **1** to accelerate; *(paso)* to quicken. **2** *fig* to speed up.

acelga *nf* chard.

acento *nm* **1** *(tilde)* accent (mark). **2** *(tónico)* stress. **3** *(pronunciación)* accent: *acento andaluz* Andalusian accent. **4** *(énfasis)* emphasis, stress. COMP **acento ortográfico** written accent, accent.

acentuación *nf* accentuation.

acentuar *vt* **1** *(tilde)* to accentuate; *(tónico)* to stress. **2** *(resaltar)* to emphasize, stress.

▶ *vpr* **acentuarse** to become more pronounced, become more marked.

acepción *nf* meaning, sense.

aceptable *adj* acceptable.

aceptación *nf* **1** acceptance. **2** *(aprobación)* approval; *(éxito)* success: *la película tuvo poca aceptación* the film wasn't popular, the film met with little success.

aceptar *vt* **1** to accept, receive. **2** *(aprobar)* to approve of.

acequia *nf* irrigation channel, ditch.

acera *nf* pavement, US sidewalk.

acerca de *adv* about, concerning, on.

acercar *vt* to bring near, bring nearer, draw up: *acércate* come closer; *¿me acercas el agua?* can you pass the water?
▶ *vpr* **acercarse 1** *(aproximarse)* to be near: *se acerca el verano* summer is near. **2** *(ir)* to go: *acércate a la esquina* go to the corner. **3** *(visitar)* to drop in, drop by.

acero *nm* steel. COMP **acero inoxidable** stainless steel.

acertado,-a *pp* → acertar.
▶ *adj* **1** *(opinión, etc)* right, correct; *(comentario)* fitting; *(idea, decisión)* clever; *(palabra)* exact. **2** *(conveniente)* suitable. LOC **estar acertado,-a** to be wise.

acertante *nm o nf* winner.

acertar *vt* **1** *(en un objetivo)* to hit. **2** *(dar con lo cierto)* to get right: *solo acertó cinco preguntas* she only got five questions right. **3** *(por azar)* to guess correctly; *(concurso, quinielas)* to win.
▶ *vi* to get right, be right.

acertijo *nm* riddle.

acético,-a *adj* acetic.

acetileno *nm* acetylene.

achacar *vt* to impute, attribute.

achaque *nm* ailment, complaint.

achatado,-a *adj* flattened.

achicar *vt* **1** *(hacerse más pequeño)* to diminish, reduce, make smaller. **2** *(agua)* to drain; *(en barco)* to bale out.
▶ *vpr* **achicarse 1** *(amenguarse)* to get smaller. **2** *(amilanarse)* to lose heart.

achicharrar *vt* to scorch; *(comida)* to burn.
▶ *vpr* **achicharrarse** to roast.

achicoria *nf* chicory.

achuchar *vt* **1** *(azuzar)* to nag at. **2** *(abrazar)* to hug, squeeze: *había una pareja achuchándose en el rincón* there was a couple having a cuddle in the corner. **3** *(empujar)* to shove.

achuchón *nm* **1** *fam (empujón)* push, shove. **2** *fam (indisposición)* ailment: *le dio un achuchón* he had a funny turn. **3** *fam (abrazo)* hug, squeeze.

acicalarse *vpr* to dress up, smarten up.

acicate *nm* spur.

acidez *nf* **1** *(sabor)* sourness, sharpness. **2** QUÍM acidity. COMP **acidez de estómago** heartburn.

ácido,-a *adj* **1** *(sabor)* sharp, tart. **2** QUÍM acidic. **3** *(tono)* harsh.
▶ *nm* **ácido** QUÍM acid. COMP **ácido sulfúrico** sulphuric acid. ‖ **ácido úrico** uric acid.

acierto *nm* **1** *(adivinación)* correct guess, right answer. **2** *(buena idea)* good choice/idea.

aclamar *vt* to acclaim.

aclaración *nf* explanation.

aclarar *vt* **1** *(cabello, color)* to lighten, make lighter. **2** *(líquido)* to thin (down). **3** *(enjuagar)* to rinse. **4** *(explicar)* to explain.
▶ *vi (mejorar el tiempo)* to clear (up).
▶ *vpr* **aclararse 1** *(entender)* to understand: *no me aclaro con esta lección* I can't understand this lesson. **2** *(decidirse)* to make up one's mind.

aclimatación *nf* acclimatization, US acclimation.

aclimatarse *vpr* to become acclimatized (a, to), become US acclimated (a, to).

acné *nf* acne.

acobardarse *vpr* to become frightened, lose one's nerve, shrink back (ante, from).

acogedor,-ra *adj* **1** *(persona)* welcoming, friendly. **2** *(lugar)* cosy, warm.

acoger *vt (recibir)* to receive; *(a invitado)* to welcome.

acogida *nf* **1** reception, welcome. **2** *(aceptación)* popularity. LOC **tener buena acogida** to be welcomed.

acometer vt 1 (embestir) to attack. 2 (emprender) to undertake.

acometida nf 1 (ataque) attack, assault. 2 (derivación) connection.

acomodado,-a adj (rico) well-to-do, well off.

acomodador,-ra nm & nf (hombre) usher; (mujer) usherette.

acompañamiento nm 1 accompaniment. 2 (guarnición de plato) accompaniment to a main dish, side dish. 3 MÚS accompaniment.

acompañante nm o nf 1 companion, escort. 2 MÚS accompanist.

acompañar vt 1 to accompany, go with: te acompaño a la puerta I'll see you to the door; nos acompañó al cine she came with us to the cinema. 2 (adjuntar) to enclose, attach. 3 MÚS to accompany. LOC acompañar en el sentimiento fml to express one's condolences to.

acondicionado,-a pp → acondicionar.
▶ adj equipped, fitted-out.

acondicionador nm conditioner. COMP acondicionador de aire air conditioner. ‖ acondicionador del cabello hair conditioner.

acondicionar vt 1 to fit up, set up. 2 (mejorar) to improve.

aconsejable adj advisable.

aconsejar vt to advise.

acontecimiento nm event, happening.

acopio LOC hacer acopio de to store up.

acoplamiento nm 1 fitting, adaptation. 2 (de naves espaciales) docking.

acoplar vt 1 (juntar) to fit (together), join, adjust. 2 TÉC to couple, connect.
▶ vpr acoplarse 1 to fit, join. 2 (naves espaciales) to dock.

acorazado,-a adj armoured (US armored), armour-plated (US armor-plated).
▶ nm acorazado battleship.

acordar vt 1 to agree. 2 (decidir) to decide.
▶ vpr acordarse to remember (de, -): no se acuerda de nada she can't remember anything.

acorde adj in agreement, agreed.
▶ nm MÚS chord.

acordeón nm accordion.

acorralar vt to corner.

acortar vt & vi to shorten, make shorter.

acosar vt to pursue, chase.

acoso nm 1 pursuit, chase. 2 fig hounding. COMP acoso sexual sexual harassment.

acostarse vpr 1 (estirarse) to lie down. 2 (irse a dormir) to go to bed: es hora de acostarse it's bedtime. LOC acostarse con fam to sleep with, go to bed with.

acostumbrado,-a pp → acostumbrar.
▶ adj 1 (persona) accustomed (a, to), used (a, to). 2 (hecho) usual, customary: es lo acostumbrado it is the custom.

acostumbrar vt 1 (habituar) to accustom to. 2 (soler) to be in the habit of.
▶ vpr acostumbrarse (habituarse) to become accustomed (a, to), get used (a, to).

acre nm (medida) acre.

acreditado,-a adj 1 (prestigioso) reputable, well-known, prestigious. 2 (representante, embajador) accredited.

acreedor,-ra adj deserving: ser/hacerse acreedor a to be worthy of.
▶ nm & nf FIN creditor.

acribillar vt to riddle, pepper.

acrílico,-a adj acrylic.

acrobacia nf acrobatics.

acróbata nm o nf acrobat.

acta nf 1 (relación) minutes pl, record (of proceedings); (publicación) transactions pl. 2 (certificado) certificate, official document. LOC levantar acta to draw up the minutes. COMP acta notarial affidavit.

actinia nf sea anemone.

actitud nf (disposición) attitude; (postura) position.

activar vt 1 TÉC to activate. 2 INFORM to enable. 3 fig (avivar) to liven up, quicken.

actividad nf activity.

activo,-a adj active: estar en activo to be on active service.
▶ nm activo FIN asset, assets pl.

acto *nm* **1** act, action. **2** *(ceremonia)* ceremony. **3** TEAT act. LOC **en el acto** at once.

actor *nm* actor.

actriz *nf* actress.

actuación *nf* **1** *(en cine, teatro)* performance. **2** *(intervención)* intervention, action.

actual *adj* **1** present, current: *dadas las circunstancias actuales* under the present circumstances. **2** *(actualizado)* up-to-date: *tiene un diseño muy actual* it has a very up-to-date design.

actualidad *nf* **1** present (time). **2** *(hechos)* current affairs *pl*; *(estado)* the current state of things: *este programa te da toda la actualidad cinematográfica* this programme gives you all the latest cinema news. LOC **en la actualidad** at present.

actualizar *vt* **1** *(poner al día)* to bring up to date, update. **2** *(filosofía)* to actualize.

actualmente *adv* *(hoy en día)* nowadays, these days; *(ahora)* at present, at the moment.

actuar *vi* **1** *(gen)* to act (como/de, as). **2** *(en obra, película)* to perform, act.

acuarela *nf* watercolour (US watercolor).

acuario *nm* aquarium.

Acuario *nm inv* Aquarius.

acuático,-a *adj* aquatic, water.

acudir *vi* **1** *(ir)* to go; *(venir)* to come, arrive. **2** *(presentarse)* to come back.

acueducto *nm* aqueduct.

acuerdo *nm* agreement. LOC **¡de acuerdo!** all right!, O.K.! ▌**de acuerdo con** in accordance with. ▌**estar de acuerdo** to agree (con, with). ▌**llegar a un acuerdo** to come to an agreement. ▌**ponerse de acuerdo** to agree.

acumulación *nf* accumulation.

acumular *vt* to accumulate; *(datos)* to gather; *(dinero)* to amass.

acunar *vt* to rock.

acuñar *vt* **1** *(monedas)* to strike, coin, mint. **2** *(una frase)* to coin.

acupuntura *nf* acupuncture.

acurrucarse *vpr* to curl up, snuggle up.

acusación *nf* **1** accusation. **2** JUR charge.

acusado,-a *pp* → acusar.
▶ *nm & nf* accused, defendant.

acusar *vt* **1** *(echar la culpa)* to accuse (de, of). **2** JUR to charge (de, with). **3** *(manifestar)* to give away.

acusativo *nm* accusative.

acuse COMP acuse de recibo acknowledgement of receipt.

acústica *nf* acoustics.

acutángulo COMP triángulo acutángulo acute triangle.

adaptación *nf* adaptation.

adaptar *vt* **1** *(acomodar)* to adapt. **2** *(ajustar)* to adjust, fit.
▶ *vpr* adaptarse *(persona)* to adapt os (a, to); *(cosa)* to fit, adjust.

adecuado,-a *pp* → adecuar.
▶ *adj* adequate, suitable.

adecuar *vt* to adapt, make suitable.

a. de J.C. *abrev* *(antes de Jesucristo)* before Christ; *(abreviatura)* BC.

adelantado,-a LOC **por adelantado** in advance.

adelantamiento *nm* overtaking. LOC **hacer un adelantamiento** to overtake.

adelantar *vt* **1** to move forward. **2** *(reloj)* to put forward. **3** *(pasar delante)* to pass. **4** AUTO to overtake. **5** *(dinero)* to pay in advance.
▶ *vi (reloj)* to be fast.
▶ *vpr* adelantarse **1** *(ir delante)* to go ahead. **2** *(llegar temprano)* to be early. **3** *(anticiparse)* to get ahead (a, of). **4** *(reloj)* to gain, be fast.

adelante *adv* forward, further.
▶ *interj* **1** *(pase)* come in! **2** *(siga)* go ahead!, carry on! LOC **de aquí en adelante** from here on. ▌**en adelante** henceforth. ▌**más adelante 1** *(tiempo)* later on. **2** *(espacio)* further on.

adelanto *nm* **1** *(avance)* advance. **2** *(tiempo)* advance. **3** *(pago)* advance; *(técnicamente)* advance payment.

adelgazar *vt* *(afinar)* to make slim.
▶ *vi (perder peso)* to slim, lose weight.

ademán *nm* *(gesto)* gesture.
▶ *nm pl* ademanes manners.

además *adv* **1** *(también)* also, as well. **2** *(es más)* furthermore, what is more: *¡y además, el coche es mío!* and what's more, the car's mine! LOC **además de** as well as, in addition to: *además de amable es guapo* as well as being kind, he's handsome.

adenoides *nm* adenoids.

adentro *adv* inside.
▸ *nm pl* **adentros** inward mind *sing*: *para sus adentros* in his heart. LOC **mar adentro** out to sea.

adepto,-a *nm & nf* follower, supporter.

aderezar *vt* *(condimentar)* to season; *(ensalada)* to dress.

adeudar *vt* **1** *(deber)* to owe, have a debt of. **2** FIN to debit, charge.

adherente *adj* adherent, adhesive.

adherir *vt* *(pegar)* to stick on.
▸ *vi* *(pegarse)* to stick (a, to).
▸ *vpr* **adherirse 1** *(pegarse)* to stick (a, to). **2** *fig* *(unirse)* to adhere to, follow.

adhesivo,-a *adj* adhesive.
▸ *nm* adhesive.

adición *nf* addiction.

adicción *nf* addition. LOC **crear adicción** to be addictive.

adicional *adj* additional.

adictivo,-a *adj* addictive.

adicto,-a *adj* addicted (a, to).
▸ *nm & nf* **1** *(drogas)* addict. **2** *(partidario)* supporter, follower.

adiestrar *vt* to train, instruct.

adinerado,-a *adj* rich, wealthy.

adiós *interj* **1** *(gen)* goodbye!; *(familiarmente)* bye!, bye-bye! **2** *(al cruzarse con alguien)* hello!
▸ *nm* goodbye.

adiposo,-a *adj* adipose.

aditivo,-a *adj* additive.
▸ *nm* additive.

adivinanza *nf* riddle, puzzle.

adivinar *vt* **1** *(descubrir)* to guess: *le adivinó el pensamiento* she read his mind. **2** *(predecir)* to forecast, foretell. **3** *(enigma)* to solve.

adivino,-a *nm & nf* fortune-teller.

adjetivo,-a *adj* adjective, adjectival.
▸ *nm* **adjetivo** adjective.

adjudicar *vt* **1** *(premio)* to award. **2** *(venta)* to sell, knock down: *¡adjudicado!* sold! **3** *(obras)* to award a contract to.
▸ *vpr* **adjudicarse 1** *(apropiarse)* to appropriate, take over. **2** *(obtener)* to win.

adjunto,-a *adj* **1** *(en carta)* enclosed. **2** *(asistente)* assistant.

administración *nf* **1** *(gen)* administration. **2** *(de medicamento)* administering. COMP **administración de lotería** lottery office. ▌ **administración pública** public administration.

administrador,-ra *nm & nf* **1** administrator. **2** *(manager)* manager. COMP **administrador,-ra de fincas** estate agent. ▌ **administrador de web** webmaster.

administrar *vt* **1** *(bienes, justicia)* to administer. **2** *(dirigir)* to manage, run. **3** *(suministrar)* to give: *le administró una aspirina* she gave him an aspirin.
▸ *vpr* **administrarse** to manage one's own money, manage one's own affairs.

administrativo,-a *adj* administrative.
▸ *nm & nf* *(funcionario)* official, civil servant; *(de empresa, banco)* office worker.

admirable *adj* admirable.

admiración *nf* **1** admiration. **2** *(signo)* exclamation mark.

admirador,-ra *nm & nf* admirer.

admirar *vt* **1** *(estimar)* to admire. **2** *(sorprender)* to amaze, surprise, astonish.

admisión *nf* **1** admission. **2** *(aceptación)* acceptance. **3** TÉC inlet, intake. LOC «Reservado el derecho de admisión» "The management reserves the right to refuse admission". COMP **plazo de admisión** closing date.

admitir *vt* **1** *(dar entrada)* to admit, let in. **2** *(aceptar)* to accept, admit: *«No se admiten propinas»* "No tipping", "Tipping not allowed". **3** *(permitir)* to allow: *su obra admite varias interpretaciones* his work is open to various interpretations. **4** *(reconocer)* to admit. **5** *(tener capacidad)* to hold.

ADN *abrev* MED *(ácido desoxirribonucleico)* desoxyribonucleic acid; *(abreviatura)* DNA.

adobar *vt* **1** CULIN to marinate, marinade. **2** *(pieles)* to tan.

adobe *nm* adobe.

adolescencia *nf* adolescence.

adolescente *adj* adolescent.
▶ *nm o nf* adolescent.

adonde *adv* where.

adónde *adv* where.

adopción *nf* adoption.

adoptar *vt* to adopt.

adoptivo,-a *adj* adoptive.

adoquín *nm* cobble, paving stone.

adorable *adj* adorable.

adoración *nf* adoration, worship.

adorar *vt* **1** REL to worship. **2** *fig* to adore.

adormecerse *vpr* to doze off.

adormilarse *vpr* to doze, drowse.

adornar *vt* to adorn, decorate.

adorno *nm* decoration, adornment.
LOC **de adorno** decorative.

adosado,-a *adj* semidetached: *casas adosadas* semidetached houses.

adquirir *vt* to acquire; *(comprar)* to buy.

adquisición *nf* acquisition; *(compra)* buy, purchase.

adrede *adv* deliberately, on purpose, purposely.

adrenalina *nf* adrenalin.

aduana *nf* **1** customs *pl.* **2** *(oficinas)* customs building. LOC **pasar (por) la aduana** to go through customs.

aducir *vt* to adduce, allege.

adueñarse *vpr* to take possession (de, of).

adulación *nf* adulation, flattery.

adular *vt* to adulate, flatter.

adulterar *vt* to adulterate.

adulterio *nm* adultery.

adulto,-a *adj* adult.
▶ *nm & nf* adult.

adverbio *nm* adverb.

adversario,-a *adj* opposing.
▶ *nm & nf* adversary, opponent.

adversidad *nf* adversity, misfortune.

adverso,-a *adj* adverse.

advertencia *nf* **1** warning. **2** *(consejo)* piece of advice.

advertir *vt* **1** *(darse cuenta)* to notice, realize. **2** *(llamar la atención)* to warn: *ya te lo advertí* I told you. **3** *(aconsejar)* to advise.

adviento *nm* Advent.

adyacente *adj* adjacent.

aéreo,-a *adj* **1** aerial. **2** AV air.

aerobic *nm* aerobics.

aerobio,-a *adj* aerobic.

aerodeslizador *nm* hovercraft.

aerodinámico,-a *adj* aerodynamic.

aeródromo *nm* aerodrome, US airfield.

aeroespacial *adj* aerospace.

aerofagia *nf* aerophagia.

aerógrafo *nm* airbrush.

aerolínea *nf* airline.

aeronáutica *nf* aeronautics.

aeronaval *adj* air-sea.

aeronave *nf* airship. COMP **aeronave espacial** spaceship.

aeroplano *nm* aeroplane, US airplane.

aeropuerto *nm* airport.

aerosol *nm* aerosol, spray.

aerostático,-a *adj* aerostatic.

aerotaxi *nm* air taxi.

afable *adj* affable, kind.

afamado,-a *adj* famous, well-known.

afán *nm* **1** *(celo)* zeal; *(interés)* keenness, eagerness. **2** *(esfuerzo)* effort.

afanar *vt* *fam* *(robar)* to nick, pinch.
▶ *vpr* **afanarse** to work with zeal. LOC **afanarse en** to work hard at. ‖ **afanarse por** to strive to, do one's best to.

afección *nf* *(enfermedad)* complaint, disease.

afectado,-a *pp* → afectar.
▶ *adj* affected.

afectar *vt* **1** *(impresionar)* to move. **2** *(dañar)* to damage. **3** *(concernir)* to concern.

afectivo,-a *adj* **1** *(sensible)* sensitive. **2** *(psicología)* affective.

afecto *nm* affection: *con todo mi afecto* with all my love. LOC **tomarle afecto a** ALGN to become fond of SB.

afectuoso,-a *adj* affectionate.

afeitar *vt* to shave.

afeminado,-a *adj* effeminate.

aferrarse *vpr* to clutch (a, to), cling (a, to).

Afganistán *nm* Afghanistan.

afgano,-a *adj* Afghan.
► *nm & nf (persona)* Afghan.
► *nm* **afgano** *(idioma)* Afghan.

afianzar *vt* **1** *(sujetar)* to strengthen, reinforce. **2** *fig* to support, back.
► *vpr* **afianzarse** *(estabilizarse)* to steady OS.

afición *nf* **1** *(inclinación)* liking, penchant: *tener afición por algo* to be fond of sth. **2 la afición** the fans *pl*, the supporters *pl*.

aficionado,-a *pp* → aficionarse.
► *adj* **1** keen, fond: *ser aficionado a algo* to be fond of STH. **2** *(no profesional)* amateur.
► *nm & nf* **1** fan, enthusiast. **2** *(no profesional)* amateur.

aficionarse *vpr* to become fond (a, of), take a liking (a, to).

afijo *nm* affix.

afilar *vt* to sharpen.

afiliarse *vpr* to join (a, to), become affiliated (a, to).

afín *adj* **1** *(semejante)* similar, kindred. **2** *(relacionado)* related. **3** *(próximo)* adjacent, next.

afinar *vt* **1** MÚS to tune. **2** *(puntería)* to sharpen.

afinidad *nf* **1** affinity. **2** QUÍM similarity.

afirmación *nf* statement, assertion.

afirmar *vt* **1** *(afianzar)* to strengthen, reinforce. **2** *(aseverar)* to state, say, declare.
► *vpr* **afirmarse** *(ratificarse)* to maintain (en, -).

afirmativo,-a *adj* affirmative. LOC **en caso afirmativo** if the answer is yes.

aflicción *nf* affliction, grief, suffering.

afligir *vt* to afflict, grieve, trouble.
► *vpr* **afligirse** to grieve, be distressed.

aflojar *vt* **1** *(soltar)* to loosen. **2** *fig (esfuerzo)* to relax. **3** *fam fig (dinero)* to pay up.

aflorar *vi* **1** *(mineral)* to crop out/up, outcrop. **2** *fig (aparecer)* to come up to the surface, appear.

afluencia *nf* inflow, influx: *afluencia de público* flow of people.

afluente *nm (río)* tributary.

afonía *nf* loss of voice.

afónico,-a *adj* hoarse, voiceless. LOC **estar afónico** to have lost one's voice.

aforo *nm (capacidad)* seating capacity.

afortunado,-a *adj* **1** lucky, fortunate: *fue una pregunta poco afortunada* it was a rather inappropriate question. **2** *(dichoso)* happy.

afrenta *nf fml* affront, outrage.

africano,-a *adj* African.
► *nm & nf* African.

afrontar *vt* to face, confront.

afterhours *nm* after-hours club.

afuera *adv* outside: *la parte de afuera* the outside; *salir afuera* to come/go out.
► *nm pl* **afueras** outskirts.

agacharse *vpr* **1** *(encogerse)* to cower. **2** *(agazaparse)* to crouch (down), squat.

agalla *nf* **1** *(de pez)* gill. **2** *(de ave)* temple. **3** BOT gall, oak apple.
► *nf pl* **agallas** *fam* courage *sing*, guts, pluck *sing*: *tener agallas* to have guts.

agarrado,-a *pp* → agarrar.
► *adj fam* stingy, tight. LOC **bailar agarrado** to dance cheek to cheek.

agarrar *vt* **1** *(con la mano)* to clutch, seize, grasp: *agárrala fuerte* hold it tight. **2** *fam (pillar)* to catch.
► *vpr* **agarrarse** *(cogerse)* to hold on, cling (a, to).

agarrotado,-a *adj (músculo)* stiff.

ágata *nf* agate.

agencia *nf* agency; *(sucursal)* branch. COMP **agencia de turismo** tourist office. ‖ **agencia de viajes** travel agency.

agenda *nf* **1** *(libro)* diary. **2** *(orden del día)* agenda.

agente *nm o nf* agent.
► *nm* agent. COMP **agente de cambio y bolsa** stockbroker. ‖ **agente de policía** **1** *(hombre)* policeman. **2** *(mujer)* policewoman.

ágil *adj* agile.

agilidad *nf* agility.

agilizar *vt* to speed up.

agitar *vt* **1** *(mover)* to agitate, shake; *(pañuelo)* to wave: «*Agítese antes de usarlo*» «Shake before use». **2** *(intranquilizar)* agitate, excite.

aglomeración *nf* **1** agglomeration. **2** *(de gente)* crowd.

aglomerado *nm (madera)* chipboard.

agnosticismo *nm* agnosticism.

agobiado,-a *pp* → agobiar.
► *adj fig (abrumado)* overwhelmed: *agobiado de trabajo* up to one's eyes in work.

agobiar *vt (abrumar)* to overwhelm.
► *vpr* **agobiarse** *(angustiarse)* to worry too much, get worked up.

agobio *nm* burden, fatigue, suffocation.

agonía *nf* 1 dying breath, last gasp: *murió después de una larga agonía* she died after a long illness; *en su agonía* on her death-bed. 2 *(sufrimiento)* agony, grief, sorrow.

agonizar *vi* to be dying: *está agonizando* she could die any moment now.

agosto *nm* August. [LOC] hacer su agosto *fig* to make a packet/pile, feather one's nest.

✎ Para ejemplos de uso, consulta marzo.

agotado,-a *pp* → agotar.
► *adj* 1 *(cansado)* exhausted, worn out. 2 *(libros)* out of print; *(mercancías)* sold out.

agotador,-ra *adj* exhausting.

agotamiento *nm* exhaustion. [COMP] agotamiento físico physical strain.

agotar *vt* to exhaust, tire/wear out.
► *vpr* **agotarse** 1 *(cansarse)* to become exhausted, become tired out. 2 COM to be sold out.

agraciado,-a *adj* 1 *(bello)* attractive, beautiful. 2 *(ganador)* winning.
► *nm & nf* lucky winner. [LOC] ser poco agraciado, -a to be unattractive/plain.

agradable *adj* nice, pleasant.

agradar *vi* to please.

agradecer *vt* 1 to thank for, be grateful for. 2 *(uso impersonal)* to be welcome: *siempre se agradece una ayuda* help is always welcome.

agradecido,-a *pp* → agradecer.
► *adj* grateful, thankful: *le quedaría muy agradecido si...* I should be very much obliged if...

agradecimiento *nm* gratefulness, gratitude, thankfulness.

agrado *nm* pleasure: *no es de su agrado* it isn't to his liking.

agrandar *vt* to enlarge, make larger.

agrario,-a *adj* agrarian, land, agricultural.

agravante *adj* aggravating.
► *nm & nf* 1 added difficulty. 2 JUR aggravating circumstance.

agravar *vt* to aggravate, worsen.
► *vpr* **agravarse** to get worse, worsen.

agravio *nm* offence, insult.

agredir *vt* to attack.

agregar *vt* to add.

agresión *nf* aggression, attack.

agresividad *nf* aggressiveness.

agresivo,-a *adj* aggressive.

agresor,-ra *nm & nf* aggressor, attacker.

agreste *adj* 1 *(salvaje)* wild. 2 *(abrupto)* rugged; *(rocoso)* rocky. 3 *(sin cultivar)* uncultivated.

agrícola *adj* agricultural, farming.

agricultor,-ra *nm & nf* farmer.

agricultura *nf* agriculture, farming.

agridulce *adj* 1 bittersweet. 2 CULIN sweet and sour.

agrietarse *vpr* to crack; *(piel)* to get chapped.

agrio,-a *adj* sour.
► *nm pl* **agrios** citrus fruits.

agronomía *nf* agronomy.

agrónomo,-a *adj* farming.
► *nm & nf* agronomist.

agropecuario,-a *adj* agricultural, farming.

agrupación *nf* 1 grouping, group. 2 *(asociación)* association.

agrupar *vt* to group, put into groups.
► *vpr* **agruparse** 1 to group together, form a group. 2 *(asociarse)* to associate.

agua *nf* 1 water: *echarse al agua* to dive in. 2 *(lluvia)* rain. 3 ARQUIT slope of a roof: *tejado a dos aguas* pitched roof. [COMP] agua dulce fresh water. ‖ agua corriente running water. ‖ agua de colonia (eau de) cologne. ‖ agua del grifo tap water. ‖ agua mineral con gas sparkling mineral water. ‖ agua oxigenada hydrogen peroxide. ‖ agua potable drinking water. ‖ aguas jurisdiccionales territorial waters.

aguacate *nm (árbol)* avocado; *(fruto)* avocado (pear).

aguacero *nm* heavy shower, downpour.

aguado,-a *pp* → aguar.
▸ *adj* watered down, wishy-washy.

aguafiestas *nm o nf inv* killjoy, spoilsport, wet blanket.

aguafuerte *nm & nf* **1** ARTE etching. **2** QUÍM nitric acid.

aguamarina *nf* aquamarine.

aguanieve *nf* sleet.

aguantar *vt* **1** (contener) to hold (back). **2** (sostener) to hold, support. **3** (soportar) to tolerate: *no aguanto más* I can't stand any more, I can't take any more.
▸ *vpr* **aguantarse 1** (contenerse) to keep back; (risa, lágrimas) to hold back. **2** (resignarse) to resign OS.

aguante *nm* **1** (paciencia) patience, endurance. **2** (fuerza) strength. LOC **tener mucho aguante 1** (paciente) to be very patient. **2** (resistente) to be strong, have a lot of stamina.

aguar *vt* to water down, add water to. LOC **aguar la fiesta a ALGN** to spoil SB's fun.

aguardar *vt* to wait (for), await.
▸ *vi* to wait.

aguardiente *nm* eau de vie, spirit, liquor.

aguarrás *nm* turpentine.

agudo,-a *adj* **1** (afilado) sharp. **2** (dolor) acute. **3** *fig* (ingenioso) witty; (mordaz) sharp. **4** (voz) high-pitched. **5** (sonido) treble, high. **6** LING (palabra) oxytone; (acento) acute. **7** MAT (ángulo) acute.

agüero *nm* omen, presage. LOC **ser de mal agüero** to be ill-omened. **I ser pájaro de mal agüero** *fig* to be bird of ill omen.

aguijón *nm* **1** ZOOL sting. **2** BOT thorn, prickle. **3** *fig* (estímulo) sting, spur.

águila *nf* eagle.

aguilucho *nm* (cría del águila) eaglet.

aguinaldo *nm* Christmas bonus/box.

aguja *nf* **1** needle; (de tricotar) knitting needle. **2** (de reloj) hand; (de tocadiscos) stylus. **3** (de arma) firing pin. **4** (de tren) point, US switch.

agujerear *vt* to make holes in.

agujero *nm* **1** hole. **2** *fig* (falta de dinero) shortfall: *encontraron un agujero de varios millones de euros* they found that several million euros were missing. COMP **agujero negro** black hole.

agujetas *nf pl* stiffness *sing*: *tener agujetas* to be stiff.

ah *interj* **1** (caer en la cuenta) ah!, oh! **2** (sorpresa, admiración) oh!

ahí *adv* there, in that place. LOC **de ahí que** hence, therefore. **I por ahí 1** (lugar) round there. **2** (aproximadamente) more or less.

ahijado,-a *nm & nf* **1** godchild; (chico) godson; (chica) goddaughter. **2** (adoptivo) adopted child.

ahínco *nm* eagerness.

ahogado,-a *pp* → ahogar.
▸ *adj* **1** drowned. **2** (asfixiado) asphyxiated, suffocated.
▸ *nm & nf* drowned person.

ahogar *vt* **1** (asfixiar) to choke, suffocate. **2** (en el agua) to drown. **3** (motor) to flood.
▸ *vpr* **ahogarse 1** to be drowned, drown: *se cayó al río y se ahogó* he fell into the river and drowned. **2** (sofocarse) to choke, suffocate. **3** (motor) to flood. LOC **ahogarse en un vaso de agua** *fig* to make a mountain out of a molehill.

ahora *adv* **1** (en este momento) now: *ahora no tengo tiempo* I haven't got time now. **2** (hace un momento) just a moment ago: *lo acabo de ver ahora* I've just seen it. **3** (dentro de un momento) in a minute, shortly: *ahora te lo preparo* I'll get it ready for you in a minute. LOC **de ahora en adelante** from now on. **I hasta ahora** until now, so far. **I por ahora** for the time being.

ahorcar *vt* to hang.
▸ *vpr* **ahorcarse** to hang oneself.

ahorrador,-ra *adj* thrifty.
▸ *nm & nf* thrifty person.

ahorrar *vt* to save.
▸ *vpr* **ahorrarse** to save OS: *te ahorrarás problemas si lo haces como yo te digo* you'll save yourself problems if you do it the way I say.

ahorro *nm* saving: *me supone un ahorro de 60 euros al mes* it represents a saving of 60 euros a month.
► *nm pl* **ahorros** savings.

ahumado,-a *pp* → ahumar.
► *adj* smoked; *(bacon)* smoky.

ahumar *vt* to smoke.

ahuyentar *vt* **1** to drive away, scare away. **2** *fig* to dismiss.

airbag® *nm* airbag®.

aire *nm* **1** air. **2** *(viento)* wind; *(corriente)* draught. **3** *fig (aspecto)* air, appearance: *tiene un aire cansado* she looks tired. **4** *fig (parecido)* resemblance, likeness: *tienen un aire de familia* there's a family likeness to them. **5** *fig (estilo)* style, manner, way: *lo hizo a su aire* he did it his way. **6** MÚS air, melody. LOC **al aire libre** in the open air, outdoors. ‖ **tomar el aire** to take the air, get some fresh air. COMP **aire acondicionado** air conditioning. ‖ **aire puro** clean air.

airear *vt* **1** *(ventilar)* to air. **2** *fig (un asunto)* to publicize.
► *vpr* **airearse** to get some fresh air.

airoso,-a LOC **salir airoso,-a** to do well, be successful: *salió airoso de la entrevista* he did well in the interview.

aislado,-a *pp* → aislar.
► *adj* **1** *(suelto)* isolated. **2** TÉC insulated.

aislante *adj* insulating.
► *nm* insulator.

aislar *vt* **1** *(dejar separado)* to isolate. **2** TÉC to insulate.

a. J.C. *abrev* → a. de J.C.

ajedrez *nm* **1** *(juego)* chess. **2** *(tablero y piezas)* chess set.

ajeno,-a *adj* **1** *(de otro)* another's, belonging to other people. **2** *(extraño)* not involved.

ajetreo *nm* activity, bustle.

ajo *nm* garlic. LOC **estar en el ajo** *fam fig* to be involved, be in the thick of it. COMP **ajo tierno** young garlic.

ajustado,-a *pp* → ajustar.
► *adj* **1** *(precio)* very low, rock-bottom; *(presupuesto)* tight. **2** *(apretado)* tight-fitting, tight.

ajustar *vt* **1** *(adaptar)* to adjust, regulate. **2** *(apretar)* to tighten. **3** *(encajar)* to fit, fit tight.

ajuste *nm* **1** *(unión)* adjustment, fitting. **2** TÉC assembly. **3** COM settlement, fixing. COMP **ajuste de cuentas** *fig* settling of scores.

al *contr* → a. LOC **al** + *inf* on + *ger*: *me lo encontré al salir de casa* I met him when I was leaving, I met him on leaving.

ala *nf* **1** wing. **2** DEP winger.
► *nf pl* **alas** *(atrevimiento)* daring *sing*. COMP **ala delta 1** *(aparato)* hang glider. **2** *(deporte)* hang gliding.

alabanza *nf* praise.

alabar *vt (elogiar)* to praise.

alabastro *nm* alabaster.

alacena *nf* cupboard.

alacrán *nm* scorpion.

alambique *nm* still.

alambre *nm* wire.

alameda *nf* **1** poplar grove. **2** *(paseo)* avenue, promenade, boulevard.

álamo *nm* poplar.

alano,-a *adj* mastiff, wolfhound.

alarde *nm* display, bragging, boasting. LOC **hacer alarde de** to flaunt, show off, parade.

alardear *vi* to boast, brag, show off.

alargador *nm* extension lead.

alargar *vt* **1** to lengthen. **2** *(estirar)* to stretch. **3** *(prolongar)* to prolong. **4** *(dar)* to hand, pass.

alarido *nm* screech, yell, shriek.

alarma *nf* alarm. LOC **dar la alarma** to give the alarm, raise the alarm.

alarmante *adj* alarming.

alarmar *vt* to alarm.
► *vpr* **alarmarse** to be alarmed, alarm os.

alarmista *nm o nf* alarmist.

alazán,-ana *adj* light chestnut, sorrel.

alba *nf* dawn, daybreak.

albacea *nm o nf* JUR *(hombre)* executor; *(mujer)* executrix.

albahaca *nf* basil.

albanés,-esa *adj* Albanian.
► *nm & nf (persona)* Albanian.
► *nm* **albanés** *(idioma)* Albanian.

Albania *nf* Albania.

albañil *nm (de ladrillos)* bricklayer; *(en general)* building worker.

albarán *nm* delivery note, despatch note.

albaricoque *nm* **1** *(fruta)* apricot. **2** *(árbol)* apricot tree.

alberca *nf* reservoir.

albergar *vt* **1** *(alojar)* to lodge, house, accommodate. **2** *fig (sentimientos)* to cherish, harbour (US harbor).

albergue *nm* **1** *(hostal)* hostel. **2** *(refugio)* shelter, refuge. COMP **albergue juvenil** youth hostel.

albino,-a *adj* albino.
► *nm & nf* albino.

albóndiga *nf* meatball.

albornoz *nm* bathrobe.

alborotador,-ra *nm & nf* troublemaker, agitator.

alborotar *vt* **1** *(agitar)* to agitate, excite. **2** *(desordenar)* to make untidy, turn upside down. **3** *(sublevar)* to incite to rebel.
► *vi* to make a racket.

alboroto *nm* **1** *(gritería)* din, racket, row. **2** *(desorden)* uproar, commotion, disturbance.

albufera *nf* lagoon.

álbum *nm* album.

albúmina *nf* albumin.

alcachofa *nf* **1** *(planta)* artichoke. **2** *(pieza)* rose, sprinkler.

alcalde *nm* mayor.

alcaldesa *nf* **1** *(cargo)* lady mayor, mayoress. **2** *(mujer del alcalde)* mayoress.

alcaldía *nf* **1** *(cargo)* mayorship. **2** *(oficina)* mayor's office, mayoralty.

alcalino,-a *adj* alkaline.

alcaloide *nm* alkaloid.

alcance *nm* **1** reach, grasp: *está al alcance de todo el mundo* it's within everyone's reach. **2** *(de arma)* range. **3** *(trascendencia)* scope, importance. **4** *(inteligencia)* intelligence: *persona de pocos alcances* person of low intelligence.

alcanfor *nm* camphor.

alcantarilla *nf* **1** *(conducto)* sewer. **2** *(boca)* drain.

alcantarillado *nm* sewer system.

alcanzar *vt* **1** *(gen)* to reach. **2** *(persona)* to catch up, catch up with. **3** *(pasar)* to pass, hand over: *alcánzame el agua* pass me some water. **4** *(conseguir)* to attain, achieve: *alcanzamos los objetivos* we achieved the goals.
► *vi* **1** *(ser suficiente)* to be sufficient (para, for), be enough (para, for): *eso no alcanza para todos* that's not enough for all of us. **2** *(ser capaz)* to manage, succeed: *no alcanzo a verlo* I can't see it.

alcaparra *nf* **1** *(fruto)* caper. **2** *(planta)* caper bush.

alcayata *nf* hook.

alcázar *nm* **1** *(fortaleza)* fortress, citadel. **2** *(palacio)* palace, castle.

alce *nm* elk, moose.

alcoba *nf* bedroom.

alcohol *nm* **1** *(sustancia)* alcohol. **2** *(bebida)* alcohol, spirits *pl*.

alcoholemia *nf* alcohol: *tasa/nivel de alcoholemia* blood alcohol level.

alcohólico,-a *adj* alcoholic.
► *nm & nf* alcoholic.

alcoholímetro *nm* breathalyzer®.

alcoholismo *nm* alcoholism.

alcornoque *nm* **1** BOT cork oak. **2** *fig* blockhead, idiot, dimwit.

aldaba *nf* **1** *(llamador)* door knocker. **2** *(barra)* bar. **3** *(pestillo)* bolt.

aldea *nf* hamlet, small village.

aldeano,-a *nm & nf* villager.

aldehído *nm* aldehyde.

aleación *nf* alloy.

aleatorio,-a *adj* random, chance.

alegar *vt* to allege, plead, claim.

alegoría *nf* allegory.

alegórico,-a *adj* allegorical, allegoric.

alegrar *vt* **1** *(causar alegría)* to make happy, make glad, cheer up. **2** *fig (avivar)* to brighten (up), enliven. **3** *fam (achispar)* to make tipsy.
► *vpr* **alegrarse 1** to be pleased, be glad. **2** *fam (achisparse)* to get tipsy.

alegre *adj* **1** *(contento)* happy, glad. **2** *(color)* bright. **3** *(música)* lively. **4** *(espacio)* cheerful, pleasant. **5** *fam (achispado)* tipsy.

alegría *nf* happiness, joy.

alejar *vt* to remove, move away.
  ► *vpr* **alejarse** to go/move away.

alemán,-ana *adj* German.
  ► *nm & nf (persona)* German.
  ► *nm* **alemán** *(idioma)* German.

Alemania *nf* Germany.

alentar *vt* **1** *(animar)* to encourage. **2** *(tener)* to harbour (US harbor), cherish.

alérgeno *nm* allergen.

alergia *nf* allergy.

alérgico,-a *adj* allergic (a, to).

alero *nm* **1** ARQUIT eaves *pl*. **2** DEP forward.

alerta *adv (vigilante)* on the alert.
  ► *nf (atención)* alert.
  ► *interj* look/watch out!

alertar *vt* to alert (de, to).

aleta *nf* **1** *(de pez)* fin; *(de mamífero, de nadador)* flipper. **2** *(de nariz)* wing, ala. **3** *(de avión)* aileron; *(de coche)* wing.

aletear *vi* **1** *(ave)* to flutter, flap its wings. **2** *(pez)* to move its fins.

alfabetizar *vt* **1** *(enseñar)* to teach to read and write. **2** *(ordenar)* to alphabetize, put in alphabetic order.

alfabeto *nm* **1** *(abecedario)* alphabet. **2** *(código)* code. COMP **alfabeto Morse** Morse code.

alfalfa *nf* alfalfa, lucerne.

alfarería *nf* **1** *(arte)* pottery. **2** *(taller)* potter's workshop.

alféizar *nm* sill, windowsill.

alférez *nm* second lieutenant.

alfil *nm* bishop.

alfiler *nm* **1** *(costura)* pin. **2** *(joya)* brooch, pin. **3** *(del pelo)* clip. **4** *(de corbata)* tiepin.

alfombra *nf* **1** carpet, rug. **2** *(de baño)* bath mat.

alfombrilla *nf* **1** rug, mat. **2** *(de ordenador)* mousemat, mousepad.

alforja *nf* saddlebag.

alga *nf* alga; *(marina)* seaweed.

algarroba *nf* **1** *(fruto)* carob bean. **2** *(planta)* vetch.

algarrobo *nm* carob tree.

álgebra *nf* algebra.

algo *pron (afirmación)* something; *(negación, interrogación)* anything: *vamos a tomar algo* let's have something to drink; *¿quieres algo?* do you want anything? LOC **algo es algo** something is better than nothing.
  ► *adv (un poco)* a bit, a little, somewhat: *te queda algo grande* it's a bit too big for you.

algodón *nm* cotton. COMP **algodón dulce/de azúcar** candyfloss, (US cotton candy). ‖ **algodón hidrófilo** cotton wool.

algoritmo *nm* algorithm.

alguacil *nm* bailiff.

alguien *pron (afirmativo)* somebody, someone; *(interrogativo, negativo)* anybody, anyone: *preguntemos a alguien* let's ask someone; *¿hay alguien?* is anyone there?

algún *adj* → alguno,-a.

alguno,-a *adj (afirmativo)* some; *(interrogativo, negativo)* any: *alguna noche voy al cine* some nights I go to the cinema; *¿ha habido alguna llamada?* has anyone phoned?, have there been any phone calls?; *el ministro no facilitó dato alguno* the minister didn't provide any information.
  ► *pron (afirmativo)* someone, somebody; *(interrogativo, negativo)* anybody: *que venga alguno que sepa francés* get someone who speaks French. LOC **alguno que otro** some, a few.

alhaja *nf* **1** jewel, gem. **2** *fig (cosa, persona)* gem, treasure.

aliado,-a *pp* → aliar.
  ► *adj* allied.
  ► *nm & nf* ally.

alianza *nf* **1** *(pacto)* alliance. **2** *(anillo)* wedding ring.

aliar *vt* to ally.
  ► *vpr* **aliarse** to become allies, form an alliance (con, with).

alias *adv* alias.
  ► *nm inv* alias.

alicates *nm pl* pliers.

aliciente *nm* incentive, inducement.

alienígena *nm o nf* alien.

aliento *nm* **1** *(respiración)* breath, breathing. **2** *fig (ánimo)* spirit, courage. LOC **quedarse sin aliento 1** *(respi-*

rando mal) to be breathless, be out of breath. **2** *(sorprendido)* to gasp.

alijo *nm* consignment: *un alijo de armas* a consignment of smuggled arms, an arms cache.

alimaña *nf* pest.

alimentación *nf* **1** *(acción)* feeding. **2** *(alimento)* food; *(dieta)* diet. **3** TÉC feed. COMP **bomba de alimentación** feed pump.

alimentar *vt* **1** *(dar alimento)* to feed. **2** *(mantener)* to keep, support. **3** *(uso técnico)* to feed.
▸ *vpr* **alimentarse** to live (de/con, on).

alimento *nm* **1** *(comida)* food. **2** *(valor nutritivo)* nutritional value, nourishment.

alineación *nf* **1** *(colocación)* alignment, lining up. **2** *(equipo)* line-up.

alinear *vt* **1** *(poner en línea)* to align, line up. **2** DEP to pick, select.

aliñar *vt* *(gen)* to season, flavour (US flavor); *(ensalada)* to dress.

aliño *nm* *(gen)* seasoning; *(para ensalada)* dressing.

alisar *vt* to smooth.

alistarse *vpr* to enlist, join up, enrol (US enroll).

aliviar *vt* **1** fig *(enfermedad, dolor)* to relieve, ease, alleviate, soothe. **2** *(consolar)* to comfort, console.

alivio *nm* **1** *(mejoría)* relief: *¡qué alivio!* what a relief! **2** *(consuelo)* comfort, consolation.

aljibe *nm* cistern, tank.

allá *adv* **1** *(lugar)* there, over there: *más allá* further (on); *allá va tu madre* there goes your mother. **2** *(tiempo)* back: *allá por los años sesenta* back in the sixties.

allanamiento COMP **allanamiento de morada 1** unlawful entry. **2** *(robo)* housebreaking, breaking and entering.

allanar *vt* **1** *(aplanar)* to level, flatten. **2** *(dificultad, etc)* to smooth out, solve, resolve.

allegado,-a *adj* close, related.
▸ *nm & nf (familia)* relative; *(amigo)* close friend.

allí *adv* **1** *(lugar)* there, over there: *allí abajo/arriba* down/up there; *por allí* over

there, round there. **2** *(tiempo)* then, at that moment.

alma *nf* soul. LOC **no había ni una alma** there wasn't a soul, there was nobody there. **I no poder** ALGN **con su alma** to be absolutely exhausted.

almacén *nm* **1** *(local)* warehouse, storehouse. **2** *(habitación)* storeroom.
▸ *nm pl* **almacenes** department store *sing*. COMP **grandes almacenes** department store *sing*.

almacenar *vt* **1** to store, warehouse. **2** *(acumular)* to store up, keep.

almeja *nf* clam.

almena *nf* merlon.
▸ *nf pl* **almenas** battlements.

almendra *nf* almond.

almendro *nm* almond tree.

almíbar *nm* syrup.

almidón *nm* starch.

almirante *nm* admiral.

almizcle *nm* musk.

almohada *nf* pillow. LOC **consultar** ALGO **con la almohada** *fam* to sleep on STH.

almohadilla *nf* **1** *(gen)* small cushion. **2** COST *(para coser)* sewing cushion; *(para alfileres)* pincushion. **3** *(de teclado)* number sign, pound. **4** *(de animal)* pad. **5** ARQUIT *(de capitel)* volute cushion.

almohadón *nm* cushion, large pillow.

almorrana *nf* fam pile.

almorzar *vi* *(al mediodía)* to have lunch; *(de desayuno)* to have breakfast; *(a media mañana)* to have elevenses, have a mid-morning snack.
▸ *vt* *(al mediodía)* to have for lunch; *(de desayuno)* to have for breakfast; *(a media mañana)* to have for elevenses, have for a mid-morning snack.

almuerzo *nm* **1** *(a mediodía)* lunch. **2** *(a media mañana)* mid-morning snack, elevenses *pl*. **3** *(desayuno)* breakfast.

alojamiento *nm* lodging, accommodation.

alojar *vt* **1** *(hospedar)* to lodge, put up, accommodate; *(dar vivienda a)* to house. **2** *(meter)* to put, place.
▸ *vpr* **alojarse** *(persona)* to stay; *(bala, etc)* to be lodged.

alondra *nf* lark.

alopecia *nf* alopecia.

alpaca¹ *nf (animal, tela)* alpaca.

alpaca² *nf (metal)* nickel silver, German silver, alpaca.

alpargata *nf* rope-soled sandal, espadrille.

Alpes *nm pl* los Alpes the Alps.

alpinismo *nm* mountaineering, mountain climbing.

alpinista *nm o nf* mountaineer, mountain climber.

alpiste *nm* birdseed, canary grass.

alquilar *vt* **1** *(dar en alquiler - período largo)* to rent, rent out, let; *(- período corto)* to hire out. **2** *(recibir en alquiler - período largo)* to rent; *(- período corto)* to hire. LOC «Se alquila» "To let".

alquiler *nm* **1** *(acción - de casa)* renting, letting; *(- de coche)* hire. **2** *(cuota - de casa)* rent; *(- de TV, etc)* rental. LOC «En alquiler» "To let", US "For rent".

alquimia *nf* alchemy.

alquitrán *nm* tar.

alrededor *adv* **1** *(lugar)* round, around: *mira alrededor* look around. **2** alrededor de *(tiempo)* around: *alrededor de las cuatro* around four o'clock. **3** *(aproximadamente)* about: *alrededor de veinte* about twenty.
▶ *nm pl* alrededores surrounding area *sing*: *en los alrededores de Sevilla* in the vicinity of Seville, just outside Seville.

alta *nf* **1** *(de un enfermo)* discharge: *dieron de/el alta al enfermo* the patient was discharged from hospital. **2** *(de un empleado)* registration *with Social Security*. **3** *(entrada, admisión)* admission; *(ingreso)* membership.

altar *nm* altar.

altavoz *nm* loudspeaker.

alteración *nf* **1** *(cambio)* alteration, change. **2** *(excitación)* agitation, uneasiness, restlessness. COMP alteración del orden público breach of the peace, disturbance of the peace.

alterar *vt* **1** *(cambiar)* to change, modify, alter. **2** *(enfadar)* to annoy, upset.
▶ *vpr* alterarse **1** *(cambiar)* to change. **2** *(enfadarse)* to lose one's temper, get upset.

altercado *nm* argument, quarrel.

alternar *vt (gen)* to alternate.
▶ *vi* **1** *(turnar)* to alternate. **2** *(relacionarse)* to meet people, socialize (con, with), mix (con, with). **3** *(en salas de fiesta, bar)* to entertain.

alternativa *nf* alternative, option, choice.

alternativo,-a *adj* alternative.

alterno,-a *adj* alternate, alternating: *días alternos* alternate days.

Alteza *nf* Highness. LOC Su Alteza Real **1** *(hombre)* His Royal Highness. **2** *(mujer)* Her Royal Highness.

altibajos *nm pl* ups and downs.

altiplano *nm* high plateau.

altitud *nf* height, altitude.

alto¹ *nm (parada)* stop: *hicieron un alto para comer* they stopped for lunch.
▶ *interj* halt!; *(policía)* stop!

alto,-a² *adj* **1** *(persona, edificio, árbol)* tall. **2** *(montaña, pared, techo, precio)* high. **3** *(elevado)* top, upper: *viven en los pisos altos* they live on the upper floors. **4** *(voz, sonido)* loud: *lo dijo en voz alta* she said it aloud. LOC a altas horas de la noche late at night. COMP alta cocina haute cuisine. ▌ alta sociedad high society.
▶ *adv* alto **1** high (up). **2** *(voz)* loud, loudly. LOC pasar por alto to pass over.
▶ *nm* **1** *(altura)* height: *solo hace dos metros de alto* it's only two metres high. **2** *(elevación)* hill, high ground. LOC en lo alto de on the top of. ▌ por todo lo alto *fig* in a grand way.

altramuz *nm* lupin.

altruismo *nm* altruism.

altura *nf* **1** *(gen)* height: *el edificio tiene una altura de 80 metros* the building is 80 metres high. **2** *(altitud)* altitude. **3** *(nivel)* level, par; *(punto)* point: *¿a qué altura de la calle vives?* how far up the street do you live? LOC estar a la altura de to measure up to, match up to, be on a par with. ▌ a estas alturas by now, at this stage.

alubia *nf* bean.

alucinación *nf* hallucination.

alucinado,-a *pp* → alucinar.
▶ *adj argot* amazed, stunned, gobsmacked.

alucinante *adj* **1** hallucinatory. **2** *argot (extraordinario)* brilliant, fantastic, amazing, incredible, mind-blowing.

alucinar *vt* **1** *(producir sensaciones)* to hallucinate. **2** *fig (cautivar)* to fascinate, amaze, astound, flip out, stun.
▶ *vi argot* to be amazed, be gobsmacked: *¡alucinas!* you're out of your mind!, you're crazy!

alud *nm* avalanche.

aludido,-a *pp* → aludir.
▶ *adj* above-mentioned, in question.
LOC **darse por aludido,-a** to take the hint.

aludir *vi* to allude (a, to), mention (a, -), refer (a, to).

alumbrado,-a *nm* lighting, lights *pl*; *(coche)* lights *pl*.

alumbramiento *nm* afterbirth.

alumbrar *vt* **1** *(iluminar)* to light, give light to, illuminate. **2** *fig (enseñar)* to enlighten.
▶ *vi* **1** *(iluminar)* to give light. **2** *(parir)* to give birth to.

aluminio *nm* aluminium, US aluminum.

alumnado *nm (de colegio)* pupils *pl*; *(de universidad)* student body.

alumno,-a *nm & nf (de colegio)* pupil; *(de universidad)* student. COMP **alumno externo** day pupil. ‖ **alumno interno** boarder. ‖ **antiguo alumno 1** *(de colegio)* old boy, former pupil. **2** *(de universidad)* old student, former student.

alunizar *vi* to land on the moon.

alusión *nf* allusion, reference.

aluvión *nm* **1** alluvion: *tierra de aluvión* alluvium, alluvial soil. **2** *fig* flood: *un aluvión de insultos* a barrage of insults.

alveolar *adj* alveolar.

alveolo *nm* **1** ANAT alveolus. **2** *(de panal)* cell.

alza *nf (aumento)* rise, increase. LOC **al alza / en alza** rising.

alzamiento *nm* **1** *(aumento)* raising, lifting. **2** *(rebelión)* uprising, insurrection.

alzar *vt* **1** *(levantar)* to raise, lift. **2** *(construir)* to build, erect. **3** *(un plano)* to draw up, make out. LOC **alzar el vuelo** to take off.

▶ *vpr* **alzarse 1** *(levantarse)* to rise up, get up. **2** *(sublevarse)* to rise, rebel.

a.m. *abrev* (ante meridiem) ante meridiem; *(abreviatura)* a.m.

ama *nf (propietaria)* landlady. COMP **ama de casa** housewife.

amabilidad *nf* kindness, affability.

amable *adj* kind, nice: *¿sería usted tan amable de...?* would you be so kind as to...?

amaestrar *vt (adiestrar)* to train; *(domar)* to tame.

amainar *vi (viento)* to die down, drop.

amamantar *vt* to breast-feed, suckle.

amanecer *vi* **1** to dawn, get light: *en verano amanece pronto* day breaks early in summer. **2** *(estar)* to be at dawn, be at daybreak: *amanecimos en Barcelona* we were in Barcelona at dawn.
▶ *nm* dawn, daybreak. LOC **al amanecer** at daybreak.

amanerado,-a *adj* affected, mannered.

amante *adj* loving, fond (de, of).
▶ *nm o nf* lover.

amañar *vt (falsear)* to fiddle, fix; *(cuentas)* to cook; *(elecciones)* to rig.

amapola *nf* poppy.

amar *vt* to love.
▶ *vpr* **amarse** to love each other, be in love (with each other).

amarar *vi (hidroavión)* to land at sea; *(nave espacial)* to splash down.

amargado,-a *pp* → amargar.
▶ *adj* embittered, resentful: *estar amargado,-a* to feel very bitter.
▶ *nm & nf* bitter person.

amargar *vi (tener sabor amargo)* to taste bitter.
▶ *vt* **1** *(hacer amargo)* to make bitter. **2** *fig (disgustos, etc)* to embitter, make bitter. **3** *fig (estropear)* to spoil, ruin: *la lluvia nos amargó el día* the rain put a damper on our day.
▶ *vpr* **amargarse** *fig* to become embittered, become bitter. LOC **a nadie le amarga un dulce** a gift is always welcome.

amargo,-a *adj* **1** *(sabor)* bitter. **2** *fig (carácter)* sour; *(experiencia)* bitter, sour, painful.

amargura *nf* **1** bitterness. **2** *(dolor)* sorrow, grief, sadness.

amarillo,-a *adj* yellow.
▶ *nm* **amarillo** yellow. COMP **prensa amarilla** sensationalist press.

amarra *nf* mooring rope.
▶ *nf pl* **amarras** *fam fig* connections. LOC **soltar las amarras 1** MAR to cast off, let go. **2** *fig* to break loose.

amarrar *vt* **1** *(atar)* to tie (up), fasten. **2** MAR to moor, tie up.

amarre *nm* mooring.

amasar *vt* **1** CULIN to knead. **2** *fig (reunir)* to amass.

amasijo *nm fam (mezcolanza)* hotchpotch, jumble.

amateur *adj* amateur.
▶ *nm o nf* amateur.

amatista *nf* amethyst.

amazona *nf* **1** *(mitología)* Amazon. **2** *(jinete)* horsewoman.

Amazonas *nm* **el Amazonas** the Amazon.

amazónico,-a *adj* Amazonian.

ámbar *nm* amber.

ambición *nf* ambition, aspiration.

ambicioso,-a *adj (plan, etc)* ambitious; *(persona)* ambitious, enterprising.

ambidextro,-a *adj* ambidextrous.
▶ *nm & nf* ambidextrous person.

ambientación *nf* **1** *(ambiente)* atmosphere. **2** *(localización)* setting.

ambientador *nm* air freshener.

ambiental *adj* **1** *(del ambiente)* environmental. **2** *(de fondo)* background.

ambientar *vt* **1** *(dar ambiente)* to give atmosphere to. **2** *(localizar)* to set.
▶ *vpr* **ambientarse** to adapt, get used (a, to).

ambiente *nm* **1** *(aire)* air, atmosphere. **2** *(entorno)* environment, atmosphere: *no hay mucho ambiente de noche* there is not much going on at night. LOC **cambiar de ambiente** to have a change of scene.

ambigüedad *nf* ambiguity.

ambiguo,-a *adj* ambiguous.

ámbito *nm* **1** *(espacio)* sphere, space. **2** *(marco)* field: *en el ámbito de la informática* in the computer science field.

ambivalente *adj* ambivalent.

ambos,-as *adj* both: *por ambos lados* on both sides.
▶ *pron* both: *me gustan ambos* I like both of them, I like them both.

ambulancia *nf* ambulance.

ambulante *adj* itinerant, travelling.

ambulatorio,-a *adj* ambulatory.
▶ *n* ambulatorio surgery, clinic.

ameba *nf* amoeba (US ameba).

amedrentar *vt* to frighten, scare.
▶ *vpr* **amedrentarse** *(asustarse)* to be frightened, be scared; *(acobardarse)* to become intimidated.

amén *nm* REL amen. LOC **decir amén a todo/todos** *fam* to agree with everything/everybody.

amenaza *nf* threat, menace.

amenazar *vt & vi* to threaten.

amenizar *vt* to liven up, make entertaining, make enjoyable.

ameno,-a *adj* lively, entertaining, enjoyable.

América *nf* America. COMP **América Central** Central America. ‖ **América del Norte** North America. ‖ **América del Sur** South America. ‖ **América Latina** Latin America.

americana *nf* jacket.

americano,-a *adj* American.
▶ *nm & nf* American.

amerizar *vi* → amarar.

ametralladora *nf* machine gun.

ametrallar *vt* **1** to machine-gun. **2** *fig (acosar)* to chase, pursue, besiege.

amianto *nm* asbestos.

amígdala *nf* tonsil.

amigdalitis *nf inv* tonsillitis.

amigo,-a *adj* **1** *(amigable)* friendly: *es muy amigo de Julio* he's very friendly with Julio. **2** *(aficionado)* fond (de, of): *no es muy amiga de discotecas* she's not keen on discos.
▶ *nm & nf* **1** friend: *una amiga mía* a friend of mine; *son amigos íntimos* they are close friends. **2** *(novio)* boyfriend; *(novia)* girlfriend. **3** *(amante)* lover.

amigote *nm fam* pal, mate, chum.

amiguismo *nm* contacts *pl*, string-pulling.

aminoácido *nm* amino acid.

aminorar *vt* to reduce, decrease. [LOC] aminorar el paso to slow down.

amistad *nf* friendship.
► *nf pl* **amistades** friends. [LOC] **hacer amistades** to make friends.

amistoso,-a *adj* friendly: *partido amistoso* friendly match.

amnesia *nf* amnesia.

amniótico,-a *adj* amniotic.

amnistía *nf* amnesty.

amo *nm* 1 *(señor)* master. 2 *(dueño)* owner. 3 *(jefe)* boss.

amoldarse *vpr* to adapt, adjust (a, to).

amonestación *nf* 1 *(represión)* reprimand, admonition, admonishment. 2 DEP caution, booking.

amonestar *vt* 1 *(reprender)* to reprimand, admonish. 2 DEP to caution, book.

amoníaco *nm* ammonia.

amontonar *vt* 1 to heap up, pile up. 2 *(juntar)* to collect, gather, accumulate.
► *vpr* **amontonarse** 1 to heap up, pile up. 2 *(gente)* to crowd together.

amor *nm* 1 *(gen)* love. 2 *(cuidado)* loving care; *(devoción)* devotion. [LOC] **con/de mil amores** *fam* willingly, with pleasure. ǀ **hacer el amor** to make love. [COMP] **amor propio** self-esteem.

amoral *adj* amoral.

amoratado,-a *adj* 1 *(de frío)* blue with cold. 2 *(de un golpe)* bruised, black and blue.

amordazar *vt (persona)* to gag; *(perro)* to muzzle.

amorfo,-a *adj* amorphous.

amoroso,-a *adj* loving, affectionate.

amortiguador *nm* 1 AUTO shock absorber. 2 TÉC damper.

amortiguar *vt (golpe)* to cushion; *(dolor)* to alleviate, ease, soothe; *(ruido)* to muffle; *(luz)* to subdue, dim.

amotinarse *vpr* 1 to rebel, rise up, riot. 2 MIL to mutiny.

amparar *vt* to protect, shelter.

► *vpr* **ampararse** 1 *(protegerse)* to take shelter, protect OS. 2 *(acogerse)* to avail OS of the protection (en, of), seek protection (en, in).

amparo *nm* protection, shelter.

amperio *nm* ampere.

ampliación *nf* 1 enlargement, extension. 2 ARQUIT extension. 3 *(fotografía)* enlargement.

ampliar *vt* 1 to enlarge, extend. 2 ARQUIT to build an extension onto. 3 *(fotografía)* to enlarge. 4 *(capital)* to increase. 5 *(estudios)* to further. 6 *(tema, idea)* to develop, expand on.

amplificación *nf* amplification.

amplio,-a *adj* 1 *(extenso)* large. 2 *(espacioso)* roomy, spacious. 3 *(ancho)* wide, broad. 4 *(holgado)* loose.

amplitud *nf* 1 *(extensión)* extent, range. 2 *(espacio)* room, space, spaciousness. 3 *(anchura)* width. 4 *(holgadura)* looseness. 5 FÍS amplitude.

ampolla *nf* 1 MED blister. 2 *(burbuja)* bubble. 3 *(tubito)* ampoule, phial.

amputar *vt* to amputate.

amueblar *vt* to furnish. [LOC] **sin amueblar** unfurnished.

amuleto *nm* amulet, charm.

amurallar *vt* to wall.

anabolizante *adj* anabolic.

anaconda *nf* anaconda.

anacoreta *nm o nf* anchorite.

anacronismo *nm* anachronism.

anaerobio,-a *adj* anaerobic.

anagrama *nm* anagram.

anal *adj* anal.

analfabetismo *nm* illiteracy.

analfabeto,-a *adj* 1 illiterate. 2 *fig* stupid.
► *nm & nf* 1 illiterate person. 2 *fig* stupid person, ignoramus.

analgésico,-a *adj* analgesic.
► *nm* **analgésico** analgesic, painkiller.

análisis *nm inv* analysis. [COMP] **análisis de orina** urine test. ǀ **análisis de sangre** blood test.

analizar *vt* to analyse (US analyze).

analogía *nf* analogy.

analógico,-a *adj* analogical.
análogo,-a *adj* analogous, similar.
anaquel *nm* shelf.
anarquía *nf* anarchy.
anárquico,-a *adj* anarchic, anarchical.
anarquista *adj* anarchist.
  ▶ *nm o nf* anarchist.
anatomía *nf* anatomy.
anca *nf* haunch. COMP **ancas de rana** frogs' legs.
ancestral *adj* ancestral, ancient.
ancho,-a *adj* **1** *(gen)* broad, wide. **2** *(prenda - holgada)* loose-fitting; *(- grande)* too big.
  ▶ *nm* **ancho 1** *(anchura)* breadth, width: *¿qué ancho tiene?* how wide is it?; *tiene cuatro metros de ancho* it's four metres wide. **2** *(en costura)* width. LOC **a sus anchas** *fam* comfortable, at ease. ‖ **estar más ancho,-a que largo,-a** to be full of os. ‖ **quedarse tan ancho, a** *fam* to behave as if nothing had happened, not bat an eyelid.
anchoa *nf* anchovy.
anchura *nf* breadth, width.
anciano,-a *adj* very old, elderly, aged.
  ▶ *nm & nf* old person, elderly person.
ancla *nf* anchor.
anclar *vi* MAR to anchor.
  ▶ *vt* TÉC to anchor.
andadas LOC **volver a las andadas** to go back to one's old tricks.
Andalucía *nf* Andalusia.
andaluz,-za *adj* Andalusian.
  ▶ *nm & nf (persona)* Andalusian.
  ▶ *nm* **andaluz** *(dialecto)* Andalusian.
andamio *nm* scaffold.
andanada *nf* MAR broadside.
andante COMP **caballero andante** knight errant.
andanzas *nf pl* adventures.
andar *vi* **1** *(moverse)* to walk. **2** *(funcionar)* to work, run, go: *este reloj no anda* this watch doesn't work. **3** *(estar)* to be: *¿cómo andas?* how are you?, how's it going? **4** *(juntarse)* to mix (con, with). LOC **andar a gatas** to crawl. ‖ **andar de puntillas** to tiptoe. ‖ **andar con rodeos** to beat about the bush. ‖ **andar con cui-**dado / **andarse con cuidado** to be careful. ‖ **andarse por las ramas** *fig* to beat about the bush.
  ▶ *interj* ¡**anda**! well!, oh!: ¡anda ya! come off it!.
andén *nm* platform.
Andes *nm pl* **los Andes** the Andes.
andino,-a *adj* Andean.
  ▶ *nm & nf* Andean.
Andorra *nm* Andorra.
andorrano,-a *adj* Andorran.
  ▶ *nm & nf* Andorran.
androide *nm* android.
anécdota *nf* anecdote.
anélido *nm* annelid.
anemia *nf* anaemia (US anemia).
anemona *nf* anemone. COMP **anemona de mar** sea anemone.
anestesia *nf* anaesthesia (US anesthesia).
anestésico,-a *adj* anaesthetic (US anesthetic).
  ▶ *nm* **anestésico** anaesthetic (US anesthetic).
anexión *nf* annexation.
anexo,-a *adj* adjoining, attached (a, to).
  ▶ *nm* **anexo** annexe (US annex).
anfetamina *nf* amphetamine.
anfibio,-a *adj* amphibious.
  ▶ *nm* **anfibio** amphibian.
  ▶ *nm pl* **los anfibios** amphibia *pl*.
anfiteatro *nm* **1** amphitheatre (US amphitheater). **2** *(en universidad)* lecture theatre (US theater). **3** *(en teatro, cine)* circle.
anfitrión,-ona *nm & nf (hombre)* host; *(mujer)* hostess.
ángel *nm* angel.
angina *nf* angina. LOC **tener anginas** to have a sore throat. COMP **angina de pecho** angina pectoris.
anglosajón,-ona *adj* Anglo-Saxon.
  ▶ *nm & nf (persona)* Anglo-Saxon.
  ▶ *nm* **anglosajón** *(idioma)* Anglo-Saxon.
Angola *nf* Angola.
angosto,-a *adj* narrow.
ángstrom *nm* angstrom.
anguila *nf* eel.

angula *nf* elver.

ángulo *nm* **1** angle. **2** *(rincón)* corner. COMP **ángulo recto** right angle.

angustia *nf* anguish, distress.

angustiar *vt* **1** *(afligir)* to distress, upset. **2** *(preocupar)* to worry, make anxious.

angustioso,-a *adj (situación)* distressing, worrying; *(mirada)* anguished.

anhelar *vt* to long for, yearn for.

anhelo *nm* longing, yearning.

anhídrido *nm* anhydride.

anilla *nf (aro)* ring.
▶ *nf pl* **anillas** DEP rings.

anillo *nm* **1** ring. **2** ARQUIT annulet. **3** *(de gusano)* annulus; *(de culebra)* coil. LOC **venir como anillo al dedo** to be just what SB needed, suit SB fine.

animación *nf* **1** *(actividad)* activity, movement, bustle. **2** *(viveza)* liveliness. **3** CINE animation.

animado,-a *pp* → animar.
▶ *adj* **1** *(movido)* animated, lively, jolly. **2** *(concurrido)* bustling, full of people. **3** *(alegre)* cheerful, in high spirits, excited.

animador,-ra *nm & nf* **1** *(artista)* entertainer. **2** *(de un equipo)* cheerleader.

animadversión *nf* antagonism, hostility, ill will, animosity.

animal *adj* animal.
▶ *nm* **1** animal. **2** *fig (basto)* rough person, brute, lout; *(necio)* dunce. COMP **animal doméstico** pet. ‖ **reino animal** animal kingdom.

animar *vt* **1** *(alegrar a algn)* to cheer up. **2** *(alegrar algo)* to brighten up, liven up. **3** *(alentar)* to encourage.
▶ *vpr* **animarse 1** *(persona)* to cheer up. **2** *(fiesta, etc)* to brighten up, liven up. **3** *(decidirse)* to make up one's mind.

ánimo *nm* **1** *(espíritu)* spirit; *(mente)* mind; *(alma)* soul. **2** *(intención)* intention, purpose: *sin ánimo de ofender* no offence intended. **3** *(valor)* courage: *no tengo ánimos de nada* I don't feel up to anything. **4** *(aliento)* encouragement.
▶ *interj* cheer up!

anión *nm* anion.

aniquilar *vt* to annihilate, destroy.

anís *nm* **1** *(planta)* anise; *(grano)* aniseed. **2** *(bebida)* anisette.

aniversario *nm* anniversary.

ano *nm* anus.

anoche *adv (late)* last night; *(early)* yesterday evening.

anochecer *vi* **1** to get dark: *cuando anocheció* when it got dark. **2** to be at nightfall, reach at nightfall.
▶ *nm* nightfall, dusk, evening. LOC **al anochecer** at nightfall, at dusk.

ánodo *nm* anode.

anofeles *nm inv* anopheles.

anomalía *nf* anomaly.

anómalo,-a *adj* anomalous.

anonimato *nm* anonymity.

anónimo,-a *adj* **1** *(desconocido)* anonymous. **2** *(sociedad)* limited, US incorporated.
▶ *nm* **anónimo** *(carta)* anonymous letter.

anorak *nm* anorak.

anorexia *nf* anorexia.

anormal *adj* **1** *(no normal)* abnormal. **2** *(inhabitual)* unusual. **3** MED subnormal.

anotación *nf* **1** *(acotación)* annotation. **2** *(nota)* note. **3** *(apunte)* noting.

anotar *vt* **1** *(acotar)* to annotate, add notes to. **2** *(apuntar)* to take down, jot down, make a note of.

ansia *nf* **1** *(ansiedad)* anxiety; *(angustia)* anguish. **2** *(deseo)* eagerness, longing, yearning: *tener ansia de poder* to be longing for power.

ansiar *vt* to long for, yearn for.

ansiedad *nf* **1** anxiety. **2** MED nervous tension.

ansioso,-a *adj* **1** *(desasosegado)* anguished, anxious, desperate. **2** *(deseoso)* eager, longing (**por/de**, to).

antagónico,-a *adj* antagonistic.

antaño *adv* formerly, in olden times, long ago.

antártico,-a *adj* Antarctic.

Antártida *nf* Antarctica.

ante¹ *prep* **1** before, in the presence of. **2** *(considerando)* in the face of: *ante estas circunstancias* under the circumstances. LOC **ante todo 1** *(primero)* first of all. **2** *(por encima de)* above all.

ante² *nm* **1** ZOOL elk, moose. **2** *(piel)* suede.

anteayer *adv* the day before yesterday.

antebrazo *nm* forearm.

antecedente *nm* **1** precedent. **2** GRAM antecedent. **3** MED history.
▶ *nm pl* **antecedentes** record *sing.*

antecesor,-ra *nm & nf* **1** *(en un cargo)* predecessor. **2** *(antepasado)* ancestor.

antelación *nf* precedence: *con cinco días de antelación* five days beforehand. LOC **con antelación** in advance.

antemano LOC **de antemano** beforehand, in advance.

antena *nf* **1** RAD TV aerial, antenna. **2** ANAT antenna, feeler. LOC **estar en antena** to be on the air. COMP **antena parabólica** satellite dish.

anteojos *nm pl* **1** *(binóculos)* binoculars, field glasses. **2** *(gafas)* glasses, spectacles.

antepasado *nm* ancestor.
▶ *nm pl* **antepasados** forefathers, forbears.

antepenúltimo,-a *adj* antepenultimate.

anteponer *vt* **1** *(poner delante)* to place in front (a, of), put in front (a, of); *(poner antes)* to put before. **2** *(preferir)* to prefer (a, to).

antera *nf* anther.

anterior *adj* **1** *(tiempo)* previous, preceding, before: *el día anterior* the day before. **2** *(lugar)* front: *la parte anterior* the front part.
▶ *nm o nf* the previous one.

anterioridad *nf* priority. LOC **con anterioridad** previously. ▌ **con anterioridad a** prior to, before.

antes *adv* **1** *(tiempo)* before, earlier: *llámame antes de salir* ring me before you leave; *deberías estar allí antes de las nueve* you should be there before nine. **2** *(en el pasado)* before, in the past. **3** *(lugar)* in front, before. LOC **antes de nada** first of all. ▌ **lo antes posible** as soon as possible.
▶ *adj* before.

antesala *nf* anteroom, antechamber.

antiadherente *adj* nonstick.

antiaéreo,-a *adj* anti-aircraft.

antibalas *adj* bullet-proof.

antibiótico,-a *adj* antibiotic.
▶ *nm* **antibiótico** antibiotic.

anticaspa *adj* anti-dandruff: *champú anticaspa* dandruff shampoo.

anticiclón *nm* anticyclone, high pressure area.

anticipación *nf* anticipation, advance. LOC **con anticipación** in advance.

anticipado,-a *pp* → anticipar.
▶ *adj* brought forward; *(temprano)* early: *gracias anticipadas* thanks in advance; *pago anticipado* payment in advance. LOC **por anticipado** in advance.

anticipar *vt* **1** to anticipate, advance, bring forward. **2** *(dinero)* to advance.
▶ *vpr* **anticiparse 1** *(llegar antes)* to come early. **2** *(adelantarse)* to beat to it: *él se me anticipó* he beat me to it.

anticipo *nm* **1** *(gen)* foretaste, preview. **2** *(pago)* advance, advance payment.

anticlinal *nm* anticline.

anticonceptivo,-a *adj* contraceptive.
▶ *nm* **anticonceptivo** contraceptive.

anticongelante *adj* antifreeze.
▶ *nm* **anticongelante** antifreeze.

anticorrosivo,-a *adj* anticorrosive.
▶ *nm* **anticorrosivo** anticorrosive.

anticuado,-a *adj* antiquated, old-fashioned, obsolete, out-of-date.

anticuario *nm* *(conocedor)* antiquary, antiquarian; *(comerciante)* antique dealer.

anticuerpo *nm* antibody.

antidepresivo,-a *adj* antidepressant.
▶ *nm* **antidepresivo** antidepressant.

antidisturbios *adj* riot. COMP **material antidisturbios** riot gear. ▌ **policía antidisturbios** riot police.

antidoping *adj* anti-doping, anti-drug.

antídoto *nm* antidote.

antifaz *nm* mask.

antígeno *nm* antigen.

antigüedad *nf* **1** *(período)* antiquity. **2** *(en empleo)* seniority. **3** *(objeto)* antique. LOC **en la antigüedad** in olden days, in former times. COMP **tienda de antigüedades** antique shop.

antiguo,-a *adj* **1** *(gen)* ancient, old; *(coche)* vintage, old. **2** *(en empleo)* senior. **3** *(pasado)* old-fashioned. **4** *(anterior)* former: *el antiguo primer ministro* the former Prime Minister.

antihéroe *nm* antihero.

antihistamínico *nm* antihistamine.

antiinflamatorio *nm* anti-inflammatory.

antílope *nm* antelope.

antimonio *nm* antimony.

antiniebla *adj inv* anti-fog. ｜COMP｜ **faros antiniebla** foglamps. ▌ **luces antiniebla** foglamps.

antipatía *nf* antipathy, dislike.

antipático,-a *adj* unfriendly, unpleasant, unkind.
▶ *nm & nf* unpleasant person.

antípoda *nm & nf (punto)* antipode, antipodes *pl*.

antirrobo *adj inv* anti-theft.

antisemitismo *nm* anti-Semitism.

antiséptico,-a *adj* antiseptic.
▶ *nm* **antiséptico** antiseptic.

antiterrorista *adj* antiterrorist.

antítesis *nf inv* antithesis.

antitetánico,-a *adj* anti-tetanus.

antitranspirante *adj* antiperspirant.
▶ *nm* antiperspirant.

antivirus *nm* **1** *(fármaco)* antivirus drug. **2** INFORM antivirus.

antojo *nm* **1** *(capricho)* whim, fancy; *(de embarazada)* craving. **2** *(en la piel)* birthmark.

antología *nf* anthology.

antónimo *nm* antonym.

antonomasia *nf* antonomasia. ｜LOC｜ **por antonomasia** par excellence.

antorcha *nf* torch.

antracita *nf* anthracite.

ántrax *nm inv* anthrax.

antro *nm* **1** *(caverna)* cavern. **2** *(tugurio)* dump, hole, dive.

antropoide *nm o nf* anthropoid.

antropología *nf* anthropology.

anual *adj* annual, yearly.

anuario *nm* yearbook.

anudar *vt (atar)* to knot, tie, fasten.

anulación *nf* **1** *(gen)* annulment, cancellation; *(de ley)* repeal; *(de sentencia)* quashing, overturning. **2** DEP *(de gol)* disallowing. ｜COMP｜ **anulación de matrimonio** annulment of marriage.

anular¹ *adj* ring-shaped.
▶ *nm* ring finger.

anular² *vt* **1** *(matrimonio)* to annul; *(una ley)* to repeal; *(una sentencia)* to quash. **2** *(un pedido, viaje)* to cancel; *(un contrato)* to invalidate, cancel. **3** DEP *(un gol)* to disallow.

anunciar *vt* **1** *(avisar)* to announce, make public. **2** *(hacer publicidad)* to advertise.
▶ *vpr* **anunciarse** to put an advert (en, in).

anuncio *nm* **1** *(aviso)* announcement; *(signo)* sign. **2** *(publicidad)* advertisement, advert, ad. **3** *(valla publicitaria)* hoarding, US billboard. ｜COMP｜ **anuncios por palabras** classified adverts, small ads.

anverso *nm* **1** *(de moneda)* obverse. **2** *(de página)* recto.

anzuelo *nm* **1** fish-hook. **2** *fig* lure, bait. ｜LOC｜ **tragar/morder/picar el anzuelo** to swallow the bait.

añadidura *nf* addition, addendum. ｜LOC｜ **por añadidura** besides, in addition.

añadir *vt* to add (a, to).

añejo,-a *adj* **1** *(vino, queso)* mature; *(jamón)* cured. **2** *(viejo)* old.

añicos *nm pl* bits, pieces. ｜LOC｜ **hacer añicos** to smash to pieces. ▌ **hacerse añicos** to shatter, smash to bits.

año *nm* year: *el año pasado* last year; *el año que viene* next year; *los años sesenta* the sixties. ｜COMP｜ **año escolar** school year. ▌ **año luz** light year.
▶ *nm pl* years, age *sing*: *¿cuántos años tienes?* how old are you?; *tengo 20 años* I'm 20 years old. ｜LOC｜ **hace años** a long time ago, years ago.

añorar *vt* **1** *(gen)* to long for, miss, yearn for. **2** *(país)* to be homesick for, miss.

aorta *nf* aorta.

aovar *vi* to lay eggs.

apacible *adj (persona)* gentle, calm, placid; *(vida)* quiet, peaceful; *(clima, tiempo)* mild; *(mar)* calm.

apaciguar *vt* to pacify, appease, placate, calm down.

apadrinar *vt* 1 *(en bautizo)* to act as godfather to. 2 *(en boda)* to be the best man for. 3 *(artista)* to sponsor.

apagar *vt* 1 *(fuego)* to extinguish, put out. 2 *(luz)* to turn out, turn off, put out. 3 *(televisión, etc)* to switch off, turn off. 4 *fig (sed)* to quench.

apagón *nm* power cut, blackout.

apaisado,-a *adj* 1 oblong. 2 INFORM landscape.

apalancarse *vpr argot* to settle OS, settle down.

apalear *vt (pegar)* to beat, cane, thrash.

apañarse LOC apañárselas to manage, get by.

apaño *nm* 1 *(remiendo, compostura)* repair, mend, patch. 2 *(acuerdo)* agreement, deal.

aparador *nm* 1 *(escaparate)* shop window. 2 *(mueble)* sideboard, cupboard, buffet.

aparato *nm* 1 *(mecanismo)* (piece of) apparatus, set; *(eléctrico)* appliance. 2 *(dispositivo)* device; *(instrumento)* instrument. 3 *(teléfono)* telephone: *está al aparato* he's on the phone. 4 *(avión)* plane. COMP aparato de radio radio set. ‖ aparato digestivo ANAT digestive system.

aparcamiento *nm* 1 *(acción)* parking. 2 *(en la calle)* place to park, parking place. 3 *(parking)* car park, US parking lot.

aparcar *vt* to park.
▶ *vi* to park. LOC «Prohibido aparcar» «No parking».

aparearse *vpr* to mate.

aparecer *vi* 1 to appear: *no aparece en la lista de invitados* she's not on the guest list. 2 *(dejarse ver)* to show up, turn up: *espero que no aparezca por mi casa* I hope he doesn't show his face near my house.

aparejador,-ra *nm & nf (de obras)* clerk of works; *(perito)* quantity surveyor.

aparentar *vt* 1 *(simular)* to pretend, affect: *aparenta indiferencia* she pretends not to care, she affects indifference. 2 *(tener aspecto de)* to look: *no aparenta la edad que tiene* he doesn't look his age.
▶ *vi* to show off.

aparente *adj* apparent.

aparición *nf* 1 appearance. 2 *(visión)* apparition.

apariencia *nf* appearance, aspect. LOC en apariencia apparently, by all appearances. ‖ guardar las apariencias *fig* to keep up appearances.

apartado,-a *pp* → apartar.
▶ *adj* 1 *(alejado)* remote, distant; *(aislado)* isolated, cut off. 2 *(retirado)* retired.
▶ *nm* apartado 1 post office box. 2 *(párrafo)* section.

apartamento *nm* small flat, apartment.

apartar *vt* 1 *(alejar)* to move away. 2 *(reservar)* to put aside, set aside.
▶ *vpr* apartarse 1 *(alejarse)* to move away. 2 *(separarse)* to withdraw, move away.

aparte *adv* apart, aside, separately
▶ *adj (distinto)* special: *eso es caso aparte* that's completely different.
▶ *nm* 1 TEAT aside. 2 LING paragraph: *punto y aparte* full stop, new paragraph. LOC aparte de *(excepto)* apart from. *(además de)* as well as, besides.

apasionante *adj* exciting, fascinating.

apasionarse *vpr* to get excited, become enthusiastic (por/de, about).

apatía *nf* apathy.

apátrida *adj* stateless.
▶ *nm o nf* stateless person.

apeadero *nm* halt.

apearse *vpr (del tren, autobús, etc.)* to get off; *(del coche)* to get out of; *(del caballo)* to dismount.

apedrear *vt* 1 *(tirar piedras)* to throw stones at. 2 *(matar a pedradas)* to stone (to death).

apego *nm* attachment, affection, liking, fondness.

apelación *nf* 1 JUR appeal. 2 *(llamamiento)* appeal, call.

apelar *vi* 1 JUR to appeal. 2 *fig (recurrir)* to resort to.

apelativo *nm* appellative, name.

apellidarse *vpr* to be called, have as a surname.

apellido *nm* family name, surname, (US last name).

apenas *adv* **1** *(casi no)* scarcely, hardly: *apenas lo conozco* I hardly know him. **2** *(con dificultad)* only just. **3** *(tan pronto como)* as soon as, no sooner: *apenas entramos, sonó el teléfono* no sooner had we had come in than the phone rang.

apéndice *nm* **1** *(órgano interno)* appendix. **2** *(de libro)* appendix.

apendicitis *nf inv* appendicitis.

aperitivo *nm* **1** *(bebida)* apéritif. **2** *(comida)* appetizer, snack.

apertura *nf* **1** *(comienzo)* opening, beginning. **2** POL liberalization.

apestar *vi* *(oler mal)* to stink.

apetecer *vi* *(agradar)* to feel like, fancy: *¿te apetece ir al teatro?* do you fancy going to the theatre?

apetecible *adj* **1** *(empleo)* desirable; *(idea)* appealing. **2** *(comida)* tasty, appetizing.

apetito *nm* appetite. LOC **abrir el apetito** to whet one's appetite.

apetitoso,-a *adj* **1** *(aspecto de comida)* appetizing; *(comida)* tasty, delicious. **2** *(oferta)* tempting.

apiadarse *vpr* to take pity *(de, on)*.

ápice *nm* **1** *(punta)* apex. **2** *fig* tiny bit, speck, iota. LOC **ni un ápice** not one bit.

apicultura *nf* beekeeping, apiculture.

apilar *vt* to pile up, heap up.

apio *nm* celery.

apisonadora *nf* steamroller, roadroller.

aplacar *vt* to placate, calm, soothe.

aplanar *vt* to smooth, level, make even.

aplastante *adj* crushing, overwhelming. COMP **triunfo/victoria aplastante** *(electoral)* landslide victory.

aplastar *vt* **1** *(gen)* to flatten, squash, crush. **2** *fig* *(destruir)* to crush, destroy.

aplaudir *vt* to clap, applaud.

aplauso *nm* applause.

aplazamiento *nm* *(gen)* adjournment, postponement; *(de pago)* deferment.

aplazar *vt* *(gen)* to adjourn, postpone, put off; *(un pago)* to defer.

aplicación *nf* application.

aplicado,-a *pp* → aplicar.
▶ *adj* *(estudioso)* studious, diligent, hard-working.

aplicar *vt* to apply.
▶ *vpr* **aplicarse** *(esforzarse)* to apply OS, work hard.

aplique *nm* **1** *(adorno)* appliqué. **2** *(lámpara)* wall light, wall lamp.

aplomo *nm* composure, self-possession.

apocado,-a *adj* **1** *(intimidado)* intimidated, frightened. **2** *(tímido)* shy, timid.

apocalipsis *nm inv* apocalypse.

apócope *nm* apocope.

apodarse *vpr* to be nicknamed.

apoderado,-a *pp* → apoderarse.
▶ *nm & nf* **1** agent, representative. **2** *(de torero, deportista)* manager.

apoderarse *vpr* to take possession **(de,** of), seize **(de, -):** *el miedo se apoderó de él* he was seized by fear.

apodo *nm* nickname.

apogeo *nm* **1** *(de órbita)* apogee. **2** *fig* *(punto culminante)* summit, height, climax, peak.

apolítico,-a *adj* apolitical.

apología *nf* apology, defence (US defense).

apoplejía *nf* apoplexy, stroke.

aporrear *vt* *(persona)* to beat, hit, thrash; *(puerta)* to bang on; *(piano)* to bang (away) on.

aportación *nf* contribution.

aportar *vt* **1** *(contribuir)* to contribute. **2** *(proporcionar)* to give, provide.

aposento *nm* **1** *(cuarto)* room. **2** *(hospedaje)* lodgings *pl*.

apósito *nm* dressing.

aposta *adv* on purpose, deliberately, intentionally.

apostar *vt* to bet *(por, on)*.
▶ *vpr* **apostarse** to bet.

apóstol *nm* **1** apostle. **2** *fig* *(defensor)* apostle, champion.

apóstrofe *nm & nf* **1** GRAM apostrophe. **2** *(reprimenda)* reprimand, rebuke.

apotema *nf* apothem.

apoteósico,-a *adj* enormous, tremendous.

A

apoyar *vt* **1** to lean, rest. **2** *(fundar)* to base, found. **3** *fig (defender algo)* to support; *(defender a alguien)* to back, support.
▶ *vpr* **apoyarse 1** *(descansar)* to lean (en, on), rest (en, on), stand (en, on). **2** *fig (basarse)* to be based (en, on).

apoyo *nm* support.

apreciable *adj* **1** *(perceptible)* appreciable, noticeable. **2** *(estimable)* valuable, precious.

apreciar *vt* **1** *(valorar)* to appraise (en, at). **2** *(sentir aprecio)* to regard highly, hold in high esteem. **3** *(reconocer valor)* to appreciate. **4** *(percibir)* to notice, see, perceive.

aprecio *nm* esteem, regard. LOC **sentir aprecio por** ALGN to be fond of SB.

aprender *vt* **1** to learn. **2** *(memorizar)* to learn by heart.
▶ *vpr* **aprenderse** learn by heart.

aprendiz,-za *nm & nf* apprentice, trainee.

aprendizaje *nm* **1** *(situación)* apprenticeship. **2** *(tiempo)* training period. **3** *(en pedagogía)* learning.

aprensión *nf (miedo)* apprehension; *(asco)* squeamishness.

aprensivo,-a *adj* apprehensive.

apresar *vt* **1** *(tomar por fuerza)* to seize, capture. **2** *(asir)* to clutch.

apresurarse *vpr* to hurry, hurry up.

apretar *vt* **1** *(estrechar)* to squeeze, hug. **2** *(tornillo)* to tighten; *(cordones, nudo)* to do up tight. **3** *(comprimir)* to compress, press together, pack tight. **4** *(botón)* to press, push.
▶ *vi* **1** *fig (aumentar)* to increase, get worse: *el calor aprieta* it's getting hotter and hotter. **2** *(prendas)* to fit tight, be tight on.

apretón COMP **apretón de manos** handshake.

aprieto *nm* tight spot, difficulty, scrape, fix. LOC **poner a** ALGN **en un aprieto** to put SB in an awkward situation.

aprisa *adv* quickly.

aprobación *nf (gen)* approval; *(ley)* passing.

aprobado,-a *pp* → aprobar.
▶ *adj* approved, passed.
▶ *nm* **aprobado** EDUC pass (mark). LOC **sacar/tener un aprobado** to get a pass.

aprobar *vt* **1** *(gen)* to approve; *(ley)* to pass. **2** *(estar de acuerdo)* to approve of. **3** EDUC *(examen, asignatura)* to pass.
▶ *vi* to pass.

apropiación *nf* appropriation. COMP **apropiación indebida** JUR theft.

apropiado,-a *pp* → apropiarse.
▶ *adj* suitable, fitting, appropriate.

apropiarse *vpr* to appropriate (de, -), take possession (de, of).

aprovechable *adj* usable.

aprovechado,-a *pp* → aprovechar.
▶ *adj* **1** *(espacio)* well-planned. **2** *pey (egoísta)* selfish; *(gorrón)* sponging, scrounging. LOC **mal aprovechado,-a** wasted.
▶ *nm & nf fam (gorrón)* sponger, scrounger; *(oportunista)* opportunist.

aprovechamiento *nm* **1** *(uso)* use, exploitation: *el aprovechamiento de los recursos naturales* the exploitation of natural resources. **2** *(provecho)* improvement, progress.

aprovechar *vt* **1** *(emplear útilmente)* to make good use of, make the most of. **2** *(sacar provecho)* to benefit from, take advantage of.
▶ *vpr* **aprovecharse** *(de alguien)* to take advantage (de, of); *(de algo)* to make the most (de, of). LOC **¡que aproveche!** enjoy your meal!

aproximación *nf* **1** *(gen)* approximation. **2** *(acercamiento)* bringing together; *(de países)* rapprochement.

aproximado,-a *pp* → aproximar.
▶ *adj* approximate, estimated. COMP **cálculo aproximado** rough estimate.

aproximar *vt* to bring near, put near.
▶ *vpr* **aproximarse** to come near, come closer.

aptitud *nf* aptitude, ability.

apto,-a *adj* **1** *(apropiado)* suitable, appropriate: *no es apto para este trabajo* he's not suitable for this job. **2** *(capaz)* capable, able.

apuesta *nf* bet, wager.

apuesto,-a *adj* (gen) good-looking; (hombre) handsome.

apuntador,-ra *nm & nf* TEAT prompter.

apuntar *vt* **1** (señalar) to point (a, at). **2** (arma) to aim. **3** (anotar) to note down, make a note of. **4** TEAT to prompt.
▶ *vpr* **apuntarse 1** (inscribirse) to enrol. **2** *fam* (participar) to take part (a, in): ¿te apuntas? are you game?

apunte *nm* **1** note. **2** (dibujo) sketch.
▶ *nm pl* **apuntes** (de clase) notes.

apuñalar *vt* to stab.

apurar *vt* **1** (terminar) to finish up. **2** AM (dar prisa) to hurry, rush.
▶ *vpr* **apurarse 1** (preocuparse) to get worried, be worried. **2** AM (darse prisa) to hurry, rush.

apuro *nm* **1** fix, tight spot; (de dinero) hardship. **2** (vergüenza) embarrassment. LOC **estar/encontrarse en un apuro** to be in a tight spot. I **pasar apuros 1** (económicos) to be hard up. **2** (dificultades) to be in a tight spot.

aquejado,-a *adj* suffering (de, from).

aquel,-ella *adj* **1** that. **2 aquellos,-as** those.

aquél,-élla *pron* **1** that one; (el anterior) the former: aquél es el mío that one is mine. **2 aquéllos,-as** those; (los anteriores) the former. LOC **aquél que...** he who... I **todo aquél que...** anyone who..., whoever...

aquella *adj* → aquel.

aquélla *pron* → aquél.

aquello *pron* that, it.

aquellos,-as *adj* → aquel,-ella.

aquéllos,-as *pron* → aquél,-éllas.

aquí *adv* **1** (lugar) here: por aquí por favor this way please. **2** (tiempo) now: de aquí en adelante from now on.

árabe *adj* (gen) Arab; (de Arabia) Arabian.
▶ *nm & nf* Arab.

Arabia *nf* Arabia. COMP **Arabia Saudita** Saudi Arabia.

arácnido *nm* arachnid.

arado *nm* plough (US plow).

arancel *nm* tariff, customs duty.

arándano *nm* bilberry, blueberry.

arandela *nf* washer.

araña *nf* **1** (arácnido) spider. **2** (pez) weever. **3** (lámpara) chandelier. COMP **araña de mar** spider crab. I **tela de araña** spider's web.

arañar *vt* **1** (raspar) to scratch. **2** *fig* (recoger) to scrape together.
▶ *vpr* **arañarse** to scratch.

arañazo *nm* scratch.

arar *vt* to plough (US plow).

arbitraje *nm* **1** (en un desacuerdo) arbitration. **2** DEP (en fútbol, boxeo) refereeing; (en cricket, tenis) umpiring.

arbitrar *vt* **1** to arbitrate. **2** DEP (en fútbol, boxeo) to referee; (en cricket, tenis) to umpire.

arbitrario,-a *adj* arbitrary.

árbitro,-a *nm & nf* **1** arbiter, arbitrator. **2** DEP (fútbol, boxeo) referee; (cricket, tenis) umpire.

árbol *nm* **1** BOT tree. **2** TÉC axle, shaft. **3** MAR mast. **4** (gráfico) tree (diagram).

arboleda *nf* grove, wood, copse.

arbusto *nm* shrub, bush.

arca *nf* chest. COMP **arca de Noé** Noah's ark. I **arcas públicas** Treasury *sing*.

arcada *nf* **1** (conjunto de arcos) arcade. **2** (de puente) arch. **3** (vómitos) retching.

arcaico,-a *adj* archaic.

arce *nm* maple (tree).

arcén *nm* side of the road, verge; (de autopista) hard shoulder.

archipiélago *nm* archipelago.

archivador *nm* (mueble) filing cabinet; (carpeta) file.

archivar *vt* **1** (ordenar) to file (away). **2** INFORM to save. **3** (arrinconar) to shelve.

archivo *nm* **1** (informe, ficha) file. **2** (documentos) files *pl*, archives *pl*. **3** INFORM file. **4** (lugar) archive. **5** (archivador) filing cabinet.

arcilla *nf* clay.

arco *nm* **1** ARQUIT arch. **2** (en geometría) arc. **3** (arma) bow. **4** (de violín, etc) bow. COMP **arco de medio punto** semicircular arch. I **arco iris** rainbow. I **arco voltaico** electric arc.

arder *vi* to burn; (completamente) to burn down; (sin llama) to smoulder.

ardid *nm* scheme, trick.

A

ardilla *nf* squirrel.

ardor *nm* **1** burning sensation, burn; *(calor)* heat. **2** *fig (ansia)* ardour (US ardor), fervour (US fervor). COMP **ardor de estómago** heartburn.

arduo,-a *adj* arduous.

área *nf* **1** *(zona)* area, zone. **2** *(medida)* are. **3** *(superficie)* area.

arena *nf* sand. COMP **arenas movedizas** quicksand *sing*.

arenisca *nf* sandstone.

arenoso,-a *adj* sandy.

arenque *nm* herring.

argamasa *nf* mortar.

Argelia *nm* Algeria.

argelino,-a *adj* Algerian.
▶ *nm & nf* Algerian.

Argentina *nf* Argentina, the Argentine.

argentino,-a *adj* Argentinian.
▶ *nm & nf* Argentinian.

argón *nm* argon.

argot *nm* **1** *(popular)* slang. **2** *(técnico)* jargon.

argucia *nf* sophism, subtlety.

argumentación *nf* **1** *(proceso)* arguing, argument. **2** *(argumento)* argument.

argumentar *vt* to deduce.

argumento *nm* **1** argument. **2** *(de novela, obra, etc)* plot.

aria *nf* aria.

aridez *nf* **1** aridity. **2** *fig* dryness.

árido,-a *adj* **1** arid. **2** *fig* dry.
▶ *nm pl* **áridos** dry goods.

Aries *nm inv* Aries.

ariete *nm* **1** *(fútbol)* centre (US center) forward. **2** *(máquina)* battering ram.

ario,-a *adj* Aryan.

arisco,-a *adj* **1** *(persona - altiva)* unsociable, unfriendly; *(- áspera)* surly, gruff; *(- huidiza)* shy. **2** *(animal)* unfriendly.

arista *nf* **1** *(línea)* edge. **2** *(filamento del trigo)* beard. **3** ARQUIT *(de viga)* arris; *(de bóveda)* groin. **4** *(de montaña)* arête.

aristocracia *nf* aristocracy.

aristócrata *nm o nf* aristocrat.

aritmético,-a *adj* arithmetical, arithmetic.

arma *nf* weapon, arm. LOC **alzarse en armas** to rise up in arms. **I ser de armas tomar** *fig* to be formidable. COMP **arma blanca** knife. **I arma de fuego** firearm.

armada *nf* navy, naval forces *pl*.

armadillo *nm* armadillo.

armador,-ra *nm & nf* shipowner.

armadura *nf* **1** *(traje)* suit of armour (US armor). **2** *(armazón)* frame. **3** ARQUIT framework.

armamento *nm* *(acción)* armament, arming.

armar *vt* **1** *(dar armas)* to arm. **2** *(cargar)* to load; *(bayoneta)* to fix. **3** *(montar - mueble)* to assemble. **4** *fam (causar, originar)* to cause, kick up, create: *armó un lío tremendo* he kicked up a tremendous fuss. LOC **armarla** *fam* to cause trouble, kick up a fuss.
▶ *vpr* **armarse 1** *(proveerse)* to provide OS *(de, with)*, arm US *(de, with)*: *se armó de pintura y pincel y se puso a pintar* he provided himself with paint and paintbrush and began to paint. **2** *(producirse)* to be, break out: *se armó un jaleo* there was a right row. LOC **armarse de paciencia** to summon up patience. **I armarse de valor** to pluck up courage.

armario *nm* *(para ropa)* wardrobe, US closet; *(de cocina)* cupboard. COMP **armario empotrado** built-in wardrobe, built-in cupboard.

armatoste *nm* *(cosa)* monstrosity; *(máquina)* useless contraption.

armazón *nm & nf* **1** frame, framework; *(de madera)* timberwork. **2** ARQUIT shell; *(de escultura)* armature.

armiño *nm* ermine.

armisticio *nm* armistice.

armonía *nf* harmony.

armónica *nf* harmonica, mouth organ.

armonioso,-a *adj* harmonious.

aro *nm* **1** hoop, ring. **2** *(juego)* hoop.

aroma *nm* aroma; *(del vino)* bouquet.

aromático,-a *adj* aromatic, fragrant.

arpa *nf* harp.

arpón *nm* harpoon.

arqueología *nf* archaeology (US archeology).

arqueólogo,-a *nm & nf* archaeologist (US archeologist).

arquero,-a *nm & nf* archer.

arquetipo *nm* archetype.

arquitecto,-a *nm & nf* architect.

arquitectura *nf* architecture.

arquitrabe *nm* architrave.

arquivolta *nf* archivolt.

arrabales *nm pl* outskirts.

arraigar *vi* to take root.
▶ *vpr* **arraigarse** *(establecerse)* to settle down.

arraigo *nm* **1** *(acción)* act of taking root. **2** *fig (raíces)* roots: *con mucho arraigo* deeply-rooted.

arrancar *vt* **1** *(árbol)* to uproot; *(flor)* to pull up. **2** *(plumas, cejas)* to pluck; *(cabello, diente)* to pull out; *(con violencia - página)* to tear out. **3** *(obtener - aplausos, sonrisa)* to get; *(- confesión, información)* to extract. **4** *(coche)* to start.
▶ *vi* **1** *(partir)* to begin, start. **2** *(salir)* to go, leave. **3** *(coche)* to start; *(tren)* to pull out.

arranque *nm* **1** TÉC starting mechanism. **2** *(comienzo)* start. **3** *fig (arrebato)* outburst, fit.

arrasar *vt* **1** *(destruir)* to raze, destroy. **2** *(allanar)* to level, smooth.
▶ *vi* *(disco, libro, película)* to be a smash hit, sweep the board; *(deportista)* to sweep to victory.

arrastrar *vt* **1** *(gen)* to drag, pull, **2** *(corriente, aire)* to sweep along. **3** *(traer como consecuencia)* to cause, bring, lead to.
▶ *vpr* **arrastrarse 1** to drag OS, crawl. **2** *fig (humillarse)* to creep, crawl.

arrastre *nm* **1** *(acción)* dragging, pulling. **2** *(telesquí)* drag lift. **3** *(en naipes)* lead.

arre *interj* gee up!, giddy up!

arrear *vt* **1** *(animales)* to spur on, urge on. **2** *(apresurar)* to hurry up. **3** *fam (pegar)* to hit: *le arreó una bofetada* she slapped him round the face.

arrebatar *vt* **1** *(quitar)* to grab, snatch. **2** *fig (cautivar)* to captivate, fascinate.

arrebato *nm (arranque)* fit, outburst.

arreciar *vi* to get stronger, get worse.

arrecife *nm* reef.

arreglado,-a *pp* → arreglar.
▶ *adj* **1** *(solucionado)* settled, fixed, sorted out. **2** *(ordenado)* tidy, neat, arranged, orderly. **3** *(bien vestido)* well-dressed, smart.

arreglar *vt* **1** *(gen)* to settle, sort out, fix. **2** *(ordenar)* to tidy up, clear up. **3** *(reparar)* to mend, fix, repair. **4** MÚS to arrange. **5** *fam* to sort out: *¡ya te arreglaré!* I'll teach you!, I'll sort you out.
▶ *vpr* **arreglarse 1** *(componerse)* to get ready, dress up; *(cabello)* to do. **2** *(solucionarse)* to get sorted out, work out; *(pareja)* to get back together again. LOC **arreglárselas** to manage, cope: *arréglatelas como puedas* do the best you can.

arreglo *nm* **1** *(acuerdo)* arrangement, agreement, settlement. **2** *(reparación)* repair. **3** MÚS arrangement. COMP **arreglo de cuentas** settling of scores, settling-up.

arremangarse *vpr* to roll up one's sleeves.

arremeter *vi* **1** *(gen)* to attack, charge; *(el toro)* to charge. **2** *(verbalmente)* to attack.

arrendamiento *nm* **1** renting, leasing, letting. **2** *(precio)* rent.

arrendar *vt* *(dar en alquiler)* to let, lease; *(tomar en alquiler)* to rent, lease.

arrendatarlo,-a *nm & nf* **1** *(que da en arriendo)* leaseholder, lessee. **2** *(inquilino)* tenant.

arrepentido,-a *pp* → arrepentirse.
▶ *adj* regretful, repentant.
▶ *nm & nf* penitent.

arrepentimiento *nm* regret, repentance.

arrepentirse *vpr* **1** *(gen)* to regret (de, -). **2** REL to repent (de, of).

arrestar *vt* **1** to arrest, detain. **2** *(poner en prisión)* to imprison, jail, put in prison.

arresto *nm* arrest.

arriar *vt* **1** *(velas)* to lower. **2** *(bandera)* to strike.

arriba *adv* **1** up; *(encima)* on (the) top: *ponlo más arriba* put it higher up. **2** *(piso)* upstairs: *vive arriba* he/she lives upstairs. **3** *(en escritos)* above: *véase más arriba* see above.

▶ *interj* up!: ¡*arriba la República!* long live the Republic!, up the Republic! LOC **de arriba abajo** from top to bottom. ‖ **hacia arriba** upwards.

arriesgado,-a *pp* → arriesgar.
▶ *adj* **1** *(peligroso)* risky, dangerous. **2** *(temerario)* bold, daring, fearless.

arriesgar *vt* **1** to risk; *(dinero)* to stake. **2** *(aventurar)* to venture.
▶ *vpr* **arriesgarse** to risk.

arrimar *vt (acercar)* to move closer.
▶ *vpr* **arrimarse** to move close, get close.

arrinconar *vt* **1** *(poner en un rincón)* to put in a corner. **2** *(retirar)* to lay aside, put away. **3** *(acorralar)* to corner.

arritmia *nf* arrhythmia.

arroba *nf* **1** *(medida de peso)* measure of weight equal to 11.502 kg, 25.3 lbs; *(medida de capacidad)* variable liquid measure. **2** *(Internet)* at, @.

arrodillarse *vpr* to kneel down, get down on one's knees.

arrogancia *nf* arrogance.

arrogante *adj* arrogant.

arrojar *vt* **1** *(tirar)* to throw, fling. **2** *(echar con violencia)* to throw out, kick out. **3** *(vomitar)* to vomit, throw up. **4** *(cuentas, etc)* to show, produce, give.
▶ *vpr* **arrojarse** to throw os.

arrojo *nm* boldness, dash, bravery, daring.

arrollador,-ra *adj* overwhelming, irresistible.

arrollar *vt* **1** *(envolver)* to roll (up). **2** *(al enemigo)* to crush, rout.

arropar *vt* to wrap up.

arroyo *nm* **1** *(corriente de agua)* stream, brook. **2** *(en la calle)* gutter.

arroz *nm* rice. COMP **arroz blanco 1** *(seco)* white rice. **2** *(hervido)* boiled rice. ‖ **arroz con leche** rice pudding. ‖ **arroz integral** brown rice.

arruga *nf (piel)* wrinkle; *(ropa)* crease.

arrugar *vt (piel)* to wrinkle; *(ropa)* to crease; *(papel)* to crumple (up).
▶ *vpr* **arrugarse 1** *(piel)* to wrinkle; *(ropa)* to crease; *(papel)* to crumple (up). **2** *fam (acobardarse)* to get the wind up.

arruinar *vt* **1** to bankrupt, ruin. **2** *(estropear)* to damage: *la tormenta ha arruinado la cosecha* the storm has ruined the crops.
▶ *vpr* **arruinarse** to be bankrupt, be ruined.

arrullar *vt* **1** *(ave)* to coo. **2** *(adormecer)* to lull.

arsenal *nm* **1** MAR shipyard. **2** *(de armas)* arsenal. **3** *fig (cantidad)* storehouse, mine.

arsénico *nm* arsenic.

arte *nm* **1** art. **2** *(habilidad)* craft, skill. **3** *(astucia)* cunning. **4** *(pesca)* fishing gear.

artefacto *nm* device, appliance; *(explosivo)* explosive device.

arteria *nf* artery. COMP **arteria carótida** carotid artery. ‖ **arteria coronaria** coronary artery.

artesa *nf* trough.

artesanal *adj (objeto)* handmade; *(comida)* home-made.

artesanía *nf* **1** *(calidad)* craftsmanship. **2** *(arte, obra)* crafts *pl*, handicrafts *pl*.

artesano,-a *adj* handmade.
▶ *nm & nf (hombre)* craftsman; *(mujer)* craftswoman.

artesonado *nm* panelled ceiling, coffered ceiling.

ártico,-a *adj* Arctic.
▶ *nm* **el Ártico** the Arctic. COMP **el Círculo Ártico** the Arctic Circle. ‖ **el océano Ártico** the Arctic Ocean.

articulación *nf* **1** LING articulation. **2** ANAT joint, articulation. **3** TÉC joint.

articulado,-a *pp* → articular.
▶ *adj* **1** *(lenguaje)* articulate. **2** *(objeto)* articulated.

articular *adj* articulated.
▶ *vt* **1** to articulate. **2** JUR to article.

artículo *nm* **1** article. **2** *(mercancía)* article, product. COMP **artículos de primera necesidad** basic commodities.

artífice *nm o nf* **1** *(artista)* craftsman, artist. **2** *(autor)* author: *Pepe ha sido el artífice de todo esto* this is all Pepe's doing.

artificial *adj* artificial.

artificioso,-a *adj* affected.

artillería *nf* artillery.

artilugio *nm* device, gadget.

artimaña *nf* artifice, trick, ruse.

artista *nm o nf* artist.

artístico,-a *adj* artistic.

artritis *nf inv* arthritis.

artrópodo *nm* arthropod.

artrosis *nf inv* arthrosis.

arzobispo *nm* archbishop.

as *nm* **1** *(naipes)* ace. **2** *(dados)* one. **3** *fig* ace, star, wizard.

asa *nf* handle.

asado,-a *pp* → asar.
▶ *adj* roast, roasted.
▶ *nm* asado roast.

asador *nm* **1** *(utensilio)* roaster. **2** *(establecimiento)* grill room, grill house.

asalariado,-a *nm & nf* wage earner, salaried worker.

asalmonado,-a *adj* salmon-pink.

asaltante *adj* assaulting, attacker.
▶ *nm o nf* attacker; *(en robo)* raider, robber.

asaltar *vt* **1** to assault, attack; *(para robar)* to raid, rob. **2** *(abordar)* to approach, come up to.

asalto *nm* **1** assault, attack; *(con robo)* raid, robbery. **2** *(boxeo)* round.

asamblea *nf* assembly, meeting.

asar *vt* to roast.
▶ *vpr* asarse **1** *(cocerse)* to roast. **2** *fig (pasar calor)* to be roasting, be boiling hot. |LOC| asar a la parrilla to grill. ‖ asar al horno to roast.

ascendencia *nf* **1** ancestry, ancestors *pl*: *era alemán, pero de ascendencia polaca* he was German, but of Polish descent. **2** *(influencia)* ascendancy.

ascender *vt* to promote.
▶ *vi* **1** *(subir)* to climb. **2** *(de categoría)* to be promoted (a, to). **3** *(sumar)* to amount (a, to).

ascendiente *nm o nf (antepasado)* ancestor.
▶ *nm (influencia)* ascendancy, power.

ascensión *nf (subida)* climb, climbing.

ascenso *nm* **1** *(subida)* climb, ascent. **2** *(aumento)* rise (de, in). **3** *(promoción)* promotion.

ascensor *nm* lift, US elevator.

asco *nm* disgust, repugnance. |LOC| dar asco to be disgusting. ‖ hacer ascos a AL-

GO to turn up one's nose at STH. ‖ ¡qué asco! how disgusting!, how revolting!

ascua *nf* live coal.

asear *vt (adecentar)* to clean, tidy up.
▶ *vpr* asearse *(arreglarse)* to wash, get washed.

asediar *vt* to besiege.

asedio *nm* siege.

asegurado,-a *pp* → asegurar.
▶ *adj* **1** *(con seguro)* insured. **2** *(garantizado)* secure: *tiene el futuro asegurado* his future is secure.

asegurar *vt* **1** *(fijar)* to secure. **2** COM to insure. **3** *(garantizar)* to assure, guarantee.
▶ *vpr* asegurarse **1** *(cerciorarse)* to make sure. **2** COM to insure OS.

asemejarse *vpr* to look like, be like.

asentir *vi* to assent, agree; *(con la cabeza)* to nod.

aseo *nm* **1** *(acción)* cleaning, tidying up. **2** *(limpieza)* cleanliness, tidiness. **3** *(habitación)* bathroom, toilet.

aséptico,-a *adj* **1** aseptic. **2** *fig* cold, indifferent.

asequible *adj* accessible: *a un precio asequible* at a reasonable price, at an affordable price.

aserrar *vt* to saw (up).

asesinar *vt* **1** to kill, murder. **2** *(a un personaje importante)* to assassinate.

asesinato *nm* **1** killing, murder. **2** *(de un pesonaje importante)* assassination.

asesino,-a *nm & nf* killer; *(hombre)* murderer; *(mujer)* murderess.

asesor,-ra *adj* advisory.
▶ *nm & nf* adviser, consultant.

asesorar *vt* **1** *(dar consejo)* to advise, give advice. **2** COM to act as a consultant to.
▶ *vpr* asesorarse *(tomar consejo)* to take advice, consult (de, -).

asesoría *nf* **1** *(cargo)* consultancy. **2** *(oficina)* consultant's office.

aseveración *nf* asseveration, assertion.

asfalto *nm* asphalt.

asfixia *nf* asphyxia, suffocation.

asfixiar *vt* to asphyxiate, suffocate.

▶ *vpr* **asfixiarse** to asphyxiate, suffocate.

así *adv* 1 *(de esta manera)* thus, (in) this way. 2 *(de esa manera)* (in) that way: *por decirlo así* so to speak; *y así sucesivamente* and so on. 3 *(tanto)* as: *así usted como yo* both you and I. 4 *(por tanto)* therefore. 5 *(tan pronto como)* as soon as: *así que lo sepa* as soon as I know. [LOC] **así así** so-so. ‖ **así que** so.
▶ *adj* such: *un hombre así* a man like that, such a man.

Asia *nf* Asia.

asiático,-a *adj* Asian.
▶ *nm & nf* Asian.

asiduidad *nf* assiduity, frequency.

asiduo,-a *adj* assiduous, frequent.

asiento *nm* 1 *(silla, etc)* seat. 2 *(emplazamiento)* site. 3 COM entry, registry. [LOC] **tomar asiento** to take a seat.

asignación *nf* 1 *(acción)* assignment, allocation. 2 *(nombramiento)* appointment, assignment. 3 *(remuneración)* allocation, allowance; *(sueldo)* wage, salary.

asignar *vt* 1 to assign, allot, allocate. 2 *(nombrar)* to appoint, assign.

asignatura *nf* subject.

asilo *nm* 1 *(institución)* asylum, home, institution. 2 *fig (protección)* protection, assistance. [LOC] **dar asilo** to shelter. [COMP] **asilo de ancianos** old people's home. ‖ **asilo político** political asylum.

asimetría *nf* asymmetry.

asimilar *vt* to assimilate.

asimismo *adv* 1 *(también)* also, as well. 2 *(de esta manera)* likewise. 3 *(además)* moreover.

asir *vt (agarrar)* to grab, seize, grasp, take hold of.

asistencia *nf* 1 *(presencia)* attendance, presence. 2 *(público)* audience. 3 *(ayuda)* assistance, help, aid. [COMP] **asistencia médica** medical assistance. ‖ **asistencia técnica** technical backup. ‖ **falta de asistencia** absence.

asistenta *nf* cleaning lady.

asistente *adj* 1 *(que está)* attending. 2 *(que ayuda)* assistant.

▶ *nm o nf* 1 *(que está)* member of the audience. 2 *(que ayuda)* assistant. [COMP] **asistente social** social worker.

asistir *vi* to attend, be present.
▶ *vt (ayudar)* to help, assist; *(a los enfermos)* to attend, care for.

asma *nf* asthma.

asno *nm* ass, donkey.

asociación *nf* association.

asociado,-a *pp* → asociar.
▶ *adj* associated, associate.
▶ *nm & nf* associate, partner.

asociar *vt* to associate (a/con, with), connect, link.
▶ *vpr* **asociarse** 1 *(relacionarse)* to be associated (a/con, with). 2 COM to form a partnership, become partners.

asociativo,-a *nf* associative. [COMP] **propiedad asociativa** associativity.

asomar *vi (empezar a aparecer)* to appear, begin to show, come out.
▶ *vt (mostrar)* to stick out.
▶ *vpr* **asomarse** 1 *(a ventana)* to stick one's head out (a, of), lean out (a, of); *(a balcón)* to come out (a, onto). 2 *(aparecer)* to appear.

asombrar *vt* to amaze, astonish.
▶ *vpr* **asombrarse** to be astonished, be amazed, be surprised.

asombro *nm* amazement, astonishment, surprise.

asombroso,-a *adj* amazing, astonishing, surprising.

asomo *nm* sign, trace, hint. [LOC] **ni por asomo** by no means.

asonante *adj* assonant.

aspa *nf* 1 *(cruz)* cross. 2 *(de molino)* sail; *(de ventilador)* blade; *(armazón)* arms *pl*.

aspaviento *nm* fuss. [LOC] **hacer aspavientos** to make a great fuss.

aspecto *nm* 1 *(faceta)* aspect, side, angle. 2 *(apariencia)* look, appearance: *¿qué aspecto tenía?* what did he look like?

aspereza *nf* roughness, coarseness.

áspero,-a *adj* 1 *(cosa)* rough, coarse. 2 *fig (persona)* surly.

aspersión *nf* sprinkling.

aspersor *nm* sprinkler.

aspiración *nf* **1** *(al respirar)* inhalation, breathing in. **2** LING aspiration. **3** TÉC intake. **4** *fig (ambición)* aspiration, ambition.

aspirador *nm* vacuum cleaner, Hoover.

aspirante *nm o nf* candidate, applicant.

aspirar *vt* **1** *(al respirar)* to inhale, breathe in. **2** *(absorber)* to suck in, draw in. **3** LING to aspirate.
▶ *vi fig (desear)* to aspire (a, to).

aspirina® *nf* aspirin.

asquear *vt* to disgust, revolt.

asqueroso,-a *adj* **1** *(sucio)* dirty, filthy. **2** *(desagradable)* disgusting, revolting, foul.
▶ *nm & nf (sucio)* filthy person, revolting person.

asta *nf* **1** *(de bandera)* staff, pole. **2** *(de lanza)* shaft; *(pica)* lance, pike. **3** *(cuerno)* horn.

asterisco *nm* asterisk.

asteroide *adj* asteroid.
▶ *nm* asteroid.

astigmatismo *nm* astigmatism.

astilla *nf* splinter, chip.

astillero *nm* shipyard, dockyard.

astrágalo *nm* **1** ANAT astragalus. **2** ARQUIT astragal.

astro *nm* star.

astrofísica *nf* astrophysics.

astrología *nf* astrology.

astrólogo,-a *nm & nf* astrologer.

astronauta *nm o nf* astronaut.

astronomía *nf* astronomy.

astrónomo,-a *nm & nf* astronomer.

astucia *nf* **1** astuteness, cunning, shrewdness. **2** *(treta)* trick, ruse.

astuto,-a *adj* astute, cunning, shrewd.

asumir *vt* to assume, take on, take upon OS.

asunto *nm* **1** *(cuestión)* matter, issue; *(tema)* subject; *(de obra)* theme: *no quiero hablar del asunto* I don't want to discuss the matter. **2** *(negocio)* affair, business: *no es asunto tuyo* it's none of your business. **3** *(aventura)* affair, love affair.
COMP **asuntos exteriores** POL Foreign Affairs.

asustado,-a *adj* frightened, scared.

asustar *vt* to frighten, scare.
▶ *vpr* **asustarse** to be frightened, be scared.

atacar *vt* to attack.

atajar *vi* to take a short cut.

atajo *nm* **1** *(camino)* short cut. **2** *fig (grupo)* bunch.

atalaya *nf (torre)* watchtower, lookout; *(mirador)* vantage point.

ataque *nm* **1** attack. **2** MED fit. COMP **ataque de nervios** nervous breakdown.

atar *vt* to tie. LOC **atar cabos** *fig* to put two and two together.

atardecer *vi* to get dark, grow dark.
▶ *nm* evening, dusk.

atareado,-a *adj* busy, occupied.

atascar *vt* **1** *(bloquear)* to block up, clog. **2** *fig (obstaculizar)* to hamper, hinder, obstruct.
▶ *vpr* **atascarse** **1** *(bloquearse)* to get blocked. **2** *(mecanismo)* to get stuck.

atasco *nm* **1** *(acción)* obstruction, blockage. **2** *(de tráfico)* traffic jam.

ataúd *nm* coffin.

ataviar *vt* **1** *(arreglar)* to dress up. **2** *(adornar)* to adorn, deck.

ateísmo *nm* atheism.

atemorizar *vt* to frighten, scare.

atención *nf* **1** *(gen)* attention. **2** *(detalle)* nice thought: *fue una atención por su parte* it was a nice thought, it was very kind of him. LOC **a la atención de** ALGN *(en cartas)* for the attention of SB. ‖ **llamar la atención** to attract attention. ‖ **llamar la atención a** ALGN to take SB to task. ‖ **prestar atención** to pay attention (a, to).
▶ *interj* **¡atención!** *(gen)* your attention please!; *(cuidado)* watch out!, look out!

atender *vt* **1** *(servir - cliente)* to serve, attend to, see to: *¿ya la atienden?* are you being served? **2** *(cuidar)* to take care of, look after. **3** *(negocio)* to take care of; *(teléfono)* to answer. **4** *(consejo, advertencia)* to heed, pay attention to; *(ruego, deseo, protesta)* to attend to; *(instrucción)* to follow, carry out.

▶ *vi* **1** *(prestar atención)* to pay attention (a, to), attend (a, to). **2** *(tener en cuenta)* to bear in mind.

atenerse *vpr* **1** *(ajustarse)* to abide (a, by), comply (a, with). **2** *(acogerse)* to rely (a, on).

atentado *nm* **1** *(ataque)* attack, assault. **2** *(afrenta)* affront. COMP **atentado terrorista** terrorist attack.

atentamente *adv* **1** attentively, carefully. **2** *(amablemente)* politely; *(en carta)* sincerely, faithfully: *«Le saluda atentamente»* "Yours sincerely", "Yours faithfully".

atentar *vi* *(físicamente - a una institución)* to attack (a/contra, -), make an attack (a/contra, on); *(- a una persona)* to attempt to kill, make an attempt on sb's life.

atento,-a *adj* **1** attentive. **2** *(amable)* polite, courteous.

atenuante *adj* **1** attenuating. **2** JUR extenuating.
▶ *nm* JUR extenuating circumstance.

atenuar *vt* **1** to attenuate. **2** JUR to extenuate.

ateo,-a *adj* atheistic.
▶ *nm & nf* atheist.

aterrador,-ra *adj* terrifying, frightful.

aterrizaje *nm* landing. COMP **aterrizaje forzoso** emergency landing.

aterrizar *vi* to land.

aterrorizar *vt* to terrify.

atesorar *vt* **1** *(acumular)* to hoard, accumulate, store up. **2** *fig* to possess.

atestado[1] *nm* JUR affidavit, statement.

atestado,-a[2] *adj* packed (de, with), crammed (de, with).

atestiguar *vt* **1** JUR to testify to, bear witness to, give evidence of. **2** *(ofrecer muestras)* to attest, testify, vouch for.

atiborrarse *vpr fam (de comida)* to stuff OS (de, with).

ático *nm* **1** *(vivienda)* penthouse, attic flat. **2** ARQUIT attic, loft.

atinar *vi* **1** *(dar con)* to hit upon, find. **2** *(acertar)* to get it right, be right, succeed.

atípico,-a *adj* atypical.

atisbo *nm* **1** *(acción)* spying, watching. **2** *fig (indicio)* inkling, slight sign.

atizar *vt* **1** *(fuego)* to poke; *(vela)* to snuff. **2** *fig (pasiones)* to rouse, excite; *(rebelión)* to stir up. **3** *(dar - golpe)* give, deal.

atlántico,-a *adj* Atlantic. COMP **el (océano) Atlántico** the Atlantic (Ocean).

atlas *nm inv* atlas.

atleta *nm o nf* athlete.

atlético,-a *adj* athletic.

atletismo *nm* athletics.

atmósfera *nf* atmosphere.

atolondrado,-a *adj* **1** *(desatinado)* scatterbrained, reckless, silly. **2** *(aturdido)* stunned, bewildered.

atómico,-a *adj* atomic.

atomizador *nm* atomizer, spray.

átomo *nm* atom.

atónito,-a *adj* astonished, amazed.

átono,-a *adj* atonic, unstressed.

atontado,-a *adj* **1** *(aturdido)* stunned, confused, bewildered. **2** *(tonto)* stupid, silly, foolish.

atormentar *vt* **1** *(torturar)* to torture. **2** *fig (causar disgusto)* to torment, harass.
▶ *vpr* **atormentarse** *(sufrir)* to torment OS.

atornillar *vt* to screw on, screw down.

atracador,-ra *nm & nf (de banco)* (bank) robber; *(en la calle)* attacker, mugger, thief.

atracar *vt* *(robar - banco, tienda)* to hold up, rob; *(- persona)* to mug.
▶ *vi* MAR *(a otra nave)* to come alongside; *(a tierra)* to tie up, dock, berth.
▶ *vpr* **atracarse** *(de comida)* to gorge OS (de, on), stuff OS (de, with).

atracción *nf (gen)* attraction.
▶ *nf pl* **atracciones** *(de feria)* rides *pl*.

atraco *nm* hold-up, robbery.

atracón *nm fam* binge, blowout.

atractivo,-a *adj* attractive, charming.
▶ *nm* **atractivo** attraction, charm, appeal.

atraer *vt* to attract.

atragantarse *vpr (no poder tragar)* to choke (con, on), swallow the wrong way.

atrapar *vt* to seize, capture, catch.

atrás *adv* **1** back: *dio un salto atrás* she jumped back. **2** *(tiempo)* ago: *días atrás* several days ago.

atrasado,-a *pp* → atrasar.
▸ *adj* **1** *(desfasado)* outdated. **2** *(pago)* overdue. **3** *(reloj)* slow. **4** *(país)* backward, underdeveloped; *(alumno)* slow, backward.

atrasar *vt (gen)* to delay, postpone, put back; *(reloj)* to put back.
▸ *vi (reloj)* to be slow.
▸ *vpr* **atrasarse 1** *(tren, etc)* to be late. **2** *(quedarse atrás)* to fall behind.

atraso *nm* **1** delay. **2** *(de reloj)* slowness: *el tren lleva mucho atraso* the train is very late. **3** *(de un país)* backwardness.

atravesar *vt* **1** *(cruzar)* to cross, go across, go over; *(pasar por)* to go through, pass through. **2** *(experimentar - gen)* to go through, experience; *(enfermedad, etc)* to suffer. **3** *(poner oblicuamente)* to put across, lay across. **4** *(con bala, etc)* to go through; *(con espada)* to run through. **5** *(situación)* to go through.

atrayente *adj* attractive.

atreverse *vpr* to dare, venture.

atrevido,-a *pp* → atreverse.
▸ *adj* **1** *(osado)* daring, bold. **2** *(insolente)* insolent, impudent. **3** *(indecoroso)* daring, risqué.

atribuir *vt* to attribute (a, to), ascribe.

atributo *nm* attribute, quality.

atril *nm (para libros)* lectern, bookrest; *(para música)* music stand.

atrio *nm* **1** *(patio)* atrium. **2** *(vestíbulo)* vestibule, entrance hall.

atrocidad *nf* **1** *(barbaridad)* atrocity, outrage. **2** *(disparate - acción)* something stupid, foolish thing; *(- dicho)* silly remark, stupid remark.

atropellar *vt* **1** AUTO to knock down, run over. **2** *(arrollar)* to trample over.

atropello *nm* **1** *(accidente)* accident, collision; *(de coche)* knocking down, running over. **2** *(apresuramiento)* haste. **3** *fig (agravio)* outrage, abuse; *(de derecho)* violation.

atroz *adj* atrocious, outrageous.

atuendo *nm* attire, dress, outfit.

atún *nm* tuna, tuna fish, tunny.

aturdido,-a *adj* **1** *(confundido)* stunned, dazed, bewildered. **2** *(atolondrado)* reckless, harebrained.

audacia *nf* audacity, boldness, daring.

audaz *adj* audacious, bold, daring.

audición *nf* **1** *(acción)* hearing; *(radio, televisión)* reception. **2** TEAT audition. **3** MÚS concert.

audiencia *nf* **1** *(recepción)* audience, hearing. **2** *(entrevista)* formal interview. **3** JUR high court. **4** *(público)* audience.

audífono *nm* hearing aid, deaf aid.

audiovisual *adj* audio-visual.
▸ *nm* audio-visual.

auditar *vt* to audit.

auditivo,-a *adj* auditory.

auditor,-ra *nm & nf* FIN auditor.

auditorio *nm* **1** *(público)* audience. **2** *(lugar)* auditorium, hall.

auge *nm* **1** *(del mercado)* boom. **2** *(de precios)* boost. **3** *(de fama, etc)* peak, summit.

augurio *nm* augury.

aula *nf (en escuela)* classroom; *(en universidad)* lecture room.

aullar *vi* to howl, yell, bay.

aullido *nm* howl, yell.

aumentar *vt* **1** to augment, increase; *(precios)* to put up; *(producción)* to step up. **2** *(óptica)* to magnify. **3** *(fotos)* to enlarge. **4** *(sonido)* to amplify.

aumento *nm* **1** increase, growth. **2** *(óptica)* magnification. **3** *(fotos)* enlargement. **4** *(sonido)* amplification. **5** *(salario)* rise, US raise.

aun *adv* even: *aun los tontos lo saben* even a fool knows that.
▸ *conj (+ gerundio o participio)* although, even though: *aun llegando tarde, lo recibieron amablemente* although he was late, he was given a warm reception. LOC **aun así** even so, even then. ▌ **aun cuando** although, even though.

aún *adv (afirmación)* still; *(negación, interrogación)* yet: *aún no ha llamado* he hasn't phoned yet. LOC **aún más** even more.

aunque *conj* **1** *(valor concesivo)* although, though; *(con énfasis)* even if, even though. **2** *(valor adversativo)* but.

aupar *vt* to help up.

aureola *nf* aureole, halo.

aurícula *nf* auricle.

auricular *adj* auricular, of the ear.
► *nm* **1** *(teléfono)* receiver, earpiece. **2** *(dedo)* little finger.
► *nm pl* **auriculares** earphones, headphones.

aurora *nf* dawn, daybreak. COMP **aurora boreal/borealis** aurora borealis, northern lights *pl*.

auscultar *vt* to sound.

ausencia *nf* absence.

ausentarse *vpr* **1** *(faltar)* to be absent. **2** *(irse)* to leave.

ausente *adj* **1** absent. **2** *(distraído)* lost in thought.
► *nm o nf* absentee.

austeridad *nf* austerity.

austero,-a *adj* austere.

Australia *nf* Australia.

australiano,-a *adj* Australian.
► *nm & nf (persona)* Australian.

australopiteco *nm* australopithecine.

Austria *nf* Austria.

austríaco,-a *adj* Austrian.
► *nm & nf* Austrian.

auténtico,-a *adj* authentic, genuine, real.

auto¹ *nm (coche)* car. COMP **autos de choque** bumper cars.

auto² *nm* **1** JUR decree, writ. **2** LIT mystery play, religious play.

autoadhesivo,-a *adj* self-adhesive.

autobiografía *nf* autobiography.

autobús *nm* bus.

autocar *nm* coach.

autocontrol *nm* self-control.

autóctono,-a *adj* indigenous.

autodefensa *nf* self-defence (US self-defense).

autodeterminación *nf* self-determination.

autodidacta *nm o nf* self-taught person.

autoescuela *nf* driving school, school of motoring.

autoestop *nm* → autostop.

autoestopista *nm o nf* → autostopista.

autógrafo,-a *nm* autograph.

autómata *nm* automaton.

automático,-a *adj* automatic.

automóvil *nm* automobile, car.

automovilismo *nm* **1** motoring. **2** DEP motor racing.

automovilista *nm o nf* motorist, driver.

automovilístico,-a *adj* car.

autonomía *nf* **1** *(gen)* autonomy. **2** *(capacidad para funcionar sin recargar)* range.

autonómico,-a *adj* autonomous, self-governing.

autónomo,-a *adj* **1** *(región)* autonomous. **2** *(trabajador)* self-employed.
► *nm & nf* COM self-employed person.

autopista *nf* motorway, US highway.

autopsia *nf* **1** autopsy, postmortem. **2** *fig* postmortem.

autor,-ra *nm & nf* **1** *(escritor)* writer, author; *(hombre)* author; *(mujer)* authoress. **2** *(responsable - gen)* person responsible; *(- de delito)* perpetrator.

autoridad *nf* authority.

autoritario,-a *adj* authoritarian.

autorización *nf* authorization.

autorizado,-a *pp* → autorizar.
► *adj* **1** *(oficial)* authorized, official. **2** *(experto)* authoritative, expert.

autorizar *vt* **1** to authorize. **2** JUR to legalize. **3** *(aprobar)* to approve of, give authority to.

autorretrato *nm* self-portrait.

autoservicio *nm* **1** *(restaurante)* self-service restaurant, cafeteria. **2** *(supermercado)* supermarket.

autostop *nm* hitchhiking.

autostopista *nm o nf* hitch-hiker.

autosuficiencia *nf* self-sufficiency.

autovía *nf* dual carriageway, US highway.

auxiliar *adj* auxiliary, assistant.
► *nm* **1** *(persona)* auxiliary, assistant. **2** GRAM *(verbo)* auxiliary.
► *vt (ayudar)* to help, assist; *(a un enfermo)* to attend; *(a un país)* to give aid to.
COMP **auxiliar administrativo** administrative assistant.

auxilio *nm* help, aid, assistance, relief.
► *interj* help! COMP **primeros auxilios** first aid *sing*.

A

aval *nm* endorsement, guarantee.

avalancha *nf* avalanche.

avalar *vt* to guarantee, endorse.

avance *nm* **1** *(acción)* advance. **2** *(pago)* advance payment. **3** *(de película)* trailer. comp **avance informativo** TV news preview, US news brief.

avanzar *vi* to advance, go forward.
► *vt* **1** *(mover adelante)* to advance, move forward. **2** *(dinero)* to advance. **3** *(una propuesta)* to put forward.

avaricia *nf* avarice.

avaro,-a *adj* *(tacaño)* avaricious, miserly, mean; *(codicioso)* greedy, avaricious.
► *nm & nf* *(tacaño)* miser; *(codicioso)* greedy person.

avasallar *vt* to subjugate, subdue.

ave *nf* bird. comp **ave de rapiña** bird of prey. ❙ **aves de corral** poultry *sing*.

avecinarse *vpr* to approach (a, -).

avellana *nf* hazelnut.

avemaría *nf* Ave Maria, Hail Mary.

avena *nf* oats *pl*.

avenida *nf* **1** *(calle)* avenue. **2** *(riada)* flood, spate.

aventajar *vt* **1** *(exceder)* to surpass, beat. **2** *(ir en cabeza)* to lead, be ahead; *(llegar)* to come first, come ahead (a, of).

aventura *nf* **1** adventure. **2** *(riesgo)* hazard, risk. **3** *(relación amorosa)* (love) affair.

aventurado,-a *pp* → aventurar.
► *adj* **1** *(arriesgado)* dangerous, risky. **2** *(atrevido)* daring, bold.

aventurar *vt* *(idea, opinión, etc)* to venture, dare, hazard.
► *vpr* **aventurarse** to venture, dare.

aventurero,-a *nm & nf* *(hombre)* adventurer; *(mujer)* adventuress.

avergonzado,-a *pp* → avergonzar.
► *adj* embarrassed, ashamed.

avergonzar *vt* *(causar vergüenza)* to shame, put to shame; *(turbar)* to embarrass.
► *vpr* **avergonzarse** to be ashamed (de, of), be embarrassed (de, about).

avería *nf* **1** *(en productos)* damage. **2** TÉC failure. **3** AUTO breakdown.

averiado,-a *pp* → averiar.
► *adj* **1** *(en productos)* damaged. **2** TÉC faulty, not working, out of order. **3** AUTO broken down.

averiar *vt* **1** *(productos)* to damage, spoil. **2** TÉC to cause to malfunction. **3** AUTO to cause a breakdown to.
► *vpr* **averiarse 1** *(productos)* to get damaged. **2** TÉC to malfunction, go wrong. **3** AUTO to break down.

averiguación *nf* inquiry, investigation.

averiguar *vt* to inquire, investigate, find out about: *averigua quién viene* find out who's coming.

aversión *nf* aversion. loc **sentir aversión por** to loathe.

avestruz *nm* ostrich.

aviación *nf* **1** aviation. **2** MIL air force. comp **accidente de aviación** air crash.

aviador,-ra *nm & nf* aviator, flier; *(hombre)* airman; *(mujer)* airwoman.

avidez *nf* avidity, eagerness.

ávido,-a *adj* avid, eager: *el chico estaba ávido de aventuras* the boy was thirsty for adventure.

avión *nm* aeroplane (US airplane), plane, aircraft.

avioneta *nf* light plane, light aircraft.

avisar *vt* **1** *(informar)* to inform, notify, announce. **2** *(advertir)* to warn. **3** *(mandar llamar)* to call for.

aviso *nm* **1** *(información)* notice. **2** *(advertencia)* warning. loc **hasta nuevo aviso** until further notice. ❙ **sin previo aviso** without prior notice.

avispa *nf* wasp.

avispero *nm* **1** *(conjunto de avispas)* swarm of wasps. **2** *(nido de avispas)* wasp's nest. **3** *fig* *(lío)* tight spot, mess.

avivar *vt* **1** *(fuego)* to stoke (up). **2** *(anhelos, deseos)* to enliven. **3** *(pasiones, dolor)* to intensify. **4** *(paso)* to quicken. **5** *(colores, luz)* to brighten up.

axial *adj* axial.

axila *nf* **1** *(del cuerpo)* armpit, underarm. **2** MED axilla. **3** *(de planta)* axil.

axioma *nm* axiom.

ay *interj* **1** *(dolor)* ouch!, ow! **2** *(pena)* alas!: *¡ay de mí!* woe is me!, poor me! **3** *(temor)* oh!

ayer *adv* **1** *(el día anterior)* yesterday. **2** *(en el pasado)* in the past, formerly.
▶ *nm* past. LOC ayer por la mañana/tarde yesterday morning/afternoon. ‖ ayer por la noche last night.

ayuda *nf* **1** help, aid, assistance. **2** *(lavativa)* enema. LOC ir en ayuda de ALGN to come to SB's assistance. ‖ prestar ayuda to help (a, -).

ayudar *vt* to help, aid, assist: *¿en qué podemos ayudarte?* how can we help you?
▶ *vpr* ayudarse *(apoyarse)* to make use (de/con, of).

ayunar *vi* to fast.

ayunas LOC en ayunas on an empty stomach: *tómalo en ayunas* take it on an empty stomach.

ayuno *nm* fast, fasting.

ayuntamiento *nm* **1** *(corporación)* town council, city council. **2** *(edificio)* town hall, city hall.

azabache *nm* jet. LOC negro,-a como el azabache jet-black.

azada *nf* hoe.

azafata *nf* **1** *(de avión)* air hostess, stewardess. **2** *(de congresos)* hostess.

azafrán *nm* saffron.

azahar *nm (de naranjo)* orange blossom; *(de limonero)* lemon blossom. COMP agua de azahar orange flower water.

azalea *nf* azalea.

azar *nm* **1** chance. **2** *(percance)* misfortune, accident. **3** *(en probabilidad)* event. LOC al azar at random. ‖ por puro azar by pure chance.

azotar *vt* **1** *(con látigo)* to whip, flog. **2** *(golpear)* to beat down on. **3** *(viento, olas)* to lash. **4** *fig (peste, hambre, etc)* to ravage.

azote *nm* **1** *(instrumento)* whip, scourge. **2** *(golpe)* lash, stroke (of the whip). **3** *(manotada)* smack. **4** *(del viento, del agua)* lashing. **5** *fig* scourge.

azotea *nf* flat roof. LOC estar mal de la azotea *fam* to have a screw loose.

azteca *adj* Aztec.
▶ *nm o nf* Aztec.

azúcar *nm & nf* sugar. COMP azúcar blanco refined sugar. ‖ azúcar moreno/negro brown sugar.

azucarado,-a *pp* → azucarar.
▶ *adj* **1** *(con azúcar)* sugared, sweetened. **2** *(como el azúcar)* sugar-like; *(dulce)* sweet. **3** *fig* sugary.

azucarero *nm (vasija)* sugar bowl.

azucarillo *nm (terrón)* sugar lump.

azucena *nf* white lily.

azufre *nm* sulphur (US sulfur).

azul *adj* blue.
▶ *nm* blue. COMP azul celeste sky blue, light blue. ‖ azul cielo sky blue, light blue. ‖ azul eléctrico electric blue. ‖ azul marino navy blue. ‖ azul turquesa turquoise. ‖ sangre azul blue blood.

azulejo *nm (baldosa)* tile, glazed tile.

azuzar *vt* to egg on.

B

B, b *nf (la letra)* B, b.

baba *nf* **1** *(de animal, adulto)* spittle, saliva; *(de niño)* dribble. **2** *(de caracol, babosa)* slime. LOC **caérsele a uno la baba** *fam* to drool.

babear *vi* **1** *(adulto, animal)* to slobber, slaver; *(niño)* to dribble. **2** *fig* to drool, slobber.

babero *nm* **1** bib. **2** *(babi)* child's overall.

babosa *nf* slug.

baca *nf* rack, roof rack, luggage rack.

bacalao *nm* cod.

bache *nm* **1** *(en carretera)* pothole. **2** *(de aire)* air pocket. **3** *fig* bad patch.

bachillerato *nm* **1** Spanish certificate of secondary education. **2** Spanish non-compulsory secondary education.

bacilo *nm* bacillus.

bacón *nm* bacon.

bacteria *nf* bacterium.

bádminton *nm* badminton.

bafle *nm* loudspeaker.

Bahamas *nf pl* **las Bahamas** the Bahamas.

bahía *nf* bay.

bailaor,-ra *nm & nf* flamenco dancer.

bailar *vt* **1** to dance. **2** *(hacer girar)* to spin: *bailó una moneda en la mesa* she spun a coin on the table.
▶ *vi* **1** to dance: *¿bailas?* do you want to dance?, would you like to dance? **2** *(girar)* to spin. **3** *(ser grande)* to be too big: *me bailan estos zapatos* these shoes are too big for me. **4** *(moverse - cosa)* to wobble; *(- persona)* to move about, fidget: *esta silla baila* this chair wobbles.

5 *(estar suelto)* to be loose: *este tornillo baila* this screw is loose.

bailarín,-ina *nm & nf* dancer.

baile *nm* **1** dance. **2** *(de etiqueta)* ball. **3** *(sala)* dance hall.

baja *nf* **1** *(descenso)* fall, drop. **2** *(por enfermedad)* sick leave.

bajada *nf* **1** *(disminución)* drop, fall. **2** *(descenso)* descent; *(de telón, barrera)* lowering. **3** *(camino)* way down. **4** *(en carretera, etc)* slope, hill.

bajar *vt* **1** *(coger algo de un lugar alto)* to get down. **2** *(dejar más abajo)* to lower. **3** *(reducir)* to lower, reduce, bring down. **4** *(recorrer de arriba abajo)* to go down. **5** *(en informática)* to download.
▶ *vi* **1** to come down. **2** *(reducirse)* to fall, drop: *ha bajado la temperatura* the temperature has dropped. **3** *(marea)* to go out. **4** *(apearse - de coche)* to get out (**de**, of); *(de bicicleta, caballo)* to get off (**de**, -).
▶ *vpr* **bajarse** to come down, to get out (**de**, -), to get off (**de**, -).

bajo,-a *adj* **1** *(gen)* low: *precios bajos* low prices. **2** *(persona)* short, not tall. **3** *(cabeza)* bowed, held low; *(ojos)* lowered, downcast. **4** *(marea)* out: *la marea está baja* the tide is out. **5** *(época)* late: *la Baja Edad Media* the late Middle Ages.

bajo *nm* **1** *(piso)* ground floor, US first floor. **2** *(de prenda)* bottoms *pl*, US cuff. **3** MÚS *(instrumento)* bass; *(contrabajo)* double bass.
▶ *nm o nf* MÚS *(músico)* bass player.
▶ *adv* low, softly, quietly.
▶ *prep* under, below.
▶ *nm pl* **bajos** ground floor;

bajura LOC **de bajura** inshore.

bala *nf* **1** bullet. **2** *(paquete)* bale.
balada *nf* ballad.
balancear *vt* to rock, swing.
▶ *vi* to rock, to swing.
▶ *vpr* **balancearse** *(mecerse)* to rock; *(columpio, brazo)* to swing.
balanceo *nm* *(gen)* swinging.
balancín *nm* **1** *(mecedora)* rocking chair. **2** *(columpio)* seesaw.
balanza *nf* *(aparato)* scales *pl*.
balar *vi* to bleat, baa.
balcón *nm* *(en edificio)* balcony.
balde *nm* bucket, pail. LOC **de balde** free, for nothing.
baldío,-a *adj* uncultivated, barren.
▶ *nm* **baldío** wasteland.
baldosa *nf* floor tile.
baldosín *nm* tile, wall tile.
balido *nm* bleat, baa.
balín *nm* pellet.
baliza *nf* **1** *(de mar)* buoy. **2** *(de tierra)* beacon.
ballena *nf* whale.
ballesta *nf* *(arma)* crossbow.
ballet *nm* ballet.
balneario,-a *adj* spa.
balón *nm* DEP ball.
baloncesto *nm* basketball.
balonmano *nm* handball.
balonvolea *nm* volleyball.
balsa *nf* **1** pool. **2** MAR raft.
bálsamo *nm* balsam, balm.
bambolear *vi* to sway.
▶ *vpr* **bambolearse** to sway.
bamboleo *nm* swaying.
bambú *nm* bamboo.
banal *adj* trivial.
banana *nf* banana.
banca *nf* **1** COM banking; *(bancos)* (the) banks *pl*. **2** *(en juego)* bank.
bancada *nf* *(banco)* long bench. **2** *(superficie)* work surface.
bancal *nm* **1** *(en pendiente)* terrace. **2** *(en llano)* plot.
bancarrota *nf* bankruptcy. LOC **estar en bancarrota** to be bankrupt.
banco *nm* **1** bank. **2** *(asiento)* bench; *(de iglesia)* pew. **3** *(mesa)* bench, work

bench. **4** *(de peces)* shoal. COMP **banco de datos** data bank.
banda¹ *nf* **1** *(faja)* sash. **2** *(lista)* band. **3** *(tira)* strip. **4** *(lado)* side. **5** *(en billar)* cushion. COMP **banda magnética** magnetic strip.
banda² *nf* **1** *(músicos)* band. **2** *(maleantes)* gang.
bandada *nf* **1** *(de pájaros)* flock; *(de insectos)* swarm; *(de peces)* shoal. **2** *(de personas)* horde.
bandeja *nf* *(gen)* tray; *(para diapositivas)* magazine.
bandera *nf* flag. COMP **bandera nacional** national flag.
banderilla *nf* **1** *(tauromaquia)* banderilla *(barbed dart stuck into the bull's back)*. **2** *(tapa)* pickled onion, carrot, gherkin, pepper, etc on a cocktail stick.
banderín *nm* pennant.
bandido,-a *nm & nf* bandit.
bando *nm* **1** *(facción)* faction, party, camp. **2** *(de aves)* flock; *(de insectos)* swarm; *(de peces)* shoal.
bandolera *nf* bandolier.
bandolero *nm* bandit.
banjo *nm* banjo.
banquero,-a *nm & nf* banker.
banqueta *nf* **1** *(taburete)* stool; *(para los pies)* footstool. **2** *(banco)* little bench.
banquete *nm* banquet, feast.
bañador *nm* *(gen)* swimsuit; *(de mujer)* swimming costume; *(de hombre)* swimming trunks *pl*.
bañar *vt* **1** *(lavar)* to bath: *me baño cada mañana* I have a bath every morning. **2** *(cubrir)* to coat: *bañó los pasteles en chocolate* she coated the cakes in chocolate.
▶ *vpr* **bañarse** to bathe; *(nadar)* to have a swim, go for a swim.
bañera *nf* bath, bathtub.
bañista *nm o nf* bather, swimmer.
baño *nm* **1** *(gen)* bath; *(en piscina, mar)* dip, swim. **2** *(cuarto)* bathroom; *(servicio)* toilet. **3** *(bañera)* bath, bathtub.
▶ *nm pl* **baños** *(balneario)* spa *sing*.
bar *nm* **1** *(cafetería)* café, snack bar; *(de bebidas alcohólicas)* bar. **2** Fís bar.
baraja *nf* *(naipes)* pack, deck.

barajar *vt (naipes)* to shuffle.

baranda *nf* handrail, banister.

barandilla *nf* handrail, banister.

barato,-a *adj* cheap.
 ► *adv* **barato** cheaply, cheap.

barba *nf* **1** ANAT chin. **2** *(pelo)* beard.

barbacoa *nf* barbecue.

barbaridad *nf* **1** *(crueldad - cualidad)* cruelty; *(- acto)* atrocity, act of cruelty. **2** *(disparate)* piece of nonsense.

barbarismo *nm* barbarism.

bárbaro,-a *adj* **1** HIST barbarian. **2** *(cruel)* barbaric, savage, cruel. **3** *fam (espléndido)* fantastic, terrific.
 ► *nm & nf* HIST barbarian.
 ► *adv* **bárbaro**: *lo pasamos bárbaro* we had a great time.

barbecho *nm* fallow land.

barbería *nf* barber's shop, barber's.

barbero *nm* barber.

barbilla *nf* chin.

barbo *nm* barbel.

barca *nf* boat, small boat.

barcaza *nf* lighter.

barco *nm (gen)* boat; *(grande)* ship.

bardo *nm* bard.

baremo *nm* **1** *(para calcular)* ready reckoner. **2** *(tarifas)* scale, table.

barítono *nm* baritone.

barman *nm* barman, US bartender.

barniz *nm (para madera)* varnish; *(para cerámica)* glaze.

barnizar *vt (madera)* to varnish; *(cerámica)* to glaze.

barómetro *nm* barometer.

barón *nm* baron.

barquero,-a *nm & nf (hombre)* boatman; *(mujer)* boatwoman.

barquillo *nm (gen)* wafer; *(cucurucho)* cornet.

barra *nf* **1** *(en bar, cafetería)* bar. **2** *(vara)* bar; *(para cortinas)* rod; *(de bicicleta)* crossbar. **3** *(de helado)* block. **4** *(de pan)* loaf. COMP **barra de labios** lipstick.

barrabasada *nf* dirty trick.

barraca *nf* **1** *(casita)* cottage *(typical in Valencia and Murcia)*. **2** *(puesto)* stall; *(caseta de feria)* booth. **3** *(chabola)* shack.

barracón *nm* hut, large hut.

barranco *nm* **1** *(precipicio)* precipice. **2** *(torrentera)* gully; *(más profunda)* ravine.

barranquismo *nm* canyoning.

barrendero,-a *nm & nf* road sweeper.

barreno *nm* **1** *(barrena)* large drill. **2** *(agujero)* drill hole, bore hole.

barreño *nm* large bowl.

barrer *vt* **1** *(suelo)* to sweep; *(hojas, migas, etc)* to sweep up. **2** *(limpiar)* to sweep away: *el viento barrió las nubes del cielo* the wind swept the clouds from the sky.

barrera *nf* **1** *(gen)* barrier. **2** *(en plaza de toros - valla)* barrier; *(- asientos)* front row. **3** *fig* obstacle.

barricada *nf* barricade.

barriga *nf* belly, stomach, tummy.

barril *nm* barrel, keg.

barrio *nm* neighbourhood (US neighborhood); *(zona)* district, area.

barrizal *nm* quagmire.

barro *nm* **1** *(lodo)* mud. **2** *(arcilla)* clay: *objetos de barro* earthenware *sing*. **3** *(objeto)* earthenware object.

barroco,-a *adj* **1** ARTE baroque. **2** *fig* ornate.

barrote *nm* **1** bar. **2** *(de escalera, silla)* rung.

barullo *nm* noise, din, racket.

basar *vt* to base *(en, on)*.
 ► *vpr* **basarse** *(cosa)* to be based *(en, on)*; *(persona)* to base oneself on.

báscula *nf (gen)* scales *pl*; *(de farmacia)* weighing machine.

bascular *vi* **1** to tilt. **2** *(oscilar)* to swing. **3** *(variar)* to swing, alternate.

base *nf* **1** *(gen)* base. **2** *fig* basis. **3** QUÍM base, alkali. **4** MAT base. **5** *(en béisbol)* base. COMP **base de datos** database.
 ► *nf pl* **bases** **1** *(de concurso)* rules. **2** *las* **bases** *(de partido, etc)* grass roots.

básico,-a *adj (gen)* basic.

basílica *nf* basilica.

basta¹ *nf* tacking stitch.

basta² *interj* enough!, stop it!

bastante *adj* **1** enough, sufficient. **2** *(abundante)* quite a lot of: *había bastante gente* there were quite a lot of people.
► *adv* **1** enough: *son lo bastante ricos como para poder permitírselo* they're rich enough to be able to afford it. **2** *(un poco)* fairly, quite. *es bastante alto* it's fairly high. **3** *(tiempo)* some time, quite a while.

bastar *vi* to be enough, be sufficient, suffice: *mi sueldo no basta para pagar el alquiler* my salary is not enough to pay the rent. LOC **bastar con** to be enough: *es muy concentrado, basta con una gota* it's highly concentrated, one drop is enough.

bastidor *nm* **1** frame. **2** *(de lienzo)* stretcher. **3** *(de coche)* chassis. **4** TEAT wing.

basto¹ *nm* ≈ club.
► *nm pl* **bastos** ≈ clubs: *el as de bastos* ≈ the ace of clubs.

basto,-a² *adj* **1** *(grosero)* coarse, rough. **2** *(sin pulimentar)* rough, unpolished.

bastón *nm* **1** stick, walking stick, US cane. **2** *(de esquí)* stick, ski stick.

basura *nf* **1** *(cosa)* rubbish, US garbage. **2** *(persona despreciable)* swine. LOC **sacar la basura** to put the rubbish out.

basurero *nm* **1** *(persona)* dustman, US garbage man. **2** *(lugar)* tip, rubbish dump.

bata *nf* **1** *(prenda ligera)* housecoat; *(albornoz)* dressing gown, US robe. **2** *(de trabajo)* overall; *(de médicos, etc)* white coat.

batalla *nf* battle.

batallar *vi* to battle, fight.

batallón *nm* **1** MIL battalion. **2** *(multitud)* horde.

batata *nf* BOT sweet potato.

bate *nm* bat.

batear *vi* to bat.
► *vt* to hit.

batería *nf* **1** *(eléctrica)* battery. **2** TEAT footlights *pl*. **3** *(conjunto de cosas)* set; *(de preguntas)* barrage. **4** MÚS drums *pl*.
► *nm o nf* drummer. LOC **recargar las baterías** to recharge one's batteries. COMP **batería de cocina** pots and pans *pl*.

batido,-a *nm* batido **1** CULIN beaten eggs. **2** *(bebida)* milk shake.

batidor,-ra *nm* CULIN *(manual)* whisk.

batidora *nf* blender, mixer.

batir *vt* **1** *(huevos)* to beat; *(nata, claras)* to whip. **2** *(palmas)* to clap. **3** *(metales)* to beat. **4** *(alas)* to flap, beat. **5** *(derribar)* to knock down. **6** *(vencer)* to beat, defeat. **7** DEP *(marca, récord)* to break.
► *vpr* **batirse** to fight.

batracio,-a *adj* batrachian.
► *nm* **batracio** batrachian.

batuta *nf* baton. LOC **llevar la batuta** to be the boss.

baúl *nm* *(cofre)* chest; *(de viaje)* trunk.

bautismo *nm* baptism, christening.

bautizar *vt* **1** to baptize, christen. **2** *(poner nombre a)* to name.

bautizo *nm* baptism, christening.

bauxita *nf* bauxite.

baya *nf* berry.

bayeta *nf* **1** baize. **2** *(paño)* cloth.

bayo,-a *adj* bay, whitish yellow.
► *nm* **bayo** *(caballo)* bay.

baza *nf* **1** *(naipes)* trick. **2** *(ventaja)* asset, advantage. **3** *(ocasión)* chance. LOC **meter baza** *fig* to butt in, stick one's oar in.

bazar *nm* **1** *(oriental)* bazaar. **2** *(tienda)* electrical goods and hardware shop.

beatificar *vt* to beatify.

beato,-a *adj* **1** *(beatificado)* blessed. **2** *(devoto)* devout.

bebé *nm* baby. COMP **bebé probeta** test-tube baby.

bebedero,-a *nm* **1** *(abrevadero)* water trough. **2** *(vasija)* drinking dish.

beber *vt* to drink.
► *vi* **1** to drink. **2** *(emborracharse)* to drink, drink heavily: *bebe mucho* he's a heavy drinker.

bebida *nf* drink, beverage.

beca *nf* *(gen)* grant; *(concedida por méritos)* scholarship, award.

becar *vt* *(gen)* to award a grant to; *(por méritos)* to award a scholarship to.

becario,-a *nm & nf* grant holder, scholarship holder.

becerro,-a *nm & nf* calf *(up to one year old)*.

bechamel *nf* béchamel sauce, white sauce.

bedel,-la *nm & nf* porter.

beduino,-a *nm & nf* Bedouin.

begonia *nf* begonia.

beicon *nm* bacon.

beige *adj* beige.
▶ *nm* beige.

béisbol *nm* baseball.

belén *nm* REL nativity scene, crib.

belga *adj* Belgian.
▶ *nm & nf* Belgian.

Bélgica *nf* Belgium.

Belice *nm* Belize.

bélico,-a *adj* military. COMP **conflicto bélico** armed conflict, war.

belleza *nf* beauty.

bello,-a *adj* beautiful.

bellota *nf* acorn.

bemol *adj* MÚS flat.
▶ *nm* MÚS flat.

bencina *nf* benzine.

bendecir *vt* to bless.

bendición *nf* blessing.
▶ *nf pl* **bendiciones** wedding ceremony *sing*.

bendito,-a *adj* 1 *(bienaventurado)* blessed. 2 *(feliz)* happy: *¡bendita la hora en que la conocí!* happy the hour I met her! 3 *(poco inteligente)* simple.
▶ *nm & nf* simple soul.

benefactor,-ra *adj* beneficent.
▶ *nm & nf (hombre)* benefactor; *(mujer)* benefactress.

beneficiar *vt* 1 to benefit, favour (US favor). 2 *(mina)* to work. 3 COM to sell below par.
▶ *vpr* **beneficiarse** 1 to benefit. 2 COM to profit. LOC **beneficiarse de** ALGO to do well out of STH, benefit from STH.

beneficiario,-a *nm & nf* beneficiary.

beneficio *nm* 1 *(ganancia)* profit. 2 *(bien)* benefit. LOC **a beneficio de** in aid of.
❙ **sacar beneficio de** to profit from.

beneficioso,-a *adj* beneficial.

benéfico,-a *adj* charitable. COMP **función benéfica** charity performance.

benevolencia *nf* 1 benevolence, kindness. 2 *(comprensión)* understanding.

benévolo,-a *adj* 1 benevolent, kind. 2 *(comprensivo)* understanding.

bengala *nf (para fiestas, etc)* sparkler.

benigno,-a *adj* 1 *(persona)* benign, gentle. 2 *(tumor)* benign. 3 *(clima)* mild.

benjamín,-ina *nm & nf (en familia - gen)* youngest child.
▶ *adj* DEP of the youngest age group *(9 or 10 years old)*.

berberecho *nm* cockle, common cockle.

berenjena *nf* aubergine, US eggplant.

berilo *nm* beryl.

bermudas *nm pl* Bermudas, Bermuda shorts.

berrear *vi* 1 *(becerro)* to bellow. 2 *(persona)* to bawl; *(niño)* to howl, bawl.

berrido *nm* 1 *(de becerro)* bellow. 2 *(de persona)* howl.

berrinche *nm* rage, tantrum, anger. LOC **coger un berrinche** to throw a tantrum.

berro *nm* watercress.

berza *nf* cabbage.

besamel *nf* bechamel, white sauce.

besar *vt* to kiss.
▶ *vpr* **besarse** *(uso recíproco)* to kiss.

beso *nm* kiss.

bestia *nf (animal)* beast.
▶ *nm o nf (persona - bruto)* brute; *(- ignorante)* ignorant fool; *(- torpe)* clumsy oaf.
▶ *adj* 1 *(bruto)* brutish. 2 *(ignorante)* ignorant; *(grosero)* rude; *(torpe)* clumsy. 3 *(asombroso)* fantastic, amazing. LOC **a lo bestia** 1 *(fuerte)* hard. 2 *(a lo loco)* like a madman. 3 *(en cantidad)* in enormous amounts.

bestial *adj* 1 *(brutal)* beastly, bestial. 2 *fam (enorme)* enormous.

bestiario *nm* bestiary.

best-seller *nm* best-seller.

besucón,-ona *adj* fond of kissing.

besugo *nm (pez)* sea bream.

besuquear *vt* to kiss again and again.

betún *nm (para zapatos)* shoe polish.

bianual *adj* biannual.

biberón *nm* baby's bottle, bottle.

Biblia *nf* Bible.

bibliografía *nf* bibliography.

biblioteca *nf* **1** library. **2** *(mueble)* bookcase, bookshelf.

bibliotecario,-a *nm & nf* librarian.

bicarbonato *nm* bicarbonate.

bicentenario,-a *nm* bicentenary, US bicentennial.

bíceps *nm inv* biceps.

bicho *nm (animal)* animal, creature; *(insecto)* bug, creepy-crawly.

bici *nf fam* bike.

bicicleta *nf* bicycle. COMP **bicicleta de carreras** racing bike. ∎ **bicicleta de montaña** mountain bike.

bicolor *adj* two-coloured (US two-colored).

bidé *nm* bidet.

bidón *nm* drum.

biela *nf* AUTO connecting rod.

bien *adv* **1** *(gen)* well: *canta bien* she sings well. **2** *(como es debido)* properly, right: *si no pronuncias bien, no te van a entender* if you don't pronounce the words properly, they won't understand you. **3** *(acertadamente)* right, correctly: *contestó bien a todas las preguntas* she answered all the questions correctly. **4** *(de acuerdo)* O.K., all right: *-ven mañana a las dos, -bien* -come tomorrow at two, -all right. **5** *(mucho)* very: *es bien sencillo* it's really simple. **6** *(de gusto, olor, aspecto, etc)* good, nice, lovely: *esta cerveza está muy bien* this beer's very good. **7** *(de salud)* well: *¿te encuentras bien?* are you feeling all right? **8** *(físicamente)* good-looking: *su novio está muy bien* her boyfriend's very good-looking. LOC **hacer bien** to do good. ∎ ¡**ya está bien!** that's enough!
▸ *nm pl* **bienes** property *sing*, possessions. COMP **bienes inmuebles** real estate *sing*.
▸ *conj* **bien... bien** either... or: *se lo enviaremos bien por correo, bien por mensajero* we'll send it to you either by post or by messenger.

bienal *adj* biennial.
▸ *nf* biennial exhibition, biennial festival.

bienestar *nm* wellbeing, welfare: *bienestar social* social welfare.

bienhechor,-ra *adj* beneficent, beneficial.

bienio *nm (periodo)* two-year period, biennium.

bienvenido,-a *adj* welcome.

bífido,-a *adj* forked.

bifocal *adj* bifocal. COMP **gafas bifocales** bifocals.

bifurcación *nf (de la carretera)* fork; *(de ferrocarril)* junction.

bigamia *nf* bigamy.

bigote *nm* **1** moustache (US mustache). **2** *(de gato)* whiskers *pl*.

bigotudo,-a *adj* mustachioed.

bikini® *nm* → biquini®.

bilabial *adj* bilabial.

bilateral *adj* bilateral.

biliar *adj* biliary, bile.

bilingüe *adj* bilingual.

bilingüismo *nm* bilingualism.

bilis *nf inv* **1** bile. **2** *fig* spleen.

billar *nm* **1** billiards. **2** *(mesa)* billiard table. COMP **billar americano** pool.
▸ *nm pl* **billares** billiard room.

billete *nm* **1** *(moneda)* note, US bill: *un billete de cincuenta euros* a fifty-euro note. **2** *(de transporte, sorteo, teatro, etc)* ticket. COMP **billete de ida y vuelta** return ticket, US round-trip ticket.

billetera *nf* wallet, US billfold.

billetero *nm* purse, US change purse.

billón *nm* trillion.

✎ El uso español coincide con el antiguo significado británico en el que un billion era a million million.

binario,-a *adj* binary.

bingo *nm* **1** *(juego)* bingo. **2** *(sala)* bingo hall. LOC ¡**bingo!** bingo!

binóculo *nm* pince-nez.

binomio *nm* binomial.

biodegradable *adj* biodegradable.

biografía *nf* biography.

biográfico,-a *adj* biographical.

biógrafo,-a *nm & nf* biographer.

biología *nf* biology.

biológico,-a *adj* biological.

biólogo,-a *nm & nf* biologist.

biomasa *nf* biomass.

biombo *nm* screen, folding screen.

biopsia *nf* biopsy.

bioquímica *nf* biochemistry.

biosfera *nf* biosphere.

bióxido *nm* dioxide.

bípedo,-a *adj* biped.

biplaza *nm* two-seater.

bipolar *adj* bipolar.

biquini *nm (traje de baño)* bikini.

Birmania *nf* Burma.

birria *nf* rubbish.

bis *adv* **1** *(en dirección):* viven en el 23 bis they live at 23A. **2** MÚS repeat, bis.

bisabuelo,-a *nm & nf* great-grandparent; *(hombre)* great-grandfather; *(mujer)* great-grandmother.

bisagra *nf* hinge.

biscote *nm* piece of Melba toast.

bisección *nf* bisection.

bisectriz *nf* bisector.

bisel *nm* bevel.

biselado,-a *adj* bevelled (US beveled).

bisiesto *adj* leap. COMP año bisiesto leap year.

bisílabo,-a *adj* two-syllabled.

bismuto *nm* bismuth.

bisnieto,-a *nm & nf* great-grandchild; *(chico)* great-grandson; *(chica)* great-granddaughter.

bisonte *nm* bison.

bistec *nm* steak.

bisturí *nm* scalpel.

bisutería *nf* costume jewellery (US jewelry).

bit *nm* bit.

biunívoco,-a *adj* one-to-one.

bivalente *adj* bivalent.

bivalvo,-a *adj* bivalve, bivalvular.

bizco,-a *adj* cross-eyed.

bizcocho *nm* sponge, sponge cake.

biznieto,-a *nm & nf* → bisnieto,-a.

bizquear *vi* to squint, be cross-eyed.

blanco,-a *adj* white.
▶ *nm & nf (gen)* white; *(hombre)* white man; *(mujer)* white woman.
▶ *nm* blanco **1** *(color)* white. **2** *(objetivo)* target, mark. **3** *fig* object: fue el blanco de todas sus críticas he was the target of all their criticism. **4** *(hueco)* blank, gap; *(en escrito)* blank space. **5** *(vino)* white wine.

blancura *nf* whiteness.

blando,-a *adj (gen)* soft.

blandura *nf* softness.

blanquear *vt* **1** to whiten, make white. **2** *(con cal)* to whitewash. **3** *(con lejía)* to bleach.
▶ *vi* to whiten, turn white.

blanquecino,-a *adj* whitish, off-white.

blanqueo *nm* **1** whitening. **2** *(con cal)* whitewashing.

bledo *nm* common amaranth. LOC me importa un bledo *fam* I don't care less, I couldn't give a damn.

blindado,-a *adj* armoured (US armored). COMP puerta blindada reinforced door.

blindaje *nm* **1** armour (US armor), armour-plating (US armor-plating). **2** *(de puerta)* reinforcing.

blindar *vt* **1** to armour-plate (US armor-plate). **2** *(puerta)* to reinforce.

bloc *nm* notepad, pad.

bloque *nm* **1** block. **2** *(papel)* pad, notepad. LOC en bloque en bloc.

bloquear *vt (gen)* to block: esto podría bloquear el proceso de paz this could block the peace process.
▶ *vpr* bloquearse *(persona)* to have a mental block.

bloqueo *nm* **1** *(gen)* blocking. **2** MIL blockade. **3** *(precios, cuenta)* freezing.

blues *nm inv* blues.

blusa *nf* blouse.

boa *nf (serpiente)* boa.

bobada *nf* silliness, foolishness. LOC decir bobadas to talk nonsense.

bobina *nf* **1** reel, bobbin. **2** ELEC coil.
bobo,-a *adj* silly, foolish.
▶ *nm & nf* fool.
boca *nf* **1** ANAT mouth. **2** *(abertura)* entrance, opening: *hay una boca de metro en la esquina* there's an entrance to the underground on the corner. LOC **boca abajo** face downwards. ▌ **callarse la boca** to shut up, shut one's mouth. COMP **boca a boca** kiss of life.
bocacalle *nf* entrance to a street.
bocadillo *nm* sandwich.
bocado *nm* **1** mouthful. **2** *(piscolabis)* snack, bite to eat. **3** *(mordedura)* bite.
bocajarro LOC **a bocajarro 1** *(disparar)* at point-blank range. **2** *(decir algo)* point-blank.
bocata *nm fam* sandwich, sarnie.
boceto *nm* sketch; *(proyecto)* outline.
bochorno *nm* **1** *(calor)* sultry weather, close weather; *(viento)* hot wind. **2** *fig (rubor)* embarrassment, shame.
bochornoso,-a *adj* **1** *(sofocante)* hot, sultry. **2** *fig (vergonzoso)* disgraceful, shameful.
bocina *nf* horn.
boda *nf* marriage, wedding.
bodega *nf* **1** *(almacén)* wine cellar. **2** *(tienda)* wine shop. **3** *(de barco)* hold.
bodegón *nm* still life.
body *nm* body.
bofetada *nf* slap, slap in the face.
bofetón *nm* hard slap.
boga *nf* vogue.
bogavante *nm* lobster.
bohemio,-a *adj (vida, etc)* bohemian.
▶ *nm & nf (artista, etc)* bohemian.
boicot *nm (no participación)* boycott.
boicotear *vt (no participar)* to boycott.
boina *nf* beret.
boj *nm* **1** *(árbol)* box tree. **2** *(madera)* boxwood.
bol *nm* bowl.
bola *nf* **1** *(gen)* ball. **2** *fam* fib, lie.
bolera *nf* bowling alley.
boletín *nm* **1** *(revista)* periodical. **2** *(de noticias)* bulletin, news bulletin. **3** *(impreso)* form. **4** *(de colegio)* report.

boleto *nm* **1** ticket. **2** *(quiniela)* coupon.
boli *nm fam* ballpen, biro.
bólido *nm fam (coche)* racing car.
bolígrafo *nm* ballpoint pen.
bolívar *nm* bolivar *(monetary unit of Venezuela)*.
Bolivia *nf* Bolivia.
boliviano,-a *adj* Bolivian.
▶ *nm & nf* Bolivian.
bollo *nm* **1** *(dulce)* pastry, bun. **2** *(abolladura)* dent.
bolo *nm* skittle, ninepin.
▶ *nm pl* **bolos** skittles.
bolsa¹ *nf (gen)* bag: *¿tiene una bolsa de plástico?* have you got a plastic bag? COMP **bolsa de aseo** toilet bag. ▌ **bolsa de deportes** sports bag.
bolsa² *nf* stock exchange.
bolsillo *nm* pocket. LOC **de bolsillo** pocket: *una calculadora de bolsillo* a pocket calculator.
bolso *nm* handbag, US purse.
bomba *nf* **1** *(explosivo)* bomb. **2** *(noticia)* bombshell. **3** pump. LOC **pasarlo bomba** to have a whale of a time.
bombardear *vt* **1** *(desde el aire)* to bomb. **2** *fig* to bombard: *me bombardearon a preguntas* they bombarded me with questions.
bombardeo *nm (desde el aire)* bombing.
bombardero *nm* bomber.
bombear *vt (agua)* to pump.
bombero,-a *nm (gen)* firefighter; *(hombre)* fireman; *(mujer)* firewoman.
bombilla *nf* light bulb, bulb.
bombín *nm (sombrero)* bowler hat.
bombo *nm (tambor)* bass drum.
bombón *nm* chocolate.
bombona *nf* cylinder. COMP **bombona de butano** butane cylinder.
bonachón,-ona *adj* kind.
bondad *nf* kindness.
bondadoso,-a *adj* kind, good.
boniato *nm* sweet potato.
bonito *nm (pez)* bonito.
bonito,-a *adj* lovely, nice.

bono *nm* **1** *(vale)* voucher. **2** *(billete)* ticket.

bonobús *nm* multiple-journey bus ticket.

bonoloto *nm* Spanish state-run lottery.

boñiga *nf* cow dung.

boquerón *nm* *(pez)* anchovy.

boquete *nm* hole.

boquiabierto,-a *adj* open-mouthed, agape.

boquilla *nf* **1** *(de pipa, instrumento)* mouthpiece. **2** *(filtro de cigarrillo)* tip.

borbotear *vi* to bubble.

borbotón *nm* bubbling.

bordado,-a *nm* embroidery.

bordar *vt* to embroider.

borde¹ *adj* *(antipático)* unpleasant.

borde² *nm* **1** *(extremo)* edge. **2** *(de vaso, taza)* rim.

bordear *vt* to skirt, go round.

bordillo *nm* kerb, US curb.

bordo *nm* MAR board. LOC **a bordo** on board.

boreal *adj* boreal, northern.

bórico,-a *adj* boric.

borla *nf* tassel.

borrachera *nf* drunken state.

borracho,-a *adj* *(persona)* drunk.
▶ *nm & nf* drunkard, drunk.

borrador *nm*. **1** *(de pizarra)* duster. **2** *(goma)* eraser, GB rubber.

borrar *vt* **1** to erase, rub out. **2** INFORM to delete.

borrasca *nf* *(tormenta)* storm.

borrego,-a *nm & nf* lamb.

borrón *nm* blot, ink blot.

borroso,-a *adj* *(visión)* blurred, hazy.

Bosnia *nf* Bosnia. COMP **Bosnia-Herzegovina** Bosnia Herzegovina.

bosnio,-a *adj* Bosnian.
▶ *nm & nf* Bosnian.

bosque *nm* wood, forest.

bosquejar *vt* to sketch, outline.

bosquejo *nm* *(dibujo)* sketch; *(plan, etc)* outline.

bostezar *vi* to yawn.

bostezo *nm* yawn.

bota¹ *nf* boot. COMP **botas de agua** gum boots, US rubber boots.

bota² *nf* *(de vino)* wineskin.

botánico,-a *adj* botanical.

botar *vi* **1** *(pelota)* to bounce. **2** *(persona)* to jump, jump up and down.

bote¹ *nm* MAR small boat. COMP **bote salvavidas** lifeboat.

bote² *nm* *(salto)* bounce.

bote³ *nm* **1** *(lata)* tin, can. **2** *(tarro)* jar. **3** *(para propinas)* jar for tips, box for tips. **4** *(fondo)* kitty.

botella *nf* **1** bottle. **2** *(de gas)* cylinder.

botellín *nm* small bottle.

botijo *nm* earthenware jar *(with spout and handle for drinking)*.

botín¹ *nm* *(zapato)* ankle boot.

botín² *nm* **1** *(de guerra)* spoils *pl*, booty. **2** *(de robo)* haul.

botiquín *nm* first-aid kit.

botón *nm* *(gen)* button.

bóveda *nf* vault.

boxeador,-ra *nm & nf* boxer.

boxear *vi* to box.

boxeo *nm* boxing.

bóxer *nm* *(perro)* boxer.

boya *nf* **1** MAR buoy. **2** *(corcho)* float.

boyante *adj* fig prosperous.

bozal *nm* muzzle.

bracear *vi* *(nadar)* to swim.

braga *nf* *(prenda)* panties *pl*, knickers *pl*.

bragueta *nf* fly, flies *pl*.

braille *nm* Braille.

bramar *vi* to bellow.

branquia *nf* gill.

brasa *nf* ember, live coal.

brasero *nm* brazier.

Brasil *nm* Brazil.

brasileño,-a *adj* Brazilian.
▶ *nm & nf* Brazilian.

bravío,-a *adj* *(animal)* wild, fierce.

bravo,-a *adj* *(fiero)* fierce, ferocious.
▶ *interj* ¡bravo! well done!, bravo!

bravura *nf* *(fiereza)* fierceness.

braza *nf* *(natación)* breaststroke.

brazada *nf* *(natación)* stroke.

brazalete *nm* bracelet, bangle.

brazo *nm* *(de persona)* arm.
▶ *nm pl* **brazos** hands, workers.

brea *nf* tar, pitch.
brebaje *nm* brew, potion.
brecha *nf* **1** break, opening. **2** *fig* breach.
breve *adj* short, brief. ☐LOC☐ **en breve** soon, shortly.
brevedad *nf* brevity, briefness.
brezo *nm* heather, heath.
bricolaje *nm* do-it-yourself, DIY.
brida *nf (de caballo)* bridle.
bridge *nm* bridge.
brigada *nf (unidad militar)* brigade.
brillante *adj* **1** *(extraordinario)* brilliant: *un alumno brillante* a brilliant student. **2** *(pelo, metal, zapatos)* shiny; *(ojos)* sparkling; *(luz, color)* bright; *(pintura)* gloss.
▶ *nm (diamante)* diamond.
brillantina *nf* brilliantine.
brillar *vi* **1** *(luz, sol, luna, pelo, zapatos)* to shine. **2** *(ojos)* to sparkle; *(estrella)* to twinkle; *(metal, dientes)* to gleam; *(cosa húmeda)* to glisten. **3** *fig* to be outstanding.
brillo *nm* **1** *(gen)* shine. **2** *(de estrella)* twinkling; *(de ojos)* sparkle; *(de pelo, zapatos)* shine. **3** *(en televisor)* brightness.
brincar *vi (cabra, etc)* to skip; *(persona)* to leap, bound.
brinco *nm (de cabra)* skip, hop; *(de persona)* leap, bound.
brindar *vi* to toast (por, to), drink (por, to): *¡brindemos por el futuro!* let's drink to the future!
▶ *vt (ofrecer)* to offer, provide.
▶ *vpr* **brindarse** to offer (a, to), volunteer (a, to).
brindis *nm inv* toast.
brisa *nf* breeze.
británico,-a *adj* British.
▶ *nm & nf* British person, Briton, Britisher.
brizna *nf (gen)* bit; *(de hierba)* blade.
broca *nf (barrena)* drill, bit.
brocha *nf* brush, paintbrush.
brochazo *nf* brushstroke.
broche *nm* **1** *(cierre)* fastener. **2** *(joya)* brooch.

broma *nf* joke: *no es broma* It's not a joke.
bromear *vi* to joke.
bromista *nm o nf* joker.
bronca *nf* **1** *(lío)* row. **2** *(riña)* quarrel; *(discusión)* argument. **3** *(reprimenda)* telling-off.
bronce *nm* bronze.
bronceado,-a *adj* bronzed.
▶ *nm* **bronceado** tan, suntan.
bronceador,-ra *nm* suntan lotion.
broncear *vt (persona)* to tan, suntan.
▶ *vpr* **broncearse** to tan, get a tan.
bronquio *nm* bronchus.
bronquitis *nf inv* bronchitis.
brotar *vi (plantas - nacer)* to sprout; *(- echar brotes)* to come into bud.
brote *nm* shoot, sprout.
broza *nf* **1** *(hojas)* dead leaves; *(ramitas)* dead twigs. **2** *(maleza)* scrub, brush.
bruces ☐LOC☐ **caerse de bruces** to fall flat on one's face.
bruja *nf (hechicera)* witch.
brujería *nf* witchcraft, sorcery.
brujo,-a *nm* wizard, sorcerer.
brújula *nf* compass.
bruma *nf* mist.
bruñido,-a *adj* burnished.
brusco,-a *adj* **1** *(repentino)* sudden. **2** *(persona)* abrupt.
brusquedad *nf* **1** *(de carácter)* abruptness. **2** *(rapidez)* suddenness.
brutal *adj (cruel)* brutal, savage.
brutalidad *nf (crueldad)* brutality.
bruto,-a *adj* **1** *(cruel)* brutal. **2** *(necio)* stupid, thick. **3** *(tosco)* rough, coarse.
▶ *nm & nf (persona - violenta)* brute, beast; *(necio)* ignoramus.
bucal *adj* oral, mouth.
bucanero *nm* buccaneer.
bucear *vi* to dive.
bucle *nm* **1** curl. **2** INFORM loop.
bucólico,-a *adj* bucolic.
budismo *nm* Buddhism.
budista *adj* Buddhist.
▶ *nm o nf* Buddhist.
buen *adj* → **bueno,-a**.

bueno,-a *adj* **1** *(gen)* good. **2** *(persona - amable)* kind; *(- agradable)* nice. **3** *(tiempo)* good, nice. **4** *(apropiado)* right, suitable. **5** *(de salud)* well.
▸ *interj* **¡bueno!** *(sorpresa)* well, very well; *(de acuerdo)* all right!

buey *nm* ox, bullock.

búfalo *nm* buffalo.

bufanda *nf* scarf.

bufar *vi (toro)* to snort.

bufé *nm* buffet.

bufete *nm (de abogado)* lawyer's office.

bufido *nm* snort.

bufón,-ona *nm & nf* buffoon, jester.

buhardilla *nf* attic.

búho *nm* owl.

buitre *nm* vulture.

bujía *nf (de motor)* spark plug.

bulbo *nm* bulb.

bulevar *nm* boulevard.

Bulgaria *nf* Bulgaria.

búlgaro,-a *adj* Bulgarian.
▸ *nm & nf (persona)* Bulgarian.
▸ *nm* **búlgaro** *(idioma)* Bulgarian.

bulldozer *nm* bulldozer.

bullicio *nm* **1** *(ruido)* noise, racket. **2** *(tumulto)* bustle, hustle and bustle.

bullicioso,-a *adj (ruidoso)* noisy.

bulto *nm* **1** *(tamaño)* volume, size, bulk. **2** *(forma)* shape, form. **3** *(abultamiento - en cosa)* bulge; *(- en piel)* lump.

bum *interj* boom!

bumerán *nm* boomerang.

bungalow *nm* bungalow.

búnker *nm* bunker.

buñuelo *nm* fritter.

BUP *abrev* EDUC (Bachillerato Unificado Polivalente) former General Certificate of Secondary Education studies.

buque *nm* MAR ship, vessel.

burbuja *nf* bubble. LOC **con burbujas** *(bebida)* fizzy.

burbujear *vi* to bubble.

burdo,-a *adj* **1** *(tejido)* coarse, rough. **2** *(persona)* coarse, crude.

burgués,-esa *nm & nf* middle-class.

burguesía *nf* middle class.

burla *nf* **1** *(mofa)* mockery, gibe. **2** *(broma)* joke. **3** *(engaño)* deception, trick.

burlar *vt* **1** to deceive, trick. **2** *(eludir)* to dodge, evade.
▸ *vpr* **burlarse** to mock (de, -), make fun (de, of), laugh (de, at).

burlón,-ona *nm & nf* joker.

burocracia *nf* bureaucracy.

burócrata *nm o nf* bureaucrat.

burrada *nf* **1** drove of asses. **2** *fam* a lot: *me gusta una burrada* I love it.

burro,-a *adj* stupid.
▸ *nm & nf* **1** *(animal)* donkey, ass. **2** *(persona ignorante)* ass.

bus *nm* **1** AUTO bus. **2** INFORM bus.

busca *nf* search, hunt.

buscapersonas *nm* bleeper, pager.

buscar *vt* **1** *(gen)* to look for, search for. **2** *(en lista, índice, etc)* to look up: *búscalo en el diccionario* look it up in the dictionary. **3** *(ir a coger)* to go and get, fetch. **4** *(recoger)* to pick up.

búsqueda *nf* search.

busto *nm (figura)* bust.

butaca *nf (sillón)* armchair.

butacón *nm* easy chair.

butano *nm* butane.

buzo *nm* diver.

buzón *nm* letter box, US mailbox.

byte *nm* INFORM byte.

C

C, c *nf (la letra)* C, c.

C¹ *sím* (Celsius) Celsius; *(símbolo)* C.

C² *sím* (centígrado) centigrade; *(símbolo)* C.

cabal *adj* **1** *(exacto)* exact, precise. **2** *fig (persona)* honest, upright.

cábala *nf* **1** *(ciencia oculta)* cabala, cabbala. **2** [en este sentido, también se usa en plural con el mismo significado] *fig (conjetura)* guess, divination. **3** *fig (intriga)* plot.

cabalgar *vi* to ride (en/sobre, -).

cabalgata *nf* cavalcade.

caballa *nf* mackerel.

caballería *nf* **1** MIL cavalry. **2** HIST knighthood.

caballero,-a *nm* **1** gentleman, sir. **2** HIST knight.

caballete *nm* easel.

caballito *nm* small horse. ▣COMP caballito de mar sea horse.
　▶ *nm pl* **caballitos** *(tiovivo)* merry-go-round *sing*, US carrousel *sing*.

caballo *nm* **1** ZOOL horse. **2** *(ajedrez)* knight.

cabaña *nf (choza)* cabin, hut, shack.

cabecear *vi* **1** to move one's head, shake one's head. **2** *(dar cabezadas)* to nod.

cabecera *nf* **1** *(gen)* top, head. **2** *(de un periódico)* headline.

cabecilla *nm o nf* leader.

cabellera *nf* hair, head of hair.

cabello *nm* hair.

caber *vi* **1** *(encajar)* to fit (en, into): *cabe ahí arriba* it'll fit up there. **2** *(pasar)* to fit, go. **3** MAT to go: *ocho entre dos caben a cuatro* two into eight goes four times, eight divided by two is four.

cabeza *nf* **1** *(gen)* head: *diez mil por cabeza* ten thousand a head. **2** *fig (juicio)* good judgement; *(talento)* talent, intelligence. ▣LOC cabeza abajo upside down. ▮ estar mal de la cabeza *fig* not to be right in the head. ▮ meterse ALGO en la cabeza *fam* to get STH into one's head. ▣COMP cabeza cuadrada *fam* bigot. ▮ cabeza de ajo bulb of garlic. ▮ cabeza rapada skinhead.

cabezada *nf (golpe recibido)* blow on the head; *(golpe dado)* butt, head butt. ▣LOC dar cabezadas *fam* to nod.

cabezal *nm* TÉC head, headstock.

cabina *nf (gen)* cabin, booth. ▣COMP cabina telefónica telephone box, US telephone booth.

cable *nm (maroma)* cable.

cabo *nm* **1** *(extremo)* end, stub. **2** *fig* end: *al cabo de un mes* in a month's time. **3** *(cuerda)* rope, line. **4** GEOG cape. ▣LOC al cabo finally. ▮ llevar a cabo to carry out.

cabra *nf* goat. ▣LOC estar como una cabra *fam* to be off one's rocker, be nuts.

cabrito *nm* ZOOL kid.

caca *nf* **1** *fam euf (excremento)* pooh. **2** *fam (en lenguaje infantil)* dirt.

cacahuete *nm (fruto)* peanut.

cacao *nm* **1** BOT cacao. **2** *(polvo, bebida)* cocoa. **3** *fam (jaleo)* mess, cockup.

cacarear *vi (gallina)* to cluck; *(gallo)* to crow.

cacatúa *nf (ave)* cockatoo.

cacería *nf* hunting, hunt.

cacerola *nf* saucepan, casserole.

cachalote *nm* sperm whale.

cacharro *nm* **1** *(de cocina)* crock, piece of crockery. **2** *fam (cosa)* piece of junk. **3** *fam pey (coche)* banger.

cachemira *nf (tejido)* cashmere.

cachete *nm (bofetada)* slap.

cacho *nm fam* bit, piece.

cachorro,-a *nm & nf (de perro)* pup, puppy; *(de gato)* kitten; *(de león, oso, zorro, tigre)* cub; *(de otros mamíferos)* young.

cacique *nm* **1** *(jefe indio)* chief, cacique. **2** POL local political boss.

caco *nm fam* thief.

cacto *nm* cactus.

cada *adj* **1** *(de dos)* each; *(de varios)* every. **2** *fam (intensificador)* such: *¡dice cada cosa!* he says such strange things! LOC **cada día** every day.

cadáver *nm* corpse, cadaver, body, dead body.

cadena *nf* **1** *(gen)* chain; *(de perro)* leash, lead. **2** *(montañosa)* range. **3** *(musical)* music centre (US center). **4** TV channel. **5** RAD chain of stations. COMP **trabajo en cadena** assembly-line work.

cadera *nf* hip.

caducar *vi* **1** *(documento, etc)* to expire: *mi pasaporte caduca este año* my passport expires this year. **2** *(alimento)* to pass its sell-by date.

caducidad *nf* expiry.

caer *vi* **1** *(gen)* to fall: *caer de espalda* to fall on one's back. **2** *(derrumbar)* to fall down, collapse. **3** *(hallarse)* to be: *el camino cae a la derecha* the road is on the right. **4** *(coincidir fechas)* to fall on, be: *el día cuatro cae en jueves* the fourth falls on a Thursday. LOC **dejar caer** to drop: *dejé caer el vaso* I dropped the glass.
▶ *vpr* **caerse 1** *(gen)* to fall, fall down. **2** *(desprenderse)* to fall out: *se le cae el pelo* he's losing his hair. LOC **caerse de sueño** *fig* to be dead on one's feet, be ready to drop.

café *nm* **1** *(gen)* coffee. **2** *(cafetería)* café, coffee bar, coffee shop. COMP **café con leche** white coffee.

cafeína *nf* caffeine.

cafetera *nf* **1** *(para hacer café)* coffee-maker. **2** *(para servir café)* coffeepot.

cafetería *nf (gen)* snack bar, coffee bar.

caimán *nm* alligator, cayman.

caja *nf* **1** *(gen)* box. **2** *(de madera)* chest; *(grande)* crate. **3** *(de bebidas)* case. **4** *(en comercio)* cash desk, till; *(en banco)* cashier's desk; *(en supermercado)* checkout. **5** *(banco)* bank: *caja de ahorros* savings bank. COMP **caja registradora** cash register.

cajero,-a *nm & nf* cashier. COMP **cajero automático** cash point, automatic cash dispenser.

cajetilla *nf* **1** *(de tabaco)* packet, US pack. **2** *(de cerillas)* box.

cajón *nm* **1** *(en mueble)* drawer. **2** *(caja grande)* crate.

cal *nf* lime. COMP **cal viva** quicklime.

cala *nf* **1** *(ensenada)* cove, creek. **2** *(planta)* arum lily.

calabacín *nm* **1** *(pequeño)* courgette, US zucchini. **2** *(grande)* marrow, US squash.

calabaza *nf* gourd, pumpkin.

calabozo *nm* **1** *(prisión)* jail, prison. **2** *(celda)* cell.

calamar *nm* squid.

calambre *nm* **1** *(contracción)* cramp. **2** *(descarga eléctrica)* electric shock.

calamidad *nf (desgracia)* calamity, disaster.

calar *vt (mojar)* to soak through, soak, drench.
▶ *vpr* **calarse 1** *(mojarse)* to get soaked. **2** AUTO to stop, stall.

calavera *nf (cabeza del esqueleto)* skull.

calcetín *nm* sock.

cálcico,-a *adj* calcium, calcic.

calcinar *vt* **1** to calcine. **2** *fig* to burn.

calcio *nm* calcium.

calcita *nf* calcite.

calcomanía *nf* transfer.

calculador,-ra *adj* calculating.
▶ *nm & nf* calculator. COMP **calculadora de bolsillo** pocket calculator.

calcular *vt* **1** to calculate, work out: *calcular una suma* to calculate a figure. **2** *(suponer)* to think, suppose, figure, guess.

cálculo *nm* calculation, estimate.

caldera *nf* boiler.

calderilla *nf* small change.

caldo *nm* **1** CULIN stock, broth. **2** *(sopa)* consommé.

calefacción *nf* heating. [COMP] **calefacción central** central heating.

calefactor *nm (máquina)* heater.

calendario *nm* calendar. [COMP] **calendario académico** school year.

calentador,-ra *nm* heater.

calentar *vt* **1** *(comida, habitación, cuerpo)* to warm up; *(agua, horno)* to heat. **2** DEP to warm up, tone up.

calibre *nm* **1** *(de arma)* calibre. **2** *fig (importancia)* importance.

calidad *nf* **1** quality. **2** *(cualidad)* kind, types. [LOC] **de primera calidad** first-class.

cálido,-a *adj* warm: *un clima cálido* a warm climate.

caliente *adj (mayor intensidad)* hot; *(menor intensidad)* warm.

calificación *nf (nota)* mark.

calificar *vt* **1** *(determinar las cualidades)* to describe, qualify. **2** EDUC to mark, grade.

caligrafía *nf* **1** *(arte)* calligraphy. **2** *(escritura de una persona)* handwriting. [COMP] **ejercicios de caligrafía** handwriting exercises.

cáliz *nm* **1** REL chalice. **2** BOT calyx. **3** *lit (copa)* cup.

caliza *nf* limestone.

callar *vi (no hablar)* to be quiet, keep quiet. [LOC] **¡cállate!** keep quiet!, be quiet!

calle *nf* **1** street, road. **2** DEP lane. [LOC] **dejar a** ALGN **en la calle 1** *(sin trabajo)* to fire SB. **2** *(sin casa)* to leave SB homeless.

callejero,-a *adj (que gusta de callejear)* fond of wandering about.
▶ *nm* **callejero** *(de calles)* street directory.

callo *nm* MED callus, corn.

calma *nf* calmness, calm, tranquillity (US tranquility). [LOC] **tomárselo con calma** to take it easy.

calmante *adj* soothing, sedative, tranquillizing (US tranquilizing).

calmar *vt* **1** *(persona)* to calm (down). **2** *(dolor)* to relieve, soothe.
▶ *vpr* **calmarse 1** *(persona)* to calm down. **2** *(dolor, etc)* to abate, ease off.

calor *nm* heat, warmth: *hace calor* it is hot.

caloría *nf* calorie.

caluroso,-a *adj* **1** *(tiempo)* warm, hot. **2** *fig* warm, enthusiastic.

calva *nf* **1** *(de la cabeza)* bald patch. **2** *(de un bosque)* clearing.

calvo,-a *adj (persona)* bald.

calzada *nf* road, US pavement.

calzado *nm* footwear, shoes *pl*.

calzar *vt* **1** *(poner calzado)* to put shoes on. **2** *(llevar calzado)* to wear: *¿qué número calzas?* what size do you take?
▶ *vpr* **calzarse** *(forma reflexiva)* to put (one's shoes) on.

calzoncillos *nm pl* pants.

cama *nf (gen)* bed. [LOC] **guardar cama** to be confined to bed, stay in bed. ▮ **hacer la cama** to make the bed. ▮ **irse a la cama** to go to bed. [COMP] **cama de matrimonio** double bed. ▮ **cama individual** single bed.

camada *nf (gen)* litter.

camaleón *nm* chameleon.

cámara *nf* **1** *(de parlamento)* house. **2** *(de rueda)* inner tube. **3** TÉC chamber. **4** *(fotográfica, de cine)* camera. **5** ANAT cavity. [COMP] **cámara alta** POL upper house. ▮ **cámara baja** POL lower house. ▮ **cámara de aire** air chamber. ▮ **cámara de cine** cine camera, (US movie camera).
▶ *nm o nf (hombre)* cameraman; *(mujer)* camerawoman.

camarero,-a *nm & nf (de bar, restaurante - hombre)* waiter; *(mujer)* waitress.

camarón *nm* common prawn.

camarote *nm* cabin.

cambiar *vt* **1** *(gen)* to change: *han cambiado las sillas* the chairs have been changed. **2** *(intercambiar)* to exchange. **3** *(moneda extranjera)* to change, exchange.

▶ *vi* **1** *(gen)* to change: *has cambiado mucho* you have changed a lot.

▶ *vpr* **cambiarse 1** *(mudarse de ropa)* to change, get changed. **2** *(mudarse de casa)* to move.

cambio *nm* **1** change, changing. **2** *(intercambio)* exchange, exchanging. LOC **a cambio de** in exchange for. **‖ en cambio** on the other hand, but, whereas.

camelia *nf* camellia.

camello *nm* ZOOL camel.

camerino *nm* dressing room.

camilla *nf (para enfermos)* stretcher.

caminar *vi (andar)* to walk.

▶ *vt (recorrer)* to cover, travel: *he caminado cinco kilómetros* I have covered five kilometres.

caminata *nf* long walk, trek.

camino *nm* **1** *(vía)* path, track. **2** *(ruta)* way, route. LOC **ir camino de** to be on one's way to. **‖ ponerse en camino** to set off (on a journey).

camión *nm* lorry, US truck. COMP **camión de mudanzas** removal van.

camionero,-a *nm & nf* lorry driver, US truck driver.

camioneta *nf* van.

camisa *nf* shirt.

camiseta *nf* **1** *(ropa interior)* vest, US undershirt. **2** *(niqui)* T-shirt. **3** DEP shirt, jersey.

camisón *nm* nightdress, nightie.

campamento *nm* **1** *(acción de acampar)* camping. **2** *(lugar)* camp.

campana *nf* **1** *(gen)* bell. **2** *fam (extractora)* extractor hood, (US stove extractor hood).

campanada *nf* stroke of a bell.

campanario *nm* belfry, bell tower.

campanilla *nf* **1** *(gen)* small bell. **2** ANAT uvula. **3** *(flor)* morning glory.

campaña *nf* **1** campaign: *campaña electoral* election campaign.

campechano,-na *adj fam* frank.

campeón,-ona *nm & nf* champion.

campeonato *nm* championship.

campesino,-a *nm & nf (gen)* peasant; *(hombre)* countryman; *(mujer)* countrywoman.

camping *nm* camp site. LOC **hacer camping / ir de camping** to go camping.

campiña *nf* countryside.

campo *nm* **1** *(campiña)* country, countryside: *vivir en el campo* to live in the country. **2** *(agricultura)* field. **3** *(de deportes)* field, pitch. **4** *(espacio)* space: *en el campo de la medicina* in the field of medicine.

campus *nm inv* campus.

camuflaje *nm* camouflage.

cana *nf* grey hair, white hair.

Canadá *nm* Canada.

canadiense *adj* Canadian.
▶ *nm & nf* Canadian.

canal *nm* **1** *(artificial)* canal. **2** *(natural)* channel.
▶ *nm & nf* TÉC channel.

canalizar *vt* to channel.

canalla *nm o nf* swine.

canalón *nm (por el borde del tejado)* gutter.

Canarias *fpl* las (islas) Canarias the Canary Islands, the Canaries.

canario,-a *adj* Canarian.
▶ *nm & nf* Canarian.
▶ *nm* **canario** *(pájaro)* canary.

canasto *nm (cesto)* basket, hamper.

cancelar *vt* **1** *(anular)* to cancel. **2** *(saldar una deuda)* to settle, pay.

cáncer *nm* cancer.

cancerígeno,-a *adj* carcinogenic.

cancha *nf (gen)* ground; *(tenis)* court.

canciller *nm* chancellor.

canción *nf* song. COMP **canción de cuna** lullaby.

candado *nm* padlock.

candidato,-a *nm & nf* candidate.

candidatura *nf* **1** *(aspiración)* candidacy, candidature: *presentó su candidatura* she put forward her candidature. **2** *(lista de candidatos)* list of candidates.

candidez *nf* ingenuousness, innocence.

cándido,-a *adj* ingenuous, innocent.

candil *nm* oil lamp.

canela *nf* cinnamon.

cangrejo *nm (de mar)* crab.

canguro *nm* ZOOL kangaroo.
▶ *nm o nf fam* baby-sitter.

caníbal *nm o nf* cannibal.

canica *nf* marble: *jugar a las canicas* to play marbles.

canino,-a *adj* canine.

canjear *vt* to exchange.

canoa *nf* canoe; *(bote)* boat.

canon *nm* **1** *(regla)* canon, norm. **2** *(cantidad de dinero)* tax.

canoso,-a *adj* grey-haired (US gray-haired).

cansado,-a *adj* **1** *(gen)* tired, weary: *estoy cansada* I'm tired. **2** *(que fatiga)* tiring: *es un trabajo muy cansado* it's a very tiring job. **3** *(harto)* tired (de, of), fed up (de, with).

cansancio *nm* tiredness, weariness.

cansar *vt* **1** *(causar cansancio)* to tire, tire out, make tired. **2** *(molestar)* to annoy; *(aburrir)* to tire, bore.
▶ *vi (causar cansancio)* to be tiring.
▶ *vpr* **cansarse** *(padecer cansancio)* to get tired, tire: *se cansó de correr* he got tired of running.

cantante *nm o nf* singer.

cantaor,-ra *nm & nf* flamenco singer.

cantar *vt* **1** to sing: *cantó una canción preciosa* she sang a beautiful song. **2** *(en juegos de naipes)* to call.
▶ *vi* **1** to sing. **2** *(pájaros)* to sing, chirp; *(insectos)* to chirp.

cántaro *nm (vasija)* pitcher. LOC **llover a cántaros** *fig* to rain cats and dogs.

cante *nm* MÚS singing.

cantera *nf (de piedra)* quarry.

cantero *nm* stonemason.

cántico *nm* canticle.

cantidad *nf (gen)* quantity; *(de dinero)* amount, sum.
▶ *adv fam* a lot: *llovía cantidad* it was pouring with rain.

cantimplora *nf* water bottle.

cantina *nf* **1** *(comedor)* canteen. **2** *(de estación)* buffet.

canto *nm* **1** *(arte)* singing. **2** *(canción)* song. **3** *(de cuchillo)* blunt edge. **4** *(esquina)* corner. **5** *(piedra)* stone, pebble. COMP **canto rodado 1** *(grande)* boulder. **2** *(pequeño)* pebble.

cantor,-ra *adj* singing. LOC **pájaro cantor** songbird.
▶ *nm & nf* singer.

caña *nf* **1** *(planta)* reed. **2** *(tallo)* cane, stem. **3** *(de pescar)* rod. **4** *(de cerveza)* small glass of draught beer. COMP **caña de azúcar** sugar cane.

cañada *nf* **1** GEOG glen, dell, hollow. **2** *(sendero)* cattle track.

cáñamo *nm* BOT hemp.

cañería *nf* piping.

caño *nm (tubo)* tube.

cañón *nm* **1** *(de artillería)* gun; *(antiguamente)* cannon. **2** *(de arma)* barrel. **3** GEOG canyon.

caoba *nf* mahogany.

caolín *nm* kaolin.

caos *nm inv* chaos.

caótico,-a *adj* chaotic.

capa *nf* **1** *(prenda)* cloak, cape. **2** GEOL stratum, layer. **3** *(de pintura)* coat; *(de polvo)* layer; *(de chocolate, etc)* coating, layer.

capacidad *nf* **1** *(gen)* capacity: *hay capacidad para cinco personas* there's room for five people. **2** *fig (habilidad)* capability, ability.

capacitar *vt* **1** *(instruir)* to train, qualify. **2** *(autorizar)* to qualify, entitle.

caparazón *nm* shell, carapace.

capataz,-za *nm & nf (hombre)* foreman; *(mujer)* forewoman.

capaz *adj* **1** *(competente)* capable, able: *es una persona muy capaz* she's very capable. **2** *(cualificado)* qualified. **3** *(capaz)* capable (de, of): *no es capaz de eso* he's incapable of doing that.

capazo *nm* **1** *(cesto)* basket. **2** *(para bebé)* carry cot.

capellán *nm* chaplain.

capicúa *adj* reversible.

capilla *nf (iglesia)* chapel.

capital *nf* capital, chief town.

capitalismo *nm* capitalism.

capitalista *adj* capitalist.
▶ *nm o nf* capitalist.

capitán,-ana *nm & nf* **1** *(oficial)* captain. **2** *(jefe)* leader, chief. **3** DEP captain.

capitanear *vt* **1** *(gen)* to lead; *(tropas)* to command. **2** *(equipo)* to captain. **3** *(buque)* to captain.

capitel *nm* capital, chapter.

capítulo *nm* **1** *(gen)* chapter. **2** *fig (tema)* subject, matter.

capó *nm* bonnet, US hood.

capota *nf (cubierta plegadiza)* folding hood, folding top.

capricho *nm (deseo)* whim, fancy.

caprichoso,-a *adj* capricious, whimsical, fanciful.
► *nm & nf* whimsical person.

cápsula *nf (gen)* capsule.

captar *vt* **1** *(ondas)* to receive. **2** *(entender)* to understand, grasp. **3** *(atraer a personas)* to attract, recruit.

captura *nf* capture.

capturar *vt* to capture, seize.

capucha *nf* hood.

capuchón *nm (de estilográfica, etc)* cap.

capullo *nm* **1** *(de insectos)* cocoon. **2** BOT bud.

caqui *adj* khaki.

cara *nf* **1** *(rostro)* face. **2** *(expresión)* face, expression. **3** *(lado)* side; *(de moneda)* right side. **4** *(superficie)* face. **5** *fig (aspecto)* look. **6** *fam fig (desvergüenza)* cheek, nerve: *¡vaya cara!* what a cheek! LOC **dar la cara** *fig* to face the consequences. **poner buena cara** to look pleased. COMP **cara de circunstancias** *fig* serious look. **cara dura** *fig* cheek, nerve.

carabina *nf (arma)* carbine, rifle.

caracol *nm (de tierra)* snail.

caracola *nf* conch.

carácter *nm* **1** *(personalidad)* character. **2** *(condición)* nature, kind. LOC **tener buen carácter** to be good-natured.

característico,-a *adj* characteristic.

carambola *nf (billar)* cannon, US carom.

caramelo *nm (dulce)* sweet, US candy.

caravana *nf (expedición)* caravan. *(atasco)* traffic jam, tailback.

caray *interj* good heavens!, God!

carbón *nm (gen)* coal.

carboncillo *nm* charcoal.

carbónico,-a *adj* carbonic. COMP **anhídrido carbónico** carbon dioxide.

carbonífero,-a *adj* carboniferous.

carbonilla *nf (residuo de carbón)* coal dust.

carbonizar *vt* **1** *(reducir a carbón)* to carbonize. **2** *(quemar)* to burn, char.

carbono *nm* carbon. COMP **dióxido de carbono** carbon dioxide.

carburador *nm* carburettor (US carburetor).

carcajada *nf* burst of laughter, guffaw. LOC **reír(se) a carcajadas** to laugh one's head off, roar with laughter.

cárcel *nf* jail, gaol, prison.

carcelero,-a *adj* prison, goal, jail.

carcoma *nf (insecto)* woodworm.

cardamomo *nm* cardamom.

cardenal *(hematoma)* bruise. *nm* REL cardinal.

cardiaco,-a *adj* cardiac, heart.

cardinal *adj* cardinal.

cardiología *nf* cardiology.

cardiólogo,-a *nm & nf* cardiologist.

cardo *nm* **1** BOT *(espinoso)* thistle; *(comestible)* cardoon.

carecer *vi* to lack (de, -).

carencia *nf* lack (de, of).

careta *nf (máscara)* mask. COMP **careta antigás** gas mask.

carey *nm* **1** *(animal)* sea turtle. **2** *(concha)* tortoiseshell.

carga *nf* **1** *(acción)* loading. **2** *(lo cargado)* load; *(de avión, barco)* cargo, freight.

cargado,-a *adj* **1** *(atmósfera)* heavy, dense. **2** *(fuerte)* strong. **3** *fig* burdened, weighed down: *cargado,-a de responsabilidades* weighed down with responsibility.

cargador,-ra *nm* **1** *(de arma)* magazine. **2** *(de batería)* battery charger. **3** *(de pluma, etc)* filler.

cargamento *nm (gen)* load; *(de avión, barco)* cargo, freight.

cargar *vt* **1** *(poner peso)* to load. **2** *(arma, máquina de fotos)* to load. **3** ELEC to charge: *cargar las pilas* to charge the batteries. **4** *(pluma, etc)* to fill. **5** INFORM to load.
► *vi* **1** *(gen)* to load. **2** *(batería)* to charge. **3** *(toro, elefante, etc)* to charge. **4** *(atacar)* to charge (contra/sobre, -). **5**

cargar con *(algo que pesa)* to carry; *(una obligación)* to shoulder, take on.
▶ *vpr* **cargarse 1** *(llenarse)* to load OS (de, with): *cargarse de trabajo* to burden OS with work. **2** ELEC to become charged. **3** EDUC *fam (suspender)* to fail. **4** *fam (destrozar)* to smash, ruin. **5** *fam (matar)* to knock off.

cargo *nm* **1** *(peso)* load, weight. **2** *(empleo)* post, position. **3** *(gobierno, custodia)* charge, responsibility. LOC **hacerse cargo de 1** *(responsabilizarse de)* to take charge of. **2** *(entender)* to realize: *me hago cargo* I realize that.

caricatura *nf* caricature.

caricia *nf* caress, stroke.

caridad *nf* charity.

caries *nf inv (enfermedad)* tooth decay, caries *pl; (lesión)* cavity.

cariño *nm* **1** *(amor)* love, affection. **2** *(esmero)* loving care. **3** *(apelativo)* darling, love, US honey. LOC **coger/tomar cariño a** ALGN/ALGO to grow fond of SB/STH.

cariñoso,-a *adj* loving, affectionate.

carisma *nm* charisma.

carismático,-a *adj* charismatic.

carmín *nm (pintalabios)* lipstick.

carnada *nf* bait.

carnaval *nm* carnival.

carne *nf* **1** ANAT flesh. **2** CULIN meat. **3** *(de fruta)* pulp. **4** *fig (cuerpo)* flesh. COMP **carne de cerdo** pork. **carne de cordero** lamb. **carne de ternera** veal. **carne de vaca** beef. **carne picada** mince, mincemeat, US ground meat, loose meat.

carné *nm* card. COMP **carné de conducir** driving licence. **carné de identidad** identity card..

carnicería *nf* butcher's, butcher's shop.

carnicero,-a *nm & nf (profesión)* butcher.

carnívoro,-a *adj* carnivorous.
▶ *nm & nf* carnivore.

caro,-a *adj (costoso)* expensive, dear.
▶ *adv* **caro** at a high price. LOC **costar caro,-a / salir caro,-a 1** *(ser costoso)* to cost a lot. **2** *(causar daño)* to cost dear.

carpa *nf* **1** *(pez)* carp. **2** *(de circo)* big top, marquee.

carpeta *nf (archivador)* folder, file; *(informática)* folder.

carpintería *nf (obra y oficio)* carpentry.

carpintero,-a *nm & nf* carpenter.

carraca *nf (instrumento)* rattle.

carrera *nf* **1** *(acción)* run. **2** *(trayecto - de desfile)* route; *(- de taxi)* ride, journey. **3** *(camino)* road. **4** DEP race. **5** *(estudios)* degree course, university education. COMP **carrera contra reloj** race against the clock. **carrera diplomática** diplomatic career.

carreta *nf* cart.

carrete *nm* **1** *(de hilo)* bobbin, reel. **2** ELEC coil. **3** *(de caña de pescar)* reel. **4** *(de película)* spool; *(de fotos)* film, roll of film. **5** *(de máquina de escribir)* cartridge.

carretera *nf* road. COMP **carretera nacional** A road, main road. **carretera de circunvalación** ring road.

carretilla *nf* wheelbarrow.

carril *nm* **1** *(de ferrocarril)* rail. **2** *(de carretera)* lane. COMP **carril bus** bus lane.

carrillo *nm* cheek.

carrito *nm (para la compra)* trolley, US cart.

carro *nm* **1** *(vehículo)* cart. **2** *(de supermercado, aeropuerto)* trolley, US cart.

carrocería *nf* body, bodywork.

carromato *nm* covered wagon.

carroña *nf* carrion.

carroñero,-a *adj* carrion-eating.

carroza *adj fam* old, old-fashioned.
▶ *nf (tirado por caballos)* coach, carriage.

carruaje *nm* carriage, coach.

carrusel *nm (tiovivo)* merry-go-round, US carrousel.

carta *nf* **1** *(misiva)* letter. **2** *(naipe)* card. **3** *(minuta)* menu. LOC **a la carta** à la carte. **echar una carta** to post a letter, US mail a letter.

cartabón *nm* set square, triangle.

cartel *nm* poster, bill.

cartelera *nf (en periódicos)* entertainment section. LOC **en cartelera** running, on.

cartera *nf* **1** *(monedero)* wallet. **2** *(de colegial)* satchel, school bag. **3** *(de ejecutivo)* briefcase.

carterista *nm o nf* pickpocket.

cartero,-a *nm & nf (hombre)* postman; *(mujer)* postwoman.

cartílago *nm* cartilage.

cartilla *nf* **1** *(para aprender)* first reader. **2** *(cuaderno)* book.

cartón *nm* **1** *(material)* cardboard. **2** *(de cigarrillos)* carton. COMP **cartón piedra** papier-mâché.

cartucho *nm (de explosivo)* cartridge.

cartulina *nf* thin cardboard.

casa *nf* **1** *(vivienda)* house. **2** *(piso)* flat. **3** *(edificio)* building. **4** *(hogar)* home: *nos quedamos en casa* we stayed at home. **5** *(empresa)* firm, company. LOC **buscar casa** to go house-hunting.

casaca *nf* fitted short coat.

casado,-a *adj* married.

casar *vt* to marry.
▶ *vi (casarse)* to marry (con, -), get married (con, to).
▶ *vpr* **casarse** to get married (con, to) marry (con, -).

cascabel *nm* bell.

cascada *nf* cascade, waterfall.

cascanueces *nm inv* nutcrackers *pl*.

cascar *vt (romper)* to crack.
▶ *vpr* **cascarse** *(romperse)* to crack.

cáscara *nf* **1** *(de huevo, nuez)* shell. **2** *(de fruta)* skin, peel.

cascarón *nm* eggshell.

cascarrabias *nm o nf inv fam* grumpy person, bad-tempered person.

casco *nm* **1** *(para la cabeza)* helmet. **2** *(envase)* empty bottle. **3** *(de barco)* hull. **4** *(de caballería)* hoof.

caserío *nm* **1** *(casa)* country house. **2** *(pueblo)* hamlet, small village.

casero,-a *adj* **1** *(persona)* home-loving. **2** *(productos)* home-made: *pan casero* home-made bread.
▶ *nm & nf (dueño - hombre)* landlord; *(mujer)* landlady.

caseta *nf* **1** *(casita)* hut, booth. **2** *(de feria)* stall, stand. **3** *(de bañistas)* bathing

hut, US bath house. **4** *(de perro)* kennel, doghouse.

casete *nm (magnetófono)* cassette player, cassette recorder.
▶ *nf (cinta)* cassette, cassette tape.

casi *adv* almost, nearly: *había casi cincuenta personas* there were almost fifty people. LOC **casi nunca** hardly ever.

casilla *nf* **1** *(casita)* hut, lodge. **2** *(de casillero)* pigeonhole. **3** *(cuadrícula)* square.

casillero *nm* pigeonholes *pl*.

casino *nm* casino.

casis *nm inv* blackcurrant bush.

caso *nm* **1** *(ocasión)* case, occasion. **2** *(gramatical)* case. LOC **en caso de que** if: *en caso de que te pierdas, llámame* if you get lost, call me. ▮ **en cualquier caso** in any case. ▮ **en todo caso** anyhow, at any rate.

caspa *nf* dandruff.

casquete *nm (prenda)* skullcap.

casquillo *nm* **1** TÉC ferrule, metal tip. **2** *(de cartucho)* case.

casta *nf (linaje)* lineage, descent.

castaña *nf* BOT chestnut.

castañetear *vi (dientes)* to chatter.

castaño,-a *adj (pelo)* brown.
▶ *nm* **castaño 1** BOT *(árbol)* chestnut tree. **2** *(madera)* chestnut.

castañuela *nf* castanet.

castellano,-a *adj* Castilian.
▶ *nm & nf (persona)* Castilian.
▶ *nm* **castellano** *(idioma)* Castilian, Spanish.

castigar *vt (aplicar una pena)* to punish.

castigo *nm* **1** *(gen)* punishment. **2** *(en deporte)* penalty.

castillo *nm* castle.

casting *nm* casting, audition.

castizo,-a *adj* pure, authentic.

casto,-a *adj* chaste.

castor *nm* beaver.

casual *adj* accidental, chance.

casualidad *nf* **1** chance, accident. **2** *(coincidencia)* coincidence. LOC **de casualidad / por casualidad** by chance.

cataclismo *nm* cataclysm.

catacumbas *nf pl* catacombs.
catalán,-ana *adj* Catalan, Catalonian.
▶ *nm & nf (persona)* Catalan.
▶ *nm* **catalán** *(idioma)* Catalan.
catalejo *nm* telescope.
catalogar *vt* **1** to catalogue (US catalog). **2** *fig* to classify, class.
catálogo *nm* catalogue (US catalog).
catamarán *nm* catamaran.
cataplasma *nf* poultice, cataplasm.
catapulta *nf* catapult.
catar *vt* **1** *(probar)* to taste. **2** *(examinar)* to examine, inspect.
catarata *nf* **1** waterfall. **2** MED cataract.
catarro *nm* cold, catarrh: *cogí un catarro* I caught a cold.
catástrofe *nf* catastrophe.
catastrófico,-a *adj* catastrophic.
catear *vt* EDUC *fam* to fail, US flunk.
catecismo *nm* catechism.
cátedra *nf (cargo de universidad)* professorship; *(de instituto)* post of head of department.
catedral *nf* cathedral.
catedrático,-a *nm & nf (de universidad)* professor; *(de instituto)* head of department.
categoría *nf* category, class; *(social)* class: *un restaurante de primera categoría* a first-class restaurant.
catequesis *nf inv* catechism.
cateto *nm (de triángulo)* side of a right-angled triangle forming the right angle.
catolicismo *nm* Catholicism.
católico,-a *adj* Catholic.
catorce *adj (cardinal)* fourteen; *(ordinal)* four
catorceavo,-a *adj* fourteenth.
▶ *nm & nf* fourteenth.
✎ Consulta también sexto,-a.

catre *nm (cama plegable)* folding bed; *(de campaña)* camp bed.
cauce *nm* **1** *(de río)* bed. **2** *fig (canal)* channel, way.
caucho *nm* rubber.

caudal *nm (de río)* flow.
caudaloso,-a *adj (río)* deep, plentiful.
causa *nf* **1** *(gen)* cause. **2** *(motivo)* cause, reason, motive. LOC **a causa de** because of, on account of.
causar *vt* **1** *(provocar)* to cause, bring about. **2** *(proporcionar)* to make, give.
cáustico,-a *adj* caustic.
cautela *nf* caution, cautiousness.
cauteloso,-a *adj* cautious, wary.
cauterizar *vt* to cauterize, fire.
cautivar *vt* to take prisoner, capture.
cautivo,-a *adj* captive.
cauto,-a *adj* cautious, wary.
cava *nm (bebida)* cava, champagne.
cavar *vt* to dig.
caverna *nf* cavern, cave.
cavernícola *nm o nf* cave dweller, caveman.
caviar *nm* caviar.
cavidad *nf* cavity.
cavilar *vi* think about, brood over.
caza *nf* **1** *(acción)* hunting. **2** *(de animales)* game. LOC **ir de caza** to go hunting.
cazador,-ra *nm & nf* hunter.
cazadora *nf (chaqueta)* jacket.
cazar *vt* **1** to hunt. **2** *fam (conseguir)* to catch, land.
cazo *nm* **1** *(cucharón)* ladle. **2** *(cacerola)* saucepan.
cazuela *nf* **1** *(utensilio)* casserole, saucepan. **2** *(guiso)* casserole, stew.
CE *abrev* **(Comunidad Europea)** European Community; *(abreviatura)* EC.
cebada *nf* barley.
cebar *vt* **1** *(animal)* to fatten, fatten up. **2** *(poner cebo)* to bait.
▶ *vpr* **cebarse** *fig (ensañarse)* to show no mercy (**en/con**, towards), take it out (**en/con**, on), vent one's anger (**en/con**, on).
cebo *nm* **1** *(para animales)* food. **2** *(para pescar)* bait.
cebolla *nf* **1** onion. **2** *(bulbo)* bulb. **3** *(de ducha)* rose, nozzle.
cebolleta *nf* **1** *(especia)* chives *pl*. **2** *(cebolla)* spring onion.

cebollino *nm* **1** *(especia)* chives *pl.* **2** *(cebolla)* spring onion.

cebra *nf* zebra. COMP **paso cebra** zebra crossing, US crosswalk.

ceceo *nm* lisp.

cecina *nf* cured meat.

ceder *vt* **1** *(dar)* to cede, give: **2** DEP *(balón)* to pass.
▶ *vi* **1** *(rendirse)* to yield (a, to), give way (a, to). **2** *(disminuir)* to diminish, slacken, go down: *la fiebre ha cedido* his temperature has gone down. LOC **ceder el paso** AUTO to give way, US yield.

cedro *nm* cedar.

CEE *abrev* (Comunidad Económica Europea) European Economic Community; *(abreviatura)* EEC.

cefalópodo,-a *adj* cephalopod.
▶ *nm* **cefalópodo** cephalopod.

cefalotórax *nm* cephalothorax.

cegar *vt* *(gen)* to blind: *el sol me cegó* the sun blinded me.
▶ *vpr* **cegarse** *fig* to become blind, be blinded.

ceguera *nf* blindness.

ceja *nf* eyebrow. LOC **tener ALGO entre ceja y ceja** *fig* to have STH in one's head.

celda *nf* cell.

celebración *nf* *(fiesta)* celebration.

celebrar *vt* **1** *(festejar)* to celebrate. **2** *(organizar)* to hold: *celebraron el debate ayer* the debate was held yesterday.
▶ *vpr* **celebrarse** *(tener lugar)* to take place, be held.

célebre *adj* famous, celebrated.

celeste *adj* *(color)* sky-blue.
▶ *nm* *(color)* sky blue.

celestial *adj* celestial, heavenly.

celibato *nm* celibacy.

celo®1 *nm fam* sellotape, US Scotch tape.

celo2 *nm* **1** *(cuidado)* zeal, fervour (US fervor). **2** BIOL *(macho)* rut; *(hembra)* heat.
▶ *nm pl* **celos** jealousy *sing.* LOC **dar celos** to make jealous.

celofán® *nm* cellophane®.

celosía *nf* **1** *(reja)* lattice. **2** *(ventana)* lattice window.

celoso,-a *adj* *(envidioso)* jealous.

Celsius *nm* Celsius.

célula *nf* cell.

celular *adj* cell, cellular.

celulosa *nf* cellulose.

cementerio *nm* cemetery.

cemento *nm* *(gen)* concrete, cement. COMP **cemento armado** reinforced concrete.

cena *nf* *(gen)* supper; *(formal)* dinner.

cenar *vi* to have supper, have dinner.
▶ *vt* to have for supper, have for dinner.

cencerro *nm* cowbell. LOC **estar como un cencerro** to be nuts, be crackers.

cenefa *nf* **1** *(sobre tejido)* edging, trimming. **2** *(sobre muro, pavimento, etc)* ornamental border, frieze.

cenicero *nm* ashtray.

cenit *nm* zenith.

ceniza *nf* ash, ashes *pl.*

censar *vt* *(hacer el censo)* to take a census of.

censo *nm* *(padrón)* census. COMP **censo electoral** electoral roll.

censura *nf* **1** censorship.

censurar *vt* to censor: *el libro fue censurado* the book was censored.

centavo,-a *nm* **1** *(parte)* hundredth, hundredth part. **2** *(moneda)* cent, centavo.

✎ Consulta también **sexto,-a.**

centella *nf* **1** *(rayo)* lightning. **2** *(chispa)* spark, flash.

centellear *vi* **1** *(gen)* to sparkle, flash. **2** *(estrellas)* to twinkle.

centena *nf* hundred.

centenar *nm* hundred. LOC **a centenares / por centenares** in hundreds.

centenario,-a *nm & nf* *(persona)* centenarian.
▶ *nm* **centenario** *(aniversario)* centenary, centennial, hundredth anniversary.

centeno *nm* rye.

centésimo,-a *adj* hundredth.
▶ *nm & nf* hundredth.

▶ *nm* **centésimo** *(moneda)* cent, centesimo.

✎ Consulta también **sexto,-a.**

centígrado,-a *adj* centigrade.

centigramo *nm* centigram, centigramme.

centilitro *nm* centilitre (US centiliter).

centímetro *nm* centimetre (US centimeter).

céntimo *nm* cent, centime. LOC **estar sin un céntimo** *fam* to be penniless.

centinela *nm & nf* **1** MIL sentry. **2** *(guardián)* watch, lookout.

centollo *nm* spider crab.

central *adj* central.
▶ *nf* **1** *(oficina principal)* head office, headquarters *pl*. **2** *(eléctrica)* power station. COMP **central telefónica** telephone exchange.

centralita *nf* switchboard.

centralizar *vt* to centralize.

centrar *vt* **1** *(gen)* to centre (US center). **2** *fig (atención, etc)* to centre (US center), focus.
▶ *vpr* **centrarse** to centre (US center) (en, on), focus (en, on): *se centró en el tema principal* he focused on the main topic.

céntrico,-a *adj* central, US downtown.

centrifugadora *nf (para ropa)* spin-dryer.

centrifugar *vt (ropa)* to spin-dry.

centrífugo,-a *adj* centrifugal.

centrípeto,-a *adj* centripetal.

centro *nm* **1** centre (US center), middle. **2** *(de ciudad)* town centre, city centre, US downtown area. **3** *(asociación)* centre (US center), association, institution. COMP **centro comercial** shopping centre, US mall. ▌ **centro cultural** cultural centre (US center).

centrocampista *nm o nf* midfield player.

céntuplo,-a *adj* centuple, hundredfold.
▶ *nm* **céntuplo** centuple, hundredfold.

centuria *nf* century.

ceñir *vt* **1** *(estrechar)* to cling to, be tight on. **2** *(rodear)* to surround, encircle.
▶ *vpr* **ceñirse 1** *(atenerse)* to keep (a, to), limit OS (a, to): *ceñirse al tema* to keep to the subject. **2** *(ajustarse una prenda)* to cling.

ceño *nm* frown. LOC **fruncir el ceño** to frown.

cepa *nf (de vid)* vine.

cepillar *vt (gen)* to brush.

cepillo *nm* **1** brush. **2** *(de carpintería)* plane. COMP **cepillo de dientes** toothbrush. ▌ **cepillo del pelo** hairbrush.

cepo *nm* **1** *(rama)* bough, branch. **2** *(de yunque)* stock. **3** *(de reo)* pillory, stocks *pl*. **4** *(trampa)* trap. **5** *(para auto)* clamp.

cera *nf* **1** wax; *(de abeja)* beeswax. **2** *(pulimento)* wax, polish.

cerámica *nf* **1** *(arte)* ceramics, pottery. **2** *(objeto)* piece of pottery.

ceramista *nm o nf* ceramist, potter.

cerca¹ *nf (vallado)* fence, wall.

cerca² *adv (lugar y tiempo)* near, close: *aquí cerca* near here. LOC **cerca de 1** *(cercano a)* near, close. **2** *(aproximadamente)* nearly, about, around.

cercado *nm* **1** *(lugar)* enclosure. **2** *(cerca)* fence, wall.

cercano,-a *adj* **1** *(inmediato)* near, close: *el fin está cercano* the end is near. **2** *(vecino)* nearby, neighbouring (US neighboring). **3** *(pariente)* close.

cercar *vt (poner una cerca)* to fence in, enclose: *cercaron la hacienda* they fenced in the property.

cerco *nm* **1** *(lo que rodea)* circle, ring. **2** *(aureola)* halo. **3** *(asedio)* siege.

cerdo,-a *nm & nf fam pey (persona sucia)* pig, slob.
▶ *nm* **cerdo 1** *(animal)* pig. **2** *(carne)* pork.

cereal *nm* cereal.

cerebro *nm* **1** ANAT brain. **2** *fig* brains *pl*: *es el cerebro de la banda* he's the brains behind the gang.

ceremonia *nf* ceremony.

ceremonial *adj* ceremonial.

ceremonioso,-a *adj* ceremonious, formal.

cereza *nf* cherry.

cerezo *nm* cherry tree.

cerilla *nf (fósforo)* match.

cero *nm* **1** MAT zero. **2** *(cifra)* nought, zero. **3** DEP nil: *ganamos tres a cero* we won three nil.

cerrado,-a *adj* **1** shut, closed. **2** LING close, closed: *vocal cerrada* close vowel. **3** *(acento)* broad, thick. **4** *(curva)* tight, sharp. **5** *fig (persona introvertida)* uncommunicative, reserved.

cerradura *nf* lock.

cerrajería *nf (negocio)* locksmith's shop.

cerrajero,-a *nm & nf* locksmith.

cerrar *vt* **1** to close, shut: *cierra la puerta* close the door. **2** *(grifo, gas)* to turn off; *(luz)* to turn off, switch off. **3** *(cremallera)* to zip (up). **4** *(frontera, puerto)* to close; *(camino)* to block. **5** *(en dominó)* to block.
▶ *vi* **1** to close, shut. **2** *(punto)* to cast off. **3** *(una herida)* to close up, heal.
▶ *vpr* **cerrarse 1** to close, shut. **2** *(una herida)* to close up, heal.

cerro *nm* hill.

cerrojo *nm* bolt. LOC **correr el cerrojo** to bolt.

certamen *nm* competition, contest.

certeza *nf* certainty.

certificado,-a *adj (envío)* registered.
▶ *nm* **certificado 1** *(documento)* certificate. **2** *(carta)* registered letter.

certificar *vt* **1** *(gen)* to certify. **2** *(carta, paquete)* to register.

cerumen *nm* earwax, cerumen.

cervato *nm* fawn.

cervecería *nf* **1** *(bar)* pub, bar. **2** *(destilería)* brewery.

cerveza *nf* beer, ale. COMP **cerveza de barril** draught (US draft) beer. ▌ **cerveza negra** stout.

cervical *adj* cervical, neck.

cesar *vi* to cease, stop: *cesó de llover* it stopped raining. LOC **sin cesar** incessantly.

cesárea *nf* caesarean (US Cesarean), Caesarean (US Cesarean) section.

cese *nm* **1** cessation. **2** *(despido)* dismissal.

cesión *nf* cession.

césped *nm* lawn, grass.

cesta *nf* **1** basket. **2** DEP *(baloncesto)* basket. COMP **cesta de la compra** shopping basket.

cesto *nm* basket. COMP **cesto de los papeles** wastepaper basket.

cetáceo,-a *nm* cetacean.

cetro *nm* sceptre (US scepter).

CFC *abrev* **(clorofluorocarbono)** chlorofluorocarbon; *(abreviatura)* CFC.

cg *sím* **(centigramo)** centigram, centigramme; *(símbolo)* cg.

chabola *nf* shack: *un barrio de chabolas* a shanty town.

chacal *nm* jackal.

chacha *nf* **1** *fam (niñera)* nanny, nursemaid. **2** *fam (sirvienta)* maid.

chacinería *nf* pork butcher's shop.

chador *nm* chuddar, chudder, chuddah.

chafar *vt* **1** *(aplastar)* to squash, crush, flatten. **2** *(arrugar)* to crumple, crease.
▶ *vpr* **chafarse** *(aplastarse)* to be squashed, be crushed, be flattened; *(arrugarse)* to become creased, become crumpled.

chaflán *nm* **1** *(bisel)* chamfer. **2** *(esquina)* corner.

chal *nm* shawl.

chalado,-a *adj (loco)* mad, crazy, nuts.

chalar *vt fam (enloquecer)* to drive crazy.
▶ *vpr* **chalarse** *fam* to go mad, go crazy, go nuts.

chaleco *nm* waistcoat, US vest. COMP **chaleco salvavidas** life jacket.

chalet *nm* **1** *(casa individual)* house, detached house. **2** *(adosado)* semidetached house.

chalupa *nf (embarcación)* boat, launch.

chamán *nm* sorcerer, wizard, shaman.

chamarra *nf (zamarra)* sheepskin jacket.

champaña *nm* champagne.

champiñón *nm* mushroom.

champú *nm* shampoo.

chamuscar *vt* to singe, scorch.
▸ *vpr* **chamuscarse** to be singed, get scorched.

chamusquina *nf* scorching, singeing.

chancho *nm* AM *(animal)* pig; *(carne)* pork.

chanchullo *nm fam* fiddle, wangle, racket.

chancla *nf (chancleta)* flip-flop.

chancleta *nf* flip-flop.

chándal *nm* track suit, jogging suit.

chanquete *nm* transparent goby.

chantaje *nm* blackmail.

chantajear *vt* to blackmail.

chao *interj fam* bye-bye!, cheerio!, so long!, ciao!

chapa *nf* 1 *(de metal)* sheet, plate. 2 *(de madera)* panel, sheet; *(contrachapado)* plywood. 3 *(tapón)* bottle top, cap. 4 *(medalla)* badge, disc.
▸ *nf pl* **chapas** game *sing* of tossing up coins.

chapado,-a *adj* 1 *(metal)* plated: *chapado,-a en plata* silver-plated. 2 *(madera)* veneered, finished.

chaparrón *nm (lluvia)* downpour, heavy shower: *cayó un buen chaparrón* there was a downpour.

chapista *nm o nf* 1 sheet metal worker. 2 AUTO panel beater.

chapotear *vi (agitar en el agua)* to splash about.

chapurrear *vt* to speak a little, have a smattering of: *chapurreo el inglés* I have a smattering of English, I speak a little English.

chapuza *nf* 1 *(trabajo sin importancia)* odd job. 2 *(trabajo mal hecho)* botched job, shoddy piece of work.

chapuzón *nm (baño)* dip. LOC **darse un chapuzón** to have a dip.

chaqueta *nf* jacket. COMP **chaqueta de punto** cardigan.

chaquetón *nm* winter jacket.

charanga *nf* 1 brass band. 2 *fam (bulla)* din, racket.

charca *nf* pool, pond.

charco *nm* puddle, pond.

charcutería *nf* pork butcher's shop, delicatessen.

charla *nf* 1 *(conversación)* talk, chat. 2 *(conferencia)* talk, informal lecture.

charlar *vi* to chat, talk.

charlatán,-ana *adj* 1 *(hablador)* talkative. 2 *(chismoso)* gossipy.
▸ *nm & nf* 1 *(parlanchín)* chatterbox. 2 *(chismoso)* gossip.

charloteo *nm fam* chatter, prattle.

chárter *adj inv* charter.
▸ *nm* charter.

chasco *nm fig (decepción)* disappointment. LOC **llevarse un chasco** to be disappointed.

chasis *nm (del coche)* chassis.

chasquear *vi* 1 *(lengua)* to click; *(dedos)* to snap. 2 *(látigo, madera)* to crack.

chasquido *nm* 1 *(de la lengua)* click; *(de los dedos)* snap. 2 *(de látigo, madera)* crack.

chat *nm* INFORM chat.

chatarra *nf* 1 *(hierro viejo)* scrap iron, scrap. 2 *fam pey (calderilla)* small change.

chatear *vi* INFORM *fam* to chat (con, with/to).

chateo *nm* INFORM *fam* chat, chatting.

chato,-a *adj (nariz)* snub; *(persona)* snub-nosed.

chaval,-la *nm & nf (joven)* kid, youngster; *(chico)* lad, boy; *(chica)* lass, girl.

chavo *nm pl* **chavos** *(dinero)* money *sing*, cash *sing*.

checo,-a *adj* Czech.
▸ *nm & nf (persona)* Czech.
▸ *nm* **checo** *(idioma)* Czech. COMP **República Checa** Czech Republic.

chef *nm* chef.

chelín *nm* shilling.

cheque *nm* cheque (US check). LOC **cobrar un cheque** to cash a cheque (US check).

chequear vt 1 *(controlar)* to check. 2 *(comprobar)* to check up on.

chequeo nm MED checkup.

Chequia nf Czechia.

chica nf girl.

chicharra nf *(cigarra)* cicada.

chicharro nm 1 *(chicharrón)* pork crackling, fried pork rind. 2 *(pez)* scad, horse mackerel.

chicharrón nm *(de cerdo)* pork crackling, fried pork rind.

chichón nm bump, lump.

chicle nm chewing gum.

chico,-a nm & nf *(gen)* kid, youngster.

chiflado,-a adj fam mad, crazy, barmy, nuts, bonkers.

chiflar vi *(silbar)* to hiss, whistle.
► vt 1 *(silbar)* to hiss, boo. 2 fam *(gustar)* to fascinate, enchant.

chiflido nm whistle, whistling.

chií adj Shiite.
► nm o nf Shiite.

chiíta adj-nm o nf → chií.

chilaba nf jellabah, jellaba.

chile nm *(pimiento)* chili, chili pepper.

Chile nm Chile.

chileno,-a adj Chilean.
► nm & nf Chilean.

chillar vi 1 *(persona)* to scream, shriek, shout: 2 *(cerdo)* to squeal; *(ratón)* to squeak; *(pájaro)* to squawk, screech. 3 *(radio)* to blare; *(frenos)* to screech, squeal. 4 *(colores)* to be loud, be gaudy, clash. 5 fam *(reñir)* to tell off.

chillido nm 1 *(de persona)* shriek, scream, cry. 2 *(de cerdo)* squeal; *(de ratón)* squeak; *(de pájaro)* squawk, screech.

chillón,-ona adj 1 *(que chilla mucho)* screaming, loud. 2 *(voz)* shrill, high-pitched; *(sonido)* harsh, strident. 3 fig *(color)* loud, gaudy.

chimenea nf 1 chimney. 2 *(hogar)* fireplace, hearth. 3 *(de barco)* funnel, stack.

chimpancé nm chimpanzee.

china nm *(piedrecita)* pebble.

China nf China.

chinchar vt fam to annoy, pester, bug.
► vpr **chincharse** fam to grin and bear it, put up with it, lump it. LOC ¡chínchate! fam hard luck!, tough luck!

chinche nm & nf ZOOL bedbug, bug.

chincheta nf drawing pin, US thumbtack.

chinchilla nf chinchilla.

chino,-a adj Chinese.
► nm & nf *(persona)* Chinese person.
► nm **chino** 1 *(idioma)* Chinese. 2 *(colador)* sieve.
► nm pl **chinos** guessing game sing.

chip nm INFORM chip.

chipirón nm baby squid.

Chipre nm Cyprus.

chipriota adj Cypriot.
► nm o nf Cypriot.

chiquillo,-a nm & nf kid, youngster.

chiquito,-a adj tiny, very small, weeny.
► nm & nf tiny tot, kid.

chirimoya nf custard apple.

chiringuito nm fam *(en playa)* refreshment stall, refreshment stand; *(en carretera)* roadside snack bar, hot food stand.

chirla nf small clam.

chirriar vi 1 *(al freír comida, etc)* to sizzle. 2 *(rueda, frenos)* to screech, squeal; *(puerta)* to creak. 3 *(aves)* to squawk.

chirrido nm 1 *(de rueda, frenos)* screech; *(de puerta)* creak, creaking. 2 *(de aves)* squawk, squawking.

chisme nm 1 *(comentario)* piece of gossip. 2 *(trasto)* knick-knack; *(de cocina, etc)* gadget; *(cosa)* thing, thingamajig.

chismoso,-a nm & nf gossip.

chispa nf 1 *(de lumbre, eléctrica, etc)* spark. 2 fig *(ingenio, gracia)* wit, sparkle; *(inteligencia)* intelligence; *(viveza)* liveliness.

chispear vi 1 *(echar chispas)* to spark, throw out sparks. 2 [en este sentido se usa sólo en tercera persona; no lleva sujeto] METEOR to drizzle, spit

chistar vi to speak. LOC sin chistar without saying a word.

chiste *nm* **1** *(dicho)* joke, funny story. **2** *(dibujo)* cartoon. `LOC` **contar un chiste** to tell a joke.

chistera *nf fig (sombrero)* top hat.

chistoso,-a *adj* **1** *(persona)* witty, funny, fond of joking. **2** *(suceso)* funny, amusing.

chivar *vt* **1** *fam (molestar)* to annoy, pester. **2** *fam (delatar)* to squeal on, tell on.
▶ *vpr* **chivarse** *fam* to tell, squeal, split.

chivato,-a *nm & nf fam (acusica)* telltale.

chivo,-a *nm & nf (cría macho)* kid, young goat; *(cría hembra)* kid, young shegoat.

choc *nm* shock.

chocar *vi* **1** *(colisionar con algo)* to collide (contra/con, with), crash (contra/con, into), run (contra/con, into). **2** *(una pelota)* to hit (contra, -), strike (contra, -).
▶ *vt* **1** *fig (sorprender)* to surprise; *(extrañar)* to shock. **2** *(las manos)* to shake.

choco *nm* small cuttlefish.

chocolate *nm* **1** *(sólido)* chocolate. **2** *(líquido)* drinking chocolate, cocoa. `COMP` **chocolate con leche** milk chocolate.

chocolatería *nf* **1** *(fábrica)* chocolate factory. **2** *(tienda)* chocolate shop. **3** *(donde se toma)* café specializing in drinking chocolate.

chocolatero,-a *adj (aficionado al chocolate)* fond of chocolate, chocolate-loving.
▶ *nm & nf* **1** *(fabricante)* chocolate maker. **2** *(vendedor)* chocolate seller.

chocolatina *nf* bar of chocolate.

chófer *nm* **1** *(particular)* chauffeur. **2** *(de autocar, etc)* driver.

chollo *nm* **1** *fam (ganga)* bargain, snip, gift. **2** *(trabajo)* cushy job.

chopera *nf* poplar grove.

chopo *nm (árbol)* poplar.

choque *nm* **1** *(gen)* collision, impact; *(de coche, tren, etc)* crash, smash, collision. **2** *(discusión)* dispute, quarrel. **3** MED shock.

chorizo,-a *nm* chorizo *(highly-seasoned pork sausage)*.

chorrear *vi* **1** *(caer a chorro)* to spout, gush, spurt. **2** *(gotear)* to drip.

chorro *nm* **1** *(de líquido)* jet, spout, spurt, gush. **2** *(de gas)* jet, blast. `LOC` **a chorros** in abundance: *tiene dinero a chorros* he's got plenty of money, he's loaded (with money).

choto,-a *nm & nf* **1** *(cabrito)* kid, young goat; *(cabrita)* female kid, young she-goat. **2** *(ternero)* sucking calf.

choza *nf* hut, shack.

christmas *nm inv* Christmas card.

chubasco *nm (chaparrón)* heavy shower, downpour.

chubasquero *nm* raincoat.

chuche *nm fam* sweet, US candy.

chuchería *nf fam (golosina)* sweet, US candy.

chucho,-a *nm & nf fam (perro)* mutt, US pooch.

chucrut *nm* sauerkraut.

chufa *nf (planta)* chufa; *(fruto)* tiger nut.

chulear *vi fam (presumir)* to brag, show off: *mira a Felipe cómo chulea con su coche nuevo* look at Felipe showing off his new car.

chuleta *nf* **1** *(costilla)* chop, cutlet. **2** *fam fig (entre estudiantes)* crib, crib note, US trot.

chulo,-a *adj* **1** *fam (descarado)* cocky, cheeky. **2** *fam (vistoso)* showy, flashy. **3** *fam (bonito)* nice, pretty.

chupado,-a *adj* **1** *fig (muy flaco)* skinny, thin; *(mejillas, cara)* hollow. **2** *argot fig (muy fácil)* dead easy.

chupar *vt* **1** to suck. **2** *(absorber)* to absorb, soak up, suck up.

chupete *nm* dummy, US pacifier.

churrería *nf* fritter shop.

churro *nm (dulce)* fritter, US cruller.

chusma *nf* riffraff, rabble, mob.

chut *nm* DEP shot, kick.

chutar *vi* DEP to shoot, kick.

chute *nm argot* fix.

cianita *nf* cyanite.

cianuro *nm* cyanide. COMP cianuro potásico potassium cyanide.

cibercafé *nm* Internet café.

ciberespacio *nm* cyberspace.

cibernauta *nm o nf* Net user.

cibernética *nf* cybernetics.

cicatriz *nf* scar.

cicatrizar *vi* to heal, cicatrize.

cíclico,-a *adj* cyclic, cyclical.

ciclismo *nm* cycling.

ciclista *adj* cycle, cycling.
► *nm o nf* cyclist.

ciclomotor *nm* moped.

ciclón *nm* cyclone.

ciego,-a *adj (persona)* blind. LOC a ciegas 1 *(sin ver)* blindly. 2 *(sin pensar)* without thinking.

cielo *nm* 1 *(gen)* sky. 2 *(clima)* weather, climate. 3 REL heaven.
► *interj* cielos good heavens! LOC llovido,-a del cielo *fig* heaven-sent. I ser un cielo (de persona) *fam* to be an angel.

ciempiés *nm inv* centipede.

cien *adj* [se usa sólo antes de los nombres en plural] one hundred, a hundred.
► *nm* one hundred, a hundred. LOC cien por cien one hundred per cent.

✎ Consulta también ciento y seis.

ciénaga *nf* marsh, bog.

ciencia *nf (disciplina)* science. COMP ciencia ficción science fiction. I ciencias naturales natural sciences.

cienmilésimo,-a *adj* hundred thousandth.
► *nm & nf* hundred thousandth.

✎ Consulta también sexto,-a.

cienmillonésimo,-a *adj* hundred millionth.
► *nm & nf* hundred millionth.

✎ Consulta también sexto,-a.

científico,-a *adj* scientific.
► *nm & nf* scientist.

ciento *adj* one hundred, a hundred:
► *nm* 1 *(número)* hundred. 2 un ciento *(centena)* about a hundred. LOC por ciento per cent.

✎ Consulta también cien.

cierre *nm* 1 *(acción)* closing, shutting; *(de fábrica)* shutdown; *(de radio, etc)* close-down. 2 *(de prenda)* fastener; *(de bolso)* clasp; *(de cinturón)* buckle, clasp. COMP cierre patronal lockout.

cierto,-a *adj* 1 *(seguro)* certain, sure. 2 *(verdadero)* true: no es cierto that's not true. LOC estar en lo cierto to be right.
I por cierto by the way.
► *adv* cierto certainly.

ciervo,-a *nm & nf (gen)* deer; *(macho)* stag, hart; *(hembra)* doe, hind.

cifra *nf* 1 *(número)* figure, number. 2 *(cantidad)* amount, number. 3 *(código)* cipher, code.

cifrar *vt (codificar)* to encode; *(en informática)* to encrypt.

cigala *nf* Dublin Bay prawn.

cigarra *nf* cicada.

cigarrillo *nm* cigarette.

cigarro *nm* 1 *(puro)* cigar. 2 *(cigarrillo)* cigarette.

cigoto *nm* zygote.

cigüeña *nf (ave)* stork.

cilindrada *nf* cylinder capacity.

cilíndrico,-a *adj* cylindric, cylindrical.

cilindro *nm* cylinder.

cima *nf* 1 *(de montaña)* summit, top; *(de árbol)* top. 2 *fig (cumbre)* summit, peak.

cimentar *vt* 1 ARQUIT to lay the foundations of. 2 *fig (afianzar)* to strengthen, consolidate.

cimiento [se usa sólo en plural con el mismo significado] *nm* 1 ARQUIT foundation, foundations *pl*. 2 *fig* basis, origin. LOC poner los cimientos to lay the foundations.

cinabrio *nm* cinnabar.

cinc *nm* zinc.

cincel *nm* chisel.

cincelar *vt* to chisel, engrave.

cincha *nf (de caballo)* girth, US cinch.

cinco *adj (cardinal)* five; *(ordinal)* fifth.
► *nm (número)* five. LOC ¡choca esos cinco! *fam* put it there!, give me five!

✎ Consulta también seis.

cincuenta *adj (cardinal)* fifty; *(ordinal)* fiftieth.
▶ *nm (número)* fifty.

✎ Consulta también seis.

cincuentavo,-a *adj* fiftieth.
▶ *nm & nf* fiftieth.

✎ Consulta también sexto,-a.

cine *nm* **1** *(local)* cinema, US movie theater: *ir al cine* to go to the cinema, US go to the movies. **2** *(arte)* cinema.

cineasta *nm o nf* film director, film-maker.

cineclub *nm* **1** *(organización)* film society, film club. **2** *(local)* cinema, US movie theater.

cinematografía *nf* film-making, cinematography, US movie-making.

cinematográfico,-a *adj* cinematographic.

cinematógrafo *nm* film projector, US movie projector.

cinética *nf* kinetics.

cinético,-a *adj* kinetic.

cínico,-a *adj* cynical.
▶ *nm & nf* cynic.

cinismo *nm* cynicism.

cinta *nf* **1** *(gen)* band, strip; *(decorativa)* ribbon. **2** COST braid, edging. **3** TÉC tape. **4** *(de máquina de escribir)* ribbon. **5** *(casete)* tape. COMP **cinta adhesiva** adhesive tape. **I cinta magnética** magnetic tape. **I cinta métrica** tape measure.

cintura *nf* waist.

cinturilla *nf* waistband.

cinturón *nm* belt. COMP **cinturón de seguridad** safety belt, seat belt.

ciprés *nm* cypress.

circo *nm* **1** *(gen)* circus. **2** GEOG cirque.

circonita *nf* zirconite.

circuito *nm* **1** *(eléctrico)* circuit. **2** *(recorrido)* tour, circuit. **3** *(de carreras)* track, circuit.

circulación *nf* **1** *(gen)* circulation. **2** *(de vehículos)* traffic. COMP **circulación sanguínea** blood circulation. **I código de (la) circulación** highway code.

circular *adj* circular.
▶ *vi* **1** *(gen)* to circulate, move, go round. **2** *(líquido, electricidad)* to circulate, flow. **3** *(coche)* to drive; *(trenes, autobuses)* to run; *(peatón)* to walk. **4** *fig (rumor, etc)* to spread, get round.

círculo *nm* *(gen)* circle. COMP **círculo familiar** family circle. **I círculo polar antártico** Antarctic Circle. **I círculo polar ártico** Arctic Circle. **I círculo vicioso** *fig* vicious circle.

circunferencia *nf* circumference.

circunflejo,-a *adj* circumflex.
▶ *nm* **circunflejo** circumflex.

circunscribir *vt* to circumscribe.
▶ *vpr* **circunscribirse** *(ceñirse)* to confine OS (a, to), limit OS (a, to).

circunscripción *nf* district, area. COMP **circunscripción electoral** constituency.

circunstancia *nf* circumstance. LOC **en estas circunstancias** under the circumstances.

circunstancial *adj* circumstantial.

circunvalar *vt* to go round.

cirio *nm* long wax candle. LOC **armar un cirio** *fam* to kick up a rumpus.

cirrosis *nf inv* cirrhosis.

ciruela *nf* plum. COMP **ciruela claudia** greengage. **I ciruela pasa** prune.

ciruelo *nm* plum tree.

cirugía *nf* surgery. COMP **cirugía estética** plastic surgery.

cirujano,-a *nm & nf* surgeon.

cisma *nm* REL schism.

cisne *nm* swan.

cisterna *nf* cistern, tank.

cita *nf* **1** *(para negocios, médico, etc)* appointment: *tengo una cita con mi abogado* I have an appointment with my lawyer. **2** *(amorosa)* date. **3** *(mención)* quotation. LOC **tener una cita** to have an appointment, have an engagement.

citación *nf* **1** *(mención)* quotation. **2** JUR citation, summons.

citar *vt* **1** *(dar cita)* to make an appointment with, arrange to meet. **2** *(mencionar)* to quote.

citoplasma *nm* cytoplasm.
cítrico,-a *adj* citric.
▶ *nm pl* **cítricos** citrus fruits.
ciudad *nf* city, town. COMP **ciudad dormitorio** dormitory town. ▍ **ciudad universitaria** university campus.
ciudadanía *nf* citizenship.
ciudadano,-a *adj* civic.
▶ *nm & nf* citizen.
ciudadela *nf* citadel, fortress.
cívico,-a *adj* civic.
civil *adj* **1** civil. **2** *(no militar)* civilian. **3** *(no eclesiástico)* lay, secular.
civilización *nf* civilization.
civilizar *vt* to civilize.
civismo *nm* **1** good citizenship, community spirit. **2** *(al servicio de los demás)* civility.
cizalla [también se usa en plural con el mismo significado.] *nf (tijeras)* metal shears *pl*, wire cutters *pl*.
cl *sím* (centilitro) centilitre (US centiliter); *(símbolo)* cl.
clamor *nm (griterío)* shouting, din, noise.
clan *nm* clan.
clandestino,-a *adj* clandestine, underground, secret.
claqué *nm* tap dancing.
claraboya *nf* skylight.
claridad *nf (luminosidad)* light, brightness. LOC **con claridad** clearly.
clarín *nm (instrumento)* bugle.
▶ *nm o nf (músico)* bugler.
clarinete *nm (instrumento)* clarinet.
clarinetista *nm o nf* clarinettist, clarinetist.
claro,-a *adj* **1** *(gen)* clear. **2** *(iluminado)* bright, well-lit. **3** *(color)* light: *azul claro* light blue. **4** *(salsa, etc)* thin; *(café, chocolate, etc)* weak. LOC **dejar** ALGO **claro** to make STH clear. ▍ **estar claro** to be clear.
▶ *adv* clearly.
▶ *interj* ¡**claro!** of course!.
clase *nf* **1** *(grupo, categoría)* class. **2** *(aula)* classroom; *(de universidad)* lecture hall. **3** *(tipo)* type, sort. LOC **asistir a clase** to attend class. COMP **clase media** middle class. ▍ **clase particular** private class, private lesson. ▍ **primera clase** first class.
clasicismo *nm* classicism.
clásico,-a *adj* **1** *(de los clásicos)* classical: *literatura clásica* classical literature. **2** *(tradicional)* classic.
▶ *nm* **clásico** classic: *este libro es un clásico de la ciencia ficción* this book is a science-fiction classic.
clasificación *nf* **1** *(gen)* classification. **2** *(distribución)* sorting, filing. **3** DEP league, table. **4** *(de discos)* top twenty, hit parade.
clasificar *vt* **1** to class, classify. **2** *(distribuir)* to sort, file.
▶ *vpr* **clasificarse 1** DEP to qualify. **2** *(llegar)* to come.
claustro *nm* ARQUIT cloister.
claustrofobia *nf* claustrophobia.
claustrofóbico,-a *adj* claustrophobic.
cláusula *nf* clause.
clausura *nf* **1** *(cierre)* closure. **2** *(acto)* closing ceremony, closing session.
clausurar *vt* **1** *(poner fin)* to close, conclude. **2** *(cerrar)* to close (down).
clavar *vt* **1** *(con clavos)* to nail. **2** *(un clavo)* to bang, hammer in; *(estaca)* to drive. **3** *fig (atención)* to fix; *(ojos)* to rivet.
▶ *vpr* **clavarse** *(gen)* to stick.
clave *nf* **1** *(de un enigma, etc)* key, clue: *la clave del éxito* the key to success. **2** *(de signos)* code, key, cipher: *un mensaje en clave* a coded message. **3** MÚS key: **4** ARQUIT keystone.
▶ *nm (instrumento)* harpsichord.
clavel *nm* carnation.
clavicémbalo *nm* harpsichord.
clavicordio *nm* clavichord.
clavícula *nf* clavicle, collarbone.
clavija *nf* **1** TÉC peg. **2** ELEC *(de enchufe)* pin.
clavo *nm* **1** nail. **2** BOT clove. LOC **dar en el clavo** *fig* to hit the nail on the head.
claxon® *nm* horn, hooter.
clemencia *nf* clemency, mercy.
clerical *adj* clerical.

clérigo *nm* priest.

clero *nm* clergy.

clic *nm* click. LOC **hacer clic 1** *(hacer ruido)* to click, go click. **2** INFORM to click.

clicar *vt* to click on.
▶ *vi* to click.

clienta *nf* client, customer.

cliente *nm o nf* client, customer.

clientela *nf* customers *pl*, clients *pl*, clientele.

clima *nm* climate.

climático,-a *adj* climatic, climatical.

climatizado,-a *adj* air-conditioned.

climatizar *vt* to air-condition.

climatología *nf* climatology.

clínica *nf* *(hospital)* clinic, private hospital.

clínico,-a *adj* clinical: *muerte clínica* clinical death.

clip *nm* **1** *(para papel)* paper clip. **2** *(para pelo)* hair-grip, US bobby pin. **3** *(pendiente)* clip-on earring.

cloaca *nf* sewer, drain.

clon *nm* clone.

clonación *nf* cloning.

clonar *vt* to clone.

clónico,-a *adj* cloned.
▶ *nm* **clónico** *(ordenador)* clone.

cloquear *vi* to cluck.

cloro *nm* chlorine.

clorofila *nf* chlorophyll.

clorofílico,-a *adj* chlorophyllous.

cloroformo *nm* chloroform.

clown *nm* clown..

club *nm* club, society. COMP **club de fútbol** football club. **club de tenis** tennis club. **club náutico** yacht club.

cm *sím* *(centímetro)* centimetre (US centimeter); *(símbolo)* cm.

coaccionar *vt* to coerce, compel.

coagular *vt* *(gen)* to coagulate, clot; *(leche)* to curdle.
▶ *vpr* **coagularse** to coagulate, clot; *(leche)* to curdle.

coágulo *nm* coagulum, clot.

coala *nm* koala, koala bear.

coartada *nf* alibi.

coba *nf fam* soft soap. LOC **dar coba a ALGN** *fam* to soft-soap SB.

cobalto *nm* cobalt.

cobarde *adj* cowardly.
▶ *nm o nf* coward.

cobardía *nf* cowardice.

cobaya *nm* guinea pig.

cobertizo *nm* shed, shack.

cobertura *nf* **1** *(gen)* cover. **2** *(de una red, servicio)* coverage. COMP **cobertura de chocolate** chocolate coating. **cobertura de seguros** insurance cover.

cobijar *vt* **1** *(cubrir)* to cover. **2** *fig* to shelter.
▶ *vpr* **cobijarse** to take shelter.

cobijo *nm* **1** *(hospedaje)* lodging. **2** *(refugio)* shelter. **3** *fig* protection, refuge.

cobol *nm* INFORM COBOL.

cobra *nf* *(serpiente)* cobra.

cobrador,-ra *nm & nf* **1** *(de luz, etc)* collector. **2** *(de transporte - hombre)* conductor; *(- mujer)* conductress.

cobrar *vt* **1** *(fijar precio por)* to charge; *(cheques)* to cash; *(salario)* to earn. **2** to get: *si no te estás quieto vas a cobrar una torta* if you don't keep still you'll get a smack. **3** *fig (adquirir)* to gain, get.
▶ *vi* to be in for it.
▶ *vpr* **cobrarse 1** *(dinero)* to take, collect. **2** *(víctimas)* to claim. **3** *(recuperar)* to recover (de, from); *(volver en sí)* to come round.

cobre *nm* *(metal)* copper.

cobro *nm* **1** *(pago)* payment. **2** *(cobranza)* collection; *(de cheque)* cashing. COMP **cobro revertido** reverse-charge, US collect.

coca *nf* **1** *(arbusto)* coca. **2** *argot* coke. **3** *fam (bebida)* Coke®.

cocción *nf* *(gen)* cooking; *(en agua)* boiling; *(en horno)* baking.

cóccix *nm inv* coccyx.

cocear *vi* to kick.

cocer *vt* *(gen)* to cook; *(hervir)* to boil; *(al horno)* to bake.
▶ *vpr* **cocerse 1** *(gen)* to cook; *(hervir)* to boil; *(al horno)* to bake. **2** *fam (de calor)* to be roasting, be boiling.

coche *nm* **1** *(automóvil)* car, automobile, motorcar: *fuimos en coche* we went by car. **2** *(de tren, de caballos)* carriage, coach. **3** *(de niño)* pram, US baby carriage. COMP **coche cama** sleeping car. ▪ **coche de alquiler** hired car, US rented car. ▪ **coche de bomberos** fire engine. ▪ **coche de carreras** racing car.

cochera *nf* depot.

cochino,-a *adj (sucio)* filthy, disgusting.
▶ *nm & nf* **1** ZOOL *(gen)* pig; *(macho)* swine; *(hembra)* sow. **2** *fam (persona)* dirty person, filthy person, pig.

cocido,-a *adj* cooked; *(en agua)* boiled; *(al horno)* baked.
▶ *nm* **cocido** CULIN stew.

cociente *nm* quotient.

cocina *nf* **1** *(lugar)* kitchen. **2** *(gastronomía)* cooking: *cocina española* Spanish cooking, Spanish cuisine. **3** *(aparato)* cooker, US stove. COMP **cocina casera** home cooking. ▪ **cocina de gas** gas cooker, US gas stove. ▪ **cocina de mercado** seasonal produce. ▪ **cocina eléctrica** electric cooker, US electric stove.

cocinar *vt* to cook.
▶ *vi* to cook.

cocinero,-a *nm & nf* cook. COMP **primer cocinero** chef.

coco¹ *nm* **1** BOT *(árbol)* coconut palm. **2** *(fruta)* coconut. COMP **coco rallado** desiccated coconut.

coco² *nm* **1** *fam (fantasma)* bogeyman. **2** *argot (cabeza)* noddle, noggin, nut. LOC **comerse el coco** *fam* to get worked up, worry about it.

cocodrilo *nm* crocodile.

cocotero *nm* coconut palm.

cóctel *nm (bebida)* cocktail.

codazo *nm (golpe)* poke with one's elbow, blow with one's elbow: *le pegó un codazo* she poked him with her elbow. LOC **abrirse paso a codazos** to elbow one's way through.

codear *vi (empujar)* to elbow.
▶ *vpr* **codearse** to rub shoulders (con, with), hobnob (con, with).

codera *nf* elbow patch.

codicia *nf* greed, coveting.

codiciar *vt* to covet, desire, crave for.

codicioso,-a *adj* covetous, greedy.

codificación *nf* **1** *(de mensajes)* encoding. **2** INFORM coding, code.

codificar *vt* **1** *(leyes)* to codify. **2** *(mensajes)* to encode. **3** INFORM to code.

código *nm* code. COMP **código de barras** bar code. ▪ **código de la circulación** highway code. ▪ **código de señales** MAR flag signals. ▪ **código Morse** Morse code.

codillo *nm* **1** *(del brazo)* elbow. **2** *(en cocina)* shoulder. **3** *(de tubería)* elbow.

codo *nm* **1** ANAT elbow. **2** TÉC bend. LOC **alzar el codo / empinar el codo** *fam* to have a few drinks, knock them back. ▪ **codo a codo / codo con codo** *fig* side by side, closely. ▪ **de codos** on one's elbows. ▪ **hablar por los codos** *fam* to talk nineteen to the dozen, talk nonstop. ▪ **romperse los codos** *fig* to study a lot, swot, cram.

codorniz *nf* quail.

coeficiente *nm* **1** MAT coefficient. **2** *(grado)* degree, rate. COMP **coeficiente de inteligencia** intelligence quotient, IQ.

cofia *nf* bonnet.

coexistir *vi* to coexist.

cofradía *nf* **1** *(hermandad)* brotherhood. **2** *(asociación)* association. **3** *(gremio)* guild.

cofre *nm (grande)* trunk, chest; *(pequeño)* box, casket.

coger *vt* **1** *(asir)* to seize, take hold of: *coge al bebé* hold the baby. **2** *(apresar)* to capture, catch. **3** *(tomar)* to take: *coge algo para beber* take a drink. **4** *(tren, etc)* to catch. **5** *(tomar prestado)* to borrow: *te he cogido el libro* I've borrowed your book. **6** *(recolectar frutos, etc)* to pick; *(del suelo)* to gather. **7** *(enfermedad, balón)* to catch: *cogí un resfriado* I caught a cold. **8** *(velocidad, fuerza)* to gather. **9** *(emisora, canal)* to pick up, get: *coger la BBC* to get the BBC. **10** *(notas)* to take, take down. **11** *(entender)* to understand, get: *no cogí el final* I didn't get the end. LOC **coger cariño a** ALGO/ALGN to become

fond of STH/SB, take a liking to STH/SB. ∎ **coger por sorpresa** to catch by surprise.
▶ *vpr* **cogerse** *(agarrarse)* to hold on: *cógete fuerte* hold on tight. LOC **cogerse un cabreo** *fam* to get very angry.

cogollo *nm (de lechuga, etc)* heart.

cogote *nm* back of the neck.

coherencia *nf* coherence, coherency.

coherente *adj* coherent, connected.

cohete *nm* rocket.

cohibir *vt* to inhibit, restrain.
▶ *vpr* **cohibirse** to feel inhibited, feel embarrassed.

coincidir *vi* **1** *(estar de acuerdo)* to agree (en, on), coincide (en, in). **2** *(ajustarse)* to coincide. **3** *(ocurrir al mismo tiempo)* to be at the same time (con, as), coincide (con, with); *(en el mismo lugar)* to meet.

cojear *vi* **1** *(persona)* to limp, hobble. **2** *(muebles)* to wobble. LOC **cojear del mismo pie** *fam* to have the same faults.

cojera *nf* limp, lameness.

cojín *nm* cushion.

cojo,-a *adj* **1** *(persona)* lame, crippled. **2** *(mueble)* wobbly. **3** *fig (defectuoso)* faulty, incomplete.

col *nf* cabbage. COMP **col de Bruselas** Brussels sprout.

cola¹ *nf* **1** *(gen)* tail. **2** *(de vestido)* train; *(de chaqueta)* tail. **3** *(fila)* queue, US line. LOC **hacer cola** to queue up, US stand in line. ∎ COMP **cola de caballo** *(peinado)* ponytail.

cola² *nf (pegamento)* glue.

colaboración *nf* **1** collaboration. **2** *(prensa)* contribution.

colaborador,-ra *adj* collaborating.
▶ *nm & nf* **1** collaborator. **2** *(prensa)* contributor.

colaborar *vi* **1** to collaborate (con, with). **2** *(prensa)* to contribute (en, to).

colada *nf* **1** *(lavado)* washing, laundry; *(con lejía)* bleaching. **2** *(ropa)* washing, wash. **3** *(volcánica)* outflow. LOC **hacer la colada** to do the washing, do the laundry.

colador *nm* **1** *(de té, café)* strainer. **2** *(de caldo, alimentos)* colander, sieve.

colapsar *vt (ciudad, aeropuerto, etc)* to paralyse; *(tráfico)* to bring to a standstill, bring to a halt.
▶ *vi* to collapse.

colar *vt (líquido)* to strain, filter.
▶ *vi fam* to wash: *veremos si cuela* we'll see if it washes.
▶ *vpr* **colarse 1** *(escabullirse)* to slip in, gatecrash. **2** *(en una cola)* to push in, jump the queue, US jump the line. **3** *fam (equivocarse)* to slip up, make a mistake.

colcha *nf* bedspread.

colchón *nm* mattress. COMP **colchón neumático** air mattress.

colchoneta *nf* small mattress.

cole *nm fam* school.

colear *vi (perro, etc)* to wag its tail; *(vaca, caballo, etc)* to swish its tail.

colección *nf* collection.

coleccionar *vt* to collect.

coleccionista *nm o nf* collector.

colectividad *nf* community.

colectivo,-a *adj* collective, group.
▶ *nm* **colectivo 1** *(asociación)* association, guild. **2** LING collective noun.

colegio *nm (escuela)* school: *van al colegio en autobús* they go to school by bus. COMP **colegio público** state school.

coleóptero *nm* coleopteran.

cólera *nf* **1** *(bilis)* bile. **2** *fig (ira)* anger, rage.
▶ *nm* MED cholera.

colérico,-a *adj* furious, irascible.

colesterol *nm* cholesterol.

coleta *nf* pigtail, ponytail.

colgado,-a *adj* hanging (de, from).

colgador *nm* (coat) hanger.

colgante *adj* hanging.
▶ *nm* **1** ARQUIT festoon. **2** *(joya)* pendant.

colgar *vt* **1** *(gen)* to hang (up). **2** *(la colada)* to hang out. **3** *(atribuir)* to pin. **4** *(el teléfono)* to put down.

▶ *vi* **1** *(estar colgado)* to hang (**de**, from): *cuelga del techo* it hangs from the ceiling. **2** *(una prenda)* to hang down, be crooked. **3** *(teléfono)* to hang up, ring off: *¡no cuelgue!* please hold!, hold the line, please!

colibrí *nm* humming bird.

cólico *nm* colic.

coliflor *nf* cauliflower.

colilla *nf* cigarette end, cigarette butt, butt.

colina *nf* hill, slope.

colirio *nm* eye drops *pl*.

colisión *nf (de vehículos)* collision, crash.

colisionar *vi (chocar)* to collide (**con/contra**, with), crash (**con/contra**, into).

colitis *nf inv* colitis.

collar *nm* **1** *(adorno)* necklace. **2** *(de animal)* collar.

colmar *vt (gen)* to fill (**de**, with); *(vaso, copa)* to fill to the brim.

colmena *nf* beehive.

colmillo *nm* **1** eye tooth, canine tooth. **2** *(de carnívoro)* fang; *(de jabalí, elefante, morsa)* tusk.

colmo *nm* height, summit. [LOC] *¡esto es el colmo!* this is the last straw!, this is the limit!

colocar *vt* **1** *(gen)* to place, put. **2** *(dar empleo)* to get a job for.
▶ *vpr* **colocarse 1** *(situarse)* to place os, put os, find os a place. **2** *(trabajar)* to find a job (**de**, as), get a job (**de**, as).

Colombia *nf* Colombia.

colombiano,-a *adj* Colombian.
▶ *nm & nf* Colombian.

colon *nm* ANAT colon.

colonia *nf* **1** *(grupo)* colony. **2** [normalmente en plural] *(vacaciones infantiles)* summer camp. **3** *(perfume)* cologne.

colonial *adj* POL colonial.

colonialismo *nm* colonialism.

colonización *nf* colonization.

colonizar *vt* to colonize, settle.

colono *nm* **1** *(habitante)* colonist, settler. **2** AGR tenant farmer.

coloquial *adj* colloquial.

coloquio *nm* talk, discussion.

color *nm* **1** colour (US color): *es de color verde* it's green. [LOC] **de color 1** *(en color)* in colour (US color), coloured (US colored). **2** *(persona)* coloured (US colored). ▌ **en color / en colores** *(cine, foto)* in colour (US color).

colorado,-a *adj* **1** coloured (US colored). **2** *(rojo)* red. [LOC] **ponerse colorado,-a** to blush, go red.

colorante *nm* colouring (US coloring), dye.

colorear *vt* to colour (US color).

colorete *nm* rouge, blusher.

colorido *nm* colour (US color).

coloso *nm* colossus.

columna *nf* **1** *(gen)* column. **2** ANAT spine. **3** *(elemento central)* backbone. [COMP] **columna vertebral** vertebral column, spinal column.

columpiar *vt* to swing.
▶ *vpr* **columpiarse** to swing (**de**, on).

columpio *nm* swing.

colza *nf* rape. [COMP] **aceite de colza** rapeseed oil, US canola oil.

coma¹ *nf* **1** *(puntuación)* comma. **2** *(en música)* comma. **3** MAT point: *cuatro coma cinco* four point five.

coma² *nm* MED coma. [LOC] **entrar en coma** to go into a coma.

comadreja *nf* weasel.

comadrona *nm & nf* midwife.

comandante *nm* **1** *(oficial)* commander, commanding officer. **2** *(graduación)* major. **3** *(piloto)* pilot.

comando *nm* **1** MIL commando. **2** INFORM command.

comarca *nf* area, region.

comba *nf* **1** *(de cuerda, cable)* bend, curve. **2** *(cuerda)* skipping rope. **3** *(juego)* skipping. [LOC] **saltar a la comba** to skip, US skip rope.

combar *vt* to bend.
▶ *vpr* **combarse** *(una cuerda)* to bend; *(viga, pared)* to sag, bulge.

combate *nm* **1** *(gen)* combat, battle. **2** MIL battle. **3** *(boxeo)* fight, contest.

combatiente *adj* fighting.
▶ *nm o nf* fighter, combatant.

combatir *vi* to fight (contra, against /-), struggle (contra, against).
▶ *vt* **1** *(luchar contra)* to fight: *combatir el cáncer* to fight cancer. **2** *fig* to combat, fight. **3** *fig (batir, golpear)* to beat, lash.
combativo,-a *adj* spirited, aggressive.
combinación *nf* **1** combination. **2** *(prenda)* slip.
combinar *vt* **1** *(gen)* to combine. **2** QUÍM to combine. **3** *(colores)* to match (con, -), go (con, with).
combustible *adj* combustible.
▶ *nm* fuel.
comedero *nm* feeding trough, manger.
comedia *nf* **1** TEAT comedy, play. **2** *fig* farce, pretence (US pretense).
comediante,-a *nm & nf* **1** *(hombre)* actor; *(mujer)* actress. **2** *fig* hypocrite, comedian.
comedor,-ra *nm (sala)* dining room; *(en una fábrica, un colegio, etc)* canteen.
comensal *nm o nf* person at the table, diner.
comentar *vt* **1** *(texto)* to comment on. **2** *(expresar una opinión)* to talk about, discuss.
comentario *nm* **1** *(observación)* remark, comment. **2** *(explicación, narración)* commentary.
▶ *nm pl* **comentarios** *(murmuración)* gossip *sing*.
comentarista *nm o nf* commentator.
comenzar *vt* to begin, start.
▶ *vi* to begin, start: *comenzó a reír* he began to laugh, he began laughing. LOC **comenzar con** to begin with. I **comenzar + ger** to start by + ger: *comenzó explicando...* he started by explaining...
comer *vt* **1** to eat. **2** *(en ajedrez)* to take, capture.
▶ *vi (gen)* to eat; *(a mediodía)* to have lunch, lunch; *(por la noche)* to have dinner, dine.
▶ *nm* eating.
▶ *vpr* **comerse 1** to eat. **2** *fig (saltarse)* to omit; *(párrafo)* to skip; *(palabra)* to swallow.

comercial *adj* **1** *(del comercio)* commercial. **2** *(de tiendas)* shopping.
▶ *nm o nf (vendedor)* seller; *(hombre)* salesman; *(mujer)* saleswoman.
comerciante *adj* business-minded.
▶ *nm o nf* **1** merchant. **2** *(interesado)* moneymaker.
comerciar *vi* **1** *(comprar y vender)* to trade, deal, buy and sell. **2** *(hacer negocios)* to do business (con, with).
comercio *nm* **1** *(ocupación)* commerce, trade. **2** *(tienda)* shop, store. LOC **comercio al por mayor** wholesale trade. COMP **comercio exterior** foreign trade. I **libre comercio** free trade.
comestible *adj* edible, eatable.
▶ *nm pl* **comestibles** groceries, food *sing*, foodstuffs *pl*.
cometa *nm (cuerpo celeste)* comet.
▶ *nf (juguete)* kite.
cometer *vt (crimen)* to commit; *(falta, error)* to make.
cómic *nm* comic.
cómico,-a *adj* **1** *(divertido)* comic, comical, funny. **2** *(de comedia)* comedy.
▶ *nm & nf (actor)* comedian, comic.
comida *nf* **1** *(alimento)* food: **2** *(desayuno, etc)* meal. **3** *(almuerzo)* lunch.
comienzo *nm* start, beginning. LOC **a comienzos de** at the beginning of. I **dar comienzo** to begin, start.
comillas *nf pl* inverted commas. LOC **entre comillas** in inverted commas.
comilona *nf* big meal, blowout.
comino *nm* BOT cumin, cummin. LOC **me importa un comino** *fam* I don't give a damn.
comisaría *nf (de policía)* police station.
comisario *nm (de policía)* police inspector.
comisión *nf* **1** *(retribución)* commission. **2** *(comité)* committee. LOC **a comisión / con comisión** on a commission basis. COMP **comisión bancaria** service charge, bank commission.
comité *nm* committee.
comitiva *nf* suite, retinue.
como *adv* **1** *(modo)* how: *lo hizo como quiso* he did it the way he wanted to. **2** *(com-*

paración) as, like: *negro como la noche* as dark as night. **3** *(en calidad de)* as: *como invitado* as a guest. **4** *(según)* as: *como dice tu amigo* as your friend says. **5** *fam (aproximadamente)* about: *había como unos cien* there were about a hundred. ⌐LOC⌐ **como quiera que 1** *(no importa cómo)* however. **2** *(ya que)* since, as, inasmuch as. ‖ **como sea** whatever happens, no matter what. ‖ **hacer como si** to pretend to +*inf*: *hace como si no viese nada* he's pretending not to see anything.

▶ *conj* **1** *(así que)* as: *como llegaban se presentaban* they introduced themselves as they arrived. **2** *(si)* if: *como lo vuelvas a hacer...* if you do it again.... **3** *(porque)* as, since: *como llegamos tarde no pudimos entrar* since we arrived late we couldn't get in.

cómo *adv* **1** *(interrogativo)* how. **2** *(por qué)* why. **3** *(admiración)* how: *¡cómo pasa el tiempo!* how time flies! ⌐LOC⌐ **¿cómo?** *fam* what? ‖ **¿cómo es que...?** how is it that...? ‖ **¡cómo no!** but of course!, certainly!

cómoda *nf* chest of drawers, commode.

comodidad *nf* **1** *(confort)* comfort. **2** *(facilidad)* convenience. ⌐LOC⌐ **con comodidad** comfortably.

comodín *nm* *(mono)* joker; *(otra carta)* wild card.

cómodo,-a *adj* **1** comfortable, cosy. **2** *(útil)* convenient, handy.

compactar *vt* to compact, compress.

compadecer *vt* to pity, feel sorry for.
▶ *vpr* **compadecerse** to take pity (de, on), pity (de, -), feel sorry (de, for).

compaginar *vt* *(combinar)* to combine, make compatible.
▶ *vpr* **compaginarse** to go together, be compatible.

compañerismo *nm* companionship, fellowship, comradeship.

compañero,-a *nm & nf* **1** *(sentimental, pareja)* partner. **2** *(colega)* companion, mate; *(camarada)* comrade. **3** *fig (guante, zapato, etc)* the other one, the one that goes with this one. ⌐COMP⌐ **compa-**

ñero,-a de colegio schoolmate. ‖ **compañero,-a de piso** flatmate. ‖ **compañero,-a de trabajo** workmate, colleague.

compañía *nf* company. ⌐LOC⌐ **en compañía de** in the company of. ‖ **hacer compañía a** ALGN to keep SB company.

comparación *nf* comparison. ⌐LOC⌐ **en comparación con** compared to, in comparison to.

comparar *vt* to compare:

comparativo,-a *adj* comparative.

compartimento *nm* compartment: *compartimento de primera clase* first-class compartment.

compartir *vt* **1** *(dividir)* to divide (up), split, share (out). **2** *(poseer en común)* to share.

compás *nm* **1** *(instrumento)* compass, compasses *pl*. **2** *(brújula)* compass. **3** MÚS *(división)* time; *(intervalo)* beat; *(ritmo)* rhythm. ⌐LOC⌐ **al compás de** in time to. ‖ **llevar el compás 1** *(con la mano)* to beat time. **2** *(al bailar)* to keep time. ‖ **perder el compás** to lose the beat.

compasión *nf* compassion, pity.

compasivo,-a *adj* compassionate, sympathetic.

compatibilidad *nf* compatibility.

compatibilizar *vt* to make compatible.

compatible *adj* compatible.

compendio *nm* summary, digest, précis, synopsis.

compenetrarse *vpr* *(uso recíproco)* to understand each other.

compensar *vt* **1** *(pérdida, error)* to make up for. **2** *(indemnizar)* to compensate, indemnify. **3** TÉC to balance, compensate. **4** *fam (merecer la pena)* to be worth one's while.

competencia *nf* **1** *(rivalidad)* competition, rivalry: **2** *(competidores)* competitors *pl*, rival company. **3** *(habilidad)* competence, ability, proficiency. **4** *(incumbencia)* responsibility.

competente *adj* **1** *(capaz)* competent, capable, proficient. **2** *(adecuado)* adequate.

competición *nf* competition, contest.

competidor,-ra *adj* **1** *(que compite)* competing. **2** *(rival)* rival.
▶ *nm & nf* **1** *(rival)* competitor. **2** *(en competición deportiva)* competitor.

competir *vi* to compete.

competitividad *nf* competitiveness.

competitivo,-a *adj* competitive.

complacer *vt* **1** *(satisfacer)* to satisfy, gratify, oblige. **2** *(agradar)* to please. **3** *fml* to please, give pleasure.

complejo,-a *adj* complex.
▶ *nm* complejo complex.

complementar *vt* to complement.
▶ *vpr* **complementarse** to complement each other, be complementary to each other.

complementario,-a *adj* complementary.

complemento *nm* **1** *(gen)* complement. **2** GRAM object, complement. COMP **complemento circunstancial** adverbial complement. ‖ **complemento directo** direct object. ‖ **complemento indirecto** indirect object.

completamente *adv* completely.

completar *vt* **1** *(gen)* to complete. **2** *(acabar)* to finish; *(perfeccionar)* to round off.

completo,-a *adj* **1** *(terminado)* finished, completed. **2** *(lleno)* full. LOC **al completo** full up, filled to capacity. ‖ **por completo** completely.

complexión *nf* constitution, build: *su hermano es de complexión fuerte* his brother is well-built.

complicación *nf* complication.

complicado,-a *adj* **1** *(gen)* complicated, complex. **2** *(carácter)* complex.

complicar *vt* **1** *(gen)* to complicate, make complicated. **2** *(implicar)* to involve (en, in).

cómplice *nm o nf* accomplice.

complicidad *nf* complicity.

complot *nm* plot, conspiracy.

componente *adj* component, constituent.
▶ *nm* **1** *(pieza)* component, constituent; *(ingrediente)* ingredient. **2** *(miembro)* member.

componer *vt* **1** *(formar)* to compose, make up, form. **2** *(reparar)* to fix, repair, mend. **3** *(adornar)* to adorn, decorate. **4** *(música, versos)* to compose.
▶ *vpr* **componerse** *(consistir)* to consist (de, of), be made up (de, of): *las palabras se componen de sílabas* words are made up of syllables.

comportamiento *nm* behaviour (US behavior), conduct.

comportar *vt* *(implica)* to involve, entail: *eso comporta un cambio de planes* that involves a change of plan.
▶ *vpr* **comportarse** *(portarse)* to behave: *se comportó mal* she misbehaved.

composición *nf* **1** *(gen)* composition. **2** *(arreglo)* arrangement.

compositor,-ra *nm & nf* composer.

compota *nf* compote.

compra *nf* purchase, buy. LOC **hacer la compra** to do the shopping, go shopping. ‖ **ir de compras** to go shopping. COMP **compra a plazos** hire purchase, US instalment buying.

comprador,-ra *nm & nf* purchaser, buyer, shopper.

comprar *vt* to buy.

compraventa *nf* buying and selling, dealing.

comprender *vt* **1** *(entender)* to understand: *lo comprendiste mal* you misunderstood it. **2** *(contener)* to comprise, include. LOC **¿comprendes?** *(en conversación)* you see?

comprensión *nf* understanding.

comprensivo,-a *adj* **1** *(tolerante)* understanding. **2** *(que comprende o incluye)* comprehensive.

compresa *nf* **1** *(higiénica)* sanitary towel. **2** *(vendaje)* compress.

comprimido,-a *adj* compressed.
▶ *nm* comprimido tablet.

comprimir *vt (apretar)* to compress; *(gente)* to cram together.

comprobante *nm (recibo)* receipt, voucher.

comprobar *vt* **1** *(verificar)* to verify, check. **2** *(observar)* to see, observe: *como podrán ustedes comprobar* as you can see for yourselves. **3** *(confirmar)* to confirm.

comprometer *vt* **1** *(exponer a riesgo)* to endanger, jeopardize, risk; *(a una persona)* to compromise. **2** *(implicar)* to involve, implicate. **3** *(obligar)* to commit. **4** *(poner en un aprieto)* to embarrass.
▶ *vpr* **comprometerse 1** *(contraer una obligación)* to commit os, pledge. **2** *(involucrarse)* to get involved. **3** *(establecer relaciones formales)* to get engaged. LOC **comprometerse a hacer** ALGO to undertake to do STH.

comprometido,-a *adj* **1** *(difícil, arriesgado)* difficult, in jeopardy. **2** *(escritor, artista, etc)* committed. **3** *(involucrado)* involved. **4** *(para casarse)* engaged.

compromiso *nm* **1** *(obligación)* commitment, obligation: *cumplió sus compromisos* she fulfilled her obligations. **2** *(cita)* appointment; *(amorosa)* date. **3** *(apuro)* difficult situation, bind. **4** *(matrimonial)* engagement.

compuesto,-a *adj (gen)* compound.

compulsar *vt* **1** *(cotejar)* to collate. **2** JUR to make a certified true copy of.

compulsivo,-a *adj* compelling, compulsive.

compungido,-a *adj* **1** *(arrepentido)* remorseful. **2** *fig (triste)* sorrowful, sad.

compungir *vt fml (entristecer)* to sadden, make sad.
▶ *vpr* **compungirse** *(entristecerse)* to be saddened, feel sad.

computación *nf* computing.

computador *nm* computer.

computadora *nf* computer.

computar *vt* **1** *(calcular)* to compute, calculate. **2** *fml (tomar en cuenta)* to take into account, count.

computarizar *vt* to computerize.

computerizar *vt* to computerize.

cómputo *nm* computation, calculation.

comulgar *vi* REL to receive Holy Communion.

común *adj* **1** *(gen)* common: *eso es poco común* that's unusual. **2** *(compartido)* shared, communal.

comuna *nf* commune.

comunal *adj* communal.

comunicación *nf* **1** *(gen)* communication. **2** *(comunicado)* communication; *(oficial)* communiqué. **3** *(telefónica)* connection. **4** *(unión)* link, connection.
▶ *nf pl* **comunicaciones** communications.

comunicado,-a *adj* served. COMP **comunicado de prensa** press release.

comunicar *vt* **1** *(hacer partícipe)* to communicate, convey, transmit. **2** *(hacer saber)* to communicate, make known, tell. **3** *(conectar)* to connect.
▶ *vi* **1** *(ponerse en comunicación)* to communicate; *(por carta)* to correspond. **2** *(teléfono)* to be engaged, US be busy. **3** *(estar conectado)* to communicate, be connected.
▶ *vpr* **comunicarse 1** *(tener relación)* to communicate; *(ponerse en contacto)* to get in touch, get in contact **(con,** with). **2** *(estar conectado)* to be connected **(con,** to).

comunicativo,-a *adj* **1** *(actitud, sentimiento)* catching, infectious. **2** *(persona)* communicative, sociable, open.

comunidad *nf* community. COMP **comunidad autónoma** autonomous region. **▎ Comunidad Económica Europea** European Economic Community.

comunión *nf* **1** communion, fellowship. **2** REL Holy Communion.

comunismo *nm* communism.

comunista *adj* communist.
▶ *nm o nf* communist.

comunitario,-a *adj (gen)* of the community, relating to the community.

con *prep* **1** *(instrumento, medio)* with. **2** *(modo, circunstancia)* in, with. **3** *(juntamente, en compañía)* with. **4** *(contenido)* with. **5** *(relación)* to. **6** *(comparación)*

compared to. **7 con +** *inf* by + *ger.*
8 *(aunque)* in spite of. ⌐LOC⌐ **con que /
con tal de que / con tal que** provided,
as long as. **I con todo (y eso)** nevertheless, even so.

concavidad *nf* concavity.

cóncavo,-a *adj* concave.

concebir *vt* **1** *(engendrar)* to conceive. **2**
fig *(comprender)* to understand.
▸ *vi* *(quedarse embarazada)* to become
pregnant, conceive.

conceder *vt* **1** *(otorgar)* to grant, concede; *(premio)* to award. **2** *(atribuir)* to
give, attach. **3** *(oportunidad, tiempo)* to
give. **4** *(admitir)* to concede, admit.

concejal,-la *nm & nf* town councillor.

concejo *nm* town council, council.

concentración *nf* **1** *(gen)* concentration. **2** *(de gente)* gathering, rally.

concentrar *vt* to concentrate.
▸ *vpr* **concentrarse 1** *(reunirse)* to concentrate. **2** *(fijar la atención)* to concentrate (en, on).

concéntrico,-a *adj* concentric.

concepción *nf* conception.

concepto *nm* **1** *(idea)* concept, conception, idea. **2** *(opinión)* opinion, view.
⌐LOC⌐ **bajo ningún concepto** under no
circumstances. **I en concepto de** by
way of.

conceptual *adj* conceptual.

concernir *vi* [se usa sólo en tercera persona de presente de indicativo, imperfecto de
indicativo y presente de subjuntivo; y en
formas impersonales] *(afectar)* to concern, touch. ⌐LOC⌐ **en lo que a mí** *(ti, él,
etc)* **concierne** as far as I am *(you are, he
is, etc)* concerned.

concertado,-a *adj* concerted.

concertar *vt* **1** *(planear)* to plan, coordinate. **2** *(entrevista)* to arrange; *(acuerdo)* to reach; *(tratado, negocio)* to conclude, settle. **3** *(precio)* to agree on.
▸ *vi* **1** *(concordar)* to agree, match up;
(números) to tally. **2** LING to agree.

concertino *nm* first violin.

concertista *nm o nf* soloist.

concesión *nf* **1** concession, granting.
2 *(de premio)* awarding.

concesionario,-a *nm & nf* concessionaire, licence holder, licensee.
▸ *nm* **concesionario** *(de coches)* dealer.

concesivo,-a *adj* LING concessive.

concha *nf* **1** *(caparazón)* shell. **2** *(carey)*
tortoiseshell. **3** *(ostra)* oyster.

conciencia *nf* **1** *(moral)* conscience. **2**
(conocimiento) consciousness, aware-
ness. ⌐LOC⌐ **a conciencia** conscientious-
ly. **I remorderle a** ALGN **la conciencia** to
weigh on SB's conscience.

concienciar *vt* to make aware (de,
of).
▸ *vpr* **concienciarse** to become aware
(de, of).

concienzudo,-a *adj* conscientious.

concierto *nm* **1** MÚS *(sesión)* concert;
(composición) concerto. **2** *(acuerdo)*
agreement. **3** *(armonía)* concert, concord.

conciliación *nf* conciliation, recon-
ciliation.

conciliador,-ra *adj* conciliatory, con-
ciliating.

conciliar *adj* conciliar.
▸ *vt* **1** *(gen)* to conciliate, bring together. **2** *(enemigos)* to reconcile.

concilio *nm* council.

concisión *nf* concision, conciseness.

conciso,-a *adj* concise, brief.

conciudadano,-a *nm & nf* fellow citizen.

concluir *vt* **1** *(terminar)* to finish. **2** *(trato,
negocio)* to close.
▸ *vi* *(finalizar)* to finish, come to an
end, conclude.

conclusión *nf* **1** *(final)* conclusion, end.
2 *(deducción)* conclusion. ⌐LOC⌐ **en conclusión** in conclusion. **I llegar a una
conclusión** to come to a conclusion.

concluyente *adj* conclusive, decisive.

concordancia *nf* **1** concordance,
agreement. **2** LING agreement.

concordante *adj* concordant.

concordar *vt* **1** *(poner de acuerdo)* to
bring into agreement, reconcile. **2**
LING to make agree.

► *vi* **1** *(convenir)* to agree, coincide, match. **2** LING to agree.

concordia *nf* concord, harmony.

concreción *nf (concisión)* concision, conciseness.

concretar *vt* **1** *(precisar)* to specify, state explicitly. **2** *(hora, precio)* to fix, set. **3** *(resumir)* to sum up.
► *vpr* **concretarse** *(tomar forma)* to take shape.

concreto,-a *adj* **1** *(real)* concrete, real. **2** *(particular)* particular, specific. LOC **en concreto** *(en particular)* in particular, specifically.

concurrencia *nf* **1** *(confluencia)* combination, concurrence. **2** *(participación)* participation.

concurrido,-a *adj* **1** *(lugar público)* busy, crowded. **2** *(espectáculo)* well-attended, popular.

concurrir *vi* **1** *(juntarse en un lugar - gente)* to gather, come together, meet. **2** *(tomar parte - concurso, etc)* to compete, take part.

concursante *nm o nf* **1** *(a concurso)* contestant, participant, competitor. **2** *(a empleo)* candidate.

concursar *vi* **1** *(competir)* to compete, take part. **2** *(para un empleo)* to be a candidate.

concurso *nm* **1** *(gen)* competition; *(de belleza, deportivo)* contest; *(en televisión)* quiz. **2** *(para puestos)* public examination: **3** *fml (concurrencia)* gathering.

condado *nm* county.

conde *nm* count.

condecoración *nf* decoration.

condecorar *vt* to decorate.

condena *nf* JUR sentence.

condenado,-a *adj* **1** JUR convicted. **2** *(sin remedio)* hopeless.

condenar *vt* **1** JUR *(declarar culpable)* to convict, find guilty. **2** JUR *(decretar condena)* to sentence, condemn. **3** *(desaprobar)* to condemn.

condensación *nf* **1** *(acción)* condensing. **2** *(efecto)* condensation.

condensado,-a *adj* condensed.

condensador,-ra *adj* condensing.

condensar *vt* to condense.

condescender *vi (adaptarse)* to comply (a, with), consent (a, to).

condescendiente *adj (complaciente)* obliging.

condición *nf* **1** *(naturaleza)* nature, condition. **2** *(carácter)* nature, character. **3** *(circunstancia)* circumstance, condition. **4** *(estado social)* status, position. **5** *(calidad)* capacity. **6** *(exigencia)* condition. LOC **a condición de que...** provided (that)... ∎ **con la condición de que...** on the condition that...
► *nf pl* **condiciones 1** *(estado)* condition *sing*, state *sing*. **2** *(aptitud)* aptitude *sing*, talent *sing*. LOC **estar en condiciones de hacer** ALGO **1** *(físicas)* to be fit to do STH. **2** *(posición, autoridad)* to be in a position to do STH.

condicionado,-a *adj* conditioned.

condicional *adj* conditional.
► *nm* conditional.

condicionar *vt* **1** *(influir en)* to condition, determine. **2** *(supeditar)* to make conditional.

condimentar *vt* to season, flavour (US flavor).

condimento *nm* seasoning, flavouring (US flavoring).

condolerse *vpr* to sympathize (de, with), feel sorry (de, for), feel pity (de, for).

cóndor *nm* condor.

conducir *vt* **1** *(guiar)* to lead, take, show. **2** *(coche, animales)* to drive.
► *vi* **1** *(un coche)* to drive. **2** *(llevar)* to lead (a, -).

conducta *nf* conduct, behaviour (US behavior).

conductividad *nf* conductivity.

conductivo,-a *adj* conductive.

conducto *nm (tubería)* pipe, conduit.

conductor,-ra *adj* FÍS conductive.
► *nm & nf* AUTO driver.
► *nm* **conductor** FÍS conductor.

conectar *vt (gen)* to connect (up).
► *vi* **1** RAD TV *(coger)* to tune in (con, to); *(dar conexión)* to tune in (con,

with). **2** *fam (llevarse bien)* to hit it off, get on well.

conector *nm* connector.

conejera *nf* **1** *(conejal)* rabbit hutch. **2** *(madriguera)* rabbit warren, rabbit burrow.

conejero,-a *nm & nf* rabbit breeder.

conejillo *nm* young rabbit. COMP conejillo de Indias guinea pig.

conejo,-a *nm & nf* rabbit.

conexión *nf* TÉC connection.

conexo,-a *adj* connected, related.

confabulación *nf* conspiracy, plot.

confabular *vi* to confabulate, discuss.
► *vpr* **confabularse** to conspire, plot.

confección *nf* **1** *(acción)* dressmaking, tailoring; *(ropa)* off-the-peg clothes *pl*, ready-to-wear clothes *pl*. **2** *(realización)* making, making up.

confeccionar *vt (vestido)* to make, make up; *(plato)* to prepare.

confederación *nf* confederation, confederacy.

confederar *vt* to confederate.

conferencia *nf* **1** *(charla)* talk, lecture. **2** POL conference, meeting. **3** *(teléfono)* long-distance call. LOC dar una conferencia sobre ALGO to lecture on STH, give a lecture on STH.

conferenciante *nm o nf* lecturer.

conferenciar *vi* to confer.

conferir *vt* **1** *(conceder)* to confer, bestow, award. **2** *(dar)* to give.

confesar *vt (reconocer)* to confess, admit.
► *vpr* **confesarse** to go to confession, confess.

confesión *nf (expresión)* confession, admission.

confesional *adj* denominational.

confesionario *nm* confessional.

confeso,-a *adj* JUR self-confessed.

confesor *nm* confessor.

confeti *nm* confetti.

confiado,-a *adj* **1** *(crédulo)* unsuspecting, gullible. **2** *(seguro)* confident, self-confident.

confianza *nf* **1** *(seguridad)* confidence. **2** *(familiaridad)* familiarity, intimacy. **3** *(presunción)* conceit. LOC de confianza **1** *(fiable)* reliable. **2** *(de responsabilidad)* trustworthy. ▌en confianza confidentially, in confidence. ▌tener confianza en uno mismo to be self-confident.

confiar *vi* **1** *(tener fe)* to trust (en, -), confide (en, in). **2** *(estar seguro)* to be confident, trust. **3** *(contar)* to count (en, on), rely (en, on).
► *vt* **1** *(depositar)* to entrust. **2** *(secretos, problemas, etc)* to confide.
► *vpr* **confiarse** *(entregarse)* to entrust os.

confidencia *nf* confidence, secret.

confidencial *adj* confidential.

confidencialidad *nf* confidentiality.

configurar *vt* **1** to form, shape. **2** INFORM to configure.

confinar *vt (recluir)* to confine.

confirmación *nf* confirmation.

confirmar *vt* to confirm.

confiscar *vt* to confiscate.

confitado,-a *adj (fruta)* candied, glacé. COMP frutas confitadas candied fruit *sing*.

confitar *vt (frutas)* to candy; *(carne)* to preserve.

confitería *nf* confectioner's, sweet shop, US candy shop.

confitero,-a *nm & nf* confectioner.

confitura *nf* preserve, jam.

conflictividad *nf* disputes *pl*.

conflictivo,-a *adj (situación)* difficult; *(tema)* controversial.

conflicto *nm* **1** *(choque)* conflict. **2** *fig (apuro)* dilemma. COMP conflicto laboral industrial dispute.

confluencia *nf* confluence.

confluir *vi (personas)* to converge, come together; *(ríos, caminos, etc)* to meet, converge.

conformar *vt* **1** *(dar forma)* to shape. **2** *(adaptar)* to conform, adjust.
► *vpr* **conformarse** *(contentarse)* to resign os (con, to), be content (con, with), make do (con, with).

conforme adj 1 (satisfecho) satisfied. 2 (de acuerdo) in accordance with, in keeping with. 3 (resignado) resigned. ⌐LOC⌐ **conforme a** in accordance with, according to.
▶ adv 1 (según, como) as. 2 (en cuanto) as soon as. 3 (a medida que) as.

conformidad nf (aprobación) approval, consent. ⌐LOC⌐ **en conformidad con** ALGO in conformity with STH, in agreement with.

conformismo nm conformism.

conformista nm o nf conformist.

confort nm comfort.

confortable adj comfortable.

confraternizar vi to fraternize.

confrontación nf (enfrentamiento) confrontation.

confrontar vt 1 (gen) to confront; (carear) to bring face to face. 2 (cotejar) to compare (con, with), collate (con, with).

confundir vt 1 (equivocar) to confuse (con, with), mistake (con, for). 2 (turbar) to confound, embarrass.
▶ vpr **confundirse 1** (mezclarse) to mingle; (colores, formas) to blend. 2 (equivocarse) to get mixed up, make a mistake. 3 (turbarse) to be confused, be embarrassed.

confusión nf 1 (desorden) confusion, chaos. 2 (equivocación) mistake, confusion.

confuso,-a adj 1 (ideas) confused. 2 (estilo, etc) obscure, confused. 3 fig (turbado) confused, embarrassed.

congelación nf 1 (gen) freezing. 2 (precios, salarios, etc) freeze. 3 MED (gen) exposure; (extremidades) frostbite.

congelado,-a adj 1 (gen) frozen. 2 MED frostbitten.
▶ nm pl **congelados** frozen food sing.

congelador nm freezer.

congelar vt 1 (gen) to freeze. 2 MED to cause frostbite on.
▶ vpr **congelarse 1** to freeze. 2 MED to get frostbite.

congeniar vi to get on.

congénito,-a adj 1 congenital. 2 fig innate.

congestión nf congestion.

congestionar vt to congest.
▶ vpr **congestionarse** to become congested.

conglomerado nm 1 TÉC conglomerate. 2 fig conglomeration, collection.

conglomerar vt to conglomerate.

congratular vt fml to congratulate on.
▶ vpr **congratularse** fml to congratulate OS (de/por, on).

congregación nf 1 (reunión) assembly. 2 REL congregation.

congregar vt to congregate, assemble.
▶ vpr **congregarse** to congregate, assemble.

congresista nm o nf 1 (que asiste a un congreso) congress participant. 2 (diputado) member of congress; (hombre) congressman; (mujer) congresswoman.

congreso nm congress. ⌐COMP⌐ **congreso de los Diputados** Parliament, US Congress.

congrio nm conger, conger eel.

congruencia nf 1 (conveniencia) congruity. 2 MAT congruence.

congruente adj 1 (coherente) coherent, suitable. 2 MAT congruent.

cónico,-a adj 1 conical. 2 (en geometría) conic.

conífera nf conifer.

conjetura nf conjecture. ⌐LOC⌐ **hacer conjeturas** to make conjectures.

conjeturar vt to conjecture.

conjugación nf conjugation.

conjugado,-a adj (enlazado) combined.

conjugar vt to conjugate.

conjunción nf conjunction.

conjuntamente adv jointly, together.

conjuntar vt to coordinate.

conjuntivitis nf inv conjunctivitis.

conjunto,-a adj 1 (compartido) joint. 2 (combinado) combined. ⌐LOC⌐ **en conjunto** altogether, on the whole.

▶ *nm* **conjunto 1** *(grupo)* group, collection. **2** *(todo)* whole: **3** *(prenda)* outfit, ensemble. **4** MÚS *(clásico)* ensemble; *(pop)* band, group. **5** MAT set. **6** DEP team.

conjura *nf* plot, conspiracy.

conjuración *nf* plot, conspiracy.

conjurar *vt (gen)* to exorcise; *(peligro)* to avert, stave off, ward off.
▶ *vi (conspirar)* to conspire (contra, against).
▶ *vpr* **conjurarse** to conspire (contra, against).

conjuro *nm* **1** *(exorcismo)* exorcism. **2** *(encantamiento)* spell, incantation.

conmemorar *vt* to commemorate.

conmemorativo,-a *adj* commemorative.

conmigo *pron* with me, to me.

conmoción *nf* **1** commotion, shock: *causar conmoción* to cause a commotion. **2** MED concussion. **3** *(levantamiento)* riot. COMP **conmoción cerebral** concussion.

conmocionar *vt* **1** to shock. **2** MED to concuss. **3** *fig* to trouble, disturb.

conmovedor,-ra *adj* moving, touching.

conmover *vt* **1** *(persona)* to move, touch. **2** *(cosa)* to shake.

conmutador *nm* switch.

conmutar *vt* **1** *(cambiar)* to exchange. **2** JUR to commute. **3** ELEC to commutate.

conmutativo,-a *adj* commutative.

connivencia *nf* connivance, collusion.

cono *nm* cone.

conocedor,-ra *nm & nf* expert (de, on), connoisseur (de, of).

conocer *vt* **1** *(gen)* to know; *(noticia)* to hear. **2** *(persona)* to meet, get to know. **3** *(reconocer)* to recognize. **4** *(país, lugar)* to have been to. LOC **dar a conocer** to make known.
▶ *vi* **1** *(saber)* to know (de, about). **2** JUR to hear (de, -).
▶ *vpr* **conocerse** *(a sí mismo)* to know os; *(dos o más personas)* to know each other; *(por primera vez)* to meet, get to know.

conocido,-a *adj* **1** known. **2** *(famoso)* well-known.

conocimiento *nm* **1** [en 1, también se usa en plural con el mismo significado] *(saber)* knowledge. **2** *(sensatez)* good sense. **3** *(conciencia)* consciousness. LOC **tener conocimiento de** ALGO to know about STH.

conquista *nf* conquest. LOC **hacer una conquista** *(amorosa)* to make a conquest.

conquistador,-ra *adj* conquering.

conquistar *vt (con las armas)* to conquer.

consagración *nf* **1** *(artista, etc)* recognition. **2** *(de una costumbre)* establishment. **3** *(dedicación)* dedication.

consagrado,-a *adj (reconocido)* recognized, established.

consagrar *vt* **1** *(palabra, expresión)* to establish. **2** *(dedicar)* to dedicate. **3** *(artista, etc)* to confirm, establish.

consanguíneo,-a *adj* consanguineous.
▶ *nm & nf* blood relation.

consanguinidad *nf* consanguinity, blood relationship.

consciente *adj* **1** conscious, aware. **2** MED conscious. **3** *(responsable)* reliable, responsible. LOC **estar consciente** to be conscious. ▍ **ser consciente de** ALGO to be aware of STH.

consecuencia *nf* **1** consequence, result. **2** *(coherencia)* consistency. LOC **a consecuencia de** as a consequence of, as a result of. ▍ **como consecuencia de** as a consequence of, as a result of.

consecuente *adj* **1** *(siguiente)* consequent. **2** *(resultante)* resulting. **3** *(coherente)* consistent.

consecutivamente *adv* consecutively.

consecutivo,-a *adj* consecutive.

conseguir *vt* **1** *(cosa)* to obtain, get; *(objetivo)* to attain, achieve. **2** *(lograr)* to manage, succeed in.

consejería *nf* **1** *(lugar)* Council. **2** *(cargo)* councillor.

consejero,-a *nm & nf* **1** *(asesor)* adviser, advisor, counsellor. **2** POL councillor.

consejo *nm* **1** *(recomendación)* advice. **2** *(junta)* council, board. [LOC] **pedir consejo a** ALGN to ask SB for advice. [COMP] **consejo de ministros** cabinet.

consenso *nm* **1** *(acuerdo)* consensus. **2** *(consentimiento)* consent, assent.

consensuar *vt* to reach a consensus on.

consentido,-a *adj* *(mimado)* spoiled, spoilt.
► *nm & nf* *(persona)* spoiled person, spoilt person; *(niño)* spoiled child, spoilt child.

consentimiento *nm* consent.

consentir *vt* **1** *(tolerar)* to allow, permit, tolerate. **2** *(mimar)* to spoil.
► *vi* **1** *(admitir)* to consent (en, to), agree (en, to). **2** *(ceder)* to weaken.

conserje *nm* **1** *(portero)* porter; *(de hotel)* hall porter. **2** *(de escuela)* caretaker.

conserva [también se usa en plural con el mismo significado] *nf* **1** *(en lata)* tinned food, canned food. **2** *(dulces)* preserves *pl*.

conservación *nf* *(de alimentos)* preservation.

conservador,-ra *adj* POL conservative.
► *nm & nf* **1** POL conservative. **2** *(de museos)* curator.

conservadurismo *nm* conservatism.

conservante *nm* preservative.

conservar *vt* **1** *(alimentos)* to preserve. **2** *(guardar)* to keep, save.
► *vpr* **conservarse 1** *(tradición, etc)* to survive. **2** *fig (mantenerse)* to keep well.

conservatorio *nm* conservatory, conservatoire, school of music.

conservero,-a *adj* canning: *industria conservera* canning industry.

considerable *adj* considerable.

considerablemente *adv* considerably.

consideración *nf* **1** *(reflexión)* consideration, attention: *este tema merece nuestra consideración* this subject deserves our attention. **2** *(respeto)* regard. [LOC] **con consideración** *(respeto)* respectfully. ▌**en consideración a** considering.

considerar *vt* *(reflexionar)* to consider, think over, think about.

consigna *nf* *(en estación, etc)* left-luggage office, US check-room.

consignar *vt* **1** *(mercancías)* to consign, ship, dispatch. **2** *(destinar - dinero, etc)* to allocate. **3** *(anotar)* to note down.

consigo *pron* **1** *(3ª persona singular - hombre)* with him; *(- mujer)* with her; *(- cosa, animal)* with it. **2** *(usted)* with you. **3** *(3ª persona plural)* with them. **4** *(ustedes)* with you.

consiguiente *adj* consequent, resulting, resultant. [LOC] **por consiguiente** therefore, consequently.

consistencia *nf* *(dureza)* consistency.

consistente *adj* **1** *(firme)* firm, solid. **2** *fig* sound, solid. **3** CULIN thick. [LOC] **consistente en** consisting of.

consistir *vi* **1** *(estribar)* to lie (en, in), consist (en, in). **2** *(estar formado)* to consist (en, of).

consistorial *adj* REL consistorial. [COMP] **casa consistorial** town hall.

consola *nf* **1** *(mueble)* console table. **2** *(de ordenador, etc)* console. [COMP] **consola de videojuegos** games console.

consolar *vt* to console, comfort.

consolidación *nf* consolidation.

consolidar *vt* to consolidate.

consomé *nm* clear soup, consommé.

consonante *nf* consonant.

consonántico,-a *adj* consonantal, consonant.

conspiración *nf* conspiracy, plot.

conspirador,-ra *nm & nf* conspirator.

conspirar *vi* to conspire, plot.

constancia *nf* **1** *(perseverancia)* constancy, perseverance. **2** *(evidencia)* evidence, proof. [LOC] **dejar constancia de** ALGO *(probar)* to prove STH.

constante *adj* **1** *(invariable)* constant. **2** *(persona)* steadfast.
► *nf* MAT constant.

constantemente *adv* constantly.

constar vi 1 (consistir en) to consist (de, of), be made up (de, of), comprise (de, -). 2 (figurar) to figure, be included, appear. 3 (ser cierto) to be a fact. 4 (quedar claro) to be clear, be known. LOC **hacer constar 1** (señalar) to point out, state. **2** (escribir) to put down, include.

constatar vt to verify, confirm.

constelación nf constellation.

consternar vt to dismay, shatter.

constipado,-a nm MED cold. LOC **estar constipado,-a** to have a cold.

constiparse vpr to catch a cold.

constitución nf constitution.

constitucional adj constitutional.

constituyente adj constituent.

construcción nf 1 construction: la industria de la construcción the construction industry. **2** (edificio) building. LOC **en construcción** under construction.

constructivo,-a adj constructive.

constructor,-ra adj construction, building.
▶ nm & nf (de edificios) builder; (de barcos) shipbuilder.

construir vt to construct, build.

consuelo nm consolation, comfort.

cónsul nm o nf consul.

consulado nm 1 (oficina) consulate. **2** (cargo) consulship.

consular adj consular.

consulta nf 1 (acción) consultation. **2** MED surgery, US doctor's office; (consultorio) consulting room. LOC **pasar consulta** to see patients, hold surgery.

consultar vt 1 (pedir opinión) to consult (con, with/-), seek advice (con, from): consulté con mis padres I consulted with my parents. **2** (buscar en un libro) to look up. LOC **consultar con un abogado** to consult a lawyer, take legal advice.

consultor,-ra nm & nf consultant.

consultorio nm MED (consulta) surgery, US doctor's office; (habitación) consulting room.

consumar vt (terminar) to complete, carry out.

consumición nf 1 consumption. **2** (bebida) drink.

consumidor,-ra nm & nf consumer.

consumir vt 1 (gastar, usar) to consume, use. **2** (destruir) to destroy, consume.
▶ vpr **consumirse 1** (extinguirse) to burn out. **2** fig (afligirse) to waste away.

consumismo nm consumerism.

consumista adj o nf consumerist.

consumo nm consumption.

contabilidad nf 1 (profesión) accountancy; (carrera) accounting. **2** (de empresa, etc) accounting, bookkeeping. LOC **llevar la contabilidad** to keep the books.

contabilizar vt to enter in the books.

contable nm o nf bookkeeper, accountant.
▶ adj countable.

contactar vt to contact, get in touch (con, with).

contacto nm 1 contact. **2** AUTO ignition. LOC **ponerse en contacto con** to get in touch with, get in contact with.

contado,-a adj few. COMP **en contadas ocasiones** seldom, rarely.

contador,-ra nm meter.

contagiar vt 1 (enfermedad) to transmit, pass on. **2** fig to infect, pass on, give.
▶ vpr **contagiarse 1** (enfermar) to get infected. **2** (transmitirse) to be contagious: esta enfermedad no se contagia this disease is not contagious.

contagio nm MED contagion, infection.

contagioso,-a adj infectious, contagious: enfermedad contagiosa infectious disease; risa contagiosa infectious laugh.

contáiner nm container.

contaminación nf contamination; (de agua, aire) pollution.

contaminante nm polluting agent.

contaminar vt to contaminate; (agua, aire) to pollute.

contar *vt* **1** *(calcular)* to count. **2** *(explicar)* to tell: *me contó un cuento* she told me a story.
▶ *vi* to count: *los niños saben contar* the children know how to count.

contemplación *nf (acción)* contemplation.

contemplar *vt (mirar)* to contemplate.

contemplativo,-a *adj* contemplative.

contemporáneo,-a *adj* contemporary.

contenedor,-ra *adj* containing.
▶ *nm* **contenedor** container.

contener *vt* **1** *(incluir)* to contain, hold. **2** *(detener)* to hold back, restrain. **3** *(respiración)* to hold.

contenido,-a *adj (moderado)* moderate, reserved.
▶ *nm* **contenido** content, contents *pl*.

contentar *vt (satisfacer)* to please, content.
▶ *vpr* **contentarse** *(conformarse)* to make do (con, with), be satisfied (con, with).

contento,-a *adj* happy, pleased: *estoy contento de conocerle* I'm pleased to meet you.

contestación *nf (respuesta)* answer, reply.

contestador *nm* answering machine.

contestar *vt (responder)* to answer.

contienda *nf* contest, dispute, struggle.

contigo *pron* with you.

contiguo,-a *adj* contiguous (a, to), adjoining, adjacent (a, to).

continental *adj* continental.

continente *nm* GEOG continent.

continuación *nf* continuation, follow-up. LOC **a continuación** next.

continuador,-ra *adj* continuing.
▶ *nm & nf* continuator.

continuamente *adv* continuously.

continuar *vt (proseguir)* to continue, carry on.

continuidad *nf* continuity.

continuo,-a *adj* **1** *(seguido)* continuous. **2** *(continuado)* continual, constant.

contornar *vt* **1** *(dar vueltas)* to skirt. **2** *(hacer los perfiles)* to trace the outline of.

contorno *nm* **1** *(perfil)* outline; *(perímetro)* perimeter. **2** *(canto)* rim, edge.

contorsionarse *vpr* to contort os, twist os.

contorsionista *nm o nf* contortionist.

contra *prep* **1** against: *tres contra uno* three against one. **2** for: *un producto contra las picaduras de mosquitos* a product for mosquito bites. LOC **en contra** against: *estaba en contra* he was against it.

contraatacar *vt* to counterattack.

contraataque *nm* counterattack.

contrabajo *nm (instrumento)* double bass.

contrabandista *nm o nf* smuggler.

contrabando *nm* **1** smuggling, contraband. **2** *(mercancías)* smuggled goods *pl*, contraband. LOC **pasar ALGO de contrabando** to smuggle STH in.

contracción *nf* contraction.

contrachapado *nm* plywood.

contracorriente *nf* crosscurrent.

contractura *nf* contracture.

contradecir *vt (decir lo contrario)* to contradict.

contradicción *nf* contradiction. LOC **estar en contradicción con** to be inconsistent with, contradictory to.

contradictorio,-a *adj* contradictory.

contraer *vt* **1** *(encoger)* to contract: *contraer un músculo* to contract a muscle. **2** *(enfermedad)* to catch. **3** *(deuda)* to contract, incur; *(hábito)* to pick up. **4** LING to contract.

contrafuerte *nm* ARQUIT buttress.

contrahecho,-a *adj* deformed, hunchbacked.

contraindicación *nf* MED contraindication.

contraindicar *vt* MED to contraindicate.

contralto *nm o nf* contralto.

contraluz *nm o nf* view against the light, back light.
LOC **a contraluz** against the light.

contraofensiva *nf* counteroffensive.

contraorden *nf* countermand.

contrapartida *nf* **1** COM balancing entry. **2** *fig* compensation.

contrapesar *vt* **1** to counterbalance, counterpoise. **2** *fig* to balance, offset.

contrapeso *nm* **1** counterweight. **2** *fig* counterbalance.

contraponer *vt* **1** *(oponer)* to set in opposition (a, to). **2** *fig (contrastar)* to contrast (a, with).

contraportada *nf* back page, back cover.

contraposición *nf* **1** *(contraste)* contrast. **2** *(oposición)* conflict, clash: *contraposición de intereses* conflict of interests. LOC **estar en contraposición** to clash.

contraprestación *nf* contractual obligation.

contraproducente *adj* counterproductive.

contrapuesto,-a *adj* opposed.

contrapunto *nm* counterpoint.

contra-reloj *adj* against the clock.
▶ *nm (en ciclismo)* time trial.

contrariamente *adv* contrary (a, to).

contrariar *vi* **1** *(oponerse)* to oppose, go against. **2** *(disgustar)* to annoy, upset: *no quería contrariarte* I didn't want to upset you.

contrario,-a *adj* **1** *(opuesto)* contrary, opposite: *iba en sentido contrario* he was going in the opposite direction. **2** *(perjudicial)* harmful (a, to), bad (a, for): *el fumar es contrario a la salud* smoking is bad for your health. LOC **al contrario** on the contrary. **I de lo contrario** otherwise. **I llevar la contraria a** ALGN to oppose SB. **I por el contrario** on the contrary. **I todo lo contrario** quite the opposite.
▶ *nm & nf* opponent, adversary, rival.

contrarreloj *adj* against the clock.
▶ *nf* race against the clock. COMP **(etapa) contrarreloj** time trial.

contrarrestar *vt (hacer frente)* to resist, oppose.

contrasentido *nm* **1** *(contradicción)* contradiction. **2** *(disparate)* piece of nonsense: *eso es un contrasentido* that's nonsense.

contraseña *nf (seña)* secret sign; *(palabra)* password.

contrastar *vi (comprobar)* to check, verify.
▶ *vi (oponerse)* to contrast (con, with).

contraste *nm (oposición)* contrast.

contratación *nf* **1** *(contrato - obrero)* hiring; *(- empleado)* engagement. **2** *(pedido)* total orders *pl*, volume of business.

contratar *vt* **1** *(servicio, etc)* to sign a contract for. **2** *(obrero)* to hire; *(empleado)* to engage.

contratiempo *nm (contrariedad)* setback, hitch; *(accidente)* mishap.

contratista *nm o nf* contractor. COMP **contratista de obras** building contractor.

contrato *nm* contract. COMP **contrato de alquiler** lease, leasing agreement. **I contrato de compraventa** contract of sale. **I contrato de trabajo** work contract. **I contrato temporal** temporary contract.

contraventana *nf* shutter.

contrayente *adj* contracting.
▶ *nm o nf (en matrimonio)* contracting party.

contribución *nf* **1** contribution. **2** *(impuesto)* tax.

contribuir *vt (pagar)* to pay.
▶ *vi* **1** *(aportar)* to contribute: *contribuir a los gastos* to contribute to the expenses. **2** *(pagar impuestos)* to pay taxes.

contribuyente *nm o nf* taxpayer.

contrincante *nm* opponent, rival.

control *nm* **1** *(gen)* control. **2** *(comprobación)* check. **3** *(sitio)* checkpoint. LOC **estar bajo control** to be under control. **I estar fuera de control** to be out of control. COMP **control a distancia** remote control. **I control de natalidad** birth control.

controlador,-ra *adj* control.
▶ *nm & nf (aéreo)* air traffic controller.

controlar vt **1** (gen) to control. **2** (comprobar) to check.
▸ vpr **controlarse** (moderarse) to control os.

contundente adj fig (categórico) convincing, overwhelming, weighty: un «no» contundente a firm «no».

contusión nf contusion, bruise.

contusionar vt to contuse, bruise.

convalecencia nf convalescence.

convalecer vi to convalesce (de, after), recover (de, from).

convaleciente adj convalescent.
▸ nm o nf convalescent.

convalidación nf **1** EDUC validation. **2** (documentos) ratification, authentication.

convalidar vt **1** EDUC to validate. **2** (documentos) to ratify, authenticate.

convencer vt **1** (de algo) to convince; (para hacer algo) to persuade: lo convencieron de su error they convinced him of his mistake. **2** fam (en frases negativas) to like, be keen on: ese color no me acaba de convencer I'm not sure about that colour.
▸ vi to be convincing: el equipo local no convenció con su actuación the local team's performance was not very convincing.
▸ vpr **convencerse** to become convinced, be convinced, convince os: se convenció de que era guapo he convinced himself that he was good-looking.

convencimiento nm conviction. LOC llegar al convencimiento de que... to be convinced that...

convención nf **1** (congreso) convention, congress. **2** (acuerdo) convention, treaty. **3** (costumbre) convention.

convencional adj conventional.

convencionalismo nm conventionalism, conventionality.

conveniencia nf **1** (utilidad) usefulness. **2** (oportunidad) suitability, advisability: la conveniencia de estas medidas the advisability of these measures. **3** (provecho) interest, benefit: solo se preocupa de su propia conveniencia he only looks out for his own interests. COMP conve-

niencias sociales social conventions. ∎ matrimonio de conveniencia marriage of convenience.

conveniente adj **1** (útil) useful. **2** (oportuno) suitable, convenient. **3** (ventajoso) advantageous. **4** (aconsejable) advisable. **5** (precio) good, fair. LOC creer conveniente to think advisable, be better.

convenientemente adv (adecuadamente) suitably; (bien) properly.

convenio nm agreement, treaty. COMP convenio colectivo / convenio laboral collective agreement.

convenir vt (acordar) to agree, arrange: convenimos el precio we agreed the price.
▸ vi **1** (acordar) to agree: convinimos en la fecha we agreed on the date. **2** (ser oportuno o conveniente) to be good for: no te conviene hacer esfuerzos it's not good for you to exert yourself. **3** (ser adecuado o propio) to suit: ese chico no te conviene that boy is not right for you. LOC conviene + inf it is as well to + inf: conviene mencionar que... it's as well to mention that... ∎ conviene que + subj it is better that, it is advisable + inf: conviene que te vayas it is better that you go.

convento nm (de monjas) convent; (de monjes) monastery.

converger vi to converge, come together.

convergir vi to converge, come together.

conversación nf conversation, talk. LOC dar conversación a ALGN to talk to SB, keep SB chatting. ∎ entablar conversación con ALGN to get into conversation with SB, engage SB in conversation.

conversador,-ra adj talkative.
▸ nm & nf conversationalist, talker.

conversar vi to converse (con, with), talk (con, to).

conversión nf conversion.

convertir vt (transformar) to change, turn, transform, convert.
▸ vpr **convertirse 1** (transformarse) to turn (en, into), change (en, into). **2** (volverse) to become (en, -), turn (en,

into): *su sueño se convirtió en realidad* his dream came true.

convexo,-a *adj* convex.

convicción *nf* conviction: *tengo la convicción de que vendrán* I firmly believe that they'll come.

convidado,-a *adj* invited.
▸ *nm & nf* guest.

convidar *vt* **1** *(invitar)* to invite: *me convidó a una fiesta* he invited me to a party. **2** *(ofrecer)* to offer: *nos convidó a pastel* he offered us some cake.

convincente *adj* convincing.

convincentemente *adv* convincingly.

convite *nm* **1** *(invitación)* invitation. **2** *(comida)* meal; *(fiesta)* party.

convivencia *nf* **1** living together. **2** *fig* coexistence.

convivir *vi* **1** to live together. **2** *fig* to coexist. LOC **saber convivir** to give and take.

convocar *vt* to convoke, summon, call together. LOC **convocar una reunión** to call a meeting.

convocatoria *nf* **1** *(citación)* convocation, summons *sing*, call to a meeting. **2** EDUC examination: *convocatoria de septiembre* (September) resits *pl*.

convoy *nm* **1** *(escolta)* convoy. **2** *(tren)* train.

conyugal *adj* conjugal. COMP **vida conyugal** married life.

cónyuge *nm o nf (gen)* spouse, partner; *(marido)* husband; *(mujer)* wife.
▸ *nm pl* **cónyuges** husband and wife, married couple *sing*.

coñac *nm* cognac, brandy.

cooperación *nf* cooperation.

cooperar *vi* to cooperate.

cooperativa *nf* cooperative.

coordenada *nf* coordinate.

coordinación *nf* coordination.

coordinador,-ra *adj* coordinating.
▸ *nm & nf* coordinator.

coordinadora *nf (comité)* coordinating committee.

coordinar *vt* to coordinate: *coordinaron la compaña* they coordinated the campaign.

copa *nf* **1** *(vaso)* glass; *(bebida)* drink: *¿te apetece una copa?* do you fancy a drink? **2** *(de árbol)* top. **3** *(trofeo)* cup.
▸ *nf pl* **copas** *(naipes)* hearts.

copete *nm* **1** *(cabello)* tuft. **2** *(penacho)* crest. **3** *(de montaña, helado)* top.

copia *nf* **1** *(gen)* copy. **2** *(de fotografía)* print. **3** *fig (persona)* image: *es la copia de su padre* he's the image of his father. LOC **sacar una copia** to make a copy.

copiadora *nf* photocopier.

copiar *vt* **1** *(gen)* to copy: *lo copió del libro* he copied it from the book. **2** EDUC to cheat, copy. **3** *(escribir)* to take down. LOC **copiar al pie de la letra** to copy word for word.

copiloto *nm* **1** AV copilot. **2** AUTO co-driver.

copioso,-a *adj* **1** *fml (abundante)* plentiful, abundant, copious. **2** *fml (lluvia)* heavy; *(cabello)* long.

copista *nm o nf* copyist.

copla *nf* **1** *(verso, estrofa)* verse, stanza. **2** *(canción)* popular folk song.

copo *nm (gen)* flake; *(de nieve)* snowflake; *(de algodón)* ball (of cotton). COMP **copos de avena** rolled oats.

coproducción *nf* co-production, joint production.

coproductor,-ra *nm & nf* co-producer.

copropiedad *nf* joint ownership.

coprotagonizar *vt* to co-star (-, in).

copulativo,-a *adj* copulative.

coque *nm* coke.

coqueta *nf* **1** *(mujer)* flirt, coquette. **2** *(mueble)* dressing table.

coquetear *vi* to flirt.

coqueteo *nm* flirtation.

coquetería *nf* coquetry, flirting, flirtation.

coraje *nm* **1** *(valor)* courage, toughness. **2** *(ira)* anger. LOC **dar coraje** *fam* to infuriate, make furious: *me da coraje que haya ganado él* it makes me furious that he won. **I** **echarle coraje a** ALGO to put some spirit into STH.

coral' *adj* MÚS choral.
▶ *nf* MÚS *(grupo)* choir, choral society.
▶ *nm* MÚS *(composición)* choral, chorale.

coral² *nm* ZOOL coral.
▶ *nm pl* **corales** coral beads.

coralina *nf* coralline.

coralino,-a *adj* coral.

Corán *nm* Koran.

coránico,-a *adj* Koranic.

coraza *nf* **1** *(armadura)* armour (US armor), cuirass. **2** *(caparazón)* shell, carapace. **3** *fig (protección)* armour (US armor), protection.

corazón *nm* **1** ANAT heart. **2** *fig (parte central)* heart, core: *en el corazón de la ciudad* in the heart of the city. **3** *(de fruta)* core. **4** *(apelativo)* darling, dear, sweetheart. LOC **abrir el corazón a** ALGN *fig* to open one's heart to SB. **I de todo corazón** *fig* sincerely, in all sincerity. **I estar con el corazón en un puño** *fig* to have one's heart in one's mouth. **I estar enfermo del corazón** to have heart trouble.
▶ *nm pl* **corazones** *(naipes)* hearts.

corazonada *nf (sentimiento)* hunch, feeling, inkling: *tuve la corazonada de que él no estaba* I had a hunch that he wasn't there.

corbata *nf* tie, US necktie: *iba con corbata* he was wearing a tie.

corcel *nm* lit steed, charger.

corchea *nf* quaver.

corchete *nm* **1** COST hook and eye, snap fastener. **2** *(signo impreso)* square bracket.

corcho *nm* **1** cork; *(corteza)* cork bark. **2** *(tapón)* cork. **3** *(para pescar, nadar)* float. **4** *(tabla)* cork mat. **5** *(tablón para anuncios, notas)* cork board.

cordada *nf* rope.

cordel *nm* rope, cord.

cordelería *nf* **1** *(oficio)* ropemaking. **2** *(cuerdas)* ropes *pl*.

cordero,-a *nm & nf* **1** lamb. **2** *fig (persona dócil)* lamb, angel.

▶ *nm* **cordero 1** *(piel)* lambskin. **2** *(carne - joven)* lamb; *(- crecido)* mutton. LOC **ser manso como un cordero** to be as gentle as a lamb.

cordial *adj (afectuoso)* cordial, friendly, warm: *una bienvenida cordial* a warm welcome.

cordialidad *nf* cordiality, warmth, friendliness.

cordialmente *adv* **1** cordially, warmly. **2** *(despedida en carta)* sincerely.

cordillera *nf* mountain range, mountain chain.

cordón *nm* **1** *(cuerda)* string. **2** *(de zapatos)* shoelace, shoestring.

cordoncillo *nm* **1** *(en tejido)* rib, ribbing. **2** *(bordado)* braid, piping.

cordura *nf* good sense. LOC **con cordura** sensibly, prudently, wisely.

Corea *nf* Korea. COMP **Corea del Norte** North Korea. **I Corea del Sur** South Korea.

coreano,-a *adj* Korean.
▶ *nm & nf (persona)* Korean.
▶ *nm* **coreano** *(idioma)* Korean.

corear *vt* **1** *(cantar)* to chorus, sing in chorus. **2** *(hablar)* to chorus, speak in chorus. **3** *fig (aclamar)* to applaud.

coreografía *nf* choreography.

coreografiar *vt* to choreograph.

coreógrafo,-a *nm & nf* choreographer.

corindón *nm* corundum.

corinto,-a *adj* maroon.
▶ *nm* **corinto** *(color)* maroon.

cormorán *nm* cormorant.

cornada *nf* goring.

cornalina *nf* cornelian, carnelian.

cornamenta *nf (gen)* horns *pl*; *(del ciervo)* antlers *pl*.

cornamusa *nf* bagpipe.

córnea *nf* cornea.

cornear *vt* to gore.

corneja *nf* crow.

cornejo *nm* dogwood.

córneo,-a *adj* hornlike, corneous.

córner *nm* DEP *(lugar)* corner; *(golpe)* corner, corner kick. LOC **lanzar un córner**

/ sacar un córner / tirar un córner to take a corner.

corneta *nf (instrumento)* bugle.

cornisa *nf* ARQUIT cornice.

coro *nm* **1** MÚS choir. **2** TEAT chorus. ⎡LOC⎤ **a coro** *fig* all together. ▪ **hacer coro** *fig* to join in the chorus.

corola *nf* corolla.

corona *nf* **1** *(aro, cerco)* crown. **2** *(de flores, etc)* wreath, garland, crown. **3** *fig (dignidad real)* King's, Queen's: *el discurso de la corona* the King's speech. **4** *fig (reino)* crown, kingdom. **5** *(aureola)* halo. **6** *(en geometría)* annulus, ring. ⎡COMP⎤ **corona solar** solar corona.

coronación *nf* **1** coronation. **2** *fig (culminación)* crowning.

coronar *vt* to crown. ▸ *vi* to crown.

coronel *nm* colonel.

coronilla *nf (parte de la cabeza)* crown of the head. ⎡LOC⎤ **estar hasta la coronilla** *fam* to be fed up (de, with).

corpiño *nm* bodice.

corporación *nf* corporation. ⎡COMP⎤ **corporación metropolitana** city corporation.

corporativo,-a *adj* corporative, corporate. ⎡COMP⎤ **imagen corporativa** corporate image.

corpulencia *nf* corpulence, stoutness.

corpulento,-a *adj* corpulent, stocky, stout.

corral *nm* **1** *(de casa)* yard, courtyard. **2** *(de granja)* farmyard, US corral.

correa *nf* **1** *(tira de piel)* strap, leather strip. **2** *(de perro)* lead, leash. **3** *(de reloj)* watchstrap. **4** *(cinturón)* belt. **5** TÉC belt.

corrección *nf* **1** *(rectificación)* correction. **2** *(educación)* courtesy, correctness, politeness, good manners *pl*. ⎡LOC⎤ **tratar con corrección** to be polite.

correccional *adj* correctional. ▸ *nm* detention centre, reformatory.

correctamente *adv* **1** *(sin errores)* correctly, accurately. **2** *(con educación)* correctly, politely, properly.

correcto,-a *adj* **1** *(sin errores)* correct, accurate. **2** *(adecuado)* suitable. **3** *(educado)* polite, courteous. **4** *(conducta)* proper.

corrector,-ra *adj* corrective. ▸ *nm & nf (de pruebas impresas)* proofreader.

corredero,-a *adj* sliding: *ventana corredera* sliding window.

corredor,-ra *adj* **1** running. **2** *(ave)* flightless: *ave corredora* flightless bird. ▸ *nm & nf* **1** DEP runner; *(de coches)* driver. **2** FIN broker. ⎡COMP⎤ **corredor,-ra de bolsa** stockbroker. ▪ **corredor,-ra de coches** racing driver. ▪ **corredor,-ra de fondo** long-distance runner. ▸ *nm* corredor *(pasillo)* corridor, gallery.

corregir *vt* **1** *(amendar)* to correct, rectify. **2** *(reprender)* to reprimand, scold, tell off. **3** EDUC to mark.

correlación *nf* correlation.

correlativo,-a *adj* correlative.

correo *nm* **1** *(servicio, correspondencia)* post, US mail. **2** *(persona)* courier. ⎡LOC⎤ **echar al correo** to post, US mail. ▪ **por correo** by post, US by mail. ⎡COMP⎤ **apartado de correos** (post office) box. ▪ **correo aéreo** airmail. ▪ **correo certificado** registered post, US registered mail. ▪ **correo electrónico** electronic mail, e-mail. ▪ **correo urgente** special delivery. ▸ *nm pl* **correos** *(oficina)* post office *sing*.

correr *vi* **1** *(gen)* to run: *se marchó corriendo* she ran off. **2** *(darse prisa)* to rush, hurry: *¡corre, es tarde!* hurry up, it's late! **3** *(viento)* to blow. **4** *(agua)* to flow, run. **5** *(tiempo)* to pass, fly. **6** *(conductor)* to drive fast. **7** *(coche)* to go fast. **8** *(puerta, ventana)* to slide. ▸ *vt* **1** *(distancia)* to cover; *(país)* to travel through. **2** *(carrera)* to run; *(caballo)* to race, run. **3** *(echar)* to close; *(cortina)* to draw; *(cerrojo)* to bolt. **4** *(mover)* to pull up, move, draw up: *corre la mesa* move the table. **5** *(estar expuesto)* to run: *correr un peligro* to run a risk. **6** *(aventura)* to have. ⎡LOC⎤ **a todo correr** at full speed. ▪ **correr mundo** to be a globe-trotter. **I correr un peligro** to be in danger.

▶ *vpr* **correrse 1** *(persona)* to move over; *(objeto)* to shift, slide. **2** *(color, tinta)* to run. **3** *(media)* to ladder. **4** *(avergonzarse)* to blush, go red.

correspondencia *nf* **1** *(gen)* correspondence. **2** *(cartas)* post, US mail. **3** *(de trenes, etc)* connection. [LOC] **mantener correspondencia con** ALGN to correspond with SB. [COMP] **curso por correspondencia** correspondence course.

corresponder *vi* **1** *(ser adecuado)* to become, befit; *(color, aspecto)* to match, go with: *los zapatos no corresponden al vestido* the shoes don't go with the dress. **2** *(encajar)* to correspond (a, to), tally (a, with); *(descripción)* to fit. **3** *(pertenecer)* to belong, pertain: *esta mesa corresponde a mi habitación* this table belongs in my bedroom.

▶ *vt* **1** *(ser el turno)* to be one's turn: *me corresponde a mí* it's my turn. **2** *(en un reparto)* to get. **3** *(incumbir)* to be the job of, be the responsibility of: *eso te corresponde a ti* that's your job. **4** *(devolver)* to return; *(amabilidad)* to repay.

▶ *vpr* **corresponderse 1** *(ajustarse)* to correspond; *(cifras)* to tally: *la dirección que te dio no se corresponde con la que yo tengo* the address he gave you doesn't correspond to the one I have. **2** *(armonizar)* to be in harmony, go with. **3** *(amarse)* to love each other.

correspondiente *adj* **1** *(que corresponde)* corresponding (a, to). **2** *(apropiado)* suitable, appropriate. **3** *(respectivo)* own.

corresponsal *nm o nf* correspondent.

corretear *vi* **1** *fam (correr)* to run about. **2** *fam (vagar)* to hang about.

corrida *nf* **1** *(carrera)* run, race. **2** *(de toros)* bullfight.

corriente *adj* **1** *(común)* ordinary, average: *personas corrientes* ordinary people. **2** *(agua)* running. **3** *(fecha)* current, present: *el cinco del corriente mes* the fifth of this month. **4** *(cuenta)* current. [LOC] **al corriente 1** *(actualizado)* up to date. **2** *(enterado)* aware. **3** *(informado)* informed, in the know: *¿estás al corriente de lo que ha pasado?* do you know what's happened? **I ir a contra corriente** *fig* to go against the tide. **I seguirle la corriente a** ALGN to humour (US humor) SB. **I tener al corriente** to keep informed. **I corriente sanguínea** bloodstream.

▶ *nm (mes)* current month, this month.

▶ *nf* **1** *(masa de agua)* current, stream, flow. **2** *(de aire)* draught (US draft). **3** ELEC current.

corrientemente *adv* usually, normally.

corro *nm* **1** *(cerco)* circle, ring. **2** *(juego)* ring-a-ring o'roses. **3** *(en la bolsa)* round enclosure.

corroer *vt* **1** *(desgastar)* to corrode. **2** GEOL to erode.

corromper *vt* **1** *(pudrir)* to turn bad. **2** *(pervertir)* to corrupt, pervert. **3** *(sobornar)* to bribe.

▶ *vpr* **corromperse 1** *(pudrirse)* to go bad, rot. **2** *(pervertirse)* to become corrupted.

corrosivo,-a *adj* **1** corrosive. **2** *fig* caustic.

▶ *nm* **corrosivo** corrosive.

corrupción *nf* **1** *(putrefacción)* rot, decay. **2** *fig* corruption, degradation. **3** *fig (soborno)* bribery.

corrupto,-a *adj* corrupt.

corruptor,-ra *adj* corrupting.

▶ *nm & nf* corrupter, perverter.

corsario,-a *adj* privateer.

▶ *nm* **corsario** privateer.

corsé *nm* corset.

corsetería *nf* ladies' underwear shop.

corta *nf* tree felling.

cortacésped *nm & nf* lawnmower.

cortacircuitos *nm inv* circuit breaker.

cortado,-a *adj* **1** *(troceado)* cut; *(en lonchas)* sliced. **2** *(leche)* sour. **3** *fam (aturdido)* dumbfounded. [LOC] **quedarse cortado,-a 1** *fam (sin palabras)* to be speechless, be lost for words. **2** *(avergonzado)* to become embarrassed.

▶ *nm* **cortado** *(café)* coffee with a dash of milk.

cortador,-ra *adj* cutting.

▶ *nm & nf (sastre, zapatero)* cutter.

cortadora *nf* cutting machine.

cortafrío *nm* cold chisel.

cortafuego *nm* **1** *(en el campo)* firebreak. **2** *(en un edificio)* firewall. **3** INFORM firewall.

cortante *adj* **1** *(que corta)* cutting, sharp. **2** *fig (aire)* biting. **3** *fig (persona, estilo)* sharp, brusque.

cortaplumas *nm inv* penknife.

cortar *vt* **1** *(gen)* to cut. **2** *(pelo)* to cut, trim. **3** *(árbol)* to cut down. **4** *(carne)* to carve. **5** *(pastel)* to cut up. **6** *(cabeza, teléfono, gas)* to cut off. **7** *(mayonesa, leche)* to curdle. **8** *(piel)* to chap, crack. **9** *(viento, frío)* to chill, bite. **10** COST to cut out. **11** *(interrumpir)* to cut off, interrupt. **12** *(bloquear)* to block: *cortaron la carretera* the road was blocked. **13** *(suprimir)* to cut out. **14** *fig (separar)* to divide, split, cut. LOC **¡corta el rollo!** *fam* knock it off! ∎ **cortar con** ALGN *fam* to split up with SB. ∎ **cortar el bacalao** *fam* to be the boss. ∎ **cortar en seco** *fig* to cut short. ∎ **cortar la digestión** to give one indigestion, upset one's stomach. ∎ **cortar la palabra** to interrupt. ∎ **cortar por lo sano** *fam* to take drastic measures.

▶ *vpr* **cortarse 1** to cut: *este metal se corta fácilmente* this metal cuts easily. **2** *(herirse)* to cut, cut os: *me he cortado* I've cut myself. **3** *(el pelo - por otro)* to have one's hair cut; *(- uno mismo)* to cut one's hair: *¿te has cortado el pelo?* have you had your hair cut? **4** *(piel)* to become chapped. **5** *(leche)* to go off, curdle; *(mayonesa)* to curdle. **6** *(comunicación)* to be cut off.

cortaúñas *nm inv* nail clippers.

corte¹ *nf* **1** *(del rey, etc)* court. **2** *(séquito)* retinue. **3** AM *(tribunal)* court.

▶ *nf pl* **las Cortes** the Spanish Parliament *sing*.

corte² *nm* **1** *(gen)* cut: *me he hecho un corte en el dedo* I've cut my finger. **2** *(filo)* edge. **3** *(sección)* section: *corte horizontal* horizontal section. **4** *(de pelo)* cut, haircut. **5** *(de helado)* wafer, US ice-cream sandwich. **6** *fam fig (vergüenza)* embarrassment: *le daba corte entrar y se quedó fuera* he was too embarrassed to go in so he stayed outside. LOC **dar un corte a** ALGN *fam* to cut SB dead.

cortejar *vt* to court.

cortejo *nm* **1** *(acompañantes)* entourage, retinue. **2** *(galanteo)* courting.

cortés *adj* courteous, polite.

cortesano,-a *adj* **1** *(de la corte)* court. **2** *(cortés)* courteous, courtly.

▶ *nm & nf (de la corte)* courtier.

cortesía *nf* **1** *(educación)* courtesy, politeness. **2** *(en cartas)* formal ending. **3** *(tratamiento)* title. **4** *(reverencia)* bow, curtsy. **5** *(regalo)* present: *esta bolsa es una cortesía de la empresa* this bag is courtesy of the company.

cortina *nf* **1** curtain. **2** *fig* curtain, screen. LOC **correr las cortinas** to draw the curtains. COMP **cortina de humo** *fig* smoke screen.

cortinaje *nm* drapery.

corto,-a *adj* **1** *(extensión)* short: *distancia corta* short distance. **2** *(duración)* short, brief: *una película corta* a short film. **3** *(escaso)* scant, meagre (US meager). **4** *fig (tonto)* thick, dim. **5** *fig (tímido)* shy, timid. LOC **corto,-a de miras** *fam* narrow-minded. ∎ **corto,-a de vista** short-sighted. ∎ **quedarse corto,-a 1** *(ropa)* to become too short: *el pantalón se me ha quedado corto* my trousers have become too short for me. **2** *(calcular mal)* to underestimate, miscalculate: *te quedaste corto con los bocadillos* you didn't make enough sandwiches.

▶ *nm* **corto** short film, short.

cortocircuito *nm* short circuit.

cortometraje *nm* short film, short.

corva *nf* back of the knee.

corzo,-a *nm & nf (macho)* roe buck; *(hembra)* roe deer.

cosa *nf* **1** *(gen)* thing: *coge tus cosas* take your things, take your stuff. **2** *(asunto)* matter, business: *es cosa tuya* it's your business. **3** *(nada)* nothing, not anything: *no hay cosa igual* there's nothing like it.

LOC **como cosa tuya** as if it were your idea. **I como si tal cosa** just like that. **I es cosa de... 1** *(tiempo)* it's time to... **2** *(cuestión)* it's a matter of... **I no valer gran cosa** not to be worth much. **I ser cosa hecha** *fam* to be no sooner said than done.

▶ *nf pl* **cosas** *fam (manías)* hang-ups: *son cosas de niños* kids do that kind of thing.

cosaco,-a *adj* Cossack.
▶ *nm* **cosaco** Cossack.

coscorrón *nm* blow on the head, knock on the head.

cosecante *nf* cosecant.

cosecha *nf* **1** harvest, crop. **2** *(tiempo)* harvest time. **3** *(año del vino)* vintage. LOC **de cosecha propia 1** *(hortalizas, fruta)* home-grown. **2** *fig (ideas, etc)* of one's own invention.

cosechadora *nf* combine harvester.

cosechar *vi* to harvest, reap.
▶ *vt* **1** *(recoger)* to harvest. **2** *(cultivar)* to grow.

coseno *nm* cosine.

coser *vt* **1** *(unir)* to sew; *(un botón)* to sew on; *(pespuntes, etc)* to stitch: *le cosí los pantalones* I sewed up her trousers. **2** MED to stitch up. **3** *(grapar)* to staple together. **4** *fig (unir)* to join.

cosido *nm* **1** sewing. **2** MED stitching.

cosificar *vt* to trivialize, belittle.

cosmética *nf* cosmetics *pl.*

cosmético,-a *adj* cosmetic.
▶ *nm* **cosmético** cosmetic.

cósmico,-a *adj* cosmic.

cosmogonía *nf* cosmogony.

cosmografía *nf* cosmography.

cosmográfico,-a *adj* cosmographic, cosmographical.

cosmología *nf* cosmology.

cosmológico,-a *adj* cosmologic, cosmological.

cosmonauta *nm o nf* cosmonaut.

cosmonave *nf* spaceship, spacecraft.

cosmopolita *adj* cosmopolitan.
▶ *nm o nf* cosmopolitan.

cosmos *nm inv* cosmos.

cosquillas *nf pl* tickling *sing.* LOC **hacer cosquillas a** ALGN to tickle SB. **I tener cosquillas** to be ticklish. **I buscarle las cosquillas a** ALGN *fam* to needle SB, annoy SB.

cosquilleo *nm* tickling.

costa¹ *nf (litoral)* coast, coastline; *(playa)* beach, seaside, US shore: *tenemos una casa en la costa* we have a house at the seaside, US we have a house on the shore.

costa² *nf* FIN cost, price. LOC **a costa de 1** *(aprovechándose)* at the expense of. **2** *(a base de)* by, by dint of, by means of: *lo consiguió a costa de muchos sacrificios* he managed it by making a lot of sacrifices. **I a toda costa** at all costs, at any price.
▶ *nf pl* **costas** JUR costs.

Costa de Marfil *nf* Ivory Coast.

costado *nm* side.
▶ *nm pl* **costados** lineage *sing.* LOC **por los cuatro costados** through and through.

costar *vi* **1** *(valer)* to cost: *¿cuánto costó?* how much was it? **2** *(ser difícil)* to be hard, be difficult; *(resultar difícil)* to be difficult for: *cuesta encontrar trabajo* it's hard to find a job. **3** *(tiempo)* to take: *me costó cuatro horas* it took me four hours. LOC **costar barato,-a** to be cheap. **I costar caro,-a 1** to be expensive, cost a lot. **2** to pay dearly for STH: *esa afirmación le costará cara* he'll pay dearly for saying that. **I costar mucho / costar trabajo** to be difficult, be hard work.

Costa Rica *nf* Costa Rica.

costarricense *adj* Costa Rican.
▶ *nm o nf* Costa Rican.

coste *nm* cost, price, expense. COMP **coste de la vida** cost of living.

costear *vt (pagar)* to pay for, afford: *su padre le costeó el viaje* his father paid for his journey.
▶ *vpr* **costearse** to pay one's way.

costero,-a *adj* coastal, coast.

costilla *nf* **1** ANAT rib. **2** CULIN cutlet.
▶ *nf pl* **costillas** *fam (espalda)* back *sing.*

costillar *nm* ribs *pl.*

costo *nm* cost, price.

costoso,-a *adj* **1** *(caro)* costly, expensive. **2** *(difícil)* hard, difficult.

costra *nf* **1** crust. **2** MED scab.

costumbre *nf* **1** *(hábito)* habit: *tengo la costumbre de comer temprano* I'm in the habit of having lunch early. **2** *(tradición)* custom: *es una costumbre rusa* it's a Russian custom. **3** JUR usage. LOC **como de costumbre** as usual. ▌ **tener por costumbre + inf** to be in the habit of + *ger*. COMP **la fuerza de la costumbre** the force of habit.
▶ *nf pl* **costumbres** *(personales)* ways, manner *sing*; *(de un pueblo)* customs.

costumbrismo *nm* folk literature.

costumbrista *adj* about local customs.
▶ *nm o nf* writer of folk literature.

costura *nf* **1** *(cosido)* sewing. **2** *(línea de puntadas)* seam: *medias sin costura* seamless stockings. **3** *(confección)* dressmaking. COMP **cesto de la costura** sewing basket.

costurera *nf* seamstress.

costurero *nm* **1** *(estuche)* sewing basket, sewing kit. **2** *(mueble)* workbox.

cota¹ *nf* *(traje)* tabard. COMP **cota de malla** coat of mail.

cota² *nf* **1** *(altura)* height above sea level: *la cota mil* one thousand metres above sea level. **2** *(número en mapa)* spot height. **3** *fig (nivel)* level: *la xenofobia está llegando a cotas muy altas* xenophobia is showing an alarming increase.

cotangente *nf* cotangent.

cotejar *vt (gen)* to compare; *(textos)* to collate, compare.

cotejo *nm (gen)* comparison; *(textos)* collation, comparison.

cotidiano,-a *adj* daily, everyday: *la vida cotidiana* everyday life.

cotiledón *nm* cotyledon.

cotilla *nf (faja)* corset.
▶ *nm o nf fam* busybody, gossip.

cotillear *vi fam* to gossip, tittle-tattle.

cotilleo *nm fam* gossip, gossiping, tittle-tattle.

cotillón *nm* **1** *(danza)* cotillion, cotillon. **2** *(fiesta)* party, celebration *especially on New Year's Eve*.

cotización *nf* **1** FIN quotation, market price. **2** *(cuota)* membership fee, subscription.

cotizar *vt* FIN to quote, price.
▶ *vi (pagar cuota)* to pay a subscription.
▶ *vpr* **cotizarse 1** *(acciones)* to sell (a, at): *las acciones del banco se cotizan a diez euros con veintitrés* the bank's shares are selling at ten euros twenty-three. **2** *fig (valorarse)* to be valued, be in demand: *este pintor se cotiza mucho* this painter is in great demand.

coto¹ *nm* **1** *(terreno)* enclosure, reserve. **2** *(poste)* boundary mark. **3** *(límite)* restriction. LOC **poner coto a** ALGO to put a stop to STH. COMP **coto de caza** game preserve.

coto² *nm (pez)* miller's thumb.

cotorra *nf* **1** *(ave)* parrot. **2** *fam fig* chatterbox. LOC **hablar como una cotorra** to be a chatterbox.

cotorrear *vi fam fig* to chatter, prattle (on).

cotorreo *nm fam fig* chatter, prattle.

COU *abrev* EDUC **(Curso de Orientación Universitaria)** ≈ *former pre-university course.*

cowboy *nm* cowboy.

coxis *nm inv* coccyx.

coyote *nm* coyote.

coyuntura *nf* **1** ANAT joint, articulation. **2** *fig (circunstancia)* moment, juncture. COMP **coyuntura económica** economic situation.

coz *nf* kick. LOC **dar una coz** to kick.

crac *nm* **1** *(quiebra)* crash, bankruptcy: *el crac de la bolsa de Nueva York* the Wall Street crash. **2** *(onomatopeya)* crack, snap: *el brazo me hizo crac* my arm gave a crack.

crack *nm (persona)* star, ace: *es un auténtico crack del fútbol* he's a crack football player.

craneal *adj* cranial.

craneano,-a *adj* cranial.

cráneo *nm* cranium, skull. LOC **ir de cráneo** *fam* to have a lot on one's plate, have one's work cut out.

cráter *nm* crater.

crawl *nm* crawl.

creación *nf* **1** *(gen)* creation. **2** *(fundación)* foundation, establishment, setting up.

creador,-ra *adj* creative.
▶ *nm & nf* creator, maker.

crear *vt* **1** *(gen)* to create: *crear problemas* to create problems. **2** *(fundar)* to found, establish; *(partido)* to set up. **3** *(inventar)* to invent.
▶ *vpr* **crearse** to make, make for os: *crearse enemigos* to make enemies for os.

creatividad *nf* creativity.

creativo,-a *adj* creative.

crecer *vi* **1** *(persona, planta)* to grow: *has crecido mucho* you've grown a lot. **2** *(incrementar)* to increase, grow, get bigger: *la población ha crecido un uno por ciento* the population has grown by one per cent. **3** *(corriente, marea)* to rise. **4** *(luna)* to wax.
▶ *vpr* **crecerse** *(tomar mayor fuerza)* to grow in confidence: *se crece ante las dificultades* he comes into his own when faced with problems.

crecido,-a *adj* **1** *(persona)* grown, grown-up. **2** *(cantidad)* big, large. **3** *(río)* in flood, in spate.

creciente *adj* **1** *(que crece)* growing; *(que aumenta)* increasing: *un interés creciente* an increasing interest. **2** *(precios)* rising. **3** *(luna)* crescent (in the first quarter).
▶ *nf (de agua)* flood, spate.

crecimiento *nm* **1** *(desarrollo)* growth, increase. **2** *(subida)* rise. **3** *(de un río)* flooding, rising.

credibilidad *nf* credibility.

crédito *nm* **1** COM credit. **2** *(confianza)* credit, belief, credence. **3** *(fama)* reputation, standing. LOC **a crédito** on credit. ▮ **dar crédito a** *(creer)* to believe (in): *no doy crédito a mis oídos* I can't believe what I'm hearing. ▮ **ser digno,-a de crédito** to be reliable. COMP **crédito hi-**

potecario debt secured by a mortgage.

credo *nm* fig *(creencias)* credo, creed.

credulidad *nf* credulity, gullibility.

crédulo,-a *adj* credulous, gullible.

creencia *nf* belief.

creer *vt* **1** *(dar por cierto)* to believe: *si no lo veo no lo creo* I've got to see it to believe it. **2** *(suponer, opinar)* to think, suppose: *¿y tú que crees?* what do you think? **3** *(tener fe)* to believe. LOC **creer a ciencia cierta** to be convinced. ▮ **¡no creas!** do you really think so?, I'm not so sure. ▮ **¡ya lo creo!** of course!
▶ *vpr* **creerse** **1** *(aceptar)* to believe: *no me lo creo* I don't believe it, I can't believe it. **2** *(considerarse)* to think: *¿quién te has creído que eres?* who do you think you are? LOC **¡que te crees tú eso!** that's what you think!

creíble *adj* credible, believable.

creído,-a *adj* arrogant, vain, conceited. LOC **ser un creído,-a** to be full of os.

crema *nf* **1** *(de leche, licor, ungüento)* cream. **2** *(natillas)* custard. **3** *(betún)* shoe polish. **4** fig *(lo mejor)* cream. COMP **crema bronceadora** suntan cream. ▮ **crema de afeitar** shaving cream. ▮ **crema hidratante** moisturizing cream.
▶ *adj* cream, cream coloured (US cream colored).

cremación *nf* cremation.

crematorio *nm* crematorium.

cremoso,-a *adj* creamy: *queso cremoso* full-fat cheese.

crepe *nf (torta)* pancake, crepe.

crepé *nm (tejido, caucho)* crepe.

crepería *nf* creperie.

crepitar *vi* to crackle.

crepúsculo *nm* twilight.

cresta *nf* **1** *(de ave)* crest; *(de gallo)* comb. **2** *(de pelo)* toupée. **3** *(de montaña, ola)* crest. LOC **estar en la cresta de la ola** *fam* to be on the crest of a wave.

Creta *nf* Crete.

cretense *adj* Cretan.
▶ *nm o nf* Cretan.

cretino,-a *adj* stupid, cretinous.
▶ *nm & nf* cretin, idiot.
creyente *adj* believing.
▶ *nm o nf* believer.
cría *nf* **1** *(acto de criar)* nursing; *(de animal)* breeding, raising. **2** *(cachorro)* young. **3** *(camada - ovíparos)* brood; *(- mamíferos)* litter.
criada *nf* maid.
criadero *nm* **1** *(de plantas)* nursery; *(de animales)* breeding farm; *(de peces)* hatchery. **2** *(mina)* seam. COMP **criadero de ostras** oyster bed.
criado,-a *adj* *(animal)* reared, raised; *(persona)* bred, brought up.
▶ *nm & nf* servant.
criador *nm & nf* breeder.
criar *vt* **1** *(educar niños)* to bring up, rear, care for: *lo crió una tía* his aunt brought him up. **2** *(nutrir)* to feed *(con, -)*; *(con pecho)* to suckle, nurse, breast-feed. **3** *(animales)* to breed, raise, rear. **4** *(producir)* to have, grow; *(vinos)* to make, mature.
▶ *vpr* **criarse 1** *(crecer)* to grow; *(formarse)* to be brought up. **2** *(producirse)* to grow.
criatura *nf* **1** creature. **2** *(niño)* baby, child. **3** *fig* baby.
cribar *vt* **1** *(colar)* to sift, sieve. **2** *fig (seleccionar)* to screen.
cric *nm* jack.
cricquet *nm* cricket.
crimen *nm* **1** *(delito)* crime. **2** *(asesinato)* murder.
criminal *adj* **1** criminal. **2** *fam (muy malo)* awful, criminal, appalling.
▶ *nm o nf* criminal.
criminalista *nm o nf (abogado)* criminal lawyer.
criminología *nf* criminology.
crin [también se usa en plural con el mismo significado] *nf* mane.
crío,-a *nm & nf fam* kid, child.
▶ *adj fam* young: *todavía eres muy crío* you're still too young. LOC **ser un crío,-a** *fam* to be childish.
criollo,-a *adj* Creole.
▶ *nm & nf (persona)* Creole.
▶ *nm (idioma)* Creole.

cripta *nf* crypt.
críquet *nm* cricket.
crisálida *nf* chrysalis.
crisantemo *nm* chrysanthemum.
crisis *nf inv* **1** *(dificultad)* crisis. **2** *(ataque)* fit, attack: *crisis de asma* asthma attack. **3** *(escasez)* shortage: *crisis de alimentos* food shortage. LOC **estar en crisis** to be in crisis, reach crisis point. COMP **crisis de gobierno** cabinet crisis. ‖ **crisis nerviosa** nervous breakdown.
crisma *nm & nf fam (cabeza)* head, nut.
crisol *nm* **1** crucible. **2** *fig* melting pot.
crispación *nf fig* tension: *un clima de crispación* a tense atmosphere.
crispar *vt fig (irritar)* to irritate, annoy, infuriate: *ese tipo me crispa* that guy infuriates me. LOC **crispar los nervios a ALGN** *fig* to get on SB's nerves.
▶ *vpr* **crisparse** *fig (irritarse)* to get annoyed, get angry.
cristal *nm* **1** *(mineral)* crystal. **2** *(vidrio)* glass. **3** *(de ventana)* window pane, pane. **4** *(de lente)* lens. **5** *(de coche)* window.
▶ *nm pl* **cristales 1** *(trozos)* glass *sing*: *ten cuidado, hay cristales por el suelo* be careful, there's some broken glass on the floor. **2** *(ventanas)* windows. COMP **botella de cristal** glass bottle. ‖ **cristal de cuarzo** quartz crystal.
cristalera *nf* **1** *(mueble)* display cabinet. **2** *(escaparate)* window, shop window. **3** *(conjunto de cristales)* windows *pl*; *(puertas)* glass doors *pl*; *(techo)* glass roof.
cristalería *nf* **1** *(fábrica)* glassworks. **2** *(tienda)* glassware shop. **3** *(conjunto)* glassware; *(vasos)* glasses *pl*.
cristalero,-a *nm & nf* glazier.
cristalino,-a *adj* transparent, crystal-clear.
▶ *nm* **cristalino** crystalline lens.
cristalización *nf* **1** crystallization. **2** *fig* consolidation.
cristalizar *vt* to crystallize.
▶ *vi* **1** to crystallize. **2** *fig* to crystallize (en, into).
▶ *vpr* **cristalizarse** to crystallize.

cristalografía *nf* crystallography.

cristiandad *nf* Christendom.

cristianismo *nm* Christianity.

cristiano,-a *adj* Christian.
▶ *nm* Christian.

criterio *nm* 1 *(en lógica)* criterion. 2 *(juicio)* judgement, discernment. 3 *(opinión)* opinion, point of view.

criticar *vt* to criticize.
▶ *vi (murmurar)* to gossip.

crítico,-a *adj* critical.
▶ *nm & nf* critic.

Croacia *nf* Croatia.

croar *vi* to croak.

croata *adj* Croatian, Croat.
▶ *nm o nf (persona)* Croat, Croatian.
▶ *nm (idioma)* Croat, Croatian.

crocante *nm* almond brittle.

crocanti *nm* almond brittle.

croché *nm* crochet.

croissant *nm* croissant.

croissantería *nf* croissant shop.

crol *nm* crawl.

cromado,-a *adj* chrome.
▶ *nm* **cromado** chroming.

cromar *vt* to chrome.

cromático,-a *adj* chromatic.

cromatismo *nm* chromatism.

cromo *nm* 1 *(metal)* chromium, chrome. 2 *(estampa)* picture card, sticker: *un álbum de cromos* a picture-card album. LOC **ir hecho,-a un cromo** *fam* to look a sight.

cromosoma *nm* chromosome.

crónica *nf* 1 *(gen)* account, chronicle. 2 *(en periódico)* article, column, feature. 3 RAD TV *(programa)* programme (US program); *(reportaje)* feature, report. 4 HIST chronicle.

crónico,-a *adj* 1 chronic. 2 *fig* deeply rooted.

cronista *nm o nf* 1 HIST chronicler. 2 *(de prensa)* columnist, feature writer. 3 RAD TV commentator.

cronología *nf* chronology.

cronológico,-a *adj* chronological.

cronometrar *vt* to time.

cronómetro *nm* 1 chronometer. 2 DEP stopwatch.

croqueta *nf* croquette.

croquis *nm inv* sketch, outline.

cros *nm inv (a pie)* cross-country race; *(en moto)* motocross race.

cruasán *nm* croissant.

cruce *nm* 1 cross, crossing. 2 AUTO crossroads. 3 *(de razas)* crossbreeding. 4 *(interferencia telefónica, etc)* crossed line: *hay un cruce* there's a crossed line. 5 ELEC short circuit.

crucero *nm* 1 *(buque)* cruiser. 2 *(viaje)* cruise.

crucial *adj* 1 crucial. 2 *fig* crucial, critical.

crucifijo *nm* crucifix.

crucifixión *nf* crucifixion.

crucigrama *nm* crossword (puzzle).

crudeza *nf* 1 *(rudeza)* crudeness, rudeness, coarseness. 2 *(del clima)* harshness.

crudo,-a *adj* 1 *(sin cocer)* raw; *(poco hecho)* underdone: *la carne está cruda* the meat is underdone, the meat isn't cooked enough. 2 *fig (duro)* crude, coarse. 3 *(color)* natural, unbleached. 4 *(clima)* harsh. LOC **verlo muy crudo** *fam* not to hold out much hope.
▶ *nm* **crudo** *(petróleo)* crude oil, crude.

cruel *adj (persona)* cruel (con/para, to).

crueldad *nf* 1 cruelty. 2 *(dureza)* harshness, severity.

cruelmente *adv* cruelly.

crujido *nm* 1 *(de puerta)* creak, creaking. 2 *(de patatas fritas)* crunching. 3 *(seda, papel)* rustle, rustling. 4 *(de dientes)* grinding.

crujiente *adj* 1 *(alimentos)* crunchy. 2 *(seda)* rustling.

crujir *vi* 1 *(puerta)* to creak. 2 *(patatas fritas)* to crunch. 3 *(seda, hojas)* to rustle. 4 *(dientes)* to grind.

crustáceo *nm* crustacean.

cruz *nf* 1 *(gen)* cross. 2 *(de moneda)* tails *pl*: *¿cara o cruz?* heads or tails?

cruzada *nf* 1 HIST crusade. 2 *(campaña)* campaign.

cruzar *vt* **1** *(gen)* to cross: *cruzar una calle* to cross a street. **2** *(poner atravesado)* to lay across; *(estar atravesado)* to lie across. **3** *(en geometría)* to intersect. **4** *(animales)* to cross. **5** *(miradas, palabras)* to exchange. `LOC` **cruzar a nado** to swim across. **cruzar los brazos** to fold one's arms.

▶ *vpr* **cruzarse 1** *(encontrarse)* to cross each other. **2** *(intercambiarse)* to exchange.

cuaderno *nm (libreta)* notebook, journal; *(escolar)* exercise book.

cuadra *nf* **1** *(establo)* stable. **2** AM *(manzana)* block, block of houses.

cuadrado,-a *adj* **1** *(forma)* square. **2** *fam (persona)* broad, stocky. **3** *fig (mente)* rigid, one-track.

▶ *nm* **cuadrado** square. `LOC` **elevar al cuadrado** to square.

cuadragésimo,-a *adj* fortieth.

▶ *nm & nf* fortieth.

✎ Consulta también **sexto,-a.**

cuadrangular *adj* quadrangular.

cuadrángulo *nm* quadrangle.

cuadrante *nm* **1** *(reloj)* sundial. **2** *(instrumento)* quadrant. **3** *(cojín)* square pillow.

cuadrar *vt* **1** *(dar figura cuadrada)* to square, make square. **2** *(geometría, matemáticas)* to square. **3** COM to balance.

▶ *vi* **1** *(coincidir)* to square, agree. **2** COM to tally, add up: *las cuentas de este mes no cuadran* the accounts don't add up this month. **3** *fig (ir bien)* to suit: *el estilo no cuadra con el tema* the style doesn't suit the subject.

cuádriceps *nm inv* quadriceps.

cuadrícula *nf* squares *pl*, grid.

cuadriculado,-a *adj* squared.

▶ *nm* **cuadriculado** squares *pl*, grid.

cuadricular *vt* to square, divide into squares.

▶ *adj* squared.

cuadrienio *nm* quadrennium.

cuadriga *nf* chariot.

cuadrilátero,-a *adj* quadrilateral, four-sided.

▶ *nm* **cuadrilátero** *(boxeo)* ring.

cuadrilla *nf* **1** *(grupo)* party, gang. **2** *(de bandidos, etc)* gang, band. **3** *(de obreros)* gang, team.

cuadro *nm* **1** *(cuadrado)* square. **2** *(pintura)* painting, picture. **3** TEAT scene. **4** *(descripción)* description, picture. **5** *(dirigentes)* leaders *pl*; *(personal)* staff. **6** *(conjunto de datos)* chart, graph. `LOC` **a cuadros** checked, US checkered: *tela a cuadros* checked (US checkered) cloth. `COMP` **cuadro clínico** clinical pattern. **cuadro sinóptico** diagram, chart.

cuadrúpedo,-a *adj* quadruped.

▶ *nm* **cuadrúpedo** quadruped.

cuádruple *adj* quadruple, fourfold.

cuadruplicar *vt* to quadruple.

▶ *vi* to quadruple.

cuajada *nf (leche)* curd; *(requesón)* cottage cheese.

cuajar *vt* **1** *(gen)* to coagulate; *(leche)* to curdle; *(sangre)* to clot. **2** *(huevo)* to set.

▶ *vi* **1** *(nieve)* to lie. **2** *fig (tener éxito)* to be a success, come off: *la cosa no cuajó* it didn't come off.

▶ *vpr* **cuajarse 1** to coagulate; *(leche)* to curdle; *(sangre)* clot. **2** *(huevo)* to set.

cual *pron* **1** *(precedido de artículo - persona)* who, whom: *la gente a la cual preguntamos* the people whom we asked. **2** *(precedido de artículo - cosa)* which: *la ciudad en la cual nací* the city where I was born. `LOC` **cada cual** everyone, everybody.

▶ *adv fml* as, like: *se enamoró cual si tuviese quince años* he fell in love like a teenager.

cuál *pron* **1** *(interrogativo)* which, which one, what: *¿cuál es el más alto?* which one is the tallest? **2** *(valor distributivo)* some. **3** *(exclamativo)* how, what: *¡cuál no sería mi asombro!* imagine my amazement! `LOC` **a cuál más** equally: *a cuál más listo* each as clever as the other.

▶ *adj (interrogativo)* which.

cualidad *nf* **1** *(de persona)* quality, attribute. **2** *(de cosa)* quality, property.

cualitativo,-a *adj* qualitative.

cualquier *adj (indefinido)* any: *cualquier otro día* any other day; *cualquier cosa* anything; *cualquier persona* anyone.

✎ Consulta también **cualquiera.**

cualquiera *adj* **1** *(indefinido)* any: *un día cualquiera* any day. **2** *(ordinario)* ordinary: *no es una corbata cualquiera* it's not an ordinary tie.
▶ *pron* **1** *(persona indeterminada)* anybody, anyone; *(cosa indeterminada)* any, any one: *cualquiera lo compraría* anybody would buy it. **2** *(nadie)* nobody: *¡cualquiera lo coge!* nobody would take it!
▶ *nf* **cualquiera que** *(persona)* whoever; *(cosa)* whatever, whichever: *cualquiera que diga eso, miente* whoever says that is lying.

cuan *adv* [se usa sólo antes de adjetivo y de adverbio] *fml* as: *cayó cuan largo era* he fell flat on the floor.

✎ Consulta también **cuanto**.

cuán *adv* [se usa sólo antes de adjetivo y de adverbio] *(interrogativo)* how: *¡cuán idiota!* how stupid!

✎ Consulta también **cuanto**.

cuando *adv* *(tiempo)* when: *cuando tenía diez años* when he was ten.
▶ *conj* **1** *(temporal)* when, whenever: *ven a verme cuando quieras* come and see me whenever you want. **2** *(condicional)* if: *cuando él lo dice* if he says so. **3** *(causal)* since. LOC **de vez en cuando** now and then, from time to time. ∥ **hasta cuando** until.
▶ *prep* during, at the time of: *cuando la guerra* during the war.

cuándo *adv* *(interrogativo)* when: *¿cuándo es tu cumpleaños?* when is your birthday?
▶ *nm* when: *no sé el cómo ni el cuándo* I don't know how or when.

cuantía *nf* **1** *(cantidad)* quantity; *(importe)* amount: *la cuantía de una factura* the amount of a bill. **2** *(dimensión)* extent: *la cuantía del desastre ecológico* the extent of the ecological disaster.

cuantitativo,-a *adj* quantitative.

cuanto *nm* FÍS quantum: *la teoría de los cuantos* the quantum theory.

cuánto,-a *adj* **1** *(pregunta singular)* how much; *(- plural)* how many: *¿cuántos años tienes?* how old are you? **2** *(exclama-*

ción) what a lot of, so many, so much: *¡cuánta gente!* there are so many people!, what a lot of people!
▶ *pron (singular)* how much; *(plural)* how many: *¿cuánto es?* how much is it?
▶ *adv* how, how much: *¡cuánto me alegro!* I'm so glad!

cuanto,-a³ *adj (singular)* as much as; *(plural)* as many as: *puedes beber cuanta agua quieras* you can drink as much water as you want. LOC **cuanto antes** as soon as possible. ∥ **en cuanto** as soon as, when: *en cuanto llegue dile...* as soon as he arrives tell him… ∥ **unos,-as cuantos,-as** some, a few.
▶ *pron* **1** *(singular)* everything, all: *escribe cuanto quieras* write as much as you want. **2** *(plural)* all who, everybody who: *cuantos entraron se asustaron* everybody who came in was frightened.

cuarcita *nf* quartzite.

cuarenta *adj (cardinal)* forty; *(ordinal)* fortieth. LOC **cantarle las cuarenta a** ALGN to give SB a piece of one's mind.
▶ *nm (número)* forty.

✎ Consulta también **seis**.

cuarentavo,-a *adj* fortieth.
▶ *nm & nf* fortieth.

✎ Consulta también **sexto,-a**.

cuarentena *nf* **1** *(exacto)* forty; *(aproximado)* about forty. **2** MED quarantine. LOC **poner a** ALGN **en cuarentena** MED to quarantine SB, put SB in quarantine.

cuaresma *nf* Lent.

cuarta *nf* **1** *(palmo)* span. **2** *(cuadrante)* quadrant.

✎ Consulta también **cuarto,-a**.

cuartear *vt* **1** *(dividir en cuatro)* to quarter, divide into four. **2** *(descuartizar)* to quarter. **3** *(rajar)* to crack.
▶ *vpr* **cuartearse** *(rajarse)* to crack, split.

cuartel *nm* MIL barracks *pl*.

cuarteto *nm* quartet.

cuartilla *nf* sheet of paper.

cuarto nm 1 (parte) quarter: un cuarto de hora a quarter of an hour. 2 (de animal) quarter. 3 (de ropa) quarter: un chaquetón tres cuartos a three-quarter length jacket. 4 (habitación) room. [LOC] de tres al cuarto fam worthless, third-rate. ▐ estar sin un cuarto fam to be broke. ▐ tres cuartos de lo mismo fam almost exactly the same. [COMP] cuarto creciente first quarter. ▐ cuarto de baño bathroom. ▐ cuartos de final DEP quarter finals.
 ▶ nm pl **cuartos** fam (dinero) money sing, dough sing.

cuarto,-a adj (ordinal) fourth: llegó cuarto he arrived in fourth place, he came fourth.
 ▶ nm & nf fourth.

✎ Consulta también sexto,-a.

cuarzo nm quartz.

cuaternario,-a adj quaternary.
 ▶ nm el cuaternario the quaternary.

cuatrienio nm quadrennium, four-year period.

cuatrimestral adj (en frecuencia) four-monthly; (en duración) four-month.

cuatrimestre nm four-month period: en el primer cuatrimestre de 2007 in the first four months of 2007.

cuatrisílabo,-a adj quadrisyllabic.
 ▶ nm cuatrisílabo quadrisyllable.

cuatro adj (cardinal) four; (ordinal) fourth. [LOC] caer cuatro gotas fam to rain very lightly, spit. ▐ decirle cuatro cosas a ALGN to tell SB off. [COMP] cuatro gatos fam just a few people, hardly anyone.
 ▶ nm (número) four.

✎ Consulta también seis.

cuatrocientos,-as adj four hundred.
 ▶ nm cuatrocientos (número) four hundred.

✎ Consulta también seis.

cuba nf cask, barrel.

Cuba nf Cuba.

cubano,-a adj Cuban.
 ▶ nm & nf Cuban.

cubertería nf cutlery.

cubeta nf 1 (rectangular) tray, tank, dish. 2 (cubo) bucket.

cúbico,-a adj cubic: raíz cúbica cube root.

cubierta nf 1 (gen) cover, covering. 2 (de libro) cover. 3 ARQUIT roof. 4 (de neumático) tyre (US tire). 5 (de barco, avión) deck. [LOC] en cubierta on deck.

cubierto,-a adj 1 (gen) covered. 2 (cielo) overcast. 3 (plaza) filled.
 ▶ nm cubierto 1 (techumbre) cover. 2 (en la mesa) place setting. [LOC] ponerse a cubierto to take cover. ▐ tener las espaldas cubiertas fam to be well-heeled.
 ▶ nm pl cubiertos cutlery sing.

cubilete nm 1 (molde) mould (US mold). 2 (de dados) dice cup, dice shaker; (juego) cup.

cubismo nm cubism.

cubista adj cubist.
 ▶ nm o nf cubist.

cubito nm 1 little cube. 2 (de hielo) ice cube.

cúbito nm cubitus.

cubo¹ nm 1 (recipiente) bucket. 2 (de rueda) hub. [COMP] cubo de la basura rubbish bin, US garbage can.

cubo² nm MAT cube. [LOC] elevar al cubo to cube.

cubrecama nm bedspread.

cubrir vt 1 (gen) to cover. 2 CULIN to coat (de, with). 3 (poner tejado) to put a roof on. 4 (niebla, etc) to shroud (de, in), cloak. 5 (ocultar) to hide. 6 (llenar) to fill (de, with), cover (de, with): cubrir de agua to fill with water. 7 (alcanzar) to come up: el agua le cubría hasta los tobillos the water came up to his ankles.
 ▶ vpr cubrirse 1 (abrigarse) to cover os. 2 (la cabeza) to put one's hat on. 3 fig (protegerse) to protect os. 4 (cielo) to become overcast. 5 (llenarse) to be filled.

cucaña nf (palo, juego) greasy pole.

cucaracha nf cockroach.

cuchara nf spoon.

cucharada *nf* spoonful. `COMP` **cucharada colmada** heaped spoonful. ‖ **cucharada rasa** level spoonful.

cucharadita *nf* teaspoonful.

cucharilla *nf* teaspoon. `COMP` **cucharilla de café** coffee spoon.

cucharita *nf* teaspoon.

cucharón *nm* ladle.

cuchichear *vi* to whisper.

cuchicheo *nm* whispering.

cuchilla *nf (hoja)* blade. `COMP` **cuchilla de afeitar** razor blade.

cuchillada *nf (golpe)* stab, slash; *(herida)* stab wound, knife wound.

cuchillería *nf* cutler's shop.

cuchillo *nm* **1** knife. **2** ARQUIT support.

cuclillas `LOC` **en cuclillas** crouching. ‖ **ponerse en cuclillas** to crouch down.

cuclillo *nm* cuckoo.

cuco *nm (insecto)* caterpillar.

cuco,-a *adj* **1** *fam (coquetón)* cute. **2** *(taimado)* shrewd, crafty.
▶ *nm* **cuco** *(ave)* cuckoo.

cucú *nm* **1** *(canto)* cuckoo. **2** *(reloj)* cuckoo clock.

cucurucho *nm* **1** *(de papel)* paper cone. **2** *(helado)* cornet, cone. **3** *(capirote)* pointed hood.

cuello *nm* **1** ANAT neck. **2** *(de camisa, vestido, abrigo)* collar; *(de jersey)* neck: *un jersey de cuello alto* a polo neck jumper, US a turtleneck jumper. **3** *(de botella)* bottleneck.

cuenca *nf* **1** *(escudilla)* wooden bowl. **2** ANAT socket. **3** GEOG basin. **4** *(minera)* coalfield.

cuenco *nm (vasija)* earthenware bowl.

cuenta *nf* **1** *(bancaria)* account. **2** *(factura)* bill. **3** *(cálculo)* count, counting. **4** *(de collar, etc)* bead. `LOC` **caer en la cuenta** to realize: *y entonces caí en la cuenta de que...* and then I realized that..., and then it dawned on me that.... ‖ **en resumidas cuentas** in short. ‖ **hacer cuentas** to do sums. ‖ **más de la cuenta** too much, too many: *comió más de la cuenta* she ate too much. ‖ **pedir cuentas** to ask for an explanation. ‖ **por la cuenta que le trae** in one's own interest. ‖

sacar cuentas to work out. ‖ **tener en cuenta** to take into account. `COMP` **cuenta atrás** countdown. ‖ **cuenta corriente** current account. ‖ **cuenta de correo electrónico** e-mail account.

cuentagotas *nm inv* dropper.

cuentakilómetros *nm inv (de velocidad)* speedometer; *(de distancia)* mileometer.

cuentarrevoluciones *nm inv* rev counter.

cuentavueltas *nm inv* rev counter.

cuentista *adj fam* overdramatic.
▶ *nm o nf* **1** *(autor)* story writer; *(narrador)* storyteller. **2** *fam (que exagera)* over-dramatic person; *(que miente)* fibber, liar.

cuento *nm* **1** *(relato)* story, tale. **2** LIT short story. **3** *fam (chisme)* gossip. **4** *fam (embuste)* fib, story. `LOC` **dejarse de cuentos 1** *fam (ir al grano)* to get to the point. **2** *(decir mentiras)* to stop telling fibs. ‖ **ir con el cuento a** ALGN to go and tell SB. ‖ **tener mucho cuento** *fam* to make a lot of fuss. ‖ **venir a cuento** to be pertinent. `COMP` **cuento chino** tall story. ‖ **cuento de hadas** fairy tale.

cuerda *nf* **1** *(cordel)* rope, string. **2** *(instrumento)* string, cord; *(voz)* voice. **3** *(de reloj)* spring: *dar cuerda a un reloj* to wind up a watch. **4** *(en geometría)* chord. **5** DEP interior. `COMP` **cuerdas vocales** vocal chords.
▶ *nf pl* **cuerdas 1** *(boxeo)* ropes. **2** MÚS strings.

cuerdo,-a *adj* **1** *(persona)* sane. **2** *(acción)* prudent, sensible.
▶ *nm & nf (persona)* sane person, person in one's right mind.

cuerno *nm* **1** horn; *(de ciervo)* antlers *pl*. **2** *(de antena)* antlers *pl*. **3** MÚS horn.
▶ *interj* golly!, gosh!

cuero *nm* **1** *(de animal)* skin, hide. **2** *(curtido)* leather: *pantalón de cuero* leather trousers. **3** *(odre)* wineskin. **4** *(balón)* ball. `LOC` **quedarse en cueros** *fam* to strip off.

cuerpo *nm* **1** ANAT body. **2** *(constitución)* build. **3** *(figura)* figure. **4** *(tronco)* trunk.

5 *(grupo)* body, force, corps: *el cuerpo de bomberos* the fire brigade (US the fire department). **6** *(cadáver)* corpse, body. **7** QUÍM substance. **8** FÍS body. **9** DEP length. LOC **cuerpo a cuerpo** hand-to-hand. **de cuerpo entero** full-length. **en cuerpo y alma** *fig* heart and soul, body and soul. COMP **cuerpo diplomático** diplomatic corps. **cuerpo geométrico** regular solid. **cuerpos celestes** heavenly bodies.

cuervo *nm (córvido en general)* crow; *(específico)* raven.

cuesta *nf (pendiente)* slope. LOC **a cuestas** on one's back, on one's shoulders. **hacérsele a uno ALGO cuesta arriba** *fig* to find STH an uphill struggle, find STH very difficult. **ir cuesta abajo** *fig* to go downhill.

cuestión *nf* **1** *(pregunta)* question. **2** *(asunto)* business, matter, question. **3** *(discusión)* dispute, quarrel, argument. LOC **en cuestión** in question. **en cuestión de...** *(tiempo)* in just a few..., in a matter of... **eso es otra cuestión** that's a whole different matter.

cuestionable *adj* questionable.

cuestionar *vt* to question.

cuestionario *nm* questionnaire.

cueva *nf* cave.

cuidado *nm* **1** *(atención)* care, carefulness. **2** *(recelo)* worry.
▶ *interj* look out!, watch out!: *¡cuidado con la moto!* mind the motorbike! LOC **andarse con cuidado** to go carefully. «**Cuidado con el perro**» «Beware of the dog». **con cuidado** carefully. **tener cuidado** to be careful. **traer sin cuidado** not to care. COMP **cuidados intensivos** intensive care *sing*.

cuidador,-ra *nm & nf* keeper.

cuidadoso,-a *adj* **1** *(atento)* careful. **2** *(celoso)* cautious.

cuidar *vt* to look after, take care of, care for.
▶ *vpr* **cuidarse** to take care of os, look after os: *¡cuídate mucho!* take good care of yourself!

culebra *nf* snake.

culinario,-a *adj* culinary, cooking: *arte culinario* cuisine.

culminación *nf* culmination, climax.

culminante *adj (momento)* culminating, climatic; *(punto)* highest.

culminar *vi* **1** to reach a peak. **2** *fig (acabar)* to finish, end.

culpa *nf* **1** *(culpabilidad)* guilt, blame. **2** *(falta)* fault: *esto es culpa mía* it's my fault. LOC **echar la culpa a ALGN** to put the blame on SB. **tener la culpa** to be to blame (de, for): *yo no tengo la culpa* I'm not to blame, it's not my fault.

culpabilidad *nf* guilt, culpability.

culpable *adj* guilty.
▶ *nm o nf* offender, culprit.

culpar *vt* **1** *(gen)* to blame (de, for). **2** *(de un delito)* to accuse (de, of).

cultivar *vt* **1** to cultivate, farm. **2** *(ejercitar facultades)* to work at, practise (US practice), improve: *cultivar la memoria* to improve one's memory. **3** *(en biología)* to produce. LOC **cultivar las amistades** *fig* to cultivate friendships.

cultivo *nm* **1** *(acción)* cultivation, farming. **2** *(cosecha)* crop. **3** BIOL culture. **4** *fig (desarrollo)* development, growth.

culto,-a *adj* **1** *(persona)* cultured, educated. **2** *(estilo)* refined.
▶ *nm* **culto** worship.

cultura *nf* culture. LOC **de cultura** educated.

cultural *adj* cultural.

cumbre *nf* **1** *(de montaña)* summit, top. **2** *fig (culminación)* pinnacle. **3** *(reunión)* summit conference, summit meeting.

cumpleaños *nm inv* birthday.

cumplido,-a *adj* **1** *(completo)* complete, full. **2** *(abundante)* large, ample. **3** *(perfecto)* perfect. **4** *(educado)* polite, courteous.
▶ *nm* **cumplido** compliment. LOC **sin cumplidos** informally.

cumplidor,-ra *adj (que cumple)* who delivers the goods: *es una chica muy cumplidora* she always delivers the goods, she always fulfils her promises.

cumplir *vt* **1** *(orden)* to carry out; *(deseo)* to fulfil (US fulfill); *(deber)* to do. **2** *(promesa)* to keep. **3** JUR *(ley)* to observe, abide by; *(pena)* to serve. **4** *(años)* to be, turn: *¡que cumplas muchos más!* many happy returns! **5** *(satisfacer)* to do, carry out, fulfil (US fulfill). LOC **cumplir con el deber** to do one's duty. **‖ cumplir con su palabra** to keep one's word. **‖ para cumplir** as a formality.
▶ *vi* **1** *(plazo)* to expire, end. **2** *(deuda, pago)* to fall due.
▶ *vpr* **cumplirse 1** *(realizarse)* to be fulfilled, come true: *se cumplió la profecía* the prophecy came true. **2** *(fecha)* to be: *se cumple una semana del comienzo del curso* it's a week since the course began.

cúmulo *nm* **1** *(montón)* load, pile, heap; *(cantidad)* series, host, string: *un cúmulo de desgracias* a series of misfortunes. **2** METEOR cumulus.

cumulonimbo *nm* cumulonimbus.

cuna *nf* **1** *(cama)* cradle. **2** *(linaje)* birth, lineage, stock. **3** *fig (origen)* cradle, birthplace: *la cuna de la filosofía* the cradle of philosophy. **4** *(lugar de nacimiento)* birthplace.

cundir *vi* **1** *(extenderse)* to spread: *cundió el pánico* panic spread. **2** *(dar de sí)* to go a long way, go far: *una hora cunde muy poco* you can't do much in an hour. **3** *(aumentar de volumen)* to swell, expand: *los fideos cunden al cocerse* noodles expand when cooked.

cuneta *nf* **1** *(de carretera)* verge. **2** *(zanja)* ditch.

cuña *nf (pieza)* wedge.

cuñado,-a *nm & nf (hombre)* brother-in-law; *(mujer)* sister-in-law.

cuño *nm* **1** *(troquel)* die, stamp. **2** *(sello)* stamp, mark.

cuota *nf* **1** *(pago)* membership fee, dues *pl*. **2** *(porción)* quota, share.

cupo *nm (cuota)* quota.

cupón *nm* **1** *(vale)* coupon, voucher. **2** *(de lotería)* ticket.

cúpula *nf* cupola, dome.

cura *nm* REL priest.
▶ *nf* **1** cure, healing. **2** *(tratamiento)* treatment: *cura de adelgazamiento* slimming treatment. LOC **hacer las primeras curas** to give first aid.

curable *adj* curable.

curación *nf* **1** *(gen)* cure. **2** *(de herida)* healing. **3** *(recuperación)* recovery.

curandero,-a *nm & nf* **1** *(charlatán)* quack. **2** *(curador)* folk healer.

curar *vt* **1** *(sanar)* to cure. **2** *(herida)* to dress; *(enfermedad)* to treat.
▶ *vi* **1** *(cuidar)* to take care (de, of). **2** *(recuperarse)* to recover, get well. **3** *(herida)* to heal (up).
▶ *vpr* **curarse 1** *(recuperarse)* to recover (de, from), get well. **2** *(herida)* to heal up.

curativo,-a *adj* curative: *poder curativo* healing power.

curia *nf* **1** REL curia. **2** JUR Bar.

curiosamente *adv* **1** *(con curiosidad)* curiously, strangely. **2** *(limpiamente)* cleanly.

curiosear *vi* **1** *(fisgar)* to pry, nose around. **2** *(mirar)* to look around.
▶ *vt (fisgar)* to pry into.

curiosidad *nf* **1** *(gen)* curiosity. **2** *(aseo)* cleanliness, tidiness. **3** *(cuidado)* care. LOC **tener curiosidad de** ALGO to be curious about STH.

currículo *nm* curriculum, curriculum vitae.

curry *nm* curry.

cursar *vt* **1** *(estudiar)* to study. **2** *(enviar)* to send, dispatch; *(orden)* to give. **3** *(tramitar)* to make an application.

cursi *adj fam (afectado)* pretentious, affected, twee.
▶ *nm o nf fam* pretentious person, affected person.

cursilada *nf* **1** *(cualidad)* affectation, pretentiousness. **2** *(hecho)* pretentious thing to do, posh thing to do. **3** *(obra, cosa)* pretentious thing: *las películas románticas me parecen una cursilada* for me romantic films are just sentimental slush.

cursillo *nm* short course, training course.

cursiva *nf (escritura)* cursive; *(tipografía)* italics *pl*.

curso *nm* **1** *(dirección)* course, direction: *el curso de los acontecimientos* the course of events. **2** EDUC *(nivel)* year, class; *(materia)* course; *(escolar)* school year: *vamos al mismo curso* we are in the same class. **3** *(río)* flow, current. COMP **curso acelerado** crash course.

cursor *nm* **1** INFORM cursor. **2** TÉC slide.

curtido,-a *adj* **1** *(por el sol)* tanned, sunburnt. **2** *(cuero)* tanned. **3** *fig (endurecido)* hardened.
▶ *nm* **curtido** *(operación)* tanning.
▶ *nm pl* **curtidos** tanned leather *sing*.

curtidor,-ra *nm & nf* tanner.

curtir *vt* **1** *(piel)* to tan. **2** *fig (acostumbrar)* to harden, toughen.
▶ *vpr* **curtirse 1** *(por el sol)* to get tanned. **2** *fig (acostumbrarse)* to become hardened.

curva *nf* **1** *(gen)* curve. **2** *(de carretera)* bend. **3** *(gráfico)* curve, graph. LOC **trazar una curva** to draw a curve.

curvar *vt* **1** *(gen)* to curve, bend. **2** *(espalda)* to arch.

curvilíneo,-a *adj* **1** curvilinear, curvilineal. **2** *fam (del cuerpo)* curvaceous, shapely.

curvo,-a *adj* curved, bent.

cuscús *nm* couscous.

cúspide *nf* **1** *(cumbre)* summit, peak. **2** *(en geometría)* apex. **3** *fig* peak.

custodia *nf* **1** custody, care. **2** REL monstrance. LOC **bajo custodia** in custody.

custodiar *vt* **1** *(proteger)* to keep, take care of. **2** *(vigilar)* to guard, watch over.

cutáneo,-a *adj* cutaneous, skin: *enfermedad cutánea* skin disease.

cúter *nm* **1** *(barco)* cutter. **2** *(cuchillo)* cutter.

cutícula *nf* cuticle.

cutis *nm inv* skin, complexion.

cuyo,-a *pron* **1** *(personas)* whose, of whom: *esta mujer, cuya hermana trabaja en Alemania...* this woman, whose sister works in Germany..., this woman, the sister of whom works in Germany... **2** *(cosas)* whose, of which: *un arbol cuyas hojas presentan esta enfermedad* a tree with leaves that show signs of this disease. LOC **en cuyo caso** in which case.

CV¹ *sím (caballos de vapor)* horse power; *(símbolo)* HP.

CV² *abrev (currículum vítae)* curriculum vitae; *(abreviatura)* CV.

D

D, d *nf (la letra)* D, d.

dado *nm* **1** *(para jugar)* die. **2** TÉC block. **3** ARQUIT dado. LOC **echar los dados** to throw the dice.

dado,-a *adj* **1** given: *dada la base y la altura, hallar la superficie* given the base and the height, find the area. **2** *(en vista de)* in view of: *dada su experiencia* in view of his experience. LOC **dado que** since, as, given that: *dado que llueve no saldremos* as it's raining we won't go out.

daga *nf* dagger.

dalai lama *nm* Dalai Lama.

dalia *nf* dahlia.

dálmata *adj* Dalmatian.
▶ *nm* Dalmatian.

daltónico,-a *adj* colour-blind, daltonic.

daltonismo *nm* colour (US color) blindness, daltonism.

dama *nf* **1** *(señora)* lady. **2** *(en el juego de damas)* king; *(en ajedrez)* queen.
▶ *nf pl* **damas** draughts, (US checkers). COMP **tablero de damas** draughtboard, (US checkerboard).

damero *nm* draughtboard, US checkerboard.

damnificar *vt* **1** *(a una persona)* to injure, harm. **2** *(cosa)* to damage.

dandy *nm* dandy.

danés,-esa *adj* Danish.
▶ *nm & nf (persona)* Dane.
▶ *nm* **danés** *(idioma)* Danish.

danza *nf* **1** *(baile)* dance. **2** *fig (negocio sucio)* shady business, shady deal; *(lío)* mess: *no te metas en esa danza* don't get mixed up in a deal like that. **3** *fam fig (riña)* row.

danzante *adj* dancing.

▶ *nm o nf* dancer.

danzar *vt (bailar)* to dance.
▶ *vi (bailar)* to dance (con, with).

danzarín,-ina *nm & nf* dancer.

dañado,-a *adj* damaged, spoiled.

dañar *vt* **1** *(causar dolor)* to hurt, harm. **2** *(estropear)* to damage, spoil. **3** *fig* to damage, stain: *ese asunto dañará su reputación* that affair will damage his reputation.
▶ *vpr* **dañarse** *(estropearse)* to get damaged, spoil; *(alimentos)* to go bad, go off.

dañino,-a *adj* harmful (para, to), damaging (para, to).

daño *nm (a persona)* harm, injury; *(a cosa)* damage; *(perjuicio)* wrong. LOC **hacer daño 1** *(doler)* to hurt. **2** *(causar dolor a ALGN)* to hurt. **3** *(ser malo para ALGO)* to damage, harm. *(ser malo para ALGN)* to do SB harm: *me hizo daño con sus palabras* her words hurt me. ‖ **hacerse daño** to hurt OS: *se hizo daño en la mano* she hurt her hand.

dar *vt* **1** *(gen)* to give: *te daré un libro* I'll give you a book. **2** *(poner en las manos, entregar)* to deliver, hand over; *(poner al alcance)* to pass, hand: *dame la sal* pass me the salt. **3** *(proporcionar, ofrecer, procurar algo no material a una persona - noticia)* to tell, announce, report; *(- consejo)* to give; *(- recuerdos, recado)* to pass on, give. **4** *(permitir tener algo, conceder)* to give. **5** *(pagar a cambio)* to give, pay: *¿cuánto me daría por esto?* how much would you give me for it? **6** *(realizar una acción)*. **7** *(producir - cosecha)* to produce, yield; *(- fruto, flores)* to bear, produce; *(- beneficio)* to produce, yield: *la higuera da higos* the fig tree bears figs. **8** *(celebrar,* *tener lugar - película)* to show, screen; *(- obra de teatro)* to perform, put on; *(- concierto)* to give, perform, put on; *(- fiesta)* to give, throw: *daremos una fiesta* we'll have a party. **9** *(pegar)* to hit. **10** *(sonar el reloj las horas)* to strike. **11** *(untar, recubrir una superficie)* to apply, give. **12** *(abrir el paso de conductos)* to turn on: *he dado el gas* I've turned the gas on. |LOC| **dar a entender que...** to give to understand that..., imply that...: *dio a entender que no vendría* she implied she wouldn't come. ‖ **dar a luz** to give birth (a, to). ‖ **dar ALGO por** to assume, consider. ‖ **dar de sí 1** *(ropa)* to stretch, give. **2** *(dinero, comida)* to go a long way. ‖ **dar igual** to be all the same, not matter: *le daba igual* it didn't matter to him, he didn't care. ‖ **dar la mano a ALGN** to shake hands with SB.

▶ *vi* **1** *(pegar, golpear)* to hit: *la pelota le dio en toda la cara* the ball hit him right in the face. **2** *(en naipes)* to deal. **3 dar a** *(botón, interruptor)* to press: *dale al botón* press the button. **4** *(mirar una cosa hacia una parte)* to look out onto, overlook. **5 dar de** *(caer)* to fall: *dio de narices en el suelo* he fell flat on his face. **6 dar de** *(suministrar)* to give. **7 dar en** *(acertar)* to find, hit on. **8 dar para** *(ser suficiente)* to be enough for, be sufficient for: *la sopa da para cuatro* the soup serves four.

dardo *nm (arma)* dart, arrow.

dársena *nf* dock, basin.

darvinismo *nm* Darwinism.

datar *vt (poner la data)* to date, put a date on.

▶ *vi (tener origen)* to date (de, from), date back (de, to): *esa iglesia data del siglo XI* that church dates from the eleventh century.

dátil *nm* date.

datilera *nf* date palm.

dativo,-a *adj* dative.

▶ *nm* **dativo** dative. |LOC| **en dativo** in the dative.

dato *nm (información)* fact, piece of information, datum. |COMP| **datos personales** personal details.

dB *sím* (decibelio) decibel; *(símbolo)* dB.

d.C. *abrev* (después de Cristo) Anno Domini; *(abreviatura)* AD.

DDT *abrev* (diclorodifeniltricloroetano) dichlorodiphenyltrichloroethane; *(abreviatura)* DDT.

de *prep* **1** *(posesión, pertenencia)* of, in: *la mesa de mi habitación* the table in my bedroom. **2** *(procedencia, origen)* from, in: *viene de Barcelona* she comes from Barcelona. **3** *(descripción)* with: *el señor del abrigo azul* the man in the blue coat. **4** *(tema)* of, on, about: *hablaron del tiempo* they talked about the weather. **5** *(materia)* made of, of: *un anillo de oro* a gold ring. **6** *(contenido)* of: *un vaso de agua* a glass of water. **7** *(oficio)* by, as: *trabaja de profesor* he works as a teacher. **8** *(modo)* on, in, as: *de pie* standing up. **9** *(tiempo)* at, by, in: *de día* by day, during the day. **10** *(lugar)* varias traducciones: *la vecina de arriba* our upstairs neighbour. **11** *(medida)* measuring: *una botella de dos litros* a two litre bottle. **12** *(causa)* with, because of, of: *llorar de alegría* to cry with joy. **13** *(agente)* by: *es una obra de Lope* a play by Lope. **14** *(con superlativo)* in, of: *el mayor de los tres* the eldest of the three. **15** *(en una aposición)* of: *la ciudad de Barcelona* the city of Barcelona.

✎ Consulta también del.

deambular *vi* to saunter, stroll.

debajo *adv* below, underneath: *el libro verde está debajo* the green book is underneath. |LOC| **por debajo** underneath: *tuvieron que pasar por debajo* they had to go underneath.

debate *nm* debate, discussion.

debatir *vt* to debate, discuss.

debe *nm* debit side.

deber *vt* **1** *(estar obligado a algo)* to owe: *debemos respeto a nuestros padres* we owe respect to our parents. **2** *(dinero, cosa)* to owe: *te debo cincuenta euros* I owe you fifty euros.

▶ *aux* **1** *(obligación presente)* must, have to, have got to: *debo ir a comprar* I must go shopping. **2** *(obligación pasada)* should, ought to: *debía haberlo comprado ayer* I should have bought it yester-

day. **3** *(obligación futura)* must, have to, have got to: *deberás tenerlo a las cinco* you must have it ready by five o'clock. **4** *(obligación moral)* should, ought to: *no deberías haberlo hecho* you shouldn't have done it. **5 deber de** *(probabilidad)* must; *(negativa)* can't: *deben de ser las seis* it must be six o'clock; *no deben de haber llegado* they can't have arrived.
▶ *vpr* **deberse 1** *(ser consecuencia)* to be due (a, to). **2** *(tener una obligación)* to have a duty (a, to).
▶ *nm* **deber** *(obligación)* duty, obligation. |LOC| **cumplir con su deber** to do one's duty. ‖ **hacer los deberes** to do one's homework.
▶ *nm pl* **deberes** *(escolares)* homework *sing.*

debidamente *adv* duly, properly.

debido,-a *adj* **1** *(merecido)* due: *con el debido respeto,...* with all due respect,... **2** *(conveniente)* right. |LOC| **como es debido 1** *(correctamente)* right, properly. **2** *(como es merecido)* deservedly: *siéntate en la silla como es debido* sit properly on the chair.

débil *adj* **1** *(persona)* weak, feeble. **2** *(ruido)* faint; *(luz)* dim, feeble. **3** LING weak.
▶ *nm o nf* weak person.

debilidad *nf* **1** *(de una persona)* weakness, feebleness. **2** *fig* weakness: *los coches de carreras son su debilidad* he has a weakness for racing cars. |LOC| **tener debilidad por 1** *(algo)* to have a weakness for. **2** *(alguien)* to have a soft spot for.

debilitamiento *nm* weakening.

debilitar *vt* to weaken, debilitate.
▶ *vpr* **debilitarse** to weaken, get weak, become weak.

debut *nm* debut, début.

debutante *nm o nf (actor)* first-time actor; *(actriz)* first-time actress.

debutar *vi* to make one's debut, make one's début.

década *nf* decade.

decadencia *nf* decadence, decline, decay.

decadente *adj* decadent.

decaedro *nm* decahedron.

decaer *vi (perder fuerzas)* to weaken; *(- entusiasmo, interés)* to flag; *(- salud)* to go down, deteriorate, decay; *(- belleza, etc)* to lose: *su interés está decayendo* his interest is flagging.

decagonal *adj* decagonal.

decágono *nm* decagon.

decagramo *nm* decagram, decagramme.

decaído,-a *adj* **1** *(débil)* weak. **2** *(triste)* sad, depressed, low.

decalitro *nm* decalitre (US decaliter).

decálogo *nm* Decalogue.

decámetro *nm* decametre (US decameter).

decano,-a *nm & nf (cargo)* dean.

decantar¹ *vt (verter)* to decant, pour off.

decantar² *vt (alabar)* to praise, laud.
▶ *vpr* **decantarse** *(preferir)* to prefer (hacia/por, -): *el público se decantó por el equipo local* the spectators were on the side of the local team.

decapar *vt (pintura)* to strip (off).

decapitar *vt* to behead, decapitate.

decápodo *nm* decapod.

decasílabo,-a *adj* decasyllabic.

decatlón *nm* decathlon.

decena *nf* **1** *(exacto)* ten. **2** *(aproximado)* about ten: *he invitado a una decena de personas* I have invited ten or so people.

decenal *adj* ten-year, decennial.

decencia *nf* **1** *(decoro)* decency, propriety. **2** *(honestidad)* honesty.

decenio *nm* decade.

decente *adj* **1** *(decoroso)* decent, proper. **2** *(honesto)* honest, upright; *(respetable)* decent, respectable.

decentemente *adv* decently.

decepción *nf* disappointment.

decepcionado,-a *adj* disappointed.

decepcionar *vt* to disappoint, let down: *no nos decepciones* don't disappoint us.

decibelio *nm* decibel.

decididamente *adv (con determinación)* resolutely, with determination: *soli-*

citó el trabajo decididamente he applied for the job with determination.

decidido,-a *adj* determined, resolute: *está decidido a acabar el trabajo* he's determined to finish the job.

decidir *vt (gen)* to decide; *(asunto)* to settle.
▶ *vi* to decide, choose: *tuvo que decidir entre los dos* she had to decide between the two.
▶ *vpr* **decidirse** to make up one's mind. LOC **decidirse por** to decide on: *se decidió por la falda roja* she decided on the red skirt.

decigramo *nm* decigram, decigramme.

decilitro *nm* decilitre (US deciliter).

décima *nf* LIT stanza of ten octosyllabic lines. LOC **tener (unas) décimas** *fam* to have a slight temperature.

decimal *adj* decimal.
▶ *nm* decimal.

decímetro *nm* decimetre (US decimeter).

décimo,-a *adj* tenth.
▶ *nm & nf* tenth.

✎ Consulta también sexto,-a.

decimoctavo,-a *adj* eighteenth.
▶ *nm & nf* eighteenth.

✎ Consulta también sexto,-a.

decimocuarto,-a *adj* fourteenth.
▶ *nm & nf* fourteenth.

✎ Consulta también sexto,-a.

decimonónico,-a *adj* nineteenth-century: *un escritor decimonónico* a nineteenth-century writer.

decimonono,-a *adj* nineteenth.
▶ *nm & nf* nineteenth.

✎ Consulta también sexto,-a.

decimonoveno,-a *adj-nm & nf* → decimonono,-a.

✎ Consulta también sexto,-a.

decimoquinto,-a *adj* fifteenth.
▶ *nm & nf* fifteenth.

✎ Consulta también sexto,-a.

decimoséptimo,-a *adj* seventeenth.
▶ *nm & nf* seventeenth.

✎ Consulta también sexto,-a.

decimosexto,-a *adj* sixteenth.
▶ *nm & nf* sixteenth.

✎ Consulta también sexto,-a.

decimotercero,-a *adj* thirteenth.
▶ *nm & nf* thirteenth.

✎ Consulta también sexto,-a.

decir *vt* **1** *(gen)* to say. **2** *(contar, revelar)* to tell: *dijo la verdad* she told the truth. **3** *(nombrar, llamar)* to call: *le dicen Cuca* she's called Cuca. **4** *(opinar)* to have to say. **5** *(un texto)* to read, say: *el texto dice lo siguiente* the text reads as follows. LOC **digo yo** in my opinion, I think. ‖ **el qué dirán** what people say. ‖ **es decir** that is (to say), ‖ **¡no me digas!** really! ‖ **querer decir** to mean: *quiero decir,...* I mean,... ‖ **se dice...** they say..., it is said...

decisión *nf* **1** *(resolución)* decision: *sus padres tuvieron que tomar una decisión* his parents had to make a decision. **2** *(determinación)* determination, resolution.

decisivo,-a *adj (importante)* decisive.

declamar *vi* to declaim, recite.
▶ *vt* to declaim, recite.

declamatorio,-a *adj* declamatory.

declaración *nf* **1** *(gen)* declaration: *declaración de renta* income tax return. **2** [también se usa en plural con el mismo significado] *(explicación pública)* statement, comment. **3** JUR evidence. **4** *(en bridge)* bid. LOC **prestar declaración** JUR to give evidence.

declarar *vt* **1** *(gen)* to declare; *(manifestar)* to state: *lo declararon vencedor* he was declared the winner. **2** JUR to find.
▶ *vi* **1** to declare. **2** JUR to testify.
▶ *vpr* **declararse** **1** *(amor)* to declare one's love (a, for). **2** *(fuego, guerra, etc)* to break out, start: *se declaró un incendio en el monte* a fire broke out on the mountain.

declinación *nf (gramatical)* declension.

declinar *vi* **1** *(disminuir)* to decline, come down. **2** *(acercarse al fin)* to end, draw to an end.
▶ *vt* GRAM to decline.

declive *nm fig (decadencia)* decline. LOC **en declive** *fig* on the decline.

decodificar *vt* to decode.

decolorar *vt (perder el color)* to discolour (US discolor).
▶ *vpr* **decolorarse** *(perder el color)* to fade, become discoloured (US discolored).

decoración *nf* **1** *(gen)* decoration. **2** TEAT scenery, set.

decorador,-ra *nm & nf* **1** decorator. **2** TEAT set designer.

decorar *vt (gen)* to decorate, adorn, embellish; *(una casa)* to decorate.

decorativo,-a *adj* decorative.

decoroso,-a *adj* **1** *(digno)* decent, respectable. **2** *(respetable)* respectable, honourable (US honorable): *un trabajo decoroso* an honourable job.

decrecer *vi (gen)* to decrease, diminish; *(aguas)* to subside, go down.

decretar *vt* **1** *(con decreto)* to decree. **2** *(ordenar)* to ordain, order.

decreto *nm* decree, order.

décuplo,-a *adj* tenfold.
▶ *nm* **décuplo** ten times.

dedal *nm* thimble.

dedicación *nf* dedication, devotion. LOC **de dedicación exclusiva** full-time.

dedicar *vt* **1** *(una dedicatoria)* to dedicate, inscribe. **2** *(tiempo, dinero)* to devote (a, to). **3** *(palabras)* to address.

dedicatoria *nf* dedication, inscription.

dedo *nm* **1** *(de la mano)* finger; *(del pie)* toe. **2** *(medida)* finger, digit. LOC **hacer dedo** *fam* to hitchhike. ▌**no tener dos dedos de frente** *fig* to be as thick as two short planks. COMP **dedo anular** ring finger, third finger. ▌**dedo gordo 1** *(de la mano)* thumb. **2** *(del pie)* big toe. ▌**dedo índice** forefinger, index finger. ▌**dedo meñique** little finger. ▌**dedo pulgar** thumb. ▌**yema del dedo** fingertip.

deducción *nf* deduction.

deducir *vt* **1** to deduce, infer. **2** *(dinero)* to deduct, subtract.
▶ *vpr* **deducirse** to follow: *de aquí se deduce que...* from this it follows that...

deductivo,-a *adj* deductive.

defecto *nm* **1** *(gen)* defect, fault; *(de una joya)* imperfection, flaw. **2** *(de persona - moral)* fault, shortcoming; *(- física)* handicap. LOC **por defecto** INFORM default: *la impresora por defecto* the default printer.

defectuoso,-a *adj* defective, faulty.

defender *vt* **1** *(gen)* to defend (contra/de, against). **2** *(mantener una opinión, afirmación)* to defend, uphold; *(respaldar a ALGN)* to stand up for, support. **3** *(proteger)* to protect (contra/de, against/from). **4** JUR *(algo)* to argue, plead; *(a alguien)* to defend.
▶ *vpr* **defenderse** *(espabilarse)* to manage, get by, get along: *¿qué tal se defiende en inglés?* how does she get by in English?, what's her English like?

defensa *nf* defence (US defense).
▶ *nm o nf* DEP *(jugador)* back, defender.

defensiva *nf* defensive. LOC **estar a la defensiva** to be on the defensive.

defensor,-ra *adj* defending.
▶ *nm & nf* **1** defender. **2** JUR counsel for the defence (US defense). COMP **defensor del pueblo** ombudsman.

deficiente *adj* **1** *(defectuoso)* deficient, faulty. **2** *(insuficiente)* lacking, insufficient.
▶ *nm o nf* mentally retarded person. COMP **deficiente mental** mentally retarded person.

déficit *nm inv* COM deficit.

deficitario,-a *adj* showing a deficit.

definición *nf* definition. LOC **por definición** by definition.

definir *vt* to define.

definitivamente *adv (para siempre)* for good, once and for all: *se marchó definitivamente* she left for good.

definitivo,-a *adj* definitive, final. LOC **en definitiva** finally, in short, all in all.

deforestación *nf* deforestation.

deforestar *vt* to deforest.

deformación *nf* deformation, distortion.

deformar *vt* (*gen*) to deform, put out of shape; (*cara*) to disfigure; (*realidad, imagen, etc*) to distort.

deforme *adj* (*persona*) deformed; (*cosa*) misshapen, out of shape; (*imagen, cara*) distorted.

deformidad *nf* deformity, malformation.

defraudar *vt* **1** (*estafar*) to defraud, cheat. **2** (*decepcionar*) to disappoint, deceive. **3** *fig* (*frustrar*) to betray: *defraudar las esperanzas* to dash one's hopes.

defunción *nf fml* death, decease.

degenerar *vi* to degenerate.

degenerativo,-a *adj* degenerative.

deglutir *vt* to swallow.
  ▸ *vi* to swallow.

degradante *adj* degrading, humiliating.

degradar *vt* to degrade, debase.
  ▸ *vpr* **degradarse** to demean os, degrade os.

degustación *nf* tasting.

degustar *vt* to taste, sample, try.

dehesa *nf* pasture, meadow.

deidad *nf* deity, divinity.

dejadez *nf* **1** (*negligencia*) negligence, carelessness. **2** (*pereza*) laziness, apathy.

dejado,-a *adj* **1** (*descuidado*) untidy, slovenly. **2** (*perezoso*) lazy.
  ▸ *nm & nf* untidy person, slovenly person.

dejar *vt* **1** (*colocar*) to leave, put. **2** (*abandonar - persona, lugar*) to leave; (*- hábito, cosa, actividad*) to give up: *dejó el tabaco* he gave up smoking. **3** (*permitir*) to allow, let: *déjale jugar* let him play. **4** (*prestar*) to lend. **5** (*ceder*) to give. **6** (*aplazar*) to put off: *dejémoslo hasta mañana* let's leave it till tomorrow. **7** (*causar un efecto*) to make: *le película me ha dejado triste* the film made me sad. **8** (*legar*) to bequeath, leave.

  ▸ *aux* **1** dejar de + *inf* (*cesar - voluntariamente*) to stop + *ger*, give up + *ger*; (*- involuntariamente*) to stop + *ger*: *ha dejado de llover* it's stopped raining. **2** no dejar de + *inf* not to fail *to + inf*: *no deja de sorprenderme* she never fails to surprise me. **3** dejar + *pp*: *lo dejó escrito en su agenda* he wrote it down in his diary.
  ▸ *vpr* **dejarse** (*olvidar*) to forget, leave behind: *me he dejado las llaves en casa* I've left my keys at home.
  ▸ *vpr* **dejarse de** (*cesar*) to stop: *déjate de tonterías* don't be silly. [LOC] dejar ALGO **por imposible** to give up on STH. ▪ **dejar en paz** to leave alone. ▪ **dejar preocupado,-a** to worry. ▪ **dejarse llevar por** ALGN to be influenced by SB.

del *contr* (*de + el*) → de.

delantal *nm* apron, pinafore.

delante *adv* **1** (*enfrente*) in front; (*adelantado*) in front, ahead. **2** de delante in front. **3** delante de in front of, ahead of, before: *delante de mis ojos* before my eyes. **4** por delante in front, ahead: *tenemos mucho tiempo por delante* we've got plenty of time ahead.

delantera *nf* **1** (*frente*) front (part). **2** DEP forward line, forwards *pl*. **3** (*ventaja*) lead, advantage. [LOC] **llevar la delantera** to be in the lead, be ahead.

delantero,-a *adj* front, front part: *el asiento delantero* the front seat.
  ▸ *nm* **delantero** DEP forward. [COMP] **delantero centro** centre (US center) forward.

delatar *vt* to inform on.
  ▸ *vpr* **delatarse** to give os away.

delator,-ra *adj* accusing, denouncing.
  ▸ *nm & nf* accuser, denouncer.

delegación *nf* **1** (*gen*) delegation. **2** (*cargo*) office.

delegado,-a *nm & nf* **1** delegate. **2** COM representative.

delegar *vt* to delegate.

deletrear *vt* to spell, spell out.

deletreo *nm* spelling (out).

delfín *nm* (*animal*) dolphin.

delgado,-a *adj* **1** (*poco ancho*) thin. **2** (*esbelto*) slim, slender. **3** (*flaco*) thin.

deliberación *nf* deliberation.
deliberadamente *adv* deliberately.
deliberar *vt* to decide.
▶ *vi* to deliberate (sobre, on).
delicadeza *nf* 1 *(finura)* delicacy, daintiness. 2 *(tacto)* thoughtfulness; *(refinamiento)* refinement.
delicado,-a *adj* 1 *(fino)* delicate; *(refinado)* refined. 2 *(difícil)* delicate, difficult: *una situación delicada* a delicate situation. 3 *(frágil)* fragile.
delicia *nf* delight, pleasure.
delicioso,-a *adj* delightful, charming; *(una comida)* delicious.
delimitar *vt* 1 *(terreno)* to delimit, mark off. 2 *(definir)* to define, specify.
delincuencia *nf* delinquency.
delincuente *nm o nf* delinquent.
delineante *nm o nf (hombre)* draughtsman; *(mujer)* draughtswoman.
delinear *vt* to delineate, outline, sketch.
delirar *vi* to be delirious.
delirio *nm* 1 *(desvarío)* delirium. 2 *fig (disparate)* nonsense.
delito *nm* offence (US offense), crime.
delta *nf* 1 *(letra)* delta. 2 *(ala delta)* hanggliding.
▶ *nm* GEOG delta.
demacrado,-a *adj (gen)* emaciated; *(cara)* haggard, drawn.
demagogia *nf* demagoguery, demagogy.
demagógico,-a *adj* demagogic, demagogical.
demagogo,-a *nm & nf* demagogue.
demanda *nf* 1 *(petición)* petition, request. 2 COM *(pedido de mercancías)* demand. 3 JUR lawsuit. [LOC] **en demanda de** asking for.
demandado,-a *nm & nf* defendant.
demandante *nm o nf* 1 JUR plaintiff. 2 *(persona que busca)* seeker, hunter. *(persona que compra)* buyer. [COMP] **demandante de empleo** job hunter.
demandar *vt* 1 *(pedir)* to request, ask for; *(desear)* to desire. 2 JUR to sue.
demarcar *vt* to demarcate.
demás *adj* other, rest of.

▶ *pron* the other, the rest: *los demás llegaron tarde* the others arrived late.
▶ *adv* besides, moreover. [LOC] **por lo demás** apart from that, otherwise. **todo lo demás** everything else.
demasiado,-a *adj (singular)* too much; *(plural)* too many.
▶ *adv (modificador de adjetivo)* too; *(modificador de verbo)* too much: *es demasiado gordo* he's too fat.
demencia *nf* 1 insanity, madness, dementia. 2 *fig (disparate)* silly thing. [COMP] **demencia senil** senile dementia.
demente *adj* mad, insane.
▶ *nm o nf* 1 *(persona enferma)* mental patient. 2 *(loco, chalado)* lunatic.
democracia *nf* democracy.
demócrata *nm o nf* democrat.
democrático,-a *adj* democratic.
demografía *nf* demography.
demográfico,-a *adj* demographic.
demoler *vt* to demolish, pull down, tear down.
demolición *nf* demolition.
demoniaco,-a *adj* demoniacal, demonic, possessed by the devil.
demonio *nm* demon, devil. [LOC] **¡demonios!** *fam* hell!, damn!
demora *nf* delay.
demorar *vt (retrasar)* to delay, hold up.
▶ *vpr* **demorarse** *(retrasarse)* to be delayed, be held up.
demostración *nf* 1 *(gen)* demonstration. 2 MAT proof.
demostrar *vt* 1 *(probar)* to prove, show. 2 *(hacer una demostración)* to demonstrate, show. 3 MAT to prove.
demostrativo,-a *adj* demonstrative.
▶ *nm* demonstrative.
denegar *vt (desestimar)* to refuse; *(negar)* to deny.
denigrante *adj* denigrating, disparaging.
denigrar *vt* 1 to denigrate, disparage, run down. 2 *(insultar)* to insult, revile.
denominación *nf* 1 *(acción)* denomination, naming. 2 *(nombre)* denomi-

nation, name. comp **denominación de origen** *(vinos)* guarantee of origin.

denominador,-ra *adj* denominative.
▶ *nm* **denominador** MAT denominator. comp **mínimo común denominador** lowest common denominator.

denominar vt to denominate, name.

densidad *nf* **1** *(gen)* density. **2** *fig (espesura)* thickness, denseness. comp **densidad de población** population density.

denso,-a *adj (gen)* dense; *(espeso)* dense, thick.

dentado,-a *adj* **1** *(con dientes)* toothed. **2** BOT dentate.

dentadura *nf* teeth *pl*, set of teeth. comp **dentadura postiza** false teeth *pl*, dentures *pl*.

dental *adj* dental. comp **cepillo dental** toothbrush.

dentellada *nf* **1** *(mordisco)* bite. **2** *(señal)* tooth mark.

dentera *nf fig (envidia)* envy. LOC **dar dentera a** ALGN **1** *(dar grima)* to set SB's teeth on edge. **2** *(dar envidia)* to make SB green with envy.

dentición *nf* **1** *(acción de dentar)* teething, dentition, cutting of the teeth. **2** *(época en que dentan los niños)* dentition.

dentífrico,-a *adj* tooth.
▶ *nm* **dentífrico** toothpaste. comp **pasta dentífrica** toothpaste.

dentista *nm o nf* dentist. LOC **ir al dentista** to go to the dentist's.

dentro *adv* inside; *(de edificio)* indoors, inside: *está ahí dentro* it's in there. LOC **dentro de 1** *(lugar)* in, inside: *dentro de la casa* in the house; *dentro de una semana* in a week, in a week's time. **2** *(tiempo)* in. ❙ **dentro de lo posible** as far as possible. ❙ **dentro de poco** soon, shortly. ❙ **por dentro 1** *(de una cosa)* (on the) inside. **2** *(de una persona)* deep down, inside, inwardly.

denuncia *nf* **1** *(acusación)* accusation, formal complaint, report. **2** JUR *(acción)* reporting; *(documento)* report. LOC **presentar una denuncia contra** ALGN to

lodge a complaint against SB, bring an action against SB, report SB.

denunciar *vt* **1** *(poner una denuncia)* to report. **2** *(dar noticia)* to denounce.

deparar *vt* **1** *(presentar)* to bring, hold in store: *nadie sabe lo que el destino nos deparará* nobody knows what fate holds in store for us. **2** *(proporcionar)* to give, afford.

departamento *nm* **1** *(sección)* department, section. **2** *(de tren)* compartment.

dependencia *nf* **1** *(hecho de depender)* dependence. **2** *(habitación)* room, outbuilding.

depender *vi* **1** to depend (de, on): *depende de ti* it's up to you. **2** *(estar bajo el mando o autoridad)* to be under, be answerable to; *(necesitar)* to be dependent on: *aún depende de sus padres* she's still dependent on her parents

dependienta *nf* shop assistant, salesgirl, saleswoman.

dependiente *adj* dependent (de, on).
▶ *nm o nf* shop assistant, salesman.

depilación *nf* depilation, hair removal. LOC **depilación a la cera** waxing.

depilar *vt* to depilate, remove the hair from; *(cejas)* to pluck.

depilatorio,-a *adj* depilatory. comp **crema depilatoria** hair-removing cream.

deplorable *adj* deplorable, regrettable.

deplorar *vt* to deplore, lament, regret deeply.

deponer *vt* **1** *(dejar)* to lay down, set aside. **2** *(destituir)* to remove from office; *(a un rey)* to depose.

deportación *nf* deportation.

deportar *vt* to deport.

deporte *nm* sport: *¿practicas algún deporte?* do you do any sport?, do you play any sport? LOC **hacer deporte** to do some sport.

deportista *adj* sporty, keen on sport.
▶ *nm o nf (hombre)* sportsman; *(mujer)* sportswoman.

deportividad *nf* sportsmanship.

deportivo,-a *adj* **1** *(aficionado al deporte)* sporting, sporty. **2** *(relacionado con el deporte)* sports: *club deportivo* sports club. **3** *(informal)* casual: *ropa deportiva* casual clothes.
▶ *nm* **deportivo** *(coche)* sports car.

depositar *vt* **1** *(dinero, joyas)* to deposit. **2** *(colocar)* to place, put. **3** *(sedimentar)* to deposit.
▶ *vpr* **depositarse** *(caer en el fondo)* to settle.

depositario,-a *nm & nf (de algo material)* depositary, trustee; *(de algo inmaterial)* repository.

depósito *nm* **1** *(recipiente)* tank. **2** *(almacén)* store, warehouse, depot. **3** *(sedimento)* deposit, sediment. LOC **en depósito** in bond. COMP **depósito de gasolina** petrol tank.

depreciar *vt* to depreciate.
▶ *vpr* **depreciarse** to depreciate.

depredador,-ra *adj* depredatory.
▶ *nm & nf* depredator, pillager.

depredar *vt* to depredate, pillage.

depresión *nf* depression: *depresión atmosférica* atmospheric depression. COMP **depresión nerviosa** nervous breakdown.

depresivo,-a *adj* **1** *(deprimente)* depressing. **2** MED depressive.

deprimente *adj* depressing.

deprimido,-a *adj* depressed.

deprimir *vt* to depress.
▶ *vpr* **deprimirse** to get depressed.

deprisa *adv* quickly.

depuración *nf (del agua)* purification; *(de la sangre)* cleansing.

depurador,-ra *adj* purifying.
▶ *nm* **depurador** *(sustancia)* depurative; *(aparato)* purifier.

depurar *vt* **1** *(purificar agua)* to purify, depurate; *(sangre)* to cleanse. **2** POL to purge. **3** *fig (perfeccionar)* to purify, refine.

derecha *nf* **1** *(mano)* right hand. **2** *(lugar)* right: *dame el de la derecha* give me the one on the right. **3** **la derecha** POL the right, the right wing.

derechista *adj* right-wing, rightist.

derecho,-a *adj* **1** right: *la mano derecha* the right hand. **2** *(recto)* straight, upright.
▶ *adv* **derecho** straight: *se fue derecho a la cama* he went straight to bed.
▶ *nm* **derecho** **1** *(leyes)* law. **2** *(privilegio)* right: *todos los niños tienen derecho a la enseñanza gratuita* all children have a right to free education. **3** *(de una tela, calcetín, etc)* right side.
▶ *nm pl* **derechos** *(impuestos)* duties, taxes; *(tarifa)* fees. LOC **¡no hay derecho!** it's not fair! **‖ tener derecho a** to be entitled to, have the right to. COMP **derecho civil** civil law. **‖ derecho de admisión** right *sing* to refuse admission. **‖ derechos de matrícula** registration fees. **‖ derechos humanos** human rights.

deriva *nf* drift. LOC **ir a la deriva** to drift.

derivada *nf* MAT derivative.

derivado,-a *adj* derived, derivative.
▶ *nm* **derivado** **1** LING derivative. **2** *(subproducto)* derivative, byproduct.

derivar *vi* **1** *(proceder)* to spring, arise, come, stem. **2** MAR to drift. **3** LING to be derived (de, from), derive (de, from).
▶ *vt* **1** *(dirigir)* to direct, divert. **2** LING to derive. **3** MAT to derive.
▶ *vpr* **derivarse** **1** *(proceder)* to result (de, from), stem (de, from). **2** LING to be derived (de, from).

dermatología *nf* dermatology.

dermatólogo,-a *nm & nf* dermatologist.

dérmico,-a *adj* dermal, dermic, skin.

dermis *nf inv* dermis.

dermoprotector,-ra *adj* which is kind to the skin.

derogar *vt* **1** JUR to abolish, repeal. **2** *(contrato)* to rescind, cancel.

derramar *vt* to pour out, spill.

derrame *nm* pouring out, spilling. COMP **derrame cerebral** MED brain haemorrhage.

derrapar *vi* to skid.

derredor *nm* surroundings *pl*. LOC **al/ en derredor** round, around.

✎ Consulta también **alrededor**.

derretir *vt (gen)* to melt; *(hielo, nieve)* to melt, thaw; *(metal)* to melt down.
▶ *vpr* **derretirse** *(fundirse)* to melt; *(hielo, nieve)* to melt, thaw.

derribar *vt* **1** *(demoler)* to pull down, demolish, knock down. **2** *(hacer caer a una persona)* to knock over; *(de un caballo)* to throw.

derribo *nm (demolición)* demolition, knocking down, pulling down.

derrocar *vt* **1** *(demoler)* to pull down, demolish, knock down. **2** *(gobierno)* to overthrow, bring down.

derrochar *vt (dilapidar)* to waste, squander.

derroche *nm (despilfarro)* waste, squandering.

derrota *nm* **1** *(de un ejército)* defeat. **2** *(fracaso)* failure, setback.

derrotar *vt* to defeat, beat: *me derrotó al tenis* he beat me at tennis.

derruido,-a *adj* in ruins.

derruir *vt* to pull down, demolish, knock down.

derrumbar *vt (demoler)* to pull down, demolish, knock down.
▶ *vpr* **derrumbarse** **1** *(un edificio)* to collapse, fall down; *(un techo)* to fall in, cave in. **2** *fig* to collapse.

desabotonar *vt (desabrochar)* to unbutton, undo.

desabrigar *vt (ropa)* to take someone's coat off.
▶ *vpr* **desabrigarse** *(uso reflexivo)* to take off one's coat.

desabrochar *vt* to undo, unfasten.
▶ *vpr* **desabrocharse** *(una prenda)* to come undone, come unfastened.

desacato *nm* **1** *(falta de respeto)* lack of respect (a, for), disrespect (a, for). **2** JUR contempt (a, for). LOC **desacato a la autoridad** contempt.

desacelerar *vi* to decelerate.

desaconsejar *vt* to advise against.

desacostumbrado,-a *adj* unusual, strange.

desacostumbrar *vt (hacer perder un uso)* to break of a habit, get out of a habit.

▶ *vpr* **desacostumbrarse** *(perder la costumbre)* to get out of the habit (de, of), lose the habit (de, of), give up (de, -).

desacreditar *vt* to discredit, bring discredit on, bring into discredit.

desactivar *vt* to defuse.

desacuerdo *nm* disagreement. LOC **estar en desacuerdo con** to be in disagreement with.

desafiar *vt* **1** *(gen)* to defy. **2** *(no hacer caso a)* to flout; *(no obedecer)* to defy. **3** *(plantar cara a - persona)* to defy, stand up to; *(- dificultad)* to brave. LOC **desafiar a ALGN a hacer ALGO** to challenge SB to do STH, dare SB to do STH.

desafilar *vt* to blunt.

desafinado,-a *adj* out of tune.

desafinar *vi (gen)* to be out of tune; *(cantar)* to sing out of tune; *(tocar)* to play out of tune.
▶ *vt* to put out of tune.

desafío *nm* **1** *(reto)* challenge. **2** *(provocación)* provocation, defiance.

desafortunadamente *adv* unfortunately.

desafortunado,-a *adj (sin suerte)* unlucky, unfortunate.

desagradable *adj* disagreeable, unpleasant.

desagradar *vi* to displease: *me desagrada su música* I don't like her music.

desagradecido,-a *adj* ungrateful.

desagrado *nm* displeasure, discontent. LOC **con desagrado** reluctantly.

desagraviar *vt (reparar el agravio)* to make amends for, make up for.

desagravio *nm* amends *pl*, compensation.

desagüe *nm* **1** *(acción)* draining, drainage. **2** *(cañería)* waste pipe, drainpipe.

desahogado,-a *adj* **1** *(espacioso)* roomy, spacious. **2** *(con dinero)* well-off, well-to-do, comfortable: *una posición desahogada* comfortable circumstances.

desahogar *vt* **1** *(consolar)* to comfort; *(aliviar)* to relieve. **2** *fig (mostrar)* to

vent, pour out: *desahogó sus penas* he vented his grief.
▸ *vpr* **desahogarse** *(desfogarse)* to let off steam: *¡desahógate!* don't bottle it up!

desahogo *nm* **1** *(alivio)* relief. **2** *fig (económico)* comfort, ease: *viven con desahogo* they live comfortably.

desahuciado,-a *adj* **1** *(enfermo)* hopeless. **2** *(inquilino)* evicted.

desahuciar *vt* **1** to deprive of all hope. **2** JUR *(inquilino)* to evict.

desahucio *nm* eviction.

desajuste *nm (mal funcionamiento)* maladjustment; *(avería)* breakdown.

desalar *vt* to desalt.

desalentador,-ra *adj* discouraging, disheartening.

desalentar *vt fig (quitar el ánimo)* to discourage, dishearten.
▸ *vpr* **desalentarse** get discouraged.

desaliento *nm* discouragement.

desalinear *vt* to put out of line.

desaliñado,-a *adj* untidy, unkempt, scruffy.

desalojar *vt* **1** *(marcharse)* to evacuate, clear, move out of. **2** *(inquilino)* to evict (de, from).

desamortización *nf* disentailment.

desamortizar *vt* to disentail.

desamparado,-a *adj (persona)* helpless, unprotected.

desamparar *vt* to abandon, desert, leave helpless.

desamparo *nm* **1** *(abandono)* abandonment, desertion. **2** *(falta de ayuda)* helplessness.

desandar *vt* to go back over, retrace.

desangrar *vt (sangrar)* to bleed.
▸ *vpr* **desangrarse** to bleed heavily, lose blood.

desanimado,-a *adj (decaído)* dejected, downhearted.

desanimar *vt* to discourage, dishearten.
▸ *vpr* **desanimarse** to be discouraged, be disheartened, lose heart.

desánimo *nm* despondency, discouragement, dejection.

desaparecer *vi (dejar de estar)* to disappear.

desaparecido,-a *adj* missing.
▸ *nm & nf* missing person: *había diez desaparecidos* there were ten missing.

desaparición *nf* disappearance.

desapasionado,-a *adj* dispassionate, objective, impartial.

desapego *nm* **1** *(indiferencia)* indifference. **2** *(falta de afecto)* coolness, lack of affection.

desapercibido,-a *adj (inadvertido)* unnoticed. LOC *pasar desapercibido,-a* to go unnoticed.

desaprensivo,-a *adj* unscrupulous.
▸ *nm & nf* unscrupulous person.

desaprobación *nf* disapproval.

desaprobar *vt* to disapprove of.

desaprovechado,-a *adj (desperdiciado)* wasted.

desaprovechar *vt* **1** *(no sacar suficiente provecho)* not to take advantage of. **2** *(desperdiciar)* to waste. LOC *desaprovechar una ocasión* to miss an opportunity, waste an opportunity.

desarmado,-a *adj* **1** *(sin armas)* unarmed. **2** *(desmontado)* dismantled, taken to pieces.

desarmar *vt* **1** *(quitar las armas)* to disarm. **2** *(desmontar)* to dismantle, take apart, take to pieces: *el mecánico desmontó el motor* the mechanic stripped the engine down.

desarme *nm* disarmament. COMP *desarme nuclear* nuclear disarmament.

desarraigado,-a *adj fig (persona)* rootless, without roots, uprooted.

desarraigar *vt (árbol, persona)* to uproot.
▸ *vpr* **desarraigarse** *fig (persona)* to pull up one's roots.

desarraigo *nm (de árbol, persona)* uprooting.

desarreglar *vt (desordenar)* make untidy, mess up, untidy.

desarrollado,-a *adj* developed: *es un país desarrollado* it's a developed country.

desarrollar *vt* **1** *(gen)* to develop. *(deshacer un rollo)* to unroll, unfold. **2** *(exponer)* to expound, explain. **3** *(llevar a cabo)* to carry out: *desarrollar un proyecto* to carry out a project. **4** MAT to expand, develop.
▶ *vpr* **desarrollarse** *(crecer)* to develop.

desarrollo *nm* **1** *(gen)* development. **2** MAT expansion.

desarticulado,-a *adj* disjointed.

desarticular *vt* **1** MED to disarticulate, put out of joint, dislocate. **2** *(un mecanismo)* to take to pieces.

desaseado,-a *adj* **1** *(sucio)* untidy, dirty. **2** *(dejado)* untidy, slovenly, unkempt, scruffy.

desasosegado,-a *adj* restless, anxious.

desasosegar *vt* to make restless, make uneasy.
▶ *vpr* **desasosegarse** to become restless, become uneasy.

desasosiego *nm* uneasiness, anxiety, restlessness.

desastrado,-a *adj (desaseado)* untidy, slovenly, unkempt, scruffy.

desastre *nm* **1** *(catástrofe)* disaster, catastrophe. **2** *fam (calamidad)* disaster, flop: *la excursión fue un desastre* the trip was a washout.

desastroso,-a *adj* disastrous.

desatar *vt* **1** *(soltar - gen)* to untie, undo, unfasten; *(- perro, etc)* to let loose: *desata al perro* let the dog loose. **2** *fig (desencadenar)* to spark off, give rise to; *(pasiones)* to unleash.
▶ *vpr* **desatarse 1** *(soltarse)* to come untied, come undone, come unfastened. **2** *fig (desencadenarse)* to break, explode: *se desató una gran tormenta* a great storm broke.

desatascador *nm* plunger.

desatascar *vt* to unblock, clear.

desatender *vt (no prestar atención)* to pay no attention to.

desatento,-a *adj (descortés)* discourteous, impolite.
▶ *nm & nf (descortés)* impolite person, discourteous person.

desatornillar *vt* to unscrew.

desautorización *nf* disapproval.

desautorizado,-a *adj* unauthorized.

desautorizar *vt* **1** *(desaprobar)* to disapprove. **2** *(prohibir)* to ban, forbid: *el gobierno desautorizó la manifestación* the Government banned the demonstration.

desavenencia *nf (desacuerdo)* disagreement, discord.

desavenir *vt* to cause to quarrel.
▶ *vpr* **desavenirse** to quarrel.

desayunar *vi* to have breakfast, breakfast.
▶ *vt* to have for breakfast.

desayuno *nm* breakfast.

desazón *nf fig (disgusto)* grief, affliction, worry.

desazonado,-a *adj* **1** *fig (disgustado)* upset. **2** *fig (inquieto)* anxious, uneasy.

desazonar *vt* **1** *fig (disgustar)* to annoy, upset. **2** *fig (inquietar)* to make uneasy, worry.
▶ *vpr* **desazonarse 1** *fig (disgustarse)* to get upset. **2** *fig (inquietarse)* to worry.

desbandada *nf* scattering.

desbandarse *vpr* to scatter, disperse.

desbaratar *vt (frustrar)* to spoil, ruin: *nos desbarató los planes* she spoilt our plans.

desbloquear *vt* **1** TÉC to free. **2** FIN to unfreeze.

desbloqueo *nm* **1** TÉC freeing. **2** FIN unfreezing.

desbocado,-a *adj (caballo)* runaway.

desbocar *vi (desembocar)* to flow (en, into).
▶ *vpr* **desbocarse** *(caballo)* to run away, bolt.

desbordar *vt* **1** *(sobrepasar)* to overflow. **2** *fig (exceder)* to surpass, exceed: *eso desborda mis conocimientos* that's way over my head.
▶ *vi (salirse)* to overflow: *el río desbordó* the river overflowed.
▶ *vpr* **desbordarse 1** *(salirse)* to overflow, flood. **2** *fig* to burst.

desbrozar *vt (terreno)* to clear of weeds, clear of undergrowth.

descabalgar *vi* to dismount.

descabellado,-a *adj fig* wild, crazy: *una idea descabellada* a crackpot idea.

descacharrar *vt fam (romper)* to break; *(estropear)* to ruin, mess up, spoil.

descafeinado,-a *adj* decaffeinated.
▶ *nm* **descafeinado** decaffeinated coffee.

descalabrar *vt (herir)* to injure; *(en la cabeza)* to injure in the head.
▶ *vpr* **descalabrarse** to injure one's head.

descalabro *nm* misfortune, damage, loss.

descalcificación *nf* decalcification.

descalcificar *vt* to decalcify.

descalificación *nf* **1** disqualification. **2** *(descrédito)* discredit.

descalificar *vt* **1** to disqualify. **2** *(desacreditar)* to discredit.

descalzar *vt (zapatos)* to take off SB's shoes.
▶ *vpr* **descalzarse** to take off one's shoes.

descalzo,-a *adj* barefoot, barefooted.

descamación *nf* desquamation.

descamarse *vpr* to desquamate.

descampado,-a *nm* open space, open field.

descansado,-a *adj* **1** rested, refreshed. **2** *(tranquilo)* easy, effortless.

descansar *vi* **1** *(gen)* to rest, have a rest; *(un momento)* to take a break. **2** *(dormir)* to sleep: *¡que descanses!* sleep well!

descansillo *nm* landing.

descanso *nm* **1** rest, break. **2** *(en un espectáculo)* interval; *(en un partido)* interval, half-time. **3** *(alivio)* relief, comfort: *¡qué descanso!* what a relief! **4** *(rellano)* landing.

descapitalizar *vt (perder el capital)* to undercapitalize.

descapotable *adj* convertible.
▶ *nm* convertible.

descarado,-a *adj (actitud)* shameless, brazen, insolent; *(persona)* cheeky.
▶ *nm & nf* shameless person, cheeky person.

descarga *nf* **1** *(acción)* unloading. **2** *(eléctrica)* discharge. **3** INFORM download.

descargar *vt* **1** *(disparar una arma)* to fire, discharge, shoot; *(vaciar una arma)* to unload. **2** INFORM to download.
▶ *vi (tormenta)* to break; *(nubes)* to burst.
▶ *vpr* **descargarse** *(pilas, baterías)* to discharge.

descargo *nm (descarga)* unloading.

descaro *nm* impudence, cheek, nerve. LOC *¡qué descaro!* what a cheek!

descarriado,-a *adj fig* lost. LOC **ser la oveja descarriada** *fig* to be the lost sheep.

descarriar *vt* **1** *(apartar del camino)* to send the wrong way, put on the wrong road, misdirect. **2** *fig* to lead astray.
▶ *vpr* **descarriarse 1** *(perderse)* to lose one's way, get lost, go the wrong way. **2** *fig* to go astray.

descarrilar *vi* to be derailed, run off the rails, go off the rails.

descartar *vt* to discard, reject, rule out: *descartamos esa posibilidad* we ruled out that possibility.

descastado,-a *adj (poco cariñoso)* unaffectionate, cold.
▶ *nm & nf (poco cariñoso)* unaffectionate person.

descendencia *nf* offspring, descendants *pl*.

descender *vi* **1** to descend, go down, come down. **2** *(temperatura, nivel, etc)* to drop, fall, go down. **3** *(ser descendiente)* to descend (de, from), issue (de, from).
▶ *vt (bajar)* to go down: *descendió la escalera muy rápidamente* he went down the stairs very quickly.

descendiente *nm o nf* descendant; *(hijos)* offspring.

descenso *nm* **1** *(acción)* descent, lowering. **2** *(de temperatura)* drop, fall. **3** *fig (declive)* decline, fall. **4** DEP *(de división)* relegation.

descentralización *nf* decentralization.

descentralizar *vt* to decentralize.

descentrar *vt fig* to disorientate, throw, put off.
▶ *vpr* **descentrarse** *fig* to become disorientated

descifrar *vt* **1** to decipher, decode. **2** *fig (llegar a comprender)* to solve, figure out.

desclavar *vt (desprender)* to take off.

descodificar *vt* to decode.

descolgar *vt* **1** *(cuadro, etc)* to take down. **2** *(bajar)* to lower, let down. **3** *(el teléfono)* to pick up, lift: *dejó el teléfono descolgado* she left the telephone off the hook.

descollar *vi* to stand out, excel.

descolonización *nf* decolonization.

descolonizar *vt* to decolonize.

descolorar *vt* to discolour (US discolor), fade.

descolorido,-a *adj* discoloured (US discolored), faded.

descombro *nm* clearing.

descompensar *vt* to unbalance, upset, throw out of kilter.

descomponer *vt* **1** *(separar)* to break down, split up. **2** *(estropear)* to break. **3** FÍS to resolve. **4** QUÍM to decompose. **5** MAT to split up. **6** *fig (molestar)* to disturb, upset; *(irritar)* irritate. **7** *(pudrir)* to rot.
▶ *vpr* **descomponerse** **1** *(pudrirse)* to decompose, rot. **2** *(estropearse)* to break down. **3** FÍS to resolve. **4** QUÍM to decompose. **5** MAT to split.

descomposición *nf* **1** *(pudrimiento)* decomposition, decay. **2** *fam (diarrea)* diarrhoea (US diarrhea).

descompresión *nf* decompression.

descomprimir *vt* to decompress, depressurize.

descompuesto,-a *adj* **1** *(podrido)* decomposed, decayed, rotten. **2** *(estropeado)* out of order, broken down. **3** *fig (alterado)* upset. [LOC] **estar descompuesto,-a** to have diarrhoea (US diarrhea).

descomunal *adj* huge, enormous.

desconcertado,-a *adj* disconcerted, confused, upset.

desconcertante *adj* disconcerting, upsetting.

desconcertar *vt (perturbar)* to disconcert, upset, disturb.
▶ *vpr* **desconcertarse** *(perturbarse)* to be disconcerted.

desconchado,-a *nm (pared)* flaking, peeling; *(loza)* chipping.

desconchar *vt (pared)* to peel off, flake; *(loza)* to chip.
▶ *vpr* **desconcharse** to peel off, flake off; *(loza)* to chip.

desconchón *nm (en pared)* bare patch.

desconcierto *nm* disorder, confusion, chaos.

desconectado,-a *adj fig* cut off (de, from).

desconectar *vt* **1** ELEC to disconnect. **2** *(un aparato)* to switch off, turn off. **3** *(desenchufar)* to unplug. **4** *fam fig* to turn off, switch off.

desconexión *nf* disconnection.

desconfiado,-a *adj* distrustful, suspicious, wary.
▶ *nm & nf* distrustful person, suspicious person, wary person.

desconfianza *nf* distrust, mistrust, suspicion.

desconfiar *vi* **1** *(faltar la confianza)* to distrust (de, -), mistrust (de, -), be suspicious (de, of). **2** *(tener cuidado)* to beware (de, of).

descongelar *vt* **1** *(comida)* to thaw, thaw out. **2** *(nevera)* to defrost.

descongestión *nf (nasal)* unblocking, clearing, decongestion.

descongestionar *vt* to clear.

desconocer *vt* not to know, be unaware of: *desconozco su nombre* I don't know her name.

desconocido,-a *adj* **1** *(no conocido)* unknown. **2** *(extraño)* strange, unfamiliar.
▶ *nm & nf* stranger, unknown person.
▶ *nm* **lo desconocido** the unknown.

desconocimiento *nm* ignorance (de, of).

desconsideración *nf* thoughtlessness .

desconsiderado,-a *adj* thoughtless.
▶ *nm & nf* thoughtless person.

desconsolado,-a *adj* disconsolate, grief-stricken, inconsolable.

desconsolar *vt* to distress, grieve.

desconsuelo *nm* affliction.

descontar *vt* (*restar*) to deduct, take off, knock off.

descontento,-a *adj* displeased, unhappy, dissatisfied, discontented.
▶ *nm & nf* malcontent.

descontrol *nm* *fam* lack of control, chaos.

descontrolado,-a *adj* 1 uncontrolled, out of control. 2 *fam fig* out of control, wild.

descontrolarse *vpr* (*persona*) to lose control.

desconvocar *vt* to cancel, call off.

descorazonador,-ra *adj* disheartening, discouraging.

descorazonar *vt* to dishearten, discourage.
▶ *vpr* **descorazonarse** to lose heart, get discouraged.

descorchar *vt* to uncork.

descorrer *vt* (*cortinas*) to draw; (*cerrojo*) to unbolt.

descortés *adj* impolite, rude, discourteous.

descortesía *nf* impoliteness, rudeness, discourtesy.

descoser *vt* to unpick.
▶ *vpr* **descoserse** to come unstitched.

descosido,-a *nm* open seam.

descoyuntar *vt* 1 (*hueso*) to dislocate, disjoint. 2 *fig* (*cansar*) to exhaust, tire out.
▶ *vpr* **descoyuntarse** to become dislocated. [LOC] **descoyuntarse de risa** *fam* to split one's sides laughing.

descreído,-a *adj* disbelieving, unbelieving.
▶ *nm & nf* disbeliever, unbeliever.

descremado,-a *adj* skimmed. [COMP] **yogur descremado** low-fat yoghurt.

describir *vt* to describe.

descripción *nf* description.

descriptivo,-a *adj* descriptive.

descrito,-a *adj* described.

descuartizar *vt* (*persona*) to quarter; (*animal*) to quarter, cut up.

descubierto,-a *adj* open, uncovered: *el cielo está descubierto* the sky is clear.

descubrimiento *nm* discovery.

descubrir *vt* 1 (*gen*) to discover; (*petróleo, oro, minas*) to find; (*conspiración*) to uncover; (*crimen*) to bring to light. 2 (*averiguar*) to find out, discover: *descubrimos sus intenciones* we found out his intentions.
▶ *vpr* **descubrirse** (*la cabeza*) to take off one's hat.

descuento *nm* 1 discount, reduction, deduction. 2 DEP injury time. [LOC] **con descuento** at a discount, on offer.

descuidado,-a *adj* 1 (*negligente*) careless, negligent. 2 (*desprevenido*) unprepared.

descuidar *vt* 1 to neglect, overlook. 2 (*distraer*) to distract.
▶ *vpr* **descuidarse** (*no tener cuidado*) to be careless. [LOC] **¡descuida!** don't worry!

descuido *nm* 1 (*negligencia*) negligence, carelessness, neglect. 2 (*distracción*) oversight, slip, mistake. [LOC] **por descuido** inadvertently, by mistake.

desde *prep* 1 (*tiempo*) since: *desde 1992* since 1992. 2 (*lugar*) from: *desde allí* from there. [LOC] **desde ahora** from now on. **‖ desde luego** 1 (*en realidad*) really. 2 (*como respuesta*) of course, certainly.

desdentado,-a *adj* toothless.

desdibujar *vt* to blur.
▶ *vpr* **desdibujarse** to become blurred, become faint.

desdicha *nf* misfortune, misery, adversity.

desdichado,-a *adj* unfortunate, wretched, unlucky.

desdoblar *vt* to unfold.

desdramatizar *vt* to make less traumatic, play down.

deseado,-a *adj* desired: *en el momento deseado* at the right time.

desear *vt* **1** *(querer)* to want: *deseo que venga* I want him to come. **2** *(anhelar)* to long for, wish for, desire; *(para alguien)* to wish: *¿qué desea?* can I help you?, what can I do for you?

desecar *vt* **1** *(gen)* to dry up. **2** *(pantano, laguna, etc)* to drain.
▶ *vpr* **desecarse** to dry up.

desechable *adj* disposable.

desechar *vt* **1** *(tirar)* to discard, throw out, throw away. **2** *(rechazar)* to refuse, reject; *(proyecto, idea)* to drop, discard.

desecho *nm* *(residuo)* reject.
▶ *nm pl* **desechos** waste *sing*, rubbish *sing.*

desembalar *vt* to unpack.

desembarazar *vt* *(dejar libre)* to free.
▶ *vpr* **desembarazarse** *(librarse)* to rid os (de, of), get rid (de, of).

desembarcar *vi* to disembark, land, go ashore.
▶ *vt* *(mercancías)* to unload; *(personas)* to disembark, put ashore.

desembarco *nm* *(mercancías)* landing, unloading; *(personas)* disembarkation, landing.

desembocadura *nf* *(de río)* mouth, outlet.

desembocar *vi* **1** *(río)* to flow (en, into). **2** *(calle)* to end (en, at), lead (en, into).

desembolso *nm* *(gasto)* expense, outlay, expenditure.

desembozar *vt* *fig* to uncover, bring out into the open.

desembrujar *vt* to remove a spell from.

desembuchar *vi* to come clean, spill the beans: *¡desembucha de una vez!* come out with it once and for all!

desempañar *vt* to wipe the steam from, demist.

desempaquetar *vt* to unpack, unwrap.

desemparejar *vt* to separate.

desempatar *vt* to break a tie between.
▶ *vi* DEP *(desempatar un resultado)* to break the deadlock.

desempate *nm* **1** tie-break, tiebreaker. **2** DEP play-off, tie-break. COMP **partido de desempate** play off, deciding match.

desempeñar *vt* **1** *(cumplir una obligación)* to discharge, fulfil (US fulfill), carry out; *(un cargo)* to fill, hold, occupy. **2** *(papel)* to play: *desempeña un papel vital* she plays a vital role.

desempeño *nm* **1** *(obligaciones, cargo)* carrying out, fulfilment (US fulfillment). **2** TEAT performance, acting.

desempleado,-a *adj* unemployed, out of work.
▶ *nm & nf* unemployed person.

desempleo *nm* unemployment. LOC **cobrar el desempleo** to be on the dole, (US be on welfare).

desempolvar *vt* **1** *(quitar el polvo)* to dust. **2** *fig (volver a usar)* to unearth.

desencadenar *vt fig (producir)* to spark off, give rise to.
▶ *vpr* **desencadenarse** **1** *(desatarse)* to break loose. **2** *(guerra, tormenta)* to break out: *se desencadenó una tormenta* a storm broke. **3** *(acontecimientos)* to start.

desencajar *vt* *(desunir)* to take apart, disjoint.
▶ *vpr* **desencajarse** *(desunirse)* to come apart, come loose.

desencallar *vt* to refloat.

desencantar *vt* *(desilusionar)* to disillusion, disappoint.
▶ *vpr* **desencantarse** to be disappointed, be disillusioned.

desencanto *nm* *(desilusión)* disillusionment, disappointment.

desenchufar *vt* to unplug, disconnect.

desencolar *vt* to unglue, unstick.
▶ *vpr* **desencolarse** to come unglued, come unstuck.

desencuadernar *vt* to unbind.
▶ *vpr* **desencuadernarse** to come unbound.

D

desenfadado,-a *adj* **1** *(despreocupado)* free and easy, carefree. **2** *(ropa)* casual.

desenfadar *vt* to calm down.
▸ *vpr* **desenfadarse** to calm down.

desenfado *nm* **1** *(soltura)* self-confidence, assurance. **2** *(franqueza)* frankness, openness.

desenfocado,-a *adj* out of focus.

desenfocar *vt* to take out of focus.

desenfoque *nm* incorrect focusing.

desenfrenado,-a *adj* *(gen)* frantic, uncontrolled, wild.

desenfreno *nm* *(falta de control)* lack of control, wild abandon.

desenfundar *vt* *(quitar)* to draw out, pull out.

desenganchar *vt* *(gen)* to unhook, unfasten; *(despegar)* to unstick.

desengañado,-a *adj* **1** *(desilusionado)* disillusioned. **2** *(decepcionado)* disappointed, let down.

desengañar *vt* **1** *(decepcionar)* to disappoint. **2** *(desilusionar)* to disillusion.
▸ *vpr* **desengañarse 1** *(ver la verdad)* to have one's eyes opened (de, about). **2** *(tener una decepción)* to be disappointed.

desengaño *nm* *(desilusión)* disillusion; *(decepción)* disappointment. LOC **sufrir un desengaño** to be disappointed.

desengrasar *vt* to remove the grease from.

desenhebrar *vt* to unthread.

desenjaular *vt* to let out of a cage, release.

desenlace *nm* **1** *(resultado)* outcome, result. **2** *(final)* end.

desenlazar *vt* *(desatar)* to untie, undo.

desenmarañar *vt* **1** *(desenredar)* to untangle, unravel. **2** *fig (poner en claro)* to unravel, clear up; *(un asunto)* to sort out.

desenmascarar *vt* to unmask.

desenredar *vt* to untangle, disentangle.
▸ *vpr* **desenredarse** to get out (de, of), extricate OS (de, from).

desenrollar *vt* to unroll, unwind.

desenroscar *vt* to unscrew, uncoil.

desentenderse *vpr* *(afectar ignorancia)* to pretend not to know (de, -/about), ignore (de, -), feign ignorance (de, of): *se desentiende de mí* she ignores me.

desenterrar *vt* *(un objeto)* to unearth, dig up; *(cadáver)* to disinter, exhume.

desentonar *vi* **1** MÚS *(instrumento)* to be out of tune; *(cantante)* to sing out of tune. **2** *fig (combinar)* not to match (con, -).

desentrenado,-a *adj* out of training.

desentrenarse *vpr* to be out of training, get out of training.

desenvainar *vt* to unsheathe, draw.

desenvoltura *nf* *fig (soltura)* confidence, assurance.

desenvolver *vt* **1** *(quitar lo que envuelve)* to unwrap. **2** *(aclarar)* to clear up.
▸ *vpr* **desenvolverse** *(manejarse)* to manage, cope: *se desenvuelve muy bien en los negocios* he manages very well in business.

desenvuelto,-a *adj* *(seguro)* confident, self-assured.

deseo *nm* wish, desire. LOC **formular un deseo** to make a wish. COMP **buenos deseos** good intentions.

deseoso,-a *adj* desirous, eager, anxious. LOC **estar deseoso,-a de hacer** ALGO to be eager to do STH.

desequilibrado,-a *adj* **1** unbalanced, out of balance. **2** *(persona)* mentally unbalanced.

desequilibrar *vt* **1** to unbalance, throw off balance. **2** *fig* to unbalance.
▸ *vpr* **desequilibrarse** *fig* to become unbalanced.

desequilibrio *nm* **1** lack of balance, imbalance. **2** *fig (mental)* unbalanced state of mind.

desertar *vi* **1** MIL to desert. **2** *fig (abandonar)* to abandon, desert.

desértico,-a *adj* desert.

desertización *nf* desertification.

desertor,-ra *nm & nf* deserter.

desesperación *nf* despair, desperation.

desesperadamente *adv* desperately, frantically.

desesperado,-a *adj (sin esperanza)* hopeless, desperate.

desesperanza *nf* despair, desperation, hopelessness.

desesperanzar *vt* to drive to despair.
▶ *vpr* **desesperanzarse** to despair, lose hope, give up hope (de, of).

desesperar *vt* 1 *(hacer perder la paciencia)* to drive to despair. 2 *(exasperar)* to exasperate.
▶ *vpr* **desesperarse** 1 *(desesperanzar)* to lose hope, despair. 2 *(irritarse)* to get irritated, become exasperated: *se desespera por todo* everything exasperates her.

desestabilización *nf* destabilization.

desestabilizar *vt* to destabilize.

desestimar *vt* to disregard, underestimate.

desfachatez *nf* cheek, nerve.

desfalco *nm* embezzlement.

desfallecer *vt (disminuir las fuerzas)* to weaken.
▶ *vi* 1 *(debilitar)* to weaken, lose strength. 2 *(decaer)* to lose heart.

desfallecido,-a *adj* weak, faint.

desfallecimiento *nm* faintness.

desfasado,-a *adj* outdated, out of date; *(persona)* old-fashioned, behind the times.

desfasar *vt* TÉC to phase out.
▶ *vpr* **desfasarse** 1 TÉC to change phase. 2 *(persona)* to be out of synch.

desfase *nm* 1 *(diferencia)* imbalance, gap. 2 TÉC phase difference. COMP **desfase horario** 1 *(entre países)* time difference. 2 *(al volar en avión)* jet lag.

desfavorable *adj* unfavourable (US unfavorable).

desfavorecer *vt (perjudicar)* to disadvantage, put at a disadvantage.

desfigurado,-a *adj (persona)* disfigured.

desfigurar *vt (cara)* to disfigure.
▶ *vpr* **desfigurarse** *(descomponerse)* to become distorted.

desfiladero *nm* defile, gorge, narrow pass.

desfilar *vi* 1 *(gen)* to march. 2 MIL to march, march past, parade. 3 *(moda)* to parade, walk up and down.

desfile *nm* 1 *(gen)* parade, procession. 2 MIL parade. 3 *(moda)* fashion show.

desfogar *vt (descargar)* to give vent to, vent.
▶ *vpr* **desfogarse** to let off steam, vent one's anger.

desgajar *vt* 1 *(rama)* to tear off; *(página)* to rip out, tear out. 2 *(romper)* to break.

desgana *nf (inapetencia)* lack of appetite. LOC **con desgana** reluctantly.

desganado,-a *adj* 1 *(sin gana)* not hungry: *está desganado* he has no appetite. 2 *(apático)* apathetic, half-hearted.

desganar *vt* 1 *(quitar el apetito)* to spoil the appetite of. 2 *(quitar las ganas)* to turn off.
▶ *vpr* **desganarse** 1 *(perder el apetito)* to lose one's appetite. 2 *(perder el interés)* to lose interest (de, in), go off (de, -).

desgañitarse *vpr* fam to shout OS hoarse, shout one's head off.

desgarbado,-a *adj* ungainly, ungraceful, clumsy.

desgarrador,-ra *adj* heartbreaking, heart-rending.

desgarrar *vt (rasgar)* to tear, rip.
▶ *vpr* **desgarrarse** *(rasgarse)* to tear, rip.

desgarro *nm (rompimiento)* tear, rip.

desgastar *vt (ropa)* to wear out, wear away; *(tacones)* to wear down.
▶ *vpr* **desgastarse** *(gastarse)* to wear out, get worn.

desgaste *nm (gen)* wear.

desglosar *vt* 1 *(escrito)* to detach. 2 *(gastos)* to break down.

desglose *nm* breakdown, separation.

desgracia *nf* 1 *(desdicha)* misfortune. 2 *(mala suerte)* bad luck, mischance. LOC **por desgracia** unfortunately.

desgraciado,-a *adj* **1** *(sin suerte)* unfortunate, unlucky. **2** *(infeliz)* unhappy.
▶ *nm & nf* wretch, unfortunate person.

desgraciar *vt (echar a perder)* to spoil.
▶ *vpr* **desgraciarse** *(malograrse)* to fail, be spoiled; *(plan, proyecto)* to fall through.

desgranar *vt (guisante, maíz)* to shell; *(trigo)* to thresh.

desgravar *vt* to deduct.

desguace *nm* **1** *(de barco)* breaking up; *(coche)* car breaking, scrapping. **2** *(lugar)* breaker's yard, scrapyard.

desguazar *vt (barco)* to break up; *(coche)* to scrap.

deshabitado,-a *adj (pueblo, lugar)* uninhabited; *(casa, piso)* unoccupied.

deshabitar *vt* to leave, abandon, vacate.

deshabituar *vt (hacer perder el hábito)* to break from the habit.
▶ *vpr* **deshabituarse** to get out of the habit (a, of), give up (a, -).

deshacer *vt* **1** *(estropear)* to ruin, damage; *(romper)* to break; *(desordenar)* to upset. **2** *(nudo)* to untie, loosen; *(paquete)* to undo, unwrap; *(cama)* to strip; *(equipaje)* to unpack; *(puntadas)* to unpick. **3** *(romper un acuerdo)* to break off. **4** *(disolver)* to dissolve; *(derretir)* to melt. **5** *(desandar)* to retrace. **6** *(planes, proyectos)* to spoil, ruin.
▶ *vpr* **deshacerse 1** *(nudo)* to come undone, come untied; *(puntada)* to come unsewn. **2** *(disolverse)* to dissolve; *(derretirse)* to melt.

desharrapado,-a *adj* ragged, in tatters.

deshecho,-a *adj* **1** *(destruido)* destroyed. **2** *(estropeado)* damaged, ruined. **3** *(nudo)* untied, undone; *(paquete)* unwrapped; *(cama)* unmade; *(equipaje)* unpacked. **4** *(disuelto)* dissolved; *(derretido)* melted.

deshelar *vt* **1** to thaw, melt. **2** *(congelador)* to defrost. **3** *(coche)* to de-ice.
▶ *vpr* **deshelarse** to thaw out, melt.

desherbar *vt* to weed.

desheredar *vt* to disinherit.

deshidratación *nf* dehydration.

deshidratado,-a *adj* dehydrated.

deshidratar *vt* to dehydrate.
▶ *vpr* **deshidratarse** to become dehydrated.

deshielo *nm* thaw; *(de congelador)* defrosting; *(de parabrisas)* de-icing.

deshilachado,-a *adj* frayed.

deshilachar *vt* to fray.

deshilvanar *vt* to untack.

deshinchado,-a *adj* **1** *(neumático, etc)* flat, deflated. **2** *(sin hinchazón)* not swollen: *la rodilla ya la tienes deshinchada* the swelling in your knee has gone down.

deshinchar *vt* **1** *(neumático, etc)* to deflate, let down. **2** *(reducir la hinchazón)* to reduce the swelling of.
▶ *vpr* **deshincharse 1** *(reducirse la hinchazón)* to deflate, go down. **2** *(reducirse la hinchazón)* to go down.

deshojar *vt (flor)* to strip the petals off; *(árbol)* to strip the leaves off.
▶ *vpr* **deshojarse** *(flor)* to lose its petals; *(árbol)* to lose its leaves.

deshollinador *nm* chimney sweep.

deshollinar *vt* to sweep.

deshonestidad *nf (sin honestidad)* dishonesty.

deshonesto,-a *adj (sin honestidad)* dishonest.

deshonra *nf* dishonour (US dishonor), disgrace.

deshonrar *vt (gen)* to dishonour (US dishonor), disgrace.

deshonroso,-a *adj* dishonourable (US dishonorable).

desidia *nf* negligence.

desierto,-a *adj (sin habitantes)* uninhabited, deserted: *una isla desierta* a desert island.
▶ *nm* **desierto** desert.

designar *vt* **1** *(denominar)* to designate. **2** *(nombrar para un cargo)* to appoint, name, assign.

desigual *adj* **1** *(gen)* unequal, uneven. **2** *(diferente)* different, unequal. **3** *(irregular)* uneven, irregular. **4** *(no liso)* uneven, rough. **5** *(variable)* changeable:

tiene un carácter muy desigual she is very changeable.

desigualdad *nf (gen)* inequality, difference.

desilusión *nf* disappointment.

desilusionar *vt* to disappoint.
► *vpr* **desilusionarse** to be disappointed.

desincrustar *vt* to descale.

desinencia *nf* ending, desinence.

desinfectante *adj* disinfectant.
► *nm* disinfectant.

desinfectar *vt* to disinfect.

desinflamar *vt* to reduce the inflammation in.
► *vpr* **desinflamarse** to go down.

desinflar *vt (gen)* to deflate; *(una rueda)* to let down.
► *vpr* **desinflarse** to go down.

desinformar *vi* to misinform.

desinsectar *vt* to fumigate.

desintegrar *vt* 1 to disintegrate. 2 *fig* to disintegrate, break up. 3 FÍS to split.
► *vpr* **desintegrarse** 1 to disintegrate. 2 *fig* to break up. 3 FÍS to split.

desinterés *nm (falta de interés)* lack of interest, indifference.

desinteresarse *vpr* 1 *(perder el interés)* to lose interest (de, in), go off (de, -). 2 *(desentenderse)* to have nothing to do (de, with).

desintoxicación *nf* detoxication.

desintoxicar *vt* to detoxicate.

desistir *vi (gen)* to desist, give up.

deslavar *vt* to half-wash.

desleal *adj* disloyal.

deslealtad *nf* disloyalty.

deslenguado,-a *adj fig (descarado)* insolent, cheeky.

desligar *vt* 1 *(desatar)* to untie, unfasten. 2 *fig (separar)* to separate (de, from). 3 *fig (librar de una obligación)* to release (de, from), free (de, from).
► *vpr* **desligarse** 1 *(desatarse)* to break away (de, from). 2 *(librarse)* to release OS (de, from), free OS (de, from).

deslindar *vt* to delimit, mark the boundaries of.

desliz *nm* 1 *(resbalón)* slide, slip. 2 *fig (error)* slip, mistake error. LOC **tener un desliz** *fig* to slip up, make a slip.

deslizamiento *nm* slipping, slip. COMP **deslizamiento de tierra** landslide.

deslizar *vt (pasar)* to slide, slip.
► *vi (resbalar)* to slide, slip.
► *vpr* **deslizarse** *(gen)* to slide; *(sobre agua)* to glide.

deslucir *vt fig (quitar la gracia)* to mar, spoil.

deslumbrar *vt* to dazzle.

deslustrar *vt (metal)* to tarnish.

desmadejar *vt fig* to tire out, exhaust.

desmagnetizar *vt* to demagnetize.

desmantelar *vt* to dismantle.

desmaquillar *vt* to remove make-up from.
► *vpr* **desmaquillarse** to remove one's make-up.

desmarcarse *vpr* 1 DEP to get into an unmarked position. 2 *(distanciarse)* to distance OS (de, from), disassociate OS (de, from).

desmayar *vt (causar desmayo)* to make faint.
► *vpr* **desmayarse** *(perder el sentido)* to faint.

desmayo *nm (pérdida del conocimiento)* faint, fainting fit. LOC **sufrir/tener un desmayo** to faint.

desmejorar *vt* to spoil, make worse, damage.
► *vi* to deteriorate, get worse, go downhill.
► *vpr* **desmejorarse** to deteriorate, get worse, go downhill.

desmelenar *vt (desgreñar)* to tousle, dishevel.
► *vpr* **desmelenarse** *fam (desmadrarse)* to let one's hair down.

desmemoriado,-a *adj* forgetful, absent-minded.

desmentir *vt* 1 *(negar)* to deny. 2 *(contradecir)* to contradict, belie.

desmenuzar *vt (gen)* to break into little pieces.

desmirriado,-a *adj fam* weedy, puny.

desmitificar *vt* to demystify.

desmoldar *vt* to remove from a mould, turn out.

desmontable *adj* that can be taken to pieces.

desmontar *vt* **1** *(desarmar)* to take to pieces, take down, dismantle. **2** *(motor)* to strip.
▶ *vi (del caballo)* to dismount (de, -).

desmoralizar *vt* to demoralize.
▶ *vpr* **desmoralizarse** to become demoralized.

desmoronamiento *nm* crumbling, disintegration, fall.

desmoronar *vt* to crumble, destroy.
▶ *vpr* **desmoronarse** to crumble, collapse, fall to pieces.

desnatado,-a *adj (leche)* skimmed; *(yogur)* low-fat.

desnaturalización *nf* **1** QUÍM denaturation. **2** *(adulteración)* adulteration.

desnaturalizar *vt* **1** *(adulterar)* to adulterate. **2** QUÍM to denature, denaturize.

desnivel *nm* **1** unevenness. **2** *(cuesta)* slope, drop. **3** *fig* difference.

desnivelar *vt* **1** *(sacar de nivel)* to make uneven. **2** *(desequilibrar)* to throw out of balance; *(balanza)* to tip.

desnudar *vt* **1** to undress. **2** *fig (despojar)* to strip.
▶ *vpr* **desnudarse** *(persona)* to get undressed, take one's clothes off.

desnudez *nf* nudity, nakedness.

desnudo,-a *adj (persona)* naked, nude; *(parte del cuerpo)* bare.

desnutrición *nf* malnutrition, undernourishment.

desnutrido,-a *adj* undernourished.

desobedecer *vt* to disobey.

desobediente *adj* disobedient.

desocupado,-a *adj* **1** *(ocioso)* free, not busy. **2** *(desempleado)* unemployed, out of work.

desocupar *vt* to vacate, leave, empty.

desodorante *nm* deodorant.

desolación *nf* **1** desolation. **2** *(tristeza)* affliction, grief.

desolado,-a *adj (triste)* distressed, heartbroken.

desolador,-ra *adj (desconsolador)* heartbreaking, devastating.

desorden *nm* disorder, disarray, mess, untidiness.

desordenado,-a *adj* **1** *(habitación, etc)* untidy, messy. **2** *(persona)* slovenly.

desordenar *vt* to untidy, disarrange, mess up.

desorganizar *vt* to disorganize, disrupt.

desorientar *vt* **1** to disorientate. **2** *fig (confundir)* to confuse.
▶ *vpr* **desorientarse** to lose one's bearings, lose one's sense of direction, get lost.

desovar *vi (insectos)* to lay eggs; *(peces)* to spawn.

desove *nm (insectos)* egg-laying; *(peces)* spawning.

desoxidante *adj* deoxidizing.

desoxirribonucleico,-a *adj* deoxyribonucleic.

despabilado,-a *adj fig (listo)* smart, sharp, quick.

despabilar *vt fig (despertar)* to wake up.
▶ *vpr* **despabilarse** **1** *(despertarse)* to wake up. **2** *(avivarse)* to wise up.

despachar *vt* **1** *(resolver)* to resolve, get through; *(tratar un asunto)* to deal with, attend. **2** *(despedir)* to dismiss, sack, fire. **3** *(en tienda)* to serve; *(vender)* to sell.

despacho *nm (oficina)* office; *(estudio)* study. COMP **despacho de billetes/localidades** ticket/box office.

despacio *adv (gen)* slowly.

desparasitar *vt (piojos)* to delouse; *(lombrices)* to worm.

desparramar *vt* to spread, scatter; *(un líquido)* to spill.

despectivo,-a *adj* **1** contemptuous, disparaging. **2** GRAM pejorative, derogatory.

despedida *nf* farewell, goodbye.

despedir *vt* **1** *(echar)* to throw out. **2** *(del trabajo)* to dismiss, fire, sack. **3**

(decir adiós) to see off, say goodbye to.

▶ *vpr* **despedirse** *(decirse adiós)* to say goodbye (de, to).

despegar *vt (desenganchar)* to unstick, take off, detach.

▶ *vi (avión)* to take off.

▶ *vpr* **despegarse** *(separarse)* to come unstuck.

despegue *nm (avión)* takeoff.

despeinar *vt* to dishevel, ruffle.

▶ *vpr* **despeinarse** to mess up one's hair.

despejar *vt* **1** *(desalojar)* to clear. **2** MAT to find. **3** INFORM to clear.

▶ *vpr* **despejarse** **1** METEOR to clear up. **2** *(espabilarse)* to wake OS up, clear one's head.

despenalizar *vt* to legalize.

despensa *nf (lugar)* pantry, larder.

despeñar *vt* to throw over a cliff.

▶ *vpr* **despeñarse** *(caer)* to fall over a cliff.

desperdiciar *vt* to waste, squander; *(oportunidad)* to throw away.

desperdicio *nm* waste.

▶ *nm pl* **desperdicios** *(basura)* rubbish *sing; (desechos)* scraps, leftovers.

desperdigar *vt* to scatter, disperse.

desperezarse *vpr* to stretch.

desperfecto *nm* **1** *(daño)* damage. **2** *(defecto)* flaw, defect.

despertador *nm* alarm clock.

despertar *vt* to wake, wake up, awaken.

▶ *vi* to wake up, awake.

▶ *vpr* **despertarse** to wake up, awake.

despiadado,-a *adj* ruthless, merciless.

despido *nm* dismissal, sacking.

despierto,-a *adj* **1** awake. **2** *(espabilado)* lively, smart, sharp, bright.

despilfarrar *vt* to waste, squander.

despilfarro *nm* waste.

despistado,-a *adj (distraído)* absent-minded.

despistar *vt fig (desorientar)* to mislead, confuse.

▶ *vpr* **despistarse** **1** *(perderse)* to get lost.. **2** *(distraerse)* to get confused.

despiste *nm* **1** *(distracción)* absent-mindedness. **2** *(error)* mistake, slip.

desplazamiento *nm (traslado)* moving, removal.

desplazar *vt* **1** *(mover)* to move, shift. **2** *fig (sustituir)* to replace, take over from.

▶ *vpr* **desplazarse** to travel.

desplegar *vt (extender)* to unfold, spread (out).

despliegue *nm fig (exhibición)* display, show, manifestation.

desplomar *vt (hacer perder la verticalidad)* to put out of plumb.

▶ *vpr* **desplomarse** *(caer algo de peso)* to fall down, collapse, topple over.

despoblar *vt* to depopulate.

▶ *vpr* **despoblarse** to become depopulated, become deserted.

despojar *vt (quitar)* to deprive (de, of), strip.

▶ *vpr* **despojarse** *(desposeerse voluntariamente)* to forsake (de, -), give up (de,-).

despojo *nm (botín)* plunder, booty.

▶ *nm pl* **despojos** *(sobras)* leavings, scraps, leftovers.

desposeer *vt (gen)* to dispossess.

déspota *nm o nf* despot, tyrant.

despreciar *vt* **1** *(desdeñar)* to despise, scorn, look down on. **2** *(ignorar)* to disregard, ignore.

desprecio *nm (desestima)* contempt, scorn, disdain.

desprender *vt* **1** *(soltar)* to release. **2** *(emanar)* to give off.

▶ *vpr* **desprenderse** *(soltarse)* to come off, come away.

desprendimiento *nm (acción de desprenderse)* detachment, loosening.

despreocupado,-a *adj (tranquilo)* unconcerned, unworried.

despreocuparse *vpr* **1** *(dejar de preocuparse)* to stop worrying. **2** *(desentenderse)* to be unconcerned (de, about), be indifferent (de, to).

desprestigiar *vt* to discredit, ruin the reputation of.

desprevenido,-a *adj* unprepared, unready. LOC **coger/pillar a** ALGN **desprevenido,-a** to catch SB unawares, take SB by surprise.

desproporcionado,-a *adj* disproportionate, out of proportion.

después *adv* **1** afterwards, later. **2** *(entonces)* then. **3** *(luego)* next. LOC **después de 1** *(tiempo)* after. **2** *(desde)* since. **3** *(+ pp)* after, once: *después de la cena* after supper. ▌ **después de todo** after all: *después de todo no está tan mal* it's not that bad after all.

despuntar *vt (quitar la punta)* to blunt, make blunt.

destacamento *nm* detachment.

destacar *vi (despuntar)* to stand out.
  ▶ *vt fig (dar énfasis)* to point out, emphasize.
  ▶ *vpr* **destacarse** to stand out.

destajo *nm* piecework. LOC **a destajo** by the piece.

destapar *vt* **1** *(gen)* to open: *destapé la caja y vi que estaba vacía* I opened the box and saw it was empty. **2** *(tapón)* to uncork; *(tapa)* to take the lid off. **3** *fig (descubrir)* to reveal, uncover.
  ▶ *vpr* **destaparse** *(en la cama)* to take the covers off.

destellar *vi (estrella)* to twinkle.

destello *nm (resplandor)* sparkle, flash; *(brillo)* gleam, shine.

destemplado,-a *adj* **1** *(carácter)* irritable, tetchy. **2** *(tiempo)* unpleasant.

desteñir *vt* to discolour (US discolor), fade.
  ▶ *vi* to lose colour (US color), fade, run.

desternillarse LOC **desternillarse de risa** *fam* to split one's sides laughing, be in stitches.

desterrar *vt* to exile, banish.

destiempo LOC **a destiempo** inopportunely, at the wrong moment: *llegó a destiempo* he arrived at the wrong moment.

destierro *nm* **1** *(pena)* banishment, exile. **2** *(lugar)* place of exile.

destilar *vt* to distil (US distill).

destilería *nf* distillery.

destinar *vt* **1** *(asignar)* to assign, set aside, destine; *(dinero)* to allocate, set aside. **2** *(persona)* to assign, post.

destinatario,-a *nm & nf* **1** *(de carta)* addressee. **2** *(de mercancías)* consignee.

destino *nm* **1** *(sino)* destiny, fate. **2** *(uso)* purpose, use. **3** *(lugar)* destination. LOC **con destino a** bound for, going to.

destitución *nf* dismissal, removal.

destituir *vt* to dismiss.

destornillador *nm* screwdriver.

destornillar *vt* to unscrew.

destrabar *vt (quitar las trabas)* to unfetter.

destreza *nf* skill.

destronar *vt* **1** to dethrone. **2** *fig* to overthrow, unseat.

destrozar *vt* **1** *(romper)* to destroy, wreck; *(despedazar)* to tear to pieces, tear to shreds. **2** *fig (causar daño moral)* to crush, shatter, devastate.

destrozo *nm (acción)* destruction.

destrucción *nf* destruction.

destruir *vt* to destroy.

desunir *vt (separar)* to divide, separate.

desuso *nm* disuse: *eso está en desuso* that's obsolete, that's outdated.

desvalido,-a *adj* needy, destitute.

desvalijar *vt* **1** *(a alguien)* to rob. **2** *(un lugar)* to burgle.

desván *nm* loft, attic.

desvanecer *vt* **1** *(hacer desaparecer)* to clear, dispel, disperse. **2** *fig (recuerdo, etc)* to dispel, banish.
  ▶ *vpr* **desvanecerse 1** *(disiparse)* to disperse, clear. **2** *fig (desaparecer)* to vanish, disappear; *(recuerdos)* to fade.

desvanecimiento *nm (desmayo)* faint, fainting fit.

desvariar *vi* to be delirious, rave.

desvarío *nm* **1** *(delirio)* delirium, raving. **2** *(disparate)* nonsense, act of madness. **3** *(capricho)* fancy, whim.

desvelar *vt* **1** *(quitar el sueño)* to keep awake. **2** *fig (revelar)* to reveal, disclose: *nos desveló el secreto* she revealed the secret to us.

▶ *vpr* **desvelarse 1** to be unable to sleep. **2** *fig (dedicarse)* to devote OS (por, to): *siempre se ha desvelado por su familia* she has always devoted herself to her family.

desvelo *nm (dedicación)* devotion, dedication.

desventaja *nf* **1** disadvantage, drawback. **2** *(problema)* problem. LOC **estar en desventaja** to be at a disadvantage.

desvergonzado,-a *adj (sinvergüenza)* shameless, brazen.

desvergüenza *nf (falta de decoro)* shamelessness.

desvestir *vt* to undress.

▶ *vpr* **desvestirse** to undress, get undressed.

desviación *nf* **1** deviation. **2** *(de carretera)* diversion, detour.

desviar *vt* **1** *(gen)* to deviate, change the course of: *desvió la mirada* she looked away. **2** *(golpe, balón)* to deflect. **3** *(carretera, río, barco, avión)* to divert. **4** *fig (tema)* to change.

▶ *vpr* **desviarse 1** *(avión, barco)* to go off course; *(coche)* to make a detour. **2** *(golpe, balón)* to be deflected. **3** *(persona, camino)* to leave.

desvío *nm* diversion, detour.

desvivirse *vpr* **1** *(desvelarse)* to do one's utmost (por, for), be devoted (por, to). **2** *(desear)* to be mad (por, about).

detallado,-a *adj* detailed, thorough.

detallar *vt* **1** to detail, give the details of, tell in detail. **2** *(especificar)* to specify.

detalle *nm* **1** *(pormenor)* detail, particular. **2** *(delicadeza)* nice gesture, nice thought. **3** *(toque decorativo)* touch. LOC **al detalle** COM retail. ▌ **tener un detalle** to be considerate, be thoughtful.

detallista *nm o nf* COM retailer, retail trader.

detectar *vt* to detect.

detective *nm o nf* detective.

detener *vt* **1** *(parar)* to stop, halt; *(proceso, negociación)* to hold up. **2** *(retener)* to keep, delay, detain.

▶ *vpr* **detenerse 1** *(pararse)* to stop, halt: *el tren se detuvo* the train stopped. **2** *(entretenerse)* to hang about, linger.

detenidamente *adv* carefully, thoroughly.

detenido,-a *adj* **1** *(parado)* held up. **2** JUR under arrest: *está detenido* he's under arrest.

▶ *nm & nf* JUR prisoner.

detergente *nm* detergent.

deteriorar *vt (estropear)* to damage, spoil; *(gastar)* to wear out.

▶ *vpr* **deteriorarse** *(estropearse)* to get damaged; *(gastarse)* to wear out.

deterioro *nm* **1** *(daño)* damage, deterioration; *(desgaste)* wear and tear. **2** *fig (empeoramiento)* deterioration, worsening.

determinado,-a *adj* **1** *(preciso)* definite, precise, certain, given, particular. **2** *(día, hora, etc)* fixed, set, appointed. **3** GRAM definite. **4** MAT determinate.

determinante *adj* decisive, determinant.

▶ *nm* MAT determinant.

determinar *vt* **1** *(decidir)* to resolve, decide, determine. **2** *(fijar)* to fix, set, appoint. **3** *(estipular)* to stipulate, specify.

▶ *vpr* **determinarse** *(decidirse)* to make up one's mind, decide.

detestar *vt* to detest, hate, abhor.

detonación *nf* detonation.

detonador *nm* detonator.

detonante *adj* detonating, explosive.

▶ *nm* **1** detonator. **2** *fig* trigger.

detrás *adv* **1** behind: *detrás de la puerta* behind the door. **2** *(en la parte posterior)* at the back, in the back. **3** *(después)* then, afterwards. LOC **ir detrás de** to go after.

deuda *nf* **1** debt. **2** REL trespass. COMP **deuda pública** national debt.

deudor,-ra *nm & nf* debtor.

devaluación *nf* devaluation.

devaluar *vt* to devalue.

devoción *nf* **1** devotion, devoutness. **2** *(afición)* devotion, dedication.

devolver *vt* **1** *(volver algo a un estado anterior)* to put back, return. **2** *(por correo)* to send back, return. **3** *(restituir un dinero)* to refund, return. **4** *(una visita, un cumplido, etc)* to return, pay back. **5** *fam (vomitar)* to vomit, throw up, bring up.
▶ *vi fam (vomitar)* to throw up, be sick.

devorar *vt* to devour.

devuelto,-a *nm (vómito)* vomit.

Dg *sím* (decagramo) decagram; *(símbolo)* Dg.

dg *sím* (decigramo) decigram; *(símbolo)* dg.

día *nm* **1** day. **2** *(con luz)* daylight, daytime: *ya es de día* it's daylight. **3** *(tiempo)* day, weather.
▶ *nm pl* **días** *(vida)* days. LOC **al día siguiente** the following day. ▌**¡buenos días!** good morning! ▌**todos los días** each day, every day. ▌**dar los buenos días** to say good morning. ▌**de día** during the day. ▌**estar al día** *fig* to be up to date. ▌**hacer buen/mal día** to be a nice/horrible day. ▌**ser de día** to be daylight. COMP **día de año nuevo** New Year's Day. ▌**día de descanso** day off. ▌**día festivo** holiday, bank holiday. ▌**día de paga** payday. ▌**día entre semana** weekday.

diabetes *nf inv* diabetes.

diabético,-a *adj* diabetic.

diablo *nm* devil, demon. COMP **un diablillo** a little devil.

diablura *nf* mischief, naughtiness.

diacrítico,-a *adj* diacritic, diacritical.

diadema *nf* **1** *(joya)* diadem. **2** *(adorno para el pelo)* hairband.

diafragma *nm* **1** ANAT diaphragm. **2** *(en fotografía)* aperture. **3** MED diaphragm, cap.

diagnóstico,-a *nm* diagnosis.

diagonal *adj* diagonal. LOC **en diagonal** diagonally.

diagrama *nm* diagram. COMP **diagrama de flujo** INFORM flow chart.

dial *nm* dial.

dialecto *nm* dialect.

dialogar *vi* **1** *(conversar)* to talk, have a conversation. **2** *fig (negociar)* to negotiate, hold talks (**sobre**, on).

diálogo *nm* dialogue, conversation.

diamante *nm* diamond.

diámetro *nm* diameter.

diana *nf* DEP *(objeto)* target; *(para dardos)* dartboard; *(blanco)* bull's eye.

diapositiva *nf* slide.

diario,-a *adj* daily, everyday.
▶ *nm* **diario** **1** *(prensa)* daily, paper, daily newspaper. **2** *(íntimo)* diary, journal. LOC **a diario** daily, every day.

diarrea *nf* diarrhoea (US diarrhea).

dibujante *nm o nf* **1** artist, drawer. **2** *(de dibujos animados)* cartoonist. **3** TÉC *(hombre)* draughtsman (US draftsman); *(mujer)* draughtswoman (US draftswoman).

dibujar *vt* **1** to draw, sketch. **2** TÉC to design. **3** *fig (describir)* to describe.

dibujo *nm* **1** *(arte)* drawing, sketching. **2** *(imagen)* drawing. **3** *(motivo)* pattern, design. COMP **dibujo artístico** artistic drawing. ▌**dibujo lineal** draughtsmanship (US draftsmanship). ▌**dibujos animados** cartoons.

diccionario *nm* dictionary.

dicho,-a *adj* said, mentioned: *dicha casa…* the said house…; *dicho esto se marchó* having said this he left. LOC **dicho y hecho** no sooner said than done.

diciembre *nm* December.

✎ Consulta también **marzo**.

dictado,-a *nm* dictation.

dictador,-ra *nm & nf* dictator.

dictadura *nf* dictatorship.

dictar *vt* **1** to dictate. **2** JUR *(ley)* to enact, decree, announce; *(sentencia)* to pronounce, pass.

didáctico,-a *adj* didactic.

diecinueve *adj (cardinal)* nineteen; *(ordinal)* nineteenth.

► *nm* **1** *(número)* nineteen. **2** *(fecha)* nineteenth.

✎ Consulta también **seis**.

dieciocho *adj (cardinal)* eighteen; *(ordinal)* eighteenth.
► *nm* **1** *(número)* eighteen. **2** *(fecha)* eighteenth

✎ Consulta también **seis**.

dieciséis *adj (cardinal)* sixteen; *(ordinal)* sixteenth.
► *nm* **1** *(número)* sixteen. **2** *(fecha)* sixteenth.

✎ Consulta también **seis**.

diecisiete *adj (cardinal)* seventeen; *(ordinal)* seventeenth.
► *nm* **1** *(número)* seventeen. **2** *(fecha)* seventeenth.

✎ Consulta también **seis**.

diente *nm* **1** *(gen)* tooth. **2** *(de ajo)* clove. LOC **echar los dientes** to teethe. ‖ **hablar entre dientes** *fig* to mumble, mutter. COMP **diente de leche** milk tooth.

diéresis *nf inv* diaeresis, dieresis.

diesel *adj* diesel.

diestro,-a *adj* **1** *lit* right. **2** *(hábil)* skilful (US skillful).

dieta *nf (régimen, alimentación)* diet.

diez *adj (cardinal)* ten; *(ordinal)* tenth.
► *nm* **1** *(número)* ten. **2** *(fecha)* tenth.

✎ Consulta también **seis**.

diezmilésimo,-a *adj* ten-thousandth.
► *nm & nf* ten-thousandth.

✎ Consulta también **sexto,-a**.

diferencia *nf* difference.

diferenciar *vt (distinguir)* to differentiate, distinguish (entre, between).
► *vpr* **diferenciarse** to differ, be different (por, because of).

diferente *adj* different.

difícil *adj* difficult, hard.

dificultad *nf* **1** difficulty. **2** *(obstáculo)* obstacle; *(problema)* trouble, problem.

difunto,-a *nm & nf* deceased.

difusión *nf* **1** *(de luz, calor)* diffusion. **2** *fig (de noticia, enfermedad, etc)* spreading. **3** RAD broadcast, broadcasting.

digestión *nf* digestion.

digestivo,-a *adj* digestive.

digital *adj* digital.

dígito *nm* digit.

dignarse *vpr* to deign (a, to), condescend (a, to).

dignidad *nf* **1** *(cualidad)* dignity. **2** *(cargo)* rank, office, post.

digno,-a *adj* **1** *(merecedor)* worthy, deserving. **2** *(respetable)* worthy, honourable (US honorable). LOC **digno,-a de admiración** worthy of admiration, admirable.

dilatado,-a *adj* **1** dilated. **2** *(vasto)* vast, extensive, large. **3** FÍS expanded.

dilatar *vt* **1** to dilate. **2** FÍS to expand. **3** *(prolongar)* to prolong, extend.

diligencia *nf* **1** *(cuidado)* diligence, care. **2** *(rapidez)* rapidity, speed. **3** *(carreta)* stagecoach.

diluir *vt* **1** *(un sólido)* to dissolve. **2** *(un líquido)* to dilute.
► *vpr* **diluirse** **1** *(un sólido)* to dissolve. **2** *(un líquido)* to dilute.

diluviar *vi* [se emplea sólo en tercera persona del singular; no lleva sujeto] to pour with rain, pour down.

diluvio *nm* flood.

dimensión *nf* **1** [también se usa en plural con el mismo significado] dimension, size. **2** *fig (importancia)* importance.

diminutivo,-a *adj* diminutive.
► *nm* **diminutivo** diminutive.

diminuto,-a *adj* tiny, minute.

dimisión *nf* resignation.

dimitir *vi* to resign (de, from).

Dinamarca *nf* Denmark.

dinamita *nf* dynamite.

dinastía *nf* dynasty.

dinero *nm* **1** money. **2** *(fortuna)* wealth. LOC **andar mal/escaso,-a de dinero** to be short of money. ‖ **tirar el dinero por la ventana** to throw money down the drain. COMP **dinero en metálico** cash.

dinosaurio *nm* dinosaur.

D

dioptría *nf* dioptre (US diopter).
dios *nm* god.
diosa *nf* goddess.
diploma *nm* diploma.
diplomacia *nf* diplomacy.
diplomático,-a *adj* diplomatic.
▶ *nm & nf* diplomat.
diptongo *nm* diphthong.
diputado,-a *nm & nf (miembro del Congreso)* deputy, *member of the Spanish Parliament.*
dique *nm (muro)* dike, breakwater.
dirección *nf (acción de dirigir)* management, running. **2** *(cargo)* directorship, position of manager. **3** *(sentido)* direction, way. **4** *(destino)* destination: *salió con dirección a Cádiz* he left for Cádiz. **5** *(domicilio)* address. **6** TÉC steering. COMP **calle de dirección única** one-way street.
directivo,-a *adj* directive, managing.
▶ *nm & nf* director, manager, board member.
directo,-a *adj* direct, straight.
▶ *nm* **directo** DEP straight hit. LOC **en directo** TV live.
director,-ra *nm & nf* **1** director, manager. **2** *(de colegio - hombre)* headmaster; *(- mujer)* headmistress. **3** *(de orquesta)* conductor. COMP **director,-ra de cine** film director.
directorio,-a *nm* **1** *(gobierno)* governing body. **2** *(de direcciones)* directory, guide. **3** INFORM directory.
dirigente *adj* leading, directing.
▶ *nm o nf* **1** leader. **2** *(de empresa)* manager.
dirigir *vt* **1** *(empresa)* to manage; *(negocio, escuela)* to run; *(un periódico)* to edit. **2** *(orquesta)* to conduct; *(película)* to direct. **3** *(coche)* to drive, steer; *(barco)* to steer; *(avión)* to pilot. **4** *(un partido)* to lead. **5** *(carta, protesta)* to address.
▶ *vpr* **dirigirse 1** *(ir)* to go (a, to), make one's way (a, to), make (a, for). **2** *(hablar)* to address (a, -), speak (a, to): *se dirigió a su padre* she addressed her father.

discapacitado,-a *adj* handicapped, disabled.
disciplina *nf* **1** *(conjunto de reglas)* discipline. **2** *(doctrina)* doctrine. **3** *(asignatura)* subject.
disciplinado,-a *adj* disciplined.
discípulo,-a *nm & nf* **1** *(seguidor)* disciple, follower. **2** *(alumno)* pupil, student.
disc-jockey *nm o nf* disc jockey, DJ.
disco *nm* **1** disc. **2** DEP discus. **3** *(de música)* record. **4** INFORM disk. COMP **disco duro** hard disk.
discoteca *nf (local)* discotheque, nightclub.
discreción *nf* **1** *(sensatez)* discretion, tact. **2** *(agudeza)* wit. LOC **a discreción** *(a voluntad)* at one's discretion.
discreto,-a *adj (prudente)* discreet, prudent, tactful.
discriminación *nf* discrimination. COMP **discriminación racial** racial discrimination.
discriminar *vt* **1** *(diferenciar)* to discriminate, distinguish. **2** *(por raza, religión, etc)* to discriminate against.
disculpa *nf* excuse, apology. LOC **pedir disculpas a** ALGN to apologize to SB.
disculpar *vt* **1** *(descargar de culpa)* to excuse: *disculpe el retraso* please excuse the delay. **2** *(perdonar)* to excuse, forgive: *¡disculpe!* excuse me!
▶ *vpr* **disculparse** to apologize (por, for), excuse OS.
discurrir *vi* **1** *(andar)* to walk, wander. **2** *(fluir)* to flow, run. **3** *(transcurrir)* to pass, go by. **4** fig *(reflexionar)* to think (sobre, about), ponder (sobre, on/over), meditate (sobre, on).
discurso *nm (conferencia)* speech.
discusión *nf* **1** *(charla)* discussion. **2** *(disputa)* argument.
discutir *vi* **1** *(examinar)* to discuss (de, -). **2** *(contender)* to argue.
diseminar *vt* to disseminate, scatter, spread.
▶ *vpr* **diseminarse** to spread.
diseñador,-ra *nm & nf* designer.
diseñar *vt* to design.

diseño *nm* design.

disfraz *nm* **1** *(para engañar)* disguise. **2** *(para una fiesta, etc)* fancy dress outfit, fancy dress costume.

disfrazar *vt (persona)* to disguise, dress up.
▶ *vpr* **disfrazarse 1** *(para engañar)* to disguise os (de, as). **2** *(para una fiesta, etc)* to dress up (de, as).

disfrutar *vt* **1** *(poseer)* to own, enjoy, possess; *(pensión, renta)* to receive. **2** *(aprovechar)* to make the most of.
▶ *vi* **1** *(poseer)* to enjoy (de, -), have (de, -), possess (de, -): *disfruta de buena salud* he enjoys good health. **2** *(gozar)* to enjoy, enjoy os: *disfruté mucho en el cine* I enjoyed myself very much at the cinema.

disgustar *vt* **1** *(molestar)* to displease, annoy, upset. **2** *(desagradar)* to dislike: *me disgusta ese sabor dulce* I don't like this sweet taste.
▶ *vpr* **disgustarse 1** *(enfadarse)* to get angry, get upset. **2** *(pelearse)* to quarrel (con, with).

disgusto *nm* **1** *(enfado)* displeasure, annoyance, anger. **2** *fig (pelea)* argument, quarrel. LOC **a disgusto** against one's will, reluctantly, unwillingly. ▌ **dar un disgusto** to upset. ▌ **llevarse un disgusto** to get upset.

disimular *vt (ocultar)* to hide, conceal.
▶ *vi* to pretend, dissemble: *no disimules* stop pretending.

disimulo *nm* pretence (US pretense), dissemblance.

dislocar *vt (sacar de lugar)* to dislocate.

disminución *nf* decrease, reduction.

disminuido,-a *adj* disabled.

disminuir *vt* **1** *(gen)* to decrease. **2** *(medidas, velocidad)* to reduce.
▶ *vi* **1** *(gen)* to diminish. **2** *(temperatura, precios)* to drop, fall.

disolución *nf* **1** *(gen)* dissolution. **2** QUÍM solution, dissolution.

disolver *vt (gen)* to dissolve.
▶ *vpr* **disolverse 1** *(gen)* to dissolve. **2** *fig* to be dissolved.

dispar *adj* unlike, different.

disparar *vt* **1** *(arma)* to fire; *(bala, flecha)* to shoot. **2** *(lanzar)* to hurl, throw. **3** DEP to shoot.

disparatado,-a *adj* absurd, foolish, ridiculous.

disparo *nm* **1** *(acción)* firing. **2** *(efecto)* shot. **3** DEP shot.

dispersar *vt (gen)* to disperse, scatter.
▶ *vpr* **dispersarse** *(gen)* to disperse, scatter.

disperso,-a *adj (esparcido)* scattered.

disponer *vt* **1** *(colocar)* to dispose, arrange, set out. **2** *(preparar)* to prepare, get ready. **3** *(ordenar)* to order, decree.
▶ *vi* **1** *(tener)* to have (de, -). **2** *(hacer uso)* to make use (de, of), have the use (de, of).
▶ *vpr* **disponerse** *(prepararse)* to get ready (a, to), prepare (a, to).

disponibilidad *nf* availability.

disponible *adj (gen)* available.

dispositivo *nm* device, gadget.

dispuesto,-a *adj* **1** *(decidido)* determined. **2** *(preparado)* prepared, ready, willing.

disputa *nf (discusión)* dispute, argument, quarrel.

disputar *vt* **1** *(competir)* to compete for, contend for. **2** DEP to play: *los equipos disputaron un partido amistoso* the teams played a friendly match.

disquete *nm* diskette, floppy disk.

disquetera *nf* disk drive.

distancia *nf* **1** distance. **2** *fig (diferencia)* difference, gap. LOC **a distancia** from a distance: *lo vimos a distancia* we saw it from a distance.

distanciar *vt* to distance, separate.
▶ *vpr* **distanciarse** to move away, become separated.

distante *adj* **1** *(en el espacio)* distant, far; *(en el tiempo)* distant, remote. **2** *fig* distant.

distinción *nf* **1** *(gen)* distinction. **2** *(elegancia)* distinction, elegance, refinement.

distinguido,-a *adj* **1** distinguished. **2** *(elegante)* elegant.

distinguir *vt* **1** *(diferenciar)* to distinguish. **2** *(caracterizar)* to mark, distinguish. **3** *(ver)* to see, make out.
▶ *vpr* **distinguirse** *(destacar)* to stand out, distinguish os.

distinto,-a *adj (diferente)* different.
▶ *adj vpr* **distintos,-as** various, several.

distracción *nf* **1** *(divertimiento)* amusement, pastime, recreation, entertainment. **2** *(despiste)* distraction, absent-mindedness.

distraer *vt* **1** *(divertir)* to amuse, entertain. **2** *(atención)* to distract.
▶ *vpr* **distraerse 1** *(divertirse)* to amuse os, enjoy os. **2** *(despistarse)* to get distracted, be inattentive, be absent-minded .

distraído,-a *adj* **1** *(desatento)* absent-minded. **2** *(entretenido)* entertaining, fun.

distribuir *vt* **1** *(repartir)* to distribute. **2** *(correo)* to deliver; *(trabajo)* to share, allot.

distrito *nm* district.

disturbio *nm* disturbance, riot.

diurno,-a *adj* daily, daytime.

divagar *vi* to digress, ramble.

diván *nm* divan, couch.

divergente *adj* divergent, diverging.

divergir *vi* to diverge.

diversidad *nf* diversity, variety.

diversificar *vt* to diversify, vary.

diversión *nf* fun, amusement, entertainment.

diverso,-a *adj* different.
▶ *adj vpr* **diversos,-as** several, various.

divertido,-a *adj* **1** *(gracioso)* funny, amusing. **2** *(entretenido)* fun, entertaining, enjoyable.

divertir *vt* to amuse, entertain.
▶ *vpr* **divertirse** to enjoy os, have a good time: *¡diviértete!* enjoy yourself!

dividir *vt* **1** to divide. **2** *(separar)* to divide, separate: *el río divide las dos comarcas* the river separates the two counties. **3** *(repartir)* to divide, split.
▶ *vpr* **dividirse** *(separarse)* to divide, split up.

divino,-a *adj* divine.

divisible *adj* **1** dividable. **2** MAT divisible.

división *nf* **1** división. **2** *fig* division, divergence.

divisor *nm* **1** divider. **2** MAT divisor.
COMP **máximo común divisor** MAT highest common factor, (US highest common denominator). ❙ **mínimo común divisor** MAT lowest common factor, (US lowest common denominator) .

divo,-a *nm & nf* star.

divorciado,-a *adj* divorced.
▶ *nm & nf (hombre)* divorcé; *(mujer)* divorcée.

divorciar *vt* to divorce.
▶ *vpr* **divorciarse** to get divorced (de, from).

divorcio *nm* divorce.

divulgar *vt* **1** *(difundir)* to divulge, spread, disclose. **2** *(por radio)* to broadcast. **3** *(propagar)* to popularize.
▶ *vpr* **divulgarse** to become known, spread.

Djibouti *nm* Djibouti, Jibouti.

dl *sím (decilitro)* decilitre (US deciliter); *(símbolo)* dl.

Dl *sím (decalitro)* decalitre (US decaliter); *(símbolo)* Dl.

dm *sím (decímetro)* decimetre (US decimeter); *(símbolo)* dm.

Dm *sím (decámetro)* decametre (US decameter); *(símbolo)* Dm.

do *nm (de solfa)* doh, do; *(de escala diatónica)* C.

dobladillo *nm* **1** *(de vestido, etc)* hem. **2** *(de pantalones)* turn-up, US cuff.

doblaje *nm* dubbing.

doblar *vt* **1** *(duplicar)* to double: *le doblo la edad* I'm twice as old as she is. **2** *(plegar)* to fold. **3** *(torcer)* to bend: *doblar un dedo* to bend a finger. **4** *(esquina)* to turn, go round. **5** *(película)* to dub.
▶ *vpr* **doblarse** *(plegarse)* to fold.

doble *adj* **1** double. **2** *(nacionalidad)* dual.
▶ *nm* **1** double: *tiene el doble que yo* he's got twice as much as I have. **2** *(duplicado)*

duplicate. $\boxed{\text{LOC}}$ **ver doble** to see double.

▶ *nm o nf* CINE stand-in, double; *(hombre)* stunt man; *(mujer)* stunt woman.

▶ *adv* double.

▶ *nm pl* **dobles** *(tenis)* doubles.

doce *adj (cardinal)* twelve; *(ordinal)* twelfth.

▶ *nm* **1** *(número)* twelve. **2** *(fecha)* twelfth.

✎ Consulta también seis.

docena *nf* dozen. $\boxed{\text{LOC}}$ **a docenas** COM by the dozen.

dócil *adj* docile, obedient.

doctor,-ra *nm & nf* doctor.

doctrina *nf* **1** doctrine. **2** *(enseñanza)* teachings *pl*.

documentación *nf* **1** documentation, documents *pl*. **2** *(para identificar)* papers *pl*, identification.

documental *adj* documentary.

▶ *nm* documentary.

documento *nm* document.

dodecaedro *nm* dodecahedron.

dodecasílabo,-a *nm* dodecasyllable, Alexandrine.

dólar *nm* dollar.

doler *vi* **1** to ache, hurt. **2** *(afligir)* to distress, sadden, upset, hurt: *me duele tal pobreza* such poverty distresses me. **3** *(sentir)* to be sorry, be sad: *me duele habérselo dicho* I'm sorry I told her about it.

dolido,-a *adj fig* hurt.

dolor *nm* **1** pain, ache. **2** *fig* pain, sorrow, grief. $\boxed{\text{COMP}}$ **dolor de cabeza** headache.

dolorido,-a *adj* sore, aching.

doloroso,-a *adj* **1** painful. **2** *fig* painful, distressing.

domador,-ra *nm & nf* tamer; *(de caballos)* horse breaker.

domar *vt* **1** to tame; *(caballos)* to break in. **2** *fig* to tame, control.

domesticar *vt* **1** to domesticate, tame. **2** *(adiestrar)* to train. **3** *fig* to subdue.

doméstico,-a *adj* domestic.

domicilio *nm* **1** residence, home, abode. **2** *(dirección)* address.

dominante *adj* dominant, dominating.

dominar *vt* **1** *(tener bajo dominio)* to dominate. **2** *(conocer a fondo)* to master: *domina el inglés* she has a good command of English.

▶ *vi* **1** *(ser superior)* to dominate. **2** *(destacar)* to stand out: *domina mucho el rojo* red is the predominant colour. **3** *(predominar)* to predominate.

▶ *vpr* **dominarse** *(controlarse)* to control os, restrain os.

domingo *nm* Sunday.

✎ Consulta también jueves.

Dominica *nf* Dominica.

dominicano,-a *adj* Dominican.

▶ *nm & nf* Dominican. $\boxed{\text{COMP}}$ **República Dominicana** Dominican Republic.

dominio *nm* **1** *(soberanía)* dominion. **2** *(poder)* power, control. **3** *(supremacía)* supremacy. **4** *(de conocimientos)* mastery, good knowledge; *(de un idioma)* good command. **5** *(territorio)* domain. **6** INFORM domain.

dominó *nm* **1** *(juego)* dominoes *pl*. **2** *(fichas)* set of dominoes.

don¹ *nm (talento)* talent, natural gift.

don² *nm* Mr: *Señor Don Juan Pérez* Mr Juan Pérez.

donante *nm o nf* donor. $\boxed{\text{COMP}}$ **donante de sangre** blood donor.

donar *vt fml* to donate, give.

donativo *nm* donation.

donde *adv* where, in which. $\boxed{\text{LOC}}$ **de donde / desde donde** from where, whence.

dónde *pron* where: *¿dónde está?* where is it?; *no sé dónde está* I don't know where it is; *¿a dónde va?* where is he going?; *¿hasta dónde?* how far?

dondequiera *adv (en cualquier parte)* anywhere; *(en todas partes)* everywhere: *dondequiera que esté lo encontraremos* wherever he is we'll find him.

dónut® *nm* doughnut.

doña *nf* Mrs: *Doña Elena Suárez* Mrs Elena Suárez.

dorado,-a *adj* golden.

dormido,-a *adj* **1** asleep. **2** *(soñoliento)* sleepy: *tengo el brazo dormido* my arm has gone numb, my arm has gone to sleep. LOC **quedarse dormido,-a 1** *(dormir)* to fall asleep. **2** *(dormirse más de la cuenta)* to oversleep.

dormir *vi* **1** to sleep: *tengo ganas de dormir* I feel sleepy. **2** *(pernoctar)* to spend the night.
▶ *vt* to put to sleep.
▶ *vpr* **dormirse 1** to fall asleep, nod off. **2** *fig* to go to sleep: *se me ha dormido el pie* my foot has gone to sleep. LOC **¡a dormir!** to bed! ‖ **dormir como un lirón** *fam* to sleep like a log. ‖ **dormir la siesta** to have a nap.

dormitorio *nm* **1** *(en una casa)* bedroom. **2** *(colectivo)* dormitory.

dorsal *adj* **1** dorsal, back. **2** LING dorsal.
▶ *nm* DEP number.

dorso *nm* back, reverse. COMP **dorso de la mano** back of the hand.

dos *adj (cardinal)* two; *(ordinal)* second: *entre ellas dos* between the two of them.
▶ *nm (número)* two; *(fecha)* second. LOC **cada dos por tres** *fam* every five minutes. COMP **dos veces** twice: *es dos veces mayor que su hermana* she's twice as old as her sister.

✎ Consulta también seis.

doscientos,-as *adj (numeral)* two hundred; *(cardinal)* two-hundredth.
▶ *nm & nf* two hundred.

✎ Consulta también seis.

dosificar *vt* **1** *(gen)* to dose. **2** *(esfuerzos, etc)* to measure.

dosis *nf inv* dose.

dotado,-a *adj* **1** *(equipado)* equipped, provided: *está dotado con airbag* it's equipped with an airbag. **2** *(con dotes)* gifted: *está muy dotado para las matemáticas* he has a talent for mathematics.

dotar *vt* **1** *(proveer de personal)* to staff (de, with); *(de material)* to equip (de, with). **2** *(bienes, dinero)* to assign. **3** *fig (dones y cualidades)* to endow (de, with), provide (de, with): *la naturaleza la dotó de un sexto sentido* nature endowed her with a sixth sense.

dragón *nm* **1** *(reptil)* flying dragon. **2** *(animal fabuloso)* dragon.

drama *nm* drama.

dramático,-a *adj* dramatic.

drenar *vt* to drain.

drive *nm* drive.

droga *nf* **1** drug. **2** *fig (cosa desagradable)* nuisance. COMP **droga blanda/dura** soft/hard drug.

drogadicto,-a *nm & nf* drug addict.

drogar *vt* to drug.
▶ *vpr* **drogarse** to take drugs.

droguería *nf* hardware shop.

dromedario *nm* dromedary.

dualidad *nf* duality.

ducentésimo,-a *adj* two-hundredth.
▶ *nm & nf* two-hundredth.

ducha *nf* shower. LOC **darse/tomar una ducha** to take a shower, have a shower.

duchar *vt* to give a shower.
▶ *vpr* **ducharse** to take a shower, have a shower.

duda *nf* doubt. LOC **no hay duda** there is no doubt. ‖ **salir de dudas** to shed one's doubts. ‖ **sin duda** no doubt, without a doubt.

dudar *vi* **1** to doubt, have doubts. **2** *(titubear)* to hesitate: *dudo entre quedarme o marcharme* I'm not sure whether to stay or leave.
▶ *vt* to doubt: *lo dudo* I doubt it. LOC **dudar de** ALGN to doubt SB, mistrust SB.

dudoso,-a *adj* **1** *(incierto)* doubtful, uncertain. **2** *(vacilante)* hesitant, undecided. **3** *(poco seguro)* questionable.

duende *nm* *(espíritu travieso)* goblin, elf.

dueño,-a *nm & nf* **1** *(propietario)* owner: *¿quién es la dueña?* who is the owner? **2** *(de casa, piso - hombre)* landlord; *(mujer)* landlady. LOC **ser dueño,-a de sí mismo,-a** to be self-possessed.

dulce *adj* **1** *(gen)* sweet. **2** *fig* soft, gentle.

▶ *nm* CULIN *(caramelo)* sweet; *(pastel)* cake. COMP **dulce de membrillo** quince jelly.

dulzura *nf* 1 sweetness. 2 *fig* softness, gentleness, sweetness.

duna *nf* dune.

dúo *nm* duet.

duodécimo,-a *adj* twelfth.
▶ *nm & nf* twelfth.

✎ Consulta también sexto,-a.

duodeno *nm* duodenum.

duplicar *vt (gen)* to duplicate; *(cantidad)* to double.
▶ *vpr* **duplicarse** to double.

duque *nm* duke.

duquesa *nf* duchess.

duración *nf* 1 duration, length: *¿cuál es la duración de la obra?* how long is the play? 2 *(coche, máquina, etc)* life. LOC **de larga duración** 1 *(periodo de tiempo)* long, long-term. 2 *(bombilla, etc)* long-life.

duradero,-a *adj* durable, lasting.

duramente *adv* 1 *(con dificultad)* hard. 2 *(con severidad)* harshly.

durante *adv* during, in, for: *viví allí durante un año* I lived there for a year.

durar *vi* 1 to last, go on for: *la película duró tres horas* the film went on for three hours. 2 *(ropa, calzado)* to wear well, last: *ese abrigo le duró mucho* he got a lot of wear out of that coat.

durazno *nm* 1 *(fruto)* peach. 2 *(árbol)* peach tree.

dureza *nf* 1 hardness, toughness. 2 *fig (de carácter)* toughness, harshness, severity. 3 *(callosidad)* corn.

duro,-a *adj* 1 hard. 2 *(carne)* tough; *(pan)* stale. 3 *(difícil)* hard, difficult.
▶ *nm* **duro** *(antiguamente)* five pesetas; *(moneda)* five-peseta coin.
▶ *adv* hard: *dale duro* hit him hard.

DVD *nm* (Disco Versátil Digital) DVD.

E

E, e *nf (la letra)* E, e.
e *conj* and.

> ✎ Usado en vez de **y** antes de palabras que empiezan por **i** o **hi**: *compramos manzanas e higos* we bought some apples and figs.

EAU *abrev (Emiratos Árabes Unidos)* United Arab Emirates; *(abreviatura)* UAE.
ebanista *nm o nf* cabinet-maker.
ebullición *nf (hervor)* boil, boiling.
echado,-a *adj (tumbado)* lying down.
echar *vt* **1** *(lanzar)* to throw. **2** *(dejar caer)* to put, drop. **3** *(líquido)* to pour; *(comida)* to give; *(sal)* to add, put in. **4** *(carta)* to post, US mail. **5** *(expulsar)* to throw out: *lo han echado del cine* he was thrown out of the cinema. **6** *(despedir de empleo)* to sack, dismiss, fire. **7** *(brotar, salir - plantas)* to sprout; *(- dientes)* to cut; *(- pelo)* to grow. **8** *(decir)* to tell. **9** *(emanar)* to give out, give off: *la caja de fusibles echa chispas* sparks are coming out of the fuse box. **10** *(suponer, calcular)* to guess: *yo le echo 40* I think she's 40. **11** *(poner, aplicar)* to put on, apply. **12** *(llave)* to lock, turn; *(cerrojo)* to bolt, fasten. **13** *fam (en el cine, teatro)* to show, put on: *echan una buena película en la tele* there's a good film on TV.
  ▶ *vi* **1** echar a + *inf (empezar)* to begin to: *echó a correr* she ran off. **2** echar de + *inf (dar)*: *echar de comer* to feed.
  ▶ *vpr* **echarse** **1** *(arrojarse)* to throw os. **2** *(tenderse)* to lie down. **3** *(ponerse)* to put on. **4** *(novio, novia)* to get os. **5** echarse a + *inf (empezar)* to begin to: *se echó a reír* he burst out laughing.

eclipsar *vt* **1** *(astro)* to eclipse. **2** *fig* to eclipse, outshine.
eclipse *nm* eclipse.
eco *nm* echo.
ecografía *nf* ultrasound scan.
ecología *nf* ecology.
ecológico,-a *adj* ecological.
ecologista *adj* ecological.
  ▶ *nm o nf* ecologist.
economato *nm* company store.
economía *nf* **1** *(administración)* economy. **2** *(ciencia)* economics. **3** *(ahorro)* economy, saving.
económico,-a *adj* **1** *(gen)* economic. **2** *(barato)* cheap, economical, inexpensive. `COMP` **crisis económica** economic crisis, recession.
economista *nm o nf* economist.
economizar *vt (ahorrar)* to economize, save.
  ▶ *vi* to economize, save.
ecosistema *nm* ecosystem.
ecuación *nf* equation. `COMP` **ecuación de primer grado** simple equation. **ǀ ecuación de segundo grado** quadratic equation.
ecuador *nm* GEOG equator.
Ecuador *nm* Ecuador.
ecuatoguineano,-a *adj* of Equatorial Guinea, from Equatorial Guinea.
  ▶ *nm & nf* person from Equatorial Guinea, inhabitant of Equatorial Guinea.
ecuatorial *adj* equatorial.
ecuatoriano,-a *adj* Ecuadorian.
  ▶ *nm & nf* Ecuadorian.
ecuestre *adj* equestrian.
edad *nf* **1** age. **2** *(tiempo, época)* time, period.
edén *nm* **1** Eden. **2** *fig* paradise, heaven.

edición *nf* **1** *(ejemplares)* edition. **2** *(publicación)* publication. **3** INFORM editing.

edificar *vt (construir)* to build, construct.

edificio *nm* building.

edil,-la *nm & nf (concejal)* town councillor.
▸ *nm* **edil** *(magistrado romano)* aedile.

edredón *nm* eiderdown, US comforter.

educación *nf* **1** *(preparación)* education. **2** *(crianza)* upbringing, breeding. **3** *(modales)* manners *pl*, politeness.

educado,-a *adj* polite.

educar *vt* **1** *(enseñar)* to educate, teach. **2** *(criar)* to bring up. **3** *(en la cortesía, etc)* to teach manners.

educativo,-a *adj* educational: *sistema educativo* education system.

edulcorar *vt* **1** to sweeten. **2** *fig* to soften, alleviate.

EE UU *abrev (Estados Unidos)* the United States of America; *(abreviatura)* USA.

efe *nf name of the letter* f.

efectivamente *adv* **1** *(realmente)* in fact, actually. **2** *(de verdad)* indeed.

efectivo,-a *adj (que tiene efecto)* effective.
▸ *nm* **efectivo** *(dinero)* cash.

efecto *nm* **1** *(resultado)* effect, result, end. **2** *(impresión)* impression: *la escena le hizo un gran efecto* the scene made a great impression on her. **3** DEP spin: *dio efecto a la pelota* he put some spin on the ball.

efectuar *vt* **1** *(gen)* to carry out, perform, make, do. **2** *(pago)* to make; *(pedido)* to place. **3** *(suma, etc)* to do. **4** *(viaje, visita, etc)* to make.

efervescente *adj* **1** *(gen)* effervescent. **2** *(bebida)* sparkling, fizzy. **3** *(pastilla)* soluble.

eficacia *nf* **1** *(persona)* efficiency, effectiveness; *(cosas)* efficacy, effectiveness. **2** *(rendimiento)* efficiency.

eficaz *adj* **1** *(eficiente)* efficient. **2** *(cosa)* efficacious, effective. **3** *(que produce rendimiento)* efficient.

eficiente *adj* efficient.

EGB *abrev* EDUC (Enseñanza General Básica) ≈ *former Primary School Education*.

egipcio,-a *adj* Egyptian.
▸ *nm & nf (persona)* Egyptian.
▸ *nm* **egipcio** *(idioma)* Egyptian.

Egipto *nm* Egypt.

egoísmo *nm* selfishness, egoism.

egoísta *adj* selfish, egoistic, egoistical.
▸ *nm o nf* egoist, selfish person.

eje *nm* **1** *(línea, recta)* axis. **2** TÉC shaft, spindle. **3** AUTO axle.

ejecución *nf* **1** *(de una orden, etc)* carrying out, execution. **2** MÚS performance. **3** *(ajusticiamiento)* execution.

ejecutar *vt* **1** *(una orden, etc)* to carry out. **2** MÚS to perform, play. **3** *(ajusticiar)* to execute. **4** INFORM to run.

ejecutivo,-a *adj* executive.
▸ *nm & nf* executive.
▸ *nm* **el ejecutivo** *(gobierno)* the government. COMP **poder ejecutivo** the executive.

ejemplar *nm (copia)* copy, number, issue.

ejemplo *nm* **1** example. **2** *(modelo)* model. LOC **dar ejemplo** to set an example. ‖ **por ejemplo** for example, for instance.

ejercer *vt* **1** *(profesión, etc)* to practise (US practice), be in practice as. **2** *(influencia)* to exert.

ejercicio *nm* **1** *(de profesión)* practice; *(de derecho)* use, exercise; *(de función)* performance. **2** EDUC exercise; *(examen)* test; *(pregunta de examen)* question; *(deberes)* homework. **3** DEP exercise.

ejército *nm* army.

el *determinante* **1** the: *el agua* water. **2 el de** the one: *el de hoy* today's. **3 el que** *(persona - sujeto)* the one who; *(- objeto)* the one, the one that, the one whom: *el que vi* the one I saw. **4** *(cosa)* the one, the one that, the one which: *el que me diste* the one (that) you gave me.

él *pron* **1** *(sujeto - persona)* he; *(- cosa, animal)* it: *él vive aquí* he lives here. **2** *(objeto - persona)* him; *(- cosa, animal)* it: *comió con él* she had lunch with him. LOC **de él** *(posesivo)* his: *es de él* It's his. ‖ **él mismo** himself.

elaborar *vt* **1** *(producto)* to make, manufacture, produce. **2** *(madera, metal, etc)* to work.

elástico,-a *adj* elastic.
▸ *nm* **elástico** elastic.

ele *nf* name of the letter l.

elección *nf* **1** *(nombramiento)* election. **2** *(opción)* choice: *lo dejamos a tu elección* we'll leave it up to you.
▶ *nf pl* **elecciones** elections.

electricidad *nf* electricity.

electricista *nm o nf* electrician.

eléctrico,-a *adj* electric, electrical.

electrodoméstico *nm* electrical appliance.

electrón *nm* electron.

electrónica *nf* electronics.

electrónico,-a *adj* electronic.

elefante,-a *nm & nf (macho)* elephant; *(hembra)* cow elephant, female elephant. COMP **elefante marino** elephant seal.

elegancia *nf* elegance.

elegante *adj* elegant, smart, stylish.

elegir *vt* **1** *(escoger)* to choose. **2** POL to elect.

elemental *adj* **1** *(del elemento)* elemental. **2** *(obvio)* elementary, basic.

elemento *nm* **1** *(gen)* element. **2** *(parte)* component, part. **3** *(individuo)* type, sort. LOC **¡menudo elemento!** *fam* he's a right one!

elevación *nf* **1** *(de terreno)* elevation, rise. **2** *(precios)* rise, raising, increasing; *(voz, tono)* raising; *(peso)* raising, lifting. **3** MAT raising.

elevado,-a *adj (gen)* high. LOC **elevado,-a a** MAT raised to: *elevado a la quinta potencia* raised to the power of five; *elevado al cubo* cubed.

elevalunas *nm inv* window winder. COMP **elevalunas eléctrico** electric window.

elevar *vt* **1** *(peso, etc)* to elevate, raise, lift. **2** *(precios)* to raise, increase, put up; *(tono, voz)* to raise. **3** MAT to raise.
▶ *vpr* **elevarse 1** *(subir)* to rise (up): *el humo se elevaba* the smoke was rising up. **2** *(alcanzar)* to reach: *se eleva hasta el techo* it reaches the ceiling.

eliminación *nf* elimination.

eliminar *vt* **1** *(gen)* to eliminate, exclude. **2** *(esperanzas, miedos, etc)* to get rid of, cast aside. **3** *fam (matar)* to kill, eliminate.

eliminatoria *nf* heat, qualifying round.

eliminatorio,-a *adj* eliminatory.

elipse *nf* ellipse.

elíptico,-a *adj* elliptic, elliptical.

elite *nf* elite.

ella *pron* **1** *(sujeto - persona)* she; *(- cosa, animal)* it. **2** *(objeto - persona)* her; *(- cosa, animal)* it: *vino con ella* he came with her.

elle *nf* name of the digraph ll.

ello *pron* it: *no me digas nada de ello* don't tell me anything about it.

ellos,-as *pron* **1** *(sujeto)* they. **2** *(objeto)* them: *vino con ellos* she came with them. LOC **de ellos,-as** theirs: *el coche es de ellos* the car is theirs. ▌ **ellos,-as mismos,-as** themselves.

elocuente *adj* eloquent.

elogiar *vt* to praise, eulogize.

elogio *nm* praise, eulogy.

eludir *vt* **1** *(responsabilidad, justicia, etc)* to evade. **2** *(pregunta)* to avoid, evade; *(persona)* to avoid.

emanar *vi* **1** *(olor, etc)* to emanate. **2** *(derivar)* to derive (de, from), come (de, from).

emancipar *vt* to emancipate, free.
▶ *vpr* **emanciparse** to become emancipated, become free.

embajada *nf (edificio)* embassy.

embajador,-ra *nm & nf* ambassador.

embalar *vt (empaquetar)* to pack, wrap.
▶ *vpr* **embalarse** *(acelerar)* to speed up.

embalse *nm* **1** *(acción)* damming. **2** *(presa)* dam, reservoir.

embarazada *adj-nf* pregnant woman.

embarazo *nm (preñez)* pregnancy.

embarazoso,-a *adj* embarrassing.

embarcación *nf (nave)* boat, vessel, craft.

embarcadero *nm* pier, jetty, quay.

embarcar *vt (personas)* to embark, put on board; *(mercancías)* to load.
▶ *vpr* **embarcarse** *(en barco)* to embark, go on board; *(en avión)* to board.

embargar vt **1** JUR to seize, sequestrate, impound. **2** *(emociones)* to overcome.

embargo nm *(de bienes)* seizure of property, sequestration. LOC **sin embargo** nevertheless, however.

embarque nm *(de personas)* boarding; *(de mercancías)* loading.

embaucar vt to deceive, trick, dupe, cheat, swindle.

embelesar vt to charm, delight, fascinate.

embellecer vt to make beautiful, beautify.
▶ vpr **embellecerse** to make os beautiful, beautify os.

embestir vt *(toro)* to charge.

émbolo nm TÉC piston; *(de cafetera)* plunger.

emborrachar vt to make drunk.
▶ vpr **emborracharse** to get drunk.

emboscada nf ambush. LOC **tender una emboscada** to lay an ambush.

embotellamiento nm AUTO *fig* traffic jam.

embrague nm clutch.

embrión nm **1** embryo. **2** *fig (idea, etc)* beginnings pl, embryo.

embrujar vt **1** *(persona)* to bewitch; *(lugar)* to haunt. **2** *fig (fascinar)* to bewitch, enchant.

embrujo nm **1** spell, charm. **2** *fig (fascinación)* fascination, attraction.

embudo nm funnel.

embuste nm *(mentira)* lie; *(engaño)* trick.

embustero,-a nm & nf liar.

embutido nm *(alimento)* processed cold meat, cold cut.

eme nf name of the letter m.

emergencia nf **1** *(imprevisto)* emergency. **2** *(salida)* emergence. LOC **en caso de emergencia** in case of emergency.

emerger vi to emerge.

emigración nf **1** emigration. **2** *(aves, pueblo)* migration.

emigrante nm o nf emigrant.

emigrar vi to emigrate; *(aves, pueblo)* to migrate.

emirato nm emirate. COMP **Emiratos Árabes Unidos** United Arab Emirates.

emisión nf **1** *(gen)* emission. **2** *(bonos, sellos, monedas)* issue. **3** RAD TV *(programa)* broadcast; *(transmisión)* transmission.

emisora nf radio station.

emitir vt **1** *(sonido, luz)* to emit; *(olor)* to give off. **2** *(manifestar)* to express. **3** *(bonos, monedas, sellos)* to issue. **4** RAD TV to broadcast, transmit.
▶ vi RAD TV to transmit.

emoción nf **1** *(sentimiento)* emotion, feeling. **2** *(excitación)* excitement.

emocionado,-a adj (deeply) moved, (deeply) touched.

emocionante adj **1** *(conmovedor)* moving, touching. **2** *(excitante)* exciting, thrilling.

emocionar vt **1** *(conmover)* to move, touch. **2** *(excitar)* to excite, thrill.
▶ vpr **emocionarse 1** *(conmoverse)* to be moved, be touched. **2** *(excitarse)* to get excited.

emoticono nm INFORM emoticon.

emotivo,-a adj *(persona)* emotional; *(acto, etc)* moving, touching; *(palabras)* emotive.

empachar vt *(comer demasiado)* to give indigestion.
▶ vpr **empacharse** *(de comer)* to have indigestion, get indigestion.

empacho nm *(indigestión)* indigestion.

empalagoso,-a adj **1** *(dulces)* too sweet, sickly. **2** *fig (persona)* sickly sweet, cloying.

empalmar vt *(unir)* to join, connect.
▶ vi **1** *(enlazar)* to join, connect. **2** *(seguir)* to follow on from.

empanada nf pasty, pie.

empanadilla nf pasty.

empañar vt *(cristal)* to steam up.
▶ vpr **empañarse** *(cristal)* to steam up.

empapar vt **1** *(humedecer)* to soak; *(penetrar)* to soak, drench. **2** *(absorber)* to soak up.

▶ *vpr* **empaparse 1** *(humedecerse)* to get soaked. **2** *(persona)* to get soaked, get drenched, be soaked, be drenched.

empapelar *vt (una pared)* to wallpaper.

empaquetar *vt (hacer paquetes)* to pack (up), wrap (up).

empastar *vt (diente)* to fill.

empaste *nm (de diente)* filling.

empatar *vt* to draw.

empate *nm (en fútbol, rugby)* draw, US tie; *(en carrera, votación)* tie: *el gol del empate* the equalizer.

empedrado,-a *adj (calle)* cobbled.
▶ *nm* **empedrado 1** *(adoquines)* cobbles *pl*, cobblestones *pl*. **2** *(acción)* cobbling, paving.

empeine *nm (pie, zapato)* instep.

empeñar *vt* **1** *(objetos)* to pawn, US hock. **2** *(palabra)* to pledge.
▶ *vpr* **empeñarse 1** *(endeudarse)* to get into debt. **2** *(insistir)* to insist (en, on).

empeño *nm (insistencia)* determination.

empeorar *vi* to worsen, deteriorate.

emperador *nm* **1** emperor. **2** *(pez)* swordfish.

emperatriz *nf* empress.

empezar *vt* to begin, start.

empinado,-a *adj (alto)* very high.

emplazar *vt (situar)* to locate, place, situate.

empleado,-a *nm & nf* employee, clerk.

emplear *vt* **1** *(dar empleo)* to employ. **2** *(usar)* to use: *empleó un cuchillo* he used a knife. **3** *(dinero)* to spend. **4** *(tiempo)* to invest, spend.
▶ *vpr* **emplearse 1** *(usarse)* to be used: *este tipo de ordenador ya no se emplea* this type of computer is no longer used. **2** *(tener trabajo)* to be employed.

empleo *nm* **1** *(trabajo)* occupation, job. **2** POL employment. **3** *(uso)* use.

empobrecer *vi* to impoverish.
▶ *vpr* **empobrecerse** to become poor, become impoverished.

empollar *vt* **1** *(huevos)* to hatch. **2** *fam (estudiar)* to swot, swot up, US bone up on.

empollón,-ona *nm & nf fam pey* swot.

emprendedor,-ra *adj* enterprising, resourceful.

emprender *vt* **1** *(gen)* to start. **2** *(misión)* to tackle; *(viaje)* to set off on; *(tarea)* to undertake. LOC **emprender el vuelo** to take flight.

empresa *nf (compañía)* firm, company. COMP **empresa multinacional** multinational company.

empresario,-a *nm & nf (gen)* employer, manager; *(hombre)* businessman, manager; *(mujer)* businesswoman, manageress.

empujar *vt* to push, shove, thrust.

empuje *nm* **1** push, thrust, drive. **2** *fig (energía)* energy, drive.

empujón *nm* push, shove. LOC **abrirse paso a empujones** to push one's way through.

en *prep* **1** *(lugar - gen)* in, at: *en Valencia* in Valencia; *en casa* at home; *en el trabajo* at work. **2** *(- en el interior)* in, inside: *en el cajón* in the drawer. **3** *(lugar - sobre)* on: *en la mesa* on the table. **4** *(año, mes, estación)* in; *(día)* on; *(época, momento)* at: *en 1994* in 1994; *en aquel momento* at that moment. **5** *(dirección)* into: *entró en su casa* he went into his house. **6** *(transporte)* by: *ir en coche* to go by car. **7** *(tema, materia)* at, in: *experto en economía* expert in economics; *bueno en ajedrez* good at chess. **8** *(modo, manera)* in: *en inglés* in English. LOC **en cuanto** as soon as. ▌ **en camino** on the way.

enajenar *vt (propiedad)* to alienate.

enamorado,-a *nm & nf* lover, sweetheart.

enamoramiento *nm* infatuation, falling in love.

enamorar *vt* to win the heart of.
▶ *vpr* **enamorarse** to fall in love (de, with).

enano,-a *adj* dwarf.
▶ *nm & nf* dwarf.

encabezamiento *nm* **1** *(gen)* heading. **2** *(fórmula)* form of address.

encabezar *vt* **1** *(carta, lista)* to head. **2** *(acaudillar)* to lead. **3** DEP *(carrera)* to lead; *(clasificación)* to head, top.

encadenar *vt* **1** *(poner cadenas)* to chain (up). **2** *fig (enlazar)* to connect, link up.

encajar *vt* **1** *(ajustar)* to fit. **2** *(recibir)* to take, withstand. **3** *(soportar)* to bear. **4** *(indirecta, comentario)* to get in. **5** *(dar un golpe)* to land: *le encajó un golpe* he landed him a blow. **6** TÉC to gear.

encaje *nm* **1** *(acto)* fit, fitting. **2** *(hueco)* socket; *(caja)* housing. **3** COST lace.

encalar *vt* to whitewash.

encallar *vi* **1** MAR to run aground. **2** *fig* to flounder, fail.

encaminar *vt (guiar, orientar)* to direct, guide, set on the right road, put on the right road.
▶ *vpr* **encaminarse** *(dirigirse)* to head (a, for) (hacia, towards). LOC **estar bien encaminado,-a** to be on the right track.

encantador,-ra *adj* enchanting, charming, delightful.

encantar *vt* **1** *(hechizar)* to cast a spell on, bewitch. **2** *fam (gustar)* to delight, love.

encanto *nm* **1** *(hechizo)* spell, enchantment, charm. **2** *fig (cosa)* delight, enchantment; *(persona)* charm.

encapricharse *vpr* **1** *(empeñarse)* to set one's mind (con/en, to). **2** *(encariñarse)* to take a fancy (con, to).

encarar *vt (afrontar)* to face, face up to, confront.
▶ *vpr* **encararse 1** *(situación, problema)* to face up (a/con, to). **2** *(persona)* to stand up (a/con, to).

encarcelar *vt* to imprison.

encarecer *vt (precios)* to put up the price of.

encargado,-a *adj* in charge.
▶ *nm & nf* **1** COM *(hombre)* manager; *(mujer)* manageress. **2** *(empleado)* person in charge.

encargar *vt* **1** *(encomendar)* to entrust, put in charge of. **2** *(recomendar)* to recommend, advise. **3** COM *(pedir)* to order, place an order for: *encargó 4 kilos de naranjas* he ordered 4 kilos of oranges.
▶ *vpr* **encargarse de** to take charge of, look after, see to, deal with.

encargo *nm* **1** *(recado)* errand. **2** COM order, commission. LOC **hacer un encargo** *(recado)* to run an errand.

encariñarse *vpr* to become fond (con, of), get attached (con, to).

encauzar *vt* **1** to channel. **2** *fig* to direct, guide.

encéfalo *nm* encephalon.

encendedor *nm* lighter.

encender *vt* **1** *(hacer arder)* to light, set fire to; *(cerilla)* to strike, light; *(vela)* to light. **2** *(luz, radio, tv)* to turn on, switch on, put on; *(gas)* to turn on, light.
▶ *vpr* **encenderse** *(luz)* to go on, come on; *(llama)* to flare up.

encerado *nm (pizarra)* blackboard.

encerar *vt* to wax, polish.

encerrar *vt* **1** *(gen)* to shut in, shut up. **2** *(con llave)* to lock in, lock up.

encestar *vt* to score a basket.

enchufado,-a *adj fam* well connected, with friends in the right places.
▶ *nm & nf fam (gen)* person with friends in the right places, US wirepuller; *(en la escuela)* teacher's pet.

enchufar *vt* **1** ELEC to connect, plug in. **2** *(unir)* to join, connect, fit. **3** *fam fig* to pull strings for: *enchufó a su hija en la empresa* he got his daughter a job in the company.

enchufe *nm* **1** ELEC *(hembra)* socket; *(macho)* plug. **2** *fam fig (trabajo)* easy job; *(influencias)* contacts *pl*, friends *pl* in high places. LOC **tener enchufe** *fam* to have contacts.

encía *nf* gum.

enciclopedia *nf* encyclopaedia, encyclopedia.

encima *adv* **1** *(más arriba)* above, overhead; *(sobre)* on top. **2** *(ropa, etc)* on, on top: *ponte algo encima* put something on. **3** *(además)* in addition, besides. **4** *fam (por si fuera poco)* what's more, on top of that, besides. LOC **encima de 1** *(a más altura)* over, above. **2** *(sobre)* on. **3** *(además)* besides, as well as, on top of that. ▮ **por encima de 1** *(más importante)* above. **2** *(más allá)* beyond: *está por encima de sus posibilidades* it's beyond her capabilities.

E

encina *nf* holm oak, evergreen oak.

encoger *vt* **1** *(contraer)* to contract. **2** *(tejido)* to shrink.
▶ *vi (tejido)* to shrink.
▶ *vpr* **encogerse 1** *(contraerse)* to contract. **2** *(tejido)* to shrink.

encolar *vt (dar cola)* to glue.

encontrar *vt* **1** *(gen)* to find. **2** *(una persona sin buscar)* to come across, meet, bump into. **3** *(dificultades)* to run into, come up against.
▶ *vpr* **encontrarse 1** *(estar)* to be: *se encuentra enfermo* he's ill. **2** *(persona)* to meet; *(por casualidad)* to bump into, run into, meet: *nos encontraremos allí* we'll meet there. **3** *(dificultades)* to run into. **4** *fig (sentirse)* to feel, be: *me encuentro mal* I feel bad.

encrucijada *nf* **1** crossroads, intersection. **2** *fig* crossroads.

encuadernación *nf (arte)* bookbinding.

encuadernar *vt* to bind.

encuadrar *vt* **1** *(cuadro, etc)* to frame. **2** *fig (encajar)* to fit in, insert.
▶ *vpr* **encuadrarse** *(incorporarse)* to join.

encuadre *nm* framing.

encubrir *vt* **1** *(ocultar)* to conceal, hide. **2** JUR *(delito)* to cover up; *(criminal)* to cover up for.

encuentro *nm* **1** *(de personas)* meeting. **2** DEP meeting, clash; *(partido)* match, game.

encuesta *nf (sondeo)* poll, survey. LOC **hacer una encuesta** to carry out an opinion poll.

encuestador,-ra *nm & nf* pollster.

encuestar *vt* to poll.

encurtidos *nm pl* pickles.

endecasílabo,-a *adj* hendecasyllabic.

enderezar *vt* **1** *(poner derecho)* to straighten out. **2** *(poner vertical)* to set upright. **3** *fig (situación, etc)* to put right.
▶ *vpr* **enderezarse** *(ponerse recto)* to straighten up.

endeudarse *vpr* to get into debt, fall into debt.

endibia *nf* endive.

endulzar *vt* to sweeten.

endurecer *vt* **1** to harden, make hard. **2** *fig* to harden, toughen.

ene *nf name of the letter* n.
▶ *adj (indeterminado)* n: *ene veces* n times.

enebro *nm* juniper.

eneldo *nm* dill.

enemigo,-a *adj* enemy, hostile.
▶ *nm & nf* enemy, foe.

enemistar *vt* to make enemies of, set at odds, cause a rift between.
▶ *vpr* **enemistarse** to become enemies.

energía *nf* **1** energy, power. **2** *fig* vigour (US vigor). COMP **energía cinética** kinetic energy.

enérgico,-a *adj* **1** energetic, vigorous. **2** *fig (decisión)* firm; *(palabra)* strong.

enero *nm* January.

✎ Consulta también marzo.

enervar *vt* **1** MED to enervate. **2** *fam (irritar)* to irritate, exasperate, get on one's nerves.
▶ *vpr* **enervarse** *fam* to get flustered, get worked up.

enfadado,-a *adj* angry, cross, annoyed, US mad.

enfadar *vt* to make angry, make cross, annoy.
▶ *vpr* **enfadarse 1** to get angry (con, with), get cross (con, with). **2** *(pelearse)* to fall out (con, with) (por, about).

enfado *nm* anger, irritation.

énfasis *nm & nf inv* emphasis, stress.

enfermar *vi* to fall ill, become ill, be taken ill.

enfermedad *nf* illness, disease, sickness. COMP **enfermedad contagiosa** contagious disease.

enfermería *nf* infirmary, sick bay.

enfermero,-a *nm & nf (hombre)* male nurse; *(mujer)* nurse.

enfermizo,-a *adj* sickly, unhealthy.

enfermo,-a *adj* sick, ill.

enfilar *vt* **1** *(poner en fila)* to line up. **2** *(una calle)* to go along, go down.

enfocar *vt* **1** to focus, focus on, get into focus. **2** *(luz)* to shine a light on.

3 *fig (problema, etc)* to focus on, approach, look at.

enfoque *nm* **1** *(acción)* focus, focusing. **2** *fig* focus, approach, angle.

enfrascarse *vpr* **1** *fig* to become absorbed (en, in), become engrossed (en, in). **2** *fig (en lectura)* to bury oo (en, in).

enfrentamiento *nm* confrontation.

enfrentar *vt* **1** *(poner frente a frente)* to bring face to face, confront. **2** *(encarar)* to face, confront.
▸ *vpr* **enfrentarse 1** *(hacer frente)* to face (a/con, -), confront (a/con, -). **2** DEP to meet (a/con, -). **3** *(pelearse)* to have an argument (a, with), fall out (a, with); *(chocar)* to clash (a/con, with).

enfrente *adv* opposite, in front, facing.

enfriar *vt* **1** to cool (down), chill. **2** *fig* to cool down.
▸ *vpr* **enfriarse 1** *(lo demasiado caliente)* to cool down. **2** *(tener frío)* to get cold; *(resfriarse)* to catch a cold, get a cold.

enfurecer *vt* to infuriate, enrage.
▸ *vpr* **enfurecerse 1** to get furious, lose one's temper. **2** *(mar)* to become rough.

enfurruñarse *vpr fam* to sulk, get in a huff.

engalanar *vt (cosa)* to festoon, deck out.
▸ *vpr* **engalanarse** *(persona)* to dress up, get dressed up.

enganchar *vt* **1** *(agarrar con gancho)* to hook. **2** *(colgar)* to hang, hang up. **3** *(vagones)* to couple.
▸ *vpr* **engancharse 1** to get caught (en, on), snag (en, on). **2** MIL to enlist, join up. **3** *argot (drogas)* to get hooked (a, on).

engañar *vt* **1** *(gen)* to deceive, mislead, fool, take in. **2** *(estafar)* to cheat, trick.
▸ *vpr* **engañarse 1** *(ilusionarse)* to deceive os. **2** *(equivocarse)* to be mistaken, be wrong.

engaño *nm* **1** deceit, deception. **2** *(estafa)* fraud, trick, swindle. **3** *(mentira)* lie.

engañoso,-a *adj (gen)* deceptive.

engarzar *vt* **1** *(perlas, etc)* to string, thread. **2** *fig (palabras, frases)* to string together.

engatusar *vt fam* to get round, coax, cajole.

engendrar *vt* to engender, beget.

engendro *nm* **1** *(feto)* foetus (US fetus). **2** *fam fig (persona)* freak. **3** *fig (cosa)* monstrosity.

englobar *vt* **1** *(incluir)* to include, comprise. **2** *(reunir)* to bring together, lump together.

engomar *vt* to gum, glue, stick.

engominarse *vpr (brillantina)* to put hair cream on; *(fijador)* to gel one's hair, put hair gel on.

engordar *vt* to fatten, fatten up, make fat.
▸ *vi* **1** *(persona)* to put on weight, get fatter. **2** *(alimento)* to be fattening.

engorroso,-a *adj fam* bothersome, annoying, awkward.

engranaje *nm* **1** TÉC gears *pl*. **2** *(de reloj)* cogs *pl*. **3** *fig* machinery.

engrasar *vt (dar grasa)* to grease, oil, lubricate.

engrescar *vt (incitar)* to cause trouble between; *(animar)* to get going, arouse, excite.
▸ *vpr* **engrescarse** to get embroiled.

engrosar *vt* **1** *(hacer grueso)* to thicken. **2** *fig (aumentar)* to increase, swell.

engullir *vt* to swallow.

enharinar *vt (cubrir)* to flour; *(manchar)* to sprinkle with flour.

enhebrar *vt* **1** to thread. **2** *fig* to connect, link.

enhorabuena *nf* congratulations *pl*.
▸ *adv* thank God.

enigma *nm* enigma, puzzle, mystery.

enigmático,-a *adj* enigmatic, mysterious, puzzling.

enjabonar *vt* **1** to soap. **2** *fig* to soft-soap, butter-up.

enjambre *nm* **1** swarm. **2** *fig* swarm, throng, crowd.

enjaular *vt* **1** to cage. **2** *fam fig* to put in jail, put inside.

enjoyar *vt* to adorn with jewels.

▶ *vpr* **enjoyarse** *fam* to put on lots of jewellery (US jewelry), be dripping with jewels.

enjuagar *vt* to rinse.

▶ *vpr* **enjuagarse** to rinse one's mouth out.

enjugar *vt (secar)* to dry, wipe (away), mop up.

enjuiciar *vt* **1** *(juzgar)* to judge; *(examinar)* to examine. **2** JUR *(civil)* to sue; *(criminal)* to indict, prosecute.

enlace *nm* **1** *(conexión)* link, connection. **2** *(boda)* marriage. **3** *(tren, etc)* connection. **4** QUÍM bond.

enlatado,-a *adj* canned, tinned.

enlatar *vt* to can, tin.

enlazar *vt* **1** *(unir)* to link, connect, tie (together). **2** *(ideas, etc)* to link, connect, relate. **3** *(carreteras, etc)* to connect.

▶ *vi (trenes, etc)* to connect (con, with).

▶ *vpr* **enlazarse 1** *(unirse)* to be linked, be connected. **2** *(casarse)* to get married, marry.

enlodar *vt* to muddy, cover with mud.

enloquecedor,-ra *adj* maddening.

enloquecer *vt* **1** *(volver loco)* to drive mad. **2** *fam (gustar)* to be mad/crazy about, be wild about.

▶ *vi (volverse loco)* to go mad/crazy, go out of one's mind.

enlosado *nm (de losas)* paving; *(de baldosas)* tiling.

enlosar *vt (losas)* to pave; *(baldosas)* to tile.

enlucir *vt (paredes, etc)* to plaster.

enmadrado,-a *adj* tied to one's mother's apron strings.

enmadrarse *vpr* to be tied to one's mother's apron strings.

enmarañar *vt* **1** *(enredar)* to tangle. **2** *fig* to embroil, muddle up, confuse.

▶ *vpr* **enmarañarse 1** *(enredarse)* to get tangled. **2** *fig* to get into a muddle, get confused.

enmarcar *vt* to frame.

enmascarado,-a *adj* masked.

▶ *nm & nf* masked person.

enmascarar *vt* **1** to mask. **2** *fig* to mask, disguise, conceal.

enmendar *vt* **1** to correct, put right. **2** *(un daño)* to repair, put right.

▶ *vpr* **enmendarse** to reform, mend one's ways.

enmienda *nf* **1** correction. **2** *(de daño)* repair, indemnity, compensation. ⌐LOC¬ **hacer propósito de enmienda** to turn over a new leaf.

enmohecer *vt (pan, queso, etc)* to make mouldy (US moldy); *(metal)* to rust.

▶ *vpr* **enmohecerse** *(pan, queso, etc)* to go mouldy (US moldy); *(metal)* to rust, go rusty.

enmoquetar *vt* to carpet.

enmudecer *vt (hacer callar)* to silence.

▶ *vi* **1** *(quedar mudo)* to be struck dumb; *(perder la voz)* to lose one's voice. **2** *(callar)* to fall silent, keep quiet.

enojado,-a *adj* angry, cross.

enojar *vt* to anger, annoy, make angry.

▶ *vpr* **enojarse** to get angry (con, with), get annoyed (con, with), lose one's temper (con, with).

enojo *nm* anger, annoyance.

enojoso,-a *adj* annoying, irritating.

enorgullecer *vt* to fill with pride.

▶ *vpr* **enorgullecerse** to be proud (de, of), pride os (de, on).

enorme *adj (grande)* enormous, huge, vast.

enormidad *nf (grandeza)* enormity, hugeness.

enquistarse *vpr* to encyst.

enrabiar *vt* to enrage, infuriate.

▶ *vpr* **enrabiarse** to become enraged.

enraizar *vi* **1** BOT to take root. **2** *fig (persona)* to put down roots.

▶ *vpr* **enraizarse** *(planta, árbol)* to take root; *(persona)* to put down roots.

enredadera *nf* creeper, climbing plant.

enredar *vt* **1** *(engatusar)* to involve, implicate. **2** *(meter cizaña)* to sow discord, cause trouble. **3** *(enmarañar)* to tangle up, entangle. **4** *fig (asunto, etc)* to confuse, complicate.

▶ *vpr* **enredarse 1** *(hacerse un lío)* to get tangled up, get entangled, get into a tangle.

enredo *nm* **1** *(maraña)* tangle. **2** *(confusión)* mess, muddle, confusion, mix-up. **3** *(engaño)* deceit. **4** *(travesura)* mischief.

enrejado *nm (reja)* railings *pl*, grating.

enrejar *vt* **1** *(puerta, ventana)* to put a grating on. **2** *(vallar)* to fence, put railings round.

enrevesado,-a *adj* complicated, difficult.

enriquecer *vt* **1** *(hacer rico)* to make rich. **2** *fig* to enrich.
▶ *vpr* **enriquecerse** to get rich.

enriquecimiento *nm* enrichment.

enrocar *vi (ajedrez)* to castle.
▶ *vt (ajedrez)* to castle.

enrojecimiento *nm (rostro)* blushing.

enrollado,-a *adj* **1** *(papel)* rolled up; *(cable)* coiled. **2** *fam (guay)* cool, great.

enrollar *vt* **1** *(papel)* to roll up; *(hilo)* to wind up. **2** *(a alguien)* to involve.
▶ *vpr* **enrollarse 1** *fam fig (hablar)* to go on and on (con, to), chatter (con, to). **2** *fam fig (tener relaciones)* to have an affair (con, with). **3** *fam fig (liarse)* to get involved (con, with).

enroque *nm* castling.

enroscar *vt (tornillo)* to screw in.
▶ *vpr* **enroscarse** to wind, coil; *(cable)* to roll up; *(serpiente)* to coil itself (up).

ensaimada *nf spiral-shaped pastry made of light dough*.

ensalada *nf* salad.

ensaladera *nf* salad bowl.

ensaladilla *nf* vegetable salad.

ensamblar *vt* to join, assemble.

ensanchar *vt* **1** *(gen)* to widen, enlarge, extend. **2** COST to let out.
▶ *vpr* **ensancharse** to get wider, expand, spread, stretch.

ensanche *nm* **1** *(gen)* widening, enlargement, extension. **2** *(de ciudad)* urban development.

ensartar *vt (cuentas)* to string (together), thread; *(aguja)* to thread.

ensayar *vt* **1** TEAT to rehearse. **2** MÚS to practise (US practice). **3** *(probar)* to try out, test.

ensayo *nm* **1** TEAT rehearsal. **2** MÚS practice. **3** *(prueba)* test, experiment, trial, attempt. **4** *(literario, etc)* essay.

enseguida *adv* at once, straight away, immediately.

✎ También se escribe en seguida.

enseñante *nm o nf* teacher.

enseñanza *nf* **1** *(educación)* education, teaching. **2** *(doctrina)* teaching, doctrine. COMP **enseñanza general básica** general basic education. ▌**enseñanza primaria** primary education.

enseñar *vt* **1** *(en escuela, etc)* to teach, train, instruct. **2** *(educar)* to educate. **3** *(mostrar, dejar ver)* to show: *me enseñó el libro* he showed me the book.

ensillar *vt* put a saddle on.

ensimismado,-a *adj* engrossed, absorbed, lost.

ensimismarse *vpr (abstraerse)* to become lost in thought.

ensoñar *vt* to daydream about.

ensordecedor,-ra *adj* deafening.

ensordecer *vt* to deafen.
▶ *vi* to go deaf.

ensortijado,-a *adj* curly.

ensuciar *vt* to dirty, make dirty.
▶ *vpr* **ensuciarse** *(mancharse)* to get dirty.

ensueño *nm* dream, fantasy. LOC **de ensueño** dream.

entablar *vt* **1** *(poner tablas)* to plank, board. **2** *(conversación)* to begin, start, open; *(amistad)* to strike up.

entallar *vt* COST to take in at the waist.

entarimado *nm* parquet floor.

ente *nm (ser)* being.

entender *nm (opinión)* understanding, opinion.
▶ *vt* **1** *(comprender)* to understand. **2** *(darse cuenta)* to realize. **3** *(discurrir)* to think, believe: *entiendo que sería mejor ir* I think it would be better to go. **4** *(interpretar)* to understand, take it.

▶ *vi (tener conocimiento)* to know (de, about).

▶ *vpr* **entenderse 1** *(comprenderse)* to be understood. **2** *fam (conocerse)* to know what one is doing: *yo ya me entiendo* I have my reasons. **3** *fam (llevarse bien)* to get along.

entendido,-a *nm & nf* expert.

entendimiento *nm* **1** *(comprensión)* understanding, comprehension. **2** *(sentido común)* understanding, sense, judgement. **3** *(inteligencia)* intelligence.

enterado,-a *nm & nf fam* expert, authority. ⌷ **darse por enterado,-a de** ALGO to be aware of STH. ▌ **estar enterado,-a** to be in the know.

enterar *vt* to inform (de, about/of); *(poner al corriente)* to acquaint (de, with), tell (de, about).

▶ *vpr* **enterarse 1** *(averiguar)* to find out (de, about). **2** *(tener conocimiento)* to learn, hear. **3** *(darse cuenta)* to realize.

enternecer *vt (conmover)* to move, touch.

▶ *vpr* **enternecerse** to be moved, be touched.

entero,-a *adj (completo)* entire, whole, complete.

▶ *nm* **entero** MAT whole number.

enterrar *vt* **1** to bury, inter. **2** *fig (olvidar)* to forget, give up.

entierro *nm* **1** *(acción)* burial. **2** *(ceremonia)* funeral.

entonar *vt* **1** *(nota)* to pitch; *(canción)* to sing, intone. **2** *(colores)* to match.

▶ *vi* **1** MÚS to intone. **2** *(colores)* to match. **3** *fig (armonizar)* to be in harmony (con, with), be in tune (con, with).

entonces *adv* **1** *(en aquel momento)* then. **2** *(en tal caso)* so, then: *entonces no lo quieres* so you don't want it. ⌷ **desde entonces** since then.

entornado,-a *adj (ojos, etc)* half-closed; *(puerta)* ajar.

entornar *vt* **1** *(ojos, etc)* to half-close. **2** *(puerta)* to leave ajar.

entorno *nm* **1** environment, surroundings *pl*. **2** INFORM environment.

entorpecer *vt* **1** to make numb, make dull. **2** *fig (dificultar)* to obstruct.

entorpecimiento *nm* **1** dullness, numbness. **2** *fig (obstrucción)* obstruction, hindrance.

entrada *nf* **1** *(gen)* entrance, entry. **2** *(vestíbulo)* hall, entrance. **3** *(billete)* ticket, admission. **4** *(público)* audience. **5** *(de libro, oración, etc)* opening; *(de año, mes)* beginning: *la entrada de la primavera* the beginning of spring. **6** *(pago inicial)* down payment, deposit. **7** CULIN entrée, starter. **8** INFORM input. **9** DEP tackle. ⌷ **de entrada 1** *(desde el principio)* straight away, from the outset. **2** *(en comida)* for starters. ▌ «**Prohibida la entrada**» "No admittance".

entramado *nm* wooden framework.

entrante *adj* entering, coming, incoming: *el año entrante* the coming year; *el mes entrante* next month.

▶ *nm* CULIN starter.

entrañable *adj* **1** *(amistad)* intimate, close. **2** *(amigo)* dear. **3** *(recuerdo)* fond.

entrar *vi* **1** *(ir adentro)* to come in, go in. **2** *(tener entrada)* to be welcome. **3** *(en una sociedad, etc)* to join; *(en una profesión)* to take up, join. **4** *(encajar, caber)* to fit: *este tornillo no entra* this screw doesn't fit. **5** *(empezar - año, estación)* to begin, start; *(- período, época)* to enter; *(- libro, carta)* to begin, open: *ya ha entrado el verano* summer has begun. **6** *(venir)* to come over, come on: *me entraron ganas de llorar* I felt like crying. **7** *(alcanzar)* to reach: *ha entrado en los cuarenta* he has reached forty. **8** INFORM to access.

▶ *vt (meter)* to put.

entre *prep* **1** *(dos términos)* between. **2** *(varios)* among, amongst: *entre los periódicos* among the newspapers. **3** *(entremedio)* somewhere between: *entre azul y verde* somewhere between blue and green. ⌷ **de entre** from among, out of: ▌ **entre tanto** meanwhile, in the meantime.

entreabierto,-a *adj (ojos, etc)* half-open; *(puerta)* ajar.

entreabrir *vt* **1** *(ojos)* to half open. **2** *(puerta, etc)* to leave ajar.

entreacto *nm* interval.

entrecejo *nm* space between the eyebrows; *(ceño)* frown.

entrecot *nm* entrecôte.

entredicho *nm* *(duda)* doubt, question. LOC poner ALGO en entredicho to have one's doubts about STH.

entrega *nf* 1 *(gen)* handing over. 2 *(de premios)* presentation. 3 COM delivery. 4 *(de posesiones)* surrender. 5 *(fascículo)* instalment (US installment), part. 6 DEP pass. COMP entrega a domicilio home delivery.

entregar *vt* 1 *(dar)* to hand over. 2 *(deberes, ejercicios)* to hand in, give in; *(premios)* to present, award. 3 COM to deliver.
▶ *vpr* **entregarse** 1 *(rendirse)* to give in (a, to), surrender. 2 *(dedicarse)* to devote os (a, to), be devoted (a, to). 3 *pey (caer en)* to give os over (a, to), take (a, to).

entrelazar *vt* to entwine, interweave, interlace.

entremedias *adv* 1 in between. 2 *(mientras tanto)* meanwhile, in the meantime. LOC entremedias de between, among.

entremés *nm* hors d'oeuvre *pl*.

entremezclar *vt* to intermingle.
▶ *vpr* **entremezclarse** to intermingle.

entrenador,-ra *nm & nf* trainer, coach.

entrenamiento *nm* training.

entrenar *vt* to train, coach.
▶ *vpr* **entrenarse** to train.

entreno *nm* training.

entresijo *nm* *fig* secret, mystery. LOC conocer todos los entresijos *fig* to know all the ins and outs.

entresuelo *nm* mezzanine, GB first floor, US second floor.

entretanto *adv* meanwhile.

entretejer *vt* to interweave, intertwine.

entretener *vt* 1 *(detener)* to hold up, detain; *(retrasar)* to delay. 2 *(ocupar)* to keep busy. 3 *(distraer)* to occupy, keep occupied. 4 *(divertir)* to entertain, amuse, distract.
▶ *vpr* **entretenerse** 1 *(retrasarse)* to be delayed, be held up. 2 *(distraerse)* to keep os occupied. 3 *(divertirse)* to amuse os.

entretenido,-a *adj* *(divertido)* entertaining, amusing.

entretenimiento *nm* *(distracción)* entertainment, distraction, amusement.

entretiempo *nm* period between seasons; *(primavera)* spring; *(otoño)* autumn. LOC un traje de entretiempo a lightweight suit.

entrevista *nf* 1 *(prensa)* interview. 2 *(reunión)* meeting. LOC hacer una entrevista a ALGN to interview SB.

entrevistador,-ra *nm & nf* interviewer.

entrevistar *vt* to interview.
▶ *vpr* **entrevistarse** 1 *(prensa)* to have an interview (con, with). 2 *(reunirse)* to have a meeting (con, with).

entristecer *vt* to make sad.
▶ *vpr* **entristecerse** to be sad (por, about).

entrometerse *vpr* to meddle, interfere.

entrometido,-a *adj* nosy.
▶ *nm & nf* meddler, nosy parker.

entroncar *vt* to relate, link, connect.
▶ *vi* *(parentesco)* to be related.

entumecido,-a *adj* numb.

entumecimiento *nm* numbness.

enturbiar *vt* 1 to make muddy, make cloudy, cloud. 2 *fig* to cloud, muddle, obscure.
▶ *vpr* **enturbiarse** 1 to get muddy, become cloudy. 2 *fig* to get confused, get muddled.

entusiasmado,-a *adj* excited.

entusiasmar *vt* 1 *(causar entusiasmo)* to fill with enthusiasm, excite. 2 *(gustar)* to like, love: *me entusiasma la ópera* I love opera.
▶ *vpr* **entusiasmarse** 1 to get enthusiastic (con, about), get excited (con, about). 2 *(gustar)* to love (con, -), like (con, -).

entusiasmo *nm* enthusiasm. LOC **con entusiasmo** keenly, enthusiastically.

entusiasta *adj* enthusiastic.

enumeración *nf (cómputo)* enumeration, count, reckoning.

enumerar *vt* to enumerate.

enunciado *nm* **1** *(teoría, etc)* enunciation. **2** LING statement. **3** *(problema, etc)* wording.

enunciar *vt* **1** *(teoría)* to enunciate. **2** *(expresar)* to express, state, word.

envalentonar *vt* to make bold, make daring.
▶ *vpr* **envalentonarse** *(volverse valiente)* to become bold, become daring.

envasado,-a *adj (bebidas)* bottled; *(conservas)* canned, tinned; *(paquetes)* packed.
▶ *nm* **envasado** *(bebidas)* bottling; *(conservas)* canning; *(paquetes)* packing. COMP **envasado al vacío** vacuum-packed.

envasar *vt (botellas)* to bottle; *(latas)* to can, tin; *(paquetes)* to pack.

envase *nm* **1** *(acción - paquetes)* packing; *(- botellas)* bottling; *(- latas)* canning. **2** *(recipiente)* container. **3** *(botella vacía)* empty. COMP **envase de cartón** carton. ‖ **envase de plástico** plastic container. ‖ **envase sin retorno** nonreturnable bottle.

envejecer *vt* to age, make look old.
▶ *vi* to get old, grow old.

envejecido,-a *adj* aged, old, old-looking: *Pablo está muy envejecido* Pablo looks very old.

envejecimiento *nm* ageing.

envenenamiento *nm* poisoning.

envenenar *vt* to poison.

envés *nm inv* **1** *(de página)* back, reverse. **2** *(de tela)* wrong side. **3** BOT reverse.

enviado,-a *nm & nf* messenger, envoy. COMP **enviado,-a especial** special correspondent.

enviar *vt* **1** *(gen)* to send. **2** COM to dispatch, remit; *(por barco)* to ship.

enviciar *vt (pervertir)* to corrupt, pervert.
▶ *vi* BOT to produce too many leaves and not enough fruit.

▶ *vpr* **enviciarse** *(pervertirse)* to become corrupted, fall into bad habits.

envidar *vi* to bid, bet.

envidia *nf* envy. LOC **dar envidia** to make envious. ‖ **tener envidia de** ALGO/ALGN to envy STH/SB.

envidiable *adj* enviable.

envidiar *vt* to envy.

envidioso,-a *adj* envious.

envío *nm* **1** *(acción)* sending, dispatch. **2** COM dispatch, shipment. **3** *(paquete)* parcel. **4** *(mensaje electrónico)* posting. LOC **hacer un envío** COM to dispatch an order. ‖ **envío contra reembolso** cash on delivery. ‖ COMP **gastos de envío** postage and packing.

envite *nm (apuesta)* bet.

enviudar *vi (hombre)* to become a widower, lose one's wife; *(mujer)* to become a widow, lose one's husband.

envoltorio *nm (de caramelo, etc)* wrapper.

envolver *vt (con papel)* to wrap, wrap up.

enyesado *nm* **1** plastering. **2** MED plaster cast.

enyesar *vt* **1** to plaster. **2** MED to put in plaster.

enzarzar *vt* **1** *(de zarzas)* to cover with brambles. **2** *fig (engrescar)* to sow discord among, set at odds.
▶ *vpr* **enzarzarse** **1** *(enredarse en zarzas)* to get entangled in brambles. **2** *fig (discusión, asunto)* to get involved (en, in).

enzima *nm & nf* enzyme.

eñe *nf* name of the letter ñ.

eoceno,-a *adj* Eocene.
▶ *nm* **eoceno** Eocene.

eólico,-a *adj* wind: *energía eólica* wind power.

épica *nf* epic poetry.

epiceno *adj* epicene.

epicentro *nm* epicentre (US epicenter).

épico,-a *adj* epic, heroic.

epicureísmo *nm* Epicureanism.

epicúreo,-a *adj* Epicurean.

epidemia *nf* epidemic.

epidémico,-a *adj* epidemic.

epidérmico,-a *adj* epidermic, skin: *enfermedad epidérmica* skin disease.

epidermis *nf inv* epidermis, skin.

epígrafe *nm* **1** *(cita)* epigraph. **2** *(título)* title, heading.

epilepsia *nf* epilepsy.

epiléptico,-a *adj* epileptic.

epílogo *nm* *(parte final)* epilogue (US epilog).

episcopado *nm* *(obispos)* episcopacy.

episcopal *adj* episcopal.

episodio *nm* **1** *(literario)* episode. **2** *(suceso)* incident, event.

epístola *nf fml* epistle, letter.

epitelio *nm* epithelium.

epíteto *nm* epithet.

época *nf* **1** time, age. **2** HIST period, epoch: *muebles de época* period furniture. **3** AGR season, time: *la época de la recolección* harvest time. LOC **por aquella época** about that time. **ser de su época** to be with the times.

epopeya *nf* **1** LIT epic poem. **2** *(hecho)* heroic deed.

equidad *nf (moderación)* fairness, reasonableness.

equidistancia *nf* equidistance.

equidistante *adj* equidistant.

equidistar *vi* to be equidistant (de, from).

equilátero,-a *adj* equilateral.

equilibrado,-a *adj* **1** balanced. **2** *(persona)* sensible, well-balanced.

equilibrar *vt* **1** to balance, poise. **2** *fig* to balance, adjust.
▶ *vpr* **equilibrarse 1** to balance (en, on). **2** *fig* to recover one's balance.

equilibrio *nm* **1** *(estabilidad)* balance: *perdió el equilibrio* he lost his balance. **2** FÍS equilibrium. **3** *fig (armonía)* balance, harmony. LOC **hacer equilibrios** *fig* to perform a balancing act. **mantener el equilibrio** to keep one's balance.

equilibrismo *nm (gen)* balancing act; *(de funámbulo)* tightrope walking.

equilibrista *nm o nf (funámbulo)* tightrope walker.

equino,-a *adj* equine, horse.

equinoccio *nm* equinox.

equinodermo *nm* echinoderm.

equipaje *nm* luggage, baggage. COMP **equipaje de mano** hand luggage.

equipar *vt* to equip, furnish.
▶ *vpr* **equiparse** *(uso reflexivo)* to kit os out (con/de, with), equip os (con/de, with).

equiparable *adj* comparable (a/con, to/with).

equiparar *vt* to compare (a/con, with), liken (a/con, to).

equipo *nm* **1** *(prestaciones)* equipment. **2** *(ropas, utensilios)* outfit, kit. **3** *(de personas)* team. COMP **equipo de alta fidelidad** hi-fi system. **equipo de fútbol** football team. **equipo de música** music centre, stereo system.

equis *nf inv* **1** *name of the letter* x. **2** MAT x, unknown quantity.

equitación *nf* horsemanship, horse riding, US horseback riding.

equitativo,-a *adj* equitable, fair.

equivalencia *nf* **1** *(igualdad)* equivalence. **2** *(sustitución)* compensation.

equivalente *adj (igual)* equivalent.
▶ *nm* equivalent.

equivaler *vi* **1** *(ser igual)* to be equivalent (a, to), be equal (a, to). **2** *(significar)* to be tantamount (a, to), amount (a, to), mean (a, -).

equivocación *nf* **1** *(error)* mistake, error. **2** *(malentendido)* misunderstanding. LOC **cometer una equivocación** to make a mistake.

equivocado,-a *adj* mistaken, wrong.

equivocar *vt* **1** to mistake, get wrong. **2** *(cambiar)* to get mixed up: *equivoqué vuestros regalos* I got your presents mixed up.
▶ *vpr* **equivocarse** to make a mistake, be mistaken, be wrong; *(de dirección, camino, etc)* to go wrong, get wrong: *me equivoqué de calle* I got the wrong street.

equívoco,-a *adj* equivocal, misleading, ambiguous.
▶ *nm* **equívoco 1** ambiguity, double meaning. **2** *(malentendido)* misunderstanding.

era *nf (tiempo)* era, age.

erario *nm* exchequer, treasury.

erasmismo *nm* Erasmianism.

ere *nf* name of the letter r.

erecto,-a *adj* erect.

eremita *nm* hermit, eremite.

ergonómico,-a *adj* ergonomic.

erguido,-a *adj* erect, upright, straight.

erguir *vt* to raise (up straight), erect, lift up.
▶ *vpr* **erguirse** *(ponerse derecho)* to straighten up, stand up straight.

erial *adj* uncultivated, untilled.
▶ *nm* uncultivated land.

erigir *vt (alzar)* to erect, build.

Eritrea *nf* Eritrea.

eritreo,-a *adj* Eritrean.
▶ *nm & nf (persona)* Eritrean.

erizado,-a *adj* bristly, prickly.

erizar *vt (pelo - animal)* to bristle; *(- persona)* make stand on end.
▶ *vpr* **erizarse** *(pelo - de animal)* to bristle; *(- de persona)* to stand on end: *el pelo se le erizó* his hair stood on end.

erizo *nm (animal)* hedgehog. COMP **erizo de mar** sea urchin.

ermita *nf* hermitage, shrine.

ermitaño,-a *adj* recluse.
▶ *nm & nf (persona solitaria)* hermit.
▶ *nm* **ermitaño** ZOOL hermit crab.

erosión *nf* erosion, wearing away.

erosionar *vt* to erode.

erosivo,-a *adj* erosive.

erradicar *vt* **1** to eradicate. **2** *(enfermedad)* to stamp out.

errado,-a *adj* mistaken, wrong.

errante *adj* wandering, errant.

errar *vt (objetivo)* to miss, get wrong.
▶ *vi* **1** *(vagar)* to wander, rove, roam. **2** *(equivocarse)* to be mistaken, be wrong.

errata *nf* erratum, misprint.

errático,-a *adj* erratic.

erre *nf* name of the digraph rr.

erróneo,-a *adj* erroneous, wrong, mistaken, unsound: *explicación errónea* wrong explanation.

error *nm* error, mistake.

eructar *vi* to belch, burp.

eructo *nm* belch, burp.

erudición *nf* erudition, learning.

erudito,-a *adj* erudite, learned.
▶ *nm & nf* scholar, expert.

erupción *nf* **1** *(volcánica)* eruption. **2** *(cutánea)* rash. LOC **entrar en erupción** to erupt.

eruptivo,-a *adj* eruptive.

esbelto,-a *adj* slim, slender.

esbozar *vt* to sketch, outline. LOC **esbozar una sonrisa** *fig* to force a smile, smile weakly.

esbozo *nm* sketch, outline.

escabechado,-a *adj* pickled, in brine.

escabechar *vt* to pickle, preserve in brine; *(arenque)* to souse, pickle.

escabeche *nm* brine, pickle.

escabechina *nf fam* massacre.

escabroso,-a *adj* **1** *(desigual)* uneven, rough: *terreno escabroso* rough terrain. **2** *fig (difícil)* tough, difficult.

escabullirse *vpr* **1** *(entre las manos)* to slip through. **2** *fig (persona)* to slip away, sneak off, disappear.

escacharrar *vt* **1** *fam (romper)* to break. **2** *fam (estropear)* to ruin, spoil.

escafandra *nf* diving suit.

escafandrista *nm o nf* diver.

escala *nf* **1** *(escalera - de mano)* ladder; *(- de tijera)* stepladder. **2** *(mapa, plano, etc)* scale: *lo dibujó a escala* he drew it to scale. **3** *(puerto)* port of call; *(aeropuerto)* stopover. **4** MÚS scale.

escalada *nf (montaña)* climb, climbing.

escalador,-ra *nm & nf* climber.

escalafón *nm (de personas)* roll, promotion list.

escalar *vt (montaña)* to climb.

escaldado,-a *adj* scalded.

escaleno *adj* scalene.

escalera *nf* **1** stairs *pl*, staircase. **2** *(escala)* ladder.

escalerilla *nf (de barco)* gangway; *(de avión)* steps *pl*.

escalfar *vt* to poach: *huevos escalfados* poached eggs.

escalinata *nf* outside steps *pl*.

escalofriante *adj* chilling, bloodcurdling, hair-raising.

escalofrío *nm* *(de frío)* shiver. LOC **tener escalofríos** to shiver.

escalón *nm* **1** *(peldaño)* step, stair; *(de escala)* rung. **2** *fig* *(grado)* degree, level, grade. **3** *fig* *(paso, medio)* stepping stone.

escalonado,-a *adj* *(espaciado)* spaced out, at regular intervals.

escalonar *vt* **1** *(espaciar)* to place at intervals, space out. **2** *(cabello)* cut in layers.

escama *nf* **1** scale. **2** *fig* *(de piel, de jabón)* flake.

escamado,-a *adj* *fam* *fig* wary, suspicious.

escamar *vt* **1** *(quitar escamas)* to scale, remove the scales from. **2** *fam* *fig* to make suspicious, make wary.

escampar *vt* to clear out.
  ▶ *vi* [se emplea sólo en tercera persona; no lleva sujeto] METEOR to stop raining, clear up.

escandalizar *vt* to shock.
  ▶ *vpr* **escandalizarse** to be shocked (de/ por, at), be scandalized (de/por, by).

escándalo *nm* **1** scandal. **2** *(alboroto)* racket, fuss, din, uproar. LOC **armar un escándalo** to kick up a fuss.

escandaloso,-a *adj* **1** scandalous, shocking, outrageous. **2** *(alborotado)* noisy, rowdy.

Escandinavia *nf* Scandinavia.

escandinavo,-a *adj* Scandinavian.
  ▶ *nm & nf* Scandinavian.

escanear *vt* to scan.

escáner *nm* scanner.

escaño *nm* **1** *(banco)* bench. **2** POL seat.

escapada *nf* **1** *fam* *(salida)* quick trip. **2** *(huida)* escape.

escapar *vi* **1** *(huir)* to escape, get away, run away. **2** *(librarse)* to escape.
  ▶ *vpr* **escaparse 1** *(huir)* to escape, run away, get away. **2** *(librarse)* to escape, avoid. **3** *(gas, etc)* to leak.

escaparate *nm* shop window.

escapatoria *nf* **1** *(huida)* escape, flight. **2** *(excusa)* excuse, way out.

escape *nm* **1** *(huida)* escape, flight, getaway. **2** *(de gas, etc)* leak.

escarabajo *nm* beetle.

escaramujo *nm* **1** *(rosal)* wild rose, dog rose. **2** *(fruto)* rosehip.

escaramuza *nf* *(riña)* run-in, squabble.

escarbar *vt* **1** *(suelo)* to scratch. **2** *(bolsillo, papeles)* to rummage in.

escarcha *nf* frost, hoarfrost.

escarlata *adj* scarlet.

escarlatina *nf* scarlet fever.

escarmentar *vt* teach a lesson to.
  ▶ *vi* to learn one's lesson: *a ver si escarmientas* that'll teach you (a lesson).

escarmiento *nm* lesson.

escarola *nf* curly endive.

escarpado,-a *adj* **1** *(inclinado)* steep, sheer. **2** *(abrupto)* craggy.

escarpia *nf* spike, hook.

escasear *vi* *(faltar)* to be scarce.

escasez *nf* *(carencia)* scarcity, lack, shortage.

escaso,-a *adj* **1** *(insuficiente)* scarce, scant, very little, small. **2** *(recursos)* slender; *(dinero)* tight; *(público)* small; *(lluvias, salario)* low; *(tiempo)* very little. **3** *(poco de algo)* few: *escasos días* few days. **4** *(que le falta poco)* hardly, scarcely, barely: *un kilo escaso* barely a kilo.

escayola *nf* **1** *(yeso)* plaster of Paris; *(estuco)* stucco. **2** MED plaster.

escayolar *vt* to put in plaster, plaster.

escena *nf* **1** TEAT *(parte)* scene; *(lugar)* stage. **2** *fig* scene.

escenario *nm* **1** TEAT stage. **2** CINE scenario. **3** *fig* scene, setting.

escenificar *vt* **1** *(novela)* to dramatize. **2** *(obra de teatro)* to stage.

escenografía *nm* **1** CINE set design. **2** TEAT stage design.

escenógrafo,-a *nm & nf* **1** CINE set designer. **2** TEAT stage designer.

escepticismo *nm* scepticism (US skepticism).

escéptico,-a *adj* sceptic (US skeptic).

escindir *vt* to split, divide.
  ▶ *vpr* **escindirse** to split (off) (en, into).

escisión *nf* **1** split, division. **2** FÍS fission. **3** MED excision.

esclavitud *nf* slavery, servitude.

esclavizar *vt* to enslave.

E

esclavo,-a *adj* enslaved.
▶ *nm & nf (gen)* slave.

esclusa *nf* lock, sluicegate, floodgate.

escoba *nf* brush, broom.

escobilla *nf* small brush.

escobón *nm* large brush.

escocer *vi* **1** to smart, sting: *le escuecen sus heridas* his cuts sting. **2** *fig* to hurt.

escocés,-a *adj* Scottish.
▶ *nm & nf (persona)* Scot; *(hombre)* Scotsman; *(mujer)* Scotswoman.
▶ *nm* **escocés** *(idioma)* Scottish Gaelic.

Escocia *nf* Scotland. COMP **Nueva Escocia** Nova Scotia.

escoger *vt* to choose, pick out, select.

escogido,-a *adj* chosen, selected; *(selecto)* choice, select.

escolar *adj* school, scholastic.
▶ *nm o nf (chico)* schoolboy; *(chica)* schoolgirl.

escolástico,-a *adj* scholastic.

escollera *nf* breakwater, jetty.

escollo *nm fig* difficulty, pitfall, snag.

escolopendra *nf* centipede.

escolta *nf* escort.

escoltar *vt* **1** to escort. **2** MAR to convoy.

escombros *nm pl* rubble *sing*, debris *sing*.

esconder *vt* to hide, conceal.
▶ *vpr* **esconderse** to hide.

escondidas LOC **hacer** ALGO **a escondidas de** ALGN to do STH behind SB's back.

escondite *nm* **1** *(lugar)* hiding place. **2** *(juego)* hide-and-seek.

escopeta *nf* shotgun.

escorpión *nm* scorpion.

escorzo *nm* foreshortening.

escote *nm* COST low neckline.

escozor *nm* **1** stinging, smarting. **2** *fig* pain, grief.

escribir *vt* **1** *(gen)* to write. **2** *(deletrear)* to spell, write.
▶ *vi* to write.
▶ *vpr* **escribirse** **1** *(deletrear)* to spell, be spelt: *¿cómo se escribe?* how do you spell it? **2** *(uso recíproco)* to write to each other. LOC **escribir a mano** to write in longhand, write by hand. I **escribir a máquina** to type.

escrito,-a *adj* written; *(mencionado)* stated.
▶ *nm* **escrito** **1** *(documento)* writing, document, text. **2** *(obra)* work, writing: *los escritos de Orwell* Orwell's writings.

escritor,-ra *nm & nf* writer.

escritorio *nm* **1** *(mueble)* writing desk, bureau. **2** *(oficina)* office.

escritura *nf* **1** *(gen)* writing: *escritura fonética* phonetic script. **2** *(caligrafía)* handwriting, writing. **3** JUR deed, document.

escrúpulo *nm* **1** [también se usa en plural con el mismo significado] *(recelo)* scruple, doubt, qualm. **2** [también se usa en plural con el mismo significado] *(aprensión)* fussiness: *eso me da escrúpulos* I'm finicky about it, I'm fussy about it. **3** *fig (cuidado)* extreme care: *lo hizo con escrúpulo* he did it with extreme care.

escrupuloso,-a *adj* **1** scrupulous. **2** *(aprensivo)* finicky, fussy. **3** *fig (exacto)* scrupulous, meticulous.

escrutinio *nm* **1** *(examen)* scrutiny, examination. **2** *(de votos)* count.

escuadra *nf* **1** *(instrumento -de dibujo)* set square; *(-de carpintería)* square; *(pieza de metal)* bracket. **2** *(de tropas)* squad; *(de buques)* squadron, fleet. **3** *(fútbol)* angle.

escuadrilla *nf* squadron.

escuadrón *nm* squadron.

escuálido,-a *adj* **1** *(delgado)* emaciated, extremely thin, skinny. **2** *(sucio)* squalid, filthy.

escucha *nf (acción)* listening. LOC **estar a la escucha de** to be listening out for. I COMP **escuchas telefónicas** phone tapping *sing*.

escuchar *vt* **1** to listen to; *(oír)* to hear. **2** *(atender)* to listen to, pay attention to: *no escuchaba mis consejos* he didn't listen to my advice.

escudo *nm* **1** *(arma)* shield. **2** *(de armas)* coat of arms. **3** *(moneda)* escudo. **4** *fig (amparo)* protection, shield.

escuela *nf* **1** *(gen)* school. **2** *(experiencia)* experience, instruction.

esculpir *vt (gen)* to sculpt, sculpture; *(madera)* to carve; *(metal)* to engrave.

escultor,-ra *nm & nf (hombre)* sculptor; *(mujer)* sculptress.

escultura *nf (gen)* sculpture; *(en madera)* carving; *(en metal)* engraving.

escupir *vt* to spit.
▶ *vt* **1** to spit out. **2** *fig (despedir)* to belch out: *la fábrica escupía humo* the factory belched out smoke.

escurreplatos *nm inv* plate rack.

escurridizo,-a *adj* **1** slippery. **2** *fig* slippery, elusive.

escurridor *nm* **1** *(colador)* strainer, colander. **2** *(de platos)* plate rack. **3** *(para ropa)* wringer, mangle.

escurrir *vt (platos, etc)* to drain; *(ropa)* to wring out; *(comida)* to strain.
▶ *vi* **1** *(destilar)* to drip, trickle. **2** *(deslizar)* to slip, slide.
▶ *vpr* **escurrirse 1** *(platos, etc)* to drain. **2** *(líquido)* to drip, trickle. **3** *(deslizarse)* to slip, slide. **4** *fam (escapar)* to run away, slip away.

esdrújulo,-a *adj* proparoxytone, stressed on the antepenultimate syllable.

ese *nf name of the letter* s.
▶ *nf pl* **eses** zigzags.

ese,-a *adj* that; *(plural)* those.

ése,-a *pron* **1** *(cosa)* that one. **2** *(hombre - sujeto)* he; *(mujer - sujeto)* she: *ése me lo dijo* he told me. **3** *(hombre - complemento)* him; *(mujer - complemento)* her: *se lo dio a ésa* he gave it to her. **4** *(anterior)* the former.

✎ Cuando no se produzca confusión con el adjetivo se puede omitir el acento.

esencia *nf* **1** essence. **2** *(perfume)* essence, perfume, scent.

esencial *adj* essential. [LOC] **lo esencial** the main thing.

esfera *nf* **1** sphere, globe. **2** *(de reloj)* dial, face. **3** *fig (campo)* field, sphere; *(ambiente)* sphere, circle.

esférico,-a *adj* spherical.
▶ *nm* **esférico** *(balón)* ball.

esfinge *nf* sphinx.

esforzar *vt* **1** *(forzar)* to strain. **2** *(animar)* to encourage, spur on.
▶ *vpr* **esforzarse** *(físicamente)* to make an effort, exert os; *(moralmente)* to try hard, strive: *se ha esforzado para llegar a la cumbre* she has striven to get to the top.

esfuerzo *nm* **1** effort, endeavour (US endeavor). **2** *(valor)* courage, spirit. [LOC] **sin esfuerzo** effortlessly.

esfumar *vt* **1** *(esfuminar)* to stump, blend. **2** *(colores)* to tone down.
▶ *vpr* **esfumarse** *fam (largarse)* to disappear, fade away.

esgrima *nf* fencing.

esguince *nm* MED sprain.

eslabón *nm* link.

eslalon *nm* slalom.

eslip *nm* **1** *(ropa interior)* men's briefs *pl*, underpants *pl*. **2** *(bañador)* trunks *pl*.
s *pl* eslips.

eslogan *nm* slogan. [COMP] **eslogan publicitario** advertising slogan.

eslovaco,-a *adj* Slovak.
▶ *nm & nf (persona)* Slovak.
▶ *nm* **eslovaco** *(idioma)* Slovak.

Eslovaquia *nf* Slovakia.

Eslovenia *nf* Slovenia.

esloveno,-a *adj* Slovene.
▶ *nm & nf (persona)* Slovene.
▶ *nm* **esloveno** *(idioma)* Slovene.

esmaltar *vt* **1** to enamel. **2** *(uñas)* to varnish. **3** *fig (adornar)* to decorate, adorn.

esmalte *nm* **1** *(gen)* enamel. **2** *(de uñas)* nail varnish, nail polish. **3** *(objeto esmaltado)* enamelled object. **4** *(color)* smalt.

esmeralda *nf* emerald.

esmerar *vt (pulir)* to polish.
▶ *vpr* **esmerarse** to do one's best (en/por, to), take great pains (en/por, over).

esmero *nm* great care, neatness.

esnob *adj (persona)* snobbish; *(lugar, etc)* posh.
▶ *nm o nf* snob.

esnobismo *nm* snobbery, snobbishness.

eso *pron* that: *eso es lo que dijo* that's what she said.

ESO *abrev* EDUC **(Enseñanza Secundaria Obligatoria)** *compulsory secondary education up to 16.*

esófago *nm* oesophagus (US esophagus), gullet.

esos,-as *adj* those.

✎ Consulta también ese,-a.

ésos,-as *pron* those (ones).

✎ Consulta también ése,-a.

espacial *adj* 1 MAT spatial, spacial. 2 *(del cosmos)* space.

espaciar *vt* to space out.

espacio *nm* 1 *(gen)* space. 2 *(que se ocupa)* space, room: *necesitamos más espacio* we need more room. 3 *(de tiempo)* period, space. 4 *(programa)* programme (US program).

espacioso,-a *adj* *(ancho)* spacious, roomy.

espada *nf* 1 *(arma)* sword. 2 *(naipe)* spade.
▶ *nf pl* **espadas** *(palo de baraja)* spades.

espaguetis *nm pl* spaghetti *sing.*

espalda *nf* 1 [también se usa en plural con el mismo significado] *(gen)* back. 2 *(natación)* backstroke.

espantapájaros *nm inv* scarecrow.

espantar *vt* 1 *(asustar)* to frighten, scare, scare off. 2 *(ahuyentar)* to frighten away.
▶ *vpr* **espantarse** 1 *(asustarse)* to be frightened, be scared. 2 *(asombrarse)* to be amazed, be astonished.

espanto *nm* 1 *(miedo)* fright, dread, terror. 2 *(asombro)* astonishment, amazement. LOC **¡qué espanto!** how awful!

espantoso,-a *adj* 1 *(terrible)* frightful, dreadful. 2 *(asombroso)* astonishing, amazing. 3 *(desmesurado)* dreadful, terrible.

España *nf* Spain.

español,-la *adj* Spanish.
▶ *nm & nf (persona)* Spaniard.
▶ *nm* **español** *(idioma)* Spanish, Castilian.

esparadrapo *nm* sticking plaster.

esparcir *vt* 1 *(desparramar)* to scatter. 2 *fig (divulgar)* to spread.
▶ *vpr* **esparcirse** 1 *(desparramarse)* to scatter, be scattered. 2 *fig (divulgarse)* to spread out.

espárrago *nm* asparagus.

esparto *nm* esparto grass.

espátula *nf* 1 *(gen)* spatula. 2 *(de pintor)* palette knife; *(de cristalero)* putty knife. 3 TÉC stripping knife. 4 *(ave)* spoonbill.

especia *nf* spice.

especial *adj* 1 *(gen)* special. 2 *(remilgado)* fussy (para, about), finicky (para, about): *es un poco especial para la comida* she's a bit finicky about food. LOC **en especial** especially.

especialidad *nf* 1 *(gen)* speciality (US specialty). 2 EDUC main subject, specialized field.

especialista *adj* specialist.
▶ *nm o nf* 1 specialist. 2 CINE stand-in; *(hombre)* stunt man; *(mujer)* stunt woman.

especialización *nf* specialization.

especialmente *adv* 1 *(exclusivamente)* specially. 2 *(particularmente)* especially.

especie *nf* 1 *(de animales, plantas)* species. 2 *(tipo)* kind, sort. 3 *(tema)* matter, notion, idea; *(noticia)* piece of news. LOC **en especie** in kind: *pagar en especie* to pay in kind.

especiero,-a *nm & nf* grocer.
▶ *nm* **especiero** spice rack.

especificar *vt* to specify.

específico,-a *adj* specific.
▶ *nm* **específico** *(medicamento)* specific; *(especialidad)* patent medicine. COMP **peso específico** specific gravity.

espécimen *nm* specimen.

espectacular *adj* spectacular.

espectáculo *nm* 1 spectacle, sight. 2 *(diversión)* entertainment. 3 *(TV, radio, etc)* performance, show.

espectador,-ra *nm & nf* 1 *(de deportes)* spectator. 2 *(de obra, película)* member of the audience; *(de televisión)* viewer.

▶ *nm pl* **espectadores** *(de obra, película)* audience *sing*; *(de programa televisivo)* viewers.

espectro *nm* **1** FÍS spectrum. **2** *(fantasma)* spectre (US specter), ghost, apparition. **3** *fig (persona)* ghost. **4** *(conjunto, serie)* range.

especulador,-ra *adj* speculating.
▶ *nm & nf* speculator.

especular *vt fig (reflexionar)* to speculate about.
▶ *vi* **1** *(comerciar)* to speculate (en, in); *(en bolsa)* to speculate (en, on). **2** *(conjeturar)* to speculate (sobre, about).

espejismo *nm* **1** mirage. **2** *fig* mirage, illusion.

espejo *nm* **1** mirror. **2** *fig (imagen)* mirror, reflection.

espeleología *nf* potholing, speleology.

espeleólogo,-a *nm & nf* potholer, speleologist.

espeluznante *adj* hair-raising, terrifying, horrifying.

espeluznar *vt* to horrify, terrify, make one's hair stand on end.

espera *nf* **1** wait, waiting. **2** *(paciencia)* patience. LOC **en espera de...** waiting for.... ▌ **estar a la espera** to be waiting, be expecting.

esperanza *nf* hope, expectance. LOC **con la esperanza de...** in the hope of.... ▌ **tener muchas esperanzas** to have high hopes. COMP **esperanza de vida** life expectancy.

esperanzador,-ra *adj* encouraging.

esperanzar *vt* to give hope to.
▶ *vpr* **esperanzarse** to have hope.

esperar *vt* **1** *(tener esperanza)* to hope for, expect: *esperan un milagro* they're hoping for a miracle. **2** *(contar, creer)* to expect: *no te esperábamos hasta mañana* we didn't expect you till tomorrow. **3** *(aguardar)* to wait for, await: *espera un momento* wait a moment. **4** *(desear)* to hope: *espero verlo* I hope to see him. **5** *fig (bebé)* to expect.
▶ *vi* to wait: *esperaré hasta que lleguen* I'll wait until they get here.

▶ *vpr* **esperarse** **1** *(aguardar)* to wait: *espérense en recepción* please wait in reception. **2** *(creer, contar)* to expect: *se espera que seas puntual* you're expected to be punctual. **3** *(desear)* to hope: *se espera que lo hayan pasado bien* we hope you've had a good time.

espermatozoide *nm* spermatozoon, sperm.

espesar *vt (salsa, etc)* to thicken; *(tejido, etc)* to make thicker.
▶ *vpr* **espesarse** **1** *(gen)* to get thicker. **2** *(salsa, etc)* to thicken.

espeso,-a *adj* **1** *(líquido, sustancia, objeto)* thick. **2** *(bosque, niebla)* thick, dense. **3** *(pasta, masa)* stiff. LOC **estar espeso,-a** *fam* not to be able to think straight.

espesor *nm* thickness.

espesura *nf* **1** *(de líquido, objeto)* thickness. **2** *(de niebla, etc)* denseness. **3** *fig (en bosque)* thicket, dense wood.

espía *nm o nf* spy.

espiar *vt* to spy on, watch.

espiga *nf* **1** *(gen)* spike; *(de trigo)* ear. **2** *(de tejido)* herringbone. **3** *(clavija)* peg, pin.

espigado,-a *adj* **1** BOT ripe. **2** *(en forma de espiga)* ear-shaped. **3** *fig (persona)* tall, lanky.

espigón *nm* **1** MAR breakwater, jetty. **2** *(punta)* sharp point, spike.

espina *nf* **1** *(de planta)* thorn. **2** *(de pez)* fishbone. **3** *(columna vertebral)* spine, backbone. **4** *fig (pesar)* sadness, sorrow, grief.

espinaca *nf* spinach.

espinal *adj* spinal: *médula espinal* spinal marrow.

espinilla *nf* **1** *(de la pierna)* shinbone. **2** *(grano)* blackhead.

espino *nm* **1** *(árbol)* hawthorn. **2** *(alambre)* barbed wire. COMP **espino albar** common hawthorn. ▌ **espino negro** blackthorn.

espinoso,-a *adj* **1** *(planta)* thorny. **2** *(pez)* spiny. **3** *fig* thorny, prickly, difficult, tricky.

espionaje *nm* spying, espionage: *película de espionaje* spy film.

espiral *adj* spiral: *escalera espiral* spiral staircase.
▶ *nf* **1** spiral. **2** *(de reloj)* hairspring.
espirar *vt* to exhale, breathe out.
▶ *vi* to breathe.
espiritismo *nm* spiritualism.
espiritista *adj* spiritualistic.
▶ *nm o nf* spiritualist.
espíritu *nm* **1** *(gen)* spirit. **2** *(alma)* soul, spirit. **3** *(fantasma)* ghost, spirit. **4** *(licores)* spirits *pl*. **5** *fig (idea central)* spirit, essence, soul.
espiritual *adj* spiritual.
espiritualidad *nf* spirituality.
espléndido,-a *adj* **1** *(magnífico)* splendid, magnificent. **2** *(generoso)* generous, lavish.
esplendor *nm* **1** *(resplandor)* brilliance, shining. **2** *fig (magnificencia)* magnificence, splendour (US splendor). **3** *(auge)* glory.
esplendoroso,-a *adj* **1** *(resplandeciente)* brilliant, radiant, shining. **2** *(grandioso)* magnificent, lavish.
espliego *nm* lavender.
espolear *vt* **1** to spur on. **2** *fig* to spur on, encourage.
espolón *nm* **1** *(de ave)* spur. **2** *(de caballería)* fetlock. **3** *(de nave)* ram. **4** *(malecón)* sea wall. **5** *fam (sabañón)* chilblain.
espolvorear *vt* **1** *(despolvorear)* to dust. **2** *(esparcir)* to powder, sprinkle.
esponja *nf* **1** sponge. **2** *fig (gorrón)* sponger.
esponjar *vt* *(ahuecar)* to fluff up; *(tierra)* to loosen.
▶ *vpr* **esponjarse 1** *fig (envanecerse)* to swell with pride. **2** *fig (físicamente)* to glow with health.
esponjoso,-a *adj (gen)* spongy; *(bizcocho)* light.
espontáneamente *adv* spontaneously.
espontaneidad *nf* spontaneity.
espontáneo,-a *adj* **1** *(cosa)* spontaneous; *(discurso)* impromptu, unprepared. **2** *(persona)* natural, unaffected.
espora *nf* spore.
esporádicamente *adv* sporadically.

esporádico,-a *adj* sporadic.
esposa *nf* wife.
esposado,-a *adj* **1** *(casado)* married. **2** *(con esposas)* handcuffed.
esposar *vt* to handcuff, put handcuffs on.
esposas *nf pl* handcuffs.
esposo *nm* husband.
esprint *nm* sprint.
esprintar *vi* to sprint.
esprínter *nm o nf* sprinter.
espuela *nf* **1** spur. **2** *fig* spur, stimulus.
espuerta *nf* two-handled rush basket.
espuma *nf* **1** *(gen)* foam; *(de jabón)* lather; *(de cerveza)* froth, head; *(olas)* surf. **2** *(impurezas)* scum. **3** *(tejido)* foam.
espumadera *nf* skimmer.
espumar *vt (quitar espuma)* to skim.
▶ *vi (hacer espuma - jabón)* to lather; *(- cerveza)* to froth; *(- vino)* to sparkle; *(- olas)* to foam.
espumillón *nm* tinsel.
espumoso,-a *adj (ola)* foamy, frothy; *(jabón)* lathery; *(vino)* sparkling.
esqueje *nm* cutting.
esquela *nf* **1** *(carta)* short letter. **2** *(mortuoria)* obituary notice.
esqueleto *nm* **1** ANAT skeleton. **2** ARQUIT framework.
esquema *nm* **1** *(gráfica)* diagram. **2** *(plan)* outline, plan.
esquemático,-a *adj* schematic, diagrammatic.
esquematizar *vt* **1** *(plan, idea)* to outline. **2** *(plano, etc)* to sketch.
esquí *nm* **1** *(tabla)* ski. **2** DEP skiing.
s *pl* esquís. COMP **esquí acuático** water-skiing. ▌ **esquí alpino** alpine skiing. ▌ **esquí náutico** water-skiing.
esquiador,-ra *nm & nf* skier.
esquiar *vi* to ski.
esquilador,-ra *nm & nf* sheepshearer.
esquiladora *nf* shears *pl*.
esquilar *vt* **1** *(pelo)* to clip. **2** *(ovejas)* to shear.
esquimal *adj* Eskimo.
▶ *nm o nf* Eskimo.
▶ *nm (idioma)* Eskimo.

esquina *nf* corner.
▷ *vt* **1** *(hacer esquina)* to form a corner with, be on the corner of. **2** *(poner en esquina)* to put in a corner.

esquinazo *nm* corner. LOC **dar el esquinazo a ALGN** *fam* to give SB the slip.

esquirla *nf* splinter.

esquirol *nm* blackleg, scab.

esquisto *nm* shale.

esquivar *vt* **1** *(persona)* to avoid, shun. **2** *(golpe)* to dodge, elude.

esquivo,-a *adj* cold, aloof.

esquizofrenia *nf* schizophrenia.

esquizofrénico,-a *adj* schizophrenic.
▷ *nm & nf* schizophrenic.

estabilidad *nf* stability.

estabilización *nf* stabilization.

estabilizar *vt* to stabilize, make stable.
▷ *vpr* **estabilizarse** to become stable, become stabilized.

estable *adj* stable, steady.

establecer *vt* **1** *(gen)* to establish; *(fundar)* to found, set up. **2** *(récord)* to set. **3** *(ordenar)* to state, lay down, establish.
▷ *vpr* **establecerse** *(en un lugar)* to settle; *(en un negocio)* to set up in business.

establecimiento *nm* **1** *(acto)* establishment, founding, setting-up. **2** *(de gente)* settlement. **3** *(local)* establishment, shop, store.

establo *nm* **1** stable, cowshed, stall. **2** *fig* filthy place, pigsty.

estabular *vt* to stable.

estaca *nf* **1** *(palo con punta)* stake, post; *(para tienda de campaña)* peg. **2** *(garrote)* stick, cudgel. **3** *(rama)* cutting. **4** *(clavo)* spike.

estacada *nf* *(obra)* fence, fencing.

estacazo *nm* blow with a stick.

estación *nf* **1** *(del año, temporada)* season. **2** *(de tren, radio)* station.

estacional *adj* seasonal.

estacionamiento *nm* **1** AUTO *(acción)* parking; *(lugar)* car park, US parking lot. **2** *fig (estancamiento)* impasse.

estacionar *vt* **1** *(colocar)* to position, place. **2** AUTO to park.
▷ *vpr* **estacionarse 1** *(estancarse)* to be stationary, remain in the same place. **2** AUTO to park.

estacionario,-a *adj* stationary, stable.

estadio *nm* **1** *(lugar)* stadium. **2** *(fase)* stage, phase. **3** *arc (medida)* stadium, furlong.

estadista *nm o nf* POL *(hombre)* statesman; *(mujer)* stateswoman. **2** MAT statistician.

estadística *nf* **1** *(ciencia)* statistics. **2** *(dato)* statistic, figure.

estadístico,-a *adj* statistical.
▷ *nm & nf* statistician.

estado *nm* **1** *(situación)* state, condition: *su estado es delicado* his condition is delicate. **2** *(en orden social)* status. **3** HIST estate. **4** POL state.

Estados Unidos *nm pl* The United States.

estadounidense *adj* American, from the United States.
▷ *nm o nf* American, person from the United States.

estafa *nf* fraud, swindle.

estafador,-ra *nm & nf* racketeer, swindler, trickster.

estafar *vt* to swindle, trick, cheat, defraud.

estafilococo *nm* staphylococcus.

estalactita *nf* stalactite.

estalagmita *nm* stalagmite.

estallar *vi* **1** *(reventar)* to explode, blow up. **2** *(neumático)* to burst; *(bomba)* to explode, go off; *(cristal)* to shatter. **3** *(volcán)* to erupt. **4** *(látigo)* to crack. **5** *fig (rebelión, epidemia)* to break out. **6** *fig (pasión, sentimientos)* to burst: *estallar en lágrimas* to burst into tears.

estallido *nm* **1** *(explosión)* explosion. **2** *(de trueno)* crash; *(de látigo)* crack. **3** *fig* outbreak.

estambre *nm* **1** COST worsted, woollen yarn (US woolen yarn). **2** BOT stamen.

estamento *nm* class, stratum.

estampa *nf* **1** *(imagen)* picture. **2** *fig (aspecto)* appearance, look, aspect.

estampación *nf* printing.

estampado,-a *adj (gen)* patterned, print; *(tela)* printed; *(metal)* stamped.
▶ *nm* **estampado** *(tela)* print.

estampar *vt* **1** *(imprimir)* to print. **2** *(metales)* to stamp. **3** *(dejar huella)* to stamp. [LOC] **estampar la firma** to sign.

estampida *nf* **1** *(ruido)* bang. **2** *(de animales)* stampede.

estampilla *nf* stamp, rubber stamp.

estampita *nf* religious print.

estancado,-a *adj* **1** *(agua)* stagnant. **2** *fig (asunto, negocio)* at a standstill; *(negociaciones)* deadlocked; *(persona)* stuck, bogged down.

estancamiento *nm* **1** stagnation. **2** *fig* deadlock, standstill.

estancar *vt* **1** *(aguas)* to hold up, hold back, dam; *(flujo)* to check. **2** *fig (progreso)* to check, block, hold up.
▶ *vpr* **estancarse 1** *(líquido)* to stagnate, become stagnant. **2** *fig* to stagnate, get bogged down.

estanco,-a *adj* watertight.
▶ *nm* **estanco** *(tienda)* tobacconist's.

estándar *adj* standard, standardized: *modelo estándar* standard model; *reglas estándar* set rules.

estandarte *nm* standard, banner.

estanque *nm* **1** *(de peces, etc)* pool, pond. **2** *(para proveer agua)* reservoir, tank.

estanquero,-a *nm & nf* tobacconist.

estante *nm* **1** *(anaquel)* shelf; *(para libros)* bookcase. **2** *(de máquina)* stand.

estantería *nf* shelving, shelves *pl*.

estaño *nm* tin.

estar *vi* **1** *(lugar, posición)* to be: *estamos en casa* we are at home. **2** *(permanecer)* to be, stay: *estuvimos allí diez días* we stayed there for ten days. **3** *(cualidades transitorias)* to be: *está cansado* he's tired. **4** *(una prenda)* to suit, be: *te está grande* it's too big for you.
▶ *aux* **1 estar + *gerundio*** to be: *estaban cantando* they were singing. **2 estar a** *(precio)* to be, sell at; *(fecha)* to be: *estamos a 15 de marzo* it's the 15th of March. **3**

estar con *(tener)* to have; *(estar de acuerdo)* to agree with: *estoy con Ana* I agree with Ana. **4 estar de** *(gen)* to be; *(trabajar)* to be, be working as; *(ir vestido)* to be, be dressed in: *estar de vacaciones* to be on holiday; *está de uniforme* he's in uniform. **5 estar en** *(consistir)* to be, lie; *(entender)* to understand; *(creer)* to think, believe; *(depender de uno)* to be up to. **6 estar para** *(estar a punto)* to be about to; *(estar acabado)* to be finished, be ready; *(estar de humor)* to feel like, be in the mood for. **7 estar por** *(no haberse ejecutado)* to remain to be; *(estar determinado)* to be for; *(ir a)* to be going to; *(a favor)* to be for. **8 estar que** *fam* to be nearly, be really, be practically: *está que se hunde* it's practically ruined. **9 estar sin + *inf*** not to have been + *pp*: *el coche está sin lavar* the car hasn't been washed, the car still needs washing.
▶ *vpr* **estarse** *(permanecer)* to spend, stay: *se estuvo todo el día leyendo* she spent all day reading.

estarcido *nm* stencil.

estarcir *vt* to stencil.

estasis *nf inv* stasis.

estatal *adj* state.

estático,-a *adj* static.

estatua *nf* statue.

estatuilla *nf* statuette, figurine.

estatura *nf* height, stature.

estatuto *nm* statute. [COMP] **estatuto de autonomía** statute of autonomy.

este *adj* **1** east, eastern. **2** *(dirección)* easterly; *(viento)* east, easterly.
▶ *nm* **1** east. **2** *(viento)* east wind.

este,-a *adj* this; *(plural)* these: *este libro* this book; *estas manzanas* these apples.

éste,-a *pron* **1** *(cosa)* this one: *dame éste* give me this one. **2** *(hombre - sujeto)* he; *(mujer - sujeto)* she: *ésta me lo dijo* she told me. **3** *(hombre - complemento)* him; *(mujer - complemento)* her: *se lo dio a éste* she gave it to him. **4** *(este último)* the latter. **5** *pey* this one.

✎ Cuando no se produzca confusión con el adjetivo se puede omitir el acento.

estela¹ *nf* **1** *(de barco)* wake, wash; *(de avión)* vapour (US vapor) trail; *(de cometa)* tail. **2** *fig* trail.

estela² *nf (monumento)* stela, stele.

estelar *adj* **1** *(sideral)* stellar. **2** *fig* star.

estenordeste *nm* **1** east-northeast. **2** *(viento)* east-northeast wind.

estepa¹ *nf (llanura)* steppe.

estepa² *nf (planta)* rockrose.

estepario,-a *adj* steppe, from the steppes.

éster *nm* ester.

estera *nf* rush mat.

estercolero *nm* **1** dunghill, dung heap. **2** *fig* pigsty.

estéreo *nm* stereo.

estereofónico,-a *adj* stereo, stereophonic.

estereoscopio *nm* stereoscope.

estereotipado,-a *adj fig* stereotyped, standard, set.

estereotipo *nm* stereotype.

estéril *adj* **1** *(tierra)* sterile, barren. **2** *(hombre)* sterile; *(mujer)* sterile, infertile. **3** *(aséptico)* sterile. **4** *fig* futile, useless.

esterilidad *nf* **1** *(de terreno)* sterility, barrenness. **2** *(de hombre)* sterility; *(de mujer)* sterility, infertility. **3** *fig* futility, uselessness.

esterilización *nf* sterilization.

esterilizador,-ra *nm* sterilizer.

esterilizar *vt* to sterilize.

esterilla *nf* **1** *(felpudo)* small mat. **2** *(de cañamazo)* rush matting, wickerwork.

esterlina *adj* sterling.
▶ *nf* sterling.

esternocleidomastoideo *nm* sternocleidomastoid.

esternón *nm* sternum, breastbone.

estesudeste *nm* **1** east-southeast. **2** *(viento)* east-southeast wind.

esteta *nm o nf* aesthete (US esthete).

estética *nf* aesthetics (US esthetics).

estéticamente *adv* aesthetically.

estético,-a *adj* aesthetic (US esthetic).

estetoscopio *nm* stethoscope.

estiércol *nm* dung, manure.

estilete *nm* **1** *(punzón)* stylus. **2** *(puñal)* stiletto. **3** MED probe.

estilismo *nm* stylism.

estilista *nm o nf* **1** *(escritor)* stylist. **2** *(diseñador)* stylist, designer.

estilístico,-a *adj* stylistic.

estilización *nf* stylization.

estilizar *vt* **1** to stylize. **2** *(hacer delgado)* to make thinner.

estilo *nm* **1** *(gen)* style. **2** *(modo)* manner, fashion. **3** GRAM speech. **4** *(natación)* stroke.

estilográfica *nf* fountain pen.

estima *nf* esteem, respect.

estimable *adj* **1** esteemed, reputable, worthy. **2** *(cantidad)* considerable.

estimación *nf* **1** *(afecto)* esteem, respect. **2** *(valoración)* estimation, evaluation. **3** *(cálculo)* estimate. COMP **propia estima** self-esteem.

estimado,-a *adj* **1** *(apreciado)* esteemed, respected. **2** *(valorado)* valued, estimated: *el precio estimado* the estimated price.

estimar *vt* **1** *(apreciar)* to esteem, respect, hold in esteem, admire. **2** *(valorar)* to value. **3** *(juzgar, creer)* to consider, think, reckon.

estimulación *nf* stimulation.

estimulante *adj* stimulating, encouraging.
▶ *nm* stimulant.

estimular *vt* **1** *(animar)* to encourage, stimulate. **2** *(apetito, pasiones)* to whet.

estímulo *nm* **1** stimulus, stimulation. **2** *fig* encouragement. **3** COM incentive.

estío *nm* summer.

estipendio *nm* stipend, fee, remuneration.

estipular *vt* to stipulate.

estirado,-a *adj* **1** *fig (en el vestir)* stiff, formal, starchy. **2** *fig (orgulloso)* stiff, conceited, haughty.
▶ *nm* **estirado 1** *(textil)* drawing. **2** *(del pelo)* straightening; *(de la piel)* lift.

estiramiento *nm* stretch.

estirar *vt* **1** *(gen)* to stretch. **2** *(cuello)* to crane. **3** *(medias)* to pull up; *(falda)* to pull down. **4** *fig (dinero)* to spin out, make go further.
▸ *vi (crecer)* to shoot up.
▸ *vpr* **estirarse 1** *(crecer)* to shoot up. **2** *(desperezarse)* to stretch.

estirón *nm* pull, jerk, tug.

estirpe *nf* stock, lineage, race.

estival *adj* summer.

esto *pron* this: *esto me gusta* I like this.

estocada *nf* stab, thrust.

estofa *nf fig* class, type.

estofado *nm* CULIN stew.

estofar *vt* CULIN to stew.

estoicismo *nm* stoicism.

estoico,-a *adj* stoic, stoical.
▸ *nm & nf* stoic.

estoma *nm* stoma.

estomacal *adj* **1** *(del estómago)* stomach, of the stomach. **2** *(digestivo)* digestive.
▸ *nm (bebida)* digestive liqueur.

estómago *nm* stomach. COMP **dolor de estómago** stomachache.

Estonia *nf* Estonia.

estonio,-a *adj* Estonian.
▸ *nm & nf (persona)* Estonian.
▸ *nm* **estonio** *(idioma)* Estonian.

estopa *nf* **1** *(fibra)* tow. **2** *(tela)* burlap. COMP **estopa de acero** steel wool.

estoque *nm (espada)* sword.

estor *nm* roller blind.

estorbar *vt* **1** *(dificultar)* to hinder, get in the way; *(obstruir)* to obstruct, block, hold up. **2** *fig (molestar)* to annoy, bother, disturb.
▸ *vi (ser obstáculo)* to be in the way.

estorbo *nm* **1** *(obstáculo)* obstruction, obstacle. **2** *(molestia)* hindrance, encumbrance; *(persona)* nuisance.

estornino *nm* starling.

estornudar *vi* to sneeze.

estornudo *nm* sneeze.

estos,-as *adj* these.

✎ Consulta también **este,-a**.

éstos,-as *pron* these (ones).

✎ Consulta también **éste,-a**.

estrabismo *nm* strabismus, squint: *tengo estrabismo* I have a squint.

estrado *nm* stage, platform; *(tarima)* dais.
▸ *nm pl* **estrados** JUR courtrooms.

estrago *nm* havoc, ruin, ravage.

estragón *nm* tarragon.

estrangular *vt* **1** *(ahogar)* to strangle. **2** MED to strangulate. **3** AUTO to throttle.

estratagema *nf* **1** MIL stratagem. **2** *fam fig* trick.

estratega *nm o nf* strategist.

estrategia *nf* strategy.

estratégicamente *adv* strategically.

estratégico,-a *adj* strategic.

estratificar *vt* to stratify.
▸ *vpr* **estratificarse** to be stratified.

estrato *nm* **1** GEOL stratum. **2** *(capa)* stratum. **3** *(nivel social)* stratum, class. **4** *(nube)* stratus.

estratosfera *nf* stratosphere.

estraza *nf* rag, piece of cloth.

estrechamente *adv* **1** *(con estrechez)* narrowly, tightly. **2** *fig (con intimidad)* closely, intimately: *están estrechamente unidos* they're very close.

estrechar *vt* **1** *(carretera)* to make narrower. **2** *(prenda)* to take in. **3** *(abrazar)* to squeeze, hug; *(mano)* to shake: *nos estrechamos las manos* we shook hands. **4** *fig (obligar)* to compel, constrain. **5** *fig (relaciones, lazos)* to strengthen.
▸ *vpr* **estrecharse 1** *(valle, etc)* to narrow, become narrower. **2** *(apretarse)* to squeeze together, squeeze up. **3** *fig (relaciones, etc)* to strengthen, get stronger.

estrechez *nf* **1** *(poco ancho)* narrowness. **2** *(falta espacio)* lack of space. **3** *(prendas)* tightness. **4** *fig (económica)* want, need. **5** *fig (amistad)* closeness, intimacy. **6** *fig (apuro)* tight spot. LOC **pasar estrecheces** *fig* to be hard up.

estrecho,-a *adj* **1** *(poco ancho)* narrow. **2** *(ropa)* tight; *(calzado)* tight, small. **3** *(habitación)* cramped, poky, small. **4** *(sin espacio)* packed, jam-packed. **5** *fig (amistad, etc)* close, intimate.
▸ *nm* **estrecho** GEOG strait, straits *pl*.

estrella *nf* **1** *(gen)* star. **2** *fig (destino)* destiny, fate.

estrellado,-a *adj* **1** *(cielo)* starry, star-spangled, full of stars. **2** *(forma)* star-shaped. **3** *(hecho pedazos)* smashed, shattered.

estrellar *vt* **1** *(llenar de estrellas)* to cover with stars. **2** *fam (hacer pedazos)* to smash (to pieces), shatter. **3** *(freír)* to fry.
▶ *vpr* **estrellarse 1** *(llenarse de estrellas)* to be full of stars. **2** *(hacerse pedazos)* to smash, shatter. **3** *(chocar)* to crash.

estremecedor,-ra *adj* **1** startling. **2** *(grito)* bloodcurdling.

estremecer *vt* **1** *(gen)* to shake. **2** *fig (asustar)* to startle, frighten.
▶ *vpr* **estremecerse 1** *(temblar)* to shake. **2** *(de miedo)* to tremble, shudder; *(de frío)* to shiver, tremble. **3** *fig* to shudder.

estrenar *vt* **1** *(gen)* to use for the first time; *(ropa)* to wear for the first time. **2** *(obra)* to perform for the first time, give the first performance of; *(película)* to release, put on release.
▶ *vpr* **estrenarse** to make one's debut.

estreno *nm* **1** *(de algo)* first use. **2** *(persona)* début, first appearance. **3** *(de obra)* first performance; *(de película)* premiere.

estreñido,-a *adj* **1** constipated. **2** *fig* mean, stingy.

estreñimiento *nm* constipation.

estreñir *vt* to constipate, make constipated.
▶ *vpr* **estreñirse** to become constipated.

estrépito *nm* **1** din, racket, clatter. **2** *fig* ostentation, fuss.

estrepitoso,-a *adj* **1** noisy, clamorous. **2** *(ruido)* deafening. **3** *fig (éxito)* resounding; *(fracaso)* spectacular.

estreptococo *nm* streptococcus.

estrés *nm* stress.

estresado,-a *adj* under stress.

estresante *adj* stressful.

estría *nf* **1** *(ranura)* groove. **2** ARQUIT flute. **3** *(en la piel)* stretch mark.

estriar *vt* **1** *(hacer ranuras)* to groove. **2** ARQUIT to flute. **3** *(piel)* to give stretch marks.
▶ *vpr* **estriarse** *(piel)* to get stretch marks.

estribillo *nm* **1** *(de poesía)* refrain; *(de canción)* chorus. **2** *(muletilla)* pet phrase, pet saying.

estribo *nm* **1** *(de jinete)* stirrup. **2** *(de carruaje, tren)* step. **3** AUTO running board; *(de moto)* footrest. **4** ARQUIT buttress; *(de puente)* pier, support. **5** *(del oído)* stirrup bone.

estribor *nm* starboard.

estricto,-a *adj* strict, rigorous.

estridencia *nf* **1** *(ruido)* stridency, shrillness. **2** *(color, etc)* loudness, garishness, gaudiness.

estridente *adj* **1** *(ruido)* strident, shrill. **2** *(color, etc)* loud, garish, gaudy.

estroboscópico,-a *adj* stroboscopic.

estroboscopio *nm* stroboscope, strobe.

estrofa *nf* stanza, verse.

estrógeno *nm* oestrogen (US estrogen).

estropajo *nm* **1** *(para fregar)* scourer. **2** *fig (desecho)* useless thing.

estropajoso,-a *adj* **1** *(lengua)* furry. **2** *(carne, etc)* gristly, tough. **3** *(pelo)* straw-like.

estropear *vt* **1** *(máquina)* to damage, break, ruin. **2** *(cosecha)* to spoil, ruin. **3** *(plan, etc)* to spoil, ruin.
▶ *vpr* **estropearse 1** *(máquina)* to break down. **2** *(cosecha)* to be spoiled, get damaged. **3** *(plan, etc)* to fail, fall through, go wrong. **4** *(comida)* to go bad.

estropicio *nm* **1** *fam (rotura)* breakage, damage; *(ruido producido)* crash, clatter, smash. **2** *fam (desorden)* mess; *(jaleo)* fuss, rumpus.

estructura *nf* **1** *(gen)* structure. **2** *(armazón)* frame, framework.

estructurado,-a *adj* structured, organized.

estructurar *vt* to structure, organize.
▶ *vpr* **estructurarse** to be structured, be organized.

estruendo *nm* **1** *(ruido)* great noise, din. **2** *(confusión)* uproar, tumult.

estruendoso,-a *adj* *(ruido)* noisy, deafening; *(aplauso)* thunderous.

estrujar *vt* **1** *(exprimir)* to squeeze. **2** *(apretar - alguien)* to crush; *(- algo)* to screw up. **3** *(ropa)* to wring. **4** *fig (sacar partido)* to drain, bleed dry.
▶ *vpr* **estrujarse** *(apretujarse)* to crowd, throng.

estuario *nm* estuary.

estucado *nm* stucco, stucco work.

estucar *vt* to stucco.

estuche *nm* **1** *(caja)* case, box. **2** *(conjunto)* set.

estuco *nm* stucco.

estudiante *nm o nf* student.

estudiar *vt* to study, learn.
▶ *vi* to study: *estudia para maestro* he's training to be a teacher.
▶ *vpr* **estudiarse** to consider.

estudio *nm* **1** *(gen)* study. **2** *(apartamento)* studio flat (US apartment), bedsit.
▶ *nm pl* **estudios** *(conocimientos)* studies, education *sing*.

estudioso,-a *adj* studious.

estufa *nf* *(calentador)* heater, stove; *(de gas, eléctrica)* fire.

estupa *nf* argot *(grupo)* drug squad.
▶ *nm o nf* *(oficial)* drug-squad officer.

estupefaciente *adj* stupefying.
▶ *nm* drug, narcotic.

estupefacto,-a *adj* astounded, dumbfounded, flabbergasted.

estupendamente *adv* marvellously (US marvelously), wonderfully.

estupendo,-a *adj* marvellous (US marvelous), wonderful, super.

estupidez *nf* stupidity, stupid thing.

estúpido,-a *adj* stupid, silly.
▶ *nm & nf* berk, idiot.

estupor *nm* stupor, amazement, astonishment. ⌐ɪoc⌐ **causar estupor** to astonish.

esturión *nm* sturgeon.

etapa *nf* **1** period, stage. **2** *(parada)* stop, stage. **3** DEP leg, stage.

éter *nm* QUÍM ether.

etéreo,-a *adj* ethereal.

eternamente *adv* eternally.

eternidad *nf* **1** eternity. **2** *fam* ages *pl*.

eternizar *vt* **1** to eternize, eternalize. **2** *fam* to prolong endlessly.
▶ *vpr* **eternizarse 1** *fam (ser interminable)* to be interminable, be endless; *(discusión)* to drag on. **2** *fam (tardar mucho)* to take ages.

eterno,-a *adj* eternal, everlasting, endless.

ética *nf* ethics *pl*, ethic.

éticamente *adv* ethically.

ético,-a *adj* ethical.

etílico,-a *adj* ethylic.

etimología *nf* etymology.

etimológico,-a *adj* etymological.

etíope *adj* Ethiopian.
▶ *nm o nf (persona)* Ethiopian.
▶ *nm* **etíope** *(idioma)* Ethiopian, Ethiopic.

Etiopía *nf* Ethiopia.

etiqueta *nf* **1** *(rótulo)* label, tag. **2** *(formalidad)* etiquette, formality, ceremony.

etiquetar *vt* to label, put a label on.

etnia *nf* ethnic group.

étnico,-a *adj* ethnic.

etnografía *nf* ethnography.

etnología *nf* ethnology.

etnólogo,-a *nm & nf* ethnologist.

eucalipto *nm* eucalyptus.

eufemismo *nm* euphemism.

euforia *nf* euphoria, elation.

eufórico,-a *adj* euphoric, elated.

eunuco *nm* eunuch.

eureka *interj* eureka!

euritmia *nf* eurythmics.

euro *nm* euro.

euroasiático,-a *adj* Eurasian.
▶ *nm & nf* Eurasian.

eurodiputado,-a *nm & nf* Member of the European Parliament, MEP, Euro MP.

Europa *nf* Europe.

europeísta *adj* pro-European.
▶ *nm o nf* pro-European.

europeo,-a *adj* European.
▶ *nm & nf* European. `COMP` **Comunidad Europea** European Community. **Unión Europea** European Union.

eurovisión *nf* Eurovision.

Euskadi *nm* the Basque Country.

euskera *nm (idioma)* Basque.

eutanasia *nf* euthanasia.

evacuación *nf* evacuation.

evacuar *vt* **1** *(lugar)* to evacuate. **2** ANAT to empty.

evadir *vt* **1** *(peligro, respuesta)* to avoid; *(responsabilidad)* to shirk. **2** *(capital, impuestos)* to evade.
▶ *vpr* **evadirse** *(escaparse)* to escape.

evaluación *nf* **1** evaluation, assessment. **2** EDUC *(acción)* assessment; *(examen)* exam.

evaluar *vt* to evaluate, assess.

evangélico,-a *adj* evangelical.

evangelio *nm* gospel.

evangelista *nm* evangelist.

evaporación *nf* evaporation.

evaporar *vt* to evaporate.
▶ *vpr* **evaporarse 1** to evaporate. **2** *fig* to vanish, disappear.

evasión *nf* **1** *(fuga)* escape, flight. **2** *fig* escape, escapism.

evasivo,-a *adj* evasive.

eventual *adj* **1** *(casual)* chance; *(probable)* possible. **2** *(trabajo)* casual, temporary, provisional. **3** *(ingresos, gastos)* incidental.
▶ *nm o nf* casual worker, temporary worker.

eventualidad *nf* eventuality, contingency.

evidencia *nf (claridad)* obviousness, clearness; *(certeza)* certainty.

evidenciar *vt* to show, make evident, prove, make obvious.

evidente *adj* evident, obvious.

evidentemente *adv* evidently, obviously.

evitar *vt* **1** *(gen)* to avoid. **2** *(impedir)* to prevent, avoid. **3** *(ahorrar)* to spare, save.

evocar *vt* **1** *(recuerdo)* to evoke, call up. **2** *(recordar)* to evoke, bring to mind.

evolución *nf* **1** *(cambio)* evolution; *(desarrollo)* development. **2** *(vuelta)* turn.

evolucionar *vi* **1** *(gen)* to evolve, develop. **2** *(dar vueltas)* to turn.

evolucionismo *nm* evolutionism.

evolutivo,-a *adj* evolutionary, evolving.

ex- *pref* ex-, former: *el ex primer ministro* the former prime minister.

exacerbar *vt* **1** *(agravar)* to exacerbate, aggravate, make worse. **2** *(irritar)* to exacerbate, exasperate, irritate.

exactamente *adv* exactly, precisely.

exactitud *nf (fidelidad)* exactness; *(precisión)* accuracy.

exacto,-a *adj* **1** *(fiel)* faithful, true; *(preciso)* accurate, exact. **2** *(verdad)* true: *eso no es exacto* that's not true.

exageración *nf* exaggeration.

exagerado,-a *adj* exaggerated.

exagerar *vt* to exaggerate.
▶ *vi* **1** to exaggerate. **2** *(abusar)* to overdo it, do too much.

exaltado,-a *adj* **1** *(discusión, etc)* heated, impassioned. **2** *(persona)* hot-headed, worked up.

exaltar *vt* **1** *(elevar)* to raise, promote. **2** *fig (alabar)* to exalt, praise, extol.
▶ *vpr* **exaltarse** *(excitarse)* to get overexcited, get worked up, get carried away.

examen *nm* **1** examination, exam. **2** *(estudio)* consideration, examination, study. `COMP` **examen final** final examination. **examen oral** oral examination.

examinar *vt (gen)* to examine.
▶ *vpr* **examinarse** to take an examination, sit an examination.

exasperante *adj* exasperating.

exasperar *vt* to exasperate.
▶ *vpr* **exasperarse** to get exasperated.

excavación *nf* **1** excavation, digging. **2** *(arqueológica)* dig.

excavadora *nf (máquina)* digger.

excavar *vt* to excavate, dig.

excedencia *nf* **1** *(de funcionario, etc)* leave. **2** *(de profesor)* sabbatical leave.

excedente *adj (sobrante)* excess, surplus.
▶ *nm* COM surplus, excess.

exceder *vt* **1** *(superar)* to excel, surpass. **2** *(sobrepasar)* to exceed, be in excess of.
▶ *vpr* **excederse 1** *(pasarse)* to overdo it, go too far. **2** *(en atenciones, etc)* to be extremely kind.

excelente *adj* excellent, first-rate.

excentricidad *nf* eccentricity.

excéntrico,-a *adj* eccentric.

excepción *nf* exception. LOC **a excepción de** with the exception of, except for. ‖ **de excepción** exceptional.

excepcional *adj* **1** *(extraordinario)* exceptional, outstanding. **2** *(raro)* exceptional, unusual.

excepto *adv* except (for), apart from, excepting.

exceptuar *vt* to except, leave out, exclude.

excesivo,-a *adj* excessive.

exceso *nm* **1** excess. **2** COM surplus. COMP **exceso de equipaje** excess baggage.

excipiente *nm* excipient.

excisión *nf* excision.

excitación *nf* **1** *(acción)* excitation. **2** *(sentimiento)* excitement.

excitante *adj* **1** exciting. **2** MED stimulating.

excitar *vt* **1** to excite. **2** *(emociones)* to stimulate, arouse.
▶ *vpr* **excitarse** to get excited, get worked up, get carried away.

exclamación *nf* exclamation; *(grito)* cry.

exclamar *vt* to exclaim, cry out.
▶ *vi* to exclaim, cry out.

exclamativo,-a *adj* exclamatory.

exclamatorio,-a *adj* exclamatory.

excluir *vt* **1** to exclude, shut out. **2** *(rechazar)* to reject; *(descartar)* to rule out; *(expulsar)* to throw out.

exclusión *nf* exclusion, shutting out.

exclusiva *nf* **1** COM sole right. **2** *(prensa)* exclusive, scoop.

exclusividad *nf* exclusiveness, exclusivity.

exclusivo,-a *adj* exclusive.

excluyente *adj* exclusive.

excremento *nf* excrement.

excretor,-ra *adj* excretory.

exculpar *vt* **1** to exonerate. **2** JUR to acquit.

excursión *nf* excursion, trip.

excursionismo *nm* hiking, rambling.

excursionista *nm o nf* tripper; *(a pie)* hiker, rambler.

excusa *nf* **1** *(pretexto)* excuse. **2** *(disculpa)* excuse, apology.

excusar *vt* **1** *(justificar)* to excuse. **2** *(disculpar)* to pardon, forgive, excuse.
▶ *vpr* **excusarse** *(justificarse)* to excuse os; *(disculparse)* to apologize.

exención *nf* exemption.

exento,-a *adj* **1** free (de, from), exempt (de, from). **2** *(descubierto)* open.

exfoliación *nf* exfoliation.

exfoliar *vt* to exfoliate.
▶ *vpr* **exfoliarse** to exfoliate.

exhalación *nf* **1** exhalation. **2** *(estrella)* shooting star; *(rayo)* flash of lightning.

exhalar *vt* **1** *(gases, vapores, etc)* to give off; *(aire)* to exhale, breathe out. **2** *fig (suspiros, etc)* to heave, let out; *(quejas)* to utter.

exhaustivo,-a *adj* exhaustive, thorough, comprehensive.

exhausto,-a *adj* exhausted.

exhibición *nf* **1** *(exposición)* exhibition, show. **2** CINE showing.

exhibicionismo *nm* exhibitionism.

exhibir *vt* **1** to exhibit, show, display. **2** *(ostentar)* to show off.
▶ *vpr* **exhibirse** *(ostentar)* to show off, make an exhibition of os.

exhortar *vt* to exhort.

exhumación *nf* exhumation.

exhumar *vt* **1** to exhume. **2** *fig* to revive, recall.

exigencia *nf* **1** demand, exigency. **2** *(requisito)* requirement.

exigente *adj* demanding, exacting.

exigir *vt* **1** *(pedir por derecho)* to demand. **2** *fig (necesitar)* to require, call for.

exilado,-a *nm & nf* exile.

exilio *nm* exile.

existencia *nf (vida)* existence, life.
▶ *nf pl* **existencias** stock *sing*, stocks.

existencial *adj* existential.

existencialismo *nm* existentialism.

existencialista *adj* existentialist.
▶ *nm o nf* existentialist.

existente *adj* **1** existing, existent. **2** COM in stock.

existir *vi* to exist, be.

éxito *nm* success.

exitoso,-a *adj* successful.

éxodo *nm* exodus.

exogamia *nf* exogamy.

exorcismo *nm* exorcism.

exorcista *nm o nf* exorcist.

exotérico,-a *adj* exoteric.

exótico,-a *adj* exotic.

exotismo *nm* exoticism.

expandir *vt* **1** *(dilatar)* to expand. **2** *fig (divulgar)* to spread.
▶ *vpr* **expandirse** **1** *(dilatarse)* to expand. **2** *fig (divulgarse)* to spread.

expansión *nf* **1** *(dilatación)* expansion. **2** *(difusión)* spreading. **3** *(aumento)* expansion, increase, growth.

expansionista *adj* expansionist.

expansivo,-a *adj* **1** *(gas, etc)* expansive. **2** *fig (franco)* expansive, open, frank.

expatriar *vt* to expatriate, banish.
▶ *vpr* **expatriarse** *(emigrar)* to emigrate, become an expatriate; *(exilarse)* to go into exile.

expectativa *nf* **1** *(esperanza)* expectation, hope. **2** *(posibilidad)* prospect.

expectoración *nf* **1** *(acción)* expectoration. **2** *(flema)* sputum, phlegm.

expectorar *vt* to expectorate.
▶ *vi* to expectorate.

expedición *nf* **1** *(gen)* expedition. **2** *(grupo de personas)* expedition, party.

3 *(acción de expedir)* dispatch, shipping; *(remesa)* shipment.

expedientar *vt* to take disciplinary action against, open a file on.

expediente *nm* **1** JUR proceedings *pl*, action: *expediente judicial* legal proceedings. **2** *(informe)* dossier, record; *(ficha)* file. **3** *(recurso)* expedient.

expedir *vt* **1** *(mercancías)* to send, dispatch, ship; *(correo)* to send, dispatch. **2** *(pasaporte, título)* to issue. **3** *(contrato, documento)* to draw up.

expeditivamente *adv* expeditiously.

expeditivo,-a *adj* expeditious.

expendedor,-ra *adj* selling, retailing, retail.
▶ *nm & nf* dealer, retailer, seller.

expender *vt* **1** *(gastar)* to spend. **2** *(vender)* to sell. **3** *(vender al menudeo)* to retail, sell.

expensas *nf pl* expenses, charges, costs.

experiencia *nf* **1** *(gen)* experience. **2** *(experimento)* experiment.

experimentación *nf* experimentation, experimenting, testing.

experimentado,-a *adj* **1** *(persona)* experienced. **2** *(método)* tested, tried.

experimental *adj* experimental.

experimentar *vt* **1** *(hacer experimentos)* to experiment, test. **2** *(probar)* to test, try out. **3** *(sentir, notar)* to experience, feel; *(- cambio)* to undergo; *(- aumento)* to show; *(- pérdida, derrota)* to suffer.

experimento *nm* experiment, test.

experto,-a *adj* expert.
▶ *nm & nf* expert.

expiar *vt* to expiate, atone for.

expirar *vi* to expire.

explanada *nf* esplanade.

explayar *vt* *fml (extender)* to extend, spread out.
▶ *vpr* **explayarse** *(dilatarse al hablar)* to dwell (en, on), talk at length (en, about).

explicable *adj* explicable, explainable.

explicación *nf* **1** explanation. **2** *(motivo)* reason.

explicar *vt* **1** *(gen)* to explain, expound, tell. **2** *(justificar)* to justify.
▶ *vpr* **explicarse** *(expresarse)* to explain os, make os understood, make os clear.

explicativo,-a *adj* explanatory.

explícito,-a *adj* explicit.

exploración *nf* **1** *(gen)* exploration. **2** TÉC scanning. **3** MIL reconnaissance.

explorador,-ra *nm & nf (persona)* explorer. **2** *(niño)* boy scout; *(niña)* girl guide, US girl scout.

explorar *vt* **1** *(gen)* to explore. **2** MED to probe. **3** MIL to reconnoitre. **4** TÉC to scan. **5** *(de mina)* to drill, prospect.

exploratorio,-a *adj* **1** exploratory. **2** MED exploratory, probing.

explosión *nf* **1** explosion, blast, blowing up. **2** *fig* outburst.

explosionar *vt* to explode.
▶ *vi* to explode, blow up.

explosiva *nf* LING plosive.

explosivo,-a *adj* **1** explosive. **2** LING plosive.
▶ *nm* **explosivo** explosive.

explotación *nf* **1** *(gen)* exploitation. **2** *(de terreno)* cultivation, farming. **3** *(de industria)* running, operating. **4** *(de recursos)* tapping, exploitation.

explotador,-ra *nm & nf pey* exploiter.

explotar *vt* **1** *(sacar provecho)* to exploit; *(mina)* to work; *(tierra)* to cultivate; *(industria)* to operate, run; *(recursos)* to tap, exploit.
▶ *vi (explosionar)* to explode, blow up.

expoliación *nf* plundering, pillaging, despoiling.

expoliar *vt* to plunder, pillage, despoil.

expolio *nm* **1** *(acción)* plundering, pillaging, despoiling. **2** *(botín)* loot, booty.

exponencial *adj* exponential.

exponente *adj* exponent, expounding.
▶ *nm* **1** MAT index, exponent. **2** *(prototipo)* exponent.

exponer *vt* **1** *(explicar)* to expound, explain; *(propuesta)* to put forward; *(hechos)* to state, set out. **2** *(mostrar)* to show, exhibit; *(mercancías)* to display. **3** *(arriesgar)* to expose, risk, endanger.
▶ *vpr* **exponerse** *(arriesgarse)* to expose os (a, to), run the risk (a, of).

exportable *adj* exportable, for exportation.

exportación *nf* export, exportation.

exportador,-ra *adj* exporting.
▶ *nm & nf* exporter.

exportar *vt* to export.

exposición *nf* **1** *(de arte)* exhibition, show; *(de mercancías)* display. **2** *(explicación)* account, explanation; *(hechos, ideas)* exposé. **3** *(al sol, etc)* exposure.

expositivo,-a *adj* explanatory.

exprés *adj* **1** *(tren)* express. **2** *(café)* expresso. **3** *(olla)* pressure.

expresar *vt* **1** *(gen)* to express. **2** *(manifestar)* to state; *(comunicar)* to convey.
▶ *vpr* **expresarse** to express os.

expresión *nf* expression.

expresionismo *nm* expressionism.

expresionista *adj* expressionist.
▶ *nm o nf* expressionist.

expresividad *nf* expressivity.

expresivo,-a *adj* **1** *(elocuente)* expressive. **2** *(mirada)* meaningful; *(silencio)* eloquent.

expreso,-a *adj (especificado)* express.

exprimidor *nm* lemon squeezer, US juicer.

exprimir *vt (fruto)* to squeeze; *(zumo)* to squeeze out.

expropiación *nf* expropriation.

expropiar *vt* to expropriate.

expuesto,-a *adj (peligroso)* dangerous, risky; *(sin protección)* exposed.

expulsar *vt* **1** *(expeler)* to expel, eject, throw out; *(humo, etc)* to belch out. **2** DEP to send off.

expulsión *nf* **1** expulsion, ejection. **2** DEP sending off. **3** *(alumno)* expulsion.

expurgar *vt* **1** to expurgate. **2** *fig* to purge.

exquisitez *nf* **1** exquisiteness. **2** *(manjar)* delicacy.

exquisito,-a *adj* **1** *(gen)* exquisite. **2** *(gusto)* refined; *(sabor)* delicious, exquisite.

extasiado,-a *adj* ecstatic.

extasiar *vt* to enrapture.
▶ *vpr* **extasiarse** to go into ecstasies, go into raptures.

éxtasis *nm inv* ecstasy, rapture.

extático,-a *adj* extatic.

extender *vt* **1** *(mapa, papel)* to spread (out), open (out). **2** *(brazo, etc)* to stretch (out); *(alas)* to spread. **3** *(mantequilla, etc)* to spread. **4** *(documento)* to draw up; *(cheque)* to make out; *(pasaporte, certificado)* to issue.
▶ *vpr* **extenderse 1** *(durar)* to extend, last. **2** *(terreno)* to stretch. **3** *fig (difundirse)* to spread, extend.

extendido,-a *adj* **1** *(difundido)* widespread. **2** *(mano, etc)* outstretched.

extensible *adj* extendable.

extensión *nf* **1** *(gen)* extension. **2** *(dimensión)* extent, size; *(superficie)* area, expanse. **3** *(duración)* duration, length.

extensivo,-a *adj* extendable, extensive.

extenso,-a *adj* **1** *(amplio)* extensive, vast; *(grande)* large. **2** *(largo)* lengthy, long.

extenuado,-a *adj* **1** *(agotado)* exhausted. **2** *(débil)* weak. **3** *(flaco)* emaciated.

extenuante *adj* exhausting.

extenuar *vt* **1** *(agotar)* to exhaust. **2** *(debilitar)* to weaken.
▶ *vpr* **extenuarse** *(agotarse)* to exhaust os, wear os out.

exterior *adj* **1** *(gen)* exterior, outer, external. **2** *(ventana, puerta)* outside; *(pared)* outer. **3** *(aspecto)* outward. **4** *(extranjero)* foreign.
▶ *nm* **1** *(superficie externa)* exterior, outside. **2** *(extranjero)* abroad, overseas. **3** *(de una persona)* appearance. **4** DEP outside.
▶ *nm pl* **exteriores** CINE location shots.

exteriorización *nf* manifestation, externalization.

exteriorizar *vt* to show, reveal, express outwardly.

exterminación *nf (supresión)* extermination, wiping out; *(destrucción)* destruction.

exterminador,-ra *adj* exterminating.
▶ *nm & nf* exterminator.

exterminar *vt (suprimir)* to exterminate, wipe out; *(destruir)* to destroy.

exterminio *nm* extermination, wiping out; *(destrucción)* destruction.

externado *nm* day school.

externo,-a *adj* **1** external, outward: *parte externa* outside. **2** *(alumno)* day.

extinción *nf* extinction.

extinguir *vt* **1** *(fuego, etc)* to extinguish, put out. **2** *(especie, deuda, epidemia)* to wipe out.
▶ *vpr* **extinguirse 1** *(fuego, etc)* to go out. **2** *(especie, etc)* to become extinct, die out. **3** *(plazo)* to expire, run out.

extintor *nm* fire extinguisher.

extirpación *nf* **1** MED removal, extraction. **2** *fig* eradication, wiping out, stamping out.

extirpar *vt* **1** MED to remove, extract. **2** *fig* to eradicate, wipe out, stamp out.

extorsión *nf* **1** *(usurpación)* extortion. **2** *fig (molestia)* inconvenience, trouble.

extorsionar *vt* **1** *(usurpar)* to extort, exact. **2** *fig (molestar)* to inconvenience, cause inconvenience to.

extra *adj* **1** *fam* extra. **2** *fam (superior)* top-quality, best-quality. **3** *(paga)* bonus.
▶ *nm* **1** *fam (gasto)* additional expense. **2** *fam (plus)* bonus.

extracción *nf* **1** *(gen)* extraction; *(de lotería)* draw. **2** *(origen)* descent, extraction. COMP **extracción de datos** INFORM data retrieval.

extracto *nm* **1** *(sustancia)* extract. **2** *(trozo)* extract, excerpt. **3** *(resumen)* summary.

extractor *nm* extractor.

extradición *nf* extradition.

extraditar *vt* to extradite.

extraer *vt* **1** *(gen)* to extract. **2** *(conclusión)* to draw.

extraescolar *adj* out of school, extracurricular. COMP **actividades extraescolares** extracurricular activities.

extrafino,-a *adj* superfine, best quality.

extralargo,-a *adj* king-size.

extralimitarse *vpr fig* to go too far, overstep.

extranjero,-a *adj* foreign, alien.
► *nm & nf* foreigner.
► *nm* **extranjero** foreign countries *pl*, abroad.

extrañar *vt* **1** *(sorprender)* to surprise. **2** *(notar extraño)* to find strange, not to be used to.
► *vpr* **extrañarse 1** *(desterrarse)* to go into exile. **2** *(sorprenderse)* to be surprised (de/por, at).

extraño,-a *adj* **1** *(no conocido)* alien, foreign. **2** *(particular)* strange, peculiar, odd, funny.

extraordinaria *nf (paga)* bonus payment.

extraordinariamente *adv* extraordinarily, unusually.

extraordinario,-a *adj* **1** *(fuera de lo común)* extraordinary, unusual; *(sorprendente)* surprising; *(admirable)* outstanding, exceptional. **2** *(raro)* queer, odd. **3** *(gastos, etc)* additional, extra; *(paga)* bonus. **4** *(revista, etc)* special.
► *nm* **extraordinario 1** *(correo)* special delivery. **2** *(revista, etc)* special issue.

extraplano,-a *adj* slimline.

extrapolar *vt* to extrapolate.

extrarradio *nm* outskirts *pl*, suburbs *pl*.

extraterrestre *adj* extramundane, extraterrestrial.
► *nm o nf* alien.

extravagancia *nf* extravagance, eccentricity.

extravagante *adj* extravagant outrageous.

extraviado,-a *adj* **1** *(disoluto)* dissolute. **2** *(perdido - persona, objeto)* missing, lost; *(- perro, niño)* stray.

extraviar *vt* **1** *(persona)* to mislead. **2** *(objeto)* to mislay, lose.
► *vpr* **extraviarse 1** *(persona)* to get lost, lose one's way. **2** *(objeto)* to get mislaid.

extravío *nm (persona)* misleading; *(cosa)* loss, mislaying.

extremado,-a *adj* extreme.

extremar *vt* to carry to extremes, carry to the limit, overdo.
► *vpr* **extremarse** to do one's best, do one's utmost, take great pains.

extremidad *nf* **1** *(parte extrema)* extremity; *(punta)* end, tip. **2** ANAT limb, extremity.

extremismo *nm* extremism.

extremista *adj* extremist.
► *nm o nf* extremist.

extremo,-a *adj* **1** *(exagerado)* extreme. **2** *(distante)* further. **3** *fig (intenso)* utmost.
► *nm* **extremo 1** *(punta)* extreme, end. **2** *(asunto, materia)* matter, question. **3** DEP wing.

extrínseco,-a *adj* extrinsic.

extrovertido,-a *adj* extroverted.
► *nm & nf* extrovert.

exuberante *adj* **1** exuberant. **2** *(vegetación)* lush, abundant.

F

F, f *nf (la letra)* F, f.

F *sím* (Fahrenheit) Fahrenheit; *(símbolo)* F.

fa *nm* F.

fabada *nf* bean stew *including pork sausage and bacon.*

fábrica *nf* **1** *(industria)* factory, plant. **2** *(fabricación)* manufacture.

fabricación *nf* manufacture, production, making.

fabricante *nm o nf* manufacturer, maker.

fabricar *vt* **1** *(producir)* to make, manufacture, produce. **2** *fig (inventar)* to fabricate, invent.

fábula *nf* **1** LIT fable. **2** *(mito)* myth, legend. **3** *(mentira)* invention.

fabular *vt* **1** *(contar fábulas)* to fable. **2** *(imaginar)* to imagine.

fabuloso,-a *adj* **1** *(fantástico)* fabulous, fantastic. **2** LIT fabulous, mythical.

faceta *nf* facet.

fachada *nf* **1** ARQUIT façade, front. **2** *fam (apariencia)* outward show.

facial *adj* facial.

fácil *adj* **1** easy. **2** *(probable)* probable, likely.

facilidad *nf* **1** *(simplicidad)* ease, facility. **2** *(aptitud)* talent, gift: *tiene facilidad para la música* he has a gift for music. COMP **facilidad de palabra** fluency.
► *nf pl* **facilidades** *(medios que facilitan)* facilities.

facilitar *vt* **1** *(simplificar)* to make easy, make easier, facilitate. **2** *(proporcionar)* to provide with, supply with.

factor *nm (gen)* factor.

factoría *nf* **1** COM trading post. **2** *(fábrica)* factory, mill.

factura *nf* invoice, bill.

facturación *nf* **1** COM invoicing. **2** *(de equipajes)* registration, check-in.

facturar *vt* **1** COM to invoice, charge for. **2** *(equipaje)* to register, check in.

facultad *nf* **1** *(capacidad)* faculty, ability. **2** *(poder)* faculty, power. **3** *(universitaria)* faculty, school.

faena *nf* **1** *(tarea)* task, job. **2** *fam (mala pasada)* dirty trick.

fagocito *nm* phagocyte.

fagot *nm (instrumento)* bassoon.
► *nm o nf (músico)* bassoonist.

faisán *nm* pheasant.

faja *nf* **1** *(cinturón)* band, belt. **2** *(ropa interior)* corset, girdle.

fajo *nm* bundle; *(de billetes)* wad.

falda *nf* **1** *(prenda)* skirt. **2** *(regazo)* lap. **3** *(ladera)* slope. **4** *(corte de carne)* brisket.

faldón *nm* **1** *(de traje)* coat-tail; *(de camisa)* shirt-tail. **2** *(prenda de bebé)* wraparound skirt. **3** *(de tejado)* gable.

falible *adj* fallible.

falla *nf* **1** *(defecto)* defect, fault. **2** GEOG fault.

fallar *vi* **1** *(premio)* to award a prize. **2** *(fracasar, no funcionar)* to fail. **3** *(puntería)* to miss; *(plan)* to go wrong.
► *vt (premio)* to award.

fallecer *vi fml* to pass away, die.

fallo *nm* **1** *(en concurso)* decision. **2** *(error)* mistake, blunder; *(fracaso)* failure. **4** *(defecto)* fault, defect.

falsear *vt (falsificar)* to counterfeit, forge.

falsedad *nf* **1** *(hipocresía)* falseness, hypocrisy. **2** *(mentira)* falsehood, lie.

falsete *nm* falsetto.

falsificador,-ra *adj (de firma, cuadro)* forging; *(de dinero)* counterfeiting.

► *nm & nf (de firma, cuadro)* forger; *(de dinero)* counterfeiter.

falsificar *vt* **1** *(gen)* to falsify. **2** *(firma, cuadro)* to forge; *(dinero)* to counterfeit, forge.

falso,-a *adj* **1** *(no verdadero)* false, untrue. **2** *(moneda)* false, counterfeit. **3** *(persona)* insincere, false.

falta *nf* **1** *(carencia)* lack: *falta de sensibilidad* lack of sensitivity. **2** *(escasez)* shortage: *existe una falta de agua* there is a water shortage. **3** *(ausencia)* absence. **4** *(error)* mistake: *has hecho una falta de ortografía* you've made a spelling mistake. **5** *(defecto)* fault, defect. **6** DEP *(fútbol)* foul; *(tenis)* fault. LOC **echar en falta** to miss. ‖ **sin falta** without fail.

faltar *vi* **1** *(haber poco)* to be lacking, be needed: *falta (más) leche* we need (more) milk. **2** *(no tener)* to lack, not have (enough). **3** *(quedar)* to remain, be left: *falta poco para que...* it won't be long till...

falto,-a LOC **estar falto,-a de** to lack, be short of, be without: *estamos faltos de dinero* we're without of money.

fama *nf (renombre)* fame, renown.

famélico,-a *adj* starving, famished.

familia *nf* **1** family. **2** *(prole)* children *pl*, family.

familiar *adj* **1** *(de la familia)* family, of the family. **2** *(conocido)* familiar, well-known. **3** LING colloquial.
► *nm o nf* relation, relative.

familiaridad *nf* familiarity.

familiarizar *vt* to familiarize (con, with), make familiar (con, with).
► *vpr* **familiarizarse** to get to know: *familiarízate con el teclado* get to know the keyboard.

familiarmente *adv* familiarly.

famoso,-a *adj* famous, well-known.

fan *nm o nf* fan, admirer. LOC **ser un,-a fan de** ALGO to be mad about STH.

fanático,-a *adj* fanatic, fanatical.

fanatismo *nm* fanaticism.

fanerógamo,-a *adj* phanerogamic, phanerogamous.

fanfarrón,-ona *adj fam* swanky.

fanfarronear *vi fam (chulear)* to show off, swank.

fango *nm (barro)* mud, mire.

fantasear *vi* **1** *(forjar en la imaginación)* to daydream, dream. **2** *(presumir)* to boast, show off.
► *vt (imaginar)* dream.

fantasía *nf* **1** fantasy. **2** fancy.

fantasioso,-a *adj* imaginative.

fantasma *nm* **1** *(espectro)* phantom, ghost. **2** *fam (fanfarrón)* braggart, show-off.

fantasmal *adj* ghostly.

fantástico,-a *adj* **1** fantastic. **2** *(estupendo)* wonderful.

fantoche *nm* **1** *(títere)* puppet, marionette. **2** *pey (fanfarrón)* braggart.

faquir *nm* fakir.

faradio *nm* farad.

farándula *nf* **1** *(compañía de teatro)* group of strolling players. **2** *(profesión, mundo del teatro)* acting, the stage.

faraón *nm* Pharaoh.

faraónico,-a *adj* Pharaonic.

fardar *vi argot (presumir)* to show off, swank.

fardo *nm (paquete)* bundle, pack.

fardón,-ona *adj argot* classy, flash.

farero,-a *nm & nf* lighthouse keeper.

faringe *nf* pharynx.

faringitis *nf inv* pharyngitis.

farmacéutico,-a *adj* pharmaceutical.
► *nm & nf* pharmacist.

farmacia *nf* **1** *(estudios)* pharmacy. **2** *(tienda)* chemist's (shop), US drugstore, pharmacy.

fármaco *nm* medicine, medication.

farmacología *nf* pharmacology.

faro *nm* **1** *(torre)* lighthouse, beacon. **2** *(coche)* headlight. **3** *fig (guía)* guiding light, guide.

farol *nm* **1** *(farola)* streetlamp, streetlight. **2** *argot (fardada)* bragging, swank.

farola *nf* streetlight, streetlamp; *(de gas)* gas lamp.

farolero,-a *adj fam* boastful.
► *nm & nf fam (fanfarrón)* show-off.
► *nm* **farolero** *(de profesión)* lamplighter.

farolillo *nm* **1** *(farol de papel)* Chinese lantern. **2** BOT Canterbury bell.

farra *nf fam* binge, spree.

farruco,-a *adj fam* conceited, cocky.

farsa *nf* TEAT farce.

farsante *adj* lying, deceitful.

fascículo *nm* instalment (US installment), fascicule, fascicle.

fascinación *nf* fascination.

fascinante *adj* fascinating.

fascinar *vt* to fascinate, captivate.

fascismo *nm* fascism.

fascista *adj* fascist.

fase *nf (etapa)* phase, stage.

fastidiado,-a *adj* **1** *(hastiado)* sickened, disgusted. **2** *(molesto)* annoyed. **3** *fam (estropeado)* ruined, spoilt. **4** *fam (mal de salud)* ill, sick, in a bad way.

fastidiar *vt* **1** *(hastiar)* to sicken, disgust. **2** *(molestar)* to annoy, bother. **3** *(partes del cuerpo)* to hurt: *le fastidia el estómago* he's got a bad stomach. **4** *fam (estropear)* to damage, ruin; *(planes)* to spoil.
▶ *vpr* **fastidiarse 1** *(aguantarse)* to put up with, grin and bear it. **2** *fam (estropearse)* to go wrong, break down: *se ha fastidiado la tele* the telly has gone wrong.

fastidio *nm* **1** *(molestia)* bother, nuisance. **2** *(aburrimiento)* boredom.

fastidioso,-a *adj* **1** *(molesto)* annoying, irksome. **2** *(aburrido)* boring, tedious.

fastuoso,-a *adj* **1** *(cosa)* splendid, lavish. **2** *(persona)* lavish, ostentatious.

fatal *adj* **1** *(inexorable)* fateful. **2** *(mortal)* deadly, fatal.
▶ *adv fam* awfully, terribly.

fatalidad *nf* **1** *(destino)* fate. **2** *(desgracia)* misfortune.

fatalismo *nm* fatalism.

fatalista *adj* fatalistic.

fatídico,-a *adj (desastroso)* disastrous, calamitous.

fatiga *nf (cansancio)* fatigue.

fatigar *vt* **1** *(cansar)* to wear out, tire. **2** *(molestar)* to annoy.

fatigoso,-a *adj (cansado)* tiring, exhausting.

fauces *nf pl (en anatomía)* gullet *sing*.

fauna *nf* fauna.

fauvismo *nm* fauvism.

fauvista *nm o nf* fauvist.

favor *nm* favour (US favor). LOC **a favor de** in favour (US favor) of. ‖ **hacer un favor** to do a favour (US favor). ‖ **por favor** please.

favorable *adj* favourable (US favorable). LOC **mostrarse favorable a** ALGO to be in favour (US favor) of STH.

favorecer *vt* **1** *(ayudar)* to favour (US favor), help. **2** *(agraciar)* suit: *el azul no me favorece* blue doesn't suit me.

favoritismo *nm* favouritism (US favoritism).

favorito,-a *adj* favourite (US favorite).

fax *nm (sistema, documento)* fax.

fe *nf* faith.

fealdad *nf* ugliness.

febrero *nm* February.

✎ Para ejemplos de uso consulta **marzo**.

febril *adj* MED feverish.

fecha *nf* **1** *(data)* date: *¿qué fecha es hoy?* what's the date today? **2** *(día)* day. LOC **fijar la fecha** to fix a date. COMP **fecha de nacimiento** date of birth.
▶ *nf pl* **fechas** *(época)* time *sing*: *por esas fechas* at that time.

fécula *nf* starch.

fecundación *nf* fertilization.

fecundar *vt* to fertilize.

fecundidad *nf (fertilidad)* fertility.

federación *nf* federation.

federal *adj* federal.

federalismo *nm* federalism.

federalista *adj* federalist.

federar *vt* to federate.

feldespato *nm* feldspar, felspar.

felicidad *nf* happiness. LOC **¡(muchas) felicidades! 1** *(éxitos)* congratulations! **2** *(cumpleaños)* happy birthday!

felicitación *nf* **1** *(acción)* congratulation. **2** *(tarjeta)* greetings card.

felicitar *vt* to congratulate (por, on).

felino,-a *adj* feline.

feliz *adj* happy.

felizmente *adv (con felicidad)* happily.

felpa *nf* plush.

felpudo,-a *adj (textil)* plushy, velvety.

femenino,-a *adj* 1 feminine. 2 *(sexo)* female; *(equipo, asociación)* women's.

feminidad *nf* femininity.

feminismo *nm* feminism.

feminista *adj* feminist.

femoral *adj* femoral.

fémur *nm* femur.

fenomenal *adj fam (fantástico)* great, terrific.
► *adv* wonderfully, marvellously.

fenómeno *nm* phenomenon.
► *adj fam (fantástico)* fantastic, terrific.

fenotipo *nm* phenotype.

feo,-a *adj* 1 *(persona - nada atractiva)* ugly; *(- poco atractiva)* plain. 2 *(aspecto, situación, tiempo, etc)* nasty, horrible, unpleasant, awful.

féretro *nm* coffin.

feria *nf* 1 COM fair. 2 *(fiesta)* fair.

fermentación *nf* fermentation.

fermentar *vi* to ferment.

fermento *nm* ferment.

ferocidad *nf* ferocity, fierceness.

feroz *adj* fierce, ferocious.

ferretería *nf* ironmonger's.

ferretero,-a *nm & nf* ironmonger.

férrico,-a *adj* ferric.

ferrocarril *nm* railway, US railroad.

ferroviario,-a *adj* railway.

fértil *adj* fertile, rich.

fertilidad *nf* fertility, fecundity.

fertilización *nf* fertilization.

fertilizante *adj* fertilizing.
► *nm (abono)* fertilizer.

fertilizar *vt* to fertilize.

ferviente *adj* fervent, passionate.

fervor *nm* fervour (US fervor).

festejar *vt (celebrar)* to celebrate.

festejo *nm* feast, entertainment.

festival *nm* festival.

festividad *nf* 1 *(fiesta)* festivity, celebration. 2 *(día)* feast day, holiday.

festivo,-a *adj* 1 *(alegre)* festive, merry. 2 *(humorístico)* witty.

fétido,-a *adj* stinking, fetid.

feto *nm* foetus (US fetus).

feudal *adj* feudal.

feudalismo *nm* feudalism.

feudo *nm* fief, feud.

fiable *adj* reliable, trustworthy.

fiambre *nm* 1 CULIN cold meat, cold cut. 2 *fam (cadáver)* stiff, corpse.

fiambrera *nf* lunch box.

fianza *nf (depósito)* deposit.

fiar *vt* 1 *(vender)* to sell on credit. 2 *(confiar)* to confide, entrust. LOC **de fiar** trustworthy, reliable.
► *vpr* **fiarse** *(confiarse)* to trust (de, -).

fibra *nf* fibre (US fiber). COMP **fibra óptica** optical fibre (US fiber).

fibroso,-a *adj* fibrous.

ficción *nf* fiction.

ficha *nf* 1 *(tarjeta)* index card, file card. 2 *(de teléfono)* token. 3 *(en juegos)* counter; *(naipes)* chip; *(ajedrez)* piece, man; *(dominó)* domino.

fichaje *nm* signing (up).

fichar *vt* 1 *(anotar)* to put on an index card; *(registrar)* to open a file on. 2 DEP to sign up, sign on.
► *vi* DEP to sign up (por, with): *finalmente fichó por el Barcelona* he finally signed up with Barcelona F.C.

fichero *nm* 1 *(archivo)* card index. 2 *(mueble)* filing cabinet, file. 3 INFORM file.

ficticio,-a *adj* fictitious.

ficus *nm inv* rubber plant.

fidelidad *nf* 1 *(lealtad)* fidelity, faithfulness. 2 *(exactitud)* accuracy. COMP **alta fidelidad** high fidelity, hi-fi.

fideo *nm* noodle.

fiebre *nf (enfermedad)* fever, temperature. LOC **tener fiebre** to have a temperature.

fiel *adj* 1 *(leal)* faithful, loyal. 2 *(exacto)* accurate.

fieltro *nm* felt.

fiera *nf* wild animal, wild beast.

fiero,-a *adj* wild, fierce, ferocious.

fiesta *nf* 1 *(día no laborable)* holiday: *el viernes es fiesta* Friday's a holiday. 2 *(reunión)* party.
► *nf pl* **fiestas** festivity, fiesta.

figura *nf* **1** *(gen)* figure. **2** *(forma)* shape.

figurar *vi* **1** *(encontrarse)* to appear, be, figure: *figura como director* he appears as director. **2** *(destacar)* to stand out, be important.
▸ *vpr* **figurarse** *(imaginarse)* to imagine, suppose.

fijador,-ra *nm (para pelo)* hairspray, hair gel.

fijar *vt (sujetar)* to fix, fasten; *(puerta)* to hang; *(ventana)* to put in.
▸ *vpr* **fijarse 1** *(darse cuenta)* to notice. **2** *(poner atención)* to pay attention, watch: *fíjate cómo se hace* watch how it's done.

fijo,-a *adj* **1** *(sujeto)* fixed, fastened. **2** *(establecido)* set, definite, firm: *fecha fija* set date. **3** *(firme)* steady, stable, firm. **4** *(permanente)* permanent.

fila *nf (línea)* file, line, row.
▸ *nf pl* **filas** *(de ejército, partido)* ranks.

filamento *nm* filament.

filete *nm (de carne, pescado)* fillet (US filet).

Filipinas *nf pl* las Filipinas the Philippines.

filipino,-a *adj* Filipino.
▸ *nm & nf (persona)* Filipino.
▸ *nm* **filipino** *(idioma)* Filipino.

film *nm* film, US movie.

filmar *vt* to film, shoot.

filmina *nf* slide, transparency.

filmoteca *nf* film institute.

filo *nm* cutting edge, edge.

filo- *pref* philo-.

filología *nf* philology.

filólogo,-a *nm & nf* philologist.

filón *nm (mineral)* seam, vein.

filosofar *vi* to philosophize.

filosofía *nf* philosophy.

filósofo,-a *nm & nf* philosopher.

filoxera *nf* phylloxera.

filtrar *vt* to filter, to leak.
▸ *vpr* **filtrarse** *(pasar a través)* to filter.

filtro *nm (material)* filter.

fin *nm* **1** *(final)* end. **2** *(objetivo)* purpose, aim. ⊔ᴏᴄ **a fin de** in order to, so as to. ▌ **a fin de que** so that. ▌ **en fin** anyway. ᴄᴏᴍᴘ **fin de semana** weekend.

final *adj (último)* final, last.
▸ *nm* end. ᴄᴏᴍᴘ **final feliz** happy ending.
▸ *nf* DEP final.

finalidad *nf* purpose, aim.

finalista *nm o nf* finalist.

finalizar *vt* to end, finish.
▸ *vi* to end, finish.

financiación *nf* financing.

financiar *vt* to finance.

finanzas *nf pl* finances.

finca *nf* property, estate. ᴄᴏᴍᴘ **finca rústica** country property.

fingir *vt* to feign, pretend: *fingió indiferencia* he feigned indifference.

finito,-a *adj* finite.

finlandés,-esa *adj* Finnish.
▸ *nm & nf (persona)* Finn.
▸ *nm* **finlandés** *(idioma)* Finnish.

Finlandia *nf* Finland.

fino,-a *adj* **1** *(delicado)* fine, delicate. **2** *(delgado)* thin. **3** *(educado)* refined, polite.

fiordo *nm* fiord, fjord.

firma *nf* **1** *(acto)* signing. **2** *(empresa)* firm.

firmamento *nm* firmament.

firmar *vt* to sign.

firme *adj (estable)* firm, steady.

firmeza *nf* firmness, steadiness.

fiscal *adj* fiscal, tax.
▸ *nm o nf* JUR public prosecutor, US district attorney.

fisco *nm* exchequer, US treasury.

fisgar *vt fam* to pry, snoop.

fisgón,-ona *adj* snooper, busybody.

fisgonear *vt* to pry, snoop.

física *nf* physics.

físico,-a *adj* physical.
▸ *nm & nf (profesión)* physicist.
▸ *nm* **físico** *(aspecto)* physique.

fisioterapeuta *nm o nf* physiotherapist.

fisioterapia *nf* physiotherapy.

fisonomía *nf* appearance.

fisura *nf* fissure.

fito- *pref* phyto-.

Fiyi *nm* Fiji.

fiyiano,-a *adj* Fijian.
▸ *nm & nf (persona)* Fijian.
▸ *nm* **fiyiano** *(idioma)* Fijian.

F

fláccido,-a *adj* flaccid, flabby.

flaco,-a *adj* 1 *(delgado)* thin, skinny. 2 *(débil)* weak, frail.

flagelo *nm* 1 whip. 2 BIOL flagellum.

flamenco,-a *adj* 1 *(gitano)* Andalusian gypsy. 2 *(música)* flamenco.
▶ *nm* flamenco 1 *(idioma)* Flemish. 2 *(música)* flamenco music. 3 *(ave)* flamingo.

flan *nm* *(dulce)* crème caramel. LOC estar como un flan to be shaking like a leaf.

flanco *nm* flank, side.

flanera *nf* mould (US mold).

flaquear *vi* to weaken, give in, to fail.

flaqueza *nf* weakness, frailty.

flash *nm* flash, flashlight.

flato *nm* *(dolor)* stitch.

flauta *nf* flute.

flautista *nm o nf* flute player.

flecha *nf* arrow.

flechazo *nm* fig *(enamoramiento)* love at first sight.

fleco *nm* *(adorno)* fringe.

flemón *nm* abscess.

flequillo *nm* fringe, US bangs *pl*.

flexibilidad *nf* flexibility.

flexible *adj* flexible.

flexionar *vt* *(cuerpo)* to bend.

flexo *nm* adjustable table lamp.

flipar *vt argot (gustar)* to drive wild.
▶ *vi* 1 *(asombrarse)* to be amazed, be stunned. 2 *(pasárselo bien)* to freak out.

flirtear *vi* to flirt.

flojear *vi* 1 *(disminuir)* to go down. 2 *(debilitarse)* to weaken, grow weak.

flojera *nf fam* weakness, faintness.

flojo,-a *adj* 1 *(suelto)* loose; *(no tensado)* slack. 2 *(débil)* weak. 3 *(mediocre)* poor: *es un estudiante flojo* he's a poor student.

flor *nf* BOT flower, bloom. LOC en flor in bloom.

florecer *vi* 1 *(plantas)* to flower, bloom; *(árboles)* to blossom. 2 *(prosperar)* to flourish, thrive.

floreciente *adj* prosperous.

florería *nf* florist's (shop).

florero *nm* vase.

florista *nm o nf* florist.

floristería *nf* florist's (shop).

flota *nf* fleet.

flotador *nm* *(de niño)* rubber ring.

flotar *vi* to float.

flote LOC a flote afloat.

fluctuar *vi* *(variar)* to fluctuate.

fluido,-a *adj* *(sin obstáculos)* fluid.
▶ *nm* fluido FÍS fluid. COMP fluido eléctrico current, power.

fluir *vi* to flow.

flúor *nm* fluorine.

fluorescente *adj* fluorescent.
▶ *nm* fluorescent light.

fluvial *adj* fluvial, river.

fobia *nf* phobia.

foca *nf* seal.

foco *nm* 1 *(en física)* focus. 2 *(lámpara)* spotlight, floodlight.

fofo,-a *adj* flabby.

fogata *nf* bonfire.

fogón *nm* *(de cocina)* kitchen range, stove.

fogueo LOC de fogueo blank.

folclore *nm* folklore.

folclórico,-a *adj* folkloric, popular.

folio *nm* folio, leaf.

folk *nm* folk music.

folleto *nm* pamphlet, leaflet, brochure; *(explicativo)* instruction leaflet.

follón *nm* 1 *fam (alboroto)* rumpus, shindy. 2 *fam (enredo, confusión)* mess, trouble. LOC armar (un) follón *fam* to kick up a rumpus.

fomentar *vt* to promote.

fonda *nf* inn.

fondo *nm* 1 *(parte más baja)* bottom: *en el fondo del pozo* at the bottom of the well. 2 *(parte más lejana)* end, back: *al fondo de la sala* at the back of the hall. 3 *(segundo término)* background. LOC a fondo 1 *(adjetival)* thorough. 2 *(adverbial)* thoroughly. ▌ en el fondo *fig* deep down, at heart. COMP fondo del mar sea bed.
▶ *nm pl* fondos funds, money *sing*.

fonema *nm* phoneme.

fonético,-a *adj* phonetic.

fónico,-a *adj* phonic.

fono- *pref* phono-.

fonología *nf* phonology.

fonoteca *nf* record library.

fontanería *nf* plumbing.

fontanero,-a *nm & nf* plumber.

footing *nm* jogging. ⌊LOC⌋ **hacer footing** to go jogging.

forastero,-a *nm & nf* stranger.

forcejear *vi* to wrestle, struggle.

forcejeo *nm* struggle, struggling.

forestal *adj* forest.

forja *nf (fragua)* forge.

forjado *nm* ARQUIT framework.

forjar *vt (metales)* to forge.

forma *nf* **1** *(gen)* form, shape: *en forma de X* X-shaped. **2** *(manera)* way. **3** DEP form. ⌊LOC⌋ **de todas formas** anyway, in any case. ▌**estar en forma** to be in shape, be fit.

formación *nf* **1** *(gen)* formation. **2** *(educación)* upbringing. ⌊COMP⌋ **formación profesional** vocational training.

formal *adj* **1** *(con los requisitos necesarios)* formal. **2** *(serio)* serious, serious-minded. **3** *(cumplidor)* reliable, dependable.

formalizar *vt* to make formal.

formalmente *adv* formally.

formar *vt* **1** *(gen)* to form. **2** *(integrar, constituir)* to form, constitute: *formar parte de algo* to be a part of sth. **3** *(educar)* to bring up.
▶ *vpr* **formarse** *(educarse)* to be educated, be trained.

formatear *vt* to format.

formato *nm (gen)* format.

formidable *adj* tremendous, formidable.

formón *nm* firmer chisel.

fórmula *nf (gen)* formula.

formular *vt* **1** *(una teoría)* to formulate. **2** *(quejas, peticiones)* to express, make.
▶ *vi* QUÍM to write formulae.

formulario,-a *nm (documento)* form: *formulario de solicitud* application form

forofo,-a *nm & nf fam* fan, supporter.

forraje *nm (pienso)* fodder, forage.

forrar *vt* **1** *(por dentro)* to line. **2** *(por fuera)* to cover. **3** *(tapizar)* to upholster.
▶ *vpr* **forrarse** *fam (de dinero)* to make a fortune, make a packet.

forro *nm* **1** *(interior)* lining. **2** *(funda)* cover, case. **3** *(tapizado)* upholstery.

fortalecer *vt* to fortify, strengthen.
▶ *vpr* **fortalecerse** to strengthen.

fortaleza *nf* **1** *(vigor)* strength. **2** *(recinto fortificado)* fortress.

fortificación *nf* fortification.

fortuito,-a *adj* chance, fortuitous.

fortuna *nf* **1** *(destino)* fortune, fate. **2** *(suerte)* luck.

forzado,-a *adj* **1** *(obligado)* forced. **2** *(rebuscado)* forced, strained. ⌊COMP⌋ **risa forzada** forced laugh.

forzar *vt* **1** *(persona)* to force, compel. **2** *(cosa)* to force open, break open.

forzoso,-a *adj* **1** *(inevitable)* inevitable, unavoidable. **2** *(obligatorio)* obligatory, compulsory.

forzudo,-a *adj* strong, brawny.

fosa *nf* **1** *(sepultura)* grave. **2** *(hoyo)* pit, hollow. **3** ANAT cavity, fossa. **4** *(en el océano)* trench, deep. ⌊COMP⌋ **fosas nasales** nostrils.

fosfato *nm* phosphate. ⌊COMP⌋ **fosfato de cal** calcium phosphate.

fosforescente *adj* phosphorescent.

fósforo *nm* **1** QUÍM phosphorus. **2** *(cerilla)* match.

fósil *nm* fossil.

foso *nm* **1** *(hoyo)* hole, pit. **2** *(de fortaleza)* moat.

foto *nf fam* photo, picture.

fotocopia *nf* photocopy.

fotocopiadora *nf* photocopier, photocopying machine.

fotocopiar *vt* to photocopy.

fotografía *nf* **1** *(proceso)* photography. **2** *(retrato)* photograph. ⌊LOC⌋ **hacer fotografías** to take photographs.

fotografiar *vt* to photograph, take a photograph of.

fotógrafo,-a *nm & nf* photographer.

fotón *nm* photon.

fotosíntesis *nf inv* photosynthesis.

FP *abrev* EDUC **(Formación Profesional)** Professional Formation *(vocational training)*.

fracasar *vi* to fail, be unsuccessful, fall through.

fracaso *nm* failure.

fracción *nf* **1** *(gen)* fraction. **2** POL faction.

fraccionar *vt* to divide, break up, split up.

fractura *nf* fracture.

fragancia *nf* fragrance.

fragata *nf* frigate.

frágil *adj* **1** *(quebradizo)* fragile, breakable. **2** *(débil)* frail, weak.

fragilidad *nf* **1** *(cualidad)* fragility. **2** *(debilidad)* frailty, weakness.

fragmento *nm* **1** *(pedazo)* fragment, piece. **2** *(literario)* passage.

fragua *nf* forge.

fraguar *vt* **1** *(metal)* to forge. **2** *fig (plan)* to dream up, fabricate; *(conspiración)* to hatch.
▶ *vi (endurecerse)* to set, harden.

fraile *nm* friar, monk.

frambuesa *nf* raspberry.

francamente *adv* frankly.

francés,-esa *adj* French.
▶ *nm & nf (persona)* French person; *(hombre)* Frenchman; *(mujer)* Frenchwoman.
▶ *nm* **francés** *(idioma)* French.

Francia *nf* France.

franco,-a[1] *nm & nf* HIST *(persona)* Frank.
▶ *nm* **franco** HIST *(idioma)* Frankish; *(moneda)* franc.

franco,-a[2] *adj* **1** *(persona)* frank, open. **2** *(cosa)* clear, obvious. **3** COM free.

francotirador,-ra *nm & nf* sniper.

franela *nf* flannel.

franja *nf* **1** *(banda)* band, strip. **2** *(de tierra)* strip. **3** COST fringe, border.

franquear *vt* **1** *(dejar libre)* to free, clear. **2** *(atravesar)* to cross. **3** *(obstáculo)* to overcome. **4** *(carta)* to frank.

franqueo *nm* postage.

franqueza *nf* **1** *(sinceridad)* frankness, openness. **2** *(confianza)* familiarity, intimacy.

frasco *nm* flask.

frase *nf* **1** *(oración)* sentence. **2** *(expresión)* phrase. COMP **frase hecha** set phrase, set expression, idiom.

fraternal *adj* fraternal, brotherly.

fraternidad *nf* fraternity, brotherhood.

fraude *nm* fraud. COMP **fraude fiscal** tax evasion.

fray *nm* Brother.

frecuencia *nf* frequency. LOC **con frecuencia** frequently, often.

frecuentar *vt* to frequent, visit.

frecuente *adj* **1** *(repetido)* frequent. **2** *(usual)* common.

frecuentemente *adv* frequently, often.

fregadero *nm* kitchen sink.

fregar *vt* **1** *(lavar)* to wash. **2** *(el suelo)* to mop. LOC **fregar los platos** to wash the dishes, GB do the washing up, wash up.

fregona *nf (utensilio)* mop.

freidora *nf* fryer, deep fryer.

freír *vt* **1** *(guisar)* to fry. **2** *fig* to annoy, exasperate.

frenar *vt* **1** to brake. **2** *fig* to restrain, check.
▶ *vi* to brake: *frenó de golpe* he jammed on the brakes.

frenazo *nm* sudden braking. LOC **dar un frenazo** to jam on the brakes.

freno *nm* **1** *(de auto)* brake. **2** *fig (contención)* curb, check. LOC **poner freno a ALGO** *fig* to curb STH.

frente *nm* **1** *(gen)* front. **2** MIL front, front line.
▶ *nf* ANAT forehead. LOC **de frente 1** *(hacia adelante)* straight ahead. **2** *(sin rodeos)* straight. ▮ **ponerse al frente de ALGO** to take command of STH.

fresa *nf* **1** *(planta)* strawberry plant. **2** *(fruto)* strawberry.
▶ *adj* strawberry.

fresco,-a *adj* **1** *(temperatura)* cool, cold: *viento fresco* cool wind; *agua fresca* cold water. **2** *(tela, vestido)* light, cool. **3** *(comida)* fresh. **4** *(reciente)* fresh, new: *noticias frescas* latest news *sing*. **5** *(desvergonzado)* cheeky, shameless.
▶ *nm* **fresco 1** *(frescor)* fresh air, cool air. **2** ARTE fresco. LOC **al fresco** in the cool. ▮ **quedarse tan fresco,-a** not to

bat an eyelid. ▌ **tomar el fresco** to get some fresh air.

frescor *nm* coolness, freshness.

frescura *nf* **1** *(frescor)* freshness, coolness. **2** *(desvergüenza)* cheek, nerve. LOC **¡qué frescura!** what a nerve!

fresno *nm* ash tree.

frialdad *nf* **1** *(frío)* coldness. **2** *(indiferencia)* coldness, indifference.

fricativo,-a *adj* fricative.

fricción *nf* **1** *(roce)* friction. **2** *(desacuerdo)* friction, discord.

frigorífico *nm* **1** *(electrodoméstico)* refrigerator, fridge. **2** *(cámara frigorífica)* cold store.

frijol *nm* bean, kidney bean.

frío,-a *adj* **1** *(gen)* cold. **2** *(indiferente)* cold, cool, indifferent; *(pasmado)* stunned: *la película me dejó frío* the film left me cold.
▶ *nm* frío cold. LOC **coger a ALGN en frío** *fig* to catch SB on the hop. ▌ **hace un frío que pela** *fam* it's freezing cold. ▌ **hacer frío** to be cold. ▌ **tener frío / pasar frío** to be cold.

friolero,-a *adj* sensitive to the cold.

friso *nm* **1** ARQUIT frieze. **2** *(zócalo)* skirting board.

frito,-a *adj* **1** CULIN fried. **2** *fam* fed up, sick: *este niño me tiene frita* I'm sick and tired of this kid.
▶ *nm* frito piece of fried food. LOC **quedarse frito,-a** *fam (dormido)* to fall fast asleep.

frívolo,-a *adj* frivolous.

frondoso,-a *adj* leafy, luxuriant.

frontera *nf* **1** frontier, border. **2** *fig* limit, bounds *pl*, borderline.

frontón *nm* **1** *(juego)* pelota. **2** *(edificio)* pelota court. **3** ARQUIT pediment.

frotar *vt* to rub. LOC **frotarse las manos** to rub one's hands together.

fruncir *vt* COST to gather. LOC **fruncir el ceño** to frown, knit one's brow.

frustración *nf* frustration.

frustrar *vt* **1** *(cosa)* to frustrate, thwart. **2** *(persona)* to disappoint.

▶ *vpr* frustrarse **1** *(proyectos, planes)* to fail, come to nothing. **2** *(persona)* to get frustrated, get disappointed.

fruta *nf* fruit.

frutería *nf* fruit shop.

frutero,-a *nm & nf* fruit seller, fruiterer.
▶ *nm* frutero fruit dish, fruit bowl.

fruto *nm* **1** *(fruta)* fruit. **2** *(resultado)* fruit, result, product. LOC **dar fruto** to bear fruit. ▌ **sacar fruto de ALGO** to profit from STH. COMP **frutos secos 1** *(almendras, etc)* nuts. **2** *(pasas, etc)* dried fruit *sing*.

fucsia *nf* fuchsia.

fuego *nm* **1** fire. **2** *(lumbre)* light. **3** *(cocina)* burner, ring. LOC **a fuego lento 1** on a low flame. **2** *(al horno)* in a slow oven. ▌ **poner las manos en el fuego por ALGO/ALGN** to stake one's life on STH/SB. ▌ **prender fuego a ALGO** to set fire to STH. COMP **fuegos artificiales** fireworks.

fuel *nm* fuel oil.

fuelle *nm (aparato)* bellows *pl*.

fuente *nf* **1** *(manantial)* spring. **2** *(artificial)* fountain. **3** *(recipiente)* serving dish, dish. **4** *fig* source.

fuera *adv* **1** *(exterior)* out, outside: *salimos fuera* we went out, we went outside. **2** *(alejado)* away; *(en el extranjero)* abroad.
▶ *interj* get out!
▶ *prep* fuera de *(un lugar)* out of; *(más allá de)* outside, beyond; *(excepto)* except for, apart from. LOC **estar fuera de sí** to be beside os. ▌ **fuera de lo normal** extraordinary, very unusual. ▌ **fuera de serie** extraordinary. COMP **fuera de juego** offside.

fuerte *adj* **1** *(gen)* strong: *tiene un sabor fuerte* it has a strong taste. **2** *(en asignatura)* strong, good: *está muy fuerte en historia* she's very strong on history. **3** *(viento)* strong; *(lluvia, nevada)* heavy; *(tormenta, seísmo)* severe; *(calor)* intense. **4** *(dolor, enfermedad)* severe, bad. **5** *(golpe)* hard, heavy. **6** *(sonido)* loud. **7** *(subida)* steep, sharp; *(bajada)* sharp: *un fuerte descenso en el precio del petróleo* a sharp fall in the price of oil. **8** *(discusión)*

heated, violent; *(aplauso)* loud, thunderous. **9** *(comida - pesado)* heavy; *(- cargado)* rich. **10** *(color)* intense.
▶ *nm* **1** *(fortificación)* fort. **2** *(punto fuerte)* forte, strong point.
▶ *adv* **1** *(mucho)* a lot. **2** *(con fuerza)* hard: *empuja fuerte* push hard. **3** *(volumen)* loud: *la música sonaba fuerte* the music was loud.

fuerza *nf* **1** *(gen)* strength. **2** *(violencia)* force, violence. **3** *(militar)* force. **4** *(en física)* force. **5** *(electricidad)* power, electric power. **6** *(poder)* power. LOC **a fuerza de** by dint of, by force of. ▌ **a la fuerza** by force. ▌ **con fuerza 1** *(gen)* strongly. **2** *(llover)* heavily. **3** *(apretar, agarrar)* tightly; *(pegar, empujar)* hard. ▌ **por fuerza** by force. COMP **fuerza de voluntad** willpower.

fuga *nf* **1** *(huida)* flight, escape. **2** *(escape)* leak.

fugarse *vpr (gen)* to flee, escape; *(de casa)* to run away from home.

fugaz *adj* fleeting, brief.

fugitivo,-a *adj (en fuga)* fleeing.
▶ *nm & nf* fugitive, runaway.

fulano,-a *nm & nf* so-and-so; *(hombre)* what's his name; *(mujer)* what's her name.
▶ *nm* fulano *fam* pey guy, GB bloke.

fulminar *vt* **1** to strike with lightning. **2** *fig* to strike dead. LOC **fulminar a** ALGN **(con la mirada)** to look daggers at SB.

fumador,-ra *nm & nf* smoker. LOC **los no fumadores** nonsmokers.

fumar *vt* to smoke.

fumigar *vt* to fumigate.

funámbulo,-a *nm & nf* tightrope walker.

función *nf* **1** *(gen)* function. **2** *(cargo)* duty. **3** *(espectáculo)* performance, show. LOC **en función de** according to. ▌ **en funciones** acting. ▌ **entrar en función** *(persona)* to take up one's post. ▌ **estar en funciones** to be in office. COMP **función de noche** evening performance. ▌ **función de tarde** matinée.

funcional *adj* functional.

funcionamiento *nm* operation, working.

funcionar *vi (desempeñar una función)* to work, function: *funciona con gasolina/diesel* it runs on petrol/diesel.

funcionario,-a *nm & nf* functionary, employee. COMP **funcionario,-a público,-a** civil servant, government employee.

funda *nf* **1** *(flexible)* cover. **2** *(rígida)* case. **3** *(de disco)* sleeve. COMP **funda de almohada** pillowcase.

fundación *nf* foundation.

fundador,-ra *nm & nf* founder.

fundamental *adj* fundamental.

fundamentalismo *nm* fundamentalism.

fundamentalista *adj* fundamentalist.
▶ *nm o nf* fundamentalist.

fundamentalmente *adv* fundamentally, basically.

fundamento *nm* **1** *(base)* basis, grounds *pl*. **2** *(seriedad)* seriousness; *(confianza)* reliability. LOC **sin fundamento** unfounded.

fundar *vt* **1** *(crear)* to found; *(erigir)* to raise: *su padre fundó la empresa* her father founded the company. **2** *(basar)* to base, found.
▶ *vpr* **fundarse 1** *(crearse)* to be founded. **2** *(teoría, afirmación)* to be based *(en,* on); *(persona)* to base os *(en,* on).

fundición *nf* **1** *(derretimiento)* melting. **2** *(de metales)* smelting. **3** *(lugar)* foundry, smelting works.

fundir *vt* **1** *(derretir)* to melt: *el sol funde la nieve* the sun melts the snow. **2** *(separar mena y metal)* to smelt. **3** *(dar forma)* to cast: *fundir una figura en bronce* to cast a figure in bronze. **4** *(bombilla, plomos)* to blow.
▶ *vpr* **fundirse 1** *(derretirse)* to melt: *la nieve se funde* snow melts. **2** *(bombilla, plomos)* to fuse, go, blow, burn out: *se han fundido los plomos* the fuses have gone. **3** *(unirse)* to merge.

fúnebre *adj* **1** *(mortuorio)* funeral. **2** *(lúgubre)* mournful, lugubrious.

funeral *nm* [también se usa en plural con el mismo significado] **1** *(entierro)* funeral. **2** *(conmemoración)* memorial service.

funerala COMP ojo a la funerala *fam* black eye.

funeraria *nf* undertaker's, US funeral parlor.

funerario,-a *adj* funerary, funeral.

funesto,-a *adj* ill-fated, fatal.

fungicida *adj* fungicidal.
▶ *nm* fungicide.

funicular *nm* funicular, funicular railway.

furgón *nm* **1** AUTO van, truck. **2** *(de tren)* (goods) wagon, US boxcar. COMP **furgón de cola** guard's van.

furgoneta *nf* van.

furia *nf* fury, rage.

furibundo,-a *adj* furious, enraged.

furiosamente *adv* furiously.

furioso,-a *adj* **1** *(colérico)* furious. **2** *(tempestad, vendaval)* raging. LOC **ponerse furioso,-a** to get angry.

furor *nm* fury, rage. LOC **hacer furor** *fig* to be all the rage.

furtivamente *adv* furtively.

furtivo,-a *adj* furtive.

furúnculo *nm* boil.

fusa *nf* demisemiquaver, US thirty-second note.

fuseaux *nm* ski pants *pl*.

fuselaje *nm* fuselage.

fusible *nm* fuse.

fusil *nm* rifle, gun.

fusilamiento *nm* shooting, execution.

fusilar *vt* **1** *(ejecutar)* to shoot, execute. **2** *(plagiar)* to plagiarize.

fusión *nf* **1** *(de metales)* fusion, melting; *(de hielo)* thawing, melting. **2** *(de intereses, partidos, ideas)* fusion. **3** *(de empresas)* merger, amalgamation.

fusionar *vt* **1** *(fundir)* to fuse. **2** *(unir)* to join, unite. **3** COM to merge: **proponen fusionar ambas empresas** they propose to merge the two companies.
▶ *vpr* **fusionarse** *(unir)* to join, unite; *(empresas)* to merge.

fusta *nf* riding whip.

fuste *nm* **1** *(palo)* stick. **2** *(de columna)* shaft.

futbito *nm* five-a-side football.

fútbol *nm* football, soccer. COMP **fútbol americano** American football.

futbolín® *nm* table football.

futbolista *nm o nf* footballer, football player, soccer player.

futbolístico,-a *adj* football.

futón *nm* futon.

futurista *adj* futuristic.

futuro,-a *adj* future.
▶ *nm* **futuro** future. LOC **en un futuro próximo** in the near future. COMP **futuro imperfecto** future. ❙ **futuro perfecto** future perfect.

G

G, g *nf (la letra)* G, g.

g *sím* (gramo) gram, gramme; *(símbolo)* g.

gabán *nm* overcoat.

gabardina *nf (impermeable)* raincoat.

gabinete *nm* **1** *(habitación)* study. **2** POL cabinet. **3** *(despacho)* office.

Gabón *nm* Gabon.

gabonés,-esa *adj* Gabonese.
▶ *nm & nf* Gabonese.

gacela *nf* gazelle.

gacha *nf (masa)* paste.
▶ *nf pl* **gachas** *(papilla)* porridge *sing*.

gafas *nf pl* **1** spectacles, glasses. **2** *(de motorista, esquí, natación)* goggles. COMP **gafas de bucear** diving mask *sing*. ‖ **gafas de sol** sunglasses.

gafe *adj fam* jinx.
▶ *nm o nf fam* jinx.

gaita *nf* **1** bagpipes *pl*, pipes *pl*. **2** *fam* bother, drag, pain.

gaitero,-a *nm & nf* MÚS piper, bagpipe player.

gajo *nm (de fruta)* segment.

gala *nf* **1** *(espectáculo)* gala. **2** *(vestido)* best dress. LOC **hacer gala de** to make a show of. COMP **cena de gala** gala dinner.
▶ *nf pl* **galas** *(adorno)* finery *sing*. LOC **lucir sus mejores galas** to be dressed in all one's finery.

galáctico,-a *adj* galactic.

galán *nm (atractivo)* handsome young man; *(mujeriego)* ladies' man.

galardón *nm* prize.

galaxia *nf* galaxy.

galera *nf (mar)* galley.

galería *nf* **1** *(gen)* gallery. **2** *(corredor descubierto)* balcony, verandah. **3** TEAT gallery, balcony. COMP **galerías comerciales** shopping centre *sing*.

galés,-a *adj* Welsh.
▶ *nm & nf (persona)* Welsh person; *(hombre)* Welshman; *(mujer)* Welshwoman.
▶ *nm* **galés** *(idioma)* Welsh.

Gales *nm* Wales. COMP **País de Gales** Wales.

galgo,-a *nm & nf* greyhound.

galleta *nf* CULIN biscuit, US cookie.

gallina *nf* hen.
▶ *nm o nf fam* chicken, coward. LOC **jugar a la gallina ciega** to play blind man's buff.

gallinero *nm* **1** henhouse. **2** *fam* bedlam, madhouse. **3** **el gallinero** TEAT the gods *pl*.

gallo *nm* **1** cock, rooster. **2** *(pez)* John Dory. **3** *fig (al cantar)* false note; *(al hablar)* squeak. LOC **en menos que canta un gallo** in a flash.

galón¹ *nm* **1** *(cinta)* braid. **2** MIL stripe, chevron.

galón² *nm (medida)* gallon.

galopar *vi* to gallop.

galope *nm* gallop. LOC **a galope / al galope 1** at a gallop. **2** *fig* in a rush. ‖ **a galope tendido** at full gallop.

gama *nf* **1** MÚS scale. **2** *(gradación, variedad)* range.

gamba¹ *nf* ZOOL prawn; *(pequeña)* shrimp.

gamba² *nf argot (pierna)* leg. LOC **meter la gamba** *fam* to put one's foot in it.

gamberrada *nf* act of hooliganism.

gamberro,-a *adj* loutish, rowdy.
▶ *nm & nf* vandal, hooligan, lout.

Gambia *nf* Gambia.

gambiano,-a *adj* Gambian.
▶ *nm & nf* Gambian.

gamo *nm* fallow deer.

gamuza *nf* **1** ZOOL chamois. **2** *(piel)* chamois leather. **3** *(paño)* duster.

gana *nf* **1** *(deseo)* wish (de, for), desire. **2** *(apetito)* appetite; *(hambre)* hunger. [LOC] **dar a** ALGN **la gana de hacer** ALGO *fam* to feel like doing STH. ‖ **tener ganas de (hacer)** ALGO to feel like (doing) STH.

ganadería *nf* **1** *(crianza)* cattle raising, stockbreeding. **2** *(ganado)* cattle, livestock.

ganadero,-a *nm & nf* **1** *(propietario)* cattle breeder, stockbreeder. **2** *(cuidador de ganado)* herdsman, US herder.

ganado *nm* livestock, stock; *(vacas)* cattle. [COMP] **ganado bovino** cattle *pl*. ‖ **ganado vacuno** cattle *pl*.

ganador,-ra *adj* winning.
▶ *nm & nf* winner.

ganancia *nf* gain, profit.

ganar *vt* **1** *(partido, concurso, premio)* to win. **2** *(dinero)* to earn: *¿cuánto ganas al año?* how much do you earn a year? **3** *(alcanzar)* to reach. **4** *(lograr)* to win.
▶ *vi* **1** *(mejorar)* to improve. **2** *(cambiar favorablemente)* to gain.
▶ *vpr* **ganarse 1** *(dinero)* to earn. **2** *(ser merecedor)* to deserve: *se lo han ganado* they deserve it. [LOC] **ganar a** ALGN **en** ALGO to be better than SB at STH.

ganchillo *nm* **1** *(aguja)* crochet hook. **2** *(labor)* crochet work. [LOC] **hacer ganchillo** to crochet.

gancho *nm* **1** hook. **2** *(para ropa)* peg. **3** *fam (atractivo)* attractiveness, charm. *(en boxeo)* hook. **4** *(en baloncesto)* hook shot. [LOC] **tener gancho** *fam* to be attractive, have charm.

gandul,-la *adj* lazy, idle.
▶ *nm & nf* idler, loafer, lazybones.

gandulear *vi* to idle, loaf around.

ganga *nf (algo barato)* bargain, good buy. [COMP] **precio de ganga** bargain price.

gángster *nm* gangster.

gansada *nf fam* silly thing to say, silly thing to do.

ganso,-a *nm & nf* ZOOL goose; *(macho)* gander.

ganzúa *nf* **1** *(garfio)* picklock. **2** *(ladrón)* burglar.

garabatear *vt (escribir)* to scribble, scrawl; *(dibujar)* to doodle.

garabato *nm* **1** *(gancho)* hook. **2** *(dibujo)* doodle; *(escritura)* scrawl, scribble.

garaje *nm* garage.

garantía *nf* **1** *(seguridad)* guarantee, security. **2** COM guarantee, warranty.

garantizado,-a *adj* guaranteed.

garantizar *vt* **1** to guarantee. **2** COM to warrant.

garbanzo *nm* chickpea.

garbeo *nm fam* walk, stroll.

garbo *nm* **1** *(airosidad al andar)* gracefulness. **2** *(gracia)* grace, stylishness.

garboso,-a *adj (airoso)* graceful.

gardenia *nf* gardenia.

garfio *nm* hook, grapple.

garganta *nf* **1** *(cuello)* throat. **2** *(desfiladero)* gorge, narrow pass.

gargantilla *nf* short necklace.

gárgola *nf* gargoyle.

garita *nf* **1** *(caseta)* box, cabin, hut; *(de centinela)* sentry box. **2** *(portería)* porter's lodge.

garito *nm* **1** *(casa de juego)* gambling dene. **2** *(antro de diversión)* dive, joint.

garra *nf (de mamífero)* paw, claw; *(de ave)* talon.
▶ *nf pl* **garras** *(poder)* clutches. [LOC] **caer en las garras de** ALGN *fig* to fall into SB's clutches. ‖ **tener garra 1** *(relato, etc)* to be compelling. **2** *(persona)* to have charisma.

garrafa *nf* carafe.

garrafal *adj* monumental, huge.

garrafón *nm* demijohn, large carafe.

garrapata *nf* tick.

garrotazo *nm* blow with a stick.

garrote *nm* thick stick, cudgel, club.

garza *nf* heron. [COMP] **garza real** grey heron.

gas *nm (gen)* gas.

G

► *nm pl* **gases** *(flatulencias)* wind *sing*, flatulence *sing*, US gas *sing*.

gasa *nf* gauze.

gaseosa *nf* GB lemonade, US soda.

gasóleo *nm* diesel oil.

gasolina *nf* petrol, US gasoline, gas. LOC **poner gasolina** to get some petrol.

gasolinera *nf* **1** petrol station, US gas station. **2** *(lancha)* motorboat.

gastado,-a *adj* **1** *(desgastado)* worn-out. **2** *(acabado)* finished, empty, used up.

gastador,-ra *adj (derrochador)* spend-thrift.

gastar *vt* **1** *(consumir dinero, tiempo)* to spend; *(gasolina, electricidad)* to use (up), consume: *este coche gasta mucha gasolina* this car uses a lot of petrol. **2** *(malgastar)* to waste. **3** *(usar perfume, jabón)* to use; *(ropa)* to wear.
► *vpr* **gastarse 1** *(desgastarse)* to wear out. **2** *(consumirse)* to run out.

gasto *nm* expenditure, expense. COMP **gastos de mantenimiento** running costs, maintenance costs. ‖ **gastos diarios** daily expenses.

gastronomía *nf* gastronomy.

gastronómico,-a *adj* gastronomic, gastronomical.

gata *nf* she-cat, cat.

✎ Véase también **gato**.

gatas LOC **a gatas** on all fours. ‖ **andar a gatas** to crawl.

gatear *vi (andar a gatas)* to crawl.

gatera *nf* cat door, cat flap.

gatillo *nm* trigger.

gatito,-a *nm & nf fam* kitty, pusy.

gato *nm* **1** cat, tomcat. **2** *(de coche)* jack. LOC **buscarle tres/cinco pies al gato** *fam* to split hairs, complicate things. ‖ **dar gato por liebre** *fam* to take SB in, con SB. ‖ **hay gato encerrado** *fam* there's something fishy going on.

gatuno,-a *adj* catlike, feline.

gavilán *nm* sparrowhawk.

gavilla *nf (de ramas, etc)* sheaf.

gaviota *nf* seagull, gull.

gay *adj* gay, homosexual.
► *nm* gay, homosexual.

gaznate *nm* gullet.

gazpacho *nm* cold soup made of tomatoes and other vegetables.

ge *nf* name of the letter g.

gel *nm* gel.

gelatina *nf* **1** *(sustancia)* gelatine. **2** *(preparado alimenticio)* jelly.

gelatinoso,-a *adj* gelatinous, jelly-like.

gélido,-a *adj* icy, icy cold.

gema *nf* **1** BOT bud. **2** *(piedra)* gem.

gemelo,-a *adj* twin.
► *nm & nf* twin.
► *nm* **gemelo** *(músculo)* calf muscle.
► *nm pl* **gemelos 1** *(botones)* cufflinks. **2** *(anteojos)* binoculars.

gemido *nm (quejido)* groan, moan.

gemir *vi (quejarse)* to moan, groan.

gen *nm* gene.

genciana *nf* gentian.

generación *nf* generation.

generacional *adj* generation, generational.

generador,-ra *nm (máquina)* generator.

general *adj* **1** general. **2** *(común)* common, usual, widespread.
► *nm (oficial)* general. LOC **en general** in general, generally.

generalidad *nf* **1** *(gen)* generality. **2** *(mayoría)* majority. **3** *(generalización)* general statement.
► *nf pl* **generalidades** *(nociones)* basic knowledge *sing*.

generalización *nf* **1** *(gen)* generalization. **2** *(extensión)* spread, spreading.

generalizado,-a *adj* widespread, common.

generalizar *vt* **1** *(gen)* to generalize. **2** *(extender)* to spread, popularize.
► *vpr* **generalizarse** to spread, become widespread, become common.

generalmente *adv* usually.

generar *vt* to generate.

genéricamente *adv* generically.

genérico,-a *adj* generic.

género nm **1** (clase) kind, sort. **2** (tela) cloth. **3** (mercancía) article. **4** GRAM gender. **5** BIOL genus.

generosamente adv generously.

generosidad nf generosity, unselfishness.

generoso,-a adj generous (con/para, to).

génesis nf inv genesis.

genética nf genetics sing.

genial adj **1** brilliant, inspired. **2** fam terrific, great, smashing.
 ▸ adv fam great.

genialidad nf **1** (idea) brilliant idea, stroke of genius. **2** (cualidad) genius.

genio nm **1** (carácter) temper, disposition. **2** (facultad) genius: Einstein fue un genio Einstein was a genius. **3** (espíritu) spirit: el genio del Renacimiento the Renaissance spirit. LOC **estar de mal genio** to be in a bad mood. ‖ **tener mal genio** to have a bad temper.

genital adj genital.
 ▸ nm pl **genitales** genitals.

genocidio nm genocide.

gente nf **1** people pl. **2** (familia) family, folks pl, people pl: me gusta estar con mi gente I like being with my family. COMP **gente menuda** fam nippers pl, kids pl.

gentil adj (amable) kind.

gentileza nf **1** (gracia) grace, elegance. **2** (cortesía) politeness, kindness.

gentilicio adj gentile.
 ▸ nm gentile.

gentío nm crowd.

gentuza nf pey mob, rabble, riffraff.

genuino,-a adj genuine, authentic.

geografía nf geography.

geógrafo,-a nm & nf geographer.

geología nf geology.

geológico,-a adj geologic, geological.

geólogo,-a nm & nf geologist.

geometría nf geometry.

geométrico,-a adj geometric, geometrical.

Georgia nf Georgia.

georgiano,-a adj Georgian.
 ▸ nm & nf (persona) Georgian.
 ▸ nm **georgiano** (idioma) Georgian.

geranio nf geranium.

gerencia nf (actividad) management.

gerente nm o nf (hombre) manager; (mujer) manageress.

geriatría nf geriatrics sing.

geriátrico,-a adj geriatric.
 ▸ nm **geriátrico** (sanatorio) geriatric hospital; (residencia) old people's home.

germano,-a adj Germanic.

germen nm germ.

germinar vi to germinate.

gerundio nm gerund.

gesta nf arc heroic deed, exploit.

gestación nf **1** gestation. **2** (período) gestation period.

gestante adj gestating.
 ▸ nf expectant mother.

gesticular vi to gesticulate.

gestión nf [también se usa en plural con el mismo significado] (trámite) step, measure, move. COMP **gestión de datos** data management.

gestionar vt **1** (negociar) to negotiate. **2** (administrar) to manage, run.

gesto nm **1** (movimiento) gesture. **2** (mueca) grimace. LOC **hacer gestos a** fam to make gestures at.

gestor,-ra nm & nf **1** (administrador) manager, director. **2** person who transacts official business on his clients' behalf, ≈ solicitor.

Ghana nf Ghana.

ghanés,-a adj Ghanaian.
 ▸ nm & nf Ghanaian.

giba nf hump, hunch.

giga nf (gigabyte) giga, gigabyte.

gigabyte nm gigabyte.

gigante nm & nf (hombre) giant; (mujer) giantess.
 ▸ adj giant, gigantic, huge.

gigantesco,-a adj giant, gigantic.

gimnasia nf gymnastics sing.

gimnasio nm gymnasium, gym.

gincana nf gymkhana.

G

ginebra *nf* gin.

ginecología *nf* gynaecology.

ginecólogo,-a *nm & nf* gynaecologist.

gineta *nf* genet.

gira *nf* tour.

girar *vi* **1** *(dar vueltas)* to rotate, whirl, spin. **2** *(torcer)* to turn: *girar a la izquierda* to turn left. **3** *fig (versar)* to deal with: *la conversación giró en torno al teatro* the conversation evolved around theatre.
▶ *vt* **1** COM to issue: *girar una letra* to issue a draft. **2** *(cambiar de sentido)* to turn, turn around: *girar el cuerpo* to turn one's body.

girasol *nm* sunflower.

giratorio,-a *adj* rotating, gyratory.

giro *nm* **1** *(vuelta)* turn, turning. **2** *(dirección)* course, direction. **3** COM draft. COMP **giro postal** money order.

gitano,-a *nm & nf* gypsy, gipsy.

glaciación *nf* glaciation.

glacial *adj* **1** glacial. **2** *fig* glacial, icy: *tuvo un recibimiento glacial* he had an icy reception.

glaciar *nm* glacier.

gladiador *nm* gladiator.

gladiolo *nm* gladiolus.

glándula *nf* gland.

glicerina *nf* glycerin, glycerine.

global *adj* global, comprehensive.

globo *nm* **1** *(esfera)* globe, sphere. **2** *(tierra)* globe. **3** *(de aire)* balloon.

glóbulo *nm* globule. COMP **glóbulo blanco** white corpuscle. ❙ **glóbulo rojo** red corpuscle.

gloria *nf* **1** *(bienaventuranza)* glory. **2** *(fama)* fame, honour (US honor).

glorieta *nf* **1** *(en un jardín)* arbour. **2** *(plazoleta)* small square.

glorificar *vt* to glorify.

glorioso,-a *adj* glorious.

glosar *vt* **1** *(explicar)* to gloss. **2** *(interpretar)* to interpret.

glosario *nm* glossary.

glotón,-ona *adj* greedy, gluttonous.
▶ *nm & nf* glutton.

glotonería *nf* gluttony, greed.

glúcido *nm* glucide.

glucosa *nf* glucose.

gluten *nm* gluten.

gnomo *nm* gnome.

gobernador,-ra *nm & nf* governor.

gobernante *adj* ruling, governing.
▶ *nm o nf* ruler, leader.

gobernar *vt* **1** *(gen)* to govern. **2** *(un país)* to rule. **3** *(un negocio)* to run, handle. **4** *(un barco)* to steer.

gobierno *nm* **1** POL government. **2** *(mando)* command, running, handling. **3** *(conducción)* direction, control; *(de un barco)* steering; *(de timón)* rudder.

goce *nm* pleasure, enjoyment.

godo,-a *adj* Gothic.
▶ *nm & nf (persona)* Goth.

gofre *nm* waffle.

gol *nm* goal.

goleador,-ra *nm & nf* scorer. COMP **el máximo goleador** the top scorer.

golear *vt* to hammer.

golf *nm (deporte)* golf.

golfista *nm o nf* golfer.

golfo *nm* gulf, large bay.

golfo,-a *nm & nf (holgazán)* good-for-nothing; *(niño)* rascal, little devil.

golondrina *nf (ave)* swallow.

golosina *nf* sweet, US candy.

goloso,-a *adj* sweet-toothed.

golpe *nm* **1** blow, knock; *(puñetazo)* punch: *le dio un golpe* he hit him. **2** *(de coche)* collision; *(fuerte)* bang; *(ligero)* bump. **3** *fig (desgracia)* blow, misfortune. LOC **de golpe** suddenly, all of a sudden. ❙ **no dar golpe** *fam* not to lift a finger, not do a blessed thing. COMP **golpe bajo** *fig* punch below the belt. ❙ **golpe de Estado** coup, coup d'état. ❙ **golpe de vista** quick glance.

golpear *vt (gen)* to hit, strike; *(personas)* to thump, hit, punch; *(puerta)* to knock on.

golpista *nm o nf* person involved in a coup d'état.

goma *nf* **1** *(material)* gum, rubber. **2** *(de borrar)* rubber, US eraser. **3** *(de pegar)* glue, gum. **4** *(banda elástica)* rubber band. COMP **goma arábiga** gum arabic. ❙ **goma de mascar** chewing gum.

gomaespuma *nf* foam rubber.
gomina *nf* hair cream.
gominola *nf* jelly bean, jelly.
gong *nm* gong.
gordo,-a *adj* **1** *(carnoso)* fat: *se puso gordo* he got fat. **2** *(grueso)* thick. **3** *(grave)* serious. **4** *(importante)* big: *¡qué mentira tan gorda!* what a big lie!
▶ *nm & nf* fat person, fatty.
▶ *nm* **gordo 1** *fam (grasa)* fat. **2 el gordo** the first prize *in the lottery*.
gordura *nf* fatness.
gorila *nm (animal)* gorilla.
gorjear *vi* to chirp, twitter.
gorra *nf* **1** *(gen)* cap. **2** *(con visera)* peaked cap. LOC **de gorra** *fam* free.
gorrión,-ona *nm & nf* sparrow.
gorro *nm* **1** cap. **2** *(de bebé)* bonnet. **3** *(de cocinero)* chef's hat.
gorrón,-ona *adj fam* scrounging, sponging.
▶ *nm & nf* sponger, scrounger.
gorronear *vi* to scrounge.
gota *nf* **1** drop. **2** *(de sudor)* bead. **3** *(de aire)* breath. LOC **caer cuatro gotas** to be spitting with rain. ‖ **gota a gota** drop by drop. ‖ **ni gota** not a bit, nothing at all. COMP **gota fría** cold air pool.
gotear *vi* **1** *(grifo)* to drip; *(tejado)* to leak. **2** [sólo se usa en tercera persona; no lleva sujeto] *(lluvia)* to drizzle.
gotera *nf* **1** *(agujero)* leak. **2** *(agua)* drip.
gótico,-a *adj* Gothic.
gozar *vi* **1** *(poseer, disfrutar)* to enjoy (de, -): *goza de muy buena salud* he enjoys very good health. **2** *(sentir placer)* to enjoy os: *gozamos con su presencia* we really enjoy her company.
gozne *nm* hinge.
gozo *nm* joy, delight, pleasure.
grabación *nf* recording.
grabado,-a *nm* **1** *(arte)* engraving. **2** *(dibujo)* picture, drawing.
grabar *vt* **1** ARTE to engrave. **2** *(registrar)* to record. **3** INFORM to save. LOC **grabarse en la memoria** *fig* to be engraved on one's memory.

gracia *nf* **1** *(favor)* favour (US favor). **2** *(atractivo)* grace, charm. **3** *(chiste)* joke. LOC **hacer gracia, tener gracia** *(diversión)* to be funny. ‖ **¡qué gracia!** how funny!
▶ *nf pl* **gracias** thank you, thanks. LOC **dar gracias a** ALGN to thank SB. ‖ **gracias a** thanks to.
gracioso,-a *adj* **1** *(atractivo)* graceful, charming. **2** *(bromista)* witty, facetious. **3** *(divertido)* funny, amusing.
▶ *nm & nf* TEAT jester, clown, fool. LOC **hacerse el gracioso** to try to be funny.
grada *nf* **1** *(peldaño)* step, stair. **2** *(gradería)* tier.
▶ *nf pl* **gradas** stands, terraces.
gradería *nf* stands *pl*, terraces *pl*.
grado *nm* **1** *(gen)* degree: *estábamos a 27 grados* it was 27 degrees. **2** *(estado)* stage. **3** EDUC *(curso)* class, year. **4** EDUC *(título)* degree. **5** *(peldaño)* step.
graduación *nf* **1** *(gen)* graduation. **2** *(de alcohol)* strength. **3** EDUC graduation.
graduado,-a *nm & nf* EDUC graduate. COMP **gafas graduadas** prescription glasses. ‖ **graduado escolar** *certificate of elementary school studies*.
gradual *adj* gradual.
graduar *vt* **1** *(termómetro)* to graduate, calibrate. **2** *(regular)* to adjust, regulate. **3** *(conceder un diploma)* to confer a degree on, US graduate. **4** *(medir)* to gauge, measure; *(la vista)* to test, check.
▶ *vpr* **graduarse** to graduate, get one's degree. LOC **graduarse la vista** to have one's eyes tested.
grafía *nf* **1** *(signo)* graphic symbol. **2** *(escritura)* writing. **3** *(ortografía)* spelling.
gráficamente *adv* graphically.
grafía *nf* graph, diagram.
gráfico,-a *adj* graphic.
▶ *nm* **gráfico** *(dibujo)* sketch, chart.
grafiti *nm pl* graffiti.
grafito *nm* graphite.
gragea *nf* pill, tablet.
grajo,-a *nm & nf* rook.

G

gramática *nf* grammar.

gramo *nm* gram, gramme.

gramófono *nm* gramophone.

gramola® *nf* gramophone.

gran *adj* [se usa delante de nombres masculinos en singular] **1** *(fuerte, intenso)* great: *se llevaron un gran susto* they were terribly shocked. **2** *(excelente)* great: *aquél era un gran libro* that was a great book.

✎ Consulta también **grande**.

granada *nf* BOT pomegranate.

granate *adj* maroon, claret.
▶ *nm* **1** *(color)* maroon, claret. **2** *(mineral)* garnet.

grande *adj* **1** *(tamaño)* large, big. **2** *(fuerte, intenso)* great: *su partida les produjo una pena muy grande* his departure caused them great sorrow. **3** *(mayor)* grown-up, old, big.
▶ *nm (de elevada jerarquía)* great. LOC **a lo grande** on a grand scale, in a big way. ❙ **estar grande una cosa a ALGN** to be too big on SB. ❙ **pasarlo en grande** *fam* to have a great time.

✎ Consulta también **gran**.

grandeza *nf* **1** *(tamaño)* size. **2** *(generosidad)* generosity.

grandioso,-a *adj* grandiose, grand, magnificent.

granel LOC **a granel 1** *(sin envase)* in bulk. **2** *(en abundancia)* lots of.

granero *nm* granary, barn.

granito *nm* granite.

granizada *nf* **1** hailstorm. **2** *fig (lluvia)* hail, shower.

granizado,-a *nm* iced drink.

granizar *vi* [sólo se usa en tercera persona; no lleva sujeto] to hail.

granizo *nm* hail, hailstone.

granja *nf* farm.

granjero,-a *nm & nf* farmer.

grano *nm* **1** grain; *(de café)* bean. **2** MED pimple, spot. LOC **ir al grano** *fam* to come to the point, get to the point.
▶ *nm pl* **granos** cereals.

granuja *nm* **1** *(pilluelo)* ragamuffin, urchin. **2** *(estafador)* crook, trickster.

granulado,-a *adj* granulated.

granuloso,-a *adj* **1** *(superficie)* granular. **2** *(piel)* pimply.

grapa *nf (para papel)* staple.

grapadora *nf* stapler.

grapar *vt* to staple.

grasa *nf* grease, fat.

grasiento,-a *adj* greasy, oily.

graso,-a *adj* greasy, oily, fatty.

gratamente *adv* pleasantly.

gratén *nm* gratin.

gratificación *nf* **1** *(satisfacción)* gratification. **2** *(recompensa)* reward.

gratificador,-ra *adj* gratifying, rewarding.

gratificante *adj* gratifying, rewarding.

gratificar *vt* **1** *(satisfacer)* to gratify. **2** *(recompensar)* to reward, tip.

gratinador *nm* grill.

gratinar *vt* to brown under the grill.

gratis *adv* free.

gratitud *nf* gratitude.

grato,-a *adj* pleasant, pleasing (para, to).

gratuidad *nf* gratuitousness.

gratuitamente *adv (de balde)* free of charge, free.

gratuito,-a *adj (de balde)* free.

grava *nf* **1** *(guijas)* gravel. **2** *(piedra machacada)* crushed stone.

gravable *adj* taxable.

gravar *vt* to tax.

grave *adj* **1** *(pesado)* heavy. **2** *(serio)* grave, serious. **3** *(voz, nota)* deep, low. LOC **estar grave** to be seriously ill.

gravedad *nf* **1** FÍS gravity. **2** *(importancia)* gravity, seriousness.

gravemente *adv* **1** *(seriamente)* seriously. **2** *(solemnemente)* solemnly, gravely.

gravilla *nf* fine gravel.

gravitar *vi* **1** FÍS to gravitate. **2** *(apoyarse en)* to rest (sobre, on).

graznar *vi* **1** *(cuervo)* to caw, croak. **2** *(oca)* to honk. **3** *(pato)* to quack.

graznido *nm* **1** *(de cuervo)* caw, croak. **2** *(de oca)* honk. **3** *(de pato)* quack.

greca *nf* fret, fretwork.

Grecia *nf* Greece.

greda *nf* fuller's earth, clay.

gregario,-a *adj* gregarious.

gremial *adj* **1** trade union, union. **2** HIST guild.

gremio *nm* **1** HIST guild, corporation. **2** *(sindicato)* union. **3** *(profesión)* profession.

greña *nf* lock of entangled hair.
▶ *nf pl* **greñas** untidy mop of hair.

gres *nm* stoneware.

gresca *nf* **1** *(bulla)* racket. **2** *(riña)* row.

griego,-a *adj* Greek.
▶ *nm & nf (persona)* Greek.
▶ *nm* **griego** *(idioma)* Greek.

grieta *nf* crack, crevice.

grifería *nf* taps *pl*, US faucets *pl*.

grifo *nm (llave)* tap, US faucet.

grill *nm* grill.

grillete *nm* shackle.

grillo *nm* ZOOL cricket.

grima *nf* displeasure, disgust.

gripal *adj* related to flu.

gripe *nf* flu, influenza. LOC **tener la gripe** to have (the) flu.

griposo,-a *adj* flu. LOC **estar griposo** to have (the) flu.

gris *adj* **1** grey (US gray). **2** *fig (mediocre)* mediocre, third-rate. **3** *fig (triste)* grey (US gray), gloomy.
▶ *nm (color)* grey (US gray).

grisáceo,-a *adj* greyish.

gritar *vi (gen)* to shout; *(chillar)* cry out, scream: ¡no me grites! don't shout at me!

griterío *nm* shouting, uproar.

grito *nm* shout; *(chillido)* cry, scream. LOC **a grito limpio** at the top of one's voice. ▌ **dar un grito 1** to shout. **2** *(chillar)* to scream. ▌ **el último grito** *fig* the latest thing, the last word. ▌ **pedir** ALGO **a gritos** *fig* to be crying out for STH, be badly in need of STH. ▌ **pegar un grito 1** to shout. **2** *(chillar)* to scream.

gritón,-ona *adj* noisy, loudmouthed.
▶ *nm & nf* loudmouth.

grogui *adj* **1** DEP punch-drunk, groggy. **2** *fig* groggy, half-asleep.

grosella *nf* redcurrant.

grosellero *nm* redcurrant bush.

groseramente *adv* crudely, rudely.

grosería *nf* **1** *(ordinariez)* rude word, rude expression. **2** *(rusticidad)* rudeness, coarseness. LOC **decir una grosería** to say something rude.

grosero,-a *adj* **1** *(tosco)* coarse, crude. **2** *(maleducado)* rude.
▶ *nm & nf* rude person.

grosor *nm* thickness.

grotesco,-a *adj* ridiculous.

grúa *nf* **1** *(construcción)* crane, derrick. **2** AUTO breakdown van, US tow truck.

gruesa *nf (doce docenas)* gross.

grueso,-a *adj* **1** *(objeto)* thick. **2** *(persona)* fat, stout.
▶ *nm* **grueso 1** *(grosor)* thickness. **2** *(parte principal)* bulk.

grulla *nf* crane.

grumete *nm* cabin boy.

grumo *nm* lump; *(de sangre)* clot; *(de leche)* curd.

grumoso,-a *adj* lumpy, clotted.

gruñido *nm* grunt, growl.

gruñir *vi* to grunt.

gruñón,-ona *adj* grumbling, grumpy.

grupa *nf* croup, hindquarters *pl*.

grupo *nm* **1** group. **2** TÉC unit, set. COMP **grupo electrógeno** power plant. ▌ **grupo sanguíneo** blood group.

gruta *nf* cavern, grotto, cave.

gua *nm* **1** *(juego)* marbles *pl*. **2** *(hoyo)* hole for the marbles.

guacamayo *nm* macaw.

guache *nm* gouache.

guadaña *nf* scythe.

guantada *nf* slap.

guantazo *nm* slap.

guante *nm* glove. LOC **echar el guante a** ALGO *fam* to nick STH.

guantera *nf* glove compartment.

guaperas *adj inv fam* good-looking.
▶ *nm o nf* good looker, looker.

guapetón,-ona *adj fam* good-looking.

guapo,-a *adj* **1** good-looking; *(hombre)* handsome; *(mujer)* beautiful, pretty. **2** *argot (bonito)* nice, smart.

guapote,-a *adj fam* good-looking.

guapura *nf fam* good looks *pl*.

guarda *nm o nf (persona)* guard, keeper. ▸ *nf (custodia)* custody, care. **2** *(de la ley, etc)* observance. **3** *(de libro)* flyleaf.

guardabarrera *nm o nf* gatekeeper.

guardabarros *nm inv* mudguard, US fender.

guardabosque *nm* forester.

guardacoches *nm o nf inv* parking attendant.

guardacostas *nm o nf inv (persona)* coastguard. ▸ *nm* coastguard vessel.

guardaespaldas *nm o nf inv* bodyguard.

guardafrenos *nm o nf inv* guard.

guardagujas *nm o nf inv (hombre)* pointsman, US switchman; *(mujer)* pointswoman, US switchwoman.

guardameta *nm o nf* goalkeeper.

guardamuebles *nm inv* furniture warehouse.

guardapolvo *nm* **1** *(cubierta)* dust cover. **2** *(mono)* overalls *pl*.

guardar *vt* **1** *(cuidar)* to keep, watch over, keep an eye on. **2** *(conservar)* to keep, hold. **3** *(la ley)* to observe, obey; *(un secreto)* to keep. **4** *(poner en un sitio)* to put away: *guárdatelo en el bolsillo* put it in your pocket. **5** *(reservar)* to save, keep: *le guardaron el mejor sitio* they saved the best seat for him. **6** INFORM to save. **7** **guardarse de** *(precaverse, evitar)* to guard against, avoid, be careful not to. LOC **guardar las formas** to be polite.

guardarropa *nm* **1** *(armario)* wardrobe. **2** *(cuarto)* cloakroom.

guardarropía *nf* wardrobe for props.

guardavía *nm (hombre)* signalman.

guardería *nf* **1** crèche, nursery. **2** *(oficio de guarda)* keeping. COMP **guardería infantil** nursery, nursery school.

guardia *nf* **1** *(vigilancia)* watch, lookout. **2** *(servicio)* duty, call. ▸ *nm o nf (hombre)* policeman; *(mujer)* policewoman. LOC **estar de guardia 1** *(doctor)* to be on duty, be on call. **2** *(soldado)* to be on guard duty. **3** *(marino)* to be on watch. COMP **farmacia de guardia** duty chemist's. ▮ **médico de guardia** doctor on duty.

guardián,-ana *nm & nf* guardian, keeper, custodian.

guarecer *vt* to take shelter (de, from), shelter (de, from).

guarida *nf* ZOOL haunt, den, lair.

guarnecer *vt* **1** *(decorar)* to adorn, decorate; *(en cocina)* to garnish. **2** *(proveer)* to provide (de, with).

guarnición *nf* **1** *(gen)* decoration, trimmings *pl*. **2** CULIN *accompaniment to a main dish*. **3** MIL garrison.

guarrada *nf* **1** *fam* something dirty, disgusting thing: *¡no hagas guarradas!* don't do such filthy things! **2** *fam (mala pasada)* dirty trick.

guarro,-a *adj* dirty, filthy. ▸ *nm & nf* pig, dirty pig.

guasa *nf* jest, fun, mockery. LOC **estar de guasa** to be joking.

guasón,-ona *adj* funny, joking. ▸ *nm & nf* jester, joker.

guata *nf* **1** *(algodón)* raw cotton. **2** *(relleno)* padding.

guateado,-a *adj* padded, quilted.

Guatemala *nf* Guatemala.

guatemalteco,-a *adj* Guatemalan. ▸ *nm & nf* Guatemalan.

guateque *nm* party.

guay *adj fam* great, cool.

gubernamental *adj* government, governmental.

gubernativo,-a *adj* government, governmental.

gubia *nf* gouge.

guepardo *nm* cheetah.

guerra *nf* war. LOC **dar guerra** *fam* to cause trouble. ▮ **declarar la guerra a** to declare war on. COMP **guerra civil** civil war. ▮ **guerra fría** cold war. ▮ **guerra mundial** world war.

guerrear *vi* to war.

guerrera *nf (chaqueta)* army jacket.

guerrero,-a *adj* **1** warlike. **2** *fam (niño)* difficult. ▸ *nm & nf* warrior, soldier.

guerrilla *nf* **1** *(guerra)* guerrilla warfare. **2** *(banda)* guerrilla band.

guerrillero,-a *nm & nf* guerrilla.

gueto *nm* ghetto.

guía *nm o nf (persona)* guide, leader.
▶ *nf* **1** *(norma)* guidance, guideline. **2** *(libro)* guidebook. COMP **guía de teléfonos** telephone directory, phone book.

guiar *vt* **1** to guide, lead. **2** *(conducir automóvil)* to drive; *(barco)* to steer; *(avión)* to pilot; *(caballo, bici)* to ride.
▶ *vpr* **guiarse** to be guided.

guijarro *nm* pebble, stone.

guillotina *nf* guillotine.

guillotinar *vt* to guillotine.

guinda *nf* **1** *(fruta)* sour cherry, morello cherry. **2** *(remate)* final touch.

guindilla *nf* **1** red pepper, chilli. **2** *fam (policía)* cop.

guindo *nm* morello cherry tree. LOC **caerse** ALGN **del guindo** *fam* to cotton on, twig.

guinea *nf* guinea.

Guinea *nf* Guinea. COMP **Guinea Ecuatorial** Equatorial Guinea. ‖ **Guinea-Bissau** Guinea-Bissau. ‖ **Nueva Guinea** New Guinea.

guineano,-a *adj* Guinean.
▶ *nm & nf* Guinean.

guiñapo *nm* **1** *(andrajo)* rag, tatter. **2** *fig (persona)* wreck.

guiñar *vt* **1** to wink: *me guiñó un ojo* he winked at me. **2** MAR to yaw.

guiño *nm* wink.

guiñol *nm* puppet theatre.

guion *nm* **1** *(esquema)* notes *pl*, sketch, outline. **2** GRAM hyphen, dash. **3** CINE script.

guionista *nm o nf* scriptwriter.

guirigay *nm* **1** *(lenguaje)* gibberish. **2** *(griterío)* racket, noise, din.

guirlache *nm* almond brittle.

guirnalda *nf* garland, wreath.

guisa *nf* manner, way.

guisado,-a *adj* cooked, stewed.
▶ *nm* **guisado** stew.

guisante *nm* pea.

guisar *vt* to cook, stew.
▶ *vpr* **guisarse** to cook, stew.

guiso *nm* stew.

guitarra *nf* guitar.

guitarrero,-a *nm & nf* **1** *(vendedor)* guitar seller. **2** *(fabricante)* guitar maker.

guitarrista *nm o nf* guitarist.

gula *nf* gluttony.

gurú *nm* guru.

gusanillo *nm* **1** little worm. **2** *(espiral)* spiral binding. **3** *(intranquilidad)* niggling doubt. LOC **matar el gusanillo** *fam* to have a snack.

gusano *nm* **1** worm; *(oruga)* caterpillar. **2** *fig (persona)* worm. COMP **gusano de seda** silkworm.

gustar *vt* **1** *(agradar)* to like. **2** *(probar)* to taste, try.

gustativo,-a *adj* gustative. COMP **papila gustativa** taste bud.

gustillo *nm* **1** *fam (regusto)* aftertaste. **2** *fam (satisfacción)* satisfaction, pleasure.

gusto *nm* **1** *(sentido, sabor)* taste. **2** *(inclinación)* liking, taste. **3** *(placer)* pleasure: *tengo el gusto de presentarle a mi hermano* may I introduce you to my brother? **4** *(capricho)* whim, fancy. LOC **con mucho gusto** with pleasure. ‖ **dar gusto** to please, delight: *me da gusto verla comer* I enjoy watching her eat. ‖ **estar a gusto** to feel comfortable, feel at ease. ‖ **hacer** ALGO **a gusto** to enjoy doing STH. ‖ **hacer** ALGO **por gusto** to do STH for fun. ‖ **¡qué gusto!** how lovely! ‖ **tanto gusto** pleased to meet you. ‖ **tener buen gusto** to have good taste.

gustosamente *adv* with pleasure, gladly, willingly.

gustoso,-a *adj* **1** *(sabroso)* tasty, savoury, palatable. **2** *(agradable)* agreeable, pleasant. **3** *(con gusto)* glad, willing, ready: *aceptó gustosa* she accepted willingly.

gutural *adj* guttural.

Guyana *nf* Guyana.

guyanés,-esa *adj* Guyanese.
▶ *nm & nf* Guyanese.

G

H

H, h *nf (la letra)* H, h.

haba *nf (legumbre)* broad bean.

haber *vi (impersonal)* to be: *hay un coche* there's a car.
▶ *aux* **1** *(en tiempos compuestos)* to have: *lo has hecho* you have done it. **2** **haber de + *inf*** *(obligación)* to have to, must, should: *han de venir hoy* they must come today. **3** **haber que + *inf*** *(obligación)* must, have to: *habrá que hacerlo* we'll have to do it. LOC **¡haberlo dicho!** why didn't you say so! ▮ **había una vez...** once upon a time there was... ▮ **¡habráse visto!** what a cheek! ▮ **¡hay que ver!** well, really!, well, I never! ▮ **no hay de qué** you're welcome, don't mention it. ▮ **no hay (nada) como...** there's nothing like... ▮ **¿qué hay?** hello!, hi!, how are you doing?
▶ *nm* COM credit, assets *pl*.
▶ *nm pl* **haberes** *(posesiones)* property *sing*, assets.

habichuela *nf (gen)* bean; *(judía blanca)* haricot bean; *(judía verde)* French bean, green bean.

hábil *adj* **1** *(diestro)* skilful (US skillful). **2** *(despabilado)* clever, smart. **3** *(acto)* clever. **4** *(apto, adecuado)* good, suitable. LOC **ser hábil en ALGO / ser hábil para ALGO** *(persona)* to be good at STH. COMP **día hábil** working day.

habilidad *nf* **1** *(aptitud)* skill. **2** *(astucia)* cleverness, smartness. LOC **tener habilidad para ALGO** to be good at STH.

habilidoso,-a *adj* skilful (US skillful).

habilitar *vt* **1** *(espacio)* to fit out; *(tiempo)* to set aside: *habilitó una habitación para consulta* he fitted a bedroom out as a consulting room. **2** *(capacitar)* to entitle, qualify; *(autorizar)* to empower.

habitable *adj* habitable, liveable.

habitación *nf* **1** *(gen)* room. **2** *(dormitorio)* bedroom. COMP **habitación doble** double room. ▮ **habitación individual** single room.

habitante *nm o nf* inhabitant.

habitar *vt* to live in, inhabit.
▶ *vi* to live.

hábitat *nm* habitat.

hábito *nm* **1** *(costumbre)* habit, custom. **2** *(vestido)* habit. LOC **tener el hábito de...** to be in the habit of...

habitual *adj* usual, habitual.

habitualmente *adv (repetidamente)* usually; *(regularmente)* regularly.

habituar *vt* to accustom (a, to).
▶ *vpr* **habituarse** to become accustomed (a, to), get used (a, to) .

habla [va precedido de el en singular] *nf* **1** *(facultad)* speech. **2** *(idioma)* language; *(dialecto)* dialect. LOC **de habla española / de habla hispana** Spanish-speaking. ▮ **estar al habla con ALGN** to be in touch with SB. ▮ **perder el habla** to lose one's power of speech.

hablado,-a *adj* spoken, oral: *francés hablado* spoken French.

hablador,-ra *adj* **1** *(parlanchín)* talkative. **2** *(chismoso)* gossipy.

habladuría [también se usa en plural con el mismo significado] *nf (chisme)* piece of gossip; *(rumor)* rumour (US rumor).

hablante *nm o nf* speaker.

hablar *vi* **1** *(gen)* to speak, talk: *habló conmigo* he spoke to me. **2** *(mencionar)* to talk, mention: *no me habló de eso* she didn't mention that. LOC **hablar a solas** to talk to os. ▮ **hablar bajo** to speak softly. ▮ **hablar claro** to speak plainly.

hablar en broma to be joking. **¡quién fue a hablar!** look who's talking!▶ *vt* **1** *(idioma)* to speak: *habla francés* he speaks French. **2** *(tratar)* to talk over, discuss: *ya lo hablaremos después* we'll discuss it later. [LOC] «Se habla inglés» "English spoken".
▶ *vpr* **hablarse** *(uso recíproco)* to speak, talk: *ayer nos hablamos por teléfono* we spoke on the 'phone yesterday. [LOC] **no hablarse con** ALGN not to be on speaking terms with SB.

hacendado,-a *nm & nf* landowner.

hacendoso,-a *adj* house-proud.

hacer *vt* **1** *(producir, fabricar, crear)* to make: *hice un pastel* I made a cake. **2** *(arreglar, disponer - uñas)* to do; *(- barba)* to trim; *(- cama)* to make; *(- maleta)* to pack. **3** *(obrar, ejecutar)* to do: *haz lo que quieras* do what you want. **4** *(conseguir - amigos, dinero)* to make. **5** *(obligar)* to make: *nos hizo leer* she made us read. **6** *(recorrer)* to do: *hacer noventa kilómetros por hora* to do ninety kilometres per hour. **7** *(en suma)* to make: *con esta hacen ochenta* that makes eighty. **8** *(ocupar un lugar)* to be: *él hace el número cuatro* he's the fourth on the list. **9** *(hacer parecer)* to make look: *ese vestido te hace mayor* that dress makes you look older. **10** *(acostumbrar)* to accustom. **11** *(practicar)* to do: *¿haces deporte?* do you do any sport? [LOC] **a medio hacer** half-done, half-finished. **¡así se hace!** that's it! **hace mucho** a long time ago. **hacer bien en...** to be right to...: *hice bien en ir* I was right to go. **hacer mal** to do the wrong thing. **hacer tiempo** to kill time.
▶ *vi* **1** *(actuar)* to play (de, -); *(representar)* to act: *hizo de abuela* she played the grandmother. **2** *(comportarse)* to pretend to be, act: *hacer el tonto* to act the fool. **3** *(clima)* to be: *hace buen día* it's a fine day. **4** *(tiempo pasado)* ago: *hace tres años* three years ago. [LOC] **hacer como que + ind** to pretend, act as if: *hizo como que no sabía nada* he acted as if he knew nothing. **hacer como si + subj** to pretend, act as if.

▶ *vpr* **hacerse 1** *(volverse)* to become, get: *hacerse rico* to get rich. **2** *(crecer)* to grow: *se ha hecho mucho* he's grown a lot. **3** *(resultar)* to become, go on, seem: *la película se hizo muy larga* the film went on too long. **4** *(simular)* to pretend: *se hizo la elegante* she pretended to be elegant. **5** *(mandar hacer)* to have made, have done: *me hice un vestido en la modista* I had a dress made at the dressmaker's. [LOC] **hacerse el/la sordo,-a** *fig* to turn a deaf ear. **hacerse una idea de** ALGO to imagine STH.

hacha [va precedido de el en singular] *nf* *(instrumento)* axe (US ax).

hache *nf (la letra)* aitch.

hacia *prep* **1** *(dirección)* towards, to. **2** *(tiempo)* at about, at around: *estaremos ahí hacia las dos* we'll be there at about two. [LOC] **hacia abajo** downward(s), down. **hacia acá** this way. **hacia adelante** forward(s): *inclínate hacia delante* lean forward. **hacia allá** that way. **hacia atrás** backward(s), back. **hacia casa** home, homeward.

hacienda *nf* **1** *(bienes)* property, wealth, possessions *pl*. **2** *(finca)* estate, property, US ranch. **3** FIN Treasury. [COMP] **hacienda pública** public funds *pl*, public finances *pl*.

hada [va precedido de el en singular] *nf* fairy.

Haití *nm* Haiti.

haitiano,-a *adj* Haitian.
▶ *nm & nf* Haitian.

halagador,-ra *adj* flattering.

halagar *vt* **1** *(lisonjear)* to flatter. **2** *(satisfacer)* to please.

halago *nm* compliment, flattery.

halcón *nm* falcon.

hallar *vt* **1** *(encontrar)* to find. **2** *(averiguar)* to find out.
▶ *vpr* **hallarse** *(estar)* to be: *se hallaba enfermo* he was ill.

hallazgo *nm* **1** *(descubrimiento)* finding, discovery. **2** *(cosa descubierta)* find.

halo *nm* halo, aura.

halógeno,-a *adj* halogenous.

H

hamaca *nf* **1** *(de red)* hammock. **2** *(tumbona)* deck chair.

hambre [va precedido de el en singular] *nf* hunger, starvation, famine. LOC **matar el hambre** *fig* to stave off hunger. ‖ **ser más listo,-a que el hambre** *fig* to be a cunning devil. ‖ **tener hambre** to be hungry.

hambriento,-a *adj* **1** hungry, starving. **2** *fig* hungry, longing: *hambriento de justicia* longing for justice.

hambruna *nf* famine.

hamburguesa *nf* hamburger.

hamburguesería *nf* hamburger restaurant.

hámster *nm* hamster.

harapiento,-a *adj* ragged, tattered.

harapo *nm* rag, tatter.

hardware *nm* hardware.

harén *nm* harem.

harina *nf* flour.

hartar *vt* **1** *(atiborrar)* to satiate, fill up. **2** *fig (deseo, etc)* to satisfy. **3** *(fastidiar)* to annoy, irritate: *me harta con sus tonterías* his silly remarks get on muy nerves. **4** *(cansar)* to tire, bore.
▶ *vpr* **hartarse 1** *(atiborrarse)* to eat one's fill, stuff os. **2** *(cansarse)* to get fed up (de, with), get tired (de, of): *me harté de esperarla* I got tired of waiting for her. LOC **hasta hartarse** to repletion.

harto,-a *adj* **1** *(repleto)* full, satiated. **2** *fam (cansado)* tired (de, of), fed up (de, with).

hasta *prep* **1** *(tiempo)* until, till, up to: *hasta el sábado* until Saturday; *desde las diez hasta las dos* from ten to two. **2** *(lugar)* as far as, up to, down to. **3** *(cantidad)* up to, as many as. **4** *(incluso)* even: *hasta sabe escribir* she even knows how to write. **5** *(como despedida)* see you: *¡hasta mañana!* see you tomorrow! LOC **desde... hasta...** from... to... ‖ **¿hasta cuándo?** until when?, how long? ‖ **hasta que** until.

hastiar *vt* to bore.
▶ *vpr* **hastiarse** to get sick (de, of), get tired (de, of).

hastío *nm* **1** *(repugnancia)* disgust. **2** *fig (aburrimiento)* boredom.

hatajo *nm fig* heap, lot, bunch: *un hatajo de disparates* a load of nonsense.

hatillo *nm* small bundle.

haya *nf* BOT beech.

hayedo *nm* beech grove.

haz *nm* **1** *(de cosas)* bundle. **2** *(de luz)* shaft, beam.

hazaña *nf* deed, exploit, heroic feat.

hazmerreír *nm* laughing stock.

hebilla *nf* buckle.

hebra *nf* **1** *(de hilo)* thread. **2** *(de carne)* sinew; *(de legumbre)* string; *(de madera)* grain; *(de planta)* strand.

hebreo,-a *adj* Hebrew.
▶ *nm & nf (persona)* Hebrew.
▶ *nm* **hebreo** *(idioma)* Hebrew.

hechicería *nf* **1** *(arte)* sorcery, witchcraft. **2** *(hechizo)* spell, charm.

hechicero,-a *nm & nf (hombre)* sorcerer, wizard; *(mujer)* sorceress, witch.

hechizar *vt* **1** *(embrujar)* cast a spell on. **2** *fig (cautivar)* to charm, bewitch.

hechizo *nm* **1** *(embrujo)* charm, spell. **2** *fig (embelesamiento)* fascination, charm.

hecho,-a *adj* **1** *(carne)* done. **2** *(persona)* mature. **3** *(frase, expresión)* set. **4** *(ropa)* ready-made. LOC **muy hecho,-a** *(carne)* well-cooked. **2** *(pasada)* overdone. ‖ **ser un hombre hecho y derecho** to be a real man.
▶ *nm* **hecho 1** *(realidad)* fact. **2** *(suceso)* event. LOC **de hecho** in fact.

hectárea *nf* hectare.

hectogramo *nm* hectogramme.

hectolitro *nm* hectolitre.

hectómetro *nm* hectometre.

hediondo,-a *adj (apestoso)* stinking, foul-smelling, smelly.

hedor *nm* stink, stench.

helada *nf* METEOR frost.

heladería *nf* ice-cream parlour.

helado,-a *adj* **1** *(gen)* frozen: *estoy helado* I'm frozen. **2** *(muy frío)* icy, freezing cold. **3** *(café, té)* iced.

▶ *nm* **helado** ice-cream. LOC **dejar a** ALGN **helado,-a** to stun SB.

helador,-ra *adj* icy, freezing.

helar *vt (congelar)* to freeze.

▶ *vi* [sólo se usa en tercera persona; no lleva sujeto] METEOR to freeze: *anoche heló* it froze last night.

▶ *vpr* **helarse 1** *(congelarse)* to freeze: *el estanque se ha helado* the pond has frozen over. **2** *(persona)* to freeze, freeze to death: *me estoy helando* I'm freezing.

helecho *nm* fern.

hélice *nf* **1** *(espiral)* helix. **2** *(propulsor)* propeller.

helicóptero *nm* helicopter.

helio *nm* helium.

helipuerto *nm* heliport.

hematoma *nm* bruise.

hembra *nf* **1** *(animal)* female. **2** *(mujer)* woman. **3** TÉC female.

hemeroteca *nf* newspaper library.

hemiciclo *nm* *(parlamento)* floor.

hemisferio *nm* hemisphere.

hemorragia *nf* haemorrhage. COMP **hemorragia nasal** nosebleed.

hemorroide *nf* haemorrhoid.

▶ *nf pl* **hemorroides** piles, haemorrhoids.

henchir *vt (llenar)* to fill (de, with), stuff (de, with), cram (de, with).

hender *vt (cortar)* to cleave, split, crack.

hendidura *nf* cleft, crack.

heno *nm* hay.

hepatitis *nf inv* hepatitis.

heptaedro *nm* heptahedron.

heptagonal *adj* heptagonal.

heptágono,-a *adj* heptagonal.

▶ *nm* **heptágono** heptagon.

heráldica *nf* heraldry.

herbario,-a *adj* herbal.

▶ *nm & nf (botánico)* botanist.

▶ *nm* **herbario** *(colección)* herbarium.

herbicida *nm* weedkiller, herbicide.

herbívoro,-a *adj* herbivorous, grass-eating.

▶ *nm & nf* herbivore.

herbolario,-a *nm & nf (persona)* herbalist.

▶ *nm* **herbolario** *(tienda)* herbalist's (shop).

herboristería *nf* herbalist's (shop).

hercio *nm* hertz.

heredad *nf (terreno)* country estate.

heredar *vt* **1** to inherit. **2** *fig* to inherit: *ha heredado los ojos de su padre* he's got his father's eyes.

heredero,-a *nm & nf (hombre)* heir; *(mujer)* heiress.

hereditario,-a *adj* hereditary.

hereje *nm o nf* heretic.

herejía *nf* heresy.

herencia *nf* **1** inheritance, legacy. **2** *(genética)* heredity.

herético,-a *adj* heretical.

herida *nf* wound.

herido,-a *adj* **1** *(físicamente)* wounded, injured, hurt: *el niño resultó herido* the boy was injured. **2** *fig (emocionalmente)* hurt, wounded. LOC **herido,-a de gravedad** badly injured.

▶ *nm & nf* wounded person, injured person.

herir *vt* **1** *(dañar)* to wound, injure, hurt. **2** *fig (ofender)* to hurt, offend.

hermafrodita *adj* hermaphrodite.

hermanado,-a *adj (ciudad, pueblo)* twinned.

hermanar *vt* **1** *(unir)* to unite, join. **2** *(combinar)* to combine. **3** *(personas)* to unite spiritually. **4** *(ciudades)* to twin.

hermanastro,-a *nm & nf (hombre)* stepbrother; *(mujer)* stepsister.

hermandad *nf (de hermanos)* fraternity, brotherhood; *(de hermanas)* fraternity, sisterhood.

hermano,-a *nm & nf (hombre)* brother; *(mujer)* sister: *¿cuántos hermanos tienes?* how many brothers and sisters have you got?

hermético,-a *adj* **1** hermetic, airtight. **2** *fig* impenetrable, secretive.

hermoso,-a *adj* **1** *(gen)* beautiful, lovely: *hace un día hermoso* it's a lovely day. **2** *(hombre)* handsome.

hermosura *adj (cualidad - de mujer, lugar)* beauty, loveliness; *(- de hombre)* handsomeness.
▶ *nf* **1** *(mujer hermosa)* beautiful woman, beauty. **2** *(persona, cosa)* beautiful thing.
hernia *nf* hernia, rupture.
héroe *nm* hero.
heroicamente *adv* heroically.
heroico,-a *adj* heroic.
heroína *nf* **1** *(mujer)* heroine. **2** *(droga)* heroin.
heroísmo *nm* heroism.
herpes *nm inv* herpes, shingles.
herradura *nf* horseshoe.
herraje *nm* iron fittings *pl*, ironwork.
herramienta *nf* tool.
herrar *vt (caballo)* to shoe.
herrería *nf* **1** *(fábrica)* ironworks *pl*. **2** *(taller)* forge, smithy, blacksmith's.
herrero *nm* blacksmith, smith.
herrumbre *nf (óxido)* rust.
hervir *vt* to boil.
▶ *vi* **1** to boil: *el agua ya hierve* the water is boiling. **2** *fig (el mar)* to surge.
hervor *nm* boiling, bubbling. LOC **dar un hervor a** ALGO to blanch STH.
heterogéneo,-a *adj* heterogeneous.
heterosexual *adj* heterosexual.
▶ *nm o nf* heterosexual.
hexaedro *nm* hexahedron.
hexagonal *adj* hexagonal.
hexágono *nm* hexagon.
hexámetro *nm* hexameter.
hiato *nm* hiatus.
hibernación *nf* hibernation.
hibernar *vi* to hibernate.
hibisco *nm* hibiscus.
híbrido,-a *adj* hybrid.
▶ *nm & nf* hybrid.
hidalgo,-a *nm* nobleman.
hidratante *adj* moisturizing.
hidratar *vt* **1** to hydrate. **2** *(piel)* to moisturize.
hidráulico,-a *adj* hydraulic.
hídrico,-a *adj* hydric.
hidroavión *nm* seaplane.
hidrocarburo *nm* hydrocarbon.

hidroeléctrico,-a *adj* hydroelectric.
hidrógeno *nm* hydrogen.
hidromasaje COMP **bañera de hidromasaje** Jacuzzi®, whirlpool bath.
hidroterapia *nf* hydrotherapy.
hiedra *nf* ivy.
hiel *nf* **1** bile. **2** *fig* bitterness, gall.
hielo *nm* **1** ice. **2** *fig (frialdad)* coldness. COMP **cubito de hielo** ice cube.
hiena *nf* hyaena, hyena.
hierático,-a *adj (rígido)* rigid.
hierba *nf* **1** grass. **2** CULIN herb. COMP **finas hierbas** mixed herbs.
hierbabuena *nf* mint.
hierro *nm (metal)* iron. COMP **hierro forjado** wrought iron. ▮ **hierro fundido** cast iron.
hígado *nm* liver.
higiene *nf* hygiene.
higiénico,-a *adj* hygienic.
higo *nm* fig. LOC **de higos a brevas** *fig* once in a blue moon. COMP **higo chumbo** prickly pear.
higuera *nf* fig tree.
hijastro,-a *nm & nf (niño, niña)* stepchild; *(hijo)* stepson; *(hija)* stepdaughter.
hijo,-a *nm & nf (niño, niña)* child; *(chico)* son; *(chica)* daughter: *tiene dos hijos y dos hijas* he has two sons and two daughters. COMP **hijo,-a único,-a 1** *(niño, niña)* only child. **2** *(chico)* only son. **3** *(chica)* only daughter.
▶ *nm pl* **hijos** children: *tiene cuatro hijos* she has four children.
hilacha *nf* **1** *(hilacho)* loose thread. **2** *(resto)* rest.
hilado,-a *adj* spun.
▶ *nm* **hilado 1** *(operación)* spinning. **2** *(hilo)* thread.
hilandería *nf* **1** *(arte)* spinning. **2** *(fábrica)* spinning mill.
hilandero,-a *nm & nf* spinner.
hilar *vt* **1** to spin. **2** *fig* to work out.
hilarante *adj* hilarious.
hilaridad *nf fml* hilarity, mirth.
hilatura *nf* **1** *(arte)* spinning. **2** *(industria)* spinning mill.
hilera *nf (línea)* line, row.

hilo *nm* **1** thread; *(grueso)* yarn. **2** *(lino)* linen. **3** *(alambre, cable)* wire. **4** *fig (de luz)* thread, thin beam; *(de líquido)* trickle, thin stream. **5** *fig (de historia, discurso)* thread; *(de pensamiento)* train. LOC **estar pendiente de un hilo** *fig* to be hanging by a thread. ‖ **mover los hilos** *fig* to pull the strings. ‖ **perder el hilo** *fig* to lose the thread.

hilvanar *vt* **1** to tack, baste. **2** *fig* to put together, outline.

himno *nm* hymn. COMP

hincapié LOC **hacer hincapié** *(insistir)* to insist on. *(subrayar)* to emphasize (en, -), stress (en, -).

hincar *vt (clavar)* to drive (in).

hincha *nm o nf* DEP fan, supporter.

hinchado,-a *adj* **1** *(inflado)* blown up. **2** *(piel)* swollen, puffed up.

hinchar *vt* **1** *(inflar)* to blow up; *(con bomba)* to pump up: *hinchar un globo* to blow up a balloon. **2** *fig (exagerar)* to blow up.
▶ *vpr* **hincharse 1** MED to swell (up): *se me ha hinchado el pie* my foot has swollen up. **2** *fam (comer)* to stuff os.

hinchazón *nf* swelling, inflation.

hindú *adj* Hindu.
▶ *nm o nf* Hindu.

hinduismo *nm* Hinduism.

hinojo *nm* BOT fennel.

hipar *vi (tener hipo)* to hiccup, have the hiccups.

hiperactivo,-a *adj* hyperactive.

hipermercado *nm* hypermarket.

hipersensible *adj* hypersensitive.

hipertensión *nf* high blood pressure.

hipertenso,-a *adj* hypertensive.
▶ *nm & nf* hypertensive.

hípica *nf* horse riding.

hípico,-a *adj* horse, equestrian.

hipnosis *nf inv* hypnosis.

hipnótico,-a *adj* hypnotic.

hipnotismo *nm* hypnotism.

hipnotizador,-ra *adj* hypnotizing.
▶ *nm & nf* hypnotist.

hipnotizar *vt* to hypnotize.

hipo *nm* hiccup. LOC **quitar el hipo** *fig* to take one's breath away.

hipocondríaco,-a *adj* hypochondriac.

hipocresía *nf* hypocrisy.

hipócrita *adj* hypocritical.
▶ *nm o nf* hypocrite.

hipódromo *nm* racetrack, racecourse.

hipopótamo *nm* hippopotamus.

hipoteca *nf* mortgage.

hipotecar *vt* to mortgage.

hipotecario,-a *adj* mortgage.

hipotensión *nf* low blood pressure.

hipotenso,-a *adj* hypotensive.

hipotenusa *nf* hypotenuse.

hipótesis *nf inv* hypothesis.

hipotético,-a *adj* hypothetic, hypothetical.

hippie *adj* hippy.
▶ *nm o nf* hippy.

hiriente *adj* **1** wounding. **2** *fig* hurtful, cutting, wounding.

hirsuto,-a *adj* **1** hairy; *(cerdoso)* bristly. **2** *fig (persona)* rough, brusque, surly.

hispánico,-a *adj* Hispanic, Spanish.

hispano,-a *adj* **1** *(de España)* Spanish, Hispanic. **2** *(de América)* Spanish-American.
▶ *nm & nf* **1** *(de España)* Spaniard. **2** *(de América)* Spanish American, US Hispanic.

hispanoamericano,-a *adj* Spanish American, Latin American.

Hispanoamérica *nf* Spanish America, Latin America.

hispanohablante *adj* Spanish-speaking.
▶ *nm o nf* Spanish speaker.

histeria *nf* hysteria.

histérico,-a *adj* hysterical.
▶ *nm & nf* hysteric. LOC **poner histérico,-a a** ALGN *fam* to drive SB mad.

histerismo *nm* hysteria.

historia *nf* **1** *(estudio)* history. **2** *(narración)* story, tale. LOC **pasar a la historia** to go down in history. COMP **historia natural** natural history. ‖ **historia universal** world history.

historiado,-a *adj fig* overelaborate.

H

historiador,-ra *nm & nf* historian.

historial *nm* **1** MED medical record, case history. **2** *(currículo)* curriculum vitae.

historiar *vt* **1** *(contar)* to tell the story of; *(acontecimientos)* to recount. **2** *(escribir)* to write the history of.

histórico,-a *adj* **1** *(relativo a la historia)* historical. **2** *(importante)* historic, memorable. **3** *(cierto)* factual, true.

historieta *nf* **1** *(cuento)* short story, anecdote. **2** *(viñetas)* comic strip.

hito *nm* **1** *(mojón)* milestone. **2** *fig (hecho importante)* milestone, landmark.

hobby *nm* hobby.

hocico *nm (de animal)* snout, muzzle.

hockey *nm* hockey. COMP **hockey sobre hielo** ice hockey.

hogar *nm* **1** *(de chimenea)* hearth, fireplace. **2** *fig (casa)* home. **3** *fig (familia)* family.

hogareño,-a *adj* **1** *(vida)* family. **2** *(persona)* home-loving, stay-at-home.

hogaza *nf* large loaf (of bread).

hoguera *nf* **1** bonfire. **2** *fig* blaze.

hoja *nf* **1** *(gen)* leaf. **2** *(pétalo)* petal. **3** *(de papel)* sheet. **4** *(de libro)* leaf, page. **5** *(de cuchillo, etc)* blade. **6** *(de puerta, ventana)* leaf: *una ventana de dos hojas* a double-leaf window. LOC **de hoja perenne** BOT evergreen. ‖ COMP **hoja de afeitar** razor blade.

hojalata *nf* tin, tin plate.

hojalatería *nf (taller, tienda)* tinsmith's.

hojalatero *nm* tinsmith.

hojaldrado,-a *adj* puff: *pasta hojaldrada* puff pastry.

hojaldre *nm & nf* [suele utilizarse más como masculino] puff pastry.

hojarasca *nf* dead leaves *pl*.

hojeada *nf* flick.

hojear *vt* to leaf through.

hola *interj fam* hello!, hullo!, US hi!

Holanda *nf* Holland.

holandés,-esa *adj* Dutch.
▸ *nm & nf (persona)* Dutch person; *(hombre)* Dutchman; *(mujer)* Dutchwoman.
▸ *nm* **holandés** *(idioma)* Dutch.

holandesa *nf (papel)* quarto sheet.

holgado,-a *adj* **1** *(ropa)* loose. **2** *(espacio)* roomy. **3** *(posición)* comfortable.

holgar *vi* **1** *(descansar)* to rest. **2** *(estar ocioso)* to be idle. LOC **huelga decir que...** needless to say (that)...

holgazán,-ana *adj* idle, lazy.
▸ *nm & nf* lazybones, layabout.

holgazanear *vi* to laze around.

holgazanería *nf* idleness, laziness.

holgura *nf* **1** *(ropa)* looseness. **2** *(espacio)* room, spaciousness. **3** *fig (bienestar)* affluence, comfort.

hollar *vt (comprimir)* to tread (on).

hollín *nm* soot.

holocausto *nm* holocaust.

hombre *nm* **1** *(individuo)* man. **2** *(especie)* man, mankind. **3** *fam (marido)* husband.
▸ *interj (asombro)* hey!, hey there!, well!: *¡hombre, Pedro, no te esperaba!* hey, Pedro, I didn't expect you! COMP **hombre orquesta** one-man band. ‖ **hombre rana** frogman.

hombrera *nf* shoulder pad.

hombría *nm* manliness, virility.

hombro *nm* shoulder. LOC **a hombros** on one's shoulders. ‖ **arrimar el hombro** to help out, lend a hand.

hombruno,-a *adj* mannish, manly.

homenaje *nm* homage, tribute. LOC **en homenaje a** in honour of. ‖ **rendir homenaje a** ALGN to pay tribute to SB.

homenajear *vt* to pay tribute to.

homeopatía *nf* homeopathy.

homicida *adj* homicidal, murder: *el arma homicida* the murder weapon.
▸ *nm o nf (hombre)* murderer; *(mujer)* murderess.

homicidio *nm* homicide, murder.

homínido *nm* hominid, hominoid.

homogéneo,-a *adj* homogeneous.

homologado,-a *adj* **1** *(centro, estudios)* officially approved, officially recognized. **2** *(productos)* authorized.

homologar *vt (comprobar)* to approve, recognize, authorize.

homosexual *adj* homosexual.
▸ *nm o nf* homosexual.

homosexualidad *nf* homosexuality.

honda *nf* sling.

hondo,-a *adj* **1** deep. **2** *fig* profound.

hondonada *nf* hollow, depression.

hondura *nf* depth.

Honduras *nm* Honduras.

hondureño,-a *adj* Honduran.
  ▶ *nm & nf* Honduran.

honestidad *nf* **1** *(honradez)* honesty, uprightness. **2** *(decencia)* decency.

honesto,-a *adj* **1** *(honrado)* honest, upright. **2** *(decente)* decent.

hongo *nm* *(gen)* fungus; *(comestible)* mushroom; *(venenoso)* toadstool.

honor *nm* *(virtud)* honour. LOC **en honor a la verdad** to be fair, in all fairness. I **hacer honor a** to live up to.
  ▶ *nm pl* **honores** *(agasajo)* honours.

honorable *adj* honourable.

honorario,-a *adj* honorary.
  ▶ *nm pl* **honorarios** fees.

honorífico,-a *adj* honorary.

honra *nf* **1** *(honor)* honour. **2** *(buena reputación)* reputation, good name.
  ▶ *nf pl* **honras** *(fúnebres)* last honours.

honradez *nf* honesty, integrity.

honrado,-a *adj* *(honesto)* honest.

honrar *vt* *(gen)* to honour: *nos honró con su presencia* he honoured us with his presence.
  ▶ *vpr* **honrarse** to be honoured.

honroso,-a *adj* **1** *(que honra)* honourable. **2** *(decoroso)* respectable.

hora *nf* **1** *(unidad de tiempo)* hour: *media hora* half an hour. **2** *(tiempo)* time: *¿qué hora es?* what time is it? **3** *(cita)* appointment: *tengo hora para las cuatro y media* I have an appointment at half past four. LOC **a altas horas** in the small hours. I **¡a buenas horas!** and about time too! I **a la hora** at the proper time, on time. I **a primera hora** first thing in the morning. I **dar la hora** to strike the hour. I **de última hora** last-minute: *una noticia de última hora* some last-minute news. I **pedir hora** to make an appointment. I **por horas** by the hour: *cobro por horas* I get paid by the

hour. COMP **hora de comer** lunch time, dinner time. I **hora punta** rush hour.

horadar *vt* **1** *(perforar)* to pierce. **2** *(taladrar)* to bore (through).

horario,-a *adj* time.
  ▶ *nm* **horario 1** timetable. **2** *(jornada laboral)* hours *pl*, timetable: *tengo horario de mañana* I work mornings. COMP **horario comercial** *(tienda)* opening hours *pl*. I **horario laboral** working hours *pl*.

horca *nf* **1** *(patíbulo)* gallows *pl*, gibbet. **2** AGR hayfork, pitchfork.

horcajadas LOC **a horcajadas** astride.

horchata *nf* sweet milky drink made from tiger nuts or almonds.

horchatería *nf* bar where *horchata* is sold.

horda *nf* **1** horde, mob. **2** *fig* gang.

horizontal *adj* horizontal.

horizonte *nm* horizon.

horma *nf* **1** mould. **2** *(de zapato)* last.

hormiga *nf* ant.

hormigón *nm* concrete. COMP **hormigón armado** reinforced concrete.

hormigonera *nf* concrete mixer.

hormiguear *vi* to itch, tingle: *me hormigueaba la mano* I had pins and needles in my hand.

hormigueo *nm* pins and needles *pl*.

hormiguero *nm* ant hill, ant's nest.

hormona *nf* hormone.

hormonal *adj* hormonal.

hornacina *nf* niche.

hornada *nf* **1** batch. **2** *fig* set, batch.

hornear *vt* to bake.

hornillo *nm* **1** TÉC small furnace. **2** *(para cocinar)* stove.

horno *nm* **1** *(de cocina)* oven. **2** TÉC furnace. **3** *(cerámica, ladrillos)* kiln. **4** *(panadería)* bakery. COMP **horno (de) microondas** microwave oven. I **horno eléctrico** electric oven.

horóscopo *nm* horoscope.

horquilla *nf* *(de pelo)* hairgrip, hairclip.

horrendo,-a *adj* horrible, awful.

hórreo *nm* granary.

horrible *adj* horrible, awful.

horripilante *adj* hair-raising, horrifying, terrifying.

horripilar *vt* to horrify, scare stiff.

horror *nm* **1** *(repulsión)* horror, terror. **2** *(temor)* hate. **3** *fig (atrocidad)* atrocity. [LOC] ¡qué horror! how awful!

horrorizar *vt (causar horror)* to horrify, terrify.
► *vpr* **horrorizarse** to be horrified.

horroroso,-a *adj* **1** *(que causa miedo)* horrifying. **2** *fam (feo)* hideous.

hortaliza *nf* vegetable.

hortelano,-a *nm & nf* market gardener.

hortensia *nf* hydrangea.

hortera *adj fam* common, tasteless.

hortícola *adj* horticultural.

horticultor,-ra *nm & nf* horticulturist.

horticultura *nf* horticulture.

hosco,-a *adj* **1** *(insociable)* sullen, surly. **2** *(lugar)* gloomy, dark.

hospedaje *nm* **1** *(acción)* lodging; *(precio)* cost of lodging. **2** *(lugar)* lodgings *pl*, accommodation.

hospedar *vt* to lodge, put up.
► *vpr* **hospedarse** to stay (en, at).

hospicio *nm* **1** *(de huérfanos)* orphanage. **2** *(de pobres)* poorhouse.

hospital *nm* hospital, infirmary.

hospitalidad *nf* hospitality.

hospitalizar *vt* to send into hospital, hospitalize.

hostal *nm* hostel, hotel.

hostelería *nf* catering.

hostia *nf* **1** REL host. **2** *tabú (choque)* bump, bash; *(torta)* slap, punch.

hostigar *vt* **1** *(azotar)* to whip. **2** *fig (perseguir)* to plague, persecute.

hostil *adj* hostile.

hostilidad *nf* hostility.
► *nf pl* **hostilidades** hostilities.

hotel *nm (establecimiento)* hotel.

hotelero,-a *adj* hotel.
► *nm & nf* hotel manager, hotelier.

hoy *adv* **1** *(día)* today. **2** *fig (actualmente)* now, nowadays. [LOC] de hoy en adelante from now on. ‖ hoy (en) día nowadays, today, these days.

hoyo *nm* **1** *(agujero)* hole, pit. **2** *(sepultura)* grave.

hoyuelo *nm* dimple.

hoz¹ *nf* agr sickle.

hoz² *nf* geog ravine, gorge.

hucha *nf* moneybox, piggy bank.

hueco,-a *adj* **1** hollow: *pared hueca* hollow wall, stud wall. **2** *(vacío)* empty. **3** *(cóncavo)* concave.
► *nm* **hueco 1** *(cavidad)* hollow, hole. **2** *(de tiempo)* slot, free time; *(de espacio)* empty space. **3** *fig (vacante)* vacancy.

huelga *nf* strike. [LOC] estar en huelga / estar de huelga to be on strike. [COMP] huelga de brazos caídos go-slow. ‖ huelga de celo work-to-rule. ‖ huelga general general strike. ‖ huelga de hambre hunger strike.

✎ Consulta también **holgar**.

huelguista *nm o nf* striker.

huella *nf* **1** *(de pie)* footprint; *(de ruedas)* track. **2** *fig (vestigio)* trace, sign: *las huellas del tiempo* the traces of time. [LOC] dejar huella to leave one's mark (en, on). [COMP] huella dactilar fingerprint.

huérfano,-a *adj* orphan, orphaned.
► *nm & nf* orphan.

huerta *nf (terreno)* market garden.

huerto *nm (de verduras)* vegetable garden; *(de frutas)* orchard.

hueso *nm* **1** ANAT bone. **2** *(de fruta)* stone, US pit. **3** *fam fig (cosa difícil)* struggle, problem: *las mates son un hueso para mí* I find maths really hard. [LOC] ser un hueso duro de roer *fig* to be a hard nut to crack.

huésped,-da *nm & nf (invitado)* guest.

hueste *nf* [también se usa en plural con el mismo significado] MIL army, host.

huesudo,-a *adj* bony.

hueva *nf* roe, spawn.

huevera *nf* **1** *(copa)* egg cup. **2** *(cartón)* egg box.

huevería *nf* egg shop.

huevero,-a *nm & nf (persona)* egg seller.

huevo *nm* egg. [COMP] huevo duro hard-boiled egg. ‖ huevo frito fried egg. ‖ huevo pasado por agua soft-boiled egg.

huida *nf* flight, escape.

huidizo,-a *adj* fleeting, elusive.

huir *vi* **1** *(escapar)* to flee, run away. **2** *(evitar)* to avoid (de, -).

hule *nm* oilcloth, oilskin.

hulla *nf* coal.

humanidad *nf* **1** *(género humano)* humanity, mankind. **2** *(cualidad)* humanity, humaneness.
▶ *nf pl* **humanidades** EDUC humanities.

humanismo *nm* humanism.

humanista *nm o nf* humanist.

humanístico,-a *adj* humanistic.

humanitario,-a *adj* humanitarian.

humanizar *vt* to humanize.
▶ *vpr* **humanizarse** to become more human.

humano,-a *adj* **1** human. **2** *(benigno)* humane.

humareda *nf* cloud of smoke.

humeante *adj* **1** *(de humo)* smoky, smoking. **2** *(de vaho)* steaming.

humear *vi* **1** *(humo)* to smoke. **2** *(vaho)* to steam.

humectante *adj* moistening.

humedad *nf* **1** humidity. **2** *(de vapor)* moisture.

humedecer *vt* to moisten, dampen.
▶ *vpr* **humedecerse** to become moist.

húmedo,-a *adj* **1** *(clima)* humid, damp. **2** *(impregnado)* damp, moist, wet.

húmero *nm* humerus.

humidificador *nm* humidifier.

humidificar *vt* to humidify.

humildad *nf* humility, humbleness.

humilde *adj* humble, modest.

humildemente *adv* humbly.

humillación *nf* humiliation.

humillante *adj* humiliating.

humillar *vt* to humiliate, humble.
▶ *vpr* **humillarse** to humble os.

humo *nm* **1** smoke. **2** *(gas)* fumes *pl*. **3** *(vapor)* steam.
▶ *nm pl* **humos** *fig* airs. LOC **bajarle los humos a** ALGN *fig* to put SB in his/her place.

humor *nm* **1** *(ánimo)* mood. **2** *(carácter)* temper. **3** *(gracia)* humour. LOC **estar de buen humor** to be in a good mood.

humorada *nf* joke, witticism.

humorismo *nm* humour.

humorista *adj* humorous.
▶ *nm o nf (cómico)* comedian.

humorístico,-a *adj* humorous.

humus *nm inv* humus.

hundible *adj* sinkable.

hundido,-a *adj* **1** *(barco, etc)* sunken. **2** *(ojos)* deep-set; *(mejillas)* hollow.

hundimiento *nm* **1** *(barco)* sinking. **2** *(tierra)* subsidence. **3** *(edificio)* collapse.

hundir *vt* **1** *(sumir)* plunge: *hundió la mano en la arena* she plunged her hand into the sand. **2** *(barco)* to sink. **3** *(derrumbar)* to demolish, ruin: *el terremoto hundió el edificio* the earthquake caused the building to collapse.
▶ *vpr* **hundirse 1** *(barco)* to sink. **2** *(derrumbarse)* to collapse, fall down.

húngaro,-a *adj* Hungarian.
▶ *nm & nf (persona)* Hungarian.
▶ *nm* **húngaro** *(idioma)* Hungarian.

Hungría *nf* Hungary.

huracán *nm* hurricane.

huracanado,-a *adj* hurricane: *vientos huracanados* hurricane winds.

huraño,-a *adj* sullen, unsociable.

hurgar *vt* **1** *(remover)* to poke, rake. **2** *(bolsillo, bolso, etc)* to rummage in.
▶ *vpr* **hurgarse** to pick.

hurón,-ona *nm (animal)* ferret.

hurra *interj* hurray!, hurrah!

hurraca *nf* magpie.

hurtadillas LOC **a hurtadillas** stealthily, on the sly.

hurtar *vt (robar)* to steal, pilfer.

hurto *nm* petty theft, pilfering.

husmeador,-ra *adj* **1** *(con la nariz)* sniffing. **2** *fig (fisgón)* prying.

husmear *vt* **1** *(con el olfato)* to sniff, scent. **2** *fig (indagar)* to pry (en, into).
▶ *vi* **1** to sniff. **2** *fig* to snoop around.

huso *nm (para hilar)* spindle, bobbin.
COMP **huso horario** time zone.

H

I

I, i *nf* (la letra) I, i.
COMP **i griega** *name of the letter* y. ▌ **i latina** *name of the letter* i.

ibérico,-a *adj* Iberian.

íbero,-a *adj* Iberian.
► *nm & nf (persona)* Iberian.

iberoamericano,-a *adj* Latin American.
► *nm & nf* Latin American.

iceberg *nm* iceberg.

icono *nm* icon.

ida *nf (acción)* going; *(salida)* departure.
LOC **de ida sola** single. ▌ **de ida y vuelta** *(billete)* return.

idea *nf* **1** idea. **2** *(noción)* notion. **3** *(ingenio)* imagination.

ideal *adj* ideal.
► *nm* ideal.

idealismo *nm* idealism.

idealista *adj* idealistic.
► *nm o nf* idealist.

idealizar *vt* to idealize.

idear *vt* **1** *(concebir)* to conceive. **2** *(inventar)* to design.

ideario *nm* ideology.

idéntico,-a *adj* identical.

identidad *nf* identity. COMP **carnet de identidad** identity card.

identificar *vt* to identify.
► *vpr* **identificarse** *(solidarizarse)* to identify (con, with).

ideología *nf* ideology.

ideólogo,-a *nm & nf* ideologist.

idílico,-a *adj* idyllic.

idilio *nm* **1** *lit* idyll. **2** *fam* romance.

idioma *nm* language.

idiosincrasia *nf* idiosyncrasy.

idiota *adj* **1** MED idiotic. **2** *fam (tonto)* stupid.
► *nm o nf* idiot.

idiotez *nf* **1** MED idiocy. **2** *(estupidez)* stupid thing to say, stupid thing to do.

idiotizar *vt* to turn into an idiot.

ido,-a *adj* **1** *(loco)* mad. **2** *(despistado)* absent-minded. LOC **estar ido,-a** **1** *fam (loco)* to be mad. **2** *(despistado)* to be miles away.

idolatrar *vt* **1** to worship. **2** *fig* to idolize.

ídolo *nm* idol.

idóneo,-a *adj* suitable.

iglesia *nf* **1** *(edificio)* church. **2** *(institución)* Church.

iglú *nm* igloo.

ignorancia *nf* ignorance.

ignorante *adj* ignorant.
► *nm o nf* ignoramus.

ignorar *vt* **1** *(desconocer)* not to know, not be aware of. **2** *(no hacer caso)* to ignore.

igual *adj* **1** *(parte)* equal. **2** *(lo mismo)* the same. **3** *(muy parecido)* just like.
► *nm (persona)* equal.
► *adv* **1** *(en comparativas)* the same. **2** *fam* maybe, perhaps: *igual no vienen* they may well not come.

igualar *vt* **1** to make equal. **2** *(allanar)* to level; *(pulir)* to smooth. **3** *(comparar)* to match: *no hay nadie que lo iguale* nobody can match him, he has no equal.
► *vpr* **igualarse** **1** *(ser iguales)* to be equal. **2** *(compararse)* to be compared.

igualdad *nf* equality.

iguana *nf* iguana.

ilegal *adj* illegal.

ilegalidad *nf* illegality.

ilegible *adj* unreadable, illegible.

ilegítimo,-a *adj* illegitimate.

ileso,-a *adj* unharmed, unhurt. LOC
salir ileso,-a to escape unharmed.

iletrado,-a *adj* illiterate.

ilícito,-a *adj* unlawful, illicit.

ilimitado,-a *adj* unlimited.

ilógico,-a *adj* illogical.

iluminación *nf (de una sala)* lighting;
(de una feria) illumination; *(de una película, un espectáculo)* lighting.

iluminar *vt* to light, light up.

ilusión *nf* **1** *(no real)* illusion. **2** *(esperanza)* hope. **3** *(emoción)* excitement.

ilusionado,-a *adj* excited.

ilusionar *vt* **1** *(crear ilusiones)* to raise
hopes. **2** *(entusiasmar)* to excite.
▶ *vpr* **ilusionarse 1** *(esperanzarse)* to
build up one's hopes. **2** *(entusiasmarse)*
to be excited (**con**, about).

ilusionismo *nm* conjuring.

ilusionista *nm o nf* conjurer, illusionist.

iluso,-a *adj* naive, gullible.

ilustración *nf* **1** *(de un texto)* illustration. **2** *(erudición)* learning. **3** la Ilustración HIST the Enlightenment.

ilustrado,-a *adj* **1** *(texto)* illustrated. **2**
(culto) learned. **3** HIST of the Enlightenment.

ilustrar *vt* **1** *(texto)* to illustrate. **2** *(instruir)* to enlighten.

ilustre *adj* **1** *(célebre)* renowned, illustrious. **2** *(distinguido)* distinguished.

imagen *nf* **1** image. **2** TV picture. LOC
ser la viva imagen de ALGN to be the
spitting image of SB.

imaginación *nf* imagination, fantasy.

imaginar *vt* **1** *(gen)* to imagine. **2** *(idear)*
to devise, think up.

✎ También se usa la forma **imaginarse**,
sobre todo en el lenguaje coloquial.

---

imaginario,-a *adj* imaginary.

imaginativo,-a *adj* imaginative.

imán¹ *nm* magnet.

imán² *nm* REL imam.

imantar *vt* to magnetize.

imbatible *adj* unbeatable.

imbécil *adj* **1** MED *(retrasado)* imbecile.
2 *fam* stupid, imbecile.
▶ *nm o nf* **1** MED imbecile. **2** *fam* idiot.

imbecilidad *nf* **1** MED imbecility. **2**
fam stupid thing to do.

imberbe *adj* beardless.

imborrable *adj* indelible.

imbuir *vt* to imbue.

imitación *nf* **1** *(copia)* imitation. **2** *(parodia)* impression.

imitador,-ra *adj* imitative.
▶ *nm & nf* **1** imitator. **2** *(cómico)* impressionist.

imitar *vt* to copy, imitate; *(gestos)* to
mimic; *(persona)* to mimic, do an impression of.

impaciencia *nf* impatience.

impacientar *vt* to make lose one's
patience, exasperate.
▶ *vpr* **impacientarse** to get impatient.

impaciente *adj* impatient, anxious.

impactado,-a *adj* impacted.

impactante *adj* striking, powerful.

impactar *vt* **1** *(físicamente)* to hit. **2** *(impresionar)* to make an impression on:
esa escena me impactó mucho that scene
made a deep impression on me.

impacto *nm* **1** *(choque)* impact. **2** *(marca)*
mark; *(agujero)* hole.

impar *adj* odd.

imparable *adj* unstoppable.

imparcial *adj* impartial, fair.

imparcialidad *nf* impartiality.

impartir *vt* *(lección)* to give.

impasible *adj* impassive.

impávido,-a *adj* dauntless.

impecable *adj* impeccable, faultless.

impedido,-a *adj* disabled.
▶ *nm & nf* disabled person.

impedimento *nm* impediment, obstacle.

impedir *vt* *(hacer imposible)* to prevent,
stop: *¿hay algo que te lo impida?* is there
anything stopping you?

impeler *vt* to drive forward, propel.

impenetrable *adj* impenetrable.

impensable *adj* unthinkable.

imperar *vi* to rule, prevail.

imperativo,-a *adj* imperative.
▶ *nm* imperativo LING imperative.
imperceptible *adj* imperceptible.
imperdible *nm* safety pin.
imperdonable *adj* unforgivable.
imperfección *nf* 1 imperfection. 2 *(defecto)* defect, fault.
imperfecto,-a *adj* 1 imperfect. 2 LING imperfect.
▶ *nm* imperfecto imperfect.
imperialismo *nm* imperialism.
imperio *nm* empire.
imperioso,-a *adj* 1 *(autoritario)* imperious. 2 *(necesario)* urgent, pressing.
impermeabilizar *vt* to waterproof.
impermeable *adj* waterproof.
▶ *nm* raincoat.
impersonal *adj* impersonal.
impertérrito,-a *adj* imperturbable.
impertinencia *nf* 1 impertinence. 2 *(palabras)* impertinent remark.
impertinente *adj* impertinent.
▶ *nm pl* impertinentes lorgnette *sing*.
imperturbable *adj* imperturbable.
ímpetu *nm* 1 *(fuerza)* vigour; *(entusiasmo)* enthusiasm; *(energía)* energy. 2 *(impulso)* impetus; *(fuerza)* force.
impetuoso,-a *adj* 1 *(persona)* impetuous. 2 *(viento)* violent.
implacable *adj* implacable, relentless.
implantar *vt* 1 to introduce. 2 MED to implant.
implante *nm* implant.
implicar *vt* 1 *(conllevar)* to imply. 2 *(involucrar)* to involve (en, in).
implícito,-a *adj* implicit.
implorar *vt* to implore, entreat, beg.
impoluto,-a *adj* spotless.
imponderable *adj* *(factor)* imponderable; *(valor)* incalculable.
imponente *adj* impressive.
imponer *vt* 1 *(ley, límite, sanción)* to impose. 2 *(respeto)* to inspire.
▶ *vi (asustar)* to be frightening.
▶ *vpr* imponerse 1 to impose one's authority (a, on). 2 *(obligarse)* to force os to. 3 *(prevalecer)* to prevail.

impopular *adj* unpopular.
importación *nf* 1 *(acción)* importation, import. 2 *(productos)* imports *pl*.
importancia *nf* importance.
importante *adj* 1 *(gen)* important; *(por su gravedad)* serious; *(por su cantidad)* considerable.
importar *vt* 1 COM *(traer de fuera)* to import. 2 *(valer)* to amount to.
▶ *vi (tener importancia)* to matter. 2 *(molestar)* to mind.
importe *nm* *(gen)* price, cost.
importunar *vt (molestar)* to pester.
imposible *adj* impossible.
imposición *nf (gen)* imposition.
impostor,-ra *nm & nf* 1 *(farsante)* impostor. 2 *(difamador)* slanderer.
impotencia *nf* impotence.
impotente *adj* impotent.
impreciso,-a *adj* imprecise, vague.
impredecible *adj (persona)* unpredictable; *(circunstancia)* unforeseeable.
imprenta *nf* 1 *(arte)* printing. 2 *(taller)* printer's, printing house.
imprescindible *adj* essential, indispensable.
impresión *nf* 1 *(en imprenta)* printing. 2 *(huella)* impression, imprint. 3 *fig (efecto)* impression; *(negativo)* shock.
impresionable *adj* impressionable.
impresionante *adj* 1 *(admirable)* impressive. 2 *fam (gen)* incredible; *(enorme)* tremendous.
impresionar *vt* 1 *(causar admiración)* to impress: *me impresionó el paisaje* the scenery impressed me. 2 *(afectar)* to affect; *(inquietar)* to disturb.
impresionismo *nm* impressionism.
impresionista *adj* impressionist.
▶ *nm o nf* impressionist.
impreso,-a *adj* printed.
▶ *nm* impreso *(formulario)* form.
impresor,-ra *nm & nf (persona)* printer.
impresora *nf (máquina)* printer.
imprevisible *adj (hecho)* unforeseeable; *(persona)* unpredictable.
imprevisto,-a *adj* unexpected.

► *nm pl* **imprevistos** *(gastos)* incidental expenses.

imprimir *vt* **1** *(gen)* to print. **2** *(dejar huella)* to stamp. **3** *fig (grabar)* to fix.

improbable *adj* improbable, unlikely.

improductivo,-a *adj* unproductive.

improperio *nm* insult.

impropio,-a *adj (inadecuado)* unsuitable, inappropriate. LOC **ser impropio,-a de ALGN** not to be worthy of SB.

improvisado,-a *adj (gen)* improvised.

improvisar *vt* to improvise.
► *vi* to improvise.

improviso LOC **de improviso** suddenly, unexpectedly.

imprudencia *nf* **1** *(falta de prudencia)* carelessness. **2** *(acción imprudente)* rash move; *(indiscreción)* indiscretion.

imprudente *adj* careless.
► *nm o nf (imprudente)* careless person; *(indiscreto)* indiscreet person.

impúdico,-a *adj (indecente)* immodest, indecent.

impuesto,-a *nm* **impuesto** tax, duty.

impugnar *vt* **1** *(resultado)* to contest. **2** *(teoría)* to refute.

impulsar *vt* **1** to impel. **2** TÉC to drive forward. **3** *(incitar)* to drive.

impulsivo,-a *adj* impulsive.
► *nm & nf* impulsive person.

impulso *nm* **1** impulse. **2** *(fuerza, velocidad)* momentum.

impune *adj* unpunished.

impunidad *nf* impunity.

impureza *nf* impurity.

impuro,-a *adj* impure.

imputación *nf* accusation.

imputar *vt* to impute.

inabarcable *adj* huge, vast.

inaccesible *adj* inaccessible.

inaceptable *adj* unacceptable.

inadaptado,-a *adj* maladjusted.
► *nm & nf* misfit.

inadvertido,-a *adj* unnoticed.

inagotable *adj* inexhaustible.

inaguantable *adj* unbearable.

inalámbrico,-a *adj* cordless.

inanición *nf* starvation.

inanimado,-a *adj* inanimate, lifeless.

inapreciable *adj* **1** *(insignificante)* imperceptible. **2** *(valioso)* invaluable.

inaudible *adj* inaudible.

inaudito,-a *adj (nunca oído)* unheard-of.

inauguración *nf* opening, inauguration.

inaugurar *vt* to inaugurate, open.

inca *adj* Inca.
► *nm o nf* Inca.

incalculable *adj* incalculable.

incalificable *adj (intolerable)* unspeakable.

incandescente *adj* incandescent.

incansable *adj* tireless.

incapacidad *nf* **1** *(gen)* incapacity, inability. **2** *(insuficiencia)* disability.

incapacitado,-a *adj (físicamente)* disabled; *(mentalmente)* incapacitated, unfit.

incapacitar *vt* **1** *(impedir)* to incapacitate.

incapaz *adj* **1** incapable (de, of). **2** *(incompetente)* incompetent.

incauto,-a *adj (crédulo)* gullible.
► *nm & nf* gullible person.

incendiar *vt* to set on fire, set fire to.
► *vpr* **incendiarse** to catch fire.

incendiario,-a *adj* incendiary.
► *nm & nf* arsonist.

incendio *nm* fire.

incentivo *nm* incentive.

incertidumbre *nf* uncertainty.

incesto *nm* incest.

incestuoso,-a *adj* incestuous.

incidente *nm* incident, event.

incidir *vi* **incidir en** **1** *(repercutir en)* to have an effect on, affect. **2** *(incurrir en)* to fall into. **3** *(tratar)* to touch upon; *(insistir en)* to stress.

incienso *nm* incense.

incierto,-a *adj* uncertain, doubtful.

incinerar *vt (basura)* to incinerate; *(cadáveres)* to cremate.

incipiente *adj* incipient.

incisión *nf* incision.

inciso,-a *nm* passing remark.

incitante *adj* **1** *(estimulante)* inciting. **2** *(provocativo)* provocative.

incitar *vt* to incite (a, to).
inclemencia *nf* harshness.
inclinación *nf* 1 *(desviación)* slant. 2 *(tendencia)* leaning. 3 *(afición)* penchant.
inclinar *vt* 1 *(ladear)* to tilt. 2 *fig (persuadir)* to dispose, move.
▶ *vpr* **inclinarse** 1 *(doblarse)* to bend, lean; *(como saludo)* to bow. 2 **inclinarse a** *fig (propender a)* to incline to. 3 **inclinarse por** *(escoger)* to choose, opt for.
incluir *vt* 1 to include. 2 *(adjuntar - en carta, etc)* to enclose.
incluso *adv* even.
▶ *prep* even.
incógnita *nf fig (misterio)* mystery.
incógnito,-a *adj* unknown.
incoherencia *nf (falta de coherencia)* incoherence.
incoherente *adj* incoherent.
incomodar *vt* 1 *(causar molestia)* to inconvenience. 2 *(fastidiar)* to annoy, bother. 3 *(enojar)* to anger.
▶ *vpr* **incomodarse** *(enfadarse)* to get annoyed, get angry.
incómodo,-a *adj* uncomfortable. [LOC] sentirse incómodo,-a to feel awkward.
incomparable *adj* incomparable.
incompetencia *nf* incompetence.
incompetente *adj* incompetent.
incompleto,-a *adj* 1 incomplete. 2 *(inacabado)* unfinished.
incomprensión *nf* lack of understanding.
incomunicado,-a *adj* 1 *(por la nieve)* cut off. 2 *(preso)* in solitary confinement.
inconcebible *adj* inconceivable.
incondicional *adj (rendición)* unconditional.
▶ *nm o nf* staunch supporter.
inconexo,-a *adj* disconnected.
inconformista *adj* nonconformist.
▶ *nm o nf* nonconformist.
inconfundible *adj* unmistakable.
incongruencia *nf* incongruity.
inconsciencia *nf* 1 MED unconsciousness. 2 *(irreflexión)* thoughtlessness.
inconsciente *adj* 1 MED unconscious. 2 *(irreflexivo)* thoughtless.

inconstante *adj (variable)* inconstant, changeable.
incontable *adj* countless.
incontinencia *nf* incontinence.
incontrolable *adj* uncontrollable.
inconveniente *adj* inappropriate.
▶ *nm (desventaja)* drawback.
incordiar *vt* to pester, bother.
incorporación *nf (llegada)* arrival; *(inclusión)* inclusion; *(unión)* joining.
incorporar *vt* 1 *(añadir)* to incorporate, include. 2 CULIN *(añadir)* to add.
▶ *vpr* **incorporarse** 1 *(levantarse)* to sit up. 2 *(a un trabajo)* to start; *(a una empresa, equipo, etc)* to join.
incorrección *nf* 1 *(falta de corrección)* incorrectness. 2 *(error)* mistake.
incorrecto,-a *adj* 1 *(inexacto)* incorrect. 2 *(descortés)* impolite.
incorregible *adj* incorrigible.
incrédulo,-a *adj* incredulous.
increíble *adj* incredible.
incrementar *vt* to increase.
incremento *nm* increase, rise.
increpar *vt (insultar)* to abuse.
incriminar *vt* to incriminate.
incrustar *vt* 1 to incrust, encrust. 2 *(arte)* to inlay.
incubar *vt* to incubate.
inculcar *vt* to inculcate, instil: *les inculcaron la necesidad de tener estudios* they instilled in them the need to study.
inculpar *vt* to accuse (de, of).
inculto,-a *adj (persona)* uneducated.
▶ *nm & nf (persona)* ignoramus.
incumbir *vi* to be incumbent (a, upon).
incumplir *vt (promesa)* to break; *(deber)* to fail to fulfil; *(contrato)* to break; *(orden)* to disobey, fail to comply with.
incurable *adj* incurable.
incurrir *vi* **incurrir en** *(error)* to fall into; *(delito)* to commit.
indagar *vt* to investigate, inquire into.
indecencia *nf* 1 indecency. 2 *(acción indecente)* scandal, outrage.
indecente *adj* 1 *(impúdico)* indecent. 2 *(indigno)* miserable.
indecible *adj* indescribable.

indecisión *nf* indecision.

indeciso,-a *adj* **1** *(persona)* indecisive, undecided. **2** *(asunto no resuelto)* undecided.

indecoroso,-a *adj* indecorous.

indefenso,-a *adj* defenceless.

indefinido,-a *adj* **1** *(período de tiempo)* indefinite; *(contrato)* open-ended. **2** *(impreciso)* indefinite. **3** LING indefinite.

indemne *adj* unharmed, unhurt.

indemnización *nf* compensation, indemnity.

indemnizar *vt* to compensate (de/por, for), indemnify (de/por, for).

independencia *nf* independence.

independiente *adj* **1** independent. **2** *(individualista)* self-sufficient.

independizar *vt* to make independent.
▶ *vpr* **independizarse** to become independent (de, of).

indeterminado,-a *adj* **1** *(gen)* indeterminate; *(en tiempo, número)* indefinite. **2** *(impreciso)* vague.

India *nf* India.

indicación *nf* **1** *(gesto, señal)* sign. **2** *(instrucción)* instruction.

indicado,-a *adj* appropriate, suitable.

indicador,-ra *adj (gen)* indicating.
▶ *nm (gen)* indicator; *(con aguja, escala)* gauge.

indicar *vt* to indicate, point out.

indicativo,-a *adj* indicative.
▶ *nm* **indicativo** LING indicative.

índice *nm* **1** *(gen)* index. **2** *(de un libro)* index, table of contents; *(catálogo)* catalogue. **3** *(dedo)* index finger.

indicio *nm* **1** *(señal)* sign. **2** *(resto)* trace.

indiferencia *nf* indifference.

indiferente *adj* indifferent.

indigente *nm o nf* poor person: *los indigentes* the needy.

indigestión *nf* indigestion.

indigesto,-a *adj (alimento)* indigestible.

indignación *nf* indignation.

indignar *vt* to infuriate.
▶ *vpr* **indignarse** to become indignant (por, at/about).

indigno,-a *adj* **1** unworthy (de, of). **2** *(vil)* low, contemptible.

indio,-a *adj* Indian.
▶ *nm & nf* Indian. LOC **hacer el indio** *fam* to play the fool.

indirecto,-a *adj* indirect.

indiscreción *nf* indiscretion.

indiscreto,-a *adj* indiscreet.
▶ *nm & nf* indiscreet person.

indispensable *adj* essential.

indisponer *vt* MED to upset, make unwell.
▶ *vpr* **indisponerse** *(enfermarse)* to be unwell.

indispuesto,-a *adj* MED indisposed, unwell.

individual *adj* individual.
▶ *nm pl* **individuales** DEP singles.

individualista *adj* individualistic.
▶ *nm o nf* individualist.

individuo,-a *nm & nf pey (gen)* character, individual.
▶ *nm* **individuo** person.

indocumentado,-a *adj (sin documentación)* without means of identification.

índole *nf* **1** *(carácter)* disposition, nature. **2** *(tipo)* type, kind.

indolente *adj* indolent.

indoloro,-a *adj* painless.

indómito,-a *adj* indomitable.

Indonesia *nf* Indonesia.

indonesio,-a *adj* Indonesian.
▶ *nm & nf* Indonesian.

inducir *vt* **1** to induce. **2** ELEC to induce.

indulgencia *nf* indulgence, leniency.

indultar *vt* JUR to pardon.

indulto *nm* pardon, amnesty.

indumentaria *nf* clothing, clothes *pl*.

industria *nf* **1** *(gen)* industry. **2** *(fábrica)* factory.

industrial *adj* industrial.
▶ *nm o nf* industrialist, manufacturer.

industrializar *vt* to industrialize.

inédito,-a *adj (libro)* unpublished.

inepto,-a *adj (persona)* incompetent.
▶ *nm & nf* incompetent person.

inercia *nf* inertia.

inerte *adj* **1** *(materia, gas)* inert. **2** *(cadáver)* lifeless.

inesperado,-a *adj* unexpected.

inestable *adj* unstable, unsteady.

inevitable *adj* inevitable.

inexistente *adj* nonexistent.

inexorable *adj* inexorable.

inexperto,-a *adj* inexperienced.

inexplicable *adj* inexplicable.

inexpresivo,-a *adj* expressionless.

infalible *adj* infallible.

infame *adj (vil)* despicable, vile.

infamia *nf* disgrace.

infancia *nf* **1** *(gen)* childhood. **2** *(los niños)* children *pl*.

infante *nm* **1** *lit (niño)* infant. **2** *(soldado)* infantryman.

infantería *nf* infantry.

infantil *adj* **1** *(literatura, juego)* children's; *(equipo)* junior. **2** *(inmaduro)* childish.

infarto *nm (de miocardio)* heart attack. COMP **infarto de miocardio** heart attack.

infatigable *adj* indefatigable, tireless.

infección *nf* infection.

infectar *vt* to infect (de, with).
▶ *vpr* **infectarse** to become infected (de, with).

infeliz *adj* **1** *(desdichado)* unhappy. **2** *(ingenuo)* ingenuous.

inferior *adj* **1** *(situado debajo)* lower. **2** *(cantidad)* less, lower. **3** *(en calidad)* inferior (a, to).
▶ *nm o nf (en rango)* subordinate; *(en calidad)* inferior.

inferioridad *nf* inferiority.

infernal *adj* infernal.

infidelidad *nf* **1** *(sexual)* infidelity, unfaithfulness. **2** *(de un amigo)* disloyalty.

infiel *adj (esposo)* unfaithful (a/con/para, to); *(amigo)* disloyal (a, to).

infiernillo *nm* portable stove.

infierno *nm* hell. LOC **¡vete al infierno!** go to hell!, get lost!

infiltrar *vt* to infiltrate.
▶ *vpr* **infiltrarse** to infiltrate (en, -).

ínfimo,-a *adj (en calidad)* lowest, poorest; *(precio)* ridiculous.

infinidad *nf* **1** *(infinito)* infinity. **2** *(gran cantidad)* infinite number.

infinitivo *nm* infinitive.

infinito,-a *adj* infinite.
▶ *nm* **el infinito** the infinite, infinity.

inflamable *adj* inflammable.

inflamación *nf* MED inflammation.

inflamar *vt* MED to inflame.
▶ *vpr* **inflamarse** MED to become inflamed.

inflar *vt* **1** *(balón)* to blow up, inflate. **2** *fig (hechos, noticias)* to exaggerate. **3** *(precios)* to inflate.
▶ *vpr* **inflarse 1** to inflate one's opinion of os. **2** *fam (hartarse de comer)* to stuff os (de, with).

inflexible *adj* inflexible.

influencia *nf* influence.

influir *vt* to influence.
▶ *vi* to have influence.

influyente *adj* influential.

información *nf* **1** *(conocimiento)* information. **2** *(noticia)* piece of news; *(conjunto de noticias)* news. **3** *(en telefónica)* directory enquiries *pl*.

informal *adj* **1** *(desenfadado)* informal. **2** *(persona)* unreliable.

informar *vt (dar noticia)* to inform (de, about).
▶ *vi* to inform (de, about), tell (de, about).
▶ *vpr* **informarse** to find out (de, about).

informática *nf* computing.

informático,-a *adj* computer.
▶ *nm & nf* computer expert.

informativo,-a *adj (ilustrativo)* informative: *una campaña con carácter informativo* a public awareness campaign.
▶ *nm* **informativo** news programme.

informatizar *vt* to computerize.

informe *nm* report.
▶ *nm pl* **informes** references.

infracción *nf* infringement.

infractor,-ra *adj* offending.
▶ *nm & nf* offender.

infraestructura *nf* infrastructure.

infranqueable *adj* **1** impassable. **2** *fig* insurmountable.

infrarrojo,-a *adj* infrared.

infravalorar *vt* to underestimate.

infrecuente *adj* infrequent.

infringir *vt (gen)* to infringe; *(ley)* to break.

infructuoso,-a *adj* fruitless, unsuccessful.

infundado,-a *adj* unfounded.

infundir *vt (respeto)* to command; *(miedo)* to fill with; *(valor)* to instil.

infusión *nf* infusion.

ingeniar *vt* to devise.
  ▶ *vpr* **ingeniárselas** to manage, find a way, contrive.

ingeniería *nf* engineering.

ingeniero,-a *nm & nf* engineer.

ingenio *nm* **1** *(talento)* talent; *(chispa)* wit. **2** *(habilidad)* ingenuity.

ingenioso,-a *adj (inteligente)* ingenious, clever; *(con chispa)* witty.

ingenuo,-a *adj* naive, ingenuous.
  ▶ *nm & nf* naive person.

ingerir *vt (alimentos)* to eat; *(bebida)* to drink.

Inglaterra *nf* England.

ingle *nf* groin.

inglés,-esa *adj* English.
  ▶ *nm & nf (persona)* English person; *(hombre)* Englishman; *(mujer)* Englishwoman.
  ▶ *nm* **inglés** *(idioma)* English.

ingratitud *nf* ingratitude, ungratefulness.

ingrato,-a *adj* **1** *(persona)* ungrateful. **2** *(trabajo, tarea)* thankless.

ingrediente *nm* ingredient.

ingresar *vt (dinero)* to pay in, deposit.
  ▶ *vi* **ingresar en 1** *(entrar)* to join. **2** *(hospital)* to be admitted in.

ingreso *nm* **1** *(en club, ejército)* joining; *(en hospital)* admission; *(en universidad)* entrance. **2** *(entrada)* entry.
  ▶ *nm pl* **ingresos** *(sueldo, renta)* income *sing*; *(beneficios)* revenue *sing*.

inhabitable *adj* uninhabitable.

inhalar *vt* to inhale, breathe in.

inherente *adj* inherent (a, in).

inhibir *vt (reprimir)* to inhibit.

▶ *vpr* **inhibirse 1** *(reprimirse)* to be inhibited. **2** *(abstenerse)* to refrain (de, from); *(negarse)* to refuse (de, to).

inhóspito,-a *adj* inhospitable.

inhumano,-a *adj* **1** *(persona)* inhuman, cruel. **2** *(dolor, sufrimiento)* inhuman.

iniciación *nf* **1** *(comienzo)* start, beginning. **2** *(de una persona)* initiation.

inicial *adj* initial.
  ▶ *nf* initial.

iniciar *vt* **1** *(empezar)* to start, begin. **2** *(introducir)* to initiate (en, in).
  ▶ *vpr* **iniciarse** *(empezar)* to start, begin.

iniciativa *nf* initiative.

inicio *nm* beginning, start.

inimitable *adj* inimitable.

injertar *vt* to graft.

injerto *nm* graft.

injuria *nf* insult, affront.

injuriar *vt (insultar)* to insult.

injusticia *nf* injustice, unfairness.

injusto,-a *adj* unfair, unjust.

inmadurez *nf* immaturity.

inmaduro,-a *adj* immature.

inmediaciones *nf pl (de una zona)* surrounding area *sing*; *(de una casa)* vicinity *sing*.

inmediato,-a *adj* **1** *(poco después)* immediate. **2** *(contiguo)* next (a, to), adjoining (a, -).

inmejorable *adj (gen)* unbeatable.

inmensidad *nf* **1** immensity. **2** *(gran cantidad)* great number.

inmenso,-a *adj* immense, vast.

inmersión *nf (gen)* immersion; *(de un buceador, submarino)* dive.

inmerso,-a *adj* immersed (en, in).

inmigración *nf* immigration.

inmigrante *adj* immigrant.
  ▶ *nm o nf* immigrant.

inmigrar *vi* to immigrate.

inminente *adj* imminent.

inmobiliario,-a *adj* property, US real estate.
  ▶ *nf* **(agencia) inmobiliaria** estate agency, US real estate company.

inmolar *vt* to immolate, sacrifice.

inmoral *adj* immoral.
inmoralidad *nf* immorality.
inmortal *adj* immortal.
inmortalidad *nf* immortality.
inmortalizar *vt* to immortalize.
inmóvil *adj* still, motionless.
inmovilizar *vt* to immobilize.
inmueble *nm* building.
inmundo,-a *adj (sucio)* dirty, filthy.
inmune *adj* MED immune (a, to).
inmunidad *nf* immunity.
inmutar *vt* to affect.
▶ *vpr* **inmutarse** to react.
innato,-a *adj* innate, inborn.
innecesario,-a *adj* unnecessary.
innegable *adj* undeniable.
innovación *nf* innovation.
innovador,-ra *adj* innovatory.
▶ *nm & nf* innovator.
innovar *vi* to innovate.
innumerable *adj* innumerable, countless.
inocencia *nf* innocence.
inocentada *nf* practical joke.
inocente *adj* **1** innocent. **2** *(ingenuo)* naive, innocent.
▶ *nm o nf* naive person, innocent person.
inocuo,-a *adj* innocuous, harmless.
inodoro,-a *adj* odourless.
▶ *nm* **inodoro** toilet.
inofensivo,-a *adj* harmless, inoffensive.
inolvidable *adj* unforgettable.
inoperante *adj* ineffective, inoperative.
inopia LOC **estar en la inopia 1** *fam (distraído)* to have one's head in the clouds. **2** *(ignorante)* to be in the dark.
inoportuno,-a *adj* inopportune.
inorgánico,-a *adj* inorganic.
inoxidable *adj* rustproof.
input *nm* input.
inquebrantable *adj (promesa)* unbreakable; *(fe)* unshakeable.
inquietante *adj* disturbing.
inquietar *vt* to worry.

▶ *vpr* **inquietarse** to worry (por, about).
inquieto,-a *adj* **1** *(agitado)* restless. **2** *(preocupado)* worried, anxious.
inquietud *nf* **1** *(agitación)* restlessness. **2** *(preocupación)* worry, anxiety.
inquilino,-a *nm & nf* tenant.
inquina *nf* animosity, antipathy. LOC **tener inquina a** ALGN to feel animosity towards SB.
insaciable *adj* insatiable.
insalubre *adj* unhealthy.
insano,-a *adj* **1** *(no sano)* unhealthy. **2** *(loco)* insane.
insatisfecho,-a *adj* dissatisfied, unsatisfied.
inscribir *vt* **1** *(grabar)* to inscribe. **2** *(apuntar)* to register; *(en un curso)* to enrol.
▶ *vpr* **inscribirse** *(gen)* to register; *(para un curso)* to enrol.
inscripción *nf* **1** *(grabado)* inscription. **2** *(registro)* registration; *(en un curso)* enrolment.
insecticida *adj* insecticidal.
▶ *nm* insecticide.
insecto *nm* insect.
inseguridad *nf* **1** *(falta de confianza)* insecurity. **2** *(duda)* uncertainty. **3** *(peligro)* lack of safety.
inseguro,-a *adj* **1** *(sin confianza)* insecure. **2** *(que duda)* uncertain. **3** *(peligroso)* unsafe.
insensato,-a *adj* foolish.
▶ *nm & nf* fool.
insensible *adj* **1** insensitive, unfeeling, thoughtless. **2** MED insensible.
inseparable *adj* inseparable.
insertar *vt* to insert (en, into).
inservible *adj* useless.
insigne *adj* distinguished, eminent.
insignia *nf (distintivo)* badge.
insignificante *adj* insignificant.
insinuación *nf* **1** *(indicación)* insinuation, hint. **2** *fam (amorosa)* overture. LOC **hacerle insinuaciones a** ALGN *(insinuarse)* to make a pass at SB.
insinuar *vt* to insinuate, hint.
insípido,-a *adj* insipid.

insistencia *nf* insistence.

insistente *adj* insistent.

insistir *vi* **1** to insist (en, on). **2** *(enfatizar)* to stress (en, -).

insobornable *adj* incorruptible.

insolación *nf* MED sunstroke.

insolencia *nf* **1** *(atrevimiento)* insolence. **2** *(palabra)* cheeky remark.

insolente *adj* **1** *(descarado)* insolent. **2** *(soberbio)* haughty.

insolidario,-a *adj* unsupportive.

insólito,-a *adj* extremely unusual.

insolvente *adj* insolvent.

insomne *adj* sleepless.
  ▶ *nm o nf* insomniac.

insomnio *nm* insomnia.

insondable *adj* unfathomable.

insonorizado,-a *adj* soundproof.

insonorizar *vt* to soundproof.

insoportable *adj* unbearable.

insospechado, -a *adj* unexpected.

insostenible *adj* untenable.

inspección *nf* *(gen)* examination, inspection; *(policial)* search.

inspeccionar *vt* *(gen)* to inspect; *(zona, lugar del crimen)* to search.

inspector,-ra *nm & nf* inspector.

inspiración *nf* **1** inspiration. **2** *(inhalación)* inhalation.

inspirado,-a *adj* inspired.

inspirar *vt* **1** *(aspirar)* to inhale, breathe in. **2** *(infundir)* to inspire.
  ▶ *vpr* **inspirarse** to be inspired (en, by).

instalación *nf* installation.
  ▶ *nf pl* **instalaciones** *(de un servicio)* facilities *pl*.

instalador,-ra *nm & nf* installer, fitter.

instalar *vt* **1** *(colocar)* to install. **2** *(equipar)* to fit out.
  ▶ *vpr* **instalarse** *(persona)* to settle; *(empresa)* to set up.

instancia *nf* *(petición)* request; *(solicitud)* form.

instantánea *nf* *(foto)* snapshot, snap.

instantáneo,-a *adj* **1** *(inmediato)* instantaneous, immediate. **2** *(momentáneo)* brief, fleeting.

instante *nm* moment, instant.

instar *vi* *(insistir)* to press, urge.

instauración *nf* establishment.

instaurar *vt* to establish.

instigar *vt* to instigate.

instintivo,-a *adj* instinctive.

instinto *nm* instinct.

institución *nf* **1** *(organismo)* institution. **2** *(creación)* establishment, institution; *(introducción)* introduction.

institucional *adj* institutional.

instituir *vt* **1** *(crear)* to institute, establish. **2** *(nombrar)* to appoint.

instituto *nm* **1** *(asociación)* institute. **2** EDUC state secondary school, US high school. COMP **instituto de bachillerato** state secondary school, US high school.

institutriz *nf* governess.

instrucción *nf* **1** *(enseñanza)* instruction; *(cultura)* education. **2** MIL military training.
  ▶ *nf pl* **instrucciones** *(indicaciones)* instructions.

instructivo,-a *adj* *(conferencia)* instructive; *(juguete)* educational.

instructor,-ra *adj* *(gen)* instructing.
  ▶ *nm & nf* instructor.

instruido,-a *adj* well-educated.

instruir *vt* **1** *(enseñar)* to instruct. **2** MIL to train. **3** JUR to investigate.

instrumental *adj* *(música)* instrumental.
  ▶ *nm* instruments *pl*.

instrumentar *vt* *(gen)* to arrange; *(para orquesta)* to orchestrate.

instrumentista *nm o nf* *(músico)* instrumentalist.

instrumento *nm* instrument.

insubordinado,-a *adj* insubordinate.
  ▶ *nm & nf* insubordinate person.

insubordinar *vt* to stir up.
  ▶ *vpr* **insubordinarse** to rebel.

insuficiente *adj* insufficient.
  ▶ *nm* EDUC fail.

insufrible *adj* insufferable.

insular *adj* insular.
  ▶ *nm o nf* islander.

insulina *nf* insulin.

insulso,-a *adj* insipid, tasteless.

insultante *adj* insulting.

insultar *vt* to insult.

insulto *nm* insult.

insumisión *nf (gen)* rebelliousness.

insumiso,-a *adj* rebellious.
► *nm & nf* MIL *person who refuses to do military service or community service in lieu.*

insuperable *adj (calidad, capacidad)* unbeatable; *(obstáculo, miedo, complejo)* unsurmountable, insuperable.

insurgente *adj* insurgent.

insurrección *nf* insurrection.

intachable *adj* irreproachable.

intacto,-a *adj* intact.

integración *nf* integration.

integral *adj* **1** *(completo)* full. **2** *(pan, pasta)* wholemeal; *(arroz)* brown.

integrante *adj* integral.
► *nm o nf* member.

integrar *vt (formar)* to make up.
► *vpr* **integrarse** to integrate.

integridad *nf* integrity.

integrismo *nm (gen)* reaction; *(religioso)* fundamentalism.

integrista *adj (gen)* reactionary; *(religioso)* fundamentalist.
► *nm o nf (gen)* reactionary; *(en religión)* fundamentalist.

íntegro,-a *adj* **1** *(completo)* whole, entire; *(versión)* unabridged. **2** *(honrado)* honest, upright.

intelecto *nm* intellect.

intelectual *adj* intellectual.
► *nm o nf* intellectual.

inteligencia *nf* intelligence. COMP **inteligencia artificial** artificial intelligence.

inteligente *adj* intelligent.

intemperie *nf* bad weather. LOC **a la intemperie** in the open (air).

intempestivo,-a *adj* inopportune.

intemporal *adj* timeless.

intención *nf (propósito)* intention.

intencionado,-a *adj* deliberatel.

intendencia *nf* MIL *(cuerpo)* ≈ service corps, US quartermaster corps.

intendente *nm* **1** supervisor. **2** MIL quartermaster general.

intensidad *nf* **1** *(gen)* intensity. **2** *(de una enfermedad)* severity; *(del dolor)* acuteness. **3** *(de la luz, del color)* brightness, intensity; *(del amor, de la fe)* strength.

intensificar *vt* to intensify.

intensivo,-a *adj* intensive.

intenso,-a *adj* **1** *(gen)* intense. **2** *(dolor)* acute. **3** *(luz, color)* bright, intense. **4** *(amor)* passionate.

intentar *vt* to try.

intento *nm* attempt, try.

interactivo,-a *adj* interactive.

intercalar *vt* to insert.

intercambiar *vt* to exchange.

intercambio *nm* exchange.

interceder *vi* to intercede.

interceptar *vt* **1** *(mensaje, correspondencia)* to intercept. **2** *(obstruir)* to block.

interceptor *adj* intercepting.
► *nm* interceptor.

intercesión *nf* intercession.

intercesor,-ra *adj* interceding.
► *nm & nf* intercessor.

interconexión *nf* interconnection.

interés *nm* **1** *(gen)* interest; *(propio)* self-interest. **2** FIN interest.

interesado,-a *adj* **1** *(gen)* interested. **2** *(egoísta)* selfish, self-interested.
► *nm & nf* **1** *(gen)* interested party. **2** *(egoísta)* selfish person.

interesante *adj* interesting.

interesar *vt* **1** to interest. **2** *(afectar)* to concern.
► *vpr* **interesarse** to take an interest (por, in).

interfaz *nf* interface.

interferencia *nf* **1** *(gen)* interference; *(intencionada)* jamming. **2** *fig* interference.

interferir *vt* **1** *(transmisión, programa)* to jam. **2** *(obstaculizar)* to interfere in.
► *vi* to meddle, interfere.

interfono *nm* intercom.

interino,-a *adj* **1** temporary, provisional. **2** *(director, presidente)* acting.
► *nm & nf (sustituto)* stand-in.

interior *adj* **1** *(bolsillo)* inside; *(habitación)* without a view, interior; *(jardín)* interior. **2** *(del país)* domestic, internal. **3** GEOG inland.

▶ *nm* **1** *(en una vivienda)* inside: *pasemos al interior* let's go inside. **2** *(conciencia)* inside. **3** GEOG interior.

interiorismo *nm* interior design.

interiorista *nm o nf* interior designer.

interiorizar *vt (creencia, principio)* to internalize.

interjección *nf* interjection.

interlocutor,-ra *nm & nf* speaker, interlocutor.

intermediario,-a *nm & nf (gen)* intermediary; *(en disputas)* mediator.

intermedio,-a *adj (gen)* intermediate; *(tamaño)* medium; *(calidad)* average; *(tiempo)* intervening; *(espacio)* between.
▶ *nm* **intermedio** *(de un espectáculo)* interval, intermission.

interminable *adj* endless, interminable.

intermitencia *nf* intermittence.

intermitente *adj (gen)* intermittent.
▶ *nm* AUTO indicator, US blinker.

internacional *adj* international.

internado *nm* boarding school.

internar *vt (en un colegio)* to send to boarding school; *(en un hospital)* to confine (en, to).
▶ *vpr* **internarse** *(penetrar)* to penetrate.

internauta *nm o nf* internaut, netsurfer.

interno,-a *adj* **1** *(órgano)* internal. **2** *(alumno)* boarding.
▶ *nm & nf* **1** *(alumno)* boarder. **2** *(médico)* intern. **3** *(preso)* prisoner.

interpelar *vt* POL to interpellate.

interponer *vt* to interpose.
▶ *vpr* **interponerse 1** *(físicamente)* to interpose os. **2** *fig* to intervene.

interpretación *nf* **1** *(gen)* interpretation. **2** *(de pieza, obra)* performance.

interpretar *vt* **1** to interpret. **2** *(obra, pieza)* to perform; *(papel)* to play.

intérprete *nm o nf* **1** *(traductor)* interpreter. **2** *(actor, músico)* performer.

interrelación *nf* interrelation.

interrelacionar *vt* to interrelate.

interrogación *nf* **1** *(acción)* interrogation, questioning. **2** *(signo)* question mark. **3** *(pregunta)* question.

interrogador,-a *nm & nf* interrogator.

interrogante *nm (incógnita)* question mark.

interrogar *vt* **1** to question. **2** *(a testigo, etc)* to interrogate.

interrogativo,-a *adj* interrogative.

interrogatorio *nm* interrogation.

interrumpir *vt* **1** *(gen)* to interrupt. **2** *(tráfico)* to block.

interrupción *nf* interruption.

interruptor *nm* switch.

intersección *nf* intersection.

interurbano,-a *adj (gen)* inter-city; *(llamada)* trunk, long-distance.

intervalo *nm* **1** *(de tiempo)* interval. **2** *(de espacio)* gap.

intervención *nf* **1** *(gen)* intervention **2** *(discurso)* speech. **3** MED operation.

intervenir *vi* **1** *(tomar parte)* to take part (en, in). **2** *(hablar)* to speak (en, at).
▶ *vt* **1** MED to operate on. **2** *(alijo, mercancía)* to seize.

interventor,-ra *nm & nf (gen)* inspector, auditor.

intestinal *adj* intestinal.

intestino *nm* intestine.

intimar *vi* to become close (con, to).

intimidación *nf* intimidation.

intimidad *nf* **1** *(amistad)* intimacy. **2** *(vida privada)* privacy, private life.

intimidar *vt* to intimidate.

íntimo,-a *adj* **1** *(vida)* private. **2** *(amigo, relación)* close. **3** *(sentimiento, emoción)* most intimate. **4** *(higiene)* personal.
▶ *nm & nf (amigo)* close friend.

intocable *adj* untouchable.

intolerable *adj* intolerable.

intolerancia *nf* intolerance: *intolerancia a la lactosa* intolerance of lactose.

intolerante *adj* intolerant.

intoxicación *nf* poisoning.

intoxicar *vt* to poison.
▶ *vpr* **intoxicarse** to poison os.

intraducible *adj* untranslatable.

intranquilidad *nf* worry, uneasiness.

intranquilizar *vt* to worry.
▶ *vpr* **intranquilizarse** to get worried.
intranquilo,-a *adj* worried, uneasy.
intransferible *adj* nontransferable.
intransigencia *nf* intransigence.
intransigente *adj* intransigent.
intransitable *adj* impassable.
intransitivo,-a *adj* intransitive.
intrascendente *adj* unimportant, insignificant.
intratable *adj (persona)* unsociable.
intrépido,-a *adj* intrepid.
intriga *nf* 1 *(maquinación secreta)* intrigue. 2 *(curiosidad)* curiosity. 3 *(de una narración, película)* intrigue.
intrigado,-a *adj* intrigued.
intrigante *adj* intriguing.
intrigar *vt (interesar)* to intrigue.
intrínseco,-a *adj* intrinsic.
introducción *nf* introduction.
introducir *vt* 1 *(gen)* to introduce; *(legislación)* to introduce, bring in. 2 *(meter)* to put, place; *(insertar)* insert. 3 *(importar)* to bring in, import.
▶ *vpr* **introducirse** *(entrar)* to get in.
intromisión *nf* interference, meddling.
introspectivo,-a *adj* introspective.
introvertido,-a *adj* introverted.
▶ *nm & nf* introvert.
intruso,-a *adj* intrusive.
▶ *nm & nf* intruder.
intuición *nf* intuition.
intuir *vt* to sense, feel.
intuitivo,-a *adj* intuitive.
inundación *nf* flood, flooding.
inundar *vt* 1 to flood. 2 *fig* to inundate.
inusitado,-a *adj* uncommon, rare.
inusual *adj* unusual.
inútil *adj* 1 *(gen)* useless. 2 *(intento)* vain.
▶ *nm o nf fam (persona)* hopeless case.
inutilizar *vt* 1 to render useless. 2 *(máquina)* to put out of action.
invadir *vt* to invade.
inválido,-a *adj* disabled, handicapped.
▶ *nm & nf* disabled person.
invariable *adj* invariable.
invasión *nf* invasion.

invasor,-ra *adj* invading.
▶ *nm & nf* invader.
invencible *adj (ejército)* invincible; *(obstáculo)* unsurmountable.
invención *nf* invention.
invendible *adj* unsaleable.
inventar *vt* 1 *(crear)* to invent. 2 *(mentir)* to make up, fabricate.
inventario *nm* inventory.
inventiva *nf* inventiveness.
invento *nm* invention.
inventor,-ra *nm & nf* inventor.
invernadero *nm* greenhouse.
invernal *adj* winter, wintry.
invernar *vi (animales)* to hibernate.
inverosímil *adj* unlikely.
inversión *nf* 1 *(gen)* inversion. 2 FIN investment.
inverso,-a *adj* inverse, opposite.
invertebrado,-a *adj* invertebrate.
▶ *nm* **invertebrado** invertebrate.
invertido,-a *adj* reversed, inverted.
invertir *vt* 1 *(orden)* to invert, reverse. 2 *(dirección)* to reverse. 3 *(tiempo)* to spend (en, on). 4 FIN to invest (en, in).
investidura *nf* investiture.
investigación *nf* 1 *(indagación)* investigation, enquiry. 2 *(estudio)* research.
investigador,-ra *adj* 1 *(que indaga)* investigating. 2 *(que estudia)* research.
▶ *nm & nf* 1 *(científico)* researcher. 2 *(detective)* investigator.
investigar *vt* 1 *(indagar)* to investigate. 2 *(campo)* to do research on.
investir *vt* to invest.
inviable *adj* non-viable, unfeasible.
invidente *adj* blind.
▶ *nm o nf* blind person.
invierno *nm* winter.
invisible *adj* invisible.
invitación *nf* invitation.
invitado,-a *adj* invited.
▶ *nm & nf* guest.
invitar *vt* to invite.
▶ *vi (incitar)* to encourage.
invocar *vt* to invoke.
involucrar *vt* to involve (en, in).

involuntario,-a *adj (reflejo, movimiento)* involuntary; *(error)* unintentional.

invulnerable *adj* invulnerable.

inyección *nf* injection.

inyectable *adj* injectable.
► *nm* injection.

inyectar *vt* to inject (en, into).

iodo *nm* iodine.

ir *vi* **1** *(gen)* to go; *(acudir)* to come. **2** *(camino, etc)* to lead. **3** *(funcionar)* to work, go. **4** *(sentar bien)* to suit; *(agradar)* to like. **5** *(tratar)* to be about.
► *aux* **ir + a + 1** going to: *voy a venderlo* I'm going to sell it. **2 ir +** : *fuimos andando* we walked, we went on foot. **3 ir +** to be: *ir cansado,-a* to be tired.
► *vpr* **irse 1** *(marcharse)* to go away, leave. **2** *(deslizarse)* to slip. **3** *(gastarse)* to go, disappear.

ira *nf* wrath, rage.

iracundo,-a *adj* irritable, irate

Irak *nm* Iraq.

Irán *nm* Iran.

iraní *adj* Iranian.
► *nm o nf* Iranian.

iranio,-a *adj* Iranian.
► *nm & nf (persona)* Iranian.
► *nm* **iranio** *(idioma)* Iranian.

iraquí *adj* Iraqi.
► *nm o nf (persona)* Iraqi.
► *nm (idioma)* Iraqi.

irascible *adj* irascible, irritable.

iris *nm inv* iris.

Irlanda *nf* Ireland. [COMP] **Irlanda del Norte** Northern Ireland.

irlandés,-esa *adj* Irish.
► *nm & nf (persona - hombre)* Irishman; *(- mujer)* Irish woman.
► *nm* **irlandés** *(idioma)* Irish.

ironía *nf* irony.

irónico,-a *adj* **1** ironic. **2** *(burlón)* mocking.

irracional *adj* irrational.

irradiar *vt* to irradiate, radiate.

irreal *adj* unreal.

irreconocible *adj* unrecognizable.

irreflexivo,-a *adj (acto)* rash; *(persona)* impetuous.

irregular *adj* irregular.

irregularidad *nf* irregularity.

irrelevante *adj* irrelevant.

irremediable *adj (daño)* irremediable.

irrepetible *adj* unrepeatable.

irreprochable *adj* irreproachable.

irresistible *adj* **1** irresistible. **2** *pey (insoportable)* unbearable.

irrespetuoso,-a *adj* disrespectful.

irresponsable *adj* irresponsible.
► *nm o nf* irresponsible person.

irreversible *adj* irreversible.

irrigar *vt* to irrigate.

irrisorio,-a *adj* derisory, ridiculous.

irritable *adj* irritable.

irritación *nf* irritation.

irritante *adj* irritating, annoying.

irritar *vt* to irritate.
► *vpr* **irritarse** to get annoyed.

irrumpir *vi* to burst (en, into).

irrupción *nf* irruption.

isla *nf* island.

islam *nm* Islam.

islámico,-a *adj* Islamic.

islandés,-esa *adj* Icelandic.
► *nm & nf (persona)* Icelander.
► *nm* **islandés** *(idioma)* Icelandic.

Islandia *nf* Iceland.

isleño,-a *adj* island.
► *nm & nf* islander.

islote *nm* small uninhabited island.

isósceles *adj* isosceles.

Israel *nm* Israel.

israelí *adj* Israeli.
► *nm o nf* Israeli.

istmo *nm* isthmus.

Italia *nf* Italy.

italiano,-a *adj* Italian.
► *nm & nf (persona)* Italian.
► *nm* **italiano** *(idioma)* Italian.

itinerante *adj* itinerant.

itinerario *nm* itinerary.

izar *vt* to hoist.

izquierda *nf* **1** *(mano)* left hand; *(pierna)* left leg. **2** POL the left.

izquierdista *adj* left-wing.

izquierdo,-a *adj* left.

J

J, j *nf (la letra)* J, j.

jabalí *nm* wild boar.

jabalina *nf* DEP javelin.

jabato *nm* ZOOL young wild boar.

jabón *nm* soap. COMP **jabón de tocador** toilet soap.

jabonera *nf* soap dish.

jabonoso,-a *adj* soapy.

jaca *nf* cob, small horse.

jacinto *nm* hyacinth.

jactarse *vpr* to boast, brag (de, about).

jacuzzi® *nm* jacuzzi®.

jade *nm* jade.

jadear *vi* to pant.

jadeo *nm* panting.

jaguar *nm* jaguar.

jalea *nf* jelly. COMP **jalea real** royal jelly.

jalear *vt* **1** *(animar)* to cheer (on), clap and shout at. **2** *(caza)* to urge on.

jaleo *nm* **1** *(alboroto)* din, racket: *no se oye nada con este jaleo* I can't hear a thing with all this racket. **2** *(escándalo)* fuss, commotion.

jalón *nm* **1** *(estaca)* stake, post. **2** *fig* milestone, landmark.

jalonar *vt (con estacas)* to stake out.

Jamaica *nf* Jamaica.

jamaicano,-a *adj* Jamaican.
▶ *nm & nf* Jamaican.

jamás *adv (+ indic)* never; *(+ subj)* ever: *jamás volveré* I shall never return. LOC **jamás de los jamases** never ever. ‖ **por siempre jamás** for ever (and ever).

jamba *nf* jamb.

jamón *nm (curado)* cured ham; *(pata del cerdo)* leg of ham. COMP **jamón de York/ jamón en dulce** boiled ham. ‖ **jamón serrano** cured ham.

Japón *nm* Japan.

japonés,-esa *adj* Japanese.
▶ *nm & nf (persona)* Japanese.
▶ *nm* **japonés** *(idioma)* Japanese.

jaque *nm* check. COMP **jaque mate** checkmate.

jaqueca *nf* migraine, headache.

jarabe *nm* MED syrup, mixture. COMP **jarabe para la tos** cough syrup.

jardín *nm* garden. COMP **jardín botánico** botanical garden. ‖ **jardín de infancia** nursery school.

jardinera *nf* **1** *(mujer)* gardener. **2** *(mueble para tiestos)* plant stand; *(en ventana)* window box.

jardinería *nf* gardening.

jardinero,-a *nm & nf* gardener.

jarra *nf* **1** *(para servir)* jug, US pitcher. **2** *(para beber)* tankard, beer mug.

jarro *nm* **1** *(recipiente)* jug. **2** *(contenido)* jugful.

jarrón *nm* **1** vase. **2** ARTE urn.

jaspeado,-a *adj* mottled, speckled.

jaula *nf* cage.

jauría *nf* pack of hounds.

Java *nf* Java.

javanés,-esa *adj* Javanese.
▶ *nm & nf* Javanese.

jazmín *nm* jasmine.

jazz *nm* jazz.

jeep® *nm* jeep.

jefatura *nf (sede)* central office; *(militar)* headquarters.

jefe,-a *nm & nf* **1** boss, head, chief. **2** COM *(hombre)* manager; *(mujer)* manageress. **3** POL leader. **4** *(de una tribu)* chief. COMP **jefe de cocina** chef. ‖ **jefe de estación** station master. ‖ **jefe de Estado** Head of State.

jengibre *nm* ginger.

jeque *nm* sheik, sheikh.

jerarquía *nf* **1** hierarchy. **2** *(grado)* scale. **3** *(categoría)* rank.

jerárquico,-a *adj* hierarchical.

jerez *nm* sherry.

jerga *nf (lenguaje)* jargon.

jergón *nm (colchón)* pallet.

jeringuilla *nf* syringe.

jeroglífico,-a *adj* hieroglyphic.
▶ *nm* jeroglífico **1** hieroglyph, hieroglyphic. **2** *(juego)* rebus.

jersey *nm* sweater, pullover, jumper.

jesuita *nm o nf* Jesuit.

jet *nm* jet.

jilguero *nm* goldfinch.

jinete *nm* rider, horseman.

jirafa *nf* giraffe.

jirón *nm* shred: *una camisa hecha jirones* a tattered shirt.

jocoso,-a *adj (persona)* jocular; *(tono)* humorous, jokey.

jofaina *nf* washbasin.

jogging *nm* jogging: *practican el jogging* they go jogging.

jolgorio *nm* **1** *(juerga)* binge. **2** *(algazara)* party.

Jordania *nf* Jordan.

jordano,-a *adj* Jordanian.
▶ *nm & nf* Jordanian.

jornada *nf* **1** *(día de trabajo)* working day: *una jornada de ocho horas* an eight-hour day. **2** *(camino recorrido)* day's journey. **3** *(en periodismo)* day: *las noticias de la jornada* today's news. COMP **media jornada** half-day.

jornal *nm* day's wage.

jornalero,-a *nm & nf* day labourer.

joroba *nf (deformidad)* hump.

jorobado,-a *adj* hunchbacked.
▶ *nm & nf* hunchback.

jorobar *vt* **1** *fam (fastidiar)* to bother, annoy. **2** *fam (romper)* to smash up, break. **3** *fam (estropear)* to ruin, wreck.

jota *nf popular Spanish dance and music.*

joven *adj* young.
▶ *nm o nf (hombre)* youth, young man; *(mujer)* young lady, girl.

jovial *adj* jovial, cheerful.

jovialidad *nf* joviality, cheerfulness.

joya *nf* jewel, piece of jewellery.

joyería *nf (tienda)* jewellery shop, jeweller's shop.

joyero,-a *nm & nf* jeweller.
▶ *nm* joyero jewellery case.

juanete *nm (en el pie)* bunion.

jubilación *nf* **1** *(acción)* retirement. **2** *(dinero)* pension.

jubilado,-a *adj* retired.
▶ *nm o nf* pensioner, retired person.

jubilar *vt* **1** *(retirar)* to retire. **2** *(persona)* to pension off; *(objeto)* to get rid of.
▶ *vpr* jubilarse *(retirarse)* to retire.

júbilo *nm* jubilation, joy.

jubiloso,-a *adj* jubilant, joyful.

jubón *nm arc* doublet.

judaico,-a *adj* Judaic.

judaísmo *nm* Judaism.

judería *nf* Jewish quarter.

judía *nf (planta)* bean. COMP **judía verde** French bean, green bean.

judicatura *nf* **1** *(profesión)* judgeship. **2** *(cuerpo)* judiciary, judicature.

judicial *adj* judicial.

judío,-a *adj (gen)* Jewish.
▶ *nm & nf (persona)* Jew.

judo *nm* judo.

judoca *nm o nf* judoka.

juego *nm* **1** *(gen)* game; *(actividad deportiva)* sport. **2** *(con dinero)* gambling. **3** *(acción de jugar)* playing. **4** *(conjunto de piezas)* set: *un juego de llaves* a set of keys. COMP **juego de azar** game of chance. ❙ **juego de café/té** coffee/tea service.

juerga *nf fam* rave-up, bash.

juerguista *adj* fun-loving.
▶ *nm o nf* raver.

jueves *nm inv* Thursday: *todos los jueves* every Thursday; *el jueves que viene* next Thursday; *el jueves pasado* last Thursday; *el jueves por la mañana/tarde/noche* Thursday morning/afternoon/night.

juez,-za *nm & nf* judge. COMP **juez de línea** linesman. ❙ **juez de paz** justice of the peace.

jugada *nf* **1** *(en ajedrez)* move; *(en billar)* shot; *(en dardos)* throw. **2** *(momento del juego)* move, piece of play. **3** *fam* dirty trick.

jugador,-ra *nm & nf* **1** player. **2** *(apostador)* gambler.

jugar *vi* to play.
▶ *vt (intervenir)* to play, go: *¿quién juega?* whose go is it?
▶ *vpr* **jugarse 1** *(arriesgar)* to risk. **2** *(apostarse)* to bet: *¿cuánto te juegas a que no viene?* what's the betting he won't come?

jugarreta *nf fam* dirty trick.

juglar *nm* minstrel.

jugo *nm* **1** *(gen)* juice. **2** *(interés)* substance.

jugoso,-a *adj (fruta, carne)* juicy.

juguete *nm* **1** toy. **2** *fig* plaything.

juguetear *vi* to play (con, with).

juguetería *nf (tienda)* toy shop.

juguetón,-ona *adj* playful.

juicio *nm* **1** *(gen)* judgement: *a mi juicio* in my opinion. **2** *(sensatez)* reason, common sense. **3** JUR trial. LOC **en su sano juicio** in one's right mind. ‖ **llevar a ALGN a juicio** to take legal action against SB. ‖ **perder el juicio** to go mad.

juicioso,-a *adj (persona)* sensible, wise.

juliana *nf* damewort.

julio¹ *nm* July.

✎ Para ejemplos de uso, consulta marzo.

julio² *nm* FÍS joule.

jumbo *nm* jumbo jet.

juncal *nm* BOT reedbed.

junco *nm* BOT rush, reed.

jungla *nf* jungle.

junio *nm* June.

✎ Para ejemplos de uso, consulta marzo.

júnior *adj* DEP junior.

junta *nf (reunión)* meeting, assembly.

juntar *vt* **1** *(unir)* to put together; *(piezas)* to assemble. **2** *(reunir - dinero)* to raise; *(- gente)* to gather together.
▶ *vpr* **juntarse 1** *(unirse)* to join, get together; *(ríos, caminos)* to meet. **2** *(acercarse)* to squeeze up: *juntaos un poco que no quepo* squeeze up, I can't get in.

junto,-a *adj* together. LOC **junto a** next to. ‖ **junto con** along with, together with.

jura *nf (acción)* oath; *(ceremonia)* swearing-in, pledge.

jurado,-a *adj* sworn.
▶ *nm* **jurado** JUR *(tribunal)* jury; *(miembro del tribunal)* juror, member of the jury.

juramentar *vt* to swear in.

juramento *nm* **1** JUR oath. **2** *(blasfemia)* swearword.

jurar *vt* to swear, take an oath.
▶ *vi (blasfemar)* to curse, swear.

jurásico,-a *adj* Jurassic.

jurel *nm* scad, horse mackerel.

jurídico,-a *adj* legal, juridical.

jurisdicción *nf* jurisdiction.

jurisprudencia *nf* jurisprudence.

jurista *nm o nf* jurist, lawyer.

justicia *nf* **1** *(equidad, derecho)* justice, fairness. **2** **la justicia** *(organismo)* the law.

justiciero,-a *adj* avenging.

justificable *adj* justifiable.

justificación *nf* justification.

justificante *adj* justifying.
▶ *nm (prueba)* written proof.

justificar *vt* **1** *(acción)* to justify. **2** *(persona)* to excuse.
▶ *vpr* **justificarse** *(persona)* to justify os; *(acción)* to be justified.

justo,-a *adj* **1** *(persona, decisión)* just, fair. **2** *(ropa)* tight. **3** *(exacto)* exact: *tengo el dinero justo para el autobús* I have the exact money for the bus. **4** *(escaso)* just enough: *me queda lo justo para llegar a fin de mes* I have just enough money to get by.
▶ *adv* **justo** *(en el preciso momento)* just; *(en el preciso lugar)* right: *vivo justo en el centro de la ciudad* I live right in the centre of town.

juvenil *adj* **1** young, youthful. **2** DEP junior, youth.

juventud *nf* **1** *(período)* youth. **2** *(los jóvenes)* young people *pl*, youth *pl*.

juzgado *nm (local)* court. COMP **juzgado de guardia** court, police court.

juzgar *vt* **1** *(formar juicio)* to judge. **2** *(considerar)* to consider, think.

K

K, k *nf (la letra)* K, k.
kaki *nm* **1** *(árbol)* persimmon tree. **2** *(fruta)* persimmon.
Kampuchea *nf* Kampuchea.
kampucheo,-a *adj* Kampuchean.
▶ *nm & nf* Kampuchean.
karst *nm* karst.
kárstico,-a *adj* karstic.
kart® *nm* go-kart, kart.
karting *nm* go-kart racing, karting.
Kathmandu *nm* Katmandu, Kathmandu.
kayac *nm* kayak.
kazajio,-a *adj* Kazakh.
▶ *nm & nf (persona)* Kazakh.
▶ *nm* **kazajio** *(idioma)* Kazakh.
Kazajstán *nm* Kazakhstan.
Kenia *nf* Kenya.
keniano,-a *adj* Kenyan.
▶ *nm & nf* Kenyan.
keroseno *nm* kerosene.
Khartum *nm* Khartoum.
kilo *nm* **1** kilogram. **2** *argot (antiguamente)* million pesetas.
kilobyte *nm* kilobyte.
kilocaloría *nf* kilocalorie.

kilogramo *nm* kilogram.
kilohertz *nm inv* kilohertz.
kilolitro *nm* kilolitre, US kiloliter.
kilometraje *nm* ≈ mileage.
kilómetro *nm* kilometre, US kilometer.
kilowatt *nm* kilowatt.
kirguís *adj* Kirghiz.
▶ *nm o nf (persona)* Kirghiz.
▶ *nm (idioma)* Kirghiz.
Kirguizistán *nm* Kirghizstan, Kirghizia.
Kiribati *nm* Kiribati.
kiwi *nm* **1** *(ave)* kiwi. **2** *(fruta)* kiwi, kiwi fruit.
km/h *abrev* **(kilómetros hora)** kilometres (US kilometers) per hour; *(abreviatura)* kph.
knock-out *nm* knockout.
koala *nm* koala.
kurdo,-a *adj* Kurdish.
▶ *nm & nf (persona)* Kurd.
▶ *nm* **kurdo** *(idioma)* Kurdish.
Kuwait *nm* Kuwait.
kuwaití *adj* Kuwaiti.
▶ *nm & nf* Kuwaiti.
kW/h *abrev* **(kilovatios hora)** kilowatts per hour; *(abreviatura)* kWh.

L

L, l *nf (la letra)* L, l.

la¹ *art def* the: *la casa* the house.

la² *pron (persona)* her; *(cosa)* it: *la invité a cenar* I invited her to supper; *no la he leído* I haven't read it.

✎ Consulta también **las**.

la³ *nm* MÚS la, lah, A.

laberíntico,-a *adj* labyrinthic.

laberinto *nm* labyrinth, maze.

labial *adj (gen)* labial.
▶ *nf* LING labial.

labio *nm* lip.

labor *nf* **1** *(gen)* work: *las labores del campo* farm work.

✎ Consulta también **las**.

laborable *adj (de trabajo)* working.

laboral *adj* labour.

laboratorio *nm* laboratory.

laborioso,-a *adj (trabajoso)* laborious.

labrador,-ra *nm & nf* farmer.

labranza *nf* farming.

labrar *vt* AGR *(campo)* to work; *(con arado)* to plough (US plow).

labriego,-a *nm & nf* farm worker.

lacio,-a *adj (cabello)* straight.

lacón *nm* ham.

lacónico,-a *adj* laconic.

lacra *nf* **1** *(señal)* mark, scar. **2** *(defecto)* fault.

lacrado,-a *adj (sobre)* sealed with wax.

lacrar *vt* to seal (with sealing wax).

lacre *nm* sealing wax.

lacrimal *adj* tear, lacrimal, lachrymal.

lacrimoso,-a *adj* tearful.

lactancia *nf* lactation.

lactante *nm o nf* unweaned baby.

lácteo,-a *adj* milk, milky. COMP productos lácteos dairy products.

láctico,-a *adj* lactic.

lactosa *nf* lactose.

lacustre *adj* lake.

ladear *vt* to tilt.

ladeo *nm* tilt.

ladera *nf* hillside.

lado *nm (gen)* side. LOC **al lado de** ALGN next to SB: *me puse a su lado* I sat next to her. ‖ **estar al lado** *(muy cerca)* to be very near. ‖ **por un lado... por otro...** on the one hand… on the other hand…

ladrador,-ra *adj* barking.

ladrar *vi* to bark.

ladrido *nm* bark.

ladrillo *nm* brick.

ladrón,-ona *nm & nf (persona - que roba)* thief; *(- que tima, engaña)* crook.

lagartija *nf* small lizard.

lagarto,-a *nm & nf (animal)* lizard.

lago *nm* lake.

lágrima *nf* tear. LOC **llorar a lágrima viva** *fam* to cry one's eyes out.

lagrimal *adj* tear, lachrymal.
▶ *nm* corner of the eye.

lagrimear *vi* to run, water.

lagrimeo *nm* watering.

lagrimón *nm* large teardrop, large tear.

laguna *nf* small lake, lagoon.

laico,-a *adj* lay, secular.

laja *nf* slab.

lama¹ *nm* REL lama.

lama² *nf* **1** *(lámina)* slat. **2** *(barro)* slime.

lamentable *adj (injusticia)* regrettable, deplorable; *(estado)* sorry, pitiful.

lamentar *vt* to regret.
▶ *vpr* **lamentarse** to complain.

lamento *nm* moan, cry.

lamer *vt* to lick.

lametazo *nm* lick.

lametón *nm* lick.

lámina *nf* **1** *(gen)* sheet, plate. **2** *(ilustración)* illustration; *(grabado)* engraving.

laminado,-a *adj* laminated.

laminar *vt* to laminate.

lámpara *nf* lamp.

lamparón *nm fam* stain.

lamprea *nf* lamprey.

lana *nf* wool. LOC **de lana** woollen (US woolen).

lanar *adj* wool-bearing.

lance *nm* **1** *(suceso)* event. **2** *(pelea)* quarrel.

lanceolado,-a *adj* lanceolate.

lancero *nm* lancer.

lanceta *nf* lancet, lance.

lancha *nf (bote)* launch, boat. COMP **lancha salvavidas** lifeboat.

landa *nf* moor.

lanero,-a *adj* wool.

langosta *nf* **1** *(crustáceo)* crawfish, spiny lobster. **2** *(insecto)* locust.

langostino *nm type of* prawn.

languidecer *vi* to languish.

languidez *nf (falta de vigor)* languor.

lánguido,-a *adj (falto de vigor)* languid, languorous.

lanilla *nf (tejido)* flannel.

lanza *nf* lance, spear.

lanzadera *nf* shuttle.

lanzado,-a *adj (impetuoso)* impetuous; *(decidido)* determined.

lanzador,-ra *nm & nf (de jabalina)* thrower; *(de béisbol)* pitcher; *(de cricket)* bowler.

lanzamiento *nm* **1** *(acción de lanzar)* throwing. **2** *(de cohete)* launching. COMP **lanzamiento de peso** shot put.

lanzar *vt* **1** *(gen)* to throw. **2** *(cohete)* to launch. **3** *fig (grito)* to let out.
▶ *vpr* **lanzarse** *(actuar decididamente)* to throw os, launch os into.

Laos *nm* Laos.

laosiano,-a *adj* Laotian.
▶ *nm & nf (persona)* Laotian.
▶ *nm* **laosiano** *(idioma)* Laotian.

lapa *nf (molusco)* limpet.

laparoscopia *nf* laparoscopy.

lapicero *nm* pencil.

lápida *nf* tombstone, slab.

lápiz *nm* pencil. COMP **lápiz de ojos** eyeliner. ▌**lápiz óptico** light pen.

lapso *nm (de tiempo)* period of time.

lapsus *nm inv (error)* slip; *(de memoria)* memory lapse, lapse of memory.

laquear *vt* to lacquer.

largar *vt* **1** *fam (dar)* to give: *le largó un discurso de media hora* he gave him a half-hour speech. **2** *fam (contar)* to tell: *esa lo larga todo* she can't keep anything to herself.
▶ *vpr* **largarse** *fam (irse)* to go, leave: *me largo* I'm off, US I'm out of here.

largo,-a *adj (en longitud)* long. LOC **a lo largo de** along, throughout: *a lo largo del año* throughout the year. ▌**dar largas a** ALGN to put SB off. ▌**pasar de largo** to pass by.
▶ *nm* **largo 1** length: *¿qué mide de largo?* how long is it?, what length is it? **2** *(de piscina)* length, US lap.

largometraje *nm* feature film.

larguero *nm (en fútbol)* crossbar.

larguirucho,-a *adj fam* lanky.

largura *nf* length.

laringe *nf* larynx.

laríngeo,-a *adj* laryngeal.

laringitis *nf inv* laryngitis.

laringología *nf* laryngology.

laringólogo,-a *nm & nf* laryngologist.

larva *nf* larva.

larvario,-a *adj* larval.

las *art def* the: *las casas* the houses.
▶ *pron (objeto directo)* them: *las vi* I saw them.

✎ Consulta también **la**.

lasca *nf* chip.

láser *nm inv* laser.

lasitud *nf* lassitude, weariness.

lástima *nf* pity.

lastimar *vt (herir)* to hurt, injure.
▶ *vpr* **lastimarse** to hurt os.

lastimero,-a *adj* pitiful.

lastimoso,-a *adj* pitiful, sorry.

L

lastrar *vt* MAR to ballast.
lastre *nm* MAR ballast.
lata *nf* 1 *(hojalata)* tin plate. 2 *(envase)* tin, can. 3 *(fastidio)* bore, drag, pain: *es una lata tener que estudiar los fines de semana* it's a pain having to study at weekends.
latente *adj* latent.
lateral *adj (gen)* side.
látex *nm inv* latex.
latido *nm* beat.
latifundio *nm (finca)* latifundium.
latigazo *nm* lash.
látigo *nm* whip.
latín *nm* Latin.
latino,-a *adj* Latin.
    ▶ *nm & nf* Latin.
Latinoamérica *nf* Latin America.
latinoamericano,-a *adj* Latin American.
    ▶ *nm & nf* Latin American.
latir *vi* to beat.
latitud *nf* latitude.
latitudinal *adj* latitudinal.
latón *nm* brass.
latoso,-a *adj fam* annoying, boring.
laúd *nm* lute.
laudatorio,-a *adj* laudatory.
laureada *nf* MIL *(insignia)* decoration.
laureado,-a *adj* prizewinning.
laurear *vt* 1 to award a prize to. 2 *(militar)* to decorate.
laurel *nm (árbol)* bay.
lava *nf* lava.
lavable *adj* washable.
lavabo *nm* 1 *(pila)* washbasin. 2 *(cuarto de baño)* washroom. 3 *(público)* toilet.
lavada *nf* big wash.
lavadero *nm* 1 *(en casa)* laundry room. 2 *(público)* public washing place.
lavado *nm* wash.
lavadora *nf* washing machine.
lavafrutas *nm inv* finger bowl.
lavamanos *nm inv* washbasin.
lavanda *nf* lavender.
lavandería *nf (automática)* launderette, US laundromat; *(con servicio)* laundry.
lavaplatos *nm inv* dishwasher.

lavar *vt* 1 *(ropa, cuerpo, etc)* to wash. 2 *(platos)* to wash up.
    ▶ *vpr* **lavarse** to wash os.
lavativa *nf* enema.
lavavajillas *nm inv* dishwasher.
laxante *nm* laxative.
laxitud *nf* laxity, laxness.
laxo,-a *adj (sin tensión)* slack.
lazada *nf* 1 *(nudo)* knot. 2 *(lazo)* bow.
lazar *vt* to lasso.
lazarillo *nm* guide. COMP **perro lazarillo** guide dog.
lazo *nm* 1 *(cinta)* ribbon; *(de adorno)* bow. 2 *fig (vínculo)* tie, bond.
le *pron* 1 *(objeto directo)* him; *(usted)* you: *¿quién le sirvió?* who served you? 2 *(objeto indirecto - a él)* him; *(- a ella)* her; *(- a usted)* you: *le regalaron un perrito* they gave him a puppy; *le repito la pregunta* I'll repeat the question for you.

✎ Consulta también **les** y **leísmo**.

leal *adj* 1 loyal, faithful. 2 *(justo)* fair.
lealtad *nf* loyalty, faithfulness.
lebrel *nm* greyhound.
lebrillo *nm* bowl.
lección *nf* lesson. LOC **dar una lección a** ALGN *fig* to teach SB a lesson.
lechada *nf* whitewash.
lechal *adj* sucking.
lechazo *nm (cordero)* sucking lamb.
leche *nf* milk. COMP **leche desnatada** skimmed milk.
lechera *nf (recipiente)* milk churn.
lechería *nf* dairy.
lechero,-a *nm* milkman, dairyman.
lecho *nm (gen)* bed; *(de un río)* river bed.
lechón *nm (animal)* piglet.
lechuga *nf* lettuce.
lechuza *nf* owl.
lectivo,-a *adj* school.
lector,-ra *nm & nf* reader. COMP **lector óptico** optical scanner.
leer *vt (gen)* to read.
    ▶ *vi* to read.
legado,-a *nm* 1 *(herencia)* legacy, bequest. 2 *(persona)* legate.
legajo *nm* dossier.

legal *adj (gen)* legal.

legalidad *nf (de una acción, etc)* legality.

legalista *adj* legalistic.

legalización *nf* **1** *(de una situación)* legalization. **2** *(de documento)* to authenticate.

legalizar *vt* **1** *(situación)* to legalize. **2** *(documento)* to authenticate.

legaña *nf* sleep.

legar *vt* to bequeath.

legendario,-a *adj* legendary.

legibilidad *nf* legibility.

legible *adj* legible.

legión *nf* MIL legion.

legionario,-a *nm* legionary.

legislación *nf* legislation.

legislador,-ra *adj* legislative.

legislar *vi* to legislate.

legislativo,-a *adj* legislative.

legislatura *nf (período)* term of office.

legitimación *nf* legitimization.

legitimar *vt* to legitimate.

legitimidad *nf* legitimacy.

legítimo,-a *adj (genuino)* real, authentic.

legua *nf (medida)* league.

legumbre *nf* **1** *(planta)* legume. **2** *(fruto)* pulse.

leguminoso,-a *nf pl* leguminous plants.

leído,-a *adj* well-read.

leísmo *nm incorrect use of* le *and* les *as direct object instead of* lo *and* los.

leísta *adj given to* leísmo.
▶ *nm o nf person who is given to* leísmo.

lejanía *nf* distance.

lejano,-a *adj (tierra, país)* distant.

lejía *nf* bleach.

lejos *adv* far, far away, far off. LOC **a lo lejos** in the distance, far away. ▌ **de lejos** from a distance.

lelo,-a *adj fam* gormless, stupid.

lema *nm (gen)* motto; *(en publicidad)* slogan.

lencería *nf (ropa interior)* lingerie.

lengua *nf* **1** ANAT tongue. **2** *(idioma)* language. LOC **irse de la lengua** *fam* to let the cat out of the bag. ▌ **tener** ALGO **en la punta de la lengua** *fig* to have

STH on the tip of one's tongue. ▌ COMP **lengua materna** mother tongue.

lenguado *nm* sole.

lenguaje *nm* **1** *(gen)* language. **2** *(habla)* speech.

lenguaraz *adj (hablador)* garrulous.

lengüeta *nf (de zapato)* tongue.

lente *nm & nf* lens.
▶ *nm pl* **lentes** lenses. COMP **lentes de contacto** contact lenses.

lenteja *nf* lentil.

lentejuela *nf* sequin.

lentilla *nf* contact lens.

lentitud *nf* slowness.

lento,-a *adj* slow.
▶ *adv* **lento** slowly.

leña *nf* wood, firewood.

leñador,-ra *nm & nf* woodcutter.

leñera *nf* woodshed.

leño *nm* log.

leñoso,-a *adj* ligneous, woody.

león,-ona *nm & nf (animal - macho)* lion; *(- hembra)* lioness. COMP **león marino** sea lion.

leonera *nf* lion's den.

leonino,-a *adj* **1** *(de león)* lion-like.

leopardo *nm* leopard.

leotardos *nm pl* thick woollen tights.

lepra *nf* leprosy.

leproso,-a *adj* leprous.

lerdo,-a *adj fam* slow-witted.

les *pron* **1** *(objeto directo)* them; *(ustedes)* you: *dice que les vio ayer* she says she saw them yesterday; *no les entiendo* I don't understand you. **2** *(objeto indirecto)* them; *(a ustedes)* you: *entraron en casa ladrones y les robaron* burglars broke in and robbed them; *les doy una oportunidad más* I'll give you one more chance.

✎ Consulta también le.

lesión *nf (daño físico)* wound, injury.

lesionado,-a *adj* injured.

lesionar *vt (herir)* to injure.
▶ *vpr* **lesionarse** to get injured.

lesivo,-a *adj* damaging, injurious.

Lesotho *nm* Lesotho.

letal *adj* lethal, deadly.

L

letanía *nf fam (lista)* long list.
letargo *nm* lethargy.
letón,-ona *adj* Latvian.
▶ *nm & nf (persona)* Latvian.
▶ *nm* **letón** *(idioma)* Latvian.
Letonia *nf* Latvia.
letra *nf* **1** *(del alfabeto)* letter. **2** *(de imprenta)* character. **3** *(escritura)* handwriting. **4** *(de canción)* lyrics *pl*, words *pl*. COMP **letra de imprenta** block capitals *pl*. ‖ **letra mayúscula** capital letter.
letrado,-a *nm & nf* lawyer.
letrero *nm* sign, notice.
letrina *nf* latrine.
leucemia *nf* leukaemia, US leukemia.
leucocito *nm* white blood cell.
leva *nf* MIL levy.
levadizo,-a *adj* which can be raised.
levadura *nf* yeast.
levantamiento *nm (de objeto, etc)* lifting.
levantar *vt (alzar)* to raise, lift: *no lo puedo levantar, pesa mucho* I can't lift it, it's heavy. LOC **levantar la vista** to look up.
▶ *vpr* **levantarse 1** *(alzarse)* to rise. **2** *(ponerse de pie)* to stand up. **3** *(dejar la cama)* get out of bed. **4** *(viento)* to get up.
levante *nm (este)* East.
levar *vt (ancla)* to weigh.
leve *adj* **1** slight, light.
levedad *nf* lightness, insignificance.
levitar *vi* to levitate.
léxico,-a *adj* lexical.
lexicón *nm (diccionario)* lexicon.
ley *nf* law.
leyenda *nf (narración)* legend.
lezna *nf* awl.
liado,-a *adj (ocupado)* busy.
liana *nf* liana.
liar *vt* **1** *(atar)* to tie up, bind; *(envolver)* to wrap up. **2** *fam (complicar)* to mix up, make a mess of; *(confundir)* to confuse: *cuéntale la verdad y no lo líes más* tell him the truth and stop messing him about.
▶ *vpr* **liarse a** + *sustantivo* to start + *ger*: *se liaron a discutir* they started arguing.
libanés,-esa *adj* Lebanese.
▶ *nm & nf* Lebanese.
Líbano *nm* **el Líbano** the Lebanon.

libar *vt (néctar)* to suck.
libélula *nf* dragonfly.
liberación *nf (de una persona)* release.
liberado,-a *adj* liberated.
liberador,-ra *adj* liberating.
liberal *adj* liberal.
▶ *nm o nf* liberal.
liberalismo *nm* liberalism.
liberalización *nf* liberalization.
liberar *vt* to free.
Liberia *nf* Liberia.
liberiano,-a *adj* Liberian.
▶ *nm & nf* Liberian.
libertad *nf (gen)* freedom, liberty. LOC **poner en libertad** to free, release. COMP **libertad de expresión** freedom of expression.
libertar *vt* to liberate.
libertario,-a *adj* libertarian.
Libia *nf* Libya.
libio,-a *adj* Libyan.
▶ *nm & nf* Libyan.
libra *nf (moneda, medida)* pound. COMP **libra esterlina** pound sterling.
librar *vt* to save (**de**, from): *me libraron de toda responsabilidad* they absolved me of all responsibility.
▶ *vi fam (tener libre)* to be off: *libro todos los lunes* I've got Mondays off.
▶ *vpr* **librarse** to escape (**de**, from).
libre *adj (gen)* free. COMP **entrada libre** free admittance.
librecambio *nm* free trade.
librería *nf (tienda)* bookshop.
librero,-a *nm & nf* bookseller.
libreta *nf (para anotar)* notebook.
libreto *nm* libretto.
libro *nm (gen)* book. COMP **libro de bolsillo** paperback. ‖ **libro de consulta** reference book. ‖ **libro de texto** textbook.
licencia *nf (permiso)* licence.
licenciado,-a *nm & nf* EDUC graduate.
licenciar *vt* EDUC to award a degree to.
▶ *vpr* **licenciarse** to graduate.
licenciatura *nf* university degree.
liceo *nm (colegio)* secondary school.
lícito,-a *adj* **1** *(legal)* licit. **2** *(justo)* fair.

licor *nm (dulce)* liqueur; *(bebida alcohólica)* liquor, spirits *pl*.

licuadora *nf* juice extractor.

licuar *vt* to liquefy.

lid *nf fig (controversia)* dispute.

líder *nm o nf* leader.

liderar *vt* to lead.

liderazgo *nm* leadership.

lidia *nf (de toros)* bullfight.

liebre *nf (animal)* hare.

Liechtenstein *nm* Liechtenstein.

lienzo *nm* ARTE *(tela)* canvas.

liga *nf* **1** *(asociación)* league, alliance. **2** DEP league.

ligadura *nf (atadura)* tie, bond.

ligamento *nm* ligament.

ligar *vt* **1** *(atar)* to tie, bind. **2** *(unir)* to link, connect.

ligero,-a *adj* **1** *(liviano)* light. **2** *(sin importancia)* minor, light.

lignito *nm* lignite.

lija *nf (papel)* sandpaper.

lijar *vt* to sand.

lila *adj (color)* lilac.
    ► *nf (flor)* lilac.

lima *nf* **1** *(herramienta)* file; *(para uñas)* nail file. **2** *(fruta)* lime; *(árbol)* lime tree.

limar *vt (pulir)* to file.

limitación *nf* limitation.

limitado,-a *adj* limited.

limitar *vt (gen)* to limit.
    ► *vi* limitar con to border with. LOC limitarse a + *inf* to restrict os to + *ger*, do no more than + *inf* : *una persona inteligente no se limita a ver la televisión* an intelligent person does not restrict himself to watching television.

límite *nm* **1** *(extremo)* limit. **2** *(frontera)* boundary. COMP **límite de velocidad** speed limit.

limítrofe *adj* bordering.

limo *nm* slime.

limón *nm* lemon.

limonada *nf* lemonade.

limonero *nm* lemon tree.

limonita *nf* limonite.

limosna *nf* alms *pl*, charity. LOC **pedir limosna** to beg.

limpiabotas *nm inv* bootblack.

limpiacristales *nm inv (producto)* window cleaning fluid.

limpiador,-ra *adj* cleaning.
    ► *nm & nf (persona)* cleaner.

limpiamente *adv* cleanly.

limpiaparabrisas *nm inv* windscreen wiper, US windshield wiper.

limpiar *vt (gen)* to clean, cleanse.

limpieza *nf (acción de limpiar)* cleaning.

limpio,-a *adj (sin suciedad)* clean.
    ► *adv* fairly: *no juegan limpio, hacen trampa* they don't play fair, they cheat.

linaje *nm (ascendencia)* lineage.

linaza *nf* linseed.

lince *nm* ZOOL lynx.

linchar *vt* to lynch.

lindar *vi* to border (con, on), adjoin (con, -).

linde *nm & nf* boundary.

lindo,-a *adj* pretty, nice, lovely.

línea *nf (gen)* line. COMP **línea aérea** airline. ▮ **línea recta** straight line.

lineal *adj* linear.

linfático,-a *adj* lymphatic.

lingote *nm* ingot.

lingüística *nf* linguistics.

lino *nm* **1** *(tela)* linen. **2** BOT flax.

linterna *nf (de pilas)* torch.

lío *nm (embrollo)* mess. LOC **hacerse un lío 1** *(uso literal)* to get tangled up. **2** *(uso figurado)* to get muddled up.

lípido *nm* lipid.

lipotimia *nf* blackout.

liquen *nm* lichen.

liquidación *nf (venta)* sale.

liquidar *vt* **1** *(deuda)* to settle, liquidate. **2** *(mercancías)* to sell off.

líquido,-a *nm* liquid.

lira *nf* **1** MÚS lyre. **2** *(moneda)* lira.

lírica *nf* poetry, lyric poetry.

lirio *nm* lily.

lirón *nm* dormouse. LOC **dormir como un lirón** to sleep like a log.

lis *nf (planta)* lily.

liso,-a *adj* **1** smooth. **2** *(pelo)* straight.

lista *nf (relación)* list.

L

listo,-a *adj* **1** *(inteligente)* clever, smart. **2** *(preparado)* ready: *¿estás lista?* are you ready?

litera *nf* bunk bed; *(tren)* couchette.

literal *adj* literal.

literario,-a *adj* literary.

literatura *nf* literature.

litigar *vi (disputar)* to argue, dispute.

litigio *nm (disputa)* dispute.

litio *nm* lithium.

litoral *nm* coast.

litosfera *nf* lithosphere.

litro *nm* litre, US liter.

Lituania *nf* Lithuania.

lituano,-a *adj* Lithuanian.
▶ *nm & nf (persona)* Lithuanian.
▶ *nm* **lituano** *(idioma)* Lithuanian.

liviano,-a *adj (ligero)* light.

lívido,-a *adj* livid.

llaga *nf (gen)* sore; *(en la boca)* ulcer.

llagar *vt* to cover with ulcers.

llama *nf* **1** *(de fuego)* flame. **2** ZOOL llama.

llamada *nf (gen)* call.

llamamiento *nm (convocatoria)* call.

llamar *vt* **1** *(gen)* to call. **2** *(dar nombre)* to name. **3** *(atraer)* to appeal to. LOC **llamar por teléfono** to call, phone, GB ring, ring up.
▶ *vi (a la puerta)* to knock; *(al timbre)* to ring; *(al teléfono)* to ring, call, phone.
▶ *vpr* **llamarse** *(tener nombre)* to be called.

llamativo,-a *adj* showy, flashy.

llamear *vi* to blaze.

llano,-a *adj* **1** *(plano)* flat. **2** *(sencillo)* simple.
▶ *nm* **llano** *(llanura)* plain.

llanta *nf* wheel rim, rim.

llanto *nm* crying, weeping.

llanura *nf (llano)* plain.

llave *nf (de puerta, etc)* key.

llavero *nm* key ring.

llegada *nf* **1** arrival. **2** DEP finishing line.

llegar *vi* **1** to arrive (a, at/in), get (a, at), reach (a, -): *llegó el primero* he arrived first. **3** *(alcanzar)* to reach: *¿llegas a ese estante?* can you reach that shelf? **4** *(ser suficiente)* to be enough, suffice:

¿te llega con diez euros? is ten euros enough? **5** *(cantidad)* to amount (a, to). **6** **llegar a** + *inf (uso enfático)*: *llegó a llamarme tonto* he even called me a silly.

llenar *vt* **1** *(espacio, recipiente)* to fill. **2** *(formulario)* to fill in. **3** *(tiempo)* to fill, occupy. **4** **llenar de** *(alegría)* to fill with.
▶ *vpr* **llenarse 1** *(gen)* to fill. **2** *(de gente)* to fill up.

lleno,-a *adj* **1** full (de, of): *está lleno de gente* it's full of people. **2** *(cubierto)* covered (de, with).

llevadero,-a *adj* bearable.

llevar *vt* **1** *(gen)* to take: *llévale esto a tu abuela* take this to your granny. **2** *(tener)* to have; *(tener encima)* to have, carry: *¿qué llevas ahí?* what's that you've got there? **3** *(prenda)* to wear, have on: *no me gusta llevar sombrero* I don't like wearing a hat. **4** *(aguantar)* to cope with. **5** *(dirigir)* to be in charge of: *¿quién lleva los pedidos?* who's in charge of orders? **6** *(conducir - coche)* to drive: *lleva un Seat azul* he drives a blue Seat. **7** *(años)* to be older: *te llevo tres años* I'm three years older than you.
▶ *vi* **1 llevar a** *(conducir)* to take, lead: *esta senda lleva a la cima* this path takes you to the summit. **2 llevar a** + *inf (inducir)* to lead to, make: *esto me lleva a pensar que...* this leads me to think that...
▶ *vpr* **llevarse 1** *(obtener)* to get; *(ganar)* to win: *los rusos se llevaron todas las medallas* the Russians won all the medals. **2** *(recibir)* to get: *se llevó un buen susto* he got quite a shock. **3** *(estar de moda)* to be fashionable: *este color ya no se lleva* this colour is not fashionable any more. **4** *(entenderse)* to get on (con, with), get along (con, with): *se lleva bien con sus padres* he gets on well with his parents. **5** MAT to carry over.

llorar *vi* to cry, weep.
▶ *vt* to mourn.

llorón,-ona *nm & nf fam* crybaby.

lloroso,-a *adj* tearful, weeping.

llover *vi* [se usa sólo en tercera persona; no lleva sujeto] to rain: *llueve* it's raining.

lloviznar *vi* [se usa sólo en tercera persona; no lleva sujeto] to drizzle.

lluvia *nf* **1** rain. **2** *fig* shower, barrage.

lo *art neut* the: *dime lo que quieres* tell me what you want. LOC **lo que** what.
▸ *pron* **1** *(objeto directo - él)* him; *(- usted)* you: *no lo conozco de nada* I don't know him from Adam. **2** *(objeto directo - cosa, animal)* it: *¿lo has probado?* have you tried it?

loar *vt* to praise, extol.

lobezno,-a *nm & nf* ZOOL wolf cub.

lobo,-a *nm & nf (macho)* wolf; *(hembra)* she-wolf.

lóbulo *nm* lobe.

local *adj* local.
▸ *nm (para negocio)* premises *pl*.

localidad *nf* **1** *(ciudad)* town. **2** TEAT *(asiento)* seat; *(billete)* ticket.

localizar *vt* **1** *(encontrar)* to locate, find. **2** *(infección, incendio)* to localize.

locativo,-a *adj* locative.

loción *nf* lotion.

loco,-a *adj (gen)* mad, crazy, insane.
▸ *nm & nf* lunatic.

locomoción *nf* locomotion.

locomotor,-ra *adj* locomotive.

locomotora *nf* locomotive.

locución *nf* phrase, locution.

locura *nf (perturbación)* madness.

locutor,-ra *nm & nf* announcer.

locutorio *nm* telephone booth.

lodo *nm* mud.

logarítmico,-a *adj* logarithmic.

logaritmo *nm* logarithm.

lógica *nf* logic.

lógico,-a *adj* **1** *(de la lógica)* logical. **2** *(natural)* normal, to be expected.

logística *nf* logistics.

logopeda *nm o nf* speech therapist.

logotipo *nm* logo, logotype.

logrado,-a *adj (conseguido)* successful.

lograr *vt (conseguir)* to get, achieve.

logro *nm (éxito)* achievement.

loísmo *nm incorrect use of* lo *and* los *as indirect objects instead of* le *and* les.

loma *nf* hill.

lombriz *nf (intestinal)* worm.

lomo *nm* **1** CULIN *(de cerdo)* loin; *(de ternera)* sirloin. **2** ANAT back.

lona *nf* canvas.

loncha *nf (de jamón, queso, etc)* slice.

londinense *adj* of London.
▸ *nm o nf* Londoner.

Londres *nm* London.

longaniza *nf cured pork sausage.*

longitud *nf* **1** length. **2** GEOG longitude.

lonja *nf (mercado)* exchange, market.

lontananza *nf (fondo)* background.

loor *nm lit* praise.

lord *nm* lord.

loriga *nf* HIST cuirass.

loro *nm (pájaro)* parrot.

los *art def* the: *los niños* the boys.
▸ *pron (objeto directo)* them; *(ustedes)* you: *los vi* I saw them; *a ustedes dos no los quiero volver a ver* I don't want to see you two again.

✎ Consulta también lo, el.

losa *nf* flagstone, slab.

loseta *nf* floor tile.

lotería *nf* lottery.

loto *nm (flor)* lotus.

loza *nf (cerámica)* china.

lozanía *nf (de persona)* healthiness.

lozano,-a *adj* **1** *(persona)* healthy, lusty. **2** *(planta)* fresh.

lubina *nf* bass.

lubricante *nm* lubricant.

lubricar *vt* to lubricate.

lucerna *nf* skylight.

lucero *nm* bright star.

lucha *nf* **1** *(gen)* fight, struggle. **2** DEP wrestling. COMP **lucha libre** free-style wrestling.

luchador,-ra *nm & nf* **1** *(gen)* fighter. **2** DEP wrestler.

luchar *vi* **1** to fight. **2** DEP to wrestle.

lucidez *nf* lucidity.

lucido,-a *adj* beautiful.

lúcido,-a *adj* lucid, clear-headed.

luciérnaga *nf* glow-worm.

lucífero,-a *adj lit* resplendent.

lucimiento *nm* showing off.

lucio *nm* pike.

lución *nm* slowworm.

lucir *vt (mostrar)* to show, display; *(ropa)* to wear, sport.
▸ *vpr* **lucirse** *(sobresalir)* to be brilliant.
lucrarse *vpr* to make a profit.
lucrativo,-a *adj* lucrative, profitable.
lucro *nm* gain, profit.
luctuoso,-a *adj lit* mournful, sorrowful.
lúdico,-a *adj* recreational.
ludópata *nm o nf* compulsive gambler.
ludopatía *nf* compulsive gambling.
luego *adv* **1** *(después)* then, afterwards, next. **2** *(más tarde)* later.
▸ *conj* so, therefore.
lugar *nm* **1** *(sitio, ciudad)* place. **2** *(posición, situación)* place, position: *llegó en quinto lugar* he finished in fifth place. **3** *(espacio)* room, space: *ya no hay lugar para más muebles* there's no room for any more furniture. LOC **en lugar de** instead of.
lugareño,-a *adj* local.
▸ *nm & nf* local.
lugarteniente *nm* deputy.
lúgubre *adj (triste)* bleak, lugubrious.
lujo *nm* luxury.
lujosamente *adv* luxuriously.
lujoso,-a *adj* luxurious.
lumbago *nm* lumbago.
lumbar *adj* lumbar.
lumbre *nf (fuego)* fire.
lumbrera *nf (persona)* genius, luminary.
luminaria *nf (en fiestas)* light.
lumínico,-a *adj* light.
luminiscencia *nf* luminiscence.
luminiscente *adj* luminiscent.
luminosidad *nf* luminosity.
luminoso,-a *adj* bright, luminous.

luminotecnia *nf* lighting.
luminotécnico,-a *adj* lighting.
luna *nf* **1** *(satélite)* moon. **2** *(cristal)* window pane; *(de ventana)* glass. **3** *(espejo)* mirror. COMP **luna llena** full moon. ▮ **luna de miel** honey moon.
lunación *nf* lunation.
lunar *adj* lunar, moon: *las fases lunares* the phases of the moon.
▸ *nm (en la piel)* beauty spot. LOC **de lunares** spotted.
lunático,-a *nm & nf* lunatic.
lunes *nm inv* Monday.

✎ Consulta también jueves.

luneta *nf car* window. COMP **luneta térmica** heated rear windscreen.
lúnula *nf* half-moon, lunule.
lupa *nf* magnifying glass. LOC **con lupa** meticulously.
lúpulo *nm* hop.
lustrabotas *nm o nf* bootblack.
lustrar *vt* to polish.
lustre *nm (brillo)* polish, shine, lustre, US luster.
lustro *nm* five years *pl*.
lustroso,-a *adj* shiny.
luto *nm* **1** mourning. **2** *fig* grief.
luxación *nf* dislocation.
Luxemburgo *nm* Luxembourg.
luxemburgués,-esa *adj* of Luxembourg, from Luxembourg.
▸ *nm & nf* Luxembourger.
luz *nf* **1** *(gen)* light. **2** *fam (electricidad)* electricity. **3** *(iluminación)* lighting. LOC **dar a luz** to give birth. ▮ **salir a la luz** to come out. COMP **luces de posición** sidelights. ▮ **luz del sol** sunlight.

M, m *nf (la letra)* M, m.

m¹ *sím* (metro) metre (US meter); *(símbolo)* m.

m² *sím* (milla) mile; *(símbolo)* m.

m³ *abrev* (minuto) minute; *(abreviatura)* min.

maca *nf (en fruta)* bruise.

macabro,-a *adj* macabre.

macaco,-a *nm & nf* ZOOL macaque.

macarrón *nm (pasta italiana)* piece of macaroni.
▶ *nm pl* **macarrones** macaroni.

macedonia *nf* fruit salad. COMP **macedonia de frutas** fruit salad.

maceración *nf (remojo - de fruta)* maceration, soaking; *(- de carne, pescado)* marinading.

macerar *vt (poner en remojo - fruta)* to macerate, soak; *(- carne, pescado)* to marinade.

maceta *nf* flowerpot.

macetero *nm* flowerpot holder.

macha *adj (almeja) type of* clam.

machacar *vt* **1** *(triturar)* to crush. **2** *fam (vencer)* to hammer, thrash. **3** *fam (insistir en)* to harp on about, go on about.
▶ *vi* **1** *(estudiar)* to swot up, cram, US grind. **2** *(insistir en)* to go on (con, about), harp on (con, about).

machacón,-ona *adj fam* insistent, repetitive.

machaque *nm* beating.

machetazo *nm* blow with a machete.

machete *nm* machete.

machihembrado,-a *nm* tongue and groove joint.

machismo *nm* male chauvinism.

machista *adj* male chauvinist.

macho *adj* **1** *(animal, planta)* male. **2** *(persona)* macho, tough.
▶ *nm* **1** *(animal, planta)* male. **2** *fam (hombre)* macho man, tough guy.

macilento,-a *adj* wan, pallid.

macizo,-a *adj* solid.
▶ *nm* **macizo** *(montañoso)* massif, mountain mass.

macro *nf* INFORM macro.

macrocefalia *nf* macrocephaly..

macrocosmos *nm inv* macrocosm.

macroeconomía *nf* macroeconomics.

macroeconómico,-a *adj* macroeconomic.

macroscópico,-a *adj* macroscopic.

mácula *nf lit* blemish.

macuto *nm* knapsack, rucksack.

Madagascar *nm* Madagascar.

madeja *nf (de lana)* skein, hank.

madera *nf (en el árbol)* wood; *(cortada)* timber, US lumber: *es de madera* it's made of wood, it's wooden.

maderero,-a *adj (industria)* timber.

madero *nm* piece of timber.

madona *nf* Madonna.

madrastra *nf* stepmother.

madraza *nf fam* doting mother.

madre *nf* mother. COMP **madre soltera** single mother.

madreselva *nf* honeysuckle.

madrigal *nm* madrigal.

madriguera *nf (de conejo)* burrow, warren; *(de zorro)* den, lair.

madrina *nf* godmother.

madroño *nm* strawberry tree.

madrugada *nf (después de medianoche)* early morning: *a las cinco de la madrugada* at five o'clock in the morning.

madrugador,-ra *nm & nf* early riser.
madrugar *vi (levantarse pronto)* to get up early.
madrugón LOC pegarse un madrugón *fam* to get up at the crack of dawn.
madurar *vi* 1 *(fruto)* to ripen. 2 *(persona)* to mature.
▶ *vt* 1 *(fruto)* to ripen. 2 *(plan, proyecto)* to think about carefully.
madurez *nf (de la persona)* maturity.
maduro,-a *adj* 1 *(persona)* mature. 2 *(fruta)* ripe.
maestre *nm* HIST master.
maestría *nf (destreza)* mastery, skill.
maestro,-a *adj (principal)* master; *(pared, viga)* main, supporting.
▶ *nm & nf* 1 *(de primaria - hombre)* schoolmaster; *(- mujer)* schoolmistress. 2 *(instructor)* teacher. COMP maestro de escuela schoolteacher.
magacín *nm (revista)* magazine.
magdalena *nf* small sponge cake.
magenta *nf* magenta.
magia *nf* magic.
mágico,-a *adj (pócima, palabra)* magic.
magisterio *nm (profesión)* teaching profession.
magistrado,-a *nm & nf (juez)* judge.
magistral *adj* masterly, masterful.
magistratura *nf (cuerpo)* judges *pl*.
magma *nf* magma.
magnanimidad *nf* magnanimity.
magnánimo,-a *adj* magnanimous.
magnate *nm* tycoon, magnate.
magnesio *nm* magnesium.
magnético,-a *adj* magnetic.
magnetismo *nm* magnetism.
magnetización *nf* magnetization.
magnetizar *vt* to magnetize.
magnetofónico,-a *adj* sound recording.
magnetófono *nm* tape recorder.
magnicidio *nm* assassination.
magnificar *vt (ensalzar)* to praise.
magnificencia *nf* magnificence, splendour.
magnífico,-a *adj* splendid.
magnitud *nf* FÍS magnitude.

magno,-a *adj* great.
magnolia *nf (árbol, flor)* magnolia.
magnolio *nm* magnolia.
mago,-a *nm & nf (gen)* magician, conjurer; *(de los cuentos)* wizard.
magro,-a *adj* lean.
magulladura *nf* bruise, contusion.
magullar *vt* to bruise.
maicena *nf* cornflour.
mailing *nm* mailshot.
maitre *nm o nf* head waiter, maître.
maíz *nm* 1 *(planta)* maize, US corn. 2 *(grano)* sweet corn, US corn.
maizal *nm* maize field, US corn field.
majada *nf* sheepfold.
majadería *nf* nonsense, balderdash.
majadero,-a *adj* stupid, dim-witted.
majar *vt* to crush.
majestad *nf (distinción)* majesty.
majestuoso,-a *adj* majestic.
majo,-a *adj (simpático)* nice.
majuelo *nm (viña)* young vine.
mal *nm* 1 evil. 2 *(daño)* harm. 3 *(enfermedad)* sickness.
▶ *adj (forma apocopada de malo)* bad.
▶ *adv* 1 *(no adecuadamente)* badly: *se portó mal con nosotros* he treated us badly. 2 *(enfermo)* ill, sick: *me encuentro mal* I feel ill, I don't feel well. 3 *(incorrectamente)* wrong: *lo has hecho mal* you've done it wrong. 4 *(en frases negativas)* bad, badly: *la película no está mal* the film's not bad.
malabarismo *nm* juggling. LOC hacer malabarismos to juggle.
malabarista *nm o nf* juggler.
malacostumbrado,-a *adj* spoilt.
malacostumbrar *vt* to spoil.
malaria *nf* malaria.
malasio,-a *adj* Malaysian.
▶ *nm & nf* Malaysian.
malaventura *nf* misfortune.
malaventurado,-a *adj* unfortunate.
Malawi *nm* Malawi.
malawiano,-a *adj* Malawian.
▶ *nm & nf* Malawian.
malayo,-a *adj* Malay.
▶ *nm & nf (persona)* Malay.
▶ *nm* malayo *(idioma)* Malay.

Malaysia *nf* Malaysia.

malcarado,-a *adj* grim-faced.

malcomer *vi* not to eat enough.

malcriado,-a *adj (mimado)* spoilt.

malcriar *vt* to spoil.

maldad *nf* **1** *(cualidad)* evil, wickedness. **2** *(acto)* evil thing, wicked thing.

maldecir *vt* to curse, damn.
▶ *vi* to curse.

maldiciente *adj* slanderous.

maldición *nf* curse.

maldito,-a *adj* damned.

Maldivas *nm* Maldives.

maldivo,-a *adj* Maldivian.
▶ *nm & nf* Maldivian.

maleabilidad *nf* malleability.

maleable *adj* malleable.

maleante *nm o nf* delinquent.

malear *vt (dañar)* to spoil, damage.

malecón *nm* mole, jetty.

maledicencia *nf* evil talk, gossip.

maleducado,-a *adj* rude.
▶ *nm & nf* rude person: *es una maleducada* she's really rude.

maleducar *vt (niño)* to spoil.

maleficio *nm* curse, evil spell.

maléfico,-a *adj* evil, harmful.

malentendido *nm* misunderstanding.

malestar *nm fig* unrest.

maleta *nf* suitcase, case. LOC **hacer la maleta 1** *(empacar)* to pack. **2** *(irse)* to pack up.

maletero *nm* AUTO boot, US trunk.

maletín *nm* briefcase.

malévolo,-a *adj* malevolent.

maleza *nf (malas hierbas)* weeds *pl*.

malformación *nf* malformation.

malgache *adj* Madagascan, Malagsy.
▶ *nm o nf* Madagascan.

malgastador,-ra *nm & nf* squanderer.

malgastar *vt* to waste, squander.

malhablado,-a *adj* foul-mouthed.

malhecho,-a *adj* deformed.

malhechor,-ra *nm & nf* criminal.

malherir *vt* to wound badly.

malhumor *nm* bad temper.

malhumorado,-a *adj* bad-tempered.
LOC **estar malhumorado,-a** to be in a bad mood.

Malí *nm* Mali.

malicia *nf (mala intención)* malice.

maliciosamente *adv* maliciously.

malicioso,-a *adj* malicious, spiteful.

maliense *adj* Malian.
▶ *nm o nf* Malian.

maligno,-a *adj* malignant.

malintencionado,-a *adj* malicious.
▶ *nm & nf* malicious person.

malinterpretar *vt* to misinterpret.

malísimo,-a *adj* terrible.

malla *nf (red)* mesh.
▶ *nf pl* **mallas** *(medias sin pie)* leggings.

malnacido,-a *nm & nf* despicable person.

malnutrición *nf* malnutrition.

malnutrido,-a *adj* malnourished.

malo,-a *adj* **1** bad: *¡qué día tan malo hace!* what dreadful weather! **2** *(malvado)* wicked, evil: *es muy mala persona* he's a nasty piece of work. **3** *(travieso)* naughty: *¡qué niño más malo!* what a naughty child! **4** *(nocivo)* harmful: *el tabaco es malo para la salud* smoking is bad for you. **5** *(enfermo)* ill, sick: *no ha venido a trabajar porque está malo con gripe* he's off sick with flu. **6** *(estropeado)* off: *este pescado ya está malo* this fish has gone off already.
▶ *nm & nf (en la ficción)* baddy, villain: *¿quién es el malo?* who's the baddy?

malogrado,-a *adj* wasted.

malograr *vt (desaprovechar)* to waste.

maloliente *adj* foul-smelling.

malparado,-a LOC **salir malparado,-a** to come off badly.

malpensado,-a *adj* nasty-minded.

malsano,-a *adj (ambiente, vida)* unhealthy; *(curiosidad)* morbid, unhealthy; *(mente)* sick.

malsonante *adj* offensive, rude.

malta *nf* malt.

Malta *nf* Malta.

maltear *vt* to malt.

maltés *adj* Maltese.
▶ *nm & nf (persona)* Maltese.
▶ *nm* **maltés** *(idioma)* Maltese.

M

maltratar *vt (tratar mal)* to ill-treat, mistreat; *(pegar)* to batter.

maltrato *nm* mistreatment.

maltrecho,-a *adj* **1** *(persona)* battered. **2** *(cosa)* damaged, destroyed.

malva *adj (color)* mauve.
▶ *nf* mallow.

malvado,-a *adj* wicked, evil.

malvarrosa *nf* hollyhock.

malvasía *nf (uva)* malvasia.

malvavisco *nm* marshmallow.

malvender *vt* to sell at a loss.

malversar *vt* to embezzle.

Malvinas *nf pl* **Islas Malvinas** Falkland Islands, Falklands.

malvinense *adj* of the Falklands.
▶ *nm o nf* Falklander, Falkland islander.

malvivir *vi* to live very badly.

mama *nf (pecho)* breast.

mamá *nf fam* mummy, US mom.

mamar *vt (succionar)* to suck.
▶ *vi (bebé)* to feed. LOC **dar de mamar** to breast-feed.

mamario,-a *adj* mammary.

mambo *nm* mambo.

mamífero,-a *adj* mammalian.

mamografía *nf* mammography.

mamotreto *nm (armatoste)* monstrosity.

mampara *nf* screen.

mampostería *nf* masonry.

mamut *nm* mammoth.

maná *nm* manna.

manada *nf (vacas, elefantes)* herd; *(ovejas)* flock; *(lobos, perros)* pack. LOC **en manada en masse**.

mánager *nm o nf* manager.

manantial *nm* spring.

manar *vi (salir)* to flow (de, from), pour (de, from), well (de, from).

manatí *nm* manatee.

manazas *adj inv* clumsy.

mancha *nf* stain, spot.

manchado,-a *adj* stained.

manchar *vt* to stain, dirty.
▶ *vpr* **mancharse** to get dirty.

mancillar *vt arc* to sully.

manco,-a *adj (sin un brazo)* one-armed; *(sin una mano)* one-handed.

mancomunidad *nf* association.

mandamiento *nm* REL commandment.

mandar *vt* **1** *(ordenar)* to order, tell. **2** *(enviar)* to send.
▶ *vi (dirigir - un grupo)* to be in charge.

mandarina *nf* mandarin, tangerine.

mandatario,-a *nm & nf* POL leader.

mandato *nm (orden)* order.

mandíbula *nf* jaw.

mandil *nm* apron.

mandioca *nf* manioc, cassava.

mando *nm* **1** *(autoridad)* command: *le han relevado en el mando* he's been dismissed. **2** *(dispositivo)* control. COMP **mando a distancia** *(sistema)* remote control.

mandolina *nf* mandolin.

mandón,-ona *adj fam* bossy.
▶ *nm & nf fam* bossy boots.

mandrágora *nf* mandrake.

mandril *nm* ZOOL mandril.

manecilla *nf (de reloj)* hand.

manejable *adj* easy-to-handle.

manejar *vt* to handle, operate, use.

manejo *nm (uso)* handling, use.

manera *nf* way, manner. LOC **de cualquier manera** **1** *(en cualquier caso)* in any case. **2** *(sin cuidado, consideración, interés)* carelessly. **de ninguna manera** certainly not. **de todas maneras** in any case.

manga *nf* sleeve: *en mangas de camisa* in shirt sleeves.

manganeso *nm* manganese.

mangar *vt fam* to pinch, nick, swipe.

manglar *nm* mangrove swamp.

mango¹ *nm* handle.

mango² *nm* BOT mango.

mangonear *vt fam* to boss about.

mangoneo *nm fam* meddling.

mangosta *nf* mongoose.

manguera *nf (de riego)* hose.

manguito *nm (de manos)* muff.

maní *nm* peanut.

manía *nf* **1** MED mania. **2** *(ojeriza)* dislike, grudge. **3** *(costumbre)* habit; *(obsesión)* obsession, mania: *tiene la manía de morderse las uñas* she has a habit of biting her nails.

maníaco,-a *adj* MED manic.
► *nm & nf fam* maniac.

maniatar *vt* to tie up.

maniático,-a *adj (raro)* cranky.
► *nm & nf (quisquilloso)* fusspot.

manicomio *nm* mental hospital.

manicura *nf* manicure.

manido,-a *adj (tema)* stale.

manifestación *nf* demonstration.

manifestante *nm o nf* demonstrator.

manifestar *vt (expresar)* to express.
► *vpr* **manifestarse** to demonstrate: *se manifestaron a favor del desarme nuclear* they demonstrated in favour of nuclear disarmament.

manifiesto,-a *adj* obvious, evident.
► *nm* **manifiesto** manifesto.

manija *nf* handle.

manilla *nf (de reloj)* hand.

manillar *nm* handlebars *pl*.

maniobra *nf* manoeuvre.

maniobrar *vi* to manoeuvre.

manipulación *nf* manipulation.

manipulador,-ra *adj* manipulative.
► *nm & nf* manipulator.

manipular *vt* to manipulate.

maniqueísmo *nm (doctrina)* Manichaeism.

maniquí *nm (muñeco)* dummy.

manirroto,-a *adj fam* spendthrift.
► *nm & nf fam* spendthrift.

manitas *nm o nf* handyman.

manivela *nf* crank, handle.

manjar *nm* delicious dish, delicacy.

mano *nf* **1** ANAT hand. **2** *(de pintura)* coat.
LOC **a mano 1** *(escrito)* handwritten, by hand. **2** *(hecho)* handmade, by hand. **3** *(cerca)* to hand, handy, near. **▌ echar una mano** to give a hand, lend a hand.

manojo *nm* bunch.

manómetro *nm* pressure gauge.

manopla *nf (guante)* mitten.

manotazo *nm* slap, smack, swipe.

mansarda *nf* attic.

mansedumbre *nf* meekness, docility.

mansión *nf* mansion.

manso,-a *adj (animal)* tame.

manta *nf (gen)* blanket.

mantear *vt* to toss in a blanket.

manteca *nf (elaborado)* lard. COMP **manteca de cacao** cocoa butter. **▌ manteca de cerdo** lard.

mantecado *nm (helado)* dairy ice cream.

mantecoso,-a *adj* greasy.

mantel *nm* tablecloth.

mantelería *nf* table linen.

mantener *vt* **1** *(conservar)* to keep. **2** *(sustentar)* to support, maintain: *ella sola mantiene a toda la familia* she supports the whole family by herself. **3** *(conversación, relaciones)* to have; *(correspondencia)* to keep up.
► *vpr* **mantenerse 1** *(sostenerse)* to remain, stand. **2** *(continuar en un estado, una posición)* to keep: *se mantuvo a distancia* she kept her distance. **3** *(sostenerse)* to manage, maintain os, ssupport os.

mantenimiento *nm* maintenance.

mantequera *nf* butter dish.

mantequería *nf (tienda)* delicatessen.

mantequilla *nf* butter.

mantilla *nf* **1** *(de mujer)* mantilla. **2** *(de niño)* shawl.

mantillo *nm (abono del suelo)* humus.

mantis *nf* mantis. COMP **mantis religiosa** praying mantis.

manto *nm (capa)* cloak.

mantón *nm* large shawl.

manual *adj* manual.
► *nm* manual, handbook.

manualidad *nf* handicraft.
► *nf pl* **manualidades** arts and crafts.

manubrio *nm* crank, crankhandle.

manufacturar *vt* to manufacture.

manuscrito,-a *adj* handwritten.
► *nm* **manuscrito** manuscript.

manutención *nf (gen)* maintenance.

manzana *nf* BOT apple.

manzanilla *nf (planta)* camomile.

manzano *nm* apple tree.

maña *nf (habilidad)* skill, knack.

mañana *nf* morning: *hace una mañana preciosa* it's a beautiful morning. LOC **por la mañana** in the morning.
► *adv* tomorrow: *mañana no tengo que ir al cole* I don't have to go to school to-

M

morrow. LOC **¡hasta mañana!** see you tomorrow!

mañoso,-a *adj (habilidoso)* skilful.

maorí *adj* Maori.
► *nm & nf (persona)* Maori.
► *nm (idioma)* Maori.

mapa *nm* map.

mapache *nm* racoon.

mapamundi *nm* map of the world.

maqueta *nf (de edificio, monumento, etc)* scale model.

maquetar *vt* to do the page layout of.

maquetista *nm o nf* **1** *(de maquetas)* model maker. **2** *(de libros)* page designer.

maquiavélico,-a *adj* Machiavellian.

maquillador,-ra *nm & nf* make-up assistant.

maquillaje *nm* make-up.

maquillar *vt* to make up.
► *vpr* **maquillarse** *(ponerse maquillaje)* to make us up.

máquina *nf* **1** *(gen)* machine. **2** *(de un tren)* engine. COMP **máquina de afeitar** shaver, electric razor. **máquina de coser** sewing machine. **máquina de escribir** typewriter. **máquina de fotos** camera. **máquina de lavar** washing machine.

maquinar *vt* to scheme, plot.

maquinaria *nf* **1** machinery. **2** mechanism.

maquinilla *nf* razor.

maquinista *nm o nf (de tren)* engine driver, US engineer.

mar *nm & nf (gen)* sea. LOC **en alta mar** on the high sea, on the open sea. **la mar de...** *(muy)* very, really.

marabunta *nf* **1** swarm of ants. **2** *fam fig* mob, crowd.

maraca *nf* maraca.

maracuyá *nf* passion fruit.

marajá *nm* maharajah.

maraña *nf (espesura)* thicket.

maratón *nm* marathon.

maratoniano,-a *adj* marathon.

maravilla *nf* wonder, marvel. LOC **de maravilla** wonderfully.

maravillar *vt* to astonish, amaze.
► *vpr* **maravillarse** to marvel (de, at).

maravilloso,-a *adj* wonderful.

marca *nf* **1** *(señal)* mark, sign. **2** *(en comestibles, productos del hogar)* brand; *(en otros productos)* make. **3** DEP record. COMP **marca registrada** registered trademark.

marcado,-a *adj* **1** *(señalado)* marked. **2** *(acento)* marked, pronounced.

marcador *nm* **1** DEP scoreboard. **2** INFORM bookmark.

marcapasos *nm inv* pacemaker.

marcar *vt* **1** *(señalar)* to mark; *(ganado)* to brand. **2** DEP *(gol, canasta)* to score. **3** *(en teléfono)* to dial.

marcha *nf* **1** *(de protesta, soldados)* march. **2** *(progreso)* course, progress. **3** *(abandono)* leaving. **4** AUTO gear. **5** DEP walk. **6** *fam (de persona)* go, energy; *(de lugar, ambiente)* life. LOC **dar marcha atrás 1** *(coche)* to reverse. **2** *(proyecto)* to fall through. **ir de marcha** *(por la noche)* go out on the town. **poner en marcha 1** *(coche)* to start. **2** *(proyecto)* to start up.

marchar *vi* **1** *(ir)* to go, walk. **2** *(funcionar)* to work, run. **3** MIL to march.
► *vpr* **marcharse** to leave.

marchitar *vt* to wither.
► *vpr* **marchitarse** to wither.

marchito,-a *adj (planta)* withered; *(belleza)* faded.

marchoso,-a *adj fam (persona)* fun-loving, wild; *(música, sitio)* lively.
► *nm & nf* raver, fun-lover.

marcial *adj* martial.

marciano,-a *adj* Martian.
► *nm & nf* Martian.

marco *nm* **1** *(de cuadro, ventana)* frame. **2** *(moneda)* mark.

marea *nf* tide. COMP **marea alta** high tide. **marea baja** low tide. **marea negra** oil slick.

mareado,-a *adj (en general)* sick: *estoy mareado* I feel sick.

mareante *adj (que marea)* sickening.

marear *vt* to make sick.
► *vpr* **marearse 1** to get sick. **2** *(sentir vértigo)* to get dizzy.

marejada *nf* swell.

marejadilla *nf* slight swell.

maremoto *nm* tidal wave.

mareo *nm* sickness.

marfil *nm* ivory.

marfileño,-a *adj (de Costa de Marfil)* of the Ivory Coast.
▸ *nm & nf* native of the Ivory Coast.

marga *nf* marl.

margarina *nf* margarine.

margarita *nf* **1** BOT daisy. **2** *(de máquina)* daisywheel.

margen *nm (del papel)* margin.

marginación *nf* exclusion.

marginado,-a *adj* marginalized.
▸ *nm & nf* social outcast.

marginal *adj* **1** *(asunto)* marginal, minor. **2** *(persona)* marginalized.

marginar *vt (persona)* exclude; *(grupo social)* marginalize.

marido *nm* husband.

marimandón,-ona *nm & nf fam* bossy boots.

marina *nf (flota)* navy.

marinar *vt* to marinate.

marine *nm* marine.

marinero,-a *nm* sailor.

marino,-a *adj (corriente, animal)* marine.

marioneta *nf* puppet. COMP **(teatro de) marionetas** puppet show.

mariposa *nf (insecto)* butterfly.

mariposear *vi (andar alrededor)* to buzz around.

mariquita *nf* ZOOL ladybird, US ladybug.

marisabidilla *nf fam* know-all.

mariscada *nf (comida)* seafood dish.

mariscal *nm* marshal.

mariscar *vi* to fish for shellfish.

marisco *nm* seafood, shellfish.

marisma *nf* salt marsh.

marismeño,-a *adj (cultivo)* marshy.

marisquería *nf* seafood restaurant.

marital *adj* marital.

marítimo,-a *adj* maritime, sea.

marketing *nm* marketing.

marmita *nf* casserole, cooking pot.

mármol *nm* marble.

marmolería *nf (taller)* marble cutter's workshop.

marmóreo,-a *adj* marmoreal.

marmota *nf* ZOOL marmot.

maroma *nf* thick rope.

marqués,-esa *nm & nf (hombre)* marquis, marquess; *(mujer)* marchioness.

marquesina *nf* bus shelter.

marquetería *nf* marquetry.

marrano,-a *adj fam* filthy, dirty.
▸ *nm & nf fam (sucio)* filthy pig, dirty pig.
▸ *nm* **marrano** ZOOL pig.

marrón *adj* brown.
▸ *nm (color)* brown.

marroquí,-ina *adj* Moroccan.
▸ *nm & nf* Moroccan.

marroquinería *nf (artículos)* leather goods *pl*.

Marruecos *nm* Morocco.

marrullero,-a *adj fam* crafty.

marsupial *nm* marsupial.

marsupio *nm* marsupium.

marta *nf* marten.

Marte *nm* Mars.

martes *nm* Tuesday.

✎ Consulta también **jueves**.

M

martillazo *nm* blow with a hammer.

martillear *vt* to hammer.

martilleo *nm* hammering.

martillo *nm* hammer.

martinete *nm (ave)* heron.

martingala *nf fam (artimaña)* ruse.

Martinica *nf* Martinique.

martín pescador *nm* kingfisher.

mártir *nm o nf* martyr.

martirio *nm* **1** martyrdom. **2** *fig* torture, torment.

martirizar *vt* **1** to martyr. **2** *fig* to torment, torture.

marzo *nm* March: *el día 16 de marzo* March the sixteenth, the sixteenth of March; *nací el 6 de marzo de 1993* I was born on March 6th 1993; *durante el mes de marzo* in March; *en marzo del año pasado* last March; *en marzo del año que viene* next March; *a principios de marzo* at the beginning of March; *a mediados de marzo* in mid-March; *a finales de marzo* at the end of March.

mas *conj* but.

más *adv* **1** *(comparativo)* more: *este año ha llovido más* it has rained more this year. **2** *(con números o cantidades)* more: *más de tres* more than three. **3** *(superlativo)* most: *es la más guapa* she's the prettiest. **4** *(después de pron interrog e indef)* else: *¿algo más?* anything else? **5** *(exclamativo)* so: *¡qué película más buena!* what a wonderful film! LOC **de más** spare, extra. ‖ **más bien** rather. ‖ **más o menos** more or less.
▶ *prep* MAT plus: *dos más dos igual a cuatro* two plus two is four.
▶ *nm* *(signo)* plus sign.

masa *nf* **1** *(en general)* mass. **2** FÍS mass: *unidad de masa* unit of mass. **3** CULIN *(para pan)* dough; *(para tartas)* pastry. **4** *(de gente)* mass, crowd.

masacre *nf* massacre.

masaje *nm* massage.

masajear *vt* to massage.

masajista *nm o nf (hombre)* masseur; *(mujer)* masseuse.
▶ *nm & nf* DEP *(en fútbol)* physiotherapist, physio.

mascar *vt* to chew.

máscara *nf (careta)* mask.

mascarilla *nf (de belleza)* face mask.

mascota *nf* **1** *(figura)* mascot. **2** *(animal doméstico)* pet.

masculinidad *nf* masculinity.

masculino,-a *adj* **1** male: *la población masculina* the male population. **2** *(propio de hombres)* masculine. **3** GRAM masculine.

mascullar *vt* to mumble, mutter.

masificado,-a *adj* overcrowded.

masilla *nf* putty.

masivo,-a *adj* mass, massive.

master *nm* EDUC Master's degree.

máster *nm (estudios)* master's degree.

masticar *vt* to chew, masticate.

mástil *nm* **1** *(asta)* mast. **2** MAR mast.

mastodóntico,-a *adj fam* enormous.

mastoides *nf inv* mastoid.

mata *nf (arbusto)* shrub, bush.

matadero *nm* slaughterhouse.

matador,-ra *adj fam (agotador)* killing.

matalahúva *nf (planta)* anise.

matamoscas *nm* **1** *(insecticida)* fly spray. **2** *(pala)* fly swat.

matanza *nf (gen)* slaughter.

matar *vt* **1** *(persona - gen)* to kill.
▶ *vpr* **matarse** *(involuntariamente)* to die; *(voluntariamente)* to kill os.

matasellos *nm inv (marca)* postmark.

mate¹ *adj (sin brillo)* matt.

mate² *nm (ajedrez)* mate.

mate³ *nm (hierba)* maté.

matemática *nf (ciencia)* mathematics.

matemáticas *nf pl* mathematics *sing*.

matemático,-a *adj* mathematical.
▶ *nm & nf* mathematician.

materia *nf* **1** *(sustancia)* matter. **2** *(asignatura)* subject. COMP **materia prima** raw material.

material *adj (en general)* material.
▶ *nm (conjunto de cosas)* equipment.

materialismo *nm* materialism.

materialista *adj* materialistic.

materializar *vt* to put into practice.

maternal *adj* maternal, motherly.

maternidad *nf* maternity.

materno,-a *adj (abuelo, etc)* maternal.

matinal *adj* morning.

matiz *nm* **1** *(color)* shade, tint. **2** *(variación)* nuance.

matizar *vt* **1** ARTE *(colores)* to blend. **2** *(sonido)* to modulate. **3** *(añadir un matiz)* to tinge *(de, with)*.

matojo *nm* small shrub, bush.

matón,-ona *nm & nf fam* bully, thug.

matorral *nm (maleza)* bushes *pl*.

matraca *nf* wooden rattle.

matraz *nm* flask.

matriarca *nf* matriarch.

matriarcado *nm* matriarchy.

matriarcal *adj* matriarchal.

matrícula *nf* **1** *(registro - de personas)* registration, enrollment: *plazo de matrícula* registration period. **2** *(tasa)* registration fee(s), tuition fee(s). **3** AUTO *(placa)* number plate, US license plate. COMP **matrícula de honor** distinction.

matricular *vt (persona)* to register.

▶ *vpr* **matricularse** to register, enroll: *me he matriculado en Informática* I've enrolled for computer science.

matrimonial *adj (derecho)* matrimonial.

matrimonio *nm* **1** *(estado)* marriage. **2** *(pareja)* married couple.

matriz *nf* **1** ANAT womb. **2** MAT matrix.

matrona *nf (comadrona)* midwife.

matutino,-a *adj* morning.
▶ *nm* **matutino** *(periódico)* morning paper.

maullar *vi* miaow, US meow.

Mauritania *nf* Mauritania.

mauritano,-a *adj* Mauritanian.
▶ *nm & nf* Mauritanian.

mausoleo *nm* mausoleum.

maxilar *nm* jaw, jawbone.

máxima *nf (temperatura)* maximum temperature.

máxime *adv fml* especially.

maximizar *vt* to maximize.

máximo,-a *adj (velocidad)* maximum; *(puntuación, condecoración)* highest.
▶ *nm* **máximo** maximum: *tenéis una hora como máximo para acabar* you must be finished in an hour.

maya *adj* Mayan.
▶ *nm o nf (persona)* Mayan.
▶ *nm* **maya** *(idioma)* Mayan.

mayestático,-a *adj* majestic.

mayo *nm* May.

✎ Para ejemplos de uso, consulta marzo.

mayólica *nf* majolica.

mayonesa *nf* mayonnaise.

mayor *adj* **1** *(comparativo)* bigger, greater, larger; *(persona)* older; *(hermanos, hijos)* elder, older. **2** *(superlativo)* biggest, greatest, largest; *(persona)* oldest; *(hermanos, hijos)* eldest, oldest. **3** *(de edad)* mature, elderly: *la gente mayor* elderly people. **4** *(adulto)* grown-up. **5** *(principal)* main. **6** MÚS major.
▶ *nm pl* **los mayores** *(adultos)* grown-ups, adults.
▶ *nm & nf* **el/la mayor** *(entre varios)* the oldest.

mayoral *nm (capataz)* foreman.

mayordomo *nm* butler.

mayoría *nf* majority: *la mayoría de los hombres...* most men...

mayorista *nm o nf* wholesaler.

mayoritario,-a *adj* majority.

mayúscula *nf* capital, capital letter.

mayúsculo,-a *adj (enorme)* enormous, gigantic.

maza *nf* HIST *(arma)* mace.

mazapán *nm* marzipan.

mazmorra *nf* dungeon.

mazo *nm (martillo)* mallet.

mazorca *nf* cob. COMP **mazorca de maíz** corncob.

me *pron* **1** me: *no me lo dijo* she didn't tell me; *dámelo* give it to me. **2** *(reflexivo)* myself: *me veo en el espejo* I can see myself in the mirror.

meandro *nm* meander.

meca *nf* mecca, Mecca.

mecánica *nf (ciencia)* mechanics.

mecánico,-a *adj* mechanical.
▶ *nm & nf* mechanic.

mecanismo *nm* mechanism.

mecanización *nf* mechanization.

mecanizado,-a *adj* mechanized.

mecanizar *vt* to mechanize.

mecano® *nm* Meccano.

mecanografía *nf* typing.

mecanografiar *vt* to type.

mecedora *nf* rocking chair.

mecenas *nm o nf* patron.

mecer *vt* to rock.
▶ *vpr* **mecerse** *(en una silla)* to rock; *(en un columpio)* to swing.

mecha *nf* **1** *(de vela)* wick. **2** MIL fuse.

mechado,-a *adj* larded.

mechar *vt (carne)* to lard.

mechero *nm (cigarette)* lighter.

mechón *nm (de pelo)* lock, strand.

medalla *nf* medal.

medallero *nm* DEP medals table.

medallista *nm o nf* DEP medal winner.

medallón *nm (joya)* medallion.

media *nf* **1** *(calcetín)* sock. **2** *(promedio)* average. **3** MAT mean. **4** **la media** *(hora)* half past, half past the hour. COMP **media aritmética** arithmetic mean.

M

▶ *nf pl* **medias** *(enteras)* tights, panti-hose; *(no enteras)* stockings.
mediación *nf* mediation.
mediado,-a *adj (recipiente)* half-empty; LOC **a mediados de** halfway through.
mediador,-ra *adj* mediating.
▶ *nm & nf* mediator.
mediana *nf* MAT median.
medianero,-a *adj* dividing.
mediano,-a *adj (de calidad)* average; *(de tamaño)* medium, medium-sized.
medianoche *nf* midnight.
mediante *adj* by means of.
mediar *vi* **1** *(interceder)* to intercede (en favor de, on behalf of). **2** *(interponerse)* to mediate (en, in), intervene (en, in). **3** *(estar en medio)* to be. **4** *(llegar a la mitad)*.
medicación *nf* medicines *pl*.
medicamento *nm* medicine, drug.
medicar *vt (recetar)* to prescribe.
▶ *vpr* **medicarse** to take medicine.
medicina *nf* medicine.
medicinal *adj* medicinal.
medición *nf (acción)* measuring.
médico,-a *adj* medical.
▶ *nm & nf* doctor. COMP **médico,-a de cabecera** general practitioner, GP. I **médico,-a de familia** family doctor.
medida *nf* **1** *(acción)* measuring; *(dato, número)* measurement. **2** *(disposición)* measure. LOC **a medida que** as.
medidor,-ra *nm* AM *(contador)* meter.
medieval *adj* medieval.
medievalista *nm o nf* medievalist.
medievo *nm* Middle Ages *pl*.
medio,-a *adj* **1** *(mitad)* half: *las dos y media* half past two; *un año y medio* a year and a half. **2** *(intermedio)* middle: *a media tarde* in the middle of the afternoon. **3** *(de promedio)* average.
▶ *adv* half: *medio terminado,-a* half-finished.
▶ *nm* **medio 1** *(mitad)* half. **2** *(centro)* middle. **3** *(contexto - físico)* environment. COMP **medio ambiente** environment.
▶ *nm pl* **medios** *(recursos)* means.
medioambiental *adj* environmental.
mediocampista *nm o nf* midfield player.

mediocre *adj* mediocre.
mediocridad *nf* mediocrity.
mediodía *nm (las doce)* midday.
mediopensionista *nm o nf* day student.
medir *vt* to measure.
▶ *vpr* **medirse** to measure os.
meditación *nf* meditation.
meditar *vt* to meditate, think.
▶ *vi* to meditate (sobre, over).
mediterráneo,-a *adj* Mediterranean.
▶ *nm & nf* Mediterranean. COMP **el (mar) Mediterráneo** the Mediterranean (Sea).
médium *nm o nf* medium.
medrar *vi (mejorar socialmente)* to get rich.
médula *nf* **1** ANAT marrow. **2** BOT pith. COMP **médula espinal** spinal cord.
medular *adj* ANAT marrow.
medusa *nf* jellyfish.
megabyte *nm* megabyte.
megafonía *nf* sound amplification.
megáfono *nm* megaphone.
megahercio *nm* megahertz.
megalítico,-a *adj* megalithic.
megalito *nm* megalith.
megalómano,-a *nm & nf* megaloma-niac.
megatón *nm* megaton.
megavatio *nm* megawatt.
megavoltio *nm* megavolt.
mejicano,-a *adj* Mexican.
▶ *nm & nf* Mexican.
Méjico *nm* Mexico.
mejilla *nf* cheek.
mejillón *nm* mussel.
mejor *adj* **1** *(comparativo)* better: *este libro es mejor que aquél* this book is better than that one. **2** *(superlativo)* best: *mi mejor amigo,-a* my best friend. LOC **a lo mejor** perhaps, maybe.
▶ *adv* **1** *(comparativo)* better: *cada vez mejor* better and better every day. **2** *(superlativo)* best.
▶ *nm & nf* **el/la mejor** the best (one).
mejora *nf (progreso)* improvement.
mejorable *adj* which could be im-proved.
mejorar *vt* to improve.

► *vi* to improve, get better.

► *vpr* **mejorarse** to get better: *¡que te mejores!* I hope you get better.

mejoría *nf* improvement.

melancolía *nf* melancholy, sadness.

melancólico,-a *adj* melancholic.

melanina *nf* melanin.

melaza *nf* molasses.

melena *nf* **1** *(de persona)* hair. **2** *(de león)* mane.

melisa *nf* lemon balm.

mella *nf* *(hendedura)* nick, notch.

mellar *vt* **1** *(objeto)* to chip, nick. **2** *fig* to dent, damage.

mellizo,-a *adj* twin.

► *nm & nf* twin.

melocotón *nm* peach.

melocotonero *nm* peach tree.

melodía *nf* melody.

melódico,-a *adj* melodic.

melodrama *nm* melodrama.

melodramático,-a *adj* melodramatic.

melómano,-a *adj* music lover.

melón *nm* *(fruto)* melon.

meloso,-a *adj* *(dulce)* sweet, honeyed.

membrana *nf* membrane.

membrillo *nm* *(fruta)* quince.

memo,-a *adj fam* stupid, dim.

memorable *adj* memorable.

memorándum *nm* *(cuaderno)* notebook.

memoria *nf* **1** *(gen)* memory. **2** *(informe)* report. **3** *(inventario)* inventory.

► *nf pl* **memorias** *(biografía)* memoirs. [LOC] **de memoria** (off) by heart, by memory. ▌ **hacer memoria** to try to remember. [COMP] **memoria RAM** RAM memory.

memorial *nm* *(acto)* conmemoration.

memorizar *vt* to memorize.

mena *nf* ore.

menaje *nm* household goods. [COMP] **menaje de cocina** kitchen equipment.

mención *nf* mention.

mencionar *vt* to mention, cite.

mendelismo *nm* Mendelism.

mendicante *adj* mendicant.

mendicidad *nf* begging.

mendigar *vi* to beg.

mendigo,-a *nm & nf* beggar.

mendrugo *nm* hard crust (of bread).

menear *vt* *(cabeza)* to shake; *(cola)* to wag; *(cuerpo, caderas)* to wiggle.

menestra *nf* vegetable stew.

mengua *nf* *(disminución)* decrease.

menguado,-a *adj* diminished.

menguante *adj* *(luna)* waning.

menguar *vi* **1** *(cantidad)* to decrease. **2** *(luna)* to wane.

menhir *nm* menhir.

meninge *nm* meninx.

meningitis *nm inv* meningitis.

menisco *nm* meniscus.

menopausia *nf* menopause.

menopáusico,-a *adj* menopausal.

menor *adj* **1** *(comparativo - en tamaño)* smaller; *(- en calidad, importancia)* lesser; *(- en edad)* younger. **2** *(superlativo - en tamaño)* smallest; *(- en calidad, importancia)* least; *(- en edad)* youngest. **3** *(inferior)* minor. **4** MÚS minor.

► *nm o nf* JUR minor. [COMP] **menor de edad** minor.

menos *adj* **1** *(comparativo - en cantidad)* less; *(- en número)* fewer: *yo tengo menos años que tú* I'm younger than you. **2** *(superlativo - de cantidad)* least; *(- de número)* fewest: *yo soy la que menos culpa tiene* I'm the least guilty.

► *adv* **1** *(comparativo - de cantidad)* less; *(- de número)* fewer: *voy al gimnasio menos que antes* I go to the gym less than before. **2** *(superlativo)* least: *es el menos guapo* he's the least good-looking. **3** *(con horas)* to: *las tres menos cuarto* a quarter to three. **4** MAT minus. [LOC] **a menos que** unless. ▌ **al menos** at least. ▌ **por lo menos** at least.

► *prep* but, except: *todo menos eso* anything but that.

► *pron* *(cantidad)* less; *(número)* fewer: *me pagó menos* he paid me less.

► *nm* MAT minus sign.

menospreciar *vt* **1** *(despreciar)* to despise, scorn. **2** *(no valorar)* to undervalue, underrate.

M

menosprecio *nm (poco aprecio)* underestimation, lack of appreciation.

mensaje *nm* 1 *(en general)* message. 2 *(envío electrónico)* posting.

mensajería *nf* courier service.

mensajero,-a *nm & nf* courier.

menstruación *nf* menstruation.

menstrual *adj* menstrual.

menstruar *vi* to menstruate.

mensual *adj* monthly.

mensualidad *nf (que se cobra)* monthly salary; *(que se paga)* monthly instalment.

mensurable *adj* measurable.

menta *nf (hierba)* mint.

mental *adj* mental.

mentalidad *nf* mentality.

mentalizar *vt* to make aware.
▶ *vpr* **mentalizarse** *(hacerse a la idea)* to get used to the idea.

mente *nf* 1 *(pensamiento)* mind. 2 *(facultades)* mind, intelligence, intellect.

mentir *vi* to lie.

mentira *nf* lie.

mentiroso,-a *nm & nf* liar.

mentón *nm* chin.

mentor *nm* mentor.

menú *nm* 1 CULIN menu. 2 INFORM menu. COMP **menú del día** set menu.

menudo,-a *adj* 1 *(pequeño)* small, tiny. 2 *(enfático)* what a…: ¡menudo lío! what a mess! LOC **a menudo** often.

meñique *adj* little. COMP **(dedo) meñique** little finger.

meollo *nm (lo esencial)* core, heart, crux.

mercader *nm arc* merchant.

mercadería *nf* merchandise.

mercadillo *nm* flea market, bazaar.

mercado *nm* market. COMP **Mercado Común** Common Market. ▮ **mercado de abastos** wholesale food market.

mercancía *nf (gen)* goods.

mercante *adj* merchant.

mercantil *adj* commercial.

mercantilismo *nm* mercantilism.

mercenario,-a *nm & nf* mercenary.

mercería *nf (tienda)* haberdasher's shop, US notions store.

mercurio *nm* QUÍM mercury.

merecedor,-ra *adj* worthy.

merecer *vt* to deserve, be worth: *merece la pena verlo* it's worth a visit.

merecido,-a *nm* (just) come-uppance. LOC **llevar su merecido** to get one's come-uppance.

merendar *vi* to have tea.
▶ *vt* to have something for tea.

merendero *nm* open-air snack bar.

merengue *nm* CULIN meringue.

meridiano,-a *nm* meridian.

meridional *adj* southern.

merienda *nf* afternoon snack, tea.

merina *nf* merino sheep.

mérito *nm (de alguien)* merit.

merluza *nf* hake.

mermar *vt* to reduce.
▶ *vi* to decrease, diminish.

mermelada *nf* jam; *(de cítricos)* marmalade.

mero *nm (pez)* grouper.

merodear *vi (curiosear)* to prowl about.

mes *nm* month.

mesa *nf (gen)* table; *(de oficina)* desk. LOC **poner la mesa** to set the table, lay the table. ▮ **quitar/recoger la mesa** to clear the table.

meseta *nf* GEOG plateau.

mesianismo *nm* Messianism.

mesías *nm inv* Messiah.

mesilla *nf* small table. COMP **mesilla de noche** bedside table.

mesocarpio *nm* mesocarp.

mesolítico,-a *nm* the Mesolithic.

mesón *nm* old-style restaurant.

mestizaje *nm* crossbreeding.

mestizo,-a *adj* of mixed race.
▶ *nm & nf* person of mixed race.

mesura *nf* restraint, moderation.

meta *nf* 1 *(en una carrera)* finishing line. 2 *(portería)* goal. 3 *fig* purpose.

metabolismo *nm* metabolism.

metabolizar *vt* to metabolize.

metafísica *nf* metaphysics.

metáfora *nf* metaphor.
metafórico,-a *adj* metaphorical.
metal *nm* metal.
metálico,-a *adj* metallic.
▶ *nm* **metálico** cash.
metalista *nm o nf* metal worker.
metalistería *nf* metal work.
metalizado,-a *adj* metallic.
metalizar *vt* to metallize (US metal-ize).
metalurgia *nf* metallurgy.
metalúrgico,-a *adj* metallurgical.
▶ *nm & nf* metallurgist.
metamórfico,-a *adj* metamorphic.
metamorfosis *nf inv* metamorphosis.
metano *nm* methane.
metanol *nm* methanol.
metástasis *nf inv* metastasis.
metatarso *nm* metatarsus.
meteórico,-a *adj* meteoric.
meteorito *nm* meteorite.
meteoro *nm* meteor.
meteorología *nf* meteorology.
meteorológico,-a *adj* meteorological.
meteorólogo,-a *nm & nf* meteorolo-gist.
metepatas *nm o nf fam* bigmouth.
meter *vt* **1** *(introducir)* to put. **2** *(implicar)* to put into (en, -), get into (en, -), in-volve in (en, -).
▶ *vpr* **meterse 1** *(introducirse en)* to get in: *se metió en la cama* he got into bed. **2** *(tomar parte - negocio)* to go into (en, -); *(involucrarse en)* to get involved (en, in/with), get mixed up (en, in/with). **3** *(introducirse)* to get involved (en, in): *me metí totalmente en el papel* I got com-pletely into the role. **4** *(ir)* to go: *¿dón-de se habrá metido?* where can he have got to?
meticuloso,-a *adj (cuidadoso)* meticu-lous.
metido,-a *adj (envuelto, implicado)* in-volved (en, in).
metileno *nm* methylene.
metílico,-a *adj* methylic.
metódico,-a *adj* methodical.
método *nm* method.

metodología *nf* methodology.
metodológico,-a *adj* methodologi-cal.
metonimia *nf* metonymy.
metraje *nm (película rodada)* footage. COMP **largo metraje** (full-length) fea-ture film.
metralla *nf* shrapnel.
metralleta *nf* sub-machine-gun.
métrica *nf* metrics *pl*.
métrico,-a *adj* **1** *(sistema, unidad)* met-ric. **2** *(del verso)* metrical, metric. COMP **sistema métrico** metric system.
metro *nm* **1** metre (US meter). **2** *(cinta)* tape measure. **3** *(transporte)* under-ground, tube, US subway. COMP **metro cuadrado** square metre.
metrónomo *nm* metronome.
metrópoli *nf* metropolis.
metropolitano,-a *adj* metropolitan.
▶ *nm* **metropolitano** *fml* underground, tube, US subway.
mexicano,-a *adj* Mexican.
▶ *nm & nf* Mexican.
México *nm* Mexico.
mezcla *nf* **1** *(acción)* mixing, blending. **2** *(producto)* mixture, blend.
mezclar *vt* **1** *(incorporar, unir)* to mix, blend. **2** *(desordenar)* to mix up.
▶ *vpr* **mezclarse 1** *(personas)* to mix (con, with). **2** *(cosas)* to get mixed up.
mezquindad *nf* **1** meanness, stingi-ness. **2** *(acción)* mean thing.
mezquino,-a *adj* low, base.
mezquita *nf* mosque.
mi *nm* MÚS E.
mí *pron* me: *éste es para mí* this one is for me.
miau *nm* miaow, meow, mew.
mica *nf* GEOL mica.
michelín *nm fam* spare tyre.
mico *nm (animal)* monkey.
micología *nf* mycology.
micosis *nf inv* mycosis.
micra *nf* micron.
micro *nm fam* mike, microphone.
microbio *nm* microbe.
microbiología *nf* microbiology.

M

microchip *nm* microchip.
microclima *nm* microclimate.
microcomputador *nm* microcomputer.
microcosmos *nm inv* microcosm.
microeconomía *nf* microeconomics.
microelectrónica *nf* microelectronics.
microfilme *nm* microfilm.
micrófono *nm* microphone.
microondas *nm* microwave. [COMP] horno microondas microwave oven.
microordenador *nm* microcomputer.
microprocesador *nm* microprocessor.
microscópico,-a *adj* microscopic.
microscopio *nm* microscope.
miedo *nm* fear. [LOC] **tener miedo** to be scared, be frightened, be afraid: *tiene miedo a la oscuridad* he's afraid of the dark.
miedoso,-a *adj* easily frightened.
miel *nf* honey.
miembro *nm* **1** *(extremidad)* limb. **2** *(socio)* member. **3** MAT member.
mientras *adv* meanwhile.
▶ *conj* **1** *(temporal)* while, whilst: *mientras estés de vacaciones no pienses en el trabajo* while you're on holiday, don't think about work. **2** *(adversativa)* whereas: *yo al menos he estudiado, mientras que tú no* at least I have studied, whereas you haven't.
miércoles *nm* Wednesday.

✎ Consulta también **jueves**.

mies *nf* corn, grain.
miga *nf (parte blanda del pan)* crumb.
migración *nf* migration.
migraña *nf* migraine.
migrar *vi* to migrate.
migratorio,-a *adj* migratory.
mijo *nm* millet.
mil *adj* **1** thousand. **2** *(milésimo)* thousandth.
▶ *nm* a thousand, one thousand.

✎ Consulta también **seis** y **sexto,-a**.

milagro *nm* miracle.
milagroso,-a *adj* miraculous.
milanesa [LOC] **a la milanesa** done in breadcrumbs.
milano *nm* kite.

milenario,-a *adj* millennial.
▶ *nm* **milenario** millennium.
milenio *nm* millennium.
milésimo,-a *adj* thousandth.
▶ *nm & nf* thousandth.

✎ Consulta también **sexto,-a**.

milhojas *nm inv* CULIN millefeuille.
mili *nf fam* military service. [LOC] **hacer la mili** *fam* to do one's military service.
milicia *nf (gente armada)* militia.
miliciano,-a *adj* of the militia.
▶ *nm & nf (hombre)* militiaman; *(mujer)* militiawoman.
miligramo *nm* milligram.
mililitro *nm* millilitre (US milliliter).
milimétrico,-a *adj* pinpoint.
milímetro *nm* millimetre (US millimeter).
militante *adj* militant.
militar *adj* military.
▶ *nm* military man, soldier.
milla *nf* mile. [COMP] **milla náutica** nautical mile.
millar *nm* thousand.
millón *nm* million.
millonario,-a *nm & nf (hombre)* millionaire; *(mujer)* millionairess.
mimar *vt (consentir)* to spoil.
mimbre *nm* wicker.
mimetismo *nm* mimicry.
mímico,-a *adj* mimic.
mimo *nm* **1** *(actor)* mime artist. **2** *(cariño)* pampering. **3** *(cuidado)* care. [LOC] **hacerle mimos a ALGN** to pamper SB.
mimosa *nf* BOT mimosa.
mimoso,-a *adj (cariñoso)* loving.
mina *nf* **1** mine. **2** *(explosivo)* mine. **3** *(de lápiz)* lead. [COMP] **mina de carbón** coal mine.
minar *vt (terreno)* to mine.
minarete *nm* minaret.
mineral *adj* mineral. [COMP] **agua mineral** mineral water.
▶ *nm* mineral.
minería *nf (técnica)* mining.
minero,-a *adj* mining.
▶ *nm & nf* miner.

miniatura *nf* miniature.

minifalda *nf* mini skirt.

minifundio *nm* smallholding.

minigolf *nm* crazy golf.

mínima *nf (temperatura)* minimum temperature.

minimizar *vt* to minimize.

mínimo,-a *adj* minimum, lowest.
▶ *nm* **mínimo** minimum: *pon el gas en el mínimo* turn the gas right down. LOC **como mínimo** at least. COMP **mínimo común múltiplo** lowest common multiple.

minino *nm fam* pussy, kitty.

minio *nm* red lead, minium.

ministerio *nm* POL ministry, US department.

ministro,-a *nm & nf* POL minister, US secretary. COMP **primer,-ra ministro,-a** prime minister.

minoría *nf* minority.

minorista *adj* retail.

minoritario,-a *adj* minority.

minucia *nf* trifle.

minucioso,-a *adj* meticulous.

minúscula *nf (letra)* small letter.

minúsculo,-a *adj (letra)* small; *(detalle)* insignificant.

minusvalía *nf* handicap, disability.

minusválido,-a *adj* disabled, handicapped.
▶ *nm & nf* disabled person.

minuta *nf (factura)* bill.

minutero *nm* minute hand.

minuto *nm* minute.

mío,-a *adj* my, of mine: *es muy amiga mía* she's a good friend of mine.
▶ *pron* mine: *este abrigo es mío* this coat is mine.

miocardio *nm* myocardium.

miope *adj* short-sighted, myopic.
▶ *nm o nf* short-sighted person.

miopía *nf* short-sightedness.

mira *nf* **1** *(dispositivo)* sight. **2** *fig* intention.

mirada *nf (gen)* look; *(vistazo)* glance.
LOC **echar una mirada a** ALGO/ALGN to take a look at STH/SB.

mirador *nm* **1** *(balcón)* glassed-in balcony. **2** *(lugar)* viewing point.

miramiento *nm* consideration.

mirar *vt* **1** *(observar)* to look at; *(con atención)* to watch. **2** *(buscar)* to look; *(registrar)* to search: *me miraron todo al pasar por la aduana* they went through everything at customs. **3** *(tener cuidado con)* to watch: *mira bien lo que haces* watch what you do.
▶ *vi* **1** *(gen)* to look. **2** *(buscar)* to look: *mira debajo de la cama* look under the bed. **3** *(tener cuidado)* to mind, watch, be careful: *mira que no te engañen* mind they don't cheat you. LOC **¡mira!** look!

miríada *nf* myriad.

mirilla *nf* peephole, spyhole.

miriópodo *nm* myriapod.

mirlo *nm* blackbird.

mirón,-ona *nm & nf fam pey (curioso)* nosy parker.

mirra *nf* myrrh.

mirto *nm* myrtle.

misa *nf* mass.

misal *nm* missal.

misántropo,-a *nm & nf* misanthrope, misanthropist.

miscelánea *nf* miscellany.

miserable *adj* **1** *(tacaño)* mean. **2** *(malvado)* wretched.
▶ *nm o nf* **1** *(malvado)* wretch. **2** *(tacaño)* miser.

miseria *nf (pobreza)* extreme poverty.

misericordia *nf* mercy.

mísero,-a *adj* miserable.

misil *nm* missile.

misión *nf (tarea)* mission, task.

misionero,-a *nm & nf* missionary.

mismo,-a *adj* **1** *(idéntico)* same: *el mismo color* the same colour. **2** *(enfático)* very: *en esta misma casa nací yo* I was born in this very house.
▶ *pron* same: *es el mismo del año pasado* it's the same one as last year.
▶ *adv* **mismo** same: *piensa lo mismo que tu* he thinks the same as you. LOC **es lo mismo 1** *(la misma cosa)* it amounts to the same thing. **2** *(no importa)* it doesn't matter.

M

misógino,-a *adj* misogynous.

míster *nm (en fútbol)* manager, coach.

misterio *nm* mystery.

misterioso,-a *adj* mysterious.

mística *nf* 1 *(misticismo)* mysticism. 2 *(teología)* mystic theology.

misticismo *nm* mysticism.

místico,-a *adj* mystic, mystical.
▶ *nm & nf (persona)* mystic.

mitad *nf* 1 half: *me llevo la mitad* I'll take half. 2 *(medio)* middle: *en mitad de la plaza* in the middle of the square.

mítico,-a *adj* mythical.

mitificar *vt (convertir en mito)* to mythicize.

mitin *nm* meeting, rally.

mito *nm* myth.

mitología *nf* mythology.

mitológico,-a *adj* mythological.

mitosis *nf inv* mitosis.

mixto,-a *adj* mixed.

mobiliario *nm* furniture.

moca *nf (café)* mocha.

mocasín *nm* moccasin.

mochila *nf* rucksack, backpack.

mochuelo *nm* ZOOL little owl.

moción *nf* motion.

moco *nm* 1 *(mucosidad)* mucus; *(familiarmente)* snot. LOC **limpiarse los mocos** *fam* to blow one's nose.

mocoso,-a *nm & nf fam* brat.

moda *nf* fashion.

modales *nm pl* manners.

modalidad *nf* form, means, way.

modelado *nm* modelling (US modeling).

modelar *vt* to model, shape.

modélico,-a *adj* model.

modelismo *nm (de arcilla, etc)* modelling.

modelo *adj* model.
▶ *nm o nf (persona)* (fashion) model.

módem *nm* modem.

moderación *nf* moderation.

moderado,-a *adj* moderate.

moderador,-ra *nm & nf (de reunión)* chairperson.

moderar *vt* to moderate.

modernismo *nm (arte, literatura)* Modernism.

modernista *adj* Modernist.
▶ *nm o nf* Modernist.

modernizar *vt* to modernize.

moderno,-a *adj* modern.

modestia *nf* modesty.

modesto,-a *adj* modest.

modificar *vt* to alter, modify.

modista *nm o nf (de ropa para mujer)* dressmaker.

modisto *nm* 1 *(diseñador)* fashion designer. 2 *(sastre)* tailor.

modo *nm* 1 way, manner. 2 LING mood: *el modo subjuntivo* the subjunctive mood. LOC **de modo que** so: *de modo que ya lo sabes* so now you know. ▌ **en cierto modo** in a way.
▶ *nm pl* **modos** manners. LOC **de todos modos** anyhow, at any rate.

modorra *nf fam* drowsiness.

modular *vt* to modulate.
▶ *adj* modular.

módulo *nm* 1 *(gen)* module. 2 *(mueble)* unit.

mofa *nf* mockery, derision.

mofarse *vpr* to scoff, mock.

mofeta *nf* skunk.

moflete *nm fam* chubby cheek.

mogollón *nm fam* loads *pl*.
▶ *adv fam* a lot: *nos gustó mogollón* it was dead brilliant.

mohair *nm* mohair.

moho *nm* mould, (US mold).

mohoso,-a *adj* mouldy (US moldy).

mojado,-a *adj (húmedo)* wet, moist.

mojama *nf* dried salted tuna.

mojar *vt* 1 *(gen)* to wet. 2 *(alimento)* to dip.
▶ *vpr* **mojarse** 1 to get wet. 2 *fam (comprometerse)* to commit os.

mojigato,-a *adj (gazmoño)* prudish.

mojón *nm (poste - de distancia)* milepost.

molar *nm (diente)* molar.

molde *nm* mould (US mold).

moldeable *adj* mouldable.

moldeado,-a *adj* moulded (US molded).

moldear *vt* ARTE *(dar forma)* to mould (US mold).

moldura *nf* moulding (US molding).
mole *nf* mass, bulk, hulk.
molécula *nf* molecule.
molecular *adj* molecular.
moler *vt* **1** *(gen)* to grind. **2** *(cansar)* to wear out.
molestar *vt* **1** *(interrumpir)* to disturb. **2** *(perturbar)* to bother, upset: *me molestan los ruidos* noise bothers me. **3** *(importunar)* to pester: *¡deja de molestarme ya!* stop pestering me! **4** *(hacer daño - apretar)* to hurt: *estos zapatos me molestan* these shoes hurt my feet.
▶ *vpr* **molestarse** to bother: *perdone que le moleste* I'm sorry to bother you.
molestia *nf* **1** *(incomodidad)* bother, trouble; *(fastidio)* nuisance. **2** MED trouble.
molesto,-a *adj* **1** annoying. **2** *(enfadado)* annoyed.
molido,-a *adj* **1** *(café)* ground. **2** *fam (cansado)* worn-out. LOC **estar molido,-a** *fam* to be worn-out.
molienda *nf* *(de café)* grinding.
moliente LOC **corriente y moliente** run of the mill, common or garden.
molinero,-a *nm & nf* miller.
molinillo *nm* grinder, mill.
molino *nm* mill. COMP **molino de viento** windmill.
molla *nf* *(pulpa)* flesh.
molleja *nf* *(de ave)* gizzard.
mollera *nf fam (inteligencia)* brains *pl*.
molón,-na *adj argot* cool, brill, fab.
molusco *nm* mollusc (US mollusk).
momentáneo,-a *adj* momentary.
momento *nm* **1** moment. **2** *(período)* time.
momia *nf* mummy.
momificación *nf* mummification.
momificar *vt* to mummify.
monacal *adj* monastic.
monacato *nm (institución)* monastic community.
Mónaco *nm* Monaco.
monada *nf (cosa bonita)* beauty, lovely thing; *(persona)* gorgeous person.
monaguillo *nm* altar boy.
monarca *nm* monarch.

monarquía *nf* monarchy.
monárquico,-a *adj* monarchic.
monasterio *nm* monastery.
monástico,-a *adj* monastic.
monda *nf (piel)* peel, skin.
mondadientes *nm inv* toothpick.
mondadura *nf (piel - de fruta)* peel.
mondar *vt (pelar)* to peel.
mondo,-a *adj (limpio)* bare.
mondongo *nm* innards *pl*.
moneda *nf (pieza)* coin.
monedero *nm* purse.
monegasco,-a *adj* Monegasque.
▶ *nm & nf* Monegasque.
monetario,-a *adj* monetary.
monetarismo *nm* monetarism.
monetarista *adj* monetarist.
mongólico,-a *adj* affected by Down's syndrome.
▶ *nm & nf* person affected by Down's syndrome.
mongolismo *nm* Down's syndrome, mongolism.
monicaco *nm fam* dodgy geezer.
monigote *nm* **1** *(figura)* rag doll, paper doll. **2** *(dibujo)* matchstick man.
monismo *nm* monism.
monista *adj* monistic.
monitor,-ra *nm & nf (profesor)* instructor.
▶ *nm* **monitor** *(pantalla)* screen.
monja *nf* nun.
monje *nm* monk.
mono,-a *adj (bonito)* nice, lovely, cute.
▶ *nm & nf* ZOOL monkey.
▶ *nm* **mono** *(prenda de trabajo)* overalls *pl*.
monocarril *nm* monorail.
monocolor *adj* monochrome.
monocorde *adj fig (monótono)* dull.
monocotiledónea *nf* monocotyledon.
monocotiledóneo,-a *adj* monocotyledonous.
monocromático,-a *adj* monochromatic.
monocromía *nf* monochrome.
monocromo,-a *adj* monochrome.
monocular *adj* monocular.
monóculo *nm* monocle.

M

monocultivo *nm* monoculture.
monódico,-a *adj* monodic.
monofásico,-a *adj* single-phase.
monofonía *nm* mono.
monofónico,-a *adj* mono.
monogamia *nf* monogamy.
monógamo,-a *adj* monogamous.
monografía *nf* monograph.
monográfico,-a *adj* monographic.
monograma *nm* monogram.
monolingüe *adj* monolingual.
monolítico,-a *adj* monolithic.
monolito *nm* monolith.
monologar *vi* to soliloquize.
monólogo *nm* (*reflexión*) monologue.
monomanía *nf* 2 *fam* obsession.
monomaníaco,-a *adj* MED monomaniac.
monomio *n* MAT monomial.
monoparental *adj* one-parent.
monopatín *nm* skateboard.
monoplano *nm* monoplane.
monoplaza *adj* single-seat.
monopolio *nm* monopoly.
monopolista *adj* monopolistic.
monopolización *nf* monopolization.
monopolizador,-ra *adj* monopolizing.
monopolizar *vt* to monopolize.
monorraíl *nm* monorail.
monosilábico,-a *adj* monosyllabic.
monosílabo,-a *adj* monosyllabic.
▶ *nm* **monosílabo** monosyllable.
monoteísmo *nm* monotheism.
monoteísta *adj* monotheistic.
▶ *nm o nf* monotheist.
monotonía *nf* monotony.
monótono,-a *adj* monotonous.
monovolumen *nm* people carrier.
monóxido *nm* monoxide. [COMP] **monóxido de carbono** carbon monoxide.
monseñor *nm* Monsignor.
monserga *nf fam* (*lección*) nagging.
monstruo *adj fam* fantastic, terrific.
▶ *nm* **1** monster. **2** *fam* (*genio*) genius.
monstruosidad *nf* (*cosa*) monstrosity.
monstruoso,-a *adj* monstrous.

monta *nf* **1** (*importancia*) value, account, importance. **2** (*de un caballo*) riding.
montacargas *nm* service lift.
montador,-ra *nm & nf* (*operario*) fitter.
montadora *nf* splicing machine.

✎ Consulta también **montador,-a.**

montaje *nm* **1** (*de piezas*) assembly. **2** (*en foto*) montage. **3** *fam* (*farsa*) setup.
montante *nm* **1** (*total*) total, total amount. **2** (*pieza vertical*) upright. **3** (*ventana*) skylight.
montaña *nf* mountain.
montañero,-a *nm & nf* mountaineer.
montañés,-esa *nm & nf* highlander.
montañismo *nm* mountaineering.
montañoso,-a *adj* mountainous.
montaplatos *nm inv* dumb waiter.
montar *vi* **1** (*subir - caballo, bicicleta*) to mount, get on; (*- coche*) to get in; (*- avión*) to get on, board. **2** (*ir en bicicleta*) to ride: *¿sabes montar en bicicleta?* can you ride bicycle?
▶ *vt* **1** (*subir - caballo*) to mount, get on. **2** (*subir - persona*) to put on: *monté al niño en la bicicleta* I lifted the kid onto his bike. **3** (*ensamblar*) to assemble, put together; (*tienda de campaña*) to put up. **4** (*nata*) to whip; (*claras*) to whisk.
▶ *vpr* **montarse 1** (*subirse*) to get on; (*- en un coche*) to get in; (*- en un caballo*) to mount, get on. **2** *fam* (*armarse*) to break out: *se montó un buen jaleo* there was a real to-do.
montaraz *adj* (*de montaña*) mountain.
monte *nm* **1** mountain, mount. **2** (*bosque*) wild, woodland.
montenegrino,-a *adj* Montenegrin.
▶ *nm & nf* Montenegrin.
Montenegro *nm* Montenegro.
montepío *nm* friendly society.
montera *nf* bullfighter's hat.
montería *nf* (*caza*) hunt.
montero,-a *nm & nf* hunter.
montés *adj* wild.
montículo *nm* mound, hillock.
monto *nm* total, total amount.
montón *nm* **1** heap, pile. **2** *fam* (*gran cantidad*) stacks *pl*, loads *pl*, heaps *pl*:

vino un montón de gente loads of people came.

montura *nf* **2** *(silla)* saddle. **3** *(armazón - de gafas)* frame.

monumental *adj* monumental.

monumento *nm* ARTE monument.

monzón *nm* monsoon.

monzónico,-a *adj* monsoon.

moña *nf fam (borrachera)* bender.

moño *nm* bun.

moquear *vi* to have a runny nose.

moqueta *nf* fitted carpet.

moquillo *nm (de perro)* distemper.

mora *nf* **1** *(de moral)* mulberry. **2** *(zarzamora)* blackberry.

morada *nf* adobe, dwelling.

morado,-a *adj (color)* purple.
▶ *nm* **morado** *(color)* purple.

morador,-ra *nm & nf* dweller.

moral¹ *adj* moral.
▶ *nf* **1** *(reglas)* morals *pl*. **2** *(ánimo)* morale, spirits *pl*.

moral² *nm* BOT mulberry tree.

moraleja *nf* moral.

moralidad *nf* morality.

moralina *nf* false morals *pl*.

moralista *adj* moralistic.

moralizador,-ra *adj* moralizing.

moralizar *vi* to moralize.
▶ *vt* to moralize.

morar *vi* to reside, dwell.

moratón *nm fam* bruise.

moratoria *nf* moratorium.

morbidez *nf* softness, tenderness.

morbo *nm fam* thrill.

morbosidad *nf (interés)* morbid curiosity.

morboso,-a *adj fam* kinky.

morcilla *nf* black pudding.

mordaz *adj* mordant, sarcastic.

mordaza *nf* gag.

mordedura *nf* bite.

morder *vt* to bite: *le ha mordido mi perro* my dog's bitten him.
▶ *vi* to bite: *ten cuidado que muerde* be careful, it bites.
▶ *vpr* **morderse** to bite. LOC **morderse la lengua** *(callarse)* to hold one's tongue.

mordida *nf fam (soborno)* bribe.

mordiente *nm* mordant.

mordisco *nm* bite.

mordisquear *vt* to nibble.

morena *nf (pez)* moray eel.

moreno,-a *adj* **1** *(pelo)* dark. **2** *(pan, azúcar)* brown.
▶ *nm* **moreno** suntan.

morera *nf* white mulberry.

moretón *nm* bruise.

morfema *nm* morpheme.

morfina *nf* morphine.

morfinómano,-a *nm & nf* morphine addict.

morfología *nf* morphology.

morfológico,-a *adj* morphological.

morganático,-a *adj* morganatic.

morgue *nf* morgue.

moribundo,-a *adj* moribund.

morir *vi (ser vivo)* to die.
▶ *vpr* **morirse** to die.

mormón,-ona *adj* Mormon.
▶ *nm & nf* Mormon.

mormónico,-a *adj* Mormon.

moro,-a *adj* Moorish.
▶ *nm & nf* Moor.

morosidad *nf* **1** *(tardanza)* delay; *(- en un pago)* arrears *pl*.

moroso,-a *adj* FIN *(cliente)* in arrears.
▶ *nm & nf* defaulter.

morral *nm* haversack.

morralla *nf* **1** *(pescado)* small fish. **2** *pey (gente)* riffraff.

morrazo LOC **pegarse un morrazo** *fam* to give os a bash.

morrena *nf* moraine.

morriña *nf* homesickness.

morrión *nm* helmet.

morro *nm* **1** *fam (de persona - boca)* lips *pl*, mouth; *(cara)* face. **2** *fam (cara dura)* cheek. **3** *(de animal)* snout, nose.

morrocotudo,-a *adj fam* terrific.

morrón *adj* COMP **pimiento morrón** sweet red pepper.

morrudo,-a *adj fam* thick-lipped.

morsa *nf* walrus.

Morse *nm* Morse code.

mortadela *nf* mortadella.

M

mortaja *nf* shroud.

mortal *adj* **1** *(criatura, ser)* mortal. **2** *(peligro, herida)* fatal. **3** *(aburrimiento, susto)* deadly.
▶ *nm o nf* mortal.

mortalidad *nf* mortality.

mortandad *nf* death toll.

mortecino,-a *adj* **1** *(luz)* faint, dull. **2** *(color)* lifeless, dull.

mortero *nm* mortar.

mortífero,-a *adj* deadly, lethal.

mortificación *nf* mortification.

mortificante *adj* mortifying.

mortificar *vt* to mortify.

mortuorio,-a *adj* mortuary.

moruno,-a *adj* Moorish.

mosaico *nm* mosaic.

mosca *nf* fly.

moscada COMP **nuez moscada** nutmeg.

moscardón *nm* **1** blowfly. **2** *(persona)* pest.

moscatel *nm* muscatel.

mosconear *vt fam* to pester.
▶ *vi fam* to be a pest, be a pain.

mosquear *vt fam* to annoy.
▶ *vpr* **mosquearse** *fam (enfadarse)* to get cross.

mosquete *nm* musket.

mosquetero *nm* musketeer.

mosquetón *nm* **1** *(arma)* short carbine. **2** *(cierre)* snap link.

mosquitera *nf* mosquito net.

mosquitero *nm* mosquito net.

mosquito *nm* mosquito.

mostacera *nf* mustard pot.

mostacho *nm* moustache.

mostaza *nf* mustard.

mosto *nm (zumo)* grape juice.

mostrador *nm (de tienda)* counter.

mostrar *vt* to show.
▶ *vpr* **mostrarse** to appear.

mostrenco,-a *adj (grande)* mammoth.

mota *nf (partícula)* speck.

mote *nm* nickname.

moteado,-a *adj* dotted, speckled.

motear *vt* to fleck, speck.

motejar *vt* to nickname.

motel *nm* motel.

motilidad *nf* motility.

motín *nm (levantamiento)* riot, uprising.

motivación *nf* motivation, motive.

motivar *vt* **1** *(causar)* to cause, give rise to. **2** *(estimular)* to motivate.

motivo *nm* motive, reason, cause.

moto *nf fam (motocicleta)* motorbike.

motocarro *nm* three-wheeled van.

motocicleta *nf* motorcycle.

motociclismo *nm* motorcycling.

motociclista *nm o nf* motorcyclist.

motocross *nm* motocross.

motocultivo *nm* mechanised agriculture.

motonáutica *nf* speedboat racing.

motonáutico,-a *adj* speedboat.

motor,-ra *adj* **1** motive. **2** BIOL motor: *función motora* motor function.
▶ *nm* **motor** TÉC engine.

motora *nf* small motorboat.

motorismo *nm* motorcycling.

motorista *nm o nf* motorcyclist.

motorizado,-a *adj* motorized.

motorizar *vt* to motorize.

motosierra *nf* power saw.

motriz *adj* [sólo se usa con nombres en femenino] motive.

mousse *nf* CULIN mousse.

mouton *nm (piel)* sheepskin.

movedizo,-a *adj (inestable)* unstable.

mover *vt* **1** to move.
▶ *vpr* **moverse 1** *(gen)* to move. **2** *fam (darse prisa)* to get a move on.

movible *adj* movable.

movida *nf fam (animación)* action.

movido,-a *adj* **1** *(día, temporada)* busy. **2** *(fiesta, concurso)* lively. **3** *(foto)* blurred.

móvil *adj* movable, mobile.
▶ *nm* **1** FÍS moving body. **2** *(motivo)* motive. **3** *(decoración, juguete)* mobile. **4** *(teléfono)* mobile (phone), cell phone.

movilidad *nf* mobility.

movilización *nf* mobilization.

movilizar *vt* to mobilize.

movimiento *nm* **1** *(gen)* movement; *(técnicamente)* motion. **2** *(de gente, ideas)* activity. **3** *(artístico, político)* movement.

moviola® *nf (máquina)* Moviola.

moza *nf (chica)* lass.

Mozambique *nm* Mozambique.

mozambiqueño,-a *adj* Mozambiquean.
▶ *nm & nf* Mozambiquean.

mozárabe *adj* Mozarab.
▶ *nm o nf* Mozarab.

mozo,-a *adj* young.
▶ *nm* **mozo 1** *(joven)* young man, lad. **2** *(camarero)* waiter. **3** *(de estación)* porter.

MP3 *abrev* (Moving Pictures Experts Group Audio Layer 3) MP3.

mu *interj (mugido)* moo.

muaré *nm* moiré.

muchacho,-a *nm & nf (chico)* boy; *(chica)* girl.

muchedumbre *nf (de personas)* crowd.

mucho,-a *adj* **1** *(singular - en afirmativas)* a lot of; *(- en negativas, interrogativas)* a lot of, much: *hicieron mucho ruido* they made a lot of noise; *no tiene mucho dinero* he hasn't got a lot of/much money. **2** *(plural - en afirmativas)* a lot of, lots of; *(- en negativas, interrogativas)* a lot of, many: *¿tienes muchos libros?* have you got a lot of/many books? **3** *(demasiado - singular)* too much; *(- plural)* too many.
▶ *pron (singular)* a lot, much; *(plural)* a lot, many: *muchos de sus amigos acudieron* many of his friends came.
▶ *adv* **1** *(de cantidad)* a lot, much: *mucho mejor/peor* much better/worse. **2** *(de tiempo)*: *mucho antes/después* much earlier/later. **3** *(de frecuencia)* often: *no vienen mucho por aquí* they don't come here often. LOC **como mucho** at the most: *te pagarán como mucho treinta euros* they'll pay you thirty euros at the most.

mucosa *nf* mucous membrane.

mucosidad *nf* mucus.

mucoso,-a *adj* mucous.

muda *nf (de ropa)* change of clothes.

mudable *adj* **1** changeable. **2** *(carácter)* fickle.

mudanza *nf (de residencia)* moving.

mudar *vt* **1** to change, alter. **2** *(plumas)* to moult (US molt). **3** *(voz)* to break: *le está mudando la voz* his voice is breaking. **4** *(piel)* to shed.
▶ *vpr* **mudarse 1** to change. **2** *(de residencia)* to move.

mudez *nf* dumbness, muteness.

mudo,-a *adj* **1** *(por defecto)* dumb; *(por voluntad)* silent, quiet. **2** *(vocal, consonante)* mute.

mueble *nm* piece of furniture.
▶ *nm pl* **muebles** furniture *sing*.

mueca *nf* **1** *(de burla)* mocking gesture, face. **2** *(de dolor)* grimace.

muela *nf (diente)* tooth, molar.

muelle *nm* **1** *(elástico)* spring. **2** MAR dock, wharf; *(malecón)* pier, jetty.

muérdago *nm* mistletoe.

muerdo *nm fam* bite.

muermo *nm fam* drag, pain, bore.

muerte *nf* **1** death. **2** *(asesinato)* murder.

muerto,-a *adj* **1** *(sin vida)* dead; *(sin actividad)* lifeless. **2** *fam (cansado)* tired.
▶ *nm & nf* dead person.

muesca *nf (corte)* nick, notch.

muesli *nm* muesli.

muestra *nf* **1** *(ejemplar)* sample. **2** *(modelo)* pattern. **3** *(señal)* proof, sign: *daba muestras de alegría* she looked happy. **4** *(exposición)* show, display.

muestrario *nm* collection of samples.

muestreo *nm (gen)* sampling.

mugido *nm (de vaca - uno)* moo.

mugir *vi (vaca)* to moo.

mugre *nf* grime, filth.

mugriento,-a *adj* grimy, filthy.

muguete *nm* lily of the valley.

mujer *nf* **1** woman. **2** *(esposa)* wife.

mujeriego,-a *adj pey* fond of the ladies.

mujerona *nf fam* big woman.

mújol *nm* grey mullet.

muladar *nm* dump.

mulato,-a *adj* mulatto.
▶ *nm & nf* mulatto.

mulero *nm* muleteer.

muleta *nf (para andar)* crutch.

M

muletilla *nf* **1** *(bastón)* cross-handled cane. **2** *(frase repetida)* pet phrase.

muletón *nm* flannelette.

mullido,-a *adj* soft, springy.

mullir *vt* *(lana)* to soften; *(almohada, colchón)* to fluff up.

mulo,-a *nm & nf* *(macho)* mule; *(hembra)* she-mule. LOC **ser más terco,-a que una mula** to be as stubborn as a mule.

multa *nf* *(gen)* fine; *(de tráfico)* ticket.

multar *vt* to fine: *¿cuánto te multaron?* how much did they fine you?

multiacceso *nm* multiaccess.

multicines *nm pl* multiplex *sing.*

multicolor *adj* multicoloured.

multicopiar *vt* to duplicate.

multicopista *nf* duplicator.

multicultural *adj* multicultural.

multidimensional *adj* multidimensional.

multidireccional *adj* multidirectional.

multidisciplinar *adj* multidisciplinary.

multifacético,-a *adj* multifaceted.

multiforme *adj* multiform.

multigrado *adj* multigrade.

multilateral *adj* multilateral.

multimedia *adj* multimedia.

multimillonario,-a *adj* *(de libras)* multimillion-pound; *(de dólares)* multimillion-dollar: *un contrato multimillonario* a multimillion-dollar contract.
▶ *nm & nf* multimillionaire.

multinacional *adj* multinational.
▶ *nf* multinational.

multípara *nf* multiparous.

múltiple *adj* **1** multiple. **2** *(muchos)* many, a number of, numerous: *opiniones múltiples* a number of opinions.

multiplicable *adj* multipliable.

multiplicación *nf* multiplication.

multiplicador,-ra *adj* multiplying.
▶ *nm* **multiplicador** multiplier.

multiplicar *vt* to multiply (por, by).

multiplicidad *nf* multiplicity.

múltiplo *adj* multiple.
▶ *nm* multiple.

multipropiedad *nf* time-share.

multirracial *adj* multiracial.

multirriesgo *adj* fully comprehensive.

multitud *nf* **1** *(de personas)* crowd. **2** *(de cosas, ideas)* multitude.

multitudinario,-a *adj* multitudinous.

multiuso *adj* multipurpose.

mundanal *adj* of the world, mundane. LOC **huir del mundanal ruido** to get away from it all.

mundano,-a *adj* of the world.

mundial *adj* worldwide, world.
▶ *nm* world championship. LOC **de fama mundial** world-famous. COMP **mundial de fútbol** World Cup.

mundialmente *adv* worldwide. LOC **mundialmente conocido,-a** world-famous.

mundillo *nm* world, circles *pl*: *el mundillo teatral* theatrical circles.

mundo *nm* world: *ha dado la vuelta al mundo dos veces* he's been around the world twice; *vive aislado en su propio mundo* he's isolated himself in his own little world; *el mundo del cine* the cinema, the world of cinema. LOC **no ser nada del otro mundo** to be nothing to write home about. **‖ por nada del mundo** not for all the world. **‖ tener mundo** to know the ways of the world. **‖ venir al mundo** to come into the world. **‖ el fin del mundo** the end of the world. COMP **el Nuevo Mundo** the New World. **‖ el Tercer Mundo** the Third World.

mundología *nf fam* worldliness.

munición *nf* ammunition.

municipal *adj* *(gobierno)* town, municipal; *(instalaciones)* council.
▶ *nm o nf* *(hombre)* policeman; *(mujer)* policewoman.
▶ *nf pl* **las municipales** local elections.

municipio *nm* **1** municipality. **2** *(ayuntamiento)* town council.

muñeca *nf* **1** ANAT wrist. **2** *(juguete)* doll. COMP **muñeca de trapo** rag doll.

muñeco *nm* *(juguete)* doll. COMP **muñeco de nieve** snowman.

muñequera *nf* wristband.

muñir *vt* *(amañar)* to fix.

muñón *nm* ANAT stump.
mural *adj* mural.
▶ *nm* mural.
muralla *nf* city wall.
murciélago *nm* bat.
murga *nf fam* nuisance. LOC **dar la murga** *fam* to be a pain in the neck.
murmullante *adj* babbling.
murmullo *nm (susurro)* whisper, whispering; *(voz baja)* murmur, murmuring.
murmuración *nf* gossip, backbiting.
murmurador,-ra *adj* gossipy.
▶ *nm & nf* gossip.
murmurar *vt (susurrar)* to murmur, whisper.
▶ *vi* **1** *(criticar)* to gossip. **2** *(decir en voz baja)* to murmur.
muro *nm* wall.
murria *nf* sadness, melancholy.
mus *nm card game in which players use signs to communicate.*
musa *nf* muse.
▶ *nf pl* **las musas** the Arts.
musaraña *nf* ZOOL shrew. LOC **estar pensando en las musarañas** to daydream.
musculación *nf* body-building.
muscular *adj* muscular.
musculatura *nf* muscles *pl*.
músculo *nm* muscle.
musculoso,-a *adj* muscular.
muselina *nf* muslin.
museo *nm* museum. COMP **museo de arte** art museum.
musgo *nm* moss. LOC **cubierto,-a de musgo** mossy, moss-covered.
musgoso,-a *adj* mossy.
música *nf* music. COMP **música de fondo** background music. ▌ **música clásica** classical music.
musical *adj* musical.
▶ *nm* musical.
musicalidad *nf* musicality.

musicar *vt* to write the music for, set to music.
músico,-a *nm & nf* musician.
musicología *nf* musicology.
musicólogo,-a *nm & nf* musicologist.
musiquilla *nf fam pey* tacky music.
musitar *vi (susurrar)* to whisper.
muslo *nm* **1** thigh. **2** CULIN *(de ave)* drumstick.
mustiarse *vi* to wilt, wither.
mustio,-a *adj* **1** *(plantas)* withered, faded. **2** *(persona)* down, downcast.
musulmán,-ana *adj* Muslim.
▶ *nm & nf* Muslim.
mutabilidad *nf* changeability.
mutable *adj* mutable.
mutación *nf* **1** change. **2** BIOL mutation.
mutante *adj* mutant.
▶ *nm o nf* mutant.
mutilación *nf* mutilation.
mutilado,-a *adj (persona)* disabled.
▶ *nm & nf* cripple.
mutilar *vt* to cripple
mutis *nm* TEAT exit.
mutismo *nm* silence.
mutua *nf* mutual benefit society. COMP **mutua de seguros** mutual insurance company.
mutualidad *nf (asociación)* mutual benefit society.
mutualista *nm o nf* member of a mutual benefit society.
mutuamente *adv* mutually: *se quieren mutuamente* they love each other.
mutuo,-a *adj* mutual, reciprocal: *por mutuo acuerdo* by mutual agreement.
muy *adv* very: *es muy difícil* it's very difficult; *se levantó muy temprano* he got up very early; *lo has hecho muy bien* you've done it very well. LOC **muy de mañana** very early in the morning. ▌ **por muy que...** however…: *por muy tarde que sea* however late it is.

M

N

N, n *nf (la letra)* N, n.
N *sím* (norte) north; *(símbolo)* N.
nabo *nm (planta)* turnip.
nácar *nm* mother-of-pearl.
nacarado,-a *adj* nacred.
nacer *vi* **1** *(persona)* to be born; *(ave)* to hatch out; *(semilla, planta)* to sprout. **2** *(río)* to rise; *(agua)* to spring; *(camino)* to start, begin. **3** *(sol)* to rise. LOC al nacer at birth.
nacido,-a *adj* born. LOC bien nacido,-a *(de buen corazón)* kind-hearted. ‖ mal nacido,-a despicable.
naciente *adj* **1** *(nuevo)* new. **2** *(creciente)* growing.
▶ *nm (este)* East.
nacimiento *nm* **1** birth. **2** *fig* origin, beginning. LOC de nacimiento from birth.
nación *nf* nation. COMP Naciones Unidas United Nations.
nacional *adj* national.
nacionalidad *nf* nationality.
nacionalismo *nm* nationalism.
nacionalista *adj* nationalist.
▶ *nm o nf* nationalist.
nacionalización *nf* naturalization.
nacionalizar *vt* **1** *(persona)* to naturalize. **2** *(empresa)* to nationalize.
▶ *vpr* **nacionalizarse** *(persona)* to become naturalized: *nacionalizarse español/británico/etc* to take up Spanish/British/etc citizenship.
nada *pron* nothing: *no quiero nada* I don't want anything.
▶ *adv* (not) at all: *no me gusta nada* I don't like it at all.
▶ *nf* nothingness. LOC de nada **1** *(no hay de qué)* don't mention it, think

nothing of it, (US you're welcome). **2** *(insignificante)* insignificant: *gracias, –de nada* thanks, – don't mention it. ‖ nada más... as soon as..., no sooner...
nadador,-ra *nm & nf* swimmer.
nadar *vi* to swim.
nadería *nf* trifle.
nadie *pron* nobody, not... anybody: *aquí no hay nadie* there's nobody here.
nado LOC a nado swimming: *cruzaron el río a nado* they swam across the river.
nafta *nf* naphtha.
naftalina *nf* naphthalene. COMP bola de naftalina mothball.
naif *adj* naïf, naive.
▶ *nm* naïf art.
nailon® *nm* nylon®.
naipe *nm* playing card.
nalga *nf* buttock.
Namibia *nf* Namibia.
namibio,-a *adj* Namibian.
▶ *nm & nf* Namibian.
nana *nf* lullaby.
naranja *nf (fruto)* orange.
▶ *adj (color)* orange.
naranjada *nf* orangeade, orange drink.
naranjal *nm* orange grove.
naranjo *nm* orange tree.
narcisismo *nm* narcissism.
narcisista *adj* narcissistic.
▶ *nm o nf* narcissist.
narciso *nm* **1** *(flor)* daffodil, narcissus. **2** *(hombre)* narcissist.
narcótico,-a *adj* narcotic.
▶ *nm* **narcótico** *(medicamento)* narcotic; *(droga)* drug.
narcotraficante *adj* drug trafficking.
▶ *nm o nf* drug trafficker.

narcotráfico *nm* drug trafficking.

nardo *nm* nard, spikenard.

narigón,-ona *adj fam* big-nosed.

nariz *nf* 1 ANAT nose. 2 *fig (sentido)* sense of smell. LOC **meter las narices en** ALGO to poke one's nose into STH.
► *interj* **¡narices!** *fam* not on your life!

narración *nf (historia)* story.

narrador,-ra *nm & nf* storyteller.

narrar *vt (gen)* to tell, relate, narrate.

narrativa *nf (género)* fiction.

narval *nm* narwhal.

nasa *nf (aparejo)* keepnet; *(cesta)* creel.

nasal *adj* nasal.
► *nf (letra)* nasal.

nata *nf* 1 cream. 2 *(de leche hervida)* skin. COMP **nata montada** whipped cream.

natación *nf* swimming.

natal *adj* native. COMP **ciudad natal** home town: **I país natal** native country.

natalicio *nm* birthday.

natalidad *nf* birth rate.

natillas *nf pl* custard *sing*.

natividad *nf* nativity.

nativo,-a *adj* native.

nato,-a *adj* born.

natural *adj* 1 *(no artificial)* natural. 2 *(fruta, flor)* fresh. LOC **al natural** CULIN in its own juice.
► *nm (nativo)* native, inhabitant. LOC **ser natural de** to be a native of, come from.

naturaleza *nf* 1 nature. 2 *(complexión)* physical constitution.

naturalidad *nf* 1 *(sencillez)* naturalness. 2 *(espontaneidad)* ease, spontaneity.

naturalismo *nm* naturalism.

naturalista *adj* naturalist.
► *nm o nf* naturalist.

naturalizar *vt* to naturalize.
► *vpr* **naturalizarse** to become naturalized: *se ha naturalizado español* he has taken up Spanish citizenship.

naturista *adj* naturist.
► *nm o nf* naturist.

naturopatía *nf* naturopathy.

naufragar *vi* 1 *(barco)* to sink, be wrecked; *(persona)* to be shipwrecked. 2 *fig* to fail.

naufragio *nm* shipwreck.

náufrago,-a *adj* shipwrecked.
► *nm & nf* shipwrecked person.

Nauru *nm* Nauru.

nauruano,-a *adj* Nauruan.
► *nm & nf* Nauruan.

náusea [también se usa en plural con el mismo significado] *nf* nausea, sickness.

nauseabundo,-a *adj* nauseating.

náutica *nf* navigation, seamanship.

náutico,-a *adj* nautical. COMP **deportes náuticos** water sports.

navaja *nf (cuchillo)* penknife.

naval *adj* naval.

nave *nf* 1 *(náutica)* ship, vessel. 2 *(espacial)* spaceship, spacecraft. 3 *(almacén)* industrial warehouse.

navegable *adj (río)* navigable.

navegación *nf (arte)* navigation.

navegador *nm (de internet)* browser.

navegante *nm o nf* navigator.

navegar *vi* 1 *(barco)* to sail. 2 *(avión)* to fly.

Navidad *nf* Christmas. LOC **felicitar las Navidades a** ALGN to wish SB a merry Christmas.

navideño,-a *adj* Christmas.

naviera *nf (empresa)* shipping company.

navío *nm* vessel, ship.

Neanderthal *adj* Neanderthal.

neblina *nf* mist.

neblinoso,-a *adj* misty.

nebulizador *nm* nebulizer.

nebulosa *nf* nebula.

nebulosidad *nf* nebulosity.

nebuloso,-a *adj* cloudy, hazy.

necedad *nf (ignorancia)* stupidity.

necesario,-a *adj* necessary.

neceser *nm (bolsa de aseo)* toilet bag.

necesidad *nf* 1 necessity, need. 2 *(pobreza)* poverty, want. LOC **pasar necesidades** to be in need.

necesitado,-a *adj* needy, poor.

necesitar *vt* to need.

necio,-a *adj* stupid.

nécora *nf* fiddler crab.

N

necrología *nf (biografía)* obituary.
necrológico,-a *adj* obituary.
▶ *nf pl* **necrológicas** *(sección prensa)* obituaries *pl*.
necrópolis *nf inv* necropolis.
necrosis *nf inv* necrosis.
néctar *nm* nectar.
nectarina *nf* nectarine.
neerlandés,-esa *adj* Dutch.
▶ *nm & nf* **1** *(persona - hombre)* Dutchman; *(- mujer)* Dutch woman. **2** *(idioma)* Dutch.
nefasto,-a *adj* unlucky, ill-fated.
nefrítico,-a *adj* nephritic. ⃞COMP cólico nefrítico nephrocolic.
negación *nf* **1** *(de un derecho)* negation. **2** refusal. **3** *(en gramática)* negative.
negado,-a *adj (inepto)* hopeless.
negar *vt* **1** *(rechazar)* to deny. **2** *(no conceder)* to refuse.
▶ *vpr* **negarse** to refuse (a, to): *se negó a devolverme el dinero* he refused to give me my money back.
negativa *nf (rechazo)* refusal.
negativo,-a *adj* negative.
▶ *nm* **negativo** *(en fotografía)* negative.
negligencia *nf* negligence.
negligente *adj* negligent.
▶ *nm o nf* negligent person.
negociable *adj* negotiable.
negociación *nf* negotiation.
negociado *nm (sección)* department.
negociador,-ra *adj* negotiating.
▶ *nm & nf* negotiator.
negociante *nm o nf* dealer, merchant.
negociar *vi (comerciar)* to do business, deal (con, in).
▶ *vt* POL to negotiate.
negocio *nm* **1** *(actividad)* business. **2** *(gestión)* deal, transaction.
negra *nf* MÚS crotchet, US quarter note.
negro,-a *adj* **1** *(gen)* black. **2** *(cine, novela)* detective.
▶ *nm & nf (hombre)* black (man); *(mujer)* black (woman).
▶ *nm* **negro** *(color)* black.
negrura *nf* blackness.
negruzco,-a *adj* blackish.

nene,-a *nm & nf* baby.
nenúfar *nm* water lily.
neoclasicismo *nm* neoclassicism.
neoclásico,-a *adj* neoclassical.
neocolonialismo *nm* neocolonialism.
neófito,-a *nm & nf* neophyte.
neolítico,-a *adj* neolithic.
▶ *nm* **neolítico** Neolithic.
neologismo *nm* neologism.
neón *nm* neon.
neonatal *adj* neonatal.
neorrealismo *nm* neorealism.
neozelandés,-esa *adj* of New Zealand, from New Zealand.
▶ *nm & nf* New Zealander.
Nepal *nm* Nepal.
nepalés,-esa *adj* Nepalese, Nepali.
▶ *nm & nf (persona)* Nepalese, Nepali.
▶ *nm* **nepalés** *(idioma)* Nepalese, Nepali.
nepotismo *nm* nepotism.
nereida *nf* nereid.
nervadura *nf* BOT nervures *pl*.
nervio *nm* ANAT nerve.
▶ *nm pl* **nervios** nerves. ⃞LOC tener los nervios de punta to be on edge.
nerviosismo *nm* nervousness.
nervioso,-a *adj (gen)* nervous. ⃞LOC ponerse nervioso,-a to get nervous.
neto,-a *adj (peso, cantidad)* net.
neumático,-a *nm* tyre (US tire).
neumonía *nf* pneumonia.
neura *nf fam* obsession.
neurálgico,-a *adj fig (fundamental)* key.
neurocirujano,-a *nm & nf* neurosurgeon.
neurología *nf* neurology.
neurólogo,-a *nm & nf* neurologist.
neurona *nf* neuron, neurone.
neurosis *nf inv* neurosis.
neurótico,-a *adj* neurotic.
▶ *nm & nf* neurotic.
neutral *adj* neutral.
neutralidad *nf* neutrality.
neutralizar *vt* to neutralize.
neutro,-a *adj* **1** neutral. **2** LING neuter.
▶ *nm* **neutro** neuter.
neutrón *nm* neutron.
nevada *nf* snowfall.

nevado,-a *adj* covered with snow.

nevar *vi* [se usa sólo en tercera persona; no lleva sujeto] to snow.

nevera *nf (eléctrica)* fridge, refrigerator.

nevero *nm* ice field.

newton *nm* newton.

nexo *nm* **1** link. **2** LING connective.

ni *conj* **1** neither, nor. **2** not even.

Nicaragua *nf* Nicaragua.

nicaragüense *adj* Nicaraguan.
▶ *nm o nf* Nicaraguan.

nicho *nm* niche.

nicotina *nf* nicotine.

nidada *nf (polluelos)* brood.

nidificar *vi* to nest.

nido *nm* nest.

niebla *nf* **1** *(nubes)* fog. **2** *fig* mist.

nieto,-a *nm & nf* grandchild; *(niño)* grandson; *(niña)* granddaughter.

nieve *nf* snow.

Nigeria *nf* Nigeria.

nigeriano,-a *adj* Nigerian.
▶ *nm & nf* Nigerian.

nigromancia *nf* necromancy.

nihilismo *nm* nihilism.

nihilista *adj* nihilistic.

nilón® *nm* nylon®.

nimbo *nm* nimbus.

nimiedad *nf (cosa nimia)* trifle.

nimio,-a *adj* insignificant, trivial.

ninfa *nf* nymph.

ningún *adj* [se usa ante un nombre masculino en singular] → **ninguno,-a**.

ninguno,-a *adj* no, not any.
▶ *pron* **1** *(persona)* nobody, no one. **2** *(objeto)* not any, none: *ninguno me gusta* I don't like any of them.

✎ Consulta también **ningún**.

niñato,-a *nm & nf fam* brat.

niñera *nf* nanny.

niñería *nf (chiquillada)* childishness.

niñez *nf (de una persona)* childhood.

niño,-a *nm & nf* **1** *(gen)* child; *(chico)* boy, little boy; *(chica)* girl, little girl.
▶ *nm pl* **niños** children, kids.

nipón,-ona *adj* Nipponese.
▶ *nm & nf* Nipponese.

níquel *nm* nickel.

niquelado,-a *adj* nickel-plated.

niquelar *vt* to nickel.

niqui *nm* T-shirt.

nirvana *nm* nirvana.

níscalo *nm* milk cap.

níspero *nm (fruto)* medlar.

nitidez *nf (transparencia)* clearness.

nítido,-a *adj (claro)* accurate.

nitrato *nm* nitrate.

nítrico,-a *adj* nitric.

nitrito *nm* nitrite.

nitrógeno *nm* nitrogen.

nitroglicerina *nf* nitroglycerine.

nitroso,-a *adj* nitrous.

nivel *nm* **1** *(altura)* level. **2** *(categoría)* standard. COMP **nivel del mar** sea level.

nivelación *nf (de un terreno)* levelling.

nivelado,-a *adj* level.

nivelar *vt (gen)* to level out, level off.

níveo,-a *adj lit* snow-white.

no *adv* no, not.
▶ *nm* no: *un no rotundo* a definite no.

nobel *nm* Nobel prize.

nobiliario,-a *adj* noble.

noble *adj (gen)* noble; *(madera)* fine.
▶ *nm o nf* noble.

nobleza *nf* **1** honesty. **2** nobility.

noche *nf* night. LOC **buenas noches 1** *(saludo)* good evening. **2** *(despedida)* good night. ❙ **por la noche** at night, after dark.

Nochebuena *nf* Christmas Eve.

Nochevieja *nf* New Year's Eve.

noción *nf* notion, idea.

nocividad *nf* noxiousness.

nocivo,-a *adj* noxious, harmful.

noctámbulo,-a *adj* nocturnal.
▶ *nm & nf fam (trasnochador)* night owl.

nocturno,-a *adj (gen)* nocturnal; *(vida)* night; *(clase)* evening.

nodo *nm* node.

nodriza *nf* wet nurse.

nodular *adj* nodular, nodulated.

nódulo *nm* nodule.

nogal *nm* walnut tree.

nogalina *nf* walnut dye.

N

nómada *adj* nomadic.
► *nm o nf* nomad.
nomadismo *nm* nomadism.
nombrado,-a *adj* well-known.
nombramiento *nm* appointment.
nombrar *vt* to name.
nombre *nm* **1** name. **2** LING noun.
nomenclatura *nf* nomenclature.
nomeolvides *nm inv (flor)* forget-me-not.
nómina *nf* pay cheque (US check).
nominación *nf* nomination.
nominal *adj* nominal.
nominalismo *nm* nominalism.
nominalista *adj* nominalist.
nominalizar *vt* to substantivize.
nominalmente *adv* nominally.
nominar *vt* to nominate.
nominativo,-a *adj* **1** *(cheque)* personal.
2 LING nominative.
non *nm* odd number.
nonagenario,-a *nm & nf* nonagenarian.
nonagésimo,-a *nm & nf* ninetieth.
► *adj* ninetieth.
nones *interj* no way!
noquear *vt* to knock out.
norcoreano,-a *adj* North Korean.
► *nm & nf* North Korean.
nordeste *nm* northeast.
nórdico,-a *adj* **1** *(del norte)* northern. **2**
(de los países del norte) Nordic.
► *nm & nf (persona)* Scandinavian.
noreste *nm* → nordeste.
noria *nf* **1** *(para agua)* water wheel.
2 *(de feria)* big wheel.
norma *nf* norm, rule.
normal *adj (habitual)* normal, usualy.
► *nf (gasolina)* two-star petrol.
normalidad *nf* normality.
normalización *nf* normalization.
normalizar *vt* to normalize.
normativa *nf* rules *pl*, regulations *pl*.
normativo,-a *adj* normative.
noroeste *nm* northwest.
norte *nm* north.
Norteamérica *nf* North America.
norteamericano,-a *adj* North American.
► *nm & nf* North American.

Noruega *nf* Norway.
noruego,-a *adj* Norwegian.
► *nm & nf (persona)* Norwegian.
► *nm* noruego *(idioma)* Norwegian.
nos *pron* **1** *(complemento)* us: *nos dijo que
no nos moviéramos* he told us not to
move. **2** *(uso reflexivo)* ourselves: *nos la-
vamos* we wash ourselves. **3** *(uso recíproco)* each other: *nos vemos mucho* we see
each other often.
nosotros,-as *pron* **1** *(sujeto)* we: *nosotros
no fuimos* we didn't go. **2** *(complemento)*
us: *con nosotros,-as* with us.
nostalgia *nf* homesickness.
nostálgico,-a *adj* nostalgic.
nota *nf* **1** *(anotación)* note. **2** *(calificación)*
mark, grade. **3** MÚS note.
notable *adj* considerable, remarkable.
notación *nf* notation.
notar *vt* **1** *(percibir)* to notice. **2** *(sentir)* to
feel: *noto un poco de calor* I feel a bit hot.
► *vpr* **notarse 1** *(percibirse)* to show:
apenas se le nota la cicatriz you can hardly
see his scar. **2** *(sentirse)* to feel.
notario,-a *nm & nf* notary public.
noticia *nf (información)* news *pl*.
► *nf pl* **las noticias** the news.
noticiario *nm* news.
notición *nm fam* bombshell.
notificación *nf* notification.
notificar *vt* to notify, inform.
notoriedad *nf (fama)* fame, prestige.
notorio,-a *adj* well-known.
novatada *nf (broma)* practical joke.
novato,-a *nm & nf (principiante)* beginner.
novecientos,-as *adj* nine hundred;
(ordinal) nine-hundredth.

✎ Consulta también seis.

novedad *nf* **1** *(cualidad)* newness. **2**
(cambio) change, innovation.
novedoso,-a *adj* novel.
novel *adj (escritor, escultor)* novice.
novela *nf* novel.
novelar *vt* to novelize.
novelesco,-a *adj (de novela)* fiction-like.
novelista *nm o nf* novelist.
novena *nf* REL novena.

noveno,-a *adj* ninth.
▶ *nm & nf* ninth.

✎ Consulta también **sexto**.

noventa *adj* ninety.
▶ *nm* ninety.

✎ Consulta también **sesenta**.

novia *nf (amiga)* girlfriend.
noviazgo *nm* engagement.
novicio,-a *nm & nf* REL novice.
noviembre *nm* November.

✎ Para ejemplos de uso, consulta **marzo**.

novillada *nf* bullfight with young bulls.
novillero,-a *nm & nf* novice bullfighter.
novillo *nm* young bull.
novio *nm* boyfriend.
nubarrón *nm* storm cloud.
nube *nf* cloud.
núbil *adj* nubile.
nublado,-a *adj* cloudy, overcast.
▶ *nm* **nublado** storm cloud.
nubosidad *nf* cloudiness.
nuboso,-a *adj* cloudy.
nuca *nf* nape (of the neck).
nuclear *adj* nuclear.
núcleo *nm* nucleus.
nudillo *nm* knuckle.
nudismo *nm* nudism.
nudo *nm* knot.
nudoso,-a *adj (madera)* knotty.
nuera *nf* daughter-in-law.
nuestro,-a *adj* our, of ours.
▶ *pron* ours.
nueva *nf* tidings *pl*, news *sing*.
nueve *adj* nine; *(noveno)* ninth.
▶ *nm* nine.

✎ Consulta también **seis**.

nuevo,-a *adj* new. LOC **de nuevo** again.
nuez *nf* BOT walnut.
nulidad *nf* **1** *(ineptitud)* incompetence. **2** JUR nullity.
nulo,-a *adj (sin valor)* invalid.

numeración *nf* **1** *(proceso)* numbering. **2** *(conjunto)* numbers *pl*. **3** *(sistema)* numbers *pl*, numerals *pl*.
numerador *nm* numerator.
numeral *adj* numeral.
▶ *nm* numeral.
numerar *vt* to number.
numérico,-a *adj* numerical.
número *nm* **1** *(gen)* number. **2** *(de una publicación)* number, issue. **3** *(de zapatos)* size: *¿qué número calzas?* what's your shoe size?, what size shoe do you take? **4** *(de un espectáculo)* act. **5** *(de lotería)* lottery ticket number. **7** LING number. COMP **número impar** odd number. **I número ordinal** ordinal number. **I número par** even number. **I número primo** prime number. **I número quebrado** fraction. **I número romano** Roman numeral.
numeroso,-a *adj* numerous: *son familia numerosa* they're a large family.
numismática *nf* numismatics.
numismático,-a *adj* numismatic.
nunca *adv* **1** never. **2** *(en interrogativa)* ever. LOC **más que nunca** more than ever. **I nunca más** never again. **I**
nupcial *adj (marcha, tarta)* wedding; *(misa)* nuptial; *(lecho)* marriage.
nupcias *nf pl fml* wedding *sing*, nuptials.
nurse *nf* nanny.
nutria *nf* otter.
nutrición *nf* nutrition.
nutrido,-a *adj (alimentado)* nourished.
nutriente *adj* nutrient.
▶ *nm* nutrient.
nutrir *vt* **1** *(alimentar)* to feed, nourish. **2** *fig* to encourage. **3** *(abastecer)* to supply (de, with).
▶ *vpr* **nutrirse 1** *(alimentarse)* to receive nourishment (de, from). **2** *fig (abastecerse)* to draw (de, on).
nutritivo,-a *adj* nutritious, nourishing. COMP **sustancia nutritiva** nutrient. **I valor nutritivo** nutritional value.

N

Ñ

Ñ, ñ *nf the fifteenth letter of the Spanish alphabet.*

ñandú *nm* AM rhea.

ñoñería *nf (tontería)* inanity, nonsense.

ñoño ,-a *adj* **1** *(soso)* insipid, dull. **2** *(tímido)* shy. **3** *(remilgado)* fussy. **4** *(poco seguro)* wet, drippy, wimpish: *no seas ñoño, no es más que un rasguño* don't be such a wimp, it's no more than a scratch. **5** AM old.

ñoqui *nm* gnocchi *pl.*

ñora *nf type of* red pepper.

ñu *nm* gnu.

O

O, o *nf (la letra)* O, o.

o *conj* **1** or: *¿té o café?* tea or coffee? **2** *(concesiva)* whether... or: *estudie o no, tiene que aprobar* whether he studies or not, he has to pass.

O *sím* (oeste) west; *(símbolo)* W.

oasis *nm inv* oasis.

obcecado,-a *adj* blind.

obcecar *vt* to blind.
► *vpr* **obcecarse** to be obstinate.

obedecer *vt (regla, ley)* to obey.
► *vi (persona)* to obey.

obediencia *nf* obedience.

obediente *adj* obedient.

obertura *nf* MÚS overture.

obesidad *nf* obesity.

obeso,-a *adj* obese.

obispo *nm* bishop.

objeción *nf* objection.

objetar *vt* to object.

objetividad *nf* objectivity.

objetivo,-a *adj* objective.
► *nm* **objetivo 1** *(fin)* aim, objective. **2** *(lente)* lens.

objeto *nm* **1** *(cosa)* object. **2** *(fin)* aim, purpose, object.

objetor,-ra *adj* objecting, dissenting.
► *nm & nf* objector.

oblea *nf* wafer.

oblicuo,-a *adj* oblique.

obligación *nf (deber)* duty, obligation.

obligado,-a *adj (forzoso)* required.

obligar *vt* to force, make.
► *vpr* **obligarse** to undertake, promise.

obligatorio,-a *adj* compulsory.

obnubilar *vt (fascinar)* to fascinate.

oboe *nm* oboe.

obra *nf* **1** *(trabajo)* work. **2** *(construcción)* building site. COMP **obra de teatro** play.
► *nf pl* **obras** *(en casa)* repairs.

obrar *vi (proceder)* to act, behave.

obrero,-a *adj* working.
► *nm & nf* worker, labourer.

obscenidad *nf* obscenity.

obsceno,-a *adj* obscene.

obscurantismo *nm* obscurantism.

obscurantista *adj* obscurantist.

obscurecer *vt* to darken.
► *vpr* **obscurecerse** *(día)* to get cloudy.

obscuridad *nf* darkness.

obscuro,-a *adj* **1** *(cielo, color)* dark. **2** *(idea, razonamiento)* obscure.

obsequiar *vt (regalar)* to give, offer.

obsequio *nm* gift, present.

observación *nf (acción)* observation.

observador,-ra *adj* observant.
► *nm & nf* observer.

observar *vt* **1** *(mirar)* to observe, watch. **2** *(notar)* to notice.

observatorio *nm* observatory.

obsesión *nf* obsession.

obsesionar *vt* to obsess.
► *vpr* **obsesionarse** to get obsessed.

obseso,-a *nm & nf* maniac.
► *adj* obsessed.

obsidiana *nf* obsidian.

obsoleto,-a *adj* obsolete.

obstáculo *nm (inconveniente)* objection.

obstante *adv* **no obstante** nevertheless, however.

obstetricia *nf* obstetrics.

obstinado,-a *adj* obstinate.

obstinarse *vpr* to persist (en, in), insist (en, on).

obstrucción *nf* obstruction.

obstruir *vt* to obstruct, block.
  ▶ *vpr* **obstruirse** to get blocked up.
obtener *vt (beca, resultados)* to get, obtain; *(premio)* to win.
obturador *nm* shutter.
obtuso,-a *adj* obtuse.
obviar *vt fml* to obviate, remove.
obvio,-a *adj* obvious.
oca *nf* goose.
ocasión *nf (oportunidad)* opportunity.
ocasional *adj (gen)* occasional.
ocasionar *vt (causar)* to cause.
ocaso *nm (anochecer)* sunset.
occidental *adj* western, occidental.
occidente *nm* the West.
Oceanía *nf* Oceania.
océano *nm* ocean.

✎ En poesía también se escribe oceano.

oceanografía *nf* oceanography.
ochenta *adj* eighty; *(octagésimo)* eightieth.
  ▶ *nm* eighty.

✎ Consulta también sesenta.

ocho *adj* eight; *(octavo)* eighth.
  ▶ *nm* eight.

✎ Consulta también seis.

ochocientos,-as *adj* eight hundred; *(ordinal)* eight hundredth.
  ▶ *nm & nf* eight hundred.
ocio *nm (tiempo libre)* leisure.
ocioso,-a *adj (desocupado)* idle.
ocre *adj* ochre.
octagonal *adj* octagonal.
octágono,-a *nm* octagon.
octano *nm* octane.
octava *nf (en música)* octave.
octavilla *nf (impreso)* pamphlet.
octavo,-a *adj* eighth: *llegó en octavo lugar* he came eighth.
  ▶ *nm & nf* eighth: *era la octava en la lista* she was the eighth on the list.
  ▶ *nm* **octavo** *(parte)* eighth.

✎ Consulta también sexto.

octeto *nm* octet.
octogésimo,-a *adj* eightieth.

octogonal *adj* octagonal.
octógono *nm* octagon.
octosílabo,-a *adj* octosyllabic.
  ▶ *nm* **octosílabo** octosyllable.
octubre *nm* October.

✎ Para ejemplos de uso, consulta marzo.

ocular *adj* eye, ocular.
oculista *nm o nf* eye specialist.
ocultar *vt (gen)* to hide, conceal.
oculto,-a *adj (escondido)* hidden.
ocupación *nf (empleo)* occupation, employment.
ocupado,-a *adj* **1** *(persona)* busy. **2** *(asiento)* taken; *(teléfono)* engaged.
ocupante *nm o nf* occupant.
ocupar *vt* **1** to occupy, take. **2** *(llenar)* to take up. **3** *(habitar)* occupy. **4** *(estar - en un cargo)* to hold, fill.
  ▶ *vpr* **ocuparse de** to take care of.
ocurrencia *nf* idea.
ocurrir *vi* to happen: *¿qué fue lo que ocurrió?* what happened?
  ▶ *vpr* **ocurrirse** to occur to: *no se me ocurre nada* nothing occurs to me.
odiar *vt* to hate, loathe.
odio *nm* hatred, loathing.
odioso,-a *adj* hateful, despicable.
odontólogo,-a *nm & nf* odontologist.
odorífico,-a *adj* odoriferous.
odre *nm* wineskin.
oeste *nm* west.
ofender *vt (herir)* to offend: *no quisiera ofenderte, pero...* no offence, but...
  ▶ *vpr* **ofenderse** to get offended.
ofendido,-a *adj* offended.
ofensa *nf* offence.
ofensivo,-a *adj* offensive.
oferta *nf* **1** offer. **2** *(suministro)* supply.
ofertar *vt (ofrecer)* to offer.
oficial *adj* official.
  ▶ *nm o nf* office worker, officer.
oficiala *nf (operaria)* assistant.
oficialmente *adv* officially.
oficiante *nm o nf* officiant.
oficiar *vi (ejercer)* to act (de, as).
oficina *nf* office.
oficinista *nm o nf* office worker, clerk.

oficio *nm (ocupación)* job.
oficioso,-a *adj (noticia)* unofficial.
ofidio *nm* snake.
ofimática *nf* office automation.
ofrecer *vt (dar)* to offer.
  ▶ *vpr* **ofrecerse** *(prestarse)* to offer.
ofrecimiento *nm* offer, offering.
ofrenda *nf* offering.
ofrendar *vt* to make an offering of.
oftalmología *nf* ophthalmology.
oftalmólogo,-a *nm & nf* eye specialist.
ofuscar *vt (confundir)* to muddle.
  ▶ *vpr* **ofuscarse** to get muddled.
ogro *nm* ogre.
oh *interj* oh!
ohm *nm* ohm.
ohmio *nm* ohm.
oídas LOC **de oídas** by hearsay.
oído *nm* **1** *(sentido)* hearing. **2** *(órgano)* ear.
oiga *interj (para llamar la atención)* excuse me!; *(por teléfono)* hello?
oír *vt* **1** *(percibir)* to hear: *no oí nada* I didn't hear anything. **2** *(atender)* to answer.
ojal *nm* buttonhole.
ojalá *interj* I hope so: *¡ojalá sea verdad!* I hope it's true!
ojeada *nf* glance, quick look.
ojear *vt (mirar)* to have a quick look at.
ojeras *nf pl* dark rings under the eyes.
ojeriza *nf fam* dislike.
ojeroso,-a *adj* haggard.
ojival *adj (arte)* ogival.
ojo *nm* **1** eye. **2** *(agujero)* hole; *(de aguja)* eye. COMP
okupa *nm o nf argot* squatter.
ola *nf* wave. COMP **ola de frío** cold spell.
oleáceo,-a *adj* oleaceous.
oleada *nf* **1** big wave. **2** *fig* wave.
oleaginoso,-a *adj* oleaginous.
oleaje *nm* swell.
oleicultura *nf (cultivo)* olive-growing.
óleo *nm (material)* oil; *(obra)* oil painting.
oleoducto *nm* pipeline.
oleoso,-a *adj* oily.
oler *vt* to smell.
  ▶ *vi* to smell: *huele a gas* it smells of gas in here.

  ▶ *vpr* **olerse** to sense: *se ha olido que nos vamos* she has sensed that we are leaving.
olfatear *vt (oler)* to sniff, smell.
olfateo *nm* sniffing.
olfativo,-a *adj* olfactory.
olfato *nm* sense of smell.
olfatorio,-a *adj* olfactory.
oligarca *nm o nf* oligarch.
oligarquía *nf* oligarchy.
oligárquico,-a *adj* oligarchic.
oligoelemento *nm* trace element.
oligofrenia *nf* **1** *(enfermedad)* mental handicap. **2** *pey* mental deficiency.
oligofrénico,-a *adj* mentally retarded.
  ▶ *nm & nf* mentally retarded person.
olimpiada *nf* HIST Olympiad.

✎ También se escribe **olimpíada**.

olisquear *vt (olfatear)* to sniff.
oliva *nf* olive.
olivar *nm* olive grove.
olivarero,-a *adj (industria)* olive.
  ▶ *nm & nf* olive grower.
olivo *nm* olive tree.
olla *nf (utensilio)* pan.
olmo *nm* elm tree.
olor *nm* smell.
oloroso,-a *adj* fragrant.
olvidadizo,-a *adj* forgetful.
olvidar *vt* to forget.
  ▶ *vpr* **olvidarse** to forget (de, -).
olvido *nm* **1** *(desmemoria)* oblivion. **2** *(lapsus)* oversight, lapse.
Omán *nm* Oman.
omaní *adj* Omani.
  ▶ *nm o nf* Omani.
ombligo *nm* navel.
omega *nf (letra)* omega.
omisión *nf* omission.
omitir *vt (no decir)* to omit, leave out.
ómnibus *nm inv* bus.
omnipotente *adj* omnipotent.
omnipresente *adj* omnipresent.
omnívoro,-a *adj* omnivorous.
omoplato *nm* shoulder blade.

✎ También se escribe **omóplato**.

once *adj* eleven; *(undécimo)* eleventh.
▶ *nm* eleven.

✎ Consulta también seis.

onceavo,-a *adj (parte)* eleventh: *la onceava parte de...* an eleventh of...
▶ *nm* eleventh: *tres onceavos* three elevenths.

✎ Consulta también sexto.

oncología *nf* oncology.
oncólogo,-a *nm & nf* oncologist.
onda *nf* wave.
ondear *vi (bandera)* to fly, flutter.
ondina *nf* water nymph, undine.
ondulación *nf* undulation, wave.
ondulado,-a *adj (pelo)* wavy.
ondulante *adj (movimiento)* rolling.
ondular *vt (pelo)* to wave.
ondulatorio,-a *adj* undulatory.
oneroso,-a *adj* onerous.
ónice *nm* onyx.
onírico,-a *adj* dream, of dreams.
ónix *nm* onyx.
onomástica *nf* saint's day.
onomástico,-a *adj* onomastic.
onomatopeya *nf* onomatopoeia.
onomatopéyico,-a *adj* onomatopoeic.
ontología *nf* ontology.
ontológico,-a *adj* ontological.
ONU *abrev* (Organización de las Naciones Unidas) United Nations Organization; *(abreviatura)* UNO.
onza *nf (peso)* ounce.
opacidad *nf* opaqueness, opacity.
opaco,-a *adj* opaque.
opalino,-a *adj (de ópalo)* opal.
ópalo *nm* opal.
opción *nf (en general)* option.
opcional *adj* optional.
open *nm inv* DEP open.
ópera *nf* opera.
operación *nf (gen)* operation.
operador,-ra *nm & nf* operator.
operando *nm* operand.
operante *adj* operative.
operar *vt* MED to operate (a, on).

▶ *vpr* **operarse** MED to have an operation.

operario,-a *nm & nf* operator, worker.
operativo,-a *adj* operative.
opereta *nf* operetta.
operístico,-a *adj* operatic.
opinable *adj* debatable.
opinar *vi* to think (de, about).
opinión *nf (juicio)* opinion.
opio *nm* opium.
opíparo,-a *adj fml* lavish.
oponente *nm o nf* opponent.
oponer *vt* to reply with.
▶ *vpr* **oponerse** *(estar en contra)* to oppose (a, -), be against (a, -).
oporto *nm* port.
oportunidad *nf* opportunity, chance.
oportunismo *nm* opportunism.
oportunista *nm o nf* opportunist.
oportuno,-a *adj (a tiempo)* opportune.
oposición *nf (antagonismo)* opposition.
opresión *nf* oppression.
opresivo,-a *adj* oppressive.
opresor,-ra *nm & nf* oppressor.
oprimido,-a *adj & nf* oppressed person.
oprimir *vt* 1 *(botón)* to press: *oprima el botón* press the button. 2 *fig* to oppress.
oprobio *nm* opprobrium.
optar *vi (elegir)* to choose (entre, from).
optativa *nf* EDUC *(asignatura)* optional subject.
optativo,-a *adj* 1 optional. 2 LING *(oración, modo)* optative.
óptica *nf* 1 *(tienda)* optician's. 2 Fís optics.
óptico,-a *nm & nf* optician.
optimismo *nm* optimism.
optimista *adj* optimistic.
optimizar *vt* to optimize.
óptimo,-a *adj* very best, optimum.
opuesto,-a *adj* 1 *(contrario)* contrary, opposed. 2 *(de enfrente)* opposite.
opulencia *nf* opulence.
opulento,-a *adj* opulent.
oquedad *nf (hueco)* cavity.
oración *nf* 1 REL *(plegaria)* prayer. 2 LING clause, sentence. COMP
oráculo *nm* oracle.

orador,-ra *nm & nf* speaker, orator.
oral *adj* oral.
orangután *nm* ZOOL orang-utan.
orar *vi* to pray.
oratoria *nf* oratory.
oratorio,-a *adj (estilo, arte)* oratorical.
orbe *nm (esfera)* orb; *(mundo)* world.
órbita *nf (de un astro)* orbit.
orbital *adj* orbital.
orca *nf* killer whale, orc.
orden *nm (ordenación)* order.
▶ *nf (mandato)* order.
ordenación *nf* arrangement.
ordenada *nf* MAT ordinate.
ordenado,-a *adj* tidy.
ordenador,-ra *nm* INFORM computer.
ordenamiento *nm* ordering.
ordenanza *nf (norma)* ordinance.
ordenar *vt* **1** *(arreglar)* to put in order; *(habitación)* to tidy up. **2** *(mandar)* to order.
ordeñar *vt* to milk.
ordinal *adj* ordinal.
▶ *nm* ordinal.
ordinariez *nf (defecto)* vulgarity.
ordinario,-a *adj* **1** *(corriente)* ordinary, common. **2** *(grosero)* vulgar, common.
orégano *nm* oregano.
oreja *nf* ear.
orejera *nf* earflap.
orejero *nm (sillón)* wing chair.
orfanato *nm* orphanage.
orfandad *nf* orphanage.
orfebre *nm* goldsmith, silversmith.
orfebrería *nf (en oro)* gold work.
orfeón *nm* choral society.
órfico,-a *adj lit* orphic.
organdí *nm* organdie.
orgánico,-a *adj* organic.
organigrama *nm* organization chart.
organillero,-a *nm & nf* organ-grinder.
organillo *nm* barrel organ.
organismo *nm* **1** *(humano)* organism. **2** *(institucional)* organization, body.
organista *nm o nf* organist.
organización *nf* organization.
organizar *vt* to organize.
organizativo,-a *adj* organizational.

órgano *nm* organ.
orgullo *nm (propia estima)* pride.
orgulloso,-a *adj* proud.
orientación *nf* aspect.
oriental *adj* eastern, oriental.
▶ *nm o nf* Oriental.
orientar *vt* **1** *(antena)* to point. **2** *(esfuerzos)* to direct. **3** *(aconsejar)* to advise.
▶ *vpr* **orientarse** to find one's bearings.
oriente *nm* East.
orificio *nm (agujero)* hole.
origen *nm (causa)* cause, origin.
original *adj (gen)* original.
▶ *nm* original.
originalidad *nf* originality.
originar *vt* to cause, give rise to.
originario,-a *adj* original.
orilla *nf* **1** *(borde)* edge. **2** *(del río)* bank; *(del mar)* shore.
orillar *vt (sortear)* to get round.
orina *nf* urine.
orinar *vi* to urinate.
oriundo,-a *adj* native of.
orla *nf (adorno)* edging.
ornamentación *nf* ornamentation.
ornamental *adj* ornamental.
ornamentar *vt* to adorn, decorate.
ornamento *nm* ornament.
ornitología *nf* ornithology.
ornitológico,-a *adj* ornithological.
ornitólogo,-a *nm & nf* ornithologist.
ornitorrinco *nm* platypus.
oro *nm* gold.
orografía *nf* orography.
orográfico,-a *adj* orographic.
orondo,-a *adj* hearty, plump.
orquesta *nf* orchestra, dance band.
orquestal *adj* orchestral.
orquestar *vt* to orchestrate.
orquídea *nf* orchid.
ortiga *nf* nettle.
ortodoncia *nf* orthodontics.
ortodoxia *nf* orthodoxy.
ortodoxo,-a *adj* orthodox.
▶ *nm & nf* orthodox.
ortografía *nf* spelling.
ortográfico,-a *adj* spelling.

O

ortopedia *nf* orthopaedics.

ortopédico,-a *adj* orthopaedic.

ortopedista *nm o nf* orthopaedist.

oruga *nf* caterpillar.

orzuelo *nm* sty.

os *pron* **1** *(complemento directo)* you: *os escucho* I am listening to you. **2** *(complemento indirecto)* you: *os traje un libro* I brought you a book. **3** *(reflexivo)* yourselves: *¿ya os estáis vistiendo?* are you getting dressed already? **4** *(recíproco)* each other: *os parecéis mucho* you look very much alike.

osadía *nf* *(audacia)* audacity, daring.

osado,-a *adj* *(audaz)* audacious.

osamenta *nf* *(esqueleto)* skeleton.

osar *vi lit* to dare, have the audacity to.

oscilación *nf* *(de precios)* fluctuation.

oscilar *vi* *(variar)* to vary, fluctuate.

oscilatorio,-a *adj* oscillating.

oscurantismo *nm* obscurantism.

oscuras LOC **a oscuras** in the dark.

óseo,-a *adj* *(tejido, estructura)* bone.

osera *nf* bear's den.

osezno *nm* bear cub.

osificación *nf* ossification.

osificar *vt* to ossify.

osmio *nm* osmium.

ósmosis *nf inv* osmosis.

oso *nm* bear.

ostentación *nf* ostentation.

ostentar *vt* *(poseer)* to hold.

ostentoso,-a *adj* ostentatious.

osteópata *nm o nf* osteopath.

osteopatía *nf* osteopathy.

osteopático,-a *adj* osteopathic.

ostra *nf* oyster.

ostracismo *nm* ostracism.

ostrero,-a *adj* oyster.

ostrícola *adj* oyster.

OTAN *abrev* (Organización del Tratado del Atlántico Norte) North Atlantic Treaty Organization; *(abreviatura)* NATO.

otear *vt* *(horizonte)* to scan.

otero *nm* hillock.

otitis *nf inv* ear infection, otitis.

otomano,-a *adj* Ottoman.
► *nm & nf* *(persona)* Ottoman.

otoñal *adj* autumnal, autumn, US fall.

otoño *nm* autumn, US fall.

otorgante *adj* *(de un premio)* awarding.

otorgar *vt* *(conceder)* to grant, give (a, to); *(premio)* to award (a, to).

otorrinolaringólogo,-a *nm & nf* ear, nose and throat specialist.

otorrinolaringología *nf* ear, nose and throat, ENT.

otro,-a *adj* other, another.
► *pron* other, another: *otros* others.

ovación *nf* ovation, applause.

ovacionar *vt* to give an ovation (a, to).

oval *adj* oval.

ovalado,-a *adj* oval.

óvalo *nm* oval.

ovario *nm* ovary.

oveja *nf* sheep, ewe.

overtura *nf* MÚS overture.

ovillar *vt* to roll into a ball.

ovillo *nm* ball of wool.

ovino,-a *adj* ovine, sheep.

ovíparo,-a *adj* oviparous.

ovulación *nf* ovulation.

ovular *adj* ovular.
► *vi* to ovulate.

óvulo *nm* ovule.

oxiacetilénico,-a *adj* oxyacetylene.

oxiacetileno *nm* oxyacetylene.

oxidable *adj* oxidizable.

oxidación *nf* **1** QUÍM oxidation. **2** *(proceso)* rusting.

oxidado,-a *adj* rusty.

oxidar *vt* to rust.
► *vpr* **oxidarse** to rust, go rusty.

óxido *nm* *(herrumbre)* rust.

oxigenado,-a *adj* QUÍM oxygenated.

oxigenar *vt* to get some fresh air in.
► *vpr* **oxigenarse** to get some fresh air.

oxígeno *nm* oxygen.

oye *interj fam* *(para llamar la atención)* hey!

oyente *nm o nf* RAD listener.

ozono *nm* ozone. COMP **capa de ozono** ozone layer.

P

P, p *nf (la letra)* P, p.
pabellón *nm (en una feria)* stand.
pabilo *nm* wick.
pábulo *nm* fuel.
pacana *nf* pecan nut.
pacer *vi* to graze.
pachón,-ona *adj (perro)* pointer.
paciencia *nf* patience.
paciente *nm o nf* patient.
pacificación *nf* pacification.
pacíficamente *adv* peacefully.
pacificar *vt* to pacify.
pacífico,-a *adj* peaceful.
pacifismo *nm* pacifism.
pacifista *adj* pacifist.
▶ *nm o nf* pacifist.
pactar *vt* to agree (to).
▶ *vi* to come to an agreement.
pacto *nm* pact, agreement.
padecer *vt* to suffer.
▶ *vi (sufrir)* to suffer (de, from).
padecimiento *nm* suffering.
padrastro *nm (padre)* stepfather.
padrazo *nm fam* loving father.
padre *nm* father.
▶ *nm pl* **padres** parents.
padrino *nm (de bautizo)* godfather.
▶ *nm pl* **padrinos** godparents.
padrón *nm (censo)* census.
paella *nf (comida)* paella.
paellera *nf* paella pan.
paga *nf* **1** *(sueldo)* pay. **2** *(de los niños)* pocket money.
pagadero,-a *adj* payable.
pagador,-ra *adj* paying.
▶ *nm & nf (gen)* payer.
paganismo *nm* paganism.
pagano,-a *nm & nf* REL pagan.

pagar *vt* to pay: *ya he pagado lo que debía* I've already paid what I owed.
▶ *vi* to pay: *en esta empresa pagan muy bien* this company pays very well.
página *nf* page.
paginación *nf* pagination.
pago *nm* payment.
paguro *nm (ermitaño)* hermit crab.
país *nm* country.
paisaje *nm* landscape.
paisajista *nm o nf (pintor)* landscape artist.
paisajístico,-a *adj* landscape.
paisano,-a *nm & nf* **1** *(compatriota)* fellow countryman. **2** *(campesino)* countryman.
paja *nf* **1** straw. **2** *fig (relleno)* waffle.
pajar *nm (lugar)* hayloft.
pajarera *nf* aviary.
pajarería *nf (tienda)* caged-bird shop.
pajarero,-a *adj* of birds.
pajarita *nf (de cuello)* bow tie.
pájaro *nm (animal)* bird.
paje *nm* page.
pajita *nf (para beber)* straw.
pajizo,-a *adj* straw-coloured (US straw-colored).
Pakistán *nm* Pakistan.
pakistaní *adj* Pakistani.
▶ *nm o nf* Pakistani.
pala *nf* **1** shovel. **2** DEP *(de ping-pong)* bat.
palabra *nf* word.
palacete *nm* mansion.
palaciego,-a *adj* palatial.
palacio *nm* palace.
palada *nf (gen)* shovelful.
paladar *nm* **1** palate. **2** *fig* taste.
paladear *vt* to savour, relish.
paladín *nm fig* champion.

palafito *nm* house on stilts.

palanca *nf (gen)* lever. LOC hacer palanca to lever.

palangana *nf* bowl.

palangre *nm (arte de pesca)* boulter.

palatal *adj* palatal.
▶ *nf* palatal.

palco *nm (en el teatro)* box.

paleografía *nf* palaeography.

paleógrafo,-a *nm & nf* palaeographer.

paleolítico,-a *adj* Palaeolithic.
▶ *nm* el paleolítico the Palaeolithic.

paleontología *nf* palaeontology.

paleontólogo,-a *nm & nf* palaeontologist.

Palestina *nf* Palestine.

palestino,-a *adj* Palestinian.
▶ *nm & nf* Palestinian.

palestra *nf* arena, forum.

paleta *nf* 1 *(de pintor)* palette. 2 *(de albañil)* trowel.

paletada *nf (de albañil)* going over with a trowel.

paletilla *nf* 1 ANAT shoulder blade. 2 CULIN shoulder.

paliar *vt* to palliate, alleviate.

paliativo,-a *adj* palliative.
▶ *nm* paliativo palliative.

palidecer *vi* 1 to turn pale. 2 *fig* to fade.

palidez *nf* paleness, pallor.

pálido,-a *adj* pale.

palillero *nm* toothpick holder.

palillo *nm (mondadientes)* toothpick.

palio *nm* canopy.

palisandro *nm* rosewood.

paliza *nf* beating, thrashing.

palma *nf* 1 BOT palm (tree). 2 *(de la mano)* palm.
▶ *nf pl* palmas *(aplausos)* clapping *sing*.

palmada *nf (golpe)* slap, pat.

palmar *nm* palm grove.

palmarés *nm (lista)* list of winners.

palmatoria *nf* candlestick.

palmeado,-a *adj* 1 BOT palmate. 2 ZOOL *(dedos)* webbed.

palmear *vi* to clap.

palmera *nf* BOT palm tree, palm.

palmeral *nm* palm grove.

palmetazo *nm* stroke of the cane.

palmípedo,-a *adj* web-footed.
▶ *nf pl* palmípedas ZOOL *(género)* web-footed birds.

palmito *nm* 1 CULIN palm heart. 2 BOT palmetto.

palmo *nm (medida)* span.

palmotear *vi* to clap.

palmoteo *nm* clapping.

palo *nm* 1 *(estaca)* stick; *(de valla)* post; *(de telégrafos)* pole. 2 *(golpe)* blow.

paloma *nf (gen)* pigeon; *(blanca)* dove.

palomar *nm* dovecote.

palometa *nf* Ray's bream.

palomilla *nf (tuerca)* wing nut.

palomino *nm* young pigeon.

palomitas COMP palomitas de maíz popcorn *sing*.

palomo *nm* cock pigeon.

palote *nm (dibujo)* stroke.

palpable *adj* palpable.

palpar *vt* MED to palpate.

palpitación *nf* palpitation.

palpitante *adj (tema, cuestión)* burning.

palpitar *vi* to palpitate, throb.

pálpito *nm* hunch, feeling.

paludismo *nm* malaria.

palurdo,-a *nm & nf* country bumpkin.

palustre *adj (de las lagunas)* lake.

pamela *nf* wide-brimmed straw hat.

pampa *nf* pampas *pl*.

pámpano *nm* vine shoot.

pamplina *nf (tontería)* daft thing.

pamplinero,-a *adj* sweet-talking.

pan *nm* 1 *(masa)* bread; *(hogaza)* loaf of bread. 2 *(alimento)* food, bread. COMP barra de pan loaf of bread. ‖ pan integral wholemeal bread.

pana *nf* corduroy.

panacea *nf* panacea.

panadería *nf* bakery, baker's.

panadero,-a *nm & nf* baker.

panal *nm* honeycomb.

Panamá *nm* Panama.

panameño,-a *adj* Panamanian.
▶ *nm & nf* Panamanian.

panamericano,-a *adj* Pan-American.

pancarta *nf* **1** placard. **2** INFORM banner.

panceta *nf* bacon.

páncreas *nm inv* pancreas.

pancreático,-a *adj* pancreatic.

panda *nm* ZOOL panda.

pandemónium *nm* pandemonium.

pandeo *nm (torcedura)* warp.

pandereta *nf* small tambourine.

pandero *nm* tambourine.

pandilla *nf* group of friends.

panecillo *nm* bread roll.

panel *nm (gen)* panel.

panera *nf* breadbasket.

panfleto *nm fig* propaganda.

pánico *nm* panic.

panificadora *nf* industrial bakery.

panocha *nf (de maíz)* corncob.

panorama *nm* panorama, view.

panorámica *nf* panorama.

panorámico,-a *adj* panoramic.

pantalla *nf* screen.

pantalón [también se usa en plural con el mismo significado] *nm* trousers *pl*, US pants. COMP **pantalón vaquero** jeans *pl*.

pantano *nm* **1** *(artificial)* reservoir. **2** *(natural)* marsh.

pantanoso,-a *adj* marshy.

panteísmo *nm* pantheism.

panteón *nm* pantheon.

pantera *nf* panther.

panties *nm pl* tights.

pantomima *nf* **1** *(representación)* pantomime, mime. **2** *fig* farce, pretence.

pantorrilla *nf* calf.

pantufla *nf* slipper.

panza *nf* belly.

panzada *nf (en el agua)* belly flop.

pañal *nm* nappy, US diaper.

pañería *nf* draper's, draper's shop.

paño *nm* cloth.

pañoleta *nf* shawl.

pañuelo *nm* handkerchief.

papa¹ *nm* **1** *fam* dad. **2 el Papa** the Pope.

papa² *nf (patata)* potato. COMP **papas fritas** chips, US French fries.

papá *nm fam* dad, daddy. COMP **Papá Noel** Santa Claus.

papada *nf* double chin.

papagayo *nm* parrot.

papaya *nf* papaya.

papayo *nm* papaya tree.

papel *nm* **1** *(gen)* paper. **2** *(en película)* role, part. COMP **papel higiénico** toilet paper. I **papel pintado** wallpaper.
▶ *nm pl* **papeles** *fam (documentación)* papers.

papeleo *nm fam* paperwork.

papelera *nf* **1** wastepaper basket. **2** *(en la calle)* litter bin.

papelería *nf* stationer's.

papelero,-a *adj (del papel)* paper: *la industria papelera* the paper industry.

papeleta *nf* **1** *(de voto)* ballot paper. **2** *(de examen)* results slip.

paperas *nf pl* mumps.

papi *nm fam* dad, daddy.

papila *nf* papilla.

papilla *nf (infantil)* baby food.

papiro *nm* papyrus.

papú *adj* Papuan.
▶ *nm o nf* Papuan.

Papúa *nf* Papua. COMP **Papúa Nueva Guinea** Papua New Guinea.

paquete *nm* **1** *(cajita)* packet, pack. **2** *(conjunto)* set, packet: *un paquete de galletas* a package of biscuits. COMP **paquete postal** parcel.

paquidermo *nm* pachyderm.

Paquistán *nm* Pakistan.

paquistaní *adj* Pakistani.
▶ *nm o nf* Pakistani.

par *adj* **1** equal. **2** MAT even.
▶ *nm (dos)* couple; *(pareja)* pair.

para *prep* **1** *(finalidad)* for: *es para su cumpleaños* it's for her birthday. **2** *(uso, utilidad)* for: *¿tienes algo para el dolor de cabeza?* have you got anything for a headache? **3** *(destino, dirección)* for, to: *¿para dónde vas?* where are you going? **4** *(tiempo, fechas límites)* by, before: *lo necesito para el viernes* I need it by Friday.
▶ *conj (finalidad)* to, in order to: *lo hice para ahorrar tiempo* I did it to save time.

parábola *nf* MAT parabola.

P

parabólica *nf* satellite dish.
parabólico,-a *adj* parabolic. COMP antena parabólica satellite dish.
parabrisas *nm inv* windscreen.
paracaídas *nm inv* parachute.
paracaidismo *nm* parachuting.
paracaidista *nm o nf* DEP parachutist.
parachoques *nm inv* AUTO bumper.
parada *nf* 1 (gen) stop, halt. 2 (de autobús, etc) stop. 3 (pausa) pause. COMP parada de autobús bus stop.
paradero *nm* whereabouts *pl*.
paradigmático,-a *adj* paradigmatic.
paradisíaco,-a *adj* heavenly.
parado,-a *adj* 1 (quieto) still. 2 (sin trabajo) unemployed.
▶ *nm & nf* unemployed person.
paradójico,-a *adj* paradoxical.
parador *nm* (hotel) state-run hotel.
parafina *nf* paraffin.
paraguas *nm inv* umbrella.
Paraguay *nm* Paraguay.
paraguaya *nf type of* peach.
paraguayo,-a *adj* Paraguayan.
▶ *nm & nf* Paraguayan.
paraíso *nm* paradise.
paraje *nm* spot.
paralela *nf* (línea) parallel line.
▶ *nf pl* **paralelas** DEP parallel bars.
paralelo,-a *adj* parallel.
▶ *nm* **paralelo** parallel.
paralelogramo *nm* parallelogram.
parálisis *nf inv* paralysis.
paralítico,-a *adj* paralytic.
▶ *nm & nf* paralytic.
paralización *nf* paralysis.
paralizar *vt* 1 MED to paralyse. 2 (circulación) to bring to a standstill.
parámetro *nm* parameter.
páramo *nm* moor.
paranoia *nf* paranoia.
paranoico,-a *nm & nf* paranoic.
parapente *nm* paragliding.
parapeto *nm* parapet.
parapléjico,-a *nm & nf* paraplegic.
parapsicología *nf* parapsychology.

parapsicológico,-a *adj* parapsychological.
parar *vt* 1 to stop. 2 DEP to save: ha parado tres disparos he's made three saves.
▶ *vi* to stop: aquí no para el tren the train doesn't stop here.
▶ *vpr* **pararse** to stop.
pararrayos *nm inv* lightning conductor.
parasitario,-a *adj* parasitic.
parásito,-a *nm* BIOL parasite.
parasol *nm* parasol, sunshade.
parcela *nf* (de tierra) plot (of land).
parcelar *vt* (finca) to divide into plots.
parche *nm* patch.
parchís *nm inv* ludo.
parcial *adj* (gen) partial.
▶ *nm* (examen) examination covering part of the course and counting towards the final mark.
parcialidad *nf* (injusticia) bias, partiality.
parco,-a *adj* (escaso) frugal, sparing.
pardo,-a *adj* (color tierra) brown.
pareado,-a *adj* (casa) semidetached.
parecer *nm* (opinión) opinion, mind.
▶ *vi* 1 to seem, look (like): parece un oso it looks like a bear. 2 (opinar) to think: ¿qué te parece? what do you think?
▶ *vpr* **parecerse** to be alike, look like: se parecen mucho they're very much alike.
parecido,-a *adj* similar.
▶ *nm* **parecido** resemblance, likeness.
pared *nf* 1 wall. 2 (de una montaña) side.
paredón *nm* execution wall.
pareja *nf* 1 (gen) pair: he perdido la pareja de este calcetín I've lost the other sock. 2 (de personas) couple; (de baile) partner.
parejo,-a *adj* (sin diferencia) the same; (por igual) even.
parentela *nf* relatives *pl*, relations *pl*.
parentesco *nm* kinship, relationship.
paréntesis *nm inv* 1 (gen) parenthesis. 2 *fig* (interrupción) break, interruption.
paria *nm o nf* pariah.
paridad *nf* (gen) parity, equality.
pariente,-a *nm & nf* relative.
parir *vt fam* to give birth to.
▶ *vi* to give birth.
parlamentario,-a *adj* parliamentary.
▶ *nm & nf* member of parliament.

parlamento *nm* parliament.

parlante *adj* talking.

parlotear *vi fam* to chatter, prattle on.

parmesan *nm (queso)* Parmesan cheese.

paro *nm* 1 stop. 2 *(desempleo)* unemployment.

parodia *nf* parody.

parodiar *vt* to parody.

paroxismo *nm* paroxysm.

parpadear *vi (ojos)* to blink, wink.

párpado *nm* eyelid.

parque *nm (jardines)* park. COMP **parque de atracciones** amusement park.

parqué *nm* parquet.

parquímetro *nm* parking meter.

parra *nf* grapevine.

parrafada *nf fam (conversación)* chat.

párrafo *nm* paragraph.

parranda *nf fam* spree.

parrilla *nf* 1 grill, US broiler, barbecue. LOC **a la parrilla** CULIN grilled.

parrillada *nf* mixed grill *(of meat or fish)*.

párroco *nm* parish priest.

parroquia *nf (iglesia)* parish church.

parsimonia *nf (lentitud)* slowness.

parsimonioso,-a *adj (tranquilo)* slow.

parte *nf* 1 *(gen)* part; *(en una partición)* portion: *divide el pastel en tres partes* cut the cake into three (slices). 2 *(en negocio)* share. 3 *(lugar)* place: *no lo venden en ninguna parte* they don't sell it anywhere. 4 *(en un conflicto)* side: *las dos partes quieren llevar la razón* both sides believe they are right.
► *nm (comunicado)* official report.
► *nf pl* **partes** *fam* privates, private parts. LOC **en parte** partly. ▌**por una parte,... por otra...** on the one hand…, on the other hand…

partera *nf* midwife.

parterre *nm* flowerbed.

partición *nf (de una herencia)* partition.

participación *nf* involvement.

participante *nm o nf* participant.

participar *vi* to participate, take part.
► *vt (notificar)* to notify, inform.

partícipe *adj* participating.
► *nm o nf* participant.

participio *nm* participle.

partícula *nf* particle.

particular *adj (concreto)* particular.
► *nm* 1 private individual. 2 *(asunto)* matter, subject.

particularidad *nf (gen)* peculiarity.

particularizar *vi* to distinguish.

partida *nf* 1 *(remesa)* consignment, lot. 2 *(documento)* certificate. 3 *(juego)* game. LOC **jugar una partida** to play a game. COMP **partida de nacimiento** birth certificate.

partidario,-a *adj* supporting.
► *nm & nf* supporter.

partidista *adj* biased, partisan.

partido,-a *adj* 1 divided. 2 *(roto)* broken.
► *nm* **partido** 1 *(grupo político)* party, group. 2 DEP *(equipo)* team; *(juego)* game, match. COMP **partido amistoso** friendly game.

partir *vt* 1 *(dividir)* to divide, cut: *voy a partir pan* I'll cut some bread. 2 *(romper)* to break; *(nueces, almendras)* to crack.
► *vi (irse)* to leave, set out, set off.
► *vpr* **partirse** to break: *se ha partido la pierna* he's broken his leg.

partitivo,-a *adj* partitive.
► *nm* partitivo partitive.

partitura *nf* score.

parto *nm* childbirth: *fue un parto difícil* it was a difficult birth. LOC **estar de parto** to be in labour (US labor).

parvulario *nm* nursery school.

párvulo,-a *nm & nf* infant.

pasa *nf* raisin.

pasable *adj* passable.

pasadizo *nm* passage.

pasado,-a *adj* 1 past. 2 *(año, semana, etc)* last. 3 *(después)* after: *pasadas las once* after eleven. 4 *(estropeado)* bad. COMP **pasado mañana** the day after tomorrow.
► *nm* pasado 1 *(tiempo)* past. 2 LING past, past tense.

pasador *nm* slide.

pasaje *nf* 1 *(tarifa)* fare, ticket. 2 *(pasajeros)* passengers *pl*. 3 *(fragmento)* passage.

pasajero,-a *nm & nf* passenger.

pasamanos *nm inv* handrail.

P

pasamontañas *nm inv* balaclava.
pasaporte *nm* passport.
pasapurés *nm inv* vegetable mill.
pasar *vi* **1** *(ir)* to pass, pass by, go: *pasa de un idioma a otro sin darse cuenta* he goes from one language to another without realizing. **2** *(tiempo)* to pass, go by: *¡cómo pasa el tiempo!* doesn't time fly! **3** *(entrar)* to come in, go in: *pasa, está abierto* come in, it's not locked. **4** *(cesar)* to pass, cease: *en cuanto pase la tormenta salimos* we'll go out when the storm has passed. **5** *(límite)* to exceed (de, -). **6** *(ocurrir)* to happen. **7** *(sufrir)* to suffer.
▶ *vt* **1** *(trasladar)* to move, transfer: *pasa este documento al otro CD* move this file to the other CD. **2** *(comunicar, dar)* to give: *pásale el informe al jefe* give this report to the boss. **3** *(cruzar)* to cross: *pasamos la frontera ayer* we crossed the border yesterday. **4** *(alcanzar)* to pass, reach: *pásame la sal, por favor* pass me the salt, please. **5** *(aventajar)* to surpass, be better than: *tu hermano ya te pasa en matemáticas* your brother is better than you at maths. **6** *(adelantar)* to overtake: *me pasó un deportivo rojo en una curva* a red sports car overtook me on a bend. **7** *(deslizar)* to run: *pasó el dedo por el estante* he ran his finger along the shelf. **8** *(tolerar)* to overlook: *esta vez te la paso, pero que no se repita* I'll overlook it this time, but don't let it happen again. **9** *(aprobar)* to pass: *pasé el examen a la primera* I passed my test first time. **10** *(proyectar)* to show: *pasaron unas diapositivas* they showed some slides. **11** *(tiempo - estar)* to spend; *(- disfrutar, padecer)* to have: *pasamos unas vacaciones estupendas* we had a wonderful holiday.
▶ *vpr* **pasarse 1** *(cambiar)* to pass over (a, to): *se ha pasado al otro bando* she's gone over to the other side. **2** *(pudrirse)* to go off. **3** *(olvidarse)* to forget: *se me pasó la fecha de entrega* I forgot about the deadline. **4** *(ir)* to go by (por, -), call in (por, at): *pásate por casa cuando quieras* pop in any time.
pasarela *nf (puente)* footbridge.
pasatiempos *nm pl* puzzles.
pascua *nf* Easter.
▶ *nf pl* **pascuas** Christmas *sing*.

pase *nm (permiso)* pass.
pasear *vi* to stroll, go for a walk.
▶ *vt* to take for a walk.
paseo *nm* **1** *(a pie)* walk; *(a caballo)* ride. **2** *(en coche)* drive; *(en bicicleta, moto)* ride. LOC **dar un paseo** to go for a walk.
pasillo *nm* corridor.
pasión *nf* passion.
pasividad *nf* passiveness, passivity.
pasmado,-a *adj* flabbergasted.
pasmar *vt* to astonish, amaze.
▶ *vpr* **pasmarse** *fam (asombrarse)* to be astonished, be amazed.
pasmo *nm (asombro)* amazement.
pasmoso,-a *adj* astonishing.
paso *nm* **1** *(movimiento)* step, footstep. **2** *(camino)* passage. LOC **abrirse paso** to force one's way through. ▌ **estar de paso** to be passing through. COMP **paso de peatones** pedestrian crossing.
pasta *nf* **1** *(masa)* paste. **2** CULIN *(italiana)* pasta. **3** *(croissant, etc)* pastry; *(de té)* biscuit.
pastar *vt* to pasture, graze.
▶ *vi* to pasture, graze.
pastel *nm* CULIN *(dulce)* cake; *(salado)* pie.
pastelería *nf (tienda)* cake shop.
pastelero,-a *nm & nf* pastrycook.
pasteurizado,-a *adj* pasteurized.
pasteurizar *vt* to pasteurize.
pastilla *nf* **1** *(medicina)* tablet, pill. **2** *(de chocolate, jabón)* bar.
pasto *nm (pastizal)* pasture.
pastor,-ra *nm & nf* shepherd.
pastoso,-a *adj (sustancia)* pasty.
pata *nf* **1** *(gen)* leg. **2** *(garra)* paw. **3** *(pezuña)* hoof. LOC **a cuatro patas** on all fours. ▌ **meter la pata** *fam* to put one's foot in it. ▌ **patas arriba** upside down.
patada *nf* kick.
patalear *vi* **1** *(con enfado)* to stamp one's feet. **2** *(protestar)* to kick up a fuss.
pataleo *nm* **1** *(con los pies)* stamping. **2** *(protesta)* complaining.
pataleta *nf fam* tantrum.
patata *nf* potato. COMP **patatas fritas 1** *(de bolsa)* crisps. **2** *(de sartén)* chips.
paté *nm* pâté.

patear vt **1** to kick. **2** (andar) to walk.

patentado,-a adj patented.

patentar vt to patent.

patente adj (evidente) obvious, patent.

patera nf boat.

paternal adj paternal.

paternalista adj paternalistic.

paternidad nf paternity.

paterno,-a adj paternal.

patético,-a adj pathetic.

patíbulo nm gallows sing.

patilla nf **1** (pata) leg. **2** (de las gafas) arm.
▶ nf pl sideboards, US sideburns.

patín nm **1** (de ruedas) roller skate, skate; (de hielo) ice skate. **2** (tabla) skateboard. **3** (patinete) scooter. **4** (en el mar) pedalo.

pátina nf patina.

patinador,-ra nm & nf skater.

patinaje nm skating. COMP **patinaje artístico** figure skating. **I patinaje sobre hielo** ice-skating. **I patinaje sobre ruedas** roller skating.

patinar vi **1** (como diversión) to skate. **2** (vehículo) to skid.

patinazo nm **1** skid. **2** fam (error) boob.

patinete nm scooter.

patio nm **1** (de una casa) courtyard; (de un colegio) playground. **2** TEAT pit.

pato,-a nm & nf (ave) duck.
▶ nm **pato** fam (persona) clumsy person.

patológico,-a adj pathological.

patria nf homeland.

patriarca nm patriarch.

patriarcado nm patriarchy.

patrimonio nm patrimony.

patrio,-a adj of one's homeland.

patriota nm o nf patriot.

patriótico,-a adj patriotic.

patriotismo nm patriotism.

patrocinador,-ra nm & nf sponsor.

patrocinar vt to sponsor.

patrocinio nm sponsorship.

patrón,-ona nm & nf **1** (dueño de una casa) landlord. **2** (jefe) employer. **3** REL patron saint.
▶ nm **patrón 1** (en costura) pattern. **2** (de barco) skipper. **3** (modelo) standard.

patronal adj (fiesta) of one's patron saint.
▶ nf (institución) employers' association.

patronato nm (patronal) employers' association.

patrulla nf (de vigilancia) patrol.

patrullar vt to patrol.

paulatino,-a adj gradual.

pausa nf **1** pause. **2** MÚS rest.

pausado,-a adj unhurried, slow.

pauta nf (norma) rule, guideline.

pavimentar vt (con losas) to pave.

pavimento nm (de losas) pavement.

pavo,-a nm & nf (ave - macho) turkey; (- hembra) turkey hen. COMP **pavo real** peacock.
▶ nm **pavo** fam (timidez) shyness.

pavonearse vpr to brag, swagger.

pavoneo nm strutting.

pavor nm terror.

pavoroso,-a adj frightful.

payasada nf **1** buffoonery. **2** fam silly thing.

payaso,-a nm & nf **1** (artista de circo) clown. **2** fam joker.

paz nf peace. LOC **dejar en paz** to leave alone. **I hacer las paces** to make up.

peaje nm **1** (dinero) toll. **2** (lugar) toll-booth.

peana nf pedestal, stand.

peatón nm pedestrian.

peatonal adj (calle, zona) pedestrian.

peca nf freckle.

pecado nm sin.

pecador,-ra nm & nf sinner.

pecaminoso,-a adj sinful, wicked.

pecar vi to sin.

pecera nf fishbowl, fish tank.

pechera nf (de camisa) shirt front.

pechina nf scallop.

pecho nm **1** (gen) chest. **2** (seno) breast. LOC **dar el pecho** to breast-feed.

pechuga nf (de un ave) breast.

pecíolo nm petiole.

pecoso,-a adj (persona) freckly.

pectina nf pectin.

pectoral nm (músculo) pectoral muscle.

P

pecuario,-a *adj* cattle.

peculiar *adj (característico)* particular.

peculiaridad *nf* peculiarity.

pecuniario,-a *adj* pecuniary.

pedagogía *nf* pedagogy.

pedagógico,-a *adj* pedagogic(al).

pedagogo,-a *nm & nf* educator.

pedal *nm* 1 pedal. 2 *fam* bender.

pedalear *vi* to pedal.

pedaleo *nm* pedalling.

pedanía *nf* hamlet.

pedante *adj* pedantic, pompous.

pedantería *nf* pedantry, pomposity.

pedazo *nm* piece, bit.

pedernal *nm* 1 *(sílex)* flint. 2 *fig* rock.

pedestal *nm* pedestal.

pedestre *adj (a pie)* on foot.

pediatra *nm o nf* paediatrician.

pediatría *nf* paediatrics.

pedicuro,-a *nm & nf* chiropodist.

pedido *nm (de mercancías)* order. LOC hacer un pedido to place an order.

pedigrí *nm* pedigree.

pedigüeño,-a *nm & nf* pest.

pedir *vt* 1 *(gen)* to ask for: *me pidió que la acompañara* she asked me to go with her. 2 *(mercancías, en restaurante)* to order: *¿qué has pedido de postre?* what did you order for dessert?
▶ *vi (por la calle)* to beg.

pedrada *nf* blow with a stone.

pedregal *nm* rocky ground.

pedregoso,-a *adj* stony, rocky.

pedrera *nf* stone quarry.

pedrería *nf* precious stones *pl*.

pedrisco *nm (granizo)* hail.

pedrusco *nm* rough stone.

pedúnculo *nm (de planta)* stem.

pega *nf fam (dificultad)* snag: *me pusieron muchas pegas* they made it difficult for me.

pegadizo,-a *adj* 1 *(canción, música)* catchy. 2 *(sustancia)* sticky, adhesive.

pegajoso,-a *adj* 1 *(mano)* sticky. 2 *pey (persona)* clingy.

pegamento *nm* glue.

pegar¹ *vt* 1 *(gen)* to stick. 2 *(contagiar)* to give: *me has pegado la gripe* you've given

me your flu. 3 *(acercar)* to move close to: *pega la estantería a la pared* move the bookcase against the wall. 4 INFORM to paste.
▶ *vi (combinar)* to match: *esta blusa no pega con la falda* this blouse doesn't go with the skirt.
▶ *vpr* **pegarse** 1 *(quemarse)* to stick: *se me ha vuelto a pegar el arroz* the rice has stuck again. 2 *(persona)* to latch onto.

pegar² *vt* 1 *(golpear)* to hit: *mamá, Pablo me ha pegado* mum, Pablo hit me. 2 *(dar)* to give: *¡vaya susto me has pegado!* you didn't half scare me!

pegatina *nf* sticker.

pego LOC dar el pego *fam* to look like the real thing.

pegote *nm fam (masa)* sticky dollop.

peinado *nm* combing.

peinado,-a *adj* combed.

peinar *vt* 1 *(gen)* to comb; *(con cepillo)* to brush. 2 *(registrar)* to comb, search.

peine *nm* comb.

peineta *nf* ornamental comb.

peladilla *nf* sugared almond.

pelado,-a *adj* 1 bald, bare. 2 *(cabeza)* hairless, bald.

peladuras *nf pl* peelings.

pelaje *nm (de animal)* coat, fur.

pelambrera *nf fam* hair.

pelapatatas *nm inv* potato peeler.

pelar *vt* 1 *(persona)* to cut sb's hair. 2 *(fruta, patata, etc)* to peel.
▶ *vpr* **pelarse** 1 *(cortarse el pelo)* to get one's hair cut. 2 *(piel)* to be peeling.

peldaño *nm* step.

pelea *nf (física)* fight; *(verbal)* quarrel.

peleador,-ra *adj* argumentative.

pelear *vi* to fight, to quarrel, argue.
▶ *vpr* **pelearse** to fight, to quarrel.

peleón,-ona *nm & nf* quarrelsome.

peletería *nf (establecimiento)* fur shop.

peletero,-a *adj (industria)* fur.
▶ *nm & nf* furrier.

peliagudo,-a *adj* tricky.

pelícano *nm* pelican.

película *nf* film. COMP **película de suspense** thriller. ▌ **película muda** silent movie.

peligrar *vi* to be in danger.

peligro *nm* danger. LOC **correr peligro de** to be in danger of. ‖ **estar fuera de peligro** to be out of danger.

peligroso,-a *adj* dangerous.

pelín *nm fam* teeny bit.

pelirrojo,-a *adj* red-haired.

pellejo *nm (piel)* skin.

pelliza *nf (forrada de piel)* fur-lined coat.

pellizcar *vt* to pinch, nip.

pellizco *nm* pinch, nip.

pelo *nm* **1** hair. **2** *(de animal)* coat, fur. **3** *fam* bit: *perdí el tren por un pelo* I missed the train by seconds. LOC **no tener un pelo de tonto,-a** *fam* to be nobody's fool. ‖ **poner los pelos de punta** to make one's hair stand on end. ‖ **tomar el pelo a** ALGN to pull sb's leg.

pelota *nf* ball. COMP **pelota de fútbol** football.
► *nm o nf fam* creep.

pelotazo *nm* blow with a ball.

pelotilla *nf* small ball.

pelotón *nm* **1** *fig (grupo)* bunch. **2** *(de ciclistas)* pack, peloton.

peltre *nm* pewter.

peluca *nf* wig.

peluche *nm (muñeco)* teddy bear.

peludo,-a *adj* hairy.

peluquería *nf* hairdresser's.

peluquero,-a *nm & nf* hairdresser.

peluquín *nm* hairpiece.

pelusa *nf (pelo)* fluff.

pélvico,-a *adj* pelvic.

pelvis *nf inv* pelvis.

pena *nf* **1** *(castigo)* sentence, punishment. **2** *(tristeza)* grief, sorrow. **3** *(lástima)* pity: *¡qué pena que no podáis venir!* it's a shame you can't make it! **4** *(dificultad)* hardship, trouble.

penado,-a *nm & nf* convict.

penal *adj (derecho)* criminal.
► *nm (prisión)* prison, US penitentiary.

penalidad *nf* trouble, hardship.

penalización *nf (acción)* penalization.

penalizar *vt* to penalize.

penalti *nm* penalty.

penar *vt (castigar)* to punish, penalize.
► *vi (padecer)* to suffer, grieve.

pender *vi* to hang (de, from).

pendiente *adj* **1** hanging. **2** *(asunto)* pending, outstanding. LOC **estar pendiente de** ALGO *(a la espera)* to be waiting for STH.
► *nf (cuesta)* slope; *(inclinación)* gradient.
► *nm (joya)* earring.

pendular *adj* pendular.

péndulo *nm* pendulum.

penetración *nf* penetration.

penetrante *adj* penetrating.

penetrar *vi* **1** *(introducirse - en un territorio)* to penetrate (en, -); *(- en propiedad)* to enter. **2** *(atravesar)* to penetrate, seep through: *la humedad ha penetrado por el suelo* damp has seeped through the floor.
► *vt (atravesar)* to penetrate; *(ruido)* to pierce.

penicilina *nf* penicillin.

península *nf* peninsula. COMP **la Península Ibérica** the Iberian Peninsula.

penique *nm* penny.

penitencia *nf* REL *(virtud)* penitence; *(castigo, sacramento)* penance.

penitenciaría *nf* penitentiary.

penitenciario,-a *adj (institución, sistema)* prison.

penoso,-a *adj (doloroso)* painful.

pensador,-ra *adj & nf* thinker.

pensamiento *nm (idea)* thought.

pensante *adj* thinking.

pensar *vi* **1** *(gen)* to think (en, of/about): *estuvo pensando en sus amigos* he was thinking about his friends. **2** *(considerar)* to consider, think (en, about). **3** *(creer)* to think, think about. **4** *(opinar)* to think (de, about). **5** *(decidir)* to decide. **6** *(tener la intención)* to intend to, plan, think of.

pensativo,-a *adj* pensive.

pensión *nf* **1** *(para jubilados)* pension. **2** *(casa de huéspedes)* boarding house. COMP **pensión completa** full board.

pensionista *nm o nf (jubilado)* pensioner.

pentagonal *adj* pentagonal.

pentágono *nm* pentagon.

pentagrama *nm* MÚS stave, staff.

pentatlón *nm* pentathlon.

penúltimo,-a *adj* penultimate.
► *nm & nf* last but one, next to last.

P

penumbra *nf (gen)* semidarkness.

penuria *nf (escasez)* shortage.

peña[1] *nf (piedra)* rock; *(monte)* crag.

peña[2] *nf (grupo)* group of friends; *(asociación)* club.

peñasco *nm* crag.

peñón *nm* craggy rock. `LOC` **el Peñón de Gibraltar** the Rock of Gibraltar.

peón *nm* **1** *(trabajador)* unskilled labourer (us laborer). **2** *(en el ajedrez)* pawn.

peonía *nf* BOT peony.

peonza *nf* top, spinning top.

peor *adj* **1** *(comparativo)* worse: *tu coche es peor que el mío* your car is worse than mine. **2** *(superlativo)* worst.

pepinillo *nm* gherkin.

pepino *nm* cucumber.

pepita *nf (de fruta)* → seed, pip.

peque *nm* kid.

pequeñez *nf* **1** *(de tamaño)* smallness. **2** *(insignificancia)* trifle.

pequeñito,-a *adj fam* teeny, wee.

pequeño,-a *adj* **1** *(de tamaño)* little, small: *este jersey me está pequeño* this jumper is too small for me. **2** *(de edad)* young. **3** *(en tiempo)* short: *nos hemos tomado unas pequeñas vacaciones* we've taken a short holiday.
▶ *nm & nf (niño)* little one: *a esta hora los pequeños tienen que estar en la cama* kids should be in bed by now. `LOC` **de pequeño,-a** as a child.

pequinés,-esa *adj* Pekinese.
▶ *nm* **pekinés** *(perro)* Pekinese.

pera *nf (fruta)* pear.

peral *nm* pear tree.

perca *nf* perch.

percance *nm* mishap.

percatarse *vpr* to notice (de, -).

percebe *nm* goose barnacle.

percepción *nf* perception.

perceptible *adj* perceptible.

perceptivo,-a *adj* perceptive.

percha *nf* **1** *(de ropa)* hanger. **2** *(perchero de pared)* rack; *(gancho)* hook.

perchero *nm (de pie)* coat stand.

percherón,-ona *adj (caballo)* Percheron.

percibir *vt (notar)* to perceive, notice.

percusión *nf* percussion.

percusionista *nm o nf* percussionist.

percutir *vt (golpear)* to strike.

perdedor,-ra *nm & nf* loser.

perder *vt* **1** *(gen)* to lose. **2** *(malgastar, desperdiciar)* to waste: *se pasa el día perdiendo el tiempo* he's always wasting time. **3** *(tren, etc)* to miss.
▶ *vi* **1** *(gen)* to lose; *(salir perdiendo)* to lose out. **2** *(empeorar)* to get worse.
▶ *vpr* **perderse 1** *(extraviarse - persona)* to get lost; *(- cosa, etc)* to go missing: *se me ha perdido un pendiente* I've lost an earring. **2** *(dejar escapar)* to miss: *¡no te lo pierdas!* don't miss it!

perdición *nf (moral)* undoing, ruin.

pérdida *nf* **1** *(daño)* loss: *las tormentas han originado muchas pérdidas materiales* the storms have caused serious damage. **2** *(desperdicio)* waste. **3** *(escape)* leak.

perdido,-a *adj* **1** *(extraviado)* lost. **2** *(desperdiciado)* wasted. **3** *(bala)* stray.

perdigón *nm* pellet.

perdiguero *nm* gun dog.

perdiz *nf* partridge.

perdón *nm* pardon, forgiveness. `LOC` **pedir perdón** to apologize, say sorry.

perdonable *adj* excusable, forgivable.

perdonar *vt* **1** *(gen)* to forgive. **2** *(excusar)* to excuse: *perdona que te interrumpa* excuse me for interrupting. **3** *(deuda)* to write off.

perdurar *vi* to last, continue to exist.

perecedero,-a *adj* perishable.

perecer *vi* to perish, die.

peregrinación *nf* pilgrimage.

peregrinar *vi* to go on a pilgrimage.

peregrino,-a *nm & nf* REL pilgrim.

perejil *nm* parsley.

perenne *adj* perennial.

pereza *nf* laziness. `LOC` **tener pereza** to feel lazy.

perezoso,-a *adj* lazy.
▶ *nm* **perezoso** ZOOL sloth.

perfección *nf* perfection. `LOC` **a la perfección** perfectly: *habla inglés a la perfección* he speaks perfect English.

perfeccionar *vt* **1** *(mejorar)* to improve. **2** *(hacer perfecto)* to perfect.

perfeccionista *adj* perfectionist.
▶ *nm o nf* perfectionist.

perfecto,-a *adj* perfect.

perfidia *nf* perfidy.

pérfido,-a *adj* perfidious.

perfil *nm* **1** *(gen)* profile. **2** *(silueta)* outline.

perfilar *vt* *(dar forma)* to outline.

perforación *nf* *(gen)* perforation.

perforadora *nf* **1** *(en una mina)* drill. **2** *(de papeles)* punch.

perforar *vt* **1** *(gen)* to perforate. **2** *(terreno)* to drill, bore. **3** *(papel)* to punch.

perfumar *vt* to perfume, scent.

perfume *nm* perfume.

perfumería *nf* *(tienda)* perfumery.

pergamino *nm* parchment.

pérgola *nf* pergola.

pericardio *nm* pericardium.

pericarpio *nm* pericarp.

pericia *nf* skill.

periferia *nf* *(de una ciudad)* outskirts *pl*.

periférico,-a *adj* **1** *(gen)* peripheral. **2** *(barrio, zona)* outlying.
▶ *nm* **periférico** INFORM peripheral unit.

perifollo *nm* BOT common chervil.

perífrasis *nf* periphrasis.

perifrástico,-a *adj* periphrastic.

perilla *nf* goatee.

perímetro *nm* perimeter.

periodicidad *nf* periodicity.

periódico,-a *adj* periodical.
▶ *nm* **periódico** newspaper.

periodismo *nm* journalism.

periodista *nm o nf* journalist.

período *nm* period.

peripecia *nf* incident.

peripuesto,-a *adj fam* all dressed up.

periquito,-a *nm o nf* parakeet.

periscopio *nm* periscope.

peristilo *nm* peristyle.

peritaje *nm* *(informe)* expert's report.

perito,-a *nm & nf (experto)* expert.

perjudicado,-a *nm & nf* person who loses out, person affected: *los más perjudicados han sido los campesinos* farmers have been worst affected.

perjudicar *vt* to adversely affect.

perjudicial *adj* harmful.

perjuicio *nm (material)* damage; *(económico)* loss.

perjurio *nm* perjury.

perla *nf* **1** pearl. **2** *fig* gem.

permanecer *vi* to stay, remain.

permanencia *nf (estancia)* stay.

permanente *adj* permanent, lasting.

permanganato *nm* permanganate.

permeabilidad *nf* permeability.

permeable *adj* permeable.

permisividad *nf* permissiveness.

permisivo,-a *adj* permissive.

permiso *nm* **1** permission. **2** *(documento)* permit. **3** leave. COMP **permiso de conducir** driving licence, US driver's licence.

permitir *vt* to allow, let: *permitió que sus hijas fueran al concierto* he let his daughters go to the concert.
▶ *vpr* **permitirse** to allow US, afford. LOC **¿me permite?** may I?

permuta *nf* exchange.

permutación *nf* permutation.

permutar *vt* **1** to exchange. **2** MAT to permute.

pernicioso,-a *adj* pernicious, harmful.

pernoctar *vi* to spend the night.

pero *conj* but.

perol *nm* cooking pot.

peroné *nm* fibula.

perorata *nf* spiel.

peróxido *nm* peroxide. COMP **peróxido de hidrógeno** hydrogen peroxide.

perpendicular *adj* perpendicular.

perpetrar *vt* to perpetrate, commit.

perpetuación *nf* perpetuation.

perpetuar *vt* to perpetuate.
▶ *vpr* **perpetuarse** to be perpetuated.

perpetuidad *nf* perpetuity.

perpetuo,-a *adj (gen)* perpetual; *(cargo)* permanent. COMP **nieves perpetuas** perpetual snows.

perplejidad *nf* perplexity.

perplejo,-a *adj* perplexed.

perrera *nf (lugar)* dog pound.

perro,-a *nm* perro ZOOL dog. [COMP] **perro caliente** hot dog. ▌ **perro pastor** sheepdog.

persecución *nf* 1 pursuit. 2 *(represión)* persecution.

perseguidor,-ora *nm & nf* pursuer.

perseguir *vt* 1 to pursue, chase. 2 *fig (seguir)* to follow: *este perro me persigue* this dog follows me everywhere.

perseverante *adj* persevering.

perseverar *vi* to persevere.

persiana *nf* blind.

persignarse *vpr* to cross OS.

persistente *adj* persistent.

persistir *vi (mantenerse firme)* to persist, persevere.

persona *nf* person. [LOC] **en persona** in person.

personaje *nm* 1 *(famoso)* celebrity. 2 *(en obra, película)* character.

personal *nm (de una empresa)* staff.

personalidad *nf (carácter)* personality.

personalizar *vt* to personalize.
▶ *vi* to get personal.

personarse *vpr* to appear in person.

personificación *nf* personification.

personificar *vt* to personify.

perspectiva *nf* 1 ARTE perspective. 2 *(posibilidad)* prospect: *este negocio presenta muy buenas perspectivas* this business has good prospects. 3 *(vista)* view, perspective. 4 *(punto de vista)* point of view.

perspicacia *nf* sharpness.

perspicaz *adj* sharp, perspicacious.

persuadir *vt* to persuade, convince.
▶ *vpr* **persuadirse** to be convinced.

persuasión *nf* persuasion.

persuasivo,-a *adj* persuasive.

pertenecer *vi* to belong (a, to).

perteneciente *adj* belonging (a, to).

pertenencia *nf* 1 *(propiedad)* property: *esto es de mi pertenencia* this belongs to me. 2 *(afiliación)* membership.
▶ *nf pl* **pertenencias** *(bienes)* belongings.

pértiga *nf* pole. [COMP] **salto de pértiga** pole vault.

pertinaz *adj* 1 *(sequía, frío)* prolonged, persistent. 2 *(persona)* obstinate.

pertinente *adj* 1 *(oportuno)* appropriate. 2 *(relevante)* pertinent, relevant.

pertrechar *vt* to supply (de, with).
▶ *vpr* **pertrecharse** to equip OS.

pertrechos *nm pl* equipment *sing.*

perturbación *nf* disruption.

perturbado,-a *adj* 1 *(trastornado)* mentally disturbed. 2 *(intranquilo)* perturbed.

perturbar *vt* 1 *(alterar)* to disturb, perturb. 2 *(inquietar)* to perturb.

Perú *nm* Peru.

peruano,-a *adj* Peruvian.
▶ *nm & nf* Peruvian.

perversidad *nf (maldad)* wickedness.

perversión *nf* disruption.

perverso,-a *adj (malvado)* evil, wicked.
▶ *nm & nf* evil person.

pervertir *vt (gen)* to corrupt.

pervivencia *nf* survival.

pervivir *vi* to live on, persist.

pesa *nf* weight.

pesadez *nf* 1 *(lentitud)* sluggishness. 2 *(molestia)* bore.

pesadilla *nf* nightmare.

pesado,-a *adj* 1 *(gen)* heavy. 2 *(molesto)* tiresome; *(aburrido)* boring.
▶ *nm & nf (persona)* bore, pain. [LOC] **ponerse pesado,-a** to get boring.

pesadumbre *nf* sorrow, grief.

pésame *nm* condolences *pl.* [LOC] **dar el pésame** to offer your condolences.

pesar *vi* 1 to weigh: *¿cuánto pesas?* how much do you weigh? 2 *(tener mucho peso)* to be heavy. 3 *(sentir)* to be sorry, regret: *me pesa mucho no haberle invitado* I really regret not having invited him.
▶ *vt* to weigh.
▶ *nm (pena)* sorrow, grief. [LOC] **a pesar de** despite, in spite of.

pesca *nf (actividad)* fishing.

pescadería *nf* fishmonger's.

pescadero,-a *nm & nf* fishmonger.

pescadilla *nf* young hake.

pescado *nm* fish. [COMP] **pescado azul** blue fish. ▌ **pescado blanco** white fish.

pescador *nm & nf* fisherman.

pescar *vi (ir a pescar)* to fish, go fishing. [LOC] **ir a pescar** to go fishing.
▶ *vt* **1** *(sacar del agua)* to get, catch. **2** *fam (agarrar)* catch: *he pescado un buen resfriado* I've caught a really nasty cold.

pescuezo *nm* neck.

pesebre *nm* manger, stall.

pesimismo *nm* pessimism.

pesimista *adj* pessimistic.
▶ *nm o nf* pessimist.

pésimo,-a *adj* dreadful, awful.

peso *nm* **1** *(gen)* weight. **2** *(balanza)* scales *pl*. **3** *(carga)* load, burden. [LOC] **de peso 1** *(pesado)* heavy. **2** *(importante)* important. **3** *(convincente)* strong, powerful.

pespunte *nm* backstitch.

pesquero,-a *nm* fishing boat.

pesquisa *nf* inquiry.

pestaña *nf (del ojo)* eyelash.

pestañear *vi* to blink.

peste *nf (mal olor)* stink, stench.

pesticida *nm* pesticide.

pestilente *adj (apestoso)* stinking.

pestillo *nm* bolt. [LOC] **cerrar con pestillo** to bolt.

pétalo *nm* petal.

petanca *nf* petanque, boules.

petardo *nm (de verbena)* firecracker.

petate *nm (de soldado, marinero)* kit bag.

petición *nf* **1** *(gen)* request. **2** plea.

petirrojo *nm* robin.

peto *nm (pantalón)* pair of dungarees.

pétreo,-a *adj* stony.

petrificar *vt (fosilizar)* to petrify.

petróleo *nm* oil.

petrolero,-a *adj* oil.
▶ *nm* **petrolero** oil tanker.

petrolífero,-a *adj* oil-bearing.

petroquímica *nf* petrochemistry.

petroquímico,-a *adj* petrochemical.

petulancia *nf* vanity.

petulante *adj* vain.

petunia *nf* petunia.

peyorativo,-a *adj* pejorative.

pez *nm* fish.

pezón *nm* nipple.

pezuña *nf* hoof.

piadoso,-a *adj* pious, devout.

pianista *nm o nf* pianist.

piano *nm* piano.

pianola® *nf* Pianola.

piar *vi* to chirp, tweet.

piara *nf* herd of pigs.

pica *nf* **1** *(lanza)* pike. **2** *(de la baraja)* spade.

picada *nf (picadura - de avispa)* sting; *(- de mosquito)* bite.

picadero *nm (escuela)* riding school.

picadillo *nm (de carne)* minced meat; *(de verduras)* chopped vegetables.

picado,-a *adj* **1** CULIN *(cortado - verdura)* finely chopped; *(- carne)* minced. **2** *(diente)* decayed. **3** *fam (ofendido)* offended.

picador *nm (minero)* face worker.

picadora *nf* mincer.

picadura *nf (de insecto, serpiente)* bite; *(de abeja, avispa)* sting.

picante *adj* **1** *(comida)* hot. **2** *fig (chiste)* spicy.

picapedrero *nm* stonecutter.

picaporte *nm* **1** *(para llamar)* door knocker. **2** *(para abrir)* door handle.

picar *vt* **1** *(morder - insecto)* to bite; *(- abeja, avispa)* to sting. **2** *(perforar - papel, tarjeta)* to punch. **3** *(dar con un pico)* to jab, goad. **4** CULIN *(cortar)* to chop finely; *(carne)* to mince. **5** *(comida)* to nibble: *vamos a salir a picar algo* we're going to get a bite to eat.
▶ *vi* **1** *(sentir escozor)* to itch: *me pica todo el cuerpo* I'm itching all over. **2** *(estar picante)* to be hot. **3** *(pez)* to bite; *(persona)* to fall for it. **4** *(comer)* to have a nibble.
▶ *vpr* **picarse 1** *(muela)* to decay, go bad. **2** *(mar)* to get choppy. **3** *(ofenderse)* to take offence.

picardía *nf (astucia)* craftiness.

picaresco,-a *nf* picaresque genre.

pícaro,-a *adj (astuto)* crafty, sly.
▶ *nm & nf (persona astuta)* slyboots.

picazón *nf (picor)* itch.

pichichi *nm (goleador)* top goal scorer.

P

pichón,-ona *nm & nf* pigeon.

pico *nm* **1** *(de ave)* beak. **2** *(herramienta)* pickaxe, pick. **3** *(de montaña)* peak. **4** *(punta)* corner. `LOC` **y pico** *(cantidad)*: *llegaremos sobre las seis y pico* we'll be there just after six.

picor *nm* itch.

picotazo *nm* **1** *(de ave)* peck. **2** *(de insecto, reptil)* bite; *(de abeja, avispa)* sting.

picotear *vt* to peck, peck at.

picoteo *nm* **1** *(de ave)* pecking. **2** *(acción de comer)* nibbling, snacking.

pictórico,-a *adj* pictorial.

picudo,-a *adj* pointed.

pie *nm* **1** ANAT foot. **2** *(base - de una lámpara)* base; *(- de una escultura)* plinth. **3** *(medida de longitud)* foot. `LOC` **a pie** on foot. **I ponerse de pie** to get to one's feet, stand up.

piedad *nf (misericordia)* pity, mercy.

piedra *nf* stone. `COMP` **piedra preciosa** gem, precious stone.

piel *nf* **1** *(de persona)* skin. **2** *(de la fruta, patatas)* peel.

pienso *nm* fodder.

pierna *nf* leg.

pieza *nf* **1** *(gen)* piece; *(de un aparato)* part. **2** MÚS piece, piece of music. **3** TEAT play. **4** *(de un juego de tablero)* piece.

pigmentación *nf* pigmentation.

pigmento *nm* pigment.

pigmeo,-a *adj (raza)* Pygmy.
► *nm & nf (raza)* Pygmy.

pijama *nm* pyjamas (US pajamas) *pl*.

pila *nf* **1** ELEC battery. **2** *(de fregar)* sink. **3** *fam (montón)* pile, heap: *tengo una pila de cosas que hacer* I've got piles of work to do. `LOC` **ponerse las pilas** *fam* to get one's act together.

pilar *nm* pillar.

pilastra *nf* pilaster.

píldora *nf* pill, tablet.

pileta *nf* AM swimming pool.

pillaje *nm* looting.

pillar *vt* **1** *(coger)* to catch. **2** *fam (robar)* to nick. **3** *fam (atropellar)* to run over. **4** *fam (entender)* to catch, get, grasp.
► *vi fam (encontrarse)* to be: *me pilla muy cerca de casa* it's very near home.

pillo,-a *nm & nf (niño)* little monkey, little devil.

pilón *nm (de una fuente)* basin.

píloro *nm* pylorus.

pilotar *vt (avión)* to pilot, fly; *(coche)* to drive; *(barco)* to sail.

pilote *nm* pile.

piloto *nm (conductor - de avión)* pilot; *(- de coche)* driver; *(- de barco)* pilot.

pimentero *nm* **1** *(recipiente)* pepper pot. **2** *(planta)* pepper plant.

pimentón *nm* paprika. `COMP` **pimentón picante** cayenne pepper.

pimienta *nf (especia)* pepper.

pimiento *nm (gen)* pepper; *(rojo)* red pepper; *(verde)* green pepper.

pinacoteca *nf* art gallery.

pináculo *nm* pinnacle.

pinar *nm* pine grove.

pincel *nm* paintbrush.

pincelada *nf* brush stroke.

pinchadiscos *nm o nf* disc jockey, DJ.

pinchar *vt* **1** *(punzar)* to prick. **2** MED *(poner inyección)* to give an injection. **3** *(sujetar)* to spear, jab. **4** *(enfadar)* to needle.

pinchazo *nm* **1** *(de neumático)* puncture. **2** *(inyección)* injection, jab, US shot.

pinche *nm & nf (de cocina)* kitchen assistant.

pincho *nm* **1** *(de una planta)* thorn. **2** *(de un erizo)* spine, prickle. **3** *(de aperitivo)* snack. **4** *(brocheta)* skewer. `COMP` **pincho moruno** shish kebab.

pineda *nf* pine grove.

pingo *nm fam (de ropa)* rag.

ping-pong *nm* table tennis, ping-pong.

pingüe *adj* substantial.

pingüino *nm* penguin.

pino *nm (árbol)* pine tree; *(madera)* pine.

pinta *nf* **1** *(mancha)* dot. **2** *(medida)* pint. **3** *fam (aspecto)* look.

pintada *nf* graffiti.

pintado,-a *adj (maquillado)* made-up.

pintalabios *nm inv* lipstick.

pintar *vt* **1** *(gen)* to paint; *(dibujar)* to draw. **2** *(maquillar)* to make up.
► *vi* **1** *(gen)* to paint. **2** *(marcar)* to write.

▶ *vpr* **pintarse** *(maquillarse)* to put one's make up on.
pintarrajear *vt fam* to daub.
pintarrajo *nm fam* daub.
pintaúñas *nm inv* nail varnish.
pinto,-a *adj* spotted.
pintor,-ra *nm & nf* artist, painter.
pintoresco,-a *adj* **1** *(lugar)* picturesque. **2** *(persona)* bizarre.
pintura *nf* **1** *(arte)* painting. **2** *(producto)* paint: *un bote de pintura* a tin of paint.
pinza *nf* **1** *(de cangrejo)* pincer. **2** *(de la ropa)* clothes peg.
▶ *nf pl* **pinzas 1** *(de depilar)* tweezers. **2** *(de servir hielo)* tongs.
pinzamiento *nm* trapped nerve.
pinzón *nm* finch.
piña *nf* **1** *(fruta)* pineapple. **2** *(del pino)* pine cone.
piñata *nf hollow figure filled with sweets (which children try to break open at parties)*.
piñón *nm (comestible)* pine nut kernel.
pío *nm* chirp.
pío,-a *adj* pious.
piojo *nm* louse.
piolet *nm* ice axe (US ax).
pionero,-a *nm & nf* pioneer.
pipa¹ *nf (de tabaco)* pipe.
pipa² *nf (de girasol)* sunflower seed.
pipeta *nf* pipette.
pique *nm (rivalidad)* rivalry, needle.
piqueta *nf* pickaxe.
piquete *nm (de huelga)* picket.
pira *nf* pyre.
pirado,-a *adj fam (loco)* loony, wacky.
piragua *nf* canoe.
piragüismo *nm* canoeing.
piragüista *nm o nf* canoeist.
piramidal *adj* pyramidal.
pirámide *nf* pyramid.
piraña *nf* piranha.
pirata *adj* pirate.
▶ *nm o nf (de la informática)* hacker.
piratear *vt* **1** *(gen)* to pirate. **2** *(informática)* to hack.
piratería *nf (gen)* piracy.
pirita *nf* pyrite.

pirómano,-a *nm & nf* pyromaniac.
piropear *vt* to make flirtatious comments to.
piropo *nm* compliment.
pirotecnia *nf* fireworks *pl*.
pirotécnico,-a *adj* pyrotechnic.
▶ *nm & nf* fireworks expert.
pirueta *nf* pirouette.
piruleta *nf* lollipop.
pirulí *nm fam (de caramelo)* lollipop.
pisada *nf (huella)* footprint.
pisapapeles *nm inv* paperweight.
pisar *vt* **1** *(gen)* to tread on. **2** *(acelerador, embrague)* to put one's foot on. **3** *fig (entrar)* to set foot in.
▶ *vi* to tread, walk, step: *no pises muy fuerte que nos oyen los vecinos* tread more quietly, the neighbours will hear us.
piscifactoría *nf* fish farm.
piscina *nf* swimming pool.
piso *nm* **1** *(para vivir)* flat. **2** *(planta)* floor.
pisotear *vt (pisar)* to trample.
pisotón *nm* stamp.
pista *nf* **1** *(rastro)* trail, track. **2** *(indicio)* clue. **3** *(de baile)* dance floor. **4** *(camino)* track. **5** *(de tenis)* court. **6** *(de circo)* ring. **7** *(de aterrizaje)* runway. COMP **pista de esquí** ski slope.
pistachero *nm* pistachio tree.
pistacho *nm* pistachio (nut).
pistilo *nm* pistil.
pistola *nf* gun.
pistolera *nf* holster.
pistolero *nm* gunman.
pistoletazo *nm* gunshot.
pistón *nm (de un motor)* piston.
pita *nf* BOT pita.
pitada *nf* **1** *(bocinazo)* hoot. **2** *(pitido)* whistle.
pitar *vi* **1** *(silbar)* to blow a whistle. **2** *(tocar la bocina)* to hoot. **3** *(abuchear)* to boo and hiss. LOC **ir/irse pitando** *fam* to rush out, dash off.
▶ *vt* DEP *(falta)* to whistle.
pitido *nm* **1** *(silbido)* whistle. **2** *(bocinazo)* hoot, honk.
pitillera *nf* cigarette case.
pitillo *nm* cigarette.

P

pito *nm (silbato)* whistle.

pitón¹ *nf* ZOOL python.

pitón² *nm (del toro)* horn.

pitonisa *nf* fortune teller.

pitorro *nm* spout.

pituitaria *nf* pituitary (gland).

pívot *nm o nf* centre.

pivotar *vi* to pivot.

pivote *nm* pivot.

pizarra *nf* 1 *(mineral)* slate. 2 *(para escribir)* blackboard.

pizca *nf fam (gen)* bit; *(de sal)* pinch.

pizza *nf* pizza.

pizzería *nf* pizzeria, pizza parlour.

placa *nf* 1 *(de metal)* sheet. 2 *(con el nombre)* plaque. 3 *(de matrícula)* number plate. 4 *(de hielo)* sheet.

placaje *nm* tackle.

placar *vt (en rugby)* to tackle.

placebo *nm* placebo.

placenta *nf* placenta.

placentero,-a *adj* pleasant.

placer *nm* pleasure.
  ▶ *vi* to please: *haz lo que te plazca* do as you please.

placidez *nf* placidity.

plácido,-a *adj* placid, calm.

plafón *nm (lámpara de techo)* ceiling light.

plaga *nf* 1 *(epidemia)* plague. 2 *(de insectos)* plague, pest. 3 *fig* invasion.

plagar *vt* to plague, infest.

plagiar *vt* to plagiarize.

plagio *nm* plagiarism.

plaguicida *nm* pesticide.

plan *nm* 1 *(intención)* plan. 2 *(programa)* project.

plana *nf (página)* page: *la noticia viene en primera plana* the news is on the front page.

plancha *nf* 1 *(de metal)* plate. 2 *(electrodoméstico)* iron. LOC **a la plancha** grilled.

planchado,-a *nm (acción)* ironing.

planchar *vt* to iron, press.

planchista *nm o nf* panel beater.

plancton *nm* plankton.

planeador *nm* glider.

planear *vt (futuro, idea)* to plan.
  ▶ *vi (en el aire)* to glide.

planeo *nm* gliding, glide.

planeta *nm* planet.

planetario,-a *adj* planetary.
  ▶ *nm* **planetario** planetarium.

planicie *nf* plain.

planificación *nf* planning.

planificador,-ra *adj* planning.
  ▶ *nm & nf* planner.

planificar *vt* to plan.

plano,-a *adj (superficie)* flat.
  ▶ *nm* **plano** 1 *(de una ciudad)* street plan, map. 2 *(de una casa)* plan. 3 *(nivel)* level. 4 MAT plane.

planta *nf* 1 BOT plant. 2 *(del pie)* sole. 3 *(de un edificio)* floor. COMP **planta baja** ground floor, US first floor.

plantación *nf* 1 *(terreno)* plantation. 2 *(acción)* planting.

plantar *vt* 1 AGR to plant. 2 *(colocar - gen)* to put, place; *(- tienda de campaña)* to pitch, put up.
  ▶ *vpr* **plantarse** *fam (colocarse)* to place OS, position OS: *se plantó en la esquina* she positioned herself on the corner.

plante *nm (laboral)* protest action.

planteamiento *nm* 1 MAT *(formulación - de un problema)* formulation.

plantear *vt* 1 *(pregunta)* to pose, raise. 2 *(problema)* to cause. 3 MAT *(problema)* to formulate.
  ▶ *vpr* **plantearse** to consider.

plantel *nm* cadre.

plantilla *nf* 1 *(patrón)* model, pattern. 2 *(personal)* staff.

plantón LOC **darle plantón a** ALGN *fam (no presentarse)* to stand SB up.

plañidero,-a *adj* plaintive, mournful.

plañir *vi* to mourn.

plaqueta *nf (de sangre)* platelet.

plasma *nm* plasma.

plasmar *vt fig* to give expression to.

plastelina *nf* Plasticine.

plástica *nf* plastic arts *pl*.

plasticidad *nf* plasticity.

plástico,-a *adj* plastic.
  ▶ *nm* **plástico** *(material)* plastic.

plastificado,-a *adj* laminated.

plastificar *vt* to laminate.

plastilina® *nf* Plasticine®.

plata *nf* silver.

plataforma *nf* platform. COMP plataforma petrolífera oil rig.

platanal *nm* banana plantation.

platanero,-a *nm* banana tree.

plátano *nm* banana.

platea *nf* stalls *pl*.

plateado,-a *adj (color)* silvery.

platear *vt* to silver-plate.

plateresco,-a *adj* plateresque.

platería *nf (taller)* silversmith's.

platero,-a *nm & nf* silversmith.

plática *nf* talk.

platicar *vi* to chat, talk.

platillo *nm* **1** *(de postre)* dessert plate; *(de café)* saucer. COMP platillo volante flying saucer.

platina *nf* MÚS → pletina.

platino *nm* platinum.

plato *nm* **1** *(recipiente)* plate, dish. **2** CULIN dish. **3** *(en comida)* course: *de primer plato hay sopa* we've got soup for starters.

plató *nm (de cine)* set, film set; *(de televisión)* floor.

platónico,-a *adj* platonic.

plausible *adj (probable)* plausible.

playa *nf* **1** *(superficie de arena)* beach. **2** *(costa)* seaside.

playeras *nf pl* canvas shoes.

plaza *nf* **1** *(de una población)* square. **2** *(mercado)* marketplace. **3** *(puesto de trabajo)* position. COMP plaza de parking parking space.

plazo *nm* **1** *(periodo de tiempo)* time. **2** *(de compra)* instalment, US installment. LOC comprar ALGO a plazos to buy STH on hire purchase, US buy STH on an installment plan.

plazoleta *nf* small square.

pleamar *nf* high tide.

plebe *nf (gen)* common people.

plebeyo,-a *nm & nf* plebeian.

plebiscito *nm* plebiscite.

plegable *adj* folding, collapsible.

plegamiento *nm* folding.

plegar *vt* to fold.
  ▶ *vpr* **plegarse** to yield, give in.

plegaria *nf* prayer.

pleitear *vi* to sue.

pleito *nm* litigation, lawsuit.

plenamente *adv* fully.

plenario,-a *adj* plenary.

plenilunio *nm* full moon.

plenitud *nf (sensación física)* fullness.

pleno,-a *adj (gen)* full, complete: *en pleno centro de la ciudad* right in the centre of the city.

pleonasmo *nm* pleonasm.

pletina *nf* deck, cassette deck.

pletórico,-a *adj* full. LOC pletórico de alegría jubilant, euphoric.

pleura *nf* pleura.

plexiglás® *nm* Perspex®.

plexo *nm* plexus.

pliego *nm (papel)* sheet of paper.

pliegue *nm* **1** fold. **2** *(en la ropa)* pleat.

plinto *nm (en gimnasia)* vaulting horse.

plisado,-a *adj* pleated.

plomada *nf* **1** *(de albañil)* plumb line. **2** *(sonda)* lead. **3** *(para pescar)* weights *pl*.

plomazo *nm o nf fam* bore.

plomizo,-a *adj (color)* lead-coloured.

plomo *nm* **1** lead. **2** *(pesa)* lead weight. **3** ELEC fuse. **4** *fam fig* bore. LOC sin plomo *(gasolina)* unleaded, lead-free.

pluma *nf* **1** *(de ave)* feather. **2** *(de escribir)* fountain pen.

plumaje *nm (de ave)* plumage.

plumero *nm (para el polvo)* feather duster.

plumilla *nf* nib.

plumón *nm* **1** *(de un ave)* down. **2** *(anorak)* down-filled anorak.

plural *adj* plural.
  ▶ *nm* plural.

pluralidad *nf (gen)* multiplicity; *(diversidad)* diversity.

pluralismo *nm* pluralism.

pluralista *adj* pluralist.

pluralizar *vt* LING to pluralize.
  ▶ *vi (generalizar)* to generalize.

pluriempleo *nm having more than one job.*

plurilingüe *adj* multilingual.

pluscuamperfecto *nm* pluperfect.

plusmarca *nf* record.

P

plusmarquista *nm o nf* record holder.
plusvalía *nf* **1** *(aumento)* appreciation. **2** *(impuesto)* capital gains tax.
plutocracia *nf* plutocracy.
Plutón *nm* Pluto.
plutonio *nm* plutonium.
pluvial *adj* rain, pluvial.
pluviómetro *nm* rain gauge.
pluviosidad *nf* rainfall.
población *nf* **1** *(número de habitantes)* population. **2** *(lugar - ciudad)* town; *(- pueblo)* village.
poblado,-a *adj* *(zona)* populated.
poblamiento *nm* settlement.
poblar *vt* **1** *(ocupar territorio)* to settle. **2** *(habitar)* to inhabit. **3** *(llenar)* to fill: *han poblado de árboles el campo* they've planted the field with trees.
pobre *adj* **1** *(gen)* poor. **2** *(infeliz)* poor.
▶ *nm o nf* **1** *(con poco dinero)* poor person; *(mendigo)* beggar. **2** *(infeliz)* poor thing: *la pobre se cree que le van a devolver el dinero* the poor thing thinks she is going to get her money back.
pobreza *nf* *(escasez de dinero)* poverty.
pocilga *nf* pigsty.
pócima *nf* *(preparado)* potion.
poción *nf* potion.
poco,-a *adj* little; *(plural)* few, not many: *hago muy poco ejercicio últimamente* I do very little exercise these days. LOC **hace poco** not long ago. ‖ **poco antes** shortly before. ‖ **poco después** shortly afterwards. ‖ **por poco** nearly.
▶ *pron* **poco** little; *(en plural)* not many: *lo poco que aprendí se me ha olvidado* what little I learned I've forgotten.
▶ *adv* little, not much: *voy poco por allí* I rarely go there.
▶ *nm* **un poco** a little, a bit: *¿me das un poco?* could you give me a little?
poda *nf* pruning.
podadera *nf* pruning shears *pl*.
podar *vt* to prune.
podenco *nm* hound.
poder *vt* **1** *(de facultad)* can, be able to: *¿puedes echarme una mano?* can you lend me a hand?; *no pude abrirlo* I couldn't open it, I was unable to open it. **2** *(de per-*

miso) may, can: *pueden pagar en efectivo o con tarjeta* you can pay in cash or by credit card; *puede retirarse* you may leave. **3** *(conjetura)* may, might: *podría haberlo dejado sobre la mesa* I may have left it on the table. **4** *(sugerencias)* can: *podríamos ir a esquiar* we could go skiing. LOC **puede que** maybe, perhaps: *puede que venga más tarde* she may come later.
▶ *vi (superar)* to be stronger than: *tú puedes a todos* you can beat all of them.
▶ *nm* **1** *(gen)* power. **2** *(posesión)* possession, hands *pl*: *la pelota está ahora en mi poder* the ball is now in my hands.
poderío *nm* *(autoridad)* power.
poderoso,-a *adj* powerful.
podio *nm* podium.
podólogo,-a *nm & nf* chiropodist.
podredumbre *nf* rottenness.
podrido,-a *adj* **1** rotten. **2** *fig* corrupt.
poema *nm* poem.
poesía *nf* **1** poetry. **2** *(poema)* poem.
poeta *nm o nf* poet.
poético,-a *adj* poetic.
poetisa *nf* poetess.
polaco,-a *adj* Polish.
▶ *nm & nf (persona)* Pole.
▶ *nm* **polaco** *(idioma)* Polish.
polar *adj* polar. COMP **estrella polar** Pole Star, Polaris.
polaridad *nf* polarity.
polarizar *vt* **1** Fís to polarize. **2** *(atención)* to focus.
polaroid® *nf* Polaroid.
polea *nf* pulley.
polémica *nf* controversy.
polémico,-a *adj* controversial.
polemizar *vi* to debate.
polen *nm* pollen.
poleo *nm* **1** *(planta)* pennyroyal. **2** *(infusión)* mint tea.
policía *nf* police, police force.
▶ *nm o nf (gen)* police officer; *(hombre)* policeman; *(mujer)* policewoman.
policíaco,-a *adj* detective.
policial *adj* police.
policromía *nf* polychromy.
policromo,-a *adj* polychrome.

polideportivo *nm* sports centre.

poliedro *nm* polyhedron.

poliéster *nm* polyester.

poliestireno *nm* polystyrene.

polietileno *nm* polythene.

polifacético,-a *adj* versatile.

polifónico,-a *adj* polyphonic.

poligamia *nf* polygamy.

polígamo,-a *adj* polygamous.
► *nm & nf* polygamist.

polígloto,-a *adj* polyglot.
► *nm & nf* polyglot.

poligonal *adj* polygonal.

polígono *nm* **1** *(figura)* polygon. **2** *(gen)* area. [COMP] **polígono industrial** industrial estate.

polígrafo,-a *nm & nf* polygraph.

poliinsaturado,-a *adj* polyunsaturated.

polilla *nf* moth.

polímero *nm* polymer.

polimorfo,-a *adj* polymorphic.

polinización *nf* pollination.

polinizar *vt* to pollinate.

polinomio *nm* polynomial.

poliomielitis *nf inv* poliomyelitis.

polisemia *nf* polysemy.

polisémico,-a *adj* polysemous.

polisílabo,-a *adj* polysyllabic.

politécnico,-a *adj* *(gen)* polytechnic.
► *nm* **politécnico** *(instituto)* technical college.

politeísmo *nm* polytheism.

politeísta *adj* polytheistic.
► *nm o nf* polytheist.

política *nf* politics.

político,-a *adj* **1** political. **2** *(por matrimonio)* -in-law: *madre política* mother-in-law; *padre político* father-in-law.
► *nm & nf* politician.

politizar *vt* to politicize.

poliuretano *nm* polyurethane.

polivalente *adj fig (versátil)* versatile.

polivinilo *nm* polyvinyl.

póliza *nf* **1** *(de seguros)* policy. **2** *(sello)* official tax stamp.

polizón *nm* stowaway.

pollera *nf* AM skirt.

pollería *nf (tienda)* poultry shop; *(sección de supermercado)* poultry section.

pollino,-a *nm & nf* ZOOL donkey.

pollo *nm* chicken.

polluelo *nm* chick.

polo *nm* **1** TÉC pole. **2** *(caramelo)* ice lolly. **3** DEP polo. [COMP] **Polo Norte** North Pole. ‖ **Polo Sur** South Pole.

Polonia *nf* Poland.

poltrona *nf* easy chair.

poltrón,-ona *adj* lazy.

polución *nf (atmosférica)* pollution.

polucionar *vt* to pollute.

polvareda *nf (de polvo)* cloud of dust.

polvera *nf* (powder) compact.

polvo *nm* **1** *(suciedad)* dust. **2** *(medicamento, etc)* powder. [LOC] **en polvo** **1** *(leche, cacao)* powdered. **2** *(nieve)* powdery. [COMP] **polvos de talco** talcum powder *sing*.

pólvora *nf* gunpowder.

polvoriento,-a *adj* dusty.

pomada *nf* cream.

pomelo *nm (fruto)* grapefruit; *(árbol)* grapefruit tree.

pómez *nf* pumice stone.

pomo *nm (de puerta)* knob.

pompa *nf* **1** *(de jabón, chicle)* bubble. **2** *(ostentación)* pomp. [COMP] **pompas de jabón** soap bubbles.

pomposo,-a *adj* pompous.

pómulo *nm* **1** *(hueso)* cheekbone. **2** *(mejilla)* cheek.

ponche *nm* punch.

ponderado,-a *adj (prudente)* measured.

ponderar *vt* **1** *(sopesar)* to ponder, consider, think over, weigh up. **2** *(alabar)* to praise highly.

ponedero *nm* nest box.

ponedora *adj (gallina)* laying.

ponencia *nf (académica)* paper; *(parlamentaria)* address, speech.

ponente *nm o nf* speaker.

poner *vt* **1** *(gen)* to place, put, set. **2** *(prenda)* to put on: *me pondré el pantalón negro* I'll put my black trousers on, I'll wear my black trousers. **3** *(encender)* to turn on, put on: *puso la radio* she put the radio on. **4** *(programar)* to set: *he*

P

puesto el despertador a las siete I've set the alarm clock for seven. **5** *(escribir)* to put, write: *pon tu nombre aquí* put your name here. **6** *(decir)* to say: *¿qué pone ese letrero?* what does that sign say? **7** *(en cine, televisión)* to show: *lo ponen mañana a las tres* it's on tomorrow at three o'clock. **8** *(dar nombre)* to name, call: *le pusieron Laura* they called her Laura. **9** *(dinero)* to put in: *pusimos veinte euros cada uno* we put in twenty euros each. **10** *(telegrama, fax)* to send; *(nota)* to leave. **11** *(deber, multa)* to give: *nos han puesto deberes para las vacaciones* they've given us homework for the holidays. **12 poner + *adj*** to make, turn: *la has puesto triste* you've made her sad.

▶ *vpr* **ponerse 1** *(sol)* to set. **2** *(volverse)* to become, get, turn: *se puso muy contenta con la noticia* the news made her very happy. **3** *(contestar al teléfono)* to answer the phone; *(hablar por teléfono)* to come to the phone: *en este momento no se puede poner* he can't come to the phone right now. **4 ponerse a + *inf*** to start + *to* + *inf*/-*ing*: *se puso a cantar* he started to sing, he started singing.

poniente *nm (dirección)* west.

pontificar *vi* to pontificate.

pontífice *nm* pope, pontiff.

pontón *nm* pontoon.

ponzoña *nf* venom.

ponzoñoso,-a *adj* venomous.

popa *nf* stern.

populacho *nm* mob, masses *pl*.

popular *adj* **1** *(del pueblo)* traditional. **2** *(muy conocido)* popular.

popularizar *vt* to popularize.

populista *adj* populist.

populoso,-a *adj* populous.

popurrí *nm* potpourri.

póquer *nm* poker.

por *prep* **1** *(gen)* for: *lo hice por ti* I did it for you. **2** *(a través de)* through, by: *iremos por la autopista* we'll go on the motorway. **3** *(calle, carretera)* along, down, up: *íbamos por la calle cuando...* we were walking along the street when... **4** *(lugar aproximado)* in, near, round: *está por aquí* it's somewhere round here. **5** *(cau-*

sa) because of: *suspendieron el concierto por la lluvia* they cancelled the concert because of the rain. **6** *(tiempo)* at, for: *nos veremos por vacaciones* I'll see you during the holidays. **7** *(medio)* by: *llegó por correo* it arrived by post. **8** *(autoría)* by: *fue escrito por Azorín* it was written by Azorín. **9** *(distribución)* per: *cinco por ciento* five per cent. **10** *(tras)* by: *les interrogó uno por uno* he interrogated each one in turn. **11** *(con pasiva)* by: *fue comprado por la reina* it was bought by the queen. **12** *(en calidad de)* as: *la tomó por esposa* he took her as his wife. **13** *(en lugar de)* instead of, in the place of: *ve tú por mí* you go in my place. **14** *(multiplicado por)* times, multiplied by: *tres por cuatro, doce* three fours are twelve, three times four is twelve. [LOC] **estar por + *inf*** *(a punto de)* to be on the point of + -*ing*. ‖ **por más que + *subj*** however much, no matter how much. ‖ **por mucho que + *subj*** however much, no matter how much.

porcelana *nf* china, porcelain: *una porcelana* a piece of china.

porcentaje *nm* percentage.

porcentual *adj* percentage.

porche *nm* veranda(h), US porch.

porcino,-a *adj* porcine. [COMP] **ganado porcino** pigs *pl*, US hogs *pl*.

porción *nf (gen)* portion, part.

pordiosero,-a *nm & nf* beggar.

porfiar *vi (insistir)* to insist (en, on).

pormenor *nm* detail. [LOC] **al pormenor** retail.

pormenorizar *vt* to detail.

poro *nm* pore.

poroso,-a *adj* porous.

porque *conj* **1** *(de causa)* because: *no voy porque no quiero* I'm not going because I don't want to. **2** *(de finalidad)* in order that, so that.

porqué *nm* cause, reason: *nunca sabremos el porqué* we'll never know why.

porquería *nf (suciedad)* dirt, filth.

porqueriza *nf* pigsty.

porra *nf (de policía)* truncheon. [LOC] **mandar a la porra a** ALGN *fam* to tell SB to get lost, send SB packing.

porrazo *nm (con bastón)* blow; *(al caer)* bump, knock.

porrón *nm typical glass drinking vessel with a thin spout used for pouring wine into the mouth.*

portaaviones *nm inv* aircraft carrier.

portada *nf (de revista, periódico)* front page; *(de libro)* title page.

portador,-ra *adj* carrying.
► *nm & nf (de un virus)* carrier.

portaequipajes *nm inv* **1** *(de un coche - maletero)* boot, US trunk; *(- en el techo)* roof rack. **2** *(de un tren)* luggage rack.

portafolios *nm inv* **1** portfolio, folder. **2** *(maletín)* briefcase.

portal *nm (entrada de edificio)* hallway.

portalámparas *nm* bulbholder.

portaminas *nm inv* propelling pencil.

portamonedas *nm inv* purse.

portar *vt* to carry.
► *vpr* **portarse** to behave. [LOC] **portarse bien** to be good, behave OS.

portátil *adj* portable.

portavoz *nm o nf (gen)* spokesperson.

portazo *nm* bang, slam *(of a door).*

porte *nm (transporte)* carriage, freight. [COMP] **portes debidos** carriage due.

porteador,-ra *nm & nf* porter.

portentoso,-a *adj* prodigious.

portería *nf* **1** *(de un edificio)* porter's lodge. **2** DEP goal.

portero,-a *nm & nf* **1** *(de un edificio)* porter. **2** DEP goalkeeper. [COMP] **portero automático** entryphone.

pórtico *nm* portico.

portillo *nm* breach.

portón *nm* large door.

Portugal *nm* Portugal.

portugués,-esa *adj* Portuguese.
► *nm & nf (persona)* Portuguese.
► *nm* **portugués** *(idioma)* Portuguese.

porvenir *nm* future.

pos [LOC] **en pos de** after, in pursuit of.

posada *nf* inn.

posar *vi (para foto, etc)* to pose.
► *vt (colocar)* to rest.
► *vpr* **posarse 1** *(pájaro)* to alight, perch, sit. **2** *(sedimento)* to settle.

posavasos *nm inv* coaster.

posdata *nf* postscript.

pose *nf (postura)* pose.

poseedor,-ra *nm & nf* owner.

poseer *vt* **1** *(propiedad)* to own. **2** *(conocimientos, talento, etc)* to have.

posesión *nf* possession. [LOC] **tomar posesión** *(de un cargo)* to take up.

posesivo,-a *adj* possessive.

poseso,-a *nm & nf* possessed person.

posguerra *nf* postwar period.

posibilidad *nf* possibility.

posible *adj* possible. [LOC] **hacer todo lo posible** to do one's best.

posición *nf (postura, situación)* position.

positivo,-a *adj* positive.

poso *nm* **1** *(del café)* dregs *pl.* **2** *fig* trace.

posología *nf* dosage.

posparto *nm* postpartum.

posponer *vt (en el tiempo)* to postpone.

posta *nf (de caballos)* change of horses. [LOC] **a posta** on purpose.

postal *nf* postcard.

poste *nm* post.

póster *nm* poster.

postergar *vt (retrasar)* to postpone.

posteridad *nf* posterity.

posterior *adj* **1** *(en el espacio)* back, rear: *en la parte posterior del edificio* at the back of the building. **2** *(en el tiempo)* later.

posteriori [LOC] **a posteriori** a posteriori.

postgrado *nm* postgraduate course.

postgraduado,-a *nm & nf* postgraduate student.

postigo *nm (de ventana)* shutter.

postilla *nf* scab.

postizo,-a *adj* false.

postor,-ra *nm & nf* bidder.

postrar *vt* to prostrate.
► *vpr* **postrarse** to prostrate OS.

postre *nm* dessert.

postular *vt (defender)* to postulate.

póstumo,-a *adj* posthumous.

postura *nf* **1** *(de un cuerpo)* posture, position. **2** *(actitud)* attitude.

P

potable *adj* drinkable.
potaje *nm* CULIN hotpot.
potasio *nm* potassium.
pote *nm (vasija)* pot.
potencia *nf* **1** *(capacidad)* power: *este coche tiene mucha potencia* this car is very powerful. **2** *(país)* power. **3** *(en matemática)* power: *elevamos seis a la tercera potencia* we raise six to the power of three.
potencial *adj* potential.
  ▶ *nm* **1** potential. **2** LING conditional tense.
potenciar *vt* to strengthen.
potentado,-a *nm* tycoon, potentate.
potente *adj* powerful.
potestad *nf* power.
potestativo,-a *adj* optional.
potingue *nm fam (crema)* face cream.
potrero *nm (lugar)* paddock.
potro,-a *nm & nf* ZOOL *(macho)* colt.
poza *nf (en un río)* pool.
pozo *nm (de agua, petróleo)* well.
práctica *nf* practice.
  ▶ *nf pl* **prácticas** practical *sing.* [LOC] **en la práctica** in practice.
practicable *adj (realizable)* feasible.
practicante *nm o nf (persona)* nurse.
practicar *vt* **1** *(gen)* to practise (US practice). **2** *(hacer)* to make; *(deporte)* to play.
  ▶ *vi* to practise (US practice).
práctico,-a *adj* **1** *(gen)* practical. **2** *(hábil)* skilful (US skillful).
pradera *nf* prairie, grassland.
prado *nf* meadow.
pragmático,-a *adj* pragmatic.
pragmatismo *nm* pragmatism.
preámbulo *nm* preamble.
preaviso *nm* notice.
precalentamiento *nm* DEP warming up.
precalentar *vt* to pre-heat.
precariedad *nf* precariousness.
precario,-a *adj* precarious.
precaución *nf* precaution.
precavido,-a *adj* cautious.
precedente *adj* preceding.
  ▶ *nm* precedent.
preceder *vt* to precede.
preceptiva *nf* precepts *pl.*

preceptivo,-a *adj* compulsory.
precepto *nm* precept.
preceptor,-ra *nm & nf* EDUC tutor.
preciado,-a *adj* precious.
preciarse *vpr* to be proud (de, of).
precintar *vt* to seal.
precinto *nm* seal.
precio *nm* **1** *(coste)* price. **2** *fig (valor)* value.
preciosidad *nf (belleza)* loveliness.
precioso,-a *adj (bello)* beautiful.
precipicio *nm* cliff, precipice.
precipitación *nf* **1** *(prisa)* rush, haste. **2** METEOR precipitation, rainfall.
precipitado,-a *adj (apresurado)* hasty.
precipitar *vt* **1** *(apresurar)* to rush. **2** QUÍM to precipitate.
  ▶ *vpr* **precipitarse 1** *(apresurarse)* to rush, be hasty. **2** *(caer)* to fall.
precisar *vt* **1** to say exactly. **2** *(necesitar)* to need.
precisión *nf* precision, accuracy.
preciso,-a *adj* **1** precise. **2** *(necesario)* necessary.
precocinado,-a *adj* precooked.
preconcebido,-a *adj* preconceived.
preconizar *vt* to advocate.
precoz *adj* **1** *(persona)* precocious. **2** *(cosecha)* early. **3** *(diagnóstico)* early.
precursor,-ra *nm & nf* precursor.
predador,-ra *adj* predatory.
predecesor,-ra *nm & nf* predecessor.
predecir *vt* to predict.
predestinado,-a *adj* predestined.
predestinar *vt* to predestine.
predeterminar *vt* to predetermine.
prédica *nf* sermon.
predicación *nf* preaching.
predicado *nm* predicate.
predicador,-ra *nm & nf* preacher.
predicar *vt* to preach.
predicativo,-a *adj* predicative.
predicción *nf* prediction.
predilección *nf* predilection.
predilecto,-a *adj* favourite.
predisponer *vt* to predispose.
predisposición *nf* predisposition.
predominante *adj* predominant.

predominar *vt* to predominate.

predominio *nm* predominance.

preeminente *adj* pre-eminent.

preescolar *adj (enseñanza, edad, etapa)* preschool, nursery-school.

preestablecer *vt* to pre-establish.

preestablecido,-a *adj* pre-established.

preestreno *nm* preview.

prefabricado,-a *adj* prefabricated.

prefacio *nm* preface.

preferencia *nf* preference.

preferente *adj* preferential.

preferible *adj* preferable.

preferido,-a *adj* favourite (US favorite).

preferir *vt* to prefer.

prefijo *nm* 1 LING prefix. 2 *(telefónico)* dialling code, US area code.

pregón *nm (discurso de fiestas)* opening address.

pregonar *vt (noticia)* to announce, make public.

pregonero *nm* town crier.

pregunta *nf* question. LOC **hacer una pregunta a** ALGN to ask SB a question.

preguntar *vt* to ask.
▶ *vpr* **preguntarse** to wonder: *me pregunto si vendrá* I wonder if he'll come.

preguntón,-ona *adj fam* inquisitive.

prehistoria *nf* prehistory.

prehistórico,-a *adj* prehistoric.

prejuicio *nm* prejudice.

prejuzgar *vt* to prejudge.

preliminar *adj* preliminary.

preludio *nm* prelude.

prematrimonial *adj* premarital.

prematuro,-a *adj* premature.

premeditación *nf* premeditation.

premeditado,-a *adj* premeditated.

premeditar *vt* to premeditate.

premiado,-a *adj* prizewinning.
▶ *nm & nf* prizewinner.

premiar *vt* to award a prize to.

premio *nm* prize.

premisa *nf* premise.

premonición *nf* premonition.

premonitorio,-a *adj* premonitory.

premura *nf (prisa)* urgency.

prenatal *adj* antenatal.

prenda *nf* 1 *(de vestir)* garment. 2 *(en juego)* forfeit.

prendarse *vpr* to fall in love (de, with).

prendedor *nm (broche)* brooch; *(alfiler)* pin.

prender *vt* 1 *(sujetar)* to attach; *(con agujas)* to pin. 2 *(encender - fuego)* to light; *(- luz)* to turn on.
▶ *vi* 1 *(arraigar - planta, costumbre)* to take root. 2 *(fuego, madera, etc)* to catch light, catch fire.

prensa *nf* 1 *(máquina)* press. 2 *(periódicos)* papers *pl*.

prensar *vt* to press.

preñado,-a *adj* pregnant.

preñar *vt (mujer)* to make pregnant; *(animal)* to impregnate.

preocupación *nf* worry.

preocupado,-a *adj* worried.

preocupar *vt* to worry.
▶ *vpr* **preocuparse** 1 *(sentir preocupación)* to worry (por, about).

preparación *nf* 1 *(gen)* preparation. 2 *(física, deportiva)* training.

preparado,-a *adj* ready, prepared.

preparador,-ra *nm & nf* DEP coach.

preparar *vt* 1 to prepare, get ready: *voy a preparar el desayuno* I'll get breakfast ready. 2 DEP *(entrenar)* to train, coach: *se está preparando para el maratón* she's training for the marathon. 3 *(estudiar)* to revise for, work for.

preparativos *nm pl* arrangements.

preposición *nf* preposition.

prepotencia *nf (arrogancia)* arrogance.

prepotente *adj* arrogant.

prerrogativa *nf* prerogative.

presa *nf* 1 *(embalse)* dam. 2 *(acción)* capture. COMP **ave de presa** bird of prey.

presagiar *vt* to be a warning of.

presagio *nm (señal)* omen.

presbítero *nm* priest.

prescindir *vi* **prescindir de** *(pasar sin)* to do without.

prescribir *vt (recetar)* to prescribe.

prescripción *nf* prescription.

P

presencia *nf (gen)* presence.

presenciar *vt (acontecimiento)* to be present at.

presentación *nf* 1 *(de un objeto, documento, etc)* presentation, showing: *la presentación del carné es imprescindible para entrar* passes must be shown to allow access. 2 *(de personas)* introduction.

presentador,-ra *nm & nf* presenter.

presentar *vt* 1 *(gen)* to present; *(mostrar)* to show. 2 *(entregar)* to hand in. 3 *(sacar al mercado)* to launch. 4 *(personas)* to introduce: *¿te han presentado ya?* have you been introduced yet? 5 TV to present.
▶ *vpr* **presentarse** 1 *(comparecer)* to turn up. 2 *(para elección)* to stand.

presente *adj* present.
▶ *nm* 1 *(tiempo)* present. 2 LING present tense. 3 *(obsequio)* gift.
▶ *nm pl* **presentes** those present.

presentimiento *nm* premonition.

presentir *vt* to have a feeling (que, that).

preservar *vt* to preserve.

preservativo *nm* condom.

presidencia *nf* 1 POL presidency. 2 *(de una empresa)* chairmanship.

presidente,-ta *nm & nf* 1 POL president. 2 chairman, US president.

presidiario,-a *nm & nf* convict.

presidio *nm* prison, penitentiary.

presidir *vt (reunión)* to chair.

presilla *nf* fastener.

presión *nf* pressure.

presionar *vt* 1 *(objeto)* to press. 2 *(persona)* to pressure, put pressure on.

preso,-a *nm & nf* prisoner.

prestación *nf* 1 *(servicio)* service. 2 *(de la Seguridad Social)* benefit, allowance. COMP **prestación por desempleo** unemployment benefit.

prestado,-a *adj* lent, on loan.

prestamista *nm o nf* moneylender.

préstamo *nm (crédito)* loan. LOC **pedir un préstamo** to ask for a loan.

prestar *vt (dejar prestado)* to lend, loan.

prestidigitador,-ra *nm & nf* conjuror.

prestigio *nm* prestige.

prestigioso,-a *adj* prestigious.

presto,-a *adj* 1 *(preparado)* ready. 2 *(rápido)* quick.

presumible *adj* probable, likely.

presumido,-a *adj (en el vestir)* vain.

presumir *vi* 1 *(vanagloriarse)* to boast (de, about), show off (de, about). 2 *(ser presumido)* to be vain.
▶ *vt (suponer)* to suppose, assume.

presunto,-a *adj* presumed, alleged.

presuntuoso,-a *adj (presumido)* vain.

presuponer *vt* to presuppose.

presupuestar *vt (proyecto)* to budget for; *(construcción, obra, etc)* to estimate.

presupuesto *nm (en finanzas)* budget; *(de una obra)* estimate.

pretencioso,-a *adj* pretentious.
▶ *nm & nf* pretentious person.

pretender *vt* 1 *(querer)* to want to: *pretende ganar el concurso* he wants to win the contest. 2 *(intentar)* to try to: *no sé qué pretende hacer* I don't know what he's trying to do. 3 *(cortejar)* to court.

pretendido,-a *adj* supposed.

pretendiente *nm (enamorado)* suitor.

pretensión *nf* 1 *(intención)* aim; *(ambición)* ambition. 2 *(derecho)* claim.

pretérito,-a *adj* past: *en tiempos pretéritos* in the past.
▶ *nm* **pretérito** simple past, preterite.

pretexto *nm* pretext.

prevalecer *vi* to prevail.

prevención *nf (precaución)* prevention.

prevenido,-a *adj* forewarned.

prevenir *vt (evitar)* to avoid, prevent.

preventivo,-a *adj (medicina)* preventive.

prever *vt (anticipar)* to foresee.

previo,-a *adj* previous.

previsible *adj* foreseeable.

previsión *nf* forecast. COMP **previsión meteorológica** weather forecast.

previsor,-ra *adj* farsighted.

prieto,-a *adj* tight.

prima *nf (gratificación)* bonus.

primacía *nf* primacy.

primar *vi (predominar)* to be important.

primaria *nf* primary education.

primario,-a *adj* primary.

primate *nm* primate.

primavera *nf* **1** spring. **2** *lit (año)* year.

primaveral *adj* spring, spring-like.

primera *nf* **1** AUTO first gear. **2** *(en transportes)* first class.

primerizo,-a *nm & nf* beginner.

primero,-a *adj* first: *el primer día del año* the first day of the year.
▶ *nm & nf* first: *es la primera de la clase* she's top of the class.
▶ *adv* **primero** *(en primer lugar)* first: *primero vamos a mirarlo en el diccionario* let's look it up in the dictionary first.

✎ Antes de los nombres masculinos en singular se usa **primer.**

primicia *nf (noticia)* scoop.

primigenio,-a *adj* original.

primitiva *nf* ≈ National Lottery.

primitivo,-a *adj* HIST primitive.

primo,-a *nm & nf (familiar)* cousin.

primogénito,-a *adj* first-born, eldest.
▶ *nm & nf* first-born, eldest.

primor *nm (delicadeza)* delicateness.

primordial *adj* essential.

primoroso,-a *adj* delicate.

princesa *nf* princess.

principado *nm* principality.

principal *adj* main: *lo principal es que duerma* the main thing is that he sleeps.
▶ *nm (piso)* first floor, US second floor.

príncipe *nm* prince.

principiante,-a *nm & nf* beginner.

principio *nm* **1** *(inicio)* beginning, start: *me voy de vacaciones a principios de mes* I'm going on holiday at the beginning of the month. **2** *(moral)* principle.

pringar *vt (ensuciar)* to make greasy: *me he puesto las manos pringando de grasa* I've got my hands covered in grease.

pringoso,-a *adj* greasy.

prior,-ra *nm & nf (hombre)* prior; *(mujer)* prioress.

prioridad *nf* priority.

prioritario,-a *adj* priority.

prisa *nf* hurry: *¡date prisa que no llegamos!* hurry up or we'll never make it! LOC co-rrer prisa to be urgent. ‖ tener prisa to be in a hurry.

prisión *nf* prison.

prisionero,-a *nm & nf* prisoner.

prisma *nm* prism.

prismáticos *nm pl* binoculars.

privacidad *nf* privacy.

privación *nf* deprivation, privation.

privado,-a *adj* private.

privar *vt (despojar)* to deprive (de, of).

privativo,-a *adj (exclusivo)* exclusive.

privatizar *vt* to privatize.

privilegiado,-a *adj* privileged.

privilegiar *vt* to privilege.

privilegio *nm* privilege.

pro *nm* advantage. COMP **los pros y los contras** the pros and cons.

proa *nf* bow, prow.

probabilidad *nf* probability.

probable *adj (posible)* probable, likely.

probado,-a *adj* proven.

probador *nm* changing room.

probar *vt* **1** *(demostrar)* to prove. **2** *(comprobar)* to test, check: *prueba el coche a ver cómo responde* check the car to see how it performs. **3** *(vino, comida, etc)* to taste, try. **4** *(prenda, zapato)* to try on.
▶ *vi* to try: *prueba a cambiarle la pila* try changing the battery.

probeta *nf* test tube.

problema *nm* problem. LOC **tener problemas con** to have trouble with.

problemático,-a *adj* problematic.

procedencia *nf* **1** origin.

procedente *adj* coming (de, from): *el tren procedente de Sevilla* the train arriving from Seville.

proceder LOC **proceder de** to come: *el queso procede de la leche* cheese comes from milk.

procedimiento *nm (método)* procedure.

procesado,-a *adj* **1** INFORM processed. **2** JUR tried.
▶ *nm & nf* **el/la procesado,-a** the accused.

procesador *nm* processor. COMP **procesador de textos** INFORM word processor.

P

procesar *vt* **1** *(gen)* to process. **2** JUR to try.

procesión *nf* procession.

proceso *nm* *(gen)* process. ⊡COMP proceso de datos data processing.

proclamar *vt* to proclaim.
▸ *vpr* **proclamarse** to proclaim OS.

proclive *adj* prone.

procreación *nf* procreation.

procrear *vi* to procreate.

procurador,-ra *nm & nf* JUR procurator.

procurar *vt* **1** to try. **2** *(proporcionar)* to get.

prodigar *vt* to be lavish with.

prodigio *nm* prodigy, miracle.

prodigioso,-a *adj* prodigious.

pródigo,-a *adj (generoso)* lavish.

producción *nf* production.

producir *vt* **1** *(gen)* to produce. **2** *(causar)* to cause.
▸ *vpr* **producirse** to happen.

productividad *nf* productivity.

productivo,-a *adj* productive.

producto *nm* *(gen)* product.

productor,-ra *adj* producing.
▸ *nm & nf* producer.

productora *nf* CINE production company.

proeza *nf* feat, heroic deed.

profanar *vt* to desecrate, profane.

profano,-a *adj (no sagrado)* profane.

profecía *nf* prophecy.

proferir *vt (palabra, sonido, etc)* to utter.

profesión *nf* profession.

profesional *adj* professional: *es futbolista profesional* he's a professional footballer.
▸ *nm o nf* professional: *es todo un profesional* he's a real professional.

profesionalidad *nf* professionalism.

profesor,-ra *nm & nf* teacher. ⊡COMP profesor,-ra particular private tutor.

profesorado *nm* teaching staff.

profeta *nm* prophet.

profético,-a *adj* prophetic.

profetizar *vt* to prophesy.

prófugo,-a *nm & nf* fugitive.

profundidad *nf* depth: *tiene cuatro metros de profundidad* it's four metres deep.

profundizar *vt* **profundizar en** *(tema, cuestión)* to look deeply into.

profundo,-a *adj (gen)* deep.

profuso,-a *adj* profuse.

progenitor,-ra *nm & nf (padre)* father; *(madre)* mother.
▸ *nm pl* **progenitores** parents.

programa *nm* **1** *(gen)* programme (US program). **2** INFORM program. **3** EDUC *(de un curso)* syllabus.

programación *nf* **1** *(de televisión, radi, etco)* programming (US programing). **2** *(de teatro)* billing. **3** INFORM programming.

programador,-ra *nm & nf* INFORM programmer.

programar *vt* **1** *(gen)* to programme (US program). **2** INFORM to program. **3** *(organizar, planear, etc)* to plan.

progresar *vi* to progress.

progresión *nf* progression. ⊡COMP progresión aritmética arithmetic progression.

progresista *adj* progressive.
▸ *nm o nf* progressive.

progresivo,-a *adj* progressive.

progreso *nm* progress.

prohibición *nf* prohibition, ban.

prohibido,-a *adj* forbidden.

prohibir *vt* to forbid.

prohibitivo,-a *adj* prohibitive.

prójimo *nm* fellow man, neighbour (US neighbor).

prole *nf* offspring.

proletariado *nm* proletariat.

proletario,-a *nm & nf* proletarian.

proliferar *vi* to proliferate.

prolijo,-a *adj (meticuloso)* meticulous.

prólogo *nm* prologue, US prolog.

prolongación *nf (gen)* prolongation.

prolongado,-a *adj (largo)* prolonged.

prolongar *vt* **1** *(en el tiempo, etc)* to prolong. **2** *(en el espacio)* to extend.
▸ *vpr* **prolongarse** to go on.

promedio *nm* average.

promesa *nf* promise.

prometedor,-ra *adj* promising.

prometer *vt* to promise: *¿lo prometes?* promise?
▸ *vi* to be promising: *esta chica es una pintora que promete* this girl is a promising artist.

prometido,-a *nm & nf (hombre)* fiancé; *(mujer)* fiancée.

prominente *adj* prominent.

promiscuo,-a *adj* promiscuous.

promoción *nf* promotion.

promocionar *vt* (to promote.

promontorio *nm* promontory.

promotor,-ra *nm & nf (inmobiliario)* developer.

promover *vt* to promote.

promulgar *vt* to enact, promulgate.

pronombre *nm* pronoun.

pronosticar *vt* to predict.

pronóstico *nm (del tiempo)* forecast.
COMP **pronóstico meteorológico** weather forecast.

pronto,-a *adv* **1** *(rápido)* soon: *no llores que pronto vendrá tu mamá* don't cry, your mummy will be here soon. **2** *(temprano)* early: *has llegado demasiado pronto* you've arrived too early. LOC **de pronto** suddenly.

pronunciación *nf* pronunciation.

pronunciado,-a *adj (marcado)* marked.

pronunciar *vt* **1** *(gen)* to pronounce. **2** *(discurso)* to make.

propagación *nf* propagation.

propaganda *nf* **1** *(publicidad)* advertising. **2** *(electoral)* propaganda.

propagar *vt* to propagate, spread.

propano *nm* propane.

propasarse *vpr* to go too far.

propensión *nf* inclination, tendency.

propenso,-a *adj* inclined. LOC **ser propenso,-a a ALGO** to be prone to sth.

propiciar *vt (favorecer)* contribute to.

propiciatorio,-a *adj* propitiatory.

propicio,-a *adj (gen)* suitable.

propiedad *nf (bien inmueble)* property.
COMP **propiedad privada** private property.

propietario,-a *nm & nf* owner.

propina *nf* tip.

propinar *vt* to give.

propio,-a *adj* **1** *(de nuestra propiedad)* own. **2** *(indicado)* appropriate. **3** *(mismo - él)* himself; *(- ella)* herself; *(- cosa, animal)* itself; *(- en plural)* themselves.

proponer *vt (persona, plan, etc)* to propose.
▸ *vpr* **proponerse** to intend.

proporción *nf* proportion.

proporcionado,-a *adj* in proportion.

proporcional *adj* proportionate.

proporcionar *vt (ayuda, etc)* to supply.

proposición *nf (idea)* proposal.

propósito *nm* **1** *(intención)* intention. **2** *(objetivo)* aim.

propuesta *nf* proposal.

propugnar *vt* to advocate.

propulsar *vt (medida, idea, etc)* to promote.

propulsión *nf* propulsion.

propulsor,-ra *nm (motor)* motor.

prórroga *nf (de un plazo)* extension.

prorrogable *adj* renewable.

prorrogar *vt (alargar)* to extend.

prosa *nf* prose.

prosaico,-a *adj* prosaic.

proscribir *vt (prohibir)* to proscribe.

proscrito,-a *nm & nf (criminal)* outlaw.

proseguir *vt* to continue, carry on.

proselitismo *nm* proselytism.

proselitista *adj* proselytic.
▸ *nm o nf* proselytizer.

prosodia *nf* prosody.

prosopopeya *nf (figura retórica)* prosopopoeia.

prospección *nf (del suelo)* surveying; *(para minerales)* prospecting.

prospecto *nm* leaflet, prospectus.

prosperar *vi* to prosper, thrive.

prosperidad *nf* prosperity.

próspero,-a *adj* prosperous.

próstata *nf* prostate, prostate gland.

prostitución *nf* prostitution.

prostituir *vt* to prostitute.
▸ *vpr* **prostituirse** to prostitute os.

prostituta *nf* prostitute.

protagonismo *nm* leading role.

P

protagonista *adj* main, leading.
► *nm o nf (de película - actor)* leading man; *(- actriz)* leading lady.

protagonizar *vt (película, etc)* to star in.

protección *nf* protection.

proteccionismo *nm* protectionism.

proteccionista *adj* protectionist.

protector,-ra *nm & nf (persona)* protector.

proteger *vt* to protect.

protegido,-a *nm & nf (hombre)* protégé; *(mujer)* protégée.

proteína *nf* protein.

proteínico,-a *adj* proteinic.

prótesis *nf* MED *(uso formal)* prosthesis. COMP **prótesis dental** denture.

protesta *nf* protest.

protestante *adj* Protestant.
► *nm o nf* Protestant.

protestar *vi (mostrar disconformidad)* to protest (contra, against).

protocolo *nm (gen)* protocol.

protón *nm* proton.

protoplasma *nm* protoplasm.

prototipo *nm* prototype.

protozoo *nm* protozoan.

protuberancia *nf* protuberance.

provecho *nm (beneficio)* benefit. LOC **¡buen provecho!** enjoy your meal!

provechoso,-a *adj (beneficioso)* beneficial.

proveedor,-ra *nm & nf* supplier.

proveer *vt (suministrar)* to provide (de, with).

provenir *vi* to come (de, from).

proverbial *adj* proverbial.

proverbio *nm* proverb, saying.

providencia *nf* JUR ruling.

providencial *adj* providential.

provincia *nf* province. LOC **de provincias** provincial.

provinciano,-a *adj pey* provincial.

provisión *nf (suministro)* provision.

provisional *adj* provisional.

provisto,-a *adj* provided (de, with), equipped (de, with).

provocación *nf (gen)* provocation.

provocar *vt* to incite, to provoke.

provocativo,-a *adj* provocative.

próximamente *adv* shortly, soon.

proximidad *nf* proximity.

próximo,-a *adj* **1** *(cerca)* near. **2** *(siguiente)* next: *el mes próximo* next month.

proyección *nf* **1** *(gen)* projection. **2** CINE screening, showing.

proyectar *vt (película)* to show.

proyectil *nm* projectile, missile.

proyecto *nm* **1** *(propósito)* plan. **2** *(plan)* project.

proyector *nm (de cine)* film projector.

prudencia *nf (cuidado)* care, caution; *(moderación)* moderation.

prudente *adj* sensible, prudent.

prueba *nf* **1** *(demostración)* proof. **2** *(experimento)* experiment, trial: *haz la prueba* try it. **3** *(examen)* test. **4** MED test. **5** DEP event. LOC **poner a prueba** to put to the test. COMP **prueba de acceso** entrance examination.

psicoanálisis *nm inv* psychoanalysis.

psicología *nf* psychology.

psicopatía *nf* psychopathy.

psicosis *nf inv* psychosis.

psique *nf* psyche.

psiquiatría *nf* psychiatry.

psiquiátrico,-a *adj* psychiatric.

psíquico,-a *adj* psychic, psychical.

pterodáctilo *nm* pterodactyl.

púa *nf* **1** *(de peine, cepillo)* tooth. **2** *(de erizo)* quill. **3** MÚS plectrum.

pubertad *nf* puberty.

pubis *nm inv* **1** pubes *pl*. **2** *(hueso)* pubis.

publicable *adj* publishable.

publicación *nf* publication.

publicar *vt (libro, etc)* to publish.

publicidad *nf (comercial)* advertising.

publicista *nm o nf* advertising executive.

publicitario,-a *adj* advertising.

público,-a *adj* public.
► *nm* **público** *(de un espectáculo)* audience; *(de televisión)* audience, viewers *pl*: *el público aplaudió entusiasmado* the audience applauded warmly. LOC **en público** in public.

publirreportaje *nm (documentary style)* television advertisement.

puchero *nm (olla)* cooking pot.

púdico,-a *adj* chaste, decent.

pudiente *adj* wealthy, rich.

pudor *nm (decencia)* decency.

pudoroso, a *adj* decent, chaste.

pudrir *vt* to rot.
  ▶ *vpr* **pudrirse** to rot.

pueblerino,-a *adj (de pueblo)* village.

pueblo *nm* 1 *(población)* village. 2 *(gente)* people.

puente *nm (sobre un río, etc)* bridge.

puerco,-a *nm & nf* pig. COMP **puerco espín** porcupine.

puericultor,-ora *nm & nf* child care specialist.

puericultura *nf* child care.

pueril *adj (infantil)* puerile, childish.

puerro *nm* leek.

puerta *nf* 1 *(gen)* door. 2 *(verja)* gate. 3 DEP *(portería)* goal. COMP **puerta de embarque** gate.

puerto *nm* 1 MAR port, harbour. 2 *(de montaña)* (mountain) pass. COMP **puerto deportivo** marina.

Puerto Rico *nm* Puerto Rico.

puertorriqueño,-a *adj* Puerto Rican.
  ▶ *nm & nf* Puerto Rican.

pues *conj* 1 *(ya que)* since, as. 2 *(por lo tanto)* therefore, so. 3 *(repetitivo)* then. 4 *(enfático)* well: *pues bien* well then; *¡pues claro!* of course!; *pues no* well no.

puesta *nf* 1 *(colocación)* setting. 2 *(de huevos)* laying. COMP **puesta de sol** sunset.

puesto,-a *nm* 1 *(sitio)* place: *ya han llegado al primer puesto* they've made it to the top. 2 *(de mercado)* stall; *(de feria, etc)* stand. 3 *(empleo)* position, post. LOC **puesto que** since, as.

púgil *nm* boxer.

pugnar *vi* to fight, struggle.

puja *nf (acción)* bidding.

pujante *adj* thriving.

pujar *vt (en subasta)* to bid higher.

pulcritud *nf* neatness.

pulcro,-a *adj* neat.

pulga *nf* flea.

pulgada *nf* inch.

pulgar *nm* thumb.

pulgón *nm* aphid.

pulimentar *vt* to polish.

pulir *vt (superficie)* to polish.

pullover *nm* pullover.

pulmón *nm* lung.

pulmonar *adj* lung, pulmonary.

pulmonía *nf* pneumonia.

pulpa *nf* pulp.

púlpito *nm* pulpit.

pulpo *nm* ZOOL octopus.

pulsación *nf* 1 pulsation. 2 *(de corazón)* beat. 3 *(en mecanografía)* stroke.

pulsador *nm (gen)* push button.

pulsar *vt* 1 *(botón, timbre, etc)* to press. 2 *(tecla - de máquina de escribir)* to tap; *(- de piano)* to play.

pulsera *nf* 1 bracelet. 2 *(de reloj)* watch strap.

pulso *nm* 1 *(presión sanguínea)* pulse: *déjame que te tome el pulso* let me take your pulse. 2 *(firmeza en la mano)* steady hand: *para dibujar hay que tener buen pulso* to be able to draw you need a steady hand.

pulular *vi* to swarm.

pulverizador *nm* spray, atomizer.

pulverizar *vt* 1 *(líquido)* to atomize, spray. 2 *(sólido)* to pulverize. 3 *(enemigo)* to crush, wipe out.

puma *nm* puma, mountain lion.

punción *nf* puncture.

punitivo,-a *adj* punitive.

punta *nf (extremo)* tip; *(extremo afilado)* point. LOC **sacar punta a** *(lápiz)* to sharpen.

puntada *nf* stitch.

puntal *nm* 1 prop. 2 *fig* support.

puntapié *nm* kick.

puntear *vt* 1 *(dibujar)* to dot. 2 MÚS to pluck.

punteo *nm* MÚS plucking, US picking.

puntera *nf (de zapato, calcetín, etc)* toe.

puntería *nf* aim: *¡qué buena puntería!* what a good shot!

puntero,-a *adj* leading.
  ▶ *nm* **puntero** *(para señalar)* pointer.

puntiagudo,-a *adj* pointed.

P

puntilla *nf* COST lace. LOC **de puntillas** on tiptoe.

puntilloso,-a *adj (exigente)* punctilious.

punto *nm* 1 *(gen)* point. 2 *(tanto)* point: *nos llevan cinco puntos de ventaja* they're five points ahead of us. 3 *(detrás de abreviatura)* dot; *(al final de la oración)* full stop, US period. 4 *(lugar)* spot: *¿en qué punto de la carretera se encuentran?* exactly where on the road are they? 5 *(tejido)* knitwear: *me he comprado una falda de punto* I bought a knitted skirt. 6 *(en costura, sutura, etc)* stitch: *me caí y me dieron tres puntos en la barbilla* I fell and needed three stitches on my chin. LOC **en punto** sharp, on the dot: *son las tres en punto* it's exactly three o'clock. COMP **dos puntos** colon. ▎ **punto cardinal** cardinal point. ▎ **punto de vista** point of view. ▎ **punto débil** weak point. ▎ **punto y coma** semicolon. ▎ **punto y seguido** full stop, new sentence, US period, new sentence.

puntuable *adj* valid.

puntuación *nf* 1 *(en ortografía)* punctuation. 2 *(acción de puntuar)* scoring; *(total de puntos)* score. 3 EDUC *(acción)* marking; *(nota)* mark: *obtuvo una puntuación muy alta* she got a very high mark.

puntual *adj (que llega a su hora)* punctual: *han llegado muy puntuales* they've arrived right on time.

puntualidad *nf* punctuality.

puntualización *nf* remark.

puntualizar *vt (especificar)* to point out.

puntuar *vt* 1 LING to punctuate. 2 EDUC to mark.
▶ *vi* DEP to score.

punzada *nf* sharp pain, stab of pain.

punzante *adj* stabbing.

punzar *vt* to prick.

punzón *nm* punch.

puñado *nm* handful.

puñal *nm* dagger.

puñalada *nf (herida)* stab wound.

puñetazo *nm* punch.

puño *nm* 1 *(mano)* fist. 2 *(de arma)* handle. 3 *(de camisa, abrigo, etc)* cuff.

pupila *nf* pupil.

pupilaje *nm (de persona)* board and lodging; *(de coche)* garaging.

pupilo,-a *nm & nf (de un tutor)* pupil.

pupitre *nm* school desk.

purasangre *adj* thoroughbred.
▶ *nm (caballo)* thoroughbred.

puré *nm (espeso)* purée; *(sopa)* thick soup: *hoy tenemos puré de zanahoria* today we've got thick carrot soup. COMP **puré de patatas** mashed potatoes.

pureza *nf* purity.

purga *nf* purge.

purgación *nf (acción)* purging.

purgante *nm* purgative, laxative.

purgar *vt* to purge (de, of).

purgatorio *nm* purgatory.

purificación *nf* purification.

purificador,-ra *adj* purifying.
▶ *nm* **purificador** purifier.

purificante *adj* purifying.

purificar *vt* to purify.

purismo *nm* purism.

purista *adj* purist.
▶ *nm o nf* purist.

puritano,-a *adj* puritan, puritanic.
▶ *nm & nf* puritan.

puro,-a *adj* 1 *(sin mezcla)* pure: *tiene un perro de pura raza* he has a purebred dog. 2 *(mero)* sheer, mere, pure: *me enteré por pura casualidad* I found out by pure chance.
▶ *nm* **puro** cigar.

púrpura *adj* purple.
▶ *nm* purple.

purulento,-a *adj* purulent.

pus *nm* pus.

pusilánime *adj* faint-hearted.

pusilanimidad *nf* faint-heartedness.

pústula *nf* pustule.

putrefacción *nf* putrefaction.

putrefacto,-a *adj* putrefied, rotten.

pútrido,-a *adj* putrefied, rotten.

puya *nf (comentario)* gibe.

puyazo *nm (comentario)* gibe.

puzzle *nm* jigsaw, puzzle.

Q, q *nf (la letra)* Q, q.
Qatar *nm* Qatar.
quásar *nm* quasar.
que¹ *pron* **1** *(sujeto, persona)* who, that; *(cosa)* that, which: *la chica que vino ayer está enferma* the girl who came yesterday is ill. **2** *(complemento, persona)* whom, who; *(cosa)* that, which: *el coche que me prestaste está ahí* the car (that) you lent me is there. **3** *prep + que (complemento circunstancial)* which; *(lugar)* where; *(tiempo)* when: *la casa en que vivía estaba lejos* the house where he lived was far away. **4** *art def + que* the one which, the one that: *ese libro es el que me gusta* that's the book I like.

que² *conj* **1** that: *dice que no vendrá* he says (that) he won't come. **2** *(en comparaciones)* than: *es más alto que su padre* he is taller than his father. **3** *(deseo, mandato):* ¡*que te diviertas!* enjoy yourself! **4** *(duda, extrañeza):* ¿*que no te hicieron pagar nada?* (you say) they didn't make you pay anything? **5** *(causal, consecutiva):* ¡*arriba, que ya son las ocho!* get up, it's eight o'clock! **6** *(tanto si... como si...)* whether... or not...: *que llueva que no llueva, iremos de excursión* whether it rains or not, we're going on a trip. **7** *(reiterativo)* and: *charla que charla se nos pasó la hora* we were so busy talking that the hour just flew by. **8** *(final)* so that: *ven aquí que te vea bien* come here so that I can see you properly. **9** *fam (condicional)* if: *que te gusta, te lo quedas; que no te gusta, lo cambias* if you like it, keep it; if you don't, you can change it. **10** *que no (adversativa)* not: *justicia pido, que no perdón* I want justice, not mercy.

qué *pron* what: *no sé qué hacer* I don't know what to do; ¿*qué querías?* what did you want?
▶ *adj* **1** *(cuál)* which: *no sé qué libro quiere* I don't know which book he wants. **2** *(en frases interrogativas)* how, what: ¿*qué años tienes?* how old are you?; ¿*qué has dicho?* what did you say? **3** *(en frases exclamativas)* how, what: ¡*qué bonito!* how nice!; ¡*qué flor más bonita!* what a lovely flower! **4** *(cantidad)* what: ¡*qué de gente!* what a crowd!

quebrada *nf* GEOL *(paso)* gorge, ravine.
quebradizo,-a *adj* **1** *(frágil)* fragile, brittle; *(pastel)* short. **2** *fig (débil moralmente)* weak, frail.
quebrado,-a *adj* **1** *(terreno)* rugged, rough, uneven; *(camino)* tortuous. **2** *(número)* fractional.
quebrantar *vt* **1** *(cascar)* to crack. **2** *(romper)* to break, shatter; *(machacar)* to grind. **3** *(debilitar)* to weaken. **4** *fig (salud, posición, fortuna)* to undermine, shatter. **5** *fig (incumplir)* to break, violate. **6** *fig (suavizar)* to take the edge off, temper; *(ablandar)* to soften. **7** *fig (causar lástima)* to wound, shatter.
▶ *vpr* **quebrantarse 1** *(cascarse)* to crack. **2** *(romperse)* to break. **3** *(la salud)* to be shattered.
quebrar *vt (romper, incumplir)* to break.
▶ *vi* **1** FIN to go bankrupt. **2** *fig (flaquear)* to weaken.
▶ *vpr* **quebrarse 1** *(romperse)* to break. **2** *(herniarse)* to rupture os. **3** *(interrumpirse)* to be broken, open up. **4** *fig (ánimo)* to break, crack.
quedar *vi* **1** *(permanecer)* to remain, stay. **2** *fig (terminar)* to end. **3** *(cita)* to arrange to meet. **4** *(resultado de algo)* to

be. **5** *(favorecer)* to look, fit. **6** *(estar situado)* to be. **7** *(restar)* to be left, remain. **8** *(faltar)* to be, be still. **9 quedar en** *(convenir)* to agree to. **10 quedar por** + *inf* not to have been + *pp*: *la cama quedó por hacer* the bed had not been made, the bed was left unmade. **11 quedar** + *ger* to be, remain: *cuando me fui el niño quedaba durmiendo* when I left the child was sleeping.

▶ *vpr* **quedarse 1** *(permanecer)* to remain, stay, be. **2** *(resultado de algo)* to be, remain. **3** *euf (morirse)* to die. **4** *(mar, viento)* to become calm; *(viento)* to drop. **5 quedarse con** *(retener algo)* to keep.

quehacer *nm* task, chore, job.

queja *nf* **1** *(descontento)* complaint. **2** *(de dolor)* moan, groan.

quejarse *vpr* **1** *(de descontento)* to complain (de, about). **2** *(de dolor)* to moan, groan.

quejido *nm* groan, moan.

quejumbroso,-a *adj* **1** *(persona)* whining, plaintive. **2** *(tono)* querulous.

quemado,-a *adj* **1** burnt; *(por el sol)* sunburnt. **2** *fig (resentido)* embittered. **3** *fam (acabado)* spent, burnt-out.

quemador,-ra *nm* burner.

quemadura *nf* **1** *(acción)* burning. **2** *(herida)* burn; *(de sol)* sunburn; *(escaldadura)* scald.

quemar *vt* **1** *(gen)* to burn; *(plantas)* to scorch. **2** *(incendiar)* to set on fire. **3** *fam (acabar)* to burn out.

▶ *vi (estar muy caliente)* to be burning hot.

▶ *vpr* **quemarse** *(persona)* to burn os; *(cosa)* to be burnt.

querella *nf* **1** JUR action, lawsuit. **2** *(queja)* complaint. **3** *(enfrentamiento)* dispute, quarrel.

querencia *nf* **1** *(acción)* love. **2** *(inclinación del animal)* homing instinct; *(inclinación del hombre)* homesickness.

querer *vt* **1** *(amar)* to love. **2** *(desear)* to want. **3** *(buscar)* to be asking for, be looking for. **4** *(petición)* would. **5** *(verificarse)* may, might.

▶ *nm* love, affection.

querido,-a *adj (amado)* dear, beloved; *(en carta)* dear.

▶ *nm & nf* **1** *(amante)* lover; *(mujer)* mistress. **2** *fam (apelativo)* darling.

quesera *nf* **1** *(fábrica)* cheese factory. **2** *(para servirlo)* cheese dish.

queso *nm* cheese.

quicio *nm* pivot hole.

quid *nm* crux.

quiebra *nf* **1** *(rotura)* break, crack. **2** *(bancarrota)* failure, bankruptcy; *(crack)* crash, collapse. **3** *(pérdida)* loss. **4** GEOG gorge. **5** *fig (fracaso)* failure.

quien *pron* **1** *(sujeto)* who: *me encontré a Toni, quien me dijo que estabas enfermo* I met Toni, who told me you were ill. **2** *(complemento)* who, whom: *las personas a quienes me encontré ayer están aquí* the people (whom) I met yesterday are here. **3** *(indefinido)* whoever, anyone who: *quien sepa la respuesta que me lo diga* anyone who knows the answer tell me.

quién *pron* **1** *(sujeto)* who: *¿quién te lo dijo?* who told you? **2** *(complemento)* who, whom: *¿con quién hablas?* who are you talking to? **3 de quién** *(posesivo)* whose: *¿de quién es esto?* whose is this?

quienquiera *pron* whoever: *entre, quienquiera que sea* come in, whoever you may be.

quieto,-a *adj* **1** *(sin movimiento)* still, motionless. **2** *fig (sosegado)* quiet, calm.

quilate *nm* **1** *(unidad de peso)* carat. **2** *(unidad del oro)* carat (US karat).

quilogramo *nm* → kilogramo.

quilométrico,-a *adj* → kilométrico,-a.

quilómetro *adj* → kilómetro.

quimera *nf* **1** *(mitología)* chimera. **2** *fig (ilusión)* wild fancy, fantasy. **3** *fig (preocupación)* worry; *(sospecha infundada)* unfounded suspicion.

quimérico,-a *adj* unrealistic, fantastic.

química *nf* chemistry.

químicamente *adv* chemically.

químico,-a *adj* chemical.

▶ *nm & nf* chemist.

quincalla *nf (objetos de metal)* cheap metalware; *(baratija)* trinket.

quincallero,-a *nm & nf (de objetos de metal)* seller of cheap metalware; *(de baratijas)* trinket seller.

quince *adj (cardinal)* fifteen; *(ordinal)* fifteenth.
▶ *nm* fifteen.

✎ Consulta también seis.

quinceañero,-a *adj* **1** *(de quince años)* fifteen-year-old. **2** *(adolescente)* teenage.
▶ *nm & nf* **1** *(de quince años)* fifteen-year-old. **2** *(adolescente)* teenager.

quinceavo,-a *adj* fifth.
▶ *nm & nf* fifth.

✎ Consulta también sexto,-a.

quincena *nf* **1** *(tiempo)* fortnight. **2** *(paga)* fortnightly pay.

quincenal *adj* fortnightly.

quincuagenario,-a *adj* quinquagenarian.
▶ *nm & nf* quinquagenarian.

quincuagésimo,-a *adj* fiftieth.
▶ *nm & nf* fiftieth.

✎ Consulta también sexto,-a.

quingentésimo,-a *adj* five hundredth.
▶ *nm & nf* five hundredth.

✎ Consulta también sexto,-a.

quiniela *nf* football pools *pl*.

quinientos,-as *adj (cardinal)* five hundred; *(ordinal)* five-hundredth.
▶ *nm* **quinientos** *(número)* five hundred.

✎ Consulta también seis.

quinina *nf* quinine.

quinqué *nm* oil lamp.

quinquenal *adj* quinquennial, five-year.

quinquenio *nm* quinquennium, five-year period.

quinta *nf* **1** *(casa)* country house. **2** *(reemplazo militar)* call-up, conscript, US draft. **3** MÚS fifth.

quintal *nm* quintal *(46 kilograms)*.

quinteto *nm* quintet.

quintilla *nf* five-line stanza.

quintillizo,-a *nm & nf* quintuplet, quin.

quinto,-a *adj* fifth.
▶ *nm & nf* fifth.
▶ *nm* **quinto** MIL conscript, recruit. **2** *fam (de cerveza)* small bottle of beer (= 20 cl).

✎ Consulta también sexto,-a.

quintuplicación *nf* quintupling.

quintuplicar *vt* to quintuple.

quíntuplo,-a *adj* quintuple.
▶ *nm* **quíntuplo** quintuple.

quinzavo,-a *adj-nm & nf* → quinceavo, -a.

quiosco *nm* kiosk; *(de periódicos)* newsstand; *(de música)* bandstand.

quiosquero,-a *nm & nf* newsagent.

quirófano *nm* operating theatre (US theater).

quirúrgico,-a *adj* surgical.

quitaesmaltes *nm inv* nail polish remover.

quitamanchas *nm inv* stain remover.

quitamiedos *nm inv* handrail.

quitanieves *nm inv* snowplough (US snowplow).

quitapinturas *nm inv* paint stripper.

quitar *vt* **1** *(separar)* to remove, take off. **2** *(sacar)* to take off, take out; *(prendas)* to take off; *(tiempo)* to take up. **3** *(apartar)* to take away, take off. **4** *(hacer desaparecer)* to remove; *(dolor)* to relieve; *(sed)* to quench. **5** *(despojar)* to take; *(robar)* to steal. **6** *(restar)* to subtract; *(descontar)* to take off. **7** *(prohibir)* to forbid, rule out. **8** *(impedir)* to prevent. **9** *(disminuir)* to take away. **10** *fam (radio, agua, etc)* to turn off.
▶ *vpr* **quitarse 1** *(desaparecer)* to go away, come out. **2 quitarse de** *(del juego, bebida, etc)* to give up.

quizá *adv* → quizás.

quizás *adv* perhaps, maybe.

Q

R

R, r *nf (la letra)* R, r.

rábano *nm* radish. LOC ¡me importa un rábano! I don't give a toss!, I couldn't care less!

rabí *nm* rabbi.

rabia *nf* **1** MED rabies. **2** *fig (enfado)* rage, fury, anger. LOC dar rabia to make furious.

rabiar *vi* **1** *(enfadarse)* to rage, be furious: *Elena está que rabia* Elena is furious. **2** *fig (padecer)* to suffer (de, from): *rabiar de dolor* to writhe in pain. LOC hacer rabiar a ALGN to make SB see red.

rabieta *nf fam* tantrum. LOC coger una rabieta *fam* to throw a tantrum.

rabillo *nm (pecíolo)* stalk, stem. LOC mirar por el rabillo del ojo to look out of the corner of one's eye.

rabino *nm* rabbi.

rabioso,-a *adj fig (airado)* furious, angry. LOC ponerse rabioso,-a to fly into a rage.

rabo *nm (gen)* tail.

rácano,-a *adj fam (tacaño)* mean, stingy.

racha *nf* **1** *(ráfaga)* gust, squall. **2** *fig (período)* spell, patch. **3** *fig (serie)* string, run, series *sing: hubo una racha de incendios* there was a series of fires. LOC a rachas in fits and starts, on and off. ∎ tener una buena racha to have a run of good luck.

racimo *nm* bunch, cluster.

ración *nf* **1** *(parte)* portion, share. **2** *(de comida)* portion, serving, helping: *«Cuatro raciones»* «Serves four».

racional *adj* rational.

racionar *vt (limitar)* to ration.

racismo *nm* racism, racialism.

radiación *nf* radiation.

radiactivo,-a *adj* radioactive.

radiador *nm* radiator.

radiante *adj fig* radiant: *radiante de alegría* radiant with joy.

radiar *vt* **1** *(irradiar)* to radiate, irradiate. **2** *(retransmitir)* to broadcast, transmit.

radical *adj* radical.

radicalizar *vt* **1** to radicalize. **2** *(postura)* to harden.
▸ *vpr* **radicalizarse 1** *(conflicto)* to intensify. **2** *(postura)* to harden.

radio¹ *nm* **1** *(de círculo)* radius: *en un radio de 10 metros* within a radius of 10 metres. **2** *(de rueda)* spoke. **3** *(campo)* scope. COMP radio de acción *fig* field of action, scope.

radio² *nf* **1** *(radiodifusión)* radio: *lo oí por la radio* I heard it on the radio. **2** *(aparato)* radio, wireless.

radioactivo,-a *adj* radioactive.

radioaficionado,-a *nm & nf* radio ham.

radiocasete *nm* radio cassette.

radiodifusión *nf* broadcasting.

radiofónico,-a *adj* radio: *concurso radiofónico* radio quiz programme.

radiografía *nf* **1** *(técnica)* radiography. **2** *(imagen)* X-ray, radiograph. LOC hacerse una radiografía to have an X-ray taken.

radionovela *nf* serial.

radiorreceptor *nm* radio, radio set.

radioterapia *nf* radiotherapy.

radiotransmisión *nf* broadcasting.

radiotransmitir *vt* to broadcast.

radioyente *nm o nf* listener.

raer *vt* to scrape (off).

ráfaga *nf* **1** *(de viento)* gust, squall. **2** *(de disparos)* burst. **3** *(de luz)* flash.

rafia *nf* raffia.

raid *nm (incursión)* raid.

raigambre *nf* **1** *(raíces)* roots *pl*, root system. **2** *fig* tradition, history.

rail *nm* rail.

raíz *nf* root. LOC **de raíz** entirely. ▪ **echar raíces 1** *(planta)* to take root. **2** *(persona)* to settle, put down roots. COMP **raíz cuadrada** square root.

raja *nf* **1** *(corte)* cut, slit. **2** *(hendidura)* crack, split. **3** *(tajada)* slice.

rajá *nm* rajah.

rajar *vt* **1** *(hender)* to split, crack. **2** *(hacer tajadas)* to slice.
▸ *vpr* **rajarse 1** *(partirse)* to split, crack. **2** *fam (desistir)* to back out, quit.

rajatabla LOC **a rajatabla** strictly.

ralentí *nm* CINE slow motion. LOC **al ralentí** *(motor)* ticking over.

ralentizar *vt* to slow down.

rallado,-a *adj (queso, etc)* grated.

rallador *nm* grater.

ralladura *nf* grated rind: *ralladura de limón* grated lemon rind.

rallar *vt* to grate.

rally *nm* rally.

rama *nf* branch. LOC **andarse por las ramas** *fam* to beat about the bush. ▪ **en rama** raw: *canela en rama* cinnamon stick.

ramaje *nm* foliage, branches *pl*.

ramal *nm (de camino, etc)* branch.

ramalazo *nm fam (ataque)* fit.

rambla *nf (paseo)* boulevard, avenue.

ramificación *nf* ramification.

ramificarse *vpr* to ramify, branch (out).

ramillete *nm* **1** posy. **2** *fig (conjunto)* bunch, group, collection.

ramo *nm* **1** *(de flores)* bunch, bouquet. **2** *fig (sector)* field: *el ramo de la alimentación* the food sector, the food industry.

rampa *nf (pendiente)* ramp. COMP **rampa de lanzamiento** launching pad.

rana *nf* frog.

rancho *nm* AM *(granja)* ranch, farm.

rancio,-a *adj* **1** *(comestibles)* stale. **2** *fig (antiguo)* old, ancient: *de rancio abolengo* of ancient lineage.

rand *nm* rand.

rango *nm* rank.

ranking *nm* ranking.

ranura *nf (para monedas, fichas)* slot.

rapapolvo *nm fam* dressing-down, ticking off, talking-to.

rapar *vt (pelo)* to crop.

rapaz *adj* ZOOL predatory, of prey: *ave rapaz* bird of prey.

rape¹ *nm (pez)* angler fish.

rape² *nm fam (rasura)* quick shave. LOC **al rape** close-cropped, short.

rapero,-a *nm & nf* rapper.

rapidez *nf* speed, rapidity: *con rapidez* quickly.

rápido,-a *adj* quick, fast.
▸ *adv* quickly: *¡rápido!* hurry up!
▸ *nm* **rápido** *(tren)* fast train.
▸ *nm pl* **rápidos** *(del río)* rapids.

rapiñar *vt fam* to pinch, steal.

rappel *nm* abseiling. LOC **hacer rappel** to abseil.

raptar *vt* to kidnap, abduct.

rapto *nm (secuestro)* kidnapping.

raqueta *nf (de tenis)* racket; *(de ping-pong)* bat, US paddle.

raquítico,-a *adj* **1** *fig (exiguo)* meagre (US meager), small. **2** *fig (débil)* weak.

rareza *nf* **1** *(poco común)* rarity, rareness. **2** *(extravagancia)* eccentricity.

raro,-a *adj* **1** *(escaso)* scarce, rare: *los gorilas albinos son animales raros* albino gorillas are rare animals. **2** *(peculiar)* odd, strange, weird: *últimamente la encuentro rara* I think she's been acting a little strange recently. LOC **¡qué raro!** how odd!, that's strange!

ras LOC **a ras de** (on a) level with. ▪ **a ras de tierra** at ground level.

rasante *adj (vuelo)* low, skimming.
▸ *nf (inclinación)* slope. COMP **cambio de rasante** brow of a hill.

rascacielos *nm inv* skyscraper.

rascador *nm (para rascar)* scraper.

rascar *vt* **1** *(la piel)* to scratch. **2** *(con rascador)* to scrape, rasp.

R

rasero *nm* strickle. [LOC] **por el mismo rasero** *fig* equally.

rasgado,-a *adj* (*roto*) torn, ripped.

rasgar *vt* to tear, rip.

rasgo *nm* 1 (*facción del rostro*) feature. 2 (*peculiaridad*) characteristic, feature. [LOC] **explicar a grandes rasgos** to outline.

rasguear *vt* (*instrumento*) to strum.

rasguñar *vt* to scratch.

rasguño *nm* (*arañazo*) scratch, scrape.

raso,-a *adj* 1 (*plano*) flat, level; (*liso*) smooth: *una cucharada rasa* a level spoonful. 2 (*atmósfera*) clear.
▶ *nm* **raso** (*tejido*) satin.

raspa *nf* (*de pescado*) bone, backbone.

raspar *vt* 1 (*rascar*) to scrape (off); (*dañar*) to scratch, graze. 2 (*rasar*) to graze, skim.

rasposo,-a *adj* rough, sharp.

rasqueta *nf* scraper.

rastra *nf* (*rastro*) trail, track. [LOC] **a rastras** 1 (*arrastrando*) dragging. 2 (*sin querer*) unwillingly, grudgingly: *llevar a rastras* to drag along.

rastrear *vt* (*seguir el rastro*) to trail, track.

rastrillar *vt* (*hojas, etc*) to rake.

rastrillo *nm* 1 (*rastro*) rake. 2 *fam* (*mercadillo*) flea market.

rastro *nm* 1 (*señal*) trace, track: *ni rastro de sangre* not a trace of blood. 2 (*vestigio*) vestige. 3 (*mercado*) flea market. [LOC] **seguir el rastro de** ALGN to follow SB's trail.

rastrojo *nm* (*paja*) stubble.

rasurar *vt* to shave.

rata *nf* ZOOL rat.

ratero,-a *nm & nf* pickpocket.

ratificar *vt* to ratify.
▶ *vpr* **ratificarse** to be confirmed.

rato *nm* 1 (*tiempo*) time, while, moment: *charlamos un rato* we chatted for a while. 2 (*espacio*) way: *hay un buen rato hasta Vigo* it's a long way to Vigo. 3 *fam* (*mucho*) very, a lot: *sabe un rato de deportes* she's a mine of information about sports. [LOC] **a ratos** at times. ▌ **pasar un buen rato** to have a good time. [COMP] **ratos libres** free time *sing*.

ratón *nm* mouse.

ratonera *nf* (*trampa*) mousetrap.

raudal *nm* 1 (*agua*) torrent, flood. 2 *fig* (*abundancia*) flood, wave. [LOC] **a raudales** in torrents.

raudo,-a *adj lit* swift, rapid.

raviolis *nm pl* ravioli.

raya¹ *nf* 1 (*línea*) line. 2 (*de color*) stripe: *pantalón a rayas* striped trousers.

raya² *nf* (*pez*) skate.

rayado,-a *adj* 1 (*tejido*) striped. 2 (*papel*) ruled.
▶ *nm* **rayado** stripes *pl*.

rayar *vt* 1 (*líneas*) to draw lines on, line, rule. 2 (*superficie*) to scratch.

rayo *nm* 1 ray, beam: *rayo de sol* sunbeam; *rayo de luz* ray of light. 2 (*relámpago*) lightning. [COMP] **rayo de luna** moonbeam. ▌ **rayos ultravioletas/UVA** ultraviolet rays. ▌ **rayos X** X-rays.

rayuela *nf* hopscotch.

raza *nf* 1 race. 2 (*animal*) breed. [LOC] **de raza** 1 (*perro*) pedigree. 2 (*caballo*) thoroughbred. [COMP] **raza humana** human race.

razón *nf* 1 (*facultad*) reason. 2 (*motivo*) reason, cause. 3 (*mensaje*) message. 4 (*justicia*) justice. 5 MAT ratio, rate. [LOC] **dar la razón a** ALGN to agree with SB, say that SB is right. ▌ **perder la razón** to lose one's reason. ▌ **tener razón** to be right.

razonable *adj* reasonable.

razonamiento *nm* reasoning.

razonar *vi* 1 (*discurrir*) to reason. 2 (*hablar*) to talk.
▶ *vt* (*explicar*) to reason out.

re *nm* re, ray, D.

reacción *nf* reaction. [LOC] **reacción en cadena** chain reaction.

reaccionar *vi* to react.

reacio,-a *adj* reluctant, unwilling.

reactivar *vt* to reactivate.

reactor *nm* 1 reactor. 2 AV jet, jet plane.

readmitir *vt* (*gen*) to readmit; (*un trabajador*) to reinstate.

reafirmar *vt* to reaffirm, reassert.

reagrupar *vt* to regroup.
▶ *vpr* **reagruparse** to regroup.

reajustar *vt* to readjust.

real¹ *adj (verdadero)* real: *en la vida real* in real life.

real² *adj (regio)* royal.

realce *nm (adorno)* relief.

realeza *nf* royalty.

realidad *nf* reality. LOC **en realidad** actually, in fact.

realista *adj (de la realidad)* realistic.
▶ *nm o nf (de la realidad)* realist.

realización *nf* **1** *(de un deseo)* fulfilment (US fulfillment). **2** *(ejecución)* execution, carrying out.

realizador,-ra *nm & nf* producer.

realizar *vt* **1** *(ambición)* to realize, fulfil, achieve; *(deseo, esperanza)* to fulfil. **2** *(llevar a cabo)* to accomplish, carry out, do, fulfil. **3** *(un viaje)* to make.
▶ *vpr* **realizarse 1** *(ambición, deseo)* to be fulfilled, be achieved; *(sueño)* to come true. **2** *(llevarse a cabo)* to be executed, be carried out.

realmente *adv* **1** *(de verdad)* really, truly. **2** *(en realidad)* actually, in fact: *realmente no hacía tanto frío* in fact it wasn't too cold.

realzar *vt* **1** *(elevar)* to raise, lift. **2** *fig (engrandecer)* to enhance, heighten.

reanimar *vt* **1** *(persona)* to revive. **2** *(fiesta, conversación)* to liven up.
▶ *vpr* **reanimarse** *(persona)* to revive.

reanudar *vt (gen)* to renew, resume.

reaparecer *vi* **1** *(gen)* to reappear. **2** *(un artista, etc)* to make a comeback. **3** *(un fenómeno)* to recur.

reavivar *vt* **1** *(fuego)* to stoke. **2** *(dolor)* to intensify; *(interés)* to revive.

rebaba *nf* rough edge.

rebaja *nf (descuento)* discount, reduction.
▶ *nf pl* **rebajas** sales.

rebajado,-a *adj* **1** *(precio)* reduced. **2** *(humillado)* humbled.

rebajar *vt* **1** *(nivel)* to lower. **2** *(precio)* to reduce. **3** *(color)* to soften. **4** *fig (humillar)* to humiliate.
▶ *vpr* **rebajarse** *fig (humillarse)* to humble os.

rebanada *nf* slice.

rebañar *vt (comida)* to finish off.

rebaño *nm (gen)* herd; *(de ovejas)* flock.

rebeca *nf* cardigan.

rebelarse *vpr* to rebel, revolt.

rebelde *adj* **1** rebellious. **2** *fig (tos, etc)* persistent.
▶ *nm o nf* rebel.

rebelión *nf* rebellion, revolt.

reblandecer *vt* to soften.
▶ *vpr* **reblandecerse** to soften.

rebobinar *vt* to rewind.

reborde *nm (de mesa)* edge; *(de taza, de tela)* edging.

rebosar *vi* **1** *(derramarse)* to overflow, brim over. **2** *fig* to brim (de, with), burst (de, with): *rebosar de alegría* to be brimming with joy.
▶ *vt fig (sentimiento)* to brim with; *(salud)* to exude.

rebotar *vi (pelota)* to bounce, rebound.

rebote *nm (de balón)* bounce, rebound. LOC **de rebote** *fig* on the rebound.

rebozado,-a *adj* coated in batter.

rebozar *vt* CULIN to coat in batter.

rebrotar *vi* to shoot, sprout.

rebuscado,-a *adj* affected, recherché.

rebuscar *vt* to search carefully for.

rebuznar *vi* to bray.

rebuzno *nm* bray, braying.

recabar *vt* **1** *(solicitar)* to ask for, entreat. **2** *(obtener)* to manage to get.

recadero,-a *nm & nf (gen)* messenger.

recado *nm* **1** *(mensaje)* message. **2** *(encargo)* errand: *me hizo un recado* she ran the errand for me.
▶ *nm pl* **recados** *(compras)* shopping *sing*.

recaer *vi (enfermedad)* to relapse, have a relapse.

recaída *nf (enfermedad)* relapse. LOC **sufrir una recaída** to have a relapse.

recalcar *vt fig* to emphasize, stress.

recalentar *vt* **1** *(volver a calentar)* to warm up. **2** *(calentar demasiado)* to overheat.

recámara *nf* **1** *(cuarto)* dressing room. **2** *(de arma)* chamber.

recambio *nm* spare, spare part; *(de pluma, bolígrafo)* refill.

recapacitar *vi* to think (sobre, over).

R

recapitular *vt* to recapitulate, sum up.

recargado,-a *adj fig (exagerado)* overelaborate, exaggerated, contrived.

recargar *vt* **1** *(volver a cargar)* to reload; *(pilas)* to recharge; *(mechero)* to refill. **2** *(sobrecargar)* to overload. **3** *fig (exagerar)* to overelaborate, exaggerate.

recargo *nm* extra charge, surcharge.

recatado,-a *adj* **1** *(prudente)* cautious, prudent. **2** *(decente)* decent.

recauchutar *vt* to retread, remould.

recaudar *vt* to collect.

recelar *vt* **1** *(sospechar)* to suspect, distrust. **2** *(temer)* to fear.
  ▶ *vi (desconfiar)* to be suspicious (de, of): *recela de todos* he is suspicious of everybody.

recelo *nm* suspicion.

recepción *nf* **1** *(gen)* reception. **2** *(de documento, carta, etc)* receipt.

recepcionista *nm o nf* receptionist.

receptivo,-a *adj* receptive (a, to).

receptor,-ra *nm & nf* receiver, recipient.
  ▶ *nm* **receptor** *(de radio, etc)* receiver.

receta *nf* **1** MED prescription. **2** CULIN recipe.

recetar *vt* to prescribe.

rechazar *vt* **1** *(gen)* to reject, turn down. **2** *(ataque)* to repel, drive back.

rechazo *nm* **1** rejection, refusal. **2** *(negativa)* denial, rejection.

rechinar *vi (madera)* to creak; *(metal)* to squeak, screech; *(dientes)* to grind.

rechistar *vi* to say, reply.

rechoncho,-a *adj fam* chubby, tubby.

rechupete LOC **de rechupete** *fam (muy bien)* super, brill, fantastic. *(comida)* delicious, scrumptious.

recibidor *nm (de casa)* entrance hall.

recibimiento *nm* reception, welcome.

recibir *vt* **1** *(gen)* to receive. **2** *(salir al encuentro)* to meet: *nos recibió en la puerta* he met us at the door.

recibo *nm* **1** *(resguardo)* receipt. **2** *(factura)* invoice, bill.

reciclar *vt (materiales)* to recycle.

recién *adv* [se usa sólo ante un participio pasado] recently, newly; *(café, pan)* freshly: *un pastel recién hecho* a freshly baked cake. LOC «**Recién pintado**» "Wet paint".

reciente *adj* recent.

recinto *nm* grounds *pl*, precincts *pl*.

recio,-a *adj (fuerte)* strong, robust.

recipiente *nm* container, receptacle.

recíproco,-a *adj* reciprocal, mutual: *un sentimiento recíproco* a mutual feeling.

recital *nm* **1** MÚS recital, concert. **2** LIT reading: *recital de poesía* poetry reading.

recitar *vt* to recite.

reclamación *nf* **1** *(demanda)* claim, demand. **2** *(queja)* complaint. LOC **presentar una reclamación** to lodge a complaint.

reclamar *vt (pedir)* to demand, claim.
  ▶ *vi (protestar)* to protest (contra, against): *reclamaron contra aquella medida* they protested against the measure.

reclamo *nm* **1** *(para cazar)* decoy bird, lure. **2** *(anuncio)* advertisement; *(eslogan)* advertising slogan.

reclinar *vt* to lean.
  ▶ *vpr* **reclinarse** to lean back, recline: *se reclinó sobre la almohada* he lent back on the pillow.

recluir *vt (encerrar)* to shut in.

recluso,-a *nm & nf* prisoner.

recluta *nm o nf* recruit.

reclutar *vt* to recruit.

recobrar *vt* **1** *(gen)* to recover. **2** *(aliento)* to get back. **3** *(tiempo)* to make up.
  ▶ *vpr* **recobrarse** *(recuperarse)* to recover (de, from).

recodo *nm* twist.

recogedor *nm* dustpan.

recoger *vt* **1** *(volver a coger)* to take again, take back. **2** *(coger)* to pick up, take back. **3** *(ir a buscar)* to pick up, collect: *me recogerá a las cuatro* he'll pick me up at four o'clock. **4** *(cosecha)* to harvest, gather; *(fruta)* to pick. **5** *(juntar)* to gather, collect. **6** *(velas)* to take in; *(cortinas)* to draw. **7** *(dar asilo)* to take in, shelter: *lo recogieron sus abuelos* he was taken in by his grandparents. **8** *(ordenar)* to clear up, tidy up.

▶ *vpr* **recogerse 1** *(irse a casa)* to go home. **2** *(irse a dormir)* to go to bed.

recolectar *vt* **1** *(reunir)* to gather, collect. **2** *(cosechar)* to harvest.

recomendar *vt* to recommend, advise: *te recomiendo que estudies más* I recommend that you study harder.

recompensa *nf* reward, recompense. LOC **en recompensa** in return.

recompensar *vt* **1** *(compensar)* to compensate. **2** *(remunerar)* to reward.

recomponer *vt* to repair, mend.

reconcentrar *vt* **1** *(concentrar)* to concentrate (en, to). **2** *(reunir)* to bring together.

▶ *vpr* **reconcentrarse** *(ensimismarse)* to become absorbed in thought, concentrate.

reconciliar *vt* to reconcile.

▶ *vpr* **reconciliarse** *(uso recíproco)* to be reconciled.

recóndito,-a *adj* hidden, secret.

reconfortar *vt* **1** *(confortar)* to comfort. **2** *(animar)* to cheer up.

reconocer *vt* **1** *(gen)* to recognize. **2** *(admitir)* to recognize, admit: *reconoció su error* she admitted her mistake. **3** *(afrontar)* to face: *reconozcámoslo* let's face it. **4** MIL *(terreno)* to reconnoitre (US reconnoiter). **5** MED *(paciente)* to examine.

▶ *vpr* **reconocerse 1** to recognize each other. **2** *(admitirse)* to admit: *se reconoció culpable* he admitted his guilt.

reconocimiento *nm* **1** *(gen)* recognition. **2** *(admisión)* admission. **3** MIL reconnaissance. **4** MED checkup.

reconstituyente *nm* tonic.

reconstruir *vt* to reconstruct.

reconvertir *vt* to restructure.

recopilar *vt* to compile, collect.

récord *adj* record: *en un tiempo récord* in record time.

▶ *nm* record.

recordar *vt* **1** *(rememorar)* to remember: *¿recuerdas?* do you remember? **2** *(traer a la memoria)* to remind (a, of): *me recuerda a mi hermano* he reminds me of my brother.

recorrer *vt* **1** *(distancia)* to cover, travel. **2** *(país)* to tour, travel over, travel round. **3** *(ciudad)* to visit, walk round.

recorrido *nm* **1** *(trayecto)* journey, trip. **2** *(distancia)* distance travelled: *un tren de largo recorrido* a long-distance train. **3** *(itinerario)* itinerary, route.

recortar *vt* **1** *(muñecos, telas, etc)* to cut out. **2** *(lo que sobra)* to cut off. **3** *(el pelo)* to trim. **4** *fig* to cut, restrict: *han recortado los gastos* expenses have been cut.

recorte *nm* **1** *(acción)* cutting. **2** *(trozo)* cutting, clipping. **3** *(de periódico)* press clipping, newspaper cutting. **4** *(de pelo)* trim, cut. **5** *fig* *(reducción)* cut, reduction: *recorte del presupuesto* budget cut.

recostar *vt* to lean.

▶ *vpr* **recostarse 1** *(apoyarse)* to lean. **2** *(tumbarse)* to lie down.

recoveco *nm* turn, bend.

recrear *vt* *(divertir)* to amuse, entertain.

▶ *vpr* **recrearse** to amuse OS, enjoy OS.

recreo *nm* *(en la escuela)* playtime, break.

recriminar *vt* **1** *(reprender)* to recriminate. **2** *(reprochar)* to reproach.

recrudecer *vi* *(empeorar)* to worsen, aggravate.

▶ *vpr* **recrudecerse 1** *(empeorar)* to worsen. **2** *(aumentar)* to be increasing.

recta *nf* **1** *(línea)* straight line. **2** *(en carretera)* straight.

rectangular *adj* rectangular.

rectángulo,-a *adj* rectangular: *triángulo rectángulo* right-angled triangle.

▶ *nm* **rectángulo** rectangle.

rectificar *vt* **1** to rectify. **2** *(corregir)* to correct.

recto,-a *adj* **1** *(derecho)* straight. **3** *(ángulo)* right.

▶ *adv* straight, straight on: *vaya todo recto* go straight on.

recuadro *nm* box.

recubrir *vt* to cover (con/de, with).

recuento *nm* recount, count.

recuerdo *nm* **1** *(imagen)* memory. **2** *(regalo)* souvenir, keepsake. LOC **en recuerdo de** in memory of.

R

► *nm pl* **recuerdos** *(saludos)* regards: *me dio recuerdos para ti* he sends you his regards.

recular *vi (retroceder)* to go back.

recuperación *nf* recovery.

recuperar *vt* **1** *(gen)* to recover. **2** *(afecto)* to win back; *(conocimiento)* to regain; *(tiempo, clases)* to make up.
► *vpr* **recuperarse** to recover (de, from).

recurrir *vi (acogerse - a algo)* to resort (a, to); *(- a algn)* to turn (a, to): *recurrió a sus padres* she turned to her parents.

recurso *nm (medio)* resort.
► *nm pl* **recursos** resources, means.

red *nf* **1** *(gen)* net. **2** *(sistema)* network, system. **3** ELEC mains *pl*. **4** INFORM network. **5** *fig (trampa)* trap. COMP **red de carreteras** road network.

redacción *nf* **1** *(escritura)* writing. **2** *(escrito)* composition, essay. **3** *(estilo)* wording. **4** *(oficina)* editorial office. **5** *(redactores)* editorial staff.

redactar *vt (escribir)* to write.

redactor,-ra *nm & nf* editor. COMP **redactor jefe** editor in chief.

redada *nf fig* raid.

redención *nf* redemption.

redescubrir *vt* to rediscover.

redil *nm* fold, sheepfold.

redimir *vt* to redeem.
► *vpr* **redimirse** to redeem OS.

redoblar *vt (aumentar)* to redouble: *redoblar esfuerzos* to redouble one's efforts.
► *vi (tambores)* to roll.

redoble *nm* roll.

redonda LOC **a la redonda** around.

redondear *vt* **1** *(poner redondo)* to round, make round. **2** *(cantidad)* to round up.

redondo,-a *adj* **1** *(circular)* round. **2** *fig (perfecto)* perfect, excellent: *un beneficio redondo* an excellent profit. **3** *fig (cantidad)* round: *en números redondos* in round figures.

reducción *nf* reduction.

reducir *vt* **1** *(gen)* to reduce: *reducir a cenizas* to reduce to ashes. **2** *(disminuir)* to reduce, cut, cut down on: *reducir gastos* to cut down on expenses.

► *vpr* **reducirse 1** *(gen)* to be reduced. **2** *(resultar)* to come down (a, to): *todo se redujo a una equivocación* it all came down to a mistake.

redundante *adj* redundant.

redundar *vi* **1** *(abundar)* to abound. **2** *(resultar)* to redound (en, to): *redundó en nuestro beneficio* it was to our advantage.

reembolsar *vt* **1** *(pagar)* to reimburse. **2** *(devolver)* to refund.

reembolso *nm* **1** *(pago)* reimbursement. **2** *(devolución)* refund. COMP **contra reembolso** cash on delivery.

reemplazar *vt* to replace.

reemplazo *nm* **1** replacement. **2** MIL call-up.

reencarnación *nf* reincarnation.

reencuentro *nm* reunion.

reestreno *nm (teatro)* revival; *(cine)* rerelease, rerun.

reestructurar *vt* to restructure.

referencia *nf (relación)* reference. LOC **hacer referencia a** ALGO to refer to STH.
► *nf pl* **referencias** *(informes)* references.

referéndum *nm inv* referendum.

referente *adj* concerning (a, -), regarding (a, -).

referir *vt* **1** *(expresar)* to tell, relate. **2** *(remitir)* to refer.
► *vpr* **referirse** to refer (a, to).

refilón LOC **mirar** ALGO **de refilón** to look at STH out of the corner of one's eye.

refinado,-a *adj (gen)* refined.

refinamiento *nm* refinement.

refinar *vt (azúcar, etc)* to refine.

refinería *nf* refinery.

reflector,-ra *adj* reflecting.
► *nm* **reflector 1** *(cuerpo)* reflector. **2** ELEC searchlight, spotlight.

reflejar *vt* **1** *(gen)* to reflect. **2** *(mostrar)* to show: *su rostro refleja sus sentimientos* her face shows her feelings.
► *vpr* **reflejarse** to be reflected.

reflejo,-a *adj (movimiento)* reflex.
► *nm* **reflejo 1** *(imagen)* reflection. **2** *(destello)* gleam, glint.

reflexión *nf* reflection.

reflexionar *vi* to reflect (sobre, on), think (sobre, about): *reflexionamos sobre el tema* we reflected on the subject.

reflexivo,-a *adj* reflective, thoughtful.

reforma *nf* **1** (gen) reform. **2** (mejora) improvement.
▶ *nf pl* **reformas** (en construcción) alterations, repairs, improvements. COMP **reforma agraria** agrarian reform.

reformar *vt* **1** (gen) to reform. **2** ARQUIT to renovate, do up.
▶ *vpr* **reformarse** (corregirse) to reform os.

reformatear *vt* INFORM to reformat.

reformatorio *nm* reformatory, reform school. COMP **reformatorio de menores** remand home.

reforzar *vt* to reinforce, strengthen.

refracción *nf* refraction. COMP **ángulo de refracción** angle of refraction.

refrán *nm* proverb, saying.

refregar *vt* **1** to rub hard. **2** *fam fig* to rub in: *me refregó mi error* he kept on about my mistake.

refrenar *vt* to restrain, curb, control.

refrescante *adj* refreshing.

refrescar *vt* **1** (poner fresco) to cool, refresh. **2** *fig* (la memoria) to refresh; (idiomas) to brush up on.
▶ *vi* **1** (el tiempo) to get cooler, cool down, turn cooler. **2** (comida, bebida) to be refreshing.
▶ *vpr* **refrescarse 1** (gen) to cool down, cool off; (lavarse) to freshen up; (tomar el fresco) to get a breath of fresh air. **2** (beber) to have a cold drink.

refresco *nm* (bebida) soft drink.

refriega *nf* (lucha) scuffle, brawl.

refrigeración *nf* **1** refrigeration. **2** (aire acondicionado) air conditioning. **3** (sistema) cooling system.

refrigerador *nm* fridge, refrigerator.

refrigerar *vt* **1** (enfriar) to refrigerate. **2** (con aire acondicionado) to air-condition.

refrigerio *nm* refreshments *pl*, snack.

refuerzo *nm* (fortalecimiento) reinforcement, strengthening.

refugiado,-a *nm & nf* refugee. COMP **refugiado político** political refugee.

refugiar *vt* to shelter, give refuge to.

▶ *vpr* **refugiarse** (gen) to take refuge; (de la lluvia) to shelter.

refugio *nm* (gen) shelter, refuge.

refunfuñar *vi fam* to grumble, moan.

refutar *vt* to refute, disprove.

regadera *nf* watering can

regadío,-a *adj* irrigable.
▶ *nm* **regadío 1** (acción) irrigation, watering. **2** (tierras) irrigated land. COMP **cultivo de regadío** irrigation farming.

regalar *vt* (dar un regalo) to give as a present: *le podemos regalar un libro para su cumpleaños* we can get him a book for his birthday.

regaliz *nm* liquorice (US licorice).

regalo *nm* **1** (obsequio) gift, present. **2** (ganga) bargain, steal.

regañadientes LOC **a regañadientes** reluctantly, grudgingly, unwillingly.

regañar *vt* to scold, tell off
▶ *vi* (reñir) to argue, quarrel, fall out: *no hacen más que regañar* they're always quarrelling.

regar *vt* **1** (plantas, tierra, río) to water. **2** (calle) to wash down, hose down.

regata *nf* MAR regatta, boat race.

regatear *vt* **1** (un precio) to haggle over, barter for. **2** (escatimar) to be sparing with. LOC **no regatear esfuerzos** to spare no effort.
▶ *vi* **1** (comerciar) to haggle, bargain. **2** DEP to dribble. **3** MAR to race.

regateo *nm* **1** (precios) haggling, bargaining. **2** DEP dribbling.

regazo *nm* lap.

regenerar *vt* to regenerate.

regentar *vt* **1** POL to govern, rule. **2** (cargo) to hold. **3** (dirigir) to manage.

regente,-a *adj* ruling, governing.
▶ *nm o nf* POL regent.

reggae *nm* reggae.

régimen *nm* **1** POL regime. **2** MED diet. **3** (condiciones) system, regime, rules *pl*. LOC **estar a régimen** to be on a diet.

regimiento *nm* regiment.

regio,-a *adj* (real) royal, regal.

región *nf* region.

regir *vt* **1** (gobernar) to govern, rule. **2** (dirigir) to manage, direct, run.

▶ *vi (ley, etc)* to be in force, apply: *esta ley aún rige* this law is still in force.

▶ *vpr* **regirse** *(guiarse)* to follow, abide (por, by), go (por, by): *se rige por la opinión de su padre* he goes by his father's opinion.

registrador,-ra *adj* registering, recording: *caja registradora* cash register.

▶ *nm & nf* registrar.

registrar *vt* **1** *(inspeccionar)* to search. **2** *(cachear)* to frisk. **3** *(inscribir)* to register, record, note.

▶ *vpr* **registrarse 1** *(matricularse)* to register, enrol (US enroll). **2** *(detectarse)* to be recorded. **3** *(ocurrir)* to happen: *se ha registrado un terremoto* there has been an earthquake.

registro *nm* **1** *(inspección)* search, inspection. **2** *(inscripción)* registration, recording. **3** JUR *(oficina)* registry. COMP **registro civil** *(oficina)* registry office.

regla *nf* **1** *(norma)* rule. **2** *(pauta)* pattern, rule. **3** *(instrumento)* ruler. **4** *(menstruación)* period. LOC **en regla** in order.

reglamentar *vt* to regulate.

reglamentario,-a *adj* statutory, prescribed, required; *(arma)* regulation.

reglamento *nm* regulations *pl*, rules *pl*.

reglar *vt (regular)* to regulate.

regocijarse *vpr* **1** *(alegrarse)* to be delighted (con, by). **2** *(regodearse)* to delight (de, in), take pleasure (de, in).

regocijo *nm (placer)* delight, joy.

regresar *vi* to return, come back, go back.

regreso *nm* return. LOC **estar de regreso** to be back.

reguero *nm* **1** *(corriente)* trickle of water. **2** *(señal)* trail, trickle.

regular *adj* **1** *(gen)* regular. **2** *fam (pasable)* so-so, average, not bad.

▶ *vt* **1** *(gen)* to regulate. **2** *(ajustar)* to adjust.

regularizar *vt* to regularize; *(normalizar)* to standardize; *(arreglar)* to sort out.

rehabilitar *vt* to rehabilitate.

▶ *nf (en rango)* to reinstate.

rehacer *vt (volver a hacer)* to do again.

▶ *vpr* **rehacerse** *(recuperarse)* to recover, recuperate.

rehén *nm o nf* hostage.

rehogar *vt* to fry lightly.

rehuir *vt* to avoid, shun.

rehusar *vt* to refuse, decline: *rehusé la invitación* I declined the invitation.

reimprimir *vt* to reprint.

reina *nf (gen)* queen.

reinado *nm* reign.

reinar *vi* **1** to reign. **2** *fig (prevalecer)* to reign, prevail: *reina el desconcierto* disorder reigns.

reincidente *adj* **1** relapsing. **2** JUR reoffending, recidivist.

▶ *nm o nf* JUR reoffender, recidivist.

reincidir *vi* **1** to relapse (en, into), fall back (en, into). **2** JUR to reoffend.

reincorporar *vt* to reincorporate.

▶ *vpr* **reincorporarse** to rejoin (a, -): *se reincorporará al trabajo el lunes* she will go back to work on Monday.

reiniciar *vt* to restart.

reino *nm* kingdom, reign.

reinserción *nf* reintegration, rehabilitation: *la reinserción social* social rehabilitation.

reinsertar *vt* to reintegrate.

▶ *vpr* **reinsertarse** to reintegrate.

reintegrar *vt* **1** *(reincorporar)* to reinstate, restore. **2** *(pagar)* to refund, reimburse.

▶ *vpr* **reintegrarse** *(volver a ejercer)* to return (a, to): *se reintegró a su puesto* he returned to his job.

reintegro *nm* **1** FIN reimbursement, repayment, refund. **2** *(de lotería)* refund of the price of the ticket.

reír *vt* to laugh at: *reír las gracias* to laugh at jokes.

▶ *vi* to laugh.

▶ *vpr* **reírse** to laugh (de, at): *¿de qué te ríes?* what are you laughing at?

reiterar *vt* to reiterate, repeat.

reiterativo,-a *adj* repetitive.

reivindicación *nf* claim, demand.

reivindicar *vt* to claim, demand.

reivindicativo,-a *adj* protest.

reja *nf (de ventana)* grill, grille, bar.

rejilla nf 1 (celosía) grill, grille. 2 (de chimenea) grate. 3 (de silla) wickerwork. 4 (de horno) grid iron. 5 (de ventilador) grill. 6 (para equipaje) luggage rack.

rejuvenecer vt to rejuvenate.
▶ vpr **rejuvenecerse** to become rejuvenated.

relación nf 1 (correspondencia) relation, relationship. 2 (conexión) link, connection. 3 (lista) list, record. 4 (relato) account, telling. 5 (en matemática) ratio.
▶ nf pl **relaciones** (conocidos) acquaintances; (contactos) contacts, connections. [LOC] **con relación a / en relación a** with regard to, regarding.

relacionar vt 1 (poner en relación) to relate, connect, associate. 2 (relatar) to tell, list.
▶ vpr **relacionarse** 1 (estar conectado) to be related (con, to), be connected (con, with). 2 (alternar) to get acquainted (con, with), mix (con, with), meet (con, -).

relajante adj relaxing.

relajar vt (gen) to relax.
▶ vpr **relajarse** (descansar) to relax.

relamer vt to lick.
▶ vpr **relamerse** to lick one's lips repeatedly.

relamido,-a adj (pulcro) prim and proper.

relámpago nm flash of lightning.

relampaguear vi [se usa sólo en tercera persona; no lleva sujeto] to flash.

relatar vt 1 (una historia) to narrate, tell. 2 (un suceso) to report, tell.

relativizar vt to lessen the importance of, play down.

relativo,-a adj relative.

relato nm 1 (narración) story, tale. 2 (informe) report, account.

relegar vt to relegate (a, to).

relente nm dew.

relevante adj 1 (significativo) relevant. 2 (importante) excellent, outstanding.

relevar vt 1 (sustituir) to relieve, take over from. 2 (eximir) to exempt (de, from). 3 (destituir) to dismiss, relieve.

relevo nm 1 MIL relief, change of the guard. 2 DEP relay.

relieve nm 1 relief. 2 fig (renombre) renown, fame. [LOC] **en relieve** in relief. ▮ **poner de relieve** fig to emphasize, highlight, underline.

religión nf religion.

religioso,-a adj religious.
▶ nm & nf (hombre) monk; (mujer) nun.

relinchar vi to neigh, whinny.

reliquia nf relic.

rellano nm landing.

rellenar vt 1 (volver a llenar) to refill, fill again. 2 (cuestionario) to fill in, fill out. 3 CULIN (ave) to stuff; (pastel) to fill.

relleno,-a adj 1 (totalmente lleno) stuffed. 2 CULIN stuffed; (pasteles) filled.
▶ nm **relleno** CULIN (aves) stuffing; (pasteles) filling.

reloj nm clock; (de pulsera) watch. [LOC] **contra reloj** against the clock. [COMP] **reloj de arena** hourglass. ▮ **reloj de pulsera** wristwatch.

relojería nf 1 (arte) watchmaking. 2 (tienda) watchmaker's, jeweller's.

relojero,-a nm & nf watchmaker.

reluciente adj shining, gleaming.

relucir vi (brillar) to shine, gleam. [LOC] **sacar a relucir** ALGO to bring up STH.

relumbrar vi to shine, dazzle, gleam.

remachar vt (clavo, etc) to clinch; (metal) to rivet.

remangar vt (mangas, pantalones) to roll up; (faldas, vestidos) to pull up, hitch up.
▶ vpr **remangarse** fig to decide quickly, make a snap decision.

remanso nm 1 (estanque) pool. 2 (lugar tranquilo) quiet place.

remar vi to row.

remarcar vt to stress, underline.

rematado,-a adj 1 absolute, utter, out-and-out. 2 convicted.

rematar vt 1 (acabar) to finish off, round off. 2 (precios) to knock down. 3 DEP to shoot.
▶ vi DEP to take a shot at goal, shoot.

remate nm 1 (final) end, finish. 2 DEP shot. [LOC] **de remate** fam utter, out-and-out, total.

R

remediar vt 1 *(poner remedio)* to remedy. 2 *(reparar)* to repair, make good. 3 *(resolver)* to solve.

remedio nm 1 *(cura)* remedy, cure. 2 *fig (solución)* solution. `LOC` **como último remedio** as a last resort. ▌**no tener más remedio que** to have no choice but to.

rememorar vt to remember, recall.

remendar vt COST to mend; *(ropas)* to patch; *(calcetines)* to darn.

remero,-a nm & nf DEP rower; *(hombre)* oarsman; *(mujer)* oarswoman.

remesa nf 1 *(de dinero)* remittance. 2 *(de mercancías)* consignment, shipment.

remeter vt *(meter adentro)* to tuck in.

remiendo nm mend, darn.

remilgado,-a adj 1 *(afectado)* affected. 2 *(con la comida)* fussy, finicky.

remite nm sender's name and address.

remitente nm o nf sender.

remitir vt 1 *(enviar)* to remit, send. 2 *(referir)* to refer.
▶ vi *(ceder)* to subside: *la fiebre ha remitido* the fever has subsided.
▶ vpr **remitirse** *(atenerse)* to refer (a, to): *se remitió a su propio acuerdo* he referred to his own agreement.

remo nm 1 *(pala)* oar, paddle. 2 DEP rowing.

remodelar vt *(modificar)* to reshape.

remojar vt *(empapar)* to soak (en, in).

remojo nm soaking. `LOC` **poner en remojo** to soak, leave to soak.

remolacha nf beetroot. `COMP` **remolacha azucarera** sugar beet.

remolcador nm 1 MAR tug, tugboat. 2 AUTO breakdown truck.

remolcar vt to tow.

remolino nm 1 *(de polvo)* whirl, cloud; *(de agua)* whirlpool, eddy; *(de aire)* whirlwind. 2 *(de pelo)* tuft.

remolón,-ona adj lazy, slack.

remolonear vi to shirk, slack.

remolque nm 1 *(acción)* towing. 2 *(vehículo)* trailer.

remontar vt 1 *(elevar)* to raise. 2 *(subir)* to go up. 3 *(río)* to sail up; *(vuelo)* to soar.
▶ vpr **remontarse** 1 *(al volar)* to soar. 2 *(datar)* to go back (a, to).

remorder vt fig *(desasosegar)* to trouble, worry.

remordimiento nm remorse.

remoto,-a adj remote, far-off.

remover vt 1 *(trasladar)* to move. 2 *(tierra)* to turn over, dig up. 3 *(líquido)* to stir. 4 *(comida)* to stir; *(ensalada)* to toss. 5 *fig (agitar)* to get moving, stir up.
▶ vpr **removerse** to stir, shift.

remunerar vt to remunerate, reward.

renacimiento nm 1 *(vuelta a nacer)* rebirth. 2 *fig* revival, renaissance. 3 **el Renacimiento** HIST the Renaissance.

renacuajo nm 1 ZOOL tadpole. 2 *fam (niño)* shrimp.

rencor nm 1 *(odio)* rancour (US rancor). 2 *(resentimiento)* resentment.

rencoroso,-a adj 1 *(hostil)* rancorous. 2 *(resentido)* resentful.

rendido,-a adj 1 *(sumiso)* humble, submissive. 2 *(muy cansado)* worn out, exhausted.

rendija nf crack, split.

rendimiento nm 1 *(producción - de terreno)* yield; *(- de máquina)* output; *(- de persona)* progress, performance; *(- de inversión)* yield, return. 2 *(trabajo - de motor, máquina)* performance.

rendir vt 1 *(vencer)* to defeat, conquer. 2 *(cansar)* to exhaust, wear out. 3 *(producir)* to yield, produce; *(progresar)* to progress.
▶ vi *(dar fruto)* to pay.
▶ vpr **rendirse** 1 *(entregarse al enemigo)* to surrender, give in. 2 *(darse por vencido)* to give up: *¡me rindo!* I give up!

renegar vt *(negar)* to deny vigorously.
▶ vi 1 *(gen)* to renounce (de, -). 2 *(protestar)* to grumble, complain.

renglón nm *(línea)* line.

reno nm reindeer.

renombre nm renown, fame.

renovación nf 1 *(de contrato, etc)* renewal. 2 *(de casa)* renovation.

renovar vt 1 *(gen)* to renew. 2 *(casa)* to renovate; *(de decoración)* to redecorate.

renta *nf* **1** *(ingresos)* income. **2** *(declaración de renta)* tax return. **3** *(beneficio)* interest, return. **4** *(alquiler)* rent. COMP **renta per cápita** per capita income.

rentable *adj* profitable.

rentar *vt* to produce, yield.

renuncia *nf* **1** renunciation. **2** *(dimisión)* resignation.

renunciar *vi* **1** *(abandonar)* to give up (a, -), abandon (a, -). **2** *(dimitir)* to resign. **3** to renounce (a, -).

reñido,-a *adj* **1** *(enemistado)* on bad terms, at odds. **2** *(de rivalidad)* bitter, tough, hard-fought.

reñir *vi* **1** *(discutir)* to quarrel, argue. **2** *(desavenirse)* to fall out.
▶ *vt (reprender)* to scold, tell off.

reojo LOC **de reojo** out of the corner of one's eye.

repantigarse *vpr fam* to lounge, loll.

reparación *nf* **1** *(arreglo)* repair. **2** *fig (desagravio)* reparation, redress *pl*.

reparar *vt* **1** *(arreglar)* to repair, mend, fix. **2** *(remediar - daño)* to make good; *(- perjuicio, insulto)* to make up for.

reparo *nm* objection. LOC **no tener reparos en** not to hesitate to.

repartición *nf* distribution.

repartidor,-ra *nm & nf (hombre)* delivery man; *(mujer)* delivery woman; *(chico)* delivery boy; *(chica)* delivery girl.

repartir *vt* **1** *(dividir)* to distribute, divide, share out. **2** *(entregar)* to give out, hand out; *(correo, leche)* to deliver; *(premios)* to give out. **3** *(comida)* to hand out. **4** *(distribuir)* to spread out.

reparto *nm* **1** *(división)* sharing out, division; *(distribución)* distribution. **2** *(de un terreno)* parcelling out; *(de un país)* partition. **3** *(entrega)* handing out; *(de mercancías)* delivery. **4** *(de obra, película)* cast.

repasar *vt (volver a examinar)* to revise, go over.

repaso *nm* check; *(lección)* review. COMP **curso de repaso** refresher course.

repatriar *vt* to repatriate.

repecho *nm* short steep slope.

repelente *adj* repellent, repulsive.

repeler *vt* **1** *(rechazar)* to repel, repulse. **2** *(repugnar)* to disgust, repel.

repente *nm* **1** *fam (movimiento)* sudden movement. **2** *fam (ataque)* fit. LOC **de repente** suddenly, all of a sudden.

repentino,-a *adj* sudden.

repercusión *nf* repercussion.

repercutir *vi fig (trascender)* to have repercussions (en, on), affect.

repertorio *nm* **1** *(resumen)* list, index. **2** TEAT repertoire, repertory.

repesca *nf fam* second chance; *(examen)* resit. LOC **hacer un examen de repesca** to resit an exam.

repetición *nf (gen)* repetition.

repetido,-a *adj* repeated.

repetidor,-ra *nm & nf* EDUC repeat student.
▶ *nm* **repetidor** TÉC relay, booster station.

repetir *vt* **1** *(gen)* to repeat: *se lo repetí dos veces* I told him twice. **2** *(volver a hacer)* to do again, do over again.
▶ *vi* **1** *(volver a servirse)* to have a second helping. **2** EDUC to repeat a year.
▶ *vpr* **repetirse 1** *(persona)* to repeat os. **2** *(hecho)* to recur.

repetitivo,-a *adj* repetitive.

repicar *vt (campanas)* to peal, ring out.

repique *nm* peal, ringing.

repisa *nf* ledge, shelf.

replantear *vt (asunto, problema)* to reconsider, rethink.

replegarse *vpr* to withdraw, retreat.

repleto,-a *adj* jam-packed (de, with).

réplica *nf* **1** *(respuesta)* answer, reply.

replicar *vt (contestar)* to answer, reply.
▶ *vi* to argue, answer back.

repliegue *nm (pliegue)* fold, crease.

repoblar *vt* to repopulate; *(bosque)* to reafforest, reforest.

repollo *nm* cabbage.

reponer *vt* **1** *(reemplazar)* to replace. **2** *(en el cine)* to rerun.
▶ *vpr* **reponerse** *(salud, susto)* to recover.

reportaje *nm* **1** *(prensa, radio)* report. **2** *(noticias)* article, news item.

reportero,-a *nm & nf* reporter.

R

reposar vi 1 *(descansar)* to rest, take a rest. 2 *(yacer)* to rest, lie, be buried. 3 *(un líquido)* to settle. LOC **dejar reposar** CULIN to leave to stand.

reposo nm 1 *(descanso)* rest. 2 *(tranquilidad)* peace.

repostar vt 1 *(provisiones)* to stock up with. 2 *(coche)* to fill up.

repostería nf *(pastas)* cakes pl; *(chocolate, bombones)* confectionery.

reprender vt to reprimand, scold.

represa nf dam.

represalia nf reprisal, retaliation.

representación nf 1 *(gen)* representation. 2 TEAT performance. LOC **en representación de** as a representative of.

representante adj representative.
▶ nm o nf representative.

representar vt 1 *(gen)* to represent. 2 *(símbolo)* to represent, stand for: *una paloma representa la paz* a dove stands for peace. 3 TEAT *(obra)* to perform; *(papel)* to play (the part of).

representativo,-a adj representative.

represión nf repression.

represivo,-a adj repressive.

reprimenda nf reprimand.

reprimido,-a adj repressed.
▶ nm & nf repressed person.

reprimir vt *(gen)* to repress, suppress.
▶ vpr **reprimirse** to control os.

reprochar vt to reproach, censure.

reproche nm reproach, criticism.

reproducción nf reproduction.

reproducir vt to reproduce, repeat.
▶ vpr **reproducirse** 1 *(gen)* to reproduce. 2 *(volver a ocurrir)* to recur.

reproductor,-ra adj 1 *(gen)* reproducing. 2 ANAT reproductive.

reptar vi *(arrastrarse)* to crawl, slither.

reptil nm reptile.

república nf republic.

republicano,-a adj republican.
▶ nm & nf republican.

repudiar vt to repudiate.

repuesto,-a nm 1 *(prevención)* store, supply, stock. 2 *(recambio)* spare, spare part. LOC **de repuesto** spare, in reserve.

repugnante adj repugnant, disgusting.

repugnar vt 1 *(negar)* to deny. 2 *(contradecir)* to contradict.

repujado,-a adj embossed, repoussé.

repujar vt to emboss.

repulsión nf repulsion, repugnance.

repulsivo,-a adj repulsive, revolting.

repuntar vi 1 *(la marea)* to turn. 2 *(economía)* to recover, pick up.

reputación nf reputation.

requemado,-a adj scorched, burnt.

requemar vt 1 *(gen)* to scorch, burn.

requerimiento nm 1 *(súplica)* request. 2 JUR *(aviso)* summons pl; *(intimación)* injunction.

requerir vt 1 *(necesitar)* to require, need: *esto requiere gran paciencia* this requires a lot of patience. 2 *(decir con autoridad)* to demand, call for. 3 *(solicitar)* to request.

requesón nm cottage cheese.

réquiem nm requiem.

requisar vt 1 MIL to requisition. 2 *fam (apropiarse)* to grab, swipe.

requisito nm requisite, requirement.

res nf *(gen)* beast, animal; *(cabeza de ganado)* head.

resaca nf 1 *(de las olas)* undertow, undercurrent. 2 *(de borrachera)* hangover.

resaltar vi fig *(distinguirse)* to stand out (de, from).
▶ vt to highlight, stress, emphasize.

resbaladizo,-a adj slippery.

resbalar vi 1 *(deslizarse)* to slide. 2 *(sin querer - persona)* to slip.

resbalón nm slip.

rescatar vt 1 *(rehén, náufrago, persona atrapada, etc)* to rescue; *(cadáver)* to recover; *(ciudad)* to recapture. 2 *(recuperar)* to recover.

rescate nm 1 *(salvamento)* rescue; *(de ciudad)* recapture. 2 *(dinero)* ransom. 3 *(recuperación)* recovery, recapture.

resecar vt to dry up.
▶ vpr **resecarse** to dry up.

reseco,-a *adj (seco)* very dry, parched.

resentido,-a *adj* resentful. LOC **estar resentido,-a con** ALGN to bear resentment towards SB.

resentimiento *nm* resentment.

reseña *nf* **1** *(crítica)* review; *(en prensa)* write-up. **2** *(descripción)* description.

reseñar *vt* **1** *(crítica)* to review. **2** *(describir)* to describe.

reserva *nf* **1** *(de plazas, entradas)* booking, reservation. **2** *(provisión)* reserve; *(existencias)* stock. **3** *(cautela)* reservation. **4** *(discreción)* discretion, reserve. **5** *(vino)* vintage. **6** *(de animales)* reserve; *(de personas)* reservation. **7** MIL reserve, reserves *pl*.
▶ *nf pl* **reservas** COM reserves, stock *sing*.

reservado,-a *adj* **1** *(persona)* reserved. **2** *(asunto)* confidential.
▶ *nm* **reservado** *(en local)* private room; *(en tren)* reserved compartment.

reservar *vt* **1** *(plazas, etc)* to book, reserve. **2** *(guardar)* to keep, save. **3** *(ocultar)* to withhold, keep to OS.
▶ *vpr* **reservarse 1** *(conservarse)* to save OS *(para, for)*. **2** to withhold, keep to OS: *se reservó su opinión* she kept her opinion to herself.

resfriado,-a *adj* with a cold.
▶ *nm* **resfriado** cold.

resfriar *vt (enfriar)* to cool.
▶ *vpr* **resfriarse** MED to catch a cold.

resguardar *vt* **1** *(proteger)* to protect *(de, from)*, shelter *(de, from)*. **2** *(salvaguardar)* to safeguard *(de, against)*.
▶ *vpr* **resguardarse** *(protegerse)* to protect OS.

resguardo *nm* **1** *(protección)* protection, shelter. **2** *(garantía)* safeguard, guarantee. **3** *(recibo)* receipt, ticket.

residencia *nf (gen)* residence. COMP **residencia de ancianos** old people's home.

residir *vi* **1** to reside *(en, in)*, live *(en, in)*. **2** *fig* to lie *(en, in)*.

residuo *nm* residue.
▶ *nm pl* **residuos** waste *sing*, refuse *sing*.

resignación *nf* resignation.

resignado,-a *adj* resigned.

resignar *vt* to resign, relinquish.
▶ *vpr* **resignarse** to resign OS *(a, to)*.

resina *nf* resin.

resistencia *nf* **1** *(gen)* resistance. **2** *(aguante)* endurance, stamina. **3** *(oposición)* resistance, opposition. **4** ELEC resistance. **5** *(de materiales)* strength.

resistente *adj* **1** *(que resiste)* resistant *(a, to)*. **2** *(fuerte)* tough, strong.

resistir *vi* **1** *(aguantar - algo)* to hold (out); *(- alguien)* to hold out, take (it), have endurance. **2** *(durar)* to endure, last. **3** *(ejército)* to hold out, resist.
▶ *vt* **1** *(soportar)* to stand, tolerate. **2** *(peso, etc)* to bear, withstand, take. **3** *(tentación, etc)* to resist.
▶ *vpr* **resistirse 1** *(rechazar)* to resist. **2** *fam (costar)* to be difficult, be hard: *la física se le resiste* he's struggling with physics. **3** *(negarse)* to refuse: *me resisto a creerlo* I find it hard to believe.

resolución *nf* **1** *(decisión)* resolution, decision; *(determinación)* determination, resolve. **2** *(solución)* solution; *(de un conflicto)* settlement; *(en técnica)* resolution.

resolver *vt* **1** *(solucionar - gen)* to resolve, solve; *(- asunto, conflicto)* to resolve, settle; *(- dificultad)* to overcome. **2** *(decidir)* to resolve, decide *(-, to)*. **3** *(deshacer)* to resolve. **4** QUÍM to dissolve.
▶ *vpr* **resolverse 1** *(solucionarse)* to be solved; *(resultar)* to work out. **2** *(reducirse)* to end up *(en, in)*, turn out.

resonancia *nf* **1** resonance. **2** *(eco)* echo. **3** *fig (importancia)* importance; *(consecuencias)* repercussions *pl*.

resorte *nm* **1** spring. **2** *fig* means *pl*.

respaldar *vt* to support, back (up).
▶ *vpr* **respaldarse 1** to lean back *(en, on)*. **2** *(apoyarse)* to lean *(en, on)*.

respaldo *nm* **1** back. **2** *fig* support, backing.

respectivamente *adv* respectively.

respectivo,-a *adj* respective. LOC **en lo respectivo a** with regard to, regarding.

respetar *vt* to respect.

respeto nm **1** (gen) respect. **2** fam (miedo) fear.
▶ nm pl **respetos** respects. COMP **falta de respeto** lack of respect.

respetuoso,-a adj respectful.

respiración nf (acción) breathing, respiration. **2** (aliento) breath more easily, breathe.

respirar vi **1** to breathe. **2** (estar vivo) to be breathing. **3** fig (relajarse) to breathe more easily, breathe a sigh of relief: al oír al doctor, respiramos when we heard what the doctor had to say we breathed a sigh of relief. LOC **sin respirar 1** (sin descanso) nonstop. **2** (con atención) attentively.
▶ vt (absorber) to breathe, breathe in, inhale.

respiratorio,-a adj respiratory.

respiro nm **1** (resuello) breathing. **2** fig (descanso) breather, break. **3** fig (alivio) relief, respite.

resplandor nm (de luz) brightness, brilliance; (de metales, cristales) gleam, glitter; (del fuego) glow, blaze.

responder vt (contestar) to answer.
▶ vi **1** (contestar) to answer, reply. **2** (replicar) to answer back. **3** (corresponder) to answer, respond to: tengo que responder a su amabilidad I have to respond to his kindness. **4** (tener el efecto deseado) to respond: el motor respondió bien the engine responded well. **5** (ser responsable) to answer (de, for), accept responsibility (de, for).

responsabilidad nf responsibility.

responsable adj responsible.
▶ nm o nf **1** (encargado) person in charge. **2** (de un crimen) perpetrator, culprit, person responsible. LOC **hacerse responsable de algo** to assume responsibility for STH.

respuesta nf **1** (gen) answer, reply. **2** (reacción) response. LOC **en respuesta a** in response to.

resquebrajar vt to crack.
▶ vpr **resquebrajarse** to crack.

resta nf subtraction.

restablecer vt (gen) to reestablish; (orden, monarquía) to restore.

▶ vpr **restablecerse 1** (gen) to be reestablished; (orden, etc) to be restored. **2** MED to recover, get better.

restablecimiento nm **1** (gen) reestablishment; (orden, etc) restoration. **2** MED recovery.

restante adj remaining.
▶ nm **lo restante** the rest, the remainder, what is left over.

restar vt **1** MAT to subtract, take (away). **2** fig (quitar) to reduce, deduct. **3** DEP to return.
▶ vi (quedar) to be left, remain. LOC **restar importancia a algo** to play STH down, play down the importance of STH.

restauración nf (restablecimiento) restoration.

restaurante nm restaurant.

restaurar vt (obra, etc) to restore.

resto nm **1** remainder, rest. **2** MAT remainder.
▶ nm pl **restos 1** (gen) remains; (ruinas) ruins. **2** (de comida) leftovers.

restricción nf restriction.

restringir vt **1** (limitar) to restrict, limit. **2** (astringir) to contract.

resucitar vt **1** to resuscitate. **2** fig to revive.
▶ vi to resuscitate.

resuelto,-a adj (decidido) resolute, determined.

resultado nm result.

resultar vi **1** (gen) to result, be the result of. **2** (ser) to be: resultó vencedor he won. **3** (acabar siendo) to turn out to be: resultó ser muy agradable he turned out to be very nice. **4** (salir) to come out, turn out, work out: todo resultó como esperábamos it all worked out as we expected. **5** (ocurrir) to turn out: resulta que está enfermo y no puede venir it turns out that he's ill and can't come. **6** (ser conveniente) to be advisable. **7** (tener éxito) to be a success, come off: el negocio resultó the business was a success. LOC **resulta que** it turns out that.

resumen nm summary.

resumir vt **1** (reducir) to summarize. **2** (concluir) to sum up: resumiendo, es una *novela excelente* in short, it's an excellent novel.

▶ *vpr* **resumirse 1** to be summarized, be summed up. **2** *(venir a ser)* to be reduced (en, to), boil down (en, to).

resurgir *vi* **1** *(volver a aparecer)* to reappear. **2** *(revivir)* to revive.

retablo *nm* altarpiece, reredos.

retaguarda *nf* rearguard. ⓁⓄⒸ **ir a la retaguarda** to bring up the rear.

retal *nm* *(de tela)* offcut, remnant.

retama *nf* broom.

retar *vt* **1** *(desafiar)* to challenge. **2** *fam (reprender)* to scold.

retazo *nm* remnant, fragment.

retención *nf* **1** *(gen)* retention. **2** FIN withholding, deduction. **3** *(de tráfico)* traffic jam, (traffic) hold-up.

retener *vt* **1** *(contener)* to restrain, hold back. **2** *(no dejar marchar)* to keep, keep back: *no quiero retenerte* I don't want to keep you. **3** *(no devolver)* to keep. **4** *(en la memoria)* to retain, remember. **5** *(detener)* to detain; *(arrestar)* to arrest. **6** FIN to deduct, withhold. **7** *(absorber)* to retain, hold: *el algodón retiene el agua* cotton holds water.

▶ *vpr* **retenerse** to restrain OS, hold OS back.

retina *nf* retina.

retirada *nf* MIL. retreat, withdrawal.

retirado,-a *adj* **1** *(apartado)* remote. **2** *(tranquilo)* secluded, quiet. **3** *(jubilado)* retired.

▶ *nm & nf* retired person, US retiree.

retirar *vt* **1** *(apartar - gen)* to take away, remove; *(- un mueble)* to move away. **2** *(un carnet)* to take away. **3** *(algo dicho)* to take back. **4** *(dinero, ley, moneda)* to withdraw. **5** *(jubilar)* to retire.

▶ *vpr* **retirarse 1** MIL to retreat, withdraw. **2** *(apartarse del mundo)* to go into seclusion. **3** *(apartarse)* to withdraw, draw back, move back: *retírate, no veo* move back, I can't see. **4** *(alejarse)* to move away: *retírate de la ventana* move away from the window. **5** *(irse a descansar)* to retire: *se retiró a su habitación* she retired to her bedroom. **7** *(jubilarse)* to

retire. ⓁⓄⒸ **no se retire** *(al teléfono)* hold on, don't hang up.

retiro *nm* **1** *(jubilación)* retirement. **2** *(pensión)* pension.

reto *nm* challenge.

retocar *vt* *(dibujo, fotografía)* to touch up, retouch.

retoque *nm* finishing touch.

retorcer *vt* **1** *(gen)* to twist. **2** *(ropa)* to wring (out).

▶ *vpr* **retorcerse 1** *(gen)* to become twisted, twist. **2** *(doblarse)* to bend. ⓁⓄⒸ **retorcerse de risa** *fig* to double up with laughter.

retorcido,-a *adj fig* twisted: *mente retorcida* warped mind.

retornable *adj* returnable. ⓁⓄⒸ «Envase no retornable» "Non-returnable".

retorno *nm* **1** return. **2** *(recompensa)* reward.

retortijón *nm* *(de tripas)* stomach cramp.

retozar *vi* to frolic, gambol.

retraído,-a *adj* **1** *(tímido)* shy, reserved. **2** *(poco comunicativo)* unsociable, withdrawn.

retraimiento *nm* *(timidez)* shyness, reserve, retiring nature.

retransmisión *nf* broadcast, transmission.

retransmitir *vt* RAD TV to broadcast. ⓁⓄⒸ **retransmitir algo en directo** to broadcast STH live.

retrasado,-a *adj* **1** *(en conocimientos, trabajo)* behind. **2** *(pagos)* late. **3** *(reloj)* slow. **4** *(tren, avión, etc)* delayed. **5** *(país)* backward, underdeveloped.

▶ *nm & nf* mentally retarded person.

retrasar *vt* **1** *(atrasar)* to delay, put off, postpone. **2** *(reloj)* to put back. **3** DEP to pass back.

▶ *vpr* **retrasarse 1** *(atrasarse)* to be late, arrive late, be delayed. **2** *(reloj)* to be slow. **3** *(trabajo, conocimientos, pagos)* to fall behind.

retraso *nm* **1** *(demora)* delay. **2** *(subdesarrollo)* backwardness, underdevelopment.

R

retratar vt 1 *(pintura)* to portray, paint a portrait of. 2 *(foto)* to photograph, take a photograph of. 3 *fig* to describe, portray, depict.
▸ vpr **retratarse** *(darse a conocer)* to be described, be portrayed.

retrato nm 1 *(pintura)* portrait. 2 *(foto)* photograph. 3 *fig (descripción)* description, depiction, portrayal. LOC **ser el vivo retrato de** ALGN to be the spitting image of SB.

retrete nm toilet, lavatory.

retribución nf 1 *(pago)* pay, payment. 2 *(recompensa)* recompense, reward.

retribuir vt 1 *(pagar)* to pay. 2 *(recompensar)* to remunerate, reward.

retroceder vi 1 *(recular)* to go back, move back. 2 *(bajar de nivel)* to go down.

retroceso nm 1 *(movimiento)* backward movement. 2 *(económico)* recession.

retrógrado,-a adj 1 *(que retrocede)* retrograde. 2 *fig (reaccionario)* reactionary.
▸ nm & nf *(reaccionario)* reactionary.

retrospectivo,-a adj retrospective.

retumbar vi 1 *(resonar)* to resound, echo. 2 *(tronar)* to thunder, boom.

reuma nm rheumatism.

reúma nm rheumatism.

reumático,-a adj rheumatic.
▸ nm & nf rheumatic.

reumatismo nm rheumatism.

reunificar vt to reunify.

reunión nf *(gen)* meeting, gathering.

reunir vt 1 *(congregar)* get together. 2 *(juntar algo)* to put together: *reunimos todos nuestros libros* we put all our books together. 3 *(recoger)* to gather (together); *(dinero)* to raise. 4 *(coleccionar)* to collect. 5 *(tener)* to have, possess. 6 *(requisitos)* to satisfy, meet, fulfil (US fulfill).
▸ vpr **reunirse** to meet (con, -), get together, have a meeting with.

reutilizar vt to reuse.

reválida nf final examination.

revalidar vt to confirm, ratify, validate.

revalorización nf *(de moneda)* revaluation; *(de precio)* appreciation, increase in value.

revalorizar vt *(moneda)* to revalue; *(precio)* to increase the value of.
▸ vpr **revalorizarse** *(moneda)* to revalue; *(precio)* to appreciate, go up in value.

revancha nf 1 revenge. 2 *(en naipes)* return game. 3 DEP return match.

revelación nf revelation.

revelado nm developing.

revelador,-ra adj revealing.
▸ nm revelador developer.

revelar vt 1 to reveal, disclose. 2 *(fotos)* to develop.

revender vt 1 *(gen)* to resell. 2 *(al por menor)* to retail. 3 *(entradas)* to tout.

reventa nf 1 *(gen)* resale. 2 *(al por menor)* retail. 3 *(de entradas)* touting.

reventar vt 1 *(gen)* to burst. 2 *(neumático)* to puncture, burst. 3 *(romper)* to break, smash. 4 *(estropear)* to ruin, spoil. 5 *fig (agotar)* to exhaust, tire out.
▸ vi 1 *fam (fastidiar)* to annoy: *me revientan sus preguntas* her questions get on my nerves. 2 *(estallar)* to burst: *la cañería reventó* the pipe burst.
▸ vpr **reventarse** 1 *(estallar)* to burst. 2 *fam (cansarse)* to tire OS out.

reventón,-ona nm 1 *(de cañería)* burst. 2 *(de neumático)* blowout.

reverendo,-a adj 1 reverend. 2 *fam (enorme)* enormous, great.
▸ nm & nf reverend.

reversible adj reversible.

reverso nm reverse, back.

revés nm 1 *(reverso)* back, reverse, wrong side; *(de tela)* wrong side. 2 *(bofetada)* slap; *(golpe)* backhander. 3 *(en tenis)* backhand (stroke). 4 *fig (contrariedad)* misfortune, setback, reverse. LOC **al revés** *(al contrario)* the other way round.

revestimiento nm covering, coating.

revestir vt 1 *(recubrir)* to cover (de, with), coat (de, with), line (de, with). 3 *fig (presentar)* to take on: *la* *ceremonia revistió gran solemnidad* the ceremony took on great solemnity.

▶ *vpr* **revestirse** to arm OS: *revestirse de paciencia* to arm OS with patience.

revisar *vt* **1** *(gen)* to revise, go through, check. **2** *(examen, etc)* to check, look over. **3** *(cuentas)* to check, audit.

revisión *nf* **1** *(gen)* revision, checking. **2** *(de billetes)* inspection. **3** *(de coche)* service, overhaul. [COMP] **revisión médica** checkup.

revisor,-ra *nm & nf* ticket inspector.

revista *nf* **1** *(publicación)* magazine, review, journal. **2** *(inspección)* inspection. **3** MIL review. **4** TEAT revue: *chica de revista* chorus girl.

revistero *nm* magazine rack.

revitalizar *vt* to revitalize.

revivir *vi* to revive.

▶ *vt* to revive, bring back to life.

revocar *vt* *(ley)* to revoke, repeal; *(orden)* to cancel, rescind.

revolcar *vt* *(derribar al suelo)* to knock down, knock over.

▶ *vpr* **revolcarse** *(echarse)* to roll about.

revolotear *vi* to fly about, flutter about, hover.

revoloteo *nm* fluttering, hovering.

revoltijo *nm* *(mezcla)* mess, clutter, jumble.

revoltoso,-a *adj* **1** *(rebelde)* rebellious.

▶ *nm & nf* rebel, troublemaker.

revolución *nf* revolution.

revolucionario,-a *adj* revolutionary.

▶ *nm & nf* revolutionary.

revolver *vt* **1** *(agitar)* to stir. **2** *(mezclar)* to mix. **3** *(ensalada)* to toss. **4** *(habitación, casa, etc)* to turn upside down. **5** *(papeles)* to rummage through; *(bolso, bolsillo, etc)* to rummage in. **6** *(producir náuseas)* to upset, turn: *le revolvió el estómago* it turned his stomach.

▶ *vpr* **revolverse 1** *(moverse)* to fidget; *(en la cama)* to toss and turn. **2** *(volverse con rapidez)* to turn around, spin round. **3** *(tiempo)* to turn stormy; *(mar)* to become rough.

revólver *nm* revolver.

revoque *nm* *(enlucido)* plastering.

revuelta *nf* *(revolución)* revolt, riot.

revuelto,-a *adj* **1** *(desordenado)* confused, mixed up, in a mess. **2** *(gente)* agitated, restless, up in arms. **3** *(tiempo)* stormy, unsettled; *(mar)* rough. **4** *(época)* turbulent: *tiempos revueltos* turbulent times.

rey *nm* king.

rezar *vi* **1** *(orar)* to pray. **2** *(decir)* to say, read.

ría *nf* *(gen)* estuary, river mouth; *(técnicamente)* ria.

riachuelo *nm* brook, stream.

riada *nf* **1** flood, flooding. **2** *fig* flood.

ribera *nf* **1** *(de río)* bank. **2** *(del mar)* shore, seashore. **3** *(tierra cercana a un río)* riverside, waterfront.

ribete *nm* *(cinta)* border, trimming, edging.

ribetear *vt* to edge, border.

ribonucleico,-a *adj* ribonucleic.

rico,-a *adj* **1** *(acaudalado)* rich, wealthy. **2** *(abundante)* rich: *rico en potasio* rich in potassium. **3** *(sabroso)* tasty, delicious. **4** *(tierra)* rich, fertile. **5** *(excelente)* rich, excellent. **6** *fam (bonito)* lovely, adorable: *tiene un niño muy rico* she's got a lovely boy.

▶ *nm & nf* rich person.

ridiculizar *vt* to ridicule, deride.

ridículo,-a *adj* ridiculous, absurd.

▶ *nm* **ridículo** ridicule. [LOC] **hacer el ridículo** to make a fool of OS.

riego *nm* irrigation, watering. [COMP] **riego sanguíneo** blood circulation.

riel *nm* rail.

rienda *nf* **1** rein. **2** *fig (control)* restraint. [LOC] **llevar las riendas** *fig* to hold the reins, be in control.

riesgo *nm* risk, danger. [LOC] **a todo riesgo** *(seguro)* fully-comprehensive.

rifa *nf* raffle.

rifar *vt* to raffle (off).

▶ *vpr* **rifarse 1** MAR to split. **2** *(solicitar, desear)* to fight over.

rifle *nm* rifle.

rigidez *nf* **1** *(dureza)* stiffness, rigidity. **2** *fig (rectitud)* strictness, firmness, inflexibility.

R

rígido,-a *adj* **1** *(duro)* rigid, stiff. **2** *fig (severo)* strict, firm, inflexible.

rigor *nm* **1** *(severidad)* rigour (US rigor), strictness, severity. **2** *(dureza)* rigour (US rigor), harshness. **3** *(exactitud)* precision, exactness.

rigurosamente *adv* **1** *(con severidad)* rigorously, severely, strictly. **2** *(con exactitud)* accurately. **3** *(minuciosamente)* meticulously. **4** *(totalmente)* absolutely.

rigurosidad *nf* rigorousness, strictness.

riguroso,-a *adj* **1** *(severo)* rigorous, severe, strict. **2** *(clima)* rigorous, severe, harsh. **3** *(exacto)* exact. **4** *(minucioso)* meticulous.

rima *nf* rhyme.
▶ *nf pl* **rimas** poem *sing*.

rimar *vt* to rhyme.
▶ *vi* to rhyme.

rincón *nm* corner.

rinconera *nf* corner unit.

ring *nm* ring.

rinoceronte *nm* rhinoceros.

riña *nf* **1** *(pelea)* fight. **2** *(discusión)* quarrel.

riñón *nm* **1** kidney.

río *nm* **1** river. **2** *fig* stream, river: *un río de sangre* a river of blood.

riqueza *nf (cualidad)* richness, wealthiness.

risa *nf* **1** laugh. **2** *(risas)* laughter. LOC **darle risa a** ALGN to make SB laugh. **entrar la risa** to begin to laugh: **ser cosa de risa** to be laughable. COMP **ataque de risa** fit of laughter.

risco *nm* crag, cliff.

ristra *nf* string.

risueño,-a *adj* **1** *(sonriente)* smiling. **2** *(animado)* cheerful.

rítmico,-a *adj* rhythmic, rhythmical.

ritmo *nm* **1** rhythm. **2** *fig* pace, speed.

rito *nm* **1** REL rite. **2** *fig (costumbre)* ritual.

ritual *adj* ritual.
▶ *nm* ritual.

rival *adj* rival.
▶ *nm o nf* rival.

rivalidad *nf* rivalry.

rivalizar *vi* to rival.

rivera *nf* brook, stream.

rizado,-a *adj* **1** *(pelo)* curly. **2** MAR choppy.
▶ *nm* **rizado** *(de pelo)* curling.

rizar *vt (pelo)* to curl.
▶ *vpr* **rizarse 1** *(pelo)* to curl, go curly. **2** *(el mar)* to ripple.

rizo *nm* **1** *(de pelo)* curl. **2** *(en el agua)* ripple. **3** *(tejido)* towelling (US toweling), terry towelling. **4** AV loop.

rizoma *nm* rhizome.

robar *vt* **1** *(banco, persona)* to rob; *(objeto)* to steal; *(casa)* to break into, burgle. **2** *(raptar)* to kidnap. **3** *(en naipes)* to draw. **4** *fig (cobrar muy caro)* to rip off. **5** *fig (corazón, alma)* to steal.

robinia *nf* robinia, false acacia.

roble *nm* oak, oak tree.

robledal *nm* oak grove, oak wood.

robo *nm* **1** *(gen)* theft, robbery; *(en casa)* burglary; *(en banco)* robbery. **2** *(en naipes)* draw. **3** *fig (estafa)* robbery.

robot *nm* robot.

robótica *nf* robotics.

robótico,-a *adj* robotic, robot-like.

robotizar *vt* to automate.

robustecer *vt* to strengthen.
▶ *vpr* **robustecerse** to grow stronger, gain strength.

robusto,-a *adj* robust, strong, sturdy.

roca *nf* rock.

roce *nm* **1** *(fricción)* rubbing; *(en piel)* chafing. **2** *(señal - en zapatos)* scuff mark; *(- en piel)* graze; *(- en coche, etc)* mark. **3** *(contacto físico)* light touch, brush. **4** *fam (trato)* contact. **5** *fam (disensión)* friction, brush.

rociar *vt* **1** *(salpicar)* to spray, sprinkle. **2** *fig (esparcir)* to scatter, strew.

rocín *nm* *(caballo)* nag, hack.

rocío *nm* dew.

rock *nm* rock.

rockero,-a *nm & nf (músico)* rock musician; *(fan)* rock fan.

rococó *adj* rococo.

rocoso,-a *adj* rocky, stony.

rodaballo *nm* turbot.

rodaja *nf* slice. LOC **en rodajas** sliced.

rodaje *nm* **1** CINE filming, shooting. **2** AUTO running-in.

rodamiento *nm* bearing.

rodapié *nm* skirting board, US baseboard.

rodar *vi* **1** *(dar vueltas)* to roll, *(rueda)* to turn. **2** *(caer rodando)* to roll down. **3** *fig (ir de un lado a otro)* to roam. **4** *(vehículos)* to run; *(velocidad)* to do.
▶ *vt* **1** *(hacer que de vueltas)* to roll. **2** CINE to film, shoot. **3** AUTO to run in. **4** *(recorrer)* to travel.

rodear *vt (cercar)* to surround, encircle.
▶ *vpr* **rodearse** to surround OS *(de,* with).

rodela *nf* round shield.

rodeno,-a *adj* red.

rodeo *nm* **1** *(desviación)* detour. **2** *fig (elusión)* evasiveness.

rodera *nf* tyre (US tire) mark, track.

rodilla *nf* **1** ANAT knee. **2** *(paño)* cloth, floorcloth.

rodillazo *nm* blow with the knee, blow to the knee.

rodillera *nf* **1** DEP knee pad. **2** COST knee patch.

rodillo *nm* **1** roller. **2** CULIN rolling pin.

rododendro *nm* rhododendron.

rodomiel *nm* rose honey.

roedor,-ra *adj* rodent.
▶ *nm* **roedor** rodent.

roer *vt* **1** *(hueso)* to gnaw. **2** *fig (desgastar)* to wear away.

rogar *vt (pedir)* to request, ask; *(implorar)* to beg, implore, plead.

rogativa *nf* rogation.

roído,-a *adj* gnawed, eaten away.

rojear *vi* to redden, turn red.

rojez *nf* redness.

rojizo,-a *adj* reddish.

rojo,-a *adj (color)* red.
▶ *nm & nf* POL *(gen)* red, Communist.
▶ *nm* **rojo** red.

rol *nm (papel)* role.

rollista *nm o nf fam (cuentista)* over-dramatic person.

rollizo,-a *adj* plump, chubby.

rollo *nm* **1** *(gen)* roll. **2** *fam (aburrimiento)* drag, bore, pain: *esta peli es un rollo* this film is a drag. **3** *fam (discurso, explicación, etc)* long drawn-out speech, boring lecture. **4** *fam (amorío)* affair. **5** *fam (asunto)* business.

romance *adj* LING Romance.
▶ *nm* **1** LING *(gen)* Romance language; *(castellano)* Spanish. **2** *(amorío)* romance.

romancero *nm* collection of romances.

románico,-a *adj* **1** *(arquitectura, arte - gen)* Romanesque. **2** *(lengua)* Romance.

romanizar *vt* to Romanize.

romanticismo *nm* romanticism.

romántico,-a *adj* romantic.
▶ *nm & nf* romantic.

rómbico,-a *adj* rhombic.

rombo *nm* **1** rhombus. **2** *(naipes)* diamond.

romboedro *nm* rhombohedron.

romboide *nm* rhomboid.

romería *nf* pilgrimage.

romero *nm* BOT rosemary.

romo,-a *adj (sin punta)* blunt, dull.

rompecabezas *nm inv* **1** *(juego)* (jigsaw) puzzle. **2** *fig (problema)* riddle, puzzle, conundrum.

rompecocos *nm inv* brain-teaser.

rompecorazones *nm o nf inv fam* heartthrob, heartbreaker.

rompehielos *nm inv* icebreaker.

rompeolas *nm inv* breakwater, jetty.

romper *vt* **1** *(gen)* to break; *(papel, tela)* to tear. **2** *(rajar, reventar)* to split. **3** *(gastar)* to wear out. **4** *fig (relaciones)* to break off. **5** *fig (ley)* to break. **6** *fig (cerca, límite)* to break through, break down.
▶ *vi* **1** *fig (acabar - con algo)* to break; *(- con alguien)* to split up, US break up. **2** *(olas, día)* to break. **3** **romper a** + *inf fig (empezar)* to burst out: *romper a reír* to burst out laughing. **4** **romper en** + *sust fig (prorrumpir)* to burst into: *romper en llanto* to burst into tears.
▶ *vpr* **romperse** **1** *(gen)* to break: *se me ha roto esta uña* I've broken this nail. **2** *(papel, tela)* to tear, rip. **3** *(rajarse, reven-*

R

tarse) to split. **4** *(desgastarse)* to wear out: *se me han roto los zapatos* my shoes are worn out. **5** *(coche)* to break down.

ron *nm* rum.

roncar *vi* to snore.

roncha *nf (en la piel)* swelling, lump, spot.

ronco,-a *adj* hoarse.

ronda *nf* **1** *(patrulla)* patrol, watch. **2** *(de policía)* beat. **3** *(vuelta)* round. **4** *(de bebidas, cartas)* round. **5** *(negociaciones)* round. LOC **hacer la ronda** to do one's rounds.

rondar *vt* **1** *(vigilar)* to patrol, do the rounds of. **2** *(merodear)* to prowl around, hang about, haunt: *siempre ronda la casa* he's always prowling around the house. **3** *fig (años)* to be about: *ronda los cincuenta* she's about fifty.
▶ *vi* **1** *(vigilar)* to patrol. **2** *(merodear)* to prowl around, roam around.

ronquera *nf* hoarseness.

ronquido *nm* snore, snoring.

ronronear *vi* to purr.

ronroneo *nm* purring.

roña *nf (suciedad)* filth, dirt.

roñería *nf fam* meanness, stinginess.

roñica *nm o nf fam* scrooge, miser.

roñoso,-a *adj* **1** *(sucio)* filthy, dirty. **2** *fam (tacaño)* mean, stingy.
▶ *nm & nf fam* scrooge, miser.

ropa *nf* clothing, clothes *pl*: *ropa de invierno* winter clothes; *ropa de esquí* ski wear. COMP **ropa blanca** linen, household linen. ❙ **ropa interior** underwear.

ropero *nm* wardrobe, US closet.

roquefort *nm (específicamente)* Roquefort; *(en general)* blue cheese.

roquero,-a *adj-nm & nf* → rockero,-a.

rosa *nf (flor)* rose.
▶ *nm (color)* pink.
▶ *adj* **1** *(color)* pink. **2** *fig (novela)* romantic. LOC **fresco,-a como una rosa** *fig* as fresh as a daisy.

rosado,-a *adj* **1** *(color)* rosy, pink. **2** *(vino)* rosé.
▶ *nm* rosado *(vino)* rosé.

rosal *nm* rosebush.

rosaleda *nf* rose garden.

rosario *nm* **1** REL rosary, beads *pl*. **2** *fig* string, series: *rosario de mentiras* string of lies. LOC **rezar el rosario** to say the rosary.

rosbif *nm* roast beef.

rosca *nf* **1** *(de tornillo)* thread. **2** CULIN doughnut. **3** *(carnosidad)* roll of fat. **4** *(anilla)* ring.

rosco *nm* ring-shaped bread roll.

roscón *nm* ring-shaped pastry; *(de Pascua)* Easter ring.

rosetón *nm* rose window.

rosquilla *nf* doughnut, ring-shaped pastry.

rostro *nm fml (cara)* face.

rotación *nf* rotation.

rotativo,-a *adj* rotary, revolving.
▶ *nm* rotativo newspaper.

roto,-a *adj* **1** *(gen)* broken. **2** *(tela, papel)* torn. **3** *(gastado)* worn out. **4** *(cansado)* tired.
▶ *nm* roto *(agujero)* hole, tear.

rotonda *nf (plaza)* roundabout, US traffic circle.

rótula *nf* ANAT kneecap.

rotulación *nf* lettering, labelling.

rotulador *nm* felt-tip pen.

rotular *vt* to label.

rotulista *nm o nf* signwriter.

rótulo *nm* **1** *(letrero)* sign; *(luminoso)* neon sign. **2** *(titular)* heading, title.

rotundo,-a *adj* **1** *(redondo)* round. **2** *fig (éxito)* resounding. **3** *(negativa)* flat, categorical; *(afirmación)* categorical, emphatic: *un no rotundo* a flat refusal.

rotura *nf* **1** *(gen)* break, breaking, crack. **2** *(en tela, papel)* tear, rip. **3** MED fracture.

roturar *vt* to plough (US plow).

roulotte *nf* caravan.

rozadura *nf* scratch, abrasion.

rozamiento *nm (roce)* rubbing, friction.

rozar *vt* **1** *(tocar ligeramente)* to touch lightly, brush. **2** *(raspar)* to rub against,

brush against; *(herir)* to graze: *el zapato me roza el pie* my shoe's rubbing my foot.
▶ *vi* **1** *(raspar)* to rub. **2** *fig (tener relación)* to border (**con**, on), verge (**con**, on).
▶ *vpr* **rozarse 1** *(rasparse)* to rub (**con**, against), brush (**con**, against). **2** *(desgastarse)* to wear (**out**). **3** *fig (tratarse)* to come into contact (**con**, with), rub shoulders (**con**, with).

Ruanda *nf* Rwanda.

ruandés,-esa *adj* Rwandan.
▶ *nm & nf* Rwandan.

rubeola *nf* German measles, rubella.

rubí *nm* ruby.

rubia *nf* blonde.

rubio,-a *adj* **1** *(cabello)* fair; *(persona)* fair-haired; *(hombre)* blond; *(mujer)* blonde. **2** *(tabaco)* Virginia.
▶ *nm & nf (hombre)* blond; *(mujer)* blonde.

rublo *nm* rouble.

rubor *nm* blush, flush.

ruborizarse *vpr* to blush, go red, redden.

rúbrica *nf* **1** *(de firma)* flourish (in signature). **2** *(título)* title, heading.

ruda *nf* rue.

rudeza *nf* roughness, coarseness.

rudimentario,-a *adj* rudimentary.

rudo,-a *adj* rough, coarse.

rueca *nf* distaff.

rueda *nf* **1** *(gen)* wheel: *de cuatro ruedas* four-wheeled. **2** *(círculo)* circle, ring. COMP **rueda de la fortuna** wheel of fortune. **I rueda de molino** millstone. **I rueda de prensa** press conference. **I rueda de recambio** spare wheel. **I rueda delantera** front wheel.

ruedo *nm (en las plazas de toros)* bullring, arena.

ruego *nm* request, petition. COMP **ruegos y preguntas** any other business.

rufián *nm (canalla)* scoundrel, villain, ruffian.

rugby *nm* rugby.

rugido *nm* roar, bellow.

rugir *vi* to roar, bellow; *(viento)* to howl; *(tripas)* to rumble.

rugosidad *nf* rugosity.

rugoso,-a *adj* rough, wrinkled.

ruibarbo *nm* rhubarb.

ruido *nm* **1** *(gen)* noise. **2** *(sonido)* sound. **3** *(jaleo)* din, row. **4** *fig* stir, commotion. LOC **hacer ruido 1** to make a noise. **2** *fig* to cause a stir. **I mucho ruido y pocas nueces** *fam* much ado about nothing.

ruidoso,-a *adj* **1** noisy, loud. **2** *fig* sensational.

ruin *adj* **1** *pey (vil)* mean, base, despicable, vile. **2** *(pequeño)* petty, insignificant. **3** *(tacaño)* stingy, mean.

ruina *nf* **1** ruin, collapse. **2** *fig* fall, end, downfall.
▶ *nf pl* **ruinas** ruins. LOC **estar hecho,-a una ruina** *fig* to be a wreck.

ruindad *nf* **1** *(maldad)* meanness, vileness. **2** *(acto)* mean act, low trick.

ruinoso,-a *adj* **1** ruinous, disastrous **2** *fig* tumbledown, dilapidated.

ruiseñor *nm* nightingale.

rular *vt (funcionar)* to work.

ruleta *nf* roulette.

rulot *nf* caravan.

Rumanía *nf* Romania.

rumano,-a *adj* Romanian, Rumanian.
▶ *nm & nf (persona)* Romanian, Rumanian.
▶ *nm* **rumano** *(idioma)* Romanian, Rumanian.

rumba *nf* rumba, rhumba.

rumbo *nm* **1** *(dirección)* course, direction. **2** *fam fig (pompa)* pomp, show. **3** *fam fig (generosidad)* lavishness, generosity. LOC **perder el rumbo 1** to go off course. **2** *fig* to lose one's bearings.

rumiante *adj* ruminant.
▶ *nm* ruminant.

rumiar *vi (animal)* to ruminate, chew the cud.
▶ *vt* **1** *(mascar)* to chew. **2** *fig (pensar)* to ruminate, chew over, reflect on.

rumor *nm* **1** *(murmullo)* murmur. **2** *(noticia, voz)* rumour (US rumor).

rumorearse *vpr* [se usa sólo en tercera persona; no lleva sujeto] to be rumoured (US rumored): *se rumorea que está enfer-*

R

mo it is rumoured that he's ill, he's rumoured to be ill.

rupestre *adj* rock. COMP **pintura rupestre** cave painting.

rupia *nf* rupee.

ruptura *nf* 1 *(rotura)* breaking, breakage, break. 2 *fig* breaking-off, break-up.

rural *adj* rural, country: *médico rural* country doctor.

Rusia *nf* Russia.

ruso,-a *adj* Russian.
▶ *nm & nf (persona)* Russian.
▶ *nm* **ruso** *(idioma)* Russian.

rústico,-a *adj* rustic, rural.
▶ *nm* **rústico** peasant. LOC **en rústica** in paperback.

ruta *nf* route, way, road. COMP **ruta aérea** air route, airway.

rutina *nf* routine: *la rutina diaria* the daily routine.

rutinario,-a *adj* 1 *(gen)* routine. 2 *(persona)* unimaginative, dull.

S

S, s *nf (la letra)* S, s.
S *sím* **(sur)** south; *(símbolo)* S.
sábado *nm* Saturday.

✎ Para ejemplos de uso, consulta **jueves**.

sábana *nf* sheet.
sabelotodo *nm o nf inv pey* know-all, know-it-all.
saber *nm* knowledge.
▶ *vt* **1** *(gen)* to know. **2** *(tener habilidad)* to be able to, know how to. **3** *(enterarse)* to learn, find out.
▶ *vi (tener sabor)* to taste (a, of).
▶ *vpr* **saberse** to know.
sabido,-a *adj* known.
sabiduría *nf* **1** *(conocimientos)* knowledge. **2** *(prudencia)* wisdom.
sabio,-a *adj* **1** *(con conocimientos)* learned, knowledgeable. **2** *(con prudencia)* wise, sensible.
▶ *nm & nf* **1** *(instruido)* learned person. **2** *(prudente)* sage, wise person.
sable *nm* sabre (US saber).
sabor *nm* **1** taste, flavour (US flavor). **2** *fig* feeling.
saborear *vt* **1** to taste. **2** *fig* to savour (US savor), relish.
sabroso,-a *adj* **1** *(con mucho sabor)* tasty, delicious. **2** *(agradable)* pleasant, delightful.
sabueso *nm* **1** *(perro)* bloodhound. **2** *fig (persona)* sleuth.
sacacorchos *nm inv* corkscrew.
sacapuntas *nm inv* pencil sharpener.
sacar *vt* **1** *(poner en el exterior)* to take out, pull out, get out. **2** *(obtener - gen)* to get; *(- premio)* to win; *(- dinero)* to get, make, earn; *(- billete)* to get, buy. **3** *(dinero del banco)* to draw, withdraw, take

out. **4** *(resolver)* to work out, solve. **5** *(encontrar)* to get, find. **6** *(enseñar)* to show. **7** *(quitar)* to remove. **8** *(extraer de algo)* to extract, obtain. **9** *(agua)* to draw. **10** *(llevar fuera)* to take out. **11** *(fotografía)* to take; *(fotocopia, copia)* to make. **12** *(producir)* to produce. **13** *(moda)* to introduce, set; *(nuevo producto)* to bring out. **14** *(publicar)* to publish, bring out. **15** *fam (ir por delante)* to be ahead. **16** *fam (ser más alto)* to be taller. **17** DEP *(tenis)* to serve; *(fútbol)* to kick off. **18** MAT *(restar)* to subtract; *(raíz)* to extract, find out. **19** *(mineral)* to extract. **20** QUÍM to extract.
▶ *vpr* **sacarse 1** *(desvestirse)* to take off. **2** *(fotografía)* to have taken.
saciar *vt* **1** *(hambre)* to satiate; *(sed)* to quench. **2** *fig (deseos)* to satisfy; *(ambiciones)* to fulfil (US fulfill).
▶ *vpr* **saciarse** to satiate os, be satiated.
saco *nm* **1** *(bolsa)* sack, bag. **2** AM *(americana)* jacket.
sacrificar *vt* **1** *(gen)* to sacrifice. **2** *fig (reses)* to slaughter; *(animal doméstico)* to destroy, put down.
▶ *vpr* **sacrificarse** to sacrifice os (por, for).
sacrificio *nm* sacrifice.
sacro,-a *adj* **1** *(sagrado)* sacred. **2** ANAT sacrum.
▶ *nm* **sacro** *(hueso)* sacrum.
sacudida *nf* **1** *(gen)* shake. **2** *(movimiento violento)* jolt, jerk. **3** *(terremoto)* earthquake.
sacudir *vt* **1** *(gen)* to shake. **2** *(alfombra, etc)* to shake out; *(polvo, arena)* to shake off. **3** *(golpear algo)* to beat. **4** *(cabeza)* to shake. **5** *(dar una paliza)* to

beat up. **6** *fig (emocionar, alterar)* to shake.

sagacidad *nf* **1** sagacity, cleverness. **2** *(astucia)* shrewdness, astuteness.

sagaz *adj* **1** clever, sagacious. **2** *(astuto)* shrewd, astute.

sagrado,-a *adj* sacred, holy.

Sáhara *nm* Sahara.

saharaui *adj* Saharaui, Sahrawi.
▶ *nm o nf* Saharaui, Sahrawi.

sahariana *nf* safari shirt, safari jacket.

sahariano,-a *adj* Saharan.

sal *nf* salt. COMP **sal fina** table salt.
▶ *nf pl* **sales** smelling salts.

sala *nf* **1** *(aposento)* room; *(grande)* hall. **2** *(sala de estar)* lounge, living room. **3** *(de hospital)* ward; *(de cine)* cinema; *(de teatro)* theatre. **4** JUR *(lugar)* courtroom; *(tribunal)* court.

salado,-a *adj* **1** *(con sal)* salted; *(con demasiada sal)* salty. **2** *fam fig (agudo)* witty; *(gracioso)* funny; *(encantador)* charming, attractive.

salamandra *nf* salamander.

salamanquesa *nf* ZOOL gecko.

salar *vt* **1** *(curar)* to salt. **2** *(sazonar)* to salt, add salt to.

salarial *adj* salary, wage.

salario *nm* salary, wages *pl*, wage.

salazón *nf* **1** *(acción)* salting. **2** *(carne)* salted meat; *(pescado)* salted fish.

salchicha *nf* sausage.

salchichón *nm* salami-type sausage.

saldo *nm* **1** *(de una cuenta)* balance. **2** *(pago)* liquidation, settlement. **3** *(resto de mercancía)* remnant, leftover, remainder. **4** *(venta a bajo precio)* sale.

salero *nm* **1** *(recipiente)* saltcellar, US salt shaker. **2** *fig (gracia)* charm, wit.

salida *nf* **1** *(partida)* departure. **2** *(puerta, etc)* exit, way out. **3** *(momento de salir)*. **4** *(viaje corto)* trip. **5** *(de un astro)* rising. **6** DEP start. **7** COM outlet, market. **8** FIN outlay, expenditure. **9** *fig (ocurrencia)* witty remark, witticism. **10** *fig (escapatoria)* solution, way out. **11** *fig (perspectiva)* opening. **12** TÉC outlet. **13** INFORM output.

saliente *adj* **1** *(que sobresale)* projecting. **2** *(cesante)* outgoing.
▶ *nm* projection, overhang, ledge.

salina *nf* **1** *(mina)* salt mine. **2** *(establecimiento)* salt works.

salir *vi* **1** *(ir hacia afuera)* to go out (de, of). **2** *(venir de dentro)* to come out. **3** *(partir)* to leave. **4** *(no estar)* to be out. **5** *(amigos, novios)* to go out. **6** *(aparecer)* to appear, be. **7** *(revista, novela, etc)* to come out; *(moda)* to come in. **8** *(proceder)* to come (de, from). **9** *(resultar)* to turn out, turn out to be. **10** *(examen, prueba)* to go, turn out. **11** *(venir a costar)* to come to, cost, work out. **12** *(sobresalir)* to project, stick out. **13** *(sol, etc)* to rise, come out; *(vegetales)* to come up; *(flores)* to come out. **14** *(granos)* to get, break out in, come out in; *(pelo)* to grow; *(diente)* to cut. **15** *(mancha)* to come out, come off. **16** *(parecerse)* to take after (a, -). **17** *(al azar)* to be drawn. **18** *(nombre, palabra)* to be able to think of. **19** *(solucionar)* to work out. **20** *(librarse)* to get out (de, of). **21** *(trabajo, oportunidad)* to come up. **22** *(dar a)* to open (a, onto), come out (a, at).
▶ *vpr* **salirse 1** *(líquido, gas)* to leak, leak out; *(río)* to overflow. **2** *(al hervir)* to boil over. **3** *(tornillo, etc)* to come off, come out. **4** *(de la carretera)* to go off (de, -).

salitre *nm* saltpetre (US saltpeter).

saliva *nf* saliva.

salmón *nm* *(pez)* salmon.
▶ *adj (color)* salmon, salmon pink.

salmonete *nm* red mullet.

Salomón *nm* Solomon. COMP **Islas Salomón** Solomon Islands.

salón *nm* **1** *(en casa)* sitting room, drawing room, lounge. **2** *(en edificio público)* hall. **3** *(exposición)* show, exhibition.

salpicar *vt* **1** *(rociar)* to sprinkle. **2** *(caer gotas)* to splash.

salpullido *nm* rash.

salsa *nf* **1** sauce. **2** *fam fig (gracia)* zest, spice. **3** MÚS salsa.

saltamontes *nm inv* grasshopper.

saltar *vi* **1** *(gen)* to jump, leap. **2** *(en paracaídas)* to parachute. **3** *(romperse)* to break; *(estallar)* to burst. **4** *(desprenderse)* to come off. **5** *(tapón, corcho)* to pop out, pop off. **6** *fig (enfadarse)* to blow up, explode. **7** *fig (de una cosa a otra)* to jump, skip, **8** *fig (decir)* to come out (con, with); *(contestar)* to answer (con, with).
▶ *vt* **1** *fig (salvar de un salto)* to jump (over), leap (over). **2** *(arrancar)* to pull off. **3** *(ajedrez, etc)* to jump. **4** *fig (omitir)* to skip, miss out.
▶ *vpr* **saltarse 1** *(ley, etc)* to ignore. **2** *(omitir)* to skip, miss out. **3** *(desprenderse)* to come off; *(- lentilla)* to fall out.

salto *nm* **1** *(gen)* jump, leap. **2** DEP jump; *(natación)* dive. **3** *(de agua)* waterfall. **4** *(despeñadero)* precipice. **5** *fig (omisión)* gap.

salubridad *nf (estado de salud)* healthiness; *(de lugar, clima)* salubriousness, salubrity.

salud *nf* health.

saludable *adj* **1** *(sano)* healthy, wholesome. **2** *fig (beneficioso)* good, beneficial.

saludar *vt* **1** *(demostrar cortesía)* to greet. **2** *(decir hola)* to say hello to. **3** MIL to salute.

saludo *nm* **1** greeting. **2** MIL salute.

salvación *nf* **1** *(gen)* salvation, rescue. **2** REL salvation.

salvado *nm* bran.

Salvador *nm* **El Salvador 1** El Salvador. **2** REL the Saviour (US Savior).

salvadoreño,-a *adj* Salvadorian, Salvadoran.
▶ *nm & nf* Salvadorian, Salvadoran.

salvaguardar *vt* to safeguard (de, from).

salvaje *adj* **1** *(planta)* wild. **2** *(animal)* wild. **3** *(pueblo, tribu)* savage, uncivilized. **4** *fam fig (violento)* savage, wild. **5** *(bruto)* uncouth, boorish.
▶ *nm o nf* **1** *(no civilizado)* savage. **2** *(bruto)* brute, boor.

salvamento *nm* rescue.

salvar *vt* **1** *(librar de peligro)* to save, rescue. **2** *(barco)* to salvage. **3** *(honor, ruina)* to save. **4** *(obstáculo)* to clear. **5** *(dificultad)* to overcome, get round. **6** *(distancia)* to cover.
▶ *vpr* **salvarse 1** *(sobrevivir)* to survive, come out alive. **2** *(escaparse)* to escape (de, from). **3** REL to be saved, save one's soul.

salvapantallas *nm inv* INFORM screensaver.

salvavidas *nm inv* life belt.

salvedad *nf (excepción)* exception.

salvia *nf* sage.

salvo,-a *adj (ileso)* unharmed, safe.
▶ *adv* **salvo** except, except for.

salvoconducto *nm* safe-conduct.

Samoa *nf* Samoa.

samoano,-a *adj* Samoan.
▶ *nm & nf (persona)* Samoan.
▶ *nm* **samoano** *(idioma)* Samoan.

san *adj* saint.

> ✎ Se usa delante de nombres de santos masculinos, excepto Tomás, Tomé, Toribio y Domingo. Consulta también **santo,-a**.

sanar *vt* to heal, cure.
▶ *vi* **1** *(enfermo)* to recover, get better. **2** *(herida)* to heal.

sanatorio *nm* clinic, nursing home; *(hospital)* hospital.

sanción *nf* **1** *(aprobación)* sanction, approval. **2** *(pena)* sanction, penalty.

sandalia *nf* sandal.

sándalo *nm* sandalwood.

sandía *nf* watermelon.

sándwich *nm* sandwich.

sanear *vt* **1** *(limpiar)* to clean; *(desinfectar)* to disinfect. **2** *(económicamente)* to make financially viable.

sangrado *nm* indention, indentation, indent.

sangrar *vt* **1** *(abrir una vena)* to bleed. **2** *(dar salida a un líquido)* to drain. **3** *fam fig (dejar sin dinero)* to bleed dry. **4** *(en impresión)* to indent.

sangre *nf* blood.

sangría *nf* **1** *(bebida)* sangria. **2** MED bleeding, bloodletting. **3** *fig (de dinero, etc)* drain.

S

sangriento,-a *adj* **1** *(que echa sangre)* bleeding. **2** *(con sangre)* bloody.

sanguijuela *nf* leech, bloodsucker.

sanidad *nf* **1** *(calidad de sano)* health, healthiness. **2** *(servicios)* health: *sanidad pública* public health.

sanitario,-a *adj* sanitary, health.
► *nm & nf* health officer.
► *nm pl* **sanitarios** bathroom fittings.

sano,-a *adj* **1** *(con salud)* healthy, fit. **2** *(saludable)* healthy, wholesome. **3** *fig (sin corrupción)* sound.

santo,-a *adj* **1** *(gen)* holy, sacred. **2** *(persona)* holy, saintly. **3** *fam (para enfatizar)* hell of a, real, right. **4** *(como título)* saint: *Santa Elena* Saint Helen.
► *nm & nf* saint.
► *nm* **santo 1** *(imagen)* image of a saint. **2** *fam (dibujo)* picture. **3** *(onomástica)* saint's day.

✎ Consulta también **san**.

santuario *nm* sanctuary, shrine.

saña *nf* **1** *(enojo)* rage, fury. **2** *(crueldad)* cruelty, viciousness.

sapiencia *nf* **1** *fml (sabiduría)* wisdom. **2** *(conocimiento)* knowledge.

saque *nm* **1** *(tenis)* service. **2** *(fútbol)* kick-off. COMP **saque de banda** *(fútbol)* throw-in.

saquear *vt (casas)* to plunder, pillage; *(casas, comercios)* to loot.

sarampión *nm* measles *pl*.

sarcasmo *nm* sarcasm.

sarcástico,-a *adj* sarcastic.

sarcófago *nm* sarcophagus.

sardina *nf* sardine.

sarga *nf* serge, twill.

sargento *nm* **1** MIL sergeant. **2** *fig* tyrant.

sarmiento *nm* vine shoot.

sarna *nf* MED *(en personas)* scabies; *(en animales)* mange.

sarpullido *nm* rash.

sarro *nm* **1** *(en los dientes)* tartar. **2** *(sedimento)* deposit.

sarta *nf* string.

sartén *nf* frying pan, US fry pan.

sastre,-a *nm & nf* tailor.

satélite *nm* satellite.

satén *nm* satin.

satisfacción *nf (gen)* satisfaction.

satisfacer *vt* **1** *(gen)* to satisfy. **2** *(deuda)* to pay. **3** *(requisitos, exigencias)* to meet, fulfil satisfy. **4** *(agravio, ofensa)* to make amends for.

satisfactorio,-a *adj* satisfactory.

satisfecho,-a *adj* **1** *(contento)* satisfied, pleased. **2** *(pagado de sí mismo)* self-satisfied.

saturación *nf* saturation.

saturado,-a *adj* **1** saturated. **2** *fig* sick, tired.

saturnismo *nm* lead poisoning.

Saturno *nm* Saturn.

sauce *nm* willow.

saúco *nm* elder.

saudí *adj* Saudi.
► *nm o nf* Saudi.

saudita *adj-nm o nf* → **saudí**.

sauna *nf* sauna.

saurio,-a *adj* saurian.
► *nm & nf* saurian.

savia *nf* **1** BOT sap. **2** *fig* sap, vitality.

saxofón *nm (instrumento)* saxophone, sax.
► *nm o nf (músico)* saxophonist, sax player.

saya *nf* **1** *(falda)* skirt. **2** *(enagua)* petticoat.

sazón *nf* **1** *(madurez)* ripeness. **2** *(sabor)* taste, flavour (US flavor). **3** *(aderezo)* seasoning.

sazonar *vt* **1** *(madurar)* to ripen, mature. **2** *(comida)* to season, flavour (US flavor).

se¹ *pron* **1** *(reflexivo - él)* himself; *(- ella)* herself; *(- usted, ustedes)* yourself, yourselves; *(- ellos, ellas)* themselves; *(- esto)* itself. **2** *(recíproco)* each other, one another: *se quieren* they love each other. **3** *(pasiva)*: *se han abierto las puertas* the doors have been opened. **4** *(impersonal)*: *se ve que no* apparently not.

se² *pron (objeto indirecto - a él)* him, to him; *(- a ella)* her, to her; *(- a ellos, ellas)* them, to them; *(- a esto)* it, to it; *(- a* *usted, ustedes)* you, to you: *se lo dije* I told her.

✎ Se usa delante de los pronombres la, las, lo y los en vez de les o las.

sé[1] *pres indic* → **saber**.
sé[2] *imperat* → **ser**.
sebo *nm* **1** *(grasa)* fat. **2** CULIN suet. **3** *(para velas)* tallow.
seca *nf (sequía)* drought.
secado *nm* drying.
secador *nm* **1** dryer, drier. **2** *(de pelo)* hairdryer.
secadora *nf* tumble dryer, dryer.
secano *nm* dry land.
secante *adj (geometría)* secant.
   ▶ *nf* secant.
secar *vt* **1** *(gen)* to dry. **2** *(lágrimas, vajilla)* to wipe; *(líquido)* to wipe up, mop up. **3** *(planta)* to wither, dry up; *(río, fuente, etc)* to dry up.
   ▶ *vpr* **secarse 1** *(gen)* to dry. **2** *(líquido, río, etc)* to dry up; *(planta)* to wither, dry up.
sección *nf* **1** *(corte)* section, cut. **2** *(geometría)* section. **3** *(departamento)* section, department. **4** *(en periódico, revista)* page, section.
seco,-a *adj* **1** *(gen)* dry. **2** *(frutos, flores)* dried. **3** *(marchito)* withered, dried up. **4** *fig (carácter)* dry; *(tono, respuesta)* curt, sharp. **5** *fig (golpe, ruido)* sharp.
secreción *nf* secretion.
secretaría *nf* **1** *(cargo)* secretaryship, office of secretary. **2** *(oficina)* secretary's office; *(en la administración)* secretariat.
secretario,-a *nm & nf* secretary.
secreteo *nm* whispering.
secreto,-a *adj* secret.
   ▶ *nm* **secreto 1** *(lo reservado)* secret. **2** *(reserva)* secrecy.
secta *nf* sect.
sector *nm* **1** *(gen)* sector. **2** *fig (zona)* area. **3** *fig (parte)* section.
secuela *nf* consequence, result.
secuencia *nf* sequence.

secuenciar *vt* to arrange in sequence, put in sequence.
secuestrar *vt* **1** *(personas)* to kidnap; *(avión)* to hijack. **2** JUR to sequester, seize, confiscate.
secuestro *nm* **1** *(personas)* kidnapping; *(de avión)* hijacking. **2** JUR sequestration, seizure, confiscation.
secundar *vt* to support, second.
secundaria *nf* EDUC secondary education.
secundario,-a *adj* secondary.
   ▶ *nm* **secundario** GEOL secondary.
secuoya *nf* sequoia, redwood.
sed *nf* thirst.
seda *nf* silk.
sede *nf* **1** *(oficina central)* headquarters, central office. **2** *(del gobierno)* seat.
sedentario,-a *adj* sedentary.
sediento,-a *adj* **1** thirsty. **2** *fig (poder, etc)* hungry (**de**, for), thirsty (**de**, for).
sedimentar *vt* to settle, deposit.
   ▶ *vpr* **sedimentarse** to settle.
sedimento *nm* sediment, deposit.
seductor,-ra *adj* **1** seductive. **2** *(atractivo)* captivating. **3** *(persuasivo)* tempting.
   ▶ *nm & nf* seducer.
segador,-ra *nm & nf* harvester, reaper.
segadora *nf* harvester, reaper; *(de césped)* lawnmower.
segar *vt* **1** *(gen)* to reap, cut; *(césped)* to mow. **2** *fig (matar)* to mow down, cut down. **3** *fig (truncar)* to cut off.
segmento *nm* **1** *(gen)* segment. **2** INFORM overlay.
segregar *vt* **1** *(separar)* to segregate. **2** *(secretar)* to secrete.
segueta *nf* fret saw.
seguido,-a *adj* **1** *(continuo)* continuous. **2** *(consecutivo)* consecutive, successive. **3** *(en línea recta)* straight, direct.
   ▶ *adv* **seguido** straight.
seguidor,-ra *nm & nf* **1** follower. **2** DEP follower, supporter, fan.
seguir *vt* **1** *(gen)* to follow. **2** *(perseguir)* to pursue, chase. **3** *(continuar)* to continue, carry on. **4** *(un camino)* to continue

S

on. **5** *(curso, etc)* to do; *(explicaciones)* to follow.

▶ *vi* **1** *(proseguir)* to go on, carry on. **2** *(continuar)* to follow on, continue. **3** *(permanecer, mantenerse)* to continue to be, be still.

▶ *vpr* **seguirse 1** *(inferirse)* to deduce. **2** *(suceder a continuación)* to follow.

según *prep* **1** *(conforme)* according to. **2** *(dependiendo)* depending on. **3** *(como)* just as. **4** *(a medida que)* as. **5** *(tal vez)* it depends.

segunda *nf* **1** *(tren, etc)* second class. **2** *(marcha del auto)* second, second gear. **3** *fig (intención)* ulterior motive.

segundero *nm* second hand.

segundo,-a *adj* second.
▶ *nm & nf* second.
▶ *nm* **segundo** *(tiempo)* second.

✎ Para ejemplos de uso, consulta **seis**.

seguridad *nf* **1** *(gen)* security. **2** *(física)* safety. **3** *(certeza)* certainty, sureness. **4** *(confianza)* confidence.

seguro,-a *adj* **1** *(asegurado)* secure. **2** *(a salvo)* safe. **3** *(firme)* firm, steady. **4** *(cierto)* certain, sure. **5** *(de fiar)* reliable. **6** *(confiado)* confident.
▶ *nm* **seguro 1** *(contrato, póliza)* insurance. **2** *(mecanismo)* safety device, safety catch.
▶ *adv* for sure, definitely.

seis *adj* **1** six: *pesa seis kilos* it weighs six kilos; *son las seis en punto* it's exactly six o'clock; *el seis de junio* the six of june; *tienen un hijo de seis años* they have a boy of six; *somos seis* there are six of us. **2** *(sexto)* sixth: *soy el seis de la lista* I'm sixth on the list.
▶ *nm* six: *el seis* number six; *seis por seis treinta y seis* six times six is thirty-six, six sixes are thirty-six.

seisavo,-a *adj-nm & nf* → **sexto,-a**.

seiscientos,-as *adj (cardinal)* six hundred; *(ordinal)* six hundredth.
▶ *nm* **seiscientos** *(número)* six hundred.

seísmo *nm (terremoto)* earthquake.

selección *nf* **1** *(gen)* selection. **2** DEP *(gen)* team; *(fútbol)* squad.

seleccionar *vt* to select.

selectividad *nf* EDUC university entrance examination.

selenio *nm* selenium.

sellar *vt* **1** *(timbrar)* to stamp; *(oficial)* to seal. **2** *(monedas, etc)* to hallmark, stamp. **3** *fig (habitación, etc)* to close (up), seal up. **4** *fig (dejar señal)* to stamp, brand. **5** *fig (concluir)* to seal, settle, conclude.
▶ *vi* to sign on.

sello *nm* **1** *(de correos)* stamp. **2** *(de estampar, precinto)* seal.

selva *nf* **1** *(bosque)* forest. **2** *(jungla)* jungle.

selvicultura *nf* forestry.

semáforo *nm* traffic lights *pl*.

semana *nf* **1** *(tiempo)* week. **2** *fig (salario)* weekly wage.

semanal *adj* weekly.

semanario,-a *adj* weekly.
▶ *nm* weekly magazine.

semántica *nf* semantics.

sembrado,-a *adj fig (cubierto)* covered (de, with), full (de, of).
▶ *nm* **sembrado** sown field.

sembrador,-ra *nm & nf* sower.

sembradora *nf* seed drill.

sembrar *vt* **1** AGR to sow. **2** *fig (esparcir)* to scatter, spread.

semejante *adj* **1** *(parecido)* similar. **2** *pey (tal)* such, like that. **3** *(geometría)* similar.
▶ *nm* fellow being.

semejanza *nf* similarity, likeness.

semen *nm* semen.

semental *nm* stud.

semestral *adj* half-yearly, semestral.

semestre *nm* **1** six-month period, semester. **2** EDUC semester.

semicírculo *nm* semicircle.

semicircunferencia *nf* semicircumference.

semiconductor *nm* semiconductor.

semicorchea *nf* semiquaver, sixteenth note.

semiesférico,-a *adj* hemispheroidal.

semifinal *nf* semifinal.

semifusa *nf* hemidemisemiquaver, sixty-fourth note.

semilla *nf* **1** seed. **2** *fig* seed, seeds.

semillero *nm* **1** seedbed. **2** *fig* hotbed, breeding ground.

seminal *adj* seminal.

semiología *nf* semiology.

semiótica *nf* semiotics.

semiseco,-a *adj* medium dry.

semitono *nm* semitone, half-step.

semivocal *adj* semivocal.
► *nf* semivowel.

sémola *nf* semolina.

senado *nm* **1** senate. **2** *fig (reunión)* assembly.

senador,-ra *nm & nf* senator.

sencillez *nf* **1** *(gen)* simplicity. **2** *(naturalidad)* simplicity, lack of affectation, unpretentiousness. **3** *(ingenuidad)* gullibility, naivety.

sencillo,-a *adj* **1** *(sin adornos)* simple, plain. **2** *(fácil)* simple, easy. **3** *(no compuesto)* single. **4** *fig (persona - natural)* natural, unaffected, unpretentious; *(- ingenua)* naive, gullible.

senderismo *nm* trekking.

sendero *nm* path.

sendos,-as *adj* each, either.

Senegal *nm* Senegal.

senegalés,-esa *adj* Senegalese.
► *nm & nf* Senegalese.

seno *nm* **1** *(pecho)* breast, bosom. **2** *(hueco entre el pecho y la ropa)* bosom. **3** *(matriz)* womb. **4** *(cavidad)* cavity, hollow, hole. **5** MAT sine. **6** ANAT sinus.

sensación *nf* **1** *(impresión)* sensation, feeling: *sensación de calor* feeling of warmth. **2** *(emoción)* sensation.

sensacional *adj* sensational.

sensatez *nf* good sense.

sensato,-a *adj* sensible.

sensibilidad *nf* **1** *(percepción, sentido artístico)* sensitivity, feeling. **2** *(emotividad)* sensibility. **3** *(precisión)* sensitivity.

sensible *adj* **1** *(capaz de sentir)* sentient. **2** *(impresionable)* sensitive. **3** *(piel, oído)* sensitive. **4** *(perceptible)* perceptible, appreciable, noticeable. **5** *(considerable)* significant, considerable, sizeable. **6** *(que causa pena)* terrible, sad. **7** TÉC *(preciso)* sensitive.

sensorial *adj* sensory.

sentado,-a *adj* **1** seated, sitting. **2** *(establecido)* established, settled.

sentar *vt* **1** *(en silla, etc)* to sit, seat. **2** *fig (establecer)* to establish.
► *vi* **1** *(color, ropa, etc)* to suit. **2** *(comida, etc)* to do; *(comentario, etc)* to take.
► *vpr* **sentarse 1** *(en silla, etc)* to sit, sit down. **2** *(líquido)* to settle. **3** *(tiempo)* to settle, settle down.

sentencia *nf* **1** JUR *(decisión)* judgement; *(condena)* sentence. **2** *(aforismo)* proverb, maxim, saying, motto.

sentenciar *vt* to sentence (a, to).

sentido,-a *adj* **1** *(muerte, etc)* deeply felt. **2** *(sensible)* touchy, sensitive.
► *nm* **sentido 1** *(gen)* sense. **2** *(significado)* sense, meaning. **3** *(conocimiento)* consciousness. **4** *(dirección)* direction.

sentimental *adj* sentimental.
► *nm o nf* sentimental person.

sentimiento *nm* **1** *(gen)* feeling. **2** *(pena)* sorrow, grief.

sentir *nm* **1** *(sentimiento)* feeling. **2** *(opinión)* opinion, view.
► *vt* **1** *(gen)* to feel. **2** *(lamentar)* to regret, be sorry about, feel sorry. **3** *(oír)* to hear. **4** *(presentir)* to feel, think, have a feeling that.
► *vpr* **sentirse** to feel.

seña *nf* **1** *(indicio, gesto)* sign. **2** *(señal)* mark.
► *nf pl* **señas** address *sing.*

señal *nf* **1** *(signo)* sign, indication. **2** *(marca)* mark; *(en libro)* bookmark. **3** *(aviso, comunicación)* signal. **4** *(placa, letrero)* sign. **5** *(vestigio)* trace. **6** *(cicatriz)* scar. **7** *(de teléfono)* tone. **8** *(de pago)* deposit.

señalado,-a *adj* **1** *(famoso)* distinguished, famous. **2** *(fijado)* appointed, fixed. **3** *(significativo)* noticeable. **4** *(marcado)* marked, scarred.

señalar *vt* **1** *(marcar)* to mark. **2** *(hacer notar)* to point out. **3** *(apuntar hacia)* to point to, show. **4** *(con el dedo)* to point at. **5** *(fijar - cita)* to arrange, make; *(fecha, lugar, precio)* to set, fix.

S

señalización *nf* **1** *(señales)* road signs *pl*; *(de aeropuerto, estación)* signposting, signs *pl*. **2** *(colocación)* signposting.

señalizar *vt* to signpost.

señor,-ra *adj* **1** *(noble)* distinguished, noble. **2** *fam* fine.
▶ *nm & nf* **1** *(hombre)* man, gentleman; *(mujer)* woman, lady. **2** *(amo - hombre)* master; *(- mujer)* mistress. **3** *(tratamiento - hombre)* sir; *(- mujer)* madam, US ma'am. **4** *(ante apellido - hombre)* Mr; *(- mujer)* Mrs.

señora *nf* *(esposa)* wife.

señorita *nf* **1** *(mujer joven)* young woman; *(con más formalidad)* young lady. **2** *(tratamiento)* Miss. **3** *fam* *(puro)* small cigar. **4** **la señorita** EDUC the teacher, Miss.

señuelo *nm* **1** decoy. **2** *fig* bait.

sépalo *nm* sepal.

separación *nf* **1** separation. **2** *(espacio)* space, gap.

separado,-a *adj* **1** separate. **2** *(divorciado)* separated. LOC **por separado** separately, individually.

separar *vt* **1** *(gen)* to separate. **2** *(hacer grupos)* to separate, sort out. **3** *(guardar aparte)* to set aside, put aside. **4** *(apartar)* to move away (de, from). **5** *(de empleo, cargo)* to remove (de, from), dismiss (de, from). **6** *fig* *(mantener alejado)* to keep away (de, from).
▶ *vpr* **separarse 1** *(tomar diferente camino)* to separate, part company. **2** *(matrimonio)* to separate. **3** *(apartarse)* to move away (de, from). **4** *(desprenderse)* to separate (de, from), come off (de, -). **5** *(de amigo, etc)* to part company (de, with). **6** **separarse de** *(dejar algo)* to part with.

sepia *nf* *(pez)* cuttlefish.

septenario,-a *adj* septenary.
▶ *nm* **septenario** septenary.

septenio *nm* septennium.

septentrional *adj* northern.

septeto *nm* septet.

septicemia *nf* septicaemia (US septicemia).

séptico,-a *adj* septic.

septiembre *nm* September.

✎ Para ejemplos de uso, consulta **marzo**.

séptimo,-a *adj* seventh.

✎ Para ejemplos de uso, consulta **sexto,-a**.

septuagenario,-a *nm & nf* septuagenarian.

septuagésimo,-a *adj* seventieth.

✎ Para ejemplos de uso, consulta **sexto,-a**.

sepulcro *nm* tomb.

sepultar *vt* to bury.

sepultura *nf* **1** *(lugar)* grave. **2** *(acto)* burial.

sequía *nf* drought.

ser *vi* **1** *(gen)* to be: *Sócrates era filósofo* Socrates was a philosopher. **2** *(pertenecer)* to be, belong (de, to): *estas sillas son nuestras* these chairs are ours. **3** *(ser propio)* to be like (de, -): *es muy de Pilar* it's just like Pilar. **4** *(costar)* to be, cost: *¿cuánto es?* how much is it? **5** *(causar)* to cause, be. **6** *(consistir en)* to lie in, consist of. **7** *(suceder)* to happen (de, to): *¿qué fue de Iván?* what happened to Iván? **8** *(ocurrir, tener lugar)* to take place, be held: *la reunión será en el salón de actos* the meeting will be held in the assembly hall. **9** **ser de** *(proceder)* to be from, come from: *Santi es de Cáceres* Santi is from Cáceres. **10** *(indica material)* to be made of: *la puerta es de madera* the door is made of wood. **11** *(devenir)* to become of: *¡qué sería de nosotros sin ti!* what would become of us without you! **12** *(estar escrito)* to be by, be written by: *es de García Márquez* it's by García Márquez. **13** **ser de + inf** *(ser digno)* to be worth: *es de ver* it's worth seeing; *es de admirar* she's to be admired.
▶ *aux (pasiva)* to be: *fue encontrado por Raúl* it was found by Raúl.
▶ *nm* **1** *(ente)* being. **2** *(esencia)* essence, substance. **3** *(valor)* core, heart. **4** *(vida)* life, existence. COMP **ser humano** human being.

serbal *nm* service tree.

serbio,-a *adj* Serb, Serbian.
▶ *nm & nf* Serb, Serbian.
▶ *nm* **serbio** *(idioma)* Serbian.

serenar *vt* **1** *(gen)* to calm. **2** *fig* *(a alguien)* to calm down.

▶ *vpr* **serenarse 1** METEOR to clear up. **2** *(mar)* to grow calm. **3** *fig (persona)* to calm down.

serenidad *nf* serenity, calm. LOC conservar la serenidad to keep calm.

sereno,-a *adj* **1** METEOR *(cielo)* clear; *(tiempo)* fine, good. **2** *fig (persona - tranquila)* calm. **3** *fig (ambiente, etc)* calm, peaceful, quiet.
▶ *nm* **sereno 1** *(vigilante)* night watchman. **2** *(ambiente de la noche)* night air, night dew.

serie *nf* **1** *(gen)* series. **2** *(conjunto)* series, string, succession.

seriedad *nf* **1** *(gravedad)* seriousness, gravity. **2** *(formalidad)* reliability, dependability. LOC **con seriedad** seriously.

serio,-a *adj* **1** *(importante)* serious, grave. **2** *(severo)* serious. **3** *(formal)* reliable, responsible, dependable. **4** *(color)* sober; *(traje, etc)* formal. LOC **tomar en serio** to take seriously.

sermón *nm* **1** REL sermon. **2** *fam* sermon, ticking-off, lecture.

seropositivo,-a *adj* **1** seropositive. **2** *(con el VIH)* HIV positive.

serpentear *vi* **1** *(gen)* to crawl, wriggle. **2** *(camino)* to wind, twist; *(río)* to wind, meander.

serpentín *nm*

serpentina *nf (de papel)* streamer.

serpiente *nf* snake.

serpol *nm* wild thyme.

serranía *nf* mountain range, mountains *pl.*

serrar *vt* to saw.

serrería *nf* sawmill.

serrín *nm* sawdust.

serrucho *nm* handsaw.

servicial *adj* obliging, helpful, accommodating.

servicio *nm* **1** *(gen)* service. **2** *(criados)* servants *pl; (asistente)* domestic help. **3** *(juego, conjunto)* set. **4** *(favor)* service, favour (US favor). **5** DEP service, serve. **6** [también **servicios.**] *(retrete)* toilet, US rest room.

servidor,-ra *nm & nf* **1** servant. **2** *euf* myself.
▶ *nm* **servidor 1** MIL gunner. **2** INFORM server.

servilleta *nf* napkin, serviette.

servio,-a *adj* Serb, Serbian.
▶ *nm & nf* Serb, Serbian.
▶ *nm* **servio** *(idioma)* Serbian.

servir *vt* **1** *(gen)* to serve. **2** *(comida, bebida)* to serve, wait on. **3** *(ayudar)* to help. **4** COM *(suministrar)* to serve, supply with; *(entregar)* to deliver.
▶ *vi* **1** *(gen)* to serve. **2** *(ser útil)* to be useful, be helpful, be a help. **3** *(objeto)* to be no good: *esto no sirve* this is no good. **4** *(estar al servicio de otro)* to be a servant, be in service. **5** *(asistir a la mesa)* to serve (en, at), wait (en, at): *servir en la mesa* to wait at table.
▶ *vpr* **servirse 1** *(comida, etc)* to serve os, help os. **2** *(usar)* to use (de, -), make use of (de, -).

sésamo *nm* sesame.

sesenta *adj (cardinal)* sixty; *(ordinal)* sixtieth.
▶ *nm (número)* sixty.

✎ Para ejemplos de uso, consulta seis.

sesentavo,-a *adj* sixtieth.

✎ Para ejemplos de uso, consulta sexto,-a.

sesión *nf* **1** *(reunión)* session, meeting. **2** CINE showing. COMP **sesión continua** continuous session. ‖ **sesión plenaria** plenary session.

seso *nm* **1** brain. **2** *fam fig* brains *pl,* grey matter, sense.
▶ *nm pl* **sesos** CULIN brains.

seta *nf (comestible)* mushroom; *(no comestible)* toadstool.

setecientos,-as *adj (cardinal)* seven hundred; *(ordinal)* seven-hundredth.
▶ *nm* **setecientos** *(número)* seven hundred.

✎ Para ejemplos de uso, consulta seis.

setenta *adj (cardinal)* seventy; *(ordinal)* seventieth.
▶ *nm (número)* seventy.

✎ Para ejemplos de uso, consulta seis.

S

setentavo,-a *adj* seventieth.
▶ *nm & nf* seventieth.

✎ Para ejemplos de uso, consulta sexto,-a.

setiembre *nm* September.

✎ Para ejemplos de uso, consulta marzo.

seto *nm* hedge.
severidad *nf* **1** *(gravedad)* severity, harshness. **2** *(rigurosidad)* strictness.
severo,-a *adj* **1** *(grave)* severe, harsh. **2** *(riguroso)* strict.
sexagenario,-a *adj* sexagenarian.
▶ *nm & nf* sexagenarian.
sexagesimal *adj* sexagesimal.
sexagésimo,-a *adj* sixtieth.
▶ *nm & nf* sixtieth.

✎ Para ejemplos de uso, consulta sexto,-a.

sexenio *nm* six-year period.
sexismo *nm* sexism.
sexista *adj* **1** sexist. **2** *(machista)* chauvinistic.
▶ *nm* **1** sexist. **2** *(machista)* male chauvinist.
sexo *nm* **1** sex. **2** *(órganos)* sexual organs *pl*, genitals *pl*.
sextante *nm* sextant.
sexteto *nm* sextet.
sexto,-a *adj* sixth: *una sexta parte* a sixth; *el siglo sexto* the sixth century; *Alfonso sexto* Alfonso the sixth; *vive en un sexto piso* he lives in a sixth-floor flat; *acabó en sexto lugar* he finished in sixth palce. **2** *(sexto)* sixth: *soy el seis de la lista* I'm sixth on the list.
▶ *nm & nf* sixth: *le correspondió un sexto del pastel* he got a sixth of the cake.
sextuplicar *vt* to multiply by six, sextuplicate.
séxtuplo,-a *adj* sextuple.
▶ *nm* séxtuplo six times as much, six times as many.
sexual *adj* *(gen)* sex; *(relaciones)* sexual: *vida sexual* sex life.
sexualidad *nf* sexuality.
Seychelles *nm pl* las (islas) Seychelles the Seychelles.
sha *nm* shah.
shérif *nm* sheriff.

si¹ *conj* **1** *(condicional)* if: *si quieres puedes venir con nosotros* you can come with us if you want to. **2** *(disyuntiva, duda)* if, whether: *no sé si decírselo (o no)* I don't know whether to tell her (or not). **3** *(énfasis)* but: *¡pero si es facilísimo!* ¡but it's really easy! LOC **como si** as if. ‖ **por si acaso** just in case: *llévatelo por si acaso* take it with you just in case.
si² *nm* MÚS ti, si, B.
sí¹ *pron* **1** *(él)* himself; *(ella)* herself; *(cosa)* itself; *(ellos, ellas)* themselves; *(usted)* yourself; *(ustedes)* yourselves: *lo hizo por sí misma* she did it by herself; *hablaban para sí* they were talking to themselves. **2** *(uno mismo)* oneself. **3** *(recíproco)* each other: *hablaban entre sí* they were talking to each other.
sí² *adv* **1** yes: *dijo que sí* she said yes. **2** *(enfático)* of course: *sí que me gusta* of course I like it. LOC **creo que sí** I think so. ‖ **porque sí 1** *(sin razón)* just because I *(you, etc)* say so. **2** *(por naturaleza)* that's the way it is: *no puedes marcharte porque sí* you can't leave just because you feel like it.
siberiano,-a *adj* Siberian.
▶ *nm & nf* Siberian.
sicoanálisis *nm inv* psychoanalysis.
sicodélico,-a *adj* psychedelic.
sicología *nf* psychology.
sida *abrev* MED (síndrome de inmunodeficiencia adquirida) acquired immune deficiency syndrome; *(abreviatura)* AIDS.
siderurgia *nf* iron and steel industry.
sidra *nf* cider, US hard cider.
siega *nf* **1** *(acción)* harvesting, reaping. **2** *(época)* harvest, harvest time. **3** *(mieses)* harvest.
siembra *nf* **1** *(acción)* sowing. **2** *(época)* sowing time. **3** *(sembrado)* sown field.
siempre *adv* always: *siempre recordaré sus palabras* I'll always remember her words.
siempreviva *nf* everlasting flower, immortelle.
sien *nf* temple.
sierra *nf* **1** TÉC saw. **2** GEOG mountain range.

Sierra Leona *nf* Sierra Leone.
sierraleonés,-esa *adj* Sierra Leonean.
▸ *nm & nf* Sierra Leonean.
siesta *nf* siesta, afternoon nap.
siete *adj (cardinal)* seven; *(séptimo)* seventh.
▸ *nm* **1** *(número)* seven. **2** *fam (rasgón)* tear.

✎ Para ejemplos de uso, consulta seis.

sigilo *nm* **1** *(secreto)* secrecy. **2** *(discreción)* discretion.
sigla *nf* acronym, abbreviation.
siglo *nm* **1** century. **2** *fig (vida mundana)* world. COMP **el Siglo de Oro** the Golden Age.
significación *nf* **1** *(sentido)* meaning. **2** *(trascendencia)* significance.
significado,-a *adj* well-known, important.
▸ *nm* **significado 1** meaning. **2** LING signifier.
significar *vt* **1** to mean: *no sé lo que significa* I don't know what it means. **2** *(hacer saber)* to make known, express.
significativo,-a *adj* **1** *(que da a entender)* meaningful. **2** *(importante)* significant.
signo *nm* **1** *(gen)* sign. **2** GRAM mark. **3** *(destino)* fate, destiny. **4** *(tendencia)* tendency.
siguiente *adj* following, next: *vamos a leer el capítulo siguiente* we're going to read the next chapter. LOC **¡el siguiente!** next, please!
sílaba *nf* syllable.
silbar *vi* **1** to whistle. **2** *(abuchear)* to hiss, boo.
silbato *nm* whistle.
silbido *nm* **1** *(acción)* whistle, whistling. **2** *(abucheo)* hissing.
silenciar *vt* **1** *(ocultar)* to hush up. **2** *(pasar por alto)* not to mention.
silencio *nm* silence. LOC **guardar silencio** to keep quiet.
silencioso,-a *adj (persona)* quiet; *(objeto)* silent.
silepsis *nf inv* syllepsis.
sílex *nm inv* flint.

silicato *nm* silicate.
sílice *nf* silica.
silíceo,-a *adj* flinty.
silícico,-a *adj* silicic.
silicio *nm* silicon.
silla *nf* **1** chair. **2** *(de montar)* saddle.
sillar *nm (piedra)* ashlar.
sillín *nm* saddle.
sillón *nm* armchair.
silueta *nf* **1** *(contorno)* silhouette. **2** *(figura)* figure, shape.
silvestre *adj* wild.
silvicultura *nf* forestry.
sima *nf* abyss, chasm.
simbiosis *nf inv* symbiosis.
simbólico,-a *adj* symbolic, symbolical.
simbolizar *vt* to symbolize.
símbolo *nm* symbol.
simetría *nf* symmetry.
simétrico,-a *adj* symmetric.
simiente *nf* seed.
simiesco,-a *adj* simian, apelike.
símil *nm* **1** *(comparación)* comparison. **2** *(semejanza)* resemblance. **3** LIT simile.
similar *adj* similar.
simio *nm* simian, monkey.
simpatía *nf* **1** *(cordialidad)* affection (por, for), liking (por, for). **2** *(amabilidad)* warmth, pleasantness. **3** *(afinidad)* affinity (por, with). **4** *(solidaridad)* sympathy (por, towards), solidarity (con, with). **5** MED sympathy.
simpático,-a *adj* **1** *(amable)* nice, likeable; *(agradable)* kind, friendly; *(encantador)* charming. **2** MED sympathetic.
simpatizante *nm o nf* supporter.
simpatizar *vi* **1** *(con persona)* to get on (con, with). **2** *(con idea, etc)* to sympathize (con, with).
simple *adj* **1** *(gen)* simple. **2** *(único)* single, just one. **3** *(mero)* mere. **4** *(persona)* simple, simple-minded.
simplicidad *nf* **1** simplicity. **2** *(ingenuidad)* naivety, ingenuousness.
simplificar *vt* to simplify.
simposio *nm* symposium.
simulación *nf* simulation.

S

simulacro *nm* sham, pretence (US pretense): *simulacro de incendio* fire drill.

simulado,-a *adj* simulated.

simulador,-ra *adj* simulative.
▸ *nm & nf* pretender.
▸ *nm* **simulador** TÉC simulator.

simular *vt* **1** to simulate. **2** *(fingir)* to pretend.

simultanear *vt* **1** *(hacer dos cosas)* to do simultaneously, do at the same time. **2** *(combinar)* to combine.

simultaneidad *nf* simultaneity.

simultáneo,-a *adj* simultaneous.

sin *prep* **1** *(carencia)* without. **2** *(además de)* not counting. [LOC] **estar sin +** *inf* not to have been + *pp*: *está sin planchar* it hasn't been ironed. ▌ **sin querer** accidentally, by mistake: *lo hizo sin querer* he didn't mean to do it.

sinagoga *nf* synagogue.

sinalefa *nf* synalepha, synaloepha, elision.

sincerarse *vpr* *(abrirse)* to open one's heart (con, to).

sinceridad *nf* sincerity.

sincero,-a *adj* sincere.

sinclinal *nm* syncline.

síncopa *nf* **1** MÚS syncopation. **2** LING syncope.

sincopado,-a *adj* MÚS syncopated.

sincopar *vt* **1** *(notas, palabras)* to syncopate. **2** *fig* *(abreviar)* to abridge.

síncope *nm* syncope.

sincretismo *nm* syncretism.

sincronía *nf* synchrony.

sincrónico,-a *adj* synchronic.

sincronismo *nm* synchronism.

sincronización *nf* synchronization.

sincronizar *vt* to synchronize.

sindicado,-a *adj* who belongs to a trade union.

sindical *adj* trade union, union.

sindicalismo *nm* trade unionism, unionism.

sindicalista *nm o nf* trade unionist, unionist.

sindicar *vt* to unionize.

▸ *vpr* **sindicarse** *(unirse a un sindicato)* to join a trade union.

sindicato *nm* trade union, union.

síndico *nm* **1** POL elected representative. **2** *(depositario)* trustee.

síndrome *nm* syndrome.

sinéresis *nf inv* syneresis, synaeresis.

sinergia *nf* synergy.

sinfín *nm* endless number.

sinfonía *nf* symphony.

sinfónico,-a *adj* symphonic.

Singapur *nm* Singapore.

singular *adj* **1** *(único)* singular, single. **2** *(excepcional)* extraordinary, exceptional.
▸ *nm* GRAM singular. [LOC] **en singular** GRAM in the singular.

singularidad *nf* **1** *(unicidad)* singularity. **2** *(excepcionalidad)* strangeness, uniqueness.

singularizar *vt* **1** *(distinguir)* to distinguish, single out. **2** GRAM to use in the singular.
▸ *vpr* **singularizarse** to distinguish os (por, by/with), stand out ((por, for).

siniestra *nf* *(izquierda)* left hand.

siniestrado,-a *adj* lit damaged.

siniestro,-a *adj* **1** *lit (izquierdo)* left, left-hand. **2** *(malo)* sinister, ominous.
▸ *nm* **siniestro** disaster, catastrophe; *(accidente)* accident; *(incendio)* fire.

sinnúmero *nm* endless number.

sino¹ *conj* **1** *(contraposición)* but: *no es blanco sino negro* it isn't white but black. **2** *(excepción)* but, except for: *nadie lo sabe sino Antonio* nobody knows except for Antonio.

sino² *nm* *(destino)* fate, destiny.

sinonimia *nf* synonymy.

sinónimo,-a *adj* synonymous.
▸ *nm* **sinónimo** synonym.

sinopsis *nf inv* synopsis.

sinóptico,-a *adj* synoptic, synoptical.

sinrazón *nf* wrong, injustice.

sinsabor *nm* fig worry, trouble, heartache.

sintáctico,-a *adj* syntactic, syntactical.

sintagma *nm* phrase. COMP **sintagma nominal** noun phrase.

sintaxis *nf inv* syntax.

síntesis *nf inv* synthesis.

sintético,-a *adj* synthetic.

sintetizador *nm* synthesizer.

sintetizar *vt* **1** to synthesize. **2** *(resumir)* to summarize: *sintetizando diría que...* to sum up, I'd like to say that...

síntoma *nm* symptom.

sintomático,-a *adj* **1** symptomatic. **2** *fig* significant.

sintomatología *nf* symptomatology.

sintonía *nf* **1** *(de radio)* tuning. **2** *(música)* signature tune. **3** *fig (armonía)* harmony. LOC **estar en sintonía con** ALGN *fig* to be in tune with SB, be on SB's wavelength.

sintonizador *nm* **1** *(botón)* tuning knob. **2** *(de cadena de sonido)* tuner.

sintonizar *vt (radio)* to tune in to: *sintonizó una emisora local* he tuned in to a local radio station.
► *vi fig (llevarse bien)* to get on well, be on the same wavelength.

sinuosidad *nf* **1** *(cualidad)* sinuosity. **2** *(curva)* bend, curve. **3** *fig (de argumento, etc)* tortuousness; *(de persona)* deviousness.

sinuoso,-a *adj* **1** *(camino)* winding. **2** *fig (argumento)* tortuous; *(persona)* devious.

sinvergüenza *nm o nf* **1** *(pícaro)* rotter, swine, louse. **2** *(descarado)* cheeky devil.

siquiatra *nm o nf* psychiatrist.

siquiatría *nf* psychiatry.

síquico,-a *adj* → psíquico,-a.

siquiera *conj* **1** *(adversativa)* even though, even if: *quisiera hablar contigo, siquiera fuera un momento* I would like to speak to you, even if it's only for a moment. **2** *(distributiva)* whether.
► *adv (por lo menos)* at least: *dame siquiera la mitad* give me at least half of it.

sirena *nf* **1** *(ninfa)* siren, mermaid. **2** *(alarma)* siren.

Siria *nf* Syria.

sirio,-a *adj* Syrian.
► *nm & nf* Syrian.

sirviente,-a *nm & nf* servant.

sisa *nf* COST armhole.

sisal *nm* sisal.

sisar *vt* **1** COST to dart, take in. **2** *(hurtar)* to pilfer, pinch, nick; *(estafar)* to cheat.

sisear *vi* to hiss.
► *vt* to hiss.

siseo *nm* hiss, hissing.

sísmico,-a *adj* seismic.

sismo *nm* earthquake, tremor.

sismógrafo *nm* seismograph.

sismología *nf* seismology.

sismólogo,-a *nm & nf* seismologist.

sistema *nm* system. COMP **sistema de ecuaciones** simultaneous equations *pl*. ‖ **sistema métrico decimal** decimal metric system. ‖ **sistema nervioso** nervous system. ‖ **sistema operativo** operative system.

sistemático,-a *adj* systematic.

sistematizar *vt* to systematize.

sístole *nf* systole.

sistólico,-a *adj* systolic.

sitiado,-a *adj* besieged.
► *nm & nf* besieged.

sitial *nm* seat of honour (US honor).

sitiar *vt* to besiege, lay siege to.

sitio *nm* **1** *(lugar)* place. **2** *(espacio)* space, room. **3** *(asiento)* seat. **4** MIL siege. COMP **sitio web** website.

sito,-a *adj fml* located, situated.

situación *nf* **1** *(circunstancia)* situation. **2** *(posición)* position. **3** *(emplazamiento)* situation, location.

situado,-a *adj* situated, located.

situar *vt* to place, locate, situate, put.
► *vpr* **situarse 1** *(colocarse)* to be placed, be located, be situated. **2** *(lograr una posición)* to get on, do well, be successful.

soasar *vt* to roast lightly.

sobaco *nm* armpit.

sobado,-a *adj* **1** *(desgastado)* worn, shabby. **2** *(manoseado)* well-thumbed, dog-eared. **3** *fig (manido)* well-worn.

S

sobar *vt* **1** *(ablandar)* to knead. **2** *fig (manosear - objeto)* to finger; *(- persona)* to grope, paw, touch up.

soberanía *nf* sovereignty.

soberano,-a *adj* **1** sovereign. **2** *fig* extreme, supreme. **3** *fam* huge, great.
▶ *nm & nf* sovereign.

soberbia *nf* **1** *(orgullo)* pride; *(arrogancia)* arrogance, haughtiness. **2** *(cólera)* rage, anger.

soberbio,-a *adj* **1** *(orgulloso)* proud; *(arrogante)* arrogant, haughty. **2** *(suntuoso)* sumptuous, magnificent. **3** *(magnífico)* superb, splendid, magnificent.

sobornable *adj* bribable, venal.

sobornar *vt* to bribe, suborn.

soborno *nm* **1** *(acción)* bribery. **2** *(regalo, etc)* bribe.

sobra *nf (exceso)* excess, surplus. [LOC] **saber** ALGO **de sobra** to know STH only too well.
▶ *nf pl* **sobras** *(desperdicios)* leftovers.

sobrado,-a *adj (que sobra)* ample, more than enough, plenty of.

sobrante *adj* leftover, remaining, spare.

sobrar *vi* **1** *(haber más de lo necesario)* to be more than enough, be too much. **2** *(estar de más)* to be superfluous, be unnecessary. **3** *(quedar)* to have left over, be left over.

sobre *prep* **1** *(encima)* on, upon, on top of. **2** *(por encima)* over, above. **3** *(acerca de)* about, on. **4** *(alrededor de)* about, around.
▶ *nm* **1** *(de correo)* envelope. **2** *(de sopa, etc)* packet. [LOC] **sobre todo** above all, especially.

sobre- *pref* super-, over-.

sobreabundancia *nf* superabundance, overabundance.

sobrealimentar *vt* to overfeed.

sobreático *nm* penthouse.

sobrecarga *nf* **1** overload. **2** *fig* additional burden, further worry.

sobrecargar *vt* **1** to overload. **2** *fig* to overburden.

sobrecogedor,-ra *adj* **1** *(conmovedor)* dramatic, awesome. **2** *(que da miedo)* frightening.

sobrecoger *vt* **1** *(coger de repente)* to startle, take by surprise. **2** *(asustar)* to frighten, scare.

sobrecubierta *nf* jacket, dust cover.

sobredosis *nf inv* overdose.

sobreentender *vt* **1** *(comprender)* to understand. **2** *(deducir)* to deduce.
▶ *vpr* **sobreentenderse** to be implied, be inferred: *se sobreentiende que su respuesta será afirmativa* one assumes that she will say yes.

sobreexcitación *nf* overexcitement.

sobreexcitar *vt* to overexcite.
▶ *vpr* **sobreexcitarse** to get overexcited.

sobreexponer *vt* to overexpose.

sobreexposición *nf* overexposure.

sobrehilar *vt* COST to whipstitch.

sobrehumano,-a *adj* superhuman.

sobreimpresión *nf* overprint.

sobrellevar *vt* to bear, endure.

sobremanera *adv* exceedingly.

sobremesa *nf* **1** *(período)* afternoon: *la programación de la sobremesa* the afternoon's television programmes. **2** *(charla)* table talk.

sobrenadar *vi* to float.

sobrenatural *adj* supernatural.

sobrenombre *nm* nickname.

sobrentender *vt-vpr* → sobreentender.

sobrepaga *nf* bonus.

sobrepasar *vt* **1** to exceed, surpass, be in excess of. **2** *(competición)* to beat.

sobrepeso *nm* **1** overload, excess weight. **2** *(de persona)* excess weight.

sobreponer *vt* to put on top (en, of), superimpose (en, on).
▶ *vpr* **sobreponerse 1** *fig (al dolor, etc)* to overcome (a, -). **2** *fig (animarse)* to pull os together.

sobreproducción *nf* excess production, overproduction.

sobresaliente *adj* **1** sticking out, protruding. **2** *fig* outstanding, excellent.
▶ *nm (calificación - colegio)* A; *(- universidad)* first, US A.

sobresalir *vi* **1** to stick out, protrude. **2** *fig* to stand out, excel.

sobresaltar *vt* to startle.
► *vpr* **sobresaltarse** to be startled.

sobresalto *nm* start; *(de temor)* fright, shock.

sobresdrújulo,-a *adj* accented on the antepenultimate syllable.

sobrestimar *vt* to overestimate.

sobretodo *nm (abrigo)* overcoat.

sobrevalorar *vt* to overestimate.

sobrevenir *vi* to happen to, befall: *no sabremos nunca lo que le sobrevino* we'll never know what happened to her.

sobreviviente *nm o nf* survivor.

sobrevivir *vi* **1** *(gen)* to survive. **2** *(a alguien)* to outlive.

sobrevolar *vt* to fly over.

sobrexcitación *nf* overexcitement.

sobrexcitar *vt-vpr* → **sobreexcitar**.

sobrexponer *vt* → **sobreexponer**.

sobriedad *nf* sobriety, moderation, restraint.

sobrino,-a *nm & nf (hombre)* nephew; *(mujer)* niece.

sobrio,-a *adj* **1** *(estilo, color, etc)* sober, plain. **2** *(persona)* sober, moderate.

socavar *vt* **1** *(excavar)* to dig under. **2** *fig* to undermine.

socavón *nm* **1** *(cueva excavada)* excavation. **2** *(bache)* hollow, hole. **3** *(de una mina)* gallery, tunnel.

sociabilidad *nf* sociability.

sociable *adj* sociable, friendly.

social *adj* social.

socialdemocracia *nf* social democracy.

socialdemócrata *adj* social democratic.
► *nm o nf* social democrat.

socialismo *nm* socialism.

socialista *adj* socialist.
► *nm o nf* socialist.

socializar *vt* **1** *(gen)* to socialize. **2** *(nacionalizar)* to nationalize.

sociedad *nf* **1** *(gen)* society. **2** COM company. **3** *(asociación)* society, association.

socio,-a *nm & nf* **1** *(miembro)* member. **2** COM partner, associate. **3** *(accionista)* shareholder, member.

socioeconómico,-a *adj* socioeconomic.

sociología *nf* sociology.

sociólogo,-a *nm & nf* sociologist.

socorrer *vt* to help, assist, come to the aid of, go to the aid of.

socorrista *nm o nf* life-saver, lifeguard.

socorro *nm* **1** *(ayuda)* help, aid, assistance. **2** *(provisiones)* supplies *pl*, provisions *pl*.
► *interj* help!

soda *nf* **1** *(bebida)* soda water. **2** QUÍM soda.

sódico,-a *adj* sodium.

sodio *nm* sodium.

sofá *nm* sofa, settee.

sofá-cama *nm* sofa bed, studio couch.

sofisticación *nf* sophistication.

sofisticado,-a *adj* sophisticated.

sofocante *adj* suffocating, stifling.

sofocar *vt* **1** *(ahogar)* to suffocate, stifle, smother. **2** *fig (incendio)* to put out, extinguish; *(rebelión)* to suppress, put down.
► *vpr* **sofocarse 1** *(de calor, etc)* to suffocate. **2** *fig (ruborizarse)* to blush.

sofoco *nm* **1** *(ahogo)* suffocation, stifling sensation. **2** *fig (vergüenza)* embarrassment; *(rubor)* blushing. **3** *fam (disgusto)* shock.

sofocón *nm fam* shock. [LOC] **llevarse un sofocón** *fam* to get into a state.

sofreír *vt* to fry lightly, brown.

sofrito *nm* fried tomato and onion sauce.

software *nm* software.

soga *nf* rope, cord.

soja *nf* soya bean, US soybean. [COMP] **salsa de soja** soy sauce.

sojuzgar *vt* to subjugate.

sol¹ *nm* **1** *(estrella)* sun. **2** *(luz)* sun, sunlight, sunshine. **3** *fam (persona)* darling. **4** *(moneda de Perú)* sol, standard monetary unit of Peru. [LOC] **hace sol** it's sunny, the sun's shining. ❚ **tomar**

S

el sol 1 *(tendido)* to sunbathe. **2** *(al caminar)* to get some sun.

sol² *nm* MÚS sol, G.

solapa *nf* **1** *(de prenda)* lapel. **2** *(de sobre, libro)* flap.

solapado,-a *adj fig* sly, evasive.

solapar *vt* **1** COST to put lapels on. **2** *fig (ocultar)* to conceal, cover up.
► *vi (cubrir)* to overlap.

solar¹ *adj (del sol)* solar.

solar² *nm* **1** *(terreno)* plot, lot; *(en obras)* building site. **2** *(casa solariega)* ancestral home.

solar³ *vt (suelo)* to floor.

solaz *nm* **1** *(esparcimiento)* recreation, entertainment. **2** *(descanso)* rest, relaxation.

solazar *vt* **1** *(entretener)* to amuse, entertain. **2** *(descansar)* to rest, relax.
► *vpr* **solazarse 1** *(divertirse)* to enjoy os. **2** *(relajarse)* to relax.

soldado *nm* soldier. COMP **soldado raso** private.

soldador,-ra *nm & nf* welder.
► *nm* **soldador** soldering iron.

soldadura *nf* **1** *(acción)* welding, soldering. **2** *(unión)* weld, soldered joint.

soldar *vt* **1** *(metal)* to weld, solder. **2** *fig (enmendar)* to mend.
► *vpr* **soldarse** *(huesos)* to knit.

soleado,-a *adj* sunny.

solear *vt* to expose to the sun, put in the sun.

soledad *nf* **1** *(estado)* solitude. **2** *(sentimiento)* loneliness. **3** *(lugar)* lonely place.

solemne *adj* **1** solemn, majestic. **2** *pey* downright: *es una solemne tontería* it's downright stupidity.

solemnidad *nf* **1** *(pompa)* solemnity, pomp, formality. **2** *(acto, ceremonia)* solemn ceremony, ceremonial occasion.

solemnizar *vt (celebrar)* to solemnize, celebrate; *(conmemorar)* to commemorate.

soler *vi (acostumbrar - presente)* to be in the habit of + *-ing*; *(- pasado)* used to:

solía venir cada martes she used to come every Tuesday.

solicitante *nm o nf* applicant.

solicitar *vt* **1** *(pedir)* to request. **2** *(trabajo)* to apply for; *(permiso, etc)* to ask for; *(votos)* to canvass for. **3** *(persona)* to chase after. **4** *(cortejar)* to woo, court.

solícito,-a *adj* obliging, attentive.

solicitud *nf* **1** *(petición)* request; *(de trabajo)* application; *(- impreso)* application form. **2** *(instancia)* petition. **3** *(diligencia)* solicitude, care. COMP **solicitud de empleo** job application.

solidaridad *nf* solidarity.

solidario,-a *adj* **1** *(ligado)* united. **2** *(responsabilidad, causa)* common.

solidarizarse *vpr* **1** *(gen)* to show one's solidarity (con, with). **2** *(apoyar)* to support (con, -).

solidez *nf (resistencia)* solidity, strength; *(firmeza)* firmness.

solidificación *nf* solidification.

solidificar *vt* **1** *(líquido)* to solidify. **2** *(pasta)* to harden, set.
► *vpr* **solidificarse 1** *(líquido)* to solidify. **2** *(pasta)* to harden, set.

sólido,-a *adj* **1** *(fuerte)* solid, strong; *(firme)* firm. **2** *fig (color)* fast. **3** *fig (principios, etc)* sound.
► *nm* **sólido** solid.

solista *nm o nf* soloist.

solitaria *nf* MED tapeworm.

solitario,-a *adj* **1** *(que está solo)* solitary, lone. **2** *(que se siente solo)* lonely. **3** *(lugar)* deserted, lonely.
► *nm & nf (persona)* solitary person.
► *nm* **solitario** *(diamante, naipes)* solitaire.

sólito,-a *adj* usual, customary.

soliviantar *vt* **1** *(inducir)* to rouse, stir up. **2** *(irritar)* to irritate.

sollozar *vi* to sob.

sólo *adv* → **solo¹**.

solo¹ *adv* [sólo se usa si se puede producir confusión con el adjetivo o con el nombre] only, just: *solo quiero café* I just want a coffee.

solo,-a *adj* **1** *(sin compañía)* alone, on one's own, by os; *(sin ayuda)* (by) os,

(for) os. **2** *(solitario)* lonely. **3** *(único)* only, sole, single. **4** *(café)* black.
▶ *nm* **solo 1** *(naipes)* solitaire. **2** *fam (café)* black coffee. **3** MÚS solo. LOC **a solas** alone, by os.

solomillo *nm* sirloin.

soltar *vt* **1** *(desasir)* to let go of, release, drop. **2** *(desatar)* to untie, unfasten, undo; *(aflojar)* to loosen. **3** *(preso)* to release, free, set free. **4** *(animal)* to let out; *(perro)* to unleash. **5** *(humo, olor)* to give off. **6** *(puntos)* to drop. **7** *(de vientre)* to loosen. **8** *fam (arrear)* to give, deal. **9** *fam (decir)* to come out with, blurt out.
▶ *vpr* **soltarse 1** *(desatarse)* to come untied, come unfastened. **2** *(desprenderse)* to come off. **3** *(tornillo, etc)* to come loose. **4** *(animal)* to get loose, break loose. **5** *(puntos)* to come undone. **6** *(vientre)* to loosen. **7** *fig (adquirir habilidad)* to become proficient, get the knack. **8** *fig (desenvolverse)* to become self-confident, loosen up.

soltero,-a *adj* single, unmarried.
▶ *nm & nf (hombre)* bachelor, single man; *(mujer)* single woman.

soluble *adj* soluble.

solución *nf* solution.

solucionar *vt* **1** *(problema)* to solve. **2** *(huelga, asunto)* to settle.

solventar *vt* **1** *(dificultad, problema)* to solve, resolve. **2** *(deuda, asunto)* to settle.

solvente *adj* **1** FIN solvent. **2** *(fiable)* reliable.
▶ *nm* QUÍM solvent.

somalí *adj* Somali.
▶ *nm o nf* Somali.

Somalia *nf* Somalia.

sombra *nf* **1** *(falta de sol)* shade. **2** *(silueta)* shadow. **3** *(espectro)* ghost, shade. **4** *fig (persona que sigue a otra)* shadow. **5** *fam fig (gracia)* wit. **6** *fig (parte pequeña)* trace, shadow, bit. **7** *fig (clandestinidad)* secrecy.

sombreado *nm* shading.

sombrero *nm* **1** *(prenda)* hat.

sombrilla *nf* parasol, sunshade.

sombrío,-a *adj* **1** *(lugar)* dark. **2** *fig (tenebroso)* gloomy, sombre (US somber). **3** *fig (persona)* gloomy, sullen.

someter *vt* **1** *(rebeldes)* to subdue, put down; *(rebelión)* to quell. **2** *(hacer recibir)* to subject (a, to). **3** *(pasiones)* to subdue. **4** *(proponer, presentar)* to submit.
▶ *vpr* **someterse 1** *(rendirse)* to surrender (a, to). **2** *(tratamiento, etc)* to undergo (a, -). LOC **someter a prueba** to test, put to the test. ∥ **someter** ALGO **a votación** to put STH to the vote.

somnolencia *nf* sleepiness, drowsiness, somnolence.

somnoliento,-a *adj* sleepy, drowsy.

son *nm* **1** *(sonido)* sound. **2** *fig (modo)* manner, way: *a mi son* my way. LOC **en son de paz** in peace.

sonado,-a *adj* **1** *(conocido)* famous. **2** *(escándalo, etc)* much talked-about. **3** *fam fig (loco)* mad, crazy.

sonámbulo,-a *nm & nf* sleepwalker, somnambulist.

sonar¹ *vi* **1** *(hacer ruido)* to sound. **2** *(timbre, teléfono, etc)* to ring. **3** *(alarma, reloj)* to go off. **4** *(instrumento)* to play. **5** *(letra)* to be pronounced.
▶ *vt* **1** *(conocer vagamente)* to sound familiar, ring a bell. **2** *(timbre, etc)* to ring; *(bocina)* to blow, sound; *(instrumento)* to play.
▶ *vpr* **sonarse** *(nariz)* to blow.

sonar² *nm* MAR sonar.

sonda *nf* **1** MED *(para intervenciones quirúrgicas)* probe; *(para evacuar líquidos)* catheter. **2** MAR sounding line. **3** *(barreno)* drill, bore. **4** *(atmosférica)* sonde; *(espacio)* probe.

sondear *vt* **1** MED to sound, probe. **2** MAR to sound. **3** *(subsuelo)* to drill, bore. **4** *fig (encuestar)* to sound out.

sondeo *nm* **1** MED sounding, probing. **2** MAR sounding. **3** *(del subsuelo)* drilling, boring. **4** *fig (encuesta)* poll.

soneto *nm* sonnet.

sónico,-a *adj* sonic.

sonido *nm* sound.

sonoridad *nf* sonority.

S

sonoro,-a *adj* **1** *(resonante)* loud, re-sounding. **2** LING sound.

sonreír *vi* to smile.
▸ *vt* **1** to smile at. **2** *fig (favorecer)* to smile on, smile upon.
▸ *vpr* **sonreírse** to smile.

sonriente *adj* smiling.

sonrisa *nf* smile.

sonrojar *vt* to make blush.
▸ *vpr* **sonrojarse** to blush.

sonsacar *vt* **1** *(gen)* to wheedle. **2** *fig (secreto)* to get out of, worm out.

soñador,-ra *nm & nf* dreamer.

soñar *vt* **1** *(al dormir)* to dream. **2** *fig (fantasear)* to daydream, dream.
▸ *vi* **1** *(al dormir)* to dream (con, about/of). **2** *fig (fantasear)* to daydream (con, about), dream (con, about/of).

soñolencia *nf* sleepiness.

soñoliento,-a *adj* drowsy, sleepy.

sopa *nf (plato)* soup.

sopesar *vt* **1** to try the weight of. **2** *fig* to weigh up.

soplar *vi* **1** *(viento, etc)* to blow. **2** *fam (denunciar)* to squeal.
▸ *vt* **1** *(polvo, etc)* to blow away, blow off; *(vela)* to blow out; *(sopa)* to blow on; *(globo)* to blow up. **2** *(vidrio)* to blow. **3** *fam fig (delatar)* to split on, grass on. **4** *fam fig (en un examen, etc)* to whisper the answer, tell the answer.

soplete *nm* blowtorch, blowlamp.

soplido *nm* blow, puff.

soplo *nm* **1** *(con la boca)* blow, puff. **2** *(de viento)* puff. **3** *fig (momento)* moment, minute. **4** MED murmur. **5** *fam (de secreto, etc)* tip-off.

soportar *vt* **1** *(aguantar)* to support, bear. **2** *fig (sufrir)* to stand, bear, endure. **3** *fig (lluvia, tormenta, etc)* to weather.

soporte *nm* support. COMP **soporte de datos** INFORM data carrier.

sorbo *nm* **1** *(acción)* sip. **2** *(trago)* gulp.

sordera *nf* deafness.

sordidez *nf* **1** *(suciedad)* squalor. **2** *(mezquindad)* meanness.

sórdido,-a *adj* **1** *(sucio)* squalid, sordid. **2** *(mezquino)* mean.

sordo,-a *adj* **1** *(persona)* deaf. **2** *(sonido, dolor, golpe)* dull. **3** LING voiceless.
▸ *nm & nf (persona)* deaf person.

sordomudez *nf* deaf-mutism.

sordomudo,-a *adj* deaf and dumb.
▸ *nm & nf* deaf mute.

sorgo *nm* sorghum.

sorprendente *adj* surprising, amazing, astonishing.

sorprender *vt* **1** *(coger desprevenido)* to catch unawares, take by surprise. **2** *fig (descubrir)* to discover; *(conversación)* to overhear. **3** *fig (maravillar)* to surprise, astonish, amaze.
▸ *vpr* **sorprenderse** *fig* to be surprised.

sorpresa *nf* surprise.

sortear *vt* **1** *(echar a suertes)* to draw lots for, cast lots for. **2** *(rifar)* to raffle. **3** MIL to draft. **4** *fig (obstáculos, dificultad)* to get round, overcome; *(preguntas)* to dodge, evade, get round.

sorteo *nm* draw; *(rifa)* raffle.

sortija *nf (anillo)* ring.

sortilegio *nm* **1** *(hechicería)* sorcery, witchcraft. **2** *(hechizo)* spell.

sosa *nf* **1** QUÍM soda. **2** BOT saltwort.

sosegado,-a *adj* calm, quiet.

sosegar *vt (aplacar)* to calm, quieten.
▸ *vpr* **sosegarse** *(calmarse)* to calm down.

sosiego *nm* calmness, peace.

soso,-a *adj* **1** *(insípido)* tasteless; *(sin sal)* unsalted. **2** *fig* dull, insipid.

sospecha *nf* suspicion.

sospechar *vt (imaginar)* to suspect, think, suppose.
▸ *vi (desconfiar)* to suspect (de, -).

sospechoso,-a *adj* suspicious.
▸ *nm & nf* suspect.

sostén *nm* **1** *(apoyo)* support. **2** *(sustento)* sustenance. **3** [también se usa en plural con el mismo significado] *(prenda)* bra.

sostener *vt* **1** *(mantener firme)* to support, hold up. **2** *(sujetar)* to hold. **3** *fig (apoyar)* to support, back. **4** *fig (afirmar)* to maintain, affirm. **5** *fig (alimentar)* to support, keep. **6** *fig (velocidad, correspondencia, relación, etc)* to keep up.
▸ *vpr* **sostenerse 1** *(mantenerse)* to support os; *(de pie)* to stand up. **2** *(permanecer)* to stay, remain.

sostenibilidad *nf* sustainability.

sostenible *adj* (gen) sustainable; (argumento) tenable.

sostenido,-a *adj* **1** (continuado) sustained; (constante) steady. **2** MÚS sharp: *fa sostenido* F sharp.
▶ *nm* **sostenido** MÚS sharp.

sota *nf* (cartas) jack, knave.

sótano *nm* (gen) basement; (de casa) cellar, basement.

sotavento *nm* lee, leeward.

soterrar *vt* **1** to bury. **2** *fig* to hide.

soto *nm* **1** (arboleda) grove, copse.

Sri Lanka *nf* Sri Lanka.

stop *nm* **1** (señal) stop sign. **2** (parada) stop.

su *adj* (de él) his; (de ella) her; (de usted, de ustedes) your; (de ellos, de ellas) their; (de animales, cosas) its; (de uno) one's.

suave *adj* **1** (agradable al tacto) soft, smooth. **2** (liso, llano) smooth, even. **3** *fig* (apacible) gentle, mild. **4** *fig* (tranquilo) easy. **5** *fig* (música, palabras, voz, luz, movimiento, viento) soft, gentle. **6** *fig* (clima) mild, clement.

suavizante *nm* **1** (de pelo) hair conditioner. **2** (de ropa) fabric softener.

suavizar *vt* **1** (hacer agradable) to soften. **2** (alisar) to smooth (out). **3** *fig* to soften.

subacuático,-a *adj* underwater.

subafluente *nm* tributary.

subalimentación *nf* undernourishment.

subalimentar *vt* to underfeed.

subalterno,-a *nm & nf* subordinate.

subasta *nf* **1** (venta) auction. **2** (adjudicación de obra) invitation to tender.

subastador,-ra *nm & nf* auctioneer.

subastar *vt* to auction (off).

subatómico,-a *adj* subatomic.

subcampeón,-ona *nm & nf* (en competición) runner-up; (en ránking) number two.

subdesarrollo *nm* underdevelopment.

subdirector,-ra *nm & nf* assistant director, assistant manager.

súbdito,-a *nm & nf* **1** (de un rey) subject. **2** (ciudadano) citizen.

subida *nf* **1** (ascenso) ascent, climb. **2** (pendiente) slope, hill. **3** *fig* (aumento - gen) increase; (- de temperatura) rise; (- de precios, salario) rise, increase.

subíndice *nm* subscript, subindex.

subir *vi* **1** (ir hacia arriba - gen) to go up, come up; (- avión) to climb. **2** (en un vehículo - coche) to get in; (autobús, avión, barco, tren) to get on, get onto. **3** (montar - bicicleta) to get on; (- caballo) to get on, mount. **4** (a un árbol) to climb up. **5** *fig* (elevarse, aumentar) to rise. **6** *fig* (categoría, puesto) to be promoted.
▶ *vt* **1** (escaleras, calle) to go up, climb; (montaña) to climb. **2** (mover arriba) to carry up, take up, bring up; (poner arriba) to put upstairs. **3** (cabeza, etc) to lift, raise. **4** (pared) to raise. **5** *fig* (precio, salario, etc) to raise, put up. **6** *fig* (subir el volumen - voz) to raise; (- aparato) to turn up. **8** *fig* (color) to strengthen.
▶ *vpr* **subirse 1** (piso, escalera) to go up. **2** (árbol, muro, etc) to climb up (a, -). **3** (en un vehículo - coche) to get in (a, -); (autobús) to get on (a, -); (avión, barco, tren) to get on (a, -), get onto (a,-): *¡súbete, súbete al coche!* get in, get into the car! **4** (en animales, bicicleta) to get on (a, -), mount. **5** (ropa, calcetines) to pull up; (cremallera) to do up, zip up; (mangas) to roll up.

súbito,-a *adj* sudden.

subjetivo,-a *adj* subjective.

subjuntivo,-a *adj* subjunctive.
▶ *nm* **subjuntivo** subjunctive.

sublevación *nf* uprising, revolt.

submarinismo *nm* skin diving.

submarinista *nm o nf* skin-diver.

submarino,-a *adj* underwater.
▶ *nm* **submarino** submarine.

submúltiplo,-a *adj* submultiple.
▶ *nm* **submúltiplo** submultiple.

suboficial *nm* **1** MIL noncommissioned officer. **2** MAR petty officer.

subordinación *nf* subordination.

subordinado,-a *adj* subordinate.
▶ *nm & nf* subordinate.

subordinar *vt* to subordinate.
▶ *vpr* **subordinarse** to subordinate os.

S

subproducto *nm* by-product.

subrayar *vt* **1** to underline. **2** *fig* to emphasize, underline, stress.

subreino *nm* subkingdom.

subrepticio,-a *adj* surreptitious.

subrogar *vt* to subrogate, substitute.

subsanar *vt* **1** *(remediar)* to rectify, correct. **2** *(dificultad, etc)* to overcome.

subscribir *vt-vpr* → suscribir.

subscriptor,-ra *nm & nf* subscriber.

subscrito,-a *adj-nm & nf* → suscrito,-a.

subsecretaría *nf* **1** *(cargo)* under-secretaryship. **2** *(oficina)* under-secretary's office.

subsecretario,-a *nm & nf* under-secretary.

subsidiario,-a *adj* subsidiary.

subsidio *nm* allowance, benefit.

subsistencia *nf* **1** *(hecho)* subsistence. **2** *(lo necesario para vivir)* sustenance.
▶ *nf pl* **subsistencias** *(provisiones)* food *sing*, provisions, supplies.

subsistir *vi* **1** *(conservarse)* to subsist, last. **2** *(vivir)* live on, survive.

substancia *nf* → sustancia.

substancial *adj* → sustancial.

substanciar *vt* to condense, abridge.

substancioso,-a *adj* → sustancioso,-a.

substantivar *vt* to use as a noun.

substantivo,-a *adj-nm* → sustantivo.

substitución *nf* substitution.

substituible *adj* replaceable.

substituir *vt* → sustituir.

substituto,-a *nm & nf* → sustituto,-a.

substracción *nf* → sustracción.

substraendo *nm* subtrahend.

substraer *vt-vpr* → sustraer.

substrato *nm* substratum.

subsuelo *nm* subsoil.

subterfugio *nm* *(escapatoria)* subterfuge; *(pretexto)* pretext.

subterráneo,-a *adj* underground.
▶ *nm* **subterráneo** underground passage, tunnel, subway.

subtítulo *nm* **1** subtitle. **2** LIT subhead.

subtotal *nm* subtotal.

subtropical *adj* subtropical.

suburbano,-a *adj* suburban.
▶ *nm* **suburbano** suburban train.

suburbio *nm* *(periferia)* suburb.

subvención *nf* subsidy, grant.

subvencionar *vt* to subsidize.

subversión *nf* subversion.

subversivo,-a *adj* subversive.

subyacente *adj* underlying.

subyacer *vi* to underlie (en, -).

subyugar *vt* **1** to subjugate. **2** *fig* to captivate.

succionar *vt* to suck up.

suceder *vi* **1** [sólo se usa en tercera persona; no lleva sujeto] *(acontecer)* to happen, occur: *¿qué sucede?* what's the matter? **2** *(seguir)* to follow (a, -), succeed (a, -). **3** *(heredar)* to succeed.
▶ *vpr* **sucederse** to follow one another.

sucesión *nf* **1** *(herencia)* succession, inheritance. **2** *(descendencia)* issue, heirs *pl*. **3** *(al trono)* succession. **4** *(serie)* series, succession.

sucesivo,-a *adj* **1** *(siguiente)* following, successive. **2** *(consecutivo)* consecutive, running.

suceso *nm* **1** *(hecho)* event, happening, occurrence. **2** *(incidente)* incident. **3** *(delito)* crime.

sucesor,-ra *nm & nf* successor.

suciedad *nf* **1** *(inmundicia)* dirt, filth. **2** *(calidad)* dirtiness, filthiness.

sucio,-a *adj* **1** *(con manchas)* dirty, filthy. **2** *(que se ensucia fácilmente)* which dirties easily. **3** *fig (deshonesto)* shady, underhand. **4** DEP *fig* foul, dirty, unfair. **5** *fig (trabajo, lenguaje)* dirty, filthy.
▶ *adv* **sucio** *fig* in an underhand way, dirty. LOC **en sucio** in rough.

sucumbir *vi* **1** *(rendirse)* to succumb (a, to), yield (a, to). **2** *(morir)* to perish. **3** *fig (tentación, etc)* to give in (a, to), yield (a, to).

sucursal *nf* **1** *(oficina)* branch, branch office. **2** *(delegación)* subsidiary.

sudadera *nf* **1** *(prenda)* sweatshirt. **2** *fam (acción)* sweat.

Sudáfrica *nf* South Africa.

sudafricano,-a *adj* South African.

Sudamérica *nf* South America.

sudamericano,-a *adj* South American.

Sudán *nm* Sudan.

sudanés,-esa *adj* Sudanese.
▶ *nm & nf* Sudanese.

sudar *vi (transpirar)* to sweat, perspire.

sudario *nm* shroud.

sudeste *adj* **1** *(del sudeste)* southeast, southeastern; *(hacia el sudeste)* southeasterly. **2** *(viento)* southeast.
▶ *nm* **1** *(punto cardinal)* southeast. **2** *(viento)* southeast wind.

sudoeste *adj* **1** *(del sudoeste)* southwest, southwestern; *(hacia el sudoeste)* southwesterly. **2** *(viento)* southwest.
▶ *nm* **1** *(punto cardinal)* southwest. **2** *(viento)* southwest wind.

sudor *nm* **1** sweat. **2** *fig* effort.

sudoríparo,-a *adj* sweat. COMP **glándulas sudoríparas** sweat glands.

sudoroso,-a *adj* sweaty.

Suecia *nf* Sweden.

sueco,-a *adj* Swedish.
▶ *nm & nf (persona)* Swede.
▶ *nm* **sueco** *(idioma)* Swedish.

suegro,-a *nm & nf (hombre)* father-in-law; *(mujer)* mother-in-law.

suela *nf (del calzado)* sole.

sueldo *nm* salary, pay, wages *pl*.

suelo *nm* **1** *(superficie)* ground; *(de interior)* floor. **2** *fig (tierra)* soil, land; *(mundo)* earth. **3** *(territorio)* soil, land. **4** *(terreno)* land. **5** *(pavimento)* surface. **6** *fig (de vasija, etc)* bottom.

suelto,-a *adj* **1** *(no sujeto)* loose. **2** *(desatado)* undone, untied. **3** *(no envasado o empaquetado)* loose. **4** *(desaparejado)* odd. **5** *(dinero)* in change. **6** *(en libertad)* free; *(huido)* at large. **7** *(disgregado)* scattered. **8** *(con diarrea)* loose. **9** *(prenda)* loose, loose-fitting. **10** *fig (ligero)* agile, nimble; *(veloz)* swift.
▶ *nm* **suelto** *(cambio)* change, small change, loose change.

sueño *nm* **1** *(acto)* sleep. **2** *(ganas de dormir)* sleepiness. **3** *(lo soñado)* dream. **4** *fig (ilusión)* dream, illusion.

suero *nm* **1** MED serum. **2** *(de la leche)* whey.

suerte *nf* **1** *(fortuna)* luck, fortune. **2** *(azar)* chance. **3** *(destino)* destiny, fate. **4** *(estado, condición)* lot, situation. **5** *fml (tipo)* sort, kind, type. LOC **¡buena suerte!** good luck!

suéter *nm* sweater.

suficiente *adj* **1** *(bastante)* sufficient, enough. **2** *(apto)* suitable. **3** *fig (engreído)* smug, complacent.

sufijo,-a *adj* suffixal.
▶ *nm* **sufijo** suffix.

sufragar *vt (costear - gastos)* to defray, pay; *(- empresa)* to finance.

sufragio *nm* **1** suffrage. **2** *(voto)* vote.

sufrido,-a *adj* **1** *(persona)* patient, long-suffering. **2** *(color)* practical; *(tejido)* hardwearing.

sufrimiento *nm* suffering.

sufrir *vt* **1** *(padecer)* to suffer. **2** *(accidente, ataque)* to have; *(operación)* to undergo. **3** *(dificultades, cambios)* to experience; *(derrota, consecuencias)* to suffer. **4** *(aguantar)* to bear put up with.
▶ *vi (padecer)* to suffer.

sugerencia *nf* suggestion.

sugerente *adj* suggestive.

sugerir *vt* **1** to suggest. **2** *(insinuar)* to hint. **3** *(suscitar)* to suggest.

sugestión *nf* suggestion.

sugestionar *vt* to influence.

sugestivo,-a *adj (que atrae)* fascinating, attractive.

suicidarse *vpr* to commit suicide.

suicidio *nm* suicide.

Suiza *nf* Switzerland.

suizo,-a *adj* Swiss.
▶ *nm & nf* Swiss.

sujeción *nf (acción)* subjection.

sujetador,-ra *adj* fastening.
▶ *nm* **sujetador** bra.

sujetar *vt* **1** *(fijar)* to fix, secure, hold. **2** *(agarrar, sostener)* hold on to. **3** *(papeles)* to fasten; *(pelo)* to hold in place. **4** *fig (dominar, someter)* to control.
▶ *vpr* **sujetarse** **1** *(agarrarse)* to hold on, hold tight. **2** *fig (someterse)* to subject os (a, to).

S

sujeto,-a *adj* **1** *(sometido)* subject (a, to), liable (a, to). **2** *(agarrado, atado)* fastened, secure.
▶ *nm* **sujeto 1** LING subject. **2** *(individuo)* fellow, individual, character.

sulfato *nm* sulphate (US sulfate).

sulfhídrico,-a *adj* sulphuretted (US sulfureted).

sulfito *nm* sulphite (US sulfite).

sulfurar *vt* **1** QUÍM to sulphurate (US sulfurate). **2** *fam fig (irritar)* to infuriate.
▶ *vpr* **sulfurarse** *fam fig* to blow one's top, lose one's rag.

sulfúrico,-a *adj* sulphuric (US sulfuric).

sulfuro *nm* sulphide (US sulfide).

sulfuroso,-a *adj* sulphurous (US sulfurous).

sultán,-ana *nm & nf (hombre)* sultan; *(mujer)* sultana.

suma *nf* **1** *(cantidad)* sum, amount. **2** MAT sum, addition. **3** *(resumen)* summary.

sumando *nm* addend.

sumar *vt* **1** MAT to add, add up. **2** *(componer una cantidad)* to total, amount to, come to. **3** *(compendiar)* to sum up.
▶ *vpr* **sumarse** *(unirse)* to join (a, in).

sumario,-a *adj* **1** summary, brief. **2** JUR summary.
▶ *nm* **sumario 1** *(resumen)* summary. **2** JUR legal proceedings *pl*, indictment.

sumergible *adj* submersible.
▶ *nm* submarine.

sumergir *vt* **1** *(meter bajo líquido)* to submerge, submerse, immerse. **2** *fig (hundir)* to plunge, sink.
▶ *vpr* **sumergirse 1** *(meterse bajo líquido)* to submerge (en, in), go underwater. **2** *fig* to become immersed (en, in).

sumidero *nm* drain, sewer.

suministrador,-ra *nm & nf* supplier.

suministrar *vt* to provide, supply.

suministro *nm* supply, supplying.

sumisión *nf* **1** *(acto)* submission. **2** *(carácter)* submissiveness.

sumiso,-a *adj* submissive, obedient.

sumo,-a *adj* **1** *(supremo)* supreme, highest. **2** *fig (muy grande)* greatest.

suntuario,-a *adj* sumptuary.

suntuoso,-a *adj* sumptuous.

supeditar *vt* **1** *(subordinar)* to subordinate (a, to). **2** *(condicionar)* to subject (a, to).
▶ *vpr* **supeditarse** *(someterse)* to subject os (a, to), bow (a, to).

súper *nm fam (supermercado)* supermarket.
▶ *nf fam (gasolina)* four-star.

superable *adj* surmountable.

superabundante *adj* superabundant.

superar *vt* **1** *(exceder)* to surpass, exceed, excel. **2** *(obstáculo, etc)* to overcome, surmount.
▶ *vpr* **superarse 1** *(sobrepasarse)* to excel os. **2** *(mejorarse)* to improve os, better os.

superconductividad *nf* superconductivity.

superconductor *nm* superconductor.

superdotado,-a *nm & nf* genius.

superestrato *nm* superstratum.

superestructura *nf* superstructure.

superficial *adj* superficial.

superficialidad *nf* superficiality.

superficie *nf* **1** *(parte externa)* surface. **2** *(área)* area.

superfluo,-a *adj* superfluous.

superhombre *nm* superman.

superíndice *nm* superscript.

superintendente *nm o nf* superintendent.

superior *adj* **1** *(encima de)* upper, top: *labio superior* upper lip. **2** *(por encima de)* greater (a, than), higher (a, than), above (a, -). **3** *fig (persona - que supera)* superior; *(- mejor)* better. **4** *fig (calidad, etc)* superior, high, excellent. **5** EDUC higher.
▶ *nm* **1** *(jefe)* superior. **2** REL superior.

superioridad *nf (persona)* superiority.

superlativo,-a *adj* superlative.
▶ *nm* **superlativo** superlative.

supermercado *nm* supermarket.

supernova *nf* supernova.

superpoblación *nf* overpopulation.

superpoblado,-a *adj* overpopulated.

superponer *vt* **1** to superimpose, lay on top. **2** *fig* to put before.

superposición *nf* superimposition.

superpotencia *nf* superpower.

superpuesto,-a *pp* → superponer.

supersónico,-a *adj* supersonic.

superstición *nf* superstition.

supersticioso,-a *adj* superstitious.

supervisar *vt* to supervise.

supervisión *nf* supervision, control.

supervisor,-ra *nm & nf* supervisor.

supervivencia *nf* survival.

superviviente *adj* surviving.
► *nm o nf* survivor.

suplemento *nm* **1** *(de revista, etc)* supplement. **2** *(de dinero)* extra charge. **3** *(geometría)* supplement.

suplencia *nf* substitution.

suplente *nm o nf* **1** *(gen)* substitute. **2** DEP reserve player. **3** TEAT understudy.

súplica *nf* **1** request, entreaty, plea. **2** JUR petition.

suplicar *vt* **1** to beseech, beg, implore. **2** JUR to appeal to.

suplicio *nm* *(castigo)* torture.

suplir *vt* **1** *(reemplazar)* to replace, substitute. **2** *(compensar)* to make up for.

suponer *vt* **1** *(gen)* to suppose, assume. **2** *(significar)* to mean. **3** *(conllevar)* to mean, entail, require. **4** *(adivinar)* to guess; *(imaginar)* to imagine, think. **5** *(creer)* to think.
► *nm fam* supposition.

suposición *nf* supposition, assumption.

suprarrenal *adj* suprarenal.

supremo,-a *adj* **1** *(gen)* supreme. **2** *(decisivo)* decisive. **3** *(último)* last, final.

suprimir *vt* **1** *(libertad, etc)* to suppress; *(ley, impuestos)* to abolish; *(dificultades)* to eliminate, remove; *(restricciones)* to lift. **2** *(tabaco, alcohol)* to cut out. **3** *(palabra)* to delete, take out, leave out. **4** *(omitir)* to omit.

supuesto,-a *adj* **1** *(que se supone)* supposed, assumed. **2** *(pretendido)* so-called, self-styled.

► *nm* **supuesto 1** *(suposición)* supposition, assumption. **2** *(hipótesis)* hypothesis.

supurar *vi* to suppurate.

sur *nm* **1** south. **2** *(viento)* south wind.

Suramérica *nf* South America.

suramericano,-a *adj-nm & nf* → sudamericano,-a.

surcar *vt* **1** AGR to plough (US plow). **2** *(agua)* to cut through, cross; *(aire)* to fly through.

surco *nm* **1** *(en tierra)* furrow. **2** *(arruga)* wrinkle. **3** *(de disco)* groove.

surcoreano,-a *adj* South Korean.
► *nm & nf* South Korean.

sureste *adj-nm* → sudeste.

surfista *nm o nf* surfer.

surgir *vi* **1** *(agua)* to spring forth, spurt up. **2** *fig (aparecer - gen)* to appear, emerge; *(- dificultades)* to crop up, arise, come up. **3** MAR to anchor.

Surinam *nm* Surinam.

suroeste *adj-nm* → sudoeste.

surtido,-a *adj* **1** *(variado)* assorted. **2** *(bien provisto)* well stocked.
► *nm* **surtido** assortment, selection.

surtidor *nm* **1** *(fuente)* fountain. **2** *(chorro)* jet, spout.

surtir *vt* *(proveer)* to supply (de, with), provide (de, with).
► *vi (brotar)* to spout, spurt.
► *vpr* **surtirse** to supply os, provide os.

susceptibilidad *nf* **1** *(gen)* susceptibility. **2** *(sensibilidad)* sensitivity.

susceptible *adj* **1** *(gen)* susceptible. **2** *(sensible)* oversensitive.

suscitar *vt* **1** *(gen)* to cause, provoke. **2** *(rebelión)* to stir up, arouse; *(discusión)* to start; *(problemas)* to cause, raise; *(interés)* to arouse.

suscribir *vt* **1** FIN to subscribe. **2** *fig (convenir con alguien)* to subscribe to, endorse. **3** *(a una revista, etc)* to take out a subscription for. **4** *fml (firmar)* to subscribe.
► *vpr* **suscribirse** *(abonarse)* to subscribe.

suscripción *nf* subscription.

suscriptor,-ra *nm & nf* subscriber.

S

suscrito,-a *adj* **1** *(abonado)* subscribed. **2** *(firmado)* undersigned.
▶ *nm & nf* undersigned.

suspender *vt* **1** *(levantar)* to hang, hang up, suspend. **2** *(aplazar - gen)* to postpone, put off, delay; *(- reunión)* to adjourn. **3** EDUC *fig* to fail. **4** *fig (pagos)* to suspend; *(servicio)* to discontinue.

suspensión *nf* **1** *(acto de levantar)* hanging, hanging up, suspension. **2** AUTO suspension. **3** *(aplazamiento - gen)* delay, postponement; *(- de reunión)* adjournment. **4** *(supresión)* suspension, discontinuation.

suspenso,-a *adj* **1** *(colgado)* hanging, suspended. **2** REL *fig (alumno)* failed. **3** *fig (asombrado)* bewildered, amazed.
▶ *nm* **suspenso** EDUC fail.

suspicacia *nf (sospecha)* suspicion.

suspicaz *adj* **1** *(desconfiado)* mistrustful, distrustful. **2** *(que sospecha)* suspicious.

suspirar *vi* to sigh.

suspiro *nm* sigh.

sustancia *nf* **1** *(gen)* substance. **2** *(esencia)* substance, essence.

sustancial *adj* **1** *(gen)* substantial. **2** *(fundamental)* essential, fundamental. **3** *(importante)* important, substantial.

sustanciar *vt* to condense, abridge.

sustancioso,-a *adj* **1** *(nutritivo)* wholesome. **2** *fig (libro, etc)* meaty.

sustantivar *vt* to use as a noun.

sustantivo,-a *nm* noun, substantive.

sustentable *adj* tenable.

sustentación *nf* **1** *(soporte)* support. **2** *(mantenimiento)* sustenance, maintenance.

sustentar *vt* **1** *(familia, etc)* to maintain, support, sustain. **2** *(sostener)* to hold up, support. **3** *(teoría, opinión)* to support, defend.

sustento *nm* **1** *(alimento)* sustenance, food. **2** *(apoyo)* support.

sustitución *nf* substitution, replacement.

sustituible *adj* replaceable, expendable.

sustituir *vt (reemplazar)* to substitute (por, with), replace (por, with).

sustitutivo,-a *adj* substitutive.
▶ *nm* sustitutivo substitute.

sustituto,-a *nm & nf* substitute, standin, replacement.

susto *nm* fright, scare, shock.

sustracción *nf* **1** *(robo)* theft. **2** MAT subtraction.

sustraendo *nm* subtrahend.

sustraer *vt* **1** *(robar)* to steal. **2** MAT to subtract.
▶ *vpr* **sustraerse** *(faltar al cumplimiento)* to evade (a, -), elude (a, -); *(tentaciones)* to resist (a, -).

sustrato *nm* substratum.

susurrar *vi* to whisper.

susurro *nm* **1** whisper. **2** *fig (agua)* murmur; *(hojas)* rustle.

sutil *adj* **1** *(delgado)* thin, fine. **2** *(aroma)* delicate; *(color)* soft. **3** *(brisa)* gentle. **4** *fig* subtle.

suturar *vt* to stitch.

suyo,-a *adj (de él)* his, of his; *(de ella)* her, of hers; *(de animales, cosas)* its; *(de usted, de ustedes)* yours, of yours; *(de ellos, de ellas)* theirs, of theirs: *este libro es suyo* this book is hers; *aquel amigo suyo* that friend of yours.
▶ *pron (de él)* his; *(de ella)* hers; *(de usted, de ustedes)* yours; *(de ellos, de ellas)* theirs: *éstos son los míos, los suyos están sobre la mesa* there are mine, hers are on the table.
▶ *nf* **la suya** *(ocasión, oportunidad)* one's chance, one's opportunity.
▶ *nm* **lo suyo 1** *(lo que toca)* what one deserves. **2** *(habilidad)* forte, one's thing: *lo suyo es el tenis* tennis is his thing. **3** *fam (mucho)* a lot: *comió lo suyo* he ate a lot.
▶ *nm pl* **los suyos** *(familiares)* his *(her, your, etc)* family *sing; (amigos)* his *(her, your, etc)* friends, his *(her, your, etc)* people.

Swazilandia *nf* Swaziland.

T

T, t *nf (la letra)* T, t.

tabaco *nm* **1** *(gen)* tobacco. **2** *(cigarrillos)* cigarettes *pl*; *(cigarro)* cigar. **3** *(enfermedad)* black rot. COMP **tabaco rubio** Virginia tobacco.

tábano *nm* horsefly.

taberna *nf* pub, bar.

tabique *nm* partition, partition wall.

tabla *nf* **1** *(de madera)* board, plank. **2** *(de piedra)* slab; *(de metal)* sheet. **3** *(estante)* shelf. **4** ARTE panel. **5** COST pleat. **6** *(índice)* index. **7** *(lista)* list; *(catálogo)* catalogue (US catalog). **8** MAT table. COMP **tabla de multiplicar** multiplication table.
    ▶ *nf pl* **tablas** **1** TEAT stage *sing*, boards. **2** *(ajedrez)* stalemate *sing*, draw *sing*.

tablado *nm* **1** *(suelo)* wooden floor. **2** *(entarimado)* wooden platform. **3** *(del escenario)* stage.

tablero *nm* **1** *(tablón)* panel, board. **2** *(en juegos)* board. **3** *(encerado)* blackboard. **4** AUTO dashboard. **5** INFORM display board. COMP **tablero de ajedrez** chessboard.

tableta *nf* **1** *(pastilla)* tablet. **2** *(de chocolate)* bar.

tablón *nm* **1** plank. **2** *(en construcción)* board. COMP **tablón de anuncios** notice board, US bulletin board.

tabulación *nf* tabulation.

tacaño,-a *adj* mean, stingy.

tacha *nf* **1** *(defecto)* flaw, blemish, defect. **2** *(descrédito)* blemish.

tachadura *nf* crossing out.

tachar *vt* **1** *(borrar)* to cross out. **2** *(culpar)* to accuse (**de**, of): *lo tachan de fascista* they accuse him of being a fascist.

tachuela *nf* tack, stud.

tacita *nf* little cup.

tácito,-a *adj* tacit.

taco *nm* **1** *(tarugo)* plug, stopper. **2** *(para pared)* plug, Rawlplug. **3** *(bloc de notas)* notepad, writing pad; *(calendario)* tear-off calendar. **4** *(de entradas)* book; *(de billetes)* wad. **5** *(de billar)* cue. **6** CULIN *(de queso, etc)* cube, piece; *(en Méjico)* taco, rolled-up tortilla. **7** *fam (palabrota)* swearword.

tacón *nm* heel.

táctica *nf* tactic, tactics *pl*, strategy.

tacto *nm* **1** *(sentido)* touch. **2** *(acción)* touch, touching. **3** *fig (delicadeza)* tact. LOC **tener tacto** to be tactful.

Tadjikistán *nm* Tadzhikistan.

tadjiko,-a *adj* Tadzhiki.
    ▶ *nm o nf (persona)* Tadzhik.
    ▶ *nm* **tadjiko** *(idioma)* Tadzhiki.

Tahití *nm* Tahiti.

tahitiano,-a *adj* Tahitian.
    ▶ *nm & nf (persona)* Tahitian.
    ▶ *nm* **tahitiano** *(idioma)* Tahitian.

tailandés,-esa *adj* Thai.
    ▶ *nm & nf (persona)* Thai.
    ▶ *nm* **tailandés** *(idioma)* Thai.

Tailandia *nf* Thailand.

Taiwan *nm* Taiwan.

taiwanés,-esa *adj* Taiwanese.
    ▶ *nm & nf* Taiwanese.

tajada *nf* **1** *(rodaja)* slice. **2** *(corte)* cut; *(cuchillada)* stab.

tajo *nm* **1** *(corte)* cut, slash. **2** *(filo)* cutting edge. **3** *(escarpa)* steep cliff.

tal *adj* **1** *(semejante)* such: *en tales condiciones* in such conditions. **2** *(tan grande)* such, so: *tal es su ignorancia que…* he is so ignorant that… **3** *(cosa sin especificar)* such and such: *tal día* such and such a

day. **4** *(persona sin especificar)* someone called, a certain: *vino un tal Alberto* someone called Alberto came.
▶ *pron (alguno - cosa)* such a thing, something; *(- persona)* someone, somebody: *yo no dije tal cosa* I didn't say such a thing.
▶ *adv (así)* in such a way, so: *tal me contestó que no supe cómo reaccionar* he answered in such a way that I didn't know how to react. LOC **tal como 1** *(ejemplos)* such as. **2** *(de la misma manera)* just as. ‖ **tal cual** just as it is.

tala *nf* tree felling.

taladrar *vt* **1** *(gen)* to drill; *(pared)* to bore through. **2** *fig (los oídos)* to pierce.

taladro *nm* **1** *(herramienta)* drill, bore. **2** *(agujero)* hole.

talar *vt* **1** *(cortar)* to fell, cut down. **2** *(destruir)* to devastate.

talento *nm* **1** *(entendimiento)* talent, intelligence. **2** *(aptitud)* gift, talent: *tiene talento para las matemáticas* she has a gift for mathematics.

talla *nf* **1** *(estatura)* height. **2** *fig (moral, intelectual)* stature. **3** *(de prenda)* size: *¿qué talla usa?* what size is he? **4** *(escultura)* carving, sculpture. **5** *(tallado - piedras)* cutting; *(- metal)* engraving.

tallar *vt* **1** *(madera, piedra)* to carve, shape; *(piedras preciosas)* to cut; *(metales)* to engrave. **2** *(medir)* to measure the height of.

talle *nm* **1** *(cintura)* waist. **2** *(figura - de hombre)* build, physique; *(- de mujer)* figure, shape.

taller *nm* **1** *(obrador)* workshop. **2** *(de artista)* studio. **3** *(en fábrica)* shop, workshop. **4** AUTO garage, repair shop.

tallo *nm* BOT stem, stalk; *(renuevo)* sprout, shoot.

talón *nm* **1** *(de pie, zapato, etc)* heel. **2** *(cheque)* cheque (US check). COMP **talón bancario** counter cheque (US check). ‖ **talón de Aquiles** Achilles' heel.

talonario *nm (de cheques)* cheque book (US check book); *(de recibos)* stub book.

tamaño,-a *adj (semejante)* such a, so big a: *no pude aguantar tamaña imperti-*

nencia I couldn't tolerate such an impertinent remark.
▶ *nm* **tamaño** *(medida)* size: *¿de qué tamaño es?* what size is it?

tamarindo *nm* tamarind.

tambalearse *vpr* **1** *(persona)* to stagger; *(mueble)* to wobble. **2** *fig* to be shaky.

también *adv* **1** *(igualmente)* also, too, as well, so: *Pedro también estaba* Pedro was also there, Pedro was there too, Pedro was there as well. **2** *(además)* besides, in addition.

tambor *nm* **1** *(instrumento)* drum. **2** *(maquinaria)* drum. **3** *(de arma)* cylinder, barrel. **4** *(de lavadora)* drum. **5** *(de freno)* brake drum.

tamiz *nm* sieve.

tamizar *vt* **1** *(harina, tierra)* to sieve. **2** *(luz)* to filter. **3** *fig (seleccionar)* to screen.

tampoco *adv* neither, nor, not… either: *no quiere estudiar y tampoco quiere ir al cine* he doesn't want to study and he doesn't want to go to the cinema either.

tan *adv* **1** *(tanto)* such, such a, so: *no seas tan cruel* don't be so cruel. **2** *(comparativo - como)* as… as, so… (that); *(- que)* so…, so… (that): *está tan gordo como tú* he's as fat as you (are). LOC **tan solo** only, just: *tan solo quiero uno* I only want one.

tanda *nf* **1** *(conjunto)* batch, lot; *(serie)* series, course. **2** *(turno)* shift. **3** *(en billar)* game.

tangente *adj* tangent.
▶ *nf* tangent.

tanque *nm* **1** *(depósito)* tank, reservoir. **2** MIL tank. **3** *(vehículo cisterna)* tanker.

tantear *vt* **1** *(calcular)* to estimate, guess. **2** *(probar medidas)* to size up. **3** *fig (ensayar)* to try out, put to the test. **4** *fig (persona)* to sound out. **5** *(dibujo)* to sketch.
▶ *vi* **1** DEP to score, keep score. **2** *(andar a tientas)* to feel one's way.

tanto,-a *adj* **1** *(incontables)* so much; *(contables)* so many: *no comas tantos caramelos* don't eat so many sweets. **2** *(comparación - incontable)* as much; *(- contables)* as many: *tengo tantos libros como tú* I've got as many books as you.

▶ *pron (incontable)* so much; *(contable)* so many: *no había tantos* there weren't so many.

▶ *adv* **1** *(cantidad)* so much: *¡te quiero tanto!* I love you so much! **2** *(tiempo)* so long: *esperamos tanto* we waited for so long. **3** *(frecuencia)* so often: *no los telefonees tanto* don't phone them so often.

▶ *nm* **tanto 1** *(punto)* point; *(fútbol)* goal. **2** *(cantidad imprecisa)* so much, a certain amount: *percibes un tanto al mes* you get so much a month. **3** *(poco)* bit: *es un tanto estrecho* it's a bit narrow. [LOC] **a las tantas** *fam* very late, at an unearthly hour. ∎ **por lo tanto** therefore.

Tanzania *nf* Tanzania.

tanzano,-a *adj* Tanzanian.
▶ *nm & nf* Tanzanian.

tapa *nf* **1** *(cubierta)* lid, top; *(de botella)* cap, top, stopper. **2** *(de libro)* cover. **3** *(de zapato)* heel-plate. **4** CULIN *(comida)* appetizer, savoury (US savory), tapa.

tapadera *nf* **1** cover, lid. **2** *fig* cover.

tapar *vt* **1** *(cubrir)* to cover; *(con tapa)* to put the lid on. **2** *(con ropas, etc)* to wrap up. **3** *(obstruir)* to obstruct; *(tubería)* to block. **4** *(ocultar)* to hide; *(a la vista)* to block. **5** *fig (encubrir)* to cover up.
▶ *vpr* **taparse 1** *(abrigarse)* to wrap up. **2** *(la nariz)* to be blocked up.

tapia *nf (cerca)* garden wall; *(de adobe)* mud wall, adobe wall.

tapiar *vt* **1** *(área)* to wall in, wall off. **2** *fig (puerta, ventana)* to wall up, close up.

tapicería *nf* **1** ARTE tapestry making. **2** *(tapices)* tapestries *pl*. **3** *(de muebles, etc)* upholstery. **4** *(tienda)* upholsterer's, upholsterer's workshop.

tapiz *nm* **1** *(de pared)* tapestry. **2** *(alfombra)* rug, carpet.

tapón *nm* **1** stopper, plug; *(de botella)* cap. **2** *(del oído)* wax in the ear. **3** *(baloncesto)* block. **4** *(embotellamiento)* traffic jam.

taponar *vt* **1** *(orificio, etc)* to plug, stop. **2** *(atascar)* to block. **3** *(poner el tapón)* to put the plug in. **4** MED to tampon, plug.

taquilla *nf* **1** *(de tren, etc)* ticket office; *(de cine, teatro)* box office. **2** *(recaudación)* takings *pl*, returns *pl*. **3** *(casillero)* pigeonholes *pl*. **4** *(armario)* locker.

tara *nf* **1** *(peso)* tare. **2** *(defecto)* defect, blemish, fault.

tardar *vt (emplear tiempo)* to take: *tardé cuatro horas* it took me four hours.
▶ *vi (demorar)* to take a long time: *se tarda más a pie* it takes longer on foot.

tarde *nf* **1** *(hasta las cinco aprox.)* afternoon. **2** *(después de las cinco aprox.)* evening.
▶ *adv* **1** *(hora avanzada)* late: *se está haciendo tarde* it's getting late. **2** *(demasiado tarde)* too late: *es tarde para salir* it's too late to go out.

tarea *nf* task, job.

tarifa *nf* **1** *(precio)* tariff, rate; *(de transporte)* fare. **2** *(lista de precios)* price list.

tarima *nf* platform, dais.

tarjeta *nf* card. [COMP] **tarjeta de crédito** credit card. ∎ **tarjeta de memoria** memory card, chip card. ∎ **tarjeta postal** postcard.

tarro *nm* **1** *(vasija)* jar, pot, tub. **2** *fam (cabeza)* bonce.

tarta *nf* flan, tart, pie: *tarta de manzana* apple pie.

tartamudear *vi* to stammer, stutter.

tartamudez *nf* stammering.

tartamudo,-a *nm & nf* stutterer.

tasa *nf* **1** *(valoración)* valuation. **2** *(precio)* fee, charge. **3** *(impuesto)* tax, levy. **4** *(límite)* limit; *(medida)* measure. **5** *(índice)* rate. [COMP] **tasa de natalidad** birth rate.

tasar *vt* **1** *(valorar)* to value. **2** *(poner precio)* to set the price of, fix the price of.

Tasmania *nf* Tasmania.

tasmano,-a *adj* Tasmanian.
▶ *nm & nf* Tasmanian.

tata *nf fam* nanny.

tatarabuelo,-a *nm & nf (hombre)* great-great-grandfather; *(mujer)* great-great-grandmother.

tataranieto,-a *nm & nf (hombre)* great-great-grandson; *(mujer)* great-great-granddaughter.

tatuaje *nm* **1** *(dibujo)* tattoo. **2** *(técnica)* tattooing.

tatuar *vt* to tattoo.

tauromaquia *nf* bullfighting, art of bullfighting, tauromachy.

taxi *nm* taxi, cab.

T

taxista *nm o nf* taxi driver.

taza *nf* **1** *(recipiente)* cup. **2** *(contenido)* cupful. **3** *(de retrete)* bowl.

te¹ *nf* **1** *name of the letter* t. **2** *(regla)* T-square.

te² *pron* **1** you, to you, for you: *te mandaré una carta* I'll send you a letter. **2** *(uso reflexivo)* yourself: *ponte el abrigo* put your coat on. **3** *(uso pronominal) no se traduce*: *vete a casa* go home.

té *nm* tea. COMP **la hora del té** teatime.

teatral *adj* **1** *(del teatro)* theatrical, dramatic. **2** *fig (exagerado)* stagy, stagey, theatrical.

teatro *nm* **1** theatre (US theater). **2** ARTE theatre (US theater), acting, stage. **3** *fig (exageración)* show, play-acting.

tebeo *nm* children's comic.

teca *nf (árbol, madera)* teak.

techo *nm* **1** *(interior)* ceiling; *(de coche, tejado)* roof. **2** *fig (límite superior)* ceiling.

tecla *nf* key.

teclado *nm* keyboard.

teclear *vi (piano)* to press the keys; *(máquina de escribir, ordenador)* to type, tap the keys.

técnica *nf* **1** *(tecnología)* technique, technology. **2** *(habilidad)* technique, method. **3** *(ingeniería)* engineering.

técnico,-a *adj* technical.
▶ *nm & nf* technician, technical expert.

tecnología *nf* technology.

tectónica *nf* tectonics.

tedio *nm* tedium, boredom.

teja *nf (de barro)* tile.

tejado *nm* roof.

tejano,-a *adj* Texan.
▶ *nm & nf* Texan.
▶ *nm pl* **tejanos** *(pantalón)* jeans.

tejar *vt* to tile.

tejer *vt* **1** *(en telar)* to weave. **2** *(hacer punto)* to knit. **3** *(araña)* to spin. **4** *fig (plan)* to weave, plot, scheme.

tejido *nm* **1** *(tela)* textile. **2** ANAT tissue.

tejo *nm (árbol)* yew tree.

tejón *nm* badger.

tela *nf* **1** *(textil)* material, fabric, cloth. **2** *(de araña)* cobweb. **3** ARTE *(lienzo)* canvas; *(cuadro)* painting. **4** *fam (dinero)* dough. **5** *fam (asunto, tema)* subject, matter. COMP **tela metálica** wire gauze.

telar *nm* **1** *(para tejer)* loom. **2** *(para encuadernar)* sewing press.

telaraña *nf* cobweb, spider's web.

tele *nf fam* telly, TV.

telecomunicación *nf* telecommunication.

telediario *nm* television news bulletin, TV news.

teleférico *nm* cable car.

telefilm *nm* TV film.

telefonear *vi* to phone.

teléfono *nm* telephone, phone. COMP **teléfono móvil** mobile phone.

telegrafiar *vt* to telegraph, wire.

telégrafo *nm* telegraph.

telegrama *nm* telegram, cable.

telemando *nm* remote control.

telenovela *nf* soap opera.

teleobjetivo *nm* telephoto lens.

telepatía *nf* telepathy.

telescopio *nm* telescope.

telesilla *nm* chair lift.

telespectador,-ra *nm & nf* TV viewer.

telesquí *nm* ski lift, drag lift.

teletexto *nm* teletext.

televisar *vt* to televise.

televisión *nf* **1** *(sistema)* television. **2** *fam (aparato)* television set.

televisor *nm* television set.

télex® *nm* telex.

telón *nm* curtain. COMP **telón de acero** POL iron curtain. ‖ **telón de fondo** TEAT backdrop.

tema *nm* **1** *(de discurso, escrito, etc)* topic, subject, theme. **2** MÚS theme.

temario *nm (de examen)* programme (US program); *(de conferencia)* agenda.

temática *nf* subject matter.

temático,-a *adj* **1** thematic. **2** LING stem.

temblar *vi* **1** *(de frío)* to shiver (de, with); *(de miedo)* to tremble (de, with). **2** *(voz)* to quiver.

temblor *nm* **1** *(gen)* tremor; *(de frío)* shivering, shivers *pl*. **2** *fig* shiver.

temer *vt* **1** *(tener miedo)* to fear, be afraid of. **2** *(sospechar)* to fear, be afraid.
▶ *vi* **1** *(tener miedo)* to be afraid. **2** *(preocuparse)* to worry.
▶ *vpr* **temerse** to be afraid: *me temo que sí* I'm afraid so.

temerario,-a *adj* reckless, rash.

temible *adj* dreadful, fearful.

temor *nm* fear.

temperamento *nm* temperament.

temperatura *nf* temperature.

tempestad *nf* **1** storm. **2** *fig* turmoil.

templado,-a *adj* **1** *(agua)* warm, lukewarm; *(clima, temperatura)* mild, temperate. **2** *(moderado)* moderate; *(sereno)* composed, unruffled. **3** *(valiente)* brave. **4** MÚS tuned. **5** *(metal)* tempered.

templar *vt* **1** *(moderar)* to moderate, temper. **2** *(algo frío)* to warm up; *(algo caliente)* to cool down. **3** *fig (cólera)* to appease; *(apaciguar)* to calm down. **4** *(cuerda, tornillo)* to tighten (up). **5** MÚS to tune. **6** TÉC to temper. **7** *(colores)* to match.
▶ *vpr* **templarse** *(contenerse)* to control os.

templo *nm* temple.

temporada *nf* **1** *(en artes, deportes, moda)* season. **2** *(período)* period, time. COMP **temporada alta** high season. ▌**temporada baja** low season.

temporal¹ *adj* **1** *(transitorio)* temporary.
▶ *nm* METEOR storm.

temporal² *adj* ANAT temporal.
▶ *nm* ANAT temporal bone.

temprano,-a *adj* early.
▶ *adv* early: *nunca se levanta temprano* he never gets up early.

tenaza *nf* [también se usa en plural con el mismo significado] *(herramienta)* pliers *pl*, pincers *pl*; *(para el fuego)* tongs *pl*.

tendedero *nm* *(cuerda)* clothesline; *(lugar)* drying place.

tendencia *nf* *(inclinación)* tendency, inclination, leaning; *(movimiento)* trend.

tender *vt* **1** *(extender - mantel, etc)* to spread; *(- red)* to cast. **2** *(puente)* to throw; *(vía, cable)* to lay; *(cuerda)* to stretch. **3** *(ropa, colada)* to hang out. **4** *(mano)* to stretch out. **5** *(emboscada, trampa)* to lay, set.

▶ *vi* *(tener tendencia)* to tend (a, to), have a tendency (a, to): *tiende al aburrimiento* it tends to be boring.
▶ *vpr* **tenderse** *(tumbarse)* to lie down.

tendero,-a *nm & nf* shopkeeper.

tendón *nm* tendon, sinew.

tenedor,-ra *nm* *(utensilio)* fork.

tener *vt* **1** *(gen)* to have, have got: *tuvimos un día estupendo* we had a wonderful day. **2** *(poseer)* to own. **3** *(sostener)* to hold: *¿qué tienes en la mano?* what are you holding? **4** *(coger)* to take: *ten tu copa* take your glass. **5** *(sensación, sentimiento)* to be, feel: *tengo hambre* I'm hungry. **6** *(mantener)* to keep: *la lluvia me ha tenido despierta toda la noche* the rain has kept me up all night. **7** *(medir)* to measure. **8** *(contener)* to hold, contain. **9** *(edad)* to be. **10** *(un hijo)* to have. **11** *(celebrar)* to hold: *tener una reunión* to hold a meeting. **12** *(considerar)* to consider, think: *lo tienen por muy listo* they think he's very smart. LOC **¡ahí tienes!** so, there you are! ▌**tener cariño a** to be fond of. ▌**tener compasión** to take pity (de, on). ▌**tener ilusión** to be enthusiastic.
▶ *aux* **tener que** *(obligación)* to have to, have got to, must: *tengo que quedarme* I must stay.
▶ *vpr* **tenerse** *(sostenerse)* to stand up. LOC **tenerse por** to consider os: *se tiene por guapo* he thinks he's handsome.

tenia *nf* tapeworm.

teniente *nm* lieutenant.

tenis *nm* *(deporte)* tenis. COMP **tenis de mesa** table tennis, ping-pong.

tenista *nm o nf* tennis player.

tensar *vt* **1** *(cable, cuerda)* to tauten. **2** *(arco)* to draw.

tensión *nf* **1** ELEC tension, voltage. **2** *(de materiales)* stress; *(de gases)* pressure. **3** MED pressure. **4** *fig (de una situación)* tension; *(de una persona)* stress, strain. COMP **alta tensión** ELEC high tension. ▌**tensión arterial** blood pressure.

tenso,-a *adj* **1** *(cuerda)* tense. **2** *fig (relaciones)* strained. **3** *fig (persona)* tense.

tentación *nf* temptation.

tentáculo *nm* tentacle.

tentador,-ra *adj* tempting, enticing.

T

tentar *vt* **1** *(palpar)* to feel, touch. **2** *(incitar)* to tempt, entice.

tentempié *nm fam (refrigerio)* snack.

teñir *vt* **1** *(dar un color)* to dye. **2** *(rebajar un color)* to tone down.
▸ *vpr* **teñirse** *(el pelo)* to dye one's hair.

teoría *nf* theory. LOC **en teoría** theoretically.

teórica *nf* theory, theoretics.

teórico,-a *adj* theoretic, theoretical.
▸ *nm & nf* theoretician, theorist.

terapeuta *nm o nf* therapist.

terapia *nf* therapy.

tercer *adj* [se usa ante nombres en masculino singular] third: *el tercer mundo* the third world.

✎ Consulta también **tercero,-a**.

tercera *nf* **1** *(clase)* third class. **2** *(marcha de auto)* third gear, third. **3** MÚS third.

tercermundista *adj* third-world.

tercero,-a *adj (ordinal)* third.
▸ *nm & nf (parte)* third.
▸ *nm* **tercero 1** *(mediador)* mediator. **2** *(persona ajena)* outsider.

✎ Consulta también **sexto,-a**.

tercio,-a *adj* third.
▸ *nm* **tercio 1** *(parte)* third. **2** *(en tauromaquia)* stage, part.

terciopelo *nm* velvet.

terco,-a *adj* obstinate, stubborn.

termal *adj* thermal.

termas *nf pl (baños)* spa *sing*, hot baths.

térmico,-a *adj* thermal.

terminación *nf* **1** *(acción)* ending, termination. **2** *(conclusión)* completion. **3** *(parte final)* end. **4** GRAM ending.

terminal *adj (último)* final, terminal.
▸ *nf* **1** *(estación)* terminus. **2** *(en aeropuerto)* terminal.
▸ *nm (de ordenador)* terminal.

terminar *vt* **1** *(acabar)* to finish, complete. **2** *(dar fin)* to end.
▸ *vi* **1** *(acabar)* to finish, end: *terminó a las cuatro* it finished at four. **2** *(acabar de)* to have just (de, -): *termina de marchar* he has just left. **3** *(final de una acción, de un estado)* to end up: *terminó por marcharse* he ended up leaving. **4** *(eliminar)* to put an

end (con, to). **5** *(estropear)* to damage (con, -), ruin (con, -): *la lluvia terminó con la cosecha* the rain damaged the crops. **6** *(reñir)* to break up (con, with). **7** *(enfermedad)* to come to the final stage.
▸ *vpr* **terminarse 1** *(acabarse)* to finish. **2** *(agotarse)* to run out: *se ha terminado el azúcar* the sugar has run out.

término *nm* **1** *(fin)* end, finish. **2** *(estación)* terminus, terminal. **3** *(límite)* limit, boundary; *(hito)* boundary marker. **4** *(plazo)* term, time, period. **5** *(palabra)* term, word: *término técnico* technical term. **6** *(estado)* condition, state. **7** *(lugar, posición)* place. **8** *(en matemáticas, gramática)* term. LOC **dar término a** ALGO to conclude STH.
▸ *nm pl* **términos** *(condiciones)* conditions, terms.

terminología *nf* terminology.

termita *nf* termite.

termitero *nm* termite's nest.

termo *nm (recipiente)* flask, thermos flask.

termómetro *nm* thermometer.

termostato *nm* thermostat.

ternera *nf* CULIN veal, beef.

ternero,-a *nm & nf (animal)* calf.

ternura *nf* tenderness, gentleness.

terraplén *nm* embankment.

terráqueo,-a *adj* earth.

terrateniente *nm o nf* landowner.

terraza *nf* **1** *(balcón)* terrace. **2** *(azotea)* roof terrace. **3** *(de un café)* terrace.

terremoto *nm* earthquake.

terrenal *adj* earthly, worldly.

terreno,-a *adj* worldly, earthly.
▸ *nm* **terreno 1** *(tierra)* land, piece of land, ground; *(solar)* plot, site. **2** GEOG terrain. **3** AGR *(de cultivo)* soil; *(campo)* field. **4** DEP field, ground.

terrestre *adj* **1** *(de la tierra)* terrestrial, earthly. **2** *(por tierra)* by land.

terrible *adj* terrible, awful.

terrícola *nm o nf (habitante)* earth dweller; *(en ciencia ficción)* earthling.

territorial *adj* territorial.

territorio *nm* territory.

terrón *nm* **1** *(de tierra)* clod. **2** *(de azúcar, etc)* lump.

terror *nm* **1** *(gen)* terror. **2** CINE horror.

terrorismo *nm* terrorism.

terrorista *adj* terrorist.
▶ *nm o nf* terrorist.

tesoro *nm* **1** *(gen)* treasure. **2** *fig* treasure.

testamento *nm* **1** JUR will, testament. **2** REL Testament. LOC **hacer testamento** to make one's will.

testarudo,-a *adj* obstinate, stubborn.

testigo *nm o nf* witness.
▶ *nm* **1** *(prueba)* proof. **2** DEP baton.

testimonio *nm* **1** JUR testimony, evidence. **2** *(prueba)* evidence, proof.

tétanos *nm inv* tetanus.

tetera *nf* teapot.

tetraedro *nm* tetrahedron.

textil *adj* textile.
▶ *nm* textile.

texto *nm* text.

textura *nf* **1** *(textil)* texture. **2** *(minerales)* structure.

tez *nf* complexion.

ti *pron* [se usa sólo después de una preposición] you: *te lo doy a ti* I'll give it to you.

tía *nf* *(pariente)* aunt.

tibio,-a *adj* **1** tepid. **2** *fig* cool.

tiburón *nm* shark.

tic *nm* **1** tic, twitch. **2** *fig* *(manía)* habit.

ticket *nm* → tique.

tiempo *nm* **1** *(gen)* time. **2** *(época)* time, period, age, days *pl*: *en tiempo de los romanos* in Roman times. **3** METEOR weather: *¿qué tiempo hace?* what's the weather like? **4** *(edad)* age: *¿qué tiempo tiene el niño?* how old is your baby? **5** *(temporada)* season: *fruta del tiempo* fruit in season. **6** *(momento)* moment, time: *no es tiempo de preguntarle eso* it's not the time to ask him that. **7** MÚS tempo, movement. **8** DEP *(parte)* half. **9** GRAM tense. **10** TÉC stroke. LOC **hacer buen tiempo** the weather is good. COMP **tiempo libre** free time.

tienda *nf* **1** *(establecimiento)* shop, US store. **2** *(de campaña)* tent. **3** *(de carro)* cover. LOC **ir de tiendas** to go shopping. COMP **tienda de campaña** tent.

tierno,-a *adj* **1** *(blando)* tender, soft. **2** *fig* *(reciente)* fresh: *pan tierno* fresh bread. **3** *fig* *(cariñoso)* affectionate.

tierra *nf* **1** *(planeta)* earth. **2** *(superficie sólida)* land. **3** *(terreno cultivado)* soil, land. **4** *(país)* country, land. **5** *(suelo)* ground. **6** ELEC earth, US ground.
▶ *nf pl* **tierras** land *sing*. LOC **tierra adentro** inland. COMP **tierra de nadie** no-man's-land. ‖ **tierra firme** terra firma.

tieso,-a *adj* **1** *(rígido)* stiff, rigid. **2** *(erguido)* upright, erect. **3** *(tenso)* taut, tight.

tiesto *nm* flowerpot.

tifón *nm* typhoon.

tigre *nm* tiger.

tijera *nf* [se suele usar en plural] *(instrumento)* scissors *pl*, pair of scissors.

tila *nf* **1** *(tilo)* lime. **2** *(flor)* lime blossom. **3** *(infusión)* lime-blossom tea.

tilde *nf* **1** *(gen)* written accent; *(de la ñ)* tilde. **2** *fig* *(tacha)* fault, flaw.

tilo *nm* lime tree.

timar *vt* to swindle, cheat, trick.

timbre *nm* **1** *(de la puerta)* bell. **2** *(sello)* stamp, seal. **3** MÚS timbre.

timidez *nf* shyness, timidity.

tímido,-a *adj* shy, timid.

timo¹ *nm* *(estafa)* swindle.

timo² *nm* *(glándula)* thymus.

timón *nm* **1** *(barco, avión)* rudder. **2** *(del arado)* beam. **3** *fig* *(negocio, etc)* helm.

Timor Oriental *nm* East Timor.

tímpano *nm* *(del oído)* eardrum.

tiniebla *nf* [también se usa en plural con el mismo significado] *(oscuridad)* darkness.
▶ *nf pl* **tinieblas** *fig* *(ignorancia)* ignorance *sing*, confusion *sing*.

tinta *nf* **1** *(gen)* ink. **2** *(tinte)* dyeing.
▶ *nf pl* **tintas** colours (US colors). COMP **tinta china** Indian ink.

tinte *nm* **1** *(colorante)* dye. **2** *(proceso)* dyeing. **3** *(tintorería)* dry-cleaner's. **4** *fig* *(aspecto)* shade.

tintero *nm* inkwell.

tintinear *vi* → tintinar.

tinto,-a *adj* **1** *(teñido)* dyed. **2** *(vino)* red.
▶ *nm* **tinto** *(vino)* red wine.

tintorería *nf* dry-cleaner's.

T

tío *nm* **1** *(pariente)* uncle. **2** *fam (hombre)* guy.
▸ *nm pl* **tíos** aunt and uncle.

tiovivo *nm* merry-go-round.

típico,-a *adj* **1** *(característico)* typical, characteristic. **2** *(pintoresco)* picturesque; *(tradicional)* traditional: *un plato típico* a traditional dish, a local dish.

tipo *nm* **1** *(clase)* type, kind. **2** FIN rate. **3** ANAT *(de hombre)* build, physique; *(de mujer)* figure. **4** *fam (persona)* guy, fellow, bloke. **5** *(en impresión)* type. COMP **tipo de interés** FIN rate of interest.

tíquet *nm* → tique.

tira *nf* **1** *(cinta, banda)* strip. **2** *(de dibujos)* comic strip. LOC **la tira** *(cantidad)* a lot, loads; *(mucho tiempo)* for yonks, for ages: *comimos la tira* we ate loads.

tirada *nf* **1** *(acción)* throw: *en la segunda tirada le salieron dos seises* he got two sixes on the second throw. **2** *(impresión)* print run: *una tirada de cinco mil ejemplares* a print run of five thousand. **3** *(distancia)* stretch: *hay una buena tirada hasta allí* it's a good few miles away. **4** *(serie)* series.

tirado,-a *adj* **1** *fam (precio)* dirt cheap. **2** *fam (problema, asunto)* dead easy. **3** *fam (abandonado)* let down.

tirador,-ra *nm & nf (persona)* shooter.
▸ *nm (de puerta, cajón)* knob, handle.

tirano,-a *nm & nf* tyrant.

tirante *adj* **1** taut. **2** *fig (situación)* tense.
▸ *nm* **1** *(de ropa en general)* strap. **2** TÉC brace, stay. **3** ARQUIT beam.
▸ *nm pl* **tirantes** *(de pantalón)* braces, US suspenders.

tirar *vt* **1** *(echar)* to throw, fling. **2** *(dejar caer)* to drop. **3** *(desechar)* to throw away. **4** *(derribar)* to knock down; *(casa, árbol)* to pull down. **5** *(derramar)* to spill. **6** *(vaso, botella)* to knock over. **7** *(estirar)* to pull. **8** *(imprimir)* to print. **9** *(un tiro)* to fire; *(una bomba)* to drop; *(cohete)* to launch. **10** DEP to take. **11** *fig (malgastar)* to waste, squander.
▸ *vi* **1** *(cuerda, puerta)* to pull (de, -). **2** *(estufa, chimenea)* to draw. **3** *(en juegos)* to be a player's move, be a player's turn: *tira él* it's his turn. **4** *fam (funcionar)* to work, run: *esto ya no tira* this doesn't work any more. **5** *fam (durar)* to last: *con esta reparación tirará un par de meses* after these repairs it'll last for a couple of months. **6** *fam fig (atraer)* to attract, appeal: *no le tira la mecánica* mechanics doesn't appeal to him. **7** *fig (inclinarse)* to be attracted (a/hacia, to), be drawn (a/hacia, to): *esta chica tira hacia las artes* this girl is drawn to the arts. **8** *fig (parecerse)* to take after (a, -): *tira a su padre* she takes after her father. **9** *fig (mantenerse)* to get by, get along: *ella tira con poco dinero* she gets by with little money. **10** *(disparar)* to shoot, fire. **11** DEP *(fútbol)* to shoot; *(ciclismo)* to set the pace.
▸ *vpr* **tirarse 1** *(lanzarse)* to throw os. **2** *(abalanzarse)* to rush (sobre, at), jump (sobre, on). **3** *(tumbarse)* to lie down. **4** *fam (tiempo)* to spend: *se tiró una hora en la ducha* he spent an hour in the shower.

tirita® *nf* sticking plaster, plaster.

tiritar *vi (gen)* to shiver, shake.

tiro *nm* **1** *(lanzamiento)* throw. **2** *(disparo, ruido)* shot. **3** *(galería de tiro)* shooting gallery. **4** DEP shooting. **5** *(caballerías)* team. **6** COST *(de pantalón)* distance between waist and crotch. **7** *(de chimenea)* draught (US draft). **8** *(fútbol, etc)* shot. COMP **tiro al blanco** target shooting.

tirón *nm* pull, tug. LOC **de un tirón** *fam* in one go.

tiroteo *nm* shooting.

títere *nm* **1** *(marioneta)* puppet, marionette. **2** *fig (persona)* puppet, dupe.
▸ *nm pl* **títeres** puppet show *sing*. LOC **no dejar títere con cabeza 1** *fam (destruir)* to break everything in sight. **2** *(criticar)* to spare nobody.

titulado,-a *adj* **1** *(llamado)* called. **2** EDUC *(diplomado)* qualified.

titular *vt* to entitle, title, call.
▸ *adj* regular.
▸ *nm o nf* **1** *(poseedor)* holder. **2** *(de un puesto)* office holder.
▸ *nm (prensa)* headline.
▸ *vpr* **titularse 1** *(llamarse)* to be called, be titled. **2** EDUC to graduate (en, in).

título *nm* **1** *(de obra)* title. **2** *(de texto legal)* heading. **3** *(dignidad)* title. **4** *(persona noble)* noble (person). **5** EDUC *(licenciatura)* degree; *(diploma)* certificate. **6** *(documento)* title. **7** *(titular de prensa)* headline.

▶ *nm pl* **títulos** *(titulación)* qualifications; *(méritos)* qualities. [COMP] **título de propiedad** deeds *pl*.

tiza *nf* chalk.

toalla *nf* towel. [COMP] **toalla de baño** bath towel.

toallero *nm* towel rail, towel rack.

tobillera *nf* ankle sock.

tobillo *nm* ankle.

tobogán *nm* **1** *(rampa)* slide, chute. **2** *(trineo)* toboggan, sledge.

tocadiscos *nm inv* record player.

tocado *nm* **1** *(peinado)* coiffure, hairdo. **2** *(prenda)* headdress, hat.

tocado,-a *adj* **1** *(fruta)* bad, rotten. **2** *fam (perturbado)* crazy, touched.

tocador *nm* **1** *(mueble)* dressing-table. **2** *(habitación)* dressing-room, boudoir.

tocar *vt* **1** *(gen)* to touch: *no tocar la mercancía* do not handle the goods. **2** *(sentir por el tacto)* to feel: *tócalo, está frío* feel it, it's cold. **3** *(revolver)* to rummage amongst, root around: *no toques mis papeles* leave my papers alone. **4** *(hacer sonar - instrumento, canción)* to play; *(timbre)* to ring; *(bocina)* to blow, honk; *(campanas)* to strike. **5** *(la hora)* to strike. **6** DEP *(diana)* to hit; *(esgrima)* to touch. **7** *fig (mencionar)* to touch on. **8** *fig (impresionar)* to touch, reach: *me tocó el corazón* he touched my heart.

▶ *vi* **1** *(ser el turno)* to be one's turn: *le toca a él* it's his turn. **2** *(corresponder)* to be up to: *le toca a él explicarse* it's up to him to explain himself. **3** *(ganar)* to win. **4** *(en un reparto, etc)* to fall. **5** *(un destino)* to be posted: *le tocó en Cartagena* he was posted to Cartagena. **6** *(tener que)* to have to: *nos tocó llevarla* we had to take her. **7** *(afectar)* to concern, affect: *le toca directamente* it directly concerns you. **8** *(entrar en contacto)* to touch.

▶ *vpr* **tocarse** *(uso reflexivo)* to touch os; *(uso recíproco)* to touch each other.

tocino *nm* **1** *(carne)* bacon. **2** *(grasa)* fat.

todavía *adv* **1** *(a pesar de ello)* still. **2** *(tiempo)* still, yet: *todavía están allí* they're still there. **3** *(para reforzar)* even: *esto todavía está mejor* this is even better.

todo,-a *adj* **1** *(sin excluir nada)* all: *todos los vecinos lo vieron* all the neighbours saw it. **2** *(verdadero)* real: *era todo un reto* it was a real challenge. **3** *(cada)* every: *todos los días* every day.

▶ *pron* **1** *(sin excluir nada)* all, everything: *llamaron todos* they all phoned. **2** *(cualquiera)* anybody: *todo el que yo diga* anybody I say.

▶ *nm* **todo** *(totalidad)* whole.

▶ *adv* completely, totally, all: *está todo mojado* it's all wet.

todoterreno *adj* four-wheel-drive.

▶ *nm* four-wheel-drive vehicle.

Togo *nm* Togo.

togolés,-esa *adj* Togolese.

▶ *nm & nf* Togolese.

toldo *nm* **1** *(cubierta)* awning. **2** *(de playa)* sunshade.

tolerancia *nf* tolerance.

tolerante *adj* tolerant, lenient.

tolerar *vt* **1** *(permitir, soportar)* to tolerate, put up with: *no te toleraré esa actitud* I won't put up with that attitude. **2** *(inconvenientes)* to stand.

toma *nf* **1** *(acción)* taking. **2** MED dose. **3** MIL capture. **4** *(de aire)* intake, inlet; *(de agua)* outlet, tap; *(de electricidad)* plug, socket. **5** *(grabación)* recording. **6** CINE take, shot. [COMP] **toma de posesión** takeover.

tomar *vt* **1** *(gen)* to take: *lo tomó en broma* she took it as a joke. **2** *(baño, ducha)* to have, take; *(foto)* to take. **3** *(comer, beber)* to have; *(beber)* to drink; *(comer)* to eat: *tómate la leche* drink your milk. **4** *(el autobús, el tren)* to catch. **5** *(aceptar)* to accept, take. **6** *(comprar)* to buy, get, have: *tomaré manzanas* I'll get some apples. **7** *(adquirir)* to acquire, get into: *tomar una costumbre* to acquire a habit. **8** MIL to capture, take.

▶ *vi* *(encaminarse)* to go, turn.

▶ *vpr* **tomarse 1** *(gen)* to take: *me tomé una aspirina* I took an aspirin. **2** *(beber)* to drink; *(comer)* to eat. [LOC] **tomarse las cosas con calma** to take it easy.

tomate *nm* *(fruto)* tomato.

tómbola *nf* tombola.

tomillo *nm* thyme.

tomo *nm (volumen)* volume.

tonel *nm* barrel, cask.

tonelada *nf* ton. COMP **tonelada métrica** metric ton, tonne.

Tonga *nf* Tonga.

tongano,-a *adj* Tongan.
► *nm & nf (persona)* Tongan.
► *nm* **tongano** *(idioma)* Tongan.

tónica *nf* 1 *(tendencia)* tendency, trend. 2 *(bebida)* tonic, tonic water.

tónico,-a *adj* 1 *(sílaba)* tonic, stressed. 2 *(nota musical)* tonic.
► *nm* **tónico** MED tonic.

tono *nm* 1 *(gen)* tone: *el tono de su discurso* the tone of her speech. 2 *(energía)* energy. LOC **fuera de tono** *fig* inappropriate, out of place.

tontear *vi (decir tonterías)* to act the clown, fool about.

tontería *nf* 1 *(calidad de tonto)* stupidity, silliness. 2 *(dicho, hecho)* silly thing, stupid thing. 3 *(insignificancia)* trifle. LOC **hacer tonterías** to mess about, fool around.

tonto,-a *adj* silly, stupid, US dumb: *¡qué idea más tonta!* what a stupid idea!
► *nm & nf* fool, idiot. LOC **hacerse el tonto** to play dumb.

topacio *nm* topaz.

topar *vi* 1 *(chocar)* to bump into: *el coche topó contra un poste* the car bumped into a pole. 2 *(encontrar - algo)* to come across, find; *(- alguien)* to bump into, run into. 3 *fig (dificultades, etc)* to come up against, run into.

tope *nm* 1 *(límite)* limit, end. 2 TÉC stop, check. 3 *(de ferrocarril)* buffer, bumping post, bumper. 4 MAR masthead.
► *adj fig* top, maximum.
► *adv argot* really, absolutely: *la fiesta fue tope divertida* the party was absolutely brilliant. LOC **a tope 1** *argot (al límite)* flat out. **2** *(lleno)* jam-packed, chock-a-block.

tópico,-a *adj* MED external: *uso tópico* external use.
► *nm* **tópico** commonplace, cliché.

topo *nm* mole.

toque *nm* 1 *(acto)* touch. 2 *(de campana)* ringing, peal, pealing; *(de trompeta)* blare, sounding; *(de claxon)* honk; *(de sirena)* hoot; *(de tambor)* beat, beating. 3 *(pincelada)* touch. 4 *fig (advertencia)* warning. LOC **dar un toque a ALGN 1** *(llamar)* to take SB to task. **2** *(llamar la atención)* to call sb's attention.

tórax *nm inv* thorax.

torcer *vt* 1 *(gen)* to twist. 2 *(doblar)* to bend; *(madera)* to warp.
► *vi (girar)* to turn: *torció a la derecha* he turned right.
► *vpr* **torcerse 1** *(gen)* to twist. **2** *(doblarse)* to bend; *(madera)* to warp. **3** *(ladearse)* to become slanted. **4** MED to sprain, twist. **5** *fig (plan)* to fall through.

torcido,-a *adj* 1 *(que no es recto)* twisted. 2 *(madera)* warped; *(metal)* bent. 3 *(ladeado)* slanted, crooked, lopsided: *el cuadro está torcido* the painting is crooked.

torear *vt* 1 *(lidiar)* to fight. 2 *fig (entretener)* to put off. 3 *fig (burlar)* to tease, confuse. 4 *fig (asunto, etc)* to tackle skilfully. 5 *fig (evitar)* to avoid.
► *vi (lidiar)* to fight.

torero,-a *nm & nf* bullfighter.

tormenta *nf* storm.

tornado *nm* tornado.

torneo *nm* 1 *(justa)* tourney, joust. 2 DEP tournament, competition.

tornillo *nm* screw, bolt.

toro *nm (animal)* bull.
► *nm pl* **los toros** *(corrida)* bullfight *sing*; *(arte)* bullfighting *sing*.

torpe *adj* 1 *(poco hábil)* clumsy. 2 *(de movimiento)* slow, awkward. 3 *(poco inteligente)* dim, thick.

torpedo *nm* MIL torpedo.

torpeza *nf* 1 *(falta de habilidad)* clumsiness, awkwardness. 2 *(mental)* dimness, stupidity. 3 *(de movimiento)* slowness, heaviness. 4 *(error)* blunder.

torre *nf* 1 *(gen)* tower. 2 *(campanario)* bell tower. 3 *(chalé)* country house, house, villa. 4 *(ajedrez)* rook, castle.

torrencial *adj* torrential.

torrente *nm* **1** *(de agua)* mountain stream. **2** *fig (abundancia)* flood, stream.

torta *nf* **1** CULIN cake. **2** *fam (golpe)* blow, crack; *(bofetada)* slap, wallop. LOC **ni torta** *fam* not a thing: *no ve ni torta* he can't see a thing.

tortazo *nm* **1** *fam (golpe)* whack, thump. **2** *fam (bofetada)* slap, punch.

tortícolis *nf inv* stiff neck.

tortilla *nf* **1** omelette (US omelet). **2** AM tortilla, pancake. COMP **tortilla de patatas** potato omelette.

tórtola *nf* → tórtolo,-a.

tortuga *nf* **1** *(de tierra)* tortoise. **2** *(marina)* turtle.

torturar *vt* to torture.

tos *nf* cough, coughing. LOC **tener tos** to have a cough.

toser *vi* to cough.

tostada *nf* toast, slice of toast.

tostador,-ra *nm & nf (de pan)* toaster, *(de café)* roaster.

tostar *vt* **1** *(pan)* to toast; *(café)* to roast; *(carnes)* to brown. **2** *fig (piel)* to tan.
▶ *vpr* **tostarse** *fig (la piel)* to get brown, turn brown, tan.

total *adj* total, complete, overall: *anestesia total* general anaesthetic.
▶ *nm* **1** *(totalidad)* whole: *el total de la población* the whole population. **2** *(suma)* total, sum.
▶ *adv* **1** *(en conclusión)* in short, so: *total, que se fueron porque quisieron* they left because they wanted to. **2** *(al fin y al cabo)* after all.

totalitario,-a *adj* totalitarian.

totalitarismo *nm* totalitarianism.

tótem *nm* totem; *(efigie)* totem pole.

tóxico,-a *adj* toxic, poisonous.
▶ *nm* **tóxico** toxicant, poison.

toxicómano,-a *nm & nf* drug addict.

tozudo,-a *adj* stubborn, obstinate.

trabajador,-ra *adj* **1** *(que trabaja)* working. **2** *(laborioso)* hard-working.
▶ *nm & nf* worker (US laborer).

trabajar *vi* **1** *(gen)* to work: *trabaja mucho* she works hard. **2** *(en obra, película)* to act, perform: *¿quién trabaja en la obra?* who's in the play?

▶ *vt* **1** *(materiales)* to work (on). **2** *(idea, idioma, etc)* to work on. **3** *(la tierra)* to till. **4** CULIN *(pasta)* to knead.

trabajo *nm* **1** *(ocupación)* work. **2** *(tarea)* task, job. **3** *(empleo)* job. **4** *(esfuerzo)* effort. **5** EDUC report.
▶ *nm pl* **trabajos** *fig (penalidades)* hardships. COMP **trabajos manuales** arts and crafts, handicrafts.

trabalenguas *nm inv* tongue twister.

trabar *vt* **1** *(unir)* to join, link. **2** *(sujetar)* to lock, fasten. **3** *(mecanismo)* to jam. **4** *(prender a alguien)* to shackle. **5** *(caballería)* to hobble. **6** *fig (empezar)* to start. **7** *fig (conversación, amistad)* to strike up. **8** *fig (impedir)* to impede.
▶ *vpr* **trabarse** *(enredarse)* to get tangled up. LOC **trabársele la lengua a** ALGN to get tongue-tied.

tractor *nm* tractor.

tradición *nf* tradition.

tradicional *adj* traditional.

traducción *nf* translation.

traducir *vt* **1** *(gen)* to translate. **2** *(expresar)* to express, show.
▶ *vpr* **traducirse** *(resulta)* to result in.

traductor,-ra *adj* translating.
▶ *nm & nf* translator.

traer *vt* **1** *(gen)* to bring. **2** *(llevar consigo)* to carry: *traía un bolso* she was carrying a bag. **3** *(vestir)* to wear: *traía una falda verde* she was wearing a green skirt. **4** *(causar)* to cause, bring: *esto le trajo muchos problemas* it caused him a lot of problems. **5** *(contener)* to contain: *el paquete trae un regalo* the package contains a gift.
▶ *vpr* **traerse** *(llevar consigo)* to bring along: *tráete al bebé* bring your baby along.

traficante *nm o nf* **1** trader, dealer. **2** *(ilegal)* trafficker.

traficar *vi* **1** to deal. **2** *(de forma ilegal)* to traffic (en, in), deal (en, in): *trafica en/con drogas* he traffics in drugs.

tráfico *nm* **1** AUTO traffic. **2** COM traffic.

tragaperras COMP **máquina tragaperras** slot machine.

tragar *vt* **1** *(ingerir)* to swallow. **2** *(absorber)* to soak up. **3** *fig (hacer desaparecer)* to swallow up. **4** *fig (gastar, consumir)*

T

to eat up, guzzle: *este coche traga mucha gasolina* this car guzzles petrol. **5** *fig (creer)* to swallow, believe. **6** *fig (aguantar)* to put up with; *(disimular)* to hide: *tuvo que tragar sus exigencias* she had to put up with his demands. **7** *fig (soportar a alguien)* to stand, stomach: *no trago a Pedro* I can't stand Pedro.
▶ *vi* to swallow, swallow up.
▶ *vpr* **tragarse** *(ingerir)* to swallow: *se tragó un botón* he swallowed a button.

tragedia *nf* tragedy.

trágico,-a *adj* tragic.

trago *nm* **1** *(sorbo)* swig, drop. **2** *fam (bebida)* drink. **3** *fam fig (adversidad)* rough time.

traición *nf* treason, betrayal. LOC *a traición* treacherously.

traicionar *vt* **1** *(gen)* to betray. **2** *fig (delatar)* to give away, betray: *su expresión traicionó sus pensamientos* his expression gave away his thoughts.

traidor,-ra *adj* treacherous.
▶ *nm & nf* traitor.

traje *nm* **1** *(de hombre)* suit. **2** *(de mujer)* dress. COMP *traje de chaqueta* tailored suit. ‖ *traje de noche* evening dress.

trama *nf* **1** *(textil)* weft, woof. **2** *(argumento)* plot.

tramar *vt* **1** *(tejidos)* to weave. **2** *fig (maquinar)* to plot, cook up.

tramitación *nf* JUR procedure.

tramitar *vt* **1** *(gestionar)* to deal with, process: *tramitaremos su pasaporte* we'll get your passport sorted out. **2** *(solicitar, negociar)* to arrange, negotiate: *tramitar un préstamo* to negotiate a loan.

trámite *nm* **1** *(paso)* step. **2** *(formalidad)* formality, requirement.

tramo *nm* **1** *(camino, etc)* stretch. **2** *(de escalera)* flight. **3** *(de terreno)* lot.

trampa *nf* **1** *(abertura)* trapdoor, hatch. **2** *(para cazar)* trap. **3** *fig (engaño)* fiddle; *(truco)* trick. **4** *fig (deuda)* debt. LOC *tender una trampa* to set a trap.

trampolín *nm* **1** *(de piscina)* springboard. **2** *(de esquí)* ski jump.

tramposo,-a *adj* deceitful, tricky.

▶ *nm & nf* trickster, cheat; *(en las cartas)* cardsharp.

trancazo *nm* **1** *(golpe)* blow with a cudgel. **2** *fam fig (resfriado)* cold; *(gripe)* flu.

trance *nm* **1** *(momento crítico)* critical moment. **2** *(dificultad)* fix, tight spot. **3** *(éxtasis)* trance.

tranquilidad *nf* *(quietud)* calmness; *(sosiego)* peace and quiet. COMP *paz y tranquilidad* peace and quiet.

tranquilizante *nm* tranquilliser (US tranquilizer).

tranquilizar *vt* **1** *(calmar)* to calm down, tranquillize (US tranquilize). **2** *(dar confianza)* to reassure, set one's mind at rest.
▶ *vpr* **tranquilizarse 1** *(calmarse)* to calm down. **2** to set one's mind at rest.

tranquilo,-a *adj* **1** *(sin inquietud)* calm, relaxed, tranquil. **2** *(sin preocupación)* reassured. **3** *(sin movimiento)* calm, still, quiet. **4** *(sin ruidos)* quiet, still, peaceful. **5** *(persona)* calm, easy-going, placid. **6** *(agua)* still; *(conciencia)* clear.

transacción *nf* transaction, deal.

transatlántico,-a *adj* transatlantic.
▶ *nm* transatlántico liner, ocean liner.

transbordar *vt* to transfer.
▶ *vi* change *(de tren, etc)*.

transbordador *nm* ferry. COMP *transbordador espacial* space shuttle.

transbordo *nm* **1** *(de vehículo)* change, US transfer. **2** *(de barco)* transshipment.

transcribir *vt* to transcribe.

transcripción *nf* transcription.

transcurrir *vi* **1** *(tiempo)* to pass, elapse. **2** *(acontecer)* to take place, go off.

transcurso *nm* **1** *(paso)* course. **2** *(duración)* space, period: *en el transcurso de dos años* in the space of two years.

transeúnte *nm o nf (peatón)* pedestrian.

transferencia *nf* FIN transfer.

transferible *adj* transferable.

transferir *vt* FIN to transfer, convey.

transformación *nf* transformation.

transformador,-ra *adj* transforming.
▶ *nm* transformador transformer.

transformar *vt* to transform, change.

▶ *vpr* **transformarse** to change, be transformed: *se transformó completamente* he was completely transformed. ⸤LOC⸥ **transformarse en 1** *(persona)* to become. **2** *(objeto)* to convert into.

transfusión *nf* transfusion. ⸤COMP⸥ **transfusión de sangre** blood transfusion.

transgénico,-a *adj* genetically modified.

transgresión *nf* transgression.

transgresor,-ra *nm & nf* transgressor, law-breaker.

transición *nf* transition.

transigencia *nf* **1** *(actitud)* tolerance, lenience. **2** *(concesión)* compromise.

transigente *adj* accommodating, tolerant, lenient.

transigir *vi* **1** *(ceder)* to compromise, give in, yield. **2** *(tolerar)* to tolerate.

transistor *nm* transistor.

transitable *adj* passable.

transitado,-a *adj* busy.

transitar *vi* **1** *(viajar)* to travel, travel about. **2** *(pasar)* to pass, go, walk.

transitivo,-a *adj* transitive.

tránsito *nm* **1** *(acción)* passage, transit, movement. **2** AUTO traffic. **3** *euf (muerte)* death, passing. **4** *(lugar de parada)* stopping place.

transitoriedad *nf* transience.

transitorio,-a *adj (pasajero)* transitory; *(de transición)* transitional, interim.

transmediterráneo,-a *adj* trans-Mediterranean.

transmisible *adj* transmissible.

transmisión *nf* **1** *(propagación)* transmission. **2** JUR transfer, transference. **3** RAD TV broadcast. **4** TÉC drive.
▶ *nf pl* **transmisiones** MIL signals. ⸤COMP⸥ **derechos de transmisión 1** JUR *(de herencia)* succession duty. **2** *(de televisión, etc)* broadcasting rights. ‖ **transmisión en directo** RAD TV live broadcast.

transmisor,-ra *adj* transmitting.
▶ *nm & nf* transmitter.

transmitir *vt* **1** *(gen)* to transmit. **2** RAD TV to broadcast. **3** *(enfermedad)* to transmit, pass on. **4** JUR to transfer, hand down.

transmutar *vt* to transmute.
▶ *vpr* **transmutarse** to change, transform.

transoceánico,-a *adj* transoceanic.

transparencia *nf* **1** transparency. **2** *(diapositiva)* transparency.

transparentar *vt fig (emociones, etc)* to reveal.
▶ *vpr* **transparentarse 1** *(ser transparente)* to be transparent, show through. **2** *fig (emociones, etc)* to show.

transparente *adj* **1** *(gen)* transparent. **2** *(tela, vestido)* transparent. **3** *fig* straight, plain.

transpiración *nf* perspiration.

transpirar *vi* to perspire, transpire.

transplantar *vt* **1** *(gen)* to transplant. **2** *(trasladar)* to transfer.

transplante *nm* transplant.

transportable *adj* transportable.

transportar *vt* **1** *(gen)* to transport. **2** *(pasajeros)* to carry; *(mercancías en barco)* to ship. **3** MAT to transfer. **4** MÚS to transpose. **5** *fig (hacer perder la razón)* to carry away, send into raptures.
▶ *vpr* **transportarse** *fig* to be transported, be enraptured.

transporte *nm* **1** *(medio)* transport. **2** *(acción)* transport, US transportation. **3** COM freight, freightage. **4** MÚS transposition. **5** *fig* transport, ecstasy, bliss. ⸤COMP⸥ **transporte público** public transport.

transportista *nm o nf* carrier.

transvasar *vt* **1** *(líquidos)* to decant. **2** *(entre ríos)* to transfer.

transvase *nm* **1** *(de líquidos)* decanting. **2** *(de ríos)* transfer.

transversal *adj* transverse.

transverso,-a *adj* transverse.

tranvía *nm* **1** *(sistema)* tramway. **2** *(vehículo)* tram, tramcar, US streetcar.

trapecio *nm* **1** DEP trapeze. **2** *(geometría)* trapezium, US trapezoid. **3** ANAT *(hueso)* trapezium; *(músculo)* trapezius.

trapecista *nm o nf* trapeze artist.

trapería *nf* secondhand clothes shop.

T

trapero,-a *nm & nf (hombre)* rag-and-bone man, US junkman; *(mujer)* rag-and-bone woman.

trapezoide *nm* trapezoid, US trapezium.

trapo *nm* 1 *(tela vieja)* rag. 2 *(paño, bayeta)* cloth. 3 MAR sails *pl*. 4 *(telón)* curtain. 5 *(del torero)* red cape.
▶ *nm pl* **trapos** clothes, rags. LOC **poner a ALGN como un trapo (sucio)** *fam* to tear SB apart. COMP **trapo del polvo** duster.

tráquea *nf* trachea, windpipe.

traqueal *adj* tracheal.

traqueotomía *nf* tracheotomy.

tras *prep* 1 *(después de)* after: *tras la salida del avión* after the departure of the plane. 2 *(detrás)* behind: *tras el muro* behind the wall. 3 *(en pos de)* after, in pursuit of: *iba siempre tras el éxito* he was always in pursuit of success. LOC **día tras día** day after day.

trasbordador *nm* ferry, car ferry.

trascendencia *nf* 1 *(importancia)* significance, importance. 2 *(filosofía)* transcendence, transcendency.

trascendental *adj* 1 *(importante)* significant, very important, consequential; *(de gran alcance)* far-reaching. 2 *(filosofía)* transcendent, transcendental.

trascendente *adj* → **trascendental**.

trascender *vi* 1 *(olor - despedir)* to smell; *(- llegar hasta)* to reach. 2 *(darse a conocer)* to become known, leak out: *el resultado trascendió* the result leaked out. 3 *(extenderse)* to spread, have a wide effect.

trascribir *vt* to transcribe.

trascripción *nf* transcription.

trasegar *vt* 1 *(mudar)* to move about, shuffle. 2 *(líquidos)* to decant.

trasero,-a *adj* back, rear.
▶ *nm* **trasero** *fam euf* bottom, bum.

trasferencia *nf* → **transferencia**.

trasferible *adj* transferable.

trasferir *vt* → **transferir**.

trasfondo *nm* 1 background. 2 *fig* undertone.

trasformación *nf* transformation.

trasformador,-ra *adj-nm* → **transformador,-ra**.

trasgresión *nf* transgression.

trasgresor,-ra *nm & nf* transgressor, law-breaker.

trashumancia *nf* transhumance, seasonal migration.

trashumante *adj* transhumant.

trasiego *nm* comings and goings *pl*, hustle and bustle.

traslación *nf* 1 *(de la Tierra)* passage, movement. 2 *(en matemáticas)* translation.

trasladar *vt* 1 *(cambiar de sitio)* to move. 2 *(de cargo, etc)* to transfer. 3 *(aplazar)* to postpone, put off.
▶ *vpr* **trasladarse** 1 *(ir)* to go. 2 *(cambiar de residencia)* to move.

traslado *nm* 1 *(cambio de lugar)* move, moving; *(de residencia)* removal. 2 *(de cargo, etc)* transfer. 3 *(copia)* copy. 4 JUR notification.

traslúcido,-a *adj* translucent, semi-transparent.

traslucir *vt fig* to show, reveal, betray.
▶ *vpr* **traslucirse** 1 *(material)* to be translucent. 2 *fig (dejar ver)* to show, show through.

trasluz *nm* diffused light, reflected light. LOC **mirar ALGO al trasluz** to look at STH against the light.

trasmano *nm o nf* second hand.

trasnochado,-a *adj* 1 *fig (viejo)* old, hackneyed. 2 *fig (desmejorado)* haggard, bleary-eyed.

trasnochador,-ra *nm & nf* night bird, nighthawk.

trasnochar *vi* to stay up late, stay up until the early hours.

traspapelado,-a *adj* mislaid, misplaced.

traspapelar *vt* to mislay, misplace.
▶ *vpr* **traspapelarse** to get mislaid, get misplaced.

traspasar *vt* 1 *(atravesar)* to go through, cross. 2 *(cambiar de lugar)* to move. 3 *(perforar)* to go through, pierce. 4 *(dar,* *pasar)* to transfer; *(vender)* to sell. **5** *fig (exceder)* to exceed, go beyond.

traspaso *nm* **1** *(de negocio, etc)* transfer, sale. **2** *(precio)* transfer fee.

traspié *nm* **1** *(tropezón)* stumble, trip. **2** *fig (equivocación)* blunder.

trasponer *vt-vpr* → transponer.

trasportista *nm o nf* carrier.

trasposición *nf* transposition.

traspuesto,-a LOC quedarse traspuesto,-a to nod off, doze off.

traspunte *nm* callboy.

trasquilado,-a *adj* **1** *(oveja)* sheared; *(pelo)* hacked, unevenly cut. **2** *fam fig* curtailed, cut down.

trasquilar *vt* **1** *(animales)* to shear. **2** *(pelo)* to hack, cut unevenly. **3** *fig* to curtail.

trastabillar *vi* **1** *(dar traspiés)* to stumble, trip. **2** *(tambalearse)* to stagger, totter.

trastada *nf fam (mala pasada)* dirty trick.

trastazo *nm fam* whack, wallop, thump. LOC **darse un trastazo** *fam* to come a cropper.

traste *nm* MÚS fret. LOC **irse al traste** *fig* to fall through.

trastear *vt* **1** MÚS to play. **2** *(revolver)* to rummage in. **3** *fig (manejar)* to twist around one's little finger.
▶ *vi (revolver)* to rummage.

trastero,-a *nm* junk room.

trastienda *nf* **1** *(de tienda)* back room. **2** *fig (astucia)* cunning.

trasto *nm* **1** *(algo inútil)* piece of junk. **2** *fam (niño)* little devil. **3** *fam (persona)* useless person, good-for-nothing, dead loss.
▶ *nm pl* **trastos** **1** *(utensilios)* tackle *sing*, gear *sing*. **2** *fam (pertenencias)* belongings, things. LOC **tirarse los trastos a la cabeza** *fig* to have a blazing row.

trastocar *vt (cambiar)* to change.
▶ *vpr* **trastocarse** *(trastornarse)* to go mad.

trastornado,-a *adj* **1** *(preocupado)* upset. **2** *(loco)* mad. **3** *(mente)* unbalanced.

trastornar *vt* **1** *(revolver)* to turn round, turn upside down. **2** *(alterar - planes)* to disrupt; *(- paz, orden)* to disturb. **3** *(estómago)* to upset. **4** *fig (enloquecer)* to drive crazy.
▶ *vpr* **trastornarse** *(perturbarse)* to go mad, go out of one's mind.

trastorno *nm* **1** *(desorden)* confusion. **2** *(molestia)* trouble, inconvenience. **3** *(perturbación)* disruption, upheaval, upset. **4** MED upset.

trastrocar *vt* **1** *(gen)* to switch around, change around. **2** *(orden)* to invert, reverse; *(significado)* to change.

trasunto *nm* **1** *(copia)* copy. **2** *(representación)* representation.

trata *nf* slave trade.

tratable *adj* friendly, congenial, easy to get along with.

tratadista *nm o nf* treatise writer.

tratado *nm* **1** *(pacto)* treaty. **2** *(estudio)* treatise.

tratamiento *nm* **1** *(gen)* treatment. **2** *(de datos, materiales)* processing. **3** *(título)* title, form of address. COMP **tratamiento de textos** word processing.

tratar *vt* **1** *(gen - objeto)* to treat, handle; *(- persona)* to treat: *nos trató bien* he treated us well. **2** *(asunto, tema)* to discuss, deal with. **3** *(gestionar)* to handle, run. **4** *(dar tratamiento)* to address as. **5** *(calificar, considerar)* to consider, call: *lo trató de idiota* she called him an idiot. **6** MED to treat. **7** *(datos, texto)* to process. **8** QUÍM to treat.
▶ *vi* **1** *(relacionarse)* to be acquainted (con, with), know (con, -). **2** *(tener tratos)* to deal (con, with). **3** *(negociar)* to negotiate (con, with). **4** *(intentar)* to try (de, to): *trata de hacerlo* try to do it. **5** *(versar)* to be about: *trata de/sobre espías* it's about spies.
▶ *vpr* **tratarse 1** *(relacionarse)* to talk to each other, be on speaking terms: *no se tratan* they're not on speaking terms. **2** *(llamarse)* to address each other as, call each other. **3** *(referirse)* to be about: *se trataba de un atraco* it was about a robbery.

T

trato *nm* **1** *(acción)* treatment. **2** *(modales)* manner. **3** *(contacto)* contact. **4** *(acuerdo)* agreement. **5** COM deal. **6** *(tratamiento)* title. LOC **cerrar un trato** to close a deal. ‖ **¡trato hecho!** it's a deal!

trauma *nm* trauma.

traumático,-a *adj* traumatic.

traumatismo *nm* traumatism.

traumatizar *vt* **1** MED to traumatize. **2** *fam* to shock.

través *nm* **1** *(inclinación)* slant. **2** *(pieza de madera)* crosspiece, crossbeam. **3** MAR beam. **4** *fig (desgracia)* misfortune. LOC **a través de 1** *(de un lado a otro)* across, over. **2** *(por dentro)* through. **3** *(mediante)* through, from.

travesaño *nm* **1** ARQUIT crosspiece. **2** DEP crossbar.

travesía *nf* **1** *(viaje)* crossing; *(por mar)* voyage, crossing. **2** *(calle)* cross-street, passage. **3** *(distancia)* distance.

travesura *nf* piece of mischief, childish prank. LOC **hacer travesuras** to get into mischief.

traviesa *nf* **1** *(de ferrocarril)* sleeper, US tie. **2** *(en construcción)* trimmer.

travieso,-a *adj* mischievous, naughty.

trayecto *nm* **1** *(distancia)* distance, way. **2** *(recorrido)* route, itinerary.

trayectoria *nf* **1** trajectory. **2** *fig* line, course, path.

traza *nf fig (apariencia)* looks *pl*, appearance.

trazado *nm* **1** *(plano)* layout, plan. **2** *(dibujo)* drawing, sketch. **3** *(de carretera, ferrocarril)* route, course.

trazar *vt* **1** *(línea, plano, dibujo)* to draw, draw up. **2** *(parque)* to lay out; *(edificio)* to design. **3** *(itinerario)* to trace. **4** *fig (plan, etc)* to outline, draft.

trazo *nm* **1** *(línea)* line. **2** *(de una letra)* stroke. **3** *fig (rasgo facial)* feature.

trébol *nm* **1** *(planta)* clover, trefoil. **2** *(naipes)* club.

trece *adj (cardinal)* thirteen; *(ordinal)* thirteenth.
▸ *nm (número)* thirteen; *(fecha)* thirteenth.

✎ Consulta también **seis**.

treceavo,-a *adj* thirteenth.
▸ *nm & nf* thirteenth.

✎ Consulta también **sexto,-a**.

trecho *nm* **1** *(espacio)* distance, way; *(tiempo)* while, time. **2** *(de camino, ruta)* stretch. **3** AGR plot, patch. **4** *fam (parte)* piece, bit.

tregua *nf* **1** truce. **2** *fig* respite, rest.

treinta *adj (cardinal)* thirty; *(ordinal)* thirtieth.
▸ *nm (número)* thirty; *(fecha)* thirtieth.

✎ Consulta también **seis**.

treintañero,-a *adj* thirty-year-old.
▸ *nm & nf* thirty-year-old person.

treintavo,-a *adj* thirtieth.
▸ *nm & nf* thirtieth.

✎ Consulta también **sexto,-a**.

treintena *nf (exacto)* thirty; *(aproximado)* about thirty.

tremendo,-a *adj* **1** *(terrible)* terrible, dreadful, frightful. **2** *(muy grande)* huge, enormous, tremendous. **3** *(travieso)* terrible. LOC **tomarse** ALGO **por la tremenda** *fig* to make a great fuss about STH.

trementina *nf* turpentine.

tremolar *vt* to wave.
▸ *vi* to wave, flutter.

trémulo,-a *adj* **1** *(tembloroso)* tremulous, quivering. **2** *(luz, llama)* flickering.

tren *nm* **1** *(ferrocarril)* train. **2** *(conjunto de máquinas)* convoy, line. **3** *fig (ritmo, modo)* speed, pace. LOC **coger el tren / tomar el tren** to catch a train. COMP **tren de alta velocidad** high-speed train.

trenca *nf (abrigo)* duffel coat, duffle coat.

trenza *nf* **1** *(peluquería)* plait, US braid. **2** COST braid.

trenzado *nm* **1** *(trenza - de pelo)* plait, US braid; *(- de costura)* braid. **2** *(en danza)* entrechat. **3** *(de caballo)* crossover step.

trenzar *vt* **1** to plait, braid. **2** *(peluquería)* to plait, US braid.

trepador,-ra *adj (planta)* climbing.
▶ *nm & nf fam pey* go-getter, social climber.

trepanación *nf* trepanation, trephination.

trepanar *vi* to trepan, trephine.

trépano *nm* **1** MED trephine. **2** TÉC bit.

trepar¹ *vt (escalar)* to climb.
▶ *vi (escalar)* to climb.

trepar² *vt* **1** *(taladrar)* to drill. **2** *(un bordado)* to trim.

trepidante *adj* **1** vibrating, shaking. **2** *fig (vida, etc)* hectic, frantic.

trepidar *vi* to vibrate, shake.

tres *adj (cardinal)* three; *(ordinal)* third.
▶ *nm (número)* three; *(fecha)* third. COMP **tres en raya** noughts and crosses, US tick-tack-toe.

✎ Consulta también **seis**.

trescientos,-as *adj (cardinal)* three hundred; *(ordinal)* three hundredth.
▶ *nm (número)* three hundred.

✎ Consulta también **seis**.

tresillo *nm (mueble)* suite, three-piece suite.

treta *nf* trick, ruse.

tríada *nf* triad.

triangular *adj* triangular.

triángulo,-a *adj* triangular.
▶ *nm* **triángulo** triangle. COMP **triángulo equilátero** equilateral triangle. ‖ **triángulo isósceles** isosceles triangle. ‖ **triángulo rectángulo** right-angled triangle.

triatlón *nm* triathlon.

tribal *adj* tribal, tribe.

tribu *nf* tribe.

tribuna *nf* **1** *(plataforma)* rostrum, dais. **2** DEP grandstand.

tribunal *nm* **1** JUR court. **2** *(de examen)* board of examiners. LOC **llevar a los tribunales** to take to court. COMP **Tribunal Supremo** High Court, US Supreme Court.

tributación *nf* taxation, levy.

tributar *vt* to pay.

tributario,-a *adj* tributary, tax.
▶ *nm & nf* taxpayer.

tributo *nm* **1** *(impuesto)* tax. **2** *(a cambio de algo)* tribute. **3** *fig (carga)* price. **4** *fig (de sentimiento)* token.

tricéfalo,-a *adj* tricephalous.

tríceps *nm inv* triceps.

triciclo *nm* tricycle.

tricornio *nm (sombrero)* three-cornered hat.

tricotar *vt* to knit.

tridente *nm* trident.

tridimensional *adj* three-dimensional.

triedro *nm* trihedron.

trienal *adj* triennial.

trienio *nm* triennium.

trifásico,-a *adj* ELEC three-phase.

trigal *nm* wheat field.

trigésimo,-a *adj* thirtieth.
▶ *nm & nf* thirtieth.

✎ Consulta también **sexto,-a**.

triglifo *nm* triglyph.

trigo *nm (cereal)* wheat.

trigonometría *nf* trigonometry.

trigonométrico,-a *adj* trigonometric, trigonometrical.

trigueño,-a *adj* **1** *(pelo)* corn-coloured (US corn-colored), dark blonde. **2** *(piel)* dark, swarthy. **3** *(persona)* olive-skinned.

triguero,-a *adj* wheat.

trilateral *adj* three-sided, trilateral.

trilingüe *adj* trilingual.

trilita *nf* TNT, trinitrotoluene.

trilla *nf* threshing.

trillado,-a *adj* **1** *(camino)* beaten, well-trodden. **2** *fig (expresión, etc)* overworked, well-worn.

trilladora *nf* threshing machine.

trillar *vt* **1** to thresh. **2** *fig* to wear out.

trillizo,-a *nm & nf* triplet.

trilogía *nf* trilogy.

trimestral *adj* quarterly, three-monthly, trimestral.

T

trimestre *nm* **1** quarter, trimester. **2** EDUC term.

trimotor *nm* three-engined aircraft.

trinar *vi* **1** *(ave)* to warble, trill. **2** MÚS to trill. **3** *fam (enfadarse)* to rage, fume: *Pedro está que trina* Pedro is fuming.

trinchar *vt* to carve, slice (up).

trinchera *nf* trench.

trineo *nm* sleigh, sled, sledge.

Trinidad *nf* Trinidad. COMP **Trinidad y Tobago** Trinidad and Tobago.

trinitrotolueno *nm* trinitrotoluene.

trino *nm* **1** *(ave)* warble, trill. **2** MÚS trill.

trino,-a *adj* trine.

trinomio *nm* trinomial.

trinquete¹ *nm (lengüeta)* pawl; *(mecanismo)* ratchet.

trinquete² *nm* **1** *(frontón)* pelota court. **2** MAR *(palo)* foremast; *(vela)* foresail.

trío *nm* trio.

tripa *nf* **1** *(intestino)* gut, intestine. **2** *(barriga)* gut, stomach. **3** *(de vasija)* belly. **4** *fam (embarazo)* belly.
▶ *nf pl* **tripas** *fam (interior)* innards.

tripartito,-a *adj* tripartite.

triple *adj* **1** triple. **2** *(tres veces)* three times: *pagamos el triple del precio real* we paid three times the real price.
▶ *nm* triple. COMP **triple salto** triple jump.

triplicado *nm* triplicate.

triplicar *vt* to triple, treble.

trípode *nm* tripod.

tríptico *nm* triptych.

triptongo *nm* triphthong.

tripulación *nf* crew.

tripulante *nm* crew member.

tripular *vt* to man.

tris *nm fam fig* bit; *(sonido)* crack. LOC **en un tris** *fam* in a jiffy: *lo hizo en un tris* he did it in a jiffy.

trisílabo,-a *adj* trisyllabic.
▶ *nm* **trisílabo** trisyllable.

triste *adj* **1** *(infeliz)* sad, unhappy; *(futuro)* bleak. **2** *(oscuro, sombrío)* gloomy, dismal. **3** *(único)* single, only: *ni un triste libro* not a single book. **4** *(insignificante)* poor, humble. LOC **es triste que...** it's a pity...: *es triste que no los podamos ayudar* it's a pity we can't help them.

tristeza *nf* sadness.
▶ *nf pl* **tristezas** problems, sufferings.

tristón,-ona *adj fam* gloomy, sad, melancholy.

tritón *nm* **1** *(anfibio)* newt. **2** Tritón *(mitología)* Triton.

triturado,-a *adj* **1** ground, crushed. **2** *fig* crumpled up.

triturador,-ra *adj* grinding, crushing, triturating.
▶ *nm* **triturador** waste disposal unit, US garbage disposal unit.

trituradora *nf* grinder, crushing machine. COMP **trituradora de papel** paper shredder.

triturar *vt* **1** to grind (up), crush; *(papel)* to shred. **2** *fig (físicamente)* to beat (up); *(moralmente)* to tear apart.

triunfador,-ra *adj* winning.
▶ *nm & nf* winner.

triunfal *adj* triumphant.

triunfalismo *nm* **1** triumphalism. **2** POL jingoism.

triunfalista *adj* **1** triumphalist. **2** POL jingoistic.
▶ *nm o nf* **1** triumphalist. **2** POL jingoist.

triunfar *vi* to triumph. LOC **triunfar en la vida** to succeed in life.

triunfo *nm* **1** *(victoria)* triumph, victory. **2** DEP win. **3** *(éxito)* success. **4** *(naipes)* trump.

trivial *adj* trivial, petty.

trivialidad *nf* triviality, pettiness.

trivializar *vt* to trivialize, minimize.

triza *nf* bit, fragment. LOC **estar hecho, -a trizas** *fam* to feel washed out.

trocar *vt* **1** *(permutar)* to exchange, swap: *trocar un lápiz por un bolígrafo* to exchange a pencil for a biro. **2** *(transformar)* to turn (en, into), convert (en, into).

trocear *vt* to cut up.

trofeo *nm* trophy.

trófico,-a *adj* food.

troglodita *nm o nf* troglodyte.

trolebús *nm* trolley bus.

tromba *nf* waterspout. COMP **tromba de agua** downpour.

trombo *nm* thrombus.

trombón *nm* MÚS trombone.
▶ *nm o nf* trombonist. COMP **trombón de varas** slide trombone.

trombosis *nf inv* thrombosis.

trompa *nf* **1** MÚS horn. **2** *(de elefante)* trunk. **3** *(de insecto)* proboscis. **4** ANAT tube. **5** *fam fig (nariz)* hooter, snout. LOC **estar trompa** *fam* to be plastered. COMP **trompa de Eustaquio** Eustachian tube. ‖ **trompa de Falopio** Fallopian tube.
▶ *nm o nf* MÚS horn player.

trompazo *nm* bump. LOC **darse un trompazo** to have a bump, have a crash.

trompeta *nf* MÚS trumpet.
▶ *nm o nf* trumpet player.

trompetista *nm o nf* trumpet player, trumpeter.

trompicón *nm* **1** *(tropezón)* trip, stumble. **2** *(golpe)* blow, hit. LOC **a trompicones** in fits and starts.

trompo *nm* top, spinning top.

tronar *vi* **1** [se usa sólo en tercera persona; no lleva sujeto] *(trueno)* to thunder. **2** *(cañón, etc)* to thunder.

tronchar *vt* **1** *(árboles)* to cut down, fell. **2** *fig* to destroy. LOC **troncharse de risa** *fam* to split one's sides with laughter.

troncho *adj* stem, stalk.

tronco *nm* **1** ANAT trunk, torso. **2** BOT *(tallo de árbol)* trunk; *(leño)* log. **3** *fig (linaje)* family stock. **4** *fig (persona inútil)* blockhead. **5** *(geometría)* frustum. **6** *argot (compañero)* mate, pal, chum. LOC **dormir como un tronco** *fam* to sleep like a log. COMP **tronco de cono** truncated cone.

tronera *nf* **1** *(de fortificación)* loophole, embrasure. **2** *(de barco)* porthole. **3** *(de billar)* pocket.

trono *nm* throne.

tropa *nf* **1** MIL troops *pl*, soldiers *pl*. **2** *(muchedumbre)* crowd.

▶ *nf pl* **tropas** MIL troops, fighting soldiers.

tropel *nm* throng, mob. LOC **en tropel** in a mad rush.

tropelía *nf* **1** *(atropello)* outrage. **2** *(tropel)* throng, mob. **3** *(delito)* crime.

tropezar *vi* **1** *(trompicar)* to trip, stumble: *tropezó con mi pie* he tripped over my foot. **2** *fig (encontrar a alguien)* to come (con, across), bump (con, into). **3** *fig (encontrar dificultades, etc)* to come up (con, against), run (con, into).

tropezón *nm* **1** *(traspié)* trip, stumble. **2** *fig (error)* slip-up, faux pas. **3** *fam (de comida)* chunk of food. LOC **dar un tropezón** to trip.

tropical *adj* tropical.

trópico *nm* tropic.
▶ *nm pl* **trópicos** tropics.

tropiezo *nm* **1** *(obstáculo)* trip. **2** *fig (error)* blunder; *(revés)* setback, mishap. **3** *(riña)* quarrel.

tropismo *nm* tropism.

tropo *nm* trope.

troposfera *nf* troposphere.

troquel *nm* die.

troqueladora *nf* stamping machine.

troquelar *vt (gen)* to stamp; *(monedas)* to strike; *(cuero)* to emboss.

trotamundos *nm o nf inv* globe-trotter; *(mochilero)* backpacker.

trotar *vi* **1** to trot. **2** *fig (andar)* to bustle, run, run about.

trote *nm* **1** *(de caballo)* trot. **2** *fam fig (actividad)* chasing about, hustle and bustle, bustle. LOC **al trote** at a trot.

trovador,-ra *nm & nf* troubadour, minstrel.

trozo *nm* piece, chunk.

trucaje *nm* trick photography.

trucar *vt* **1** *(foto, etc)* to doctor, alter, tamper with. **2** AUTO to soup up.

trucha *nf* trout.

truco *nm* **1** *(ardid)* trick. **2** *(fotográfico)* trick effect, trick camera shot. **3** *(tranquillo)* knack. LOC **coger el truco a ALGO** *fam* to get the knack of STH, get the hang of STH.

T

truculencia *nf* **1** cruelty. **2** *fig* sensationalism.

truculento,-a *adj* **1** *(cruel)* cruel. **2** *fig (excesivo)* sensationalistic.

trueno *nm* **1** thunder, thunderclap. **2** *fam (joven)* hare brain.

trueque *nm* exchange, swap.

trufa *nf* **1** *(hongo)* truffle. **2** *(de chocolate)* chocolate truffle.

trufar *vt* to stuff with truffles.
▶ *vi fig* to tell lies.*f*

truhan,-ana *nm & nf* rogue, crook.

truncado,-a *adj (geometría)* truncated.

truncar *vt* **1** *(cortar)* to truncate. **2** *fig (ilusiones, esperanzas)* to shatter, cut short. **3** *fig (escrito)* to leave unfinished; *(sentido)* to upset.
▶ *vpr* **truncarse** *fig (ilusiones, etc)* to cut short.

trust *nm* trust, cartel.

tu *adj* your: *tu coche* your car; *tus coches* your cars.

tú *pron* **1** you. **2** REL Thou. LOC **tratar de tú** to address as *tú*.

tuareg *adj* Tuareg.
▶ *nm* Tuareg.

tuba *nf* tuba.

tubérculo *nm* **1** BOT tuber. **2** MED tubercle.

tuberculosis *nf inv* tuberculosis.

tuberculoso,-a *adj* **1** BOT tuberous. **2** MED tubercular, tuberculous.

tubería *nf* **1** *(de agua)* piping, pipes *pl*, plumbing. **2** *(de gas, petróleo)* pipeline.

tuberoso,-a *adj* tuberous.

tubo *nm* **1** *(de ensayo, etc)* tube. **2** *(tubería)* pipe. **3** ANAT tube. COMP **tubo de ensayo** test tube. ‖ **tubo de escape** exhaust pipe, exhaust. ‖ **tubo digestivo** alimentary canal.

tubular *adj* tubular.
▶ *nm* bicycle tyre.

tucán *nm* toucan.

tuerca *nf* nut.

tuerto,-a *adj* one-eyed, blind in one eye.
▶ *nm & nf* one-eyed person.

tuétano *nm* **1** marrow. **2** *fig* essence, core.

tufo *nm* **1** *(mal olor)* pong, foul smell, stink. **2** *(emanación)* fume, vapour (US vapor).

tugurio *nm* **1** *(choza)* shepherd's hut. **2** *(casucha)* hovel, shack. **3** *fig* hole, dive.

tul *nm* tulle.

tulipa *nf* **1** *(bot)* small tulip. **2** *(lámpara)* tulip-shaped lampshade.

tulipán *nm* tulip.

tullido,-a *adj* crippled, disabled.
▶ *nm & nf* cripple.

tumbado,-a *adj (estirado)* lying, stretched out: *tumbado al sol* lying in the sun.

tumbar *vt* **1** *(derribar)* to knock out, knock over. **2** EDUC *fam* to fail.
▶ *vpr* **tumbarse** *(acostarse)* to lie down, stretch out.

tumbo *nm* jolt, bump. LOC **dar tumbos** to jolt, bump along.

tumbona *nf* **1** *(hamaca)* deck-chair. **2** *(silla extensible)* lounger.

tumor *nm* tumour (US tumor).

túmulo *nm* **1** *(montecillo)* tumulus, burial mound, barrow. **2** *(catafalco)* catafalque.

tumulto *nm* tumult, commotion.

tumultuoso,-a *adj* tumultuous, riotous.

tuna *nf* student minstrel group.

tunda *nf* **1** *fam* thrashing, beating. **2** *fig (trabajo agotador)* exhausting job, drag.

tundra *nf* tundra.

tunecino,-a *adj* Tunisian.
▶ *nm & nf* Tunisian.

túnel *nm* tunnel.

Túnez *nm* **1** *(ciudad)* Tunis. **2** *(país)* Tunisia.

tungsteno *nm* tungsten.

túnica *nf* tunic.

tuno *nm* BOT prickly pear.

tupí *adj* Tupi.
▶ *nm & nf* Tupi.
▶ *nm (idioma)* Tupi.

tupido,-a *adj* **1** dense, thick. **2** *fig (torpe)* clumsy, dense.

tupir *vi (apretar)* to pack tight, press down.
  ▶ *vpr* **tupirse 1** *(comiendo)* to stuff os. **2** *(ofuscarse)* to get muddled up, get in a muddle.

turba[1] *nf* **1** *(combustible)* peat, turf. **2** *(abono)* peat, peat moss.

turba[2] *nf (muchedumbre)* mob, crowd.

turbación *nf* **1** *(alteración)* disturbance. **2** *(preocupación)* anxiety, worry. **3** *(desconcierto)* confusion, uneasiness.

turbado,-a *adj* **1** *(alterado)* disturbed, unsettled. **2** *(preocupado)* worried, upset. **3** *(desconcertado)* confused.

turbador,-ra *adj* **1** *(que altera)* disturbing, unsettling. **2** *(preocupante)* worrying, upsetting. **3** *(desconcertante)* confusing, disconcerting.

turbante *nm* turban.

turbar *vt* **1** *(alterar)* to unsettle, disturb. **2** *(enturbiar)* to stir up. **3** *(preocupar)* to upset, worry. **4** *(desconcertar)* to baffle, put off.
  ▶ *vpr* **turbarse 1** *(preocuparse)* to be upset, become upset. **2** *(desconcertarse)* to be confused, be baffled.

turbera *nf* peat bog.

turbina *nf* turbine.

turbio,-a *adj* **1** *(oscurecido)* cloudy, muddy, turbid. **2** *fig (dudoso)* shady, dubious. **3** *fig (turbulento)* turbulent. **4** *fig (confuso)* confused. **5** *fig (vista)* blurred.

turbo *nm* turbo.

turbogenerador *nm* turbogenerator.

turbohélice *nm* turboprop.

turborreactor *nm* turbojet, turbojet engine.

turbulencia *nf* turbulence.

turbulento,-a *adj* turbulent, troubled.

turco,-a *adj* Turkish.
  ▶ *nm & nf (persona)* Turk.
  ▶ *nm* **turco** *(idioma)* Turkish.

turgencia *nf* turgidity, turgidness.

turgente *adj* turgid.

turismo *nm* **1** *(gen)* tourism. **2** *(industria)* tourist trade, tourist industry. **3** AUTO private car, saloon. LOC **hacer**

turismo 1 *(país)* to go touring. **2** *(ciudad, pueblo)* to go sightseeing.

turista *nm o nf* tourist.

turístico,-a *adj* tourist. LOC **de interés turístico** of interest to tourists.

Turkmenistán *nm* Turkmenistan.

túrmix® *nm inv* liquidizer, blender.

turnar *vi* to alternate.
  ▶ *vpr* **turnarse** to take turns.

turno *nm* **1** *(tanda)* turn, go: *es mi turno* it's my turn; *¿a quién le toca el turno?* who's next? **2** *(período de trabajo)* shift. LOC **estar de turno** to be on duty. COMP **turno de día / turno de noche** day shift / night shift.

turquesa *adj* turquoise.
  ▶ *nf (piedra)* turquoise.
  ▶ *nm (color)* turquoise.

Turquía *nf* Turkey.

turrón *nm type of* nougat.

turronería *nf* shop selling nougat.

tute *nm* **1** *(naipes)* card game. **2** *fig (esfuerzo)* beating, thrashing.

tutear *vt* **1** to address as *tú*. **2** *fig* to be on familiar terms with.
  ▶ *vpr* **tutearse** *(uso recíproco)* to address each other as *tú*.

tutela *nf* **1** JUR guardianship, tutelage. **2** *fig* protection, guidance. LOC **bajo la tutela de** under the protection of.

tutelar *adj* tutelary.

tuteo *nm* use of the *tú* form of address.

tutor,-ra *nm & nf* **1** JUR guardian. **2** *fig* protector, guide. **3** EDUC tutor.
  ▶ *nm* **tutor** AGR stake, prop.

tutoría *nf* **1** JUR guardianship, tutelage. **2** EDUC post of tutor.

Tuvalu *nm* Tuvalu.

tuyo,-a *adj* of yours, one of your: *¿es primo tuyo?* is he a cousin of yours?, is he your cousin?
  ▶ *pron* yours, your own: *el tuyo está allí* yours is there.
  ▶ *nm* **lo tuyo** *(lo que es tuyo)* what is yours; *(lo que te concierne)* your business, your own business.
  ▶ *nm pl* **los tuyos** *(familiares)* your family *sing*; *(amigos)* your friends.

T

U

U, u *nf (la letra)* U, u.
u [se usa ante palabras que empiezan por o u ho] *conj* or: *diez u once* ten or eleven.

✎ Consulta también **o**.

ubre *nf* udder.
ucraniano,-a *adj* Ukrainian.
▶ *nm & nf (persona)* Ukrainian.
Uganda *nf* Uganda.
ugandés,-esa *adj* Ugandan.
▶ *nm & nf* Ugandan.
úlcera *nf* ulcer. COMP **úlcera de estómago** stomach ulcer.
ulceración *nf* ulceration.
ultimar *vt* to finish, complete.
ultimátum *nm inv* **1** ultimatum. **2** *fam* final word.
último,-a *adj* **1** last. **2** *(más reciente)* latest; *(de dos)* latter. **3** *(más alejado)* furthest; *(más abajo)* bottom, lowest; *(más arriba)* top; *(más atrás)* back. **4** *(definitivo)* final. LOC **por último** finally.
ultraje *nm* outrage, insult.
ultraligero *adj* ultralight.
▶ *nm* **ultraligero** *(avión)* microlight.
ultramar *nm* overseas: *viene de ultramar* it comes from overseas, it's imported.
ultramarino,-a *adj* overseas.
▶ *nm pl* **ultramarinos** groceries.
ultrasonido *nm* ultrasound.
ultravioleta *adj inv* ultraviolet.
ulular *vi* **1** *(animal)* to howl; *(búho)* to hoot. **2** *fig* to howl.
umbilical *adj* umbilical.
umbral *nm* **1** threshold. **2** *fig* threshold, outset.
un,-na *art indef* a, an: *un libro* a book; *un ojo* an eye.

▶ *adj* **1** *(numeral)* one: *tiene un año* he's one year old. **2** *(indef)* some: *un día volverá* he'll come some day.

✎ Consulta también **uno,-a**.

unánime *adj* unanimous.
unanimidad *nf* unanimity.
undécimo,-a *adj* eleventh.
▶ *nm & nf (ordinal, partitivo)* eleventh.

✎ Consulta también **sexto,-a**.

ungüento *nm* ointment.
ungulado,-a *adj* ungulate, hoofed.
▶ *nm* **ungulado** ungulate.
unicelular *adj* unicellular, single-cell.
único,-a *adj* **1** *(solo)* only, sole: *la única persona* the only person. **2** *(extraordinario)* unique.
unicornio *nm* unicorn.
unidad *nf* **1** unit. **2** *(barco)* vessel; *(avión)* aircraft; *(de tren)* carriage, coach. **3** *(cohesión)* unity.
unido,-a *adj* **1** *(junto)* united. **2** *(avenido)* attached: *estar muy unidos* to be very close.
unifamiliar COMP **vivienda unifamiliar** detached house.
unificación *nf* unification.
unificador,-ra *adj* unifying.
▶ *nm & nf* unifier.
unificar *vt* to unify.
uniformado,-a *adj* in uniform.
uniformar *vt* **1** *(igualar)* to make uniform, standardize. **2** *(poner un uniforme)* to put into uniform, give a uniform.
uniforme *adj* **1** uniform. **2** *(superficie)* even.
▶ *nm (prenda)* uniform.
uniformidad *nf* **1** *(igualdad)* uniformity. **2** *(de superficie)* evenness.
uniformizar *vt* to standardize.
unilateral *adj* unilateral.

unión *nf* **1** union. **2** TÉC *(acoplamiento)* joining; *(junta)* joint.

unir *vt* **1** *(juntar)* to unite, join. **2** *(combinar)* to combine (a, with).

unitario,-a *adj* unitary.

univalvo,-a *adj* univalve.

universal *adj* universal.

universidad *nf* university.

universitario,-a *adj* university.
 ► *nm & nf (que está estudiando)* university student; *(licenciado)* university graduate.

universo *nm* universe.

unívoco,-a *adj* univocal.

uno,-a *adj (numeral)* one: *el número uno* number one.
 ► *pron* **1** one: *uno (de ellos)* one of them. **2** *(impersonal)* one, you: *uno tiene que velar por sus intereses* one has to look after one's own interests. **3** *fam (persona)* someone, somebody: *estaba hablando con una* he was talking to some woman.
 ► *nm* **uno** *(número)* one.
 ► *nf* **la una** *(hora)* one o'clock.
 ► *adj vpr* **unos,-as** *(indefinido)* some; *(aproximado)* about, around: *unas cajas* some boxes; *habrá unos treinta* there must be around thirty. LOC **a (la) una** together. **I de uno,-a en uno,-a** one by one.

untar *vt* **1** to grease, smear: *untar pan con mantequilla* to spread butter on bread. **2** *fam (sobornar)* to bribe.

uña *nf* **1** nail; *(del dedo)* fingernail; *(del dedo del pie)* toenail. **2** *(garra)* claw; *(pezuña)* hoof.

uralita® *nf* uralite.

uranio *nm* uranium.

Urano *nm* Uranus.

urbanismo *nm* town planning.

urbanización *nf* **1** *(proceso)* urbanization. **2** *(conjunto residencial)* housing development, housing estate.

urbanizar *vt* to urbanize, develop.

urbano,-a *adj* urban, city.

urbe *nf* large city, metropolis.

uréter *nm* ureter.

uretra *nf* urethra.

urgencia *nf* urgency, emergency.
 ► *nf pl* **urgencias** *(servicio)* casualty department *sing*, casualty *sing*, US emer-

gency room. LOC **en (un) caso de urgencia** in an emergency.

urgente *adj* **1** urgent. **2** *(correo)* express (post, US mail), first-class (post, US mail).

urgir *vi* to be urgent, be pressing.

urinario,-a *adj* urinary.
 ► *nm* **urinario** *(retrete)* urinal.

urna *nf* **1** POL ballot box. **2** *(vasija)* urn. **3** *(caja)* glass case.

urraca *nf* **1** magpie. **2** *fig (cotorra)* chatterbox.

urticaria *nf* hives *pl*, urticaria.

Uruguay *nm* Uruguay.

uruguayo,-a *adj* Uruguayan.
 ► *nm & nf* Uruguayan.

usado,-a *adj* **1** *(gastado)* worn out, old. **2** *(de segunda mano)* second-hand, used.

usar *vt* **1** to use. **2** *(prenda)* to wear.
 ► *vi* to use (de, -).
 ► *vpr* **usarse** *(estar de moda)* to be used, be in fashion.

uso *nm* **1** use. **2** *(ejercicio)* exercise. **3** *(de prenda)* wearing. **4** *(costumbre)* usage, custom. **5** GRAM usage.

usted *pron fml* you.

usual *adj* usual, common.

usuario,-a *nm & nf* user.

usurero,-a *nm & nf* usurer.

usurpar *vt* to usurp.

utensilio *nm* **1** *(herramienta)* tool, utensil. **2** *(aparato)* device, implement.

uterino,-a *adj* uterine.

útero *nm* uterus, womb.

útil¹ *adj* useful.

útil² *nm (herramienta)* tool, instrument.

utilidad *nf* **1** utility, usefulness. **2** *(beneficio)* profit.

utilitario,-a *adj* utilitarian.
 ► *nm* **utilitario** *(coche)* utility vehicle.

utilizar *vt* to use, make use of.

utopía *nf* utopia.

utópico,-a *adj* utopian.

uva *nf* grape.

uve *nf* name of the letter v.

uzbeco,-a *adj* Uzbek.
 ► *nm & nf (persona)* Uzbek.
 ► *nm* **uzbeco** *(idioma)* Uzbek.

Uzbekistán *nm* Uzbekistan.

U

V

V, v *nf (la letra)* V, v.

V *sím* **(voltio)** volt; *(símbolo)* V.

vaca *nf* **1** *(animal)* cow. **2** *(carne)* beef. **3** *(cuero)* cowhide.

vacaciones *nf pl* holiday, holidays *pl*, US vacation: *se fueron de vacaciones a Mallorca* they went to Majorca for their holidays. LOC **irse de vacaciones** to go on holiday.

vacante *adj* vacant.
▶ *nf* vacancy.

vaciar *vt* **1** *(recipiente)* to empty; *(local)* to empty, clear. **2** *(contenido)* to pour away. **3** *(dejar hueco)* to hollow out. **4** *(moldear)* to cast, mould (US mold).

vacilación *nf* **1** *(duda)* hesitation. **2** *(oscilación)* swaying, vacillation.

vacilar *vi* **1** *(oscilar)* to sway, vacillate. **2** *(estar poco firme)* to wobble. **3** *(al andar)* to sway, stagger; *(al hablar)* to falter. **4** *(luz)* to flicker. **5** *fig (dudar)* to hesitate, waver. **6** *fam (tomar el pelo)* to joke, tease: *¡no me vaciles!* don't tease me! **7** *fam (presumir)* to show off.

vacío,-a *adj* **1** *(gen)* empty: *el cine está vacío* the cinema is empty. **2** *(no ocupado)* vacant, unoccupied; *(sin muebles)* unfurnished. **3** *(hueco)* hollow.
▶ *nm* **vacío 1** *(gen)* emptiness, void. **2** *(hueco)* gap; *(espacio)* space, empty space; *(espacio en blanco)* blank space. **3** *(vacante)* vacancy. **4** FÍS vacuum. **5** *fig (falta)* emptiness, void.

vacuna *nf* MED vaccine.

vacunación *nf* MED vaccination.

vado *nm* **1** *(de río)* ford. **2** *(de acera)* dropped kerb. COMP **«Vado permanente»** "Keep clear".

vagabundo,-a *adj* **1** wandering, roving. **2** *pey* vagrant.

▶ *nm & nf* **1** *(trotamundos)* wanderer, rover. **2** *pey* vagrant, tramp, US hobo. **3** *(sin casa)* tramp, US hobo.

vagar¹ *vi (estar ocioso)* to idle about.

vagar² *vi (errar)* to wander (por, about), roam (por, about): *pasa su tiempo vagando por el pueblo* he spends his time wandering about town.

vago,-a¹ *adj* **1** *(vacío)* empty; *(desocupado)* vacant. **2** *(holgazán)* lazy, idle.

vago,-a² *adj (impreciso)* vague: *idea vaga* vague idea.

vagón *nm* **1** *(para pasajeros)* carriage, coach, US car. **2** *(para mercancías)* wagon, goods van, truck, US boxcar.

vaho *nm* **1** *(vapor)* vapour (US vapor), steam. **2** *(aliento)* breath.

vaina *nf* **1** *(de espada, etc)* sheath. **2** *(de instrumento, etc)* case. **3** BOT pod.

vainilla *nf* vanilla.

vajilla *nf* tableware, dishes *pl*, crockery. COMP **una vajilla** a dinner service.

vale *nm* **1** *(comprobante)* voucher; *(recibo)* receipt. **2** *(pagaré)* promissory note.
▶ *interj fam* OK!

valedor,-ra *nm & nf* protector.

valentía *nf (valor)* bravery, courage.

valer *vt* **1** *(tener un valor de)* to be worth: *no vale nada* it is worthless. **2** *(costar)* to cost, be: *vale siete euros el kilo* it costs seven euros a kilo **3** *(hacer merecedor)* to win, earn, get: *el suspenso le valió un rapapolvo* failing the exam earned him a good ticking-off. **4** *(ocasionar)* to cause: *me ha valido muchos problemas* he's caused me a lot of problems. **5** MAT to equal.
▶ *vi* **1** *(tener un valor de)* to be worth. **2** *(ser útil, adecuado)* to be useful, be of use, be good for: *¿te vale este libro?* is this book any use (to you)? **3** *(costar)* to cost,

be worth. **4** *(ser válido, contar)* to count. **5** *(tener validez)* to be valid; *(monedas)* to be legal tender: *ese billete aún vale* that ticket is still valid. **6** *(ser suficiente, bastar)* to do, be enough: *con esto ya me vale* this will be enough for me. **7** *(estar permitido)* to be allowed, be permitted.
▶ *nm (valía)* value.
▶ *vpr* **valerse 1** *(utilizar)* to use (de, of), make use (de, of): *se valió de un bastón* he used a stick. **2** *(espabilarse)* to manage, cope. ⎡LOC⎤ **valerse por sí mismo** to be able to manage on one's own.

valeroso,-a *adj* courageous, brave.

validez *nf* validity.

válido,-a *adj* valid.

valiente *adj* **1** *(valeroso)* brave, courageous, bold. **2** *(fuerte)* strong.

valioso,-a *adj* valuable, precious.

valla *nf* **1** *(cerca)* fence; *(construcción)* wall. **2** MIL stockade. **3** DEP hurdle. **4** *(para publicidad)* hoarding, US billboard. **5** *fig* obstacle. ⎡COMP⎤ **valla publicitaria** hoarding, US billboard.

vallado *nm* **1** *(cerca)* fence. **2** MIL stockade.

vallar *vt* to fence (in).

valle *nm* valley.

valor *nm* **1** *(valía)* value, worth, merit: *una persona de gran valor* a person of great merit. **2** *(precio)* price. **3** *(validez)* value: *estas monedas dejarán de tener valor muy pronto* these coins will soon be of no value. **4** *(importancia)* importance. **5** *(coraje)* courage. **6** MAT value.
▶ *nm pl* **valores 1** FIN securities, bonds. **2** *(principios)* values.

valorar *vt* **1** *(tasar)* to value, calculate the value of. **2** *(aumentar el valor)* to raise the value of.

vals *nm* waltz.

válvula *nf* valve. ⎡COMP⎤ **válvula de seguridad** safety valve.

vampiro *nm* **1** *(espectro)* vampire. **2** *(mamífero)* vampire bat. **3** *fig* parasite.

vandalismo *nm* vandalism.

vándalo,-a *adj* Vandal.
▶ *nm & nf* **1** Vandal. **2** *fig* vandal.

vanidad *nf* vanity, conceit.

vanidoso,-a *adj* vain, conceited.

Vanuatu *nm* Vanuatu.

vapor *nm* **1** *(gas)* vapour (US vapor), steam. **2** *(barco)* steamship, steamer. ⎡LOC⎤ **al vapor** CULIN steamed. ⎡COMP⎤ **vapor de agua** water vapour (US vapor).

vaquero,-a *adj* cow, cattle.
▶ *nm & nf (pastor)* cowherd, US cowboy; *(pastora)* cowherd, US cowgirl.
▶ *nm pl* **vaqueros** *(pantalones)* jeans, pair of jeans.

vara *nf* **1** *(palo)* staff, rod, pole. **2** *(de mando)* staff, mace. **3** *(medida de longitud)* unit of length equal to approximately 33 inches. **4** *(tauromaquia)* lance, pike.

variable *adj* variable, changeable.
▶ *nf* MAT variable.

variación *nf* variation, change.

variado,-a *adj* **1** varied, mixed. **2** *(galletas, helados)* assorted.

variante *adj* variable.
▶ *nf* **1** *(versión)* variant. **2** *(diferencia)* difference.

variar *vt* **1** *(cambiar)* to change. **2** *(dar variedad)* to vary, give some variety to.
▶ *vi* **1** *(cambiar)* to change: *han variado de planes* they have changed their plans. **2** *(diferir)* to be different (de, to), differ (de, from): *lo que dices varía de tus primeras declaraciones* what you're saying differs from your first statement. **3** MAT to vary. ⎡LOC⎤ **para variar** *irón* as usual, just for a change.

varicela *nf* MED chickenpox, varicella.

variedad *nf* **1** *(diversidad)* variety, diversity: *una gran variedad de productos* a wide variety of products. **2** *(clase, tipo)* variety.
▶ *nf pl* **variedades** *(espectáculo)* variety show *sing*.

varilla *nf* **1** *(vara)* stick, rod. **2** *(de paraguas, abanico)* rib; *(de corsé)* stay.

vario,-a *adj* **1** *(diverso)* different, diverse. **2** *(variado)* varied, assorted. **3** *(mudable)* changeable, variable.
▶ *nm pl* **varios** *(algunos)* some, several.

varita *nf* small stick. ⎡COMP⎤ **varita mágica** magic wand.

varón *nm* **1** *(hombre)* man; *(chico)* boy. **2** *(sexo)* male.

V

vasco,-a *adj* Basque.
▶ *nm & nf (persona)* Basque.
▶ *nm* **vasco** *(idioma)* Basque. COMP **País Vasco** Basque Country.

vasija *nf* vessel, pot, jar.

vaso *nm* **1** *(para beber)* glass. **2** *(para flores)* vase. **3** ANAT vessel. COMP **vaso capilar** capillary. ❘ **vasos sanguíneos** blood vessels.

vasto,-a *adj* vast, immense, huge.

váter *nm fam* toilet.

vatio *nm* watt.

vaya *interj* what a: *¡vaya idea!* what an idea!

vecindario *nm* **1** *(lugar)* neighbourhood (US neighborhood). **2** *(vecinos)* neighbours *pl* (US neighbors *pl*), community, residents *pl*.

vecino,-a *adj* nearby, next, neighbouring (US neighboring).
▶ *nm & nf* **1** *(del barrio)* neighbour (US neighbor). **2** *(residente)* resident. **3** *(habitante)* inhabitant.

vegetación *nf* vegetation.
▶ *nf pl* **vegetaciones** MED adenoids.

vegetal *adj* vegetable.
▶ *nm* **1** vegetable, plant. **2** *(persona)* vegetable.

vegetariano,-a *adj* vegetarian.
▶ *nm & nf* vegetarian.

vehículo *nm* **1** *(gen)* vehicle. **2** *(coche)* car. **3** *fig* vehicle. **4** *fig (enfermedades)* transmitter, carrier.

veinte *adj (cardinal)* twenty; *(vigésimo)* twentieth.
▶ *nm (número)* twenty; *(fecha)* twentieth. COMP **los años veinte** the twenties.

✎ Consulta también **seis**.

veinteavo,-a *adj* twentieth.
▶ *nm & nf* twentieth.

✎ Consulta también **sexto**.

veintena *nf (exacto)* twenty; *(aproximado)* about twenty.

veinticinco *adj (cardinal)* twenty-five; *(ordinal)* twenty-fifth.
▶ *nm (número)* twenty-five; *(fecha)* twenty-fifth.

veinticuatro *adj (cardinal)* twenty-four; *(ordinal)* twenty-fourth.
▶ *nm (número)* twenty-four; *(fecha)* twenty-fourth.

veintidós *adj (cardinal)* twenty-two; *(ordinal)* twenty-second.
▶ *nm (número)* twenty-two; *(fecha)* twenty-second.

veintinueve *adj (cardinal)* twenty-nine; *(ordinal)* twenty-ninth.
▶ *nm (número)* twenty-nine; *(fecha)* twenty-ninth.

veintiocho *adj (cardinal)* twenty-eight; *(ordinal)* twenty-eighth.
▶ *nm (número)* twenty-eight; *(fecha)* twenty-eighth.

veintiséis *adj (cardinal)* twenty-six; *(ordinal)* twenty-sixth.
▶ *nm (número)* twenty-six; *(fecha)* twenty-sixth.

veintisiete *adj (cardinal)* twenty-seven; *(ordinal)* twenty-seventh.
▶ *nm (número)* twenty-seven; *(fecha)* twenty-seventh.

veintitrés *adj (cardinal)* twenty-three; *(ordinal)* twenty-third.
▶ *nm (número)* twenty-three; *(fecha)* twenty-third.

veintiún *adj* [se usa sólo ante nombres en masculino] twenty-one.

veintiuna *nf* pontoon, blackjack.

veintiuno,-a *adj (cardinal)* twenty-one; *(ordinal)* twenty-first.
▶ *nm (número)* twenty-one; *(fecha)* twenty-first.

vejar *vt* **1** *(molestar)* to vex, annoy. **2** *(humillar)* to humiliate.

vejez *nf* old age.

vejiga *nf* bladder.

vela¹ *nf* **1** *(vigilia)* watch, vigil; *(de muerto)* wake. **2** *(desvelo)* wakefulness. **3** *(candela)* candle. LOC **pasar la noche en vela** to have a sleepless night.

vela² *nf* **1** *(de barco)* sail. **2** DEP sailing. **3** *fig (barco de vela)* sailing ship.

velamen *nm* sails *pl*.

velar¹ *vi* **1** *(no dormir)* to stay awake; *(no acostarse)* to stay up. **2** *fig (cuidar)* to watch (por, over), look (por, after): *velaron por él* they looked after him.

▶ *vt (enfermo)* to sit up with, watch over; *(muerto)* to keep vigil over.

velar² *adj* LING velar.

▶ *vt* **1** *fig (cubrir)* to hide, cover, veil. **2** *(fotografía)* to fog. **3** *(pintura)* to glaze.

▶ *vpr* **velarse** *(fotografía)* to become fogged, get exposed

velero,-a *nm & nf (fabricante de velas)* sailmaker.

▶ *nm* **velero** sailing ship, sailing boat.

veleta *nf (para el viento)* weathercock, weather vane.

▶ *nm o nf fam fig (persona)* fickle person.

vello *nm* **1** *(de persona - pelusa)* down; *(-en las piernas, etc)* hair. **2** *(de fruta, planta)* down, bloom.

velo *nm* **1** *(gen)* veil. **2** ANAT velum.

velocidad *nf* **1** *(rapidez)* speed, velocity. **2** AUTO *(marcha)* gear. [COMP] **velocidad de la luz** speed of light. ‖ **velocidad de transmisión** INFORM bit rate.

velocímetro *nm* speedometer.

velódromo *nm* cycle track, US velodrome.

veloz *adj* fast, quick, swift, rapid.

vena *nf* **1** ANAT vein. **2** *(yacimiento)* vein, seam. **3** BOT vein. **4** *(en mármol, etc)* vein, streak. **5** *fig (disposición)* mood. [LOC] **tener vena de...** to have a gift for…: *tiene vena de cantante* he has a gift for singing.

venado *nm* **1** ZOOL stag, deer. **2** CULIN venison.

vencedor,-ra *adj* winning.

▶ *nm & nf* **1** *(equipo, etc)* winner, victor.

vencejo *nm (ave)* swift.

vencer *vt* **1** DEP to beat. **2** *(exceder)* to outdo, surpass: *la vence en belleza* she surpasses her in beauty. **3** *(problema, etc)* to overcome, surmount. **4** *(ser dominado)* to overcome: *la venció el cansancio* she was overcome by tiredness.

▶ *vi* **1** *(ganar)* to win. **2** *(deuda, etc)* to fall due, be payable. **3** *(plazo)* to expire.

▶ *vpr* **vencerse** **1** *(romperse)* to break; *(doblarse)* to bend, incline. **2** *fig (reprimir)* to control OS.

venda *nf* bandage.

vendaje *nm* dressing.

vendar *vt* to bandage.

vendaval *nm* strong wind, gale.

vendedor,-ra *adj* selling.

▶ *nm & nf* **1** *(gen)* seller; *(hombre)* salesman; *(mujer)* saleswoman. **2** *(dependiente)* shop assistant.

vender *vt* **1** *(gen)* to sell. **2** *fig (traicionar)* to betray.

▶ *vpr* **venderse** **1** *(uso impersonal)* to be on sale, be sold: *se vende en farmacias* on sale at your chemist's. **2** *(dejarse sobornar)* to sell OS. [LOC] **«Se vende»** "For sale".

vendimia *nf (cosecha)* grape harvest.

veneno *nm (química, vegetal)* poison; *(animal)* venom.

venenoso,-a *adj* **1** poisonous, venomous. **2** *fig* spiteful, venomous.

venezolano,-a *adj* Venezuelan.

▶ *nm & nf* Venezuelan.

Venezuela *nf* Venezuela.

venganza *nf* revenge, vengeance.

vengar *vt* to avenge.

▶ *vpr* **vengarse** to take revenge (de, on).

venir *vi* **1** *(gen)* to come: *el mes que viene* next month. **2** *(llegar)* to arrive: *vino tarde* he arrived late. **3** *(proceder)* to come (de, from): *viene de París* it comes from Paris. **4** *(estar, aparecer)* to be, come: *las explicaciones vienen en español* the instructions are in Spanish. **5** *(ser)* to be: *eso te viene grande* that's too big for you.

▶ *aux* **1** **venir a** + *inf (aproximación)* to be about; *(alcanzar, llegar a)* to arrive at; *(terminar por)* to end up. **2** **venir** + *ger (acción durativa)*: *lo venía avisando desde hace tiempo* he has been warning us about it for a long time. **3** **venir** + *pp (ser, estar)* to be: *eso viene motivado por la inflación* it's caused by inflation.

▶ *vpr* **venirse** to come back, go back.

venoso,-a *adj* **1** *(sangre)* venous. **2** *(manos, etc)* veined, veiny.

venta *nf* **1** *(acción)* sale, selling. **2** *(hostal)* country inn; *(restaurante)* restaurant.

ventaja *nf* **1** *(gen)* advantage. **2** *(provecho)* profit. [LOC] **llevar ventaja a** ALGN to have the advantage over SB.

ventajoso,-a *adj* **1** advantageous. **2** *(beneficioso)* profitable.

ventana *nf* **1** ARQUIT window. **2** *(de la nariz)* nostril.

V

ventanilla *nf* **1** *(banco, coche, sobre, etc)* window. **2** *(barco)* porthole. **3** *(de taquilla)* window, ticket window.

ventilación *nf* ventilation.

ventilador *nm* ventilator, fan.

ventilar *vt* **1** *(lugar)* to air, ventilate. **2** *(agitar al viento)* to air. **3** *fig (dar a conocer)* to air. **4** *fig (discutir)* to discuss, clear up.
▶ *vpr* **ventilarse 1** *(lugar)* to be ventilated. **2** *(objeto)* to be aired. **3** *fam (terminar)* to finish off: *se ventiló el pastel en un minuto* he finished off the cake in a minute.

ventisca *nf* snowstorm, blizzard.

ventoso,-a *adj* windy.

ver *vt* **1** *(gen)* to see: *no te veo* I can't see you. **2** *(mirar)* to look (at). **3** *(televisión)* to watch. **4** *fig (entender)* understand: *no veo por qué lo hizo* I can't understand why she did it. **5** *(visitar)* to visit, see: *ven a verme* come and see me. **6** JUR to try, hear. **7** *(parecer)* to look: *te veo triste* you look sad. LOC **a ver** let's see, let me see.
▶ *nm* **1** *(vista)* sight, vision. **2** *(apariencia)* looks *pl*, appearance.
▶ *vpr* **verse 1** *(ser visto)* to be seen: *aquí dentro no se ve nada* you can't see a thing in here. **2** *(con algn)* to meet, see each other. **3** *(en una situación, etc)* to find OS, be: *se vio en un apuro* he was in a fix. **4** *(imaginarse)* to imagine OS.

veranear *vi* to spend the summer (holiday) (en, in/at).

veraneo *nm* summer holiday. LOC **ir de veraneo** to go on holiday.

veraniego,-a *adj* summer, summery.

verano *nm* summer.

veras LOC **de veras** really, seriously.

veraz *adj* truthful, veracious.

verbal *adj* verbal, oral.

verbena *nf* **1** BOT verbena. **2** *(fiesta)* night party.

verbo *nm* verb.

verdad *nf* **1** truth, truthfulness: *es verdad* it's true. **2** *(confirmación)*: *es bonita, ¿verdad?* she's pretty, isn't she?

verdadero,-a *adj* true, real.

verde *adj* **1** *(color)* green. **2** *(fruta)* unripe, green; *(madera)* unseasoned. **3** *fig (persona)* green, immature. **4** *fam (chiste)* blue, dirty.
▶ *nm* **1** *(color)* green. **2** *(hierba)* grass. **3** POL green: *los verdes* the Greens.

verdugo *nm* **1** *(persona)* executioner. **2** *(prenda)* balaclava, balaclava helmet.

verdulera *nf fig* coarse woman, foul-mouthed woman.

verdulería *nf* greengrocer's (shop).

verdulero,-a *nm & nf* greengrocer.

verdura *nf* **1** *(hortaliza)* vegetables *pl*, greens *pl*. **2** *(color)* greenness, greenery.

vereda *nf* footpath, path.

veredicto *nm* verdict.

vergonzoso,-a *adj* **1** *(acto)* shameful, shocking: *un asunto vergonzoso* a shocking business. **2** *(persona)* bashful, shy.

vergüenza *nf* **1** *(deshonor, etc)* shame, sense of shame: *sus palabras me dan vergüenza* her words make me feel ashamed. **2** *(timidez)* bashfulness, shyness; *(turbación)* embarrassment: *me da vergüenza bailar* I'm too shy to dance. **3** *(escándalo)* disgrace, shame: *lo que han hecho es una vergüenza* what they did is a disgrace. LOC **¡qué vergüenza!** it's a disgrace!, how disgraceful!

verídico,-a *adj* truthful, true.

verificar *vt* **1** *(comprobar)* to verify, check. **2** *(probar)* to prove. **3** *(efectuar)* to carry out, perform.
▶ *vpr* **verificarse 1** *(comprobarse)* to come true. **2** *(efectuarse)* to take place.

verja *nf* **1** *(reja)* grating, grille. **2** *(cerca)* railing, railings *pl*. **3** *(puerta)* iron gate.

verruga *nf* wart.

versión *nf* **1** *(gen)* version, account. **2** *(traducción)* translation. **3** *(adaptación)* adaptation. LOC **en versión original** in the original language.

verso *nm* **1** LIT verse. **2** *fam (poema)* poem.

vértebra *nf* vertebra.

vertebrado,-a *adj* vertebrate.
▶ *nm pl* **los vertebrados** the vertebrates.

vertebral *adj* vertebral, spinal.

vertedero *nm* rubbish dump, rubbish tip.

verter *vt* **1** *(líquido - voluntariamente)* to pour, pour out. **2** *(derramar)* to spill. **3** *(vaciar)* to empty, empty out. **4** *(basura)* to dump. **5** *fig (conceptos, ideas, etc)* to express, voice.

vertical *adj* vertical: *lo puso vertical* she put it upright.
▶ *nf* vertical, vertical line.
▶ *nm* vertical.

vértice *nm* vertex.

vertiente *nf* **1** *(gen)* slope. **2** *fig (aspecto)* angle.

vértigo *nm* **1** MED vertigo. **2** *(mareo)* dizziness, giddiness: *me da vértigo* it makes me feel dizzy. **3** *fig* frenzy.

vesícula *nf* vesicle. COMP **vesícula biliar** gall bladder.

vestíbulo *nm* **1** *(de casa)* hall, entrance. **2** *(de hotel, etc)* hall, lobby, vestibule, foyer.

vestido,-a *adj* dressed. *vestida de blanco* dressed in white.
▶ *nm* **vestido 1** *(indumentaria)* clothes *pl*, dress, costume. **2** *(de mujer)* dress; *(de hombre)* suit.

vestigio *nm* vestige, trace, remains *pl*.

vestimenta *nf* clothes *pl*, garments *pl*.

vestir *vt* **1** *(llevar)* to wear, be dressed in: *vestía un vestido rojo* she was wearing a red dress. **2** *(ayudar a vestirse)* to dress; *(hacer vestidos)* to make clothes for: *la vistió su madre* her mother dressed her. **3** *(cubrir)* to cover (de, with).
▶ *vi* **1** to dress: *vestir de negro* to dress in black. **2** *(ser elegante, lucir)* to be classy, look smart: *esa falda viste mucho* that skirt is very classy.
▶ *vpr* **vestirse 1** *(uso reflexivo)* to dress os, get dressed. **2** *(comprarse la ropa)* to buy one's clothes: *se viste en Milán* she buys her clothes in Milan.

vestuario *nm* **1** *(ropas)* wardrobe, clothes *pl*. **2** TEAT *(ropa)* wardrobe, costumes *pl*; *(camerino)* dressing room. **3** DEP changing room.

veta *nf* **1** *(de mármol, roca)* seam, vein; *(de madera)* streak. **2** *fig* streak.

vetar *vt* to veto, put a veto on.

veterinario,-a *adj* veterinary.

▶ *nm & nf* veterinary surgeon, vet, US veterinarian.

veto *nm* veto. LOC **poner el veto a** to put a veto on, veto.

vez *nf* **1** time: *fue la única vez que la vi* it was the only time I saw her; *una vez* once; *dos veces* twice; *cuatro veces* four times. **2** *(turno)* turn; *(ocasión)* occasion. LOC **a veces** sometimes. ‖ **otra vez** again.

vía *nf* **1** *(camino)* road, way; *(calle)* street; *(carril)* lane. **2** *(de tren)* track, line; *(en la estación)* platform: *el tren de la vía uno* the train at platform one. **3** ANAT passage, canal, track. **4** *fig (modo)* way, manner, means. **5** JUR procedure. **6** *(rumbo, dirección)* via, through: *Barcelona-Singapur vía Frankfurt* Barcelona-Singapore via Frankfurt. LOC **dar vía libre a** to leave the way open for. ‖ **por vía aérea 1** *(gen)* by air. **2** *(correo)* airmail. COMP **transmisión vía satélite** satellite transmission.

viajante *nm* commercial traveller (US traveler), travelling (US traveling) salesman.

viajar *vi* to travel: *ha viajado por el mundo entero* she's travelled all over the world.

viaje *nm* **1** *(gen)* journey, trip. **2** *(en coche)* drive, journey. **3** *(travesía por mar)* voyage. **4** [se suele usar en plural] *(concepto de viajar)* travel. **5** *(carga)* load. LOC **¡buen viaje!** bon voyage!, have a good trip! ‖ **estar de viaje** to be away, be away on a trip. COMP **viaje de ida y vuelta** return trip, US round trip.

viajero,-a *adj* travelling (US traveling).
▶ *nm & nf* **1** traveller (US traveler). **2** *(en transporte público)* passenger.

víbora *nf* viper.

vibración *nf* **1** vibration. **2** LING rolling, trilling.

vibrar *vi* **1** *(gen)* to vibrate; *(pulsar)* to throb, pulsate: *toda la ciudad vibraba de actividad* the whole city throbbed with activity. **2** *fig (conmoverse)* to be moved, be overcome with emotion: *el cantante hizo vibrar al público* the singer thrilled the audience. **3** LING to roll, trill.

vibratorio,-a *adj* vibratory.

V

viciar *vt* **1** *(corromper)* to corrupt, lead astray. **2** *(aire)* to pollute.
► *vpr* **viciarse 1** *(enviciarse)* to take to vice, become corrupted. **2** *(objeto)* to go out of shape.

vicio *nm* **1** *(corrupción)* vice, corruption. **2** *(mala costumbre)* bad habit; *(inmoralidad)* vice. **3** *(del lenguaje)* incorrect usage. **4** *(defecto)* defect.

vicioso,-a *adj* **1** *(cosa)* faulty, defective. **2** *(persona)* depraved, perverted.
► *nm & nf* depraved person.

víctima *nf* victim, casualty.

victoria *nf* victory, triumph. LOC **cantar victoria** to proclaim a victory.

victorioso,-a *adj* victorious, triumphant.

vid *nf* grapevine, vine.

vida *nf* **1** *(gen)* life. **2** *(viveza)* liveliness. **3** *(tiempo)* lifetime, life. **4** *(modo de vivir)* life, way of life. **5** *(medios)* living, livelihood. LOC **darse la gran vida / pegarse la gran vida / darse la vida padre** *fam* to live it up. I **de por vida** for life. I **de toda la vida** lifelong: *un amigo de toda la vida* a lifelong friend. I **estar con vida / estar sin vida** to be alive / be dead. I **ganarse la vida** to earn one's living. I **quitarle la vida a** ALGN to take SB's life. COMP **vida familiar** family life.

vídeo *nm* *(aparato)* video, video recorder; *(cinta)* video, video tape.

videoconferencia *nf* videoconference.

videoclip *nm* video, pop video.

videoclub *nm* video club.

videojuego *nm* video game.

vidriera *nf* **1** *(ventana)* picture window. **2** *(puerta)* glass door. **3** *(de balcón, galería)* French window. **4** *(vitral)* stained-glass window. **5** *(escaparate)* shop window.

vidriero,-a *nm & nf* **1** *(fabricante)* glassmaker. **2** *(colocador)* glazier.

vidrio *nm* *(material)* glass.

viejo,-a *adj* **1** *(gen)* old: *un coche viejo* an old car. **2** *(desgastado)* old, worn-out. **3** *(antiguo)* old, ancient.
► *nm & nf (hombre)* old man; *(mujer)* old woman. LOC **hacerse viejo,-a** to grow old.

viento *nm* **1** *(gen)* wind. **2** *(rumbo)* direction. **3** *(de caza)* scent. **4** *(cuerda)* rope, guy. **5** *fam (flatulencia)* wind, flatulence. LOC **contra viento y marea** *fig* come hell or high water. I **hacer viento / soplar viento** to be windy. I **ir viento en popa 1** MAR to sail before the wind. **2** *fig* to do very well.

vientre *nm* **1** ANAT belly, abdomen. **2** *(vísceras)* bowels *pl.* **3** *(de embarazada)* womb.

viernes *nm inv* Friday. COMP **Viernes Santo** Good Friday.

✎ Consulta también jueves.

Vietnam *nm* Vietnam.

vietnamita *adj* Vietnamese.
► *nm & nf (persona)* Vietnamese.
► *nm* **vietnamita** *(idioma)* Vietnamese.

viga *nf* **1** *(de madera)* beam, rafter. **2** *(de acero, etc)* girder.

vigésimo,-a *adj* twentieth: *vigésimo primero* twenty-first.
► *nm & nf* twentieth.

✎ Consulta también sexto,-a.

vigía *nm o nf* lookout.

vigilante *adj* **1** *(que vigila)* vigilant, watchful. **2** *(alerta)* alert.
► *nm o nf (hombre)* guard, watchman; *(mujer)* guard. COMP **vigilante nocturno** night watchman.

vigilar *vt* **1** *(cuidar)* to watch (over), look after: *vigila al niño* look after the baby. **2** *(con armas, etc)* to guard. **3** *(supervisar)* to oversee. **4** *(estar atento)* to keep an eye on, take care of: *vigila la puerta, que no entre nadie* keep an eye on the door and see nobody gets in.
► *vi (gen)* to keep watch.

vigor *nm* **1** *(fuerza)* vigour (US vigor), strength. **2** *(validez)* force, effect. LOC **en vigor** in force.

vigoroso,-a *adj* vigorous, strong.

VIH *abrev* MED *(virus de inmunodeficiencia humana)* Human Immune Deficiency Virus; *(abreviatura)* HIV.

vil *adj* vile, base, despicable.

vileza *nf* **1** *(cualidad)* vileness, baseness. **2** *(acto)* vile act, despicable deed.

villa *nf* **1** *(casa)* villa, country house. **2** *(pueblo)* small town; *(ciudad)* town.

villancico *nm* carol, Christmas carol.

villano,-a *nm & nf* **1** HIST villein, serf. **2** *fig (persona ruin)* villain.

vinagre *nm* **1** vinegar. **2** *fig* sourpuss.

vinculación *nf* **1** *(acción)* linking, binding. **2** *(vínculo)* link, bond.

vincular *vt* **1** *(unir)* to link (a, to), bind (a, to). **2** *(relacionar)* to relate (con, to), connect (con, with), link (con, with). **3** JUR to entail.
▶ *vpr* **vincularse** to link OS (a, to).

vínculo *nm* **1** tie, bond, link. **2** *fig* link.

vinícola *adj* wine-producing.

vinicultor,-ra *nm & nf* wine producer.

vinicultura *nf* wine production, wine growing.

vino *nm* wine. COMP **vino blanco** white wine. I **vino tinto** red wine.

viña *nf* vineyard.

viñedo *nm* vineyard.

viñeta *nf* **1** *(en impresión)* vignette. **2** *(dibujo humorístico)* cartoon.

viola *nf* viola.

violáceo,-a *adj* violaceous, violet.

violencia *nf* **1** *(fuerza)* violence. **2** *(embarazo)* embarrassment. **3** *(situación embarazosa)* embarrassing situation. **4** *(violación)* rape.

violentar *vt* **1** *(forzar algo)* to force, break open. **2** *(obligar a alguien)* to force, use force on. **3** *fig (entrar)* to break into, enter by force.
▶ *vpr* **violentarse 1** *fig (molestarse)* to get annoyed. **2** *fig (avergonzarse)* to feel ashamed.

violento,-a *adj* **1** *(gen)* violent. **2** *(molesto)* embarrassed, awkward, ill at ease.

violeta *adj (color)* violet.
▶ *nm (color)* violet.
▶ *nf* BOT violet.

violín *nm* violin.

violinista *nm o nf* violinist.

violón *nm* double bass.

violoncelista *nm o nf* cellist.

violoncelo *nm* cello.

violonchelista *nm o nf* cellist.

violonchelo *nm* cello.

viraje *nm* **1** *(curva)* turn, bend. **2** *(en coche)* turn. **3** MAR tack. **4** *(fotografía)* toning.

viral *adj* viral.

virar *vi* **1** MAR to tack, put about. **2** AUTO to turn round.

virgen *adj* **1** *(persona)* virgin. **2** *(puro)* virgin, pure.
▶ *nm o nf* virgin. COMP **la Santísima Virgen** the Blessed Virgin.

vírico,-a *adj* viral.

virtual *adj* virtual.

virtud *nf* **1** *(cualidad)* virtue. **2** *(propiedad, eficacia)* property, quality: *con virtudes curativas* with medicinal properties. LOC **en virtud de** by virtue of.

virtuosismo *nm* virtuosity.

virtuoso,-a *adj* virtuous.
▶ *nm & nf* virtuous person.

viruela *nf* **1** MED smallpox. **2** *(marca)* pockmark. LOC **picado,-a de viruelas** pockmarked.

virulencia *nf* virulence.

virulento,-a *adj* virulent.

virus *nm inv* virus.

viruta *nf* shaving.

visado,-a *adj* endorsed with a visa.
▶ *nm* **visado** visa.

visar *vt* **1** *(pasaporte)* to endorse with a visa. **2** *(documento)* to endorse, approve.

víscera *nf* internal organ.
▶ *nf pl* **vísceras** viscera, entrails.

visceral *adj* **1** visceral. **2** *fig* profound, deep-rooted.

viscosa *nf* viscose.

viscoso,-a *adj* viscous.

visera *nf* **1** *(de gorra)* peak; *(de casco)* visor. **2** *(suelta)* eyeshade. **3** AUTO sun visor.

visibilidad *nf* visibility.

visigodo,-a *nm & nf* Visigoth.

visillo *nm* small lace curtain.

visión *nf* **1** *(acción)* vision. **2** *(vista)* sight. **3** *(ilusión)* vision. **4** *fig (persona fea)*

V

fright, sight. LOC **ver visiones** to dream, see things.

visita *nf* **1** *(acción)* visit. **2** *(invitado)* visitor, guest; *(invitados)* visitors *pl*, guests *pl*. LOC **estar de visita en** to be visiting. COMP **horas de visita** MED surgery hours.

visitante *nm o nf* visitor.

visitar *vt* **1** *(ir a ver a alguien)* to visit, pay a visit to, call on, go and see: *vamos a ver a la abuela* let's go and visit grandma. **2** *(lugar)* to visit, see. **3** *(inspeccionar)* to inspect, visit, examine.

vislumbrar *vt* **1** *(ver)* to glimpse, catch a glimpse of, make out. **2** *fig (conjeturar)* to begin to see: *vislumbraron una solución al problema* they began to see a solution to the problem.

viso *nm* **1** *(reflejo)* sheen, shimmer. **2** *(ropa interior)* underskirt. **3** *fig (apariencia)* appearance. LOC **tener visos de** to seem, appear.

visón *nm* mink.

visor *nm* **1** *(de arma)* sight. **2** *(de máquina fotográfica)* viewfinder.

víspera *nf* **1** *(día anterior)* day before. **2** *(de fiesta)* eve.
▶ *nf pl* **vísperas** REL vespers.

vista *nf* **1** *(visión)* sight, vision. **2** *(ojo)* eye, eyes *pl*. **3** *(panorama)* view. **4** *(aspecto)* appearance, aspect, look. **5** *(dibujo, cuadro, foto)* view. **6** *(intención)* intention. **7** *(propósito)* outlook, prospect. **8** JUR trial, hearing.
▶ *nf pl* **vistas** view *sing*: *la habitación tiene vistas al mar* the room has a view of the sea. LOC **a primera vista / a simple vista** at first sight: *a primera vista parecía más complicado* at first sight it looked more complicated. **I con vistas a 1** *(hacia)* overlooking. **2** *(pensando en)* with a view to, in anticipation of. **I en vista de** in view of, considering. **I hacer la vista gorda** *fam* to turn a blind eye. **I ser corto,-a de vista** to be shortsighted. **I tener vista de lince** *fig* to be eagle-eyed, have eyes like a hawk.

vistazo *nm* glance. LOC **dar un vistazo a** ALGO **/ echar un vistazo a** ALGO **1** *(mirar)* to

have a look at STH. **2** *(vigilar)* to keep an eye on.

visto,-a *adj* **1** *(anticuado)* old-fashioned. **2** *(dado)* in view of, considering. **3** *(corriente)* common. **4** *(ladrillo, viga, obra)* exposed. **5** JUR *(dictaminado)*: *el caso está visto para sentencia* the case has been heard and a verdict may be decided upon.
▶ *nm* **visto** approval. LOC **dar el visto bueno a** ALGO to approve STH, O.K. STH. **I estar bien visto,-a** to be well looked upon, be considered acceptable. **I por lo visto** apparently. **I visto que...** in view of the fact that..., given that..., seeing that...

vistoso,-a *adj* **1** *(llamativo)* showy, flashy. **2** *(colorido)* bright, colourful (US colorful).

visual *adj* visual.
▶ *nf (línea)* line of vision, line of sight.

visualización *nf* display.

visualizar *vt* **1** to visualize. **2** INFORM to display.

vital *adj* **1** *(de la vida)* vital. **2** *fig (esencial)* essential, vital.

vitalicio,-a *adj* life, for life: *un cargo vitalicio* a post held for life.

vitalidad *nf* vitality.

vitalizar *vt* to vitalize.

vitamina *nf* vitamin.

vitícola *adj* wine-growing, wine-producing, viticultural.

viticultor,-ra *nm & nf* wine grower, viticulturist.

viticultura *nf* wine-growing, viticulture.

vitorear *vt (aclamar)* to cheer, acclaim.

vitral *nm* stained-glass window.

vítreo,-a *adj* vitreous.

vitrina *nf* **1** *(armario)* glass cabinet, display cabinet. **2** *(de exposición)* glass case, showcase. **3** *(escaparate)* shop window.

vitro *loc* in vitro in vitro. COMP **fecundación in vitro** in vitro fertilization.

vitrocerámica COMP **encimera vitrocerámica** ceramic hob.

vitualla *nf* [generalmente se usa en plural] provisions *pl*, food.

viudedad *nf* **1** *(estado)* widowhood. **2** *(pensión - hombre)* widower's pension; *(- mujer)* widow's pension.

viudez *nf* widowhood.

viudo,-a *adj* widowed.
▶ *nm & nf (hombre)* widower; *(mujer)* widow.

viva *nm* cheer, shout.

vivaz *adj* **1** *(vivo)* vivacious, lively. **2** *(perspicaz)* sharp, quick-witted.

víveres *nm pl* food *sing*, provisions, supplies.

vivero *nm* **1** *(de plantas)* nursery. **2** *(de peces)* fish farm, fish hatchery; *(de moluscos)* bed.

viveza *nf* **1** *(persona)* liveliness, vivacity. **2** *(color, relato)* vividness. **3** *(al hablar)* vehemence. **4** *(agudeza)* sharpness, quick-wittedness.

vivienda *nf* **1** *(gen)* housing, accommodation. **2** *(morada)* dwelling. **3** *(casa)* house. **4** *(piso)* flat.

vivir *vi* **1** *(tener vida)* to live; *(estar vivo)* to be alive: *vivió hasta los ochenta años* he lived to the age of eighty. **2** *(habitar)* to live: *vive en Barcelona* she lives in Barcelona. **3** *(mantenerse)* to live, live on, make a living: *ese trabajo no le da para vivir* he can't live on what that job pays. **4** *fig (durar)* to last, live on.
▶ *vt (pasar por, experimentar)* to live through, go through, experience: *mi abuelo vivió la guerra* my grandfather lived through the war.

vivo,-a *adj* **1** *(que tiene vida)* living; *(que está)* alive: *materia viva* living matter; *Pepe está vivo* Pepe is alive. **2** *(fuego, llama)* live, burning. **3** *(lengua)* living. **4** *fig (color, etc)* bright, vivid. **5** *fig (animado)* lively, vivacious. **6** *fig (dolor, emoción, etc)* acute, deep, intense. **7** *fig (descripción)* lively, graphic. **8** *fig (carácter)* quick, irritable. **9** *fig (listo)* quick-witted. **10** *fig (astuto)* shrewd, sly. **11** *fig (llaga, herida)* open. LOC **en vivo** TV live.
▶ *nm & nf* **1** living person: *los vivos* the living. **2** *fam fig (astuto)* quick-witted person.

vocablo *nm* word, term.

vocabulario *nm* vocabulary.

vocación *nf* vocation, calling.

vocacional *adj* vocational.

vocal *adj* vocal.
▶ *nf* vowel.
▶ *nm o nf (de junta, etc)* member.

vocativo *nm* vocative.

vocear *vi (dar voces)* to shout, cry out.
▶ *vt* **1** *(divulgar)* to publish. **2** *(gritar)* to shout, cry out. **3** *(divulgar)* to publish, proclaim. **4** *(aclamar)* to cheer, acclaim.

vocero,-a *nm & nf (gen)* spokesperson; *(hombre)* spokesman; *(mujer)* spokeswoman.

voladizo,-a *adj* projecting, jutting out.
▶ *nm* voladizo projection.

volador,-ra *adj* flying.

volante *adj (que vuela)* flying.
▶ *nm* **1** COST flounce; *(adorno)* frill, ruffle. **2** AUTO steering wheel. **3** TÉC flywheel.

volar *vi* **1** *(ir por el aire)* to fly. **2** *fig (papeles, etc)* to be blown away. **3** *fig (ir deprisa)* to fly: *el tiempo vuela* time flies. **4** *fam fig (desaparecer)* to disappear, vanish. **5** *fig (sobresalir de un edificio)* to jut out, project. **6** *fig (noticia, etc)* to spread rapidly.
▶ *vt* **1** *fig (hacer explotar - edificio)* to blow up, demolish; *(- caja fuerte)* to blow open; *(- en minería)* to blast. **2** *fig (en impresión)* to raise. **3** *(en caza)* to flush.
▶ *vpr* **volarse** *(papeles, etc)* to be blown away. LOC **echarse a volar** to fly away, fly off.

volcán *nm* volcano.

volcánico,-a *adj* volcanic.

volcar *vi* **1** *(coche, etc)* to turn over, overturn. **2** MAR to capsize.
▶ *vt* **1** *(gen)* to turn over, knock over, upset. **2** *(vaciar)* to empty out, pour out. **3** *fig (hacer cambiar de parecer)* to make change one's mind.
▶ *vpr* **volcarse** *fig (entregarse)* to do one's utmost.

volear *vt* to volley.

V

voleibol *nm* volleyball.

voleo *nm* DEP volley. [LOC] **a voleo / al voleo** *fig* at random, haphazardly.

volquete *nm* dumper-truck.

voltaje *nm* voltage.

voltear *vt* 1 *(dar vueltas)* to whirl, twirl. 2 *(poner al revés)* to turn over, toss. 3 *(campanas)* to peal, ring out. 4 *(a una persona)* to toss up in the air.

voltereta *nf* somersault. [LOC] **dar volteretas** to do somersaults.

voltímetro *nm* voltmeter.

voltio *nm* volt.

voluble *adj* changeable, fickle.

volumen *nm* 1 *(gen)* volume. 2 *(tamaño)* size. [COMP] **volumen de negocios** turnover.

voluminoso,-a *adj* 1 voluminous. 2 *(enorme)* bulky, massive.

voluntad *nf* 1 *(cualidad)* will. 2 *(fuerza de voluntad)* willpower: *tiene mucha voluntad* she's very strong-willed. 3 *(deseo)* wish. 4 *(propósito)* intention, purpose: *tiene buena voluntad* her intentions are good. 5 *(afecto)* affection. [LOC] **a voluntad** at will. ∎ **buena voluntad** goodwill. [COMP] **voluntad de hierro / voluntad férrea** will of iron, iron will.

voluntariado *nm* 1 MIL voluntary enlistment. 2 *(civil)* group of volunteers.

voluntario,-a *adj* voluntary.
▶ *nm & nf* volunteer.

voluntarioso,-a *adj (con voluntad)* willing.

voluta *nf* 1 ARQUIT volute, scroll. 2 *(espiral)* spiral, column. 3 *(de humo)* ring.

volver *vt* 1 *(dar vuelta a)* to turn, turn over; *(hacia abajo)* to turn upside down; *(de dentro afuera)* to turn inside out; *(lo de atrás hacia delante)* to turn back to front: *volver la tortilla* to turn the omelette. 2 *(convertir)* to turn, make, change: *el dinero ha vuelto tonto a Paco* money has made Paco foolish. 3 *(devolver)* to give back; *(a su lugar)* to put back.
▶ *vi* 1 *(regresar)* to return; *(ir)* to go back; *(venir)* to come back: *vuelve cuando quieras* come back whenever you want. 2 *(a un tema, etc)* to return, revert. 3 **volver a** *(hacer otra vez)* to do again: *volver a leer* to read again. [LOC] **volver a las andadas** to fall back into one's old habits. ∎ **volver del revés** to turn inside out. ∎ **volver en sí** to regain consciousness, come round. ∎
▶ *vpr* **volverse** 1 *(regresar - ir)* to go back; *(- venir)* to come back. 2 *(darse la vuelta)* to turn. 3 *(convertirse)* to turn, become. [LOC] **volverse atrás** *fig* to go back on one's word, back out. ∎ **volverse en contra de** ALGN to turn against SB.

vomitar *vt* 1 to vomit, bring up. 2 *fig* to belch, spew out.
▶ *vi* to be sick, vomit: *tengo ganas de vomitar* I feel sick.

vómito *nm* 1 *(resultado)* vomit. 2 *(acción)* vomiting.

voracidad *nf* voracity, voraciousness.

vorágine *nf* vortex, whirlpool.

voraz *adj* 1 voracious. 2 *fig* fierce, raging.

vórtice *nf* 1 vortex, whirlpool. 2 *(de ciclón)* centre (US center) of a cyclone.

vos *pron* 1 *arc (usted)* thou, you. 2 AM *(tú)* you.

vosotros,-as *pron (sujeto)* you; *(objeto)* you, yourselves: *con vosotros* with you; *entre vosotras* among yourselves; *¿cómo lo sabéis vosotros?* how do you know?

votación *nf* 1 *(voto)* vote, ballot. 2 *(acto)* vote, voting. [LOC] **someter** ALGO **a votación** to put STH to the vote, take a ballot on STH. [COMP] **votación a mano alzada** voting by a show of hands.

votante *nm o nf* voter.

votar *vi (dar el voto)* to vote.
▶ *vt (proponer para aprobar)* to pass.

voto *nm* 1 *(gen)* vote: *tres votos a favor* three votes for. 2 REL vow. 3 *(deseo)* wish. 4 *(blasfemia)* curse, oath. [COMP] **derecho al voto** the right to vote. ∎ **voto de censura** vote of no confidence. ∎ **voto de confianza** vote of confidence.

voz *nf* **1** *(sonido)* voice. **2** *(grito)* shout. **3** *(vocablo, palabra)* word. **4** GRAM voice: *voz activa* active voice. **5** MÚS *(de instrumento)* tone; *(cantante)* voice· *canción a tres voces* three-part song. **6** *fig (rumor)* rumour (US rumor). **7** *fig (en asamblea - facultad de hablar)* voice, say; *(- voto)* vote. LOC **alzar la voz / levantar la voz** to raise one's voice. ▌**dar voces** to shout. ▌**en voz alta** aloud. ▌**en voz baja** in a low voice. ▌**tener voz y voto 1** *fam* to have a say. **2** *fml* to be a voting member.

vuelco *nm* **1** *(gen)* tumble, upset. **2** *(barco)* capsizing. **3** *fig* change. LOC **dar un vuelco 1** *(coche)* to overturn. **2** *(empresa)* to go to ruin. ▌**me dio un vuelco el corazón** my heart missed a beat.

vuelo *nm* **1** *(acto, espacio, etc)* flight. **2** *(acción)* flying. **3** ARQUIT *(voladizo)* projection. LOC **al vuelo** in flight. ▌**alzar el vuelo / emprender el vuelo / levantar el vuelo** to take flight. ▌**cazarlas al vuelo / cogerlas al vuelo** *fig* to be quick on the uptake. COMP **vuelo chárter / vuelo regular** charter flight / scheduled flight.

vuelta *nf* **1** *(giro)* turn. **2** *(en un circuito)* lap, circuit. **3** *(paseo)* walk, stroll: *vamos a dar una vuelta* let's go for a walk. **4** *(regreso, retorno)* return; *(viaje de regreso)* return journey, journey back: *a la vuelta de las vacaciones* after the holidays. **5** *(dinero de cambio)* change: *quédese con la vuelta* keep the change. **6** *(curva)* bend, curve. **7** *(reverso)* back, reverse. **8** *(de torneo, etc)* round. **9** *(cambio)* change, alteration. **10** COST *(de pantalón)* turn-up; *(forro)* lining. **11** *(al hacer punto)* row. LOC **a vuelta de correo** by return of post. ▌**dar la vuelta a 1** *(alrededor)* to go round. **2** *(girar)* to turn (round). **3** *(de arriba abajo)* to turn upside down. **4** *(de dentro a fuera)* to turn inside out. **5** *(cambiar de lado)* to turn over. ▌**dar la vuelta al mundo** to go round the world. ▌**dar vueltas a** ALGO *fig* to worry about STH: *¡no lo des más vueltas!* don't worry about it! ▌**dar media vuelta** to turn round. ▌**estar de vuelta de todo** to have seen it all before. ▌**¡hasta la vuelta!** see you when I get back! COMP **la vuelta al colegio 1** *(en publicidad)* "Back to school". **2** *(primer día)* first day back at school.

vuelto,-a *adj (cuello)* roll: *jersey de cuello vuelto* roll-neck sweater.

vuestro,-a *adj* your, of yours: *vuestra casa* your house; *un amigo vuestro* a friend of yours.
▸ *pron* yours: *éstas son las vuestras* these are yours.
▸ *nm* **lo vuestro** what is yours, what belongs to you.

vulgar *adj* **1** *(grosero)* vulgar, coarse, common: *lenguaje vulgar* coarse language. **2** *(general)* common, general. **3** *(banal)* banal, ordinary; *(idea)* commonplace. **4** *(no técnico)* lay: *término vulgar* lay term.

vulgaridad *nf* **1** *(grosería)* vulgarity, coarseness. **2** *(banalidad)* banality, triviality.

vulgarismo *nm* vulgarism.

vulgarización *nf* vulgarization, popularization.

vulgarizar *vt* **1** *(popularizar)* to popularize, vulgarize. **2** *(hacer vulgar)* to make common.
▸ *vpr* **vulgarizarse** *(popular)* to become popular, become common; *(grosero)* to become vulgar, become common.

vulgo *nm pey* common people *pl*, masses *pl*.

vulnerable *adj* vulnerable.

vulneración *nf* **1** *(gen)* violation. **2** *fig (reputación)* damaging, harming.

vulnerar *vt* **1** *(ley, etc)* to violate. **2** *fig (honor, etc)* to damage, harm.

V

W, w *nf (la letra)* W, w.
W *sím* **(vatio)** watt; *(símbolo)* W.
wáter *nm fam* toilet.
waterpolo *nm* water polo.
watt *nm* watt.

✎ Consulta también **vatio**.

web *nf* website.
whisky *nm* whisky; *(irlandés)* whiskey.
COMP **whisky escocés** Scotch, Scotch whisky.
windsurfing *nm* windsurfing.
wolframio *nm* wolfram.

X, x *nf (la letra)* X, x.
xenofobia *nf* xenophobia.
xenófobo,-a *adj* xenophobic.
▶ *nm & nf* xenophobe.

xerocopia *nf* Xerox, photocopy.
xerografía *nf* xerography.
xilófono *nm* xylophone.
xilografía *nf* xylography.

Y, y *nf (la letra)* Y, y.

y *conj* **1** and: *Alberto y María* Alberto and María. **2** *(hora)* past: *son las tres y cuarto* it's a quarter past three. **3** *(en pregunta)* what about: *¿y Pepe, se viene?* what about Pepe, is he coming? **4** *(repetición)* after: *veces y veces* time after time, time and time again. LOC **y eso que** even though. ▪ **¿y (qué)?** so (what)? ▪ **¿y si...?** what if... ? ▪ **¡y tanto!** you bet!, and how!

✎ Consulta también **e**.

ya *adv* **1** already: *esa película ya la he visto* I've already seen that film. **2** *(más tarde)* later: *ya lo haré* I'll do it later. **3** *(ahora mismo)* at once, right now, straightaway: *tienes que mandarlo ya* you must send it at once. **4** *(ahora)* now: *ya viven en el piso nuevo* they're living in the new flat now. **5** *(uso enfático)*: *ya lo sé* I know that; *es facilísimo, ya verás* it's dead easy, you'll see. **6** *(denota satisfacción)*: *¡ya tenemos coche nuevo!* we've got the new car! **7** *(con tono amenazante)*: *¡ya verás ya!* just you wait! **8** *(con indignación)*: *¡ya está bien!* enough is enough! **9** *(para tranquilizar)*: *ya encontrarás trabajo, ya verás como sí* you'll find a job, you'll see. **10** *(para afirmar)* I know, yes: *tienes que estudiar –ya, pero...* you have to study – I know, but... LOC **¡ya está!** there we are!, all done! ▪ **ya que** since, seeing that: *ya que estás aquí, quédate a cenar* seeing that you're here, why don't you stay for supper?
▶ *interj irón* oh yes!

yacer [92] *vi* **1** *(estar enterrado)* to lie. **2** *fml (hallarse)* to lie. **3** *lit (dormir)* to be lying; *(acostarse)* to lie (**con**, with): *Aquí yace...* Here lies...

yacimiento *nm* bed, deposit. COMP **yacimiento petrolífero** oilfield.

yarda *nf* yard.

yate *nm* yacht.

yedra *nf* ivy.

yegua *nf* mare.

yeísmo *nm* pronunciation of ll as y.

yema *nf* **1** *(de huevo)* yolk. **2** BOT bud. **3** *(del dedo)* fingertip. COMP **yema de huevo** egg yolk.

Yemen *nm* Yemen.

yemení *adj* Yemeni.
▶ *nm o nf* Yemeni.

yerba *nf* → **hierba**.

yermo ,-a *adj* **1** *(estéril)* barren. **2** *(despoblado)* deserted, uninhabited.

yerno *nm* son-in-law.

yesca *nf* tinder.

yeso *nm* **1** *(mineral)* gypsum. **2** *(para la construcción)* plaster. **3** *(tiza)* chalk. **4** *(escultura)* plaster cast.

yeyuno *nm* jejunum.

yihad *nf* jihad.

yo *pron* I: *el jefe soy yo* I'm the boss; *soy yo* it's me; *entre tú y yo* between you and me; *yo en tu lugar...* if I were you...; *yo que tú...* if I were you...
▶ *nm* **el yo** the ego, the self.

yodo *nm* iodine.

yogur *nm* yoghurt.
▶ *pl* yogures.

yogurt *nm* yoghurt.
▶ *pl* yogurts.

yóquey *nm* jockey.

yugo *nm* yoke.

yugular *adj* jugular.
▶ *nf* jugular vein.

yunque *nm* anvil.

yunta *nf* team of oxen, yoke.

yuxtaposición *nf* juxtaposition.

Z

Z, z *nf (la letra)* Z, z.

zafarrancho *nm* **1** MIL clearing for action. **2** *(jaleo)* commotion. **3** *(desorden)* mess.

zafarse *vpr* to get away (de, from), free os (de, from), escape (de, from): *logró zafarse de la policía* he managed to get away from the police.

zafiro *nm* sapphire.

zaga *nf* **1** rear. **2** *(en deporte)* defence (US defense). LOC **a la zaga** behind. ▌ **no irle a la zaga a** ALGN not to lag behind SB: *es muy travieso, pero su hermano no le va a la zaga* he's really naughty, but his brother's every bit as bad.

zagal,-la *nm & nf* **1** *(muchacho)* lad; *(muchacha)* lass. **2** *(pastor)* shepherd; *(pastora)* shepherdess.

zaguán *nm* hall, hallway.

zaherir *vt* **1** to wound, hurt. **2** *(sentimientos)* to hurt.

Zaire *nm* Zaire.

zaireño,-a *adj* Zairean.
▶ *nm & nf* Zairean.

zalamero,-a *adj* charming, winning.
▶ *nm & nf* charmer. LOC **ponerse zalamero,-a** to turn on the charm.

zamarra *nf* sheepskin jacket.

Zambia *nf* Zambia.

zambiano,-a *adj* Zambian.
▶ *nm & nf* Zambian.

zambo,-a *adj* knock-kneed.
▶ *nm (mono)* spider monkey.

zambullida *nf* plunge, dive. LOC **darse una zambullida** to take a dip.

zambullir *vt* to plunge.

zampar *vi fam* to stuff oneself.

zampoña *nf* panpipes.

zanahoria *nf* carrot.

zanca *nf (de pájaro)* leg; *(de persona)* long leg.

zancada *nf* stride. LOC **en dos zancadas** in two shakes.

zancadilla *nf* **1** trip. **2** *fam (engaño)* ruse, trick. LOC **ponerle la zancadilla a** ALGN to trip SB up.

zanco *nm* stilt.

zancudo,-a *adj* **1** long-legged. **2** *(ave)* wading. COMP **aves zancudas** waders, wading birds.
▶ *nm* **zancudo** AM mosquito.

zángano,-a *nm & nf fam (persona)* loafer.
▶ *nm (insecto)* drone.

zanja *nf* trench. LOC **abrir una zanja** to dig a trench.

zanjar *vt fig (asunto)* to settle.

zapata *nf* **1** *(arandela)* washer. **2** TÉC shoe. **3** *(de cámara fotográfica)* hot shoe. COMP **zapata de freno** brake shoe.

zapatear *vi (bailar)* to stamp one's feet rhythmically.

zapateo *nm* rhythmic stamping.

zapatería *nf* **1** *(tienda)* shoe shop. **2** *(taller de reparación)* shoe repairer's, cobbler's; *(taller de fabricación)* shoemaker's. **3** *(oficio)* shoemaking.

zapatero,-a *nm & nf* **1** *(que arregla)* shoe repairer, cobbler. **2** *(que fabrica)* shoemaker. **3** *(que vende)* shoe seller. COMP **zapatero remendón** cobbler.

zapatilla *nf* **1** *(de estar en casa)* slipper. **2** *(de loneta)* plimsoll. COMP **zapatilla de ballet** ballet shoe. ▌ **zapatilla de deporte** trainer, running shoe.

zapato *nm* shoe. COMP **zapatos de tacón** high-heeled shoes.

zar *nm* tsar, czar.

zarabanda *nf* **1** MÚS saraband. **2** *fam (jaleo)* bustle, confusion.

zarandear *vt* **1** *(sacudir)* to shake; *(empujar)* to jostle, knock about. **2** *(cribar)* to sieve.

zarandeo *nm* **1** *(sacudida)* shaking; *(empujones)* jostling about. **2** *(criba)* sieving. **3** *(contoneo)* swaggering, strutting.

zarcillo *nm* **1** *(pendiente)* earring. **2** BOT tendril.

zarigüeya *nf* opossum.

zarina *nf* tsarina, czarina.

zarpa *nf* claw, paw. LOC echarle la zarpa a ALGO **1** *(animal)* to pounce on STH. **2** *(persona)* to grab STH.

zarpar *vi* to weigh anchor, set sail.

zarza *nf* bramble, blackberry bush.

zarzal *nm* bramble patch.

zarzamora *nf (zarza)* blackberry bush; *(fruto)* blackberry.

zarzuela *nf* **1** MÚS zarzuela, *Spanish operetta*. **2** CULIN fish stew.

zenit *nm* zenith.

zeta *nf (letra)* zed, US zee.
▸ *nm argot* police car.

Zimbabwe *nm* Zimbabwe.

zimbabwense *adj* Zimbabwean.
▸ *nm o nf* Zimbabwean.

zinc *nm* zinc.

zócalo *nm* **1** *(de habitación)* skirting board; *(de edificio)* plinth course, plinth. **2** *(pedestal)* plinth, socle.

zodiaco *nm* zodiac.

zona *nf* **1** area. **2** *(fronteriza, militar)* zone.
▸ *nm* MED *(herpes)* shingles. COMP zona azul parking meter zone. ∎ zona edificada built-up area. ∎ zona fronteriza border zone. ∎ zona glacial frigid zone. ∎ zona templada temperate zone. ∎ zona tórrida torrid zone. ∎ zona verde green zone.

zoología *nf* zoology.

zoológico,-a *adj* zoological.
▸ *nm* zoo.

zoólogo,-a *nm & nf* zoologist.

zorra *nf* **1** *(animal)* vixen. **2** *tabú (mujer)* bitch.

zorro,-a *adj (astuto)* cunning, sly.
▸ *nm* zorro **1** *(animal)* fox; *(macho)* dog fox, fox. **2** *(piel)* fox-fur, fox-skin. **3** *(persona)* old fox. COMP zorro viejo sly old fox.
▸ *nm pl* zorros *(para el polvo)* duster *sing*.

zorzal *nm (ave)* thrush.

zozobrar *vi* **1** *(barco)* to sink, capsize. **2** *(persona)* to worry, be anxious. **3** *(proyecto)* to fail, be ruined.

zueco *nm* clog.

zulo *nm* hide-out.

zumbar *vi (abejorro, oídos)* to buzz: me zumban los oídos my ears are buzzing.
▸ *vt fam (pegar)* to thrash.

zumo *nm* juice: zumo de naranja orange juice.

zurcir *vt* to darn, mend.

zurdo,-a *adj (persona)* left-handed; *(mano)* left.
▸ *nm & nf* left-hander, left-handed person.
▸ *nf (mano)* left hand: un golpe con la zurda a left-handed blow.

zurra *nf fam* thrashing.

zurrar *vt* **1** *fam* to thrash. **2** *fam (cuero)* to tan.

zurrón *nm* shepherd's pouch, shepherd's bag.